Goldmine

RECORD ALBUM

PRICE GUIDE

TIM NEELY

Published by

 **krause
publications**

700 E. State Street • Iola, WI 54990-0001
Telephone: 715/445-2214

Please call or write for our free catalog of music publications.
Our toll-free number to place an order or obtain a free catalog is 800-258-0929
or please use our regular business telephone 715-445-2214
for editorial comment and further information.

ISBN: 0-87341-780-1
Printed in the United States of America

Contents

Introduction

Before I dig into the meat of the introductory material and the listings, I'd like to state what the new *Goldmine Record Album Price Guide* is NOT.

Please read the following carefully before writing to ask why your common pressing of *Rumours* or *Thriller* or *Hotel California* is not listed in here:

This book is not, nor is it meant to serve as, a complete listing (i.e. discography) of anyone's albums! By the very definition of this book, which I am about to state, any complete discographies listed within are purely coincidental. There will be missing albums. It's not that we don't know about them; we most likely do. But until they reach a certain threshold, they won't be listed in here. If you want a book with more complete discographies, I recommend the *Standard Catalog Of American Records 1950-1975*, which should be available where you bought this book. If an album is not listed in THAT book, and it's by an artist who began recording in 1975 or earlier, then we need to know.

So what is this book then?

It lists between 35,000 and 40,000 albums that have **a current market value of at least $20 in near-mint condition**. It is meant to serve the need of the collector and dealer who doesn't want to wade through what sports card collectors and dealers would call "commons" (and what some record collectors and dealers would call "junk") to find the material that has value above the trivial.

Will there be some titles not listed that go for $20 or more? Of course. We may even have made some truly glaring omissions. For example, we found some listings of private label albums that could go for hundreds or even thousands – but we couldn't independently confirm their existence. We couldn't find them on prominent want lists or sale lists, for example. We also don't have every sought-after jazz album listed. (Much of that will be rectified in a new jazz albums price guide, which should be out in early 2000.) And, even though we've added literally thousands of listings in the areas of soundtracks and various artists collections, we've probably missed some important items there as well.

And naturally, some of the items we have listed for $20 or more may trade for less in your experience. (That's why this is a "guide" rather than the law.)

But for the most part, if an album came out in the 1960s, 1970s or 1980s, and it was issued on one of the major labels of the era, and it's not listed in this book, then it brings very little on the collector's market.

Why such a restriction? Why not just list everything by an artist as we do in other books?

Well, we considered it. But we wanted to make this book different.

We wanted to add more different kinds of music to this book. In addition to rock, R&B and soul, we've got listings for country, pop vocalists, some jazz, and even – for the first time in a *Goldmine* price guide – selected classical albums. If we had to list every common album by every common artist, we would have been unable to do this.

So what else sets this book apart?

For starters, as opposed to previous *Goldmine* album price guides, this book is 8 x 11 in format, so there are more albums in fewer pages. Therefore, there's plenty of room for expansion in the future should the LP market warrant massive additions.

It's the first album price guide to feature a checklist format, so you can use it to keep track of those LPs you have and don't have.

And as with most of the other *Goldmine* price guides, we don't generalize. All albums are listed individually. When applicable, mono, stereo and quadraphonic versions are listed separately.

We also have the most complete listing anywhere of record label variations. In our "Record Label Identifier" section, we list over 150 different labels and we tell you how to tell a first pressing album from later editions.

In addition, we have – for the first time in any price guide – a "Reissue Identifier," which will tell you which numbers and prefixes indicate whether your record is a (relatively) worthless reissue or an original, especially in the confusing 1970s and 1980s.

Finally, we have the "$1,000 Club," a popular addition to our *Goldmine Price Guide To 45 RPM Records* that we've carried over to this new book. We list 255 different albums that, should copies be found in near-mint condition, would fetch $1,000 or more.

The album market: What's up?

When I began work on this volume, and during the early stages of its completion, I thought the scenario was going to be somewhere between mixed and glum.

Over the past several years, the markets – and as a result, the prices – for 45s and picture sleeves have grown substantially. At first, I didn't see that with albums. When I started researching the going rates of albums, I naturally started comparing to other books. For many items, I just wasn't seeing the kind of prices listed in the past. Maybe it's because the listed prices were too high to begin with. Regardless, the rare, and not-so-rare, album market seemed not to have fully recovered from the "album glut" of the early 1990s, when unprecedented numbers of LPs hit the used record bins because of the numbers of people "upgrading" their music collections to compact disc.

Then I got a phone call from a dealer in Michigan. I explained what I saw based on my research. And he caused me to re-assess my entire theory.

"Y'know, I used to routinely cut the prices in the price guide 40 to 50 percent, 'cause that's all I could sell them for," he said. "Now I only need to cut the prices about 10 to 15 percent. And there are some things, like blues records, where I can get book value for them. Sometimes more."

Of course, this forced me to open my eyes a bit. And while it's not 100 percent true everywhere, our dealer in Michigan seems to be on to something. Prices at the basic layer of record collecting – the neighborhood used record store – are starting to creep upward.

Don't get me wrong. There are still a lot of cheap albums out there. But a good percentage of the stuff in the bargain bins is either extremely common or well short of near-mint condition. The proverbial "good stuff" is much harder to find in those places.

So what conclusions can be drawn? Basically, the album market seems to be working in three waves:

The common, cheap stuff is still common and cheap. (However, still sealed, original, non-cutout versions of common albums can get $10-$15. I saw a never-opened American copy of AC/DC's *Back In Black*, by all accounts a common LP, go for $15 at auction. And I know a dealer in New York who can easily sell still-sealed copies of *Thriller* by Michael Jackson for $10, not to mention other dance classics such as *Saturday Night Fever*.)

The stuff in the middle seems to be creeping upward, probably affected by the upward trend in rare items.

And the really rare stuff? A lot of it was overpriced in older books, and even though the listed values seem to be lower than they used to be, the *actual* selling prices are higher than they were in most cases. Sure, it's possible that some dealers can get more than the prices listed here. But most dealers won't.

In conclusion, our hope is that you won't be able to take this book and automatically slash the prices by 40 percent because they're way too high. We hope that these are closer to what is really happening rather than what we *wish* was happening.

As far as specific genres of music go, here's where the most upward action has been:

■ **The blues.** Just as is true with singles, the album market for the blues is red-hot. Almost nothing has gone down, and even people who used to feel otherwise can now easily get the former "book values" for top-condition blues albums. Just about anything on the original (non-trident logo) Prestige

Bluesville label from the early 1960s is in the $80-$120 range in near-mint or more.

- **Elvis Presley.** One of the more interesting surprises was how often I raised the prices of Elvis Presley albums to reflect new market realities. Prices went up for almost all pressings before 1977. Only those that were commonly available during the run on the retail market immediately after his death remain cheap. (These include black label, dog near top pressings and Pickwick pressings.) Oddly, too, late 1980s compilations are also starting to escalate in interest. For starters, these were mostly well-conceived and well-done, as opposed to some of the strange compilations that came out in the early post-death years. Also, only the completists were buying the vinyl versions of such releases as *Elvis: The Great Performances; The Complete Million Dollar Quartet*; and the *Time-Life Elvis The King* set. Today, these are going up in value as a result. Compact disc versions of these are relatively plentiful, but the vinyl pressings are not.

- **Television-related records.** Soundtracks, incidental music, cartoon albums, "celebrity vocals"-type releases by people who had no business singing – it all seems to be hot. This is especially true if there's some baby-boomer nostalgia attached. For example, any album related to the Brady Bunch sells today – they generally were flops to begin with, and now they are quite hard to find. Television shows of the 1960s also are sought after. And the albums on Colpix and Hanna-Barbera relating to cartoon characters of the 1960s? As Ralph Kramden used to say, "To the moon!" As always, though, finding them in suitably collectible condition is not always easy. Recognizing this, we've put in a separate section in the back simply called "Television Albums" that we've segregated from soundtracks and original casts.

- Certain albums of the 1990s. Would you pay $200 or more for the first edition of an album from 1994? Well, that's the going rate for the Smashing Pumpkins' *Pisces Iscariot* first edition, a numbered pressing of 2,000 copies that contains a bonus 45 not found in later editions. There are many albums from the early and mid 1990s that predate the recent "vinyl revival," many of which are utterly unknown to collectors. The most action is in "alternative" acts such as Smashing Pumpkins and Nirvana. But there's also starting to be some action in early-1990s record club pressings that were not issued on vinyl anywhere else, at least not in the U.S. Many of those are listed in this book for the first time anywhere since the record club catalogs discontinued them.

There's been plenintrotty of other activity in record album collecting, and we encourage you to explore the pages of this book to see what's been going on.

Collecting questions

I've got some of the items in here, but no one will give me what they are "worth"! They want to give me pennies on the dollar! What's up?

Too many people treat books like this way too literally, and with delusions of grandeur.

What the values in here reflect are **retail** prices – what a collector might pay for the item from a dealer, and **not** what a dealer will pay a collector for resale. Too many non-collectors (and even some collectors) don't understand that.

I know one dealer who has told me that he won't buy records from someone who tells him they consulted a price guide first. While that is extreme, it shows the distrust some dealers have for books like this and how the public uses (and abuses) them.

Just as importantly, the highest values are for records in the best condition (see the section on "Grading your records" below). And there is a reason for that: Truly pristine records are very difficult to find! Many collectors are willing to pay handsomely for them – but for many of the records in this book, Near Mint examples aren't even known to exist!

One reason we've expanded the price listing to three grades of condition is to reflect that. There's a tendency to look at the highest price listed for something and assume that's what your record is worth. More realistically, though, such a small percentage of records are truly Near Mint – especially from the 1950s and 1960s – that your own records, if you were a typical accumulator and not a collector, are considerably less than Near Mint.

The price guide tells me that my Elvis records are worth something, but the used record store in the local strip mall treats them as if they are by Mantovani. What's up?

To get the most from a dealer, make sure the kind of music you're trying to sell matches his/her main inventory focus.

Many dealers today are specialists within the vast world of record collecting. And they aren't interested in other things, no matter how valuable they might be.

I know of a classical music dealer who intentionally undervalues Elvis Presley records in his "wanted to buy" lists for a very simple reason: His clientele doesn't buy them, so he doesn't want them! The same Elvis records would get a lot more from someone who focuses on Elvis. Keep that in mind when you try to sell your punk singles to a store that specializes in vocal groups, or your Orioles 45s to an alternative shop.

I still think I can get the most for what I have. How do I do so?

There is only one way you'll be able to get anything close to the prices listed for most items, and that's to sell them direct to the collector.

The "old-fashioned" way is through record collecting magazines. The oldest and most widely read remains *Goldmine*, which was founded in 1974. Published every two weeks, the magazine is loaded with ads from people selling records of all kinds and from all eras. *Goldmine* has advertising salespeople who will help you put your ad together for maximum impact. To see what *Goldmine* is about, pick up a copy. It is available at all Tower Records stores in the U.S., most Barnes and Noble and Borders bookstores and hundreds of independent record dealers. If you still can't find a copy, call 1-800-258-0929.

A rapidly growing way to sell records and other memorabilia is over the Internet, more on which later.

Now, one from the other side of the equation, the record seller.

You've got to be kidding! I'm a dealer, and I can't sell my records at these prices. If I try, they just sit until I reduce them. What gives?

Basically, how much you get for a record depends on what kind of a dealer you are.

In general, the highest prices for records are obtained by those dealers who sell mostly or entirely through mail-order to a targeted audience. These are people who sell items through auctions in *Goldmine* and sometimes through their own private auction lists. They cater to record collectors, often those from abroad (who, like it or not, often set the prices on rare items because they have to have something more than an American does). They have built reputations for sterling customer service, and their clientele is willing to pay more for the knowledge that they, indeed, are getting what they bought. They will usually get something approaching the prices in this book, and often they can get more.

But most dealers don't fit in that category.

Anyone who sells records in a store or a stand, by definition, has a larger potential market than a mail-order dealer (an area's entire population that might want to buy music), but a less targeted one. Therefore, it's going to be difficult for Joe's Collectible Records in Appleton, Wisconsin (a hypothetical example – there is no such store) to

get the same for a record that a well-known, well-established dealer will. The average customer at our fictional Joe's will have less knowledge of what collectible records sell for from an educated dealer to an educated consumer.

That's why we have price guides: to help educate average people about what their records may sell for. And after all, that's all it is: a guide. (How many times have we said that now?) You may know from your own experience that you can't sell at these prices; adjust accordingly. You also may know that some of these prices are too low (it does happen); you know your market as well as anyone.

Grading your records

When it comes to records, and how much you'll get for them, remember this above all:

Condition is (almost) everything!

Yes, it's possible to get a high price for a beat-up record, if it's exceptionally rare. But for common material, if it's not in at least Very Good condition – and preferably closer to Near Mint – you won't get many buyers. Or at least you won't the second time around. So accurately grading your discs is important, whether you're selling your records to a dealer or selling them to another collector.

Visual or play grading? In an ideal world, every record would be played before it is graded. But the time involved makes it impractical for most dealers, and anyway, it's rare that you get a chance to hear a record before you buy through the mail. Some advertisers play-grade everything and say so. But unless otherwise noted, records are visually graded.

How to grade. Look at everything about a record -- its playing surface, its label, its edges -- under a strong light. Then, based on your overall impression, give it a grade based on the following criteria:

Mint (M): Absolutely perfect in every way -- certainly never played, possibly even still sealed. (More on still sealed under "Other considerations.") Should be used sparingly as a grade, if at all.

Near Mint (NM or M-): A nearly perfect record. Many dealers won't give a grade higher than this, implying (perhaps correctly) that no record is ever truly perfect.

The record should show no obvious signs of wear. An LP jacket should have no creases, folds, seam splits or any other noticeable similar defect. No cut-out holes, either. And of course, the same should be true of any other inserts, such as posters, lyric sleeves and the like.

Basically, an LP in Near Mint condition looks as if you just got it home from a new record store and removed the shrink wrap.

Near Mint is the highest price listed in all *Goldmine* price guides. Anything that exceeds this grade, in the opinion of both buyer and seller, is worth significantly more than the highest *Goldmine* book value.

Very Good Plus (VG+): Generally worth 50 percent of the Near Mint value.

A Very Good Plus record will show some signs that it was played and otherwise handled by a previous owner who took good care of it.

Record surfaces may show some slight signs of wear and may have slight scuffs or very light scratches that don't affect one's listening experience. Slight warps that do not affect the sound are OK.

The label may have some ring wear or discoloration, but it should be barely noticeable. The center hole will not have been misshapen by repeated play.

LP inner sleeves will have some slight ring wear, lightly turned-up corners, or a slight seam split. An LP jacket may have slight signs of wear also and may be marred by a cut-out hole, indentation or corner indicating it was taken out of print and sold at a discount.

In general, if not for a couple minor things wrong with it, this would be Near Mint. All but the most mint-crazy collectors will find a Very Good Plus record highly acceptable.

A synonym used by some collectors and dealers for "Very Good Plus" is "Excellent."

Very Good (VG): Generally worth 25 percent of the Near Mint value.

Many of the defects found in a VG+ record will be more pronounced in a VG disc.

Surface noise will be evident upon playing, especially in soft passages and during a song's intro and fade, but will not overpower the music otherwise. Groove wear will start to be noticeable, as will light scratches (deep enough to feel with a fingernail) that will affect the sound.

Labels may be marred by writing, or have tape or stickers (or their residue) attached. The same will be true of picture sleeves or LP covers. However, it will not have all of these problems at the same time, only two or three of them.

This *Goldmine* price guide lists Very Good as the lowest price. This, *not* the Near Mint price, should be your guide when determining how much a record is worth, as that is the price a dealer will normally pay you for a Near Mint record.

Good (G), Good Plus (G+): Generally worth 10-15 percent of the Near Mint value.

Good does not mean Bad! A record in Good or Good Plus condition can be put onto a turntable and will play through without skipping. But it will have significant surface noise and scratches and visible groove wear (on a styrene record, the groove will be starting to turn white).

A jacket or sleeve will have seam splits, especially at the bottom or on the spine. Tape, writing, ring wear or other defects will start to overwhelm the object.

If it's a common item, you'll probably find another copy in better shape eventually. Pass it up. But if it's something you have been seeking for years, and the price is right, get it... but keep looking to upgrade.

Poor (P), Fair (F): Generally worth 0-5 percent of the Near Mint price.

The record is cracked, badly warped, and won't play through without skipping or repeating. The LP jacket barely keeps the LP inside it. Inner sleeves are fully seam split, crinkled, and written upon.

Except for impossibly rare records otherwise unattainable, records in this condition should be bought or sold for no more than a few cents each.

Other grading considerations. Most dealers give a separate grade to the record and its cover. In an ad, a record's grade is listed first, followed by that of the jacket, unless noted otherwise.

With **Still Sealed (SS)** records, let the buyer beware, unless it's a U.S. pressing from the last 10-15 years or so. It's too easy to re-seal one. Yes, some legitimately never-opened LPs from the 1960s still exist, and some of them bring rather fancy prices. But if you're looking for a specific pressing, the only way you can know for sure is to open the record. Also, European imports are not factory-sealed, so if you see them advertised as sealed, someone other than the manufacturer sealed them.

Common collecting abbreviations

In addition to the letters used to designate a record's grade, it's not uncommon to see other abbreviations used in dealer advertisements. Knowing the more common ones helps to prevent confusion. Here are some that pertain to albums:

boot: bootleg (illegal pressing)
cc: cut corner
co: cutout
coh: cut-out hole
cov, cv, cvr: cover
dh: drill hole
dj: disc jockey (promotional) record
gf: gatefold (cover)
imp: import
ins: insert
lbl: label
m, mo: monaural (mono)
nap: (does) not affect play
noc: number on cover

nol: number on label

obi: not actually an abbreviation, "obi" is the Japanese word for "sash" and is used to describe the strip of paper usually wrapped around Japanese (and occasional US) pressings of LPs.

orig: original

pr, pro, promo: promotional record

q: quadraphonic

re: reissue

rec: record

ri: reissue

rw: ring wear

s: stereo

sl: slight

sm: saw mark

soc: sticker on cover

sol: sticker on label

ss: still sealed

s/t: self-titled

st: stereo

sw: shrink wrap

toc: tape on cover

tol: tape on label

ts: taped seam

w/: with

wlp: white label promo

wobc: writing on back cover

woc: writing on cover

wofc: writing on front cover

wol: writing on label

wr: wear

wrp: warp

xol: "x" on label

Some notes on the pricing

The prices listed in here were determined from many sources.

The more common items reflect a consensus of used record shops and collectors, plus prices in ads and online over the past few months. In some ways, these items are more difficult to get a handle on; they sell without much publicity because of their low value, thus they aren't reported as often.

The rarer items are often the matter of conjecture because they so rarely come up for public sale. A high auction price for a truly rare piece can be the only way such an item's "worth" can be gauged, no matter what someone says about the value being inflated. Records, as with all collectibles, are only worth what someone will pay for them.

Because of the inexact nature of this undertaking, that's why we always urge you to use a book such as this as a guide and not as the final word on pricing.

We, too, can always use more input on the subject. See the **How you can help** section for more information.

And by the way, the publisher of the book does not engage in the buying and selling of records. So the prices listed in here should not be construed as "offers to buy" or "offers to sell" from Krause Publications.

Some notes on promotional records

To list every promotional version of every album in this book would be a consumption of space better used for unique listings. It would come close to doubling the length of the book. Some selected promos are listed, either because they are unique – in other words, the only version of the album is promotional – or because there is a significant, verifiable price difference between the promo and stock copies.

That said, however, we have noticed in recent years a growth in the collectibility of certain promo albums, especially of hit albums. I've heard of cases where promo versions of, say, Carole King's *Tapestry* or

Ted Nugent's *Cat Scratch Fever* have gone for twice as much as the stock copy!

Not all promos are created equal, however.

It's probably easier to say which promotional copies are *not* going to fetch that kind of premium. Those are copies that are otherwise identical to stock copies – the same label, the same number, the same everything – but are merely stamped on the front or back cover with (usually) a gold "For Promotional Only" indicator. There's nothing special about these records for the most part; any time the record company wants to create a promo, it can take a stock copy and gold-stamp it!

These are known as "designate promos" and rarely get more than 10 percent above the price of a regular stock copy, if that. For some sought-after rare items, such as Tori Amos' early album *Y Kant Tori Read*, designate promos go for much, much less than copies not so designated.

Some albums that appear to be "designate promos" do have collector value. These are copies pressed on special "audiophile vinyl," the most notable of which are the "Quiex II" pressings from the Warner-Reprise-Geffen family. Some of these fetch as much as 4-5 times the regular editions! These will *always* be marked on the cover with a sticker advertising the "Quiex II" record within. Capitol also did some promo-only audiophile vinyl, which is distinguishable because it altered the covers on most of these. Elektra did some in the late 1980s also, most notably on a couple 10,000 Maniacs albums. These could become more collectible as their presence becomes more known.

Other promos of little collector value are those with a hole punch in the corner. This was Capitol's preferred method of creating promos during much of the 1970s. These are never worth more than the stock copy, and usually go for less.

Also, Columbia for a time merely used a "timing strip" on the front or back cover to designate a promo; these, too, also have little extra value above the stock copy. There is a major exception, though: The earliest promos for Bruce Springsteen's *Greetings From Asbury Park, N.J.* included both an attached timing strip *and* a glossy 8-1/2 x 11 "Bruce Springsteen Fact Sheet" glued to the back cover along the top. By the way, no white-label promos were ever pressed of this title.

Promos that *do* attract interest are those with custom promotional labels. Most of the time, these are white versions of the regular label, thus the term "white label promo." Of course, the label isn't always white; sometimes it's yellow or blue or pink or some other color. But it will always have as part of the label typesetting, "Promotional Copy" or "Audition Copy" or "Demonstration" or some other such term. Sometimes, the label will be almost identical to the stock versions, but some sort of words alluding to the promotional nature of the record will have been added to the typeset copy.

What makes these promos special? They are far more likely to have been mastered from the actual master mixdown tape, rather than a several-generations-removed copy, thus making them of higher sonic quality than later editions. They are among the first to come off the presses – after all, promos get sent out before stock copies Sometimes they are specially mastered to sound better over the air or through a store's loudspeakers. Regardless, they are sought after, and their value ranges from the same as a stock copy to as much as twice that of a stock copy.

Some notes on imports

If you think adding a lot of promotional listings would make this book unwieldy, think about all the non-U.S. pressings of the albums in this book!

(First, a clarification. In the 1980s, it was not uncommon for American record companies, especially independent ones such as Enigma, to have their LPs pressed in Canada. In fact, every BMG Direct Marketing, i.e., record club, album pressed after 1987 was made in Canada, and they say so on the jacket. Because these albums were designed to be sold in the U.S., we don't consider them imports.)

Imports first became an attractive collecting area to Americans in the 1970s. As the sales of U.S. albums increased, the quality control decreased, and the record companies seemed not to care. Meanwhile,

overseas, pressings were smaller and done with more care. Often, too, the covers were better and more informative, and the albums had extra goodies not found in the domestic counterparts. With some artists, a record released outside the States might never be released here, or would show up in a radically different form. (Elvis Costello's early catalog is an example.) Import sales have directly led to U.S. releases of several albums, most notably *Cheap Trick At Budokan*, which originally was not going to be released outside Japan!

Most imports, by definition, are scarce. Few other countries have the size of market that the United States does. A "gold" record in other countries requires much fewer sales than the same award in the U.S. Imports manufactured before the 1970s, when they started to appear more often in specialty shops in the States, are almost impossible to find here.

But just because the scarcity is there doesn't mean that the demand is. The collecting market for imports is much smaller than the market for domestic records. It is generally true that, in any given country, most of the collecting interest is in records manufactured and/or marketed in the homeland. That said, though, records from other countries can often bring much more in another country than in the originating country!

As much as a certain minority of readers would like to see them, long listings of imports likely will remain outside the scope of the *Goldmine Record Album Price Guide*.

Making sense of the main listings

We've told you about most of the features in the book. Let's break down a listing to see what a line means.

The artist's name is in bold, all capital letters. They are mostly alphabetized the way our computer did, so blame any things that seem out of order on it. I think we caught most of the way-out things, but if not, let us know and we'll get 'em the next time.

Underneath some artists are cross-references or other information we feel is helpful. Cross-references to other artists in the book are in all capital letters.

Then we have grouped the discographies by record label. Under each record label are individual listings in numerical order, ignoring prefixes. This may result in some things appearing to be way out of order. For example, because they have numbers approximately 6,800 apart, mono and stereo versions of the same albums on Columbia will rarely be adjacent to each other. This is also true of other labels with separate mono and stereo numbering systems, such as Mercury, Liberty, Imperial, London, and many more. However, as the RCA Victor label used the same numbers for mono and stereo, those versions are usually listed next to each other.

Each line starts with a check box, which you can use to keep track of what you have. Then comes the record number. You'll also find the title of the record as best as we can determine (you'd be surprised how often the title differs between the record and the jacket!); the year of release; and the value in Very Good, Very Good-Plus and Near Mint condition.

For many listings, you'll see a letter or two in brackets after the record number. These designate something special about the listing as follows:

B: the album is listed as stereo, but some of the tracks are in mono (the "B" means "both" stereo and mono)

DJ: some sort of promotional copy, usually for radio stations, and not meant for public sale

EP: a 12-inch extended play album, usually with only four to six tracks. It normally is no more than half the length of a regular album. Rarely used to describe 12-inch records until the 1980s; before that, it refers to similar 7-inch records.

M: mono record (all 12-inch albums released either in mono only or in both mono and stereo before 1968)

P: the album is listed as stereo, but only part of it is "true" two-channel stereo

PD: picture disc (graphics actually appear as part of the record; these were popular in the late 1970s to early 1980s and, for some artists, are their only valuable albums today)

Q: quadraphonic record (mostly from the years 1972-76, these were usually remixed, sometimes radically, to play on systems with four separate speakers)

R: the album is listed as stereo, but actually is all, or almost all, rechanneled stereo (called "Duophonic" by Capitol or "Enhanced for Stereo" or "Simulated Stereo" by Decca); these almost always are less sought-after than the same material in "true mono"

S: stereo record (again, when the record was pressed both in mono and stereo). If we're not sure of an album's "true" stereo content, or if we know an album is all, or almost all, true stereo, we use "S."

10: a 10-inch album, most of which are from the early years of LPs, 1948-54, and quite difficult to find in top condition

(x) where x is a number: the number of records in a set

Finally, some items have lines in italics following them. That defines something about the item listed above, such as who also is on the record, or a color of label or vinyl.

Making sense of the listings in back

Because of the nature of these items, we've used a slightly different format for the four sections that appear after the letter Z. These four sections are "Original Cast Recordings," "Soundtracks," "Television Albums" and "Various Artists Collections."

Within each category, these are arranged alphabetically by the title of the release, again as our computer did them, and ignoring the words "A," "An" or "The." The exception is if the title begins with a number. Computers have this nasty tendency to put these first, before things beginning with "A." We've moved them to where they would be if the number were spelled out. For example, if an album begins with the number "10," we moved it as if it were actually "Ten."

Underneath each title are the applicable releases, arranged alphabetically and numerically by label. Those lines start with a check box, then are followed by the label and number listed together; any applicable abbreviations in brackets (which are the same as in the rest of the book – M for mono, S for stereo, etc.); the year of release; and the prices in three grades of condition.

The Wild, Wild Web: The online market

Among the many sources for pricing used in this book, this is the first record collecting price guide we know of that uses online set sales and auction results as a source. We do so with some trepidation, as some weird things can happen online that don't happen "in real life." But it's become too important a vehicle for selling to ignore anymore.

A dealer from New York raves about the stuff he can move online that just sits in his store – often for much higher prices than he can get in his store, if it ever sells them at all without a discount. In searching the results of LP auctions on the best-known of the auction sites, eBay (www.ebay.com), some albums that certain dealers have for $10 in their catalogs have gone for over $100 at auction! So who's right?

Online selling seems to draw two widely different audiences. One is very much the same audience as a stand-alone record store, except on a global scale rather than a regional one. Browsers who know next to nothing about record collecting and the relative scarcity of the listed pieces are common. These are people who can sometimes be fooled into paying too much for a common piece, especially certain million-selling compact discs, because of three magic letters: "OOP," short for "out of print." Just because something's out of print doesn't mean it has vanished off the face of the earth!

The other audience drawn to online sales are the hyper-specialists, and this is often where items can justifiably go for much larger sums than in a retail store. Thanks to search engines on most of the better sites, a fan of, say, Garth Brooks can type in the words "Garth Brooks" and find nothing but the Garth Brooks-related material. People who specialize in one artist will usually pay more – sometimes a *lot* more – than someone who collects a more broad range of artists. But because they are specialists, they also know which items are common, so they don't get taken on the easy stuff.

Remember that album I mentioned earlier that went for $100 online that I'd seen in a dealer's catalog for $10? That album was the obscure 1986 Columbia release by country singer Marty Stuart. (The vinyl version, too, not the CD.) It's hard to know whether every Marty Stuart fan would pay that much for it if they could find it, but two of them got into a bidding war over it, thus the $100 price tag. (No, I didn't value it at $100 in this book, though I considered it. Just be alerted that it *has* sold for that much and it could again.)

I have bought records over the web, and have yet to have significant problems. It's faster than "snail mail" and less expensive than a long-distance telephone call. But it's not perfect. Just as in real life, it pays to be wary.

As a seller, you are reaching a larger audience than you would in a record collecting magazine, but also a much less targeted one. The Internet seems to be a good place to sell lower-priced items that might take up valuable space in an expensive print ad. But many more valuable pieces sit or fetch less than they might through more traditional means.

As a buyer, you have to watch out for overgraded, under-described items. Photos of the items help. Also, buying from someone who deals in records as a primary area rather than as an obvious sideline to his/her Beanie Baby business is recommended. Look for dealers with strong feedback ratings; that is a sign of satisfied customers. Also, check for use of something resembling the *Goldmine* grading system. People who say their albums are in "good condition" don't know record collecting, because "good" is a low grade in the world of records (as it is in some other collecting areas, such as coins).

Listing recommended web sites is like trying to catch the wind, as Donovan sang; they come and go and move with alarming frequency. We recommend using a search engine and typing in the words "vinyl records" or "auction" or even the title or artist of the item you may be looking for. Or search the pages of a current *Goldmine* magazine; most of the major dealers advertise, and those who have web sites will list their addresses.

We feel the online world will continue to grow in importance over time. At some point it may become the biggest market for collectible records. So we'll continue to keep an eye on it for future *Goldmine* price guides.

Introducing the counterfeit Beatles

Several albums are the source of constant questions to the *Goldmine* office. Certainly one that brings the most, because some copies of it are extremely rare and valuable, is *Introducing The Beatles*, the debut album on the Vee Jay label.

Today, as was true earlier in Beatles history, the most sought-after version is the so-called "Ad Back" version. The very first printings of this album, made at the dawn of Beatlemania, have a back cover with photos of 25 other Vee Jay albums in lieu of any other liner notes. We list the stereo version of this album at $12,000 in near-mint condition.

A few years ago, the collecting world was sent into a frenzy after a different variation, at the time the only known legitimate copy of this variation, sold for the equivalent of $25,000. Since that time, somewhere between six and 10 copies of this rare variant have been discovered to exist, and the price has dropped to about $8,000 or so in near-mint condition.

The problem is that, superficially, everyone thinks that they have this rare version. It's the pressing of *Introducing The Beatles* with a "STEREOPHONIC" banner across the top of the front cover, and on the back cover, the contents list "Love Me Do" as the last song on side one and "P.S. I Love You" as the first song on side two.

Here's the rub: From the late 1960s to the late 1970s, record stores around the country were flooded with hundreds of thousands of unauthorized reproductions of the album. It used to be easy to know if you had a fake; today, even most of the fakes have been in collections for 20 or more years.

So in the interests of awareness, we'll give you some of the more obvious ways to tell whether that *Introducing The Beatles* you have is an original.

On The Cover: Raise a warning flag if the album claims to be "Stereo" or "Stereophonic" on the cover and has a list of songs on the back that include "Love Me Do" and "P.S. I Love You." This is the most common counterfeit version.

Most authentic front covers don't say "Stereophonic" on them; in the lower right corner they will say "LP 1062." Authentic copies of *Introducing The Beatles* in stereo have always been scarce; they were even scarce in 1964! If your back cover either has ads for other albums, is completely blank, or has a list of songs claiming that "Please Please Me" and "Ask Me Why" are on the record, it's probably authentic.

If your cover has a brown border around the front cover photo, stop right there; it's fake.

If there is no shadow accompanying George Harrison, who is at the far right of the cover photo, you have a fake.

If the cover has a yellow tint and has the word "Stereo" in the upper left, it's counterfeit.

There are some very well-done counterfeit covers; another giveaway is if you have a counterfeit record inside the jacket. Unless someone who owned both put an authentic record into a phony cover (it happens), a phony record implies a phony cover.

On The Record: Let's assume your record passes the first test or has too good a fake cover to be certain. Now, check the record, because this is where the originals stick out from the fakes.

First, does the record say "Stereo" on the label? While some authentic copies say stereo and actually play mono, the reverse is not true. If it doesn't say "Stereo," it's not stereo.

Second, where are the words "Introducing The Beatles" and "The Beatles"? Both real and phony copies have them. But on an authentic copy, the words "The Beatles" are directly underneath "Introducing The Beatles," and both lines are above the center hole. If the center hole separates "Introducing The Beatles" and "The Beatles," it's a counterfeit.

Almost all real copies of the record have some sort of machine stamping in the dead wax, usually the words "Audio Matrix," the letters "MR" in a circle, or the letters "ARP." Some (not all) originals also have a numerical date scrawled in the dead wax (such as 2-12-64). No phonies have any of the above. Also, phonies often will be on flimsy vinyl as opposed to the sturdier 1960s vinyl.

The Play Test: If you're still not sure whether your "stereo" *Introducing The Beatles* is the real thing, put Side 1, Song 1 on your turntable. "I Saw Her Standing There," as well as the next four tracks, will be in clean, crisp, true stereo, with plenty of separation. If the record is mono or very poorly rechanneled stereo, and the record doesn't say "Stereo" on it, it's an authentic mono copy or a phony.

The Who's mis-Leeds-ing packaging

How can I tell that new blood is entering the record collecting field? When things that used to be common knowledge aren't so common anymore.

Several times in the past year, and also on the Internet, I've come across people telling me that they had an intriguing collection of papers, letters and other odds and sods relating to The Who. Each of them thought they had a one-of-a-kind find, and each was wondering what they could be worth.

Those of us who know what this stuff is had to tell the disappointed inquirers that their items are not worth much. All of these "documents" exist hundreds of thousands of times over, although they look convincing enough to fool the novice.

In 1970, the Who released their first legitimate live album, *Live At Leeds*. Even by the standards of the day, it had quite elaborate packaging. The album cover itself was about as simple as it gets: The Decca originals were packaged like an advance press kit, with the album cover opening up into a 12x12 folder. The record, in a brown generic sleeve with a faux handwritten label, was in one of the two flaps inside the package. And in the other flap was an assortment of extremely well reproduced items from all phases of The Who's history. Among them:

■ A contract for the band's appearance at Woodstock;

- A rejection letter from EMI Records to The High Numbers' manager, Kit Lambert, dated "22nd October 1964" (the High Numbers were the early Who);
- A lyric sheet for "My Generation";
- A letter informing the band of the cancellation of a ballroom gig in 1965;
- Notes of the payments for certain gigs.

The album also has a poster and photos, 12 items in all. Also, some copies have a rectangular sticker at the upper left corner of the front cover stating, "It Is The Best Live Rock Album Ever Made… – *The New York Times*."

It is not difficult to find Decca pressings of *Live At Leeds*. Finding one with all the pieces is a different matter entirely. The most likely missing item is the poster, as many consumers took it out of the package to hang it on their wall, thus irreparably separating it from its source. All in all, a near-mint copy of the entire package on Decca can go for $40 or so.

When MCA reissued the album in 1973, after consolidating all its labels (Decca, Kapp and Uni most prominent among them) into one, it deleted all the goodies and packaged the album in a more normal LP cover. So for more than 20 years, the *Live At Leeds* package was incomplete. In 1995, the original release was expanded to twice its prior length on a CD reissue; early pressings came in a 12x12 box that reproduced all the goodies that had been in the original LP, at full size no less, not postage-stamp CD size.

So no, these contracts and things are not a rare find. Presumably, the true originals reside wherever The Who keeps such items.

Elvis' Moody Blue: Black is beautiful

Thumb through this book, and you'll notice many rare and valuable albums listed that were released on colored vinyl. Most of the time, colored vinyl issues are, indeed, scarcer and thus more valuable than their black-vinyl counterparts.

But there are exceptions, and the major exception is the colored vinyl album everyone seems to have – Elvis Presley's *Moody Blue* on blue vinyl.

Even before Elvis died August 16, 1977, *Moody Blue* was poised to be his most successful album of new material in some years. The title song, released months in advance of the album, had become Elvis' first No. 1 country song in almost 20 years. The second single, "Way Down," would become his second consecutive No. 1 country hit; it peaked there the week ending August 20, 1977, the *Billboard* issue that was on the stands the week he died.

To help spur sales of the new album, RCA decided to press the first run on blue vinyl. On the shrink wrap, these were called "The Blue Album." The original plan was then to start making *Moody Blue* albums on black vinyl once the blue ones ran out. The gimmick seemed to work: Even before posthumous sales kicked in, the new album had reached No. 21 on the *Billboard* album charts, his highest peaking album since *Aloha From Hawaii Via Satellite* in 1973.

Then Elvis keeled over that fateful Tuesday.

Not long before Presley's death, the first black vinyl versions began to appear on the market. Then RCA made a fateful decision: It chose to resume printing *Moody Blue* on blue vinyl. All the rest of the copies with the number AFL1-2428 were pressed in blue. Thus, what could have been a legitimate collector's item became the most common colored vinyl album in recorded music history.

Moody Blue was eventually certified double platinum for the sales of 2 million copies by the Recording Industry Association of America, though it probably sold even more than that. Nearly all the vinyl copies are on translucent blue vinyl.

The *real* collector's item when it comes to Moody Blue, not including some custom-made test pressings in vinyl colors other than blue, is the commercial black vinyl version. In near-mint condition it can go for $200. The blue vinyl? At *most* $10, and that's for a still-sealed copy, unless you can find a sucker.

Collecting stereo classical music: A primer

I get many suggestions from readers, collectors and dealers about the books in the *Goldmine* line. Also, I hear about the ones we haven't done. One of the most requested items is some kind of guide to classical music.

Based on the size of the market, it's tough to see us doing a complete guide to classical records any time soon. What we can do, though, is feature some of the most collectible classical LPs in this album price guide. And that we have done, as there are at least several hundred of the most collectible classical albums listed in this book. That's still a tiny fraction of the entire universe of classical records, most of which trade for no more than the average common pop LP.

In preparing information for this article, I spoke to David Canfield, who is one of the world's leading sources for mail-order classical music. He has, for years, published privately his *Canfield Guide To Classical Recordings*, a massive two-volume set of classical record prices, which are based on the prices he gets in his business. He admits that some big-city dealers can get more than he does for certain classical titles, but his clientele won't pay big-city prices. They will, however, pay good prices when the content warrants. (As with all the prices in this book, the values for classical LPs reflect a variety of sources, not merely Canfield's opinion.)

As with rock, country and other genres, there are many rare and sought-after classical recordings, but the percentage in that category is tiny. "The most collectible American LPs are those with recognized musical value that didn't sell very well," Canfield says. "It's a small handful that can bring big money."

The ones that get the most attention, those that even most casual collectors at least have a passing notion about, are the early stereo albums on RCA Victor, Mercury and London. Audiophiles who are classical music buffs have long lusted after the earliest pressings of these albums; at the same time, most popular and rock collectors had no idea of the rarities they were passing up. Most important to these collectors, they sound incredible on a great stereo system. They sound good even on an average system.

The RCA Victor albums are usually called "shaded dogs." That's because of the dark red area behind the Nipper logo on these otherwise bright red labeled albums. The rarest of these have been known to bring hundreds of dollars; a couple have crossed the $1,000 mark. The mystique of some of these is so great than an entire record company was started specifically to reissue the rarest and most musically important of these on brand-new, 180-gram vinyl editions. That label is called Classic Records, and their new LP versions of the original RCA Victor "shaded dogs" have received generally (though not universally) favorable reviews.

To identify the first editions of these records, look for the words "LIVING STEREO" at the bottom of the label. The earliest stereo LPs will also have these words in a one-inch banner across the top of the front jacket. To really get picky, look in the trail-off wax at the stamper numbers. The closer they are to ending in "1S," the more desirable they are. A "1S" pressing on both sides of a Living Stereo shaded dog is a classical audiophile's dream album! Remember, too, that near-mint albums are even more important here than usual.

The "shaded dog" era lasted from 1958 to about 1963. That year, RCA introduced its so-called "Dynagroove" system, which received savage reviews from the audiophile magazines of the day and ended the "golden age of stereo."

At the same time as the RCA "shaded dogs" came the "Mercury Living Presence" series. These, too, are renowned for their sound. Original pressings of this series continued to emerge until at least the mid-1960s. The first editions of the labels will be a deep, dark red with the word "Mercury" along the top, standing alone. The 1958-63 era originals will NOT have a notation on the label stating "Vendor: Mercury Record Corporation." This line was added around 1963.

The most sought-after of this series is an album called *Hi-Fi A La Española* by the Eastman-Rochester "Pops" Orchestra conducted by Frederick Fennell (SR 90144). If you don't want to pay the $1,000 or so a near-mint original could set you back, Classic Records has reissued this

for about $30 – although that reissue will soon be out of print, too, if it isn't already.

Early classical London stereo albums were leased from the British Decca label, which also has a sterling reputation among audiophiles. The original early stereo U.K. pressings on Decca are highly collectible, though outside the scope of a book such as this that focuses mostly on American issues. The first pressings of these London stereos have a light blue back cover rather than the usual white, thus they are known as "blue backs" among audiophiles.

The vast majority of the classical albums covered in this book are of the early stereo variety. We've included extensive listings of RCA Victor "shaded dogs" and Mercury Living Presence albums. We hope in the future to add some London "blue back" listings and other assorted classical albums that have verifiable collector interest.

To keep the book consistent, these are listed by artist (usually the orchestra name) rather than by their label.

By the way, you may have noticed that we focused on stereo albums. The reason is that most of the mono versions of the above RCA Victor and Mercury albums have little collector value. Unless they do, we don't list the mono versions.

One word of warning: Classical record collecting is a highly specialized and rather small collecting area, just as the audience for classical music radio, concerts and current CDs is. Even though certain classical albums can go for three and four figures, it can take a lot more work to get that kind of sum than it will for, let's say, a Beatles *Yesterday And Today* butcher cover. Although who knows – maybe just by shedding some light on the most sought-after titles, the demand for them will increase. Most of these albums contain fine music and performances worthy of greater exposure.

For more information on the *Canfield Guide To Classical Recordings*, you can contact Canfield at Ars Antiqua, 3378 Disc Drive, Elletsville, IN 47429. You can also call him at (812) 876-6553. The newest edition, the fifth, of his classical music guide (the last edition cost $79.95, so be prepared) should be ready by the time you read this.

How you can help

Conservatively speaking, this book has between 35,000 and 40,000 listings by thousands of artists. All of this information is located in a growing database of records, which will make both future price guides and *Goldmine* magazine better products in the long run.

But as you look through this first *Goldmine Record Album Price Guide*, you'll see that we need help in several areas. Certain parts of this book aren't as good as they could be, and we know you can help.

Remember, as we told you in the beginning, **this book is not, nor is it meant to serve as, a discography book.** If an artist's complete discography appears, it is by happenstance, not by design! Because we list only those albums that have a near-mint value of $20 or more, a lot of common albums have been omitted. Do not, I repeat, do not, tell us about these – we know about them! You will be wasting both your time and ours.

If an album from the 1960s, 1970s and 1980s is not listed, and it's by a major artist on a major label, it's probably common, and unless demand for it increases, it isn't going to be listed in here. As we said earlier, please check the *Standard Catalog Of American Records 1950-1975* for this information. If it's missing from *there*, then let us know.

Given the above, here's the kind of information we can use to make future editions better:

Late mono LPs. In 1967 and 1968, record companies somewhat abruptly stopped making monaural albums. Some of the mono albums are quite rare now. We're interested in what might exist that we don't have listed. We're also interested in deleting listings of mono albums that really don't exist.

Private label LPs. In the process of researching this book, we came upon listings for many private label albums. These usually fit in the categories of garage, psychedelic, progressive or punk; all of these, by definition, are rare, and many are highly collectible. As we couldn't confirm the existence of every such LP title we came upon, we can use help with adding more titles, and appropriate pricing, to the list.

Some of the private-label records we *do* list are members of the $1,000 Club. We'd like to know more about those, too, so we can accurately describe them to the collector. If you have any of these, or you've heard them, or you're an expert in the field, we'd like to hear from you.

Pop albums of the 1950s. We list a lot of albums by non-rock performers of the 1950s that you won't find in any other price guide. But we're sure that we didn't find them all. These are definitely an exception to the above rule about unlisted albums. If, for example, you have a 1950s album by Doris Day or Percy Faith or Vaughn Monroe that's not listed – say, we list two different numbers but it falls in between them – we *do* want to know about that. Especially if it's an early 10-inch album. (That is, one record with four or so songs on each side, not four records with one song on each side. The latter are 78s and outside the scope of this book.)

The Folkways label. Perhaps the most confusing American record label ever was Folkways. It used a dizzying array of prefixes and numbering systems, usually simultaneously and seemingly with little rhyme or reason. Not only that, to this day, every song ever issued on the label is in print, either on compact disc or via a cassette copy recorded from the original, which can be done for a fee.

Much music of lasting value, both historically and to collectors, was issued on Folkways, but we have found no reliable sources that tell us about label variations, cover variations or other things that help determine collectibility. For example, the label was at one time under the aegis of Scholastic Book Services. We know nothing about how those editions differ from earlier ones, if at all. We'd love more information on this very important label. (And please don't steer us to the Smithsonian Folkways web site – we've been there. It's excellent for what it is, but we need more.)

American pressings meant for other markets. Just as some albums on the London label proudly claim to be "Made in England," even though they were meant for sale in the United States, the opposite is true of some albums meant for sale overseas. Though sold in places like England and Germany, they will say on the labels "Made in U.S.A." We need to know more about these.

On a related subject, we found out quite by accident a few years ago that some labels made special, often unique, compilations that were meant for sale only on military bases overseas. (The At Ease label, manufactured by ABC in the 1970s, was one such imprint.) We'd like to know more about these American albums, too.

And finally, some of the larger American record companies had (and still have) separate divisions that market Spanish-language music to areas with large Hispanic populations, both in the United States and in Latin America. Most of these albums, too, are U.S. pressings, on labels such as CBS International, and some of these can be highly collectible. (Check the listings for Miami Sound Machine.) We can use more information on this little-known area of album collecting.

Photos. Sending us photos, photocopies or computer scans of items helps us, as these serve to prove the existence of the item in question.

We hope that future editions of this, and all, *Goldmine* price guides can have some cool photos of rarities. We also can accept computer scans e-mailed to us as attachments or sent on a disc. Some of our photos in this book and others came from computer scans. You can contact us for more information if you think you have something that might be worth putting in a future edition of any of our books.

We receive many contributions and suggestions, so not everyone's help can be acknowledged. But rest assured that even your one little correction helps in the long run.

Anything else of value. Did we miss an album (not including imports) that you know you always sell for $20 or more in mint condition? We'd like to know about that.

You may contact the author by mail:

Tim Neely
Goldmine Record Album Price Guide
700 E. State St.
Iola, WI 54990

or by phone:
(715) 445-2214 or 4612, ext. 782

or by e-mail:
neelyt@krause.com

If you write or e-mail, enclose a daytime phone number or return e-mail where I can reply in case I have any questions.

I can also be reached via fax at (715) 445-4087, but I prefer that you write or call before faxing me any large contributions.

Acknowledgments

Even though only one person's name is on the front cover, a book like this would not have been possible if not for a lot of input from others.

First, at Krause Publications I'd like to thank Greg Loescher, the editor of *Goldmine*, for his continued support of this and other books. He also supplied some album covers from his own collection to add to the ones we'd already received from elsewhere. Also, big kudos go to the Krause proofreading staff and design staff for getting this together and offering helpful suggestions. And, too, thanks to Don Gulbrandsen, books division managing editor, for his patience, which I admit I sometimes tax.

Once again, many of the photos of rare records come to us courtesy of Good Rockin' Tonight, the auction house in California. Four times a year, the company holds auctions of "rare and important" rock 'n' roll, R&B and blues records and memorabilia; call 1-800-531-1899 or e-mail info@goodrockintonight.com.

Others who played a role in getting this price guide together, with listings, corrections from older books and pricing suggestions, include:
- Tom Grosh of Very English and Rolling Stone, Lancaster, Pennsylvania. He never ceases to amaze with the rare material he turns up that no one's ever seen before.
- Gordon Wrubel of Good Rockin' Tonight. Several years ago, before there was yet such a thing as Good Rockin' Tonight,

he gave me a marked copy of a prior *Goldmine* price guide, including some photos of previously unlisted items. Finally, we've added that material to this book.
- Michael Sharritt of Athens, Alabama. Always an enthusiastic contributor, I learn from him often.
- Bill Hamilton of San Diego, California. A big help on pop albums of the 1950s and an encouraging voice during times that I struggle.
- John Beznik of Illinois. For several years, he's been keeping an eye out for interesting albums while serving as a volunteer for the Mammoth Music Mart in Skokie, Ill. I've lost count of the corrections and additions we've been able to make as a result.
- Rick at Quality Vinyl and CD Outlet of South Riding, Virginia. He helped revamp and update the listings and pricing on audiophile pressings.
- David Canfield of Ars Antiqua, Ellettsville, Indiana, for his time and expertise on classical music collecting.

Dozens, if not hundreds, of others, offered a listing here, a correction or addition there, a suggestion somewhere else. You all know who you are; pat yourself on the back for a job well done.

I'd also like to thank all the record companies that still produce, or have resumed producing, vinyl albums, and also to those artists who insist on making it available. Many of these are of the highest quality, and they help keep vinyl alive, not only for aging boomers, but for younger folks just discovering the wonderful world of records. As I write this, a new version of the Beach Boys' classic *Pet Sounds* album has been released – in true stereo, and on 180-gram vinyl!

Thanks, finally, to family and friends – you all know who you are by now – and to God, for making it all possible.

Tim Neely
July 1999

Record Label Identifier

For the most part, the most collectible records are original pressings. Those are the ones that presumably were available at the time the album was first issued.

Of course, not every copy of *Elvis' Golden Records* is created equal, no matter how similar the covers may look from pressing to pressing. Copyright dates on liner notes are meaningless. A 1958 date on the cover can be attached to a pressing from the 1980s!

To tell for sure, you have to know the labels.

As opposed to 45s, which often were deleted quickly and replaced by "golden oldies" reissues, albums could stay in print in covers looking ostensibly the same for years, sometimes decades! With only some superficial differences, the same album cover can contain a copy of *Meet The Beatles!* that was pressed in 1964, 1974 or 1984. The same is true of an album such as *Johnny's Greatest Hits* by Johnny Mathis; it was in print from 1958 until vinyl was phased out. In that time, Columbia went through several different label designs. It's only the originals that are most sought after.

Thus this rough guide to many of the most common and collectible labels.

Eventually, with your help, we'd like this to be even more thorough. Instead of listing label variations by approximate year of changeover, we'd like to nail down exact numbers where a label changed from one to another. Sometimes, because of printing plant overlap, this will not be possible. But the closer we get, the better the guide gets.

We'd also like information on labels we chose to omit this time around, either because we don't know or because the information we do have is confusing.

By the way, this guide does not attempt to delve into the various promotional labels record companies used. Most of the time, though, they are white versions of the labels that were in use at the time. Not every label used promo labels; others used them at some times, but not at all times. Columbia, for example, went through a period in the mid 1970s where it had no white-label promos. (Bruce Springsteen's *Greetings From Asbury Park, N.J.,* for example, was never issued as a white label promo.)

Enough ado, let's go:

A&M
1963-73: Brown label.

1974-86: Silver gray label with fading A&M logo.

1986-end: Black label with white strip through center hole and A&M logo at right.

ABC; ABC-PARAMOUNT
1956-61: Black label, "ABC-Paramount" multi-color logo at top, "A Product of Am-Par Record Corp." in white at bottom.

1962-66: Black label, "ABC-Paramount" multi-color logo at top, "A Product of ABC-Paramount Records Inc." in white at bottom.

1966-67: Possible transition label with "abc" in a white circle at top of label, but not in a multi-colored box.

1967-72: "abc" in a white circle at top of label surrounded by a multi-colored box.

1973: "ABC" in a white triangle spelled out in children's blocks. Very short-lived label. Quickly replaced by 1967-72 label again until another new label was created.

1974-77: Multi-colored (yellow, orange, purple) "target" label with "abc Records" at top of label between two lines.

1977-79: Multi-colored (yellow, orange, purple) "target" label with "abc" in an eighth note at top of label. In 1979, the label was bought by MCA, which gradually replaced ABC albums with MCA pressings.

ABC DUNHILL – See DUNHILL.

ABKCO
Allan Klein's reissue label, albums have light blue labels with a darker blue logo above the center hole.

ABNER
Only three albums came out on Abner, and all three exist on three different labels. One label is black with a logo of a falcon on a glove; the other is maroon with the same logo of a falcon on a glove. Abner records also were released on Vee Jay with the same catalog numbers in Abner jackets.

ACE
1958-62: Black label, silver print.

1962: Dark blue label, white at top, "ACE" in blue oval.

1971 (2020-21): Yellow label, black print.

1975 (2022): Red label, black print.

Custom labels were used on 1007 and 1008.

APPLE
1968-75: Green "Granny Smith" apple label on one side, sliced apple on the other. Some, though not all, albums from 1968-70 had a line of small white print on the sliced side with "A Subsidiary of Capitol Industries, Inc." along the bottom and a tiny Capitol logo. The small print appears only to have been used at one Capitol pressing plant, so two albums could both be originals, yet one will have the "Capitol logo" and the other won't.

1975: "All Rights Reserved" disclaimer added to the label print.

Apple 34001 was originally issued with a red apple label. Custom labels exist on many numbers.

ARGO
Early mono editions had a greenish label, some with gold print, some with silver print, with "ULTRA HIGH FIDELITY" adjacent to the vertical "ARGO." Later mono editions are known to have a silver label with black print or a black label with silver print, also with "ULTRA HIGH FIDELITY."

Early stereo editions have dark blue labels with silver print.

The next label was silver with black print, but without the words "ULTRA HIGH FIDELITY."

The final Argo label (to the end of 1965) was a brown label with a pink and white "ARGO" in an oval at left. The Argo label was replaced by Cadet in 1965.

ARISTA
1975-76 (AL 4001 to 4105?): Light blue label, white Arista logo with "Arista Records" beneath.

1976-77: Light blue label, white Arista logo with "Arista" beneath.

1977-79: Black label, light blue Arista logo, "Arista" underneath.

1979-84: Fading blue label, three-dimensional Arista logo at top, "Arista" at left side of logo slanting upward.

1984-90: Black label, "ARISTA" above multicolor mountain skyline.

1990-end: Black label, "ARISTA" above white mountain skyline.

Custom labels were used on some releases.

ASYLUM
1972-73 (SD 5051 to SD 5066?): White label, "door-in-a-circle" logo at top of label.

1973-84: "Clouds" label. Around 1975, a small "W" (Warner Communications) logo was added to the label print.

1976: Some 45s in this era were issued with a solid blue label with a small "a" at the top. It's unknown if any LPs exist with this label.

1985-end: Split black and yellow label.

Custom labels were used on some releases.

ATCO

1958-61 (33-101 to 33-138): Yellow label with a harp at the upper left

1961-68 mono: Gold and gray label, "AT" to left of center hole, "CO" to right of center hole in white background.

1961-68 stereo (SD 33-139 to SD 33-256): Purple and brown label, "AT" to left of center hole, "CO" to right of center hole in white background.

1969-77: Yellow label, "Atco" logo at left. Earlier labels have a "1841 Broadway" address, later ones have a "75 Rockefeller Plaza" address and add a small "W" (Warner Communications) logo in the small print.

1978-84: Gray label, logo at top.

1985-end: Whitish label, "ATCO" in different colored letters at an angle at top with many smaller "ATCO"s in the background.

ATLANTIC

1950-60 mono: Black label, silver print.

1959-60 stereo: Green label, silver print.

1960: So-called "bullseye" label. Monos have orange, purple and black fan around the center hole and "Atlantic" in orange and purple band at top; stereos have blue and green fan around the center hole and "Atlantic" in blue and green band at top.

1960-61: "White fan logo" issues. Monos were orange and purple, stereos were green and blue. Through the center hole is a white strip; on the right side of the center hole, a white "fan" in a black background can be found.

1961-68: "Black fan logo" issues. The "fan" at right switches to a black logo inside a white box.

1969-end: Red and green label with Atlantic logo at top. Early editions have an "1841 Broadway" address along the lower rim; later on, the address was changed and a small "W" (Warner Communications) logo was added.

Custom labels were used for some releases.

AUDIO LAB

A budget label created by Syd Nathan of King Records, all Audio Lab LPs have blue labels with silver print.

B.T. PUPPY

Black label, silver print, "B.T. Puppy Records" in red at top with cocker spaniel head underneath.

BANG

1966-73 (211-227): Mostly red label, white at top, with "BANG records" gun logo centered in a yellow background.

1974-78 (400-410): Sky blue label with clouds and stylized "BANG" curving around the top.

1979-82 (Columbia distribution): Light brown label, red logo on top.

BARNABY

1970-73 (CBS distribution): Light blue label, treble clef logo at left.

1973 (15007-15008, MGM distribution): White label with line drawing.

1974-79 (4000, 5000, 6000 series, distributed by GRT/Janus): Multicolor label, yellow rim, vinyl record hanging limply from tree.

BEARSVILLE

The label had the same basic design throughout its history; only the distribution changed.

1971: "Distributed by Ampex" at the bottom.

1972-76: "Distributed by Warner Bros. Records" at the bottom.

1976-81: No distribution notice at bottom of label.

1981-82: "3300 Warner Blvd." address added to bottom of label.

BELL

1965-69: Blue label, silver print.

1970-74: Silver label, black print.

BELTONE

Only one album was released on the label, and it is mostly orange with black printing.

BIG TREE

1970-71: Red and yellow label.

1971-74: Red and white label.

1974-76: Light blue and red label.

1976-80: Multicolor label.

BIG TOP

All releases have a black label with silver print.

BLUE THUMB

1969 (first four LPs): Black label.

1969-74 (Gulf & Western distribution): Off-white, almost gray label, with blue thumb print at upper left.

1974-end: Multi-colored (yellow, orange, purple) "target" label with "abc Blue Thumb" at top of label between two lines and a blue thumb print at upper left.

BLUESVILLE

1960-63: Bright blue label with silver print.

1964-end: Lighter blue label with Prestige trident logo at right side.

BLUESWAY

1967-68: Blue label.

1968-74: Black label, blue rim around outside.

BROTHER

1967 (9001): Brown label with large horseman and "Brother records" at top.

1970-75: Light yellow label, yellow rim around outside, "A Licensee of Warner Bros. Inc." at bottom.

1976-78: Same as 1970-75, but print changes to "A Division of Warner Bros. Records Inc."

BRUNSWICK

1950-63: Black label, silver print.

1963-72: Black label, color band through center, "A Division of Decca Records" in fine print.

1972-end: Black label, color band through center, "Manufactured by Brunswick Record Corp." along rim.

BUDDAH

1967-72: Multi-color kaleidoscope label with black drawing of Buddha at bottom and "BUDDAH RECORDS" on either side of drawing.

1972-76: Maroon label with smiling Buddha figure, "BUDDAH RECORDS" in white at top.

1977-end: Black label with Arista logo added at bottom.

BUENA VISTA

Best known as the label of Annette, it actually predates her hits slightly.

The first series was BV-1300; these have turquoise labels with silver print.

The BV-3300 series, where the Annette records are, were first issued with a black label, silver print. Later ones were issued with a half black, half mostly yellow label with a slight rainbow effect, "Buena Vista" in black over the yellow section.

The BV-4000 series was a continuation of the Disneyland WDL-4000 series (see Disneyland listing for more detail). 4022-4025 were

originally issued on black labels, silver print; 4026-4048 first came out on the half black, half yellow label mentioned in the BV-3300 series.

The 1980s issues in the 62000 series have a blue and red label with a white strip just above the center hole that goes through the middle of the center hole. The "Buena Vista" logo is in red at the upper left.

CADENCE

1954-61 (1000 series, 3000-3051?, 4000s, 5000s, 25000 series to 25051?): Maroon lower two-thirds of label; upper third is silver with "cadence" in lowercase and a metronome logo.

1961-64 (3052?-3068, 25052?-25068): Red label, black rim with "CADENCE RECORDS" inside in white.

CADET

Cadet replaced the Argo label in 1965. Many Argo titles were reissued in Argo covers with Cadet labels.
The first label was an all light blue label with "CADET" across the top in black.

The second label was a fading blue label with "CADET" across the top in fading red, white and blue letters.

1971-end (50000 and 60000 series, GRT distribution): Yellow label, red rim, horizontal red stripe through center hole, "CADET" at left.

CADET CONCEPT

All issues have a gray label with black print, "CADET" in pink, "CONCEPT" in orange (red).

CAMDEN – See RCA CAMDEN.

CAMEO

1958 (1001): Black label, brown print, cameo at top.
1958-60 (1002-1007?): Orange label, black print, cameo at top.
1960-68: Red and black label, white cameo in yellow border at left.
1968 (20,000): Purple label, white at top, "Cameo" across the top in an arc, cameo logo inside "o."

CANADIAN-AMERICAN

1959-61 (1001-1005?): Black label, silver print.
1961-65 (1006?-1018): Black label, five color bars across top of label.

CAPITOL

As you might gather, Capitol is at times a confusing label. For now, we're sticking to the regular pop series in this label roundup. Especially in the 1980s, the budget labels used different color schemes; for now, we're ignoring them, but we do appreciate more information.

1949-54 (10-inch albums, most with "H" prefix): Purple label with silver print. Some labels have a silver ring near the outer rim, some do not. Also, some exist with a red label and gold print and/or an "L" prefix.

1954-58 (12-inch mono albums): Turquoise label, with or without silver ring near outer rim. Some albums were issued with a gray label. There doesn't seem to be much rhyme or reason as to which releases have turquoise labels and which have gray, so in the listings we don't distinguish them.

1958-59 (mono and stereo, approx. 1021-1225): Black label, rainbow ring around outside rim (usually called the "black colorband label") with white Capitol logo and "Long Playing High Fidelity" at the left of the label.

1959-62 (mono and stereo, approx. 1226-1660?): Same as 1958-59, except a white line replaces the words "Long Playing High Fidelity."

1962-68 (approx. 1660-2999): Black colorband label, Capitol logo moved to top of label.

1968-69 (approx. 101-200s in new numbering system): Black colorband label, Capitol logo at top, with extra print along the edge of the colorband "A Subsidiary of Capitol Industries, Inc." added to "Mfd. By Capitol Records Inc."

1969-71 (200s into the 700s?): Lime green label, "Capitol" at upper left, new Capitol "target" logo at top.

1971-72 (700s into early 11000s): Red label, "Capitol" at upper left, purple Capitol "target" logo at top. Sometimes assumed to be a country label only, it was used on all Capitol releases for this short period.

1972-78 (Early 11000s into 11800s): Orange label, "Capitol" in greenish letters across bottom of label. Some issues geared toward the R&B market have a red label with "Capitol" in black letters across the bottom.

1978-83 (11800s into 12200s): Purple label with huge white "Capitol" logo dominating the top third of the label.

1983-88: The black colorband label, logo at top, returns, except that the perimeter print is in black, inside the color ring, instead of outside it in white as in the 1960s.

1988-present: Purple label with much smaller Capitol logo at top of label and a long ring of unbroken type around the outer rim.

Custom labels were used on many titles, and especially from 1978 to the present, older labels were often used out of sequence to create a nostalgic feel.

CAPRICORN

1970: Yellow Atco label with "Capricorn Series" at bottom.
1970-71: Pink label.
1972-74: Plain tan label, "CAPRICORN RECORDS" across the top.
1975-78: Light brown label, large goat facing right.
1978-end (Polygram distribution): Light brown label, large goat facing left.

CARLTON

All labels are tan with a black "C" around the center ring and a white strip to the right with a black "Carlton" in it.

CASABLANCA

1974 (9000 series): Dark blue label with Bogart mug and "Manufactured and Distributed by Warner Bros. Records Inc." in white along the bottom.

1974-76 (7000-7020s): Dark blue label with Bogart mug, "Manufactured and Distributed by Casablanca Records Inc." in white along the bottom.

1976-77 (7020s-7050s?): Tan label, desert scene at top, "Casablanca" at top.

1977-81 (7050s?-7100s): Tan label, desert scene at top, "Casablanca Record and FilmWorks" at top.

1981-end (7100s into six-digit numbers): "Manufactured and Distributed by Polygram" at bottom.

CHALLENGE

1958-63 mono (600-617): Blue label, silver print, "Challenge" logo in oval at top.

1960-65 stereo (2500-2521): Black label, silver print, "Challenge" logo in oval at top.

1963-65 mono (618-621): Blue-green label, silver print, "Challenge" logo in oval at top.

1966-67 (622-624, 2522-2524): Black label, silver print, "CHALLENGE" in block letters across the top.

1969-end (2000 series): Black label, white coat of arms logo at top, "Challenge" in red.

CHANCELLOR

1958-59 (5001-5003): Pink label, black print.
1959-63 (5004-5032): Black label, silver print, "Chancellor" in red across top of label.

CHECKER

1957-65 (1400s and 2971-2995): Black label, silver print, "CHECKER" at left of center hole in vertical block letters. Some issues

have maroon label with silver print that are otherwise identical to the black label versions.

1965-66 (2996-3001): Light blue label with alternating red and black checkers at top of label.

1966-71 (3002-3017): Fading blue label with "CHECKER" across the top in fading red, white and blue letters.

1971-end (reissues): Blue label, purple rim, purple stripe through center hole, "CHECKER" at left.

CHESS

1956-1963 (1425-1482): Black label, silver print, "CHESS" at left of center hole in vertical block letters. Some issues have blue label with silver print that are otherwise identical to the black label versions. Those few stereo releases in this time had gold labels with black print.

1963-65 (1483?-1500?): Black label, "CHESS" across the top in gold with a four-color knight chess piece in back. This basic label design also exists on a blue label with all-silver print and no four-color graphics.

1965 (1490s): Fading blue label, "CHESS" across the top in all white letters.

1965-71 (1500-1553 and 400 series): Fading blue label with "CHESS" across the top in fading red, white and blue letters.

1971-76 (50000 and 60000 series, later 200, 400 and 700 series): Orange label, light blue rim, light blue stripe through center hole, "CHESS" at left.

1982-89 (8200, 8300, 8400, 8500, 9000 series): Dark blue label, silver print, "CHESS RECORDS" in arc at top, checkerboard motif around lower edge.

CHRYSALIS

1972-77: Green label, red butterfly at lower left, "Chrysalis" in red along bottom.

1977-87: White label fading to blue at bottom, white butterfly at lower left, "Chrysalis" in white along bottom. During this time, distribution changed from independent to the CBS family of labels; reissues of 1300-series albums have a new prefix, usually "PV," and the number "4" before the four digits.

1987-89: White label, colored butterfly at left.

1989-end: Off-white label, different butterfly logo.

CLASS

1957-58 (5001-5002): Black label, silver print.

1959 (5003-5004): Maroon label, silver print.

CO & CE

Three albums came out on this label, two by the Vogues and one by Lou Christie, all in mono only. The labels are yellow with a white hourglass at left.

COED

1960 (901): Yellow label, black print.

1960 (902): Black label, silver print.

1961-63 (903-906): Red label, black and white print.

COLGEMS

1966-67: Red label, white area at top in which "COLGEMS" appears in red, "TM of Colgems Records" appears underneath the top logo.

1967-70: Same as above, "TM of Colgems Records" is deleted.

COLPIX

1958-62?: Gold label, "COLPIX" in red curving around top of label with line drawing of Statue of Liberty underneath.

1962?-64?: Gold label, strip of movie film with "COLPIX RECORDS" in white background within.

1964?-66?: Light blue label, strip of movie film with "COLPIX RECORDS" in light blue background within.

1966 (4001, stereo only): Dark blue label, silver print, no strip of movie film.

COLUMBIA (pop)

Another long and storied label, its history is less confusing if you break it into its pop and "Masterworks" divisions. The below only apply to pop (GL, CL, CS series before 1970, prefixes ending in "C" after 1970) releases.

10-Inch LPs:
1948-54 (6000 series): Maroon label, gold print, "Long Playing" at bottom.

1955 (10-inch LPs, 2500 House Party Series): Red and black label with six white "eye" logos, three at left, three at right.

12-Inch Mono LPs:
1951-53 (501-525): Black label, silver print, "Long Playing" at bottom. Originals have a "GL" prefix.

1953-55 (525-600s): Maroon label, gold print, "Long Playing" at bottom.

1955-62 (600s-no earlier than 1779): Red and black label with six white "eye" logos, three at left, three at right.

1962-65 (1780?-2300s): Red label, "COLUMBIA" in white along the top, "GUARANTEED HIGH FIDELITY" in black along bottom.

1965-68 (2300s-2800s): Red label, "COLUMBIA" in white along the top, "360 SOUND MONO 360 SOUND" in white along the bottom.

12-Inch Stereo LPs:
1958-62 (8000-no earlier than 8579): Red and black label with six white "eye" logos, three at left, three at right, "STEREO FIDELITY" in white along the bottom.

1962-63 (8580?-unknown): Red label, "COLUMBIA" in white along the top, "360 SOUND STEREO 360 SOUND" in black along bottom, no arrows.

1963-65 (range unknown): Red label, "COLUMBIA" in white along the top, "360 SOUND STEREO 360 SOUND" in black along bottom, arrows added to left of first "360" and right of second "SOUND."

1965-70 (9100s-9999, CS 1000 series, 30000-30050?): Red label, "COLUMBIA" in white along the top, "360 SOUND STEREO 360 SOUND" in white along the bottom.

1970-90: Orange label, gold "COLUMBIA" six times in ring along outer edge.

1990-present: Red label, "COLUMBIA" in white along top, all other label print in black.

Custom labels were used for some releases.

COLUMBIA MASTERWORKS (classical, shows)

Before 1970, classical releases had an "ML" or "MS" prefix; movie and stage play releases had "OL" and "OS" prefixes (sometimes with a "K" before the first two letters).

10-Inch LPs:
Two different labels exist: Some have a green label, gold print, "Long Playing" at bottom, and others have a dark blue label, gold print, "Long Playing" at bottom.

12-Inch Mono LPs:
1948-54 (4001-?): Dark blue label, gold print, "Long Playing" at bottom. Some also have green labels with gold print and "Long Playing" at bottom.

1955-62: Gray and black label with six white "eye" logos, three at left, three at right.

1962-65: Gray label, "COLUMBIA" in white along the top, "GUARANTEED HIGH FIDELITY" in black along bottom.

1965-68: Gray label, "COLUMBIA" in white along the top, "360 SOUND MONO 360 SOUND" in white along the bottom.

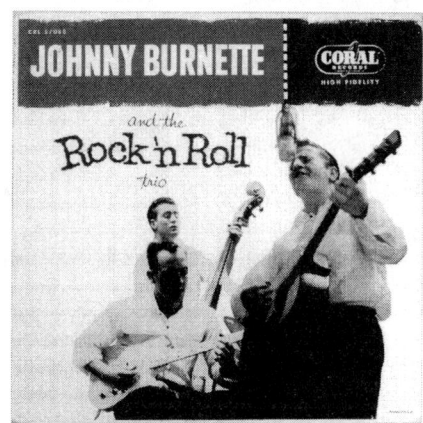

12-Inch Stereo LPs:

1958-62: Gray and black label with six white "eye" logos, three at left, three at right, "STEREO FIDELITY" in white along the bottom.

1962-63: Gray label, "COLUMBIA" in white along the top, "360 SOUND STEREO 360 SOUND" in black along bottom, no arrows.

1963-65: Gray label, "COLUMBIA" in white along the top, "360 SOUND STEREO 360 SOUND" in black along bottom, arrows added to left of first "360" and right of second "SOUND."

1965-70: Gray label, "COLUMBIA" in white along the top, "360 SOUND STEREO 360 SOUND" in white along the bottom.

1970-early 1980s: Olive label, gold "COLUMBIA" six times in ring along outer edge.

Later variations include the "COLUMBIA" being replaced by "CBS," a large "FM" on labels, a special label for digital recordings, and a green label with "CBS" around the outer rim in white. By the end of the 1980s, no more vinyl was coming out in this series. Today this label is known as Sony Classical.

COLUMBIA SPECIAL PRODUCTS (CSP)

Late 1950s-1970: Red label, black strip curving along the top of the label, "COLUMBIA SPECIAL PRODUCTS" in white over the black.

1971-82?: Orange label, "CSP" in yellow at top of label, "COLUMBIA SPECIAL PRODUCTS" in smaller print beneath.

1982?-early 1990s: Orange label, "CBS SPECIAL PRODUCTS" in three lines to the left of the center hole.

Early 1990s: Orange label, "Sony Music Special Products" in two lines to the left of the center hole.

CORAL

1950s-1963: Maroon label, silver print.

1963-68: Black label, rainbow ring near center, "A Subsidiary of Decca Records" in fine print.

1968-70: Black label, rainbow ring near center, "A Division of MCA Records" in fine print.

COTILLION

1969-72: Grayish label, "Cotillion" in box at top.

1976-80s: Reactivated label; purple with a round "C" logo at top.

CROWN

This was a budget label. It began by putting some rare R&B and blues sides on LP, but eventually its issues became cheesier and cheesier.

1950s-60: Black label, gold or silver print. Some of the early Crown titles also exist on red vinyl.

1960-mid 60s: Gray label, black print.

Mid 60s-late 60s: Black label, each letter of "CROWN" in a different color.

DAKAR

1969-70 (9000s): Black label with wide rainbow colorband along the edge.

1972-76 (76900s): White label, black print.

DECCA

1949-54 (10-inch LPs in the 5000 series plus 12-inch LPs in the 8000 series): Black label, gold print. Earliest pressings have a "DLP" prefix, which was quickly replaced by "DL."

1954-60 (later 10-inch LPs and 12-inch LPs from around 8100 to 8981): Black label, silver print. Stereo pressings, which added a "7" to the mono number, had maroon labels with silver print.

1960-66 (4000-4830s, 74000-74830s): Black label with rainbow stripe through center hole and "Mfrd. By Decca Records" in the fine print.

1967-71 (4830s to end of mono, 74830 into some 75000s and 79000s): Black label with rainbow stripe through center hole and "A Division of MCA" in the fine print.

1972-73: Black label with rainbow stripe through center hole and "Mfrd. By MCA" in the fine print.

In addition to the regular series, Decca had a "Gold Label Series" of classical music; these have gold labels with black print.

MCA merged Decca, Uni and Kapp in January 1973 and closed down all three.

DEL-FI

1959 (1201): Light blue, black printing, blue circles on a black background around the outside of the label.

1959 (1202-1204): Light blue label, gold and black diamonds around the outside of the label.

1959-64 (1205-1249): Black label, blue and gold diamonds around the outside of the label.

DERAM

The basic label is white at the bottom, brown at the top with "DERAM" in white letters over the brown background.

DIONN

The only album on this label has an orange label with black print.

DISNEYLAND

One of the most confusing labels out there. Albums were issued in several numerical series, sometimes simultaneously.

The first LPs on the label were in the WDL-4000 series. Early pressings have yellow labels and black print with "A Disneyland Record" underneath the center hole. Later editions have red labels with silver print and "Disneyland" in an arc above the center hole.

The WDL-3000 series came next. 3001 was issued with the above yellow label; it was reissued, and all others had their original issue, with a purple label, silver print, and "Disneyland" along the upper edge of the label.

Next were the ST-3900 series. Original editions were issued with purple labels, silver print. Some were reissued in the 1970s with a yellow label, a rainbow band curving along the top edge and "Disneyland" in white on the rainbow.

The next series was in the ST-1900 range. Original editions of these have light blue labels with black print; some later originals and first reissues have a darker blue label; the final reissues have green labels. The next, and most common, series was the DQ-1200 and 1300 series. Original issues have yellow labels with black print, "Disneyland" curving along the top. Reissues from the 1970s and 1980s have the yellow rainbow label and usually omit the "DQ."

A 1970s and 1980s line was the 2500 series; all of these come with the yellow rainbow label.

Further clarifications are welcome.

DOLTON

1959-62: Light blue label, dark blue print with fish logos at left of center hole.

1962-65: Darker blue label, multicolor fish logo to the left of the center hole.

1966-68: Mostly black label, blue section to left of center hole with stylized red-and-black "D" in white background.

DORE

1960s: Light blue label, feather at top.

1970s: Dark blue label, larger feather on top.

1970s: Black label, multicolor logo.

DOT

1954-56: Maroon label with "Gallatin, Tennessee" in fine print. A possible transition label, maroon with "Hollywood, Cal." in fine print, may exist. (45s exist with this label.)

1956-68: Black label, multicolored cursive "Dot" logo at top.

1968-70: Black label, both "DOT" and Paramount logos appear at top of label.

1971-74: Purple and orange label, "DOT" in box at top of label.

1974-75: Multi-colored (yellow, orange, purple) "target" label with "abc Dot Records" at top of label between two lines.

1976-77: Multi-colored (yellow, orange, purple) "target" label with "abc Dot" at top of label between two lines.

DUKE

1955 (70): Yellow and purple label, "DUKE" in yellow on purple background.

1957-62 (71-75): Yellow and purple label, "DUKE" in yellow on purple background, purple stripe around the outside of the yellow part of the label.

1963-70 (76-92): Orange label, fading to yellow toward the center hole.

1970s (reissues): Green label.

DUNHILL

1965-68 (50000-50030s): Black label, "DUNHILL" in white with gold border at top.

1968-72 (50030s-50170s): Black label, "DUNHILL" and "abc" in multi-colored boxes at top.

1973: "DUNHILL" in a white rectangle spelled out in children's blocks. Very short-lived label. Quickly replaced by 1968-72 label again until another new label was created.

1974-75: Multi-colored (yellow, orange, purple) "target" label with "abc Dunhill" at top of label between two lines.

ELEKTRA

1950s: White label with "electron" logo.

Late 1950s-1961?: Gray label, small guitar player at top.

1961?-1966?: Gold label, large guitar player at top.

1966-69: Gold (tan) label with large stylized "E" at top.

1969-70: Red label with large stylized "E" at top.

1971-74: Dark greenish label with butterfly holding white stylized "E" at left, "13 Columbus Circle" address along outer edge.

1975-79: Lighter greenish label with butterfly holding white stylized "E" at left, "W" (Warner Communications) logo added to the fine print.

1980-83: Red label, small white stylized "E" logo at top.

1984-89: Black and red label, "ELEKTRA" across top.

1989-91: Gray label.

1991-present: Tan label.

Custom labels were used for some releases.

EMBER

1958 (100, 200, 300, 400): Red label, black print.

1959 (401, reissues of earlier titles): White label, black print, eight circles around the outside of the label. The word "EMBER" is depicted in burning logs.

1960s (reissues): Black label, silver print.

1960s (800 series): Black label, "EMBER" logo at left with red flames emanating from it.

END

All End LPs (301-316) were issued with a gray label, a front end of a dog at top left, the back end of a dog at top right, and "end" in red letters. The words "A Product of End Music Inc., New York, N.Y." is at the bottom.

Reissues have the same basic label design, but "A Division of Roulette Records, Inc." is the new fine print.

Still later reissues have a light blue label with an orange band through the center hole and the word "END" in blue on either end of the band.

ENJOY

The only album issued on this label has a gold label with blue print.

ENTERPRISE

1967-68 (13-100 series): Blue label, rainbow at top with "Enterprise" in black over the rainbow. These were distributed by Atlantic.

1968-72 (1001-1024, 5000-5002): Black label, "ENTERPRISE" in yellow at top.

1972-74 (1025-1038, 5003-5007, 7501-7510): Black label, "ENTERPRISE" in white directly above center hole, large rainbow-colored stylized "E" above that.

EPIC

1955-62: Yellow label with series of short black lines around the perimeter and "Epic" on top. Some early labels also are gold with a similar design. Stereo issues (1959-62) have the same label but with "Stereorama" above the word "Epic" on the top of the label.

1962-63: Yellow label with "Epic" appearing eight times around the perimeter (mono); yellow label with "Epic Stereo" appearing three times around the perimeter (stereo)

1963-65 (24040s-24160s mono, 26040s-26160s stereo): Yellow label, "A Product of CBS" as part of the fine print.

1965-73 (all later monos, stereos into the 31000s): Yellow label, no "A Product of CBS" at bottom.

1973-79: Orange label with white concentric circles, Epic logo in white at top.

1979-present: Dark blue label, "Epic" in cursive letters across top.

EXCELLO

1960-mid 1960s (8000-8005?): Orange label, blue print.

Mid 1960s-early 1970s: White label, black print, pink and green arrows at top of label.

Early 1970s-1976: Light blue label, "excello" in white background in box.

FAMOUS

A reissue label for Keen material, the label was blue with silver print.

FEDERAL

Early 10-inch albums have all-green labels, "Federal" in silver across the top.

Albums in the 500 series have black labels with silver print and the word "Federal" straight across the top of the label. These are among the rarest and most valuable albums in all of record collecting. Federal albums with green labels and silver top appear to be bootlegs.

FELSTED

All Felsted albums have orange labels with black print.

FIRE

1959-60 (100-101): White label, red print.

1960-62 (102-105): Red label, black print.

FLIP

Two albums, both various artists sets, were released on Flip. Both are blue labels with silver print.

FORUM/FORUM CIRCLE

A budget label that reissued material that first appeared on the Roulette label.

1960 (16000 series): Black label, gold print.

1961-63 (9000 series): Mono issues have maroon labels; stereo issues have red labels.

1964 (Forum Circle series): Mono issues have light blue labels, stereo issues have yellow labels.

FRATERNITY

1950s (1001-1012?): Light blue label.

Early 1960s (1013?-1018?): Red label, black print.

Mid to late 1960s and beyond (1019?-1028): Maroon label, silver print.

FURY

Two albums were issued on this label. Both have yellow labels with black print and a horse-in-a-tornado logo.

GEE

1956-59 (701-704): Red label, black print, "GEE" in large red letters in a black background at top.

1961-62 (705-707): Gray label, "GEE RECORDS" across the bottom.

GEFFEN

1980-85: White label with horizontal pinstripes.

1985-1990s: Black label.

GOLDEN WORLD

One label was issued on this label; it has a yellow label with black print.

GOLDWAX

Only two albums are known to have been released on this label in the U.S. Both are yellow with black print.

GONE

All albums on this label, which had LP releases from 1958-61, have pink and tan labels.

GORDY

1962-67 (901-927?): Purple label, "Gordy" in cursive yellow letters at top superimposed over and oval with the slogan "IT'S WHAT'S IN THE GROOVES THAT COUNT."

1968-1980s (928? forward): Purple label, "GORDY" in purple to left of center hole, yellow wedge going through center hole from left to right.

GUARANTEED

The only album issued on this label has a white label with black print and "GUARANTEED" in red, arc-shaped, at the top of the label.

GUYDEN

Three albums on this label, all with purple labels with silver strip at the top, in which "Guyden Records" appears in purple print next to a torch.

HARMONY

This was Columbia's budget label from the mid 1950s until the early 1970s.

1957-early 1960s: Maroon label, silver print.

Early 1960s-late 1960s: Black label, silver print.

Late 1960s-early 1970s: Brown label.

Early 1970s: Gold label, Harmony logo in red.

HERALD

1955-58 (0100-0111): "Spokes label": Multi-colored spokes emanate from the center hole to the outside. Above the center hole is a yellow trumpet with a yellow banner and "HERALD" in black print.

1960 (1012): Black label, silver print.

1960-62 (1013-1015): Yellow label, silver print.

HICKORY

1960-62 (100-110?): Black label, silver print, "Hickory" slants upward at top of label.

1963-73 (111?-168): Black label, rainbow at upper left.

1973-75 (4501-4524): Brown label, rainbow at upper left, "MGM Records" lion at right of center hole.

1976-77 (44001-44009?): Multi-colored (yellow, orange, purple) "target" label with "abc Records" at top of label between two lines and the "Hickory" logo at left of center hole.

1977-79 (44010?-44017): Multi-colored (yellow, orange, purple) "target" label with "abc" in an eighth note at top of label, and "Hickory" logo to the right of the note.

HIFI

Standard issues had silver labels with "HIFIRECORD" three times around the perimeter. The word "HIFI" was in silver, "RECORD" was in red.

Also see LIFE.

HIP

Four albums came out on this label from 1969-72. The label is red and pink with "Hip" in blue print bordered in black.

HORIZON

The folk music label of 1961-64 issued its mono albums on black labels with silver print (sometimes white print) and its stereo albums on dark blue labels with silver print.

HULL

Exactly three albums came out on this label, all of them highly desirable. Each had a different label thus:

1000: Dark red label, black print.

1001: Light blue label, black print.

1002: Red label, black print, "Hull Records Inc." in gold above the center hole.

IMPACT

Exactly one album was released on Impact. Its label is red with black print.

IMPERIAL

1950-56 (10-inch LPs; 12-inch LPs in the 100 series): Blue label, "IMPERIAL" in script print at top.

1956-57 (9001-9041?): Maroon label, "IMPERIAL" in silver block letters at top.

1957-64 (9042?-9267?, mono): Black label with colored rays emanating from Imperial logo at top.

1959-64 (12001-12267?, stereo): Black label, silver print, with "IMPERIAL STEREO" directly above the center hole. Some of the later 12250-12267 issues had the mono "colored rays" label with the word "Stereo" added.

1964-66 (9268?-9320s?, 12268?-12320s?): Black label, "IR/Imperial" to left of center hole, white area above logo, pink area below logo.

1966-70 (9320s? to end of monos, 12320s?-12457): Black label, "IR/Imperial" logo to left of center hole in white with red background; green areas above and below logo, which has been enlarged.

INTERPHON

Exactly one label came out on this label. It has a light blue label with red logo to the left of the center hole.

INDIGO

Black label, silver print, the word "Indigo" in indigo (purple) and "Records" next to it in blue.

INFINITY (pop)

In business for just over a year (late 1978 to late 1979), it lasted long enough to have two label variations. The earliest LPs have a primarily white label with "optical illusion" logo at the top. Later LPs have a primarily brown label with a slightly different rendering of the optical illusion logo.

ISLAND

Since the label was first set up as a U.S. entity in 1972, it's been distributed by Capitol, independently, by Warner Bros. and Atco (at the same time for different artists!) and PolyGram. The labels have changed even more often than the distribution, and it's possible we missed a variation or two.

1972-74: Sunray label, "ISLAND" along bottom of label in stylized letters.

1974-75: Yellow background on label, "water skier" offshore, "island" along top.

1975-77: Black label with "I" logo at bottom and "Island Records" underneath.

1977-80: Orange and blue label.

1981-82: Light blue label with darker blue ring around the outside.

1982-83: Dark purple label with skyscraper at left and "Island" slanting upward.

1983-84: Light blue label, "Island" in red across top.

1985-90: Black label.

Custom labels were used for some issues.

JAMIE

1958: Yellow label.

1959-67: White and gold label.

1970 (3034): Orange and black label.

JANUS

1970-76 (3000s, early 7000s): Brownish gold label.

1977-78 (later 7000s): Reddish orange label.

JOSIE

The first label was cream colored with blue print and "josie" at the top of the label in a blue oval.

The second label was tan with black print with the "josie" logo in a black oval. The logo sits atop a group of multi-colored stripes emanating vertically from a horizontal white line that goes through the center hole.

The third label was tan with black print, "JOSIE" spelled in five different colors vertically to the left of the center hole.

JUBILEE

1950s (10-inch LPs from 1-25, 12-inch LPs from 1000-1014?): Pink label, black print.

1956-59 (1015?-1104?): Blue label, silver print.

1959-61 (1105?-1121?): Flat black label, silver print, "jubilee" in silver spiked oval at top of label.

1961-64 (5001-5055): Glossy black label, silver print, "jubilee" in large colored spiked oval at top of label.

1965-69 (8001-8031): Glossy black label, silver print, "jubilee" in much smaller colored spiked oval at top of label.

JUDD

The one album on this label has a purple label with silver print.

KAMA SUTRA

1965-69: Yellow label.

1970-71: Pink label.

1972-74: Light blue label, Garden of Eden scene at top.

KAPP

1955-59: Maroon label, silver print. Some issues have a blue label, silver print.

1959-62: Black and blue label with red "K" at top of label and "KAPP" underneath.

1962-64: Black and blue label with white major's hat and "KAPP" underneath.

1964-71: Black label with major's hat and "KAPP" underneath.

1971-73: Orange and purple label.

MCA merged Decca, Uni and Kapp in January 1973 and closed down all three.

Custom labels were used on some issues. For example, there are some early Christmas releases with silver labels and red and green holly leaves adorning the label.

KEEN

1958-59 (2000 series): Colored vertical stripes with letters of "KEEN" in individual gray circles.

1959-60 (86100 series): Black label, "KEEN" to left of center hole, five-color vertical stripe next to it.

KING

One of the most confusing labels at first glance, it's made even more so because of the often wide disparity in asking prices for what appear to be insignificant differences in the size and style of logo. Read on.

Early to mid 1950s (10-inch LPs): Maroon label, silver print. "KING" is in a straight line at the top of the label.

1955-early 1960s (500-late 600s): Black label, silver print, "KING" curves along the outside and is about two inches wide at the top of the label.

Early 1960s-mid 1960s (Late 600s-unknown): Black label, silver print, "KING" curves along the outside and is about three inches wide at the top of the label (the letters are thicker and more stretched out than the earlier version).

Late 1950s-mid 1960s (stereo releases): Blue label, silver print, "KING" curves along the outside and is about three inches wide at the top of the label.

Mid 1960s-early 1970s: Blue label, silver print, "KING" straight across the top with a crown centered above the "I" and "N."

Late 1960s: James Brown LPs had a custom brown and orange label with his face on it.

Early 1970s (1146-1154): Yellow label with sitting king right of the center hole.

Mid 1970s (16000 series): Yellow label with "KING" vertically at top of label and two protrusions to form a stylized letter "K" coming from it.

Late 1970s (5000 series): Restores blue crowned King label of the mid- to late-1960s.

KIRSHNER

Successor to Calendar Records.

1969-mid 1970s: Orange label, "KIRSHNER" in individual boxes across the top.

Mid 1970s-early 1980s (CBS distribution): White label with multi-color top.

Custom labels were used on some CBS albums.

KOKO

Mostly a custom label for Luther Ingram, these albums have white labels with the word "KOKO" on both sides of the center hole in alternating yellow, red, purple and blue letters.

LAURIE

1959 (1000-1002): Gold label, black print.

1960-1980s (1003-1010, 2002-2052, 4000 series): Gold "pentagram" in center of label with black background surrounding it. Early pressings tend to be quite firm and substantial, and some seem to be almost brittle; later pressings tend to have glossier labels and flimsier wax.

LEGRAND

Original issues have red and gold labels with no crown on top. LeGrand reissued most of its LPs in the 1980s, and these are easily distinguishable by the white band through the center hole and the crown on the label.

LIBERTY

1956-60 (3001-3140? mono): Turquoise label, silver print, "LIBERTY" at top of label with drawing of Statue of Liberty above.

1958-60 (early 7000s stereo to 7140?): Black label, silver print, "LIBERTY" at top of label with drawing of Statue of Liberty above, huge word "STEREO" just below the logo.

1960-66 (3141?-3420?, 7141?-7420?): Black label, rainbow colored area left of center hole, "LIBERTY" in white over a gold crest left of center hole.

1960-69 (12000 and 14000 "Premier Series"): Gold label, black print, design similar to above except that black lines replace the rainbow area.

1966-69 (3421?-end of mono, 7421?-7620?): Black label, rainbow colored area left of center hole, white vertical line abutting rainbow area, "LIBERTY" in black inside a rounded white box with a Statue of Liberty graphic.

1970-71 (7620?-end of original series): Black label, rainbow colored area left of center hole, white vertical line abutting rainbow area, "LIBERTY" in black inside a squared-off white box with a Statue of Liberty graphic, "Liberty/UA Inc." at bottom of label.

1980-86 (reactivated label, 1000-51100 series and 10000 reissue series): Gray label, multi-colored "Liberty" across top.

Custom labels were used for some issues, most notably 1960s issues by the Chipmunks, which have black labels with cartoon renditions of Alvin, Theodore, Simon and David Seville.

LIFE (HIFI)

Actually the "Hifi Life Series," but because of the prominence of the word "Life" on the label, most collectors call this the Life label.

Original issues have a red label with the word "Life" in cursive white letters. Later issues have either yellow or gold labels with a smaller "Life" in black letters.

LONDON (pop)

London releases can be quite confusing. At times, its records for release in the U.S. were pressed both in the U.S. and in England, and different labels were used in each country. The following applies to pop issues only – classical releases are another ballgame entirely. By the 1980s, almost all, if not all, London classical releases were being pressed in Europe, even those meant for sale in the U.S.

10-Inch Albums

Early to mid 1950s: Some have deep blue labels with gold print; some have red labels with gold print.

12-Inch Mono Albums

Mid 1950s-1964 ("LL" prefix until about 3380): Deep red label, silver print, "LONDON" in cursive capital letters across the top with an "ffrr" ear above the "LONDON." Two horizontal silver lines go through the center hole; between these lines are the words "Full Frequency Range Recording."

1964-65 (about 3380-3430): Deep red label, silver print, "LONDON" in a box with the "ffrr" ear logo to the right of this. All of these pressings have print that says "Made in England by the Decca Record Co., Ltd." and will have upside-down matrix numbers on the label.

1964-65 (about 3380-3460): Deep red label, silver print, "LONDON" stands alone, unboxed, above the center hole. All these labels have print that says "Made in U.S.A." Both the above two series ran at the same time, and neither is more "original" than the other, but the "ffrr" pressings are much more rare.

1966-68 (about 3460 to end): Varying shades of red labels (1966s tend to be bright red, 1967s almost maroon) with "LONDON" in a box at the top of the label.

Stereo Albums

1959-64 (PS series to about 379): Deep blue label, silver print, "LONDON" in cursive capital letters across the top with an "ffss" ear above the "LONDON." Two horizontal silver lines go through the center hole; between these lines are the words "Full Frequency Range Recording." The earliest stereos have blue shaded back covers; these are known among audiophiles as "blue backs" and demand a premium.

1964-65 (about 380-430): Deep blue label, silver print, "LONDON" in a box with the "ffss" ear logo to the right of this. All of these pressings have print that says "Made in England by the Decca Record Co., Ltd." and will have upside-down matrix numbers on the label.

1964-65 (about 380-460): Deep blue label, silver print, "LONDON" stands alone, unboxed, above the center hole. All these labels have print that says "Made in U.S.A." Both the above two series ran at the same time, and neither is more "original" than the other, but the "ffss" pressings are much more rare.

1966-78 (about 460-early 700s): Varying shades of blue labels (earlier ones are much richer blue than later ones) with "LONDON" in a box at the top of the label.

A "sunrise" label was used on 45s starting around 1976 until about 1983; it's unknown if this was used on LPs, but if it was, it certainly wasn't used until after 1978. Later London pop labels are white with red trim and "LONDON" in white inside a black upside-down triangle.

LUCKY ELEVEN

One album was issued on this label. It has a yellowish label with a greenish horseshoe in the background.

LUNIVERSE

One album was issued on this label. It has a yellow label with black print.

MAINSTREAM

1960s: Silvery-blue label.

1970s: Red and black label, "Red Lion Productions" at upper right, "Mainstream" at upper left.

MCA

1973 (2100): All-black label, white print; appears to have been used only on this number.

1973-77: Black label, silver print, rainbow at upper left.

1977-79: Tan label, darker tan ring around rim.

1980-late 1990s: Blue label, black print, rainbow at upper left.

Late 1990s: White label, new "MCA/Music Corporation of America" logo left of center hole.

Custom labels were used on some releases.

MERCURY (pop)

1949-1955 (25000 series, all 10-inch LPs): Black label, silver print, "MERCURY" curving around outside of top of label.

1955-early 1960s (12-inch mono, 20000-20700s, also stereo from 60000 to 60700s): Black label, silver print, "MERCURY" stands alone at top, no print along lower edge of label.

Early 1960s-1965 (20700s-20900s; 60700s-60900s): Black label, silver print, "Mercury" in an oval. Some of these issues add "Vendor: Mercury Record Corporation" along lower edge of label.

1965-68 (20900s-end, 60900s-61200?): Red label, "MERCURY" in all capital letters across top with Mercury head at upper left.

1968-72 (61200?-61300s? and early SRM-1 series to 670 or so): Bright red label, twelve "Mercury" logos along the outer rim of the label.

1973-74 (SRM-1-670 to 999?): Bright red label, seven "Mercury" logos along the outer rim of the label.

1974-83: Chicago skyline label.

1983-90s: Black label, "Mercury" in glowing red letters across the top.

1990s: Black label, "Mercury" logo in white inside a red diamond at top of label.

Custom labels exist for some issues.

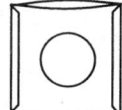

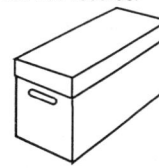
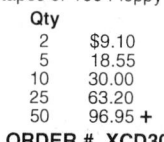 

MERCURY (classical Living Presence)

1950s-early 1960s: Flat maroon label, "MERCURY" stands alone, no print along lower rim of label.

Early 1960s-mid 1960s: Flat maroon label, "MERCURY" stands alone, "Vendor: Mercury Record Corporation" added to label print.

Mid 1960s-early 1970s: Glossy maroon label, "Mercury" in oval logo at top of label.

MGM

1949-59 (10-inch LPs and 12-inch LPs to approximately 3770): Yellow label, black trim and print.

1960-68 (3771?-4515?): Black label, multi-color letters across top.

1968-76 (4516? into 5000s): Blue and gold swirl label.

Except for a very few releases, MGM ceased to exist as a record label in 1976; its material became part of the growing PolyGram empire.

MINIT

1961-63 (0001-0004): Orange label, black print.

1964-68 (24005-24023?, 40005-40023?): Black label, silver print, "MINIT" logo to left of center hole, "A Product of Liberty Records" along bottom.

1968-89 (40024?-40028): Same as above, but "Liberty/UA Records" is the new perimeter print.

MONUMENT

1959 (4000 and 14000 only): White label, gray to black vertical stripes, "MONUMENT" above center hole in black with gold trim.

1960-62 (4001-4009, 14001-14009): White and copper swirl label, "Monument" at top, Washington Monument right of center hole.

1963 (8000-8004?, 18000-18004?): White and multicolor swirl label, "Monument" at top, Washington Monument right of center hole.

1963-71 (8005?-end, 18005?-18147): Light green label, gold band around rim, stylized blue, pink and yellow Washington monument above "monument" at top of label.

1971-76 (30000 series, CBS distribution): Dark orange, almost brown, label.

1977-81 (6600, 7600, 8600 series): Black label with "MONU-MENT" spelled out in simulated stone-carved letters across the top.

1982-83 (38000 series): Silver label.

MOTOWN

1961 (1000): White label, blue print, large blue "M" at top center that serves to turn the two O's in "MOTOWN" on their sides.

1961-62 (1001-1006): Blue label with map on upper half of the label. The original map stretches from western Kansas to the Atlantic coast with a red star over Detroit.

1962-1980s (1007 on): Blue label with map on upper half of the label. This map stretches only from mid-Indiana to mid-Pennsylvania. This design remained basically unchanged into the 1980s, with only changes in perimeter print. There is also more yellow in the word "MOTOWN" in 1970s and 1980s pressings than in 1960s pressings, where the letters fade from red to yellow to blue. Later pressings never make it all the way to the same rich blue as earlier versions.

MOWEST

A short-lived Motown label of the early 1970s, all of its LPs have a beach-at-sunset label with the top and bottom parts in orange and the middle in light blue.

MUSE

From the Ember-Herald family, this one-off label was black with silver print.

MUSICOR

1962: Brown label.

1962-69: Black label.

1970-75?: Tan label.

1976?-end: Green and yellow label.

MUSTANG

Red label, black print. Two albums were issued on this label, both by the Bobby Fuller Four.

NASCO

This label apparently didn't issue LPs until the late 1960s; several of these are sought after by psychedelic music collectors. The label is black with silver print.

ODE

1967-70: Yellow label, "Ode" logo in black print left of the center hole.

1970-71: White and silver label, "Ode 70" at upper right.

1971-75: White and silver label, "Ode Records Inc." at upper right.

1975-78: Tan label with both Ode and Epic logos.

OKEH

Although active for a long time, Okeh LPs were only issued from 1962 through 1969. All labels are purple with the familiar "Okeh" logo in gold above the center hole.

PARAMOUNT

Not to be confused with ABC-Paramount, this was an entirely different label established around 1969.

Most, if not all, original issues have a gray label with Paramount logo to the left of the center hole in black. Some 1970s reissues, after ABC bought the rights to the label, have a blue label with a white "Paramount" logo at the top.

PARKWAY

1960-61 (7001-7005?): Orange label, "PARKWAY" in uneven black letters across the top.

1961-67 (7006?-7057): Orange and yellow label, "PARKWAY" in white letters straight across the top.

1967 (50,000): Gold label.

PARROT

Except for some subtle perimeter print changes, this label was the same from 1964-76: Black with a colored bird left of center hole and the word "parrot" in yellow at the upper right.

PEACOCK

Almost entirely a gospel label, it had three distinct label designs. The first label was black with silver print, "PEACOCK" in silver above the center hole, a drawing of a peacock in black over the logo. The second label, after ABC picked up distribution, was also black with silver print, but "PEACOCK" was now in white and the peacock drawing was in color.

In 1974, the label changed to an unknown design with "abc Peacock" at top of label between two lines.

PHIL-L.A. OF SOUL

Two albums were issued, both with white labels and black print.

PHILIPS (pop)

The below does not apply to classical LPs issued on the Philips label in the 1980s. Most of those were pressed overseas, usually in The Netherlands, then exported to the U.S. for sale.

The basic label stayed the same from 1962 through the early 1970s: It was black with the "PHILIPS" shield above the center hole. The changes all had to do with the perimeter print, as follows:

1962-63: "Chicago 1, Illinois" at the bottom

1963-66: "Vendor: Mercury Record Corporation" at the bottom.

1966-70: No perimeter print at bottom.

1970-74: "Manufactured and Distributed by Mercury" at the bottom.

PHILLES

1962-63 (4001-4005): Light blue label with black print
1964-66 (4006-4011): Yellow and red label, black print.

PHILLIPS INTERNATIONAL

All the LPs issued on this label have a blue world map with a red, white and blue banner across the top. Over the banner it says "Sam C. Phillips International Corp."

PICKWICK

A budget label, most of the albums on this label are common and rarely fetch more than single digits in any condition – and that includes the Elvis ones! The biggest exception is a 1967 Simon and Garfunkel compilation.

From the mid-1960s to about 1976, the label was silver with black print. Starting around 1976 into the early 1980s, the label was black with a multi-colored Pickwick logo.

POLYDOR

Labels are red from 1969 into the 1990s, with the only changes taking place in the perimeter print.

PORTRAIT

1976-early 80s: Gray label.
1980s: Black label.
Custom labels were used on some releases.

RAMA

Labels are dark blue with silver print.

RARE EARTH

1969 (505-509): The lower half of the label is white. The upper half has an orange background, a drawing of a tree and the words "RARE EARTH" in white. This label was later used as the promo label, but for the first editions of these early LPs, it also was the stock label.

1970-76 (511-550): All-orange label with a drawing of a tree and the words "RARE EARTH" in white.

RCA CAMDEN

This was RCA Victor's budget label.
1954-57: Pink label.
1957-64: Blue label, purple perimeter.
1964-68: Light blue label, dark blue perimeter.
1969-75: All-blue label with "RCA" turned on its side at left and "Camden" right of the center hole.

Most Camden titles still in print in 1975 were reissued with the same number on Pickwick.

RCA SPECIAL PRODUCTS

Before 1973, there was no label with this official name. Special-products issues on RCA were easily identifiable by the prefix "PR," "PRM" or "PRS" and a three-digit number.

The earliest of these (early 1960s-1968) have a flat black label and silver print, "RCA Victor" in silver and an outline of the Nipper logo in silver underneath.

The next series of these (1968-73) have a tan, almost maize, label, with "RCA" on its side at the left of the center hole, "Victor" to the right of the center hole, and no dog.

When the entire RCA catalog began using alphanumeric prefixes in 1973, RCA Special Products got its own series beginning, for the most part, with "DPL1." Early label colors vary; some are green, some are light blue. By 1977 the label was black with the dog near top, "RCA Special Products" on two lines in white to the left of the dog.

RCA VICTOR (pop)

Another long and involved label with sometimes overlapping label designs. We welcome any corrections and clarifications. The below apply only to pop albums; Red Seal records are treated elsewhere.

10-Inch Albums

1951-55: Most pop albums have black labels with silver print. A silver ring goes all the way around the label. The words "RCA VICTOR" are along the upper edge above the silver ring. An outline of Nipper is under the silver ring at top. Some albums of this period also had green labels with silver print; reissues of older material had silver-gray labels with red print.

Mono 12-Inch Albums

Before 1955 (early 1000s): Black labels with silver print; silver ring all the way around the label; "RCA VICTOR" along upper edge above the ring; outline of Nipper at top under ring.

1955-63 (mid 1000s-2700s): Shiny black label, "RCA VICTOR" in white with full-bodied Nipper logo underneath. The bottom of the label says "LONG 33 1/3 PLAY."

1963-64 (2700s-2999): Shiny black label, "RCA VICTOR" in white with full Nipper logo. The bottom of the label says "MONO" in some cases; others have an extra-bold "DYNAGROOVE" across the bottom with the word "MONO" in much smaller print on either side.

1965-68 (3300-3900s): Shiny black label, "RCA VICTOR" is much larger along top of label, the Nipper logo is slightly smaller underneath. Along the bottom is either "MONAURAL" or "MONO DYNA-GROOVE."

Stereo 12-Inch Albums

1958-63 (2000s-2700s): Shiny black label, "RCA VICTOR" in white with full-bodied Nipper logo underneath. The bottom of the label says "LIVING STEREO."

1963-64 (2700s-2999): Shiny black label, "RCA VICTOR" in white with full-bodied Nipper logo underneath. The bottom of the label says "STEREO" in some cases; others have an extra-bold "DYNA-GROOVE" across the bottom with the word "STEREO" in much smaller print on either side. This series also had the first rechanneled stereo releases, all of which had numbers before 2000; these have the extra bold word "STEREO" at the bottom with "Electronically Reprocessed" underneath.

1965-68 (3300s-early 4000s): Shiny black label, "RCA VICTOR" is much larger along top of label, the Nipper logo is slightly smaller underneath. Along the bottom is either "STEREO," "STEREO DYNA-GROOVE" or "STEREO Electronically Reprocessed."

1969-71 (early 4000s-about 4460): Orange label on rigid, non-flexible vinyl, "RCA" on its side to left of center hole, "Victor" to right of center hole, no dog logo.

1971-76 (4460?-APL1-1000 or so): Orange label on so-called "Dynaflex" vinyl, "RCA" on its side to left of center hole, "Victor" to right of center hole, no dog logo.

1974-76 (early APL1 series): Tan label, released simultaneously with above orange label. Tan labels were used in Indianapolis, which explains why more of these are found in the East, and the orange labels were used in Hollywood, which explains why more of these are found in the West.

1976-late 1980s: Black label, Nipper logo is restored and added to upper right. "RCA" is now above the center hole to the left of Nipper, "Victor" is on its side to the left of the center hole.

Late 1980s-1990s: Mostly red label with circular "RCA" logo in black background at top. There are other variations of this label as well. It was not until this label that the word "Victor" was dropped from pop LPs.

RCA VICTOR RED SEAL (classical)

10-Inch Albums

1951-55: Red labels with silver print. A silver ring goes all the way around the label. The words "RCA VICTOR" are along the upper edge above the silver ring. Just under the silver ring are the words "RED SEAL RECORD." Under that is an outline of Nipper.

Mono 12-Inch Albums

Before 1955: Red labels with silver print; silver ring all the way around the label; "RCA VICTOR" along upper edge above the ring; "RED SEAL RECORD" just under the ring; outline of Nipper at top under those words.

1955-63: Deep red label, "RCA VICTOR" in white with full-bodied Nipper logo underneath. Behind the Nipper logo is a darker red area, thus lending the nickname "shaded dog" to these pressings. The bottom of the label says "LONG 33 1/3 PLAY."

1963-64: Deep red label, "RCA VICTOR" in white with full Nipper logo. The bottom of the label says "MONO" in some cases; others have an extra-bold "DYNAGROOVE" across the bottom with the word "MONO" in much smaller print on either side.

1965-68: Red label, "RCA VICTOR" is much larger along top of label, the Nipper logo is slightly smaller underneath, and there is no shading behind it. Along the bottom is either "MONAURAL" or "MONO DYNAGROOVE." Collectors call these "white dog" pressings.

Stereo 12-Inch Albums

1958-63: Shiny red label, "RCA VICTOR" in white with full-bodied Nipper logo underneath. The bottom of the label says "LIVING STEREO." Behind the Nipper logo is a darker red area, thus lending the nickname "shaded dog" to these pressings. These stereo pressings are among the most collected stereo albums in the world!

1963-64: Shiny red label, "RCA VICTOR" in white with full-bodied Nipper logo underneath. The bottom of the label says "STEREO" in some cases; others have an extra-bold "DYNAGROOVE" across the bottom with the word "STEREO" in much smaller print on either side. This series also had the first rechanneled stereo releases, all of which had numbers before 2000; these have the extra bold word "STEREO" at the bottom with "Electronically Reprocessed" underneath. Although these still have the "shaded dog" motif, they are not as collectible as the "LIVING STEREO" originals.

1965-68: Shiny black label, "RCA VICTOR" is much larger along top of label, the Nipper logo is slightly smaller underneath, and there is no shading behind it. Along the bottom is either "STEREO," "STEREO DYNAGROOVE" or "STEREO Electronically Reprocessed." Collectors call these "white dog" pressings.

1969-71: Red label on rigid, non-flexible vinyl, "RCA" on its side to left of center hole, "Red Seal" to right of center hole, no dog logo. This and the next variation are known as "no dog" pressings.

1971-76: Red label on so-called "Dynaflex" vinyl, "RCA" on its side to left of center hole, "Red Seal" to right of center hole, no dog logo.

1976-late 1980s: Black label, Nipper logo is restored and added to upper right. "RCA" is now above the center hole to the left of Nipper, "Red Seal" is on its side to the left of the center hole. These are known as "late dog" pressings.

RED BIRD

A short-lived label, Red Bird released albums from 1964 to 1966. All have yellow labels with black print. A red bird is above the center hole, and the words "Red" and "Bird" are on either side of it in black.

RENDEZVOUS

1958-60 (1301-1310?): Brown label, silver print.

1960-end (1311?-1314): Black label, silver print, "rendezvous records" in white above center hole.

REPRISE

1961-67 (6001-6280?, 1000-1022?; 2000-2015?): Pink, gold and green label with a large steamboat at the upper left corner and the word "reprise:" on the label at upper right. Albums in the 1000 series, which were mostly for Frank Sinatra, had his photo on the label instead of the steamboat.

1968-70 (6281?-6400s; 1024-1029; 2016?-2025?): Two-tone orange label (rich orange at top, duller orange on bottom) with a smaller steamboat, an "r:" logo in a red circle with a "W7" logo overlapping it at its left.

1970-early 1980s (6400s on, 2026?-2200s): All-tan (dull orange) label with steamboat, the "W7" logo is gone, though the "r:" remains, this time in a box rather than a circle.

Mid 1980s: Black and red label.

Late 1980s-present: Light blue and maize label.

RIC-TIC

Exactly one album was released on this Detroit label. It has a red label with black print.

RISING SONS

A short-lived subsidiary of Monument, this label was black with silver print and four colored arrows at upper left.

ROLLING STONES

1971 (59100): Earliest stock copies of the first album on the label have white labels.

1971-84 (all others): Yellow label with red "lips and tongue" logo left of the center hole.

Custom labels exist for some releases.

ROULETTE

1957 (25001-25003): Black label, silver print, "ROULETTE" in silver along top, silver roulette wheel underneath label name.

1957-59 (25004-25045?): Black label, silver print, 'ROULETTE" in white along top, red roulette wheel underneath label name.

1959-62 (25046?-25180s?): White label, black print, "ROULETTE" in black along top, blue, red, yellow and green "spokes" through center hole.

1962-63 (25180s?-25230s?): Left side of label is orange, right side is pink, black print, "ROULETTE" in white to left of center hole between two white lines.

1963-1970s (25230-25361; 42000 and 3000 series): Alternating orange and yellow label in the pattern of a roulette wheel, "ROULETTE" in black near the top of the label.

1980s (59000 series): Alternating orange and yellow label in the pattern of a roulette wheel, "ROULETTE" in green near the top of the label.

Roulette had many other numbering systems, most notably the 52000 series for jazz. We'd appreciate help in placing those series within the above time frame.

RSO

1973-75: Peach label, distributed by Atco.

1976-78: Tan label, distributed by Polydor (has Polydor logo in fine print).

1978-81: Tan label, distributed by Polygram (no Polydor logo in fine print).

1981-83: Silver label.

SAVOY

1950-1960s: Maroon label.

1970s (reissues): Brown label, "Distributed by Arista."

SCEPTER

1961 (501): Red label, "Scepter" in black script and a silver outline.

1962-71: Red label, black wedge through center hole, "SCEPTER RECORDS" in white in two lines at the left of the center hole.

Late 1960s-1973: Kaleidoscopic label, "SCEPTER RECORDS" in black inside white oval at top of label. There may be some overlap between this label and the earlier one, as there also was in 45s.

1974-76: Dark blue label, "SCEPTER" in white.

SCORE

A reissue label for Aladdin material, many of these are quite rare, though not nearly as rare as the Aladdin originals. All of these have maroon labels with "SCORE" above the center hole in an oval.

SHELTER

1971-72 (8900-8910?): Red label with an upside-down Superman logo at left.

1972-73: Red label with blacked-out upside-down Superman logo on top.

1974-76 (MCA distribution): Yellow label.

1977-78 (ABC distribution): Orange label with crescent moon at left.

SIRE

1968-70 (97000 series): White label, both Sire and London logos at top of label.

1970-71: Yellow label, blue stylized "S" at top, "Distributed by Polydor Records" in fine print.

1972-74: Yellow label, blue stylized "S" at top, "Distributed by Famous Music, A G+W Company" in fine print.

1974-76: Yellow label, blue stylized "S" at top, "Distributed by ABC Records Inc." in fine print.

1977-1980s: Yellow label, blue stylized "S" at top, makes reference to distribution by Warner Bros.

SMASH

1961-68: Flat red label, "SMASH" at top of label.

1968-71: Red label, both "SMASH" and Mercury logos at top of label.

SOUL

1965-66 (701-702): White label, black print, "SOUL" printed vertically in purple to the left of the center hole in a light purple background.

1966-78 (703-751): Label has three circles with three shades of purple. The "SOUL" logo is in white, centered at the top of the label.

SOUND STAGE 7

1963-66 (5000-5003?, 15000-15003?): Red label, black print, "SOUND 7 STAGE" above center hole.

1968-70 (15004?-15009): Black label, "SOUND STAGE" in two rows in white print over a blue "7."

1972-75 (30000 series): Gold label.

SPECIALTY

1957 (100): White label with wide black ring around the outside and a narrow yellow ring between the white and black areas. "Specialty" is in cursive letters in yellow over the black ring at the top of the label.

1957-70 (2100-2140s?): Gold label, black print, "Specialty" in gold letters across the top over a black background.

1971-89 (2140s-end): Black and white label, "Specialty" in large yellow letters over the black part of the label. Similar in spirit to the design of 1950s 45 rpm labels.

STAX

1962-68 (701-726): Mono releases have light blue labels with black "Stax" logo at top and stack of records over it. Stereo releases have yellow labels with the same "Stax" records logo.

1968-72 (2000-2045, 3001): Yellow label with "finger-snapping" logo in blue tint at the left of center hole.

1972-75 (2046-2047; 3002-3024, 5500 series): Yellow label with "finger-snapping" logo in brown at left of center hole.

1976-late 1980s (4100 and 8500 series): Purple fading to white label, "finger-snapping" logo in black at left of center hole.

STRAND

Mostly a budget label, its labels were orange with black print.

SUE

Early 1960s: Orange label, black print, "Sue RECORDS" in white print left of center hole.

Mid 1960s: Orange label, black print, "Sue RECORDS" in black print left of center hole.

1969 (8801): Red label, black print.

SUN

1956-65 (1220-1275): Yellow label, brown print. Musical notes ring the outer edge of the label. Alternating brown and yellow rays emanate from the center hole area. The letters "SUN" are in yellow over the rays. At the bottom of the label, in yellow print with brown background, are the words "Memphis, Tennessee."

1969-86 (100-148, 1000-1035): Yellow label, brown print. Four "targets" are visible in the lower half of the label. The music notes only go around half the label instead of nearly all of it, and at the bottom is "Sun International Corp., A Division of the Shelby Singleton Corp., Nashville, U.S.A."

SUNSET

This was Liberty Records' budget label. It has a black label with a light blue area at the left of the label; the "SUNSET" logo is to the left of the center hole.

SWAN

1959-63 (501-512?): White label, red print.

1964-end (513?-517): Black label, silver print.

TAMLA

1961-62 (220-231?): White label, black print. Above the center hole is an overlapping globe-record logo with "TAMLA" in an arc above the globe. The oceans of the world and center hole of the record are colored purple.

1962 (229?-233?): Yellow label, black print, same as above except that the oceans and record hole are colored brown.

1963-67 (236?-280?): Yellow label, black print, side-by-side record and globe at top of label, "TAMLA" in yellow over the globe.

1968-1980s (281?-end): Yellow label, black print, brown areas at upper left and upper right of label, "TAMLA" logo, with flattened globe above, in box centered at top.

TEEM

Ace imprint; purple label with silver print.

THREE BROTHERS

A short-lived label, its only release was a 1973 Lou Christie album. It was mostly blue with yellow and white circles that share the same border.

THRESHOLD

1970-73 (1-10?): White label, purple logo.

1974-83 (11?-end): Dark blue label.

TOP RANK

On mono labels, the upper left quadrant of the label is white with a drawing in gold of a man hitting a gong; the other three quadrants of the label are red.

On stereo labels, the upper left quadrant of the label is white with a drawing in red of a man hitting a gong; the other three quadrants of the label are gold.

TOWER

1965-68: Orange label.

1968-69: Multi-colored, striped label.

TRACK

1970-71: Black label, distributed by Atlantic.

1972: Silver label with Decca logo.

1973-75: Brown label, distributed by MCA.

20TH CENTURY/20TH FOX

1958-early 1960s: Light blue "clouds" label, "20th Fox" logo in red at top of label.

Mid 1960s-early 1970s: Black label with gold border, "20th Century Fox Records" logo at top of label. Most of these issues were distributed by ABC.

1972-77: Light blue label, "20th Century" logo in white at top of label.

1978-early 1980s: Light brown label with added spotlights, logo again changes to "20th Century Fox."

UNI

This label had two distinct incarnations.

From 1967-72 it was a quasi-independent division of the MCA family of labels. Labels are yellow with several colored stripes and "uni" at the upper right. Uni, Kapp and Decca were folded at the end of 1972 into the new, all-encompassing MCA label.

In the mid-1980s, MCA briefly reactivated Uni. These labels are blue with "uni RECORDS" in two lines in black above the center hole.

UNITED ARTISTS

1958-59: Red and black label, "UNITED" to left of center hole, "ARTISTS" to right of center hole.

1959: Mono albums had an all-red label; stereo albums had blue labels.

1960: Black label, large "UA" logo on top.

1960-68: Black label, blue, gold, white and red circles along upper edge of label, "UNITED" in gold, "ARTISTS" underneath in white, both words in a rounded-off rectangle.

1968-70: Pink and orange label.

1970-71: Black label, orange area at left of center hole, "UA/United Artists" logo in box directly left of center hole.

1971-77: Tan label with "UA" in brown at top.

1977-80: Multi-colored "sunrise" label.

UNIVERSAL

A country label that lasted for exactly one year (1989). The earliest albums had black and pale yellow labels; later albums have black and red labels.

V.I.P.

This Motown label had a brown, tan, orange, yellow and white label. The "V.I.P." logo is printed vertically to the left of the center hole, inside an oval with an orange background.

VALIANT

Early 1960s: Purple label.

Mid 1960s: Red and black label.

VANGUARD

Early years through 1963: Mono issues were maroon with silver print.

Late 1958s-mid 1960s: Stereo issues were black with silver print.

Mid 1960s-early 1970s: Silvery gray to bronze label with white horseman logo on bottom.

Other labels also existed; we appreciate more information, as many Vanguard releases stayed in print for two decades or more.

VEE JAY

Pre-bankruptcy issues:

1957-60 (1001-1016; 1022; 5001-5005?): Maroon label, silver print with a squiggly line under the words "Vee-Jay RECORDS." A silver band is around the outside of the label. In this number range, stereo issues were gray with black print with otherwise identical graphics.

1960-64 (1019-21; 1023-1070s?, 5006?-5053?, 3004-3037): Black label, silver print, "Vee Jay" logo in white with a treble clef between the two words, surrounded by a red oval. The outer rim of the label has a rainbow band.

1964-65 (1070s-1154; 5054?-5083; 2501-2509): Black label, silver print, "VJ" in white, "VEE-JAY RECORDS" underneath that in two lines in white, all surrounded by two white brackets. The outer rim of the label has a rainbow band.

1964-65 (various, as needed): Black label, silver print, no rainbow band. The letters "VJ" stand alone with "VEE JAY RECORDS" underneath, all in silver print, no brackets.

Post-bankruptcy issues:

Late 1960s-early 1970s: Black label, silver print. Most have the "VJ" and "VEE-JAY RECORDS" in brackets, all in silver print. Some have "VJ" on one line and "RECORDS" on another with no brackets, still all in silver print. Although these records were issued in stereo jackets, they generally play mono!

(This may be the source and time period of most of the "best" illegitimate *Introducing The Beatles* albums, as they match this description. The Beatles albums are considered "counterfeits" because Vee-Jay did not have the rights to reproduce them after 1964. The material Vee-Jay actually owned and reissued at this time, such as *Duke Of Earl* by Gene Chandler, is considered legitimate product, though less valuable than the originals.)

1972-74 (1001-1011 and 2-1000 to 2-1008): Red label, silver print, similar to original maroon Vee-Jay label. At least one of these (1002) was issued on a pink label with black print.

1977 (VJ International): Orange label, black "VJ International" logo in white circle.

VERVE

1956-60 (8000 series mono, 6000 series stereo): Black label, silver print, "Verve Records, Inc." at bottom, "MGV" prefix.

1961-early 1970s (8000 series): Black label, silver print, "MGM Records" at bottom, "V" prefix for mono, "V6" for stereo.

1966-early 1970s (5000 series): Dark blue label, silver print, "V" prefix for mono, "V6" for stereo.

Early 1970s-1975: White label with both "Verve" and "MGM" logos at top of label.

Various labels were used after Verve was reactivated in the early 1980s.

VIK

A 1950s RCA subsidiary, its issues were black with a multi-color "Vik" logo across the top.

VIRGIN

Virgin's American history is spotty at times; for some years there was no Virgin Records in America, but material that came out on Virgin U.K. was leased to other labels.

1973-75: White label, "two virgins" painting at top of label, distributed by Atlantic.

1976-78: Unknown label design, distributed by CBS.

1979-80: White label, "Virgin" in red letters, again distributed by Atlantic.

1981: Unknown design, distributed by RSO.

1983-86: Black label, "Virgin" and "Epic" logos on label. (All of these were Culture Club albums.)

1987-89: Black label, blue upside-down triangle logo at top of label.

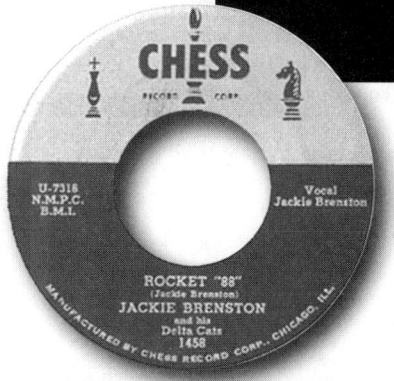

VOLT

1965-68 (411-419): Yellow label, black print, "VOLT RECORDS" above center hole, yellow lightning bolt in black background beneath that.

1969-72 (6001-6017): Dark blue label, black print.

1972-74 (6018-6023 and 9500 series): Orange label, black print.

WAND

1960s: White with black top.

Early 1970s: Kaleidoscope label, "Wand" in black across top of label.

WARNER BROS.

Mono Albums

1958-62 (1200-1470?): Gray label, black "WB" shield at top, "WB" letters in shield are in gold print.

1962-66 (1470?-1620?): Gray label, black "WB" shield at top, "WB" letters in shield are in white print.

1966-67 (1620?-1700s): Gold label.

Stereo Albums

1958-67 (1200-1730?): Gold label.

1968-70 (1730?-1840?): Green label, "Warner Bros.-Seven Arts Records" along top edge, "W7" logo boxed underneath that.

1970-73 (1840?-1890?; 2500-2700?): Green label, "Warner Bros. Records" along top edge, "WB" shield logo underneath that.

1973-78 (2700?-3150?): So-called "Burbank palm trees" label. "Burbank, Home of Warner Bros. Records" along top edge, black "WB" shield underneath that, lined boulevard of palm trees comprises the label design.

1978-83? (3150?-25000?): Tan label, narrow horizontal lines every quarter inch or so, large "WB" shield at top of label.

1983?-present (25000?-on): White label, no horizontal lines, large "WB" shield remains at top.

WARWICK

Original mono labels were white with a green filled-in circle in the middle of the label. Four yellow circles are on the left of the label; four blue circles tend toward the right of the label. At the top is a Warwick crest logo with a green shield. Original stereo labels were also white, but instead of the green filled-in circle, a blue dot is to the right of the center hole and a yellow dot to the left of the center hole. Concentric like-colored circles surround each dot.

The second version of the mono label was plain white with black print and the Warwick logo in black. Stereo labels were purple with silver print and the Warwick logo in silver.

WEED

Exactly one album came out on this short-lived Motown imprint. The label is black with silver print with "WEED" in yellow and two fingers giving the peace sign above that. The label's slogan, which, alas, is not on the record, was "Your Favorite Artists Are On Weed."

WHITE WHALE

1965-67 (100-120?, 7100-7120?): Dark blue label.

1967-70 (7120?-end): Lighter blue label with concentric white circles.

"X"

This subsidiary of RCA Victor released albums from 1954 through 1956. The label is white with red print and a big red "X" at the top of the label.

Dating RCA albums

On all albums pressed by RCA Victor from the early 1950s through 1972, there is an eight-digit master number, four of which are to the left of a hyphen, four of which are to the right.

For albums first released before 1955, you can tell what year the record was mastered by looking at the first two digits. For albums mastered from 1955-72, you can tell the year by looking at the first digit, which will always be a letter.

This list won't tell you what year the album was actually *pressed*; for that, you still need to see the label guide.

The following works on all RCA family albums, including Red Seal, Camden, Bluebird and Victrola. It also works on non-RCA albums that were pressed at the RCA plants, including custom pressings. So you might want to check some albums on such labels as 20th Fox, Cadence and Motown, just to name three, to see if they have RCA-style master numbers.

Here is the RCA code.

1951-54: The first two digits of the master number correspond to the following years.

E1: 1951
E2: 1952
E3: 1953
E4: 1954

1955-72: RCA altered the code so that only the first digit corresponded to the year.

F: 1955
G: 1956
H: 1957
J: 1958
K: 1959
L: 1960
M: 1961
N: 1962
P: 1963
R: 1964
S: 1965
T: 1966
U: 1967
W: 1968
X: 1969
Z: 1970
A: 1971
B: 1972

After 1972: RCA changed its published master numbers to the same number as the record number, with an added "A" for side 1 and a "B" for side 2. You can no longer tell the year based on the master number.

Reissue Identifier

Even without knowing what the label looks like, there are ways to tell if some albums are reissues because of either the number or the prefix attached to it.

Especially in the 1980s, record companies constantly finagled with the list prices of their albums. Once an album stopped selling, it was often put into a "budget line" series if it had been popular enough. Many times, the original pressings ended up in the lower-priced section, but stickers were added to the covers to make the change rather than "waste" a good record. These stickers on the record reduce the value to the level of the reissue. (You can try to remove them, but they don't come off very easily!)

Below are some of the labels known to reissue material by changing either the number or the prefix. With the exception of a few solo Beatles outings on Capitol, these reissues *always* trade for less than the original editions. The following guide is meant as a supplement to the label variation guide, not as a substitute. And, of course, we appreciate additions and clarifications to the guide.

A&M
The SP-3100 and SP-3200 series are reissues. Originals of these have numbers in the 4000s.

ARISTA
If a record was originally issued in the 4000s, 9500s or 9600s, the same title in the 8000s is a reissue. Not all 8000s are reissues, though!

ATLANTIC
If a record was originally issued in the 7200s, 8000s or 18000s, the same title in the 19000s is a reissue.

CAPITOL
If a record has an "SM" prefix and a number lower than 3000, it is a reissue.

Albums in the 16000 series, most with "SN" prefixes, are almost always reissues. A handful (mostly Christmas albums) had their first release in this series, though.

CHRYSALIS
If a record has a "PV" prefix, it is a reissue.

If a record was originally released with a four-digit number (usually 1000 to around 1400) and you have it with a "4" before it, it's a reissue.

COLUMBIA (pop)
All of the following are reissues:
- A record with a four-digit number and a "PC" prefix.
- Records with a "PC" prefix, if first issued with a "C," "KC," "JC," "FC," "NJC," "BFC," "TC," "QC," or "OC" prefix. (Note: Some original pressings from 1973 through 1977 have a "PC" prefix. It's not 100 percent foolproof, but check the back cover for a bar code. If there is no bar code, it's probably original if it didn't first have a "KC.")
- Albums first issued before 1979 with a bar code on the back cover.
- Albums with an extended bar code on the back cover; the last two digits will be "02" or "03."

DOLTON
Some Dolton covers exist with Liberty labels inside; these are reissues.

EPIC
All of the following are reissues:
- A record with a number in the 26000s and a "PE" prefix.
- Records with a "PE" prefix, if first issued with an "E," "KE," "JE," "FE," "NJE," "BFE," "TE," "QE," or "OE" prefix. (Note: Some original pressings from 1973 through 1977 have a "PE" prefix. If it didn't first have a "KE," these will have orange labels.)
- Albums first issued before 1979 with a bar code on the back cover.
- Albums with an extended bar code on the back cover; the last two digits will be "02" or "03."

MCA
Any MCA album with a number embossed in gold on the front cover is a reissue, and the value of the record is reduced accordingly. This is even though everything else about the LP – cover art, inner sleeve and the record – will all have the original issue numbers.

Albums in the 2000 series (up to 2099) are reissues of material from other labels.

Albums in the 37000 series are reissues.

MERCURY
Albums originally issued with three- or five-digit numbers that have a six-digit number beginning with "8" are reissues. These usually will have a bar code on back – another sign of a reissue.

MOTOWN
Albums in the "M5-100" series (later changed to 5000 series) are reissues.

RCA VICTOR (pop)
All of the following are reissues:
- Albums with a small "RE" somewhere on the front or back cover. This indicates that the cover art has somehow been changed since the first pressing. Sometimes the changes are subtle, such as the location of the number on the front cover. Other times, the changes are significant. Some covers are known to have been changed as many as six times!
- Albums from the 1960s by country artists that are part of the "Country Music Hall of Fame Series."
- Albums originally issued with an "LSP" prefix that have an "AFL1" or "ANL1" prefix instead.
- Albums with an "AYL1" prefix. A small handful of these are not reissues, but the vast majority are.
- Albums with "Best Buy Series" on the cover.
- Albums with a sticker around the upper spine that covers up the old number with a new one.

REPRISE
In 1977, when the top list price of LPs went from $6.98 to $7.98, several older popular albums had their numbers changed. (One of them was *Fleetwood Mac* by Fleetwood Mac.) Originals of these have an "MS" prefix; the reissues have an "MSK" prefix.

ROLLING STONES
Check the numbers carefully! Several issues had their numbers changed when their list price changed. The best thing to do here is to know the original numbers:

59100 is original; 39105 is a reissue.
59101 is original; 39106 is a reissue.
79102 is original; 39107 is a reissue.

Also, if the prefix is "FC" instead of "COC," it is a reissue. (The change occurred when distribution went from Atlantic/Atco to CBS.)

SWAN SONG
Several albums' numbers changed when their list prices changed in 1977:

8410 is original; 8501 is a reissue.
8413 is original; 8502 is a reissue.
8415 is original; 8503 is a reissue.

WARNER BROS.
In 1977, when the top list price of LPs went from $6.98 to $7.98, several older popular albums had their numbers changed. (One of them was *Best Of The Doobies* by the Doobie Brothers.) Originals of these have a "BS" prefix; the reissues have a "BSK" prefix.

The $1,000 Club

While compiling this book, we couldn't help notice that a significant number of albums belong to a mythical club. These are those records that, assuming a near-mint record and cover, would most likely fetch four figures in open auction.

We call it The $1,000 Club.

In all, 255 of the albums listed in the following pages fit the bill. Certainly there are more that aren't listed, but as we've mentioned elsewhere, some genres are less completely represented in this book than others are.

The total dollar value of our mythical list is $686,500, a pretty fair chunk of change.

Why do we call it "mythical"? Because, frankly, some of the albums mentioned in the below list are not known to exist in near-mint condition! The "value" we list is extrapolated based on sales of lesser-condition albums.

Remember, in comparing your own albums to the below list, everything must match *exactly*. The number, type (mono or stereo), and all the descriptive material must be identical. If your copy of *The Freewheelin' Bob Dylan* or *Introducing The Beatles* or *Ram* doesn't match the description 100 percent, it's not in this league! To help you, we'll mention some of the more common variations to the below to help you rule out your copy. All three of the above exist as common or counterfeit versions in addition to rare versions. So keep this in mind! The prices also apply only to U.S. pressings of the albums, unless noted otherwise. Canadian pressings need not apply, eh?

That said, here's the club, with the most valuable listed first. In case of ties, the albums are listed alphabetically by artist, then by title.

30,000   **Dylan, Bob**
The Freewheelin' Bob Dylan (Columbia CS 8786) Stereo
"360 Sound Stereo" in black on label (no arrows); record plays, and label lists, "Let Me Die in My Footsteps," "Rocks and Gravel," "Talkin' John Birch Blues" and "Gamblin' Willie's Dead Man's Hand." No known stereo copies play these without listing them.

18,000   **Beatles, The**
Hear the Beatles Tell All (Vee Jay PRO 202) Mono
White label promo with blue print; only two copies are known.

15,000   **Presley, Elvis**
Elvis' Christmas Album (RCA Victor LOC-1035) Mono
This is for a unique "Long Play" label pressing on red vinyl.

13,000   **Ward, Billy, and the Dominoes**
Billy Ward and His Dominoes (Federal 295-94) 10-inch LP

12,000   **Beatles, The**
The Beatles and Frank Ifield on Stage
(Vee Jay SR 1085) Stereo
The cover features a portrait of the Beatles; both the cover and label of the record say "Stereo."

12,000   **Beatles, The**
A Hard Day's Night (United Artists UAS 6366) Stereo
Pink vinyl; only one copy known, probably privately (and secretly) done by a pressing-plant employee.

12,000   **Beatles, The**
Introducing the Beatles (Vee Jay SR 1062) Stereo
This version contains advertisements for 25 other Vee Jay albums on the back cover (thus it's known as the "ad back" cover to collectors); the record contains "Love Me Do" and "P.S. I Love You" and is only known to exist on the oval Vee Jay logo with colorband.

12,000   **Dylan, Bob**
The Freewheelin' Bob Dylan (Columbia CL 1986) Mono
"Guaranteed High Fidelity" on label; plays "Let Me Die in My Footsteps," "Rocks and Gravel," "Talkin' John Birch Blues" and "Gamblin' Willie's Dead Man's Hand." Label does NOT list these. In dead wax, matrix number ends in "–1" followed by a letter.

10,000   **Rolling Stones, The**
12 x 5 (London LL 3402) Mono
Maroon label with "London" unboxed at top; possibly unique blue vinyl pressing.

10,000   **Rolling Stones, The**
Let It Bleed (London NPS-5) Stereo
One-of-a-kind red/yellow/blue/green vinyl pressing (all on the same record!).

10,000   **Rolling Stones, The**
Beggars Banquet (London PS 539) Stereo
Original "toilet graffiti" cover; not to be confused with the 1986 reissue, which says "Digitally Remastered from Original Master Recording" and "100% Virgin Vinyl" on the back cover.

10,000   **Soundtrack**
The Caine Mutiny (RCA Victor LOC-1013) Mono
The "holy grail" to collectors of soundtracks; it was scheduled for release in 1954 and canceled at the last minute, but a few copies were pressed and escaped.

8,000   **Beatles, The**
The Beatles Again (Apple SO-385) Cover slick
Regular copies of this album have no title on the cover except on the spine, and that title is "Hey Jude." Prototypes, however, with "The Beatles Again" on the cover, are known to exist. This is also NOT to be confused with the versions that have records stating "The Beatles Again"; these are common. Almost all the value here is for the cover, which was not released to the general public.

8,000   **Beatles, The**
Introducing the Beatles (Vee Jay SR 1062) Stereo
This version contains "Love Me Do" and "P.S. I Love You" and lists the titles on the back cover. The only known legitimate copies are on the oval Vee Jay logo with colorband. WARNING! This is the most counterfeited album in the history of recorded music. In order to be authentic, the LABEL of the record must say "STEREO" on it.

8,000   **Beatles, The**
Yesterday and Today (Capitol ST 2553) Stereo
"First state" butcher cover (never had other cover on top); cover will be the same size as other Capitol Beatles LPs, whereas "third state" covers (peeled version) will be slightly narrower than most LPs.

8,000   **Midnighters, The**
Their Greatest Hits (Federal 295-90) 10-inch LP

8,000   **Milburn, Amos**
Rockin' the Boogie (Aladdin LP-704) 10-inch LP
This is for the version with a blue cover and red vinyl.

8,000   **Milburn, Amos/Wynonie Harris/etc.**
Party After Hours (Aladdin LP-703) 10-inch LP
Blue cover, red vinyl. Aladdin 10-inch albums are among the rarest albums anywhere.

8,000   **Rolling Stones, The**
Big Hits (High Tide and Green Grass)
(London NP 1) Mono
With two lines of type on the front cover, all in small letters. This is not to be confused with the regular edition of this cover, which has the letters on the front cover all in capitals.

8,000   **Turner, Ike and Tina**
River Deep -- Mountain High (Philles PHLP 4011) Mono
Some records were pressed for this album, but the cover never was before Phil Spector decided to close down his record label. The album later saw wider release on the A&M label in America and London in the U.K., but this is for a yellow and red Philles pressing with no cover!

7,500   **Brown, Charles**
Mood Music (Aladdin LP-702) 10-inch LP
Red vinyl; another rare Aladdin release.

6,000   **Burnette, Johnny**
Johnny Burnette & the Rock 'N' Roll Trio
(Coral CRL 57080) Mono
Originals have maroon labels, printing on jacket's spine and "Made in U.S.A." in lower right of back cover. The most sought-after rockabilly album in the world.

6,000 Lewis, Smiley
I Hear You Knocking (Imperial LP-9141) Mono
This is for a possibly unique edition on green vinyl.

6,000 Rolling Stones, The
Through the Past, Darkly (Big Hits Vol. 2)
(London NPS 3) Picture disc
Prototype picture discs that used the cover art from "Big Hits (High Tide and Green Grass)" either on one or both sides.

5,000 Ballard, Frank
Rhythm-Blues Party (Phillips International 1985) Mono

5,000 Beatles, The
The Beatles and Frank Ifield on Stage
(Vee Jay LP 1085) Mono
The cover has a portrait of the Beatles on it; counterfeits are poorly reproduced and have no spine print, whereas authentic copies DO have print on the spine.

5,000 Dylan, Bob
Blood on the Tracks (Columbia PC 33235) Test pressing
Test pressing with radically different versions of five songs including "Idiot Wind" and "Tangled Up in Blue." This will be clearly identified as a test pressing.

5,000 Jefferson Airplane
Jefferson Airplane Takes Off!
(RCA Victor LSP-3584) Stereo
Version 1: With "Runnin' 'Round This World" as the last song on side 1. Count the number of bands on Side 1 of the record; don't rely on the cover listing, as some jackets list the title when it's not on the record.

5,000 Moore, Gatemouth
Gatemouth Moore Sings Blues (King 684) Mono
The world's most valuable 12-inch blues album.

5,000 Presley, Elvis
Aloha from Hawaii Via Satellite
(RCA Victor VPSX-6089) (2 records) Quad
Not to be confused with common pressings of this album, this rare version was specially made for employees of Stokely-Van Camp. It has a Saturn-shaped sticker on the front cover with "Chicken of the Sea" and mermaid logo.

4,000 Ace, Johnny
Memorial Album for Johnny Ace (Duke DLP-71) Mono
Playing card cover; red vinyl.

4,000 Bachs, The
Out of the Bachs (Raio (no #))
Among the most highly sought-after and rare albums are privately pressed garage and psychedelic records. Many of these develop a reputation far greater than any pretentions the bands had at the time. This is arguably the most legendary of all of these records.

4,000 Beatles, The
Yesterday and Today (Capitol T 2553) Mono
"First state" butcher cover (never had other cover on top); cover will be the same size as other Capitol Beatles LPs, whereas "third state" covers (peeled version) will be slightly narrower than most LPs.

4,000 Beatles, The
Introducing the Beatles (Vee Jay LP 1062) Mono
This is the mono version of the "ad back" (25 photos of other Vee Jay albums on back) cover. The record has "Love Me Do" and "P.S. I Love You" on it.

4,000 Bennett, Boyd
Boyd Bennett (King 395-594) Mono
An extremely rare artifact of early rock 'n' roll.

4,000 Bowie, David
Diamond Dogs (RCA Victor CPL1-0576) Stereo
Original copies have a cover with the dog's genitals clearly visible. (So you know, they look like a man's genitals.) Almost all were destroyed prior to release. Regular issues have the area darkly shaded. Also, in 1990 the original cover was reissued, but on the Ryko Analogue label and not the RCA label, so there is no way to confuse them.

4,000 Brown, Charles
Mood Music (Aladdin LP-702) 10-inch vinyl
Black vinyl version of the red-vinyl release listed higher.

4,000 Dylan, Bob
Bob Dylan In Concert
(Columbia CL 2302/CS 9102) Cover slick
Scheduled for release in 1965 but never pressed. This value is for the cover slick, which would have been pasted onto LP jackets if the release had gone ahead as originally planned.

4,000 Fendermen, The
Mule Skinner Blues (Soma MG-1240) Mono
Blue vinyl version.

4,000 Five Royales, The
The Rockin' 5 Royales (Apollo LP-488) Mono
The first pressings of this album have a purple label.

4,000 Hendrix, Jimi
Electric Ladyland (Reprise 2R 6307) (2 records) Mono
Common in stereo, this is for a white-label promotional copy that plays in mono. It was only sent to radio stations.

4,000 Jan and Dean
Save for a Rainy Day (Columbia CS 9461) Stereo
Actually a Dean Torrence solo album recorded while Jan Berry was recuperating from his near-fatal auto accident. It was scheduled for release on Columbia, but never was. This value is for an acetate or test pressing of the above. (Dean also pressed up some copies privately, but those are not included above, either.)

4,000 Mann, Rev. Columbus
They Shall Be Mine (Tamla T-227) Mono
This gospel album is the rarest of all Motown LPs and also the rarest of gospel albums. It may have received no distribution outside of Detroit.

4,000 McCartney, Paul and Linda
Ram (Apple MAS-3375) Mono
Credited to "Paul and Linda McCartney"; mono record in stereo cover for radio station use only. The record will clearly be marked "Mono" and will have the "MAS" prefix on it.

4,000 Milburn, Amos
Rockin' the Boogie (Aladdin LP-704) 10-inch LP
Black vinyl edition of red-vinyl rarity mentioned earlier.

4,000 Milburn, Amos/Wynonie Harris/etc.
Party After Hours (Aladdin LP-703) 10-inch LP
Black vinyl edition of red-vinyl rarity mentioned earlier.

4,000 Parker, Charlie
The Bird Blows the Blues (Dial LP-1) Mono
This very early long-play record (1949) was available only via mail-order. The most sought-after jazz album on the planet. The Dial Records that recorded early Bird was not the same Dial that recorded Joe Tex; this label was already history by the early 1950s.

4,000 Phillips, Esther
Memory Lane (King 622) Mono

4,000 Sinatra, Frank
SinatraJobim (Reprise FS 1028) Stereo test pressing
This unreleased album is confusing, because there WAS a released collaboration between the two in 1967. That album was called Francis Albert Sinatra & Antonio Carlos Jobim, and it is common. This album was to be a follow-up, but it was shelved. Test pressings of the unreleased album exist, and this value is for one of these. Also, 8-track tapes of this exist (Sinatra stands behind a Greyhound bus on the slick) and are 10% of this value.

3,000 Beatles, The
The Beatles vs. The Four Seasons
(Vee Jay DXS-30) (2 records) Stereo
Combines Introducing the Beatles (Vee Jay 1062) with Golden Hits of the Four Seasons (Vee Jay 1065). Both albums are in stereo and are clearly identified as such on the label. Add another $300 if the enclosed poster is there.

3,000   Beatles, The
A Hard Day's Night
(United Artists UAL 3366) Mono promo
White label promo pressing of this otherwise fairly common LP.

3,000   Beatles, The
United Artists Presents Help!
(United Artists UA-Help-Show)
One-sided interview record with script (blue label).

3,000   Christopher
What'cha Gonna Do (Chris-Tee 12411)

3,000   Damon
Song of a Gypsy (Ankh 968)
This is for the gatefold cover edition.

3,000   Dylan, Bob
Ceremonies of the Horsemen
(Asylum 7E-1003) Cover only
No records were pressed with this title, but never-glued covers exist, of which 3 or 4 are known. Value is for one of these covers. The album was scrapped and became Planet Waves.

3,000   Dylan, Bob
The Freewheelin' Bob Dylan
(Columbia CL 1986) Mono promo
White label promo; label and timing strip list the deleted tracks but record plays the "correct" tracks.

3,000   Frost, Frank
Hey Boss Man! (Phillips International PLP-1975) Mono

3,000   Glenn, Lloyd
Lloyd Glenn (Swing Time 1901) 10-inch LP

3,000   Gospel Stars, The
The Great Gospel Stars (Tamla TM-222) Mono
The rarest gospel group album, another Motown gem that may not have been distributed outside of the Detroit area.

3,000   Index
The Index (DC 71)
Black label; issued with black and white jacket; number is from dead wax. This Detroit-area garage band actually did two distinct albums, a fact not generally known to the collecting community until an interview with the band's former manager in 1996.

3,000   Jefferson Airplane
Jefferson Airplane Takes Off!
(RCA Victor LPM-3584) Mono
Version 1: With "Runnin' 'Round This World" as last song on side 1. Count the number of bands on Side 1 of the record; don't rely on the cover listing, as some jackets list the title when it's not on the record.

3,000   McNeely, Big Jay
Big Jay McNeely (Federal 295-96) 10-inch LP

3,000   Patron Saints, The
Fohhob Bohob ((no label) JT-1001) Stereo
100 copies were pressed. This is such a legendary private album that the members of the band have created a web site in its honor!

3,000   Phaphner
Overdrive (Dragon LP-101) Stereo

3,000   Presley, Elvis
Moody Blue (RCA Victor AFK1-2428) Cover slick
Alternate cover slick (never put on an actual cover), with the words "Moody Blue" inside the large word "Elvis." See any late-1970s Elvis inner sleeve for a black and white photo of the scrapped cover. For unknown reasons, the known copies of this slick have the letter "K" in the catalog number where there should be an "L."

3,000   Prince
The Black Album (Paisley Park 25677DJ) (2) Promo
This is the legendary, formerly unreleased album from 1988. This version is the entire album on two 12-inch records that play at 45 RPM.

3,000   Rolling Stones, The
England's Newest Hit Makers -- The Rolling Stones
(London LL 3375) Promo
This is for the white label promo edition.

3,000   Rolling Stones, The
The Rolling Stones -- The Promotional Album
(London RSD-1) Promo
Album also exists as an import, but this is for a "Made in U.S.A." version.

3,000   Rolling Stones, The
Songs of the Rolling Stones (Abkco MPD-1) Promo
There are two versions of the cover of this rare promo-only album. This is for what is known as the "Rock and Roll Circus" cover, as it contains a photo from the then-unreleased TV special.

2,500   Beatles, The
Introducing the Beatles (Vee Jay SR 1062) Stereo
Probably a transitional cover, the back is completely blank – no ads, no titles, nothing. The record contains "Love Me Do" and "P.S. I Love You"; the label must say "STEREO" on it.

2,500   Brown, Roy / Wynonie Harris / Eddie Vinson
Battle of the Blues, Volume 4 (King 668) Mono

2,500   Hendrix, Jimi
Axis: Bold As Love (Reprise R 6281) Mono
Not to be confused with the far, far more common stereo version. This is for a stock copy on the two-tone orange "r:" and "W7" label.

2,500   Mariani
Perpetuum Mobile (Sonobeat 1001) Stereo
This private press was not issued with a cover.

2,500   Presley, Elvis
International Hotel, Las Vegas Nevada,
Presents Elvis, 1969 (RCA Victor (no #))
Gift box to guests at Elvis' July 31-Aug, 1, 1969 shows. Includes LPM-4088 and LSP-4155; press release; 1969 catalog; three photos; and thank-you note from Elvis and the Colonel. Most of the value is for the box.

2,500   Presley, Elvis
International Hotel, Las Vegas Nevada,
Presents Elvis, 1970 (RCA Victor (no #))
Gift box to guests at Elvis' Jan. 28, 1970 show. Includes LSP-6020 and 47-9791; press release; 1970 catalog; photo; booklet; and dinner menu. Most of the value is for the box.

2,400   Beatles, The
Songs, Pictures and Stories of the Fabulous Beatles
(Vee Jay VJS 1092) Stereo
All copies have gatefold cover with 2/3 width on front; also, all copies have "Introducing the Beatles" records. This is for labels with the oval Vee Jay logo with colorband.

2,400   Beatles, The
Songs, Pictures and Stories of the Fabulous Beatles
(Vee Jay VJS 1092) Stereo
All copies have gatefold cover with 2/3 width on front; also, all copies have "Introducing the Beatles" records. This is for labels with the brackets Vee Jay logo with colorband.

2,400   Beatles, The
Songs, Pictures and Stories of the Fabulous Beatles
(Vee Jay VJS 1092) Stereo
All copies have gatefold cover with 2/3 width on front; also, all copies have "Introducing the Beatles" records. This is for labels with the plain Vee Jay logo on a solid black (no colorband) label. NOTE: Any non-gatefold copy of the above three, or any copy called "Songs and Pictures of the Fabulous Beatles," is a counterfeit.

2,400   Champs, The
Go Champs Go (Challenge CHL-601) Mono
Rare edition on blue vinyl.

2,000   Beatles, The
The Beatles 10th Anniversary Box Set
(Apple/Capitol (no #)) (17 records)
A 1974 issue, mostly used as an in-house promotion and not offered for sale. It contains all the original American issues of

the Beatles LPs except A Hard Day's Night and Let It Be, on green Apple labels.

2,000 **Beatles, The**
United Artists Presents A Hard Day's Night
(United Artists SP-2359/60) Promo
Open-end interview with script.

2,000 **Beatles, The**
United Artists Presents Help!
(United Artists UA-Help-INT) Promo
Open-end interview with script (red label).

2,000 **Beatles, The**
The Yellow Submarine (A United Artists Release)
(Apple Films KAL 004) Promo
One-sided LP with radio spots for movie.

2,000 **Brigade, The**
Last Laugh (Band'n Vocal 1066)
Private pressing.

2,000 **Browne, Jackson**
"Jackson Browne's First Album"
((No label) (no #)) (2 records) Mono
Recorded in 1967, this is a publisher's demo in a plain cardboard jacket. Few, if any, of these songs were recorded by Jackson Browne again.

2,000 **Brute Force**
Extemporaneous (B.T. Puppy BTPS-1015) Stereo
Legendary psych album from The Tokens' label.

2,000 **Dylan, Bob**
The Freewheelin' Bob Dylan (Columbia CL 1986) Mono
White label promo; label lists deleted tracks; timing strip lists, and record plays, "correct" tracks.

2,000 **Five Keys, The**
The Best of the Five Keys (Aladdin LP-806) Mono
Copies of Aladdin 806 entitled "On the Town" are bootlegs.

2,000 **Five Royales, The**
The Rockin' 5 Royales (Apollo LP-488) Mono
Green label second edition.

2,000 **Five Satins, The**
The Five Satins Sing (Ember ELP-100) Mono
Red label; group pictured on front cover; blue vinyl

2,000 **Fraction**
Moon Blood (Angelus 571)

2,000 **Glenn, Lloyd**
Chica-Boo (Aladdin LP-808) Mono
Red vinyl version.

2,000 **Hi-Lites, The**
For Your Precious Love (Dandee DLP-206) Mono

2,000 **Index**
The Index (DC 4736)
Red label; issued with generic white jacket, though sometimes found in first LP's jacket; number in dead wax. This is not the same album as the other Index release, though some of the contents overlap.

2,000 **Iveys, The**
Maybe Tomorrow (Apple ST-3355) Cover slick
This album was not released in the U.S. The value above is for a cover slick, copies of which do exist. The Iveys later recorded as Badfinger.

2,000 **Jacks, The**
Jumpin' with the Jacks (RPM LRP-3006) Mono

2,000 **Johnson, Lonnie**
Lonesome Road (King 395-520) Mono

2,000 **Lennon, John**
Double Fantasy (Nautilus NR-47)
Not to be confused with any release on Geffen or Capitol, or even the regular Nautilus audiophile issue. This copy has an experimental cover, which ended up not being used, with a yellow background drawn around the photo of John and Yoko and a red heart added to the bottom center of the cover.

2,000 **McNeely, Big Jay**
A Rhythm and Blues Concert
(Savoy MG-15045) 10-inch LP

2,000 **Misfits, The**
Legacy of Brutality (Plan 9 PL9-06)
Exactly 16 copies were pressed on pink vinyl. These evidently were transitional issues made as the presses were gradually changing from white to red vinyl. Some of these are more pink than others, but none are purely red or white.

2,000 **Music Emporium, The**
The Music Emporium (Sentinel 69001)

2,000 **New Tweedy Brothers, The**
The New Tweedy Brothers (Ridon 234)
With oversized hexagonal cover designed to look like a sugar cube.

2,000 **Presley, Elvis**
Aloha from Hawaii Via Satellite
(RCA Victor VPSX-6089) (2) Promo
Orange or dark orange labels; with white timing sticker on front cover.

2,000 **Presley, Elvis**
Elvis' Gold Records, Volume 4
(RCA Victor LPM-3921) Mono
"Monaural" on label; this was an extremely late mono issue from 1968 and as such is extraordinarily rare.

2,000 **Presley, Elvis**
Elvis Country ("I'm 10,000 Years Old")
(RCA Victor LSP-4460)
Green vinyl, probably a one-of-a-kind pressing from around the time of Elvis' death. The label is the post-1976 black label, dog near top.

2,000 **Presley, Elvis**
Moody Blue (RCA Victor AFL1-2428) Test pressing
Experimental colored vinyl pressings (with no cover), any color or combination except blue or black.

2,000 **Presley, Elvis**
Speedway (RCA Victor LPM-3989) Mono
"Monaural" on label; this was an extremely late mono issue from 1968 and as such is extraordinarily rare.

2,000 **Prince**
The Black Album (Paisley Park 25677) Stereo
Withdrawn prior to its scheduled 1988 release, though a few copies escaped. This is for the entire album on one record with the above number. This is not to be confused with promotional editions made in 1994 when the album got its legitimate release (Warner Bros. PRO-A-7330 and 45793). Nor is it to be confused with the numerous vinyl counterfeits, which were pressed on other labels and on colored vinyl and allegedly come from other countries (they're all boots).

2,000 **Reed, Lula**
Blue and Moody (King 604) Mono

2,000 **Reeves, Jim**
Jim Reeves Sings (Abbott LP-5001) Mono
The world's most valuable country & western album.

2,000 **Royal Opera House Orchestra**
(Ernest Ansermet, conductor)
The Royal Ballet Gala Performances
(RCA Victor Red Seal LDS-6065) (2 records) Stereo
Original with "shaded dog" labels; the most valuable classical album listed in this book.

2,000 **Search Party**
Montgomery Chapel (Century 32013)

2,000 **Shaggs, The**
Philosophy of the World (Third World 3001)
Legendary private-label release, it later was reissued on Rounder after its DIY reputation grew.

2,000   **Smack, The**
        The Smack (Audio House (# unknown))

2,000   **Touch**
        Street Suite (Mainline PS-70-116-7)

2,000   **Various Artists**
        Robert W. Sarnoff – 25 Years of RCA Leadership
        (RCA Victor RWS-0001) Promo
        Souvenir record handed out at Sarnoff's retirement party in 1973. The most valuable various-artists set. It contains four Elvis Presley tracks.

2,000   **West Coast Pop Art Experimental Band, The**
        West Coast Pop Art Experimental Band (Fifo M 101)
        With regular cover. This was their first album, privately pressed.

1,800   **Jefferson Airplane**
        Jefferson Airplane Takes Off!
        (RCA Victor LSP-3584) Stereo
        Version 2: No "Runnin' 'Round This World", but "questionable" lyrics remain in "Let Me In" ("Don't tell me you want money") and "Run Around" ("That sway as you lay under me"). Until the exact matrix numbers are known, it must be heard to confirm.

1,600   **Beatles, The**
        Introducing the Beatles (Vee Jay SR 1062) Stereo
        Song titles cover; with "Please Please Me" and "Ask Me Why"; oval Vee Jay logo with colorband.

1,600   **Beatles, The**
        Introducing the Beatles (Vee Jay SR 1062) Stereo
        Song titles cover; with "Please Please Me" and "Ask Me Why"; plain Vee Jay logo on solid black label.

1,600   **Platters, The**
        The Platters (Federal 549) Mono
        A collection of material they made before they became famous, this album is extremely rare.

1,600   **Shannon, Del**
        Runaway (Big Top 12-1303) Stereo
        Still one of the most sought-after albums among collectors of stereo rock 'n' roll.

1,500   **Beatles, The**
        Beatlemania Tour Coverage
        (I-N-S Radio News DOC-1) Promo
        Promo-only open-end interview with script in plain white jacket.

1,500   **Beatles, The**
        A Hard Day's Night (United Artists T 90828) Mono
        This is for the Capitol Record Club edition, much rarer in mono than in stereo.

1,500   **Beatles, The**
        Introducing the Beatles (Vee Jay SR 1062) Stereo
        Song titles cover; with "Please Please Me" and "Ask Me Why"; brackets Vee Jay logo with colorband.

1,500   **Beatles, The**
        The Savage Young Beatles (Savage BM-69) Mono
        Yellow label, glossy orange cover.

1,500   **Beatles, The**
        United Artists Presents A Hard Day's Night
        (United Artists SP-2362/3) Promo
        Radio spots for movie.

1,500   **Beatles, The**
        United Artists Presents Help!
        (United Artists UA-Help-A/B) Promo
        Radio spots for movie.

1,500   **Beatles, The**
        Yesterday and Today (Capitol ST 2553) Stereo
        "Third state" butcher cover (trunk cover removed, leaving butcher cover intact); cover will be about 3/16-inch narrower than other Capitol Beatles LPs; value is highly negotiable depending upon the success of removing the paste-over.

1,500   **C.A. Quintet, The**
        A Trip Through Hell (Candy Floss 7764)

1,500   **Chantels, The**
        We're the Chantels (End LP-301) Mono
        Group photo on front cover.

1,500   **Damon**
        Song of a Gypsy (Ankh 968)
        Regular cover; gatefold covers go for more.

1,500   **Dylan, Bob**
        Bob Dylan (Warner/7 Arts 221567) Promo
        Publisher's demo with 12 Dylan performances of then-unreleased songs from the "Basement Tapes" era.

1,500   **Ebon-Knights, The**
        First Date (Stepheny 4001) Mono

1,500   **Fugitives, The, and Others**
        Friday at the Cage A-Go-Go (Westchester 1005) Mono

1,500   **Grandma's Rockers**
        Homemade Apple Pie (Fredlo 6727)

1,500   **Hawkins, Dale**
        Oh! Susie-Q (Chess LP-1429) Mono

1,500   **Haymarket Square**
        Magic Lantern (Chaparral 201)

1,500   **Holly, Buddy**
        That'll Be the Day (Decca DL 8707) Mono
        Black label with silver print.

1,500   **Hopkins, Lightnin'**
        Lightnin' and the Blues (Herald LP 1012) Mono
        Black label.

1,500   **Hopkins, Lightnin'**
        Mojo Hand (Fire FLP 104) Mono

1,500   **McCartney, Paul**
        Band on the Run Radio Interview Special
        (National Features Corp. 2955/6) Promo
        Promo-only interview disc.

1,500   **Midnighters, The**
        Their Greatest Hits (Federal 395-541) Mono
        Red cover.

1,500   **Night Shadows, The**
        The Square Root of Two (Spectrum 2001)
        There are four versions of this limited-edition album. Some copies come with an added 45 and a poster; some with only a poster; some with only a 45; some with neither 45 nor poster. This is the rarest version, with both 45 and poster.

1,500   **Other Half, The**
        The Other Half (7/2 (no #))
        Album has been counterfeited, but those records are translucent when held to a light, originals are not.

1,500   **Paragons, The & The Jesters**
        The Paragons Meet the Jesters (Jubilee JLP-1098) Mono
        Multi-color splash vinyl.

1,500   **Penguins, The**
        The Best Vocal Groups...Rhythm and Blues
        (Dootone DTL-204) Mono
        Usually considered the Penguins' first album, it also includes tracks by the Medallions, Don Julian and the Meadowlarks, and the Dootones. This is for the first pressing on a flat maroon label.

1,500   **Presley, Elvis**
        Kissin' Cousins (RCA Victor LSP-2894) Stereo
        Another "experimental" near-death pressing, this one comes on blue vinyl with the 1976 black label, dog near top.

1,500   **Residents, The**
        The Third Reich 'N' Roll (Ralph RR 1075)
        Numbered box set on marbled vinyl, silkscreened cover and lithographs inside.

1,500   **Rhodes, Todd**
        Todd Rhodes Playing His Greatest Hits
        (King 295-88) 10-inch LP

1,500   **Shaggs, The**
        Wink (MCM 6311)
        Of all things, this is not the same group as on the $2,000 Philosophy Of The World, though the albums were recorded within a year of each other. It's highly likely that neither group ever heard of the other.

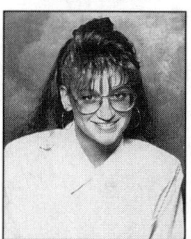

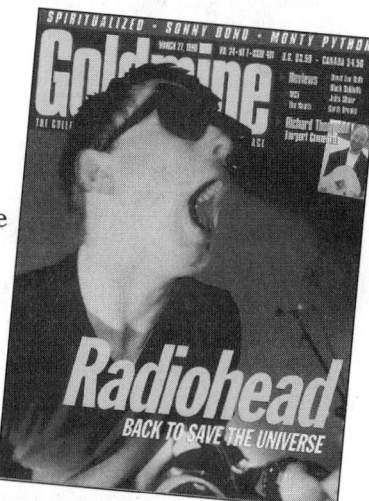

1,500 **Shannon, Del**
Little Town Flirt (Big Top 12-1308) Stereo
Stereo copies are not identified as such on either cover or label; some, but not all, copies have an "S" in the dead wax. Playing is the best way to identify. This, by the way, is for copies that are stereo on both sides (some copies have one side in stereo and one side in mono). Del Shannon never knew this was released in stereo until an interviewer from Goldmine magazine told him it had been!

1,500 **Shirley and Lee**
Let the Good Times Roll (Aladdin 807) Mono

1,500 **Soundtrack**
Rock, Rock, Rock ((no label) (no #)) Mono
Demo version, 20 tracks.

1,500 **Various Artists**
Rock & Roll with Rhythm & Blues (Aladdin LP-710) Mono
One of the two most sought-after commercially released various-artists collections.

1,500 **Various Artists**
Your Favorite Singing Groups (Hull 1002) Mono
One of the two most sought-after commercially released various-artists collections.

1,500 **Various Artists**
The Phil Spector Spectacular (Philles PHLP 100) Promo
This mysterious item was not generally known in the collector's market until the early 1990s. It's a greatest-hits collection probably meant for radio, as a way to re-introduce Phil Spector. It's been dated anywhere from 1966 to 1972 – the label credits the Righteous Brothers tracks as "courtesy of MGM Records," so it's probably closer to 1972 than 1966 – and was not issued with a cover.

1,500 **Vinson, Eddie "Cleanhead"/Jimmy Witherspoon**
Battle of the Blues, Volume 3 (King 634) Mono

1,500 **Ward, Billy, and the Dominoes**
Billy Ward and His Dominoes (Federal 548) Mono

1,500 **Waters, Muddy**
The Best of Muddy Waters (Chess LP-1427) Promo
White label promo.

1,500 **Wild Country**
Wild Country (LSI 0275)
The 1975 private-label debut by the group that became Alabama.

1,200 **Ace, Johnny**
Memorial Album for Johnny Ace
(Duke DLP-70) 10-inch LP

1,200 **Beatles, The**
The Beatles Special Limited Edition
(Apple/Capitol (no #)) (10 records)
Another in-house promotional item from 1974, this box set contains Apple-label editions of Meet The Beatles, Something New, Beatles '65, The Early Beatles, Rubber Soul, Revolver, Sgt. Pepper's Lonely Hearts Club Band, Magical Mystery Tour, Abbey Road, and Hey Jude.

1,200 **Beatles, The**
Introducing the Beatles (Vee Jay LP 1062) Mono
Probably a transitional cover, the back is completely blank – no ads, no titles, nothing. The record contains "Love Me Do" and "P.S. I Love You."

1,200 **Beatles, The**
Yesterday and Today (Capitol T 2553) Mono
"Third state" butcher cover (trunk cover removed, leaving butcher cover intact); cover will be about 3/16-inch narrower than other Capitol Beatles LPs; value is highly negotiable depending upon the success of removing the paste-over.

1,200 **Brown, James**
Please Please Please (King 610) Mono
"Woman's and man's legs" cover; "King" on label is two inches wide. This is the first edition of this rare album.

1,200 **Cleftones, The**
For Sentimental Reasons (Gee SGLP-707) Stereo

1,200 **Crystals, The**
Twist Uptown (Philles DT-90722) Rechanneled stereo
Not released to the general public in any form of stereo, even rechanneled, this is the rechanneled Capitol Record Club edition.

1,200 **Fendermen, The**
Mule Skinner Blues (Soma MG-1240) Mono
Regular edition on black vinyl.

1,200 **Fugitives, The**
The Fugitives at Dave's Hideout (Hideout 1001) Mono

1,200 **Hawkins, Screamin' Jay**
At Home with Screamin' Jay Hawkins
(Epic LN 3448) Mono

1,200 **Hopkins, Lightnin'**
Lightnin' Hopkins Strums the Blues
(Score SLP-4022) Mono
Score was an Aladdin reissue label, and many Score albums are quite rare, though not as rare as the Aladdins.

1,200 **Jones, George**
The Grand Ole Opry's New Star (Starday SLP 101) Mono
Possum's first album, and also the first album on the legendary Nashville independent label. Originals have yellow labels.

1,200 **Kreed**
Kreed (Vision of Sound 71-56)

1,200 **Lazy Smoke**
Corridor of Faces (Onyx 6003)

1,200 **Marvelettes, The**
Smash Hits of 62' (Tamla T-229) Mono
This is the title as it is listed on the front cover; the cover has a large black "M" with song titles in circles.

1,200 **Midnighters, The**
The Midnighters, Volume 2 (Federal 395-581) Mono

1,200 **Night Shadows, The**
The Square Root of Two (Spectrum 2001)
There are four versions of this limited-edition album. Some copies come with an added 45 and a poster; some with only a poster; some with only a 45; some with neither 45 nor poster. This is the version with a poster, but no 45.

1,200 **Perkins, Carl**
The Dance Album of Carl Perkins (Sun SLP-1225) Mono
The most sought-after on the Sun label, though a couple on the Phillips International subsidiary are far more rare.

1,200 **Presley, Elvis**
Special Christmas Programming
(RCA Victor UNRM-5697/8) Promo
White label promo. Add 25% for script.

1,200 **Revere, Paul, and the Raiders**
Paul Revere and the Raiders (Sande S-1001) Mono
Original version with "Sande" and no mention of "Etiquette" in trail-off area.

1,200 **Rising Storm, The**
Calm Before the Rising Storm (Remnant BBA-3571)
For years, THE sought-after private-label psych recording. A reissue sated the demand from the curious, but the original is still very rare.

1,200 **Shep and the Limelites**
Our Anniversary (Hull 1001) Mono

1,200 **Springsteen, Bruce**
Born to Run (Columbia PC 33795) Test pressing
Test pressing with "Bruce Springsteen -- Born to Run" in script print. Also includes mailing envelope, letter from CBS and orange patch. This does not look like any other edition of this album!

1,200 **Soundtrack**
Jurassic Park (MCA/BMG (no #)) Picture disc
Custom-made picture disc for in-house use; promo only. This is the newest release in the $1,000 Club, as it was pressed in 1993.

1,200 **Soundtrack**
Jamboree! (Warner Bros. (no #)) Mono
Album has been counterfeited. Originals have front cover slicks and back cover notes printed on the cardboard, and the records have "Jam 1" and "Jam 2" stamped (not etched) in the dead wax.

1,200 **Teddy Bears, The**
The Teddy Bears Sing! (Imperial LP-12010) Stereo
Demand has gone up and down for this, the first full-length album involving Phil Spector. It's still extremely rare.

1,200 **Ward, Billy, and the Dominoes**
Clyde McPhatter with Billy Ward and His Dominoes (Federal 559) Mono

1,200 **Wild Country**
Deuces Wild (LSI 0177)
The second album by the group that became Alabama.

1,100 **Night Shadows, The**
The Square Root of Two (Spectrum 2001)
There are four versions of this limited-edition album. Some copies come with an added 45 and a poster; some with only a poster; some with only a 45; some with neither 45 nor poster. This is the version with a bonus 45, but no poster.

1,000 **Annette / Hayley Mills**
Annette and Hayley Mills (Singing 10 of Their Greatest All-Time Hits) (Disneyland DL-3508) Mono
TV offer; issued with paper jacket. Though the cover says "Buena Vista Records Presents," the label is the yellow Disneyland label. The most valuable album related to the Walt Disney empire.

1,000 **Astaire, Fred**
The Fred Astaire Story (Mercury MGC-1001/4) (4 records) Mono
Spiral-bound four-record set, pressed on blue vinyl, autographed by Fred Astaire.

1,000 **Beach Boys, The**
Smile (Capitol T/DT 2580) Cover slick
The most famous unreleased album of all time. This price is for a legitimate cover slick not attached to a sleeve. These items have been counterfeited, some more obviously than others.

1,000 **Beatles, The**
Ain't She Sweet (Atco 33-169) Promo
White label promo version of this shameless cash-in record.

1,000 **Beatles, The**
Introducing the Beatles (Vee Jay LP 1062) Mono
This album shouldn't exist, but it does. This is the transitional all-white "blank back" cover, but the record contains "Please Please Me" and "Ask Me Why."

1,000 **Beatles, The**
Introducing the Beatles (Vee Jay LP 1062) Mono
Song titles cover; with "Please Please Me" and "Ask Me Why"; brackets Vee Jay logo on solid black label (no colorband).

1,000 **Beatles, The**
Yesterday and Today (Capitol ST 2553) Stereo
"Second state" butcher cover (trunk cover pasted over original cover). As the number of these "second state" covers continues to decrease, because of the temptation to remove the outer cover to see the "treasure" below, intact copies can only become more valuable.

1,000 **Beatles, The**
Yesterday and Today (Capitol T 2553) Mono
"Second state" butcher cover (trunk cover pasted over original cover). As the number of these "second state" covers continues to decrease, because of the temptation to remove the outer cover to see the "treasure" below, intact copies can only become more valuable.

1,000 **Bolder Damn**
Mourning (Hit HRI-5061)

1,000 **Bow Street Runners, The**
The Bow Street Runners (B.T. Puppy BTPS-1026)
Another impossibly rare psych album from the Tokens' label.

1,000 **Bradshaw, Tiny**
Off and On (King 295-74) 10-inch LP

1,000 **Brown, James**
Please Please Please (King 610) Mono
"Woman's and man's legs" cover; "King" on label is three inches wide (this is an early second pressing)

1,000 **Clap**
Have You Reached Yet? (Nova Sol 1001)

1,000 **Country Joe and the Fish**
Joe McDonald (Custom Fidelity CFS-2348)
Recorded in 1964, 200 copies were pressed for Joe McDonald's personal use.

1,000 **Doors, The**
Waiting for the Sun (Elektra EKL-4024) Mono
Yes, this album exists on mono stock copies, and they are the rarest items in the Doors' catalog.

1,000 **Dylan, Bob**
Blonde on Blonde (Columbia C2L 41) (2 records) Mono
White label promo copy.

1,000 **Dylan, Bob**
The Freewheelin' Bob Dylan (Columbia CS 8786) Stereo
From the 1970s, an unauthorized red vinyl pressing exists on the orange label.

1,000 **Eastman-Rochester "Pops" Orchestra**
(Frederick Fennell, cond.)
Hi-Fi A La Española
(Mercury Living Presence SR 90144) Stereo
The rarest of all "Mercury Living Presence" albums; maroon label, no "Vendor: Mercury Record Corporation."

1,000 **Esquerita**
Esquerita (Capitol T 1186) Mono

1,000 **Fantastic Dee Jays, The**
The Fantastic Dee Jays (Stone SLP-4003)

1,000 **Fapardokly**
Fapardokly (U.I.P. 2250)
Merrill Fankhauser was in this group.

1,000 **Five Royales, The**
The Rockin' 5 Royales (Apollo LP-488) Mono
This is the third pressing on a yellow label.

1,000 **Gaye, Marvin**
The Soulful Moods of Marvin Gaye (Tamla T 221) Mono
His first, rarest and most sought-after album.

1,000 **Glenn, Lloyd**
Chica-Boo (Aladdin LP-808) Mono
Black vinyl.

1,000 **Glenn, Lloyd**
Lloyd Glenn (Score SLP-4006) Mono

1,000 **Glenn, Lloyd**
After Hours (Score SLP-4020) Mono

1,000 **Jefferson Airplane**
Jefferson Airplane Takes Off!
(RCA Victor LPM-3584) Mono
Version 2: No "Runnin' 'Round This World", but "questionable" lyrics remain in "Let Me In" ("Don't tell me you want money") and "Run Around" ("That sway as you lay under me"). Until the exact matrix numbers are known, it must be heard to confirm.

1,000 **John, Little Willie**
Fever (King 395-564) Mono
This is for the original "nurse with thermometer" cover

1,000   Kenny and the Kasuals
The Impact Sound of Kenny and the Kasuals Live at the Studio Club (Mark 5000) Mono

1,000   Kerouac, Jack
Poetry for the Beat Generation (Dot DLP-3154) Mono
Acknowledged to be extremely rare; the same performance is on Hanover 5000.

1,000   Khazad Doom
Level 6 1/2 (LPL 892)

1,000   Led Zeppelin
Houses of the Holy (Atlantic 7255) Mono promo
As late as 1973, some albums were stilll released to radio in mono, five years after it was discontinued to the general public. This is for a white-label promo copy with no "SD" prefix.

1,000   Lennon, John
John Lennon Sings the Great Rock & Roll Hits (Roots) (Adam VIII A-8018)
The album that forced Apple to release the Rock 'n' Roll project. Counterfeits abound on the Adam VIII issue. On authentic copies, cover is posterboard (not slicks); labels are normal size (not overly large); printing on cover is sharp, not blurry; and the word "Greatest" does NOT appear on the spine (it's "Great"). Also, authentic copies usually have an inner sleeve advertising other Adam VIII albums.

1,000   Lennon, John
Some Time in New York City (Apple SVBB-3392) (2 records) Promo
White label promo, NOT a designate promo.

1,000   Marble Phrogg, The
The Marble Phrogg (Derrick 8868)

1,000   Midnighters, The
Their Greatest Hits (Federal 395-541) Mono
Yellow cover.

1,000   Mystic Siva
Mystic Siva (VO 19713)

1,000   Nelson, Ricky
More Songs by Ricky (Imperial LP 12059) Promo
Promo copy on blue vinyl. Add 20 percent for enclosed poster.

1,000   New Dawn, The
There's a New Dawn (Hoot GR 70-4569)

1,000   Night Shadows, The
The Square Root of Two (Spectrum 2001)
There are four versions of this limited-edition album. Some copies come with an added 45 and a poster; some with only a poster; some with only a 45; some with neither 45 nor poster. This version has neither the bonus 45 nor psychedelic poster.

1,000   Police, The
Ghost in the Machine (A&M SP-3730) Promo picture disc
Special prototype picture disc that lights up when placed on a turntable.

1,000   Presley, Elvis
Blue Hawaii (RCA Victor LSP-2426) Stereo
The RCA gremlins at work again, this is a blue vinyl edition with the black label, dog near top label that is on most posthumous Elvis LPs.

1,000   Robbins, Marty
Rock 'N Roll 'N Robbins (Columbia CL 2601) 10-inch LP

1,000   Rolling Stones, The
Hot Rocks 1964-1971 (London 2PS 606/7) (2 records) Stereo
With alternate mixes of "Brown Sugar" and "Wild Horses" unavailable elsewhere. The date "11-5-71" is in the Side 4 trail-off area.

1,000   Royal Opera House Orchestra (Alexander Gibson, conductor) Gounod: Ballet Music of Faust; Bizet: Carmen (RCA Victor Red Seal LSC-2449) Stereo
Original with "shaded dog" label, this is the rarest single-record classical "Living Stereo" release.

1,000   Rubber Memory
Welcome (R.P.C. 69401)

1,000   Shannon, Del
Little Town Flirt (Big Top 12-1308) Stereo & mono
One side is mono, one side is stereo; again, should be played to confirm with 100 percent accuracy.

1,000   Smothers, Smokey
The Backporch Blues (King 779) Mono

1,000   Soundtrack
Go, Johnny, Go! ((No label) (no number)) Promo
This legendary rock 'n' roll soundtrack only exists as a promo.

1,000   Summer Sounds, The
Up Down (Laurel 90973)

1,000   Trammell, Bobby Lee
Arkansas Twist (Atlanta 1503) Mono

1,000   Various Artists
Christmas Programming from RCA Victor (RCA Victor SP-33-66) Promo
Promo-only collection; has been counterfeited, but originals have color covers and phonies have black and white covers.

1,000   Vincent, Gene
Bluejean Bop! (Capitol T 764) Mono
Black label promo.

1,000   Vincent, Gene
Bluejean Bop! (Capitol T 764) Mono
Yellow label promo.

1,000   Vincent, Gene
Gene Vincent and the Blue Caps (Capitol T 811) Mono
Black label promo.

1,000   Vincent, Gene
Gene Vincent and the Blue Caps (Capitol T 811) Mono
Yellow label promo.

1,000   Vincent, Gene
A Gene Vincent Record Date (Capitol T 1059) Mono
Black label promo.

1,000   Vincent, Gene
A Gene Vincent Record Date (Capitol T 1059) Mono
Yellow label promo.

1,000   Vincent, Gene
Gene Vincent Rocks! And the Blue Caps Roll (Capitol T 970) Mono
Yellow label promo.

1,000   Vincent, Gene
Gene Vincent Rocks! And the Blue Caps Roll (Capitol T 970) Mono
Black label promo.

1,000   Walker, T-Bone
Classics in Jazz (Capitol H 370) 10-inch LP

1,000   Waters, Muddy
Muddy Waters Sings Big Bill (Chess LP-1444) Promo
White label promo.

1,000   Williams, Otis, and His Charms
Their All Time Hits (DeLuxe 570) Mono

1,000   Wonder, Stevie
Workout Stevie, Workout (Tamla T 248) Test pressing
Was supposed to be released in 1964, but was not; only test pressings and/or acetates are known to exist.

1,000   Young, Neil
Ode to the Wind (Reprise MSK 2266) Test pressing
No cover, just a plain white jacket with inserts. When it was revamped and redone, the title of this 1978 test had been changed to Comes A Time for commercial release.

Number	Title	Yr	VG	VG+	NM

A

A.F.O. EXECUTIVES WITH TAMI LYNN
A.F.O.
❏ 5002 [M]	A Compendium	1962	37.50	75.00	150.00

ABBA
ATLANTIC
❏ PR 300 [DJ]	Abba	1978	7.50	15.00	30.00
❏ PR 432 [DJ]	A Collection of Hits	1982	7.50	15.00	30.00
❏ PR 436 [(2) DJ]	The Abba Special	1983	12.50	25.00	50.00
NAUTILUS
❏ NR-20	Arrival	1981	7.50	15.00	30.00
-- *Audiophile vinyl*					

ABBEY TAVERN SINGERS, THE
V.I.P.
❏ 402 [M]	We're Off to Dublin in the Green	1966	10.00	20.00	40.00
❏ S-402 [S]	We're Off to Dublin in the Green	1966	12.50	25.00	50.00

AC/DC
ATLANTIC
❏ LAAS-001 [DJ]	Live at the Atlantic Studios	1977	15.00	30.00	60.00
-- *This album has been counterfeited*					
❏ PR 562 [DJ]	Flick of the Switch Interview Album	1983	10.00	20.00	40.00

ACE, JOHNNY
ABC DUKE
❏ DLPX-71	Memorial Album	1974	5.00	10.00	20.00
DUKE
❏ DLP-70 [10]	Memorial Album for Johnny Ace	1955	400.00	800.00	1,200.
❏ DLP-71 [M]	Memorial Album for Johnny Ace	1956	125.00	250.00	500.00
-- *With no playing card on front cover*					
❏ DLP-71 [M]	Memorial Album for Johnny Ace	1961	2,000.	3,000.	4,000.
-- *Playing card cover; red vinyl*					
❏ DLP-71 [M]	Memorial Album for Johnny Ace	1961	50.00	100.00	200.00
-- *With playing card on front cover*					

ACKLIN, BARBARA
BRUNSWICK
❏ BL 754129	Great Soul Hits	1967	6.25	12.50	25.00
❏ BL 754137	Love Makes a Woman	1968	5.00	10.00	20.00
❏ BL 754148	Seven Days of Night	1969	5.00	10.00	20.00
❏ BL 754156	Someone Else's Arms	1970	5.00	10.00	20.00
❏ BL 754166	I Did It	1971	5.00	10.00	20.00
❏ BL 754187	I Call It Trouble	1972	5.00	10.00	20.00

ACUFF, ROY
CAPITOL
❏ T 617 [M]	Songs of the Smoky Mountains	1955	15.00	30.00	60.00
❏ DT 1870 [R]	The Best of Roy Acuff	1963	5.00	10.00	20.00
❏ T 1870 [M]	The Best of Roy Acuff	1963	7.50	15.00	30.00
❏ T 2103 [M]	The Great Roy Acuff	1964	6.25	12.50	25.00
❏ ST 2276 [S]	The Voice of Country Music	1965	10.00	20.00	40.00
❏ T 2276 [M]	The Voice of Country Music	1965	7.50	15.00	30.00
COLUMBIA
❏ CL 9004 [10]	Songs of the Smoky Mountains	1949	50.00	100.00	200.00
❏ CL 9010 [10]	Old Time Barn Dance	1949	37.50	75.00	150.00
❏ CL 9013 [10]	Songs of the Saddle	1950	37.50	75.00	150.00
ELEKTRA
❏ E-C 10-1-78	An Interview with Roy Acuff	1978	6.25	12.50	25.00
HARMONY
❏ HL 7082 [M]	Great Speckled Bird	1958	6.25	12.50	25.00
❏ HL 7294 [M]	That Glory Bound Train	1961	5.00	10.00	20.00
HICKORY
❏ LPM-H-101 [M]	Once More It's Roy Acuff	1961	7.50	15.00	30.00
❏ LPM-109 [M]	King of Country Music -- All-Time Greatest Hits	1962	6.25	12.50	25.00
❏ LPM-113 [M]	Roy Acuff -- Star of the Grand Ole Opry	1963	6.25	12.50	25.00
❏ LPM-114 [M]	The World Is His Stage	1963	6.25	12.50	25.00
❏ LPM-115 [M]	Roy Acuff Sings American Folk Songs	1963	6.25	12.50	25.00
❏ LPM-117 [M]	Hand-Clapping Gospel Songs	1963	6.25	12.50	25.00
❏ LPM-119 [M]	Country Music Hall of Fame	1964	5.00	10.00	20.00
❏ LPM-125 [M]	Great Train Songs	1965	5.00	10.00	20.00
❏ LPM-134 [M]	Roy Acuff Sings Hank Williams	1966	10.00	20.00	40.00
❏ LPS-134 [S]	Roy Acuff Sings Hank Williams	1966	10.00	20.00	40.00
❏ LPS-139	Famous Opry Favorites	1967	5.00	10.00	20.00

❏ LPS-145	Living Legend	1968	5.00	10.00	20.00
❏ LPS-147	Treasury of Country Hits	1969	5.00	10.00	20.00
❏ LPS-156	Roy Acuff Time	1970	5.00	10.00	20.00
❏ DT-90698 [R]	Great Train Songs	1965	6.25	12.50	25.00
-- *Capitol Record Club edition*					
MGM
❏ E-3707 [M]	Favorite Hymns	1958	12.50	25.00	50.00
❏ E-4044 [M]	Hymn Time	1962	6.25	12.50	25.00
❏ SE-4044 [R]	Hymn Time	196?	5.00	10.00	20.00

ADAMS, EDIE
DECCA
❏ DL 4488 [M]	Behind Those Swingin' Doors	1964	5.00	10.00	20.00
❏ DL 74488 [S]	Behind Those Swingin' Doors	1964	6.25	12.50	25.00
MGM
❏ E-3751 [M]	Music to Listen to Records To	1959	10.00	20.00	40.00
❏ SE-3751 [S]	Music to Listen to Records To	1959	15.00	30.00	60.00

ADAMS, FAYE
WARWICK
❏ W 2031 [M]	Shake a Hand	1961	150.00	300.00	600.00

ADAMS, KAY
TOWER
❏ ST 5033 [S]	Wheels & Tears	1966	7.50	15.00	30.00
❏ T 5033 [M]	Wheels & Tears	1966	6.25	12.50	25.00
❏ ST 5069 [S]	Make Mine Country	1967	5.00	10.00	20.00
❏ T 5069 [M]	Make Mine Country	1967	6.25	12.50	25.00
❏ ST 5087	Alcohol & Tears	1968	5.00	10.00	20.00

ADAMS, MIKE, AND THE RED JACKETS
CROWN
❏ CST-255 [S]	Twist Contest	1962	7.50	15.00	30.00
❏ CST-312 [S]	Surfer's Beat	1963	7.50	15.00	30.00
-- *Black vinyl*					
❏ CST-312 [S]	Surfer's Beat	1963	25.00	50.00	100.00
-- *Red vinyl*					
❏ CLP-5255 [M]	Twist Contest	1962	6.25	12.50	25.00
❏ CLP-5312 [M]	Surfer's Beat	1963	6.25	12.50	25.00

ADDEO, LEO
RCA CAMDEN
❏ CAS-510 [S]	Hawaii in Stereo	1960	5.00	10.00	20.00
❏ CAS-594 [S]	More Hawaii in Hi-Fi	1961	5.00	10.00	20.00
RCA VICTOR
❏ LSA-2414 [S]	Paradise Regained	1961	7.50	15.00	30.00

ADDERLEY, CANNONBALL
BLUE NOTE
❏ BLP-1595 [M]	Somethin' Else	1958	37.50	75.00	150.00
-- *"Deep groove" version (deep indentation under label on both sides)*					
❏ BLP-1595 [M]	Somethin' Else	1958	25.00	50.00	100.00
-- *Regular version with W. 63rd St. address on label*					
❏ BLP-1595 [M]	Somethin' Else	1963	6.25	12.50	25.00
-- *With New York, USA address on label*					
❏ BST-1595 [S]	Somethin' Else	1959	25.00	50.00	100.00
-- *"Deep groove" version (deep indentation under label on both sides)*					
❏ BST-1595 [S]	Somethin' Else	1959	18.75	37.50	75.00
-- *Regular version with W. 63rd St. address on label*					
❏ B1-46338	Somethin' Else	1997	5.00	10.00	20.00
-- *Audiophile reissue*					
❏ BST-81595 [S]	Somethin' Else	1963	5.00	10.00	20.00
-- *With New York, USA address on label*					
CAPITOL
❏ ST 2203 [S]	Domination	1964	5.00	10.00	20.00
❏ ST 2216 [S]	Fiddler on the Roof	1965	5.00	10.00	20.00
❏ ST 2284 [S]	Live Session	1965	5.00	10.00	20.00
❏ ST 2399 [S]	Cannonball Adderley -- Live!	1965	5.00	10.00	20.00
❏ ST 2531 [S]	Great Love Themes	1966	5.00	10.00	20.00
❏ ST 2617 [S]	Why Am I Treated So Bad?	1966	5.00	10.00	20.00
❏ T 2663 [M]	Mercy, Mercy, Mercy!	1967	6.25	12.50	25.00
❏ T 2822 [M]	74 Miles Away -- Walk Tall	1967	6.25	12.50	25.00
EMARCY
❏ MG-36043 [M]	Julian "Cannonball" Adderley	1955	15.00	30.00	60.00
❏ MG-36063 [M]	Julian "Cannonball" Adderley and Strings	1956	15.00	30.00	60.00
❏ MG-36077 [M]	In the Land of Hi-Fi	1956	15.00	30.00	60.00
❏ MG-36110 [M]	Sophisticated Swing	1957	15.00	30.00	60.00
❏ MG-36135 [M]	Cannonball's Sharpshooters	1958	15.00	30.00	60.00
❏ MG-36146 [M]	Jump for Joy	1958	15.00	30.00	60.00
FANTASY
❏ FSP 2 [DJ]	Big Man Sampler	1975	5.00	10.00	20.00

Number	Title	Yr	VG	VG+	NM
LIMELIGHT					
❏ LM 82009 [M] Cannonball and Coltrane		1964	6.25	12.50	25.00
-- *Reissue of Mercury 20449*					
❏ LM 82032 [M] Them Adderleys		1964	6.25	12.50	25.00
❏ LS 86009 [S] Cannonball and Coltrane		1964	5.00	10.00	20.00
-- *Reissue of Mercury 60449*					
❏ LS 86032 [S] Them Adderleys		1964	5.00	10.00	20.00
MERCURY					
❏ MG-20449 [M] Cannonball Adderley Quintet in Chicago		1959	12.50	25.00	50.00
❏ MG-20530 [M] Jump for Joy		1960	10.00	20.00	40.00
-- *Reissue of EmArcy 36146*					
❏ MG-20531 [M] Cannonball's Sharpshooters		1960	10.00	20.00	40.00
-- *Reissue of EmArcy 36135*					
❏ MG-20616 [M] Cannonball En Route		1961	10.00	20.00	40.00
❏ MG-20652 [M] The Lush Side of Cannonball Adderley		1961	10.00	20.00	40.00
-- *Reissue of EmArcy 36063*					
❏ SR-60449 [S] Cannonball Adderley Quintet in Chicago		1960	10.00	20.00	40.00
❏ SR-60530 [S] Jump for Joy		1960	7.50	15.00	30.00
❏ SR-60531 [S] Cannonball's Sharpshooters		1960	7.50	15.00	30.00
❏ SR-60616 [S] Cannonball En Route		1961	7.50	15.00	30.00
❏ SR-60652 [R] The Lush Side of Cannonball Adderley		1961	7.50	15.00	30.00
RIVERSIDE					
❏ RLP 12-269 [M] Portrait of Cannonball		1958	12.50	25.00	50.00
❏ RLP 12-286 [M] Things Are Getting Better		1959	12.50	25.00	50.00
❏ RLP 12-303 [M] Cannonball Takes Charge		1959	12.50	25.00	50.00
❏ RLP 12-311 [M] Cannonball Adderley Quintet in San Francisco		1959	12.50	25.00	50.00
❏ RLP 12-322 [M] Them Dirty Blues		1960	12.50	25.00	50.00
❏ RLP 344 [M] Cannonball Adderley Quintet at the Lighthouse		1960	10.00	20.00	40.00
❏ RLP 355 [M] Cannonball Adderley and the Poll-Winners		1960	10.00	20.00	40.00
❏ RLP 377 [M] African Waltz		1961	10.00	20.00	40.00
❏ RLP 388 [M] Cannonball Adderley Quintet Plus		1961	10.00	20.00	40.00
❏ RLP 404 [M] Cannonball Adderley Sextet In New York		1962	7.50	15.00	30.00
❏ RLP 416 [M] Cannonball's Greatest Hits		1962	10.00	20.00	40.00
❏ RLP 433 [M] Know What I Mean?		1962	7.50	15.00	30.00
❏ RLP 444 [M] Jazz Workshop Revisited		1963	7.50	15.00	30.00
❏ RLP 455 [M] Cannonball's Bossa Nova		1963	7.50	15.00	30.00
❏ RLP 477 [M] Nippon Soul -- Recorded in Concert in Tokyo		1964	6.25	12.50	25.00
❏ RM 499 [M] Cannonball in Europe		1967	5.00	10.00	20.00
❏ RLP 1128 [S] Things Are Getting Better		1959	10.00	20.00	40.00
❏ RLP 1148 [S] Cannonball Takes Charge		1959	10.00	20.00	40.00
❏ RLP 1157 [S] Cannonball Adderley Quintet in San Francisco		1959	10.00	20.00	40.00
❏ RLP 1170 [S] Them Dirty Blues		1960	10.00	20.00	40.00
❏ RS 9344 [S] Cannonball Adderley Quintet at the Lighthouse		1960	7.50	15.00	30.00
❏ RS 9355 [S] Cannonball Adderley and the Poll-Winners		1960	7.50	15.00	30.00
❏ RS 9377 [S] African Waltz		1961	7.50	15.00	30.00
❏ RS 9388 [S] Cannonball Adderley Quintet Plus		1961	7.50	15.00	30.00
❏ RS 9404 [S] Cannonball Adderley Sextet In New York		1962	7.50	15.00	30.00
❏ RS 9416 [S] Cannonball's Greatest Hits		1962	7.50	15.00	30.00
❏ RS 9433 [S] Know What I Mean?		1962	7.50	15.00	30.00
❏ RS 9444 [S] Jazz Workshop Revisited		1963	7.50	15.00	30.00
❏ RS 9455 [S] Cannonball's Bossa Nova		1963	7.50	15.00	30.00
❏ RS 9477 [S] Nippon Soul -- Recorded in Concert in Tokyo		1964	6.25	12.50	25.00
SAVOY					
❏ MG-12018 [M] Presenting Cannonball		1955	20.00	40.00	80.00

ADRIAN AND THE SUNSETS

Number	Title	Yr	VG	VG+	NM
SUNSET					
❏ 63-601 [M] Breakthrough		1963	37.50	75.00	150.00
-- *Multi-color vinyl*					
❏ 63-601 [M] Breakthrough		1963	20.00	40.00	80.00
-- *Black vinyl*					
❏ SD 63-601 [S] Breakthrough		1963	75.00	150.00	300.00
-- *Multi-color vinyl*					
❏ SD 63-601 [S] Breakthrough		1963	37.50	75.00	150.00
-- *Black vinyl*					

ADVANCEMENT, THE

Number	Title	Yr	VG	VG+	NM
PHILIPS					
❏ PHS 600-328 The Advancement		1969	10.00	20.00	40.00

ADVENTURERS, THE

Number	Title	Yr	VG	VG+	NM
COLUMBIA					
❏ CL 1747 [M] Can't Stop Twistin'		1961	15.00	30.00	60.00
❏ CS 8547 [S] Can't Stop Twistin'		1961	20.00	40.00	80.00

AEROSMITH

Number	Title	Yr	VG	VG+	NM
COLUMBIA					
❏ A3S 187 [DJ] Pure Gold from Rock 'n' Roll's Golden Boys		1976	12.50	25.00	50.00
-- *Promo-only compilation of the first three albums*					
❏ KC 32005 Aerosmith		1973	5.00	10.00	20.00
-- *Orange cover with back cover typo "Walking The Dig"*					
❏ KCQ 32847 [Q] Get Your Wings		1974	6.25	12.50	25.00
❏ PCQ 33749 [Q] Toys in the Attic		1975	6.25	12.50	25.00
❏ PCQ 34165 [Q] Rocks		1976	6.25	12.50	25.00

AESOP'S FABLES

Number	Title	Yr	VG	VG+	NM
CADET CONCEPT					
❏ LPS-323 In Due Time		1969	5.00	10.00	20.00

AFDEM, JEFF, AND THE SPRINGFIELD FLUTE

Number	Title	Yr	VG	VG+	NM
BURDETTE					
❏ 5162 Something		1969	10.00	20.00	40.00

AFFECTION COLLECTION, THE

Number	Title	Yr	VG	VG+	NM
EVOLUTION					
❏ 2007 The Affection Collection		1969	5.00	10.00	20.00

AFFINITY

Number	Title	Yr	VG	VG+	NM
PARAMOUNT					
❏ PAS-5027 Affinity		1970	6.25	12.50	25.00

AFGHAN WHIGS

Number	Title	Yr	VG	VG+	NM
SUB POP					
❏ 60 Up In It		1990	6.25	12.50	25.00
-- *First pressings have orange vinyl and a different sleeve than the black vinyl version*					
❏ 130 Congregation		1992	5.00	10.00	20.00
-- *Import only; made in Germany (no U.S. vinyl)*					

AFRIKA CORPS

Number	Title	Yr	VG	VG+	NM
IRON CROSS/DACOIT					
❏ (# unknown) Music to Kill By		1977	15.00	30.00	60.00
KLEEN KUT/LIMP					
❏ (# unknown) Hello World!		1978	5.00	10.00	20.00
-- *As "The Korps"; blue vinyl*					

AGAPE

Number	Title	Yr	VG	VG+	NM
MARK					
❏ MRS-2170 Gospel Hard Rock		1971	25.00	50.00	100.00
RENRUT					
❏ 101 Victims of Tradition		1972	30.00	60.00	120.00

AGE OF REASON, THE

Number	Title	Yr	VG	VG+	NM
GEORGETOWNE					
❏ (no #) The Age of Reason		1969	37.50	75.00	150.00

AGGREGATION, THE

Number	Title	Yr	VG	VG+	NM
L.H.I.					
❏ 12008 Mind Odyssey		1967	75.00	150.00	300.00

AHBEZ, EDEN

Number	Title	Yr	VG	VG+	NM
DEL-FI					
❏ DFLP-1211 [M] Eden's Island		1960	37.50	75.00	150.00
❏ DFST-1211 [S] Eden's Island		1960	50.00	100.00	200.00

AIR SUPPLY

Number	Title	Yr	VG	VG+	NM
MOBILE FIDELITY					
❏ 1-113 The One That You Love		1983	5.00	10.00	20.00
-- *Audiophile vinyl*					
NAUTILUS					
❏ NR-31 Lost in Love		1982	5.00	10.00	20.00
-- *Audiophile vinyl*					

AKENS, JEWEL

Number	Title	Yr	VG	VG+	NM
ERA					
❏ EL-110 [M] The Birds and the Bees		1965	7.50	15.00	30.00
❏ ES-110 [S] The Birds and the Bees		1965	25.00	50.00	100.00

Number	Title	Yr	VG	VG+	NM

ALABAMA
ALABAMA
| ❏ ALA-78-9-01 | The Alabama Band | 1978 | 100.00 | 200.00 | 400.00 |

LSI
| ❏ 0177 | Deuces Wild | 1977 | 300.00 | 600.00 | 1,200. |
-- As "Wild Country"
| ❏ 0275 | Wild Country | 1975 | 750.00 | 1,125. | 1,500. |
-- As "Wild Country"

PLANTATION
| ❏ 44 | Wild Country | 1981 | 15.00 | 30.00 | 60.00 |

RCA
| ❏ 9574-1-RDJ | Open-Ended Interview | 1988 | 7.50 | 15.00 | 30.00 |

ALAIMO, STEVE
ABC-PARAMOUNT
❏ 501 [M]	Starring Steve Alaimo	1965	10.00	20.00	40.00
❏ S-501 [S]	Starring Steve Alaimo	1965	12.50	25.00	50.00
❏ 531 [M]	Where the Action Is	1965	10.00	20.00	40.00
❏ S-531 [S]	Where the Action Is	1965	12.50	25.00	50.00
❏ 551 [M]	Steve Alaimo Sings and Swings	1966	10.00	20.00	40.00
❏ S-551 [S]	Steve Alaimo Sings and Swings	1966	12.50	25.00	50.00

CHECKER
❏ LP-2981 [M]	Twist with Steve Alaimo	1962	37.50	75.00	150.00
❏ LP-2983 [M]	Mashed Potatoes	1962	37.50	75.00	150.00
❏ LP-2986 [M]	Every Day I Have to Cry	1963	37.50	75.00	150.00

CROWN
| ❏ CLP-5382 [M] | Steve Alaimo | 1963 | 6.25 | 12.50 | 25.00 |

ALBERGHETTI, ANNA MARIA
CAPITOL
❏ T 887 [M]	I Can't Resist You	1957	7.50	15.00	30.00
❏ ST 1379 [S]	Warm and Willing	1960	7.50	15.00	30.00
❏ T 1379 [M]	Warm and Willing	1960	5.00	10.00	20.00

MERCURY
| ❏ MG-20056 [M] | Songs by Anna Maria Alberghetti | 1955 | 7.50 | 15.00 | 30.00 |

MGM
| ❏ E-4001 [M] | Love Makes the World Go 'Round | 1962 | 5.00 | 10.00 | 20.00 |
| ❏ SE-4001 [S] | Love Makes the World Go 'Round | 1962 | 6.25 | 12.50 | 25.00 |

ALBERT, EDDIE
COLUMBIA
| ❏ CL 2599 [M] | The Eddie Albert Album | 1967 | 5.00 | 10.00 | 20.00 |
| ❏ CS 9399 [S] | The Eddie Albert Album | 1967 | 5.00 | 10.00 | 20.00 |

DOT
| ❏ DLP-3109 [M] | High Upon a Mountain | 1958 | 5.00 | 10.00 | 20.00 |
| ❏ DLP-25109 [S] | High Upon a Mountain | 1958 | 6.25 | 12.50 | 25.00 |

KAPP
❏ KL-1000 [M]	One God	1954	7.50	15.00	30.00
❏ KL-1017 [M]	Eddie Albert and Margo	1956	7.50	15.00	30.00
❏ KL-1083 [M]	September Song	1958	6.25	12.50	25.00

ALBERT, THE
PERCEPTION
| ❏ 9 | The Albert | 1971 | 5.00 | 10.00 | 20.00 |

ALBERTS, AL
Also see FOUR ACES.
CORAL
| ❏ CRL 57259 [M] | A Man Has Got to Sing | 1959 | 6.25 | 12.50 | 25.00 |
| ❏ CRL 757259 [S] | A Man Has Got to Sing | 1959 | 7.50 | 15.00 | 30.00 |

ALBRIGHT, LOLA
COLUMBIA
| ❏ CL 1327 [M] | Dreamsville | 1959 | 7.50 | 15.00 | 30.00 |
| ❏ CS 8133 [S] | Dreamsville | 1959 | 10.00 | 20.00 | 40.00 |

ALDA, ROBERT
ROULETTE
| ❏ R-25006 [M] | Robert Alda | 1959 | 6.25 | 12.50 | 25.00 |
| ❏ SR-25006 [S] | Robert Alda | 1959 | 7.50 | 15.00 | 30.00 |

ALEONG, ALI, AND THE NOBLES
REPRISE
❏ R-6011 [M]	Twistin' the Hits	1962	6.25	12.50	25.00
❏ R9-6011 [S]	Twistin' the Hits	1962	7.50	15.00	30.00
❏ R-6020 [M]	C'mon Baby, Let's Dance	1962	6.25	12.50	25.00
❏ R9-6020 [S]	C'mon Baby, Let's Dance	1962	7.50	15.00	30.00

VEE JAY
| ❏ LP-1060 [M] | Come Surf with Me | 1963 | 7.50 | 15.00 | 30.00 |
| ❏ SR-1060 [S] | Come Surf with Me | 1963 | 12.50 | 25.00 | 50.00 |

ALEXANDER'S TIMELESS BLOOZBAND
SMASK
| ❏ 1001 [M] | Alexander's Timeless Bloozband | 1967 | 50.00 | 100.00 | 200.00 |

UNI
| ❏ 73021 | For Sale | 1968 | 6.25 | 12.50 | 25.00 |

ALEXANDER, ARTHUR
DOT
| ❏ DLP 3434 [M] | You Better Move On | 1962 | 25.00 | 50.00 | 100.00 |
| ❏ DLP 25434 [S] | You Better Move On | 1962 | 40.00 | 80.00 | 160.00 |

WARNER BROS.
| ❏ BS 2592 | Arthur Alexander | 1972 | 6.25 | 12.50 | 25.00 |

ALICE IN CHAINS
COLUMBIA
| ❏ CAS 2192 [DJ] | We Die Young | 1990 | 5.00 | 10.00 | 20.00 |
-- Five-song promo-only EP from the Facelift LP
| ❏ C2 57804 [(2)] | Jar of Flies/Sap | 1994 | 5.00 | 10.00 | 20.00 |
-- Two cassette/CD EP releases in one vinyl package

ALIOTTA-HAYNES-JEREMIAH
AMPEX
| ❏ A-10108 | Aliotta-Haynes Music | 1970 | 5.00 | 10.00 | 20.00 |
-- As "Aliotta-Haynes"
| ❏ A-10119 | Aliotta-Haynes-Jeremiah | 1970 | 5.00 | 10.00 | 20.00 |

BIG FOOT
| ❏ 714 | Lake Shore Drive | 1978 | 6.25 | 12.50 | 25.00 |

LITTLE FOOT
| ❏ 711 | Slippin' Away | 1977 | 5.00 | 10.00 | 20.00 |

ALIVE AND KICKING
ROULETTE
| ❏ SR 42052 | Alive and Kicking | 1970 | 5.00 | 10.00 | 20.00 |

ALL AMERICAN RUMBLERS, THE
GONE
| ❏ LP-5006 [M] | Destination Dixie | 1959 | 12.50 | 25.00 | 50.00 |

ALL STARS, THE
GRAMOPHONE
| ❏ 20192 | Boogie Woogie | 196? | 12.50 | 25.00 | 50.00 |

ALLAN, DAVIE, AND THE ARROWS
TOWER
❏ DT 5002 [R]	Apache '65	1965	7.50	15.00	30.00
❏ T 5002 [M]	Apache '65	1965	10.00	20.00	40.00
❏ DT 5043 [R]	The Wild Angels	1966	5.00	10.00	20.00
❏ T 5043 [M]	The Wild Angels	1966	7.50	15.00	30.00
❏ DT 5056 [R]	The Wild Angels, Vol. II	1967	5.00	10.00	20.00
❏ T 5056 [M]	The Wild Angels, Vol. II	1967	7.50	5.00	30.00
❏ DT 5074 [R]	Devil's Angel	1967	5.00	10.00	20.00
❏ T 5074 [M]	Devil's Angel	1967	7.50	15.00	30.00
❏ DT 5078 [R]	Blues Theme	1967	10.00	20.00	40.00
❏ T 5078 [M]	Blues Theme	1967	12.50	25.00	50.00
❏ DT 5083 [R]	Mondo Hollywood	1968	5.00	10.00	20.00
❏ T 5083 [M]	Mondo Hollywood	1968	7.50	15.00	30.00
❏ DT 5094	Cycledelic Sounds	1968	12.50	25.00	50.00

ALLEN AND ROSSI
ABC-PARAMOUNT
| ❏ ABC-270 [M] | Hello Dere | 1962 | 5.00 | 10.00 | 20.00 |
| ❏ ABC-445 [M] | One More Time Hello Dere | 1963 | 5.00 | 10.00 | 20.00 |

MERCURY
| ❏ MG-21077 [M] | The Adventures of Batman and Rubin | 1966 | 10.00 | 20.00 | 40.00 |
| ❏ SR-61077 [S] | The Adventures of Batman and Rubin | 1966 | 12.50 | 25.00 | 50.00 |
-- The above LP was written by "Batman" creator Bob Kane as a parody of his own comic book

REPRISE
| ❏ R-6104 [M] | Too Funny for Words | 1964 | 5.00 | 10.00 | 20.00 |

ROULETTE
| ❏ R-507 [M] | The Truth About the Green Hornet | 1966 | 5.00 | 10.00 | 20.00 |
| ❏ R-508 [M] | Dedicated to Our Armed Forces | 1967 | 5.00 | 10.00 | 20.00 |

Number	Title	Yr	VG	VG+	NM

ALLEN, DAVE
INTERNATIONAL ARTISTS
❏ 11	Color Blind	1969	15.00	30.00	60.00
-- Original pressing					
❏ 11	Color Blind	1979	5.00	10.00	20.00
-- Repressing with "RE2" and "Masterfonics" in dead wax					

ALLEN, DAYTON
GRAND AWARD
❏ GA 33-424 [M]	Why Not?	1960	6.25	12.50	25.00

ALLEN, LEE
EMBER
❏ ELP-200 [M]	Walkin' with Mr. Lee	1958	125.00	250.00	500.00
-- Red label					
❏ ELP-200 [M]	Walkin' with Mr. Lee	1959	50.00	100.00	200.00
-- White "logs" label					
❏ ELP-200 [M]	Walkin' with Mr. Lee	1961	25.00	50.00	100.00
-- Red and black label					

ALLEN, PHYLICIA
Later known as Phylicia Ayers-Allen and Phylicia Rashad.
CASABLANCA
❏ NBLP-7108	Josephine Superstar	1978	6.25	12.50	25.00

ALLEN, RAY, AND THE UPBEATS
BLAST
❏ BLP-6804 [M]	A Tribute to Six	1962	30.00	60.00	120.00

ALLEN, REX
BUENA VISTA
❏ BV-3307 [M]	Rex Allen Sings 16 Golden Hits	1961	10.00	20.00	40.00
DECCA
❏ DL 8402 [M]	Under Western Skies	1956	12.50	25.00	50.00
❏ DL 8776 [M]	Mister Cowboy	1959	10.00	20.00	40.00
❏ DL 75011 [S]	The Smooth Country Sound of Rex Allen	1968	5.00	10.00	20.00
❏ DL 75205	The Touch of God's Hand	1970	5.00	10.00	20.00
❏ DL 78776 [S]	Mister Cowboy	1959	15.00	30.00	60.00
HACIENDA
❏ WWLP-101 [M]	Rex Allen Sings	1960	50.00	100.00	200.00
MERCURY
❏ MG-20719 [M]	Faith of a Man	1962	6.25	12.50	25.00
❏ MG-20752 [M]	Rex Allen Sings and Tells Tales	1963	6.25	12.50	25.00
❏ SR-60719 [S]	Faith of a Man	1962	7.50	15.00	30.00
❏ SR-60752 [S]	Rex Allen Sings and Tells Tales	1963	7.50	15.00	30.00

ALLEN, RICHIE
IMPERIAL
❏ LP-9212 [M]	Stranger from Durango	1962	10.00	20.00	40.00
❏ LP-9229 [M]	The Rising Surf	1963	20.00	40.00	80.00
❏ LP-9243 [M]	Surfer's Slide	1963	20.00	40.00	80.00
❏ LP-12212 [S]	Stranger from Durango	1962	12.50	25.00	50.00
❏ LP-12229 [S]	The Rising Surf	1963	37.50	75.00	150.00
❏ LP-12243 [S]	Surfer's Slide	1963	37.50	75.00	150.00

ALLEN, ROSALIE
GRAND AWARD
❏ GA-33-330 [M]	Songs of the Golden West	1957	10.00	20.00	40.00
RCA VICTOR
❏ LPM-2313 [M]	Rosalie Allen	1961	5.00	10.00	20.00
❏ LSP-2313 [S]	Rosalie Allen	1961	6.25	12.50	25.00
WALDORF
❏ 150 [10]	Rosalie Allen Sings Country and Western	1955	20.00	40.00	80.00

ALLEN, STEVE
CORAL
❏ CRL 57004 [M]	Music for Tonight	1955	6.25	12.50	25.00
❏ CRL 57015 [M]	Tonight at Midnight	1956	6.25	12.50	25.00
❏ CRL 57018 [M]	Jazz for Tonight	1956	6.25	12.50	25.00
❏ CRL 57019 [M]	Steve Sings	1956	6.25	12.50	25.00
❏ CRL 57028 [M]	Let's Dance	1956	6.25	12.50	25.00
❏ CRL 57048 [M]	Allen Plays Allen	1956	6.25	12.50	25.00
❏ CRL 57070 [M]	The Steve Allen Show	1957	6.25	12.50	25.00
❏ CRL 57138 [M]	Romantic Rendezvous	1957	5.00	10.00	20.00
DECCA
❏ DL 8151 [M]	Steve Allen's All Star Jazz Concert, Vol. 1	1955	7.50	15.00	30.00
❏ DL 8152 [M]	Steve Allen's All Star Jazz Concert, Vol. 2	1955	7.50	15.00	30.00
DOT
❏ DLP 3194 [M]	...And All That Jazz	1959	6.25	12.50	25.00
❏ DLP 3472 [M]	Funny Fone Calls	1963	5.00	10.00	20.00
❏ DLP 3473 [M]	12 Greatest Hits	1963	5.00	10.00	20.00
❏ DLP 3517 [M]	More Funny Fone Calls	1963	5.00	10.00	20.00
❏ DLP 25194 [S]	...And All That Jazz	1959	5.00	10.00	20.00
❏ DLP 25380 [S]	Bossa Nova Jazz	1963	5.00	10.00	20.00
❏ DLP 25515 [S]	Gravy Waltz and 11 Current Hits!	1963	5.00	10.00	20.00
❏ DLP 25519 [S]	Steve Allen Plays the Piano Greats	1963	5.00	10.00	20.00
❏ DLP 25530 [S]	Steve Allen Sings	1963	5.00	10.00	20.00
❏ DLP 25538 [S]	Cuando Caliente El Sol and More	1963	5.00	10.00	20.00
❏ DLP 25560 [S]	Great Ragtime Hits	1963	5.00	10.00	20.00
FORUM
❏ F-9014 [M]	Steve Allen at the Round Table	196?	5.00	10.00	20.00
ROULETTE
❏ R-25053 [M]	Steve Allen at the Round Table	1959	6.25	12.50	25.00
❏ SR-25053 [S]	Steve Allen at the Round Table	1959	5.00	10.00	20.00
SIGNATURE
❏ 1004 [M]	Man in the Street	1959	7.50	15.00	30.00

ALLEN, TONY
CROWN
❏ CST-240 [S]	Rock and Roll with Tony Allen	1961	25.00	50.00	100.00
❏ CLP-5231 [M]	Rock and Roll with Tony Allen	1960	25.00	50.00	100.00
-- Black label					
❏ CLP-5231 [M]	Rock and Roll with Tony Allen	1961	15.00	30.00	60.00
-- Gray label					

ALLEN, WOODY
BELL
❏ 6008	The Wonderful Wacky World of Woody Allen	1967	5.00	10.00	20.00
CAPITOL
❏ ST 2986	The Third Woody Allen Album	1968	6.25	12.50	25.00
COLPIX
❏ CP 488 [M]	Woody Allen 2	1965	7.50	15.00	30.00
❏ CP 518 [M]	Woody Allen	1964	7.50	15.00	30.00
❏ SCP 488 [R]	Woody Allen 2	1965	6.25	12.50	25.00
UNITED ARTISTS
❏ UA-LA849-J2 [(2)]	Woody Allen: Stand-Up Comic 1964-1968	1977	5.00	10.00	20.00
-- Compilation of material from Colpix and Capitol LPs (different from UA 9968)					
❏ UAS 9968 [(2)]	Woody Allen: The Nightclub Years	1972	5.00	10.00	20.00
-- Compilation of material from Colpix and Capitol LPs					

ALLIN, GG
BLACK & BLUE
❏ 006053-X	Always Was, Is and Always Shall Be	1985	12.50	25.00	50.00
-- Reissue of Orange original					
BLOOD
❏ (# unknown)	Eat My Fuc	198?	12.50	25.00	50.00
-- Hand-decorated plain cover					
ORANGE
❏ (# unknown)	Always Was, Is and Always Shall Be	1980	25.00	50.00	100.00

ALLISON, GENE
VEE JAY
❏ LP-1009 [M]	Gene Allison	1959	75.00	150.00	300.00
-- Maroon label					
❏ LP-1009 [M]	Gene Allison	196?	25.00	50.00	100.00
-- Black label, oval or brackets logo					

ALLISON, KEITH
COLUMBIA
❏ CL 2641 [M]	Keith Allison In Action	1967	6.25	12.50	25.00
❏ CS 9441 [S]	Keith Allison In Action	1967	6.25	12.50	25.00

ALLISON, LUTHER
DELMARK
❏ DS-625	Love Me, Mama	1969	6.25	12.50	25.00

ALLMAN BROTHERS BAND, THE
Also see DUANE ALLMAN; DUANE AND GREGG ALLMAN; THE HOUR GLASS.
ATCO
❏ SD 2-805 [(2)]	Beginnings	1973	5.00	10.00	20.00

Number	Title	Yr	VG	VG+	NM

CAPRICORN
- ❑ CX4 0102 [(2) Q] Eat a Peach — 1974 — 7.50 — 15.00 — 30.00
- ❑ CX4 0131 [(2) Q] The Allman Brothers Band at Fillmore East — 1974 — 7.50 — 15.00 — 30.00
- ❑ SD 2-802 [(2)] The Allman Brothers Band at Fillmore East — 1971 — 5.00 — 10.00 — 20.00

MOBILE FIDELITY
- ❑ 1-157 [(2)] Eat a Peach — 1984 — 50.00 — 100.00 — 200.00
  -- *Audiophile vinyl*
- ❑ 1-213 Brothers and Sisters — 1994 — 7.50 — 15.00 — 30.00
  -- *Audiophile vinyl*

NAUTILUS
- ❑ NR-30 [(2)] The Allman Brothers Band at Fillmore East — 1982 — 25.00 — 50.00 — 100.00
  -- *Audiophile vinyl*

POLYDOR
- ❑ 839 417-1 [(6)] Dreams — 1989 — 10.00 — 20.00 — 40.00

ALLMAN, DUANE
Also see THE ALLMAN BROTHERS BAND.
CAPRICORN
- ❑ 2CP 0108 [(2)] An Anthology — 1972 — 5.00 — 10.00 — 20.00
- ❑ 2CP 0139 [(2)] An Anthology, Vol. II — 1974 — 5.00 — 10.00 — 20.00

ALLMAN, DUANE AND GREGG
Also see THE ALLMAN BROTHERS BAND.
BOLD
- ❑ 33-301 Duane and Gregg Allman — 1972 — 6.25 — 12.50 — 25.00
  -- *Gatefold cover*

ALLMAN, SHELDON
DEL-FI
- ❑ DFLP-1213 [M] Sing Along with Drac — 1961 — 10.00 — 20.00 — 40.00
HIFI
- ❑ R-415 [M] Folk Songs for the 21st Century — 1960 — 10.00 — 20.00 — 40.00
- ❑ R-415 [M] Folk Songs for the 21st Century — 1960 — 7.50 — 15.00 — 30.00

ALLSUP, TOMMY
GRT
- ❑ 20004 Tommy Allsup and the Tennessee Saxes Play the Hits of Tammy Wynette — 1970 — 5.00 — 10.00 — 20.00
METROMEDIA
- ❑ MM 1004 Tommy Allsup and the Nashville Survey Play the Hits of Charley Pride — 1969 — 6.25 — 12.50 — 25.00
REPRISE
- ❑ R 6182 [M] Tommy Allsup Plays the Buddy Holly Songbook — 1965 — 10.00 — 20.00 — 40.00
- ❑ RS 6182 [S] Tommy Allsup Plays the Buddy Holly Songbook — 1965 — 12.50 — 25.00 — 50.00

ALMEIDA, LAURINDO
CAPITOL
- ❑ H-193 [10] Guitar Concert — 1950 — 20.00 — 40.00 — 80.00
- ❑ ST 1759 [S] Viva Bossa Nova! — 1962 — 5.00 — 10.00 — 20.00
- ❑ ST 1872 [S] Ole! Bossa Nova — 1963 — 5.00 — 10.00 — 20.00
- ❑ ST 1946 [S] It's a Bossa Nova World — 1963 — 5.00 — 10.00 — 20.00
- ❑ SP 8482 [S] Songs of Enchantment — 196? — 5.00 — 10.00 — 20.00
CORAL
- ❑ CRL 56049 [10] A Guitar Recital of Famous Serenades — 1952 — 20.00 — 40.00 — 80.00
- ❑ CRL 56086 [10] Latin Melodies — 1952 — 20.00 — 40.00 — 80.00
- ❑ CRL 57056 [M] A Guitar Recital of Famous Serenades — 1956 — 12.50 — 25.00 — 50.00
CRYSTAL CLEAR
- ❑ CCS-8001 Virtuoso Guitar — 1978 — 6.25 — 12.50 — 25.00
  -- *Direct-to-disc recording; plays at 45 rpm*
- ❑ CCS-8007 New Directions — 1979 — 6.25 — 12.50 — 25.00
  -- *Direct-to-disc recording*
PACIFIC JAZZ
- ❑ PJLP-7 [10] Laurindo Almeida Quartet — 1953 — 30.00 — 60.00 — 120.00
- ❑ PJLP-13 [10] Laurindo Almeida Quartet, Vol. 2 — 1954 — 30.00 — 60.00 — 120.00
- ❑ PJ-1204 [M] Laurindo Almeida Quartet Featuring Bud Shank — 1955 — 20.00 — 40.00 — 80.00
  -- *Reissue of 10-inch Pacific Jazz LPs*
WORLD PACIFIC
- ❑ WP-1204 [M] Laurindo Almeida Quartet Featuring Bud Shank — 1958 — 12.50 — 25.00 — 50.00
  -- *Reissue of Pacific Jazz 1204*
- ❑ WP-1412 [M] Brazilliance, Vol. 1 — 1962 — 7.50 — 15.00 — 30.00
  -- *Reissue of World Pacific 1204*
- ❑ ST-1419 [S] Brazilliance, Vol. 2 — 1962 — 6.25 — 12.50 — 25.00
- ❑ WP-1419 [M] Brazilliance, Vol. 2 — 1962 — 7.50 — 15.00 — 30.00
- ❑ ST-1425 [S] Brazilliance, Vol. 3 — 1962 — 6.25 — 12.50 — 25.00
- ❑ WP-1425 [M] Brazilliance, Vol. 3 — 1962 — 7.50 — 15.00 — 30.00

ALPERT, HERB
MOBILE FIDELITY
- ❑ 1-053 Rise — 1981 — 6.25 — 12.50 — 25.00
  -- *Audiophile vinyl*

AMAZING RHYTHM ACES
ABC
- ❑ D-913 Stacked Deck — 1975 — 5.00 — 10.00 — 20.00
- ❑ AA-1123 The Amazing Rhythm Aces — 1979 — 5.00 — 10.00 — 20.00

AMBASSADORS, THE
ARCTIC
- ❑ ALPS-1005 Soul Summit — 1969 — 6.25 — 12.50 — 25.00

AMBOY DUKES, THE
Also see TED NUGENT.
MAINSTREAM
- ❑ S-421 Ted Nugent and the Amboy Dukes — 1976 — 7.50 — 15.00 — 30.00
  -- *Reissue of early material*
- ❑ S-2-801 [(2)] Journeys and Migrations — 1974 — 7.50 — 15.00 — 30.00
  -- *Reissue of 6112 and 6118*
- ❑ S-6104 [S] The Amboy Dukes — 1967 — 10.00 — 20.00 — 40.00
- ❑ S-6112 Journey to the Center of the Mind — 1968 — 10.00 — 20.00 — 40.00
- ❑ S-6118 Migration — 1968 — 10.00 — 20.00 — 40.00
- ❑ S-6125 The Best of the Original Amboy Dukes — 1969 — 7.50 — 15.00 — 30.00
- ❑ 56104 [M] The Amboy Dukes — 1967 — 20.00 — 40.00 — 80.00
POLYDOR
- ❑ 24-4012 Marriage on the Rocks/ Rock Bottom — 1970 — 6.25 — 12.50 — 25.00
- ❑ 24-4035 Survival of the Fittest/Live — 1971 — 6.25 — 12.50 — 25.00
  -- *As "Ted Nugent and the Amboy Dukes"*

AMBROSE, AMANDA
DUNWICH
- ❑ S-668 [S] Amanda — 1966 — 5.00 — 10.00 — 20.00

AMBROSIA
NAUTILUS
- ❑ NR-23 Life Beyond L.A. — 1981 — 7.50 — 5.00 — 30.00
  -- *Audiophile vinyl*

AMECHE, DON, AND FRANCES LANGFORD
COLUMBIA
- ❑ CL 1692 The Bickersons — 1962 — 5.00 — 10.00 — 20.00
  -- *Live-in-the-studio recordings from 1961*
- ❑ CL 1883 The Bickersons Fight Back — 1962 — 5.00 — 10.00 — 20.00
  -- *More live-in-the-studio recordings from 1961*
RADIOLA/MURRAY HILL
- ❑ 3MH 36721 [(3)] Return of the Bickersons — 1987 — 5.00 — 10.00 — 20.00
  -- *Compilation of radio shows*

AMERICA
WARNER BROS.
- ❑ BS 2576 America — 1971 — 6.25 — 12.50 — 25.00
  -- *Allegedly, first pressings omit "A Horse with No Name."*
- ❑ BS4 2808 [Q] Holiday — 1974 — 5.00 — 10.00 — 20.00
- ❑ BS4 2852 [Q] Hearts — 1975 — 5.00 — 10.00 — 20.00

AMERICAN BLUES EXCHANGE, THE
TAYL
- ❑ TLS-1 Blueprint — 1969 — 100.00 — 200.00 — 400.00

AMERICAN BLUES, THE
Early incarnation of ZZ TOP.
KARMA
- ❑ 1001 The American Blues Is Here — 1967 — 100.00 — 200.00 — 400.00
UNI
- ❑ 73044 The American Blues Do Their Thing — 1968 — 15.00 — 30.00 — 60.00

AMERICAN BREED, THE
ACTA
- ❑ 8002 [M] The American Breed — 1967 — 5.00 — 10.00 — 20.00
- ❑ 8003 [M] Bend Me, Shape Me — 1968 — 5.00 — 10.00 — 20.00
- ❑ 38002 [S] The American Breed — 1967 — 6.25 — 12.50 — 25.00

Number	Title	Yr	VG	VG+	NM
❑ 38003 [S]	Bend Me, Shape Me	1968	6.25	12.50	25.00
❑ 38006	Pumpkin, Powder, Scarlet & Green	1968	5.00	10.00	20.00
❑ 38008	Lonely Side of the City	1969	5.00	10.00	20.00

AMERICAN DREAM, THE
AMPEX
Number	Title	Yr	VG	VG+	NM
❑ A-10101	The American Dream	1970	5.00	10.00	20.00

-- Produced by Todd Rundgren

AMERICAN EAGLE
DECCA
Number	Title	Yr	VG	VG+	NM
❑ DL 75258	American Eagle	1971	5.00	10.00	20.00

AMERICAN REVOLUTION
FLICK DISC
Number	Title	Yr	VG	VG+	NM
❑ FLS-54002	American Revolution	1968	6.25	12.50	25.00

AMES BROTHERS, THE
Also see ED AMES.
CORAL
Number	Title	Yr	VG	VG+	NM
❑ CRL 56014 [10]	Sing a Song of Christmas	1950	12.50	25.00	50.00
❑ CRL 56017 [10]	In the Evening by the Moonlight	1951	12.50	25.00	50.00
❑ CRL 56024 [10]	Sentimental Me	1951	12.50	25.00	50.00
❑ CRL 56025 [10]	Hoop-De-Hoo	1951	12.50	25.00	50.00
❑ CRL 56042 [10]	Sweet Leilani	1951	12.50	25.00	50.00
❑ CRL 56050 [10]	Favorite Spirituals	1952	12.50	25.00	50.00
❑ CRL 56079 [10]	Home on the Range	1952	12.50	25.00	50.00
❑ CRL 56080 [10]	Merry Christmas	1952	12.50	25.00	50.00
❑ CRL 56097 [10]	Favorite Songs	1954	12.50	25.00	50.00
❑ CRL 57031 [M]	Ames Brothers Concert	1956	7.50	15.00	30.00
❑ CRL 57054 [M]	Love's Old Sweet Song	1956	7.50	15.00	30.00
❑ CRL 57166 [M]	Sounds of Christmas Harmony	1957	7.50	15.00	30.00
❑ CRL 57176 [M]	Love Serenade	1958	7.50	15.00	30.00
❑ CRL 57338 [M]	Our Golden Favorites	1960	7.50	15.00	30.00

EPIC
Number	Title	Yr	VG	VG+	NM
❑ BN 26036 [S]	Hello Italy	1962	5.00	10.00	20.00
❑ BN 26069 [S]	Knees Up Mother Brown	1963	5.00	10.00	20.00

RCA VICTOR
Number	Title	Yr	VG	VG+	NM
❑ LPM-1142 [M]	Exactly Like You	1955	7.50	15.00	30.00
❑ LPM-1157 [M]	Four Brothers	1955	7.50	15.00	30.00
❑ LPM-1228 [M]	The Ames Brothers with Hugo Winterhalter	1956	7.50	15.00	30.00
❑ LPM-1487 [M]	Sweet Seventeen	1957	7.50	15.00	30.00
❑ LPM-1541 [M]	There'll Always Be a Christmas	1957	7.50	15.00	30.00
❑ LPM-1680 [M]	Destination Moon	1958	6.25	12.50	25.00
❑ LSP-1680 [S]	Destination Moon	1958	7.50	15.00	30.00
❑ LPM-1855 [M]	Smoochin' Time	1958	6.25	12.50	25.00
❑ LSP-1855 [S]	Smoochin' Time	1958	7.50	15.00	30.00
❑ LPM-1859 [M]	The Best of the Ames Brothers	1958	6.25	12.50	25.00
❑ LSP-1859(e) [R]	The Best of the Ames Brothers	196?	5.00	10.00	20.00
❑ LPM-1954 [M]	Famous Hits of Famous Quartets	1959	5.00	10.00	20.00
❑ LSP-1954 [S]	Famous Hits of Famous Quartets	1959	6.25	12.50	25.00
❑ LPM-1998 [M]	The Ames Brothers Sing the Best in the Country	1959	5.00	10.00	20.00
❑ LSP-1998 [S]	The Ames Brothers Sing the Best in the Country	1959	6.25	12.50	25.00
❑ LPM-2009 [M]	Words and Music	1959	5.00	10.00	20.00
❑ LSP-2009 [S]	Words and Music	1959	6.25	12.50	25.00
❑ LPM-2100 [M]	Hello, Amigos	1960	5.00	10.00	20.00
❑ LSP-2100 [S]	Hello, Amigos	1960	6.25	12.50	25.00
❑ LPM-2182 [M]	The Blend and the Beat	1960	5.00	10.00	20.00
❑ LSP-2182 [S]	The Blend and the Beat	1960	6.25	12.50	25.00
❑ LPM-2273 [M]	The Best of the Bands	1960	5.00	10.00	20.00
❑ LSP-2273 [S]	The Best of the Bands	1960	6.25	12.50	25.00
❑ LPM-3186 [10]	It Must Be True	1954	12.50	25.00	50.00

AMES, ED
Also see THE AMES BROTHERS.
RCA VICTOR
Number	Title	Yr	VG	VG+	NM
❑ LPM-4028 [M]	Apologize	1968	5.00	10.00	20.00

AMES, NANCY
LIBERTY
Number	Title	Yr	VG	VG+	NM
❑ LST-7276 [S]	The Incredible Nancy Ames	1963	5.00	10.00	20.00
❑ LST-7299 [S]	Portrait of Nancy	1963	5.00	10.00	20.00
❑ LST-7329 [S]	I Never Will Marry	1964	5.00	10.00	20.00
❑ LST-7369 [S]	This Is the Girl That Is	1964	5.00	10.00	20.00
❑ LST-7400 [S]	Let It Be Me	1965	5.00	10.00	20.00

AMISH, THE
SUSSEX
Number	Title	Yr	VG	VG+	NM
❑ SUX-7016	The Amish	1972	6.25	12.50	25.00

AMMONS, ALBERT
MERCURY
Number	Title	Yr	VG	VG+	NM
❑ MG-25012 [10]	Boogie Woogie Piano	1950	37.50	75.00	150.00

AMMONS, GENE
ARGO
Number	Title	Yr	VG	VG+	NM
❑ 697 [M]	Dig Him	1962	7.50	15.00	30.00
❑ S-697 [S]	Dig Him	1962	6.25	12.50	25.00
❑ 698 [M]	Just Jug	1962	7.50	15.00	30.00
❑ S-698 [S]	Just Jug	1962	6.25	12.50	25.00

CADET
Number	Title	Yr	VG	VG+	NM
❑ LP-783 [M]	Make It Happen	1967	6.25	12.50	25.00

CHESS
Number	Title	Yr	VG	VG+	NM
❑ LP 1442 [M]	Soulful Saxophone	1959	10.00	20.00	40.00

EMARCY
Number	Title	Yr	VG	VG+	NM
❑ MG-26031 [10]	With or Without	1954	30.00	60.00	120.00

MOODSVILLE
Number	Title	Yr	VG	VG+	NM
❑ MVLP-18 [M]	Nice and Cool	1961	12.50	25.00	50.00

-- Originals have green label

Number	Title	Yr	VG	VG+	NM
❑ MVLP-18 [M]	Nice and Cool	1965	6.25	12.50	25.00

-- Second editions have blue label with trident at right

Number	Title	Yr	VG	VG+	NM
❑ MVLP-28 [M]	The Soulful Moods of Gene Ammons	1963	12.50	25.00	50.00

-- Originals have green label

Number	Title	Yr	VG	VG+	NM
❑ MVLP-28 [M]	The Soulful Moods of Gene Ammons	1965	6.25	12.50	25.00

-- Second editions have blue label with trident at right

Number	Title	Yr	VG	VG+	NM
❑ MVST-28 [S]	The Soulful Moods of Gene Ammons	1963	10.00	20.00	40.00

PRESTIGE
Number	Title	Yr	VG	VG+	NM
❑ PRLP-107 [10]	Gene Ammons	1951	50.00	100.00	200.00
❑ PRLP-112 [10]	Tenor Sax Favorites, Volume 1	1951	50.00	100.00	200.00
❑ PRLP-127 [10]	Gene Ammons Favorites, Volume 2	1952	50.00	100.00	200.00
❑ PRLP-149 [10]	Gene Ammons Favorites, Volume 3	1953	50.00	100.00	200.00
❑ PRLP-211 [10]	Gene Ammons Jazz Session	1955	50.00	100.00	200.00
❑ PRLP-7039 [M]	Hi Fidelity Jam Session	1956	25.00	50.00	100.00
❑ PRLP-7039 [M]	The Happy Blues	1960	12.50	25.00	50.00

-- Retitled version of "Hi Fidelity Jam Session"

Number	Title	Yr	VG	VG+	NM
❑ PRLP-7050 [M]	Gene Ammons All Star Session	1956	25.00	50.00	100.00

-- Compilation of Prestige 107 and 127

Number	Title	Yr	VG	VG+	NM
❑ PRLP-7050 [M]	Woofin' and Tweetin'	1960	12.50	25.00	50.00

-- Retitled version of "Gene Ammons All Star Session"

Number	Title	Yr	VG	VG+	NM
❑ PRLP-7060 [M]	Jammin' with Gene	1956	25.00	50.00	100.00
❑ PRLP-7060 [M]	Not Really the Blues	1960	12.50	25.00	50.00

-- Retitled version of "Jammin' with Gene"

Number	Title	Yr	VG	VG+	NM
❑ PRLP-7083 [M]	Funky	1957	25.00	50.00	100.00

-- Originals have yellow label, "W. 50th St., NYC" address

Number	Title	Yr	VG	VG+	NM
❑ PRLP-7110 [M]	Jammin' in Hi-Fi with Gene Ammons	1957	25.00	50.00	100.00

-- Originals have yellow label, "W. 50th St., NYC" address

Number	Title	Yr	VG	VG+	NM
❑ PRLP-7132 [M]	The Big Sound	1958	25.00	50.00	100.00

-- Originals have yellow label, "W. 50th St., NYC" address

Number	Title	Yr	VG	VG+	NM
❑ PRLP-7146 [M]	Blue Gene	1958	12.50	25.00	50.00

-- Originals have yellow label, Bergenfield, N.J. address

Number	Title	Yr	VG	VG+	NM
❑ PRLP-7176 [M]	The Twister	1960	12.50	25.00	50.00

-- Originals have yellow label, Bergenfield, N.J. address; reissue of 7110

Number	Title	Yr	VG	VG+	NM
❑ PRLP-7180 [M]	Boss Tenor	1960	12.50	25.00	50.00

-- Originals have yellow label, Bergenfield, N.J. address

Number	Title	Yr	VG	VG+	NM
❑ PRST-7180 [S]	Boss Tenor	1960	10.00	20.00	40.00

-- Originals have silver label

Number	Title	Yr	VG	VG+	NM
❑ PRLP-7192 [M]	Jug	1960	12.50	25.00	50.00

-- Originals have yellow label, Bergenfield, N.J. address

Number	Title	Yr	VG	VG+	NM
❑ PRST-7192 [S]	Jug	1960	10.00	20.00	40.00

-- Originals have silver label

Number	Title	Yr	VG	VG+	NM
❑ PRLP-7201 [M]	Groove Blues	1961	12.50	25.00	50.00

-- Originals have yellow label, Bergenfield, N.J. address

Number	Title	Yr	VG	VG+	NM
❑ PRLP-7208 [M]	Up Tight!	1961	12.50	25.00	50.00

-- Originals have yellow label, Bergenfield, N.J. address

Number	Title	Yr	VG	VG+	NM
❑ PRST-7208 [S]	Up Tight!	1961	10.00	20.00	40.00

-- Originals have silver label

Number	Title	Yr	VG	VG+	NM
❑ PRLP-7238 [M]	Twistin' the Jug	1962	12.50	25.00	50.00

-- Originals have yellow label, Bergenfield, N.J. address

Number	Title	Yr	VG	VG+	NM
❑ PRST-7238 [S]	Twistin' the Jug	1962	10.00	20.00	40.00

-- Originals have silver label

Number	Title	Yr	VG	VG+	NM
❑ PRLP-7257 [M]	Bad! Bossa Nova	1962	7.50	15.00	30.00

-- Originals have yellow label, Bergenfield, N.J. address

Number	Title	Yr	VG	VG+	NM
❑ PRST-7257 [S]	Bad! Bossa Nova	1962	10.00	20.00	40.00

-- Originals have silver label

Number	Title	Yr	VG	VG+	NM
❑ PRLP-7270 [M]	Preachin'	1963	7.50	15.00	30.00

-- Originals have silver label

Number	Title	Yr	VG	VG+	NM
❑ PRST-7270 [S]	Preachin'	1963	10.00	20.00	40.00

-- Originals have silver label

Number	Title	Yr	VG	VG+	NM
❑ PRLP-7275 [M]	Soul Summit, Volume 2	1963	7.50	15.00	30.00

-- Originals have yellow label, Bergenfield, N.J. address

Number	Title	Yr	VG	VG+	NM
❑ PRST-7275 [S]	Soul Summit, Volume 2	1963	10.00	20.00	40.00

-- Originals have silver label

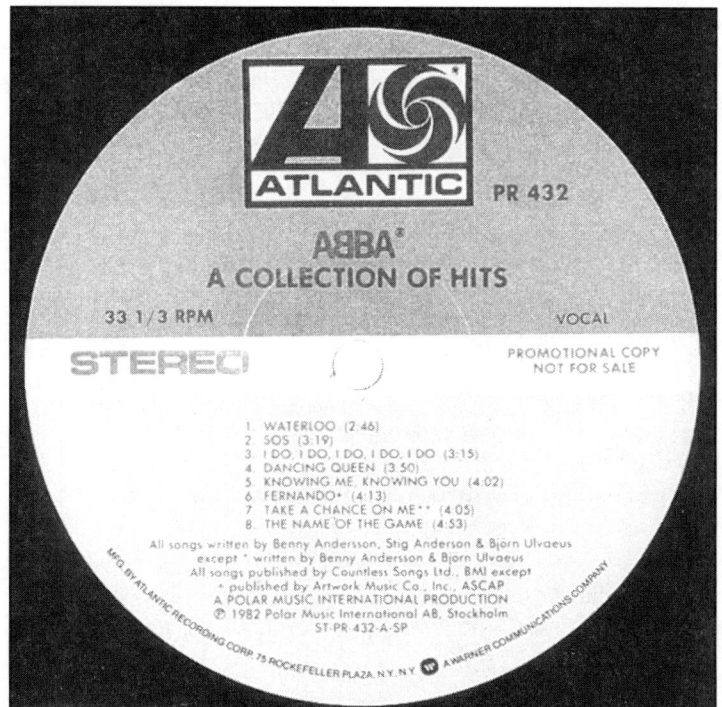

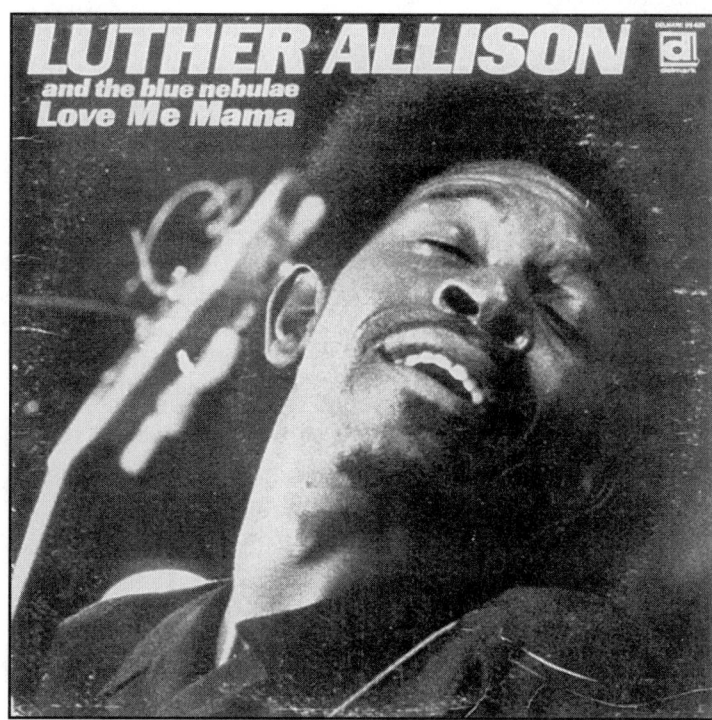

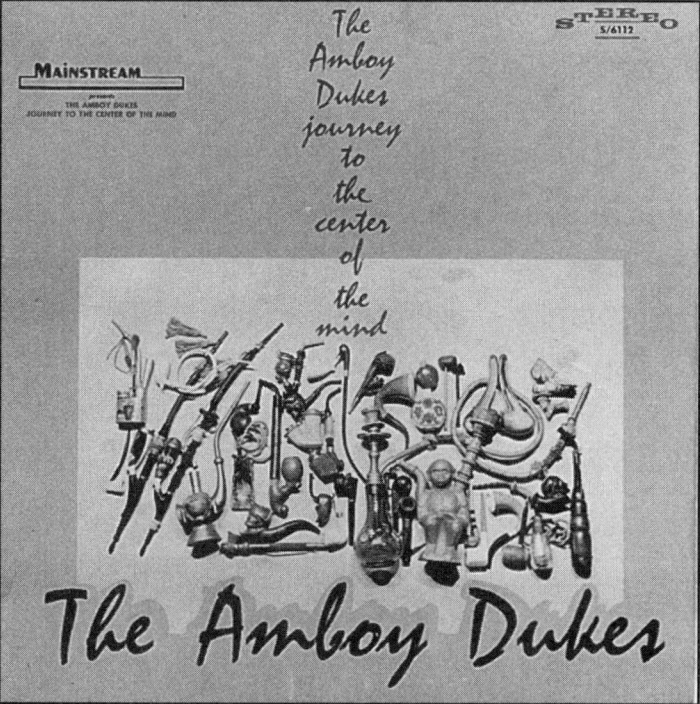

(Top left) One of the more collectible American releases by Abba is this promotional-only album, *A Collection Of Hits*, which was released to radio around 1982. (Top right) When Aerosmith's first album came out in 1973, it featured this cover. Some copies have a typographical error on the back, in which "Walking The Dog" is listed as "Walking The Dig." (Bottom left) Bluesman Luther Allison recorded his debut album for the Chicago jazz and blues label Delmark in 1969. It is now his most collectible LP. (Bottom right) The second album for the Amboy Dukes featured their only hit, the title track. The Dukes are best known for giving us Ted Nugent.

Number	Title	Yr	VG	VG+	NM
❏ PRLP-7287 [M] Late Hour Special		1964	7.50	15.00	30.00
-- Originals have yellow label, Bergenfield, N.J. address					
❏ PRST-7287 [S] Late Hour Special		1964	10.00	20.00	40.00
-- Originals have silver label					
❏ PRLP-7320 [M] Velvet Soul		1964	7.50	15.00	30.00
-- Originals have yellow label, Bergenfield, N.J. address					
❏ PRST-7320 [S] Velvet Soul		1964	10.00	20.00	40.00
-- Originals have silver label					
❏ PRLP-7369 [M] Angel Eyes		1965	6.25	12.50	25.00
-- Originals have blue label with trident at right					
❏ PRST-7369 [S] Angel Eyes		1965	7.50	15.00	30.00
-- Originals have blue label with trident at right					
❏ PRLP-7400 [M] Sock!		1966	6.25	12.50	25.00
-- Originals have blue label with trident at right					
❏ PRST-7400 [S] Sock!		1966	7.50	15.00	30.00
-- Originals have blue label with trident at right					
❏ PRLP-7445 [M] Boss Soul!		1967	6.25	12.50	25.00
-- Originals have blue label with trident at right					
❏ PRST-7445 [S] Boss Soul!		1967	7.50	15.00	30.00
-- Originals have blue label with trident at right					
❏ PRLP-7495 [M] Gene Ammons Live in Chicago		1967	5.00	10.00	20.00
-- Originals have blue label with trident at right					
❏ PRST-7495 [S] Gene Ammons Live in Chicago		1967	6.25	12.50	25.00
❏ PRLP-7534 [M] Boss Tenor		1967	6.25	12.50	25.00
-- Originals have blue label with trident at right					
❏ PRST-7534 [S] Boss Tenor		1967	5.00	10.00	20.00
-- Originals have blue label with trident at right					
❏ PRST-7552 Jungle Soul		1968	5.00	10.00	20.00
-- Reissue of 7257					
❏ PRST-7708 The Best of Gene Ammons for Beautiful People		1969	5.00	10.00	20.00
❏ PRST-7739 The Boss Is Back!		1970	5.00	10.00	20.00
❏ PRST-7774 The Best of Gene Ammons		1970	5.00	10.00	20.00
SAVOY					
❏ MG-14033 [M] Golden Saxophone		1961	7.50	15.00	30.00
VEE JAY					
❏ LP-3024 [M] Juggin' Around		1961	10.00	20.00	40.00
❏ LPS-3024 [S] Juggin' Around		1961	7.50	15.00	30.00

AMMONS, GENE, AND RICHARD "GROOVE" HOLMES
PACIFIC JAZZ

Number	Title	Yr	VG	VG+	NM
❏ PJ-32 [M]	Groovin' with Jug	1961	10.00	20.00	40.00
❏ ST-32 [S]	Groovin' with Jug	1961	7.50	15.00	30.00

AMMONS, GENE, AND SONNY STITT
CADET

Number	Title	Yr	VG	VG+	NM
❏ LP-785 [M]	Jug and Sonny	1967	5.00	10.00	20.00
CHESS					
❏ LP 1455 [M]	Jug and Sonny	1960	10.00	20.00	40.00
PRESTIGE					
❏ PRLP-7234 [M]	Soul Summit	1962	12.50	25.00	50.00
❏ PRST-7234 [S]	Soul Summit	1962	10.00	20.00	40.00
❏ PRLP-7454 [M]	Soul Summit	1967	5.00	10.00	20.00
VERVE					
❏ V-8426 [M]	Boss Tenors	1962	5.00	10.00	20.00
❏ V6-8426 [S]	Boss Tenors	1962	6.25	12.50	25.00
❏ V-8468 [M]	Boss Tenors in Orbit	1962	5.00	10.00	20.00
❏ V6-8468 [S]	Boss Tenors in Orbit	1962	6.25	12.50	25.00

AMON DUUL
PROPHESY

Number	Title	Yr	VG	VG+	NM
❏ PHS-1003	Amon Duul	1969	6.25	12.50	25.00

ANCIENT GREASE
MERCURY

Number	Title	Yr	VG	VG+	NM
❏ SR-61305	Women and Children First	1970	7.50	15.00	30.00

ANDERS & PONCIA
WARNER BROS.

Number	Title	Yr	VG	VG+	NM
❏ WS 1778	The Anders & Poncia Album	1969	7.50	15.00	30.00

ANDERSEN, ERIC
VANGUARD

Number	Title	Yr	VG	VG+	NM
❏ VSD 79157 [S]	Today Is the Highway	1965	5.00	10.00	20.00
❏ VSD 79206 [S]	'Bout Changes and Things	1966	5.00	10.00	20.00

ANDERSON, AL
Also see NRBQ; THE WILDWEEDS.
VANGUARD

Number	Title	Yr	VG	VG+	NM
❏ VSD-79324	Al Anderson	1973	5.00	10.00	20.00

ANDERSON, BILL
DECCA

Number	Title	Yr	VG	VG+	NM
❏ DL 4192 [M]	Bill Anderson Sings Country Songs	1962	5.00	10.00	20.00
❏ DL 4427 [M]	Still	1963	5.00	10.00	20.00
❏ DL 4859 [M]	Bill Anderson's Greatest Hits	1967	5.00	10.00	20.00
❏ DL 4886 [M]	I Can Do Nothing Alone	1967	6.25	12.50	25.00
❏ DL 74192 [S]	Bill Anderson Sings Country Songs	1962	6.25	12.50	25.00
❏ DL 74427 [S]	Still	1963	6.25	12.50	25.00
❏ DL 74499 [S]	Bill Anderson Sings	1964	5.00	10.00	20.00
❏ DL 74600 [S]	Bill Anderson Showcase	1964	5.00	10.00	20.00
❏ DL 74646 [S]	From This Pen	1965	5.00	10.00	20.00
❏ DL 74686 [S]	Bright Lights and Country Music	1965	5.00	10.00	20.00
❏ DL 74771 [S]	I Love You Drops	1966	5.00	10.00	20.00
❏ DL 74855 [S]	Get While the Gettin's Good	1967	5.00	10.00	20.00
❏ DL 74859 [S]	Bill Anderson's Greatest Hits	1967	5.00	10.00	20.00
❏ DL 74886 [S]	I Can Do Nothing Alone	1967	5.00	10.00	20.00

ANDERSON, BILL, AND JAN HOWARD
Also see each artist's individual listings.
DECCA

Number	Title	Yr	VG	VG+	NM
❏ DL 4959 [M]	For Loving You	1967	6.25	12.50	25.00
❏ DL 74959 [S]	For Loving You	1967	5.00	10.00	20.00
❏ DL 75184	If It's All the Same to You	1970	5.00	10.00	20.00
❏ DL 75293	Bill & Jan (Or Jan & Bill)	1972	5.00	10.00	20.00

ANDERSON, CASEY
ATCO

Number	Title	Yr	VG	VG+	NM
❏ 33-149 [M]	The Bag I'm In	1962	5.00	10.00	20.00
❏ SD 33-149 [S]	The Bag I'm In	1962	6.25	12.50	25.00
❏ 33-166 [M]	More Pretty Girls Than One	1964	5.00	10.00	20.00
❏ SD 33-166 [S]	More Pretty Girls Than One	1964	6.25	12.50	25.00
❏ 33-172 [M]	Live at the Ice House	1965	5.00	10.00	20.00
❏ SD 33-172 [S]	Live at the Ice House	1965	6.25	12.50	25.00
❏ 33-176 [M]	Blues Is a Woman Gone	1965	5.00	10.00	20.00
❏ SD 33-176 [S]	Blues Is a Woman Gone	1965	6.25	12.50	25.00
ELEKTRA					
❏ EKL-192 [M]	Goin' Places	1960	5.00	10.00	20.00
❏ EKS-7192 [S]	Goin' Places	1960	6.25	12.50	25.00

ANDERSON, ERNESTINE
MERCURY

Number	Title	Yr	VG	VG+	NM
❏ MG-20354 [M]	Hot Cargo	1958	10.00	20.00	40.00
❏ MG-20400 [M]	Ernestine Anderson	1959	10.00	20.00	40.00
❏ MG-20492 [M]	Fascinating Ernestine	1959	10.00	20.00	40.00
❏ MG-20496 [M]	My Kinda Swing	1959	10.00	20.00	40.00
❏ MG-20582 [M]	Moanin'	1960	10.00	20.00	40.00
❏ SR-60074 [S]	Ernestine Anderson	1959	12.50	25.00	50.00
❏ SR-60171 [S]	Fascinating Ernestine	1959	12.50	25.00	50.00
❏ SR-60175 [S]	My Kinda Swing	1959	12.50	25.00	50.00
❏ SR-60242 [S]	Moanin'	1960	12.50	25.00	50.00
SUE					
❏ LP 1015 [M]	The New Sound of Ernestine Anderson	1963	5.00	10.00	20.00

ANDERSON, HERB OSCAR
VERVE

Number	Title	Yr	VG	VG+	NM
❏ V-5021 [M]	What Would I Be	1967	5.00	10.00	20.00
❏ V6-5021 [S]	What Would I Be	1967	6.25	12.50	25.00

ANDERSON, LAURIE
WARNER BROS.

Number	Title	Yr	VG	VG+	NM
❏ 25192 [(5)]	The United States Live	1984	7.50	15.00	30.00
-- Boxed set					
❏ WBMS-134-2 [(2) DJ]	Home of the Brave Interview	1986	7.50	15.00	30.00
-- Part of the Warner Bros. Music Show series					

ANDERSON, LEROY
DECCA

Number	Title	Yr	VG	VG+	NM
❏ DL 7509 [10]	Leroy Anderson, Volume 1	195?	7.50	15.00	30.00
❏ DL 7519 [10]	Leroy Anderson, Volume 2	195?	7.50	15.00	30.00
❏ DL 8121 [M]	Blue Tango and Other Favorites	1955	5.00	10.00	20.00
❏ DL 8193 [M]	Christmas Carols	1955	5.00	10.00	20.00
❏ DL 8954 [M]	Leroy Anderson Conducts His Music	1959	5.00	10.00	20.00
❏ DL 9749 [M]	Leroy Anderson "Pops" Concert	195?	5.00	10.00	20.00
❏ DL 74335 [S]	New Music of Leroy Anderson	1962	5.00	10.00	20.00
❏ DL 78865 [S]	Leroy Anderson Conducts Leroy Anderson	1958	5.00	10.00	20.00
❏ DL 78954 [S]	Leroy Anderson Conducts His Music	1959	6.25	12.50	25.00

Number	Title	Yr	VG	VG+	NM

ANDERSON, LIZ
RCA VICTOR

Number	Title	Yr	VG	VG+	NM
❏ LPM-3769 [M]	Liz Anderson Sings	1967	7.50	15.00	30.00
❏ LSP-3769 [S]	Liz Anderson Sings	1967	5.00	10.00	20.00
❏ LPM-3852 [M]	Cookin' Up Hits	1967	7.50	15.00	30.00
❏ LSP-3852 [S]	Cookin' Up Hits	1967	5.00	10.00	20.00
❏ LPM-3908 [M]	Liz Anderson Sings Her Favorites	1968	10.00	20.00	40.00
❏ LSP-3908 [S]	Liz Anderson Sings Her Favorites	1968	5.00	10.00	20.00
❏ LSP-4014	Like a Merry-Go-Round	1968	5.00	10.00	20.00
❏ LSP-4222	If the Creek Don't Rise	1969	5.00	10.00	20.00
❏ LSP-4346	Husband Hunting	1970	5.00	10.00	20.00

ANDERSON, LYNN
CHART

Number	Title	Yr	VG	VG+	NM
❏ CHM-1001 [M]	Ride, Ride, Ride	1967	5.00	10.00	20.00
❏ CHM-1004 [M]	Promises, Promises	1968	5.00	10.00	20.00

ANDERSON, MARIAN
RCA VICTOR RED SEAL

Number	Title	Yr	VG	VG+	NM
❏ LM-110 [10]	Spirituals	195?	25.00	50.00	100.00
❏ LM-2032 [M]	Spirituals	195?	20.00	40.00	80.00
❏ LSC-2592 [S]	He's Got the Whole World in His Hands	1962	5.00	10.00	20.00
-- Originals with "shaded dog" label					
❏ LSC-2613 [S]	Marian Anderson Sings Christmas Carols	1961	6.25	12.50	25.00
-- Originals with "shaded dog" label					
❏ LRM-7006 [10]	Eleven Great Sprituals	1951	25.00	50.00	100.00
❏ LM 7008 [10]	Marian Anderson Sings Christmas Carols	1954	15.00	30.00	60.00

ANDERSON, MILDRED
BLUESVILLE

Number	Title	Yr	VG	VG+	NM
❏ BVLP-1004 [M]	Person to Person	1960	12.50	25.00	50.00
-- Blue and silver label					
❏ BVLP-1004 [M]	Person to Person	1964	6.25	12.50	25.00
-- Blue label with trident logo					
❏ BVLP-1017 [M]	No More in Life	1961	12.50	25.00	50.00
-- Blue and silver label					
❏ BVLP-1017 [M]	No More in Life	1964	6.25	12.50	25.00
-- Blue label with trident logo					

ANDERSON, PINK
BLUESVILLE

Number	Title	Yr	VG	VG+	NM
❏ BVLP-1038 [M]	Carolina Blues Man	1961	30.00	60.00	120.00
-- Blue label, silver print					
❏ BVLP-1038 [M]	Carolina Blues Man	1964	7.50	15.00	30.00
-- Blue label with trident logo					
❏ BVLP-1051 [M]	Medicine Show Man	1962	25.00	50.00	100.00
-- Blue label, silver print					
❏ BVLP-1051 [M]	Medicine Show Man	1964	7.50	15.00	30.00
-- Blue label with trident logo					
❏ BVLP-1071 [M]	Ballad and Folk Singer	1963	25.00	50.00	100.00
-- Blue label, silver print					
❏ BVLP-1071 [M]	Ballad and Folk Singer	1964	7.50	15.00	30.00
-- Blue label with trident logo					

ANDERSON, PINK, AND REV. GARY DAVIS
Also see each artist's individual listings.
RIVERSIDE

Number	Title	Yr	VG	VG+	NM
❏ RLP 12-611 [M]	Carolina Street Ballads/ Harlem Street Spirituals	196?	15.00	30.00	60.00

ANDREWS SISTERS, THE
Also see BING CROSBY.
CAPITOL

Number	Title	Yr	VG	VG+	NM
❏ T 790 [M]	The Andrews Sisters in Hi-Fi	1957	7.50	15.00	30.00
❏ T 860 [M]	Fresh and Fancy Free	1957	7.50	15.00	30.00
❏ T 973 [M]	The Dancing Twenties	1957	7.50	15.00	30.00
❏ T 1924 [M]	The Hits of the Andrews Sisters	1963	5.00	10.00	20.00
DECCA					
❏ DL 4019 [M]	Curtain Call	1956	7.50	15.00	30.00
❏ DL 5065 [10]	Tropical Songs	1950	10.00	20.00	40.00
❏ DL 5120 [10]	The Andrews Sisters	1951	10.00	20.00	40.00
❏ DL 5155 [10]	Club 15	1951	10.00	20.00	40.00
❏ DL 5264 [10]	Berlin Songs	1951	10.00	20.00	40.00
❏ DL 5282 [10]	Christmas Cheer	1950	10.00	20.00	40.00
❏ DL 5306 [10]	I Love to Tell the Story	1952	10.00	20.00	40.00
❏ DL 5423 [10]	My Isle of Golden Dreams	1953	10.00	20.00	40.00
❏ DL 5438 [10]	Sing, Sing, Sing	1953	10.00	20.00	40.00
❏ DL 8354 [M]	Jingle Bells	1956	7.50	15.00	30.00
❏ DL 8360 [M]	The Andrews Sisters -- By Popular Demand	1957	7.50	15.00	30.00

DOT

Number	Title	Yr	VG	VG+	NM
❏ DLP 25406 [S]	The Andrews Sisters' Greatest Hits	1962	5.00	10.00	20.00
❏ DLP 25452 [S]	Great Golden Hits	1962	5.00	10.00	20.00

ANDREWS, ERNIE
GENE NORMAN PRESENTS

Number	Title	Yr	VG	VG+	NM
❏ GNP-28 [M]	In the Dark	1957	10.00	20.00	40.00
❏ GNP-42 [M]	Ernie Andrews	1959	10.00	20.00	40.00
❏ GNP-43 [M]	Travelin' Light	1959	10.00	20.00	40.00

ANDREWS, JULIE
COLUMBIA

Number	Title	Yr	VG	VG+	NM
❏ CL 1712 [M]	Broadway's Fair Julie	1962	5.00	10.00	20.00
-- Red and black label with six "eye" logos					
❏ CL 1886 [M]	Don't Go In the Lion's Cage Tonight	1963	5.00	10.00	20.00
❏ CS 8512 [S]	Broadway's Fair Julie	1962	6.25	12.50	25.00
-- Red and black label with six "eye" logos					
❏ CS 8686 [S]	Don't Go In the Lion's Cage Tonight	1963	6.25	12.50	25.00
RCA VICTOR					
❏ LPM-1403 [M]	The Lass with the Delicate Air	1957	10.00	20.00	40.00
-- With pale blue jacket and the words "Julie Andrews" in a picture frame					
❏ LPM-1403 [M]	The Lass with the Delicate Air	1958	7.50	15.00	30.00
-- With altered cover; "RE" on jacket					
❏ LSP-1403 [S]	The Lass with the Delicate Air	1958	15.00	30.00	60.00
❏ LPM-1681 [M]	Julie Andrews Sings	1958	7.50	15.00	30.00
❏ LSP-1681 [S]	Julie Andrews Sings	1958	12.50	25.00	50.00

ANDREWS, LEE, AND THE HEARTS
LOST-NITE

Number	Title	Yr	VG	VG+	NM
❏ LP-101 [M]	Biggest Hits	1964	25.00	50.00	100.00
-- Yellow vinyl					
❏ LP-101 [M]	Biggest Hits	1964	12.50	25.00	50.00
-- Black vinyl					
❏ LP-113 [M]	Lee Andrews and the Hearts Live	1965	12.50	25.00	50.00

ANGELI, PIER
ROULETTE

Number	Title	Yr	VG	VG+	NM
❏ R-25051 [M]	Italia Con Pier Angeli	1959	6.25	12.50	25.00
❏ SR-25051 [S]	Italia Con Pier Angeli	1959	7.50	15.00	30.00

ANGELOU, MAYA
LIBERTY

Number	Title	Yr	VG	VG+	NM
❏ LRP-3028 [M]	Miss Calypso	1958	12.50	25.00	50.00

ANGELS, THE
ASCOT

Number	Title	Yr	VG	VG+	NM
❏ AM 13009 [M]	Twelve of Their Greatest Hits	1964	6.25	12.50	25.00
❏ AS 16009 [S]	Twelve of Their Greatest Hits	1964	7.50	15.00	30.00
CAPRICE					
❏ LP 1001 [M]	...And the Angels Sing	1962	30.00	60.00	120.00
❏ SLP 1001 [S]	...And the Angels Sing	1962	50.00	100.00	200.00
SMASH					
❏ MGS-27039 [M]	My Boyfriend's Back	1963	10.00	20.00	40.00
❏ MGS-27048 [M]	A Halo to You	1964	10.00	20.00	40.00
❏ SRS-67039 [S]	My Boyfriend's Back	1963	15.00	30.00	60.00
❏ SRS-67048 [S]	A Halo to You	1964	15.00	30.00	60.00

ANGRY SAMOANS
BAD TRIP

Number	Title	Yr	VG	VG+	NM
❏ (# unknown)	Back from Samoa	1982	7.50	15.00	30.00
❏ 001 [EP]	Different World/Unhinged + 4	1986	6.25	12.50	25.00
❏ 002	The Mistaken	1987	6.25	12.50	25.00
-- As "The Mistaken"; 1,000 copies made					
❏ 201 [EP]	Inside My Brain	1981	7.50	15.00	30.00
-- Original with heavy gray cardboard cover					

ANIMALS, THE
Also see ERIC BURDON; ALAN PRICE.
MGM

Number	Title	Yr	VG	VG+	NM
❏ E-4264 [M]	The Animals	1964	7.50	15.00	30.00
-- "The House of the Rising Sun" is the edited 45 version					
❏ E-4264 [M-DJ]	The Animals	1964	25.00	50.00	100.00
-- Yellow label promo					
❏ SE-4264 [R]	The Animals	1964	6.25	12.50	25.00
-- "The House of the Rising Sun" is the edited 45 version (rechanneled, like the rest of the LP)					
❏ E-4281 [M]	The Animals On Tour	1965	7.50	15.00	30.00
❏ E-4281 [M-DJ]	The Animals On Tour	1965	25.00	50.00	100.00
-- Yellow label promo					
❏ SE-4281 [R]	The Animals On Tour	1965	6.25	12.50	25.00
❏ E-4305 [M]	Animal Tracks	1965	10.00	20.00	40.00
❏ E-4305 [M-DJ]	Animal Tracks	1965	37.50	75.00	150.00
-- Yellow label promo					

Number	Title	Yr	VG	VG+	NM
❏ SE-4305 [R]	Animal Tracks	1965	7.50	15.00	30.00
❏ E-4324 [M]	The Best of the Animals	1966	5.00	10.00	20.00
-- This album was the first to contain the full-length version of "House of the Rising Sun."					
❏ E-4324 [M-DJ]	The Best of the Animals	1966	20.00	40.00	80.00
-- Yellow label promo					
❏ SE-4324 [R]	The Best of the Animals	1966	6.25	12.50	25.00
❏ E-4384 [M]	Animalization	1966	6.25	12.50	25.00
❏ E-4384 [M-DJ]	Animalization	1966	25.00	50.00	100.00
-- Yellow label promo					
❏ SE-4384 [P]	Animalization	1966	7.50	15.00	30.00
-- All stereo except "Inside Looking Out," which is rechanneled.					
❏ E-4414 [M]	Animalism	1966	6.25	12.50	25.00
❏ E-4414 [M-DJ]	Animalism	1966	25.00	50.00	100.00
-- Yellow label promo					
❏ SE-4414 [S]	Animalism	1966	7.50	15.00	30.00
❏ SE-4433 [S]	Eric Is Here	1967	5.00	10.00	20.00
❏ E-4454 [M]	The Best of Eric Burdon and the Animals, Vol. 2	1967	5.00	10.00	20.00
❏ SE-4454 [P]	The Best of Eric Burdon and the Animals, Vol. 2	1967	5.00	10.00	20.00
❏ E-4484 [M]	Winds of Change	1967	5.00	10.00	20.00
❏ SE-4484 [S]	Winds of Change	1967	6.25	12.50	25.00
❏ E-4537 [M]	The Twain Shall Meet	1968	5.00	10.00	20.00
❏ SE-4537 [S]	The Twain Shall Meet	1968	6.25	12.50	25.00
❏ SE-4553	Every One of Us	1968	6.25	12.50	25.00
❏ SE-4591 [(2)]	Love Is	1968	12.50	25.00	50.00
❏ ST 90414 [R]	The Animals on Tour	1965	10.00	20.00	40.00
-- Capitol Record Club edition					
❏ T 90414 [M]	The Animals on Tour	1965	12.50	25.00	50.00
-- Capitol Record Club edition					
❏ T 90571 [M]	Animal Tracks	1965	12.50	25.00	50.00
-- Capitol Record Club edition					
❏ KAO 90622 [M]	The Best of the Animals	1966	10.00	20.00	40.00
-- Capitol Record Club edition					
❏ SKAO 90622 [R]	The Best of the Animals	1966	10.00	20.00	40.00
-- Capitol Record Club edition					
❏ T 90687 [M]	The Animals	1966	12.50	25.00	50.00
-- Capitol Record Club edition					
❏ ST 90923 [P]	Animalization	1966	12.50	25.00	50.00
-- Capitol Record Club edition					
❏ T 90923 [M]	Animalization	1966	12.50	25.00	50.00
-- Capitol Record Club edition					

ANIMATED EGG, THE
ALSHIRE

Number	Title	Yr	VG	VG+	NM
❏ SF-5104	The Animated Egg	1967	12.50	25.00	50.00

ANKA, PAUL
ABC-PARAMOUNT

Number	Title	Yr	VG	VG+	NM
❏ 240 [M]	Paul Anka	1958	12.50	25.00	50.00
❏ 296 [M]	My Heart Sings	1959	7.50	15.00	30.00
❏ S-296 [S]	My Heart Sings	1959	12.50	25.00	50.00
❏ 323 [M]	Paul Anka Sings His Big 15	1960	12.50	25.00	50.00
❏ S-323 [R]	Paul Anka Sings His Big 15	196?	7.50	15.00	30.00
❏ 347 [M]	Paul Anka Swings for Young Lovers	1960	7.50	15.00	30.00
❏ S-347 [S]	Paul Anka Swings for Young Lovers	1960	10.00	20.00	40.00
❏ 353 [M]	Anka at the Copa	1960	7.50	15.00	30.00
❏ S-353 [S]	Anka at the Copa	1960	10.00	20.00	40.00
❏ 360 [M]	It's Christmas Everywhere	1960	7.50	15.00	30.00
❏ S 360 [S]	It's Christmas Everywhere	1960	10.00	20.00	40.00
❏ 371 [M]	Strictly Instrumental	1961	7.00	15.00	30.00
❏ S-371 [S]	Strictly Instrumental	1961	10.00	20.00	40.00
❏ 390 [M]	Paul Anka Sings His Big 15, Vol. 2	1961	7.50	15.00	30.00
❏ S-390 [S]	Paul Anka Sings His Big 15, Vol. 2	1961	10.00	20.00	40.00
❏ 409 [M]	Paul Anka Sings His Big 15, Vol. 3	1962	6.25	12.50	25.00
❏ S-409 [S]	Paul Anka Sings His Big 15, Vol. 3	1962	7.50	15.00	30.00
❏ 420 [M]	Diana	1962	6.25	12.50	25.00
❏ S-420 [S]	Diana	1962	7.50	15.00	30.00

RCA VICTOR

Number	Title	Yr	VG	VG+	NM
❏ LPM-2502 [M]	Young, Alive and In Love!	1962	6.25	12.50	25.00
-- With portrait of Paul Anka on front cover					
❏ LSP-2502 [S]	Young, Alive and In Love!	1962	7.50	15.00	30.00
-- With portrait of Paul Anka on front cover					
❏ LSP-2502 [S]	Young, Alive and In Love!	1962	5.00	10.00	20.00
-- With portrait of Paul Anka on back cover					
❏ LPM-2575 [M]	Let's Sit This One Out	1962	5.00	10.00	20.00
❏ LSP-2575 [S]	Let's Sit This One Out	1962	6.25	12.50	25.00
❏ LPM-2614 [M]	Our Man Around the World	1963	5.00	10.00	20.00
❏ LSP-2614 [S]	Our Man Around the World	1963	6.25	12.50	25.00
❏ LPM-2691 [M]	Paul Anka's 21 Golden Hits	1963	5.00	10.00	20.00
❏ LSP-2691 [S]	Paul Anka's 21 Golden Hits	1963	6.25	12.50	25.00
-- LPM/LSP-2691 has re-recorded versions of ABC-Paramount hits					
❏ LSP-2744 [S]	Songs I Wish I'd Written	1963	5.00	10.00	20.00
❏ LSP-2996 [S]	Excitement on Park Avenue	1964	5.00	10.00	20.00
❏ LSP-3580 [S]	Strictly Nashville	1966	5.00	10.00	20.00
❏ LSP-3875 [S]	Paul Anka Live	1967	5.00	10.00	20.00

RIVIERA

Number	Title	Yr	VG	VG+	NM
❏ 0047 [M]	Paul Anka and Others	1959	37.50	75.00	150.00
-- With Paul Anka's RPM recordings plus tracks by other artists					

ANN-MARGRET
Also see AL HIRT AND ANN-MARGRET.
RCA VICTOR

Number	Title	Yr	VG	VG+	NM
❏ LPM-2399 [M]	And Here She Is...	1961	7.50	15.00	30.00
❏ LPM-2453 [M]	On the Way Up	1961	7.50	15.00	30.00
❏ LPM-2551 [M]	The Vivacious One	1962	7.50	15.00	30.00
❏ LPM-2659 [M]	Bachelor's Paradise	1963	7.50	15.00	30.00
❏ LPM-3710 [M]	Songs from The Swinger and Others	1966	15.00	30.00	60.00
❏ LSP-2399 [S]	And Here She Is...	1961	10.00	20.00	40.00
❏ LSP-2453 [S]	On the Way Up	1961	10.00	20.00	40.00
❏ LSP-2551 [S]	The Vivacious One	1962	10.00	20.00	40.00
❏ LSP-2659 [S]	Bachelor's Paradise	1963	10.00	20.00	40.00
❏ LSP-3710 [S]	Songs from The Swinger and Others	1966	20.00	40.00	80.00

ANNETTE
BUENA VISTA

Number	Title	Yr	VG	VG+	NM
❏ BV-3301 [M]	Annette	1959	30.00	60.00	120.00
❏ BV-3302 [M]	Annette Sings Anka	1960	25.00	50.00	100.00
❏ BV-3303 [M]	Hawaiiannette	1960	18.75	37.50	75.00
❏ BV-3304 [M]	Italiannette	1960	18.75	37.50	75.00
❏ BV-3305 [M]	Dance Annette	1961	18.75	37.50	75.00
❏ BV-3312 [M]	The Story of My Teens	1962	18.75	37.50	75.00
❏ BV-3313 [M]	Teen Street	1962	18.75	37.50	75.00
❏ BV-3314 [M]	Muscle Beach Party	1963	18.75	37.50	75.00
❏ STER-3314 [S]	Muscle Beach Party	1963	37.50	75.00	150.00
❏ BV-3316 [M]	Beach Party	1963	15.00	30.00	60.00
❏ STER-3316 [S]	Beach Party	1963	25.00	50.00	100.00
❏ BV-3320 [M]	Annette on Campus	1964	12.50	25.00	50.00
❏ STER-3320 [S]	Annette on Campus	1964	25.00	50.00	100.00
❏ BV-3324 [M]	Annette at Bikini Beach	1964	12.50	25.00	50.00
❏ STER-3324 [S]	Annette at Bikini Beach	1964	25.00	50.00	100.00
❏ BV-3325 [M]	Annette's Pajama Party	1964	10.00	20.00	40.00
❏ STER-3325 [S]	Annette's Pajama Party	1964	25.00	50.00	100.00
❏ BV-3327 [M]	Annette Sings Golden Surfin' Hits	1964	25.00	50.00	100.00
❏ STER-3327 [S]	Annette Sings Golden Surfin' Hits	1964	37.50	75.00	150.00
❏ BV-3328 [M]	Something Borrowed, Something Blue	1964	15.00	30.00	60.00
❏ STER-3328 [P]	Something Borrowed, Something Blue	1964	25.00	50.00	100.00
❏ BV-4037	Annette Funicello	1972	12.50	25.00	50.00

RHINO

Number	Title	Yr	VG	VG+	NM
❏ RNLP-702 [PD]	The Best of Annette	1984	6.25	12.50	25.00

ANNETTE / HAYLEY MILLS
Also see each artist's individual listings.
DISNEYLAND

Number	Title	Yr	VG	VG+	NM
❏ DL-3508 [M]	Annette and Hayley Mills (Singing 10 of Their Greatest All-Time Hits)	1964	250.00	500.00	1,000.
-- TV offer; issued with paper jacket. Though the cover says "Buena Vista Records Presents," the label is the yellow Disneyland label					

ANONYMOUS
A-MAJOR

Number	Title	Yr	VG	VG+	NM
❏ AMLS-1002	Inside the Shadow	1976	62.50	125.00	250.00

ANT TRIP CEREMONY
C.R.C.

Number	Title	Yr	VG	VG+	NM
❏ 2129	24 Hours	1970	150.00	300.00	600.00

ANTHEM
BUDDAH

Number	Title	Yr	VG	VG+	NM
❏ BDS-5071	Anthem	1971	5.00	10.00	20.00

ANTHONY, RAY
CAPITOL

Number	Title	Yr	VG	VG+	NM
❏ T 749 [M]	Jazz Session at the Tower	1956	10.00	20.00	40.00

AORTA
COLUMBIA

Number	Title	Yr	VG	VG+	NM
❏ CS 9785	Aorta	1969	7.50	15.00	30.00

HAPPY TIGER

Number	Title	Yr	VG	VG+	NM
❏ HT-1010	Aorta 2	1970	10.00	20.00	40.00

Number	Title	Yr	VG	VG+	NM
APHRODITE'S CHILD					
VERTIGO					
❑ VEL-2-500 [(2)] 666 (The Apocalypse of John)		1972	5.00	10.00	20.00
APPEL, DAVE					
CAMEO					
❑ C-1004 [M]	Alone Together	1958	7.50	15.00	30.00
APPLE PIE MOTHERHOOD BAND, THE					
ATLANTIC					
❑ SD 8189	The Apple Pie Motherhood Band	1968	6.25	12.50	25.00
❑ SD 8233	Apple Pie	1969	6.25	12.50	25.00
APPLETREE THEATRE CO.					
VERVE FORECAST					
❑ FTS-3042	Playback	1968	7.50	15.00	30.00
-- RICK NELSON appears on this album					
APRIL WINE					
BIG TREE					
❑ BTS 2012	April Wine	1972	5.00	10.00	20.00
AQUATONES, THE					
FARGO					
❑ 3001 [M]	The Aquatones Sing	1964	125.00	250.00	500.00
ARBORS, THE					
DATE					
❑ TEM 3011 [M] Valley of the Dolls		1967	5.00	10.00	20.00
ARCHER, FRANCES, AND BEVERLY GILE					
DISNEYLAND					
❑ WDL-1008 [M] A Child's Garden of Verses		1959	5.00	10.00	20.00
-- Reissue of 3004					
❑ DQ-1226 [M] Songs from All Around the World		1962	5.00	10.00	20.00
-- Black and white back cover (original)					
❑ DQ-1241 [M] A Child's Garden of Verses		1964	5.00	10.00	20.00
-- Reissue of 1008					
❑ EB-1347/8 [10]A Child's Garden of Verses		1955	37.50	75.00	150.00
-- The very first LP released on Disneyland Records					
❑ WDL-3004 [M] A Child's Garden of Verses		1956	6.25	12.50	25.00
-- Reissue of 1347/8					
❑ WDL-3006 [M] Folk Songs from the Far Corners		1957	6.25	12.50	25.00
❑ WDL-3023 [M] Community Concert		1958	7.50	15.00	30.00
❑ ST-3802 [M] A Child's Garden of Verses		1971	6.25	12.50	25.00
-- Reissue of 1241					
ARCHIES, THE					
CALENDAR					
❑ KES-101	The Archies	1968	6.25	12.50	25.00
❑ KES-103	Everything's Archie	1969	6.25	12.50	25.00
KIRSHNER					
❑ KES-103 [DJ]	Everything's Archie Box	1969	25.00	50.00	100.00
-- Box with LP, photos, press kit and buttons					
❑ KES-105	Jingle Jangle	1969	6.25	12.50	25.00
❑ KES-107	Sunshine	1970	6.25	12.50	25.00
❑ KES-109	The Archies Grestest Hits	1970	6.25	12.50	25.00
ARDEN, TONI					
DECCA					
❑ DL 8651 [M]	Miss Toni Arden	1957	7.50	15.00	30.00
-- Black label, silver print					
❑ DL 8765 [M]	Sing a Song of Italy	1958	6.25	12.50	25.00
-- Black label, silver print					
❑ DL 8875 [M]	Besame	1959	5.00	10.00	20.00
-- Black label, silver print					
❑ DL 78765 [S]	Sing a Song of Italy	1959	7.50	15.00	30.00
-- Maroon label, silver print					
❑ DL 78875 [S]	Besame	1959	7.50	15.00	30.00
-- Maroon label, silver print					
AREA CODE 615					
POLYDOR					
❑ 24-4002	Area Code 615	1969	5.00	10.00	20.00
❑ 24-4025	A Trip in the Country	1970	5.00	10.00	20.00
ARGENT					
EPIC					
❑ BN 26525	Argent	1970	5.00	10.00	20.00
-- Yellow label					

Number	Title	Yr	VG	VG+	NM
❑ KE 30128	A Ring of Hands	1971	5.00	10.00	20.00
-- Yellow label					
❑ KE 31556	All Together Now	1972	5.00	10.00	20.00
-- Yellow label					
❑ KE 32195	In Deep	1973	5.00	10.00	20.00
-- Orange label					
❑ PEQ 32195 [Q] In Deep		1974	7.50	15.00	30.00
❑ PE 32573	Nexus	1974	5.00	10.00	20.00
-- Orange label					
❑ KEG 33079 [(2)]Encore -- Live in Concert		1975	5.00	10.00	20.00
-- Orange labels					
❑ PE 33422	Circus	1975	5.00	10.00	20.00
-- Orange label					
ARISTOCATS, THE					
HIFI					
❑ J-610 [M]	Boogie and Blues	1959	7.50	15.00	30.00
❑ JS-610 [S]	Boogie and Blues	1959	10.00	20.00	40.00
ARLEN, HAROLD, AND "FRIEND"					
The "Friend" is BARBRA STREISAND.					
COLUMBIA MASTERWORKS					
❑ OL 6520 [M]	Harold Sings Arlen	1966	7.50	15.00	30.00
❑ OS 2920 [S]	Harold Sings Arlen	1966	10.00	20.00	40.00
-- Gray label with "360 Sound" in white					
ARMAGEDDON					
Two different groups.					
A&M					
❑ SP-4513	Armageddon	1975	5.00	10.00	20.00
-- With Keith Relf, ex-YARDBIRDS					
AMOS					
❑ 73075	Armageddon	1970	6.25	12.50	25.00
ARMSTRONG, LOUIS					
ABC					
❑ S-650	What a Wonderful World	1968	7.50	15.00	30.00
AUDIO FIDELITY					
❑ AFLP-1930 [M] Louis Armstrong Plays King Oliver		1960	7.50	15.00	30.00
❑ AFSD-5930 [S] Louis Armstrong Plays King Oliver		1960	10.00	20.00	40.00
❑ AFSD-6128 [S] Ain't Gonna Give Nobody None of My Jelly Roll		1964	5.00	10.00	20.00
❑ AFSD-6132 [S] The Best of Louis Armstrong		1964	5.00	10.00	20.00
BRUNSWICK					
❑ BL 58004 [10] Armstrong Classics		1950	25.00	50.00	100.00
BUENA VISTA					
❑ BV-4044	Disney Swings the Satchmo Way	1968	10.00	20.00	40.00
COLUMBIA					
❑ CL 591 [M]	Louis Armstrong Plays W.C. Handy	1954	10.00	20.00	40.00
❑ CL 708 [M]	Satch Plays Fats	1955	10.00	20.00	40.00
❑ CL 840 [M]	Ambassador Satch	1956	10.00	20.00	40.00
❑ CL 851 [M]	The Louis Armstrong Story, Volume 1	1956	7.50	15.00	30.00
❑ CL 852 [M]	The Louis Armstrong Story, Volume 2	1956	7.50	15.00	30.00
❑ CL 853 [M]	The Louis Armstrong Story, Volume 3	1956	7.50	15.00	30.00
❑ CL 854 [M]	The Louis Armstrong Story, Volume 4	1956	7.50	15.00	30.00
❑ CL 1077 [M]	Satchmo the Great	1957	7.50	15.00	30.00
❑ CL 2638 [M]	Louis Armstrong's Greatest Hits	1967	5.00	10.00	20.00
❑ ML 4383 [M]	The Louis Armstrong Story, Volume 1	1951	12.50	25.00	50.00
❑ ML 4384 [M]	The Louis Armstrong Story, Volume 2	1951	12.50	25.00	50.00
❑ ML 4385 [M]	The Louis Armstrong Story, Volume 3	1951	12.50	25.00	50.00
❑ ML 4386 [M]	The Louis Armstrong Story, Volume 4	1951	12.50	25.00	50.00
❑ CL 6335 [10]	Louis Armstrong Plays W.C. Handy, Volume 2	1955	10.00	20.00	40.00
DECCA					
❑ DX 108 [(2) M] Satchmo at Symphony Hall		1954	18.75	37.50	75.00
-- Black labels, silver print					
❑ DX 155 [(4) M] Satchmo, A Musical Autobiography		1956	25.00	50.00	100.00
-- Black labels, silver print					
❑ DXM 155 [(4) M] Satchmo, A Musical Autobiography		1960	10.00	20.00	40.00
-- Black labels with color bars					
❑ DXB 183 [(2) M]The Best of Louis Armstrong		196?	7.50	15.00	30.00
❑ DL 4137 [M]	Satchmo's Golden Favorites	1961	5.00	10.00	20.00
❑ DL 4227 [M]	I Love Jazz	1962	5.00	10.00	20.00
❑ DL 4230 [M]	Satchmo, A Musical Autobiography, 1926-1927	1962	6.25	12.50	25.00

Number	Title	Yr	VG	VG+	NM
❑ DL 4245 [M]	King Louis	1962	5.00	10.00	20.00
❑ DL 4330 [M]	Satchmo, A Musical Autobiography, 1928-1930	1962	6.25	12.50	25.00
❑ DL 4331 [M]	Satchmo, A Musical Autobiography, 1930-1934	1962	6.25	12.50	25.00
❑ DL 5225 [10]	New Orleans to New York	1950	18.75	37.50	75.00
❑ DL 5279 [10]	New Orleans Days	1950	18.75	37.50	75.00
❑ DL 5280 [10]	Jazz Concert	1950	18.75	37.50	75.00
❑ DL 5401 [10]	Satchmo Serenades	1952	18.75	37.50	75.00
❑ DL 5532 [10]	Latter-Day Louis	1954	18.75	37.50	75.00
❑ DL 5536 [10]	Louis Armstrong-Gordon Jenkins	1954	18.75	37.50	75.00
❑ DL 8037 [M]	Satchmo at Symphony Hall, Volume 1	1954	10.00	20.00	40.00
-- Black label, silver print					
❑ DL 8038 [M]	Satchmo at Symphony Hall, Volume 2	1954	10.00	20.00	40.00
-- Black label, silver print					
❑ DL 8041 [M]	Satchmo at Pasadena	1954	10.00	20.00	40.00
-- Black label, silver print					
❑ DL 8126 [M]	Satchmo Sings	1955	10.00	20.00	40.00
-- Black label, silver print					
❑ DL 8168 [M]	Louis Armstrong at the Crescendo, Volume 1	1955	10.00	20.00	40.00
-- Black label, silver print					
❑ DL 8169 [M]	Louis Armstrong at the Crescendo, Volume 2	1955	10.00	20.00	40.00
-- Black label, silver print					
❑ DL 8211 [M]	Satchmo Serenades	1956	10.00	20.00	40.00
-- Black label, silver print					
❑ DL 8283 [M]	New Orleans Jazz	1956	10.00	20.00	40.00
-- Black label, silver print					
❑ DL 8284 [M]	Jazz Classics	1956	10.00	20.00	40.00
-- Black label, silver print					
❑ DL 8327 [M]	Satchmo's Collector's Items	1957	10.00	20.00	40.00
-- Black label, silver print					
❑ DL 8329 [M]	New Orleans Nights	1957	10.00	20.00	40.00
-- Black label, silver print					
❑ DL 8330 [M]	Satchmo on Stage	1957	10.00	20.00	40.00
-- Black label, silver print					
❑ DL 8488 [M]	Louis and the Angels	1957	10.00	20.00	40.00
-- Black label, silver print					
❑ DL 8781 [M]	Louis and the Good Book	1958	10.00	20.00	40.00
-- Black label, silver print					
❑ DL 8840 [M]	Satchmo in Style	1958	10.00	20.00	40.00
-- Black label, silver print					
❑ DL 8963 [M]	Satchmo, A Musical Autobiography, 1923-1925	1960	6.25	12.50	25.00
❑ DL 9225 [M]	Rare Items (1935-1944)	196?	5.00	10.00	20.00
❑ DL 9233 [M]	Young Louis the Sideman (1924-1927)	196?	5.00	10.00	20.00

MCA

Number	Title	Yr	VG	VG+	NM
❑ 10006 [(4)]	Satchmo, A Musical Autobiography	197?	6.25	12.50	25.00
-- Reissue of Decca 155					

RCA VICTOR

Number	Title	Yr	VG	VG+	NM
❑ WPT 9 [10]	Town Hall Concert '48	1951	20.00	40.00	80.00
❑ LJM-1005 [M]	Louis Armstrong Sings the Blues	1954	12.50	25.00	50.00
❑ LPM-1443 [M]	Town Hall Concert Plus	1957	12.50	25.00	50.00
❑ LPM-2322 [M]	A Rare Batch of Satch	1961	6.25	12.50	25.00
❑ LPM-2971 [M]	Louis Armstrong in the '30s/ in the '40s	1964	5.00	10.00	20.00
❑ VPM-6044 [(2)]	July 4, 1900/July 6, 1971	1971	5.00	10.00	20.00

RIVERSIDE

Number	Title	Yr	VG	VG+	NM
❑ RLP 12-101 [M]	The Young Louis Armstrong	195?	10.00	20.00	40.00
-- Blue label					
❑ RLP 12-101 [M]	The Young Louis Armstrong	1956	20.00	40.00	80.00
-- White label, blue print					
❑ RLP 12-122 [M]	Louis Armstrong 1923	195?	10.00	20.00	40.00
-- Blue label					
❑ RLP 12-122 [M]	Louis Armstrong 1923	1956	20.00	40.00	80.00
-- White label, blue print					
❑ RLP-1001 [10]	Louis Armstrong Plays the Blues	1953	25.00	50.00	100.00
❑ RLP-1029 [10]	Louis Armstrong with King Oliver's Creole Jazz Band 1923	1953	25.00	50.00	100.00

VERVE

Number	Title	Yr	VG	VG+	NM
❑ MGV-4012 [M]	Louis Under the Stars	1957	12.50	25.00	50.00
❑ V-4012 [M]	Louis Under the Stars	1961	5.00	10.00	20.00
❑ MGV-4035 [M]	I've Got the World on a String	1959	12.50	25.00	50.00
❑ V-4035 [M]	I've Got the World on a String	1961	5.00	10.00	20.00
❑ MGVS-6044 [S]	Louis Under the Stars	1960	10.00	20.00	40.00
❑ MGVS-6101 [S]	I've Got the World on a String	1960	10.00	20.00	40.00

ARMSTRONG, LOUIS, AND DUKE ELLINGTON
Also see each artist's individual listings.
MOBILE FIDELITY

Number	Title	Yr	VG	VG+	NM
❑ 2-155 [(2)]	The Great Reunion	1984	20.00	40.00	80.00
-- Audiophile vinyl					

ROULETTE

Number	Title	Yr	VG	VG+	NM
❑ R 52074 [M]	Together for the First Time	1961	6.25	12.50	25.00
❑ SR 52074 [S]	Together for the First Time	1961	5.00	10.00	20.00
❑ R 52103 [M]	The Great Reunion	1963	5.00	10.00	20.00
❑ SR 52103 [S]	The Great Reunion	1963	6.25	12.50	25.00

ARMSTRONG, LOUIS, AND THE MILLS BROTHERS
Also see each artist's individual listings.
DECCA

Number	Title	Yr	VG	VG+	NM
❑ DL 5509 [10]	Louis Armstrong and the Mills Brothers	1954	15.00	30.00	60.00

ARMSTRONG, LOUIS, AND OSCAR PETERSON
Also see each artist's individual listings.
VERVE

Number	Title	Yr	VG	VG+	NM
❑ MGV-8322 [M]	Louis Armstrong Meets Oscar Peterson	1959	12.50	25.00	50.00
❑ MGVS-6062 [S]	Louis Armstrong Meets Oscar Peterson	1960	10.00	20.00	40.00
❑ V-8322 [M]	Louis Armstrong Meets Oscar Peterson	1961	5.00	10.00	20.00

ARNAZ, DESI
RCA VICTOR

Number	Title	Yr	VG	VG+	NM
❑ LPM-3096 [10]	Babalu!	1954	30.00	60.00	120.00

ARNOLD, BILLY BOY
PRESTIGE

Number	Title	Yr	VG	VG+	NM
❑ PRLP-7389 [M]	Blues on the South Side	1965	7.50	15.00	30.00
❑ PRST-7389 [S]	Blues on the South Side	1965	10.00	20.00	40.00

ARNOLD, EDDY
RCA CAMDEN

Number	Title	Yr	VG	VG+	NM
❑ CAL-471 [M]	Eddy Arnold (That's How Much I Love You)	1959	5.00	10.00	20.00
❑ CAL-563 [M]	More Eddy Arnold	1960	5.00	10.00	20.00

RCA VICTOR

Number	Title	Yr	VG	VG+	NM
❑ LPM-1111 [M]	Wanderin' with Eddy Arnold	1955	12.50	25.00	50.00
❑ LPM-1223 [M]	All-Time Favorites	1955	12.50	25.00	50.00
-- New version of LPM 3117					
❑ LPM-1224 [M]	Anytime	1955	12.50	25.00	50.00
-- New version of LPM 3027					
❑ LPM-1225 [M]	The Chapel on the Hill	1955	12.50	25.00	50.00
-- New version of LPM 3031					
❑ LPM-1293 [M]	A Dozen Hits	1956	12.50	25.00	50.00
❑ LPM-1377 [M]	A Little on the Lonely Side	1956	12.50	25.00	50.00
❑ LPM-1484 [M]	When They Were Young	1956	12.50	25.00	50.00
❑ LPM-1575 [M]	My Darling, My Darling	1957	10.00	20.00	40.00
❑ LPM-1733 [M]	Praise Him, Praise Him	1958	10.00	20.00	40.00
❑ LPM-1928 [M]	Have Guitar, Will Travel	1959	6.25	12.50	25.00
❑ LSP-1928 [S]	Have Guitar, Will Travel	1959	7.50	15.00	30.00
❑ LPM-2036 [M]	Thereby Hangs a Tale	1959	6.25	12.50	25.00
❑ LSP-2036 [S]	Thereby Hangs a Tale	1959	7.50	15.00	30.00
❑ LPM-2185 [M]	Eddy Arnold Sings Them Again	1960	6.25	12.50	25.00
❑ LSP-2185 [S]	Eddy Arnold Sings Them Again	1960	7.50	15.00	30.00
❑ LPM-2268 [M]	You Gotta Have Love	1960	6.25	12.50	25.00
❑ LSP-2268 [S]	You Gotta Have Love	1960	7.50	15.00	30.00
❑ LPM-2337 [M]	Let's Make Memories Tonight	1961	5.00	10.00	20.00
❑ LSP-2337 [S]	Let's Make Memories Tonight	1961	6.25	12.50	25.00
❑ LPM-2471 [M]	One More Time	1961	5.00	10.00	20.00
❑ LSP-2471 [S]	One More Time	1961	6.25	12.50	25.00
❑ LPM-2554 [M]	Christmas with Eddy Arnold	1962	5.00	10.00	20.00
❑ LSP-2554 [S]	Christmas with Eddy Arnold	1962	6.25	12.50	25.00
❑ LPM-2578 [M]	Cattle Call	1962	6.25	12.50	25.00
❑ LSP-2578 [S]	Cattle Call	1962	7.50	15.00	30.00
❑ LPM-2596 [M]	Our Man Down South	1962	6.25	12.50	25.00
❑ LSP-2596 [S]	Our Man Down South	1962	7.50	15.00	30.00
❑ LPM-2629 [M]	Faithfully Yours	1963	6.25	12.50	25.00
❑ LSP-2629 [S]	Faithfully Yours	1963	7.50	15.00	30.00
❑ LPM-2811 [M]	Folk Song Book	1964	5.00	10.00	20.00
❑ LSP-2811 [S]	Folk Song Book	1964	6.25	12.50	25.00
❑ LPM-2909 [M]	Sometimes I'm Happy, Sometimes I'm Blue	1964	5.00	10.00	20.00
❑ LSP-2909 [S]	Sometimes I'm Happy, Sometimes I'm Blue	1964	6.25	12.50	25.00
❑ LPM-2951 [M]	Pop Hits from the Country Side	1964	5.00	10.00	20.00
❑ LSP-2951 [S]	Pop Hits from the Country Side	1964	6.25	12.50	25.00
❑ LPM-3027 [10]	Anytime	1952	30.00	60.00	120.00
-- Label calls this "Country Classics"					
❑ LPM-3031 [10]	All-Time Hits from the Hills	1952	25.00	50.00	100.00
❑ LPM-3117 [10]	All-Time Favorites	1953	25.00	50.00	100.00
❑ LPM-3219 [10]	The Chapel on the Hill	1954	25.00	50.00	100.00
❑ LPM-3230 [10]	An American Institution	1954	25.00	50.00	100.00
❑ LPM-3230	An American Institution Booklet	1954	12.50	25.00	50.00

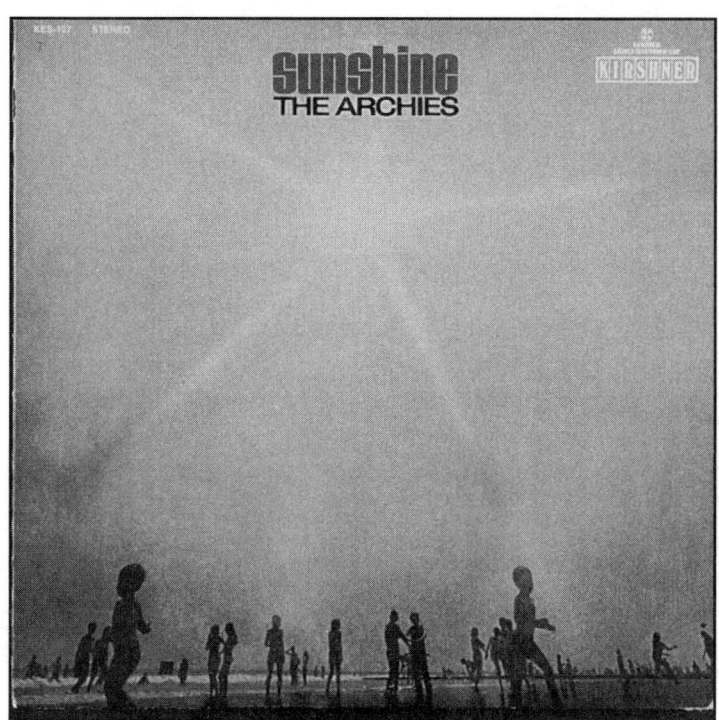

(Top left) The cover may claim it "sounds great in stereo," but *The Best Of The Animals*, the MGM version (the later Abkco issue has a similar cover but different contents), is entirely rechanneled. (Top right) Paul Anka was one of the few "teen idols" to write most of his own material. His ABC-Paramount albums, including this early hits collection, are not that easy to find. (Bottom left) By far, the biggest-selling of the late 1960s-early 1970s "cartoon bands" was the Archies, which is one reason why their records aren't as pricey as, say, those of the Banana Splits or Josie and the Pussycats. *Sunshine* was their fourth album, a milestone none of the other cartoon bands achieved. (Bottom right) Chet Atkins was one of the architects of the Nashville country sound; in addition to his own albums such as the above *Teensville*, he was a session musician on literally hundreds of other records, and his influence was enormous.

Number	Title	Yr	VG	VG+	NM
❑ LSP-3361 [S]	The Easy Way	1965	5.00	10.00	20.00
❑ LPM-3565 [M]	The Best of Eddy Arnold	1967	5.00	10.00	20.00
❑ LPM-3753 [M]	Lonely Again	1967	5.00	10.00	20.00
❑ LPM-3869 [M]	Turn the World Around	1967	5.00	10.00	20.00
❑ LPM-3931 [M]	The Everlovin' World of Eddy Arnold	1968	10.00	20.00	40.00

ART OF LOVIN'
MAINSTREAM
❑ S-6113	Art of Lovin'	1968	50.00	100.00	200.00

ARTHUR
LHI
❑ 12000	Dreams and Images	1968	10.00	20.00	40.00

ARTISTICS, THE
BRUNSWICK
❑ BL 54123 [M]	I'm Gonna Miss You	1967	6.25	12.50	25.00
❑ BL 754123 [S]	I'm Gonna Miss You	1967	6.25	12.50	25.00
❑ BL 754139	The Articulate Artistics	1968	6.25	12.50	25.00
❑ BL 754153	What Happened	1969	6.25	12.50	25.00
❑ BL 754168	I Want You to Make My Life Over	1970	6.25	12.50	25.00
❑ BL 754195	Look Out	1973	5.00	10.00	20.00
OKEH
❑ OKM-12119 [M]	Get My Hands on Some Lovin'	1967	20.00	40.00	80.00
❑ OKS-14119 [S]	Get My Hands on Some Lovin'	1967	20.00	40.00	80.00

ARTISTS UNITED AGAINST APARTHEID
MANHATTAN
❑ SPRO-9538	Voices of Sun City	1985	8.75	17.50	35.00
-- Promo album of interviews with participants					

ARZACHEL
ROULETTE
❑ SR 42036	Arzachel	1969	37.50	75.00	150.00

ASGAERD
THRESHOLD
❑ THS 6	In the Realm of Asgaerd	1972	5.00	10.00	20.00

ASHES
VAULT
❑ 125	Ashes	1968	12.50	25.00	50.00

ASHKAN
SIRE
❑ SES-97107	In from the Cold	1970	6.25	12.50	25.00

ASHLEY, LEON
RCA VICTOR
❑ LPM-3900 [M]	Laura (What's He Got That I Ain't Got)	1967	7.50	15.00	30.00
❑ LSP-3900 [S]	Laura (What's He Got That I Ain't Got)	1967	5.00	10.00	20.00

ASHWORTH, ERNEST
HICKORY
❑ LPM-118 [M]	Hits of Today and Tomorrow	1964	6.25	12.50	25.00

ASIA
Includes members of KING CRIMSON and YES.
GEFFEN
❑ GHS 2008 [DJ]	Asia	1982	5.00	10.00	20.00
-- Promo on Quiex II vinyl					
❑ GHS 4008 [DJ]	Alpha	1983	5.00	10.00	20.00
-- Promo on Quiex II vinyl					

ASLEEP AT THE WHEEL
EPIC
❑ BG 33782 [(2)]	Fathers and Sons	1974	6.25	12.50	25.00
-- With Bob Wills					
UNITED ARTISTS
❑ UA-LA038-F	Comin' Right At Ya!	1973	5.00	10.00	20.00

ASSOCIATION, THE
VALIANT
❑ VLM-5002 [M]	And Then…Along Comes The Association	1966	5.00	10.00	20.00

Number	Title	Yr	VG	VG+	NM
❑ VLM-5004 [M]	Renaissance	1966	5.00	10.00	20.00
-- With no blurb for "No Fair at All" on cover					
❑ VLS-25002 [S]	And Then…Along Comes The Association	1966	6.25	12.50	25.00
❑ VLS-25004 [S]	Renaissance	1966	6.25	12.50	25.00
-- With no blurb for "No Fair at All" on cover					
❑ VLS-25004 [S]	Renaissance	1967	5.00	10.00	20.00
-- With blurb for "No Fair at All" on cover					
WARNER BROS.
❑ WS 1696 [S]	Insight Out	1967	5.00	10.00	20.00
-- Gold label					
❑ ST-91586	Greatest Hits	1968	5.00	10.00	20.00
-- Capitol Record Club edition					

ASTAIRE, FRED
CHOREO
❑ A-1 [M]	Three Evenings with Fred Astaire	1961	10.00	20.00	40.00
CLEF
❑ MGC-662 [M]	The Fred Astaire Story, Volume 1	1955	12.50	25.00	50.00
-- Reissue of Mercury 1001					
❑ MGC-663 [M]	The Fred Astaire Story, Volume 2	1955	12.50	25.00	50.00
-- Reissue of Mercury 1002					
❑ MGC-664 [M]	The Fred Astaire Story, Volume 3	1955	12.50	25.00	50.00
-- Reissue of Mercury 1003					
❑ MGC-665 [M]	The Fred Astaire Story, Volume 4	1955	12.50	25.00	50.00
-- Reissue of Mercury 1004					
EPIC
❑ LN 3103 [M]	Nothing Thrilled Us Half As Much	1955	12.50	25.00	50.00
❑ LN 3137 [M]	The Best of Fred Astaire	1955	12.50	25.00	50.00
❑ FLM 13103 [M]	Nothing Thrilled Us Half As Much	196?	5.00	10.00	20.00
-- Reissue of 3103					
KAPP
❑ KL-1165 [M]	Fred Astaire Now	1959	6.25	12.50	25.00
❑ KS-3165 [S]	Fred Astaire Now	1959	7.50	15.00	30.00
MERCURY
❑ MGC-1001 [M]	The Fred Astaire Story, Volume 1	1954	25.00	50.00	100.00
❑ MGC-1001/4 [(4) M]	The Fred Astaire Story	1953	250.00	500.00	1,000.
-- Spiral-bound four-record set, pressed on blue vinyl, autographed by Fred Astaire					
❑ MGC-1002 [M]	The Fred Astaire Story, Volume 2	1954	25.00	50.00	100.00
❑ MGC-1003 [M]	The Fred Astaire Story, Volume 3	1954	25.00	50.00	100.00
❑ MGC-1004 [M]	The Fred Astaire Story, Volume 4	1954	25.00	50.00	100.00
VERVE
❑ MGV-2010 [M]	Mr. Top Hat	1956	12.50	25.00	50.00
❑ MGV-2114 [M]	Easy to Dance With	1958	12.50	25.00	50.00

ASTRONAUTS, THE
RCA VICTOR
❑ PRM-183 [M]	Rockin' with the Astronauts	1965	7.50	15.00	30.00
❑ LPM-2760 [M]	Surfin' with the Astronauts	1963	15.00	30.00	60.00
❑ LSP-2760 [S]	Surfin' with the Astronauts	1963	20.00	40.00	80.00
❑ LPM-2782 [M]	Everything Is A-OK!	1964	12.50	25.00	50.00
❑ LSP-2782 [S]	Everything Is A-OK!	1964	15.00	30.00	60.00
❑ LPM-2858 [M]	Competition Coupe	1964	15.00	30.00	60.00
❑ LSP-2858 [S]	Competition Coupe	1964	20.00	40.00	80.00
❑ LPM-2903 [M]	The Astronauts Orbit Kampus	1964	10.00	20.00	40.00
❑ LSP-2903 [S]	The Astronauts Orbit Kampus	1964	12.50	25.00	50.00
❑ LPM-3307 [M]	The Astronauts Go, Go, Go	1965	7.50	15.00	30.00
❑ LSP-3307 [S]	The Astronauts Go, Go, Go	1965	10.00	20.00	40.00
❑ LPM-3359 [M]	Favorites for You from Us	1965	7.50	15.00	30.00
❑ LSP-3359 [S]	Favorites for You from Us	1965	10.00	20.00	40.00
❑ LPM-3454 [M]	Down the Line	1966	7.50	15.00	30.00
❑ LSP-3454 [S]	Down the Line	1966	10.00	20.00	40.00
❑ LPM-3733 [M]	Travelin' Men	1967	12.50	25.00	50.00
❑ LSP-3733 [S]	Travelin' Men	1967	7.50	15.00	30.00

ASTRONAUTS, THE / THE LIVERPOOL FIVE
RCA VICTOR
❑ PRS-251 [S]	Stereo Festival	1967	25.00	50.00	100.00
-- Special-products edition					

ASYLUM CHOIR -- See LEON RUSSELL AND MARC BENNO.

ATCHER, BOBBY
COLUMBIA
❑ CL 2232 [M]	The Dean of Cowboy Singers	1964	6.25	12.50	25.00
❑ HL 9006 [10]	Early American Folk Songs	1949	20.00	40.00	80.00
❑ HL 9013 [10]	Songs of the Saddle	1949	20.00	40.00	80.00
HARMONY
❑ HL 7313 [M]	Early American Folk Songs	1964	5.00	10.00	20.00

Number	Title	Yr	VG	VG+	NM

ATKINS, CHET

DOLTON

Number	Title	Yr	VG	VG+	NM
❏ BLP-16506 [M]	Play Guitar with Chet Atkins	1967	6.25	12.50	25.00
❏ BST-17506 [S]	Play Guitar with Chet Atkins	1967	7.50	15.00	30.00

RCA RED SEAL

❏ LSC-2870 [S]	The "Pops" Goes Country	1966	5.00	10.00	20.00

-- Above with the Boston Pops Orchestra, Arthur Fiedler, conductor

RCA VICTOR

❏ LPM-1090 [M]	A Session with Chet Atkins	1954	15.00	30.00	60.00

-- Red cover

❏ LPM-1090 [M]	A Session with Chet Atkins	1961	5.00	10.00	20.00

-- Woman and guitars cover

❏ LPM-1197 [M]	Chet Atkins in Three Dimensions	1956	12.50	52.00	50.00

-- Black-and-white guitar cover

❏ LPM-1197 [M]	Chet Atkins in Three Dimensions	1961	5.00	10.00	20.00

-- Red guitar cover

❏ LPM-1236 [M]	Stringin' Along with Chet Atkins	1956	12.50	25.00	50.00

-- Orange cover

❏ LPM-1236 [M]	Stringin' Along with Chet Atkins	1961	5.00	10.00	20.00

-- Full-color cover

❏ LPM-1383 [M]	Finger Style Guitar	1956	12.50	25.00	50.00

-- Chet's face not visible on cover

❏ LPM-1383 [M]	Finger Style Guitar	1961	5.00	10.00	20.00

-- Chet's face visible on cover

❏ LPM-1544 [M]	Chet Atkins at Home	1957	12.50	25.00	50.00

-- Title in block letters on cover

❏ LPM-1544 [M]	Chet Atkins at Home	1961	5.00	10.00	20.00

-- Title in script on cover

❏ LPM-1577 [M]	Hi-Fi in Focus	1957	12.50	25.00	50.00

-- No guitars on cover

❏ LPM-1577 [M]	Hi-Fi in Focus	1957	5.00	10.00	20.00

-- Guitar on cover

❏ LPM-1993 [M]	Chet Atkins in Hollywood	1959	7.50	15.00	30.00

-- Night-time cover

❏ LPM-1993 [M]	Chet Atkins in Hollywood	1961	5.00	10.00	20.00

-- Daylight "blonde" cover

❏ LSP-1993 [S]	Chet Atkins in Hollywood	1959	12.50	25.00	50.00

-- Night-time cover

❏ LSP-1993 [S]	Chet Atkins in Hollywood	1961	7.50	15.00	30.00

-- Daylight "blonde" cover

❏ LPM-2025 [M]	Hum & Strum Along	1959	6.25	12.50	25.00

-- Add $10 NM if instruction book is included

❏ LSP-2025 [S]	Hum & Strum Along	1959	10.00	20.00	40.00

-- Add $10 NM if instruction book is included

❏ LPM-2103 [M]	Mister Guitar	1959	7.50	15.00	30.00

-- Lone guitar on cover

❏ LPM-2103 [M]	Mister Guitar	1961	5.00	10.00	20.00

-- Guitar and woman on cover

❏ LSP-2103 [S]	Mister Guitar	1959	12.50	25.00	50.00

-- Lone guitar on cover

❏ LSP-2103 [S]	Mister Guitar	1961	7.50	15.00	30.00

-- Guitar and woman on cover

❏ LPM-2161 [M]	Teensville	1960	7.50	15.00	30.00

-- Title overlaps cover photo

❏ LPM-2161 [M]	Teensville	1961	5.00	10.00	20.00

-- Title in black strip at top of cover photo

❏ LSP-2161 [S]	Teensville	1960	12.50	25.00	50.00

-- Title overlaps cover photo

❏ LSP-2161 [S]	Teensville	1961	7.50	15.00	30.00

-- Title in black strip at top of cover photo

❏ LPM-2175 [M]	The Other Chet Atkins	1960	5.00	10.00	20.00
❏ LSP-2175 [S]	The Other Chet Atkins	1960	7.50	15.00	30.00
❏ LPM-2232 [M]	Chet Atkins' Workshop	1961	5.00	10.00	20.00
❏ LSP-2232 [S]	Chet Atkins' Workshop	1961	7.50	15.00	30.00
❏ LPM-2346 [M]	The Most Popular Guitar	1961	5.00	10.00	20.00
❏ LSP-2346 [S]	The Most Popular Guitar	1961	7.50	15.00	30.00
❏ LPM-2423 [M]	Christmas with Chet Atkins	1961	5.00	10.00	20.00
❏ LSP-2423 [S]	Christmas with Chet Atkins	1961	7.50	15.00	30.00
❏ LPM-2450 [M]	Down Home	1962	5.00	10.00	20.00
❏ LSP-2450 [S]	Down Home	1962	6.25	12.50	25.00
❏ LPM-2549 [M]	Caribbean Guitar	1962	5.00	10.00	20.00
❏ LSP-2549 [S]	Caribbean Guitar	1962	6.25	12.50	25.00
❏ LPM-2601 [M]	Back Home Hymns	1962	5.00	10.00	20.00
❏ LSP-2601 [S]	Back Home Hymns	1962	6.25	12.50	25.00
❏ LPM-2616 [M]	Our Man in Nashville	1963	5.00	10.00	20.00
❏ LSP-2616 [S]	Our Man in Nashville	1963	6.25	12.50	25.00
❏ LPM-2678 [M]	Travelin'	1963	5.00	10.00	20.00
❏ LSP-2678 [S]	Travelin'	1963	6.25	12.50	25.00
❏ LPM-2719 [M]	Teen Scene	1963	5.00	10.00	20.00
❏ LSP-2719 [S]	Teen Scene	1963	6.25	12.50	25.00
❏ LSP-2783 [S]	Guitar Country	1964	5.00	10.00	20.00
❏ LSP-2887 [S]	The Best of Chet Atkins	1964	5.00	10.00	20.00
❏ LSP-2908 [S]	Progressive Pickin'	1964	5.00	10.00	20.00
❏ LPM-3079 [10]	Chet Atkins' Gallopin' Guitar	1952	37.50	75.00	150.00
❏ LPM-3169 [10]	Stringin' Along with Chet Atkins	1953	25.00	50.00	100.00
❏ LSP-3316 [S]	My Favorite Guitars	1965	5.00	10.00	20.00
❏ LSP-3429 [S]	More of That "Guitar Country"	1965	5.00	10.00	20.00
❏ LPM-3531 [M]	Chet Atkins Picks On the Beatles	1966	6.25	12.50	25.00
❏ LSP-3531 [S]	Chet Atkins Picks On the Beatles	1966	7.50	15.00	30.00
❏ LPM-3728 [M]	It's a Guitar World	1967	7.50	15.00	30.00
❏ LPM-3818 [M]	Chet Atkins Picks the Best	1967	7.50	15.00	30.00
❏ LPM-3885 [M]	Class Guitar	1967	7.50	15.00	30.00
❏ LPM-3992 [M]	Solo Flights	1968	12.50	25.00	50.00

ATLANTA RHYTHM SECTION

DECCA

Number	Title	Yr	VG	VG+	NM
❏ DL 75265	Atlanta Rhythm Section	1972	6.25	12.50	25.00
❏ DL 75390	Back Up Against the Wall	1973	6.25	12.50	25.00

MOBILE FIDELITY

❏ 1-038	Champagne Jam	1981	10.00	20.00	40.00

-- Audiophile vinyl

ATOMIC ROOSTER

ELEKTRA

Number	Title	Yr	VG	VG+	NM
❏ EKS-74094	Death Walks Behind You	1971	5.00	10.00	20.00
❏ EKS-74109	In Hearing Of Atomic Rooster	1971	5.00	10.00	20.00
❏ EKS-75039	Made in England	1972	5.00	10.00	20.00

ATTILA

Also see BILLY JOEL.

EPIC

❏ E 30030	Attila	1970	7.50	15.00	30.00

AU GO-GO SINGERS, THE

With Stephen Stills and Richie Furay, later of BUFFALO SPRINGFIELD.

ROULETTE

Number	Title	Yr	VG	VG+	NM
❏ R 25280 [M]	They Call Us the Au Go-Go Singers	1964	12.50	25.00	50.00
❏ SR 25280 [S]	They Call Us the Au Go-Go Singers	1964	17.50	35.00	70.00

AUGER, BRIAN, TRINITY

ATCO

❏ SD 2-701 [(2)]	Streetnoise	1969	5.00	10.00	20.00

AUGUST SONS

EYES IN THE WOODS

❏ (# unknown) [EP]	I Am Not a Vampire	1989	8.75	17.50	35.00

AUGUST, JAN

MERCURY

❏ MG 20160 [M]	Christmas Favorites	1955	6.25	12.50	25.00

AUM

FILLMORE

❏ Z 30002	Resurrection	1970	7.50	15.00	30.00

SIRE

❏ SES-97007	Bluesvibes	1969	10.00	20.00	40.00

AUSTIN, BOBBY

CAPITOL

Number	Title	Yr	VG	VG+	NM
❏ ST 2773 [S]	Apartment No. 9	1967	5.00	10.00	20.00
❏ T 2773 [M]	Apartment No. 9	1967	6.25	12.50	25.00
❏ ST 2915	Old Love Never Dies	1968	5.00	10.00	20.00

AUSTIN, DONALD

EASTBOUND

❏ EB-9005	Crazy Legs	1973	7.50	15.00	30.00

AUSTIN, GENE

DECCA

❏ DL 8433 [M]	My Blue Heaven	1957	10.00	20.00	40.00

DOT

❏ DLP 25300 [S]	Great Hits	1960	6.25	12.50	25.00
❏ DLP 3300 [M]	Great Hits	1960	5.00	10.00	20.00

RCA VICTOR

❏ LPM-3200 [10]	My Blue Heaven	1953	15.00	30.00	60.00

"X"

❏ LVA-1007 [M]	Gene Austin Sings All-Time	1954	10.00	20.00	40.00

AUSTIN, SIL

MERCURY

Number	Title	Yr	VG	VG+	NM
❏ MG-20237 [M]	Slow Walk Rock	1957	17.50	35.00	70.00
❏ MG-20320 [M]	Everything Is Shakin'	1958	17.50	35.00	70.00
❏ MG-20424 [M]	Sil Austin Plays Pretty for the People	1959	10.00	20.00	40.00
❏ MG-20576 [M]	Soft, Plaintive and Moody	1960	10.00	20.00	40.00

Number	Title	Yr	VG	VG+	NM
❏ MG-20663 [M]	Golden Saxophone Hits	1961	6.25	12.50	25.00
❏ MG-20925 [M]	Sil Austin Plays Pretty Melodies of the World	1964	5.00	10.00	20.00
❏ MG-21126 [M]	Sil Austin Plays Pretty for the People Again	1967	5.00	10.00	20.00
❏ SR-60096 [S]	Sil Austin Plays Pretty for the People	1959	15.00	30.00	60.00
❏ SR-60236 [S]	Soft, Plaintive and Moody	1960	15.00	30.00	60.00
❏ SR-60663 [S]	Golden Saxophone Hits	1961	7.50	15.00	30.00
❏ SR-61126 [S]	Sil Austin Plays Pretty for the People Again	1967	5.00	10.00	20.00
❏ SR-90925 [S]	Sil Austin Plays Pretty Melodies of the World	1964	6.25	12.50	25.00

AUTOSALVAGE
RCA VICTOR
❏ LPM-3940 [M]	Autosalvage	1968	10.00	20.00	40.00
❏ LSP-3940 [S]	Autosalvage	1968	10.00	20.00	40.00

AUTRY, GENE
CHALLENGE
❏ CHL-600 [M]	Christmas with Gene Autry	1958	12.50	25.00	50.00

COLUMBIA
❏ CL 677 [M]	Gene Autry and Champion -- Western Adventures	1955	30.00	60.00	120.00
❏ CL 1575 [M]	Gene Autry's Greatest Hits	1961	7.50	15.00	30.00
-- Red and black label with six "eye" logos					
❏ CL 2547 [10]	Merry Christmas with Gene Autry	1954	30.00	60.00	120.00
-- "House Party Series" release					
❏ CL 2568 [10]	Gene Autry Sings Peter Cottontail	1955	30.00	60.00	120.00
❏ CL 6020 [10]	Easter Favorites	1949	37.50	75.00	150.00
❏ CL 6137 [10]	Merry Christmas	1950	37.50	75.00	150.00
❏ JL 8001 [10]	Gene Autry at the Rodeo	1949	37.50	75.00	150.00
❏ JL 8009 [10]	Stampede	1949	37.50	75.00	150.00
❏ JL 8012 [10]	Champion	1950	37.50	75.00	150.00
❏ CL 9001 [10]	Western Classics, Volume 1	1949	37.50	75.00	150.00
❏ CL 9002 [10]	Western Classics, Volume 2	1949	37.50	75.00	150.00

GRAND PRIX
❏ KS-X11 [S]	The Original Gene Autry Sings Rudolph the Red-Nosed Reindeer and Other Christmas Favorites	1961	5.00	10.00	20.00

HARMONY
❏ HL 7332 [M]	Gene Autry's Great Western Hits	1965	7.50	15.00	30.00
❏ HL 7376 [M]	Back in the Saddle Again	1966	5.00	10.00	20.00
❏ HL 7399 [M]	Gene Autry Sings	1966	5.00	10.00	20.00
❏ HL 9505 [M]	Gene Autry and Champion -- Western Adventures	1959	7.50	15.00	30.00
❏ HL 9550 [M]	The Original Rudolph the Red-Nosed Reindeer and Other Children's Christmas Favorites	1964	6.25	12.50	25.00

MELODY RANCH
❏ 101 [M]	Melody Ranch	1965	10.00	20.00	40.00

MURRAY HILL
❏ 897296 [(4)]	Melody Ranch Radio Show	197?	15.00	30.00	60.00
-- Compilation of some of Gene's radio shows in a box set					

RCA VICTOR
❏ LPM-2623 [M]	Gene Autry's Golden Hits	1962	7.50	15.00	30.00
❏ LSP-2623 [S]	Gene Autry's Golden Hits	1962	10.00	20.00	40.00

REPUBLIC
❏ 6011	South of the Border, All American Cowboy	1976	5.00	10.00	20.00
❏ 6012	Cowboy Hall of Fame	1976	5.00	10.00	20.00

AVALANCHES, THE
WARNER BROS.
❏ W 1525 [M]	Ski Surfin'	1963	10.00	20.00	40.00
❏ WS 1525 [S]	Ski Surfin'	1963	15.00	30.00	60.00

AVALON, FRANKIE
CHANCELLOR
❏ CHL 5001 [M]	Frankie Avalon	1958	12.50	25.00	50.00
-- Pink label					
❏ CHL 5001 [M]	Frankie Avalon	1959	10.00	20.00	40.00
-- Black label					
❏ CHL 5002 [M]	The Young Frankie Avalon	1959	12.50	25.00	50.00
-- Pink label					
❏ CHL 5002 [M]	The Young Frankie Avalon	1959	10.00	20.00	40.00
-- Black label					
❏ CHLS 5002 [S]	The Young Frankie Avalon	1959	15.00	30.00	60.00
-- Pink label					
❏ CHLS 5002 [S]	The Young Frankie Avalon	1959	12.50	25.00	50.00
-- Black label					
❏ CHLX 5004 [M]	Swingin' on a Rainbow	1959	10.00	20.00	40.00
❏ CHLXS 5004 [S]	Swingin' on a Rainbow	1959	12.50	25.00	50.00
❏ CHL 5011 [M]	Summer Scene	1960	7.50	15.00	30.00

Number	Title	Yr	VG	VG+	NM
❏ CHLS 5011 [S]	Summer Scene	1960	10.00	20.00	40.00
❏ CHL 5018 [M]	A Whole Lotta Frankie	1961	7.50	15.00	30.00
❏ CHL 5022 [M]	And Now About Mr. Avalon	1961	7.50	15.00	30.00
❏ CHLS 5022 [S]	And Now About Mr. Avalon	1961	10.00	20.00	40.00
❏ CHL 5025 [M]	Italiano	1962	7.50	15.00	30.00
❏ CHLS 5025 [S]	Italiano	1962	10.00	20.00	40.00
❏ CHL 5027 [M]	You're Mine	1962	7.50	15.00	30.00
❏ CHLS 5027 [S]	You're Mine	1962	10.00	20.00	40.00
❏ CHL 5031 [M]	Frankie Avalon's Christmas Album	1962	7.50	15.00	30.00
❏ CHLS 5031 [S]	Frankie Avalon's Christmas Album	1962	10.00	20.00	40.00
❏ CHL 5032 [M]	Cleopatra Plus 13 Other Great Hits	1963	7.50	15.00	30.00
❏ CHLS 5032 [S]	Cleopatra Plus 13 Other Great Hits	1963	10.00	20.00	40.00
❏ 69801 [M]	Young and In Love	1960	20.00	40.00	80.00
-- LP in felt cover and 3-D portrait, all in box					
❏ 69801 [M]	Young and In Love	1960	10.00	20.00	40.00
-- LP without the box					

UNITED ARTISTS
❏ UAL-3371 [M]	Songs from Muscle Beach Party	1964	6.25	12.50	25.00
❏ UAL-3382 [M]	Frankie Avalon's 15 Greatest Hits	1964	5.00	10.00	20.00
❏ UAS-6371 [S]	Songs from Muscle Beach Party	1964	7.50	15.00	30.00
❏ UAS-6382 [S]	Frankie Avalon's 15 Greatest Hits	1964	6.25	12.50	25.00

AVENGERS
CD PRESENTS
❏ 007	Avengers	1983	5.00	10.00	20.00
-- Red vinyl					

GO
❏ 005	Avengers	1983	30.00	60.00	120.00

WHITE NOISE
❏ 002 [EP]	Avengers	1978	5.00	10.00	20.00

AVENGERS VI, THE
MARK 56
❏ (# unknown)	Good Humor Presents Real Cool Hits	1966	62.50	125.00	250.00
-- Custom pressing for the Good Humor ice cream company					

AVERAGE WHITE BAND
ATLANTIC
❏ QD 7308 [Q]	Average White Band	1975	5.00	10.00	20.00

MCA
❏ 345	Show Your Hands	1973	6.25	12.50	25.00

MOBILE FIDELITY
❏ 1-245	Average White Band	1996	5.00	10.00	20.00
-- Audiophile vinyl					

AVONS, THE
HULL
❏ HLP-1000 [M]	The Avons	1960	175.00	350.00	700.00

AXTON, HOYT
EXODUS
❏ EX-301 [M]	Hoyt Axton Sings Bessie Smith	1966	5.00	10.00	20.00
❏ EXS-321 [M]	Saturday's Child	1966	5.00	10.00	20.00
-- Cover says stereo, record plays mono					

HORIZON
❏ WP-1601 [M]	The Balladeer	1962	6.25	12.50	25.00
-- Black label					
❏ WP-1601 [S]	The Balladeer	1962	7.50	15.00	30.00
-- Same number as mono, but with blue label					
❏ WP-1601 [M]	Greenback Dollar	1963	5.00	10.00	20.00
-- Black label; two fewer songs than "The Balladeer"					
❏ WP-1601 [S]	Greenback Dollar	1963	6.25	12.50	25.00
-- Blue label; two fewer songs than "The Balladeer"					
❏ WP-1613 [M]	Thunder 'N Lightnin'	1963	6.25	12.50	25.00
❏ SWP-1613 [S]	Thunder 'N Lightnin'	1963	7.50	15.00	30.00
❏ WP-1621 [M]	Saturday's Child	1963	6.25	12.50	25.00
❏ SWP-1621 [S]	Saturday's Child	1963	7.50	15.00	30.00

SURREY
❏ S-1005 [M]	Mr. Greenback Dollar Man	1965	5.00	10.00	20.00
❏ SS-1005 [S]	Mr. Greenback Dollar Man	1965	6.25	12.50	25.00

VEE JAY
❏ LP-1098 [M]	Hoyt Axton Explodes!	1964	6.25	12.50	25.00
❏ LPS-1098 [R]	Hoyt Axton Explodes!	1964	5.00	10.00	20.00
❏ LP-1118 [M]	The Best of Hoyt Axton	1965	5.00	10.00	20.00
❏ LPS-1118 [S]	The Best of Hoyt Axton	1965	6.25	12.50	25.00
❏ LP-1126 [M]	Greenback Dollar	1965	5.00	10.00	20.00
❏ LPS-1126 [S]	Greenback Dollar	1965	6.25	12.50	25.00
❏ LP-1127 [M]	Saturday's Child	1965	5.00	10.00	20.00
❏ LPS-1127 [S]	Saturday's Child	1965	6.25	12.50	25.00
-- Reissue of Horizon 1621					
❏ LP-1128 [M]	Thunder 'N Lightnin'	1965	5.00	10.00	20.00

Number	Title	Yr	VG	VG+	NM
❏ LPS-1128 [S] Thunder 'N Lightnin'		1965	6.25	12.50	25.00
-- *Reissue of Horizon 1613*					

VEE JAY INTERNATIONAL

Number	Title	Yr	VG	VG+	NM
❏ VJS-2-1005 [(2)] Gold		1974	5.00	10.00	20.00
-- *Compilation of older Vee Jay material*					

AYCOCK, EARL
MERCURY

Number	Title	Yr	VG	VG+	NM
❏ MG-20282 [M] Earl Aycock		1958	6.25	12.50	25.00

AYERS, ROY
ATLANTIC

Number	Title	Yr	VG	VG+	NM
❏ 1488 [M]	Virgo Vibes	1967	5.00	10.00	20.00
❏ SD 1514	Stoned Soul Picnic	1968	5.00	10.00	20.00
❏ SD 1538	Daddy Bug	1969	5.00	10.00	20.00

UNITED ARTISTS

Number	Title	Yr	VG	VG+	NM
❏ UAL-3325 [M] West Coast Vibes		1964	5.00	10.00	20.00
❏ UAS-6325 [S] West Coast Vibes		1964	6.25	12.50	25.00

AZITIS
ELCO

Number	Title	Yr	VG	VG+	NM
❏ SC-EC-5555	Help!	197?	125.00	250.00	500.00

AZTECA
COLUMBIA

Number	Title	Yr	VG	VG+	NM
❏ CQ 31776 [Q] Azteca		1974	5.00	10.00	20.00

AZTECS, THE
WORLD ARTISTS

Number	Title	Yr	VG	VG+	NM
❏ WAM-2001 [M] Live at the Ad Lib Club of London	1964	15.00	30.00	60.00

B

BABY
LONE STARR

Number	Title	Yr	VG	VG+	NM
❏ 9782	Baby	1974	6.25	12.50	25.00

BABY GRAND
ARISTA

Number	Title	Yr	VG	VG+	NM
❏ AL 4148	Baby Grand	1977	5.00	10.00	20.00

BABY HUEY
CURTOM

Number	Title	Yr	VG	VG+	NM
❏ CRS-8007	The Living Legend	1970	10.00	20.00	40.00

BABY RAY
IMPERIAL

Number	Title	Yr	VG	VG+	NM
❏ LP-9335 [M]	Where Soul Lives	1967	6.25	12.50	25.00
❏ LP-12335 [S]	Where Soul Lives	1967	7.50	15.00	30.00

BACHAUER, GINA
MERCURY LIVING PRESENCE

Number	Title	Yr	VG	VG+	NM
❏ SR 90301 [S]	Brahms: Piano Concerto No. 2	196?	6.25	12.50	25.00
-- *With Stanislaw Skrowaczewski/London Symphony Orchestra; maroon label, no "Vendor: Mercury Record Corporation"*					
❏ SR 90321 [S]	Beethoven: Piano Concerto No. 5 "Emperor"	196?	17.50	35.00	70.00
-- *With Stanislaw Skrowaczewski/London Symphony Orchestra; maroon label, no "Vendor: Mercury Record Corporation"*					
❏ SR 90368 [S]	Chopin: Piano Concerto No. 1; xNocturne; Three Etudes	196?	7.50	15.00	30.00
-- *Maroon label, no "Vendor: Mercury Record Corporation"*					
❏ SR 90368 [S]	Chopin: Piano Concerto No. 1; Nocturne; Three Etudes	196?	7.50	15.00	30.00
-- *Maroon label, with "Vendor: Mercury Record Corporation"*					
❏ SR 90381 [S]	Beethoven: Piano Concerto No. 4; Piano Sonata in E	196?	6.25	12.50	25.00
-- *With Antal Dorati/London Symphony Orchestra; maroon label, no "Vendor: Mercury Record Corporation"*					
❏ SR 90432 [S]	Chopin: Piano Concerto No. 2 in F; Fantasy in F	1965	10.00	20.00	40.00
-- *Maroon label, no "Vendor: Mercury Record Corporation"*					

BACHAUER, GINA, AND SIR JOHN GIELGUD
MERCURY LIVING PRESENCE

Number	Title	Yr	VG	VG+	NM
❏ SR 90391 [S]	Collaboration in Poetry and Music	196?	5.00	10.00	20.00
-- *Maroon label, no "Vendor: Mercury Record Corporation"*					

BACHELORS, THE
LONDON

Number	Title	Yr	VG	VG+	NM
❏ PS 353 [S]	Presenting the Bachelors	1964	5.00	10.00	20.00
❏ PS 393 [P]	Back Again	1964	5.00	10.00	20.00
-- *"I Wouldn't Trade You for the World" is rechanneled.*					
❏ PS 418 [S]	No Arms Can Ever Hold You	1965	5.00	10.00	20.00
❏ PS 435 [P]	Marie	1965	5.00	10.00	20.00
-- *"Marie" is rechanneled*					
❏ PS 460 [S]	Hits of the 60's	1966	5.00	10.00	20.00

BACHS, THE
RAIO

Number	Title	Yr	VG	VG+	NM
❏ (no #)	Out of the Bachs	1967	2,000.	3,000.	4,000.

BACK PORCH MAJORITY, THE
EPIC

Number	Title	Yr	VG	VG+	NM
❏ LN 24319 [M]	Willy Nilly Wonder of Illusion	1967	5.00	10.00	20.00
❏ BN 26134 [S]	Live from Ledbetter's	1965	5.00	10.00	20.00
❏ BN 26149 [S]	Riverboat Days	1965	5.00	10.00	20.00
❏ BN 26184 [S]	That's the Way It's Gonna Be	1966	5.00	10.00	20.00

BACKUS, JIM
RCA VICTOR

Number	Title	Yr	VG	VG+	NM
❏ LPM-1362 [M]	Mr. Magoo in Hi-Fi	1957	12.50	25.00	50.00

BACON FAT
BLUE HORIZON

Number	Title	Yr	VG	VG+	NM
❏ BH-4807	Grease One for Me	1970	6.25	12.50	25.00

BAD BRAINS
BAD BRAINS

Number	Title	Yr	VG	VG+	NM
❏ 003 [EP]	I and I Survive/Destroy Babylon	1983	5.00	10.00	20.00

Number	Title	Yr	VG	VG+	NM

PVC
❑ 8917	Rock for Light	1983	5.00	10.00	20.00

BAD RELIGION
EPITAPH
| ❑ EPI-BRLP-1 | How Could Hell Be Any Worse? | 1982 | 7.50 | 15.00 | 30.00 |

BADFINGER
APPLE
❑ ST 3364	Magic Christian Music	1970	7.50	15.00	30.00
-- With Capitol logo on Side 2 bottom					
❑ ST 3364	Magic Christian Music	1970	5.00	10.00	20.00
❑ SKAO 3367	No Dice	1970	7.50	15.00	30.00
❑ SW 3387	Straight Up	1971	15.00	30.00	60.00
❑ SW 3411	Ass	1973	5.00	10.00	20.00
RYKO ANALOGUE
| ❑ RALP 10189 | Day After Day | 1990 | 5.00 | 10.00 | 20.00 |
| -- Limited edition on clear vinyl with obi | | | | | |

BAEZ, JOAN
A&M
| ❑ QU-54339 [Q] | Come From the Shadows | 1974 | 5.00 | 10.00 | 20.00 |
| ❑ QU-54527 [Q] | Diamonds and Rust | 1975 | 5.00 | 10.00 | 20.00 |
MOBILE FIDELITY
| ❑ 1-238 | Diamonds and Rust | 1996 | 15.00 | 30.00 | 60.00 |
| -- Audiophile vinyl | | | | | |
NAUTILUS
| ❑ NR-12 | Diamonds and Rust | 1980 | 10.00 | 20.00 | 40.00 |
| -- Audiophile vinyl | | | | | |
SQUIRE
| ❑ SQ-33001 [M] | The Best of Joan Baez | 1963 | 5.00 | 10.00 | 20.00 |
VANGUARD
❑ VRS-9078 [M]	Joan Baez	1960	5.00	10.00	20.00
❑ VRS-9094 [M]	Joan Baez, Vol. 2	1961	5.00	10.00	20.00
❑ VRS-9112 [M]	Joan Baez In Concert	1962	5.00	10.00	20.00
❑ VRS-9113 [M]	Joan Baez In Concert, Part 2	1963	5.00	10.00	20.00
❑ VSD-2077 [S]	Joan Baez	1960	6.25	12.50	25.00
❑ VSD-2097 [S]	Joan Baez, Vol. 2	1961	6.25	12.50	25.00
❑ VSD-2122 [S]	Joan Baez In Concert	1962	6.25	12.50	25.00
❑ VSD-2123 [S]	Joan Baez In Concert, Part 2	1963	6.25	12.50	25.00
❑ VSQ-40001/2	Blessed Are	1973	6.25	12.50	25.00
[(2) Q]					
❑ VSQ-40032 [Q]	Hits/Greatest & Others	1973	5.00	10.00	20.00
❑ VSD-79160 [S]	Joan Baez/5	1964	5.00	10.00	20.00
❑ VSD-79200 [S]	Farewell, Angelina	1965	5.00	10.00	20.00
❑ VSD-79230 [S]	Noel	1966	5.00	10.00	20.00
❑ VSD-79240 [S]	Joan	1967	5.00	10.00	20.00
❑ VSD-79275	Baptism	1968	5.00	10.00	20.00
❑ VSD-79306/7 [(2)]	Any Day Now	1969	6.25	12.50	25.00

BAGDASARIAN, ROSS
Also see THE CHIPMUNKS; DAVID SEVILLE.
LIBERTY
| ❑ LRP-3451 [M] | The Crazy, Mixed-Up World of Ross Bagdasarian | 1966 | 10.00 | 20.00 | 40.00 |
| ❑ LST-7451 [S] | The Crazy, Mixed-Up World of Ross Bagdasarian | 1966 | 12.50 | 25.00 | 50.00 |

BAILES BROTHERS, THE
AUDIO LAB
| ❑ AL-1511 [M] | Avenues of Prayer | 1959 | 50.00 | 100.00 | 200.00 |

BAILEY, MILDRED
COLUMBIA
❑ C3L 22 [(3)]	Her Greatest Performances	1962	12.50	25.00	50.00
-- With booklet; originals have red and black labels with six "eye" logos					
❑ CL 6094 [10]	Serenade	1950	15.00	30.00	60.00
DECCA
| ❑ DL 5133 [10] | Mildred Bailey Memorial Album | 1950 | 15.00 | 30.00 | 60.00 |
| ❑ DL 5387 [10] | The Rockin' Chair Lady | 195? | 15.00 | 30.00 | 60.00 |

BAILEY, PEARL
COLUMBIA
| ❑ CL 6099 [10] | Pearl Bailey Entertains | 1950 | 12.50 | 25.00 | 50.00 |
CORAL
❑ CRL 56068 [10]	Say Si Si	1953	12.50	25.00	50.00
❑ CRL 56078 [10]	I'm with You	1954	12.50	25.00	50.00
❑ CRL 57037 [M]	Pearl Bailey	1957	10.00	20.00	40.00
❑ CRL 57162 [M]	Cultured Pearl	1958	10.00	20.00	40.00

MERCURY
| ❑ MG-20187 [M] | The One and Only Pearl Bailey Sings | 1956 | 10.00 | 20.00 | 40.00 |
| ❑ MG-20277 [M] | The Intoxicating Pearl Bailey | 1957 | 10.00 | 20.00 | 40.00 |
ROULETTE
❑ R-25012 [M]	Pearl Bailey A Broad	1957	7.50	15.00	30.00
-- Black label original					
❑ R-25016 [M]	Pearl Bailey Sings for Adults Only	1959	5.00	10.00	20.00
-- Originals have a white label with colored spokes					
❑ SR-25016 [S]	Pearl Bailey Sings for Adults Only	1959	6.25	12.50	25.00
-- Originals have a white label with colored spokes					
❑ R-25037 [M]	St. Louis Blues	1958	7.50	15.00	30.00
-- Black label original					
❑ SR-25037 [S]	St. Louis Blues	1959	7.50	15.00	30.00
-- Originals have a white label with colored spokes					
❑ R-25063 [M]	Pearl Bailey Sings Porgy and Bess and Other Gershwin Melodies	1959	5.00	10.00	20.00
-- Originals have a white label with colored spokes					
❑ SR-25063 [S]	Pearl Bailey Sings Porgy and Bess and Other Gershwin Melodies	1959	6.25	12.50	25.00
-- Originals have a white label with colored spokes					
❑ R-25101 [M]	More Songs for Adults Only	1960	5.00	10.00	20.00
-- Originals have a white label with colored spokes					
❑ SR-25101 [S]	More Songs for Adults Only	1960	6.25	12.50	25.00
-- Originals have a white label with colored spokes					
❑ R-25116 [M]	Songs of the Bad Old Days	1960	5.00	10.00	20.00
-- Originals have a white label with colored spokes					
❑ SR-25116 [S]	Songs of the Bad Old Days	1960	6.25	12.50	25.00
-- Originals have a white label with colored spokes					
❑ R-25125 [M]	Naughty But Nice	1960	5.00	10.00	20.00
-- Originals have a white label with colored spokes					
❑ SR-25125 [S]	Naughty But Nice	1960	6.25	12.50	25.00
-- Originals have a white label with colored spokes					
❑ R-25144 [M]	The Best of Pearl Bailey	1961	5.00	10.00	20.00
-- Originals have a white label with colored spokes					
❑ SR-25144 [S]	The Best of Pearl Bailey	1961	6.25	12.50	25.00
-- Originals have a white label with colored spokes					
❑ R-25155 [M]	Pearl Bailey Sings Songs of Harold Arlen	1961	5.00	10.00	20.00
-- Originals have a white label with colored spokes					
❑ SR-25155 [S]	Pearl Bailey Sings Songs of Harold Arlen	1961	6.25	12.50	25.00
-- Originals have a white label with colored spokes					
❑ R-25181 [M]	Come On, Let's Play with Pearlie	1962	5.00	10.00	20.00
-- Originals have a white label with colored spokes					
❑ SR-25181 [S]	Come On, Let's Play with Pearlie	1962	6.25	12.50	25.00
-- Originals have a white label with colored spokes					
❑ R-25195 [M]	About Good Little Girls and Bad Little Boys	1963	5.00	10.00	20.00
-- Originals have a pink and orange label					
❑ SR-25195 [S]	About Good Little Girls and Bad Little Boys	1963	6.25	12.50	25.00
-- Originals have a pink and orange label					
❑ R-25222 [M]	C'est La Vie	1963	5.00	10.00	20.00
-- Originals have a pink and orange label					
❑ SR-25222 [S]	C'est La Vie	1963	6.25	12.50	25.00
-- Originals have a pink and orange label					
❑ SR-25259 [S]	The Risque World of Pearl Bailey	1964	5.00	10.00	20.00
❑ SR-25271 [S]	Songs by James Van Heusen	1964	5.00	10.00	20.00
❑ SR-25300 [S]	For Women Only	1965	5.00	10.00	20.00
VOCALION
| ❑ VL 3621 [M] | Gems by Pearl Bailey | 1958 | 6.25 | 12.50 | 25.00 |

BAILLARGEON, HELENE
FOLKWAYS
| ❑ FW 829 [10] | Christmas Songs of French Canada | 195? | 12.50 | 25.00 | 50.00 |
| ❑ FC 7229 | Christmas Songs of French Canada | 195? | 12.50 | 25.00 | 50.00 |

BAIN, BOB
CAPITOL
❑ T 965 [M]	Rockin', Rollin' and Strollin'	1958	20.00	40.00	80.00
❑ ST 1201 [S]	Latin Love	1959	10.00	20.00	40.00
❑ T 1201 [M]	Latin Love	1959	7.50	15.00	30.00
❑ ST 1500 [S]	Guitar De Amor	1961	10.00	20.00	40.00
❑ T 1500 [M]	Guitar De Amor	1961	7.50	15.00	30.00

BAKER, GEORGE, SELECTION
COLOSSUS
| ❑ CS-1002 | Little Green Bag | 1970 | 5.00 | 10.00 | 20.00 |

BAKER, GINGER, 'S AIR FORCE
Also see CREAM.
ATCO
| ❑ SD 2-703 [(2)] | Ginger Baker's Air Force | 1970 | 5.00 | 10.00 | 20.00 |

Number	Title	Yr	VG	VG+	NM

BAKER, JOSEPHINE
RCA VICTOR RED SEAL
❏ LSC-2427 [S]	The Fabulous Josephine Baker	1960	10.00	20.00	40.00
-- Original with "shaded dog" label					

BAKER, LAVERN
ATLANTIC
❏ 1281 [M]	LaVern Baker Sings Bessie Smith	1958	30.00	60.00	120.00
-- Black label					
❏ 1281 [M]	LaVern Baker Sings Bessie Smith	1960	7.50	15.00	30.00
-- Red and purple label, "fan" logo in white					
❏ 1281 [M]	LaVern Baker Sings Bessie Smith	1960	5.00	10.00	20.00
-- Red and purple label, "fan" logo in black					
❏ SD 1281 [S]	LaVern Baker Sings Bessie Smith	1959	37.50	75.00	150.00
-- Green label					
❏ SD 1281 [S]	LaVern Baker Sings Bessie Smith	1960	10.00	20.00	40.00
-- Green and blue label, "fan" logo in white					
❏ SD 1281 [S]	LaVern Baker Sings Bessie Smith	1963	6.25	12.50	25.00
-- Green and blue label, "fan" logo in black					
❏ 8002 [M]	LaVern	1956	62.50	125.00	250.00
-- Black label					
❏ 8002 [M]	LaVern	1960	7.50	15.00	30.00
-- Red and purple label, "fan" logo in white					
❏ 8002 [M]	LaVern	1963	5.00	10.00	20.00
-- Red and purple label, "fan" logo in black					
❏ 8007 [M]	LaVern Baker	1957	62.50	125.00	250.00
-- Black label					
❏ 8007 [M]	LaVern Baker	1960	7.50	15.00	30.00
-- Red and purple label, "fan" logo in white					
❏ 8007 [M]	LaVern Baker	1963	5.00	10.00	20.00
-- Red and purple label, "fan" logo in black					
❏ 8030 [M]	Blues Ballads	1959	50.00	100.00	200.00
-- Black label					
❏ 8030 [M]	Blues Ballads	1960	37.50	75.00	150.00
-- White "bullseye" label					
❏ 8030 [M]	Blues Ballads	1960	7.50	15.00	30.00
-- Red and purple label, "fan" logo in white					
❏ 8030 [M]	Blues Ballads	1963	5.00	10.00	20.00
-- Red and purple label, "fan" logo in black					
❏ 8036 [M]	Precious Memories	1959	50.00	100.00	200.00
-- Black label					
❏ 8036 [M]	Precious Memories	1960	37.50	75.00	150.00
-- White "bullseye" label					
❏ 8036 [M]	Precious Memories	1960	7.50	15.00	30.00
-- Red and purple label, "fan" logo in white					
❏ 8036 [M]	Precious Memories	1963	5.00	10.00	20.00
-- Red and purple label, "fan" logo in black					
❏ SD 8036 [S]	Precious Memories	1959	75.00	150.00	300.00
-- Green label					
❏ SD 8036 [S]	Precious Memories	1960	50.00	100.00	200.00
-- White "bullseye" label					
❏ SD 8036 [S]	Precious Memories	1960	10.00	20.00	40.00
-- Green and blue label, "fan" logo in white					
❏ SD 8036 [S]	Precious Memories	1963	6.25	12.50	25.00
-- Green and blue label, "fan" logo in black					
❏ 8050 [M]	Saved	1961	25.00	50.00	100.00
-- Red and purple label, "fan" logo in white					
❏ 8050 [M]	Saved	1963	5.00	10.00	20.00
-- Red and purple label, "fan" logo in black					
❏ SD 8050 [S]	Saved	1961	37.50	75.00	150.00
-- Green and blue label, "fan" logo in white					
❏ SD 8050 [S]	Saved	1963	6.25	12.50	25.00
-- Green and blue label, "fan" logo in black					
❏ 8071 [M]	See See Rider	1962	25.00	50.00	100.00
-- Red and purple label, "fan" logo in white					
❏ 8071 [M]	See See Rider	1963	5.00	10.00	20.00
-- Red and purple label, "fan" logo in black					
❏ SD 8071 [S]	See See Rider	1962	37.50	75.00	150.00
-- Green and blue label, "fan" logo in white					
❏ SD 8071 [S]	See See Rider	1963	6.25	12.50	25.00
-- Green and blue label, "fan" logo in black					
❏ 8078 [M]	The Best of LaVern Baker	1963	37.50	75.00	150.00
-- Red and purple label, "fan" logo in black					
BRUNSWICK
❏ BL 754160	Let Me Belong to You	1970	5.00	10.00	20.00

BAKER, MICKEY "GUITAR"
Also see MICKEY AND SYLVIA.
ATLANTIC
❏ 8035 [M]	The Wildest Guitar	1959	37.50	75.00	150.00
-- Black label					
❏ 8035 [M]	The Wildest Guitar	1960	12.50	25.00	50.00
-- Red and purple label, "fan" logo in white					
❏ SD 8035 [S]	The Wildest Guitar	1959	62.50	125.00	250.00
-- Green label					
❏ SD 8035 [S]	The Wildest Guitar	1960	20.00	40.00	80.00
-- Green and blue label, "fan" logo in white					

KING
❏ 839 [M]	But Wild	196?	20.00	40.00	80.00
-- Blue label with crown					
❏ 839 [M]	But Wild	1963	100.00	200.00	400.00
-- Black label, no crown					
❏ S-839 [R]	But Wild	196?	10.00	20.00	40.00

BAKER, RONNIE
WARNER BROS.
❏ W 1212 [M]	Oh, Johnny!	1958	7.50	15.00	30.00
❏ WS 1212 [S]	Oh, Johnny!	1959	12.50	25.00	50.00

BALDRY, LONG JOHN
ASCOT
❏ AM-13022 [M]	Long John's Blues	1965	12.50	25.00	50.00
❏ AS-16022 [R]	Long John's Blues	1965	10.00	20.00	40.00

BALIN, MARTY
Also see JEFFERSON AIRPLANE; JEFFERSON STARSHIP.
EMI AMERICA
❏ SPRO-9673	Balin	1981	5.00	10.00	20.00
-- Red vinyl					

BALL, KENNY
KAPP
❏ KL-1276 [M]	Midnight in Moscow	1962	5.00	10.00	20.00
❏ KL-1285 [M]	It's Trad	1962	5.00	10.00	20.00
❏ KL-1294 [M]	Recorded Live	1962	5.00	10.00	20.00
❏ KS-3276 [S]	Midnight in Moscow	1962	5.00	10.00	20.00
❏ KS-3285 [S]	It's Trad	1962	5.00	10.00	20.00
❏ KS-3294 [S]	Recorded Live	1962	5.00	10.00	20.00
❏ KS-3314 [S]	More	1963	5.00	10.00	20.00
❏ KS-3340 [S]	Big Ones	1963	5.00	10.00	20.00
❏ KS-3348 [S]	Washington Square and the Best of Kenny Ball	1964	5.00	10.00	20.00
❏ KS-3392 [S]	For the Jet Set	1964	5.00	10.00	20.00

BALLADEERS, THE
DEL-FI
❏ DFLP-1204 [M]	Alive-O!	1959	10.00	20.00	40.00

BALLARD, FRANK
PHILLIPS INTERNATIONAL
❏ 1985 [M]	Rhythm-Blues Party	1962	2,500.	3,750.	5,000.

BALLARD, HANK, AND THE MIDNIGHTERS
Also see THE MIDNIGHTERS.
KING
❏ 618 [M]	Singin' and Swingin'	1959	62.50	125.00	250.00
❏ 674 [M]	The One and Only Hank Ballard	1959	62.50	125.00	250.00
-- Brown cover					
❏ 674 [M]	The One and Only Hank Ballard	1960	37.50	75.00	150.00
-- Green cover					
❏ 700 [M]	Finger Poppin' Time	1960	37.50	75.00	150.00
❏ 740 [M]	Spotlight on Hank Ballard	1961	37.50	75.00	150.00
❏ KS-740 [S]	Spotlight on Hank Ballard	1961	75.00	150.00	300.00
❏ 748 [M]	Let's Go Again	1961	30.00	60.00	120.00
❏ 759 [M]	Dance Along	1961	30.00	60.00	120.00
❏ 781 [M]	The Twistin' Fools	1962	25.00	50.00	100.00
❏ 793 [M]	Jumpin' Hank Ballard	1962	25.00	50.00	100.00
❏ 815 [M]	The 1963 Sound of Hank Ballard	1963	25.00	50.00	100.00
❏ 867 [M]	Biggest Hits	1963	25.00	50.00	100.00
❏ 896 [M]	A Star in Your Eyes	1964	25.00	50.00	100.00
❏ 913 [M]	Those Lazy, Lazy Days	1965	17.50	35.00	70.00
❏ 927 [M]	Glad Songs, Sad Songs	1965	17.50	35.00	70.00
❏ 950 [M]	24 Hit Tunes	1966	15.00	30.00	60.00
❏ 981 [M]	24 Great Songs	1968	10.00	20.00	40.00
❏ KSD-1052	You Can't Keep a Good Man Down	1969	12.50	25.00	50.00

BALLARD, KAYE
UNITED ARTISTS
❏ UAL-3043 [M]	Kaye Ballard Swings	1959	5.00	10.00	20.00
❏ UAL-3155 [M]	Kaye Ballard Live?	1960	5.00	10.00	20.00
❏ UAL-3165 [M]	Ha-Ha Boo-Hoo	1960	5.00	10.00	20.00
❏ UAS-6043 [S]	Kaye Ballard Swings	1959	6.25	12.50	25.00
❏ UAS-6155 [S]	Kaye Ballard Live?	1960	6.25	12.50	25.00
❏ UAS-6165 [S]	Ha-Ha Boo-Hoo	1960	6.25	12.50	25.00

BANANA SPLITS, THE
DECCA
❏ DL 75075	We're the Banana Splits	1969	50.00	100.00	200.00

Number	Title	Yr	VG	VG+	NM

BANCHEE
ATLANTIC
| ❏ SD 8240 | Banchee | 1969 | 5.00 | 10.00 | 20.00 |
POLYDOR
| ❏ 24-4066 | Thinkin' | 1971 | 12.50 | 25.00 | 50.00 |

BAND, THE
Also see BOB DYLAN; RONNIE HAWKINS.
CAPITOL
❏ SKAO 2955	Music from Big Pink	1968	6.25	12.50	25.00
-- Black label with colorband					
❏ SABB-11045 [(2)]	Rock of Ages	1972	5.00	10.00	20.00
MOBILE FIDELITY
| ❏ 1-039 | Music from Big Pink | 1981 | 12.50 | 25.00 | 50.00 |
| -- Audiophile vinyl | | | | | |
WARNER BROS.
| ❏ PRO-A-737 [DJ] | The Last Waltz Sampler | 1978 | 5.00 | 10.00 | 20.00 |
| ❏ 3WS 3146 [(3)] | The Last Waltz | 1978 | 5.00 | 10.00 | 20.00 |

BANDITS, THE
WORLD PACIFIC
| ❏ ST-1833 [S] | The Electric 12 String | 1964 | 6.25 | 12.50 | 25.00 |
| ❏ T-1833 [M] | The Electric 12 String | 1964 | 5.00 | 10.00 | 20.00 |

BANDWAGON, THE
EPIC
| ❏ BN 26426 | Johnny Johnson and the Bandwagon | 1969 | 5.00 | 10.00 | 20.00 |

BANG
CAPITOL
| ❏ ST-11190 | Music | 1973 | 5.00 | 10.00 | 20.00 |

BANGLES
COLUMBIA
| ❏ CAS 2270 [DJ] | Interchords | 1986 | 5.00 | 10.00 | 20.00 |
| -- Promo-only interview album | | | | | |
FAULTY PRODUCTS
| ❏ FEP 1302 [EP] | Bangles | 1982 | 5.00 | 10.00 | 20.00 |

BANKS, DARRELL
ATCO
| ❏ 33-216 [M] | Darrell Banks Is Here | 1967 | 6.25 | 12.50 | 25.00 |
| ❏ SD 33-216 [S] | Darrell Banks Is Here | 1967 | 7.50 | 15.00 | 30.00 |
VOLT
| ❏ VOS-6002 | Here to Stay | 1969 | 6.25 | 12.50 | 25.00 |

BANTAMS, THE
WARNER BROS.
| ❏ W 1625 [M] | Beware the Bantams | 1966 | 5.00 | 10.00 | 20.00 |
| ❏ WS 1625 [S] | Beware the Bantams | 1966 | 6.25 | 12.50 | 25.00 |

BAR-KAYS, THE
ATCO
| ❏ SD 33-289 | Soul Finger | 1968 | 6.25 | 12.50 | 25.00 |
VOLT
❏ 417 [M]	Soul Finger	1967	10.00	20.00	40.00
❏ S-417 [S]	Soul Finger	1967	10.00	20.00	40.00
❏ 6004	Gotta Groove	1969	7.50	15.00	30.00
❏ 6011	Black Rock	1971	6.25	12.50	25.00
❏ VOS-8001	Do You See What I See	1972	6.25	12.50	25.00
❏ 9504	Cold Blooded	1974	6.25	12.50	25.00

BARBARIANS, THE
LAURIE
| ❏ LLP-2033 [M] | Are You a Boy or Are You a Girl? | 1966 | 37.50 | 75.00 | 150.00 |
| ❏ SLP-2033 [S] | Are You a Boy or Are You a Girl? | 1966 | 50.00 | 100.00 | 200.00 |

BARBARY, RICHARD
A&M
| ❏ SP-3010 | Soul Machine | 1968 | 5.00 | 10.00 | 20.00 |

BARBER, CHRIS, 'S JAZZ BAND
ATLANTIC
| ❏ 1292 [M] | Here Is Chris Barber | 1959 | 10.00 | 20.00 | 40.00 |
COLPIX
| ❏ CP-404 [M] | Petite But Great | 1959 | 7.50 | 15.00 | 30.00 |

LAURIE
❏ 1001 [M]	Petite Fleur	1959	10.00	20.00	40.00
❏ LLP-1003 [M]	Trad Jazz Volume 1	1960	7.50	15.00	30.00
❏ LLP-1009 [M]	Chris Barber's "American" Jazz Band	1962	7.50	15.00	30.00

BARBIERI, GATO
ESP-DISK'
| ❏ 1049 | In Search of the Mystery | 1968 | 5.00 | 10.00 | 20.00 |

BARBOUR, KEITH
EPIC
| ❏ BN 26485 | Echo Park | 1969 | 5.00 | 10.00 | 20.00 |

BARCLAY JAMES HARVEST
SIRE
| ❏ SES-97026 | Barclay James Harvest | 1970 | 5.00 | 10.00 | 20.00 |

BARDOT, BRIGITTE
DOT
| ❏ DLP-3120 [M] | La Belle Bardot | 1958 | 25.00 | 50.00 | 100.00 |
PHILIPS
| ❏ PCC 204 [M] | Brigitte Bardot Sings | 1963 | 7.50 | 15.00 | 30.00 |
| ❏ PCC 604 [S] | Brigitte Bardot Sings | 1963 | 10.00 | 20.00 | 40.00 |

BARE, BOBBY
MERCURY
❏ SR-61290	This Is Bare Country	1970	5.00	10.00	20.00
❏ SR-61316	Where Have All the Seasons Gone	1971	5.00	10.00	20.00
❏ SR-61363	What Am I Gonna Do?	1972	5.00	10.00	20.00
RCA VICTOR
❏ CPL2-0290 [(2)]	Bobby Bare Sings Lullabys, Legends and Lies	1973	5.00	10.00	20.00
❏ LPM-2776 [M]	"Detroit City" and Other Hits	1963	5.00	10.00	20.00
❏ LSP-2776 [S]	"Detroit City" and Other Hits	1963	6.25	12.50	25.00
❏ LPM-2835 [M]	500 Miles Away from Home	1964	5.00	10.00	20.00
❏ LSP-2835 [S]	500 Miles Away from Home	1964	6.25	12.50	25.00
❏ LPM-2955 [M]	The Travelin' Bare	1964	5.00	10.00	20.00
❏ LSP-2955 [S]	The Travelin' Bare	1964	6.25	12.50	25.00
❏ LPM-3395 [M]	Constant Sorrow	1965	5.00	10.00	20.00
❏ LSP-3395 [S]	Constant Sorrow	1965	6.25	12.50	25.00
❏ LPM-3479 [M]	The Best of Bobby Bare	1965	5.00	10.00	20.00
❏ LSP-3479 [S]	The Best of Bobby Bare	1965	6.25	12.50	25.00
❏ LPM-3515 [M]	Talk Me Some Sense	1966	5.00	10.00	20.00
❏ LSP-3515 [S]	Talk Me Some Sense	1966	6.25	12.50	25.00
❏ LPM-3618 [M]	The Streets of Baltimore	1966	5.00	10.00	20.00
❏ LSP-3618 [S]	The Streets of Baltimore	1966	6.25	12.50	25.00
❏ LPM-3688 [M]	This I Believe	1966	5.00	10.00	20.00
❏ LSP-3688 [S]	This I Believe	1966	6.25	12.50	25.00
❏ LPM-3831 [M]	A Bird Named Yesterday	1967	6.25	12.50	25.00
❏ LSP-3831 [S]	A Bird Named Yesterday	1967	5.00	10.00	20.00
❏ LPM-3896 [M]	The English Country Side	1967	10.00	20.00	40.00
❏ LSP-3896 [S]	The English Country Side	1967	5.00	10.00	20.00
❏ LPM-3994 [M]	The Best of Bobby Bare -- Volume 2	1968	10.00	20.00	40.00
❏ LSP-3994 [S]	The Best of Bobby Bare -- Volume 2	1968	5.00	10.00	20.00
❏ LSP-4177	(Margie's At) The Lincoln Park Inn (And Other Controversial Country Songs)	1969	5.00	10.00	20.00
❏ VPS-6090 [(2)]	This Is Bobby Bare	1972	5.00	10.00	20.00

BARE, BOBBY, AND SKEETER DAVIS
Also see each artist's individual listings.
RCA VICTOR
| ❏ LPM-3336 [M] | Tunes for Two | 1965 | 5.00 | 10.00 | 20.00 |
| ❏ LSP-3336 [S] | Tunes for Two | 1965 | 6.25 | 12.50 | 25.00 |

BARE, BOBBY, NORMA JEAN, & LIZ ANDERSON
Also see each artist's individual listings.
RCA VICTOR
| ❏ LPM-3764 [M] | The Game of Triangles | 1967 | 6.25 | 12.50 | 25.00 |
| ❏ LSP-3764 [S] | The Game of Triangles | 1967 | 5.00 | 10.00 | 20.00 |

BARGE, GENE
CHECKER
| ❏ LP-2994 [M] | Dance with Daddy G | 1965 | 12.50 | 25.00 | 50.00 |

BARKER, WARREN
WARNER BROS.
| ❏ W 1205 [M] | "The King and I" for Orchestra | 1958 | 5.00 | 10.00 | 20.00 |

Number	Title	Yr	VG	VG+	NM
❑ WS 1205 [S]	"The King and I" for Orchestra	1958	6.25	12.50	25.00

BARNES, GEORGE
DECCA

Number	Title	Yr	VG	VG+	NM
❑ DL 8658 [M]	Guitars -- By George	1957	10.00	20.00	40.00
-- Black label, silver print					

MERCURY

Number	Title	Yr	VG	VG+	NM
❑ MG-20956 [M]	Guitar Galaxies	1962	6.25	12.50	25.00
❑ SR-60956 [S]	Guitar Galaxies	1962	7.50	15.00	30.00

BARNES, J.J.
VOLT

Number	Title	Yr	VG	VG+	NM
❑ VOS-6001	Rare Stamps	1969	7.50	15.00	30.00
-- With Steve Mancha					

BARNETT, BOBBY
SIMS

Number	Title	Yr	VG	VG+	NM
❑ LP-198 [M]	Bobby Barnett at the World Famous Crystal Palace, Tombstone, Arizona	1964	6.25	12.50	25.00

BARNUM, H.B.
CAPITOL

Number	Title	Yr	VG	VG+	NM
❑ ST 2278 [S]	Golden Boy	1965	5.00	10.00	20.00
❑ ST 2289 [S]	Big Hits of Detroit	1965	5.00	10.00	20.00
❑ ST 2583 [S]	Pop and Ice Cream Sodas	1966	5.00	10.00	20.00

BAROQUE ENSEMBLE OF THE MERSEYSIDE KAMMERMUSIKGESELLSCHAFT, THE
ELEKTRA

Number	Title	Yr	VG	VG+	NM
❑ EKL-306 [M]	The Baroque Beatles Book	1966	6.25	12.50	25.00
❑ EKS-7306 [S]	The Baroque Beatles Book	1966	7.50	15.00	30.00

BAROQUES, THE
CHESS

Number	Title	Yr	VG	VG+	NM
❑ LP-1516 [M]	The Baroques	1967	20.00	40.00	80.00
❑ LPS-1516 [S]	The Baroques	1967	25.00	50.00	100.00

BARRACUDAS, THE
JUSTICE

Number	Title	Yr	VG	VG+	NM
❑ JLP-143	A Plane View	1968	125.00	250.00	500.00

BARRETT, RONA
MISS RONA

Number	Title	Yr	VG	VG+	NM
❑ MRR 1001	Miss Rona Sings Hollywood's Greatest Hits	1974	10.00	20.00	40.00

BARRETT, SUSAN
RCA VICTOR

Number	Title	Yr	VG	VG+	NM
❑ LPM-3738 [M]	Susan Barrett	1967	10.00	20.00	40.00
❑ LSP-3738 [S]	Susan Barrett	1967	7.50	15.00	30.00

BARRETT, SYD
Also see PINK FLOYD.
CAPITOL

Number	Title	Yr	VG	VG+	NM
❑ C1-91206	Opel	1989	5.00	10.00	20.00

HARVEST

Number	Title	Yr	VG	VG+	NM
❑ SABB-11314 [(2)]	The Madcap Laughs/Barrett	1974	6.25	12.50	25.00

BARRY AND BARRY -- See BARRY McGUIRE AND BARRY KANE.

BARRY AND THE TAMERLANES
VALIANT

Number	Title	Yr	VG	VG+	NM
❑ LP-406 [M]	I Wonder What She's Doing Tonight	1963	37.50	75.00	150.00
❑ LPS-406 [S]	I Wonder What She's Doing Tonight	1963	75.00	150.00	300.00

BARRY, GENE
RCA VICTOR

Number	Title	Yr	VG	VG+	NM
❑ LPM-2975 [M]	The Star of "Burke's Law" Sings of Love and Things	1964	6.25	12.50	25.00
❑ LSP-2975 [S]	The Star of "Burke's Law" Sings of Love and Things	1964	7.50	15.00	30.00

BARRY, JOHN
COLUMBIA

Number	Title	Yr	VG	VG+	NM
❑ CS 9293 [S]	Great Movie Sounds of John Barry	1966	5.00	10.00	20.00
❑ CS 9508 [S]	You Only Live Twice	1967	5.00	10.00	20.00

BARRY, LEN
DECCA

Number	Title	Yr	VG	VG+	NM
❑ DL 4720 [M]	1-2-3	1965	7.50	15.00	30.00
❑ DL 74720 [S]	1-2-3	1965	10.00	20.00	40.00

RCA VICTOR

Number	Title	Yr	VG	VG+	NM
❑ LPM-3823 [M]	My Kind of Soul	1967	6.25	12.50	25.00
❑ LSP-3823 [S]	My Kind of Soul	1967	5.00	10.00	20.00

BARRYMORE, LIONEL, AS EBENEZER SCROOGE
MGM

Number	Title	Yr	VG	VG+	NM
❑ CH 112 [10]	A Christmas Carol	1952	10.00	20.00	40.00

BARTHOLOMEW, DAVE
IMPERIAL

Number	Title	Yr	VG	VG+	NM
❑ LP-9162 [M]	Fats Domino Presents Dave Bartholomew	1961	25.00	50.00	100.00
❑ LP-9217 [M]	New Orleans House Party	1963	25.00	50.00	100.00
❑ LP-12076 [S]	Fats Domino Presents Dave Bartholomew	1961	37.50	75.00	150.00
❑ LP-12217 [S]	New Orleans House Party	1963	37.50	75.00	150.00

BASIE, COUNT
Also see TONY BENNETT; TERESA BREWER; ELLA FITZGERALD; ARTHUR PRYSOCK; FRANK SINATRA; SARAH VAUGHAN; JACKIE WILSON.
ABC

Number	Title	Yr	VG	VG+	NM
❑ 570 [M]	Basie's Swingin' -- Voices Singin'	1966	5.00	10.00	20.00
❑ S-570 [S]	Basie's Swingin' -- Voices Singin'	1966	6.25	12.50	25.00

AMERICAN RECORDING SOCIETY

Number	Title	Yr	VG	VG+	NM
❑ G-401 [M]	Count Basie	1956	10.00	20.00	40.00
❑ G-422 [M]	Basie's Best	1957	10.00	20.00	40.00

BRUNSWICK

Number	Title	Yr	VG	VG+	NM
❑ BL 54012 [M]	Count Basie	1957	10.00	20.00	40.00

CLEF

Number	Title	Yr	VG	VG+	NM
❑ MCG-120 [10]	Count Basie and His Orchestra Collates	1953	50.00	100.00	200.00
❑ MCG-146 [10]	Count Basie Sextet	1954	50.00	100.00	200.00
❑ MGC-148 [10]	Count Basie Big Band	1954	50.00	100.00	200.00
❑ MGC-626 [M]	Count Basie Dance Session #1	1954	25.00	50.00	100.00
❑ MGC-633 [M]	Basie Jazz	1954	25.00	50.00	100.00
❑ MGC-647 [M]	Count Basie Jazz Session #2	1955	25.00	50.00	100.00
❑ MGC-666 [M]	Basie	1955	25.00	50.00	100.00
❑ MGC-685 [M]	The Count	1956	20.00	40.00	80.00
❑ MGC-706 [M]	The Swinging Count	1956	15.00	30.00	60.00
❑ MGC-722 [M]	The Band of Distinction	1956	15.00	30.00	60.00
❑ MGC-723 [M]	Basie Roars Again	1956	15.00	30.00	60.00
❑ MGC-724 [M]	The King of Swing	1956	15.00	30.00	60.00
❑ MGC-729 [M]	Basie Rides Again!	1956	15.00	30.00	60.00

COLUMBIA

Number	Title	Yr	VG	VG+	NM
❑ CL 754 [M]	Classics	1955	10.00	20.00	40.00
❑ CL 901 [M]	Blues By Basie	1956	10.00	20.00	40.00
❑ CL 997 [M]	One O'Clock Jump	1956	10.00	20.00	40.00
❑ CL 2560 [10]	Basie Bash	1956	12.50	25.00	50.00
❑ CL 6079 [10]	Dance Parade	1949	25.00	50.00	100.00

COMMAND

Number	Title	Yr	VG	VG+	NM
❑ CQ-40004 [Q]	Broadway Basie's…Way	1972	5.00	10.00	20.00

DECCA

Number	Title	Yr	VG	VG+	NM
❑ DL 5111 [10]	Count Basie at the Piano	1950	25.00	50.00	100.00
❑ DL 8049 [M]	Count Basie and His Orchestra	1954	12.50	25.00	50.00
❑ DXB 170 [(2) M]	The Best of Count Basie	196?	6.25	12.50	25.00

EMARCY

Number	Title	Yr	VG	VG+	NM
❑ MG-26023 [10]	Jazz Royalty	1954	17.50	35.00	70.00

EPIC

Number	Title	Yr	VG	VG+	NM
❑ LG 1021 [10]	The Old Count and the New Count -- Basie	1954	17.50	35.00	70.00
❑ LN 1117 [10]	Rock the Blues	1955	17.50	35.00	70.00
❑ LN 3107 [M]	Lester Leaps In	1955	12.50	25.00	50.00
-- With Lester Young					
❑ LN 3168 [M]	Let's Go to Prez	1955	12.50	25.00	50.00
-- With Lester Young					
❑ LN 3169 [M]	Basie's Back in Town	1955	12.50	25.00	50.00

IMPULSE!

Number	Title	Yr	VG	VG+	NM
❑ A-15 [M]	Count Basie and the Kansas City Seven	1962	7.50	15.00	30.00
❑ AS-15 [S]	Count Basie and the Kansas City Seven	1962	10.00	20.00	40.00

JAZZ PANORAMA

Number	Title	Yr	VG	VG+	NM
❑ 1803 [10]	Count Basie and Lester Young	1951	25.00	50.00	100.00

Number	Title	Yr	VG	VG+	NM

MERCURY

Number	Title	Yr	VG	VG+	NM
❏ MGC-120 [10]	Count Basie and His Orchestra Collates	1952	55.00	110.00	220.00
❏ MG-25105 [10]	Count Basie and His Kansas City Seven	1952	25.00	50.00	100.00

MOBILE FIDELITY

Number	Title	Yr	VG	VG+	NM
❏ 1-129	Basie Plays Hefti	1985	20.00	40.00	80.00
-- Audiophile vinyl					
❏ 1-237	April in Paris	1995	10.00	20.00	40.00
-- Audiophile vinyl					

RCA CAMDEN

Number	Title	Yr	VG	VG+	NM
❏ CAL-395 [M]	The Count	1958	6.25	12.50	25.00
❏ CAL-497 [M]	Basie's Basement	1959	6.25	12.50	25.00
❏ CAL-514 [M]	Count Basie in Kansas City	1959	6.25	12.50	25.00

RCA VICTOR

Number	Title	Yr	VG	VG+	NM
❏ LPM-1112 [M]	Count Basie	1955	12.50	25.00	50.00

REPRISE

Number	Title	Yr	VG	VG+	NM
❏ R-6070 [M]	This Time by Basie! Hits of the 50's and 60's	1963	5.00	10.00	20.00
❏ R9-6070 [S]	This Time by Basie! Hits of the 50's and 60's	1963	6.25	12.50	25.00
❏ RS-6153 [S]	Pop Goes the Basie	1965	5.00	10.00	20.00

ROULETTE

Number	Title	Yr	VG	VG+	NM
❏ RB-1 [(2) M]	The Count Basie Story	1960	10.00	20.00	40.00
❏ SRB-1 [(2) S]	The Count Basie Story	1960	12.50	25.00	50.00
❏ R 52003 [M]	Basie	1958	7.50	15.00	30.00
❏ SR 52003 [S]	Basie	1958	7.50	15.00	30.00
-- Black vinyl					
❏ SR 52003 [S]	Basie	1958	25.00	50.00	100.00
-- Red vinyl					
❏ R 52011 [M]	Basie Plays Hefti	1958	7.50	15.00	30.00
❏ SR 52011 [S]	Basie Plays Hefti	1958	7.50	15.00	30.00
❏ R 52024 [M]	One More Time	1959	7.50	15.00	30.00
❏ SR 52024 [S]	One More Time	1959	7.50	15.00	30.00
❏ R 52028 [M]	Breakfast Dance & Barbecue	1959	7.50	15.00	30.00
❏ SR 52028 [S]	Breakfast Dance & Barbecue	1959	7.50	15.00	30.00
❏ R 52032 [M]	Chairman of the Board	1959	7.50	15.00	30.00
❏ SR 52032 [S]	Chairman of the Board	1959	7.50	15.00	30.00
❏ R 52036 [M]	Dance with Basie	1959	7.50	15.00	30.00
❏ SR 52036 [S]	Dance with Basie	1959	7.50	15.00	30.00
❏ R 52044 [M]	Not Now -- I'll Tell You When	1960	6.25	12.50	25.00
❏ SR 52044 [S]	Not Now -- I'll Tell You When	1960	7.50	15.00	30.00
❏ R 52051 [M]	String Along with Basie	1960	6.25	12.50	25.00
❏ SR 52051 [S]	String Along with Basie	1960	7.50	15.00	30.00
❏ R 52056 [M]	Benny Carter's Kansas City Suite	1960	6.25	12.50	25.00
❏ SR 52056 [S]	Benny Carter's Kansas City Suite	1960	7.50	15.00	30.00
❏ R 52065 [M]	Basie at Birdland	1961	6.25	12.50	25.00
❏ SR 52065 [S]	Basie at Birdland	1961	7.50	15.00	30.00
❏ SR 52081 [S]	The Best of Basie	1962	5.00	10.00	20.00
❏ R 52086 [M]	The Legend	1962	5.00	10.00	20.00
❏ SR 52086 [S]	The Legend	1962	6.25	12.50	25.00
❏ SR 52089 [S]	The Best of Basie, Volume 2	1962	5.00	10.00	20.00
❏ R 52099 [M]	Count Basie in Sweden	1963	5.00	10.00	20.00
❏ SR 52099 [S]	Count Basie in Sweden	1963	6.25	12.50	25.00
❏ R 52106 [M]	Easin' It	1963	5.00	10.00	20.00
❏ SR 52106 [S]	Easin' It	1963	6.25	12.50	25.00
❏ R 52111/2/3 [(3) M]	The World of Count Basie	1964	10.00	20.00	40.00
❏ SR 52111/2/3 [(3) S]	The World of Count Basie	1964	12.50	25.00	50.00

UNITED ARTISTS

Number	Title	Yr	VG	VG+	NM
❏ UAL-3480 [M]	Basie Meets Bond	1966	6.25	12.50	25.00
❏ UAS-6480 [S]	Basie Meets Bond	1966	7.50	15.00	30.00

VERVE

Number	Title	Yr	VG	VG+	NM
❏ VSPS-12 [S]	Inside Outside	1966	5.00	10.00	20.00
❏ MGVS-6024 [S]	Count Basie at Newport	1960	12.50	25.00	50.00
❏ MGV-8012 [M]	April in Paris	1957	12.50	25.00	50.00
❏ V-8012 [M]	April in Paris	1961	5.00	10.00	20.00
❏ MGV-8018 [M]	Basie Roars Again	1957	12.50	25.00	50.00
-- Reissue of Clef 723					
❏ V-8018 [M]	Basie Roars Again	1961	5.00	10.00	20.00
❏ MGV-8070 [M]	The Count	1957	12.50	25.00	50.00
-- Reissue of Clef 120					
❏ V-8070 [M]	The Count	1961	5.00	10.00	20.00
❏ MGV-8090 [M]	The Swinging Count!	1957	12.50	25.00	50.00
-- Reissue of Clef 706					
❏ V-8090 [M]	The Swinging Count!	1961	5.00	10.00	20.00
❏ MGV-8103 [M]	The Band of Distinction	1957	12.50	25.00	50.00
-- Reissue of Clef 722					
❏ V-8103 [M]	The Band of Distinction	1961	5.00	10.00	20.00
❏ MGV-8104 [M]	The King of Swing	1957	12.50	25.00	50.00
-- Reissue of Clef 724					
❏ V-8104 [M]	The King of Swing	1961	5.00	10.00	20.00

Number	Title	Yr	VG	VG+	NM
❏ MGV-8108 [M]	Basie Rides Again!	1957	12.50	25.00	50.00
-- Reissue of Clef 729					
❏ V-8108 [M]	Basie Rides Again!	1961	5.00	10.00	20.00
❏ V-8199 [M]	Basie in London	1961	5.00	10.00	20.00
❏ MGV-8199 [M]	Basie in London	1957	12.50	25.00	50.00
❏ MGV-8243 [M]	Count Basie at Newport	1958	12.50	25.00	50.00
❏ V-8243 [M]	Count Basie at Newport	1961	5.00	10.00	20.00
❏ V6-8243 [S]	Count Basie at Newport	1961	5.00	10.00	20.00
❏ MGV-8291 [M]	Hall of Fame	1958	12.50	25.00	50.00
❏ V-8291 [M]	Hall of Fame	1961	5.00	10.00	20.00
❏ V6-8407 [S]	The Essential Count Basie	1961	5.00	10.00	20.00
❏ V6-8511 [S]	On My Way and Shoutin' Again!	1963	5.00	10.00	20.00
❏ V6-8549 [S]	Li'l Ol' Groovemaker…Basie!	1963	5.00	10.00	20.00
❏ V6-8563 [S]	More Hits of the 50's and 60's	1963	5.00	10.00	20.00
❏ V6-8596 [S]	Verve's Choice -- Best of Count	1964	5.00	10.00	20.00
❏ V6-8597 [S]	Basie Land	1964	5.00	10.00	20.00
❏ V6-8616 [S]	Basie Picks the Winners	1965	5.00	10.00	20.00
❏ V-8659 [M]	Basie's Beatle Bag	1966	7.50	15.00	30.00
❏ V6-8659 [S]	Basie's Beatle Bag	1966	10.00	20.00	40.00
❏ V-8687 [M]	Basie's Beat	1967	5.00	10.00	20.00

BASIE, COUNT, AND SAMMY DAVIS, JR.
Also see each artist's individual listings.

VERVE

Number	Title	Yr	VG	VG+	NM
❏ V6-8605 [S]	Our Shining Hour	1965	5.00	10.00	20.00

BASIE, COUNT, AND BILLY ECKSTINE
Also see each artist's individual listings.

ROULETTE

Number	Title	Yr	VG	VG+	NM
❏ R 52029 [M]	Basie/Eckstine, Inc.	1959	6.25	12.50	25.00
❏ SR 52029 [S]	Basie/Eckstine, Inc.	1959	7.50	15.00	30.00

BASIE, COUNT, AND DIZZY GILLESPIE
Also see each artist's individual listings.

VERVE

Number	Title	Yr	VG	VG+	NM
❏ V-8560 [M]	The Count Basie Band and the Dizzy Gillespie Band at Newport	1963	5.00	10.00	20.00
❏ V6-8560 [S]	The Count Basie Band and the Dizzy Gillespie Band at Newport	1963	6.25	12.50	25.00

BASIE, COUNT, AND JOE WILLIAMS

CLEF

Number	Title	Yr	VG	VG+	NM
❏ MGC-678 [M]	Count Basie Swings/ Joe Williams Sings	1955	12.50	25.00	50.00

ROULETTE

Number	Title	Yr	VG	VG+	NM
❏ R 52021 [M]	Memories Ad Lib	1959	7.50	15.00	30.00
❏ SR 52021 [S]	Memories Ad Lib	1959	10.00	20.00	40.00
❏ R 52033 [M]	Everyday I Have the Blues	1959	7.50	15.00	30.00
❏ SR 52033 [S]	Everyday I Have the Blues	1959	10.00	20.00	40.00
❏ R 52054 [M]	Just the Blues	1960	7.50	15.00	30.00
❏ SR 52054 [S]	Just the Blues	1960	10.00	20.00	40.00

VANGUARD

Number	Title	Yr	VG	VG+	NM
❏ VRS-8508 [M]	A Night at Count Basie's	1955	12.50	25.00	50.00

VERVE

Number	Title	Yr	VG	VG+	NM
❏ MGV-2016 [M]	The Greatest! Count Basie Swings/ Joe Williams Sings Standards	1956	12.50	25.00	50.00
❏ MGVS-6006 [S]	The Greatest! Count Basie Swings/ Joe Williams Sings Standards	1960	10.00	20.00	40.00
❏ MGV-8063 [M]	Count Basie Swings/ Joe Williams Sings	1957	10.00	20.00	40.00
-- Reissue of Clef 678					
❏ V-8488 [M]	Count Basie Swings/ Joe Williams Sings	1962	6.25	12.50	25.00
-- Reissue of 8063					

BASKERVILLE HOUNDS, THE

DOT

Number	Title	Yr	VG	VG+	NM
❏ DLP-3823 [M]	The Baskerville Hounds (Featuring Space Rock, Part 2)	1967	12.50	25.00	50.00
❏ DLP-25823 [S]	The Baskerville Hounds (Featuring Space Rock, Part 2)	1967	20.00	40.00	80.00

BASS, FONTELLA

CHECKER

Number	Title	Yr	VG	VG+	NM
❏ LP-2997 [M]	The "New" Look	1966	15.00	30.00	60.00
-- Blue label with red and black checkers					
❏ LP-2997 [M]	The "New" Look	1967	7.50	15.00	30.00
-- Blue and white label					
❏ LPS-2997 [S]	The "New" Look	1966	20.00	40.00	80.00
-- Blue label with red and black checkers					
❏ LPS-2997 [S]	The "New" Look	1967	10.00	20.00	40.00
-- Blue and white label					

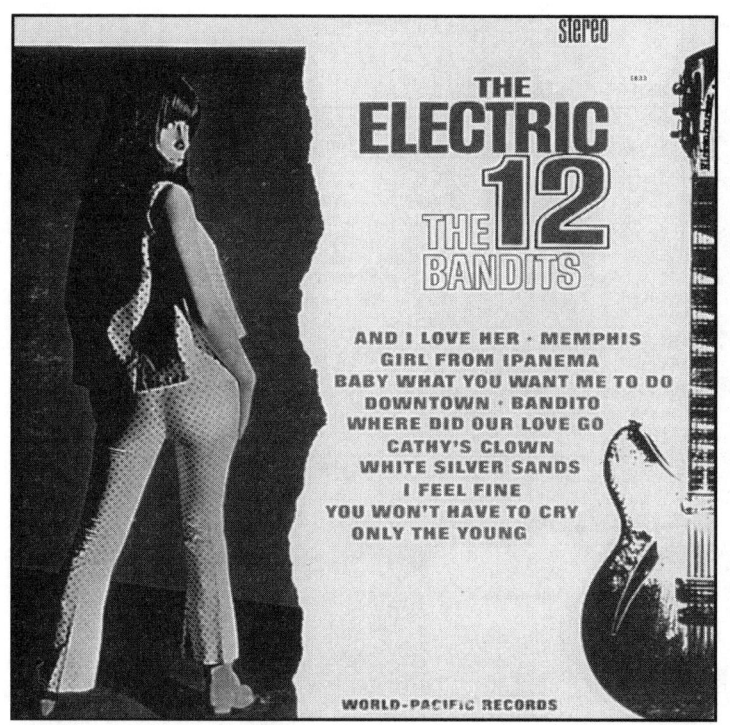

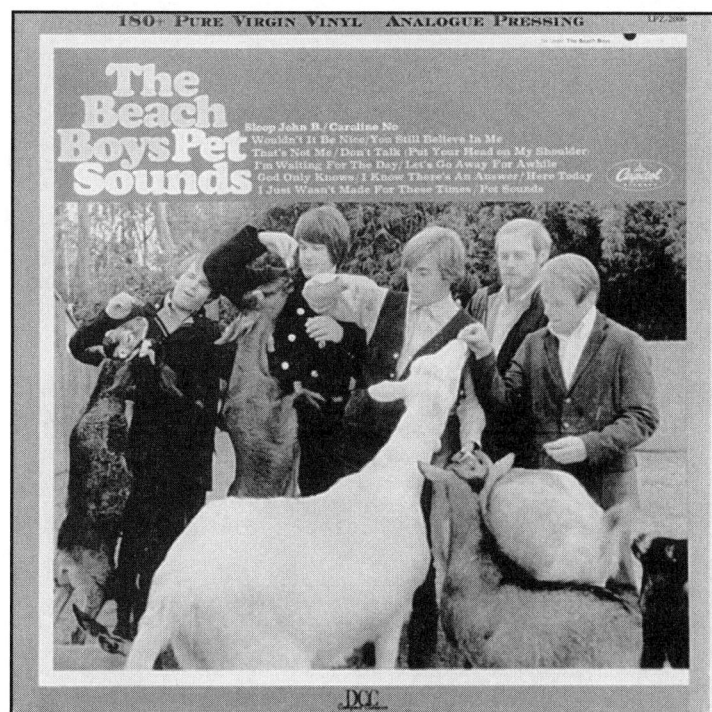

(Top left) The Bandits were a studio group that featured Glen Campbell among its pickers. This is their only album. (Top right) Many Beach Boys albums are highly sought-after, but one of the most collectible is this pressing of *Sunflower.* This is the Capitol Record Club edition with a different catalog number. (Bottom left) The Beach Boys' magnum opus, *Pet Sounds,* has been released numerous times on vinyl. For the ultimate experience, get this pressing by DCC Compact Classics. It'll set you back $20-$25, but it's worth it. Also recommended is the new (summer 1999) vinyl pressing of the album in true stereo. In fact, get 'em both. There are both subtle and significant differences, most notably in the lead vocals on "Wouldn't It Be Nice." (Bottom right) For the most part, Harry Belafonte's albums have been ignored by mainstream collectors. But audiophiles have long paid much higher than "book value" for certain releases, including this one, *Jump Up Calypso.* Several of Belafonte's LPs have been reissued by audiophile labels.

Number	Title	Yr	VG	VG+	NM

BASSEY, SHIRLEY
EPIC
❏ LN 3834 [M]	The Bewitching Shirley Bassey	1962	5.00	10.00	20.00

MGM
❏ E-3862 [M]	The Fabulous Shirley Bassey	1960	5.00	10.00	20.00
❏ SE-3862 [S]	The Fabulous Shirley Bassey	1960	6.25	12.50	25.00

UNITED ARTISTS
❏ UAS 6169 [S]	Shirley Bassey	1962	5.00	10.00	20.00
❏ UAS 6237 [S]	Shirley Bassey Sings the Hits from "Oliver"	1962	5.00	10.00	20.00

BASTARDS, THE
TREEHOUSE
❏ 016	Monticallo	1989	6.25	12.50	25.00

BATTERED ORNAMENTS
HARVEST
❏ SKAO-422	Mantle-Piece	1970	10.00	20.00	40.00

BAUGH, PHIL
ERA
❏ ES-801	California Guitar	1969	6.25	12.50	25.00

LONGHORN
❏ LP-02 [M]	Country Guitar	1965	12.50	25.00	50.00

TORO
❏ T-502 [M]	Country Guitar II	1965	10.00	20.00	40.00

BAUHAUS
A&M
❏ SP 4918	The Sky's Gone Out	1982	5.00	10.00	20.00
❏ SP-4953	Burning from the Inside	1983	5.00	10.00	20.00

RCA
❏ 9804-1-R [(2)]	Swing the Heartache/The BBC Sessions	1989	5.00	10.00	20.00

BAXTER
PARAMOUNT
❏ PAS-6050	Baxter	1973	5.00	10.00	20.00

BAXTER, LES
CAPITOL
❏ H 288 [10]	Le Sacre Du Sauvage	1952	20.00	40.00	80.00
❏ T 288 [M]	Le Sacre Du Sauvage	1954	10.00	20.00	40.00
❏ H 3?? [10]	Music for Peace of Mind	1953	20.00	40.00	80.00
❏ H 3?? [10]	Music Out of the Moon	1953	20.00	40.00	80.00
❏ T 390 [M]	Music Out of the Moon/ Music for Peace of Mind	1954	10.00	20.00	40.00
❏ H 474 [10]	Thinking of You	1954	12.50	25.00	50.00
❏ T 474 [M]	Thinking of You	1954	10.00	20.00	40.00
❏ LAL 486 [M]	The Passions	1954	10.00	20.00	40.00
❏ T 594 [M]	Kaleidoscope	1955	10.00	20.00	40.00
❏ T 655 [M]	Tamboo!	1955	10.00	20.00	40.00
❏ T 733 [M]	Caribbean Moonlight	1956	10.00	20.00	40.00
❏ T 774 [M]	Skins!	1957	10.00	20.00	40.00
❏ T 780 [M]	'Round the World	1957	10.00	20.00	40.00
❏ T 843 [M]	Midnight on the Cliffs	1957	10.00	20.00	40.00
❏ T 868 [M]	Ports of Pleasure	1957	10.00	20.00	40.00
❏ T 968 [M]	Space Escapade	1958	10.00	20.00	40.00
❏ T 1012 [M]	Selections from "South Pacific"	1958	10.00	20.00	40.00
❏ T 1388 [M]	Baxter's Best	1960	7.50	15.00	30.00
❏ ST 1537 [S]	Jewels of the Sea	1961	7.50	15.00	30.00
❏ T 1537 [M]	Jewels of the Sea	1961	6.25	12.50	25.00
❏ ST 1661 [S]	The Sensational Les Baxter	1962	7.50	15.00	30.00
❏ T 1661 [M]	The Sensational Les Baxter	1962	6.25	12.50	25.00
❏ ST 1846 [S]	The Original Quiet Village	1963	6.25	12.50	25.00
❏ T 1846 [M]	The Original Quiet Village	1963	5.00	10.00	20.00
❏ T 10015 [M]	La Femme	1956	10.00	20.00	40.00

REPRISE
❏ R9-6036 [S]	Voices in Rhythm	1961	5.00	10.00	20.00
❏ R9-6049 [S]	The Primitive and the Passionate	1962	5.00	10.00	20.00
❏ R9-6079 [S]	Academy Award Winners '63	1963	5.00	10.00	20.00
❏ R9-6100 [S]	The Soul of the Drums	1963	5.00	10.00	20.00

BAYSIDERS, THE
EVEREST
❏ BRST-1124 [S]	Over the Rainbow	1961	75.00	150.00	300.00
❏ LPBR-5124 [M]	Over the Rainbow	1961	50.00	100.00	200.00

BBC SYMPHONY ORCHESTRA (ANTAL DORATI, COND.)
MERCURY LIVING PRESENCE
❏ SR 90416 [S]	Bartok: The Miraculous Mandarin	196?	17.50	35.00	70.00
-- Maroon label, no "Vendor: Mercury Record Corporation"					
❏ SR 90416 [S]	Bartok: The Miraculous Mandarin	196?	12.50	25.00	50.00
-- Maroon label, with "Vendor: Mercury Record Corporation"					
❏ SR 90416 [S]	Bartok: The Miraculous Mandarin	196?	5.00	10.00	20.00
-- Third edition: Dark red (not maroon) label					

BE-BOP DELUXE
CAPITOL
❏ SPRO-8486	Sunburst Finish	1975	6.25	12.50	25.00
-- Specially banded version for radio					

HARVEST
❏ SPRO-8531	Be-Bop's Biggest	1978	7.50	15.00	30.00
-- Promo-only compilation					

BEACH BOYS, THE
ASYLUM
❏ R 113793	Surf's Up	1972	37.50	75.00	150.00
-- RCA Record Club edition, pressed with wrong labels					

BROTHER
❏ ST 9001 [R]	Smiley Smile	1967	5.00	10.00	20.00
-- No mention of Barry Turnbull on cover					
❏ T 9001 [M]	Smiley Smile	1967	10.00	20.00	40.00
-- No mention of Barry Turnbull on cover					
❏ T 9001 [M]	Smiley Smile	1967	7.50	15.00	30.00
-- "Title for this album by Barry Turnbull" on back cover					

BROTHER/REPRISE
❏ 2MS 2083 [(2)]	Carl and the Passions "So Tough"/ Pet Sounds	1972	7.50	15.00	30.00
❏ 2MS 2083 [(2) DJ]	Carl and the Passions "So Tough"/ Pet Sounds	1972	12.50	25.00	50.00
-- White label promo					
❏ MS 2118 [DJ]	Holland	1973	125.00	250.00	500.00
-- Test pressing with "We Got Love," deleted from promos and stock copies					
❏ MS 2118 [DJ]	Holland	1973	10.00	20.00	40.00
-- White label promo; includes bonus white-label promo EP, "Mount Vernon and Fairway," in picture sleeve, taped to back cover					
❏ MS 2197 [M]	Pet Sounds	1974	5.00	10.00	20.00
❏ RS 6453	Surf's Up	1971	5.00	10.00	20.00
❏ RS 6453 [DJ]	Surf's Up	1971	10.00	20.00	40.00
-- White label promo					
❏ RS-6382	Sunflower	1970	6.25	12.50	25.00
❏ RS-6382 [DJ]	Sunflower	1970	12.50	25.00	50.00
-- White label promo					
❏ 2RS 6484 [(2)]	The Beach Boys In Concert	1973	5.00	10.00	20.00
❏ 2RS 6484 [(2) DJ]	The Beach Boys In Concert	1973	10.00	20.00	40.00
-- White label promo					
❏ SKAO-93352	Sunflower	1970	50.00	100.00	200.00
-- Capitol Record Club edition					
❏ R 113793	Surf's Up	1972	6.25	12.50	25.00
-- RCA Record Club edition					
❏ R 223569 [(2)]	The Beach Boys In Concert	1973	6.25	12.50	25.00
-- RCA Record Club edition					

CAPITOL
❏ SKAO-133	20/20	1969	5.00	10.00	20.00
-- Black label with colorband					
❏ SKAO-8-0133	20/20	1969	7.50	15.00	30.00
-- Capitol Record Club edition; black label					
❏ SKAO-8-0133	20/20	1970	10.00	20.00	40.00
-- Capitol Record Club edition; lime label					
❏ SWBB-253 [(2)]	Close-Up	1969	7.50	15.00	30.00
-- Reissue of "Surfin' U.S.A." and "All Summer Long" in one package; black labels with colorband					
❏ SWBB-253 [(2)]	Close-Up	1970	10.00	20.00	40.00
-- Lime labels					
❏ ST-442	Good Vibrations	1970	5.00	10.00	20.00
-- Lime label (original)					
❏ ST-442	Good Vibrations	1972	6.25	12.50	25.00
-- Red or orange label					
❏ ST-8-0442	Good Vibrations	1970	7.50	15.00	30.00
-- Capitol Record Club edition					
❏ STBB-500 [(2)]	All Summer Long/California Girls	1970	5.00	10.00	20.00
-- Lime labels; "Special Double Play" pack; two separate LPs (abridged versions of "All Summer Long" and "Summer Days [And Summer Nights!!]") bound together					
❏ STBB-500 [(2)]	All Summer Long/California Girls	1971	6.25	12.50	25.00
-- Red labels; "Special Double Play" pack; two separate LPs (abridged versions of "All Summer Long" and "Summer Days [And Summer Nights!!]") bound together					
❏ STBB-701 [(2)]	Fun, Fun, Fun/Dance, Dance,	1970	5.00	10.00	20.00
-- Lime labels; "Special Double Play" pack; two separate LPs (abridged versions of "Shut Down, Volume 2" and "The Beach Boys Today!") bound together					
❏ STBB-701 [(2)]	Fun, Fun, Fun/Dance, Dance,	1971	6.25	12.50	25.00
-- Red labels; "Special Double Play" pack; two separate LPs (abridged versions of "Shut Down, Volume 2" and "The Beach Boys Today!") bound together					

Number	Title	Yr	VG	VG+	NM
❏ DT 1808 [R]　Surfin' Safari		1962	6.25	12.50	25.00
-- With only the "Duophonic" banner at top					
❏ DT 1808 [R]　Surfin' Safari		1962	20.00	40.00	80.00
-- With "Capitol Full Dimensional Stereo" banner under the "Duophonic" banner					
❏ T 1808 [M]　Surfin' Safari		1962	10.00	20.00	40.00
❏ ST 1890 [S]　Surfin' U.S.A.		1963	12.50	25.00	50.00
❏ T 1890 [M]　Surfin' U.S.A.		1963	10.00	20.00	40.00
❏ ST 1981 [S]　Surfer Girl		1963	12.50	25.00	50.00
-- With reference to The Four Freshmen in liner notes					
❏ ST 1981 [S]　Surfer Girl		1963	12.50	25.00	50.00
-- With reference to "their other new single record, 'Little Deuce Coupe'" in liner notes					
❏ T 1981 [M]　Surfer Girl		1963	10.00	20.00	40.00
-- With reference to The Four Freshmen in liner notes					
❏ T 1981 [M]　Surfer Girl		1963	10.00	20.00	40.00
-- With reference to "their other new single record, 'Little Deuce Coupe'" in liner notes					
❏ ST 1998 [S]　Little Deuce Coupe		1963	10.00	20.00	40.00
❏ T 1998 [M]　Little Deuce Coupe		1963	10.00	20.00	40.00
❏ ST 2027 [P]　Shut Down, Volume 2		1964	10.00	20.00	40.00
❏ T 2027 [M]　Shut Down, Volume 2		1964	10.00	20.00	40.00
❏ ST 2110 [S]　All Summer Long		1964	12.50	25.00	50.00
-- With "Don't Break Down" erroneously listed on front cover					
❏ ST 2110 [S]　All Summer Long		1964	7.50	15.00	30.00
-- With "Don't Back Down" correctly listed on front cover					
❏ T 2110 [M]　All Summer Long		1964	12.50	25.00	50.00
-- With "Don't Break Down" erroneously listed on front cover					
❏ T 2110 [M]　All Summer Long		1964	7.50	15.00	30.00
-- With "Don't Back Down" correctly listed on front cover					
❏ ST 2164 [S]　The Beach Boys' Christmas Album		1964	12.50	25.00	50.00
❏ T 2164 [M]　The Beach Boys' Christmas Album		1964	12.50	25.00	50.00
❏ STAO 2198 [S] Beach Boys Concert		1964	7.50	15.00	30.00
-- With bound-in booklet					
❏ STAO-8-2198 [S] Beach Boys Concert		196?	20.00	40.00	80.00
-- Capitol Record Club edition					
❏ TAO 2198 [M]　Beach Boys Concert		1964	7.50	15.00	30.00
-- With bound-in booklet					
❏ DT 2269 [R]　The Beach Boys Today!		1965	6.25	12.50	25.00
❏ DT-8-2269 [R] The Beach Boys Today!		1965	20.00	40.00	80.00
-- Capitol Record Club edition					
❏ T 2269 [M]　The Beach Boys Today!		1965	7.50	15.00	30.00
❏ DT 2354 [R]　Summer Days (And Summer Nights!)	1965	12.50	25.00	50.00
-- With "New Improved Full Dimensional Stereo" banner					
❏ DT 2354 [R]　Summer Days (And Summer Nights!)	1965	6.25	12.50	25.00
-- With "Duophonic" banner					
❏ T 2354 [M]　Summer Days (And Summer Nights!)	1965	7.50	15.00	30.00
❏ DMAS 2398 [R]Beach Boys Party!		1965	7.50	15.00	30.00
-- With sheet of photos					
❏ DMAS 2398 [R]Beach Boys Party!		1965	6.25	12.50	25.00
-- Without sheet of photos					
❏ MAS 2398 [M]　Beach Boys Party!		1965	10.00	20.00	40.00
-- With sheet of photos					
❏ MAS 2398 [M]　Beach Boys Party!		1965	7.50	15.00	30.00
-- Without sheet of photos					
❏ DT 2458 [R]　Pet Sounds		1966	7.50	15.00	30.00
❏ T 2458 [M]　Pet Sounds		1966	10.00	20.00	40.00
❏ T 2545 [M]　Best of the Beach Boys		1966	5.00	10.00	20.00
-- Black label with colorband					
❏ T 2545 [M]　Best of the Beach Boys		1967	7.50	15.00	30.00
-- Red and white "Starline" label					
❏ T/DT 2580　Smile		1966	250.00	500.00	1,000.
-- Unreleased; price is for cover slick, which has been counterfeited					
❏ T/DT 2580　Smile Booklet		1966	75.00	150.00	300.00
-- Printed for insertion into unreleased "Smile" LP; counterfeits exist					
❏ T 2706 [M]　Best of the Beach Boys, Vol. 2		1967	6.25	12.50	25.00
❏ DTCL 2813 [(3) R] The Beach Boys Deluxe Set		1967	12.50	25.00	50.00
-- Maroon border on box; custom pressings of LPs with "DTCL" prefixes					
❏ DTCL-8-2813　The Beach Boys Deluxe Set [(3) R]		1967	37.50	75.00	150.00
-- Capitol Record Club edition; blue border on box; custom pressings of LPs with "DTCL" prefixes					
❏ TCL 2813 [(3) M]The Beach Boys Deluxe Set		1967	62.50	125.00	250.00
-- Black border on box; albums have "T" prefixes					
❏ ST 2859 [S]　Wild Honey		1967	5.00	10.00	20.00
❏ T 2859 [M]　Wild Honey		1967	10.00	20.00	40.00
❏ ST-8-2891 [R]　Smiley Smile		1968	75.00	150.00	300.00
-- Capitol Record Club edition					
❏ DKAO 2893　Stack-o-Tracks		1968	25.00	50.00	100.00
-- With sheet music booklet					
❏ DKAO 2893　Stack-o-Tracks		1968	12.50	25.00	50.00
-- Without sheet music booklet					
❏ DKAO-8-2893　Stack-o-Tracks		1968	50.00	100.00	200.00
-- Capitol Record Club edition					
❏ ST 2895　Friends		1968	6.25	12.50	25.00
❏ DKAO 2945 [P] The Best of the Beach Boys, Vol. 3	1969	5.00	10.00	20.00
-- "Starline" label					
❏ PRO 3133 [DJ] Silver Platter Service from Hollywood: The Beach Boys Christmas Special		1964	50.00	100.00	200.00
❏ SVBB-11307 [(2)] Endless Summer		1974	5.00	10.00	20.00
-- Orange labels, "Capitol" on bottom; with poster					

Number	Title	Yr	VG	VG+	NM
❏ R 223559 [(2)] Endless Summer		197?	6.25	12.50	25.00
-- RCA Music Service edition					
❏ R 233593 [(2)] American Summer		1975	6.25	12.50	25.00
-- RCA Music Service exclusive					
❏ SVBB-511307 [(2)] Endless Summer		197?	6.25	12.50	25.00
-- Columbia Record Club edition					
❏ SVBB-511384 [(2)] Spirit of America		1975	5.00	10.00	20.00
-- Columbia Record Club edition					
CAPITOL SPECIAL MARKETS					
❏ SLB-6994 [(2)] Golden Years of the Beach Boys		1975	5.00	10.00	20.00
❏ SLB-8134 [(2)] The Beach Boys		1980	5.00	10.00	20.00
DCC COMPACT CLASSICS					
❏ LPZ-2006 [M]　Pet Sounds		1995	6.25	12.50	25.00
-- Audiophile vinyl					
MOBILE FIDELITY					
❏ 1-116　Surfer Girl		1984	7.50	15.00	30.00
-- Audiophile vinyl					
SEARS					
❏ SPS-609　Summertime Blues		1970	12.50	25.00	50.00

BEACON STREET UNION, THE
MGM

Number	Title	Yr	VG	VG+	NM
❏ E-4517 [M]　The Eyes of the Beacon Street		1967	7.50	15.00	30.00
❏ SE-4517 [S]　The Eyes of the Beacon Street		1967	6.25	12.50	25.00
❏ SE-4568　The Clown Died in Marvin Gardens	1968	6.25	12.50	25.00

BEANS
AVALANCHE

Number	Title	Yr	VG	VG+	NM
❏ 9200　Beans		1971	5.00	10.00	20.00

BEASLEY, JIMMY
CROWN

Number	Title	Yr	VG	VG+	NM
❏ CLP-5014 [M]　The Fabulous Jimmy Beasley		1957	37.50	75.00	150.00
-- Black label					
❏ CLP-5247 [M]　Twist with Jimmy Beasley		1962	10.00	20.00	40.00
-- Gray label					
MODERN					
❏ MLP-1214 [M]　The Fabulous Jimmy Beasley		1956	100.00	200.00	400.00

BEASTIE BOYS
CAPITOL

Number	Title	Yr	VG	VG+	NM
❏ SPRO 79461 [(2) DJ] Hip Hop Sampler		1994	12.50	25.00	50.00
-- Promo-only compilation of remixes and things					
❏ C1-92844　Paul's Boutique		1989	5.00	10.00	20.00
-- Multi-gatefold edition (number on record is 91743, the same as single gatefold edition)					
❏ C1-98938 [(2)] Check Your Head		1992	5.00	10.00	20.00
GRAND ROYAL					
❏ GR 061 [(2)]　Hello Nasty		1998	5.00	10.00	20.00
-- Limited edition on yellow vinyl					
RAT CAGE					
❏ 026 [EP]　Cookypuss		1983	10.00	20.00	40.00

BEAT FARMERS
CURB

Number	Title	Yr	VG	VG+	NM
❏ 17381 [EP]　Home of Country Dick		1987	6.25	12.50	25.00
-- Promo only with four non-LP songs					

BEAT OF THE EARTH, THE
ARDISH

Number	Title	Yr	VG	VG+	NM
❏ AS-0001　The Beat of the Earth		1968	100.00	200.00	400.00
❏ AS-001　The Beat of the Earth		1968	75.00	150.00	300.00

BEATLE BUDDIES, THE
DIPLOMAT

Number	Title	Yr	VG	VG+	NM
❏ DS-2313 [S]　The Beatle Buddies		1964	5.00	10.00	20.00

BEATLES, THE
Also see PETE BEST; GEORGE HARRISON; JOHN LENNON; PAUL McCARTNEY; RINGO STARR.
APPLE

Number	Title	Yr	VG	VG+	NM
❏ SBC-100 [M]　The Beatles' Christmas Album		1970	100.00	200.00	400.00
-- Fan club issue of the seven Christmas messages; very good counterfeits exist					
❏ SWBO-101 [(2)] The Beatles		1968	37.50	75.00	200.00
-- Numbered copy; includes four individual photos and large poster (included in value); because the white cover shows ring wear so readily, this is an EXTREMELY difficult album to find in near-mint condition					
❏ SWBO-101 [(2)] The Beatles		197?	15.00	30.00	60.00
-- Un-numbered copy; includes four individual photos and large poster (included in value)					

Number	Title	Yr	VG	VG+	NM
❑ SWBO-101 [(2)] The Beatles		1975	17.50	35.00	70.00
-- With "All Rights Reserved" on labels; title in black on cover; photos and poster of thinner stock than originals					
❑ SW-153 [P]	Yellow Submarine	1969	12.50	25.00	50.00
-- With Capitol logo on Side 2 bottom. "Only a Northern Song" is rechanneled.					
❑ SW-153 [P]	Yellow Submarine	1971	5.00	10.00	20.00
-- With "Mfd. by Apple" on label					
❑ SW-153 [P]	Yellow Submarine	1975	6.25	12.50	25.00
-- With "All Rights Reserved" on label					
❑ SO-383	Abbey Road	1969	18.75	37.50	75.00
-- With Capitol logo on Side 2 bottom; "Her Majesty" is NOT listed on either the jacket or the label					
❑ SO-383	Abbey Road	1969	10.00	20.00	40.00
-- With Capitol logo on Side 2 bottom; "Her Majesty" IS listed on both the jacket and the label					
❑ SO-383	Abbey Road	1969	5.00	10.00	20.00
-- With "Mfd. by Apple" on label; "Her Majesty" is NOT listed on the label					
❑ SO-383	Abbey Road	1969	5.00	10.00	20.00
-- With "Mfd. by Apple" on label; "Her Majesty" IS listed on the label					
❑ SO-383	Abbey Road	1975	6.25	12.50	25.00
-- With "All Rights Reserved" on label					
❑ SO-385 [DJ]	The Beatles Again	1970	4,000.	6,000.	8,000.
-- Prototype covers with "The Beatles Again" on cover; not released to the general public					
❑ SW-385	Hey Jude	1970	10.00	20.00	40.00
-- Label calls the LP "The Beatles Again"; record is "SO-385" (this could be found in retail stores as late as 1973)					
❑ SW-385	Hey Jude	1970	6.25	12.50	25.00
-- Label calls the LP "The Beatles Again"; record is "SW-385"					
❑ SW-385	Hey Jude	1970	18.75	37.50	75.00
-- With Capitol logo on Side 2 bottom; label calls the LP "Hey Jude"					
❑ SW-385	Hey Jude	1970	5.00	10.00	20.00
-- With "Mfd. by Apple" on label; label calls the LP "Hey Jude"					
❑ SW-385	Hey Jude	1975	6.25	12.50	25.00
-- With "All Rights Reserved" on label; label calls the LP "Hey Jude"					
❑ SKBO-3403 [P] The Beatles 1962-1966		1973	7.50	15.00	30.00
-- Custom red Apple labels. "Love Me Do" and "I Want to Hold Your Hand" are rechanneled; "She Loves You," "A Hard Day's Night," "I Feel Fine" and "Ticket to Ride" are mono; "From Me to You," "Can't Buy Me Love" and everything else is stereo.					
❑ SKBO-3403 [P] The Beatles 1962-1966		1975	12.50	25.00	50.00
-- Custom red Apple labels with "All Rights Reserved" on labels					
❑ SKBO-3404 [B] The Beatles 1967-1970		1973	7.50	15.00	30.00
-- Custom blue Apple labels. "Hello Goodbye" and "Penny Lane" are mono, all others stereo.					
❑ SKBO-3404 [B] The Beatles 1967-1970		1975	12.50	25.00	50.00
-- Custom blue Apple labels with "All Rights Reserved" on labels					
❑ SPRO 11206/7 [EP] Anthology 2 Sampler		1996	37.50	75.00	150.00
-- Promo-only collection sent to college radio stations					
❑ C1-8-31796 [(2)] Live at the BBC		1994	12.50	25.00	50.00
❑ AR-34001	Let It Be	1970	6.25	12.50	25.00
-- Red Apple label; originals have "Bell Sound" stamped in trail-off area, counterfeits do not					
❑ C1-8-34445 [(3)] Anthology 1		1995	10.00	20.00	40.00
-- All copies distributed in the U.S. were manufactured in the U.K. with no distinguishing marks (some LPs imported directly from the U.K. have "Made in England" stickers, which can be removed easily)					
❑ C1-8-34448 [(3)] Anthology 2		1996	10.00	20.00	40.00
❑ C1-8-34451 [(3)] Anthology 3		1996	7.50	15.00	30.00
❑ C1-97036 [B]	The Beatles 1962-1966	1993	6.25	12.50	25.00
-- Custom red Apple labels; red vinyl; all copies pressed in U.K; U.S. versions have a bar-code sticker over the international bar code on back cover. "Love Me Do," "Please Please Me," "From Me to You" and "She Loves You," all others are stereo.					
❑ C1-97039	The Beatles 1967-1970	1993	6.25	12.50	25.00
-- Custom blue Apple labels; blue vinyl; all copies pressed in U.K.; U.S. versions have a bar-code sticker over the international bar code on back cover					

APPLE FILMS

❑ KAL 004 [DJ]	The Yellow Submarine (A United Artists Release)	1969	1,000.	1,500.	2,000.
-- One-sided LP with radio spots for movie					

APPLE/CAPITOL (APPLE LABEL, CAPITOL COVER)

❑ (no #) [(10)]	The Beatles Special Limited Edition	1974	300.00	600.00	1,200.
❑ (no #) [(17)]	The Beatles 10th Anniversary Box Set	1974	1,000.	1,500.	2,000.
❑ ST 2047 [P]	Meet the Beatles!	1968	10.00	20.00	40.00
-- With Capitol logo on Side 2 bottom					
❑ ST 2047 [P]	Meet the Beatles!	1971	5.00	10.00	20.00
-- With "Mfd. by Apple" on label					
❑ ST 2047 [P]	Meet the Beatles!	1975	6.25	12.50	25.00
-- With "All Rights Reserved" on label					
❑ ST 2080 [P]	The Beatles' Second Album	1968	10.00	20.00	40.00
-- With Capitol logo on Side 2 bottom					
❑ ST 2080 [P]	The Beatles' Second Album	1971	5.00	10.00	20.00
-- With "Mfd. by Apple" on label					
❑ ST 2080 [P]	The Beatles' Second Album	1975	6.25	12.50	25.00
-- With "All Rights Reserved" on label					
❑ ST 2108 [S]	Something New	1968	10.00	20.00	40.00
-- With Capitol logo on Side 2 bottom					
❑ ST 2108 [S]	Something New	1971	5.00	10.00	20.00
-- With "Mfd. by Apple" on label					
❑ ST 2108 [S]	Something New	1975	6.25	2.50	25.00
-- With "All Rights Reserved" on label					
❑ STBO 2222 [(2) P] The Beatles' Story		1968	12.50	25.00	50.00
-- With Capitol logo on bottom of B-side of both records					

Number	Title	Yr	VG	VG+	NM
❑ STBO 2222 [(2) P] The Beatles' Story		1971	7.50	15.00	30.00
-- With "Mfd. by Apple" on labels					
❑ STBO 2222 [(2) P] The Beatles' Story		1975	10.00	20.00	40.00
-- With "All Rights Reserved" on labels					
❑ ST 2228 [P]	Beatles '65	1968	10.00	20.00	40.00
-- With Capitol logo on Side 2 bottom					
❑ ST 2228 [P]	Beatles '65	1971	5.00	10.00	20.00
-- With "Mfd. by Apple" on label					
❑ ST 2228 [P]	Beatles '65	1975	6.25	12.50	25.00
-- With "All Rights Reserved" on label					
❑ ST 2309 [P]	The Early Beatles	1969	10.00	20.00	40.00
-- With Capitol logo on Side 2 bottom					
❑ ST 2309 [P]	The Early Beatles	1971	5.00	10.00	20.00
-- With "Mfd. by Apple" on label					
❑ ST 2309 [P]	The Early Beatles	1975	6.25	12.50	25.00
-- With "All Rights Reserved" on label					
❑ ST 2358 [P]	Beatles VI	1969	10.00	20.00	40.00
-- With Capitol logo on Side 2 bottom					
❑ ST 2358 [P]	Beatles VI	1971	5.00	10.00	20.00
-- With "Mfd. by Apple" on label					
❑ ST 2358 [P]	Beatles VI	1975	6.25	12.50	25.00
-- With "All Rights Reserved" on label					
❑ SMAS 2386 [P] Help!		1969	10.00	20.00	40.00
-- With Capitol logo on Side 2 bottom					
❑ SMAS 2386 [P] Help!		1971	5.00	10.00	20.00
-- With "Mfd. by Apple" on label					
❑ SMAS 2386 [P] Help!		1975	6.25	12.50	25.00
-- With "All Rights Reserved" on label					
❑ ST 2442 [S]	Rubber Soul	1969	10.00	20.00	40.00
-- With Capitol logo on Side 2 bottom					
❑ ST 2442 [S]	Rubber Soul	1971	5.00	10.00	20.00
-- With "Mfd. by Apple" on label					
❑ ST 2442 [S]	Rubber Soul	1975	6.25	12.50	25.00
-- With "All Rights Reserved" on label					
❑ ST 2553 [P]	Yesterday and Today	1969	10.00	20.00	40.00
-- With Capitol logo on Side 2 bottom					
❑ ST 2553 [P]	Yesterday and Today	1971	5.00	10.00	20.00
-- With "Mfd. by Apple" on label					
❑ ST 2553 [S]	Yesterday and Today	1971	6.25	12.50	25.00
-- With "Mfd. by Apple" on label; all 11 tracks are in true stereo. Check for a triangle in the record's trail-off area.					
❑ ST 2553 [P]	Yesterday and Today	1975	6.25	12.50	25.00
-- With "All Rights Reserved" on label					
❑ ST 2576 [S]	Revolver	1969	10.00	20.00	40.00
-- With Capitol logo on Side 2 bottom					
❑ ST 2576 [S]	Revolver	1971	5.00	10.00	20.00
-- With "Mfd. by Apple" on label					
❑ ST 2576 [S]	Revolver	1975	6.25	12.50	25.00
-- With "All Rights Reserved" on label					
❑ SMAS 2653 [S] Sgt. Pepper's Lonely Hearts Club Band		1969	10.00	20.00	40.00
-- With Capitol logo on Side 2 bottom					
❑ SMAS 2653 [S] Sgt. Pepper's Lonely Hearts Club Band		1971	6.25	12.50	25.00
-- With "Mfd. by Apple" on label					
❑ SMAS 2653 [S] Sgt. Pepper's Lonely Hearts Club Band		1975	6.25	12.50	25.00
-- With "All Rights Reserved" on label					
❑ SMAL 2835 [P] Magical Mystery Tour		1969	10.00	20.00	40.00
-- With Capitol logo on Side 2 bottom; with 24-page booklet					
❑ SMAL 2835 [P] Magical Mystery Tour		1971	5.00	10.00	20.00
-- With "Mfd. by Apple" on label; with 24-page booklet					
❑ SMAL 2835 [P] Magical Mystery Tour		1975	6.25	12.50	25.00
-- With "All Rights Reserved" on label; with 24-page booklet					

ATCO

❑ 33-169 [M]	Ain't She Sweet	1964	50.00	100.00	200.00
❑ 33-169 [M-DJ] Ain't She Sweet		1964	250.00	500.00	1,000.
-- White label promo					
❑ SD 33-169 [P] Ain't She Sweet		1964	100.00	200.00	400.00
-- Tan and purple label; all four Beatles tracks are rechanneled					
❑ SD 33-169 [P] Ain't She Sweet		1969	125.00	250.00	500.00
-- Yellow label					

AUDIOFIDELITY

❑ PD-339 [M]	First Movement	1982	7.50	15.00	30.00
-- Contains eight Decca audition tracks; picture disc					

BACKSTAGE

❑ 2-201 [(2) M]	Like Dreamers Do	1982	10.00	20.00	40.00
-- Gatefold package, individually numbered (numbers under 100 increase value significantly)					
❑ 2-201 [(2) M]	Like Dreamers Do	1982	12.50	25.00	50.00
-- Non-gatefold package					
❑ BSR-1111 [(3) M] Like Dreamers Do		1982	15.00	30.00	60.00
-- Two picture discs (10 of 15 Decca audition tracks on one, interviews on the other) and one white-vinyl record (same contests as musical picture disc)					
❑ BSR-1111 [(3) M] Like Dreamers Do		1982	25.00	50.00	100.00
-- Same as above, except colored-vinyl LP is gray					
❑ BSR-1111 [DJ] Like Dreamers Do		1982	12.50	25.00	50.00
-- White vinyl promo in white sleeve					

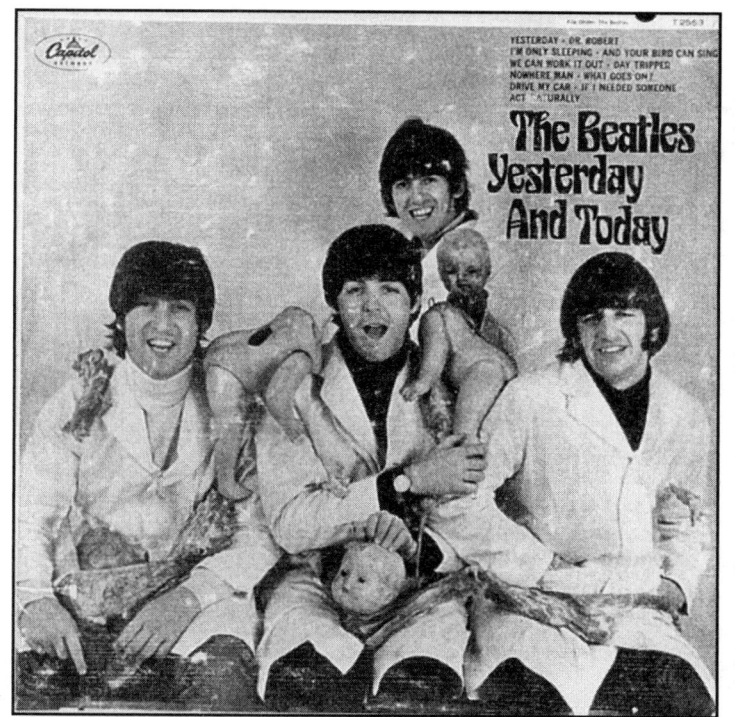

(Top left) Ah yes, the Beatles resplendent in butcher smocks, raw meat and decapitated baby dolls. The *Yesterday And Today* album with this cover was quickly pulled from the market. There has been much discussion about how rare this album really is, but even with thousands of surviving copies, the demand far outpaces the supply. This is a "third state" (peeled) mono copy; recommendations today are to leave the album covered, as more and more of the top layers are being removed to reveal the "butcher cover" below. (Top right) The version of *Yesterday And Today* the vast majority of record buyers saw – the Beatles are in and around a trunk. Thanks to the white background, it's easy to see if you have a paste-over "butcher cover," because the "V" of Ringo's turtleneck will show through the white background several inches under the lettering. (Bottom left) Most original U.S. copies of *Sgt. Pepper's Lonely Hearts Club Band* have a yellow strip across the top with the word "STEREO" in it. This is one of the sought-after mono pressings, which is often cited as closer to the way the Beatles themselves wanted the album to sound. (Bottom right) Even rarer still is the mono copies of *Magical Mystery Tour,* identifiable by how high the graphics are on the front cover. On the stereo cover, the graphics are not nearly so close to the top edge.

Number	Title	Yr	VG	VG+	NM
❏ BSR-1111 [DJ] Like Dreamers Do		1982	12.50	25.00	50.00
-- Gray vinyl promo in white sleeve					
❏ BSR-1165 [PD] The Beatles Talk with Jerry G.		1982	6.25	12.50	25.00
-- Picture disc					
❏ BSR-1175 [PD] The Beatles Talk with Jerry G., Vol. 2		1983	6.25	12.50	25.00
-- Picture disc					
CAPITOL					
❏ (no #) [(18)]	The Beatles Collection Platinum Series	1984	200.00	400.00	800.00
❏ BC-13 [(14)]	The Beatles Collection	1978	62.50	125.00	250.00
-- American versions have "EMI" and "BC-13" on box spine; imports go for less					
❏ SWBO-101 [(2)]	The Beatles	1976	7.50	15.00	30.00
-- Orange label; with photos and poster					
❏ SWBO-101 [(2)]	The Beatles	1978	7.50	15.00	30.00
-- Purple label, large Capitol logo; with photos and poster (some copies have four photos as one perforated sheet)					
❏ SWBO-101 [(2)]	The Beatles	1983	10.00	20.00	40.00
-- Black label, print in colorband; with photos and poster (some copies have four photos as one perforated sheet)					
❏ SJ-383	Abbey Road	1984	7.50	15.00	30.00
-- New prefix; black label, print in colorband					
❏ SJ-385	Hey Jude	1984	7.50	15.00	30.00
-- New prefix; black label, print in colorband					
❏ SW-385	Hey Jude	1983	12.50	25.00	50.00
-- Black label, print in colorband					
❏ ST 2047 [P]	Meet the Beatles!	1964	37.50	75.00	150.00
-- Black label with colorband; "Beatles!" on cover in tan to brown print. "I Want to Hold Your Hand" and "This Boy" are rechanneled, the other 10 tracks are true stereo					
❏ ST 2047 [P]	Meet the Beatles!	1964	18.75	37.50	75.00
-- Black label with colorband; "Beatles!" on cover in green print					
❏ ST 2047 [P]	Meet the Beatles!	1969	10.00	20.00	40.00
-- Lime green label					
❏ T 2047 [M]	Meet the Beatles!	1964	50.00	100.00	200.00
-- Black label with colorband; "Beatles!" on cover in tan to brown print					
❏ T 2047 [M]	Meet the Beatles!	1964	25.00	50.00	100.00
-- Black label with colorband; "Beatles!" on cover in green print					
❏ ST-8-2047 [P]	Meet the Beatles!	1964	125.00	250.00	500.00
-- Capitol Record Club edition; black label with colorband					
❏ ST-8-2047 [P]	Meet the Beatles!	1969	50.00	100.00	200.00
-- Capitol Record Club edition; lime green label					
❏ ST 2080 [P]	The Beatles' Second Album	1964	25.00	50.00	100.00
-- Black label with colorband. "She Loves You," "I'll Get You" and "You Can't Do That" are rechanneled					
❏ ST 2080 [P]	The Beatles' Second Album	1969	10.00	20.00	40.00
-- Lime green label					
❏ T 2080 [M]	The Beatles' Second Album	1964	45.00	90.00	180.00
❏ ST-8-2080 [P]	The Beatles' Second Album	1964	125.00	250.00	500.00
-- Capitol Record Club edition; black label with colorband					
❏ ST-8-2080 [P]	The Beatles' Second Album	1969	75.00	150.00	300.00
-- Capitol Record Club edition; lime green label					
❏ ST 2108 [S]	Something New	1964	20.00	40.00	80.00
-- Black label with colorband					
❏ ST 2108 [S]	Something New	1969	10.00	20.00	40.00
-- Lime green label					
❏ T 2108 [M]	Something New	1964	37.50	75.00	150.00
❏ ST-8-2108 [S]	Something New	1964	75.00	150.00	300.00
-- Capitol Record Club edition; black label with colorband					
❏ ST-8-2108 [S]	Something New	1969	37.50	75.00	150.00
-- Capitol Record Club edition; lime green label					
❏ ST-8-2108 [S]	Something New	1969	75.00	150.00	300.00
-- Longines Symphonette edition (will be stated on label); lime green label					
❏ STBO 2222 [(2) P]	The Beatles' Story	1964	37.50	75.00	150.00
-- Black label with colorband. Some of the musical snippets are rechanneled.					
❏ STBO 2222 [(2) P]	The Beatles' Story	1969	12.50	25.00	50.00
-- Lime green label					
❏ STBO 2222 [(2) P]	The Beatles' Story	1976	5.00	10.00	20.00
-- Orange label					
❏ STBO 2222 [(2) P]	The Beatles' Story	1978	5.00	10.00	20.00
-- Purple label, large Capitol logo					
❏ STBO 2222 [(2) P]	The Beatles' Story	1983	10.00	20.00	40.00
-- Black label, print in colorband					
❏ TBO 2222 [(2) M]	The Beatles' Story	1964	50.00	100.00	200.00
❏ ST 2228 [P]	Beatles '65	1964	20.00	40.00	80.00
-- Black label with colorband. "She's a Woman" and "I Feel Fine" are rechanneled.					
❏ ST 2228 [P]	Beatles '65	1969	10.00	20.00	40.00
-- Lime green label					
❏ T 2228 [M]	Beatles '65	1964	30.00	60.00	120.00
❏ ST 2309 [P]	The Early Beatles	1965	25.00	50.00	100.00
-- Black label with colorband. "Love Me Do" and "P.S. I Love You" are rechanneled.					
❏ ST 2309 [P]	The Early Beatles	1969	10.00	20.00	40.00
-- Lime green label					
❏ ST 2309 [P]	The Early Beatles	1983	6.25	12.50	25.00
-- Black label, print in colorband					
❏ T 2309 [M]	The Early Beatles	1965	50.00	100.00	200.00
❏ ST 2358 [P]	Beatles VI	1965	20.00	40.00	80.00
-- Black label with colorband; with "See label for correct playing order" on back cover					
❏ ST 2358 [P]	Beatles VI	1965	18.75	37.50	75.00
-- Black label with colorband; with song titles listed in correct order on back cover. "Yes It Is" is rechanneled.					
❏ ST 2358 [P]	Beatles VI	1969	10.00	20.00	40.00
-- Lime green label					
❏ ST 2358 [M]	Beatles VI	1988	20.00	40.00	80.00
-- Purple label, small Capitol logo; plays in mono despite label designation					
❏ T 2358 [M]	Beatles VI	1965	30.00	60.00	120.00
-- With "See label for correct playing order" on back cover					
❏ T 2358 [M]	Beatles VI	1965	25.00	50.00	100.00
-- With song titles listed in correct order on back cover					
❏ ST-8-2358 [P]	Beatles VI	1965	125.00	250.00	500.00
-- Capitol Record Club edition; black label with colorband					
❏ ST-8-2358 [P]	Beatles VI	1969	100.00	200.00	400.00
-- Capitol Record Club edition; lime green label					
❏ MAS 2386 [M]	Help!	1965	37.50	75.00	150.00
❏ SMAS 2386 [P]	Help!	1965	18.75	37.50	75.00
-- Black label with colorband. Has incidental music by George Martin. "Ticket to Ride" is rechanneled.					
❏ SMAS 2386 [P]	Help!	1969	10.00	20.00	40.00
-- Lime green label					
❏ SMAS-8-2386 [P]	Help!	1965	175.00	350.00	700.00
-- Longines Symphonette edition; with "Mfd. by Longines" and "8" on cover					
❏ SMAS-8-2386 [P]	Help!	1965	150.00	300.00	600.00
-- Capitol Record Club edition; black label with colorband; with "8" on cover					
❏ SMAS-8-2386 [P]	Help!	1965	100.00	200.00	400.00
-- Capitol Record Club edition; black label with colorband; no "8" on cover					
❏ SMAS-8-2386 [P]	Help!	1969	100.00	200.00	400.00
-- Capitol Record Club edition; lime green label; with "8" on cover					
❏ SMAS-8-2386 [P]	Help!	1969	50.00	100.00	200.00
-- Capitol Record Club edition; lime green label; no "8" on cover					
❏ ST 2442 [S]	Rubber Soul	1965	15.00	30.00	60.00
-- Black label with colorband					
❏ ST 2442 [S]	Rubber Soul	1969	10.00	20.00	40.00
-- Lime green label					
❏ T 2442 [M]	Rubber Soul	1965	30.00	60.00	120.00
❏ ST-8-2442 [S]	Rubber Soul	1965	75.00	150.00	300.00
-- Capitol Record Club edition; black label with colorband					
❏ ST-8-2442 [S]	Rubber Soul	1969	50.00	100.00	200.00
-- Capitol Record Club edition; lime green label					
❏ ST-8-2442 [S]	Rubber Soul	1969	62.50	125.00	250.00
-- Longines Symphonette edition (will be stated on label); lime green label					
❏ ST 2553 [P]	Yesterday and Today	1966	4,000.	6,000.	8,000.
-- "First state" butcher cover (never had other cover on top); cover will be the same size as other Capitol Beatles LPs					
❏ ST 2553 [P]	Yesterday and Today	1966	500.00	750.00	1,000.
-- "Second state" butcher cover (trunk cover pasted over original cover)					
❏ ST 2553 [P]	Yesterday and Today	1966	375.00	750.00	1,500.
-- "Third state" butcher cover (trunk cover removed, leaving butcher cover intact); cover will be about 3/16-inch narrower than other Capitol Beatles LPs; value is highly negotiable depending upon the success of removing the paste-over					
❏ ST 2553 [P]	Yesterday and Today	1966	20.00	40.00	80.00
-- Trunk cover; black label with colorband (all later variations have the trunk cover). "I'm Only Sleeping," "Dr. Robert" and "And Your Bird Can Sing" are rechanneled.					
❏ ST 2553 [P]	Yesterday and Today	1969	10.00	20.00	40.00
-- Lime green label					
❏ T 2553 [M]	Yesterday and Today	1966	2,000.	3,000.	4,000.
-- "First state" butcher cover (never had other cover on top); cover will be the same size as other Capitol Beatles LPs					
❏ T 2553 [M]	Yesterday and Today	1966	250.00	500.00	1,000.
-- "Second state" butcher cover (trunk cover pasted over original cover)					
❏ T 2553 [M]	Yesterday and Today	1966	400.00	800.00	1,200.
-- "Third state" butcher cover (trunk cover removed, leaving butcher cover intact); cover will be about 3/16-inch narrower than other Capitol Beatles LPs; value is highly negotiable depending upon the success of removing the paste-over					
❏ T 2553 [M]	Yesterday and Today	1966	37.50	75.00	150.00
-- Trunk cover					
❏ ST-8-2553 [P]	Yesterday and Today	1966	75.00	150.00	300.00
-- Capitol Record Club edition; black label with colorband					
❏ ST-8-2553 [P]	Yesterday and Today	1969	37.50	75.00	150.00
-- Capitol Record Club edition; lime green label; all 11 tracks are in true stereo! (We don't know if the same is true of the black label version.)					
❏ ST 2576 [S]	Revolver	1966	25.00	50.00	100.00
-- Black label with colorband					
❏ ST 2576 [S]	Revolver	1969	10.00	20.00	40.00
-- Lime green label					
❏ ST 2576 [S]	Revolver	1970	75.00	150.00	300.00
-- Red label with "target" Capitol at top (same design as lime green label)					
❏ T 2576 [M]	Revolver	1966	50.00	100.00	200.00
❏ ST-8-2576 [S]	Revolver	1966	100.00	200.00	400.00
-- Capitol Record Club edition; black label with colorband					
❏ ST-8-2576 [S]	Revolver	1969	30.00	60.00	120.00
-- Capitol Record Club edition; lime green label					
❏ ST-8-2576 [S]	Revolver	1973?	50.00	100.00	200.00
-- Capitol Record Club edition; orange label (a very late issue, as Capitol Record Club closed in 1973)					
❏ MAS 2653 [M]	Sgt. Pepper's Lonely Hearts Club Band	1967	75.00	150.00	300.00
❏ SMAS 2653 [S]	Sgt. Pepper's Lonely Hearts Club Band	1967	25.00	50.00	100.00
-- Black label with colorband					
❏ SMAS 2653 [S]	Sgt. Pepper's Lonely Hearts Club Band	1969	12.50	25.00	50.00
-- Lime green label					

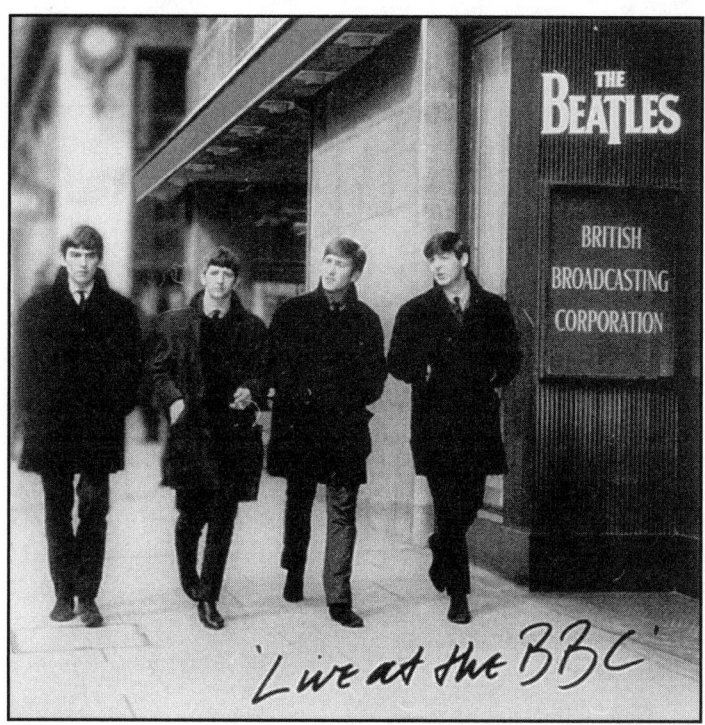

(Top left) In 1970, the Beatles Fan Club sent its U.S. members *The Beatles Christmas Album*, a compilation of the Beatles' seven Christmas messages to their fans. It's never been released to the general public legitimately, and bootlegs abound, but legitimate copies can sell in the hundreds. (Top right) In 1994, EMI finally gave the public some previously unreleased Beatles music in the form of *Live At The BBC*. The American vinyl version was hard to find in 1994, and it's even harder to find now. (Bottom) Here are two of the early versions of the album that was to become *Rarities*. At left is the purple label pressing with the SPRO number that appeared in the U.S. version of the box set *The Beatles Collection*. At right is the record that was going to be released, with the exact contents as the album in the box. Then Capitol realized that, to American audiences, the songs on this record weren't exactly "rarities," so it was pulled before release and replaced with a different collection of the same name.

Number	Title	Yr	VG	VG+	NM
2653	Sgt. Pepper's Lonely Hearts Club Band Special Inner Sleeve	1967	3.75	7.50	15.00
	-- Red-pink psychedelic sleeve only issued with 1967 (mono and stereo) editions				
2653	Sgt. Pepper's Lonely Hearts Club Band Cut-Out Inserts	1967	---	---	3.00
MAL 2835 [M]	Magical Mystery Tour	1967	75.00	150.00	300.00
	-- With 24-page book bound into center of gatefold				
SMAL 2835 [P]	Magical Mystery Tour	1967	25.00	50.00	100.00
	-- Black label with colorband; with 24-page booklet. "Penny Lane," "Baby You're a Rich Man" and "All You Need Is Love" is rechanneled, as is the second half of "I Am the Walrus" (every "stereo" version of "Walrus" is this way)				
SMAL 2835 [P]	Magical Mystery Tour	1969	12.50	25.00	50.00
	-- Lime green label; with 24-page booklet				
SKBO-3403 [P]	The Beatles 1962-1966	1976	5.00	10.00	20.00
	-- Red labels				
SKBO-3403 [P]	The Beatles 1962-1966	1976	7.50	15.00	30.00
	-- Blue labels (error pressing)				
SKBO-3404 [B]	The Beatles 1967-1970	1976	5.00	10.00	20.00
	-- Blue labels				
SPRO-8969	Rarities	1978	12.50	25.00	50.00
	-- Purple label, large Capitol logo; part of the U.S. box set The Beatles Collection (BC-13)				
SKBO-11537 [(2)]	Rock 'n' Roll Music	1976	6.25	12.50	25.00
SMAS-11638	The Beatles at the Hollywood Bowl	1977	5.00	10.00	20.00
	-- Originals with embossed title and ticket on front cover				
SMAS-11638 [DJ]	The Beatles at the Hollywood Bowl	1977	125.00	250.00	500.00
	-- Advance tan label promo in plain white jacket				
SMAS-11638	The Beatles at the Hollywood Bowl	1989	10.00	20.00	40.00
	-- With UPC code on back cover				
SKBL-11711[(2) P]	Love Songs	1977	5.00	10.00	20.00
	-- With booklet and embossed, leather-like cover. "P.S. I Love You" and "Yes It Is" are rechanneled.				
SKBL-11711[(2) P]	Love Songs	1988	7.50	15.00	30.00
	-- With booklet, but without embossed cover				
SEAX-11840 [PD]	Sgt. Pepper's Lonely Hearts Club Band	1978	5.00	10.00	20.00
	-- Picture disc; deduct 25% for cut-outs				
SEBX-11841 [(2)]	The Beatles	1978	12.50	25.00	50.00
	-- White vinyl; with photos and poster (with number "SEBX-11841" on each)				
SEBX-11842 [P]	The Beatles 1962-1966	1978	10.00	20.00	40.00
	-- Red vinyl				
SEBX-11843 [B]	The Beatles 1967-1970	1978	10.00	20.00	40.00
	-- Blue vinyl				
SEAX-11900 [PD]	Abbey Road	1978	10.00	20.00	40.00
	-- Picture disc; deduct 25% for cut-outs				
SW-11921 [P]	A Hard Day's Night	1988	6.25	12.50	25.00
	-- Purple label, small Capitol logo				
SW-11922	Let It Be	1988	6.25	12.50	25.00
	-- Purple label, small Capitol logo; add 20% if poster and custom innersleeve are included				
SN-12009 [DJ]	Rarities	1979	75.00	150.00	300.00
	-- Green label; withdrawn before official release; all known copies have a plain white sleeve				
SHAL-12080 [B]	Rarities	1980	5.00	10.00	20.00
	-- Completely different LP than 12009; black label with colorband. First pressing says that "There's a Place" debuts in stereo (false) and that the screaming at the end of "Helter Skelter" was a "classic Lennon statement" (it's actually Ringo).				
SV-12199 [DJ]	Reel Music	1982	10.00	20.00	40.00
	-- Yellow vinyl promo; numbered back cover with 12-page booklet				
SV-12199 [DJ]	Reel Music	1982	5.00	10.00	20.00
	-- Yellow vinyl promo; plain white cover with 12-page booklet				
SV-12245 [P]	20 Greatest Hits	1982	5.00	10.00	20.00
	-- Purple label, large Capitol logo. "Love Me Do" and "She Loves You" are rechanneled, the other 18 tracks are stereo				
SV-12245 [P]	20 Greatest Hits	1983	5.00	10.00	20.00
	-- Black label, print in colorband				
SV-12245 [P]	20 Greatest Hits	1988	6.25	12.50	25.00
	-- Purple label, small Capitol logo				
CLJ-46435 [M]	Please Please Me	1987	5.00	10.00	20.00
	-- Black label, print in colorband; first Capitol version of original British LP				
CLJ-46435 [M]	Please Please Me	1988	6.25	12.50	25.00
	-- Purple label, small Capitol logo				
CLJ-46436 [M]	With the Beatles	1987	5.00	10.00	20.00
	-- Black label, print in colorband; first Capitol version of original British LP				
CLJ-46436 [M]	With the Beatles	1988	6.25	12.50	25.00
	-- Purple label, small Capitol logo				
CLJ-46437 [M]	A Hard Day's Night	1987	5.00	10.00	20.00
	-- Black label, print in colorband; first Capitol version of original British LP				
CLJ-46437 [M]	A Hard Day's Night	1988	6.25	12.50	25.00
	-- Purple label, small Capitol logo				
CLJ-46438 [M]	Beatles for Sale	1987	5.00	10.00	20.00
	-- Black label, print in colorband; first Capitol version of original British LP				
CLJ-46438 [M]	Beatles for Sale	1988	6.25	12.50	25.00
	-- Purple label, small Capitol logo				
CLJ-46439 [S]	Help!	1987	5.00	10.00	20.00
	-- Black label, print in colorband; first Capitol version of original British LP				
CLJ-46439 [S]	Help!	1988	6.25	12.50	25.00
	-- Purple label, small Capitol logo				
CLJ-46440 [S]	Rubber Soul	1987	5.00	10.00	20.00
	-- Black label, print in colorband; first Capitol version of original British LP				
CLJ-46440 [S]	Rubber Soul	1988	6.25	12.50	25.00
	-- Purple label, small Capitol logo				
CLJ-46441 [S]	Revolver	1987	5.00	10.00	20.00
	-- Black label, print in colorband; first Capitol version of original British LP				
CLJ-46441 [S]	Revolver	1988	6.25	12.50	25.00
	-- Purple label, small Capitol logo				
C1-46442 [S]	Sgt. Pepper's Lonely Hearts Club Band	1988	6.25	12.50	25.00
	-- New number; purple label, small Capitol logo				
C1-46443 [ ]		1988	12.50	25.00	50.00
	-- New number; purple label, small Capitol logo; with photos and poster (some copies have four photos as one perforated sheet)				
C1-46443 [(2)]	The Beatles	1995	5.00	10.00	20.00
	-- With Apple logo on back cover				
C1-46445 [P]	Yellow Submarine	1988	6.25	12.50	25.00
	-- New number; purple label, small Capitol logo				
C1-46446	Abbey Road	1988	6.25	12.50	25.00
	-- New number; purple label, small Capitol logo				
C1-48062 [P]	Magical Mystery Tour	1988	6.25	12.50	25.00
	-- New number; purple label, small Capitol logo; no booklet				
C1-90435 [P]	The Beatles 1962-1966	1988	7.50	15.00	30.00
	-- New number; purple labels, small Capitol logo				
C1-90438 [B]	The Beatles 1967-1970	1988	7.50	15.00	30.00
	-- New number; purple labels, small Capitol logo				
C1-90441 [P]	Meet the Beatles!	1988	6.25	12.50	25.00
	-- New number; purple label, small Capitol logo				
C1-90442	Hey Jude	1988	6.25	12.50	25.00
	-- New number; purple label, small Capitol logo				
C1-90443 [S]	Something New	1988	6.25	12.50	25.00
	-- New number; purple label, small Capitol logo				
C1-90444 [P]	The Beatles' Second Album	1988	6.25	12.50	25.00
	-- New number; purple label, small Capitol logo				
C1-90445 [M]	Beatles VI	1988	6.25	12.50	25.00
	-- New number; purple label, small Capitol logo; plays in mono despite label designation				
C1-90446 [P]	Beatles '65	1988	6.25	12.50	25.00
	-- New number; purple label, small Capitol logo				
C1-90447 [P]	Yesterday and Today	1988	6.25	12.50	25.00
	-- New number; purple label, small Capitol logo; stereo content uncertain				
C1-90452 [S]	Revolver	1988	6.25	12.50	25.00
	-- New number; purple label, small Capitol logo				
C1-90453 [S]	Rubber Soul	1988	6.25	12.50	25.00
	-- New number; purple label, small Capitol logo				
C1-90454 [P]	Help!	1988	6.25	12.50	25.00
	-- New number; purple label, small Capitol logo				
C1-91135 [(2) B]	Past Masters Volume 1 and 2	1988	6.25	12.50	25.00
	-- Some early tracks are in mono, but "This Boy," "She's a Woman." "Yes It Is," and "The Inner Light" are in stereo.				
BBX1-91302 [(14)]	The Beatles Deluxe Box Set	1988	75.00	150.00	300.00

CLARION

Number	Title	Yr	VG	VG+	NM
601 [M]	The Amazing Beatles and Other Great English Group Sounds	1966	25.00	50.00	100.00
SD 601 [P]	The Amazing Beatles and Other Great English Group Sounds	1966	50.00	100.00	200.00
	-- All four Beatles tracks are rechanneled				

GREAT NORTHWEST

Number	Title	Yr	VG	VG+	NM
GNW 4007	Beatle Talk	1978	12.50	25.00	50.00
	-- Columbia Record Club edition; "CRC" on spine				

HALL OF MUSIC

Number	Title	Yr	VG	VG+	NM
HM-1-2200 [(2) M]	Live 1962, Hamburg, Germany	1981	12.50	25.00	50.00
	-- Only American LP with the original European contents -- "I Saw Her Standing There," "Twist and Shout," "Ask Me Why" and "Reminiscing" replace the four songs listed with the Lingasong issue				

I-N-S RADIO NEWS

Number	Title	Yr	VG	VG+	NM
DOC-1 [DJ]	Beatlemania Tour Coverage	1964	750.00	1,125.	1,500.
	-- Promo-only open-end interview with script in plain white jacket				

LINGASONG

Number	Title	Yr	VG	VG+	NM
LS-2-7001 [(2) DJ]	Live at the Star Club in Hamburg, Germany, 1962	1977	50.00	100.00	200.00
	-- Promo only on red vinyl				
LS-2-7001 [(2) DJ]	Live at the Star Club in Hamburg, Germany, 1962	1977	75.00	150.00	300.00
	-- Promo only on blue vinyl				
LS-2-7001 [(2) DJ]	Live at the Star Club in Hamburg, Germany, 1962	1977	10.00	20.00	40.00
	-- Promo on black vinyl; "D.J. Copy Not for Sale" on labels				
LS-2-7001 [(2) R]	Live at the Star Club in Hamburg, Germany, 1962	1977	5.00	10.00	20.00
	-- American version contains "I'm Gonna Sit Right Down and Cry," "Where Have You Been All My Life," "Till There Was You," and "Sheila," not on imports				

LLOYDS

Number	Title	Yr	VG	VG+	NM
ER-MC-LTD	The Great American Tour -- 1965 Live Beatlemania Concert	1965	150.00	300.00	600.00
	-- Another interview album from the Ed Rudy people, with a live Beatles show in the background and the songs poorly overdubbed by the Liverpool Lads				

METRO

Number	Title	Yr	VG	VG+	NM
M-563 [M]	This Is Where It Started	1966	25.00	50.00	100.00
	-- Reissue of MGM album with two of the "others" tracks deleted				
MS-563 [R]	This Is Where It Started	1966	50.00	100.00	200.00
	-- In mono cover with "Stereo" sticker				

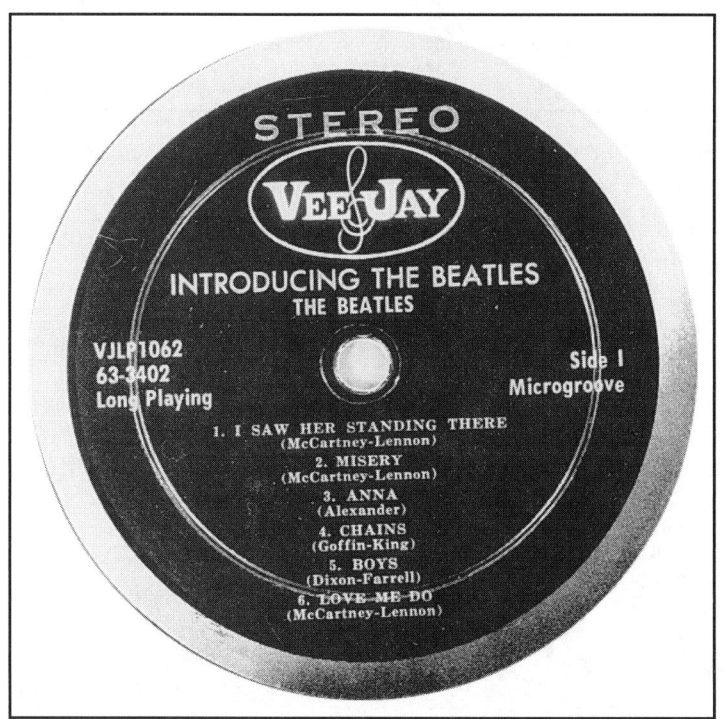

Most of the Beatles' albums on Vee Jay records are among their most sought-after. But most of them have been counterfeited, especially the first one, so you need to beware before paying a lot for a "too good to be true" copy. (Top left) Here's a legitimate stereo pressing of *Introducing The Beatles* with "Love Me Do" as the last song on side 1. Notice the word "STEREO" above the oval Vee Jay logo. If your copy is in a stereo cover and the record *doesn't* say "stereo" on it, either there or at one of the sides, it's not legitimate. (Top right) The most common legitimate *Introducing The Beatles* pressings have a rainbow color band, the Vee Jay brackets logo in white, the rest of the print in silver, and "Ask Me Why" as the last song on side 1. Oh yes, it's also mono. Vee Jay made very few stereo records, and they were scarce even in 1964. (Bottom left) Perhaps the rarest of all American Beatles albums, not including promos, is the "portrait cover" of *The Beatles And Frank Ifield On Stage*. Near-mint copies in stereo have been known to fetch close to five figures. (Bottom right) Only two copies are known of the white-label promo version of *Hear The Beatles Tell All*. Copies were sent to the two men who did the interviews, and perhaps others were sent out, but they were recalled when it was discovered that the credit for each interview was switched! Stock copies on black labels corrected the error.

Number	Title	Yr	VG	VG+	NM
❏ MS-563 [R]	This Is Where It Started	1966	37.50	75.00	150.00
-- In stereo cover					

MGM

Number	Title	Yr	VG	VG+	NM
❏ E-4215 [M]	The Beatles with Tony Sheridan and Their Guests	1964	50.00	100.00	200.00
-- Without "And Guests" on cover					
❏ E-4215 [M]	The Beatles with Tony Sheridan and Their Guests	1964	62.50	125.00	250.00
-- With "And Guests" on cover					
❏ SE-4215 [R]	The Beatles with Tony Sheridan and Their Guests	1964	200.00	400.00	800.00
-- Without "And Guests" on cover					
❏ SE-4215 [R]	The Beatles with Tony Sheridan and Their Guests	1964	150.00	300.00	600.00
-- With "And Guests" on cover					

MOBILE FIDELITY

Number	Title	Yr	VG	VG+	NM
❏ BC-1 [(13)]	The Beatles Collection	1982	125.00	250.00	500.00
❏ 1-023	Abbey Road	1979	12.50	25.00	50.00
-- Audiophile vinyl					
❏ 1-047 [P]	Magical Mystery Tour	1980	15.00	30.00	60.00
-- Audiophile vinyl; yes, this contains the rechanneled stereo versions of "Penny Lane," "Baby You're a Rich Man" and "All You Need Is Love"					
❏ 2-072 [(2)]	The Beatles	1982	12.50	25.00	50.00
-- Audiophile vinyl; not issued with photos or poster					
❏ 1-100 [S]	Sgt. Pepper's Lonely Hearts Club Band	1985	10.00	20.00	40.00
-- Audiophile vinyl					
❏ UHQR-1-100 [S]	Sgt. Pepper's Lonely Hearts Club Band	1982	75.00	150.00	300.00
-- Ultra High Quality release with special cover; numbered edition of 5,000; numbers under 100 fetch even more					
❏ 1-101 [P]	Please Please Me	1986	10.00	20.00	40.00
-- Audiophile vinyl; British version of album. "Love Me Do" and "P.S. I Love You" are rechanneled.					
❏ 1-102 [S]	With the Beatles	1986	37.50	75.00	150.00
-- Audiophile vinyl; British version of album. Limited run because of a damaged stamper that was not replaced.					
❏ 1-103 [S]	A Hard Day's Night	1987	10.00	20.00	40.00
-- Audiophile vinyl; British version of album					
❏ 1-104 [S]	Beatles for Sale	1986	10.00	20.00	40.00
-- Audiophile vinyl; British version of album					
❏ 1-105 [S]	Help!	1985	10.00	20.00	40.00
-- Audiophile vinyl; British version of album					
❏ 1-106 [S]	Rubber Soul	1985	10.00	20.00	40.00
-- Audiophile vinyl; British version of album					
❏ 1-107 [S]	Revolver	1986	10.00	20.00	40.00
-- Audiophile vinyl; British version of album					
❏ 1-108 [P]	Yellow Submarine	1987	15.00	30.00	60.00
-- Audiophile vinyl					
❏ 1-109	Let It Be	1987	50.00	100.00	200.00
-- Audiophile vinyl; regular cover					
❏ 1-109	Let It Be	1987	10.00	20.00	40.00
-- Audiophile vinyl; gatefold cover					

ORANGE

Number	Title	Yr	VG	VG+	NM
❏ ORC-12880	The Silver Beatles	1985	100.00	200.00	400.00
-- Test pressing; full cover cover slick folded around a white cover. Both contain all 15 Decca audition tracks					
❏ ORC-12880	The Silver Beatles	1985	75.00	150.00	300.00
-- Test pressing; white cover with title sticker					

PBR INTERNATIONAL

Number	Title	Yr	VG	VG+	NM
❏ 7005/6 [(2)]	The David Wigg Interviews (The Beatles Tapes)	1978	20.00	40.00	80.00
-- Blue vinyl					
❏ 7005/6 [(2)]	The David Wigg Interviews (The Beatles Tapes)	1980	15.00	30.00	60.00
-- Black vinyl					

PHOENIX

Number	Title	Yr	VG	VG+	NM
❏ P20-623	20 Hits, Beatles	1983	5.00	10.00	20.00
-- With 12 Decca audition tracks, four Beatles/Tony Sheridan tracks, and four Tony Sheridan solo tracks					
❏ P20-629	20 Hits, Beatles	1983	5.00	10.00	20.00
-- With 20 live Hamburg tracks					

PICKWICK

Number	Title	Yr	VG	VG+	NM
❏ BAN-90051 [M]	Recorded Live in Hamburg, Vol. 1	1978	7.50	15.00	30.00
❏ BAN-90061 [M]	Recorded Live in Hamburg, Vol. 2	1978	7.50	15.00	30.00
❏ BAN-90071 [M]	Recorded Live in Hamburg, Vol. 3	1978	10.00	20.00	40.00

POLYDOR

Number	Title	Yr	VG	VG+	NM
❏ 24-4504 [R]	The Beatles -- Circa 1960 -- In the Beginning Featuring Tony Sheridan	197?	10.00	20.00	40.00
-- Some copies of the record contain only the title "The Beatles -- In the Beginning"					
❏ 24-4504 [R]	The Beatles -- Circa 1960 -- In the Beginning Featuring Tony Sheridan	1970	6.25	12.50	25.00
-- Originals have gatefold cover					
❏ SKAO-93199 [R]	The Beatles -- Circa 1960 -- In the Beginning Featuring Tony Sheridan	1970	10.00	20.00	40.00
-- Capitol Record Club edition					

Number	Title	Yr	VG	VG+	NM
❏ 825 073-1 [R]	The Beatles -- Circa 1960 -- In the Beginning Featuring Tony Sheridan	1988	5.00	10.00	20.00
-- Reissue with new number					

RADIO PULSEBEAT NEWS

Number	Title	Yr	VG	VG+	NM
❏ 2	The American Tour with Ed Rudy	1964	25.00	50.00	100.00
-- Yellow label; some copies came with a special edition of Teen Talk magazine (add 50%)					
❏ 2	The American Tour with Ed Rudy	1980	6.25	12.50	25.00
-- Blue label; authorized reissue with Beatles' photo on cover					
❏ 3	1965 Talk Album -- Ed Rudy with New U.S. Tour	1965	37.50	75.00	150.00
-- "The Beatles" in black print under front cover photo (other versions appear to be bootlegs)					

RAVEN/PVC

Number	Title	Yr	VG	VG+	NM
❏ 8911 [DJ]	Talk Downunder	1981	20.00	40.00	80.00
-- Promo only in white cover with title sticker. Label reads "For Radio Play Only"					

SAVAGE

Number	Title	Yr	VG	VG+	NM
❏ BM-69 [M]	The Savage Young Beatles	1964	37.50	75.00	150.00
-- Orange label; no legitimate copy says "Stereo" on cover					
❏ BM-69 [M]	The Savage Young Beatles	1964	375.00	750.00	1,500.
-- Yellow label, glossy orange cover					

SILHOUETTE

Number	Title	Yr	VG	VG+	NM
❏ SM-10004 [PD]	Timeless	1981	6.25	12.50	25.00
-- Picture disc with interviews plus remakes of "Imagine" and "Let It Be" (by non-Beatles)					
❏ SM-10004 [PD]	Timeless	1981	5.00	10.00	20.00
-- Picture disc with all interviews					
❏ SM-10010 [PD]	Timeless II	1982	5.00	10.00	20.00
-- Picture disc with mostly interviews					
❏ SM-10013	The British Are Coming	1984	20.00	40.00	80.00
-- Same as above, but red vinyl					
❏ SM-10013 [DJ]	The British Are Coming	1984	10.00	20.00	40.00
-- White label promo; no numbered sticker					
❏ SM-10015	Golden Beatles	1985	20.00	40.00	80.00
-- Gold vinyl					
❏ PD-83010 [PD]	The British Are Coming	1985	7.50	15.00	30.00
-- Picture disc					

STERLING

Number	Title	Yr	VG	VG+	NM
❏ 8895-6481	I Apologize	1966	100.00	200.00	400.00
-- One-sided LP with John Lennon's "apology" for supposed anti-Christian remarks; includes photo					
❏ 8895-6481	I Apologize	1966	75.00	150.00	300.00
-- Same as above, but without photo					

UNITED ARTISTS

Number	Title	Yr	VG	VG+	NM
❏ UA-Help-A/B [DJ]	United Artists Presents Help!	1965	500.00	1,000.	1,500.
-- Radio spots for movie					
❏ UA-Help-INT [DJ]	United Artists Presents Help!	1965	1,000.	1,500.	2,000.
-- Open-end interview with script (red label)					
❏ UA-Help-Show [DJ]	United Artists Presents Help!	1965	1,500.	2,250.	3,000.
-- One-sided interview with script (blue label)					
❏ SP-2359/60 [DJ]	United Artists Presents A Hard Day's Night	1964	1,000.	1,500.	2,000.
-- Open-end interview with script					
❏ SP-2362/3 [DJ]	United Artists Presents A Hard Day's Night	1964	375.00	750.00	1,500.
-- Radio spots for movie					
❏ UAL 3366 [M]	A Hard Day's Night	1964	62.50	125.00	250.00
-- With "I'll Cry Instead" listing					
❏ UAL 3366 [M]	A Hard Day's Night	1964	50.00	100.00	200.00
-- With "I Cry Instead" listing					
❏ UAL 3366 [M-DJ]	A Hard Day's Night	1964	750.00	1,500.	3,000.
-- White label promo					
❏ UAS 6366 [P]	A Hard Day's Night	1964	62.50	125.00	250.00
-- With "I'll Cry Instead" listing. Has incidental music by George Martin. All eight Beatles tracks are rechanneled; Martin's are in true stereo.					
❏ UAS 6366 [P]	A Hard Day's Night	1964	6,000.	9,000.	12,000.
-- Pink vinyl; only one copy known, probably privately (and secretly) done by a pressing-plant employee					
❏ UAS 6366 [P]	A Hard Day's Night	1964	50.00	100.00	200.00
-- With "I Cry Instead" listing					
❏ UAS 6366 [P]	A Hard Day's Night	1968	12.50	25.00	50.00
-- Pink and orange label					
❏ UAS 6366 [P]	A Hard Day's Night	1970	12.50	25.00	50.00
-- Black and orange label					
❏ UAS 6366 [P]	A Hard Day's Night	1971	5.00	10.00	20.00
-- Tan label					
❏ UAS 6366 [P]	A Hard Day's Night	1975	5.00	10.00	20.00
-- Tan label with "All Rights Reserved" in perimeter print					
❏ UAS 6366 [P]	A Hard Day's Night	1977	5.00	10.00	20.00
-- Sunrise label. Note: Any of the variations from 1968 on can have titles of songs incorrectly listed as "I Cry Instead" and "Tell Me Who," or only one can be wrong, or neither can be wrong. No difference in value at this time.					
❏ ST 90828 [P]	A Hard Day's Night	1964	187.50	375.00	750.00
-- Capitol Record Club edition					
❏ T 90828 [M]	A Hard Day's Night	1964	750.00	1,125.	1,500.
-- Capitol Record Club edition					

UNITED DISTRIBUTORS

Number	Title	Yr	VG	VG+	NM
❏ UDL-2333 [M]	Dawn of the Silver Beatles	1981	15.00	30.00	60.00
-- Hand-stamped numbers on back cover and label; contains 10 Decca audition tracks					

Number	Title	Yr	VG	VG+	NM
❑ UDL-2333 [M] Dawn of the Silver Beatles		1981	12.50	25.00	50.00
-- With numbered registration card (deduct 20% if missing)					
❑ UDL-2382 [M] Lightning Strikes Twice		1981	15.00	30.00	60.00
-- Side 1 has five Beatles' Decca audition tracks; Side 2 has live Elvis Presley performances from 1955					

VEE JAY

Number	Title	Yr	VG	VG+	NM
❑ DX-30 [(2) M]	The Beatles vs. The Four Seasons	1964	200.00	400.00	800.00
-- Combines "Introducing the Beatles" with "Golden Hits of the Four Seasons" (Vee Jay 1065)					
❑ DXS-30 [(2) S]	The Beatles vs. The Four Seasons	1964	1,500.	2,250.	3,000.
-- Combines "Introducing the Beatles" with "Golden Hits of the Four Seasons" (Vee Jay 1065)					
❑ DX(S)-30	The Beatles vs. The Four Seasons Poster	1964	75.00	150.00	300.00
❑ 202 [M]	Hear the Beatles Tell All	1964	75.00	150.00	300.00
-- Without "PRO" prefic on label					
❑ PRO 202 [DJ]	Hear the Beatles Tell All	1964	6,000.	12,000.	18,000.
-- White label promo with blue print					
❑ PRO 202 [M]	Hear the Beatles Tell All	1964	50.00	100.00	200.00
-- With "PRO" prefix on label					
❑ PRO 202 [PD]	Hear the Beatles Tell All	1987	5.00	10.00	20.00
-- Shaped picture disc with same recordings as the black vinyl versions					
❑ LP 1062 [M]	Introducing the Beatles	1964	1,500.	2,750.	4,000.
-- "Ad back" cover; with "Love Me Do" and "P.S. I Love You"					
❑ LP 1062 [M]	Introducing the Beatles	1964	400.00	800.00	1,200.
-- Blank back cover; with "Love Me Do" and "P.S. I Love You"					
❑ LP 1062 [M]	Introducing the Beatles	1964	200.00	400.00	800.00
-- Song titles cover; with "Love Me Do" and "P.S. I Love You" (Note: Mono records inside stereo jackets, with "Introducing The Beatles" above the center hole and "The Beatles" below the center hole, are all counterfeits and have little collector value)					
❑ LP 1062 [M]	Introducing the Beatles	1964	250.00	500.00	1,000.
-- Blank back cover; with "Please Please Me" and "Ask Me Why"					
❑ LP 1062 [M]	Introducing the Beatles	1964	75.00	150.00	300.00
-- Song titles cover; with "Please Please Me" and "Ask Me Why"; oval Vee Jay logo on colorband					
❑ LP 1062 [M]	Introducing the Beatles	1964	75.00	150.00	300.00
-- Song titles cover; with "Please Please Me" and "Ask Me Why"; oval Vee Jay logo on solid black label					
❑ LP 1062 [M]	Introducing the Beatles	1964	62.50	125.00	250.00
-- Song titles cover; with "Please Please Me" and "Ask Me Why"; brackets Vee Jay logo with colorband (most common authentic version)					
❑ LP 1062 [M]	Introducing the Beatles	1964	250.00	500.00	1,000.
-- Song titles cover; with "Please Please Me" and "Ask Me Why"; brackets Vee Jay logo on solid black label					
❑ LP 1062 [M]	Introducing the Beatles	1964	62.50	125.00	250.00
-- Song titles cover; with "Please Please Me" and "Ask Me Why"; plain Vee Jay logo on solid black label					
❑ SR 1062 [B]	Introducing the Beatles	1964	4,000.	8,000.	12,000.
-- "Ad back" cover; with "Love Me Do" and "P.S. I Love You" (both mono); oval Vee Jay logo with colorband only!					
❑ SR 1062 [B]	Introducing the Beatles	1964	625.00	1,250.	2,500.
-- Blank back cover; with "Love Me Do" and "P.S. I Love You"; oval Vee Jay logo with colorband only!					
❑ SR 1062 [B]	Introducing the Beatles	1964	3,000.	5,500.	8,000.
-- Song titles cover; with "Love Me Do" and "P.S. I Love You"; oval Vee Jay logo with colorband only! Approximately 10 authentic copies are known, with hundreds of thousands of counterfeits (to be authentic, record must have the word "STEREO" on the label, plus both of the lines "Introducing The Beatles" and "The Beatles" must be above the center hole)					
❑ SR 1062 [S]	Introducing the Beatles	1964	400.00	800.00	1,600.
-- Song titles cover; with "Please Please Me" and "Ask Me Why"; oval Vee Jay logo with colorband					
❑ SR 1062 [S]	Introducing the Beatles	1964	375.00	750.00	1,500.
-- Song titles cover; with "Please Please Me" and "Ask Me Why"; brackets Vee Jay logo with colorband					
❑ SR 1062 [S]	Introducing the Beatles	1964	400.00	800.00	1,600.
-- Song titles cover; with "Please Please Me" and "Ask Me Why"; plain Vee Jay logo on solid black label					
❑ LP 1085 [M]	The Beatles and Frank Ifield on Stage	1964	2,000.	3,500.	5,000.
-- Portrait of Beatles cover; counterfeits are poorly reproduced and have no spine print					
❑ SR 1085 [B]	The Beatles and Frank Ifield on Stage	1964	4,000.	8,000.	12,000.
-- Portrait of Beatles cover; "Stereo" on both cover and label					
❑ LP 1085 [M]	Jolly What! The Beatles and Frank Ifield on Stage	1964	62.50	125.00	250.00
-- Man in Beatle wig cover; originals have printing on spine and a dark blue/purple background (counterfeits have a black background and no spine print)					
❑ SR 1085 [B]	Jolly What! The Beatles and Frank Ifield on Stage	1964	125.00	250.00	500.00
-- Man in Beatle wig cover; "Stereo" on both cover and label. "From Me to You" is mono.					
❑ LP 1092 [M]	Songs, Pictures and Stories of the Fabulous Beatles	1964	125.00	250.00	500.00
-- All copies have gatefold cover with 2/3 width on front; also, all copies have "Introducing the Beatles" records. Oval Vee Jay logo with colorband.					
❑ LP 1092 [M]	Songs, Pictures and Stories of the Fabulous Beatles	1964	125.00	250.00	500.00
-- See above; oval Vee Jay logo on solid black label					
❑ LP 1092 [M]	Songs, Pictures and Stories of the Fabulous Beatles	1964	125.00	250.00	500.00
-- See above; brackets Vee Jay logo with colorband					
❑ LP 1092 [M]	Songs, Pictures and Stories of the Fabulous Beatles	1964	125.00	250.00	500.00
-- See above; plain Vee Jay logo on solid black label					
❑ VJS 1092 [S]	Songs, Pictures and Stories of the Fabulous Beatles	1964	800.00	1,600.	2,400.
-- All copies have gatefold cover with 2/3 width on front; also, all copies have "Introducing the Beatles" records. Oval Vee Jay logo with colorband.					
❑ VJS 1092 [S]	Songs, Pictures and Stories of the Fabulous Beatles	1964	800.00	1,600.	2,400.
-- See above; brackets Vee Jay logo with colorband					

Number	Title	Yr	VG	VG+	NM
❑ VJS 1092 [S]	Songs, Pictures and Stories of the Fabulous Beatles	1964	800.00	1,600.	2,400.
-- See above; plain Vee Jay logo on solid black label. NOTE: Any non-gatefold copy or any copy called "Songs and Pictures of the Fabulous Beatles" is a counterfeit.					

BEAU BRUMMELS, THE
AUTUMN

Number	Title	Yr	VG	VG+	NM
❑ LP 103 [M]	Introducing the Beau Brummels	1965	12.50	25.00	50.00
❑ SLP 103 [S]	Introducing the Beau Brummels	1965	15.00	30.00	60.00
❑ LP 104 [M]	The Beau Brummels, Volume 2	1965	10.00	20.00	40.00
❑ SLP 104 [S]	The Beau Brummels, Volume 2	1965	12.50	25.00	50.00

VAULT

Number	Title	Yr	VG	VG+	NM
❑ LP-114 [M]	Best of the Beau Brummels	1967	6.25	12.50	25.00
❑ SLP-114 [S]	Best of the Beau Brummels	1967	6.25	12.50	25.00
❑ SLP-121	Beau Brummels, Vol. 44	1968	6.25	12.50	25.00

WARNER BROS.

Number	Title	Yr	VG	VG+	NM
❑ W 1644 [M]	Beau Brummels '66	1966	5.00	10.00	20.00
❑ W 1692 [M]	Triangle	1967	5.00	10.00	20.00
❑ WS 1644 [S]	Beau Brummels '66	1966	6.25	12.50	25.00
❑ WS 1692 [S]	Triangle	1967	6.25	12.50	25.00
❑ WS 1760	Bradley's Barn	1968	6.25	12.50	25.00
❑ BS 2842	The Beau Brummels	1975	5.00	10.00	20.00

BEAUREGARDE
EMPIRE

Number	Title	Yr	VG	VG+	NM
❑ (no #)	Beauregarde	1969	25.00	50.00	100.00

SOUND

Number	Title	Yr	VG	VG+	NM
❑ 7104	Beauregarde	1969	20.00	40.00	80.00

BEAVER AND KRAUSE
LIMELIGHT

Number	Title	Yr	VG	VG+	NM
❑ 86069	Ragnarok -- Electronic Funk	1969	7.50	15.00	30.00

BEAVER, PAUL
RAPTURE

Number	Title	Yr	VG	VG+	NM
❑ 11111	Perchance to Dream	196?	12.50	25.00	50.00

BECK
FINGERPAINT

Number	Title	Yr	VG	VG+	NM
❑ 02 [10]	A Western Harvest Field by Moonlight	1992	5.00	10.00	20.00
-- With fingerpainting insert					

BECK, BOGERT & APPICE
Also see JEFF BECK; Tim Bogert and Carmen Appice were in VANILLA FUDGE.
EPIC

Number	Title	Yr	VG	VG+	NM
❑ CQ 32140 [Q]	Beck, Bogert & Appice	1973	5.00	10.00	20.00

BECK, JEFF
Also see BECK, BOGERT AND APPICE; THE YARDBIRDS.
EPIC

Number	Title	Yr	VG	VG+	NM
❑ AS 151 [DJ]	Everything You Always Wanted to Hear by Jeff Beck But Were Afraid to Ask For	1977	5.00	10.00	20.00
-- Promo-only sampler					
❑ A2S 850 [(2)]	Then and Now	1981	6.25	12.50	25.00
-- Promo-only sampler					
❑ EQ 30993 [Q]	Rough and Ready	1972	5.00	10.00	20.00
❑ EQ 31331 [Q]	Jeff Beck Group	1972	5.00	10.00	20.00
❑ PEQ 33409 [Q]	Blow by Blow	1975	5.00	10.00	20.00
❑ PEQ 33849 [Q]	Wired	1976	5.00	10.00	20.00
❑ HE 43409	Blow by Blow	1980	12.50	25.00	50.00
-- Half-speed mastered edition					

BEDIENT, JACK
EXECUTIVE PRODUCTIONS

Number	Title	Yr	VG	VG+	NM
❑ (no #) [M]	Jack Bedient	196?	20.00	40.00	80.00

FANTASY

Number	Title	Yr	VG	VG+	NM
❑ 3365 [M]	Live at Harvey's	1965	15.00	30.00	60.00

SATORI

Number	Title	Yr	VG	VG+	NM
❑ LP 1001 [M]	Where Did She Go?	1966	15.00	30.00	60.00

TROPHY

Number	Title	Yr	VG	VG+	NM
❑ 101 [M]	Two Sides of Jack Bedient	1964	15.00	30.00	60.00

BEDLAM
CHRYSALIS

Number	Title	Yr	VG	VG+	NM
❑ CHR-1048	Bedlam	1973	6.25	12.50	25.00

Number	Title	Yr	VG	VG+	NM

BEE GEES
Also see ROBIN GIBB.
ATCO

Number	Title	Yr	VG	VG+	NM
❑ 33-223 [M]	Bee Gees' 1st	1967	7.50	15.00	30.00
❑ SD 33-223 [S]	Bee Gees' 1st	1967	5.00	10.00	20.00
-- Brown and purple label original					
❑ 33-233 [M]	Horizontal	1968	7.50	15.00	30.00
❑ SD 33-233 [S]	Horizontal	1968	5.00	10.00	20.00
-- Brown and purple label original					
❑ 33-253 [M]	Idea	1968	12.50	25.00	50.00
-- White label promo only					
❑ SD 33-253 [S]	Idea	1968	5.00	10.00	20.00
-- Brown and purple label original					
❑ 33-264 [M]	Rare, Precious & Beautiful	1968	7.50	15.00	30.00
-- White label promo only					
❑ 33-292 [M]	Best of Bee Gees	1969	7.50	15.00	30.00
-- White label promo only					
❑ 33-321 [M]	Rare, Precious & Beautiful, Volume	1970	7.50	15.00	30.00
-- White label promo only					
❑ SD 2-702 [(2)]	Odessa	1969	20.00	40.00	80.00
-- Record club editions with plain red cover					
❑ SD 2-702 [(2)]	Odessa	1969	10.00	20.00	40.00
-- Red felt cover					

MOBILE FIDELITY

Number	Title	Yr	VG	VG+	NM
❑ 1-263	Trafalgar	1996	10.00	20.00	40.00
-- Audiophile vinyl					

NAUTILUS

Number	Title	Yr	VG	VG+	NM
❑ NR-17	Spirits Having Flown	1981	7.50	15.00	30.00
❑ NR-42	Living Eyes	1982	25.00	50.00	100.00
-- Record was never released; value is for test pressings					

RSO

Number	Title	Yr	VG	VG+	NM
❑ SMP-1 [DJ]	The Words and Music of Maurice, Barry and Robin Gibb	1979	12.50	25.00	50.00
-- Promo-only publisher's sampler					
❑ PRO 033 [DJ]	Saturday Night Fever Special Disco Versions	1978	12.50	25.00	50.00
-- Promo-only sampler; contains an otherwise unavailable extended version of "Stayin' Alive"					
❑ PRO ??? [DJ]	Select Disco Cuts from "Spirits Having Flown"	1979	7.50	15.00	30.00
❑ PUB-1000 [DJ]	Unichappell Publisher's Sampler	1980	12.50	25.00	50.00

BEE, MOLLY
CAPITOL

Number	Title	Yr	VG	VG+	NM
❑ T 1097 [M]	Young Romance	1958	10.00	20.00	40.00

MGM

Number	Title	Yr	VG	VG+	NM
❑ E-4303 [M]	It's Great, It's Molly Bee	1965	5.00	10.00	20.00
❑ SE-4303 [S]	It's Great, It's Molly Bee	1965	6.25	12.50	25.00
❑ E-4423 [M]	Swingin' Country	1967	5.00	10.00	20.00
❑ SE-4423 [S]	Swingin' Country	1967	6.25	12.50	25.00

BEETHOVEN SOUL
DOT

Number	Title	Yr	VG	VG+	NM
❑ DLP-3821 [M]	Beethoven Soul	1967	6.25	12.50	25.00
❑ DLP-25821 [S]	Beethoven Soul	1967	6.25	12.50	25.00

BEGINNING OF THE END, THE
ALSTON

Number	Title	Yr	VG	VG+	NM
❑ SD 33-379	Funky Nassau	1971	5.00	10.00	20.00

BEL-AIRE GIRLS, THE
EVEREST

Number	Title	Yr	VG	VG+	NM
❑ BRST-1081 [S]	The Bel-Aire Girls Sing Along with the Teen-Agers	1960	20.00	40.00	80.00
❑ LPBR-5081 [M]	The Bel-Aire Girls Sing Along with the Teen-Agers	1960	15.00	30.00	60.00

BEL-AIRE POPS ORCHESTRA, THE
LIBERTY

Number	Title	Yr	VG	VG+	NM
❑ LRP-3414 [M]	Jan and Dean's Pop Symphony No. 1	1965	30.00	60.00	120.00
❑ LST-7414 [S]	Jan and Dean's Pop Symphony No. 1	1965	50.00	100.00	200.00

BELAFONTE, HARRY
DCC COMPACT CLASSICS

Number	Title	Yr	VG	VG+	NM
❑ LPZ-2039	Jump Up Calypso	1997	6.25	12.50	25.00
-- Audiophile vinyl					

RCA VICTOR

Number	Title	Yr	VG	VG+	NM
❑ LPM-1006 [M]	Belafonte Sings the Blues	1954	12.50	25.00	50.00
-- Reissued in 1958 with the same number, then re-recorded in 1959					
❑ LPM-1022 [M]	"Mark Twain" and Other Folk Favorites	1954	12.50	25.00	50.00
❑ LPM-1150 [M]	Belafonte	1955	12.50	25.00	50.00
❑ LPM-1248 [M]	Calypso	1956	7.50	15.00	30.00

Number	Title	Yr	VG	VG+	NM
❑ LPM-1402 [M]	An Evening with Belafonte	1957	6.25	12.50	25.00
❑ LPM-1505 [M]	Belafonte Sings of the Caribbean	1957	7.50	15.00	30.00
❑ LOC-1507 [M]	Porgy and Bess	1959	5.00	10.00	20.00
❑ LSO-1507 [S]	Porgy and Bess	1959	6.25	12.50	25.00
-- With Lena Horne					
❑ LPM-1887 [M]	To Wish You a Merry Christmas	1958	6.25	12.50	25.00
❑ LSP-1887 [S]	To Wish You a Merry Christmas	1958	10.00	20.00	40.00
❑ LPM-1927 [M]	Love Is a Gentle Thing	1959	5.00	10.00	20.00
❑ LSP-1927 [S]	Love Is a Gentle Thing	1959	6.25	12.50	25.00
❑ LPM-1972 [M]	Belafonte Sings the Blues	1959	5.00	10.00	20.00
❑ LSP-1972 [S]	Belafonte Sings the Blues	1959	6.25	12.50	25.00
❑ LPM-2022 [M]	My Lord What a Mornin'	1960	5.00	10.00	20.00
❑ LSP-2022 [S]	My Lord What a Mornin'	1960	6.25	12.50	25.00
❑ LPM-2194 [M]	Swing Dat Hammer	1961	5.00	10.00	20.00
❑ LSP-2194 [S]	Swing Dat Hammer	1961	6.25	12.50	25.00
❑ LPM-2309 [M]	At Home and Abroad	1961	5.00	10.00	20.00
❑ LSP-2309 [S]	At Home and Abroad	1961	6.25	12.50	25.00
❑ LPM-2388 [M]	Jump Up Calypso	1961	5.00	10.00	20.00
❑ LSP-2388 [S]	Jump Up Calypso	1961	6.25	12.50	25.00
❑ LPM-2449 [M]	The Midnight Special	1962	7.50	15.00	30.00
❑ LSP-2449 [S]	The Midnight Special	1962	10.00	20.00	40.00
-- The above LP features Bob Dylan on harmonica on the title track, his first appearance on record					
❑ LPM-2574 [M]	The Many Moods of Belafonte	1962	5.00	10.00	20.00
❑ LSP-2574 [S]	The Many Moods of Belafonte	1962	6.25	12.50	25.00
❑ LPM-2626 [M]	To Wish You a Merry Christmas	1962	5.00	10.00	20.00
❑ LSP-2626 [S]	To Wish You a Merry Christmas	1962	6.25	12.50	25.00
-- Reissue of LPM-1887 with new cover and one additional track					
❑ LPM-2695 [M]	Streets I Have Walked	1963	5.00	10.00	20.00
❑ LSP-2695 [S]	Streets I Have Walked	1963	6.25	12.50	25.00
❑ LSP-2953 [S]	Ballads, Blues and Boasters	1964	5.00	10.00	20.00
❑ LSP-3415 [S]	An Evening with Belafonte/Mouskouri	1966	5.00	10.00	20.00
-- With Nana Mouskouri					
❑ LSP-3420 [S]	An Evening with Belafonte/Makeba	1965	5.00	10.00	20.00
-- With Miriam Makeba					
❑ LOC-6006 [(2) M]	Belafonte at Carnegie Hall	1959	6.25	12.50	25.00
❑ LSO-6006 [(2) S]	Belafonte at Carnegie Hall	1959	12.50	25.00	50.00
❑ LOC-6007 [(2) M]	Belafonte Returns to Carnegie Hall	1960	5.00	10.00	20.00
❑ LSO-6007 [(2) S]	Belafonte Returns to Carnegie Hall	1960	15.00	30.00	60.00
-- The above LP also has tracks by Odetta, Miriam Makeba and The Chad Mitchell Trio (the latter for the first time on record)					
❑ LOC-6009 [(2) M]	Belafonte at the Greek Theatre	1964	5.00	10.00	20.00
❑ LSO-6009 [(2) S]	Belafonte at the Greek Theatre	1964	10.00	20.00	40.00

RCA VICTOR/CLASSIC

Number	Title	Yr	VG	VG+	NM
❑ LSP-1972	Belafonte Sings the Blues	199?	6.25	12.50	25.00
-- Audiophile vinyl					
❑ LSO-6006 [(2)]	Belafonte at Carnegie Hall	1996	10.00	20.00	40.00
-- Audiophile vinyl					
❑ LSO-6007 [(2)]	Belafonte Returns to Carnegie Hall	1996	10.00	20.00	40.00
-- Audiophile vinyl					

BELEW, CARL
DECCA

Number	Title	Yr	VG	VG+	NM
❑ DL 4074 [M]	Carl Belew	1960	6.25	12.50	25.00
❑ DL 74074 [S]	Carl Belew	1960	7.50	15.00	30.00

HILLTOP

Number	Title	Yr	VG	VG+	NM
❑ JM-6013 [M]	Another Lonely Night	1965	5.00	10.00	20.00
❑ JS-6013 [S]	Another Lonely Night	1965	5.00	10.00	20.00

RCA VICTOR

Number	Title	Yr	VG	VG+	NM
❑ LPM-2848 [M]	Hello Out There	1964	5.00	10.00	20.00
❑ LSP-2848 [S]	Hello Out There	1964	6.25	12.50	25.00
❑ LPM-3381 [M]	Am I That Easy to Forget?	1965	5.00	10.00	20.00
❑ LSP-3381 [S]	Am I That Easy to Forget?	1965	6.25	12.50	25.00
❑ LPM-3919 [M]	Twelve Shades of Belew	1968	12.50	25.00	50.00
❑ LSP-3919 [S]	Twelve Shades of Belew	1968	5.00	10.00	20.00

WRANGLER

Number	Title	Yr	VG	VG+	NM
❑ WR 1007 [M]	Carl Belew	1962	7.50	15.00	30.00
❑ WRS 31007 [S]	Carl Belew	1962	10.00	20.00	40.00

BELL, ARCHIE, AND THE DRELLS
ATLANTIC

Number	Title	Yr	VG	VG+	NM
❑ 8181 [M]	Tighten Up	1968	12.50	25.00	50.00
❑ SD 8181 [S]	Tighten Up	1968	7.50	15.00	30.00
❑ SD 8204	I Can't Stop Dancing	1968	7.50	15.00	30.00
❑ SD 8226	There's Gonna Be a Showdown	1969	7.50	15.00	30.00

BELL, FREDDIE, AND THE BELL BOYS
20TH FOX

Number	Title	Yr	VG	VG+	NM
❑ TF-4146 [M]	Bells Are Swinging	1964	6.25	12.50	25.00
❑ TFS-4146 [S]	Bells Are Swinging	1964	7.50	15.00	30.00

MERCURY

Number	Title	Yr	VG	VG+	NM
❑ MG-20289 [M]	Rock and Roll... All Flavors	1957	50.00	100.00	200.00

Number	Title	Yr	VG	VG+	NM

BELL, VINCENT
DECCA
| ❑ DL 4938 [M] | Pop Goes the Electric Sitar | 1967 | 5.00 | 10.00 | 20.00 |

MUSICOR
| ❑ MS-3009 [S] | 51 Motion Picture Favorites | 1963 | 5.00 | 10.00 | 20.00 |
| ❑ MS-3047 [S] | Big 16 Guitar Favorites | 1965 | 5.00 | 10.00 | 20.00 |

VERVE
| ❑ V6-8574 [S] | Whistle Stop | 1964 | 5.00 | 10.00 | 20.00 |

BELL, WILLIAM
STAX
❑ 719 [M]	Soul of a Bell	1967	10.00	20.00	40.00
❑ S-719 [S]	Soul of a Bell	1967	12.50	25.00	50.00
❑ ST-2014 [M]	Bound to Happen	1969	12.50	25.00	50.00
-- Mono is promo only					
❑ STS-2014 [S]	Bound to Happen	1969	7.50	15.00	30.00
❑ STS-2037	Wow...	1971	7.50	15.00	30.00
❑ STS-3005	Phases of Reality	1973	5.00	10.00	20.00
❑ STS-5502	Relating	1974	5.00	10.00	20.00

BELLUS, TONY
NRC
❑ LPA-8 [M]	Robbin' the Cradle	1960	50.00	100.00	200.00
-- Blue label					
❑ LPA-8 [M]	Robbin' the Cradle	1960	25.00	50.00	100.00
-- Black label					

BELMONTS, THE
Also see DION; DION AND THE BELMONTS.
BUDDAH
| ❑ BDS-5123 | Cigars, Acapella, Candy | 1972 | 12.50 | 25.00 | 50.00 |

DOT
| ❑ DLP-25949 | Summer Love | 1969 | 7.50 | 15.00 | 30.00 |

SABINA
| ❑ SALP-5001 [M] | The Belmonts' Carnival of Hits | 1962 | 37.50 | 75.00 | 150.00 |

BELVIN, JESSE
CROWN
❑ CLP-5145 [M]	The Casual Jesse Belvin	1959	17.50	35.00	70.00
-- Black label					
❑ CLP-5187 [M]	The Unforgettable Jesse Belvin	1959	17.50	35.00	70.00
-- Black label					

RCA VICTOR
❑ LPM-2089 [M]	Just Jesse Belvin	1959	10.00	20.00	40.00
❑ LSP-2089 [S]	Just Jesse Belvin	1959	15.00	30.00	60.00
❑ LPM-2105 [M]	Mr. Easy	1960	7.50	15.00	30.00
❑ LSP-2105 [S]	Mr. Easy	1960	10.00	20.00	40.00

BENATAR, PAT
MOBILE FIDELITY
| ❑ 1-057 | In the Heat of the Night | 1981 | 6.25 | 12.50 | 25.00 |
| -- Audiophile vinyl | | | | | |

BENAY, BEN
CAPITOL
| ❑ ST 2484 [S] | The Big Blues Harmonica of Ben Benay | 1966 | 6.25 | 12.50 | 25.00 |
| ❑ T 2484 [M] | The Big Blues Harmonica of Ben Benay | 1966 | 5.00 | 10.00 | 20.00 |

BENDIX, WILLIAM
CRICKET
| ❑ CR-30 [M] | William Bendix Sings and Tells Famous Pirate Stories | 1959 | 10.00 | 20.00 | 40.00 |

BENET, VICKI
DECCA
❑ DL 8233 [M]	Woman of Paris	1956	10.00	20.00	40.00
❑ DL 8381 [M]	The French Touch	1957	10.00	20.00	40.00
❑ DL 8987 [M]	Vicki Benet a Paris	1959	7.50	15.00	30.00
❑ DL 78987 [S]	Vicki Benet a Paris	1959	10.00	20.00	40.00

LIBERTY
| ❑ LRP-3103 [M] | Sing to Me of Love | 1960 | 6.25 | 12.50 | 25.00 |
| ❑ LST-7103 [S] | Sing to Me of Love | 1960 | 7.50 | 15.00 | 30.00 |

BENNETT, BOYD
KING
| ❑ 395-594 [M] | Boyd Bennett | 1955 | 1,500. | 2,750. | 4,000. |

BENNETT, CONNIE, WITH BILL SMITH AND THE HARLEM-AIRES
HOLLYWOOD
| ❑ LPH-30 [M] | Rhythm 'N Blues in the Night | 1957 | 125.00 | 250.00 | 500.00 |
| -- Photo of Julie "Catwoman" Newmar on front cover | | | | | |

BENNETT, TONY
COLUMBIA
❑ C2L 23 [(2) M]	Tony Bennett at Carnegie Hall	1962	5.00	10.00	20.00
❑ CL 621 [M]	Cloud Seven	1955	10.00	20.00	40.00
❑ C2S 823 [(2) S]	Tony Bennett at Carnegie Hall	1962	6.25	12.50	25.00
❑ CL 938 [M]	Tony	1956	7.50	15.00	30.00
❑ CL 1079 [M]	The Beat of My Heart	1957	7.50	15.00	30.00
❑ CL 1186 [M]	Long Ago and Far Away	1958	7.50	15.00	30.00
❑ CL 1229 [M]	Tony's Greatest Hits	1958	7.50	15.00	30.00
❑ CL 1292 [M]	Blue Velvet	1958	7.50	15.00	30.00
❑ CL 1294 [M]	Tony Bennett In Person	1959	6.25	12.50	25.00
❑ CL 1301 [M]	Hometown, My Hometown	1959	6.25	12.50	25.00
❑ CL 1429 [M]	To My Wonderful One	1960	6.25	12.50	25.00
❑ CL 1446 [M]	Tony Sings for Two	1960	6.25	12.50	25.00
❑ CL 1471 [M]	Alone Together	1960	6.25	12.50	25.00
❑ CL 1535 [M]	More Tony's Greatest Hits	1961	5.00	10.00	20.00
❑ CL 1559 [M]	A String of Harold Arlen	1961	5.00	10.00	20.00
❑ CL 1658 [M]	My Heart Sings	1961	5.00	10.00	20.00
❑ CL 2507 [10]	Alone at Last with Tony Bennett	1955	15.00	30.00	60.00
❑ CL 2550 [10]	Because of You	1956	15.00	30.00	60.00
❑ CL 6221 [10]	Because of You	1952	20.00	40.00	80.00
❑ CS 8104 [S]	Tony Bennett In Person	1959	10.00	20.00	40.00
❑ CS 8107 [S]	Hometown, My Hometown	1959	10.00	20.00	40.00
❑ CS 8226 [S]	To My Wonderful One	1960	10.00	20.00	40.00
❑ CS 8242 [S]	Tony Sings for Two	1960	10.00	20.00	40.00
❑ CS 8262 [S]	Alone Together	1960	10.00	20.00	40.00
❑ CS 8335 [S]	More Tony's Greatest Hits	1961	6.25	12.50	25.00
❑ CS 8359 [S]	A String of Harold Arlen	1961	6.25	12.50	25.00
❑ CS 8458 [S]	My Heart Sings	1961	6.25	12.50	25.00
❑ CS 8563 [S]	Mr. Broadway	1962	5.00	10.00	20.00
❑ CS 8669 [S]	I Left My Heart in San Francisco	1962	5.00	10.00	20.00
❑ CS 8800 [S]	I Wanna Be Around	1963	6.25	12.50	25.00
❑ CS 8856 [S]	This Is All I Ask	1963	5.00	10.00	20.00
❑ CS 8941 [S]	The Many Moods of Tony	1964	5.00	10.00	20.00
❑ CS 8975 [S]	When Lights Are Low	1964	5.00	10.00	20.00
❑ CS 9085 [S]	Who Can I Turn To	1964	5.00	10.00	20.00

COLUMBIA SPECIAL PRODUCTS
| ❑ CSS 552 [S] | Singer Presents Tony Bennett | 1966 | 5.00 | 10.00 | 20.00 |

BENNETT, TONY, AND COUNT BASIE
ROULETTE
❑ R 25072 [M]	Count Basie Swings/Tony Sings	1961	6.25	12.50	25.00
❑ SR 25072 [S]	Count Basie Swings/Tony Sings	1961	7.50	15.00	30.00
❑ R 25231 [M]	Bennett and Basie Strike Up the Band	1963	5.00	10.00	20.00
❑ SR 25231 [S]	Bennett and Basie Strike Up the Band	1963	6.25	12.50	25.00

BENNETT, TONY, AND BILL EVANS
MOBILE FIDELITY
| ❑ 1-117 | The Tony Bennett/Bill Evans Album | 1981 | 10.00 | 20.00 | 40.00 |
| -- Audiophile vinyl | | | | | |

BENSON, GEORGE
A&M
❑ SP-3014	Shape of Things to Come	1969	5.00	10.00	20.00
-- Brown label					
❑ SP-3020	Tell It Like It Is	1969	5.00	10.00	20.00
-- Brown label					
❑ SP-3028	The Other Side of Abbey Road	1970	6.25	12.50	25.00
-- Brown label					

COLUMBIA
❑ CL 2525 [M]	The Most Exciting New Guitarist on the Jazz Scene Today -- It's Uptown	1966	5.00	10.00	20.00
❑ CL 2613 [M]	The George Benson Cook Book	1967	5.00	10.00	20.00
❑ CS 9325 [S]	The Most Exciting New Guitarist on the Jazz Scene Today -- It's Uptown	1966	5.00	10.00	20.00
-- Red "360 Sound" label					
❑ CS 9413 [S]	The George Benson Cook Book	1967	5.00	10.00	20.00
-- Red "360 Sound" label					

MOBILE FIDELITY
| ❑ 1-011 | Breezin' | 1979 | 15.00 | 30.00 | 60.00 |
| -- Audiophile vinyl | | | | | |

PRESTIGE
| ❑ PRLP-7310 [M] | The New Boss Guitar of George Benson | 1964 | 6.25 | 12.50 | 25.00 |

Number	Title	Yr	VG	VG+	NM
❏ PRST-7310 [S]	The New Boss Guitar of George Benson	1964	7.50	15.00	30.00
VERVE					
❏ V6-8749	Giblet Gravy	1968	5.00	10.00	20.00
❏ V6-8771	Goodies	1969	5.00	10.00	20.00

BENTON, BROOK
EPIC

Number	Title	Yr	VG	VG+	NM
❏ LN 3573 [M]	Brook Benton At His Best	1959	12.50	25.00	50.00
MERCURY					
❏ MG-20421 [M]	It's Just a Matter of Time	1959	10.00	20.00	40.00
❏ MG-20464 [M]	Endlessly	1959	7.50	15.00	30.00
❏ MG-20565 [M]	So Many Ways I Love You	1960	7.50	15.00	30.00
❏ MG-20602 [M]	Songs I Love to Sing	1960	7.50	15.00	30.00
❏ MG-20607 [M]	Golden Hits	1961	5.00	10.00	20.00
❏ MG-20619 [M]	If You Believe	1961	5.00	10.00	20.00
❏ MG-20641 [M]	The Boll Weevil Song and 11 Other Great Hits	1961	5.00	10.00	20.00
❏ MG-20673 [M]	There Goes That Song Again	1962	5.00	10.00	20.00
❏ MG-20740 [M]	Singing the Blues -- Lie to Me	1962	5.00	10.00	20.00
❏ MG-20774 [M]	Golden Hits, Volume 2	1963	5.00	10.00	20.00
❏ MG-20830 [M]	Best Ballads of Broadway	1963	5.00	10.00	20.00
❏ MG-20886 [M]	Born to Sing the Blues	1964	5.00	10.00	20.00
❏ SR-60077 [S]	It's Just a Matter of Time	1959	12.50	25.00	50.00
❏ SR-60146 [S]	Endlessly	1959	10.00	20.00	40.00
❏ SR-60225 [S]	So Many Ways I Love You	1960	10.00	20.00	40.00
❏ SR-60602 [S]	Songs I Love to Sing	1960	10.00	20.00	40.00
❏ SR-60607 [S]	Golden Hits	1961	7.50	15.00	30.00
❏ SR-60619 [S]	If You Believe	1961	7.50	15.00	30.00
❏ SR-60641 [S]	The Boll Weevil Song and 11 Other Great Hits	1961	7.50	15.00	30.00
❏ SR-60673 [S]	There Goes That Song Again	1962	7.50	15.00	30.00
❏ SR-60740 [S]	Singing the Blues -- Lie to Me	1962	7.50	15.00	30.00
❏ SR-60774 [S]	Golden Hits, Volume 2	1963	7.50	15.00	30.00
❏ SR-60830 [S]	Best Ballads of Broadway	1963	6.25	12.50	25.00
❏ SR-60886 [S]	Born to Sing the Blues	1964	6.25	12.50	25.00
❏ SR-60918 [S]	On the Country Side	1964	5.00	10.00	20.00
❏ SR-60934 [S]	This Bitter Earth	1964	5.00	10.00	20.00
RCA VICTOR					
❏ LSP-3514 [S]	That Old Feeling	1966	5.00	10.00	20.00
❏ LSP-3526 [S]	Mother Nature, Father Time	1965	5.00	10.00	20.00
❏ LSP-3590 [S]	My Country	1966	5.00	10.00	20.00
REPRISE					
❏ R-6268 [M]	Laura (What's He Got That I Ain't Got)	1967	5.00	10.00	20.00

BERBERIAN, JOHN, WITH THE ROCK EAST ENSEMBLE
MAINSTREAM

Number	Title	Yr	VG	VG+	NM
❏ S-6123	Impressions East	1969	30.00	60.00	120.00
VERVE FORECAST					
❏ FTS-3073	Middle Eastern Rock	1969	12.50	25.00	50.00

BERG, GERTRUDE
AMY

Number	Title	Yr	VG	VG+	NM
❏ 8007 [M]	How to Be a Jewish Mother	1965	6.25	12.50	25.00

BERGEN, FRANCES
COLUMBIA

Number	Title	Yr	VG	VG+	NM
❏ CL 873 [M]	The Beguiling Miss Bergen	1956	7.50	15.00	30.00

BERGEN, POLLY
COLUMBIA

Number	Title	Yr	VG	VG+	NM
❏ CL 994 [M]	Bergen Sings Morgan	1957	7.50	15.00	30.00
❏ CL 1031 [M]	The Party's Over	1957	7.50	15.00	30.00
❏ CL 1138 [M]	Polly and Her Pop	1958	6.25	12.50	25.00
❏ CL 1218 [M]	My Heart Sings	1959	5.00	10.00	20.00
❏ CL 1300 [M]	All Alone by the Telephone	1959	5.00	10.00	20.00
❏ CL 1481 [M]	Four Seasons of Love	1960	5.00	10.00	20.00
❏ CL 1632 [M]	"Do Re Mi" and "Annie Get Your Gun"	1961	5.00	10.00	20.00
❏ CS 80?? [S]	All Alone by the Telephone	1959	6.25	12.50	25.00
❏ CS 8018 [S]	My Heart Sings	1959	6.25	12.50	25.00
❏ CS 8246 [S]	Four Seasons of Love	1960	6.25	12.50	25.00
❏ CS 8432 [S]	"Do Re Mi" and "Annie Get Your Gun"	1961	6.25	12.50	25.00
JUBILEE					
❏ JGL-14 [10]	Polly Bergen	1955	12.50	25.00	50.00
PHILIPS					
❏ PHS 600-084 [S]	Act One -- Sing, Too	1963	5.00	10.00	20.00

BERLE, MILTON
FORUM

Number	Title	Yr	VG	VG+	NM
❏ F-9005 [M]	Songs My Mother Loved	1963	5.00	10.00	20.00
ROULETTE					
❏ R-25018 [M]	Songs My Mother Loved	1957	10.00	20.00	40.00

BERLIN
ENIGMA

Number	Title	Yr	VG	VG+	NM
❏ 3 [EP]	Pleasure Victim	1982	6.25	12.50	25.00

BERMAN, SHELLEY
VERVE

Number	Title	Yr	VG	VG+	NM
❏ MGV-15003 [M]	Inside Shelley Berman	1959	6.25	12.50	25.00
❏ MGV-15007 [M]	Outside Shelley Berman	1959	6.25	12.50	25.00
❏ MGV-15008-2 [(2) M]	Inside and Outside Shelley Berman	1959	7.50	15.00	30.00
❏ V-15008-2 [(2) M]	Inside and Outside Shelley Berman	1962	5.00	10.00	20.00
❏ MGV-15013 [M]	The Edge of Shelley Berman	1960	6.25	12.50	25.00
❏ MGV-15027 [M]	A Personal Appearance	1961	5.00	10.00	20.00
❏ V-15043 [M]	The Sex Life of the Primate (And Other Bits of Gossip)	1964	5.00	10.00	20.00
❏ V-15048 [M]	Great Moments in Comedy	1965	5.00	10.00	20.00

BERNARD, ROD
JIN

Number	Title	Yr	VG	VG+	NM
❏ LP-4007 [M]	Rod Bernard	196?	15.00	30.00	60.00

BERNARDI, HERSCHEL
COLUMBIA

Number	Title	Yr	VG	VG+	NM
❏ C 30004	Show Stopper	1970	5.00	10.00	20.00
COLUMBIA MASTERWORKS					
❏ OS 3010 [S]	Fiddler on the Roof	1966	6.25	12.50	25.00
❏ OL 6610 [M]	Fiddler on the Roof	1966	5.00	10.00	20.00

BERRY, BROOKS, AND SCRAPPER BLACKWELL
BLUESVILLE

Number	Title	Yr	VG	VG+	NM
❏ BVLP-1074 [M]	My Heart Struck Sorrow	1963	20.00	40.00	80.00
-- Blue label, silver print					
❏ BVLP-1074 [M]	My Heart Struck Sorrow	1964	6.25	12.50	25.00
-- Blue label with trident logo					

BERRY, CHUCK
CHESS

Number	Title	Yr	VG	VG+	NM
❏ LP-1426 [M]	After School Session	1958	50.00	100.00	200.00
❏ LP-1432 [M]	One Dozen Berrys	1958	50.00	100.00	200.00
❏ LP-1435 [M]	Chuck Berry Is On Top	1959	45.00	90.00	180.00
❏ LP-1448 [M]	Rockin' at the Hops	1960	45.00	90.00	180.00
❏ LP-1456 [M]	New Juke Box Hits	1961	45.00	90.00	180.00
❏ LP-1465 [M]	Chuck Berry Twist	1962	25.00	50.00	100.00
❏ LP-1465 [M]	More Chuck Berry	1963	30.00	60.00	120.00
-- Retitled version of above					
❏ LP-1480 [M]	Chuck Berry On Stage	1963	30.00	60.00	120.00
❏ LP-1485 [M]	Chuck Berry's Greatest Hits	1964	30.00	60.00	120.00
❏ LP-1488 [M]	St. Louis to Liverpool	1964	15.00	30.00	60.00
❏ LPS-1488 [S]	St. Louis to Liverpool	1964	20.00	40.00	80.00
❏ LP-1495 [M]	Chuck Berry in London	1965	7.50	15.00	30.00
❏ LPS-1495 [S]	Chuck Berry in London	1965	10.00	20.00	40.00
❏ LP-1498 [M]	Fresh Berry's	1965	7.50	15.00	30.00
❏ LPS-1498 [S]	Fresh Berry's	1965	10.00	20.00	40.00
❏ LP-1514 [(2) M]	Chuck Berry's Golden Decade	1967	10.00	20.00	40.00
❏ LPS-1514 [(2) S]	Chuck Berry's Golden Decade	1967	5.00	10.00	20.00
-- Old cover does not have a pink radio					
❏ LPS-1550	Back Home	1970	5.00	10.00	20.00
❏ CH-50008	San Fransisco Dues	1971	5.00	10.00	20.00
❏ CH-50043	Chuck Berry/Bio	1973	5.00	10.00	20.00
❏ CH-60020	The London Chuck Berry Sessions	1972	5.00	10.00	20.00
❏ 2CH-60023 [(2)]	Chuck Berry's Golden Decade, Vol. 2	1973	6.25	12.50	25.00
❏ 2CH-60028 [(2)]	Chuck Berry's Golden Decade, Vol. 3	1974	6.25	12.50	25.00
❏ CH6-80001 [(6)]	The Chess Box	1989	12.50	25.00	50.00
MERCURY					
❏ SRM-2-6501 [(2)]	St. Louis to Frisco to Memphis	1972	5.00	10.00	20.00
❏ MG-21138 [M]	Love at the Fillmore Auditorium	1967	5.00	10.00	20.00
❏ SR-61138 [S]	Love at the Fillmore Auditorium	1967	5.00	10.00	20.00
❏ SR-61176	From St. Louis to Frisco	1968	5.00	10.00	20.00
❏ SR-61223	Concerto in B Goode	1969	5.00	10.00	20.00

Number	Title	Yr	VG	VG+	NM
BERRY, KEN					
BARNABY					
❏ Z 30014	R.F.D.	1970	6.25	12.50	25.00
❏ Z 30094	Ken Berry, R.F.D.	1970	7.50	15.00	30.00
BERRY, RICHARD					
CROWN					
❏ CST-371 [R]	Richard Berry and the Dreamers	1963	7.50	15.00	30.00
❏ CLP-5371 [M]	Richard Berry and the Dreamers	1963	15.00	30.00	60.00
PAM					
❏ 1001	Live at the Century Restaurant	1968	10.00	20.00	40.00
❏ 1002	Wild Berry	196?	10.00	20.00	40.00
BEST, PETER					
Also see THE BEATLES.					
SAVAGE					
❏ BM-71	Best of the Beatles	1966	50.00	100.00	200.00
-- Authentic copies have white circle around the word "Savage" and white circle around Pete Best's head on the album cover.					
BEVERLY HILL BILLIES, THE					
Also see ELTON BRITT.					
RAR-ARTS					
❏ 1000 [M]	Those Fabulous Beverly Hill Billies	1961	25.00	50.00	100.00
-- Gold vinyl					
BIANCO					
RCA/READER'S DIGEST					
❏ CSP-104 [S]	Joy to the World	1962	5.00	10.00	20.00
BIG BEATS, THE					
LIBERTY					
❏ LRP-3407 [M]	The Big Beats Live	1965	7.50	15.00	30.00
❏ LST-7407 [S]	The Big Beats Live	1965	10.00	20.00	40.00
BIG BOPPER					
MERCURY					
❏ MG-20402 [M]	Chantilly Lace	1959	125.00	250.00	500.00
-- Black label					
❏ MG-20402 [M]	Chantilly Lace	1964	50.00	100.00	200.00
-- Red label with black or black & white Mercury logo at top					
❏ MG-20402 [M]	Chantilly Lace	196?	6.25	12.50	25.00
-- Red label with twelve Mercury logos on label edge					
BIG BOYS					
MOMENT					
❏ 001	Fun, Fun, Fun	1982	10.00	20.00	40.00
❏ 002	Lullabys Help the Brain Go	1983	10.00	20.00	40.00
RADICAL					
❏ RRR 80351	Recorded Live at Raul's	1980	15.00	30.00	60.00
-- One side features the Big Boys; the other side, the Dicks					
WASTED TALENT					
❏ 3405	Industry Standard	1981	10.00	20.00	40.00
BIG BROTHER					
ALL-AMERICAN					
❏ 5770	Big Brother	1970	37.50	75.00	150.00
BIG BROTHER AND THE HOLDING COMPANY					
Also see JANIS JOPLIN.					
COLUMBIA					
❏ KCL 2900 [M]	Cheap Thrills	1968	75.00	150.00	300.00
-- Red label stock copy has been confirmed					
❏ KCS 9700 [M]	Cheap Thrills	1968	25.00	50.00	100.00
-- White label "Special Mono Radio Station Copy" with stereo number					
❏ KCS 9700 [S]	Cheap Thrills	1968	6.25	12.50	25.00
-- Red "360 Sound" label					
❏ C 30222	Be a Brother	1970	5.00	10.00	20.00
❏ C 30631	Big Brother and the Holding Company	1971	5.00	10.00	20.00
-- Reissue of Mainstream LP with two extra tracks					
❏ C 30738	How Hard It Is	1971	5.00	10.00	20.00
MAINSTREAM					
❏ S-6099 [S]	Big Brother and the Holding Company	1967	12.50	25.00	50.00
❏ 56099 [M]	Big Brother and the Holding Company	1967	25.00	50.00	100.00
BIG DADDY					
REGENT					
❏ MG-6106 [M]	Twist Party	1962	17.50	35.00	70.00

Number	Title	Yr	VG	VG+	NM
BIG FOOT					
WINRO					
❏ 1004	Big Foot	1969	7.50	15.00	30.00
BIG MAYBELLE					
BRUNSWICK					
❏ BL 54107 [M]	What More Can a Woman Do	1962	12.50	25.00	50.00
❏ BL 754107 [S]	What More Can a Woman Do	1962	17.50	35.00	70.00
❏ BL 754142	The Gospel Soul of Big Maybelle	1968	10.00	20.00	40.00
EPIC					
❏ EE 22011 [M]	Gabbin' Blues	196?	7.50	15.00	30.00
-- Reissue of Okeh recordings					
PARAMOUNT					
❏ PAS-1011 [(2)]	The Last of Big Maybelle	1973	6.25	12.50	25.00
ROJAC					
❏ RS 123	Saga of the Good Life and Hard Times	196?	10.00	20.00	40.00
❏ R 522 [M]	Got a Brand New Bag	1967	10.00	20.00	40.00
❏ RS 522 [S]	Got a Brand New Bag	1967	10.00	20.00	40.00
SAVOY					
❏ MG-14005 [M]	Big Maybelle Sings	1957	75.00	150.00	300.00
❏ MG-14011 [M]	Blues, Candy and Big Maybelle	1958	75.00	150.00	300.00
SCEPTER					
❏ S-522 [M]	The Soul of Big Maybelle	1964	10.00	20.00	40.00
❏ SS-522 [S]	The Soul of Big Maybelle	1964	12.50	25.00	50.00
BIG STAR					
Leader Alex Chilton also sang with THE BOX TOPS.					
ARDENT					
❏ ADS-1501	Radio City	1974	7.50	15.00	30.00
❏ ADS-2803	#1 Record	1972	6.25	12.50	25.00
PVC					
❏ 7903	Big Star's Third	1978	6.25	12.50	25.00
BIG THREE, THE					
Also see CASS ELLIOT.					
FM					
❏ 307 [M]	The Big Three	1963	7.50	15.00	30.00
❏ S-307 [S]	The Big Three	1963	10.00	20.00	40.00
❏ 311 [M]	Live at the Recording Studio	1964	7.50	15.00	30.00
❏ S-311 [S]	Live at the Recording Studio	1964	10.00	20.00	40.00
ROULETTE					
❏ R-42000 [M]	The Big Three Featuring Cass Elliot	1967	5.00	10.00	20.00
❏ SR-42000 [S]	The Big Three Featuring Cass Elliot	1967	6.25	12.50	25.00
BIGELOW, ARTHUR LYNDS					
COLUMBIA					
❏ CL 750 [M]	Christmas Carillon	1955	6.25	12.50	25.00
BIGGS, E. POWER					
COLUMBIA MASTERWORKS					
❏ MS 6167 [S]	Joyeaux Noel: Twelve Noels by Louis Clark Daquin	1960	5.00	10.00	20.00
BIGGS, RICHARD KEYS					
CAPITOL					
❏ T 9013 [M]	Christmas Bells	1954	5.00	10.00	20.00
COLUMBIA					
❏ CL 6076 [10]	An Organ Concert of Carols	1950	10.00	20.00	40.00
BILK, MR. ACKER					
ATCO					
❏ SD 33-129 [S]	Stranger on the Shore	1961	5.00	10.00	20.00
❏ SD 33-144 [S]	Above the Stars	1962	5.00	10.00	20.00
❏ SD 33-150 [S]	Only You	1963	5.00	10.00	20.00
❏ SD 33-158 [S]	Call Me Mister	1963	5.00	10.00	20.00
REPRISE					
❏ R-6031 [M]	A Stranger No More	1962	5.00	10.00	20.00
BILLION DOLLAR BABIES					
POLYDOR					
❏ PRO 022 [DJ]	Battle Axe	1977	5.00	10.00	20.00
-- Promo-only sampler					
BIRKIN, JANE, AND SERGE GAINSBOURG					
FONTANA					
❏ SRF-67610	Je T'aime	1970	5.00	10.00	20.00

Number	Title	Yr	VG	VG+	NM

BIRTH CONTROL
PROPHESY

Number	Title	Yr	VG	VG+	NM
❑ PRS-1002	Birth Control: A New German Rock Group	1970	7.50	15.00	30.00

BISHOP, ELVIN
FILLMORE

❑ F 30001	Elvin Bishop Group	1969	5.00	10.00	20.00
❑ Z 30239	Feel It	1970	5.00	10.00	20.00

BISHOP, JOEY
ABC

❑ ABCS-656	Joey Bishop Sings Country and Western	1968	7.50	15.00	30.00

BIT 'A SWEET
ABC

❑ S-640	Hypnotic 1	1968	10.00	20.00	40.00

BJOERLING, JUSSI
RCA VICTOR RED SEAL

❑ LSC-2570 [S]	The Incomparable Jussi Bjoerling	1962	5.00	10.00	20.00
-- Original with "shaded dog" label					

BLACK LIGHTNING
TOWER

❑ ST 5129	Shades of Black Lightning	1968	5.00	10.00	20.00

BLACK MERDA
CHESS

❑ LP-1551	Black Merda	1970	12.50	25.00	50.00

BLACK OAK ARKANSAS
ATCO

❑ QD 7019 [Q]	Raunch 'n' Roll/Live	1974	5.00	10.00	20.00

BLACK PEARL
ATLANTIC

❑ SD 8220	Black Pearl	1969	6.25	12.50	25.00
PROPHESY					
❑ PRS-1001	Black Pearl -- Live!	1970	6.25	12.50	25.00

BLACK RANDY AND THE METROSQUAD
DANGERHOUSE

❑ PCP 725	"Pass the Dust, I Think I'm Bowie"	1980	12.50	25.00	50.00

BLACK SABBATH
WARNER BROS.

❑ WS4 1887 [Q]	Paranoid	1974	7.50	15.00	30.00
-- All quad copies have "Burbank" palm trees label					
❑ 2BS 2923 [(2)]	We Sold Our Souls for Rock 'N' Roll	1975	5.00	10.00	20.00
-- "Burbank" palm trees label					

BLACK SHEEP
CAPITOL

❑ ST-11369	Black Sheep	1974	5.00	10.00	20.00
❑ ST-11447	Encouraging Words	1975	5.00	10.00	20.00

BLACK VELVET
OKEH

❑ OKS 14130	Love City	1969	5.00	10.00	20.00

BLACK, BILL, 'S COMBO
HI

❑ HL-12001 [M]	Smokie	1960	15.00	30.00	60.00
-- Black label with red and silver logo					
❑ HL-12001 [M]	Smokie	1960	10.00	20.00	40.00
-- Orange and white label					
❑ HL-12002 [M]	Saxy Jazz	1960	10.00	20.00	40.00
❑ HL-12003 [M]	Solid and Raunchy	1960	10.00	20.00	40.00
❑ HL-12004 [M]	That Wonderful Feeling	1961	5.00	10.00	20.00
❑ HL-12005 [M]	Movin'	1961	5.00	10.00	20.00
❑ HL-12006 [M]	Bill Black's Record Hop	1961	6.25	12.50	25.00
❑ SHL-32001 [R]	Smokie	1964	5.00	10.00	20.00
❑ SHL-32002 [R]	Saxy Jazz	1964	5.00	10.00	20.00
❑ SHL-32003 [R]	Solid and Raunchy	1964	5.00	10.00	20.00
❑ SHL-32004 [S]	That Wonderful Feeling	1961	6.25	12.50	25.00
❑ SHL-32005 [S]	Movin'	1961	6.25	12.50	25.00
❑ SHL-32006 [S]	Bill Black's Record Hop	1961	7.50	15.00	30.00
❑ SHL-32006 [S]	Let's Twist Her	1961	5.00	10.00	20.00
-- Retitled version of above					
❑ SHL-32009 [S]	The Untouchable Sound of Bill Black	1962	5.00	10.00	20.00
❑ SHL-32012 [S]	Bill Black's Greatest Hits	1963	5.00	10.00	20.00
❑ SHL-32013 [S]	Bill Black's Combo Goes West	1963	5.00	10.00	20.00
❑ SHL-32015 [S]	Bill Black Plays the Blues	1964	5.00	10.00	20.00
❑ SHL-32017 [S]	Bill Black Plays Tunes by Chuck Berry	1964	5.00	10.00	20.00
❑ SHL-32020 [S]	Bill Black's Combo Goes Big Band	1964	5.00	10.00	20.00
❑ SHL-32023 [S]	More Solid and Raunchy	1965	5.00	10.00	20.00
❑ SHL-32027 [S]	Mr. Beat	1965	5.00	10.00	20.00

BLACK, CILLA
CAPITOL

❑ ST 2308 [S]	Is It Love?	1965	10.00	20.00	40.00
❑ T 2308 [M]	Is It Love?	1965	6.25	12.50	25.00

BLACK, CLINT
RCA

❑ R 124690	Put Yourself in My Place	1990	5.00	10.00	20.00
-- Released on vinyl only through BMG Direct Marketing					

BLACK, JEANNE
CAPITOL

❑ ST 1513 [S]	A Little Bit Lonely	1961	6.25	12.50	25.00
❑ T 1513 [M]	A Little Bit Lonely	1961	5.00	10.00	20.00

BLACKBYRDS, THE
FANTASY

❑ FPM-4004 [Q]	Flying Start	1975	6.25	12.50	25.00

BLACKFOOT, J.D.
FANTASY

❑ F-9468	Song of Crazy Horse	1974	5.00	10.00	20.00
❑ F-9487	Southbound and Gone	1975	5.00	10.00	20.00
MERCURY					
❑ SR-61288	The Ultimate Prophecy	1970	15.00	30.00	60.00

BLACKHORSE
DSDA

❑ 001	Blackhorse	1979	15.00	30.00	60.00

BLACKMAN, HONOR
LONDON

❑ PS 408 [S]	Everything I've Got	1964	10.00	20.00	40.00
❑ LL 3408 [M]	Everything I've Got	1964	7.50	15.00	30.00

BLACKWELL, OTIS
DAVIS

❑ 109 [M]	Singin' the Blues	1956	125.00	250.00	500.00
INNER CITY					
❑ 1032	These Are My Songs	1977	5.00	10.00	20.00

BLACKWELL, SCRAPPER
BLUESVILLE

❑ BVLP-1047	Mr. Scrapper's Blues	1962	45.00	90.00	180.00
-- Blue label, silver print					
❑ BVLP-1047	Mr. Scrapper's Blues	1964	10.00	20.00	40.00
-- Blue label with trident logo					

BLADES, JIMMY, AND CHARLES SMART
LONDON

❑ LB 82 [10]	Christmas Chimes	195?	10.00	20.00	40.00
-- Back cover with liner notes and no reference to other LPs					
❑ LB 82 [10]	Christmas Chimes	195?	7.50	15.00	30.00
-- Back cover with liner notes and other Christmas LPs mentioned					

BLAINE, HAL
ABC DUNHILL

❑ DS-50035	Have Fun!!! Play Drums!!!	1968	12.50	25.00	50.00
-- With instruction booklet					
❑ DS-50035	Have Fun!!! Play Drums!!!	1968	10.00	20.00	40.00
-- Without instruction booklet					
DUNHILL					
❑ D-50002 [M]	Drums! Drums! A-Go-Go	1966	7.50	15.00	30.00
❑ DS-50002 [S]	Drums! Drums! A-Go-Go	1966	10.00	20.00	40.00
❑ D-50019 [M]	Psychedelic Percussion	1967	10.00	20.00	40.00
❑ DS-50019 [S]	Psychedelic Percussion	1967	15.00	30.00	60.00

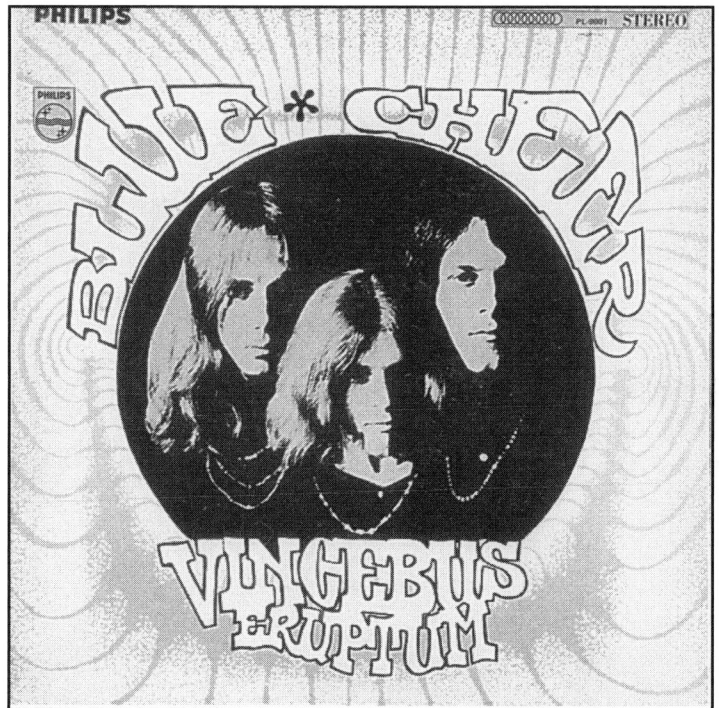

Top left) The Big Bopper is usually thought of as a one-hit wonder. But he did record an entire album. Not only that, it actually came back into print – on vinyl, no less – in the late 1980s! (Top right) Blind Faith's only album was the subject of controversy here in the States. The pictured "nude girl" cover was not acceptable to most retailers, so it was replaced by a cover with the band's photo on the front and the album's lyrics on the back. The back cover of the "nude girl" version has the same background but no girl.

(Bottom left) Blue Cheer is regarded as one of the first heavy-metal bands, mostly on the reputation of their hard version of "Summertime Blues." This is their debut album, which is more highly sought after in mono than the pictured stereo. (Bottom right) The Blues Project was an underappreciated mid-1960s band; two of its members, Steve Katz and Al Kooper, became charter members of Blood, Sweat and Tears.

Number	Title	Yr	VG	VG+	NM

RCA VICTOR
- ❏ LPM-2834 [M]   Deuces, "T's," Roadsters & Drums   1963   25.00   50.00   100.00
- ❏ LSP-2834 [S]   Deuces, "T's," Roadsters & Drums   1963   37.50   75.00   150.00

BLAKE BABIES
Juliana Hatfield was in this group. None of her solo albums exist on US vinyl.
CHEWBUD
- ❏ 001   Nicely, Nicely   1987   10.00   20.00   40.00

BLANC, MEL
CAPITOL
- ❏ H-436 [10]   Party Panic   1953   25.00   50.00   100.00

BLAND, BOBBY
ABC DUKE
- ❏ DLP 92-2 [(2)]   Introspective of the Early Years   1974   5.00   10.00   20.00
DUKE
- ❏ DLP-74 [M]   Two Steps from the Blues   1961   62.50   125.00   250.00
  -- *Purple and yellow label*
- ❏ DLP-74 [M]   Two Steps from the Blues   1962   62.50   125.00   250.00
  -- *Orange label, red vinyl*
- ❏ DLP-74 [M]   Two Steps from the Blues   1962   25.00   50.00   100.00
  -- *Orange label, black vinyl*
- ❏ DLPS-74 [R]   Two Steps from the Blues   196?   15.00   30.00   60.00
- ❏ DLP-75 [M]   Here's the Man!!!   1962   50.00   100.00   200.00
  -- *Purple and yellow label*
- ❏ DLP-75 [M]   Here's the Man!!!   1962   25.00   50.00   100.00
  -- *Orange label*
- ❏ DLPS-75 [S]   Here's the Man!!!   1962   50.00   100.00   200.00
  -- *With spoken intro to "36-22-36"*
- ❏ DLPS-75 [S]   Here's the Man!!!   196?   25.00   50.00   100.00
  -- *Without spoken intro to "36-22-36"*
- ❏ DLP-77 [M]   Call On Me/That's the Way Love Is   1963   25.00   50.00   100.00
- ❏ DLPS-77 [S]   Call On Me/That's the Way Love Is   1963   37.50   75.00   150.00
- ❏ DLP-78 [M]   Ain't Nothing You Can Do   1964   20.00   40.00   80.00
- ❏ DLPS-78 [S]   Ain't Nothing You Can Do   1964   30.00   60.00   120.00
- ❏ DLP-79 [M]   The Soul of the Man   1966   20.00   40.00   80.00
- ❏ DLPS-79 [S]   The Soul of the Man   1966   30.00   60.00   120.00
- ❏ DLP-84 [M]   The Best of Bobby Bland   1967   5.00   10.00   20.00
- ❏ DLPS-84 [P]   The Best of Bobby Bland   1967   6.25   12.50   25.00
- ❏ DLP-86 [M]   The Best of Bobby Bland, Volume 2   1968   6.25   12.50   25.00
- ❏ DLPS-86 [P]   The Best of Bobby Bland, Volume 2   1968   5.00   10.00   20.00
- ❏ DLP-88 [M]   A Touch of the Blues   1968   6.25   12.50   25.00
- ❏ DLPS-88 [S]   A Touch of the Blues   1968   5.00   10.00   20.00
- ❏ DLPS-89   Spotlighting the Man   1969   5.00   10.00   20.00
- ❏ DLPS-90   If Loving You Is Wrong   1970   5.00   10.00   20.00

BLAND, BOBBY, AND B.B. KING
Also see each artist's individual listings.
COMMAND
- ❏ CQDY-40012   Together for the First Time...Live   1974   6.25   12.50   25.00
  [(2) Q]

BLASSIE, FRED
RHINO
- ❏ RNLP-813 [PD]   I Bite the Songs   1985   5.00   10.00   20.00

BLASTERS, THE
The Crown group is not the same as the others.
CROWN
- ❏ CST-392 [S]   Sounds of the Drags   1963   6.25   12.50   25.00
- ❏ CLP-5392 [M]   Sounds of the Drags   1963   5.00   10.00   20.00
ROLLIN' ROCK
- ❏ 021   American Music   1980   12.50   25.00   50.00
WARNER BROS.
- ❏ WBMS-130 [DJ]   The Warner Bros. Music Show   1985   5.00   10.00   20.00
  -- *One side: The Blasters; the other side: The Smiths*

BLESSED END
TNS
- ❏ 248   Movin' On   1971   75.00   150.00   300.00

BLEYER, ARCHIE
CADENCE
- ❏ CLP-3044 [M]   Moonlight Serenade   1962   5.00   10.00   20.00
- ❏ CLP-25044 [S]   Moonlight Serenade   1962   6.25   12.50   25.00

BLIND FAITH
Also see ERIC CLAPTON; STEVE WINWOOD.
ATCO
- ❏ 33-304A [M]   Blind Faith   1969   50.00   100.00   200.00
  -- *White label promo only*
- ❏ SD 33-304A [S]   Blind Faith   1969   6.25   12.50   25.00
  -- *Cover with naked girl on Side 1 and same scene without girl on Side 2*
MOBILE FIDELITY
- ❏ 1-186   Blind Faith   1985   10.00   20.00   40.00
  -- *Audiophile vinyl*

BLOCKER, DAN
Also see LORNE GREENE, MICHAEL LANDON AND DAN BLOCKER.
TREY
- ❏ TLP-903 [M]   Tales for Young 'Uns   1961   12.50   25.00   50.00

BLOCKER, DAN, AND JOHN MITCHUM
RCA VICTOR
- ❏ LPM-2896 [M]   Our Land -- Our Heritage   1964   7.50   15.00   30.00
- ❏ LSP-2896 [S]   Our Land -- Our Heritage   1964   10.00   20.00   40.00

BLOND
FONTANA
- ❏ SRF-67067   Blond   1969   5.00   10.00   20.00

BLONDE ON BLONDE
JANUS
- ❏ JLP-3003   Contrasts   1969   6.25   12.50   25.00

BLONDIE
CHRYSALIS
- ❏ CHS 24 PDJ [DJ]   At Home with Debbie Harry and Chris Stein   1981   12.50   25.00   50.00
  -- *Open-end interview with script*
- ❏ CHP 5001 [PD]   Parallel Lines   1979   6.25   12.50   25.00
  -- *Picture disc*
MOBILE FIDELITY
- ❏ 1-050   Parallel Lines   1980   7.50   15.00   30.00
  -- *Audiophile vinyl*
PRIVATE STOCK
- ❏ PS-2023   Blondie   1976   6.25   12.50   25.00

BLOOD, SWEAT AND TEARS
COLUMBIA
- ❏ CQ 30994 [Q]   Blood, Sweat and Tears   1972   5.00   10.00   20.00
- ❏ CQ 31170 [Q]   Blood, Sweat and Tears' Greatest Hits   1972   5.00   10.00   20.00
- ❏ CQ 32929 [Q]   Mirror Image   1974   5.00   10.00   20.00
- ❏ HC 49619   Child Is Father to the Man   1981   20.00   40.00   80.00
  -- *Half-speed mastered edition*
DIRECT DISK
- ❏ SD-16605   Blood, Sweat and Tears   1981   15.00   30.00   60.00
MOBILE FIDELITY
- ❏ 1-251   Blood, Sweat and Tears   1996   30.00   60.00   120.00
  -- *Audiophile vinyl; fewer than 2,000 pressed*

BLOODROCK
CAPITOL
- ❏ SVBB-11038 [(2)]   Bloodrock Live   1972   5.00   10.00   20.00

BLOODY MARY
FAMILY PRODUCTIONS
- ❏ FPS-2707   Bloody Mary   1972   6.25   12.50   25.00

BLOOMFIELD, MIKE, AND AL KOOPER
Also see AL KOOPER.
COLUMBIA
- ❏ KGP 6 [(2)]   The Live Adventures of Mike Bloomfield & Al Kooper   1969   6.25   12.50   25.00
  -- *Red "360 Sound" labels*

BLOOMFIELD, MIKE/AL KOOPER/STEVE STILLS
COLUMBIA
- ❏ CS 9701   Super Session   1968   5.00   10.00   20.00
  -- *Red "360 Sound" label*
- ❏ CQ 30991 [Q]   Super Session   1971   5.00   10.00   20.00

Number	Title	Yr	VG	VG+	NM
MOBILE FIDELITY					
❑ 1-178	Super Session	198?	10.00	20.00	40.00
-- Audiophile vinyl					
BLUE ANGEL					
With Cyndi Lauper on lead vocals.					
POLYDOR					
❑ PD1-6300	Blue Angel	1980	5.00	10.00	20.00
BLUE BARONS, THE					
PHILIPS					
❑ PHM 200-017 [M]	Twist to the Great Blues Hits	1962	5.00	10.00	20.00
❑ PHS 600-017 [S]	Twist to the Great Blues Hits	1962	6.25	12.50	25.00
BLUE BEATS, THE					
A.A.					
❑ 133 [M]	The Beatle Beat	1964	10.00	20.00	40.00
BLUE BOYS, THE					
RCA VICTOR					
❑ LPM-3331 [M]	We Remember Jim	1965	6.25	12.50	25.00
❑ LSP-3331 [S]	We Remember Jim	1965	7.50	15.00	30.00
❑ LPM-3529 [M]	Sounds of Jim Reeves	1966	5.00	10.00	20.00
❑ LSP-3529 [S]	Sounds of Jim Reeves	1966	6.25	12.50	25.00
❑ LPM-3696 [M]	The Blue Boys in Person	1967	5.00	10.00	20.00
❑ LSP-3696 [S]	The Blue Boys in Person	1967	6.25	12.50	25.00
❑ LPM-3794 [M]	Hit After Hit	1967	6.25	12.50	25.00
❑ LSP-3794 [S]	Hit After Hit	1967	5.00	10.00	20.00
BLUE CHEER					
PHILIPS					
❑ PHM 200-264 [M]	Vincebus Eruptum	1968	20.00	40.00	80.00
❑ PHS 600-264 [S]	Vincebus Eruptum	1968	10.00	20.00	40.00
❑ PHS 600-278	Outsideinside	1968	10.00	20.00	40.00
❑ PHS 600-305	New! Improved! Blue Cheer	1969	10.00	20.00	40.00
❑ PHS 600-333	Blue Cheer	1970	10.00	20.00	40.00
❑ PHS 600-347	The Original Human Being	1970	10.00	20.00	40.00
❑ PHS 600-350	Oh! Pleasant Hope	1971	10.00	20.00	40.00
BLUE DIAMONDS, THE					
LONDON					
❑ LL 3235 [M]	Ramona1	1963	6.25	12.50	25.00
BLUE JAYS, THE					
MILESTONE					
❑ 1001 [M]	The Blue Jays Meet Little Caesar and the Romans	1962	25.00	50.00	100.00
BLUE OYSTER CULT					
COLUMBIA					
❑ CQ 32017 [Q]	Tyranny and Mutation	1973	7.50	15.00	30.00
❑ CQ 32858 [Q]	Secret Treaties	1974	7.50	15.00	30.00
BLUE RIDGE MOUNTAIN BOYS, THE					
TIME					
❑ ST-2083 [S]	Hootenanny and Bluegrass	1963	5.00	10.00	20.00
❑ ST-2103 [S]	Bluegrass Down Home	1963	5.00	10.00	20.00
BLUE SKY BOYS, THE					
CAPITOL					
❑ ST 2483 [S]	Presenting the Blue Sky Boys	1966	6.25	12.50	25.00
❑ T 2483 [M]	Presenting the Blue Sky Boys	1966	5.00	10.00	20.00
RCA CAMDEN					
❑ CAL-797 [M]	The Blue Sky Boys	1963	5.00	10.00	20.00
STARDAY					
❑ SLP-205 [M]	Rare Treasury of Old Song Gems	1962	10.00	20.00	40.00
❑ SLP-257 [M]	Together Again	1963	10.00	20.00	40.00
❑ SLP-269 [M]	The Blue Sky Boys	1964	10.00	20.00	40.00
BLUE THINGS, THE					
RCA VICTOR					
❑ LPM-3603 [M]	The Blue Things	1966	30.00	60.00	120.00
❑ LSP-3603 [S]	The Blue Things	1966	45.00	90.00	180.00
BLUE VELVET BAND, THE					
WARNER BROS.					
❑ WS 1802	Sweet Moments	1969	7.50	15.00	30.00

Number	Title	Yr	VG	VG+	NM
BLUE, DAVID					
ELEKTRA					
❑ EKM-4003 [M]	David Blue	1966	5.00	10.00	20.00
❑ EKS-74003 [S]	David Blue	1966	5.00	10.00	20.00
BLUEGRASS HOPPERS, THE					
CUCA					
❑ 1160	The Country's Come to Town	196?	6.25	12.50	25.00
BLUES CLIMAX					
HORNE					
❑ JC-333	Blues Climax	1969	15.00	30.00	60.00
BLUES IMAGE					
ATCO					
❑ SD 33-300	Blues Image	1969	6.25	12.50	25.00
❑ SD 33-317	Open	1970	5.00	10.00	20.00
❑ SD 33-346	Red, White and Blues Image	1971	5.00	10.00	20.00
BLUES MAGOOS					
ABC					
❑ S-697	Never Goin' Back to Georgia	1969	5.00	10.00	20.00
❑ S-710	Gulf Coast Bound	1970	5.00	10.00	20.00
MERCURY					
❑ MG-21096 [M]	Psychedelic Lollipop	1966	10.00	20.00	40.00
❑ MG-21104 [M]	Electric Comic Book	1967	7.50	15.00	30.00
❑ 21104/61104	Electric Comic Book Comic Book	1967	3.75	7.50	15.00
❑ SR-61096 [S]	Psychedelic Lollipop	1966	12.50	25.00	50.00
❑ SR-61104 [S]	Electric Comic Book	1967	10.00	20.00	40.00
❑ SR-61167	Basic Blues Magoos	1968	7.50	15.00	30.00
BLUES PROJECT, THE					
SOUNDS OF THE SOUTH					
❑ MCA2-8003 [(2)]	Reunion in Central Park	1973	5.00	10.00	20.00
-- Yellow labels					
VERVE FOLKWAYS					
❑ FT-3000 [M]	Live at the Café a Go Go	1966	5.00	10.00	20.00
❑ FTS-3000 [S]	Live at the Café a Go Go	1966	6.25	12.50	25.00
❑ FT-3008 [M]	Projections	1966	5.00	10.00	20.00
❑ FTS-3008 [S]	Projections	1966	6.25	12.50	25.00
VERVE FORECAST					
❑ FTS-3000 [S]	Live at the Café a Go Go	1967	5.00	10.00	20.00
-- Reissue of Verve Folkways 3000					
❑ FTS-3008 [S]	Projections	1967	5.00	10.00	20.00
-- Reissue of Verve Folkways 3008					
❑ FT-3025 [M]	The Blues Project Live at Town Hall	1967	5.00	10.00	20.00
BLYTH, ANN					
EVEREST					
❑ SDBR-1113 [S]	Hail Mary	1960	10.00	20.00	40.00
❑ LPBR-5113 [M]	Hail Mary	1960	7.50	15.00	30.00
BLYTHE, STERLING					
CROWN					
❑ CLP-5179 [M]	Sterling Blythe Sings	1963	5.00	10.00	20.00
SAGE & SAND					
❑ C-14 [M]	A Night at the Showboat	196?	6.25	12.50	25.00
-- Red vinyl; label print is multi-colored					
❑ C-14 [M]	A Night at the Showboat	1962	10.00	20.00	40.00
-- Red vinyl; label print is red and black					
BO GRUMPUS					
ATCO					
❑ 33-246 [M]	Bo Grumpus	1968	7.50	15.00	30.00
❑ SD 33-246 [S]	Bo Grumpus	1968	5.00	10.00	20.00
BOA					
SNAKEFIELD					
❑ SN-001	Wrong Road	1969	62.50	125.00	250.00
BOB AND EARL					
CRESTVIEW					
❑ CRS-3055	Bob & Earl	1969	6.25	12.50	25.00
TIP					
❑ TLP-1011 [M]	Harlem Shuffle	1964	7.50	15.00	30.00
❑ TLS-9011 [S]	Harlem Shuffle	1964	12.50	25.00	50.00

Number	Title	Yr	VG	VG+	NM

BOB AND RAY
RCA VICTOR
Number	Title	Yr	VG	VG+	NM
❏ LPM-1773 [M]	Bob and Ray Throw a Stereo Spectacular	1958	7.50	15.00	30.00
❏ LSP-1773 [S]	Bob and Ray Throw a Stereo Spectacular	1958	30.00	60.00	120.00
❏ LPM-2131 [M]	Bob and Ray on a Platter	1960	7.50	15.00	30.00
❏ LSP-2131 [S]	Bob and Ray on a Platter	1960	12.50	25.00	50.00

RCA VICTOR/CLASSIC
Number	Title	Yr	VG	VG+	NM
❏ LSP-1773 [S]	Bob and Ray Throw a Stereo Spectacular	199?	6.25	12.50	25.00

-- Audiophile vinyl

UNICORN
Number	Title	Yr	VG	VG+	NM
❏ UN 1001 [10]	Write If You Get Work	1954	15.00	30.00	60.00

BOB B. SOXX AND THE BLUE JEANS
PHILLIES
Number	Title	Yr	VG	VG+	NM
❏ PHLP-4002 [M]	Zip-a-Dee Doo-Dah	1963	125.00	250.00	500.00

BOBO, WILLIE
ROULETTE
Number	Title	Yr	VG	VG+	NM
❏ R-52097 [M]	Bobo's Beat	1962	6.25	12.50	25.00
❏ SR-52097 [S]	Bobo's Beat	1962	7.50	15.00	30.00

TICO
Number	Title	Yr	VG	VG+	NM
❏ ST-1108 [S]	Do That Thing	1963	7.50	15.00	30.00
❏ T-1108 [M]	Do That Thing	1963	6.25	12.50	25.00

VERVE
Number	Title	Yr	VG	VG+	NM
❏ V6-8631 [S]	Spanish Grease	1965	5.00	10.00	20.00
❏ V6-8648 [S]	Uno, Dos, Tres	1966	5.00	10.00	20.00
❏ V6-8669 [S]	Feelin' So Good	1966	5.00	10.00	20.00
❏ V-8685 [M]	Juicy	1967	5.00	10.00	20.00
❏ V6-8685 [S]	Juicy	1967	5.00	10.00	20.00
❏ V-8699 [M]	Bobo Motion	1967	5.00	10.00	20.00
❏ V6-8699 [S]	Bobo Motion	1967	5.00	10.00	20.00
❏ V6-8736	Spanish Blues Band	1968	5.00	10.00	20.00

BOETCHER, CURT
ELEKTRA
Number	Title	Yr	VG	VG+	NM
❏ EKS-75037	There's an Innocent Face	1972	5.00	10.00	20.00

BOFFALONGO
UNITED ARTISTS
Number	Title	Yr	VG	VG+	NM
❏ UAS-6726	Boffalongo	1969	5.00	10.00	20.00
❏ UAS-6770	Beyond Your Head	1970	5.00	10.00	20.00

BOGARDE, DIRK
LONDON
Number	Title	Yr	VG	VG+	NM
❏ PS 210 [S]	Lyrics for Lovers	1960	7.50	15.00	30.00
❏ LL 3187 [M]	Lyrics for Lovers	1960	6.25	12.50	25.00

BOHEMIAN VENDETTA
MAINSTREAM
Number	Title	Yr	VG	VG+	NM
❏ S-6106 [S]	Bohemian Vendetta	1968	50.00	100.00	200.00
❏ 56106 [M]	Bohemian Vendetta	1968	30.00	60.00	120.00

BOLDER DAMN
HIT
Number	Title	Yr	VG	VG+	NM
❏ HRI-5061	Mourning	1971	250.00	500.00	1,000.

BOLGER, RAY
DISNEYLAND
Number	Title	Yr	VG	VG+	NM
❏ ST-3930 [M]	The Story of the Scarecrow of Oz	1965	7.50	15.00	30.00

BOLIN, TOMMY
GEFFEN
Number	Title	Yr	VG	VG+	NM
❏ 3GHS 24248 [(3)]	The Ultimate Tommy Bolin	1989	7.50	15.00	30.00

BOLOTIN, MICHAEL
Later recorded as Michael Bolton.
RCA VICTOR
Number	Title	Yr	VG	VG+	NM
❏ APL1-0992	Michael Bolotin	1975	5.00	10.00	20.00
❏ APL1-1551	Every Day of My Life	1976	5.00	10.00	20.00

BONADUCE, DANNY
LION
Number	Title	Yr	VG	VG+	NM
❏ LN-1015	Danny Bonaduce	1973	15.00	30.00	60.00

BOND, EDDIE
PHILLIPS INT'L.
Number	Title	Yr	VG	VG+	NM
❏ PLP-1980 [M]	The Greatest Country Gospel Hits	1961	100.00	200.00	400.00

BOND, GRAHAM
MERCURY
Number	Title	Yr	VG	VG+	NM
❏ SRM-1-612	We Put Our Magick on You	1971	5.00	10.00	20.00
❏ SR-61327	Holy Magick	1970	5.00	10.00	20.00

PULSAR
Number	Title	Yr	VG	VG+	NM
❏ 10604	Love Is the Law	1969	6.25	12.50	25.00
❏ 10606	Mighty Graham Bond	1969	6.25	12.50	25.00

WARNER BROS.
Number	Title	Yr	VG	VG+	NM
❏ 2LS 2555 [(2)]	Solid Bond	1971	5.00	10.00	20.00

BOND, JOHNNY
HARMONY
Number	Title	Yr	VG	VG+	NM
❏ HL 7308 [M]	Johnny Bond's Best	1964	5.00	10.00	20.00
❏ HL 7353 [M]	Bottled in Bond	1965	5.00	10.00	20.00

STARDAY
Number	Title	Yr	VG	VG+	NM
❏ SLP-147 [M]	That Wild, Wicked But Wonderful West	1961	12.50	25.00	50.00
❏ SLP-227 [M]	Songs That Made Him Famous	1963	10.00	20.00	40.00
❏ SLP-298 [M]	Hot Rod Lincoln	1964	12.50	25.00	50.00
❏ 333 [M]	Ten Little Bottles	1965	10.00	20.00	40.00
❏ SLP-333 [S]	Ten Little Bottles	1965	7.50	15.00	30.00
❏ 354 [M]	Famous Hot Rodders I Have Known	1965	20.00	40.00	80.00
❏ SLP-354 [S]	Famous Hot Rodders I Have Known	1965	10.00	20.00	40.00
❏ 368 [M]	The Man Who Comes Around	1966	5.00	10.00	20.00
❏ SLP-368 [S]	The Man Who Comes Around	1966	6.25	12.50	25.00
❏ 378 [M]	Bottles Up	1966	5.00	10.00	20.00
❏ SLP-378 [S]	Bottles Up	1966	6.25	12.50	25.00
❏ SLP-388 [S]	The Branded Stock of Johnny Bond	1966	5.00	10.00	20.00
❏ SLP-402 [S]	Ten Nights in a Barroom	1967	5.00	10.00	20.00

BONDS, GARY U.S.
LEGRAND
Number	Title	Yr	VG	VG+	NM
❏ LLP-3001 [M]	Dance 'Til Quarter to Three	1961	25.00	50.00	100.00
❏ LLP-3002 [M]	Twist Up Calypso	1962	17.50	35.00	70.00
❏ LLP-3003 [M]	Greatest Hits of Gary U.S. Bonds	1962	17.50	35.00	70.00

BONFIRE, MARS
UNI
Number	Title	Yr	VG	VG+	NM
❏ 73027	Mars Bonfire	1968	5.00	10.00	20.00

BONNEVILLES, THE
Two different groups.
DRUM BOY
Number	Title	Yr	VG	VG+	NM
❏ DLM-1001 [M]	Meet the Bonnevilles	1963	25.00	50.00	100.00
❏ DLS-1001 [S]	Meet the Bonnevilles	1963	37.50	75.00	150.00

JUSTICE
Number	Title	Yr	VG	VG+	NM
❏ JLP-146	Bringing It Home	196?	125.00	250.00	500.00

BONNIE LOU
KING
Number	Title	Yr	VG	VG+	NM
❏ 595 [M]	Bonnie Lou Sings	1958	35.00	70.00	140.00

BONNIWELL, T.S.
Also see THE MUSIC MACHINE.
CAPITOL
Number	Title	Yr	VG	VG+	NM
❏ ST-377	Close	1969	5.00	10.00	20.00

BONZO DOG BAND, THE
IMPERIAL
Number	Title	Yr	VG	VG+	NM
❏ LP 9370 [M]	Gorilla	1968	7.50	15.00	30.00
-- With booklet					
❏ LP 9370 [M]	Gorilla	1968	5.00	10.00	20.00
-- Without booklet					
❏ LP 12370 [S]	Gorilla	1968	7.50	15.00	30.00
-- With booklet					
❏ LP 12370 [S]	Gorilla	1968	5.00	10.00	20.00
-- Without booklet					
❏ LP 12432	Urban Spaceman	1968	7.50	15.00	30.00
-- With booklet					
❏ LP 12432	Urban Spaceman	1968	5.00	10.00	20.00
-- Without booklet					
❏ LP 12445	Tadpoles	1969	5.00	10.00	20.00
❏ LP 12457	Keynsham	1969	5.00	10.00	20.00

Number	Title	Yr	VG	VG+	NM

BOOGIE KINGS, THE
MONTEL
| ❏ LP-104 [M] | The Boogie Kings | 1966 | 6.25 | 12.50 | 25.00 |
| ❏ LP-109 [M] | Blue Eyed Soul | 1967 | 6.25 | 12.50 | 25.00 |

BOOKER T. AND THE MG'S
ATLANTIC
| ❏ SD 8202 | The Best of Booker T. and the MG's | 1968 | 5.00 | 10.00 | 20.00 |

STAX
❏ ST-701 [M]	Green Onions	1962	17.50	35.00	70.00
❏ STS-701 [R]	Green Onions	1966	12.50	25.00	50.00
❏ ST-705 [M]	Soul Dressing	1965	17.50	35.00	70.00
❏ STS-705 [R]	Soul Dressing	1966	12.50	25.00	50.00
❏ ST-711 [M]	And Now...Booker T. and the MG's	1966	12.50	25.00	50.00
❏ STS-711 [S]	And Now...Booker T. and the MG's	1966	20.00	40.00	80.00
❏ ST-713 [M]	In the Christmas Spirit	1966	100.00	200.00	400.00
-- Fingers and piano keys cover					
❏ ST-713 [M]	In the Christmas Spirit	1967	50.00	100.00	200.00
-- Santa Claus cover					
❏ STS-713 [S]	In the Christmas Spirit	1966	100.00	200.00	400.00
-- Fingers and piano keys cover					
❏ STS-713 [S]	In the Christmas Spirit	1967	50.00	100.00	200.00
-- Santa Claus cover					
❏ ST-717 [M]	Hip Hug-Her	1967	10.00	20.00	40.00
❏ STS-717 [S]	Hip Hug-Her	1967	12.50	25.00	50.00
❏ STS-724	Doin' Our Thing	1968	12.50	25.00	50.00
❏ STS-2001	Soul Limbo	1968	6.25	12.50	25.00
❏ STS-2006	Uptight	1969	6.25	12.50	25.00
❏ STS-2009	The Booker T. Set	1969	6.25	12.50	25.00
❏ STS-2027	McLemore Avenue	1970	6.25	12.50	25.00

BOOMERANG
RCA VICTOR
| ❏ LSP-4577 | Boomerang | 1971 | 5.00 | 10.00 | 20.00 |

BOONE, PAT
DOT
❏ DLP-3012 [M]	Pat Boone	1956	12.50	25.00	50.00
-- Maroon label					
❏ DLP-3012 [M]	Pat Boone	1957	6.25	12.50	25.00
-- Black label					
❏ DLP-3030 [M]	Howdy!	1956	12.50	25.00	50.00
-- Maroon label					
❏ DLP-3030 [M]	Howdy!	1957	6.25	12.50	25.00
-- Black label					
❏ DLP-3050 [M]	Pat	1957	6.25	12.50	25.00
❏ DLP-3068 [M]	Hymns We Love	1957	6.25	12.50	25.00
❏ DLP-3071 [M]	Pat's Great Hits	1957	6.25	12.50	25.00
❏ DLP-3077 [M]	Pat Boone Sings Irving Berlin	1958	5.00	10.00	20.00
❏ DLP-3118 [M]	Star Dust	1958	5.00	10.00	20.00
❏ DLP-3121 [M]	Yes Indeed!	1958	5.00	10.00	20.00
❏ DLP-3158 [M]	Pat Boone Sings	1959	5.00	10.00	20.00
❏ DLP-3180 [M]	Tenderly	1959	5.00	10.00	20.00
❏ DLP-3199 [M]	Side by Side	1959	5.00	10.00	20.00
❏ DLP-3222 [M]	White Christmas	1959	6.25	12.50	25.00
❏ DLP-3501 [M]	Pat Boone Sings Guess Who?	1963	12.50	25.00	50.00
❏ DLP-25068 [S]	Hymns We Love	1959	7.50	15.00	30.00
❏ DLP-25071 [P]	Pat's Great Hits	1959	7.50	15.00	30.00
❏ DLP-25077 [S]	Pat Boone Sings Irving Berlin	1959	6.25	12.50	25.00
❏ DLP-25118 [S]	Star Dust	1959	6.25	12.50	25.00
❏ DLP-25121 [S]	Yes Indeed!	1959	6.25	12.50	25.00
❏ DLP-25158 [S]	Pat Boone Sings	1959	6.25	12.50	25.00
❏ DLP-25180 [S]	Tenderly	1959	6.25	12.50	25.00
❏ DLP-25199 [S]	Side by Side	1959	6.25	12.50	25.00
❏ DLP-25222 [S]	White Christmas	1959	7.50	15.00	30.00
❏ DLP-25234 [S]	He Leadeth Me	1960	5.00	10.00	20.00
❏ DLP-25261 [S]	Pat's Great Hits Volume 2	1960	5.00	10.00	20.00
❏ DLP-25270 [S]	Moonglow	1960	12.50	25.00	50.00
-- Blue vinyl					
❏ DLP-25270 [S]	Moonglow	1960	5.00	10.00	20.00
-- Black vinyl					
❏ DLP-25285 [S]	This and That	1960	5.00	10.00	20.00
❏ DLP-25346 [S]	Great! Great! Great!	1961	5.00	10.00	20.00
❏ DLP-25501 [S]	Pat Boone Sings Guess Who?	1963	20.00	40.00	80.00

BOONE, RANDY
DECCA
❏ DL 4619 [M]	Singing Star of The Virginian	1965	6.25	12.50	25.00
❏ DL 4663 [M]	Ramblin' Randy	1965	5.00	10.00	20.00
❏ DL 74619 [S]	Singing Star of The Virginian	1965	8.75	17.50	35.00
❏ DL 74663 [S]	Ramblin' Randy	1965	7.50	15.00	30.00

BOOT
AGAPE
| ❏ 2601 | Boot | 1972 | 6.25 | 12.50 | 25.00 |

BORDERSONG
REAL GOOD
| ❏ 1001 | Morning | 1975 | 12.50 | 25.00 | 50.00 |
| -- With Ann and Nancy Wilson, later of HEART | | | | | |

BORODIN STRING QUARTET
MERCURY LIVING PRESENCE
| ❏ SR 90309 [S] | Shostakovich: String Quartets No. 4 and 8 | 196? | 25.00 | 50.00 | 100.00 |
| -- Maroon label, no "Vendor: Mercury Record Corporation" | | | | | |

BOSTIC, EARL
KING
❏ 295-64 [10]	Earl Bostic and His Alto Sax	1951	50.00	100.00	200.00
-- Black vinyl					
❏ 295-64 [10]	Earl Bostic and His Alto Sax	1951	100.00	200.00	400.00
-- Red vinyl					
❏ 295-65 [10]	Earl Bostic and His Alto Sax	1951	100.00	200.00	400.00
-- Red vinyl					
❏ 295-65 [10]	Earl Bostic and His Alto Sax	1951	50.00	100.00	200.00
-- Black vinyl					
❏ 295-66 [10]	Earl Bostic and His Alto Sax	1951	50.00	100.00	200.00
-- Black vinyl					
❏ 295-66 [10]	Earl Bostic and His Alto Sax	1951	100.00	200.00	400.00
-- Red vinyl					
❏ 295-72 [10]	Earl Bostic and His Alto Sax	1952	50.00	100.00	200.00
❏ 295-76 [10]	Earl Bostic and His Alto Sax	1952	50.00	100.00	200.00
❏ 295-77 [10]	Earl Bostic and His Alto Sax	1952	50.00	100.00	200.00
❏ 295-78 [10]	Earl Bostic and His Alto Sax	1952	50.00	100.00	200.00
❏ 295-79 [10]	Earl Bostic and His Alto Sax	1952	50.00	100.00	200.00
❏ 295-95 [10]	Earl Bostic Plays Old Standards	1954	50.00	100.00	200.00
❏ 295-103 [10]	Earl Bostic and His Alto Sax	1954	50.00	100.00	200.00
❏ 395-500 [M]	The Best of Earl Bostic	1956	25.00	50.00	100.00
❏ 395-503 [M]	Bostic for You	1956	25.00	50.00	100.00
❏ 395-515 [M]	Alto-Tude	1957	25.00	50.00	100.00
❏ 395-525 [M]	Dance Time	1957	20.00	40.00	80.00
❏ 395-529 [M]	Let's Dance with Earl Bostic	1957	20.00	40.00	80.00
❏ 395-547 [M]	Invitation to Dance	1958	20.00	40.00	80.00
❏ 558 [M]	C'mon and Dance with Earl Bostic	1958	20.00	40.00	80.00
❏ KS-558 [S]	C'mon and Dance with Earl Bostic	1959	37.50	75.00	150.00
❏ 571 [M]	Bostic Rocks	1958	20.00	40.00	80.00
❏ 583 [M]	Showcase of Swinging Dance Hits	1958	20.00	40.00	80.00
❏ 597 [M]	Alto Magic in Hi-Fi	1958	20.00	40.00	80.00
❏ 602 [M]	Sweet Tunes of the Fantastic Fifties	1959	12.50	25.00	50.00
❏ 613 [M]	Workshop	1959	12.50	25.00	50.00
❏ 620 [M]	Sweet Tunes from the Roaring Twenties	1959	12.50	25.00	50.00
❏ 632 [M]	Sweet Tunes of the Swinging Forties	1959	12.50	25.00	50.00
❏ 640 [M]	Sweet Tunes of the Sentimental Forties	1960	12.50	25.00	50.00
❏ 662 [M]	Musical Pearls	1960	12.50	25.00	50.00
❏ 705 [M]	Hit Tunes of Big Broadway Shows	1960	12.50	25.00	50.00
❏ 725 [M]	25 Years of Rhythm and Blues Hits	1961	12.50	25.00	50.00
❏ 786 [M]	By Popular Demand	1961	12.50	25.00	50.00
❏ 827 [M]	Earl Bostic Plays Bossa Nova	1963	12.50	25.00	50.00
❏ 838 [M]	The Fantastic Fifties	1963	12.50	25.00	50.00
❏ 846 [M]	Jazz As I Feel It	1963	12.50	25.00	50.00
❏ 881 [M]	The Best of Earl Bostic	1964	12.50	25.00	50.00
❏ 900 [M]	The New Sound	1964	12.50	25.00	50.00
❏ 921 [M]	The Great Hits of 1964	1964	12.50	25.00	50.00
❏ KS-1048 [S]	Harlem Nocturne	1969	6.25	12.50	25.00

PHILIPS
| ❏ PHM 200-262 [M] | The Song Is Not Ended | 1967 | 6.25 | 12.50 | 25.00 |
| ❏ PHS 600-262 [S] | The Song Is Not Ended | 1967 | 6.25 | 12.50 | 25.00 |

BOSTON
EPIC
❏ HE 34188	Boston	1981	12.50	25.00	50.00
-- Half-speed mastered edition, original issue					
❏ HE 44188	Boston	1982	10.00	20.00	40.00
-- Half-speed mastered edition, second pressing					
❏ HE 45050	Don't Look Back	1982	20.00	40.00	80.00
-- Half-speed mastered edition					

MOBILE FIDELITY
| ❏ 1-249 | Boston | 1996 | 6.25 | 12.50 | 25.00 |
| -- Audiophile vinyl | | | | | |

Number	Title	Yr	VG	VG+	NM

BOSTON POPS ORCHESTRA (ARTHUR FIEDLER, CONDUCTOR)

Perhaps the most popular orchestra and conductor in American history, Fiedler and the Pops released literally hundreds of albums, of which the below are a sample. Most of these are from the "golden age of stereo" and also exist in monaural, but are much less in demand than the stereo pressings.

RCA VICTOR RED SEAL

Number	Title	Yr	VG	VG+	NM
❏ LSC-1817 [S]	Offenbach: Gaite Parisienne	1958	75.00	150.00	300.00
-- *Original with "shaded dog" label*					
❏ LSC-1817 [S]	Offenbach: Gaite Parisienne	199?	6.25	12.50	25.00
-- *Classic Records reissue*					
❏ LSC-1990 [S]	Offenbach: In America	1958	30.00	60.00	120.00
-- *Original with "shaded dog" label*					
❏ LSC-1990 [S]	Offenbach: In America	1964	50.00	100.00	200.00
-- *Second pressing with "white dog" label; a rare case where the second edition is more desirable than the first*					
❏ LSC-2028 [S]	Waltzes by the Strauss Family	1958	5.00	10.00	20.00
-- *Original with "shaded dog" label*					
❏ LSC-2052 [S]	Tchaikovsky: The Nutcracker (selections)	1958	5.00	10.00	20.00
-- *Original with "shaded dog" label*					
❏ LSC-2084 [S]	Rossini-Respighi: La Boutique Fantasque	1958	37.50	75.00	150.00
-- *Original with "shaded dog" label*					
❏ LSC-2100 [S]	Hi-Fi Fiedler	1958	15.00	30.00	60.00
-- *Original with "shaded dog" label*					
❏ LSC-2125 [S]	Grieg: Music from Peer Gynt	1958	10.00	20.00	40.00
-- *Original with "shaded dog" label*					
❏ LSC-2130 [S]	Strauss, Johann: Orchestral Music from Gypsy Baron and Die Fledermaus	1958	7.50	15.00	30.00
-- *Original with "shaded dog" label*					
❏ LSC-2202 [S]	Pops Caviar	1959	10.00	20.00	40.00
-- *Original with "shaded dog" label*					
❏ LSC-2213 [S]	Boston Tea Party	1959	5.00	10.00	20.00
-- *Original with "shaded dog" label*					
❏ LSC-2229 [S]	Marches in Hi-Fi	1959	5.00	10.00	20.00
-- *Original with "shaded dog" label*					
❏ LSC-2235 [S]	Good Music to Have Fun With	1959	7.50	15.00	30.00
-- *Original with "shaded dog" label*					
❏ LSC-2240 [S]	Kay, Hershey: Stars and Stripes	1959	10.00	20.00	40.00
-- *Original with "shaded dog" label*					
❏ LSC-2267 [S]	Offenbach: Gaite Parisienne; Khachatourian: Gayne Suite	1959	5.00	10.00	20.00
-- *Original with "shaded dog" label*					
❏ LSC-2270 [S]	Pops Stoppers	1959	5.00	10.00	20.00
-- *Original with "shaded dog" label*					
❏ LSC-2294 [S]	Rodgers: Slaughter on Tenth Avenue	1959	5.00	10.00	20.00
-- *Original with "shaded dog" label*					
❏ LSC-2320 [S]	Song of India	1959	15.00	30.00	60.00
-- *Original with "shaded dog" label*					
❏ LSC-2329 [S]	Pops Christmas Party	1959	20.00	40.00	80.00
-- *Original copies have "shaded dog" with small "RCA Victor" logo; large "Living Stereo" on front cover*					
❏ LSC-2329 [S]	Pops Christmas Party	1964	7.50	15.00	30.00
-- *Second editions have "white dog" with large "RCA Victor" logo; small "Living Stereo" on front cover*					
❏ LSC-2367 [S]	Gershwin: Rhapsody in Blue; An American in Paris	1960	5.00	10.00	20.00
-- *Earl Wild, piano; originals with "shaded dog" label*					
❏ LSC-2380 [S]	Music from Million Dollar Movies	1960	5.00	10.00	20.00
-- *Original with "shaded dog" label*					
❏ LSC-2439 [S]	All-Time Favorites	1960	6.25	12.50	25.00
-- *Original with "shaded dog" label*					
❏ LSC-2442 [S]	The Music of Franz Liszt	1960	6.25	12.50	25.00
-- *Original with "shaded dog" label*					
❏ LSC-2470 [S]	More Classical Music for People Who Hate Classical Music	1961	7.50	15.00	30.00
-- *Original with "shaded dog" label*					
❏ LSC-2486 [S]	Music of Frank Loesser	1961	12.50	25.00	50.00
-- *Original with "shaded dog" label*					
❏ LSC-2549 [S]	Family Fun	1961	7.50	15.00	30.00
-- *Original with "shaded dog" label*					
❏ LSC-2586 [S]	Gershwin: Piano Concerto	1962	7.50	15.00	30.00
-- *Earl Wild, piano; originals with "shaded dog" label*					
❏ LSC-2586 [S]	Gershwin: Piano Concerto	199?	6.25	12.50	25.00
-- *Earl Wild, piano; Classic Records reissue*					
❏ LSC-2596 [S]	Saint-Saens: Carnival of the Animals; Britten: Young Person's Guide to the Orchestra	1962	7.50	15.00	30.00
-- *Original with "shaded dog" label*					
❏ LSC-2621 [S]	Chopin: Les Sylphides; Prokofiev: Love for Three Oranges	1962	10.00	20.00	40.00
❏ LSC-2637 [S]	Rodgers: No Strings; State Fair	1962	5.00	10.00	20.00
-- *Original with "shaded dog" label*					
❏ LSC-2702 [S]	Milhaud: A Frenchman in New York; Gershwin: An American in Paris	1963	10.00	20.00	40.00
-- *Original with "shaded dog" label*					
❏ LSC-6082 [(2)]	Everything But the Beer	1959	30.00	60.00	120.00
-- *Original with "shaded dog" label*					

BOSTON SYMPHONY ORCHESTRA (AARON COPLAND, CONDUCTOR)

RCA VICTOR RED SEAL

Number	Title	Yr	VG	VG+	NM
❏ LSC-2401 [S]	Copland: Appalachian Spring; The Tender Land Suite	1960	6.25	12.50	25.00
-- *Original with "shaded dog" label*					

BOSTON SYMPHONY ORCHESTRA (ERICH LEINSDORF, CONDUCTOR)

RCA VICTOR RED SEAL

Number	Title	Yr	VG	VG+	NM
❏ LSC-2707 [S]	Prokofiev: Symphony No. 5	1963	6.25	12.50	25.00
-- *Original with "shaded dog" label*					

BOSTON SYMPHONY ORCHESTRA (PIERRE MONTEUX, CONDUCTOR)

RCA VICTOR RED SEAL

Number	Title	Yr	VG	VG+	NM
❏ LSC-1901 [S]	Tchaikovsky: Symphony No. 6 "Pathetique"	1958	12.50	25.00	50.00
-- *Original with "shaded dog" label*					
❏ LSC-1901 [S]	Tchaikovsky: Symphony No. 6 "Pathetique"	199?	6.25	12.50	25.00
-- *Classic Records reissue*					
❏ LSC-2239 [S]	Tchaikovsky: Symphony No. 5	1959	10.00	20.00	40.00
-- *Original with "shaded dog" label*					
❏ LSC-2239 [S]	Tchaikovsky: Symphony No. 5	1964	10.00	20.00	40.00
-- *Second edition with "white dog" label*					
❏ LSC-2369 [S]	Tchaikovsky: Symphony No. 4	1959	12.50	25.00	50.00
-- *Original with "shaded dog" label*					
❏ LSC-2369 [S]	Tchaikovsky: Symphony No. 4	199?	6.25	12.50	25.00
-- *Classic Records reissue*					
❏ LSC-2376 [S]	Stravinsky: Petrouchka	1960	17.50	35.00	70.00
-- *Original with "shaded dog" label*					
❏ LSC-2376 [S]	Stravinsky: Petrouchka	1964	12.50	25.00	50.00
-- *Second edition with "white dog" label*					

BOSTON SYMPHONY ORCHESTRA (CHARLES MUNCH, CONDUCTOR)

RCA VICTOR RED SEAL

Number	Title	Yr	VG	VG+	NM
❏ LSC-1893 [S]	Ravel: Daphne and Chloe	1958	75.00	150.00	300.00
-- *Original with "shaded dog" label*					
❏ LSC-1893 [S]	Ravel: Daphne and Chloe	199?	6.25	12.50	25.00
-- *Classic Records reissue*					
❏ LSC-1900 [S]	Berlioz: Symphonie Fantastique	199?	6.25	12.50	25.00
-- *Classic Records issue. This album is not known to have been issued in stereo before this.*					
❏ LSC-1984 [S]	Ravel: Bolero; La Valse; Rapsodie Espagnole; Debussy: Prelude	1958	15.00	30.00	60.00
-- *Original with "shaded dog" label*					
❏ LSC-2097 [S]	Brahms: Symphony No. 1	1958	20.00	40.00	80.00
-- *Original with "shaded dog" label*					
❏ LSC-2105 [S]	Tchaikovsky: Serenade for Strings	1958	17.50	35.00	70.00
-- *Original with "shaded dog" label*					
❏ LSC-2111 [S]	Debussy: La Mer	1958	20.00	40.00	80.00
-- *Original with "shaded dog" label*					
❏ LSC-2131 [S]	Franck: Symphony in D	1958	5.00	10.00	20.00
-- *Original with "shaded dog" label*					
❏ LSC-2221 [S]	Mendelssohn: Symphony No. 4 and No. 5	1959	6.25	12.50	25.00
-- *Original with "shaded dog" label*					
❏ LSC-2228 [S]	Berlioz: Harold in Italy	1959	10.00	20.00	40.00
-- *Original with "shaded dog" label*					
❏ LSC-2233 [S]	Beethoven: Symphony No. 3	1959	15.00	30.00	60.00
-- *Original with "shaded dog" label*					
❏ LSC-2271 [S]	Ravel: Concerto in G; d'Indy: Symphony on a French Mountain Air	1959	37.50	75.00	150.00
-- *Original with "shaded dog" label*					
❏ LSC-2271 [S]	Ravel: Concerto in G; d'Indy: Symphony on a French Mountain Air	199?	6.25	12.50	25.00
-- *Classic Records reissue*					
❏ LM-2282 [M]	Debussy: Images	1959	5.00	10.00	20.00
❏ LSC-2282 [S]	Debussy: Images	1959	37.50	75.00	150.00
❏ LSC-2292 [S]	The French Touch	1959	40.00	80.00	160.00
-- *Original with "shaded dog" label*					
❏ LSC-2297 [S]	Brahms: Symphony No. 4	1959	10.00	20.00	40.00
-- *Original with "shaded dog" label*					
❏ LSC-2341 [S]	Saint-Saens: Symphony No. 3	1960	5.00	10.00	20.00
-- *Original with "shaded dog" label*					
❏ LSC-2344 [S]	Schubert: Symphony No. 9	1960	25.00	50.00	100.00
-- *Original with "shaded dog" label*					
❏ LSC-2344 [S]	Schubert: Symphony No. 9	1964	10.00	20.00	40.00
-- *Second edition with "white dog" label*					
❏ LM-2352 [M]	Blackwood: Symphony No. 1; Haieff: Symphony No. 2	1960	5.00	10.00	20.00

Number	Title	Yr	VG	VG+	NM
❏ LSC-2352 [S]	Blackwood: Symphony No. 1; Haieff: Symphony No. 2	1960	37.50	75.00	150.00
-- Original with "shaded dog" label					
❏ LSC-2371 [S]	Mahler: Songs of a Wayfarer	1960	10.00	20.00	40.00
-- Original with "shaded dog" label					
❏ LSC-2438 [S]	Berlioz: Overtures	1960	12.50	25.00	50.00
-- Original with "shaded dog" label					
❏ LSC-2474 [S]	Schumann: Symphony No. 1	1961	6.25	12.50	25.00
-- Original with "shaded dog" label					
❏ LSC-2520 [S]	Mendelssohn: Symphony No. 3 "Scotch"; Scherzo from Octet in E-flat	1961	7.50	15.00	30.00
-- Original with "shaded dog" label					
❏ LSC-2522 [S]	Schubert: Symphony No. 2; Beethoven: Prometheus Ballet Excerpts	1961	7.50	15.00	30.00
-- Original with "shaded dog" label					
❏ LSC-2565 [S]	Tchaikovsky: Romeo and Juliet; Strauss, Richard: Till Eulenspiegel	1961	7.50	15.00	30.00
-- Original with "shaded dog" label					
❏ LSC-2567 [S]	Poulenc: Organ Concerto; Stravinsky: Jeu de Cartes	1961	6.25	12.50	25.00
-- Original with "shaded dog" label					
❏ LSC-2568 [S]	Ravel: Daphnis et Chloe	1961	10.00	20.00	40.00
-- Original with "shaded dog" label					
❏ LSC-2608 [S]	Berlioz: Symphonie Fantastique	1962	12.50	25.00	50.00
-- Original with "shaded dog" label					
❏ LSC-2625 [S]	Milhaude: La Creation du Monde; Suite Provencale	1962	50.00	100.00	200.00
❏ LSC-2625 [S]	Milhaude: La Creation Du Monde	1962	37.50	75.00	150.00
-- With "white dog" label					
❏ LSC-2625 [S]	Milhaude: La Creation Du Monde	199?	6.25	12.50	25.00
-- Classic Records reissue					
❏ LSC-2629 [S]	Dvorak: Symphony No. 4 (8) in G	1962	10.00	20.00	40.00
-- Original with "shaded dog" label					
❏ LSC-2647 [S]	Chausson: Symphony in B-flat; Franck: Le Chasseur Maudit	1962	7.50	15.00	30.00
-- Original with "shaded dog" label					
❏ LSC-2683 [S]	Tchaikovsky: Symphony No. 6	1962	5.00	10.00	20.00
-- Original with "shaded dog" label					
❏ LSC-6140 [(3)]	Bach: Brandenburg Concertos No. 1-6	196?	25.00	50.00	100.00
-- Original with "shaded dog" label					

BOSTON TEA PARTY, THE
FLICK DISC

Number	Title	Yr	VG	VG+	NM
❏ 45,000	The Boston Tea Party	1968	15.00	30.00	60.00

BOW STREET RUNNERS, THE
B.T. PUPPY

Number	Title	Yr	VG	VG+	NM
❏ BTPS-1026	The Bow Street Runners	1969	500.00	750.00	1,000.

BOW WOW WOW
RCA

Number	Title	Yr	VG	VG+	NM
❏ DJL1-4193 [DJ]	RCA Radio Special	1981	6.25	12.50	25.00

BOWEN, JIMMY
REPRISE

Number	Title	Yr	VG	VG+	NM
❏ R-6210 [M]	Sunday Morning with the Comics	1966	7.50	15.00	30.00
❏ RS-6210 [S]	Sunday Morning with the Comics	1966	10.00	20.00	40.00

ROULETTE

Number	Title	Yr	VG	VG+	NM
❏ R 25004 [M]	Jimmy Bowen	1957	75.00	150.00	300.00
-- Black and silver label					
❏ R 25004 [M]	Jimmy Bowen	1958	37.50	75.00	150.00
-- Red label					

BOWIE, DAVID
DERAM

Number	Title	Yr	VG	VG+	NM
❏ DE 16003 [M]	David Bowie	1967	30.00	60.00	120.00
❏ DES 18003 [S]	David Bowie	1967	37.50	75.00	150.00

EMI AMERICA

Number	Title	Yr	VG	VG+	NM
❏ SPRO 9960/1 [(2) DJ]	Let's Talk	1983	6.25	12.50	25.00
-- Promo-only interview album					
❏ SPRO-79112/3 [DJ]	Never Let Me Down: The Interview	1987	6.25	12.50	25.00

LONDON

Number	Title	Yr	VG	VG+	NM
❏ PS 628/629 [(2)]	Images 1966-1967	1973	12.50	25.00	50.00
-- Original pressings have dark blue and silver labels. Later pressings, if any, are worth at least 50% less.					

MERCURY

Number	Title	Yr	VG	VG+	NM
❏ SR 61246	Man of Words, Man of Music	1969	37.50	75.00	150.00
❏ SR 61325	The Man Who Sold the World	1970	10.00	20.00	40.00
-- An often-counterfeited album; originals have matrix numbers stamped in the trail-off area					

MOBILE FIDELITY

Number	Title	Yr	VG	VG+	NM
❏ 1-064	The Rise and Fall of Ziggy Stardust and the Spiders from Mars	1983	12.50	25.00	50.00
-- Audiophile vinyl					
❏ 1-083	Let's Dance	1984	7.50	15.00	30.00
-- Audiophile vinyl					

RCA RED SEAL

Number	Title	Yr	VG	VG+	NM
❏ ARL1-2743	Peter and the Wolf	1978	5.00	10.00	20.00
-- With the Philadelphia Orchestra conducted by Eugene Ormandy; black vinyl					
❏ ARL1-2743	Peter and the Wolf	1978	5.00	10.00	20.00
-- With the Philadelphia Orchestra conducted by Eugene Ormandy; green vinyl					

RCA VICTOR

Number	Title	Yr	VG	VG+	NM
❏ APL1-0291	Pin Ups	1973	5.00	10.00	20.00
❏ CPL1-0576	Diamond Dogs	1974	1,000.	2,000.	4,000.
-- Original copies have cover with dog's genitals clearly visible. Almost all were destroyed prior to release.					
❏ CPL1-0576	Diamond Dogs	1974	5.00	10.00	20.00
-- Standard issue, with dog's genitals airbrushed					
❏ CPL2-0771 [(2)]	David Live	1974	5.00	10.00	20.00
-- At time of release, available with either orange or tan labels					
❏ DJL1-2697 [DJ]	Bowie Now	1978	18.75	37.50	75.00
❏ CPL2-2913 [(2)]	Stage	1978	5.00	10.00	20.00
❏ DJL1-3016 [DJ]	An Evening with David Bowie	1978	12.50	25.00	50.00
-- Live concert for "Superstars Radio Network"					
❏ DJL1-3545 [DJ]	1980 All Clear	1980	5.00	10.00	20.00
❏ DJL1-3829 [DJ]	Special Radio Series, Volume 1	1980	6.25	12.50	25.00
❏ DJL1-3840 [DJ]	Scary Monsters Interview	1980	5.00	10.00	20.00
❏ LSP-4623	Hunky Dory	1972	5.00	10.00	20.00
❏ LSP-4702	The Rise and Fall of Ziggy Stardust and the Spiders from Mars	1972	5.00	10.00	20.00
❏ LSP-4813	Space Oddity	1973	5.00	10.00	20.00
-- Reissue of Mercury SR-61246; add 1/3 if bonus poster is enclosed					
❏ LSP-4816	The Man Who Sold the World	1973	5.00	10.00	20.00
-- Reissue of Mercury SR-61325; add 1/3 if bonus poster is enclosed					
❏ LSP-4852	Aladdin Sane	1973	5.00	10.00	20.00
-- Orange label is original (deduct 50% for tan labels)					
❏ CPL2-4862 [(2)]	Ziggy Stardust, The Motion Picture	1983	5.00	10.00	20.00
❏ CPL2-4862 [(2) DJ]	Ziggy Stardust, The Motion Picture	1983	12.50	25.00	50.00
-- Promo version on clear vinyl					

RYKO ANALOGUE

Number	Title	Yr	VG	VG+	NM
❏ RALP 0120/1/2 [(6)]	Sound + Vision	1989	20.00	40.00	80.00
-- Six-LP box set on clear vinyl with three gatefold cardboard inner sleeves					
❏ RALP 0131 [(2)]	Space Oddity	1990	5.00	10.00	20.00
-- Clear vinyl with "Limited Edition" obi					
❏ RALP 0132 [(2)]	The Man Who Sold the World	1990	5.00	10.00	20.00
-- Clear vinyl with "Limited Edition" obi					
❏ RALP 0133 [(2)]	Hunky Dory	1990	5.00	10.00	20.00
-- Clear vinyl with "Limited Edition" obi					
❏ RALP 0134 [(2)]	The Rise and Fall of Ziggy Stardust and the Spiders from Mars	1990	5.00	10.00	20.00
-- Clear vinyl with "Limited Edition" obi					
❏ RALP 0135	Aladdin Sane	1990	5.00	10.00	20.00
-- Clear vinyl with "Limited Edition" obi					
❏ RALP 0136	Pin Ups	1990	5.00	10.00	20.00
-- Clear vinyl with "Limited Edition" obi					
❏ RALP 0137	Diamond Dogs	1990	5.00	10.00	20.00
-- Clear vinyl with "Limited Edition" obi; genitals on dog are restored					
❏ RALP 0138/9 [(2)]	David Live	1990	5.00	10.00	20.00
-- Clear vinyl with "Limited Edition" obi					
❏ RALP 0171 [(2)]	Changesbowie	1990	5.00	10.00	20.00
-- Clear vinyl with "Limited Edition" obi					
❏ LSD-4702 [DJ]	The Rise and Fall of Ziggy Stardust and the Spiders from Mars	1990	25.00	50.00	100.00
-- Special promo-only package with both the LP and CD versions					

BOWMAN, DON
RCA VICTOR

Number	Title	Yr	VG	VG+	NM
❏ LPM-2831 [M]	Our Man in Trouble	1964	5.00	10.00	20.00
❏ LSP-2831 [S]	Our Man in Trouble	1964	6.25	12.50	25.00
❏ LPM-3345 [M]	Fresh from the Funny Farm	1965	5.00	10.00	20.00
❏ LSP-3345 [S]	Fresh from the Funny Farm	1965	6.25	12.50	25.00
❏ LPM-3646 [M]	Don Bowman Recorded Almost Live	1966	5.00	10.00	20.00
❏ LSP-3646 [S]	Don Bowman Recorded Almost Live	1966	6.25	12.50	25.00
❏ LPM-3795 [M]	From Mexico with Laughs Featuring the Tijuana Drum and Bugle Corps	1967	6.25	12.50	25.00
❏ LSP-3795 [S]	From Mexico with Laughs Featuring the Tijuana Drum and Bugle Corps	1967	5.00	10.00	20.00
❏ LPM-3920 [M]	Funny Folk Flops	1968	12.50	25.00	50.00
❏ LSP-3920 [S]	Funny Folk Flops	1968	5.00	10.00	20.00

Number	Title	Yr	VG	VG+	NM

BOX TOPS, THE
BELL
❑ 6011 [M]	The Letter/Neon Rainbow	1967	6.25	12.50	25.00
❑ S-6011 [S]	The Letter/Neon Rainbow	1967	5.00	10.00	20.00
❑ S-6017	Cry Like a Baby	1968	5.00	10.00	20.00
❑ S-6023	Non-Stop	1968	5.00	10.00	20.00
❑ S-6025	The Box Tops Super Hits	1968	5.00	10.00	20.00
❑ S-6032	Dimensions	1969	5.00	10.00	20.00

BOXCAR WILLIE
AHMC
❑ AA 118	Marty Martin Sings Country Music	1976	12.50	25.00	50.00

-- Marty Martin changed his name to "Boxcar Willie" after one of his early songs

BOYCE, TOMMY
RCA CAMDEN
❑ CAL-2202 [M]	Tommy Boyce	1967	5.00	10.00	20.00
❑ CAS-2202 [S]	Tommy Boyce	1967	6.25	12.50	25.00

BOYCE, TOMMY, AND BOBBY HART
A&M
❑ LP-126 [M]	Test Patterns	1967	5.00	10.00	20.00
❑ LP-143 [M]	I Wonder What She's Doing Tonite?	1968	7.50	15.00	30.00
❑ SP-4126 [S]	Test Patterns	1967	5.00	10.00	20.00
❑ SP-4143 [S]	I Wonder What She's Doing Tonite?	1968	5.00	10.00	20.00
❑ SP-4162	It's All Happening on the Inside	1968	5.00	10.00	20.00

BOYD, BILLY
CROWN
❑ CST-196 [R]	Twangy Guitars	196?	12.50	25.00	50.00

-- Red vinyl
❑ CLP-5170 [M]	Twangy Guitars	1960	15.00	30.00	60.00

-- Black label, silver print
❑ CLP-5170 [M]	Twangy Guitars	1961	5.00	10.00	20.00

-- Gray label

BOYD, EDDIE
EPIC
❑ BN 26409	7936 South Rhodes	1968	7.50	15.00	30.00

LONDON
❑ PS 554	I'll Dust My Broom	1969	7.50	15.00	30.00

BOYD, JIMMY
COLUMBIA
❑ CL 2543 [10]	I Saw Mommy Kissing Santa Claus	1955	10.00	20.00	40.00

-- "House Party Series" reissue
❑ CL 6270 [10]	Christmas with Jimmy Boyd	1953	25.00	50.00	100.00

BOYER, CHARLES
VALIANT
❑ VLM-5001 [M]	Where Does Love Go?	1966	6.25	12.50	25.00
❑ VLS-25001 [S]	Where Does Love Go?	1966	7.50	15.00	30.00

BOYS TOWN CHOIR, THE
MASTERTONE
❑ MS-102	Christmas at Boys Town	1964	5.00	10.00	20.00

-- Some copies contain a concert program

BOYZ II MEN
MOTOWN
❑ 31453 0323-1 [DJ]	II	1994	6.25	12.50	25.00

-- Vinyl is promo only; in Motown company cover

BRADFORD, ALEX
CHECKER
❑ LP-10041 [M]	Alex Bradford	196?	6.25	12.50	25.00

SPECIALTY
❑ SP-2108 [M]	Too Close to Heaven	1959	25.00	50.00	100.00

VEE JAY
❑ LP-5023 [M]	One Step	1962	10.00	20.00	40.00
❑ LP-5056 [M]	The Soul of Alex Bradford	1964	10.00	20.00	40.00

BRADFORD, SCOTT
PROBE
❑ 4509	Rock Slides	1969	5.00	10.00	20.00

BRADLEY, OWEN
CORAL
❑ CRL 56012 [10]	Christmas Time	1950	20.00	40.00	80.00
❑ CRL 56022 [10]	Strauss Waltzes	195?	15.00	30.00	60.00
❑ CRL 56035 [10]	Lazy River	195?	15.00	30.00	60.00
❑ CRL 56047 [10]	Singin' in the Rain	195?	15.00	30.00	60.00
❑ CRL 56065 [10]	Cherished Hymns	195?	15.00	30.00	60.00
❑ CRL 57071 [M]	Organ and Chimes Played by Owen Bradley	1956	7.50	15.00	30.00

DECCA
❑ DL 4078 [M]	Paradise Island	1960	5.00	10.00	20.00
❑ DL 8652 [M]	Joyous Bells of Christmas	1957	7.50	15.00	30.00
❑ DL 8724 [M]	Bandstand Hop	1958	7.50	15.00	30.00
❑ DL 8868 [M]	Big Guitar	1958	7.50	15.00	30.00
❑ DL 74078 [S]	Paradise Island	1960	6.25	12.50	25.00
❑ DL 78868 [S]	Big Guitar	1958	10.00	20.00	40.00

BRADSHAW, TERRY
MERCURY
❑ SRM-1-1073	I'm So Lonesome I Could Cry	1976	5.00	10.00	20.00

BRADSHAW, TINY
KING
❑ 295-74 [10]	Off and On	1955	250.00	500.00	1,000.
❑ 395-501 [M]	Selections	1956	175.00	350.00	700.00
❑ 653 [M]	Great Composer	1960	75.00	150.00	300.00
❑ 953 [M]	24 Great Songs	1966	10.00	20.00	40.00

BRADY BUNCH, THE
PARAMOUNT
❑ PAS-5026	Merry Christmas from the Brady Bunch	1971	20.00	40.00	80.00
❑ PAS-6032	Meet the Brady Bunch	1972	12.50	25.00	50.00
❑ PAS-6037	The Kids from the Brady Bunch	1972	10.00	20.00	40.00
❑ PAS-6058	The Brady Bunch Phonograph Record	1973	20.00	40.00	80.00

BRAND, OSCAR
ABC-PARAMOUNT
❑ ABC-388 [M]	Oscar Brand Sings for Adults	1961	6.25	12.50	25.00
❑ ABCS-388 [S]	Oscar Brand Sings for Adults	1961	7.50	15.00	30.00

AUDIO FIDELITY
❑ AFLP-1806 [M]	Bawdy Songs and Backroom Ballads, Vol. II	195?	6.25	12.50	25.00
❑ AFLP-1824 [M]	Bawdy Songs and Backroom Ballads, Vol. III	195?	6.25	12.50	25.00
❑ AFLP-1847 [M]	Bawdy Songs and Backroom Ballads, Vol. IV	195?	6.25	12.50	25.00
❑ AFLP-1884 [M]	Bawdy Sea Shanties (Vol. 5)	1959	6.25	12.50	25.00
❑ AFLP-1906 [M]	Bawdy Songs and Backroom Ballads, Vol. I	195?	6.25	12.50	25.00
❑ AFLP-1920 [M]	Bawdy Western Songs (Vol. VI)	1960	6.25	12.50	25.00
❑ AFLP-1952 [M]	Bawdy Songs Goes to College	1961	6.25	12.50	25.00
❑ AFLP-1966 [M]	Rollicking Sea Shanties	1962	6.25	12.50	25.00
❑ AFLP-1971 [M]	Sing Along Bawdy Songs and Backroom Ballads	1962	6.25	12.50	25.00
❑ AFLP-2121 [M]	Bawdy Hootenanny	1964	5.00	10.00	20.00
❑ AFSD-5824 [S]	Bawdy Songs and Backroom Ballads, Vol. III	196?	6.25	12.50	25.00
❑ AFSD-5847 [S]	Bawdy Songs and Backroom Ballads, Vol. IV	195?	6.25	12.50	25.00
❑ AFSD-5884 [S]	Bawdy Sea Shanties (Vol. 5)	1959	7.50	15.00	30.00
❑ AFSD-5920 [S]	Bawdy Western Songs (Vol. VI)	1960	7.50	15.00	30.00
❑ AFSD-5952 [S]	Bawdy Songs Goes to College	1961	7.50	15.00	30.00
❑ AFSD-5966 [S]	Rollicking Sea Shanties	1962	7.50	15.00	30.00
❑ AFSD-5971 [S]	Sing Along Bawdy Songs and Backroom Ballads	1962	7.50	15.00	30.00
❑ AFSD-6121 [S]	Bawdy Hootenanny	1964	6.25	12.50	25.00

CHESTERFIELD
❑ CMS-101 [10]	Backroom Ballads	195?	12.50	25.00	50.00

DECCA
❑ DL 4275 [M]	Folk Songs for Fun	1962	5.00	10.00	20.00
❑ DL 74275 [S]	Folk Songs for Fun	1962	6.25	12.50	25.00

ELEKTRA
❑ EKL-168 [M]	The Wild Blue Yonder	1959	5.00	10.00	20.00
❑ EKL-169 [M]	Every Inch a Sailor	1960	5.00	10.00	20.00
❑ EKL-174 [M]	Tell It to the Marines	1960	5.00	10.00	20.00
❑ EKL-178 [M]	Out of the Blue: Songs of a Fighting Airforce	1960	5.00	10.00	20.00
❑ EKL-183 [M]	Boating Songs and All That Bilge	1960	5.00	10.00	20.00
❑ EKL-188 [M]	Sports Car Songs for Big Wheels	1960	6.25	12.50	25.00

Number	Title	Yr	VG	VG+	NM
❑ EKL-198 [M]	Up in the Air: Songs for the Madcap Airman	1961	5.00	10.00	20.00
❑ EKL-204 [M]	For Doctors Only	1961	5.00	10.00	20.00
❑ EKL-228 [M]	A Snow Job for Skiers	1963	5.00	10.00	20.00
❑ EKL-237 [M]	Songs Fore Golfers	1963	5.00	10.00	20.00
❑ EKL-242 [M]	Cough: Army Songs Out of the Barracks Bag	1963	5.00	10.00	20.00
❑ EKS-7168 [S]	The Wild Blue Yonder	1959	6.25	12.50	25.00
❑ EKS-7169 [S]	Every Inch a Sailor	1960	6.25	12.50	25.00
❑ EKS-7174 [S]	Tell It to the Marines	1960	6.25	12.50	25.00
❑ EKS-7178 [S]	Out of the Blue: Songs of a Fighting Airforce	1960	6.25	12.50	25.00
❑ EKS-7183 [S]	Boating Songs and All That Bilge	1960	6.25	12.50	25.00
❑ EKS-7188 [S]	Sports Car Songs for Big Wheels	1960	7.50	15.00	30.00
❑ EKS-7198 [S]	Up in the Air: Songs for the Madcap Airman	1961	6.25	12.50	25.00
❑ EKS-7204 [S]	For Doctors Only	1961	6.25	12.50	25.00
❑ EKS-7228 [S]	A Snow Job for Skiers	1963	6.25	12.50	25.00
❑ EKS-7237 [S]	Songs Fore Golfers	1963	6.25	12.50	25.00
❑ EKS-7242 [S]	Cough: Army Songs Out of the Barracks Bag	1963	6.25	12.50	25.00

FOLKWAYS

Number	Title	Yr	VG	VG+	NM
❑ FA 5280 [M]	Election Songs of the United States	1960	6.25	12.50	25.00

RIVERSIDE

Number	Title	Yr	VG	VG+	NM
❑ RLP 12-630 [M]	American Drinking Songs	1956	7.50	15.00	30.00
❑ RLP 12-639 [M]	G.I. -- American Army Songs	195?	7.50	15.00	30.00
❑ RLP 12-825 [M]	Absolute Nonsense	195?	7.50	15.00	30.00
❑ RLP 12-835 [M]	Songs Inane Only	1959	7.50	15.00	30.00
❑ RLP 12-844 [M]	Songs of the U.S. Army	1960	7.50	15.00	30.00

TRADITION

Number	Title	Yr	VG	VG+	NM
❑ RLP 1014 [M]	Laughing America	195?	7.50	15.00	30.00
❑ TLP 1022 [M]	Pie in the Sky	195?	7.50	15.00	30.00
❑ TLP 2053	The Best of Oscar Brand	1967	5.00	10.00	20.00

BRANDMEIER, JONATHON
BRANDMEIER

Number	Title	Yr	VG	VG+	NM
❑ BPI 2004	Almost Live	1984	5.00	10.00	20.00

BRASSELLE, KEEFE
CORAL

Number	Title	Yr	VG	VG+	NM
❑ CRL 57295 [M]	Minstrel Man	1959	5.00	10.00	20.00
❑ CRL 757295 [S]	Minstrel Man	1959	6.25	12.50	25.00

BRAUN, BOB
DECCA

Number	Title	Yr	VG	VG+	NM
❑ DL 4339 [M]	Till Death Do Us Part	1962	5.00	10.00	20.00
❑ DL 74339 [S]	Till Death Do Us Part	1962	6.25	12.50	25.00

BRAUTIGAN, RICHARD
HARVEST

Number	Title	Yr	VG	VG+	NM
❑ ST-424	Listening to Richard Brautigan	1970	7.50	15.00	30.00

BRAZOS VALLEY BOYS, THE
WARNER BROS.

Number	Title	Yr	VG	VG+	NM
❑ W 1664 [M]	Where Is the Circus	1966	5.00	10.00	20.00
❑ WS 1664 [S]	Where Is the Circus	1966	6.25	12.50	25.00
❑ W 1679 [M]	The Countrypolitan Sound	1967	5.00	10.00	20.00
❑ WS 1679 [S]	The Countrypolitan Sound	1967	6.25	12.50	25.00
❑ W 1686 [M]	The Gold Standard Collection	1967	5.00	10.00	20.00
❑ WS 1686 [S]	The Gold Standard Collection	1967	6.25	12.50	25.00

BREAD
ELEKTRA

Number	Title	Yr	VG	VG+	NM
❑ BRD-1 [DJ]	Bread	1971	5.00	10.00	20.00

-- *In-store sampler; very similar to the future LP "The Best of Bread"*

Number	Title	Yr	VG	VG+	NM
❑ EQ-5015 [Q]	Baby I'm-a Want You	1974	5.00	10.00	20.00
❑ EQ-5056 [Q]	The Best of Bread	1973	5.00	10.00	20.00

BREAD, LOVE AND DREAMS
LONDON

Number	Title	Yr	VG	VG+	NM
❑ PS 566	Bread, Love and Dreams	1969	7.50	15.00	30.00

BREAM, JULIAN
RCA VICTOR RED SEAL

Number	Title	Yr	VG	VG+	NM
❑ LSC-2448 [S]	The Art of Julian Bream	1960	7.50	15.00	30.00

-- *Original with "shaded dog" label*

Number	Title	Yr	VG	VG+	NM
❑ LSC-2487 [S]	Giuliani: Guitar Concerto; Arnold: Guitar Concerto	1961	25.00	50.00	100.00

-- *Original with "shaded dog" label*

Number	Title	Yr	VG	VG+	NM
❑ LSC-2560 [S]	The Golden Age of English Lute Music	1961	6.25	12.50	25.00

-- *Original with "shaded dog" label*

Number	Title	Yr	VG	VG+	NM
❑ LSC-2606 [S]	Popular Classics for Spanish Guitar	1962	6.25	12.50	25.00

-- *Original with "shaded dog" label*

Number	Title	Yr	VG	VG+	NM
❑ LSC-2656 [S]	An Evening of Elizabethan Music	1962	15.00	30.00	60.00

-- *Original with "shaded dog" labe*

BREEDLOVE, JIMMY
RCA CAMDEN

Number	Title	Yr	VG	VG+	NM
❑ CAL-430 [M]	Rock 'N' Roll Hits	1958	10.00	20.00	40.00

BREEN, BOBBY
LONDON

Number	Title	Yr	VG	VG+	NM
❑ LB 270 [10]	Songs at Yuletide	1953	12.50	25.00	50.00

BRENDA AND THE TABULATIONS
DIONN

Number	Title	Yr	VG	VG+	NM
❑ LPM-2000 [M]	Dry Your Eyes	1967	10.00	20.00	40.00
❑ LPS-2000 [S]	Dry Your Eyes	1967	12.50	25.00	50.00

TOM & BOTTOM

Number	Title	Yr	VG	VG+	NM
❑ 100	Brenda and the Tabulations	1970	5.00	10.00	20.00

BRENNAN, WALTER
DOT

Number	Title	Yr	VG	VG+	NM
❑ DLP-3309 [M]	Dutchman's Gold	1960	6.25	12.50	25.00
❑ DLP-25309 [S]	Dutchman's Gold	1960	7.50	15.00	30.00

EVEREST

Number	Title	Yr	VG	VG+	NM
❑ SDBR-1103 [S]	World of Miracles	1960	7.50	15.00	30.00
❑ SDBR-1123 [S]	The President: A Musical Biography of Our Chief Executive	1960	7.50	15.00	30.00
❑ LPBR-5103 [M]	World of Miracles	1960	6.25	12.50	25.00
❑ LPBR-5123 [M]	The President: A Musical Biography of Our Chief Executive	1960	6.25	12.50	25.00

LIBERTY

Number	Title	Yr	VG	VG+	NM
❑ LRP-3233 [M]	Old Rivers	1962	5.00	10.00	20.00
❑ LRP-3257 [M]	'Twas the Night Before Christmas Back Home	1962	5.00	10.00	20.00
❑ LRP-3266 [M]	Mama Sang a Song	1963	5.00	10.00	20.00
❑ LRP-3317 [M]	Talkin' from the Heart	1964	5.00	10.00	20.00
❑ LRP-3372 [M]	Gunfight at the O.K. Corral	1964	5.00	10.00	20.00
❑ LST-7233 [S]	Old Rivers	1962	6.25	12.50	25.00
❑ LST-7241 [S]	The President: A Musical Biography of Our Chief Executive	1962	5.00	10.00	20.00

-- *Reissue of Everest 1123*

Number	Title	Yr	VG	VG+	NM
❑ LST-7244 [S]	World of Miracles	1962	5.00	10.00	20.00

-- *Reissue of Everest 1103*

Number	Title	Yr	VG	VG+	NM
❑ LST-7257 [S]	'Twas the Night Before Christmas Back Home	1962	6.25	12.50	25.00
❑ LST-7266 [S]	Mama Sang a Song	1963	6.25	12.50	25.00
❑ LST-7317 [S]	Talkin' from the Heart	1964	6.25	12.50	25.00
❑ LST-7372 [S]	Gunfight at the O.K. Corral	1964	6.25	12.50	25.00

R.P.C.

Number	Title	Yr	VG	VG+	NM
❑ 108 [M]	By the Fireside	1961	7.50	15.00	30.00
❑ 108S [S]	By the Fireside	1961	10.00	20.00	40.00

BREW
ABC

Number	Title	Yr	VG	VG+	NM
❑ ABCS-672	Very Strange Brew	1969	5.00	10.00	20.00

BREWER, TERESA
CORAL

Number	Title	Yr	VG	VG+	NM
❑ CXB 7 [(2) M]	The Best of Teresa Brewer	1965	5.00	10.00	20.00
❑ CXSB 7 [(2) P]	The Best of Teresa Brewer	1965	5.00	10.00	20.00
❑ CRL 56072 [10]	A Bouquet of Hits	1952	10.00	20.00	40.00
❑ CRL 56093 [10]	Till I Waltz Again with You	1953	10.00	20.00	40.00
❑ CRL 57027 [M]	Music, Music, Music	1955	7.50	15.00	30.00
❑ CRL 57053 [M]	Teresa	1956	7.50	15.00	30.00
❑ CRL 57135 [M]	For Teenagers in Love	1957	7.50	15.00	30.00
❑ CRL 57144 [M]	Teresa Brewer At Christmas Time	1957	7.50	15.00	30.00
❑ CRL 57179 [M]	Miss Music	1958	7.50	15.00	30.00
❑ CRL 57232 [M]	Time for Teresa	1958	7.50	15.00	30.00
❑ CRL 57245 [M]	Teresa Brewer and the Dixieland Band	1958	5.00	10.00	20.00
❑ CRL 57297 [M]	When Your Lover Has Gone	1959	5.00	10.00	20.00
❑ CRL 57315 [M]	Ridin' High	1960	5.00	10.00	20.00
❑ CRL 57329 [M]	Naughty, Naughty, Naughty	1960	5.00	10.00	20.00
❑ CRL 57351 [M]	My Golden Favorites	1960	5.00	10.00	20.00
❑ CRL 57361 [M]	Songs Everybody Knows	1961	5.00	10.00	20.00
❑ CRL 57374 [M]	Aloha from Teresa	1961	5.00	10.00	20.00

Number	Title	Yr	VG	VG+	NM
❑ CRL 57414 [M] Don't Mess with Tess		1962	5.00	10.00	20.00
❑ CRL 757245 [S] Teresa Brewer and the		1958	7.50	15.00	30.00
Dixieland Band					
❑ CRL 757297 [S] When Your Lover Has Gone		1959	7.50	15.00	30.00
❑ CRL 757315 [S] Ridin' High		1960	6.25	12.50	25.00
❑ CRL 757329 [S] Naughty, Naughty, Naughty		1960	6.25	12.50	25.00
❑ CRL 757351 [R] My Golden Favorites		1960	5.00	10.00	20.00
❑ CRL 757361 [S] Songs Everybody Knows		1961	6.25	12.50	25.00
❑ CRL 757374 [S] Aloha from Teresa		1961	6.25	12.50	25.00
❑ CRL 757414 [S] Don't Mess with Tess		1962	6.25	12.50	25.00
LONDON					
❑ APB-1006 [10] Teresa Brewer		1951	12.50	25.00	50.00
PHILIPS					
❑ PHS 600-062 [S] Teresa Brewer's Greatest Hits		1962	5.00	10.00	20.00
❑ PHS 600-099 [S] Terrific Teresa		1963	5.00	10.00	20.00

BRIGADE, THE
BAND'N VOCAL

Number	Title	Yr	VG	VG+	NM
❑ 1066	Last Laugh	1970	1,000.	1,500.	2,000.

BRIGG
SUSQUEHANNA

Number	Title	Yr	VG	VG+	NM
❑ LP-301	Brigg	1973	45.00	90.00	180.00

BRIGMAN, GEORGE
SOLID

Number	Title	Yr	VG	VG+	NM
❑ SR-001	Jungle Rot	1975	30.00	60.00	120.00

BRILL, MARTY
MERCURY

Number	Title	Yr	VG	VG+	NM
❑ MG-20178 [M] The Roving Balladeer		1957	6.25	12.50	25.00

BRIMSTONE
BRIMSTONE

Number	Title	Yr	VG	VG+	NM
❑ (no #)	Paper Winged Dreams	1968	50.00	100.00	200.00

BRINSLEY SCHWARZ
Featuring Nick Lowe and Ian Gomm.
CAPITOL

Number	Title	Yr	VG	VG+	NM
❑ ST-589	Brinsley Schwarz	1970	5.00	10.00	20.00
❑ ST-744	Despite It All	1971	5.00	10.00	20.00

BRITT, ELTON
Also see THE BEVERLY HILL BILLIES.
ABC-PARAMOUNT

Number	Title	Yr	VG	VG+	NM
❑ ABC-293 [M]	The Wandering Cowboy	1959	6.25	12.50	25.00
❑ ABCS-293 [S]	The Wandering Cowboy	1959	10.00	20.00	40.00
❑ ABC-322 [M]	Beyond the Sunset	1960	6.25	12.50	25.00
❑ ABCS-322 [S]	Beyond the Sunset	1960	10.00	20.00	40.00
❑ ABC-331 [M]	I Heard a Forest Praying	1960	6.25	12.50	25.00
❑ ABCS-331 [S]	I Heard a Forest Praying	1960	10.00	20.00	40.00
❑ ABC-521 [M]	The Singing Hills	1965	6.25	12.50	25.00
❑ ABCS-521 [S]	The Singing Hills	1965	10.00	20.00	40.00
❑ ABC-566 [M]	Somethin' for Everybody	1966	6.25	12.50	25.00
❑ ABCS-566 [S]	Somethin' for Everybody	1966	10.00	20.00	40.00
RCA VICTOR					
❑ LPM-1288 [M]	Yodel Songs	1956	15.00	30.00	60.00
❑ LPM-2669 [M]	The Best of Elton Britt	1963	6.25	12.50	25.00
❑ LPM-3222 [10]	Yodel Songs	1954	30.00	60.00	120.00

BRITT, TINA
MINIT

Number	Title	Yr	VG	VG+	NM
❑ LP-24023	Blue All the Way	1968	5.00	10.00	20.00

BROCAS HELM
GARGOYLE

Number	Title	Yr	VG	VG+	NM
❑ 138801	Black Death	1988	12.50	25.00	50.00

BROCK, B., AND THE SULTANS
CROWN

Number	Title	Yr	VG	VG+	NM
❑ CST-399 [S]	Do the Beetle	1964	12.50	25.00	50.00
❑ CLP-5399 [M]	Do the Beetle	1964	10.00	20.00	40.00

BROLIN, JAMES
ARTCO

Number	Title	Yr	VG	VG+	NM
❑ LPC-1099	James Brolin Sings	1974	6.25	12.50	25.00

BROOKLYN BRIDGE, THE
BUDDAH

Number	Title	Yr	VG	VG+	NM
❑ BDS-5034	Brooklyn Bridge	1969	5.00	10.00	20.00
❑ BDS-5042	The Second Brooklyn Bridge	1969	5.00	10.00	20.00
❑ BDS-5065	The Brooklyn Bridge	1970	5.00	10.00	20.00
❑ BDS-5107	Bridge in Blue	1972	5.00	10.00	20.00

BROOKS, DONNIE
ERA

Number	Title	Yr	VG	VG+	NM
❑ EL-105 [M]	The Happiest	1961	37.50	75.00	150.00

BROOKS, GARTH
CAPITOL

Number	Title	Yr	VG	VG+	NM
❑ C1-90897	Garth Brooks	1989	6.25	12.50	25.00
-- Non-record club edition					
❑ C1-590897	Garth Brooks	1989	5.00	10.00	20.00
-- Columbia House edition					
CAPITOL NASHVILLE					
❑ R 173266	No Fences	1990	12.50	25.00	50.00
-- Only released on U.S. vinyl by BMG Direct Marketing					
❑ C1-596330	Ropin' the Wind	1991	12.50	25.00	50.00
-- Only released on U.S. vinyl by Columbia House					

BROOKS, HADDA
CROWN

Number	Title	Yr	VG	VG+	NM
❑ CLP-5010 [M]	Femme Fatale	1957	15.00	30.00	60.00
-- Black label; reissue of Modern LP					
❑ CLP-5374 [M]	Hadda Brooks Sings and Swings	1963	6.25	12.50	25.00
-- Gray label					
MODERN					
❑ MLP-1210 [M]	Femme Fatale	1956	50.00	100.00	200.00

BROOKS, HADDA / PETE JOHNSON
CROWN

Number	Title	Yr	VG	VG+	NM
❑ CLP-5058 [M]	Boogie	1958	12.50	25.00	50.00

BROONZY, BIG BILL
CHESS

Number	Title	Yr	VG	VG+	NM
❑ LP-1468 [M]	Big Bill Broonzy and	1962	40.00	80.00	160.00
	Washboard Sam				
COLUMBIA					
❑ WL 111 [M]	Big Bill's Blues	1958	25.00	50.00	100.00
DIAL					
❑ LP-306 [10]	Blues Concert	1952	37.50	75.00	150.00
EMARCY					
❑ MG-26034 [10]	Folk Blues	1954	30.00	60.00	120.00
❑ MG-36137 [M]	Blues by Broonzy	1958	25.00	50.00	100.00
EPIC					
❑ EE 22017 [M]	Big Bill's Blues	196?	5.00	10.00	20.00
FOLKWAYS					
❑ FA-2315 [M]	Big Bill Broonzy	1957	12.50	25.00	50.00
❑ FA-2326 [M]	Country Blues	1957	12.50	25.00	50.00
❑ FG-3586 [M]	His Songs and Story	195?	12.50	25.00	50.00
MERCURY					
❑ MG-20822 [M]	Big Bill Broonzy -- Memorial	1963	7.50	15.00	30.00
❑ MG-20905 [M]	Remembering Big Bill Broonzy	1964	7.50	15.00	30.00
❑ SR-60822 [R]	Big Bill Broonzy -- Memorial	1963	5.00	10.00	20.00
❑ SR-60905 [R]	Remembering Big Bill Broonzy	1964	5.00	10.00	20.00
PERIOD					
❑ SLP-1114 [M]	Big Bill Broonzy Sings (Blues)	1956	37.50	75.00	150.00
❑ SLP-1209 [M]	Big Bill Broonzy Sings and Josh	1958	17.50	35.00	70.00
	White Comes a-Visiting				
VERVE					
❑ MGV-3000-5 [(5)M]	The Big Bill Broonzy Story	1959	50.00	100.00	200.00
❑ MGV-3001 [M]	Last Session, Vol. 1	1959	12.50	25.00	50.00
❑ MGV-3002 [M]	Last Session, Vol. 2	1959	12.50	25.00	50.00
❑ MGV-3003 [M]	Last Session, Vol. 3	1959	12.50	25.00	50.00

BROTH
MERCURY

Number	Title	Yr	VG	VG+	NM
❑ SR-61298	Broth	1970	5.00	10.00	20.00

BROTHER FOX AND TAR BABY
CAPITOL

Number	Title	Yr	VG	VG+	NM
❑ ST-544	Brother Fox and Tar Baby	1970	7.50	15.00	30.00
ORACLE					
❑ 1001	Brother Fox and Tar Baby	1969	7.50	15.00	30.00

Number	Title	Yr	VG	VG+	NM
BROTHERS FOUR, THE					
COLUMBIA					
❏ CS 9302 [S]	A Beatles' Songbook (The Brothers Four Sing Lennon/McCartney)	1966	5.00	10.00	20.00
BROWN'S FERRY FOUR, THE					
KING					
❏ 551 [M]	Sacred Songs	1957	20.00	40.00	80.00
❏ 590 [M]	Sacred Songs	1958	20.00	40.00	80.00
❏ 943	Wonderful Sacred Songs	1964	7.50	15.00	30.00
BROWN, AL					
AMY					
❏ A-1 [M]	Madison Dance Party	1960	10.00	20.00	40.00
❏ AS-1 [S]	Madison Dance Party	1960	12.50	25.00	50.00
BROWN, ARTHUR, THE CRAZY WORLD OF					
TRACK					
❏ SD 8198	The Crazy World of Arthur Brown	1968	6.25	12.50	25.00
BROWN, BOBBY					
DESTINY					
❏ 4001	Bobby Brown Live	1972	25.00	50.00	100.00
❏ 4002	The Enlightening Beam of Axonda	1972	30.00	60.00	120.00
BROWN, BOOTS					
GROOVE					
❏ LG-1000 [M]	Rock That Beat	1955	75.00	150.00	300.00
BROWN, BUSTER					
FIRE					
❏ FLP-102 [M]	The New King of the Blues	1961	175.00	350.00	700.00
-- White and red label					
❏ FLP-102 [M]	The New King of the Blues	1961	75.00	150.00	300.00
-- Red and black label, white cover					
❏ FLP-102 [M]	The New King of the Blues	1961	100.00	200.00	400.00
-- Red and black label, purple cover					
BROWN, CHARLES					
ALADDIN					
❏ LP-702 [10]	Mood Music	1953	1,500.	2,750.	4,000.
-- Black vinyl					
❏ LP-702 [10]	Mood Music	1953	3,000.	5,250.	7,500.
-- Red vinyl					
BLUESWAY					
❏ BLS-6039	Charles Brown -- Legend	1970	6.25	12.50	25.00
BULLSEYE BLUES					
❏ BB-9501	All My Life	1990	5.00	10.00	20.00
IMPERIAL					
❏ LP-9178 [M]	Charles Brown Sings Million Sellers	1961	100.00	200.00	400.00
KING					
❏ 775 [M]	Charles Brown Sings Christmas Songs	1961	37.50	75.00	150.00
❏ KS-775 [S]	Charles Brown Sings Christmas Songs	1963	75.00	150.00	300.00
-- Stereo copies (whether true stereo or rechanneled, we don't know) exist on blue labels with "King" in block letters (no crown).					
❏ 878 [M]	The Great Charles Brown	1963	50.00	100.00	200.00
MAINSTREAM					
❏ S-6007 [S]	Boss of the Blues	1965	7.50	15.00	30.00
❏ S-6035 [S]	Ballads My Way	1965	7.50	15.00	30.00
❏ 56007 [M]	Boss of the Blues	1965	5.00	10.00	20.00
❏ 56035 [M]	Ballads My Way	1965	5.00	10.00	20.00
SCORE					
❏ SLP-4011 [M]	Driftin' Blues	1958	100.00	200.00	400.00
BROWN, HYLO					
CAPITOL					
❏ T 1168 [M]	Hylo Brown	1959	20.00	40.00	80.00
STARDAY					
❏ SLP-185 [M]	Bluegrass Balladeer	1962	10.00	20.00	40.00
❏ SLP-204 [M]	Bluegrass Goes to College	1962	10.00	20.00	40.00
❏ SLP-220 [M]	Hylo Brown Meets the Lonesome Pine Fiddlers	1963	10.00	20.00	40.00
❏ SLP-249 [M]	Sing Me a Bluegrass Song	1963	10.00	20.00	40.00

Number	Title	Yr	VG	VG+	NM
BROWN, JAMES					
HRB					
❏ 1004 [(2)]	The Fabulous James Brown	1974	6.25	12.50	25.00
KING					
❏ 610 [M]	Please Please Please	1958	300.00	600.00	1,200.
-- "Woman's and man's legs" cover; "King" on label is two inches wide					
❏ 610 [M]	Please Please Please	1961	250.00	500.00	1,000.
-- "Woman's and man's legs" cover; "King" on label is three inches wide					
❏ 635 [M]	Try Me!	1959	225.00	450.00	900.00
-- "Woman with cigarette and gun" cover; "King" on label is two inches wide					
❏ 635 [M]	Try Me!	1961	150.00	300.00	600.00
-- "Woman with cigarette and gun" cover; "King" on label is three inches wide					
❏ 683 [M]	Think!	1960	225.00	450.00	900.00
-- "Baby" cover; "King" on label is two inches wide					
❏ 683 [M]	Think!	1961	150.00	300.00	600.00
-- "Baby" cover; "King" on label is three inches wide					
❏ 683 [M]	Think!	1963	25.00	50.00	100.00
-- James Brown photo cover; "crownless" King label					
❏ 683 [M]	Think!	1966	12.50	25.00	50.00
-- James Brown photo cover; "crown" King label					
❏ 743 [M]	The Amazing James Brown	1961	125.00	250.00	500.00
-- "James Brown in suit" cover					
❏ 743 [M]	The Amazing James Brown	1963	37.50	75.00	150.00
-- White title cover; "crownless" King label					
❏ 743 [M]	The Amazing James Brown	1966	125.00	250.00	500.00
-- White title cover with "James Brown" in huge letters; "crown" King label					
❏ 771 [M]	Night Train	1961	75.00	150.00	300.00
-- Original title					
❏ 771 [M]	Twist Around	1962	62.50	125.00	250.00
-- Second title					
❏ 771 [M]	Jump Around	1963	50.00	100.00	200.00
-- Third title					
❏ KS-771 [S]	Jump Around	1963	75.00	150.00	300.00
-- Stereo copies of King 771 only exist with this title					
❏ 780 [M]	Shout and Shimmy	1962	62.50	125.00	250.00
-- "Shout and Shimmy" on both cover and label					
❏ 780 [M]	Good Good Twistin'	1962	50.00	100.00	200.00
-- "Good Good Twistin' " on either label or cover, or both					
❏ 780 [M]	Excitement	1963	37.50	75.00	150.00
-- Third title; "crownless" King label					
❏ 780 [M]	Excitement	1966	12.50	25.00	50.00
-- Third title; "crown" King label					
❏ 804 [M]	James Brown & His Famous Flames Tour the U.S.A.	1962	37.50	125.00	250.00
-- "Crownless" King label					
❏ 804 [M]	James Brown & His Famous Flames Tour the U.S.A.	1966	12.50	25.00	50.00
-- "Crown" King label					
❏ 826 [M]	Live at the Apollo	1963	50.00	100.00	200.00
-- Custom back cover; "crownless" King label					
❏ 826 [M]	Live at the Apollo	1963	37.50	75.00	150.00
-- Other King albums on back cover; "crownless" King label					
❏ 826 [M]	Live at the Apollo	1966	12.50	25.00	50.00
-- "Crown" King label					
❏ KS-826 [S]	Live at the Apollo	1963	75.00	150.00	300.00
-- Custom back cover; "crownless" King label					
❏ KS-826 [S]	Live at the Apollo	1963	50.00	100.00	200.00
-- Other King albums on back cover; "crownless" King label					
❏ KS-826 [S]	Live at the Apollo	1966	17.50	35.00	70.00
-- "Crown" King label					
❏ 851 [M]	Prisoner of Love	1963	50.00	100.00	200.00
-- Custom back cover; "crownless" King label					
❏ 851 [M]	Prisoner of Love	1963	25.00	50.00	100.00
-- Other King albums on back cover; "crownless" King label					
❏ 851 [M]	Prisoner of Love	1966	12.50	25.00	50.00
-- "Crown" King label					
❏ 883 [M]	Pure Dynamite! Live at the Royal	1964	50.00	100.00	200.00
-- "Crownless" King label					
❏ 883 [M]	Pure Dynamite! Live at the Royal	1966	12.50	25.00	50.00
-- "Crown" King label					
❏ 883 [M-DJ]	Pure Dynamite! Live at the Royal	1964	200.00	400.00	800.00
-- White label promo; banded for airplay					
❏ 909 [M]	Please Please Please	1964	25.00	50.00	100.00
-- Reissue of 610; "crownless" King label					
❏ 909 [M]	Please Please Please	1966	12.50	25.00	50.00
-- "Crown" King label					
❏ 919 [M]	The Unbeatable James Brown -- 16 Hits	1964	25.00	50.00	100.00
-- Reissue of 635; "crownless" King label					
❏ 919 [M]	The Unbeatable James Brown -- 16 Hits	1966	12.50	25.00	50.00
-- "Crown" King label					
❏ 938 [M]	Papa's Got a Brand New Bag	1965	20.00	40.00	80.00
-- Red cover; "crownless" King label					
❏ 938 [M]	Papa's Got a Brand New Bag	1966	12.50	25.00	50.00
-- Green cover; "crownless" King label					
❏ 938 [M]	Papa's Got a Brand New Bag	1966	10.00	20.00	40.00
-- "Crown" King label					

Number	Title	Yr	VG	VG+	NM
LPS-938 [P]	Papa's Got a Brand New Bag	1965	25.00	50.00	100.00
-- Red cover; "crownless" King label					
LPS-938 [P]	Papa's Got a Brand New Bag	1966	15.00	30.00	60.00
-- Green cover; "crownless" King label					
LPS-938 [P]	Papa's Got a Brand New Bag	1966	12.50	25.00	50.00
-- "Crown" King label					
946 [M]	I Got You (I Feel Good)	1966	25.00	50.00	100.00
-- "Crownless" King label					
946 [M]	I Got You (I Feel Good)	1966	10.00	20.00	40.00
-- "Crown" King label					
LPS-946 [S]	I Got You (I Feel Good)	1966	37.50	75.00	150.00
-- "Crownless" King label					
LPS-946 [S]	I Got You (I Feel Good)	1966	12.50	25.00	50.00
-- "Crown" King label					
961 [M]	Mighty Instrumentals	1966	25.00	50.00	100.00
LPS-961 [S]	Mighty Instrumentals	1966	37.50	75.00	150.00
985 [M]	It's a Man's Man's Man's World	1966	12.50	25.00	50.00
KS-985 [S]	It's a Man's Man's Man's World	1966	17.50	35.00	70.00
1010 [M]	Christmas Songs	1966	25.00	50.00	100.00
-- Wreath on gray wall, no song titles on back					
1010 [M]	Christmas Songs	1967	20.00	40.00	80.00
-- Wreath on white wall, song titles are on back					
KS-1010 [S]	Christmas Songs	1966	37.50	75.00	150.00
-- Wreath on gray wall, no song titles on back					
KS-1010 [S]	Christmas Songs	1967	25.00	50.00	100.00
-- Wreath on white wall, song titles are on back					
1016 [M]	Raw Soul	1967	12.50	25.00	50.00
KS-1016 [P]	Raw Soul	1967	17.50	35.00	70.00
1018 [M]	Live at the Garden	1967	20.00	40.00	80.00
1018 [M]	Live at the Garden	1967	100.00	200.00	400.00
-- Black label promo; banded for airplay					
KS-1018 [S]	Live at the Garden	1967	25.00	50.00	100.00
1020 [M]	Cold Sweat	1967	12.50	25.00	50.00
KS-1020 [S]	Cold Sweat	1967	17.50	35.00	70.00
KS-1040	A Soulful Christmas	1968	20.00	40.00	80.00
KS-1047	Say It Loud -- I'm Black and I'm Proud	1969	12.50	25.00	50.00
KS-1051	Gettin' Down To It	1969	12.50	25.00	50.00
KSD-1055	James Brown Plays & Directs The Popcorn	1969	10.00	20.00	40.00
KSD-1063	It's a Mother	1969	10.00	20.00	40.00
KSD-1092	Ain't It Funky	1970	10.00	20.00	40.00
KSD-1095	It's a New Day So Let a Man Come In	1970	10.00	20.00	40.00
KSD-1100	Soul on Top	1970	10.00	20.00	40.00
KSD-1110	Sho Is Funky Down Here	1971	10.00	20.00	40.00
KSD-1115 [(2)]	Sex Machine	1970	12.50	25.00	50.00
KSD-1124	Hey America!	1970	10.00	20.00	40.00
KSD-1127	Super Bad	1971	10.00	20.00	40.00
LPS-1022 [(2)]	Live at the Apollo, Volume II	1968	17.50	35.00	70.00
LPS-1024	James Brown Presents His Show of Tomorrow	1968	12.50	25.00	50.00
-- Various-artists album					
LPS-1030	I Can't Stand Myself (When You Touch Me)	1968	12.50	25.00	50.00
LPS-1031	I Got the Feelin'	1968	12.50	25.00	50.00
LPS-1034	James Brown Plays Nothing But	1968	12.50	25.00	50.00
LPS-1038	Thinking About Little Willie John and a Few Nice Things	1968	12.50	25.00	50.00
POLYDOR					
25-3003 [(2)]	Revolution of the Mind -- Live at the Apollo, Volume III	1971	15.00	30.00	60.00
PD2-3004 [(2)]	Get On the Good Foot	1972	15.00	30.00	60.00
PD2-3007 [(2)]	The Payback	1973	12.50	25.00	50.00
24-4054	Hot Pants	1971	10.00	20.00	40.00
PD-5028	There It Is	1972	10.00	20.00	40.00
SC-5401	James Brown Soul Classics	1972	6.25	12.50	25.00
SC-5402	Soul Classics, Volume 2	1973	6.25	12.50	25.00
PD-6014	Black Caesar	1973	12.50	25.00	50.00
PD-6015	Slaughter's Big Rip-Off	1973	12.50	25.00	50.00
PD-1-6039	Reality	1975	10.00	20.00	40.00
PD-1-6042	Sex Machine Today	1975	10.00	20.00	40.00
PD-1-6054	Everybody's Doin' the Hustle & Dead On the Double Bump	1975	10.00	20.00	40.00
PD-1-6059	Hot	1976	10.00	20.00	40.00
PD-1-6071	Get Up Offa That Thing	1976	10.00	20.00	40.00
PD-1-6093	Bodyheat	1976	10.00	20.00	40.00
PD-1-6111	Mutha's Nature	1977	10.00	20.00	40.00
PD-1-6140	Jam/1980s	1978	10.00	20.00	40.00
PD-1-6181	Take a Look at Those Cakes	1978	7.50	15.00	30.00
PD-1-6212	The Original Disco Man	1979	7.50	15.00	30.00
PD-1-6258	People	1980	7.50	15.00	30.00
PD-1-6318	Nonstop!	1981	7.50	15.00	30.00
PD-1-6340	The Best of James Brown	1981	5.00	10.00	20.00
PD-2-6290 [(2)]	James Brown...Live/Hot on the One	1980	12.50	25.00	50.00

Number	Title	Yr	VG	VG+	NM
PD-2-9001 [(2)]	Hell	1974	20.00	40.00	80.00
PD-2-9004 [(2)]	Sex Machine Live	1976	12.50	25.00	50.00
829 254-1 [(2)]	Solid Gold: 30 Golden Hits	1985	5.00	10.00	20.00
SCOTTI BROTHERS					
75225-1	Love Overdue	1991	5.00	10.00	20.00
SMASH					
MGS-27054 [M]	Showtime	1964	7.50	15.00	30.00
MGS-27057 [M]	Grits & Soul	1965	7.50	15.00	30.00
MGS-27058 [M]	Out of Sight	1965	25.00	50.00	100.00
MGS-27072 [M]	James Brown Plays James Brown -- Today & Yesterday	1965	7.50	15.00	30.00
MGS-27080 [M]	James Brown Plays New Breed	1966	7.50	15.00	30.00
MGS-27084 [M]	Handful of Soul	1966	7.50	15.00	30.00
MGS-27087 [M]	The James Brown Show	1967	7.50	15.00	30.00
-- Various-artists LP					
MGS-27093 [M]	James Brown Plays the Real Thing	1967	7.50	15.00	30.00
SRS-67054 [S]	Showtime	1964	10.00	2.00	40.00
SRS-67057 [S]	Grits & Soul	1965	10.00	20.00	40.00
SRS-67058 [S]	Out of Sight	1965	37.50	75.00	150.00
SRS-67072 [S]	James Brown Plays James Brown -- Today & Yesterday	1965	10.00	20.00	40.00
SRS-67080 [S]	James Brown Plays New Breed	1966	10.00	2.00	40.00
SRS-67084 [S]	Handful of Soul	1966	10.00	20.00	40.00
SRS-67087 [S]	The James Brown Show	1967	10.00	2.00	40.00
-- Various-artists LP					
SRS-67093 [S]	James Brown Plays the Real Thing	1967	10.00	20.00	40.00
SRS-67109	James Brown Sings Out of Sight	1968	7.50	15.00	30.00
-- Abridged reissue of 67058					
T.K.					
615	Soul Syndrome	1980	7.50	15.00	30.00
BROWN, JIM ED					
Also see THE BROWNS.					
RCA VICTOR					
LPM-3569 [M]	Alone with You	1966	5.00	10.00	20.00
LSP-3569 [S]	Alone with You	1966	6.25	12.50	25.00
LPM-3744 [M]	Just Jim	1967	6.25	12.50	25.00
LSP-3744 [S]	Just Jim	1967	5.00	10.00	20.00
LPM-3853 [M]	Gems by Jim	1967	6.25	12.50	25.00
LSP-3853 [S]	Gems by Jim	1967	5.00	10.00	20.00
LPM-3942 [M]	Bottle, Bottle	1968	10.00	20.00	40.00
LSP-3942 [S]	Bottle, Bottle	1968	5.00	10.00	20.00
LSP-4011	Country's Best on Record	1968	5.00	10.00	20.00
LSP-4130	This Is My Best!	1968	5.00	10.00	20.00
LSP-4175	Jim Ed Sings the Browns	1969	5.00	10.00	20.00
BROWN, MAXINE					
COMMONWEALTH UNITED					
CU-6001	We'll Cry Together	1969	5.00	10.00	20.00
WAND					
WD-656 [M]	The Fabulous Sound of Maxine Brown	1963	12.50	25.00	50.00
WDS-656 [S]	The Fabulous Sound of Maxine Brown	1963	15.00	30.00	60.00
WD-663 [M]	Spotlight on Maxine Brown	1965	7.50	15.00	30.00
WDS-663 [S]	Spotlight on Maxine Brown	1965	10.00	20.00	40.00
WD-684 [M]	Maxine Brown's Greatest Hits	1967	5.00	10.00	20.00
WDS-684 [S]	Maxine Brown's Greatest Hits	1967	6.25	12.50	25.00
BROWN, NAPPY					
SAVOY					
MG-14002 [M]	Nappy Brown Sings	1958	100.00	200.00	400.00
MG-14025 [M]	The Right Time	1960	62.50	125.00	250.00
BROWN, ODELL					
ABC IMPULSE!					
AS-9140	3 for Shepp	1968	5.00	10.00	20.00
CADET					
LPS-775 [S]	Raising the Roof	1966	5.00	10.00	20.00
LP-788 [M]	Mellow Yellow	1967	5.00	10.00	20.00
LP-800 [M]	Ducky	1967	5.00	10.00	20.00
BROWN, ROY					
BLUESWAY					
BLS-6019	The Blues Are Brown	1968	6.25	12.50	25.00
BLS-6056	Hard Times	1973	6.25	12.50	25.00
EPIC					
E 30473	Live at Monterey	1971	6.25	12.50	25.00

Number	Title	Yr	VG	VG+	NM

KING
- ❏ 956 [M] — Roy Brown Sings 24 Hits — 1966 — 12.50 — 25.00 — 50.00
- ❏ KS-956 [R] — Roy Brown Sings 24 Hits — 1966 — 12.50 — 25.00 — 50.00
- ❏ KS-1130 — Hard Luck Blues — 1971 — 6.25 — 12.50 — 25.00

BROWN, ROY / WYNONIE HARRIS
Also see each artist's individual listings.
KING
- ❏ 607 [M] — Battle of the Blues — 1958 — 150.00 — 300.00 — 600.00
- ❏ 627 [M] — Battle of the Blues, Volume 2 — 1959 — 200.00 — 400.00 — 800.00

BROWN, ROY / WYNONIE HARRIS / EDDIE VINSON
Also see each artist's individual listings.
KING
- ❏ 668 [M] — Battle of the Blues, Volume 4 — 1960 — 625.00 — 1,250. — 2,500.

BROWN, RUTH
ATLANTIC
- ❏ 1308 [M] — Last Date with Ruth Brown — 1959 — 50.00 — 100.00 — 200.00
  -- Black label
- ❏ 1308 [M] — Last Date with Ruth Brown — 1961 — 12.50 — 25.00 — 50.00
  -- Red and purple label, "fan" logo in white
- ❏ SD 1308 [S] — Last Date with Ruth Brown — 1959 — 75.00 — 150.00 — 300.00
  -- Green label
- ❏ SD 1308 [S] — Last Date with Ruth Brown — 1961 — 15.00 — 30.00 — 60.00
  -- Blue and green label, "fan" logo in white
- ❏ 8004 [M] — Ruth Brown — 1957 — 50.00 — 100.00 — 200.00
  -- Black label
- ❏ 8004 [M] — Ruth Brown — 1960 — 37.50 — 75.00 — 150.00
  -- White "bullseye" label
- ❏ 8004 [M] — Ruth Brown — 1961 — 12.50 — 25.00 — 50.00
  -- Red and purple label, "fan" logo in white
- ❏ 8026 [M] — Miss Rhythm — 1959 — 50.00 — 100.00 — 200.00
  -- Black label
- ❏ 8026 [M] — Miss Rhythm — 1960 — 37.50 — 75.00 — 150.00
  -- White "bullseye" label
- ❏ 8026 [M] — Miss Rhythm — 1961 — 12.50 — 25.00 — 50.00
  -- Red and purple label, "fan" logo in white
- ❏ 8080 [M] — The Best of Ruth Brown — 1963 — 10.00 — 20.00 — 40.00

MAINSTREAM
- ❏ S-6034 [S] — Ruth Brown '65 — 1965 — 7.50 — 15.00 — 30.00
- ❏ 56034 [M] — Ruth Brown '65 — 1965 — 6.25 — 12.50 — 25.00

PHILIPS
- ❏ PHM 200-028 [M] — Along Comes Ruth — 1962 — 10.00 — 20.00 — 40.00
- ❏ PHM 200-065 [M] — Gospel Time — 1962 — 7.50 — 15.00 — 30.00
- ❏ PHS 600-028 [S] — Along Comes Ruth — 1962 — 12.50 — 25.00 — 50.00
- ❏ PHS 600-065 [S] — Gospel Time — 1962 — 10.00 — 20.00 — 40.00

BROWNE, JACKSON
(NO LABEL)
- ❏ (no #) [(2)] — "Jackson Browne's First Album" — 1967 — 1,000. — 1,500. — 2,000.
  -- Publisher's demo in plain cardboard jacket

ASYLUM
- ❏ EQ-1017 [Q] — Late for the Sky — 1974 — 7.50 — 15.00 — 30.00
- ❏ SD 5051 — Jackson Browne (Saturate Before Using) — 1972 — 5.00 — 10.00 — 20.00
  -- Burlap cover, opens at top; white label with "Asylum Records" logo in a circle at top

MOBILE FIDELITY
- ❏ 1-055 — The Pretender — 1981 — 6.25 — 12.50 — 25.00
  -- Audiophile vinyl

BROWNS, THE
Also see JIM ED BROWN.
RCA VICTOR
- ❏ LPM-1438 [M] — Jim Edward, Maxine and Bonnie Brown — 1957 — 12.50 — 25.00 — 50.00
- ❏ LPM-2144 [M] — Sweet Sounds by the Browns — 1959 — 7.50 — 15.00 — 30.00
- ❏ LSP-2144 [S] — Sweet Sounds by the Browns — 1959 — 10.00 — 20.00 — 40.00
- ❏ LPM-2174 [M] — Town and Country — 1960 — 5.00 — 10.00 — 20.00
- ❏ LSP-2174 [S] — Town and Country — 1960 — 6.25 — 12.50 — 25.00
- ❏ LPM-2260 [M] — The Browns Sing Their Hits — 1960 — 5.00 — 10.00 — 20.00
- ❏ LSP-2260 [S] — The Browns Sing Their Hits — 1960 — 6.25 — 12.50 — 25.00
- ❏ LPM-2333 [M] — Our Favorite Folk Songs — 1961 — 5.00 — 10.00 — 20.00
- ❏ LSP-2333 [S] — Our Favorite Folk Songs — 1961 — 6.25 — 12.50 — 25.00
- ❏ LPM-2345 [M] — The Little Brown Church Hymnal — 1961 — 5.00 — 10.00 — 20.00
- ❏ LSP-2345 [S] — The Little Brown Church Hymnal — 1961 — 6.25 — 12.50 — 25.00
- ❏ LSP-2784 [S] — Grand Ole Opry Favorites — 1963 — 5.00 — 10.00 — 20.00
- ❏ LSP-2860 [S] — This Young Land — 1964 — 5.00 — 10.00 — 20.00
- ❏ LSP-2987 [S] — Three Shades of Brown — 1964 — 5.00 — 10.00 — 20.00
- ❏ LSP-3423 [S] — When Love Is Gone — 1965 — 5.00 — 10.00 — 20.00
- ❏ LSP-3561 [S] — The Best of the Browns — 1966 — 5.00 — 10.00 — 20.00
- ❏ LSP-3668 [S] — Our Kind of Country — 1966 — 5.00 — 10.00 — 20.00

- ❏ LPM-3798 [M] — The Old Country Church — 1967 — 5.00 — 10.00 — 20.00

BROWNSVILLE STATION
EPIC
- ❏ JE 35606 — Air Special — 1978 — 5.00 — 10.00 — 20.00
  -- Orange vinyl promo

PALLADIUM
- ❏ P-1004 — Brownsville Station — 1970 — 7.50 — 15.00 — 30.00

BRUBECK, DAVE
COLUMBIA
- ❏ C2L 26 [(2) M] — The Dave Brubeck Quartet at Carnegie Hall — 1963 — 6.25 — 12.50 — 25.00
  -- Red "Guaranteed High Fidelity" label
- ❏ CL 566 [M] — Jazz Goes to College — 1954 — 20.00 — 40.00 — 80.00
  -- Dark red label, gold print; released at the same time as 6321 and 6322
- ❏ CL 566 [M] — Jazz Goes to College — 1955 — 12.50 — 25.00 — 50.00
  -- Red/black label with six "eye" logos
- ❏ CL 566 [M] — Jazz Goes to College — 1962 — 5.00 — 10.00 — 20.00
  -- Red "Guaranteed High Fidelity" label
- ❏ CL 590 [M] — Dave Brubeck at Storyville: 1954 — 1954 — 20.00 — 40.00 — 80.00
  -- Dark red label, gold print; released at the same time as 6330 and 6331
- ❏ CL 590 [M] — Dave Brubeck at Storyville: 1954 — 1955 — 12.50 — 25.00 — 50.00
  -- Red/black label with six "eye" logos
- ❏ CL 590 [M] — Dave Brubeck at Storyville: 1954 — 1962 — 5.00 — 10.00 — 20.00
  -- Red "Guaranteed High Fidelity" label
- ❏ CL 622 [M] — Brubeck Time — 1955 — 15.00 — 30.00 — 60.00
  -- Red/black label with six "eye" logos
- ❏ CL 622 [M] — Brubeck Time — 1962 — 5.00 — 10.00 — 20.00
  -- Red "Guaranteed High Fidelity" label
- ❏ CL 699 [M] — Jazz: Red Hot and Cool — 1955 — 15.00 — 30.00 — 60.00
  -- Red/black label with six "eye" logos
- ❏ CL 699 [M] — Jazz: Red Hot and Cool — 1962 — 5.00 — 10.00 — 20.00
  -- Red "Guaranteed High Fidelity" label
- ❏ C2S 826 [(2) S] — The Dave Brubeck Quartet at Carnegie Hall — 1963 — 7.50 — 15.00 — 30.00
  -- Red label, "360 Sound" in black
- ❏ C2S 826 [(2) S] — The Dave Brubeck Quartet at Carnegie Hall — 1966 — 5.00 — 10.00 — 20.00
  -- Red label, "360 Sound" in white
- ❏ CL 878 [M] — Brubeck Plays Brubeck — 1956 — 15.00 — 30.00 — 60.00
  -- Red/black label with six "eye" logos
- ❏ CL 878 [M] — Brubeck Plays Brubeck — 1962 — 5.00 — 10.00 — 20.00
  -- Red "Guaranteed High Fidelity" label
- ❏ CL 932 [M] — American Jazz Festival at Newport '56 — 1956 — 12.50 — 25.00 — 50.00
  -- Red/black label with six "eye" logos
- ❏ CL 932 [M] — American Jazz Festival at Newport '56 — 1962 — 5.00 — 10.00 — 20.00
  -- Red "Guaranteed High Fidelity" label
- ❏ CL 984 [M] — Jazz Impressions of the U.S.A. — 1957 — 12.50 — 25.00 — 50.00
  -- Red/black label with six "eye" logos
- ❏ CL 984 [M] — Jazz Impressions of the U.S.A. — 1962 — 5.00 — 10.00 — 20.00
  -- Red "Guaranteed High Fidelity" label
- ❏ CL 1034 [M] — Jazz Goes to Junior College — 1957 — 10.00 — 20.00 — 40.00
  -- Red/black label with six "eye" logos
- ❏ CL 1034 [M] — Jazz Goes to Junior College — 1962 — 5.00 — 10.00 — 20.00
  -- Red "Guaranteed High Fidelity" label
- ❏ CL 1059 [M] — Dave Digs Disney — 1957 — 10.00 — 20.00 — 40.00
  -- Red/black label with six "eye" logos
- ❏ CL 1059 [M] — Dave Digs Disney — 1962 — 5.00 — 10.00 — 20.00
  -- Red "Guaranteed High Fidelity" label
- ❏ CL 1169 [M] — Dave Brubeck Quartet in Europe — 1958 — 10.00 — 20.00 — 40.00
  -- Red/black label with six "eye" logos
- ❏ CL 1169 [M] — Dave Brubeck Quartet in Europe — 1962 — 5.00 — 10.00 — 20.00
  -- Red "Guaranteed High Fidelity" label
- ❏ CL 1249 [M] — Newport 1958 — 1958 — 10.00 — 20.00 — 40.00
  -- Red/black label with six "eye" logos
- ❏ CL 1249 [M] — Newport 1958 — 1962 — 5.00 — 10.00 — 20.00
  -- Red "Guaranteed High Fidelity" label
- ❏ CL 1251 [M] — Jazz Impressions of Eurasia — 1958 — 10.00 — 20.00 — 40.00
  -- Red/black label with six "eye" logos
- ❏ CL 1251 [M] — Jazz Impressions of Eurasia — 1962 — 5.00 — 10.00 — 20.00
  -- Red "Guaranteed High Fidelity" label
- ❏ CL 1347 [M] — Gone with the Wind — 1959 — 10.00 — 20.00 — 40.00
  -- Red/black label with six "eye" logos
- ❏ CL 1347 [M] — Gone with the Wind — 1962 — 5.00 — 10.00 — 20.00
  -- Red "Guaranteed High Fidelity" label
- ❏ CL 1397 [M] — Time Out — 1960 — 10.00 — 20.00 — 40.00
  -- Red/black label with six "eye" logos; front cover does NOT say "Featuring Take Five"
- ❏ CL 1397 [M] — Time Out Featuring "Take Five" — 1960 — 6.25 — 12.50 — 25.00
  -- Red/black label with six "eye" logos
- ❏ CL 1439 [M] — Southern Scene — 1960 — 6.25 — 12.50 — 25.00
- ❏ CL 1454 [M] — The Riddle — 1960 — 6.25 — 12.50 — 25.00
  -- Red/black label with six "eye" logos

Number	Title	Yr	VG	VG+	NM
❑ CL 1466 [M]	Bernstein Plays Brubeck Plays Bernstein	1960	6.25	12.50	25.00
-- Red/black label with six "eye" logos					
❑ CL 1553 [M]	Brubeck and Rushing	1961	6.25	12.50	25.00
-- Red/black label with six "eye" logos					
❑ CL 1609 [M]	Tonight Only!	1961	6.25	12.50	25.00
-- Red/black label with six "eye" logos					
❑ CL 1690 [M]	Time Further Out	1961	6.25	12.50	25.00
-- Red/black label with six "eye" logos					
❑ CL 1775 [M]	Countdown -- Time in Outer Space	1962	7.50	15.00	30.00
-- Red/black label with six "eye" logos					
❑ CL 1963 [M]	Brandenburg Gate Revisited	1963	5.00	10.00	20.00
-- Red "Guaranteed High Fidelity" label					
❑ CL 1998 [M]	Bossa Nova U.S.A.	1963	5.00	10.00	20.00
-- Red "Guaranteed High Fidelity" label					
❑ CL 2127 [M]	Time Changes	1964	5.00	10.00	20.00
-- Red "Guaranteed High Fidelity" label					
❑ CL 2212 [M]	Jazz Impressions of Japan	1964	5.00	10.00	20.00
-- Red "Guaranteed High Fidelity" label					
❑ CL 2275 [M]	Jazz Impressions of New York	1965	5.00	10.00	20.00
-- Red "Guaranteed High Fidelity" label					
❑ CL 2316 [M]	Take Five	1965	5.00	10.00	20.00
-- Red "Guaranteed High Fidelity" label					
❑ CL 2348 [M]	Angel Eyes	1965	5.00	10.00	20.00
-- Red "Guaranteed High Fidelity" label					
❑ CL 2695 [M]	Bravo Brubeck!	1967	5.00	10.00	20.00
❑ CL 2712 [M]	Jackpot	1967	5.00	10.00	20.00
❑ CL 6321 [10]	Jazz Goes to College, Volume 1	1954	25.00	50.00	100.00
❑ CL 6322 [10]	Jazz Goes to College, Volume 2	1954	25.00	50.00	100.00
❑ CL 6330 [10]	Dave Brubeck at Storyville: 1954, Volume 1	1954	20.00	40.00	80.00
❑ CL 6331 [10]	Dave Brubeck at Storyville: 1954, Volume 2	1954	20.00	40.00	80.00
❑ CS 8058 [S]	Jazz Impressions of Eurasia	1959	12.50	25.00	50.00
-- Red/black label with six "eye" logos					
❑ CS 8058 [S]	Jazz Impressions of Eurasia	1962	6.25	12.50	25.00
-- Red label, "360 Sound" in black					
❑ CS 8082 [S]	Newport 1958	1959	12.50	25.00	50.00
-- Red/black label with six "eye" logos					
❑ CS 8082 [S]	Newport 1958	1962	6.25	12.50	25.00
-- Red label, "360 Sound" in black					
❑ CS 8090 [S]	Dave Digs Disney	1959	12.50	25.00	50.00
-- Red/black label with six "eye" logos					
❑ CS 8090 [S]	Dave Digs Disney	1962	6.25	12.50	25.00
-- Red label, "360 Sound" in black					
❑ CS 8156 [S]	Gone with the Wind	1959	12.50	25.00	50.00
-- Red/black label with six "eye" logos					
❑ CS 8156 [S]	Gone with the Wind	1962	6.25	12.50	25.00
-- Red label, "360 Sound" in black					
❑ CS 8192 [S]	Time Out	1960	12.50	25.00	50.00
-- Red/black label with six "eye" logos; front cover does NOT say "Featuring Take Five"					
❑ CS 8192 [S]	Time Out Featuring "Take Five"	1960	7.50	15.00	30.00
-- Red/black label with six "eye" logos					
❑ CS 8192 [S]	Time Out Featuring "Take Five"	1962	5.00	10.00	20.00
-- Red label, "360 Sound" in black					
❑ CS 8235 [S]	Southern Scene	1960	7.50	15.00	30.00
-- Red/black label with six "eye" logos					
❑ CS 8235 [S]	Southern Scene	1962	5.00	10.00	20.00
-- Red label, "360 Sound" in black					
❑ CS 8248 [S]	The Riddle	1960	7.50	15.00	30.00
-- Red/black label with six "eye" logos					
❑ CS 8248 [S]	The Riddle	1962	5.00	10.00	20.00
-- Red label, "360 Sound" in black					
❑ CS 8257 [S]	Brubeck Plays Bernstein Plays Brubeck	1960	7.50	15.00	30.00
-- Red/black label with six "eye" logos					
❑ CS 8257 [S]	Brubeck Plays Bernstein Plays Brubeck	1962	5.00	10.00	20.00
-- Red label, "360 Sound" in black					
❑ CS 8353 [S]	Brubeck and Rushing	1961	7.50	15.00	30.00
-- Red/black label with six "eye" logos					
❑ CS 8353 [S]	Brubeck and Rushing	1962	5.00	10.00	20.00
-- Red label, "360 Sound" in black					
❑ CS 8409 [S]	Tonight Only!	1961	7.50	15.00	30.00
-- Red/black label with six "eye" logos					
❑ CS 8409 [S]	Tonight Only!	1962	5.00	10.00	20.00
-- Red label, "360 Sound" in black					
❑ CS 8490 [S]	Time Further Out	1961	7.50	15.00	30.00
-- Red/black label with six "eye" logos					
❑ CS 8490 [S]	Time Further Out	1962	5.00	10.00	20.00
-- Red label, "360 Sound" in black					
❑ CS 8575 [S]	Countdown -- Time in Outer Space	1962	5.00	10.00	20.00
-- Red label, "360 Sound" in black					
❑ CS 8575 [S]	Countdown -- Time in Outer Space	1962	10.00	20.00	40.00
-- Red/black label with six "eye" logos					
❑ CS 8763 [S]	Brandenburg Gate Revisited	1963	6.25	12.50	25.00
-- Red label, "360 Sound" in black					
❑ CS 8798 [S]	Bossa Nova U.S.A.	1963	6.25	12.50	25.00
-- Red label, "360 Sound" in black					

Number	Title	Yr	VG	VG+	NM
❑ CS 8927 [S]	Time Changes	1964	6.25	12.50	25.00
-- Red label, "360 Sound" in black					
❑ CS 9012 [S]	Jazz Impressions of Japan	1964	6.25	12.50	25.00
-- Red label, "360 Sound" in black					
❑ CS 9075 [S]	Jazz Impressions of New York	1965	6.25	12.50	25.00
-- Red label, "360 Sound" in black					
❑ CS 9116 [S]	Take Five	1965	6.25	12.50	25.00
-- Red label, "360 Sound" in black					
❑ CS 9148 [S]	Angel Eyes	1965	6.25	12.50	25.00
-- Red label, "360 Sound" in black					
❑ CS 9237 [S]	My Favorite Things	1966	5.00	10.00	20.00
-- Red "360 Sound" label					
❑ CS 9284 [S]	Dave Brubeck's Greatest Hits	1966	5.00	10.00	20.00
-- Red "360 Sound" label					
❑ CS 9312 [S]	Time In	1966	5.00	10.00	20.00
-- Red "360 Sound" label					
❑ CS 9402 [S]	Anything Goes! Dave Brubeck Quartet Plays Cole Porter	1966	5.00	10.00	20.00
-- Red "360 Sound" label					

COLUMBIA/CLASSIC

❑ CS 8192	Time Out	1995	6.25	12.50	25.00
-- Audiophile vinyl					

DIRECT DISK

❑ 106 [(2)]	A Cut Above	1979	6.25	12.50	25.00

FANTASY

❑ 3-1 [10]	Dave Brubeck Trio	1951	37.50	75.00	150.00
❑ 3-2 [10]	Dave Brubeck Trio	1951	37.50	75.00	150.00
❑ 3-3 [10]	Dave Brubeck Octet	1951	37.50	75.00	150.00
❑ 3-4 [10]	Dave Brubeck Trio	1952	37.50	75.00	150.00
❑ 3-5 [10]	Dave Brubeck Quartet with Paul Desmond	1952	37.50	75.00	150.00
❑ 3-7 [10]	Dave Brubeck Quartet with Paul Desmond	1952	37.50	75.00	150.00
❑ 3-8 [10]	Jazz at Storyville	1953	37.50	75.00	150.00
❑ 3-10 [10]	Jazz at the Blackhawk	1953	37.50	75.00	150.00
❑ 3-11 [10]	Jazz at Oberlin	1953	37.50	75.00	150.00
❑ 3-13 [10]	Jazz at the College of the Pacific	1954	37.50	75.00	150.00
❑ 3-16 [10]	Old Sounds from San Francisco	1954	37.50	75.00	150.00
❑ 3-20 [10]	Paul and Dave's Jazz Interwoven	1955	37.50	75.00	150.00
❑ 3204 [M]	Dave Brubeck Trio	1956	25.00	50.00	100.00
-- Dark red vinyl; reissue of 3-1					
❑ 3204 [M]	Dave Brubeck Trio	195?	15.00	30.00	60.00
-- Black vinyl, red label, non-flexible vinyl					
❑ 3204 [M]	Dave Brubeck Trio	196?	10.00	20.00	40.00
-- Black vinyl, red label, flexible vinyl					
❑ 3205 [M]	Dave Brubeck Trio: Distinctive Rhythm Instrumentals	1956	25.00	50.00	100.00
-- Dark red vinyl; reissue of 3-2					
❑ 3205 [M]	Dave Brubeck Trio: Distinctive Rhythm Instrumentals	195?	15.00	30.00	60.00
-- Black vinyl, red label, non-flexible vinyl					
❑ 3205 [M]	Dave Brubeck Trio: Distinctive Rhythm Instrumentals	196?	10.00	20.00	40.00
-- Black vinyl, red label, flexible vinyl					
❑ 3210 [M]	Jazz at the Blackhawk	1956	25.00	50.00	100.00
-- Dark red vinyl; reissue of 3-10					
❑ 3210 [M]	Jazz at the Blackhawk	195?	15.00	30.00	60.00
-- Black vinyl, red label, non-flexible vinyl					
❑ 3210 [M]	Jazz at the Blackhawk	196?	10.00	20.00	40.00
-- Black vinyl, red label, flexible vinyl					
❑ 3223 [M]	Jazz at the College of the Pacific	1956	25.00	50.00	100.00
-- Dark red vinyl; reissue of 3-13					
❑ 3223 [M]	Jazz at the College of the Pacific	195?	15.00	30.00	60.00
-- Black vinyl, red label, non-flexible vinyl					
❑ 3223 [M]	Jazz at the College of the Pacific	196?	10.00	20.00	40.00
-- Black vinyl, red label, flexible vinyl					
❑ 3229 [M]	Brubeck-Desmond	1956	25.00	50.00	100.00
-- Dark red vinyl; reissue of 3-5					
❑ 3229 [M]	Brubeck-Desmond	195?	15.00	30.00	60.00
-- Black vinyl, red label, non-flexible vinyl					
❑ 3229 [M]	Brubeck-Desmond	196?	10.00	20.00	40.00
-- Black vinyl, red label, flexible vinyl					
❑ 3230 [M]	Dave Brubeck Quartet	1956	25.00	50.00	100.00
-- Dark red vinyl; reissue of 3-7					
❑ 3230 [M]	Dave Brubeck Quartet	195?	15.00	30.00	60.00
-- Black vinyl, red label, non-flexible vinyl					
❑ 3230 [M]	Dave Brubeck Quartet	196?	10.00	20.00	40.00
-- Black vinyl, red label, flexible vinyl					
❑ 3239 [M]	Dave Brubeck Octet	1956	25.00	50.00	100.00
-- Dark red vinyl; reissue of 3-3					
❑ 3239 [M]	Dave Brubeck Octet	195?	15.00	30.00	60.00
-- Black vinyl, red label, non-flexible vinyl					
❑ 3239 [M]	Dave Brubeck Octet	196?	10.00	20.00	40.00
-- Black vinyl, red label, flexible vinyl					
❑ 3240 [M]	Brubeck Desmond: Jazz at Storyville	1957	25.00	50.00	100.00
-- Dark red vinyl; reissue of 3-8					

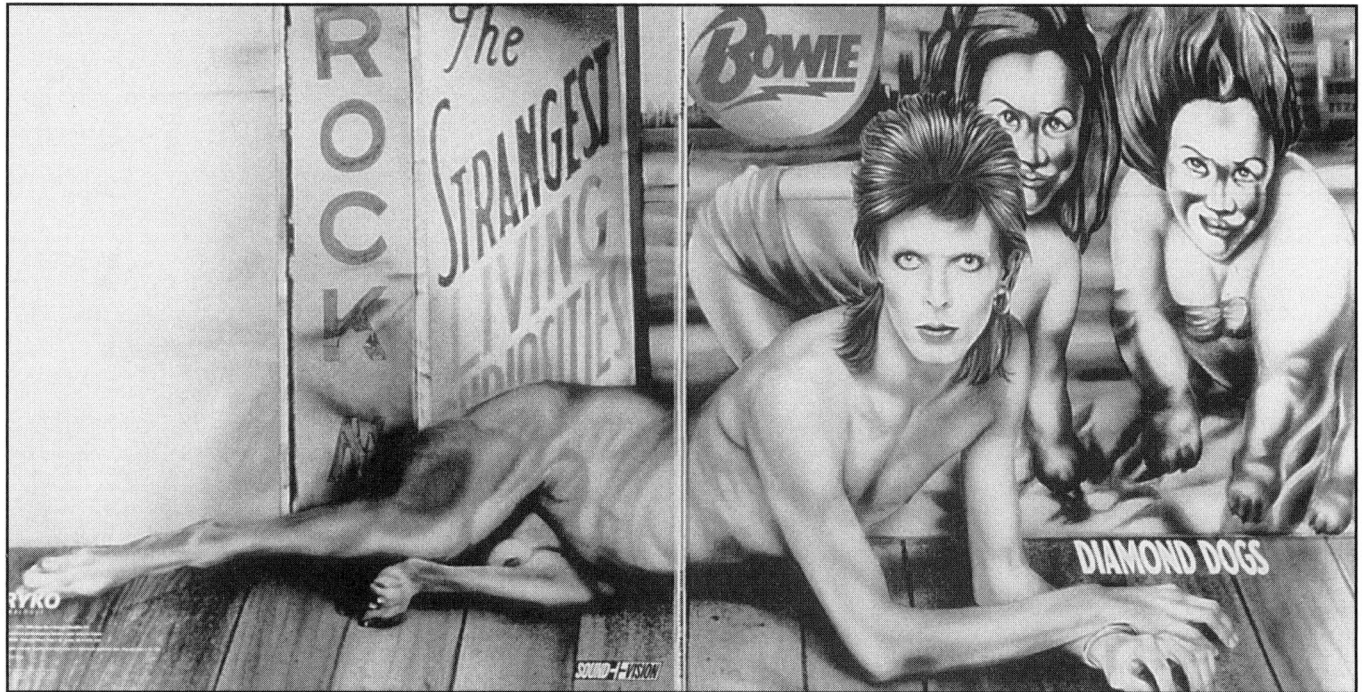

(Top) In 1990, when Rykodisc reissued the early David Bowie catalog on both vinyl and compact disc, it gave buyers a bonus. It restored the original cover of *Diamond Dogs,* on which Bowie's genitals are clearly visible. Original pressings of this album on RCA can go for thousands; the Ryko version goes for about $20 in near-mint condition. (Bottom left) Bordersong was an obscure Pacific Northwest rock band. Their debut album, released in 1975, features, on one track, Ann and Nancy Wilson on vocals. The two, of course, would later form the band Heart. (Bottom right) The most collectible album by Bread is this 1971 promotional item that was a collection of its hits and selected album tracks to that time. The 1973 album *The Best Of Bread* turned out to be fairly similar.

Number	Title	Yr	VG	VG+	NM
❏ 3240 [M]	Brubeck Desmond: Jazz at Storyville	195?	15.00	30.00	60.00
-- Black vinyl, red label, non-flexible vinyl					
❏ 3240 [M]	Brubeck Desmond: Jazz at Storyville	196?	10.00	20.00	40.00
-- Black vinyl, red label, flexible vinyl					
❏ 3245 [M]	Jazz at Oberlin	1957	25.00	50.00	100.00
-- Dark red vinyl; reissue of 3-11					
❏ 3245 [M]	Jazz at Oberlin	195?	15.00	30.00	60.00
-- Black vinyl, red label, non-flexible vinyl					
❏ 3245 [M]	Jazz at Oberlin	196?	10.00	20.00	40.00
-- Black vinyl, red label, flexible vinyl					
❏ 3249 [M]	Brubeck & Desmond at Wilshire-Ebell	1957	25.00	50.00	100.00
-- Dark red vinyl					
❏ 3249 [M]	Brubeck & Desmond at Wilshire-Ebell	195?	15.00	30.00	60.00
-- Black vinyl, red label, non-flexible vinyl					
❏ 3249 [M]	Brubeck & Desmond at Wilshire-Ebell	196?	10.00	20.00	40.00
-- Black vinyl, red label, flexible vinyl					
❏ 3259 [M]	Dave Brubeck Plays and Plays and Plays and Plays and...	1958	15.00	30.00	60.00
-- Red vinyl					
❏ 3259 [M]	Dave Brubeck Plays and Plays and Plays and Plays and...	195?	10.00	20.00	40.00
-- Black vinyl, red label, non-flexible vinyl					
❏ 3259 [M]	Dave Brubeck Plays and Plays and Plays and Plays and...	196?	7.50	15.00	30.00
-- Black vinyl, red label, flexible vinyl					
❏ 3268 [M]	Re-Union	1958	15.00	30.00	60.00
-- Red vinyl					
❏ 3268 [M]	Re-Union	195?	10.00	20.00	40.00
-- Black vinyl, red label, non-flexible vinyl					
❏ 3268 [M]	Re-Union	196?	7.50	15.00	30.00
-- Black vinyl, red label, flexible vinyl					
❏ 3298 [M]	Two Knights at the Black Hawk	1959	15.00	30.00	60.00
-- Red vinyl					
❏ 3298 [M]	Two Knights at the Black Hawk	1959	10.00	20.00	40.00
-- Black vinyl, red label, non-flexible vinyl					
❏ 3298 [M]	Two Knights at the Black Hawk	196?	7.50	15.00	30.00
-- Black vinyl, red label, flexible vinyl					
❏ 3301 [M]	Brubeck A La Mode	1960	15.00	30.00	60.00
-- Red vinyl					
❏ 3301 [M]	Brubeck A La Mode	1960	10.00	20.00	40.00
-- Black vinyl, red label, non-flexible vinyl					
❏ 3301 [M]	Brubeck A La Mode	196?	7.50	15.00	30.00
-- Black vinyl, red label, flexible vinyl					
❏ 3319 [M]	Near-Myth	1961	15.00	30.00	60.00
-- Red vinyl					
❏ 3319 [M]	Near-Myth	1961	10.00	20.00	40.00
-- Black vinyl, red label, non-flexible vinyl					
❏ 3319 [M]	Near-Myth	196?	7.50	15.00	30.00
-- Black vinyl, red label, flexible vinyl					
❏ 3331 [M]	Dave Brubeck Trio Featuring Cal Tjader	1962	15.00	30.00	60.00
-- Red vinyl					
❏ 3331 [M]	Dave Brubeck Trio Featuring Cal Tjader	1962	10.00	20.00	40.00
-- Black vinyl, red label, non-flexible vinyl					
❏ 3331 [M]	Dave Brubeck Trio Featuring Cal Tjader	196?	7.50	15.00	30.00
-- Black vinyl, red label, flexible vinyl					
❏ 3332 [M]	Brubeck Tjader	1962	10.00	20.00	40.00
-- Black vinyl, red label, non-flexible vinyl					
❏ 3332 [M]	Brubeck Tjader	1962	15.00	30.00	60.00
-- Red vinyl					
❏ 3332 [M]	Brubeck Tjader	196?	7.50	15.00	30.00
-- Black vinyl, red label, flexible vinyl					
❏ 8007 [S]	Re-Union	1962	12.50	25.00	50.00
-- Blue vinyl					
❏ 8007 [S]	Re-Union	196?	7.50	15.00	30.00
-- Black vinyl, blue label, non-flexible vinyl					
❏ 8007 [S]	Re-Union	196?	5.00	10.00	20.00
-- Black vinyl, blue label, flexible vinyl					
❏ 8047 [S]	Brubeck A La Mode	1962	12.50	25.00	50.00
-- Blue vinyl					
❏ 8047 [S]	Brubeck A La Mode	196?	7.50	15.00	30.00
-- Black vinyl, blue label, non-flexible vinyl					
❏ 8047 [S]	Brubeck A La Mode	196?	5.00	10.00	20.00
-- Black vinyl, blue label, flexible vinyl					
❏ 8063 [S]	Near-Myth	1962	12.50	25.00	50.00
-- Blue vinyl					
❏ 8063 [S]	Near-Myth	196?	7.50	15.00	30.00
-- Black vinyl, blue label, non-flexible vinyl					
❏ 8063 [S]	Near-Myth	196?	5.00	10.00	20.00
-- Black vinyl, blue label, flexible vinyl					
❏ 8069 [R]	Jazz at Oberlin	1962	10.00	20.00	40.00
-- Blue vinyl					

Number	Title	Yr	VG	VG+	NM
❏ 8069 [R]	Jazz at Oberlin	196?	5.00	10.00	20.00
-- Black vinyl, blue label, non-flexible vinyl					
❏ 8073 [R]	Dave Brubeck Trio Featuring Cal Tjader	1962	10.00	20.00	40.00
-- Blue vinyl					
❏ 8073 [R]	Dave Brubeck Trio Featuring Cal Tjader	1962	5.00	10.00	20.00
-- Black vinyl, blue label, non-flexible vinyl					
❏ 8074 [R]	Brubeck Tjader	1962	10.00	20.00	40.00
-- Blue vinyl					
❏ 8074 [R]	Brubeck Tjader	1962	5.00	10.00	20.00
-- Black vinyl, blue label, non-flexible vinyl					
❏ 8078 [R]	Jazz at the College of the Pacific	1962	10.00	20.00	40.00
-- Blue vinyl					
❏ 8078 [R]	Jazz at the College of the Pacific	196?	5.00	10.00	20.00
-- Black vinyl, blue label, non-flexible vinyl					
❏ 8080 [R]	Jazz at Storyville	1962	10.00	20.00	40.00
-- Blue vinyl					
❏ 8080 [R]	Jazz at Storyville	1962	5.00	10.00	20.00
-- Black vinyl, blue label, non-flexible vinyl					
❏ 8081 [R]	Two Knights at the Blackhawk	1962	10.00	20.00	40.00
-- Blue vinyl					
❏ 8081 [R]	Two Knights at the Blackhawk	1962	5.00	10.00	20.00
-- Black vinyl, blue label, non-flexible vinyl					
❏ 8092 [R]	Brubeck-Desmond	1962	10.00	20.00	40.00
-- Blue vinyl					
❏ 8092 [R]	Brubeck-Desmond	1962	5.00	10.00	20.00
-- Black vinyl, blue label, non-flexible vinyl					
❏ 8093 [R]	Dave Brubeck Quartet	1962	10.00	2.00	40.00
-- Blue vinyl					
❏ 8093 [R]	Dave Brubeck Quartet	1962	5.00	10.00	20.00
-- Black vinyl, blue label, non-flexible vinyl					
❏ 8094 [R]	Dave Brubeck Octet	1962	10.00	20.00	40.00
-- Blue vinyl					
❏ 8094 [R]	Dave Brubeck Octet	1962	5.00	10.00	20.00
-- Black vinyl, blue label, non-flexible vinyl					
❏ 8095 [S]	Brubeck and Desmond at Wilshire-Ebell	1962	12.50	25.00	50.00
-- Blue vinyl					
❏ 8095 [S]	Brubeck and Desmond at Wilshire-Ebell	1962	7.50	15.00	30.00
-- Black vinyl, blue label, non-flexible vinyl					
❏ 8095 [S]	Brubeck and Desmond at Wilshire-Ebell	196?	5.00	10.00	20.00
-- Black vinyl, blue label, flexible vinyl					

MOBILE FIDELITY

Number	Title	Yr	VG	VG+	NM
❏ 1-216	We're All Together Again for the First Time	1994	15.00	30.00	60.00
-- Audiophile vinyl					

MOON

Number	Title	Yr	VG	VG+	NM
❏ 028	St. Louis Blues	1992	5.00	10.00	20.00

BRUCE, ED
MONUMENT

Number	Title	Yr	VG	VG+	NM
❏ SLP-18118	Shades	1969	5.00	10.00	20.00

RCA VICTOR

Number	Title	Yr	VG	VG+	NM
❏ LPM-3948 [M]	If I Could Just Go Home	1968	12.50	25.00	50.00
❏ LSP-3948 [S]	If I Could Just Go Home	1968	6.25	12.50	25.00

BRUCE, LENNY
BIZARRE

Number	Title	Yr	VG	VG+	NM
❏ 2XS 6329 [(2)]	The Berkeley Concert	1969	6.25	12.50	25.00

DOUGLAS

Number	Title	Yr	VG	VG+	NM
❏ 2	To Is a Preposition, Come Is a Verb	196?	5.00	10.00	20.00
❏ 788	The Essential Lenny Bruce Politics	1968	5.00	10.00	20.00

FANTASY

Number	Title	Yr	VG	VG+	NM
❏ 7001 [M]	Interviews of Our Times	1959	25.00	50.00	100.00
-- Opaque, non-flexible red vinyl; tan cover with Lenny Bruce's name blacked out throughout the back					
❏ 7001 [M]	Interviews of Our Times	1959	10.00	20.00	40.00
-- Non-flexible black vinyl; cover changed to blue tint					
❏ 7001 [M]	Interviews of Our Times	1962	10.00	20.00	40.00
-- Translucent, flexible red vinyl					
❏ 7001 [M]	Interviews of Our Times	1962	5.00	10.00	20.00
-- Flexible black vinyl					
❏ 7003 [M]	The Sick Humor of Lenny Bruce	1959	25.00	50.00	100.00
-- Opaque, non-flexible red vinyl					
❏ 7003 [M]	The Sick Humor of Lenny Bruce	1959	10.00	20.00	40.00
-- Non-flexible black vinyl					
❏ 7003 [M]	The Sick Humor of Lenny Bruce	1962	10.00	20.00	40.00
-- Translucent, flexible red vinyl					
❏ 7003 [M]	The Sick Humor of Lenny Bruce	1962	5.00	10.00	20.00
-- Flexible black vinyl					
❏ 7007 [M]	I Am Not a Nut, Elect Me	1960	25.00	50.00	100.00
-- Opaque, non-flexible red vinyl					

Number	Title	Yr	VG	VG+	NM
❏ 7007 [M]	I Am Not a Nut, Elect Me	1960	10.00	20.00	40.00
-- Non-flexible black vinyl					
❏ 7007 [M]	I Am Not a Nut, Elect Me	1962	10.00	20.00	40.00
-- Translucent, flexible red vinyl					
❏ 7007 [M]	I Am Not a Nut, Elect Me	1962	5.00	10.00	20.00
-- Flexible black vinyl					
❏ 7011 [M]	Lenny Bruce, American	1961	25.00	50.00	100.00
-- Opaque, non-flexible red vinyl					
❏ 7011 [M]	Lenny Bruce, American	1961	10.00	20.00	40.00
-- Non-flexible black vinyl					
❏ 7011 [M]	Lenny Bruce, American	1962	10.00	20.00	40.00
-- Translucent, flexible red vinyl					
❏ 7011 [M]	Lenny Bruce, American	1962	5.00	10.00	20.00
-- Flexible black vinyl					
❏ 7012 [M]	The Best of Lenny Bruce	1962	12.50	25.00	50.00
-- Red vinyl					
❏ 7012 [M]	The Best of Lenny Bruce	1962	5.00	10.00	20.00
-- Black vinyl					
❏ 34201 [(3)]	Lenny Bruce at the Curran Theater	1971	10.00	20.00	40.00
❏ 79003 [(2)]	The Real Lenny Bruce	1975	5.00	10.00	20.00

LENNY BRUCE

Number	Title	Yr	VG	VG+	NM
❏ LB-3001/2 [M]	Lenny Bruce Is Out Again	196?	75.00	150.00	300.00
-- Privately pressed version with white labels and Lenny's address on cover					
❏ LB-9001/2 [10]	Warning: Sale of This Album...	1962	125.00	250.00	500.00
-- Privately pressed LP with routines used as evidence in Lenny's obscenity trial					

PHILLIES

Number	Title	Yr	VG	VG+	NM
❏ PHLP-4010 [M]	Lenny Bruce Is Out Again	1966	25.00	50.00	100.00
-- Reissue of Lenny Bruce 3001/2					

UNITED ARTISTS

Number	Title	Yr	VG	VG+	NM
❏ UAL 3580 [M]	The Midnight Concert	1967	6.25	12.50	25.00
❏ UAS 6580	The Midnight Concert	1967	5.00	10.00	20.00
❏ UAS 9800 [(3)]	Lenny Bruce/Carnegie Hall	1972	6.25	12.50	25.00

BRUNSON, FRANKIE
GEE

Number	Title	Yr	VG	VG+	NM
❏ GLP-704 [M]	Big Daddy's Blues	1959	20.00	40.00	80.00
❏ SGLP-704 [S]	Big Daddy's Blues	1959	30.00	60.00	120.00

BRUTE FORCE
B.T. PUPPY

Number	Title	Yr	VG	VG+	NM
❏ BTPS-1015	Extemporaneous	1971	1,000.	1,500.	2,000.

COLUMBIA

Number	Title	Yr	VG	VG+	NM
❏ CL 2615 [M]	I, Brute Force -- Confections of Love	1967	5.00	10.00	20.00
❏ CS 9415 [S]	I, Brute Force -- Confections of Love	1967	5.00	10.00	20.00

EMBRYO

Number	Title	Yr	VG	VG+	NM
❏ 522	Brute Force	1970	5.00	10.00	20.00

BRYANT, ANITA
CARLTON

Number	Title	Yr	VG	VG+	NM
❏ LP-118 [M]	Anita Bryant	1959	5.00	10.00	20.00
❏ STLP-118 [S]	Anita Bryant	1959	7.50	15.00	30.00
❏ LP-127 [M]	Hear Anita Bryant in Your Home Tonight	1960	5.00	10.00	20.00
❏ STLP-127 [S]	Hear Anita Bryant in Your Home Tonight	1960	6.25	12.50	25.00
❏ LP-132 [M]	In My Little Corner of the World	1961	5.00	10.00	20.00
❏ STLP-132 [S]	In My Little Corner of the World	1961	6.25	12.50	25.00

COLUMBIA

Number	Title	Yr	VG	VG+	NM
❏ CS 8519 [S]	Kisses Sweeter Than Wine	1961	5.00	10.00	20.00
❏ CS 8567 [S]	Abiding Love	1962	5.00	10.00	20.00

BRYANT, BOUDLEAUX
MONUMENT

Number	Title	Yr	VG	VG+	NM
❏ MLP-8007 [M]	Boudleaux Bryant's Best Sellers	1963	5.00	10.00	20.00
❏ SLP-18007 [S]	Boudleaux Bryant's Best Sellers	1963	6.25	12.50	25.00

BRYANT, JIMMY
CAPITOL

Number	Title	Yr	VG	VG+	NM
❏ ST 1314 [S]	Country Cabin Jazz	1960	25.00	50.00	100.00
❏ T 1314 [M]	Country Cabin Jazz	1960	20.00	40.00	80.00

DOLTON

Number	Title	Yr	VG	VG+	NM
❏ BLP-16505 [M]	Play Country Guitar with Jimmy Bryant	196?	6.25	12.50	25.00
❏ BST-17505 [S]	Play Country Guitar with Jimmy Bryant	196?	7.50	15.00	30.00

IMPERIAL

Number	Title	Yr	VG	VG+	NM
❏ LP-9310 [M]	Bryant's Back in Town	1966	5.00	10.00	20.00
❏ LP-9315 [M]	Laughing Guitar, Crying Guitar	1966	5.00	10.00	20.00
❏ LP-9338 [M]	We Are Young	1967	5.00	10.00	20.00
❏ LP-9360 [M]	That Fastest Guitar in the Country	1967	6.25	12.50	25.00
❏ LP-12310 [S]	Bryant's Back in Town	1966	6.25	12.50	25.00
❏ LP-12315 [S]	Laughing Guitar, Crying Guitar	1966	6.25	12.50	25.00
❏ LP-12338 [S]	We Are Young	1967	6.25	12.50	25.00
❏ LP-12360 [S]	That Fastest Guitar in the Country	1967	5.00	10.00	20.00

BRYANT, RAY
CADET

Number	Title	Yr	VG	VG+	NM
❏ LPS-767 [S]	Gotta Travel On	1966	5.00	10.00	20.00
❏ LPS-778 [S]	Lonesome Traveler	1966	5.00	10.00	20.00
❏ LPS-781 [S]	Slow Freight	1967	5.00	10.00	20.00
❏ LP-793 [M]	The Ray Bryant Touch	1967	5.00	10.00	20.00
❏ LP-801 [M]	Take a Bryant Step	1967	5.00	10.00	20.00

COLUMBIA

Number	Title	Yr	VG	VG+	NM
❏ CL 1449 [M]	Little Susie	1960	5.00	10.00	20.00
❏ CL 1476 [M]	The Madison Time	1960	6.25	12.50	25.00
❏ CL 1633 [M]	Con Alma	1961	5.00	10.00	20.00
❏ CL 1746 [M]	Dancing the Big Twist	1962	5.00	10.00	20.00
❏ CL 1867 [M]	Hollywood Jazz Beat	1962	5.00	10.00	20.00
❏ CS 8244 [S]	Little Susie	1960	6.25	12.50	25.00
❏ CS 8276 [S]	The Madison Time	1960	7.50	15.00	30.00
❏ CS 8433 [S]	Con Alma	1961	6.25	12.50	25.00
❏ CS 8546 [S]	Dancing the Big Twist	1962	6.25	12.50	25.00
❏ CS 8667 [S]	Hollywood Jazz Beat	1962	6.25	12.50	25.00

EPIC

Number	Title	Yr	VG	VG+	NM
❏ LN 3279 [M]	Ray Bryant Trio	1956	17.50	35.00	70.00

NEW JAZZ

Number	Title	Yr	VG	VG+	NM
❏ NJLP-8213 [M]	Alone with the Blues	1959	12.50	25.00	50.00
-- Purple label					
❏ NJLP-8213 [M]	Alone with the Blues	1965	6.25	12.50	25.00
-- Blue label with trident logo					
❏ NJLP-8227 [M]	Ray Bryant Trio	1959	12.50	25.00	50.00
-- Purple label; reissue of Prestige 7098					
❏ NJLP-8227 [M]	Ray Bryant Trio	1965	6.25	12.50	25.00
-- Blue label with trident logo					

PRESTIGE

Number	Title	Yr	VG	VG+	NM
❏ PRLP-7098 [M]	Ray Bryant Trio	1957	17.50	35.00	70.00

SIGNATURE

Number	Title	Yr	VG	VG+	NM
❏ SM-6008 [M]	Ray Bryant Plays	1960	50.00	100.00	200.00
❏ SS-6008 [S]	Ray Bryant Plays	1960	62.50	125.00	250.00

SUE

Number	Title	Yr	VG	VG+	NM
❏ LP-1016 [M]	Groove House	1963	10.00	20.00	40.00
❏ LPS-1016 [S]	Groove House	1963	12.50	25.00	50.00
❏ LP-1019 [M]	Live at Basin Street	1964	10.00	20.00	40.00
❏ LPS-1019 [S]	Live at Basin Street	1964	12.50	25.00	50.00
❏ LP-1032 [M]	Cold Turkey	1964	10.00	20.00	40.00
❏ LPS-1032 [S]	Cold Turkey	1964	12.50	25.00	50.00
❏ LP-1036 [M]	Ray Bryant Soul	1965	10.00	20.00	40.00
❏ LPS-1036 [S]	Ray Bryant Soul	1965	12.50	25.00	50.00

BRYNNER, YUL
VANGUARD

Number	Title	Yr	VG	VG+	NM
❏ VRS-9256 [M]	The Gypsy and I	1967	7.50	15.00	30.00
❏ VSD-79256 [S]	The Gypsy and I	1967	10.00	20.00	40.00

BUA, GENE
HERITAGE

Number	Title	Yr	VG	VG+	NM
❏ 35,004	Love of Life	1973	5.00	10.00	20.00

BUBBLE GUM MACHINE, THE
SENATE

Number	Title	Yr	VG	VG+	NM
❏ 21002 [M]	The Bubble Gum Machine	1968	6.25	12.50	25.00
❏ S-21002 [S]	The Bubble Gum Machine	1968	7.50	15.00	30.00

BUBBLE PUPPY, THE
INTERNATIONAL ARTISTS

Number	Title	Yr	VG	VG+	NM
❏ 10	A Gathering of Promises	1969	25.00	50.00	100.00
-- Original does not have "Masterfonics" in the dead wax					
❏ 10	A Gathering of Promises	1979	6.25	12.50	25.00
-- Reissue has "Masterfonics" in the dead wax					

BUBBLES, JOHN W.
VEE JAY

Number	Title	Yr	VG	VG+	NM
❏ VJ-1109 [M]	Bubbles, John W., That Is	1964	5.00	10.00	20.00

BUCHANAN BROTHERS
EVENT

Number	Title	Yr	VG	VG+	NM
❏ ES-101	Medicine Man	1969	6.25	12.50	25.00

Number	Title	Yr	VG	VG+	NM

BUCHANAN, ROY
BIOYA
❑ MM-519	Buch and the Snake Stretchers	1971	50.00	100.00	200.00

BUCKAROOS, THE
Also see BUCK OWENS.
CAPITOL
❑ ST-194	Anywhere U.S.A.	1969	6.25	12.50	25.00
❑ ST-321	Roll Your Own with Buck Owens' Buckaroos	1969	6.25	12.50	25.00
❑ ST-440	Rompin' and Stompin'	1970	5.00	10.00	20.00
❑ ST-767	The Buckaroos Play the Hits	1971	5.00	10.00	20.00
❑ ST-860	The Buckaroos Play the Songs of Merle Haggard	1971	6.25	12.50	25.00
❑ ST 2436 [S]	The Buck Owens Song Book	1966	6.25	12.50	25.00
❑ T 2436 [M]	The Buck Owens Song Book	1966	5.00	10.00	20.00
❑ ST 2722 [S]	America's Most Wanted Band	1967	6.25	12.50	25.00
❑ T 2722 [M]	America's Most Wanted Band	1967	5.00	10.00	20.00
❑ ST 2828 [S]	The Buck Owens' Buckaroos Strike Again!	1967	6.25	12.50	25.00
❑ T 2828 [M]	The Buck Owens' Buckaroos Strike Again!	1967	6.25	12.50	25.00
❑ ST 2902	A Night on the Town with Buck Owens' Buckaroos	1968	6.25	12.50	25.00
❑ ST 2973	Meanwhile Back at the Ranch	1968	6.25	12.50	25.00

BUCKINGHAM NICKS
Also see FLEETWOOD MAC; STEVIE NICKS.
POLYDOR
❑ PD-5058	Buckingham Nicks	1973	10.00	20.00	40.00
-- Gatefold cover					

BUCKINGHAMS, THE
COLUMBIA
❑ CL 2669 [M]	Time & Charges	1967	6.25	12.50	25.00
❑ CL 2798 [M]	Portraits	1968	6.25	12.50	25.00
❑ CS 9469 [S]	Time & Charges	1967	5.00	10.00	20.00
❑ CS 9598 [S]	Portraits	1968	5.00	10.00	20.00
❑ CS 9703	In One Ear and Gone Tomorrow	1968	5.00	10.00	20.00
❑ CS 9812	The Buckinghams Greatest Hits	1969	5.00	10.00	20.00
-- Red "360 Sound" label					

U.S.A.
❑ 107 [M]	Kind of a Drag	1967	150.00	300.00	600.00
-- With "I'm a Man"					
❑ 107 [M]	Kind of a Drag	1967	7.50	15.00	30.00
-- Without "I'm a Man"					
❑ 107 [S]	Kind of a Drag	1967	10.00	20.00	40.00
-- No known stereo copy has "I'm a Man"					

BUCKLEY, LORD
CRESTVIEW
❑ CRV-801 [M]	The Best of Lord Buckley	1963	12.50	25.00	50.00
❑ CRV7-801 [S]	The Best of Lord Buckley	1963	15.00	30.00	60.00

ELEKTRA
❑ EKS-74047	The Best of Lord Buckley	1969	6.25	12.50	25.00
-- Reissue of Crestview 7-801					

RCA VICTOR
❑ LPM-3246 [10]	Hipsters, Flipsters and Finger Poppin' Daddies, Knock Me Your Lobes	1955	75.00	150.00	300.00

REPRISE
❑ RS 6389	A Most Immaculately Hip Aristocrat	1970	6.25	12.50	25.00
-- Reissue of Straight 1054					

STRAIGHT
❑ STS-1054	A Most Immaculately Hip Aristocrat	1970	10.00	20.00	40.00

VAYA
❑ 101/2 [M]	Euphoria, Volume 1	1955	37.50	75.00	150.00
❑ 107/8 [M]	Euphoria, Volume 2	1955	50.00	100.00	200.00
❑ 1715 [10]	Euphoria	195?	75.00	150.00	300.00
-- Red vinyl					

WORLD PACIFIC
❑ WP-1279 [M]	The Way Out Humor of Lord Buckley	1959	30.00	60.00	120.00
-- With "Far Out Humor" on the back cover					
❑ WP-1279 [M]	The Way Out Humor of Lord Buckley	1959	25.00	50.00	100.00
-- With correct "Way Out Humor" on the back cover					
❑ WP-1815 [M]	Lord Buckley in Concert	1964	12.50	25.00	50.00
-- Reissue of 1279					
❑ WP-1849 [M]	Blowing His Mind (and Yours, Too)	1966	12.50	25.00	50.00
❑ WPS-21879	Buckley's Best	1968	10.00	20.00	40.00
❑ WPS-21889	Bad Rapping of the Marquis de Sade	1969	7.50	15.00	30.00

BUCKLEY, TIM
ELEKTRA
❑ EKL-4018 [M]	Goodbye and Hello	1967	6.25	12.50	25.00
❑ EKS-74004 [S]	Tim Buckley	1966	5.00	10.00	20.00
❑ EKS-74018 [S]	Goodbye and Hello	1967	5.00	10.00	20.00
❑ EKS-74045	Happy Sad	1969	5.00	10.00	20.00
❑ EKS-74074	Lorca	1970	5.00	10.00	20.00

STRAIGHT
❑ STS-1060	Blue Afternoon	1969	7.50	15.00	30.00

BUD AND TRAVIS
LIBERTY
❑ LRP-3125 [M]	Bud and Travis	1959	7.50	15.00	30.00
❑ LRP-3138 [M]	Spotlight On Bud and Travis	1960	5.00	10.00	20.00
❑ LRP-3222 [M]	Bud and Travis...In Concert, Volume 2	1961	5.00	10.00	20.00
❑ LRP-3295 [M]	Naturally	1963	5.00	10.00	20.00
❑ LRP-3341 [M]	Perspective on Bud and Travis	1964	5.00	10.00	20.00
❑ LRP-3386 [M]	Bud and Travis In Person (At the Cellar Door)	1964	5.00	10.00	20.00
❑ LRP-3398 [M]	The Latin Album	1965	5.00	10.00	20.00
❑ LST-7125 [S]	Bud and Travis	1959	10.00	20.00	40.00
❑ LST-7138 [S]	Spotlight On Bud and Travis	1960	6.25	12.50	25.00
❑ LST-7222 [S]	Bud and Travis...In Concert, Volume 2	1961	6.25	12.50	25.00
❑ LST-7295 [S]	Naturally	1963	6.25	12.50	25.00
❑ LST-7341 [S]	Perspective on Bud and Travis	1964	6.25	12.50	25.00
❑ LST-7386 [S]	Bud and Travis In Person (At the Cellar Door)	1964	6.25	12.50	25.00
❑ LST-7398 [S]	The Latin Album	1965	6.25	12.50	25.00
❑ LDM-11001 [(2) M]	Bud and Travis...In Concert	1960	6.25	12.50	25.00
❑ LDS-12001 [(2) S]	Bud and Travis...In Concert	1960	7.50	15.00	30.00

BUDDIES, THE
WING
❑ MGW-12293 [M]	The Buddies and the Compacts	1965	12.50	25.00	50.00
❑ MGW-12306 [M]	Go Go with the Buddies	1965	12.50	25.00	50.00
❑ SRW-16293 [S]	The Buddies and the Compacts	1965	20.00	40.00	80.00
❑ SRW-16306 [S]	Go Go with the Buddies	1965	20.00	40.00	80.00

BUDGIE
KAPP
❑ KS-3656	Budgie	1971	7.50	15.00	30.00
❑ KS-3669	Squawk	1972	7.50	15.00	30.00

MCA
❑ 429	In for the Kill	1973	5.00	10.00	20.00

BUFFALO NICKEL JUGBAND, THE
HAPPY TIGER
❑ 1018	The Buffalo Nickel Jugband	1971	6.25	12.50	25.00

BUFFALO SPRINGFIELD
ATCO
❑ 33-200 [M]	Buffalo Springfield	1967	50.00	100.00	200.00
-- With "Baby Don't Scold Me"					
❑ SD 33-200 [S]	Buffalo Springfield	1967	50.00	100.00	200.00
-- With "Baby Don't Scold Me"					
❑ 33-200A [M]	Buffalo Springfield	1967	6.25	12.50	25.00
-- With "For What It's Worth" replacing "Baby Don't Scold Me"					
❑ SD 33-200A [S]	Buffalo Springfield	1967	6.25	12.50	25.00
-- With "For What It's Worth" replacing "Baby Don't Scold Me"; purple and brown label					
❑ 33-226 [M]	Buffalo Springfield Again	1967	20.00	40.00	80.00
❑ SD 33-226 [S]	Buffalo Springfield Again	1967	6.25	12.50	25.00
-- Purple and brown label					
❑ 33-256 [M]	Last Time Around	1968	30.00	60.00	120.00
-- White label promo only					
❑ SD 33-256 [S]	Last Time Around	1968	7.50	15.00	30.00
-- Purple and brown label					
❑ 33-283 [M]	Retrospective/The Best of Buffalo Springfield	1969	25.00	50.00	100.00
-- White label promo only					
❑ SD 33-283 [S]	Retrospective/The Best of Buffalo Springfield	1969	5.00	10.00	20.00
-- Yellow label					
❑ SD 2-806 [(2)]	Buffalo Springfield	1973	5.00	10.00	20.00
-- Yellow label					

Number	Title	Yr	VG	VG+	NM

BUFFETT, JIMMY
ABC
| ❏ SPDJ-43 [DJ] | Special Jimmy Buffett Sampler | 1978 | 5.00 | 10.00 | 20.00 |

BARNABY
| ❏ BR-6014 | High Cumberland Jubilee | 1975 | 10.00 | 20.00 | 40.00 |
| ❏ Z 30093 | Down to Earth | 1970 | 25.00 | 50.00 | 100.00 |

BUGALOOS, THE
CAPITOL
| ❏ SW-621 | The Bugaloos | 1970 | 7.50 | 15.00 | 30.00 |

BUGGS, THE
CORONET
| ❏ CXS-212 [S] | The Beatle Beat | 1964 | 5.00 | 10.00 | 20.00 |

BULLDOG
DECCA
| ❏ DL 75370 | Bulldog | 1972 | 5.00 | 10.00 | 20.00 |

BUNCH, THE
A&M
| ❏ SP-4354 | The Bunch | 1973 | 6.25 | 12.50 | 25.00 |

BUNKERS, THE
Also see CARROLL O'CONNOR.
RCA VICTOR
| ❏ APL1-0102 | Archie and Edith Side by Side | 1973 | 5.00 | 10.00 | 20.00 |

BUOYS, THE
SCEPTER
| ❏ SPS-593 | Timothy | 1971 | 6.25 | 12.50 | 25.00 |

BURDON, ERIC
Also see THE ANIMALS.
CAPITOL
| ❏ S?A?-11426 | Stop | 1975 | 5.00 | 10.00 | 20.00 |
-- Cover shaped like a hexagon

BURDON, ERIC, AND WAR
Also see ERIC BURDON; WAR.
MGM
| ❏ SE-4710 | The Black Man's Burdon | 1970 | 5.00 | 10.00 | 20.00 |

BURGESS, WILMA
DECCA
❏ DL 4935 [M]	Tear Time	1967	6.25	12.50	25.00
❏ DL 74788 [S]	Don't Touch Me	1966	5.00	10.00	20.00
❏ DL 74852 [S]	Wilma Burgess Sings Misty Blue	1967	5.00	10.00	20.00
❏ DL 74935 [S]	Tear Time	1967	5.00	10.00	20.00
❏ DL 75024	The Tender Lovin' Country Sound	1968	5.00	10.00	20.00
❏ DL 75090	Parting Is Such Sweet Sorrow	1968	5.00	10.00	20.00

BURGHOFF, GARY
SHALOM
| ❏ 651 | Gary Burghoff and His Mardi Gras Celebration Band | 1983 | 10.00 | 20.00 | 40.00 |

BURKE, SOLOMON
APOLLO
| ❏ ALP-498 [M] | Solomon Burke | 1962 | 125.00 | 250.00 | 500.00 |
ATLANTIC
❏ 8067 [M]	Solomon Burke's Greatest Hits	1962	12.50	25.00	50.00
❏ SD 8067 [S]	Solomon Burke's Greatest Hits	1962	20.00	40.00	80.00
❏ 8085 [M]	If You Need Me	1963	12.50	25.00	50.00
❏ SD 8085 [S]	If You Need Me	1963	20.00	40.00	80.00
❏ 8096 [M]	Rock N' Soul	1964	12.50	25.00	50.00
❏ SD 8096 [S]	Rock N' Soul	1964	20.00	40.00	80.00
❏ 8109 [M]	The Best of Solomon Burke	1965	7.50	15.00	30.00
❏ SD 8109 [S]	The Best of Solomon Burke	1965	10.00	20.00	40.00
❏ SD 8158	King Solomon	1968	6.25	12.50	25.00
❏ SD 8185	I Wish I Knew	1968	6.25	12.50	25.00
BELL
❏ 6033	Proud Mary	1969	5.00	10.00	20.00
CLARION
❏ 607 [M]	I Almost Lost My Mind	1966	5.00	10.00	20.00
❏ SD 607 [S]	I Almost Lost My Mind	1966	6.25	12.50	25.00

KENWOOD
| ❏ LP-498 [M] | Solomon Burke | 1964 | 50.00 | 100.00 | 200.00 |
-- Reissue of Apollo 498

BURNETT, CAROL
DECCA
❏ DL 4049 [M]	Carol Burnett Remembers How They Stopped the Show	1960	7.50	15.00	30.00
❏ DL 4437 [M]	Let Me Entertain You	1964	5.00	10.00	20.00
❏ DL 74049 [S]	Carol Burnett Remembers How They Stopped the Show	1960	10.00	20.00	40.00
❏ DL 74437 [S]	Let Me Entertain You	1964	6.25	12.50	25.00
RCA VICTOR
❏ LPM-3839 [M]	Carol Burnett Sings	1967	5.00	10.00	20.00
❏ LSP-3839 [S]	Carol Burnett Sings	1967	5.00	10.00	20.00

BURNETT, J. HENRY -- See T-BONE BURNETT.

BURNETT, T-BONE
UNI
| ❏ 73125 | The B-52 Band and the Fabulous Skyhawks | 1972 | 7.50 | 15.00 | 30.00 |
-- As "J. Henry Burnett"

BURNETTE, BILLY
ENTRANCE
| ❏ Z 31228 | Billy Burnette | 1972 | 5.00 | 10.00 | 20.00 |

BURNETTE, DORSEY
DOT
| ❏ DLP-3456 [M] | Dorsey Burnette Sings | 1963 | 10.00 | 20.00 | 40.00 |
| ❏ DLP-25456 [S] | Dorsey Burnette Sings | 1963 | 12.50 | 25.00 | 50.00 |
ERA
❏ EL-102 [M]	Tall Oak Tree	1960	37.50	75.00	150.00
❏ ES-102 [S]	Tall Oak Tree	1960	75.00	150.00	300.00
❏ ES-800 [M]	Dorsey Burnette's Greatest Hits	1969	6.25	12.50	25.00

BURNETTE, JOHNNY
CORAL
| ❏ CRL 57080 [M] | Johnny Burnette & the Rock 'N' Roll Trio | 1956 | 2,000. | 4,000. | 6,000. |
-- Originals have maroon labels, printing on jacket's spine and "Made in U.S.A." in lower right of back cover
LIBERTY
❏ LRP-3179 [M]	Dreamin'	1960	10.00	20.00	40.00
❏ LRP-3183 [M]	Johnny Burnette	1961	10.00	20.00	40.00
❏ LRP-3190 [M]	Johnny Burnette Sings	1961	10.00	20.00	40.00
❏ LRP-3206 [M]	Johnny Burnette's Hits and Other Favorites	1962	10.00	20.00	40.00
❏ LRP-3255 [M]	Roses Are Red	1962	10.00	20.00	40.00
❏ LRP-3389 [M]	The Johnny Burnette Story	1964	10.00	20.00	40.00
❏ LST-7179 [S]	Dreamin'	1960	15.00	30.00	60.00
❏ LST-7183 [S]	Johnny Burnette	1961	15.00	30.00	60.00
❏ LST-7190 [S]	Johnny Burnette Sings	1961	15.00	30.00	60.00
❏ LST-7206 [S]	Johnny Burnette's Hits and Other Favorites	1962	12.50	25.00	50.00
❏ LST-7255 [S]	Roses Are Red	1962	12.50	25.00	50.00
❏ LST-7389 [S]	The Johnny Burnette Story	1964	12.50	25.00	50.00
SOLID SMOKE
❏ SS-8001	Tear It Up	1978	7.50	15.00	30.00
-- Blue vinyl
SUNSET
| ❏ SUS-5179 [S] | Dreamin' | 1967 | 5.00 | 10.00 | 20.00 |

BURNETTE, SMILEY
CRICKET
| ❏ CR-11 [M] | Rodeo Songaree | 1959 | 7.50 | 15.00 | 30.00 |
STARDAY
| ❏ SLP-191 [M] | Ole Frog | 1962 | 10.00 | 20.00 | 40.00 |

BURNS, RANDY
ESP-DISK'
| ❏ 1039 | Songs of Love and War | 1966 | 6.25 | 12.50 | 25.00 |
| ❏ 1089 | Evening of the Magician | 1968 | 6.25 | 12.50 | 25.00 |

BURNT SUITE
B.J.W.
| ❏ 9 | Burnt Suite | 1967 | 50.00 | 100.00 | 200.00 |

Number	Title	Yr	VG	VG+	NM

BURRELL, KENNY

ARGO
Number	Title	Yr	VG	VG+	NM
❑ LP-655 [M]	A Night at the Vanguard	1959	7.50	15.00	30.00
❑ LPS-655 [S]	A Night at the Vanguard	1959	10.00	20.00	40.00

BLUE NOTE
| ❑ BLP-1523 [M] | Introducing Kenny Burrell | 1956 | 50.00 | 100.00 | 200.00 |
| -- "Deep groove" version (deep indentation under label on both sides) |
| ❑ BLP-1523 [M] | Introducing Kenny Burrell | 1956 | 37.50 | 75.00 | 150.00 |
| -- Regular version, Lexington Ave. address on label |
| ❑ BLP-1523 [M] | Introducing Kenny Burrell | 1957 | 12.50 | 25.00 | 50.00 |
| -- W. 63rd St., NYC address on label |
| ❑ BLP-1523 [M] | Introducing Kenny Burrell | 1963 | 6.25 | 12.50 | 25.00 |
| -- New York, USA address on label |
| ❑ BLP-1543 [M] | Kenny Burrell, Volume 2 | 1957 | 50.00 | 100.00 | 200.00 |
| -- "Deep groove" version (deep indentation under label on both sides) |
| ❑ BLP-1543 [M] | Kenny Burrell, Volume 2 | 1957 | 37.50 | 75.00 | 150.00 |
| -- Regular version, Lexington Ave. address on label |
| ❑ BLP-1543 [M] | Kenny Burrell, Volume 2 | 1957 | 12.50 | 25.00 | 50.00 |
| -- W. 63rd St., NYC address on label |
| ❑ BLP-1543 [M] | Kenny Burrell, Volume 2 | 1963 | 6.25 | 12.50 | 25.00 |
| -- New York, USA address on label |
| ❑ BLP-1596 [M] | Blue Lights, Volume 1 | 1958 | 25.00 | 50.00 | 100.00 |
| -- "Deep groove" version (deep indentation under label on both sides) |
| ❑ BLP-1596 [M] | Blue Lights, Volume 1 | 1958 | 17.50 | 35.00 | 70.00 |
| -- Regular version, W. 63rd St., NYC address on label |
| ❑ BLP-1596 [M] | Blue Lights, Volume 1 | 1963 | 6.25 | 12.50 | 25.00 |
| -- New York, USA address on label |
| ❑ BST-1596 [S] | Blue Lights, Volume 1 | 1959 | 25.00 | 50.00 | 100.00 |
| -- "Deep groove" version (deep indentation under label on both sides) |
| ❑ BST-1596 [S] | Blue Lights, Volume 1 | 1959 | 17.50 | 35.00 | 70.00 |
| -- Regular version, W. 63rd St., NYC address on label |
| ❑ BST-1596 [S] | Blue Lights, Volume 1 | 1963 | 6.25 | 12.50 | 25.00 |
| -- New York, USA address on label |
| ❑ BLP-1597 [M] | Blue Lights, Volume 2 | 1958 | 25.00 | 50.00 | 100.00 |
| -- "Deep groove" version (deep indentation under label on both sides) |
| ❑ BLP-1597 [M] | Blue Lights, Volume 2 | 1958 | 17.50 | 35.00 | 70.00 |
| -- Regular version, W. 63rd St., NYC address on label |
| ❑ BLP-1597 [M] | Blue Lights, Volume 2 | 1963 | 6.25 | 12.50 | 25.00 |
| -- New York, USA address on label |
| ❑ BST-1597 [S] | Blue Lights, Volume 2 | 1959 | 25.00 | 50.00 | 100.00 |
| -- "Deep groove" version (deep indentation under label on both sides) |
| ❑ BST-1597 [S] | Blue Lights, Volume 2 | 1959 | 17.50 | 35.00 | 70.00 |
| -- Regular version, W. 63rd St., NYC address on label |
| ❑ BST-1597 [S] | Blue Lights, Volume 2 | 1963 | 6.25 | 12.50 | 25.00 |
| -- New York, USA address on label |
| ❑ BLP-4021 [M] | On View at the Five Spot Café | 1960 | 25.00 | 50.00 | 100.00 |
| -- "Deep groove" version (deep indentation under label on both sides) |
| ❑ BLP-4021 [M] | On View at the Five Spot Café | 1960 | 17.50 | 35.00 | 70.00 |
| -- Regular version, W. 63rd St., NYC address on label |
| ❑ BLP-4021 [M] | On View at the Five Spot Café | 1963 | 6.25 | 12.50 | 25.00 |
| -- New York, USA address on label |
| ❑ BLP-4123 [M] | Midnight Blue | 1963 | 7.50 | 15.00 | 30.00 |
| -- New York, USA address on label |
| ❑ BST-84021 [S] | On View at the Five Spot Café | 1960 | 15.00 | 30.00 | 60.00 |
| -- W. 63rd St., NYC address on label |
| ❑ BST-84021 [S] | On View at the Five Spot Café | 1963 | 6.25 | 12.50 | 25.00 |
| -- New York, USA address on label |
| ❑ BST-84123 [S] | Midnight Blue | 1963 | 10.00 | 20.00 | 40.00 |
| -- New York, USA address on label |

CADET
| ❑ LP-798 [M] | Ode to 52nd Street | 1967 | 5.00 | 10.00 | 20.00 |
| ❑ LPS-769 [S] | Men at Work | 1965 | 5.00 | 10.00 | 20.00 |
| -- Reissue of Argo 655 |
| ❑ LPS-772 [S] | The Tender Gender | 1966 | 5.00 | 10.00 | 20.00 |
| ❑ LPS-779 [S] | Have Yourself a Soulful Little Christmas | 1966 | 5.00 | 10.00 | 20.00 |

COLUMBIA
| ❑ CL 1703 [M] | Weaver of Dreams | 1961 | 5.00 | 10.00 | 20.00 |
| ❑ CS 8503 [S] | Weaver of Dreams | 1961 | 6.25 | 12.50 | 25.00 |

KAPP
| ❑ KL-1326 [M] | Lotta Bossa Nova | 1962 | 5.00 | 10.00 | 20.00 |
| ❑ KS-3326 [S] | Lotta Bossa Nova | 1962 | 6.25 | 12.50 | 25.00 |

MOODSVILLE
| ❑ MVLP-29 [M] | Bluesy Burrell | 1963 | 10.00 | 20.00 | 40.00 |
| -- Green label |
| ❑ MVLP-29 [M] | Bluesy Burrell | 1965 | 5.00 | 10.00 | 20.00 |
| -- Blue label with trident logo |
| ❑ MVST-29 [S] | Bluesy Burrell | 1963 | 10.00 | 20.00 | 40.00 |
| -- Green label |
| ❑ MVST-29 [S] | Bluesy Burrell | 1965 | 6.25 | 12.50 | 25.00 |
| -- Blue label with trident logo |

PRESTIGE
| ❑ PRLP-7073 [M] | All Night Long | 1957 | 25.00 | 50.00 | 100.00 |
| -- Actually an all-star session; reissued as a Kenny Burrell album, thus it is listed here |
| ❑ PRLP-7081 [M] | All Day Long | 1957 | 25.00 | 50.00 | 100.00 |
| -- Actually an all-star session; reissued as a Kenny Burrell album, thus it is listed here |
| ❑ PRLP-7088 [M] | Kenny Burrell | 1957 | 20.00 | 40.00 | 80.00 |
| ❑ PRLP-7277 [M] | All Day Long | 1963 | 12.50 | 25.00 | 50.00 |
| -- Reissue of 7081 |
| ❑ PRST-7277 [R] | All Day Long | 1963 | 5.00 | 10.00 | 20.00 |
| ❑ PRLP-7289 [M] | All Night Long | 1964 | 12.50 | 25.00 | 50.00 |
| -- Reissue of 7073 |
| ❑ PRST-7289 [R] | All Night Long | 1964 | 5.00 | 10.00 | 20.00 |
| ❑ PRLP-7308 [M] | Blue Moods | 1964 | 7.50 | 15.00 | 30.00 |
| -- Reissue of 7088 |
❑ PRST-7308 [R]	Blue Moods	1964	5.00	10.00	20.00
❑ PRLP-7315 [M]	Soul Call	1964	6.25	12.50	25.00
❑ PRST-7315 [S]	Soul Call	1964	7.50	15.00	30.00
❑ PRLP-7347 [M]	Crash	1964	6.25	12.50	25.00
❑ PRST-7347 [S]	Crash	1964	7.50	15.00	30.00
❑ PRLP-7448 [M]	The Best of Kenny Burrell	1967	7.50	15.00	30.00
❑ PRST-7448 [S]	The Best of Kenny Burrell	1967	5.00	10.00	20.00

VERVE
❑ V-8553 [M]	Blue Bash!	1963	5.00	10.00	20.00
❑ V6-8553 [S]	Blue Bash!	1963	6.25	12.50	25.00
❑ V-8746 [M]	Blues-- The Common Ground	1968	5.00	10.00	20.00
❑ V6-8612 [S]	Guitar Forms	1965	5.00	10.00	20.00
❑ V6-8656 [S]	A Generation Ago Today	1966	5.00	10.00	20.00

BURRELL, KENNY, AND JOHN COLTRANE
Also see each artist's individual listings.

NEW JAZZ
| ❑ NJLP-8217 [M] | The Cats | 1959 | 20.00 | 40.00 | 80.00 |
| -- Purple label |
| ❑ NJLP-8217 [M] | The Cats | 1965 | 6.25 | 12.50 | 25.00 |
| -- Blue label with trident logo |
| ❑ NJLP-8276 [M] | Kenny Burrell with John Coltrane | 1962 | 15.00 | 30.00 | 60.00 |
| -- Purple label |
| ❑ NJLP-8276 [M] | Kenny Burrell with John Coltrane | 1965 | 6.25 | 12.50 | 25.00 |
| -- Blue label with trident logo |

PRESTIGE
| ❑ PRLP-7532 [M] | Kenny Burrell Quintet with John Coltrane | 1967 | 7.50 | 15.00 | 30.00 |
| ❑ PRST-7532 [S] | Kenny Burrell Quintet with John Coltrane | 1967 | 5.00 | 10.00 | 20.00 |

BURRITO BROTHERS, THE -- See THE FLYING BURRITO BROTHERS.

BURROUGHS, WILLIAM
ESP-DISK'
| ❑ 1050 [M] | Call Me Burroughs | 1967 | 25.00 | 50.00 | 100.00 |

BURROWS, ABE
COLUMBIA
| ❑ CL 6128 [10] | Abe Burrows Sings? | 1950 | 10.00 | 20.00 | 40.00 |
DECCA
| ❑ DL 5288 [10] | The Girl with the 3 Blue Eyes | 1951 | 10.00 | 20.00 | 40.00 |

BURTON, JAMES
A&M
| ❑ SP-4293 | James Burton | 1971 | 6.25 | 12.50 | 25.00 |

BUSH, JOHNNY
MILLION
| ❑ 1001 | The Best of Johnny Bush | 1972 | 6.25 | 12.50 | 25.00 |
STOP
❑ 10002	Sound of a Heartache	1968	6.25	12.50	25.00
❑ 10005	Undo the Night	1968	5.00	10.00	20.00
❑ 10008	You Gave Me a Mountain	1969	5.00	10.00	20.00
❑ 10014	Johnny Bush	1970	5.00	10.00	20.00

BUSH, KATE
EMI AMERICA
| ❑ ST-17171 | Hounds of Love | 1985 | 7.50 | 15.00 | 30.00 |
| -- Marbled vinyl |
HARVEST
| ❑ ST-11762 | The Kick Inside | 1978 | 6.25 | 12.50 | 25.00 |

BUTERA, SAM, AND THE WITNESSES
CAPITOL
❑ ST 1098 [S]	The Big Horn	1959	10.00	20.00	40.00
❑ T 1098 [M]	The Big Horn	1958	7.50	15.00	30.00
❑ ST 1521 [S]	The Big Sax and the Big Voice	1960	7.50	15.00	30.00
❑ T 1521 [M]	The Big Sax and the Big Voice	1960	6.25	12.50	25.00
DOT
| ❑ DLP-3272 [M] | The Wildest Clan | 1960 | 5.00 | 10.00 | 20.00 |

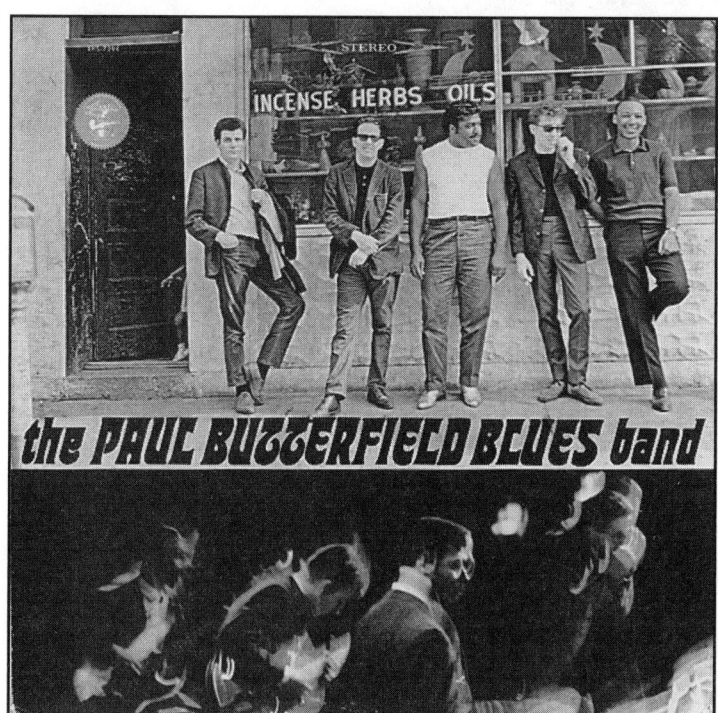

(Top left) Take a poll of classic-rock fans and ask them what album they'd like to see on CD that isn't there legitimately yet, and *Buckingham Nicks* usually finishes in the top three. This was the album that first interested Mick Fleetwood in the two then-lovers, and they joined Fleetwood Mac in 1974. The rest, as they say, is history. (Top right) One of the most valuable albums in the world, and the top dollar item among rockabilly fans, is *Johnny Burnette And The Rock 'n Roll Trio*, released on Coral in the late 1950s. (Bottom left) The debut album from the Paul Butterfield Blues Band, another underrated 1960s artifact, features not only Butterfield but the talents of Elvin Bishop and Mike Bloomfield. (Bottom right) In 1969, a small record label called Together released this collection of Byrds demos recorded in 1964 and called it *Preflyte*. This is the original cover; in 1973, Columbia reissued the material in a completely different cover that is not as sought-after as the first edition.

Number	Title	Yr	VG	VG+	NM
❑ DLP-3381 [M] Apache		1961	5.00	10.00	20.00
❑ DLP-25272 [S] The Wildest Clan		1960	6.25	12.50	25.00
❑ DLP-25381 [S] Apache		1961	6.25	12.50	25.00

BUTLER, BILLY
OKEH
Number	Title	Yr	VG	VG+	NM
❑ OKM 12115 [M] Right Track		1966	5.00	10.00	20.00
❑ OKS 14115 [S] Right Track		1966	6.25	12.50	25.00

BUTLER, CARL
COLUMBIA
Number	Title	Yr	VG	VG+	NM
❑ CL 2002 [M]	Don't Let Me Cross Over	1963	5.00	10.00	20.00
❑ CS 8802 [S]	Don't Let Me Cross Over	1963	6.25	12.50	25.00

BUTLER, CARL, AND PEARL
COLUMBIA
Number	Title	Yr	VG	VG+	NM
❑ CL 2125 [M]	Loving Arms	1964	5.00	10.00	20.00
❑ CL 2640 [M]	Avenue of Prayer	1967	5.00	10.00	20.00
❑ CS 8925 [S]	Loving Arms	1964	6.25	12.50	25.00
❑ CS 9108 [S]	The Old and the New	1965	5.00	10.00	20.00

BUTLER, FREDDIE
KAPP
Number	Title	Yr	VG	VG+	NM
❑ KS-3519	With a Dab of Soul	1968	7.50	15.00	30.00

BUTLER, JERRY
ABNER
Number	Title	Yr	VG	VG+	NM
❑ R-2001 [M]	Jerry Butler, Esquire	1959	100.00	200.00	400.00

MERCURY
Number	Title	Yr	VG	VG+	NM
❑ SRM-2-7502 [(2)] The Spice of Life		1972	5.00	10.00	20.00
❑ MG-21005 [M] The Soul Artistry of Jerry Butler		1967	5.00	10.00	20.00
❑ MG-21146 [M] Mr. Dream Merchant		1967	5.00	10.00	20.00

VEE JAY
Number	Title	Yr	VG	VG+	NM
❑ LP-1027 [M]	Jerry Butler, Esquire	1960	37.50	75.00	150.00
-- Reissue of Abner 2001					
❑ LP-1029 [M]	He Will Break Your Heart	1960	20.00	40.00	80.00
❑ LP-1034 [M]	Love Me	1961	12.50	25.00	50.00
-- Reissue of 1027					
❑ LP-1038 [M]	Aware of Love	1961	10.00	20.00	40.00
❑ SR-1038 [S]	Aware of Love	1961	12.50	25.00	50.00
❑ LP-1046 [M]	Moon River	1962	10.00	20.00	40.00
❑ SR-1046 [S]	Moon River	1962	12.50	25.00	50.00
❑ LP-1048 [M]	The Best of Jerry Butler	1962	6.25	12.50	25.00
❑ SR-1048 [P]	The Best of Jerry Butler	1962	7.50	15.00	30.00
❑ LP-1057 [M]	Folk Songs	1963	6.25	12.50	25.00
❑ SR-1057 [S]	Folk Songs	1963	7.50	15.00	30.00
❑ LP-1075 [M]	For Your Precious Love	1963	6.25	12.50	25.00
❑ SR-1075 [S]	For Your Precious Love	1963	7.50	15.00	30.00
❑ LP-1076 [M]	Giving Up On Love/Need to Belong	1963	6.25	12.50	25.00
❑ VJS-1076 [S]	Giving Up On Love/Need to Belong	1963	7.50	15.00	30.00
❑ LP-1119 [M]	More of the Best of Jerry Butler	1965	6.25	12.50	25.00
❑ VJS-1119 [S]	More of the Best of Jerry Butler	1965	7.50	15.00	30.00

BUTTERFIELD, PAUL
ELEKTRA
Number	Title	Yr	VG	VG+	NM
❑ EKL-294 [M]	The Paul Butterfield Blues Band	1965	5.00	10.00	20.00
-- Gold label with guitar player					
❑ EKL-315 [M]	East-West	1966	5.00	10.00	20.00
-- Gold label with guitar player					
❑ 7E-2001 [(2)]	The Butterfield Blues Band/Live	1970	6.25	12.50	25.00
❑ 7E-2005 [(2)]	Golden Butter/The Best of the Paul Butterfield Blues Band	1972	6.25	12.50	25.00
❑ EKL-4015 [M]	The Resurrection of Pigboy Crabshaw	1967	7.50	15.00	30.00
❑ EKS-7294 [S]	The Paul Butterfield Blues Band	1965	6.25	12.50	25.00
-- Gold label with guitar player					
❑ EKS-7294 [S]	The Paul Butterfield Blues Band	1966	5.00	10.00	20.00
-- Brown label					
❑ EKS-7315 [S]	East-West	1966	6.25	12.50	25.00
-- Gold label with guitar player					
❑ EKS-7315 [S]	East-West	1967	5.00	10.00	20.00
-- Brown label					
❑ EKS-74015 [S]	The Resurrection of Pigboy Crabshaw	1967	5.00	10.00	20.00
-- Brown label					
❑ EKS-74025	In My Own Dream	1968	5.00	10.00	20.00
-- Brown label					
❑ EKS-74053	Keep On Moving	1969	5.00	10.00	20.00
-- Red label with large stylized "E"					
❑ EKS-75013	Sometimes I Just Feel Like Smilin'	1971	5.00	10.00	20.00

BUTTHOLE SURFERS
ALTERNATIVE TENTACLES
Number	Title	Yr	VG	VG+	NM
❑ VIRUS 32 [EP] Butthole Surfers		1983	6.25	12.50	25.00
-- Original pressing of debut EP with no title					
❑ VIRUS 32 [EP] Brown Reason to Live		1983	5.00	10.00	20.00
-- Retitled version of debut EP with brown swirl vinyl					

TOUCH & GO
Number	Title	Yr	VG	VG+	NM
❑ 5	Psychic...Powerless... Another Man's Sac	1985	5.00	10.00	20.00
-- Original on clear vinyl					
❑ 8	Rembrandt Pussyhorse	1986	10.00	20.00	40.00
-- Red vinyl; supposedly only 100 were pressed					
❑ 14	Cream Corn from the Socket of Devils	1985	5.00	10.00	20.00
-- Red vinyl					

BYRD, BILLY
REPRISE
Number	Title	Yr	VG	VG+	NM
❑ R-6040 [M]	Lonesome Country Songs	1962	5.00	10.00	20.00
❑ R9-6040 [S]	Lonesome Country Songs	1962	6.25	12.50	25.00

WARNER BROS.
Number	Title	Yr	VG	VG+	NM
❑ W 1327 [M]	I Love a Guitar	1960	5.00	10.00	20.00
❑ WS 1327 [S]	I Love a Guitar	1960	6.25	12.50	25.00
❑ W 1576 [M]	The Golden Guitar of Billy Byrd	1964	5.00	10.00	20.00
❑ WS 1576 [S]	The Golden Guitar of Billy Byrd	1964	6.25	12.50	25.00

BYRD, BOBBY
KING
Number	Title	Yr	VG	VG+	NM
❑ KS-1118	I Need Help	1970	50.00	100.00	200.00

BYRD, CHARLIE
COLUMBIA
Number	Title	Yr	VG	VG+	NM
❑ CL 2592 [M]	Byrdland	1967	5.00	10.00	20.00
❑ CL 2652 [M]	Hollywood Byrd	1967	5.00	10.00	20.00
❑ CL 2692 [M]	More Brazilian Byrd	1967	5.00	10.00	20.00
❑ CS 9137 [S]	Brazilian Byrd	1965	5.00	10.00	20.00
-- Red label, "360 Sound" in black					
❑ CS 9355 [S]	Christmas Carols for Solo Guitar	1966	5.00	10.00	20.00
❑ CS 9627 [M]	Hit Trip	1968	6.25	12.50	25.00
-- "Special Mono Radio Station Copy" with white label					

CRYSTAL CLEAR
Number	Title	Yr	VG	VG+	NM
❑ 8002	Charlie Byrd	1979	7.50	15.00	30.00
-- Direct-to-disc recording; plays at 45 rpm					

MOBILE FIDELITY
Number	Title	Yr	VG	VG+	NM
❑ 1-515	Byrd at the Gate	1982	10.00	20.00	40.00
-- Audiophile vinyl					

OFFBEAT
Number	Title	Yr	VG	VG+	NM
❑ OLB-3001 [M]	Jazz at the Show Boat, Volume 1	1959	6.25	12.50	25.00
❑ OLB-3005 [M]	Jazz at the Show Boat, Volume 2	1959	6.25	12.50	25.00
❑ OLB-3006 [M]	Jazz at the Show Boat, Volume 3	1959	6.25	12.50	25.00
❑ OLB-3007 [M]	Charlie's Choice	1960	6.25	12.50	25.00
❑ OS-93001 [S]	Jazz at the Show Boat, Volume 1	1959	7.50	15.00	30.00
❑ OS-93005 [S]	Jazz at the Show Boat, Volume 2	1959	7.50	15.00	30.00
❑ OS-93006 [S]	Jazz at the Show Boat, Volume 3	1959	7.50	15.00	30.00
❑ OS-93007 [S]	Charlie's Choice	1960	7.50	15.00	30.00

RIVERSIDE
Number	Title	Yr	VG	VG+	NM
❑ RM-427 [M]	Latin Impressions	1962	5.00	10.00	20.00
❑ RM-436 [M]	Bossa Nova Pelos Passaros	1962	5.00	10.00	20.00
❑ RM-448 [M]	Byrd's Word	1963	5.00	10.00	20.00
❑ RM-449 [M]	Byrd in the Wind	1963	5.00	10.00	20.00
❑ RM-450 [M]	Mr. Guitar	1963	5.00	10.00	20.00
❑ RM-451 [M]	The Guitar Artistry of Charlie Byrd	1963	5.00	10.00	20.00
❑ RM-452 [M]	Charlie Byrd at the Village Vanguard	1963	5.00	10.00	20.00
❑ RM-453 [M]	Blues Sonata	1963	5.00	10.00	20.00
❑ RM-454 [M]	Once More! Bossa Nova	1963	5.00	10.00	20.00
❑ RM-467 [M]	Byrd at the Gate	1964	5.00	10.00	20.00
❑ RM-498 [M]	Solo Flight	1967	5.00	10.00	20.00
❑ RS-9427 [S]	Latin Impressions	1962	6.25	12.50	25.00
❑ RS-9436 [S]	Bossa Nova Pelos Passaros	1962	6.25	12.50	25.00
❑ RS-9448 [S]	Byrd's Word	1963	6.25	12.50	25.00
❑ RS-9449 [S]	Byrd in the Wind	1963	6.25	12.50	25.00
❑ RS-9450 [S]	Mr. Guitar	1963	6.25	12.50	25.00
❑ RS-9451 [S]	The Guitar Artistry of Charlie Byrd	1963	6.25	12.50	25.00
❑ RS-9452 [S]	Charlie Byrd at the Village Vanguard	1963	6.25	12.50	25.00
❑ RS-9453 [S]	Blues Sonata	1963	6.25	12.50	25.00
❑ RS-9454 [S]	Once More! Bossa Nova	1963	6.25	12.50	25.00
❑ RS-9467 [S]	Byrd at the Gate	1964	6.25	12.50	25.00
❑ RS-9481 [S]	Byrd Song	1966	5.00	10.00	20.00

Number	Title	Yr	VG	VG+	NM

SAVOY
| ❏ MG-12099 [M] | Jazz Recital | 1957 | 10.00 | 20.00 | 40.00 |
| ❏ MG-12116 [M] | Blues for Night People | 1957 | 10.00 | 20.00 | 40.00 |

BYRD, CHARLIE, AND FATHER MALCOLM BOYD
COLUMBIA
| ❏ CS 9348 [S] | Are You Running With Me, Jesus? | 1966 | 5.00 | 10.00 | 20.00 |

BYRD, CHARLIE, HERB ELLIS & BARNEY KESSEL
CONCORD JAZZ
| ❏ CJD-1002 | Straight Tracks | 1986 | 5.00 | 10.00 | 20.00 |

-- *Direct-to-disc recording*

BYRD, DONALD
BLUE NOTE
| ❏ BLP-4007 [M] | Off to the Races | 1959 | 30.00 | 60.00 | 120.00 |

-- *"Deep groove" version (deep indentation under label on both sides)*
| ❏ BLP-4007 [M] | Off to the Races | 1959 | 20.00 | 40.00 | 80.00 |

-- *W. 63rd St., NYC address on label*
| ❏ BLP-4007 [M] | Off to the Races | 1963 | 6.25 | 12.50 | 25.00 |

-- *"New York, USA" address on label*
| ❏ BST-4007 [S] | Off to the Races | 1959 | 20.00 | 40.00 | 80.00 |

-- *"Deep groove" version (deep indentation under label on both sides)*
| ❏ BST-4007 [S] | Off to the Races | 1959 | 15.00 | 30.00 | 60.00 |

-- *W. 63rd St., NYC address on label*
| ❏ BST-4007 [S] | Off to the Races | 1963 | 6.25 | 12.50 | 25.00 |

-- *"New York, USA" address on label*
| ❏ BLP-4019 [M] | Byrd in Hand | 1959 | 30.00 | 60.00 | 120.00 |

-- *"Deep groove" version (deep indentation under label on both sides)*
| ❏ BLP-4019 [M] | Byrd in Hand | 1959 | 20.00 | 40.00 | 80.00 |

-- *W. 63rd St., NYC address on label*
| ❏ BLP-4019 [M] | Byrd in Hand | 1963 | 6.25 | 12.50 | 25.00 |

-- *"New York, USA" address on label*
| ❏ BLP-4026 [M] | Fuego | 1960 | 30.00 | 60.00 | 120.00 |

-- *"Deep groove" version (deep indentation under label on both sides)*
| ❏ BLP-4026 [M] | Fuego | 1960 | 20.00 | 40.00 | 80.00 |

-- *W. 63rd St., NYC address on label*
| ❏ BLP-4026 [M] | Fuego | 1963 | 6.25 | 12.50 | 25.00 |

-- *"New York, USA" address on label*
| ❏ BLP-4048 [M] | Byrd in Flight | 1960 | 30.00 | 60.00 | 120.00 |

-- *"Deep groove" version (deep indentation under label on both sides)*
| ❏ BLP-4048 [M] | Byrd in Flight | 1960 | 20.00 | 40.00 | 80.00 |

-- *W. 63rd St., NYC address on label*
| ❏ BLP-4048 [M] | Byrd in Flight | 1963 | 6.25 | 12.50 | 25.00 |

-- *"New York, USA" address on label*
| ❏ BLP-4060 [M] | Donald Byrd at the Half Note Café, Volume 1 | 1961 | 20.00 | 40.00 | 80.00 |

-- *W. 63rd St., NYC address on label*
| ❏ BLP-4060 [M] | Donald Byrd at the Half Note Café, Volume 1 | 1963 | 6.25 | 12.50 | 25.00 |

-- *"New York, USA" address on label*
| ❏ BLP-4061 [M] | Donald Byrd at the Half Note Café, Volume 2 | 1961 | 20.00 | 40.00 | 80.00 |

-- *W. 63rd St., NYC address on label*
| ❏ BLP-4061 [M] | Donald Byrd at the Half Note Café, Volume 2 | 1963 | 6.25 | 12.50 | 25.00 |

-- *"New York, USA" address on label*
| ❏ BLP-4075 [M] | The Cat Walk | 1961 | 20.00 | 40.00 | 80.00 |

-- *61st St, New York address on label*
| ❏ BLP-4075 [M] | The Cat Walk | 1963 | 6.25 | 12.50 | 25.00 |

-- *"New York, USA" address on label*
❏ BLP-4101 [M]	Royal Flush	1962	5.00	10.00	20.00
❏ BLP-4118 [M]	Free Form	1963	5.00	10.00	20.00
❏ BLP-4124 [M]	A New Perspective	1964	5.00	10.00	20.00
❏ BLP-4188 [M]	I'm Tryin' to Get Home	1965	5.00	10.00	20.00
❏ BLP-4238 [M]	Mustang!	1966	5.00	10.00	20.00
❏ BLP-4259 [M]	Blackjack	1967	6.25	12.50	25.00
❏ BST-84019 [S]	Byrd in Hand	1959	15.00	30.00	60.00

-- *W. 63rd St., NYC address on label*
| ❏ BST-84019 [S] | Byrd in Hand | 1963 | 6.25 | 12.50 | 25.00 |

-- *"New York, USA" address on label*
| ❏ BST-84026 [S] | Fuego | 1959 | 15.00 | 30.00 | 60.00 |

-- *W. 63rd St., NYC address on label*
| ❏ BST-84026 [S] | Fuego | 1963 | 6.25 | 12.50 | 25.00 |

-- *"New York, USA" address on label*
| ❏ BST-84048 [S] | Byrd in Flight | 1960 | 15.00 | 30.00 | 60.00 |

-- *W. 63rd St., NYC address on label*
| ❏ BST-84048 [S] | Byrd in Flight | 1963 | 6.25 | 12.50 | 25.00 |

-- *"New York, USA" address on label*
| ❏ BST-84060 [S] | Donald Byrd at the Half Note Café, Volume 1 | 1961 | 15.00 | 30.00 | 60.00 |

-- *W. 63rd St., NYC address on label*
| ❏ BST-84060 [S] | Donald Byrd at the Half Note Café, Volume 1 | 1963 | 6.25 | 12.50 | 25.00 |

| ❏ BST-84061 [S] | Donald Byrd at the Half Note Café, Volume 2 | 1961 | 15.00 | 30.00 | 60.00 |

-- *W. 63rd St., NYC address on label*
| ❏ BST-84061 [S] | Donald Byrd at the Half Note Café, Volume 2 | 1963 | 6.25 | 12.50 | 25.00 |

-- *"New York, USA" address on label*
| ❏ BST-84075 [S] | The Cat Walk | 1961 | 15.00 | 30.00 | 60.00 |

-- *61st St, New York address on label*
| ❏ BST-84075 [S] | The Cat Walk | 1963 | 6.25 | 12.50 | 25.00 |

-- *"New York, USA" address on label*
| ❏ BST-84101 [S] | Royal Flush | 1962 | 6.25 | 12.50 | 25.00 |

-- *"New York, USA" address on label*
| ❏ BST-84118 [S] | Free Form | 1963 | 6.25 | 12.50 | 25.00 |

-- *"New York, USA" address on label*
| ❏ BST-84124 [S] | A New Perspective | 1964 | 6.25 | 12.50 | 25.00 |

-- *"New York, USA" address on label*
| ❏ BST-84188 [S] | I'm Tryin' to Get Home | 1965 | 6.25 | 12.50 | 25.00 |

-- *"New York, USA" address on label*
| ❏ BST-84238 [S] | Mustang! | 1966 | 6.25 | 12.50 | 25.00 |

-- *"New York, USA" address on label*
❏ BST-84259 [S]	Blackjack	1967	5.00	10.00	20.00
❏ BST-84292	Slow Drag	1968	5.00	10.00	20.00
❏ BST-84319	Fancy Free	1969	5.00	10.00	20.00
❏ BST-84349	Electric	1970	5.00	10.00	20.00
❏ BST-84380	Ethiopian Nights	1972	5.00	10.00	20.00

SAVOY
| ❏ MG-12032 [M] | Byrd's Word | 1956 | 25.00 | 50.00 | 100.00 |
| ❏ MG-12064 [M] | The Jazz Message of Donald Byrd | 1956 | 30.00 | 60.00 | 120.00 |

TRANSITION
❏ TRLP-4 [M]	Byrd's Eye View	1956	150.00	300.00	600.00
❏ TRLP-5 [M]	Byrd Jazz	1956	150.00	300.00	600.00
❏ TRLP-17 [M]	Byrd Blows on Beacon Hill	1956	150.00	300.00	600.00

VERVE
| ❏ V-8609 [M] | Up with Donald Byrd | 1965 | 5.00 | 10.00 | 20.00 |
| ❏ V6-8609 [S] | Up with Donald Byrd | 1965 | 6.25 | 12.50 | 25.00 |

BYRD, JERRY
DECCA
❏ DL 4078 [M]	Paradise Island	1961	5.00	10.00	20.00
❏ DL 8643 [M]	Hi-Fi Guitar	1958	10.00	20.00	40.00
❏ DL 74078 [S]	Paradise Island	1961	6.25	12.50	25.00

MERCURY
❏ MG-20230 [M]	On the Shores of Waikiki	1960	7.50	15.00	30.00
❏ MG-20345 [M]	Steel Guitar Favorites	1961	7.50	15.00	30.00
❏ MG-20693 [M]	Hawaiian Golden Hits	1962	7.50	15.00	30.00
❏ MG-20856 [M]	Blue Hawaiian Steel Guitar	1963	7.50	15.00	30.00
❏ MG-20932 [M]	The Man of Steel	1964	5.00	10.00	20.00
❏ MG-25077 [10]	Nani Hawaii	1953	20.00	40.00	80.00
❏ MG-25134 [10]	Guitar Magic	1954	20.00	40.00	80.00
❏ MG-25169 [10]	Byrd's Expedition	1954	20.00	40.00	80.00
❏ SR-60230 [S]	On the Shores of Waikiki	1960	10.00	20.00	40.00
❏ SR-60345 [S]	Steel Guitar Favorites	1961	10.00	20.00	40.00
❏ SR-60693 [S]	Hawaiian Golden Hits	1962	10.00	20.00	40.00
❏ SR-60856 [S]	Blue Hawaiian Steel Guitar	1963	10.00	20.00	40.00
❏ SR-60932 [S]	The Man of Steel	1964	6.25	12.50	25.00

MONUMENT
❏ MLP-4008 [M]	Memories of Maria	1962	5.00	10.00	20.00
❏ MLP-8009 [M]	Byrd of Paradise	1962	5.00	10.00	20.00
❏ MLP-8018 [M]	Admirable Byrd	1963	5.00	10.00	20.00
❏ SLP-14008 [S]	Memories of Maria	1962	6.25	12.50	25.00
❏ SLP-18009 [S]	Byrd of Paradise	1962	6.25	12.50	25.00
❏ SLP-18018 [S]	Admirable Byrd	1963	6.25	12.50	25.00

BYRD, JOE, AND THE FIELD HIPPIES
COLUMBIA MASTERWORKS
| ❏ MS 7317 | The American Metaphysical Circus | 1969 | 10.00 | 20.00 | 40.00 |

BYRD, SENATOR ROBERT
COUNTY
| ❏ 769 | Mountain Fiddler | 1978 | 6.25 | 12.50 | 25.00 |

BYRDS, THE
COLUMBIA
| ❏ CL 2372 [M] | Mr. Tambourine Man | 1965 | 10.00 | 20.00 | 40.00 |

-- *"Guaranteed High Fidelity" on label*
| ❏ CL 2372 [M] | Mr. Tambourine Man | 1966 | 7.50 | 15.00 | 30.00 |

-- *"360 Sound Mono" on label*
❏ CL 2454 [M]	Turn! Turn! Turn!	1965	7.50	15.00	30.00
❏ CL 2549 [M]	Fifth Dimension (5D)	1966	7.50	15.00	30.00
❏ CL 2642 [M]	Younger Than Yesterday	1967	7.50	15.00	30.00
❏ CL 2716 [M]	The Byrds' Greatest Hits	1967	7.50	15.00	30.00
❏ CL 2775 [M]	The Notorious Byrd Brothers	1968	12.50	25.00	50.00

Number	Title	Yr	VG	VG+	NM
❏ CS 9172 [S]	Mr. Tambourine Man	1965	10.00	20.00	40.00
-- Red label, "360 Sound" in black					
❏ CS 9172 [S]	Mr. Tambourine Man	1966	6.25	12.50	25.00
-- Red label, "360 Sound" in white					
❏ CS 9254 [S]	Turn! Turn! Turn!	1965	6.25	12.50	25.00
-- Red "360 Sound" label					
❏ CS 9349 [S]	Fifth Dimension (5D)	1966	6.25	12.50	25.00
-- Red "360 Sound" label					
❏ CS 9442 [S]	Younger Than Yesterday	1967	6.25	12.50	25.00
-- Red "360 Sound" label					
❏ CS 9516 [S]	The Byrds' Greatest Hits	1967	5.00	10.00	20.00
-- Red "360 Sound" label					
❏ CS 9575 [S]	The Notorious Byrd Brothers	1968	5.00	10.00	20.00
-- Red "360 Sound" label					
❏ CS 9670 [M]	Sweetheart of the Rodeo	1968	25.00	50.00	100.00
-- "Special Mono Radio Station Copy" with white label					
❏ CS 9670 [S]	Sweetheart of the Rodeo	1968	5.00	10.00	20.00
-- Red "360 Sound" label					
❏ CS 9755 [S]	Dr. Byrds and Mr. Hyde	1969	5.00	10.00	20.00
-- Red "360 Sound" label					
❏ CS 9942 [S]	Ballad of Easy Rider	1969	5.00	10.00	20.00
-- Red "360 Sound" label					
❏ G 30127 [(2)]	The Byrds (Untitled)	1970	5.00	10.00	20.00
-- With "Kathleen" listed on back cover (it is not on the set)					
TOGETHER					
❏ ST-1-1001	Preflyte	1969	6.25	12.50	25.00

BYRNE, DAVID, AND RYUICHI SAKAMOTO
VIRGIN

Number	Title	Yr	VG	VG+	NM
❏ 2204 [DJ]	The Making of The Last Emperor: An Interview with David Byrne and Ryuchi Sakamoto	1988	6.25	12.50	25.00

BYRNES, EDD
WARNER BROS.

Number	Title	Yr	VG	VG+	NM
❏ W 1309 [M]	Kookie	1959	25.00	50.00	100.00
❏ WS 1309 [S]	Kookie	1959	30.00	60.00	120.00
❏ W/WS 1309	Kookie Bonus Photo	1959	12.50	25.00	50.00

C

C.A. QUINTET, THE
CANDY FLOSS

Number	Title	Yr	VG	VG+	NM
❏ 7764	A Trip Through Hell	1969	500.00	1,000.	1,500.

C.C.S.
RAK

❏ Z 30559	Whole Lotta Love	1971	5.00	10.00	20.00
❏ KZ 31569	C.C.S.	1972	5.00	10.00	20.00

C.K. STRONG
EPIC

❏ BN 26473	C.K. Strong	1969	5.00	10.00	20.00

CABARET VOLTAIRE
ROUGH TRADE

❏ ROUGH US 9	The Voice of America	1980	5.00	10.00	20.00
❏ ROUGH US 15	Red Mecca	1981	5.00	10.00	20.00
❏ ROUGH US 24	Hai! Live in Japan	1982	5.00	10.00	20.00

CABOT, SEBASTIAN
MGM

❏ E-4431 [M]	Sebastian Cabot, Actor; Bob Dylan, Poet: A Dramatic Reading with Music	1967	7.50	15.00	30.00
❏ SE-4431 [S]	Sebastian Cabot, Actor; Bob Dylan, Poet: A Dramatic Reading with Music	1967	10.00	20.00	40.00

CACTUS
With Tim Bogert and Carmen Appice, ex-VANILLA FUDGE.
ATCO

❏ SD 33-340	Cactus	1970	5.00	10.00	20.00
❏ SD 33-356	One Way...Or Another	1971	5.00	10.00	20.00
❏ SD 33-377	Restrictions	1971	5.00	10.00	20.00
❏ SD 7011	'Ot 'N' Sweaty	1972	5.00	10.00	20.00

CADETS, THE
CROWN

❏ CST-370 [R]	The Cadets	1963	25.00	50.00	100.00
❏ CLP-5015 [M]	Rockin' 'n' Reelin'	1957	62.50	125.00	250.00
-- Black label					
❏ CLP-5370 [M]	The Cadets	1963	37.50	75.00	150.00

CADILLACS, THE
JUBILEE

❏ JGM-1045 [M]	The Fabulous Cadillacs	1957	100.00	200.00	400.00
-- Blue label					
❏ JGM-1045 [M]	The Fabulous Cadillacs	1959	62.50	125.00	250.00
-- Flat black label					
❏ JGM-1045 [M]	The Fabulous Cadillacs	1960	25.00	50.00	100.00
-- Glossy black label					
❏ JGM-1089 [M]	The Crazy Cadillacs	1959	75.00	150.00	300.00
-- Flat black label					
❏ JGM-1089 [M]	The Crazy Cadillacs	1960	25.00	50.00	100.00
-- Glossy black label					
❏ JGM-5009 [M]	Twisting with the Cadillacs	1962	50.00	100.00	200.00
MURRAY HILL					
❏ 1285 [(5)]	The Cadillacs	198?	10.00	20.00	40.00
-- Box set					

CADILLACS, THE/ THE ORIOLES
JUBILEE

❏ JGM-1117 [M]	The Cadillacs Meet the Orioles	1961	50.00	100.00	200.00

CAGLE, BUDDY
IMPERIAL

❏ LP-9318 [M]	The Way You Like It	1966	5.00	10.00	20.00
❏ LP-9348 [M]	Mi Casa, Tu Casa	1967	5.00	10.00	20.00
❏ LP-9361 [M]	Longtime Traveling	1967	7.50	15.00	30.00
❏ LP-12318 [S]	The Way You Like It	1966	6.25	12.50	25.00
❏ LP-12348 [S]	Mi Casa, Tu Casa	1967	6.25	12.50	25.00
❏ LP-12361 [S]	Longtime Traveling	1967	6.25	12.50	25.00
❏ LP-12374	Through a Crack in a Boxcar Door	1968	6.25	12.50	25.00

CAIN
A.S.I.

❏ 204	A Pound of Flesh	1974	15.00	30.00	60.00
❏ 214	Stinger	1975	10.00	20.00	40.00

Number	Title	Yr	VG	VG+	NM

CAIOLA, AL
ATCO
Number	Title	Yr	VG	VG+	NM
❑ 33-117 [M]	Music for Space Squirrels	1960	6.25	12.50	25.00
❑ SD 33-117 [S]	Music for Space Squirrels	1960	7.50	15.00	30.00

CHANCELLOR
❑ CHL-5008 [M]	Great Pickin'	1960	6.25	12.50	25.00
❑ CHS-5008 [S]	Great Pickin'	1960	7.50	15.00	30.00

RCA VICTOR
❑ LPM-2031 [M]	High Strung	1959	6.25	12.50	25.00
❑ LSP-2031 [S]	High Strung	1959	7.50	15.00	30.00

ROULETTE
❑ R 25108 [M]	Salute Italia	1960	5.00	10.00	20.00
❑ SR 25108 [S]	Salute Italia	1960	6.25	12.50	25.00

SAVOY
❑ MG-12033 [M]	Deep in a Dream	1955	10.00	20.00	40.00
❑ MG-12057 [M]	Serenade in Blue	1956	10.00	20.00	40.00

TIME
❑ S-2000 [S]	Percussion and Guitars	1960	6.25	12.50	25.00
❑ S-2006 [S]	Percussion Espanol	1960	6.25	12.50	25.00
❑ S-2026 [S]	Percussion Espanol, Vol. 2	1960	6.25	12.50	25.00
❑ S-2039 [S]	Spanish Guitars	1960	6.25	12.50	25.00
❑ S-2101 [S]	Gershwin and Guitars	1961	6.25	12.50	25.00
❑ 52000 [M]	Percussion and Guitars	1960	5.00	10.00	20.00
❑ 52006 [M]	Percussion Espanol	1960	5.00	10.00	20.00
❑ 52026 [M]	Percussion Espanol, Vol. 2	1960	5.00	10.00	20.00
❑ 52039 [M]	Spanish Guitars	1960	5.00	10.00	20.00
❑ 52101 [M]	Gershwin and Guitars	1961	5.00	10.00	20.00

UNITED ARTISTS
❑ UAL-3133 [M]	The Magnificent Seven	1960	5.00	10.00	20.00
❑ UAL-3299 [M]	Cleopatra and All That Jazz	1963	6.25	12.50	25.00
❑ UAS-6133 [S]	The Magnificent Seven	1960	6.25	12.50	25.00
❑ UAS-6161 [S]	Hit Instrumentals from TV	1961	5.00	10.00	20.00
❑ UAS-6299 [S]	Cleopatra and All That Jazz	1963	7.50	15.00	30.00
❑ UAS-6435 [S]	Sounds for Spies and Private	1965	5.00	10.00	20.00

CAJUN PETE
MERCURY
❑ MG-20633 [M]	Tales of the Bayou	1961	5.00	10.00	20.00
❑ SR-60633 [S]	Tales of the Bayou	1961	6.25	12.50	25.00

CAKE, THE
DECCA
❑ DL 4927 [M]	The Cake	1967	5.00	10.00	20.00
❑ DL 74927 [S]	The Cake	1967	6.25	12.50	25.00
❑ DL 75039	A Slice of the Cake	1968	6.25	12.50	25.00

CALDWELL, LOUISE HARRISON
RECAR
❑ 2012 [M]	All About the Beatles	1965	50.00	100.00	200.00
-- With insert					
❑ 2012 [M]	All About the Beatles	1965	37.50	75.00	150.00
-- Without insert					

CALE, JOHN
Also see THE VELVET UNDERGROUND.
COLUMBIA
❑ CS 1037	Vintage Violence	1970	5.00	10.00	20.00
-- Red "360 Sound" label; orange labels go for less					

ISLAND
❑ IXP-2 [DJ]	Hear Fear	1975	12.50	25.00	50.00
-- Promo-only interview album					
❑ ILPS 9301	Fear	1975	5.00	10.00	20.00
❑ ILPS 9459	Guts	1977	5.00	10.00	20.00

REPRISE
❑ MS 2131	Paris, 1919	1973	6.25	12.50	25.00

CALIFORNIA POPPY PICKERS, THE
ALSHIRE
❑ S-5153	Hair-Aquarius	1969	7.50	15.00	30.00
❑ S-5167	Honky Tonk Women	1970	10.00	20.00	40.00

CALIFORNIA, RANDY
Also see SPIRIT.
EPIC
❑ KE 31755	Kapt. Kopter & the Fabulous Twirly Birds	1972	6.25	12.50	25.00
-- Yellow label					

CALLENDER, BOBBY
MGM
❑ SE-4557	Rainbow	1968	37.50	75.00	150.00

CALLIOPE
BUDDAH
Number	Title	Yr	VG	VG+	NM
❑ BDS-5023	Steamed	1968	5.00	10.00	20.00

CALLOWAY, CAB
BRUNSWICK
❑ BL 58101 [10]	Cab Calloway	1954	25.00	50.00	100.00

COLUMBIA
❑ CG 32593 [(2)]	The Hi De Ho Man	1973	5.00	10.00	20.00

CORAL
❑ CRL 57408 [M]	Blues Make Me Happy	1962	6.25	12.50	25.00
❑ CRL 757408 [S]	Blues Make Me Happy	1962	7.50	15.00	30.00

EPIC
❑ LN 3265 [M]	Cab Calloway	1957	12.50	25.00	50.00

P.I.P.
❑ 6801	Cab Calloway '68	1968	5.00	10.00	20.00

RCA VICTOR
❑ LPM-2021 [M]	Hi De Hi De Ho	1958	7.50	15.00	30.00
❑ LSP-2021 [S]	Hi De Hi De Ho	1958	10.00	20.00	40.00

CAMARATA
BUENA VISTA
❑ BV-3319 [M]	33 Great Walt Disney Motion Picture Melodies	1963	6.25	12.50	25.00
❑ STER-3319 [S]	33 Great Walt Disney Motion Picture Melodies	1963	7.50	15.00	30.00
❑ BV-3321 [M]	The Changing Seasons	1964	5.00	10.00	20.00
❑ STER-3321 [S]	The Changing Seasons	1964	7.50	15.00	30.00
❑ BV-3322 [M]	In the Still of the Night	1959	5.00	10.00	20.00
❑ STER-3322 [S]	In the Still of the Night	1960	7.50	15.00	30.00
❑ BV-3330 [M]	Tinpanorama	1965	5.00	10.00	20.00
❑ BV-4023 [M]	Camarata Conducts a Modern Interpretation of Snow White and the Seven Dwarfs	1963	7.50	15.00	30.00
-- Gatefold cover					
❑ STER-4023 [S]	Camarata Conducts a Modern Interpretation of Snow White and the Seven Dwarfs	1963	10.00	20.00	40.00
-- Gatefold cover					
❑ BV-4023 [M]	Camarata Conducts a Modern Interpretation of Snow White and the Seven Dwarfs	1967	5.00	10.00	20.00
-- Regular cover					
❑ STER-4023 [S]	Camarata Conducts a Modern Interpretation of Snow White and the Seven Dwarfs	1967	6.25	12.50	25.00
-- Regular cover					
❑ BV-4047	Camarata Featuring Tutti's Trumpets	1970	5.00	10.00	20.00
-- Reissue of Disneyland 3011					
❑ BV-4048	Camarata Featuring Tutti's Trombones	1970	5.00	10.00	20.00

DISNEYLAND
❑ (# unknown) [(4) M]	Music of the Seasons	1959	10.00	20.00	40.00
-- Box set with mono versions of 3021, 3026, 3027 and 3032					
❑ (# unknown) [(4) S]	Music of the Seasons	1959	20.00	40.00	80.00
-- Box set with stereo versions of 3021, 3026, 3027 and 3032					
❑ DQ-1232 [M]	A Child's Introduction to Melody and Instruments of the Orchestra	1963	5.00	10.00	20.00
❑ STER-3011 [S]	Tutti's Trumpets	1959	7.50	15.00	30.00
❑ WDL-3011 [M]	Tutti's Trumpets	1957	5.00	10.00	20.00
❑ STER-3021 [S]	Autumn	1959	7.50	15.00	30.00
❑ WDL-3021 [M]	Autumn	1958	5.00	10.00	20.00
❑ STER-3026 [S]	Winter	1959	7.50	15.00	30.00
❑ WDL-3026 [M]	Winter	1958	5.00	10.00	20.00
❑ STER-3027 [S]	Summer	1959	6.25	12.50	25.00
❑ WDL-3027 [M]	Summer	1958	5.00	10.00	20.00
❑ STER-3032 [S]	Spring	1959	6.25	12.50	25.00
❑ WDL-3032 [M]	Spring	1958	5.00	10.00	20.00
❑ WDL-4009 [M]	Camarata Interprets Music from Cinderella and Bambi	1957	15.00	30.00	60.00

CAMBRIDGE, GODFREY
EPIC
❑ FLM 13101 [M]	Ready or Not...Here's Godfrey Cambridge	1964	5.00	10.00	20.00
❑ FLM 13102 [M]	Them Cotton Pickin' Days Is Over	1965	5.00	10.00	20.00
❑ FLM 13108 [M]	Godfrey Cambridge Toys with the World	1966	5.00	10.00	20.00
❑ FLM 13115 [M]	The Godfrey Cambridge Show Live at the Aladdin	1968	5.00	10.00	20.00
❑ FLS 15101 [S]	Ready or Not...Here's Godfrey Cambridge	1964	5.00	10.00	20.00
❑ FLS 15102 [S]	Them Cotton Pickin' Days Is Over	1965	5.00	10.00	20.00
❑ FLS 15108 [S]	Godfrey Cambridge Toys with the World	1966	5.00	10.00	20.00
❑ FLS 15115 [S]	The Godfrey Cambridge Show Live at the Aladdin	1968	5.00	10.00	20.00

Number	Title	Yr	VG	VG+	NM

CAMP, HAMILTON
ELEKTRA
❏ EKL-278 [M]	Paths of Victory	1965	6.25	12.50	25.00
❏ EKS-7278 [S]	Paths of Victory	1965	7.50	15.00	30.00

CAMPBELL, ALEX
STARDAY
❏ SLP-214 [M]	16 Radio Favorites	1963	6.25	12.50	25.00
❏ SLP-342 [M]	Travel On	1965	6.25	12.50	25.00

CAMPBELL, ARCHIE
RCA VICTOR
❏ LPM-3504 [M]	Have a Laugh on Me	1966	5.00	10.00	20.00
❏ LSP-3504 [S]	Have a Laugh on Me	1966	6.25	2.50	25.00
❏ LPM-3699 [M]	The Cockfight and Other Tall Tales	1967	5.00	10.00	20.00
❏ LSP-3699 [S]	The Cockfight and Other Tall Tales	1967	6.25	12.50	25.00
❏ LPM-3780 [M]	Kids I Love 'Em	1967	6.25	12.50	25.00
❏ LSP-3780 [S]	Kids I Love 'Em	1967	5.00	10.00	20.00
❏ LPM-3892 [M]	The Golden Years	1967	6.25	12.50	25.00
❏ LSP-3892 [S]	The Golden Years	1967	5.00	10.00	20.00
STARDAY
❏ SLP-162 [M]	Make Friends with Archie Campbell	1962	7.50	15.00	30.00
❏ SLP-167 [M]	Bedtime Stories for Adults	1962	7.50	15.00	30.00
❏ SLP-223 [M]	The Joker Is Wild	1963	7.50	15.00	30.00
❏ SLP-377 [M]	The Grand Ole Opry's Good Humor Man	1966	6.25	12.50	25.00

CAMPBELL, ARCHIE, AND LORENE MANN
RCA VICTOR
❏ LSP-4068	Tell It Like It Is	1968	5.00	10.00	20.00

CAMPBELL, CECIL
STARDAY
❏ SLP-254 [M]	Steel Guitar Jamboree	1963	10.00	20.00	40.00

CAMPBELL, CHOKER
MOTOWN
❏ M-620 [M]	Hits of the Sixties	1964	25.00	50.00	100.00

CAMPBELL, DICK
MERCURY
❏ MG-21060 [M]	Dick Campbell Sings Where It's At	1966	7.50	15.00	30.00
❏ SR-61060 [S]	Dick Campbell Sings Where It's At	1966	10.00	20.00	40.00

CAMPBELL, GLEN
CAPITOL
❏ STBO-268	Glen Campbell -- "Live"	1969	5.00	10.00	20.00
❏ ST 1810 [S]	Big Bluegrass Special	1962	25.00	50.00	100.00
-- As "The Green River Boys Featuring Glen Campbell"					
❏ T 1810 [M]	Big Bluegrass Special	1962	20.00	40.00	80.00
-- As "The Green River Boys Featuring Glen Campbell"					
❏ ST 1881 [S]	Too Late to Worry, Too Blue to	1963	6.25	12.50	25.00
❏ T 1881 [M]	Too Late to Worry, Too Blue to	1963	5.00	10.00	20.00
❏ ST 2023 [S]	The Astounding 12-String Guitar of Glen Campbell	1964	5.00	10.00	20.00
❏ ST 2392 [S]	The Big Bad Rock Guitar of Glen Campbell	1965	5.00	10.00	20.00
❏ SWAK-93157	Limited Collector's Edition	1970	5.00	10.00	20.00
-- Capitol Record Club exclusive; includes tour program					

CAMPBELL, JO ANN
ABC-PARAMOUNT
❏ 393 [M]	Twistin' and Listenin'	1962	20.00	40.00	80.00
❏ S-393 [S]	Twistin' and Listenin'	1962	25.00	50.00	100.00
CAMEO
❏ C-1026 [M]	All the Hits of Jo Ann Campbell	1962	12.50	25.00	50.00
❏ SC-1026 [S]	All the Hits of Jo Ann Campbell	1962	25.00	50.00	100.00
CORONET
❏ CX-199 [M]	Starring Jo Ann Campbell	196?	5.00	10.00	20.00
END
❏ LP-306 [M]	I'm Nobody's Baby	1959	37.50	75.00	150.00

CAMPER VAN BEETHOVEN
INDEPENDENT PROJECT
❏ 016	Telephone Free Landslide Victory	1985	10.00	20.00	40.00
-- Version 1: Handmade covers, letterpress design, with inserts					
❏ 016	Telephone Free Landslide Victory	1985	5.00	10.00	20.00
-- Version 2: With normal covers; 1,175 pressed					

CAMPUS SINGERS, THE
ARGO
❏ LP-4023 [M]	The Campus Singers at the Fickle Pickle	1963	5.00	10.00	20.00
❏ LPS-4023 [S]	The Campus Singers at the Fickle Pickle	1963	6.25	12.50	25.00
❏ LP-4033 [M]	Road of Blue	1964	5.00	10.00	20.00
❏ LPS-4033 [S]	Road of Blue	1964	6.25	12.50	25.00

CAN
MUTE
❏ 9033-1 [(3)]	Sacrilege	1997	6.25	12.50	25.00
-- Album of remixes					

CANADIAN BEADLES, THE
TIDE
❏ 2005 [M]	Three Faces North	1964	12.50	25.00	50.00

CANADIAN SWEETHEARTS, THE
A&M
❏ LP-106 [M]	Introducing the Canadian Sweethearts	1964	10.00	20.00	40.00
❏ SP-4106 [S]	Introducing the Canadian Sweethearts	1964	12.50	25.00	50.00

CANARIES, THE
B.T. PUPPY
❏ BTS-1007	Flying High with the Canaries	1970	25.00	50.00	100.00

CANDY STORE, THE
DECCA
❏ DL 75147	Turned-On Christmas	1969	6.25	12.50	25.00

CANDYMEN, THE
ABC
❏ 616 [M]	The Candymen	1967	6.25	12.50	25.00
❏ S-616 [S]	The Candymen	1967	5.00	10.00	20.00
❏ S-633	The Candymen Bring You Candypower	1968	5.00	10.00	20.00

CANNED HEAT
LIBERTY
❏ LRP-3526 [M]	Canned Heat	1967	6.25	12.50	25.00
❏ LST-7526 [S]	Canned Heat	1967	5.00	10.00	20.00
❏ LST-7541	Boogie with Canned Heat	1968	5.00	10.00	20.00
❏ LST-7618	Hallelujah	1969	5.00	10.00	20.00
❏ LST-11000	Canned Heat Cook Book (The Best of Canned Heat)	1969	5.00	10.00	20.00
❏ LST-27200 [(2)]	Living the Blues	1968	6.25	12.50	25.00
UNITED ARTISTS
❏ UAS-9955 [(2)]	Living the Blues	1971	5.00	10.00	20.00
-- Reissue of Liberty 27200					
WAND
❏ WDS-693	Live at Topanga Canyon	1970	6.25	12.50	25.00

CANNED HEAT AND JOHN LEE HOOKER -- See JOHN LEE HOOKER AND CANNED HEAT.

CANNIBAL AND THE HEADHUNTERS
DATE
❏ TEM 3001 [M]	Land of 1000 Dances	1966	7.50	15.00	30.00
❏ TES 4001 [S]	Land of 1000 Dances	1966	10.00	20.00	40.00
RAMPART
❏ RM-3302 [M]	Land of 1000 Dances	1965	12.50	25.00	50.00
❏ RS-3302 [S]	Land of 1000 Dances	1965	17.50	35.00	70.00

CANNON, ACE
HI
❏ HL-12007 [M]	Tuff Sax	1962	6.25	12.50	25.00
❏ HL-12008 [M]	Looking Back	1962	6.25	12.50	25.00
❏ HL-12014 [M]	The Moanin' Sax of Ace Cannon	1963	6.25	12.50	25.00
❏ HL-12016 [M]	Aces Hi	1964	5.00	10.00	20.00
❏ HL-12019 [M]	The Great Show Tunes	1964	5.00	10.00	20.00
❏ HL-12022 [M]	Christmas Cheer	1964	5.00	10.00	20.00
❏ HL-12035 [M]	The Misty Sax of Ace Cannon	1967	5.00	10.00	20.00
❏ HL-12040 [M]	Memphis Golden Hits	1967	5.00	10.00	20.00
❏ SHL-32007 [S]	Tuff Sax	1962	7.50	15.00	30.00
❏ SHL-32008 [S]	Looking Back	1962	7.50	15.00	30.00
❏ SHL-32014 [S]	The Moanin' Sax of Ace Cannon	1963	7.50	15.00	30.00

Number	Title	Yr	VG	VG+	NM
❑ SHL-32016 [S] Aces Hi		1964	6.25	12.50	25.00
❑ SHL-32019 [S] The Great Show Tunes		1964	6.25	12.50	25.00
❑ SHL-32022 [S] Christmas Cheer		1964	6.25	12.50	25.00
❑ SHL-32025 [S] Ace Cannon Live		1965	5.00	10.00	20.00
❑ SHL-32028 [S] Nashville Hits		1965	5.00	10.00	20.00
❑ SHL-32030 [S] Sweet and Tuff		1966	5.00	10.00	20.00

CANNON, FREDDIE
SWAN

Number	Title	Yr	VG	VG+	NM
❑ LP-502 [M]	The Explosive! Freddy Cannon	1960	30.00	60.00	120.00
❑ LPS-502 [S]	The Explosive! Freddy Cannon	1960	75.00	150.00	300.00
❑ LP-504 [M]	Happy Shades of Blue	1960	37.50	75.00	150.00
❑ LP-505 [M]	Solid Gold Hits	1961	37.50	75.00	150.00
❑ LP-507 [M]	Freddy Cannon at Palisades Park	1962	37.50	75.00	150.00
❑ LP-511 [M]	Freddy Cannon Steps Out	1963	37.50	75.00	150.00

WARNER BROS.

Number	Title	Yr	VG	VG+	NM
❑ W 1544 [M]	Freddie Cannon	1964	7.50	15.00	30.00
❑ WS 1544 [S]	Freddie Cannon	1964	10.00	20.00	40.00
❑ W 1612 [M]	Action!	1965	7.50	15.00	30.00
❑ WS 1612 [S]	Action!	1965	10.00	20.00	40.00
❑ W 1628 [M]	Freddie Cannon's Greatest Hits	1966	7.50	15.00	30.00
❑ WS 1628 [S]	Freddie Cannon's Greatest Hits	1966	10.00	20.00	40.00

CANNON, GUS
STAX

Number	Title	Yr	VG	VG+	NM
❑ ST-702 [M]	Walk Right In	1962	150.00	300.00	600.00

CANTELON, WILLARD
SUPREME

Number	Title	Yr	VG	VG+	NM
❑ M-113 [M]	L.S.D. Battle for the Mind	1966	7.50	15.00	30.00
❑ S-113 [S]	L.S.D. Battle for the Mind	1966	10.00	20.00	40.00

CANTOR, EDDIE
VIK

Number	Title	Yr	VG	VG+	NM
❑ LXA-1119 [M]	The Best of Eddie Cantor	1957	12.50	25.00	50.00

CAPITAL CITY ROCKETS
ELEKTRA

Number	Title	Yr	VG	VG+	NM
❑ EKS-75079	Capital City Rockets	1973	5.00	10.00	20.00

CAPITOLS, THE
ATCO

Number	Title	Yr	VG	VG+	NM
❑ 33-190 [M]	Dance the Cool Jerk	1966	10.00	20.00	40.00
❑ SD 33-190 [S]	Dance the Cool Jerk	1966	12.50	25.00	50.00
❑ 33-201 [M]	We Got a Thing That's In the Groove	1966	10.00	20.00	40.00
❑ SD 33-201 [S]	We Got a Thing That's In the Groove	1966	12.50	25.00	50.00

CAPTAIN BEEFHEART
BLUE THUMB

Number	Title	Yr	VG	VG+	NM
❑ BTS-1	Strictly Personal	1968	12.50	25.00	50.00
-- Black label, unbanded sides					
❑ BTS-1	Strictly Personal	1969	7.50	15.00	30.00
-- White label, unbanded sides					
❑ BTS-1	Strictly Personal	197?	5.00	10.00	20.00
-- White label, banded sides					

BUDDAH

Number	Title	Yr	VG	VG+	NM
❑ BDM-1001 [M]	Safe As Milk	1967	25.00	50.00	100.00
❑ BDS-5001 [S]	Safe As Milk	1967	15.00	30.00	60.00
❑ 1001/5001	Safe As Milk "Baby Jesus" Bumper Sticker	1967	6.25	12.50	25.00
❑ BDS-5063	Safe As Milk	1969	6.25	12.50	25.00
❑ BDS-5077	Mirror Man	1971	12.50	25.00	50.00
-- Die-cut gatefold cover					
❑ BDS-5077	Mirror Man	197?	6.25	12.50	25.00
-- Regular cover					

MERCURY

Number	Title	Yr	VG	VG+	NM
❑ SRM-1-1018	Bluejeans and Moonbeams	1975	5.00	10.00	20.00

REPRISE

Number	Title	Yr	VG	VG+	NM
❑ 2MS 2027 [(2)] Trout Mask Replica		1970	7.50	15.00	30.00
-- Stock copy with 2027 labels and 2027 jacket					
❑ MS 2050	The Spotlight Kid	1971	5.00	10.00	20.00
❑ MS 2115	Clear Spot	1972	5.00	10.00	20.00
❑ RS 6420	Lick My Decals Off, Baby	1970	5.00	10.00	20.00

STRAIGHT

Number	Title	Yr	VG	VG+	NM
❑ 2STS-1053 [(2)] Trout Mask Replica		1969	62.50	125.00	250.00
-- Stock copy with 1053 labels labels (this has been confirmed to exist)					
❑ 2STS-1053 [(2) DJ] Trout Mask Replica		1969	50.00	100.00	200.00
-- White label promo with 1053 labels					
❑ 2MS 2027 [(2)] Trout Mask Replica		1969	15.00	30.00	60.00
-- Stock copy with 2027 labels inside 1053 jacket					
❑ 2MS 2027 [(2) DJ] Trout Mask Replica		1969	37.50	75.00	150.00
-- White label promo with 2027 labels inside 1053 jacket					
❑ RS 6420	Lick My Decals Off, Baby	1970	12.50	25.00	50.00

WARNER BROS.

Number	Title	Yr	VG	VG+	NM
❑ (no #)	Bat Chain Puller	1978	100.00	200.00	400.00
-- Test pressing with different selections than stock version					

CAPTAIN BEYOND
CAPRICORN

Number	Title	Yr	VG	VG+	NM
❑ CP 0105	Captain Beyond	1972	7.50	15.00	30.00
-- Original covers are 3-D					

CARAVAN
VERVE FORECAST

Number	Title	Yr	VG	VG+	NM
❑ FTS-3066	Caravan	1969	10.00	20.00	40.00

CARAVAN, JIMMY
TOWER

Number	Title	Yr	VG	VG+	NM
❑ ST 5103	Look Into the Flower	1968	5.00	10.00	20.00

VAULT

Number	Title	Yr	VG	VG+	NM
❑ 9007	Hey Jude	1969	5.00	10.00	20.00

CARAVELLES, THE
SMASH

Number	Title	Yr	VG	VG+	NM
❑ MGS-27044 [M]	You Don't Have to Be a Baby to Cry	1963	15.00	30.00	60.00
❑ SRS-67044 [R]	You Don't Have to Be a Baby to Cry	1963	15.00	30.00	60.00

CARE PACKAGE
LIBERTY

Number	Title	Yr	VG	VG+	NM
❑ LST-7647	Keep On Keepin' On	1970	6.25	12.50	25.00

CAREFREES, THE
LONDON

Number	Title	Yr	VG	VG+	NM
❑ PS 379 [S]	From England! The Carefrees	1964	25.00	50.00	100.00
❑ LL 3379 [M]	From England! The Carefrees	1964	20.00	40.00	80.00

CARGILL, HENSON
MONUMENT

Number	Title	Yr	VG	VG+	NM
❑ SLP-18094	Skip a Rope	1968	5.00	10.00	20.00
❑ SLP-18103	Coming On Strong	1968	5.00	10.00	20.00
❑ SLP-18117	None of My Business	1969	5.00	10.00	20.00
❑ SLP-18137	Uncomplicated	1970	5.00	10.00	20.00

CARLIN, GEORGE
ERA

Number	Title	Yr	VG	VG+	NM
❑ EL 103 [M]	George Carlin and Jack Burns At the Playboy Club Tonight	1960	6.25	12.50	25.00

RCA VICTOR

Number	Title	Yr	VG	VG+	NM
❑ LPM-3772 [M]	Take-Offs and Put-Ons	1967	5.00	10.00	20.00

CARLISLES, THE
KING

Number	Title	Yr	VG	VG+	NM
❑ 643 [M]	Fresh from the Country	1959	12.50	25.00	50.00

MERCURY

Number	Title	Yr	VG	VG+	NM
❑ MG-20359 [M]	On Stage with the Carlisles	1958	12.50	25.00	50.00

CARLOS, WALTER
COLUMBIA MASTERWORKS

Number	Title	Yr	VG	VG+	NM
❑ HM 45950	Switched-On Brandenburgs Vol. 1	1980	6.25	12.50	25.00
-- Half-speed mastered edition					

CARLTON, LARRY
UNI

Number	Title	Yr	VG	VG+	NM
❑ 73036	With a Little Help from My Friends	1968	5.00	10.00	20.00

CARMEN
EPIC

Number	Title	Yr	VG	VG+	NM
❑ BN 26479	Carmen	1969	5.00	10.00	20.00

CARMICHAEL, HOAGY
BOOK-OF-THE-MONTH

Number	Title	Yr	VG	VG+	NM
❑ 61-5450 [(3)]	Hoagy Carmichael	1984	7.50	15.00	30.00

DECCA

Number	Title	Yr	VG	VG+	NM
❑ DL 5068 [10]	Stardust Road	1950	20.00	40.00	80.00
❑ DL 8588 [M]	Stardust Road	1958	7.50	15.00	30.00

GOLDEN

Number	Title	Yr	VG	VG+	NM
❑ LP-198-18 [M]	Havin' a Party	1958	7.50	15.00	30.00

Number	Title	Yr	VG	VG+	NM
JAZZTONE					
❑ J-1266 [M]	Hoagy Sings Carmichael	1957	7.50	15.00	30.00
KIMBERLY					
❑ 2023 [M]	The Legend of Hoagy Carmichael	1962	6.25	12.50	25.00
❑ 11023 [R]	The Legend of Hoagy Carmichael	196?	5.00	10.00	20.00
PACIFIC JAZZ					
❑ PJ-1223 [M]	Hoagy Sings Carmichael	1956	15.00	30.00	60.00
RCA VICTOR					
❑ LPT-3072 [10]	Old Rockin' Chair	1953	20.00	40.00	80.00

CARNES, KIM
AMOS					
❑ AAS 7016	Rest on Me	1971	5.00	10.00	20.00
MOBILE FIDELITY					
❑ 1-073	Mistaken Identity	1982	6.25	12.50	25.00
-- Audiophile vinyl					

CARNEY, ART
COLUMBIA					
❑ CL 2595 [10]	Doodle-Li-Boops and Rhinocelopes	1955	20.00	40.00	80.00

CAROLEERS, THE
ALLEGRO ROYALE					
❑ 1295 [M]	An Hour of Christmas Music	195?	5.00	10.00	20.00
-- B-side by anonymous "Organ and Chimes"					

CAROLINA SLIM
SHARP					
❑ 2002 [M]	Blues from the Cotton Fields	195?	62.50	125.00	250.00

CARP
Actor Gary Busey was in this group.
EPIC					
❑ E 30212	Carp	1970	6.25	12.50	25.00

CARPENTER, IKE
ALADDIN					
❑ LP-811 [M]	Lights Out	1957	—	—	—
-- Unreleased					
DISCOVERY					
❑ DL 3003 [10]	Dancers in Love	1949	75.00	150.00	300.00
INTRO					
❑ 950 [10]	Lights Out	1952	75.00	150.00	300.00
SCORE					
❑ SLP-4010 [M]	Lights Out	1957	37.50	75.00	150.00

CARPENTERS
A&M					
❑ SP-4205	Offering	1969	10.00	20.00	40.00
❑ QU-53502 [Q]	Carpenters	1974	5.00	10.00	20.00
❑ QU-53511 [Q]	A Song for You	1974	5.00	10.00	20.00
❑ QU-53519 [Q]	Now & Then	1974	5.00	10.00	20.00
❑ QU-53601 [Q]	The Singles 1969-1973	1974	5.00	10.00	20.00
❑ QU-54271 [Q]	Close to You	1974	5.00	10.00	20.00
❑ QU-54530 [Q]	Horizon	1975	5.00	10.00	20.00

CARR, CATHY
DOT					
❑ DLP-3674 [M]	Ivory Tower	1966	6.25	12.50	25.00
❑ DLP-25674 [S]	Ivory Tower	1966	6.25	12.50	25.00
FRATERNITY					
❑ 1005 [M]	Ivory Tower	1957	30.00	60.00	120.00
ROULETTE					
❑ R 25077 [M]	Shy	1959	10.00	20.00	40.00
❑ SR 25077 [S]	Shy	1959	12.50	25.00	50.00

CARR, JAMES
GOLDWAX					
❑ 3001S	You Got My Mind Messed Up	1968	37.50	75.00	150.00
❑ 3002S	A Man Needs a Woman	1968	37.50	75.00	150.00

CARR, JOE "FINGERS"
CAPITOL					
❑ T 280 [M]	Bar Room Piano	1952	7.50	15.00	30.00
❑ T 345 [M]	Roughhouse Piano	1953	7.50	15.00	30.00
❑ T 443 [M]	Joe "Fingers" Carr and His Ragtime Band	1954	7.50	15.00	30.00
❑ T 527 [M]	Fireman's Ball	1954	7.50	15.00	30.00

Number	Title	Yr	VG	VG+	NM
❑ ST 1151 [S]	"Fingers" and the Flapper	1959	6.25	12.50	25.00
❑ T 1151 [M]	"Fingers" and the Flapper	1959	5.00	10.00	20.00
❑ ST 1217 [S]	Joe "Fingers" Carr and His Swingin' String Band	1959	6.25	12.50	25.00
❑ T 1217 [M]	Joe "Fingers" Carr and His Swingin' String Band	1959	5.00	10.00	20.00
WARNER BROS.					
❑ WS 1386 [S]	The World's Greatest Ragtime Piano Player	1960	5.00	10.00	20.00

CARR, LEROY
COLUMBIA					
❑ CL 1911 [M]	Blues Before Sunrise	1962	7.50	15.00	30.00
❑ CS 8511 [R]	Blues Before Sunrise	1962	5.00	10.00	20.00

CARR, VIKKI
LIBERTY					
❑ LRP-3506 [M]	Intimate Excitement	1967	5.00	10.00	20.00
❑ LRP-3533 [M]	It Must Be Him	1967	5.00	10.00	20.00
❑ LST-7314 [S]	Color Her Great	1963	5.00	10.00	20.00
❑ LST-7354 [S]	Discovery!	1964	5.00	10.00	20.00
❑ LST-7383 [S]	Discovery! Volume Two	1964	5.00	10.00	20.00
❑ LST-7420 [S]	The Anatomy of Love	1965	5.00	10.00	20.00
❑ LST-7456 [S]	The Way of Today	1966	5.00	10.00	20.00

CARROLL BROTHERS, THE
CAMEO					
❑ C-1015 [M]	College Twist Party	1962	6.25	12.50	25.00
❑ SC-1015 [S]	College Twist Party	1962	10.00	20.00	40.00

CARROLL, ANDREA /BEVERLY WARREN
B.T. PUPPY					
❑ BTS-1017	Andrea Carroll and Beverly Warren Side By Side	1971	37.50	75.00	150.00

CARROLL, DIAHANN
ATLANTIC					
❑ 8048 [M]	Fun Life	1961	5.00	10.00	20.00
❑ SD 8048 [S]	Fun Life	1961	6.25	12.50	25.00
RCA VICTOR					
❑ LPM-1467 [M]	Diahann Carroll Sings Harold Arlen	1957	10.00	20.00	40.00
UNITED ARTISTS					
❑ UAL 3080 [M]	Diahann Carroll at the Persian Room	1960	5.00	10.00	20.00
❑ UAS 6080 [S]	Diahann Carroll at the Persian Room	1960	6.25	12.50	25.00
VIK					
❑ LXA-1131 [M]	Best Beat Forward	1958	7.50	15.00	30.00

CARROLL, DIAHANN, AND ANDRE PREVIN
Also see each artist's individual listings.
UNITED ARTISTS					
❑ UAL 3069 [M]	Diahann Carroll and Andre Previn	1960	5.00	10.00	20.00
❑ UAL 4021 [M]	Porgy and Bess	1959	5.00	10.00	20.00
❑ UAS 5021 [S]	Porgy and Bess	1959	6.25	12.50	25.00
❑ UAS 6069 [S]	Diahann Carroll and Andre Previn	1960	6.25	12.50	25.00

CARROLL, JIM, BAND
ATLANTIC					
❑ 80123	I Write Your Name	1984	5.00	10.00	20.00

CARS, THE
DCC COMPACT CLASSICS					
❑ LPZ-2056	The Cars Greatest Hits	1998	6.25	12.50	25.00
-- Audiophile vinyl					
ELEKTRA					
❑ 5E-567 [PD]	Shake It Up	1981	12.50	25.00	50.00
-- Promo-only picture disc with "KMET-FM" imprinted on back					
❑ 5E-567 [PD]	Shake It Up	1981	10.00	20.00	40.00
-- Promo-only picture disc with blank back					
NAUTILUS					
❑ NR-14	The Cars	1981	7.50	15.00	30.00
-- Audiophile vinyl					
❑ NR-49	Candy-O	1982	7.50	15.00	30.00
-- Audiophile vinyl					

CARSON, MARTHA
CAPITOL					
❑ ST 1507 [S]	Satisfied	1960	7.50	15.00	30.00

Number	Title	Yr	VG	VG+	NM
❏ T 1507 [M]	Satisfied	1960	6.25	12.50	25.00
❏ ST 1607 [S]	A Talk with the Lord	1961	7.50	15.00	30.00
❏ T 1607 [M]	A Talk with the Lord	1961	6.25	12.50	25.00

RCA VICTOR

Number	Title	Yr	VG	VG+	NM
❏ LPM-1145 [M]	Journey to the Sky	1955	10.00	20.00	40.00
❏ LPM-1490 [M]	Rock-a My Soul	1957	12.50	25.00	50.00

SIMS

Number	Title	Yr	VG	VG+	NM
❏ LP-100 [M]	Martha Carson	196?	6.25	12.50	25.00

CARTER FAMILY, THE
Also see MOTHER MAYBELLE CARTER.

ACME

Number	Title	Yr	VG	VG+	NM
❏ LP-1 [M]	All Time Favorites	1960	50.00	100.00	200.00
❏ LP-2 [M]	In Memory of A.P. Carter	1960	50.00	100.00	200.00

COLUMBIA

Number	Title	Yr	VG	VG+	NM
❏ CL 2617 [M]	Country Album	1967	6.25	12.50	25.00
❏ CS 9119 [S]	The Best of the Carter Family	1965	5.00	10.00	20.00
❏ CS 9417 [S]	Country Album	1967	5.00	10.00	20.00
❏ KC 31454	Travelin' Minstrel Band	1972	5.00	10.00	20.00
❏ KC 33084	Three Generations	1974	5.00	10.00	20.00
❏ KC 34266	Country's First Family	1976	5.00	10.00	20.00

DECCA

Number	Title	Yr	VG	VG+	NM
❏ DL 4404 [M]	A Collection of Favorites by the Carter Family	1963	7.50	15.00	30.00
❏ DL 4557 [M]	More Favorites by the Carter Family	1964	7.50	15.00	30.00

LIBERTY

Number	Title	Yr	VG	VG+	NM
❏ LRP-3230 [M]	The Carter Family Album	1962	7.50	15.00	30.00
❏ LST-7230 [S]	The Carter Family Album	1962	10.00	20.00	40.00

RCA VICTOR

Number	Title	Yr	VG	VG+	NM
❏ LPM-2772 [M]	'Mid the Green Fields of Virginia	1963	10.00	20.00	40.00
❏ LSP-2772 [R]	'Mid the Green Fields of Virginia	1963	5.00	10.00	20.00

STARDAY

Number	Title	Yr	VG	VG+	NM
❏ SLP-248 [M]	Echoes of the Carter Family	1963	10.00	20.00	40.00

CARTER, ANITA
MERCURY

Number	Title	Yr	VG	VG+	NM
❏ MG-20770 [M]	Folk Songs Old and New	1963	6.25	12.50	25.00
❏ MG-20847 [M]	Anita of the Carter Family	1964	6.25	12.50	25.00
❏ SR-60770 [S]	Folk Songs Old and New	1963	7.50	15.00	30.00
❏ SR-60847 [S]	Anita of the Carter Family	1964	7.50	15.00	30.00

CARTER, CALVIN
VEE JAY

Number	Title	Yr	VG	VG+	NM
❏ LP-1041 [M]	Twist with Calvin Carter	1962	25.00	50.00	100.00
❏ SR-1041 [S]	Twist with Calvin Carter	1962	37.50	75.00	150.00

CARTER, CLARENCE
ATLANTIC

Number	Title	Yr	VG	VG+	NM
❏ SD 8192	This Is Clarence Carter	1968	7.50	15.00	30.00
❏ SD 8199	The Dynamic Clarence Carter	1969	7.50	15.00	30.00
❏ SD 8238	Testifyin'	1969	7.50	15.00	30.00
❏ SD 8267	Patches	1970	7.50	15.00	30.00
❏ SD 8282	The Best of Clarence Carter	1971	5.00	10.00	20.00

CARTER, JACK
AAMCO

Number	Title	Yr	VG	VG+	NM
❏ ALP-316 [M]	Broadway A La Carter	1958	6.25	12.50	25.00

CARTER, LYNDA
EPIC

Number	Title	Yr	VG	VG+	NM
❏ 35308 [PD]	Portrait	1978	15.00	30.00	60.00

-- Value is for picture disc; regular LP goes for much less

CARTER, MEL
DERBY

Number	Title	Yr	VG	VG+	NM
❏ LPM-702 [M]	When a Boy Falls in Love	1963	75.00	150.00	300.00

IMPERIAL

Number	Title	Yr	VG	VG+	NM
❏ LP-12289 [S]	Hold Me, Thrill Me, Kiss Me	1965	5.00	10.00	20.00
❏ LP-12300 [S]	All of a Sudden My Heart Sings	1966	5.00	10.00	20.00
❏ LP-12319 [S]	Easy Listening	1966	5.00	10.00	20.00

CARTER, MOTHER MAYBELLE
Also see THE CARTER FAMILY.

AMBASSADOR

Number	Title	Yr	VG	VG+	NM
❏ 98069 [M]	Mother Maybelle Carter	195?	37.50	75.00	150.00

COLUMBIA

Number	Title	Yr	VG	VG+	NM
❏ CL 2475 [M]	A Living Legend	1965	5.00	10.00	20.00
❏ CS 9275 [S]	A Living Legend	1965	6.25	12.50	25.00

Number	Title	Yr	VG	VG+	NM
❏ KG 32436 [(2)]	Mother Maybelle Carter	1973	6.25	12.50	25.00

KAPP

Number	Title	Yr	VG	VG+	NM
❏ KL-1413 [M]	Queen of the Autoharp	1964	5.00	10.00	20.00
❏ KS-3413 [S]	Queen of the Autoharp	1964	6.25	12.50	25.00

SMASH

Number	Title	Yr	VG	VG+	NM
❏ MGS-27025 [M]	Mother Maybelle Carter and Her Autoharp	1963	5.00	10.00	20.00
❏ MGS-27041 [M]	Pickin' and Singin'	1963	5.00	10.00	20.00
❏ SRS-67025 [S]	Mother Maybelle Carter and Her Autoharp	1963	6.25	12.50	25.00
❏ SRS-67041 [S]	Pickin' and Singin'	1963	6.25	12.50	25.00

CARTER, WILF -- See MONTANA SLIM.

CARTOONE
ATLANTIC

Number	Title	Yr	VG	VG+	NM
❏ SD 8219	Cartoone	1969	5.00	10.00	20.00

CARTWRIGHT, ANGELA
STAR-BRIGHT

Number	Title	Yr	VG	VG+	NM
❏ HLP-102 [M]	Angela Cartwright Sings	1959	12.50	25.00	50.00

CARVER, JOHNNY
IMPERIAL

Number	Title	Yr	VG	VG+	NM
❏ LP-9347 [M]	Really Country	1967	7.50	15.00	30.00
❏ LP-12347 [S]	Really Country	1967	5.00	10.00	20.00
❏ LP-12380	You're in Good Hands with Johnny Carver	1968	5.00	10.00	20.00
❏ LP-12412	Leaving Again	1968	5.00	10.00	20.00

CASADESUS, JEAN
RCA VICTOR RED SEAL

Number	Title	Yr	VG	VG+	NM
❏ LSC-2415 [S]	Debussy: Preludes, Book 1	1960	10.00	20.00	40.00

-- Original with "shaded dog" label

CASCADES, THE
UNI

Number	Title	Yr	VG	VG+	NM
❏ 73069	Maybe the Rain Will Fall	1969	6.25	12.50	25.00

VALIANT

Number	Title	Yr	VG	VG+	NM
❏ W 405 [M]	Rhythm of the Rain	1963	37.50	75.00	150.00
❏ WS 405 [S]	Rhythm of the Rain	1963	75.00	150.00	300.00

CASE, ALLEN
COLUMBIA

Number	Title	Yr	VG	VG+	NM
❏ CL 1406 [M]	"The Deputy" Sings	1960	5.00	10.00	20.00
❏ CS 8202 [S]	"The Deputy" Sings	1960	7.50	15.00	30.00

CASEY, AL
STACY

Number	Title	Yr	VG	VG+	NM
❏ STM-100 [M]	Surfin' Hootenanny	1963	75.00	150.00	300.00
❏ STS-100 [S]	Surfin' Hootenanny	1963	100.00	200.00	400.00

CASH, ALVIN
MAR-V-LUS

Number	Title	Yr	VG	VG+	NM
❏ 1827 [M]	Twine Time	1965	7.50	15.00	30.00

CASH, JOHNNY
COLUMBIA

Number	Title	Yr	VG	VG+	NM
❏ C2L 38 [(2) M]	Ballads of the True West	1965	6.25	12.50	25.00
❏ C2S 838 [(2) S]	Ballads of the True West	1965	6.25	12.50	25.00
❏ CL 1253 [M]	The Fabulous Johnny Cash	1958	5.00	10.00	20.00
❏ CL 1284 [M]	Hymns by Johnny Cash	1959	6.25	12.50	25.00
❏ CL 1339 [M]	Songs of Our Soil	1959	6.25	12.50	25.00
❏ CL 1463 [M]	Now, There Was a Song!	1960	6.25	12.50	25.00
❏ CL 1464 [M]	Ride This Train	1960	6.25	12.50	25.00
❏ CL 1622 [M]	The Lure of the Grand Canyon	1961	10.00	20.00	40.00
	-- Cash narrates; with Andre Kostelanetz and His Orchestra				
❏ CL 1722 [M]	Hymns from the Heart	1962	5.00	10.00	20.00
❏ CL 1802 [M]	The Sound of Johnny Cash	1962	5.00	10.00	20.00
❏ CL 1930 [M]	Blood, Sweat & Tears	1963	5.00	10.00	20.00
❏ CL 2052 [M]	Ring of Fire (The Best of Johnny Cash)	1963	5.00	10.00	20.00
❏ CL 2117 [M]	The Christmas Spirit	1963	6.25	12.50	25.00
❏ CL 2647 [M]	From Sea to Shining Sea	1967	5.00	10.00	20.00
❏ CL 2678 [M]	Johnny Cash's Greatest Hits, Volume 1	1967	5.00	10.00	20.00
❏ CS 8122 [S]	The Fabulous Johnny Cash	1959	10.00	20.00	40.00
❏ CS 8125 [S]	Hymns by Johnny Cash	1959	10.00	20.00	40.00
❏ CS 8148 [S]	Songs of Our Soil	1959	10.00	20.00	40.00
❏ CS 8254 [S]	Now, There Was a Song!	1960	10.00	20.00	40.00

Number	Title	Yr	VG	VG+	NM
❑ CS 8255 [S]	Ride This Train	1960	10.00	20.00	40.00
❑ CS 8422 [S]	The Lure of the Grand Canyon	1961	12.50	25.00	50.00
-- Cash narrates; with Andre Kostelanetz and His Orchestra					
❑ CS 8522 [S]	Hymns from the Heart	1962	7.50	15.00	30.00
❑ CS 8602 [S]	The Sound of Johnny Cash	1962	7.50	15.00	30.00
❑ CS 8730 [S]	Blood, Sweat & Tears	1963	6.25	12.50	25.00
❑ CS 8852 [S]	Ring of Fire (The Best of Johnny Cash)	1963	6.25	12.50	25.00
❑ CS 8917 [S]	The Christmas Spirit	1963	7.50	15.00	30.00
❑ CS 8990 [S]	I Walk the Line	1964	5.00	10.00	20.00
❑ CS 9048 [S]	Bitter Tears (Ballads of the American Indian)	1964	5.00	10.00	20.00
❑ CS 9109 [S]	Orange Blossom Special	1965	5.00	10.00	20.00
❑ CS 9246 [S]	Mean as Hell	1965	5.00	10.00	20.00
❑ CS 9292 [S]	Everybody Loves a Nut	1966	5.00	10.00	20.00
❑ CS 9337 [S]	That's What You Get for Lovin' Me	1966	5.00	10.00	20.00
❑ CS 9447 [S]	From Sea to Shining Sea	1967	5.00	10.00	20.00
❑ CS 9478 [S]	Johnny Cash's Greatest Hits, Volume 1	1967	5.00	10.00	20.00
❑ CS 9639	Johnny Cash at Folsom Prison	1968	5.00	10.00	20.00
❑ CQ 30961 [Q]	Johnny Cash at San Quentin	1971	5.00	10.00	20.00
❑ CG 32253 [(2)]	The Gospel Road	1973	6.25	12.50	25.00

COLUMBIA SPECIAL PRODUCTS

Number	Title	Yr	VG	VG+	NM
❑ 363	Legends and Love Songs	196?	5.00	10.00	20.00

DORAL/CSP

Number	Title	Yr	VG	VG+	NM
❑ (# unknown)	Doral Presents Johnny Cash	1972	10.00	20.00	40.00
-- Mail-order offer from Doral cigarettes					

SUN

Number	Title	Yr	VG	VG+	NM
❑ LP-118 [(2)]	Johnny Cash -- The Legend	1970	5.00	10.00	20.00
❑ LP-126 [(2)]	Johnny Cash: The Man, The World, His Music	1971	5.00	10.00	20.00
❑ SLP-1220 [M]	Johnny Cash with His Hot and Blue Guitar	1956	25.00	50.00	100.00
❑ SLP-1235 [M]	The Songs That Made Him	1958	25.00	50.00	100.00
❑ SLP-1240 [M]	Johnny Cash's Greatest!	1959	12.50	25.00	50.00
❑ SLP-1245 [M]	Johnny Cash Sings Hank Williams	1960	12.50	25.00	50.00
❑ SLP-1255 [M]	Now Here's Johnny Cash	1961	12.50	25.00	50.00
❑ SLP-1270 [M]	All Aboard the Blue Train	1963	12.50	25.00	50.00
❑ SLP-1275 [M]	The Original Sun Sound of Johnny Cash	1965	12.50	25.00	50.00

CASH, JOHNNY, AND JUNE CARTER
COLUMBIA

Number	Title	Yr	VG	VG+	NM
❑ CL 2728 [M]	Carryin' On with Johnny Cash and June Carter	1967	5.00	10.00	20.00
❑ CS 9528 [S]	Carryin' On with Johnny Cash and June Carter	1967	5.00	10.00	20.00

CASH, ROSEANNE
COLUMBIA

Number	Title	Yr	VG	VG+	NM
❑ AS 1527 [DJ]	Interview with Martha Hume	1982	7.50	15.00	30.00
-- Generic cover with sticker					
❑ HC 46965	Seven Year Ache	1981	6.25	12.50	25.00
-- "Half-Speed Master"					

CASH, TOMMY
EPIC

Number	Title	Yr	VG	VG+	NM
❑ BN 26484	Your Lovin' Takes the Leavin' Out of Me	1969	5.00	10.00	20.00

UNITED ARTISTS

Number	Title	Yr	VG	VG+	NM
❑ UAS-6628	Here Comes Tommy Cash	1968	5.00	10.00	20.00

CASHMAN, PISTILLI, AND WEST
ABC

Number	Title	Yr	VG	VG+	NM
❑ S-629	Bound to Happen	1968	5.00	10.00	20.00

CASINOS, THE
FRATERNITY

Number	Title	Yr	VG	VG+	NM
❑ LP-1019 [M]	Then You Can Tell Me Goodbye	1967	10.00	20.00	40.00
❑ LPS-1019 [S]	Then You Can Tell Me Goodbye	1967	15.00	30.00	60.00

CASSELL, PETE
HILLTOP

Number	Title	Yr	VG	VG+	NM
❑ 6023	The Legend of Pete Cassell	1965	6.25	12.50	25.00

CASSIDY, DAVID
Also see THE PARTRIDGE FAMILY.
BELL

Number	Title	Yr	VG	VG+	NM
❑ 1109	Rock Me Baby	1972	5.00	10.00	20.00
❑ 1132	Dreams Are Nothing More Than Wishes	1973	5.00	10.00	20.00
❑ 1312	Cassidy Live	1974	6.25	12.50	25.00

Number	Title	Yr	VG	VG+	NM
❑ 6070	Cherish	1972	5.00	10.00	20.00

RCA VICTOR

Number	Title	Yr	VG	VG+	NM
❑ APL1-1066	The Higher They Climb...	1975	25.00	50.00	100.00
-- Blue vinyl					
❑ APL1-1852	Gettin' It in the Street	1976	10.00	20.00	40.00

CASTELLS, THE
ERA

Number	Title	Yr	VG	VG+	NM
❑ EL-109 [M]	So This Is Love	1962	30.00	60.00	120.00
❑ ES-109 [S]	So This Is Love	1962	100.00	200.00	400.00

CASTOR, JIMMY, BUNCH
RCA VICTOR

Number	Title	Yr	VG	VG+	NM
❑ APD1-0103 [Q]	Dimension III	1973	5.00	10.00	20.00

SMASH

Number	Title	Yr	VG	VG+	NM
❑ MGS-27091 [M]	Hey Leroy!	1967	10.00	20.00	40.00
❑ SRS-67091 [S]	Hey Leroy!	1967	10.00	20.00	40.00

CAT MOTHER AND THE ALL NIGHT NEWS BOYS
POLYDOR

Number	Title	Yr	VG	VG+	NM
❑ 24-4001	The Street Giveth...And the Street Taketh Away	1969	6.25	12.50	25.00
-- Produced by Jimi Hendrix					

CATALINAS, THE
RIC

Number	Title	Yr	VG	VG+	NM
❑ M-1006 [M]	Fun, Fun, Fun	1964	25.00	50.00	100.00
❑ S-1006 [S]	Fun, Fun, Fun	1964	37.50	75.00	150.00

CATANOOGA CATS, THE
FORWARD

Number	Title	Yr	VG	VG+	NM
❑ ST-F-1018	The Catanooga Cats	1969	10.00	20.00	40.00

CATAPILLA
VERTIGO

Number	Title	Yr	VG	VG+	NM
❑ 1006	Catapilla	1971	7.50	15.00	30.00

CATHY JEAN AND THE ROOMATES
VALMOR

Number	Title	Yr	VG	VG+	NM
❑ 78 [M]	Great Oldies	1962	200.00	400.00	800.00
-- Reissue with titles on cover and no group shot					
❑ 789 [M]	At the Hop!	1961	225.00	450.00	900.00

CAUTHEN, STEVE
BAREBACK

Number	Title	Yr	VG	VG+	NM
❑ BB 3334	...And Steve Cauthen Sings Too!	1977	5.00	10.00	20.00

CENTAURUS
AZRA

Number	Title	Yr	VG	VG+	NM
❑ 61549	Centaurus	1978	12.50	25.00	50.00
-- Issued on clear vinyl					

CENTRAL NERVOUS SYSTEM
MUSIC FACTORY

Number	Title	Yr	VG	VG+	NM
❑ MFS-12003	I Could Have Danced All Night	1968	5.00	10.00	20.00

CENTURIONS, THE
DEL-FI

Number	Title	Yr	VG	VG+	NM
❑ DFLP-1228 [M]	Surfer's Pajama Party	1963	25.00	50.00	100.00
❑ DFST-1228 [S]	Surfer's Pajama Party	1963	50.00	100.00	200.00
-- Above has the same title and number, and almost the same cover, as the album of the same name by Bruce Johnston, but the contents are different					

CESANA
MODERN

Number	Title	Yr	VG	VG+	NM
❑ M-100 [M]	Tender Emotions	1964	5.00	10.00	20.00

CEYLEIB PEOPLE, THE
VAULT

Number	Title	Yr	VG	VG+	NM
❑ LP-117	Tanyet	1968	15.00	30.00	60.00

CHAD AND JEREMY
COLUMBIA

Number	Title	Yr	VG	VG+	NM
❑ CL 2374 [M]	Before and After	1965	5.00	10.00	20.00
❑ CL 2398 [M]	I Don't Want to Lose You Baby	1966	6.25	12.50	25.00
❑ CL 2564 [M]	Distant Shores	1966	5.00	10.00	20.00
❑ CL 2671 [M]	Of Cabbages and Kings	1967	5.00	10.00	20.00

Number	Title	Yr	VG	VG+	NM
❏ CL 2899 [M]	The Ark	1968	6.25	12.50	25.00
❏ CS 9174 [S]	Before and After	1965	7.50	15.00	30.00
❏ CS 9198 [S]	I Don't Want to Lose You Baby	1966	10.00	20.00	40.00
❏ CS 9364 [P]	Distant Shores	1966	6.25	12.50	25.00
-- "Distant Shores" is rechanneled					
❏ CS 9471 [S]	Of Cabbages and Kings	1967	6.25	12.50	25.00
❏ CS 9699 [S]	The Arc	1968	6.25	12.50	25.00
-- Some copies spell the LP title this way on the cover					
❏ CS 9699 [S]	The Ark	1968	6.25	12.50	25.00
-- Correct spelling of LP title on cover					

CHAIRMEN OF THE BOARD
INVICTUS

Number	Title	Yr	VG	VG+	NM
❏ ST-7300	Give Me Just a Little More Time	1970	10.00	20.00	40.00
❏ SKAO-7304	In Session	1970	10.00	20.00	40.00
❏ ST-9801	Bittersweet	1972	10.00	20.00	40.00
❏ KZ 32526	The Skin I'm In	1974	10.00	20.00	40.00

CHAKIRIS, GEORGE
CAPITOL

Number	Title	Yr	VG	VG+	NM
❏ ST 1750 [S]	George Chakiris	1962	5.00	10.00	20.00
❏ ST 1813 [S]	Memories Are Made of These	1963	5.00	10.00	20.00

HORIZON

Number	Title	Yr	VG	VG+	NM
❏ ST-1610 [S]	The Gershwin Songbook	1962	5.00	10.00	20.00

CHALKER, CURLY
COLUMBIA

Number	Title	Yr	VG	VG+	NM
❏ CL 2596 [M]	Big Hits on Big Steel	1965	5.00	10.00	20.00
❏ CS 9396 [S]	Big Hits on Big Steel	1965	7.50	15.00	30.00

CHALLENGERS, THE
GNP CRESCENDO

Number	Title	Yr	VG	VG+	NM
❏ GNP-609 [(2) M]	25 Great Instrumental Hits	1967	6.25	12.50	25.00
❏ GNPS-609 [(2) S]	25 Great Instrumental Hits	1967	5.00	10.00	20.00
❏ GNP-2010 [M]	The Challengers at the Teenage Fair	1965	5.00	10.00	20.00
❏ GNPS-2010 [S]	The Challengers at the Teenage Fair	1965	6.25	12.50	25.00
❏ GNP-2018 [M]	The Man from U.N.C.L.E.	1965	5.00	10.00	20.00
❏ GNPS-2018 [S]	The Man from U.N.C.L.E.	1965	6.25	12.50	25.00
❏ GNP-2025 [M]	California Kicks	1966	5.00	10.00	20.00
❏ GNPS-2025 [S]	California Kicks	1966	6.25	12.50	25.00
❏ GNP-2030 [M]	Billy Strange and the Challengers	1966	5.00	10.00	20.00
❏ GNPS-2030 [S]	Billy Strange and the Challengers	1966	6.25	12.50	25.00
❏ GNP-2031 [M]	Wipe Out	1966	5.00	10.00	20.00
❏ GNPS-2031 [S]	Wipe Out	1966	6.25	12.50	25.00
❏ GNPS-2045	Light My Fire with Classical Gas	1968	5.00	10.00	20.00
❏ GNPS-2056	Vanilla Funk	1970	5.00	10.00	20.00

TRIUMPH

Number	Title	Yr	VG	VG+	NM
❏ TR-100 [M]	The Challengers Go Sidewalk Surfing	1965	5.00	10.00	20.00
❏ TRS-100 [S]	The Challengers Go Sidewalk Surfing	1965	6.25	12.50	25.00

VAULT

Number	Title	Yr	VG	VG+	NM
❏ LP-100 [M]	Surfbeat	1963	12.50	25.00	50.00
❏ VS-100 [S]	Surfbeat	1963	20.00	40.00	80.00
-- Black vinyl					
❏ VS-100 [S]	Surfbeat	1963	62.50	125.00	250.00
-- Red vinyl					
❏ VS-100 [S]	Surfbeat	1963	62.50	12.50	250.00
-- Orange vinyl					
❏ VS-100 [S]	Surfbeat	1963	62.50	125.00	250.00
-- Yellow vinyl					
❏ LP-101 [M]	Lloyd Thaxton Goes Surfin' with the Challengers	1963	15.00	30.00	60.00
-- Original title					
❏ VS-101 [S]	Lloyd Thaxton Goes Surfin' with the Challengers	1963	25.00	50.00	100.00
-- Original title; black vinyl					
❏ VS-101 [S]	(Lloyd Thaxton Goes) Surfin' with the Challengers	1963	62.50	125.00	250.00
-- Either title; blue vinyl					
❏ VS-101 [S]	(Lloyd Thaxton Goes) Surfin' with the Challengers	1963	62.50	125.00	250.00
-- Either title; red vinyl					
❏ VS-101 [S]	(Lloyd Thaxton Goes) Surfin' with the Challengers	1963	62.50	125.00	250.00
-- Either title; orange vinyl					
❏ VS-101 [S]	(Lloyd Thaxton Goes) Surfin' with the Challengers	1963	62.50	125.00	250.00
-- Either title; yellow vinyl					
❏ LP-101 [M]	Surfin' with the Challengers	1963	12.50	25.00	50.00
-- Altered title					
❏ VS-101 [S]	Surfin' with the Challengers	1963	20.00	40.00	80.00
-- Altered title; black vinyl					
❏ LP-102 [M]	The Challengers On The Move	1963	10.00	20.00	40.00
❏ VS-102 [S]	The Challengers On The Move	1963	15.00	30.00	60.00

Number	Title	Yr	VG	VG+	NM
❏ LP-107 [M]	K-39	1964	20.00	40.00	80.00
❏ LP-109 [M]	The Surf's Up	1965	10.00	20.00	40.00
❏ VS-109 [S]	The Surf's Up	1965	15.00	30.00	60.00
❏ LP-110 [M]	The Challengers A-Go-Go	1966	7.50	15.00	30.00
❏ VS-110 [S]	The Challengers A-Go-Go	1966	10.00	20.00	40.00
❏ LP-111 [M]	The Challengers' Greatest Hits	1967	6.25	12.50	25.00
❏ VS-111 [S]	The Challengers' Greatest Hits	1967	6.25	12.50	25.00

CHAMAELEON CHURCH
Chevy Chase was in this group.
MGM

Number	Title	Yr	VG	VG+	NM
❏ SE-4574	Chamaeleon Church	1968	5.00	10.00	20.00

CHAMBERLAIN, RICHARD
MGM

Number	Title	Yr	VG	VG+	NM
❏ SE-4088 [S]	Richard Chamberlain Sings	1962	5.00	10.00	20.00
❏ SE-4185 [S]	Twilight of Honor	1963	5.00	10.00	20.00
❏ SE-4287 [S]	Joy in the Morning	1965	5.00	10.00	20.00
❏ ST 90512 [S]	Richard Chamberlain Sings	1965	7.50	15.00	30.00
-- Capitol Record Club edition					
❏ T 90512 [S]	Richard Chamberlain Sings	1965	6.25	12.50	25.00
-- Capitol Record Club edition					

CHAMBERS BROTHERS, THE
AVCO

Number	Title	Yr	VG	VG+	NM
❏ 69003	Night Move	1975	5.00	10.00	20.00

COLUMBIA

Number	Title	Yr	VG	VG+	NM
❏ KGP 20 [(2)]	Love, Peace and Happiness	1969	6.25	12.50	25.00
❏ CL 2722 [M]	The Time Has Come	1967	7.50	15.00	30.00
❏ CS 9522 [S]	The Time Has Come	1967	5.00	10.00	20.00
-- Red "360 Sound" label					
❏ CS 9671	A New Time -- A New Day	1968	5.00	10.00	20.00

ROXBURY

Number	Title	Yr	VG	VG+	NM
❏ RLX-106	Live In Concert on Mars	1976	7.50	15.00	30.00

VAULT

Number	Title	Yr	VG	VG+	NM
❏ VS-135 [(2)]	The Chambers Brothers Greatest Hits	1970	5.00	10.00	20.00
❏ LP-9003 [M]	People Get Ready	1966	5.00	10.00	20.00
❏ LPS-9003 [S]	People Get Ready	1966	6.25	12.50	25.00

CHAMPS, THE
CHALLENGE

Number	Title	Yr	VG	VG+	NM
❏ CHL-601 [M]	Go Champs Go	1958	62.50	125.00	250.00
❏ CHL-601 [M]	Go Champs Go	1958	800.00	1,600.	2,400.
-- Blue vinyl					
❏ CHL-605 [M]	Everybody's Rockin' with the Champs	1959	50.00	100.00	200.00
❏ CHL-613 [M]	Great Dance Hits	1962	30.00	60.00	120.00
❏ CHL-614 [M]	All American Music from the Champs	1962	30.00	60.00	120.00
❏ CHS-2500 [S]	Everybody's Rockin' with the Champs	1959	75.00	150.00	300.00
❏ CHS-2513 [S]	Great Dance Hits	1962	50.00	100.00	200.00
❏ CHS-2514 [S]	All American Music from the Champs	1962	50.00	100.00	200.00

CHANDLER, GENE
BRUNSWICK

Number	Title	Yr	VG	VG+	NM
❏ BL 54124 [M]	The Girl Don't Care	1967	6.25	12.50	25.00
❏ BL 754124 [S]	The Girl Don't Care	1967	5.00	10.00	20.00
❏ BL 754131	There Was a Time	1968	5.00	10.00	20.00
❏ BL 754149	The Two Sides of Gene Chandler	1969	5.00	10.00	20.00

CHECKER

Number	Title	Yr	VG	VG+	NM
❏ LP-3003 [M]	The Duke of Soul	1967	12.50	25.00	50.00
❏ LPS-3003 [R]	The Duke of Soul	1967	7.50	15.00	30.00

CONSTELLATION

Number	Title	Yr	VG	VG+	NM
❏ LP 1421 [M]	Greatest Hits by Gene Chandler	1964	12.50	25.00	50.00
❏ LP 1423 [M]	Just Be True	1964	12.50	25.00	50.00
❏ LP 1425 [M]	Gene Chandler -- Live On Stage in '65	1965	12.50	25.00	50.00

VEE JAY

Number	Title	Yr	VG	VG+	NM
❏ LP-1040 [M]	The Duke of Earl	1962	30.00	60.00	120.00
❏ SR-1040 [S]	The Duke of Earl	1962	200.00	400.00	800.00
-- "Stereophonic" on front cover; top back cover contains note that begins: "Important Notice...This Is a Stereophonic Record"; "Stereo" on record labels					
❏ SR-1040 [S]	The Duke of Earl	1962	62.50	125.00	250.00
-- "Stereo" sticker on mono cover; "Stereo" on record labels					
❏ SR-1040 [S/M]	The Duke of Earl	196?	12.50	25.00	50.00
-- "Stereophonic" on front; no "Important Notice..." on back; record plays mono. Most labels are all-black with "VJ" in brackets. This was a semi-authorized reissue after ex-Vee Jay executives bought the company's remnants in bankruptcy court in 1966.					

Number	Title	Yr	VG	VG+	NM

CHANDLER, JEFF
LIBERTY
❑ LRP-3067 [M]	Jeff Chandler Sings to You	1957	10.00	20.00	40.00
❑ LRP-3074 [M]	Warm and Easy	1958	10.00	20.00	40.00

CHANNEL, BRUCE
SMASH
❑ MGS-27008 [M]	Hey! Baby (And 11 Other Songs About Your Baby)	1962	25.00	50.00	100.00
❑ SRS-67008 [R]	Hey! Baby (And 11 Other Songs About Your Baby)	1962	15.00	30.00	60.00

CHANNING, CAROL
COMMAND
❑ 880 SD [S]	Carol Channing Entertains	1966	5.00	10.00	20.00
PLANTATION
❑ PLP-527	Carol Channing With the Original Country Cast	1978	5.00	10.00	20.00
VANGUARD
❑ VSD-2041 [S]	Carol Channing	1959	10.00	20.00	40.00
❑ VRS-9056 [M]	Carol Channing	1959	7.50	15.00	30.00

CHANTAY'S
DOT
❑ DLP 3516 [M]	Pipeline	1963	12.50	25.00	50.00
❑ DLP 3771 [M]	Two Sides of the Chantays	1966	12.50	25.00	50.00
❑ DLP 25516 [S]	Pipeline	1963	20.00	40.00	80.00
❑ DLP 25771 [S]	Two Sides of the Chantays	1966	20.00	40.00	80.00
DOWNEY
❑ DLP-1002 [M]	Pipeline	1963	55.00	110.00	220.00
❑ DLPS-1002 [S]	Pipeline	1963	87.50	175.00	350.00

CHANTELS, THE
CARLTON
❑ LP-144 [M]	The Chantels On Tour/ Look in My Eyes	1962	50.00	100.00	200.00
❑ STLP-144 [S]	The Chantels On Tour/ Look in My Eyes	1962	100.00	200.00	400.00
END
❑ LP-301 [M]	We're the Chantels	1958	500.00	1,000.	1,500.
-- Group photo on front cover					
❑ LP-301 [M]	We're the Chantels	1959	100.00	200.00	400.00
-- Jukebox on front cover, "1962" not in trail-off wax					
❑ LP-301 [M]	We're the Chantels	1962	50.00	100.00	200.00
-- Jukebox on front cover, "1962" in trail-off wax					
❑ LP-312 [M]	There's Our Song Again	1962	30.00	60.00	120.00
FORUM
❑ F-9104 [M]	The Chantels Sing Their Favorites	1964	12.50	25.00	50.00
❑ FS-9104 [R]	The Chantels Sing Their Favorites	1964	6.25	12.50	25.00

CHAPIN BROTHERS, THE
ROCK-LAND
❑ RR-66 [M]	Chapin Music	1966	7.50	15.00	30.00

CHARIOT
NATIONAL GENERAL
❑ NG-2003	Chariot	1971	12.50	25.00	50.00

CHARIOTEERS, THE
COLUMBIA
❑ CL 6014 [10]	Sweet and Low	1949	75.00	150.00	300.00
HARMONY
❑ HL 7089 [M]	The Charioteers with Billy Williams	1957	25.00	50.00	100.00

CHARISMA
ROULETTE
❑ SR-42037	Charisma	1970	5.00	10.00	20.00

CHARITY
UNI
❑ 73061	Charity Now	1969	6.25	12.50	25.00

CHARLATANS, THE
PHILIPS
❑ PHS 600-309	The Charlatans	1969	25.00	50.00	100.00

CHARLENE
PRODIGAL
❑ P6-10015	Charlene	1976	5.00	10.00	20.00

Number	Title	Yr	VG	VG+	NM
❑ P6-10018	Songs of Love	1977	5.00	10.00	20.00

CHARLES RIVER VALLEY BOYS, THE
ELEKTRA
❑ EKL-4006 [M]	Beatle Country	1967	5.00	10.00	20.00
❑ EKS-74006 [S]	Beatle Country	1967	6.25	12.50	25.00

CHARLES, RAY
ABC
❑ S-590X [(2) S]	A Man and His Soul	1967	5.00	10.00	20.00
❑ 595 [M]	Ray Charles Invites You to Listen	1967	5.00	10.00	20.00
❑ SQBO-91036 [(2)]	The Ray Charles Story	1967	6.25	12.50	25.00
-- Capitol Record Club exclusive					
ABC-PARAMOUNT
❑ 335 [M]	The Genius Hits the Road	1960	5.00	10.00	20.00
❑ S-335 [S]	The Genius Hits the Road	1960	7.50	15.00	30.00
❑ 355 [M]	Dedicated to You	1961	5.00	10.00	20.00
❑ S-355 [S]	Dedicated to You	1961	7.50	15.00	30.00
❑ 410 [M]	Modern Sounds in Country and Western Music	1962	6.25	12.50	25.00
❑ S-410 [S]	Modern Sounds in Country and Western Music	1962	7.50	15.00	30.00
❑ 415 [M]	Ray Charles' Greatest Hits	1962	5.00	10.00	20.00
❑ S-415 [S]	Ray Charles' Greatest Hits	1962	6.25	12.50	25.00
❑ 435 [M]	Modern Sounds in Country and Western Music (Volume Two)	1962	5.00	10.00	20.00
❑ S-435 [S]	Modern Sounds in Country and Western Music (Volume Two)	1962	6.25	12.50	25.00
❑ 465 [M]	Ingredients in a Recipe for Soul	1963	5.00	10.00	20.00
❑ S-465 [S]	Ingredients in a Recipe for Soul	1963	6.25	12.50	25.00
❑ 480 [M]	Sweet & Sour Tears	1964	5.00	10.00	20.00
❑ S-480 [S]	Sweet & Sour Tears	1964	6.25	12.50	25.00
❑ 495 [M]	Have a Smile with Me	1964	5.00	10.00	20.00
❑ S-495 [S]	Have a Smile with Me	1964	6.25	12.50	25.00
❑ S-500 [S]	Ray Charles Live in Concert	1965	5.00	10.00	20.00
❑ S-520 [S]	Country & Western Meets Rhythm & Blues	1965	5.00	10.00	20.00
❑ S-544 [S]	Crying Time	1966	5.00	10.00	20.00
❑ ST-90144 [S]	Ray Charles Live in Concert	1965	5.00	10.00	20.00
-- Capitol Record Club edition					
❑ T-90144 [M]	Ray Charles Live in Concert	1965	5.00	10.00	20.00
-- Capitol Record Club edition					
❑ ST-90625 [S]	Crying Time	1966	5.00	10.00	20.00
-- Capitol Record Club edition					
❑ T-90625 [M]	Crying Time	1966	5.00	10.00	20.00
-- Capitol Record Club edition					
ATLANTIC
❑ 2-900 [(2) M]	The Ray Charles Story	1962	10.00	20.00	40.00
❑ 1259 [M]	The Great Ray Charles	1957	12.50	25.00	50.00
-- Black label					
❑ 1259 [M]	The Great Ray Charles	1960	6.25	12.50	25.00
-- Red and white label, white fan logo on right					
❑ 1259 [M]	The Great Ray Charles	1962	5.00	10.00	20.00
-- Red and white label, black fan logo on right					
❑ SD 1259 [S]	The Great Ray Charles	1959	12.50	25.00	50.00
-- Green label					
❑ SD 1259 [S]	The Great Ray Charles	1960	6.25	12.50	25.00
-- Blue and green label, white fan logo on right					
❑ SD 1259 [S]	The Great Ray Charles	1962	5.00	10.00	20.00
-- Blue and green label, black fan logo on right					
❑ 1289 [M]	Ray Charles at Newport	1958	12.50	25.00	50.00
-- Black label					
❑ 1289 [M]	Ray Charles at Newport	1960	6.25	12.50	25.00
-- Red and white label, white fan logo on right					
❑ 1289 [M]	Ray Charles at Newport	1962	5.00	10.00	20.00
-- Red and white label, black fan logo on right					
❑ SD 1289 [S]	Ray Charles at Newport	1959	12.50	25.00	50.00
-- Green label					
❑ SD 1289 [S]	Ray Charles at Newport	1960	6.25	12.50	25.00
-- Blue and green label, white fan logo on right					
❑ SD 1289 [S]	Ray Charles at Newport	1962	5.00	10.00	20.00
-- Blue and green label, black fan logo on right					
❑ 1312 [M]	The Genius of Ray Charles	1960	10.00	20.00	40.00
-- Black label					
❑ 1312 [M]	The Genius of Ray Charles	1960	10.00	20.00	40.00
-- White "bullseye" label					
❑ 1312 [M]	The Genius of Ray Charles	1960	6.25	12.50	25.00
-- Red and white label, white fan logo on right					
❑ 1312 [M]	The Genius of Ray Charles	1962	5.00	10.00	20.00
-- Red and white label, black fan logo on right					
❑ SD 1312 [S]	The Genius of Ray Charles	1960	12.50	25.00	50.00
-- Green label					
❑ SD 1312 [S]	The Genius of Ray Charles	1960	12.50	25.00	50.00
-- White "bullseye" label					
❑ SD 1312 [S]	The Genius of Ray Charles	1960	6.25	12.50	25.00
-- Blue and green label, white fan logo on right					

Number	Title	Yr	VG	VG+	NM
❑ SD 1312 [S]	The Genius of Ray Charles	1962	5.00	10.00	20.00
-- Blue and green label, black fan logo on right					
❑ SD 1312 [S]	The Genius of Ray Charles	1968	5.00	10.00	20.00
-- Brown and purple label					
❑ 1369 [M]	The Genius After Hours	1961	6.25	12.50	25.00
-- Red and white label, white fan logo on right					
❑ 1369 [M]	The Genius After Hours	1962	5.00	10.00	20.00
-- Red and white label, black fan logo on right					
❑ SD 1369 [S]	The Genius After Hours	1961	7.50	15.00	30.00
-- Blue and green label, white fan logo on right					
❑ SD 1369 [S]	The Genius After Hours	1962	6.25	12.50	25.00
-- Blue and green label, black fan logo on right					
❑ 3700 [(6)]	Ray Charles: A Life in Music	198?	12.50	25.00	50.00
❑ SD 7101 [S]	The Great Hits of Ray Charles Recorded on 8-Track Stereo	1966	6.25	12.50	25.00
❑ 8006 [M]	Ray Charles (Rock and Roll)	1957	22.50	45.00	90.00
-- Black label					
❑ 8006 [M]	Ray Charles (Rock and Roll)	1960	6.25	12.50	25.00
-- Red and white label, white fan logo on right					
❑ 8006 [M]	Hallelujah! I Love Her So	1962	5.00	10.00	20.00
-- Red and white label, black fan logo on right; retitled version					
❑ 8025 [M]	Yes, Indeed!	1958	12.50	25.00	50.00
-- Black label; cover has screaming girls					
❑ 8025 [M]	Yes, Indeed!	1960	6.25	12.50	25.00
-- Red and white label, white fan logo on right; cover has screaming girls					
❑ 8025 [M]	Yes, Indeed!	1962	5.00	10.00	20.00
-- Red and white label, black fan logo on right; cover has Ray on it					
❑ 8029 [M]	What'd I Say	1959	12.50	25.00	50.00
-- Black label					
❑ 8029 [M]	What'd I Say	1960	10.00	20.00	40.00
-- White "bullseye" label					
❑ 8029 [M]	What'd I Say	1960	6.25	12.50	25.00
-- Red and white label, white fan logo on right					
❑ 8029 [M]	What'd I Say	1962	5.00	10.00	20.00
-- Red and white label, black fan logo on right					
❑ 8039 [M]	Ray Charles In Person	1960	6.25	12.50	25.00
-- Red and white label, white fan logo on right					
❑ 8039 [M]	Ray Charles In Person	1960	10.00	20.00	40.00
-- Black label					
❑ 8039 [M]	Ray Charles In Person	1962	5.00	10.00	20.00
-- Red and white label, black fan logo on right					
❑ 8052 [M]	The Genius Sings the Blues	1961	6.25	12.50	25.00
-- Red and white label, white fan logo on right					
❑ 8052 [M]	The Genius Sings the Blues	1962	5.00	10.00	20.00
-- Red and white label, black fan logo on right					
❑ 8054 [M]	Do the Twist!	1961	6.25	12.50	25.00
-- Red and white label, white fan logo on right					
❑ 8054 [M]	Do the Twist!	1962	5.00	10.00	20.00
-- Red and white label, black fan logo on right					
❑ 8063 [M]	The Ray Charles Story, Volume 1	1962	5.00	10.00	20.00
❑ 8064 [M]	The Ray Charles Story, Volume 2	1962	5.00	10.00	20.00
❑ 8083 [M]	The Ray Charles Story, Volume 3	1963	5.00	10.00	20.00
❑ 8094 [M]	The Ray Charles Story, Volume 4	1964	5.00	10.00	20.00
❑ SD 8094 [S]	The Ray Charles Story, Volume 4	1964	6.25	12.50	25.00
COLUMBIA					
❑ AS 1920 [DJ]	Friendship Radio Show	1984	5.00	10.00	20.00
DCC COMPACT CLASSICS					
❑ LPZ-2012	Greatest Country and Western Hits	1995	17.50	35.00	70.00
-- Audiophile vinyl					
HOLLYWOOD					
❑ 504 [M]	The Original Ray Charles	1959	37.50	75.00	150.00
❑ 505 [M]	The Fabuolus Ray Charles	1959	37.50	75.00	150.00
IMPULSE!					
❑ A-2 [M]	Genius + Soul = Jazz	1961	6.25	12.50	25.00
❑ AS-2 [S]	Genius + Soul = Jazz	1961	7.50	15.00	30.00
LONGINES SYMPHONETTE					
❑ 95647 [(5)]	The Greatest Hits of Ray Charles	1974	10.00	20.00	40.00

CHARLES, RAY, AND BETTY CARTER
ABC

Number	Title	Yr	VG	VG+	NM
❑ S-385 [S]	Ray Charles and Betty Carter	1967	5.00	10.00	20.00
ABC-PARAMOUNT					
❑ 385 [M]	Ray Charles and Betty Carter	1961	10.00	20.00	40.00
❑ S-385 [S]	Ray Charles and Betty Carter	1961	15.00	30.00	60.00
DCC COMPACT CLASSICS					
❑ LPZ-2005	Ray Charles and Betty Carter	1995	20.00	40.00	80.00
-- Audiophile vinyl					

CHARLES, RAY & MILT JACKSON
ATLANTIC

Number	Title	Yr	VG	VG+	NM
❑ 1279 [M]	Soul Brothers	1958	12.50	25.00	50.00
-- Black label					
❑ 1279 [M]	Soul Brothers	1960	6.25	12.50	25.00
-- Red and white label, white fan logo on right					
❑ 1279 [M]	Soul Brothers	1962	5.00	10.00	20.00
-- Red and white label, black fan logo on right					

Number	Title	Yr	VG	VG+	NM
❑ SD 1279 [S]	Soul Brothers	1959	12.50	25.00	50.00
-- Green label					
❑ SD 1279 [S]	Soul Brothers	1960	6.25	12.50	25.00
-- Blue and green label, white fan logo on right					
❑ SD 1279 [S]	Soul Brothers	1962	5.00	10.00	20.00
-- Blue and green label, black fan logo on right					
❑ 1360 [M]	Soul Meeting	1961	6.25	12.50	25.00
-- Red and white label, white fan logo on right					
❑ 1360 [M]	Soul Meeting	1962	5.00	10.00	20.00
-- Red and white label, black fan logo on right					
❑ SD 1360 [S]	Soul Meeting	1961	7.50	15.00	30.00
-- Blue and green label, white fan logo on right					
❑ SD 1360 [S]	Soul Meeting	1962	6.25	12.50	25.00
-- Blue and green label, black fan logo on right					

CHARLES, RAY, AND CLEO LAINE
RCA VICTOR

Number	Title	Yr	VG	VG+	NM
❑ DJL1-2163 [(2)]	Porgy & Bess	1976	5.00	10.00	20.00
-- Promo-only excerpts from 2-record set					

CHASE
EPIC

Number	Title	Yr	VG	VG+	NM
❑ EQ 30472 [Q]	Chase	1973	5.00	10.00	20.00
❑ EQ 32572 [Q]	Pure Music	1974	5.00	10.00	20.00

CHASE, LINCOLN
LIBERTY

Number	Title	Yr	VG	VG+	NM
❑ LRP-3076 [M]	The Explosive Lincoln Chase	1958	12.50	25.00	50.00

CHEAP TRICK
EPIC

Number	Title	Yr	VG	VG+	NM
❑ AS 518 [DJ]	From Tokyo to You	1979	7.50	15.00	30.00
-- Promo-only sampler from Cheap Trick at Budokan					

CHECKER, CHUBBY
ABKCO

Number	Title	Yr	VG	VG+	NM
❑ 4219 [(2)]	Chubby Checker's Greatest Hits	1972	5.00	10.00	20.00
PARKWAY					
❑ P 7001 [M]	Twist with Chubby Checker	1960	10.00	20.00	40.00
-- All-orange label					
❑ P 7001 [M]	Twist with Chubby Checker	1962	7.50	15.00	30.00
-- Orange and yellow label					
❑ P 7002 [M]	For Twisters Only	1960	10.00	20.00	40.00
-- All-orange label					
❑ P 7002 [M]	For Twisters Only	1962	7.50	15.00	30.00
-- Orange and yellow label					
❑ P 7003 [M]	It's Pony Time	1961	10.00	20.00	40.00
-- All-orange label					
❑ P 7003 [M]	It's Pony Time	1962	7.50	15.00	30.00
-- Orange and yellow label					
❑ P 7004 [M]	Let's Twist Again	1961	10.00	20.00	40.00
-- All-orange label					
❑ P 7004 [M]	Let's Twist Again	1962	7.50	15.00	30.00
-- Orange and yellow label					
❑ P 7007 [M]	Your Twist Party	1961	10.00	20.00	40.00
-- All-orange label					
❑ P 7007 [M]	Your Twist Party	1962	7.50	15.00	30.00
-- Orange and yellow label					
❑ P 7008 [M]	Twistin' Round the World	1962	7.50	15.00	30.00
❑ SP 7008 [B]	Twistin' Round the World	1962	10.00	20.00	40.00
❑ P 7009 [M]	For Teen Twisters Only	1962	7.50	15.00	30.00
❑ SP 7009 [S]	For Teen Twisters Only	1962	10.00	20.00	40.00
❑ P 7014 [M]	All the Hits (For Your Dancin' Party)	1962	7.50	15.00	30.00
❑ P 7020 [M]	Limbo Party	1962	7.50	15.00	30.00
❑ SP 7020 [S]	Limbo Party	1962	10.00	20.00	40.00
❑ P 7022 [M]	Chubby Checker's Biggest Hits	1962	7.50	15.00	30.00
❑ SP 7022 [R]	Chubby Checker's Biggest Hits	1962	7.50	15.00	30.00
❑ P 7026 [M]	Chubby Checker In Person	1963	7.50	15.00	30.00
❑ SP 7026 [S]	Chubby Checker In Person	1963	10.00	20.00	40.00
-- The above record is labeled "Twist It Up"					
❑ P 7027 [M]	Let's Limbo Some More	1963	7.50	15.00	30.00
❑ SP 7027 [S]	Let's Limbo Some More	1963	10.00	20.00	40.00
❑ P 7030 [M]	Beach Party	1963	7.50	15.00	30.00
❑ SP 7030 [S]	Beach Party	1963	10.00	20.00	40.00
❑ P 7036 [M]	Chubby Checker With Sy Oliver and His Orchestra	1964	7.50	15.00	30.00
❑ SP 7036 [S]	Chubby Checker With Sy Oliver and His Orchestra	1964	10.00	20.00	40.00
❑ P 7040 [M]	Folk Album	1964	7.50	15.00	30.00
❑ SP 7040 [S]	Folk Album	1964	10.00	20.00	40.00
❑ P 7045 [M]	Discotheque	1965	7.50	15.00	30.00
❑ SP 7045 [S]	Discotheque	1965	10.00	20.00	40.00
❑ P 7048 [M]	Chubby Checker's Eighteen Golden Hits	1966	7.50	15.00	30.00

Number	Title	Yr	VG	VG+	NM
❏ SP 7048 [P]	Chubby Checker's Eighteen Golden Hits	1966	10.00	20.00	40.00

CHECKMATES, THE
JUSTICE
❏ JLP-149	The Checkmates	1966	100.00	200.00	400.00

CHECKMATES LTD., THE
A&M
❏ SP-4183	Love Is All I Have to Give	1969	6.25	12.50	25.00
CAPITOL
❏ ST 2840 [S]	Live at Caesar's Palace	1968	5.00	10.00	20.00
❏ T 2840 [M]	Live at Caesar's Palace	1968	7.50	15.00	30.00

CHELSEA
Future KISS member PETER CRISS (as "Peter Cris") played drums on this LP.
DECCA
❏ DL 75262	The Chelsea Album	1972	37.50	75.00	150.00

CHER
Also see SONNY & CHER.
ATCO
❏ SD 33-298	3614 Jackson Highway	1969	5.00	10.00	20.00
CASABLANCA
❏ NBPIX-7133 [PD]	Take Me Home	1979	12.50	25.00	50.00
IMPERIAL
❏ LP-9292 [M]	All I Really Want to Do	1965	5.00	10.00	20.00
❏ LP-9301 [M]	The Sonny Side of Cher	1966	5.00	10.00	20.00
❏ LP-12292 [S]	All I Really Want to Do	1965	6.25	12.50	25.00
❏ LP-12301 [S]	The Sonny Side of Cher	1966	6.25	12.50	25.00
❏ LP-12320 [S]	Cher	1966	5.00	10.00	20.00
❏ LP-12358 [S]	With Love -- Cher	1967	5.00	10.00	20.00
❏ LP-12373	Backstage	1968	5.00	10.00	20.00
❏ LP-12406	Cher's Golden Greats	1968	5.00	10.00	20.00
KAPP
❏ KRS-3649	Cher	1971	5.00	10.00	20.00
-- Original title of LP (renamed "Gypsys, Tramps & Thieves")					
UNITED ARTISTS
❏ UXS-88 [(2)]	Cher Superpak	1971	5.00	10.00	20.00
❏ UXS-89 [(2)]	Cher Superpak, Vol. II	1972	5.00	10.00	20.00
-- The above are reissues of Imperial recordings					

CHEROKEE
ABC
❏ ABCS-719	Cherokee	1970	5.00	10.00	20.00

CHERRY PEOPLE, THE
HERITAGE
❏ HTS 35,000	The Cherry People	1968	5.00	10.00	20.00

CHERRY, DON
COLUMBIA
❏ CL 893 [M]	Swingin' for Two	1956	6.25	12.50	25.00

CHESS, TUBBY, AND HIS CANDY STRIPE TWISTERS
GRAND PRIX
❏ KS-187 [S]	Do the Twist	1962	5.00	10.00	20.00

CHESTER, GARY
DCP
❏ DCL 3803 [M]	Yeah, Yeah, Yeah	1964	5.00	10.00	20.00
❏ DCS 6803 [S]	Yeah, Yeah, Yeah	1964	6.25	12.50	25.00

CHEVALIER, MAURICE
CAPITOL
❏ T 10360 [M]	The Young Chevalier	196?	5.00	10.00	20.00
EPIC
❏ FXS 15117	Maurice Chevalier at 80	1968	5.00	10.00	20.00
LONDON
❏ GH 46001/4 [(4) M]	60 Years of Song	1966	10.00	20.00	40.00
❏ GHS 56001/4 [(4) S]	60 Years of Song	1966	12.50	25.00	50.00
MGM
❏ 2E-5 [(2) M]	Yesterday...Today	1958	10.00	20.00	40.00
-- Yellow label original; also released separately as 3702 and 3703					
❏ 2SE-5 [(2) S]	Yesterday...Today	1958	15.00	30.00	60.00
-- Yellow label original; also released separately as 3702 and 3703					
❏ E-3702 [M]	Yesterday	1958	6.25	12.50	25.00
-- Yellow label original					
❏ SE-3702 [S]	Yesterday	1958	7.50	15.00	30.00
-- Yellow label original					
❏ E-3703 [M]	Today	1958	6.25	12.50	25.00
-- Yellow label original					
❏ SE-3703 [S]	Today	1958	7.50	15.00	30.00
-- Yellow label original					
❏ E-3738 [M]	Maurice Chevalier Sings Broadway	1959	6.25	12.50	25.00
-- Yellow label original					
❏ SE-3738 [S]	Maurice Chevalier Sings Broadway	1959	7.50	15.00	30.00
-- Yellow label original					
❏ E-3773 [M]	A Tribute to Al Jolson	1959	6.25	12.50	25.00
-- Yellow label original					
❏ SE-3773 [S]	A Tribute to Al Jolson	1959	7.50	15.00	30.00
-- Yellow label original					
❏ E-3801 [M]	Life Is Just a Bowl of Cherries	1960	5.00	10.00	20.00
❏ SE-3801 [S]	Life Is Just a Bowl of Cherries	1960	6.25	12.50	25.00
❏ E-3835 [M]	Thank Heaven for Little Girls	1960	5.00	10.00	20.00
❏ SE-3835 [S]	Thank Heaven for Little Girls	1960	6.25	12.50	25.00
❏ E-4015 [M]	Maurice Chevalier Sings Lerner, Loewe & Chevalier	1962	5.00	10.00	20.00
❏ SE-4015 [S]	Maurice Chevalier Sings Lerner, Loewe & Chevalier	1962	6.25	12.50	25.00
❏ E-4120 [M]	Paris to Broadway	1963	5.00	10.00	20.00
❏ SE-4120 [S]	Paris to Broadway	1963	6.25	12.50	25.00
❏ SE-4205 [S]	The Very Best of Maurice Chevalier	1964	5.00	10.00	20.00
RCA VICTOR
❏ LPM-2076 [M]	Thank Heaven for Maurice Chevalier	1960	6.25	12.50	25.00
❏ LSP-2076 [S]	Thank Heaven for Maurice Chevalier	1960	7.50	15.00	30.00
TIME
❏ S-2072 [S]	Maurice Chevalier	1963	6.25	12.50	25.00
❏ 52072 [M]	Maurice Chevalier	1963	5.00	10.00	20.00

CHEVRONS, THE
TIME
❏ T-10008 [M]	Sing-a-Long Rock & Roll	1961	20.00	40.00	80.00

CHI-LITES, THE
BRUNSWICK
❏ BL 754152	Give It Away	1969	6.25	12.50	25.00
❏ BL 754165	I Like Your Lovin', Do You Like Mine?	1970	6.25	12.50	25.00
❏ BL 754170	(For God's Sake) Give More Power to the People	1971	6.25	12.50	25.00
❏ BL 754179	A Lonely Man	1972	6.25	12.50	25.00
❏ BL 754184	The Chi-Lites Greatest Hits	1972	6.25	12.50	25.00
❏ BL 754188	A Letter to Myself	1973	6.25	12.50	25.00
❏ BL 754197	Chi-Lites	1973	6.25	12.50	25.00
❏ BL 754200	Toby	1974	6.25	12.50	25.00
❏ BL 754204	Half a Love	1975	6.25	12.50	25.00
❏ BL 754208	The Chi-Lites Greatest Hits, Volume 2	1976	6.25	12.50	25.00

CHICAGO
COLUMBIA
❏ (no #) [(17)]	Chicago	1976	62.50	125.00	250.00
-- Promo-only set: The first 10 Chicago LPs with gold stamps on covers, box, side panel and wraparound					
❏ GP 8 [(2)]	Chicago Transit Authority	1969	6.25	12.50	25.00
-- Red labels with "360 Sound" at bottom					
❏ GP 8 [(2)]	Chicago Transit Authority	1970	5.00	10.00	20.00
-- Orange labels; most copies add a Roman numeral "I" to the title on spine					
❏ KGP 24 [(2)]	Chicago II	1970	10.00	20.00	40.00
-- Red labels with "360 Sound" at bottom					
❏ KGP 24 [(2)]	Chicago II	1970	5.00	10.00	20.00
-- Orange labels					
❏ C2 30110 [(2)]	Chicago III	1971	5.00	10.00	20.00
❏ C2Q 30110 [(2) Q]	Chicago III	1974	7.50	15.00	30.00
❏ C2G 30863 [(2)]	Chicago at Carnegie Hall, Vol. 1 & 2	1971	5.00	10.00	20.00
-- First half of the 4-LP box, possibly for Columbia Record Club only					
❏ C2G 30864 [(2)]	Chicago at Carnegie Hall, Vol. 3 & 4	1971	5.00	10.00	20.00
-- Second half of the 4-LP box, possibly for Columbia Record Club only					
❏ C4Q 30865 [(4) Q]	Chicago at Carnegie Hall	1971	12.50	25.00	50.00
❏ C4X 30865 [(4)]	Chicago at Carnegie Hall	1971	10.00	20.00	40.00
-- With box, 4 posters and program. Deduct for missing items.					
❏ CQ 31102 [Q]	Chicago V	1974	6.25	12.50	25.00
❏ KC 31102	Chicago V	1972	5.00	10.00	20.00
❏ CQ 32400 [Q]	Chicago VI	1974	6.25	12.50	25.00
❏ C2 32810 [(2)]	Chicago VII	1974	5.00	10.00	20.00
❏ C2Q 32810 [(2) Q]	Chicago VII	1974	7.50	15.00	30.00
❏ PCQ 33100 [Q]	Chicago VIII	1975	6.25	12.50	25.00
❏ GQ 33255 [(2) Q]	Chicago Transit Authority	1975	6.25	12.50	25.00
❏ GQ 33258 [(2) Q]	Chicago II	1975	6.25	12.50	25.00

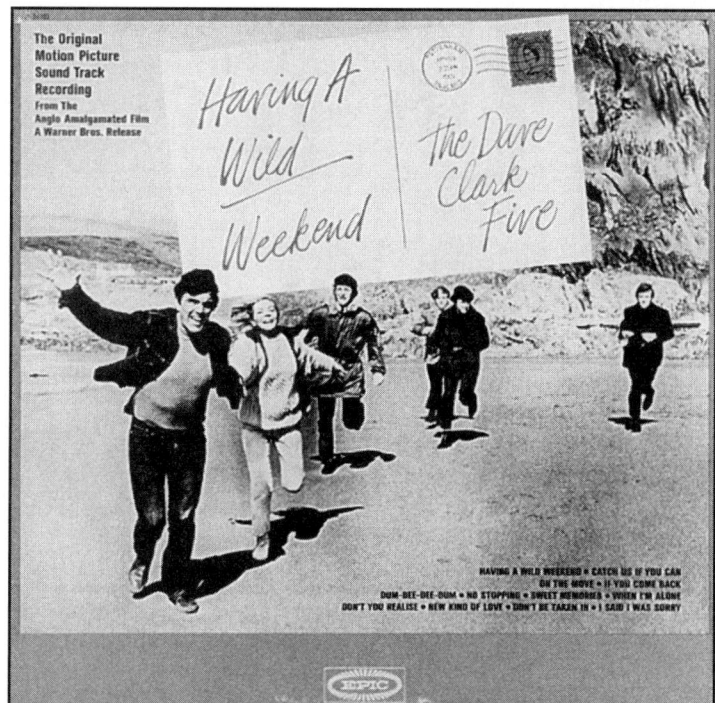

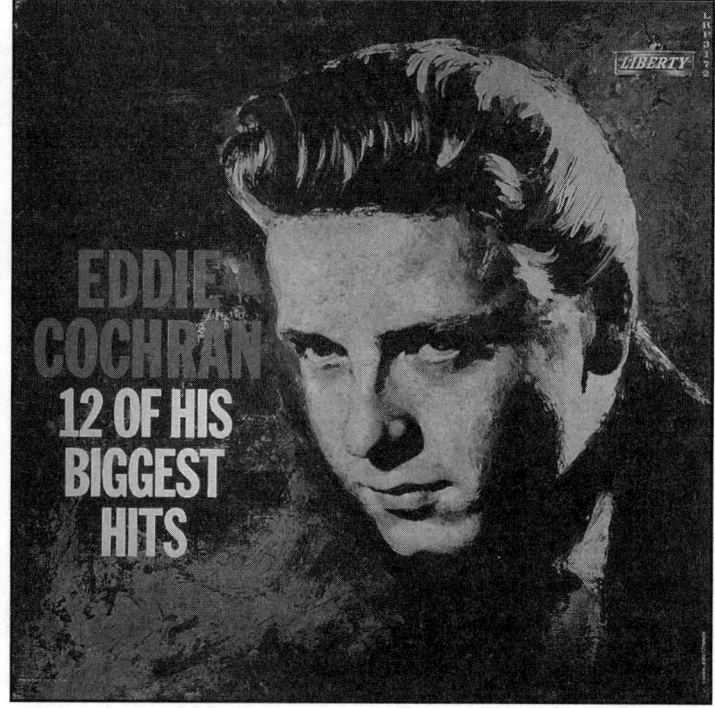

(Top left) Before he became a singing storyteller in the 1970s, Harry Chapin recorded this album on the tiny Rock-Land label with his brothers Steve and Tom. It's rarer than its value indicates. (Top right) Thanks to a change in rights ownership, DCC Compact Classics was forced to delete this fine 1996 Ray Charles vinyl compilation after it had been out for no more than a year. Today it brings several times its original selling price. (Bottom left) Among the many hit albums by the Dave Clark Five in the mid-1960s was the soundtrack album from *Having A Wild Weekend*, which featured the hit single "Catch Us If You Can." DC5 albums from this period are always more collectible in mono, as all the stereo until around 1967 was rechanneled. (Bottom right) Original Eddie Cochran albums on Liberty, including this one, are quite hard to find and bring good money in top condition.

Number	Title	Yr	VG	VG+	NM
❑ PCQ 33900 [Q]	Chicago IX -- Chicago's Greatest Hits	1975	6.25	12.50	25.00
❑ PCQ 34200 [Q]	Chicago X	1976	6.25	12.50	25.00
❑ HC 43900	Chicago IX -- Chicago's Greatest Hits	1982	7.50	15.00	30.00
-- Half-speed mastered edition					
❑ HC 44200	Chicago X	1982	7.50	15.00	30.00
-- Half-speed mastered edition					

MAGNUM

Number	Title	Yr	VG	VG+	NM
❑ MR 604	Chicago Transit Authority Live in Concert	1978	5.00	10.00	20.00
-- Taken from their 1969 Toronto Rock 'n Roll Revival performance					

MOBILE FIDELITY

Number	Title	Yr	VG	VG+	NM
❑ 2-128 [(2)]	Chicago Transit Authority	1983	20.00	40.00	80.00
-- Audiophile vinyl					

REPRISE

Number	Title	Yr	VG	VG+	NM
❑ R 110533	Twenty 1	1991	5.00	10.00	20.00
-- BMG Direct Marketing version					

WARNER BROS.

Number	Title	Yr	VG	VG+	NM
❑ 25060 [DJ]	Chicago 17	1984	5.00	10.00	20.00
-- Promo pressing on Quiex II vinyl					

CHICAGO SYMPHONY ORCHESTRA (PIERRE MONTEUX, CONDUCTOR)
RCA VICTOR RED SEAL

Number	Title	Yr	VG	VG+	NM
❑ LSC-2514 [S]	Franck: Symphony in D	1961	12.50	25.00	50.00
-- Original with "shaded dog" label					

CHICAGO SYMPHONY ORCHESTRA (FRITZ REINER, CONDUCTOR)
RCA VICTOR RED SEAL

Number	Title	Yr	VG	VG+	NM
❑ LSC-1806 [S]	Strauss: Also Sprach Zarathustra	1958	37.50	75.00	150.00
-- Original with "shaded dog" label					
❑ LSC-1806 [S]	Strauss: Also Sprach Zarathustra	199?	6.25	12.50	25.00
-- Classic Records reissue					
❑ LSC-1934 [S]	Bartok: Concerto for Orchestra	1958	30.00	60.00	120.00
-- Original with "shaded dog" label					
❑ LSC-1934 [S]	Bartok: Concerto for Orchestra	199?	6.25	12.50	25.00
-- Classic Records reissue					
❑ LSC-1991 [S]	Beethoven: Symphony No. 7	1958	12.50	25.00	50.00
-- Original with "shaded dog" label					
❑ LSC-2112 [S]	Vienna	1958	18.75	37.50	75.00
-- Original with "shaded dog" label					
❑ LSC-2150 [S]	Prokofiev: Lieutenant Kije; Stravinsky: Song of the Nightingale	1958	10.00	20.00	40.00
-- Original with "shaded dog" label					
❑ LSC-2150 [S]	Prokofiev: Lieutenant Kije; Stravinsky: Song of the Nightingale	1964	15.00	30.00	60.00
-- Second edition with "white dog" label					
❑ LSC-2183 [S]	The Reiner Sound	1958	20.00	40.00	80.00
-- Original with "shaded dog" label					
❑ LSC-2183 [S]	The Reiner Sound	199?	6.25	12.50	25.00
-- Classic Records reissue					
❑ LSC-2201 [S]	Mussorgsky-Ravel: Pictures at an Exhibition	1959	20.00	40.00	80.00
-- Original with "shaded dog" label					
❑ LSC-2201 [S]	Mussorgsky-Ravel: Pictures at an Exhibition	1964	7.50	15.00	30.00
-- Second edition with "white dog" label					
❑ LSC-2209 [S]	Brahms: Symphony No. 3	1959	17.50	35.00	70.00
-- Original with "shaded dog" label					
❑ LSC-2209 [S]	Brahms: Symphony No. 3	1964	17.50	35.00	70.00
-- Second edition with "white dog" label					
❑ LSC-2214 [S]	Dvorak: Symphony No. 9 "From the New World"	1959	5.00	10.00	20.00
-- Original with "shaded dog" label					
❑ LSC-2216 [S]	Tchaikovsky: Symphony No. 6 "Pathetique"	1959	10.00	20.00	40.00
-- Original with "shaded dog" label					
❑ LSC-2222 [S]	Debussy: Iberia	1958	50.00	100.00	200.00
-- Original with "shaded dog" label					
❑ LSC-2222 [S]	Debussy: Iberia	199?	6.25	12.50	25.00
-- Classic Records reissue					
❑ LSC-2230 [S]	Spain	1958	10.00	20.00	40.00
-- Original with "shaded dog" label					
❑ LSC-2230 [S]	Spain	1964	12.50	25.00	50.00
-- Second issue with "white dog" label					
❑ LSC-2230 [S]	Spain	199?	6.25	12.50	25.00
-- Classic Records reissue					
❑ LSC-2241 [S]	Tchaikovsky: 1812 Overture	1958	125.00	250.00	500.00
-- Original with "shaded dog" label					
❑ LSC-2241 [S]	Tchaikovsky: 1812 Overture	199?	6.25	12.50	25.00
-- Classic Records reissue					
❑ LSC-2251 [S]	Hovhaness: Mysterious Mountain; Stravinsky: Divertimento	1959	30.00	60.00	120.00
-- Original with "shaded dog" label					

Number	Title	Yr	VG	VG+	NM
❑ LSC-2251 [S]	Hovhaness: Mysterious Mountain; Stravinsky: Divertimento	1964	17.50	35.00	70.00
-- Second edition with "white dog" label					
❑ LSC-2318 [S]	Rossini: Overtures	1959	12.50	25.00	50.00
-- Original with "shaded dog" label					
❑ LSC-2328 [S]	Tchaikovsky: The Nutcracker	1959	7.50	15.00	30.00
-- Original with "shaded dog" label					
❑ LSC-2343 [S]	Beethoven: Symphony No. 5	1960	12.50	25.00	50.00
-- Original with "shaded dog" label					
❑ LSC-2364 [S]	Mahler: Symphony No. 4	1960	20.00	40.00	80.00
-- Original with "shaded dog" label					
❑ LSC-2364 [S]	Mahler: Symphony No. 4	199?	6.25	12.50	25.00
-- Classic Records reissue					
❑ LSC-2374 [S]	Bartok: Music for Strings, Percussion and Celesta	1959	20.00	40.00	80.00
-- Original with "shaded dog" label					
❑ LSC-2374 [S]	Bartok: Music for Strings, Percussion and Celesta	199?	6.25	12.50	25.00
-- Classic Records reissue					
❑ LDS-2384 [S]	Strauss, Richard: Don Quixote	1960	12.50	25.00	50.00
-- Original with "shaded dog" label					
❑ LSS-2384 [S]	Strauss, Richard: Don Quixote	1960	30.00	60.00	120.00
-- Original with "shaded dog" label; limited edition of 200 in box with booklet					
❑ LSC-2395 [S]	Prokofiev: Alexander Nevsky	1960	12.50	25.00	50.00
-- Original with "shaded dog" label					
❑ LSC-2395 [S]	Prokofiev: Alexander Nevsky	1964	10.00	20.00	40.00
-- Second edition with "white dog" label					
❑ LSC-2423 [S]	Festival	1960	50.00	100.00	200.00
-- Original with "shaded dog" label					
❑ LSC-2423 [S]	Festival	199?	6.25	12.50	25.00
-- Classic Records reissue					
❑ LSC-2436 [S]	Respighi: Pines of Rome; Fountains of Rome	1960	20.00	40.00	80.00
-- Original with "shaded dog" label					
❑ LSC-2436 [S]	Respighi: Pines of Rome; Fountains of Rome	199?	6.25	12.50	25.00
-- Classic Records reissue					
❑ LSC-2441 [S]	Reiner Conducts Wagner	1960	12.50	25.00	50.00
-- Original with "shaded dog" label					
❑ LSC-2441 [S]	Reiner Conducts Wagner	1964	10.00	20.00	40.00
-- Second edition with "white dog" label					
❑ LSC-2446 [S]	Rimsky-Korsakov: Scheherazade	1960	30.00	60.00	120.00
-- Original with "shaded dog" label					
❑ LSC-2446 [S]	Rimsky-Korsakov: Scheherazade	199?	6.25	12.50	25.00
-- Classic Records reissue					
❑ LSC-2462 [S]	Debussy: La Mer; Strauss, Richard: Don Juan	1961	10.00	20.00	40.00
-- Original with "shaded dog" label					
❑ LSC-2462 [S]	Debussy: La Mer; Strauss, Richard: Don Juan	1964	10.00	20.00	40.00
-- Second edition with "white dog" label					
❑ LSC-2496 [S]	The Heart of the Symphony	1961	10.00	20.00	40.00
-- Original with "shaded dog" label					
❑ LSC-2500 [S]	Strauss: Waltzes	1960	25.00	50.00	100.00
-- Original with "shaded dog" label					
❑ LSC-2500 [S]	Strauss: Waltzes	199?	6.25	12.50	25.00
-- Classic Records reissue					
❑ LSC-2516 [S]	Schubert: Symphonies No. 5 and 8	1961	5.00	10.00	20.00
-- Original with "shaded dog" label					
❑ LSC-2609 [S]	Strauss, Richard: Also Sprach Zarathustra	1962	10.00	20.00	40.00
-- Original with "shaded dog" label					
❑ LSC-2609 [S]	Strauss, Richard: Also Sprach Zarathustra	1964	5.00	10.00	20.00
-- Second edition with "white dog" label					
❑ LMD-2614 [M]	Beethoven: Symphony No. 6 "Pastorale"	1962	10.00	20.00	40.00
-- Gatefold with bound-in booklet					
❑ LSC-2614 [S]	Beethoven: Symphony No. 6 "Pastorale"	1962	5.00	10.00	20.00
-- Original with "shaded dog" label; non-gatefold edition					
❑ LSCD-2614 [S]	Beethoven: Symphony No. 6 "Pastorale"	1962	25.00	50.00	100.00
-- Gatefold with bound-in booklet					

CHICKEN SHACK
BLUE HORIZON

Number	Title	Yr	VG	VG+	NM
❑ BH 4809	Accept Chicken Shack	1970	6.25	12.50	25.00
❑ BH 7705	O.K. Ken?	1969	6.25	12.50	25.00
❑ BH 7706	100-Ton Chicken	1969	6.25	12.50	25.00

DERAM

Number	Title	Yr	VG	VG+	NM
❑ DES 18063	Imagination Lady	1972	5.00	10.00	20.00

EPIC

Number	Title	Yr	VG	VG+	NM
❑ LN 24414 [M]	Forty Blue Fingers, Freshly Packed and Ready to Serve	1968	25.00	50.00	100.00
❑ BN 26414 [S]	Forty Blue Fingers, Freshly Packed and Ready to Serve	1968	7.50	15.00	30.00

Number	Title	Yr	VG	VG+	NM
LONDON					
☐ XPS 632	Unlucky Boy	1973	5.00	10.00	20.00
CHIFFONS, THE					
B.T. PUPPY					
☐ S-1011	My Secret Love	1970	100.00	200.00	400.00
LAURIE					
☐ LLP-2018 [M]	He's So Fine	1963	30.00	60.00	120.00
☐ LLP-2020 [M]	One Fine Day	1963	50.00	100.00	200.00
☐ LLP-2036 [M]	Sweet Talkin' Guy	1966	25.00	50.00	100.00
☐ SLP-2036 [S]	Sweet Talkin' Guy	1966	37.50	75.00	150.00
☐ 4001	Everything You Always Wanted to Hear by the Chiffons	1975	5.00	10.00	20.00
☐ DT-90075 [R]	He's So Fine	1965	50.00	100.00	200.00
-- Capitol Record Club edition					
☐ ST-90779 [S]	Sweet Talkin' Guy	1966	50.00	100.00	200.00
-- Capitol Record Club edition					
CHILDRE, LEW					
STARDAY					
☐ SLP-153 [M]	Old Time Get Together	1961	6.25	12.50	25.00
CHILDREN'S CHOIR OF ALL NATIONS, THE					
WARNER BROS.					
☐ W 1231 [M]	Some Children See Him	1958	5.00	10.00	20.00
CHILDREN, THE					
ATCO					
☐ SD 33-271	Rebirth	1968	6.25	12.50	25.00
CINEMA					
☐ CLP-1	Rebirth	1968	37.50	75.00	150.00
CHILLIWACK					
A&M					
☐ SP-3509 [(2)]	Chilliwack	1971	5.00	10.00	20.00
PARROT					
☐ PAS 71040	Chilliwack	1970	5.00	10.00	20.00
CHIPMUNKS, THE, DAVID SEVILLE AND					
Also see ROSS BAGDASARIAN; DAVID SEVILLE.					
LIBERTY					
☐ LRP-3132 [M]	Let's All Sing with the Chipmunks	1959	7.50	15.00	30.00
-- Black vinyl; original cover features "realistic" chipmunks and no reference to "The Alvin Show"					
☐ LRP-3132 [M]	Let's All Sing with the Chipmunks	1959	15.00	30.00	60.00
-- Red vinyl					
☐ LRP-3132 [M]	Let's All Sing with the Chipmunks	1961	5.00	10.00	20.00
-- Second cover features the "cartoon" Chipmunks and a reference to "The Alvin Show"					
☐ LRP-3159 [M]	Sing Again with the Chipmunks	1960	10.00	20.00	40.00
-- Original cover features "realistic" chipmunks					
☐ LRP-3159 [M]	Sing Again with the Chipmunks	1961	5.00	10.00	20.00
-- Second cover features the "cartoon" Chipmunks					
☐ LRP-3170 [M]	Around the World with the Chipmunks	1960	10.00	20.00	40.00
-- Original cover features "realistic" chipmunks on and near a plane					
☐ LRP-3170 [M]	Around the World with the Chipmunks	1961	5.00	10.00	20.00
-- Second cover features the "cartoon" Chipmunks on and near a camel					
☐ LRP-3209 [M]	The Alvin Show	1961	6.25	12.50	25.00
☐ LRP-3229 [M]	The Chipmunks Songbook	1962	6.25	12.50	25.00
☐ LRP-3256 [M]	Christmas with the Chipmunks	1962	6.25	12.50	25.00
☐ LRP-3334 [M]	Christmas with the Chipmunks, Vol. 2	1963	6.25	12.50	25.00
☐ LRP-3388 [M]	The Chipmunks Sing the Beatles Hits	1964	7.50	15.00	30.00
☐ LRP-3405 [M]	The Chipmunks Sing with Children	1965	5.00	10.00	20.00
☐ LRP-3424 [M]	The Chipmunks A-Go-Go	1965	5.00	10.00	20.00
☐ LST-7132 [S]	Let's All Sing with the Chipmunks	1959	20.00	40.00	80.00
-- Red vinyl					
☐ LST-7132 [S]	Let's All Sing with the Chipmunks	1959	10.00	20.00	40.00
-- Black vinyl; original cover features "realistic" chipmunks and no reference to "The Alvin Show"					
☐ LST-7132 [S]	Let's All Sing with the Chipmunks	1961	6.25	12.50	25.00
-- Second cover features the "cartoon" Chipmunks and a reference to "The Alvin Show"					
☐ LST-7159 [S]	Sing Again with the Chipmunks	1960	12.50	25.00	50.00
-- Original cover features "realistic" chipmunks					
☐ LST-7159 [S]	Sing Again with the Chipmunks	1961	6.25	12.50	25.00
-- Second cover features the "cartoon" Chipmunks					
☐ LST-7170 [S]	Around the World with the Chipmunks	1960	12.50	25.00	50.00
-- Original covers have "realistic" chipmunks on and near a plane.					
☐ LST-7170 [S]	Around the World with the Chipmunks	1960	6.25	12.50	25.00
-- Second cover features the "cartoon" Chipmunks on and near a camel					
☐ LST-7209 [S]	The Alvin Show	1961	7.50	15.00	30.00
☐ LST-7229 [S]	The Chipmunks Songbook	1962	7.50	15.00	30.00

Number	Title	Yr	VG	VG+	NM
☐ LST-7256 [S]	Christmas with the Chipmunks	1962	7.50	15.00	30.00
☐ LST-7334 [S]	Christmas with the Chipmunks, Vol. 2	1963	7.50	15.00	30.00
☐ LST-7388 [S]	The Chipmunks Sing the Beatles Hits	1964	10.00	20.00	40.00
☐ LST-7405 [S]	The Chipmunks Sing with Children	1965	6.25	12.50	25.00
☐ LST-7424 [S]	The Chipmunks A-Go-Go	1965	6.25	12.50	25.00
SUNSET					
☐ LST-7334 [S]	Christmas with the Chipmunks, Vol. 2	1968	5.00	10.00	20.00
-- Budget-line reissue of Liberty LST-7334					
UNITED ARTISTS					
☐ UA-LA352-E2 [(2)]	Christmas with the Chipmunks	1974	5.00	10.00	20.00
-- Entire contents of both original Liberty LPs					
CHOATES, HARRY					
D					
☐ 7000 [M]	Jole Blon	196?	10.00	20.00	40.00
CHOCO AND HIS MALIMBA DRUM RHYTHMS					
AUDIO FIDELITY					
☐ AFLP-2102 [M]	African Latin Voodoo Drums	1962	5.00	10.00	20.00
☐ AFSD-6102 [S]	African Latin Voodoo Drums	1962	7.50	15.00	30.00
CHOCOLATE WATCH BAND, THE					
TOWER					
☐ ST 5096 [S]	No Way Out	1967	100.00	200.00	400.00
☐ T 5096 [M]	No Way Out	1967	75.00	150.00	300.00
☐ ST 5106 [S]	The Inner Mystique	1968	75.00	150.00	300.00
☐ T 5106 [M]	The Inner Mystique	1968	100.00	200.00	400.00
☐ ST 5153	One Step Beyond	1969	75.00	150.00	300.00
CHORDETTES, THE					
CADENCE					
☐ CLP-1002 [10]	Close Harmony	1955	12.50	25.00	50.00
☐ CLP-3001 [M]	The Chordettes	1957	10.00	20.00	40.00
☐ CLP-3020 [M]	Barbershop Harmony	1958	10.00	20.00	40.00
☐ CLP-3056 [M]	Never on Sunday	1962	5.00	10.00	20.00
☐ CLP-25056 [S]	Never on Sunday	1962	7.50	15.00	30.00
COLUMBIA					
☐ CL 956 [M]	Listen	1955	12.50	25.00	50.00
☐ CL 2519 [10]	The Chordettes	1955	10.00	20.00	40.00
☐ CL 6111 [10]	Harmony Time	1950	12.50	25.00	50.00
☐ CL 6170 [10]	Harmony Time, Vol. 2	1951	12.50	25.00	50.00
☐ CL 6218 [10]	Harmony Encores	1952	12.50	25.00	50.00
☐ CL 6285 [10]	Your Requests	1953	12.50	25.00	50.00
CHOSEN FEW, THE					
MAPLE					
☐ 6000	Takin' All the Love I Can	196?	5.00	10.00	20.00
RCA VICTOR					
☐ LSP-4242	The Chosen Few	1969	5.00	10.00	20.00
CHRISTIE, LOU					
CO & CE					
☐ LP-1231 [M]	Lou Christie Strikes Back	1966	10.00	20.00	40.00
☐ LPS-1231 [S]	Lou Christie Strikes Back	1966	15.00	30.00	60.00
COLPIX					
☐ CP-4001 [M]	Lou Christie Strikes Again	1966	7.50	5.00	30.00
☐ SCP-4001 [S]	Lou Christie Strikes Again	1966	12.50	25.00	50.00
MGM					
☐ SE-4360 [S]	Lightnin' Strikes	1966	5.00	10.00	20.00
☐ SE-4394 [S]	Painter of Hits	1966	5.00	10.00	20.00
ROULETTE					
☐ R 25208 [M]	Lou Christie	1963	12.50	25.00	50.00
-- Blue background on front cover					
☐ R 25208 [M]	Lou Christie	1963	10.00	20.00	40.00
-- White wall in background on front cover					
☐ SR 25208 [S]	Lou Christie	1963	20.00	40.00	80.00
-- Blue background on front cover					
☐ SR 25208 [S]	Lou Christie	1963	15.00	30.00	60.00
-- White wall in background on front cover					
☐ R 25332 [M]	Lou Christie Strikes Again	1966	6.25	12.50	25.00
☐ SR 25332 [S]	Lou Christie Strikes Again	1966	7.50	15.00	30.00
SPIN-O-RAMA					
☐ M-173 [M]	Starring Lou Christie and the Classics	1966	5.00	10.00	20.00
THREE BROTHERS					
☐ THB-2000	Lou Christie	1973	5.00	10.00	20.00

Number	Title	Yr	VG	VG+	NM

CHRISTOPHER
BELL
| ❏ 1203 | R.P.M. | 1970 | 5.00 | 10.00 | 20.00 |

CHRIS-TEE
| ❏ 12411 | What'cha Gonna Do | 1970 | 1,500. | 2,250. | 3,000. |

METROMEDIA
| ❏ 1024 | Christopher | 1970 | 75.00 | 150.00 | 300.00 |

CHRISTY, JUNE
CAPITOL
❏ H 516 [10]	Something Cool	1954	20.00	40.00	80.00
❏ T 516 [M]	Something Cool	1955	12.50	25.00	50.00
-- Turquoise label					
❏ T 516 [M]	Something Cool	1959	6.25	12.50	25.00
-- Black label with colorband					
❏ T 656 [M]	Duets	1955	10.00	20.00	40.00
-- Turquoise label					
❏ T 725 [M]	The Misty Miss Christy	1956	10.00	20.00	40.00
-- Turquoise label					
❏ T 833 [M]	June -- Fair and Warmer!	1957	10.00	20.00	40.00
-- Turquoise label					
❏ T 902 [M]	Gone for the Day	1957	10.00	20.00	40.00
-- Turquoise label					
❏ T 1006 [M]	This Is June Christy!	1958	10.00	20.00	40.00
-- Turquoise label					
❏ ST 1076 [S]	June's Got Rhythm	1958	10.00	20.00	40.00
-- Black label with colorband, Capitol logo at left					
❏ T 1076 [M]	June's Got Rhythm	1958	7.50	15.00	30.00
-- Black label with colorband, Capitol logo at left					
❏ ST 1114 [S]	The Song Is June!	1959	10.00	20.00	40.00
-- Black label with colorband, Capitol logo at left					
❏ T 1114 [M]	The Song Is June!	1959	7.50	15.00	30.00
-- Black label with colorband, Capitol logo at left					
❏ ST 1202 [S]	June Christy Recalls Those Kenton Days	1959	10.00	20.00	40.00
-- Black label with colorband, Capitol logo at left					
❏ T 1202 [M]	June Christy Recalls Those Kenton Days	1959	7.50	15.00	30.00
-- Black label with colorband, Capitol logo at left					
❏ ST 1308 [S]	Ballads for Night People	1959	10.00	20.00	40.00
-- Black label with colorband, Capitol logo at left					
❏ T 1308 [M]	Ballads for Night People	1959	7.50	15.00	30.00
-- Black label with colorband, Capitol logo at left					
❏ STBO 1327 [(2) S]	Road Show	1960	10.00	20.00	40.00
-- Black label with colorband, Capitol logo at left					
❏ TBO 1327 [(2) M]	Road Show	1960	7.50	15.00	30.00
-- Black label with colorband, Capitol logo at left					
❏ ST 1398 [S]	The Cool School	1960	10.00	20.00	40.00
-- Black label with colorband, Capitol logo at left					
❏ T 1398 [M]	The Cool School	1960	7.50	15.00	30.00
-- Black label with colorband, Capitol logo at left					
❏ ST 1498 [S]	Off Beat	1961	12.50	25.00	50.00
-- Black label with colorband, Capitol logo at left					
❏ T 1498 [M]	Off Beat	1961	10.00	20.00	40.00
-- Black label with colorband, Capitol logo at left					
❏ ST 1586 [S]	Do-Re-Mi	1961	12.50	25.00	50.00
-- Black label with colorband, Capitol logo at left					
❏ T 1586 [M]	Do-Re-Mi	1961	10.00	20.00	40.00
-- Black label with colorband, Capitol logo at left					
❏ ST 1605 [S]	That Time of Year	1961	12.50	25.00	50.00
-- Black label with colorband, Capitol logo at left					
❏ T 1605 [M]	That Time of Year	1961	10.00	20.00	40.00
❏ ST 1693 [S]	The Best of June Christy	1962	7.50	15.00	30.00
-- Black logo with colorband					
❏ T 1693 [M]	The Best of June Christy	1962	6.25	12.50	25.00
-- Black label with colorband					
❏ ST 1845 [S]	Big Band Specials	1962	6.25	12.50	25.00
❏ T 1845 [M]	Big Band Specials	1962	5.00	10.00	20.00
❏ ST 1953 [S]	The Intimate June Christy	1963	6.25	12.50	25.00
❏ T 1953 [M]	The Intimate June Christy	1963	5.00	10.00	20.00
❏ ST 2410 [S]	Something Broadway, Something Latin	1965	7.50	15.00	30.00
❏ T 2410 [M]	Something Broadway, Something Latin	1965	6.25	12.50	25.00

CHRYSALIS
MGM
| ❏ SE-4547 | Definition | 1968 | 7.50 | 15.00 | 30.00 |

CHURCH, THE
ARISTA
| ❏ ADP 9713 [DJ] | Sum of the Parts | 1988 | 10.00 | 20.00 | 40.00 |
| -- Interviews and live acoustic tracks | | | | | |

CIRCUS
METROMEDIA
| ❏ 7401 | Circus | 1973 | 7.50 | 15.00 | 30.00 |

CIRCUS MAXIMUS
Also see JERRY JEFF WALKER.
VANGUARD
❏ VRS-9260 [M]	Circus Maximus	1967	5.00	10.00	20.00
❏ VSD-79260 [S]	Circus Maximus	1967	6.25	12.50	25.00
❏ VSD-79274	Neverland Revisited	1968	6.25	12.50	25.00

CITY, THE
❏ Also see CAROLE KING.
ODE
| ❏ Z12 44012 | Now That Everything's Been Said | 1968 | 20.00 | 40.00 | 80.00 |
| -- Color front cover | | | | | |

CLANTON, JIMMY
ACE
❏ DLP-100 [M]	Jimmy's Happy/Jimmy's Blue	1960	100.00	200.00	400.00
-- The "Happy" album is red vinyl, the "Blue" album is blue					
❏ DLP-100 [M]	Jimmy's Happy/Jimmy's Blue	1960	37.50	75.00	150.00
-- Black vinyl; also released as two separate albums, 1007 and 1008					
❏ DLP-100	Jimmy's Happy/Jimmy's Blue Poster	1960	20.00	40.00	80.00
❏ 1001 [M]	Just a Dream	1959	30.00	60.00	120.00
❏ 1007 [M]	Jimmy's Happy	1960	10.00	20.00	40.00
❏ 1008 [M]	Jimmy's Blue	1960	10.00	20.00	40.00
❏ 1011 [M]	My Best to You	1960	25.00	50.00	100.00
❏ 1014 [M]	Teenage Millionaire	1961	25.00	50.00	100.00
❏ 1026 [M]	Venus in Blue Jeans	1962	25.00	50.00	100.00
PHILIPS
| ❏ PHM 200-154 [M] | The Best of Jimmy Clanton | 1964 | 6.25 | 12.50 | 25.00 |
| ❏ PHS 600-154 [S] | The Best of Jimmy Clanton | 1964 | 7.50 | 15.00 | 30.00 |

CLAP
NOVA SOL
| ❏ 1001 | Have You Reached Yet? | 1970 | 250.00 | 500.00 | 1,000. |

CLAPTON, ERIC
ATCO
❏ 33-329 [DJ]	Eric Clapton	1970	25.00	50.00	100.00
-- Mono pressing is promo only					
❏ SD 33-329	Eric Clapton	1970	5.00	10.00	20.00
❏ SD 33-329	Eric Clapton	1970	50.00	100.00	200.00
-- Odd pressing with alternate takes of "After Midnight" and "Blues Power" plus remixes of other tracks. Look for "CTH" in trail-off area.					
❏ SD 2-803 [(2)]	History of Eric Clapton	1972	5.00	10.00	20.00
-- Contains tracks from the Yardbirds, John Mayall's Bluesbreakers, Cream, Blind Faith, and solo records					
DUCK
| ❏ W1-26420 [(2)] | 24 Nights | 1991 | 6.25 | 12.50 | 25.00 |
| -- Vinyl copies released only through Columbia House | | | | | |
MOBILE FIDELITY
❏ 1-030	Slowhand	1980	17.50	35.00	70.00
-- Audiophile vinyl					
❏ 1-220	Eric Clapton	1995	6.25	12.50	25.00
-- Audiophile vinyl					
NAUTILUS
| ❏ NR-32 [(2)] | Just One Night | 1981 | 37.50 | 75.00 | 150.00 |
| -- Audiophile vinyl | | | | | |
POLYDOR
❏ 24-3503 [(2)]	Eric Clapton at His Best	1972	5.00	10.00	20.00
-- Compiles tracks from his first solo album plus Derek and the Dominos					
❏ 835 261-1 [(6)]	Crossroads	1988	12.50	25.00	50.00
-- Box set; contains material from all phases of his career					
RSO
❏ 035 [DJ]	Slowhand	1977	6.25	12.50	25.00
-- White vinyl promo					
❏ 1009 [DJ]	Limited Backless	1978	10.00	20.00	40.00
-- White vinyl promo					
❏ QD 4801 [Q]	461 Ocean Boulevard	1974	6.25	12.50	25.00
❏ QD 4806 [Q]	There's One in Every Crowd	1975	6.25	12.50	25.00

CLARK SISTERS, THE
CORAL
| ❏ CRL 57290 [M] | Beauty Shop Beat | 1960 | 5.00 | 10.00 | 20.00 |
| ❏ CRL 757290 [S] | Beauty Shop Beat | 1960 | 6.25 | 12.50 | 25.00 |
DOT
❏ DLP-3104 [M]	Sing, Sing, Sing	1957	7.50	15.00	30.00
❏ DLP-3137 [M]	The Clark Sisters Swing Again	1958	6.25	12.50	25.00
❏ DLP 25137 [S]	The Clark Sisters Swing Again	1958	7.50	15.00	30.00

Number	Title	Yr	VG	VG+	NM

CLARK, CHRIS
MOTOWN

Number	Title	Yr	VG	VG+	NM
❑ M-664 [M]	Soul Sounds	1967	12.50	25.00	50.00
❑ MS-664 [S]	Soul Sounds	1967	15.00	30.00	60.00

WEED

| ❑ 801 | C.C. Rides Again | 1969 | 20.00 | 40.00 | 80.00 |

CLARK, CLAUDINE
CHANCELLOR

| ❑ CHL-5029 [M] | Party Lights | 1962 | 62.50 | 125.00 | 250.00 |

CLARK, DAVE, FIVE
CORTLEIGH

| ❑ C-1073 [M] | The Dave Clark Five with Ricky Astor | 1964 | 7.50 | 15.00 | 30.00 |

-- With two early DC5 tracks and assorted other stuff by other artists

CROWN

| ❑ CLP-5400 [M] | The Dave Clark Five with the Playbacks | 1964 | 7.50 | 15.00 | 30.00 |

-- With two early DC5 tracks and assorted other stuff by other artists

| ❑ CLP-5473 [M] | Chaquita/In Your Heart | 1964 | 7.50 | 15.00 | 30.00 |

-- With two early DC5 tracks and assorted other stuff by other artists

EPIC

| ❑ LN 24093 [M] | Glad All Over | 1964 | 20.00 | 40.00 | 80.00 |

-- Group photo, no instruments

| ❑ LN 24093 [M] | Glad All Over | 1964 | 10.00 | 20.00 | 40.00 |

-- Group photo with instruments

❑ LN 24104 [M]	The Dave Clark Five Return	1964	10.00	20.00	40.00
❑ LN 24117 [M]	American Tour	1964	10.00	20.00	40.00
❑ LN 24128 [M]	Coast to Coast	1965	10.00	20.00	40.00
❑ LN 24139 [M]	Weekend in London	1965	10.00	20.00	40.00
❑ LN 24162 [M]	Having a Wild Weekend	1965	10.00	20.00	40.00
❑ LN 24178 [M]	I Like It Like That	1965	10.00	20.00	40.00
❑ LN 24185 [M]	The Dave Clark Five's Greatest Hits	1966	6.25	12.50	25.00
❑ LN 24198 [M]	Try Too Hard	1966	7.50	15.00	30.00
❑ LN 24212 [M]	Satisfied with You	1966	7.50	15.00	30.00
❑ LN 24221 [M]	More Greatest Hits	1966	6.25	12.50	25.00
❑ LN 24236 [M]	5 by 5	1967	7.50	15.00	30.00
❑ LN 24312 [M]	You Got What It Takes	1967	7.50	15.00	30.00
❑ LN 24354 [M]	Everybody Knows	1968	7.50	15.00	30.00
❑ BN 26093 [R]	Glad All Over	1964	12.50	25.00	50.00

-- Group photo, no instruments

| ❑ BN 26093 [R] | Glad All Over | 1964 | 7.50 | 15.00 | 30.00 |

-- Group photo with instruments

❑ BN 26104 [R]	The Dave Clark Five Return	1964	7.50	15.00	30.00
❑ BN 26117 [R]	American Tour	1964	7.50	15.00	30.00
❑ BN 26128 [R]	Coast to Coast	1965	7.50	15.00	30.00
❑ BN 26139 [R]	Weekend in London	1965	7.50	15.00	30.00
❑ BN 26162 [R]	Having a Wild Weekend	1965	7.50	15.00	30.00
❑ BN 26178 [R]	I Like It Like That	1965	7.50	15.00	30.00
❑ BN 26185 [R]	The Dave Clark Five's Greatest Hits	1966	5.00	10.00	20.00

-- Yellow label

| ❑ BN 26185 [R] | The Dave Clark Five's Greatest Hits | 1973 | 10.00 | 20.00 | 40.00 |

-- Orange label

❑ BN 26198 [R]	Try Too Hard	1966	6.25	12.50	25.00
❑ BN 26212 [R]	Satisfied with You	1966	6.25	12.50	25.00
❑ BN 26221 [R]	More Greatest Hits	1966	5.00	10.00	20.00
❑ BN 26236 [S]	5 by 5	1967	10.00	20.00	40.00
❑ BN 26312 [S]	You Got What It Takes	1967	10.00	20.00	40.00
❑ BN 26354 [S]	Everybody Knows	1968	10.00	20.00	40.00
❑ EG 30434 [(2)]	The Dave Clark Five	1971	25.00	50.00	100.00

-- Twenty hits and near-hits, all in true stereo! Yellow label.

| ❑ EG 30434 [(2)] | The Dave Clark Five | 1973 | 20.00 | 40.00 | 80.00 |

-- Twenty hits and near-hits, all in true stereo! Orange label.

| ❑ KEG 33459 [(2) M] | Glad All Over Again | 1975 | 12.50 | 25.00 | 50.00 |
| ❑ XEM 77238/9 [DJ] | The Dave Clark Five Interview | 1964 | 150.00 | 300.00 | 600.00 |

CLARK, DEE
ABNER

❑ LP-2000 [M]	Dee Clark	1959	30.00	60.00	120.00
❑ SR-2000 [S]	Dee Clark	1959	87.50	175.00	350.00
❑ LP-2002 [M]	How About That	1960	20.00	40.00	80.00
❑ SR-2002 [S]	How About That	1960	30.00	60.00	120.00

VEE JAY

❑ LP-1019 [M]	You're Looking Good	1960	12.50	25.00	50.00
❑ LP-1037 [M]	Hold On, It's Dee Clark	1961	12.50	25.00	50.00
❑ SR-1037 [S]	Hold On, It's Dee Clark	1961	25.00	50.00	100.00
❑ LP-1047 [M]	The Best of Dee Clark	1964	12.50	25.00	50.00
❑ SR-1047 [S]	The Best of Dee Clark	1964	25.00	50.00	100.00

CLARK, DICK -- See VARIOUS ARTISTS COLLECTIONS (back of book).

CLARK, DOUG, AND THE HOT NUTS
GROSS

❑ 101	Nuts to You	196?	7.50	15.00	30.00
❑ 102	On Campus	196?	7.50	15.00	30.00
❑ 103	Homecoming	196?	7.50	15.00	30.00
❑ 104	Rush Week	1967	7.50	15.00	30.00
❑ 105	Panty Raid	196?	7.50	15.00	30.00
❑ 106	Summer Session	196?	7.50	15.00	30.00
❑ 107	Hell Night	196?	7.50	15.00	30.00
❑ 108	Freak Out	196?	7.50	15.00	30.00
❑ 109	With a Hat On	196?	7.50	15.00	30.00

CLARK, GENE
Also see THE BYRDS.
COLUMBIA

| ❑ CL 2618 [M] | Gene Clark with the Gosdin Brothers | 1967 | 7.50 | 15.00 | 30.00 |
| ❑ CS 9418 [S] | Gene Clark with the Gosdin Brothers | 1967 | 12.50 | 25.00 | 50.00 |

RSO

| ❑ RS-1-3011 | Two Sides to Every Story | 1976 | 5.00 | 10.00 | 20.00 |

CLARK, GUY
RCA VICTOR

| ❑ APL1-1303 | Old No. 1 | 1976 | 5.00 | 10.00 | 20.00 |
| ❑ APL1-1944 | Texas Cookin' | 1976 | 5.00 | 10.00 | 20.00 |

CLARK, KEN, AND DON ANTHONY
STARDAY

| ❑ SLP-114 [M] | Fiddlin' Country Style | 1959 | 10.00 | 20.00 | 40.00 |

CLARK, PETULA
COCA-COLA

| ❑ 103 [DJ] | Petula Clark Swings the Jingle | 1966 | 37.50 | 75.00 | 150.00 |

IMPERIAL

| ❑ LP-9079 [M] | Pet Clark | 1959 | 12.50 | 25.00 | 50.00 |
| ❑ LP-9281 [M] | Uptown with Petula Clark | 1965 | 5.00 | 10.00 | 20.00 |

-- Reissue of Imperial 9079

| ❑ LP-12079 [S] | Pet Clark | 1959 | 20.00 | 40.00 | 80.00 |
| ❑ LP-12281 [S] | Uptown with Petula Clark | 1965 | 6.25 | 12.50 | 25.00 |

-- Reissue of Imperial 12079

LAURIE

| ❑ ST-90497 [S] | In Love! | 1965 | 5.00 | 10.00 | 20.00 |

-- Capitol Record Club edition

ROULETTE

| ❑ 1 [(3)] | Petula | 1975 | 5.00 | 10.00 | 20.00 |

WARNER BROS.

| ❑ WS 1590 [S] | Downtown | 1965 | 5.00 | 10.00 | 20.00 |

-- Originals have gold labels

| ❑ WS 1598 [S] | I Know a Place | 1965 | 5.00 | 10.00 | 20.00 |

-- Originals have gold labels

| ❑ WS 1608 [S] | The World's Greatest International Hits | 1965 | 5.00 | 10.00 | 20.00 |

-- Originals have gold labels

| ❑ ST-93215 [(2) P] | Hits...My Way | 1969 | 6.25 | 12.50 | 25.00 |

-- Capitol Record Club exclusive; "The Other Man's Grass Is Always Greener" is rechanneled.

CLARK, ROY
CAPITOL

❑ ST 1780 [S]	The Lightning Fingers of Roy	1962	6.25	12.50	25.00
❑ T 1780 [M]	The Lightning Fingers of Roy	1962	5.00	10.00	20.00
❑ ST 1972 [S]	The Tip of My Fingers	1963	6.25	12.50	25.00
❑ T 1972 [M]	The Tip of My Fingers	1963	5.00	10.00	20.00
❑ ST 2031 [S]	Happy to Be Unhappy	1964	6.25	12.50	25.00
❑ T 2031 [M]	Happy to Be Unhappy	1964	5.00	10.00	20.00
❑ ST 2425 [S]	The Roy Clark Guitar Spectacular	1965	6.25	12.50	25.00
❑ T 2425 [M]	The Roy Clark Guitar Spectacular	1965	5.00	10.00	20.00
❑ ST 2452 [S]	Roy Clark Sings Lonesome Love Ballads	1966	6.25	12.50	25.00
❑ T 2452 [M]	Roy Clark Sings Lonesome Love Ballads	1966	5.00	10.00	20.00
❑ ST 2535 [S]	Stringing Along with the Blues	1966	6.25	12.50	25.00
❑ T 2535 [M]	Stringing Along with the Blues	1966	5.00	10.00	20.00

TOWER

| ❑ ST 5055 [S] | Roy Clark Live | 1967 | 5.00 | 10.00 | 20.00 |

CLARK, SANFORD
LHI

| ❑ 12003 | Return of the Fool | 1968 | 15.00 | 30.00 | 60.00 |

CLARK, YODELING SLIM
CONTINENTAL

| ❑ C-1505 [M] | Cowboy and Yodel Songs | 1962 | 10.00 | 20.00 | 40.00 |

MASTERSEAL

| ❑ MS-57 [M] | Cowboy Songs | 1963 | 6.25 | 12.50 | 25.00 |

Number	Title	Yr	VG	VG+	NM
❏ MS-112 [M]	Songs by Yodeling Slim Clark	1964	6.25	12.50	25.00
❏ MS-135 [M]	Cowboy Songs Vol. 2	1964	6.25	12.50	25.00
PALOMINO					
❏ 300 [M]	Yodeling Slim Clark Sings the Legendary Jimmie Rodgers Songs	1966	15.00	30.00	60.00
❏ 301 [M]	Yodeling Slim Clark Sings and Yodels Favorite Montana Slim Songs of the Mountains and Plains, Vol. 1	1966	15.00	30.00	60.00
❏ 303 [M]	Yodeling Slim Clark Sings and Yodels Favorite Montana Slim Songs of the Mountains and Plains, Vol. 2	1966	10.00	20.00	40.00
❏ 306 [M]	I Feel a Trip Coming On	1966	10.00	20.00	40.00
❏ 307 [M]	Old Chestnuts	1967	10.00	20.00	40.00
❏ 310 [M]	Yodeling Slim Clark Happens Again	1967	10.00	20.00	40.00
❏ 311 [M]	The Ballad of Billy Venero	1968	10.00	20.00	40.00
❏ 314 [M]	Yodeling Slim Clark's 50th Anniversary Album	1968	12.50	25.00	50.00
-- Gold vinyl					
PLAYHOUSE					
❏ 2017 [10]	Western Songs and Dances	1954	12.50	25.00	50.00

CLARY, ROBERT
ATLANTIC

Number	Title	Yr	VG	VG+	NM
❏ 8053 [M]	Livin' It Up at the Playboy Club	1961	7.50	15.00	30.00
❏ SD 8053 [S]	Livin' It Up at the Playboy Club	1961	10.00	20.00	40.00
EPIC					
❏ LN 3171 [M]	Meet Robert Clary	1955	6.25	12.50	25.00
❏ LN 3281 [M]	Hooray for Love	1956	6.25	12.50	25.00
MERCURY					
❏ MG-20367 [M]	Gigi Sung by Robert Clary	1958	5.00	10.00	20.00
❏ SR-60042 [S]	Gigi Sung by Robert Clary	1958	7.50	15.00	30.00

CLASH, THE
EPIC

Number	Title	Yr	VG	VG+	NM
❏ AS 913 [DJ]	Sandinista Now!	1981	5.00	10.00	20.00
-- Promo-only sampler					
❏ AS 952 [DJ]	If Music Could Talk (Interchords)	1981	7.50	15.00	30.00
-- Promo-only interview record					
❏ AS 99-1592 [PD]	Combat Rock	1982	10.00	20.00	40.00
-- Promo-only picture disc					
❏ AS 1594 [DJ]	The World According to the Clash	1982	10.00	20.00	40.00
-- Promo-only sampler					
❏ AS 99-1595 [DJ]	Combat Rock	1982	7.50	15.00	30.00
-- Camouflage green vinyl promo					
❏ JE 35543 [DJ]	Give 'Em Enough Rope	1978	7.50	15.00	30.00
-- White label promo; timing strip; back cover has one incorrect song title					
❏ E2 36238 [DJ]	London Calling	1980	6.25	12.50	25.00
-- White label promo					
❏ E3X 37037 [(3)]	Sandinista!	1981	5.00	10.00	20.00
EPIC LEGACY					
❏ E3 53191 [(3) 10]	Super Black Market Clash	1993	5.00	10.00	20.00

CLASS-AIRES, THE
HONEY BEE

Number	Title	Yr	VG	VG+	NM
❏ (# unknown)	Tears Start to Fall	195?	75.00	150.00	300.00

CLASSICS IV
IMPERIAL

Number	Title	Yr	VG	VG+	NM
❏ LP-12371	Spooky	1968	5.00	10.00	20.00
❏ LP-12407	Mamas and Papas/Soul Train	1969	5.00	10.00	20.00
❏ LP-12429	Traces	1969	5.00	10.00	20.00
❏ LP-16000	Dennis Yost & the Classics IV/ Golden Greats - Volume I	1969	5.00	10.00	20.00

CLAUSON, WILLIAM
CAPITOL

Number	Title	Yr	VG	VG+	NM
❏ T 10158 [M]	Concert	195?	6.25	12.50	25.00
❏ T 10176 [M]	Scandinavia	195?	6.25	12.50	25.00
RCA VICTOR					
❏ LPM-1286 [M]	Folk Songs	1956	7.50	15.00	30.00

CLAY, CASSIUS
COLUMBIA

Number	Title	Yr	VG	VG+	NM
❏ CL 2093 [M]	I Am the Greatest!	1963	10.00	20.00	40.00
❏ CS 8893 [S]	I Am the Greatest!	1963	12.50	25.00	50.00

CLAY, OTIS
HI

Number	Title	Yr	VG	VG+	NM
❏ SHL 32075	Trying to Live My Life Without You	1972	5.00	10.00	20.00

CLAYTON, PAUL
ELEKTRA

Number	Title	Yr	VG	VG+	NM
❏ EKL-147 [M]	Unholy Matrimony	1958	7.50	15.00	30.00
❏ EKL-155 [M]	Bobby Burns' Merry Muses	1958	7.50	15.00	30.00
FOLKWAYS					
❏ FA-2007 [M]	Cumberland Mountain Folksongs	1957	15.00	30.00	60.00
❏ FA-2106 [M]	Bay State Ballads	1956	15.00	30.00	60.00
❏ FA-2110 [M]	Folksongs and Ballads of Virginia	1956	15.00	30.00	60.00
❏ FA-2310 [M]	Folk Ballads of the English-Speaking World	1956	15.00	30.00	60.00
❏ FA-2429 [M]	Foc'sle Songs and Shanties	1959	7.50	15.00	30.00
❏ FW-8708 [M]	British Broadside Ballads in Popular Tradition	1957	10.00	20.00	40.00
MONUMENT					
❏ MLP-8017 [M]	Folk Singer	1965	5.00	10.00	20.00
❏ SLP-18017 [S]	Folk Singer	1965	6.25	12.50	25.00
RIVERSIDE					
❏ RLP 12-615 [M]	Bloody Ballads	1957	7.50	15.00	30.00
❏ RLP 12-640 [M]	Wanted for Murder -- American Folksongs of Outlaws and Desperadoes	1958	7.50	15.00	30.00
❏ RLP 12-648 [M]	Timber-r-r! -- Folk Songs and Ballads of the Lumberjack	1958	7.50	15.00	30.00
STINSON					
❏ SLP-69 [10]	Whaling Songs and Ballads	1958	10.00	20.00	40.00
❏ SLP-70 [10]	Waters of Tyme -- English North Country Songs	1958	10.00	20.00	40.00
TRADITION					
❏ TLP-1005 [M]	Whaling and Sailing Songs from the Days of Moby Dick	1956	7.50	15.00	30.00

CLAYTON-THOMAS, DAVID
Also see BLOOD, SWEAT AND TEARS.
DECCA

Number	Title	Yr	VG	VG+	NM
❏ DL 75146	David Clayton-Thomas!	1969	5.00	10.00	20.00
RCA VICTOR					
❏ APD1-0173 [Q]	Harmony Junction	1973	5.00	10.00	20.00

CLEANLINESS AND GODLINESS SKIFFLE BAND, THE
Also see THE MASKED MARAUDERS.
VANGUARD

Number	Title	Yr	VG	VG+	NM
❏ VSD-79285	Greatest Hits	1968	6.25	12.50	25.00

CLEAR LIGHT
Cliff DeYoung was in this group.
ELEKTRA

Number	Title	Yr	VG	VG+	NM
❏ EKL-4011 [M]	Clear Light	1967	6.25	12.50	25.00
❏ EKS-74011 [S]	Clear Light	1967	6.25	12.50	25.00

CLEARY, DON
PALOMINO

Number	Title	Yr	VG	VG+	NM
❏ 302 [M]	Don Cleary Sings Traditional Cowboy Songs	1966	12.50	25.00	50.00

CLEAVER, ELDRIDGE
MORE

Number	Title	Yr	VG	VG+	NM
❏ 4000 [M]	Soul On Wax	1968	6.25	12.50	25.00

CLEFTONES, THE
GEE

Number	Title	Yr	VG	VG+	NM
❏ GLP-705 [M]	Heart and Soul	1961	50.00	100.00	200.00
❏ SGLP-705 [S]	Heart and Soul	1961	125.00	250.00	500.00
❏ GLP-707 [M]	For Sentimental Reasons	1961	62.50	125.00	250.00
❏ SGLP-707 [S]	For Sentimental Reasons	1961	300.00	600.00	1,200.

CLIBURN, VAN
RCA VICTOR RED SEAL

Number	Title	Yr	VG	VG+	NM
❏ LM-2252 [M]	Tchaikovsky: Piano Concerto No. 1	1958	6.25	12.50	25.00
❏ LSC-2252 [S]	Tchaikovsky: Piano Concerto No. 1	1958	7.50	15.00	30.00
-- "Shaded dog" pressing ("Living Stereo" on label)					
❏ LSC-2252 [S]	Tchaikovsky: Piano Concerto No. 1	1965	5.00	10.00	20.00
-- "White dog" pressing ("Stereo" on label)					
❏ LM-2355 [M]	Rachmaninoff: Piano Concerto No. 3	1959	6.25	12.50	25.00
❏ LSC-2355 [S]	Rachmaninoff: Piano Concerto No. 3	1959	7.50	15.00	30.00
-- "Shaded dog" pressing ("Living Stereo" on label)					
❏ LSC-2355 [S]	Rachmaninoff: Piano Concerto No. 3	1965	5.00	10.00	20.00
-- "White dog" pressing ("Stereo" on label)					

Number	Title	Yr	VG	VG+	NM
❏ LSC-2455 [S]	Schumann: Piano Concerto in A Minor	1960	7.50	15.00	30.00
-- "Shaded dog" pressing ("Living Stereo" on label)					
❏ LSC-2455 [S]	Schumann: Piano Concerto in A Minor	1965	5.00	10.00	20.00
-- "White dog" pressing ("Stereo" on label)					
❏ LSC-2507 [S]	Prokofiev: Piano Concerto No. 3; MacDowell: Piano Concerto No. 2	1961	12.50	25.00	50.00
-- "Shaded dog" pressing ("Living Stereo" on label)					
❏ LSC-2507 [S]	Prokofiev: Piano Concerto No. 3; MacDowell: Piano Concerto No. 2	1965	5.00	10.00	20.00
-- "White dog" pressing ("Stereo" on label)					
❏ LSC-2562 [S]	Beethoven: Piano Concerto No. 5 (Emperor Concerto)	1961	5.00	10.00	20.00
-- "Shaded dog" pressing ("Living Stereo" on label)					
❏ LSC-2562 [S]	Beethoven: Piano Concerto No. 5 (Emperor Concerto)	1964	5.00	10.00	20.00
-- "White dog" pressing ("Stereo" on label)					
❏ LSC-2576 [S]	My Favorite Chopin	1962	5.00	10.00	20.00
-- "Shaded dog" pressing ("Living Stereo" on label)					
❏ LSC-2581 [S]	Brahms: Piano Concerto No. 2	1962	5.00	10.00	20.00
-- "Shaded dog" pressing ("Living Stereo" on label)					
❏ LSC-2601 [S]	Rachmaninoff: Piano Concerto No. 2	1962	5.00	10.00	20.00
-- "Shaded dog" pressing ("Living Stereo" on label)					

CLIFF, JIMMY
A&M
| ❏ SP-4251 | Wonderful World, Beautiful People | 1970 | 6.25 | 12.50 | 25.00 |
ISLAND
| ❏ SW-9343 | Struggling Man | 1973 | 5.00 | 10.00 | 20.00 |
VEEP
| ❏ VPS-16536 | Can't Get Enough of It | 1969 | 10.00 | 20.00 | 40.00 |

CLIFFORD, BUZZ
COLUMBIA
| ❏ CL 1616 [M] | Baby Sittin' with Buzz | 1961 | 25.00 | 50.00 | 100.00 |
| ❏ CS 8416 [S] | Baby Sittin' with Buzz | 1961 | 37.50 | 75.00 | 150.00 |
DOT
| ❏ DLP-25965 | See Your Way Clear | 1969 | 7.50 | 15.00 | 30.00 |

CLIFFORD, MIKE
UNITED ARTISTS
| ❏ UAL-3409 [M] | For the Love of Mike | 1965 | 5.00 | 10.00 | 20.00 |
| ❏ UAS-6409 [S] | For the Love of Mike | 1965 | 6.25 | 12.50 | 25.00 |

CLIFTON, BILL, AND THE DIXIE MOUNTAIN BOYS
STARDAY
❏ SLP-111 [M]	Mountain Folk Songs	1959	10.00	20.00	40.00
❏ SLP-146 [M]	The Carter Family Memorial Album	1961	7.50	15.00	30.00
❏ SLP-159 [M]	The Bluegrass Sound of Bill Clifton	1961	7.50	15.00	30.00
❏ SLP-213 [M]	Soldier, Sing Me a Song	1963	6.25	12.50	25.00
❏ SLP-271 [M]	Code of the Mountains	1965	6.25	12.50	25.00

CLINE, PATSY
DECCA
❏ DXB 176 [(2) M]	The Patsy Cline Story	1963	10.00	20.00	40.00
❏ DL 4202 [M]	Patsy Cline Showcase	1961	10.00	20.00	40.00
❏ DL 4282 [M]	Sentimentally Yours	1962	7.50	15.00	30.00
❏ DL 4508 [M]	A Portrait of Patsy Cline	1964	7.50	15.00	30.00
❏ DL 4586 [M]	That's How a Heartache Begins	1964	7.50	15.00	30.00
❏ DL 4854 [M]	Patsy Cline's Greatest Hits	1967	5.00	10.00	20.00
❏ DXSB 7176 [(2) S]	The Patsy Cline Story	1963	12.50	25.00	50.00
❏ DL 8611 [M]	Patsy Cline	1957	25.00	50.00	100.00
-- Black label with silver print					
❏ DL 8611 [M]	Patsy Cline	1960	12.50	25.00	50.00
-- Black label with color bars					
❏ DL 74202 [S]	Patsy Cline Showcase	1961	12.50	25.00	50.00
❏ DL 74282 [S]	Sentimentally Yours	1962	10.00	20.00	40.00
❏ DL 74508 [S]	A Portrait of Patsy Cline	1964	10.00	20.00	40.00
❏ DL 74586 [S]	That's How a Heartache Begins	1964	10.00	20.00	40.00
❏ DL 74854 [S]	Patsy Cline's Greatest Hits	1967	6.25	12.50	25.00
EVEREST
❏ 5200 [M]	Golden Hits	1962	5.00	10.00	20.00
❏ 5204 [M]	Encores	1962	5.00	10.00	20.00
❏ 5217 [M]	In Memoriam	1963	5.00	10.00	20.00
❏ 5223 [M]	Legend	1963	5.00	10.00	20.00
❏ 5229 [M]	Reflections	1964	5.00	10.00	20.00
SEARS
| ❏ SRS-127 | In Care of the Blues | 1968 | 6.25 | 12.50 | 25.00 |

CLINTON, GEORGE
Also see FUNKADELIC; PARLIAMENT.
INVICTUS
| ❏ ST-9815 | Black Vampire | 1973 | 5.00 | 10.00 | 20.00 |

CLIQUE, THE
WHITE WHALE
| ❏ WWS-7126 | The Clique | 1969 | 5.00 | 10.00 | 20.00 |

CLOONEY SISTERS, THE
Also see ROSEMARY CLOONEY.
EPIC
| ❏ LN 3160 [M] | The Clooney Sisters with Tony Pastor | 1956 | 15.00 | 30.00 | 60.00 |

CLOONEY, ROSEMARY
COLUMBIA
❏ CL 585 [M]	Hollywood's Best	1955	12.50	25.00	50.00
❏ CL 872 [M]	Blue Rose	1956	10.00	20.00	40.00
❏ CL 969 [M]	Clooney Tunes	1957	20.00	40.00	80.00
❏ CL 1006 [M]	Ring Around the Rosie	1957	10.00	20.00	40.00
-- With the Hi-Lo's					
❏ CL 1230 [M]	Rosie's Greatest Hits	1958	10.00	20.00	40.00
-- Six "eye" logos on label					
❏ CL 1230 [M]	Rosie's Greatest Hits	1962	6.25	12.50	25.00
-- "Guaranteed High Fidelity" on label					
❏ CL 2525 [10]	Tenderly	1955	12.50	25.00	50.00
❏ CL 2569 [10]	Children's Favorites	1955	12.50	25.00	50.00
❏ CL 2572 [10]	A Date with the King	1956	12.50	25.00	50.00
❏ CL 2581 [10]	On Stage	1956	12.50	25.00	50.00
❏ CL 2597 [10]	My Fair Lady	1956	12.50	25.00	50.00
❏ CL 6224 [10]	Hollywood's Best	1952	15.00	30.00	60.00
❏ CL 6297 [10]	Rosemary Clooney (While We're Young)	1954	15.00	30.00	60.00
❏ CL 6338 [10]	White Christmas	1954	15.00	30.00	60.00
CORAL
| ❏ CRL 57266 [M] | Swing Around Rosie | 1959 | 7.50 | 15.00 | 30.00 |
| ❏ CRL 757266 [S] | Swing Around Rosie | 1959 | 10.00 | 20.00 | 40.00 |
HARMONY
❏ HL 7123 [M]	Rosemary Clooney in High	195?	6.25	12.50	25.00
❏ HL 7213 [M]	Hollywood Hits	195?	6.25	12.50	25.00
❏ HL 7454 [M]	Mixed Emotions	1968	5.00	10.00	20.00
❏ HL 9501 [M]	Rosemary Clooney Sings for Children	196?	5.00	10.00	20.00
MGM
❏ E-3687 [M]	Oh, Captain!	1958	10.00	20.00	40.00
❏ E-3782 [M]	Hymns from the Heart	1959	7.50	15.00	30.00
❏ SE-3782 [S]	Hymns from the Heart	1959	10.00	20.00	40.00
❏ E-3834 [M]	Rosie Clooney Swings Softly	1960	7.50	15.00	30.00
❏ SE-3834 [S]	Rosie Clooney Swings Softly	1960	10.00	20.00	40.00
RCA VICTOR
❏ LPM-2133 [M]	A Touch of Tabasco	1960	5.00	10.00	20.00
❏ LSP-2133 [S]	A Touch of Tabasco	1960	7.50	15.00	30.00
❏ LPM-2212 [M]	Clap Hands, Here Comes Rosie	1960	5.00	10.00	20.00
❏ LSP-2212 [S]	Clap Hands, Here Comes Rosie	1960	7.50	15.00	30.00
❏ LPM-2265 [M]	Rosie Solves the Swingin' Riddle	1961	5.00	10.00	20.00
❏ LSP-2265 [S]	Rosie Solves the Swingin' Riddle	1961	7.50	15.00	30.00
❏ LPM-2565 [M]	Country Hits from the Heart	1963	5.00	10.00	20.00
❏ LSP-2565 [S]	Country Hits from the Heart	1963	7.50	15.00	30.00
REPRISE
❏ R-6088 [M]	Love	1963	7.50	15.00	30.00
❏ R9-6088 [S]	Love	1963	10.00	20.00	40.00
❏ R-6108 [M]	Thanks for Nothing	1964	7.50	15.00	30.00
❏ RS-6108 [S]	Thanks for Nothing	1964	10.00	20.00	40.00

CLOONEY, ROSEMARY, AND BING CROSBY
Also see each artist's individual listings.
CAPITOL
| ❏ ST 2300 [S] | That Travelin' Two-Beat | 1965 | 7.50 | 15.00 | 30.00 |
| ❏ T 2300 [M] | That Travelin' Two-Beat | 1965 | 5.00 | 10.00 | 20.00 |
RCA VICTOR
| ❏ LPM-1854 [M] | Fancy Meeting You Here | 1958 | 5.00 | 10.00 | 20.00 |
| ❏ LSP-1854 [S] | Fancy Meeting You Here | 1958 | 7.50 | 15.00 | 30.00 |

CLOUD, BRUCE
CAPITOL
| ❏ ST-343 | California Soul | 1969 | 5.00 | 10.00 | 20.00 |

CLOVER
FANTASY
| ❏ 8395 | Clover | 1969 | 6.25 | 12.50 | 25.00 |

Number	Title	Yr	VG	VG+	NM
❑ 8405	Forty-Niner	1970	6.25	12.50	25.00

CLOVER, TIMOTHY
TOWER
❑ ST 5114	A Harvard Square Affair	1968	5.00	10.00	20.00

CLOVERS, THE
ATLANTIC
❑ 1248 [M]	The Clovers	1956	150.00	300.00	600.00
❑ 8009 [M]	The Clovers	1957	100.00	200.00	400.00
-- Reissue of 1248 on the "pop" series; black label					
❑ 8009 [M]	The Clovers	1960	75.00	150.00	300.00
-- White "bullseye" label					
❑ 8009 [M]	The Clovers	1961	50.00	100.00	200.00
-- Red and white label					
❑ 8034 [M]	Dance Party	1959	100.00	200.00	400.00
-- Black label					
❑ 8034 [M]	Dance Party	1960	75.00	150.00	300.00
-- White "bullseye" label					
❑ 8034 [M]	Dance Party	1961	50.00	100.00	200.00
-- Red and white label					

GRAND PRIX
❑ K-428 [M]	The Original Love Potion Number Nine	1964	7.50	15.00	30.00

POPLAR
❑ 1001 [M]	The Clovers In Clover	1958	100.00	200.00	400.00

UNITED ARTISTS
❑ UAL-3033 [M]	The Clovers In Clover	1959	75.00	150.00	300.00
❑ UAL-3099 [M]	Love Potion Number Nine	1959	62.50	125.00	250.00
❑ UAS-6033 [R]	The Clovers In Clover	196?	50.00	100.00	200.00
❑ UAS-6099 [S]	Love Potion Number Nine	1959	125.00	250.00	500.00

COASTERS, THE
ATCO
❑ 33-101 [M]	The Coasters	1958	75.00	150.00	300.00
-- Yellow "harp" label					
❑ 33-101 [M]	The Coasters	196?	15.00	30.00	60.00
-- Gold and dark blue label					
❑ 33-111 [M]	The Coasters' Greatest Hits	1959	37.50	75.00	150.00
-- Yellow "harp" label					
❑ 33-111 [M]	The Coasters' Greatest Hits	196?	15.00	30.00	60.00
-- Gold and gray label					
❑ 33-123 [M]	One By One	1960	37.50	75.00	150.00
-- Yellow "harp" label					
❑ 33-123 [M]	One By One	196?	15.00	30.00	60.00
-- Gold and gray label					
❑ SD 33-123 [S]	One By One	1960	100.00	200.00	400.00
-- Yellow "harp" label					
❑ SD 33-123 [S]	One By One	196?	37.50	75.00	150.00
-- Purple and brown label					
❑ 33-135 [M]	Coast Along with the Coasters	1962	25.00	50.00	100.00
-- Gold and gray label					
❑ SD 33-135 [S]	Coast Along with the Coasters	1962	37.50	75.00	150.00
-- Purple and brown label					
❑ SD 33-371	Their Greatest Recordings/ The Early Years	1971	5.00	10.00	20.00

CLARION
❑ 605 [M]	That Is Rock and Roll	1965	10.00	20.00	40.00
❑ SD 605 [S]	That Is Rock and Roll	1965	12.50	25.00	50.00

KING
❑ KS-1146	The Coasters On Broadway	1971	6.25	12.50	25.00

COCHRAN, EDDIE
LIBERTY
❑ LRP-3061 [M]	Singin' to My Baby	1957	200.00	400.00	800.00
-- Green label					
❑ LRP-3061 [M]	Singin' to My Baby	1960	75.00	150.00	300.00
-- Black label					
❑ LRP-3172 [M]	Eddie Cochran (12 of His Biggest Hits)	1960	30.00	60.00	120.00
❑ LRP-3220 [M]	Never to Be Forgotten	1962	25.00	50.00	100.00

SUNSET
❑ SUM-1123 [M]	Summertime Blues	1966	10.00	20.00	40.00
❑ SUS-5123 [R]	Summertime Blues	1966	6.25	12.50	25.00

UNITED ARTISTS
❑ UAS-9959 [(2)]	Legendary Masters Series #4	1972	6.25	12.50	25.00

COCHRAN, HANK
MONUMENT
❑ SLP-18089	The Heart of Hank	1968	5.00	10.00	20.00

RCA VICTOR
❑ LPM-3303 [M]	Hits from the Heart	1965	5.00	10.00	20.00

Number	Title	Yr	VG	VG+	NM
❑ LSP-3303 [S]	Hits from the Heart	1965	6.25	12.50	25.00
❑ LPM-3431 [M]	Going in Training	1965	5.00	10.00	20.00
❑ LSP-3431 [S]	Going in Training	1965	6.25	12.50	25.00

COCHRAN, WAYNE
CHESS
❑ LPS-1519	Wayne Cochran!	1968	10.00	20.00	40.00

KING
❑ KS-1116	Alive and Well	1970	5.00	10.00	20.00

COCKER, JOE
A&M
❑ QU-54182 [Q]	With a Little Help from My Friends	1974	5.00	10.00	20.00
❑ QU-54224 [Q]	Joe Cocker!	1974	5.00	10.00	20.00

MOBILE FIDELITY
❑ 1-223	Sheffield Steel	1995	10.00	20.00	40.00
-- Audiophile vinyl					

COCTEAU TWINS
CAPITOL
❑ SPRO 79066/7 [DJ]	Sampler	1991	12.50	25.00	50.00
-- Promo-only 10-song collection					

COE, DAVID ALLAN
SSS INTERNATIONAL
❑ 9	Penitentiary Blues	1977	20.00	40.00	80.00

COHEN, LEONARD
COLUMBIA
❑ CL 2733 [M]	Leonard Cohen	1967	6.25	12.50	25.00

COHEN, MYRON
AUDIO FIDELITY
❑ 701 [M]	Myron Cohen	196?	5.00	10.00	20.00

COLD BLOOD
SAN FRANCISCO
❑ 200	Cold Blood	1969	5.00	10.00	20.00
❑ 205	Sisyphus	1970	5.00	10.00	20.00

COLDER, BEN -- See SHEB WOOLEY.

COLE, BUDDY
COLUMBIA
❑ CL 1224 [M]	Pipes & Chimes of Christmas	1958	5.00	10.00	20.00
-- Red label with six "eye" logos					
❑ CS 8032 [S]	Pipes & Chimes of Christmas	1958	6.25	12.50	25.00
-- Red and black label with six "eye" logos					

COLE, COZY
AUDITION
❑ 33-5943 [M]	Cozy Cole	1955	12.50	25.00	50.00

BETHLEHEM
❑ BCP-21 [M]	Jazz at the Metropole Café	1955	12.50	25.00	50.00

CHARLIE PARKER
❑ PLP-403 [M]	A Cozy Conaption of Carmen	1962	5.00	10.00	20.00
❑ PLP-403S [S]	A Cozy Conaption of Carmen	1962	6.25	12.50	25.00

COLUMBIA
❑ CS 9353 [S]	It's a Rockin' Thing	1965	5.00	10.00	20.00

CORAL
❑ CRL 757423 [S]	Drum Beat Dancing Feet	1962	5.00	10.00	20.00
❑ CRL 757457 [S]	It's a Cozy World	1964	5.00	10.00	20.00

FELSTED
❑ 2002 [S]	Cozy's Caravan/Earl's Backroom	1958	10.00	20.00	40.00
❑ 7002 [M]	Cozy's Caravan/Earl's Backroom	1958	12.50	25.00	50.00

GRAND AWARD
❑ GA 33-334 [M]	After Hours	1956	10.00	20.00	40.00

KING
❑ 673 [M]	Cozy Cole	1959	15.00	30.00	60.00

LOVE
❑ 500M [M]	Topsy	1959	25.00	50.00	100.00
❑ 500S [S]	Topsy	1959	50.00	100.00	200.00

PARIS
❑ 122 [M]	Cozy Cole and His All-Stars	1958	12.50	25.00	50.00

Number	Title	Yr	VG	VG+	NM

COLE, IKE
DEE GEE
Number	Title	Yr	VG	VG+	NM
❏ 4001	Ike Cole's Tribute to His Brother Nat	1966	10.00	20.00	40.00

COLE, JERRY
CAPITOL
Number	Title	Yr	VG	VG+	NM
❏ ST 2044 [S]	Outer Limits	1963	20.00	40.00	80.00
❏ T 2044 [M]	Outer Limits	1963	12.50	25.00	50.00
❏ ST 2061 [S]	Hot Rod Dance Party	1964	25.00	50.00	100.00
❏ T 2061 [M]	Hot Rod Dance Party	1964	20.00	40.00	80.00
❏ (S)T 2061	Hot Rod Dance Party Bonus Photo	1964	6.25	12.50	25.00
❏ ST 2112 [S]	Surf Age	1964	30.00	60.00	120.00
-- With bonus single by Dick Dale, "Thunder Wave"/"Spanish Kiss"					
❏ T 2112 [M]	Surf Age	1964	25.00	50.00	100.00
-- With bonus single by Dick Dale, "Thunder Wave"/"Spanish Kiss"					
❏ ST 2112 [S]	Surf Age	1964	25.00	50.00	100.00
-- With bonus single missing					
❏ T 2112 [M]	Surf Age	1964	20.00	40.00	80.00
-- With bonus single missing					
LIBERTY
Number	Title	Yr	VG	VG+	NM
❏ LRP-3362 [M]	Sounds of the Big Irons	1964	12.50	25.00	50.00
❏ LST-7362 [S]	Sounds of the Big Irons	1964	15.00	30.00	60.00

COLE, MARIA
KAPP
Number	Title	Yr	VG	VG+	NM
❏ 102 [10]	Maria Cole	1954	12.50	25.00	50.00

COLE, NAT KING
CAPITOL
Number	Title	Yr	VG	VG+	NM
❏ H 8 [10]	The King Cole Trio	1950	25.00	50.00	100.00
❏ H 29 [10]	The King Cole Trio, Volume 2	1950	25.00	50.00	100.00
❏ H 59 [10]	The King Cole Trio, Volume 3	1950	25.00	50.00	100.00
❏ H 156 [10]	Nat King Cole at the Piano	1950	25.00	50.00	100.00
❏ H 177 [10]	The King Cole Trio, Volume 4	1950	17.50	35.00	70.00
❏ H 213 [10]	Harvest of Hits	1950	17.50	35.00	70.00
❏ H 220 [10]	The Nat King Cole Trio	1950	15.00	30.00	60.00
❏ H 332 [10]	Penthouse Serenade	1951	15.00	30.00	60.00
❏ T 332 [M]	Penthouse Serenade	1955	10.00	20.00	40.00
❏ H 357 [10]	Unforgettable	1952	15.00	30.00	60.00
❏ T 357 [M]	Unforgettable	1955	10.00	20.00	40.00
-- Turquoise label					
❏ T 357 [M]	Unforgettable	1958	7.50	15.00	30.00
-- Black label with colorband, "Capitol" at left					
❏ T 357 [M]	Unforgettable	1962	5.00	10.00	20.00
-- Black label with colorband, "Capitol" at top					
❏ H 420 [10]	Nat King Cole Sings for Two in Love	1953	12.50	25.00	50.00
❏ T 420 [M]	Nat King Cole Sings for Two in Love	1955	10.00	20.00	40.00
-- Turquoise label					
❏ T 420 [M]	Nat King Cole Sings for Two in Love	1958	7.50	15.00	30.00
-- Black label with colorband, "Capitol" at left					
❏ T 420 [M]	Nat King Cole Sings for Two in Love	1962	5.00	10.00	20.00
-- Black label with colorband, "Capitol" at top					
❏ H 514 [10]	Tenth Anniversary Album	1954	12.50	25.00	50.00
❏ W 514 [M]	Tenth Anniversary Album	1955	10.00	20.00	40.00
❏ T 591 [M]	Vocal Classics	1955	10.00	20.00	40.00
❏ T 592 [M]	Instrumental Classics	1955	10.00	20.00	40.00
❏ T 680 [M]	Ballads of the Day	1956	10.00	20.00	40.00
-- Turquoise label					
❏ T 680 [M]	Ballads of the Day	1958	7.50	15.00	30.00
-- Black label with colorband, "Capitol" at left					
❏ T 680 [M]	Ballads of the Day	1962	5.00	10.00	20.00
-- Black label with colorband, "Capitol" at top					
❏ W 689 [M]	The Piano Style of Nat King Cole	1956	10.00	20.00	40.00
-- Turquoise label					
❏ W 689 [M]	The Piano Style of Nat King Cole	1958	7.50	15.00	30.00
-- Black label with colorband, "Capitol" at left					
❏ W 689 [M]	The Piano Style of Nat King Cole	1962	5.00	10.00	20.00
-- Black label with colorband, "Capitol" at top					
❏ W 782 [M]	After Midnight	1956	10.00	20.00	40.00
-- Turquoise label					
❏ W 782 [M]	After Midnight	1958	7.50	15.00	30.00
-- Black label with colorband, "Capitol" at left					
❏ W 782 [M]	After Midnight	1962	5.00	10.00	20.00
-- Black label with colorband, "Capitol" at top					
❏ SW 824 [S]	Love Is the Thing	1959	7.50	15.00	30.00
-- Black label with colorband, "Capitol" at left					
❏ SW 824 [S]	Love Is the Thing	1962	5.00	10.00	20.00
-- Black label with colorband, "Capitol" at top					
❏ W 824 [M]	Love Is the Thing	1957	10.00	20.00	40.00
-- Turquoise or gray label					
❏ W 824 [M]	Love Is the Thing	1958	7.50	15.00	30.00
-- Black label with colorband, "Capitol" at left					
❏ W 824 [M]	Love Is the Thing	1962	5.00	10.00	20.00
-- Black label with colorband, "Capitol" at top					
❏ T 870 [M]	This Is Nat "King" Cole	1957	10.00	20.00	40.00
-- Turquoise or gray label					
❏ T 870 [M]	This Is Nat "King" Cole	1958	7.50	15.00	30.00
-- Black label with colorband, "Capitol" at left					
❏ T 870 [M]	This Is Nat "King" Cole	1962	5.00	10.00	20.00
-- Black label with colorband, "Capitol" at top					
❏ SW 903 [S]	Just One of Those Things	1959	7.50	15.00	30.00
-- Black label with colorband, "Capitol" at left					
❏ SW 903 [S]	Just One of Those Things	1962	5.00	10.00	20.00
-- Black label with colorband, "Capitol" at top					
❏ W 903 [M]	Just One of Those Things	1957	10.00	20.00	40.00
-- Turquoise or gray label					
❏ W 903 [M]	Just One of Those Things	1958	7.50	15.00	30.00
-- Black label with colorband, "Capitol" at left					
❏ W 903 [M]	Just One of Those Things	1962	5.00	10.00	20.00
-- Black label with colorband, "Capitol" at top					
❏ SW 993 [S]	St. Louis Blues	1959	12.50	25.00	50.00
-- Black label with colorband, "Capitol" at left					
❏ W 993 [M]	St. Louis Blues	1958	12.50	25.00	50.00
-- Turquoise or gray label					
❏ W 993 [M]	St. Louis Blues	1962	10.00	20.00	40.00
-- Black label with colorband, "Capitol" at left					
❏ W 1031 [M]	Cole Espanol	1958	7.50	15.00	30.00
-- Black label with colorband, "Capitol" at left					
❏ W 1031 [M]	Cole Espanol	1962	5.00	10.00	20.00
-- Black label with colorband, "Capitol" at top					
❏ SW 1084 [S]	The Very Thought of You	1959	7.50	15.00	30.00
-- Black label with colorband, "Capitol" at left					
❏ SW 1084 [S]	The Very Thought of You	1962	5.00	10.00	20.00
-- Black label with colorband, "Capitol" at top					
❏ W 1084 [M]	The Very Thought of You	1958	7.50	15.00	30.00
-- Black label with colorband, "Capitol" at left					
❏ W 1084 [M]	The Very Thought of You	1962	5.00	10.00	20.00
-- Black label with colorband, "Capitol" at left					
❏ SW 1120 [S]	Welcome to the Club	1959	10.00	20.00	40.00
-- Black label with colorband, "Capitol" at left					
❏ W 1120 [M]	Welcome to the Club	1959	7.50	15.00	30.00
-- Black label with colorband, "Capitol" at left					
❏ SW 1190 [S]	To Whom It May Concern	1959	10.00	20.00	40.00
-- Black label with colorband, "Capitol" at left					
❏ W 1190 [M]	To Whom It May Concern	1959	7.50	15.00	30.00
-- Black label with colorband, "Capitol" at left					
❏ SW 1220 [S]	A Mis Amigos	1959	10.00	20.00	40.00
-- Black label with colorband, "Capitol" at left					
❏ SW 1220 [S]	A Mis Amigos	1962	6.25	12.50	25.00
-- Black label with colorband, "Capitol" at top					
❏ W 1220 [M]	A Mis Amigos	1959	7.50	15.00	30.00
-- Black label with colorband, "Capitol" at left					
❏ W 1220 [M]	A Mis Amigos	1962	5.00	10.00	20.00
-- Black label with colorband, "Capitol" at top					
❏ ST 1249 [S]	Every Time I Feel the Spirit	1960	7.50	15.00	30.00
-- Black label with colorband, "Capitol" at left					
❏ T 1249 [M]	Every Time I Feel the Spirit	1960	6.25	12.50	25.00
-- Black label with colorband, "Capitol" at left					
❏ SW 1331 [S]	Tell Me About Yourself	1960	7.50	15.00	30.00
-- Black label with colorband, "Capitol" at left					
❏ W 1331 [M]	Tell Me About Yourself	1960	6.25	12.50	25.00
-- Black label with colorband, "Capitol" at left					
❏ SWAK 1392 [S]	Wild Is Love	1960	7.50	15.00	30.00
-- Black label with colorband, "Capitol" at left					
❏ WAK 1392 [M]	Wild Is Love	1960	6.25	12.50	25.00
-- Black label with colorband, "Capitol" at left					
❏ SW 1444 [S]	The Magic of Christmas	1960	5.00	10.00	20.00
❏ W 1444 [M]	The Magic of Christmas	1960	5.00	10.00	20.00
❏ SW 1574 [S]	The Touch of Your Lips	1961	6.25	12.50	25.00
-- Black label with colorband, "Capitol" at left					
❏ SW 1574 [S]	The Touch of Your Lips	1962	5.00	10.00	20.00
-- Black label with colorband, "Capitol" at top					
❏ W 1574 [M]	The Touch of Your Lips	1961	5.00	10.00	20.00
-- Black label with colorband, "Capitol" at left					
❏ SWCL 1613 [(3) S]	The Nat King Cole Story	1961	7.50	15.00	30.00
❏ WCL 1613 [(3) M]	The Nat King Cole Story	1961	6.25	12.50	25.00
❏ SW 1675 [S]	Nat King Cole Sings/ George Shearing Plays	1962	7.50	15.00	30.00
-- Black label with colorband, "Capitol" at left					
❏ SW 1675 [S]	Nat King Cole Sings/ George Shearing Plays	1963	5.00	10.00	20.00
-- Black label with colorband, "Capitol" at top					
❏ W 1675 [M]	Nat King Cole Sings/ George Shearing Plays	1962	6.25	12.50	25.00
-- Black label with colorband, "Capitol" at left					
❏ SW 1713 [S]	Nat King Cole Sings the Blues	1962	6.25	12.50	25.00
-- Black label with colorband, "Capitol" at left					
❏ W 1713 [M]	Nat King Cole Sings the Blues	1962	5.00	10.00	20.00
-- Black label with colorband, "Capitol" at left					
❏ SW 1749 [S]	More Cole Espanol	1962	7.50	15.00	30.00
-- Black label with colorband, "Capitol" at left					
❏ SW 1749 [S]	More Cole Espanol	1963	5.00	10.00	20.00
-- Black label with colorband, "Capitol" at top					
❏ W 1749 [M]	More Cole Espanol	1962	6.25	12.50	25.00
-- Black label with colorband, "Capitol" at left					
❏ ST 1793 [S]	Ramblin' Rose	1962	5.00	10.00	20.00

Number	Title	Yr	VG	VG+	NM
❑ ST 1838 [S]	Dear Lonely Hearts	1962	5.00	10.00	20.00
❑ SW 1859 [S]	Where Did Everyone Go?	1963	5.00	10.00	20.00
❑ SW 1929 [S]	Nat King Cole Sings the Blues, Volume 2	1963	5.00	10.00	20.00
❑ ST 1932 [S]	Those Lazy-Hazy-Crazy Days of Summer	1963	5.00	10.00	20.00
❑ SW 2008 [S]	Let's Face the Music	1963	5.00	10.00	20.00
❑ SW 2117 [S]	My Fair Lady	1964	5.00	10.00	20.00
-- Black label with colorband					
❑ ST 2118 [S]	I Don't Want to Be Hurt Anymore	1964	5.00	10.00	20.00
❑ ST 2195 [S]	L-O-V-E	1965	5.00	10.00	20.00
❑ STCL 2873 [(3) P]	The Nat King Cole Deluxe Set	1968	6.25	12.50	25.00
❑ TCL 2873 [(3) M]	The Nat King Cole Deluxe Set	1968	7.50	15.00	30.00
❑ H 9110 [10]	Eight Top Pops	1954	12.50	25.00	50.00
❑ SQBO 90938 [(2)]	The Velvet Moods of Nat King Cole	1967	6.25	12.50	25.00
-- Capitol Record Club exclusive					
DCC COMPACT CLASSICS					
❑ LPZ-2029	Love Is the Thing	1997	6.25	12.50	25.00
-- Audiophile vinyl					
❑ LPZ-2047	The Very Thought of You	1998	6.25	12.50	25.00
-- Audiophile vinyl					
❑ LPZ-2061 [(2)]	The Greatest Hits	1998	8.75	17.50	35.00
-- Audiophile vinyl					
DECCA					
❑ DL 8260 [M]	In the Beginning	1956	10.00	20.00	40.00
-- Black label, silver print					
❑ DL 8260 [M]	In the Beginning	1960	6.25	12.50	25.00
-- Black label with color bars					
MOBILE FIDELITY					
❑ 1-081	Nat King Cole Sings/ George Shearing Plays	1981	10.00	20.00	40.00
-- Audiophile vinyl					
SCORE					
❑ SLP-4019 [M]	The King Cole Trio and Lester Young	1957	20.00	40.00	80.00

COLE, NATALIE
ELEKTRA

Number	Title	Yr	VG	VG+	NM
❑ 61049 [(2)]	Unforgettable	1991	5.00	10.00	20.00
MOBILE FIDELITY					
❑ 1-032	Thankful	1980	5.00	10.00	20.00
-- Audiophile vinyl					

COLLAGE, THE
SMASH

Number	Title	Yr	VG	VG+	NM
❑ SRS-67101	The Collage	1968	5.00	10.00	20.00

COLLECTORS, THE
WARNER BROS.

Number	Title	Yr	VG	VG+	NM
❑ WS 1746	The Collectors	1968	6.25	12.50	25.00
❑ WS 1774	Grass and Wild Strawberries	1969	6.25	12.50	25.00

COLLEGIANS, THE
WINLEY

Number	Title	Yr	VG	VG+	NM
❑ LP-6004 [M]	Sing Along with the Collegians	195?	100.00	200.00	400.00

COLLIER, MITTY
CHESS

Number	Title	Yr	VG	VG+	NM
❑ LP-1492 [M]	Shades of a Genius	1965	10.00	20.00	40.00
❑ LPS-1492 [S]	Shades of a Genius	1965	15.00	30.00	60.00

COLLINS, AARON
CROWN

Number	Title	Yr	VG	VG+	NM
❑ CLP-5028 [M]	Calypso U.S.A.	1958	150.00	300.00	600.00

COLLINS, ALBERT
BLUE THUMB

Number	Title	Yr	VG	VG+	NM
❑ BTS 8	Truckin' with Albert Collins	1969	6.25	12.50	25.00
-- Reissue of TCF Hall LP					
IMPERIAL					
❑ LP-12428	Love Can Be Found Anywhere	1968	7.50	15.00	30.00
❑ LP-12438	Trash Talkin'	1969	7.50	15.00	30.00
❑ LP-12449	The Complete Albert Collins	1969	7.50	15.00	30.00
MOBILE FIDELITY					
❑ 1-217	Showdown!	1995	7.50	15.00	30.00
-- With Robert Cray and Johnny Copeland; audiophile vinyl					
❑ 1-226	Cold Snap	1995	5.00	10.00	20.00
-- Audiophile vinyl					
TCF HALL					
❑ 8002 [M]	The Cool Sound of Albert Collins	1965	75.00	150.00	300.00

COLLINS, DOROTHY
CORAL

Number	Title	Yr	VG	VG+	NM
❑ CRL 57105 [M]	Dorothy Collins at Home	1957	6.25	12.50	25.00
❑ CRL 57106 [M]	Songs by Dorothy Collins	1957	6.25	12.50	25.00
❑ CRL 57150 [M]	Picnic	1958	6.25	12.50	25.00
EVEREST					
❑ SDBR-1026 [S]	Singing and Swinging	196?	6.25	12.50	25.00
❑ LPBR-5026 [M]	Singing and Swinging	196?	5.00	10.00	20.00
TOP RANK					
❑ TM-340 [M]	A New Way to Travel	1959	6.25	12.50	25.00

COLLINS, JUDY
DIRECT DISK

Number	Title	Yr	VG	VG+	NM
❑ SD-16607	Judith	1980	10.00	20.00	40.00
-- Audiophile vinyl					
ELEKTRA					
❑ EKL-209 [M]	Maid of Constant Sorrow	1961	10.00	20.00	40.00
-- "Guitar player" label					
❑ EKL-209 [M]	Maid of Constant Sorrow	1966	5.00	10.00	20.00
-- Gold/tan label					
❑ EKL-222 [M]	Golden Apples of the Sun	1962	7.50	15.00	30.00
-- "Guitar player" label					
❑ EKL-222 [M]	Golden Apples of the Sun	1966	5.00	10.00	20.00
-- Gold/tan label					
❑ EKL-243 [M]	Judy Collins #3	1963	7.50	15.00	30.00
-- "Guitar player" label					
❑ EKL-243 [M]	Judy Collins #3	1966	5.00	10.00	20.00
-- Gold/tan label					
❑ EKL-280 [M]	Judy Collins' Concert	1964	7.50	15.00	30.00
-- "Guitar player" label					
❑ EKL-280 [M]	Judy Collins' Concert	1966	5.00	10.00	20.00
-- Gold/tan label					
❑ EKL-300 [M]	Judy Collins' Fifth Album	1965	7.50	15.00	30.00
-- "Guitar player" label					
❑ EKL-300 [M]	Judy Collins' Fifth Album	1966	5.00	10.00	20.00
-- Gold/tan label					
❑ EKL-320 [M]	In My Life	1966	5.00	10.00	20.00
❑ EQ-1032 [Q]	Judith	1975	5.00	10.00	20.00
❑ EKL-4012 [M]	Wildflowers	1967	6.25	12.50	25.00
❑ EQ-5030 [Q]	Colors of the Day/ The Best of Judy Collins	1973	5.00	10.00	20.00
❑ EKS-7243 [S]	Judy Collins #3	1963	10.00	20.00	40.00
-- "Guitar player" label					
❑ EKS-7243 [S]	Judy Collins #3	1966	6.25	12.50	25.00
-- Gold/tan label					
❑ EKS-7280 [S]	Judy Collins' Concert	1964	10.00	20.00	40.00
-- "Guitar player" label					
❑ EKS-7280 [S]	Judy Collins' Concert	1966	6.25	12.50	25.00
-- Gold/tan label					
❑ EKS-7300 [S]	Judy Collins' Fifth Album	1965	10.00	20.00	40.00
-- "Guitar player" label					
❑ EKS-7300 [S]	Judy Collins' Fifth Album	1966	6.25	12.50	25.00
-- Gold/tan label					
❑ EKS-7320 [S]	In My Life	1966	6.25	12.50	25.00
❑ EKS-74012 [S]	Wildflowers	1967	5.00	10.00	20.00
-- Gold/tan label					
❑ EKS-74027	In My Life	1968	5.00	10.00	20.00
-- Reissue of 7320; gold/tan label					
❑ EKS-74033	Who Knows Where the Time Goes	1968	5.00	10.00	20.00
-- Gold/tan label					

COLLINS, LYN
PEOPLE

Number	Title	Yr	VG	VG+	NM
❑ PE-5602	Think (About It)	1972	6.25	12.50	25.00
❑ PE-6605	Check Me Out	1975	6.25	12.50	25.00

COLLINS, SHIRLEY AND DOROTHY
HARVEST

Number	Title	Yr	VG	VG+	NM
❑ SKAO-370	Anthems in Eden	1969	12.50	25.00	50.00

COLLINS, TOMMY
CAPITOL

Number	Title	Yr	VG	VG+	NM
❑ T 776 [M]	Words and Music Country Style	1957	25.00	50.00	100.00
❑ T 1125 [M]	Light of the Lord	1959	25.00	50.00	100.00
❑ T 1196 [M]	This Is Tommy Collins	1959	15.00	30.00	60.00
❑ T 1436 [M]	Songs I Love to Sing	1961	12.50	25.00	50.00
❑ ST 1436 [S]	Songs I Love to Sing	1961	15.00	30.00	60.00
COLUMBIA					
❑ CL 2510 [M]	The Dynamic Tommy Collins	1966	7.50	15.00	30.00
❑ CL 2778 [M]	Tommy Collins On Tour -- His Most Requested Songs	1968	15.00	30.00	60.00
❑ CS 9310 [S]	The Dynamic Tommy Collins	1966	10.00	20.00	40.00
❑ CS 9578 [S]	Tommy Collins On Tour -- His Most Requested Songs	1968	7.50	15.00	30.00

Number	Title	Yr	VG	VG+	NM
STARDAY					
❑ SLP-474	Tommy Collins Callin'	1972	5.00	10.00	20.00
TOWER					
❑ DT 5021 [R]	Let's Live a Little	1966	5.00	10.00	20.00
❑ T 5021 [M]	Let's Live a Little	1966	7.50	15.00	30.00
❑ DT 5107 [R]	Shindig	1967	5.00	10.00	20.00
❑ T 5107 [M]	Shindig	1967	10.00	20.00	40.00

COLMAN, RONALD/ CHARLES LAUGHTON
DECCA
❑ DLP 8010 [M]	A Christmas Carol/ Mr. Pickwick's Christmas	1949	5.00	10.00	20.00

COLONNA, JERRY
DECCA
❑ DL 5540 [10]	Music? For Screaming!!!	1955	15.00	30.00	60.00
LIBERTY					
❑ LRP-3046 [M]	Let's All Sing with Jerry Colonna	1957	10.00	20.00	40.00
❑ LRP-9004 [M]	Along the Dixieland Hi-Fi Way	1956	10.00	20.00	40.00

COLOSSEUM
ABC DUNHILL
❑ DS-50062	Those Who Are About to Die Salute You	1969	5.00	10.00	20.00
❑ DS-50079	The Grass Is Green	1970	5.00	10.00	20.00

COLOURS
DOT
❑ DLP-25854	Colours	1968	6.25	12.50	25.00
❑ DLP-25935	Atmosphere	1969	6.25	12.50	25.00

COLTER, JESSI
RCA VICTOR
❑ LSP-4333	Country Star	1970	5.00	10.00	20.00

COLTRANE, JOHN
ABC IMPULSE!
❑ AS-9148	Cosmic Music	1969	5.00	10.00	20.00
-- Reissue of Coltrane LP					
❑ AS-9161	Selflessness	1969	5.00	10.00	20.00
❑ AS-9165	Transition	1969	5.00	10.00	20.00
❑ AS-9200 [(2)]	Greatest Years	1971	5.00	10.00	20.00
❑ AS-9202 [(2)]	Live in Seattle	1971	5.00	10.00	20.00
❑ AS-9211	Sun Ship	1971	5.00	10.00	20.00
ATLANTIC					
❑ 1311 [M]	Giant Steps	1959	12.50	25.00	50.00
-- Black label					
❑ 1311 [M]	Giant Steps	1960	6.25	12.50	25.00
-- Orange and purple label, white fan logo					
❑ SD 1311 [S]	Giant Steps	1959	15.00	30.00	60.00
-- Green label					
❑ SD 1311 [S]	Giant Steps	1960	6.25	12.50	25.00
-- Green and blue label, white fan logo					
❑ 1354 [M]	Coltrane Jazz	1960	7.50	15.00	30.00
-- Orange and purple label, white fan logo					
❑ SD 1354 [S]	Coltrane Jazz	1960	7.50	15.00	30.00
-- Green and blue label, white fan logo					
❑ 1361 [M]	My Favorite Things	1961	7.50	15.00	30.00
-- Orange and purple label, white fan logo					
❑ SD 1361 [S]	My Favorite Things	1961	7.50	15.00	30.00
-- Green and blue label, white fan logo					
❑ 1373 [M]	Ole' Coltrane	1961	7.50	15.00	30.00
-- Orange and purple label, white fan logo					
❑ SD 1373 [S]	Ole' Coltrane	1961	7.50	15.00	30.00
-- Green and blue label, white fan logo					
❑ 1382 [M]	Coltrane Plays the Blues	1962	7.50	15.00	30.00
❑ SD 1382 [S]	Coltrane Plays the Blues	1962	7.50	51.00	30.00
-- Green and blue label, black fan logo					
❑ 1419 [M]	Coltrane's Sound	1964	6.25	12.50	25.00
❑ SD 1419 [S]	Coltrane's Sound	1964	6.25	12.50	25.00
-- Green and blue label, black fan logo					
❑ 1451 [M]	The Avant Garde	1966	6.25	12.50	25.00
❑ SD 1451 [S]	The Avant Garde	1966	6.25	12.50	25.00
-- Green and blue label, black fan logo					
ATLANTIC/RHINO					
❑ R1-71984 [(12)]	The Heavyweight Champion: The Complete Atlantic Recordings	1995	50.00	100.00	200.00
BLUE NOTE					
❑ BLP-1577 [M]	Blue Train	1957	37.50	75.00	150.00
-- "Deep groove" version (deep indentation under label on both sides)					
❑ BLP-1577 [M]	Blue Train	1957	25.00	50.00	100.00
-- Regular version, W. 63rd St., NYC address on label					

Number	Title	Yr	VG	VG+	NM
❑ BLP-1577 [M]	Blue Train	196?	7.50	15.00	30.00
-- New York, USA address on label					
❑ BST-1577 [S]	Blue Train	1959	30.00	60.00	120.00
-- "Deep groove" version (deep indentation under label on both sides)					
❑ BST-1577 [S]	Blue Train	1959	20.00	40.00	80.00
-- Regular version, W. 63rd St., NYC address on label					
❑ BST-1577 [S]	Blue Train	196?	6.25	12.50	25.00
-- New York, USA address on label					
COLTRANE					
❑ AU-4950	Cosmic Music	1966	75.00	150.00	300.00
❑ AU-5000	Cosmic Music	1966	50.00	100.00	200.00
DCC COMPACT CLASSICS					
❑ LPZ-2032	Lush Life	1997	6.25	12.50	25.00
-- Audiophile vinyl					
IMPULSE!					
❑ A-6 [M]	Africa/Brass	1961	7.50	15.00	30.00
❑ AS-6 [S]	Africa/Brass	1961	10.00	20.00	40.00
❑ A-10 [M]	Live at the Village Vanguard	1962	7.50	15.00	30.00
❑ AS-10 [S]	Live at the Village Vanguard	1962	10.00	20.00	40.00
❑ A-21 [M]	Coltrane	1962	7.50	15.00	30.00
❑ AS-21 [S]	Coltrane	1962	10.00	20.00	40.00
❑ A-30 [M]	Duke Ellington and John Coltrane	1963	7.50	15.00	30.00
❑ AS-30 [S]	Duke Ellington and John Coltrane	1963	10.00	20.00	40.00
❑ A-32 [M]	Ballads	1963	7.50	15.00	30.00
❑ AS-32 [S]	Ballads	1963	10.00	20.00	40.00
❑ A-40 [M]	John Coltrane + Johnny Hartman	1963	10.00	20.00	40.00
❑ AS-40 [S]	John Coltrane + Johnny Hartman	1963	12.50	25.00	50.00
❑ A-42 [M]	Impressions	1963	6.25	12.50	25.00
❑ AS-42 [S]	Impressions	1963	7.50	15.00	30.00
❑ A-50 [M]	Coltrane Live at Birdland	1963	6.25	12.50	25.00
❑ AS-50 [S]	Coltrane Live at Birdland	1963	7.50	15.00	30.00
❑ A-66 [M]	Crescent	1964	6.25	12.50	25.00
❑ AS-66 [S]	Crescent	1964	7.50	15.00	30.00
❑ A-77 [M]	A Love Supreme	1965	7.50	15.00	30.00
❑ AS-77 [S]	A Love Supreme	1965	10.00	20.00	40.00
❑ A-85 [M]	The John Coltrane Quartet Plays	1965	6.25	12.50	25.00
❑ AS-85 [S]	The John Coltrane Quartet Plays	1965	7.50	15.00	30.00
❑ A-94 [M]	New Thing at Newport	1965	6.25	12.50	25.00
❑ AS-94 [S]	New Thing at Newport	1965	7.50	15.00	30.00
❑ A-95 [M]	Ascension	1965	20.00	40.00	80.00
-- Without "Edition II" in dead wax					
❑ A-95 [M]	Ascension	1966	6.25	12.50	25.00
-- With "Edition II" in dead wax					
❑ AS-95 [S]	Ascension	1965	25.00	50.00	100.00
-- Without "Edition II" in dead wax					
❑ AS-95 [S]	Ascension	1966	7.50	15.00	30.00
-- With "Edition II" in dead wax					
❑ A-9106 [M]	Kulu Se Mama	1966	6.25	12.50	25.00
❑ AS-9106 [S]	Kulu Se Mama	1966	7.50	15.00	30.00
❑ A-9110 [M]	Meditations	1966	6.25	12.50	25.00
❑ AS-9110 [S]	Meditations	1966	7.50	15.00	30.00
❑ A-9120 [M]	Expression	1967	7.50	15.00	30.00
❑ AS-9120 [S]	Expression	1967	6.25	12.50	25.00
❑ A-9124 [M]	Live at the Village Vanguard Again!	1967	7.50	15.00	30.00
❑ AS-9124 [S]	Live at the Village Vanguard Again!	1967	6.25	12.50	25.00
❑ A-9140 [M]	Om	1967	7.50	15.00	30.00
❑ AS-9140 [S]	Om	1967	6.25	12.50	25.00
PRESTIGE					
❑ PRLP-7105 [M]	Coltrane	1957	25.00	50.00	100.00
-- Yellow label					
❑ PRLP-7105 [M]	Coltrane	1964	7.50	15.00	30.00
-- Blue label with trident logo					
❑ PRLP-7123 [M]	John Coltrane and the Red Garland Trio	1957	25.00	50.00	100.00
-- Yellow label					
❑ PRLP-7123 [M]	Traneing In	1964	7.50	15.00	30.00
-- Blue label with trident logo; reissue with new title					
❑ PRLP-7142 [M]	Soultrane	1958	20.00	40.00	80.00
-- Yellow label					
❑ PRLP-7142 [M]	Soultrane	1964	6.25	12.50	25.00
-- Blue label with trident logo					
❑ PRLP-7158 [M]	Cattin' with Coltrane and Quinichette	1959	20.00	40.00	80.00
-- Yellow label					
❑ PRLP-7158 [M]	Cattin' with Coltrane and Quinichette	1964	6.25	12.50	25.00
-- Blue label with trident logo					
❑ PRLP-7188 [M]	Lush Life	1960	20.00	40.00	80.00
-- Yellow label					
❑ PRLP-7188 [M]	Lush Life	1964	6.25	12.50	25.00
-- Blue label with trident logo					
❑ PRLP-7213 [M]	Settin' the Pace	1961	20.00	40.00	80.00
-- Yellow label					
❑ PRLP-7213 [M]	Settin' the Pace	1964	6.25	12.50	25.00
-- Blue label with trident logo					
❑ PRLP-7243 [M]	Standard Coltrane	1962	10.00	20.00	40.00
-- Yellow label					

Number	Title	Yr	VG	VG+	NM
❏ PRLP-7243 [M] Standard Coltrane		1964	6.25	12.50	25.00
-- Blue label with trident logo					
❏ PRST-7243 [S] Standard Coltrane		1962	12.50	25.00	50.00
-- Silver label					
❏ PRST-7243 [S] Standard Coltrane		1964	6.25	12.50	25.00
-- Blue label with trident logo					
❏ PRLP-7247 [M] Mating Call		1962	10.00	20.00	40.00
-- Yellow label					
❏ PRLP-7247 [M] Mating Call		1964	6.25	12.50	25.00
-- Blue label with trident logo					
❏ PRST-7247 [R] Mating Call		196?	6.25	12.50	25.00
-- Silver label					
❏ PRST-7247 [R] Mating Call		1964	5.00	10.00	20.00
-- Blue label with trident logo					
❏ PRLP-7249 [M] Tenor Conclave		1962	10.00	20.00	40.00
-- Yellow label					
❏ PRLP-7249 [M] Tenor Conclave		1964	6.25	12.50	25.00
-- Blue label with trident logo					
❏ PRST-7249 [R] Tenor Conclave		196?	6.25	12.50	25.00
-- Silver label					
❏ PRST-7249 [R] Tenor Conclave		1964	5.00	10.00	20.00
-- Blue label with trident logo					
❏ PRLP-7268 [M] Stardust		1963	10.00	20.00	40.00
-- Yellow label					
❏ PRLP-7268 [M] Stardust		1964	6.25	12.50	25.00
-- Blue label with trident logo					
❏ PRST-7268 [S] Stardust		1963	10.00	20.00	40.00
-- Silver label					
❏ PRST-7268 [S] Stardust		1964	6.25	12.50	25.00
-- Blue label with trident logo					
❏ PRLP-7280 [M] Dakar		1963	10.00	20.00	40.00
-- Yellow label					
❏ PRLP-7280 [M] Dakar		1964	6.25	12.50	25.00
-- Blue label with trident logo					
❏ PRST-7280 [S] Dakar		1963	10.00	20.00	40.00
-- Silver label					
❏ PRST-7280 [S] Dakar		1964	6.25	12.50	25.00
-- Blue label with trident logo					
❏ PRLP-7292 [M] The Believer		1964	6.25	12.50	25.00
-- Blue label with trident logo					
❏ PRLP-7292 [M] The Believer		1964	10.00	20.00	40.00
-- Yellow label					
❏ PRST-7292 [S] The Believer		1964	10.00	20.00	40.00
-- Silver label					
❏ PRST-7292 [S] The Believer		1964	6.25	12.50	25.00
-- Blue label with trident logo					
❏ PRLP-7316 [M] Black Pearls		1964	10.00	20.00	40.00
-- Yellow label					
❏ PRLP-7316 [M] Black Pearls		1964	6.25	12.50	25.00
-- Blue label with trident logo					
❏ PRST-7316 [S] Black Pearls		1964	6.25	12.50	25.00
-- Blue label with trident logo					
❏ PRST-7316 [S] Black Pearls		1964	10.00	20.00	40.00
-- Silver label					
❏ PRLP-7353 [M] Bahia		1965	6.25	12.50	25.00
❏ PRST-7353 [S] Bahia		1965	6.25	12.50	25.00
❏ PRLP-7378 [M] The Last Trane		1965	6.25	12.50	25.00
❏ PRST-7378 [S] The Last Trane		1965	6.25	12.50	25.00
❏ PRLP-7426 [M] John Coltrane Plays for Lovers		1966	6.25	12.50	25.00
❏ PRST-7426 [S] John Coltrane Plays for Lovers		1966	6.25	12.50	25.00
❏ PRLP-7531 [M] Soultrane		1967	6.25	12.50	25.00

SOLID STATE

Number	Title	Yr	VG	VG+	NM
❏ SM-17025 [M] Coltrane Time		1968	6.25	12.50	25.00

UNITED ARTISTS

Number	Title	Yr	VG	VG+	NM
❏ UAJ-14001 [M] Coltrane Time		1962	10.00	20.00	40.00
❏ UAJS-15001 [S] Coltrane Time		1962	12.50	25.00	50.00

COLUMBIA CHOIR, THE
COLUMBIA

Number	Title	Yr	VG	VG+	NM
❏ CL 1051 [M] The Christmas Mood		1957	7.50	15.00	30.00
-- Expanded version of 10-inch LP with B-side instrumentals					
❏ CL 2546 [10] The Christmas Mood		1955	10.00	20.00	40.00
-- "House Party Series" reissue					
❏ CL 6??? [10] The Christmas Mood		1955	12.50	25.00	50.00
-- First appearance of the "Albert Burt Carols" on record					

COLUMBUS BOYCHOIR
DECCA

Number	Title	Yr	VG	VG+	NM
❏ DL 78920 [S] Joy to the World		1959	5.00	10.00	20.00

COLWELL-WINFIELD BLUES BAND, THE
VERVE FORECAST

Number	Title	Yr	VG	VG+	NM
❏ FTS-3056	Cold Wind Blues	1968	5.00	10.00	20.00

ZA-ZOO

Number	Title	Yr	VG	VG+	NM
❏ 1	Live Bust	1971	7.50	15.00	30.00

COLYER, KEN
LONDON

Number	Title	Yr	VG	VG+	NM
❏ PB 904 [10]	New Orleans to London	1954	12.50	25.00	50.00
❏ LL 1340 [M]	Back to the Delta	1956	10.00	20.00	40.00
❏ LL 1618 [M]	Club Session with Colyer	1957	10.00	20.00	40.00

COMFORTABLE CHAIR, THE
ODE

Number	Title	Yr	VG	VG+	NM
❏ Z12 44005	The Comfortable Chair	1968	5.00	10.00	20.00

COMMON PEOPLE, THE
CAPITOL

Number	Title	Yr	VG	VG+	NM
❏ ST-266	Of the People/By the People/For the People/From the Common People	1969	25.00	50.00	100.00

COMO, PERRY
RCA CAMDEN

Number	Title	Yr	VG	VG+	NM
❏ CAL-403 [M]	Dream Along with Me	1957	5.00	10.00	20.00
❏ CAL-511 [M]	Como's Wednesday Night Music Hall	1959	5.00	10.00	20.00

RCA VICTOR

Number	Title	Yr	VG	VG+	NM
❏ LPM-51 [10]	Merry Christmas	1951	10.00	20.00	40.00
❏ LOP-1004 [M]	Saturday Night with Mr. C.	1958	6.25	12.50	25.00
❏ LOP-1007 [M]	Como's Golden Records	1958	6.25	12.50	25.00
❏ LPM-1085 [M]	So Smooth	1955	7.50	15.00	30.00
❏ LPM-1172 [M]	I Believe	1956	7.50	15.00	30.00
❏ LPM-1176 [M]	Relaxing with Perry Como	1956	7.50	15.00	30.00
❏ LPM-1177 [M]	A Sentimental Date with Perry Como	1956	7.50	15.00	30.00
❏ LPM-1191 [M]	Hits from Broadway Shows	1956	7.50	15.00	30.00
❏ LPM-1243 [M]	Perry Como Sings Merry Christmas Music	1956	7.50	15.00	30.00
❏ LPM-1463 [M]	We Get Letters	1957	6.25	12.50	25.00
❏ LPM-1885 [M]	When You Come to the End of the Day	1958	5.00	10.00	20.00
❏ LSP-1885 [S]	When You Come to the End of the Day	1958	7.50	15.00	30.00
❏ LPM-1971 [M]	Saturday Night with Mr. C.	1959	5.00	10.00	20.00
-- Reissue of LOP-1004					
❏ LPM-1981 [M]	Como's Golden Records	1959	5.00	10.00	20.00
-- Reissue of LOP-1007					
❏ LPM-2010 [M]	Como Swings	1959	5.00	10.00	20.00
❏ LSP-2010 [S]	Como Swings	1959	6.25	12.50	25.00
❏ LPM-2066 [M]	Season's Greetings from Perry Como	1959	6.25	12.50	25.00
-- Original front covers have "LPM-2066" in lower left corner					
❏ LPM-2066 [M]	Season's Greetings from Perry Como	1959	5.00	10.00	20.00
-- Later front covers have "LPM-2066" in upper right, inside RCA Victor box					
❏ LSP-2066 [S]	Season's Greetings from Perry Como	1959	6.25	12.50	25.00
❏ LSP-2343 [S]	For the Young at Heart	1960	5.00	10.00	20.00
❏ LSP-2390 [S]	Sing to Me, Mr. C.	1961	5.00	10.00	20.00
❏ LSP-2567 [S]	By Request	1962	5.00	10.00	20.00
❏ LSP-2630 [S]	The Best of Irving Berlin's Songs from "Mr. President"	1962	5.00	10.00	20.00
❏ LSP-2708 [S]	The Songs I Love	1963	5.00	10.00	20.00
❏ LPM-3013 [10]	TV Favorites	1952	10.00	20.00	40.00
❏ LPM-3035 [10]	A Sentimental Date with Perry Como	1952	10.00	20.00	40.00
❏ LPM-3044 [10]	Supper Club Favorites	1952	10.00	20.00	40.00
❏ LPM-3124 [10]	Hits from Broadway Shows	1953	10.00	20.00	40.00
❏ LPM-3133 [10]	Around the Christmas Tree	1953	10.00	20.00	40.00
❏ LPM-3188 [10]	I Believe	1954	10.00	20.00	40.00
❏ LPM-3224 [10]	Como's Golden Records	1954	10.00	20.00	40.00

COMPETITORS, THE
DOT

Number	Title	Yr	VG	VG+	NM
❏ DLP-3542 [M]	Hits of the Street and Strip	1963	37.50	75.00	150.00
❏ DLP-25542 [S]	Hits of the Street and Strip	1963	50.00	100.00	200.00

COMSTOCK, BOBBY
ASCOT

Number	Title	Yr	VG	VG+	NM
❏ AM-13026 [M]	Out of Sight	1966	6.25	12.50	25.00
❏ AS-16026 [S]	Out of Sight	1966	7.50	15.00	30.00

CONCRETE BLONDE
I.R.S.

Number	Title	Yr	VG	VG+	NM
❏ X1-13037	Bloodletting	1990	5.00	10.00	20.00
-- Red vinyl					
❏ 82037 [DJ]	Bloodletting	1990	6.25	12.50	25.00
-- Promo-only, sticker on generic cover, black vinyl					

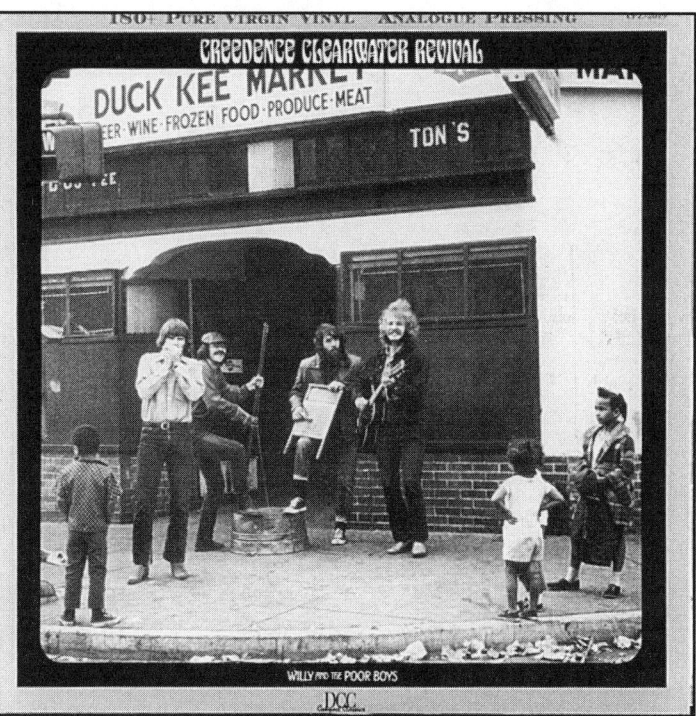

(Top left) *Bloodletting* was Concrete Blonde's biggest album, spurred by the success of their only hit single, "Joey," in 1990. Originally, the album was only released on vinyl as a promo. When the I.R.S. label's distribution changed from MCA to Capitol, the new company did a very limited stock vinyl version on blood red vinyl. (Top right) Most Ray Conniff albums are not that sought-after. This is the exception: *Dance The Bop,* a "cash-in" on the rock 'n' roll "craze," also included a booklet of dance instructions. The value listed in this book may be conservative for this 1956 release. (Bottom left) Here's a tough one: Cream's *Disraeli Gears,* released in 1967, sold a lot of copies. But very few of those sales were of the mono version, pictured here. (Bottom right) In 1996, one of Creedence Clearwater Revival's finest albums, *Willie and the Poor Boys,* received the 180-gram vinyl treatment from DCC Compact Classics.

Number	Title	Yr	VG	VG+	NM

CONDELLO
SCEPTER
❑ SPS-542	Phase 1	1968	10.00	20.00	40.00

CONLEY, ARTHUR
ATCO
❑ 33-215 [M]	Sweet Soul Music	1967	10.00	20.00	40.00
❑ SD 33-215 [S]	Sweet Soul Music	1967	7.50	15.00	30.00
❑ 33-220 [M]	Shake, Rattle & Roll	1967	10.00	20.00	40.00
❑ SD 33-220 [S]	Shake, Rattle & Roll	1967	7.50	15.00	30.00
❑ SD 33-243	Soul Directions	1968	7.50	15.00	30.00
❑ SD 33-276	More Sweet Soul	1969	7.50	15.00	30.00

CONNELLY, PEGGY
BETHLEHEM
❑ BCP-53 [M]	Peggy Connelly	1956	25.00	50.00	100.00

CONNIFF, RAY
COLUMBIA
❑ CL 925 [M]	'S Wonderful!	1956	5.00	10.00	20.00
-- Red and black label with six "eye" logos					
❑ CL 1004 [M]	Dance the Bop	1957	7.50	15.00	30.00
-- Red and black label with six "eye" logos; includes instruction booklet					
❑ CL 1346 [M]	Conniff Meets Butterfield	1959	5.00	10.00	20.00
-- Red and black label with six "eye" logos					
❑ CS 8001 [S]	'S Awful Nice	1958	5.00	10.00	20.00
-- Red and black label with six "eye" logos					
❑ CS 8022 [S]	Concert in Rhythm	1958	5.00	10.00	20.00
-- Red and black label with six "eye" logos					
❑ CS 8037 [S]	'S Marvelous	1958	5.00	10.00	20.00
-- Red and black label with six "eye" logos					
❑ CS 8064 [S]	Broadway in Rhythm	1959	5.00	10.00	20.00
-- Red and black label with six "eye" logos					
❑ CS 8117 [S]	Hollywood in Rhythm	1959	5.00	10.00	20.00
-- Red and black label with six "eye" logos					
❑ CS 8155 [S]	Conniff Meets Butterfield	1959	6.25	12.50	25.00
-- Red and black label with six "eye" logos					

CONNOR, CHRIS
ABC
❑ ABC-585 [M]	Chris Connor Now	1966	5.00	10.00	20.00
❑ ABCS-585 [S]	Chris Connor Now	1966	6.25	12.50	25.00
ABC-PARAMOUNT
❑ ABC-529 [M]	Gentle Bossa Nova	1965	5.00	10.00	20.00
❑ ABCS-529 [S]	Gentle Bossa Nova	1965	6.25	12.50	25.00
ATLANTIC
❑ 2-601 [(2) M]	Chris Connor Sings the George Gershwin Almanac of Song	1957	25.00	50.00	100.00
-- Black label					
❑ 2-601 [(2) M]	Chris Connor Sings the George Gershwin Almanac of Song	196?	10.00	20.00	40.00
-- Multi-color label, white "fan" logo					
❑ 2-601 [(2) M]	Chris Connor Sings the George Gershwin Almanac of Song	196?	5.00	10.00	20.00
-- Multi-color label, black "fan" logo					
❑ 1228 [M]	Chris Connor	1956	12.50	25.00	50.00
-- Black label					
❑ 1228 [M]	Chris Connor	196?	5.00	10.00	20.00
-- Multi-color label, white "fan" logo					
❑ SD 1228 [S]	Chris Connor	1958	15.00	30.00	60.00
-- Green label					
❑ SD 1228 [S]	Chris Connor	196?	6.25	12.50	25.00
-- Multi-color label, white "fan" logo					
❑ 1240 [M]	He Loves Me, He Loves Me Not	1956	12.50	25.00	50.00
-- Black label					
❑ 1240 [M]	He Loves Me, He Loves Me Not	196?	5.00	10.00	20.00
-- Multi-color label, white "fan" logo					
❑ 1240 [M]	He Loves Me, He Loves Me Not	1960	10.00	20.00	40.00
-- White "bullseye" label					
❑ SD 1240 [S]	He Loves Me, He Loves Me Not	1958	15.00	30.00	60.00
-- Green label					
❑ SD 1240 [S]	He Loves Me, He Loves Me Not	1960	12.50	25.00	50.00
-- White "bullseye" label					
❑ SD 1240 [S]	He Loves Me, He Loves Me Not	196?	6.25	12.50	25.00
-- Multi-color label, white "fan" logo					
❑ 1286 [M]	A Jazz Date with Chris Connor	1958	12.50	25.00	50.00
-- Black label					
❑ 1286 [M]	A Jazz Date with Chris Connor	196?	5.00	10.00	20.00
-- Multi-color label, white "fan" logo					
❑ 1290 [M]	Chris Craft	1958	12.50	25.00	50.00
-- Black label					
❑ 1290 [M]	Chris Craft	196?	5.00	10.00	20.00
-- Multi-color label, white "fan" logo					
❑ 1307 [M]	Ballads of the Sad Café	1959	12.50	25.00	50.00
-- Black label					
❑ 1307 [M]	Ballads of the Sad Café	196?	5.00	10.00	20.00
-- Multi-color label, white "fan" logo					
❑ SD 1307 [S]	Ballads of the Sad Café	1959	15.00	30.00	60.00
-- Green label					
❑ SD 1307 [S]	Ballads of the Sad Café	196?	6.25	12.50	25.00
-- Multi-color label, white "fan" logo					
❑ 1309 [M]	Chris Connor Sings the George Gershwin Almanac of Song, Vol. 1	1959	10.00	20.00	40.00
-- Black label					
❑ 1309 [M]	Chris Connor Sings the George Gershwin Almanac of Song, Vol. 1	196?	5.00	10.00	20.00
-- Multi-color label, white "fan" logo					
❑ 1310 [M]	Chris Connor Sings the George Gershwin Almanac of Song, Vol. 2	1959	10.00	20.00	40.00
-- Black label					
❑ 1310 [M]	Chris Connor Sings the George Gershwin Almanac of Song, Vol. 2	196?	5.00	10.00	20.00
-- Multi-color label, white "fan" logo					
❑ 8014 [M]	I Miss You So	1957	12.50	25.00	50.00
-- Black label					
❑ 8014 [M]	I Miss You So	196?	5.00	10.00	20.00
-- Multi-color label, white "fan" logo					
❑ 8014 [M]	I Miss You So	1960	10.00	20.00	40.00
-- White "bullseye" label					
❑ 8032 [M]	Witchcraft	1959	12.50	25.00	50.00
-- Black label					
❑ 8032 [M]	Witchcraft	196?	5.00	10.00	20.00
-- Multi-color label, white "fan" logo					
❑ SD 8032 [S]	Witchcraft	1959	15.00	30.00	60.00
-- Green label					
❑ SD 8032 [S]	Witchcraft	196?	6.25	12.50	25.00
-- Multi-color label, white "fan" logo					
❑ 8040 [M]	Chris In Person	1959	12.50	25.00	50.00
-- Black label					
❑ 8040 [M]	Chris In Person	196?	5.00	10.00	20.00
-- Multi-color label, white "fan" logo					
❑ SD 8040 [S]	Chris In Person	1959	15.00	30.00	60.00
-- Green label					
❑ SD 8040 [S]	Chris In Person	196?	6.25	12.50	25.00
-- Multi-color label, white "fan" logo					
❑ 8046 [M]	A Portrait of Chris	1960	10.00	20.00	40.00
-- Multi-color label, white "fan" logo					
❑ SD 8046 [S]	A Portrait of Chris	1960	12.50	25.00	50.00
-- Multi-color label, white "fan" logo					
❑ 8061 [M]	Free Spirits	1962	7.50	15.00	30.00
-- Multi-color label, black "fan" logo					
❑ SD 8061 [S]	Free Spirits	1962	10.00	20.00	40.00
-- Multi-color label, black "fan" logo					
BETHLEHEM
❑ BCP-20 [M]	This Is Chris	1955	15.00	30.00	60.00
❑ BCP-56 [M]	Chris	1957	15.00	30.00	60.00
❑ BCP-1001 [10]	Chris Connor Sings Lullabys of Birdland	1954	20.00	40.00	80.00
❑ BCP-1002 [10]	Chris Connor Sings Lullabys for Lovers	1954	20.00	40.00	80.00
❑ BCP-6004 [M]	Chris Connor Sings Lullabys of Birdland	1955	12.50	25.00	50.00
FM
❑ 300 [M]	Chris Connor at the Village Gate	1963	12.50	25.00	50.00
❑ S-300 [S]	Chris Connor at the Village Gate	1963	15.00	30.00	60.00
❑ 312 [M]	A Weekend in Paris	1964	12.50	25.00	50.00
❑ S-312 [S]	A Weekend in Paris	1964	15.00	30.00	60.00

CONNOR, CHRIS, AND MAYNARD FERGUSON
Also see each artist's individual listings.
ATLANTIC
❑ 8049 [M]	Double Exposure	1961	7.50	15.00	30.00
-- Multi-color label, white "fan" logo					
❑ SD 8049 [S]	Double Exposure	1961	10.00	20.00	40.00
-- Multi-color label, white "fan" logo					
ROULETTE
❑ R 52068 [M]	Two's Company	1961	7.50	15.00	30.00
-- White label with colored spokes					
❑ SR 52068 [S]	Two's Company	1961	10.00	20.00	40.00
-- White label with colored spokes					

CONNY
CAPITOL
❑ T 10253 [M]	Germany's Greatest Record Star	1960	7.50	15.00	30.00

CONSTANTINE, EDDIE
KAPP
❑ KL-1018 [M]	La Grande Sensation de la Paris	1957	7.50	15.00	30.00

Number	Title	Yr	VG	VG+	NM
MERCURY					
❑ MG-20339 [M]	The Rage of Paris	1958	6.25	12.50	25.00
CONTOURS, THE					
GORDY					
❑ G 901 [M]	Do You Love Me?	1962	125.00	250.00	500.00
CONWAY, JULIE					
HARMONY					
❑ HL 7143 [M]	Good Housekeeping's Plan for Reducing Off-the-Record	1960	5.00	10.00	20.00
COODER, RY					
MOBILE FIDELITY					
❑ 1-085	Jazz	198?	100.00	200.00	400.00
-- Audiophile vinyl					
REPRISE					
❑ PRO 588 [DJ]	The Ry Cooder Radio Show	1976	25.00	50.00	100.00
COOKE, ALISTAIR					
COLUMBIA MASTERWORKS					
❑ ML 4970 [M]	An Evening with Alistair Cooke	1955	10.00	20.00	40.00
COOKE, SAM					
FAMOUS					
❑ 502	Sam's Songs	1969	10.00	20.00	40.00
❑ 505	Only Sixteen	1969	10.00	20.00	40.00
❑ 508	So Wonderful	1969	10.00	20.00	40.00
❑ 509	You Send Me	1969	10.00	20.00	40.00
❑ 512	Cha-Cha-Cha	1969	10.00	20.00	40.00
KEEN					
❑ A-2001 [M]	Sam Cooke	1958	50.00	100.00	200.00
❑ A-2003 [M]	Encore	1958	50.00	100.00	200.00
❑ A-2004 [M]	Tribute to the Lady	1959	37.50	75.00	150.00
❑ AS-2004 [S]	Tribute to the Lady	1959	50.00	100.00	200.00
❑ 86101 [M]	Hit Kit	1959	62.50	125.00	250.00
❑ 86103 [M]	I Thank God	1960	100.00	200.00	400.00
❑ 86106 [M]	The Wonderful World of Sam Cooke	1960	87.50	175.00	350.00
RCA CAMDEN					
❑ CAL-2264 [M]	The One and Only Sam Cooke	1967	5.00	10.00	20.00
RCA VICTOR					
❑ LPM-2221 [M]	Cooke's Tour	1960	10.00	20.00	40.00
❑ LSP-2221 [S]	Cooke's Tour	1960	12.50	25.00	50.00
❑ LPM-2236 [M]	Hits of the 50's	1960	10.00	20.00	40.00
❑ LSP-2236 [S]	Hits of the 50's	1960	12.50	25.00	50.00
❑ LPM-2293 [M]	Swing Low	1960	10.00	20.00	40.00
❑ LSP-2293 [S]	Swing Low	1960	12.50	25.00	50.00
❑ LPM-2392 [M]	My Kind of Blues	1961	10.00	20.00	40.00
❑ LSP-2392 [S]	My Kind of Blues	1961	12.50	25.00	50.00
❑ LPM-2555 [M]	Twistin' the Night Away	1962	10.00	20.00	40.00
❑ LSP-2555 [S]	Twistin' the Night Away	1962	12.50	25.00	50.00
❑ LPM-2625 [M]	The Best of Sam Cooke	1962	7.50	15.00	30.00
❑ LSP-2625 [R]	The Best of Sam Cooke	1962	5.00	10.00	20.00
❑ LPM-2673 [M]	Mr. Soul	1963	7.50	15.00	30.00
❑ LSP-2673 [S]	Mr. Soul	1963	10.00	20.00	40.00
❑ LPM-2709 [M]	Night Beat	1963	7.50	15.00	30.00
❑ LSP-2709 [S]	Night Beat	1963	10.00	20.00	40.00
❑ LPM-2899 [M]	Ain't That Good News	1964	7.50	15.00	30.00
❑ LSP-2899 [S]	Ain't That Good News	1964	10.00	20.00	40.00
❑ LPM-2970 [M]	Sam Cooke at the Copa	1964	7.50	15.00	30.00
❑ LSP-2970 [S]	Sam Cooke at the Copa	1964	10.00	20.00	40.00
❑ LPM-3367 [M]	Shake	1965	6.25	12.50	25.00
❑ LSP-3367 [S]	Shake	1965	7.50	15.00	30.00
❑ LPM-3373 [M]	The Best of Sam Cooke, Volume 2	1965	6.25	12.50	25.00
❑ LSP-3373 [S]	The Best of Sam Cooke, Volume 2	1965	7.50	15.00	30.00
❑ LPM-3435 [M]	Try a Little Love	1965	6.25	12.50	25.00
❑ LSP-3435 [S]	Try a Little Love	1965	7.50	15.00	30.00
❑ LPM-3517 [M]	The Unforgettable Sam Cooke	1966	5.00	10.00	20.00
❑ LSP-3517 [S]	The Unforgettable Sam Cooke	1966	6.25	12.50	25.00
❑ LSP-3991 [S]	The Man Who Invented Soul	1968	6.25	12.50	25.00
❑ VPS-6027 [(2)]	This Is Sam Cooke	1970	5.00	10.00	20.00
COOKIES, THE/LITTLE EVA/CAROLE KING					
DIMENSION					
❑ DLP-6001 [M]	The Dimension Dolls, Vol. 1	1964	62.50	125.00	250.00
COOL, CALVIN, AND THE SURF KNOBS					
CHARTER					
❑ CLP-103 [M]	The Surfer's Beat	1963	10.00	20.00	40.00
❑ CLS-103 [S]	The Surfer's Beat	1963	12.50	25.00	50.00

Number	Title	Yr	VG	VG+	NM
COOLEY, SPADE					
COLUMBIA					
❑ CL 9007 [10]	Sagebrush Swing	1949	50.00	100.00	200.00
DECCA					
❑ DL 5563 [10]	Dance-O-Rama	1955	75.00	150.00	300.00
RAYNOTE					
❑ R-5007 [M]	Fidoolin'	1959	10.00	20.00	40.00
❑ RS-5007 [S]	Fidoolin'	1959	12.50	25.00	50.00
ROULETTE					
❑ R 25145 [M]	Fidoolin'	1961	7.50	15.00	30.00
❑ SR 25145 [S]	Fidoolin'	1961	10.00	20.00	40.00
COOLIDGE, RITA					
NAUTILUS					
❑ NR-16	Anytime...Anywhere	1981	6.25	12.50	25.00
-- Audiophile vinyl					
COOPER, ALICE					
MOBILE FIDELITY					
❑ 1-063	Welcome to My Nightmare	1980	12.50	25.00	50.00
-- Audiophile vinyl					
STRAIGHT					
❑ STS-1051	Pretties for You	1969	37.50	75.00	150.00
-- Yellow label stock copy					
❑ STS-1051	Pretties for You	1970	15.00	30.00	60.00
-- Pink label stock copy					
❑ STS-1051 [DJ]	Pretties for You	1969	50.00	100.00	200.00
-- White label promo					
❑ WS 1845	Easy Action	1970	12.50	25.00	50.00
-- Pink label stock copy; "Alice Cooper" in black on cover					
❑ WS 1845	Easy Action	1970	7.50	15.00	30.00
-- Pink label stock copy; "Alice Cooper" in white on cover					
❑ WS 1845 [DJ]	Easy Action	1970	25.00	50.00	100.00
-- White label promo					
❑ WS 1883	Love It to Death	1971	12.50	25.00	50.00
-- Pink label stock copy					
❑ WS 1883 [DJ]	Love It to Death	1971	25.00	50.00	100.00
-- White label promo					
WARNER BROS.					
❑ PRO 789 [DJ]	The Alice Cooper Radio Show	1978	6.25	12.50	25.00
❑ WS 1883	Love It to Death	1971	7.50	15.00	30.00
-- Version 1: Green "WB" label; cover has Alice's thumb sticking out in such a way that it appears to be another part of the body					
❑ WS 1883	Love It to Death	1971	5.00	10.00	20.00
-- Version 2: Green "WB" label; same as above, but has a white box reading "Contains the Hit 'I'm Eighteen' " (versions with Alice's thumb missing go for less)					
❑ WS 1883	Love It to Death	1971	5.00	10.00	20.00
-- Version 3: Green "WB" label; cover has large white areas at top and bottom with lower half of the photo cropped out					
❑ BS 2567	Killer	1971	7.50	15.00	30.00
-- Early copies have an attached 1972 calendar/poster					
❑ BS 2623	School's Out	1972	7.50	15.00	30.00
-- With paper panties intact; back cover lists song titles					
❑ BS 2623	School's Out	1972	5.00	10.00	20.00
-- Back cover does not list song titles, but panties are missing					
❑ BS 2623	School's Out	1972	10.00	20.00	40.00
-- With paper panties intact; back cover does not list song titles					
❑ BS4 2685 [Q]	Billion Dollar Babies	1974	6.25	12.50	25.00
❑ BS4 2748 [Q]	Muscle of Love	1974	6.25	12.50	25.00
❑ BS4 2803 [Q]	Alice Cooper's Greatest Hits	1974	6.25	12.50	25.00
COOPER, JACKIE					
DOT					
❑ DLP-3146 [M]	The Movies Swing!	1958	7.50	15.00	30.00
COOPER, LES, AND THE SOUL ROCKERS					
EVERLAST					
❑ ELP-202 [M]	Wiggle Wobble	1963	12.50	25.00	50.00
COOPER, WILMA LEE AND STONEY					
DECCA					
❑ DL 4784 [M]	Wilma Lee and Stoney Cooper Sing	1966	5.00	10.00	20.00
❑ DL 74784 [S]	Wilma Lee and Stoney Cooper Sing	1966	6.25	12.50	25.00
HARMONY					
❑ HL 7233 [M]	Sacred Songs	1960	6.25	12.50	25.00
HICKORY					
❑ LP-100 [M]	There's a Big Wheel	1960	12.50	25.00	50.00
❑ LP-106 [M]	Family Favorites	1962	10.00	20.00	40.00
❑ LP-112 [M]	New Songs of Inspiration	1962	10.00	20.00	40.00

Number	Title	Yr	VG	VG+	NM
COPAS, COWBOY					
KING					
❏ 553 [M]	Cowboy Copas Sings His All-Time Hits	1957	25.00	50.00	100.00
❏ 556 [M]	Favorite Sacred Songs	1957	20.00	40.00	80.00
❏ 619 [M]	Sacred Songs by Cowboy Copas	1959	20.00	40.00	80.00
❏ 714 [M]	Tragic Tales of Love and Life	1960	20.00	40.00	80.00
❏ 720 [M]	Broken Hearted Melodies	1960	20.00	40.00	80.00
❏ 817 [M]	Country Gentleman of Song	1963	10.00	20.00	40.00
❏ 824 [M]	As You Remember Cowboy	1963	10.00	20.00	40.00
❏ 894 [M]	Cowboy Copas Hymns	1964	10.00	20.00	40.00
STARDAY					
❏ SLP-118 [M]	All Time Country Music Great	1960	10.00	20.00	40.00
❏ SLP-133 [M]	Inspirational Songs	1961	10.00	20.00	40.00
❏ SLP-144 [M]	Cowboy Copas	1961	10.00	20.00	40.00
❏ SLP-157 [M]	Opry Star Spotlight on Cowboy Copas	1962	10.00	20.00	40.00
❏ SLP-175 [M]	Mister Country Music	1962	10.00	20.00	40.00
❏ SLP-184 [M]	Songs That Made Him Famous	1962	10.00	20.00	40.00
❏ SLP-208 [M]	Country Music Entertainer #1	1963	10.00	20.00	40.00
❏ SLP-212 [M]	Beyond the Sunset	1963	10.00	20.00	40.00
❏ SLP-234 [M]	The Unforgettable Cowboy Copas	1963	10.00	20.00	40.00
❏ SLP-247 [M]	Star of the Grand Ole Opry	1963	10.00	20.00	40.00
❏ SLP-268 [M]	Cowboy Copas and His Friends	1964	10.00	20.00	40.00
❏ SLP-317 [M]	The Legend Lives On	1965	7.50	15.00	30.00
❏ SLP-347 [(2) M]	The Cowboy Copas Story	1965	7.50	15.00	30.00
COPAS, COWBOY, AND HAWKSHAW HAWKINS					
Also see each artist's individual listings.					
KING					
❏ 835 [M]	In Memory	1963	10.00	20.00	40.00
❏ 850 [M]	The Legend of Cowboy Copas and Hawkshaw Hawkins	1964	10.00	20.00	40.00
❏ 984 [M]	24 Great Hits	1968	6.25	12.50	25.00
COPAS, COWBOY/ HAWKSHAW HAWKINS/ PATSY CLINE					
Also see each artist's individual listings.					
STARDAY					
❏ SLP-346 [M]	Gone But Not Forgotten	1965	7.50	15.00	30.00
COPPER PLATED INTEGRATED CIRCUIT, THE					
COMMAND					
❏ RS-945 SD	Plugged In Pop	1969	6.25	12.50	25.00
COPPERPENNY					
RCA VICTOR					
❏ LSP-4291	Copperpenny	1970	5.00	10.00	20.00
CORDIALS, THE					
CATAMOUNT					
❏ 902	Blue Eyed Soul	1967	6.25	12.50	25.00
COREA, CHICK					
BLUE NOTE					
❏ BST-84353	Song of Singing	1970	5.00	10.00	20.00
GROOVE MERCHANT					
❏ 2202	Sundance	1972	5.00	10.00	20.00
SOLID STATE					
❏ SS-18039	Now He Sings, Now He Sobs	1969	5.00	10.00	20.00
❏ SS-18055	Chick Corea "Is"	1969	5.00	10.00	20.00
VORTEX					
❏ 2004	Tones	1971	5.00	10.00	20.00
COREY, JILL					
COLUMBIA					
❏ CL 1095 [M]	Sometimes I'm Happy, Sometimes I'm Blue	1957	7.50	15.00	30.00
CORNELL, DON					
CORAL					
❏ CRL 57055 [M]	Don	1955	7.50	15.00	30.00
❏ CRL 57133 [M]	For Teenagers Only	1957	7.50	15.00	30.00
DOT					
❏ DLP-25160 [S]	Don Cornell's Great Hits	1959	7.50	15.00	30.00
❏ DLP-3160 [M]	Don Cornell's Great Hits	1959	6.25	12.50	25.00
SIGNATURE					
❏ SM-1001 [M]	Don Cornell Sings Love Songs	1960	5.00	10.00	20.00
❏ SS-1001 [S]	Don Cornell Sings Love Songs	1960	6.25	12.50	25.00

Number	Title	Yr	VG	VG+	NM
CORNELLS, THE					
GAREX					
❏ LPGA-100 [M]	Beach Bound	1963	125.00	250.00	500.00
CORPORATION, THE					
AGE OF AQUARIUS					
❏ 4150	Get On Our Swing	1968	7.50	15.00	30.00
❏ 4250	Hassles in My Mind	1969	7.50	15.00	30.00
CAPITOL					
❏ ST-175	The Corporation	1969	12.50	25.00	50.00
CORPUS					
ACORN					
❏ 1001	Creation: A Child	1971	75.00	150.00	300.00
CORTEZ, DAVE "BABY"					
CHESS					
❏ LP-1473 [M]	Rinky Dink	1962	12.50	25.00	50.00
CLOCK					
❏ C-331 [M]	Dave "Baby" Cortez	1960	10.00	20.00	40.00
❏ CS-331 [S]	Dave "Baby" Cortez	1960	12.50	25.00	50.00
❏ MGC-20647 [M]	Dave "Baby" Cortez	1961	7.50	15.00	30.00
❏ SRC-60647 [S]	Dave "Baby" Cortez	1961	10.00	20.00	40.00
RCA VICTOR					
❏ LPM-2099 [M]	The Happy Organ	1959	20.00	40.00	80.00
❏ LSP-2099 [S]	The Happy Organ	1959	25.00	50.00	100.00
ROULETTE					
❏ R-25298 [M]	Organ Shindig	1965	5.00	10.00	20.00
❏ SR-25298 [S]	Organ Shindig	1965	6.25	12.50	25.00
❏ R-25315 [M]	Tweety Pie	1966	5.00	10.00	20.00
❏ SR-25315 [S]	Tweety Pie	1966	6.25	12.50	25.00
❏ R-25328 [M]	In Orbit with Dave "Baby" Cortez	1966	5.00	10.00	20.00
❏ SR-25328 [S]	In Orbit with Dave "Baby" Cortez	1966	6.25	12.50	25.00
T-NECK					
❏ TNS-3005	The Isley Brothers Way	1970	5.00	10.00	20.00
COSBY, BILL					
TETRAGRAMMATON					
❏ T-5100 [(2)]	8:15 12:15	1969	5.00	10.00	20.00
WARNER BROS.					
❏ PRO 249 [DJ]	Radio Sampler Album -- The Best of Bill Cosby	1969	5.00	10.00	20.00
-- Promo LP with edits of 12 tracks for radio use					
COSTELLO, ELVIS					
COLUMBIA					
❏ (no #) [PD]	My Aim Is True/This Year's Model	1978	12.50	25.00	50.00
-- Promo-only picture disc; one side is dedicated to each album					
❏ AS 529 [EP]	Live at Hollywood High	1978	5.00	10.00	20.00
-- Promo-only 12-inch version of 7-inch single					
❏ AS 958 [DJ]	Tom Snyder Interview	1981	5.00	10.00	20.00
❏ AS 1318 [DJ]	Almost Blue	1981	10.00	20.00	40.00
-- Radio sampler with introductions by Elvis before each track					
❏ HC 48157	Imperial Bedroom	1982	10.00	20.00	40.00
-- Half-Speed Mastered edition					
WARNER BROS.					
❏ PRO-A-3488 [(2) DJ]	Spike -- The Elvis Costello Hour	1989	7.50	15.00	30.00
-- Music and conversation; generic gatefold sleeve with sticker on cover					
COTTON PICKERS, THE					
PHILIPS					
❏ PHM 200-025 [M]	Country Guitar	1962	5.00	10.00	20.00
❏ PHS 600-025 [S]	Country Guitar	1962	6.25	12.50	25.00
COTTON, JAMES					
VERVE FORECAST					
❏ FT-3023 [M]	The James Cotton Blues Band	1967	6.25	12.50	25.00
❏ FTS-3023 [S]	The James Cotton Blues Band	1967	5.00	10.00	20.00
❏ FTS-3038	Pure Cotton	1968	5.00	10.00	20.00
COUCH, ORVILLE					
VEE JAY					
❏ VJ-1087 [M]	Hello Trouble	1964	5.00	10.00	20.00
❏ VJS-1087 [S]	Hello Trouble	1964	10.00	20.00	40.00
COUNT FIVE, THE					
DOUBLE SHOT					
❏ DSM-1001 [M]	Psychotic Reaction	1966	10.00	20.00	40.00

Number	Title	Yr	VG	VG+	NM
❑ DSS-5001 [R]	Psychotic Reaction	1966	6.25	12.50	25.00

COUNTRY ALL-STARS, THE
Includes CHET ATKINS.
RCA VICTOR

❑ LPM-3167 [10]	String Dustin'	1953	37.50	75.00	150.00

COUNTRY CUT-UPS, THE
TOWN HOUSE

❑ 1000 [M]	The Country Cut-Ups Go to College	195?	20.00	40.00	80.00

COUNTRY GENTLEMEN, THE
CIMARRON

❑ 2001 [M]	Songs of the Pioneers	1962	10.00	20.00	40.00

MERCURY

❑ MG-20858 [M]	Folk Session Inside	1963	5.00	10.00	20.00
❑ SR-60858 [S]	Folk Session Inside	1963	6.25	12.50	25.00

STARDAY

❑ SLP-109 [M]	Traveling Dobro Blues	1959	12.50	25.00	50.00
❑ SLP-174 [M]	Bluegrass at Carnegie Hall	1962	10.00	20.00	40.00
❑ SLP-311 [M]	Songs of the Pioneers	1965	6.25	12.50	25.00

COUNTRY GOSPELAIRES, THE
STARDAY

❑ SLP-105 [M]	The Church Back Home	1959	7.50	15.00	30.00

COUNTRY JOE AND THE FISH
Includes Joe McDonald as a solo act.
CUSTOM FIDELITY

❑ CFS-2348	Joe McDonald	1968	500.00	750.00	1,000.
-- Recorded in 1964, 200 copies were pressed for Joe McDonald.					

MOBILE FIDELITY

❑ 1-056	Paradise with an Ocean View	1981	7.50	15.00	30.00
-- Audiophile vinyl					

VANGUARD

❑ VSD-27/28 [(2)]	The Life and Times of Country Joe & the Fish From Haight-Ashbury to Woodstock	1971	5.00	10.00	20.00
❑ VSD-6545	Country Joe & The Fish/Greatest Hits	1969	5.00	10.00	20.00
❑ VSD-6555	C.J. Fish	1970	5.00	10.00	20.00
❑ VRS-9244 [M]	Electric Music for the Mind and Body	1967	25.00	50.00	100.00
-- Black label					
❑ VRS-9244 [M]	Electric Music for the Mind and Body	1967	5.00	10.00	20.00
-- Gold label					
❑ VRS-9266 [M]	I-Feel-Like-I'm-Fixin'-to-Die	1967	5.00	10.00	20.00
❑ VSD-79244 [S]	Electric Music for the Mind and Body	1967	5.00	10.00	20.00
-- Gold label					
❑ VSD-79244 [S]	Electric Music for the Mind and Body	1967	12.50	25.00	50.00
-- Black label					
❑ VSD-79266 [S]	I-Feel-Like-I'm-Fixin'-to-Die	1967	5.00	10.00	20.00
❑ 7/9266	I-Feel-Like-I'm-Fixin'-to-Die "Fish Game" Poster	1967	2.50	5.00	10.00
❑ VSD-79277	Together	1968	5.00	10.00	20.00
❑ VSD-79299	Here We Are Again	1969	5.00	10.00	20.00

COUNTS, THE
AWARE

❑ 2002	Love Sign	1973	6.25	12.50	25.00
❑ 2006	Funk Pump	1975	5.00	10.00	20.00

WESTBOUND

❑ 2011	What's Up Front That Counts	1972	7.50	15.00	30.00

COURTNEY, LOU
RIVERSIDE

❑ 92000	Skate Now (Shing-a-Ling)	1967	6.25	12.50	25.00

COUSIN WILBUR
C.W.

❑ 100 [M]	The Cousin Wilbur Show	195?	12.50	25.00	50.00

COUSINS, THE
PARKWAY

❑ P-7005 [M]	Music of the Strip	1961	5.00	10.00	20.00
❑ SP-7005 [S]	Music of the Strip	1961	6.25	12.50	25.00

COVAY, DON
ATLANTIC

❑ 8104 [M]	Mercy	1965	10.00	20.00	40.00
❑ SD 8104 [S]	Mercy	1965	12.50	25.00	50.00
❑ 8120 [M]	See Saw	1966	10.00	20.00	40.00
❑ SD 8120 [S]	See Saw	1966	12.50	25.00	50.00
❑ SD 8237	The House of Blue Lights	1969	6.25	12.50	25.00

COWARD, NOEL
COLUMBIA MASTERWORKS

❑ ML 5063 [M]	Noel Coward at Las Vegas	1955	7.50	15.00	30.00

COWARD, NOEL, AND GERTRUDE LAWRENCE
RCA VICTOR

❑ LPM-1156 [M]	Noel and Gertie	1955	7.50	15.00	30.00

COWBOY JUNKIES
LATENT RECORDINGS

❑ LATEX 4	Whites Off Earth Now!!	1986	7.50	15.00	30.00
-- Canada-only release					

RCA/CLASSIC

❑ 8568-1-R	The Trinity Session	1997	5.00	10.00	20.00
-- Reissue on audiophile vinyl					

COWSILLS, THE
LONDON

❑ PS 587	On My Side	1971	7.50	15.00	30.00

MGM

❑ E-4498 [M]	The Cowsills	1967	5.00	10.00	20.00
❑ SE-4639	II X II	1969	5.00	10.00	20.00

COX, DANNY
PIONEER

❑ 2125	Sunny	196?	7.50	15.00	30.00

TOGETHER

❑ 1011	Birth Announcement	1970	7.50	15.00	30.00

COXON'S ARMY
Early PAT BENATAR.
TRACE

❑ (# unknown)	Coxon's Army	1975	100.00	200.00	400.00

CRADDOCK, BILLY "CRASH"
ABC

❑ X-777	Afraid I'll Want to Love Her One More Time	1973	6.25	12.50	25.00

CARTWHEEL

❑ 193	Knock Three Times	1971	5.00	10.00	20.00
❑ 05001	You Better Move On	1972	5.00	10.00	20.00

KING

❑ 912 [M]	I'm Tore Up	1964	25.00	50.00	100.00

CRAMER, FLOYD
MGM

❑ E-3502 [M]	That Honky-Tonk Piano	1957	10.00	20.00	40.00

RCA VICTOR

❑ LSP-2151 [S]	Hello Blues	1960	5.00	10.00	20.00
❑ LPM-2350 [M]	Last Date	1961	5.00	10.00	20.00
❑ LSP-2350 [S]	Last Date	1961	6.25	12.50	25.00
❑ LSP-2359 [S]	On the Rebound	1961	5.00	10.00	20.00
❑ LSP-2428 [S]	Floyd Cramer Gets Organ-ized	1962	5.00	10.00	20.00
❑ LSP-2466 [S]	America's Biggest Selling Pianist	1962	5.00	10.00	20.00
❑ LSP-2544 [S]	I Remember Hank Williams	1962	5.00	10.00	20.00
❑ LSP-2642 [S]	Swing Along	1963	5.00	10.00	20.00
❑ LSP-2701 [S]	Comin' On	1963	5.00	10.00	20.00
❑ LSP-2800 [S]	Country Piano -- City Strings	1964	5.00	10.00	20.00
❑ LSP-2883 [S]	Cramer at the Console	1964	5.00	10.00	20.00
❑ LSP-3318 [S]	Hits from the Country Hall of Fame	1965	5.00	10.00	20.00
❑ LPM-3828 [M]	We Wish You a Merry Christmas	1967	7.50	15.00	30.00
❑ LPM-3925 [M]	Floyd Cramer Plays Country Classics	1968	5.00	10.00	20.00
❑ VPS-6031 [(2)]	This Is Floyd Cramer	1970	5.00	10.00	20.00

CRAMPS, THE
ENIGMA

❑ 268 [DJ]	Stay Sick!	1990	5.00	10.00	20.00
-- Promo-only version					

I.R.S.

❑ SP-501 [EP]	Gravest Hits	1979	6.25	12.50	25.00

Number	Title	Yr	VG	VG+	NM

CRANE, BOB
EPIC
❑ LN 24224 [M]	The Funny Side of TV	1966	6.25	12.50	25.00
❑ BN 26224 [S]	The Funny Side of TV	1966	7.50	15.00	30.00

CRAWFORD, HANK
ATLANTIC
❑ 1356 [M]	More Soul	1960	5.00	10.00	20.00
-- Purple and red label, white fan logo					
❑ SD 1356 [S]	More Soul	1960	6.25	12.50	25.00
-- Green and blue label, white fan logo					
❑ 1372 [M]	The Soul Clinic	1961	5.00	10.00	20.00
-- Purple and red label, white fan logo					
❑ SD 1372 [S]	The Soul Clinic	1961	6.25	12.50	25.00
-- Green and blue label, white fan logo					
❑ SD 1387 [S]	From the Heart	1962	5.00	10.00	20.00
❑ SD 1405 [S]	Soul of the Ballad	1963	5.00	10.00	20.00
❑ SD 1423 [S]	True Blue	1964	5.00	10.00	20.00
❑ SD 1436 [S]	Dig These Blues	1965	5.00	10.00	20.00
❑ SD 1455 [S]	After Hours	1966	5.00	10.00	20.00
❑ 1470 [M]	Mr. Blues	1967	5.00	10.00	20.00

MOBILE FIDELITY
❑ 1-224	Soul of the Ballad	1995	6.25	12.50	25.00
-- Audiophile vinyl					

CRAWFORD, JOHNNY
DEL-FI
❑ DFLP-1220 [M]	The Captivating Johnny Crawford	1962	10.00	20.00	40.00
❑ DFLP-1223 [M]	A Young Man's Fancy	1962	7.50	15.00	30.00
❑ DFST-1223 [S]	A Young Man's Fancy	1962	10.00	20.00	40.00
❑ DFLP-1224 [M]	Rumors	1963	7.50	15.00	30.00
❑ DFST-1224 [S]	Rumors	1963	10.00	20.00	40.00
❑ DFLP-1229 [M]	His Greatest Hits	1963	7.50	15.00	30.00
❑ DFST-1229 [S]	His Greatest Hits	1963	10.00	20.00	40.00
❑ DFLP-1248 [M]	Greatest Hits, Volume 2	1964	5.00	10.00	20.00
❑ DFST-1248 [S]	Greatest Hits, Volume 2	1964	6.25	12.50	25.00

GUEST STAR
❑ GS-1470 [M]	Johnny Crawford	196?	5.00	10.00	20.00
❑ GSS-1470 [S]	Johnny Crawford	196?	6.25	12.50	25.00

SUPREME
❑ M-110 [M]	Songs from "The Restless Ones"	1965	5.00	10.00	20.00
❑ MS-210 [S]	Songs from "The Restless Ones"	1965	6.25	12.50	25.00

CRAYTON, PEE WEE
CROWN
❑ CLP-5175 [M]	Pee Wee Crayton	1959	25.00	50.00	100.00
-- Black label					
❑ CLP-5175 [M]	Pee Wee Crayton	196?	5.00	10.00	20.00
-- Gray label					

CRAZY ELEPHANT
BELL
❑ 6034	Crazy Elephant	1969	5.00	10.00	20.00

CRAZY OTTO
DECCA
❑ DL 8113 [M]	Crazy Otto	1955	5.00	10.00	20.00
-- Black label, silver print					
❑ DL 8163 [M]	Crazy Otto Rides Again	1956	5.00	10.00	20.00
❑ DL 74157 [S]	Have Piano, Will Travel	1961	5.00	10.00	20.00
❑ DL 78919 [S]	Golden Award Songs	1960	5.00	10.00	20.00

CREAM
Also see GINGER BAKER'S AIR FORCE; BLIND FAITH; ERIC CLAPTON.
ATCO
❑ 33-206 [M]	Fresh Cream	1967	12.50	25.00	50.00
❑ SD 33-206 [S]	Fresh Cream	1967	7.50	15.00	30.00
-- Purple and brown labels					
❑ 33-232 [M]	Disraeli Gears	1967	12.50	25.00	50.00
❑ SD 33-232 [S]	Disraeli Gears	1967	7.50	15.00	30.00
-- Purple and brown labels					
❑ SD 33-291	Best of Cream	1969	6.25	12.50	25.00
❑ SD 33-328	Live Cream	1970	6.25	12.50	25.00
❑ 2-700 [(2) M]	Wheels of Fire	1968	50.00	100.00	200.00
-- White label promo; no stock copies are mono					
❑ SD 2-700 [(2) S]	Wheels of Fire	1968	12.50	25.00	50.00
-- Purple and brown labels; foil-like cover					
❑ SD 2-700 [(2) S]	Wheels of Fire	1969	5.00	10.00	20.00
-- Yellow labels; dull gray cover					
❑ SD 7001	Goodbye	1969	7.50	15.00	30.00
-- Purple and brown labels; deduct 33% if poster is missing					
❑ SD 7005	Live Cream -- Volume II	1972	6.25	12.50	25.00

DCC COMPACT CLASSICS
❑ LPZ-2015	Fresh Cream	1996	7.50	15.00	30.00
-- Audiophile vinyl					

MOBILE FIDELITY
❑ 2-066 [(2)]	Wheels of Fire	1980	22.50	45.00	90.00
-- Audiophile vinyl					

RSO
❑ 015 [(2) DJ]	Classic Cuts	1978	10.00	20.00	40.00
-- Promo-only compilation					

CREATION OF SUNLIGHT
WINDI
❑ 1001	Creation of Sunlight	1968	150.00	300.00	600.00

CREEDENCE CLEARWATER REVIVAL
DCC COMPACT CLASSICS
❑ LPZ-2019	Willie and the Poor Boys	1996	5.00	10.00	20.00
-- Audiophile vinyl					

FANTASY
❑ F-8382	Creedence Clearwater Revival	1968	6.25	12.50	25.00
-- With no reference to "Susie Q" on the front cover					
❑ F-8382 [DJ]	Creedence Clearwater Revival	1968	20.00	40.00	80.00
-- White label promo					
❑ F-8387 [DJ]	Bayou Country	1969	20.00	40.00	80.00
-- White label promo					
❑ F-8393 [DJ]	Green River	1969	20.00	40.00	80.00
-- White label promo					
❑ F-8397 [DJ]	Willy and the Poor Boys	1969	20.00	40.00	80.00
-- White label promo					
❑ F-8402 [DJ]	Cosmo's Factory	1970	20.00	40.00	80.00
-- White label promo					

MOBILE FIDELITY
❑ 1-037	Cosmo's Factory	1979	17.50	35.00	70.00
-- Audiophile vinyl					

CREME SODA
TRINITY
❑ CST-11	Tricky Zingers	197?	25.00	50.00	100.00
-- With photo of group on cover					
❑ CST-11	Tricky Zingers	197?	10.00	20.00	40.00
-- With white cover					

CRESCENDOS, THE
GUEST STAR
❑ G-1453 [M]	Oh Julie	1962	12.50	25.00	50.00
❑ GS-1453 [R]	Oh Julie	1962	5.00	10.00	20.00

CRESTS, THE
COED
❑ LPC-901 [M]	The Crests Sing All Biggies	1960	50.00	100.00	200.00
-- Red label					
❑ LPC-901 [M]	The Crests Sing All Biggies	1960	100.00	200.00	400.00
-- Yellow label, black print					
❑ LPC-904 [M]	The Best of the Crests	1961	100.00	200.00	400.00

POST
❑ 3000	The Crests Sing	196?	10.00	20.00	40.00

CREW CUTS, THE
CAMAY
❑ CA-1002 [M]	The Crew Cuts Sing Folk	196?	5.00	10.00	20.00
❑ CA-3002 [S]	The Crew Cuts Sing Folk	196?	6.25	12.50	25.00

MERCURY
❑ MG-20067 [M]	The Crew Cuts Go Longhair	1955	12.50	25.00	50.00
❑ MG-20140 [M]	The Crew Cuts On Campus	1956	12.50	25.00	50.00
❑ MG-20143 [M]	Crew Cut Capers	1956	12.50	25.00	50.00
❑ MG-20144 [M]	Rock and Roll Bash	1956	20.00	40.00	80.00
❑ MG-20199 [M]	Music A La Carte	1957	12.50	25.00	50.00
❑ MG-25200 [10]	The Crew Cuts On Campus	1956	20.00	40.00	80.00

RCA VICTOR
❑ PR-102 [M]	The Crew Cuts Sing Out!	1960	6.25	12.50	25.00
❑ PR-129 [M]	The Crew Cuts Have a Ball	1960	6.25	12.50	25.00
-- Produced for Ebonite bowling balls; Side 2 has "Bowling Tips by Top Stars"					
❑ LPM-1933 [M]	Surprise Package	1958	7.50	15.00	30.00
❑ LSP-1933 [S]	Surprise Package	1959	10.00	20.00	40.00
❑ LPM-2037 [M]	The Crew Cuts Sing	1959	7.50	15.00	30.00
❑ LSP-2037 [S]	The Crew Cuts Sing	1959	10.00	20.00	40.00
❑ LPM-2067 [M]	You Must Have Been a Beautiful Baby	1960	7.50	15.00	30.00
❑ LSP-2067 [S]	You Must Have Been a Beautiful Baby	1960	10.00	20.00	40.00

WING
❑ MGW-12125 [M]	Rock and Roll Bash	196?	6.25	12.50	25.00

Number	Title	Yr	VG	VG+	NM
❏ MGW-12145 [M] The Crew Cuts On Campus		196?	5.00	10.00	20.00
❏ MGW-12177 [M] The Crew Cuts		196?	5.00	10.00	20.00
❏ MGW-12180 [M] High School Favorites		196?	5.00	10.00	20.00
❏ MGW-12195 [M] The Crew Cuts Sing the Masters		196?	5.00	10.00	20.00

CREWE, BOB
PHILIPS

Number	Title	Yr	VG	VG+	NM
❏ PHM 200-150 [M]	All the Song Hits of the Four Seasons	1964	6.25	12.50	25.00
❏ PHM 200-238 [M]	Bob Crewe Plays the Four Seasons' Hits	1967	5.00	10.00	20.00
❏ PHS 600-150 [S]	All the Song Hits of the Four Seasons	1964	7.50	15.00	30.00

WARWICK

Number	Title	Yr	VG	VG+	NM
❏ W-2009 [M]	Kicks	1960	6.25	12.50	25.00
❏ WST-2009 [S]	Kicks	1960	12.50	25.00	50.00
❏ W-2034 [M]	Crazy in the Heart	1961	6.25	12.50	25.00
❏ WST-2034 [S]	Crazy in the Heart	1961	12.50	25.00	50.00

CRICKETS, THE
Also see TOMMY ALLSUP; SONNY CURTIS; BUDDY HOLLY.
BARNABY

Number	Title	Yr	VG	VG+	NM
❏ Z 30268	Rockin' 50's Rock 'N' Roll	1970	6.25	12.50	25.00

BRUNSWICK

Number	Title	Yr	VG	VG+	NM
❏ BL 54038 [M]	The "Chirping" Crickets	1957	200.00	400.00	800.00
-- Textured cover					
❏ BL 54038 [M]	The "Chirping" Crickets	1958	150.00	300.00	600.00
-- Regular cover					

CORAL

Number	Title	Yr	VG	VG+	NM
❏ CRL 57230 [M]	In Style with the Crickets	1960	50.00	100.00	200.00
❏ CRL 757230 [S]	In Style with the Crickets	1960	100.00	200.00	400.00

LIBERTY

Number	Title	Yr	VG	VG+	NM
❏ LRP-3272 [M]	Something Old, Something New, Something Blue, Somethin' Else	1962	37.50	75.00	150.00
❏ LRP-3351 [M]	California Sun/She Loves You	1964	25.00	50.00	100.00
❏ LST-7272 [S]	Something Old, Something New, Something Blue, Somethin' Else	1962	50.00	100.00	200.00
❏ LST-7351 [S]	California Sun/She Loves You	1964	37.50	75.00	150.00

VERTIGO

Number	Title	Yr	VG	VG+	NM
❏ VEL-1020	Remnants	1973	5.00	10.00	20.00

CRISS, PETER
Also see CHELSEA; KISS.
CASABLANCA

Number	Title	Yr	VG	VG+	NM
❏ NBLP-7122	Peter Criss	1978	5.00	10.00	20.00
❏ NBPIX-7122 [PD]	Peter Criss	1978	12.50	25.00	50.00
❏ NBLP-7240	Out of Control	1980	6.25	12.50	25.00

CRITTERS, THE
KAPP

Number	Title	Yr	VG	VG+	NM
❏ KL-1485 [M]	Younger Girl	1966	7.50	15.00	30.00
❏ KS-3485 [S]	Younger Girl	1966	10.00	20.00	40.00

PROJECT 3

Number	Title	Yr	VG	VG+	NM
❏ PR 4001SD	Touch 'n Go with the Critters	1968	7.50	15.00	30.00
❏ PR 4002SD	The Critters	1969	7.50	15.00	30.00

CRITTERS, THE /THE YOUNG RASCALS/LOU CHRISTIE
BOUTIQUE

Number	Title	Yr	VG	VG+	NM
❏ CA-1079 [M]	A Taste of the Critters & The Young Rascals & Lou Christie	1966	10.00	20.00	40.00

CROCE, JIM
ABC

Number	Title	Yr	VG	VG+	NM
❏ ABCX-756	You Don't Mess Around with Jim	1972	5.00	10.00	20.00
-- Original covers have no green box advertising "Time in a Bottle"					

CAPITOL

Number	Title	Yr	VG	VG+	NM
❏ SMAS-315	Jim and Ingrid Croce	1970	7.50	15.00	30.00

COMMAND

Number	Title	Yr	VG	VG+	NM
❏ QD-40006 [Q]	You Don't Mess Around with Jim	1974	6.25	12.50	25.00
❏ QD-40007 [Q]	Life and Times	1974	6.25	12.50	25.00
❏ QD-40008 [Q]	I Got a Name	1974	6.25	12.50	25.00
❏ QD-40020 [Q]	Photographs & Memories/ His Greatest Hits	1974	6.25	12.50	25.00

CROCE

Number	Title	Yr	VG	VG+	NM
❏ 101	Facets	1966	75.00	150.00	300.00

DCC COMPACT CLASSICS

Number	Title	Yr	VG	VG+	NM
❏ LPZ-2054	His Greatest Recordings	1998	5.00	10.00	20.00
-- Audiophile vinyl					

MOBILE FIDELITY

Number	Title	Yr	VG	VG+	NM
❏ 1-079	You Don't Mess Around with Jim	1981	10.00	20.00	40.00
-- Audiophile vinyl					

CROME SYRCUS, THE
COMMAND

Number	Title	Yr	VG	VG+	NM
❏ RS 925 SD	The Love Cycle	1968	10.00	20.00	40.00

CROSBY, BING
BRUNSWICK

Number	Title	Yr	VG	VG+	NM
❏ BL 54005 [M]	The Voice of Bing in the 1930s	1957	6.25	12.50	25.00
❏ BL 58000 [10]	Bing Crosby, Volume 1	1950	12.50	25.00	50.00
❏ BL 58001 [10]	Bing Crosby, Volume 2	1950	12.50	25.00	50.00

CAPITOL

Number	Title	Yr	VG	VG+	NM
❏ ST 2300 [S]	That Travelin' Two-Beat	1965	5.00	10.00	20.00
❏ ST 2346 [S]	Great Country Hits	1965	5.00	10.00	20.00

COLUMBIA

Number	Title	Yr	VG	VG+	NM
❏ CL 2502 [10]	Der Bingle	1955	10.00	20.00	40.00
❏ CL 6027 [10]	Crosby Classics	1949	12.50	25.00	50.00
❏ CL 6105 [10]	Crosby Classics, Volume 2	1950	12.50	25.00	50.00
❏ C4X 44229 [(4)]	The Crooner: The Columbia Years	1988	10.00	20.00	40.00

DECCA

Number	Title	Yr	VG	VG+	NM
❏ DX 151 [(5) M]	Bing: A Musical Autobiography	195?	37.50	75.00	150.00
❏ DX 152 [(3) M]	Old Masters	195?	37.50	75.00	150.00
❏ DXB 184 [(2) M]	The Best of Bing	1965	6.25	12.50	25.00
❏ DL 4086 [M]	My Golden Favorites	1961	6.25	12.50	25.00
❏ DL 4250 [M]	Bing's Hollywood: Easy to Remember	1962	6.25	12.50	25.00
❏ DL 4251 [M]	Bing's Hollywood: Pennies from Heaven	1962	6.25	12.50	25.00
❏ DL 4252 [M]	Bing's Hollywood: Pocket Full of Dreams	1962	6.25	12.50	25.00
❏ DL 4253 [M]	Bing's Hollywood: East Side of Heaven	1962	6.25	12.50	25.00
❏ DL 4254 [M]	Bing's Hollywood: The Road Begins	1962	6.25	12.50	25.00
❏ DL 4255 [M]	Bing's Hollywood: Only Forever	1962	6.25	12.50	25.00
❏ DL 4256 [M]	Bing's Hollywood: Holiday Inn	1962	6.25	12.50	25.00
❏ DL 4257 [M]	Bing's Hollywood: Swinging on a Star	1962	6.25	12.50	25.00
❏ DL 4258 [M]	Bing's Hollywood: Accentuate the Positive	1962	6.25	12.50	25.00
❏ DL 4259 [M]	Bing's Hollywood: Blue Skies	1962	6.25	12.50	25.00
❏ DL 4260 [M]	Bing's Hollywood: But Beautiful	1962	6.25	12.50	25.00
❏ DL 4261 [M]	Bing's Hollywood: Sunshine Cake	1962	6.25	12.50	25.00
❏ DL 4262 [M]	Bing's Hollywood: Cool of the Evening	1962	6.25	12.50	25.00
❏ DL 4263 [M]	Bing's Hollywood: Zing a Little Zong	1962	6.25	12.50	25.00
❏ DL 4264 [M]	Bing's Hollywood: Anything Goes	1962	6.25	12.50	25.00
❏ DL 4281 [M]	Holiday in Europe	1962	6.25	12.50	25.00
❏ DL 4283 [M]	Two Favorite Stories by Bing Crosby	1962	6.25	12.50	25.00
❏ DL 4415 [M]	Songs Everybody Knows	1964	6.25	12.50	25.00
❏ DLP 5000 [10]	Hits from Musical Comedies	1949	12.50	25.00	50.00
❏ DLP 5001 [10]	Jerome Kern Songs	1949	12.50	25.00	50.00
❏ DLP 5010 [10]	Stephen Foster Songs	1949	12.50	25.00	50.00
❏ DLP 5011 [10]	El Bingo	1949	12.50	25.00	50.00
❏ DLP 5019 [10]	Merry Christmas	1949	15.00	30.00	60.00
❏ DLP 5020 [10]	Christmas Greetings	1949	15.00	30.00	60.00
❏ DL 5028 [10]	Auld Lang Syne	1950	12.50	25.00	50.00
❏ DL 5037 [10]	St. Patrick's Day	1950	12.50	25.00	50.00
❏ DL 5039 [10]	St. Valentine's Day	1950	12.50	25.00	50.00
❏ DL 5042 [10]	Blue Skies	1950	12.50	25.00	50.00
❏ DL 5052 [10]	Going My Way/The Bells of St. Mary's	1950	15.00	30.00	60.00
❏ DL 5063 [10]	Don't Fence Me In	1950	12.50	25.00	50.00
❏ DL 5064 [10]	Cole Porter Songs	1950	12.50	25.00	50.00
❏ DL 5081 [10]	Songs by Gershwin	1950	12.50	25.00	50.00
❏ DL 5102 [10]	Blue of the Night	1950	12.50	25.00	50.00
❏ DL 5107 [10]	Cowboy Songs	1950	12.50	25.00	50.00
❏ DL 5119 [10]	Drifting and Dreaming	1950	12.50	25.00	50.00
❏ DL 5122 [10]	Hawaiian Songs	1950	12.50	25.00	50.00
❏ DL 5126 [10]	Stardust	1950	12.50	25.00	50.00
❏ DL 5129 [10]	Cowboy Songs, Volume 2	1950	12.50	25.00	50.00
❏ DL 5220 [10]	Bing Sings Hits	1950	12.50	25.00	50.00
❏ DL 5272 [10]	Top o' the Morning/ The Emperor Waltz	1950	12.50	25.00	50.00
❏ DL 5284 [10]	Mr. Music	1950	12.50	25.00	50.00
❏ DL 5298 [10]	Hits from Broadway Shows	1951	12.50	25.00	50.00
❏ DL 5299 [10]	Favorite Hawaiian Songs	1951	12.50	25.00	50.00
❏ DL 5302 [10]	Go West, Young Man	1951	12.50	25.00	50.00
❏ DL 5310 [10]	Way Back Home	1951	12.50	25.00	50.00
❏ DL 5323 [10]	Bing and the Dixieland Bands	1951	12.50	25.00	50.00
❏ DL 5326 [10]	Yours Is My Heart Alone	1951	12.50	25.00	50.00
❏ DL 5331 [10]	Country Style	1951	12.50	25.00	50.00
❏ DL 5340 [10]	Down Memory Lane	1951	12.50	25.00	50.00
❏ DL 5343 [10]	Down Memory Lane, Volume 2	1951	12.50	25.00	50.00
❏ DL 5351 [10]	Beloved Hymns	1951	12.50	25.00	50.00
❏ DL 5355 [10]	Bing Sings Victor Herbert	1951	12.50	25.00	50.00
❏ DL 5390 [10]	Bing and Connee	1953	12.50	25.00	50.00
-- With Connee Boswell					

Number	Title	Yr	VG	VG+	NM
❏ DL 5403 [10]	When Irish Eyes Are Smiling	1952	12.50	25.00	50.00
❏ DL 5417 [10]	Just for You	1952	12.50	25.00	50.00
❏ DL 5444 [10]	The Road to Bali	1952	15.00	30.00	60.00
❏ DL 5499 [10]	Song Hits of Paris/Le Bing	1953	12.50	25.00	50.00
❏ DL 5508 [10]	Some Fine Old Chestnuts	1953	12.50	25.00	50.00
❏ DL 5520 [10]	Bing Sings the Hits	1954	12.50	25.00	50.00
❏ DL 5556 [10]	Country Girl/Little Boy Lost/ Anything Goes	1954	12.50	25.00	50.00
❏ DL 6000 [10]	Two Favorite Stories by Bing Crosby	1950	15.00	30.00	60.00
❏ DL 6001 [10]	Ichabod/Rip Van Winkle	1950	12.50	25.00	50.00
❏ DL 6008 [10]	Collector's Classics: Mississippi/Here Is My Heart	1951	15.00	30.00	60.00
❏ DL 6009 [10]	Collector's Classics: Anything Goes/Two for Tonight	1951	15.00	30.00	60.00
❏ DL 6010 [10]	Collector's Classics: Rhythm on the Range/Pennies from Heaven	1951	15.00	30.00	60.00
❏ DL 6011 [10]	Collector's Classics: Waikiki Wedding	1951	15.00	30.00	60.00
❏ DL 6012 [10]	Collector's Classics: Paris Honeymoon	1951	15.00	30.00	60.00
❏ DL 6013 [10]	Collector's Classics: The Star Maker/Doctor Rhythm	1951	15.00	30.00	60.00
❏ DL 6014 [10]	Collector's Classics: Big Broadcast of 1936	1951	15.00	30.00	60.00
❏ DL 6015 [10]	Collector's Classics: The Road to Singapore/If I Had My Way	1951	15.00	30.00	60.00
❏ DL 8020 [M]	The Man Without a Country/ What So Proudly We Hail	1950	10.00	20.00	40.00
❏ DL 8110 [M]	Lullaby Time	1955	10.00	20.00	40.00
❏ DL 8128 [M]	Merry Christmas	1955	10.00	20.00	40.00
-- Expanded version of 10-inch LP; all-black label					
❏ DL 8128 [M]	Merry Christmas	1960	6.25	12.50	25.00
-- Reissue on black label with color bars					
❏ DL 8128 [M]	Merry Christmas	1960	15.00	30.00	60.00
-- Black label with color bars; at least one copy is known to exist on red vinyl					
❏ DL 8207 [M]	Shillelaghs and Shamrocks	1956	10.00	20.00	40.00
❏ DL 8210 [M]	Home on the Range	1956	10.00	20.00	40.00
❏ DL 8262 [M]	When Irish Eyes Are Smiling	1956	10.00	20.00	40.00
❏ DL 8268 [M]	Drifting and Dreaming	1956	10.00	20.00	40.00
❏ DL 8269 [M]	Blue Hawaii	1956	10.00	20.00	40.00
❏ DL 8318 [M]	Anything Goes	1956	12.50	25.00	50.00
❏ DL 8352 [M]	Song I Wish I Had Sung... The First Time Around	1956	10.00	20.00	40.00
❏ DL 8365 [M]	Twilight on the Trail	1957	10.00	20.00	40.00
❏ DL 8374 [M]	Some Fine Old Chestnuts	1957	10.00	20.00	40.00
❏ DL 8419 [M]	A Christmas Sing with Bing Around the World	1957	10.00	20.00	40.00
❏ DL 8493 [M]	Bing and the Dixieland Bands	1957	10.00	20.00	40.00
❏ DL 8575 [M]	New Tricks	1957	10.00	20.00	40.00
❏ DL 8687 [M]	Around the World	1958	10.00	20.00	40.00
❏ DL 8780 [M]	Bing in Paris	1958	10.00	20.00	40.00
❏ DL 8781 [M]	That Christmas Feeling	1958	7.50	15.00	30.00
-- Expanded version of DL 5020; all-black label, textured cover					
❏ DL 8781 [M]	That Christmas Feeling	1960	5.00	10.00	20.00
-- Reissue on black label with color bars, smooth cover					
❏ DL 8846 [M]	In a Little Spanish Town	1959	7.50	15.00	30.00
❏ DL 9054 [M]	Bing: A Musical Autobiography 1927-1934	1961	10.00	20.00	40.00
❏ DL 9064 [M]	Bing: A Musical Autobiography 1934-1941	1961	10.00	20.00	40.00
❏ DL 9067 [M]	Bing: A Musical Autobiography 1941-44	1961	10.00	20.00	40.00
❏ DL 9077 [M]	Bing: A Musical Autobiography 1944-47	1961	10.00	20.00	40.00
❏ DL 9078 [M]	Bing: A Musical Autobiography 1947-1953	1961	10.00	20.00	40.00
❏ DL 9106 [M]	Ichabod/Rip Van Winkle	1962	6.25	12.50	25.00
GOLDEN					
❏ A298:20 [M]	Ali Baba and the 40 Thieves	1957	6.25	12.50	25.00
❏ A298:21 [M]	How Lovely Is Christmas/ A Christmas Story	195?	6.25	12.50	25.00
MGM					
❏ SE-3890 [S]	Senor Bing	1961	5.00	10.00	20.00
❏ SE-4129 [S]	The Great Standards	1963	5.00	10.00	20.00
❏ SE-4203 [S]	The Very Best of Bing Crosby	1964	5.00	10.00	20.00
MOBILE FIDELITY					
❏ 1-260	Bing Sings Whilst Bregman Swings	1996	5.00	10.00	20.00
-- Audiophile vinyl					
RCA VICTOR					
❏ LPM-1473 [M]	Bing with a Beat	1957	6.25	12.50	25.00
❏ LPM-1854 [M]	Fancy Meeting You Here	1958	5.00	10.00	20.00
❏ LSP-1854 [S]	Fancy Meeting You Here	1958	7.50	15.00	30.00
❏ LPM-2071 [M]	Young Bing Crosby	1959	5.00	10.00	20.00
REPRISE					
❏ R9-6106 [S]	Return to Paradise Islands	1964	5.00	10.00	20.00
VERVE					
❏ MGV 2020 [M]	Bing Sings Whilst Bregman Swings	1956	12.50	25.00	50.00

Number	Title	Yr	VG	VG+	NM
❏ V-2020 [M]	Bing Sings Whilst Bregman Swings	1961	6.25	12.50	25.00
WARNER BROS.					
❏ 2W 1401 [(2) M]	101 Gang Songs	1961	5.00	10.00	20.00
❏ 2WS 1401 [(2) S]	101 Gang Songs	1961	6.25	12.50	25.00
❏ WS 1363 [S]	Join with Bing and Sing Along	1960	5.00	10.00	20.00
❏ WS 1422 [S]	Join Bing in a Gang Song Sing-Along	1961	5.00	10.00	20.00
❏ WS 1435 [S]	Join Bing and Sing Along	1962	5.00	10.00	20.00
❏ WS 1482 [S]	On the Happy Side	1962	5.00	10.00	20.00
❏ WS 1484 [S]	I Wish You a Merry Christmas	1962	5.00	10.00	20.00
"X"					
❏ XLVA-4250 [M]	Young Bing Crosby	1955	12.50	25.00	50.00

CROSBY, BING, AND LOUIS ARMSTRONG
Also see each artist's individual listings.

Number	Title	Yr	VG	VG+	NM
MGM					
❏ SE-3882 [S]	Bing and Satchmo	1960	5.00	10.00	20.00

CROSBY, STILLS & NASH
Also see STEPHEN STILLS.

Number	Title	Yr	VG	VG+	NM
ATLANTIC					
❏ SD 8229	Crosby, Stills & Nash	1969	5.00	10.00	20.00
NAUTILUS					
❏ NR-48	Crosby, Stills & Nash	1982	37.50	75.00	150.00
-- Audiophile vinyl					

CROSBY, STILLS, NASH & YOUNG
Also see STEPHEN STILLS; NEIL YOUNG.

Number	Title	Yr	VG	VG+	NM
ATLANTIC					
❏ PR 165 [M-DJ]	Celebration/CSNY Month	1974	25.00	50.00	100.00
-- Promo-only LP in mono					
❏ PR 165 [S-DJ]	Celebration/CSNY Month	1974	12.50	25.00	50.00
-- Promo-only LP in stereo					
❏ 2-902 [(2) M]	4 Way Street	1971	25.00	50.00	100.00
-- White label promo; no stock copies are mono					
❏ SD 2-902 [(2)]	4 Way Street	1971	5.00	10.00	20.00
❏ SD 2-902 [(2) DJ]	4 Way Street	1971	12.50	25.00	50.00
-- White label stereo promo					
❏ 7200 [M]	Deja Vu	1970	37.50	75.00	150.00
-- White label promo; no stock copies are mono					
❏ SD 7200 [DJ]	Deja Vu	1970	15.00	30.00	60.00
-- White label stereo promo					
❏ PR 18102 [DJ]	A Rap with C, S, N & Y	1974	12.50	25.00	50.00
-- Promo-only interview album					

CROSSFIRES, THE

Number	Title	Yr	VG	VG+	NM
STRAND					
❏ SL-1083 [M]	Limbo Rock	1963	5.00	10.00	20.00
❏ SLS-1083 [S]	Limbo Rock	1963	6.25	12.50	25.00

CROSTON, JILL -- See LACY J. DALTON.

CROTHERS, SCATMAN

Number	Title	Yr	VG	VG+	NM
CRAFTSMAN					
❏ 8036 [M]	Gone with the Scat Man	1960	7.50	15.00	30.00
DOOTO					
❏ DTL 814 [M]	Comedy Sweepstakes	1961	6.25	12.50	25.00
MOTOWN					
❏ M 777L	Big Ben Sings	1973	5.00	10.00	20.00
TOPS					
❏ 1511 [M]	Rock and Roll with Scat Man	1956	20.00	40.00	80.00

CROW

Number	Title	Yr	VG	VG+	NM
AMARET					
❏ ST-5002	Crow Music	1969	5.00	10.00	20.00
❏ ST-5006	Crow By Crow	1970	5.00	10.00	20.00
❏ ST-5009	Mosaic	1971	5.00	10.00	20.00

CROWS, THE / THE HARPTONES

Number	Title	Yr	VG	VG+	NM
ROULETTE					
❏ RE-114 [(2)]	Echoes of a Rock Era: The	1973	5.00	10.00	20.00

CRUCIFIX

Number	Title	Yr	VG	VG+	NM
UNIVERSAL					
❏ RON 2 [EP]	Crucifix	1982	10.00	20.00	40.00

CRUDUP, ARTHUR

Number	Title	Yr	VG	VG+	NM
DELMARK					
❏ DS-614	Look on Yonder's Wall	1969	10.00	20.00	40.00

Number	Title	Yr	VG	VG+	NM
❏ DS-621	Crudup's Mood	1969	10.00	20.00	40.00

FIRE

Number	Title	Yr	VG	VG+	NM
❏ 103 [M]	Mean Ol' Frisco	1960	300.00	600.00	900.00

RCA VICTOR

Number	Title	Yr	VG	VG+	NM
❏ LVP-573	Father of Rock and Roll	1971	5.00	10.00	20.00

CRUM, SIMON -- See FERLIN HUSKY.

CRUSADERS, THE
Includes listings for The Jazz Crusaders.

CRUSADERS

Number	Title	Yr	VG	VG+	NM
❏ 16000	Street Life	1982	6.25	12.50	25.00
-- Audiophile vinyl					
❏ 16002	Ongaku-Kai: Live in Japan	1982	6.25	12.50	25.00
-- Audiophile vinyl					

MOBILE FIDELITY

Number	Title	Yr	VG	VG+	NM
❏ 1-010	Chain Reaction	1979	5.00	10.00	20.00
-- Audiophile vinyl					

PACIFIC JAZZ

Number	Title	Yr	VG	VG+	NM
❏ PJ-27 [M]	Freedom Sound	1961	6.25	12.50	25.00
❏ ST-27 [S]	Freedom Sound	1961	7.50	15.00	30.00
❏ PJ-43 [M]	Lookin' Ahead	1962	6.25	12.50	25.00
❏ ST-43 [S]	Lookin' Ahead	1962	7.50	15.00	30.00
❏ PJ-57 [M]	The Jazz Crusaders at the Lighthouse	1962	6.25	12.50	25.00
❏ ST-57 [S]	The Jazz Crusaders at the Lighthouse	1962	7.50	15.00	30.00
❏ PJ-68 [M]	Tough Talk	1963	6.25	12.50	25.00
❏ ST-68 [S]	Tough Talk	1963	7.50	15.00	30.00
❏ PJ-76 [M]	Heat Wave	1963	6.25	12.50	25.00
❏ ST-76 [S]	Heat Wave	1963	7.50	15.00	30.00
❏ PJ-83 [M]	Stretchin' Out	1964	6.25	12.50	25.00
❏ ST-83 [S]	Stretchin' Out	1964	7.50	15.00	30.00
❏ PJ-87 [M]	The Thing	1964	6.25	12.50	25.00
❏ ST-87 [S]	The Thing	1964	7.50	15.00	30.00
❏ PJ-10092 [M]	Chili Con Soul	1965	5.00	10.00	20.00
❏ PJ-10098 [M]	The Jazz Crusaders at the Lighthouse '66	1966	5.00	10.00	20.00
❏ PJ-10106 [M]	Talk That Talk	1966	5.00	10.00	20.00
❏ PJ-10115 [M]	The Festival Album	1967	6.25	12.50	25.00
❏ PJ-10124	Uh Huh	1967	6.25	12.50	25.00
❏ ST-20092 [S]	Chili Con Soul	1965	6.25	12.50	25.00
❏ ST-20098 [S]	The Jazz Crusaders at the Lighthouse '66	1966	6.25	12.50	25.00
❏ ST-20106 [S]	Talk That Talk	1966	6.25	12.50	25.00
❏ ST-20115 [S]	The Festival Album	1967	5.00	10.00	20.00
❏ ST-20124	Uh Huh	1967	5.00	10.00	20.00
❏ ST-20131	The Jazz Crusaders at the Lighthouse '68	1968	5.00	10.00	20.00
❏ ST-20136	Powerhouse	1968	5.00	10.00	20.00
❏ ST-20165	The Jazz Crusaders at the Lighthouse '69	1969	5.00	10.00	20.00
❏ ST-20175	The Best of the Jazz Crusaders	1969	5.00	10.00	20.00

CRYAN' SHAMES, THE
COLUMBIA

Number	Title	Yr	VG	VG+	NM
❏ CL 2589 [M]	Sugar & Spice	1967	5.00	10.00	20.00
❏ CL 2786 [M]	A Scratch in the Sky	1967	6.25	12.50	25.00
❏ CS 9389 [S]	Sugar & Spice	1967	6.25	12.50	25.00
❏ CS 9586 [S]	A Scratch in the Sky	1967	5.00	10.00	20.00
❏ CS 9719	Synthesis	1969	5.00	10.00	20.00

CRYSTAL MANSION, THE
CAPITOL

Number	Title	Yr	VG	VG+	NM
❏ ST-227	The Crystal Mansion	1969	5.00	10.00	20.00

CRYSTALS, THE
PHILLES

Number	Title	Yr	VG	VG+	NM
❏ PHLP-4000 [M]	Twist Uptown	1962	150.00	300.00	600.00
❏ PHLP-4001 [M]	He's a Rebel	1963	150.00	300.00	600.00
❏ PHLP-4003 [M]	The Crystals Sing the Greatest Hits, Vol. 1	1963	150.00	300.00	600.00
❏ DT-90722 [R]	Twist Uptown	1965	300.00	600.00	1,200.
-- Capitol Record Club edition					
❏ T-90722 [M]	Twist Uptown	1965	150.00	300.00	600.00
-- Capitol Record Club edition					

CUBY AND THE BLIZZARDS
PHILIPS

Number	Title	Yr	VG	VG+	NM
❏ PHS 600-307	Cuby and the Blizzards Live	1969	5.00	10.00	20.00
❏ PHS 600-331	King of the World	1970	5.00	10.00	20.00

CUFF LINKS, THE
DECCA

Number	Title	Yr	VG	VG+	NM
❏ DL 75160	Tracy	1969	5.00	10.00	20.00
❏ DL 75235	The Cuff Links	1970	5.00	10.00	20.00

CUGAT, XAVIER
COLUMBIA

Number	Title	Yr	VG	VG+	NM
❏ CL 515 [M]	Relaxing with Cugat (Quiet Music, Volume VI)	1953	10.00	20.00	40.00
-- Second editions have maroon label, gold print and a "CL" prefix					
❏ GL 515 [M]	Relaxing with Cugat (Quiet Music, Volume VI)	1952	12.50	25.00	50.00
-- Original copies have black label, silver print and a "GL" prefix					
❏ CL 537 [M]	Dance with Cugat	1953	10.00	20.00	40.00
-- Maroon label, gold print					
❏ CL 537 [M]	Dance with Cugat	1955	6.25	12.50	25.00
-- Red and black label with six "eye" logos					
❏ CL 579 [M]	Favorite Rhumbas	1954	10.00	20.00	40.00
-- Maroon label, gold print					
❏ CL 579 [M]	Favorite Rhumbas	1955	6.25	12.50	25.00
-- Red and black label with six "eye" logos					
❏ CL 610 [M]	Ole	1955	10.00	20.00	40.00
-- Maroon label, gold print					
❏ CL 610 [M]	Ole	1955	6.25	12.50	25.00
-- Red and black label with six "eye" logos					
❏ CL 626 [M]	Mucho Mucho Mambo	1955	10.00	20.00	40.00
-- Maroon label, gold print					
❏ CL 626 [M]	Mucho Mucho Mambo	1955	6.25	12.50	25.00
-- Red and black label with six "eye" logos					
❏ CL 718 [M]	Cha Cha Cha	1956	7.50	15.00	30.00
-- Red and black label with six "eye" logos					
❏ CL 732 [M]	Mambo at the Waldorf	1956	7.50	15.00	30.00
-- Red and black label with six "eye" logos					
❏ CL 733 [M]	Merengue by Cugat	1956	7.50	15.00	30.00
-- Red and black label with six "eye" logos					
❏ CL 1064 [M]	Bread, Love and Cha Cha Cha	1957	6.25	12.50	25.00
❏ CL 1094 [M]	Cugar Cavalcade	1958	6.25	12.50	25.00
-- Red and black label with six "eye" logos					
❏ CL 1143 [M]	Waltzes! But By Cugat	1959	6.25	12.50	25.00
-- Red and black label with six "eye" logos					
❏ CL 2506 [10]	Mambo!	1955	12.50	25.00	50.00
❏ CL 6005 [10]	Cugat's Rhumba	1948	12.50	25.00	50.00
❏ CL 6021 [10]	Cugat's Favorite Rhumbas	1949	12.50	25.00	50.00
❏ CL 6036 [10]	Rhumba with Cugat	1949	12.50	25.00	50.00
❏ CL 6077 [10]	Conga with Cugat	1949	12.50	25.00	50.00
❏ CL 6086 [10]	Tropical Bouquet	1950	12.50	25.00	50.00
❏ CL 6121 [10]	Dance Date	1950	12.50	25.00	50.00
❏ CL 6213 [10]	Mambo at the Waldorf	1951	12.50	25.00	50.00
❏ CL 6234 [10]	Tango with Cugat	1951	12.50	25.00	50.00
❏ CL 6236 [10]	Samba with Cugat	1951	12.50	25.00	50.00
❏ CS 8055 [S]	Cugar Cavalcade	1959	7.50	15.00	30.00
-- Red and black label with six "eye" logos					
❏ CS 8059 [S]	Waltzes! But By Cugat	1959	7.50	15.00	30.00
-- Red and black label with six "eye" logos					

DECCA

Number	Title	Yr	VG	VG+	NM
❏ DL 74672 [S]	Feeling Good	1965	5.00	10.00	20.00
❏ DL 74740 [S]	Dance Party	1966	5.00	10.00	20.00
❏ DL 74799 [S]	Bang Bang	1966	5.00	10.00	20.00
❏ DL 74851 [S]	Xavier Cugat Today	1967	5.00	10.00	20.00

MERCURY

Number	Title	Yr	VG	VG+	NM
❏ PPS-2003 [M]	Viva Cugat!	1961	5.00	10.00	20.00
❏ PPS-2015 [M]	The Best of Cugat	1961	5.00	10.00	20.00
❏ PPS-2021 [M]	Cugat Plays Continental Favorites	1961	5.00	10.00	20.00
❏ PPS-6003 [S]	Viva Cugat!	1961	6.25	12.50	25.00
❏ PPS-6015 [S]	The Best of Cugat	1961	6.25	12.50	25.00
❏ PPS-6021 [S]	Cugat Plays Continental Favorites	1961	6.25	12.50	25.00
❏ MG 20065 [M]	Cugat's Favorites	1955	7.50	15.00	30.00
❏ MG 20108 [M]	Mambo!/Music for Latin Lovers	1957	7.50	15.00	30.00
❏ MG-20705 [M]	Twist with Cugat	1962	5.00	10.00	20.00
❏ MG-20745 [M]	The Most Popular Movie Themes As Styled by Cugat	1961	5.00	10.00	20.00
❏ MG-20798 [M]	Cugat's Golden Goodies	1963	5.00	10.00	20.00
❏ MG-20832 [M]	Cugi's Cocktails	1963	5.00	10.00	20.00
❏ MG 25120 [10]	Here's Cugat	195?	10.00	20.00	40.00
❏ MG 25149 [10]	Dance with Cugat/The Great Latin-American Rhythms of Xavier Cugat	195?	10.00	20.00	40.00
❏ MG 25168 [10]	Mambos by Cugat	195?	10.00	20.00	40.00
❏ SR-60705 [S]	Twist with Cugat	1962	6.25	12.50	25.00
❏ SR-60745 [S]	The Most Popular Movie Themes As Styled by Cugat	1961	6.25	12.50	25.00
❏ SR-60798 [S]	Cugat's Golden Goodies	1963	6.25	12.50	25.00
❏ SR-60832 [S]	Cugi's Cocktails	1963	6.25	12.50	25.00
❏ SR-60868 [S]	Viva Cugat!	1964	5.00	10.00	20.00
-- Reissue of 6003					
❏ SR-60870 [S]	The Best of Cugat	1964	5.00	10.00	20.00
-- Reissue of 6015					
❏ SR-60888 [S]	Cugat Caricatures	1964	5.00	10.00	20.00

Number	Title	Yr	VG	VG+	NM

RCA VICTOR

Number	Title	Yr	VG	VG+	NM
❏ LPT-11 [10]	Tangos	195?	10.00	20.00	40.00
❏ LPM-1882 [M]	The King Plays Some Aces	1958	5.00	10.00	20.00
❏ LSP-1882 [S]	The King Plays Some Aces	1958	6.25	12.50	25.00
❏ LPM-1894 [M]	Cugat in Spain	1959	5.00	10.00	20.00
❏ LSP-1894 [S]	Cugat in Spain	1959	6.25	12.50	25.00
❏ LPM-1987 [M]	Chili Con Cugie	1959	5.00	10.00	20.00
❏ LSP-1987 [S]	Chili Con Cugie	1959	6.25	12.50	25.00
❏ LPM-2173 [M]	Cugat in France, Spain and Italy	1960	5.00	10.00	20.00
❏ LSP-2173 [S]	Cugat in France, Spain and Italy	1960	6.25	12.50	25.00

CULLEY, FRANK "FLOORSHOW"
BATON

Number	Title	Yr	VG	VG+	NM
❏ BL 1201 [M]	Rock 'n Roll: Instrumentals for Dancing the Lindy Hop	1955	150.00	300.00	600.00

-- B-side tracks by Buddy Tate Orchestra; this LP does exist, contrary to prior reports

CULT, THE
WARNER BROS.

Number	Title	Yr	VG	VG+	NM
❏ WBMS-147 [DJ]	Electric Interview	1987	10.00	20.00	40.00

CULTURE CLUB
VIRGIN/EPIC

Number	Title	Yr	VG	VG+	NM
❏ 9E9-39237 [PD]	Colour By Numbers	1983	6.25	12.50	25.00
❏ 9E9-40005 [PD]	Waking Up with the House on Fire	1984	6.25	12.50	25.00

CUMBERLAND THREE, THE
Also see JOHN STEWART.
ROULETTE

Number	Title	Yr	VG	VG+	NM
❏ R 25121 [M]	Folk Scene U.S.A.	1960	5.00	10.00	20.00
❏ SR 25121 [S]	Folk Scene U.S.A.	1960	6.25	12.50	25.00
❏ R 25132 [M]	Civil War Almanac, Volume 1: The Yankees	1960	5.00	10.00	20.00
❏ SR 25132 [S]	Civil War Almanac, Volume 1: The Yankees	1960	6.25	12.50	25.00
❏ R 25133 [M]	Civil War Almanac, Volume 2: The Rebels	1960	5.00	10.00	20.00
❏ SR 25133 [S]	Civil War Almanac, Volume 2: The Rebels	1960	6.25	12.50	25.00

CURE, THE
A&M

Number	Title	Yr	VG	VG+	NM
❏ SP-6020 [(2)]	Happily Ever After	1981	7.50	15.00	30.00

ELEKTRA

Number	Title	Yr	VG	VG+	NM
❏ 60737 [(2) DJ]	Kiss Me, Kiss Me, Kiss Me	1987	7.50	15.00	30.00

-- Promo-only audiophile pressing

Number	Title	Yr	VG	VG+	NM
❏ 60978 [(2)]	Mixed Up	1990	5.00	10.00	20.00

-- LP version has one extra track not on CD or cassette

Number	Title	Yr	VG	VG+	NM
❏ R 274190	Mixed Up	1990	6.25	12.50	25.00

-- BMG Direct Marketing edition

CURLESS, DICK
CAPITOL

Number	Title	Yr	VG	VG+	NM
❏ ST-552	Hard, Hard Travelin' Man	1970	5.00	10.00	20.00
❏ ST-689	Doggin' It	1971	5.00	10.00	20.00
❏ ST-792	Comin' On Country	1971	5.00	10.00	20.00
❏ ST-11087	Stonin' Around	1972	5.00	10.00	20.00
❏ ST-11119	Live at the Wheeling Truck Driver's Jamboree	1973	5.00	10.00	20.00
❏ ST-11211	The Last Blues Song	1973	7.50	15.00	30.00

-- First cover shows Dick Curless with an eye patch

Number	Title	Yr	VG	VG+	NM
❏ ST-11211	The Last Blues Song	1973	5.00	10.00	20.00

-- Second cover shows Dick Curless with no eye patch

TIFFANY

Number	Title	Yr	VG	VG+	NM
❏ 1016 [M]	Dick Curless Sings Songs of the Open Country	1958	25.00	50.00	100.00
❏ 1028 [M]	Singing Just for Fun	1959	25.00	50.00	100.00
❏ 1033 [M]	I Love to Tell a Story	1960	25.00	50.00	100.00

TOWER

Number	Title	Yr	VG	VG+	NM
❏ DT 5005 [R]	Tombstone Every Mile	1965	5.00	10.00	20.00
❏ T 5005 [M]	Tombstone Every Mile	1965	7.50	15.00	30.00
❏ DT 5012 [R]	Hymns	1965	5.00	10.00	20.00
❏ T 5012 [M]	Hymns	1965	7.50	15.00	30.00
❏ DT 5013 [R]	The Soul of Dick Curless	1966	5.00	10.00	20.00
❏ T 5013 [M]	The Soul of Dick Curless	1966	7.50	15.00	30.00
❏ DT 5015 [R]	Travelin' Man	1966	5.00	10.00	20.00
❏ T 5015 [M]	Travelin' Man	1966	7.50	15.00	30.00
❏ DT 5016 [R]	At Home with Dick Curless	1966	5.00	10.00	20.00
❏ T 5016 [M]	At Home with Dick Curless	1966	7.50	15.00	30.00
❏ ST 5066 [S]	All of Me Belongs to You	1967	7.50	15.00	30.00
❏ T 5066 [M]	All of Me Belongs to You	1967	7.50	15.00	30.00
❏ ST 5089 [S]	Ramblin' Country	1967	7.50	15.00	30.00
❏ T 5089 [M]	Ramblin' Country	1967	7.50	15.00	30.00
❏ ST 5108	The Long Lonesome Road	1968	7.50	15.00	30.00
❏ ST 5139	The Wild Side of Town	1969	7.50	15.00	30.00

CURLESS, DICK, AND KAY ADAMS
Also see each artist's individual listings.
TOWER

Number	Title	Yr	VG	VG+	NM
❏ DT 5025 [R]	A Devil Like Me Needs an Angel Like You	1966	5.00	10.00	20.00
❏ T 5025 [M]	A Devil Like Me Needs an Angel Like You	1966	7.50	15.00	30.00

CURRIE, CHERIE AND MARIE
CAPITOL

Number	Title	Yr	VG	VG+	NM
❏ ST-12022	Messin' with the Boys	1979	5.00	10.00	20.00

CURTIS, KEN
CAPITOL

Number	Title	Yr	VG	VG+	NM
❏ ST 2418 [S]	Gunsmoke's Festus	1965	10.00	20.00	40.00
❏ T 2418 [M]	Gunsmoke's Festus	1965	7.50	15.00	30.00

DOT

Number	Title	Yr	VG	VG+	NM
❏ DLP-25859	Gunsmoke's Festus Calls Out Ken Curtis	1968	7.50	15.00	30.00

CURTIS, MAC
EPIC

Number	Title	Yr	VG	VG+	NM
❏ BN 26419	The Sunshine Man	1969	5.00	10.00	20.00

CURTIS, SONNY
Also see THE CRICKETS.
IMPERIAL

Number	Title	Yr	VG	VG+	NM
❏ LP-9276 [M]	Beatle Hits Flamenco Style	1964	10.00	20.00	40.00
❏ LP-12276 [S]	Beatle Hits Flamenco Style	1964	12.50	25.00	50.00

VIVA

Number	Title	Yr	VG	VG+	NM
❏ V-36012	The First of Sonny Curtis	1968	6.25	12.50	25.00
❏ V-36021	The Sonny Curtis Style	1969	6.25	12.50	25.00

CYKLE, THE
LABEL

Number	Title	Yr	VG	VG+	NM
❏ 9-261	The Cykle	1969	125.00	250.00	500.00

CYMBAL, JOHNNY
KAPP

Number	Title	Yr	VG	VG+	NM
❏ KL-1324 [M]	Mr. Bass Man	1963	12.50	25.00	50.00
❏ KS-3324 [S]	Mr. Bass Man	1963	17.50	35.00	70.00

CYRKLE, THE
COLUMBIA

Number	Title	Yr	VG	VG+	NM
❏ CL 2544 [M]	Red Rubber Ball	1966	5.00	10.00	20.00
❏ CS 9344 [S]	Red Rubber Ball	1966	7.50	15.00	30.00
❏ CS 9432 [S]	Neon	1967	5.00	10.00	20.00

CYRUS, BILLY RAY
MERCURY

Number	Title	Yr	VG	VG+	NM
❏ 1P-8218	Some Gave All	1992	6.25	12.50	25.00

-- Only released on vinyl through Columbia House

Number	Title	Yr	VG	VG+	NM

D

DADDY COOL
REPRISE
| ☐ MS 2088 | Teenage Heaven | 1972 | 5.00 | 10.00 | 20.00 |

DADDY DEWDROP
SUNFLOWER
| ☐ SNF-5006 | Daddy Dewdrop | 1971 | 5.00 | 10.00 | 20.00 |

DAILEY, DON
CROWN
| ☐ CLP-5314 [M] | Surf Stompin' | 1963 | 7.50 | 15.00 | 30.00 |

DAKUS, WES, AND THE REBELS
KAPP
| ☐ KL-1536 [M] | Wes Dakus' Rebels | 1967 | 5.00 | 10.00 | 20.00 |
| ☐ KS-3536 [S] | Wes Dakus' Rebels | 1967 | 6.25 | 12.50 | 25.00 |

DALE AND GRACE
MICHELLE
| ☐ 100 [M] | I'm Leaving It Up to You | 1964 | 37.50 | 75.00 | 150.00 |
MONTEL
| ☐ 100 [M] | I'm Leaving It Up to You | 1964 | 37.50 | 75.00 | 150.00 |

DALE, DICK, AND THE DEL-TONES
CAPITOL
☐ ST 1930 [S]	King of the Surf Guitar	1963	25.00	50.00	100.00
☐ T 1930 [M]	King of the Surf Guitar	1963	15.00	30.00	60.00
☐ ST 2002 [S]	Checkered Flag	1963	20.00	40.00	80.00
☐ T 2002 [M]	Checkered Flag	1963	12.50	25.00	50.00
☐ ST 2053 [S]	Mr. Eliminator	1964	20.00	40.00	80.00
☐ T 2053 [M]	Mr. Eliminator	1964	12.50	25.00	50.00
☐ ST 2111 [S]	Summer Surf	1964	30.00	60.00	120.00
-- With bonus single by Jerry Cole, "Racing Waves"/"Movin' Surf," in front cover pocket					
☐ ST 2111 [S]	Summer Surf	1964	17.50	35.00	70.00
-- Without bonus single					
☐ T 2111 [M]	Summer Surf	1964	25.00	50.00	100.00
-- With bonus single by Jerry Cole, "Racing Waves"/"Movin' Surf," in front cover pocket					
☐ T 2111 [M]	Summer Surf	1964	12.50	25.00	50.00
-- Without bonus single					
☐ ST 2293 [S]	Rock Out -- Live at Ciro's	1965	37.50	75.00	150.00
☐ T 2293 [M]	Rock Out -- Live at Ciro's	1965	25.00	50.00	100.00
CLOISTER
☐ CLP-6301 [M]	Silver Sounds of the Surf	1963	50.00	100.00	200.00
-- With tracks by the Stompers					
DELTONE
☐ LPM-1001 [M]	Surfer's Choice	1962	37.50	75.00	150.00
☐ DT 1886 [R]	Surfer's Choice	1962	10.00	20.00	40.00
☐ T 1886 [M]	Surfer's Choice	1962	15.00	30.00	60.00
DUB TONE
☐ LP-1246 [M]	The Surf Family	1964	7.50	15.00	30.00
-- With tracks by the Hollywood Surfers					

DALLAS, DEAN, AND THE DOUGHBOYS
CUMBERLAND
| ☐ MGC-29516 [M] | Golden Country Hits | 1965 | 5.00 | 10.00 | 20.00 |
| ☐ SRC-69516 [S] | Golden Country Hits | 1965 | 6.25 | 12.50 | 25.00 |

DALLAS, MARIA
RCA VICTOR
| ☐ LPM-3950 [M] | Tumblin' Down | 1968 | 10.00 | 20.00 | 40.00 |
| ☐ LSP-3950 [S] | Tumblin' Down | 1968 | 5.00 | 10.00 | 20.00 |

DALTON, LACY J.
HARBOR
| ☐ 001 | Jill Croston | 1978 | 6.25 | 12.50 | 25.00 |
| -- As "Jill Croston" | | | | | |

DAMIN EIH, A.L.K. AND BROTHER CLARK
DEMELOT
| ☐ 7310 | Never Mind | 1973 | 37.50 | 75.00 | 150.00 |

DAMITA JO
ABC-PARAMOUNT
| ☐ 378 [M] | The Big Fifteen | 1961 | 20.00 | 40.00 | 80.00 |
| ☐ S-378 [S] | The Big Fifteen | 1961 | 25.00 | 50.00 | 100.00 |

EPIC
☐ BN 26131 [S]	This Is Damita Jo	1965	5.00	10.00	20.00
☐ BN 26164 [S]	One More Time with Feeling	1965	5.00	10.00	20.00
☐ BN 26202 [S]	Midnight Session	1966	5.00	10.00	20.00
☐ LN 24244 [M]	If You Go Away	1967	5.00	10.00	20.00
MERCURY
☐ MG-20642 [M]	I'll Save the Last Dance for You	1961	7.50	15.00	30.00
☐ MG-20703 [M]	Damita Jo at the Diplomat	1962	6.25	12.50	25.00
☐ MG-20734 [M]	Sing a Country Song	1962	6.25	12.50	25.00
☐ MG-20818 [M]	This One's for Me	1963	5.00	10.00	20.00
☐ SR-60642 [S]	I'll Save the Last Dance for You	1961	10.00	20.00	40.00
☐ SR-60703 [S]	Damita Jo at the Diplomat	1962	7.50	15.00	30.00
☐ SR-60734 [S]	Sing a Country Song	1962	7.50	15.00	30.00
☐ SR-60818 [S]	This One's for Me	1963	6.25	12.50	25.00
VEE JAY
☐ LP-1137 [M]	Damita Jo Sings	1965	6.25	12.50	25.00
☐ LPS-1137 [S]	Damita Jo Sings	1965	12.50	25.00	50.00

DAMNATION OF ADAM BLESSING, THE
UNITED ARTISTS
☐ UAS-5533	Which Is the Justice, Which Is the Thief	1971	5.00	10.00	20.00
☐ UAS-6738	The Damnation of Adam Blessing	1970	5.00	10.00	20.00
☐ UAS-6773	The Second Damnation	1970	5.00	10.00	20.00

DAMON
ANKH
☐ 968	Song of a Gypsy	1970	1,500.	2,250.	3,000.
-- Gatefold cover					
☐ 968	Song of a Gypsy	1970	500.00	1,000.	1,500.
-- Regular cover					

DAMONE, VIC
COLUMBIA
☐ CL 900 [M]	That Towering Feeling!	1956	6.25	12.50	25.00
☐ CL 1088 [M]	Angela Mia	1957	5.00	10.00	20.00
☐ CL 1??? [M]	Closer Than a Kiss	195?	5.00	10.00	20.00
☐ CS 8019 [S]	Closer Than a Kiss	1959	7.50	15.00	30.00
☐ CS 8046 [S]	Angela Mia	1959	7.50	15.00	30.00
☐ CS 8169 [S]	This Game of Love	1960	5.00	10.00	20.00
☐ CS 8373 [S]	On the Swingin' Side	1961	5.00	10.00	20.00
MERCURY
☐ MG-20163 [M]	Yours for a Song	1957	6.25	12.50	25.00
☐ MG-20193 [M]	My Favorites	1957	6.25	12.50	25.00
☐ MG-25028 [10]	Vic Damone	1950	10.00	20.00	40.00
☐ MG-25029 [10]	Vic Damone	1950	10.00	20.00	40.00
☐ MG-25045 [10]	Vic Damone	1950	10.00	20.00	40.00
☐ MG-25054 [10]	Song Hits	1950	10.00	20.00	40.00
☐ MG-25092 [10]	Christmas Favorites	1951	10.00	20.00	40.00
☐ MG-25100 [10]	Vic Damone and Others	1952	10.00	20.00	40.00
☐ MG-25131 [10]	The Night Has a Thousand Eyes	1952	10.00	20.00	40.00
☐ MG-25132 [10]	Vocals by Vic	1952	10.00	20.00	40.00
☐ MG-25133 [10]	April in Paris	1952	10.00	20.00	40.00
☐ MG-25156 [10]	Vic Damone	1952	10.00	20.00	40.00

DAN AND DALE
TIFTON
| ☐ M-8002 [M] | Batman and Robin | 1966 | 7.50 | 15.00 | 30.00 |
| ☐ S-78002 [S] | Batman and Robin | 1966 | 10.00 | 20.00 | 40.00 |

DANA, BILL -- See JOSE JIMENEZ.

DANA, VIC
DOLTON
☐ BLP-2013 [M]	This Is Bill Dana	1961	5.00	10.00	20.00
☐ BST-8013 [S]	This Is Bill Dana	1961	7.50	15.00	30.00
☐ BST-8015 [S]	Warm and Wild	1962	5.00	10.00	20.00
☐ BST-8026 [S]	More	1963	5.00	10.00	20.00
☐ BST-8028 [S]	Shangri-La	1964	5.00	10.00	20.00
☐ BST-8032 [S]	Now	1964	5.00	10.00	20.00
☐ BST-8034 [S]	Red Roses for a Blue Lady	1965	5.00	10.00	20.00
☐ BST-8036 [S]	Moonlight and Roses	1965	5.00	10.00	20.00
☐ BST-8041 [S]	Crystal Chandelier	1966	5.00	10.00	20.00
☐ BST-8046 [S]	Town and Country	1966	5.00	10.00	20.00
☐ BST-8048 [S]	Golden Greats	1966	5.00	10.00	20.00
☐ BST-8049 [S]	Little Altar Boy and Other Christmas Songs	1966	5.00	10.00	20.00

DANE, BARBARA
CAPITOL
| ☐ ST 1758 [S] | On My Way | 1962 | 10.00 | 20.00 | 40.00 |
| ☐ T 1758 [M] | On My Way | 1962 | 7.50 | 15.00 | 30.00 |

Number	Title	Yr	VG	VG+	NM
DOT					
❑ DLP-3177 [M]	Livin' with the Blues	1959	7.50	15.00	30.00
❑ DLP-25177 [S]	Livin' with the Blues	1959	10.00	20.00	40.00
FOLKWAYS					
❑ FA-2468	Barbara Dane and the Chambers Brothers	1966	12.50	25.00	50.00
❑ FA-2471	Folk Songs	1966	7.50	15.00	30.00

DANIELS, CHARLIE, BAND
Number	Title	Yr	VG	VG+	NM
EPIC					
❑ HE 44365	Fire on the Mountain	1982	7.50	15.00	30.00
-- Half-speed mastered edition					
❑ HE 45751	Million Mile Reflections	1982	7.50	15.00	30.00
-- Half-speed mastered edition					
MOBILE FIDELITY					
❑ 1-176	Million Mile Reflections	1984	7.50	15.00	30.00
-- Audiophile vinyl					

DANIELS, SLOPPY
Number	Title	Yr	VG	VG+	NM
DOOTO					
❑ DTL-266 [M]	Sloppy's House Party	1959	6.25	12.50	25.00

DANTE AND THE EVERGREENS
Number	Title	Yr	VG	VG+	NM
MADISON					
❑ MA-1002 [M]	Dante and the Evergreens	1961	125.00	250.00	500.00

DANTE, RON
Also see THE ARCHIES; THE DETERGENTS.

Number	Title	Yr	VG	VG+	NM
KIRSHNER					
❑ KES-106	Ron Dante Brings You Up	1970	5.00	10.00	20.00

DARCEL, DENISE
Number	Title	Yr	VG	VG+	NM
CAMEO					
❑ C-1002 [M]	Banned in Boston	1958	10.00	20.00	40.00

DARIN, BOBBY
Number	Title	Yr	VG	VG+	NM
ATCO					
❑ 33-102 [M]	Bobby Darin	1958	25.00	50.00	100.00
-- Yellow "harp" label					
❑ 33-102 [M]	Bobby Darin	1962	7.50	15.00	30.00
-- Gold and dark blue label					
❑ 33-104 [M]	That's All	1959	10.00	20.00	40.00
-- Yellow "harp" label					
❑ 33-104 [M]	That's All	1962	5.00	10.00	20.00
-- Gold and dark blue label					
❑ SD 33-104 [S]	That's All	1959	25.00	50.00	100.00
-- Yellow "harp" label					
❑ SD 33-104 [S]	That's All	1962	6.25	12.50	25.00
-- Purple and brown label					
❑ 33-115 [M]	This Is Darin	1960	10.00	20.00	40.00
-- Yellow "harp" label					
❑ 33-115 [M]	This Is Darin	1962	5.00	10.00	20.00
-- Gold and dark blue label					
❑ SD 33-115 [S]	This Is Darin	1960	20.00	40.00	80.00
-- Yellow "harp" label					
❑ SD 33-115 [S]	This Is Darin	1960	6.25	12.50	25.00
-- Purple and brown label					
❑ 33-122 [M]	Darin at the Copa	1960	10.00	20.00	40.00
-- Yellow "harp" label					
❑ 33-122 [M]	Darin at the Copa	1962	5.00	10.00	20.00
-- Gold and dark blue label					
❑ SD 33-122 [S]	Darin at the Copa	1960	20.00	40.00	80.00
-- Yellow "harp" label					
❑ SD 33-122 [S]	Darin at the Copa	1962	6.25	12.50	25.00
-- Purple and brown label					
❑ 33-124 [M]	It's You or No One	1960	10.00	20.00	40.00
-- Yellow "harp" label					
❑ 33-124 [M]	It's You or No One	1962	5.00	10.00	20.00
-- Gold and dark blue label					
❑ SD 33-124 [S]	It's You or No One	1960	20.00	40.00	80.00
-- Yellow "harp" label					
❑ SD 33-124 [S]	It's You or No One	1962	6.25	12.50	25.00
-- Purple and brown label					
❑ 33-125 [M]	The 25th Day of December	1960	12.50	25.00	50.00
-- Yellow "harp" label					
❑ 33-125 [M]	The 25th Day of December	1962	5.00	10.00	20.00
-- Gold and dark blue label					
❑ SD 33-125 [S]	The 25th Day of December	1960	15.00	30.00	60.00
-- Yellow "harp" label					
❑ SD 33-125 [S]	The 25th Day of December	1962	6.25	12.50	25.00
-- Purple and brown label					
❑ 33-126 [M]	Two of a Kind	1961	10.00	20.00	40.00
-- Yellow "harp" label					
❑ 33-126 [M]	Two of a Kind	1962	5.00	10.00	20.00
-- Gold and dark blue label					

Number	Title	Yr	VG	VG+	NM
❑ SD 33-126 [S]	Two of a Kind	1961	12.50	25.00	50.00
-- Yellow "harp" label					
❑ SD 33-126 [S]	Two of a Kind	1962	6.25	12.50	25.00
-- Purple and brown label					
❑ 33-131 [M]	The Bobby Darin Story	1961	10.00	20.00	40.00
-- Yellow "harp" label; white cover					
❑ 33-131 [M]	The Bobby Darin Story	1962	5.00	10.00	20.00
-- Gold and dark blue label; black cover					
❑ SD 33-131 [S]	The Bobby Darin Story	1961	12.50	25.00	50.00
-- Yellow "harp" label; white cover					
❑ SD 33-131 [S]	The Bobby Darin Story	1962	6.25	12.50	25.00
-- Purple and brown label; black cover					
❑ 33-134 [M]	Love Swings	1961	10.00	20.00	40.00
-- Yellow "harp" label					
❑ 33-134 [M]	Love Swings	1962	5.00	10.00	20.00
-- Gold and dark blue label					
❑ SD 33-134 [S]	Love Swings	1961	12.50	25.00	50.00
-- Yellow "harp" label					
❑ SD 33-134 [S]	Love Swings	1962	6.25	12.50	25.00
-- Purple and brown label					
❑ 33-138 [M]	Twist with Bobby Darin	1961	10.00	20.00	40.00
-- Yellow "harp" label					
❑ 33-138 [M]	Twist with Bobby Darin	1962	5.00	10.00	20.00
-- Gold and dark blue label					
❑ SD 33-138 [S]	Twist with Bobby Darin	1961	12.50	25.00	50.00
-- Yellow "harp" label					
❑ SD 33-138 [S]	Twist with Bobby Darin	1962	6.25	12.50	25.00
-- Purple and brown label					
❑ 33-140 [M]	Bobby Darin Sings Ray Charles	1962	6.25	12.50	25.00
❑ SD 33-140 [S]	Bobby Darin Sings Ray Charles	1962	7.50	15.00	30.00
❑ 33-146 [M]	Things & Other Things	1962	6.25	12.50	25.00
❑ SD 33-146 [S]	Things & Other Things	1962	7.50	15.00	30.00
❑ 33-167 [M]	Winners	1964	6.25	12.50	25.00
❑ SD 33-167 [S]	Winners	1964	7.50	15.00	30.00
❑ SP 1001 [M]	For Teenagers Only	1960	37.50	75.00	150.00
-- Gatefold with fold-open poster and paper insert					
❑ SP 1001 [M]	For Teenagers Only	1960	18.75	37.50	75.00
-- With extras missing					
ATLANTIC					
❑ SD 8121 [S]	The Shadow of Your Smile	1966	5.00	10.00	20.00
❑ SD 8126 [S]	In a Broadway Bag	1966	5.00	10.00	20.00
❑ SD 8135 [S]	If I Were a Carpenter	1967	12.50	25.00	50.00
-- Inexplicably rare in stereo					
❑ SD 8142 [S]	Inside Out	1967	7.50	15.00	30.00
CAPITOL					
❑ ST 1791 [S]	Oh! Look at Me Now	1962	5.00	10.00	20.00
❑ SW 1791 [S]	Oh! Look at Me Now	1962	6.25	12.50	25.00
❑ W 1791 [M]	Oh! Look at Me Now	1962	5.00	10.00	20.00
❑ ST 1826 [S]	Earthy	1963	5.00	10.00	20.00
❑ ST 1866 [S]	You're the Reason I'm Living	1963	5.00	10.00	20.00
❑ ST 1942 [S]	18 Yellow Roses	1963	5.00	10.00	20.00
❑ ST 2007 [S]	Golden Folk Hits	1963	5.00	10.00	20.00
❑ ST 2194 [S]	From Hello Dolly to Goodbye Charlie	1964	5.00	10.00	20.00
❑ ST 2322 [S]	Venice Blue	1965	5.00	10.00	20.00
CLARION					
❑ 603 [M]	Clementine	1966	5.00	10.00	20.00
❑ SD 603 [S]	Clementine	1966	6.25	12.50	25.00
DIRECTION					
❑ 1936	Born Walden Robert Cassotto	1968	6.25	12.50	25.00
❑ 1937	Committment	1969	6.25	12.50	25.00
MOTOWN					
❑ MS-739	Finally	1972	125.00	250.00	500.00
-- Unreleased; value is for RCA test pressing					
❑ M 753L	Bobby Darin	1972	5.00	10.00	20.00

DARIUS
Number	Title	Yr	VG	VG+	NM
CHARTMAKER					
❑ 1102	Darius	1969	62.50	125.00	250.00

DARLING, DENVER
Number	Title	Yr	VG	VG+	NM
AUDIO LAB					
❑ AL-1507 [M]	Songs of the Trail	1958	25.00	50.00	100.00

DARNEL, BILL
Number	Title	Yr	VG	VG+	NM
"X"					
❑ LVA-30?? [10]	Bill Darnel Sings	1955	10.00	20.00	40.00

DARRELL, JOHNNY
Number	Title	Yr	VG	VG+	NM
UNITED ARTISTS					
❑ UAL 3594 [M]	Ruby, Don't Take Your Love to Town	1967	6.25	12.50	25.00
❑ UAS 6594 [S]	Ruby, Don't Take Your Love to Town	1967	5.00	10.00	20.00
❑ UAS 6634	The Son of Hickory Holler's Tramp	1968	5.00	10.00	20.00
❑ UAS 6660	With Pen in Hand	1968	5.00	10.00	20.00

Number	Title	Yr	VG	VG+	NM
❑ UAS 6707	Why You Been Gone So Long	1969	5.00	10.00	20.00
❑ UAS 6752	California Stop-Over	1970	5.00	10.00	20.00

DARREN, JAMES
COLPIX

Number	Title	Yr	VG	VG+	NM
❑ CLP-406 [M]	James Darren (Album No. 1)	1960	37.50	75.00	150.00
-- Green vinyl					
❑ CLP-406 [M]	James Darren (Album No. 1)	1960	10.00	20.00	40.00
❑ CLP-418 [M]	Gidget Goes Hawaiian (James Darren Sings the Movies)	1961	7.50	15.00	30.00
❑ SCP-418 [S]	Gidget Goes Hawaiian (James Darren Sings the Movies)	1961	10.00	20.00	40.00
❑ CLP-424 [M]	James Darren Sings for All Sizes	1962	7.50	15.00	30.00
❑ SCP-424 [S]	James Darren Sings for All Sizes	1962	10.00	20.00	40.00
❑ CLP-428 [M]	Love Among the Young	1962	7.50	15.00	30.00
❑ SCP-428 [S]	Love Among the Young	1962	10.00	20.00	40.00

WARNER BROS.

Number	Title	Yr	VG	VG+	NM
❑ WS 1668 [S]	James Darren/All	1967	5.00	10.00	20.00

DARREN, JAMES/ SHELLEY FABARES/PAUL PETERSEN
COLPIX

Number	Title	Yr	VG	VG+	NM
❑ CP-444 [M]	Teenage Triangle	1963	10.00	20.00	40.00
❑ SCP-444 [R]	Teenage Triangle	1963	10.00	20.00	40.00
❑ CP-468 [M]	More Teenage Triangle	1964	10.00	20.00	40.00
❑ SCP-468 [P]	More Teenage Triangle	1964	15.00	30.00	60.00

DARRIEU, DANIELLE
CAPITOL

Number	Title	Yr	VG	VG+	NM
❑ ST 10319 [S]	Danielle Darrieux	1963	7.50	15.00	30.00
❑ T 10319 [M]	Danielle Darrieux	1963	5.00	10.00	20.00

LONDON

Number	Title	Yr	VG	VG+	NM
❑ LB-616 [10]	Le Voix de France	1954	12.50	25.00	50.00

DARTELLS, THE
DOT

Number	Title	Yr	VG	VG+	NM
❑ DLP-3522 [M]	Hot Pastrami	1963	7.50	15.00	30.00
❑ DLP-25522 [S]	Hot Pastrami	1963	10.00	20.00	40.00

DARTS, THE
DEL-FI

Number	Title	Yr	VG	VG+	NM
❑ DFLP-1244 [M]	Hollywood Drag	1963	10.00	20.00	40.00
❑ DFST-1244 [S]	Hollywood Drag	1963	12.50	25.00	50.00

DASHIEL, BUD, AND THE KINSMEN
WARNER BROS.

Number	Title	Yr	VG	VG+	NM
❑ W 1429 [M]	Folk Music in a Contemporary Manner	1961	6.25	12.50	25.00
❑ WS 1429 [S]	Folk Music in a Contemporary Manner	1961	7.50	15.00	30.00
❑ W 1432 [M]	Live Concert Extraordinaire -- Bud Dashiel and the Kinsmen Sing Everybody's Hits	1961	6.25	12.50	25.00
❑ WS 1432 [S]	Live Concert Extraordinaire -- Bud Dashiel and the Kinsmen Sing Everybody's Hits	1961	7.50	15.00	30.00

DAUGHTERS OF ALBION, THE
FONTANA

Number	Title	Yr	VG	VG+	NM
❑ SRF-67586	The Daughters of Albion	1968	5.00	10.00	20.00

DAVE DEE, DOZY, BEAKY, MICK & TICH
FONTANA

Number	Title	Yr	VG	VG+	NM
❑ MGF-27567 [M]	Greatest Hits	1967	7.50	15.00	30.00
❑ SRF-67567 [P]	Greatest Hits	1967	10.00	20.00	40.00
-- "Bend It" and "Hold Tight" are rechanneled.					

IMPERIAL

Number	Title	Yr	VG	VG+	NM
❑ LP-12402 [P]	Time to Take Off	1968	10.00	20.00	40.00
-- "Zabadak" is rechanneled.					

DAVEY AND THE BADMEN
GOTHIC

Number	Title	Yr	VG	VG+	NM
❑ KRW-054	Wanted	1963	50.00	100.00	200.00

DAVID AND JONATHAN
CAPITOL

Number	Title	Yr	VG	VG+	NM
❑ ST 2473 [S]	Michelle	1966	5.00	10.00	20.00

DAVID, THE
V.M.C.

Number	Title	Yr	VG	VG+	NM
❑ 124	Another Day, Another Lifetime	1968	25.00	50.00	100.00

DAVIE, HUTCH
ATCO

Number	Title	Yr	VG	VG+	NM
❑ 33-105 [M]	Much Hutch	1958	12.50	25.00	50.00

DAVIS, JIMMIE
DECCA

Number	Title	Yr	VG	VG+	NM
❑ DL 8174 [M]	Near the Cross	1955	6.25	12.50	25.00
❑ DL 8572 [M]	Hymn Time	1957	6.25	12.50	25.00
❑ DL 8729 [M]	The Door Is Always Open	1958	6.25	12.50	25.00
❑ DL 8786 [M]	Hail Him with a Song	1958	6.25	12.50	25.00
❑ DL 8896 [M]	You Are My Sunshine	1959	5.00	10.00	20.00
❑ DL 8953 [M]	Suppertime	1960	5.00	10.00	20.00
❑ DL 78896 [S]	You Are My Sunshine	1959	6.25	12.50	25.00
❑ DL 78953 [S]	Suppertime	1960	6.25	12.50	25.00

DAVIS, LINK
MERCURY

Number	Title	Yr	VG	VG+	NM
❑ SR-61243	Cajun Crawdaddy	1969	5.00	10.00	20.00

DAVIS, MARTHA
Also see THE MOTELS.
CAPITOL

Number	Title	Yr	VG	VG+	NM
❑ CLT-79197/8 [DJ]	Policy (Radio Cue Card)	1987	6.25	12.50	25.00

DAVIS, MAXWELL
ALADDIN

Number	Title	Yr	VG	VG+	NM
❑ LP-709 [10]	Maxwell Davis	1955	100.00	200.00	400.00
❑ LP-804 [M]	Maxwell Davis	1956	50.00	100.00	200.00

SCORE

Number	Title	Yr	VG	VG+	NM
❑ SLP-4106 [M]	Blue Tango	1957	50.00	100.00	200.00

DAVIS, MILES
BLUE NOTE

Number	Title	Yr	VG	VG+	NM
❑ BLP-1501 [M]	Miles Davis, Volume 1	1955	50.00	100.00	200.00
-- "Deep groove" version (deep indentation under label on both sides)					
❑ BLP-1501 [M]	Miles Davis, Volume 1	1955	37.50	75.00	150.00
-- Regular version with Lexington Ave. address on label					
❑ BLP-1501 [M]	Miles Davis, Volume 1	1958	12.50	25.00	50.00
-- Regular version with W. 63rd St. address on label					
❑ BLP-1501 [M]	Miles Davis, Volume 1	1963	6.25	12.50	25.00
-- With New York, USA address on label					
❑ BLP-1502 [M]	Miles Davis, Volume 2	1955	50.00	100.00	200.00
-- "Deep groove" version (deep indentation under label on both sides)					
❑ BLP-1502 [M]	Miles Davis, Volume 2	1955	37.50	75.00	150.00
-- Regular version with Lexington Ave. address on label					
❑ BLP-1502 [M]	Miles Davis, Volume 2	1958	12.50	25.00	50.00
-- Regular version with W. 63rd St. address on label					
❑ BLP-1502 [M]	Miles Davis, Volume 2	1963	6.25	12.50	25.00
-- With New York, USA address on label					
❑ BLP-5013 [10]	Miles Davis (Young Man with a Horn)	1952	75.00	150.00	300.00
❑ BLP-5022 [10]	Miles Davis, Vol. 2	1953	75.00	150.00	300.00
❑ BLP-5040 [10]	Miles Davis, Vol. 3	1954	75.00	150.00	300.00

CAPITOL

Number	Title	Yr	VG	VG+	NM
❑ H 459 [10]	Jeru	1954	62.50	125.00	250.00
-- First 33 1/3 rpm issue of some of the "Birth of the Cool" sessions					
❑ T 762 [M]	Birth of the Cool	1956	37.50	75.00	150.00
❑ T 1974 [M]	Birth of the Cool	1963	7.50	15.00	30.00
-- Reissue of 762					

COLUMBIA

Number	Title	Yr	VG	VG+	NM
❑ C2L 20 [(2) M]	Miles Davis in Person (Friday & Saturday Nights at the Blackhawk, San Francisco)	1961	12.50	25.00	50.00
-- Six "eye" logos on label					
❑ C2L 20 [(2) M]	Miles Davis in Person (Friday & Saturday Nights at the Blackhawk, San Francisco)	1963	7.50	15.00	30.00
-- "Guaranteed High Fidelity" on label					
❑ C2L 20 [(2) M]	Miles Davis in Person (Friday & Saturday Nights at the Blackhawk, San Francisco)	1965	6.25	12.50	25.00
-- "Mono" on label					
❑ GP 26 [(2)]	Bitches Brew	1970	10.00	20.00	40.00
-- "360 Sound Stereo" on red labels					
❑ C2S 820 [(2) S]	Miles Davis in Person (Friday & Saturday Nights at the Blackhawk, San Francisco)	1961	12.50	25.00	50.00
-- Six "eye" logos on label					
❑ C2S 820 [(2) S]	Miles Davis in Person (Friday & Saturday Nights at the Blackhawk, San Francisco)	1963	7.50	15.00	30.00
-- "360 Sound Stereo" in black on label					
❑ C2S 820 [(2) S]	Miles Davis in Person (Friday & Saturday Nights at the Blackhawk, San Francisco)	1965	6.25	12.50	25.00
-- "360 Sound Stereo" in white on label					
❑ CL 949 [M]	'Round About Midnight	1957	12.50	25.00	50.00
-- Six "eye" logos on label					
❑ CL 949 [M]	'Round About Midnight	1963	6.25	12.50	25.00
-- "Guaranteed High Fidelity" on label					

Number	Title	Yr	VG	VG+	NM
❏ CL 949 [M]	'Round About Midnight	1965	5.00	10.00	20.00
-- "Mono" on label					
❏ CL 1041 [M]	Miles Ahead	1957	20.00	40.00	80.00
-- Six "eye" logos on label; cover has a white woman and her child on a sailboat					
❏ CL 1041 [M]	Miles Ahead	1957	12.50	25.00	50.00
-- Six "eye" logos on label; cover has Miles Davis on a sailboat					
❏ CL 1041 [M]	Miles Ahead	1963	6.25	12.50	25.00
-- "Guaranteed High Fidelity" on label					
❏ CL 1041 [M]	Miles Ahead	1965	5.00	10.00	20.00
-- "Mono" on label					
❏ CL 1193 [M]	Milestones	1958	12.50	25.00	50.00
-- Six "eye" logos on label					
❏ CL 1193 [M]	Milestones	1963	6.25	12.50	25.00
-- "Guaranteed High Fidelity" on label					
❏ CL 1193 [M]	Milestones	1965	5.00	10.00	20.00
-- "Mono" on label					
❏ CL 1268 [M]	Jazz Track	1958	20.00	40.00	80.00
-- Six "eye" logos on label; with abstract drawing on cover					
❏ CL 1268 [M]	Jazz Track	1958	12.50	25.00	50.00
-- Six "eye" logos on label; with Miles and a woman on cover					
❏ CL 1274 [M]	Porgy and Bess	1958	12.50	25.00	50.00
-- Six "eye" logos on label					
❏ CL 1274 [M]	Porgy and Bess	1963	6.25	12.50	25.00
-- "Guaranteed High Fidelity" on label					
❏ CL 1274 [M]	Porgy and Bess	1965	5.00	10.00	20.00
-- "Mono" on label					
❏ CL 1355 [M]	Kind of Blue	1959	15.00	30.00	60.00
-- Six "eye" logos on label					
❏ CL 1355 [M]	Kind of Blue	1963	6.25	12.50	25.00
-- "Guaranteed High Fidelity" on label					
❏ CL 1355 [M]	Kind of Blue	1965	5.00	10.00	20.00
-- "Mono" on label					
❏ CL 1480 [M]	Sketches of Spain	1960	12.50	25.00	50.00
-- Six "eye" logos on label					
❏ CL 1480 [M]	Sketches of Spain	1963	6.25	12.50	25.00
-- "Guaranteed High Fidelity" on label					
❏ CL 1480 [M]	Sketches of Spain	1965	5.00	10.00	20.00
-- "Mono" on label					
❏ CL 1656 [M]	Someday My Prince Will Come	1961	10.00	20.00	40.00
-- Six "eye" logos on label					
❏ CL 1656 [M]	Someday My Prince Will Come	1963	6.25	12.50	25.00
-- "Guaranteed High Fidelity" on label					
❏ CL 1656 [M]	Someday My Prince Will Come	1965	5.00	10.00	20.00
-- "Mono" on label					
❏ CL 1669 [M]	Miles Davis in Person, Vol. 1 (Friday Nights at the Blackhawk, San Francisco)	1961	7.50	15.00	30.00
-- Six "eye" logos on label; later pressings may exist					
❏ CL 1670 [M]	Miles Davis in Person, Vol. 2 (Saturday Nights at the Blackhawk, San Francisco)	1961	7.50	15.00	30.00
-- Six "eye" logos on label; later pressings may exist					
❏ CL 1812 [M]	Miles Davis at Carnegie Hall	1962	12.50	25.00	50.00
-- Six "eye" logos on label					
❏ CL 1812 [M]	Miles Davis at Carnegie Hall	1963	6.25	12.50	25.00
-- "Guaranteed High Fidelity" on label					
❏ CL 1812 [M]	Miles Davis at Carnegie Hall	1965	5.00	10.00	20.00
-- "Mono" on label					
❏ CL 2051 [M]	Seven Steps to Heaven	1963	6.25	12.50	25.00
-- "Guaranteed High Fidelity" on label					
❏ CL 2051 [M]	Seven Steps to Heaven	1965	5.00	10.00	20.00
-- "Mono" on label					
❏ CL 2106 [M]	Quiet Nights	1964	6.25	12.50	25.00
-- "Guaranteed High Fidelity" on label					
❏ CL 2106 [M]	Quiet Nights	1965	5.00	10.00	20.00
-- "Mono" on label					
❏ CL 2183 [M]	Miles Davis in Europe	1964	6.25	12.50	25.00
-- "Guaranteed High Fidelity" on label					
❏ CL 2183 [M]	Miles Davis in Europe	1965	5.00	10.00	20.00
-- "Mono" on label					
❏ CL 2306 [M]	My Funny Valentine	1965	5.00	10.00	20.00
-- "Mono" on label					
❏ CL 2306 [M]	My Funny Valentine	1965	6.25	12.50	25.00
-- "Guaranteed High Fidelity" on label					
❏ CL 2350 [M]	E.S.P.	1965	6.25	12.50	25.00
-- "Guaranteed High Fidelity" on label					
❏ CL 2350 [M]	E.S.P.	1965	5.00	10.00	20.00
-- "Mono" on label					
❏ CL 2453 [M]	"Four" & More -- Recorded Live in Concert	1966	5.00	10.00	20.00
❏ CL 2601 [M]	Miles Smiles	1966	5.00	10.00	20.00
❏ CL 2628 [M]	Milestones	1967	7.50	15.00	30.00
-- Reissue of 1193?					
❏ CL 2732 [M]	Sorcerer	1967	7.50	15.00	30.00
❏ CL 2794 [M]	Nefertiti	1968	12.50	25.00	50.00
❏ CL 2828 [M]	Miles in the Sky	1968	20.00	40.00	80.00
❏ CS 8021 [S]	Milestones	1959	12.50	25.00	50.00
-- Six "eye" logos on label					
❏ CS 8021 [S]	Milestones	1963	6.25	12.50	25.00
-- "360 Sound Stereo" in black on label					
❏ CS 8021 [S]	Milestones	1965	5.00	10.00	20.00
-- "360 Sound Stereo" in white on label					
❏ CS 8085 [S]	Porgy and Bess	1959	12.50	25.00	50.00
-- Six "eye" logos on label					
❏ CS 8085 [S]	Porgy and Bess	1963	6.25	12.50	25.00
-- "360 Sound Stereo" in black on label					
❏ CS 8085 [S]	Porgy and Bess	1965	5.00	10.00	20.00
-- "360 Sound Stereo" in white on label					
❏ CS 8163 [S]	Kind of Blue	1959	30.00	60.00	120.00
-- Six "eye" logos on label					
❏ CS 8163 [S]	Kind of Blue	1963	6.25	12.50	25.00
-- "360 Sound Stereo" in black on label					
❏ CS 8163 [S]	Kind of Blue	1965	5.00	10.00	20.00
-- "360 Sound Stereo" in white on label					
❏ CS 8271 [S]	Sketches of Spain	1960	20.00	40.00	80.00
-- Six "eye" logos on label					
❏ CS 8271 [S]	Sketches of Spain	1963	6.25	12.50	25.00
-- "360 Sound Stereo" in black on label					
❏ CS 8271 [S]	Sketches of Spain	1965	5.00	10.00	20.00
-- "360 Sound Stereo" in white on label					
❏ CS 8456 [S]	Someday My Prince Will Come	1961	10.00	20.00	40.00
-- Six "eye" logos on label					
❏ CS 8456 [S]	Someday My Prince Will Come	1963	6.25	12.50	25.00
-- "360 Sound Stereo" in black on label					
❏ CS 8456 [S]	Someday My Prince Will Come	1965	5.00	10.00	20.00
-- "360 Sound Stereo" in white on label					
❏ CS 8469 [S]	Miles Davis in Person, Vol. 1 (Friday Nights at the Blackhawk, San Francisco)	1961	7.50	15.00	30.00
-- Six "eye" logos on label; later pressings may exist					
❏ CS 8470 [S]	Miles Davis in Person, Vol. 2 (Saturday Nights at the Blackhawk, San Francisco)	1961	7.50	15.00	30.00
-- Six "eye" logos on label; later pressings may exist					
❏ CS 8612 [S]	Miles Davis at Carnegie Hall	1962	12.50	25.00	50.00
-- Six "eye" logos on label					
❏ CS 8612 [S]	Miles Davis at Carnegie Hall	1962	6.25	12.50	25.00
-- "360 Sound Stereo" in black on label					
❏ CS 8612 [S]	Miles Davis at Carnegie Hall	1965	5.00	10.00	20.00
-- "360 Sound Stereo" in white on label					
❏ CS 8851 [S]	Seven Steps to Heaven	1963	6.25	12.50	25.00
-- "360 Sound Stereo" in black on label					
❏ CS 8851 [S]	Seven Steps to Heaven	1965	5.00	10.00	20.00
-- "360 Sound Stereo" in white on label					
❏ CS 8906 [S]	Quiet Nights	1964	6.25	12.50	25.00
-- "360 Sound Stereo" in black on label					
❏ CS 8906 [S]	Quiet Nights	1965	5.00	10.00	20.00
-- "360 Sound Stereo" in white on label					
❏ CS 8983 [S]	Miles Davis in Europe	1964	6.25	12.50	25.00
-- "360 Sound Stereo" in black on label					
❏ CS 8983 [S]	Miles Davis in Europe	1965	5.00	10.00	20.00
-- "360 Sound Stereo" in white on label					
❏ CS 9106 [S]	My Funny Valentine	1965	6.25	12.50	25.00
-- "360 Sound Stereo" in black on label					
❏ CS 9106 [S]	My Funny Valentine	1965	5.00	10.00	20.00
-- "360 Sound Stereo" in white on label					
❏ CS 9150 [S]	E.S.P.	1965	6.25	12.50	25.00
-- "360 Sound Stereo" in black on label					
❏ CS 9150 [S]	E.S.P.	1965	5.00	10.00	20.00
-- "360 Sound Stereo" in white on label					
❏ CS 9253 [S]	"Four" & More -- Recorded Live in Concert	1966	5.00	10.00	20.00
-- "360 Sound Stereo" on red label					
❏ CS 9401 [S]	Miles Smiles	1966	5.00	10.00	20.00
-- "360 Sound Stereo" on red label					
❏ CS 9428 [S]	Milestones	1967	5.00	10.00	20.00
-- "360 Sound Stereo" on red label; reissue of 8021?					
❏ CS 9532 [S]	Sorcerer	1967	5.00	10.00	20.00
-- "360 Sound Stereo" on red label					
❏ CS 9594 [S]	Nefertiti	1968	5.00	10.00	20.00
-- "360 Sound Stereo" on red label					
❏ CS 9628 [S]	Miles in the Sky	1968	5.00	10.00	20.00
-- "360 Sound Stereo" on red label					
❏ CS 9750	Filles de Kilimanjaro	1969	5.00	10.00	20.00
-- "360 Sound Stereo" on red label					
❏ CS 9808	Miles Davis' Greatest Hits	1969	5.00	10.00	20.00
-- "360 Sound Stereo" on red label					
❏ CS 9875	In a Silent Way	1969	5.00	10.00	20.00
❏ GQ 30954 [(2) Q]	Live-Evil	1973	7.50	15.00	30.00
❏ GQ 30997 [(2) Q]	Bitches Brew	1972	10.00	20.00	40.00
❏ C6X 36976 [(6)]	The Miles Davis Collection Vol. 1: 12 Sides of Miles	1980	12.50	25.00	50.00
❏ HC 46790	The Man with the Horn	1982	7.50	15.00	30.00
-- Half-speed mastered edition					

COLUMBIA/CLASSIC

Number	Title	Yr	VG	VG+	NM
❏ CS 8163 [(2)]	Kind of Blue	1997	10.00	20.00	40.00
-- Reissue; contains both the original Side 1, which was mastered slightly fast, and the "correct" Side 1 (as Side 3)					
❏ CS 8271 [S]	Sketches of Spain	1999	6.25	12.50	25.00
-- Audiophile reissue					

DEBUT

Number	Title	Yr	VG	VG+	NM
❏ DEB 120 [M]	Blue Moods	1955	62.50	125.00	250.00

Number	Title	Yr	VG	VG+	NM

FANTASY

Number	Title	Yr	VG	VG+	NM
❑ 6001 [M]	Blue Moods	1962	12.50	25.00	50.00
-- *Reissue of Debut album; red vinyl*					
❑ 6001 [M]	Blue Moods	1963	7.50	15.00	30.00
-- *Black vinyl, red label*					
❑ 86001 [R]	Blue Moods	1962	7.50	15.00	30.00
-- *Blue vinyl*					

MOBILE FIDELITY

Number	Title	Yr	VG	VG+	NM
❑ 1-177	Someday My Prince Will Come	1985	20.00	40.00	80.00
-- *Audiophile vinyl*					

MOSAIC

Number	Title	Yr	VG	VG+	NM
❑ MQ10-158 [(10)]	The Complete Plugged Nickel Sessions	199?	37.50	75.00	150.00
❑ MQ11-164 [(11)]	Miles Davis & Gil Evans: The Complete Columbia Studio Recordings	199?	50.00	100.00	200.00
❑ MQ10-177 [(10)]	The Complete Studio Recordings of the Miles Davis Quintet 1965-June 1968	1998	37.50	75.00	150.00
❑ MQ6-183 [(6)]	The Complete Bitches Brew Sessions	1999	25.00	50.00	100.00

PRESTIGE

Number	Title	Yr	VG	VG+	NM
❑ P-12 [(12)]	Chronicle: The Complete Prestige Recordings	198?	25.00	50.00	100.00
❑ PRLP-124 [10]	The New Sounds of Miles Davis	1952	62.50	125.00	250.00
❑ PRLP-140 [10]	Blue Period	1953	62.50	125.00	250.00
❑ PRLP-154 [10]	Miles Davis Plays Al Cohn Compositions	1953	62.50	125.00	250.00
❑ PRLP-161 [10]	Miles Davis Featuring Sonny Rollins	1953	62.50	125.00	250.00
❑ PRLP-182 [10]	Miles Davis Sextet	1954	62.50	125.00	250.00
❑ PRLP-185 [10]	Miles Davis Quintet	1954	62.50	125.00	250.00
❑ PRLP-187 [10]	Miles Davis Quintet Featuring Sonny Rollins	1954	62.50	125.00	250.00
❑ PRLP-196 [10]	Miles Davis All Stars, Volume 1	1955	62.50	125.00	250.00
❑ PRLP-200 [10]	Miles Davis All Stars, Volume 2	1955	62.50	125.00	250.00
❑ PRLP-7007 [M]	The Musings of Miles	1955	37.50	75.00	150.00
❑ PRLP-7012 [M]	Dig Miles Davis/Sonny Rollins	1956	37.50	75.00	150.00
-- *Gray cover*					
❑ PRLP-7012 [M]	Dig Miles Davis/Sonny Rollins	1957	30.00	60.00	120.00
-- *Color cover*					
❑ PRLP-7014 [M]	Miles -- The New Miles Davis Quintet	1956	37.50	75.00	150.00
❑ PRLP-7025 [M]	Miles Davis and Horns	1956	37.50	75.00	150.00
❑ PRLP-7034 [M]	Miles Davis and the Milt Jackson Quintet/Sextet	1956	37.50	75.00	150.00
-- *With W. 50th St. address on yellow label*					
❑ PRLP-7034 [M]	Miles Davis and the Milt Jackson Quintet/Sextet	196?	7.50	15.00	30.00
-- *With trident on blue label*					
❑ PRLP-7044 [M]	Collectors' Item	1956	30.00	60.00	120.00
-- *With W. 50th St. address on yellow label*					
❑ PRLP-7044 [M]	Collectors' Item	196?	7.50	15.00	30.00
-- *With trident on blue label*					
❑ PRLP-7054 [M]	Blue Haze	1956	30.00	60.00	120.00
-- *With W. 50th St. address on yellow label*					
❑ PRLP-7054 [M]	Blue Haze	196?	7.50	15.00	30.00
-- *With trident on blue label*					
❑ PRLP-7076 [M]	Walkin'	1957	25.00	50.00	100.00
-- *With W. 50th St. address on yellow label*					
❑ PRLP-7076 [M]	Walkin'	196?	7.50	15.00	30.00
-- *With trident on blue label*					
❑ PRLP-7094 [M]	Cookin' with the Miles Davis Quintet	1957	25.00	50.00	100.00
-- *With W. 50th St. address on yellow label*					
❑ PRLP-7094 [M]	Cookin' with the Miles Davis Quintet	196?	7.50	15.00	30.00
-- *With trident on blue label*					
❑ PRLP-7109 [M]	Bags Groove	1957	25.00	50.00	100.00
-- *With W. 50th St. address on yellow label*					
❑ PRLP-7109 [M]	Bags Groove	196?	7.50	15.00	30.00
-- *With trident on blue label*					
❑ PRLP-7129 [M]	Relaxin' with the Miles Davis Quintet	1957	25.00	50.00	100.00
-- *With W. 50th St. address on yellow label*					
❑ PRLP-7129 [M]	Relaxin' with the Miles Davis Quintet	196?	7.50	15.00	30.00
-- *With trident on blue label*					
❑ PRLP-7150 [M]	Miles Davis and the Modern Jazz Giants	1958	20.00	40.00	80.00
-- *With Bergenfield, NJ address on yellow label*					
❑ PRLP-7150 [M]	Miles Davis and the Modern Jazz Giants	196?	7.50	15.00	30.00
-- *With trident on blue label*					
❑ PRLP-7166 [M]	Workin' with the Miles Davis Quintet	1959	20.00	40.00	80.00
-- *With Bergenfield, NJ address on yellow label*					

Number	Title	Yr	VG	VG+	NM
❑ PRLP-7166 [M]	Workin' with the Miles Davis Quintet	196?	7.50	15.00	30.00
-- *With trident on blue label*					
❑ PRLP-7168 [M]	Early Miles	1959	20.00	40.00	80.00
-- *Reissue of 7025; with Bergenfield, NJ address on yellow label*					
❑ PRLP-7168 [M]	Early Miles	196?	7.50	15.00	30.00
-- *With trident on blue label*					
❑ PRLP-7200 [M]	Steamin' with the Miles Davis Quintet	1961	20.00	40.00	80.00
-- *With Bergenfield, NJ address on yellow label*					
❑ PRLP-7200 [M]	Steamin' with the Miles Davis Quintet	196?	7.50	15.00	30.00
-- *With trident on blue label*					
❑ PRLP-7221 [M]	The Beginning	1962	12.50	25.00	50.00
-- *Reissue of 7007; with Bergenfield, NJ address on yellow label*					
❑ PRLP-7221 [M]	The Beginning	196?	7.50	15.00	30.00
-- *With trident on blue label*					
❑ PRLP-7254 [M]	The Original Quintet	1963	12.50	25.00	50.00
-- *Reissue of 7014; with Bergenfield, NJ address on yellow label*					
❑ PRLP-7254 [M]	The Original Quintet	196?	7.50	15.00	30.00
-- *With trident on blue label*					
❑ PRST-7254 [R]	The Original Quintet	1963	5.00	10.00	20.00
❑ PRLP-7281 [M]	Diggin'	1963	12.50	25.00	50.00
-- *Reissue of 7012; with Bergenfield, NJ address on yellow label*					
❑ PRLP-7281 [M]	Diggin'	196?	7.50	15.00	30.00
-- *With trident on blue label*					
❑ PRST-7281 [R]	Diggin'	1963	5.00	10.00	20.00
❑ PRLP-7322 [M]	Miles Davis Plays Richard	1964	7.50	15.00	30.00
❑ PRST-7322 [R]	Miles Davis Plays Richard	1964	5.00	10.00	20.00
❑ PRLP-7352 [M]	Miles Davis Plays for Lovers	1965	7.50	15.00	30.00
❑ PRST-7352 [R]	Miles Davis Plays for Lovers	1965	5.00	10.00	20.00
❑ PRLP-7373 [M]	Jazz Classics	1965	7.50	15.00	30.00
❑ PRST-7373 [R]	Jazz Classics	1965	5.00	10.00	20.00
❑ PRLP-7457 [M]	Miles Davis' Greatest Hits	1967	5.00	10.00	20.00

DAVIS, MILES, AND THELONIOUS MONK
Also see each artist's individual listings.

COLUMBIA

Number	Title	Yr	VG	VG+	NM
❑ CL 2178 [M]	Miles and Monk at Newport	1964	6.25	12.50	25.00
-- *"Guaranteed High Fidelity" on label*					
❑ CL 2178 [M]	Miles and Monk at Newport	1965	5.00	10.00	20.00
-- *"Mono" on label*					
❑ CS 8978 [S]	Miles and Monk at Newport	1964	6.25	12.50	25.00
-- *"360 Sound Stereo" in black on label*					
❑ CS 8978 [S]	Miles and Monk at Newport	1965	5.00	10.00	20.00
-- *"360 Sound Stereo" in white on label*					

DAVIS, PAUL

BANG

Number	Title	Yr	VG	VG+	NM
❑ BLPS-223	A Little Bit of Paul Davis	1970	10.00	20.00	40.00

DAVIS, REVEREND GARY
Also see PINK ANDERSON AND REVEREND GARY DAVIS.

BLUESVILLE

Number	Title	Yr	VG	VG+	NM
❑ BVLP-1015 [M]	Harlem Street Singer	1961	25.00	50.00	100.00
-- *Blue label, silver print*					
❑ BVLP-1015 [M]	Harlem Street Singer	1964	7.50	15.00	30.00
-- *Blue label with trident logo*					
❑ BVLP-1032 [M]	A Little More Faith	1961	25.00	50.00	100.00
-- *Blue label, silver print*					
❑ BVLP-1032 [M]	A Little More Faith	1964	7.50	15.00	30.00
-- *Blue label with trident logo*					
❑ BVLP-1049 [M]	Say No to the Devil	1962	25.00	50.00	100.00
-- *Blue label, silver print*					
❑ BVLP 1049 [M]	Say No to the Devil	1964	7.50	15.00	30.00
-- *Blue label with trident logo*					

FOLKLORE

Number	Title	Yr	VG	VG+	NM
❑ F-14028 [M]	Pure Religion	196?	10.00	20.00	40.00
❑ F-14033 [M]	Guitar and Banjo	196?	10.00	20.00	40.00

STINSON

Number	Title	Yr	VG	VG+	NM
❑ SLP-56 [10]	The Singing Reverend	195?	25.00	50.00	100.00

DAVIS, SAMMY, JR.

DECCA

Number	Title	Yr	VG	VG+	NM
❑ DXSB 7192 [(2) S]	The Best of Sammy Davis, Jr.	1966	5.00	10.00	20.00
❑ DL 8118 [M]	Starring Sammy Davis, Jr.	1955	7.50	15.00	30.00
❑ DL 8170 [M]	Just for Lovers	1955	7.50	15.00	30.00
❑ DL 8351 [M]	Here's Looking at You	1956	6.25	12.50	25.00
❑ DL 8486 [M]	Sammy Swings	1957	6.25	12.50	25.00
❑ DL 8641 [M]	It's All Over But the Swingin'	1957	6.25	12.50	25.00
❑ DL 8676 [M]	Mood to Be Wooed	1958	6.25	12.50	25.00
❑ DL 8779 [M]	All the Way And Then Some	1958	6.25	12.50	25.00
❑ DL 8841 [M]	Sammy Davis, Jr., at Town Hall	1959	5.00	10.00	20.00
❑ DL 8854 [M]	Porgy and Bess	1959	5.00	10.00	20.00
❑ DL 8921 [M]	The Sammy Awards	1960	5.00	10.00	20.00

Number	Title	Yr	VG	VG+	NM
❑ DL 8981 [M]	I Got a Right to Swing	1960	5.00	10.00	20.00
❑ DL 74153 [S]	Mr. Entertainment	1961	5.00	10.00	20.00
❑ DL 74381 [S]	Forget-Me-Nots for First Nighters	1963	5.00	10.00	20.00
❑ DL 78841 [S]	Sammy Davis, Jr., at Town Hall	1959	6.25	12.50	25.00
❑ DL 78854 [S]	Porgy and Bess	1959	6.25	12.50	25.00
❑ DL 78921 [S]	The Sammy Awards	1960	6.25	12.50	25.00
❑ DL 78981 [S]	I Got a Right to Swing	1960	6.25	12.50	25.00

REPRISE

Number	Title	Yr	VG	VG+	NM
❑ R9-2003 [S]	The Wham of Sam	1961	5.00	10.00	20.00
❑ R9-2010 [S]	Sammy Davis, Jr., Belts the Best of Broadway	1962	5.00	10.00	20.00
❑ R9-6033 [S]	All Star Spectacular	1962	5.00	10.00	20.00
❑ R9-6051 [S]	What Kind of Fool Am I and Other Show-Stoppers	1962	5.00	10.00	20.00
❑ R-6063 [(2) M]	Sammy Davis Jr. at the Cocoanut Grove	1963	5.00	10.00	20.00
❑ R9-6063 [(2) S]	Sammy Davis Jr. at the Cocoanut Grove	1963	6.25	12.50	25.00
❑ R9-6082 [S]	As Long As She Needs Me	1963	5.00	10.00	20.00
❑ R9-6095 [S]	Sammy Davis Jr. Salutes the Stars of the London Palladium	1964	5.00	10.00	20.00
❑ R9-6096 [S]	Treasury of Golden Hits	1964	5.00	10.00	20.00
❑ R9-6114 [S]	The Shelter of Your Arms	1964	5.00	10.00	20.00
❑ R9-6126 [S]	California Suite	1964	5.00	10.00	20.00
❑ RS-6237 [(2) S]	That's All	1967	5.00	10.00	20.00

DAVIS, SAMMY, JR. AND CARMEN McRAE
DECCA

Number	Title	Yr	VG	VG+	NM
❑ DL 8490 [M]	Boy Meets Girl	1957	7.50	15.00	30.00

DAVIS, SKEETER
RCA VICTOR

Number	Title	Yr	VG	VG+	NM
❑ LPM-2197 [M]	I'll Sing You a Song and Harmonize, Too	1960	6.25	12.50	25.00
❑ LSP-2197 [S]	I'll Sing You a Song and Harmonize, Too	1960	7.50	15.00	30.00
❑ LPM-2327 [M]	Here's the Answer	1961	6.25	12.50	25.00
❑ LSP-2327 [S]	Here's the Answer	1961	7.50	15.00	30.00
❑ LPM-2699 [M]	The End of the World	1963	6.25	12.50	25.00
❑ LSP-2699 [S]	The End of the World	1963	7.50	15.00	30.00
❑ LPM-2736 [M]	Cloudy, With Occasional Tears	1963	6.25	12.50	25.00
❑ LSP-2736 [S]	Cloudy, With Occasional Tears	1963	7.50	15.00	30.00
❑ LPM-2980 [M]	Let Me Get Close to You	1964	5.00	10.00	20.00
❑ LSP-2980 [S]	Let Me Get Close to You	1964	6.25	12.50	25.00
❑ LPM-3374 [M]	The Best of Skeeter Davis	1965	5.00	10.00	20.00
❑ LSP-3374 [S]	The Best of Skeeter Davis	1965	6.25	12.50	25.00
❑ LPM-3382 [M]	Written by the Stars	1965	5.00	10.00	20.00
❑ LSP-3382 [S]	Written by the Stars	1965	6.25	12.50	25.00
❑ LPM-3463 [M]	Skeeter Sings Standards	1965	5.00	10.00	20.00
❑ LSP-3463 [S]	Skeeter Sings Standards	1965	6.25	12.50	25.00
❑ LPM-3567 [M]	Singin' in the Summer Sun	1966	5.00	10.00	20.00
❑ LSP-3567 [S]	Singin' in the Summer Sun	1966	6.25	12.50	25.00
❑ LPM-3667 [M]	My Heart's in the Country	1966	5.00	10.00	20.00
❑ LSP-3667 [S]	My Heart's in the Country	1966	6.25	12.50	25.00
❑ LPM-3763 [M]	Hand in Hand with Jesus	1967	7.50	15.00	30.00
❑ LSP-3763 [M]	Hand in Hand with Jesus	1967	5.00	10.00	20.00
❑ LPM-3790 [M]	Skeeter Davis Sings Buddy Holly	1967	12.50	25.00	50.00
❑ LSP-3790 [S]	Skeeter Davis Sings Buddy Holly	1967	10.00	20.00	40.00
❑ LPM-3876 [M]	What Does It Take (To Keep a Man Like You Satisfied)	1967	7.50	15.00	30.00
❑ LSP-3876 [S]	What Does It Take (To Keep a Man Like You Satisfied)	1967	5.00	10.00	20.00
❑ LPM-3960 [M]	Why So Lonely?	1968	12.50	25.00	50.00
❑ LSP-3960 [S]	Why So Lonely?	1968	5.00	10.00	20.00
❑ LSP-4055	I Love Flatt & Scruggs	1968	5.00	10.00	20.00
❑ LSP-4124	The Closest Thing to Love	1969	5.00	10.00	20.00
❑ LSP-4200	Maryfrances	1969	5.00	10.00	20.00

DAVIS, SPENCER, GROUP
UNITED ARTISTS

Number	Title	Yr	VG	VG+	NM
❑ UAL 3578 [M]	Gimme Some Lovin'	1967	12.50	25.00	50.00
❑ UAL 3589 [M]	I'm a Man	1967	10.00	20.00	40.00
❑ UAS 6578 [R]	Gimme Some Lovin'	1967	10.00	20.00	40.00
❑ UAS 6589 [P]	I'm a Man	1967	12.50	25.00	50.00
❑ UAS 6641 [P]	The Spencer Davis Group's Greatest Hits	1968	6.25	12.50	25.00
❑ UAS 6652	With Their New Face On	1968	5.00	10.00	20.00
❑ UAS 6691	Heavies	1969	5.00	10.00	20.00

DAVIS, TYRONE
DAKAR

Number	Title	Yr	VG	VG+	NM
❑ DK-9005	Can I Change My Mind	1969	7.50	15.00	30.00
❑ DK-9027	Turn Back the Hands of Time	1970	7.50	15.00	30.00
❑ DK-76901	I Had It All the Time	1972	7.50	15.00	30.00
❑ DK-76902	Tyrone Davis' Greatest Hits	1972	6.25	12.50	25.00
❑ DK-76904	Without You in My Life	1973	6.25	12.50	25.00

Number	Title	Yr	VG	VG+	NM
❑ DK-76909	It's All in the Game	1974	5.00	10.00	20.00
❑ DK-76915	Homewrecker	1975	5.00	10.00	20.00
❑ DK-76918	Turning Point	1976	5.00	10.00	20.00

DAWE, TIM
Also see IRON BUTTERFLY.
STRAIGHT

Number	Title	Yr	VG	VG+	NM
❑ STS-1058	Penrod	1969	7.50	15.00	30.00

DAY BLINDNESS
STUDIO 10

Number	Title	Yr	VG	VG+	NM
❑ DBX-101	Day Blindness	1969	15.00	30.00	60.00

DAY, BOBBY
CLASS

Number	Title	Yr	VG	VG+	NM
❑ LP-5002 [M]	Rockin' with Robin	1959	100.00	200.00	400.00

RENDEZVOUS

Number	Title	Yr	VG	VG+	NM
❑ M-1312 [M]	Rockin' with Robin	196?	20.00	40.00	80.00

DAY, DENNIS
DESIGN

Number	Title	Yr	VG	VG+	NM
❑ DLPX-1 [M]	Dennis Day Sings "Christmas Is for the Family"	195?	5.00	10.00	20.00

-- Cover features Jack Benny as Santa; he also appears briefly on the LP

STEREO SPECTRUM

Number	Title	Yr	VG	VG+	NM
❑ SDLPX-1 [S]	Dennis Day Sings "Christmas Is for the Family"	195?	7.50	15.00	30.00

-- Same as Design 1

DAY, DORIS
COLUMBIA

Number	Title	Yr	VG	VG+	NM
❑ DD 1 [M]	Listen to Day	1960	5.00	10.00	20.00
❑ DDS 1 [S]	Listen to Day	1960	6.25	12.50	25.00
❑ C2L 5 [(2) M]	Hooray for Hollywood	1959	10.00	20.00	40.00
❑ CL 582 [M]	Young Man with a Horn	1954	10.00	20.00	40.00
-- Reissue of 6106; red label, gold print					
❑ CL 624 [M]	Day Dreams	1955	10.00	20.00	40.00
-- Red label, gold print					
❑ CL 624 [M]	Day Dreams	1956	6.25	12.50	25.00
-- Six "eye" logos on label					
❑ CL 710 [M]	Love Me or Leave Me	1955	12.50	25.00	50.00
-- Red label, gold print					
❑ CL 710 [M]	Love Me or Leave Me	1956	6.25	12.50	25.00
-- Six "eye" logos on label					
❑ CL 749 [M]	Day in Hollywood	1956	7.50	15.00	30.00
❑ C2S 805 [(2) S]	Hooray for Hollywood	1959	12.50	25.00	50.00
❑ CL 942 [M]	Day By Day	1957	7.50	15.00	30.00
❑ CL 1053 [M]	Day By Night	1958	5.00	10.00	20.00
❑ CL 1210 [M]	Doris Day's Greatest Hits	1958	7.50	15.00	30.00
-- Six "eye" logos on label					
❑ CL 1232 [M]	Cuttin' Capers	1959	5.00	10.00	20.00
❑ CL 1??? [M]	Hooray for Hollywood, Volume 1	1959	5.00	10.00	20.00
❑ CL 1??? [M]	Hooray for Hollywood, Volume 2	1959	5.00	10.00	20.00
❑ CL 14?? [M]	What Every Girl Should Know	1960	5.00	10.00	20.00
❑ CL 1461 [M]	Show Time	1960	5.00	10.00	20.00
❑ CL 1660 [M]	I Have Dreamed	1961	5.00	10.00	20.00
❑ CL 1752 [M]	Duet	1962	5.00	10.00	20.00
-- With Andre Previn					
❑ CL 2518 [M]	Lights, Camera, Action	1955	12.50	25.00	50.00
❑ CL 6071 [10]	You're My Thrill	1949	15.00	30.00	60.00
❑ CL 6106 [10]	Young Man with a Horn	1950	25.00	50.00	100.00
❑ CL 6149 [10]	Tea for Two	1950	15.00	30.00	60.00
❑ CL 6168 [10]	Lullaby of Broadway	1951	15.00	30.00	60.00
❑ CL 6186 [10]	On Moonlight Bay	1951	15.00	30.00	60.00
❑ CL 6198 [10]	I'll See You in My Dreams	1951	15.00	30.00	60.00
❑ CL 6248 [10]	By the Light of the Silvery Moon	1953	15.00	30.00	60.00
❑ CL 6273 [10]	Calamity Jane	1953	15.00	30.00	60.00
❑ CL 6339 [10]	Young at Heart	1954	15.00	30.00	60.00
-- Six songs by Doris Day, two by Frank Sinatra					
❑ CS 8066 [S]	Hooray for Hollywood, Volume 1	1959	6.25	12.50	25.00
❑ CS 8067 [S]	Hooray for Hollywood, Volume 2	1959	6.25	12.50	25.00
❑ CS 8078 [S]	Cuttin' Capers	1959	6.25	12.50	25.00
❑ CS 8089 [S]	Day By Day	1959	6.25	12.50	25.00
❑ CS 8234 [S]	What Every Girl Should Know	1960	6.25	12.50	25.00
❑ CS 8261 [S]	Show Time	1960	5.00	10.00	20.00
❑ CS 8460 [S]	I Have Dreamed	1961	6.25	12.50	25.00
❑ CS 8552 [S]	Duet	1962	6.25	12.50	25.00
-- With Andre Previn					
❑ CS 8704 [S]	You'll Never Walk Alone	1962	5.00	10.00	20.00
❑ CS 8931 [S]	Love Him!	1964	5.00	10.00	20.00

COLUMBIA SPECIAL PRODUCTS

Number	Title	Yr	VG	VG+	NM
❑ XTV 82021/2 [M]	Wonderful Day	1961	10.00	20.00	40.00

Number	Title	Yr	VG	VG+	NM

DAY, JIMMY
PHILIPS
❏ PHM 200-016 [M] Golden Steel Guitar Hits		1962	6.25	12.50	25.00
❏ PHM 200-075 [M] Steel and Strings		1963	6.25	12.50	25.00
❏ PHS 600-016 [S] Golden Steel Guitar Hits		1962	7.50	15.00	30.00
❏ PHS 600-075 [S] Steel and Strings		1963	7.50	15.00	30.00

DE LA SOUL
TOMMY BOY
❏ 1041 [(2) DJ] De La Soul Is Dead		1991	6.25	12.50	25.00
-- Promo-only two-record set					

DE-FENDERS, THE
DEL-FI
❏ DFLP-1242 [M]	Drag Beat	1963	12.50	25.00	50.00
❏ DFST-1242 [S]	Drag Beat	1963	15.00	30.00	60.00
WORLD PACIFIC
❏ ST-1810 [S]	The De-Fenders Play the Big Ones	1963	17.50	35.00	70.00
-- Black vinyl					
❏ ST-1810 [S]	The De-Fenders Play the Big Ones	1963	37.50	75.00	150.00
-- Green vinyl					
❏ ST-1810 [S]	The De-Fenders Play the Big Ones	1963	37.50	75.00	150.00
-- Red vinyl					
❏ WP-1810 [M]	The De-Fenders Play the Big Ones	1963	12.50	25.00	50.00

DEAD BOYS
SIRE
❏ SR-6038	Young, Loud & Snotty	1977	6.25	12.50	25.00
❏ SRK-6054	We Have Come for Your Children	1978	6.25	12.50	25.00

DEAD KENNEDYS
FAULTY
❏ 70014	Fresh Fruit for Rotting Vegetables	1982	10.00	20.00	40.00
-- With nursing home photo on back cover, no reference to I.R.S. on label or cover					
I.R.S./FAULTY PRODUCTS
❏ SP-70014	Fresh Fruit for Rotting Vegetables	1980	5.00	10.00	20.00
-- Originals have an orange cover "to distinguish it from imports"					

DEADLY ONES, THE
VEE JAY
❏ LP-1090 [M]	It's Monster Surfing Time	1964	25.00	50.00	100.00
❏ LPS-1090 [S]	It's Monster Surfing Time	1964	30.00	60.00	120.00

DEAL, BILL, AND THE RHONDELS
HERITAGE
❏ HTS 35003	Vintage Rock	1969	7.50	15.00	30.00
❏ HTS 35006	The Best of Bill Deal and the Rhondels	1970	7.50	15.00	30.00

DEAN, EDDIE
SAGE AND SAND
❏ C-1 [M]	Greatest Westerns	1956	12.50	25.00	50.00
❏ C-5 [M]	Hi-Country	1957	12.50	25.00	50.00
❏ C-16 [M]	Hillbilly Heaven	1961	7.50	15.00	30.00
SOUND
❏ LP-603 [M]	Greatest Westerns	1957	7.50	15.00	30.00

DEAN, JIMMY
COLUMBIA
❏ CL 1025 [M]	Jimmy Dean's Hour of Prayer	1957	10.00	20.00	40.00
❏ CL 1735 [M]	Big Bad John and Other Fabulous Songs and Tales	1961	5.00	10.00	20.00
❏ CL 1894 [M]	Portrait of Jimmy Dean	1962	5.00	10.00	20.00
❏ CS 8535 [S]	Big Bad John and Other Fabulous Songs and Tales	1961	6.25	12.50	25.00
❏ CS 8694 [S]	Portrait of Jimmy Dean	1962	6.25	12.50	25.00
❏ CS 8827 [S]	Everybody's Favorite	1963	5.00	10.00	20.00
❏ CS 8988 [S]	Songs We All Love Best	1964	5.00	10.00	20.00
❏ CS 9201 [S]	The First Thing Every Morning	1965	5.00	10.00	20.00
KING
❏ 686 [M]	Favorites of Jimmy Dean	1961	15.00	30.00	60.00
MERCURY
❏ MG-20319 [M]	Jimmy Dean Sings His Television Favorites	1957	10.00	20.00	40.00
RCA VICTOR
❏ LPM-3824 [M]	Most Richly Blesed	1967	5.00	10.00	20.00
❏ LPM-3890 [M]	The Jimmy Dean Show	1967	5.00	10.00	20.00
❏ LPM-3999 [M]	A Thing Called Love	1968	7.50	15.00	30.00

DEAN, JIMMY / JOHNNY HORTON
LA BREA
❏ L 8014 [M]	Bummin' Around with Jimmy Dean and Johnny Horton	1961	20.00	40.00	80.00
STARDAY
❏ SLP-325 [M]	Bummin' Around with Jimmy Dean and Johnny Horton	1965	7.50	15.00	30.00

DEARIE, BLOSSOM
Known to some as one of the singers on the "Schoolhouse Rock" ABC cartoon series.
VERVE
❏ MGV-2037 [M]	Blossom Dearie	1957	15.00	30.00	60.00
❏ V-2037 [M]	Blossom Dearie	1961	5.00	10.00	20.00
❏ MGV-2081 [M]	Give Him the Ooh-La-La	1958	15.00	30.00	60.00
❏ V-2081 [M]	Give Him the Ooh-La-La	1961	5.00	10.00	20.00
❏ MGV-2109 [M]	Blossom Dearie Sings Comden & Green	1959	15.00	30.00	60.00
❏ V-2109 [M]	Blossom Dearie Sings Comden & Green	1961	5.00	10.00	20.00
❏ V6-2109 [S]	Blossom Dearie Sings Comden & Green	1961	6.25	12.50	25.00
❏ MGV-2111 [M]	Once Upon a Summertime	1958	15.00	30.00	60.00
❏ V-2111 [M]	Once Upon a Summertime	1961	5.00	10.00	20.00
❏ V6-2111 [S]	Once Upon a Summertime	1961	6.25	12.50	25.00
❏ MGV-2125 [M]	My Gentleman Friend	1959	15.00	30.00	60.00
❏ V-2125 [M]	My Gentleman Friend	1961	5.00	10.00	20.00
❏ V6-2125 [S]	My Gentleman Friend	1961	6.25	12.50	25.00
❏ MGV-2133 [M]	Broadway Song Hits	1960	12.50	25.00	50.00
❏ V-2133 [M]	Broadway Song Hits	1961	5.00	10.00	20.00
❏ V6-2133 [S]	Broadway Song Hits	1961	6.25	12.50	25.00
❏ MGVS-6020 [S]	Once Upon a Summertime	1960	12.50	25.00	50.00
❏ MGVS-6050 [S]	Blossom Dearie Sings Comden & Green	1960	12.50	25.00	50.00
❏ MGVS-6112 [S]	My Gentleman Friend	1960	12.50	25.00	50.00
❏ MGVS-6139 [S]	Broadway Song Hits	1960	15.00	30.00	60.00

DEAUVILLE, RONNIE
ERA
❏ 20002 [M]	Smoke Dreams	1957	10.00	20.00	40.00
IMPERIAL
❏ LP-9060 [M]	Romance	1959	6.25	12.50	25.00
❏ LP-12009 [S]	Romance	1959	7.50	15.00	30.00

DEBRIS
STATIC DISPOSAL
❏ 0000	Debris	1976	20.00	40.00	80.00

DeCARLO, YVONNE
MASTERSEAL
❏ 33-1869/70 [M] Yvonne DeCarlo Sings		1957	20.00	40.00	80.00

DeCASTRO SISTERS, THE
ABBOTT
❏ 5002 [M]	The DeCastro Sisters	1956	15.00	30.00	60.00
CAPITOL
❏ ST 1402 [S]	The DeCastros Sing	1960	7.50	15.00	30.00
❏ T 1402 [M]	The DeCastros Sing	1960	6.25	12.50	25.00
❏ ST 1501 [S]	The Rockin' Beat	1961	7.50	15.00	30.00
❏ T 1501 [M]	The Rockin' Beat	1961	6.25	12.50	25.00

DECEMBER'S CHILDREN
MAINSTREAM
❏ S-6128	December's Children	1970	12.50	25.00	50.00

DEE, JOEY, AND THE STARLITERS
JUBILEE
❏ JLP-8000 [M]	Hitsville	1966	5.00	10.00	20.00
❏ JLS-8000 [S]	Hitsville	1966	6.25	12.50	25.00
ROULETTE
❏ R-25166 [M]	Doin' the Twist at the Peppermint Lounge	1961	10.00	20.00	40.00
❏ SR-25166 [S]	Doin' the Twist at the Peppermint Lounge	1961	12.50	25.00	50.00
❏ R-25171 [M]	All the World Is Twistin'	1962	7.50	15.00	30.00
❏ SR-25171 [S]	All the World Is Twistin'	1962	10.00	20.00	40.00
❏ R-25173 [M]	Back at the Peppermint Lounge -- Twistin'	1962	7.50	15.00	30.00
❏ SR-25173 [S]	Back at the Peppermint Lounge -- Twistin'	1962	10.00	20.00	40.00
❏ R-25197 [M]	Joey Dee	1963	6.25	12.50	25.00
❏ SR-25197 [S]	Joey Dee	1963	7.50	15.00	30.00

Number	Title	Yr	VG	VG+	NM
❑ R-25221 [M]	Dance, Dance, Dance	1963	6.25	12.50	25.00
❑ SR-25221 [S]	Dance, Dance, Dance	1963	7.50	15.00	30.00
SCEPTER					
❑ S 503 [M]	The Peppermint Twisters	1962	6.25	12.50	25.00
❑ SS 503 [S]	The Peppermint Twisters	1962	7.50	15.00	30.00

DEEP PURPLE
DCC COMPACT CLASSICS

Number	Title	Yr	VG	VG+	NM
❑ LPZ-2052 [(2)]	Made in Japan	1998	10.00	20.00	40.00
-- Audiophile vinyl					
TETRAGRAMMATON					
❑ T-102	Shades of Deep Purple	1968	7.50	15.00	30.00
❑ T-107	The Book of Taliesyn	1968	7.50	15.00	30.00
❑ T-119	Deep Purple	1969	7.50	15.00	30.00
❑ T-131	Concerto for Group and Orchestra	1970	75.00	150.00	300.00
WARNER BROS.					
❑ BS4 2607 [Q]	Machine Head	1974	6.25	12.50	25.00
WARNER BROS./PURPLE					
❑ PR4 2832 [Q]	Stormbringer	1974	6.25	12.50	25.00

DEEP RIVER BOYS, THE
QUE

Number	Title	Yr	VG	VG+	NM
❑ FLS-104 [M]	Midnight Magic	1957	37.50	75.00	150.00
RCA CAMDEN					
❑ CAL-303 [M]	Presenting the Deep River Boys	1957	15.00	30.00	60.00
-- Reissue of "X" album					
WALDORF MUSIC HALL					
❑ MH 33-108 [10]	The Deep River Boys Sing Songs of Jubilee	195?	37.50	75.00	150.00
-- Cartoon on cover					
❑ MH 33-108 [10]	The Deep River Boys Sing Songs of Jubilee	1954	75.00	150.00	300.00
-- Photo of group on cover					
"X"					
❑ LXA-1019 [M]	Presenting the Deep River Boys	1956	30.00	60.00	120.00

DEEP, THE
PARKWAY

Number	Title	Yr	VG	VG+	NM
❑ P 7051 [M]	Psychedelic Moods	1966	62.50	125.00	250.00
❑ SP 7051 [S]	Psychedelic Moods	1966	125.00	250.00	500.00

DEEP SIX, THE
LIBERTY

Number	Title	Yr	VG	VG+	NM
❑ LST-7475 [S]	The Deep Six	1966	5.00	10.00	20.00

DEERFIELD
FLAT ROCK

Number	Title	Yr	VG	VG+	NM
❑ FRS-1	Nil Desperandum	1971	30.00	60.00	120.00

DeJOHN SISTERS, THE
EPIC

Number	Title	Yr	VG	VG+	NM
❑ LN 1116 [M]	The DeJohn Sisters	195?	7.50	15.00	30.00
UNITED ARTISTS					
❑ UAL-3103 [M]	Yes Indeed	1960	5.00	10.00	20.00
❑ UAS-6103 [S]	Yes Indeed	1960	6.25	12.50	25.00

DEKKER, DESMOND, AND THE ACES
UNI

Number	Title	Yr	VG	VG+	NM
❑ 73059	Israelites	1969	7.50	15.00	30.00

DEL SATINS
B.T. PUPPY

Number	Title	Yr	VG	VG+	NM
❑ BTS-1019	Out to Lunch	1972	75.00	150.00	300.00

DEL VIKINGS, THE
DOT

Number	Title	Yr	VG	VG+	NM
❑ DLP-3685 [M]	Come Go with Me	1966	50.00	100.00	200.00
❑ DLP-25685 [R]	Come Go with Me	1966	37.50	75.00	150.00
LUNIVERSE					
❑ LP-1000 [M]	Come Go with the Del Vikings	1957	125.00	250.00	500.00
-- Eight tracks, cover is composed of slicks. Counterfeits have more tracks and a preprinted cover (not slicks)					
MERCURY					
❑ MG-20314 [M]	They Sing -- They Swing	1957	75.00	150.00	300.00
❑ MG-20353 [M]	A Swinging, Singing Record Session	1958	50.00	100.00	200.00

DEL VIKINGS, THE / THE SONNETS
CROWN

Number	Title	Yr	VG	VG+	NM
❑ CLP-5368 [M]	The Del Vikings and the Sonnets	1963	10.00	20.00	40.00

DELANEY AND BONNIE
ATCO

Number	Title	Yr	VG	VG+	NM
❑ SD 33-326	Delaney & Bonnie & Friends On Tour with Eric Clapton	1970	6.25	12.50	25.00
-- Yellow label original					
❑ SD 33-341	To Bonnie from Delaney	1970	6.25	12.50	25.00
❑ SD 33-358	Motel Shot	1971	6.25	12.50	25.00
❑ SD 33-383	Country Life	1972	5.00	10.00	20.00
❑ SD 7014	The Best of Delaney and Bonnie	1972	5.00	10.00	20.00
COLUMBIA					
❑ KC 31377	D&B Together	1972	5.00	10.00	20.00
ELEKTRA					
❑ EKS-74039	Accept No Substitute -- The Original Delaney & Bonnie & Friends	1969	7.50	15.00	30.00
GNP CRESCENDO					
❑ GNPS-2054	Genesis	1970	5.00	10.00	20.00
STAX					
❑ STS-2026	Home	1969	7.50	15.00	30.00

DELEGATES, THE
MAINSTREAM

Number	Title	Yr	VG	VG+	NM
❑ 100	The Delegates	1973	5.00	10.00	20.00

DELFONICS, THE
PHILLY GROOVE

Number	Title	Yr	VG	VG+	NM
❑ 1150	La La Means I Love You	1968	20.00	40.00	80.00
❑ 1151	The Sexy Sound of Soul	1969	20.00	40.00	80.00
❑ 1152	The Delfonics Super Hits	1969	12.50	25.00	50.00
❑ 1153	The Delfonics	1970	12.50	25.00	50.00
❑ 1154	Tell Me This is a Dream	1972	12.50	25.00	50.00
❑ 1501	Alive & Kicking	1974	12.50	25.00	50.00

DELLER, ALFRED
VANGUARD

Number	Title	Yr	VG	VG+	NM
❑ VRS-479 [M]	The Three Ravens	195?	10.00	20.00	40.00
❑ VRS-499 [M]	The Holly and the Ivy -- Christmas Songs of Old England	1956	10.00	20.00	40.00

DELLS, THE
CADET

Number	Title	Yr	VG	VG+	NM
❑ LPS-804	There Is	1968	12.50	25.00	50.00
❑ LPS-822	The Dells Musical Menu/ Always Together	1969	12.50	25.00	50.00
❑ LPS-824	The Dells Greatest Hits	1969	12.50	25.00	50.00
❑ LPS-829	Love Is Blue	1969	12.50	25.00	50.00
❑ LPS-837	Like It Is, Like It Was	1970	12.50	25.00	50.00
❑ 50004	Freedom Means	1971	6.25	12.50	25.00
❑ 50017	The Dells Sing Dionne Warwicke's Greatest Hits	1972	6.25	12.50	25.00
❑ 50021	Sweet As Funk Can Be	1972	6.25	12.50	25.00
❑ 50037	Give Your Baby a Standing	1973	6.25	12.50	25.00
❑ 50046	The Dells	1973	6.25	12.50	25.00
❑ 60030	The Mighty Mighty Dells	1974	6.25	12.50	25.00
❑ 60036	The Dells' Greatest Hits, Vol. 2	1975	5.00	10.00	20.00
VEE JAY					
❑ LP 1010 [M]	Oh What a Nite	1959	200.00	400.00	800.00
-- Maroon label					
❑ LP 1010 [M]	Oh What a Nite	1961	75.00	150.00	300.00
-- Black label with colorband					
❑ LP 1141 [M]	It's Not Unusual	1965	25.00	50.00	100.00
❑ LPS 1141 [S]	It's Not Unusual	1965	37.50	75.00	150.00

DELLS, THE, AND THE DRAMATICS
Also see each artist's individual listings.
CADET

Number	Title	Yr	VG	VG+	NM
❑ 60027	The Dells Vs. the Dramatics	1974	6.25	12.50	25.00

DELMORE BROTHERS, THE
KING

Number	Title	Yr	VG	VG+	NM
❑ 589 [M]	Songs by the Delmore Brothers	1958	37.50	75.00	150.00
❑ 785 [M]	30th Anniversary Album	1962	20.00	40.00	80.00
❑ 910 [M]	In Memory	1964	10.00	20.00	40.00
❑ 920 [M]	In Memory, Volume 2	1964	10.00	20.00	40.00
❑ 983 [M]	24 Great Country Songs	1966	7.50	15.00	30.00
❑ KS-983 [R]	24 Great Country Songs	1966	5.00	10.00	20.00

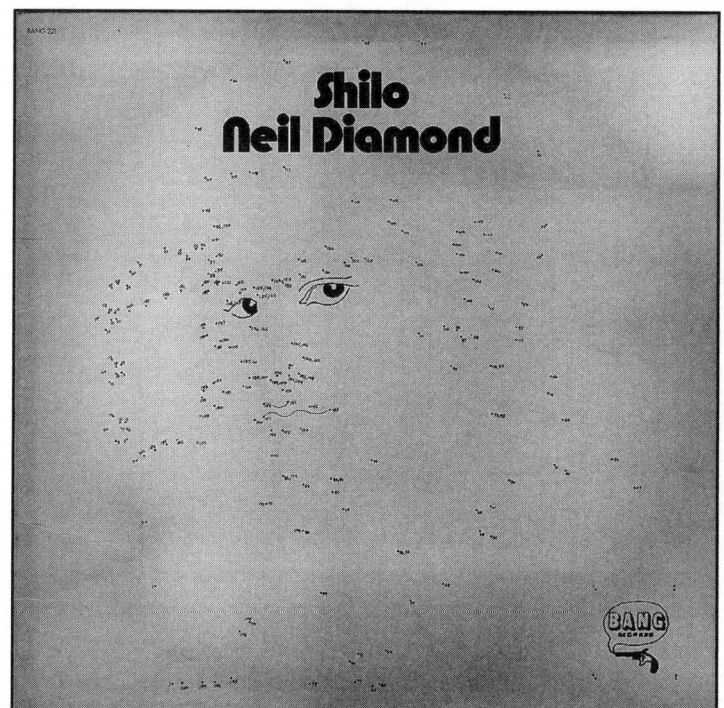

(Top left) Dave Dee, Dozy, Beaky, Mick & Tich were much bigger in England than in the U.S. But Imperial Records still issued an entire album, which failed to chart, that featured their only Hot 100 hit "Zabadak." (Top right) When Joey Dee hit it big with "Peppermint Twist," Scepter Records, his label prior to Roulette, created this cash-in album called *The Peppermint Twisters*. (Bottom left) One of the many compilations of Neil Diamond recordings issued on the Bang label, *Shilo* is rarely found in its pure state as this copy is. Most consumers connected the dots on the cover! It's said that Columbia, Diamond's label at the time, bought Bang in 1979 to gain control of his early masters and get all the dubious compilations off the market. (Bottom right) Doug Dillard of the Dillards and Gene Clark of the Byrds got together to form Dillard & Clark. Their most collectible album, on the A&M brown label, is *The Fantastic Expedition of Dillard & Clark*.

Number	Title	Yr	VG	VG+	NM

DEMENSIONS, THE
CORAL
❑ CRL 57430 [M] My Foolish Heart	1963	37.50	75.00	150.00
❑ CRL 757430 [S] My Foolish Heart	1963	75.00	150.00	300.00

DEMIAN
Includes members of THE BUBBLE PUPPY.
ABC
❑ ABCS-718	Demian	1970	15.00	30.00	60.00

DENNY, MARTIN
LIBERTY
❑ LRP-3034 [M]	Exotica	1957	10.00	20.00	40.00
-- Turquoise label					
❑ LRP-3034 [M]	Exotica	1960	6.25	12.50	25.00
-- Black rainbow label					
❑ LRP-3077 [M]	Exotica, Volume II	1957	7.50	15.00	30.00
-- Turquoise label					
❑ LRP-3077 [M]	Exotica, Volume II	1960	5.00	10.00	20.00
-- Black rainbow label					
❑ LRP-3081 [M]	Forbidden Island	1958	7.50	15.00	30.00
-- Turquoise label; woman in jungle on cover					
❑ LRP-3081 [M]	Forbidden Island	1960	5.00	10.00	20.00
-- Black rainbow label; white foil on cover					
❑ LRP-3087 [M]	Primitiva	1958	7.50	15.00	30.00
-- Turquoise label					
❑ LRP-3087 [M]	Primitiva	1960	5.00	10.00	20.00
-- Black rainbow label					
❑ LRP-3102 [M]	Hypnotique	1958	7.50	15.00	30.00
-- Turquoise label					
❑ LRP-3102 [M]	Hypnotique	1960	5.00	10.00	20.00
-- Black rainbow label					
❑ LRP-3111 [M]	Afro-Desia	1959	7.50	15.00	30.00
-- Turquoise label					
❑ LRP-3111 [M]	Afro-Desia	1960	5.00	10.00	20.00
-- Black rainbow label					
❑ LRP-3116 [M]	Exotica, Vol. III	1959	7.50	15.00	30.00
-- Turquoise label					
❑ LRP-3116 [M]	Exotica, Vol. III	1960	5.00	10.00	20.00
-- Black rainbow label					
❑ LRP-3122 [M]	Quiet Village	1959	7.50	15.00	30.00
-- Turquoise label					
❑ LRP-3122 [M]	Quiet Village	1960	5.00	10.00	20.00
-- Black rainbow label					
❑ LRP-3141 [M]	The Enchanted Sea	1959	7.50	15.00	30.00
-- Turquoise label					
❑ LRP-3141 [M]	The Enchanted Sea	1960	5.00	10.00	20.00
-- Black rainbow label					
❑ LRP-3158 [M]	Exotic Sounds from the Silver Screen	1960	5.00	10.00	20.00
❑ LRP-3163 [M]	Exotic Sounds Visit Broadway	1960	5.00	10.00	20.00
❑ LRP-3168 [M]	Exotic Percussion	1961	5.00	10.00	20.00
❑ LST-7001 [S]	Forbidden Island	1958	10.00	20.00	40.00
-- All-black label; woman in jungle on cover					
❑ LST-7001 [S]	Forbidden Island	1960	6.25	12.50	25.00
-- Black rainbow label; white foil on cover					
❑ LST-7006 [S]	Exotica, Volume II	1958	10.00	20.00	40.00
-- All-black label					
❑ LST-7006 [S]	Exotica, Volume II	1960	6.25	12.50	25.00
-- Black rainbow label					
❑ LST-7023 [S]	Primitiva	1958	10.00	20.00	40.00
-- All-black label					
❑ LST-7023 [S]	Primitiva	1960	6.25	12.50	25.00
-- Black rainbow label					
❑ LST-7034 [R]	Exotica	1958	6.25	12.50	25.00
-- All-black label					
❑ LST-7034 [R]	Exotica	1960	5.00	10.00	20.00
-- Black rainbow label					
❑ LST-7102 [S]	Hypnotique	1958	10.00	20.00	40.00
-- All-black label					
❑ LST-7102 [S]	Hypnotique	1960	6.25	12.50	25.00
-- Black rainbow label					
❑ LST-7111 [S]	Afro-Desia	1959	10.00	20.00	40.00
-- All-black label					
❑ LST-7111 [S]	Afro-Desia	1960	6.25	12.50	25.00
-- Black rainbow label					
❑ LST-7116 [S]	Exotica, Vol. III	1959	10.00	20.00	40.00
-- All-black label					
❑ LST-7116 [S]	Exotica, Vol. III	1960	6.25	12.50	25.00
-- Black rainbow label					
❑ LST-7122 [S]	Quiet Village	1959	10.00	20.00	40.00
-- All-black label					
❑ LST-7122 [S]	Quiet Village	1960	6.25	12.50	25.00
-- Black rainbow label					
❑ LST-7141 [S]	The Enchanted Sea	1959	10.00	20.00	40.00
-- All-black label					
❑ LST-7141 [S]	The Enchanted Sea	1960	6.25	12.50	25.00
-- Black rainbow label					
❑ LST-7158 [S]	Exotic Sounds from the Silver Screen	1960	6.25	12.50	25.00
❑ LST-7163 [S]	Exotic Sounds Visit Broadway	1960	6.25	12.50	25.00
❑ LST-7168 [S]	Exotic Percussion	1961	6.25	12.50	25.00
❑ LST-7224 [S]	The Exotic Sounds of Martin Denny In Person	1962	5.00	10.00	20.00
❑ LST-7237 [S]	A Taste of Honey	1962	5.00	10.00	20.00
❑ LST-7277 [S]	Another Taste of Honey	1963	5.00	10.00	20.00
❑ LST-7307 [S]	The Versatile Martin Denny	1963	5.00	10.00	20.00
❑ LST-7621	Exotic Moog	1969	10.00	20.00	40.00

DENNY, SANDY
Also see FAIRPORT CONVENTION.
HANNIBAL
❑ HNBX-5301 [(3)]	Who Knows Where the Time Goes	198?	5.00	10.00	20.00

DENVER, JOHN
Also see THE MITCHELL TRIO.
HJD
❑ 66	John Denver Sings	1966	125.00	250.00	500.00
-- Private issue of 300 or so, made by JD as Christmas gifts to friends.					

MERCURY
❑ SRM-1-704	Beginnings	1972	5.00	10.00	20.00
-- With illustration on cover					

RCA VICTOR
❑ APL2-1263 [(2)]	The John Denver Gift Pak	1974	7.50	15.00	30.00
-- Contains "Rocky Mountain Christmas" and "Windsong" in a special Christmas sleeve.					
❑ DJL1-0075 [DJ]	The John Denver Radio Show	1973	7.50	15.00	30.00
❑ DJL1-0683 [DJ]	The Second John Denver Radio Show	1974	7.50	15.00	30.00
❑ DJL1-5398 [DJ]	The John Denver Holiday Radio Show	1984	5.00	10.00	20.00

DePAUR CHORUS, THE
COLUMBIA
❑ CL 725 [M]	The Spirit of Christmas/ God Is With Us	1955	7.50	15.00	30.00
❑ CL 923 [M]	Calypso Christmas	1956	10.00	20.00	40.00

COLUMBIA MASTERWORKS
❑ AL 45 [10]	Swing Low	1953	15.00	30.00	60.00
❑ ML 2119 [10]	Work Songs and Spirituals	195?	15.00	30.00	60.00

MERCURY LIVING PRESENCE
❑ SR 90382 [S]	Songs of New Nations	196?	15.00	30.00	60.00
-- Maroon label, no "Vendor: Mercury Record Corporation"					
❑ SR 90382 [S]	Songs of New Nations	196?	12.50	25.00	50.00
-- Maroon label, with "Vendor: Mercury Record Corporation"					
❑ SR 90418 [S]	Danse Calinda! Creole Songs, Work Songs and Spirituals	196?	12.50	25.00	50.00
-- Maroon label, no "Vendor: Mercury Record Corporation"					
❑ SR 90418 [S]	Danse Calinda! Creole Songs, Work Songs and Spirituals	196?	7.50	15.00	30.00
-- Maroon label, with "Vendor: Mercury Record Corporation"					

DEPECHE MODE
MUTE
❑ MUTEL 5 [(3)]	The Singles 86-98	1998	7.50	15.00	30.00
-- Numbered, limited box set pressed in England with U.S. bar code sticker					

SIRE
❑ PRO-A-5192 [(2) DJ]	Selections from the Commercially Available Box Sets One and Two	1991	6.25	12.50	25.00
❑ PRO-A-5242 [(2) DJ]	Selections from the Commercially Available Box Set Three	1991	10.00	20.00	40.00
-- Above two are promo-only samplers					

DEPENDABLES, THE
UNITED ARTISTS
❑ UAS-6799	Klaatu Berrada Niktu	1971	5.00	10.00	20.00

DEPUTIES, THE
Backing group for FARON YOUNG.
FARON YOUNG
❑ 002 [M]	Sounds of the Deputies	1965	7.50	15.00	30.00

DEREK AND THE DOMINOS
Also see ERIC CLAPTON.
ATCO
❑ 2-704 [(2) M]	Layla and Other Assorted Love Songs	1970	75.00	150.00	300.00
-- White label promo only					

Number	Title	Yr	VG	VG+	NM
❑ SD 2-704[(2) DJ] Layla and Other Assorted Love Songs		1970	50.00	100.00	200.00
-- White label promo					
❑ SD 2-704 [(2) S] Layla and Other Assorted Love Songs		1970	7.50	15.00	30.00
DIRECT DISK					
❑ SD-16629 [(2)] Layla and Other Assorted Love Songs		1981	37.50	75.00	150.00
-- Audiophile vinyl					
MOBILE FIDELITY					
❑ 2-239 [(2)] Derek and the Dominos In Concert		1996	12.50	25.00	50.00
-- Audiophile vinyl					
POLYDOR					
❑ PD2-3501 [(2)] Layla and Other Assorted Love Songs		1972	5.00	10.00	20.00
RSO					
❑ SO 2-8800 [(2)] Derek and the Dominos in Concert		1973	5.00	10.00	20.00

DERRINGER, RICK
Also see THE McCOYS.
BLUE SKY

Number	Title	Yr	VG	VG+	NM
❑ ZQ 32481 [Q] All American Boy		1974	5.00	10.00	20.00

DeSANTO, SUGAR PIE
CHECKER

❑ LP-2979 [M] Sugar Pie DeSanto		1961	50.00	100.00	200.00

DeSHANNON, JACKIE
IMPERIAL

Number	Title	Yr	VG	VG+	NM
❑ LP-9286 [M] This Is Jackie DeShannon		1965	5.00	10.00	20.00
-- Black and pink label					
❑ LP-9294 [M] You Won't Forget Me		1965	5.00	10.00	20.00
-- Black and pink label					
❑ LP-9296 [M] In the Wind		1965	5.00	10.00	20.00
-- Black and pink label					
❑ LP-12286 [S] This Is Jackie DeShannon		1965	6.25	12.50	25.00
-- Black and pink label					
❑ LP-12286 [S] This Is Jackie DeShannon		1966	5.00	10.00	20.00
-- Black and green label					
❑ LP-12294 [S] You Won't Forget Me		1965	6.25	12.50	25.00
-- Black and pink label					
❑ LP-12294 [S] You Won't Forget Me		1966	5.00	10.00	20.00
-- Black and green label					
❑ LP-12296 [S] In the Wind		1965	6.25	12.50	25.00
-- Black and pink label					
❑ LP-12296 [S] In the Wind		1966	5.00	10.00	20.00
-- Black and green label					
❑ LP-12328 [S] Are You Ready for This?		1966	5.00	10.00	20.00
❑ LP-12344 [S] New Image		1967	5.00	10.00	20.00
❑ LP-12352 [S] For You		1967	5.00	10.00	20.00
LIBERTY					
❑ LRP-3320 [M] Jackie DeShannon		1963	10.00	2.00	40.00
❑ LRP-3390 [M] Breakin' It Up on the Beatles Tour!		1964	10.00	20.00	40.00
❑ LST-7320 [S] Jackie DeShannon		1963	12.50	25.00	50.00
❑ LST-7390 [S] Breakin' It Up on the Beatles Tour!		1964	12.50	25.00	50.00

DESMOND, JOHNNY
COLUMBIA

Number	Title	Yr	VG	VG+	NM
❑ CL 1??? [M] Once Upon a Time		1959	5.00	10.00	20.00
❑ CS 8194 [S] Once Upon a Time		1959	6.25	12.50	25.00

DESMOND, PAUL
Also see DAVE BRUBECK.
FANTASY

Number	Title	Yr	VG	VG+	NM
❑ 3-21 [10] Paul Desmond		1955	25.00	50.00	100.00
❑ 3235 [M] Paul Desmond Quartet Featuring Don Elliott		1956	20.00	40.00	80.00
-- Red vinyl					
❑ 3235 [M] Paul Desmond Quartet Featuring Don Elliott		1957	10.00	20.00	40.00
-- Black vinyl, red label, non-flexible vinyl					
❑ 3235 [M] Paul Desmond Quartet Featuring Don Elliott		1962	5.00	10.00	20.00
-- Black vinyl, red label, flexible vinyl					
RCA VICTOR					
❑ LPM-2438 [M] Desmond Blue		1961	7.50	15.00	30.00
❑ LSP-2438 [S] Desmond Blue		1961	7.50	15.00	30.00
❑ LPM-2569 [M] Take Ten		1962	6.25	12.50	25.00
❑ LSP-2569 [S] Take Ten		1962	7.50	15.00	30.00
❑ LPM-2654 [M] Two of a Mind		1963	6.25	12.50	25.00
❑ LSP-2654 [S] Two of a Mind		1963	7.50	15.00	30.00
❑ LPM-3320 [M] Boss Antigua		1965	5.00	10.00	20.00
❑ LSP-3320 [S] Boss Antigua		1965	6.25	12.50	25.00

Number	Title	Yr	VG	VG+	NM
❑ LPM-3407 [M] Glad to Be Unhappy		1965	5.00	10.00	20.00
❑ LSP-3407 [S] Glad to Be Unhappy		1965	6.25	12.50	25.00
❑ LPM-3480 [M] Easy Living		1965	5.00	10.00	20.00
❑ LSP-3480 [S] Easy Living		1965	6.25	12.50	25.00
WARNER BROS.					
❑ W 1356 [M] First Place Again		1960	7.50	15.00	30.00
❑ WS 1356 [S] First Place Again		1960	7.50	15.00	30.00

DETERGENTS, THE
Also see RON DANTE.
ROULETTE

Number	Title	Yr	VG	VG+	NM
❑ R 25308 [M] The Many Faces of the		1965	30.00	60.00	120.00
❑ SR 25308 [R] The Many Faces of the		1965	25.00	50.00	100.00

DETROIT CITY LIMITS, THE
OKEH

❑ OKS 14127 98c + Tax		1968	7.50	15.00	30.00

DETROIT EMERALDS
WESTBOUND

Number	Title	Yr	VG	VG+	NM
❑ 2006 Do Me Right		1971	10.00	20.00	40.00
❑ 2013 You Want It, You Got It		1972	10.00	20.00	40.00
❑ 2018 I'm in Love with You		1973	10.00	20.00	40.00

DETROIT SYMPHONY ORCHESTRA (PAUL PARAY, COND.)
MERCURY LIVING PRESENCE

Number	Title	Yr	VG	VG+	NM
❑ SR 90001 [S] Bizet: Carmen Suite		1959	10.00	20.00	40.00
-- Maroon label, no "Vendor: Mercury Record Corporation"					
❑ SR 90005 [S] Ravel: Bolero; Ma Mere L'Oye; Chabrier: Bourree Fantasque		1959	6.25	12.50	25.00
-- Maroon label, no "Vendor: Mercury Record Corporation"					
❑ SR 90010 [S] Debussy: La Mer; Iberia		1959	50.00	100.00	200.00
-- Maroon label, no "Vendor: Mercury Record Corporation"					
❑ SR 90012 [S] Saint-Saens: Symphony No. 3		1959	18.75	37.50	75.00
-- Maroon label, no "Vendor: Mercury Record Corporation"					
❑ SR 90017 [S] Chausson: Symphony in B-flat		1959	7.50	15.00	30.00
-- Maroon label, no "Vendor: Mercury Record Corporation"					
❑ SR 90019 [S] Rachmaninoff: Symphony No. 2		1959	5.00	10.00	20.00
-- Maroon label, no "Vendor: Mercury Record Corporation"					
❑ SR 90102 [S] Schumann: Symphony No. 2		196?	6.25	12.50	25.00
-- Maroon label, with "Vendor: Mercury Record Corporation"					
❑ SR 90102 [S] Schumann: Symphony No. 2		1960	10.00	20.00	40.00
-- Maroon label, no "Vendor: Mercury Record Corporation"					
❑ SR 90107 [S] Wagner: Dawn & Sigfried's Rhine Journey, etc.		196?	12.50	25.00	50.00
-- Maroon label, no "Vendor: Mercury Record Corporation"					
❑ SR 90128 [S] Paray: Mass for Joan of Arc		1960	10.00	20.00	40.00
-- Maroon label, no "Vendor: Mercury Record Corporation"					
❑ SR 90129 [S] Haydn: Symphony No. 96; Mozart: Symphony No. 35		1960	5.00	10.00	20.00
-- Maroon label, no "Vendor: Mercury Record Corporation"					
❑ SR 90133 [S] Schumann: Symphony No. 3 "Rhenish"		1960	7.50	15.00	30.00
-- Maroon label, no "Vendor: Mercury Record Corporation"					
❑ SR 90174 [S] Mendelssohn: A Midsummer Night's Dream; Symphony No. 5		196?	12.50	25.00	50.00
-- Maroon label, no "Vendor: Mercury Record Corporation"					
❑ SR 90174 [S] Mendelssohn: A Midsummer Night's Dream; Symphony No. 5		196?	6.25	12.50	25.00
-- Maroon label, with "Vendor: Mercury Record Corporation"					
❑ SR 90177 [S] Schmitt: Tragedie de Salome; Strauss, Richard: Salome-Dance; Lalo: Namouna, Suite 1		196?	30.00	60.00	120.00
-- Maroon label, no "Vendor: Mercury Record Corporation"					
❑ SR 90191 [S] Ouvertures Francaises		196?	30.00	60.00	120.00
-- Maroon label, no "Vendor: Mercury Record Corporation"					
❑ SR 90198 [S] Schumann: Symphony No. 1; Manfred Overture		196?	5.00	10.00	20.00
-- Maroon label, no "Vendor: Mercury Record Corporation"					
❑ SR 90203 [S] Bouquet de Paray		196?	7.50	15.00	30.00
-- Maroon label, with "Vendor: Mercury Record Corporation"					
❑ SR 90203 [S] Bouquet de Paray		196?	15.00	30.00	60.00
-- Maroon label, no "Vendor: Mercury Record Corporation"					
❑ SR 90204 [S] Sibelius: Symphony No. 2		196?	25.00	50.00	100.00
-- Maroon label, no "Vendor: Mercury Record Corporation"					
❑ SR 90204 [S] Sibelius: Symphony No. 2		196?	12.50	25.00	50.00
-- Maroon label, with "Vendor: Mercury Record Corporation"					
❑ SR 90204 [S] Sibelius: Symphony No. 2		196?	5.00	10.00	20.00
-- Third edition: Dark red (not maroon) label					
❑ SR 90205 [S] Beethoven: Symphonies No. 1 and 2		196?	25.00	50.00	100.00
-- Maroon label, no "Vendor: Mercury Record Corporation"					
❑ SR 90211 [S] Vive La Marche!		196?	10.00	20.00	40.00
-- Maroon label, no "Vendor: Mercury Record Corporation"					
❑ SR 90212 [S] Chabrier: Espana; Suite Pastorale; Fete Polonaise; Overture to "Gwendoline"; Danse Slave		196?	37.50	75.00	150.00
-- Maroon label, no "Vendor: Mercury Record Corporation"					

Number	Title	Yr	VG	VG+	NM
❏ SR 90212 [S]	Chabrier: Espana; Suite Pastorale; Fete Polonaise; Overture to "Gwendoline"; Danse Slave	199?	6.25	12.50	25.00
-- Classic Records reissue					
❏ SR 90213 [S]	Ravel: La Tombeau de Couperin; Valses Nobles et Sentimentales; Debussy: Petite Suite; Prelude	196?	62.50	125.00	250.00
-- Maroon label, no "Vendor: Mercury Record Corporation"					
❏ SR 90215 [S]	Overtures	196?	15.00	30.00	60.00
-- Maroon label, no "Vendor: Mercury Record Corporation"					
❏ SR 90232 [S]	Wagner: Rienzi Overture; Magic Fire Music; Flying Dutchman Overture; Meistersinger Excerpts	196?	10.00	20.00	40.00
❏ SR 90247 [S]	French Overtures	196?	20.00	40.00	80.00
-- Maroon label, no "Vendor: Mercury Record Corporation"					
❏ SR 90254 [S]	Berlioz: Symphonie Fantastique	196?	30.00	60.00	120.00
-- Maroon label, no "Vendor: Mercury Record Corporation"					
❏ SR 90254 [S]	Berlioz: Symphonie Fantastique	196?	7.50	15.00	30.00
-- Maroon label, with "Vendor: Mercury Record Corporation"					
❏ SR 90262 [S]	Dvorak: Symphony No. 9 "From the New World"	196?	37.50	75.00	150.00
-- Maroon label, no "Vendor: Mercury Record Corporation"					
❏ SR 90269 [S]	Suppe: Overtures	196?	10.00	20.00	40.00
-- Maroon label, no "Vendor: Mercury Record Corporation"					
❏ SR 90269 [S]	Suppe: Overtures	196?	6.25	12.50	25.00
-- Maroon label, with "Vendor: Mercury Record Corporation"					
❏ SR 90281 [S]	Debussy: Nocturnes; Ravel: Daphnis et Chloe Suite 2	196?	62.50	125.00	250.00
-- Maroon label, no "Vendor: Mercury Record Corporation"					
❏ SR 90285 [S]	Franck: Symphony in D	196?	17.50	35.00	70.00
-- Maroon label, no "Vendor: Mercury Record Corporation"					
❏ SR 90285 [S]	Franck: Symphony in D	196?	7.50	15.00	30.00
-- Maroon label, with "Vendor: Mercury Record Corporation"					
❏ SR 90313 [S]	Ravel: Rapsodie Espagnole; La Valse; Pavane; Alborada; Ibert: Escales	196?	125.00	250.00	500.00
-- Maroon label, no "Vendor: Mercury Record Corporation"					
❏ SR 90318 [S]	Ballet Highlights from French Opera	196?	30.00	60.00	120.00
-- Maroon label, no "Vendor: Mercury Record Corporation"					
❏ SR 90318 [S]	Ballet Highlights from French Opera	196?	25.00	50.00	100.00
-- Maroon label, with "Vendor: Mercury Record Corporation"					
❏ SR 90330 [S]	Schumann: Symphonies No. 1 and 3	196?	6.25	12.50	25.00
-- Maroon label, with "Vendor: Mercury Record Corporation"					
❏ SR 90330 [S]	Schumann: Symphonies No. 1 and 3	196?	10.00	20.00	40.00
-- Maroon label, no "Vendor: Mercury Record Corporation"					
❏ SR 90331 [S]	Saint-Saens: Symphony No. 3; Chausson: Symphony in B-flat	196?	7.50	15.00	30.00
-- Maroon label, no "Vendor: Mercury Record Corporation"					
❏ SR 90359 [S]	Curtain Up! Heroic Overtures	196?	7.50	15.00	30.00
-- Maroon label, no "Vendor: Mercury Record Corporation"					
❏ SR 90372 [S]	Debussy: La Mer; Petite Suite; Iberia; Prelude	196?	10.00	20.00	40.00
-- Maroon label, no "Vendor: Mercury Record Corporation"					
❏ SR 90373 [S]	Ravel: Ma Mere L'Oye; Pavane; Tombeau de Couperin; Valses Nobles et Sentimentales	196?	10.00	20.00	40.00
-- Maroon label, no "Vendor: Mercury Record Corporation"					
❏ SR 90374 [S]	Bizet: Carmen Suite; L'Arlesienne Suites No. 1 and 2; Chabrier: Espana; Bourree; Marche	196?	5.00	10.00	20.00
-- Maroon label, no "Vendor: Mercury Record Corporation"					
❏ SR 90375 [S]	Berlioz: Symphonie Fantastique; Le Corsair Overture; Royal Hunt and Storm	196?	7.50	15.00	30.00
-- Maroon label, no "Vendor: Mercury Record Corporation"					
❏ SR 90377 [S]	Overtures and Excerpts from French Opera	196?	10.00	20.00	40.00
-- Maroon label, no "Vendor: Mercury Record Corporation"					

DEUCE COUPES, THE
Two different groups?
CROWN

Number	Title	Yr	VG	VG+	NM
❏ CST-393 [S]	The Shut Downs	1963	6.25	12.50	25.00
❏ CLP-5393 [M]	The Shut Downs	1963	5.00	10.00	20.00

DEL-FI

❏ DFLP-1243 [M]	Hotrodder's Choice	1963	12.50	25.00	50.00
❏ DFST-1243 [S]	Hotrodder's Choice	1963	15.00	30.00	60.00

DEVIANTS, THE
SIRE

❏ SES-97001	Ptoof!	1968	15.00	30.00	60.00
❏ SES-97005	Disposable	1969	15.00	30.00	60.00
❏ SES-97016	No. 3	1969	15.00	30.00	60.00

DEVIL'S ANVIL, THE
COLUMBIA

❏ CL 2664 [M]	Hard Rock from the Middle East	1967	6.25	12.50	25.00
❏ CS 9464 [S]	Hard Rock from the Middle East	1967	7.50	15.00	30.00

Number	Title	Yr	VG	VG+	NM

DEVILED HAM
SUPER K

❏ SKS-6003	I Had Too Much to Dream Last Night	1968	6.25	12.50	25.00

DEVO
ENIGMA

❏ EPRO 326 [DJ]	Smooth Noodle Maps	1990	5.00	10.00	20.00
-- Promo only, no picture cover					

DeVOL, FRANK
COLUMBIA

❏ C2L 12 [(2) M]	The Columbia Album of Irving Berlin	1958	7.50	15.00	30.00
❏ C2S 812 [(2) S]	The Columbia Album of Irving Berlin	1958	10.00	20.00	40.00
❏ CS 8172 [S]	Fabulous Hollywood	1959	5.00	10.00	20.00
❏ CS 82?? [S]	Four Seasons of Love	1960	5.00	10.00	20.00
❏ CS 8209 [S]	The Old Sweet Songs	1960	5.00	10.00	20.00
❏ CS 8273 [S]	More Old Sweet Songs	1960	5.00	10.00	20.00

DEVROE, BILLY, AND THE DEVILAIRES
TAMPA

❏ TP-31 [M]	Billy Devroe and the Devilaires, Vol. 1	1957	10.00	20.00	40.00
❏ TP-39 [M]	Billy Devroe and the Devilaires, Vol. 2	1958	10.00	20.00	40.00

DeWITT, GEORGE
EPIC

❏ BN 531 [S]	George DeWitt Sings That Tune	1959	7.50	15.00	30.00
❏ LN 3562 [M]	George DeWitt Sings That Tune	1959	5.00	10.00	20.00

DEXTER, AL
CAPITOL

❏ ST 1701 [S]	Al Dexter Sings and Plays His Greatest Hits	1962	10.00	20.00	40.00
❏ T 1701 [M]	Al Dexter Sings and Plays His Greatest Hits	1962	7.50	15.00	30.00

COLUMBIA

❏ CL 9005 [10]	Songs of the Southwest	195?	12.50	25.00	50.00

HARMONY

❏ HL 7293 [M]	Pistol Packin' Mama	1961	5.00	10.00	20.00

DIALOGUE
COLD

❏ (no #)	Dialogue	1968	75.00	150.00	300.00
-- White cover with insert					
❏ (no #)	Dialogue	1968	25.00	50.00	100.00
-- Orange cover with insert					

DIALS, THE
TIME

❏ S-2100 [S]	It's Monkey Time	1964	7.50	15.00	30.00
❏ 52100 [M]	It's Monkey Time	1964	6.25	12.50	25.00

DIAMOND, LEO
RCA VICTOR

❏ LPM-1165 [M]	Skin Diver Suite and Other Selections	1955	15.00	30.00	60.00

REPRISE

❏ R-6002 [M]	Exciting Sounds of the South Seas	1961	6.25	12.50	25.00
❏ R9-6002 [S]	Exciting Sounds of the South Seas	1961	7.50	15.00	30.00
❏ R-6009 [M]	Themes from Great Foreign Films	1961	6.25	12.50	25.00
❏ R9-6009 [S]	Themes from Great Foreign Films	1961	7.50	15.00	30.00
❏ R-6024 [M]	Off Shore	1962	6.25	12.50	25.00
❏ R9-6024 [S]	Off Shore	1962	7.50	15.00	30.00

DIAMOND, NEIL
BANG

❏ BLP 214 [M]	The Feel of Neil Diamond	1966	15.00	30.00	60.00
-- All tracks play mono					
❏ BLP 214 [P]	The Feel of Neil Diamond	1966	20.00	40.00	80.00
-- Album is labeled mono, but plays in stereo					
❏ BLPS 214 [P]	The Feel of Neil Diamond	1966	25.00	50.00	100.00
-- Album is labeled stereo and plays in stereo (except "Solitary Man," "Do It," "I'll Come Running" are rechanneled)					
❏ BLP 217 [M]	Just For You	1967	10.00	20.00	40.00
-- With blurb for "Thank the Lord for the Night Time" on cover					

Number	Title	Yr	VG	VG+	NM
❑ BLPS 217 [P]	Just For You	1967	12.50	25.00	50.00
-- With blurb for "Thank the Lord for the Night Time" on cover					
❑ BLPS 217 [P]	Just For You	1968	10.00	20.00	40.00
-- With blurb for "Shilo" pasted over "Thank the Lord for the Night Time" blurb					
❑ BLPS 217 [P]	Just For You	1970	5.00	10.00	20.00
-- With blurb for "Shilo" imprinted on cover					
❑ BLPS 219 [P]	Neil Diamond's Greatest Hits	1968	10.00	20.00	40.00
-- First editions have the single version of "Solitary Man" in rechanneled stereo					
❑ BLPS 219 [P]	Neil Diamond's Greatest Hits	196?	5.00	10.00	20.00
-- Later editions have an alternate take of "Solitary Man" in true stereo					
❑ BLPS 221 [S]	Shilo	1970	10.00	20.00	40.00
❑ BLPS 224 [P]	Do It!	1971	7.50	15.00	30.00
❑ BLPS-227 [(2) S]	Double Gold	1973	10.00	20.00	40.00
COLUMBIA					
❑ PCQ 32919 [Q]	Serenade	1974	6.25	12.50	25.00
❑ 9C9 39915 [PD]	Primitive	1984	5.00	10.00	20.00
❑ HC 42550	Jonathan Livingston Seagull	1982	12.50	25.00	50.00
-- Half-speed mastered edition					
❑ HC 45625	You Don't Bring Me Flowers	1982	7.50	15.00	30.00
-- Half-speed mastered edition					
❑ HC 47628	On the Way to the Sky	1982	7.50	15.00	30.00
-- Half-speed mastered edition					
❑ HC 48068	12 Greatest Hits, Vol. II	1982	7.50	15.00	30.00
❑ HC 48359	Heartlight	1982	7.50	15.00	30.00
-- Half-speed mastered edition					
DIRECT DISK					
❑ SD 16612	His 12 Greatest Hits	1982	12.50	25.00	50.00
-- Audiophile vinyl					
FROG KING					
❑ AAR-1	Early Classics	1972	10.00	20.00	40.00
-- Compilation of Bang material for Columbia Record Club; includes songbook (deduct 25% if missing)					
MCA					
❑ 8000 [(2)]	Hot August Night	1972	5.00	10.00	20.00
MOBILE FIDELITY					
❑ 2-024 [(2)]	Hot August Night	1979	10.00	20.00	40.00
-- Audiophile vinyl					
❑ 1-071	The Jazz Singer	1981	7.50	15.00	30.00
-- Audiophile vinyl					
UNI					
❑ ND-11 [DJ]	Neil Diamond DJ Sampler	1970	50.00	100.00	200.00
❑ 1913 [DJ]	Open-End Interview with Neil Diamond	1971	75.00	150.00	300.00
❑ 73030	Velvet Gloves and Spit	1968	7.50	15.00	30.00
-- First editions do not include "Shilo"					
❑ 73030	Velvet Gloves and Spit	1970	5.00	10.00	20.00
-- Later editions add a new recording of "Shilo"					
❑ 73047	Brother Love's Travelling Salvation Show	1969	7.50	15.00	30.00
-- First editions do not include "Sweet Caroline"					
❑ 73047	Brother Love's Travelling Salvation Show	1969	5.00	10.00	20.00
-- Later editions add "Sweet Caroline"					
❑ 73071	Touching You Touching Me	1969	5.00	10.00	20.00
❑ 73084	Neil Diamond/Gold	1970	5.00	10.00	20.00
❑ 73092	Tap Root Manuscript	1970	5.00	10.00	20.00
❑ 93106	Stones	1971	5.00	10.00	20.00
❑ 93136	Moods	1972	5.00	10.00	20.00
❑ ST-93501	Tap Root Manuscript	1970	6.25	12.50	25.00
-- Capitol Record Club issue					

DIAMONDS, THE
MERCURY

Number	Title	Yr	VG	VG+	NM
❑ MG-20213 [M]	Collection of Golden Hits	1956	30.00	60.00	120.00
❑ MG-20309 [M]	The Diamonds	1957	30.00	60.00	120.00
❑ MG-20368 [M]	The Diamonds Meet Pete Rugolo	1958	20.00	40.00	80.00
❑ MG-20480 [M]	Songs from the Old West	1959	20.00	40.00	80.00
❑ SR-60076 [S]	The Diamonds Meet Pete Rugolo	1959	30.00	60.00	120.00
❑ SR-60159 [S]	Songs from the Old West	1959	30.00	60.00	120.00
WING					
❑ MGW-12114 [M]	The Diamonds: America's Famous Song Stylists	1959	7.50	15.00	30.00
❑ MGW-12178 [M]	Pop Hits by the Diamonds	1962	7.50	15.00	30.00

DICK AND DEEDEE
LIBERTY

Number	Title	Yr	VG	VG+	NM
❑ LRP-3236 [M]	Tell Me/The Mountain's High	1962	12.50	25.00	50.00
❑ LST-7236 [R]	Tell Me/The Mountain's High	1962	10.00	20.00	40.00
WARNER BROS.					
❑ W 1500 [M]	Young and In Love	1963	6.25	12.50	25.00
❑ WS 1500 [S]	Young and In Love	1963	7.50	15.00	30.00
❑ W 1538 [M]	Turn Around	1964	6.25	12.50	25.00
❑ WS 1538 [S]	Turn Around	1964	7.50	15.00	30.00
❑ W 1586 [M]	Thou Shalt Not Steal	1965	6.25	12.50	25.00
❑ WS 1586 [S]	Thou Shalt Not Steal	1965	7.50	15.00	30.00

Number	Title	Yr	VG	VG+	NM
❑ W 1623 [M]	Song We've Sung on "Shindig"	1966	6.25	12.50	25.00
❑ WS 1623 [S]	Song We've Sung on "Shindig"	1966	7.50	15.00	30.00

DICKENS, LITTLE JIMMY
COLUMBIA

Number	Title	Yr	VG	VG+	NM
❑ CL 1047 [M]	Raisin' the Dickens	1957	20.00	40.00	80.00
❑ CL 1545 [M]	Big Songs by Little Jimmy	1960	7.50	15.00	30.00
❑ CL 1887 [M]	Little Jimmy Dickens Sings Out Behind the Barn	1962	7.50	15.00	30.00
❑ CL 2288 [M]	Handle with Care	1964	6.25	12.50	25.00
❑ CL 2442 [M]	May the Bird of Paradise Fly Up Your Nose	1965	6.25	12.50	25.00
❑ CL 2551 [M]	Little Jimmy Dickens' Greatest	1966	6.25	12.50	25.00
❑ CS 8345 [S]	Big Songs by Little Jimmy	1960	10.00	20.00	40.00
❑ CS 8687 [S]	Little Jimmy Dickens Sings Out Behind the Barn	1962	10.00	20.00	40.00
❑ CL 9053 [10]	The Old Country Church	1954	30.00	60.00	120.00
❑ CS 9088 [S]	Handle with Care	1964	7.50	15.00	30.00
❑ CS 9242 [S]	May the Bird of Paradise Fly Up Your Nose	1965	7.50	15.00	30.00
❑ CS 9351 [S]	Little Jimmy Dickens' Greatest	1966	7.50	15.00	30.00
DECCA					
❑ DL 4967 [M]	Jimmy Dickens Sings	1967	7.50	15.00	30.00
❑ DL 74967 [S]	Jimmy Dickens Sings	1967	5.00	10.00	20.00
❑ DL 75091	Jimmy Dickens Comes Callin'	1968	5.00	10.00	20.00
❑ DL 75133	Jimmy Dickens' Greatest Hits	1969	5.00	10.00	20.00

DICKIES, THE
A&M

Number	Title	Yr	VG	VG+	NM
❑ SP-4742	The Incredible Shrinking Dickies	1979	5.00	10.00	20.00
-- First pressing on yellow vinyl					

DICKS, THE
RADICAL

Number	Title	Yr	VG	VG+	NM
❑ RRR 80351	Recorded Live at Raul's	1980	15.00	30.00	60.00
-- One side features the Big Boys; the other side, the Dicks					
SST					
❑ 017	Kill from the Heart	1983	6.25	12.50	25.00

DICKY DOO AND THE DON'TS
UNITED ARTISTS

Number	Title	Yr	VG	VG+	NM
❑ UAL-3094 [M]	The Madison and Other Dances	1959	10.00	20.00	40.00
❑ UAL-3097 [M]	Teen Scene	1959	10.00	20.00	40.00
❑ UAS-6094 [S]	The Madison and Other Dances	1959	12.50	25.00	50.00
❑ UAS-6097 [S]	Teen Scene	1959	12.50	25.00	50.00

DIDDLEY, BO
ACCORD

Number	Title	Yr	VG	VG+	NM
❑ SN-7182	Toronto Rock and Roll Revival, Vol. 5	1982	5.00	10.00	20.00
CHECKER					
❑ LP 1431 [M]	Bo Diddley	1958	50.00	100.00	200.00
❑ LP 1436 [M]	Go Bo Diddley	1959	37.50	75.00	150.00
❑ LP 2974 [M]	Have Guitar, Will Travel	1960	37.50	75.00	150.00
❑ LP 2976 [M]	Spotlight on Bo Diddley	1960	37.50	75.00	150.00
❑ LP 2977 [M]	Bo Diddley Is a Gunslinger	1961	37.50	75.00	150.00
❑ LP 2980 [M]	Bo Diddley Is a Lover	1961	37.50	75.00	150.00
❑ LP 2982 [M]	Bo Diddley's a Twister	1962	25.00	50.00	100.00
❑ LP 2982 [M]	Road Runner	1967	20.00	40.00	80.00
-- Reissue of "Bo Diddley's a Twister"					
❑ LP 2984 [M]	Bo Diddley	1962	25.00	50.00	100.00
❑ LP 2985 [M]	Bo Diddley and Company	1963	40.00	80.00	120.00
❑ LP 2987 [M]	Surfin' with Bo Diddley	1964	40.00	80.00	120.00
❑ LPS 2987 [R]	Surfin' with Bo Diddley	1964	7.50	15.00	30.00
❑ LP 2988 [M]	Bo Diddley's Beach Party	1963	25.00	50.00	100.00
❑ LP 2989 [M]	16 All Time Greatest Hits	1964	12.50	25.00	50.00
❑ LPS 2989 [R]	16 All Time Greatest Hits	1964	7.50	15.00	30.00
❑ LP 2992 [M]	Hey! Good Lookin'	1965	15.00	30.00	60.00
❑ LPS 2992 [R]	Hey! Good Lookin'	1965	7.50	15.00	30.00
❑ LP 2996 [M]	500% More Man	1965	15.00	30.00	60.00
❑ LPS 2996 [R]	500% More Man	1965	7.50	15.00	30.00
❑ LP 3001 [M]	The Originator	1966	7.50	15.00	30.00
❑ LPS 3001 [S]	The Originator	1966	10.00	20.00	40.00
❑ LP 3006 [M]	Go Bo Diddley	1967	12.50	25.00	50.00
-- Reissue of 1436					
❑ LPS 3006 [R]	Go Bo Diddley	1967	10.00	20.00	40.00
❑ LP 3007 [M]	Boss Man	1967	20.00	40.00	80.00
-- Reissue of Chess 1431					
❑ LPS 3007 [R]	Boss Man	1967	12.50	25.00	50.00
❑ LPS 3013	The Black Gladiator	1968	7.50	15.00	30.00
CHESS					
❑ CH3-19502 [(3)]	The Chess Box	1990	10.00	20.00	40.00
❑ CH 50001	Another Dimension	1971	10.00	20.00	40.00
❑ CH 50016	Where It All Began	1972	10.00	20.00	40.00

Number	Title	Yr	VG	VG+	NM
❏ CH 50029	The London Bo Diddley Sessions	1973	6.25	12.50	25.00
❏ CH 50047	Big Bad Bo	1974	6.25	12.50	25.00
❏ 2CH 60005 [(2)]	Got My Own Bag of Tricks	1972	6.25	12.50	25.00

RCA VICTOR

Number	Title	Yr	VG	VG+	NM
❏ APL1-1229	The 20th Anniversary of Rock and Roll	1976	5.00	10.00	20.00

DIDDLEY, BO/CHUCK BERRY
Also see each artist's individual listings.
CHECKER

Number	Title	Yr	VG	VG+	NM
❏ LP 2991 [M]	Two Great Guitars	1964	15.00	30.00	60.00
❏ LPS 2991 [R]	Two Great Guitars	1964	10.00	20.00	40.00

DIDDLEY, BO/MUDDY WATERS/HOWLIN' WOLF
Also see each artist's individual listings.
CHECKER

Number	Title	Yr	VG	VG+	NM
❏ LP 3010 [M]	Super, Super Blues Band	1968	12.50	25.00	50.00
❏ LPS 3010 [S]	Super, Super Blues Band	1968	10.00	20.00	40.00

DIDDLEY, BO/MUDDY WATERS/LITTLE WALTER
Also see each artist's individual listings.
CHECKER

Number	Title	Yr	VG	VG+	NM
❏ LP 3008 [M]	Super Blues Band	1968	12.50	25.00	50.00
❏ LPS 3008 [S]	Super Blues Band	1968	10.00	20.00	40.00

DIETRICH, MARLENE
CAPITOL

Number	Title	Yr	VG	VG+	NM
❏ STCR-300 [(3)]	The Magic of Marlene	1969	10.00	20.00	40.00
-- All three of her Capitol LPs in one box					
❏ ST 10282 [S]	Wiedersehn Mit Marlene	1961	6.25	12.50	25.00
❏ T 10282 [M]	Wiedersehn Mit Marlene	1961	5.00	10.00	20.00
❏ ST 10397 [S]	Marlene (Songs in German by the Inimitable Dietrich)	1965	6.25	12.50	25.00
❏ T 10397 [M]	Marlene (Songs in German by the Inimitable Dietrich)	1965	5.00	10.00	20.00
❏ ST 10443 [S]	Marlene Dietrich's Berlin	1966	6.25	12.50	25.00
❏ T 10443 [M]	Marlene Dietrich's Berlin	1966	5.00	10.00	20.00

COLUMBIA

Number	Title	Yr	VG	VG+	NM
❏ CL 105 [10]	Overseas -- Songs for the O.S.S.	1953	25.00	50.00	100.00
❏ CL 1275 [M]	Lili Marlene	1959	12.50	25.00	50.00

COLUMBIA MASTERWORKS

Number	Title	Yr	VG	VG+	NM
❏ WL 164 [M]	Dietrich in Rio	195?	10.00	20.00	40.00
❏ WS 316 [S]	Dietrich in Rio	195?	12.50	25.00	50.00
❏ OS 2830 [S]	Dietrich in London	1966	7.50	15.00	30.00
❏ ML 4975 [M]	At the Café de Paris	1955	12.50	25.00	50.00
❏ OL 6430 [M]	Dietrich in London	1966	6.25	12.50	25.00

DECCA

Number	Title	Yr	VG	VG+	NM
❏ DL 5100 [10]	Souvenir Album	1950	20.00	40.00	80.00
❏ DL 8465 [M]	Marlene Dietrich	1957	10.00	20.00	40.00
-- Black label, silver print					
❏ DL 8465 [M]	Marlene Dietrich	196?	6.25	12.50	25.00
-- Black label with color bars					
❏ DL 78465 [R]	Marlene Dietrich	196?	5.00	10.00	20.00

MURRAY HILL/CSP

Number	Title	Yr	VG	VG+	NM
❏ P3 14689 [(3)]	The Legendary Marlene Dietrich	1978	7.50	15.00	30.00

VOX

Number	Title	Yr	VG	VG+	NM
❏ VS-3040 [10]	Marlene Dietrich Sings	1950	20.00	40.00	80.00

DIGA RHYTHM BAND, THE
Also see THE GRATEFUL DEAD.
ROUND

Number	Title	Yr	VG	VG+	NM
❏ RX-110	The Diga Rhythm Band	1976	6.25	12.50	25.00

DILL, DANNY
LIBERTY

Number	Title	Yr	VG	VG+	NM
❏ LRP-3301 [M]	Folk Songs from the Country	1963	5.00	10.00	20.00
❏ LST-7301 [S]	Folk Songs from the Country	1963	6.25	12.50	25.00

MGM

Number	Title	Yr	VG	VG+	NM
❏ E-3819 [M]	Folk Songs from the Wild West	1960	5.00	10.00	20.00
❏ SE-3819 [S]	Folk Songs from the Wild West	1960	6.25	12.50	25.00

DILLARD AND CLARK
A&M

Number	Title	Yr	VG	VG+	NM
❏ SP-4158	The Fantastic Expedition of Dillard and Clark	1968	5.00	10.00	20.00
-- Brown label					

DILLARD, DOUG
TOGETHER

Number	Title	Yr	VG	VG+	NM
❏ STT-1003	The Banjo Album	1970	20.00	40.00	80.00

DILLARDS, THE
CRYSTAL CLEAR

Number	Title	Yr	VG	VG+	NM
❏ CCS-5007	Mountain Rock	1979	6.25	12.50	25.00
-- Direct-to-disc recording					

ELEKTRA

Number	Title	Yr	VG	VG+	NM
❏ EKL-232 [M]	Back Porch Bluegrass	1963	6.25	12.50	25.00
❏ EKL-265 [M]	The Dillards, Live!!! Almost!!!	1964	5.00	10.00	20.00
❏ EKL-285 [M]	Pickin' and Fiddlin'	1965	5.00	10.00	20.00
❏ EKS-7232 [S]	Back Porch Bluegrass	1963	7.50	5.00	30.00
-- Mandolin-player label					
❏ EKS-7265 [S]	The Dillards, Live!!! Almost!!!	1964	6.25	12.50	25.00
-- Mandolin-player label					
❏ EKS-7285 [S]	Pickin' and Fiddlin'	1965	6.25	12.50	25.00
-- Mandolin-player label					
❏ EKS-74035	Wheatstraw Suite	1968	5.00	10.00	20.00
-- Tan label with large stylized "E" on top					
❏ EKS-74054	Copperfields	1969	5.00	10.00	20.00
-- Red label with large stylized "E" on top					

DILLER, PHYLLIS
COLUMBIA

Number	Title	Yr	VG	VG+	NM
❏ CS 9623	Born to Sing	1969	5.00	10.00	20.00

DIMENSIONS, THE
SAHARA

Number	Title	Yr	VG	VG+	NM
❏ (# unknown)	From All Dimensions	1966	200.00	400.00	800.00

DINNING SISTERS, THE
CAPITOL

Number	Title	Yr	VG	VG+	NM
❏ H 318 [10]	The Dinning Sisters	195?	12.50	25.00	50.00

DINNING, MARK
MGM

Number	Title	Yr	VG	VG+	NM
❏ E-3828 [M]	Teen Angel	1960	20.00	40.00	80.00
❏ SE-3828 [S]	Teen Angel	1960	37.50	75.00	150.00
❏ E-3855 [M]	Wanderin'	1960	20.00	40.00	80.00
❏ SE-3855 [S]	Wanderin'	1960	30.00	60.00	120.00

DINO, DESI AND BILLY
REPRISE

Number	Title	Yr	VG	VG+	NM
❏ R 6176 [M]	I'm a Fool	1965	5.00	10.00	20.00
❏ RS 6176 [S]	I'm a Fool	1965	6.25	12.50	25.00
❏ R 6194 [M]	Our Time's Coming	1966	5.00	10.00	20.00
❏ RS 6194 [S]	Our Time's Coming	1966	6.25	12.50	25.00
❏ R 6198 [M]	Memories Are Made of This	1966	5.00	10.00	20.00
❏ RS 6198 [S]	Memories Are Made of This	1966	6.25	12.50	25.00
❏ R 6224 [M]	Souvenir	1966	5.00	10.00	20.00
❏ RS 6224 [S]	Souvenir	1966	6.25	12.50	25.00

DINOSAUR JR
HOMESTEAD

Number	Title	Yr	VG	VG+	NM
❏ 015-2	Dinosaur	1985	5.00	10.00	20.00
-- Released under the name "Dinosaur"					

SST

Number	Title	Yr	VG	VG+	NM
❏ 130	You're Living All Over Me	1987	5.00	10.00	20.00
-- First released under the name "Dinosaur"					

DION
Also see DION AND THE BELMONTS.
COLUMBIA

Number	Title	Yr	VG	VG+	NM
❏ CL 2010 [M]	Ruby Baby	1963	7.50	15.00	30.00
❏ CL 2107 [M]	Donna the Prima Donna	1963	7.50	15.00	30.00
❏ CS 8810 [S]	Ruby Baby	1963	10.00	20.00	40.00
❏ CS 8907 [S]	Donna the Prima Donna	1963	10.00	20.00	40.00
❏ CS 9773	Wonder Where I'm Bound	1969	5.00	10.00	20.00
❏ KC 31942	Dion's Greatest Hits	1973	5.00	10.00	20.00

LAURIE

Number	Title	Yr	VG	VG+	NM
❏ LLP 2004 [M]	Alone with Dion	1960	50.00	100.00	200.00
-- With four wallet-size photos on inside strip (deduct 50% if missing)					
❏ LLP 2009 [M]	Runaround Sue	1961	25.00	50.00	100.00
-- Black vinyl					
❏ LLP 2009 [M]	Runaround Sue	1961	200.00	400.00	800.00
-- Colored vinyl (gold, green or blue)					
❏ LLP 2012 [M]	Lovers Who Wander	1962	17.50	35.00	70.00
❏ LLP 2013 [M]	Dion Sings His Greatest Hits	1962	17.50	35.00	70.00
❏ SLP 2013 [R]	Dion Sings His Greatest Hits	196?	12.50	25.00	50.00
❏ LLP 2015 [M]	Love Came to Me	1963	17.50	35.00	70.00
❏ LLP 2017 [M]	Dion Sings to Sandy (And All His Other Girls)	1963	12.50	25.00	50.00
❏ LLP 2019 [M]	Dion Sings the 15 Million Sellers	1963	12.50	25.00	50.00
❏ SLP 2019 [R]	Dion Sings the 15 Million Sellers	196?	7.50	15.00	30.00
❏ LLP 2022 [M]	More of Dion's Greatest Hits	1964	12.50	25.00	50.00

Number	Title	Yr	VG	VG+	NM
❑ SLP 2022 [R]	More of Dion's Greatest Hits	196?	7.50	15.00	30.00
❑ SLP 2047	Dion	1968	5.00	10.00	20.00
❑ DT-90386 [R]	Dion Sings His Greatest Hits	1965	30.00	60.00	120.00
-- Capitol Record Club edition					
❑ T-90386 [M]	Dion Sings His Greatest Hits	1965	30.00	60.00	120.00
-- Capitol Record Club edition					
❑ DT-91027 [R]	Runaround Sue	196?	30.00	60.00	120.00
-- Capitol Record Club edition					
❑ T-91027 [M]	Runaround Sue	196?	30.00	60.00	120.00
-- Capitol Record Club edition					
❑ DT-91128 [R]	More of Dion's Greatest Hits	196?	30.00	60.00	120.00
-- Capitol Record Club edition					
❑ T-91128 [M]	More of Dion's Greatest Hits	196?	30.00	60.00	120.00
-- Capitol Record Club edition					
❑ ST-91577	Dion	1968	6.25	12.50	25.00
-- Capitol Record Club edition					
WARNER BROS.					
❑ WS 1826	Sit Down, Old Friend	1969	5.00	10.00	20.00

DION AND THE BELMONTS
ABC

Number	Title	Yr	VG	VG+	NM
❑ 599 [M]	Together Again	1967	7.50	15.00	30.00
❑ S-599 [S]	Together Again	1967	10.00	20.00	40.00
LAURIE					
❑ LLP 1002 [M]	Presenting Dion & The Belmonts	1959	62.50	125.00	250.00
❑ LLP 2002 [M]	Presenting Dion & The Belmonts	1960	37.50	75.00	150.00
❑ SLP 2002 [R]	Presenting Dion & The Belmonts	196?	300.00	600.00	900.00
-- Despite its rechanneled stereo sound, this record is collectible because of its utter rarity					
❑ LLP 2006 [M]	Wish Upon a Star	1960	37.50	75.00	150.00
❑ LLP 2016 [M]	"Together" On Records -- By Special Request	1963	12.50	25.00	50.00
❑ SLP 6000 [(3)]	60 Greatest Hits	197?	7.50	15.00	30.00
-- In box					
❑ SLP 6000 [(3)]	60 Greatest Hits	197?	5.00	10.00	20.00
-- In regular cover					

DIRE STRAITS
WARNER BROS.

Number	Title	Yr	VG	VG+	NM
❑ WBMS-109 [DJ]	Dire Straits Live	1980	12.50	25.00	50.00
-- "The Warner Bros. Music Show" promo					
❑ 23728 [DJ]	Love Over Gold	1982	12.50	25.00	50.00
-- Promo on Quiex II vinyl; the times of the songs also are listed differently than on stock copies					
❑ 25085 [(2) DJ]	Dire Straits Live -- Alchemy	1984	12.50	25.00	50.00
-- Promo on Quiex II vinyl					
❑ 25264 [DJ]	Brothers in Arms	1985	12.50	25.00	50.00
-- Promo on Quiex II vinyl					

DIRKSEN, SENATOR EVERETT MCKINLEY
CAPITOL

Number	Title	Yr	VG	VG+	NM
❑ T 2754 [M]	Man Is Not Alone	1967	5.00	10.00	20.00
❑ ST 2792 [S]	Everett McKinley Dirksen at Christmas Time	1967	5.00	10.00	20.00

DIRT BAND, THE -- See NITTY GRITTY DIRT BAND.

DIRTY BLUES BAND, THE
BLUESWAY

Number	Title	Yr	VG	VG+	NM
❑ BLS-6010	The Dirty Blues Band	1968	5.00	10.00	20.00
❑ BLS-6020	Stone Dirt	1968	5.00	10.00	20.00

DIVINYLS
CHRYSALIS

Number	Title	Yr	VG	VG+	NM
❑ BFV 41627	Temperamental	1989	5.00	10.00	20.00
-- Reissued as 21627, which goes for less					

DIXIE CUPS, THE
ABC-PARAMOUNT

Number	Title	Yr	VG	VG+	NM
❑ 525 [M]	Riding High	1965	15.00	30.00	60.00
❑ S-525 [S]	Riding High	1965	20.00	40.00	80.00
RED BIRD					
❑ RB-20-100 [M]	Chapel of Love	1964	15.00	30.00	60.00
❑ RBS-20-100 [S]	Chapel of Love	1964	20.00	40.00	80.00
❑ RB-20-103 [M]	Iko Iko	1965	37.50	75.00	150.00

DIXIE DREGS, THE
DIRECT DISK

Number	Title	Yr	VG	VG+	NM
❑ SD-16620	Dregs of the Earth	1980	10.00	20.00	40.00
-- Audiophile vinyl					

DIXIEBELLES, THE
SOUND STAGE 7

Number	Title	Yr	VG	VG+	NM
❑ SSM-5000 [M]	Down at Papa Joe's	1963	10.00	20.00	40.00
❑ SSS-15000 [R]	Down at Papa Joe's	1963	7.50	15.00	30.00

DIXON, WILLIE
BLUESVILLE

Number	Title	Yr	VG	VG+	NM
❑ BVLP-1003 [M]	Willie's Blues	1960	37.50	75.00	150.00
-- Blue and silver label					
❑ BVLP-1003 [M]	Willie's Blues	1964	10.00	20.00	40.00
-- Blue label, trident logo at right					
CHESS					
❑ CH3-16500 [(3)]	The Chess Box: Willie Dixon	1988	7.50	15.00	30.00
COLUMBIA					
❑ CS 9987	I Am the Blues	1970	6.25	12.50	25.00
-- Red label, "360 Sound"					

DIXON, WILLIE, AND MEMPHIS SLIM
BATTLE

Number	Title	Yr	VG	VG+	NM
❑ BV-6122 [M]	In Paris	1963	7.50	15.00	30.00
❑ BVS-6122 [S]	In Paris	1963	10.00	20.00	40.00
VERVE					
❑ MGV-3007 [M]	Blues Every Which Way	1961	30.00	60.00	120.00

DOBKINS, CARL, JR.
DECCA

Number	Title	Yr	VG	VG+	NM
❑ DL 8938 [M]	Carl Dobkins, Jr.	1959	25.00	50.00	100.00
❑ DL 78938 [S]	Carl Dobkins, Jr.	1959	37.50	75.00	150.00

DOC HOLLIDAY
METROMEDIA

Number	Title	Yr	VG	VG+	NM
❑ 1017	Doc Holliday	1973	5.00	10.00	20.00

DR. FEELGOOD AND THE INTERNS
OKEH

Number	Title	Yr	VG	VG+	NM
❑ OKM 12101 [M]	Dr. Feelgood and the Interns	1962	25.00	50.00	100.00
❑ OKS 14101 [S]	Dr. Feelgood and the Interns	1962	50.00	100.00	200.00

DR. JOHN
ATCO

Number	Title	Yr	VG	VG+	NM
❑ SD 33-234	Gris-Gris	1968	7.50	15.00	30.00
-- Purple and brown label					

DR. ROSS
FORTUNE

Number	Title	Yr	VG	VG+	NM
❑ F-3011 [M]	Doctor Ross, The Harmonica Boss	1962	12.50	25.00	50.00
❑ FS-3011 [S]	Doctor Ross, The Harmonica Boss	1962	25.00	50.00	100.00
TESTAMENT					
❑ 2206 [M]	Doctor Ross	196?	5.00	10.00	20.00

DR. WEST'S MEDICINE SHOW AND JUG BAND
Also see NORMAN GREENBAUM.
GO GO

Number	Title	Yr	VG	VG+	NM
❑ 22-17-002	The Eggplant That Ate Chicago	1967	6.25	12.50	25.00
GREGAR					
❑ GG-101	Norman Greenbaum with Dr. West's Medicine Show and Jug Band	1970	5.00	10.00	20.00

DODD, DICK
TOWER

Number	Title	Yr	VG	VG+	NM
❑ ST 5142	The First Evolution of Dick Dodd	1968	12.50	25.00	50.00

DODD, JIMMIE
DISNEYLAND

Number	Title	Yr	VG	VG+	NM
❑ WDL-1014 [M]	Jimmie Dodd Sings His Favorite Hymns	1959	6.25	12.50	25.00
-- Reissue of 3014 with new number					
❑ DQ-1235 [M]	Sing Along with Jimmie Dodd	1963	7.50	15.00	30.00
❑ WDL-3014 [M]	Jimmie Dodd Sings His Favorite Hymns	1958	6.25	12.50	25.00
IMPERIAL					
❑ LP-9089 [M]	Lonely Guitar	1959	10.00	20.00	40.00
❑ LP-9121 [M]	Swing-A-Spell	1960	10.00	20.00	40.00
❑ LP-12058 [S]	Swing-A-Spell	1960	12.50	25.00	50.00

Number	Title	Yr	VG	VG+	NM

DODD, KEN
LIBERTY
| ❏ LST-7442 [S] | Tears and The River | 1966 | 5.00 | 10.00 | 20.00 |

DODSON, MARGE
COLUMBIA
❏ CL 1309 [M]	In the Still of the Night	1959	7.50	15.00	30.00
❏ CL 1458 [M]	New Voice in Town	1960	7.50	15.00	30.00
❏ CS 8258 [S]	New Voice in Town	1960	10.00	20.00	40.00

DOGGETT, BILL
ABC-PARAMOUNT
| ❏ 507 [M] | Wow! | 1965 | 5.00 | 10.00 | 20.00 |
| ❏ S-507 [S] | Wow! | 1965 | 6.25 | 12.50 | 25.00 |
COLUMBIA
❏ CL 1814 [M]	Oops!	1962	5.00	10.00	20.00
❏ CL 1942 [M]	Prelude to the Blues	1963	5.00	10.00	20.00
❏ CL 2082 [M]	Fingertips	1963	5.00	10.00	20.00
❏ CS 8614 [S]	Oops!	1962	6.25	12.50	25.00
❏ CS 8742 [S]	Prelude to the Blues	1963	6.25	12.50	25.00
❏ CS 8882 [S]	Fingertips	1963	6.25	12.50	25.00
KING
❏ 295-82 [10]	Bill Doggett -- His Organ and Combo	1955	37.50	75.00	150.00
❏ 295-83 [10]	Bill Doggett -- His Organ and Combo, Volume 2	1955	37.50	75.00	150.00
❏ 295-89 [10]	All-Time Christmas Favorites	1955	50.00	100.00	200.00
❏ 295-102 [10]	Sentimentally Yours	1956	37.50	75.00	150.00
❏ 395-502 [M]	Moondust	1957	15.00	30.00	60.00
❏ 395-514 [M]	Hot Doggett	1957	15.00	30.00	60.00
❏ 395-523 [M]	As You Desire	1957	15.00	30.00	60.00
❏ 395-531 [M]	Everybody Dance to the Honky Tonk	1958	15.00	30.00	60.00
❏ 395-532 [M]	Dame Dreaming	1958	15.00	30.00	60.00
❏ 395-533 [M]	A Salute to Ellington	1958	15.00	30.00	60.00
❏ 395-557 [M]	The Doggett Beat for Dancing	1958	15.00	30.00	60.00
❏ 395-563 [M]	Candle Glow	1958	15.00	30.00	60.00
❏ 395-582 [M]	Swingin' Easy	1959	15.00	30.00	60.00
❏ 395-585 [M]	Dance Awhile	1959	15.00	30.00	60.00
❏ 395-600 [M]	A Bill Doggett Christmas	1959	10.00	20.00	40.00
❏ 395-609 [M]	Hold It	1959	15.00	30.00	60.00
❏ 633 [M]	High and Wide	1959	12.50	25.00	50.00
❏ 641 [M]	Big City Dance Party	1959	12.50	25.00	50.00
❏ 667 [M]	Bill Doggett On Tour	1959	12.50	25.00	50.00
❏ 706 [M]	For Reminiscent Lovers, Romantic Songs	1960	12.50	25.00	50.00
❏ 723 [M]	Back Again with More	1960	12.50	25.00	50.00
❏ 759 [M]	Bonanza of 24 Songs	1960	12.50	25.00	50.00
❏ 778 [M]	The Many Moods of Bill Doggett	1960	12.50	25.00	50.00
❏ 830 [M]	American Songs in the Bossa Nova Style	1963	10.00	20.00	40.00
❏ 868 [M]	Impressions	1964	10.00	20.00	40.00
❏ 908 [M]	The Best of Bill Doggett	1964	10.00	20.00	40.00
❏ 959 [M]	Bonanza of 24 Hit Songs	1966	7.50	15.00	30.00
❏ KS-1078	Honky Tonk Popcorn	1969	12.50	25.00	50.00
❏ KS-1097	The Nearness of You	1970	6.25	12.50	25.00
❏ KS-1101	Ram-Bunk-Shush	1970	6.25	12.50	25.00
❏ KS-1104	Sentimental Journey	1970	6.25	12.50	25.00
❏ KS-1108	Soft	1970	6.25	12.50	25.00
ROULETTE
| ❏ R 25330 [M] | Honky Tonk A La Mod | 1966 | 5.00 | 10.00 | 20.00 |
| ❏ SR 25330 [S] | Honky Tonk A La Mod | 1966 | 6.25 | 12.50 | 25.00 |
WARNER BROS.
❏ W 1404 [M]	3,046 People Danced 'Til 4 AM	1960	5.00	10.00	20.00
❏ WS 1404 [S]	3,046 People Danced 'Til 4 AM	1960	6.25	12.50	25.00
❏ W 1421 [M]	The Band with the Beat	1961	5.00	10.00	20.00
❏ WS 1421 [S]	The Band with the Beat	1961	6.25	12.50	25.00
❏ W 1452 [M]	Bill Doggett Swings	1962	5.00	10.00	20.00
❏ WS 1452 [S]	Bill Doggett Swings	1962	6.25	12.50	25.00

DOJO
ECLIPSE
| ❏ ES-7309 | Down for the Last Time | 1971 | 6.25 | 12.50 | 25.00 |

DOLLAR, JOHNNY
DATE
| ❏ TEM 3009 [M] | Johnny Dollar | 1967 | 6.25 | 12.50 | 25.00 |
| ❏ TES 4009 [S] | Johnny Dollar | 1967 | 5.00 | 10.00 | 20.00 |

DOMINO, FATS
ABC-PARAMOUNT
❏ 455 [M]	Here Comes... Fats Domino	1963	5.00	10.00	20.00
❏ S-455 [S]	Here Comes... Fats Domino	1963	6.25	12.50	25.00
❏ 479 [M]	Fats in the Fire	1964	5.00	10.00	20.00
❏ S-479 [S]	Fats in the Fire	1964	6.25	12.50	25.00
❏ 510 [M]	Get Away with Fats Domino	1965	5.00	10.00	20.00
❏ S-510 [S]	Get Away with Fats Domino	1965	6.25	12.50	25.00
❏ ST-90167 [S]	Get Away with Fats Domino	1965	7.50	15.00	30.00
-- Capitol Record Club edition					
❏ T-90167 [M]	Get Away with Fats Domino	1965	6.25	12.50	25.00
-- Capitol Record Club edition					
GRAND AWARD
| ❏ 267 [M] | Fats Domino | 196? | 5.00 | 10.00 | 20.00 |
IMPERIAL
❏ LP-9004 [M]	Rock and Rollin' with Fats Domino	1956	37.50	75.00	150.00
-- Maroon label					
❏ LP-9004 [M]	Rock and Rollin' with Fats Domino	1958	20.00	40.00	80.00
-- Black label with stars on top					
❏ LP-9004 [M]	Rock and Rollin' with Fats Domino	1964	6.25	12.50	25.00
-- Black and pink label					
❏ LP-9004 [M]	Rock and Rollin' with Fats Domino	1967	5.00	10.00	20.00
-- Black and green label					
❏ LP-9009 [M]	Fats Domino Rock and Rollin'	1956	37.50	75.00	150.00
-- Maroon label					
❏ LP-9009 [M]	Fats Domino Rock and Rollin'	1958	20.00	40.00	80.00
-- Black label with stars on top					
❏ LP-9009 [M]	Fats Domino Rock and Rollin'	1964	6.25	12.50	25.00
-- Black and pink label					
❏ LP-9009 [M]	Fats Domino Rock and Rollin'	1967	5.00	10.00	20.00
-- Black and green label					
❏ LP-9028 [M]	This Is Fats Domino!	1957	37.50	75.00	150.00
-- Maroon label					
❏ LP-9028 [M]	This Is Fats Domino!	1958	20.00	40.00	80.00
-- Black label with stars on top					
❏ LP-9028 [M]	This Is Fats Domino!	1964	6.25	12.50	25.00
-- Black and pink label					
❏ LP-9028 [M]	This Is Fats Domino!	1967	5.00	10.00	20.00
-- Black and green label					
❏ LP-9038 [M]	Here Stands Fats Domino	1957	37.50	75.00	150.00
-- Maroon label					
❏ LP-9038 [M]	Here Stands Fats Domino	1958	20.00	40.00	80.00
-- Black label with stars on top					
❏ LP-9038 [M]	Here Stands Fats Domino	1964	6.25	12.50	25.00
-- Black and pink label					
❏ LP-9038 [M]	Here Stands Fats Domino	1967	5.00	10.00	20.00
-- Black and green label					
❏ LP-9040 [M]	This Is Fats	1957	37.50	75.00	150.00
-- Maroon label					
❏ LP-9040 [M]	This Is Fats	1958	20.00	40.00	80.00
-- Black label with stars on top					
❏ LP-9040 [M]	This Is Fats	1964	6.25	12.50	25.00
-- Black and pink label					
❏ LP-9040 [M]	This Is Fats	1967	5.00	10.00	20.00
-- Black and green label					
❏ LP-9055 [M]	The Fabulous Mr. D.	1958	25.00	50.00	100.00
-- Black label with stars on top					
❏ LP-9055 [M]	The Fabulous Mr. D.	1964	7.50	15.00	30.00
-- Black and pink label					
❏ LP-9055 [M]	The Fabulous Mr. D.	1967	5.00	10.00	20.00
-- Black and green label					
❏ LP-9062 [M]	Fats Domino Swings	1959	25.00	50.00	100.00
-- Black label with stars on top					
❏ LP-9062 [M]	Fats Domino Swings	1964	7.50	15.00	30.00
-- Black and pink label					
❏ LP-9062 [M]	Fats Domino Swings	1967	5.00	10.00	20.00
-- Black and green label					
❏ LP-9065 [M]	Let's Play Fats Domino	1959	25.00	50.00	100.00
-- Black label with stars on top					
❏ LP-9065 [M]	Let's Play Fats Domino	1964	7.50	15.00	30.00
-- Black and pink label					
❏ LP-9065 [M]	Let's Play Fats Domino	1967	5.00	10.00	20.00
-- Black and green label					
❏ LP-9103 [M]	Million Record Hits	1960	25.00	50.00	100.00
-- Black label with stars on top					
❏ LP-9103 [M]	Million Record Hits	1964	7.50	15.00	30.00
-- Black and pink label					
❏ LP-9103 [M]	Million Record Hits	1967	5.00	10.00	20.00
-- Black and green label					
❏ LP-9127 [M]	A Lot of Dominos	1960	25.00	50.00	100.00
-- Black label with stars on top					
❏ LP-9127 [M]	A Lot of Dominos	1964	7.50	15.00	30.00
-- Black and pink label					
❏ LP-9127 [M]	A Lot of Dominos	1967	5.00	10.00	20.00
-- Black and green label					
❏ LP-9138 [M]	I Miss You So	1961	25.00	50.00	100.00
-- Black label with stars on top					
❏ LP-9138 [M]	I Miss You So	1964	7.50	15.00	30.00
-- Black and pink label					

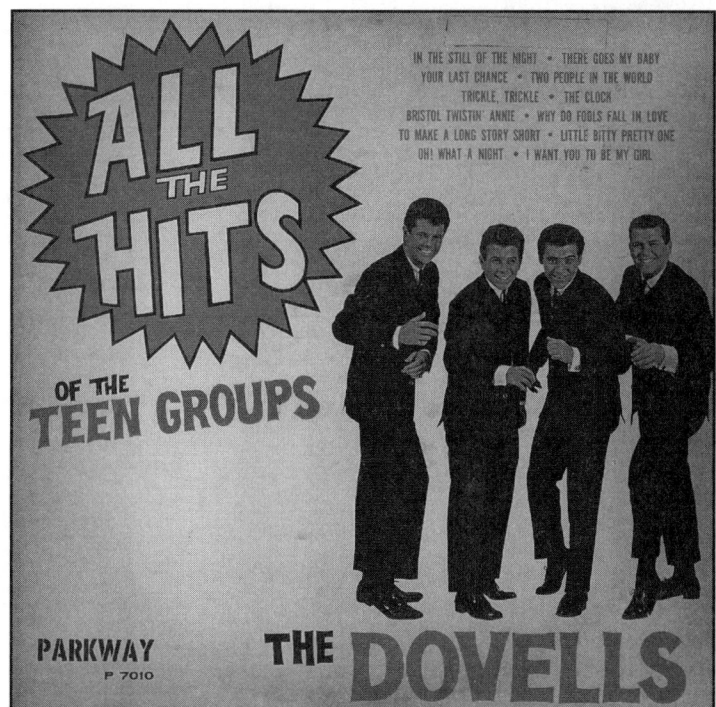

(Top left) Keyboardist Bill Doggett recorded a lot of albums in his long career, but his biggest hit single by far was "Honky Tonk (Parts 1 and 2)" in 1956. This is the album with both parts on it; unfortunately, the fade between parts is still on this album version! (Top right) Donovan's *A Gift From a Flower to a Garden* was a fairly elaborate package, consisting of a box, two records and a folder containing the lyrics to the songs on individual sheets of paper. The two records inside also were issued individually at the same time, under the names *Wear Your Love Like Heaven* and *For Little Ones*. (Bottom left) It was not unusual in the early 1960s for performers to cover or re-make other artists' hits for albums. Here's the Dovells' album full of songs that had been hits for others. (Bottom right) *The Freewheelin' Bob Dylan* by Bob Dylan. If you have a near-mint stereo copy that contains four songs that were deleted from later editions, you have an album that could fetch as much as $30,000! Please, please, though, check the listing to find out the characteristics of this album before you become convinced you have the rare version. Only two copies are known, and neither is in near-mint condition.

Number	Title	Yr	VG	VG+	NM
❑ LP-9138 [M]	I Miss You So	1967	5.00	10.00	20.00
-- Black and green label					
❑ LP-9153 [M]	Let the Four Winds Blow	1961	25.00	50.00	100.00
-- Black label with stars on top					
❑ LP-9153 [M]	Let the Four Winds Blow	1964	7.50	15.00	30.00
-- Black and pink label					
❑ LP-9153 [M]	Let the Four Winds Blow	1967	5.00	10.00	20.00
-- Black and green label					
❑ LP-9164 [M]	What a Party	1962	15.00	30.00	60.00
-- Black label with stars on top					
❑ LP-9164 [M]	What a Party	1964	7.50	15.00	30.00
-- Black and pink label					
❑ LP-9164 [M]	What a Party	1967	5.00	10.00	20.00
-- Black and green label					
❑ LP-9170 [M]	Twistin' the Stomp	1962	15.00	30.00	60.00
-- Black label with stars on top					
❑ LP-9170 [M]	Twistin' the Stomp	1964	7.50	15.00	30.00
-- Black and pink label					
❑ LP-9170 [M]	Twistin' the Stomp	1967	5.00	10.00	20.00
-- Black and green label					
❑ LP-9195 [M]	Million Sellers by Fats	1962	12.50	25.00	50.00
-- Black label with stars on top					
❑ LP-9195 [M]	Million Sellers by Fats	1964	7.50	15.00	30.00
-- Black and pink label					
❑ LP-9195 [M]	Million Sellers by Fats	1967	5.00	10.00	20.00
-- Black and green label					
❑ LP-9208 [M]	Just Domino	1962	12.50	25.00	50.00
-- Black label with stars on top					
❑ LP-9208 [M]	Just Domino	1964	7.50	15.00	30.00
-- Black and pink label					
❑ LP-9208 [M]	Just Domino	1967	5.00	10.00	20.00
-- Black and green label					
❑ LP-9227 [M]	Walking to New Orleans	1963	12.50	25.00	50.00
-- Black label with stars on top					
❑ LP-9227 [M]	Walking to New Orleans	1964	7.50	15.00	30.00
-- Black and pink label					
❑ LP-9227 [M]	Walking to New Orleans	1967	5.00	10.00	20.00
-- Black and green label					
❑ LP-9239 [M]	Let's Dance with Domino	1963	12.50	25.00	50.00
-- Black label with stars on top					
❑ LP-9239 [M]	Let's Dance with Domino	1964	7.50	15.00	30.00
-- Black and pink label					
❑ LP-9239 [M]	Let's Dance with Domino	1967	5.00	10.00	20.00
-- Black and green label					
❑ LP-9248 [M]	Here He Comes Again	1963	12.50	25.00	50.00
-- Black label with stars on top					
❑ LP-9248 [M]	Here He Comes Again	1964	7.50	15.00	30.00
-- Black and pink label					
❑ LP-9248 [M]	Here He Comes Again	1967	5.00	10.00	20.00
-- Black and green label					
❑ LP-12066 [S]	A Lot of Dominos	1961	37.50	75.00	150.00
-- Black label with silver top					
❑ LP-12066 [S]	A Lot of Dominos	1964	10.00	20.00	40.00
-- Black and pink label					
❑ LP-12066 [S]	A Lot of Dominos	1967	6.25	12.50	25.00
-- Black and green label					
❑ LP-12073 [S]	Let the Four Winds Blow	1961	37.50	75.00	150.00
-- Black label with silver top					
❑ LP-12073 [S]	Let the Four Winds Blow	1964	10.00	20.00	40.00
-- Black and pink label					
❑ LP-12073 [S]	Let the Four Winds Blow	1967	6.25	12.50	25.00
-- Black and green label					
❑ LP-12091 [R]	Fats Domino Swings	1964	5.00	10.00	20.00
-- Black and pink label					
❑ LP-12103 [R]	Million Record Hits	1964	5.00	10.00	20.00
-- Black and pink label					
❑ LP-12195 [R]	Million Sellers by Fats	1964	5.00	10.00	20.00
-- Black and pink label					
❑ LP-12227 [R]	Walking to New Orleans	1964	5.00	10.00	20.00
-- Black and pink label					
❑ LP-12248 [R]	Here He Comes Again	1964	5.00	10.00	20.00
-- Black and pink label					
MERCURY					
❑ MG-21039 [M]	Fats Domino '65	1965	6.25	12.50	25.00
❑ SR-61039 [S]	Fats Domino '65	1965	10.00	20.00	40.00
REPRISE					
❑ RS 6304	Fats Is Back	1968	7.50	15.00	30.00
❑ RS 6439	Fats	1970	125.00	250.00	500.00
-- Officially unreleased, test pressings and coverless stock copies are known to exist					
SUNSET					
❑ SUS-5200 [P]	Trouble in Mind	1968	5.00	10.00	20.00
UNITED ARTISTS					
❑ UAMG-104 [DJ]	The Fats Domino Sound	1973	10.00	20.00	40.00
-- Promo compilation of 30 excerpts of Fats hits					
❑ UA-LA122-F2 [(2)]	Cookin' with Fats (Superpak)	1974	7.50	15.00	30.00
❑ UA-LA122-F2 [(2) DJ]	Cookin' with Fats (Superpak)	1974	75.00	150.00	300.00
-- Promo with one black vinyl record and one colored vinyl record					

DOMINOES, THE -- See BILLY WARD AND THE DOMINOES.

DON AND DEWEY
SPECIALTY

Number	Title	Yr	VG	VG+	NM
❑ SPS-2131	They're Rockin' Til Midnight, Rollin' Til Dawn	1970	7.50	15.00	30.00
-- Original labels are black and gold					

DON AND EDDIE
MODERN

Number	Title	Yr	VG	VG+	NM
❑ PLP-814 [M]	Rock and Roll Party	1963	10.00	20.00	40.00
❑ PLP-814S [S]	Rock and Roll Party	1963	12.50	25.00	50.00

DON AND THE GOODTIMES
BURDETTE

Number	Title	Yr	VG	VG+	NM
❑ 300 [M]	Don and the Goodtimes' Greatest Hits	1966	37.50	75.00	150.00
❑ 300S [R]	Don and the Goodtimes' Greatest Hits	1966	25.00	50.00	100.00
-- LP plays rechanneled stereo					
❑ 300S [S]	Don and the Goodtimes' Greatest Hits	1966	75.00	150.00	300.00
-- LP plays true stereo					
EPIC					
❑ LN 24311 [M]	So Good	1967	5.00	10.00	20.00
❑ BN 26311 [S]	So Good	1967	5.00	10.00	20.00
PICCADILLY					
❑ 3394	Goodtime Rock 'n' Roll	1980	6.25	12.50	25.00
WAND					
❑ WDS-679	Where the Action Is	1969	7.50	15.00	30.00

DON, DICK & JIMMY
CROWN

Number	Title	Yr	VG	VG+	NM
❑ CLP-5005 [M]	Spring Fever	1958	10.00	20.00	40.00
DOT					
❑ DLP-3152 [M]	Don, Dick & Jimmy	1959	7.50	15.00	30.00
MODERN					
❑ MLP-1205 [M]	Spring Fever	1957	30.00	60.00	120.00
VERVE					
❑ MGV-2084 [M]	Medium Rare	1958	10.00	20.00	40.00
❑ MGV-2107 [M]	Songs for the Hearth	1959	10.00	20.00	40.00

DONALDSON, LOU
ARGO

Number	Title	Yr	VG	VG+	NM
❑ LP-724 [M]	Signifyin'	1963	6.25	12.50	25.00
❑ LPS-724 [S]	Signifyin'	1963	6.25	12.50	25.00
❑ LP-734 [M]	Possum Head	1964	6.25	12.50	25.00
❑ LPS-734 [S]	Possum Head	1964	6.25	12.50	25.00
❑ LP-747 [M]	Cole Slaw	1965	6.25	12.50	25.00
❑ LPS-747 [S]	Cole Slaw	1965	6.25	12.50	25.00
BLUE NOTE					
❑ BLP-1537 [M]	Lou Donaldson Quartet/Quintet/Sextet	1957	50.00	100.00	200.00
-- "Deep groove" version (deep indentation under label on both sides)					
❑ BLP-1537 [M]	Lou Donaldson Quartet/Quintet/Sextet	1957	10.00	20.00	40.00
-- Regular version with W. 63rd St. address on label					
❑ BLP-1537 [M]	Lou Donaldson Quartet/Quintet/Sextet	1957	37.50	75.00	150.00
-- Regular version with Lexington Ave. address on label					
❑ BLP-1537 [M]	Lou Donaldson Quartet/Quintet/Sextet	1963	6.25	12.50	25.00
-- With New York, USA address on label					
❑ BLP-1545 [M]	Wailing with Lou	1957	30.00	60.00	120.00
-- "Deep groove" version (deep indentation under label on both sides)					
❑ BLP-1545 [M]	Wailing with Lou	1957	20.00	40.00	80.00
-- Regular version with W. 63rd St. address on label					
❑ BLP-1545 [M]	Wailing with Lou	1963	6.25	12.50	25.00
-- With New York, USA address on label					
❑ BLP-1566 [M]	Swing and Soul	1957	30.00	60.00	120.00
-- "Deep groove" version (deep indentation under label on both sides)					
❑ BLP-1566 [M]	Swing and Soul	1957	20.00	40.00	80.00
-- Regular version with W. 63rd St. address on label					
❑ BLP-1566 [M]	Swing and Soul	1963	6.25	12.50	25.00
-- With New York, USA address on label					
❑ BST-1566 [S]	Swing and Soul	1959	20.00	40.00	80.00
-- "Deep groove" version (deep indentation under label on both sides)					
❑ BST-1566 [S]	Swing and Soul	1959	12.50	25.00	50.00
-- Regular version with W. 63rd St. address on label					
❑ BST-1566 [S]	Swing and Soul	1963	5.00	10.00	20.00
-- With New York, USA address on label					
❑ BLP-1591 [M]	Lou Takes Off	1958	30.00	60.00	120.00
-- "Deep groove" version (deep indentation under label on both sides)					

Number	Title	Yr	VG	VG+	NM
❑ BLP-1591 [M]	Lou Takes Off	1958	20.00	40.00	80.00
-- Regular version with W. 63rd St. address on label					
❑ BLP-1591 [M]	Lou Takes Off	1963	6.25	12.50	25.00
-- With New York, USA address on label					
❑ BST-1591 [S]	Lou Takes Off	1959	20.00	40.00	80.00
-- "Deep groove" version (deep indentation under label on both sides)					
❑ BST-1591 [S]	Lou Takes Off	1959	12.50	25.00	50.00
-- Regular version with W. 63rd St. address on label					
❑ BST-1591 [S]	Lou Takes Off	1963	5.00	10.00	20.00
-- With New York, USA address on label					
❑ BLP-1593 [M]	Blues Walk	1958	30.00	60.00	120.00
-- "Deep groove" version (deep indentation under label on both sides)					
❑ BLP-1593 [M]	Blues Walk	1958	20.00	40.00	80.00
-- Regular version with W. 63rd St. address on label					
❑ BLP-1593 [M]	Blues Walk	1963	6.25	12.50	25.00
-- With New York, USA address on label					
❑ BST-1593 [S]	Blues Walk	1959	20.00	40.00	80.00
-- "Deep groove" version (deep indentation under label on both sides)					
❑ BST-1593 [S]	Blues Walk	1959	12.50	25.00	50.00
-- Regular version with W. 63rd St. address on label					
❑ BST-1593 [S]	Blues Walk	1963	5.00	10.00	20.00
-- With New York, USA address on label					
❑ BLP-4012 [M]	LD + 3	1959	30.00	60.00	120.00
-- "Deep groove" version (deep indentation under label on both sides)					
❑ BLP-4012 [M]	LD + 3	1959	20.00	40.00	80.00
-- Regular version with W. 63rd St. address on label					
❑ BLP-4012 [M]	LD + 3	1963	6.25	12.50	25.00
-- With New York, USA address on label					
❑ BST-4012 [S]	LD + 3	1960	20.00	40.00	80.00
-- "Deep groove" version (deep indentation under label on both sides)					
❑ BST-4012 [S]	LD + 3	1960	12.50	25.00	50.00
-- Regular version with W. 63rd St. address on label					
❑ BST-4012 [S]	LD + 3	1963	5.00	10.00	20.00
-- With New York, USA address on label					
❑ BLP-4025 [M]	The Time Is Right	1960	30.00	60.00	120.00
-- "Deep groove" version (deep indentation under label on both sides)					
❑ BLP-4025 [M]	The Time Is Right	1960	20.00	40.00	80.00
-- Regular version with W. 63rd St. address on label					
❑ BLP-4025 [M]	The Time Is Right	1963	6.25	12.50	25.00
-- With New York, USA address on label					
❑ BLP-4036 [M]	Sunny Side Up	1960	30.00	60.00	120.00
-- "Deep groove" version (deep indentation under label on both sides)					
❑ BLP-4036 [M]	Sunny Side Up	1960	20.00	40.00	80.00
-- Regular version with W. 63rd St. address on label					
❑ BLP-4036 [M]	Sunny Side Up	1963	6.25	12.50	25.00
-- With New York, USA address on label					
❑ BLP-4053 [M]	Light Foot	1960	20.00	40.00	80.00
-- With W. 63rd St. address on label					
❑ BLP-4053 [M]	Light Foot	1963	6.25	12.50	25.00
-- With New York, USA address on label					
❑ BLP-4066 [M]	Here 'Tis	1961	20.00	40.00	80.00
-- With W. 63rd St. address on label					
❑ BLP-4066 [M]	Here 'Tis	1963	6.25	12.50	25.00
-- With New York, USA address on label					
❑ BLP-4079 [M]	Gravy Train	1962	20.00	40.00	80.00
-- With 61st St. address on label					
❑ BLP-4079 [M]	Gravy Train	1963	6.25	12.50	25.00
-- With New York, USA address on label					
❑ BLP-4108 [M]	The Natural Soul	1963	6.25	12.50	25.00
❑ BLP-4125 [M]	Good Gracious	1963	6.25	12.50	25.00
❑ BLP-4263 [M]	Alligator Boogaloo	1967	7.50	15.00	30.00
❑ BLP-4271 [M]	Mr. Shing-a-Ling	1968	7.50	15.00	30.00
❑ BLP-5021 [10]	Lou Donaldson Quintet/Quartet	1953	50.00	100.00	200.00
❑ BLP-5030 [10]	Lou Donaldson-Clifford Brown	1954	50.00	100.00	200.00
❑ BLP-5055 [10]	Lou Donaldson Sextet, Volume 2	1955	50.00	100.00	200.00
❑ BST-84025 [S]	The Time Is Right	1960	12.50	25.00	50.00
-- With W. 63rd St. address on label					
❑ BST-84025 [S]	The Time Is Right	1963	5.00	10.00	20.00
-- With New York, USA address on label					
❑ BST-84036 [S]	Sunny Side Up	1960	12.50	25.00	50.00
-- With New York, USA address on label					
❑ BST-84036 [S]	Sunny Side Up	1963	5.00	10.00	20.00
-- With New York, USA address on label					
❑ BST-84053 [S]	Light Foot	1960	12.50	25.00	50.00
-- With W. 63rd St. address on label					
❑ BST-84053 [S]	Light Foot	1963	5.00	10.00	20.00
-- With New York, USA address on label					
❑ BST-84066 [S]	Here 'Tis	1961	12.50	25.00	50.00
-- With W. 63rd St. address on label					
❑ BST-84066 [S]	Here 'Tis	1963	5.00	10.00	20.00
-- With New York, USA address on label					
❑ BST-84079 [S]	Gravy Train	1962	12.50	25.00	50.00
-- With W. 63rd St. address on label					
❑ BST-84079 [S]	Gravy Train	1963	5.00	10.00	20.00
-- With New York, USA address on label					
❑ BST-84108 [S]	The Natural Soul	1963	6.25	12.50	25.00
❑ BST-84125 [S]	Good Gracious	1963	6.25	12.50	25.00
❑ BST-84263 [S]	Alligator Boogaloo	1967	5.00	10.00	20.00
❑ BST-84271 [S]	Mr. Shing-a-Ling	1968	5.00	10.00	20.00
❑ BST-84280	Midnight Creeper	1968	5.00	10.00	20.00

Number	Title	Yr	VG	VG+	NM
❑ BST-84299	Say It Loud!	1969	5.00	10.00	20.00
❑ BST-84318	Hot Dog	1969	5.00	10.00	20.00
CADET					
❑ LP-724 [M]	Signifyin'	1966	5.00	10.00	20.00
-- Reissue of Argo 724					
❑ LP-734 [M]	Possum Head	1966	5.00	10.00	20.00
-- Reissue of Argo 734					
❑ LP-747 [M]	Cole Slaw	1966	5.00	10.00	20.00
-- Reissue of Argo 747					
❑ LP-759 [M]	Musty Rusty	1966	6.25	12.50	25.00
❑ LPS-759 [S]	Musty Rusty	1966	6.25	12.50	25.00
❑ LP-768 [M]	Rough House Blues	1966	6.25	12.50	25.00
❑ LPS-768 [S]	Rough House Blues	1966	6.25	12.50	25.00
❑ LP-789 [M]	Blowin' in the Wind	1967	6.25	12.50	25.00
❑ LPS-789 [S]	Blowin' in the Wind	1967	5.00	10.00	20.00
❑ LPS-815	Lou Donaldson At His Best	1969	5.00	10.00	20.00
❑ LPS-842	Fried Buzzard -- Lou Donaldson Live	1970	5.00	10.00	20.00

DONEGAN, LONNIE

Number	Title	Yr	VG	VG+	NM
ABC-PARAMOUNT					
❑ 433 [M]	Sing Hallelujah	1963	5.00	10.00	20.00
❑ S-433 [S]	Sing Hallelujah	1963	6.25	12.50	25.00
ATLANTIC					
❑ 8038 [M]	Skiffle Folk Songs	1960	10.00	20.00	40.00
❑ SD 8038 [S]	Skiffle Folk Songs	1960	12.50	25.00	50.00
DOT					
❑ DLP-3159 [M]	Lonnie Donegan	1959	10.00	20.00	40.00
MERCURY					
❑ MG-20229 [M]	An Englishman Sings American Folk Songs	1957	12.50	25.00	50.00

DONNER, RAL

Number	Title	Yr	VG	VG+	NM
GONE					
❑ LP-5012 [M]	Takin' Care of Business	1961	75.00	150.00	300.00

DONNER, RAL /RAY SMITH /BOBBY DALE

Number	Title	Yr	VG	VG+	NM
CROWN					
❑ CST-335 [R]	Ral Donner, Ray Smith and Bobby Dale	1963	5.00	10.00	20.00
❑ CLP-5335 [M]	Ral Donner, Ray Smith and Bobby Dale	1963	10.00	20.00	40.00

DONNIE AND THE DELCHORDS

Number	Title	Yr	VG	VG+	NM
TAURUS					
❑ 1000	Sing with Triple Stereo	1967	75.00	150.00	300.00

DONOVAN

Number	Title	Yr	VG	VG+	NM
EPIC					
❑ B2N 171 [(2) S]	A Gift from a Flower to a Garden	1967	6.25	12.50	25.00
-- Boxed set of two LPs with portfolio of lyrics and drawings. The two records also were issued separately as Epic 26349 and 26350.					
❑ L2N 6071 [(2)]	A Gift from a Flower to a Garden	1967	12.50	25.00	50.00
-- Boxed set of two LPs with portfolio of lyrics and drawings. The two records also were issued separately as Epic 24349 and 24350.					
❑ LN 24217 [M]	Sunshine Superman	1966	7.50	15.00	30.00
-- Contains the single version of "Sunshine Superman"					
❑ LN 24239 [M]	Mellow Yellow	1967	7.50	15.00	30.00
HICKORY					
❑ LPM-123 [M]	Catch the Wind	1965	6.25	12.50	25.00
❑ LPS-123 [R]	Catch the Wind	1965	—	—	—
-- Not known to exist					
❑ LPM-127 [M]	Fairy Tale	1965	5.00	10.00	20.00
❑ LPS-127 [P]	Fairy Tale	1965	6.25	12.50	25.00
-- "Colours" is rechanneled					
❑ LPM-135 [M]	The Real Donovan	1966	5.00	10.00	20.00
❑ LPS-135 [P]	The Real Donovan	1966	6.25	12.50	25.00
-- Half stereo, including "Colours," the rest rechanneled.					
❑ LPS-143 [P]	Like It Is, Was and Evermore Shall Be	1968	5.00	10.00	20.00
❑ LPS-149 [P]	The Best of Donovan	1969	5.00	10.00	20.00

DOOBIE BROTHERS, THE

Number	Title	Yr	VG	VG+	NM
DCC COMPACT CLASSICS					
❑ LPZ-2053	Best of the Doobies	1998	6.25	12.50	25.00
-- Audiophile vinyl					
MOBILE FIDELITY					
❑ 1-122	Takin' It to the Streets	1983	10.00	20.00	40.00
-- Audiophile vinyl					
NAUTILUS					
❑ NR-5	The Captain and Me	1980	10.00	20.00	40.00
-- Audiophile vinyl					

Number	Title	Yr	VG	VG+	NM
❑ NR-18	Minute by Minute	1981	7.50	15.00	30.00
-- Audiophile vinyl					
PICKWICK					
❑ SPC-3721	Introducing the Doobie Brothers	1980	5.00	10.00	20.00
-- Pre-Warner Bros. recordings; withdrawn shortly after release					
WARNER BROS.					
❑ BS4 2634 [Q]	The Captain and Me	1974	5.00	10.00	20.00
❑ BS4 2750 [Q]	What Were Once Vices Are Now Habits	1974	5.00	10.00	20.00
❑ BS4 2835 [Q]	Stampede	1975	5.00	10.00	20.00

DOORS, THE
DCC COMPACT CLASSICS

Number	Title	Yr	VG	VG+	NM
❑ LPZ-2045	Strange Days	1997	6.25	12.50	25.00
-- Audiophile vinyl					
❑ LPZ-2046	The Doors	1997	6.25	12.50	25.00
-- Audiophile vinyl					
❑ LPZ-2049	Waiting for the Sun	1998	6.25	12.50	25.00
-- Audiophile vinyl					
❑ LPZ-2050	L.A. Woman	1998	6.25	12.50	25.00
-- Audiophile vinyl					
ELEKTRA					
❑ EKL-4007 [M]	The Doors	1967	50.00	100.00	200.00
❑ EKL-4014 [M]	Strange Days	1967	150.00	300.00	600.00
❑ EKL-4024 [M]	Waiting for the Sun	1968	250.00	500.00	1,000.
❑ EQ-5035 [Q]	Best of the Doors	1973	5.00	10.00	20.00
-- Butterfly labels					
❑ 8E-6001 [(2)]	Weird Scenes Inside the Gold Mine	1972	5.00	10.00	20.00
-- Butterfly labels					
❑ EKS-9002 [(2)]	Absolutely Live	1970	6.25	12.50	25.00
-- Butterfly labels					
❑ EKS-9002 [(2) DJ]	Absolutely Live	1970	20.00	40.00	80.00
-- White label promo					
❑ 60345 [(2)]	The Best of the Doors	1985	10.00	20.00	40.00
-- White label promo on audiophile vinyl					
❑ E1-61047	The Doors	1991	5.00	10.00	20.00
-- Soundtrack from the movie; only available on US vinyl from Columbia House					
❑ EKS-74007 [S]	The Doors	1967	12.50	25.00	50.00
-- Brown labels					
❑ EKS-74014 [S]	Strange Days	1967	10.00	20.00	40.00
-- Brown labels					
❑ EKS-74024 [S]	Waiting for the Sun	1968	7.50	15.00	30.00
-- Brown labels					
❑ EKS-74024 [S-DJ]	Waiting for the Sun	1968	37.50	75.00	150.00
-- White label promo					
❑ EKS-74079 [DJ]	13	1970	10.00	20.00	40.00
-- White label promo					
❑ EKS-75005	The Soft Parade	1969	12.50	25.00	50.00
-- Brown labels					
❑ EKS-75005	The Soft Parade	1969	5.00	10.00	20.00
-- Red labels with large stylized "E"					
❑ EKS-75007	Morrison Hotel/Hard Rock Café	1970	6.25	12.50	25.00
-- Red labels with large stylized "E"					
❑ EKS-75007 [DJ]	Morrison Hotel/Hard Rock Café	1970	25.00	50.00	100.00
-- White label promo					
❑ EKS-75011	L.A. Woman	1971	12.50	25.00	50.00
-- With see-through window on cover and yellow innersleeve with photo of Jim Morrison on a cross					
❑ EKS-75011 [DJ]	L.A. Woman	1971	25.00	50.00	100.00
-- White label promo					
MOBILE FIDELITY					
❑ 1-051	The Doors	1980	15.00	30.00	60.00
-- Audiophile vinyl					

DORFMAN, ANIA
RCA VICTOR RED SEAL

Number	Title	Yr	VG	VG+	NM
❑ LSC-2207 [S]	Schumann: Carnaval	1959	10.00	20.00	40.00
-- Original with "shaded dog" label					

DORS, DIANA
COLUMBIA

Number	Title	Yr	VG	VG+	NM
❑ CL 1436 [M]	Swingin' Dors	1960	20.00	40.00	80.00
❑ CS 8232 [S]	Swingin' Dors	1960	25.00	50.00	100.00

DORSEY, JIMMY
COLUMBIA

Number	Title	Yr	VG	VG+	NM
❑ CL 608 [M]	Dixie by Dorsey	1955	7.50	15.00	30.00
-- Red and black label with six "eye" logos					
❑ CL 608 [M]	Dixie by Dorsey	1955	10.00	20.00	40.00
-- Maroon label with gold print					
❑ CL 6095 [10]	Dixie by Dorsey	1950	12.50	25.00	50.00
❑ CL 6114 [10]	Dorseyland Band	1950	12.50	25.00	50.00
CORAL					
❑ CRL 56004 [10]	Contrasting Music, Volume 1	1950	12.50	25.00	50.00
❑ CRL 56008 [10]	Contrasting Music, Volume 2	1950	12.50	25.00	50.00
❑ CRL 56033 [10]	Gershwin Music	1950	12.50	25.00	50.00

Number	Title	Yr	VG	VG+	NM
DECCA					
❑ DL 5091 [10]	Latin American Favorites	1950	12.50	25.00	50.00
❑ DL 8153 [M]	Latin American Favorites	1955	7.50	15.00	30.00
-- Black label, silver print					
❑ DL 8609 [M]	The Great Jimmy Dorsey	1957	6.25	12.50	25.00
-- Black label, silver print					
DOT					
❑ DLP-3437 [M]	So Rare	1962	5.00	10.00	20.00
-- Reissue of Fraternity LP					
FRATERNITY					
❑ F-1008 [M]	Fabulous Jimmy Dorsey	1957	7.50	15.00	30.00

DORSEY, LEE
AMY

Number	Title	Yr	VG	VG+	NM
❑ 8010 [M]	Ride Your Pony	1966	7.50	15.00	30.00
❑ S-8010 [S]	Ride Your Pony	1966	10.00	20.00	40.00
❑ 8011 [M]	The New Lee Dorsey	1966	6.25	12.50	25.00
❑ S-8011 [S]	The New Lee Dorsey	1966	7.50	15.00	30.00
FURY					
❑ 1002 [M]	Ya Ya	1962	75.00	150.00	300.00
SPHERE SOUND					
❑ SR-7003 [M]	Ya Ya	196?	25.00	50.00	100.00
-- Reissue of Fury 1002					
❑ SSR-7003 [R]	Ya Ya	196?	12.50	25.00	50.00
-- Rechanneled reissue of Fury 1002					

DORSEY, TOMMY
On titles with asterisks (*), some of the tracks feature FRANK SINATRA as vocalist.
20TH CENTURY FOX

Number	Title	Yr	VG	VG+	NM
❑ TCF 101/2 [(2) M]	Tommy Dorsey's Greatest Band	1959	7.50	15.00	30.00
❑ TFM-3157 [M]	This Is Tommy Dorsey and His Greatest Band	196?	5.00	10.00	20.00
DECCA					
❑ DL 5317 [10]	Tommy Dorsey Plays Howard	1951	12.50	25.00	50.00
❑ DL 5448 [10]	In a Sentimental Mood	1952	12.50	25.00	50.00
❑ DL 5449 [10]	Tenderly	1952	12.50	25.00	50.00
❑ DL 5452 [10]	Your Invitation to Dance	1952	12.50	25.00	50.00
RCA VICTOR					
❑ LPT-10 [M]	Getting Sentimental with Tommy Dorsey*	1951	20.00	40.00	80.00
❑ ALPT-15 [M]	All Time Hits*	1951	20.00	40.00	80.00
❑ LPM-22 [10]	Tommy Dorsey Plays Cole Porter for Dancing	1951	12.50	25.00	50.00
❑ LPM-1229 [M]	Yes Indeed*	1956	12.50	25.00	50.00
❑ LPM-1425 [M]	Tommy Dorsey Plays Cole Porter and Jerome Kern	1956	6.25	12.50	25.00
❑ LPM-1432 [M]	Tribute to Dorsey, Volume 1*	1956	10.00	20.00	40.00
❑ LPM-1433 [M]	Tribute to Dorsey, Volume 2*	1956	10.00	20.00	40.00
❑ LPM-1643 [M]	Having a Wonderful Time*	1958	10.00	20.00	40.00
❑ LPT-3005 [10]	This Is Tommy Dorsey*	1952	20.00	40.00	80.00
❑ LPT-3018 [10]	This Is Tommy Dorsey*	1952	12.50	25.00	50.00
❑ LPM-3674 [M]	The Best of Tommy Dorsey*	1966	5.00	10.00	20.00
❑ LPM-6003 [(2) M]	That Sentimental Gentleman*	1957	20.00	40.00	80.00
-- Box set					
❑ VPM-6038 [(2)]	This Is Tommy Dorsey*	197?	6.25	12.50	25.00
❑ VPM-6064 [(2)]	This Is Tommy Dorsey, Volume 2*	197?	6.25	12.50	25.00

DOUGLAS, GLENN
DECCA

Number	Title	Yr	VG	VG+	NM
❑ DL 8748 [M]	Heartbreak Alley	1958	12.50	25.00	50.00

DOUGLAS, K.C.
BLUESVILLE

Number	Title	Yr	VG	VG+	NM
❑ BVLP-1023 [M]	K.C.'s Blues	1961	20.00	40.00	80.00
-- Blue label, silver print					
❑ BVLP-1023 [M]	K.C.'s Blues	1964	7.50	15.00	30.00
-- Blue label, trident logo at right					
❑ BVLP-1050 [M]	Big Road Blues	1962	20.00	40.00	80.00
-- Blue label, silver print					
❑ BVLP-1050 [M]	Big Road Blues	1964	7.50	15.00	30.00
-- Blue label, trident logo at right					
COOK ROAD					
❑ 5002 [M]	A Dead Beat Guitar and the Mississippi Blues	1956	125.00	250.00	500.00

DOUGLAS, LEW
CARLTON

Number	Title	Yr	VG	VG+	NM
❑ LP 12-126 [M]	Themes from Motion Pictures and TV	1960	6.25	12.50	25.00

DOUGLAS, STEVE
CROWN

Number	Title	Yr	VG	VG+	NM
❑ CLP-5251 [M]	Twist with Steve Douglas and the Rebel Rousers	1962	5.00	10.00	20.00

Number	Title	Yr	VG	VG+	NM
MERCURY					
❏ SR-61217	Reflections in a Golden Horn	1969	6.25	12.50	25.00
DOVAL, JIM, AND THE GAUCHOS					
ABC-PARAMOUNT					
❏ ABC-506 [M]	The Gauchos Featuring Jim Doval	1965	7.50	15.00	30.00
❏ ABCS-506 [S]	The Gauchos Featuring Jim Doval	1965	10.00	20.00	40.00
DOVE, RONNIE					
DIAMOND					
❏ D 5002 [M]	Right Or Wrong	1964	5.00	10.00	20.00
❏ DS 5002 [S]	Right Or Wrong	1964	6.25	12.50	25.00
❏ D 5003 [M]	One Kiss for Old Times' Sake	1965	5.00	10.00	20.00
❏ DS 5003 [S]	One Kiss for Old Times' Sake	1965	6.25	12.50	25.00
❏ D 5004 [M]	I'll Make All Your Dreams Come True	1965	5.00	10.00	20.00
❏ DS 5004 [S]	I'll Make All Your Dreams Come True	1965	6.25	12.50	25.00
❏ DS 5005 [S]	The Best of Ronnie Dove	1966	5.00	10.00	20.00
❏ DS 5006 [S]	Ronnie Dove Sings the Hits for You	1966	5.00	10.00	20.00
❏ DS 5007 [S]	Cry	1967	5.00	10.00	20.00
DOVELLS, THE					
CAMEO					
❏ C-1082 [M]	Len Barry Sings with the Dovells	1965	7.50	15.00	30.00
❏ SC-1082 [S]	Len Barry Sings with the Dovells	1965	12.50	25.00	50.00
PARKWAY					
❏ P 7006 [M]	The Bristol Stomp	1961	20.00	40.00	80.00
-- Light orange label					
❏ P 7006 [M]	The Bristol Stomp	1962	12.50	25.00	50.00
-- Dark orange and yellow label					
❏ P 7010 [M]	All the Hits of the Teen Groups	1962	12.50	25.00	50.00
❏ P 7021 [M]	For Your Hully Gully Party	1962	12.50	25.00	50.00
❏ P 7025 [M]	You Can't Sit Down	1963	12.50	25.00	50.00
WYNCOTE					
❏ W 9052 [M]	Discotheque	1965	5.00	10.00	20.00
❏ W 9114 [M]	The Dovells' Biggest Hits	1965	5.00	10.00	20.00
DOWELL, JOE					
SMASH					
❏ MGS-27000 [M]	Wooden Heart	1961	10.00	20.00	40.00
❏ MGS-27011 [M]	German American Hits	1962	6.25	12.50	25.00
❏ SRS-67000 [S]	Wooden Heart	1961	12.50	25.00	50.00
❏ SRS-67011 [S]	German American Hits	1962	7.50	15.00	30.00
WING					
❏ MGW-12328 [M]	Wooden Heart	196?	5.00	10.00	20.00
❏ SRW-16328 [S]	Wooden Heart	196?	5.00	10.00	20.00
DOWLING, CHET, AND BILL MINKIN					
COLUMBIA					
❏ CL 2776 [M]	Senator Bobby's Christmas Party	1967	5.00	10.00	20.00
❏ CS 9576 [S]	Senator Bobby's Christmas Party	1967	5.00	10.00	20.00
DOWNS, HUGH					
EPIC					
❏ BN 541 [S]	An Evening with Hugh Downs	1961	7.50	15.00	30.00
❏ LN 3597 [M]	An Evening with Hugh Downs	1961	6.25	12.50	25.00
DOYLE, BOBBY, THREE					
KENNY ROGERS was in this group.					
COLUMBIA					
❏ CL 1858 [M]	In a Most Unusual Way	1962	10.00	20.00	40.00
❏ CS 8658 [S]	In a Most Unusual Way	1962	12.50	25.00	50.00
DOYLE, MIKE					
FLEETWOOD					
❏ FLP-3018 [M]	The Secrets of Surfing	1963	30.00	60.00	120.00
DOZIER, GENE, AND THE BROTHERHOOD					
MINIT					
❏ 24010 [S]	Blues Power	1967	6.25	12.50	25.00
❏ 40010 [M]	Blues Power	1967	6.25	12.50	25.00
DRAGONFLY					
MEGAPHONE					
❏ MS-1202	Dragonfly	1968	50.00	100.00	200.00
DRAGSTERS, THE					
WING					
❏ MGW-12269 [M]	Hey Little Cobra/Drag City	1964	20.00	40.00	80.00
❏ SRW-16269 [S]	Hey Little Cobra/Drag City	1964	25.00	50.00	100.00

Number	Title	Yr	VG	VG+	NM
DRAKE, GUY					
ROYAL AMERICAN					
❏ 1001	Welfare Cadillac	1970	6.25	12.50	25.00
DRAKE, NICK					
HANNIBAL					
❏ HNBX-5302 [(3)]	Fruit Tree	198?	6.25	12.50	25.00
ISLAND					
❏ SMAS-9307	Nick Drake	1971	6.25	12.50	25.00
❏ SMAS-9318	Pink Moon	1972	6.25	12.50	25.00
DRAKE, PETE					
CANAAN					
❏ 9640 [S]	Steel Away	1967	5.00	10.00	20.00
CUMBERLAND					
❏ MGC-29053 [M]	Country Steel Guitar	1963	5.00	10.00	20.00
❏ SRC-69053 [S]	Country Steel Guitar	1963	6.25	12.50	25.00
SMASH					
❏ SRS-67053 [S]	Forever	1964	5.00	10.00	20.00
❏ SRS-67060 [S]	Talking Steel Guitar	1965	5.00	10.00	20.00
❏ SRS-67064 [S]	Talking Steel and Singing Strings	1965	5.00	10.00	20.00
STARDAY					
❏ SLP-180 [M]	The Fabulous Steel Guitar of Pete Drake	1962	10.00	20.00	40.00
❏ SLP-319 [M]	The Amazing Incredible Pete Drake	1964	7.50	15.00	30.00
DRAMATICS, THE					
VOLT					
❏ VOS-6018	Whatcha See Is Whatcha Get	1972	6.25	12.50	25.00
❏ VOS-6019	A Dramatic Experience	1973	6.25	12.50	25.00
❏ VOS-9501	Dramatically Yours	1974	6.25	12.50	25.00
DRAPER, RUSTY					
MERCURY					
❏ MG-20068 [M]	Music for a Rainy Night	1956	7.50	15.00	30.00
❏ MG-20117 [M]	Encores	1957	7.50	15.00	30.00
❏ MG-20118 [M]	Rusty Draper Sings	1957	7.50	15.00	30.00
❏ MG-20173 [M]	Rusty Meets Hoagy	1957	7.50	15.00	30.00
❏ MG-20499 [M]	Hits That Sold a Million	1960	7.50	15.00	30.00
❏ MG-20657 [M]	Country and Western Golden Greats	1961	7.50	15.00	30.00
❏ SR-60176 [S]	Hits That Sold a Million	1960	10.00	20.00	40.00
❏ SR-60657 [S]	Country and Western Golden Greats	1961	10.00	20.00	40.00
MONUMENT					
❏ SLP-18005 [S]	Greatest Hits	1964	5.00	10.00	20.00
❏ SLP-18018 [S]	Night Life	1964	5.00	10.00	20.00
❏ SLP-18026 [S]	Rusty Draper Plays Guitar	1965	5.00	10.00	20.00
DREAD ZEPPELIN					
I.R.S.					
❏ X1-13048	Un-Led-Ed	1990	5.00	10.00	20.00
-- All copies on gold vinyl					
DREAM 6					
With Johnette Napolitano, later of CONCRETE BLONDE.					
HAPPY HERMIT					
❏ 1983 [EP]	Dream 6	1983	10.00	20.00	40.00
DREAM SYNDICATE, THE					
DOWN THERE					
❏ 2 [EP]	Sure Thing + 3	1982	5.00	10.00	20.00
RUBY					
❏ 807	The Days of Wine and Roses	1982	5.00	10.00	20.00
DREAMLOVERS, THE					
COLUMBIA					
❏ CL 2020 [M]	The Bird and Other Golden Dancing Grooves	1963	10.00	20.00	40.00
❏ CS 8820 [S]	The Bird and Other Golden Dancing Grooves	1963	12.50	25.00	50.00
DREAMS AND ILLUSIONS					
VERVE FORECAST					
❏ FTS-3040	Dreams and Illusions	1968	5.00	10.00	20.00
DREW, DORIS					
MODE					
❏ MOD-126 [M]	The Delightful Doris Drew	1957	20.00	40.00	80.00

Number	Title	Yr	VG	VG+	NM

DREW, PATTI
CAPITOL
❏ ST-156	I've Been Here All the Time	1969	5.00	10.00	20.00
❏ ST-408	Wild Is Love	1970	5.00	10.00	20.00
❏ ST 2804 [S]	Tell Him	1968	7.50	15.00	30.00
❏ T 2804 [M]	Tell Him	1968	7.50	15.00	30.00

DRIFTERS, THE
Also see BEN E. KING; CLYDE McPHATTER.
ATLANTIC
❏ 8003 [M]	Clyde McPhatter and the Drifters	1956	125.00	250.00	500.00
-- Black label					
❏ 8003 [M]	Clyde McPhatter and the Drifters	1959	15.00	30.00	60.00
-- Mostly red label					
❏ 8022 [M]	Rockin' and Driftin'	1958	150.00	300.00	600.00
-- Black label					
❏ 8022 [M]	Rockin' and Driftin'	1958	125.00	250.00	500.00
-- White "bullseye" label					
❏ 8022 [M]	Rockin' and Driftin'	1959	15.00	30.00	60.00
-- Mostly red label					
❏ 8041 [M]	The Drifters' Greatest Hits	1960	150.00	300.00	600.00
-- Black label					
❏ 8041 [M]	The Drifters' Greatest Hits	1960	25.00	50.00	100.00
-- Mostly red label, white "fan" logo					
❏ 8059 [M]	Save the Last Dance for Me	1962	30.00	60.00	120.00
-- Mostly red label, white "fan" logo					
❏ SD 8059 [S]	Save the Last Dance for Me	1962	50.00	100.00	200.00
-- Mostly red label, white "fan" logo					
❏ 8073 [M]	Up on the Roof -- The Best of the Drifters	1963	25.00	50.00	100.00
-- Mostly red label, black "fan" logo					
❏ SD 8073 [S]	Up on the Roof -- The Best of the Drifters	1963	37.50	75.00	150.00
-- Mostly red label, black "fan" logo					
❏ 8093 [M]	Our Biggest Hits	1964	15.00	30.00	60.00
-- Mostly red label, black "fan" logo					
❏ SD 8093 [S]	Our Biggest Hits	1964	20.00	40.00	80.00
-- Mostly red label, black "fan" logo					
❏ 8099 [M]	Under the Boardwalk	1964	20.00	40.00	80.00
-- Black and white photo of group on cover					
❏ 8099 [M]	Under the Boardwalk	1964	12.50	25.00	50.00
-- Color photo of group on cover					
❏ SD 8099 [S]	Under the Boardwalk	1964	30.00	60.00	120.00
-- Black and white photo of group on cover					
❏ SD 8099 [S]	Under the Boardwalk	1964	15.00	30.00	60.00
-- Color photo of group on cover					
❏ 8103 [M]	The Good Life with the Drifters	1965	10.00	20.00	40.00
❏ SD 8103 [S]	The Good Life with the Drifters	1965	12.50	25.00	50.00
❏ 8113 [M]	I'll Take You Where the Music's Playing	1965	10.00	20.00	40.00
❏ SD 8113 [S]	I'll Take You Where the Music's Playing	1965	12.50	25.00	50.00
❏ 8153 [M]	The Drifters' Golden Hits	1968	7.50	15.00	30.00
❏ SD 8153 [P]	The Drifters' Golden Hits	1968	7.50	15.00	30.00
-- Green and blue label					
CLARION
| ❏ 608 [M] | The Drifters | 1964 | 5.00 | 10.00 | 20.00 |
| ❏ SD 608 [P] | The Drifters | 1964 | 7.50 | 15.00 | 30.00 |

DRIFTIN' SLIM
MILESTONE
| ❏ MLS-93004 [(2)] | Driftin' Slim and His Blues Band | 1968 | 6.25 | 12.50 | 25.00 |

DRIFTWOOD, JIMMY
MONUMENT
❏ MLP-8006 [M]	Voice of the People	1963	5.00	10.00	20.00
❏ MLP-8019 [M]	Down in the Arkansas	1965	5.00	10.00	20.00
❏ SLP-18006 [S]	Voice of the People	1963	6.25	12.50	25.00
❏ SLP-18019 [S]	Down in the Arkansas	1965	6.25	12.50	25.00
RCA VICTOR
❏ LPM-1635 [M]	Newly Discovered Early American Folk Songs	1958	12.50	25.00	50.00
❏ LPM-1994 [M]	Jimmie Driftwood and the Wilderness Road	1959	7.50	15.00	30.00
❏ LSP-1994 [S]	Jimmie Driftwood and the Wilderness Road	1959	10.00	20.00	40.00
❏ LPM-2171 [M]	The Westward Movement	1960	7.50	15.00	30.00
❏ LSP-2171 [S]	The Westward Movement	1960	10.00	20.00	40.00
❏ LPM-2228 [M]	Tall Tales in Song	1960	7.50	15.00	30.00
❏ LSP-2228 [S]	Tall Tales in Song	1960	10.00	20.00	40.00
❏ LPM-2316 [M]	Songs of Billy Yank and Johnny Reb	1961	7.50	15.00	30.00
❏ LSP-2316 [S]	Songs of Billy Yank and Johnny Reb	1961	10.00	20.00	40.00
❏ LPM-2443 [M]	Driftwood at Sea	1962	7.50	15.00	30.00
❏ LSP-2443 [S]	Driftwood at Sea	1962	10.00	20.00	40.00

DRUIDS OF STONEHENGE, THE
UNI
| ❏ 3004 [M] | Creation | 1967 | 15.00 | 30.00 | 60.00 |
| ❏ 73004 [S] | Creation | 1967 | 20.00 | 40.00 | 80.00 |

DRUSKY, ROY
DECCA
❏ DL 4160 [M]	Anymore with Roy Drusky	1961	6.25	12.50	25.00
❏ DL 4340 [M]	It's My Way	1962	5.00	10.00	20.00
❏ DL 74160 [S]	Anymore with Roy Drusky	1961	7.50	15.00	30.00
❏ DL 74340 [S]	It's My Way	1962	6.25	12.50	25.00
MERCURY
❏ MG-20883 [M]	Songs of the Cities	1963	5.00	10.00	20.00
❏ MG-20919 [M]	Yesterday's Gone	1964	5.00	10.00	20.00
❏ MG-20973 [M]	The Pick of the Country	1964	5.00	10.00	20.00
❏ MG-21006 [M]	Country Music All Around the World	1965	5.00	10.00	20.00
❏ MG-21052 [M]	Roy Drusky's Greatest Hits	1965	5.00	10.00	20.00
❏ MG-21083 [M]	In a New Dimension	1966	5.00	10.00	20.00
❏ MG-21097 [M]	If the Whole World Stopped Lovin'	1966	5.00	10.00	20.00
❏ MG-21118 [M]	Now Is a Lonely Time	1967	6.25	12.50	25.00
❏ SR-60883 [S]	Songs of the Cities	1963	6.25	12.50	25.00
❏ SR-60919 [S]	Yesterday's Gone	1964	6.25	12.50	25.00
❏ SR-60973 [S]	The Pick of the Country	1964	6.25	12.50	25.00
❏ SR-61006 [S]	Country Music All Around the World	1965	6.25	12.50	25.00
❏ SR-61052 [S]	Roy Drusky's Greatest Hits	1965	6.25	12.50	25.00
❏ SR-61083 [S]	In a New Dimension	1966	6.25	12.50	25.00
❏ SR-61097 [S]	If the Whole World Stopped Lovin'	1966	6.25	12.50	25.00
❏ SR-61118 [S]	Now Is a Lonely Time	1967	5.00	10.00	20.00
❏ SR-61145	Roy Drusky's Greatest Hits Vol. 2	1968	5.00	10.00	20.00
❏ SR-61173	Jody and the Kid	1968	5.00	10.00	20.00
❏ SR-61206	Portrait of Roy Drusky	1969	5.00	10.00	20.00
❏ SR-61233	My Grass Is Green	1969	5.00	10.00	20.00
❏ SR-61260	I'll Make Amends	1970	5.00	10.00	20.00
❏ SR-61266	The Best of Roy Drusky	1970	5.00	10.00	20.00
❏ SR-61306	All My Hard Times	1970	5.00	10.00	20.00
❏ SR-61336	I Love the Way That You've Been Lovin' Me	1971	5.00	10.00	20.00

DRUSKY, ROY, AND PRISCILLA MITCHELL
MERCURY
| ❏ MG-21078 [M] | Together Again | 1966 | 5.00 | 10.00 | 20.00 |
| ❏ SR-61078 [S] | Together Again | 1966 | 6.25 | 12.50 | 25.00 |

DRY CITY SCAT BAND, THE
ELEKTRA
| ❏ EKL-292 [M] | The Dry City Scat Band | 1965 | 6.25 | 12.50 | 25.00 |
| ❏ EKS-7292 [S] | The Dry City Scat Band | 1965 | 7.50 | 15.00 | 30.00 |

DUALS, THE
SUE
❏ LP-2002 [M]	Stick Shift	1961	100.00	200.00	400.00
-- Cartoon cover					
❏ LP-2002 [M]	Stick Shift	1964	50.00	100.00	200.00
-- Photo cover					

DUBS, THE / THE SHELLS
JOSIE
| ❏ JM-4001 [M] | The Dubs Meet the Shells | 1962 | 75.00 | 150.00 | 300.00 |
| ❏ JSS-4001 [S] | The Dubs Meet the Shells | 1962 | 150.00 | 300.00 | 600.00 |

DUDLEY, DAVE
GOLDEN RING
| ❏ GR 110 [M] | Dave Dudley Sings Six Days on the Road | 1963 | 20.00 | 40.00 | 80.00 |
MERCURY
❏ MG-20899 [M]	Songs About the Working Man	1964	5.00	10.00	20.00
❏ MG-20927 [M]	Travelin' with Dave Dudley	1964	5.00	10.00	20.00
❏ MG-20970 [M]	Talk of the Town	1964	5.00	10.00	20.00
❏ MG-20999 [M]	Rural Route #1	1965	5.00	10.00	20.00
❏ MG-21028 [M]	Truck Drivin' Son-of-a-Gun	1965	5.00	10.00	20.00
❏ MG-21046 [M]	Dave Dudley's Greatest Hits	1965	5.00	10.00	20.00
❏ MG-21057 [M]	There's a Star Spangled Banner Waving Somewhere	1966	5.00	10.00	20.00
❏ MG-21074 [M]	Lonelyville	1966	5.00	10.00	20.00
❏ MG-21098 [M]	Free and Easy	1966	5.00	10.00	20.00
❏ MG-21133 [M]	Dave Dudley Country	1967	6.25	12.50	25.00
❏ MG-21144 [M]	Greatest Hits Vol. 2	1968	7.50	15.00	30.00
❏ SR-60899 [S]	Songs About the Working Man	1964	6.25	12.50	25.00
❏ SR-60927 [S]	Travelin' with Dave Dudley	1964	6.25	12.50	25.00
❏ SR-60970 [S]	Talk of the Town	1964	6.25	12.50	25.00
❏ SR-60999 [S]	Rural Route #1	1965	6.25	12.50	25.00
❏ SR-61028 [S]	Truck Drivin' Son-of-a-Gun	1965	6.25	12.50	25.00

Number	Title	Yr	VG	VG+	NM
❑ SR-61046 [S]	Dave Dudley's Greatest Hits	1965	6.25	12.50	25.00
❑ SR-61057 [S]	There's a Star Spangled Banner Waving Somewhere	1966	6.25	12.50	25.00
❑ SR-61074 [S]	Lonelyville	1966	6.25	12.50	25.00
❑ SR-61098 [S]	Free and Easy	1966	5.00	10.00	20.00
❑ SR-61133 [S]	Dave Dudley Country	1967	5.00	10.00	20.00
❑ SR-61144 [S]	Greatest Hits Vol. 2	1968	5.00	10.00	20.00
❑ SR-61172 [S]	Thanks for All the Miles	1968	5.00	10.00	20.00
❑ SR-61215	One More Mile	1969	5.00	10.00	20.00

DUKE OF IRON, THE
PRESTIGE
❑ PRLP-13068 [M]	Limbo, Limbo, Limbo	1963	7.50	15.00	30.00

DUKE OF PADUCAH, THE
STARDAY
❑ SLP-148 [M]	Button Shoes, Belly Laughs and Monkey Business	1961	10.00	20.00	40.00

DUKE, PATTY
UNITED ARTISTS
❑ UAL-3452 [M]	Don't Just Stand There	1965	5.00	10.00	20.00
❑ UAL-3492 [M]	Patty	1966	5.00	10.00	20.00
❑ UAS-6452 [S]	Don't Just Stand There	1965	7.50	15.00	30.00
❑ UAS-6492 [S]	Patty	1966	7.50	15.00	30.00
❑ UAS-6535 [S]	Patty Duke's Greatest Hits	1966	6.25	12.50	25.00
❑ UAS-6632	Songs from the Valley of the Dolls	1968	6.25	12.50	25.00

DUKE, PATTY, WITH NORMAN VINCENT PEALE
GUIDEPOSTS
❑ GP-101 [M]	Guideposts for Christmas	1963	20.00	40.00	80.00

DUKE, VERNON
ATLANTIC
❑ 407 [10]	Vernon Duke Plays Vernon Duke	1954	25.00	50.00	100.00

DUKES OF DIXIELAND, THE
AUDIO FIDELITY
❑ AFSD-5823 [S]	You Have to Hear It to Believe It -- The Dukes of Dixieland, Vol. 1	196?	5.00	10.00	20.00
❑ AFSD-5840 [S]	You Have to Hear It to Believe It -- The Dukes of Dixieland, Vol. 2	196?	5.00	10.00	20.00
❑ AFSD-5851 [S]	Marching Along with the Dukes of Dixieland, Vol. 3	196?	5.00	10.00	20.00
❑ AFSD-5860 [S]	The Dukes of Dixieland On Bourbon Street, Vol. 4	196?	5.00	10.00	20.00
❑ AFSD-5862 [S]	Mardi Gras Time	1958	5.00	10.00	20.00
❑ AFSD-5891 [S]	The Dukes of Dixieland On Campus	1959	5.00	10.00	20.00
❑ AFSD-5892 [S]	Up the Mississippi	1959	5.00	10.00	20.00
VIK
❑ LX-1025 [M]	The Dukes of Dixieland at the Jazz Band Ball	1956	7.50	15.00	30.00

DUNBAR, AYNSLEY
Also see JEFFERSON AIRPLANE; JOURNEY; JOHN MAYALL.
BLUE THUMB
❑ BTS-4	The Aynsley Dunbar Retaliation	1968	6.25	12.50	25.00
❑ BTS-6	Doctor Dunbar's Prescription	1969	6.25	12.50	25.00
❑ BTS-16	To Mum From Aynsley and the Boys	1970	6.25	12.50	25.00

DUNCAN, BILL
KING
❑ 825 [M]	A Scene Near My Country Home	1962	7.50	15.00	30.00

DUNCAN, JOHNNY
COLUMBIA
❑ CS 9824	Johnny One Time	1969	5.00	10.00	20.00

DUNHAM, KATHERINE
AUDIO FIDELITY
❑ AFLP-1803 [M]	The Singing Gods-Drum Rhythms of Cuba, Haiti, Brazil	1957	10.00	20.00	40.00
DECCA
❑ DL 5251 [10]	Afro-Caribbean Songs and Rhythms	1951	15.00	30.00	60.00

DUPRE, MARCEL
MERCURY LIVING PRESENCE
❑ SR 90168 [S]	Franck: Piece Heroique; 3	196?	12.50	25.00	50.00
-- Maroon label, no "Vendor: Mercury Record Corporation"					
❑ SR 90168 [S]	Franck: Piece Heroique; 3	196?	15.00	30.00	60.00
-- Maroon label, with "Vendor: Mercury Record Corporation"					

Number	Title	Yr	VG	VG+	NM
❑ SR 90168 [S]	Franck: Piece Heroique; 3	196?	7.50	15.00	30.00
-- Third edition: Dark red (not maroon) label					
❑ SR 90169 [S]	Organ Recital	196?	30.00	60.00	120.00
-- Maroon label, no "Vendor: Mercury Record Corporation"					
❑ SR 90169 [S]	Organ Recital	196?	60.00	120.00	240.00
-- Maroon label, with "Vendor: Mercury Record Corporation"					
❑ SR 90227 [S]	Dupre at Saint-Sulpice, Vol. 1	196?	15.00	30.00	60.00
-- Maroon label, no "Vendor: Mercury Record Corporation"					
❑ SR 90228 [S]	Dupre at Saint-Sulpice, Vol. 3	196?	12.50	25.00	50.00
-- Maroon label, no "Vendor: Mercury Record Corporation"					
❑ SR 90228 [S]	Dupre at Saint-Sulpice, Vol. 3	196?	10.00	20.00	40.00
-- Maroon label, with "Vendor: Mercury Record Corporation"					
❑ SR 90229 [S]	Dupre at Saint-Sulpice, Vol. 2	196?	25.00	50.00	100.00
-- Maroon label, no "Vendor: Mercury Record Corporation"					
❑ SR 90229 [S]	Dupre at Saint-Sulpice, Vol. 2	196?	15.00	30.00	60.00
-- Maroon label, with "Vendor: Mercury Record Corporation"					
❑ SR 90230 [S]	Dupre at Saint-Sulpice, Vol. 4	196?	30.00	60.00	120.00
-- Maroon label, no "Vendor: Mercury Record Corporation"					
❑ SR 90230 [S]	Dupre at Saint-Sulpice, Vol. 4	196?	12.50	25.00	50.00
-- Maroon label, with "Vendor: Mercury Record Corporation"					
❑ SR 90231 [S]	Dupre at Saint-Sulpice, Vol. 5	196?	12.50	25.00	50.00
-- Maroon label, no "Vendor: Mercury Record Corporation"					

DUPREE, CHAMPION JACK
ATLANTIC
❑ 8019 [M]	Blues from the Gutter	1959	37.50	75.00	150.00
-- Black label					
❑ 8019 [M]	Blues from the Gutter	1960	12.50	25.00	50.00
-- White "fan" logo at right of label					
❑ 8019 [M]	Blues from the Gutter	1963	5.00	10.00	20.00
-- Black "fan" logo at right of label					
❑ SD 8019 [S]	Blues from the Gutter	1959	50.00	100.00	200.00
-- Green label					
❑ SD 8019 [S]	Blues from the Gutter	1960	15.00	30.00	60.00
-- Green and blue label, white "fan" logo at right of label					
❑ SD 8019 [S]	Blues from the Gutter	1963	6.25	12.50	25.00
-- Green and blue label, black "fan" logo at right of label					
❑ 8045 [M]	Natural and Soulful Blues	1961	12.50	25.00	50.00
-- White "fan" logo at right of label					
❑ 8045 [M]	Natural and Soulful Blues	1963	5.00	10.00	20.00
-- Black "fan" logo at right of label					
❑ SD 8045 [S]	Natural and Soulful Blues	1961	15.00	30.00	60.00
-- Green and blue label, white "fan" logo at right of label					
❑ SD 8045 [S]	Natural and Soulful Blues	1963	6.25	12.50	25.00
-- Green and blue label, black "fan" logo at right of label					
❑ 8056 [M]	Champion of the Blues	1961	12.50	25.00	50.00
-- White "fan" logo at right of label					
❑ 8056 [M]	Champion of the Blues	1963	5.00	10.00	20.00
-- Black "fan" logo at right of label					
BLUE HORIZON
❑ 7702	When You Feel the Feeling	1969	6.25	12.50	25.00
CONTINENTAL
❑ CLP-16002 [M]	Low Down Blues	1961	62.50	125.00	250.00
FOLKWAYS
❑ FS-3825 [M]	Women Blues of Champion Jack Dupree	1961	6.25	12.50	25.00
KING
❑ 735 [M]	Champion Jack Dupree Sings the Blues	1961	75.00	150.00	300.00
LONDON
❑ PS 553	From New Orleans to Chicago	1969	5.00	10.00	20.00
OKEH
❑ OKM 12103 [M]	Cabbage Greens	1963	7.50	15.00	30.00

DUPREE, CHAMPION JACK, AND MICKEY BAKER
SIRE
❑ SES-97010	In Heavy Blues	1969	7.50	15.00	30.00

DUPREE, CHAMPION JACK, AND JIMMY RUSHING
AUDIO LAB
❑ AL-1512 [M]	Two Shades of Blue	1958	50.00	100.00	200.00

DUPREE, SIMON, AND THE BIG SOUND
TOWER
❑ ST-5097	Without Reservations	1968	10.00	20.00	40.00

DUPREES, THE
COED
❑ LPC-905 [M]	You Belong to Me	1962	75.00	150.00	300.00
❑ LPC-906 [M]	Have You Heard	1963	50.00	100.00	200.00
COLOSSUS
❑ 5000	Duprees Gold	1970	7.50	15.00	30.00
-- As "The Italian Asphalt & Pavement Co."					

Number	Title	Yr	VG	VG+	NM
HERITAGE					
❑ HTS-35002	Total Recall	1968	7.50	15.00	30.00
POST					
❑ 1000	The Duprees Sing	196?	7.50	15.00	30.00

DURAN DURAN

Number	Title	Yr	VG	VG+	NM
CAPITOL					
❑ SPRO-79097/8 [EP]	Duran Goes Dutch	1987	12.50	25.00	50.00
-- Promo-only five-song EP recorded live in Rotterdam					
HARVEST					
❑ MLP-15006 [EP]	Carnival	1982	6.25	12.50	25.00
-- Imports of this are relatively common and worth much less.					
MOBILE FIDELITY					
❑ 1-182	Seven and the Ragged Tiger	1985	5.00	10.00	20.00
-- Audiophile vinyl					

DURANTE, JIMMY

Number	Title	Yr	VG	VG+	NM
DECCA					
❑ DL 5116 [10]	Jimmy Durante	195?	12.50	25.00	50.00
❑ DL 9049 [M]	Club Durante	195?	6.25	12.50	25.00
❑ DL 78884 [S]	Jimmy Durante at the Piano	1959	5.00	10.00	20.00
LION					
❑ L-70053 [M]	Jimmy Durante in Person	195?	7.50	15.00	30.00
MGM					
❑ E-3242 [M]	Jimmy Durante in Person	1955	7.50	15.00	30.00
ROULETTE					
❑ R-25123 [M]	Jimmy Durante at the	1961	5.00	10.00	20.00
❑ SR-25123 [S]	Jimmy Durante at the	1961	6.25	12.50	25.00
WARNER BROS.					
❑ WS 1506 [S]	September Song	1963	5.00	10.00	20.00
❑ WS 1531 [S]	Hello Young Lovers	1964	5.00	10.00	20.00
❑ WS 1577 [S]	Jimmy Durante's Way of Life	1965	5.00	10.00	20.00
❑ WS 1655 [S]	One of Those Songs	1966	5.00	10.00	20.00
❑ WS 1713 [S]	Songs for Sunday	1967	5.00	10.00	20.00

DURBIN, DEANNA

Number	Title	Yr	VG	VG+	NM
DECCA					
❑ DL 8785 [M]	Deanna Durbin	1958	12.50	25.00	50.00

DUST

Number	Title	Yr	VG	VG+	NM
KAMA SUTRA					
❑ KSBS-2041	Dust	1971	6.25	12.50	25.00
-- Pink label					
❑ KSBS-2059	Hard Attack	1972	6.25	12.50	25.00
-- Pink label					

DUVAL, DENISE / GEORGES PRETRE

Number	Title	Yr	VG	VG+	NM
RCA VICTOR RED SEAL					
❑ LSS-2385 [S]	Poulenc: La Voix Humana	1960	12.50	25.00	50.00
-- Original with "shaded dog" label					

DWARVES

Number	Title	Yr	VG	VG+	NM
SUB POP					
❑ 67	Blood, Guts and Pussy	1990	5.00	10.00	20.00
-- First 1,000 on red vinyl					

DYKE AND THE BLAZERS

Number	Title	Yr	VG	VG+	NM
ORIGINAL SOUND					
❑ LP 8876 [M]	The Funky Broadway	1967	12.50	25.00	50.00
❑ LPS 8876 [S]	The Funky Broadway	1967	18.75	37.50	75.00
❑ LPS 8877	Dyke's Greatest Hits	1968	18.75	37.50	75.00

DYLAN, BOB

Number	Title	Yr	VG	VG+	NM
ASYLUM					
❑ AB-201 [(2)]	Before the Flood	1974	5.00	10.00	20.00
❑ AB-201 [(2) DJ]	Before the Flood	1974	12.50	25.00	50.00
-- White label promo					
❑ 7E-1003	Ceremonies of the Horsemen	1974	1,500.	2,250.	3,000.
-- Original title of "Planet Waves"; no records were pressed with this title, but never-glued covers exist, of which 3 or 4 are known. Value is for one of these covers.					
❑ 7E-1003	Planet Waves	1974	5.00	10.00	20.00
-- With wraparound (olive green) second cover					
❑ 7E-1003 [DJ]	Planet Waves	1974	12.50	25.00	50.00
-- White label promo					
❑ EQ-1003 [Q]	Planet Waves	1974	12.50	25.00	50.00
COLUMBIA					
❑ C2L 41 [(2) M]	Blonde on Blonde	1966	25.00	50.00	100.00
-- "Female photos" inner gatefold with two women pictured					
❑ C2L 41 [(2) M]	Blonde on Blonde	1968	75.00	150.00	300.00
-- No photos of women inside gatefold					

Number	Title	Yr	VG	VG+	NM
❑ C2L 41 [(2) M]	Blonde on Blonde	1966	250.00	500.00	1,000.
-- White label promo					
❑ AS 422 [DJ]	Renaldo and Clara	1976	12.50	25.00	50.00
-- Promo-only sampler from the movie. Authentic copies have a sticker on a white cover; counterfeits have the title printed on the cover.					
❑ AS 798 [DJ]	Saved	1980	6.25	12.50	25.00
-- Promo sampler from LP					
❑ C2S 841 [(2) S]	Blonde on Blonde	1966	15.00	30.00	60.00
-- "Female photos" inner gatefold with two women pictured					
❑ C2S 841 [(2) S]	Blonde on Blonde	1968	7.50	15.00	30.00
-- No photos of women inside gatefold; "360 Sound Stereo" on label					
❑ AS 1259 [DJ]	The Dylan London Interview, July 1981	1981	6.25	12.50	25.00
❑ AS 1471 [DJ]	Electric Lunch	1982	6.25	12.50	25.00
-- Promo-only sampler					
❑ AS 1770 [DJ]	Infidels	1983	5.00	10.00	20.00
-- Promo-only sampler					
❑ CL 1779 [M]	Bob Dylan	1962	62.50	125.00	250.00
-- Six "eye" logos on label; stock copy					
❑ CL 1779 [M]	Bob Dylan	1962	125.00	250.00	500.00
-- Six "eye" logos on label; "A New Star on Columbia" sticker on cover and promo stamp on label					
❑ CL 1779 [M]	Bob Dylan	1963	10.00	20.00	40.00
-- "Guaranteed High Fidelity" on label					
❑ CL 1779 [M]	Bob Dylan	1966	7.50	15.00	30.00
-- "Mono" on label					
❑ CL 1986 [M]	The Freewheelin' Bob Dylan	1963	4,000.	8,000.	12,000.
-- "Guaranteed High Fidelity" on label; plays "Let Me Die in My Footsteps," "Rocks and Gravel," "Talkin' John Birch Blues" and "Gamblin' Willie's Dead Man's Hand." Label does NOT list these. In dead wax, matrix number ends in "--1" followed by a letter (usually, if not always, "A")					
❑ CL 1986 [M]	The Freewheelin' Bob Dylan	1963	1,000.	2,000.	3,000.
-- White label promo; label and timing strip list the deleted tracks but record plays the "correct" tracks					
❑ CL 1986 [M]	The Freewheelin' Bob Dylan	1963	500.00	1,000.	2,000.
-- White label promo; label lists deleted tracks; timing strip lists, and record plays, "correct" tracks					
❑ CL 1986 [M]	The Freewheelin' Bob Dylan	1963	200.00	400.00	800.00
-- White label promo; timing strip lists deleted tracks; label lists, and record plays, "correct" tracks					
❑ CL 1986 [M]	The Freewheelin' Bob Dylan	1963	125.00	250.00	500.00
-- White label promo; label AND timing strip list, and record plays, "correct" tracks					
❑ CL 1986 [M]	The Freewheelin' Bob Dylan	1963	10.00	20.00	40.00
-- "Guaranteed High Fidelity" on label; corrected version (record plays what label says)					
❑ CL 1986 [M]	The Freewheelin' Bob Dylan	1966	7.50	15.00	30.00
-- "Mono" on label					
❑ CAS 2222 [DJ]	Time Passes Slowly	1985	6.25	12.50	25.00
-- Promo-only sampler from Biograph box set					
❑ CL 2105 [M]	The Times They Are a-Changin'	1964	10.00	20.00	40.00
-- "Guaranteed High Fidelity" on label					
❑ CL 2105 [M]	The Times They Are a-Changin'	1964	100.00	200.00	400.00
-- White label promo					
❑ CL 2105 [M]	The Times They Are a-Changin'	1965	7.50	15.00	30.00
-- "Mono" on label					
❑ CL 2193 [M]	Another Side of Bob Dylan	1964	10.00	20.00	40.00
-- "Guaranteed High Fidelity" on label					
❑ CL 2193 [M]	Another Side of Bob Dylan	1964	100.00	200.00	400.00
-- White label promo					
❑ CL 2193 [M]	Another Side of Bob Dylan	1965	7.50	15.00	30.00
-- "Mono" on label					
❑ 2302/9102	Bob Dylan In Concert	1965	2,000.	3,000.	4,000.
-- Never pressed; value is for a cover slick, some of which were printed					
❑ CL 2328 [M]	Bringing It All Back Home	1965	75.00	150.00	300.00
-- White label promo					
❑ CL 2328 [M]	Bringing It All Back Home	1965	12.50	25.00	50.00
-- "Guaranteed High Fidelity" on label					
❑ CL 2328 [M]	Bringing It All Back Home	1965	7.50	15.00	30.00
-- "Mono" on label					
❑ CL 2389 [M]	Highway 61 Revisited	1965	20.00	40.00	80.00
❑ CL 2389 [M]	Highway 61 Revisited	1965	100.00	200.00	400.00
-- White label promo					
❑ KCL 2663 [M]	Bob Dylan's Greatest Hits	1967	12.50	25.00	50.00
❑ CL 2804 [M]	John Wesley Harding	1968	37.50	75.00	150.00
❑ CS 8579 [S]	Bob Dylan	1962	100.00	200.00	400.00
-- Six "eye" logos on label; stock copy					
❑ CS 8579 [S]	Bob Dylan	1962	150.00	300.00	600.00
-- Six "eye" logos on label; "A New Star on Columbia" sticker on cover and promo stamp on label					
❑ CS 8579 [S]	Bob Dylan	1963	10.00	20.00	40.00
-- "360 Sound Stereo" in black on label					
❑ CS 8579 [S]	Bob Dylan	1965	6.25	12.50	25.00
-- "360 Sound Stereo" in white on label					
❑ CS 8786 [S]	The Freewheelin' Bob Dylan	1963	15,000.	22,500.	30,000.
-- "360 Sound Stereo" in black on label (no arrows); record plays, and label lists, "Let Me Die in My Footsteps," "Rocks and Gravel," "Talkin' John Birch Blues" and "Gamblin' Willie's Dead Man's Hand." No known stereo copies play these without listing them.					
❑ CS 8786 [S]	The Freewheelin' Bob Dylan	1963	12.50	25.00	50.00
-- "360 Sound Stereo" in black on label (no arrows)					
❑ CS 8786 [S]	The Freewheelin' Bob Dylan	1964	10.00	20.00	40.00
-- "360 Sound Stereo" in black on label (with arrows)					
❑ CS 8786 [S]	The Freewheelin' Bob Dylan	1965	6.25	12.50	25.00
-- "360 Sound Stereo" in white on label					
❑ CS 8786 [S]	The Freewheelin' Bob Dylan	197?	250.00	500.00	1,000.
-- Orange label; unauthorized red vinyl pressing					
❑ CS 8905 [S]	The Times They Are a-Changin'	1964	10.00	20.00	40.00
-- "360 Sound Stereo" in black on label					

Number	Title	Yr	VG	VG+	NM
❏ CS 8905 [S]	The Times They Are a-Changin'	1965	6.25	12.50	25.00
-- "360 Sound Stereo" in white on label					
❏ CS 8993 [S]	Another Side of Bob Dylan	1964	10.00	20.00	40.00
-- "360 Sound Stereo" in black on label					
❏ CS 8993 [S]	Another Side of Bob Dylan	1965	6.25	12.50	25.00
-- "360 Sound Stereo" in white on label					
❏ CS 9128 [S]	Bringing It All Back Home	1965	10.00	20.00	40.00
-- "360 Sound Stereo" in black on label					
❏ CS 9128 [S]	Bringing It All Back Home	1965	6.25	12.50	25.00
-- "360 Sound Stereo" in white on label					
❏ CS 9189 [S]	Highway 61 Revisited	1965	62.50	125.00	250.00
-- With alternate take of "From a Buick 6." Matrix number on Side 1 will end in "--1" plus a letter					
❏ CS 9189 [S]	Highway 61 Revisited	1965	7.50	15.00	30.00
-- With "regular" take of "From a Buick 6." Matrix number on Side 1 will end in "--2" or higher, plus a letter; "360 Sound Stereo" on label					
❏ CS 9604 [S]	John Wesley Harding	1968	5.00	10.00	20.00
-- "360 Sound Stereo" label					
❏ KCS 9825	Nashville Skyline	1969	7.50	15.00	30.00
-- "360 Sound Stereo" label					
❏ C2X 30050 [(2)]	Self Portrait	1970	37.50	75.00	150.00
-- "360 Sound Stereo" labels					
❏ C2X 30050 [(2)]	Self Portrait	1970	5.00	10.00	20.00
-- Orange labels					
❏ KCQ 32825 [Q]	Nashville Skyline	1973	7.50	15.00	30.00
❏ PC 33235 [DJ]	Blood on the Tracks	1975	2,500.	3,750.	5,000.
-- Test pressing with radically different versions of five songs including "Idiot Wind" and "Tangled Up in Blue"					
❏ PC 33235 [DJ]	Blood on the Tracks	1975	7.50	15.00	30.00
-- Regular white label promo					
❏ PC2 33682 [(2)]	The Basement Tapes	1975	5.00	10.00	20.00
❏ PC2 33682 [(2) DJ]	The Basement Tapes	1975	10.00	20.00	40.00
-- White label promo					
❏ PC 33893 [DJ]	Desire	1976	7.50	15.00	30.00
-- White label promo					
❏ PCQ 33893 [Q]	Desire	1976	7.50	15.00	30.00
❏ PC 34349 [DJ]	Hard Rain	1976	7.50	15.00	30.00
-- White label promo					
❏ JC 35453 [DJ]	Street Legal	1978	6.25	12.50	25.00
-- White label promo					
❏ PC2 36067 [(2) DJ]	Bob Dylan at Budokan	1979	7.50	15.00	30.00
-- White label promo					
❏ FC 36120 [DJ]	Slow Train Coming	1979	6.25	12.50	25.00
-- White label promo					
❏ C5X 38830 [(5)]	Biograph	1985	7.50	15.00	30.00
❏ HC 43235	Blood on the Tracks	198?	20.00	40.00	80.00
-- Half-speed mastered edition					
❏ HC 49825	Nashville Skyline	198?	20.00	40.00	80.00
-- Half-speed mastered edition					
❏ C 53200	Good As I Been to You	1992	5.00	10.00	20.00
❏ 474000 [(3)]	Bob Dylan -- The 30th Anniversary Concert Celebration	1993	7.50	15.00	30.00
-- Albums pressed in US for export to Europe; some stayed here					

COLUMBIA/CLASSIC

❏ CK2-65759-1[(2)]	The Bootleg Series Vol. 4: Bob Dylan Live 1966, The "Royal Albert Hall" Concert	1999	12.50	25.00	50.00
-- Box set with 12x12 booklet and two records individually packaged in cardboard jackets and sleeves					

ISLAND

❏ AB-201 [(2)]	Before the Flood	1974	10.00	20.00	40.00
-- Error pressing with wrong labels (should be Asylum)					

MOBILE FIDELITY

❏ 1-114	The Times They Are a-Changin'	1982	12.50	25.00	50.00
-- Audiophile vinyl					

WARNER/7 ARTS

❏ 221567 [DJ]	Bob Dylan	1967	375.00	750.00	1,500.
-- Publisher's demo with 12 Dylan performances of then-unreleased songs from the "Basement Tapes" era					

DYLAN, BOB, AND ALAN J. WEBERMAN
FOLKWAYS

❏ FB-5322 [M]	Bob Dylan vs. A.J. Weberman	1977	75.00	150.00	300.00
-- No music, but a tape-recorded phone conversation; quickly withdrawn from the market					

DYNAMICS, THE
BOLO

❏ BLP-8001 [M]	The Dynamics with Jimmy Hanna	1964	12.50	25.00	50.00

DYNATONES, THE
HANNA-BARBERA

❏ HLP-8509 [M]	The Fife Piper	1966	5.00	10.00	20.00
❏ HST-8509 [S]	The Fife Piper	1966	6.25	12.50	25.00

E

EAGLE
JANUS

Number	Title	Yr	VG	VG+	NM
❏ JLS-3011	Come Under Nancy's Tent	1970	5.00	10.00	20.00

EAGLES
Also see JOE WALSH.
ASYLUM

❏ EQ 1004 [Q]	On the Border	1974	5.00	10.00	20.00
❏ EQ 1039 [Q]	One of These Nights	1975	5.00	10.00	20.00

DCC COMPACT CLASSICS

❏ LPZ-2043	Hotel California	1997	6.25	12.50	25.00
-- Audiophile vinyl					
❏ LPZ-2051	Their Greatest Hits 1971-1975	1998	6.25	12.50	25.00
-- Audiophile vinyl					

MOBILE FIDELITY

❏ 1-126	Hotel California	1984	25.00	50.00	100.00
-- Audiophile vinyl					

EAGLIN, SNOOKS
BLUESVILLE

❏ BVLP-1046 [M]	That's All Right	1962	15.00	30.00	60.00
-- Blue label, silver print					
❏ BVLP-1046 [M]	That's All Right	1964	6.25	12.50	25.00
-- Blue label, trident logo at right					

FOLKWAYS

❏ FA-2476 [M]	New Orleans Street Singer	1959	10.00	20.00	40.00

EARLS, THE
OLD TOWN

❏ LP-104 [M]	Remember Me Baby	1963	125.00	250.00	500.00
-- Counterfeit identification: Counterfeits have more than 1-inch trailoffs; legitimate copies have 5/8-inch trailoff					

EARTH ISLAND
PHILPS

❏ PHS 600-340	We Must Survive	1970	6.25	12.50	25.00

EARTH OPERA
ELEKTRA

❏ EKS-74016	Earth Opera	1968	5.00	10.00	20.00
❏ EKS-74038	The Great American Eagle Tragedy	1969	5.00	10.00	20.00

EARTH, WIND & FIRE
ARC

❏ HC 45647	The Best of Earth, Wind & Fire, Vol. 1	1981	10.00	20.00	40.00
-- Half-speed mastered edition					
❏ HC 45730	I Am	1981	7.50	15.00	30.00
-- Half-speed mastered edition					
❏ HC 47548	Raise!	1982	7.50	15.00	30.00
-- Half-speed mastered edition					

COLUMBIA

❏ CQ 32194 [Q]	Head to the Sky	1973	5.00	10.00	20.00
❏ CQ 32712 [Q]	Open Our Eyes	1974	5.00	10.00	20.00
❏ PCQ 34241 [Q]	Spirit	1976	6.25	12.50	25.00
❏ HC 48367	Powerlight	1983	7.50	15.00	30.00
-- Half-speed mastered edition					

MOBILE FIDELITY

❏ 1-159	That's the Way of the World	198?	7.50	15.00	30.00
-- Audiophile vinyl					

WARNER BROS.

❏ WS 1905	Earth, Wind, and Fire	1971	5.00	10.00	20.00
-- Green label					
❏ WS 1958	The Need of Love	1971	5.00	10.00	20.00
-- Green label					
❏ 2WS 2798 [(2)]	Another Time	1974	5.00	10.00	20.00
-- "Burbank" palm trees labels					

EAST
CAPITOL

❏ ST-11083	East	1972	6.25	12.50	25.00

EAST OF EDEN
DERAM

❏ DES 18023	Mercator Projected	1969	5.00	10.00	20.00
❏ DES 18043	Snafu	1970	5.00	10.00	20.00

Number	Title	Yr	VG	VG+	NM

HARVEST

Number	Title	Yr	VG	VG+	NM
❏ SW-806	East of Eden	1971	5.00	10.00	20.00

EAST SIDE KIDS, THE
UNI

❏ 73032	The Tiger and the Lamb	1968	6.25	12.50	25.00

EASTMAN-ROCHESTER "POPS" ORCHESTRA (FREDERICK FENNELL, CONDUCTOR)
MERCURY LIVING PRESENCE

❏ SR 90043 [S]	Music of Leroy Anderson, Vol. 2	1959	7.50	15.00	30.00
-- *Maroon label, no "Vendor: Mercury Record Corporation"*					
❏ SR 90043 [S]	Music of Leroy Anderson, Vol. 2	196?	5.00	10.00	20.00
-- *Maroon label, with "Vendor: Mercury Record Corporation"*					
❏ SR 90144 [S]	Hi-Fi A La Espanola	196?	250.00	500.00	1,000.
-- *Maroon label, no "Vendor: Mercury Record Corporation"*					
❏ SR 90144 [S]	Hi-Fi A La Espanola	199?	6.25	12.50	25.00
-- *Classic Records reissue*					
❏ SR 90219 [S]	Grainger: Country Gardens	196?	12.50	25.00	50.00
-- *Maroon label, no "Vendor: Mercury Record Corporation"*					
❏ SR 90222 [S]	Popovers	196?	6.25	12.50	25.00
-- *Maroon label, no "Vendor: Mercury Record Corporation"*					
❏ SR 90271 [S]	Marches for Orchestra	196?	5.00	10.00	20.00
-- *Maroon label, no "Vendor: Mercury Record Corporation"*					
❏ SR 90271 [S]	Marches for Orchestra	196?	6.25	12.50	25.00
-- *Maroon label, with "Vendor: Mercury Record Corporation" (second edition is more sought after than the first)*					
❏ SR 90400 [S]	Music of Leroy Anderson, Volume	196?	37.50	75.00	150.00

EASTMAN-ROCHESTER ORCHESTRA (HOWARD HANSON, CONDUCTOR)
MERCURY LIVING PRESENCE

❏ SR 90018 [S]	Chadwick: Symphonic Sketches	1959	15.00	30.00	60.00
-- *Maroon label, no "Vendor: Mercury Record Corporation"*					
❏ SR 90049 [S]	Grofe: Grand Canyon Suite; Mississippi Suite	1959	12.50	25.00	50.00
-- *Maroon label, no "Vendor: Mercury Record Corporation"*					
❏ SR 90053 [S]	Music for Quiet Listening	1959	20.00	40.00	80.00
-- *Maroon label, no "Vendor: Mercury Record Corporation"*					
❏ SR 90053 [S]	Music for Quiet Listening	196?	10.00	20.00	40.00
-- *Maroon label, with "Vendor: Mercury Record Corporation"*					
❏ SR 90103 [S]	McPhee: Tabuh-Tauhan; Sessions: The Black Masters	196?	62.50	125.00	250.00
-- *Maroon label, no "Vendor: Mercury Record Corporation"*					
❏ SR 90134 [S]	Fiesta in Hi-Fi	1960	25.00	50.00	100.00
-- *Maroon label, no "Vendor: Mercury Record Corporation"*					
❏ SR 90136 [S]	Carpenter: Adventures in a Perambulator; Phillips: Selections from McGuffey's Readers	1960	12.50	25.00	50.00
-- *Maroon label, no "Vendor: Mercury Record Corporation"*					
❏ SR 90147 [S]	Kennan: Three Pieces; Rogers: Once Upon a Time; Bergama: Gold and the Senor Commandante	196?	50.00	100.00	200.00
-- *Maroon label, no "Vendor: Mercury Record Corporation"*					
❏ SR 90149 [S]	Ives: Three Places in New England; Symphony No. 3	196?	10.00	20.00	40.00
-- *Maroon label, no "Vendor: Mercury Record Corporation"*					
❏ SR 90149 [S]	Ives: Three Places in New England; Symphony No. 3	196?	6.25	12.50	25.00
-- *Maroon label, with "Vendor: Mercury Record Corporation"*					
❏ SR 90150 [S]	Hanson: Elegy in Memory of Koussevitzky; Song of Democracy; Lane: 4 Songs	196?	50.00	100.00	200.00
-- *Maroon label, no "Vendor: Mercury Record Corporation"*					
❏ SR 90150 [S]	Hanson: Elegy in Memory of Koussevitzky; Song of Democracy; Lane: 4 Songs	196?	22.50	45.00	90.00
-- *Maroon label, with "Vendor: Mercury Record Corporation"*					
❏ SR 90163 [S]	Herbert: Cello Concerto; Peter: Sinfonia in G	196?	17.50	35.00	70.00
-- *Maroon label, no "Vendor: Mercury Record Corporation"*					
❏ SR 90165 [S]	Hanson: Symphony No. 1 "Nordic"; Fantasy Variations on a Theme of Youth	196?	12.50	25.00	50.00
-- *Maroon label, no "Vendor: Mercury Record Corporation"*					
❏ SR 90165 [S]	Hanson: Symphony No. 1 "Nordic"; Fantasy Variations on a Theme of Youth	196?	5.00	10.00	20.00
-- *Maroon label, with "Vendor: Mercury Record Corporation"*					
❏ SR 90175 [S]	The Composer and His Orchestra	196?	17.50	35.00	70.00
-- *Maroon label, no "Vendor: Mercury Record Corporation"*					
❏ SR 90175 [S]	The Composer and His Orchestra	196?	6.25	12.50	25.00
-- *Maroon label, with "Vendor: Mercury Record Corporation"*					
❏ SR 90192 [S]	Hanson: Symphony No. 2 "Romantic"; Lament for Beowulf	196?	15.00	30.00	60.00
-- *Maroon label, no "Vendor: Mercury Record Corporation"*					
❏ SR 90192 [S]	Hanson: Symphony No. 2 "Romantic"; Lament for Beowulf	196?	6.25	12.50	25.00
-- *Maroon label, with "Vendor: Mercury Record Corporation"*					
❏ SR 90206 [S]	Piston: The Incredible Flutist; Moore: Pageant of P.T. Barnum	196?	17.50	35.00	70.00

❏ SR 90206 [S]	Piston: The Incredible Flutist; Moore: Pageant of P.T. Barnum	196?	10.00	20.00	40.00
❏ SR 90223 [S]	Bloch: Concerti Grossi No. 1 and 2	196?	17.50	35.00	70.00
-- *Maroon label, no "Vendor: Mercury Record Corporation"*					
❏ SR 90223 [S]	Bloch: Concerti Grossi No. 1 and 2	196?	12.50	25.00	50.00
-- *Maroon label, with "Vendor: Mercury Record Corporation"*					
❏ SR 90223 [S]	Bloch: Concerti Grossi No. 1 and 2	196?	7.50	15.00	30.00
-- *Third edition: Dark red (not maroon) label*					
❏ SR 90224 [S]	Barber: Medea; Capricorn	196?	7.50	15.00	30.00
-- *Maroon label, no "Vendor: Mercury Record Corporation"*					
❏ SR 90257 [S]	Ginastera: Overture to a Creole "Faust"; Guarnieri: Three Dances; Still: Sahdji Ballet	196?	62.50	125.00	250.00
-- *Maroon label, no "Vendor: Mercury Record Corporation"*					
❏ SR 90263 [S]	Gould, Morton: Fall River Legend; Spirituals	196?	17.50	35.00	70.00
-- *Maroon label, no "Vendor: Mercury Record Corporation"*					
❏ SR 90263 [S]	Gould, Morton: Fall River Legend; Spirituals	196?	7.50	15.00	30.00
-- *Maroon label, with "Vendor: Mercury Record Corporation"*					
❏ SR 90267 [S]	The Composer and His Orchestra, Volume 2	196?	17.50	35.00	70.00
-- *Maroon label, no "Vendor: Mercury Record Corporation"*					
❏ SR 90267 [S]	The Composer and His Orchestra, Volume 2	196?	5.00	10.00	20.00
-- *Maroon label, with "Vendor: Mercury Record Corporation"*					
❏ SR 90277 [S]	Loeffler: Deux Rapsodies; Barlow: Night Song; McCauley: Five Miniatures	196?	75.00	150.00	300.00
-- *Maroon label, no "Vendor: Mercury Record Corporation"*					
❏ SR 90286 [S]	Bloch: Schelomo; Herbert: Cello Concerto No. 2	196?	12.50	25.00	50.00
-- *Maroon label, no "Vendor: Mercury Record Corporation"*					
❏ SR 90379 [S]	Schuman: New England Tripytch; Mennin: Symphony No. 5; Griffes: Poem for Flute and Orchestra	196?	10.00	20.00	40.00
-- *Maroon label, no "Vendor: Mercury Record Corporation"*					
❏ SR 90379 [S]	Schuman: New England Tripytch; Mennin: Symphony No. 5; Griffes: Poem for Flute and Orchestra	196?	5.00	10.00	20.00
-- *Maroon label, with "Vendor: Mercury Record Corporation"*					
❏ SR 90429 [S]	Thomson: Symphony on a Hymn Tune; The Feast of Love; Hanson: Four Psalms	196?	10.00	20.00	40.00
-- *Maroon label, no "Vendor: Mercury Record Corporation"*					
❏ SR 90429 [S]	Thomson: Symphony on a Hymn Tune; The Feast of Love; Hanson: Four Psalms	196?	7.50	15.00	30.00
-- *Maroon label, with "Vendor: Mercury Record Corporation"*					
❏ SR 90429 [S]	Thomson: Symphony on a Hymn Tune; The Feast of Love; Hanson: Four Psalms	196?	5.00	10.00	20.00
-- *Third edition: Dark red (not maroon) label*					
❏ SR 90430 [S]	Hanson: Piano Concerto; Mosaics; LaMontaine: Birds of Paradise	196?	7.50	15.00	30.00
-- *Maroon label, no "Vendor: Mercury Record Corporation"*					
❏ SR 90430 [S]	Hanson: Piano Concerto; Mosaics; LaMontaine: Birds of Paradise	1965	17.50	35.00	70.00
-- *Maroon label, with "Vendor: Mercury Record Corporation"*					
❏ SR 90449 [S]	Hanson: Symphony No. 3; MacDowell: Symphony No. 1	1965	10.00	20.00	40.00
-- *Maroon label, with "Vendor: Mercury Record Corporation"*					

EASTMAN-ROCHESTER PHILHARMONIA (HOWARD HANSON, CONDUCTOR)
MERCURY LIVING PRESENCE

❏ SR 90299 [S]	Musical Diplomats USA	196?	10.00	20.00	40.00
-- *Maroon label, no "Vendor: Mercury Record Corporation"*					
❏ SR 90357 [S]	The Composer and His Orchestra, Volume 3	196?	6.25	12.50	25.00
-- *Maroon label, no "Vendor: Mercury Record Corporation"*					

EASTMAN-ROCHESTER WIND ENSEMBLE (FREDERICK FENNELL, CONDUCTOR)
MERCURY LIVING PRESENCE

❏ SR 90105 [S]	Marching Along	1960	5.00	10.00	20.00
-- *Maroon label, no "Vendor: Mercury Record Corporation"*					
❏ SR 90111 [S]	Spirit of '76: Music for Fifes and Drums	1960	7.50	15.00	30.00
-- *Maroon label, no "Vendor: Mercury Record Corporation"*					
❏ SR 90112 [S]	Ruffles and Flourishes	1960	10.00	20.00	40.00
-- *Maroon label, no "Vendor: Mercury Record Corporation"*					
❏ SR 90143 [S]	Hindemith: Symphony in B-flat; Schoenberg: Theme and Variations; Stravinsky: Symphony of Wind Instruments	196?	20.00	40.00	80.00
-- *Maroon label, no "Vendor: Mercury Record Corporation"*					
❏ SR 90143 [S]	Hindemith: Symphony in B-flat; Schoenberg: Theme and Variations; Stravinsky: Symphony of Wind Instruments	196?	10.00	20.00	40.00
-- *Maroon label, with "Vendor: Mercury Record Corporation"*					
❏ SR 90170 [S]	March Time	196?	7.50	15.00	30.00
-- *Maroon label, no "Vendor: Mercury Record Corporation"*					
❏ SR 90173 [S]	Winds in Hi-Fi	196?	25.00	50.00	100.00
-- *Maroon label, no "Vendor: Mercury Record Corporation"*					

Number	Title	Yr	VG	VG+	NM
❑ SR 90173 [S]	Winds in Hi-Fi	196?	12.50	25.00	50.00
-- *Maroon label, with "Vendor: Mercury Record Corporation"*					
❑ SR 90173 [S]	Winds in Hi-Fi	196?	6.25	12.50	25.00
-- *Third edition: Dark red (not maroon) label*					
❑ SR 90176 [S]	Mozart: Serenade No. 10 in E-flat	196?	12.50	25.00	50.00
-- *Maroon label, no "Vendor: Mercury Record Corporation"*					
❑ SR 90176 [S]	Mozart: Serenade No. 10 in E-flat	196?	5.00	10.00	20.00
-- *Maroon label, with "Vendor: Mercury Record Corporation"*					
❑ SR 90197 [S]	British Band Classics, Vol. 2	196?	18.75	37.50	75.00
-- *Maroon label, no "Vendor: Mercury Record Corporation"*					
❑ SR 90197 [S]	British Band Classics, Vol. 2	196?	15.00	30.00	60.00
-- *Maroon label, with "Vendor: Mercury Record Corporation"*					
❑ SR 90197 [S]	British Band Classics, Vol. 2	196?	7.50	15.00	30.00
-- *Third edition: Dark red (not maroon) label*					
❑ SR 90207 [S]	Hands Across the Sea	196?	12.50	25.00	50.00
-- *Maroon label, no "Vendor: Mercury Record Corporation"*					
❑ SR 90220 [S]	Gould: West Point Symphony; Bennett: Songs; Williams: Fanfare and Allegro; Work: Autumn Walk	196?	15.00	30.00	60.00
-- *Maroon label, with "Vendor: Mercury Record Corporation"*					
❑ SR 90220 [S]	Gould: West Point Symphony; Bennett: Songs; Williams: Fanfare and Allegro; Work: Autumn Walk	196?	50.00	100.00	200.00
-- *Maroon label, no "Vendor: Mercury Record Corporation"*					
❑ SR 90221 [S]	Diverse Winds	196?	25.00	50.00	100.00
-- *Maroon label, no "Vendor: Mercury Record Corporation"*					
❑ SR 90245 [S]	Gabrieli Music for Wind	196?	10.00	20.00	40.00
-- *Maroon label, no "Vendor: Mercury Record Corporation"*					
❑ SR 90256 [S]	Ballet for Band	196?	25.00	50.00	100.00
-- *Maroon label, no "Vendor: Mercury Record Corporation"*					
❑ SR 90264 [S]	Sousa Sound Off	196?	6.25	12.50	25.00
-- *Maroon label, no "Vendor: Mercury Record Corporation"*					
❑ SR 90276 [S]	Wagner for Band	196?	37.50	75.00	150.00
-- *Maroon label, no "Vendor: Mercury Record Corporation"*					
❑ SR 90276 [S]	Wagner for Band	196?	25.00	50.00	100.00
-- *Maroon label, with "Vendor: Mercury Record Corporation" (second edition is more sought after than the first)*					
❑ SR 90276 [S]	Wagner for Band	196?	10.00	20.00	40.00
-- *Third edition: Dark red (not maroon) label*					
❑ SR 90284 [S]	Sousa on Review	196?	30.00	60.00	120.00
-- *Maroon label, no "Vendor: Mercury Record Corporation"*					
❑ SR 90284 [S]	Sousa on Review	196?	20.00	40.00	80.00
-- *Maroon label, with "Vendor: Mercury Record Corporation"*					
❑ SR 90314 [S]	Screamers (Circus Marches)	196?	10.00	20.00	40.00
-- *Maroon label, no "Vendor: Mercury Record Corporation"*					
❑ SR 90314 [S]	Screamers (Circus Marches)	196?	6.25	12.50	25.00
-- *Maroon label, with "Vendor: Mercury Record Corporation"*					
❑ SR 90390 [S]	Broadway Marches	196?	6.25	12.50	25.00
-- *Maroon label, no "Vendor: Mercury Record Corporation"*					

EASTMAN-ROCHESTER WIND ENSEMBLE (A. CLYDE ROLLER, CONDUCTOR)
MERCURY LIVING PRESENCE

Number	Title	Yr	VG	VG+	NM
❑ SR 90366 [S]	Hovhaness: Symphony No. 4; Giannini: Symphony No. 3	196?	37.50	75.00	150.00
-- *Maroon label, no "Vendor: Mercury Record Corporation"*					
❑ SR 90366 [S]	Hovhaness: Symphony No. 4; Giannini: Symphony No. 3	196?	30.00	60.00	120.00
-- *Maroon label, with "Vendor: Mercury Record Corporation"*					
❑ SR 90366 [S]	Hovhaness: Symphony No. 4; Giannini: Symphony No. 3	196?	12.50	25.00	50.00
-- *Third edition: Dark red (not maroon) label*					

EASTWOOD, CLINT
CAMEO

Number	Title	Yr	VG	VG+	NM
❑ C-1056 [M]	Clint Eastwood Sings Cowboy Favorites	1963	25.00	50.00	100.00
❑ SC-1056 [S]	Clint Eastwood Sings Cowboy Favorites	1963	37.50	75.00	150.00

EASY RIDERS, THE -- See TERRY GILKYSON.

EASYBEATS, THE
UNITED ARTISTS

Number	Title	Yr	VG	VG+	NM
❑ UAL 3588 [M]	Friday on My Mind	1967	10.00	20.00	40.00
❑ UAS 6588 [P]	Friday on My Mind	1967	12.50	25.00	50.00
-- *"Make You Feel Alright" is rechanneled.*					
❑ UAS 6667 [P]	Falling Off the Edge of the World	1968	10.00	20.00	40.00
-- *"Women" is rechanneled.*					

EBON-KNIGHTS, THE
STEPHENY

Number	Title	Yr	VG	VG+	NM
❑ 4001 [M]	First Date	1959	375.00	750.00	1,500.

EBSEN, BUDDY
REPRISE

Number	Title	Yr	VG	VG+	NM
❑ R-6174 [M]	Buddy Ebsen Sings Howdy!	1965	7.50	15.00	30.00

Number	Title	Yr	VG	VG+	NM
❑ RS-6174 [S]	Buddy Ebsen Sings Howdy!	1965	10.00	20.00	40.00

ECKSTINE, BILLY
AUDIO LAB

Number	Title	Yr	VG	VG+	NM
❑ AL-1549 [M]	Mr. B	1960	30.00	60.00	120.00

DELUXE

| ❑ FA-2010 [M] | Billy Eckstine and His Orchestra | 195? | 20.00 | 40.00 | 80.00 |

EMARCY

❑ MG-26025 [10]	Blues for Sale	1954	30.00	60.00	120.00
❑ MG-26027 [10]	The Love Songs of Mr. B	1954	30.00	60.00	120.00
❑ MG-36010 [M]	I Surrender, Dear	1955	20.00	40.00	80.00
❑ MG-36029 [M]	Blues for Sale	1955	20.00	40.00	80.00
❑ MG-36030 [M]	The Love Songs of Mr. B	1955	20.00	40.00	80.00
❑ MG-36129 [M]	Billy Eckstine's Imagination	1958	15.00	30.00	60.00

KING

| ❑ 295-12 [10] | The Great Mr. B | 1953 | 75.00 | 150.00 | 300.00 |

LION

| ❑ L-70057 [M] | The Best of Billy Eckstine | 1958 | 6.25 | 12.50 | 25.00 |

MERCURY

❑ MG-20333 [M]	Billy's Best	1958	10.00	20.00	40.00
❑ MG-20637 [M]	Broadway, Bongos and Mr. B	1961	6.25	12.50	25.00
❑ MG-20674 [M]	Billy Eckstine and Quincy Jones at Basin St. East	1962	6.25	12.50	25.00
❑ MG-20736 [M]	Don't Worry 'Bout Me	1962	6.25	12.50	25.00
❑ SR-60086 [S]	Billy's Best	1958	12.50	25.00	50.00
❑ SR-60637 [S]	Broadway, Bongos and Mr. B	1961	7.50	15.00	30.00
❑ SR-60674 [S]	Billy Eckstine and Quincy Jones at Basin St. East	1962	7.50	15.00	30.00
❑ SR-60736 [S]	Don't Worry 'Bout Me	1962	7.50	15.00	30.00
❑ SR-60796 [S]	The Golden Hits of Billy Eckstine	1963	5.00	10.00	20.00

MGM

❑ E-153 [10]	Billy Eckstine Sings Rodgers & Hammerstein	1952	37.50	75.00	150.00
❑ E-219 [10]	Tenderly	1953	37.50	75.00	150.00
❑ E-257 [10]	I Let a Song Go Out of My Heart	1954	37.50	75.00	150.00
❑ E-523 [10]	Songs by Billy Eckstine	1951	40.00	80.00	160.00
❑ E-548 [10]	Favorites	1951	40.00	80.00	160.00
❑ E-3176 [M]	Mr. B with a Beat	1955	12.50	25.00	50.00
❑ E-3209 [M]	Rendezvous	1955	12.50	25.00	50.00
❑ E-3275 [M]	That Old Feeling	1956	12.50	25.00	50.00

MOTOWN

❑ M 632 [M]	Prime of My Life	1965	5.00	10.00	20.00
❑ MS 632 [S]	Prime of My Life	1965	6.25	12.50	25.00
❑ M 646 [M]	My Way	1966	5.00	10.00	20.00
❑ MS 646 [S]	My Way	1966	6.25	12.50	25.00
❑ MS 677	For Love of Ivy	1969	6.25	12.50	25.00

NATIONAL

| ❑ NLP-2001 [10] | Billy Eckstine Sings | 1949 | 50.00 | 100.00 | 200.00 |

REGENT

❑ MG-6052 [M]	Prisoner of Love	1957	12.50	25.00	50.00
❑ MG-6053 [M]	The Duke, the Blues and Me	1957	12.50	25.00	50.00
❑ MG-6054 [M]	My Deep Blue Dream	1957	12.50	25.00	50.00
❑ MG-6058 [M]	You Call It Madness	1957	12.50	25.00	50.00

ROULETTE

❑ R-25052 [M]	No Cover, No Minimum	1961	6.25	12.50	25.00
❑ SR-25052 [S]	No Cover, No Minimum	1961	7.50	15.00	30.00
❑ R-25104 [M]	Once More with Feeling	1962	6.25	12.50	25.00
❑ SR-25104 [S]	Once More with Feeling	1962	7.50	15.00	30.00

EDDIE AND BETTY
WARNER BROS.

| ❑ W 1350 [M] | Nightlife for Daydreamers | 1959 | 6.25 | 12.50 | 25.00 |
| ❑ WS 1350 [S] | Nightlife for Daydreamers | 1959 | 7.50 | 15.00 | 30.00 |

EDDIE AND THE SUBTITLES
(NO LABEL)

| ❑ (no #) | Skeletons in the Closet | 1981 | 10.00 | 20.00 | 40.00 |

13TH STORY

| ❑ MR 3301 | Dead Drunks Don't Dance | 1983 | 6.25 | 12.50 | 25.00 |

EDDY, DUANE
COLPIX

❑ CP-490 [M]	Duane A-Go-Go	1965	7.50	15.00	30.00
❑ CPS-490 [S]	Duane A-Go-Go	1965	10.00	20.00	40.00
❑ CP-494 [M]	Duane Eddy Does Bob Dylan	1965	7.50	15.00	30.00
❑ CPS-494 [S]	Duane Eddy Does Bob Dylan	1965	10.00	20.00	40.00

JAMIE

| ❑ JLP-3000 [M] | Have "Twangy" Guitar -- Will Travel | 1958 | 30.00 | 60.00 | 120.00 |
| -- *Duane sitting with guitar case, title on cover in white (1st)* | | | | | |

Number	Title	Yr	VG	VG+	NM
❏ JLP-3000 [M]	Have "Twangy" Guitar -- Will Travel	1959	25.00	50.00	100.00
-- *Duane sitting with guitar case, title on cover in green and red (2nd)*					
❏ JLP-3000 [M]	Have "Twangy" Guitar -- Will Travel	1959	12.50	25.00	50.00
-- *Duane standing with guitar (3rd)*					
❏ JLPS-3000 [S]	Have "Twangy" Guitar -- Will Travel	1958	100.00	200.00	400.00
-- *Duane sitting with guitar case, title on cover in white (1st)*					
❏ JLPS-3000 [S]	Have "Twangy" Guitar -- Will Travel	1959	75.00	150.00	300.00
-- *Duane sitting with guitar case, title on cover in green and red (2nd)*					
❏ JLPS-3000 [S]	Have "Twangy" Guitar -- Will Travel	1959	25.00	50.00	100.00
-- *Duane standing with guitar (3rd), album plays true stereo*					
❏ JLPS-3000 [R]	Have "Twangy" Guitar -- Will Travel	196?	12.50	25.00	50.00
-- *Duane standing with guitar (3rd), album plays fake stereo*					
❏ JLPM-3006 [M]	Especially for You...	1959	10.00	20.00	40.00
❏ JLPS-3006 [S]	Especially for You...	1959	15.00	30.00	60.00
❏ JLPM-3009 [M]	The "Twangs" The "Thang"	1959	10.00	20.00	40.00
❏ JLPS-3009 [S]	The "Twangs" The "Thang"	1959	15.00	30.00	60.00
❏ JLPM-3011 [M]	Songs of Our Heritage	1960	20.00	40.00	80.00
-- *Gatefold cover*					
❏ JLPM-3011 [M]	Songs of Our Heritage	196?	7.50	15.00	30.00
-- *Regular cover*					
❏ JLPS-3011 [S]	Songs of Our Heritage	1960	25.00	50.00	100.00
-- *Gatefold cover*					
❏ JLPS-3011 [S]	Songs of Our Heritage	1960	125.00	250.00	500.00
-- *Gatefold cover, blue vinyl*					
❏ JLPS-3011 [S]	Songs of Our Heritage	1960	125.00	250.00	500.00
-- *Gatefold cover, red vinyl*					
❏ JLPS-3011 [S]	Songs of Our Heritage	196?	10.00	20.00	40.00
-- *Regular cover*					
❏ JLPM-3014 [M]	$1,000,000.00 Worth of Twang	1960	10.00	20.00	40.00
❏ JLPS-3014 [R]	$1,000,000.00 Worth of Twang	1960	7.50	15.00	30.00
❏ JLPM-3019 [M]	Girls! Girls! Girls!	1961	10.00	20.00	40.00
❏ JLPS-3019 [R]	Girls! Girls! Girls!	1961	7.50	15.00	30.00
❏ JLPM-3021 [M]	$1,000,000.00 Worth of Twang, Volume 2	1962	10.00	20.00	40.00
❏ JLPS-3021 [R]	$1,000,000.00 Worth of Twang, Volume 2	1962	7.50	15.00	30.00
❏ JLPM-3022 [M]	Twistin' with Duane Eddy	1962	10.00	20.00	40.00
❏ JLPS-3022 [P]	Twistin' with Duane Eddy	1962	10.00	20.00	40.00
❏ JLPM-3024 [M]	Surfin'	1963	12.50	25.00	50.00
❏ JLPS-3024 [S]	Surfin'	1963	20.00	40.00	80.00
❏ JLPM-3025 [M]	Duane Eddy & The Rebels -- In Person	1963	7.50	15.00	30.00
❏ JLPS-3025 [S]	Duane Eddy & The Rebels -- In Person	1963	10.00	20.00	40.00
❏ JLPM-3026 [M]	16 Greatest Hits	1964	10.00	20.00	40.00
❏ JLPS-3026 [R]	16 Greatest Hits	1964	7.50	15.00	30.00
❏ ST-90663 [S]	Duane Eddy & The Rebels -- In Person	1965	12.50	25.00	50.00
❏ T-90663 [M]	Duane Eddy & The Rebels -- In Person	1965	10.00	20.00	40.00
-- *Capitol Record Club edition*					
❏ ST-90682 [S]	Have "Twangy" Guitar -- Will Travel	1965	20.00	40.00	80.00
-- *Capitol Record Club edition*					
❏ T-90682 [M]	Have "Twangy" Guitar -- Will Travel	1965	15.00	30.00	60.00
-- *Capitol Record Club edition*					
❏ ST-91301 [S]	The "Twangs" The "Thang"	1966	15.00	30.00	60.00
-- *Capitol Record Club edition*					
❏ T-91301 [M]	The "Twangs" The "Thang"	1966	15.00	30.00	60.00
-- *Capitol Record Club edition*					
RCA VICTOR					
❏ LPM-2525 [M]	Twistin' 'N' Twangin'	1962	6.25	12.50	25.00
❏ LSP-2525 [S]	Twistin' 'N' Twangin'	1962	10.00	20.00	40.00
❏ LPM-2576 [M]	Twangy Guitar -- Silky Strings	1962	6.25	12.50	25.00
❏ LSP-2576 [S]	Twangy Guitar -- Silky Strings	1962	10.00	20.00	40.00
❏ LPM-2648 [M]	Dance with the Guitar Man	1962	6.25	12.50	25.00
❏ LSP-2648 [S]	Dance with the Guitar Man	1962	10.00	20.00	40.00
❏ LPM-2681 [M]	Twang a Country Song	1963	6.25	12.50	25.00
❏ LSP-2681 [S]	Twang a Country Song	1963	10.00	20.00	40.00
❏ LPM-2700 [M]	"Twangin' " Up a Storm!	1963	6.25	12.50	25.00
❏ LSP-2700 [S]	"Twangin' " Up a Storm!	1963	10.00	20.00	40.00
❏ LPM-2798 [M]	Lonely Guitar	1964	5.00	10.00	20.00
❏ LSP-2798 [S]	Lonely Guitar	1964	7.50	15.00	30.00
❏ LPM-2918 [M]	Water Skiing	1964	5.00	10.00	20.00
❏ LSP-2918 [S]	Water Skiing	1964	7.50	15.00	30.00
❏ LPM-2993 [M]	Twangin' the Golden Hits	1965	5.00	10.00	20.00
❏ LSP-2993 [S]	Twangin' the Golden Hits	1965	7.50	15.00	30.00
❏ LPM-3432 [M]	Twangsville	1965	5.00	10.00	20.00
❏ LSP-3432 [S]	Twangsville	1965	7.50	15.00	30.00
❏ LPM-3477 [M]	The Best of Duane Eddy	1965	5.00	10.00	20.00

Number	Title	Yr	VG	VG+	NM
❏ LSP-3477 [P]	The Best of Duane Eddy	1965	6.25	12.50	25.00
-- *Black "Stereo" label*					
REPRISE					
❏ R-6218 [M]	The Biggest Twang of Them All	1966	7.50	15.00	30.00
❏ RS-6218 [S]	The Biggest Twang of Them All	1966	10.00	20.00	40.00
❏ R-6240 [M]	The Roaring Twangies	1967	7.50	15.00	30.00
❏ RS-6240 [S]	The Roaring Twangies	1967	10.00	20.00	40.00
SIRE					
❏ SASH-3702 [(2)]	The Vintage Years	1975	6.25	12.50	25.00

EDDY, NELSON
HARMONY

Number	Title	Yr	VG	VG+	NM
❏ HL 7201 [M]	Nelson Eddy Sings the Best Loved Carols of Christmas	195?	5.00	10.00	20.00

EDEN'S CHILDREN
ABC

Number	Title	Yr	VG	VG+	NM
❏ 624 [M]	Eden's Children	1968	10.00	20.00	40.00
❏ S-624 [S]	Eden's Children	1968	6.25	12.50	25.00
❏ S-652	Sure Looks Real	1968	5.00	10.00	20.00

EDEN, BARBARA
DOT

Number	Title	Yr	VG	VG+	NM
❏ DLP-3795 [M]	Miss Barbara Eden	1967	10.00	20.00	40.00
❏ DLP-25795 [S]	Miss Barbara Eden	1967	12.50	25.00	50.00

EDGE, THE
NOSE

Number	Title	Yr	VG	VG+	NM
❏ NRS-48003	The Edge	1970	10.00	20.00	40.00

EDMONSON, TRAVIS
Also see BUD AND TRAVIS.
HORIZON

Number	Title	Yr	VG	VG+	NM
❏ WP-1606 [M]	Travis On Cue	1962	5.00	10.00	20.00
❏ WPS-1606 [S]	Travis On Cue	1962	6.25	12.50	25.00
REPRISE					
❏ R-6035 [M]	Travis On His Own	1962	6.25	12.50	25.00
❏ R9-6035 [S]	Travis On His Own	1962	7.50	15.00	30.00

EDMUNDS, DAVE
ATLANTIC

Number	Title	Yr	VG	VG+	NM
❏ PR 320 [DJ]	College Network	1978	12.50	25.00	50.00
-- *Promo-only interview album*					
COLUMBIA					
❏ AS99 1725 [PD]	Information	1983	6.25	12.50	25.00
-- *Promo-only picture disc*					
MAM					
❏ 3	Rockpile	1972	10.00	20.00	40.00

EDWARDS, JONATHAN AND DARLENE
Actually JO STAFFORD and PAUL WESTON.
COLUMBIA

Number	Title	Yr	VG	VG+	NM
❏ CL 1024 [M]	The Piano Artistry of Jonathan Edwards	1955	12.50	25.00	50.00
❏ CL 1513 [M]	Jonathan and Darlene Edwards In Paris	1960	6.25	12.50	25.00
❏ CS 8313 [S]	Jonathan and Darlene Edwards In Paris	1960	7.50	15.00	30.00
DOT					
❏ DLP-25792 [S]	Songs for Sheiks and Flappers	1967	5.00	10.00	20.00
RCA VICTOR					
❏ LPM-2495 [M]	Sing Along with Jonathan and Darlene	1962	5.00	10.00	20.00
❏ LSP-2495 [S]	Sing Along with Jonathan and Darlene	1962	6.25	12.50	25.00

EDWARDS, STONEY
CAPITOL

Number	Title	Yr	VG	VG+	NM
❏ ST-741	Country Singer	1970	6.25	12.50	25.00
❏ ST-834	Down Home in the Country	1971	5.00	10.00	20.00
❏ ST-11090	Stoney Edwards	1972	5.00	10.00	20.00
❏ ST-11173	She's My Rock	1973	5.00	10.00	20.00
❏ ST-11401	Mississippi on My Mind	1975	5.00	10.00	20.00
❏ ST-11499	Blackbird	1976	5.00	10.00	20.00

EDWARDS, TOMMY
LION

Number	Title	Yr	VG	VG+	NM
❏ L-70120 [M]	Tommy Edwards	1959	7.50	15.00	30.00

Number	Title	Yr	VG	VG+	NM
MGM					
❑ E-3732 [M]	It's All in the Game	1958	7.50	15.00	30.00
-- Yellow label					
❑ E-3732 [M]	It's All in the Game	1960	5.00	10.00	20.00
-- Black label					
❑ SE-3732 [S]	It's All in the Game	1959	10.00	20.00	40.00
-- Yellow label					
❑ SE-3732 [S]	It's All in the Game	1960	6.25	12.50	25.00
-- Black label					
❑ E-3760 [M]	For Young Lovers	1959	7.50	15.00	30.00
-- Yellow label					
❑ E-3760 [M]	For Young Lovers	1960	5.00	10.00	20.00
-- Black label					
❑ SE-3760 [S]	For Young Lovers	1959	10.00	20.00	40.00
-- Yellow label					
❑ SE-3760 [S]	For Young Lovers	1960	6.25	12.50	25.00
-- Black label					
❑ E-3805 [M]	You Started Me Dreaming	1960	5.00	10.00	20.00
❑ SE-3805 [S]	You Started Me Dreaming	1960	6.25	12.50	25.00
❑ E-3822 [M]	Step Out Singing	1960	5.00	10.00	20.00
❑ SE-3822 [S]	Step Out Singing	1960	6.25	12.50	25.00
❑ E-3838 [M]	Tommy Edwards in Hawaii	1960	5.00	10.00	20.00
❑ SE-3838 [S]	Tommy Edwards in Hawaii	1960	6.25	12.50	25.00
❑ E-3884 [M]	Tommy Edwards' Greatest Hits	1961	5.00	10.00	20.00
❑ SE-3884 [S]	Tommy Edwards' Greatest Hits	1961	6.25	12.50	25.00
❑ E-3959 [M]	Golden Country Hits	1961	5.00	10.00	20.00
❑ SE-3959 [S]	Golden Country Hits	1961	6.25	12.50	25.00
❑ E-4020 [M]	Stardust	1962	5.00	10.00	20.00
❑ SE-4020 [S]	Stardust	1962	6.25	12.50	25.00
❑ E-4060 [M]	Soft Strings and Two Guitars	1962	5.00	10.00	20.00
❑ SE-4060 [S]	Soft Strings and Two Guitars	1962	6.25	12.50	25.00
❑ SE-4141 [S]	The Very Best of Tommy Edwards	1963	5.00	10.00	20.00
REGENT					
❑ MG-6096 [M]	Tommy Edwards Sings	1958	15.00	30.00	60.00

EDWARDS, VINCENT
DECCA

Number	Title	Yr	VG	VG+	NM
❑ DL 4311 [M]	Vincent Edwards Sings	1962	5.00	10.00	20.00
❑ DL 4336 [M]	Sometimes I'm Happy... Sometimes I'm Blue	1962	5.00	10.00	20.00
❑ DL 4399 [M]	In Person at the Riviera	1963	5.00	10.00	20.00
❑ DL 74311 [S]	Vincent Edwards Sings	1962	6.25	12.50	25.00
❑ DL 74336 [S]	Sometimes I'm Happy... Sometimes I'm Blue	1962	6.25	12.50	25.00
❑ DL 74399 [S]	In Person at the Riviera	1963	6.25	12.50	25.00

EIRE APPARENT, THE
BUDDAH

Number	Title	Yr	VG	VG+	NM
❑ BDS-5031	Sunrise	1969	10.00	20.00	40.00
-- Produced by JIMI HENDRIX.					

EL CAMPO JADES, THE
GOLDEN EAGLE

Number	Title	Yr	VG	VG+	NM
❑ LP-101 [M]	The El Campo Jades	1966	12.50	25.00	50.00

EL DORADOS
VEE JAY

Number	Title	Yr	VG	VG+	NM
❑ LP-1001 [M]	Crazy Little Mama	1959	200.00	400.00	800.00
-- Maroon label, thick silver band					
❑ LP-1001 [M]	Crazy Little Mama	1960	100.00	200.00	400.00
-- Maroon label, thin silver band					
❑ LP-1001 [M]	Crazy Little Mama	1962	62.50	125.00	250.00
-- Black label with colorband					

ELBERT, DONNIE
ALL PLATINUM

Number	Title	Yr	VG	VG+	NM
❑ 3007	Where Did Our Love Go	1971	6.25	12.50	25.00
❑ 3019	Dancin' the Night Away	1977	6.25	12.50	25.00
DELUXE					
❑ 12003	Have I Sinned	1971	6.25	12.50	25.00
KING					
❑ 629 [M]	The Sensational Donnie Elbert Sings	1959	100.00	200.00	400.00

ELECTRIC LIGHT ORCHESTRA
JET

Number	Title	Yr	VG	VG+	NM
❑ JT-LA823-L2 [(2)DJ]	Out of the Blue	1977	6.25	12.50	25.00
-- Promo only on blue vinyl					
❑ Z4X 36966 [(4)]	A Box of Their Best	1980	6.25	12.50	25.00
❑ HZ 45789	Discovery	1980	7.50	15.00	30.00
-- Half-speed mastered edition					
❑ HZ 46310	ELO's Greatest Hits	1981	10.00	20.00	40.00
-- Half-speed mastered edition					

Number	Title	Yr	VG	VG+	NM
❑ HZ 47371	Time	1982	7.50	15.00	30.00
-- Half-speed mastered edition					
❑ HZ 48490	Secret Messages	1983	7.50	15.00	30.00
-- Half-speed mastered edition					
UNITED ARTISTS					
❑ SP-123 [DJ]	Ole Elo	1976	25.00	50.00	100.00
-- Gold vinyl, cover similar to the released version except for the single line "Ole Elo" (no "Electric Light Orchestra" underneath) at the top of the front cover					
❑ SP-123 [DJ]	Ole Elo	1976	12.50	25.00	50.00
-- Gold vinyl promo with generic cover					
❑ SP-123 [DJ]	Ole Elo	1976	20.00	40.00	80.00
-- Red, blue or white vinyl promos with generic cover					
❑ UA-LA546-DJ [DJ]	Face the Music	1975	6.25	12.50	25.00
-- Promo only, banded for airplay					

ELECTRIC PRUNES, THE
REPRISE

Number	Title	Yr	VG	VG+	NM
❑ R-6248 [M]	The Electric Prunes	1967	12.50	25.00	50.00
❑ RS-6248 [S]	The Electric Prunes	1967	10.00	20.00	40.00
❑ R-6262 [M]	Underground	1967	12.50	25.00	50.00
❑ RS-6262 [S]	Underground	1967	10.00	20.00	40.00
❑ R-6275 [M]	Mass in F Minor	1967	10.00	20.00	40.00
❑ RS-6275 [S]	Mass in F Minor	1967	7.50	15.00	30.00
❑ RS-6316	Release of an Oath	1968	7.50	15.00	30.00
❑ RS-6342	Just Good Rock 'n Roll	1969	7.50	15.00	30.00

ELECTRIC TOILET, THE
NASCO

Number	Title	Yr	VG	VG+	NM
❑ 9004	In the Hands of Karma	1970	50.00	100.00	200.00

ELECTRIC UNDERGROUND, THE
PREMIER

Number	Title	Yr	VG	VG+	NM
❑ P-9060 [M]	Guitar Explosion	1967	12.50	25.00	50.00
❑ PS-9060 [S]	Guitar Explosion	1967	12.50	25.00	50.00

ELECTROSONICS, THE
PHILIPS

Number	Title	Yr	VG	VG+	NM
❑ PHM 200-047 [M]	Electronic Music	1962	17.50	35.00	70.00
❑ PHS 600-047 [S]	Electronic Music	1962	22.50	45.00	90.00

ELEPHANTS MEMORY
APPLE

Number	Title	Yr	VG	VG+	NM
❑ SMAS-3389	Elephants Memory	1972	6.25	12.50	25.00
METROMEDIA					
❑ MD-1035	Take It to the Streets	1970	5.00	10.00	20.00

ELEVENTH HOUSE, THE (WITH LARRY CORYELL)
VANGUARD

Number	Title	Yr	VG	VG+	NM
❑ VSQ-40036 [Q]	Introducing the Eleventh House with Larry Coryell	1974	6.25	12.50	25.00

ELF
EPIC

Number	Title	Yr	VG	VG+	NM
❑ KE 31789	Elf	1972	5.00	10.00	20.00

ELGART, LARRY
BRUNSWICK

Number	Title	Yr	VG	VG+	NM
❑ BL 58054 [10]	Impressions of Outer Space	1954	15.00	30.00	60.00
DECCA					
❑ DL 8034 [M]	Music for Barefoot Ballerinas	1955	10.00	20.00	40.00

ELGART, LES
COLUMBIA

Number	Title	Yr	VG	VG+	NM
❑ CL 536 [M]	Sophisticated Swing	1953	7.50	15.00	30.00
-- Maroon label, gold print					
❑ CL 594 [M]	Just One More Dance	1954	7.50	15.00	30.00
-- Maroon label, gold print					
❑ CL 619 [M]	Band of the Year	1955	10.00	20.00	40.00
-- Maroon label, gold print; first LP appearance of "Bandstand Boogie"					
❑ CL 684 [M]	The Dancing Sound	1955	7.50	15.00	30.00
-- Red and black label, six "eye" logos					
❑ CL 803 [M]	For Dancers Only	1956	7.50	15.00	30.00
-- Red and black label, six "eye" logos					
❑ CL 873 [M]	The Elgart Touch	1956	7.50	15.00	30.00
-- Red and black label, six "eye" logos					
❑ CL 1008 [M]	For Dancers Also	1957	6.25	12.50	25.00
❑ CL 1350 [M]	The Great Sound of Les Elgart	1959	5.00	10.00	20.00
❑ CL 1450 [M]	The Band with That Sound	1960	5.00	10.00	20.00
❑ CL 1500 [M]	Designs for Dancing	1960	5.00	10.00	20.00
❑ CL 1567 [M]	Half Satin - Half Latin	1961	5.00	10.00	20.00
❑ CL 1659 [M]	It's De-Lovely	1961	5.00	10.00	20.00

Number	Title	Yr	VG	VG+	NM
❑ CL 1785 [M]	The Twist Goes to College	1962	5.00	10.00	20.00
❑ CL 1890 [M]	Best Band on Campus	1963	5.00	10.00	20.00
❑ CL 6287 [10]	Just One More Dance	195?	10.00	20.00	40.00
❑ CS 8159 [S]	The Great Sound of Les Elgart	1959	6.25	12.50	25.00
❑ CS 8245 [S]	The Band with That Sound	1960	6.25	12.50	25.00
❑ CS 8291 [S]	Designs for Dancing	1960	6.25	12.50	25.00
❑ CS 8367 [S]	Half Satin - Half Latin	1961	6.25	12.50	25.00
❑ CS 8459 [S]	It's De-Lovely	1961	6.25	12.50	25.00
❑ CS 8585 [S]	The Twist Goes to College	1962	6.25	12.50	25.00
❑ CS 8690 [S]	Best Band on Campus	1963	6.25	12.50	25.00

ELGINS, THE
V.I.P.

Number	Title	Yr	VG	VG+	NM
❑ 400 [M]	Darling Baby	1966	12.50	25.00	50.00
❑ S-400 [S]	Darling Baby	1966	20.00	40.00	80.00

ELIAS, ROSALIND, AND GIORGIO TOZZI
RCA VICTOR RED SEAL

Number	Title	Yr	VG	VG+	NM
❑ LSC-2350 [S]	A Yuletide Song Fest	1959	15.00	30.00	60.00
-- Original with "shaded dog" label					

ELIGIBLES, THE
CAPITOL

Number	Title	Yr	VG	VG+	NM
❑ ST 1310 [S]	Along the Trail	1960	7.50	15.00	30.00
❑ T 1310 [M]	Along the Trail	1960	6.25	12.50	25.00
❑ ST 1411 [S]	Love Is a Gamble	1960	7.50	15.00	30.00
❑ T 1411 [M]	Love Is a Gamble	1960	6.25	12.50	25.00

ELIMINATORS, THE
LIBERTY

Number	Title	Yr	VG	VG+	NM
❑ LRP-3365 [M]	Liverpool! Dragsters! Cycles! Surfing!	1964	20.00	40.00	80.00
❑ LST-7365 [S]	Liverpool! Dragsters! Cycles! Surfing!	1964	25.00	50.00	100.00

ELIZABETH
VANGUARD

Number	Title	Yr	VG	VG+	NM
❑ VSD-6501	Elizabeth	1968	15.00	30.00	60.00

ELLIE POP
MAINSTREAM

Number	Title	Yr	VG	VG+	NM
❑ S-6115	Ellie Pop	1968	10.00	20.00	40.00

ELLINGTON, DUKE
ALLEGRO

Number	Title	Yr	VG	VG+	NM
❑ 1591 [M]	Duke Ellington and His Orchestra Play	1955	12.50	25.00	50.00
❑ 3082 [M]	Duke Ellington	1953	12.50	25.00	50.00
❑ 4014 [10]	Duke Ellington and His Orchestra Play	1954	25.00	50.00	100.00
❑ 4038 [10]	Duke Ellington and His Orchestra Play	1954	25.00	50.00	100.00

ATLANTIC

Number	Title	Yr	VG	VG+	NM
❑ QD 1580 [Q]	New Orleans Suite	1974	6.25	12.50	25.00

BETHLEHEM

Number	Title	Yr	VG	VG+	NM
❑ BCP-60 [M]	Historically Speaking, The Duke	1956	15.00	30.00	60.00
❑ BCP-6005 [M]	Duke Ellington Presents	1956	15.00	30.00	60.00

BLUEBIRD

Number	Title	Yr	VG	VG+	NM
❑ 5659-1-RB [(4)]	Duke Ellington: The Blanton-Webster Band	1986	6.25	12.50	25.00
❑ 6641-1-RB [(4)]	Black, Brown and Beige	1988	6.25	12.50	25.00

BRUNSWICK

Number	Title	Yr	VG	VG+	NM
❑ BL 54007 [M]	Early Ellington	1954	12.50	25.00	50.00
❑ BL 58002 [10]	Ellingtonia, Volume 1	1950	25.00	50.00	100.00
❑ BL 58012 [10]	Ellingtonia, Volume 2	1950	25.00	50.00	100.00

CAPITOL

Number	Title	Yr	VG	VG+	NM
❑ H 440 [10]	Premiered by Ellington	1953	25.00	50.00	100.00
❑ H 477 [10]	Ellington Plays Ellington	1954	25.00	50.00	100.00
❑ T 477 [M]	The Duke Plays Ellington	1954	10.00	20.00	40.00
-- Turquoise label					
❑ T 477 [M]	The Duke Plays Ellington	1958	5.00	10.00	20.00
-- Black label with colorband, logo at left					
❑ T 521 [M]	Ellington '55	1955	10.00	20.00	40.00
-- Turquoise label					
❑ T 521 [M]	Ellington '55	1958	5.00	10.00	20.00
-- Black label with colorband, logo at left					
❑ T 637 [M]	Dance to the Duke	1955	10.00	20.00	40.00
-- Turquoise label					
❑ T 637 [M]	Dance to the Duke	1958	5.00	10.00	20.00
-- Black label with colorband, logo at left					

Number	Title	Yr	VG	VG+	NM
❑ T 679 [M]	Ellington Showcase	1956	10.00	20.00	40.00
-- Turquoise label					
❑ T 679 [M]	Ellington Showcase	1958	5.00	10.00	20.00
-- Black label with colorband, logo at left					
❑ T 1602 [M]	The Best of Duke Ellington	1961	5.00	10.00	20.00

COLUMBIA

Number	Title	Yr	VG	VG+	NM
❑ C3L 27 [M (3)]	The Ellington Era, Vol. 1	1963	10.00	20.00	40.00
❑ C3L 39 [M (3)]	The Ellington Era, Vol. 2	1964	10.00	20.00	40.00
❑ CL 558 [M]	The Music of Duke Ellington	1954	12.50	25.00	50.00
-- Maroon label with gold print					
❑ CL 558 [M]	The Music of Duke Ellington	1956	10.00	20.00	40.00
-- Red and black label with six "eye" logos					
❑ CL 663 [M]	Blue Light	1955	10.00	20.00	40.00
❑ CL 825 [M]	Masterpieces by Ellington	1956	10.00	20.00	40.00
-- Reissue of Columbia Masterworks 4418					
❑ CL 830 [M]	Hi-Fi Ellington Uptown	1956	10.00	20.00	40.00
❑ CL 848 [M]	Liberian Suite	1956	10.00	20.00	40.00
-- Reissue of Columbia 6073					
❑ CL 934 [M]	Ellington at Newport	1957	10.00	20.00	40.00
-- Red and black label with six "eye" logos					
❑ LSC-951 [S]	A Drum Is a Woman	1957	10.00	20.00	40.00
❑ CL 951 [M]	A Drum Is a Woman	1957	10.00	20.00	40.00
❑ CL 1033 [M]	Such Sweet Thunder	1957	10.00	20.00	40.00
❑ CL 1085 [M]	Ellington Indigos	1958	6.25	12.50	25.00
❑ CL 1162 [M]	Brown, Black and Beige	1958	6.25	12.50	25.00
❑ CL 1198 [M]	The Cosmic Scene	1959	20.00	40.00	80.00
❑ CL 1245 [M]	Newport 1958	1959	6.25	12.50	25.00
❑ CL 1282 [M]	Duke Ellington at the Bal Masque	1959	6.25	12.50	25.00
❑ CL 1323 [M]	Duke Ellington Jazz Party	1959	6.25	12.50	25.00
❑ CL 1400 [M]	Festival Session	1960	6.25	12.50	25.00
❑ CL 1445 [M]	Blues in Orbit	1960	6.25	12.50	25.00
❑ CL 1541 [M]	The Nutcracker Suite	1960	7.50	15.00	30.00
❑ CL 1546 [M]	Piano in the Background	1960	7.50	15.00	30.00
❑ CL 1597 [M]	Peer Gynt Suite/Suite Thursday	1961	6.25	12.50	25.00
❑ CL 1715 [M]	First Time	1962	6.25	12.50	25.00
❑ CL 1790 [M]	All American	1962	5.00	10.00	20.00
❑ CL 1907 [M]	Midnight in Paris	1963	5.00	10.00	20.00
❑ CL 2522 [10]	Duke's Mixture	1955	20.00	40.00	80.00
❑ CL 2562 [10]	Here's the Duke	1955	20.00	40.00	80.00
❑ CL 2593 [10]	Al Hibbler with the Duke	1956	20.00	40.00	80.00
❑ CL 6024 [10]	Mood Ellington	1949	25.00	50.00	100.00
❑ CL 6073 [10]	Liberian Suite	1949	25.00	50.00	100.00
❑ CS 8015 [S]	Brown, Black and Beige	1958	7.50	15.00	30.00
❑ CS 8053 [S]	Ellington Indigos	1958	7.50	15.00	30.00
❑ CS 8072 [S]	Newport 1958	1959	7.50	15.00	30.00
❑ CS 8098 [S]	Duke Ellington at the Bal Masque	1959	7.50	15.00	30.00
❑ CS 8127 [S]	Duke Ellington Jazz Party	1959	7.50	15.00	30.00
❑ CS 8241 [S]	Blues in Orbit	1960	7.50	15.00	30.00
❑ CS 8341 [S]	The Nutcracker Suite	1960	10.00	20.00	40.00
❑ CS 8346 [S]	Piano in the Background	1960	10.00	20.00	40.00
❑ CS 8397 [S]	Peer Gynt Suite/Suite Thursday	1961	7.50	15.00	30.00
❑ CS 8515 [S]	First Time	1962	7.50	15.00	30.00
❑ CS 8590 [S]	All American	1962	6.25	12.50	25.00
❑ CS 8829 [S]	Midnight in Paris	1963	6.25	12.50	25.00

COLUMBIA MASTERWORKS

Number	Title	Yr	VG	VG+	NM
❑ ML 4418 [M]	Masterpieces by Ellington	1951	25.00	50.00	100.00
❑ ML 4639 [M]	Ellington Uptown	1951	25.00	50.00	100.00

DECCA

Number	Title	Yr	VG	VG+	NM
❑ DL 9224 [M]	Duke Ellington, Volume 1 -- In the Beginning	1958	10.00	20.00	40.00
-- Black label, silver print					
❑ DL 9224 [M]	Duke Ellington, Volume 1 -- In the Beginning	1961	6.25	12.50	25.00
-- Black label with color bars					
❑ DL 9241 [M]	Duke Ellington, Volume 2 -- Hot in Harlem	1959	10.00	20.00	40.00
-- Black label, silver print					
❑ DL 9241 [M]	Duke Ellington, Volume 2 -- Hot in Harlem	1961	6.25	12.50	25.00
-- Black label with color bars					
❑ DL 9247 [M]	Duke Ellington, Volume 3 -- Rockin' in Rhythm	1959	10.00	20.00	40.00
-- Black label, silver print					
❑ DL 9247 [M]	Duke Ellington, Volume 3 -- Rockin' in Rhythm	1961	6.25	12.50	25.00
-- Black label with color bars					
❑ DL 79224 [R]	Duke Ellington, Volume 1 -- In the Beginning	1958	6.25	12.50	25.00
-- Black label, silver print					
❑ DL 79241 [R]	Duke Ellington, Volume 2 -- Hot in Harlem	1959	6.25	12.50	25.00
-- Black label, silver print					
❑ DL 79247 [R]	Duke Ellington, Volume 3 -- Rockin' in Rhythm	1959	6.25	12.50	25.00
-- Black label, silver print					

HALL OF FAME

Number	Title	Yr	VG	VG+	NM
❑ 625/6/7 [(3)]	The Immortal Duke Ellington	197?	5.00	10.00	20.00

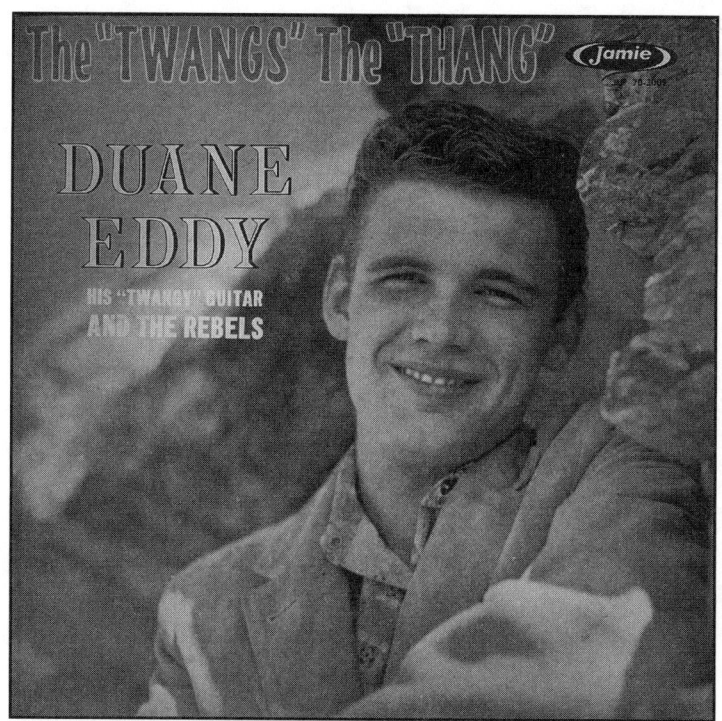

(Top left) Duane Eddy was one of the most successful instrumentalists in the early rock era. *The "Twangs" The "Thang"* was his third album, and he would record many more before his career petered out. (Top right) Not to be confused with the folkie who had a hit with "Sunshine," this Jonathan Edwards was actually Paul Weston. He did parody albums with his wife, Jo Stafford, who sang under the name "Darlene Edwards" on these albums. Notice that the same hand appears twice on the piano in the album cover! (Bottom left) Cass Elliot didn't like being called "Mama Cass" after the Mamas and the Papas broke up, which helped to precipitate her eventual move from the Dunhill label to RCA. This, her second album, was later reissued, with an extra song, as *Make Your Own Kind of Music*. (Bottom right) Here is the album of Shirley, Shirley, bo-birley… you know the rest … based around her best-remembered hit "The Name Game." The song may say there isn't any name that you can't rhyme, but you might want to be careful about "Bart" and "Chuck"!

Number	Title	Yr	VG	VG+	NM
JAZZ PANORAMA					
❑ 1802 [10]	Duke Ellington -- Vol. 1	1951	25.00	50.00	100.00
❑ 1811 [10]	Duke Ellington -- Vol. 2	1951	25.00	50.00	100.00
❑ 1816 [10]	Duke Ellington -- Vol. 3	1951	25.00	50.00	100.00
LONDON					
❑ AL-3551 [10]	The Duke -- 1926	195?	25.00	50.00	100.00
MOBILE FIDELITY					
❑ 1-214	Anatomy of a Murder	1995	10.00	20.00	40.00
-- Audiophile vinyl					
MOSAIC					
❑ MQ8-160 [(8)]	The Complete Capitol Recordings of Duke Ellington	199?	37.50	75.00	150.00
PRESTIGE					
❑ 34003 [(3)]	The Carnegie Hall Concerts: January 1943	197?	5.00	10.00	20.00
RCA CAMDEN					
❑ CAL-394 [M]	Duke Ellington at Tanglewood	1958	5.00	10.00	20.00
❑ CAL-459 [M]	Duke Ellington at the Cotton Club	1959	5.00	10.00	20.00
RCA VICTOR					
❑ WPT-11 [10]	Duke Ellington	1951	25.00	50.00	100.00
❑ LPV-506 [M]	Daybreak Express	1964	5.00	10.00	20.00
❑ LPV-517 [M]	Jumpin' Punkins	1965	5.00	10.00	20.00
❑ LPV-541 [M]	Johnny Come Lately	1967	5.00	10.00	20.00
❑ LPV-553 [M]	Pretty Woman	1968	5.00	10.00	20.00
❑ LPV-568 [M]	Flaming Youth	1969	5.00	10.00	20.00
❑ LJM-1002 [M]	Seattle Concert	1954	12.50	25.00	50.00
❑ LPT-1004 [M]	Ellington's Greatest	1954	10.00	20.00	40.00
❑ LPM-1092 [M]	Duke and His Men	1955	10.00	20.00	40.00
❑ LPM-1364 [M]	In a Mellotone	1957	10.00	20.00	40.00
❑ LPM-1715 [M]	Duke Ellington at His Very Best	1958	10.00	20.00	40.00
❑ LPT-3017 [10]	This Is Duke Ellington and His Orchestra	1952	25.00	50.00	100.00
❑ LPT-3067 [10]	Duke Ellington Plays the Blues	1952	25.00	50.00	100.00
❑ LSP-3576 [S]	The Popular Duke Ellington	1966	5.00	10.00	20.00
❑ LSP-3582 [S]	Concert of Sacred Music	1966	5.00	10.00	20.00
❑ LPM-3782 [M]	Far East Suite	1967	6.25	12.50	25.00
❑ LPM-3906 [M]	And His Mother Called Him Bill	1968	12.50	25.00	50.00
❑ LPM-6009 [(2) M]	The Indispensible Duke Ellington	1961	12.50	25.00	50.00
RCA VICTOR RED SEAL					
❑ LSC-2857 [S]	The Duke at Tanglewood	1966	5.00	10.00	20.00
REPRISE					
❑ R-6069 [M]	Afro-Bossa	1962	5.00	10.00	20.00
❑ R9-6069 [S]	Afro-Bossa	1962	5.00	10.00	20.00
❑ R-6097 [M]	The Symphonic Ellington	1963	5.00	10.00	20.00
❑ R9-6097 [S]	The Symphonic Ellington	1963	5.00	10.00	20.00
❑ R-6122 [M]	Ellington '65: Hits of the '60s/ This Time by Ellington	1964	5.00	10.00	20.00
❑ RS-6122 [S]	Ellington '65: Hits of the '60s/ This Time by Ellington	1964	5.00	10.00	20.00
❑ R-6141 [M]	Mary Poppins	1964	5.00	10.00	20.00
❑ RS-6141 [S]	Mary Poppins	1964	5.00	10.00	20.00
❑ R-6154 [M]	Ellington '66	1965	5.00	10.00	20.00
❑ R-6168 [M]	Will Big Bands Ever Come Back?	1965	5.00	10.00	20.00
❑ R-6185 [M]	Concert in the Virgin Islands	1965	5.00	10.00	20.00
❑ R-6234 [M]	Duke Ellington's Greatest Hits	1967	5.00	10.00	20.00
RIVERSIDE					
❑ RLP-12-129 [M]	Birth of Big Band Jazz	195?	7.50	15.00	30.00
-- Blue label with mike logo					
❑ RLP-12-129 [M]	Birth of Big Band Jazz	1956	15.00	30.00	60.00
-- White label, blue print					
❑ RLP-475 [M]	Great Times!	1963	6.25	12.50	25.00
❑ RS-9475 [S]	Great Times!	1963	6.25	12.50	25.00
RONDO-LETTE					
❑ A-7 [M]	Duke Ellington and Orchestra	1958	7.50	15.00	30.00
ROYALE					
❑ 18143 [10]	Duke Ellington and His Orchestra	195?	12.50	25.00	50.00
❑ 18152 [10]	Duke Ellington Plays Ellington	195?	12.50	25.00	50.00
SOLID STATE					
❑ SS-19000 [(2)]	75th Birthday	1970	5.00	10.00	20.00
TREND					
❑ 529	The Symphonic Ellington	1982	5.00	10.00	20.00
UNITED ARTISTS					
❑ UAJ-14017 [M]	Money Jungle	1962	10.00	20.00	40.00
❑ UAJS-15017 [S]	Money Jungle	1962	10.00	20.00	40.00
"X"					
❑ LVA-3037 [10]	Duke Ellington Plays	1955	25.00	50.00	100.00
ELLINGTON, HARVEY					
STEPHENY					
❑ MF-4010 [M]	I Can't Hide the Blues	1959	20.00	40.00	80.00

Number	Title	Yr	VG	VG+	NM
ELLIOT, CASS					
Also see THE MAMAS AND THE PAPAS.					
ABC DUNHILL					
❑ DS-50040	Dream a Little Dream	1968	5.00	10.00	20.00
❑ DS-50055	Bubble Gum, Lemonade &...Something for Mama	1969	5.00	10.00	20.00
ELLIOTT, DEAN					
CAPITOL					
❑ ST 1834 [S]	Zounds! What Sounds!	1962	12.50	25.00	50.00
❑ T 1834 [M]	Zounds! What Sounds!	1962	10.00	20.00	40.00
❑ ST 1864 [S]	Heartstrings	1962	6.25	12.50	25.00
❑ T 1864 [M]	Heartstrings	1962	5.00	10.00	20.00
ELLIOTT, RAMBLIN' JACK					
FOLKLORE					
❑ FL 14011 [M]	The Songs of Woody Guthrie	1964	5.00	10.00	20.00
❑ FL 14014 [M]	Ramblin'	1964	5.00	10.00	20.00
❑ FL 14019 [M]	Hootenanny with Jack Elliott	1964	5.00	10.00	20.00
❑ FL 14029 [M]	Country Style	1964	5.00	10.00	20.00
MONITOR					
❑ MF-379 [M]	Ramblin' Cowboy	1962	6.25	12.50	25.00
❑ MF-380 [M]	Jack Elliott Sings Woody Guthrie and Jimmie Rodgers	1962	6.25	12.50	25.00
❑ MS-380 [S]	Jack Elliott Sings Woody Guthrie and Jimmie Rodgers	1962	7.50	15.00	30.00
PRESTIGE					
❑ PRLP-13016 [M]	The Songs of Woody Guthrie	1961	7.50	15.00	30.00
❑ PRLP-13033 [M]	Ramblin'	1961	7.50	15.00	30.00
❑ PRLP-13045 [M]	Country Style	1962	7.50	15.00	30.00
❑ PRLP-13065 [M]	Jack Elliott at the Second Fret	1962	7.50	15.00	30.00
TOPIC					
❑ T-15 [10]	Jack Takes the Floor	195?	10.00	20.00	40.00
VANGUARD					
❑ VRS-9151 [M]	Jack Elliott	1964	5.00	10.00	20.00
❑ VSD-79151 [S]	Jack Elliott	1964	6.25	12.50	25.00
ELLIS, ANITA					
ELEKTRA					
❑ EKL-179 [M]	The World in My Arms	1959	10.00	20.00	40.00
EPIC					
❑ LN 3280 [M]	I Wonder What Became of Me	1956	10.00	20.00	40.00
❑ LN 3419 [M]	Him	1958	10.00	20.00	40.00
ELLIS, JIMMY					
❑ Also see ORION.					
BOBLO					
❑ 78-829	By Request Jimmy Sings Elvis	1978	25.00	50.00	100.00
ELLIS, RED					
STARDAY					
❑ SLP-168 [M]	Holy Cry from the Cross	1962	6.25	12.50	25.00
❑ SLP-203 [M]	The Sacred Sound of Bluegrass Music	1962	6.25	12.50	25.00
❑ SLP-273 [M]	Old Time Religion Bluegrass Style	1963	6.25	12.50	25.00
ELLIS, SHIRLEY					
COLUMBIA					
❑ CL 2679 [M]	Sugar, Let's Shing-a-Ling	1967	5.00	10.00	20.00
❑ CS 9479 [S]	Sugar, Let's Shing-a-Ling	1967	6.25	12.50	25.00
CONGRESS					
❑ CGL-3002 [M]	Shirley Ellis In Action	1964	6.25	12.50	25.00
❑ CGS-3002 [S]	Shirley Ellis In Action	1964	7.50	15.00	30.00
❑ CGL-3003 [M]	The Name Game	1965	6.25	12.50	25.00
❑ CGS-3003 [S]	The Name Game	1965	7.50	15.00	30.00
ELLIS, STEVE, AND THE STARFIRES					
I.G.L.					
❑ 105	The Steve Ellis Songbook	1967	125.00	250.00	500.00
ELMER GANTRY'S VELVET OPERA					
EPIC					
❑ BN 26415	Elmer Gantry's Velvet Opera	1968	12.50	25.00	50.00
ELMORE, ROBERT					
MERCURY LIVING PRESENCE					
❑ SR 90109 [S]	Boardwalk Pipes	196?	25.00	50.00	100.00
-- Maroon label, no "Vendor: Mercury Record Corporation"					

Number	Title	Yr	VG	VG+	NM
❑ SR 90127 [S]	Bach on the Biggest	1960	7.50	15.00	30.00
-- Maroon label, no "Vendor: Mercury Record Corporation"					

EMANUELE, VITTORIO
RCA VICTOR RED SEAL
❑ LSC-2424 [S]	Vivaldi: The Four Seasons	1960	10.00	20.00	40.00
-- With the Societa Corelli; original with "shaded dog" label					

EMBERS, THE
JCP
❑ 2006 [M]	The Embers Roll Eleven	1965	50.00	100.00	200.00
❑ 2009 [M]	Just for the Birds	1966	37.50	75.00	150.00

EMERSON'S OLD-TIMEY CUSTARD-SUCKIN' BAND
ESP-DISK'
❑ 2006	Emerson's Old-Timey Custard-Suckin' Band	1970	7.50	15.00	30.00

EMERSON, KEITH
Also see EMERSON, LAKE AND PALMER; THE NICE.
EMERSON
❑ KEITH LP1	The Christmas Album	1993	5.00	10.00	20.00
-- British import only					

EMERSON, LAKE AND PALMER
Also see KEITH EMERSON.
ATLANTIC
❑ PR 281 [DJ]	On Tour with Emerson, Lake and Palmer	1977	10.00	20.00	40.00
MANTICORE
❑ SD 3-200 [(3)]	Welcome Back, My Friends, to the Show That Never Ends, Ladies and Gentlemen	1974	5.00	10.00	20.00
MOBILE FIDELITY
❑ 1-031	Pictures at an Exhibition	1980	7.50	15.00	30.00
-- Audiophile vinyl					
❑ 1-203	Tarkus	1994	6.25	12.50	25.00
-- Audiophile vinyl					
❑ 1-218	Trilogy	1994	10.00	20.00	40.00
-- Audiophile vinyl					

EMMONS, BOBBY
HI
❑ HL-32024 [M]	Blues with a Beat	1965	6.25	12.50	25.00
❑ SHL-32024 [S]	Blues with a Beat	1965	7.50	15.00	30.00

EMMONS, BUDDY
MERCURY
❑ MG-20843 [M]	Steel Guitar Jazz	1963	20.00	40.00	80.00
❑ SR-60843 [S]	Steel Guitar Jazz	1963	25.00	50.00	100.00

EMMONS, BUDDY, AND SHOT JACKSON
STARDAY
❑ SLP-230 [M]	Singing Strings of Steel and Dobro	196?	10.00	20.00	40.00

EMOTIONS
VOLT
❑ VOS-6008	So I Can Love You	1971	6.25	12.50	25.00
❑ VOS-6015	Untouched	1972	6.25	12.50	25.00

END, THE
LONDON
❑ PS 560	Introspection	1969	12.50	25.00	50.00

ENGEL, SCOTT, AND JOHN STEWART -- See THE WALKER BROTHERS.

ENNIS, ETHEL
CAPITOL
❑ T 941	Change of Scenery	1957	10.00	20.00	40.00
JUBILEE
❑ JLP-1021 [M]	Lullabies for Losers	1956	12.50	25.00	50.00
❑ JLP-5024 [M]	Ethel Ennis Sings	1963	5.00	10.00	20.00
❑ SJLP-5024 [S]	Ethel Ennis Sings	1963	6.25	12.50	25.00
RCA VICTOR
❑ LPM-2786 [M]	This Is Ethel Ennis	1964	5.00	10.00	20.00
❑ LSP-2786 [S]	This Is Ethel Ennis	1964	6.25	12.50	25.00
❑ LPM-2984 [M]	Eyes for You	1964	5.00	10.00	20.00
❑ LSP-2984 [S]	Eyes for You	1964	6.25	12.50	25.00

Number	Title	Yr	VG	VG+	NM

ENO, BRIAN
Also see ROXY MUSIC.
EDITIONS EG
❑ EGBS-2 [(11)]	Working Backwards: 1983-1973	1984	15.00	30.00	60.00
-- Boxed set of nine albums plus Music For Films II and Rarities 12"					
JEM
❑ ENO DJ [DJ]	Music for Airplay	1981	12.50	25.00	50.00
-- Promo-only 10-track sampler					

ENTWISTLE, JOHN
Also see THE WHO.
DECCA
❑ DL 79183	Smash Your Head Against the Wall	1971	6.25	12.50	25.00
TRACK
❑ DL 79190	Whistle Rymes	1972	6.25	12.50	25.00
❑ L33-1926 [DJ]	Who's Ox	1975	12.50	25.00	50.00
-- Promo-only sampler					

EPIC CHOIR, THE
EPIC
❑ LC 3144 [M]	The Story of Christmas	1954	6.25	12.50	25.00
-- Gatefold cover with bound-in booklet					

EPPS, PRESTON
ORIGINAL SOUND
❑ LPM-5002 [M]	Bongo, Bongo, Bongo	1960	12.50	25.00	50.00
❑ LPM-5009 [M]	Surfin' Bongos	1963	10.00	20.00	40.00
❑ LPS-8851 [S]	Bongo, Bongo, Bongo	1960	20.00	40.00	80.00
❑ LPS-8872 [S]	Surfin' Bongos	1963	12.50	25.00	50.00
TOP RANK
❑ RM-349 [M]	Bongola	1961	10.00	20.00	40.00
❑ RS-349 [S]	Bongola	1961	12.50	25.00	50.00

EQUALS, THE
LAURIE
❑ LLP-2045 [M]	Unequalled	1967	6.25	12.50	25.00
❑ SLP-2045 [S]	Unequalled	1967	7.50	15.00	30.00
PRESIDENT
❑ PTL-1015	Equal Sensation	1968	6.25	12.50	25.00
❑ PTL-1020	The Sensational Equals	1968	6.25	12.50	25.00
❑ PTL-1025	Equals Supreme	1968	6.25	12.50	25.00
❑ PTL-1030	Strikeback	1969	6.25	12.50	25.00
RCA VICTOR
❑ LSP-4078	Baby Come Back	1968	6.25	12.50	25.00

ERASURE
MUTE/ELEKTRA
❑ 5621 [DJ]	Abba-esque (Remixes)	1992	6.25	12.50	25.00
-- Promo-only vinyl; remixes of 4-song EP; no special jacket					

ERICA
ESP-DISK'
❑ 1099	You Used to Think	1968	15.00	30.00	60.00

ERIK
VANGUARD
❑ VRS-9267 [M]	Look Where I Am	1967	5.00	10.00	20.00
❑ VSD-79267 [S]	Look Where I Am	1967	5.00	10.00	20.00

ERIK AND THE VIKINGS
KARATE
❑ KLP-1401 [M]	Sing A-Long Rock 'n Roll	1965	50.00	100.00	200.00

ERVIN, SENATOR SAM
COLUMBIA
❑ KC 32756	Senator Sam at Home	1973	6.25	12.50	25.00

ESCORTS, THE
TEO
❑ LPM-5000 [M]	The Escorts Bring Down the House	1966	30.00	60.00	120.00

ESP
DREAM
❑ DRE 187301	The Future Is Now	1986	12.50	25.00	50.00

ESQUERITA
CAPITOL
❑ T 1186 [M]	Esquerita	1959	250.00	500.00	1,000.

Number	Title	Yr	VG	VG+	NM

ESQUIRES, THE
BUNKY
❑ 300	Get On Up and Get Away	1968	8.75	17.50	35.00

ESQUIVEL
RCA VICTOR
❑ LPM-1345 [M]	To Love Again	1957	12.50	25.00	50.00
❑ LPM-1749 [M]	Four Corners of the World	1958	6.25	12.50	25.00
❑ LSP-1749 [S]	Four Corners of the World	1958	12.50	25.00	50.00
❑ LPM-1753 [M]	Other Worlds, Other Sounds	1959	6.25	12.50	25.00
❑ LSP-1753 [S]	Other Worlds, Other Sounds	1959	12.50	25.00	50.00
❑ LPM-1978 [M]	Exploring New Sounds in Hi-Fi	1959	7.50	15.00	30.00
❑ LSP-1978 [S]	Exploring New Sounds in Hi-Fi	1959	15.00	30.00	60.00
❑ LPM-1988 [M]	Strings Aflame	1959	6.25	12.50	25.00
❑ LSP-1988 [S]	Strings Aflame	1959	12.50	25.00	50.00
❑ LPM-2225 [M]	Infinity in Sound	1960	7.50	15.00	30.00
❑ LSP-2225 [S]	Infinity in Sound	1960	15.00	30.00	60.00
❑ LPM-2296 [M]	Infinity in Sound, Vol. 2	1961	7.50	15.00	30.00
❑ LSP-2296 [S]	Infinity in Sound, Vol. 2	1961	15.00	30.00	60.00
❑ LPM-2418 [M]	Latin-esque	1962	5.00	10.00	20.00
❑ LSP-2418 [S]	Latin-esque	1962	15.00	30.00	60.00
-- Die-cut cover that reveals inner sleeve					
❑ LSP-2418 [S]	Latin-esque	1962	10.00	20.00	40.00
-- Standard cover					
❑ LPM-3502 [M]	The Best of Esquivel	1966	5.00	10.00	20.00
❑ LSP-3502 [S]	The Best of Esquivel	1966	7.50	15.00	30.00
❑ LPM-3697 [M]	The Genius of Esquivel	1967	5.00	10.00	20.00
❑ LSP-3697 [S]	The Genius of Esquivel	1967	7.50	15.00	30.00
REPRISE
❑ R-6046 [M]	More of Other Worlds, Other Sounds	1962	6.25	12.50	25.00
❑ R9-6046 [S]	More of Other Worlds, Other Sounds	1962	7.50	15.00	30.00

ESSEX, DAVID
COLUMBIA
❑ CQ 32560 [Q]	Rock On	1974	7.50	15.00	30.00
❑ KC 32560	Rock On	1974	5.00	10.00	20.00

ESSEX, THE
ROULETTE
❑ R-25234 [M]	Easier Said Than Done	1963	10.00	20.00	40.00
❑ SR-25234 [S]	Easier Said Than Done	1963	12.50	25.00	50.00
❑ R-25235 [M]	A Walkin' Miracle	1963	10.00	20.00	40.00
❑ SR-25235 [S]	A Walkin' Miracle	1963	12.50	25.00	50.00
❑ R-25246 [M]	Young and Lively	1964	10.00	20.00	40.00
❑ SR-25246 [S]	Young and Lively	1964	12.50	25.00	50.00

ETC.
WINDI
❑ WLPS-1011	Etc. Is the Name of the Band!	1976	6.25	12.50	25.00

ETERNITY'S CHILDREN
TOWER
❑ ST-5123	Eternity's Children	1968	6.25	12.50	25.00
❑ ST-5144	Timeless	1969	7.50	15.00	30.00

EUPHONIOUS WAIL
KAPP
❑ KS-3668	Euphonious Wail	1973	10.00	20.00	40.00

EUPHORIA
CAPITOL
❑ SKAO-363	A Gift from Euphoria	1969	30.00	60.00	120.00
HERITAGE
❑ HTS 35,005	Euphoria	1971	7.50	15.00	30.00
RAINBOW
❑ 1003	Lost in a Trance	1973	75.00	150.00	300.00

EURYTHMICS
RCA VICTOR
❑ DJL1-5707 [DJ]	Rough and Tough -- Live at the Roxy	1986	7.50	15.00	30.00
-- Promo-only 4-song live album					

EVANS, DALE
Also see ROY ROGERS AND DALE EVANS.
CAPITOL
❑ ST 2772 [S]	It's Real	1967	6.25	12.50	25.00
❑ T 2772 [M]	It's Real	1967	6.25	12.50	25.00

EVANS, PAUL
CARLTON
❑ STLP-129 [S]	Hear Paul Evans in Your Home Tonight	1961	15.00	30.00	60.00
❑ TLP-129 [M]	Hear Paul Evans in Your Home Tonight	1961	10.00	20.00	40.00
❑ STLP-130 [S]	Folk Songs of Many Lands	1961	15.00	30.00	60.00
❑ TLP-130 [M]	Folk Songs of Many Lands	1961	10.00	20.00	40.00
GUARANTEED
❑ GUL-1000 [M]	Fabulous Teens	1960	17.50	35.00	70.00
❑ GUS-1000 [S]	Fabulous Teens	1960	20.00	40.00	80.00
KAPP
❑ KL-1346 [M]	21 Years in a Tennessee Jail	1964	6.25	12.50	25.00
❑ KL-1475 [M]	Another Town, Another Jail	1966	6.25	12.50	25.00
❑ KS-3346 [S]	21 Years in a Tennessee Jail	1964	10.00	20.00	40.00
❑ KS-3475 [S]	Another Town, Another Jail	1966	7.50	15.00	30.00

EVEN DOZEN JUG BAND, THE
Among the group members were John Sebastian and Maria D'Amato (later Muldaur).
ELEKTRA
❑ EKL-246 [M]	The Even Dozen Jug Band	1964	7.50	15.00	30.00
❑ EKS-7246 [S]	The Even Dozen Jug Band	1964	12.50	25.00	50.00

EVERETT, BETTY
UNI
❑ 73048	There'll Come a Time	1969	6.25	12.50	25.00
VEE JAY
❑ LP 1077 [M]	You're No Good	1964	10.00	20.00	40.00
❑ SR 1077 [S]	You're No Good	1964	17.50	35.00	70.00
❑ LP 1077 [M]	It's In His Kiss	1964	7.50	15.00	30.00
❑ SR 1077 [S]	It's In His Kiss	1964	12.50	25.00	50.00
❑ LP 1122 [M]	The Very Best of Betty Everett	1965	10.00	20.00	40.00
❑ VJS 1122 [S]	The Very Best of Betty Everett	1965	12.50	25.00	50.00

EVERETT, BETTY, AND JERRY BUTLER
VEE JAY
❑ LP 1099 [M]	Delicious Together	1964	5.00	10.00	20.00
❑ VJS 1099 [S]	Delicious Together	1964	6.25	12.50	25.00

EVERETTE, LEON
TRUE
❑ 1002	Goodbye King of Rock and Roll	1977	6.25	12.50	25.00
-- Deduct 40% if poster of Elvis Presley is missing					

EVERGREEN BLUES, THE
MERCURY
❑ SR-61157	7 Do 11	1968	5.00	10.00	20.00

EVERLY BROTHERS, THE
BARNABY
❑ BGP-350 [(2)]	The Everly Brothers' Original Golden Hits	1970	5.00	10.00	20.00
CADENCE
❑ CLP-3003 [M]	The Everly Brothers	1958	25.00	50.00	100.00
-- Maroon label with metronome logo					
❑ CLP-3003 [M]	The Everly Brothers	1962	15.00	30.00	60.00
-- Red label with black border					
❑ CLP-3016 [M]	Songs Our Daddy Taught Us	1958	25.00	50.00	100.00
-- Maroon label with metronome logo					
❑ CLP-3016 [M]	Songs Our Daddy Taught Us	1962	15.00	30.00	60.00
-- Red label with black border					
❑ CLP-3025 [M]	The Everly Brothers' Best	1959	22.50	45.00	90.00
-- Maroon label with metronome logo					
❑ CLP-3025 [M]	The Everly Brothers' Best	1962	15.00	30.00	60.00
-- Red label with black border					
❑ CLP-3040 [M]	The Fabulous Style of the Everly Brothers	1960	20.00	40.00	80.00
-- Maroon label with metronome logo					
❑ CLP-3040 [M]	The Fabulous Style of the Everly Brothers	1962	12.50	25.00	50.00
-- Red label with black border					
❑ CLP-3059 [M]	Folk Songs of the Everly Brothers	1963	12.50	25.00	50.00
-- Reissue of 3016					
❑ CLP-3062 [M]	15 Everly Hits 15	1963	10.00	20.00	40.00
❑ CLP-25040 [P]	The Fabulous Style of the Everly Brothers	1960	30.00	60.00	120.00
-- Maroon label with metronome logo					
❑ CLP-25040 [P]	The Fabulous Style of the Everly Brothers	1962	15.00	30.00	60.00
-- Red label with black border					
❑ CLP-25059 [R]	Folk Songs of the Everly Brothers	1963	10.00	20.00	40.00

Number	Title	Yr	VG	VG+	NM
❑ CLP-25062 [P]	15 Everly Hits 15	1963	12.50	25.00	50.00

HARMONY

Number	Title	Yr	VG	VG+	NM
❑ HS 11350	Christmas with the Everly Brothers and the Boys Town Choir	1969	5.00	10.00	20.00

RHINO

Number	Title	Yr	VG	VG+	NM
❑ RNDF-258 [PD]	Heartaches and Harmonies	1985	5.00	10.00	20.00

TIME-LIFE

Number	Title	Yr	VG	VG+	NM
❑ SRNR-09 [(2)]	The Everly Brothers: 1957-1962	1986	5.00	10.00	20.00
	-- Part of "The Rock 'n' Roll Era" series; box set with insert				

WARNER BROS.

Number	Title	Yr	VG	VG+	NM
❑ PRO 134 [10]	It's Everly Time!	1960	150.00	300.00	600.00
	-- Promo "souvenir sampler" from their debut on WB				
❑ W 1381 [M]	It's Everly Time!	1960	7.50	15.00	30.00
❑ WS 1381 [S]	It's Everly Time!	1960	10.00	20.00	40.00
❑ W 1395 [M]	A Date with the Everly Brothers	1960	12.50	25.00	50.00
	-- Gatefold edition with poster and wallet-size photos				
❑ W 1395 [M]	A Date with the Everly Brothers	1960	10.00	20.00	40.00
	-- Gatefold edition without poster or photos				
❑ W 1395 [M]	A Date with the Everly Brothers	1961	7.50	15.00	30.00
	-- Regular edition				
❑ WS 1395 [S]	A Date with the Everly Brothers	1960	18.75	37.50	75.00
	-- Gatefold edition with poster and wallet-size photos				
❑ WS 1395 [S]	A Date with the Everly Brothers	1960	12.50	25.00	50.00
	-- Gatefold edition without poster or photos				
❑ WS 1395 [S]	A Date with the Everly Brothers	1961	10.00	20.00	40.00
	-- Regular edition				
❑ W 1418 [M]	Both Sides of an Evening	1961	7.50	15.00	30.00
❑ WS 1418 [S]	Both Sides of an Evening	1961	10.00	20.00	40.00
❑ W 1430 [M]	Instant Party!	1962	7.50	15.00	30.00
❑ WS 1430 [S]	Instant Party!	1962	10.00	20.00	40.00
❑ W 1471 [M]	The Golden Hits of the Everly Brothers	1962	7.50	15.00	30.00
❑ WS 1471 [S]	The Golden Hits of the Everly Brothers	1962	10.00	20.00	40.00
	-- Gold label				
❑ WS 1471	The Golden Hits of the Everly Brothers	1967	5.00	10.00	20.00
	-- Green "W7" label				
❑ W 1483 [M]	Christmas with the Everly Brothers and the Boys Town Choir	1962	10.00	20.00	40.00
❑ WS 1483 [S]	Christmas with the Everly Brothers and the Boys Town Choir	1962	12.50	25.00	50.00
❑ W 1513 [M]	Great Country Hits	1963	10.00	20.00	40.00
❑ WS 1513 [S]	Great Country Hits	1963	12.50	25.00	50.00
❑ W 1554 [M]	The Very Best of the Everly Brothers	1964	7.50	15.00	30.00
	-- Originals have yellow covers				
❑ W 1554 [M]	The Very Best of the Everly Brothers	1965	5.00	10.00	20.00
	-- Later pressings have white covers				
❑ WS 1554 [S]	The Very Best of the Everly Brothers	1964	10.00	20.00	40.00
	-- Originals have yellow covers				
❑ WS 1554 [S]	The Very Best of the Everly Brothers	1965	6.25	12.50	25.00
	-- White cover; gold label				
❑ WS 1554	The Very Best of the Everly Brothers	1967	5.00	10.00	20.00
	-- Green "W7" label				
❑ W 1578 [M]	Rock & Soul	1964	10.00	20.00	40.00
❑ WS 1578 [S]	Rock & Soul	1964	12.50	25.00	50.00
❑ W 1585 [M]	Gone, Gone, Gone	1965	10.00	20.00	40.00
❑ WS 1585 [S]	Gone, Gone, Gone	1965	12.50	25.00	50.00
❑ W 1605 [M]	Beat & Soul	1965	10.00	20.00	40.00
❑ WS 1605 [S]	Beat & Soul	1965	12.50	25.00	50.00
❑ W 1620 [M]	In Our Image	1966	10.00	20.00	40.00
❑ WS 1620 [S]	In Our Image	1966	12.50	25.00	50.00
❑ W 1646 [M]	Two Yanks in London	1966	10.00	20.00	40.00
❑ WS 1646 [S]	Two Yanks in London	1966	12.50	25.00	50.00
❑ W 1676 [M]	The Hit Sound of the Everly Brothers	1967	12.50	25.00	50.00
❑ WS 1676 [S]	The Hit Sound of the Everly Brothers	1967	10.00	20.00	40.00
❑ W 1708 [M]	The Everly Brothers Sing	1967	12.50	25.00	50.00
❑ WS 1708 [S]	The Everly Brothers Sing	1967	10.00	20.00	40.00
❑ WS 1752	Roots	1968	10.00	20.00	40.00
❑ WS 1858	The Everly Brothers Show	1970	7.50	15.00	30.00
❑ ST-91343 [S]	The Very Best of the Everly Brothers	1967	10.00	20.00	40.00
	-- Capitol Record Club edition				
❑ ST-91601	Roots	1968	12.50	25.00	50.00
	-- Capitol Record Club edition				
❑ STAO-93286	The Everly Brothers Show	1970	10.00	20.00	40.00
	-- Capitol Record Club edition				

EVERPRESENT FULLNESS, THE

WHITE WHALE

Number	Title	Yr	VG	VG+	NM
❑ 7132	The Everpresent Fullness	1970	6.25	12.50	25.00

EVERY MOTHER'S SON

MGM

Number	Title	Yr	VG	VG+	NM
❑ E-4471 [M]	Every Mother's Son	1967	5.00	10.00	20.00
❑ SE-4471 [S]	Every Mother's Son	1967	5.00	10.00	20.00
❑ E-4504 [M]	Every Mother's Son's Back	1967	5.00	10.00	20.00
❑ SE-4504 [S]	Every Mother's Son's Back	1967	5.00	10.00	20.00

EVERYTHING IS EVERYTHING

VANGUARD

Number	Title	Yr	VG	VG+	NM
❑ VSD-6512	Everything Is Everything	1969	6.25	12.50	25.00

EXCITERS, THE

RCA VICTOR

Number	Title	Yr	VG	VG+	NM
❑ LSP-4211	Caviar and Chitlins	1969	7.50	15.00	30.00

ROULETTE

Number	Title	Yr	VG	VG+	NM
❑ R 25326 [M]	The Exciters	1966	7.50	15.00	30.00
❑ SR 25326 [S]	The Exciters	1966	10.00	20.00	40.00

TODAY

Number	Title	Yr	VG	VG+	NM
❑ 1001	Black Beauty	1971	5.00	10.00	20.00

UNITED ARTISTS

Number	Title	Yr	VG	VG+	NM
❑ UAL-3264 [M]	Tell Him	1963	17.50	35.00	70.00
❑ UAS-6264 [S]	Tell Him	1963	37.50	75.00	150.00

EYES OF BLUE

MERCURY

Number	Title	Yr	VG	VG+	NM
❑ SR-61184	Crossroads of Time	1968	7.50	15.00	30.00
❑ SR-61220	In Fields of Ardath	1969	7.50	15.00	30.00

Number	Title	Yr	VG	VG+	NM

F

FABARES, SHELLEY
Also see JAMES DARREN/SHELLEY FABARES/PAUL PETERSEN.
COLPIX

Number	Title	Yr	VG	VG+	NM
❏ CLP-426 [M]	Shelley!	1962	37.50	75.00	150.00
❏ CST-426 [S]	Shelley!	1962	150.00	300.00	600.00
❏ CLP-431 [M]	The Things We Did Last Summer	1962	25.00	50.00	100.00
❏ CST-431 [S]	The Things We Did Last Summer	1962	100.00	200.00	400.00

FABIAN
CHANCELLOR

Number	Title	Yr	VG	VG+	NM
❏ CHL-5003 [M]	Hold That Tiger!	1959	25.00	50.00	100.00
-- Pink label					
❏ CHL-5003 [M]	Hold That Tiger!	1959	12.50	25.00	50.00
-- Black label					
❏ CHLS-5003 [S]	Hold That Tiger!	1959	37.50	75.00	150.00
-- Pink label					
❏ CHLS-5003 [S]	Hold That Tiger!	1959	18.75	37.50	75.00
-- Black label					
❏ CHL-5005 [M]	Fabulous Fabian	1959	12.50	25.00	50.00
❏ CHLS-5005 [S]	Fabulous Fabian	1959	18.75	37.50	75.00
❏ CHL-5012 [M]	The Good Old Summertime	1960	12.50	25.00	50.00
❏ CHLS-5012 [S]	The Good Old Summertime	1960	18.75	37.50	75.00
❏ CHL-5019 [M]	Rockin' Hot	1961	18.75	37.50	75.00
❏ CHL-5024 [M]	Fabian's 16 Fabulous Hits	1962	18.75	37.50	75.00
❏ CHL-69802 [M]	The Fabian Facade: Young and Wonderful	1960	20.00	40.00	80.00
-- Felt gatefold cover with die-cut window					

FABIAN / FRANKIE AVALON
Also see each artist's individual listings.
CHANCELLOR

Number	Title	Yr	VG	VG+	NM
❏ CHL-5009 [M]	The Hit Makers	1960	25.00	50.00	100.00

FABRIC, BENT
ATCO

Number	Title	Yr	VG	VG+	NM
❏ SD 33-148 [S]	Alley Cat	1962	5.00	10.00	20.00

FABULOUS FLIPPERS, THE
VERITAS

Number	Title	Yr	VG	VG+	NM
❏ VS-2570	Something Tangible	1970	6.25	12.50	25.00

FABULOUS JOKERS, THE
MONUMENT

Number	Title	Yr	VG	VG+	NM
❏ MLP-8059 [M]	Guitars Extraordinaire	1966	25.00	50.00	100.00
❏ SLP-18059 [S]	Guitars Extraordinaire	1966	37.50	75.00	150.00

FACENDA, JOHN (NARRATOR)
RCA VICTOR

Number	Title	Yr	VG	VG+	NM
❏ LOP-1504 [M]	The Nativity	1958	7.50	15.00	30.00
-- Gatefold with 12-page booklet					

FACES
Also see ROD STEWART; SMALL FACES.
WARNER BROS.

Number	Title	Yr	VG	VG+	NM
❏ WS 1851	First Step	1970	5.00	10.00	20.00
-- First pressings have "small faces." on front cover					

FAGEN, DONALD
Also see STEELY DAN.
MOBILE FIDELITY

Number	Title	Yr	VG	VG+	NM
❏ 1-120	The Nightfly	1982	10.00	20.00	40.00
-- Audiophile vinyl					

FAHEY, JOHN
REPRISE

Number	Title	Yr	VG	VG+	NM
❏ MS 2089	Of Rivers and Religions	1972	5.00	10.00	20.00
❏ MS 2145	After the Ball	1973	5.00	10.00	20.00

TAKOMA

Number	Title	Yr	VG	VG+	NM
❏ C-1002	The Transfiguration of Blind Joe Death	196?	10.00	20.00	40.00
❏ C-1003	Death Chants, Breakdowns and Military Waltzes	196?	10.00	20.00	40.00
❏ C-1004	Dance of Death and Other Plantation Favorites	196?	10.00	20.00	40.00
❏ C-1008	The Great San Bernardino Birthday Party	196?	7.50	15.00	30.00
❏ C-1014	Volume 6	196?	7.50	15.00	30.00

Number	Title	Yr	VG	VG+	NM
❏ C-1019	Voice of the Turtle	1971	7.50	15.00	30.00
-- With gatefold jacket and booklet					
❏ C-1020	The New Possibility: John Fahey's Guitar Soli Christmas Album	1971	6.25	12.50	25.00
-- Originals with gatefold and booklet					
❏ C-1030	America	1972	6.25	12.50	25.00
-- With gatefold jacket and booklet					
❏ C-1035	Fare Forward Voyagers	1973	5.00	10.00	20.00

VANGUARD

Number	Title	Yr	VG	VG+	NM
❏ VSD 55/56 [(2)]	Essential John Fahey	1974	5.00	10.00	20.00
❏ VRS-9259 [M]	Requia	1968	6.25	12.50	25.00
❏ VSD-79259 [S]	Requia	1968	5.00	10.00	20.00
❏ VSD-79293	The Yellow Princess	1969	5.00	10.00	20.00

FAIRPORT CONVENTION
Also see SANDY DENNY.
COTILLION

Number	Title	Yr	VG	VG+	NM
❏ SD 9024	Fairport Convention	1968	7.50	15.00	30.00

FAITH NO MORE
MORDAM

Number	Title	Yr	VG	VG+	NM
❏ FNM 1	We Care a Lot	1985	5.00	10.00	20.00

FAITH, ADAM
AMY

Number	Title	Yr	VG	VG+	NM
❏ 8005 [M]	Adam Faith	1965	6.25	12.50	25.00
❏ S-8005 [S]	Adam Faith	1965	7.50	15.00	30.00

MGM

Number	Title	Yr	VG	VG+	NM
❏ E-3951 [M]	England's Top Singer	1961	10.00	20.00	40.00
❏ SE-3951 [S]	England's Top Singer	1961	12.50	25.00	50.00

FAITH, PERCY
COLUMBIA

Number	Title	Yr	VG	VG+	NM
❏ C2L 15 [(2) M]	The Columbia Album of Christmas Music	1958	7.50	15.00	30.00
-- Combines CL 588 and CL 1187 into one gatefold package					
❏ CL 525 [M]	Continental Music	1955	5.00	10.00	20.00
❏ CL 550 [M]	Kismet	1955	5.00	10.00	20.00
❏ CL 577 [M]	Music from Hollywood	1955	5.00	10.00	20.00
❏ CL 588 [M]	Music of Christmas	1955	6.25	12.50	25.00
❏ CL 640 [M]	House of Flowers	1956	5.00	10.00	20.00
❏ CL 681 [M]	Delicado	1956	5.00	10.00	20.00
❏ CL 705 [M]	Music for Her	1956	5.00	10.00	20.00
❏ CL 880 [M]	Passport to Romance	1956	5.00	10.00	20.00
❏ CL 895 [M]	My Fair Lady	1957	5.00	10.00	20.00
❏ CL 955 [M]	L'il Abner	1957	5.00	10.00	20.00
❏ CL 1010 [M]	Adventure in the Sun	1957	5.00	10.00	20.00
❏ CL 1075 [M]	Viva!	1957	5.00	10.00	20.00
❏ CL 1182 [M]	Touchdown!	1957	5.00	10.00	20.00
❏ CL 1187 [M]	Hallelujah!	1957	5.00	10.00	20.00
❏ CL 1188 [M]	Jubliation!	1957	5.00	10.00	20.00
❏ CL 1267 [M]	Malaguena	1958	5.00	10.00	20.00
❏ CL 1381 [M]	Music of Christmas	1959	5.00	10.00	20.00
-- Re-recorded version of CL 588 with same track order					
❏ CL 2810 [M]	For Those in Love	1968	5.00	10.00	20.00
❏ CS 8005 [S]	South Pacific	1958	6.25	12.50	25.00
❏ CS 8033 [S]	Hallelujah!	1958	6.25	12.50	25.00
❏ CS 8038 [S]	Viva!	1958	6.25	12.50	25.00
❏ CS 8081 [S]	Malaguena	1958	6.25	12.50	25.00
❏ CS 8105 [S]	Porgy and Bess	1959	5.00	10.00	20.00
❏ CS 8108 [S]	A Night with Sigmund Romberg	1959	5.00	10.00	20.00
❏ CS 8181 [S]	A Night with Jerome Kern	1959	5.00	10.00	20.00

FAITHFULL, MARIANNE
ISLAND

Number	Title	Yr	VG	VG+	NM
❏ PRO 794 [EP]	Blazing Away Sampler	1990	5.00	10.00	20.00
-- Promo-only sampler for radio					

LONDON

Number	Title	Yr	VG	VG+	NM
❏ PS 452 [S]	Go Away from My World	1965	5.00	10.00	20.00
❏ PS 482 [S]	Faithfull Forever	1966	5.00	10.00	20.00
❏ LL 3423 [M]	Marianne Faithfull	1965	5.00	10.00	20.00

MOBILE FIDELITY

Number	Title	Yr	VG	VG+	NM
❏ 1-235	Broken English	1995	6.25	12.50	25.00
-- Audiophile vinyl					

FALL, THE
I.R.S.

Number	Title	Yr	VG	VG+	NM
❏ SP-003	Live at the Witch Trials	1979	5.00	10.00	20.00

FALLEN ANGELS, THE
ROULETTE

Number	Title	Yr	VG	VG+	NM
❏ R 25358 [M]	The Fallen Angels	1967	7.50	15.00	30.00

Number	Title	Yr	VG	VG+	NM
❏ SR 25358 [S]	The Fallen Angels	1967	10.00	20.00	40.00
❏ SR 42011	It's a Long Way Down	1968	25.00	50.00	100.00

FAME GANG, THE
FAME
| ❏ SKAO-4200 | Solid Gold from Muscle Shoals | 1969 | 6.25 | 12.50 | 25.00 |

FAME, GEORGIE
EPIC
| ❏ BN 26368 | The Ballad of Bonnie and Clyde | 1968 | 6.25 | 12.50 | 25.00 |
IMPERIAL
❏ LP-9282 [M]	Yeh, Yeh	1965	6.25	12.50	25.00
❏ LP-9331 [M]	Get Away	1966	6.25	12.50	25.00
❏ LP-12282 [P]	Yeh, Yeh	1965	7.50	15.00	30.00
-- Entire album is stereo except "Yeh, Yeh" (rechanneled)
| ❏ LP-12331 [R] | Get Away | 1966 | 5.00 | 10.00 | 20.00 |

FAMILY
REPRISE
| ❏ RS-6313 | Music in a Doll's House | 1968 | 5.00 | 10.00 | 20.00 |

FAMILY DOGG
BUDDAH
| ❏ BDS-5100 | The View from Rowland's Head | 1972 | 6.25 | 12.50 | 25.00 |

FANKHAUSER, MERRILL
Also see FAPARDOKLY.
MAUI
| ❏ 101 | Merrill Fankhauser | 1976 | 12.50 | 25.00 | 50.00 |
SHAMLEY
| ❏ SS-701 | Things Going Round in My Mind | 1968 | 20.00 | 40.00 | 80.00 |

FANTASTIC BAGGYS, THE
IMPERIAL
| ❏ LP-9270 [M] | Tell 'Em I'm Surfin' | 1964 | 37.50 | 75.00 | 150.00 |
| ❏ LP-12270 [S] | Tell 'Em I'm Surfin' | 1964 | 75.00 | 150.00 | 300.00 |

FANTASTIC DEE JAYS, THE
STONE
| ❏ SLP-4003 | The Fantastic Dee Jays | 1966 | 250.00 | 500.00 | 1,000. |

FANTASTIC FOUR, THE
SOUL
| ❏ SS-717 | The Best of the Fantastic Four | 1969 | 10.00 | 20.00 | 40.00 |

FANTASTIC JOHNNY C, THE
PHIL-LA OF SOUL
| ❏ 4000 | Boogaloo Down Broadway | 1968 | 20.00 | 40.00 | 80.00 |

FANTASY
LIBERTY
| ❏ LSP-7643 | Fantasy | 1970 | 5.00 | 10.00 | 20.00 |

FAPARDOKLY
Also see MERRILL FANKHAUSER.
U.I.P.
| ❏ 2250 | Fapardokly | 1967 | 250.00 | 500.00 | 1,000. |

FAR CRY
VANGUARD
| ❏ VSD-6510 | Far Cry | 1969 | 6.25 | 12.50 | 25.00 |

FARDON, DON
GNP CRESCENDO
| ❏ GNPS-2044 | Indian Reservation | 1968 | 5.00 | 10.00 | 20.00 |

FARLOWE, CHRIS
COLUMBIA
| ❏ CL 2593 [M] | The Fabulous Chris Farlowe | 1966 | 10.00 | 20.00 | 40.00 |
| ❏ CS 9393 [R] | The Fabulous Chris Farlowe | 1966 | 6.25 | 12.50 | 25.00 |
IMMEDIATE
| ❏ Z12 52010 | Paint It Farlowe | 1968 | 5.00 | 10.00 | 20.00 |

FARM BAND, THE
MANTRA
| ❏ 777 [(2)] | The Farm Band | 1972 | 7.50 | 15.00 | 30.00 |
-- With poster

FARNER, MARK, AND DON BREWER
Also see GRAND FUNK RAILROAD.
QUADICO
| ❏ 7401 [PD] | Monumental Funk | 1977 | 5.00 | 10.00 | 20.00 |
-- Picture disc

FARRELL, RICHARD
MERCURY LIVING PRESENCE
| ❏ SR 90126 [S] | Lizst: Piano Concerto No. 1; Grieg: Piano Concerto in A | 1960 | 6.25 | 12.50 | 25.00 |
-- Maroon label, no "Vendor: Mercury Record Corporation"

FAT CITY
ABC PROBE
| ❏ 4508 | Reincarnation | 1969 | 5.00 | 10.00 | 20.00 |

FAT MATTRESS
ATCO
| ❏ SD 33-309 | Fat Mattress | 1969 | 5.00 | 10.00 | 20.00 |

FATHER YOD AND THE SPIRIT OF '76 -- See YA HO WA 13.

FAUN
GREGAR
| ❏ 7000 | Faun | 1969 | 12.50 | 25.00 | 50.00 |

FAY, FRANK
BALLY
| ❏ BAL-10215 [M] | Be Frank with Fay | 1957 | 10.00 | 20.00 | 40.00 |

FEAR
SLASH
| ❏ SR 111 | The Record | 1982 | 5.00 | 10.00 | 20.00 |

FEAR ITSELF
DOT
| ❏ DLP-25942 | Fear Itself | 1969 | 5.00 | 10.00 | 20.00 |

FEDERAL DUCK
MUSICOR
| ❏ MS-3162 | Federal Duck | 1968 | 5.00 | 10.00 | 20.00 |

FEELIES, THE
STIFF
| ❏ USE-4 | Crazy Rhythms | 1980 | 7.50 | 15.00 | 30.00 |
-- Price is for an actual U.S. pressing. Most copies sold in U.S. were U.K. copies with stickers.

FELDMAN, VICTOR
AVA
| ❏ A-19 [M] | Soviet Jazz Themes | 1963 | 6.25 | 12.50 | 25.00 |
| ❏ AS-19 [S] | Soviet Jazz Themes | 1963 | 6.25 | 12.50 | 25.00 |
CONTEMPORARY
❏ C-3541 [M]	Suite Sixteen	1957	10.00	20.00	40.00
❏ C-3549 [M]	The Arrival of Victor Feldman	1958	10.00	20.00	40.00
❏ C-5005 [M]	Latinsville	1960	10.00	20.00	40.00
❏ S-7541 [S]	Suite Sixteen	1959	7.50	15.00	30.00
❏ S-7549 [S]	The Arrival of Victor Feldman	1959	7.50	15.00	30.00
❏ S-9005 [S]	Latinsville	1960	7.50	15.00	30.00
INTERLUDE
❏ MO-510 [M]	With Mallets Aforethought	1959	10.00	20.00	40.00
-- Reissue of Mode LP
MODE
| ❏ LP-120 [M] | Victor Feldman on Vibes | 1957 | 15.00 | 30.00 | 60.00 |
NAUTILUS
| ❏ NR-50 | The Secret of the Andes | 1982 | 5.00 | 10.00 | 20.00 |
-- Audiophile vinyl
RIVERSIDE
| ❏ RLP-366 [M] | Merry Ole Soul | 1961 | 6.25 | 12.50 | 25.00 |
| ❏ RS-9366 [S] | Merry Ole Soul | 1961 | 6.25 | 12.50 | 25.00 |
VEE JAY
| ❏ LP-1096 [M] | Love Me with All Your Heart | 1964 | 7.50 | 15.00 | 30.00 |
| ❏ LP-2507 [M] | It's a Wonderful World | 1965 | 5.00 | 10.00 | 20.00 |
WORLD PACIFIC
| ❏ ST-1807 [S] | Stop the World, I Want to Get Off | 1962 | 5.00 | 10.00 | 20.00 |
| ❏ WP-1807 [M] | Stop the World, I Want to Get Off | 1962 | 7.50 | 15.00 | 30.00 |

FELICE, DEE
BETHLEHEM
| ❏ B-10000 | In Heat | 1969 | 12.50 | 25.00 | 50.00 |
-- Produced by JAMES BROWN.

Number	Title	Yr	VG	VG+	NM

FELICIANO, JOSE
RCA VICTOR

Number	Title	Yr	VG	VG+	NM
❏ LSP-3358 [S]	The Voice and Guitar of Jose Feliciano	1965	5.00	10.00	20.00
❏ LSP-3503 [S]	Bag Full of Soul (Folk, Rock and Blues)	1966	5.00	10.00	20.00
❏ LSP-3581 [S]	Fantastic Feliciano	1966	5.00	10.00	20.00
❏ LPM-3957 [M]	Feliciano!	1968	6.25	12.50	25.00

FELT
NASCO

Number	Title	Yr	VG	VG+	NM
❏ 9006	Felt	1971	50.00	100.00	200.00

FEMININE COMPLEX, THE
ATHENA

Number	Title	Yr	VG	VG+	NM
❏ 600	The Feminine Complex	1969	7.50	15.00	30.00

FENDERMEN, THE
SOMA

Number	Title	Yr	VG	VG+	NM
❏ MG-1240 [M] -- Black vinyl	Mule Skinner Blues	1960	300.00	600.00	1,200.
❏ MG-1240 [M] -- Blue vinyl	Mule Skinner Blues	1960	2,000.	3,000.	4,000.

FERGUSON, MAYNARD
CAMEO

Number	Title	Yr	VG	VG+	NM
❏ C-1046 [M]	The New Sounds of Maynard Ferguson	1963	5.00	10.00	20.00
❏ SC-1046 [S]	The New Sounds of Maynard Ferguson	1963	6.25	12.50	25.00
❏ C-1066 [M]	Come Blow Your Horn	1964	5.00	10.00	20.00
❏ SC-1066 [S]	Come Blow Your Horn	1964	6.25	12.50	25.00

COLUMBIA

Number	Title	Yr	VG	VG+	NM
❏ PCQ 34457 [Q]	Conquistador	1977	5.00	10.00	20.00
❏ HC 44457 -- Half-speed mastered edition	Conquistador	1982	7.50	15.00	30.00

EMARCY

Number	Title	Yr	VG	VG+	NM
❏ MG-26017 [10]	Maynard Ferguson's Hollywood Party	1954	25.00	50.00	100.00
❏ MG-26024 [10]	Dimensions	1954	25.00	50.00	100.00
❏ MG-36009 [M]	Jam Session Featuring Maynard Ferguson	1955	12.50	25.00	50.00
❏ MG-36021 [M]	Maynard Ferguson Octet	1955	15.00	30.00	60.00
❏ MG-36044 [M]	Dimensions	1956	12.50	25.00	50.00
❏ MG-36046 [M]	Maynard Ferguson's Hollywood Party	1956	12.50	25.00	50.00
❏ MG-36076 [M]	Around the Horn with Maynard Ferguson	1956	12.50	25.00	50.00
❏ MG-36114 [M]	Boy with Lots of Brass	1957	12.50	25.00	50.00

MAINSTREAM

Number	Title	Yr	VG	VG+	NM
❏ S-6031 [S]	Color Him Wild	1965	5.00	10.00	20.00
❏ S-6045 [S]	The Blues Roar	1965	5.00	10.00	20.00
❏ S-6060 [S]	Maynard Ferguson Sextet	1966	5.00	10.00	20.00

MERCURY

Number	Title	Yr	VG	VG+	NM
❏ MG-20556 [M]	Boy with Lots of Brass	1960	7.50	15.00	30.00
❏ SR-60124 [S]	Boy with Lots of Brass	1960	7.50	15.00	30.00

NAUTILUS

Number	Title	Yr	VG	VG+	NM
❏ NR-57 -- Audiophile vinyl	Storm	1983	10.00	20.00	40.00

ROULETTE

Number	Title	Yr	VG	VG+	NM
❏ R 52012 [M]	A Message from Newport	1958	6.25	12.50	25.00
❏ SR 52012 [S]	A Message from Newport	1958	6.25	12.50	25.00
❏ R 52027 [M]	A Message from Birdland	1959	6.25	12.50	25.00
❏ SR 52027 [S]	A Message from Birdland	1959	6.25	12.50	25.00
❏ R 52038 [M]	Maynard Ferguson Plays Jazz for Dancing	1959	6.25	12.50	25.00
❏ SR 52038 [S]	Maynard Ferguson Plays Jazz for Dancing	1959	6.25	12.50	25.00
❏ R 52047 [M]	Newport Suite	1960	6.25	12.50	25.00
❏ SR 52047 [S]	Newport Suite	1960	6.25	12.50	25.00
❏ R 52055 [M]	Let's Face the Music and Dance	1960	6.25	12.50	25.00
❏ SR 52055 [S]	Let's Face the Music and Dance	1960	6.25	12.50	25.00
❏ R 52058 [M]	Swingin' My Way Through College	1960	6.25	12.50	25.00
❏ SR 52058 [S]	Swingin' My Way Through College	1960	6.25	12.50	25.00
❏ R 52064 [M]	Maynard '61	1961	6.25	12.50	25.00
❏ SR 52064 [S]	Maynard '61	1961	6.25	12.50	25.00
❏ SR 52083 [S]	Maynard '62	1962	5.00	10.00	20.00
❏ SR 52084 [S]	Si! Si! M.F.	1962	5.00	10.00	20.00
❏ SR 52097 [S]	Maynard '63	1963	5.00	10.00	20.00
❏ SR 52107 [S]	Maynard '64	1964	5.00	10.00	20.00
❏ SR 52110 [S]	The World of Maynard Ferguson	1964	5.00	10.00	20.00

FERLINGHETTI, LAWRENCE
FANTASY

Number	Title	Yr	VG	VG+	NM
❏ 7004 [M] -- Red vinyl	The Impeachment of Eisenhower	1958	50.00	100.00	200.00
❏ 7004 [M] -- Black vinyl	The Impeachment of Eisenhower	1958	25.00	50.00	100.00

FERRANTE AND TEICHER
ABC-PARAMOUNT

Number	Title	Yr	VG	VG+	NM
❏ S-221 [S]	Heavenly Sounds in Hi-Fi	1958	5.00	10.00	20.00
❏ S-248 [S]	Ferrante and Teicher with Percussion	1958	5.00	10.00	20.00
❏ S-285 [S]	Ferrante and Teicher Blast Off	1959	5.00	10.00	20.00
❏ S-313 [S]	Ferrante and Teicher Play Light Classics	1960	5.00	10.00	20.00
❏ S-336 [S]	Themes from Broadway Shows	1960	5.00	10.00	20.00

COLUMBIA

Number	Title	Yr	VG	VG+	NM
❏ CL 573 [M]	Hi-Fire Works	1955	6.25	12.50	25.00

UNITED ARTISTS

Number	Title	Yr	VG	VG+	NM
❏ UA-LA831-P [(4)]	For You with Love	1978	5.00	10.00	20.00

WESTMINSTER

Number	Title	Yr	VG	VG+	NM
❏ SW 1045 [S]	Soundproof	195?	6.25	12.50	25.00
❏ SW 1048 [S]	Latin American Adventure	195?	6.25	12.50	25.00
❏ WL 3044 [M]	Christmas Hi-Fi Favorites	195?	5.00	10.00	20.00
❏ WP 6001 [M]	Postcards from Paris	195?	5.00	10.00	20.00
❏ WP 6021 [M]	Adventure in Carols	195?	5.00	10.00	20.00

FESTIVAL CHAMBER ORCHESTRA (ANTAL DORATI, COND.)
MERCURY LIVING PRESENCE

Number	Title	Yr	VG	VG+	NM
❏ SR 90436 [S] -- Maroon label, with "Vendor: Mercury Record Corporation"	Haydn: Symphonies No. 59 and 81	1965	6.25	12.50	25.00
❏ SR 90438 [S] -- Maroon label, with "Vendor: Mercury Record Corporation"	Mozart: Marches; Lucio Silva Overture; Menuet; German Dances	1965	6.25	12.50	25.00

FESTIVAL QUARTET
RCA VICTOR RED SEAL

Number	Title	Yr	VG	VG+	NM
❏ LSC-2147 [S] -- Original with "shaded dog" label	Schubert: Trout Quintet	1958	37.50	75.00	150.00
❏ LSC-2147 [S] -- Second edition with "white dog" label	Schubert: Trout Quintet	1964	30.00	60.00	120.00
❏ LSC-2330 [S] -- Original with "shaded dog" label	Brahms: Piano Quartet in C	1959	12.50	25.00	50.00
❏ LSC-2473 [S] -- Originals with "shaded dog" label	Brahms: Piano Quartet in G	1961	15.00	30.00	60.00
❏ LSC-2517 [S] -- Originals with "shaded dog" label	Brahms: Piano Quartet in A	1961	15.00	30.00	60.00
❏ LSC-2735 [S] -- Original with "shaded dog" label	Faure: Piano Quartet in G	1963	12.50	25.00	50.00

FEVER TREE
AMPEX

Number	Title	Yr	VG	VG+	NM
❏ A-10113	For Sale	1970	6.25	12.50	25.00

UNI

Number	Title	Yr	VG	VG+	NM
❏ 73024	Fever Tree	1968	6.25	12.50	25.00
❏ 73040	Another Time, Another Place	1968	6.25	12.50	25.00
❏ 73067	Creation	1970	6.25	12.50	25.00

FIELD, SALLY
COLGEMS

Number	Title	Yr	VG	VG+	NM
❏ COM-106 [M]	The Flying Nun	1967	7.50	15.00	30.00
❏ COS-106 [S]	The Flying Nun	1967	6.25	12.50	25.00

FIELDS, ERNIE
RENDEZVOUS

Number	Title	Yr	VG	VG+	NM
❏ 1309 [M]	In the Mood	1960	12.50	25.00	50.00

FIELDS, GRACIE
LIBERTY

Number	Title	Yr	VG	VG+	NM
❏ LRP-3059 [M]	Our Gracie	1957	10.00	20.00	40.00

FIELDS, IRVING
ABC-PARAMOUNT

Number	Title	Yr	VG	VG+	NM
❏ ABC-187 [M]	Irving Fields at the St. Moritz	1956	7.50	15.00	30.00

DECCA

Number	Title	Yr	VG	VG+	NM
❏ DL 4114 [M]	More Bagels and Bongos	1961	5.00	10.00	20.00
❏ DL 4174 [M]	Pizzas and Bongos	1961	5.00	10.00	20.00
❏ DL 4238 [M]	Champagne and Bongos	1962	5.00	10.00	20.00
❏ DL 4323 [M]	Bikinis and Bongos	1962	5.00	10.00	20.00
❏ DL 8856 [M]	Bagels and Bongos	1959	5.00	10.00	20.00

Number	Title	Yr	VG	VG+	NM
❏ DL 8901 [M]	At the Emerald Room, Hotel Astor	1959	5.00	10.00	20.00
❏ DL 74114 [S]	More Bagels and Bongos	1961	6.25	12.50	25.00
❏ DL 74174 [S]	Pizzas and Bongos	1961	6.25	12.50	25.00
❏ DL 74238 [S]	Champagne and Bongos	1962	6.25	12.00	25.00
❏ DL 74323 [S]	Bikinis and Bongos	1962	6.25	12.00	25.00
❏ DL 78856 [S]	Bagels and Bongos	1959	7.50	15.00	30.00
❏ DL 78901 [S]	At the Emerald Room, Hotel Astor	1959	7.50	15.00	30.00

EVEREST

Number	Title	Yr	VG	VG+	NM
❏ SDBR-1134 [S]	Twisting	1962	6.25	12.50	25.00
❏ LPBR-5134 [M]	Twisting	1962	5.00	10.00	20.00

FIESTA

Number	Title	Yr	VG	VG+	NM
❏ FLP-1228 [M]	Fabulous Fingers	195?	7.50	15.00	30.00

GONE

Number	Title	Yr	VG	VG+	NM
❏ LP-5003 [M]	Fabulous Touch	1959	6.25	12.50	25.00

KING

Number	Title	Yr	VG	VG+	NM
❏ 703 [M]	Irving Fields Favorites	1960	7.50	15.00	30.00
❏ 709 [M]	Live It Up	1960	7.50	15.00	30.00
❏ 724 [M]	Classics Go Latin	1960	5.00	10.00	20.00
❏ 724-S [S]	Classics Go Latin	1960	7.50	15.00	30.00
❏ 742 [M]	Lox, Latin and Bongos	1960	5.00	10.00	20.00
❏ 742-S [S]	Lox, Latin and Bongos	1960	7.50	15.00	30.00

RCA VICTOR

Number	Title	Yr	VG	VG+	NM
❏ LPT-38 [10]	Fields Favorites	195?	12.50	25.00	50.00

TOPS

Number	Title	Yr	VG	VG+	NM
❏ L-1562 [M]	Irving Fields Plays Irving Berlin	1957	7.50	15.00	30.00

FIELDS, THE
UNI

Number	Title	Yr	VG	VG+	NM
❏ 73050	The Fields	1969	12.50	25.00	50.00

FIFTH DIMENSION, THE
SOUL CITY

Number	Title	Yr	VG	VG+	NM
❏ SCM-92000 [M]	Up, Up and Away	1967	5.00	10.00	20.00
❏ SCM-92001 [M]	The Magic Garden	1967	5.00	10.00	20.00

FIFTH ESTATE, THE
JUBILEE

Number	Title	Yr	VG	VG+	NM
❏ JGM-8005 [M]	Ding Dong! The Witch Is Dead	1967	6.25	12.50	25.00
❏ JGS-8005 [S]	Ding Dong! The Witch Is Dead	1967	7.50	15.00	30.00

FIFTY FOOT HOSE
LIMELIGHT

Number	Title	Yr	VG	VG+	NM
❏ 86062	Cauldron	1968	25.00	50.00	100.00

FILETS OF SOUL
SQUID

Number	Title	Yr	VG	VG+	NM
❏ 4857	Freedom	1968	25.00	50.00	100.00

FINCHLEY BOYS, THE
GOLDEN THROAT

Number	Title	Yr	VG	VG+	NM
❏ 200-19	Everlasting Tribute	1971	50.00	100.00	200.00

FINNEY, ALBERT
MOTOWN

Number	Title	Yr	VG	VG+	NM
❏ M6-889	The Albert Finney Album	1977	5.00	10.00	20.00

FIRE
ABC

Number	Title	Yr	VG	VG+	NM
❏ S-661	Fire	1969	5.00	10.00	20.00

FIRE & ICE LTD.
CAPITOL

Number	Title	Yr	VG	VG+	NM
❏ ST 2577 [S]	The Happening	1966	10.00	20.00	40.00
❏ T 2577 [M]	The Happening	1966	7.50	15.00	30.00

FIRE ESCAPE, THE
GNP CRESCENDO

Number	Title	Yr	VG	VG+	NM
❏ GNP-2034 [M]	Psychotic Reaction	1967	10.00	20.00	40.00
❏ GNPS-2034 [S]	Psychotic Reaction	1967	7.50	15.00	30.00

FIREBALLS, THE
Includes Jimmy Gilmer and the Fireballs.
ATCO

Number	Title	Yr	VG	VG+	NM
❏ SD 33-239	Bottle of Wine	1968	6.25	12.50	25.00
❏ SD 33-275	Come On, React!	1969	6.25	12.50	25.00

CROWN

Number	Title	Yr	VG	VG+	NM
❏ CST-376 [R]	Jimmy Gilmer and the Fireballs & The Sugar Shackers	1963	6.25	12.50	25.00
❏ CST-387 [R]	The Sensational Jimmy Gilmer & The Fireballs	1964	6.25	12.50	25.00
❏ CLP-5376 [M]	Jimmy Gilmer and the Fireballs & The Sugar Shackers	1963	6.25	12.50	25.00
❏ CLP-5387 [M]	The Sensational Jimmy Gilmer & The Fireballs	1964	6.25	12.50	25.00

DOT

Number	Title	Yr	VG	VG+	NM
❏ DLP-3512 [M]	Torquay	1963	12.50	25.00	50.00
❏ DLP-3545 [M]	Sugar Shack	1963	10.00	20.00	40.00
-- Jimmy Gilmer and the Fireballs					
❏ DLP-3577 [M]	Buddy's Buddy	1964	12.50	25.00	50.00
-- Jimmy Gilmer and the Fireballs					
❏ DLP-3643 [M]	Lucky 'Leven	1965	7.50	15.00	30.00
❏ DLP-3668 [M]	Folkbeat	1965	7.50	15.00	30.00
❏ DLP-3709 [M]	Campusology	1966	7.50	15.00	30.00
❏ DLP-25512 [S]	Torquay	1963	20.00	40.00	80.00
❏ DLP-25545 [S]	Sugar Shack	1963	15.00	30.00	60.00
-- Jimmy Gilmer and the Fireballs					
❏ DLP-25577 [S]	Buddy's Buddy	1964	20.00	40.00	80.00
-- Jimmy Gilmer and the Fireballs					
❏ DLP-25643 [S]	Lucky 'Leven	1965	10.00	20.00	40.00
❏ DLP-25668 [S]	Folkbeat	1965	10.00	20.00	40.00
❏ DLP-25709 [S]	Campusology	1966	10.00	20.00	40.00
❏ DLP-25856	Firewater	1968	6.25	12.50	25.00

TOP RANK

Number	Title	Yr	VG	VG+	NM
❏ RM-324 [M]	The Fireballs	1960	37.50	75.00	150.00
❏ RM-343 [M]	Vaquero	1960	37.50	75.00	150.00
❏ RS-643 [S]	Vaquero	1960	50.00	100.00	200.00

WARWICK

Number	Title	Yr	VG	VG+	NM
❏ W-2042 [M]	Here Are the Fireballs	1961	37.50	75.00	150.00
❏ WST-2042 [S]	Here Are the Fireballs	1961	62.50	125.00	250.00

FIREBIRDS, THE
CROWN

Number	Title	Yr	VG	VG+	NM
❏ CST-589	Light My Fire	1968	17.50	35.00	70.00

FIREFLIES, THE
TAURUS

Number	Title	Yr	VG	VG+	NM
❏ 1002 [M]	You Were Mine	196?	25.00	50.00	100.00
❏ S-1002 [S]	You Were Mine	196?	75.00	150.00	300.00

FIRESIGN THEATRE, THE
COLUMBIA

Number	Title	Yr	VG	VG+	NM
❏ CL 2719 [M]	Waiting for the Electrician	1968	6.25	12.50	25.00
❏ CQ 30737 [Q]	I Think We're All Bozos on This Bus	1972	5.00	10.00	20.00
❏ KG 31099 [(2)]	Dear Friends	1972	5.00	10.00	20.00
❏ CQ 33141 [Q]	Everything You Know Is Wrong	1974	5.00	10.00	20.00

FIRST EDITION, THE
Also see KENNY ROGERS.
REPRISE

Number	Title	Yr	VG	VG+	NM
❏ MS 2039	Transition	1971	5.00	10.00	20.00
❏ 2SX 6476 [(2)]	The Ballad of Calico	1972	6.25	12.50	25.00
❏ R-6276 [M]	The First Edition	1967	7.50	15.00	30.00
❏ RS-6276 [S]	The First Edition	1967	6.25	12.50	25.00
❏ RS-6302	The First Edition's Second	1968	6.25	12.50	25.00
❏ RS-6328	The First Edition '69	1969	6.25	12.50	25.00
❏ RS-6352	Ruby, Don't Take Your Love to Town	1969	5.00	10.00	20.00
-- Starting here, as "Kenny Rogers and the First Edition"					
❏ RS-6385	Something's Burning	1970	5.00	10.00	20.00
❏ RS-6412	Tell It All Brother	1970	5.00	10.00	20.00
❏ RS-6437	Greatest Hits	1971	5.00	10.00	20.00

FISCHER, WILD MAN
REPRISE

Number	Title	Yr	VG	VG+	NM
❏ 2XS 6332 [(2)]	An Evening with Wild Man Fischer	1969	12.50	25.00	50.00

FISHER, AL, AND LOU MARKS
CAMEO

Number	Title	Yr	VG	VG+	NM
❏ C-1081 [M]	Rome on the Range	1964	5.00	10.00	20.00

SWAN

Number	Title	Yr	VG	VG+	NM
❏ SLP-514 [M]	It's a Beatle (Coo-Coo) World	1964	10.00	20.00	40.00

FISHER, CHIP
RCA VICTOR

Number	Title	Yr	VG	VG+	NM
❏ LPM-1797 [M]	Chipper at the Sugar Bowl	1958	10.00	20.00	40.00
❏ LSP-1797 [S]	Chipper at the Sugar Bowl	1958	12.50	25.00	50.00

FISHER, EDDIE
DOT

Number	Title	Yr	VG	VG+	NM
❏ DLP-25658 [S]	Mary Christmas	1965	5.00	10.00	20.00

Number	Title	Yr	VG	VG+	NM
RAMROD					
❏ RRS-1 [(2) S]	Eddie Fisher at the Winter Garden	1963	5.00	10.00	20.00
RCA VICTOR					
❏ LOC-1024 [M]	Academy Award Winners	1955	10.00	20.00	40.00
❏ LPM-1097 [M]	I Love You	1955	7.50	15.00	30.00
❏ LPM-1180 [M]	I'm in the Mood for Love	1955	7.50	15.00	30.00
❏ LPM-1181 [M]	May I Sing to You?	1955	7.50	15.00	30.00
❏ LPM-1399 [M]	Bundle of Joy	1957	7.50	15.00	30.00
❏ LPM-1548 [M]	Thinking of You	1957	7.50	15.00	30.00
❏ LPM-1647 [M]	As Long As There's Music	1958	7.50	15.00	30.00
❏ LSP-1647 [S]	As Long As There's Music	1958	12.50	25.00	50.00
❏ LSP-2504 [S]	Eddie Fisher's Greatest Hits	1962	5.00	10.00	20.00
❏ LPM-3025 [10]	Fisher Sings	1952	12.50	25.00	50.00
❏ LPM-3058 [10]	I'm in the Mood for Love	1952	12.50	25.00	50.00
❏ LPM-3065 [10]	Christmas with Fisher	1952	12.50	25.00	50.00
❏ LPM-3122 [10]	Irving Berlin Favorites	1953	12.50	25.00	50.00
❏ LPM-3185 [10]	May I Sing to You?	1953	12.50	25.00	50.00
❏ LPM-3820 [M]	People Like You	1967	5.00	10.00	20.00

FISHER, TONI

SIGNET

Number	Title	Yr	VG	VG+	NM
❏ WP-509 [S]	The Big Hurt	1960	12.50	25.00	50.00
-- Issued in "Stereomonic"					

FITZGERALD, ELLA

CAPITOL

Number	Title	Yr	VG	VG+	NM
❏ T 2685 [M]	Brighten the Corner	1967	5.00	10.00	20.00
❏ T 2805 [M]	Ella Fitzgerald's Christmas	1967	5.00	10.00	20.00
DECCA					
❏ DXB 156 [(2) M]	The Best of Ella	1959	10.00	20.00	40.00
-- Black labels, silver print					
❏ DXB 156 [(2) M]	The Best of Ella	1961	6.25	12.50	25.00
-- Black labels with color bars					
❏ DL 4129 [M]	Golden Favorites	1961	5.00	10.00	20.00
❏ DL 5084 [10]	Souvenir Album	1950	30.00	60.00	120.00
❏ DL 5300 [10]	Ella Fitzgerald Sings Gershwin Songs	1951	30.00	60.00	120.00
❏ DXSB 7156 [(2) R]	The Best of Ella	196?	5.00	10.00	20.00
❏ DL 8068 [M]	Songs in a Mellow Mood	1954	12.50	25.00	50.00
❏ DL 8149 [M]	Lullabies of Birdland	1955	12.50	25.00	50.00
❏ DL 8155 [M]	Sweet and Hot	1955	12.50	25.00	50.00
❏ DL 8378 [M]	Ella Sings Gershwin	1957	10.00	20.00	40.00
❏ DL 8477 [M]	Ella and Her Fellas	1957	10.00	20.00	40.00
❏ DL 8695 [M]	The First Lady of Song	1958	10.00	20.00	40.00
❏ DL 8696 [M]	Miss Ella Fitzgerald and Mr. NelsonRiddle Invite You to Listen and Relax	1958	10.00	20.00	40.00
❏ DL 8832 [M]	For Sentimental Reasons	1958	10.00	20.00	40.00
VERVE					
❏ V-10-4 [(4) M]	Ella Fitzgerald Sings the Duke Ellington Song Book	196?	12.50	25.00	50.00
❏ V-29-5 [(5) M]	Ella Fitzgerald Sings the George and Ira Gershwin Song Book	196?	25.00	50.00	100.00
-- Reissue of MGV-4029					
❏ V6-29-5 [(5) S]	Ella Fitzgerald Sings the George and Ira Gershwin Song Book	196?	25.00	50.00	100.00
-- Reissue of MGVS-6082					
❏ MGV-4001-2 [(2) M]	Ella Fitzgerald Sings the Cole Porter Song Book	1956	20.00	40.00	80.00
❏ V-4001-2 [(2) M]	Ella Fitzgerald Sings the Cole Porter Song Book	1961	6.25	12.50	25.00
❏ MGV-4002-2 [(2) M]	Ella Fitzgerald Sings the Rodgers & Hart Song Book	1956	20.00	40.00	80.00
❏ V-4002-2 [(2) M]	Ella Fitzgerald Sings the Rodgers and Hart Song Book	1961	6.25	12.50	25.00
❏ MGV-4004 [M]	Like Someone in Love	1957	12.50	25.00	50.00
❏ V-4004 [M]	Like Someone in Love	1961	5.00	10.00	20.00
❏ V6-4004 [S]	Like Someone in Love	1961	5.00	10.00	20.00
❏ MGV-4008-2 [(2) M]	Ella Fitzgerald Sings the Duke Ellington Song Book, Vol. 1	1957	20.00	40.00	80.00
❏ V-4008-2 [(2) M]	Ella Fitzgerald Sings the Duke Ellington Song Book, Vol. 1	1961	6.25	12.50	25.00
❏ MGV-4009-2 [(2) M]	Ella Fitzgerald Sings the Duke Ellington Song Book, Vol. 2	1957	20.00	40.00	80.00
❏ V-4009-2 [(2) M]	Ella Fitzgerald Sings the Duke Ellington Song Book, Vol. 2	1961	6.25	12.50	25.00
❏ MGV-4010-4 [(4) M]	Ella Fitzgerald Sings the Duke Ellington Song Book	1957	37.50	75.00	150.00
-- Combines 4008 and 4009 into one package					
❏ MGV-4013 [M]	Ella Fitzgerald Sings the Gershwin Song Book	1957	12.50	25.00	50.00
❏ MGV-4019-2 [(2) M]	Ella Fitzgerald Sings the Irving Berlin Song Book	1958	20.00	40.00	80.00
❏ V-4019-2 [(2) M]	Ella Fitzgerald Sings the Irving Berlin Song Book	1961	6.25	12.50	25.00

Number	Title	Yr	VG	VG+	NM
❏ V6-4019-2 [(2) S]	Ella Fitzgerald Sings the Irving Berlin Song Book	1961	6.25	12.50	25.00
❏ MGV-4021 [M]	Ella Swings Lightly	1958	12.50	25.00	50.00
❏ V-4021 [M]	Ella Swings Lightly	1961	5.00	10.00	20.00
❏ V6-4021 [S]	Ella Swings Lightly	1961	5.00	10.00	20.00
❏ MGV-4022 [M]	Ella Fitzgerald Sings the Rodgers & Hart Song Book, Vol. 1	1959	12.50	25.00	50.00
❏ V-4022 [M]	Ella Fitzgerald Sings the Rodgers & Hart Song Book, Vol. 1	1961	5.00	10.00	20.00
❏ V6-4022 [S]	Ella Fitzgerald Sings the Rodgers & Hart Song Book, Vol. 1	1961	5.00	10.00	20.00
❏ MGV-4023 [M]	Ella Fitzgerald Sings the Rodgers & Hart Song Book, Vol. 2	1959	12.50	25.00	50.00
❏ V-4023 [M]	Ella Fitzgerald Sings the Rodgers & Hart Song Book, Vol. 2	1961	5.00	10.00	20.00
❏ V6-4023 [S]	Ella Fitzgerald Sings the Rodgers & Hart Song Book, Vol. 2	1961	5.00	10.00	20.00
❏ MGV-4024 [M]	Ella Fitzgerald Sings the George and Ira Gershwin Song Book, Vol. 1	1959	12.50	25.00	50.00
❏ V-4024 [M]	Ella Fitzgerald Sings the George and Ira Gershwin Song Book, Vol. 1	1961	5.00	10.00	20.00
❏ V6-4024 [S]	Ella Fitzgerald Sings the George and Ira Gershwin Song Book, Vol. 1	1961	5.00	10.00	20.00
❏ MGV-4025 [M]	Ella Fitzgerald Sings the George and Ira Gershwin Song Book, Vol. 2	1959	12.50	25.00	50.00
❏ V-4025 [M]	Ella Fitzgerald Sings the George and Ira Gershwin Song Book, Vol. 2	1961	5.00	10.00	20.00
❏ V6-4025 [S]	Ella Fitzgerald Sings the George and Ira Gershwin Song Book, Vol. 2	1961	5.00	10.00	20.00
❏ MGV-4026 [M]	Ella Fitzgerald Sings the George and Ira Gershwin Song Book, Vol. 3	1959	12.50	25.00	50.00
❏ V-4026 [M]	Ella Fitzgerald Sings the George and Ira Gershwin Song Book, Vol. 3	1961	5.00	10.00	20.00
❏ V6-4026 [S]	Ella Fitzgerald Sings the George and Ira Gershwin Song Book, Vol. 3	1961	5.00	10.00	20.00
❏ MGV-4027 [M]	Ella Fitzgerald Sings the George and Ira Gershwin Song Book, Vol. 4	1959	12.50	25.00	50.00
❏ V-4027 [M]	Ella Fitzgerald Sings the George and Ira Gershwin Song Book, Vol. 4	1961	5.00	10.00	20.00
❏ V6-4027 [S]	Ella Fitzgerald Sings the George and Ira Gershwin Song Book, Vol. 4	1961	5.00	10.00	20.00
❏ MGV-4028 [M]	Ella Fitzgerald Sings the George and Ira Gershwin Song Book, Vol. 5	1959	12.50	25.00	50.00
❏ V-4028 [M]	Ella Fitzgerald Sings the George and Ira Gershwin Song Book, Vol. 5	1961	5.00	10.00	20.00
❏ V6-4028 [S]	Ella Fitzgerald Sings the George and Ira Gershwin Song Book, Vol. 5	1961	5.00	10.00	20.00
❏ MGV-4029-5 [(5) M]	Ella Fitzgerald Sings the George	1959	125.00	250.00	500.00
-- Box set with 4024 through 4028 plus bonus 10-inch LP, all in walnut box with leather pockets					
❏ MGV-4029-5 [(5) M]	Ella Fitzgerald Sings the George and Ira Gershwin Song Book	1959	62.50	125.00	250.00
-- Box set with 4024 through 4028 plus bonus 10-inch LP					
❏ MGV-4030 [M]	Ella Fitzgerald Sings the Irving Berlin Song Book, Vol. 1	1959	12.50	25.00	50.00
❏ V-4030 [M]	Ella Fitzgerald Sings the Irving Berlin Song Book, Vol. 1	1961	5.00	10.00	20.00
❏ V6-4030 [S]	Ella Fitzgerald Sings the Irving Berlin Song Book, Vol. 1	1961	5.00	10.00	20.00
❏ MGV-4031 [M]	Ella Fitzgerald Sings the Irving Berlin Song Book, Vol. 2	1959	12.50	25.00	50.00
❏ V-4031 [M]	Ella Fitzgerald Sings the Irving Berlin Song Book, Vol. 2	1961	5.00	10.00	20.00
❏ V6-4031 [S]	Ella Fitzgerald Sings the Irving Berlin Song Book, Vol. 2	1961	5.00	10.00	20.00
❏ MGV-4032 [M]	Sweet Songs for Swingers	1959	12.50	25.00	50.00
❏ V-4032 [M]	Sweet Songs for Swingers	1961	5.00	10.00	20.00
❏ V6-4032 [S]	Sweet Songs for Swingers	1961	5.00	10.00	20.00
❏ MGV-4034 [M]	Hello, Love	1959	12.50	25.00	50.00
❏ V-4034 [M]	Hello, Love	1961	5.00	10.00	20.00
❏ V6-4034 [S]	Hello, Love	1961	5.00	10.00	20.00
❏ MGV-4036 [M]	Get Happy!	1960	10.00	20.00	40.00
❏ V-4036 [M]	Get Happy!	1961	5.00	10.00	20.00
❏ V6-4036 [S]	Get Happy!	1961	5.00	10.00	20.00
❏ MGV-4041 [M]	Mack the Knife -- Ella in Berlin	1960	10.00	20.00	40.00
❏ V-4041 [M]	Mack the Knife -- Ella in Berlin	1961	5.00	10.00	20.00
❏ V6-4041 [S]	Mack the Knife -- Ella in Berlin	1961	5.00	10.00	20.00
❏ MGV 4042 [M]	Ella Wishes You a Swinging Christmas	1960	12.50	25.00	50.00
❏ MGVS 4042 [S]	Ella Wishes You a Swinging Christmas	1960	15.00	30.00	60.00
❏ V 4042 [M]	Ella Wishes You a Swinging Christmas	1961	10.00	20.00	40.00
❏ V6 4042 [S]	Ella Wishes You a Swinging Christmas	1961	12.50	25.00	50.00
❏ MGV-4043 [M]	Let No Man Write My Epitaph	1961	10.00	20.00	40.00
❏ V-4043 [M]	Let No Man Write My Epitaph	1961	5.00	10.00	20.00
❏ V6-4043 [S]	Let No Man Write My Epitaph	1961	5.00	10.00	20.00

Number	Title	Yr	VG	VG+	NM
❏ MGV-4046-2 [(2) M]	Ella Fitzgerald Sings the Harold Arlen Song Book	1961	15.00	30.00	60.00
❏ MGV-4049 [M]	Ella Fitzgerald Sings Cole Porter	1961	10.00	20.00	40.00
❏ V-4049 [M]	Ella Fitzgerald Sings Cole Porter	1961	5.00	10.00	20.00
❏ MGV-4050 [M]	Ella Fitzgerald Sings More Cole Porter	1961	10.00	20.00	40.00
❏ V-4050 [M]	Ella Fitzgerald Sings More Cole Porter	1961	5.00	10.00	20.00
❏ MGV-4052 [M]	Ella in Hollywood	1961	10.00	20.00	40.00
❏ V-4052 [M]	Ella in Hollywood	1961	5.00	10.00	20.00
❏ V-4053 [M]	Clap Hands, Here Comes Charley	1962	10.00	20.00	40.00
❏ V6-4053 [S]	Clap Hands, Here Comes Charley	1962	37.50	75.00	150.00
❏ V-4054 [M]	Ella Swings Brightly with Nelson	1962	7.50	15.00	30.00
❏ V6-4054 [S]	Ella Swings Brightly with Nelson	1962	7.50	15.00	30.00
❏ V-4055 [M]	Ella Swings Gently with Nelson	1962	7.50	15.00	30.00
❏ V6-4055 [S]	Ella Swings Gently with Nelson	1962	7.50	15.00	30.00
❏ V-4056 [M]	Rhythm Is My Business	1962	7.50	15.00	30.00
❏ V6-4056 [S]	Rhythm Is My Business	1962	7.50	15.00	30.00
❏ V-4057 [M]	Ella Fitzgerald Sings the Harold Arlen Song Book, Vol. 1	1962	7.50	15.00	30.00
❏ V6-4057 [S]	Ella Fitzgerald Sings the Harold Arlen Song Book, Vol. 1	1962	7.50	15.00	30.00
❏ V-4058 [M]	Ella Fitzgerald Sings the Harold Arlen Song Book, Vol. 2	1962	7.50	15.00	30.00
❏ V6-4058 [S]	Ella Fitzgerald Sings the Harold Arlen Song Book, Vol. 2	1962	7.50	15.00	30.00
❏ V-4059 [M]	Ella Sings Broadway	1963	6.25	12.50	25.00
❏ V6-4059 [S]	Ella Sings Broadway	1963	6.25	12.50	25.00
❏ V-4060 [M]	Ella Fitzgerald Sings the Jerome Kern Song Book	1963	6.25	12.50	25.00
❏ V6-4060 [S]	Ella Fitzgerald Sings the Jerome Kern Song Book	1963	6.25	12.50	25.00
❏ V-4061 [M]	Ella and Basie!	1963	6.25	12.50	25.00
❏ V6-4061 [S]	Ella and Basie!	1963	6.25	12.50	25.00
❏ V-4062 [M]	These Are the Blues	1963	6.25	12.50	25.00
❏ V6-4062 [S]	These Are the Blues	1963	6.25	12.50	25.00
❏ V-4064 [M]	Hello, Dolly!	1964	6.25	12.50	25.00
❏ V6-4064 [S]	Hello, Dolly!	1964	6.25	12.50	25.00
❏ V-4065 [M]	Ella at Juan Les Pins	1964	6.25	12.50	25.00
❏ V6-4065 [S]	Ella at Juan Les Pins	1964	6.25	12.50	25.00
❏ V-4066 [M]	A Tribute to Cole Porter	1964	6.25	12.50	25.00
❏ V6-4066 [S]	A Tribute to Cole Porter	1964	6.25	12.50	25.00
❏ V-4067 [M]	Ella Fitzgerald Sings the Johnny Mercer Song Book	1965	5.00	10.00	20.00
❏ V6-4067 [S]	Ella Fitzgerald Sings the Johnny Mercer Song Book	1965	5.00	10.00	20.00
❏ V-4068 [M]	Porgy & Bess	1965	5.00	10.00	20.00
❏ V6-4068 [S]	Porgy & Bess	1965	5.00	10.00	20.00
❏ V-4069 [M]	Ella in Hamburg	1966	5.00	10.00	20.00
❏ V6-4069 [S]	Ella in Hamburg	1966	5.00	10.00	20.00
❏ V-4070 [M]	Ella at Duke's Place	1966	5.00	10.00	20.00
❏ V6-4070 [S]	Ella at Duke's Place	1966	5.00	10.00	20.00
❏ V-4071 [M]	Whisper Not	1966	5.00	10.00	20.00
❏ V6-4071 [S]	Whisper Not	1966	5.00	10.00	20.00
❏ V-4072 [M]	Ella & Duke at Cote d'Azur	1967	6.25	12.50	25.00
❏ MGVS-6000 [S]	Like Someone in Love	1960	10.00	20.00	40.00
❏ MGVS-6005-2 [(2) S]	Ella Fitzgerald Sings the Irving Berlin Song Book	1960	15.00	30.00	60.00
❏ MGVS-6009 [S]	Ella Fitzgerald Sings the Rodgers & Hart Song Book, Vol. 1	1960	10.00	20.00	40.00
❏ MGVS-6010 [S]	Ella Fitzgerald Sings the Rodgers & Hart Song Book, Vol. 2	1960	10.00	20.00	40.00
❏ MGVS-6019 [S]	Ella Swings Lightly	1960	10.00	20.00	40.00
❏ MGVS-6026 [S]	Ella Fitzgerald at the Opera House	1960	10.00	20.00	40.00
❏ MGVS-6052 [S]	Ella Fitzgerald Sings the Irving Berlin Song Book, Vol. 1	1960	10.00	20.00	40.00
❏ MGVS-6053 [S]	Ella Fitzgerald Sings the Irving Berlin Song Book, Vol. 2	1960	10.00	20.00	40.00
❏ MGVS-6072 [S]	Sweet Songs for Swingers	1960	10.00	20.00	40.00
❏ MGVS-6077 [S]	Ella Fitzgerald Sings the George and Ira Gershwin Song Book, Vol. 1	1960	10.00	20.00	40.00
❏ MGVS-6078 [S]	Ella Fitzgerald Sings the George and Ira Gershwin Song Book, Vol. 2	1960	10.00	20.00	40.00
❏ MGVS-6079 [S]	Ella Fitzgerald Sings the George and Ira Gershwin Song Book, Vol. 3	1960	10.00	20.00	40.00
❏ MGVS-6080 [S]	Ella Fitzgerald Sings the George and Ira Gershwin Song Book, Vol. 4	1960	10.00	20.00	40.00
❏ MGVS-6081 [S]	Ella Fitzgerald Sings the George and Ira Gershwin Song Book, Vol. 5	1960	10.00	20.00	40.00
❏ MGVS-6082-5 [(5) S]	Ella Fitzgerald Sings the George and Ira Gershwin Song Book	1960	50.00	100.00	200.00
-- Box set with 6077 through 6081 plus bonus 10-inch LP					
❏ MGVS-6100 [S]	Hello, Love	1960	10.00	20.00	40.00
❏ MGVS-6102 [S]	Get Happy!	1960	10.00	20.00	40.00
❏ MGVS-6163 [S]	Mack the Knife -- Ella in Berlin	1960	10.00	20.00	40.00
❏ MGV-8264 [M]	Ella Fitzgerald at the Opera House	1958	12.50	25.00	50.00
❏ V-8264 [M]	Ella Fitzgerald at the Opera House	1961	5.00	10.00	20.00
❏ V6-8264 [S]	Ella Fitzgerald at the Opera House	1961	5.00	10.00	20.00
❏ MGV-8288 [M]	One O'Clock Jump	1958	12.50	25.00	50.00
❏ V-8288 [M]	One O'Clock Jump	1961	5.00	10.00	20.00
❏ V-8745 [M]	Ella "Live"	1968	7.50	15.00	30.00
❏ 825 024-1 [(5)]	The George and Ira Gershwin Songbook (Complete)	198?	6.25	12.50	25.00

FITZGERALD, ELLA, AND LOUIS ARMSTRONG
Also see each artist's individual listings.
MOBILE FIDELITY

Number	Title	Yr	VG	VG+	NM
❏ 2-248 [(2)]	Ella and Louis Again	1996	37.50	75.00	150.00
-- Audiophile vinyl					

VERVE
❏ MGV-4003 [M]	Ella and Louis	1956	12.50	25.00	50.00
❏ V-4003 [M]	Ella and Louis	1961	5.00	10.00	20.00
❏ MGV-4006-2 [(2) M]	Ella and Louis Again	1956	20.00	40.00	80.00
❏ V-4006-2 [(2) M]	Ella and Louis Again	1961	6.25	12.50	25.00
❏ MGV-4011-2 [(2) M]	Porgy and Bess	1957	20.00	40.00	80.00
❏ V-4011-2 [(2) M]	Porgy and Bess	1961	6.25	12.50	25.00
❏ V6-4011-2 [(2) S]	Porgy and Bess	1961	6.25	12.50	25.00
❏ MGV-4017 [M]	Ella and Louis Again, Vol. 1	1958	12.50	25.00	50.00
❏ V-4017 [M]	Ella and Louis Again, Vol. 1	1961	5.00	10.00	20.00
❏ MGV-4018 [M]	Ella and Louis Again, Vol. 2	1958	12.50	25.00	50.00
❏ V-4018 [M]	Ella and Louis Again, Vol. 2	1961	5.00	10.00	20.00
❏ MGVS-6040-2 [(2) S]	Porgy and Bess	1960	15.00	30.00	60.00

FITZGERALD, ELLA, AND BILLIE HOLIDAY
Also see each artist's individual listings.
AMERICAN RECORDING SOCIETY
| ❏ G-433 [M] | Ella Fitzgerald and Billie Holiday at Newport | 1957 | 10.00 | 20.00 | 40.00 |

VERVE
❏ MGVS-6022 [S]	Ella Fitzgerald and Billie Holiday at Newport	1960	10.00	20.00	40.00
❏ MGV-8234 [M]	Ella Fitzgerald and Billie Holiday at Newport	1958	12.50	25.00	50.00
❏ V-8234 [M]	Ella Fitzgerald and Billie Holiday at Newport	1961	5.00	10.00	20.00
❏ V6-8234 [S]	Ella Fitzgerald and Billie Holiday at Newport	1961	5.00	10.00	20.00

FIVE AMERICANS, THE
ABNAK
❏ AB-1967 [M]	Western Union/Sound of Love	1967	5.00	10.00	20.00
❏ AB-1969 [M]	Progressions	1967	5.00	10.00	20.00
❏ ABST-2067 [S]	Western Union/Sound of Love	1967	7.50	15.00	30.00
❏ ABST-2069 [S]	Progressions	1967	7.50	15.00	30.00
❏ ABST-2071 [(2)]	Now and Then	1968	6.25	12.50	25.00

HANNA-BARBERA
| ❏ HLP-9503 [M] | I See the Light | 1966 | 10.00 | 20.00 | 40.00 |

FIVE BY FIVE
PAULA
| ❏ LPS-2202 | Next Exit | 1969 | 6.25 | 12.50 | 25.00 |

FIVE DISCS, THE
MAGIC CARPET
| ❏ 1002 | The Five Discs Sing Again | 1991 | 5.00 | 10.00 | 20.00 |
| -- Dark blue cover | | | | | |

FIVE EMPREES, THE
FREEPORT
❏ 3001 [M]	The Five Emprees	1965	12.50	25.00	50.00
❏ 3001 [M]	Little Miss Sad	1966	7.50	15.00	30.00
-- Same LP, new title					
❏ 4001 [S]	The Five Emprees	1965	15.00	30.00	60.00
❏ 4001 [S]	Little Miss Sad	1966	10.00	20.00	40.00
-- Same LP, new title					

FIVE KEYS, THE
ALADDIN
| ❏ LP-806 [M] | The Best of the Five Keys | 1956 | 1,000. | 1,500. | 2,000. |
| -- Copies of Aladdin 806 entitled "On the Town" are bootlegs. | | | | | |

CAPITOL
❏ T 828 [M]	The Five Keys On Stage!	1957	75.00	150.00	300.00
-- On cover, the far left singer has his thumb sticking out (inadvertently?) in a phallic way					
❏ T 828 [M]	The Five Keys On Stage!	1957	125.00	250.00	500.00
-- On cover, the far left singer's "offending" thumb is airbrushed out					
❏ M-1769	The Fantastic Five Keys	1977	5.00	10.00	20.00
-- Reissue with new prefix					

Number	Title	Yr	VG	VG+	NM
❏ T 1769 [M]	The Fantastic Five Keys	1962	75.00	150.00	300.00
KING					
❏ 688 [M]	The Five Keys	1960	200.00	400.00	800.00
❏ 692 [M]	Rhythm and Blues Hits, Past and Present	1960	150.00	300.00	600.00
SCORE					
❏ LP-4003 [M]	The Five Keys On the Town	1957	200.00	400.00	800.00
-- Reissue of Aladdin 806.					

FIVE MAN ELECTRICAL BAND
CAPITOL

Number	Title	Yr	VG	VG+	NM
❏ ST-165	Five Man Electrical Band	1969	5.00	10.00	20.00
LION					
❏ LN-1009	Sweet Paradise	1973	5.00	10.00	20.00
LIONEL					
❏ LRS-1100	Good-Byes & Butterflies	1970	7.50	15.00	30.00
❏ LRS-1101	Coming of Age	1971	5.00	10.00	20.00

FIVE ROYALES, THE
APOLLO

Number	Title	Yr	VG	VG+	NM
❏ LP-488 [M]	The Rockin' 5 Royales	1956	2,000.	3,000.	4,000.
-- Purple label					
❏ LP-488 [M]	The Rockin' 5 Royales	1956	1,000.	1,500.	2,000.
-- Green label					
❏ LP-488 [M]	The Rockin' 5 Royales	1956	250.00	500.00	1,000.
-- Yellow label					
KING					
❏ 580 [M]	Dedicated to You	1957	125.00	250.00	500.00
❏ 616 [M]	The 5 Royales Sing for You	1959	100.00	200.00	400.00
❏ 678 [M]	The Five Royales	1960	62.50	125.00	250.00
❏ 955 [M]	24 All Time Hits	1966	25.00	50.00	100.00

FIVE SATINS, THE
CELEBRITY SHOWCASE

Number	Title	Yr	VG	VG+	NM
❏ JB-7671	The Best of the Five Satins	1970	5.00	10.00	20.00
EMBER					
❏ ELP-100 [M]	The Five Satins Sing	1957	1,000.	1,500.	2,000.
-- Red label; group pictured on front cover; blue vinyl					
❏ ELP-100 [M]	The Five Satins Sing	1957	150.00	300.00	600.00
-- Red label; group pictured on front cover; black vinyl					
❏ ELP-100 [M]	The Five Satins Sing	1959	75.00	150.00	300.00
-- Mostly white "logs" label; group pictured on front cover					
❏ ELP-100 [M]	The Five Satins Sing	1959	50.00	100.00	200.00
-- Mostly white "logs" label; no picture on cover					
❏ ELP-100 [M]	The Five Satins Sing	1961	25.00	50.00	100.00
-- Black label; no picture on cover					
❏ ELP-401 [M]	The Five Satins Encore	1960	50.00	100.00	200.00
-- Mostly white "logs" label					
❏ ELP-401 [M]	The Five Satins Encore	1961	25.00	50.00	100.00
-- Black label					
MOUNT VERNON					
❏ 108	The Five Satins Sing	196?	7.50	15.00	30.00

FIVE STAIRSTEPS, THE
BUDDAH

Number	Title	Yr	VG	VG+	NM
❏ BDS-5008	Our Family Portrait	1967	5.00	10.00	20.00
CURTOM					
❏ 8002	Love's Happening	1969	5.00	10.00	20.00
WINDY C					
❏ 6000 [M]	The Five Stairsteps	1967	6.25	12.50	25.00
❏ S-6000 [S]	The Five Stairsteps	1967	6.25	12.50	25.00

FLAGG, FANNIE
RCA VICTOR

Number	Title	Yr	VG	VG+	NM
❏ LPM-3856 [M]	Rally 'Round the Flagg	1967	5.00	10.00	20.00

FLAIRS, THE
CROWN

Number	Title	Yr	VG	VG+	NM
❏ CLP-5356 [M]	The Flairs	1963	20.00	40.00	80.00

FLAME, THE
BROTHER

Number	Title	Yr	VG	VG+	NM
❏ BR-2500	The Flame	1970	7.50	15.00	30.00
-- Deduct 1/3 if poster is missing					

FLAMIN' GROOVIES, THE
EPIC

Number	Title	Yr	VG	VG+	NM
❏ BN 26487	Supersnazz	1969	12.50	25.00	50.00

KAMA SUTRA

Number	Title	Yr	VG	VG+	NM
❏ KSBS-2021	Flamingo	1970	7.50	15.00	30.00
-- Pink label					
❏ KSBS-2031	Teenage Head	1971	7.50	15.00	30.00
-- Pink label					
SNAZZ					
❏ R-2371 [10]	Sneekers	1969	25.00	50.00	100.00
-- This album has been counterfeited					

FLAMING LIPS, THE
LOVELY SORTS OF DEATH

Number	Title	Yr	VG	VG+	NM
❏ (# unknown) [EP]	The Flaming Lips (Bag Full of Thoughts)	1984	12.50	25.00	50.00
-- Red vinyl; black background on jacket					
❏ (# unknown) [EP]	The Flaming Lips (Bag Full of Thoughts)	1984	17.50	35.00	70.00
-- Green vinyl; dark brown background on jacket					
PINK DUST					
❏ 72173	Hear It Is	1986	8.75	17.50	35.00
-- Originals on white vinyl					
❏ 72188 [EP]	The Flaming Lips	1985	6.25	12.50	25.00
-- Originals on lavender vinyl; reissue of Lovely Sorts of Death EP					
RESTLESS					
❏ 72207	Oh My Gawd, The Flaming Lips	1987	5.00	10.00	20.00
-- Clear vinyl, gatefold sleeve					

FLAMING YOUTH
Phil Collins was in this group.
UNI

Number	Title	Yr	VG	VG+	NM
❏ 73075	Ark 2	1969	10.00	20.00	40.00

FLAMINGO, JOHNNY
DIADON

Number	Title	Yr	VG	VG+	NM
❏ 201 [M]	Johnny Flamingo Sings In the Wee Small Hours	1961	25.00	50.00	100.00

FLAMINGOS, THE
CHECKER

Number	Title	Yr	VG	VG+	NM
❏ LP-1433 [M]	The Flamingos	1959	100.00	200.00	400.00
-- Black label					
❏ LP-1433 [M]	The Flamingos	196?	37.50	75.00	150.00
-- Blue label					
❏ LPS-3005 [R]	The Flamingos	1966	6.25	12.50	25.00
-- Rechanneled reissue of 1433					
CONSTELLATION					
❏ CS-3 [M]	Collectors Showcase: The Flamingos	1964	25.00	50.00	100.00
-- With hot pink lettering on cover					
❏ CS-3 [M]	Collectors Showcase: The Flamingos	1964	12.50	25.00	50.00
-- With more restrained pink lettering on cover					
END					
❏ LP-304 [M]	Flamingo Serenade	1959	50.00	100.00	200.00
-- Gray label with dog					
❏ LP-304 [M]	Flamingo Serenade	1959	100.00	200.00	400.00
-- Black label with shadow print logo					
❏ LPS-304 [S]	Flamingo Serenade	1959	125.00	250.00	500.00
-- Cover says "Stereo"					
❏ LPS-304 [S]	Flamingo Serenade	196?	50.00	100.00	200.00
-- Cover says "Rechanneled Stereo" (only one track is)					
❏ LP-307 [M]	Flamingo Favorites	1960	25.00	50.00	100.00
❏ LPS-307 [R]	Flamingo Favorites	1960	17.50	35.00	70.00
❏ LP-308 [M]	Requestfully Yours	1960	25.00	50.00	100.00
❏ LPS-308 [R]	Requestfully Yours	1960	17.50	35.00	70.00
❏ LP-316 [M]	The Sound of the Flamingos	1962	25.00	50.00	100.00
❏ LPS-316 [S]	The Sound of the Flamingos	1962	50.00	100.00	200.00
-- "Stereo" at upper right corner of front cover					
❏ LPS-316 [R]	The Sound of the Flamingos	1962	17.50	35.00	70.00
PHILIPS					
❏ PHM 200-206 [M]	Their Hits -- Then and Now	1966	6.25	12.50	25.00
❏ PHS 600-206 [S]	Their Hits -- Then and Now	1966	7.50	15.00	30.00

FLAMINGOS, THE, AND THE MOONGLOWS
Also see each artist's individual listings.
VEE JAY

Number	Title	Yr	VG	VG+	NM
❏ LP-1052 [M]	The Flamingos Meet the Moonglows on the Dusty Road of Hits	1962	37.50	75.00	150.00

FLANDERS AND SWANN
ANGEL

Number	Title	Yr	VG	VG+	NM
❏ 35797 [M]	At the Drop of a Hat	196?	5.00	10.00	20.00
❏ S 35797 [S]	At the Drop of a Hat	196?	6.25	12.50	25.00

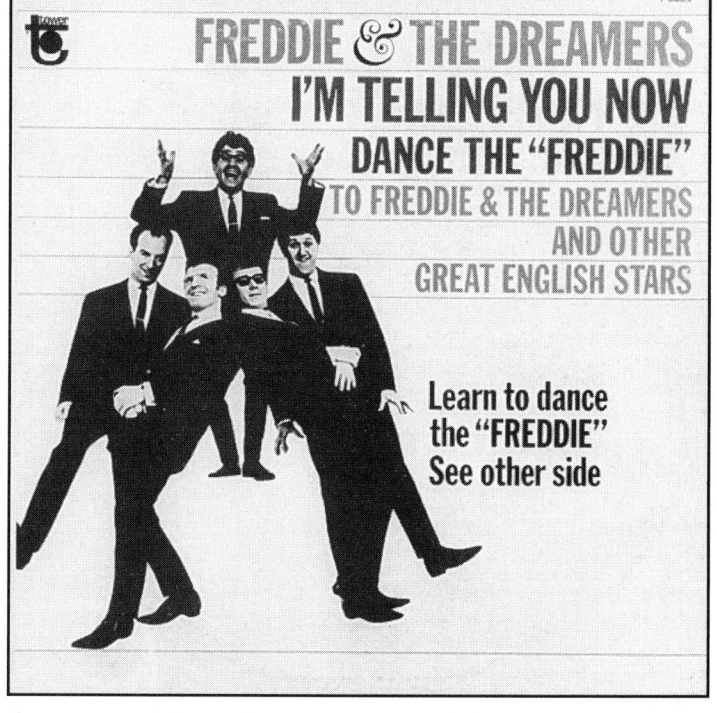

(Top left) Any album on the Aladdin label is scarce; most are rare; some are almost impossible. Here's *The Best of the Five Keys*, a collection of some of their best-loved records that in top condition can sell for a four-figure sum. (Top right) How about another mega-rarity for you? *The Rockin' Five Royales* was this vocal group's lone Apollo album. The rarest version has a purple label; the medium-rare version has a green label; the least rare version has a yellow label. But none is easy to find. (Bottom left) In 1967, when *Four Tops Reach Out* was released, it was still common for albums to have one or two hits and mostly filler after that. But six different songs on this album made the Top 20 on the *Billboard* charts! (Bottom right) The Tower label owned the rights to exactly four songs by Freddie and the Dreamers. Regardless, it created this album in 1965 after "I'm Telling You Now," one of the four songs, hit No. 1 on the charts. Only two of the Freddie and the Dreamers songs even made it to this album! The rest was filled out with tracks by other British acts, none of whom ever had an American album (or hit): Four Just Men; Heinz; Linda Laine and the Sinners; Mike Rabin and the Demons; and The Toggery Five.

Number	Title	Yr	VG	VG+	NM
❑ 36112 [M]	The Bestiary of Flanders and Swann	196?	5.00	10.00	20.00
❑ S 36112 [S]	The Bestiary of Flanders and Swann	196?	6.25	12.50	25.00
❑ 36388 [M]	At the Drop of Another Hat	1966	5.00	10.00	20.00
❑ S 36388 [S]	At the Drop of Another Hat	1966	6.25	12.50	25.00
❑ 65042 [M]	At the Drop of a Hat	1959	6.25	12.50	25.00
-- Original issue					

FLANDERS, TOMMY
VERVE FORECAST

Number	Title	Yr	VG	VG+	NM
❑ FTS-3075	Moonstone	1969	5.00	10.00	20.00

FLARES, THE
PRESS

Number	Title	Yr	VG	VG+	NM
❑ PR 73001 [M]	Encore of Foot Stompin' Hits	196?	20.00	40.00	80.00
❑ PRS 83001 [S]	Encore of Foot Stompin' Hits	196?	30.00	60.00	120.00

FLAT EARTH SOCIETY, THE
FLEETWOOD

Number	Title	Yr	VG	VG+	NM
❑ 3027	Waleeco	1968	75.00	150.00	300.00

FLATT AND SCRUGGS
COLUMBIA

Number	Title	Yr	VG	VG+	NM
❑ GP 30 [(2)]	20 All-Time Great Recordings	1970	5.00	10.00	20.00
❑ CL 1019 [M]	Foggy Mountain Jamboree	1957	12.50	25.00	50.00
❑ CL 1424 [M]	Songs of Glory	1960	5.00	10.00	20.00
❑ CL 1564 [M]	Foggy Mountain Banjo	1961	5.00	10.00	20.00
❑ CL 1664 [M]	Songs of the Famous Carter	1961	5.00	10.00	20.00
❑ CL 1830 [M]	Folk Songs of Our Land	1962	5.00	10.00	20.00
❑ CL 1951 [M]	Hard Travelin' Featuring The Ballad of Jed Clampett	1963	5.00	10.00	20.00
❑ CL 2045 [M]	Flatt and Scruggs at Carnegie Hall	1963	5.00	10.00	20.00
❑ CL 2134 [M]	Recorded Live at Vanderbilt University	1964	5.00	10.00	20.00
❑ CL 2255 [M]	The Fabulous Sound of Flatt & Scruggs	1964	5.00	10.00	20.00
❑ CL 2643 [M]	Strictly Instrumental	1967	5.00	10.00	20.00
❑ CL 2686 [M]	Hear the Whistle Blow	1967	5.00	10.00	20.00
❑ CS 8221 [S]	Songs of Glory	1960	6.25	12.50	25.00
❑ CS 8364 [S]	Foggy Mountain Banjo	1961	6.25	12.50	25.00
❑ CS 8464 [S]	Songs of the Famous Carter	1961	6.25	12.50	25.00
❑ CS 8630 [S]	Folk Songs of Our Land	1962	6.25	12.50	25.00
❑ CS 8751 [S]	Hard Travelin' Featuring The Ballad of Jed Clampett	1963	6.25	12.50	25.00
❑ CS 8845 [S]	Flatt and Scruggs at Carnegie Hall	1963	6.25	12.50	25.00
❑ CS 8934 [S]	Recorded Live at Vanderbilt University	1964	6.25	12.50	25.00
❑ CS 9055 [S]	The Fabulous Sound of Flatt & Scruggs	1964	6.25	12.50	25.00
❑ CS 9154 [S]	Pickin' Strummin' and Singin'	1965	5.00	10.00	20.00
❑ CS 9243 [S]	Town and Country	1966	5.00	10.00	20.00
❑ CS 9313 [S]	When the Saints Go Marching In	1966	5.00	10.00	20.00
❑ CS 9370 [S]	Flatt and Scruggs' Greatest Hits	1966	5.00	10.00	20.00
❑ CS 9443 [S]	Strictly Instrumental	1967	5.00	10.00	20.00
❑ CS 9486 [S]	Hear the Whistle Blow	1967	5.00	10.00	20.00
❑ CS 9596	Changin' Times Featuring Foggy Mountain Breakdown	1968	5.00	10.00	20.00
❑ CS 9649	The Story of Bonnie & Clyde	1968	5.00	10.00	20.00
❑ CS 9741	Nashville Airplane	1969	5.00	10.00	20.00

MERCURY

Number	Title	Yr	VG	VG+	NM
❑ MG-20358 [M]	Country Music	1958	10.00	20.00	40.00
❑ MG-20542 [M]	Lester Flatt & Earl Scruggs	1959	10.00	20.00	40.00
❑ MG-20773 [M]	The Original Sound of Flatt & Scruggs	1963	6.25	12.50	25.00
❑ SR-61162	Original Theme from Bonnie & Clyde	1968	5.00	10.00	20.00

STARDAY

Number	Title	Yr	VG	VG+	NM
❑ SLP-365 [M]	Stars of the Grand Ol' Opry	1966	6.25	12.50	25.00
-- With Jim and Jesse					

FLEETWOOD MAC
Also see BUCKINGHAM NICKS; PETER GREEN; STEVIE NICKS.
BLUE HORIZON

Number	Title	Yr	VG	VG+	NM
❑ BH-3801 [(2)]	Fleetwood Mac in Chicago	1970	7.50	15.00	30.00

EPIC

Number	Title	Yr	VG	VG+	NM
❑ LN 24402 [M]	Fleetwood Mac	1968	25.00	50.00	100.00
-- White label promo only					
❑ LN 24446 [M]	English Rose	1969	25.00	50.00	100.00
-- White label promo only					
❑ BN 26402 [S]	Fleetwood Mac	1968	7.50	15.00	30.00
❑ BN 26406 [S]	English Rose	1969	7.50	15.00	30.00
❑ KE 30632 [(2)]	Black Magic Woman	1971	5.00	10.00	20.00

MOBILE FIDELITY

Number	Title	Yr	VG	VG+	NM
❑ 1-012	Fleetwood Mac	1980	10.00	20.00	40.00
-- Audiophile vinyl					
❑ 1-119	Mirage	1984	10.00	20.00	40.00
-- Audiophile vinyl					

NAUTILUS

Number	Title	Yr	VG	VG+	NM
❑ NR-8	Rumours	1980	10.00	20.00	40.00
-- Audiophile vinyl					

REPRISE

Number	Title	Yr	VG	VG+	NM
❑ MS 2158	Mystery to Me	1973	5.00	10.00	20.00
-- With "Good Things Come to Those Who Wait"					
❑ RS 6368	Then Play On	1969	5.00	10.00	20.00
-- First pressings have "When You Say" and "My Dream."					
❑ RS 6465	Future Games	1971	6.25	12.50	25.00
-- Originals have a pale yellow cover					

WARNER BROS.

Number	Title	Yr	VG	VG+	NM
❑ PRO-A-866 [DJ]	Tusk Remix	1979	5.00	10.00	20.00
-- Promo-only EP					
❑ 23607 [DJ]	Mirage	1982	5.00	10.00	20.00
-- Promo on Quiex II vinyl					

FLEETWOODS, THE
DOLTON

Number	Title	Yr	VG	VG+	NM
❑ BLP-2001 [M] Mr. Blue		1959	20.00	40.00	80.00
-- Pale blue label with dolphins on top					
❑ BLP-2001 [M] Mr. Blue		1963	5.00	10.00	20.00
-- Dark label, logo on left					
❑ BLP-2002 [M] The Fleetwoods		1960	12.50	25.00	50.00
-- Pale blue label with dolphins on top					
❑ BLP-2002 [M] The Fleetwoods		1963	5.00	10.00	20.00
-- Dark label, logo on left					
❑ BLP-2005 [M] Softly		1961	12.50	25.00	50.00
-- Pale blue label with dolphins on top					
❑ BLP-2005 [M] Softly		1963	5.00	10.00	20.00
-- Dark label, logo on left					
❑ BLP-2007 [M] Deep in a Dream		1961	10.00	20.00	40.00
-- Pale blue label with dolphins on top					
❑ BLP-2007 [M] Deep in a Dream		1963	5.00	10.00	20.00
-- Dark label, logo on left					
❑ BLP-2011 [M] The Best of the Oldies		1962	10.00	20.00	40.00
-- Pale blue label with dolphins on top					
❑ BLP-2011 [M] The Best of the Oldies		1963	5.00	10.00	20.00
-- Dark label, logo on left					
❑ BLP-2018 [M] The Fleetwoods' Greatest Hits		1962	6.25	12.50	25.00
❑ BLP-2020 [M] The Fleetwoods Sing for Lovers by Night		1963	7.50	15.00	30.00
❑ BLP-2025 [M] Goodnight My Love		1963	7.50	15.00	30.00
❑ BLP-2030 [M] Before and After		1965	7.50	15.00	30.00
❑ BLP-2039 [M] Folk Rock		1965	7.50	15.00	30.00
❑ BST-8001 [S] Mr. Blue		1959	25.00	50.00	100.00
-- Pale blue label with dolphins on top					
❑ BST-8001 [S] Mr. Blue		1963	6.25	12.50	25.00
-- Dark label, logo on left					
❑ BST-8002 [S] The Fleetwoods		1960	17.50	35.00	70.00
-- Pale blue label with dolphins on top					
❑ BST-8002 [S] The Fleetwoods		1963	6.25	12.50	25.00
-- Dark label, logo on left					
❑ BST-8005 [S] Softly		1961	17.50	35.00	70.00
-- Pale blue label with dolphins on top					
❑ BST-8005 [S] Softly		1963	6.25	12.50	25.00
-- Dark label, logo on left					
❑ BST-8007 [S] Deep in a Dream		1961	12.50	25.00	50.00
-- Pale blue label with dolphins on top					
❑ BST-8007 [S] Deep in a Dream		1963	6.25	12.50	25.00
-- Dark label, logo on left					
❑ BST-8011 [S] The Best of the Oldies		1962	12.50	25.00	50.00
-- Pale blue label with dolphins on top					
❑ BST-8011 [S] The Best of the Oldies		1963	6.25	12.50	25.00
-- Dark label, logo on left					
❑ BST-8018 [S] The Fleetwoods' Greatest Hits		1962	7.50	15.00	30.00
❑ BST-8020 [S] The Fleetwoods Sing for Lovers by Night		1963	10.00	20.00	40.00
❑ BST-8025 [S] Goodnight My Love		1963	10.00	20.00	40.00
❑ BST-8030 [S] Before and After		1965	10.00	20.00	40.00
❑ BST-8039 [S] Folk Rock		1965	10.00	20.00	40.00

FLEMING, RHONDA
COLUMBIA

Number	Title	Yr	VG	VG+	NM
❑ CL 1080 [M]	Rhonda	1958	15.00	30.00	60.00

FLEMONS, WADE
VEE JAY

Number	Title	Yr	VG	VG+	NM
❑ LP-1011 [M]	Wade Flemons	1959	37.50	75.00	150.00
-- Maroon label					
❑ LP-1011 [M]	Wade Flemons	196?	20.00	40.00	80.00
-- Black label					

Number	Title	Yr	VG	VG+	NM

FLESH FOR LULU
CAPITOL
❑ SPRO 79992 [DJ] Final Vinyl		1989	5.00	10.00	20.00
(Every Little Word + 7 Live)					
-- Red vinyl; sticker on generic cover					

FLESHEATERS
RUBY
❑ JRR-101	A Minute to Pray, a Second to Die	1981	5.00	10.00	20.00
❑ JRR 805	Forever Came Today	1982	5.00	10.00	20.00
UPSETTER
| ❑ UPCJ-34 | No Questions Asked | 1980 | 10.00 | 20.00 | 40.00 |
| ❑ UP 56 | A Hard Road to Follow | 1983 | 7.50 | 15.00 | 30.00 |

FLETCHER, SAM
VAULT
❑ LP-116 [M]	The Look of Love, the Sound of Soul	1967	7.50	15.00	30.00
❑ VS-116 [S]	The Look of Love, the Sound of Soul	1967	7.50	15.00	30.00
VEE JAY
| ❑ LP-1094 [M] | Sam Fletcher Sings | 1964 | 10.00 | 20.00 | 40.00 |

FLINT, SHELBY
VALIANT
❑ LP-401 [M]	Shelby Flint -- The Quiet Girl	1961	10.00	20.00	40.00
❑ LP-403 [M]	Shelby Flint Sings Folk	1962	10.00	20.00	40.00
❑ LPS-403 [S]	Shelby Flint Sings Folk	1962	12.50	25.00	50.00
❑ VL-5003 [M]	Cast Your Fate to the Wind	1966	6.25	12.50	25.00
❑ VLS-25003 [S]	Cast Your Fate to the Wind	1966	7.50	15.00	30.00

FLIRTATIONS, THE
DERAM
❑ DES-18028	Nothing But a Heartache	1969	5.00	10.00	20.00

FLO AND EDDIE
REPRISE
❑ MS 2099	The Phlorescent Leech and Eddie	1972	5.00	10.00	20.00
❑ MS 2141	Flo and Eddie	1973	5.00	10.00	20.00
RHINO
| ❑ RNTA-1999 [(3)] | History of Flo & Eddie | 198? | 5.00 | 10.00 | 20.00 |

FLOATING BRIDGE, THE
VAULT
❑ VS-124	The Floating Bridge	1969	7.50	15.00	30.00

FLOCK, THE
COLUMBIA
❑ CS 9911	The Flock	1969	5.00	10.00	20.00
-- "360 Sound" label					
❑ C 30007	Dinosaur Swamps	1970	5.00	10.00	20.00
-- "360 Sound" label					

FLOW
CTI
❑ 1003	Flow	1970	5.00	10.00	20.00

FLOWERS, PHIL
GUEST STAR
❑ G-1456 [M]	I Am the Greatest	1964	7.50	15.00	30.00
❑ GS-1456 [S]	I Am the Greatest	1964	10.00	20.00	40.00
❑ G-1457 [M]	Phil Flowers Sings a Tribute	1964	7.50	15.00	30.00
❑ GS-1457 [S]	Phil Flowers Sings a Tribute	1964	10.00	20.00	40.00
MOUNT VERNON
| ❑ 154 [M] | Rhythm and Blues | 196? | 6.25 | 12.50 | 25.00 |

FLOYD, EDDIE
STAX
❑ 714 [M]	Knock on Wood	1967	17.50	35.00	70.00
❑ ST 714 [S]	Knock on Wood	1967	17.50	35.00	70.00
❑ STS-2002	I've Never Found a Girl	1968	7.50	15.00	30.00
❑ STS-2011	Rare Stamps	1969	6.25	12.50	25.00
❑ STS-2017	You've Got to Have Eddie	1969	6.25	12.50	25.00
❑ STS-2029	California Girl	1970	6.25	12.50	25.00
❑ STS-2041	Down to Earth	1971	6.25	12.50	25.00
❑ STS-3016	Baby Lay Your Head Down	1973	6.25	12.50	25.00
❑ STS-5512	Soul Street	1974	6.25	12.50	25.00

FLYING BURRITO BROTHERS, THE
A&M
❑ SP-4175	The Gilded Palace of Sin	1969	5.00	10.00	20.00
-- Brown label					
❑ SP-8070 [DJ]	Hot Burrito	1975	10.00	20.00	40.00
-- Promo-only issue with poster					

FOCUS
SIRE
❑ SES-97027	In and Out of Focus	1970	5.00	10.00	20.00

FOGELBERG, DAN
FULL MOON/EPIC
❑ A2S 1335 [(2) DJ] Interchords		1982	6.25	12.50	25.00
-- Promo-only release					
❑ PEQ 33499 [Q] Captured Angel		1975	5.00	10.00	20.00
❑ HE 45634	Phoenix	1981	6.25	12.50	25.00
-- Half-speed mastered edition					
❑ HE 48308	Dan Fogelberg/Greatest Hits	1983	6.25	12.50	25.00
-- Half-speed mastered edition					

FOGERTY, JOHN
Also see CREEDENCE CLEARWATER REVIVAL.
WARNER BROS.
❑ 25203-1 [DJ]	Centerfield	1985	5.00	10.00	20.00
-- Promo versions on Quiex II audiophile vinyl					

FOLEY, LORD ADRIAN
MGM
❑ E-3358 [M]	Lord Adrian Foley at the Piano	1955	10.00	20.00	40.00

FOLEY, RED
DECCA
❑ DXB 177 [(2) M] The Red Foley Story		1964	6.25	12.50	25.00
❑ DL 4107 [M]	Red Foley's Golden Favorites	1961	5.00	10.00	20.00
❑ DL 4140 [M]	Company's Comin'	1961	5.00	10.00	20.00
❑ DL 4198 [M]	Songs of Devotion	1961	5.00	10.00	20.00
❑ DL 4290 [M]	Dear Hearts and Gentle People	1962	5.00	10.00	20.00
❑ DL 4341 [M]	The Red Foley Show	1963	5.00	10.00	20.00
❑ DL 4603 [M]	Songs Everybody Knows	1965	5.00	10.00	20.00
❑ DL 4849 [M]	Songs for the Soul	1967	6.25	12.50	25.00
❑ DL 5303 [10]	Red Foley Souvenir Album	1951	20.00	40.00	80.00
❑ DL 5338 [10]	Lift Up Your Voice	1952	20.00	40.00	80.00
❑ DXSB 7177 [(2) S] The Red Foley Story		1964	7.50	15.00	30.00
❑ DL 8294 [M]	Red Foley Souvenir Album	1956	12.50	25.00	50.00
❑ DL 8296 [M]	Beyond the Sunset	1956	12.50	25.00	50.00
❑ DL 8767 [M]	He Walks with Thee	1958	12.50	25.00	50.00
❑ DL 8806 [M]	My Keepsake Album	1958	12.50	25.00	50.00
❑ DL 8847 [M]	Let's All Sing with Red Foley	1959	10.00	20.00	40.00
❑ DL 8903 [M]	Let's All Sing to Him	1959	10.00	20.00	40.00
❑ DL 38068 [M]	Gratefully	1958	25.00	50.00	100.00
-- Special-products issue for Dickies clothing					
❑ DL 74107 [S]	Red Foley's Golden Favorites	1961	6.25	12.50	25.00
❑ DL 74140 [S]	Company's Comin'	1961	6.25	12.50	25.00
❑ DL 74198 [S]	Songs of Devotion	1961	6.25	12.50	25.00
❑ DL 74290 [S]	Dear Hearts and Gentle People	1962	6.25	12.50	25.00
❑ DL 74341 [S]	The Red Foley Show	1963	6.25	12.50	25.00
❑ DL 74603 [S]	Songs Everybody Knows	1965	6.25	12.50	25.00
❑ DL 74849 [S]	Songs for the Soul	1967	5.00	10.00	20.00
❑ DL 78847 [S]	Let's All Sing with Red Foley	1959	12.50	25.00	50.00
❑ DL 78903 [S]	Let's All Sing to Him	1959	12.50	25.00	50.00

FOLK SINGERS, THE
ELEKTRA
❑ EKL-157 [M]	The Folk Singers	1958	7.50	15.00	30.00

FOLKNIKS, THE
HIFI-LIFE SERIES
❑ L-1017 [M]	The Sound of Twelve-String Guitar and Banjo	1964	5.00	10.00	20.00
❑ SL-1017 [S]	The Sound of Twelve-String Guitar and Banjo	1964	6.25	12.50	25.00

FOLKSWINGERS, THE
WORLD PACIFIC
❑ ST-1812 [S]	12 String Guitar!	1963	7.50	15.00	30.00
-- Black vinyl					
❑ ST-1812 [S]	12 String Guitar!	1963	15.00	30.00	60.00
-- Red vinyl					
❑ WP-1812 [M]	12 String Guitar!	1963	6.25	12.50	25.00
❑ ST-1814 [S]	12 String Guitar, Volume 2	1963	7.50	15.00	30.00
❑ WP-1814 [M]	12 String Guitar, Volume 2	1963	6.25	12.50	25.00

Number	Title	Yr	VG	VG+	NM
❏ ST-1846 [S]	Raga Rock	1966	7.50	15.00	30.00
❏ WP-1846 [M]	Raga Rock	1966	6.25	12.50	25.00

FONDA, HENRY
CORAL
| ❏ CRL 57308 [M] | Voices of the 20th Century | 1958 | 15.00 | 30.00 | 60.00 |

FONTAINE, FRANK
ABC-PARAMOUNT
❏ S-442 [S]	Songs I Sing on the Jackie Gleason Show	1963	5.00	10.00	20.00
❏ S-460 [S]	Sings Like Crazy	1963	5.00	10.00	20.00
❏ S-470 [S]	How Sweet It Is	1964	5.00	10.00	20.00
❏ S-490 [S]	More Songs I Sing on the Jackie Gleason Show	1964	5.00	10.00	20.00
❏ S-514 [S]	I'm Counting on You	1965	5.00	10.00	20.00
❏ S-541 [S]	All Time Great Hits	1966	5.00	10.00	20.00

FONTANA, WAYNE
MGM
| ❏ E-4459 [M] | Wayne Fontana | 1967 | 5.00 | 10.00 | 20.00 |
| ❏ SE-4459 [S] | Wayne Fontana | 1967 | 6.25 | 12.50 | 25.00 |

FONTANA, WAYNE, AND THE MINDBENDERS
Also see THE MINDBENDERS.
FONTANA
| ❏ MGF-27542 [M] | The Game of Love | 1965 | 7.50 | 15.00 | 30.00 |
| ❏ SRF-67542 [R] | The Game of Love | 1965 | 6.25 | 12.50 | 25.00 |

FONTANE SISTERS, THE
DOT
❏ DLP-104 [10]	The Fontane Sisters	1955	12.50	25.00	50.00
❏ DLP-3004 [M]	The Fontane Sisters	1956	10.00	20.00	40.00
-- Maroon label					
❏ DLP-3004 [M]	The Fontane Sisters	1957	6.25	12.50	25.00
-- Black label					
❏ DLP-3042 [M]	The Fontanes Sing	1957	7.50	15.00	30.00
❏ DLP-25531 [S]	The Tips of My Fingers	1963	5.00	10.00	20.00

FOOD
CAPITOL
| ❏ ST-304 | Forever Is a Dream | 1969 | 15.00 | 30.00 | 60.00 |

FOOL, THE
MERCURY
| ❏ SR-61178 | The Fool | 1968 | 7.50 | 15.00 | 30.00 |

FORBES, GRAHAM
PHILLIPS INTERNATIONAL
| ❏ PLP-1955 [M] | The Martini Set | 1959 | 200.00 | 400.00 | 800.00 |

FORD THEATRE, THE
ABC
| ❏ S-658 | Trilogy | 1968 | 6.25 | 12.50 | 25.00 |
| ❏ S-681 | Time Changes | 1969 | 5.00 | 10.00 | 20.00 |

FORD, FRANKIE
ACE
| ❏ LP 1005 [M] | Let's Take a Sea Cruise | 1959 | 75.00 | 150.00 | 300.00 |

FORD, LITA
Also see THE RUNAWAYS.
MERCURY
| ❏ 810 331-1 | Out for Blood | 1984 | 6.25 | 12.50 | 25.00 |
| -- Original cover has a bloody guitar on it | | | | | |

FORD, MARY
Also see LES PAUL AND MARY FORD.
CHALLENGE
| ❏ CHL-623 [M] | A Brand New Ford | 1966 | 6.25 | 12.50 | 25.00 |
| ❏ CHS-2623 [S] | A Brand New Ford | 1966 | 7.50 | 15.00 | 30.00 |

FORD, NEAL, AND THE FANATICS
HICKORY
| ❏ LPS-141 | Neal Ford and the Fanatics | 1968 | 6.25 | 12.50 | 25.00 |

FORD, RITA
COLUMBIA
| ❏ CL 1698 [M] | A Music Box Christmas | 1961 | 5.00 | 10.00 | 20.00 |
| -- Black and red label with six "eye" logos | | | | | |

Number	Title	Yr	VG	VG+	NM
EPIC					
❏ LN 24022 [M]	Music Box Wonderland Christmas with Rita Ford's Music Boxes	1962	5.00	10.00	20.00

FORD, ROCKY BILLY
AUDIO LAB
| ❏ AL-1561 [M] | A New Singing Star | 1960 | 37.50 | 75.00 | 150.00 |

FORD, TENNESSEE ERNIE
CAPITOL
❏ T 700 [M]	This Lusty Land	1956	6.25	12.50	25.00
-- Turquoise or gray label					
❏ T 700 [M]	This Lusty Land	1959	5.00	10.00	20.00
-- Black label with colorband, logo at left					
❏ T 756 [M]	Hymns	1956	6.25	12.50	25.00
-- Turquoise or gray label					
❏ T 756 [M]	Hymns	1959	5.00	10.00	20.00
-- Black label with colorband, logo at left					
❏ T 818 [M]	Spirituals	1957	6.25	12.50	25.00
-- Turquoise or gray label					
❏ T 818 [M]	Spirituals	1959	5.00	10.00	20.00
-- Black label with colorband, logo at left					
❏ T 841 [M]	Tennessee Ernie Ford Favorites	1958	5.00	10.00	20.00
-- Black label with colorband, logo at left					
❏ T 888 [M]	Ol' Rockin' Ern	1957	12.50	25.00	50.00
-- Turquoise or gray label					
❏ ST 1005 [S]	Nearer the Cross	1959	6.25	12.50	25.00
-- Black label with colorband, logo at left					
❏ ST 1005 [S]	Nearer the Cross	1962	5.00	10.00	20.00
-- Black label with colorband, logo at top					
❏ T 1005 [M]	Nearer the Cross	1958	5.00	10.00	20.00
-- Black label with colorband, logo at left					
❏ ST 1071 [S]	The Star Carol	1958	7.50	15.00	30.00
-- Black label with colorband, logo at left					
❏ ST 1071 [S]	The Star Carol	1962	5.00	10.00	20.00
-- Black label with colorband, logo at top					
❏ T 1071 [M]	The Star Carol	1958	6.25	12.50	25.00
-- Black label with colorband, logo at left					
❏ ST 1227 [S]	Gather 'Round	1959	5.00	10.00	20.00
❏ ST 1272 [S]	A Friend We Have	1959	5.00	10.00	20.00
❏ STAO 1332 [S]	Sing a Hymn with Me	1960	6.25	12.50	25.00
-- With hymnal					
❏ TAO 1332 [M]	Sing a Hymn with Me	1960	5.00	10.00	20.00
-- With hymnal					
❏ ST 1539 [S]	Civil War Songs of the North	1961	5.00	10.00	20.00
❏ ST 1540 [S]	Civil War Songs of the South	1961	5.00	10.00	20.00
❏ ST 1794 [S]	Book of Favorite Hymns	1962	5.00	10.00	20.00
❏ ST 1994 [S]	The Story of Christmas	1963	5.00	10.00	20.00
❏ STBL 2183 [(2) S]	The World's Best Loved Hymns	1964	6.25	12.50	25.00
❏ TBL 2183 [(2) M]	The World's Best Loved Hymns	1964	5.00	10.00	20.00
❏ T 2845 [M]	Our Garden of Hymns	1968	5.00	10.00	20.00
❏ STCL 2942 [(3)]	The Tennessee Ernie Ford Deluxe Set	1968	5.00	10.00	20.00

FOREIGNER
ATLANTIC
| ❏ A1-82299 | Unusual Heat | 1990 | 5.00 | 10.00 | 20.00 |
| -- U.S. vinyl available only through Columbia House | | | | | |
MOBILE FIDELITY
| ❏ 1-052 | Double Vision | 1981 | 7.50 | 15.00 | 30.00 |
| -- Audiophile vinyl | | | | | |

FOREST
HARVEST
| ❏ SKAO-419 | Forest | 1970 | 12.50 | 25.00 | 50.00 |

FORGOTTEN CHILD
BLUE LAMPION
| ❏ BLM 10001 | Forgotten Child | 1986 | 15.00 | 30.00 | 60.00 |

FORMULA V
BURLINGUEN
| ❏ (# unknown) | Formula V | 197? | 6.25 | 12.50 | 25.00 |
MIAMI
| ❏ 6076 | Formula V | 197? | 6.25 | 12.50 | 25.00 |

FORREST, HELEN
CAPITOL
| ❏ T 704 [M] | Voice of the Name Bands | 1956 | 12.50 | 25.00 | 50.00 |

FORREST, JIMMY
NEW JAZZ
| ❏ NJLP-8250 [M] | Forrest Fire | 1960 | 15.00 | 30.00 | 60.00 |
| -- Purple label | | | | | |

Number	Title	Yr	VG	VG+	NM
❑ NJLP-8250 [M] Forrest Fire		1965	7.50	15.00	30.00
-- Blue label with trident logo at right					
❑ NJLP-8293 [M] Soul Street		1962	15.00	30.00	60.00
-- Purple label					
❑ NJLP-8293 [M] Soul Street		1965	7.50	15.00	30.00
-- Blue label with trident logo at right					

PRESTIGE

Number	Title	Yr	VG	VG+	NM
❑ PRLP-7202 [M] Out of the Forrest		1961	10.00	20.00	40.00
-- Yellow label					
❑ PRLP-7202 [M] Out of the Forrest		1965	5.00	10.00	20.00
-- Blue label with trident logo at right					
❑ PRLP-7218 [M] Most Much!		1961	10.00	20.00	40.00
-- Yellow label					
❑ PRLP-7218 [M] Most Much!		1965	5.00	10.00	20.00
-- Blue label with trident logo at right					
❑ PRLP-7235 [M] Sit Down and Relax with Jimmy Forrest		1962	10.00	20.00	40.00
-- Yellow label					
❑ PRLP-7235 [M] Sit Down and Relax with Jimmy Forrest		1965	5.00	10.00	20.00
-- Blue label with trident logo at right					
❑ PRST-7235 [S] Sit Down and Relax with Jimmy Forrest		1962	15.00	30.00	60.00
-- Silver label					
❑ PRST-7235 [S] Sit Down and Relax with Jimmy Forrest		1965	6.25	12.50	25.00
-- Blue label with trident logo at right					

UNITED

Number	Title	Yr	VG	VG+	NM
❑ 002 [10]	Night Train	195?	30.00	60.00	120.00

FORRESTER, HOWDY
CUB

Number	Title	Yr	VG	VG+	NM
❑ 8008 [M]	Fancy Fiddlin' Country Style	1960	10.00	20.00	40.00

MGM

Number	Title	Yr	VG	VG+	NM
❑ E-4035 [M]	Fancy Fiddlin' Country Style	1962	7.50	15.00	30.00
-- Reissue of Cub LP					

UNITED ARTISTS

Number	Title	Yr	VG	VG+	NM
❑ UAL-3295 [M]	Fiddlin' Country Style	1963	5.00	10.00	20.00
❑ UAS-6295 [S]	Fiddlin' Country Style	1963	6.25	12.50	25.00

FORRESTER, MAUREEN
RCA VICTOR RED SEAL

Number	Title	Yr	VG	VG+	NM
❑ LSC-2275 [S]	Brahms, Schumann: Lieder	1959	5.00	10.00	20.00
-- Original with "shaded dog" label					

FORT MUDGE MEMORIAL DUMP, THE
MERCURY

Number	Title	Yr	VG	VG+	NM
❑ SR-61256	The Fort Mudge Memorial Dump	1970	7.50	15.00	30.00

FORTUNE, JOHNNY
PARK AVENUE

Number	Title	Yr	VG	VG+	NM
❑ S-401 [S]	Soul Surfer	1963	75.00	150.00	300.00
❑ P-1301 [M]	Soul Surfer	1963	50.00	100.00	200.00

FORTUNES, THE
CAPITOL

Number	Title	Yr	VG	VG+	NM
❑ ST-809	Here Comes That Rainy Day Feeling Again	1971	5.00	10.00	20.00

COCA-COLA

Number	Title	Yr	VG	VG+	NM
❑ (no #) [DJ]	It's the Real Thing	1969	15.00	30.00	60.00

PRESS

Number	Title	Yr	VG	VG+	NM
❑ PR 73002 [M]	The Fortunes	1965	8.75	17.50	35.00
❑ PRS 83002 [S]	The Fortunes	1965	12.50	25.00	50.00

49TH PARALLEL, THE
MAVERICK

Number	Title	Yr	VG	VG+	NM
❑ MAS-7001	The 49th Parallel	1969	62.50	125.00	250.00

FORUM, THE
MIRA

Number	Title	Yr	VG	VG+	NM
❑ MLPS-301 [S]	The River Is Wide	1967	5.00	10.00	20.00

FOSTER, CHUCK
PHILLIPS INTERNATIONAL

Number	Title	Yr	VG	VG+	NM
❑ PLP-1965 [M]	Chuck Foster at the Hotel	1961	50.00	100.00	200.00

FOSTER, DAVID
MOBILE FIDELITY

Number	Title	Yr	VG	VG+	NM
❑ 1-123	The Best of Me	1982	5.00	10.00	20.00
-- Audiophile vinyl					

FOSTER, PAT
COUNTERPOINT

Number	Title	Yr	VG	VG+	NM
❑ CPT-560 [M]	Documentary Talking Blues	195?	10.00	20.00	40.00

RIVERSIDE

Number	Title	Yr	VG	VG+	NM
❑ RLP-12-654 [M]	Gold Rush Songs	195?	10.00	20.00	40.00

FOUL DOGS, THE
RHYTHM SOUND

Number	Title	Yr	VG	VG+	NM
❑ GA-481	No. 1	1968	75.00	150.00	300.00

FOUNDATIONS, THE
UNI

Number	Title	Yr	VG	VG+	NM
❑ 73016	Baby Now That I've Found You	1968	7.50	15.00	30.00
❑ 73043	Build Me Up Buttercup	1969	7.50	15.00	30.00
❑ 73058	Digging the Foundations	1969	7.50	15.00	30.00

FOUNTAIN, PETE
CORAL

Number	Title	Yr	VG	VG+	NM
❑ CRL 57200 [M]	Lawrence Welk Presents Pete Fountain	1958	5.00	10.00	20.00
❑ CRL 757282 [S]	Pete Fountain's New Orleans	1959	5.00	10.00	20.00
❑ CRL 757284 [S]	The Blues	1959	5.00	10.00	20.00
❑ CRL 757313 [S]	Pete Fountain Day	1960	5.00	10.00	20.00
❑ CRL 757314 [S]	Pete Fountain at the Bateau Lounge	1960	5.00	10.00	20.00
❑ CRL 757333 [S]	Pete Fountain Salutes the Great Clarinetists	1960	5.00	10.00	20.00
❑ CRL 757357 [S]	Pete Fountain On Tour	1961	5.00	10.00	20.00
❑ CRL 757359 [S]	Pete Fountain's French Quarter	1961	5.00	10.00	20.00
❑ CRL 757378 [S]	I Love Paris	1961	5.00	10.00	20.00
❑ CRL 757394 [S]	Swing Low Sweet Chariot	1962	5.00	10.00	20.00
❑ CRL 757401 [S]	Pete Fountain's Music from Dixie	1962	5.00	10.00	20.00
❑ CRL 757419 [S]	New Orleans Scene	1963	5.00	10.00	20.00

RCA VICTOR

Number	Title	Yr	VG	VG+	NM
❑ LSP-2097 [S]	Pete Fountain at the Jazz Band Ball	1960	5.00	10.00	20.00

FOUNTAIN, PETE, AND "BIG" TINY LITTLE
CORAL

Number	Title	Yr	VG	VG+	NM
❑ CRL 757334 [S]	Mr. New Orleans Meets Mr. Honky Tonk	1961	5.00	10.00	20.00

FOUNTAIN, PETE, AND AL HIRT
Also see each artist's individual listings.
CORAL

Number	Title	Yr	VG	VG+	NM
❑ CRL 757389 [S]	Bourbon Street	1962	5.00	10.00	20.00

FOUR ACES
Also see AL ALBERTS.
DECCA

Number	Title	Yr	VG	VG+	NM
❑ DL 4013 [M]	The Golden Hits of the Four Aces	1960	5.00	10.00	20.00
❑ DL 5429 [10]	The Four Aces	1952	20.00	40.00	80.00
❑ DL 8122 [M]	The Mood for Love	1955	12.50	25.00	50.00
-- All-black label, silver print					
❑ DL 8122 [M]	The Mood for Love	196?	5.00	10.00	20.00
-- Black label with color bars					
❑ DL 8191 [M]	Merry Christmas	1956	12.50	25.00	50.00
❑ DL 8227 [M]	Sentimental Souvenirs	1956	12.50	25.00	50.00
-- All-black label, silver print					
❑ DL 8227 [M]	Sentimental Souvenirs	196?	5.00	10.00	20.00
-- Black label with color bars					
❑ DL 8228 [M]	Heart and Soul	1956	12.50	25.00	50.00
-- All-black label, silver print					
❑ DL 8228 [M]	Heart and Soul	196?	5.00	10.00	20.00
-- Black label with color bars					
❑ DL 8312 [M]	She Sees All the Hollywood Hits	1957	12.50	25.00	50.00
❑ DL 8567 [M]	Shuffling Along	1957	12.50	25.00	50.00
-- All-black label, silver print					
❑ DL 8567 [M]	Shuffling Along	196?	5.00	10.00	20.00
-- Black label with color bars					
❑ DL 8693 [M]	Hits from Hollywood	1958	12.50	25.00	50.00
-- All-black label, silver print					
❑ DL 8693 [M]	Hits from Hollywood	196?	5.00	10.00	20.00
-- Black label with color bars					
❑ DL 8766 [M]	The Swingin' Aces	1958	10.00	20.00	40.00
-- All-black label, silver print					
❑ DL 8766 [M]	The Swingin' Aces	196?	5.00	10.00	20.00
-- Black label with color bars					
❑ DL 8855 [M]	Hits from Broadway	1959	10.00	20.00	40.00
❑ DL 8855 [M]	Hits from Broadway	196?	5.00	10.00	20.00
-- Black label with color bars					
❑ DL 8944 [M]	Beyond the Blue Horizon	1959	10.00	20.00	40.00
-- All-black label, silver print					

Number	Title	Yr	VG	VG+	NM
❏ DL 8944 [M]	Beyond the Blue Horizon	196?	5.00	10.00	20.00
-- Black label with color bars					
❏ DL 74013 [S]	The Golden Hits of the Four Aces	1960	6.25	12.50	25.00
❏ DL 78766 [S]	The Swingin' Aces	1958	12.50	25.00	50.00
-- All-black label, silver print					
❏ DL 78766 [S]	The Swingin' Aces	196?	6.25	12.50	25.00
-- Black label with color bars					
❏ DL 78855 [S]	Hits from Broadway	1959	12.50	25.00	50.00
-- All-black label, silver print					
❏ DL 78855 [S]	Hits from Broadway	196?	6.25	12.50	25.00
-- Black label with color bars					
❏ DL 78944 [S]	Beyond the Blue Horizon	1959	12.50	25.00	50.00
-- All-black label, silver print					
❏ DL 78944 [S]	Beyond the Blue Horizon	196?	6.25	12.50	25.00
-- Black label with color bars					
UNITED ARTISTS					
❏ UAL-3337 [M]	Record Oldies	1963	5.00	10.00	20.00
❏ UAS-6337 [S]	Record Oldies	1963	6.25	12.50	25.00

FOUR COINS, THE
EPIC

Number	Title	Yr	VG	VG+	NM
❏ LN 1104 [M]	The Four Coins	1955	12.50	25.00	50.00
❏ LN 3445 [M]	The Four Coins in Shangri-La	1958	7.50	15.00	30.00
MGM					
❏ SE-3944 [S]	Greek Songs	1961	5.00	10.00	20.00
ROULETTE					
❏ SR-25288 [S]	Greek Songs Mama Never Taught Me	1965	5.00	10.00	20.00

FOUR FRESHMEN, THE
CAPITOL

Number	Title	Yr	VG	VG+	NM
❏ H 522 [10]	Voices in Modern	1955	12.50	25.00	50.00
❏ T 522 [M]	Voices in Modern	1955	10.00	20.00	40.00
❏ T 683 [M]	Four Freshmen and Five Trombones	1956	10.00	20.00	40.00
❏ T 743 [M]	Freshmen Favorites	1956	10.00	20.00	40.00
❏ T 763 [M]	4 Freshmen and 5 Trumpets	1957	10.00	20.00	40.00
❏ T 844 [M]	Four Freshmen and Five Saxes	1957	10.00	20.00	40.00
❏ T 992 [M]	Voices in Latin	1958	7.50	15.00	30.00
❏ ST 1008 [S]	The Four Freshmen In Person	1958	10.00	20.00	40.00
❏ T 1008 [M]	The Four Freshmen In Person	1958	7.50	15.00	30.00
❏ ST 1074 [S]	Voices in Love	1958	7.50	15.00	30.00
❏ T 1074 [M]	Voices in Love	1958	5.00	10.00	20.00
❏ ST 1103 [S]	Freshmen Favorites, Vol. 2	1959	7.50	15.00	30.00
❏ T 1103 [M]	Freshmen Favorites, Vol. 2	1959	5.00	10.00	20.00
❏ ST 1189 [S]	Love Lost	1959	7.50	15.00	30.00
❏ T 1189 [M]	Love Lost	1959	5.00	10.00	20.00
❏ ST 1255 [S]	The Four Freshmen and Five Guitars	1959	7.50	15.00	30.00
❏ T 1255 [M]	The Four Freshmen and Five Guitars	1959	5.00	10.00	20.00
❏ ST 1295 [S]	Voices and Brass	1960	7.50	15.00	30.00
❏ T 1295 [M]	Voices and Brass	1960	5.00	10.00	20.00
❏ ST 1378 [S]	First Affair	1960	7.50	15.00	30.00
❏ T 1378 [M]	First Affair	1960	5.00	10.00	20.00
❏ ST 1485 [S]	Freshmen Year	1961	6.25	12.50	25.00
❏ T 1485 [M]	Freshmen Year	1961	5.00	10.00	20.00
❏ ST 1543 [S]	Voices in Fun	1961	6.25	12.50	25.00
❏ T 1543 [M]	Voices in Fun	1961	5.00	10.00	20.00
❏ ST 1640 [S]	The Best of the Four Freshmen	1962	6.25	12.50	25.00
❏ T 1640 [M]	The Best of the Four Freshmen	1962	5.00	10.00	20.00
❏ ST 1682 [S]	Stars in Our Eyes	1962	6.25	12.50	25.00
❏ T 1682 [M]	Stars in Our Eyes	1962	5.00	10.00	20.00
❏ ST 1753 [S]	Swingers	1963	5.00	10.00	20.00
❏ ST 1860 [S]	The Four Freshmen In Person, Volume 2	1963	5.00	10.00	20.00
❏ ST 1950 [S]	Got That Feelin'	1963	5.00	10.00	20.00
❏ ST 2067 [S]	Funny How Time Slips Away	1964	5.00	10.00	20.00
❏ ST 2168 [S]	More Four Freshmen and Five Trombones	1964	5.00	10.00	20.00
CREATIVE WORLD					
❏ ST-1059 [(2)]	Stan Kenton and the Four Freshmen at Butler University	1972	5.00	10.00	20.00

FOUR GIRLS, THE
CORAL

Number	Title	Yr	VG	VG+	NM
❏ CRL 57158 [M]	Make a Joyful Noise Unto the	1957	15.00	30.00	60.00

FOUR KNIGHTS, THE
CAPITOL

Number	Title	Yr	VG	VG+	NM
❏ H 346 [10]	Spotlight Songs	1953	50.00	100.00	200.00
❏ T 346 [M]	Spotlight Songs	1956	37.50	75.00	150.00

CORAL

Number	Title	Yr	VG	VG+	NM
❏ CRL 57221 [M]	The Four Knights	1959	25.00	50.00	100.00
❏ CRL 57309 [M]	Million Dollar Baby	1960	15.00	30.00	60.00
❏ CRL 757309 [S]	Million Dollar Baby	1960	20.00	40.00	80.00

FOUR LADS, THE
COLUMBIA

Number	Title	Yr	VG	VG+	NM
❏ CL 861 [M]	The Four Lads with Frankie Laine	1956	10.00	20.00	40.00
❏ CL 912 [M]	On the Sunny Side	1956	10.00	20.00	40.00
❏ CL 1045 [M]	The Four Lads Sing Frank Loesser	1957	10.00	20.00	40.00
❏ CL 1111 [M]	Four on the Aisle	1958	6.25	12.50	25.00
❏ CL 1223 [M]	Breezin' Along	1958	6.25	12.50	25.00
❏ CL 1235 [M]	The Four Lads' Greatest Hits	1958	6.25	12.50	25.00
❏ CL 1299 [M]	The Four Lads Swing Along	1959	6.25	12.50	25.00
❏ CL 1407 [M]	High Spirits!	1959	6.25	12.50	25.00
❏ CL 2545 [10]	The Four Lads Sing Frank Loesser	1956	12.50	25.00	50.00
❏ CL 2577 [10]	Stage Show	1956	12.50	25.00	50.00
❏ CL 6329 [10]	Stage Show	1954	12.50	25.00	50.00
❏ CS 8035 [S]	Breezin' Along	1958	7.50	15.00	30.00
❏ CS 8047 [S]	Four on the Aisle	1958	7.50	15.00	30.00
❏ CS 8106 [S]	The Four Lads Swing Along	1959	7.50	15.00	30.00
❏ CS 8203 [S]	High Spirits!	1959	7.50	15.00	30.00
❏ CS 8293 [S]	Love Affair	1960	5.00	10.00	20.00
❏ CS 8350 [S]	Everything Goes	1960	5.00	10.00	20.00
DOT					
❏ DLP-25438 [S]	Hits of the 60's	1962	5.00	10.00	20.00
❏ DLP-25533 [S]	Oh Happy Day	1963	5.00	10.00	20.00
KAPP					
❏ KS-3224 [S]	Twelve Hits	1961	5.00	10.00	20.00
❏ KS-3254 [S]	Dixieland Doin's	1961	5.00	10.00	20.00
UNITED ARTISTS					
❏ UAS-6356 [S]	This Year's Top Movie Hits	1964	5.00	10.00	20.00
❏ UAS-6399 [S]	Songs of World War I	1964	5.00	10.00	20.00

FOUR LOVERS, THE
Also see THE FOUR SEASONS.
RCA VICTOR

Number	Title	Yr	VG	VG+	NM
❏ LPM-1317 [M]	Joyride	1956	175.00	350.00	700.00

FOUR PREPS, THE
CAPITOL

Number	Title	Yr	VG	VG+	NM
❏ T 994 [M]	The Four Preps	1958	7.50	15.00	30.00
❏ T 1090 [M]	The Things We Did Last Summer	1958	6.25	12.50	25.00
❏ ST 1216 [S]	Dancing and Dreaming	1959	6.25	12.50	25.00
❏ T 1216 [M]	Dancing and Dreaming	1959	5.00	10.00	20.00
❏ T 1291 [M]	Early in the Morning	1960	6.25	12.50	25.00
❏ ST 1566 [S]	The Four Preps on Campus	1961	6.25	12.50	25.00
❏ T 1566 [M]	The Four Preps on Campus	1961	5.00	10.00	20.00
❏ ST 1647 [S]	Campus Encore	1962	6.25	12.50	25.00
❏ T 1647 [M]	Campus Encore	1962	5.00	10.00	20.00
❏ ST 1814 [S]	Campus Confidential	1963	5.00	10.00	20.00
❏ ST 1976 [S]	Songs for a Campus Party	1963	5.00	10.00	20.00
❏ ST 2169 [S]	How to Succeed in Love	1964	5.00	10.00	20.00

FOUR SEASONS, THE
Also see FRANKIE VALLI.
PHILIPS

Number	Title	Yr	VG	VG+	NM
❏ PHM 200-124 [M]	Dawn (Go Away) and 11 Other Great Songs	1964	5.00	10.00	20.00
❏ PHM 200-129 [M]	Born to Wander	1964	5.00	10.00	20.00
❏ PHM 200-146 [M]	Rag Doll	1964	5.00	10.00	20.00
-- With yellow seal noting presence of "Save It For Me"					
❏ PHM 200-146 [M]	Rag Doll	1964	5.00	10.00	20.00
-- Without yellow seal noting presence of "Save It For Me"					
❏ PHM 200-150 [M]	All the Song Hits of the Four Seasons	1964	5.00	10.00	20.00
❏ PHM 200-164 [M]	The 4 Seasons Entertain You	1965	5.00	10.00	20.00
-- With orange seal noting presence of "Bye Bye Baby" and "Toy Soldier"					
❏ PHM 200-164 [M]	The 4 Seasons Entertain You	1965	5.00	10.00	20.00
-- With orange seal noting presence of "Bye Bye Baby"					
❏ PHM 200-193 [M]	Big Hits by Burt Bacharach... Hal David...Bob Dylan	1965	5.00	10.00	20.00
-- "Open book" cover					
❏ PHM 200-193 [M]	Big Hits by Burt Bacharach... Hal David...Bob Dylan	1966	7.50	15.00	30.00
-- Group photos on cover					
❏ PHM 200-196 [M]	The 4 Seasons' Gold Vault of Hits	1965	5.00	10.00	20.00
-- Title in red print with no border					
❏ PHM 200-201 [M]	Working My Way Back to You	1966	5.00	10.00	20.00
❏ PHM 200-222 [M]	Lookin' Back	1966	5.00	10.00	20.00
❏ PHM 200-223 [M]	The Four Seasons' Christmas Album	1966	6.25	12.50	25.00
-- Reissue of Vee Jay album (same contents and order) with new cover					

Number	Title	Yr	VG	VG+	NM
❏ PHM 200-243 [M] New Gold Hits		1967	5.00	10.00	20.00
❏ PHS 600-124 [S] Dawn (Go Away) and		1964	6.25	12.50	25.00
11 Other Great Songs					
❏ PHS 600-129 [S] Born to Wander		1964	6.25	12.50	25.00
❏ PHS 600-146 [S] Rag Doll		1964	6.25	12.50	25.00
-- Without yellow seal noting presence of "Save It For Me"					
❏ PHS 600-146 [S] Rag Doll		1964	6.25	12.50	25.00
-- With yellow seal noting presence of "Save It For Me"					
❏ PHS 600-150 [S] All the Song Hits of		1964	6.25	12.50	25.00
the Four Seasons					
❏ PHS 600-164 [S] The 4 Seasons Entertain You		1965	5.00	10.00	20.00
-- With blue seal noting presence of "Bye Bye Baby" and "Toy Soldier"					
❏ PHS 600-164 [S] The 4 Seasons Entertain You		1965	6.25	12.50	25.00
-- With orange seal noting presence of "Bye Bye Baby" and "Toy Soldier"					
❏ PHS 600-164 [S] The 4 Seasons Entertain You		1965	6.25	12.50	25.00
-- With orange seal noting presence of "Bye Bye Baby"					
❏ PHS 600-193 [S] Big Hits by Burt Bacharach...		1965	6.25	12.50	25.00
Hal David...Bob Dylan					
-- "Open book" cover					
❏ PHS 600-193 [S] Big Hits by Burt Bacharach...		1966	10.00	20.00	40.00
Hal David...Bob Dylan					
-- Group photos on cover					
❏ PHS 600-196 [S] The 4 Seasons' Gold Vault of Hits		1965	5.00	10.00	20.00
-- Title in red print with black border					
❏ PHS 600-196 [S] The 4 Seasons' Gold Vault of Hits		1965	6.25	12.50	25.00
-- Title in red print with no border					
❏ PHS 600-201 [S] Working My Way Back to You		1966	6.25	12.50	25.00
❏ PHS 600-221 [S] 2nd Vault of Golden Hits		1966	5.00	10.00	20.00
❏ PHS 600-222 [S] Lookin' Back		1966	6.25	12.50	25.00
❏ PHS 600-223 [S] The Four Seasons'		1966	7.50	15.00	30.00
Christmas Album					
❏ PHS 600-243 [S] New Gold Hits		1967	6.25	12.50	25.00
❏ PHS 600-290 The Genuine Imitation Life Gazette		1969	6.25	12.50	25.00
-- Yellow newspaper					
❏ PHS 600-341 Half & Half		1970	5.00	10.00	20.00
❏ PHS-2-6501 [(2)] Edizione d'Oro		1968	7.50	15.00	30.00
-- Number "4" on cover is white on gold foil					
❏ PHS-2-6501 [(2)] Edizione d'Oro		1968	6.25	12.50	25.00
-- Number "4" on cover is red on gold foil					
❏ PHS-2-6501 [(2)] Edizione d'Oro		1969	6.25	12.50	25.00
-- Number "4" on cover is white on gold board					
RHINO					
❏ RNRP-72998 [(4)] 25th Anniversary Collection		1987	6.25	12.50	25.00
SEARS					
❏ SPS-609	Brotherhood of Man	1970	6.25	12.50	25.00
VEE JAY					
❏ LP-1053 [M]	Sherry & 11 Others	1962	7.50	15.00	30.00
❏ SR-1053 [S]	Sherry & 11 Others	1962	10.00	20.00	40.00
❏ LP 1055 [M]	The Four Seasons Greetings	1962	7.50	15.00	30.00
❏ SR 1055 [S]	The Four Seasons Greetings	1962	10.00	20.00	40.00
❏ LP-1056 [M]	Big Girls Don't Cry and	1963	7.50	15.00	30.00
	Twelve Others				
❏ SR-1056 [S]	Big Girls Don't Cry and	1963	10.00	20.00	40.00
	Twelve Others				
❏ LP-1059 [M]	Ain't That a Shame and 11 Others	1963	7.50	15.00	30.00
❏ SR-1059 [S]	Ain't That a Shame and 11 Others	1963	10.00	20.00	40.00
❏ LP-1065 [M]	Golden Hits of the Four Seasons	1963	7.50	15.00	30.00
❏ SR-1065 [S]	Golden Hits of the Four Seasons	1963	10.00	20.00	40.00
❏ LP-1082 [M]	Folk-Nanny	1964	7.50	15.00	30.00
❏ SR-1082 [S]	Folk-Nanny	1964	10.00	20.00	40.00
❏ LP-1082 [M]	Stay & Other Great Hits	1964	6.25	12.50	25.00
-- Retitled version of Folk-Nanny					
❏ SR-1082 [S]	Stay & Other Great Hits	1964	7.50	15.00	30.00
-- Retitled version of Folk-Nanny					
❏ LP-1088 [M]	More Golden Hits by the	1964	7.50	15.00	30.00
	Four Seasons				
-- With "Long Lonely Nights" on record					
❏ LP-1088 [M]	More Golden Hits by the	1964	5.00	10.00	20.00
	Four Seasons				
-- With "Apple of My Eye" on record					
❏ SR-1088 [S]	More Golden Hits by the	1964	6.25	12.50	25.00
	Four Seasons				
-- With "Apple of My Eye" on record					
❏ SR-1088 [S]	More Golden Hits by the	1964	10.00	20.00	40.00
	Four Seasons				
-- With "Long Lonely Nights" on record					
❏ LP-1121 [M]	We Love Girls	1965	7.50	15.00	30.00
❏ LPS-1121 [S]	We Love Girls	1965	10.00	20.00	40.00
❏ LP-1154 [M]	Recorded Live on Stage	1965	7.50	15.00	30.00
❏ LPS-1154 [S]	Recorded Live on Stage	1965	10.00	20.00	40.00

FOUR TOPS, THE
COMMAND

❏ CQD-40011 [Q]	Keeper of the Castle	1974	5.00	10.00	20.00
❏ CQD-40012 [Q]	Main Street People	1974	5.00	10.00	20.00

MOTOWN

❏ 622 [M]	Four Tops	1964	7.50	15.00	30.00

Number	Title	Yr	VG	VG+	NM
❏ MS-622 [S]	Four Tops	1964	10.00	20.00	40.00
❏ 634 [M]	Four Tops Second Album	1965	6.25	12.50	25.00
❏ MS-634 [S]	Four Tops Second Album	1965	7.50	15.00	30.00
❏ 647 [M]	4 Tops On Top	1966	6.25	12.50	25.00
❏ MS-647 [S]	4 Tops On Top	1966	7.50	15.00	30.00
❏ 654 [M]	Four Tops Live!	1966	6.25	12.50	25.00
❏ MS-654 [S]	Four Tops Live!	1966	7.50	15.00	30.00
❏ 657 [M]	4 Tops on Broadway	1967	6.25	12.50	25.00
❏ MS-657 [S]	4 Tops on Broadway	1967	7.50	15.00	30.00
❏ 660 [M]	Four Tops Reach Out	1967	7.50	15.00	30.00
❏ MS-660 [S]	Four Tops Reach Out	1967	6.25	12.50	25.00
❏ 662 [M]	The Four Tops Greatest Hits	1967	7.50	15.00	30.00
❏ MS-662 [S]	The Four Tops Greatest Hits	1967	5.00	10.00	20.00
❏ 669 [M]	Yesterday's Dreams	1968	7.50	15.00	30.00
❏ MS-669 [S]	Yesterday's Dreams	1968	5.00	10.00	20.00
❏ MS-675	Four Tops Now!	1969	5.00	10.00	20.00
❏ MS-695	Soul Spin	1969	5.00	10.00	20.00
❏ MS-704	Still Waters Run Deep	1970	5.00	10.00	20.00
❏ MS-721	Changing Times	1970	5.00	10.00	20.00
❏ MS-740	Four Tops Greatest Hits, Vol. 2	1971	5.00	10.00	20.00
❏ MS-748	Nature Planned It	1972	5.00	10.00	20.00
❏ M9-809 [(3)]	Anthology	1974	5.00	10.00	20.00

WORKSHOP JAZZ

❏ 217 [M]	Breakin' Through	1962	---	---	---
-- This album is pictured on some early Motown inner sleeves, but is not known to exist					

FOUR TUNES, THE
JUBILEE

❏ LP-1039 [M]	12 x 4	1957	62.50	125.00	250.00

FOURTH CEKCION, THE
SOLAR

❏ 110	The Fourth Cekcion	1970	15.00	30.00	60.00

FOURTH WAY, THE
CAPITOL

❏ ST-317	The Fourth Way	1969	5.00	10.00	20.00

FOWLER, WALLY
DECCA

❏ DL 8560 [M]	Call of the Cross	1958	10.00	20.00	40.00

DOVE

❏ 1000	A Tribute to Elvis Presley	1977	5.00	10.00	20.00

KING

❏ 702 [M]	Gospel Song Festival	1960	25.00	50.00	100.00

STARDAY

❏ SLP-112 [M]	All Nite Singing Gospel Concert	1960	10.00	20.00	40.00
❏ SLP-301 [M]	All Nite Singing Concert	1964	7.50	15.00	30.00

FOWLEY, KIM
CAPITOL

❏ ST-11075	I'm Bad	1972	5.00	10.00	20.00
❏ ST-11159	International Heroes	1973	5.00	10.00	20.00
❏ ST-11248	Automatic	1974	5.00	10.00	20.00

IMPERIAL

❏ LP-12413	Born to Be Wild	1968	10.00	20.00	40.00
❏ LP-12423	Outrageous	1969	10.00	20.00	40.00
❏ LP-12443	Good Clean Fun	1969	10.00	20.00	40.00

TOWER

❏ ST 5080 [S]	Love Is Alive and Well	1967	10.00	20.00	40.00
❏ T 5080 [M]	Love Is Alive and Well	1967	7.50	15.00	30.00

FOX, CURLY
HARMONY

❏ HL 7302 [M]	Traveling Blues	1963	5.00	10.00	20.00

STARDAY

❏ SLP-235 [M]	Curly Fox and Texas Ruby	1963	7.50	15.00	30.00

FOXX, INEZ (AND CHARLIE)
DYNAMO

❏ D-7000 [M]	Come By Here	1967	7.50	15.00	30.00
❏ D-7002 [M]	Inez and Charlie Foxx's Greatest	1967	7.50	15.00	30.00
	Hits				
❏ DS-8000 [S]	Come By Here	1967	10.00	20.00	40.00
❏ DS-8002 [S]	Inez and Charlie Foxx's Greatest	1967	10.00	20.00	40.00
	Hits				
❏ DS-8003	Swingin' Mockin' Band	1968	7.50	15.00	30.00

SUE

❏ LP-1027 [M]	Mockingbird	1966	25.00	50.00	100.00

Number	Title	Yr	VG	VG+	NM

SYMBOL

| ❏ SYM-4400 [M] | Mockingbird | 1963 | 37.50 | 75.00 | 150.00 |

FRACTION
ANGELUS

| ❏ 571 | Moon Blood | 1971 | 1,000. | 1,500. | 2,000. |

FRAGER, MALCOLM
RCA VICTOR RED SEAL

| ❏ LSC-2465 [S] | Prokofiev: Piano Concerto No. 2 | 1961 | 25.00 | 50.00 | 100.00 |

-- *Originals with "shaded dog" label*

FRAMPTON, PETER
MOBILE FIDELITY

| ❏ 2-262 [(2)] | Frampton Comes Alive! | 1996 | 10.00 | 20.00 | 40.00 |

-- *Audiophile vinyl*

SWEET THUNDER

| ❏ 6 [(2)] | Frampton Comes Alive! | 198? | 25.00 | 50.00 | 100.00 |

-- *Audiophile edition*

FRANCIS, CONNIE
LEO

| ❏ LE-903 [M] | Connie Francis and the Kids Next Door | 1967 | 12.50 | 25.00 | 50.00 |
| ❏ LES-903 [S] | Connie Francis and the Kids Next Door | 1967 | 15.00 | 30.00 | 60.00 |

MATI-MOR

| ❏ 8002 [M] | Sing Along wth Connie Francis | 1961 | 10.00 | 20.00 | 40.00 |

-- *Made for Brylcreem*

METRO

❏ M-519 [M]	Connie Francis	1964	5.00	10.00	20.00
❏ MS-519 [S]	Connie Francis	1964	6.25	12.50	25.00
❏ M-538 [M]	Folk Favorites	1965	5.00	10.00	20.00
❏ MS-538 [S]	Folk Favorites	1965	6.25	12.50	25.00
❏ M-571 [M]	Songs of Love	1966	5.00	10.00	20.00
❏ MS-571 [S]	Songs of Love	1966	6.25	12.50	25.00
❏ M-603 [M]	The Incomparable Connie Francis	1967	5.00	10.00	20.00
❏ MS-603 [S]	The Incomparable Connie Francis	1967	6.25	12.50	25.00

MGM

| ❏ GAS-109 | Greatest Golden Groovie Goodies (Golden Archive Series) | 1970 | 6.25 | 12.50 | 25.00 |
| ❏ E-3686 [M] | Who's Sorry Now? | 1958 | 25.00 | 50.00 | 100.00 |

-- *Yellow label*

| ❏ E-3686 [M] | Who's Sorry Now? | 1960 | 10.00 | 20.00 | 40.00 |

-- *Black label*

| ❏ E-3761 [M] | The Exciting Connie Francis | 1959 | 20.00 | 40.00 | 80.00 |

-- *Yellow label*

| ❏ E-3761 [M] | The Exciting Connie Francis | 1959 | 7.50 | 15.00 | 30.00 |

-- *Black label*

| ❏ SE-3761 [S] | The Exciting Connie Francis | 1959 | 10.00 | 20.00 | 40.00 |

-- *Black label*

| ❏ SE-3761 [S] | The Exciting Connie Francis | 1959 | 25.00 | 50.00 | 100.00 |

-- *Yellow label*

❏ E-3776 [M]	My Thanks to You	1959	7.50	15.00	30.00
❏ SE-3776 [S]	My Thanks to You	1959	10.00	20.00	40.00
❏ E-3791 [M]	Italian Favorites	1959	7.50	15.00	30.00
❏ SE-3791 [S]	Italian Favorites	1959	10.00	20.00	40.00
❏ E-3792 [M]	Christmas in My Heart	1959	7.50	15.00	30.00
❏ SE-3792 [S]	Christmas in My Heart	1959	10.00	20.00	40.00
❏ E-3793 [M]	Connie's Greatest Hits	1960	7.50	15.00	30.00
❏ E-3794 [M]	Rock 'N' Roll Million Sellers	1960	7.50	15.00	30.00
❏ SE-3794 [S]	Rock 'N' Roll Million Sellers	1960	10.00	20.00	40.00
❏ E-3795 [M]	Country and Western Golden Hits	1960	7.50	15.00	30.00
❏ SE-3795 [S]	Country and Western Golden Hits	1960	10.00	20.00	40.00
❏ E-3853 [M]	Spanish and Latin American Favorites	1960	7.50	15.00	30.00
❏ SE-3853 [S]	Spanish and Latin American Favorites	1960	10.00	20.00	40.00
❏ E-3869 [M]	Jewish Favorites	1961	7.50	15.00	30.00
❏ SE-3869 [S]	Jewish Favorites	1961	10.00	20.00	40.00
❏ E-3871 [M]	More Italian Favorites	1960	7.50	15.00	30.00
❏ SE-3871 [S]	More Italian Favorites	1960	10.00	20.00	40.00
❏ E-3893 [M]	Songs to a Swinging Band	1961	7.50	15.00	30.00
❏ SE-3893 [S]	Songs to a Swinging Band	1961	10.00	20.00	40.00
❏ E-3913 [M]	Connie Francis at the Copa	1961	7.50	15.00	30.00
❏ SE-3913 [S]	Connie Francis at the Copa	1961	10.00	20.00	40.00
❏ E-3942 [M]	More Greatest Hits	1961	7.50	15.00	30.00
❏ SE-3942 [S]	More Greatest Hits	1961	10.00	20.00	40.00
❏ E-3965 [M]	Never on Sunday and Other Title Songs from Motion Pictures	1961	7.50	15.00	30.00
❏ SE-3965 [S]	Never on Sunday and Other Title Songs from Motion Pictures	1961	10.00	20.00	40.00
❏ E-3969 [M]	Folk Song Favorites	1961	7.50	15.00	30.00
❏ SE-3969 [S]	Folk Song Favorites	1961	10.00	20.00	40.00
❏ E-4013 [M]	Irish Favorites	1962	7.50	15.00	30.00

Number	Title	Yr	VG	VG+	NM
❏ SE-4013 [S]	Irish Favorites	1962	10.00	20.00	40.00
❏ E-4022 [M]	Do the Twist	1962	7.50	15.00	30.00
❏ SE-4022 [S]	Do the Twist	1962	10.00	20.00	40.00
❏ E-4022 [M]	Dance Party	196?	6.25	12.50	25.00

-- *Retitled version of "Do the Twist"*

| ❏ SE-4022 [S] | Dance Party | 196? | 7.50 | 15.00 | 30.00 |

-- *Retitled version of "Do the Twist"*

❏ E-4023 [M]	Fun Songs for Children	1962	12.50	25.00	50.00
❏ E-4048 [M]	Award Winning Motion Picture Hits	1963	6.25	12.50	25.00
❏ SE-4048 [S]	Award Winning Motion Picture Hits	1963	7.50	15.00	30.00
❏ E-4049 [M]	Connie Francis Sings Second Hand Love and Other Hits	1962	6.25	12.50	25.00
❏ SE-4049 [S]	Connie Francis Sings Second Hand Love and Other Hits	1962	7.50	15.00	30.00
❏ E-4079 [M]	Country Music Connie Style	1962	6.25	12.50	25.00
❏ SE-4079 [S]	Country Music Connie Style	1962	7.50	15.00	30.00
❏ E-4102 [M]	Modern Italian Hits	1963	6.25	12.50	25.00
❏ SE-4102 [S]	Modern Italian Hits	1963	7.50	15.00	30.00
❏ E-4123 [M]	Follow the Boys	1963	6.25	12.50	25.00
❏ SE-4123 [S]	Follow the Boys	1963	7.50	15.00	30.00
❏ E-4124 [M]	German Favorites	1963	6.25	12.50	25.00
❏ SE-4124 [S]	German Favorites	1963	7.50	15.00	30.00
❏ E-4145 [M]	Greatest American Waltzes	1963	6.25	12.50	25.00
❏ SE-4145 [S]	Greatest American Waltzes	1963	7.50	15.00	30.00
❏ E-4161 [M]	Mala Femmena & Connie's Big Hits from Italy	1963	6.25	12.50	25.00
❏ SE-4161 [S]	Mala Femmena & Connie's Big Hits from Italy	1963	7.50	15.00	30.00
❏ E-4167 [M]	The Very Best of Connie Francis	1963	6.25	12.50	25.00
❏ SE-4167 [S]	The Very Best of Connie Francis	1963	7.50	15.00	30.00
❏ E-4210 [M]	In the Summer of His Years	1964	6.25	12.50	25.00
❏ SE-4210 [S]	In the Summer of His Years	1964	7.50	15.00	30.00
❏ E-4229 [M]	Looking for Love	1964	6.25	12.50	25.00
❏ SE-4229 [S]	Looking for Love	1964	7.50	15.00	30.00
❏ E-4253 [M]	A New Kind of Connie	1964	6.25	12.50	25.00
❏ SE-4253 [S]	A New Kind of Connie	1964	7.50	15.00	30.00
❏ E-4294 [M]	Connie Francis Sings For Mama	1965	6.25	12.50	25.00
❏ SE-4294 [S]	Connie Francis Sings For Mama	1965	7.50	15.00	30.00
❏ E-4298 [M]	All Time International Hits	1965	6.25	12.50	25.00
❏ SE-4298 [S]	All Time International Hits	1965	7.50	15.00	30.00
❏ E-4355 [M]	Jealous Heart	1966	6.25	12.50	25.00
❏ SE-4355 [S]	Jealous Heart	1966	7.50	15.00	30.00
❏ E-4382 [M]	Movie Greats of the 60's	1966	6.25	12.50	25.00
❏ SE-4382 [S]	Movie Greats of the 60's	1966	7.50	15.00	30.00
❏ E-4399 [M]	Connie's Christmas	1966	6.25	12.50	25.00
❏ SE-4399 [S]	Connie's Christmas	1966	7.50	15.00	30.00
❏ E-4411 [M]	Live at the Sahara in Las Vegas	1967	6.25	12.50	25.00
❏ SE-4411 [S]	Live at the Sahara in Las Vegas	1967	7.50	15.00	30.00
❏ E-4448 [M]	Love, Italian Style	1967	6.25	12.50	25.00
❏ SE-4448 [S]	Love, Italian Style	1967	7.50	15.00	30.00
❏ E-4472 [M]	Connie Francis On Broadway Today	1967	6.25	12.50	25.00
❏ SE-4472 [S]	Connie Francis On Broadway Today	1967	7.50	15.00	30.00
❏ E-4474 [M]	Grandes Exitos del Cine de los Anos 60	1967	6.25	12.50	25.00
❏ SE-4474 [S]	Grandes Exitos del Cine de los Anos 60	1967	7.50	15.00	30.00
❏ E-4487 [M]	My Heart Cries for You	1967	7.50	15.00	30.00
❏ SE-4487 [S]	My Heart Cries for You	1967	6.25	12.50	25.00
❏ E-4522 [M]	Hawaii: Connie	1968	25.00	50.00	100.00
❏ SE-4522 [S]	Hawaii: Connie	1968	6.25	12.50	25.00
❏ SE-4573	Connie & Clyde	1968	6.25	12.50	25.00
❏ SE-4585	Connie Francis Sings Bacharach & David	1968	6.25	12.50	25.00
❏ SE-4637	The Wedding Cake	1969	6.25	12.50	25.00
❏ SE-4655	The Songs of Les Reed	1969	6.25	12.50	25.00
❏ ST 90510 [S]	The Very Best of Connie Francis	1965	10.00	20.00	40.00

-- *Capitol Record Club edition*

| ❏ T 90510 [M] | The Very Best of Connie Francis | 1965 | 10.00 | 20.00 | 40.00 |

-- *Capitol Record Club edition*

| ❏ ST-91145 | My Best to You | 1968 | 7.50 | 15.00 | 30.00 |

-- *Capitol Record Club*

FRANKLIN, ALAN, EXPLOSION
ALADDIN

| ❏ 104049 | Come Home Baby | 1969 | 20.00 | 40.00 | 80.00 |

HORNE

| ❏ JC-888 | The Blues Climax | 1970 | 20.00 | 40.00 | 80.00 |

FRANKLIN, ARETHA
ATLANTIC

❏ SD 2-906 [(2)]	Amazing Grace	1972	5.00	10.00	20.00
❏ 8139 [M]	I Never Loved a Man the Way I Love You	1967	6.25	12.50	25.00
❏ SD 8139 [S]	I Never Loved a Man the Way I Love You	1967	5.00	10.00	20.00

-- *Green and blue label*

Number	Title	Yr	VG	VG+	NM
❏ 8150 [M]	Aretha Arrives	1967	6.25	12.50	25.00
❏ SD 8150 [S]	Aretha Arrives	1967	5.00	10.00	20.00
-- Green and blue label					
❏ 8176 [M]	Aretha: Lady Soul	1968	7.50	15.00	30.00
❏ SD 8176 [S]	Aretha: Lady Soul	1968	5.00	10.00	20.00
-- Green and blue label					
❏ SD 8186	Aretha Now	1968	5.00	10.00	20.00
-- Green and blue label					
❏ QD 8305 [Q]	The Best of Aretha Franklin	1974	5.00	10.00	20.00
CHECKER					
❏ 10009 [M]	Gospel Soul	196?	5.00	10.00	20.00
COLUMBIA					
❏ CL 1612 [M]	Aretha	1961	12.50	25.00	50.00
-- Red and black label with six "eye" logos					
❏ CL 1612 [M]	Aretha	1963	5.00	10.00	20.00
-- "Guaranteed High Fidelity" on label					
❏ CL 1761 [M]	The Electrifying Aretha Franklin	1962	10.00	20.00	40.00
-- Red and black label with six "eye" logos					
❏ CL 1761 [M]	The Electrifying Aretha Franklin	1963	5.00	10.00	20.00
-- "Guaranteed High Fidelity" on label					
❏ CL 1876 [M]	The Tender, The Moving, The Swinging Aretha Franklin	1962	10.00	20.00	40.00
-- Red and black label with six "eye" logos					
❏ CL 1876 [M]	The Tender, The Moving, The Swinging Aretha Franklin	1963	5.00	10.00	20.00
-- "Guaranteed High Fidelity" on label					
❏ CL 2079 [M]	Laughing on the Outside	1963	5.00	10.00	20.00
-- "Guaranteed High Fidelity" on label					
❏ CL 2163 [M]	Unforgettable	1964	5.00	10.00	20.00
-- "Guaranteed High Fidelity" on label					
❏ CL 2281 [M]	Runnin' Out of Fools	1964	5.00	10.00	20.00
-- "Guaranteed High Fidelity" on label					
❏ CL 2351 [M]	Yeah!!!	1965	5.00	10.00	20.00
-- "Guaranteed High Fidelity" on label					
❏ CL 2521 [M]	Soul Sister	1966	5.00	10.00	20.00
❏ CL 2629 [M]	Take It Like You Give It	1967	6.25	12.50	25.00
❏ CL 2673 [M]	Aretha Franklin's Greatest Hits	1967	6.25	12.50	25.00
❏ CL 2754 [M]	Take a Look	1967	7.50	15.00	30.00
❏ CS 8412 [S]	Aretha	1961	20.00	40.00	80.00
-- Red and black label with six "eye" logos					
❏ CS 8412 [S]	Aretha	1963	6.25	12.50	25.00
-- "360 Sound Stereo" on label					
❏ CS 8561 [S]	The Electrifying Aretha Franklin	1962	12.50	25.00	50.00
-- Red and black label with six "eye" logos					
❏ CS 8561 [S]	The Electrifying Aretha Franklin	1963	6.25	12.50	25.00
-- "360 Sound Stereo" on label					
❏ CS 8676 [S]	The Tender, The Moving, The Swinging Aretha Franklin	1962	12.50	25.00	50.00
-- Red and black label with six "eye" logos					
❏ CS 8676 [S]	The Tender, The Moving, The Swinging Aretha Franklin	1963	6.25	12.50	25.00
-- "360 Sound Stereo" on label					
❏ CS 8879 [S]	Laughing on the Outside	1963	6.25	12.50	25.00
-- "360 Sound Stereo" on label					
❏ CS 8963 [S]	Unforgettable	1964	6.25	12.50	25.00
-- "360 Sound Stereo" on label					
❏ CS 9081 [S]	Runnin' Out of Fools	1964	6.25	12.50	25.00
-- "360 Sound Stereo" on label					
❏ CS 9151 [S]	Yeah!!!	1965	6.25	12.50	25.00
-- "360 Sound Stereo" on label					
❏ CS 9321 [S]	Soul Sister	1966	6.25	12.50	25.00
-- "360 Sound Stereo" on label					
❏ CS 9429 [S]	Take It Like You Give It	1967	5.00	10.00	20.00
-- "360 Sound Stereo" on label					
❏ CS 9473 [S]	Aretha Franklin's Greatest Hits	1967	5.00	10.00	20.00
-- "360 Sound Stereo" on label					
❏ CS 9554 [S]	Take a Look	1967	5.00	10.00	20.00
-- "360 Sound Stereo" on label					
❏ CS 9601	Aretha Franklin's Greatest Hits, Volume 2	1968	5.00	10.00	20.00
-- "360 Sound Stereo" on label					
❏ CS 9776	Soft and Beautiful	1969	5.00	10.00	20.00
-- "360 Sound Stereo" on label					
❏ KG 31355 [(2)]	In the Beginning/The World of Aretha Franklin 1960-1967	1972	5.00	10.00	20.00

FRANKLIN, CAROLYN
RCA VICTOR

Number	Title	Yr	VG	VG+	NM
❏ LSP-4160	Baby Dynamite	1969	5.00	10.00	20.00
❏ LSP-4317	Chain Reaction	1970	5.00	10.00	20.00
❏ LSP-4411	I'd Rather Be Lonely	1973	5.00	10.00	20.00

FRANKLIN, ERMA
BRUNSWICK

Number	Title	Yr	VG	VG+	NM
❏ BL 754147	Soul Sister	1969	5.00	10.00	20.00
EPIC					
❏ BN 619 [S]	Her Name Is Erma	1962	10.00	20.00	40.00
❏ LN 3824 [M]	Her Name Is Erma	1962	7.50	15.00	30.00

FRANKS, MICHAEL
DIRECT DISK

Number	Title	Yr	VG	VG+	NM
❏ SD-16611	Tiger in the Rain	1980	7.50	15.00	30.00
-- Audiophile vinyl					

FRANTIC
LIZARD

Number	Title	Yr	VG	VG+	NM
❏ 20103	Conception	1971	6.25	12.50	25.00

FRATERNITY OF MAN, THE
ABC

Number	Title	Yr	VG	VG+	NM
❏ S-647	The Fraternity of Man	1968	7.50	15.00	30.00
DOT					
❏ DLP-25955	Get It On	1969	6.25	12.50	25.00

FRAWLEY, WILLIAM
DOT

Number	Title	Yr	VG	VG+	NM
❏ DLP-3061 [M]	William Frawley Sings the Old Ones	1958	10.00	20.00	40.00

FRAZIER, DALLAS
CAPITOL

Number	Title	Yr	VG	VG+	NM
❏ ST 2552 [S]	Elvira	1966	6.25	12.50	25.00
❏ T 2552 [M]	Elvira	1966	5.00	10.00	20.00
❏ ST 2764 [S]	Tell It Like It Is	1967	5.00	10.00	20.00
❏ T 2764 [M]	Tell It Like It Is	1967	6.25	12.50	25.00

FREAK SCENE, THE
COLUMBIA

Number	Title	Yr	VG	VG+	NM
❏ CL 2656 [M]	Psychedelic Psoul	1967	17.50	35.00	70.00
❏ CS 9456 [S]	Psychedelic Psoul	1967	25.00	50.00	100.00

FREBERG, STAN
CAPITOL

Number	Title	Yr	VG	VG+	NM
❏ T 777 [M]	A Child's Garden of Freberg	1957	12.50	25.00	50.00
-- Turquoise label					
❏ WBO 1035 [(2) M]	The Best of the Stan Freberg Shows	1958	15.00	30.00	60.00
❏ T 1242 [M]	Stan Freberg with the Original Cast	1959	7.50	15.00	30.00
❏ SW 1573 [S]	Stan Freberg Presents the United States of America	1961	7.50	15.00	30.00
❏ W 1573 [M]	Stan Freberg Presents the United States of America	1961	6.25	12.50	25.00
❏ T 1694 [M]	Face the Funnies	1962	6.25	12.50	25.00
❏ T 1816 [M]	Madison Ave. Werewolf	1962	6.25	12.50	25.00
❏ T 2020 [M]	The Best of Stan Freberg	1964	6.25	12.50	25.00
❏ ST 2551 [S]	The Stan Freberg Underground Show #1	1966	6.25	12.50	25.00
❏ T 2551 [M]	The Stan Freberg Underground Show #1	1966	5.00	10.00	20.00

FRED, JOHN, AND HIS PLAYBOY BAND
PAULA

Number	Title	Yr	VG	VG+	NM
❏ LP-2191 [M]	John Fred and His Playboys	1966	5.00	10.00	20.00
❏ LPS-2191 [S]	John Fred and His Playboys	1966	6.25	12.50	25.00
❏ LP-2193 [M]	34:40 of John Fred and His Playboys	1967	5.00	10.00	20.00
❏ LPS-2193 [S]	34:40 of John Fred and His Playboys	1967	6.25	12.50	25.00
❏ LP-2197 [M]	Agnes English	1967	6.25	12.50	25.00
❏ LPS-2197 [S]	Agnes English	1967	5.00	10.00	20.00
❏ LPS-2197 [S]	Judy in Disguise with Glasses	1968	5.00	10.00	20.00
-- Retitled version of "Agnes English"					
❏ LPS-2201	Permanently Stated	1969	5.00	10.00	20.00
UNI					
❏ 73077	Love in My Soul	1970	10.00	20.00	40.00

FREDDIE AND THE DREAMERS
MERCURY

Number	Title	Yr	VG	VG+	NM
❏ MG-21017 [M]	Freddie and the Dreamers	1965	6.25	12.50	25.00
❏ MG-21026 [M]	Do the Freddie	1965	5.00	10.00	20.00
❏ MG-21031 [M]	Seaside Swingers	1965	5.00	10.00	20.00
❏ SR-61017 [R]	Freddie and the Dreamers	1965	5.00	10.00	20.00
❏ SR-61026 [S]	Do the Freddie	1965	6.25	12.50	25.00
❏ SR-61031 [S]	Seaside Swingers	1965	6.25	12.50	25.00
❏ SR-61053 [S]	Frantic Freddie	1965	5.00	10.00	20.00
❏ SR-61061 [S]	Fun Lovin' Freddie	1966	5.00	10.00	20.00
TOWER					
❏ DT 5003 [R]	I'm Telling You Now	1965	5.00	10.00	20.00
❏ T 5003 [M]	I'm Telling You Now	1965	6.25	12.50	25.00
-- Contains only two Freddie and the Dreamers songs, but the group's picture is on the cover. Also includes Four Just Men (2), Heinz (2), Linda Laine and the Sinners (2), Mike Rabin and the Demons (2) and The Toggery Five (2)					

Number	Title	Yr	VG	VG+	NM

FREDRIC
FORTE
❏ 80461	Phases and Faces	1968	200.00	400.00	800.00

FREE BAND, THE
VANGUARD
❏ VSD-6507	The Free Band	1969	5.00	10.00	20.00

FREE DESIGN, THE
AMBROTYPE
❏ 1016	There Is a Song	1972	12.50	25.00	50.00

PROJECT 3
❏ PR 4006 SD	The Free Design Sing for Very Important People	1970	6.25	12.50	25.00
❏ PR-5019 SD	Kites Are Fun	1967	6.25	12.50	25.00
❏ PR-5031 SD	You Could Be Born Again	1968	6.25	12.50	25.00
❏ PR-5037 SD	Heaven/Earth	1969	6.25	12.50	25.00
❏ PR-5045 SD	Stars/Times/Bubbles/Love	1971	6.25	12.50	25.00
❏ PR-5061 SD	One By One	1971	6.25	12.50	25.00

FREEBORNE
MONITOR
❏ MPS-607	Peak Impressions	1967	25.00	50.00	100.00

FREED, ALAN
Also see VARIOUS ARTISTS COLLECTIONS.
BRUNSWICK
❏ BL 54043 [M]	The Alan Freed Rock 'n' Roll Show	1959	37.50	75.00	150.00

CORAL
❏ CRL 57063 [M]	Alan Freed's Rock 'n' Roll Dance Party, Vol. 1	1956	37.50	75.00	150.00
❏ CRL 57115 [M]	Alan Freed's Rock 'n' Roll Dance Party, Vol. 2	1957	37.50	75.00	150.00
❏ CRL 57177 [M]	Go Go Go -- Alan Freed's TV Record Hop	1957	37.50	75.00	150.00
❏ CRL 57213 [M]	Rock Around the Block	1958	37.50	75.00	150.00
❏ CRL 57216 [M]	Alan Freed Presents the King's Henchmen	1958	37.50	75.00	150.00

MGM
❏ E-293 [10]	The Big Beat	195?	50.00	100.00	200.00

FREEMAN, BOBBY
AUTUMN
❏ LP 102 [M]	C'mon and S-W-I-M	1964	12.50	25.00	50.00

JOSIE
❏ JM-4007 [M]	Get In the Swim with Bobby Freeman	1965	7.50	15.00	30.00
❏ JS-4007 [R]	Get In the Swim with Bobby Freeman	1965	6.25	12.50	25.00

JUBILEE
❏ JLP-1086 [M]	Do You Wanna Dance?	1959	35.00	70.00	140.00
❏ JLPS-1086 [S]	Do You Wanna Dance?	1959	50.00	100.00	200.00
❏ JGM-5010 [M]	Twist with Bobby Freeman	1962	25.00	50.00	100.00

KING
❏ 930 [M]	The Lovable Style of Bobby Freeman	1965	62.50	125.00	250.00

FREEMAN, ERNIE
IMPERIAL
❏ LP-9022 [M]	Ernie Freeman Plays Irving Berlin	1957	12.50	25.00	50.00
❏ LP-9030 [M]	Jivin' Around	1957	12.50	25.00	50.00
❏ LP-9057 [M]	Ernie Freeman	1958	12.50	25.00	50.00
❏ LP-9133 [M]	Dark at the Top of the Stairs	1959	7.50	15.00	30.00
❏ LP-9148 [M]	Raunchy	1960	12.50	25.00	50.00
❏ LP-9157 [M]	Twistin' Time	1961	7.50	15.00	30.00
❏ LP-9193 [M]	The Stripper	1962	5.00	10.00	20.00
❏ LP-12067 [S]	Dark at the Top of the Stairs	1959	10.00	20.00	40.00
❏ LP-12081 [S]	Twistin' Time	1961	10.00	20.00	40.00
❏ LP-12193 [S]	The Stripper	1962	6.25	12.50	25.00

LIBERTY
❏ LRP-3283 [M]	Limbo Dance Party	1962	5.00	10.00	20.00
❏ LRP-3331 [M]	Comin' Home Baby	1963	5.00	10.00	20.00
❏ LST-7263 [S]	Limbo Dance Party	1962	6.25	12.50	25.00
❏ LST-7331 [S]	Comin' Home Baby	1963	6.25	12.50	25.00

FREEMAN, EVELYN
IMPERIAL
❏ LP-9101 [M]	Sky High	1960	5.00	10.00	20.00
❏ LP-12043 [S]	Sky High	1960	7.50	15.00	30.00

UNITED ARTISTS
❏ UAL-3178 [M]	Didn't It Rain	1962	5.00	10.00	20.00
❏ UAS-6178 [S]	Didn't It Rain	1962	6.25	12.50	25.00

FREEPORT
MAINSTREAM
❏ S-6130	Freeport	1970	12.50	25.00	50.00

FREES, PAUL
MGM
❏ SE-4735	Paul Frees and the Poster People	1969	6.25	12.50	25.00

FREHLEY, ACE
Also see KISS.
CASABLANCA
❏ NBLP-7121	Ace Frehley	1978	5.00	10.00	20.00
❏ NBPIX-7121 [PD]	Ace Frehley	1978	12.50	25.00	50.00

FRIAR TUCK
MERCURY
❏ MG-21111 [M]	Friar Tuck and His Psychedelic Guitar	1967	10.00	20.00	40.00
❏ SR-61111 [S]	Friar Tuck and His Psychedelic Guitar	1967	12.50	25.00	50.00

FRICKE, JANIE
COLUMBIA
❏ AS99 1535 [DJ]	Janie Fricke On Tour	1982	15.00	30.00	60.00
-- Promo-only picture disc					

FRIEDMAN, ERICK
RCA VICTOR RED SEAL
❏ LSC-2610 [S]	Paganini: Violin Concerto No. 1; Saint-Saens: Intro and Rondo Capriccioso	1962	10.00	20.00	40.00
-- Original with "shaded dog" label					
❏ LSC-2610 [S]	Paganini: Violin Concerto No. 1; Saint-Saens: Intro and Rondo Capriccioso	1964	5.00	10.00	20.00
-- Second edition with "white dog" label					

FRIEND AND LOVER
VERVE FORECAST
❏ FTS-3055	Reach Out of the Darkness	1968	5.00	10.00	20.00

FRIENDS OF DISTINCTION, THE
RCA VICTOR
❏ APD1-0276	Greatest Hits	1973	5.00	10.00	20.00

FRIJID PINK
LION
❏ LN-1004	Earth Omen	1972	5.00	10.00	20.00

PARROT
❏ PAS 71033	Frijid Pink	1970	6.25	12.50	25.00
❏ PAS 71041	Defrosted	1970	6.25	12.50	25.00

FRIZZELL, LEFTY
ABC
❏ ABCX-799	Lefty	1974	7.50	15.00	30.00
-- Original title					
❏ ABCX-799	The Legendary Lefty Frizzell	1974	5.00	10.00	20.00
-- Revised title					
❏ AC-30035	The ABC Collection	1976	5.00	10.00	20.00

COLUMBIA
❏ CL 1342 [M]	The One and Only Lefty Frizzell	1959	30.00	60.00	120.00
❏ CL 2169 [M]	Saginaw, Michigan	1964	7.50	15.00	30.00
❏ CL 2386 [M]	The Sad Side of Love	1965	7.50	15.00	30.00
❏ CL 2488 [M]	Lefty Frizzell's Greatest Hits	1966	7.50	15.00	30.00
❏ CL 2772 [M]	Puttin' On	1967	12.50	25.00	50.00
❏ CS 8969 [S]	Saginaw, Michigan	1964	10.00	20.00	40.00
❏ CL 9019 [10]	Lefty Frizzell Sings the Songs of Jimmie Rodgers	1951	62.50	125.00	250.00
❏ CL 9021 [10]	Listen to Lefty	1952	62.50	125.00	250.00
❏ CS 9186 [S]	The Sad Side of Love	1965	10.00	20.00	40.00
❏ CS 9288 [S]	Lefty Frizzell's Greatest Hits	1966	10.00	20.00	40.00
-- Red label, "360 Sound Stereo" at bottom					
❏ CS 9572 [S]	Puttin' On	1967	10.00	20.00	40.00
❏ C 32249	Lefty Frizzell Sings the Songs of Jimmie Rodgers	1973	5.00	10.00	20.00
❏ PC 33882	Remembering...The Greatest Hits of Lefty Frizzell	1975	5.00	10.00	20.00

Number	Title	Yr	VG	VG+	NM
HARMONY					
❑ HL 7241 [M]	Lefty Frizzell Sings the Songs of Jimmie Rodgers	1960	7.50	15.00	30.00
FROGGIE BEAVER					
FROGGIE BEAVER					
❑ 7301	From the Pond	1973	12.50	25.00	50.00
FROLK HEAVEN					
LRS					
❑ RF-6023	At the Apex of High	197?	100.00	200.00	400.00
FROMAN, JANE					
CAPITOL					
❑ H 354 [10]	Yours Alone	1952	10.00	20.00	40.00
❑ T 726 [M]	Faith	1956	6.25	12.50	25.00
❑ T 889 [M]	Songs at Sunset	1957	6.25	12.50	25.00
DECCA					
❑ DL 6021 [10]	Souvenirs	1952	10.00	20.00	40.00
RCA VICTOR					
❑ LPT-3055 [10]	Gems from Gershwin	1952	10.00	20.00	40.00
FROST, FRANK					
PHILLIPS INTERNATIONAL					
❑ PLP-1975 [M]	Hey Boss Man!	1961	1,500.	2,250.	3,000.
FROST, MAX, AND THE TROOPERS					
TOWER					
❑ ST-5147	Shape of Things to Come	1968	12.50	25.00	50.00
FROST, THE					
VANGUARD					
❑ VSD-6520	Frost Music	1969	5.00	10.00	20.00
❑ VSD-6541	Rock and Roll Music	1969	5.00	10.00	20.00
❑ VSD-6556	Through the Eyes of Love	1970	5.00	10.00	20.00
FRUT					
TRASH					
❑ (# unknown)	Keep On Truckin'	1971	20.00	40.00	80.00
-- Originals on yellow vinyl					
WESTBOUND					
❑ WB-2005	Keep On Truckin'	1971	7.50	15.00	30.00
-- Reissue of Trash LP					
❑ WB-2008	Spoiled Rotten	1972	7.50	15.00	30.00
FUGITIVES, THE					
HIDEOUT					
❑ 1001 [M]	The Fugitives at Dave's Hideout	1965	300.00	600.00	1,200.
JUSTICE					
❑ JLP-141	The Fugitives On the Run	1967	75.00	150.00	300.00
FUGITIVES, THE, AND OTHERS					
WESTCHESTER					
❑ 1005 [M]	Friday at the Cage A-Go-Go	1965	375.00	750.00	1,500.
FUGS, THE					
BROADSIDE					
❑ 304 [M]	The Village Fugs Sing Ballads of Contemporary Protest, Point of View, and General Dissatisfaction	1965	125.00	250.00	500.00
-- With insert					
❑ 304 [M]	The Village Fugs Sing Ballads of Contemporary Protest, Point of View, and General Dissatisfaction	1965	100.00	200.00	400.00
-- Without insert					
ESP-DISK					
❑ 1018 [M]	The Fugs First Album	1966	37.50	75.00	150.00
-- Turquoise and black cover, different from all other versions					
❑ 1018 [M]	The Fugs First Album	1966	10.00	20.00	40.00
-- "Reissue of Broadside 304" on cover					
❑ 1018 [M]	The Fugs First Album	1967	7.50	15.00	30.00
-- No reference to reissue on cover					
❑ 1028 [S]	The Fugs	1966	20.00	40.00	80.00
-- Psychedelic color shield on cover					
❑ 1028 [S]	The Fugs	1966	12.50	25.00	50.00
-- Black and white cover, back cover photos staggered					
❑ 1028 [S]	The Fugs	1966	7.50	5.00	30.00
-- Black and white cover, back cover photos aligned					
❑ 1038 [S]	Virgin Fugs	1967	25.00	50.00	100.00
-- "For Adult Minds" sticker on cover; with poster, book and stickers					
❑ 1038 [S]	Virgin Fugs	1967	7.50	15.00	30.00
-- "For Adult Minds" printed on cover					
❑ 1038 [S]	Virgin Fugs	1967	12.50	25.00	50.00
-- "For Adult Minds" sticker, no inserts					

Number	Title	Yr	VG	VG+	NM
❑ 1038 [S]	Virgin Fugs	1967	12.50	25.00	50.00
-- "For Adult Minds" stamped on cover					
❑ 2018	Fugs 4, Rounders Score	196?	20.00	40.00	80.00
REPRISE					
❑ R-6280 [M]	Tenderness Junction	1968	10.00	20.00	40.00
❑ RS-6280 [S]	Tenderness Junction	1968	7.50	15.00	30.00
❑ RS-6305	It Crawled Into My Hand, Honest	1968	6.25	12.50	25.00
❑ RS-6359	Belle of Avenue A	1969	6.25	12.50	25.00
❑ RS-6396	Golden Fifth	1970	6.25	12.50	25.00
FULLER, BOBBY, FOUR					
MUSTANG					
❑ M-900 [M]	KRLA King of the Wheels	1965	37.50	75.00	150.00
❑ MS-900 [S]	KRLA King of the Wheels	1965	50.00	100.00	200.00
❑ M-901 [M]	The Bobby Fuller Four (I Fought the Law)	1966	20.00	40.00	80.00
❑ MS-901 [S]	The Bobby Fuller Four (I Fought the Law)	1966	37.50	75.00	150.00
FULLER, JERRY					
LIN					
❑ 100 [M]	Teenage Love	1960	62.50	125.00	250.00
FULSON, LOWELL					
ARHOOLIE					
❑ R-2003	Early Recordings	1962	7.50	15.00	30.00
KENT					
❑ KST-516 [S]	Lowell Fulsom	1965	10.00	20.00	40.00
❑ KST-520 [S]	Tramp	1967	10.00	20.00	40.00
❑ KST-531	Lowell Fulsom Now	1969	7.50	15.00	30.00
❑ KLP-5016 [M]	Lowell Fulsom	1965	7.50	15.00	30.00
❑ KLP-5020 [M]	Tramp	1967	7.50	15.00	30.00
FUN AND GAMES					
UNI					
❑ 73042	Elephant Candy	1968	6.25	12.50	25.00
FUNKADELIC					
Also see GEORGE CLINTON; PARLIAMENT.					
WARNER BROS.					
❑ BS 2973	Hardcore Jollies	1976	6.25	12.50	25.00
❑ BS 3209	One Nation Under a Groove	1978	6.25	12.50	25.00
-- Includes bonus 7-inch single with small hole (deduct 20% if missing)					
❑ BSK 3371	Uncle Jam Wants You	1979	6.25	12.50	25.00
❑ BSK 3482	The Electric Spanking of War Babies	1981	6.25	12.50	25.00
WESTBOUND					
❑ 208	Standing on the Verge of Getting It On	1975	6.25	12.50	25.00
-- Reissue of Westbound 1001					
❑ 215	Let's Take It to the Stage	1975	12.50	25.00	50.00
❑ 216	Funkadelic	1975	7.50	15.00	30.00
-- Reissue of Westbound 2000					
❑ 217	Free Your Mind... And Your Ass Will Follow	1975	6.25	12.50	25.00
-- Reissue of Westbound 2001					
❑ 218	Maggot Brain	1975	6.25	12.50	25.00
-- Reissue of Westbound 2007					
❑ 221 [(2)]	America Eats Its Young	1976	6.25	12.50	25.00
-- Reissue of Westbound 2020					
❑ 223	Cosmic Slop	1976	6.25	12.50	25.00
-- Reissue of Westbound 2022					
❑ 227	Tales of Kidd Funkadelic	1976	12.50	25.00	50.00
❑ 303	Best of the Early Years	197?	10.00	20.00	40.00
❑ 1001	Standing on the Verge of Getting It On	1974	12.50	25.00	50.00
❑ 1004	Funkadelic's Greatest Hits	1975	12.50	25.00	50.00
❑ 2000	Funkadelic	1970	12.50	25.00	50.00
❑ 2001	Free Your Mind... And Your Ass Will Follow	1970	12.50	25.00	50.00
❑ 2007	Maggot Brain	1971	12.50	25.00	50.00
❑ 2020 [(2)]	America Eats Its Young	1972	15.00	30.00	60.00
❑ 2020 [(2)]	America Eats Its Young	1991	5.00	10.00	20.00
-- Reissue with bar code					
❑ 2022	Cosmic Slop	1973	12.50	25.00	50.00
FUSE					
Also see CHEAP TRICK.					
EPIC					
❑ BN 26502	Fuse	1970	20.00	40.00	80.00
FUTURE, THE					
SHAMLEY					
❑ 703	Down the Country Road	1969	5.00	10.00	20.00

Number	Title	Yr	VG	VG+	NM

G

G.T.O.'S
REPRISE
❑ RS 6390	Permanent Damage	1970	17.50	35.00	70.00
-- With booklet					
❑ RS 6390	Permanent Damage	1970	12.50	25.00	50.00
-- Without booklet					

STRAIGHT
❑ STS-1059	Permanent Damage	1969	25.00	50.00	100.00
-- With booklet					
❑ STS-1059	Permanent Damage	1969	20.00	40.00	80.00
-- Without booklet					

GABRIEL BONDAGE
DHARMA
❑ D-804	Angel Dust	1975	12.50	25.00	50.00
❑ D-808	Another Trip to Earth	1977	5.00	10.00	20.00
-- Exists on white, red, or blue vinyl; each of similar value					

GABRIEL, PETER
Also see GENESIS.
DIRECT DISK
❑ SD-16615	Peter Gabriel	1980	20.00	40.00	80.00
-- The "Solsbury Hill" album; contains a long version of "Slowburn" not available elsewhere					

GAILLARD, SLIM
CLEF
❑ MGC-126 [10]	Mish Mash	1953	25.00	50.00	100.00
❑ MGC-138 [10]	Slim Cavorts	1953	25.00	50.00	100.00

DOT
❑ DLP-3190 [M]	Slim Gaillard Rides Again	1959	7.50	15.00	30.00
❑ DLP-25190 [S]	Slim Gaillard Rides Again	1959	10.00	20.00	40.00

KING
❑ 295-80 [10]	Slim Gaillard/Boogie	195?	25.00	50.00	100.00

NORGRAN
❑ MGN-13 [10]	Slim Gaillard and His Musical Aggregation Wherever They May Be	1954	25.00	50.00	100.00

VERVE
❑ MGV-2013 [M]	Smorgasbord, Help Yourself	1956	12.50	25.00	50.00
❑ V-2013 [M]	Smorgasbord, Help Yourself	1961	5.00	10.00	20.00

GAITHER, BILL, TRIO
HEART WARMING
❑ R 3197	Christmas…Back Home in Indiana	1972	5.00	10.00	20.00

GALAHADS, THE
LIBERTY
❑ LRP-3371 [M]	Hello, Galahads	1964	5.00	10.00	20.00
❑ LST-7371 [S]	Hello, Galahads	1964	6.25	12.50	25.00

GALE, SUNNY
CANADIAN AMERICAN
❑ CALP-1015 [M]	Goldies by the Girls	1964	6.25	12.50	25.00

RCA VICTOR
❑ LPM-1277 [M]	Sunny and Blue	1956	10.00	20.00	40.00

WARWICK
❑ W-2018 [M]	Sunny	1960	7.50	15.00	30.00

GALLOP, FRANK
MUSICOR
❑ (# unknown) [S]	Frank Gallop Sings	1966	5.00	10.00	20.00

GALS & PALS
FONTANA
❑ SRF-67538 [S]	Gals & Pals (The Exciting Vocal Sounds of Europe's Newest "In" Group)	1965	5.00	10.00	20.00
❑ SRF-67557 [S]	Gals & Pals Sing Something for Everybody	1966	5.00	10.00	20.00

GAME
FAITHFUL VIRTUE
❑ 2003	Game	1969	5.00	10.00	20.00

GANDALF
CAPITOL
❑ ST-121	Gandalf	1969	50.00	100.00	200.00

GANDALF THE GREY
G.W.R.
❑ 7	The Grey Wizard Am I	1972	75.00	150.00	300.00

GANT, CECIL
KING
❑ 671 [M]	Cecil Gant	1960	20.00	40.00	80.00

RED MILL
❑ (no #) [M]	Cecil Gant	1956	125.00	250.00	500.00
-- Red vinyl					

SOUND
❑ 601 [M]	The Incomparable Cecil Gant	1958	25.00	50.00	100.00

GANTS, THE
LIBERTY
❑ LRP-3432 [M]	Road Runner	1965	7.50	15.00	30.00
❑ LRP-3455 [M]	The Gants Galore	1966	7.50	15.00	30.00
❑ LRP-3473 [M]	The Gants Again	1966	7.50	15.00	30.00
❑ LST-7432 [S]	Road Runner	1965	10.00	20.00	40.00
❑ LST-7455 [S]	The Gants Galore	1966	10.00	20.00	40.00
❑ LST-7473 [S]	The Gants Again	1966	10.00	20.00	40.00

GARAGIOLA, JOE
UNITED ARTISTS
❑ UAL-3032 [M]	That Holler Guy!	1959	10.00	20.00	40.00
❑ UAS-6032 [S]	That Holler Guy!	1959	12.50	25.00	50.00

GARBER, JAN
DECCA
❑ DL 8482 [M]	Dance at Home	195?	5.00	10.00	20.00
-- Black label, silver print					
❑ DL 8483 [M]	In a Dancing Mood	195?	5.00	10.00	20.00
-- Black label, silver print					
❑ DL 8484 [M]	Designed for Dancing	195?	5.00	10.00	20.00
-- Black label, silver print					
❑ DL 78793 [S]	Music from the Blue Room, Roosevelt Hotel, New Orleans	195?	5.00	10.00	20.00
-- Black label, silver print					
❑ DL 78824 [S]	Waltzes	195?	5.00	10.00	20.00
-- Black label, silver print					
❑ DL 78867 [S]	Jan Garber in Danceland	195?	5.00	10.00	20.00
-- Black label, silver print					
❑ DL 78932 [S]	Christmas Dance Party	1959	5.00	10.00	20.00
-- Black label, silver print					

GARBO, GRETA
MGM
❑ E-4201 [M]	Garbo	1964	10.00	20.00	40.00

GARCIA, JERRY
Also see THE GRATEFUL DEAD.
ROUND
❑ RX-102	Garcia	1974	6.25	12.50	25.00
❑ RX-107	Reflections	1975	7.50	15.00	30.00
❑ RN-LA565-G	Reflections	1976	5.00	10.00	20.00
-- Reissue of Round 107 with United Artists distribution					

WARNER BROS.
❑ BS 2582	Garcia	1972	10.00	20.00	40.00
-- Green label with "WB" logo					

GARDNER, BROTHER DAVE
CAPITOL
❑ ST 1867 [S]	It Don't Make No Difference	1963	6.25	12.50	25.00
❑ T 1867 [M]	It Don't Make No Difference	1963	5.00	10.00	20.00
❑ ST 2055 [S]	It's All in How You Look at It	1964	6.25	12.50	25.00
❑ T 2055 [M]	It's All in How You Look at It	1964	5.00	10.00	20.00

4 STAR
❑ 4S 75003	Brother Dave Gardner's New Comedy Album	1976	5.00	10.00	20.00

RCA VICTOR
❑ LPM-2083 [M]	Rejoice, Dear Hearts!	1960	5.00	10.00	20.00
❑ LSP-2083(e) [S]	Rejoice, Dear Hearts!	196?	6.25	12.50	25.00
❑ LPM-2239 [M]	Kick Thy Own Self	1960	5.00	10.00	20.00
❑ LSP-2239(e) [S]	Kick Thy Own Self	196?	6.25	12.50	25.00
❑ LPM-2335 [M]	Ain't That Weird?	1961	5.00	10.00	20.00
❑ LSP-2335 [S]	Ain't That Weird?	1961	6.25	12.50	25.00
❑ LPM-2498 [M]	Did You Ever?	1962	5.00	10.00	20.00
❑ LSP-2498 [S]	Did You Ever?	1962	6.25	12.50	25.00
❑ LPM-2628 [M]	All Seriousness Aside	1963	5.00	10.00	20.00
❑ LSP-2628 [S]	All Seriousness Aside	1963	6.25	12.50	25.00
❑ LPM-2761 [M]	It's Bigger Than Both of Us	1963	5.00	10.00	20.00

Number	Title	Yr	VG	VG+	NM
❑ LSP-2761 [S]	It's Bigger Than Both of Us	1963	6.25	12.50	25.00
❑ LPM-2852 [M]	Best of Dave Gardner	1964	5.00	10.00	20.00
❑ LSP-2852 [S]	Best of Dave Gardner	1964	6.25	12.50	25.00

TONKA

❑ TLP 713	Out Front	1969	5.00	10.00	20.00

TOWER

❑ ST 5050 [S]	Hip-ocracy	1966	5.00	10.00	20.00
❑ ST 5075 [S]	It Don't Make No Difference	1967	5.00	10.00	20.00

GARDNER, DON, AND DEE DEE FORD
FIRE

❑ LP-105 [M]	Need Your Lovin'	1962	100.00	200.00	400.00

SUE

❑ LP-1044 [M]	Don Gardner and Dee Dee Ford In Sweden	1965	30.00	60.00	120.00

GARDNERS, THE
PRESTIGE INT'L.

❑ PRLP-13062 [M]	Folk Songs Far and Near	1962	7.50	15.00	30.00

GARFUNKEL, ART
Also see SIMON AND GARFUNKEL.
COLUMBIA

❑ CQ 31474 [Q]	Angel Clare	1973	5.00	10.00	20.00
❑ PCQ 33700 [Q]	Breakaway	1975	5.00	10.00	20.00
❑ JC 34975	Watermark	1978	25.00	50.00	100.00
-- Stock copy with "Fingerpaint" on side 2					
❑ JC 34975 [DJ]	Watermark	1978	15.00	30.00	60.00
-- Test pressing or white label promo with "Fingerpaint" on side 2					

GARLAND, HANK
COLUMBIA

❑ CL 1572 [M]	Jazz Winds from a New Direction	1961	7.50	15.00	30.00
❑ CL 1913 [M]	The Unforgettable Guitar of Hank Garland	1962	7.50	15.00	30.00
❑ CS 8372 [S]	Jazz Winds from a New Direction	1961	10.00	20.00	40.00
❑ CS 8713 [S]	The Unforgettable Guitar of Hank Garland	1962	10.00	20.00	40.00

HARMONY

❑ HL 7231 [M]	Velvet Guitar	196?	5.00	10.00	20.00
❑ HS 11028 [S]	Velvet Guitar	196?	6.25	12.50	25.00

GARLAND, JUDY
ABC

❑ 620 [M]	Judy Garland At Home at the Palace -- Opening Night	1967	5.00	10.00	20.00
❑ S-620 [S]	Judy Garland At Home at the Palace -- Opening Night	1967	6.25	12.50	25.00

CAPITOL

❑ W 676 [M]	Miss Show Business	1955	10.00	20.00	40.00
❑ T 734 [M]	Judy	1956	10.00	20.00	40.00
❑ T 835 [M]	Alone	1957	10.00	20.00	40.00
❑ ST 1036 [S]	Judy in Love	1959	10.00	20.00	40.00
❑ T 1036 [M]	Judy in Love	1958	6.25	12.50	25.00
❑ ST 1118 [S]	Garland at the Grove	1959	10.00	20.00	40.00
❑ T 1118 [M]	Garland at the Grove	1959	6.25	12.50	25.00
❑ ST 1188 [S]	The Letter	1959	10.00	20.00	40.00
❑ T 1188 [M]	The Letter	1959	6.25	12.50	25.00
-- Add 80% if letter is on cover					
❑ ST 1467 [S]	Judy -- That's Entertainment	1960	10.00	20.00	40.00
❑ T 1467 [M]	Judy -- That's Entertainment	1960	6.25	12.50	25.00
❑ SWBO 1569 [(2) S]	Judy at Carnegie Hall	1961	12.50	25.00	50.00
❑ WBO 1569 [(2) M]	Judy at Carnegie Hall	1961	10.00	20.00	40.00
❑ SW 1710 [S]	The Garland Touch	1962	7.50	15.00	30.00
❑ W 1710 [M]	The Garland Touch	1962	5.00	10.00	20.00
❑ SW 1861 [S]	I Could Go On Singing	1963	15.00	30.00	60.00
❑ W 1861 [M]	I Could Go On Singing	1963	10.00	20.00	40.00
❑ ST 1941 [S]	Our Love Letter	1963	7.50	15.00	30.00
❑ T 1941 [M]	Our Love Letter	1963	5.00	10.00	20.00
❑ ST 1999 [S]	The Hits of Judy Garland	1964	7.50	15.00	30.00
❑ T 1999 [M]	The Hits of Judy Garland	1964	5.00	10.00	20.00
❑ W 2062 [M]	Just for Openers	1964	5.00	10.00	20.00
❑ STCL 2988 [(3)]	The Judy Garland Deluxe Set	1968	10.00	20.00	40.00

DECCA

❑ DXB 172 [(2) M]	The Best of Judy Garland	1963	5.00	10.00	20.00
❑ DL 4199 [M]	The Magic of Judy Garland	1961	7.50	15.00	30.00
❑ DL 6020 [10]	Judy at the Palace	1952	25.00	50.00	100.00
❑ DXSB 7172 [(2) R]	The Best of Judy Garland	1963	5.00	10.00	20.00
❑ DL 8190 [M]	Judy Garland's Greatest Performances	1955	10.00	20.00	40.00

MARK 56

❑ 632 [PD]	In Concert: San Francisco	1978	15.00	30.00	60.00

METRO

Number	Title	Yr	VG	VG+	NM
❑ MS-506 [S]	Judy Garland	1965	5.00	10.00	20.00
❑ MS-581 [S]	Judy Garland in Song	1966	5.00	10.00	20.00

MGM

❑ SDP-1 [(2)]	Golden Years at MGM	1969	7.50	15.00	30.00
❑ E-82 [10]	Judy Garland Sings	1951	25.00	50.00	100.00
❑ E-3149 [M]	If You Feel Like Singing, Sing	1955	15.00	30.00	60.00
❑ E-3989 [M]	The Judy Garland Story Vol. 1: The Star Years	1961	7.50	15.00	30.00
❑ E-4005 [M]	The Judy Garland Story Vol. 2: The Hollywood Years	1962	7.50	15.00	30.00
❑ E-4204 [M]	The Very Best of Judy Garland	1964	7.50	15.00	30.00

GARLAND, JUDY, AND LIZA MINNELLI
Also see each artist's individual listings.
CAPITOL

❑ SWBO 2295 [(2) S]	"Live" at the London Palladium	1965	7.50	15.00	30.00
❑ WBO 2295 [(2) M]	"Live" at the London Palladium	1965	6.25	12.50	25.00

MOBILE FIDELITY

❑ 1-048	"Live" at the London Palladium	1981	6.25	12.50	25.00
-- Audiophile vinyl					

GARNER, ERROLL
ABC-PARAMOUNT

❑ 365 [M]	Dreamstreet	1961	5.00	10.00	20.00
❑ S-365 [S]	Dreamstreet	1961	6.25	12.50	25.00
❑ 395 [M]	Closeup in Swing	1961	5.00	10.00	20.00
❑ S-395 [S]	Closeup in Swing	1961	6.25	12.50	25.00

ATLANTIC

❑ ALR-109 [10]	Rhapsody	1950	20.00	40.00	80.00
❑ ALR-112 [10]	Erroll Garner at the Piano	1951	20.00	40.00	80.00
❑ ALR-128 [10]	Passport to Fame	1952	25.00	50.00	100.00
❑ ALR-135 [10]	Piano Solos, Volume 2	1952	20.00	40.00	80.00
❑ 1227 [M]	The Greatest Garner	1956	10.00	20.00	40.00
-- Black label					
❑ 1315 [M]	Perpetual Motion	1959	10.00	20.00	40.00
-- Black label					

BLUE NOTE

❑ BLP-5007 [10]	Overture to Dawn, Volume 1	1952	50.00	100.00	200.00
❑ BLP-5008 [10]	Overture to Dawn, Volume 2	1952	50.00	100.00	200.00
❑ BLP-5014 [10]	Overture to Dawn, Volume 3	1953	50.00	100.00	200.00
❑ BLP-5015 [10]	Overture to Dawn, Volume 4	1953	50.00	100.00	200.00
❑ BLP-5016 [10]	Overture to Dawn, Volume 5	1953	50.00	100.00	200.00

COLUMBIA

❑ C2L 9 [(2) M]	Paris Impressions	1958	10.00	20.00	40.00
❑ CL 535 [M]	Erroll Garner at the Piano	1953	15.00	30.00	60.00
-- Red label with gold print					
❑ CL 535 [M]	Erroll Garner at the Piano	1956	7.50	15.00	30.00
-- Red and black label with six "eye" logos					
❑ CL 583 [M]	Gems	1954	15.00	30.00	60.00
-- Red label with gold print					
❑ CL 583 [M]	Gems	1956	7.50	15.00	30.00
-- Red and black label with six "eye" logos					
❑ CL 617 [M]	Gone Garner Gonest	1955	15.00	30.00	60.00
-- Red label with gold print					
❑ CL 617 [M]	Gone Garner Gonest	1956	7.50	15.00	30.00
-- Red and black label with six "eye" logos					
❑ CL 667 [M]	Erroll Garner Plays for Dancing	1956	7.50	15.00	30.00
❑ CL 883 [M]	Concert by the Sea	1956	7.50	15.00	30.00
❑ CL 939 [M]	The Most Happy Piano	1957	7.50	15.00	30.00
❑ CL 1014 [M]	Other Voices	1957	7.50	15.00	30.00
❑ CL 1060 [M]	Soliloquy	1957	7.50	15.00	30.00
❑ CL 1141 [M]	Encores in Hi-Fi	1958	7.50	15.00	30.00
❑ CL 1216 [M]	Paris Impressions, Volume 1	1958	5.00	10.00	20.00
❑ CL 1217 [M]	Paris Impressions, Volume 2	1958	5.00	10.00	20.00
❑ CL 1452 [M]	The One and Only Erroll Garner	1960	5.00	10.00	20.00
❑ CL 1512 [M]	Swinging Solos	1960	5.00	10.00	20.00
❑ CL 1587 [M]	The Provocative Erroll Garner	1961	5.00	10.00	20.00
❑ CL 2540 [10]	Garnerland	1955	15.00	30.00	60.00
❑ CL 2606 [10]	He's Here! He's Gone! He's	1956	15.00	30.00	60.00
❑ CL 6139 [10]	Piano Moods	1950	20.00	40.00	80.00
❑ CL 6173 [10]	Gems	1951	20.00	40.00	80.00
❑ CL 6209 [10]	Solo Flight	1952	20.00	40.00	80.00
❑ CL 6259 [10]	Erroll Garner Plays for Dancing	1953	20.00	40.00	80.00
❑ CS 8252 [S]	The One and Only Erroll Garner	1960	6.25	12.50	25.00
❑ CS 8312 [S]	Swinging Solos	1960	6.25	12.50	25.00
❑ CS 8387 [S]	The Provocative Erroll Garner	1961	6.25	12.50	25.00

DIAL

❑ LP-205 [10]	Erroll Garner, Volume 1	1950	50.00	100.00	200.00
❑ LP-902 [M]	Free Piano Improvisations Recorded by Baron Timme Rosenkranz at One of His Famous Gaslight Jazz Sessions	1949	75.00	150.00	300.00

EMARCY

❑ MG-26016 [10]	Garnering	1954	20.00	40.00	80.00

Number	Title	Yr	VG	VG+	NM
❏ MG-26042 [10] Gone with Garner		1954	20.00	40.00	80.00
❏ MG-36001 [M] Contrasts		1955	7.50	15.00	30.00
❏ MG-36026 [M] Garnering		1955	7.50	15.00	30.00
❏ MG-36069 [M] Erroll!		1956	7.50	15.00	30.00

JAZZTONE

Number	Title	Yr	VG	VG+	NM
❏ J-1269 [M] Early Erroll		1957	10.00	20.00	40.00

KING

Number	Title	Yr	VG	VG+	NM
❏ 295-17 [10] Piano Stylist		1952	20.00	40.00	80.00
❏ 395-540 [M] Piano Variations		1958	12.50	25.00	50.00

MERCURY

Number	Title	Yr	VG	VG+	NM
❏ MG-20009 [M] Erroll Garner at the Piano		1953	12.50	25.00	50.00
❏ MG-20055 [M] Mambo Moves Garner		1954	12.50	25.00	50.00
❏ MG-20063 [M] Solitaire		1954	12.50	25.00	50.00
❏ MG-20090 [M] Afternoon of an Elf		1955	12.50	25.00	50.00
❏ MG-25117 [10] Erroll Garner at the Piano		1951	20.00	40.00	80.00
❏ MG-25157 [10] Gone with Garner		1951	20.00	40.00	80.00
❏ SR-60662 [S] Erroll Garner Plays Misty		1962	5.00	10.00	20.00
❏ SR-60803 [S] The Best of Erroll Garner		1963	5.00	10.00	20.00
❏ SR-60859 [S] New Kind of Love		1963	5.00	10.00	20.00
❏ SR-61308 [S] Feeling Is Believing		1964	5.00	10.00	20.00

REPRISE

Number	Title	Yr	VG	VG+	NM
❏ R 6080 [M] One World Concert		1963	5.00	10.00	20.00
❏ RS 6080 [S] One World Concert		1963	6.25	12.50	25.00

RONDO-LETTE

Number	Title	Yr	VG	VG+	NM
❏ A-15 [M] Erroll Garner		1958	6.25	12.50	25.00

SAVOY

Number	Title	Yr	VG	VG+	NM
❏ MG-12002 [M] Penthouse Serenade		1955	7.50	15.00	30.00
❏ MG-12003 [M] Serenade to "Laura"		1955	7.50	15.00	30.00
❏ MG-15000 [10] Erroll Garner Plays Piano Solos		1950	20.00	40.00	80.00
❏ MG-15001 [10] Erroll Garner Plays Piano Solos, Volume 2		1950	20.00	40.00	80.00
❏ MG-15002 [10] Erroll Garner Plays Piano Solos, Volume 3		1950	20.00	40.00	80.00
❏ MG-15003 [10] Erroll Garner Plays Piano Solos, Volume 4		1950	20.00	40.00	80.00
❏ MG-15026 [10] Erroll Garner at the Piano		1953	20.00	40.00	80.00

GARNETT, GALE
COLUMBIA

Number	Title	Yr	VG	VG+	NM
❏ CL 2825 [M] An Audience with the King of Wands		1968	5.00	10.00	20.00

RCA VICTOR

Number	Title	Yr	VG	VG+	NM
❏ LPM-2833 [M] My Kind of Folk Songs		1964	10.00	20.00	40.00
-- Black and white/blueish cover					
❏ LSP-2833 [S] My Kind of Folk Songs		1964	12.50	25.00	50.00
-- Black and white/blueish cover					
❏ LSP-2833 [S] My Kind of Folk Songs		1965	5.00	10.00	20.00
-- Color photo on cover					
❏ LSP-3305 [S] Lovin' Place		1965	5.00	10.00	20.00
❏ LSP-3325 [S] The Many Faces of Gale Garnett		1965	5.00	10.00	20.00
❏ LSP-3498 [S] Variety Is the Spice of Gale		1966	5.00	10.00	20.00
❏ LSP-3586 [S] New Adventures		1966	5.00	10.00	20.00
❏ LPM-3747 [M] Flying and Rainbows and Love		1967	6.25	12.50	25.00
❏ LSP-3747 [S] Flying and Rainbows and Love		1967	5.00	10.00	20.00

GARROWAY, DAVE
CAMEO

Number	Title	Yr	VG	VG+	NM
❏ C-1001 [M] An Adventure in Hi-Fi Music		1958	10.00	20.00	40.00
-- Black label, brown print, cameo figure at top					

GARSON, GREER
LION

Number	Title	Yr	VG	VG+	NM
❏ L-70102 [M] Greer Garson Babysits with Stories and Songs		1958	7.50	15.00	30.00

GARVIN, REX, AND THE MIGHTY CRAVERS
TOWER

Number	Title	Yr	VG	VG+	NM
❏ ST 5130 Raw Funky Earth		1968	7.50	15.00	30.00

GARY, JOHN
LA BREA

Number	Title	Yr	VG	VG+	NM
❏ 8010 [M] John Gary		1961	6.25	12.50	25.00
❏ S-8010 [S] John Gary		1961	7.50	15.00	30.00

RCA VICTOR

Number	Title	Yr	VG	VG+	NM
❏ LOC-1139 [M] The John Gary Carnegie Hall Concert		1967	5.00	10.00	20.00
❏ LSP-2745 [S] Catch a Rising Star		1963	5.00	10.00	20.00
❏ LSP-2804 [S] Encore		1964	5.00	10.00	20.00
❏ LSP-2922 [S] So Tenderly		1964	5.00	10.00	20.00
❏ LSP-2940 [S] The John Gary Christmas Album		1964	5.00	10.00	20.00
❏ LPM-3928 [M] John Gary On Broadway		1968	5.00	10.00	20.00
❏ LPM-3992 [M] John Gary Sings/John Gary		1968	5.00	10.00	20.00

GARY, SAM
TRANSITION

Number	Title	Yr	VG	VG+	NM
❏ TRLP-F-1 [M] Spirituals and Work Songs		1958	7.50	15.00	30.00

GAS MASK
TONSIL

Number	Title	Yr	VG	VG+	NM
❏ 4001 Gas Mask		1970	5.00	10.00	20.00

GATES, DAVID
Also see BREAD.
ELEKTRA

Number	Title	Yr	VG	VG+	NM
❏ EQ-5066 [Q] First		1973	5.00	10.00	20.00

GATES, HEN
MASTERSEAL

Number	Title	Yr	VG	VG+	NM
❏ MLP-700 [M] Let's All Dance to Rock and Roll		1956	25.00	50.00	100.00

PALACE

Number	Title	Yr	VG	VG+	NM
❏ P-700 [M] Let's All Dance to Rock and Roll		1958	15.00	30.00	60.00
-- Reissue of Masterseal 700					
❏ PST-700 [S] Let's All Dance to Rock and Roll		1958	20.00	40.00	80.00
-- Labeled stereo, but plays in mono					

PARIS

Number	Title	Yr	VG	VG+	NM
❏ (# unknown) [M] Rock and Roll Festival		1957	15.00	30.00	60.00

PLYMOUTH

Number	Title	Yr	VG	VG+	NM
❏ R12-144 [M] Rock and Roll		1956	15.00	30.00	60.00
❏ R12-149 [M] Rock and Roll, No. 2		1957	15.00	30.00	60.00

GATEWAY SINGERS, THE
DECCA

Number	Title	Yr	VG	VG+	NM
❏ DL 8413 [M] Puttin' On the Style		1956	10.00	20.00	40.00
❏ DL 8671 [M] The Gateway Singers at the Hungry I		1958	7.50	15.00	30.00
❏ DL 8742 [M] The Gateway Singers in Hi-Fi		1958	7.50	15.00	30.00

MGM

Number	Title	Yr	VG	VG+	NM
❏ E-3905 [M] Down in the Valley		1961	5.00	10.00	20.00
❏ SE-3905 [S] Down in the Valley		1961	6.25	12.50	25.00
❏ E-4154 [M] Hootenanny		1963	5.00	10.00	20.00
❏ SE-4154 [S] Hootenanny		1963	6.25	12.50	25.00

WARNER BROS.

Number	Title	Yr	VG	VG+	NM
❏ W 1295 [M] The Gateway Singers on the Lot		1959	6.25	12.50	25.00
❏ WS 1295 [S] The Gateway Singers on the Lot		1959	7.50	15.00	30.00
❏ W 1334 [M] Wagons West		1960	6.25	12.50	25.00
❏ WS 1334 [S] Wagons West		1960	7.50	15.00	30.00

GATEWAY TRIO, THE
CAPITOL

Number	Title	Yr	VG	VG+	NM
❏ ST 1868 [S] The Mad, Mad, Mad Gateway Trio		1963	5.00	10.00	20.00
❏ ST 2184 [S] The Gateway Trio		1964	5.00	10.00	20.00

GATLIN, LARRY, AND THE GATLIN BROTHERS BAND
COLUMBIA

Number	Title	Yr	VG	VG+	NM
❏ HC 48135 Sure Feels Like Love		1982	62.50	125.00	250.00
-- Half-speed mastered edition					

SWORD & SHIELD

Number	Title	Yr	VG	VG+	NM
❏ 9009 [M] The Old Country Church		1961	25.00	50.00	100.00
-- As "The Gatlin Quartet" (with sister Donna joining Larry, Rudy and Steve)					

GAUCHOS, THE -- See JIM DOVAL AND THE GAUCHOS.

GAVIN, KEVIN
CHARLIE PARKER

Number	Title	Yr	VG	VG+	NM
❏ PLP-810 [M] Hey! This Is Kevin Gavin		1962	7.50	15.00	30.00
❏ PLP-810S [S] Hey! This Is Kevin Gavin		1962	10.00	20.00	40.00

GAYE, MARVIN
COLUMBIA

Number	Title	Yr	VG	VG+	NM
❏ 9C9 40133 [PD] Dream of a Lifetime		1985	5.00	10.00	20.00
❏ HC 48197 Midnight Love		1984	10.00	20.00	40.00
-- Half-speed mastered edition					

MOTOWN

Number	Title	Yr	VG	VG+	NM
❏ M9-791A3 [(3)]Anthology		1974	5.00	10.00	20.00
❏ 37463 1296-1 [DJ] The Master 1961-1984		1995	5.00	10.00	20.00
-- Vinyl is promo only; 8-song sampler from box set					

TAMLA

Number	Title	Yr	VG	VG+	NM
❏ T 221 [M] The Soulful Moods of Marvin Gaye		1961	250.00	500.00	1,000.
❏ T 239 [M] That Stubborn Kinda' Fella		1963	150.00	300.00	600.00
❏ T 242 [M] Recorded Live -- Marvin Gaye on Stage		1963	75.00	150.00	300.00
❏ T 251 [M] When I'm Alone I Cry		1964	62.50	125.00	250.00

Number	Title	Yr	VG	VG+	NM
❏ T 252 [M]	Marvin Gaye/Greatest Hits	1964	7.50	15.00	30.00
❏ TS 252 [S]	Marvin Gaye/Greatest Hits	1964	10.00	20.00	40.00
❏ T 258 [M]	How Sweet It Is to Be Loved by You	1965	10.00	20.00	40.00
❏ TS 258 [S]	How Sweet It Is to Be Loved by You	1965	12.50	25.00	50.00
❏ T 259 [M]	Hello Broadway, This Is Marvin	1965	10.00	20.00	40.00
❏ TS 259 [S]	Hello Broadway, This Is Marvin	1965	12.50	25.00	50.00
❏ T 261 [M]	A Tribute to the Greate Nat King Cole	1965	10.00	20.00	40.00
❏ TS 261 [S]	A Tribute to the Greae Nat King Cole	1965	12.50	25.00	50.00t
❏ T 266 [M]	Moods of Marvin Gaye	1966	10.00	20.00	40.00
❏ TS 266 [S]	Moods of Marvin Gaye	1966	12.50	25.00	50.00
❏ T 278 [M]	Marvin Gaye/Greatest Hits, Vol. 2	1967	6.25	12.50	25.00
❏ TS 278 [S]	Marvin Gaye/Greatest Hits, Vol. 2	1967	5.00	10.00	20.00
❏ T 285 [M]	In the Groove	1968	12.50	25.00	50.00
❏ TS 285 [S]	In the Groove	1968	6.25	12.50	25.00
❏ TS 285 [S]	I Heard It Through the Grapevine	1969	5.00	10.00	20.00
-- Retitled version of "In the Groove"					
❏ TS 292	M.P.G.	1969	5.00	10.00	20.00
❏ TS 293	Marvin Gaye and His Girls	1969	5.00	10.00	20.00
-- Includes duets with Tammi Terrell, Mary Wells, Kim Weston					
❏ TS 299	That's the Way Love Is	1969	5.00	10.00	20.00
❏ TS 300	Marvin Gaye Super Hits	1970	5.00	10.00	20.00

GAYE, MARVIN, AND KIM WESTON
Also see each artist's individual listings.
TAMLA

Number	Title	Yr	VG	VG+	NM
❏ T 270 [M]	Take Two	1966	7.50	15.00	30.00
❏ TS 270 [S]	Take Two	1966	10.00	20.00	40.00

GAYE, MARVIN, AND MARY WELLS
Also see each artist's individual listings.
MOTOWN

Number	Title	Yr	VG	VG+	NM
❏ M 613 [M]	Together	1964	12.50	25.00	50.00

GAYE, MARVIN, AND TAMMI TERRELL
Also see each artist's individual listings.
TAMLA

Number	Title	Yr	VG	VG+	NM
❏ T 277 [M]	United	1967	7.50	15.00	30.00
❏ TS 277 [S]	United	1967	6.25	12.50	25.00
❏ T 284 [M]	You're All I Need	1968	12.50	25.00	50.00
❏ TS 284 [S]	You're All I Need	1968	5.00	10.00	20.00
❏ TS 294	Easy	1969	5.00	10.00	20.00
❏ TS 302	Marvin Gaye & Tammi Terrell/Greatest Hits	1970	5.00	10.00	20.00

GAYLE, CRYSTAL
MOBILE FIDELITY

Number	Title	Yr	VG	VG+	NM
❏ 1-043	We Must Believe in Magic	1981	5.00	10.00	20.00
-- Audiophile vinyl					

NAUTILUS

Number	Title	Yr	VG	VG+	NM
❏ NR-36	When I Dream	198?	7.50	15.00	30.00
-- Audiophile vinyl					

GAYLORDS, THE
MERCURY

Number	Title	Yr	VG	VG+	NM
❏ MG-20186 [M]	Italia	1957	7.50	15.00	30.00
❏ MG-20213 [M]	Collection of Golden Hits	1957	7.50	15.00	30.00
❏ MG-20356 [M]	Let's Have a Pizza Party	1958	5.00	10.00	20.00
❏ MG-20430 [M]	That's Amore	1959	5.00	10.00	20.00
❏ MG-20620 [M]	American Hits in Italian	1961	5.00	10.00	20.00
❏ MG-20695 [M]	The Gaylords at the Shamrock	1962	5.00	10.00	20.00
❏ MG-20742 [M]	Party Style	1963	5.00	10.00	20.00
❏ MG-25198 [10]	By Request	1955	12.50	25.00	50.00
❏ SR-60075 [S]	Let's Have a Pizza Party	1959	7.50	15.00	30.00
❏ SR-60102 [S]	That's Amore	1959	7.50	15.00	30.00
❏ SR-60620 [S]	American Hits in Italian	1961	7.50	15.00	30.00
❏ SR-60695 [S]	The Gaylords at the Shamrock	1962	6.25	12.50	25.00
❏ SR-60742 [S]	Party Style	1963	6.25	12.50	25.00

TIME

Number	Title	Yr	VG	VG+	NM
❏ S-2109 [S]	Live at Lake Tahoe	196?	5.00	10.00	20.00
❏ S-2127 [S]	Bella Italia	196?	5.00	10.00	20.00

GAYNOR, MITZI
VERVE

Number	Title	Yr	VG	VG+	NM
❏ MGV-2110 [M]	Mitzi	1959	7.50	15.00	30.00
❏ MGV-2115 [M]	Mitzi Gaynor Sings the Lyrics of Ira Gershwin	1959	7.50	15.00	30.00
❏ MGVS-6014 [S]	Mitzi	1959	10.00	20.00	40.00
❏ MGVS-6049 [S]	Mitzi Gaynor Sings the Lyrics of Ira Gershwin	1959	10.00	20.00	40.00

GEARS, THE
PLAYGEMS

Number	Title	Yr	VG	VG+	NM
❏ GS 6471	Rockin' at Ground Zero	1980	7.50	15.00	30.00

GEEZINSLAW BROTHERS, THE
CAPITOL

Number	Title	Yr	VG	VG+	NM
❏ ST-130	The Geezinslaw Brothers Are Alive	1969	5.00	10.00	20.00
❏ ST 2570 [S]	Can You Believe... The Geezinslaw Brothers!	1966	6.25	12.50	25.00
❏ T 2570 [M]	Can You Believe... The Geezinslaw Brothers!	1966	5.00	10.00	20.00
❏ ST 2771 [S]	My Dirty, Lowdown, Rotten, Cotton-Pickin' Little Darlin'	1967	6.25	12.50	25.00
❏ T 2771 [M]	My Dirty, Lowdown, Rotten, Cotton-Pickin' Little Darlin'	1967	5.00	10.00	20.00
❏ ST 2885	The Geezinslaw Brothers & "Chubby"	1968	6.25	12.50	25.00

COLUMBIA

Number	Title	Yr	VG	VG+	NM
❏ CL 2100 [M]	The Kooky World of the Geezinslaw Brothers	1963	6.25	12.50	25.00
❏ CS 8900 [S]	The Kooky World of the Geezinslaw Brothers	1963	7.50	15.00	30.00

GEILS, J., BAND
ATLANTIC

Number	Title	Yr	VG	VG+	NM
❏ QD 7260 [Q]	Bloodshot	1973	5.00	10.00	20.00
❏ SD 7260	Bloodshot	1973	5.00	10.00	20.00
-- Red vinyl					
❏ QD 7286 [Q]	Ladies Invited	1973	5.00	10.00	20.00
❏ QD 18107 [Q]	Nightmares and Other Tales from the Vinyl Jungle	1974	5.00	10.00	20.00

NAUTILUS

Number	Title	Yr	VG	VG+	NM
❏ NR-25	Love Stinks	1982	5.00	10.00	20.00
-- Audiophile vinyl					

GENE AND DEBBE
TRX

Number	Title	Yr	VG	VG+	NM
❏ 1001	Here and Now	1968	6.25	12.50	25.00

GENE LOVES JEZEBEL
GEFFEN

Number	Title	Yr	VG	VG+	NM
❏ 141 [DJ]	Discover Interview	1986	6.25	12.50	25.00
❏ 4192 [EP]	Remix Sampler	1990	5.00	10.00	20.00
-- Promo-only collection					

GENESIS
Also see PETER GABRIEL.
ABC IMPULSE!

Number	Title	Yr	VG	VG+	NM
❏ ASD-9205	Trespass	1971	7.50	15.00	30.00

LONDON

Number	Title	Yr	VG	VG+	NM
❏ PS 643	From Genesis to Revelation	1974	5.00	10.00	20.00
-- First US release of debut album					

MOBILE FIDELITY

Number	Title	Yr	VG	VG+	NM
❏ 1-062	A Trick of the Tail	1981	12.50	25.00	50.00
-- Audiophile vinyl					

GENTLE SOUL
EPIC

Number	Title	Yr	VG	VG+	NM
❏ BN 26374	Gentle Soul	1969	25.00	50.00	100.00

GENTRY, BOBBIE
CAPITOL

Number	Title	Yr	VG	VG+	NM
❏ T 2830 [M]	Ode to Billie Joe	1967	5.00	10.00	20.00

GENTRYS, THE
MGM

Number	Title	Yr	VG	VG+	NM
❏ GAS-127	The Gentrys (Golden Archive Series)	1970	5.00	10.00	20.00
❏ E-4336 [M]	Keep On Dancing	1965	6.25	12.50	25.00
❏ E-4346 [M]	Gentry Time	1966	5.00	10.00	20.00
❏ SE-4336 [P]	Keep On Dancing	1965	7.50	15.00	30.00
❏ SE-4346 [S]	Gentry Time	1966	6.25	12.50	25.00

SUN

Number	Title	Yr	VG	VG+	NM
❏ LP-117	The Gentrys	1970	7.50	15.00	30.00

GEORDIE
MGM

Number	Title	Yr	VG	VG+	NM
❏ SE-4903	Hope You Like It	1973	7.50	15.00	30.00

GEORGE, BARBARA
A.F.O.

Number	Title	Yr	VG	VG+	NM
❏ 5001 [M]	I Know (You Don't Love Me No More)	1962	62.50	125.00	250.00

Number	Title	Yr	VG	VG+	NM

GERHARD, RAMONA
SOMA
| ❏ MG 1202 | Christmas in Hi-Fi with Ramona Gerhard | 195? | 5.00 | 10.00 | 20.00 |

-- Red vinyl

GERMS, THE
MOHAWK
| ❏ SCALP-001 | Recorded Live at the Whiskey, June, 1977 | 1981 | 12.50 | 25.00 | 50.00 |

-- First edition: Numbered edition, with sticker
| ❏ SCALP-001 | Recorded Live at the Whiskey, June, 1977 | 1981 | 5.00 | 10.00 | 20.00 |

-- Second edition: Un-numbered edition, with sticker

GERONIMO BLACK
UNI
| ❏ 73132 | Geronimo Black | 1972 | 6.25 | 12.50 | 25.00 |

GERRY AND THE PACEMAKERS
LAURIE
❏ LLP-2024 [M]	Don't Let the Sun Catch You Crying	1964	7.50	15.00	30.00
❏ SLP-2024 [R]	Don't Let the Sun Catch You Crying	1964	6.25	12.50	25.00
❏ LLP-2027 [M]	Gerry and the Pacemakers' Second Album	1964	7.50	15.00	30.00
❏ SLP-2027 [R]	Gerry and the Pacemakers' Second Album	1964	6.25	12.50	25.00
❏ LLP-2030 [M]	I'll Be There	1964	7.50	15.00	30.00
❏ SLP-2030 [R]	I'll Be There	1964	6.25	12.50	25.00
❏ LLP-2031 [M]	Greatest Hits	1965	6.25	12.50	25.00
❏ LLP-2037 [M]	Girl on a Swing	1966	6.25	12.50	25.00
❏ SLP-2037 [S]	Girl on a Swing	1966	5.00	10.00	20.00
❏ DT 90384 [R]	Greatest Hits	1965	6.25	12.50	25.00

-- Capitol Record Club edition
| ❏ T 90384 [M] | Greatest Hits | 1965 | 6.25 | 12.50 | 25.00 |

-- Capitol Record Club edition
| ❏ DT 90555 [R] | Don't Let the Sun Catch You Crying | 1964 | 7.50 | 15.00 | 30.00 |

-- Capitol Record Club edition
| ❏ T 90555 [M] | Don't Let the Sun Catch You Crying | 1964 | 10.00 | 20.00 | 40.00 |

-- Capitol Record Club edition
UNITED ARTISTS
| ❏ UAL 3387 [M] | Ferry Cross the Mersey | 1965 | 6.25 | 12.50 | 25.00 |

-- Also contains incidental music by George Martin
| ❏ UAS 6387 [S] | Ferry Cross the Mersey | 1965 | 10.00 | 20.00 | 40.00 |
| ❏ ST 90812 [S] | Ferry Cross the Mersey | 1965 | 12.50 | 25.00 | 50.00 |

-- Capitol Record Club edition
| ❏ T 90812 [M] | Ferry Cross the Mersey | 1965 | 10.00 | 20.00 | 40.00 |

-- Capitol Record Club edition

GETZ, STAN
Also see HOLIDAY, BILLIE, AND STAN GETZ; TJADER, CAL, AND STAN GETZ.
AMERICAN RECORDING SOCIETY
❏ G-407 [M]	Stan Getz	1956	10.00	20.00	40.00
❏ G-428 [M]	Intimate Portrait	1957	10.00	20.00	40.00
❏ G-443 [M]	Stan Getz	1957	10.00	20.00	40.00
BLUE RIBBON
| ❏ BR-8012 [M] | Rhythms | 1961 | 5.00 | 10.00 | 20.00 |
CLEF
| ❏ MGC-137 [10] | Stan Getz Plays | 1953 | 50.00 | 100.00 | 200.00 |
| ❏ MGC-143 [10] | The Artistry of Stan Getz | 1953 | 50.00 | 100.00 | 200.00 |
CROWN
| ❏ CLP-5002 [M] | Groovin' High | 1957 | 10.00 | 20.00 | 40.00 |

-- Reissue of Modern 1202
DALE
| ❏ 21 [10] | In Retrospect | 1951 | 75.00 | 150.00 | 300.00 |
JAZZTONE
| ❏ J-1230 [M] | Stan Getz' Most Famous | 1956 | 10.00 | 20.00 | 40.00 |
METRONOME
| ❏ BLP-6 [M] | The Sound | 1956 | 12.50 | 25.00 | 50.00 |
MODERN
| ❏ MLP-1202 [M] | Groovin' High | 1956 | 37.50 | 75.00 | 150.00 |
NEW JAZZ
| ❏ NJLP-8214 [M] | Long Island Sound | 1959 | 15.00 | 30.00 | 60.00 |

-- Reissue of Prestige 7002; purple label
| ❏ NJLP-8214 [M] | Long Island Sound | 1965 | 6.25 | 12.50 | 25.00 |

-- Blue label with trident logo on right
NORGRAN
❏ MGN-1000 [M]	Interpretations by the Stan Getz Quintet	1954	30.00	60.00	120.00
❏ MGN-1008 [M]	Interpretations by the Stan Getz Quintet #2	1954	30.00	60.00	120.00
❏ MGN-1029 [M]	Interpretations by the Stan Getz Quintet #3	1955	37.50	75.00	150.00
❏ MGN-1032 [M]	West Coast Jazz	1955	37.50	75.00	150.00
❏ MGN-1042 [M]	Stan Getz Plays	1955	25.00	50.00	100.00

-- Reissue of Clef 137 and 143 on one 12-inch LP
❏ MGN-1087 [M]	Stan Getz '56	1956	25.00	50.00	100.00
❏ MGN-1088 [M]	More West Coast Jazz with Stan Getz	1956	25.00	50.00	100.00
❏ MGN-2000-2 [(2)M]	Stan Getz at the Shrine	1955	50.00	100.00	200.00

-- Boxed set with booklet
PRESTIGE
❏ PRLP-102 [10]	Stan Getz and the Tenor Sax Stars	1951	50.00	100.00	200.00
❏ PRLP-104 [10]	Stan Getz, Volume 2	1951	50.00	100.00	200.00
❏ PRLP-108 [10]	Stan Getz-Lee Konitz	1951	50.00	100.00	200.00
❏ PRLP-7002 [M]	Stan Getz Quartets	1955	25.00	50.00	100.00
❏ PRLP-7255 [M]	Early Stan	1963	10.00	20.00	40.00
❏ PRST-7255 [R]	Early Stan	1963	5.00	10.00	20.00
❏ PRLP-7256 [M]	Stan Getz' Greatest Hits	1963	10.00	20.00	40.00
❏ PRST-7256 [R]	Stan Getz' Greatest Hits	1963	5.00	10.00	20.00
❏ PRLP-7337 [M]	Stan Getz' Greatest Hits	1967	6.25	12.50	25.00

-- Reissue of PRLP 7256
| ❏ PRLP-7434 [M] | Getz Plays Jazz Classics | 1967 | 6.25 | 12.50 | 25.00 |

-- Reissue of PRLP 7255
| ❏ PRLP-7516 [M] | Preservation | 1967 | 6.25 | 12.50 | 25.00 |
ROOST
❏ RK-103 [(2) M]	The Stan Getz Years	1964	10.00	20.00	40.00
❏ RKS-103 [(2) R]	The Stan Getz Years	1964	6.25	12.50	25.00
❏ R-402 [10]	Stan Getz	1950	50.00	100.00	200.00
❏ R-404 [10]	Stan Getz and the Swedish All Stars	1951	50.00	100.00	200.00
❏ R-407 [10]	Jazz at Storyville	1952	37.50	75.00	150.00
❏ R-411 [10]	Jazz at Storyville, Volume 2	1952	37.50	75.00	150.00
❏ R-417 [10]	Chamber Music	1953	37.50	75.00	150.00
❏ R-420 [10]	Jazz at Storyville, Volume 3	1954	37.50	75.00	150.00
❏ R-423 [10]	Split Kick	1954	37.50	75.00	150.00
❏ LP-2207 [M]	The Sounds of Stan Getz	1956	20.00	40.00	80.00

-- Reissue of R-402
| ❏ LP-2209 [M] | Storyville | 1956 | 20.00 | 40.00 | 80.00 |

-- Reissue of R-407 and half of R-411
| ❏ LP-2225 [M] | Storyville, Volume 2 | 1957 | 20.00 | 40.00 | 80.00 |

-- Reissue of R-423 and the other half of R-411
❏ LP-2249 [M]	The Greatest of Stan Getz	1963	7.50	15.00	30.00
❏ LP-2251 [M]	Moonlight in Vermont	1963	7.50	15.00	30.00
❏ LP-2255 [M]	Modern World	1963	7.50	15.00	30.00
❏ LP-2258 [M]	Getz Age	1963	7.50	15.00	30.00
SAVOY
| ❏ MG-9004 [10] | New Sounds in Modern Music | 1951 | 75.00 | 150.00 | 300.00 |
VERVE
| ❏ MGV-8028 [M] | West Coast Jazz | 1957 | 12.50 | 25.00 | 50.00 |

-- Reissue of Norgran 1032
| ❏ V-8028 [M] | West Coast Jazz | 1961 | 5.00 | 10.00 | 20.00 |

-- Reissue of MGV-8028
| ❏ MGV-8029 [M] | Stan Getz '57 | 1957 | 12.50 | 25.00 | 50.00 |

-- Reissue of Norgran 1087 with revised title
| ❏ V-8029 [M] | Stan Getz '57 | 1961 | 5.00 | 10.00 | 20.00 |

-- Reissue of MGV-8029
| ❏ MGV-8122 [M] | Interpretations by the Stan Getz Quintet #3 | 1957 | 12.50 | 25.00 | 50.00 |

-- Reissue of Norgran 1029
| ❏ V-8122 [M] | Interpretations by the Stan Getz Quintet #3 | 1961 | 5.00 | 10.00 | 20.00 |

-- Reissue of MGV-8122
| ❏ MGV-8133 [M] | Stan Getz Plays | 1957 | 12.50 | 25.00 | 50.00 |

-- Reissue of Norgran 1042
| ❏ V-8133 [M] | Stan Getz Plays | 1961 | 5.00 | 10.00 | 20.00 |

-- Reissue of MGV-8133
| ❏ MGV-8177 [M] | More West Coast Jazz with Stan Getz | 1957 | 12.50 | 25.00 | 50.00 |

-- Reissue of Norgran 1088
| ❏ V-8177 [M] | More West Coast Jazz with Stan Getz | 1961 | 5.00 | 10.00 | 20.00 |

-- Reissue of MGV-8177
| ❏ MGV-8188-2 [M] | Stan Getz at the Shrine | 1957 | 25.00 | 50.00 | 100.00 |

-- Reissue of Norgran 2000-2
| ❏ V-8188-2 [(2) M] | Stan Getz at the Shrine | 1961 | 6.25 | 12.50 | 25.00 |

-- Reissue of MGV-8188-2
| ❏ MGV-8200 [M] | Stan Getz and the Cool Sounds | 1957 | 12.50 | 25.00 | 50.00 |

-- Reissue of American Recording Society 407 with new name
| ❏ V-8200 [M] | Stan Getz and the Cool Sounds | 1961 | 5.00 | 10.00 | 20.00 |

-- Reissue of MGV-8200
| ❏ MGV-8213 [M] | Stan Getz in Stockholm | 1958 | 12.50 | 25.00 | 50.00 |

-- Reissue of American Recording Society 428 with new name
| ❏ V-8213 [M] | Stan Getz in Stockholm | 1961 | 5.00 | 10.00 | 20.00 |

-- Reissue of MGV-8213
| ❏ MGV-8263 [M] | Stan Meets Chet | 1958 | 15.00 | 30.00 | 60.00 |

-- With Chet Baker
| ❏ V-8263 [M] | Stan Meets Chet | 1961 | 5.00 | 10.00 | 20.00 |

-- Reissue of MGV-8263

Number	Title	Yr	VG	VG+	NM
❑ MGV-8294 [M] The Steamer		1959	12.50	25.00	50.00
❑ V-8294 [M] The Steamer		1961	5.00	10.00	20.00
-- Reissue of MGV-8294					
❑ MGV-8296 [M] Award Winner		1959	12.50	25.00	50.00
❑ V-8296 [M] Award Winner		1961	5.00	10.00	20.00
-- Reissue of MGV-8296					
❑ MGV-8321 [M] The Soft Swing		1959	12.50	25.00	50.00
❑ V-8321 [M] The Soft Swing		1961	5.00	10.00	20.00
-- Reissue of MGV-8321					
❑ MGV-8331 [M] Imported from Europe		1959	12.50	25.00	50.00
❑ V-8331 [M] Imported from Europe		1961	5.00	10.00	20.00
-- Reissue of MGV-8331					
❑ MGV-8379 [M] Cool Velvet -- Stan Getz and Strings		1960	12.50	25.00	50.00
❑ V-8379 [M] Cool Velvet -- Stan Getz and Strings		1961	5.00	10.00	20.00
-- Reissue of MGV-8379					
❑ V6-8379 [S] Cool Velvet -- Stan Getz and Strings		1961	5.00	10.00	20.00
❑ MGV-8393-2 [(2) M] Stan Getz At Large		1960	15.00	30.00	60.00
❑ V-8393-2 [(2) M] Stan Getz At Large		1961	6.25	12.50	25.00
-- Reissue of MGV-8393-2					
❑ V-8412 [M] Focus		1961	6.25	12.50	25.00
❑ V6-8412 [S] Focus		1961	5.00	10.00	20.00
❑ V-8494 [M] Big Band Bossa Nova		1962	5.00	10.00	20.00
❑ V6-8494 [S] Big Band Bossa Nova		1962	6.25	12.50	25.00
❑ V-8523 [M] Jazz Samba Encore!		1963	5.00	10.00	20.00
❑ V6-8523 [S] Jazz Samba Encore!		1963	6.25	12.50	25.00
❑ V6-8554 [S] Reflections		1964	5.00	10.00	20.00
❑ V6-8600 [S] Getz Au Go Go		1964	5.00	10.00	20.00
❑ V-8693 [M] Sweet Rain		1967	6.25	12.50	25.00
❑ V-8707 [M] Voices		1967	6.25	12.50	25.00
❑ V-8719 [M] The Best of Stan Getz		1967	6.25	12.50	25.00
❑ V-8752 [M] What the World Needs Now -- Stan Getz Plays Bacharach and David		1968	7.50	15.00	30.00
❑ V6-8802-2 [(2)] Dynasty		1971	5.00	10.00	20.00
❑ 823 611-1 [(5)] The Girl from Ipanema: The Bossa Nova Years		1984	12.50	25.00	50.00

GETZ, STAN, AND LAURINDO ALMEIDA
Also see each artist's individual listings.
VERVE

Number	Title	Yr	VG	VG+	NM
❑ V6-8665 [S]	Stan Getz with Guest Artist Laurindo Almeida	1965	5.00	10.00	20.00

GETZ, STAN, AND BOB BROOKMEYER
VERVE

Number	Title	Yr	VG	VG+	NM
❑ V-8418 [M]	Stan Getz and Bob Brookmeyer (Recorded Fall 1961)	1961	5.00	10.00	20.00
❑ V6-8418 [S]	Stan Getz and Bob Brookmeyer (Recorded Fall 1961)	1961	5.00	10.00	20.00

GETZ, STAN, AND CHARLIE BYRD
Also see each artist's individual listings.
DCC COMPACT CLASSICS

Number	Title	Yr	VG	VG+	NM
❑ LPZ-2011	Jazz Samba	1995	6.25	12.50	25.00
-- Audiophile vinyl					

VERVE

Number	Title	Yr	VG	VG+	NM
❑ V-8432 [M]	Jazz Samba	1962	5.00	10.00	20.00
❑ V6-8432 [S]	Jazz Samba	1962	6.25	12.50	25.00

GETZ, STAN, AND JOAO GILBERTO
MOBILE FIDELITY

Number	Title	Yr	VG	VG+	NM
❑ 1-208	Getz/Gilberto	1994	12.50	25.00	50.00
-- Audiophile vinyl					

VERVE

Number	Title	Yr	VG	VG+	NM
❑ V6-8545 [S]	Getz/Gilberto	1964	5.00	10.00	20.00
❑ V6-8623 [S]	Getz/Gilberto #2	1965	5.00	10.00	20.00

GETZ, STAN, AND J.J. JOHNSON
VERVE

Number	Title	Yr	VG	VG+	NM
❑ MGVS-6027 [S]	Stan Getz and J.J. Johnson at the Opera House	1960	10.00	20.00	40.00
❑ MGV-8265 [M]	Stan Getz and J.J. Johnson at the Opera House	1958	12.50	25.00	50.00
❑ V-8265 [M]	Stan Getz and J.J. Johnson at the Opera House	1961	5.00	10.00	20.00

GETZ, STAN, AND OSCAR PETERSON
VERVE

Number	Title	Yr	VG	VG+	NM
❑ MGV-8251 [M]	Stan Getz and the Oscar Peterson Trio	1958	12.50	25.00	50.00
❑ V-8251 [M]	Stan Getz and the Oscar Peterson Trio	1961	5.00	10.00	20.00
-- Reissue of MGV-8251					

Number	Title	Yr	VG	VG+	NM
❑ MGV-8348 [M]	Stan Getz with Gerry Mulligan and the Oscar Peterson Trio	1959	12.50	25.00	50.00
❑ V-8348 [M]	Stan Getz with Gerry Mulligan and the Oscar Peterson Trio	1961	5.00	10.00	20.00
-- Reissue of MGV-8348					

GHOULS, THE
CAPITOL

Number	Title	Yr	VG	VG+	NM
❑ ST 2215 [S]	Dracula's Deuce	1965	37.50	75.00	150.00
❑ T 2215 [M]	Dracula's Deuce	1965	30.00	60.00	120.00

GIANT CRAB, THE
UNI

Number	Title	Yr	VG	VG+	NM
❑ 73037	A Giant Crab Comes Forth	1968	6.25	12.50	25.00
❑ 73057	Cool It, Helios	1969	6.25	12.50	25.00

GIBB, ROBIN
Also see BEE GEES.
ATCO

Number	Title	Yr	VG	VG+	NM
❑ SD 33-323	Robin's Reign	1969	5.00	10.00	20.00

GIBBS, GEORGIA
BELL

Number	Title	Yr	VG	VG+	NM
❑ 6000S [S]	Call Me Georgia Gibbs	1966	5.00	10.00	20.00

CORAL

Number	Title	Yr	VG	VG+	NM
❑ CRL 56037 [10]	Ballin' the Jack	1951	12.50	25.00	50.00
❑ CRL 57183 [M]	Her Nibs	1957	10.00	20.00	40.00

EMARCY

Number	Title	Yr	VG	VG+	NM
❑ MG-36103 [M]	Swingin' with Gibbs	1957	7.50	15.00	30.00

EPIC

Number	Title	Yr	VG	VG+	NM
❑ BN 26059 [S]	Georgia Gibbs' Greatest Hits	1963	5.00	10.00	20.00

IMPERIAL

Number	Title	Yr	VG	VG+	NM
❑ LP-9107 [M]	Something's Gotta Give	1960	5.00	10.00	20.00
❑ LP-12064 [S]	Something's Gotta Give	1960	6.25	12.50	25.00

MERCURY

Number	Title	Yr	VG	VG+	NM
❑ MG-20071 [M]	Music and Memories	1955	10.00	20.00	40.00
❑ MG-20114 [M]	Song Favorites	1956	10.00	20.00	40.00
❑ MG-20170 [M]	Swingin' with Her Nibs	1956	10.00	20.00	40.00
❑ MG-25175 [10]	Georgia Gibbs Sings Oldies	1953	12.50	25.00	50.00
❑ MG-25199 [10]	The Man That Got Away	1954	12.50	25.00	50.00

GIBSON, ALTHEA
DOT

Number	Title	Yr	VG	VG+	NM
❑ DLP-3105 [M]	Althea Gibson Sings	1959	10.00	20.00	40.00
❑ DLP-25105 [S]	Althea Gibson Sings	1959	12.50	25.00	50.00

GIBSON, BOB
ELEKTRA

Number	Title	Yr	VG	VG+	NM
❑ EKL-177 [M]	Ski Songs	1959	6.25	12.50	25.00
❑ EKL-197 [M]	Yes I See	1961	5.00	10.00	20.00
❑ EKL-239 [M]	Where I'm Bound	1964	5.00	10.00	20.00
❑ EKS-7177 [S]	Ski Songs	1959	7.50	15.00	30.00
❑ EKS-7197 [S]	Yes I See	1961	6.25	12.50	25.00
❑ EKS-7239 [S]	Where I'm Bound	1964	6.25	12.50	25.00

RIVERSIDE

Number	Title	Yr	VG	VG+	NM
❑ RLP 12-802 [M]	Offbeat Folk Songs	1956	10.00	20.00	40.00
❑ RLP 12-806 [M]	I Come For to Sing	1957	10.00	20.00	40.00
❑ RLP 12-816 [M]	Carnegie Concert	1958	10.00	20.00	40.00
❑ RLP 12-830 [M]	There's a Meetin' Here Tonight	1958	10.00	20.00	40.00
❑ RLP-1111 [S]	There's a Meetin' Here Tonight	1959	12.50	25.00	50.00
❑ RM 7542 [M]	Hootenanny at Carnegie	1963	5.00	10.00	20.00
-- Reissue of 12-816 with slightly altered lineup					

STINSON

Number	Title	Yr	VG	VG+	NM
❑ SLP-76 [10]	Folksongs of Ohio	1954	12.50	25.00	50.00

GIBSON, BOB, AND BOB CAMP
ELEKTRA

Number	Title	Yr	VG	VG+	NM
❑ EKL-207 [M]	Gibson and Camp at the Gate of Horn	1961	5.00	10.00	20.00
❑ EKS-7207 [S]	Gibson and Camp at the Gate of Horn	1961	6.25	12.50	25.00

GIBSON, DON
LION

Number	Title	Yr	VG	VG+	NM
❑ L-70069 [M]	Songs by Don Gibson	1958	20.00	40.00	80.00

RCA VICTOR

Number	Title	Yr	VG	VG+	NM
❑ LPM-1743 [M]	Oh Lonesome Me	1958	12.50	25.00	50.00
❑ LPM-1918 [M]	No One Stands Alone	1959	7.50	15.00	30.00
❑ LSP-1918 [S]	No One Stands Alone	1959	10.00	20.00	40.00

Number	Title	Yr	VG	VG+	NM
❏ LPM-2038 [M]	That Gibson Boy	1959	7.50	15.00	30.00
❏ LSP-2038 [S]	That Gibson Boy	1959	10.00	20.00	40.00
❏ LPM-2184 [M]	Look Who's Blue	1960	7.50	15.00	30.00
❏ LSP-2184 [S]	Look Who's Blue	1960	10.00	20.00	40.00
❏ LPM-2269 [M]	Sweet Dreams	1960	7.50	15.00	30.00
❏ LSP-2269 [S]	Sweet Dreams	1960	10.00	20.00	40.00
❏ LPM-2361 [M]	Girls, Guitars and Gibson	1961	7.50	15.00	30.00
❏ LSP-2361 [S]	Girls, Guitars and Gibson	1961	10.00	20.00	40.00
❏ LPM-2448 [M]	Some Favorites of Mine	1962	7.50	15.00	30.00
❏ LSP-2448 [S]	Some Favorites of Mine	1962	10.00	20.00	40.00
❏ LPM-2702 [M]	I Wrote a Song	1963	7.50	15.00	30.00
❏ LSP-2702 [S]	I Wrote a Song	1963	10.00	20.00	40.00
❏ LPM-2878 [M]	God Walks These Hills	1964	5.00	10.00	20.00
❏ LSP-2878 [S]	God Walks These Hills	1964	6.25	12.50	25.00
❏ LPM-3376 [M]	The Best of Don Gibson	1965	5.00	10.00	20.00
❏ LSP-3376 [S]	The Best of Don Gibson	1965	6.25	12.50	25.00
❏ LPM-3470 [M]	Too Much Hurt	1965	5.00	10.00	20.00
❏ LSP-3470 [S]	Too Much Hurt	1965	6.25	12.50	25.00
❏ LPM-3594 [M]	Don Gibson with Spanish Guitars	1966	5.00	10.00	20.00
❏ LSP-3594 [S]	Don Gibson with Spanish Guitars	1966	6.25	12.50	25.00
❏ LPM-3680 [M]	Great Country Songs	1966	5.00	10.00	20.00
❏ LSP-3680 [S]	Great Country Songs	1966	6.25	12.50	25.00
❏ LPM-3843 [M]	All My Love	1967	5.00	10.00	20.00
❏ LSP-3843 [S]	All My Love	1967	6.25	12.50	25.00
❏ LPM-3974 [M]	The King of Country Soul	1968	12.50	25.00	50.00
❏ LSP-3974 [S]	The King of Country Soul	1968	5.00	10.00	20.00
❏ LSP-4053	More Country Soul	1968	5.00	10.00	20.00

GIBSON, STEVE, AND THE RED CAPS
MERCURY

Number	Title	Yr	VG	VG+	NM
❏ MG-25115 [10]	You're Driving Me Crazy (Harmony Time)	1952	100.00	200.00	400.00
❏ MG-25116 [10]	Blueberry Hill (Singing & Swinging)	1952	100.00	200.00	400.00

GIFFORD, KATHIE LEE
HEARTLAND

Number	Title	Yr	VG	VG+	NM
❏ HL-3046 [(2)]	Christmas with Kathie Lee Gifford	1993	5.00	10.00	20.00

GILBERT, ANN
GROOVE

Number	Title	Yr	VG	VG+	NM
❏ LG-1004 [M]	The Many Moods of Ann	1956	12.50	25.00	50.00

GILBERT, RONNIE
Also see THE WEAVERS.
MERCURY

Number	Title	Yr	VG	VG+	NM
❏ MG-20917 [M]	Alone with Ronnie Gilbert	1964	5.00	10.00	20.00
❏ SR-60917 [S]	Alone with Ronnie Gilbert	1964	6.25	12.50	25.00

GILELS, EMIL
RCA VICTOR RED SEAL

Number	Title	Yr	VG	VG+	NM
❏ LSC-2219 [S]	Brahms: Piano Concerto No. 2	1959	25.00	50.00	100.00
-- With Fritz Reiner/Chicago Symphony Orchestra; original with "shaded dog" label					
❏ LSC-2493 [S]	Schubert: Piano Sonata, op. 53	1961	10.00	20.00	40.00
-- Original with "shaded dog" label					

GILES, GILES & FRIPP
DERAM

Number	Title	Yr	VG	VG+	NM
❏ DES 18019	The Cheerful Insanity of Giles, Giles & Fripp	1968	15.00	30.00	60.00

GILKYSON, TERRY
COLUMBIA

Number	Title	Yr	VG	VG+	NM
❏ CL 990 [M]	Marianne and Other Songs	1957	12.50	25.00	50.00
❏ CL 1302 [M]	Wanderin' Folk Songs	1959	7.50	15.00	30.00

DECCA

Number	Title	Yr	VG	VG+	NM
❏ DL 5263 [10]	Folk Songs	1950	12.50	25.00	50.00
❏ DL 5457 [10]	Golden Minutes of Folk Music	1952	12.50	25.00	50.00

KAPP

Number	Title	Yr	VG	VG+	NM
❏ KS 3196 [S]	Rollin'	1960	5.00	10.00	20.00
❏ KS 3327 [S]	The Cry of the Wild Goose	1963	5.00	10.00	20.00

GILL, VINCE
MCA

Number	Title	Yr	VG	VG+	NM
❏ R 173599	Pocket Full of Gold	1991	5.00	10.00	20.00
-- Only released on vinyl through BMG Direct Marketing					

GILLESPIE, DANA
LONDON

Number	Title	Yr	VG	VG+	NM
❏ PS 540	Foolish Seasons	1968	5.00	10.00	20.00

GILLESPIE, DARLENE
DISNEYLAND

Number	Title	Yr	VG	VG+	NM
❏ WDL-1010 [M]	Top Tunes of the '50's -- Darlene Gillespie Sings TV Favorites	1959	10.00	20.00	40.00
-- Reissue of 3010					
❏ DQ-1228 [M]	Sleeping Beauty	1962	5.00	10.00	20.00
-- Cover is black and white; later pressings, which go for less, are shaded blue on the back					
❏ WDL-3010 [M]	Darlene of the Teens	1957	20.00	40.00	80.00
❏ WDL-3010 [M]	Top Tunes of the '50's -- Darlene Gillespie Sings TV Favorites	1958	12.50	25.00	50.00
-- Reissue with new title and cover					

MICKEY MOUSE CLUB

Number	Title	Yr	VG	VG+	NM
❏ MM-32 [M]	Sleeping Beauty	1959	10.00	20.00	40.00

GILLESPIE, DIZZY
ALLEGRO

Number	Title	Yr	VG	VG+	NM
❏ 3017 [M]	Dizzy Gillespie Plays	195?	30.00	60.00	120.00
❏ 3083 [M]	Dizzy Gillespie	195?	30.00	60.00	120.00
❏ 4023 [10]	Dizzy Gillespie	195?	50.00	100.00	200.00
❏ 4108 [10]	Dizzy Gillespie Plays	195?	50.00	100.00	200.00

AMERICAN RECORDING SOCIETY

Number	Title	Yr	VG	VG+	NM
❏ G-405 [M]	Jazz Creations/Dizzy Gillespie	1955	25.00	50.00	100.00
❏ G-423 [M]	Big Band Jazz	1955	25.00	50.00	100.00

ATLANTIC

Number	Title	Yr	VG	VG+	NM
❏ ALR-138 [10]	Dizzy Gillespie	1952	100.00	200.00	400.00
❏ ALR-142 [10]	Dizzy Gillespie, Vol. 2	1952	100.00	200.00	400.00
❏ 1257 [M]	Dizzy at Home and Abroad	1957	25.00	50.00	100.00
-- Black label					
❏ 1257 [M]	Dizzy at Home and Abroad	1961	7.50	15.00	30.00
-- Multi-color label with white "fan" logo					

BARONET

Number	Title	Yr	VG	VG+	NM
❏ 105 [M]	A Handful of Modern Jazz	1961	10.00	20.00	40.00

BLUE NOTE

Number	Title	Yr	VG	VG+	NM
❏ BLP-5017 [10]	Horn of Plenty	1953	75.00	150.00	300.00

CLEF

Number	Title	Yr	VG	VG+	NM
❏ MGC-136 [10]	Dizzy Gillespie with Strings	1953	50.00	100.00	200.00

CONTEMPORARY

Number	Title	Yr	VG	VG+	NM
❏ C-2504 [10]	Dizzy in Paris	1953	50.00	100.00	200.00

DEE GEE

Number	Title	Yr	VG	VG+	NM
❏ LP-1000 [10]	Dizzy Gillespie	1950	75.00	150.00	300.00

DIAL

Number	Title	Yr	VG	VG+	NM
❏ 212 [10]	Modern Trumpets	1952	100.00	200.00	400.00

DISCOVERY

Number	Title	Yr	VG	VG+	NM
❏ DL-3013 [10]	Dizzy Gillespie Plays, Johnny Richards Conducts	1950	75.00	150.00	300.00

GNP

Number	Title	Yr	VG	VG+	NM
❏ GNP-23 [M]	Dizzy Gillespie and His Big Band	1957	20.00	40.00	80.00
❏ GNP-4 [10]	Dizzy Gillespie with His Original Big Band	195?	50.00	100.00	200.00

IMPULSE!

Number	Title	Yr	VG	VG+	NM
❏ AS-9149	Swing Low, Sweet Cadillac!	1967	5.00	10.00	20.00

LIMELIGHT

Number	Title	Yr	VG	VG+	NM
❏ LM-82007 [M]	Jambo Caribe	1964	5.00	10.00	20.00
❏ LM-82022 [M]	The New Continent	1965	5.00	10.00	20.00
❏ LM-82042 [M]	The Melody Lingers On	1967	5.00	10.00	20.00
❏ LS-86007 [S]	Jambo Caribe	1964	6.25	12.50	25.00
❏ LS-86022 [S]	The New Continent	1965	6.25	12.50	25.00
❏ LS-86042 [S]	The Melody Lingers On	1967	6.25	12.50	25.00

NORGRAN

Number	Title	Yr	VG	VG+	NM
❏ MGN-1003 [M]	Afro Dizzy	1954	30.00	60.00	120.00
❏ MGN-1023 [M]	Dizzy and Strings	1955	30.00	60.00	120.00
❏ MGN-1083 [M]	Jazz Recital	1956	30.00	60.00	120.00
❏ MGN-1084 [M]	World Statesman	1956	30.00	60.00	120.00
❏ MGN-1090 [M]	Diz Big Band	1956	30.00	60.00	120.00

PHILIPS

Number	Title	Yr	VG	VG+	NM
❏ PHM 200-048 [M]	Dizzy at the French Riviera	1962	5.00	10.00	20.00
❏ PHM 200-070 [M]	New Wave!	1962	5.00	10.00	20.00
❏ PHM 200-091 [M]	Something Old, Something New	1963	5.00	10.00	20.00
❏ PHM 200-106 [M]	Dizzy Gillespie and the Double Six	1963	5.00	10.00	20.00
❏ PHM 200-123 [M]	Dizzy Gillespie Goes Hollywood	1964	5.00	10.00	20.00
❏ PHS 600-048 [S]	Dizzy at the French Riviera	1962	6.25	12.50	25.00
❏ PHS 600-070 [S]	New Wave!	1962	6.25	12.50	25.00
❏ PHS 600-091 [S]	Something Old, Something New	1963	6.25	12.50	25.00
❏ PHS 600-106 [S]	Dizzy Gillespie and the Double Six	1963	6.25	12.50	25.00
❏ PHS 600-123 [S]	Dizzy Gillespie Goes Hollywood	1964	6.25	12.50	25.00

RCA VICTOR

Number	Title	Yr	VG	VG+	NM
❏ LPV-530 [M]	Dizzy Gillespie	1966	6.25	12.50	25.00
❏ LJM-1009 [M]	Dizzier and Dizzier	1954	30.00	60.00	120.00
❏ LPM-2398 [M]	The Greatest of Dizzy Gillespie	1961	12.50	25.00	50.00
-- "Long Play" on label					

Number	Title	Yr	VG	VG+	NM
REGENT					
❑ MG-6043 [M]	School Days	1957	25.00	50.00	100.00
REPRISE					
❑ R-6072 [M]	Dateline: Europe	1963	5.00	10.00	20.00
❑ R9-6072 [S]	Dateline: Europe	1963	6.25	12.50	25.00
ROOST					
❑ LP-2214 [M]	Concert in Paris	1957	30.00	60.00	120.00
❑ R-414 [10]	Dizzy Over Paris	1953	62.50	125.00	250.00
SAVOY					
❑ MG-12020 [M]	Groovin' High	1955	15.00	30.00	60.00
❑ MG-12047 [M]	The Champ	1956	15.00	30.00	60.00
❑ MG-12110 [M]	The Dizzy Gillespie Story	1957	15.00	30.00	60.00
SOLID STATE					
❑ SS-18034	Live at the Village Vanguard	1968	5.00	10.00	20.00
❑ SS-18054	My Way	1969	5.00	10.00	20.00
❑ SS-18061	Cornucopia	1969	5.00	10.00	20.00
VERVE					
❑ MGVS-6023 [S]	Dizzy Gillespie at Newport	1960	15.00	30.00	60.00
❑ MGVS-6047 [S]	Have Trumpet, Will Excite	1960	15.00	30.00	60.00
❑ MGVS-6068 [S]	The Ebullient Mr. Gillespie	1960	15.00	30.00	60.00
❑ MGVS-6117 [S]	Greatest Trumpet of Them All	1960	15.00	30.00	60.00
❑ MGV-8017 [M]	Dizzy in Greece	1957	15.00	30.00	60.00
❑ V-8017 [M]	Dizzy in Greece	1961	6.25	12.50	25.00
❑ MGV-8173 [M]	Jazz Recital	1957	15.00	30.00	60.00
❑ V-8173 [M]	Jazz Recital	1961	6.25	12.50	25.00
❑ MGV-8174 [M]	World Statesman	1957	15.00	30.00	60.00
❑ V-8174 [M]	World Statesman	1961	6.25	12.50	25.00
❑ MGV-8178 [M]	Diz Big Band	1957	17.50	35.00	70.00
❑ V-8178 [M]	Diz Big Band	1961	6.25	12.50	25.00
❑ MGV-8191 [M]	Afro Dizzy	1957	15.00	30.00	60.00
❑ MGV-8208 [M]	Manteca	1958	15.00	30.00	60.00
❑ V-8208 [M]	Manteca	1961	6.25	12.50	25.00
❑ MGV-8214 [M]	Dizzy Gillespie and Stuff Smith	1958	15.00	30.00	60.00
❑ V-8214 [M]	Dizzy Gillespie and Stuff Smith	1961	6.25	12.50	25.00
❑ MGV-8242 [M]	Dizzy Gillespie at Newport	1958	15.00	30.00	60.00
❑ V-8242 [M]	Dizzy Gillespie at Newport	1961	6.25	12.50	25.00
❑ V6-8242 [S]	Dizzy Gillespie at Newport	1961	6.25	12.50	25.00
❑ MGV-8260 [M]	Duets	1958	15.00	30.00	60.00
-- With Sonny Rollins and Sonny Stitt					
❑ MGV-8313 [M]	Have Trumpet, Will Excite	1959	15.00	30.00	60.00
❑ V-8313 [M]	Have Trumpet, Will Excite	1961	6.25	12.50	25.00
❑ V6-8313 [S]	Have Trumpet, Will Excite	1961	6.25	12.50	25.00
❑ MGV-8328 [M]	The Ebullient Mr. Gillespie	1959	15.00	30.00	60.00
❑ V-8328 [M]	The Ebullient Mr. Gillespie	1961	6.25	12.50	25.00
❑ V6-8328 [S]	The Ebullient Mr. Gillespie	1961	6.25	12.50	25.00
❑ MGV-8352 [M]	Greatest Trumpet of Them All	1959	15.00	30.00	60.00
❑ V-8352 [M]	Greatest Trumpet of Them All	1961	6.25	12.50	25.00
❑ V6-8352 [S]	Greatest Trumpet of Them All	1961	6.25	12.50	25.00
❑ MGV-8386 [M]	Portrait of Duke Ellington	1960	15.00	30.00	60.00
❑ V-8386 [M]	Portrait of Duke Ellington	1961	6.25	12.50	25.00
❑ MGV-8394 [M]	Gillespiana	1960	15.00	30.00	60.00
❑ V-8394 [M]	Gillespiana	1961	6.25	12.50	25.00
❑ V6-8394 [S]	Gillespiana	1961	6.25	12.50	25.00
❑ V-8401 [M]	An Electrifying Evening with the Dizzy Gillespie Quintet	1961	5.00	10.00	20.00
❑ V6-8401 [S]	An Electrifying Evening with the Dizzy Gillespie Quintet	1961	6.25	12.50	25.00
❑ V-8411 [M]	Perceptions	1961	5.00	10.00	20.00
❑ V6-8411 [S]	Perceptions	1961	6.25	12.50	25.00
❑ V-8423 [M]	Carnegie Hall Concert	1962	5.00	10.00	20.00
❑ V6-8423 [S]	Carnegie Hall Concert	1962	6.25	12.50	25.00
❑ V-8477 [M]	Dizzy, Rollins & Stitt	1962	5.00	10.00	20.00
-- Reissue of MGV-8260					
❑ V6-8477 [S]	Dizzy, Rollins & Stitt	1962	6.25	12.50	25.00
❑ V-8560 [M]	Dizzy at Newport	1964	5.00	10.00	20.00
❑ V6-8560 [S]	Dizzy at Newport	1964	6.25	12.50	25.00
❑ V-8566 [M]	The Essential Dizzy Gillespie	1964	5.00	10.00	20.00
❑ V6-8566 [S]	The Essential Dizzy Gillespie	1964	6.25	12.50	25.00

GILLESPIE, DIZZY, AND STAN GETZ
Also see each artist's individual listings.

Number	Title	Yr	VG	VG+	NM
NORGRAN					
❑ MGN-2 [10]	The Dizzy Gillespie-Stan Getz Sextet #1	1954	75.00	150.00	300.00
❑ MGN-18 [10]	The Dizzy Gillespie-Stan Getz Sextet #2	1954	75.00	150.00	300.00
❑ MGN-1050 [M]	Diz and Getz	1956	30.00	60.00	120.00
VERVE					
❑ MGV-8141 [M]	Diz and Getz	1957	20.00	40.00	80.00
-- Reissue of Norgran 1050					
❑ V-8141 [M]	Diz and Getz	1961	6.25	12.50	25.00

GILLESPIE, DIZZY, AND CHARLIE PARKER
Also see each artist's individual listings.

Number	Title	Yr	VG	VG+	NM
ROOST					
❑ SK-106 [(2) M]	The Beginning: Diz and Bird	1960	25.00	50.00	100.00
❑ LP-2234 [M]	Diz 'n' Bird In Concert	1959	20.00	40.00	80.00

GILLESPIE, DIZZY, AND DJANGO REINHARDT

Number	Title	Yr	VG	VG+	NM
VERVE					
❑ MGV-8015 [M]	Jazz from Paris	1957	15.00	30.00	60.00
❑ V-8015 [M]	Jazz from Paris	1961	6.25	12.50	25.00

GILLEY, MICKEY

Number	Title	Yr	VG	VG+	NM
ASTRO					
❑ 101 [M]	Lonely Wine	1964	75.00	150.00	300.00
PAULA					
❑ LP-2195 [M]	Down the Line	1967	10.00	20.00	40.00
❑ LPS-2195 [S]	Down the Line	1967	10.00	20.00	40.00
PLAYBOY					
❑ PB-128	Room Full of Roses	1974	5.00	10.00	20.00
❑ PB-403	City Lights	1974	5.00	10.00	20.00

GILMER, JIMMY, AND THE FIREBALLS -- See THE FIREBALLS.

GILMER, JULIA ANN

Number	Title	Yr	VG	VG+	NM
ABC-PARAMOUNT					
❑ ABC-168 [M]	Cads, Blackguards and False True-Loves	1956	7.50	15.00	30.00

GIN BLOSSOMS

Number	Title	Yr	VG	VG+	NM
SAN JACINTO					
❑ DRAM 019	Dusted	1989	5.00	10.00	20.00
-- With picture insert and biographical material					

GINNY AND THE GALLIONS

Number	Title	Yr	VG	VG+	NM
DOWNEY					
❑ D-1003 [M]	Two Sides of Ginny and the Gallions	1964	7.50	15.00	30.00
❑ DS-1003 [S]	Two Sides of Ginny and the Gallions	1964	10.00	20.00	40.00

GINSBERG, ALLEN

Number	Title	Yr	VG	VG+	NM
ATLANTIC					
❑ 4001 [M]	Allen Ginsburg Reads Kaddish	1966	7.50	15.00	30.00
FANTASY					
❑ F-7006 [M]	Howl and Other Poems	1959	100.00	200.00	400.00
-- Red vinyl					
❑ F-7006 [M]	Howl and Other Poems	1959	50.00	100.00	200.00
-- Black non-flexible vinyl					

GITS, THE

Number	Title	Yr	VG	VG+	NM
C/Z					
❑ 051	Frenching the Bully	199?	6.25	12.50	25.00
-- Originals on red vinyl					

GLACIERS, THE

Number	Title	Yr	VG	VG+	NM
MERCURY					
❑ MG-20895 [M]	From Sea to Ski	1964	12.50	25.00	50.00
❑ SR-60895 [S]	From Sea to Ski	1964	15.00	30.00	60.00

GLAD
Timothy Schmit, later of POCO and EAGLES, was in this group.

Number	Title	Yr	VG	VG+	NM
ABC					
❑ S-655	Feelin' Glad	1969	6.25	12.50	25.00

GLASER, JIM

Number	Title	Yr	VG	VG+	NM
STARDAY					
❑ SLP-158 [M]	Just Looking for a Home	1961	10.00	20.00	40.00

GLASER, TOMPALL

Number	Title	Yr	VG	VG+	NM
DECCA					
❑ DL 4041 [M]	This Land Folk Songs	1960	7.50	15.00	30.00
❑ DL 74041 [S]	This Land Folk Songs	1960	10.00	20.00	40.00
MGM					
❑ E-4465 [M]	Tompall & the Glaser Brothers	1967	6.25	12.50	25.00
❑ SE-4465 [S]	Tompall & the Glaser Brothers	1967	5.00	10.00	20.00

GLASS HARP

Number	Title	Yr	VG	VG+	NM
DECCA					
❑ DL 75261	Glass Harp	1971	6.25	12.50	25.00
❑ DL 75306	Synergy	1971	6.25	12.50	25.00
❑ DL 75358	It Makes Me Glad	1972	6.25	12.50	25.00

GLAZER, TOM

Number	Title	Yr	VG	VG+	NM
UNITED ARTISTS					
❑ UAL 3540 [M]	The Ballad of Namu the Killer Whale And Other Ballads of Adventure	1966	6.25	12.50	25.00

Number	Title	Yr	VG	VG+	NM
❏ UAS 6540 [S]	The Ballad of Namu the Killer Whale And Other Ballads of Adventure	1966	10.00	20.00	40.00

WASHINGTON

Number	Title	Yr	VG	VG+	NM
❏ WC-301 [M]	The Tom Glazer Concert For and With Children	1959	6.25	12.50	25.00

GLEASON, JACKIE
CAPITOL

Number	Title	Yr	VG	VG+	NM
❏ H 352 [10]	Music for Lovers Only	1952	7.50	15.00	30.00
❏ W 352 [M]	Music for Lovers Only	1953	6.25	12.50	25.00
❏ H 366 [10]	Lover's Rhapsody	1953	7.50	15.00	30.00
❏ H 455 [10]	Music to Make You Misty	1954	7.50	15.00	30.00
❏ W 455 [M]	Music to Make You Misty	1954	6.25	12.50	25.00
❏ L 471 [10]	Tawny	1954	7.50	15.00	.30.00
❏ W 471 [M]	Tawny	1954	6.25	12.50	25.00
❏ WAO 475 [(2) M]	Music for Lovers Only/ Music to Make You Misty	1954	10.00	20.00	40.00
❏ W 509 [M]	Music, Martini and Memories	1954	6.25	12.50	25.00
❏ H 511 [10]	And Awaaay We Go!	1954	20.00	40.00	80.00
❏ W 511 [M]	And Awaaay We Go!	1955	10.00	20.00	40.00
❏ W 568 [M]	Romantic Jazz	1955	6.25	12.50	25.00
❏ W 570 [M]	Music to Remember Her	1955	6.25	12.50	25.00
❏ H 627 [10]	Lonesome Echo	1955	7.50	15.00	30.00
❏ W 627 [M]	Lonesome Echo	1955	6.25	12.50	25.00
❏ W 632 [M]	Music to Change Her Mind	1956	6.25	12.50	25.00
❏ W 717 [M]	Night Winds	1956	6.25	12.50	25.00
❏ W 758 [M]	Merry Christmas	1956	6.25	12.50	25.00
❏ W 816 [M]	Music for the Love Hours	1957	6.25	12.50	25.00
❏ W 859 [M]	Velvet Brass	1957	6.25	12.50	25.00
❏ SW 859 [S]	Velvet Brass	1959	6.25	12.50	25.00
-- We haven't confirmed if this is in true stereo or not.					
❏ W 905 [M]	Jackie Gleason Presents "Oooo!"	1957	6.25	12.50	25.00
❏ SW 905 [S]	Jackie Gleason Presents "Oooo!"	1959	6.25	12.50	25.00
-- We haven't confirmed if this is in true stereo or not.					
❏ W 961 [M]	The Torch with Blue Flame	1958	5.00	10.00	20.00
❏ SW 961 [S]	The Torch with Blue Flame	1959	6.25	12.50	25.00
❏ SW 1020 [S]	Riff Jazz	1959	6.25	12.50	25.00
❏ W 1020 [M]	Riff Jazz	1958	5.00	10.00	20.00
❏ SW 1075 [S]	Rebound	1959	6.25	12.50	25.00
❏ W 1075 [M]	Rebound	1959	5.00	10.00	20.00
❏ SW 1147 [S]	That Moment	1959	6.25	12.50	25.00
❏ W 1147 [M]	That Moment	1959	5.00	10.00	20.00
❏ SW 1250 [S]	Aphrodisia	1960	6.25	12.50	25.00
❏ W 1250 [M]	Aphrodisia	1960	5.00	10.00	20.00
❏ SW 1315 [S]	Opiate D'Amour	1960	5.00	10.00	20.00
❏ SW 1439 [S]	Lazy Lively Love	1961	6.25	12.50	25.00
❏ W 1439 [M]	Lazy Lively Love	1961	5.00	10.00	20.00
❏ SW 1519 [S]	The Gentle Touch	1961	6.25	12.50	25.00
❏ W 1519 [M]	The Gentle Touch	1961	5.00	10.00	20.00
❏ SWBO 1619 [(2)S]	A Lover's Portfolio	1962	6.25	12.50	25.00
❏ WBO 1619 [(2) M]	A Lover's Portfolio	1962	5.00	10.00	20.00
❏ SW 1689 [S]	Love, Embers and Flame	1962	5.00	10.00	20.00
❏ T 2791 [M]	'Tis the Season	1967	5.00	10.00	20.00
❏ STCL 2816 [(3) S]	The Jackie Gleason Deluxe Set	1968	6.25	12.50	25.00
-- Reissue of three complete LPs (titles unknown)					
❏ TCL 2816 [(3) M]	The Jackie Gleason Deluxe Set	1968	6.25	12.50	25.00

GLENN, DARRELL
NRC

Number	Title	Yr	VG	VG+	NM
❏ LPA-5 [M]	Crying in the Chapel	1959	6.25	12.50	25.00
❏ SLPA-5 [S]	Crying in the Chapel	1959	7.50	15.00	30.00

GLENN, LLOYD
ALADDIN

Number	Title	Yr	VG	VG+	NM
❏ LP-808 [M]	Chica-Boo	1956	250.00	500.00	1,000.
-- Black vinyl					
❏ LP-808 [M]	Chica-Boo	1956	1,000.	1,500.	2,000.
-- Red vinyl					

IMPERIAL

Number	Title	Yr	VG	VG+	NM
❏ LP-9174 [M]	Chica-Boo	1962	37.50	75.00	150.00
❏ LP-9175 [M]	After Hours	1962	37.50	75.00	150.00
❏ LP-12174 [S]	Chica-Boo	1962	50.00	100.00	200.00
❏ LP-12175 [S]	After Hours	1962	50.00	100.00	200.00

SCORE

Number	Title	Yr	VG	VG+	NM
❏ SLP-4006 [M]	Lloyd Glenn	1957	250.00	500.00	1,000.
❏ SLP-4020 [M]	After Hours	1958	250.00	500.00	1,000.

SWING TIME

Number	Title	Yr	VG	VG+	NM
❏ 1901 [10]	Lloyd Glenn	1954	1,500.	2,250.	3,000.

GLITTERHOUSE
DYNOVOICE

Number	Title	Yr	VG	VG+	NM
❏ 31905	Color Bland	1968	5.00	10.00	20.00

GLOBETROTTERS
KIRSHNER

Number	Title	Yr	VG	VG+	NM
❏ KES-108	Globetrotters	1971	5.00	10.00	20.00

GLORY
TEXAS REVOLUTION

Number	Title	Yr	VG	VG+	NM
❏ CFS-2531	A Meat Music Sampler	1969	25.00	50.00	100.00

GO-GO'S, THE
RCA VICTOR

Number	Title	Yr	VG	VG+	NM
❏ LPM-2930 [M]	Swim with the Go-Go's	1964	6.25	12.50	25.00
❏ LSP-2930 [S]	Swim with the Go-Go's	1964	7.50	15.00	30.00

GODCHAUX, KEITH AND DONNA -- See KEITH AND DONNA.

GODZ, THE
ESP-DISK'

Number	Title	Yr	VG	VG+	NM
❏ 1037 [M]	Contact High with the Godz	1967	15.00	30.00	60.00
❏ S-1037 [S]	Contact High with the Godz	1967	12.50	25.00	50.00
❏ 1047	Godz 2	1968	12.50	25.00	50.00
❏ 1077	Third Testament	1969	12.50	25.00	50.00
❏ 2017	Godzundheit	1970	12.50	25.00	50.00

GOLDBERG, BARRY
BUDDAH

Number	Title	Yr	VG	VG+	NM
❏ BDS-5012	The Barry Goldberg Reunion	1968	6.25	12.50	25.00
❏ BDS-5029	Two Jews Blues	1969	6.25	12.50	25.00

EPIC

Number	Title	Yr	VG	VG+	NM
❏ LN 24199 [M]	Blowing My Mind	1966	7.50	15.00	30.00
❏ BN 26199 [S]	Blowing My Mind	1966	10.00	20.00	40.00

GOLDEBRIARS, THE
EPIC

Number	Title	Yr	VG	VG+	NM
❏ BN 26087 [S]	The Goldebriars	1964	5.00	10.00	20.00
❏ BN 26114 [S]	Straight Ahead	1964	5.00	10.00	20.00

GOLDEN DAWN
INTERNATIONAL ARTISTS

Number	Title	Yr	VG	VG+	NM
❏ 4	Power Plant	1968	25.00	50.00	100.00

GOLDEN EARRING
ATLANTIC

Number	Title	Yr	VG	VG+	NM
❏ SD 8244	Eight Miles High	1970	6.25	12.50	25.00

CAPITOL

Number	Title	Yr	VG	VG+	NM
❏ ST-164	Miracle Mirror	1969	10.00	20.00	40.00
❏ ST 2823 [S]	Winter Harvest	1967	6.25	12.50	25.00
❏ T 2823 [M]	Winter Harvest	1967	12.50	25.00	50.00

DWARF

Number	Title	Yr	VG	VG+	NM
❏ 2000	Golden Earring	1971	6.25	12.50	25.00

TRACK

Number	Title	Yr	VG	VG+	NM
❏ 396	Moontan	1974	6.25	12.50	25.00
-- Original cover with nude dancer					

GOLDEN GATE QUARTET, THE
COLUMBIA

Number	Title	Yr	VG	VG+	NM
❏ CL 6102 [10]	Golden Gate Spirituals	1950	37.50	75.00	150.00

HARMONY

Number	Title	Yr	VG	VG+	NM
❏ HL 7018 [M]	The Golden Chariot	1957	20.00	40.00	80.00
-- Original pressing has maroon labels					
❏ HL 7018 [M]	The Golden Chariot	195?	6.25	12.50	25.00
-- Second pressing has black labels					

MERCURY

Number	Title	Yr	VG	VG+	NM
❏ MG-25063 [10]	Spirituals	1951	37.50	75.00	150.00

RCA CAMDEN

Number	Title	Yr	VG	VG+	NM
❏ CAL-308 [M]	The Golden Gate Quartet	1956	20.00	40.00	80.00

GOLDENROD
CHARTMAKER

Number	Title	Yr	VG	VG+	NM
❏ CSG-1101	Goldenrod	1968	50.00	100.00	200.00

GOLDSBORO, BOBBY
UNITED ARTISTS

Number	Title	Yr	VG	VG+	NM
❏ SP-58 [DJ]	The Bobby Goldsboro Family Album	1971	12.50	25.00	50.00
-- Promo-only compilation					
❏ UA-LA311-H2 [(2)]	Bobby Goldsboro's 10th Anniversary Album	1974	5.00	10.00	20.00
❏ UAL 3358 [M]	The Bobby Goldsbob Album	1964	5.00	10.00	20.00

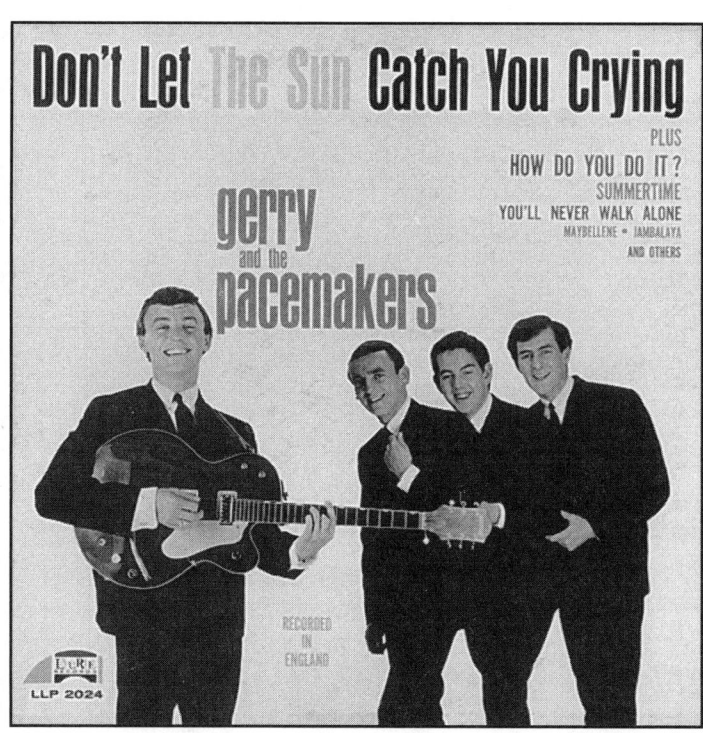

(Top left) Little is known about the circumstances of this Cecil Gant album. It came out in 1954 or so on a Chicago label called Red Mill on red vinyl. The cover is a textured red with gold print. Nonetheless, in near-mint condition it's at least a $500 piece. (Top right) Just as with the Dave Clark Five, the early albums by Gerry and the Pacemakers in America are more sought-after in mono than stereo because all the albums on Laurie were rechanneled. True stereo versions of most of their hits came out years later, once the rights to their material reverted to Capitol. (Bottom left) The first album by bluesman Lloyd Glenn was this extremely rare 1954 10-inch piece on the Swing Time label, which was soon gone. (Bottom right) Years before they had a thing called radar love, Golden Earring's records came out on several American labels without success. One of the toughest to find is this Atlantic album with their remake of the Byrds' "Eight Miles High" serving as the title track.

Number	Title	Yr	VG	VG+	NM
❏ UAL 3381 [M]	I Can't Stop Loving You	1964	5.00	10.00	20.00
❏ UAL 3425 [M]	Little Things	1965	5.00	10.00	20.00
❏ UAL 3471 [M]	Broomstick Cowboy	1966	5.00	10.00	20.00
❏ UAL 3486 [M]	It's Too Late	1966	5.00	10.00	20.00
❏ UAL 3552 [M]	Blue Autumn	1967	5.00	10.00	20.00
❏ UAL 3561 [M]	Sold Goldsboro/ Bobby Goldsboro's Greatest Hits	1967	5.00	10.00	20.00
❏ UAL 3599 [M]	Romantic, Soulful, Wacky	1967	5.00	10.00	20.00
❏ UAS 5502	Bobby Goldsboro's Greatest Hits	1970	5.00	10.00	20.00
❏ UAS 6358 [S]	I Can't Stop Loving You	1964	6.25	12.50	25.00
❏ UAS 6358 [S]	The Bobby Goldsbob Album	1964	6.25	12.50	25.00
❏ UAS 6425 [S]	Little Things	1965	6.25	12.50	25.00
❏ UAS 6471 [S]	Broomstick Cowboy	1966	6.25	12.50	25.00
❏ UAS 6486 [S]	It's Too Late	1966	6.25	12.50	25.00
❏ UAS 6552 [S]	Blue Autumn	1967	6.25	12.50	25.00
❏ UAS 6561 [S]	Sold Goldsboro/Bobby Goldsboro's Greatest Hits	1967	5.00	10.00	20.00
❏ UAS 6599 [S]	Romantic, Soulful, Wacky	1967	5.00	10.00	20.00
❏ UAS 6642	Honey	1968	5.00	10.00	20.00
❏ UAS 6657	Word Pictures Featuring Autumn of My Life	1968	5.00	10.00	20.00
❏ UAS 6704	Today	1969	5.00	10.00	20.00
❏ UAS 6735	Muddy Mississippi Line	1969	5.00	10.00	20.00
❏ UAS 6777	We Gotta Start Lovin'	1970	5.00	10.00	20.00

GOLDSBORO, BOBBY, AND DEL REEVES
UNITED ARTISTS

Number	Title	Yr	VG	VG+	NM
❏ UAL 3615 [M]	Our Way of Life	1967	5.00	10.00	20.00
❏ UAS 6615 [S]	Our Way of Life	1967	5.00	10.00	20.00

GOLDTONES, THE
LABREA

Number	Title	Yr	VG	VG+	NM
❏ L-8011 [M]	The Goldtones	1961	10.00	20.00	40.00
❏ LS-8011 [S]	The Goldtones	1961	12.50	25.00	50.00

GOLLIWOGS, THE
Also see CREEDENCE CLEARWATER REVIVAL.
FANTASY

Number	Title	Yr	VG	VG+	NM
❏ F-9474	Pre-Creedence	1975	7.50	15.00	30.00
-- Reissue of Fantasy and Scorpio sides					

GOMEZ, VICENTE
DECCA

Number	Title	Yr	VG	VG+	NM
❏ DL 8017 [M]	Spanish Guitar Recital	195?	7.50	15.00	30.00
-- Black label, silver print					
❏ DL 8439 [M]	Romantic Guitar	1957	6.25	12.50	25.00
-- Black label, silver print					
❏ DL 8918 [M]	Vicente Gomez	1959	5.00	10.00	20.00
-- Black label, silver print					
❏ DL 8965 [M]	The Artistry of Vicente Gomez	1959	5.00	10.00	20.00
-- Black label, silver print					
❏ DL 74088 [S]	Concerto Flamenco	1960	5.00	10.00	20.00
❏ DL 74156 [S]	Rio Flamenco	1961	5.00	10.00	20.00
❏ DL 74312 [S]	Guitar Extraordinary	1962	5.00	10.00	20.00
❏ DL 78918 [S]	Vicente Gomez	1959	6.25	12.50	25.00
-- Maroon or black label					
❏ DL 78965 [S]	The Artistry of Vicente Gomez	1959	6.25	12.50	25.00
-- Maroon or black label					

GOO GOO DOLLS
ENIGMA

Number	Title	Yr	VG	VG+	NM
❏ 7 73406-1	JED	1989	5.00	10.00	20.00

MERCENARY

Number	Title	Yr	VG	VG+	NM
❏ MER-2102	Goo Goo Dolls	1987	7.50	15.00	30.00

GOOD AND PLENTY
SENATE

Number	Title	Yr	VG	VG+	NM
❏ LP-21001 [M]	The World of Good and Plenty	1967	7.50	15.00	30.00
❏ LPS-21001 [S]	The World of Good and Plenty	1967	7.50	15.00	30.00

GOOD GUYS, THE
GNP CRESCENDO

Number	Title	Yr	VG	VG+	NM
❏ GNP-2001 [M]	Sidewalk Surfing	1964	7.50	15.00	30.00
❏ GNPS-2001 [S]	Sidewalk Surfing	1964	10.00	20.00	40.00

UNITED ARTISTS

Number	Title	Yr	VG	VG+	NM
❏ UAS-6370 [S]	The Good Guys Sing	1964	5.00	10.00	20.00

GOOD RATS, THE
KAPP

Number	Title	Yr	VG	VG+	NM
❏ KS-3580	The Good Rats	1969	10.00	20.00	40.00

PASSPORT

Number	Title	Yr	VG	VG+	NM
❏ SP-20 [DJ]	Rats the Way You Like It (Live)	1978	15.00	30.00	60.00

RAT CITY

Number	Title	Yr	VG	VG+	NM
❏ RCR-8001	Rat City in Blue	1975	5.00	10.00	20.00

WARNER BROS.

Number	Title	Yr	VG	VG+	NM
❏ BS 2813	Tasty	1974	7.50	15.00	30.00

GOOD TIMES, THE
KAMA SUTRA

Number	Title	Yr	VG	VG+	NM
❏ KSLP-8052 [S]	The Good Times	1966	5.00	10.00	20.00

GOODEES, THE
HIP

Number	Title	Yr	VG	VG+	NM
❏ HIS-7002	Candy Coated Goodees	1969	6.25	12.50	25.00

GOODMAN, BENNY
BRUNSWICK

Number	Title	Yr	VG	VG+	NM
❏ BL 54010 [M]	Benny Goodman 1927-34	1954	7.50	15.00	30.00
❏ BL 58015 [10]	Chicago Jazz Classics	1950	12.50	25.00	50.00

CAPITOL

Number	Title	Yr	VG	VG+	NM
❏ H 202 [10]	Session for Six	1950	12.50	25.00	50.00
❏ H 295 [10]	Easy Does It	1952	12.50	25.00	50.00
❏ H 343 [10]	The Benny Goodman Trio	1952	12.50	25.00	50.00
❏ T 395 [M]	Session for Six	1953	10.00	20.00	40.00
-- Turquoise label					
❏ T 395 [M]	Session for Six	1958	5.00	10.00	20.00
-- Black label with colorband, Capitol logo on left					
❏ H 409 [M]	The Benny Goodman Band	1953	12.50	25.00	50.00
❏ T 409 [M]	The Benny Goodman Band	1953	10.00	20.00	40.00
-- Turquoise label					
❏ T 409 [M]	The Benny Goodman Band	1958	5.00	10.00	20.00
-- Black label with colorband, Capitol logo on left					
❏ H 441 [10]	The Goodman Touch	1953	12.50	25.00	50.00
❏ T 441 [M]	The Goodman Touch	1953	10.00	20.00	40.00
-- Turquoise label					
❏ T 441 [M]	The Goodman Touch	1958	5.00	10.00	20.00
-- Black label with colorband, Capitol logo on left					
❏ H 479 [10]	Small Combo 1947	1954	12.50	25.00	50.00
❏ H1-565 [10]	B.G. in Hi-Fi (Volume 1)	1955	7.50	15.00	30.00
❏ H2-565 [10]	B.G. in Hi-Fi (Volume 2)	1955	7.50	15.00	30.00
❏ W 565 [M]	B.G. in Hi-Fi	1955	10.00	20.00	40.00
-- Turquoise label					
❏ W 565 [M]	B.G. in Hi-Fi	1958	5.00	10.00	20.00
-- Black label with colorband, Capitol logo on left					
❏ T 668 [M]	Mostly Sextets	1956	7.50	15.00	30.00
-- Turquoise label					
❏ T 668 [M]	Mostly Sextets	1958	5.00	10.00	20.00
-- Black label with colorband, Capitol logo on left					
❏ T 669 [M]	Benny Goodman Combos	1956	7.50	15.00	30.00
-- Turquoise label					
❏ T 669 [M]	Benny Goodman Combos	1958	5.00	10.00	20.00
-- Black label with colorband, Capitol logo on left					
❏ S 706 [M]	Selections Featured in "The Benny Goodman Story"	1956	7.50	15.00	30.00
-- Turquoise label					
❏ S 706 [M]	Selections Featured in "The Benny Goodman Story"	1958	5.00	10.00	20.00
-- Black label with colorband, Capitol logo on left					
❏ T 1514 [M]	The Hits of Benny Goodman	1961	5.00	10.00	20.00
-- Black label with colorband, Capitol logo on left					

CENTURY

Number	Title	Yr	VG	VG+	NM
❏ 1150	The King of Swing Direct to Disc	1979	7.50	15.00	30.00
-- Direct-to-disc audiophile recording					

CHESS

Number	Title	Yr	VG	VG+	NM
❏ LP-1440 [DJ]	Benny Rides Again	1960	25.00	50.00	100.00
-- Multi-color swirl vinyl					
❏ LP-1440 [M]	Benny Rides Again	1960	12.50	25.00	50.00
❏ LPS-1440 [S]	Benny Rides Again	1960	7.50	15.00	30.00

CLASSICS RECORD LIBRARY

Number	Title	Yr	VG	VG+	NM
❏ RL-7673 [(3) M]	An Album of Swing Classics	1967	12.50	25.00	50.00
❏ RLS-7673 [(3) S]	An Album of Swing Classics	1967	10.00	20.00	40.00
-- Above two were compiled for Book-of-the-Month Club					

COLUMBIA

Number	Title	Yr	VG	VG+	NM
❏ GL 102 [10]	Let's Hear the Melody	1950	15.00	30.00	60.00
❏ CL 500 [M]	The Golden Era: Combos	1954	10.00	20.00	40.00
-- Red label with gold print					
❏ CL 500 [M]	The Golden Era: Combos	1955	7.50	15.00	30.00
-- Red and black label with six "eye" logos					
❏ CL 501 [M]	The Golden Era: Bands	1954	10.00	20.00	40.00
-- Red label with gold print					
❏ CL 501 [M]	The Golden Era: Bands	1955	7.50	15.00	30.00
-- Red and black label with six "eye" logos					
❏ CL 516 [M]	The Benny Goodman Trio Plays for the Fletcher Henderson Fund	1954	10.00	20.00	40.00
-- Reissue of Martin Block 1000; red label with gold print					
❏ CL 516 [M]	The Benny Goodman Trio Plays for the Fletcher Henderson Fund	1955	7.50	15.00	30.00
-- Red and black label with six "eye" logos					
❏ CL 523 [M]	Benny Goodman Presents Eddie Sauter Arrangements	1954	10.00	20.00	40.00
-- Red label with gold print					

Number	Title	Yr	VG	VG+	NM
❑ CL 523 [M]	Benny Goodman Presents Eddie Sauter Arrangements	1955	7.50	15.00	30.00
-- Red and black label with six "eye" logos					
❑ CL 524 [M]	Benny Goodman Presents Fletcher Henderson Arrangements	1954	10.00	20.00	40.00
-- Red label with gold print					
❑ CL 524 [M]	Benny Goodman Presents Fletcher Henderson Arrangements	1955	7.50	15.00	30.00
-- Red and black label with six "eye" logos					
❑ CL 534 [M]	Benny Goodman and His	1954	10.00	20.00	40.00
-- Red label with gold print					
❑ CL 534 [M]	Benny Goodman and His	1955	7.50	15.00	30.00
-- Red and black label with six "eye" logos					
❑ CL 552 [M]	The New Benny Goodman Sextet	1954	10.00	20.00	40.00
-- Red label with gold print					
❑ CL 552 [M]	The New Benny Goodman Sextet	1955	7.50	15.00	30.00
-- Red and black label with six "eye" logos					
❑ CL 652 [M]	The Benny Goodman Sextet and Orchestra with Charlie Christian	1955	7.50	15.00	30.00
-- Red and black label with six "eye" logos					
❑ CL 652 [M]	The Benny Goodman Sextet and Orchestra with Charlie Christian	1963	5.00	10.00	20.00
-- Red label with "Guaranteed High Fidelity" or "Mono" at bottom					
❑ CL 814 [M]	Carnegie Hall Jazz Concert, Volume 1	1956	7.50	15.00	30.00
-- Red and black label with six "eye" logos					
❑ CL 814 [M]	Carnegie Hall Jazz Concert, Volume 1	1963	5.00	10.00	20.00
-- Red label with "Guaranteed High Fidelity" or "Mono" at bottom					
❑ CL 815 [M]	Carnegie Hall Jazz Concert, Volume 2	1956	7.50	15.00	30.00
-- Red and black label with six "eye" logos					
❑ CL 815 [M]	Carnegie Hall Jazz Concert, Volume 2	1963	5.00	10.00	20.00
-- Red label with "Guaranteed High Fidelity" or "Mono" at bottom					
❑ CL 816 [M]	Carnegie Hall Jazz Concert, Volume 3	1956	7.50	15.00	30.00
-- Red and black label with six "eye" logos					
❑ CL 816 [M]	Carnegie Hall Jazz Concert, Volume 3	1963	5.00	10.00	20.00
-- Red label with "Guaranteed High Fidelity" or "Mono" at bottom					
❑ CL 817 [M]	The King of Swing, Volume 1	1956	7.50	15.00	30.00
❑ CL 818 [M]	The King of Swing, Volume 2	1956	7.50	15.00	30.00
❑ CL 819 [M]	The King of Swing, Volume 3	1956	7.50	15.00	30.00
❑ CL 820 [M]	The Great Benny Goodman	1956	7.50	15.00	30.00
-- Red and black label with six "eye" logos					
❑ CL 820 [M]	The Great Benny Goodman	1963	5.00	10.00	20.00
-- Red label with "Guaranteed High Fidelity" or "Mono" at bottom					
❑ CL 821 [M]	The Vintage Benny Goodman	1956	7.50	15.00	30.00
❑ CL 1247 [M]	Benny Goodman in Brussels, Volume 1	1958	7.50	15.00	30.00
❑ CL 1248 [M]	Benny Goodman in Brussels, Volume 2	1958	7.50	15.00	30.00
❑ CL 1324 [M]	The Happy Session	1959	7.50	15.00	30.00
❑ CL 1579 [M]	Benny Goodman Swings Again	1960	7.50	15.00	30.00
❑ CL 2533 [10]	Benny at the Ballroom	1955	10.00	20.00	40.00
-- Retitled reissue of 6100					
❑ CL 2564 [10]	The Benny Goodman Six	1955	10.00	20.00	40.00
-- Retitled reissue of 6052					
❑ CL 6033 [10]	Benny Goodman and Peggy Lee	1949	20.00	40.00	80.00
❑ CL 6048 [10]	Dance Parade	1949	12.50	25.00	50.00
❑ CL 6052 [10]	Goodman Sextet Session	1949	12.50	25.00	50.00
❑ CL 6100 [10]	Dance Parade, Volume 2	1950	12.50	25.00	50.00
❑ CL 6302 [10]	Let's Hear the Melody	1951	12.50	25.00	50.00
-- Reissue of GL 102					
❑ CS 8075 [S]	Benny Goodman in Brussels, Volume ?	1959	10.00	20.00	40.00
❑ CS 8129 [S]	The Happy Session	1959	6.25	12.50	25.00
❑ CS 8379 [S]	Benny Goodman Swings Again	1960	6.25	12.50	25.00
❑ XTV 28995/6 [M]	Swing Into Spring	1959	5.00	10.00	20.00
-- Special item made for Texaco service stations					

COLUMBIA MASTERWORKS

Number	Title	Yr	VG	VG+	NM
❑ OSL 160 [(2) M]	Carnegie Hall Jazz Concert	1956	18.75	37.50	75.00
-- Gray and black labels with six "eye" logos					
❑ OSL 160 [(2) M]	Carnegie Hall Jazz Concert	1963	10.00	20.00	40.00
-- Gray labels with "Columbia" at top					
❑ SL 160 [(2) M]	Carnegie Hall Jazz Concert	1950	25.00	50.00	100.00
-- Green labels					
❑ SL 176 [(6) M]	King of Swing	1950	37.50	75.00	150.00
❑ OSL 180 [(2) M]	The King of Swing	1956	18.75	37.50	75.00
-- Gray and black labels with six "eye" logos					
❑ OSL 180 [(2) M]	The King of Swing	1963	10.00	20.00	40.00
-- Gray labels with "Columbia" at top					
❑ SL 180 [(2) M]	1937-38 Jazz Concert No. 2	1950	18.75	37.50	75.00
❑ ML 4358 [M]	Carnegie Hall Jazz Concert, Volume 1	1950	10.00	20.00	40.00
❑ ML 4359 [M]	Carnegie Hall Jazz Concert, Volume 2	1950	10.00	20.00	40.00
❑ ML 4590 [M]	1937-38 Jazz Concert No. 2, Volume 1	1950	10.00	20.00	40.00
❑ ML 4591 [M]	1937-38 Jazz Concert No. 2, Volume 2	1950	10.00	20.00	40.00
❑ ML 4613 [M]	King of Swing, Volume 1	1950	10.00	20.00	40.00
❑ ML 4614 [M]	King of Swing, Volume 2	1950	10.00	20.00	40.00
❑ MS 6805 [S]	Meeting at the Summit	1961	5.00	10.00	20.00
-- With the Columbia Jazz Combo and the Columbia Orchestra					

DECCA

Number	Title	Yr	VG	VG+	NM
❑ DXB 188 [(2) M]	The Benny Goodman Story	1956	15.00	30.00	60.00
-- Black label, silver print					
❑ DXB 188 [(2) M]	The Benny Goodman Story	1961	10.00	20.00	40.00
-- Black label with color bars					
❑ DL 8252 [M]	The Benny Goodman Story, Volume 1	1956	7.50	15.00	30.00
-- Black label, silver print					
❑ DL 8252 [M]	The Benny Goodman Story, Volume 1	1961	5.00	10.00	20.00
-- Black label with color bars					
❑ DL 8253 [M]	The Benny Goodman Story, Volume 2	1956	7.50	15.00	30.00
-- Black label, silver print					
❑ DL 8253 [M]	The Benny Goodman Story, Volume 2	1961	5.00	10.00	20.00
-- Black label with color bars					

HARMONY

Number	Title	Yr	VG	VG+	NM
❑ HL 7005 [M]	Peggy Lee Sings with Benny Goodman	1957	5.00	10.00	20.00

MARTIN BLOCK

Number	Title	Yr	VG	VG+	NM
❑ MB-1000 [M]	The Benny Goodman Trio Plays for the Fletcher Henderson Fund	1951	12.50	25.00	50.00

MGM

Number	Title	Yr	VG	VG+	NM
❑ 3E-9 [(3) M]	The Benny Goodman Treasure Chest	1959	37.50	75.00	150.00
❑ E-3788 [M]	Performance Recordings, Volume 1	1959	6.25	12.50	25.00
❑ E-3789 [M]	Performance Recordings, Volume 2	1959	6.25	12.50	25.00
❑ E-3790 [M]	Performance Recordings, Volume 3	1959	6.25	12.50	25.00
❑ E-3810 [M]	The Sound of Music	1960	5.00	10.00	20.00
❑ SE-3810 [S]	The Sound of Music	1960	6.25	12.50	25.00

RCA VICTOR

Number	Title	Yr	VG	VG+	NM
❑ WPT 12 [10]	Benny Goodman	1951	12.50	25.00	50.00
❑ WPT 26 [10]	Immortal Performances	1952	12.50	25.00	50.00
❑ LPT-1005 [M]	Benny Goodman	1954	10.00	20.00	40.00
❑ LPM-1099 [M]	The Golden Age of Benny Goodman	1955	10.00	20.00	40.00
❑ LPM-1226 [M]	The Benny Goodman Trio/Quartet/Quintet	1956	10.00	20.00	40.00
❑ LPM-1239 [M]	This Is Benny Goodman	1956	10.00	20.00	40.00
❑ LPM-2247 [M]	The Kingdom of Swing	1960	5.00	10.00	20.00
❑ LSP-2247 [S]	The Kingdom of Swing	1960	6.25	12.50	25.00
❑ LSP-2968 [S]	Together Again	1964	5.00	10.00	20.00
❑ LPT-3004 [10]	Benny Goodman Quartet	1952	12.50	25.00	50.00
❑ LPT-3056 [10]	Benny Goodman 1937-39	1954	12.50	25.00	50.00
❑ LOC-6008 [(2) M]	Benny Goodman in Moscow	1962	5.00	10.00	20.00
❑ LSO-6008 [(2) S]	Benny Goodman in Moscow	1962	6.25	12.50	25.00
❑ LPT-6703 [(5) M]	The Golden Age of Swing	1956	150.00	300.00	600.00
-- Five-record set in white vinyl binder with bound-in booklet					

SUNBEAM

Number	Title	Yr	VG	VG+	NM
❑ 116/27 [(12)]	Manhattan Room 1937	197?	15.00	30.00	60.00
❑ 128/32 [(5)]	From the Congress Hotel, Chicago, 1935-36	197?	6.25	12.50	25.00

WESTINGHOUSE

Number	Title	Yr	VG	VG+	NM
❑ (no #) [(5) M]	Benny in Brussels	1958	25.00	50.00	100.00
❑ (no #) [M]	Benny Goodman Plays World Favorites in High Fidelity	1958	7.50	15.00	30.00

GOODMAN, DICKIE

CASH

Number	Title	Yr	VG	VG+	NM
❑ CR 6000	Mr. Jaws and Other Fables	1975	6.25	12.50	25.00

COMET

Number	Title	Yr	VG	VG+	NM
❑ 69	My Son, the Joke	1963	10.00	20.00	40.00

IX CHAINS

Number	Title	Yr	VG	VG+	NM
❑ NCS 9000	The Original Flying Saucers	1973	10.00	20.00	40.00

RORI

Number	Title	Yr	VG	VG+	NM
❑ 3301	The Many Heads of Dickie Goodman	1962	20.00	40.00	80.00

GOODMAN, DODY

CORAL

Number	Title	Yr	VG	VG+	NM
❑ CRL 57196 [M]	Dody Goodman Sings?	1958	7.50	15.00	30.00

GORDON 'N ROGERS' INTER-URBAN ELECTRIC A&E PIT CREW & RHYTHM BAND

CAPITOL

Number	Title	Yr	VG	VG+	NM
❑ STAO-276	Bug In!	1969	5.00	10.00	20.00

Number	Title	Yr	VG	VG+	NM

GORDON, JUSTIN
DOT
- ❏ DLP-3214 [M]   Justin Gordon Swings | 1959 | 10.00 | 20.00 | 40.00 |

GORDON, KELLY
CAPITOL
- ❏ ST-201   Defunked | 1969 | 5.00 | 10.00 | 20.00 |

GORDON, ROBERT
RCA VICTOR
- ❏ AFL1-3294   Rock Billy Boogie | 1979 | 5.00 | 10.00 | 20.00 |
-- Original pressing on white vinyl
- ❏ DJL1-3411 [DJ]   Essential Robert Gordon | 1979 | 7.50 | 15.00 | 30.00 |
-- Promo-only live album with tracks from Tuff Darts

GORE, CHARLIE
AUDIO LAB
- ❏ AL-1526 [M]   The Country Gentleman | 1959 | 50.00 | 100.00 | 200.00 |

GORE, LESLEY
MERCURY
- ❏ MG 20805 [M]   I'll Cry If I Want To | 1963 | 7.50 | 15.00 | 30.00 |
-- With no blurb for "It's My Party"
- ❏ MG 20805 [M]   I'll Cry If I Want To | 1964 | 5.00 | 10.00 | 20.00 |
-- With blurb for "It's My Party"
- ❏ MG 20849 [M]   Lesley Gore Sings of Mixed-Up Hearts | 1963 | 7.50 | 15.00 | 30.00 |
- ❏ MG 20901 [M]   Boys, Boys, Boys | 1964 | 7.50 | 15.00 | 30.00 |
- ❏ MG 20943 [M]   Girl Talk | 1964 | 7.50 | 15.00 | 30.00 |
- ❏ MG 21024 [M]   The Golden Hits of Lesley Gore | 1965 | 7.50 | 15.00 | 30.00 |
- ❏ MG 21042 [M]   My Town, My Guy & Me | 1965 | 7.50 | 15.00 | 30.00 |
- ❏ MG 21066 [M]   All About Love | 1966 | 7.50 | 15.00 | 30.00 |
- ❏ MG 21120 [M]   California Nights | 1967 | 7.50 | 15.00 | 30.00 |
- ❏ SR 60805 [S]   I'll Cry If I Want To | 1963 | 10.00 | 20.00 | 40.00 |
-- With no blurb for "It's My Party"
- ❏ SR 60805 [S]   I'll Cry If I Want To | 1964 | 7.50 | 15.00 | 30.00 |
-- With blurb for "It's My Party"
- ❏ SR 60849 [S]   Lesley Gore Sings of Mixed-Up Hearts | 1963 | 10.00 | 20.00 | 40.00 |
- ❏ SR 60901 [S]   Boys, Boys, Boys | 1964 | 10.00 | 20.00 | 40.00 |
- ❏ SR 60943 [S]   Girl Talk | 1964 | 10.00 | 20.00 | 40.00 |
- ❏ SR 61024 [S]   The Golden Hits of Lesley Gore | 1965 | 10.00 | 20.00 | 40.00 |
-- Originals have 12 tracks
- ❏ SR 61042 [S]   My Town, My Guy & Me | 1965 | 10.00 | 20.00 | 40.00 |
- ❏ SR 61066 [S]   All About Love | 1966 | 10.00 | 20.00 | 40.00 |
-- Stereo version has a different cover and liner notes than the mono version
- ❏ SR 61120 [S]   California Nights | 1967 | 10.00 | 20.00 | 40.00 |
- ❏ SR 61185   The Golden Hits of Lesley Gore, Vol. 2 | 1968 | 10.00 | 20.00 | 40.00 |
WING
- ❏ PRW-2-119 [(2)]The Sound of Young Love | 1969 | 5.00 | 10.00 | 20.00 |

GORME, EYDIE
Also see STEVE LAWRENCE AND EYDIE GORME.
ABC-PARAMOUNT
- ❏ 150 [M]   Eydie Gorme | 1957 | 7.50 | 15.00 | 30.00 |
- ❏ 192 [M]   Eydie Swings the Blues | 1957 | 7.50 | 15.00 | 30.00 |
- ❏ 218 [M]   Eydie Gorme Vamps the Roaring 20's | 1958 | 7.50 | 15.00 | 30.00 |
- ❏ 246 [M]   Eydie in Love | 1958 | 7.50 | 15.00 | 30.00 |
- ❏ 254 [M]   Show Stoppers | 1959 | 6.25 | 12.50 | 25.00 |
- ❏ S-254 [S]   Show Stoppers | 1959 | 7.50 | 15.00 | 30.00 |
- ❏ 273 [M]   Love Is a Season | 1959 | 6.25 | 12.50 | 25.00 |
- ❏ S-273 [S]   Love Is a Season | 1959 | 7.50 | 15.00 | 30.00 |
- ❏ 307 [M]   On Stage | 1959 | 6.25 | 12.50 | 25.00 |
- ❏ S-307 [S]   On Stage | 1959 | 7.50 | 15.00 | 30.00 |
- ❏ 343 [M]   Eydie in Dixieland | 1960 | 6.25 | 12.50 | 25.00 |
- ❏ S-343 [S]   Eydie in Dixieland | 1960 | 7.50 | 15.00 | 30.00 |
- ❏ S-512 [S]   The Best of Romance, Ballads, Blues, Dixieland, Roaring 20's, Showstoppers | 1965 | 5.00 | 10.00 | 20.00 |
COLUMBIA
- ❏ CL 2764 [M]   Eydie Gorme's Greatest Hits | 1967 | 5.00 | 10.00 | 20.00 |
- ❏ CS 8812 [S]   Blame It on the Bossa Nova | 1963 | 5.00 | 10.00 | 20.00 |
- ❏ CS 8865 [S]   Let the Good Times Roll | 1963 | 5.00 | 10.00 | 20.00 |
- ❏ CS 8920 [S]   Gorme Country Style | 1964 | 5.00 | 10.00 | 20.00 |
- ❏ CS 9003 [S]   Amor | 1964 | 5.00 | 10.00 | 20.00 |
- ❏ CS 9100 [S]   The Sound of Music (And Other Broadway Hits) | 1965 | 5.00 | 10.00 | 20.00 |
- ❏ CS 9176 [S]   More Amor | 1965 | 5.00 | 10.00 | 20.00 |
- ❏ CS 9276 [S]   Don't Go to Strangers | 1966 | 5.00 | 10.00 | 20.00 |
- ❏ CS 9394 [S]   Softly, As I Leave You | 1967 | 5.00 | 10.00 | 20.00 |
CORAL
- ❏ CRL 57109 [M]Delight | 1957 | 10.00 | 20.00 | 40.00 |

UNITED ARTISTS
- ❏ UAL 3143 [M]   Come Sing with Me | 1961 | 5.00 | 10.00 | 20.00 |
- ❏ UAL 3152 [M]   I Feel So Spanish | 1961 | 5.00 | 10.00 | 20.00 |
- ❏ UAL 3189 [M]   The Very Best of Eydie | 1962 | 5.00 | 10.00 | 20.00 |
- ❏ UAS 6143 [S]   Come Sing with Me | 1961 | 6.25 | 12.50 | 25.00 |
- ❏ UAS 6152 [S]   I Feel So Spanish | 1961 | 6.25 | 12.50 | 25.00 |
- ❏ UAS 6189 [S]   The Very Best of Eydie | 1962 | 6.25 | 12.50 | 25.00 |

GOSDIN BROTHERS, THE
CAPITOL
- ❏ ST 2852   Sounds of Goodbye | 1968 | 5.00 | 10.00 | 20.00 |

GOSPEL STARS, THE
TAMLA
- ❏ TM-222 [M]   The Great Gospel Stars | 1961 | 1,000. | 2,000. | 3,000. |

GOSSETT, LOU
B.T. PUPPY
- ❏ BTS-1013   From Me to You | 1970 | 10.00 | 20.00 | 40.00 |

GOULD, MORTON
COLUMBIA MASTERWORKS
- ❏ ML 2065 [10]   Christmas Music for Orchestra | 1949 | 7.50 | 15.00 | 30.00 |
RCA VICTOR RED SEAL
- ❏ LSC-1994 [S]   Jungle Drums | 1958 | 10.00 | 20.00 | 40.00 |
-- Original with "shaded dog" label
- ❏ LSC-2080 [S]   Brass and Percussion | 1958 | 6.25 | 12.50 | 25.00 |
-- Original with "shaded dog" label
- ❏ LSC-2104 [S]   Blues in the Night | 1958 | 10.00 | 20.00 | 40.00 |
-- Original with "shaded dog" label
- ❏ LSC-2195 [S]   Copland: Billy the Kid; Rodeo | 1959 | 17.50 | 35.00 | 70.00 |
-- Original with "shaded dog" label
- ❏ LSC-2217 [S]   Baton and Bows | 1959 | 6.25 | 12.50 | 25.00 |
-- Original with "shaded dog" label
- ❏ LSC-2224 [S]   Where's the Melody? | 1959 | 5.00 | 10.00 | 20.00 |
-- Original with "shaded dog" label
- ❏ LSC-2232 [S]   Moon, Wind and Stars | 1959 | 6.25 | 12.50 | 25.00 |
-- Original with "shaded dog" label
- ❏ LSC-2308 [S]   Doubling in Brass | 1959 | 12.50 | 25.00 | 50.00 |
-- Original with "shaded dog" label
- ❏ LSC-2317 [S]   Living Strings | 1959 | 5.00 | 10.00 | 20.00 |
-- Original with "shaded dog" label
- ❏ LSC-2345 [S]   Tchaikovsky: 1812 Overture; Ravel: Bolero | 1960 | 5.00 | 10.00 | 20.00 |
-- Original with "shaded dog" label
- ❏ LSC-2437 [S]   Bizet: Carmen for Orchestra | 1960 | 6.25 | 12.50 | 25.00 |
-- Original with "shaded dog" label
- ❏ LSC-2532 [S]   Fall River Legend | 1961 | 12.50 | 25.00 | 50.00 |
-- Original with "shaded dog" label
- ❏ LSC-2559 [S]   Jerome Kern and Cole Porter Favorites | 1961 | 5.00 | 10.00 | 20.00 |
-- Original with "shaded dog" label
- ❏ LSC-2579 [S]   Piano Favorites | 1962 | 12.50 | 25.00 | 50.00 |
-- Original with "shaded dog" label
- ❏ LSC-2686 [S]   Spirituals for Strings | 1962 | 7.50 | 15.00 | 30.00 |
-- Original with "shaded dog" label

GOULDMAN, GRAHAM
RCA VICTOR
- ❏ LPM-3954 [M]   The Graham Gouldman Thing | 1968 | 12.50 | 25.00 | 50.00 |
- ❏ LSP-3954 [S]   The Graham Gouldman Thing | 1968 | 12.50 | 25.00 | 50.00 |

GRACIOUS
PAUL DAVIS was in this group.
CAPITOL
- ❏ ST-602   Gracious | 1970 | 10.00 | 20.00 | 40.00 |

GRAFFITI
ABC
- ❏ S-663   Graffiti | 1968 | 50.00 | 100.00 | 200.00 |

GRAFFMAN, GARY
RCA VICTOR RED SEAL
- ❏ LSC-2274 [S]   Brahms: Piano Concerto No. 1 | 1959 | 25.00 | 50.00 | 100.00 |
-- With Charles Munch/Boston Symphony Orchestra; original with "shaded dog" label
- ❏ LSC-2304 [S]   Chopin: Ballades | 1959 | 5.00 | 10.00 | 20.00 |
-- Original with "shaded dog" label
- ❏ LSC-2396 [S]   Beethoven: Piano Concerto No. 3 | 1960 | 45.00 | 90.00 | 180.00 |
-- Original with "shaded dog" label
- ❏ LSC-2468 [S]   Chopin: Concerto No. 1; Mendelssohn: Capriccio Brilliant | 1961 | 25.00 | 50.00 | 100.00 |
-- Original with "shaded dog" label

Number	Title	Yr	VG	VG+	NM

GRAMMER, BILLY
DECCA
❑ DL 74212 [S]	Gospel Guitar	1962	5.00	10.00	20.00
MONUMENT
❑ MLP-4000 [M]	Travelin' On	1959	10.00	20.00	40.00
❑ MLP-8039 [M]	Travelin' On	1965	6.25	12.50	25.00
❑ SLP-18039 [P]	Travelin' On	1965	7.50	15.00	30.00

GRANATA, ROCCO
LAURIE
| ❑ LLP-2003 [M] | Marina and Other Italian Favorites | 1960 | 6.25 | 12.50 | 25.00 |

GRAND FUNK RAILROAD
Also see MARK FARNER AND DON BREWER.
CAPITOL
❑ SMAS-11207	We're An American Band	1973	7.50	15.00	30.00
	-- Gold vinyl with sheet of four stickers				
❑ SMAS-11207	We're An American Band	1973	5.00	10.00	20.00
	-- Gold vinyl without sheet of four stickers				

GRANDMA'S ROCKERS
FREDLO
| ❑ 6727 | Homemade Apple Pie | 1967 | 500.00 | 1,000. | 1,500. |

GRANT, AMY
MYRRH
| ❑ MSB-6768 [PD] | A Christmas Album | 1983 | 20.00 | 40.00 | 80.00 |
| | -- Promo-only picture disc | | | | |

GRANT, EARL
DECCA
❑ DL 4937 [M]	Gently Swingin'	1968	5.00	10.00	20.00
❑ DL 4974 [M]	Spanish Eyes	1968	6.25	12.50	25.00
❑ DXS 7204 [(2)]	The Best of Earl Grant	1969	5.00	10.00	20.00
❑ DL 8672 [M]	The Versatile Earl Grant	1958	5.00	10.00	20.00
❑ DL 78830 [S]	The End	1959	5.00	10.00	20.00
❑ DL 78905 [S]	Grant Takes Rhythm	1959	5.00	10.00	20.00
❑ DL 78916 [S]	Nothing But the Blues	1960	5.00	10.00	20.00
❑ DL 78935 [S]	Paris Is My Beat	1960	5.00	10.00	20.00

GRANT, GOGI
ERA
❑ EL-106 [M]	The Wayward Wind	196?	6.25	12.50	25.00
❑ 20001 [M]	Suddenly There's Gogi Grant	1956	25.00	50.00	100.00
	-- Red vinyl				
❑ 20001 [M]	Suddenly There's Gogi Grant	1956	15.00	30.00	60.00
	-- Black vinyl				
LIBERTY
| ❑ LRP-3144 [M] | If You Want to Get to Heaven, Shout | 1960 | 7.50 | 15.00 | 30.00 |
| ❑ LST-7144 [S] | If You Want to Get to Heaven, Shout | 1960 | 10.00 | 20.00 | 40.00 |
RCA VICTOR
❑ LOC-1030 [M]	The Helen Morgan Story	1957	15.00	30.00	60.00
❑ LPM-1717 [M]	Welcome to My Heart	1958	10.00	20.00	40.00
❑ LPM-1940 [M]	Torch Time	1959	7.50	15.00	30.00
❑ LSP-1940 [S]	Torch Time	1959	10.00	20.00	40.00
❑ LPM-2000 [M]	Granted... It's Gogi	1960	7.50	15.00	30.00
❑ LSP-2000 [S]	Granted... It's Gogi	1960	10.00	20.00	40.00

GRAPEFRUIT
ABC DUNHILL
| ❑ DS-50050 | Around Grapefruit | 1968 | 5.00 | 10.00 | 20.00 |

GRAPPELLI, STEPHANE, AND BARNEY KESSEL
MOBILE FIDELITY
| ❑ 1-111 | I Remember Django | 1984 | 12.50 | 25.00 | 50.00 |
| | -- Audiophile vinyl | | | | |

GRASS ROOTS, THE
ABC DUNHILL
❑ DS-50047	Golden Grass	1968	5.00	10.00	20.00
❑ DS-50052	Lovin' Things	1969	5.00	10.00	20.00
❑ DS-50067	Leaving It All Behind	1969	5.00	10.00	20.00
❑ DS-50087	More Golden Grass	1970	5.00	10.00	20.00
❑ DSX-50107	Their 16 Greatest Hits	1971	5.00	10.00	20.00
COMMAND
| ❑ QD-40013 [Q] | Their 16 Greatest Hits | 1974 | 7.50 | 15.00 | 30.00 |

DUNHILL
❑ D-50011 [M]	Where Were You When I Needed You	1966	37.50	75.00	150.00
❑ DS-50011 [S]	Where Were You When I Needed You	1966	25.00	50.00	100.00
❑ D-50020 [M]	Let's Live for Today	1967	6.25	12.50	25.00
❑ DS-50020 [S]	Let's Live for Today	1967	7.50	15.00	30.00
❑ D-50027 [M]	Feelings	1968	7.50	15.00	30.00
❑ DS-50027 [S]	Feelings	1968	5.00	10.00	20.00

GRATEFUL DEAD, THE
ARISTA
❑ SP-35 [DJ]	Grateful Dead Sampler	1978	7.50	15.00	30.00
❑ AL 7001 [DJ]	Terrapin Station	1977	12.50	25.00	50.00
	-- Radio station promos are banded for airplay				
❑ AL3 8634 [(3)]	Without a Net	1990	6.25	12.50	25.00
DIRECT DISK
| ❑ SD-16619 | Terrapin Station | 1980 | 25.00 | 50.00 | 100.00 |
| | -- Audiophile vinyl | | | | |
GRATEFUL DEAD
❑ GD-01	Wake of the Flood	1973	5.00	10.00	20.00
	-- With no contributing artists on back cover				
❑ GD-01 [DJ]	Wake of the Flood	1973	100.00	200.00	400.00
	-- Green vinyl meant for fan-club members; ironically, most copies were damaged in a flood before distribution				
❑ GD-102	Grateful Dead from the Mars Hotel	1974	5.00	10.00	20.00
	-- Without United Artists distribution				
❑ GD-LA494-G	Blues for Allah	1975	5.00	10.00	20.00
❑ GD-LA620-J2 [(2)]	Steal Your Face	1976	6.25	12.50	25.00
MOBILE FIDELITY
❑ 1-014	American Beauty	1980	12.50	25.00	50.00
	-- Audiophile vinyl				
❑ 1-172	Grateful Dead from the Mars Hotel	1984	10.00	20.00	40.00
	-- Audiophile vinyl				
SUNFLOWER
❑ SUN-5001	Vintage Dead	1970	10.00	20.00	40.00
	-- Album has been counterfeited, but bogus covers are 1/4" shorter than normal LP cover				
❑ SNF-5004	Historic Dead	1971	10.00	20.00	40.00
WARNER BROS.
❑ W 1689 [M]	The Grateful Dead	1967	50.00	100.00	200.00
❑ WS 1689 [S]	The Grateful Dead	1967	20.00	40.00	80.00
	-- Gold label				
❑ WS 1689 [S]	The Grateful Dead	1968	6.25	12.50	25.00
	-- Green label with "W7" logo				
❑ WS 1749	Anthem of the Sun	1968	7.50	15.00	30.00
	-- Green label with "W7" logo				
❑ WS 1749	Anthem of the Sun	197?	12.50	25.00	50.00
	-- Green label with "WB" logo, white background on cover with radically remixed version of LP				
❑ WS 1790	Aoxomoxoa	1969	7.50	15.00	30.00
	-- Green label with "W7" logo				
❑ 2WS 1830 [(2)]	Live/Dead	1969	10.00	20.00	40.00
	-- Green labels with "W7" logo				
❑ 2WS 1830 [(2)]	Live/Dead	1970	5.00	10.00	20.00
	-- Green labels with "WB" logo				
❑ WS 1869	Workingman's Dead	1970	6.25	12.50	25.00
	-- Green label with "WB" logo; textured cover with back cover slick upside down				
❑ WS 1893	American Beauty	1970	6.25	12.50	25.00
	-- Green label with "WB" logo				
❑ 2WS 1935 [(2)]	Grateful Dead	1971	7.50	15.00	30.00
	-- Green labels with "WB" logo				
❑ 3WX 2668 [(3)]	Europe '72	1972	10.00	20.00	40.00
	-- Green labels with "WB" logo				
❑ 3WX 2668 [(3)]	Europe '72	1973	5.00	10.00	20.00
	-- "Burbank" palm-trees labels				
❑ BS 2721	History of the Grateful Dead, Vol. 1 (Bear's Choice)	1973	5.00	10.00	20.00
	-- "Burbank" palm-trees labels				
❑ BS 2764	The Best of/Skeletons from the Closet	1974	5.00	10.00	20.00
	-- "Burbank" palm-trees labels				
❑ 2WS 3091 [(2)]	What a Long Strange Trip It's Been: The Best of the Grateful Dead	1977	5.00	10.00	20.00
	-- "Burbank" palm-trees labels				

GRAVES, TERESA
KIRSHNER
| ❑ KOS-104 | Teresa Graves | 1970 | 6.25 | 12.50 | 25.00 |

GRAVITY ADJUSTERS EXPANSION BAND
NOCTURNE
| ❑ NRS-302 | One | 1973 | 75.00 | 150.00 | 300.00 |

Number	Title	Yr	VG	VG+	NM

GRAY, BILLY
DECCA

❏ DL 5567 [10]	Dance-O-Rama	1956	50.00	100.00	200.00

GRAY, CLAUDE
DECCA

❏ DL 4882 [M]	Claude Gray Sings	1967	6.25	12.50	25.00
❏ DL 74882 [S]	Claude Gray Sings	1967	5.00	10.00	20.00
❏ DL 74963	The Easy Way of Claude Gray	1968	5.00	10.00	20.00

MERCURY

❏ MG-20658 [M]	Songs of Broken Love Affairs	1962	5.00	10.00	20.00
❏ MG-20718 [M]	Country Goes to Town	1962	5.00	10.00	20.00
❏ SR-60658 [S]	Songs of Broken Love Affairs	1962	6.25	12.50	25.00
❏ SR-60718 [S]	Country Goes to Town	1962	6.25	12.50	25.00

GRAY, DOBIE
CHARGER

❏ CHR-M-2002 [M]	Dobie Gray Sings for "In" Crowders That Go "Go Go"	1965	10.00	20.00	40.00
❏ CHR-S-2002 [S]	Dobie Gray Sings for "In" Crowders That Go "Go Go"	1965	30.00	60.00	120.00

STRIPE

❏ LPM 2001 [M]	Look -- Dobie Gray	1963	25.00	50.00	100.00

GRAY, DOLORES
CAPITOL

❏ T 897 [M]	Warm Brandy	1957	7.50	15.00	30.00

GRAY, GLEN, AND THE CASA LOMA ORCHESTRA
CAPITOL

❏ W 747 [M]	Casa Loma in Hi-Fi!	1956	6.25	12.50	25.00

CORAL

❏ CRL 56006 [10]	Hoagy Carmichael Songs	1950	12.50	25.00	50.00
❏ CRL 56009 [10]	Glen Gray Souvenirs	1950	12.50	25.00	50.00

DECCA

❏ DL 5089 [10]	Musical Smoke Rings	1950	12.50	25.00	50.00
❏ DL 5397 [10]	No-Name Jive	1953	12.50	25.00	50.00
❏ DL 8570 [M]	Smoke Rings	1957	5.00	10.00	20.00

HARMONY

❏ HL 7045 [M]	The Great Recordings of Glen	1957	5.00	10.00	20.00

GREAT SOCIETY, THE
Also see GRACE SLICK.
COLUMBIA

❏ CS 9627 [M]	Conspicuous Only In Its Absence	1968	12.50	25.00	50.00

-- White label promo only; "Special Mono Radio Station Copy" sticker on front; same number as stereo version

❏ CS 9627 [S]	Conspicuous Only In Its Absence	1968	6.25	12.50	25.00

-- Red label, "360 Sound Stereo"

❏ CS 9702	How It Was	1968	6.25	12.50	25.00

-- Red label, "360 Sound Stereo"

GREAT SPECKLED BIRD
AMPEX

❏ A-10103	Great Speckled Bird	1970	5.00	10.00	20.00

GREAVES, R.B.
ATCO

❏ SD 33-311	R.B. Greaves	1969	5.00	10.00	20.00

GRECO, BUDDY
CORAL

❏ CRL 57022 [M]	Buddy Greco at Mister Kelly's	1956	6.25	12.50	25.00

GRECO, JULIETTE
COLUMBIA

❏ CL 569 [M]	St. Germain-des-Pres	1954	7.50	15.00	30.00

-- Maroon label, gold print

GREEK FOUNTAIN RIVER FRONT BAND, THE
MONTEL

❏ 110 [M]	The Greek Fountain River Band Takes Requests	1965	30.00	60.00	120.00

GREELEY, GEORGE
WARNER BROS.

❏ WS 1249 [S]	The World's Greatest Popular Piano Concertos	1959	5.00	10.00	20.00
❏ WS 1291 [S]	World Renowned Popular Piano Concertos	1959	5.00	10.00	20.00
❏ WS 1319 [S]	The Greatest Motion Picture Piano Concertos	1959	5.00	10.00	20.00
❏ WS 1338 [S]	22 Best Loved Christmas Piano Concertos	1959	5.00	10.00	20.00

GREEN BULLFROG
DECCA

❏ DL 75269	Green Bullfrog	1971	6.25	12.50	25.00

GREEN DAY
REPRISE

❏ 45529 [DJ]	Dookie	1994	8.75	17.50	35.00

-- Promo version on clear green vinyl in plain white cover

❏ 45529 [DJ]	Dookie	1994	7.50	15.00	30.00

-- Promo version on milky pale-green vinyl

GREEN RIVER
Members of this band later joined Mudhoney, Mother Love Bone and Pearl Jam.
SUB POP

❏ 11 [EP]	Dry as a Bone	1987	12.50	25.00	50.00

-- First 2,000 copies have yellow inserts

❏ 11 [EP]	Dry as a Bone	1987	8.75	17.50	35.00

-- Later copies have pink inserts

❏ 15 [EP]	Rehab Doll	1988	8.75	17.50	35.00

-- First 1,000 copies on green vinyl

❏ 15 [EP]	Rehab Doll	1988	6.25	12.50	25.00

GREEN, AL
BELL

❏ 6076	Al Green	1972	5.00	10.00	20.00

-- Reissue of Hot Line LP

HOT LINE

❏ 1500 [M]	Back Up Train	1967	12.50	25.00	50.00

-- As "Al Greene"

❏ S-1500 [S]	Back Up Train	1967	20.00	40.00	80.00

-- As "Al Greene"

GREEN, BERNIE, WITH THE STEREO MAD-MEN
RCA VICTOR

❏ LPM-1929 [M]	Musically Mad	1959	15.00	30.00	60.00
❏ LSP-1929 [S]	Musically Mad	1959	30.00	60.00	120.00

GREEN, GARLAND
UNI

❏ 73073	Jealous Kind of Fellow	1969	5.00	10.00	20.00

GREEN, GRANT
BLUE NOTE

❏ BN-LA037-G [(2)]	Live at the Lighthouse	1973	5.00	10.00	20.00
❏ BLP-4064 [M]	Grant's First Stand	1961	20.00	40.00	80.00

-- With W. 63rd St. address on label

❏ BLP-4064 [M]	Grant's First Stand	1963	6.25	12.50	25.00

-- With New York, USA address on label

❏ BLP-4071 [M]	Green Street	1961	15.00	30.00	60.00

-- With W. 63rd St. address on label

❏ BLP-4071 [M]	Green Street	1963	6.25	12.50	25.00

-- With New York, USA address on label

❏ BLP-4086 [M]	Grant Stand	1962	15.00	30.00	60.00

-- With W. 63rd St. address on label and 61st St. address on jacket

❏ BLP-4086 [M]	Grant Stand	1963	6.25	12.50	25.00

-- With New York, USA address on label

❏ BLP-4099 [M]	Sunday Mornin'	1962	15.00	30.00	60.00

-- With 61st St. address on label

❏ BLP-4099 [M]	Sunday Mornin'	1963	6.25	12.50	25.00

-- With New York, USA address on label

❏ BLP-4111 [M]	The Latin Bit	1962	10.00	20.00	40.00
❏ BLP-4132 [M]	Feelin' the Spirit	1963	10.00	20.00	40.00
❏ BLP-4139 [M]	Am I Blue	1963	10.00	20.00	40.00
❏ BLP-4154 [M]	Idle Moments	1964	10.00	20.00	40.00
❏ BLP-4183 [M]	Talkin' About!	1964	10.00	20.00	40.00
❏ BLP-4202 [M]	I Want to Hold Your Hand	1964	10.00	20.00	40.00
❏ BLP-4253 [M]	Street of Dreams	1967	12.50	25.00	50.00
❏ BLP-84064 [S]	Grant's First Stand	1961	15.00	30.00	60.00

-- With W. 63rd St. address on label

❏ BLP-84064 [S]	Grant's First Stand	1963	5.00	10.00	20.00

-- With New York, USA address on label

Number	Title	Yr	VG	VG+	NM
❏ BLP-84071 [S] Green Street		1961	12.50	25.00	50.00
-- With W. 63rd St. addresss on label					
❏ BLP-84071 [S] Green Street		1963	5.00	10.00	20.00
-- With New York, USA address on label					
❏ BLP-84086 [S] Grant Stand		1962	12.50	25.00	50.00
-- With 61st St. address on label					
❏ BLP-84086 [S] Grant Stand		1963	5.00	10.00	20.00
-- With New York, USA address on label					
❏ BLP-84099 [S] Sunday Mornin'		1962	12.50	25.00	50.00
-- With 61st St. address on label					
❏ BLP-84099 [S] Sunday Mornin'		1963	5.00	10.00	20.00
-- With New York, USA address on label					
❏ BLP-84111 [S] The Latin Bit		1962	10.00	20.00	40.00
-- With New York, USA address on label					
❏ BLP-84132 [S] Feelin' the Spirit		1963	10.00	20.00	40.00
-- With New York, USA address on label					
❏ BLP-84139 [S] Am I Blue		1963	10.00	20.00	40.00
-- With New York, USA address on label					
❏ BLP-84154 [S] Idle Moments		1964	10.00	20.00	40.00
-- With New York, USA address on label					
❏ BLP-84183 [S] Talkin' About!		1964	10.00	20.00	40.00
-- With New York, USA address on label					
❏ BLP-84202 [S] I Want to Hold Your Hand		1964	10.00	20.00	40.00
-- With New York, USA address on label					
❏ BLP-84253 [S] Street of Dreams		1967	10.00	20.00	40.00
❏ BLP-84310 Goin' West		1969	10.00	20.00	40.00
❏ BLP-84327 Carryin' On		1969	10.00	20.00	40.00
❏ BLP-84340 Green Is Beautiful		1970	6.25	12.50	25.00
❏ BLP-84360 Alive!		1970	6.25	12.50	25.00
❏ BLP-84373 Visions		1971	5.00	10.00	20.00
❏ BLP-84413 Shades of Green		1972	5.00	10.00	20.00
DELMARK					
❏ DL-404 [M] All the Gin Is Gone		1966	6.25	12.50	25.00
❏ DL-427 [M] Black Forrest		1966	6.25	12.50	25.00
❏ DS-404 [S] All the Gin Is Gone		1966	6.25	12.50	25.00
❏ DS-427 [S] Black Forrest		1966	6.25	12.50	25.00
VERVE					
❏ V-8627 [M] His Majesty, King Funk		1965	7.50	15.00	30.00
❏ V6-8627 [S] His Majesty, King Funk		1965	7.50	15.00	30.00

GREEN, LLOYD
CHART
Number	Title	Yr	VG	VG+	NM
❏ 1006	Mr. Nashville	1968	6.25	12.50	25.00
❏ 1024	Moody River	1970	6.25	12.50	25.00
TIME
| ❏ ST-2152 [S] | Big Steel Guitar | 1964 | 10.00 | 20.00 | 40.00 |
| ❏ T-2152 [M] | Big Steel Guitar | 1964 | 7.50 | 15.00 | 30.00 |

GREEN, PETER
REPRISE
Number	Title	Yr	VG	VG+	NM
❏ RS 6436	The End of the Game	1970	5.00	10.00	20.00

GREENBAUM, NORMAN
REPRISE
Number	Title	Yr	VG	VG+	NM
❏ RS 6365	Spirit in the Sky	1969	5.00	10.00	20.00

GREENBRIAR BOYS, THE
ELEKTRA
Number	Title	Yr	VG	VG+	NM
❏ EKL-233 [M]	Dian and the Greenbriar Boys	1963	6.25	12.50	25.00
❏ EKS-7233 [S]	Dian and the Greenbriar Boys	1963	7.50	15.00	30.00
VANGUARD
❏ VRS-9104 [M]	The Greenbriar Boys	1962	6.25	12.50	25.00
❏ VRS-9159 [M]	Ragged But Right	1964	5.00	10.00	20.00
❏ VRS-9233 [M]	Better Late Than Never	1966	5.00	10.00	20.00
❏ VSD-79159 [S]	Ragged But Right	1964	6.25	12.50	25.00
❏ VSD-79233 [S]	Better Late Than Never	1966	6.25	12.50	25.00

GREENE, JACK
DECCA
Number	Title	Yr	VG	VG+	NM
❏ DL 4845 [M]	There Goes My Everything	1967	5.00	10.00	20.00
❏ DL 4904 [M]	All the Time	1967	5.00	10.00	20.00
❏ DL 4939 [M]	What Locks the Door	1968	6.25	12.50	25.00
❏ DL 4979 [M]	You Are My Treasure	1968	7.50	15.00	30.00

GREENE, LORNE
RCA CAMDEN
Number	Title	Yr	VG	VG+	NM
❏ CAS-2391	Five Card Stud	1970	6.25	12.50	25.00
RCA VICTOR
❏ SP-33-327 [DJ]	Palaver with The Man	1965	12.50	25.00	50.00
-- Promo-only interview record with script					
❏ LPM-2661 [M]	Young at Heart	1963	6.25	12.50	25.00
❏ LSP-2661 [S]	Young at Heart	1963	7.50	15.00	30.00
❏ LPM-2843 [M]	Welcome to the Ponderosa	1964	6.25	12.50	25.00
❏ LSP-2843 [S]	Welcome to the Ponderosa	1964	7.50	15.00	30.00
❏ LPM-3302 [M]	The Man	1965	6.25	12.50	25.00
❏ LSP-3302 [S]	The Man	1965	7.50	15.00	30.00
❏ LPM-3409 [M]	Lorne Greene's American West	1965	6.25	12.50	25.00
❏ LSP-3409 [S]	Lorne Greene's American West	1965	7.50	15.00	30.00
❏ LPM-3410 [M]	Have a Happy Holiday	1965	6.25	12.50	25.00
❏ LSP-3410 [S]	Have a Happy Holiday	1965	7.50	15.00	30.00
❏ LPM-3678 [M]	Portrait of the West	1966	6.25	12.50	25.00
❏ LSP-3678 [S]	Portrait of the West	1966	7.50	15.00	30.00
RCA VICTOR RED SEAL					
❏ LM-2783 [M]	Peter and the Wolf	1964	6.25	12.50	25.00
❏ LSC-2783 [S]	Peter and the Wolf	1964	7.50	15.00	30.00
-- Above with the London Symphony Orchestra					

GREENE, LORNE; MICHAEL LANDON; DAN BLOCKER
RCA VICTOR
Number	Title	Yr	VG	VG+	NM
❏ LPM-2583 [M]	Bonanza -- Ponderosa Party Time!	1962	7.50	15.00	30.00
❏ LSP-2583 [S]	Bonanza -- Ponderosa Party Time!	1962	10.00	20.00	40.00
❏ LPM-2757 [M]	Christmas on the Ponderosa	1963	6.25	12.50	25.00
❏ LSP-2757 [S]	Christmas on the Ponderosa	1963	7.50	15.00	30.00

GREENSLEEVES, EDDIE
CAMEO
Number	Title	Yr	VG	VG+	NM
❏ C-1031 [M]	Humorous Folk Songs	1963	5.00	10.00	20.00
❏ SC-1031 [S]	Humorous Folk Songs	1963	6.25	12.50	25.00

GREENWICH, ELLIE
UNITED ARTISTS
Number	Title	Yr	VG	VG+	NM
❏ UAS-6648	Ellie Greenwich Composes, Produces and Sings	1968	12.50	25.00	50.00
VERVE
| ❏ V6-5091 | Let It Be Written, Let It Be Sung | 1973 | 6.25 | 12.50 | 25.00 |

GREER, PAULA
WORKSHOP JAZZ
Number	Title	Yr	VG	VG+	NM
❏ WSJ 203 [M]	Introducing Miss Paula Greer	1963	62.50	125.00	250.00

GREGG, BOBBY
EPIC
Number	Title	Yr	VG	VG+	NM
❏ LN 24051 [M]	Let's Stomp and Wild Weekend	1963	7.50	15.00	30.00
❏ BN 26051 [S]	Let's Stomp and Wild Weekend	1963	10.00	20.00	40.00

GREGORY, DICK
COLPIX
Number	Title	Yr	VG	VG+	NM
❏ CP 417 [M]	In Living Black and White	1961	6.25	12.50	25.00
❏ CP 420 [M]	East and West	1961	6.25	12.50	25.00
❏ CP 480 [M]	We All Have Problems	1964	6.25	12.50	25.00
GATEWAY					
❏ GLP 9007 [M]	My Brother's Keeper	1963	10.00	20.00	40.00
POPPY					
❏ PYS 60001 [(2)]	The Light Side: The Dark Side	1969	5.00	10.00	20.00
TOMATO					
❏ 9001 [(3)]	The Best of Dick Gregory	1978	5.00	10.00	20.00
VEE JAY					
❏ LP 1093 [M]	Running for President	1964	6.25	12.50	25.00
❏ LP 4001 [M]	Dick Gregory Talks Turkey	1962	6.25	12.50	25.00
❏ LP 4005 [M]	Two Sides of Dick Gregory	1963	6.25	12.50	25.00

GRENFELL, JOYCE
ELEKTRA
Number	Title	Yr	VG	VG+	NM
❏ EKL-184 [M]	Presenting Joyce Grenfell	1960	7.50	15.00	30.00

GRIER, ROOSEVELT
RIC
Number	Title	Yr	VG	VG+	NM
❏ M-1008 [M]	Soul City	1964	5.00	10.00	20.00
❏ S-1008 [S]	Soul City	1964	6.25	12.50	25.00

GRIFF, RAY
DOT
Number	Title	Yr	VG	VG+	NM
❏ DLP-25868	A Ray of Sunshine	1968	5.00	10.00	20.00

GRIFFIN, JIMMY
Also see BREAD.
REPRISE
Number	Title	Yr	VG	VG+	NM
❏ R-6091 [M]	Summer Holiday	1963	12.50	25.00	50.00
❏ R9-6091 [S]	Summer Holiday	1963	15.00	30.00	60.00

Number	Title	Yr	VG	VG+	NM

GRIFFIN, KEN
COLUMBIA

Number	Title	Yr	VG	VG+	NM
❏ CL 692 [M]	The Organ Plays at Christmas	1955	6.25	12.50	25.00
-- Red and black label with six "eye" logos					
❏ CL 6130 [10]	Christmas Carols by Ken Griffin	1950	7.50	15.00	30.00

GRIFFIN, MERV
CAMEO

| ❏ C-1060 [M] | My Favorite Songs | 1964 | 5.00 | 10.00 | 20.00 |
| ❏ SC-1060 [S] | My Favorite Songs | 1964 | 6.25 | 12.50 | 25.00 |

CARLTON

| ❏ LP-12-134 [M] | Merv Griffin's Dance Party | 1961 | 7.50 | 15.00 | 30.00 |
| ❏ STLP-12-134 [S] | Merv Griffin's Dance Party | 1961 | 10.00 | 20.00 | 40.00 |

GRIFFITH, ANDY
CAPITOL

❏ T 962 [M]	Just for Laughs	1958	10.00	20.00	40.00
❏ ST 1105 [S]	Andy Griffith Shouts the Blues and Old Timey Songs	1959	12.50	25.00	50.00
❏ T 1105 [M]	Andy Griffith Shouts the Blues and Old Timey Songs	1959	10.00	20.00	40.00
❏ ST 1215 [S]	This Here Andy Griffith	1959	10.00	20.00	40.00
❏ T 1215 [M]	This Here Andy Griffith	1959	7.50	15.00	30.00
❏ ST 1611 [S]	Songs, Themes and Laughs from The Andy Griffith Show	1961	30.00	60.00	120.00
❏ T 1611 [M]	Songs, Themes and Laughs from The Andy Griffith Show	1961	20.00	40.00	80.00
❏ ST 2066 [S]	Andy and Cleopatra	1964	6.25	12.50	25.00
❏ T 2066 [M]	Andy and Cleopatra	1964	5.00	10.00	20.00

GRIFFITH, JOHNNY, TRIO
WORKSHOP JAZZ

| ❏ WSJ 205 [M] | Jazz | 1963 | 50.00 | 100.00 | 200.00 |

GRIFFITH, SHIRLEY
BLUESVILLE

❏ BVLP-1087 [M]	The Blues of Shirley Griffith	1964	12.50	25.00	50.00
-- Blue label, silver print					
❏ BVLP-1087 [M]	The Blues of Shirley Griffith	1964	6.25	12.50	25.00
-- Blue label, trident logo at right					

GRIMES, GARY
DIRECT DISK

| ❏ SD-16630 | Starhand Visions | 198? | 7.50 | 15.00 | 30.00 |
| -- Audiophile vinyl | | | | | |

GRISMAN, DAVID
KALEIDOSCOPE

| ❏ 5 | David Grisman Quintet | 1977 | 5.00 | 10.00 | 20.00 |

GRISSOM, JIMMY
ARGO

| ❏ LP-729 [M] | World of Trouble | 1964 | 6.25 | 12.50 | 25.00 |

GRODECK WHIPPERJENNY
PEOPLE

| ❏ 3000 | Grodeck Whipperjenny | 1969 | 50.00 | 100.00 | 200.00 |

GROOV-U
GATEWAY

| ❏ GLP-3010 | Groov-U On Campus | 196? | 10.00 | 20.00 | 40.00 |

GROOVIE GOOLIES, THE
RCA VICTOR

| ❏ LSP-4420 | The Groovie Goolies | 1970 | 6.25 | 12.50 | 25.00 |

GROUNDHOGS, THE
CLEVE

| ❏ CH-82871 | The Groundhogs with John Lee Hooker and John Mayall | 196? | 25.00 | 50.00 | 100.00 |

IMPERIAL

| ❏ LP-12452 | Blues Obituary | 1969 | 10.00 | 20.00 | 40.00 |

LIBERTY

| ❏ LST-7644 | Thank Christ for the Bomb | 1970 | 7.50 | 15.00 | 30.00 |

UNITED ARTISTS

❏ UA-LA008-F	Hogwash	1973	5.00	10.00	20.00
❏ UA-LA603-G	Crosscut Saw	1976	5.00	10.00	20.00
❏ UA-LA680-G	Black Diamond	1976	5.00	10.00	20.00
❏ UAS-5513	The Groundhogs Split	1971	5.00	10.00	20.00
❏ UAS-5570	Who Will Save the World	1972	5.00	10.00	20.00

WORLD PACIFIC

Number	Title	Yr	VG	VG+	NM
❏ WPS-21892	Scratching the Surface	1968	10.00	20.00	40.00

GROUP IMAGE, THE
COMMUNITY

| ❏ A-101 | A Mouth in the Clouds | 1968 | 7.50 | 15.00 | 30.00 |

GROUP ONE
RCA VICTOR

| ❏ LSP-3524 [S] | Brothers Go to Mothers and Others | 1966 | 5.00 | 10.00 | 20.00 |

GROUP THERAPY
RCA VICTOR

| ❏ LSP-3976 [S] | People Get Ready for Group Therapy | 1968 | 5.00 | 10.00 | 20.00 |

GROUP, THE
BELL

| ❏ 6038 | The Group | 1970 | 5.00 | 10.00 | 20.00 |

RCA VICTOR

| ❏ LPM-2663 [M] | The Group | 1963 | 5.00 | 10.00 | 20.00 |
| ❏ LSP-2663 [S] | The Group | 1963 | 6.25 | 12.50 | 25.00 |

GROVE, BOBBY
KING

| ❏ 831 [M] | It Was for You | 1963 | 10.00 | 20.00 | 40.00 |

GROWING CONCERN, THE
MAINSTREAM

| ❏ S-6108 [S] | The Growing Concern | 1968 | 30.00 | 60.00 | 120.00 |
| ❏ 56108 [M] | The Growing Concern | 1968 | 20.00 | 40.00 | 80.00 |

GROWL
DISCREET

| ❏ DS 2209 | Growl | 1974 | 5.00 | 10.00 | 20.00 |

GRUSIN, DAVE
COLUMBIA

| ❏ CL 2344 [M] | Kaleidoscope | 1965 | 5.00 | 10.00 | 20.00 |
| ❏ CS 9144 [S] | Kaleidoscope | 1965 | 6.25 | 12.50 | 25.00 |

EPIC

| ❏ BN 622 [S] | Subways Are for Sleeping | 1962 | 6.25 | 12.50 | 25.00 |
| ❏ LN 3829 [M] | Subways Are for Sleeping | 1962 | 5.00 | 10.00 | 20.00 |

GRYPHON
(NO LABEL)

| ❏ 12497 | Gryphon | 197? | 20.00 | 40.00 | 80.00 |

GUADALCANAL DIARY
DB

| ❏ 73 | Walking in the Shadow of the Big Man | 1984 | 5.00 | 10.00 | 20.00 |

ENTERTAINMENT ON DISC

| ❏ EOD 102 [EP] | Watusi Rodeo | 1983 | 5.00 | 10.00 | 20.00 |

GUARALDI, VINCE, TRIO
FANTASY

❏ 3213 [M]	Modern Music from San Francisco	1956	12.50	25.00	50.00
-- Red vinyl					
❏ 3213 [M]	Modern Music from San Francisco	195?	6.25	12.50	25.00
-- Black vinyl, red label, non-flexible vinyl					
❏ 3225 [M]	Vince Guaraldi Trio	1956	12.50	25.00	50.00
-- Red vinyl					
❏ 3225 [M]	Vince Guaraldi Trio	195?	6.25	12.50	25.00
-- Black vinyl, red label, non-flexible vinyl					
❏ 3257 [M]	A Flower Is a Lovesome Thing	1958	10.00	20.00	40.00
-- Red vinyl					
❏ 3257 [M]	A Flower Is a Lovesome Thing	195?	6.25	12.50	25.00
-- Black vinyl, red label, non-flexible vinyl					
❏ 3337 [M]	Jazz Impressions of Black Orpheus (Cast Your Fate to the Wind)	1962	10.00	20.00	40.00
-- Red vinyl					
❏ 3337 [M]	Jazz Impressions of Black Orpheus (Cast Your Fate to the Wind)	1962	6.25	12.50	25.00
-- Black vinyl, red label, non-flexible vinyl					
❏ 3352 [M]	Vince Guaraldi in Person	1963	6.25	12.50	25.00
❏ 3356 [M]	Vince Guaraldi and Bola Sete and Friends	1964	6.25	12.50	25.00
❏ 3358 [M]	Tour de Force	1964	6.25	12.50	25.00
❏ 3359 [M]	Jazz Impressions	1965	6.25	12.50	25.00

Number	Title	Yr	VG	VG+	NM
❑ 3360 [M]	The Latin Side of Vince Guaraldi	1965	6.25	12.50	25.00
❑ 3362 [M]	From All Sides	1966	5.00	10.00	20.00
❑ 3367 [M]	Vince Guaraldi at Grace Cathedral	1967	5.00	10.00	20.00
❑ 3371 [M]	Live at the El Matador	1967	5.00	10.00	20.00
❑ 5019 [M]	A Charlie Brown Christmas	1964	7.50	15.00	30.00
❑ 8089 [S]	Jazz Impressions of Black Orpheus (Cast Your Fate to the Wind)	1962	10.00	20.00	40.00
-- Blue vinyl					
❑ 8089 [S]	Jazz Impressions of Black Orpheus (Cast Your Fate to the Wind)	1962	6.25	12.50	25.00
-- Black vinyl, blue label, non-flexible vinyl					
❑ 8352 [S]	Vince Guaraldi in Person	1963	6.25	12.50	25.00
❑ 8356 [S]	Vince Guaraldi and Bola Sete and Friends	1964	6.25	12.50	25.00
❑ 8358 [S]	Tour de Force	1964	6.25	12.50	25.00
❑ 8359 [S]	Jazz Impressions	1965	6.25	12.50	25.00
❑ 8360 [S]	The Latin Side of Vince Guaraldi	1965	6.25	12.50	25.00
❑ 8362 [S]	From All Sides	1966	5.00	10.00	20.00
❑ 8367 [S]	Vince Guaraldi at Grace Cathedral	1967	5.00	10.00	20.00
❑ 8371 [S]	Live at the El Matador	1967	5.00	10.00	20.00
❑ 8377	Live-Live-Live	1968	5.00	10.00	20.00
❑ 8430	A Boy Named Charlie Brown -- Jazz Impressions	1971	5.00	10.00	20.00
-- Reissue of 85017					
❑ 8431	A Charlie Brown Christmas	1971	6.25	12.50	25.00
-- Reissue of 85019; dark blue label					
❑ 85017	A Boy Named Charlie Brown -- Jazz Impressions	196?	6.25	12.50	25.00
❑ 85019 [S]	A Charlie Brown Christmas	1964	10.00	20.00	40.00
MOBILE FIDELITY					
❑ 1-112	Jazz Impressions of Black Orpheus (Cast Your Fate to the Wind)	1983	12.50	25.00	50.00
-- Audiophile vinyl					
WARNER BROS.					
❑ WS 1747	Oh Good Grief!	1968	5.00	10.00	20.00

GUARD, DAVE, AND THE WHISKEYHILL SINGERS
Dave Guard had been with THE KINGSTON TRIO.
CAPITOL

Number	Title	Yr	VG	VG+	NM
❑ ST 1728 [S]	Dave Guard and the Whiskeyhill Singers	1962	6.25	12.50	25.00
❑ T 1728 [M]	Dave Guard and the Whiskeyhill Singers	1962	5.00	10.00	20.00

GUESS WHO, THE
COMPLEAT

Number	Title	Yr	VG	VG+	NM
❑ 672012-1 [(2)]	The Best of the Gues Who, Live	1986	5.00	10.00	20.00
RCA VICTOR					
❑ APD1-0130 [Q]	#10	1974	6.25	12.50	25.00
❑ APD1-0269 [Q]	The Best of the Guess Who, Volume II	1974	6.25	12.50	25.00
❑ APD1-0405 [Q]	Road Food	1974	6.25	12.50	25.00
❑ CPD1-0636 [Q]	Flavours	1975	6.25	12.50	25.00
❑ LSP-4141	Wheatfield Soul	1969	5.00	10.00	20.00
-- Orange label, non-flexible vinyl					
❑ LSP-4157	Canned Wheat Packed By the Guess Who	1969	5.00	10.00	20.00
-- Orange label, non-flexible vinyl					
❑ LSP-4266	American Woman	1970	5.00	10.00	20.00
-- Orange label, non-flexible vinyl					
❑ LSP-4359	Share the Land	1970	5.00	10.00	20.00
-- Orange label, non-flexible vinyl					
❑ LSP-4779	Live at the Paramount (Seattle)	1972	6.25	12.50	25.00
SCEPTER					
❑ SP-533 [M]	Shakin' All Over	1966	10.00	20.00	40.00
❑ SPS-533 [P]	Shakin' All Over	1966	6.25	12.50	25.00
-- The above lists the artist as "The Guess Who's Chad Allan & The Expressions" on the cover					

GUIDED BY VOICES
E RECORDS

Number	Title	Yr	VG	VG+	NM
❑ GBV 0001	Devil Between My Toes	1987	30.00	60.00	120.00
HALO					
❑ 1	Sandbox	1987	10.00	20.00	40.00
❑ 2	Self Inflicted Aerial Nostalgia	1989	10.00	20.00	40.00
I WANNA					
❑ (no #) [EP]	Forever Since Breakfast	1986	25.00	50.00	100.00
ROCKATHON					
❑ (no #)	Propeller	1992	12.50	25.00	50.00
-- Hand-colored cover with nature-book paste-on					
ROCKET #9					
❑ (no #)	Same Place the Fly Got Smashed	1990	10.00	20.00	40.00

GUITAR RAMBLERS, THE
COLUMBIA

Number	Title	Yr	VG	VG+	NM
❑ CL 2067 [M]	The Happy, Youthful New Sounds of the Guitar Ramblers	1964	6.25	12.50	25.00
❑ CS 8867 [S]	The Happy, Youthful New Sounds of the Guitar Ramblers	1964	7.50	15.00	30.00

GUITAR SLIM
SPECIALTY

Number	Title	Yr	VG	VG+	NM
❑ SP-2130	Things That I Used to Do	1969	5.00	10.00	20.00

GUITAR, BONNIE
DOT

Number	Title	Yr	VG	VG+	NM
❑ DLP-3069 [M]	Moonlight and Shadows	1957	12.50	25.00	50.00
❑ DLP-3151 [M]	Whispering Hope	1958	10.00	20.00	40.00
❑ DLP-3335 [M]	Dark Moon	1961	6.25	12.50	25.00
❑ DLP-3696 [M]	Two Worlds	1966	5.00	10.00	20.00
❑ DLP-3737 [M]	Miss Bonnie Guitar	1966	5.00	10.00	20.00
❑ DLP-3746 [M]	Merry Christmas from Bonnie Guitar	1966	5.00	10.00	20.00
❑ DLP-3793 [M]	Award Winner	1967	5.00	10.00	20.00
❑ DLP-25151 [S]	Whispering Hope	1958	12.50	25.00	50.00
❑ DLP-25696 [S]	Two Worlds	1966	6.25	12.50	25.00
❑ DLP-25737 [S]	Miss Bonnie Guitar	1966	6.25	12.50	25.00
❑ DLP-25746 [S]	Merry Christmas from Bonnie Guitar	1966	6.25	12.50	25.00
❑ DLP-25793 [S]	Award Winner	1967	5.00	10.00	20.00
❑ DLP-25840	Bonnie Guitar	1968	5.00	10.00	20.00
❑ DLP-25947	Bonnie Guitar Affair!	1969	5.00	10.00	20.00

GULLIVER
Also see DARYL HALL AND JOHN OATES.
ELEKTRA

Number	Title	Yr	VG	VG+	NM
❑ EKS-74070	Gulliver	1970	5.00	10.00	20.00

GUN
EPIC

Number	Title	Yr	VG	VG+	NM
❑ BN 26468	Gun	1969	5.00	10.00	20.00
❑ BN 26551	Gunsight	1970	6.25	12.50	25.00

GUNS N' ROSES
GEFFEN

Number	Title	Yr	VG	VG+	NM
❑ XXXG 24148	Appetite for Destruction	1988	12.50	25.00	50.00
-- Original "rape cover"; the XXXG prefix is on the cover only; all copies of the record use the GHS prefix					
❑ GEF 24415 [(2)]	Use Your Illusion I	1991	5.00	10.00	20.00
❑ GEF 24420 [(2)]	Use Your Illusion II	1991	5.00	10.00	20.00
UZI SUICIDE					
❑ USR 001 [EP]	Live ?!*@ Like a Suicide	1986	30.00	60.00	120.00

GUNTER, ARTHUR
EXCELLO

Number	Title	Yr	VG	VG+	NM
❑ LPS-8017	Black and Blues	1971	6.25	12.50	25.00

GUTHRIE, ARLO
REPRISE

Number	Title	Yr	VG	VG+	NM
❑ MS4 2142 [Q]	Last of the Brooklyn Cowboys	1973	5.00	10.00	20.00
❑ R 6267 [M]	Alice's Restaurant	1967	5.00	10.00	20.00

GUTHRIE, JACK
CAPITOL

Number	Title	Yr	VG	VG+	NM
❑ T 2456 [M]	Jack Guthrie's Greatest Songs	1966	6.25	12.50	25.00

GUTHRIE, WOODY
ELEKTRA

Number	Title	Yr	VG	VG+	NM
❑ EKL-271/2 [(3) M]	The Library of Congress Recordings	1964	10.00	20.00	40.00
-- Original pressing has "guitar player" labels					
FOLKWAYS					
❑ FP-11 [10]	Dust Bowl Ballads	1950	150.00	300.00	600.00
❑ FP-715 [10]	Songs to Grow On For Mother and Child	195?	150.00	30.00	600.00
❑ FA-2011 [10]	Dust Bowl Ballads	195?	125.00	250.00	500.00
-- Reissue of FP-11					
❑ FA-2481 [M]	Bound for Glory: Songs and Stories of Woody Guthrie	1956	37.50	75.00	150.00
❑ FA-2483 [M]	Woody Guthrie Sings Folk Songs	1964	12.50	25.00	50.00
❑ FA-2484 [M]	Woody Guthrie Sings Folk Songs, Vol. 2	1964	12.50	25.00	50.00
❑ FA-2485 [M]	Struggle	1964	12.50	25.00	50.00
❑ FH-5212 [M]	Dust Bowl Ballads	1964	7.50	15.00	30.00

Number	Title	Yr	VG	VG+	NM
❑ FH-5485 [M]	Ballds of Sacco and Vanzetti	196?	7.50	15.00	30.00
❑ FC-7015 [10]	Songs to Grow On For Mother and Child	1953	125.00	250.00	500.00
-- Reissue of FP-715					
❑ FC-7027 [10]	Songs to Grow On Vol. 3	1951	125.00	250.00	500.00
RCA VICTOR					
❑ LPV-502 [M]	Dust Bowl Ballads	1964	6.25	12.50	25.00
VERVE FOLKWAYS					
❑ FV-9007 [M]	Bed on the Floor	1965	7.50	15.00	30.00
❑ FV-9036 [M]	Bonneville Dam & Other Columbia River Songs	1965	7.50	15.00	30.00
❑ FVS-9007 [R]	Bed on the Floor	1965	5.00	10.00	20.00
❑ FVS-9036 [R]	Bonneville Dam & Other Columbia River Songs	1965	5.00	10.00	20.00

GUTHRIE, WOODY, AND CISCO HOUSTON
STINSON

Number	Title	Yr	VG	VG+	NM
❑ SLP-32 [10]	Cowboy Songs	195?	50.00	100.00	200.00
❑ SLP-44 [10]	Folk Songs, Vol. 1	195?	50.00	100.00	200.00
❑ SLP-53 [10]	More Songs	195?	50.00	100.00	200.00

GUTHRIE, WOODY; SONNY TERRY; ALEX STEWART
STINSON

Number	Title	Yr	VG	VG+	NM
❑ SLP-7 [10]	Chain Gang, Vol. 1	195?	50.00	100.00	200.00
❑ SLP-8 [10]	Chain Gang, Vol. 2	195?	50.00	100.00	200.00

GUY, BUDDY
BLUE THUMB

Number	Title	Yr	VG	VG+	NM
❑ BTS 20	Buddy and the Juniors	1970	6.25	12.50	25.00
CHESS					
❑ LP-409	I Was Walking Through the Woods	1970	5.00	10.00	20.00
❑ LP-1527 [M]	I Left My Blues in San Francisco	1968	7.50	15.00	30.00
MCA					
❑ 11165	I Was Walking Through the Woods	1995	6.25	12.50	25.00
-- "Heavy Vinyl" audiophile reissue					
VANGUARD					
❑ VSD-79272	A Man and the Blues	1968	6.25	12.50	25.00
❑ VSD-79290	This Is Buddy Guy	1969	6.25	12.50	25.00
❑ VSD-79323	Hold That Plane!	1972	5.00	10.00	20.00

GUY, CHARLES
CAPITOL

Number	Title	Yr	VG	VG+	NM
❑ ST 1920 [S]	Prisoner's Dream	1963	6.25	12.50	25.00
❑ T 1920 [M]	Prisoner's Dream	1963	5.00	10.00	20.00

GYPSY
METROMEDIA

Number	Title	Yr	VG	VG+	NM
❑ MD-1031 [(2)]	Gypsy	1970	5.00	10.00	20.00

H

H.P. LOVECRAFT
PHILIPS

Number	Title	Yr	VG	VG+	NM
❑ PHM 200-252 [M]	H.P. Lovecraft	1967	5.00	10.00	20.00
❑ PHS 600-252 [S]	H.P. Lovecraft	1967	6.25	12.50	25.00
❑ PHS 600-279	Lovecraft II	1968	6.25	12.50	25.00
REPRISE					
❑ RS 6419	Valley of the Moon	1970	5.00	10.00	20.00

H.Y. SLEDGE
SSS INTERNATIONAL

Number	Title	Yr	VG	VG+	NM
❑ 22	Bootleg Music	1971	5.00	10.00	20.00

HA'PENNYS, THE
FERSCH

Number	Title	Yr	VG	VG+	NM
❑ FL-1110	Love Is Not the Same	1968	50.00	100.00	200.00

HAGAR, ERNIE
SAGE AND SAND

Number	Title	Yr	VG	VG+	NM
❑ C-42 [M]	Swinging Steel Guitar	1965	7.50	15.00	30.00

HAGGARD, MERLE
CAPITOL

Number	Title	Yr	VG	VG+	NM
❑ SKAO-168	Pride In What I Am	1969	6.25	12.50	25.00
❑ SWBB-223 [(2)]	Same Train, A Different Time	1969	7.50	15.00	30.00
❑ SWBB-259 [(2)]	Close-Up	1969	7.50	15.00	30.00
-- Reissue in one package of "Strangers" and "Swinging Doors"					
❑ ST-319	A Portrait of Merle Haggard	1969	5.00	10.00	20.00
❑ ST-384	Okie from Muskogee	1970	5.00	10.00	20.00
❑ ST-451	The Fightin' Side of Me	1970	5.00	10.00	20.00
❑ ST-638	A Tribute to the Best Damn Fiddle Player in the World (Or, My Salute to Bob Wills)	1970	6.25	12.50	25.00
❑ STBB-707 [(2)]	Sing a Sad Song/High on a Hilltop	1971	7.50	15.00	30.00
❑ SWBO-803 [(2)]	The Land of Many Churches	1971	15.00	30.00	60.00
❑ ST-823	Truly the Best of Merle Haggard	1971	10.00	20.00	40.00
❑ ST-835	Someday We'll Look Back	1971	5.00	10.00	20.00
❑ ST-882	Let Me Tell You About a Song	1972	5.00	10.00	20.00
❑ ST 2373 [S]	Strangers	1965	7.50	15.00	30.00
❑ T 2373 [M]	Strangers	1965	6.25	12.50	25.00
❑ ST 2585 [S]	Swinging Doors	1966	7.50	15.00	30.00
❑ T 2585 [M]	Swinging Doors	1966	6.25	12.50	25.00
❑ ST 2702 [S]	I'm a Lonesome Fugitive	1967	7.50	15.00	30.00
❑ T 2702 [M]	I'm a Lonesome Fugitive	1967	6.25	12.50	25.00
❑ ST 2789 [S]	Branded Man	1967	7.50	15.00	30.00
❑ T 2789 [M]	Branded Man	1967	6.25	12.50	25.00
❑ ST 2848 [S]	Sing Me Back Home	1968	6.25	12.50	25.00
❑ T 2848 [M]	Sing Me Back Home	1968	7.50	15.00	30.00
❑ ST 2912	The Legend of Bonnie and Clyde	1968	6.25	12.50	25.00
❑ SKAO 2951	The Best of Merle Haggard	1968	6.25	12.50	25.00
❑ ST 2972	Mama Tried	1968	6.25	12.50	25.00
CAPITOL SPECIAL MARKETS					
❑ SL-8086 [(2)]	Songs I'll Always Sing	1977	5.00	10.00	20.00

HAGGARD, MERLE, AND BONNIE OWENS
Also see each artist's individual listings.
CAPITOL

Number	Title	Yr	VG	VG+	NM
❑ ST 2453 [S]	Just Between the Two of Us	1966	7.50	15.00	30.00
❑ T 2453 [M]	Just Between the Two of Us	1966	6.25	12.50	25.00

HAINES, CONNIE
CORAL

Number	Title	Yr	VG	VG+	NM
❑ CRL 56055 [10]	Connie Haines Sings	1955	30.00	60.00	120.00
RCA VICTOR					
❑ LPM-2264 [M]	Faith, Hope and Charity	1961	5.00	10.00	20.00
❑ LSP-2264 [S]	Faith, Hope and Charity	1961	7.50	15.00	30.00
TOPS					
❑ L-1606 [M]	Connie Haines Sings Helen Morgan	1959	7.50	15.00	30.00

HALEY, BILL, AND HIS COMETS
DECCA

Number	Title	Yr	VG	VG+	NM
❑ DL 5560 [10]	Shake, Rattle and Roll	1955	200.00	400.00	800.00
❑ DL 8225 [M]	Rock Around the Clock	1955	37.50	75.00	150.00
-- All-black label with silver print					
❑ DL 8225 [M]	Rock Around the Clock	1960	12.50	25.00	50.00
-- Black label with colorband, no mention of MCA on label					
❑ DL 8225 [M]	Rock Around the Clock	1967	7.50	15.00	30.00
-- Black label with colorband, "A Division of MCA" on label					
❑ DL 8315 [M]	Music for the Boyfriend	1956	37.50	75.00	150.00

Number	Title	Yr	VG	VG+	NM
❏ DL 8345 [M]	Rock 'n Roll Stage Show	1956	37.50	75.00	150.00
❏ DL 8569 [M]	Rockin' the Oldies	1957	37.50	75.00	150.00
❏ DL 8692 [M]	Rockin' Around the World	1958	37.50	75.00	150.00
❏ DL 8775 [M]	Rockin' the Joint	1958	37.50	75.00	150.00
❏ DL 8821 [M]	Bill Haley's Chicks	1959	25.00	50.00	100.00
❏ DL 8964 [M]	Strictly Instrumental	1960	25.00	50.00	100.00
❏ DL 78225 [R]	Rock Around the Clock	1959	18.75	37.50	75.00
-- All-black label with silver print					
❏ DL 78225 [R]	Rock Around the Clock	1960	6.25	12.50	25.00
-- Black label with colorband, no mention of MCA on label					
❏ DL 78821 [S]	Bill Haley's Chicks	1959	37.50	75.00	150.00
❏ DL 78964 [S]	Strictly Instrumental	1960	37.50	75.00	150.00
ESSEX					
❏ LP 202 [M]	Rock with Bill Haley and the Comets	1955	125.00	250.00	500.00
JANUS					
❏ 3035	Travelin' Band	1972	6.25	12.50	25.00
KAMA SUTRA					
❏ KLPS-2014	Scrapbook	1970	7.50	15.00	30.00
ROULETTE					
❏ R 25174 [M]	Twistin' Knights at the Roundtable	1962	20.00	40.00	80.00
❏ SR 25174 [S]	Twistin' Knights at the Roundtable	1962	25.00	50.00	100.00
SOMERSET					
❏ P-4600 [M]	Rock with Bill Haley and the Comets	1958	37.50	75.00	150.00
TRANS WORLD					
❏ LP 202 [M]	Rock with Bill Haley and the Comets	1956	75.00	150.00	300.00
VOCALION					
❏ VL 3696 [M]	Bill Haley and the Comets	1963	6.25	12.50	25.00
WARNER BROS.					
❏ W 1378 [M]	Bill Haley and His Comets	1959	12.50	25.00	50.00
❏ W 1391 [M]	Bill Haley's Jukebox	1960	12.50	25.00	50.00
❏ WS 1378 [S]	Bill Haley and His Comets	1959	17.50	35.00	70.00
❏ WS 1391 [S]	Bill Haley's Jukebox	1960	17.50	35.00	70.00
❏ ST-9????	Rock 'N' Roll Revival	1970	6.25	12.50	25.00
-- Capitol Record Club edition					

HALFNELSON -- See SPARKS.

HALL, BECKY
AAMCO

Number	Title	Yr	VG	VG+	NM
❏ ALP-324 [M]	A Tribute to Bessie Smith	1958	7.50	15.00	30.00

HALL, CONNIE
DECCA

Number	Title	Yr	VG	VG+	NM
❏ DL 4??? [M]	Connie Hall	1962	6.25	12.50	25.00
❏ DL 74??? [S]	Connie Hall	1962	7.50	15.00	30.00
VOCALION					
❏ VL 3752 [M]	Country Songs	1965	5.00	10.00	20.00
❏ VL 3801 [M]	Country Style	1968	5.00	10.00	20.00
❏ VL 73752 [S]	Country Songs	1965	6.25	12.50	25.00
❏ VL 73801 [S]	Country Style	1968	5.00	10.00	20.00

HALL, DARYL, AND JOHN OATES
MOBILE FIDELITY

Number	Title	Yr	VG	VG+	NM
❏ 1-069	Abandoned Luncheonette	1982	5.00	10.00	20.00
-- Audiophile vinyl					
RCA VICTOR					
❏ DJL1-3512 [DJ]	Post Static	1979	5.00	10.00	20.00
-- Promo-only one-sided 4-song sampler					

HALL, DICKSON
EPIC

Number	Title	Yr	VG	VG+	NM
❏ LN 3427 [M]	25 All-Time Country and Western Hits	1958	6.25	12.50	25.00
KAPP					
❏ KL-1067 [M]	Fabulous Country Hits Way Out West	1957	7.50	15.00	30.00
❏ KL-1464 [M]	24 Fabulous Country Hits	1966	5.00	10.00	20.00
❏ KS-3464 [S]	24 Fabulous Country Hits	1966	6.25	12.50	25.00
MGM					
❏ E-329 [10]	Outlaws of the Old West	1954	15.00	30.00	60.00
❏ E-3263 [M]	Outlaws of the Old West	1956	10.00	20.00	40.00
PERFECT					
❏ P-14016 [M]	Country & Western Million Sellers	1960	5.00	10.00	20.00
❏ PS-14016 [S]	Country & Western Million Sellers	1960	6.25	12.50	25.00

HALL, JOANIE
SAGE AND SAND

Number	Title	Yr	VG	VG+	NM
❏ C-34 [M]	Western Meets Country	1962	6.25	12.50	25.00

HALL, JUANITA
COUNTERPOINT

Number	Title	Yr	VG	VG+	NM
❏ 558 [S]	Juanita Hall Sings the Blues	1959	37.50	75.00	150.00

HALL, LARRY
STRAND

Number	Title	Yr	VG	VG+	NM
❏ SL-1005 [M]	Sandy	1960	37.50	75.00	150.00
❏ SLS-1005 [S]	Sandy	1960	50.00	100.00	200.00

HALL, TOM T.
MERCURY

Number	Title	Yr	VG	VG+	NM
❏ SR-61211	Ballad of Forty Dollars	1969	5.00	10.00	20.00
❏ SR-61247	Homecoming	1969	5.00	10.00	20.00
❏ SR-61277	Witness Life	1970	5.00	10.00	20.00
❏ SR-61307	100 Children	1970	5.00	10.00	20.00

HALLE ORCHESTRA (JOHN BARBIROLLI, COND.)
MERCURY LIVING PRESENCE

Number	Title	Yr	VG	VG+	NM
❏ SR 90115 [S]	Williams, Vaughan: Symphony No. 8; Bax: Garden of Fand; Butterworth: Shropshire Lad	1960	12.50	25.00	50.00
-- Maroon label, no "Vendor: Mercury Record Corporation"					
❏ SR 90124 [S]	Viennese Night at the Proms	1960	5.00	10.00	20.00
-- Maroon label, no "Vendor: Mercury Record Corporation"					
❏ SR 90125 [S]	Elgar: Enigma Variations; Purcell: Suite for Strings	1960	5.00	10.00	20.00
-- Maroon label, no "Vendor: Mercury Record Corporation"					
❏ SR 90160 [S]	Suppe: Overtures	196?	12.50	25.00	50.00
-- Maroon label, no "Vendor: Mercury Record Corporation"					
❏ SR 90161 [S]	Encore Please, Sir John!	196?	15.00	30.00	60.00
-- Maroon label, no "Vendor: Mercury Record Corporation"					
❏ SR 90164 [S]	Grieg: Peer Gynt Suite; Symphonic Dances; Elegiac Melodies	196?	25.00	50.00	100.00
-- Maroon label, no "Vendor: Mercury Record Corporation"					

HALLE ORCHESTRA (GEORGE WELDON, COND.)
MERCURY LIVING PRESENCE

Number	Title	Yr	VG	VG+	NM
❏ SR 90137 [S]	Khachaturian: Gayne Ballet Suite; Mussorgsky: Night on Bare Mountain	196?	7.50	15.00	30.00
-- Maroon label, no "Vendor: Mercury Record Corporation"					

HALLYDAY, JOHNNY
PHILIPS

Number	Title	Yr	VG	VG+	NM
❏ PHM 200-019 [M]	America's Rockin' Hits	1962	20.00	40.00	80.00
❏ PHS 600-019 [S]	America's Rockin' Hits	1962	25.00	50.00	100.00

HALOS, THE
WARWICK

Number	Title	Yr	VG	VG+	NM
❏ W-2046 [M]	The Halos	1962	100.00	200.00	400.00

HAMBLEN, STUART
COLUMBIA

Number	Title	Yr	VG	VG+	NM
❏ CL 1588 [M]	The Spell of the Yukon	1961	5.00	10.00	20.00
❏ CL 1769 [M]	Of God I Sing	1962	5.00	10.00	20.00
❏ CS 8388 [S]	The Spell of the Yukon	1961	6.25	12.50	25.00
❏ CS 8569 [S]	Of God I Sing	1962	6.25	12.50	25.00
CORAL					
❏ CRL 57254 [M]	Remember Me	1960	6.25	12.50	25.00
HARMONY					
❏ HL 7009 [M]	Hymns	1957	6.25	12.50	25.00
RCA CAMDEN					
❏ CAL-537 [M]	Beyond the Sun	1959	6.25	12.50	25.00
RCA VICTOR					
❏ LPM-1253 [M]	It Is No Secret	1956	10.00	20.00	40.00
❏ LPM-1436 [M]	Grand Old Hymns	1957	10.00	20.00	40.00
❏ LPM-3265 [10]	It Is No Secret	1954	15.00	30.00	60.00

HAMILTON STREETCAR
DOT

Number	Title	Yr	VG	VG+	NM
❏ DLP-25939	Hamilton Streetcar	1969	6.25	12.50	25.00

HAMILTON, CHICO
ABC IMPULSE!

Number	Title	Yr	VG	VG+	NM
❏ AS-9213 [(2)]	His Great Hits	1971	5.00	10.00	20.00
COLUMBIA					
❏ CL 1590 [M]	Selections from "Bye Bye Birdie"	1961	5.00	10.00	20.00
❏ CL 1619 [M]	Chico Hamilton Special	1961	5.00	10.00	20.00
❏ CL 1807 [M]	Drumfusion	1962	5.00	10.00	20.00
❏ CS 8390 [S]	Selections from "Bye Bye Birdie"	1961	6.25	12.50	25.00
❏ CS 8419 [S]	Chico Hamilton Special	1961	6.25	12.50	25.00
❏ CS 8607 [S]	Drumfusion	1962	6.25	12.50	25.00

Number	Title	Yr	VG	VG+	NM
DECCA					
❑ DL 8614 [M]	Jazz from the Sweet Smell of Success	1957	12.50	25.00	50.00
IMPULSE!					
❑ A-29 [M]	Passin' Thru	1963	6.25	12.50	25.00
❑ AS-29 [S]	Passin' Thru	1963	7.50	15.00	30.00
❑ A-59 [M]	Man from Two Worlds	1964	6.25	12.50	25.00
❑ AS-59 [S]	Man from Two Worlds	1964	7.50	15.00	30.00
❑ A-82 [M]	Chi Chi Chico	1965	5.00	10.00	20.00
❑ AS-82 [S]	Chi Chi Chico	1965	6.25	12.50	25.00
❑ A-9102 [M]	El Chico	1965	5.00	10.00	20.00
❑ AS-9102 [S]	El Chico	1965	6.25	12.50	25.00
❑ A-9114 [M]	The Further Adventures of El Chico	1966	5.00	10.00	20.00
❑ AS-9114 [S]	The Further Adventures of El Chico	1966	6.25	12.50	25.00
❑ A-9130 [M]	The Dealer	1966	5.00	10.00	20.00
❑ AS-9130 [S]	The Dealer	1966	6.25	12.50	25.00
NAUTILUS					
❑ NR-13	Reaching for the Top	1981	7.50	15.00	30.00
-- Audiophile vinyl					
PACIFIC JAZZ					
❑ PJLP-17 [10]	Chico Hamilton Trio	1955	25.00	50.00	100.00
❑ PJ-39 [M]	Spectacular	1962	6.25	12.50	25.00
-- Reissue of 1209					
❑ PJ-1209 [M]	Chico Hamilton Quintet	1955	18.75	37.50	75.00
❑ PJ-1216 [M]	Chico Hamilton Quintet In Hi-Fi	1956	18.75	37.50	75.00
❑ PJ-1220 [M]	Chico Hamilton Trio	1956	18.75	37.50	75.00
❑ PJ-1225 [M]	Chico Hamilton Quintet	1957	18.75	37.50	75.00
❑ PJ-1231 [M]	Chico Hamilton Plays the Music of Fred Katz	1957	18.75	37.50	75.00
REPRISE					
❑ R-6078 [M]	A Different Journey	1963	7.50	15.00	30.00
❑ R9-6078 [S]	A Different Journey	1963	10.00	20.00	40.00
WARNER BROS.					
❑ W 1245 [M]	Chico Hamilton Quintet with Strings Attached	1958	12.50	25.00	50.00
❑ WS 1245 [S]	Chico Hamilton Quintet with Strings Attached	1958	15.00	30.00	60.00
❑ W 1271 [M]	Gongs East	1958	12.50	25.00	50.00
❑ WS 1271 [S]	Gongs East	1958	15.00	30.00	60.00
❑ W 1344 [M]	The Three Faces of Chico	1959	12.50	25.00	50.00
❑ WS 1344 [S]	The Three Faces of Chico	1959	15.00	30.00	60.00
WORLD PACIFIC					
❑ ST-1003 [S]	South Pacific in Hi-Fi	1958	10.00	20.00	40.00
❑ ST-1005 [S]	Chico Hamilton Quintet	1958	10.00	20.00	40.00
❑ ST-1008 [S]	The Chico Hamilton Trio Featuring Freddie Gambrell	1958	10.00	20.00	40.00
❑ ST-1016 [S]	Ellington Suite	1959	10.00	20.00	40.00
❑ WP-1216 [M]	Chico Hamilton Quintet In Hi-Fi	1958	12.50	25.00	50.00
❑ WP-1225 [M]	Chico Hamilton Quintet	1958	12.50	25.00	50.00
❑ WP-1231 [M]	Chico Hamilton Plays the Music of Fred Katz	1958	12.50	25.00	50.00
❑ PJ-1238 [M]	South Pacific in Hi-Fi	1957	12.50	25.00	50.00
❑ WP-1238 [M]	South Pacific in Hi-Fi	1958	10.00	20.00	40.00
❑ PJ-1242 [M]	The Chico Hamilton Trio Featuring Freddie Gambrell	1957	12.50	25.00	50.00
❑ WP-1242 [M]	The Chico Hamilton Trio Featuring Freddie Gambrell	1958	10.00	20.00	40.00
❑ WP-1258 [M]	Ellington Suite	1959	12.50	25.00	50.00
❑ WP-1287 [M]	The Original Hamilton Quintet	1960	12.50	25.00	50.00

HAMILTON, GEORGE
ABC-PARAMOUNT

Number	Title	Yr	VG	VG+	NM
❑ 535 [M]	By George	1966	5.00	10.00	20.00
❑ S-535 [S]	By George	1966	6.25	12.50	25.00

HAMILTON, GEORGE, IV
ABC-PARAMOUNT

Number	Title	Yr	VG	VG+	NM
❑ 220 [M]	On Campus	1958	10.00	20.00	40.00
❑ S-220 [S]	On Campus	1958	12.50	25.00	50.00
❑ 251 [M]	Sing Me a Sad Song (A Tribute to Hank Williams)	1958	10.00	20.00	40.00
❑ S-251 [S]	Sing Me a Sad Song (A Tribute to Hank Williams)	1958	12.50	25.00	50.00
❑ 461 [M]	George Hamilton IV's Big 15	1963	7.50	15.00	30.00
❑ S-461 [P]	George Hamilton IV's Big 15	1963	10.00	20.00	40.00
RCA VICTOR					
❑ LPM-2373 [M]	To You and Yours from Me and Mine	1961	6.25	12.50	25.00
❑ LSP-2373 [S]	To You and Yours from Me and Mine	1961	7.50	15.00	30.00
❑ LPM-2778 [M]	Abilene	1963	6.25	12.50	25.00
❑ LSP-2778 [S]	Abilene	1963	7.50	15.00	30.00
❑ LPM-2972 [M]	Fort Worth, Dallas or Houston	1964	6.25	12.50	25.00
❑ LSP-2972 [S]	Fort Worth, Dallas or Houston	1964	7.50	15.00	30.00

Number	Title	Yr	VG	VG+	NM
❑ LPM-3371 [M]	Mister Sincerity... A Tribute to Ernest Tubb	1965	6.25	12.50	25.00
❑ LSP-3371 [S]	Mister Sincerity... A Tribute to Ernest Tubb	1965	7.50	15.00	30.00
❑ LPM-3510 [M]	Coast Country	1966	6.25	12.50	25.00
❑ LSP-3510 [S]	Coast Country	1966	7.50	15.00	30.00
❑ LPM-3601 [M]	Steel Rail Blues	1966	5.00	10.00	20.00
❑ LSP-3601 [S]	Steel Rail Blues	1966	5.00	10.00	20.00
❑ LPM-3752 [M]	Folk Country Classics	1967	6.25	12.50	25.00
❑ LSP-3752 [S]	Folk Country Classics	1967	5.00	10.00	20.00
❑ LPM-3854 [M]	Folksy	1967	6.25	12.50	25.00
❑ LSP-3854 [S]	Folksy	1967	5.00	10.00	20.00
❑ LPM-3962 [M]	The Gentle Country Sound of George Hamilton IV	1968	10.00	20.00	40.00
❑ LSP-3962 [S]	The Gentle Country Sound of George Hamilton IV	1968	5.00	10.00	20.00
❑ LSP-4066	In the 4th Dimension	1968	5.00	10.00	20.00

HAMILTON, ROY
EPIC

Number	Title	Yr	VG	VG+	NM
❑ BN 518 [S]	With All My Love	1958	10.00	20.00	40.00
❑ BN 525 [S]	Why Fight The Feeling?	1959	7.50	15.00	30.00
❑ BN 530 [S]	Come Out Swingin'	1959	7.50	15.00	30.00
❑ BN 535 [S]	Have Blues, Must Travel	1959	7.50	15.00	30.00
❑ BN 551 [S]	Spirituals	1960	7.50	15.00	30.00
❑ BN 578 [S]	Soft 'n Warm	1960	7.50	15.00	30.00
❑ BN 595 [S]	You Can Have Her	1961	10.00	20.00	40.00
❑ BN 610 [S]	Only You	1961	7.50	15.00	30.00
❑ BN 632 [R]	You'll Never Walk Alone	1962	5.00	10.00	20.00
❑ LN 1023 [10]	You'll Never Walk Alone	1954	50.00	100.00	200.00
❑ LN 1103 [10]	The Voice of Roy Hamilton	1954	50.00	100.00	200.00
❑ LN 3176 [M]	Roy Hamilton	1955	15.00	30.00	60.00
❑ LN 3294 [M]	You'll Never Walk Alone	1956	17.50	35.00	70.00
❑ LN 3364 [M]	Golden Boy	1957	12.50	25.00	50.00
❑ LN 3519 [M]	With All My Love	1958	7.50	15.00	30.00
❑ LN 3545 [M]	Why Fight The Feeling?	1959	6.25	12.50	25.00
❑ LN 3561 [M]	Come Out Swingin'	1959	6.25	12.50	25.00
❑ LN 3580 [M]	Have Blues, Must Travel	1959	6.25	12.50	25.00
❑ LN 3628 [M]	Roy Hamilton At His Best	1960	10.00	20.00	40.00
❑ LN 3654 [M]	Spirituals	1960	6.25	12.50	25.00
❑ LN 3717 [M]	Soft 'n Warm	1960	6.25	12.50	25.00
❑ LN 3775 [M]	You Can Have Her	1961	7.50	15.00	30.00
❑ LN 3807 [M]	Only You	1961	6.25	12.50	25.00
❑ LN 24000 [M]	Mr. Rock and Soul	1962	6.25	12.50	25.00
❑ LN 24009 [M]	Roy Hamilton's Greatest Hits	1962	5.00	10.00	20.00
❑ LN 24316 [M]	Roy Hamilton's Greatest Hits, Vol. 2	1967	5.00	10.00	20.00
❑ BN 26000 [S]	Mr. Rock and Soul	1962	7.50	15.00	30.00
❑ BN 26009 [S]	Roy Hamilton's Greatest Hits	1962	6.25	12.50	25.00
❑ BN 26316 [S]	Roy Hamilton's Greatest Hits, Vol. 2	1967	6.25	12.50	25.00
MGM					
❑ SE-4139 [S]	Warm and Soul	1963	5.00	10.00	20.00
❑ SE-4233 [S]	Sentimental, Lonely & Blue	1964	5.00	10.00	20.00
RCA VICTOR					
❑ LSP-3552 [S]	The Impossible Dream	1966	5.00	10.00	20.00

HAMILTON, RUSS
KAPP

Number	Title	Yr	VG	VG+	NM
❑ KL-1076 [M]	Rainbow	1957	20.00	40.00	80.00

HAMMER
SAN FRANCISCO

Number	Title	Yr	VG	VG+	NM
❑ SD 203	Hammer	1970	5.00	10.00	20.00

HAMMER, JACK
WARWICK

Number	Title	Yr	VG	VG+	NM
❑ W-2014 [M]	Rebellion: Jack Hammer Sings and Reads Songs and Poems of the Beat Generation	1960	20.00	40.00	80.00

HAMMOND, JOHN
ATLANTIC

Number	Title	Yr	VG	VG+	NM
❑ 8152 [M]	I Can Tell	1967	7.50	15.00	30.00
❑ SD 8152 [S]	I Can Tell	1967	7.50	15.00	30.00
VANGUARD					
❑ VSD-2148 [S]	John Hammond	1964	10.00	20.00	40.00
❑ VRS-9132 [M]	John Hammond	1964	7.50	15.00	30.00
❑ VRS-9153 [M]	Big City Blues	1964	7.50	15.00	30.00
❑ VRS-9178 [M]	So Many Roads	1965	7.50	15.00	30.00
❑ VRS-9198 [M]	Country Blues	1966	7.50	15.00	30.00
❑ VRS-9245 [M]	Mirrors	1967	7.50	15.00	30.00
❑ VSD-79153 [S]	Big City Blues	1964	10.00	20.00	40.00
❑ VSD-79178 [S]	So Many Roads	1965	10.00	20.00	40.00
❑ VSD-79198 [S]	Country Blues	1966	10.00	20.00	40.00
❑ VSD-79245 [S]	Mirrors	1967	7.50	15.00	30.00

Number	Title	Yr	VG	VG+	NM

HAMMOND, JOHNNY
NEW JAZZ
Number	Title	Yr	VG	VG+	NM
❑ NJLP-8221 [M] All Soul		1959	12.50	25.00	50.00
-- Purple label					
❑ NJLP-8221 [M] All Soul		1965	6.25	12.50	25.00
-- Blue label with trident logo					
❑ NJLP-8229 [M] That Good Feelin'		1959	12.50	25.00	50.00
-- Purple label					
❑ NJLP-8229 [M] That Good Feelin'		1965	6.25	12.50	25.00
-- Blue label with trident logo					
❑ NJLP-8241 [M] Talk That Talk		1960	12.50	25.00	50.00
-- Purple label					
❑ NJLP-8241 [M] Talk That Talk		1965	6.25	12.50	25.00
-- Blue label with trident logo					
❑ NJLP-8288 [M] Look Out!		1962	12.50	25.00	50.00
-- Purple label					
❑ NJLP-8288 [M] Look Out!		1965	6.25	12.50	25.00
-- Blue label with trident logo					

PRESTIGE
Number	Title	Yr	VG	VG+	NM
❑ PRLP-7203 [M] Stimulation		1961	10.00	20.00	40.00
-- Yellow label					
❑ PRLP-7203 [M] Stimulation		1965	6.25	12.50	25.00
-- Blue label with trident logo					
❑ PRLP-7217 [M] Gettin' the Message		1961	10.00	20.00	40.00
-- Yellow label					
❑ PRLP-7217 [M] Gettin' the Message		1965	6.25	12.50	25.00
-- Blue label with trident logo					
❑ PRLP-7408 [M] The Stinger		1965	5.00	10.00	20.00
❑ PRST-7408 [S] The Stinger		1965	6.25	12.50	25.00
❑ PRLP-7420 [M] Opus de Funk		1966	5.00	10.00	20.00
❑ PRST-7420 [S] Opus de Funk		1966	6.25	12.50	25.00
❑ PRLP-7464 [M] The Stinger Meets the Golden Thrush		1966	5.00	10.00	20.00
❑ PRST-7464 [S] The Stinger Meets the Golden Thrush		1966	6.25	12.50	25.00
❑ PRLP-7482 [M] Love Potion #9		1967	6.25	12.50	25.00
❑ PRST-7482 [S] Love Potion #9		1967	5.00	10.00	20.00
❑ PRLP-7494 [M] Ebb Tide		1967	6.25	12.50	25.00
❑ PRST-7494 [S] Ebb Tide		1967	5.00	10.00	20.00
❑ PRST-7549 Soul Flowers		1968	5.00	10.00	20.00
❑ PRST-7564 Dirty Grape		1968	5.00	10.00	20.00
❑ PRST-7588 Nasty		1968	5.00	10.00	20.00
❑ PRST-7681 Soul Talk		1969	5.00	10.00	20.00

RIVERSIDE
Number	Title	Yr	VG	VG+	NM
❑ RLP-442 [M] Black Coffee		1963	6.25	12.50	25.00
❑ RLP-466 [M] Mr. Wonderful		1963	6.25	12.50	25.00
❑ RLP-482 [M] Open House!		1965	5.00	10.00	20.00
❑ RLP-496 [M] A Little Taste		1965	5.00	10.00	20.00
❑ RS-9442 [S] Black Coffee		1963	7.50	15.00	30.00
❑ RS-9466 [S] Mr. Wonderful		1963	7.50	15.00	30.00
❑ RS-9482 [S] Open House!		1965	6.25	12.50	25.00
❑ RS-9496 [S] A Little Taste		1965	6.25	12.50	25.00

HANCOCK, HERBIE
BLUE NOTE
Number	Title	Yr	VG	VG+	NM
❑ BLP-4109 [M] Takin' Off		1962	12.50	25.00	50.00
❑ BLP-4126 [M] My Point of View		1963	8.75	17.50	35.00
❑ BLP-4147 [M] Inventions and Dimensions		1963	8.75	17.50	35.00
❑ BLP-4175 [M] Empyrean Isles		1964	8.75	17.50	35.00
❑ BLP-4195 [M] Maiden Voyage		1965	8.75	17.50	35.00
❑ B1-46339 Maiden Voyage		1997	5.00	10.00	20.00
-- Audiophile reissue					
❑ BST-84109 [S] Takin' Off		1962	10.00	20.00	40.00
-- With New York, USA address on label					
❑ BST-84126 [S] My Point of View		1963	8.75	17.50	35.00
-- With New York, USA address on label					
❑ BST-84147 [S] Inventions and Dimensions		1963	8.75	17.50	35.00
-- With New York, USA address on label					
❑ BST-84175 [S] Empyrean Isles		1964	8.75	17.50	35.00
-- With New York, USA address on label					
❑ BST-84195 [S] Maiden Voyage		1965	8.75	17.50	35.00
-- With New York, USA address on label					

COLUMBIA
Number	Title	Yr	VG	VG+	NM
❑ CQ 32371 [Q] Head Hunters		1973	6.25	12.50	25.00
❑ PCQ 32965 [Q] Thrust		1974	6.25	12.50	25.00
❑ PCQ 34280 [Q] Secrets		1976	6.25	12.50	25.00

MGM
Number	Title	Yr	VG	VG+	NM
❑ E-4447 [M] Blow-Up		1967	8.75	17.50	35.00
❑ SE-4447 [S] Blow-Up		1967	10.00	20.00	40.00
-- Also includes one track by the Yardbirds					

HANDY, JOHN
ROULETTE
Number	Title	Yr	VG	VG+	NM
❑ R 52042 [M] In the Ver-nac'-u-lar		1960	5.00	10.00	20.00
❑ SR 52042 [S] In the Ver-nac'-u-lar		1960	6.25	12.50	25.00
❑ R 52088 [M] No Coast Jazz		1962	5.00	10.00	20.00
❑ SR 52088 [S] No Coast Jazz		1962	6.25	12.50	25.00
❑ SR 52121 [S] John Handy Jazz		1964	5.00	10.00	20.00
❑ SR 52124 [S] Quote, Unquote		1964	5.00	10.00	20.00

HANGMEN, THE
MONUMENT
Number	Title	Yr	VG	VG+	NM
❑ MLP-8077 [M] Bitter Sweet		1967	7.50	15.00	30.00
❑ SLP-18077 [S] Bitter Sweet		1967	10.00	20.00	40.00

HANKINS, ESCO
AUDIO LAB
Number	Title	Yr	VG	VG+	NM
❑ AL-1547 [M] Country Style		1961	50.00	100.00	200.00

HAPPENINGS, THE
Also see THE TOKENS & THE HAPPENINGS.
B.T. PUPPY
Number	Title	Yr	VG	VG+	NM
❑ BT-1001 [M] The Happenings (Bye-Bye, So Long, Farewell...See You in September)		1966	6.25	12.50	25.00
❑ BTS-1001 [S] The Happenings (Bye-Bye, So Long, Farewell...See You in September)		1966	7.50	15.00	30.00
❑ BT-1003 [M] Psycle		1967	6.25	12.50	25.00
❑ BTS-1003 [S] Psycle		1967	7.50	15.00	30.00
❑ BTS-1004 The Happenings Golden Hits!		1968	10.00	20.00	40.00

JUBILEE
Number	Title	Yr	VG	VG+	NM
❑ JGS-8028 Piece of Mind		1969	6.25	12.50	25.00
❑ JGS-8030 The Happenings' Greatest Hits		1969	6.25	12.50	25.00

HAPPY CHIPMUNKS, THE
HOLIDAY
Number	Title	Yr	VG	VG+	NM
❑ HDY-1950 Merry Christmas from the Happy Chipmunks		1982	6.25	12.50	25.00
-- Record quickly pulled from market because of unauthorized use of the name "Chipmunks"					

HAPPY DRAGON BAND, THE
FIDDLER'S MUSIC
Number	Title	Yr	VG	VG+	NM
❑ 1157 The Happy Dragon Band		1977	20.00	40.00	80.00

HAPSHASH AND THE COLOURED COAT
IMPERIAL
Number	Title	Yr	VG	VG+	NM
❑ LP-9377 [M] Hapshash and the Coloured Coat		1968	12.50	25.00	50.00
❑ LP-12377 [S] Hapshash and the Coloured Coat		1968	10.00	20.00	40.00
❑ LP-12430 Western Flyer		1969	10.00	20.00	40.00

HARD TIMES, THE
WORLD PACIFIC
Number	Title	Yr	VG	VG+	NM
❑ WP-1867 [M] Blew Mind		1968	6.25	12.50	25.00
❑ WPS-21867 [S] Blew Mind		1968	7.50	15.00	30.00

HARDEN TRIO, THE
COLUMBIA
Number	Title	Yr	VG	VG+	NM
❑ CL 2506 [M] Tippy Toeing		1966	5.00	10.00	20.00
❑ CS 9306 [S] Tippy Toeing		1966	6.25	12.50	25.00

HARDEN, ARLENE
COLUMBIA
Number	Title	Yr	VG	VG+	NM
❑ CL 2833 [M] Sing Me Back Home		1967	7.50	15.00	30.00
❑ CS 9633 [S] Sing Me Back Home		1967	5.00	10.00	20.00
❑ CS 9674 What Can I Say		1968	5.00	10.00	20.00

HARDIN, TIM
ATCO
Number	Title	Yr	VG	VG+	NM
❑ 33-210 [M] This Is Tim Hardin		1967	6.25	12.50	25.00
❑ SD 33-210 [S] This Is Tim Hardin		1967	5.00	10.00	20.00

COLUMBIA
Number	Title	Yr	VG	VG+	NM
❑ CS 9787 Suite for Susan Moore and Damion -- We Are -- One, One, All in One		1969	6.25	12.50	25.00
-- "360 Sound" label					
❑ C 30551 Bird on a Wire		1971	5.00	10.00	20.00
❑ KC 31764 Painted Head		1972	5.00	10.00	20.00

MGM
Number	Title	Yr	VG	VG+	NM
❑ GAS-104 Tim Hardin (Golden Archive Series)		1970	5.00	10.00	20.00

VERVE FOLKWAYS
Number	Title	Yr	VG	VG+	NM
❑ FT-3004 [M] Tim Hardin/1		1966	6.25	12.50	25.00
❑ FTS-3004 [S] Tim Hardin/1		1966	7.50	15.00	30.00

VERVE FORECAST
Number	Title	Yr	VG	VG+	NM
❑ FTS-3004 [S] Tim Hardin/1		1967	5.00	10.00	20.00
❑ FTS-3022 Tim Hardin/2		1967	6.25	12.50	25.00
❑ FTS-3049 Tim Hardin/3 -- Live in Concert		1968	6.25	12.50	25.00
❑ FTS-3064 Tim Hardin/4		1969	6.25	12.50	25.00
❑ FTS-3078 The Best of Tim Hardin		1970	5.00	10.00	20.00

Number	Title	Yr	VG	VG+	NM

HARDWATER
CAPITOL
| ❑ ST-2954 | Hardwater | 1968 | 10.00 | 20.00 | 40.00 |

HARDY BOYS, THE
RCA VICTOR
| ❑ LSP-4217 | Here Come the Hardy Boys | 1969 | 5.00 | 10.00 | 20.00 |
| ❑ LSP-4315 | Wheels | 1970 | 5.00 | 10.00 | 20.00 |

HARDY, FRANCOISE
4 CORNERS OF THE WORLD
❑ FCL-4208 [M]	The "Yeh Yeh" Girl from Paris!	196?	5.00	10.00	20.00
❑ FCS-4208 [S]	The "Yeh Yeh" Girl from Paris!	196?	6.25	12.50	25.00
❑ FCL-4219 [M]	Maid in Paris	196?	5.00	10.00	20.00
❑ FCS-4219 [S]	Maid in Paris	196?	6.25	12.50	25.00
❑ FCL-4231 [M]	Francoise…	196?	5.00	10.00	20.00
❑ FCS-4231 [S]	Francoise…	196?	6.25	12.50	25.00
❑ FCL-4238 [M]	Je Vous Aime	196?	5.00	10.00	20.00
❑ FCS-4238 [S]	Je Vous Aime	196?	6.25	12.50	25.00
REPRISE
❑ RS 6290	Francoise Hardy	1968	6.25	12.50	25.00
❑ RS 6318	Loving	1969	5.00	10.00	20.00
❑ RS 6345	Mon Amour, Adieu	1969	5.00	10.00	20.00

HARMONAIRES MALE QUINTET, THE
VARSITY
| ❑ 6915 [10] | Spirituals | 195? | 20.00 | 40.00 | 80.00 |

HARMONY BLAZERS, THE
HARMONY
❑ HL 7103 [M]	Ten Big Hits	1959	10.00	20.00	40.00
❑ HL 7126 [M]	Rock & Roll Vol. II	1959	10.00	20.00	40.00
❑ HL 7200 [M]	The Big Ten	1959	10.00	20.00	40.00

HARNELL, JOE
EPIC
| ❑ BN 573 [S] | I Want to Be Happy | 1960 | 5.00 | 10.00 | 20.00 |
KAPP
❑ KS 3318 [S]	Fly Me to the Moon and the Bossa Nova Pops	1962	5.00	10.00	20.00
❑ KS 3325 [S]	More Joe Harnell, More Bossa Nova Pops	1963	5.00	10.00	20.00
❑ KS 3339 [S]	Joe Harnell	1963	5.00	10.00	20.00
MOTOWN
❑ MS-698	Moving On!!	1969	10.00	20.00	40.00

HARPER, JANICE
CAPITOL
| ❑ ST 1337 [S] | Embers of Love | 1960 | 6.25 | 12.50 | 25.00 |
| ❑ T 1337 [M] | Embers of Love | 1960 | 5.00 | 10.00 | 20.00 |

HARPER, ROY
CHRYSALIS
| ❑ PRO-620 [DJ] | Introduction to Roy Harper | 1976 | 7.50 | 15.00 | 30.00 |
HARVEST
| ❑ SKAO-418 | Flat Baroque and Berserk | 1970 | 5.00 | 10.00 | 20.00 |
WORLD PACIFIC
| ❑ WPS-21888 | Folkjokeopus | 1969 | 6.25 | 12.50 | 25.00 |

HARPERS BIZARRE
WARNER BROS.
❑ W 1693 [M]	Feelin' Groovy	1967	6.25	12.50	25.00
❑ WS 1693 [S]	Feelin' Groovy	1967	5.00	10.00	20.00
-- Gold label					
❑ WS 1716	Anything Goes	1967	5.00	10.00	20.00
❑ WS 1739	The Secret Life of Harpers Bizarre	1968	5.00	10.00	20.00
❑ WS 1784	Harpers Bizarre Four	1969	5.00	10.00	20.00
❑ ST-91351	Anything Goes	1968	6.25	12.50	25.00
-- Capitol Record Club edition					

HARPO, SLIM
EXCELLO
❑ LP-8003 [M]	Raining in My Heart	1961	62.50	125.00	250.00
-- Orange and blue label					
❑ LPS-8003 [M]	Raining in My Heart	196?	25.00	50.00	100.00
-- All-blue label					
❑ LP-8005 [M]	Baby Scratch My Back	1966	50.00	100.00	200.00
-- Orange and blue label					
❑ LPS-8005 [M]	Baby Scratch My Back	196?	25.00	50.00	100.00
-- All-blue label					
❑ LPS-8008 [M]	Tip On In	1968	12.50	25.00	50.00

Number	Title	Yr	VG	VG+	NM
❑ LPS-8010 [M]	The Best of Slim Harpo	1969	12.50	25.00	50.00
❑ LPS-8013 [M]	Slim Harpo Knew the Blues	1970	12.50	25.00	50.00

HARRIS, DAVE
DECCA
| ❑ DL 4113 [M] | Dinner Music for a Pack of Hungry Cannibals | 1961 | 5.00 | 10.00 | 20.00 |
| ❑ DL 74113 [S] | Dinner Music for a Pack of Hungry Cannibals | 1961 | 6.25 | 12.50 | 25.00 |

HARRIS, EDDIE
COLUMBIA
❑ CS 8968 [S]	Cool Sax, Warm Heart	1964	5.00	10.00	20.00
❑ CS 9095 [S]	Cool Sax from Hollywood to Broadway	1965	5.00	10.00	20.00
❑ CS 9681 [M]	Here Comes the Judge	1968	6.25	12.50	25.00
-- Mono copies are promo only					
VEE JAY
❑ VJLPS 1081 [S]	The Theme from Exodus and Other Film Spectaculars	1964	5.00	10.00	20.00
❑ LP 3016 [M]	Exodus to Jazz	1961	7.50	15.00	30.00
❑ LPS 3016 [S]	Exodus to Jazz	1961	10.00	20.00	40.00
❑ LP 3025 [M]	Mighty Like a Rose	1961	7.50	15.00	30.00
❑ LPS 3025 [S]	Mighty Like a Rose	1961	10.00	20.00	40.00
❑ LP 3027 [M]	Jazz for "Breakfast at Tiffany's"	1961	7.50	15.00	30.00
❑ LPS 3027 [S]	Jazz for "Breakfast at Tiffany's"	1961	10.00	20.00	40.00
❑ LP 3028 [M]	A Study in Jazz	1962	5.00	10.00	20.00
❑ LPS 3028 [S]	A Study in Jazz	1962	7.50	15.00	30.00
❑ LP 3031 [M]	Eddie Harris Goes to the Movies	1962	5.00	10.00	20.00
❑ LPS 3031 [S]	Eddie Harris Goes to the Movies	1962	7.50	15.00	30.00
❑ LP 3034 [M]	Bossa Nova	1963	5.00	10.00	20.00
❑ LPS 3034 [S]	Bossa Nova	1963	7.50	15.00	30.00

HARRIS, EMMYLOU
JUBILEE
| ❑ JGS-8031 | Gliding Bird | 1969 | 30.00 | 60.00 | 120.00 |
| -- Originals have color covers; counterfeit covers are black and white | | | | | |
MOBILE FIDELITY
| ❑ 1-015 | Quarter Moon in a Ten Cent Town | 1979 | 10.00 | 20.00 | 40.00 |
| -- Audiophile vinyl | | | | | |

HARRIS, PEPPERMINT
TIME
| ❑ 5 [M] | Peppermint Harris | 1962 | 50.00 | 100.00 | 200.00 |

HARRIS, PHIL
RCA VICTOR
| ❑ LPM-1985 [M] | The South Shall Rise Again | 1959 | 6.25 | 12.50 | 25.00 |
| ❑ LPM-3037 [10] | Phil Harris On the Record | 1952 | 10.00 | 20.00 | 40.00 |

HARRIS, RICHARD
ATLANTIC
| ❑ QD 18120 [Q] | The Prophet by Kahlil Gibran | 1974 | 5.00 | 10.00 | 20.00 |
| -- Spoken-word recording | | | | | |

HARRIS, ROLF
EPIC
❑ LN 24053 [M]	Tie Me Kangaroo Down, Sport & Sun Arise	1963	5.00	10.00	20.00
❑ LN 24110 [M]	Join Rolf Harris Singing The Count of King Caractacus (And Other Fun Songs)	1964	5.00	10.00	20.00
❑ BN 26053 [S]	Tie Me Kangaroo Down, Sport & Sun Arise	1963	6.25	12.50	25.00
❑ BN 26110 [S]	Join Rolf Harris Singing The Count of King Caractacus (And Other Fun Songs)	1964	6.25	12.50	25.00

HARRIS, SHAUN
Also see THE WEST COAST POP ART EXPERIMENTAL BAND.
CAPITOL
| ❑ ST-11168 | Shaun Harris | 1973 | 7.50 | 15.00 | 30.00 |

HARRIS, WYNONIE
KING
| ❑ KS-1086 | Good Rockin' Blues | 1970 | 6.25 | 12.50 | 25.00 |

HARRISON, GEORGE
Also see THE BEATLES; TRAVELING WILBURYS.
APPLE
| ❑ STCH-639 [(3)] | All Things Must Pass | 1970 | 10.00 | 20.00 | 40.00 |
| -- Apple labels on first two records and "Apple Jam" labels on third; includes poster and lyric innersleeves | | | | | |

Number	Title	Yr	VG	VG+	NM
❏ ST-3350	Wonderwall Music	1968	37.50	75.00	150.00
-- With Capitol logo on Side 2 bottom					
❏ ST-3350	Wonderwall Music	1968	6.25	12.50	25.00
-- With "Mfd. by Apple" on label					
❏ ST-3350	Wonderwall Music Bonus Photo	1968	---	2.50	5.00
CAPITOL					
❏ STCH-639 [(3)] All Things Must Pass		1976	7.50	15.00	30.00
-- Orange labels with poster and lyric innersleeves					
❏ STCH-639 [(3)] All Things Must Pass		1978	6.25	12.50	25.00
-- Purple labels with poster and lyric innersleeves					
❏ STCH-639 [(3)] All Things Must Pass		1983	25.00	50.00	100.00
-- Black labels, print in colorband, with poster and lyric innersleeves					
❏ ST-11578	The Best of George Harrison	1976	45.00	90.00	180.00
-- Orange label					
❏ ST-11578	The Best of George Harrison	1983	6.25	12.50	25.00
-- Black label, print in colorband					
❏ ST-11578	The Best of George Harrison	1988	6.25	12.50	25.00
-- Odd reissue with custom label; large stand-alone "S" in trail-off area; bar code on cover					
❏ ST-11578	The Best of George Harrison	1989	20.00	40.00	80.00
-- Purple label, small Capitol logo					
❏ SN-16216	Living in the Material World	1980	5.00	10.00	20.00
-- Budget-line reissue					
❏ SN-16217	Extra Texture (Read All About It)	1980	6.25	12.50	25.00
-- Budget-line reissue					
CAPITOL/APPLE					
❏ STCH-639 [(3)] All Things Must Pass		1988	20.00	40.00	80.00
-- Odd pressing with Apple labels and Capitol cover (look for stand-alone "S" in trail-off wax); with large sticker on back cover					
DARK HORSE					
❏ (no #) [DJ]	Dark Horse Radio Special	1974	100.00	200.00	400.00
-- Promo-only; George Harrison introduces his new record label and artists					
❏ PRO 649 [DJ]	A Personal Music Dialogue at Thirty Three and 1/3	1976	12.50	25.00	50.00
❏ DHK 3255	George Harrison	1979	10.00	20.00	40.00
-- Columbia House edition (back cover says "Manufactured by Columbia House Under License")					
❏ 23724 [DJ]	Gone Troppo	1982	6.25	12.50	25.00
-- Promo on Quiex II vinyl					
❏ 25726	Best of Dark Horse 1976-1989	1989	6.25	12.50	25.00
ZAPPLE					
❏ ST-3358	Electronic Sound	1969	10.00	20.00	40.00

HARRISON, GEORGE, AND FRIENDS

Also see BADFINGER; BOB DYLAN; GEORGE HARRISON; LEON RUSSELL; RAVI SHANKAR; RINGO STARR.

Number	Title	Yr	VG	VG+	NM
APPLE					
❏ STCX-3385 [(3)] The Concert for Bangla Desh		1971	10.00	20.00	40.00
-- With 64-page booklet and custom innersleeves					
❏ STCX-3385 [(3)] The Concert for Bangla Desh		1975	12.50	25.00	50.00
-- As above, but with "All Rights Reserved" on labels					
CAPITOL					
❏ SABB-12248 [(2)] The Concert for Bangla Desh		1982	75.00	150.00	300.00
-- Scheduled reissue that was never officially released, though a few copies got out by mistake					

HARRISON, NOEL

Number	Title	Yr	VG	VG+	NM
LONDON					
❏ PS 459 [S]	Noel Harrison	1966	6.25	12.50	25.00
❏ LL 3459 [M]	Noel Harrison	1966	5.00	10.00	20.00
REPRISE					
❏ RS-6263 [S]	Collage	1967	5.00	10.00	20.00

HARRISON, WES

Number	Title	Yr	VG	VG+	NM
PHILIPS					
❏ PHM 200-103 [M] You Won't Believe Your Ears		1963	5.00	10.00	20.00
❏ PHS 600-103 [S] You Won't Believe Your Ears		1963	6.25	12.50	25.00

HARRISON, WILBERT

Number	Title	Yr	VG	VG+	NM
BUDDAH					
❏ BDS-5002	Wilbert Harrison	1971	7.50	15.00	30.00
CHELSEA					
❏ CH 523	Wilbert Harrison	1977	5.00	10.00	20.00
JUGGERNAUT					
❏ ST-8803	Shoot You Full of Love	1971	12.50	25.00	50.00
SPHERE SOUND					
❏ SSR-7000 [M]	Kansas City	1965	62.50	125.00	250.00
❏ SSSR-7000 [R]	Kansas City	1965	50.00	100.00	200.00
SUE					
❏ SSLP-8801	Let's Work Together	1970	12.50	25.00	50.00
WET SOUL					
❏ 1001	Anything You Want	197?	12.50	25.00	50.00

HART, FREDDIE

Number	Title	Yr	VG	VG+	NM
COLUMBIA					
❏ CL 1792 [M]	The Spirited Freddie Hart	1962	10.00	20.00	40.00
KAPP					
❏ KL-1513 [M]	Hurtin' Man	1967	5.00	10.00	20.00
❏ KL-1539 [M]	The Neon and the Rain	1967	5.00	10.00	20.00
❏ KS-3456 [S]	The Hart of Country Music	1966	5.00	10.00	20.00
❏ KS-3492 [S]	Straight from the Heart	1966	5.00	10.00	20.00
❏ KS-3513 [S]	Hurtin' Man	1967	5.00	10.00	20.00
❏ KS-3539 [S]	The Neon and the Rain	1967	5.00	10.00	20.00
❏ KS-3546	Togetherness	1968	5.00	10.00	20.00
❏ KS-3568	Born a Fool	1968	5.00	10.00	20.00

HART, MICKEY

Also see THE GRATEFUL DEAD.

Number	Title	Yr	VG	VG+	NM
WARNER BROS.					
❏ BS 2635	Rolling Thunder	1972	7.50	15.00	30.00

HARTFORD, JOHN

Number	Title	Yr	VG	VG+	NM
RCA VICTOR					
❏ LPM-3687 [M]	John Hartford Looks at Life	1966	5.00	10.00	20.00
❏ LPM-3796 [M]	Earthwords and Music	1967	6.25	12.50	25.00
❏ LPM-3884 [M]	The Love Album	1967	6.25	12.50	25.00

HARTMAN, LISA

Number	Title	Yr	VG	VG+	NM
KIRSHNER					
❏ PZ 34109	Lisa Hartman	1976	10.00	20.00	40.00
❏ JZ 35609	Hold On	1978	5.00	10.00	20.00

HARUMI

Number	Title	Yr	VG	VG+	NM
VERVE FORECAST					
❏ FTS-3030	Harumi	1968	6.25	12.50	25.00

HARVEY, LAURENCE

Number	Title	Yr	VG	VG+	NM
ATLANTIC					
❏ 1367 [M]	This Is My Beloved	1962	10.00	20.00	40.00
❏ SD 1367 [S]	This Is My Beloved	1962	12.50	25.00	50.00

HASKELL, JACK

Number	Title	Yr	VG	VG+	NM
STRAND					
❏ SL-1020 [M]	Jack Haskell Swings for Jack Paar	1961	5.00	10.00	20.00
❏ SLS-1020 [S]	Jack Haskell Swings for Jack Paar	1961	7.50	15.00	30.00

HASKELL, JIMMIE

Number	Title	Yr	VG	VG+	NM
IMPERIAL					
❏ LP-9068 [M]	Countdown	1959	7.50	15.00	30.00
❏ LP-12015 [S]	Countdown	1959	12.50	25.00	50.00

HASKILL, CLARA

Number	Title	Yr	VG	VG+	NM
MERCURY LIVING PRESENCE					
❏ SR 90413 [S]	Mozart: Piano Concertos No. 20 and 23; Rondo in A	196?	7.50	15.00	30.00
-- Maroon label, no "Vendor: Mercury Record Corporation"					
❏ SR 90413 [S]	Mozart: Piano Concertos No. 20 and 23; Rondo in A	196?	10.00	20.00	40.00
-- Maroon label, with "Vendor: Mercury Record Corporation" (second edition is more sought after than the first)					

HASSLES, THE

Also see ATTILA; BILLY JOEL.

Number	Title	Yr	VG	VG+	NM
UNITED ARTISTS					
❏ UAS-6631	The Hassles	1968	6.25	12.50	25.00
❏ UAS-6699	Hour of the Wolf	1969	6.25	12.50	25.00

HAVENS, RICHIE

Number	Title	Yr	VG	VG+	NM
DOUGLAS					
❏ SD-779 [S]	Richie Havens' Record	1966	5.00	10.00	20.00
❏ D-780 [M]	Electric Havens	1966	6.25	12.50	25.00
❏ SD-780 [S]	Electric Havens	1966	5.00	10.00	20.00
MGM					
❏ SE-4700 [(2)]	Richard P. Havens, 1963	1970	5.00	10.00	20.00
-- Reissue of Verve Forecast 3047					
VERVE FOLKWAYS					
❏ FT-3006 [M]	Mixed Bag	1967	6.25	12.50	25.00
❏ FTS-3006 [S]	Mixed Bag	1967	5.00	10.00	20.00
VERVE FORECAST					
❏ FTS-3034	Something Else Again	1968	5.00	10.00	20.00
❏ FTS-3047 [(2)]	Richard P. Havens, 1983	1968	6.25	12.50	25.00

Number	Title	Yr	VG	VG+	NM

HAWKINS, DALE
BELL
| ❏ 6036 | L.A., Memphis and Tyler, Texas | 1969 | 10.00 | 20.00 | 40.00 |

CHESS
| ❏ LP-1429 [M] | Oh! Susie-Q | 1958 | 500.00 | 1,000. | 1,500. |

ROULETTE
| ❏ R 25175 [M] | Let's All Twist at the Miami Beach Peppermint Lounge | 1962 | 50.00 | 100.00 | 200.00 |
| ❏ SR 25175 [S] | Let's All Twist at the Miami Beach Peppermint Lounge | 1962 | 75.00 | 150.00 | 300.00 |

HAWKINS, DOLORES
EPIC
| ❏ LN 1119 [M] | Meet Dolores Hawkins | 1955 | 10.00 | 20.00 | 40.00 |
| ❏ LN 3250 [M] | Dolores | 1957 | 10.00 | 20.00 | 40.00 |

HAWKINS, ERSKINE
CORAL
| ❏ CRL 56051 [10] | After Hours | 1954 | 30.00 | 60.00 | 120.00 |

DECCA
| ❏ DL 4081 [M] | The Hawk Blows at Midnight | 1960 | 7.50 | 15.00 | 30.00 |
| ❏ DL 74081 [S] | The Hawk Blows at Midnight | 1960 | 10.00 | 20.00 | 40.00 |

IMPERIAL
❏ LP-9191 [M]	25 Golden Years of Jazz, Volume 1	1962	6.25	12.50	25.00
❏ LP-9197 [M]	25 Golden Years of Jazz, Volume 2	1962	6.25	12.50	25.00
❏ LP-12191 [S]	25 Golden Years of Jazz, Volume 1	1962	7.50	15.00	30.00
❏ LP-12197 [S]	25 Golden Years of Jazz, Volume 2	1962	7.50	15.00	30.00

RCA VICTOR
| ❏ LPM-2227 [M] | After Hours | 1960 | 10.00 | 20.00 | 40.00 |

HAWKINS, HAWKSHAW
GLADWYNNE
| ❏ G-2006 [M] | Country Western Cavalcade with Hawkshaw Hawkins | 195? | 30.00 | 60.00 | 120.00 |

HARMONY
| ❏ HL 7301 [M] | The Great Hawkshaw Hawkins | 1963 | 5.00 | 10.00 | 20.00 |

KING
❏ 587 [M]	Hawkshaw Hawkins	1958	25.00	50.00	100.00
❏ 592 [M]	Grand Ole Opry Favorites	1958	25.00	50.00	100.00
❏ 599 [M]	Hawkshaw Hawkins	1959	25.00	50.00	100.00
❏ 808 [M]	The All New Hawkshaw Hawkins	1963	20.00	40.00	80.00
❏ KS-808 [S]	The All New Hawkshaw Hawkins	1963	25.00	50.00	100.00
❏ 858 [M]	Taken From Our Vaults, Volume 1	1963	10.00	20.00	40.00
❏ 870 [M]	Taken From Our Vaults, Volume 2	1963	10.00	20.00	40.00
❏ 873 [M]	Taken From Our Vaults, Volume 3	1964	10.00	20.00	40.00

LABREA
| ❏ 8020 [M] | Hawkshaw Hawkins | 195? | 25.00 | 50.00 | 100.00 |

RCA CAMDEN
| ❏ CAL-808 [M] | Hawkshaw Hawkins Sings | 1964 | 5.00 | 10.00 | 20.00 |
| ❏ CAL-931 [M] | The Country Gentleman | 1966 | 5.00 | 10.00 | 20.00 |

HAWKINS, JENNELL
AMAZON
| ❏ 1001 [M] | The Many Moods of Jenny | 1961 | 37.50 | 75.00 | 150.00 |
| ❏ 1002 [M] | Moments to Remember | 1962 | 37.50 | 75.00 | 150.00 |

HAWKINS, RONNIE
ROULETTE
❏ R 25078 [M]	Ronnie Hawkins	1959	37.50	75.00	150.00
-- White label with spokes					
❏ R 25078 [M]	Ronnie Hawkins	1964	12.50	25.00	50.00
-- Orange/yellow label					
❏ SR 25078 [S]	Ronnie Hawkins	1959	50.00	100.00	200.00
-- White label with spokes; black vinyl					
❏ SR 25078 [S]	Ronnie Hawkins	1959	150.00	300.00	600.00
-- White label with spokes; red vinyl					
❏ R 25102 [M]	Mr. Dynamo	1960	37.50	75.00	150.00
❏ SR 25102 [S]	Mr. Dynamo	1960	50.00	100.00	200.00
-- Black vinyl					
❏ SR 25102 [S]	Mr. Dynamo	1960	150.00	300.00	600.00
-- Red vinyl					
❏ R 25120 [M]	The Folk Ballads of Ronnie Hawkins	1960	25.00	50.00	100.00
❏ R 25137 [M]	The Songs of Hank Williams	1960	25.00	50.00	100.00
❏ SR 25078 [S]	Ronnie Hawkins	1964	15.00	30.00	60.00
-- Orange/yellow label					
❏ SR 25120 [S]	The Folk Ballads of Ronnie Hawkins	1960	37.50	75.00	150.00
❏ SR 25137 [S]	The Songs of Hank Williams	1960	37.50	75.00	150.00
❏ SR 42045	The Best of Ronnie Hawkins and His Band	1970	6.25	12.50	25.00

HAWKINS, SCREAMIN' JAY
EPIC
❏ LN 3448 [M]	At Home with Screamin' Jay Hawkins	1958	300.00	600.00	1,200.
❏ LN 3457 [M]	I Put a Spell on You	1958	125.00	250.00	500.00
❏ BN 26457 [R]	I Put a Spell on You	1969	15.00	30.00	60.00

PHILIPS
| ❏ PHS 600-319 | What That Is | 1969 | 10.00 | 20.00 | 40.00 |
| ❏ PHS 600-336 | Screamin' Jay Hawkins | 1970 | 10.00 | 20.00 | 40.00 |

SOUNDS OF HAWAII
| ❏ 5015 | A Night at Forbidden City | 196? | 12.50 | 25.00 | 50.00 |

HAWKS, BILLY
PRESTIGE
| ❏ PRLP-7501 [M] | New Genius of the Blues | 1967 | 6.25 | 12.50 | 25.00 |
| ❏ PRST-7501 [S] | New Genius of the Blues | 1967 | 5.00 | 10.00 | 20.00 |

HAWKWIND
UNITED ARTISTS
| ❏ UA-LA120-H [(2)] | Space Ritual/ Alive in Liverpool and London | 1973 | 5.00 | 10.00 | 20.00 |

HAWN, GOLDIE
REPRISE
| ❏ MS 2061 | Goldie | 1972 | 6.25 | 12.50 | 25.00 |

HAYDEN, WILLIE
DOOTO
❏ DTL-293 [M]	Blame It on the Blues	1960	125.00	250.00	500.00
-- Maroon label					
❏ DTL-293 [M]	Blame It on the Blues	196?	50.00	100.00	200.00
-- Multi-color label					

HAYES, BILL
ABC-PARAMOUNT
| ❏ 194 [M] | Bill Hayes Sings the Best of Disney | 1957 | 10.00 | 20.00 | 40.00 |

DAYBREAK
| ❏ DR-2020 | The Look of Love | 1972 | 6.25 | 12.50 | 25.00 |

KAPP
| ❏ KL-1106 [M] | Jimmy Crack Corn | 1958 | 6.25 | 12.50 | 25.00 |

HAYES, ISAAC
ENTERPRISE
❏ E-100 [M]	Presenting Isaac Hayes	1968	10.00	20.00	40.00
❏ ES-100 [S]	Presenting Isaac Hayes	1968	7.50	15.00	30.00
❏ ENS-1001	Hot Buttered Soul	1969	5.00	10.00	20.00
❏ ENS-1010	The Isaac Hayes Movement	1970	5.00	10.00	20.00
❏ ENS-1014	To Be Continued	1970	5.00	10.00	20.00
❏ ENS-5002 [(2)]	Shaft	1971	5.00	10.00	20.00
❏ ENS-5003 [(2)]	Black Moses	1971	5.00	10.00	20.00

HAYES, ROLAND
VANGUARD
❏ VRS-462 [M]	The Life of Christ in Folk Song	1954	7.50	15.00	30.00
❏ VRS-494 [M]	My Songs, Aframerican Religious Folk Songs	1955	7.50	15.00	30.00
❏ VRS-7016 [10]	Christmas Carols of the Nations	195?	12.50	25.00	50.00

HAYMARKET SQUARE
CHAPARRAL
| ❏ 201 | Magic Lantern | 1968 | 375.00 | 750.00 | 1,500. |

HAYMES, DICK
CAPITOL
| ❏ T 713 [M] | Rain or Shine | 1956 | 7.50 | 15.00 | 30.00 |
| ❏ T 787 [M] | Moondreams | 1956 | 7.50 | 15.00 | 30.00 |

DECCA
❏ DL 5012 [10]	Souvenir Album	1949	12.50	25.00	50.00
❏ DL 5022 [10]	Christmas Songs	1949	12.50	25.00	50.00
❏ DL 5023 [10]	Dick Haymes Sings Irving Berlin	1949	12.50	25.00	50.00
❏ DL 5038 [10]	Little Shamrocks	1950	12.50	25.00	50.00
❏ DL 5243 [10]	Dick Haymes Sings with Helen Forrest, Volume 1	195?	12.50	25.00	50.00
❏ DL 8773 [M]	Little White Lies	1959	10.00	20.00	40.00

WARWICK
| ❏ W-2023 [M] | Richard the Lion-Hearted | 1960 | 7.50 | 15.00 | 30.00 |

Number	Title	Yr	VG	VG+	NM

HAYWARD, JUSTIN, AND JOHN LODGE
Also see THE MOODY BLUES.
THRESHOLD
Number	Title	Yr	VG	VG+	NM
❑ THSX 101 [DJ]	Blue Jays	1975	12.50	25.00	50.00

-- Open-end interview with script; used to promote the LP of the same name

HAYWOOD, LEON
DECCA
❑ DL 74949	It's Got to Be Mellow	1969	5.00	10.00	20.00

GALAXY
❑ 8206	Mellow, Mellow	196?	5.00	10.00	20.00

HAZEL, EDDIE
Member of PARLIAMENT/ FUNKADELIC.
WARNER BROS.
❑ BSK 3058	Games, Dames and Guitar Thangs	1977	10.00	20.00	40.00

HAZLEWOOD, LEE
Also see NANCY SINATRA AND LEE HAZLEWOOD.
MERCURY
❑ MG-20860 [M]	Trouble Is a Lonesome Town	1964	5.00	10.00	20.00
❑ SR-60860 [S]	Trouble Is a Lonesome Town	1964	6.25	12.50	25.00

MGM
❑ SE-4362 [S]	The World of Lee Hazlewood	1966	5.00	10.00	20.00
❑ SE-4403 [S]	Lee Hazlewoodism - Its Cause and Cure	1966	5.00	10.00	20.00

HEAD
BUDDAH
❑ BDS-5062	Head	1970	7.50	15.00	30.00

-- With coloring book (deduct 1/3 if missing)

HEAD OVER HEELS
CAPITOL
❑ ST-797	Head Over Heels	1971	7.50	15.00	30.00

HEAD SHOP, THE
EPIC
❑ BN 26476	The Head Shop	1969	15.00	30.00	60.00

HEAD, JIM, AND HIS DEL RAYS
HP
❑ 22893 [M]	Jim Head and His Del Rays	1963	75.00	150.00	300.00

HEAD, ROY
ABC DUNHILL
❑ DS-50080	Same People	1970	5.00	10.00	20.00

SCEPTER
❑ S-532 [M]	Treat Me Right	1965	7.50	15.00	30.00
❑ SS-532 [S]	Treat Me Right	1965	10.00	20.00	40.00

TNT
❑ 101 [M]	Roy Head and the Traits	1965	37.50	75.00	150.00

-- Counterfeit alert: Authentics do NOT contain the hit "Treat Her Right."

HEADS, HANDS AND FEET
ATCO
❑ SD 7025	Old Soldiers Never Die	1973	5.00	10.00	20.00

CAPITOL
❑ SVBB-680 [(2)]	Heads, Hands and Feet	1971	6.25	12.50	25.00
❑ ST-11051	Tracks	1972	5.00	10.00	20.00

HEADS, THE
LIBERTY
❑ LST-7581	Heads Up	1968	6.25	12.50	25.00

HEADSTONE
STARR
❑ (# unknown)	Still Looking	1974	37.50	75.00	150.00

HEART
EPIC
❑ AS 884 [DJ]	Heart	1980	5.00	10.00	20.00

-- Promo-only sampler from "Greatest Hits/Live"
MUSHROOM
❑ MRS-1-SP [PD]	Magazine	1978	5.00	10.00	20.00
❑ MRS-2-SP [PD]	Dreamboat Annie	1978	6.25	12.50	25.00

❑ MRS-5008	Magazine	1977	15.00	30.00	60.00

-- Side 2, Track 3 is "Blues Medley (Mother Earth) (You Shook Me Babe)." Also, at the bottom of the back cover is a lengthy statement beginning "Mushroom Records regrets that a contractural dispute..."
NAUTILUS
❑ NR-3	Dreamboat Annie	1980	10.00	20.00	40.00

-- Audiophile pressing
PORTRAIT
❑ HR 44799	Little Queen	1981	12.50	25.00	50.00

-- Half-speed mastered edition

HEARTBEATS, THE
EMUS
❑ ES-12033	A Thousand Miles Away	1979	6.25	12.50	25.00

ROULETTE
❑ R 25107 [M]	A Thousand Miles Away	1960	100.00	200.00	400.00

HEARTS AND FLOWERS
CAPITOL
❑ ST 2762 [S]	Now Is the Time for Hearts and Flowers	1967	10.00	20.00	40.00
❑ T 2762 [M]	Now Is the Time for Hearts and Flowers	1967	10.00	20.00	40.00
❑ ST 2868	Of Horses, Kids and Forgotten Women	1968	12.50	25.00	50.00

HEARTS OF STONE
V.I.P.
❑ VIPS-404	Stop the World...We Wanna Get On	1970	10.00	20.00	40.00

HEARTS, THE
ZELLA
❑ 337 [M]	I Feel Good	1963	100.00	200.00	400.00

HEATHER BLACK
AMERICAN PLAYBOY
❑ 1001	Heather Black Live	197?	15.00	30.00	60.00
❑ 1001 [(2)]	Heather Black Live	197?	37.50	75.00	150.00

-- Evidently, some copies of this were 2-record sets
DOUBLE BAYOU
❑ 2000	Heather Black	197?	7.50	15.00	30.00

HEATS, THE
ALBATROSS
❑ 1001	The Heats	1980	6.25	12.50	25.00

HEAVY BALLOON, THE
ELEPHANT
❑ EVS-104	32,000 Lbs.	1969	17.50	35.00	70.00

HEBB, BOBBY
PHILIPS
❑ PHM 200-212 [M]	Sunny	1966	6.25	12.50	25.00
❑ PHS 600-212 [S]	Sunny	1966	7.50	15.00	30.00

HEFTI, NEAL
COLUMBIA
❑ CL 1516 [M]	Light and Right	1960	5.00	10.00	20.00
❑ CS 8316 [S]	Light and Right	1960	6.25	12.50	25.00

CORAL
❑ CX 2 [(2) M]	Hollywood Song Book	1959	10.00	20.00	40.00
❑ 7CX 2 [(2) S]	Hollywood Song Book	1959	15.00	30.00	60.00
❑ CRL 56083 [10]	Swingin' on a Coral Reef	1953	12.50	25.00	50.00
❑ CRL 57241 [M]	Hollywood Song Book, Volume 1	1958	5.00	10.00	20.00
❑ CRL 57242 [M]	Hollywood Song Book, Volume 2	1958	5.00	10.00	20.00
❑ CRL 57256 [M]	Music U.S.A.	1959	5.00	10.00	20.00
❑ CRL 757241 [S]	Hollywood Song Book, Volume 1	1959	7.50	15.00	30.00
❑ CRL 757242 [S]	Hollywood Song Book, Volume 2	1959	7.50	15.00	30.00
❑ CRL 757256 [S]	Music U.S.A.	1959	7.50	15.00	30.00

EPIC
❑ LN 3113 [M]	Singing Instrumentals	1956	12.50	25.00	50.00

RCA VICTOR
❑ LPM-3573 [M]	Batman Theme (and 11 Other Bat-Songs)	1966	12.50	25.00	50.00
❑ LSP-3573 [S]	Batman Theme (and 11 Other Bat-Songs)	1966	15.00	30.00	60.00
❑ LPM-3621 [M]	Hefti in Gotham City	1966	12.50	25.00	50.00
❑ LSP-3621 [S]	Hefti in Gotham City	1966	15.00	30.00	60.00

Number	Title	Yr	VG	VG+	NM

REPRISE

Number	Title	Yr	VG	VG+	NM
❑ R-6018 [M]	Themes from TV's Top 12	1962	6.25	12.50	25.00
❑ R9-6018 [S]	Themes from TV's Top 12	1962	7.50	15.00	30.00
❑ R-6039 [M]	Jazz Pops	1962	5.00	10.00	20.00
❑ R9-6039 [S]	Jazz Pops	1962	6.25	12.50	25.00

"X"

❑ LXA-3021 [10]	Music of Rudolf Frimi	1954	12.50	25.00	50.00

HEIFETZ, JASCHA
RCA VICTOR RED SEAL

❑ LSC-1903 [S]	Brahms: Violin Concerto	1958	20.00	40.00	80.00
-- With Fritz Reiner/Chicago Symphony Orchestra; original with "shaded dog" label					
❑ LSC-1992 [S]	Beethoven: Violin Concerto in D	1958	20.00	40.00	80.00
-- With Charles Munch/Boston Symphony Orchestra					
❑ LSC-2129 [S]	Tchaikovsky: Violin Concerto	1958	7.50	15.00	30.00
-- With Fritz Reiner/Chicago Symphony Orchestra; original with "shaded dog" label					
❑ LSC-2129 [S]	Tchaikovsky: Violin Concerto	1999	6.25	12.50	25.00
-- Classic Records reissue					
❑ LSC-2314 [S]	Mendelsohn: Violin Concerto in E; Prokofiev: Violin Concerton in G	1959	10.00	20.00	40.00
-- With Charles Munch/Boston Symphony Orchestra					
❑ LSC-2435 [S]	Sibelius: Violin Concerto	1960	20.00	40.00	80.00
-- Originals with "shaded dog" label					
❑ LSC-2577 [S]	Bach: Concerto for Two Violins; Beethoven: Kreutzer Sonata	1962	22.50	45.00	90.00
-- Original with "shaded dog" label					
❑ LSC-2603 [S]	Bruch: Scottish Fantasy; Vieuxtemps; Violin Concerto No. 5	1962	6.25	12.50	25.00
-- Original with "shaded dog" label					
❑ LSC-2652 [S]	Bruch: Violin Concerto No. 1 in G; Mozart: Violin Concerto No. 4 in D	1962	15.00	30.00	60.00
-- Original with "shaded dog" label					
❑ LSC-2734 [S]	Glazunov: Violin Concerto; Mozart: Sinfonia Concertante	1963	25.00	50.00	100.00
-- Original with "shaded dog" label					

HEIFETZ, JASCHA, AND GREGOR PIATIGORSKI
RCA VICTOR RED SEAL

❑ LSC-2513 [S]	Brahms: Double Concerto	1961	10.00	20.00	40.00
-- Originals with "shaded dog" label					

HEIFETZ, JASCHA; WILLIAM PRIMROSE; GREGOR PIATIGORSKI
RCA VICTOR RED SEAL

❑ LSC-2550 [S]	Beethoven: Serenade, op. 8; Kodaly: Duo	1961	12.50	25.00	50.00
-- Originals with "shaded dog" label					
❑ LSC-2563 [S]	Beethoven: Trio in D; Bach: Three Sinfonias; Schubert: Trio No. 2	1961	10.00	20.00	40.00
-- Original with "shaded dog" label					

HEINDORF, RAY
DCC COMPACT CLASSICS

❑ LPZ-2023	For Whom the Bell Tolls	1996	6.25	12.50	25.00
-- Audiophile vinyl					

WARNER BROS.

❑ B 1201 [M]	For Whom the Bell Tolls	1958	7.50	15.00	30.00
-- Re-recording of 1943 movie score; the first LP on Warner Bros. Records					
❑ BS 1201 [S]	For Whom the Bell Tolls	1959	10.00	20.00	40.00
-- Gold label					
❑ W 1213 [M]	Spellbound	1958	7.50	15.00	30.00
-- Re-recording of 1945 movie score					
❑ WS 1213 [S]	Spellbound	1959	10.00	20.00	40.00
-- Gold label					

HELL, RICHARD, AND THE VOIDOIDS
SIRE

❑ SRK 6037	Blank Generation	1977	6.25	12.50	25.00

HELLERS, THE
COMMAND

❑ RS 934 SD	Singers, Talkers, Players, Swingers and Doers	1968	10.00	20.00	40.00

HELMS, BOBBY
COLUMBIA

❑ CL 2060 [M]	The Best of Bobby Helms	1963	6.25	12.50	25.00
❑ CS 8860 [S]	The Best of Bobby Helms	1963	7.50	15.00	30.00

DECCA

❑ DL 8638 [M]	Bobby Helms Sings to My Special Angel	1957	30.00	60.00	120.00

KAPP

❑ KS 3463 [S]	I'm the Man	1966	5.00	10.00	20.00
❑ KS 3505 [S]	Sorry My Name Isn't Fred	1966	5.00	10.00	20.00

LITTLE DARLIN'

Number	Title	Yr	VG	VG+	NM
❑ 8088	All New Just for You	1968	6.25	12.50	25.00

HELMS, DON
SMASH

❑ MGS-27001 [M]	The Steel Guitar Sounds of Hank Williams	1962	5.00	10.00	20.00
❑ MGS-27019 [M]	Don Helms' Steel Guitar	1962	5.00	10.00	20.00
❑ SRS-67001 [S]	The Steel Guitar Sounds of Hank Williams	1962	6.25	12.50	25.00
❑ SRS-67019 [S]	Don Helms' Steel Guitar	1962	6.25	12.50	25.00

HELP
DECCA

❑ DL 75257	Help	1970	7.50	15.00	30.00
❑ DL 75304	Second Coming	1971	7.50	15.00	30.00

HENDERSON, BILL
MGM

❑ E-4128 [M]	Bill Henderson with the Oscar Peterson Trio	1963	6.25	12.50	25.00
❑ SE-4128 [S]	Bill Henderson with the Oscar Peterson Trio	1963	7.50	15.00	30.00

VEE JAY

❑ LP-1015 [M]	Bill Henderson Sings	1959	6.25	12.50	25.00
❑ SR-1015 [S]	Bill Henderson Sings	1959	10.00	20.00	40.00
❑ LP-1031 [M]	Bill Henderson	1961	6.25	12.50	25.00
❑ SR-1031 [S]	Bill Henderson	1961	10.00	20.00	40.00

VERVE

❑ V-8619 [M]	When My Dreamboat Comes Home	1965	5.00	10.00	20.00
❑ V6-8619 [S]	When My Dreamboat Comes Home	1965	6.25	12.50	25.00

HENDERSON, BUGS
ARMADILLO

❑ LP-78-1	The Bugs Henderson Group At Last	1978	10.00	20.00	40.00

HENDERSON, JOE
TODD

❑ MT-2701 [M]	Snap Your Fingers	1962	12.50	25.00	50.00
❑ ST-2701 [S]	Snap Your Fingers	1962	17.50	35.00	70.00

HENDERSON, SKITCH
CAPITOL

❑ H 110 [10]	Keyboard Sketches	1950	12.50	25.00	50.00

HENDRIX, JIMI
CAPITOL

❑ STAO-472	Band of Gypsys	1970	5.00	10.00	20.00
❑ SWBB-659 [(2)]	Get That Feeling/Flashing	1971	6.25	12.50	25.00
❑ ST 2856 [S]	Get That Feeling	1967	10.00	20.00	40.00
❑ T 2856 [M]	Get That Feeling	1967	20.00	40.00	80.00
❑ ST 2894 [S]	Flashing	1968	10.00	20.00	40.00
❑ T 2894 [M]	Flashing	1968	25.00	50.00	100.00
❑ SJ-12416	Band of Gypsys 2	1986	37.50	75.00	150.00
-- Side 2 lists three songs, but plays four completely different songs. Four bands are visible on the record.					

EXPERIENCE HENDRIX/CAPITOL

❑ ST-472	Band of Gypsys	1997	6.25	12.50	25.00
-- Limited edition on "heavy vinyl" with booklet; distributed by Classic Records					

EXPERIENCE HENDRIX/MCA

❑ 11599 [(2)]	First Rays of the New Rising Sun	1997	12.50	25.00	50.00
-- Limited edition on "heavy vinyl" with booklet					
❑ 11600 [(2)]	Electric Ladyland	1997	10.00	20.00	40.00
-- Limited edition on "heavy vinyl" with booklet					
❑ 11601	Axis: Bold As Love	1997	12.50	25.00	50.00
-- Limited edition on "heavy vinyl" with booklet					
❑ 11602 [(2)]	Are You Experienced?	1997	12.50	25.00	50.00
-- Limited edition on "heavy vinyl" with booklet					
❑ 11607	Band of Gypsys	1997	6.25	12.50	25.00
-- Limited edition on "heavy vinyl" with booklet; pressed in U.S. for export to Europe					
❑ 11608	Are You Experienced?	1997	10.00	20.00	40.00
-- Limited edition on "heavy vinyl" with booklet; pressed in U.S. for export to Europe; has different cover than US version					
❑ 11671 [(2)]	Experience Hendrix: The Best of Jimi Hendrix	1998	6.25	12.50	25.00
-- Despite lower number, was released after South Saturn Delta					
❑ 11684 [(2)]	South Saturn Delta	1997	6.25	12.50	25.00
-- Numbered, limited edition on "heavy vinyl"					
❑ 11742 [(3)]	BBC Sessions	1998	7.50	15.00	30.00
❑ 11931 [(3)]	Live at the Fillmore East	1999	7.50	15.00	30.00
❑ 11987 [(3)]	Live at Woodstock	1999	7.50	15.00	30.00

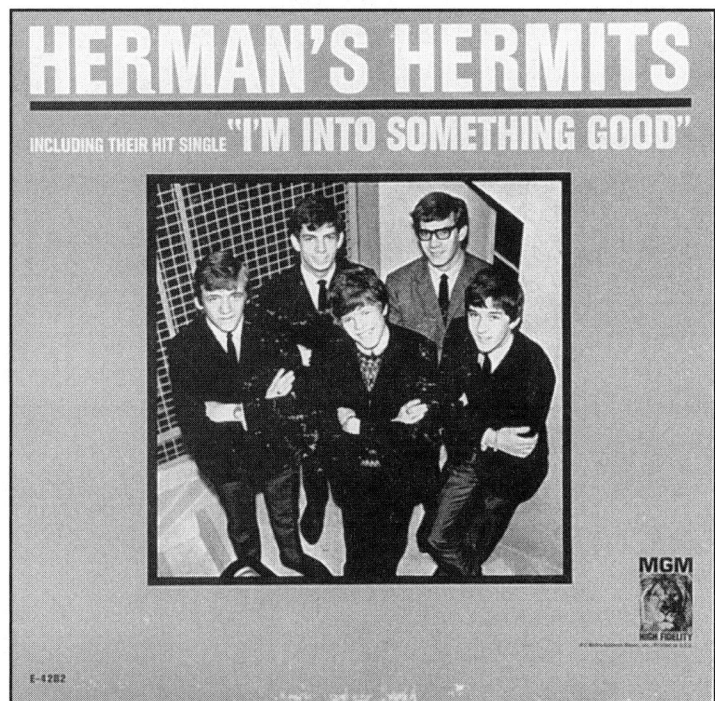

(Top left) Among the first solo Beatles albums was *Wonderwall Music,* the George Harrison-composed soundtrack to a seldom-seen movie. (Top right) "Sunny" was a big enough hit single that Philips had Bobby Hebb record an album with the hit as the lead song. (Bottom left) One of the few truly uncommon Herman's Hermits albums is this 1965 issue. The first edition of *Introducing Herman's Hermits*, pictured above, said that it featured "I'm Into Something Good." Shortly after its issue, a different song, one not even released as a single in the U.K., became the lead track – "Mrs. Brown You've Got a Lovely Daughter." (Bottom right) Early albums by the Hollies, of which *Hear! Here!* is one, are not easy to find today.

Number	Title	Yr	VG	VG+	NM
NUTMEG					
❏ 1001	High, Live 'N' Dirty	1978	6.25	12.50	25.00
-- Black vinyl					
❏ 1001	High, Live 'N' Dirty	1978	6.25	12.50	25.00
-- Red vinyl					
REPRISE					
❏ MS 2025	Smash Hits	1969	10.00	20.00	40.00
-- With "W7" and "r:" logos on two-tone orange label					
❏ MS 2025	Smash Hits Bonus Poster	1969	10.00	20.00	40.00
❏ MS 2029	Historic Performances As Recorded at the Monterey International Pop Festival	1970	5.00	10.00	20.00
-- Side 1: Jimi Hendrix; Side 2: Otis Redding					
❏ MS 2034	The Cry of Love	1971	125.00	250.00	500.00
-- With "W7" and "r:" logos on two-tone orange label					
❏ MS 2040	Rainbow Bridge	1971	5.00	10.00	20.00
❏ MS 2049	Hendrix in the West	1972	5.00	10.00	20.00
❏ MS 2103	War Heroes	1972	5.00	10.00	20.00
❏ 2RS 2245 [(2)]	The Essential Jimi Hendrix	1978	5.00	10.00	20.00
❏ R 6261 [M]	Are You Experienced?	1967	50.00	100.00	200.00
❏ RS 6261 [S]	Are You Experienced?	1967	12.50	25.00	50.00
-- Pink, gold and green label					
❏ RS 6261 [S]	Are You Experienced?	1968	6.25	12.50	25.00
-- With "W7" and "r:" logos on two-tone orange label					
❏ R 6281 [M]	Axis: Bold As Love	1968	625.00	1,250.	2,500.
❏ RS 6281 [S]	Axis: Bold As Love	1968	20.00	40.00	80.00
-- Pink, gold and green label					
❏ RS 6281 [S]	Axis: Bold As Love	1968	6.25	12.50	25.00
-- With "W7" and "r:" logos on two-tone orange label					
❏ 2R 6307 [(2) M]	Electric Ladyland	1968	2,000.	3,000.	4,000.
-- Mono is promo only					
❏ 2RS 6307 [(2)]	Electric Ladyland	1968	25.00	50.00	100.00
-- With "W7" and "r:" logos on two-tone orange label					
❏ 2RS 6481 [(2)]	Soundtrack Recordings from the Film Jimi Hendrix	1973	6.25	12.50	25.00
❏ SMAS-93972	Rainbow Bridge	1971	12.50	25.00	50.00
-- Capitol Record Club edition					
RHINO					
❏ RNDF-254 [PD]	The Jimi Hendrix Interview	1982	6.25	12.50	25.00

HENDRIX, JIMI, AND LONNIE YOUNGBLOOD

Number	Title	Yr	VG	VG+	NM
MAPLE					
❏ 6004	Two Great Experiences Together	1971	12.50	25.00	50.00

HENRY TREE

Number	Title	Yr	VG	VG+	NM
MAINSTREAM					
❏ S-6129	Electric Holy Man	1968	7.50	15.00	30.00

HENRY, CLARENCE

Number	Title	Yr	VG	VG+	NM
ARGO					
❏ LP-4009 [M]	You Always Hurt the One You Love	1961	75.00	125.00	250.00
CADET					
❏ LP-4009 [M]	You Always Hurt the One You Love	1966	12.50	25.00	50.00
-- Includes copies of Cadet LP in Argo sleeves					
ROULETTE					
❏ SR 42039	Alive and Well and Living in New Orleans	1969	6.25	12.50	25.00

HENSKE, JUDY

Number	Title	Yr	VG	VG+	NM
ELEKTRA					
❏ EKL-231 [M]	Judy Henske	1963	5.00	10.00	20.00
❏ EKL-241 [M]	High Flying Bird	1964	5.00	10.00	20.00
❏ EKL-7241 [S]	High Flying Bird	1964	6.25	12.50	25.00
❏ EKS-7231 [S]	Judy Henske	1963	6.25	12.50	25.00
MERCURY					
❏ MG-21010 [M]	Little Bit of Sunshine... Little Bit of Rain	1965	5.00	10.00	20.00
❏ SR-61010 [S]	Little Bit of Sunshine... Little Bit of Rain	1965	6.25	12.50	25.00
REPRISE					
❏ R-6203 [M]	The Death Defying Judy Henske: The First Concert Album	1966	5.00	10.00	20.00
❏ RS-6203 [S]	The Death Defying Judy Henske: The First Concert Album	1966	6.25	12.50	25.00

HENSKE, JUDY, AND JERRY YESTER

Number	Title	Yr	VG	VG+	NM
REPRISE					
❏ RS-6388	Farewell Aldebaran	1969	5.00	10.00	20.00
STRAIGHT					
❏ STS-1052	Farewell Aldebaran	1968	7.50	15.00	30.00

HENSLEY, WALTER

Number	Title	Yr	VG	VG+	NM
CAPITOL					
❏ ST 2149 [S]	The Five-String Banjo Today	1964	5.00	10.00	20.00

HERD, THE

Number	Title	Yr	VG	VG+	NM
FONTANA					
❏ SRF-67579	Lookin' Thru You	1968	6.25	12.50	25.00

HERMAN'S HERMITS

Number	Title	Yr	VG	VG+	NM
MGM					
❏ E-4282 [M]	Introducing Herman's Hermits	1965	6.25	12.50	25.00
-- Version 1: With "Including Their Hit Single 'I'm Into Something Good' " on front cover					
❏ E-4282 [M]	Introducing Herman's Hermits	1965	5.00	10.00	20.00
-- Version 2: Same as above, but with a sticker that says "Featuring "Mrs. Brown You Have a Lovely Daughter"."					
❏ SE-4282 [R]	Introducing Herman's Hermits	1965	5.00	10.00	20.00
-- Version 1: With "Including Their Hit Single 'I'm Into Something Good' " on front cover					
❏ ST 90416 [S]	Introducing Herman's Hermits	1965	5.00	10.00	20.00
-- Capitol Record Club edition					
❏ T 90416 [M]	Introducing Herman's Hermits	1965	6.25	12.50	25.00
-- Capitol Record Club edition					

HERMAN, JERRY

Number	Title	Yr	VG	VG+	NM
UNITED ARTISTS					
❏ UAL-3432 [M]	Hello, Jerry!	1965	5.00	10.00	20.00
❏ UAS-6432 [S]	Hello, Jerry!	1965	6.25	12.50	25.00

HERMAN, WOODY

Number	Title	Yr	VG	VG+	NM
AMERICAN RECORDING SOCIETY					
❏ G-410 [M]	The Progressive Big Band Sound	1956	10.00	20.00	40.00
ATLANTIC					
❏ 1328 [M]	Woody Herman at the Monterey Jazz Festival	1960	10.00	20.00	40.00
❏ SD 1328 [S]	Woody Herman at the Monterey Jazz Festival	1960	7.50	15.00	30.00
BRUNSWICK					
❏ BL 54024 [M]	The Swinging Herman Herd	1957	10.00	20.00	40.00
CAPITOL					
❏ H 324 [10]	Classics in Jazz	1952	17.50	35.00	70.00
❏ T 324 [M]	Classics in Jazz	1955	10.00	20.00	40.00
❏ T 560 [M]	The Woody Herman Band	1955	10.00	20.00	40.00
❏ T 658 [M]	Road Band	1955	10.00	20.00	40.00
❏ T 748 [M]	Jackpot!	1956	10.00	20.00	40.00
❏ T 784 [M]	Blues Groove	1956	10.00	20.00	40.00
❏ T 1554 [M]	The Hits of Woody Herman	1961	5.00	10.00	20.00
CENTURY					
❏ 1080	Road Father	1979	6.25	12.50	25.00
-- Direct-to-disc recording					
CLEF					
❏ MGC-745 [M]	Jazz, the Utmost!	1956	20.00	40.00	80.00
COLUMBIA					
❏ C3L 25 [(3) M]	The Thundering Herds	1963	12.50	25.00	50.00
❏ CL 592 [M]	The Three Herds	1955	12.50	25.00	50.00
-- Maroon label with gold print					
❏ CL 592 [M]	The Three Herds	1956	7.50	15.00	30.00
-- Red and black label with six "eye" logos					
❏ CL 651 [M]	Music for Tired Lovers	1955	10.00	20.00	40.00
❏ CL 2509 [10]	Ridin' Herd	1955	15.00	30.00	60.00
❏ CL 2563 [10]	Woody!	1955	15.00	30.00	60.00
❏ CL 6026 [10]	Sequence in Jazz	1949	17.50	35.00	70.00
❏ CL 6049 [10]	Dance Parade	1949	17.50	35.00	70.00
❏ CL 6092 [10]	Woody Herman and His Woodchoppers	1950	17.50	35.00	70.00
CORAL					
❏ CRL 56005 [10]	Blue Prelude	1950	17.50	35.00	70.00
❏ CRL 56010 [10]	Woody Herman Souvenirs	1950	17.50	35.00	70.00
❏ CRL 56090 [10]	Woody's Best	1953	17.50	35.00	70.00
CROWN					
❏ CLP 5180 [M]	The New Swingin' Herman Band	1960	5.00	10.00	20.00
DECCA					
❏ DL 8133 [M]	Woodchopper's Ball	1955	10.00	20.00	40.00
DIAL					
❏ LP-210 [10]	Swinging with the Woodchoppers	1950	37.50	75.00	150.00
EVEREST					
❏ LPBR-1032 [M]	Moody Woody	1958	7.50	15.00	30.00
❏ LPBR-5003 [M]	The Herd Rides Again	1958	7.50	15.00	30.00
❏ SDBR-1003 [S]	The Herd Rides Again...In Stereo	1958	10.00	20.00	40.00
❏ SDBR-5032 [S]	Moody Woody	1958	10.00	20.00	40.00
❏ EV-5222 [S]	The Best of Woody Herman	1963	5.00	10.00	20.00
FANTASY					
❏ FPM-4003 [Q]	Children of Lima	1975	5.00	10.00	20.00
FORUM					
❏ F-9016 [M]	Woody Herman Sextet at the Round Table	196?	5.00	10.00	20.00
❏ FS-9016 [S]	Woody Herman Sextet at the Round Table	196?	6.25	12.50	25.00

Number	Title	Yr	VG	VG+	NM
HARMONY					
❏ HL 7013 [M]	Bijou	1957	5.00	10.00	20.00
❏ HL 7093 [M]	Summer Sequence	1957	5.00	10.00	20.00
JAZZLAND					
❏ JLP-17 [M]	The Fourth Herd	1960	6.25	12.50	25.00
❏ JLP-917 [S]	The Fourth Herd	1960	6.25	12.50	25.00
LION					
❏ L-70059 [M]	The Herman Herd at Carnegie Hall	1958	6.25	12.50	25.00
MARS					
❏ MRX-1 [10]	Dance Date on Mars	1952	37.50	75.00	150.00
❏ MRX-2 [10]	Woody Herman Goes Native	1953	37.50	75.00	150.00
MGM					
❏ E-158 [10]	Woody Herman at Carnegie Hall, 1946, Vol. 1	1952	17.50	35.00	70.00
❏ E-159 [10]	Woody Herman at Carnegie Hall, 1946, Vol. 2	1952	17.50	35.00	70.00
❏ E-192 [10]	The Third Herd	1953	17.50	35.00	70.00
❏ E-284 [10]	Blue Flame	1955	17.50	35.00	70.00
❏ E-3043 [M]	Carnegie Hall 1946	1953	12.50	25.00	50.00
-- Compiles 158 and 159 on one 12-inch LP					
❏ E-3385 [M]	Hi-Fi-ing Herd	1956	10.00	20.00	40.00
MOBILE FIDELITY					
❏ 1-219	The Fourth Herd	1994	7.50	15.00	30.00
-- Audiophile vinyl					
PHILIPS					
❏ PHS 600-004 [S]	Swing Low, Sweet Chariot	1962	5.00	10.00	20.00
❏ PHS 600-065 [S]	Woody Herman 1963	1963	5.00	10.00	20.00
❏ PHS 600-092 [S]	Encore: Woody Herman 1963	1963	5.00	10.00	20.00
❏ PHS 600-118 [S]	Woody Herman: 1964	1964	5.00	10.00	20.00
❏ PHS 600-131 [S]	The Swinging Herman Herd Recorded Live	1964	5.00	10.00	20.00
❏ PHS 600-171 [S]	Woody's Big Band Goodies	1965	5.00	10.00	20.00
ROULETTE					
❏ R 25067 [M]	Woody Herman Sextet at the Round Table	1959	7.50	15.00	30.00
❏ SR 25067 [S]	Woody Herman Sextet at the Round Table	1959	10.00	20.00	40.00
VERVE					
❏ MGV-2030 [M]	Early Autumn	1957	10.00	20.00	40.00
❏ MGV-2069 [M]	Songs for Hip Lovers	1957	10.00	20.00	40.00
❏ MGV-2096 [M]	Love Is the Sweetest Thing -- Sometimes	1958	10.00	20.00	40.00
❏ MGV-8014 [M]	Jazz, the Utmost!	1957	10.00	20.00	40.00
-- Reissue of Clef LP					
❏ MGV-8216 [M]	Men from Mars	1958	10.00	20.00	40.00
❏ MGV-8255 [M]	Woody Herman '58	1958	10.00	20.00	40.00
❏ V-8558 [M]	Hey! Heard the Herd?	1963	5.00	10.00	20.00
-- Reissue of Verve 8216					
❏ V6-8764	Concerto for Herd	1968	5.00	10.00	20.00
HERON, MIKE					
ELEKTRA					
❏ EKS-74093	Smiling Men with Bad Reputations	1971	5.00	10.00	20.00
HERRMANN, BERNARD					
MOBILE FIDELITY					
❏ 1-240	The Fantasy Film World of Bernard Herrmann	1996	5.00	10.00	20.00
-- Audiophile vinyl					
❏ 1-255	The Four Faces of Jazz	1996	5.00	10.00	20.00
-- Audiophile vinyl					
HESITATIONS, THE					
KAPP					
❏ KL-1525 [M]	Soul Superman	1967	7.50	15.00	30.00
❏ KS-3525 [S]	Soul Superman	1967	6.25	12.50	25.00
❏ KS-3548	The New Born Free	1968	6.25	12.50	25.00
❏ KS-3561	Where We're At	1968	6.25	12.50	25.00
❏ KS-3574	Solid Gold	1969	6.25	12.50	25.00
HESS, CHUCK					
STRAND					
❏ SL-1084 [M]	Country & Western Favorites	1960	5.00	10.00	20.00
❏ SLS-1084 [S]	Country & Western Favorites	1960	6.25	12.50	25.00
HESTER, CAROLYN					
COLUMBIA					
❏ CL 1796 [M]	Carolyn Hester	1962	15.00	30.00	60.00
-- With Bob Dylan on harmonica on three tracks; black and red label with six "eye" logos					
❏ CL 1796 [M]	Carolyn Hester	1963	5.00	10.00	20.00
-- Red label with "Guaranteed High Fidelity"					
❏ CL 2032 [M]	This Life I'm Living	1963	5.00	10.00	20.00

Number	Title	Yr	VG	VG+	NM
❏ CS 8596 [S]	Carolyn Hester	1962	20.00	40.00	80.00
-- With Bob Dylan on harmonica on three tracks; black and red label with six "eye" logos					
❏ CS 8596 [S]	Carolyn Hester	1963	6.25	12.50	25.00
-- Red label, "360 Sound Stereo" in black					
❏ CS 8832 [S]	This Life I'm Living	1963	6.25	12.50	25.00
CORAL					
❏ CRL 57143 [M]	Scarlet Ribbons	1957	12.50	25.00	50.00
DOT					
❏ DLP-25604 [S]	That's My Song	1964	5.00	10.00	20.00
❏ DLP-25638 [S]	Carolyn Hester at Town Hall One	1965	5.00	10.00	20.00
❏ DLP-25649 [S]	Carolyn Hester at Town Hall Two	1965	5.00	10.00	20.00
FOLK ODYSSEY					
❏ 32-16-0264	Simply Carolyn Hester	196?	5.00	10.00	20.00
METROMEDIA					
❏ MD-1001	The Carolyn Hester Coalition	1969	5.00	10.00	20.00
❏ MD-1022	Magazine	1970	15.00	30.00	60.00
RCA VICTOR					
❏ APD1-0086 [Q]	Carolyn Hester	1973	5.00	10.00	20.00
-- Only released in quadraphonic					
TRADITION					
❏ TLP-1043 [M]	Carolyn Hester	1961	10.00	20.00	40.00
HEYWOOD, EDDIE					
BRUNSWICK					
❏ BL 58036 [10]	Eddie Heywood '45	1953	12.50	25.00	50.00
COLUMBIA					
❏ CL 6157 [10]	Piano Moods	1951	12.50	25.00	50.00
COMMODORE					
❏ FL-20007 [10]	Eight Selections	1950	18.75	37.50	75.00
CORAL					
❏ CRL 57095 [M]	Featuring Eddie Heywood	1957	10.00	20.00	40.00
DECCA					
❏ DL 8202 [M]	Lightly and Politely	1956	7.50	15.00	30.00
❏ DL 8270 [M]	Swing Low Sweet Heywood	1956	7.50	15.00	30.00
EMARCY					
❏ MG-36042 [M]	Eddie Heywood	1955	10.00	20.00	40.00
EPIC					
❏ LN 3327 [M]	Eddie Heywood at Twilight	1956	7.50	15.00	30.00
MERCURY					
❏ MG-20445 [M]	Breezin' Along with the Breeze	1959	5.00	10.00	20.00
❏ MG-20590 [M]	Eddie Heywood at the Piano	1960	5.00	10.00	20.00
❏ MG-20632 [M]	One for My Baby	1960	5.00	10.00	20.00
❏ SR-60115 [S]	Breezin' Along with the Breeze	1959	6.25	12.50	25.00
❏ SR-60248 [S]	Eddie Heywood at the Piano	1960	6.25	12.50	25.00
❏ SR-60632 [S]	One for My Baby	1960	6.25	12.50	25.00
MGM					
❏ E-135 [10]	It's Easy to Remember	1952	12.50	25.00	50.00
❏ E-3093 [M]	Pianorama	1955	10.00	20.00	40.00
❏ E-3260 [M]	Eddie Heywood	1956	10.00	20.00	40.00
RCA VICTOR					
❏ LPM-1466 [M]	The Touch of Eddie Heywood	1957	7.50	15.00	30.00
❏ LPM-1529 [M]	Canadian Sunset	1957	7.50	15.00	30.00
❏ LPM-1900 [M]	The Keys and I	1958	7.50	15.00	30.00
HI-LITES, THE					
DANDEE					
❏ DLP-206 [M]	For Your Precious Love	1958	500.00	1,000.	2,000.
HI-LO'S, THE					
COLUMBIA					
❏ CL 952 [M]	Suddenly It's the Hi-Lo's	1957	7.50	15.00	30.00
❏ CL 1023 [M]	Now Hear This	1957	7.50	15.00	30.00
❏ CL 1259 [M]	The Hi-Lo's and All That Jazz	1958	7.50	15.00	30.00
❏ CL 1416 [M]	Broadway Playbill	1959	7.50	15.00	30.00
❏ CL 1509 [M]	All Over the Place	1960	6.25	12.50	25.00
❏ CL 1723 [M]	This Time It's Love	1962	6.25	12.50	25.00
❏ CS 8057 [S]	Love Nest	1958	10.00	20.00	40.00
❏ CS 8077 [S]	The Hi-Lo's and All That Jazz	1958	10.00	20.00	40.00
❏ CS 8213 [S]	Broadway Playbill	1959	10.00	20.00	40.00
❏ CS 8300 [S]	All Over the Place	1960	7.50	15.00	30.00
❏ CS 8523 [S]	This Time It's Love	1962	7.50	15.00	30.00
KAPP					
❏ KL 1027 [M]	The Hi-Lo's and the Jerry Fielding Band	1956	7.50	15.00	30.00
❏ KL 1184 [M]	Under Glass	1959	6.25	12.50	25.00
-- Reissue of Starlite 7005					
❏ KL 1194 [M]	On Hand	1960	6.25	12.50	25.00
-- Reissue of Starlite 7008					
OMEGA					
❏ OSL-11 [S]	The Hi-Lo's in Stereo	195?	7.50	15.00	30.00

Number	Title	Yr	VG	VG+	NM
REPRISE					
❑ R-6066 [M]	The Hi-Lo's Happen to Bossa Nova	1963	5.00	10.00	20.00
❑ R9-6066 [S]	The Hi-Lo's Happen to Bossa Nova	1963	6.25	12.50	25.00
STARLITE					
❑ 6004 [10]	Listen!	1955	15.00	30.00	60.00
❑ 6005 [10]	The Hi-Lo's, I Presume	1955	15.00	30.00	60.00
❑ 7005 [M]	Under Glass	1956	10.00	20.00	40.00
❑ 7006 [M]	Listen!	1956	10.00	20.00	40.00
-- Reissue of 6004					
❑ 7007 [M]	The Hi-Lo's. I Presume	1956	10.00	20.00	40.00
-- Reissue of 6005					
❑ 7008 [M]	On Hand	1956	10.00	20.00	40.00

HI-TONES, THE

Number	Title	Yr	VG	VG+	NM
HI					
❑ HL-31011 [M]	Raunchy Sounds	1963	5.00	10.00	20.00
❑ SHL-32011 [S]	Raunchy Sounds	1963	6.25	12.50	25.00
L&M					
❑ 223	I'm So Sorry	196?	50.00	100.00	200.00

HIATT, JOHN

Number	Title	Yr	VG	VG+	NM
MOBILE FIDEILTY					
❑ 1-210	Bring the Family	1994	12.50	25.00	50.00
-- Audiophile vinyl					

HIBBLER, AL

Number	Title	Yr	VG	VG+	NM
ARGO					
❑ LP-601 [M]	Melodies by Al Hibbler	1956	10.00	20.00	40.00
-- Reissue of Marterry LP					
ATLANTIC					
❑ 1251 [M]	After the Lights Go Down Low	1957	12.50	25.00	50.00
-- Black label					
❑ 1251 [M]	After the Lights Go Down Low	1961	6.25	12.50	25.00
-- Mostly red label, white fan logo					
❑ 1251 [M]	After the Lights Go Down Low	1963	5.00	10.00	20.00
-- Mostly red label, black fan logo					
BRUNSWICK					
❑ BL 54036 [M]	Al Hibbler with the Ellingtonians	1957	12.50	25.00	50.00
DECCA					
❑ DL 8328 [M]	Starring Al Hibbler	1956	7.50	15.00	30.00
❑ DL 8420 [M]	Here's Hibbler	1957	7.50	15.00	30.00
❑ DL 8697 [M]	Torchy and Blue	1958	7.50	15.00	30.00
❑ DL 8757 [M]	Hits by Hibbler	1958	7.50	15.00	30.00
❑ DL 8862 [M]	Al Hibbler Remembers the Big Songs of the Big Bands	1959	7.50	15.00	30.00
❑ DL 78862 [S]	Al Hibbler Remembers the Big Songs of the Big Bands	1959	10.00	20.00	40.00
LMI					
❑ 10001 [M]	Early One Morning	1964	7.50	15.00	30.00
MARTERRY					
❑ LP-601 [M]	Melodies by Al Hibbler	1956	20.00	40.00	80.00
NORGRAN					
❑ MGN-4 [10]	Al Hibbler Favorites	1954	37.50	75.00	150.00
❑ MGN-15 [10]	Al Hibbler Sings Duke Ellington	1954	37.50	75.00	150.00
REPRISE					
❑ R-2005 [M]	It's Monday Every Day	1961	7.50	15.00	30.00
❑ R9-2005 [S]	It's Monday Every Day	1961	10.00	20.00	40.00
SCORE					
❑ SLP-4013 [M]	I Surrender, Dear	1957	25.00	50.00	100.00
VERVE					
❑ MGV-4000 [M]	Al Hibbler Sings Love Songs	1956	15.00	30.00	60.00
❑ V-4000 [M]	Al Hibbler Sings Love Songs	1961	5.00	10.00	20.00

HICKEY, ERSEL

Number	Title	Yr	VG	VG+	NM
BACK-TRAC					
❑ P 18750	The Rockin' Bluebird	1985	15.00	30.00	60.00
-- Allegedly, only 200 copies of this were pressed					

HICKMAN, DWAYNE

Number	Title	Yr	VG	VG+	NM
CAPITOL					
❑ ST 1441 [S]	Dobie!	1960	12.50	25.00	50.00
❑ T 1441 [M]	Dobie!	1960	10.00	20.00	40.00

HIGGINS, CHUCK

Number	Title	Yr	VG	VG+	NM
COMBO					
❑ LP-300 [M]	Pachuko Hop	195?	200.00	400.00	800.00
-- "Naked woman" cover (well, she's wearing a scarf)					
❑ LP-300 [M]	Pachuko Hop	195?	100.00	200.00	40.00
-- Chuck Higgins on cover, fully clothed					

HIGH TIDE

Number	Title	Yr	VG	VG+	NM
LIBERTY					
❑ LST-7638	Sea Shanties	1969	6.25	12.50	25.00

HIGH TREASON

Number	Title	Yr	VG	VG+	NM
ABBOTT					
❑ ABS-1209	High Treason	1968	15.00	30.00	60.00

HIGHTOWER, DEAN

Number	Title	Yr	VG	VG+	NM
ABC-PARAMOUNT					
❑ ABC-312 [M]	Twangy Guitar with a Beat	1959	6.25	12.50	25.00
❑ ABCS-312 [S]	Twangy Guitar with a Beat	1959	7.50	15.00	30.00

HIGHTOWER, DONNA

Number	Title	Yr	VG	VG+	NM
CAPITOL					
❑ ST 1133 [S]	Take One	1959	12.50	25.00	50.00
❑ T 1133 [M]	Take One	1959	10.00	20.00	40.00
❑ ST 1273 [S]	Gee Baby…Ain't I Good to You	1959	12.50	25.00	50.00
❑ T 1273 [M]	Gee Baby…Ain't I Good to You	1959	10.00	20.00	40.00

HIGHWAYMEN, THE

Number	Title	Yr	VG	VG+	NM
UNITED ARTISTS					
❑ UAS 6125 [S]	The Highwaymen	1961	5.00	10.00	20.00
❑ UAS 6168 [S]	Standing Room Only!	1962	5.00	10.00	20.00
❑ UAS 6225 [S]	Encore!	1962	5.00	10.00	20.00
❑ UAS 6245 [S]	March On, Brothers	1963	5.00	10.00	20.00
❑ UAS 6294 [S]	Hootenanny with the Highwaymen	1963	5.00	10.00	20.00
❑ UAS 6323 [S]	One More Time	1964	5.00	10.00	20.00
❑ UAS 6348 [S]	Homecoming	1964	5.00	10.00	20.00

HILDEGARDE

Number	Title	Yr	VG	VG+	NM
DECCA					
❑ DL 8656 [M]	Souvenir Album	1958	7.50	15.00	30.00
-- Black label, silver print					

HILL, GOLDIE

Number	Title	Yr	VG	VG+	NM
DECCA					
❑ DL 4034 [M]	Goldie Hill	1960	6.25	12.50	25.00
❑ DL 4148 [M]	Lonely Heartaches	1961	5.00	10.00	20.00
❑ DL 4219 [M]	According to My Heart	1962	5.00	10.00	20.00
❑ DL 4492 [M]	Country Hit Parade	1964	5.00	10.00	20.00
❑ DL 74034 [S]	Goldie Hill	1960	7.50	15.00	30.00
❑ DL 74148 [S]	Lonely Heartaches	1961	6.25	12.50	25.00
❑ DL 74219 [S]	According to My Heart	1962	6.25	12.50	25.00
❑ DL 74492 [S]	Country Hit Parade	1964	6.25	12.50	25.00

HILL, TINY

Number	Title	Yr	VG	VG+	NM
MERCURY					
❑ MG-25126 [10]	Tiny Hill	1952	12.50	25.00	50.00

HILL, VINCE

Number	Title	Yr	VG	VG+	NM
TOWER					
❑ T 5064 [M]	At the Club	1966	6.25	12.50	25.00

HILLMEN, THE

Number	Title	Yr	VG	VG+	NM
TOGETHER					
❑ STT-1012	The Hillmen	1970	20.00	40.00	80.00

HILLOW HAMMET

Number	Title	Yr	VG	VG+	NM
HOUSE OF FOX					
❑ 2	Hammer	1968	37.50	75.00	150.00

HILLTOPPERS, THE

Number	Title	Yr	VG	VG+	NM
DOT					
❑ DLP-105 [10]	The Hilltoppers	1954	15.00	30.00	60.00
❑ DLP-106 [10]	The Hilltoppers	1954	15.00	30.00	60.00
❑ DLP-3003 [M]	The Hilltoppers Present Tops in Pops	1955	12.50	25.00	50.00
-- Cartoon of female fan on cover					
❑ DLP-3003 [M]	The Hilltoppers Present Tops in Pops	1956	7.50	15.00	30.00
-- Four caps with "W" on them on cover					
❑ DLP-3029 [M]	The Towering Hilltoppers	1957	7.50	15.00	30.00
❑ DLP-3073 [M]	Love in Bloom	1958	7.50	15.00	30.00

HINES, ERNIE

Number	Title	Yr	VG	VG+	NM
WE PRODUCE					
❑ 1902	Electrified	1972	12.50	25.00	50.00

Number	Title	Yr	VG	VG+	NM
HINES, HINES & DAD					
COLUMBIA					
❑ CS 9679	Pandemonium	1968	5.00	10.00	20.00
HINES, MIMI					
DECCA					
❑ DL 4709 [M]	Mimi Hines Sings	1966	5.00	10.00	20.00
❑ DL 4834 [M]	Mimi Hines Is a Happening	1967	6.25	12.50	25.00
❑ DL 74709 [S]	Mimi Hines Sings	1966	6.25	12.50	25.00
❑ DL 74834 [S]	Mimi Hines Is a Happening	1967	5.00	10.00	20.00
HINSON, DON, AND THE RIGAMORTICIANS					
CAPITOL					
❑ ST 2219 [S]	Monster Dance Party	1964	10.00	20.00	40.00
❑ T 2219 [M]	Monster Dance Party	1964	7.50	15.00	30.00
HINTON, JOE					
BACK BEAT					
❑ B-60 [M]	Funny (How Time Slips Away)	1965	12.50	25.00	50.00
❑ BS-60 [S]	Funny (How Time Slips Away)	1965	17.50	35.00	70.00
DUKE					
❑ DLPS-91	Duke-Peacock Remembers Joe Hinton	1969	5.00	10.00	20.00
HINTON, SAM					
DECCA					
❑ DL 8108 [M]	Singing Across the Land	1955	10.00	20.00	40.00
❑ DL 8418 [M]	A Family Tree of Folk Songs	1957	7.50	15.00	30.00
HIRT, AL					
AUDIO FIDELITY					
❑ AFSD-5877 [S]	Swingin' Dixie (At Dan's Pier 600 in New Orleans)	1959	5.00	10.00	20.00
❑ AFSD-5878 [S]	Swingin' Dixie	1959	5.00	10.00	20.00
❑ AFSD-5926 [S]	Swingin' Dixie (Vol. 3)	1961	5.00	10.00	20.00
❑ AFSD-5927 [S]	Swingin' Dixie	1961	5.00	10.00	20.00
RCA VICTOR					
❑ LSC-2729 [S]	"Pops" Goes the Trumpet	1964	5.00	10.00	20.00
-- With the Boston Pops Orchestra conducted by Arthur Fiedler					
❑ LPM-3917 [M]	Al Hirt Plays Bert Kaempfert	1968	5.00	10.00	20.00
❑ LPM-3979 [M]	Unforgettable	1968	6.25	12.50	25.00
VERVE					
❑ MGV-1012 [M]	Swinging Dixie from Dan's Pier	1957	12.50	25.00	50.00
❑ MGV-1027 [M]	Blockbustin' Dixie!	195?	10.00	20.00	40.00
❑ V-1027 [M]	Blockbustin' Dixie!	1961	5.00	10.00	20.00
HIRT, AL, AND ANN-MARGRET					
Also see each artist's individual listings.					
RCA VICTOR					
❑ LPM-2690 [M]	Beauty and the Beard	1964	6.25	12.50	25.00
❑ LSP-2690 [S]	Beauty and the Beard	1964	7.50	15.00	30.00
HITCHCOCK, STAN					
EPIC					
❑ LN 24138 [M]	Just Call Me Lonesome	1965	5.00	10.00	20.00
❑ BN 26138 [S]	Just Call Me Lonesome	1965	6.25	12.50	25.00
❑ BN 26408	I'm Easy to Love	1968	5.00	10.00	20.00
❑ BN 26438	Softly and Tenderly	1969	5.00	10.00	20.00
HOBBITS, THE					
DECCA					
❑ DL 4920 [M]	Down to Middle-Earth	1967	10.00	20.00	40.00
❑ DL 74920 [S]	Down to Middle-Earth	1967	12.50	25.00	50.00
❑ DL 75009	Men and Doors	1968	7.50	15.00	30.00
HOFFMAN, ABBIE					
BIG TOE					
❑ 1	Wake Up, America!	196?	7.50	15.00	30.00
HOFNER, ADOLPH					
COLUMBIA					
❑ CL 9017 [10]	Dude Ranch Dances	1951	50.00	100.00	200.00
DECCA					
❑ DL 5564 [10]	Dance-O-Rama	1955	100.00	200.00	400.00
HOG HEAVEN					
Also see TOMMY JAMES AND THE SHONDELLS.					
ROULETTE					
❑ SR 42057	Hog Heaven	1971	5.00	10.00	20.00
HOGAN, CLAIRE					
MGM					
❑ E-4501 [M]	Boozers and Losers	1967	5.00	10.00	20.00
❑ SE-4501 [S]	Boozers and Losers	1967	6.25	12.50	25.00
HOGAN, SILAS					
EXCELLO					
❑ LPS-8019	Trouble at Home	1972	5.00	10.00	20.00
HOGG, SMOKEY					
CROWN					
❑ CLP-5226 [M]	Smokey Hogg Sings the Blues	1962	12.50	25.00	50.00
TIME					
❑ 6 [M]	Smokey Hogg	1962	20.00	40.00	80.00
HOLDEN, RANDY					
HOBBIT					
❑ 5002	Population II	1968	50.00	100.00	200.00
HOLDEN, RON					
DONNA					
❑ DLP-2111 [M]	I Love You So	1960	62.50	125.00	250.00
❑ DLPS-2111 [M]	I Love You So	1960	75.00	150.00	300.00
-- Stereo records not known to exist; this is for a mono record in a stereo cover					
HOLIDAY, BILLIE					
AMERICAN RECORDING SOCIETY					
❑ G-409 [M]	Billie Holiday Sings	1956	15.00	30.00	60.00
-- Reissue of Clef 713					
❑ G-431 [M]	Lady Sings the Blues	1957	15.00	30.00	60.00
-- Reissue of Clef 721					
CLEF					
❑ MGC-118 [10]	Billie Holiday Sings	1953	45.00	90.00	180.00
❑ MGC-144 [10]	An Evening with Billie Holiday	1954	45.00	90.00	180.00
❑ MGC-161 [10]	Billie Holiday Favorites	1954	45.00	90.00	180.00
❑ MGC-169 [10]	Billie Holiday at Jazz at the Philharmonic	1955	45.00	90.00	180.00
❑ MGC-669 [M]	Music for Torching	1955	25.00	50.00	100.00
❑ MGC-686 [M]	A Recital by Billie Holiday	1956	30.00	60.00	120.00
-- Reissue of 144 and 161 as one 12-inch LP					
❑ MGC-690 [M]	Solitude -- Songs by Billie Holiday	1956	30.00	60.00	120.00
-- Reissue of 118					
❑ MGC-713 [M]	Velvet Moods	1956	30.00	60.00	120.00
❑ MGC-721 [M]	Lady Sings the Blues	1956	30.00	60.00	120.00
COLUMBIA					
❑ C3L 21 [(3) M]	The Golden Years	1962	12.50	25.00	50.00
-- Red and black label with six "eye" logos					
❑ C3L 21 [(3) M]	The Golden Years	1963	6.25	12.50	25.00
-- Red "Guaranteed High Fidelity" or "360 Sound" label					
❑ C3L 40 [(3) M]	The Golden Years, Volume 2	1966	7.50	15.00	30.00
❑ CL 637 [M]	Lady Day	1954	17.50	35.00	70.00
-- Maroon label, gold print					
❑ CL 637 [M]	Lady Day	1956	10.00	20.00	40.00
-- Red and black label with six "eye" logos					
❑ CL 1157 [M]	Lady in Satin	1958	10.00	20.00	40.00
-- Red and black label with six "eye" logos					
❑ CL 6129 [10]	Billie Holiday Sings	1950	50.00	100.00	200.00
❑ CL 6163 [10]	Billie Holiday Favorites	1951	50.00	100.00	200.00
❑ CS 8048 [S]	Lady in Satin	1958	10.00	20.00	40.00
-- Red and black label with six "eye" logos					
❑ G 30782 [(2)]	God Bless the Child	1972	5.00	10.00	20.00
COMMODORE					
❑ FL-20005 [10]	Billie Holiday, Volume 1	1950	62.50	125.00	250.00
❑ FL-20006 [10]	Billie Holiday, Volume 2	1950	62.50	125.00	250.00
❑ DL-30008 [M]	Billie Holiday	1959	12.50	25.00	50.00
-- Reissue of 20006					
❑ DL-30011 [M]	Billie Holiday with Eddie Heywood and His Orchestra	1959	12.50	25.00	50.00
-- Reissue of 20005					
DECCA					
❑ DXB-161 [(2) M]	The Billie Holiday Story	1959	5.00	10.00	20.00
❑ DL 5345 [10]	Lover Man	1951	50.00	100.00	200.00
❑ DL 8215 [M]	The Lady Sings	1956	15.00	30.00	60.00
❑ DL 8701 [M]	*The Blues Are Brewin'	1958	15.00	30.00	60.00
❑ DL 8702 [M]	Lover Man	1958	15.00	30.00	60.00
JAZZTONE					
❑ J-1209 [M]	Billie Holiday Sings	1955	12.50	25.00	50.00
-- Reissue of Commodore 20005					
JOLLY ROGER					
❑ 5020 [10]	Billie Holiday, Volume 1	1954	25.00	50.00	100.00
❑ 5021 [10]	Billie Holiday, Volume 2	1954	25.00	50.00	100.00
❑ 5022 [10]	Billie Holiday, Volume 3	1954	25.00	50.00	100.00

Number	Title	Yr	VG	VG+	NM
MAINSTREAM					
❏ 56000 [M]	The Commodore Recordings	1965	6.25	12.50	25.00
❏ 56022 [M]	Once Upon a Time	1965	6.25	12.50	25.00
MGM					
❏ E-3764 [M]	Billie Holiday	1959	10.00	20.00	40.00
❏ SE-3764 [S]	Billie Holiday	1959	12.50	25.00	50.00
MOBILE FIDELITY					
❏ 1-247	Body and Soul	1996	30.00	60.00	120.00
-- Audiophile vinyl					
RIC					
❏ R-2001 [M]	Rare Live Recordings	1964	6.25	12.50	25.00
SCORE					
❏ SLP-4014 [M]	Billie Holiday Sings the Blues	1957	30.00	60.00	120.00
UNITED ARTISTS					
❏ UAJ-14014 [M]	Lady Love	1962	10.00	20.00	40.00
❏ UASJ-15014 [S]	Lady Love	1962	12.50	25.00	50.00
VERVE					
❏ MGVS-6021 [S]	Songs for Distingue Lovers	1960	15.00	30.00	60.00
❏ MGV-8026 [M]	Music for Torching	1957	10.00	20.00	40.00
-- Reissue of Clef 669					
❏ V-8026 [M]	Music for Torching	1961	5.00	10.00	20.00
❏ MGV-8027 [M]	A Recital by Billie Holiday	1957	10.00	20.00	40.00
-- Reissue of Clef 686					
❏ V-8027 [M]	A Recital by Billie Holiday	1961	5.00	10.00	20.00
❏ MGV-8074 [M]	Solitude -- Songs by Billie Holiday	1957	10.00	20.00	40.00
-- Reissue of Clef 690					
❏ V-8074 [M]	Solitude -- Songs by Billie Holiday	1961	5.00	10.00	20.00
❏ MGV-8096 [M]	Velvet Moods	1957	10.00	20.00	40.00
-- Reissue of Clef 713					
❏ V-8096 [M]	Velvet Moods	1961	5.00	10.00	20.00
❏ MGV-8099 [M]	Lady Sings the Blues	1957	10.00	20.00	40.00
-- Reissue of Clef 721					
❏ V-8099 [M]	Lady Sings the Blues	1957	5.00	10.00	20.00
❏ MGV-8197 [M]	Body and Soul	1957	15.00	30.00	60.00
❏ V-8197 [M]	Body and Soul	1961	5.00	10.00	20.00
❏ MGV-8257 [M]	Songs for Distingue Lovers	1958	15.00	30.00	60.00
❏ V-8257 [M]	Songs for Distingue Lovers	1961	5.00	10.00	20.00
❏ MGV-8302 [M]	Stay with Me	1959	12.50	25.00	50.00
❏ V-8302 [M]	Stay with Me	1961	5.00	10.00	20.00
❏ MGV-8329 [M]	All or Nothing at All	1959	12.50	25.00	50.00
❏ V-8329 [M]	All or Nothing at All	1959	5.00	10.00	20.00
❏ MGV-8338-2 [(2)M]	The Unforgettable Lady Day	1959	20.00	40.00	80.00
❏ V-8338-2 [(2) M]	The Unforgettable Lady Day	1961	6.25	12.50	25.00
❏ V-8410 [M]	The Essential Billie Holiday	1961	5.00	10.00	20.00
❏ V-8505 [M]	The Essential Jazz Vocals	1963	5.00	10.00	20.00
❏ V6-8257 [S]	Songs for Distingue Lovers	1961	6.25	12.50	25.00

HOLIDAY, BILLIE, AND STAN GETZ
Also see each artist's individual listings.

Number	Title	Yr	VG	VG+	NM
DALE					
❏ 25 [10]	Billie and Stan	1951	100.00	200.00	400.00

HOLIDAY, JIMMY

Number	Title	Yr	VG	VG+	NM
MINIT					
❏ LP-24005 [M]	Turning Point	1966	7.50	15.00	30.00
❏ LP-40005 [S]	Turning Point	1966	10.00	20.00	40.00

HOLLAND, EDDIE

Number	Title	Yr	VG	VG+	NM
MOTOWN					
❏ 604 [M]	Eddie Holland	1963	100.00	200.00	400.00

HOLLIDAY, JUDY

Number	Title	Yr	VG	VG+	NM
COLUMBIA					
❏ CL 1153 [M]	Trouble Is a Man	1958	7.50	15.00	30.00
❏ CS 8041 [S]	Trouble Is a Man	1959	10.00	20.00	40.00

HOLLIES, THE

Number	Title	Yr	VG	VG+	NM
EPIC					
❏ AS 138 [DJ]	Everything You Always Wanted to Hear by the Hollies But Were Afraid to Ask For	1976	5.00	10.00	20.00
-- Promo-only sampler album					
❏ LN 24315 [M]	Evolution	1967	7.50	15.00	30.00
❏ LN 24344 [M]	Dear Eloise/King Midas in Reverse	1967	7.50	15.00	30.00
❏ BN 26315 [S]	Evolution	1967	6.25	12.50	25.00
❏ BN 26344 [S]	Dear Eloise/King Midas in Reverse	1967	6.25	12.50	25.00
❏ BN 26538	He Ain't Heavy, He's My Brother	1970	5.00	10.00	20.00
❏ E 30255	Moving Finger	1970	5.00	10.00	20.00
IMPERIAL					
❏ LP-9265 [M]	Here I Go Again	1964	37.50	75.00	150.00
-- Black label with stars					
❏ LP-9265 [M]	Here I Go Again	1964	12.50	25.00	50.00
-- Black and pink label					

Number	Title	Yr	VG	VG+	NM
❏ LP-9299 [M]	Hear! Here!	1965	12.50	25.00	50.00
❏ LP-9312 [M]	The Hollies -- Beat Group	1966	7.50	15.00	30.00
❏ LP-9330 [M]	Bus Stop	1966	7.50	15.00	30.00
-- Black and pink label					
❏ LP-9330 [M]	Bus Stop	1966	6.25	12.50	25.00
-- Black and green label					
❏ LP-9339 [M]	Stop! Stop! Stop!	1966	6.25	12.50	25.00
❏ LP-9350 [M]	The Hollies' Greatest Hits	1967	5.00	10.00	20.00
❏ LP-12265 [R]	Here I Go Again	1964	25.00	50.00	100.00
-- Black label with silver print					
❏ LP-12265 [R]	Here I Go Again	1964	7.50	15.00	30.00
-- Black and pink label					
❏ LP-12299 [R]	Hear! Here!	1965	7.50	15.00	30.00
❏ LP-12312 [S]	The Hollies -- Beat Group	1966	10.00	20.00	40.00
❏ LP-12330 [R]	Bus Stop	1966	6.25	12.50	25.00
-- Black and pink label					
❏ LP-12330 [R]	Bus Stop	1966	5.00	10.00	20.00
-- Black and green label					
❏ LP-12339 [S]	Stop! Stop! Stop!	1966	7.50	15.00	30.00
❏ LP-12350 [P]	The Hollies' Greatest Hits	1967	6.25	12.50	25.00

HOLLOWAY, BRENDA

Number	Title	Yr	VG	VG+	NM
TAMLA					
❏ T 257 [M]	Every Little Bit Hurts	1964	50.00	100.00	200.00
❏ TS 257 [R]	Every Little Bit Hurts	1964	37.50	75.00	150.00

HOLLOWAY, LOLEATTA

Number	Title	Yr	VG	VG+	NM
GOLD MIND					
❏ 7500	Loleatta	1977	5.00	10.00	20.00
❏ A-9501	Queen of the Night	1978	5.00	10.00	20.00
❏ GA-9506	Love Sensation	1979	5.00	10.00	20.00

HOLLY, BUDDY
Also see THE CRICKETS.

Number	Title	Yr	VG	VG+	NM
CORAL					
❏ CXB 8 [(2) M]	The Best of Buddy Holly	1966	20.00	40.00	80.00
❏ CXSB 8 [(2) R]	The Best of Buddy Holly	1966	12.50	25.00	50.00
❏ CRL 57210 [M]	Buddy Holly	1958	100.00	200.00	400.00
-- Maroon label					
❏ CRL 57210 [M]	Buddy Holly	1964	25.00	50.00	100.00
-- Black label with color bars					
❏ CRL 57279 [M]	The Buddy Holly Story	1959	75.00	150.00	300.00
-- Maroon label; back color print in black and red					
❏ CRL 57279 [M]	The Buddy Holly Story	1959	37.50	75.00	150.00
-- Maroon label; back color print in all black					
❏ CRL 57279 [M]	The Buddy Holly Story	1963	20.00	40.00	80.00
-- Black label with color bars					
❏ CRL 57326 [M]	The Buddy Holly Story, Vol. 2	1959	50.00	100.00	200.00
-- Maroon label					
❏ CRL 57326 [M]	The Buddy Holly Story, Vol. 2	1963	20.00	40.00	80.00
-- Black label with color bars					
❏ CRL 57405 [M]	Buddy Holly and the Crickets	1962	37.50	75.00	150.00
-- Reissue of the Crickets LP on Brunswick 54038					
❏ CRL 57426 [M]	Reminiscing	1963	50.00	100.00	200.00
-- Maroon label					
❏ CRL 57426 [M]	Reminiscing	1964	20.00	40.00	80.00
-- Black label with color bars					
❏ CRL 57450 [M]	Buddy Holly Showcase	1964	25.00	50.00	100.00
❏ CRL 57463 [M]	Holly in the Hills	1965	30.00	60.00	120.00
❏ CRL 57492 [M]	Buddy Holly's Greatest Hits	1967	20.00	40.00	80.00
❏ CRL 757279 [R]	The Buddy Holly Story	1963	10.00	20.00	40.00
❏ CRL 757326 [R]	The Buddy Holly Story, Vol. 2	1963	10.00	20.00	40.00
❏ CRL 757405 [R]	Buddy Holly and the Crickets	1963	10.00	20.00	40.00
❏ CRL 757426 [R]	Reminiscing	1964	10.00	20.00	40.00
❏ CRL 757450 [R]	Buddy Holly Showcase	1964	20.00	40.00	80.00
❏ CRL 757463 [R]	Holly in the Hills	1965	25.00	50.00	100.00
❏ CRL 757492 [P]	Buddy Holly's Greatest Hits	1967	12.50	25.00	50.00
❏ CRL 757504 [S]	Giant	1969	12.50	25.00	50.00
CRICKET					
❏ C001000	Buddy Holly Live -- Volume 1	197?	5.00	10.00	20.00
❏ C001001	Buddy Holly Live -- Volume 1	197?	5.00	10.00	20.00
DECCA					
❏ DXSE 7207 [(2)]	A Rock 'n' Roll Collection	1972	10.00	20.00	40.00
❏ DL 8707 [M]	That'll Be the Day	1958	375.00	750.00	1,500.
-- Black label with silver print					
❏ DL 8707 [M]	That'll Be the Day	1961	75.00	150.00	300.00
-- Black label with color bars					
MCA					
❏ 4009 [(2)]	A Rock 'n' Roll Collection	1973	5.00	10.00	20.00
-- Black labels with rainbow					
❏ 4184 [(2)]	Legend	1985	5.00	10.00	20.00
❏ 5540 [(2)]	From the Original Master Tapes	1986	6.25	12.50	25.00
❏ 11161	Buddy Holly	1995	10.00	20.00	40.00
-- Audiophile "Heavy Vinyl" reissue with gatefold cover					
❏ 80000 [(6)]	The Complete Buddy Holly	1981	12.50	25.00	50.00
-- Box set with booklet and custom innersleeves					

Number	Title	Yr	VG	VG+	NM
VOCALION					
❏ VL 3811 [M]	The Great Buddy Holly	1967	20.00	40.00	80.00
❏ VL 73811 [R]	The Great Buddy Holly	1967	12.50	25.00	50.00
❏ VL 73923	Good Rockin'	1971	30.00	60.00	120.00
HOLLYRIDGE STRINGS, THE					
CAPITOL					
❏ ST 2116 [S]	The Beatles Song Book	1964	5.00	10.00	20.00
❏ ST 2156 [S]	The Beach Boys Song Book	1964	5.00	10.00	20.00
❏ ST 2199 [S]	Hits Made Famous by the Four Seasons	1965	5.00	10.00	20.00
❏ ST 2202 [S]	The Beatles Song Book, Vol. 2	1965	5.00	10.00	20.00
❏ ST 2221 [S]	Hits Made Famous by Elvis	1965	5.00	10.00	20.00
❏ ST 2310 [S]	The Nat King Cole Song Book	1965	5.00	10.00	20.00
❏ ST 2429 [S]	The New Beatles Song Book	1966	5.00	10.00	20.00
❏ ST 2564 [S]	Oldies But Goldies	1966	5.00	10.00	20.00
❏ ST 2611 [S]	Skyscraper	1966	5.00	10.00	20.00
❏ T 2656 [M]	The Beatles Song Book, Vol. 4	1967	5.00	10.00	20.00
❏ T 2749 [M]	The Beach Boys Song Book, Vol.	1967	5.00	10.00	20.00
HOLLYWOOD ARGYLES, THE					
LUTE					
❏ L-9001 [M]	The Hollywood Argyles (Alley Oop)	1960	175.00	350.00	700.00
HOLLYWOOD PERSUADERS, THE					
ORIGINAL SOUND					
❏ LPM-5013 [M]	Drums a-Go-Go	1965	12.50	25.00	50.00
❏ LPS-8874 [S]	Drums a-Go-Go	1965	15.00	30.00	60.00
HOLMAN, EDDIE					
ABC					
❏ S-701	I Love You	1970	7.50	15.00	30.00
HOLMBERG, JIM					
ESP-DISK'					
❏ 1098	MIJ	196?	5.00	10.00	20.00
HOLMES, JAKE					
TOWER					
❏ T 5079 [M]	Above Ground	1967	5.00	10.00	20.00
HOLMES, MARVIN					
BROWN DOOR					
❏ MH-6573	Summer of '73	1973	6.25	12.50	25.00
❏ MH-6581	Honor Thy Father	1975	6.25	12.50	25.00
UNI					
❏ 73046	Ooh, Ooh, The Dragon And Other Monsters	1969	7.50	15.00	30.00
HOLMES, RICHARD "GROOVE"					
PACIFIC JAZZ					
❏ PJ-23 [M]	Richard "Groove" Holmes	1961	6.25	12.50	25.00
❏ ST-23 [S]	Richard "Groove" Holmes	1961	7.50	15.00	30.00
❏ PJ-32 [M]	Groovin' with Jug	1961	7.50	15.00	30.00
❏ ST-32 [S]	Groovin' with Jug	1961	10.00	20.00	40.00
❏ PJ-51 [M]	Somethin' Special	1962	5.00	10.00	20.00
❏ ST-51 [S]	Somethin' Special	1962	6.25	12.50	25.00
❏ PJ-59 [M]	After Hours	1962	5.00	10.00	20.00
❏ ST-59 [S]	After Hours	1962	6.25	12.50	25.00
❏ ST-20105 [S]	Tell It Like It Tis	1966	5.00	10.00	20.00
PRESTIGE					
❏ PRST-7435 [S]	Soul Message	1966	5.00	10.00	20.00
❏ PRST-7468 [S]	Living Soul	1966	5.00	10.00	20.00
❏ PRST-7485 [S]	Misty	1966	5.00	10.00	20.00
❏ PRLP-7493 [M]	Spicy	1967	5.00	10.00	20.00
❏ PRLP-7497 [M]	Super Cool	1967	5.00	10.00	20.00
❏ PRLP-7514 [M]	Get Up and Get It	1967	5.00	10.00	20.00
WARNER BROS.					
❏ W 1553 [M]	Book of the Blues	1964	5.00	10.00	20.00
❏ WS 1553 [S]	Book of the Blues	1964	6.25	12.50	25.00
HOLY MACKEREL					
REPRISE					
❏ RS-6311	Holy Mackerel	1968	6.25	12.50	25.00
HOLY MODAL ROUNDERS, THE					
ELEKTRA					
❏ EKS-74026	The Moray Eels Eat the Holy Modal Rounders	1968	7.50	15.00	30.00

Number	Title	Yr	VG	VG+	NM
ESP-DISK'					
❏ 1068 [M]	Indian War Whoop	1967	10.00	20.00	40.00
❏ 1068-S [S]	Indian War Whoop	1967	10.00	20.00	40.00
FANTASY					
❏ F-24711	Stampfel and Weber	1972	5.00	10.00	20.00
FOLKLORE					
❏ FRLP-14031 [M]	The Holy Modal Rounders	1964	20.00	40.00	80.00
METROMEDIA					
❏ MD-1039	Good Taste Is Timeless	1970	7.50	15.00	30.00
PRESTIGE					
❏ PRLP-7410 [M]	The Holy Modal Rounders 2	1965	10.00	20.00	40.00
❏ PRLP-7451 [M]	The Holy Modal Rounders	1966	10.00	20.00	40.00
-- Reissue of Folklore LP					
❏ PR-7720	The Holy Modal Rounders	1969	6.25	12.50	25.00
HOMBRES, THE					
VERVE FORECAST					
❏ FT-3036 [M]	Let It Out (Let It All Hang Out)	1967	7.50	15.00	30.00
❏ FTS-3036 [S]	Let It Out (Let It All Hang Out)	1967	6.25	12.50	25.00
HOMER					
UNITED					
❏ HS-101	Grown in U.S.A.	1970	62.50	125.00	250.00
HOMER AND JETHRO					
AUDIO LAB					
❏ AL-1513 [M]	Musical Madness	1958	25.00	50.00	100.00
KING					
❏ 639 [M]	They Sure Are Corny	1959	25.00	50.00	100.00
❏ 848 [M]	Cornier Than Corn	1963	17.50	35.00	70.00
❏ KS-1005	24 Great Songs in the Homer & Jethro Style	1967	5.00	10.00	20.00
RCA VICTOR					
❏ LPM-1412 [M]	Barefoot Ballads	1957	12.50	25.00	50.00
❏ LPM-1560 [M]	The Worst of Homer & Jethro	1958	12.50	25.00	50.00
❏ LPM-1880 [M]	Life Can Be Miserable	1958	7.50	15.00	30.00
❏ LSP-1880 [S]	Life Can Be Miserable	1958	12.50	25.00	50.00
❏ LPM-2181 [M]	Homer and Jethro at the Country Club	1960	6.25	12.50	25.00
❏ LSP-2181 [S]	Homer and Jethro at the Country Club	1960	10.00	20.00	40.00
❏ LPM-2286 [M]	Songs My Mother Never Sang	1961	6.25	12.50	25.00
❏ LSP-2286 [S]	Songs My Mother Never Sang	1961	7.50	15.00	30.00
❏ LPM-2455 [M]	Zany Songs of the '30s	1962	6.25	12.50	25.00
❏ LSP-2455 [S]	Zany Songs of the '30s	1962	7.50	15.00	30.00
❏ LPM-2459 [M]	Playing It Straight	1962	6.25	12.50	25.00
❏ LSP-2459 [S]	Playing It Straight	1962	7.50	15.00	30.00
❏ LPM-2492 [M]	Homer and Jethro at the Convention	1962	6.25	12.50	25.00
❏ LSP-2492 [S]	Homer and Jethro at the Convention	1962	7.50	15.00	30.00
❏ LPM-2674 [M]	Homer and Jethro Go West	1963	6.25	12.50	25.00
❏ LSP-2674 [S]	Homer and Jethro Go West	1963	7.50	15.00	30.00
❏ LPM-2743 [M]	Ooh, That's Corny	1963	6.25	12.50	25.00
❏ LSP-2743 [S]	Ooh, That's Corny	1963	7.50	15.00	30.00
❏ LPM-2928 [M]	Cornfucius Say	1964	6.25	12.50	25.00
❏ LSP-2928 [S]	Cornfucius Say	1964	7.50	15.00	30.00
❏ LPM-2954 [M]	Fractured Folk Songs	1964	6.25	12.50	25.00
❏ LSP-2954 [S]	Fractured Folk Songs	1964	7.50	15.00	30.00
❏ LPM-3112 [10]	Homer & Jethro Fracture Frank Loesser	1953	37.50	75.00	150.00
❏ LPM-3357 [M]	Homer and Jethro Sing Tenderly	1965	6.25	12.50	25.00
❏ LSP-3357 [S]	Homer and Jethro Sing Tenderly	1965	7.50	15.00	30.00
❏ LPM-3462 [M]	The Old Crusty Minstrels	1965	6.25	12.50	25.00
❏ LSP-3462 [S]	The Old Crusty Minstrels	1965	7.50	15.00	30.00
❏ LPM-3474 [M]	The Best of Homer and Jethro	1966	6.25	12.50	25.00
❏ LSP-3474 [S]	The Best of Homer and Jethro	1966	7.50	15.00	30.00
❏ LPM-3538 [M]	Any News from Nashville?	1966	6.25	12.50	25.00
❏ LSP-3538 [S]	Any News from Nashville?	1966	7.50	15.00	30.00
❏ LPM-3673 [M]	Wanted for Murder	1966	6.25	12.50	25.00
❏ LSP-3673 [S]	Wanted for Murder	1966	7.50	15.00	30.00
❏ LPM-3701 [M]	It Ain't Necessarily Square	1967	7.50	15.00	30.00
❏ LSP-3701 [S]	It Ain't Necessarily Square	1967	6.25	12.50	25.00
❏ LPM-3822 [M]	Nashville Cats	1967	10.00	20.00	40.00
❏ LSP-3822 [S]	Nashville Cats	1967	6.25	12.50	25.00
❏ LPM-3877 [M]	Somethin' Stupid	1967	12.50	25.00	50.00
❏ LSP-3877 [S]	Somethin' Stupid	1967	6.25	12.50	25.00
❏ LPM-3973 [M]	There's Nothing Like an Old Hippie	1968	25.00	50.00	100.00
❏ LSP-3973 [S]	There's Nothing Like an Old Hippie	1968	6.25	12.50	25.00
❏ LSP-4001	Cool, Crazy Christmas	1968	5.00	10.00	20.00
❏ LSP-4024	Homer and Jethro at Vanderbilt U.	1969	5.00	10.00	20.00
❏ LSP-4148	Homer and Jethro's Next Album	1969	5.00	10.00	20.00

Number	Title	Yr	VG	VG+	NM

HOMESICK JAMES
PRESTIGE
❑ PRLP-7388 [M]	Homesick James	1965	7.50	15.00	30.00

HONDELLS, THE
MERCURY
❑ MG-20940 [M]	Go Little Honda	1964	10.00	20.00	40.00
❑ MG-20982 [M]	The Hondells	1965	12.50	25.00	50.00
❑ SR-60940 [S]	Go Little Honda	1964	15.00	30.00	60.00
❑ SR-60982 [S]	The Hondells	1965	20.00	40.00	80.00

HONEY AND THE BEES
JOSIE
❑ JOS-4013	Love	1970	5.00	10.00	20.00

HONEYCOMBS, THE
INTERPHON
❑ IN-88001 [M]	Here Are the Honeycombs	1964	10.00	20.00	40.00
❑ IN-88001 [R]	Here Are the Honeycombs	1964	7.50	15.00	30.00
VEE JAY
❑ IN-88001 [M]	Here Are the Honeycombs	1964	12.50	25.00	50.00
❑ IN-88001 [R]	Here Are the Honeycombs	1964	10.00	20.00	40.00

HOODOO RHYTHM DEVILS, THE
CAPITOL
❑ ST-842	The Hoodoo Rhythm Devils	1971	5.00	10.00	20.00

HOOK, THE
UNI
❑ 73023	The Hook Will Grab You	1968	6.25	12.50	25.00
❑ 73038	Hooked	1969	6.25	12.50	25.00

HOOKER, EARL
BLUE THUMB
❑ BTS 12	Sweet Black Angel	1969	5.00	10.00	20.00
BLUESWAY
❑ BLS-6032	Don't Have to Worry	1969	5.00	10.00	20.00
❑ BLS-6038	If You Miss Him	1970	5.00	10.00	20.00
CUCA
❑ 3400 [M]	The Genius of Earl Hooker	1965	37.50	75.00	150.00

HOOKER, JOHN LEE
ABC
❑ S-720 [(2)]	Endless Boogie	1971	5.00	10.00	20.00
❑ X-736	Never Get Out of These Blues	1972	5.00	10.00	20.00
❑ XQ-736 [Q]	Never Get Out of These Blues	1974	6.25	12.50	25.00
❑ X-761	Live at Soledad Prison	1972	5.00	10.00	20.00
❑ XQ-761 [Q]	Live at Soledad Prison	1974	6.25	12.50	25.00
❑ X-768	Born in Mississippi, Raised Up in Tennessee	1973	5.00	10.00	20.00
❑ XQ-768 [Q]	Born in Mississippi, Raised Up in Tennessee	1974	6.25	12.50	25.00
❑ XQ-838 [Q]	Free Beer and Chicken	1974	6.25	12.50	25.00
ATCO
❑ 33-151 [M]	Don't Turn Me From Your Door	1963	25.00	50.00	100.00
❑ SD 33-151 [R]	Don't Turn Me From Your Door	1967	12.50	25.00	50.00
ATLANTIC
❑ SD 7228	Detroit Special	1972	5.00	10.00	20.00
BATTLE
❑ BLP-6113 [M]	John Lee Hooker	196?	37.50	75.00	150.00
❑ BLP-6114 [M]	How Long Blues	196?	37.50	75.00	150.00
BLUESWAY
❑ BL-6002 [M]	Live at Café A-Go-Go	1967	6.25	12.50	25.00
❑ BLS-6002 [S]	Live at Café A-Go-Go	1967	5.00	10.00	20.00
❑ BL-6012 [M]	Urban Blues	1967	6.25	12.50	25.00
❑ BLS-6012 [S]	Urban Blues	1967	5.00	10.00	20.00
❑ BLS-6023	Simply the Truth	1968	5.00	10.00	20.00
❑ BLS-6038	If You Miss 'Em	1969	5.00	10.00	20.00
❑ BLQ-6052 [Q]	Live at Kabuki-Wuki	1974	6.25	12.50	25.00
CHESS
❑ LP-1438 [M]	House of the Blues	1960	75.00	150.00	300.00
-- Black label					
❑ LP-1438 [M]	House of the Blues	1966	12.50	25.00	50.00
-- Blue and white label					
❑ LP-1454 [M]	John Lee Hooker Plays and Sings the Blues	1961	75.00	150.00	300.00
-- Black label					
❑ LP-1454 [M]	John Lee Hooker Plays and Sings the Blues	1966	12.50	25.00	50.00
-- Blue and white label					

❑ LP-1508 [M]	Real Folk Blues	1966	12.50	25.00	50.00
❑ LPS-1508 [R]	Real Folk Blues	1966	7.50	15.00	30.00
❑ 60011 [(2)]	Mad Man Blues	1973	5.00	10.00	20.00
CROWN
❑ CLP-5157 [M]	The Blues	1960	25.00	50.00	100.00
-- Black label with silver "Crown"					
❑ CLP-5157 [M]	The Blues	1962	7.50	15.00	30.00
-- Gray label					
❑ CLP-5232 [M]	John Lee Hooker Sings the Blues	1962	25.00	50.00	100.00
-- Black label with silver "Crown"					
❑ CLP-5232 [M]	John Lee Hooker Sings the Blues	1962	7.50	15.00	30.00
-- Gray label					
❑ CLP-5295 [M]	Folk Blues	1962	7.50	15.00	30.00
-- Gray label					
❑ CLP-5353 [M]	The Great John Lee Hooker	1963	7.50	15.00	30.00
-- Gray label					
EXODUS
❑ 325 [M]	Is He the World's Greatest Blues Singer?	1966	6.25	12.50	25.00
GALAXY
❑ 8201 [M]	I'm John Lee Hooker	1962	62.50	125.00	250.00
❑ 8205 [M]	Live at Sugar Hill	196?	62.50	125.00	250.00
IMPULSE!
❑ A-9103 [M]	It Serves You Right to Suffer	1966	7.50	15.00	30.00
❑ AS-9103 [S]	It Serves You Right to Suffer	1966	10.00	20.00	40.00
KING
❑ 727 [M]	John Lee Hooker Sings the Blues	1960	125.00	250.00	500.00
❑ KS-1085	Moanin' and Stompin' Blues	1970	6.25	12.50	25.00
RIVERSIDE
❑ RLP-12-321 [M]	That's My Story	1960	25.00	50.00	100.00
❑ RLP-12-838 [M]	The Country Blues of John Lee Hooker	1959	25.00	50.00	100.00
SPECIALTY
❑ SPS-2125	Alone	1970	7.50	15.00	30.00
❑ SPS-2127	Going Down Highway 51	1970	7.50	15.00	30.00
UNITED ARTISTS
❑ UA-LA127-J	John Lee Hooker's Detroit	1974	6.25	12.50	25.00
VEE JAY
❑ LP-1007 [M]	I'm John Lee Hooker	1959	75.00	150.00	300.00
-- Maroon label					
❑ LP-1007 [M]	I'm John Lee Hooker	1960	20.00	40.00	80.00
-- Black label with colorband					
❑ LP-1023 [M]	Travelin'	1960	20.00	40.00	80.00
❑ LP-1033 [M]	The Folk Lore of John Lee Hooker	1961	12.50	25.00	50.00
❑ SR-1033 [S]	The Folk Lore of John Lee Hooker	1961	20.00	40.00	80.00
❑ LP-1043 [M]	Burnin'	1962	12.50	25.00	50.00
❑ SR-1043 [S]	Burnin'	1962	37.50	75.00	150.00
❑ LP-1049 [M]	The Best of John Lee Hooker	1962	12.50	25.00	50.00
❑ SR-1049 [P]	The Best of John Lee Hooker	1962	20.00	40.00	80.00
❑ LP-1058 [M]	The Big Soul of John Lee Hooker	1963	12.50	25.00	50.00
❑ SR-1058 [S]	The Big Soul of John Lee Hooker	1963	37.50	75.00	150.00
❑ LP-1066 [M]	John Lee Hooker On Campus	1963	12.50	25.00	50.00
❑ SR-1066 [S]	John Lee Hooker On Campus	1963	37.50	75.00	150.00
❑ LP-1078 [M]	John Lee Hooker at Newport	1964	12.50	25.00	50.00
❑ SR-1078 [S]	John Lee Hooker at Newport	1964	37.50	75.00	150.00
❑ LP-8502 [M]	Is He the World's Greatest Folk/Blues Singer	1965	10.00	20.00	40.00
VERVE FOLKWAYS
❑ FT-3003 [M]	John Lee Hooker and Seven	1965	6.25	12.50	25.00
❑ FTS-3003 [S]	John Lee Hooker and Seven	1965	10.00	20.00	40.00

HOOKER, JOHN LEE, AND CANNED HEAT
Also see each artist's individual listings.
LIBERTY
❑ 35002	Hooker 'n' Heat	1971	5.00	10.00	20.00

HOOTCH
PROGRESS
❑ PRS-4844	Hootch	1974	150.00	300.00	600.00

HOOTERS
ANTENNA
❑ HOO 83	Amore	1983	5.00	10.00	20.00

HOPE, BOB
DECCA
❑ DL 4396 [M]	Hope in Russia and One Other Place	1963	5.00	10.00	20.00
❑ DL 74396 [S]	Hope in Russia and One Other Place	1963	6.25	12.50	25.00

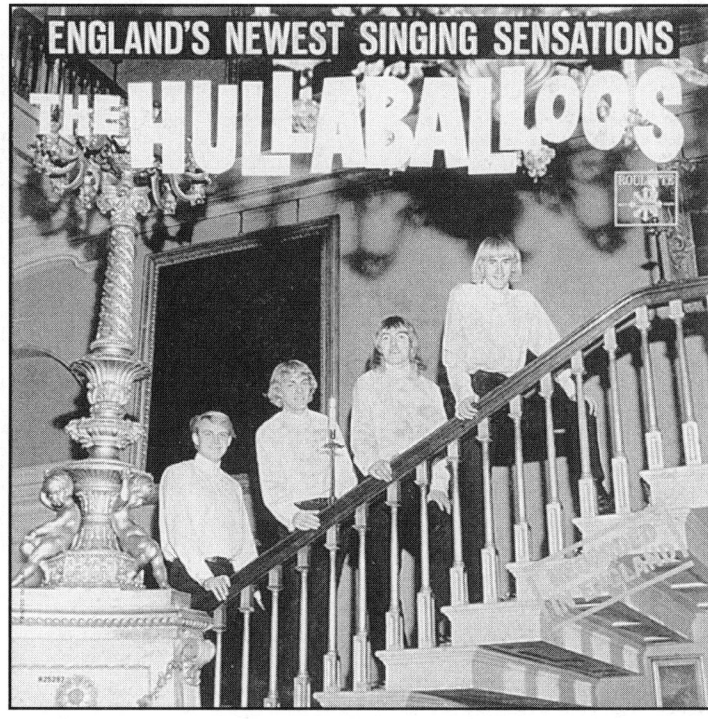

(Top left) *Buddy Holly* was the only album to be released under his name during his lifetime. The original on Coral is highly sought after. This 1995 reissue, on the short-lived MCA "Heavy Vinyl" series, has become collectible in its own right. (Top right) Best known for the novelty of their female drummer, the Honeycombs did have one big American hit, "Have I the Right." That led to the only album to be released on the Interphon label. (Bottom left) The first album by blues singer Howlin' Wolf, *Moanin' in the Moonlight*, is a major blues rarity and can go for $600 in near-mint condition. (Bottom right) Their biggest American hit was a remake of Buddy Holly's "I'm Gonna Love You Too," but Roulette not only issued the above album by the Hullaballoos, they issued a second one as well.

Number	Title	Yr	VG	VG+	NM
HOPE, LYNN					
ALADDIN					
❏ LP-707 [10]	Lynn Hope and His Tenor Sax	1953	150.00	300.00	600.00
❏ LP-805 [M]	Lynn Hope and His Tenor Sax	1955	125.00	250.00	500.00
IMPERIAL					
❏ LP-9177 [M]	Tenderly	1962	10.00	20.00	40.00
❏ LP-12177 [S]	Tenderly	1962	15.00	30.00	60.00
KING					
❏ 717 [M]	Maharajah of the Saxophone	1961	30.00	60.00	120.00
SCORE					
❏ SLP-4015 [M]	Tenderly	1957	50.00	100.00	200.00
HOPKIN, MARY					
APPLE					
❏ SW-3351	Post Card	1969	6.25	12.50	25.00
❏ SW-5-3351	Post Card	1969	7.50	15.00	30.00
-- Capitol Record Club edition					
❏ SMAS-3381	Earth Song/Ocean Song	1970	6.25	12.50	25.00
❏ SW-3395	Those Were the Days	1972	10.00	20.00	40.00
HOPKINS, LIGHTNIN'					
ANALOGUE PRODUCTIONS					
❏ AAPB-014	Goin' Away	199?	10.00	20.00	40.00
-- Audiophile reissue					
ARHOOLIE					
❏ 1011	Lightnin' Hopkins and His Guitar	196?	5.00	10.00	20.00
❏ 1022	Lightnin' Hopkins, His Brother and Barbara Dane	196?	5.00	10.00	20.00
BLUESVILLE					
❏ BVLP-1019 [M]	Lightnin'	1961	25.00	50.00	100.00
-- Blue label, silver print					
❏ BVLP-1019 [M]	Lightnin'	1964	7.50	15.00	30.00
-- Blue label, trident logo on right					
❏ BVLP-1029 [M]	Last Night Blues	1961	25.00	50.00	100.00
-- Blue label, silver print					
❏ BVLP-1045 [M]	Blues in My Bottle	1962	25.00	50.00	100.00
-- Blue label, silver print					
❏ BVLP-1045 [M]	Blues in My Bottle	1964	7.50	15.00	30.00
-- Blue label, trident logo on right					
❏ BVLP-1057 [M]	Walkin' This Street	1962	25.00	50.00	100.00
-- Blue label, silver print					
❏ BVLP-1057 [M]	Walkin' This Street	1964	7.50	15.00	30.00
-- Blue label, trident logo on right					
❏ BVLP-1061 [M]	Lightnin' & Co.	1963	25.00	50.00	100.00
-- Blue label, silver print					
❏ BVLP-1061 [M]	Lightnin' & Co.	1964	7.50	15.00	30.00
-- Blue label, trident logo on right					
❏ BVLP-1070 [M]	Smokes Like Lightnin'	1963	25.00	50.00	100.00
-- Blue label, silver print					
❏ BVLP-1070 [M]	Smokes Like Lightnin'	1964	7.50	15.00	30.00
-- Blue label, trident logo on right					
❏ BVLP-1073 [M]	Goin' Away	1963	25.00	50.00	100.00
-- Blue label, silver print					
❏ BVLP-1073 [M]	Goin' Away	1964	7.50	15.00	30.00
-- Blue label, trident logo on right					
❏ BVLP-1081 [M]	Gotta Move Your Baby	1964	7.50	15.00	30.00
-- Blue label, trident logo on right					
❏ BVLP-1084 [M]	Lightnin' Hopkins' Greatest Hits	1964	10.00	20.00	40.00
❏ BVLP-1086 [M]	Down Home Blues	1964	6.25	12.50	25.00
BLUESWAY					
❏ S-6039	If You Miss 'Im	1969	5.00	10.00	20.00
CANDID					
❏ CM-8010 [M]	Lightnin' in New York	1961	30.00	60.00	120.00
❏ CS-9010 [S]	Lightnin' in New York	1961	37.50	75.00	150.00
CROWN					
❏ CLP-5224 [M]	Lightnin' Hopkins Sings the Blues	1962	25.00	50.00	100.00
-- Black label, silver "Crown"					
❏ CLP-5224 [M]	Lightnin' Hopkins Sings the Blues	1962	12.50	25.00	50.00
-- Gray label					
❏ CLP-5224 [M]	Lightnin' Hopkins Sings the Blues	196?	6.25	12.50	25.00
-- Black label, multi-color logo					
DART					
❏ D-8000 [M]	Lightning Strikes Again	1960	100.00	200.00	400.00
❏ D-8000 [M]	Blues Underground	196?	50.00	100.00	200.00
-- Retitled version of above					
FANTASY					
❏ 24702 [(2)]	Double Blues	1972	5.00	10.00	20.00
FIRE					
❏ FLP 104 [M]	Mojo Hand	1960	375.00	750.00	1,500.
FOLKLORE					
❏ FRLP-14021 [M]	Hootin' the Blues	1964	15.00	30.00	60.00
❏ FRST-14021 [S]	Hootin' the Blues	1964	17.50	35.00	70.00

Number	Title	Yr	VG	VG+	NM
FOLKWAYS					
❏ FS-3822 [M]	Lightnin' Hopkins	1962	10.00	20.00	40.00
GUEST STAR					
❏ G-1458 [M]	"Live" at the Bird Lounge, Houston, Texas	1964	7.50	15.00	30.00
❏ GS-1458 [R]	"Live" at the Bird Lounge, Houston, Texas	1964	5.00	10.00	20.00
HERALD					
❏ LP 1012 [M]	Lightnin' and the Blues	1959	750.00	1,125.	1,500.
-- Black label					
❏ LP 1012 [M]	Lightnin' and the Blues	1959	200.00	400.00	800.00
-- Yellow label					
❏ LP 1012 [M]	Lightnin' and the Blues	196?	125.00	250.00	500.00
-- Multi-color label					
IMPERIAL					
❏ LP-9180 [M]	Lightnin' Hopkins On Stage	1962	75.00	150.00	300.00
❏ LP-9186 [M]	Lightnin' Hopkins Sings the Blues	1962	75.00	150.00	300.00
❏ LP-9211 [M]	Lightnin' Hopkins and the Blues	1963	50.00	100.00	200.00
❏ LP-12211 [R]	Lightnin' Hopkins and the Blues	1963	25.00	50.00	100.00
INTERNATIONAL ARTISTS					
❏ IA-6	Free Form Patterns	1968	50.00	100.00	200.00
-- With photo on cover					
❏ IA-6	Free Form Patterns	1968	12.50	25.00	50.00
-- With psychedelic art on cover					
MAINSTREAM					
❏ S-6040 [S]	Blues	196?	7.50	15.00	30.00
❏ 56040 [M]	Blues	196?	6.25	12.50	25.00
MOUNT VERNON					
❏ 104 [M]	Nothin' But the Blues	196?	6.25	12.50	25.00
POPPY					
❏ 60002 [(2)]	Lightnin'!	1969	6.25	12.50	25.00
PRESTIGE					
❏ PRLPT-7370 [(2)M]	My Life with the Blues	1965	15.00	30.00	60.00
❏ PRST-7370 [(2) S]	My Life with the Blues	1965	17.50	35.00	70.00
❏ PRLP-7377 [M]	Soul Blues	1966	12.50	25.00	50.00
❏ PRST-7377 [S]	Soul Blues	1966	15.00	30.00	60.00
SCORE					
❏ SLP-4022 [M]	Lightnin' Hopkins Strums the Blues	1958	300.00	600.00	1,200.
SPHERE SOUND					
❏ SSR-7001 [M]	Lightnin' Hopkins	1964	100.00	200.00	400.00
❏ SSSR-7001 [R]	Lightnin' Hopkins	1964	75.00	150.00	300.00
TIME					
❏ 1 [M]	Blues/Folk	1960	30.00	60.00	120.00
❏ 2 [M]	Blues/Folk Volume 2	1960	30.00	60.00	120.00
❏ ST-70004 [S]	Last of the Great Blues Singers	1962	30.00	60.00	120.00
❏ T-70004 [M]	Last of the Great Blues Singers	1962	30.00	60.00	120.00
TRADITION					
❏ TLP-1035 [M]	Country Blues	1960	7.50	15.00	30.00
❏ TLP-1040 [M]	Autobiography in Blues	1961	7.50	15.00	30.00
❏ TLP-2056 [M]	The Best of Lightnin' Hopkins	1967	5.00	10.00	20.00
VAULT					
❏ 129	California Mudslide	1969	6.25	12.50	25.00
VEE JAY					
❏ LP 1044 [M]	Lightnin' Strikes	1962	12.50	25.00	50.00
VERVE					
❏ V-8453 [M]	Fast Life Woman	1962	10.00	20.00	40.00
VERVE FOLKWAYS					
❏ FV-9000 [M]	The Roots of Lightnin' Hopkins	1965	6.25	12.50	25.00
❏ FVS-9000 [S]	The Roots of Lightnin' Hopkins	1965	7.50	15.00	30.00
❏ FV-9022 [M]	Lightnin' Strikes	1965	6.25	12.50	25.00
❏ FVS-9022 [S]	Lightnin' Strikes	1965	7.50	15.00	30.00
VERVE FORECAST					
❏ FT-3013 [M]	Something Blue	1967	5.00	10.00	20.00
❏ FTS-3013 [S]	Something Blue	1967	6.25	12.50	25.00
❏ FTS-3031	Lightnin' Strikes	1968	5.00	10.00	20.00
WORLD PACIFIC					
❏ ST-1817 [S]	First Meetin'	1963	20.00	40.00	80.00
-- Red vinyl					
❏ ST-1817 [S]	First Meetin'	1963	10.00	20.00	40.00
-- Black vinyl					
❏ WP-1817 [M]	First Meetin'	1963	7.50	15.00	30.00
HOPKINS, NICKY					
COLUMBIA					
❏ KC 32074	The Tin Man Was a Dreamer	1973	5.00	10.00	20.00
HOPNEY					
ILLUSION					
❏ CM-1032	End and Means	197?	62.50	125.00	250.00
❏ CM-1033	Perils of Love	197?	62.50	125.00	250.00
❏ CM-1034	Cosmic Rockout	197?	125.00	250.00	500.00

Number	Title	Yr	VG	VG+	NM
HORNE, LENA					
CHARTER					
❑ CLS-101 [S]	Lena Sings Your Requests	1963	5.00	10.00	20.00
❑ CLS-106 [S]	Like Latin	1964	5.00	10.00	20.00
JAZZTONE					
❑ J-1262 [M]	Lena and Ivie	1957	12.50	25.00	50.00
LION					
❑ L-70050 [M]	I Feel So Smoochie	1959	5.00	10.00	20.00
MGM					
❑ E-545 [10]	Lena Horne Sings	1952	12.50	25.00	50.00
MOBILE FIDELITY					
❑ 2-094 [(2)]	Lena Horne: The Lady and Her Music	1982	10.00	20.00	40.00
-- Audiophile vinyl					
MOVIETONE					
❑ MTS 72005 [S]	Once in a Lifetime	196?	5.00	10.00	20.00
RCA VICTOR					
❑ LOC-1028 [M]	Lena Horne at the Waldorf Astoria	1957	7.50	15.00	30.00
❑ LSO-1028 [S]	Lena Horne at the Waldorf Astoria	1957	10.00	20.00	40.00
❑ LPM-1148 [M]	It's Love	1955	12.50	25.00	50.00
❑ LPM-1375 [M]	Stormy Weather	1956	12.50	25.00	50.00
❑ LPM-1879 [M]	Give the Lady What She Wants	1958	7.50	15.00	30.00
❑ LSP-1879 [S]	Give the Lady What She Wants	1958	10.00	20.00	40.00
❑ LPM-1895 [M]	Songs of Burke and Van Heusen	1959	7.50	15.00	30.00
❑ LSP-1895 [S]	Songs of Burke and Van Heusen	1959	10.00	20.00	40.00
❑ LPM-2364 [M]	Lena Horne at the Sands	1961	6.25	12.50	25.00
❑ LSP-2364 [S]	Lena Horne at the Sands	1961	7.50	15.00	30.00
❑ LPM-2465 [M]	Lena on the Blue Side	1962	6.25	12.50	25.00
❑ LSP-2465 [S]	Lena on the Blue Side	1962	7.50	15.00	30.00
❑ LPM-2587 [M]	Lena...Lovely and Alive	1963	6.25	12.50	25.00
❑ LSP-2587 [S]	Lena...Lovely and Alive	1963	7.50	15.00	30.00
❑ LPT-3061 [10]	This Is Lena Horne	1952	12.50	25.00	50.00
TOPS					
❑ L-910 [10]	Moanin' Low	195?	10.00	20.00	40.00
❑ L-931 [10]	Lena Horne Sings	195?	10.00	20.00	40.00
❑ L-1502 [M]	Lena Horne	1958	5.00	10.00	20.00
20TH CENTURY FOX					
❑ TFS-4115 [S]	Here's Lena Now	1964	5.00	10.00	20.00
UNITED ARTISTS					
❑ UAS 6433 [S]	Feelin' Good	1965	5.00	10.00	20.00
❑ UAS 6470 [S]	Lena in Hollywood	1966	5.00	10.00	20.00
❑ UAS 6496 [S]	Soul	1966	5.00	10.00	20.00
HORNE, LENA, AND HARRY BELAFONTE					
Also see each artist's individual listings.					
RCA VICTOR					
❑ LOC-1507 [M]	Porgy and Bess	1959	6.25	12.50	25.00
❑ LSO-1507 [S]	Porgy and Bess	1959	10.00	20.00	40.00
HORNETS, THE					
LIBERTY					
❑ LRP-3348 [M]	Motorcycles U.S.A.	1963	10.00	20.00	40.00
❑ LRP-3364 [M]	Big Drag Boats U.S.A.	1964	12.50	25.00	50.00
❑ LST-7348 [S]	Motorcycles U.S.A.	1963	12.50	25.00	50.00
❑ LST-7364 [S]	Big Drag Boats U.S.A.	1964	15.00	30.00	60.00
HOROWITZ, VLADIMIR					
RCA VICTOR RED SEAL					
❑ LSC-2366 [S]	Beethoven: Piano Sonata in D "Appassionata"	1960	6.25	12.50	25.00
-- Originals with "shaded dog" label					
HORSES					
Don Johnson of "Miami Vice" and "Nash Bridges" fame was in this band.					
WHITE WHALE					
❑ WWS-7121	Horses	1970	10.00	20.00	40.00
HORTON, JOHNNY					
BRIAR					
❑ 104 [M]	Done Rovin'	196?	37.50	75.00	150.00
COLUMBIA					
❑ CL 1362 [M]	The Spectacular Johnny Horton	1959	7.50	15.00	30.00
❑ CL 1478 [M]	Johnny Horton Makes History	1960	7.50	15.00	30.00
❑ CL 1596 [M]	Johnny Horton's Greatest Hits	1961	6.25	12.50	25.00
❑ CL 1721 [M]	Honky-Tonk Man	1962	7.50	15.00	30.00
❑ CL 2299 [M]	I Can't Forget You	1965	6.25	12.50	25.00
❑ CL 2566 [M]	Johnny Horton on Stage at the Louisiana Hayride	1966	5.00	10.00	20.00
❑ CS 8167 [S]	The Spectacular Johnny Horton	1959	10.00	20.00	40.00
❑ CS 8269 [S]	Johnny Horton Makes History	1960	10.00	20.00	40.00
❑ CS 8396 [S]	Johnny Horton's Greatest Hits	1961	7.50	15.00	30.00

Number	Title	Yr	VG	VG+	NM
❑ CS 9366 [S]	Johnny Horton on Stage at the Louisiana Hayride	1966	6.25	12.50	25.00
DOT					
❑ DLP 3221 [M]	Johnny Horton	1962	7.50	15.00	30.00
MERCURY					
❑ MG-20478 [M]	The Fantastic Johnny Horton	1959	12.50	25.00	50.00
SESAC					
❑ 1201 [M]	Free and Easy Songs	1959	37.50	75.00	150.00
HORTON, ROBERT					
COLUMBIA					
❑ CL 2202 [M]	The Very Thought of You	1964	6.25	12.50	25.00
❑ CL 2408 [M]	A Man Called Shenandoah	1966	6.25	12.50	25.00
❑ CS 9002 [S]	The Very Thought of You	1964	7.50	15.00	30.00
❑ CS 9208 [S]	A Man Called Shenandoah	1966	7.50	15.00	30.00
HORTON, WALTER "SHAKEY"					
ARGO					
❑ LP-4037 [M]	The Soul of Blues Harmonica	1964	37.50	75.00	150.00
❑ LPS-4037 [S]	The Soul of Blues Harmonica	1964	62.50	125.00	250.00
HOT BUTTER					
MUSICOR					
❑ MS-3242	Popcorn	1972	5.00	10.00	20.00
-- Die-cut cover					
HOT DOGGERS, THE					
BRUCE JOHNSTON was in this group.					
EPIC					
❑ BN 26054 [S]	Surfin' U.S.A.	1963	50.00	100.00	200.00
❑ LN 24054 [M]	Surfin' U.S.A.	1963	37.50	75.00	150.00
HOT POOP					
HOT POOP					
❑ 3072	Hot Poop Does Their Own Thing	197?	75.00	150.00	300.00
HOT RODDERS, THE					
CROWN					
❑ CST-378 [S]	Big Hot Rod	1963	6.25	12.50	25.00
❑ CLP-5378 [M]	Big Hot Rod	1963	5.00	10.00	20.00
HOT TUNA					
With members of JEFFERSON AIRPLANE.					
GRUNT					
❑ BFD1-0820 [Q]	America's Choice	1975	6.25	12.50	25.00
❑ BFD1-1238 [Q]	Yellow Fever	1975	6.25	12.50	25.00
❑ CYL2-2545 [(2)]	Double Dose	1978	5.00	10.00	20.00
HOTHOUSE FLOWERS					
LONDON					
❑ PRO 884-1 [DJ]	Live	1990	6.25	12.50	25.00
-- Six-song promo-only live EP					
HOTLEGS					
Members later were in 10CC.					
CAPITOL					
❑ ST-587	Hotlegs Thinks: School Stinks	1970	6.25	12.50	25.00
HOUK, RALPH					
CARLTON					
❑ HH-16 [M]	Hear How to Play Better Baseball	1961	10.00	20.00	40.00
HOUR GLASS, THE					
Also see THE ALLMAN BROTHERS BAND.					
LIBERTY					
❑ LRP-3536 [M]	The Hour Glass	1967	6.25	12.50	25.00
❑ LST-7536 [S]	The Hour Glass	1967	7.50	15.00	30.00
❑ LST-7555	The Power of Love	1968	7.50	15.00	30.00
HOUSE, SON					
COLUMBIA					
❑ CL 2417 [M]	Father of the Folk Blues	1965	5.00	10.00	20.00
❑ CS 9217 [S]	Father of the Folk Blues	1965	6.25	12.50	25.00
-- Red "360 Sound" label					
HOUSE, SON, AND J.D. SHORT					
VERVE FOLKWAYS					
❑ FV-9035 [M]	Blues from the Mississippi Delta	1966	10.00	20.00	40.00
❑ FVS-9035 [R]	Blues from the Mississippi Delta	1966	5.00	10.00	20.00

Number	Title	Yr	VG	VG+	NM
HOUSTON FEARLESS					
IMPERIAL					
❑ LP-12421	Houston Fearless	1969	5.00	10.00	20.00
HOUSTON, DAVID					
EPIC					
❑ EGP 502 [(2)]	The World of David Houston	1970	5.00	10.00	20.00
❑ LN 24303 [M]	A Loser's Cathedral	1967	5.00	10.00	20.00
❑ LN 24320 [M]	Golden Hymns	1967	5.00	10.00	20.00
❑ LN 24338 [M]	You Mean the World to Me	1967	5.00	10.00	20.00
❑ LN 24342 [M]	David Houston's Greatest Hits	1968	7.50	15.00	30.00
❑ BN 26112 [S]	New Voice from Nashville	1964	5.00	10.00	20.00
❑ BN 26156 [S]	12 Great Country Hits	1965	5.00	10.00	20.00
❑ BN 26213 [S]	Almost Persuaded	1966	5.00	10.00	20.00
HOUSTON, DAVID, AND TAMMY WYNETTE					
Also see each artist's individual listings.					
EPIC					
❑ LN 24325 [M]	My Elusive Dreams	1967	5.00	10.00	20.00
HOUSTON, JOE					
COMBO					
❑ LP-100 [M]	Joe Houston	195?	100.00	200.00	400.00
-- Silver cover with "J" in the shape of a saxophone					
❑ LP-100 [M]	Joe Houston	195?	100.00	200.00	400.00
-- Color photo of Joe Houston on cover					
❑ LP-400 [M]	Rockin' at the Drive In	195?	75.00	150.00	300.00
-- Black ink on front and back covers					
❑ LP-400 [M]	Rockin' at the Drive In	195?	50.00	100.00	200.00
-- Blue ink on front and back covers					
CROWN					
❑ CST-313 [R]	Surf Rockin'	1963	7.50	15.00	30.00
❑ CST-319 [R]	Limbo	1963	7.50	15.00	30.00
❑ CLP-5006 [M]	Joe Houston Rock and Rolls All Night Long	195?	25.00	50.00	100.00
-- Black label, gold print					
❑ CLP-5006 [M]	Joe Houston Rock and Rolls All Night Long	196?	10.00	20.00	40.00
-- Gray label, black print					
❑ CLP-5203 [M]	Wild Man of the Tenor Sax	1962	10.00	20.00	40.00
❑ CLP-5246 [M]	Doin' the Twist	1962	10.00	20.00	40.00
❑ CLP-5313 [M]	Surf Rockin'	1963	10.00	20.00	40.00
❑ CLP-5319 [M]	Limbo	1963	10.00	20.00	40.00
MODERN					
❑ LMP-1206 [M]	Joe Houston Blows All Night Long	1956	75.00	150.00	300.00
TOPS					
❑ L-1518 [M]	Rock and Roll	195?	20.00	40.00	80.00
HOUSTON, THELMA					
ABC DUNHILL					
❑ DS-50054	Sun Shower	1969	6.25	12.50	25.00
MOWEST					
❑ MW-102	Thelma Houston	1972	5.00	10.00	20.00
SHEFFIELD LABS					
❑ 2	I've Got the Music in Me	1975	10.00	20.00	40.00
SHEFFIELD TREASURY					
❑ ST-200	I've Got the Music in Me	1983	5.00	10.00	20.00
-- Reissue of Sheffield Labs 2					
HOWARD, DAVE					
CHOREO					
❑ 5 [M]	I Love Everybody	1962	6.25	12.50	25.00
❑ S-5 [S]	I Love Everybody	1962	7.50	15.00	30.00
HOWARD, EDDY					
MERCURY					
❑ MG-20112 [M]	Singing in the Rain	195?	6.25	12.50	25.00
❑ MG-20312 [M]	Paradise Isle	195?	6.25	12.50	25.00
❑ MG-20432 [M]	Great for Dancing	1958	5.00	10.00	20.00
❑ SR-60104 [S]	Great for Dancing	1959	6.25	12.50	25.00
❑ SR-60562 [S]	Eddy Howard's Golden Hits	1961	5.00	10.00	20.00
❑ SR-60593 [S]	More Eddy Howard's Golden Hits	1962	5.00	10.00	20.00
❑ SR-60665 [S]	Eddy Howard Sings and Plays the Great Old Waltzes	1962	5.00	10.00	20.00
❑ SR-60817 [S]	Eddy Howard Sings and Plays the Great Band Hits	196?	5.00	10.00	20.00
❑ SR-60910 [S]	Intimately Yours	1965	5.00	10.00	20.00
❑ SR-61014 [S]	Softly and Sincerely	196?	5.00	10.00	20.00
HOWARD, HARLAN					
CAPITOL					
❑ ST 1631 [S]	Harlan Howard Sings Harlan Howard	1961	10.00	20.00	40.00

Number	Title	Yr	VG	VG+	NM
❑ T 1631 [M]	Harlan Howard Sings Harlan Howard	1961	7.50	15.00	30.00
MONUMENT					
❑ MLP-8038 [M]	All-Time Favorite Country Songwriter	1965	6.25	12.50	25.00
❑ SLP-18038 [S]	All-Time Favorite Country Songwriter	1965	7.50	15.00	30.00
RCA VICTOR					
❑ LPM-3729 [M]	Mr. Songwriter	1967	6.25	12.50	25.00
❑ LSP-3729 [S]	Mr. Songwriter	1967	5.00	10.00	20.00
❑ LPM-3886 [M]	Down to Earth	1968	12.50	25.00	50.00
❑ LSP-3886 [S]	Down to Earth	1968	5.00	10.00	20.00
HOWARD, JAN					
CAPITOL					
❑ ST 1779 [S]	Sweet and Sentimental	1962	6.25	12.50	25.00
❑ T 1779 [M]	Sweet and Sentimental	1962	5.00	10.00	20.00
DECCA					
❑ DL 4931 [M]	This Is Jan Howard Country	1967	6.25	12.50	25.00
❑ DL 74793 [S]	Jan Howard Sings Evil on Your Mind	1966	5.00	10.00	20.00
❑ DL 74832 [S]	Bad Seed	1966	5.00	10.00	20.00
❑ DL 74931 [S]	This Is Jan Howard Country	1967	5.00	10.00	20.00
❑ DL 75012	Count Your Blessings, Woman	1968	5.00	10.00	20.00
❑ DL 75130	Jan Howard	1969	5.00	10.00	20.00
❑ DL 75166	For God and Country	1969	6.25	12.50	25.00
❑ DL 75207	Rock Me Back to Little Rock	1970	5.00	10.00	20.00
❑ DL 75293	Love Is Like a Spinning Wheel	1972	5.00	10.00	20.00
TOWER					
❑ ST 5068 [S]	Lonely Country	1967	5.00	10.00	20.00
❑ T 5068 [M]	Lonely Country	1967	5.00	10.00	20.00
WRANGLER					
❑ 1005 [M]	Jan Howard	1962	6.25	12.50	25.00
❑ S-1005 [S]	Jan Howard	1962	7.50	15.00	30.00
HOWL THE GOOD					
RARE EARTH					
❑ RS-537	Howl the Good	1972	5.00	10.00	20.00
HOWLIN' WOLF					
CADET					
❑ LPS-319	This Is Howlin' Wolf's New Album	1969	6.25	12.50	25.00
CHESS					
❑ LP-1434 [M]	Moanin' in the Moonlight	1958	150.00	300.00	600.00
❑ LP-1469 [M]	Howlin' Wolf	1962	150.00	300.00	600.00
❑ LP-1502 [M]	The Real Folk Blues	1966	12.50	25.00	50.00
❑ LP-1512 [M]	More Real Folk Blues	1966	12.50	25.00	50.00
❑ LP-1540	Evil	1969	6.25	12.50	25.00
❑ CH5-9332 [(5)]	The Chess Box	1991	10.00	20.00	40.00
❑ CH-50002	Message to the Young	1971	5.00	10.00	20.00
❑ CH-50015	Live and Cookin'	1972	5.00	10.00	20.00
❑ CH-50045	Back Door Wolf	1974	5.00	10.00	20.00
❑ CH-60008	The London Howlin' Wolf Sessions	1971	5.00	10.00	20.00
❑ CH-60016 [(2)]	Howlin' Wolf, AKA Chester Burnett	1972	6.25	12.50	25.00
CROWN					
❑ CLP-5240 [M]	Howlin' Wolf Sings the Blues	1962	6.25	12.50	25.00
CUSTOM					
❑ CM-2055 [M]	Big City Blues	196?	10.00	20.00	40.00
❑ CS-2055 [R]	Big City Blues	196?	5.00	10.00	20.00
HUBBARD, FREDDIE					
ATLANTIC					
❑ 1477 [M]	Backlash	1967	6.25	12.50	25.00
BLUE NOTE					
❑ BLP-4040 [M]	Open Sesame	1960	30.00	60.00	120.00
-- "Deep groove" version (deep indentation under label on both sides)					
❑ BLP-4040 [M]	Open Sesame	1960	20.00	40.00	80.00
-- Regular version with W. 63rd St. address on label					
❑ BLP-4040 [M]	Open Sesame	1963	5.00	10.00	20.00
-- With New York, USA address on label					
❑ BLP-4056 [M]	Goin' Up	1960	20.00	40.00	80.00
-- With W. 63rd St. address on label					
❑ BLP-4056 [M]	Goin' Up	1963	5.00	10.00	20.00
-- With New York, USA address on label					
❑ BLP-4073 [M]	Hub Cap	1961	20.00	40.00	80.00
-- With W. 63rd St. address on label					
❑ BLP-4073 [M]	Hub Cap	1963	5.00	10.00	20.00
-- With New York, USA address on label					
❑ BLP-4085 [M]	Ready for Freddie	1961	20.00	40.00	80.00
-- With 61st St. address on label					
❑ BLP-4085 [M]	Ready for Freddie	1963	5.00	10.00	20.00
-- With New York, USA address on label					

Number	Title	Yr	VG	VG+	NM
❏ BLP-4115 [M]	Hub Tones	1962	6.25	12.50	25.00
❏ BLP-4172 [M]	Breaking Point	1964	6.25	12.50	25.00
❏ BLP-4196 [M]	Blue Spirits	1965	6.25	12.50	25.00
❏ BLP-4207 [M]	The Night of the Cookers -- Live at Club Le Marchal, Vol. 1	1965	6.25	12.50	25.00
❏ BLP-4208 [M]	The Night of the Cookers -- Live at Club Le Marchal, Vol. 2	1965	6.25	12.50	25.00
❏ BST-84040 [S]	Open Sesame	1960	15.00	30.00	60.00
-- With W. 63rd St. addresss on label					
❏ BST-84040 [S]	Open Sesame	1963	6.25	12.50	25.00
-- With New York, USA address on label					
❏ BST-84056 [S]	Goin' Up	1960	15.00	30.00	60.00
-- With W. 63rd St. addresss on label					
❏ BST-84056 [S]	Goin' Up	1963	6.25	12.50	25.00
-- With New York, USA address on label					
❏ BST-84073 [S]	Hub Cap	1961	15.00	30.00	60.00
-- With W. 63rd St. addresss on label					
❏ BST-84073 [S]	Hub Cap	1963	6.25	12.50	25.00
-- With New York, USA address on label					
❏ BST-84085 [S]	Ready for Freddie	1961	15.00	30.00	60.00
-- With 61st St. addresss on label					
❏ BST-84085 [S]	Ready for Freddie	1963	6.25	12.50	25.00
-- With New York, USA address on label					
❏ BST-84115 [S]	Hub-Tones	1962	7.50	15.00	30.00
-- With New York, USA address on label					
❏ BST-84172 [S]	Breaking Point	1964	7.50	15.00	30.00
-- With New York, USA address on label					
❏ BST-84196 [S]	Blue Spirits	1965	7.50	15.00	30.00
-- With New York, USA address on label					
❏ BST-84207 [S]	The Night of the Cookers -- Live at Club Le Marchal, Vol. 1	1965	7.50	15.00	30.00
-- With New York, USA address on label					
❏ BST-84208 [S]	The Night of the Cookers -- Live at Club Le Marchal, Vol. 2	1965	7.50	15.00	30.00
-- With New York, USA address on label					

IMPULSE!

Number	Title	Yr	VG	VG+	NM
❏ A-27 [M]	The Artistry of Freddie Hubbard	1962	6.25	12.50	25.00
❏ AS-27 [S]	The Artistry of Freddie Hubbard	1962	7.50	15.00	30.00
❏ A-38 [M]	The Body and Soul of Freddie Hubbard	1963	6.25	12.50	25.00
❏ AS-38 [S]	The Body and Soul of Freddie Hubbard	1963	7.50	15.00	30.00

HUDSON AND LANDRY
DORE

Number	Title	Yr	VG	VG+	NM
❏ 324	Hanging In There	1971	5.00	10.00	20.00
❏ 326	Losing Their Heads	1971	5.00	10.00	20.00
❏ 329	Right-Off!	1972	5.00	10.00	20.00
❏ 331	Weird Kingdom	1973	5.00	10.00	20.00

HUDSON, ROCK
STANYAN

Number	Title	Yr	VG	VG+	NM
❏ SR-10014	Rock Gently	1971	6.25	12.50	25.00

HUGHES, FRED
WAND

Number	Title	Yr	VG	VG+	NM
❏ WD-664 [M]	Send My Baby Back	1965	5.00	10.00	20.00
❏ WDS-664 [S]	Send My Baby Back	1965	6.25	12.50	25.00

HUGHES, JIMMY
ATCO

Number	Title	Yr	VG	VG+	NM
❏ 33-209 [M]	Why Not Tonight	1967	5.00	10.00	20.00
❏ SD 33-209 [S]	Why Not Tonight	1967	5.00	10.00	20.00

VEE JAY

Number	Title	Yr	VG	VG+	NM
❏ VJ-1102 [M]	Steal Away	1965	6.25	12.50	25.00
❏ VJS-1102 [R]	Steal Away	1965	6.25	12.50	25.00

VOLT

Number	Title	Yr	VG	VG+	NM
❏ VOS-6003	Something Special	1969	5.00	10.00	20.00

HUGHES, LANGSTON
MGM

Number	Title	Yr	VG	VG+	NM
❏ E-3697 [M]	The Weary Blues	1958	12.50	25.00	50.00
-- Yellow label					

HUGO AND LUIGI
RCA VICTOR

Number	Title	Yr	VG	VG+	NM
❏ LSP-2254 [S]	The Sound of Children at Christmas	1960	5.00	10.00	20.00

ROULETTE

Number	Title	Yr	VG	VG+	NM
❏ R-25044 [M]	When Good Fellows Get Together	1959	5.00	10.00	20.00

HULLABALLOOS, THE
ROULETTE

Number	Title	Yr	VG	VG+	NM
❏ R-25297 [M]	England's Newest Singing Sensations	1965	12.50	25.00	50.00
❏ SR-25297 [P]	England's Newest Singing Sensations	1965	18.75	37.50	75.00
❏ R-25310 [M]	The Hullabaloos on Hullabaloo	1965	12.50	25.00	50.00
❏ SR-25310 [P]	The Hullabaloos on Hullabaloo	1965	18.75	37.50	75.00

HULLABALOO SINGERS AND ORCHESTRA, THE
COLUMBIA

Number	Title	Yr	VG	VG+	NM
❏ CL 2410 [M]	The Hullabaloo Show	1965	5.00	10.00	20.00
❏ CS 9210 [S]	The Hullabaloo Show	1965	6.25	12.50	25.00

HUMAN BEINZ, THE
CAPITOL

Number	Title	Yr	VG	VG+	NM
❏ ST 2906	Nobody But Me	1968	7.50	15.00	30.00
❏ ST 2926	Evolutions	1968	10.00	20.00	40.00

GATEWAY

Number	Title	Yr	VG	VG+	NM
❏ GLP-3012	Nobody But Me	1968	10.00	20.00	40.00
-- With added tracks by The Mammals					

HUMBLEBUMS, THE
GERRY RAFFERTY was in this group.
LIBERTY

Number	Title	Yr	VG	VG+	NM
❏ LST-7636	The Humblebums	1969	7.50	15.00	30.00
❏ LST-7656	Open Up the Door	1970	7.50	15.00	30.00

HUMES, ANITA -- See THE ESSEX.

HUMPERDINCK, ENGELBERT
EPIC

Number	Title	Yr	VG	VG+	NM
❏ (no #) [PD]	Last of the Romantics	1978	6.25	12.50	25.00

PARROT

Number	Title	Yr	VG	VG+	NM
❏ PA 61012 [M]	Release Me	1967	5.00	10.00	20.00
❏ PA 61015 [M]	The Last Waltz	1967	5.00	10.00	20.00

HUNGER
PUBLIC

Number	Title	Yr	VG	VG+	NM
❏ 1006	Strictly from Hunger	1969	150.00	300.00	600.00

HUNT, TOMMY
DYNAMO

Number	Title	Yr	VG	VG+	NM
❏ D-7001 [M]	Tommy Hunt's Greatest Hits	1967	5.00	10.00	20.00
❏ DS-8001 [S]	Tommy Hunt's Greatest Hits	1967	6.25	12.50	25.00

SCEPTER

Number	Title	Yr	VG	VG+	NM
❏ 506 [M]	I Just Don't Know What to Do with Myself	1962	12.50	25.00	50.00
❏ SS-506 [S]	I Just Don't Know What to Do with Myself	1962	15.00	30.00	60.00

HUNTER MUSKETT
BRADLEY

Number	Title	Yr	VG	VG+	NM
❏ 1003	Hunter Muskett	197?	20.00	40.00	80.00

HUNTER, IVORY JOE
ATLANTIC

Number	Title	Yr	VG	VG+	NM
❏ 8008 [M]	Ivory Joe Hunter	1957	50.00	100.00	200.00
-- Black label					
❏ 8008 [M]	Ivory Joe Hunter	1960	25.00	50.00	100.00
-- Purple and red label					
❏ 8015 [M]	The Old and the New	1958	50.00	100.00	200.00
-- Black label					
❏ 8015 [M]	The Old and the New	1960	25.00	50.00	100.00
-- Purple and red label					

DOT

Number	Title	Yr	VG	VG+	NM
❏ DLP-3569 [M]	This Is Ivory Joe Hunter	1964	10.00	20.00	40.00
❏ DLP-25569 [S]	This Is Ivory Joe Hunter	1964	12.50	25.00	50.00

EPIC

Number	Title	Yr	VG	VG+	NM
❏ E 30348	The Return of Ivory Joe Hunter	1971	5.00	10.00	20.00

GOLDISC

Number	Title	Yr	VG	VG+	NM
❏ 403 [M]	The Fabulous Ivory Joe Hunter	1961	15.00	30.00	60.00

KING

Number	Title	Yr	VG	VG+	NM
❏ 605 [M]	16 of His Greatest Hits	1958	100.00	200.00	400.00

LION

Number	Title	Yr	VG	VG+	NM
❏ L-70068 [M]	I Need You So	1959	15.00	30.00	60.00

MGM

Number	Title	Yr	VG	VG+	NM
❏ E-3488 [M]	I Get That Lonesome Feeling	1957	75.00	150.00	300.00

SMASH

Number	Title	Yr	VG	VG+	NM
❏ MGS-27037 [M]	Ivory Joe Hunter's Golden Hits	1963	10.00	20.00	40.00
❏ SRS-67037 [S]	Ivory Joe Hunter's Golden Hits	1963	12.50	25.00	50.00

SOUND

Number	Title	Yr	VG	VG+	NM
❏ M-603 [M]	Ivory Joe Hunter	1959	37.50	75.00	150.00

Number	Title	Yr	VG	VG+	NM
STRAND					
❏ SL-1123 [M]	The Artistry of Ivory Joe Hunter	196?	10.00	20.00	40.00
❏ SLS-1123 [S]	The Artistry of Ivory Joe Hunter	196?	12.50	25.00	50.00

HUNTER, ROBERT

Number	Title	Yr	VG	VG+	NM
RELIX					
❏ 2002 [PD]	Promontory Rider	1982	5.00	10.00	20.00
-- Limited edition of 1,000 picture discs					
ROUND					
❏ RX-101	Tales of the Great Rum Runners	1974	10.00	20.00	40.00
❏ RX-105	Tiger Rose	1975	10.00	20.00	40.00

HUNTER, TAB

Number	Title	Yr	VG	VG+	NM
DOT					
❏ DLP-3370 [M]	Young Love	1961	7.50	15.00	30.00
❏ DLP-25370 [S]	Young Love	1961	7.50	15.00	30.00
WARNER BROS.					
❏ W 1221 [M]	Tab Hunter	1958	7.50	15.00	30.00
❏ WS 1221 [S]	Tab Hunter	1958	10.00	20.00	40.00
❏ W 1292 [M]	When I Fall in Love	1959	7.50	15.00	30.00
❏ WS 1292 [S]	When I Fall in Love	1959	10.00	20.00	40.00
❏ W 1367 [M]	R.F.D. Tab Hunter	1960	7.50	15.00	30.00
❏ WS 1367 [S]	R.F.D. Tab Hunter	1960	10.00	20.00	40.00

HURT, MISSISSIPPI JOHN

Number	Title	Yr	VG	VG+	NM
BIOGRAPH					
❏ C-4 [M]	1928: His First Recordings	1972	6.25	12.50	25.00
PIEDMONT					
❏ PLP-13157 [M]	Folk Songs and Blues	1963	20.00	40.00	80.00
❏ PLP-13181 [M]	Worried Blues	1964	20.00	40.00	80.00
VANGUARD					
❏ VSD-19/20 [(2)]	The Best of Mississippi John Hurt	197?	6.25	12.50	25.00
❏ VRS-9145 [M]	Blues at Newport	1965	6.25	12.50	25.00
❏ VRS-9220 [M]	Mississippi John Hurt/Today	1966	6.25	12.50	25.00
❏ VRS-9248 [M]	The Immortal Mississippi John	1967	6.25	12.50	25.00
❏ VSD-79145 [S]	Blues at Newport	1965	7.50	15.00	30.00
❏ VSD-79220 [S]	Mississippi John Hurt/Today	1966	7.50	15.00	30.00
❏ VSD-79248 [S]	The Immortal Mississippi John	1967	7.50	15.00	30.00
❏ VSD-79327	The Last Session	1972	5.00	10.00	20.00

HURVITZ, SANDY

Number	Title	Yr	VG	VG+	NM
VERVE					
❏ V6-5064	Sandy's Album Is Here at Last	1968	7.50	15.00	30.00
-- Produced by FRANK ZAPPA					

HUSKER DU

Number	Title	Yr	VG	VG+	NM
NEW ALLIANCE					
❏ 007	Land Speed Record	1982	6.25	12.50	25.00
-- No reference to SST on cover					
REFLEX					
❏ #D	Everything Falls Apart	1982	10.00	20.00	40.00
SST					
❏ PSST E27 [DJ]	Eight Miles High/6 from Zen Arcade	1984	7.50	15.00	30.00
-- Promo sampler, etched design on side 1, sticker cover					
WARNER BROS.					
❏ WBMS-145 [DJ]	The Warehouse Interview	1987	6.25	12.50	25.00
-- Promo only, part of the Warner Bros. Music Show series					

HUSKY, FERLIN

Number	Title	Yr	VG	VG+	NM
CAPITOL					
❏ T 718 [M]	Songs of the Home and Heart	1956	15.00	30.00	60.00
-- Turquoise label					
❏ T 718 [M]	Songs of the Home and Heart	1959	10.00	20.00	40.00
-- Black colorband label, Capitol logo at left					
❏ T 718 [M]	Songs of the Home and Heart	1962	6.25	12.50	25.00
-- Black colorband label, Capitol logo at top					
❏ T 880 [M]	Boulevard of Broken Dreams	1957	15.00	30.00	60.00
-- Turquoise label					
❏ T 976 [M]	Sittin' On a Rainbow	1958	15.00	30.00	60.00
-- Turquoise label					
❏ T 1204 [M]	Born to Lose	1959	10.00	20.00	40.00
-- Black colorband label, Capitol logo at left					
❏ T 1204 [M]	Born to Lose	1962	6.25	12.50	25.00
-- Black colorband label, Capitol logo at top					
❏ T 1280 [M]	Ferlin's Favorites	1960	10.00	20.00	40.00
-- Black colorband label, Capitol logo at left					
❏ T 1280 [M]	Ferlin's Favorites	1962	6.25	12.50	25.00
-- Black colorband label, Capitol logo at top					
❏ T 1383 [M]	Gone	1960	10.00	20.00	40.00
-- Black colorband label, Capitol logo at left					
❏ T 1383 [M]	Gone	1962	6.25	12.50	25.00
-- Black colorband label, Capitol logo at top					

Number	Title	Yr	VG	VG+	NM
❏ ST 1546 [S]	Walkin' and Hummin'	1961	7.50	15.00	30.00
-- Black colorband label, Capitol logo at left					
❏ ST 1546 [S]	Walkin' and Hummin'	1962	5.00	10.00	20.00
-- Black colorband label, Capitol logo at top					
❏ T 1546 [M]	Walkin' and Hummin'	1961	6.25	12.50	25.00
-- Black colorband label, Capitol logo at left					
❏ ST 1633 [S]	Memories of Home	1961	7.50	15.00	30.00
-- Black colorband label, Capitol logo at left					
❏ ST 1633 [S]	Memories of Home	1962	5.00	10.00	20.00
-- Black colorband label, Capitol logo at top					
❏ T 1633 [M]	Memories of Home	1961	6.25	12.50	25.00
-- Black colorband label, Capitol logo at left					
❏ ST 1720 [S]	Some of My Favorites	1962	5.00	10.00	20.00
❏ ST 1885 [S]	The Heart and Soul of Ferlin	1963	5.00	10.00	20.00
❏ ST 2101 [S]	By Request	1964	5.00	10.00	20.00
❏ ST 2305 [S]	True, True Lovin'	1965	5.00	10.00	20.00
❏ ST 2439 [S]	Ferlin Husky Sings the Songs of Music City, U.S.A.	1966	5.00	10.00	20.00
❏ ST 2548 [S]	I Could Sing All Night	1966	5.00	10.00	20.00
❏ T 2705 [M]	What Am I Gonna Do Now?	1967	5.00	10.00	20.00
KING					
❏ 647 [M]	Country Tunes Sung from the	1959	17.50	35.00	70.00
❏ 728 [M]	Easy Livin'	1960	17.50	35.00	70.00

HUTTON, BETTY

Number	Title	Yr	VG	VG+	NM
CAPITOL					
❏ H 256 [10]	Square in the Social Circle	1950	15.00	30.00	60.00
WARNER BROS.					
❏ W 1267 [M]	Betty Hutton at the Saints and Sinners Ball	1959	5.00	10.00	20.00
❏ WS 1267 [S]	Betty Hutton at the Saints and Sinners Ball	1959	6.25	12.50	25.00

HUTTON, DANNY

Also see THREE DOG NIGHT.

Number	Title	Yr	VG	VG+	NM
MGM					
❏ SE-4664	Pre-Dog Night	1970	7.50	15.00	30.00

HYLAND, BRIAN

Number	Title	Yr	VG	VG+	NM
ABC-PARAMOUNT					
❏ 400 [M]	Let Me Belong to You	1961	7.50	15.00	30.00
❏ S-400 [S]	Let Me Belong to You	1961	10.00	20.00	40.00
❏ 431 [M]	Sealed with a Kiss	1962	7.50	15.00	30.00
❏ S-431 [S]	Sealed with a Kiss	1962	10.00	20.00	40.00
❏ 463 [M]	Country Meets Folk	1964	7.50	15.00	30.00
❏ S-463 [S]	Country Meets Folk	1964	10.00	20.00	40.00
KAPP					
❏ KL 1202 [M]	The Bashful Blonde	1960	12.50	25.00	50.00
❏ KS 3202 [S]	The Bashful Blonde	1960	20.00	40.00	80.00
PHILIPS					
❏ PHM 200-136 [M]	Here's to Our Love	1964	5.00	10.00	20.00
❏ PHM 200-158 [M]	Rockin' Folk	1965	5.00	10.00	20.00
❏ PHM 200-217 [M]	The Joker Went Wild	1966	5.00	10.00	20.00
❏ PHS 600-136 [S]	Here's to Our Love	1964	6.25	12.50	25.00
❏ PHS 600-158 [S]	Rockin' Folk	1965	6.25	12.50	25.00
❏ PHS 600-217 [S]	The Joker Went Wild	1966	6.25	12.50	25.00

HYMAN, DICK

Number	Title	Yr	VG	VG+	NM
COMMAND					
❏ RS 811 SD [S]	Provocative Piano	1960	5.00	10.00	20.00
❏ RS 824 SD [S]	Provocative Piano Volume 2	1961	5.00	10.00	20.00
❏ RS 832 SD [S]	The Dick Hyman Trio	1961	5.00	10.00	20.00
❏ RS 856 SD [S]	Electrodynamics	1963	5.00	10.00	20.00
❏ RS 862 SD [S]	Fabulous	1963	5.00	10.00	20.00
❏ RS 875 SD [S]	Keyboard Kaleidoscope	1964	5.00	10.00	20.00
❏ RS 33-891 [M]	The Man from O.R.G.A.N.	1965	5.00	10.00	20.00
❏ RS 891 SD [S]	The Man from O.R.G.A.N.	1965	6.25	12.50	25.00
❏ RS 899 SD [S]	Happening!	1966	5.00	10.00	20.00
❏ RS 911 SD [S]	Brazilian Impressions	1966	5.00	10.00	20.00
❏ RS 938 SD	Mirrors	1967	5.00	10.00	20.00
❏ RS 938 SD	Moog -- The Electric Eclectics of Dick Hyman	1968	7.50	15.00	30.00
❏ RS 946 SD	The Age of Electronicus	1969	7.50	15.00	30.00
❏ RS 951 SD	Concerto Electro	1970	7.50	15.00	30.00
MGM					
❏ E-3280 [M]	The Dick Hyman Trio Swings	1954	6.25	12.50	25.00
-- Yellow label					
❏ E-3329 [M]	The "Unforgettable" Sound of the Dick Hyman Trio	1955	6.25	12.50	25.00
-- Yellow label					
❏ E-3379 [M]	Behind a Shady Nook	1956	6.25	12.50	25.00
-- Yellow label					
❏ E-3483 [M]	Red Sails in the Sunset	1957	6.25	12.50	25.00
-- Yellow label					

Number	Title	Yr	VG	VG+	NM
❑ E-3494 [M]	Hi-Fi Suite	1957	6.25	12.50	25.00
-- Yellow label					
❑ E-3535 [M]	60 Great All-Time Songs, Vol. 1	1957	5.00	10.00	20.00
-- Yellow label					
❑ E-3536 [M]	60 Great All-Time Songs, Vol. 2	1957	5.00	10.00	20.00
-- Yellow label					
❑ E-3537 [M]	60 Great All-Time Songs, Vol. 3	1957	5.00	10.00	20.00
-- Yellow label					
❑ E-3553 [M]	Rockin' Sax and Rollin' Organ	1958	6.25	12.50	25.00
-- Yellow label					
❑ E-3586 [M]	60 Great All-Time Songs, Vol. 4	1958	5.00	10.00	20.00
-- Yellow label					
❑ E-3587 [M]	60 Great All-Time Songs, Vol. 5	1958	5.00	10.00	20.00
-- Yellow label					
❑ E-3588 [M]	60 Great All-Time Songs, Vol. 6	1958	5.00	10.00	20.00
-- Yellow label					
❑ E-3606 [M]	Dick Hyman and Harpsichord in Hi-Fi	1958	5.00	10.00	20.00
-- Yellow label					
❑ E-3642 [M]	Gigi	1958	5.00	10.00	20.00
-- Yellow label					
❑ E-3724 [M]	60 Great Songs That Say "I Love You"	1959	5.00	10.00	20.00
-- Yellow label					
❑ E-3725 [M]	60 Great Songs from Broadway Musicals	1959	5.00	10.00	20.00
-- Yellow label					
❑ E-3747 [M]	Whoop-Up!	1959	5.00	10.00	20.00
-- Yellow label					
❑ E-3808 [M]	Strictly Organic	1960	5.00	10.00	20.00
❑ E-4119 [M]	Moon Gas	1963	5.00	10.00	20.00
❑ SE-4119 [S]	Moon Gas	1963	7.50	15.00	30.00

I

IAN AND SYLVIA
AMPEX

Number	Title	Yr	VG	VG+	NM
❑ A-10103	Great Speckled Bird	1970	5.00	10.00	20.00

MGM

Number	Title	Yr	VG	VG+	NM
❑ E-4388 [M]	Lovin' Sound	1967	5.00	10.00	20.00
❑ SE-4550	Full Circle	1968	5.00	10.00	20.00

VANGUARD

Number	Title	Yr	VG	VG+	NM
❑ VSD-2113 [S]	Ian and Sylvia	1963	7.50	15.00	30.00
❑ VSD-2149 [S]	Four Strong Winds	1963	6.25	12.50	25.00
❑ VRS-9109 [M]	Ian and Sylvia	1963	6.25	12.50	25.00
❑ VRS-9133 [M]	Four Strong Winds	1963	5.00	10.00	20.00
❑ VRS-9154 [M]	Northern Journey	1964	5.00	10.00	20.00
❑ VRS-9175 [M]	Early Morning Rain	1965	5.00	10.00	20.00
❑ VRS-9215 [M]	Play One More	1966	5.00	10.00	20.00
❑ VRS-9241 [M]	So Much for Dreaming	1967	5.00	10.00	20.00
❑ VSD-79154 [S]	Northern Journey	1964	6.25	12.50	25.00
❑ VSD-79175 [S]	Early Morning Rain	1965	6.25	12.50	25.00
❑ VSD-79215 [S]	Play One More	1966	6.25	12.50	25.00
❑ VSD-79241 [S]	So Much for Dreaming	1967	6.25	12.50	25.00

IAN AND THE ZODIACS
PHILIPS

Number	Title	Yr	VG	VG+	NM
❑ PHM 200-176 [M]	Ian and the Zodiacs	1965	10.00	20.00	40.00
❑ PHS 600-176 [S]	Ian and the Zodiacs	1965	12.50	25.00	50.00

IAN, JANIS
ANALOGUE PRODUCTIONS

Number	Title	Yr	VG	VG+	NM
❑ AAP 027	Breaking Silence	1995	6.25	12.50	25.00
-- Audiophile vinyl					

MGM

Number	Title	Yr	VG	VG+	NM
❑ GAS-121	Janis Ian (Golden Archive Series)	1970	6.25	12.50	25.00

VERVE FORECAST

Number	Title	Yr	VG	VG+	NM
❑ FT-3017 [M]	Janis Ian	1967	5.00	10.00	20.00
❑ FT-3024 [M]	For All the Seasons of Your Mind	1967	5.00	10.00	20.00

ICE-T
SIRE

Number	Title	Yr	VG	VG+	NM
❑ PRO-A-4959 [(2) DJ]	O.G. Original Gangster	1991	10.00	20.00	40.00
-- Promo-only radio-ready version of album otherwise unavailable on U.S. vinyl					

ID, THE
❑ Two different groups.
AURA

Number	Title	Yr	VG	VG+	NM
❑ 1000	Where Are We Going?	1976	12.50	25.00	50.00

RCA VICTOR

Number	Title	Yr	VG	VG+	NM
❑ LPM-3805 [M]	The Inner Sound of the Id	1967	10.00	20.00	40.00
❑ LSP-3805 [S]	The Inner Sound of the Id	1967	10.00	20.00	40.00

IDES OF MARCH, THE
WARNER BROS.

Number	Title	Yr	VG	VG+	NM
❑ WS 1863	Vehicle	1970	5.00	10.00	20.00
-- Green "W7" label					

IDLE RACE, THE
Jeff Lynne, later of ELECTRIC LIGHT ORCHESTRA, was in this group.
LIBERTY

Number	Title	Yr	VG	VG+	NM
❑ LST-7603	Birthday Party	1969	12.50	25.00	50.00

IF
CAPITOL

Number	Title	Yr	VG	VG+	NM
❑ ST-539	If	1970	5.00	10.00	20.00
❑ SW-676	If2	1971	5.00	10.00	20.00
❑ SMAS-820	If3	1971	5.00	10.00	20.00

IFIELD, FRANK
CAPITOL

Number	Title	Yr	VG	VG+	NM
❑ ST 10356 [S]	I'm Confessin'	1963	6.25	12.50	25.00
❑ T 10356 [M]	I'm Confessin'	1963	5.00	10.00	20.00

HICKORY

Number	Title	Yr	VG	VG+	NM
❑ LPM-132 [M]	The Best of Frank Ifield	1966	5.00	10.00	20.00
❑ LPS-132 [P]	The Best of Frank Ifield	1966	5.00	10.00	20.00
❑ LPS-136 [S]	Tale of Two Cities	1967	5.00	10.00	20.00
❑ ST-90753 [S]	The Best of Frank Ifield	1966	6.25	12.50	25.00
-- Capitol Record Club edition					
❑ T-90753 [M]	The Best of Frank Ifield	1966	6.25	12.50	25.00
-- Capitol Record Club edition					

Number	Title	Yr	VG	VG+	NM
VEE JAY					
❑ LP 1054 [M]	I Remember You	1962	7.50	15.00	30.00
❑ SR 1054 [S]	I Remember You	1962	12.50	25.00	50.00
IGGY AND THE STOOGES					
Also includes The Stooges.					
COLUMBIA					
❑ KC 32111	Raw Power	1973	12.50	25.00	50.00
ELEKTRA					
❑ EKS 74051	The Stooges	1969	12.50	25.00	50.00
-- By "The Stooges"; red label with large stylized "E" (butterfly label, deduct 60%)					
❑ EKS 74101	Fun House	1970	12.50	25.00	50.00
-- By "The Stooges"; red label with large stylized "E" (butterfly label, deduct 60%)					
IGGY POP					
Also see IGGY AND THE STOOGES.					
A&M					
❑ SP-17641 [DJ]	Live at the Channel 7/19/88	1988	10.00	20.00	40.00
-- Numbered, rubber-stamped promo-only edition					
IKETTES, THE					
MODERN					
❑ M-102 [M]	Soul Hits	1965	7.50	15.00	30.00
❑ MST-102 [S]	Soul Hits	1965	10.00	20.00	40.00
ILL WIND, THE					
ABC					
❑ S-641	Flashes	1968	25.00	50.00	100.00
ILLUSION, THE					
STEED					
❑ ST-37003	The Illusion	1969	5.00	10.00	20.00
ILLUSTRATION					
JANUS					
❑ JLP-3010	Illustration	1969	6.25	12.50	25.00
ILMO SMOKEHOUSE					
BEAUTIFUL SOUND					
❑ 3002	Ilmo Smokehouse	1971	10.00	20.00	40.00
ROULETTE					
❑ RS-3002	Ilmo Smokehouse	1971	5.00	10.00	20.00
IMPACS, THE					
KING					
❑ 886 [M]	Impact!	1964	50.00	100.00	200.00
❑ KS-886 [S]	Impact!	1964	75.00	150.00	300.00
❑ 916 [M]	A Weekend with the Impacs	1964	50.00	100.00	200.00
❑ KS-916 [S]	A Weekend with the Impacs	1964	75.00	150.00	300.00
IMPACTS, THE					
DEL-FI					
❑ DFLP-1234 [M]	Wipe Out	1963	15.00	30.00	60.00
❑ DFS-1234 [S]	Wipe Out	1963	20.00	40.00	80.00
IMPALA SYNDROME, THE					
PARALLAX					
❑ 4002	The Impala Syndrome	1970	25.00	50.00	100.00
IMPALAS, THE					
CUB					
❑ 8003 [M]	Sorry (I Ran All the Way Home)	1959	100.00	200.00	400.00
❑ S-8003 [S]	Sorry (I Ran All the Way Home)	1959	150.00	300.00	600.00
IMPRESSIONS, THE					
Also see JERRY BUTLER; CURTIS MAYFIELD.					
ABC					
❑ 606 [M]	The Fabulous Impressions	1967	6.25	12.50	25.00
❑ S-606 [S]	The Fabulous Impressions	1967	5.00	10.00	20.00
❑ D-780 [(2)]	Curtis Mayfield/His Early Years with the Impressions	1973	5.00	10.00	20.00
ABC-PARAMOUNT					
❑ 450 [M]	The Impressions	1963	7.50	15.00	30.00
❑ S-450 [S]	The Impressions	1963	10.00	20.00	40.00
❑ 468 [M]	The Never Ending Impressions	1964	7.50	15.00	30.00
❑ S-468 [S]	The Never Ending Impressions	1964	10.00	20.00	40.00
❑ 493 [M]	Keep On Pushing	1964	7.50	15.00	30.00
❑ S-493 [S]	Keep On Pushing	1964	10.00	20.00	40.00

Number	Title	Yr	VG	VG+	NM
❑ 505 [M]	People Get Ready	1965	7.50	15.00	30.00
❑ S-505 [S]	People Get Ready	1965	10.00	20.00	40.00
❑ 515 [M]	The Impressions' Greatest Hits	1965	5.00	10.00	20.00
❑ S-515 [S]	The Impressions' Greatest Hits	1965	6.25	12.50	25.00
❑ 523 [M]	One By One	1965	5.00	10.00	20.00
❑ S-523 [S]	One By One	1965	6.25	12.50	25.00
❑ 545 [M]	Ridin' High	1966	5.00	10.00	20.00
❑ S-545 [S]	Ridin' High	1966	6.25	12.50	25.00
❑ ST-90520 [S]	One By One	1965	7.50	15.00	30.00
-- Capitol Record Club edition					
❑ T-90520 [M]	One By One	1965	6.25	12.50	25.00
-- Capitol Record Club edition					
IMPROVISATION CHAMBER ENSEMBLE					
RCA VICTOR RED SEAL					
❑ LSC-2558 [S]	Studies in Improvisation	1961	7.50	15.00	30.00
-- Original with "shaded dog" label					
IMUS, DON					
BANG					
❑ 407	This Honky's Nuts	1974	6.25	12.50	25.00
RCA VICTOR					
❑ LSP-4699	1200 Hamburgers to Go	1972	6.25	12.50	25.00
❑ LSP-4819	One Sacred Chicken to Go	1973	6.25	12.50	25.00
IN GROUP, THE					
IN					
❑ I-1002 [M]	Swinging 12 String	1964	5.00	10.00	20.00
❑ IS-1002 [S]	Swinging 12 String	1964	6.25	12.50	25.00
IN-SECT, THE					
RCA CAMDEN					
❑ CAL-909 [M]	Introducing the In-Sect Direct from England	1964	10.00	20.00	40.00
❑ CAS-909 [S]	Introducing the In-Sect Direct from England	1964	12.50	25.00	50.00
INCREDIBLE STRING BAND, THE					
ELEKTRA					
❑ EKM-322 [M]	The Incredible String Band	1967	7.50	15.00	30.00
❑ 7E-2002 [(2)]	'U'	1971	6.25	12.50	25.00
-- Butterfly label					
❑ 7E-2004 [(2)]	Relics of the Incredible String Band	1971	5.00	10.00	20.00
-- Butterfly label					
❑ EKM-4010 [M]	The 5,000 Spirits	1967	7.50	15.00	30.00
❑ EKS-7322 [S]	The Incredible String Band	1967	5.00	10.00	20.00
-- Brown label					
❑ EKS-74010 [S]	The 5,000 Spirits	1967	5.00	10.00	20.00
-- Brown label					
❑ EKS-74021	The Hangman's Beautiful Daughter	1968	5.00	10.00	20.00
-- Brown label					
❑ EKS-74036	Wee Tam	1969	5.00	10.00	20.00
-- Brown label					
❑ EKS-74037	The Big Huge	1969	5.00	10.00	20.00
-- Brown label					
INCREDIBLES, THE					
AUDIO ARTS					
❑ AAS-7000	Heart and Soul	1970	5.00	10.00	20.00
INDEPENDENTS, THE					
WAND					
❑ WDS-694	The First Time We Met	1973	6.25	12.50	25.00
❑ WDS-696	The Independents	1973	6.25	12.50	25.00
❑ WDS-699	Discs of Gold	1974	6.25	12.50	25.00
INDEX					
DC					
❑ 71	The Index	1968	1,500.	2,250.	3,000.
-- Black label; issued with black and white jacket; number is from dead wax					
❑ 4736	The Index	1968	1,000.	1,500.	2,000.
-- Red label; issued with generic white jacket, though sometimes found in first LP's jacket; number in dead wax					
INDIAN SUMMER					
RCA/NEON					
❑ NE-3	Indian Summer	1971	5.00	10.00	20.00
INDIGO GIRLS					
DRAGON PATH					
❑ LMM-I [EP]	Indigo Girls	1986	37.50	75.00	150.00
-- Black vinyl					
❑ LMM-I [EP]	Indigo Girls	1986	50.00	100.00	200.00
-- Blue or clear vinyl (each of equal value)					

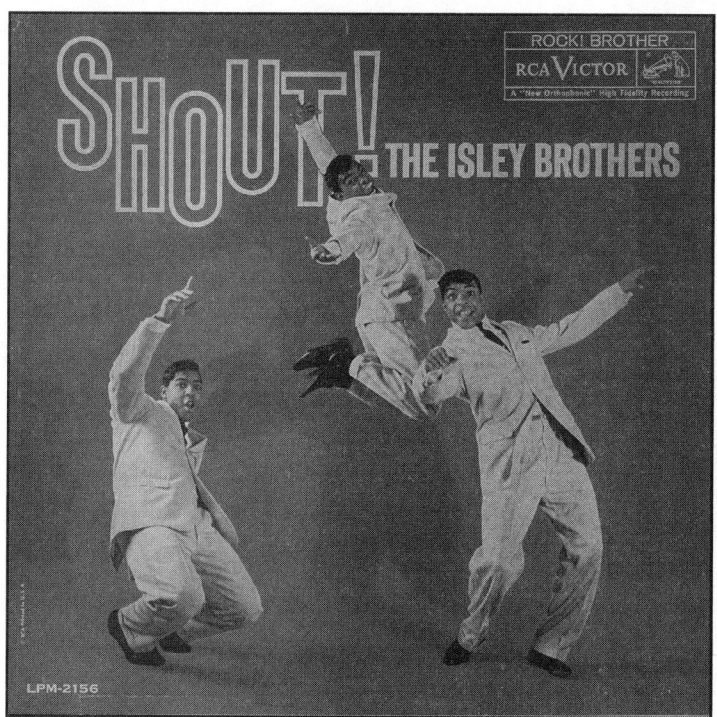

(Top left) Janis Ian's debut album from 1967, featuring the hit "Society's Child," is harder to find in mono than in stereo. (Top right) The International Submarine Band was unknown during its time, but one of its members, Gram Parsons, became a leader in the burgeoning country-rock sound, both as a member of the Byrds and with the Flying Burrito Brothers. This album has become an important artifact in retrospect. (Bottom left) The Isley Brothers' first album, based around their first hit single "Shout," is one of the more memorable LP covers out there. (Bottom right) It's A Beautiful Day was the name of the band as well as the album. It contains the FM radio staple "White Bird" and is not easy to find today, especially on its original red "360 Sound" pressing.

Number	Title	Yr	VG	VG+	NM
EPIC					
❏ EAS 1481 [EP]	Kid Fears/Closer to Fine/ Center Stage/Prince of Darkness	1989	7.50	15.00	30.00
-- Promo-only with tour-dates sticker on white cardboard cover					
❏ EAS 1861 [DJ]	Land of Canaan Plus Five Live	1989	10.00	20.00	40.00
-- Promo-only item with five live tracks on B-side					
❏ EAS 2201 [DJ]	Shades of Indigo: An Interview by Shawn Colvin	1990	10.00	20.00	40.00
❏ EAS 4020 [DJ]	Indigo Girls Live	1991	10.00	20.00	40.00
-- Promo-only version of "Back on the Bus Y'All"					
❏ FE 45044	Indigo Girls	1989	5.00	10.00	20.00
❏ FE 45427	Strange Fire	1989	5.00	10.00	20.00
-- Reissue of Indigo release					
❏ E 46820	Nomads*Indians*Saints	1990	5.00	10.00	20.00
❏ E 57621	Swamp Ophelia	1994	7.50	15.00	30.00
-- Black vinyl; all copies autographed on the label by the Indigo Girls					
❏ E 57621	Swamp Ophelia	1994	10.00	20.00	40.00
-- Green vinyl; all copies autographed on the label by the Indigo Girls					
INDIGO					
❏ LMM-II	Strange Fire	1987	37.50	75.00	150.00
-- Black vinyl					
❏ LMM-II	Strange Fire	1987	50.00	100.00	200.00
-- Blue, clear or red vinyl (each of equal value)					

INFLUENCE
ABC

Number	Title	Yr	VG	VG+	NM
❏ ABCS-630	Influence	1968	7.50	15.00	30.00

INGMANN, JORGEN
ATCO

Number	Title	Yr	VG	VG+	NM
❏ 33-130 [M]	Apache	1961	10.00	20.00	40.00
❏ 33-139 [M]	The Many Guitars of Jorgen Ingmann	1962	10.00	20.00	40.00
MERCURY					
❏ MG-20200 [M]	Swinging Guitar	1956	15.00	30.00	60.00
❏ MG-20292 [M]	Swing Softly	1956	15.00	30.00	60.00

INK SPOTS, THE
COLORTONE

Number	Title	Yr	VG	VG+	NM
❏ 4901 [M]	The Ink Spots	1958	15.00	30.00	60.00
❏ 4947 [M]	The Ink Spots, Vol. 2	1959	15.00	30.00	60.00
CROWN					
❏ CST-144 [S]	The Ink Spots' Greatest Hits	1959	12.50	25.00	50.00
-- Red vinyl					
❏ CST-144 [S]	The Ink Spots' Greatest Hits	1959	6.25	12.50	25.00
-- Black vinyl					
❏ CST-175 [S]	The Ink Spots	1961	12.50	25.00	50.00
-- Red vinyl					
❏ CST-175 [S]	The Ink Spots	1961	6.25	12.50	25.00
-- Black vinyl					
❏ CST-217 [S]	The Sensational Ink Spots	1962	6.25	12.50	25.00
❏ CLP-5112 [M]	The Ink Spots' Greatest Hits	1959	5.00	10.00	20.00
❏ CLP-5142 [M]	The Ink Spots	1961	5.00	10.00	20.00
❏ CLP-5187 [M]	The Sensational Ink Spots	1962	5.00	10.00	20.00
DECCA					
❏ DXB 182 [(2) M]	The Best of the Ink Spots	1965	7.50	15.00	30.00
❏ DL 4297 [M]	Our Golden Favorites	1962	6.25	12.50	25.00
❏ DL 5056 [10]	The Ink Spots	1950	12.50	25.00	50.00
❏ DI 5071 [10]	The Ink Spots, Vol. 2	1950	12.50	25.00	50.00
❏ DL 5333 [10]	Precious Memories	1951	12.50	25.00	50.00
❏ DL 5541 [10]	Street of Dreams	1954	12.50	25.00	50.00
❏ DXSB 7182 [(2) P]	The Best of the Ink Spots	1965	5.00	10.00	20.00
❏ DL 8154 [M]	The Best of the Ink Spots	1955	10.00	20.00	40.00
-- Black label, silver print					
❏ DL 8232 [M]	Time Out for Tears	1956	10.00	20.00	40.00
-- Black label, silver print					
❏ DL 8768 [M]	Torch Time	1958	10.00	20.00	40.00
-- Black label, silver print					
❏ DL 74297 [S]	Our Golden Favorites	1962	5.00	10.00	20.00
GRAND AWARD					
❏ GA 232 SD [S]	The Ink Spots' Greatest, Volume 3	1959	10.00	20.00	40.00
❏ GA 33-328 [M]	The Ink Spots' Greatest, Volume 1	1958	6.25	12.50	25.00
❏ GA 33-354 [M]	The Ink Spots' Greatest, Volume 2	1958	6.25	12.50	25.00
❏ GA 33-396 [M]	The Ink Spots' Greatest, Volume 3	1959	6.25	12.50	25.00
KING					
❏ 535 [M]	Something Old, Something New	1956	100.00	200.00	400.00
❏ 642 [M]	Songs That Will Live Forever	1959	75.00	150.00	300.00
-- Reissue of 535					
TOPS					
❏ L-1561 [M]	The Ink Spots	1957	10.00	20.00	40.00
❏ L-1668 [M]	The Ink Spots, Vol. 2	1959	10.00	20.00	40.00
VERVE					
❏ MGV-2124 [M]	The Ink Spots' Favorites	1959	6.25	12.50	25.00
❏ MGVS-6096 [S]	The Ink Spots' Favorites	1959	10.00	20.00	40.00
WALDORF MUSIC HALL					
❏ MH 33-144 [10]	Songs of the South Seas	195?	20.00	40.00	80.00
❏ MH 33-152 [10]	The Ink Spots Quartet	195?	20.00	40.00	80.00

INMAN, AUTRY
JUBILEE

Number	Title	Yr	VG	VG+	NM
❏ JGM-2055 [M]	Discotheque Saturday Night	1964	5.00	10.00	20.00
❏ JGS-2055 [S]	Discotheque Saturday Night	1964	6.25	12.50	25.00
❏ JGM-2056 [M]	New Year's Eve with Autry Inman	1964	5.00	10.00	20.00
❏ JGS-2056 [S]	New Year's Eve with Autry Inman	1964	6.25	12.50	25.00
MOUNTAIN DEW					
❏ 7022 [M]	Autry Inman	1963	5.00	10.00	20.00
❏ S-7022 [S]	Autry Inman	1963	6.25	12.50	25.00
SIMS					
❏ 107 [M]	Autry Inman at the Frontier Club	1964	5.00	10.00	20.00
❏ S-107 [S]	Autry Inman at the Frontier Club	1964	6.25	12.50	25.00

INNOCENCE, THE
KAMA SUTRA

Number	Title	Yr	VG	VG+	NM
❏ KLP-8059 [M]	The Innocence	1967	5.00	10.00	20.00
❏ KLPS-8059 [S]	The Innocence	1967	7.50	15.00	30.00

INNOCENT, THE
With Trent Reznor, pre-NINE INCH NAILS.
RED LABEL

Number	Title	Yr	VG	VG+	NM
❏ 7300	Livin' in the Street	1985	15.00	30.00	60.00

INNOCENTS, THE
INDIGO

Number	Title	Yr	VG	VG+	NM
❏ 503 [M]	Innocently Yours	1961	20.00	40.00	80.00
❏ 503 [M-DJ]	Innocently Yours	1961	125.00	250.00	500.00
-- Plain white cover					

INSECT TRUST, THE
ATCO

Number	Title	Yr	VG	VG+	NM
❏ SD 33-313	Hoboken Saturday Night	1970	10.00	20.00	40.00
CAPITOL					
❏ SKAO-109	The Insect Trust	1968	10.00	20.00	40.00

INSIDE OUT
FREDLO

Number	Title	Yr	VG	VG+	NM
❏ 6834	Bringing It All Back	1968	50.00	100.00	200.00

INTERNATIONAL SUBMARINE BAND, THE
With Gram Parsons, later of THE BYRDS and THE FLYING BURRITO BROTHERS.
LHI

Number	Title	Yr	VG	VG+	NM
❏ 12001	Safe at Home	1968	25.00	50.00	100.00
-- Counterfeits have white labels, legitimate copies have multi-color labels					

INTERPRETERS, THE
CADET

Number	Title	Yr	VG	VG+	NM
❏ LPS-762 [S]	The Knack	1966	5.00	10.00	20.00

INTRIGUES, THE
YEW

Number	Title	Yr	VG	VG+	NM
❏ YS-777	In a Moment	1970	7.50	15.00	30.00

INTRUDERS, THE
GAMBLE

Number	Title	Yr	VG	VG+	NM
❏ G-5001 [M]	The Intruders Are Together	1967	10.00	20.00	40.00
❏ GS-5001 [S]	The Intruders Are Together	1967	12.50	25.00	50.00
❏ GS-5004	Cowboys to Girls	1968	12.50	25.00	50.00
❏ GS-5005	The Intruders Greatest Hits	1969	10.00	20.00	40.00
❏ GS-5008	When We Get Married	1970	12.50	25.00	50.00
❏ KZ 31991	Save the Children	1973	5.00	10.00	20.00
❏ KZ 32131	Super Hits	1973	5.00	10.00	20.00

INVADERS, THE
JUSTICE

Number	Title	Yr	VG	VG+	NM
❏ JLP-125	On the Right Track	196?	75.00	150.00	300.00

INVICTAS, THE
20TH CENTURY FOX

Number	Title	Yr	VG	VG+	NM
❏ TCF-3152 [M]	The Invictas	1964	10.00	20.00	40.00
INVICTAS					
❏ M80P-5816/7 [M]	The Invictas	196?	62.50	125.00	250.00
SAHARA					
❏ 101 [M]	The Invictas A-Go-Go	1965	30.00	60.00	120.00

Number	Title	Yr	VG	VG+	NM
INVISIBLE MAN'S BAND, THE					
Successor to THE FIVE STAIRSTEPS.					
BOARDWALK					
❏ NB1-33238	Really Wanna See Ya	1981	5.00	10.00	20.00
INXS					
ATLANTIC					
❏ A1-82294 [(2)]	Live Baby Live	1991	5.00	10.00	20.00
-- Columbia House version (only U.S. vinyl pressing)					
IRISH ROVERS, THE					
DECCA					
❏ DL 4835 [M]	First	1967	5.00	10.00	20.00
❏ DL 4951 [M]	The Unicorn	1968	6.25	12.50	25.00
IRON BUTTERFLY					
ATCO					
❏ 33-227 [M]	Heavy	1967	7.50	15.00	30.00
❏ SD 33-227 [S]	Heavy	1967	6.25	12.50	25.00
-- Brown and purple label					
❏ 33-250 [M]	In-A-Gadda-Da-Vida	1968	12.50	25.00	50.00
❏ SD 33-250 [S]	In-A-Gadda-Da-Vida	1968	6.25	12.50	25.00
-- Brown and purple label					
IRON MAIDEN					
CAPITOL					
❏ SEAX-12219 [PD]	The Number of the Beast	1982	12.50	25.00	50.00
❏ SEAX-12306 [PD]	Piece of Mind	1983	15.00	30.00	60.00
❏ 53185 [(4)]	Best of the Beast	1996	20.00	40.00	80.00
-- Box set with booklet; probably a UK pressing stickered with US bar code					
EPIC					
❏ E 46905	No Prayer for the Dying	1990	6.25	12.50	25.00
-- Red vinyl					
ISLEY BROTHERS, THE					
ISLAND					
❏ 7243 [(2) DJ]	Mission to Please	1996	5.00	10.00	20.00
-- Promo-only vinyl in generic cover					
RCA VICTOR					
❏ LPM-2156 [M]	Shout!	1959	30.00	60.00	120.00
-- "Long Play" label					
❏ LSP-2156 [S]	Shout!	1959	50.00	100.00	200.00
-- "Living Stereo" label					
SCEPTER					
❏ SC-552 [M]	Take Some Time Out for the Isley Brothers	1966	7.50	15.00	30.00
❏ SCS-552 [S]	Take Some Time Out for the Isley Brothers	1966	10.00	20.00	40.00
T-NECK					
❏ ASZ 137 [DJ]	Everything You Always Wanted to Hear by the Isley Brothers But Were Afraid to Ask For	1976	5.00	10.00	20.00
-- Promo-only compilation					
❏ TNS-3001	It's Our Thing	1969	5.00	10.00	20.00
❏ TNS-3002	The Brothers: Isley	1969	5.00	10.00	20.00
❏ TNS-3007	In the Beginning (With Jimi Hendrix)	1970	5.00	10.00	20.00
❏ TNS-3010 [(2)]	The Isleys Live	1973	5.00	10.00	20.00
❏ ZQ 32453 [Q]	3 + 3	1974	5.00	10.00	20.00
❏ PZQ 33070 [Q]	Live It Up	1974	5.00	10.00	20.00
❏ PZQ 33809 [Q]	Harvest for the World	1976	5.00	10.00	20.00
❏ PZQ 34432 [Q]	Go for Your Guns	1977	5.00	10.00	20.00
TAMLA					
❏ T-269 [M]	This Old Heart of Mine	1966	6.25	12.50	25.00
❏ TS-269 [S]	This Old Heart of Mine	1966	7.50	15.00	30.00
❏ T-275 [M]	Soul on the Rocks	1967	6.25	12.50	25.00
❏ TS-275 [S]	Soul on the Rocks	1967	7.50	15.00	30.00
❏ TS-287	Doin' Their Thing (Best of the Isley Brothers)	1969	5.00	10.00	20.00
UNITED ARTISTS					
❏ UAL-3313 [M]	The Famous Isley Brothers	1963	12.50	25.00	50.00
❏ UAS-6313 [S]	The Famous Isley Brothers	1963	15.00	30.00	60.00
WAND					
❏ WD-653 [M]	Twist & Shout	1962	20.00	40.00	80.00
❏ WDS-653 [S]	Twist & Shout	1962	25.00	50.00	100.00
IT'S A BEAUTIFUL DAY					
COLUMBIA					
❏ CS 1058	Marrying Maiden	1970	7.50	15.00	30.00
-- Red "360 Sound" label					
❏ CS 9768	It's A Beautiful Day	1969	7.50	15.00	30.00
-- Red "360 Sound" label					
❏ CS 9768	It's A Beautiful Day	1970	5.00	10.00	20.00
-- Orange label					
❏ KC 32660 [DJ]	A Thousand and One Nights	1973	12.50	25.00	50.00
-- Canceled before commercial release?					
SAN FRANCISCO SOUND					
❏ 11790	It's a Beautiful Day	1985	6.25	12.50	25.00
-- Limited reissue					
IVERS, PETER					
EPIC					
❏ BN 26500	Knight of the Blue Communion	1970	10.00	20.00	40.00
IVES, BURL					
COLUMBIA					
❏ CL 628 [M]	The Wayfaring Stranger	1955	7.50	15.00	30.00
❏ CL 980 [M]	Burl Ives Sings Songs for All Ages	1956	7.50	15.00	30.00
❏ CL 1459 [M]	Return of the Wayfaring Stranger	1960	7.50	15.00	30.00
❏ CL 2570 [10]	Children's Favorites	1955	10.00	20.00	40.00
-- "House Party Series" issue					
❏ CL 6058 [10]	The Return of the Wayfaring Stranger	1949	12.50	25.00	50.00
❏ CL 6109 [10]	The Wayfaring Stranger	1950	12.50	25.00	50.00
❏ CL 6144 [10]	More Folk Songs	1950	12.50	25.00	50.00
DECCA					
❏ DXB 167 [(2) M]	The Best of Burl Ives	1961	6.25	12.50	25.00
❏ DL 5013 [10]	Ballads and Folk Songs	1949	12.50	25.00	50.00
❏ DL 5080 [10]	Ballads and Folk Songs, Volume 2	1949	12.50	25.00	50.00
❏ DL 5093 [10]	Ballads, Folk and Country Songs	1949	12.50	25.00	50.00
❏ DL 5428 [10]	Christmas Day in the Morning	1952	12.50	25.00	50.00
❏ DL 5467 [10]	Folk Songs Dramatic and Dangerous	1953	12.50	25.00	50.00
❏ DL 5490 [10]	Women: Folk Songs About the Fair Sex	1954	12.50	25.00	50.00
❏ DXSB 7167 [(2) S]	The Best of Burl Ives	1961	7.50	15.00	30.00
❏ DL 8080 [M]	Coronation Concert	1953	10.00	20.00	40.00
❏ DL 8107 [M]	The Wild Side of Life	1955	6.25	12.50	25.00
❏ DL 8125 [M]	Men	1956	6.25	12.50	25.00
❏ DL 8245 [M]	Down to the Sea in Ships	1956	6.25	12.50	25.00
❏ DL 8246 [M]	Women	1956	6.25	12.50	25.00
❏ DL 8247 [M]	In the Quiet of Night	1956	6.25	12.50	25.00
❏ DL 8248 [M]	Burl Ives Sings for Fun	1956	6.25	12.50	25.00
❏ DL 8391 [M]	Christmas Eve	1957	6.25	12.50	25.00
❏ DL 8444 [M]	Songs of Ireland	1958	6.25	12.50	25.00
❏ DL 8587 [M]	Captain Burl Ives' Ark	1958	6.25	12.50	25.00
❏ DL 8637 [M]	Old Time Varieties	1958	6.25	12.50	25.00
❏ DL 8749 [M]	Australian Folk Songs	1959	6.25	12.50	25.00
❏ DL 8886 [M]	Cheers	1959	6.25	12.50	25.00
❏ DL 74152 [S]	The Versatile Burl Ives	1961	5.00	10.00	20.00
❏ DL 74179 [S]	Songs of the West	1961	5.00	10.00	20.00
❏ DL 74279 [S]	It's Just My Funny Way of	1962	5.00	10.00	20.00
❏ DL 74304 [S]	Sing Out, Sweet Land	1962	5.00	10.00	20.00
❏ DL 74320 [S]	Sunshine in My Soul	1962	5.00	10.00	20.00
❏ DL 74361 [S]	Burl	1963	5.00	10.00	20.00
❏ DL 74390 [S]	The Best of Burl's for Boys and Girls	1963	5.00	10.00	20.00
❏ DL 74433 [S]	Singin' Easy	1964	5.00	10.00	20.00
❏ DL 74533 [S]	True Love	1964	5.00	10.00	20.00
❏ DL 74578 [S]	Pearly Shells	1964	5.00	10.00	20.00
❏ DL 78886 [S]	Cheers	1959	7.50	15.00	30.00
DISNEYLAND					
❏ STER-3927 [S]	Chim Chim Chiree and Other Children's Choices	1964	5.00	10.00	20.00
STINSON					
❏ SLP-1 [10]	The Wayfaring Stranger	1949	15.00	30.00	60.00
UNITED ARTISTS					
❏ UAS 6060 [S]	Ballads	1959	5.00	10.00	20.00
WORD					
❏ 8140 [S]	Faith and Joy	196?	5.00	10.00	20.00
IVEYS, THE					
APPLE					
❏ ST-3355	Maybe Tomorrow	1969	500.00	1,000.	2,000.
-- Album not released in US; price is for an LP slick, which does exist					
IVORY					
TETRAGRAMMATON					
❏ T-104	Ivory	1968	5.00	10.00	20.00
IVORY, JACKIE					
ATCO					
❏ 33-178 [M]	Soul Discovery	1965	5.00	10.00	20.00
❏ SD 33-178 [S]	Soul Discovery	1965	6.25	12.50	25.00
IVY LEAGUE, THE					
CAMEO					
❏ C 2000 [M]	Tossing and Turning	1965	7.50	15.00	30.00
❏ CS 2000 [R]	Tossing and Turning	1965	7.50	15.00	30.00

Number	Title	Yr	VG	VG+	NM

J

J.B.'S, THE -- See FRED WESLEY.

J.K. AND COMPANY
WHITE WHALE
❑ WWS-7117	Suddenly One Summer	1969	6.25	12.50	25.00

JACKS, THE
CROWN
❑ CLP-5021 [M]	Jumpin' with the Jacks	1960	50.00	100.00	200.00
❑ CLP-5372 [M]	Jumpin' with the Jacks	1962	25.00	50.00	100.00
❑ CST-372 [R]	Jumpin' with the Jacks	1962	12.50	25.00	50.00

RPM
❑ LRP-3006 [M]	Jumpin' with the Jacks	1956	1,000.	1,500.	2,000.

JACKSON HEIGHTS
MERCURY
❑ SR-61331	King Progress	1970	6.25	12.00	25.00

VERVE
❑ V6-5089	Jackson Heights	1973	5.00	10.00	20.00

JACKSON, ALAN
ARISTA
❑ AS 8623	Here in the Real World	1990	5.00	10.00	20.00
❑ AS 8681	Don't Rock the Jukebox	1991	6.25	12.50	25.00

-- Columbia House vinyl edition
❑ R 143877	Don't Rock the Jukebox	1991	6.25	12.50	25.00

-- BMG Direct Marketing vinyl version. The two record club versions are the only vinyl versions.

JACKSON, BULL MOOSE
AUDIO LAB
❑ AL-1524 [M]	Bull Moose Jackson	1959	150.00	300.00	600.00

JACKSON, CHUCK
GUEST STAR
❑ GS-1912 [M]	Chuck Jackson	196?	5.00	10.00	20.00

MOTOWN
❑ M-667 [M]	Chuck Jackson Arrives!	1967	10.00	20.00	40.00
❑ MS-667 [S]	Chuck Jackson Arrives!	1967	6.25	12.50	25.00
❑ MS-687	Goin' Back to Chuck Jackson	1969	6.25	12.50	25.00

SPIN-O-RAMA
❑ 123 [M]	Starring Chuck Jackson	196?	5.00	10.00	20.00

STRAND
❑ SL-1125 [M]	The Great Chuck Jackson	196?	6.25	12.50	25.00
❑ SLS-1125 [S]	The Great Chuck Jackson	196?	7.50	15.00	30.00

V.I.P.
❑ 403	Teardrops Keep Fallin' on My	1970	10.00	20.00	40.00

WAND
❑ WD-650 [M]	I Don't Want to Cry	1961	10.00	20.00	40.00
❑ WD-654 [M]	Any Day Now	1962	10.00	20.00	40.00
❑ WD-655 [M]	Encore	1963	10.00	20.00	40.00
❑ WD-658 [M]	Chuck Jackson On Tour	1964	10.00	20.00	40.00
❑ WD-667 [M]	Mr. Everything	1965	7.50	15.00	30.00
❑ WDS-667 [S]	Mr. Everything	1965	10.00	20.00	40.00
❑ WD-673 [M]	A Tribute to Rhythm and Blues	1966	7.50	15.00	30.00
❑ WDS-673 [S]	A Tribute to Rhythm and Blues	1966	10.00	20.00	40.00
❑ WD-676 [M]	A Tribute to Rhythm and Blues, Volume 2	1966	7.50	15.00	30.00
❑ WDS-676 [S]	A Tribute to Rhythm and Blues, Volume 2	1966	10.00	20.00	40.00
❑ WD-680 [M]	Dedicated to the King!!	1966	10.00	20.00	40.00
❑ WDS-680 [S]	Dedicated to the King!!	1966	12.50	25.00	50.00
❑ WD-683 [M]	Chuck Jackson's Greatest Hits	1967	5.00	10.00	20.00
❑ WDS-683 [S]	Chuck Jackson's Greatest Hits	1967	6.25	12.50	25.00

JACKSON, CHUCK, AND MAXINE BROWN
Also see each artist's individual listings.
WAND
❑ WD-669 [M]	Say Something	1965	7.50	15.00	30.00
❑ WDS-669 [S]	Say Something	1965	10.00	20.00	40.00
❑ WD-678 [M]	Hold On, We're Coming	1966	7.50	15.00	30.00
❑ WDS-678 [S]	Hold On, We're Coming	1966	10.00	20.00	40.00

JACKSON, CHUCK, AND TAMMI TERRELL
Also see each artist's individual listings.
WAND
❑ WD-682 [M]	The Early Show	1967	7.50	15.00	30.00

Number	Title	Yr	VG	VG+	NM
❑ WDS-682 [S]	The Early Show	1967	7.50	15.00	30.00

JACKSON, DEON
ATCO
❑ 33-188 [M]	Love Makes the World Go Round	1966	7.50	15.00	30.00
❑ SD 33-188 [S]	Love Makes the World Go Round	1966	10.00	20.00	40.00

JACKSON, J.J.
CALLA
❑ C-1101 [M]	But It's Alright/I Dig Girls	1967	5.00	10.00	20.00
❑ CS-1101 [S]	But It's Alright/I Dig Girls	1967	6.25	12.50	25.00

CONGRESS
❑ CS-7000	The Greatest Little Soul Band in the World	1968	6.25	12.50	25.00

WARNER BROS.
❑ WS 1797	The Great J.J. Jackson	1969	5.00	10.00	20.00

JACKSON, JOE
A&M
❑ SP-3666 [(2)]	Look Sharp!	1979	5.00	10.00	20.00

-- Two 10-inch records in gatefold sleeve with button
MOBILE FIDELITY
❑ 1-080	Night and Day	1982	7.50	15.00	30.00

-- Audiophile vinyl

JACKSON, LIL' SON
ARHOOLIE
❑ 1004 [M]	Lil' Son Jackson	1960	6.25	12.50	25.00

IMPERIAL
❑ LP-9142 [M]	Rockin' and Rollin'	1961	100.00	200.00	400.00

JACKSON, MAHALIA
APOLLO
❑ 1001/2 [M]	Command Performance	1961	6.25	12.50	25.00
❑ 201/202 [M]	Spirituals	1954	7.50	15.00	30.00
❑ 482 [M]	No Matter How You Pray	1959	6.25	12.50	25.00
❑ 499 [M]	Mahalia Jackson	1962	6.25	12.50	25.00

COLUMBIA
❑ CL 644 [M]	Mahalia Jackson	1955	10.00	20.00	40.00
❑ CL 702 [M]	Sweet Little Jesus Boy	1955	10.00	20.00	40.00
❑ CL 899 [M]	Bless This House	1956	7.50	15.00	30.00
❑ CL 1244 [M]	Newport 1958	1959	5.00	10.00	20.00
❑ CL 1343 [M]	That Great Gettin' Up Morning	1959	5.00	10.00	20.00
❑ CL 1428 [M]	Come On Children, Let's Sing	1960	5.00	10.00	20.00
❑ CL 1473 [M]	The Power and the Glory	1960	5.00	10.00	20.00
❑ CS 8071 [S]	Newport 1958	1959	7.50	15.00	30.00
❑ CS 8153 [S]	That Great Gettin' Up Morning	1959	6.25	12.50	25.00
❑ CS 8225 [S]	Come On Children, Let's Sing	1960	6.25	12.50	25.00
❑ CS 8264 [S]	The Power and the Glory	1960	6.25	12.50	25.00
❑ CS 8349 [S]	I Believe	1960	5.00	10.00	20.00
❑ CS 8443 [S]	Every Time I Feel the Spirit	1961	5.00	10.00	20.00
❑ CS 8526 [S]	Recorded in Europe During Her Latest Concert Tour	1962	5.00	10.00	20.00
❑ CS 8624 [S]	Great Songs of Love and Faith	1962	5.00	10.00	20.00
❑ CS 8703 [S]	Silent Night	1962	5.00	10.00	20.00
❑ CS 8736 [S]	Make a Joyful Noise Unto the Lord	1962	5.00	10.00	20.00

GRAND AWARD
❑ GA 33-326 [M]	Mahalia Jackson	1955	7.50	15.00	30.00
❑ GA 33-390 [M]	Mahalia Jackson	195?	7.50	15.00	30.00

KENWOOD
❑ 1001/2 [(2)]	Command Performance	196?	5.00	10.00	20.00

JACKSON, MICHAEL
Also see THE JACKSONS.
EPIC
❑ E3 59000 [(3)]	HIStory: Past, Present and Future -- Book I	1995	5.00	10.00	20.00

-- Box set with 12x12 booklet
❑ HE 47545	Off the Wall	1982	10.00	20.00	40.00

-- Half-speed mastered edition
❑ HE 48112	Thriller	1982	10.00	20.00	40.00

-- Half-speed mastered edition
MOTOWN
❑ M 755	Ben	1972	15.00	30.00	60.00

-- With Michael Jackson on top half of cover, rats on the bottom half

JACKSON, SAMMY
ARVEE
❑ A-434 [M]	Ladies Man	1962	12.50	25.00	50.00
❑ SA-434 [S]	Ladies Man	1962	15.00	30.00	60.00

Number	Title	Yr	VG	VG+	NM

JACKSON, SHOT
CUMBERLAND
❑ MGC-29513 [M] Bluegrass Dobro		1965	5.00	10.00	20.00
❑ SRC-69513 [S] Bluegrass Dobro		1965	6.25	12.00	25.00

STARDAY
❑ SLP-230 [M]	The Singing Strings of Steel Guitar and Dobro	1962	7.50	15.00	30.00

JACKSON, STONEWALL
COLUMBIA
❑ CL 1391 [M]	The Dynamic Stonewall Jackson	1959	6.25	12.50	25.00
❑ CL 1770 [M]	Sadness in a Song	1962	5.00	10.00	20.00
❑ CL 2059 [M]	I Love a Song	1963	5.00	10.00	20.00
❑ CL 2674 [M]	Help Stamp Out Loneliness	1967	6.25	12.50	25.00
❑ CL 2762 [M]	Stonewall Jackson Country	1967	6.25	12.50	25.00
❑ CS 8186 [S]	The Dynamic Stonewall Jackson	1959	7.50	15.00	30.00
❑ CS 8570 [S]	Sadness in a Song	1962	6.25	12.50	25.00
❑ CS 8859 [S]	I Love a Song	1963	6.25	12.50	25.00
❑ CS 9078 [S]	Trouble & Me	1964	5.00	10.00	20.00
❑ CS 9177 [S]	Stonewall Jackson's Greatest Hits	1965	5.00	10.00	20.00
❑ CS 9309 [S]	All's Fair in Love 'n' War	1966	5.00	10.00	20.00
❑ CS 9474 [S]	Help Stamp Out Loneliness	1967	5.00	10.00	20.00
❑ CS 9562 [S]	Stonewall Jackson Country	1967	5.00	10.00	20.00
❑ CS 9669	Nothing Takes the Place of Loving You	1968	5.00	10.00	20.00
❑ CS 9708	The Great Old Songs	1968	5.00	10.00	20.00
❑ CS 9754	The Old Country Church	1969	6.25	12.50	25.00
❑ CS 9880	Tribute to Hank Williams	1969	5.00	10.00	20.00

JACKSON, TOMMY
DECCA
❑ DL 8950 [M]	Square Dances Without Calls	1959	5.00	10.00	20.00
❑ DL 78950 [S]	Square Dances Without Calls	1959	6.25	12.50	25.00

DOT
❑ DLP-3015 [M]	Popular Square Dance Music	1957	7.50	15.00	30.00
❑ DLP-3085 [M]	Square Dance Tonight!	1958	6.25	12.50	25.00
❑ DLP-3163 [M]	Do-Si-Do	1959	5.00	10.00	20.00
❑ DLP-3330 [M]	Square Dance Festival, Vol. 1	1960	5.00	10.00	20.00
❑ DLP-3331 [M]	Square Dance Festival, Vol. 2	1960	5.00	10.00	20.00
❑ DLP-3471 [M]	Greatest Bluegrass Hits	1962	5.00	10.00	20.00
❑ DLP-3532 [M]	Square Dance Festival, Vol. 3	1961	5.00	10.00	20.00
❑ DLP-25380 [S]	Square Dances	1963	5.00	10.00	20.00
❑ DLP-25454 [S]	Swing Your Partner	1962	5.00	10.00	20.00
❑ DLP-25471 [S]	Greatest Bluegrass Hits	1962	6.25	12.50	25.00

MERCURY
❑ MG-20346 [M]	Square Dance Fiddle Favorites	1958	6.25	12.50	25.00

JACKSON, WALTER
OKEH
❑ OKM 12107 [M]	It's All Over	1965	6.25	12.50	25.00
❑ OKM 12108 [M]	Welcome Home	1966	6.25	12.50	25.00
❑ OKM 12120 [M]	Speak Her Name	1967	6.25	12.50	25.00
❑ OKS 14107 [S]	It's All Over	1965	7.50	15.00	30.00
❑ OKS 14108 [S]	Welcome Home	1966	7.50	15.00	30.00
❑ OKS 14120 [S]	Speak Her Name	1967	7.50	15.00	30.00

JACKSON, WANDA
CAPITOL
❑ T 1041 [M]	Wanda Jackson	1958	75.00	150.00	300.00
-- Black colorband label, Capitol logo at left					
❑ T 1041 [M]	Wanda Jackson	1962	25.00	50.00	100.00
-- Black colorband label, Capitol logo at top					
❑ T 1384 [M]	Rockin' with Wanda	1960	100.00	200.00	400.00
-- Black colorband label, Capitol logo at left					
❑ T 1384 [M]	Rockin' with Wanda	1962	62.50	125.00	250.00
-- Gold "Star Line" label					
❑ T 1384 [M]	Rockin' with Wanda	1963	37.50	75.00	150.00
-- Black "Star Line" label					
❑ ST 1511 [S]	There's a Party Goin' On	1961	100.00	200.00	400.00
-- Black colorband label, Capitol logo at left					
❑ T 1511 [M]	There's a Party Goin' On	1961	62.50	125.00	250.00
-- Black colorband label, Capitol logo at left					
❑ ST 1596 [S]	Right or Wrong	1961	12.50	25.00	50.00
-- Black colorband label, Capitol logo at left					
❑ ST 1596 [S]	Right or Wrong	1962	6.25	12.50	25.00
-- Black colorband label, Capitol logo at top					
❑ T 1596 [M]	Right or Wrong	1961	10.00	20.00	40.00
-- Black colorband label, Capitol logo at left					
❑ T 1596 [M]	Right or Wrong	1962	5.00	10.00	20.00
-- Black colorband label, Capitol logo at top					
❑ ST 1776 [S]	Wonderful Wanda	1962	7.50	15.00	30.00
❑ T 1776 [M]	Wonderful Wanda	1962	6.25	12.50	25.00
❑ ST 1911 [S]	Love Me Forever	1963	7.50	15.00	30.00
❑ T 1911 [M]	Love Me Forever	1963	6.25	12.50	25.00
❑ ST 2030 [S]	Two Sides of Wanda	1964	7.50	15.00	30.00
❑ T 2030 [M]	Two Sides of Wanda	1964	6.25	12.50	25.00
❑ ST 2306 [S]	Blues in My Heart	1965	7.50	15.00	30.00
❑ T 2306 [M]	Blues in My Heart	1965	6.25	12.50	25.00
❑ ST 2438 [S]	Wanda Jackson Sings Country Songs	1965	7.50	15.00	30.00
❑ T 2438 [M]	Wanda Jackson Sings Country Songs	1965	6.25	12.50	25.00
❑ ST 2606 [S]	Wanda Jackson Salutes the Country Music Hall of Fame	1966	5.00	10.00	20.00
❑ T 2704 [M]	Reckless Love Affair	1967	5.00	10.00	20.00
❑ T 2812 [M]	You'll Always Have My Love	1967	5.00	10.00	20.00

DECCA
❑ DL 4224 [M]	Lovin' Country Style	1962	12.50	25.00	50.00

JACKSONS, THE
Includes the Jackson Five. Also see MICHAEL JACKSON.
EPIC
❑ HE 46424	Triumph	1982	15.00	30.00	60.00
-- Half-speed mastered edition					

MOTOWN
❑ MS 700	Diana Ross Presents the Jackson 5	1969	6.25	12.50	25.00
❑ MS 709	ABC	1970	6.25	12.50	25.00
❑ MS 713	Christmas Album	1970	6.25	12.50	25.00
❑ M7-868 [(3)]	Anthology	1976	5.00	10.00	20.00
❑ 37463 1294-1 [DJ] Soulsation!		1995	5.00	10.00	20.00
-- Vinyl is promo only; 4-song sampler from box set					

JACOBI, LOU
CAPITOL
❑ ST 2596 [S]	Al Tijuana and His Jewish Brass	1966	5.00	10.00	20.00

JACOBS, DICK
CORAL
❑ CRL 57381 [M]	The Electro-Sonic Orchestra Presenting a New Concept in Sound	1958	5.00	10.00	20.00
❑ CRL 757381 [S]	The Electro-Sonic Orchestra Presenting a New Concept in Sound	1958	7.50	15.00	30.00

JACOBS, FREDDIE
WESTMINSTER
❑ WP-6087 [M]	Swingin' Folk Tunes	195?	7.50	15.00	30.00

JACOBS, HANK
SUE
❑ LP-1023 [M]	So Far Away	1964	20.00	40.00	80.00

JADE
GENERAL AMERICAN
❑ 11311	The Faces of Jade	1968	20.00	40.00	80.00

JADE, FAINE
RSVP
❑ 8002	Introspection: A Faine Jade Recital	1968	100.00	200.00	400.00

JADES, THE
JARRETT
❑ 21517 [M]	Live at the Disco a-Go-Go	1965	30.00	60.00	120.00

JAG PANZER
AZRA IRON WORKS
❑ 1001 [PD]	Ample Destruction	1985	6.25	12.00	25.00
-- Allegedly, 250 were pressed as picture discs					

JAGGERZ, THE
GAMBLE
❑ GS-5006	Introducing the Jaggerz	1969	5.00	10.00	20.00

JAIM
ETHEREAL
❑ 1001	Prophecy Fulfilled	1970	12.50	25.00	50.00

JALOPY FIVE, THE
MODERN SOUND
❑ M-561 [M]	I Love That West Coast Sound	1965	12.50	25.00	50.00
❑ MS-561 [S]	I Love That West Coast Sound	1965	12.50	25.00	50.00

JAM, THE
POLYDOR
❑ PD1-6110	In the City	1977	6.25	12.50	25.00
❑ PD1-6129	This Is the Modern World	1978	5.00	10.00	20.00

Number	Title	Yr	VG	VG+	NM
JAMAL, AHMAD					
ARGO					
❏ LP-602 [M]	Chamber Music of New Jazz	1956	7.50	15.00	30.00
-- Reissue of Creative 602					
❏ LP-610 [M]	Count 'Em 88	1957	7.50	15.00	30.00
❏ LP-628 [M]	But Not for Me/Ahmad Jamal at the Pershing	1958	7.50	15.00	30.00
❏ LPS-628 [S]	But Not for Me/Ahmad Jamal at the Pershing	1958	10.00	20.00	40.00
❏ LP-636 [M]	Ahmad Jamal, Volume IV	1958	7.50	15.00	30.00
❏ LPS-636 [S]	Ahmad Jamal, Volume IV	1958	10.00	20.00	40.00
❏ LP-638 [(2) M]	Portfolio of Ahmad Jamal	1959	10.00	20.00	40.00
❏ LPS-638 [(2) S]	Portfolio of Ahmad Jamal	1959	12.50	25.00	50.00
❏ LP-646 [M]	Jamal at the Penthouse	1959	7.50	15.00	30.00
❏ LPS-646 [S]	Jamal at the Penthouse	1959	10.00	20.00	40.00
❏ LP-662 [M]	Happy Mood	1960	5.00	10.00	20.00
❏ LPS-662 [S]	Happy Mood	1960	6.25	12.50	25.00
❏ LP-667 [M]	Ahmad Jamal at the Pershing Volume 2	1961	5.00	10.00	20.00
❏ LPS-667 [S]	Ahmad Jamal at the Pershing Volume 2	1961	6.25	12.50	25.00
❏ LP-673 [M]	Listen to Ahmad Jamal	1961	5.00	10.00	20.00
❏ LPS-673 [S]	Listen to Ahmad Jamal	1961	6.25	12.50	25.00
❏ LP-685 [M]	Alhambra	1961	5.00	10.00	20.00
❏ LPS-685 [S]	Alhambra	1961	6.25	12.50	25.00
❏ LP-691 [M]	All of You	1962	5.00	10.00	20.00
❏ LPS-691 [S]	All of You	1962	6.25	12.50	25.00
❏ LP-703 [M]	Ahmad Jamal at the Blackhawk	1962	5.00	10.00	20.00
❏ LPS-703 [S]	Ahmad Jamal at the Blackhawk	1962	6.25	12.50	25.00
❏ LP-712 [M]	Macanudo	1963	5.00	10.00	20.00
❏ LPS-712 [S]	Macanudo	1963	6.25	12.50	25.00
❏ LP-719 [M]	Poin'-ci-an'a	1963	5.00	10.00	20.00
❏ LPS-719 [S]	Poin'-ci-an'a	1963	6.25	12.50	25.00
❏ LP-733 [M]	"Naked City" Theme	1964	5.00	10.00	20.00
❏ LPS-733 [S]	"Naked City" Theme	1964	6.25	12.50	25.00
❏ LP-751 [M]	The Roar of the Greasepaint	1965	5.00	10.00	20.00
❏ LPS-751 [S]	The Roar of the Greasepaint	1965	6.25	12.50	25.00
❏ LP-758 [M]	Extensions	1965	5.00	10.00	20.00
❏ LPS-758 [S]	Extensions	1965	6.25	12.50	25.00
CADET					
❏ LPS-638 [(2) S]	Portfolio of Ahmad Jamal	1966	5.00	10.00	20.00
❏ LPS-764 [S]	Rhapsody	1966	5.00	10.00	20.00
❏ LPS-777 [S]	Heat Wave	1966	5.00	10.00	20.00
❏ LPS-786 [S]	Standard Eyes	1967	5.00	10.00	20.00
❏ LP-792 [M]	Cry Young	1967	5.00	10.00	20.00
CREATIVE					
❏ LP-602 [M]	Chamber Music of New Jazz	1956	12.50	25.00	50.00
EPIC					
❏ BN 627 [R]	Ahmad Jamal Trio	196?	5.00	10.00	20.00
❏ BN 634 [S]	The Piano Scene of Ahmad Jamal	1959	5.00	10.00	20.00
❏ LN 3212 [M]	Ahmad Jamal Trio	1956	12.50	25.00	50.00
-- Yellow label with lines around rim					
❏ LN 3212 [M]	Ahmad Jamal Trio	1963	6.25	12.50	25.00
-- Yellow label, no lines around rim					
❏ LN 3631 [M]	The Piano Scene of Ahmad Jamal	1959	7.50	15.00	30.00
JAMES GANG, THE					
Also see TOMMY BOLIN; JOE WALSH.					
ABC					
❏ S-711 [DJ]	James Gang Rides Again	1970	6.25	12.50	25.00
-- First pressing with a short version of Ravel's "Bolero"; possibly only on some promo copies					
JAMES, BOB					
ESP-DISK'					
❏ 1009 [M]	Explosions	1965	5.00	10.00	20.00
❏ S-1009 [S]	Explosions	1965	6.25	12.50	25.00
MERCURY					
❏ MG-20768 [M]	Bold Conceptions	1963	5.00	10.00	20.00
❏ SR-60768 [S]	Bold Conceptions	1963	6.25	12.50	25.00
TAPPAN ZEE					
❏ HC 45594	Touchdown	1982	7.50	15.00	30.00
-- Half-speed mastered edition					
❏ HC 47495	Sign of the Times	1982	7.50	15.00	30.00
-- Half-speed mastered edition					
JAMES, BOB, AND EARL KLUGH					
MOBILE FIDELITY					
❏ 1-124	Two of a Kind	1984	10.00	20.00	40.00
-- Audiophile vinyl					
TAPPAN ZEE					
❏ HC 46241	One on One	198?	7.50	15.00	30.00
-- Half-speed mastered edition					

Number	Title	Yr	VG	VG+	NM
JAMES, DENNIS					
KAPP					
❏ KL-1009 [M]	Let's All Sing a Song for Christmas	1955	7.50	15.00	30.00
JAMES, ELMORE					
BELL					
❏ 6037	Elmore James	1969	6.25	12.50	25.00
CHESS					
❏ LP-1537	Whose Muddy Shoes	1969	6.25	12.50	25.00
CROWN					
❏ CLP-5168 [M]	Blues After Hours	1961	62.50	125.00	250.00
-- Black label, silver "Crown"					
❏ CLP-5168 [M]	Blues After Hours	1962	12.50	25.00	50.00
-- Gray label					
KENT					
❏ KST-522 [R]	Original Folk Blues	1964	6.25	12.50	25.00
❏ KLP-5022 [M]	Original Folk Blues	1964	10.00	20.00	40.00
❏ KLP-9001	Anthology of the Blues Legend	196?	6.25	12.50	25.00
❏ KLP-9010	The Resurrection of Elmore James	196?	6.25	12.50	25.00
SPHERE SOUND					
❏ SR-7002 [M]	The Sky Is Crying	1965	45.00	90.00	180.00
❏ SSR-7002 [R]	The Sky Is Crying	1965	30.00	60.00	120.00
❏ SR-7008 [M]	I Need You	1966	37.50	75.00	150.00
❏ SSR-7008 [R]	I Need You	1966	30.00	60.00	120.00
JAMES, ETTA					
ARGO					
❏ LP-4003 [M]	At Last!	1961	10.00	20.00	40.00
❏ LPS-4003 [S]	At Last!	1961	15.00	30.00	60.00
❏ LP-4011 [M]	The Second Time Around	1961	7.50	15.00	30.00
❏ LPS-4011 [S]	The Second Time Around	1961	10.00	20.00	40.00
❏ LP-4013 [M]	Etta James	1962	7.50	15.00	30.00
❏ LPS-4013 [S]	Etta James	1962	10.00	20.00	40.00
❏ LP-4018 [M]	Etta James Sings for Lovers	1962	7.50	15.00	30.00
❏ LPS-4018 [S]	Etta James Sings for Lovers	1962	10.00	20.00	40.00
❏ LP-4025 [M]	Etta James Top Ten	1963	7.50	15.00	30.00
❏ LPS-4025 [S]	Etta James Top Ten	1963	10.00	20.00	40.00
❏ LP-4032 [M]	Etta James Rocks the House	1964	25.00	50.00	100.00
❏ LPS-4032 [S]	Etta James Rocks the House	1964	37.50	75.00	150.00
❏ LP-4040 [M]	The Queen of Soul	1965	7.50	15.00	30.00
❏ LPS-4040 [S]	The Queen of Soul	1965	10.00	20.00	40.00
CADET					
❏ LP-802 [M]	Tell Mama	1968	6.25	12.50	25.00
❏ LPS-802 [S]	Tell Mama	1968	5.00	10.00	20.00
❏ LPS-832	Funk	1969	5.00	10.00	20.00
❏ LPS-4055 [S]	Call My Name	1967	5.00	10.00	20.00
CHESS					
❏ 2CH-60004 [(2)]	Peaches	1971	5.00	10.00	20.00
CROWN					
❏ CST-360 [R]	Etta James	1963	5.00	10.00	20.00
-- With Etta somber on cover					
❏ CST-360 [R]	Etta James	1963	5.00	10.00	20.00
-- With Etta smiling on cover					
❏ CLP-5209 [M]	Miss Etta James	1961	25.00	50.00	100.00
-- First edition, with framed picture on cover					
❏ CLP-5209 [M]	Miss Etta James	1962	15.00	30.00	60.00
-- Second edition, all-white cover with "Miss Etta James"					
❏ CLP-5234 [M]	The Best of Etta James	1962	15.00	30.00	60.00
-- Black label					
❏ CLP-5234 [M]	The Best of Etta James	1963	7.50	15.00	30.00
-- Gray label					
❏ CLP-5250 [M]	Twist with Etta James	1962	15.00	30.00	60.00
-- Black label					
❏ CLP-5250 [M]	Twist with Etta James	1963	7.50	15.00	30.00
-- Gray label					
❏ CLP-5360 [M]	Etta James	1963	7.50	15.00	30.00
-- With Etta somber on cover					
❏ CLP-5360 [M]	Etta James	1963	7.50	15.00	30.00
-- With Etta smiling on cover					
KENT					
❏ KST-500 [R]	Miss Etta James	1964	20.00	40.00	80.00
-- Red vinyl					
❏ KST-500 [R]	Miss Etta James	1964	6.25	12.50	25.00
-- Black vinyl					
❏ KLP-5000 [M]	Miss Etta James	1964	7.50	15.00	30.00
JAMES, HARRY					
On titles with asterisks (*), at least one track has FRANK SINATRA as lead vocalist.					
CAPITOL					
❏ W 654 [M]	Harry James in Hi-Fi	1955	7.50	15.00	30.00
❏ W 712 [M]	More Harry James in Hi-Fi	1956	7.50	15.00	30.00
❏ T 874 [M]	Wild About Harry	1957	7.50	15.00	30.00
❏ T 1093 [M]	Harry's Choice	1958	7.50	15.00	30.00

COLUMBIA

Number	Title	Yr	VG	VG+	NM
CL 522 [M]	One Night Stand	1953	10.00	20.00	40.00
-- Maroon label, gold print					
GL 522 [M]	One Night Stand	1953	12.50	25.00	50.00
-- Black label, silver print; first edition					
CL 553 [M]	Trumpet After Midnight	1954	10.00	20.00	40.00
-- Maroon label, gold print					
CL 562 [M]	Dancing in Person with Harry James at the Hollywood Palladium	1954	10.00	20.00	40.00
-- Maroon label, gold print					
CL 581 [M]	Soft Lights, Sweet Trumpet	1954	10.00	20.00	40.00
-- Maroon label, gold print					
CL 615 [M]	Juke Box Jamboree	1955	10.00	20.00	40.00
-- Maroon label, gold print					
CL 655 [M]	*All Time Favorites	1955	10.00	20.00	40.00
-- Maroon label, gold print					
CL 2527 [10]	The Man with the Horn	1955	12.50	25.00	50.00
CL 6009 [10]	*All Time Favorites	1949	12.50	25.00	50.00
CL 6044 [10]	Trumpet Time	1950	12.50	25.00	50.00
CL 6088 [10]	Dance Parade	1950	12.50	25.00	50.00
CL 6138 [10]	Your Dance Date	1951	12.50	25.00	50.00
CL 6207 [10]	Soft Lights, Sweet Trumpet	1952	12.50	25.00	50.00

JAMES, JIMMY, AND THE VAGABONDS
ATCO

Number	Title	Yr	VG	VG+	NM
33-222 [M]	The New Religion	1967	5.00	10.00	20.00
SD 33-222 [S]	The New Religion	1967	5.00	10.00	20.00

JAMES, JONI
MGM

Number	Title	Yr	VG	VG+	NM
E-222 [10]	Let There Be Love	1953	50.00	100.00	200.00
E-234 [10]	Award Winning Album	1954	50.00	100.00	200.00
E-272 [10]	Little Girl Blue	1955	50.00	100.00	200.00
E-3240 [M]	When I Fall in Love	1955	20.00	40.00	80.00
-- Yellow label					
E-3240 [M]	When I Fall in Love	1960	10.00	20.00	40.00
-- Black label					
E-3328 [M]	In the Still of the Night	1956	20.00	40.00	80.00
-- Yellow label					
E-3328 [M]	In the Still of the Night	1960	10.00	20.00	40.00
-- Black label					
E-3346 [M]	Award Winning Album	1956	20.00	40.00	80.00
-- Yellow label					
E-3346 [M]	Award Winning Album	1960	10.00	20.00	40.00
-- Black label					
E-3347 [M]	Little Girl Blue	1956	20.00	40.00	80.00
-- Yellow label					
E-3347 [M]	Little Girl Blue	1960	10.00	20.00	40.00
-- Black label					
E-3348 [M]	Let There Be Love	1956	20.00	40.00	80.00
-- Yellow label					
E-3348 [M]	Let There Be Love	1960	10.00	20.00	40.00
-- Black label					
E-3449 [M]	Songs by Victor Young and Frank Loesser	1956	20.00	40.00	80.00
-- Yellow label					
E-3449 [M]	Songs by Victor Young and Frank Loesser	1960	10.00	20.00	40.00
-- Black label					
E-3468 [M]	Merry Christmas from Joni	1956	30.00	60.00	120.00
-- Yellow label original					
E-3468 [M]	Merry Christmas from Joni	1960	15.00	30.00	60.00
-- Black label reissue					
E-3528 [M]	Give Us This Day	1957	20.00	40.00	80.00
-- Yellow label					
E-3528 [M]	Give Us This Day	1960	10.00	20.00	40.00
-- Black label					
E-3533 [M]	Songs by Jerome Kern and Harry Warren	1957	20.00	40.00	80.00
-- Yellow label					
E-3533 [M]	Songs by Jerome Kern and Harry Warren	1960	10.00	20.00	40.00
-- Black label					
E-3602 [M]	Among My Souvenirs	1958	20.00	40.00	80.00
-- Yellow label					
E-3602 [M]	Among My Souvenirs	1960	10.00	20.00	40.00
-- Black label					
E-3623 [M]	Ti Voglio Bene	1958	20.00	40.00	80.00
-- Yellow label					
E-3623 [M]	Ti Voglio Bene	1960	10.00	20.00	40.00
-- Black label					
E-3702 [M]	Award Winning Album, Volume 2	1958	20.00	40.00	80.00
-- Yellow label					
E-3702 [M]	Award Winning Album, Volume 2	1960	10.00	20.00	40.00
-- Black label					
E-3718 [M]	Je T'aime (I Love You)	1958	20.00	40.00	80.00
-- Yellow label					
E-3718 [M]	Je T'aime (I Love You)	1960	10.00	20.00	40.00
-- Black label					
SE-3718 [S]	Je T'aime (I Love You)	1958	30.00	60.00	120.00
-- Yellow label					
SE-3718 [S]	Je T'aime (I Love You)	1960	12.50	25.00	50.00
-- Black label					
E-3739 [M]	Songs of Hank Williams	1959	20.00	40.00	80.00
-- Yellow label					
E-3739 [M]	Songs of Hank Williams	1960	10.00	20.00	40.00
-- Black label					
SE-3739 [S]	Songs of Hank Williams	1959	30.00	60.00	120.00
-- Yellow label					
SE-3739 [S]	Songs of Hank Williams	1960	12.50	25.00	50.00
-- Black label					
E-3749 [M]	Irish Favorites	1959	20.00	40.00	80.00
-- Yellow label					
E-3749 [M]	Irish Favorites	1960	10.00	20.00	40.00
-- Black label					
SE-3749 [S]	Irish Favorites	1959	30.00	60.00	120.00
-- Yellow label					
SE-3749 [S]	Irish Favorites	1960	12.50	25.00	50.00
-- Black label					
E-3755 [M]	100 Strings and Joni	1959	20.00	40.00	80.00
-- Yellow label					
E-3755 [M]	100 Strings and Joni	1960	10.00	20.00	40.00
-- Black label					
SE-3755 [S]	100 Strings and Joni	1959	30.00	60.00	120.00
-- Yellow label					
SE-3755 [S]	100 Strings and Joni	1960	12.50	25.00	50.00
-- Black label					
E-3772 [M]	Joni James Swings Sweet	1959	15.00	30.00	60.00
SE-3772 [S]	Joni James Swings Sweet	1959	20.00	40.00	80.00
E-3800 [M]	Joni James at Carnegie Hall	1959	15.00	30.00	60.00
SE-3800 [S]	Joni James at Carnegie Hall	1959	20.00	40.00	80.00
E-3837 [M]	I'm In the Mood for Love	1960	15.00	30.00	60.00
SE-3837 [S]	I'm In the Mood for Love	1960	20.00	40.00	80.00
E-3839 [M]	100 Strings and Joni On Broadway	1960	15.00	30.00	60.00
SE-3839 [S]	100 Strings and Joni On Broadway	1960	17.50	35.00	70.00
E-3840 [M]	100 Strings and Joni In Hollywood	1960	15.00	30.00	60.00
SE-3840 [S]	100 Strings and Joni In Hollywood	1960	17.50	35.00	70.00
E-3885 [M]	More Joni Hits	1960	12.50	25.00	50.00
SE-3885 [S]	More Joni Hits	1960	15.00	30.00	60.00
E-3892 [M]	100 Voices, 100 Strings	1960	12.50	25.00	50.00
SE-3892 [S]	100 Voices, 100 Strings	1960	15.00	30.00	60.00
E-3958 [M]	Folk Songs by Joni James	1961	12.50	25.00	50.00
SE-3958 [S]	Folk Songs by Joni James	1961	15.00	30.00	60.00
E-3987 [M]	The Mood Is Swinging	1961	12.50	25.00	50.00
SE-3987 [S]	The Mood Is Swinging	1961	15.00	30.00	60.00
E-3990 [M]	The Mood Is Romance	1961	12.50	25.00	50.00
SE-3990 [S]	The Mood Is Romance	1961	15.00	30.00	60.00
E-3991 [M]	The Mood Is Blue	1961	12.50	25.00	50.00
SE-3991 [S]	The Mood Is Blue	1961	15.00	30.00	60.00
E-4053 [M]	I Feel a Song Comin' On	1962	12.50	25.00	50.00
SE-4053 [S]	I Feel a Song Comin' On	1962	15.00	30.00	60.00
E-4054 [M]	I'm Your Girl	1962	12.50	25.00	50.00
SE-4054 [S]	I'm Your Girl	1962	15.00	30.00	60.00
E-4088 [M]	After Hours	1962	12.50	25.00	50.00
SE-4088 [S]	After Hours	1962	15.00	30.00	60.00
E-4101 [M]	Country Girl Style	1962	12.50	25.00	50.00
SE-4101 [S]	Country Girl Style	1962	15.00	30.00	60.00
E-4151 [M]	The Very Best of Joni James	1963	10.00	20.00	40.00
SE-4151 [S]	The Very Best of Joni James	1963	12.50	25.00	50.00
E-4158 [M]	Something for the Boys	1963	10.00	20.00	40.00
SE-4158 [S]	Something for the Boys	1963	12.50	25.00	50.00
E-4182 [M]	Three O'Clock in the Morning	1963	10.00	20.00	40.00
SE-4182 [S]	Three O'Clock in the Morning	1963	12.50	25.00	50.00
E-4200 [M]	My Favorite Things	1963	10.00	20.00	40.00
SE-4200 [S]	My Favorite Things	1963	12.50	25.00	50.00
E-4208 [M]	Italianissime!	1963	10.00	20.00	40.00
SE-4208 [S]	Italianissime!	1963	12.50	25.00	50.00
E-4248 [M]	Put On a Happy Face	1964	10.00	20.00	40.00
SE-4248 [S]	Put On a Happy Face	1964	12.50	25.00	50.00
E-4255 [M]	Joni James Sings the Gershwins	1964	10.00	20.00	40.00
SE-4255 [S]	Joni James Sings the Gershwins	1964	12.50	25.00	50.00
E-4263 [M]	Beyond the Reef	1964	10.00	20.00	40.00
SE-4263 [S]	Beyond the Reef	1964	12.50	25.00	50.00
E-4286 [M]	Bossa Nova Style	1965	10.00	20.00	40.00
SE-4286 [S]	Bossa Nova Style	1965	12.50	25.00	50.00

JAMES, LEONARD
DECCA

Number	Title	Yr	VG	VG+	NM
DL 8772 [M]	Boppin' and a-Strollin'	1958	12.50	25.00	50.00

JAMES, SKIP
VANGUARD

Number	Title	Yr	VG	VG+	NM
VRS-9219 [M]	Skip James Today!	1966	7.50	15.00	30.00
VSD-79219 [S]	Skip James Today!	1966	6.25	12.50	25.00
VSD-79273	Devil Got My Woman	1968	6.25	12.50	25.00

Number	Title	Yr	VG	VG+	NM

JAMES, SONNY
CAPITOL

Number	Title	Yr	VG	VG+	NM
❏ SWBB-258 [(2)] Close-Up		1969	5.00	10.00	20.00
-- Combines ST 2500 and ST 2788 in one package					
❏ STBB-535 [(2)] You're the Only World I Know/ I'll Never Find Another You		1970	5.00	10.00	20.00
-- Combines the two listed albums in one package					
❏ T 779 [M]	The Southern Gentleman	1957	12.50	25.00	50.00
-- Turquoise label					
❏ T 779 [M]	The Southern Gentleman	1964	5.00	10.00	20.00
-- Black label with colorband, logo on top					
❏ T 887 [M]	Sonny	1957	12.50	25.00	50.00
-- Turquoise label					
❏ T 887 [M]	Sonny	1964	5.00	10.00	20.00
-- Black label with colorband, logo on top					
❏ T 988 [M]	Honey	1958	12.50	25.00	50.00
-- Turquoise label					
❏ T 988 [M]	Honey	1964	5.00	10.00	20.00
-- Black label with colorband, logo on top					
❏ T 1178 [M]	This Is Sonny James	1959	10.00	20.00	40.00
-- Black label with colorband, logo at left					
❏ T 1178 [M]	This Is Sonny James	1964	5.00	10.00	20.00
-- Black label with colorband, logo on top					
❏ ST 2017 [S]	The Minute You're Gone	1964	6.25	12.50	25.00
❏ T 2017 [M]	The Minute You're Gone	1964	5.00	10.00	20.00
❏ ST 2209 [S]	You're the Only World I Know	1965	6.25	12.50	25.00
❏ T 2209 [M]	You're the Only World I Know	1965	5.00	10.00	20.00
❏ ST 2317 [S]	I'll Keep Holding On	1965	6.25	12.50	25.00
❏ T 2317 [M]	I'll Keep Holding On	1965	5.00	10.00	20.00
❏ ST 2415 [S]	Behind the Tear	1965	6.25	12.50	25.00
❏ T 2415 [M]	Behind the Tear	1965	5.00	10.00	20.00
❏ ST 2500 [S]	True Love's a Blessing	1966	6.25	12.50	25.00
❏ T 2500 [M]	True Love's a Blessing	1966	5.00	10.00	20.00
❏ ST 2561 [S]	Till the Last Leaf Shall Fall	1966	6.25	12.50	25.00
❏ T 2561 [M]	Till the Last Leaf Shall Fall	1966	5.00	10.00	20.00
❏ ST 2589 [S]	My Christmas Dream	1966	6.25	12.50	25.00
❏ T 2589 [M]	My Christmas Dream	1966	5.00	10.00	20.00
❏ ST 2615 [S]	The Best of Sonny James	1966	5.00	10.00	20.00
-- Black Starline label					
❏ T 2703 [M]	Need You	1967	5.00	10.00	20.00
❏ T 2788 [M]	I'll Never Find Another You	1967	5.00	10.00	20.00
❏ T 2884 [M]	A World of Our Own	1968	6.25	12.50	25.00

DOT

Number	Title	Yr	VG	VG+	NM
❏ DLP 3462 [M] Young Love		1962	10.00	20.00	40.00
❏ DLP 25462 [S] Young Love		1962	12.50	25.00	50.00

JAMES, TOMMY, AND THE SHONDELLS
ROULETTE

Number	Title	Yr	VG	VG+	NM
❏ R 25336 [M]	Hanky Panky	1966	5.00	10.00	20.00
❏ SR 25336 [P]	Hanky Panky	1966	6.25	12.50	25.00
-- "Hanky Panky" is rechanneled					
❏ R 25344 [M]	It's Only Love	1967	7.50	15.00	30.00
❏ SR 25344 [S]	It's Only Love	1967	6.25	12.50	25.00
❏ R 25353 [M]	I Think We're Alone Now	1967	7.50	15.00	30.00
❏ SR 25353 [P]	I Think We're Alone Now	1967	6.25	12.50	25.00
-- Footprints cover; "I Think We're Alone Now" is rechanneled					
❏ SR 25355	Something Special! The Best of Tommy James & The Shondells	1968	6.25	12.50	25.00
❏ SR 25357	Gettin' Together	1968	6.25	12.50	25.00
❏ SR 42012	Mony Mony	1968	5.00	10.00	20.00
❏ SR 42023	Crimson and Clover	1969	5.00	10.00	20.00
❏ SR 42030	Cellophane Symphony	1969	5.00	10.00	20.00
❏ SR 42040	The Best of Tommy James & The Shondells	1969	5.00	10.00	20.00
-- Original versions are in a Unipak (gatefold must be opened to remove record)					

JAMME
ABC DUNHILL

Number	Title	Yr	VG	VG+	NM
❏ DS-50072	Jamme	1970	5.00	10.00	20.00

JAN AND DEAN
COLUMBIA

Number	Title	Yr	VG	VG+	NM
❏ CS 9461 [S]	Save for a Rainy Day	1967	2,000.	3,000.	4,000.
-- LP not known to exist, but an acetate does, and possibly an import on this label and number					

DEADMAN'S CURVE

Number	Title	Yr	VG	VG+	NM
❏ (no #)	Live at the Keystone Berkeley	1981	6.25	12.50	25.00
-- With front and back covers pasted on					
❏ (no #)	Live at the Keystone Berkeley	1981	12.50	25.00	50.00
-- Plain jacket with front and back cover inserts					

DORE

Number	Title	Yr	VG	VG+	NM
❏ LP-101 [M]	Jan and Dean	1960	100.00	200.00	400.00
-- Original with blue label					
❏ LP-101	Jan and Dean Bonus Photo	1960	30.00	60.00	120.00

J&D

Number	Title	Yr	VG	VG+	NM
❏ 101 [M]	Save for a Rainy Day	1967	75.00	150.00	300.00
-- Private pressing by Dean Torrence of unreleased Columbia album					

LIBERTY

Number	Title	Yr	VG	VG+	NM
❏ LRP-3248 [M]	Jan and Dean's Golden Hits	1962	7.50	15.00	30.00
❏ LRP-3294 [M]	Jan and Dean Take Linda Surfin'	1963	12.50	25.00	50.00
❏ LRP-3314 [M]	Surf City and Other Swingin' Cities	1963	10.00	20.00	40.00
❏ LRP-3339 [M]	Drag City	1963	10.00	20.00	40.00
❏ LRP-3361 [M]	Dead Man's Curve/ The New Girl in School	1964	10.00	20.00	40.00
-- Black and white cover with pink tint					
❏ LRP-3361 [M]	Dead Man's Curve/ The New Girl in School	1964	7.50	15.00	30.00
-- Full-color cover					
❏ LRP-3361 [M]	The New Girl in School/ Dead Man's Curve	1964	5.00	10.00	20.00
-- Reissue with reversed title					
❏ LRP-3368 [M]	Ride the Wild Surf	1964	7.50	15.00	30.00
❏ LRP-3377 [M]	The Little Old Lady from Pasadena	1964	7.50	15.00	30.00
❏ LRP-3403 [M]	Command Performance/ Live in Person	1965	7.50	15.00	30.00
❏ LRP-3417 [M]	Jan and Dean's Golden Hits, Volume 2	1965	6.25	12.50	25.00
❏ LRP-3431 [M]	Folk 'N' Roll	1965	7.50	15.00	30.00
❏ LRP-3441 [M]	Filet of Soul	1966	7.50	15.00	30.00
❏ LRP-3444 [M]	Jan and Dean Meet Batman	1966	12.50	25.00	50.00
❏ LRP-3458 [M]	Popsicle	1966	7.50	15.00	30.00
❏ LRP-3460 [M]	Jan and Dean's Golden Hits, Volume 3	1966	6.25	12.50	25.00
❏ LST-7248 [S]	Jan and Dean's Golden Hits	1962	10.00	20.00	40.00
❏ LST-7294 [S]	Jan and Dean Take Linda Surfin'	1963	20.00	40.00	80.00
❏ LST-7314 [S]	Surf City and Other Swingin' Cities	1963	12.50	25.00	50.00
❏ LST-7339 [S]	Drag City	1963	12.50	25.00	50.00
❏ LST-7361 [S]	Dead Man's Curve/ The New Girl in School	1964	10.00	2.00	40.00
-- Full-color cover					
❏ LST-7361 [S]	Dead Man's Curve/ The New Girl in School	1964	12.50	25.00	50.00
-- Black and white cover with pink tint					
❏ LST-7361 [S]	The New Girl in School/ Dead Man's Curve	1964	7.50	15.00	30.00
-- Reissue with reversed title					
❏ LST-7368 [S]	Ride the Wild Surf	1964	10.00	20.00	40.00
❏ LST-7377 [S]	The Little Old Lady from Pasadena	1964	10.00	20.00	40.00
❏ LST-7403 [S]	Command Performance/ Live in Person	1965	10.00	20.00	40.00
❏ LST-7417 [S]	Jan and Dean's Golden Hits, Volume 2	1965	7.50	15.00	30.00
❏ LST-7431 [S]	Folk 'N' Roll	1965	10.00	20.00	40.00
❏ LST-7441 [S]	Filet of Soul	1966	10.00	20.00	40.00
❏ LST-7444 [S]	Jan and Dean Meet Batman	1966	17.50	35.00	70.00
❏ LST-7458 [S]	Popsicle	1966	10.00	20.00	40.00
❏ LST-7460 [S]	Jan and Dean's Golden Hits, Volume 3	1966	7.50	15.00	30.00

RHINO

Number	Title	Yr	VG	VG+	NM
❏ RNDA 1498	One Summer Night -- Live	1982	5.00	10.00	20.00

UNITED ARTISTS

Number	Title	Yr	VG	VG+	NM
❏ UAS-9961 [(2)] Anthology (Legendary Masters Series, Vol. 3)		1971	6.25	12.50	25.00

JAN AND KJELD
KAPP

Number	Title	Yr	VG	VG+	NM
❏ KL-1190 [M]	Banjo Boy	1960	7.50	15.00	30.00

JAN AND LORRAINE
ABC

Number	Title	Yr	VG	VG+	NM
❏ S-691	Gypsy People	1969	6.25	12.50	25.00

JANE'S ADDICTION
WARNER BROS.

Number	Title	Yr	VG	VG+	NM
❏ PRO-A-3369 [DJ] Words and Music		1988	10.00	20.00	40.00
-- Promo-only interview album					

JANIGRO, ANTONIO
RCA VICTOR RED SEAL

Number	Title	Yr	VG	VG+	NM
❏ LSC-2365 [S]	Cello Concertos	1960	12.50	25.00	50.00
-- Original with "shaded dog" label					
❏ LSC-2460 [S]	Bach: Suite No. 2 in B; Brandenburg Concerto No. 5	1961	7.50	15.00	30.00
-- Original with "shaded dog" label					
❏ LSC-2653 [S]	Music for Strings	1962	12.50	25.00	50.00
-- Original with "shaded dog" label					

JANIS, BYRON
MERCURY LIVING PRSENSCE

Number	Title	Yr	VG	VG+	NM
❏ SR 90260 [S]	Rachmaninoff: Piano Concerto No. 2; Preludes in C# and E-flat	196?	15.00	30.00	60.00
-- With Antal Dorati/Minneapolis Symphony Orchestra; maroon label, no "Vendor: Mercury Record Corporation"					

(Top left) Best known among rockabilly fans for her raucous "Let's Have a Party," Wanda Jackson recorded for many years after that, later having some success on the country charts. Here is her 1962 album *Wonderful Wanda,* which came toward the end of her rocking years. (Top right) Elmore James' only album for Chess was *Whose Muddy Shoes,* issued in 1969. (Bottom left) It's been over 30 years since Joni James made a record, but she's still fondly recalled, and collected, by fans of female vocal music. All of her albums, especially early stereo gems such as *100 Strings and Joni*, are sought-after today. (Bottom right) From Eastern Pennsylvania came Jay and the Techniques and two Top 20 hits, "Apples, Peaches, Pumpkin Pie" and "Keep the Ball Rollin'." This album, *Love Lost and Found,* post-dates their hits.

Number	Title	Yr	VG	VG+	NM
❏ SR 90260 [S]	Rachmaninoff: Piano Concerto No. 2; Preludes in C# and E-flat	196?	6.25	12.50	25.00
-- With Antal Dorati/Minneapolis Symphony Orchestra; maroon label, with "Vendor: Mercury Record Corporation"					
❏ SR 90266 [S]	Tchaikovsky: Piano Concerto No. 1	196?	6.25	12.50	25.00
-- With Herbert Menges/London Symphony Orchestra; maroon label, with "Vendor: Mercury Record Corporation"					
❏ SR 90266 [S]	Tchaikovsky: Piano Concerto No. 1	196?	15.00	30.00	60.00
-- With Herbert Menges/London Symphony Orchestra; maroon label, no "Vendor: Mercury Record Corporation"					
❏ SR 90283 [S]	Rachmaninoff: Piano Concerto No. 3	196?	12.50	25.00	50.00
-- With Antal Dorati/London Symphony Orchestra; maroon label, with "Vendor: Mercury Record Corporation"					
❏ SR 90283 [S]	Rachmaninoff: Piano Concerto No. 3	196?	15.00	30.00	60.00
-- With Antal Dorati/London Symphony Orchestra; maroon label, no "Vendor: Mercury Record Corporation"					
❏ SR 90300 [S]	Prokofiev: Piano Concerto No. 2; Rachmaninoff: Piano Concerto No. 1	196?	7.50	15.00	30.00
-- Maroon label, no "Vendor: Mercury Record Corporation"					
❏ SR 90300 [S]	Prokofiev: Piano Concerto No. 2; Rachmaninoff: Piano Concerto No. 1	196?	7.50	15.00	30.00
-- Maroon label, with "Vendor: Mercury Record Corporation"					
❏ SR 90300 [S]	Prokofiev: Piano Concerto No. 2; Rachmaninoff: Piano Concerto No. 1	196?	7.50	15.00	30.00
-- Third edition: Dark red (not maroon) label					
❏ SR 90305 [S]	Encore	196?	30.00	60.00	120.00
-- Maroon label, no "Vendor: Mercury Record Corporation"					
❏ SR 90329 [S]	Liszt: Piano Concertos No. 1 and 2	196?	10.00	20.00	40.00
-- Maroon label, no "Vendor: Mercury Record Corporation"					
❏ SR 90383 [S]	Schumann: Piano Concerto; Arabesque; Wieck Variations	196?	12.50	25.00	50.00
-- With Stanislaw Skrowaczewski/London Symphony Orchestra; maroon label, no "Vendor: Mercury Record Corporation"					

RCA VICTOR

Number	Title	Yr	VG	VG+	NM
❏ LSC-2541 [S]	Liszt: Todtentanz; Rachmaninoff: Piano Concerto No. 1	1961	50.00	100.00	200.00
-- With Fritz Reiner/Chicago Symphony Orch.; originals with "shaded dog" label					
❏ LSC-2541 [S]	Liszt: Todtentanz; Rachmaninoff: Piano Concerto No. 1	1961	6.25	12.50	25.00
-- With Fritz Reiner/Chicago Symphony Orch.; Classic Records reissue					

RCA VICTOR RED SEAL

Number	Title	Yr	VG	VG+	NM
❏ LSC-2237 [S]	Rachmaninoff: Piano Concerto No. 3	1959	75.00	150.00	300.00
-- With Charles Munch/Boston Symphony Orchestra; original with "shaded dog" label					

JANIS, JOHNNY
ABC-PARAMOUNT

Number	Title	Yr	VG	VG+	NM
❏ ABC-140 [M]	For the First Time	1956	15.00	30.00	60.00

COLUMBIA

| ❏ CL 1674 [M] | The Start of Something Big | 1961 | 6.25 | 12.50 | 25.00 |
| ❏ CS 8474 [S] | The Start of Something Big | 1961 | 7.50 | 15.00 | 30.00 |

MONUMENT

| ❏ SLP-18036 [S] | Once in a Blue Moon | 1965 | 5.00 | 10.00 | 20.00 |

JANSSEN, DAVID
EPIC

| ❏ LN 24150 [M] | Hidden Island | 1965 | 5.00 | 10.00 | 20.00 |
| ❏ BN 26150 [S] | Hidden Island | 1965 | 6.25 | 12.50 | 25.00 |

JAPAN
ARIOLA AMERICA

| ❏ SW-50037 | Adolescent Sex | 1978 | 5.00 | 10.00 | 20.00 |

JARRE, JEAN-MICHEL
MOBILE FIDELITY

❏ 1-212	Oxygene	1995	5.00	10.00	20.00
-- Audiophile vinyl					
❏ 1-227	Equinoxe	1995	5.00	10.00	20.00
-- Audiophile vinyl					

JARREAU, AL
MOBILE FIDELITY

| ❏ 1-019 | All Fly Home | 1980 | 5.00 | 10.00 | 20.00 |
| -- Audiophile vinyl | | | | | |

JARRETT, KEITH
ECM

❏ 1035/6/7 [(3)]	Solo Concerts	1974	5.00	10.00	20.00
❏ 1100 [(10)]	The Sun Bear Concerts	1977	20.00	40.00	80.00
❏ 1227 [(3)]	Concerts	1982	5.00	10.00	20.00

VORTEX

❏ 2006	Life Between the Exit Signs	1969	5.00	10.00	20.00
❏ 2008	Restoration Ruin	1969	5.00	10.00	20.00
❏ 2012	Somewhere Before	1970	5.00	10.00	20.00

JASPER WRATH
SUNFLOWER

Number	Title	Yr	VG	VG+	NM
❏ SNF-5003	Jasper Wrath	1971	10.00	20.00	40.00

JAY AND THE AMERICANS
UNITED ARTISTS

❏ UAL-3222 [M]	She Cried	1962	12.50	25.00	50.00
❏ UAL-3300 [M]	At the Café Wha?	1963	12.50	25.00	50.00
❏ UAL-3407 [M]	Come a Little Bit Closer	1964	6.25	12.50	25.00
❏ UAL-3417 [M]	Blockbusters	1965	6.25	12.50	25.00
❏ UAL-3453 [M]	Jay and the Americans Greatest Hits	1965	5.00	10.00	20.00
❏ UAL-3474 [M]	Sunday and Me	1966	5.00	10.00	20.00
❏ UAL-3534 [M]	Livin' Above Your Head	1966	5.00	10.00	20.00
❏ UAL-3555 [M]	Jay and the Americans Greatest Hits, Volume 2	1966	5.00	10.00	20.00
❏ UAL-3562 [M]	Try Some of This	1967	5.00	10.00	20.00
❏ UAS-6222 [S]	She Cried	1962	25.00	50.00	100.00
❏ UAS-6300 [S]	At the Café Wha?	1963	25.00	50.00	100.00
❏ UAS-6407 [S]	Come a Little Bit Closer	1964	7.50	15.00	30.00
❏ UAS-6417 [S]	Blockbusters	1965	7.50	15.00	30.00
❏ UAS-6453 [S]	Jay and the Americans Greatest Hits	1965	6.25	12.50	25.00
❏ UAS-6474 [S]	Sunday and Me	1966	6.25	12.50	25.00
❏ UAS-6534 [S]	Livin' Above Your Head	1966	6.25	12.50	25.00
❏ UAS-6555 [S]	Jay and the Americans Greatest Hits, Volume 2	1966	5.00	10.00	20.00
❏ UAS-6582 [S]	Try Some of This	1967	5.00	10.00	20.00
❏ UAS-6671	Sands of Time	1969	5.00	10.00	20.00
❏ UAS-6719	Wax Museum	1970	5.00	10.00	20.00
❏ UAS-6751	Wax Museum, Volume 2	1970	5.00	10.00	20.00
❏ UAS-6762	Capture the Moment	1970	5.00	10.00	20.00
❏ ST-90814 [S]	Jay and the Americans Greatest Hits	1966	7.50	15.00	30.00
-- Capitol Record Club edition					
❏ ST-90815 [S]	Jay and the Americans Greatest Hits, Volume 2	1966	7.50	15.00	30.00
-- Capitol Record Club edition					

JAY AND THE TECHNIQUES
SMASH

❏ MGS-27095 [M]	Apples, Peaches, Pumpkin Pie	1967	7.50	15.00	30.00
❏ SRS-67095 [S]	Apples, Peaches, Pumpkin Pie	1967	7.50	15.00	30.00
-- First cover with "live" photo of the band					
❏ SRS-67095 [S]	Apples, Peaches, Pumpkin Pie	1968	5.00	10.00	20.00
-- Second cover with "posed" photo of the band					
❏ SRS-67102	Love Lost and Found	1968	7.50	15.00	30.00

JAYE, JERRY
HI

| ❏ HL-12038 [M] | My Girl Josephine | 1967 | 5.00 | 10.00 | 20.00 |
| ❏ SHL-32038 [S] | My Girl Josephine | 1967 | 5.00 | 10.00 | 20.00 |

JAYNETTS, THE
TUFF

| ❏ LP 13 [M] | Sally Go 'Round the Roses | 1963 | 75.00 | 150.00 | 300.00 |

JAZZ CRUSADERS, THE -- See THE CRUSADERS.

JAZZY JEFF AND THE FRESH PRINCE
WORD UP

| ❏ WDLP-0001 | Rock the House | 1985 | 6.25 | 12.50 | 25.00 |

JEFFERSON
JANUS

| ❏ JLS-3006 | Baby, Take Me in Your Arms | 1969 | 6.25 | 12.50 | 25.00 |

JEFFERSON AIRPLANE
Also see MARTY BALIN; JEFFERSON STARSHIP; PAUL KANTNER; GRACE SLICK.
DCC COMPACT CLASSICS

| ❏ LPZ-2033 | Surrealistic Pillow | 1997 | 6.25 | 12.50 | 25.00 |
| -- Audiophile vinyl | | | | | |

MOBILE FIDELITY

| ❏ 1-148 | Crown of Creation | 1984 | 5.00 | 10.00 | 20.00 |
| -- Audiophile vinyl | | | | | |

RCA VICTOR

❏ APD1-0320 [Q]	Volunteers	1973	20.00	40.00	80.00
-- Yellow/orange label					
❏ APD1-0320 [Q]	Volunteers	1975	12.50	25.00	50.00
-- Tan label					
❏ LOP-1511 [M]	After Bathing at Baxter's	1967	12.50	25.00	50.00

Number	Title	Yr	VG	VG+	NM
❑ LSO-1511 [S]　After Bathing at Baxter's		1967	5.00	10.00	20.00
-- Black label, dog on top					
❑ LPM-3584 [M]　Jefferson Airplane Takes Off!		1966	1,500.	2,250.	3,000.
-- Version 1: With "Runnin' 'Round This World" as last song on side 1. Count the number of bands on Side 1 of the record; don't rely on the cover listing, as some jackets list the title when it's not on the record					
❑ LPM-3584 [M]　Jefferson Airplane Takes Off!		1966	250.00	500.00	1,000.
-- Version 2: No "Runnin' 'Round This World", but "questionable" lyrics remain in "Let Me In" ("Don't tell me you want money") and "Run Around" ("That sway as you lay under me"). Until the exact matrix numbers are known, it must be heard to confirm.					
❑ LPM-3584 [M]　Jefferson Airplane Takes Off!		1966	6.25	12.50	25.00
-- Version 3: No "Runnin' 'Round This World", altered lyrics to "Let Me In" ("Don't tell me it's so funny") and "Run Around ("That sway as you stay here by me"). All later versions confirm to Version 3.					
❑ LSP-3584 [S]　Jefferson Airplane Takes Off!		1966	2,000.	3,500.	5,000.
-- Version 1: See Version 1 note under mono version					
❑ LSP-3584 [S]　Jefferson Airplane Takes Off!		1966	450.00	900.00	1,800.
-- Version 2: See Version 2 note under mono version					
❑ LSP-3584 [S]　Jefferson Airplane Takes Off!		1966	6.25	12.50	25.00
-- Version 3: See Version 3 note under mono version					
❑ LPM-3766 [M]　Surrealistic Pillow		1967	15.00	30.00	60.00
❑ LSP-3766 [S]　Surrealistic Pillow		1967	7.50	15.00	30.00
-- Black label, dog on top					
❑ LSP-4048　Crown of Creation		1968	7.50	15.00	30.00
-- Black label, dog on top					

JEFFERSON STARSHIP
See cross-references under JEFFERSON AIRPLANE.
DCC COMPACT CLASSICS

Number	Title	Yr	VG	VG+	NM
❑ LPZ-2036　Red Octopus		1997	6.25	12.50	25.00
-- Audiophile vinyl					

JEFFERSON, BLIND LEMON
MILESTONE

Number	Title	Yr	VG	VG+	NM
❑ MLP-2004 [M]　The Immortal Blind Lemon Jefferson		1968	6.25	12.50	25.00
❑ MLP-2007 [M]　The Immortal Blind Lemon Jefferson, Vol. 2		1969	6.25	12.50	25.00
❑ MLP-2013 [M]　Black Snake Moan		1970	6.25	12.50	25.00

RIVERSIDE

Number	Title	Yr	VG	VG+	NM
❑ RLP 12-125 [M]　Blind Lemon Jefferson -- Classic Folk Blues		1957	30.00	60.00	120.00
❑ RLP 12-136 [M]　Blind Lemon Jefferson, Volume 2		1958	30.00	60.00	120.00
❑ 1014 [10]　The Folk Blues of Blind Lemon Jefferson		1953	62.50	125.00	250.00
❑ 1053 [10]　Penitentiary Blues		1955	62.50	125.00	250.00

JEFFREY, JOE, GROUP
WAND

Number	Title	Yr	VG	VG+	NM
❑ WDS-686　My Pledge of Love		1969	7.50	15.00	30.00

JEFFRIES, FRAN
WARWICK

Number	Title	Yr	VG	VG+	NM
❑ W-2020 [M]　Fran Can Really Hang You Up the Most		1960	5.00	10.00	20.00

JEFFRIES, HERB
BETHLEHEM

Number	Title	Yr	VG	VG+	NM
❑ BCP-72 [M]　Say It Isn't So		1957	15.00	30.00	60.00

CORAL

Number	Title	Yr	VG	VG+	NM
❑ CRL 56044 [10]　Time on My Hands		1951	25.00	50.00	100.00

MERCURY

Number	Title	Yr	VG	VG+	NM
❑ MG-25089 [10]　Magenta Moods		1950	25.00	50.00	100.00
❑ MG-25091 [10]　Just Jeffries		1950	25.00	50.00	100.00

JELLY BEAN BANDITS, THE
MAINSTREAM

Number	Title	Yr	VG	VG+	NM
❑ S-6103 [S]　The Jelly Bean Bandits		1967	37.50	75.00	150.00
❑ 56103 [M]　The Jelly Bean Bandits		1967	25.00	50.00	100.00

JELLYBREAD
BLUE HORIZON

Number	Title	Yr	VG	VG+	NM
❑ BH-4801　First Slice		1970	7.50	15.00	30.00

JELVING, AKE
CAPITOL

Number	Title	Yr	VG	VG+	NM
❑ T 10079 [M]　Christmas in Sweden		1957	7.50	15.00	30.00
-- Turquoise label					
❑ T 10079 [M]　Christmas in Sweden		195?	5.00	10.00	20.00
-- Black label with colorband, logo on left					

JENKINS, FLORENCE FOSTER
The 1940s version of MRS. MILLER, except she tried to sing arias and not pop.
RCA VICTOR

Number	Title	Yr	VG	VG+	NM
❑ LM-2597 [M]　The Glory (????) of the Human Voice		1961	5.00	10.00	20.00
❑ LRT-7001 [10]　A Florence! Foster!! Jenkins!!! Recital!!!!		195?	10.00	20.00	40.00

JENKINS, GORDON
CAPITOL

Number	Title	Yr	VG	VG+	NM
❑ T 766 [M]　The Complete Manhattan Tower		1956	7.50	15.00	30.00
-- Turquoise or gray label					

DECCA

Number	Title	Yr	VG	VG+	NM
❑ DL 8011 [M]　Manhattan Tower/ California (The Golden State)		1951	7.50	15.00	30.00
-- Black label, gold print					

JENNIFER
Later recorded as JENNIFER WARNES.
PARROT

Number	Title	Yr	VG	VG+	NM
❑ PAS-71020　I Can Remember Anything		1968	5.00	10.00	20.00
❑ PAS-71034　See Me		1970	5.00	10.00	20.00

JENNINGS, BILL
AUDIO LAB

Number	Title	Yr	VG	VG+	NM
❑ AL-1514 [M]　Guitar/Vibes		1959	25.00	50.00	100.00

KING

Number	Title	Yr	VG	VG+	NM
❑ 295-105 [10]　Jazz Interlude		195?	62.50	125.00	250.00
❑ 295-106 [10]　The Fabulous Guitar of Bill Jennings		195?	62.50	125.00	250.00
❑ 398-508 [M]　Mood Indigo		1955	25.00	50.00	100.00
❑ 398-527 [M]　Billy in the Lion's Den		1956	25.00	50.00	100.00

PRESTIGE

Number	Title	Yr	VG	VG+	NM
❑ PRLP-7164 [M]　Enough Said!		1959	12.50	25.00	50.00
❑ PRLP-7177 [M]　Glide On		1960	12.50	25.00	50.00

JENNINGS, WAYLON
Also see WAYLON AND WILLIE.
A&M

Number	Title	Yr	VG	VG+	NM
❑ SP-4238　Don't Think Twice		1969	10.00	20.00	40.00

BAT

Number	Title	Yr	VG	VG+	NM
❑ 1001 [M]　Waylon Jennings at JD's		1964	175.00	350.00	700.00
-- Approximately 500 copies pressed					

RCA VICTOR

Number	Title	Yr	VG	VG+	NM
❑ LPM-3523 [M]　Folk-Country		1966	7.50	15.00	30.00
❑ LSP-3523 [S]　Folk-Country		1966	10.00	20.00	40.00
❑ LPM-3620 [M]　Leavin' Town		1966	7.50	15.00	30.00
❑ LSP-3620 [S]　Leavin' Town		1966	10.00	20.00	40.00
❑ LPM-3660 [M]　Waylon Sings Ol' Harlan		1967	7.50	15.00	30.00
❑ LSP-3660 [S]　Waylon Sings Ol' Harlan		1967	10.00	20.00	40.00
❑ LPM-3736 [M]　Nashville Rebel		1967	10.00	20.00	40.00
❑ LSP-3736 [S]　Nashville Rebel		1967	12.50	25.00	50.00
❑ LPM-3825 [M]　Love of the Common People		1967	7.50	15.00	30.00
❑ LSP-3825 [S]　Love of the Common People		1967	6.25	12.50	25.00
❑ LPM-3918 [M]　Hangin' On		1968	25.00	50.00	100.00
❑ LSP-3918 [S]　Hangin' On		1968	6.25	12.50	25.00
❑ LSP-4023 [S]　Only the Greatest		1968	6.25	12.50	25.00
❑ LSP-4085　Jewels		1968	6.25	12.50	25.00
❑ LSP-4137　Just to Satisfy You		1969	6.25	12.50	25.00
❑ LSP-4180　Country-Folk		1969	6.25	12.50	25.00
❑ LSP-4260　Waylon		1970	5.00	10.00	20.00
❑ LSP-4341　The Best of Waylon Jennings		1970	5.00	10.00	20.00
❑ LSP-4418　Singer of Sad Songs		1970	5.00	10.00	20.00
❑ LSP-4487　The Taker/Tulsa		1971	5.00	10.00	20.00
❑ LSP-4567　Cedartown, Georgia		1971	5.00	10.00	20.00
❑ LSP-4647　Good Hearted Woman		1972	5.00	10.00	20.00
❑ LSP-4751　Ladies Love Outlaws		1972	5.00	10.00	20.00

SOUNDS

Number	Title	Yr	VG	VG+	NM
❑ 1001 [M]　Waylon Jennings at JD's		1964	125.00	250.00	500.00
-- Approximately 500 copies pressed; reissue of Bat 1001					

VOCALION

Number	Title	Yr	VG	VG+	NM
❑ DL 73873　Waylon Jennings		1969	6.25	12.50	25.00

JENSEN, KRIS
HICKORY

Number	Title	Yr	VG	VG+	NM
❑ LP 110 [M]　Torture		1963	20.00	40.00	80.00

JENSEN, KURT
HOLLYWOOD

Number	Title	Yr	VG	VG+	NM
❑ LPH-137 [M]　An Evening with Jayne		195?	15.00	30.00	60.00
-- Collectible for its "cheesecake" cover of Jayne Mansfield					

JEREMY AND THE SATYRS
REPRISE

Number	Title	Yr	VG	VG+	NM
❑ RS-6282　Jeremy and the Satyrs		1968	5.00	10.00	20.00

JEREMY'S FRIENDS
Alan Arkin was a member of this group.
WARWICK

Number	Title	Yr	VG	VG+	NM
❑ W-2019 [M]　Jeremy's Friends		1960	12.50	12.00	50.00

Number	Title	Yr	VG	VG+	NM

JERICHO
AMPEX
❏ A-10112	Jericho	1971	6.25	12.50	25.00

JESSE J. AND THE BANDITS
RECAR
❏ 2001 [M]	Top Teen Hits	1965	25.00	50.00	100.00

JESUS JONES
SBK
❏ 05348 [DJ]	A Conversation with Jesus	1990	5.00	10.00	20.00
-- Generic cover with sticker					

JETHRO TULL
CHRYSALIS
❏ PRO 623 [DJ]	The Jethro Tull Radio Show	1975	12.50	25.00	50.00
❏ 2CH 1035 [(2)]	Living in the Past	1972	5.00	10.00	20.00
-- Two-record set with booklet; green labels					
❏ CH4 1044 [Q]	Aqualung	1974	10.00	20.00	40.00
❏ CH4 1067 [Q]	War Child	1974	10.00	20.00	40.00
❏ V5X 41653 [(5)]	20 Years of Jethro Tull	1988	20.00	40.00	80.00
❏ VX2 41655 [(2)]	20 Years of Jethro Tull	1989	6.25	12.50	25.00
-- Abridged version of Chrysalis 41653					

DCC COMPACT CLASSICS
❏ LPZ 2033	Aqualung	1997	6.25	12.50	25.00
-- Audiophile vinyl					
❏ LPZ-2059	Original Masters	1998	6.25	12.50	25.00
-- Audiophile vinyl					

MOBILE FIDELITY
❏ 1-061	Aqualung	1980	17.50	35.00	70.00
-- Audiophile vinyl					
❏ 1-092	The Broadsword and the Beast	1982	10.00	20.00	40.00
-- Audiophile vinyl					
❏ 1-187	Thick as a Brick	1985	7.50	15.00	30.00
-- Audiophile vinyl					

REPRISE
❏ 2MS 2106 [(2)]	Living in the Past	1972	6.25	12.50	25.00
-- Two-record set with booklet; original edition, rather than using cardboard outer sleeve for the records, has record sleeves attached to enclosed booklet, and thus is difficult to find intact					
❏ RS 6336	This Was	1969	5.00	10.00	20.00
-- Two-tone orange label with "r:" and "W7" logos on label					
❏ RS 6360	Stand Up	1969	5.00	10.00	20.00
-- Two-tone orange label with "r:" and "W7" logos on label; band "stands up" when gatefold is opened					
❏ RS 6400	Benefit	1970	5.00	10.00	20.00
-- Two-tone orange label with "r:" and "W7" logos on label					

JETT, JOAN
BLACKHEART
❏ JJ 707	Joan Jett	1980	12.50	25.00	50.00

JIM & JESSE
EPIC
❏ LN 24031 [M]	Bluegrass Special	1963	5.00	10.00	20.00
❏ LN 24074 [M]	Bluegrass Classics	1963	5.00	10.00	20.00
❏ LN 24107 [M]	The Old Country Church	1964	5.00	10.00	20.00
❏ LN 24144 [M]	Y'All Come	1964	5.00	10.00	20.00
❏ LN 24176 [M]	Berry Pickin' the Country	1965	5.00	10.00	20.00
❏ LN 24204 [M]	Sing Unto Him	1966	5.00	10.00	20.00
❏ LN 24314 [M]	Diesel on My Tail	1967	5.00	10.00	20.00
❏ BN 26031 [S]	Bluegrass Special	1963	6.25	12.50	25.00
❏ BN 26074 [S]	Bluegrass Classics	1963	6.25	12.50	25.00
❏ BN 26107 [S]	The Old Country Church	1964	6.25	12.50	25.00
❏ BN 26144 [S]	Y'All Come	1964	6.25	12.50	25.00
❏ BN 26176 [S]	Berry Pickin' the Country	1965	6.25	12.50	25.00
❏ BN 26204 [S]	Sing Unto Him	1966	6.25	12.50	25.00
❏ BN 26314 [S]	Diesel on My Tail	1967	6.25	12.50	25.00
❏ BN 26394	All-Time Great Country Instrumentals	1968	5.00	10.00	20.00
❏ BN 26465	Saluting the Louvin Brothers	1969	5.00	10.00	20.00

JIMENEZ, JOSE
KAPP
❏ KL 1215 [M]	Jose Jimenez the Submarine Officer	1961	6.25	12.50	25.00
-- Original title					
❏ KL 1215 [M]	More Jose Jimenez	1961	5.00	10.00	20.00
❏ KL 1238 [M]	Jose Jimenez -- The Astronaut (The First Man in Space)	1961	5.00	10.00	20.00
❏ KL 1304 [M]	Jose Jimenez Talks to Teenagers of All Ages	1962	5.00	10.00	20.00
❏ KL-1257 [M]	Jose Jimenez in Orbit -- Bill Dana on Earth	1961	5.00	10.00	20.00
❏ KL-1320 [M]	Jose Jimenez -- Our Secret Weapon	1963	5.00	10.00	20.00
❏ KL-1332 [M]	Jose Jimenez in Jollywood	1963	5.00	10.00	20.00
❏ KL-1402 [M]	Bill Dana in Las Vegas	1964	5.00	10.00	20.00
❏ KS-3332 [S]	Jose Jimenez in Jollywood	1963	6.25	12.50	25.00

Number	Title	Yr	VG	VG+	NM

ROULETTE
❏ R 25161 [M]	My Name...Jose Jimenez	1961	5.00	10.00	20.00
-- Reissue of Signature LP					

SIGNATURE
❏ SM 1013 [M]	My Name...Jose Jimenez	1960	6.25	12.50	25.00

JIVE FIVE, THE
UNITED ARTISTS
❏ UAL-3455 [M]	The Jive Five	1965	12.50	25.00	50.00
❏ UAS-6455 [S]	The Jive Five	1965	18.75	37.50	75.00

JOE & EDDIE
GNP CRESCENDO
❏ GNP-75 [M]	Joe & Eddie	1963	5.00	10.00	20.00
❏ GNP-86 [M]	There's a Meetin' Here Tonite	1963	5.00	10.00	20.00
❏ GNP-96 [M]	Coast to Coast	1964	5.00	10.00	20.00
❏ GNPS-96 [S]	Coast to Coast	1964	6.25	12.50	25.00
❏ GNP-99 [M]	Joe & Eddie, Volume 4	1964	5.00	10.00	20.00
❏ GNPS-99 [S]	Joe & Eddie, Volume 4	1964	6.25	12.50	25.00
❏ GNPS-2005 [S]	Tear Down the Walls	1965	5.00	10.00	20.00
❏ GNPS-2007 [S]	Joe & Eddie Live in Hollywood	1965	5.00	10.00	20.00
❏ GNPS-2014 [S]	Walkin' Down the Line	1965	5.00	10.00	20.00
❏ GNPS-2021 [S]	The Magic of Their Singing	1966	5.00	10.00	20.00

JOEL, BILLY
COLUMBIA
❏ AS 326 [DJ]	Souvenir	1976	7.50	15.00	30.00
-- Promo-only LP with one side live, one side a compilation of studio tracks					
❏ AS 1343 [DJ]	Billy Joel Interview	1982	6.25	12.50	25.00
❏ CQ 32544 [Q]	Piano Man	1974	5.00	10.00	20.00
❏ PCQ 33146 [Q]	Streetlife Serenade	1975	5.00	10.00	20.00
❏ PCQ 33848 [Q]	Turnstiles	1976	5.00	10.00	20.00
❏ HC 34987	The Stranger	1981	7.50	15.00	30.00
-- Half-speed mastered edition (original)					
❏ HC 44987	The Stranger	1982	6.25	12.50	25.00
-- Half-speed mastered edition (reissue)					
❏ HC 45609	52nd Street	1982	6.25	12.50	25.00
-- Half-speed mastered edition					
❏ HC 47461	Songs in the Attic	1982	17.50	35.00	70.00
-- Half-speed mastered edition					
❏ HC 48837	An Innocent Man	1983	7.50	15.00	30.00
-- Half-speed mastered edition					

FAMILY PRODUCTIONS
❏ FPS-2700	Cold Spring Harbor	1971	10.00	20.00	40.00
-- Authentic copies have mostly dark blue labels; when reissued on Columbia, the entire LP was remixed and remastered, and "You Can Make Me Free" was shortened by three minutes					

JOHANSEN, DAVID
Also see NEW YORK DOLLS.
BLUE SKY
❏ AS 519 [DJ]	The David Johansen Group Live	1978	7.50	15.00	30.00

JOHN'S CHILDREN
WHITE WHALE
❏ WWS 7128	Orgasm	1970	50.00	100.00	200.00

JOHN, ELTON
DCC COMPACT CLASSICS
❏ LPZ-2004	Madman Across the Water	1994	5.00	10.00	20.00
-- Audiophile vinyl					
❏ LPZ-2013	Elton John's Greatest Hits	1995	5.00	10.00	20.00
-- Audiophile vinyl					

DIRECT DISC
❏ SD-16614 [(2)]	Goodbye Yellow Brick Road	1980	12.50	25.00	50.00
-- Audiophile vinyl					

GEFFEN
❏ GHS 24031 [DJ]	Breaking Hearts	1984	5.00	10.00	20.00
-- Promo pressing on Quiex II vinyl					

MCA
❏ L33-1995 [PD]	A Single Man	1978	10.00	20.00	40.00
-- Promo picture disc					
❏ 2100	Don't Shoot Me, I'm Only the Piano Player	1973	5.00	10.00	20.00
-- With all-black label (no rainbow) and booklet					
❏ 2142 [DJ]	Captain Fantastic and the Brown Dirt Cowboy	1975	75.00	150.00	300.00
-- Brown vinyl promo, autographed by Elton John and Bernie Taupin					
❏ 14951 [PD]	A Single Man	1978	5.00	10.00	20.00
-- Stock picture disc					

MOBILE FIDELITY
❏ 2-160 [(2)]	Goodbye Yellow Brick Road	1984	10.00	20.00	40.00
-- Audiophile vinyl					

Number	Title	Yr	VG	VG+	NM
NAUTILUS					
❏ NR-42	Elton John's Greatest Hits	198?	25.00	50.00	100.00
-- *Audiophile vinyl*					
ROCKET					
❏ 526 915-1	Made in England	1995	5.00	10.00	20.00
-- *U.S. version is on 180-gram vinyl, distributed by Classic Records*					

JOHN, LITTLE WILLIE
BLUESWAY

❏ BLS-6069	Free at Last	1973	6.25	12.50	25.00
KING					
❏ 395-564 [M]	Fever	1956	250.00	500.00	1,000.
-- *"Nurse with thermometer" cover*					
❏ 564 [M]	Fever	1957	150.00	300.00	600.00
-- *White cover with "Fever" in large colorful letters*					
❏ 596 [M]	Talk to Me	1958	75.00	150.00	300.00
❏ 603 [M]	Mister Little Willie John	1958	62.50	125.00	250.00
❏ 691 [M]	Little Willie John In Action	1960	62.50	125.00	250.00
❏ 739 [M]	Sure Things	1961	37.50	75.00	150.00
❏ 767 [M]	The Sweet, the Hot, the Teenage Beat	1961	37.50	75.00	150.00
❏ 802 [M]	Come On and Join Little Willie	1962	30.00	60.00	120.00
❏ 895 [M]	These Are My Favorite Songs	1964	25.00	50.00	100.00
❏ 949 [M]	Little Willie Sings All Originals	1966	25.00	50.00	100.00
❏ KS-949 [S]	Little Willie Sings All Originals	1966	37.50	75.00	150.00
❏ KS-1081	Free at Last	1970	10.00	20.00	40.00

JOHN, ROBERT
COLUMBIA

❏ CS 9687	If You Don't Want My Love	1968	5.00	10.00	20.00

JOHNNIE & JACK
DECCA

❏ DL 4308 [M]	Smiles and Tears	1962	5.00	10.00	20.00
❏ DL 74308 [S]	Smiles and Tears	1962	6.25	12.50	25.00
RCA CAMDEN					
❏ CAL-747 [M]	Johnny & Jack Sing "Poison Love" and Other Country Favorites	1963	6.25	12.50	25.00
❏ CAL-822 [M]	Sincerely	1964	6.25	12.50	25.00
RCA VICTOR					
❏ LPM-1587 [M]	The Tennessee Mountain Boys	1957	10.00	20.00	40.00
❏ LPM-2017 [M]	Hits by Johnnie & Jack	1959	7.50	15.00	30.00
❏ LSP-2017 [R]	Hits by Johnnie & Jack	1959	5.00	10.00	20.00
❏ VPM-6022 [(2)]	All the Best of Johnnie & Jack	1970	6.25	12.50	25.00

JOHNNY AND THE BLUE BEATS
WINSOR

❏ 1001	Smile	196?	10.00	20.00	40.00

JOHNNY AND THE HURRICANES
ATILA

❏ 1030 [M]	Live at the Star-Club	1964	75.00	150.00	300.00
BIG TOP					
❏ 13-1302 [M]	The Big Sound of Johnny and the Hurricanes	1960	62.50	125.00	250.00
❏ ST 13-1302 [S]	The Big Sound of Johnny and the Hurricanes	1960	75.00	150.00	300.00
WARWICK					
❏ W-2007 [M]	Johnny and the Hurricanes	1959	37.50	75.00	150.00
❏ W-2007ST [S]	Johnny and the Hurricanes	1959	75.00	150.00	300.00
❏ W-2010 [M]	Stormsville	1960	37.50	75.00	150.00
❏ W-2010ST [S]	Stormsville	1960	62.50	125.00	250.00

JOHNSON FAMILY SINGERS, THE
RCA VICTOR

❏ LPM-1128 [M]	Old Time Religion	1955	6.25	12.50	25.00

JOHNSON, BETTY
ATLANTIC

❏ 8017 [M]	Betty Johnson	1958	12.50	25.00	50.00
❏ 8027 [M]	The Song You Heard When You Fell in Love	1959	12.50	25.00	50.00
-- *Black label*					
❏ 8027 [M]	The Song You Heard When You Fell in Love	1960	5.00	10.00	20.00
-- *White "fan" logo on right*					
❏ SD 8027 [S]	The Song You Heard When You Fell in Love	1959	20.00	40.00	80.00
-- *Green label*					
❏ SD 8027 [S]	The Song You Heard When You Fell in Love	1960	6.25	12.50	25.00
-- *White "fan" logo on right*					

Number	Title	Yr	VG	VG+	NM
JOHNSON, BLIND WILLIE					
FOLKWAYS					
❏ FG-3585 [M]	Blind Willie Johnson: His Story	1957	25.00	50.00	100.00
RBF					
❏ 10 [M]	Blind Willie Johnson 1927-1930	1965	17.50	35.00	70.00

JOHNSON, BOB, AND THE LONESOME TRAVELERS
PARKWAY

❏ P-7017 [M]	12 Shades of Bluegrass	1962	12.50	25.00	50.00

JOHNSON, BUBBER
KING

❏ 569 [M]	Come Home	1957	50.00	100.00	200.00
❏ 624 [M]	Bubber Johnson Sings Sweet Love Songs	1959	37.50	75.00	150.00

JOHNSON, BUDDY
MERCURY

❏ MG-20209 [M]	Rock 'n' Roll	195?	20.00	40.00	80.00
❏ MG-20322 [M]	Walkin'	195?	20.00	40.00	80.00
❏ MG-20330 [M]	Buddy Johnson Wails	195?	20.00	40.00	80.00
❏ SR-60072 [S]	Buddy Johnson Wails	195?	25.00	50.00	100.00
WING					
❏ MGW-12005 [M]	Rock 'n' Roll	1956	37.50	75.00	150.00
❏ MGW-12111 [M]	Rock 'n' Roll Stage Show	1963	10.00	20.00	40.00

JOHNSON, BUDDY & ELLA
MERCURY

❏ MG-20347 [M]	Swing Me	195?	20.00	40.00	80.00
ROULETTE					
❏ R 25085 [M]	Go Ahead and Rock and Roll	1959	20.00	40.00	80.00
❏ SR 25085 [S]	Go Ahead and Rock and Roll	1959	30.00	60.00	120.00

JOHNSON, CANDY
CANJO

❏ LP-1001 [M]	The Candy Johnson Show	1964	10.00	20.00	40.00
❏ LP-1002 [M]	Bikini Beach	1964	10.00	20.00	40.00

JOHNSON, LAURIE
COLPIX

❏ CP 471 [M]	England's New Big Band	1964	5.00	10.00	20.00

JOHNSON, LONNIE
BLUESVILLE

❏ BVLP-1007 [M]	Blues by Lonnie	1960	50.00	100.00	200.00
-- *Blue label, silver print*					
❏ BVLP-1007 [M]	Blues by Lonnie	1964	15.00	30.00	60.00
-- *Blue label with trident logo at right*					
❏ BVLP-1011 [M]	Blues and Ballads	1960	50.00	100.00	200.00
-- *Blue label, silver print*					
❏ BVLP-1011 [M]	Blues and Ballads	1964	15.00	30.00	60.00
-- *Blue label with trident logo at right*					
❏ BVLP-1024 [M]	Losing Game	1961	50.00	100.00	200.00
-- *Blue label, silver print*					
❏ BVLP-1024 [M]	Losing Game	1964	15.00	30.00	60.00
-- *Blue label with trident logo at right*					
❏ BVLP-1062 [M]	Another Night to Cry	1963	50.00	100.00	200.00
-- *Blue label, silver print*					
❏ BVLP-1062 [M]	Another Night to Cry	1964	15.00	30.00	60.00
-- *Blue label with trident logo at right*					
COLUMBIA					
❏ C 46221	Steppin' On the Blues	1990	5.00	10.00	20.00
KING					
❏ 395-520 [M]	Lonesome Road	1958	750.00	1,375.	2,000.
❏ 958 [M]	Lonnie Johnson 24 Twelve-Bar Blues	1966	15.00	30.00	60.00
❏ KS-958 [R]	Lonnie Johnson 24 Twelve-Bar Blues	1966	15.00	30.00	60.00
❏ KS-1083	Tomorrow Night	1970	6.25	12.50	25.00
PRESTIGE					
❏ PRST-7724	The Blues of Lonnie Johnson	1970	5.00	10.00	20.00

JOHNSON, LONNIE, AND VICTORIA SPIVEY
BLUESVILLE

❏ BVLP-1044 [M]	Idle Hours	1962	37.50	75.00	150.00
-- *Blue label, silver print*					
❏ BVLP-1044 [M]	Idle Hours	1964	12.50	25.00	50.00
-- *Blue label with trident logo at right*					
❏ BVLP-1054 [M]	Woman Blues	1962	37.50	75.00	150.00
-- *Blue label, silver print*					
❏ BVLP-1054 [M]	Woman Blues	1964	12.50	25.00	50.00
-- *Blue label with trident logo at right*					

Number	Title	Yr	VG	VG+	NM

JOHNSON, MARV
UNITED ARTISTS

Number	Title	Yr	VG	VG+	NM
❏ UAL 3081 [M]	Marvelous Marv Johnson	1960	37.50	75.00	150.00
❏ UAL 3118 [M]	More Marv Johnson	1961	37.50	75.00	150.00
❏ UAL 3187 [M]	I Believe	1962	37.50	75.00	150.00
❏ UAS 6081 [S]	Marvelous Marv Johnson	1960	50.00	100.00	200.00
❏ UAS 6118 [S]	More Marv Johnson	1961	50.00	100.00	200.00
❏ UAS 6187 [S]	I Believe	1962	50.00	100.00	200.00

JOHNSON, OSIE
BETHLEHEM

Number	Title	Yr	VG	VG+	NM
❏ BCP-66 [M]	The Happy Jazz of Osie Johnson	1957	12.50	25.00	50.00

RCA VICTOR

❏ LPM-1369 [M]	A Bit of the Blues	1957	10.00	20.00	40.00

JOHNSON, ROBERT
COLUMBIA

Number	Title	Yr	VG	VG+	NM
❏ CL 1654 [M]	King of the Delta Blues Singers	1961	125.00	250.00	500.00
-- Red and black label with six "eye" logos					
❏ CL 1654 [M]	King of the Delta Blues Singers	1963	12.50	25.00	50.00
-- "Guaranteed High Fidelity" label					
❏ CL 1654 [M]	King of the Delta Blues Singers	1965	6.25	12.50	25.00
-- "360 Sound Mono" label					
❏ C 30034 [M]	King of the Delta Blues Singers, Volume 2	1970	5.00	10.00	20.00
❏ C3 46222 [(3)]	Robert Johnson -- The Complete Recordings	1990	12.50	25.00	50.00

JOHNSON, SYL
TWINIGHT

Number	Title	Yr	VG	VG+	NM
❏ LPS-1002	Is It Because I'm Black?	1968	7.50	15.00	30.00

JOHNSTON, BRUCE
Also see THE BEACH BOYS; THE CENTURIONS.
COLUMBIA

Number	Title	Yr	VG	VG+	NM
❏ CL 2057 [M]	Surfin' 'Round the World	1963	37.50	75.00	150.00
❏ CS 8857 [S]	Surfin' 'Round the World	1963	75.00	150.00	300.00

DEL-FI

❏ DFLP-1228 [M]	Surfers' Pajama Party	1963	25.00	50.00	100.00
❏ DFST-1228 [S]	Surfers' Pajama Party	1963	50.00	100.00	200.00

JOHNSTON, COLONEL JUBILATION B., AND THE MYSTIC KNIGHTS BAND AND STREET SINGERS
COLUMBIA

Number	Title	Yr	VG	VG+	NM
❏ CL 2532 [M]	Moldy Goldies	1966	6.25	12.50	25.00
❏ CS 9332 [S]	Moldy Goldies	1966	7.50	15.00	30.00

JOLLY, PETE
AVA

Number	Title	Yr	VG	VG+	NM
❏ A-22 [M]	Little Bird	1963	5.00	10.00	20.00
❏ AS-22 [S]	Little Bird	1963	6.25	12.50	25.00
❏ A-39 [M]	Sweet September	1963	5.00	10.00	20.00
❏ AS-39 [S]	Sweet September	1963	6.25	12.50	25.00

CHARLIE PARKER

❏ PLP-825 [M]	Pete Jolly Gasses Everybody	1962	5.00	10.00	20.00
❏ PLP-825S [S]	Pete Jolly Gasses Everybody	1962	6.25	12.50	25.00

COLUMBIA

❏ CL 2397 [M]	Too Much, Baby	1965	5.00	10.00	20.00
❏ CS 9197 [S]	Too Much, Baby	1965	6.25	12.50	25.00

METROJAZZ

❏ E-1014 [M]	Impossible	1958	8.75	17.50	35.00
❏ SE-1014 [S]	Impossible	1958	8.75	17.50	35.00

MGM

❏ E-4127 [M]	5 O'Clock Shadows	1963	5.00	10.00	20.00
❏ SE-4127 [S]	5 O'Clock Shadows	1963	6.25	12.50	25.00

RCA VICTOR

❏ LPM-1105 [M]	Jolly Jumps In	1955	12.50	25.00	50.00
❏ LPM-1125 [M]	Duo, Trio, Quartet	1955	12.50	25.00	50.00
❏ LPM-1367 [M]	When Lights Are Low	1957	12.50	25.00	50.00

STEREO FIDELITY

❏ SFS-11000 [S]	Continental Jazz	1960	6.25	12.50	25.00

JOLSON, AL
DECCA

Number	Title	Yr	VG	VG+	NM
❏ DXA 169 [(2) M]	The Best of Jolson	196?	6.25	12.50	25.00
❏ DLP 5006 [10]	Jolson Sings Again	1949	7.50	15.00	30.00
❏ DLP 5026 [10]	Al Jolson In Songs He Made Famous	1949	7.50	15.00	30.00
❏ DLP 5029 [10]	Souvenir Album, Vol. II	1949	7.50	15.00	30.00

Number	Title	Yr	VG	VG+	NM
❏ DLP 5030 [10]	Al Jolson, Vol. III	1949	7.50	15.00	30.00
❏ DLP 5031 [10]	Souvenir Album, Vol. IV	1949	7.50	15.00	30.00
❏ DL 5308 [10]	Stephen Foster Songs	1950	25.00	50.00	100.00
❏ DL 5314 [10]	Souvenir Album, Vol. V	1951	7.50	15.00	30.00
❏ DL 5315 [10]	Souvenir Album, Vol. VI	1951	7.50	15.00	30.00
❏ DL 9034 [M]	You Made Me Love You	1957	6.25	12.50	25.00
-- Black label, silver print					
❏ DL 9035 [M]	Rock-a-Bye Your Baby	1957	6.25	12.50	25.00
-- Black label, silver print					
❏ DL 9036 [M]	Rainbow 'Round My Shoulder	1957	6.25	12.50	25.00
-- Black label, silver print					
❏ DL 9037 [M]	You Ain't Heard Nothin' Yet!	1957	6.25	12.50	25.00
-- Black label, silver print					
❏ DL 9038 [M]	Memories	1957	6.25	12.50	25.00
-- Black label, silver print					
❏ DL 9063 [M]	The Immortal Al Jolson	1958	6.25	12.50	25.00
-- Black label, silver print					
❏ DL 9070 [M]	Overseas	1959	7.50	15.00	30.00
-- Black label, silver print					
❏ DL 9074 [M]	The World's Greatest Entertainer	1959	6.25	12.50	25.00
-- Black label, silver print					
❏ DL 9095 [M]	Al Jolson with Oscar Levant at the Piano	1961	7.50	15.00	30.00
❏ DL 9099 [M]	Jolie	196?	6.25	12.50	25.00

JON AND ROBIN AND THE IN CROWD
ABNAK

Number	Title	Yr	VG	VG+	NM
❏ ABM-2068 [M]	Soul of a Boy and Girl	1967	5.00	10.00	20.00
❏ ABST-2068 [S]	Soul of a Boy and Girl	1967	5.00	10.00	20.00
❏ ABST-2070	Elastic Event	1968	5.00	10.00	20.00

JONES BOYS, THE
MUSICOR

Number	Title	Yr	VG	VG+	NM
❏ MM-2017 [M]	Country and Western Songbook	1964	6.25	12.50	25.00
❏ MS-3017 [S]	Country and Western Songbook	1964	7.50	15.00	30.00
❏ MS-3182	My Boys, the Jones Boys	1970	5.00	10.00	20.00

JONES, ANN, AND HER AMERICAN SWEETHEARTS
AUDIO LAB

Number	Title	Yr	VG	VG+	NM
❏ AL-1521 [M]	Ann Jones and Her American Sweethearts	1959	37.50	75.00	150.00
❏ AL-1556 [M]	Hit and Run	1960	37.50	75.00	150.00

JONES, BRIAN
Also see THE ROLLING STONES.
ROLLING STONES

Number	Title	Yr	VG	VG+	NM
❏ COC 49100	Brian Jones Presents the Pipes of Pan at Joujouka	1971	15.00	30.00	60.00

JONES, CURTIS
BLUESVILLE

Number	Title	Yr	VG	VG+	NM
❏ BVLP-1022 [M]	Trouble Blues	1961	20.00	40.00	80.00
-- Blue label, silver print					
❏ BVLP-1022 [M]	Trouble Blues	1964	6.25	12.50	25.00
-- Blue label, trident logo at right					

DELMARK

❏ DL-605 [M]	Lonesome Bedroom Blues	1963	10.00	20.00	40.00

JONES, DAVY
BELL

Number	Title	Yr	VG	VG+	NM
❏ 6067	Davy Jones	1971	5.00	10.00	20.00

COLPIX

❏ CP 493 [M]	David Jones	1965	6.25	12.50	25.00
❏ CPS 493 [S]	David Jones	1965	10.00	20.00	40.00
-- This album charted in 1967 thanks to the singer's membership in The Monkees					

JONES, DEAN
VALIANT

Number	Title	Yr	VG	VG+	NM
❏ VLM-407 [M]	Introducing Dean Jones	196?	5.00	10.00	20.00
❏ VLS-407 [S]	Introducing Dean Jones	196?	5.00	10.00	20.00

JONES, ETTA
KING

Number	Title	Yr	VG	VG+	NM
❏ 544 [M]	The Jones Girl...Etta	1956	25.00	50.00	100.00
❏ 707 [M]	Etta Jones Sings	1960	12.50	25.00	50.00

PRESTIGE

❏ PRLP-7186 [M]	Don't Go to Strangers	1960	10.00	20.00	40.00
-- Yellow label					
❏ PRLP-7186 [M]	Don't Go to Strangers	1964	5.00	10.00	20.00
-- Blue label, trident logo at right					
❏ PRST-7186 [S]	Don't Go to Strangers	1960	12.50	25.00	50.00
-- Silver label					

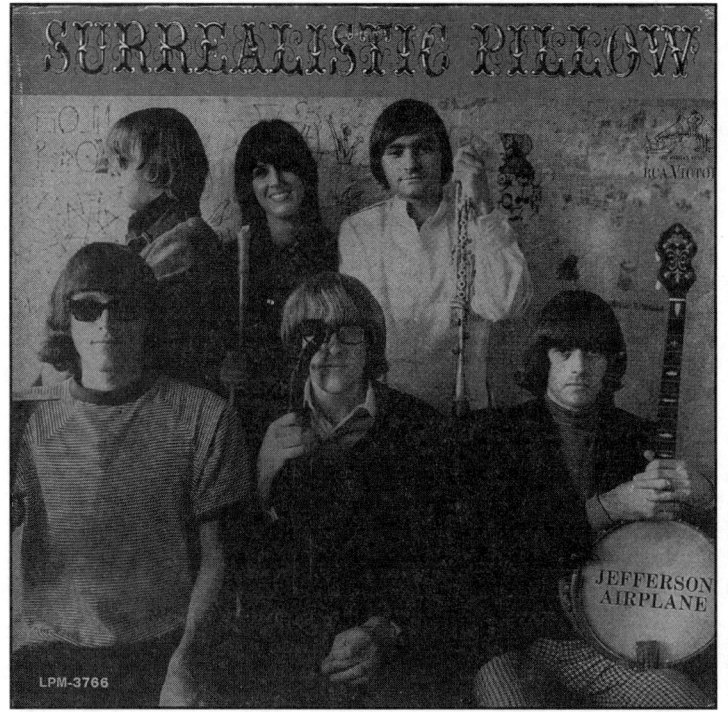
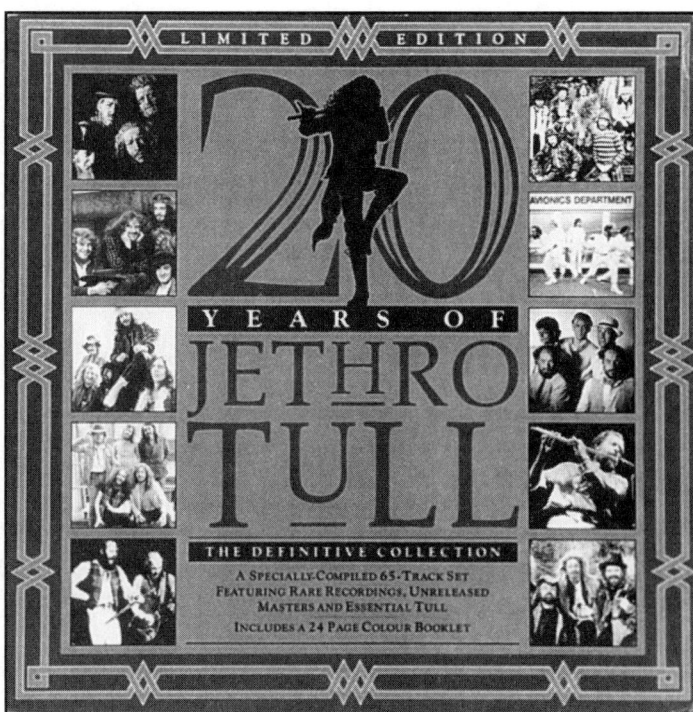

(Top left) Sought after for its different, less echo-laden, mix, the mono version of Jefferson Airplane's *Surrealistic Pillow* continues to grow in stature. (Top right) In the early days of the compact-disc-inspired box set boom, most of the boxes also came out in vinyl. Many of these vinyl boxes are now quite scarce, including *20 Years Of Jethro Tull,* issued in 1988. (Bottom left) Every major, and most minor, record labels turned her down at least once. So in 1979, Joan Jett released her debut album on her own Blackheart Records. Within a year, almost the exact album was issued on Neil Bogart's Boardwalk Records under the name *Bad Reputation*. (Bottom right) Billy Joel's first album, *Cold Spring Harbor*, is worth finding on the original dark blue Family Productions label despite the mis-mastering that caused his voice to sound higher-pitched than in real life. The main reason: The reissue on Columbia, although getting the pitch right, has several songs remixed, sometimes radically. And one song, "You Can Make Me Free," was shortened by almost three minutes.

Number	Title	Yr	VG	VG+	NM
❑ PRST-7186 [S] Don't Go to Strangers		1964	6.25	12.50	25.00
-- Blue label, trident logo at right					
❑ PRLP-7194 [M] Something Nice		1961	12.50	25.00	50.00
-- Yellow label					
❑ PRLP-7194 [M] Something Nice		1964	6.25	12.50	25.00
-- Blue label, trident logo at right					
❑ PRLP-7204 [M] So Warm -- Etta Jones and Strings		1961	10.00	20.00	40.00
-- Yellow label					
❑ PRLP-7204 [M] So Warm -- Etta Jones and Strings		1964	5.00	10.00	20.00
-- Blue label, trident logo at right					
❑ PRST-7204 [S] So Warm -- Etta Jones and Strings		1961	12.50	25.00	50.00
-- Silver label					
❑ PRST-7204 [S] So Warm -- Etta Jones and Strings		1964	6.25	12.50	25.00
-- Blue label, trident logo at right					
❑ PRLP-7214 [M] From the Heart		1961	10.00	20.00	40.00
-- Yellow label					
❑ PRLP-7214 [M] From the Heart		1964	5.00	10.00	20.00
-- Blue label, trident logo at right					
❑ PRST-7214 [S] From the Heart		1961	12.50	25.00	50.00
-- Silver label					
❑ PRST-7214 [S] From the Heart		1964	6.25	12.50	25.00
-- Blue label, trident logo at right					
❑ PRLP-7241 [M] Lonely and Blue		1962	10.00	20.00	40.00
-- Yellow label					
❑ PRLP-7241 [M] Lonely and Blue		1964	5.00	10.00	20.00
-- Blue label, trident logo at right					
❑ PRST-7241 [S] Lonely and Blue		1962	12.50	25.00	50.00
-- Silver label					
❑ PRST-7241 [S] Lonely and Blue		1964	6.25	12.50	25.00
-- Blue label, trident logo at right					
❑ PRLP-7272 [M] Love Shout		1963	10.00	20.00	40.00
-- Yellow label					
❑ PRLP-7272 [M] Love Shout		1964	5.00	10.00	20.00
-- Blue label, trident logo at right					
❑ PRST-7272 [S] Love Shout		1963	12.50	25.00	50.00
-- Silver label					
❑ PRST-7272 [S] Love Shout		1964	6.25	12.50	25.00
-- Blue label, trident logo at right					
❑ PRLP-7284 [M] Holler!		1963	10.00	20.00	40.00
-- Yellow label					
❑ PRLP-7284 [M] Holler!		1964	5.00	10.00	20.00
-- Blue label, trident logo at right					
❑ PRST-7284 [S] Holler!		1963	12.50	25.00	50.00
-- Silver label					
❑ PRST-7284 [S] Holler!		1964	6.25	12.50	25.00
-- Blue label, trident logo at right					
❑ PRLP-7442 [M] Etta Jones' Greatest Hits		1967	6.25	12.50	25.00
❑ PRST-7442 [S] Etta Jones' Greatest Hits		1967	5.00	10.00	20.00

ROULETTE

Number	Title	Yr	VG	VG+	NM
❑ R-25329 [M]	Etta Jones Sings	1965	5.00	10.00	20.00
❑ SR-25329 [S]	Etta Jones Sings	1965	6.25	12.50	25.00

JONES, GEORGE

MCA

Number	Title	Yr	VG	VG+	NM
❑ 10398	And Along Came Jones	1991	5.00	10.00	20.00
-- Vinyl issued only through Columbia House					

MERCURY

Number	Title	Yr	VG	VG+	NM
❑ MG-20282 [M]	Hillbilly Hit Parade, Volume 1	1957	37.50	75.00	150.00
-- Five tracks by George Jones, one by George Jones with Benny Barnes, and four by other artists					
❑ MG-20306 [M]	14 Country Favorites	1957	37.50	75.00	150.00
❑ MG-20462 [M]	Country Church Time	1959	50.00	100.00	200.00
❑ MG-20477 [M]	George Jones Sings White Lightning and Other Favorites	1959	37.50	75.00	150.00
❑ MG-20596 [M]	George Jones Salutes Hank Williams	1960	20.00	40.00	80.00
❑ MG-20621 [M]	George Jones' Greatest Hits	1961	10.00	20.00	40.00
❑ MG-20624 [M]	Country and Western Hits	1961	10.00	20.00	40.00
❑ MG-20694 [M]	George Jones Sings From the Heart	1962	10.00	20.00	40.00
❑ MG-20793 [M]	The Novelty Side of George Jones	1963	20.00	40.00	80.00
❑ MG-20836 [M]	The Ballad Side of George Jones	1963	10.00	20.00	40.00
❑ MG-20906 [M]	Blue and Lonesome	1964	6.25	12.50	25.00
❑ MG-20937 [M]	Country and Western No. 1 Male Singer	1964	6.25	12.50	25.00
❑ MG-20990 [M]	Heartaches and Tears	1965	6.25	12.50	25.00
❑ MG-21029 [M]	Singing the Blues	1965	6.25	12.50	25.00
❑ MG-21048 [M]	George Jones' Greatest Hits Volume 2	1965	6.25	12.50	25.00
❑ SR-60257 [S]	George Jones Salutes Hank Williams	1960	25.00	50.00	100.00
❑ SR-60621 [P]	George Jones' Greatest Hits	1961	12.50	25.00	50.00
❑ SR-60624 [P]	Country and Western Hits	1961	12.50	25.00	50.00
❑ SR-60694 [S]	George Jones Sings From the Heart	1962	12.50	25.00	50.00
❑ SR-60793 [S]	The Novelty Side of George Jones	1963	25.00	50.00	100.00
❑ SR-60836 [S]	The Ballad Side of George Jones	1963	12.50	25.00	50.00
❑ SR-60906 [S]	Blue and Lonesome	1964	7.50	15.00	30.00
❑ SR-60937 [S]	Country and Western No. 1 Male Singer	1964	7.50	15.00	30.00
❑ SR-60990 [S]	Heartaches and Tears	1965	7.50	15.00	30.00
❑ SR-61029 [S]	Singing the Blues	1965	7.50	15.00	30.00
❑ SR-61048 [S]	George Jones' Greatest Hits Volume 2	1965	7.50	15.00	30.00

MUSICOR

Number	Title	Yr	VG	VG+	NM
❑ MM-2046 [M]	Mr. Country and Western Music	1965	7.50	15.00	30.00
❑ MM-2060 [M]	New Country Hits	1965	7.50	15.00	30.00
❑ MM-2061 [M]	Old Brush Arbors	1966	7.50	15.00	30.00
❑ MM-2088 [M]	Love Bug	1966	7.50	15.00	30.00
❑ MM-2099 [M]	I'm a People	1966	6.25	12.50	25.00
❑ MM-2106 [M]	We Found Heaven Right Here on Earth	1966	6.25	12.50	25.00
❑ MM-2116 [M]	George Jones' Greatest Hits	1967	6.25	12.50	25.00
❑ MM-2119 [M]	Walk Through This World with Me	1967	7.50	15.00	30.00
❑ MM-2124 [M]	Cup of Loneliness	1967	7.50	15.00	30.00
❑ MM-2128 [M]	Hits by George	1967	7.50	15.00	30.00
❑ MS-3046 [S]	Mr. Country and Western Music	1965	10.00	20.00	40.00
❑ MS-3060 [S]	New Country Hits	1965	10.00	20.00	40.00
❑ MS-3061 [S]	Old Brush Arbors	1966	10.00	20.00	40.00
❑ MS-3088 [S]	Love Bug	1966	10.00	20.00	40.00
❑ MS-3099 [S]	I'm a People	1966	7.50	15.00	30.00
❑ MS-3106 [S]	We Found Heaven Right Here on Earth	1966	7.50	15.00	30.00
❑ MS-3116 [S]	George Jones' Greatest Hits	1967	6.25	12.50	25.00
❑ MS-3119 [S]	Walk Through This World with Me	1967	5.00	10.00	20.00
❑ MS-3124 [S]	Cup of Loneliness	1967	5.00	10.00	20.00
❑ MS-3128 [S]	Hits by George	1967	5.00	10.00	20.00
❑ MS-3149	The Songs of Dallas Frazier	1968	5.00	10.00	20.00
❑ MS-3158	If My Heart Had Windows	1968	5.00	10.00	20.00
❑ M2S-3159 [(2)]	The George Jones Story: The Musical Loves, Life and Sorrows of America's Great Country Star	1968	7.50	15.00	30.00
❑ M2S-3169 [(2)]	My Country	1969	7.50	15.00	30.00
❑ MS-3177	I'll Share My World with You	1969	5.00	10.00	20.00
❑ MS-3181	Where Grass Won't Grow	1969	5.00	10.00	20.00
❑ MS-3188	Will You Visit Me on Sunday?	1970	5.00	10.00	20.00
❑ MS-3191	The Best of George Jones	1970	5.00	10.00	20.00
❑ MS-3194	George Jones With Love	1971	5.00	10.00	20.00
❑ MS-3203	The Best of Sacred Music	1971	5.00	10.00	20.00
❑ MS-3204	The Great Songs of Leon Payne	1971	5.00	10.00	20.00

SEARS

Number	Title	Yr	VG	VG+	NM
❑ SPS-125	Maybe, Little Baby	196?	5.00	10.00	20.00

STARDAY

Number	Title	Yr	VG	VG+	NM
❑ SLP 101 [M]	The Grand Ole Opry's New Star	1958	300.00	600.00	1,200.
❑ SLP 125 [M]	The Crown Prince of Country	1960	40.00	80.00	160.00
❑ SLP 150 [M]	George Jones Sings His Greatest Hits	1962	12.50	25.00	50.00
❑ SLP 151 [M]	The Fabulous Country Music Sound of George Jones	1962	12.50	25.00	50.00
❑ SLP 335 [M]	George Jones	1965	10.00	20.00	40.00
❑ SLP 344 [M]	Long Live King George	1965	10.00	20.00	40.00
❑ SLP 366 [(2) M]	The George Jones Story	1966	7.50	15.00	30.00
❑ SLP 366	The George Jones Story Bonus Photo	1966	5.00	10.00	20.00
❑ SLP 401	The George Jones Song Book & Picture Album	1967	12.50	25.00	50.00
-- With book					
❑ SLP 401 [M]	The George Jones Song Book & Picture Album	1967	7.50	15.00	30.00
-- Without book					
❑ SLP 440 [M]	The Golden Country Hits of George Jones	1969	7.50	15.00	30.00
❑ DT-90080 [R]	George Jones Sings His Greatest Hits	1964	20.00	40.00	80.00
-- Capitol Record Club edition					

UNITED ARTISTS

Number	Title	Yr	VG	VG+	NM
❑ UXS-85 [(2)]	George Jones Superpak	1972	5.00	10.00	20.00
❑ UAL-3193 [M]	The New Favorites of George Jones	1962	7.50	15.00	30.00
❑ UAL-3218 [M]	George Jones Sings the Hits of His Country Cousins	1962	7.50	15.00	30.00
❑ UAL-3219 [M]	Homecoming in Heaven	1962	7.50	15.00	30.00
❑ UAL-3220 [M]	My Favorites of Hank Williams	1962	7.50	15.00	30.00
❑ UAL-3221 [M]	George Jones Sings Bob Wills	1962	10.00	20.00	40.00
❑ UAL-3270 [M]	I Wish the Night Would Never End	1963	6.25	12.50	25.00
❑ UAL-3291 [M]	The Best of George Jones	1963	6.25	12.50	25.00
❑ UAL-3338 [M]	More New Favorites	1964	6.25	12.50	25.00
❑ UAL-3364 [M]	George Jones Sings Like the Dickens	1964	10.00	20.00	40.00
❑ UAL-3388 [M]	I Get Lonely in a Hurry	1964	7.50	15.00	30.00
❑ UAL-3408 [M]	Trouble in Mind	1965	7.50	15.00	30.00
❑ UAL-3422 [M]	The Race Is On	1965	7.50	15.00	30.00
-- With photo of George Jones on front					
❑ UAL-3422 [M]	The Race Is On	1965	5.00	10.00	20.00
-- With cartoon on front					
❑ UAL-3442 [M]	King of Broken Hearts	1965	7.50	15.00	30.00
❑ UAL-3457 [M]	The Great George Jones	1966	7.50	15.00	30.00
❑ UAL-3532 [M]	George Jones' Golden Hits, Volume 1	1966	5.00	10.00	20.00
❑ UAL-3558 [M]	The Young George Jones	1967	7.50	15.00	30.00

Number	Title	Yr	VG	VG+	NM
❏ UAL-3566 [M]	George Jones' Golden Hits, Volume 2	1967	7.50	15.00	30.00
❏ UAS-6193 [S]	The New Favorites of George Jones	1962	10.00	20.00	40.00
❏ UAS-6218 [S]	George Jones Sings the Hits of His Country Cousins	1962	10.00	20.00	40.00
❏ UAS-6219 [S]	Homecoming in Heaven	1962	10.00	20.00	40.00
❏ UAS-6220 [S]	My Favorites of Hank Williams	1962	10.00	20.00	40.00
❏ UAS-6221 [S]	George Jones Sings Bob Wills	1962	12.50	25.00	50.00
❏ UAS-6270 [S]	I Wish the Night Would Never End	1963	7.50	15.00	30.00
❏ UAS-6291 [S]	The Best of George Jones	1963	7.50	15.00	30.00
❏ UAS-6328 [S]	More New Favorites	1964	7.50	15.00	30.00
❏ UAS-6364 [S]	George Jones Sings Like the Dickens	1964	12.50	25.00	50.00
❏ UAS-6388 [S]	I Get Lonely in a Hurry	1964	10.00	20.00	40.00
❏ UAS-6408 [S]	Trouble in Mind	1965	10.00	20.00	40.00
❏ UAS-6422 [S]	The Race Is On	1965	10.00	20.00	40.00
-- With photo of George Jones on front					
❏ UAS-6422 [S]	The Race Is On	1965	6.25	12.50	25.00
-- With cartoon on front					
❏ UAS-6442 [S]	King of Broken Hearts	1965	10.00	20.00	40.00
❏ UAS-6457 [S]	The Great George Jones	1966	10.00	20.00	40.00
❏ UAS-6532 [S]	George Jones' Golden Hits, Volume 1	1966	6.25	12.50	25.00
❏ UAS-6558 [S]	The Young George Jones	1967	5.00	10.00	20.00
❏ UAS-6566 [S]	George Jones' Golden Hits, Volume 2	1967	5.00	10.00	20.00

JONES, GEORGE, AND MELBA MONTGOMERY
Also see each artist's individual listings.
MUSICOR

Number	Title	Yr	VG	VG+	NM
❏ MM-2109 [M]	Close Together (As You and Me)	1966	5.00	10.00	20.00
❏ MM-2127 [M]	Boy Meets Girl	1967	7.50	15.00	30.00
-- Alternate title					
❏ MM-2127 [M]	Let's Get Together	1967	7.50	15.00	30.00
❏ MS-3109 [S]	Close Together (As You and Me)	1966	6.25	12.50	25.00
❏ MS-3127 [S]	Boy Meets Girl	1967	5.00	10.00	20.00
-- Alternate title					
❏ MS-3127 [S]	Let's Get Together	1967	5.00	10.00	20.00

UNITED ARTISTS

Number	Title	Yr	VG	VG+	NM
❏ UAL-3301 [M]	Singing What's In Our Heart	1963	6.25	12.50	25.00
❏ UAL-3352 [M]	Bluegrass Hootenanny	1964	6.25	12.50	25.00
❏ UAL-3472 [M]	Blue Moon of Kentucky	1966	5.00	10.00	20.00
❏ UAS-6301 [S]	Singing What's In Our Heart	1963	7.50	15.00	30.00
❏ UAS-6352 [S]	Bluegrass Hootenanny	1964	7.50	15.00	30.00
❏ UAS-6472 [S]	Blue Moon of Kentucky	1966	6.25	12.50	25.00

JONES, GEORGE; MELBA MONTGOMERY; JUDY LYNN
Also see each artist's individual listings.
UNITED ARTISTS

Number	Title	Yr	VG	VG+	NM
❏ UAL-3367 [M]	A King and Two Queens	1964	5.00	10.00	20.00
❏ UAS-6367 [S]	A King and Two Queens	1964	6.25	12.50	25.00

JONES, GEORGE; MELBA MONTGOMERY; GENE PITNEY
Also see each artist's individual listings.
MUSICOR

Number	Title	Yr	VG	VG+	NM
❏ MM-2079 [M]	Famous Country Duets	1965	5.00	10.00	20.00
❏ MS-3079 [S]	Famous Country Duets	1965	6.25	12.50	25.00

JONES, GEORGE, AND MARGIE SINGLETON
Also see GEORGE JONES.
MERCURY

Number	Title	Yr	VG	VG+	NM
❏ MG-20747 [M]	Duets Country Style	1962	7.50	15.00	30.00
❏ SR-60747 [S]	Duets Country Style	1962	10.00	20.00	40.00

JONES, GRANDPA
DECCA

Number	Title	Yr	VG	VG+	NM
❏ DL 4364 [M]	An Evening with Grandpa Jones	1963	6.25	12.50	25.00
❏ DL 74364 [S]	An Evening with Grandpa Jones	1963	7.50	15.00	30.00

KING

Number	Title	Yr	VG	VG+	NM
❏ 554 [M]	Grandpa Jones Sings His Biggest Hits	1958	25.00	50.00	100.00
❏ 625 [M]	Strictly Country Tunes	1959	25.00	50.00	100.00
❏ 809 [M]	Rollin' Along with Grandpa Jones	1963	15.00	30.00	60.00
❏ 822 [M]	16 Sacred Gospel Songs	1963	15.00	30.00	60.00
❏ 845 [M]	Do You Remember?	1963	15.00	30.00	60.00
❏ 888 [M]	The Other Side of Grandpa Jones	1964	15.00	30.00	60.00
❏ KS-1042	The Living Legend of Country Music	1969	5.00	10.00	20.00

MONUMENT

Number	Title	Yr	VG	VG+	NM
❏ MLP-4006 [M]	Grandpa Jones Makes the Rafters Ring	1962	6.25	12.50	25.00
❏ MLP-8001 [M]	Yodeling Hits	1963	5.00	10.00	20.00
❏ MLP-8021 [M]	Real Folk Songs	1964	5.00	10.00	20.00
❏ MLP-8041 [M]	Grandpa Jones Remembers the Brown's Ferry Four	1966	6.25	12.50	25.00

Number	Title	Yr	VG	VG+	NM
❏ SLP-14006 [S]	Grandpa Jones Makes the Rafters Ring	1962	7.50	15.00	30.00
❏ SLP-18001 [S]	Yodeling Hits	1963	6.25	12.50	25.00
❏ SLP-18021 [S]	Real Folk Songs	1964	6.25	12.50	25.00
❏ SLP-18041 [S]	Grandpa Jones Remembers the Brown's Ferry Four	1966	7.50	15.00	30.00
❏ SLP-18083	Everybody's Grandpa	1968	5.00	10.00	20.00
❏ SLP-18131	Grandpa Jones Sings Hits from Hee Haw	1969	5.00	10.00	20.00

JONES, JACK
CAPITOL

Number	Title	Yr	VG	VG+	NM
❏ ST 1274 [S]	This Love of Mine	1959	7.50	15.00	30.00
❏ T 1274 [M]	This Love of Mine	1959	6.25	12.50	25.00
❏ ST 2100 [S]	In Love	1964	5.00	10.00	20.00
-- Reissue of 1274					

RCA VICTOR

Number	Title	Yr	VG	VG+	NM
❏ LPM-3911 [M]	Without Her	1967	5.00	10.00	20.00
❏ LPM-3969 [M]	If You Ever Leave Me	1968	5.00	10.00	20.00

JONES, JIMMY
MGM

Number	Title	Yr	VG	VG+	NM
❏ E-3847 [M]	Good Timin'	1960	30.00	60.00	120.00
❏ SE-3847 [S]	Good Timin'	1960	40.00	80.00	160.00

JONES, JOE
ROULETTE

Number	Title	Yr	VG	VG+	NM
❏ R 25143 [M]	You Talk Too Much	1961	37.50	75.00	150.00
❏ SR 25143 [R]	You Talk Too Much	1961	25.00	50.00	100.00

JONES, JOHN PAUL
Also see LED ZEPPELIN.
COLUMBIA

Number	Title	Yr	VG	VG+	NM
❏ KC 32047	John Paul Jones	1973	5.00	10.00	20.00

JONES, JONAH
ANGEL

Number	Title	Yr	VG	VG+	NM
❏ ANG.60005 [10]	Jonah Wails -- 1st Blast	1954	18.75	37.50	75.00
❏ ANG.60006 [10]	Jonah Wails -- 2nd Blast	1954	18.75	37.50	75.00

BETHLEHEM

Number	Title	Yr	VG	VG+	NM
❏ BCP-1014 [10]	Jonah Jones Sextet	1954	20.00	40.00	80.00

CAPITOL

Number	Title	Yr	VG	VG+	NM
❏ T 839 [M]	Muted Jazz	1957	10.00	20.00	40.00
❏ T 963 [M]	Swingin' On Broadway	1958	10.00	20.00	40.00
❏ ST 1039 [S]	Jumpin' with Jonah	1958	7.50	15.00	30.00
❏ T 1039 [M]	Jumpin' with Jonah	1958	6.25	12.50	25.00
❏ ST 1083 [S]	Swingin' at the Cinema	1958	7.50	15.00	30.00
❏ T 1083 [M]	Swingin' at the Cinema	1958	6.25	12.50	25.00
❏ ST 1115 [S]	Jonah Jumps Again	1959	7.50	15.00	30.00
❏ T 1115 [M]	Jonah Jumps Again	1959	6.25	12.50	25.00
❏ ST 1193 [S]	I Dig Chicks	1959	6.25	12.50	25.00
❏ T 1193 [M]	I Dig Chicks	1959	5.00	10.00	20.00
❏ ST 1237 [S]	Swingin' 'Round the World	1959	6.25	12.50	25.00
❏ T 1237 [M]	Swingin' 'Round the World	1959	5.00	10.00	20.00
❏ ST 1375 [S]	Hit Me Again!	1960	6.25	12.50	25.00
❏ T 1375 [M]	Hit Me Again!	1960	5.00	10.00	20.00
❏ ST 1405 [S]	A Touch of Blue	1960	6.25	12.50	25.00
❏ T 1405 [M]	A Touch of Blue	1960	5.00	10.00	20.00
❏ ST 1532 [S]	The Unsinkable Molly Brown	1961	6.25	12.50	25.00
❏ T 1532 [M]	The Unsinkable Molly Brown	1961	5.00	10.00	20.00
❏ ST 1557 [S]	Great Instrumental Hits Styled by Jonah Jones	1961	6.25	12.50	25.00
❏ T 1557 [M]	Great Instrumental Hits Styled by Jonah Jones	1961	5.00	10.00	20.00
❏ ST 1641 [S]	Broadway Swings Again	1961	6.25	12.50	25.00
❏ T 1641 [M]	Broadway Swings Again	1961	5.00	10.00	20.00
❏ ST 1660 [S]	Jonah Jones/Glenn Gray	1961	6.25	12.50	25.00
❏ T 1660 [M]	Jonah Jones/Glenn Gray	1961	5.00	10.00	20.00
❏ ST 1773 [S]	Jazz Bonus	1962	5.00	10.00	20.00
❏ ST 1948 [S]	And Now, In Person -- Jonah	1963	5.00	10.00	20.00
❏ ST 2087 [S]	Blowin' Up a Storm	1964	5.00	10.00	20.00

GROOVE

Number	Title	Yr	VG	VG+	NM
❏ LG-1001 [M]	Jonah Jones at the Embers	1956	12.50	25.00	50.00

MOTOWN

Number	Title	Yr	VG	VG+	NM
❏ M-683	Along Came Jonah	1969	10.00	20.00	40.00
❏ M-690	Little Dis, Little Dat	1970	10.00	20.00	40.00

RCA VICTOR

Number	Title	Yr	VG	VG+	NM
❏ LPM-2004 [M]	Jonah Jones at the Embers	1959	10.00	20.00	40.00
-- Reissue of Groove and Vik LP					

VIK

Number	Title	Yr	VG	VG+	NM
❏ LXA-1135 [M]	Jonah Jones at the Embers	1958	10.00	20.00	40.00
-- Reissue of Groove LP					

Number	Title	Yr	VG	VG+	NM

JONES, LINDA
LOMA
| ❑ 5907 | Hypnotized | 1967 | 7.50 | 15.00 | 30.00 |

TURBO
| ❑ 7007 | Your Precious Love | 1972 | 5.00 | 10.00 | 20.00 |

JONES, PAUL
Also see MANFRED MANN.
CAPITOL
| ❑ ST 2795 [S] | Paul Jones Sings Songs from the Film "Privilege" and Others | 1967 | 7.50 | 15.00 | 30.00 |
| ❑ T 2795 [M] | Paul Jones Sings Songs from the Film "Privilege" and Others | 1967 | 7.50 | 15.00 | 30.00 |

JONES, QUINCY
Includes some of his soundtrack work.
A&M
❑ QU-53041 [Q]	You've Got It Bad Girl	1974	5.00	10.00	20.00
❑ QU-53617 [Q]	Body Heat	1974	5.00	10.00	20.00
❑ QU-54526 [Q]	Mellow Madness	1975	5.00	10.00	20.00

ABC-PARAMOUNT
| ❑ 149 [M] | This Is How I Feel About Jazz | 1956 | 25.00 | 50.00 | 100.00 |
| ❑ 186 [M] | Go West, Man! | 1957 | 25.00 | 50.00 | 100.00 |

COLGEMS
| ❑ COM-107 [M] | In Cold Blood | 1967 | 5.00 | 10.00 | 20.00 |
| ❑ COS-107 [S] | In Cold Blood | 1967 | 6.25 | 12.50 | 25.00 |

EMARCY
| ❑ MG-36083 [M] | Jazz Abroad | 1956 | 25.00 | 50.00 | 100.00 |

IMPULSE!
| ❑ A-11 [M] | The Quintessence | 1962 | 7.50 | 15.00 | 30.00 |
| ❑ AS-11 [S] | The Quintessence | 1962 | 10.00 | 20.00 | 40.00 |

LIBERTY
| ❑ LOM-16004 [M] | Enter Laughing | 1967 | 6.25 | 12.50 | 25.00 |
| ❑ LOS-17004 [S] | Enter Laughing | 1967 | 7.50 | 15.00 | 30.00 |

MERCURY
❑ MG-20444 [M]	Birth of a Band	1959	12.50	25.00	50.00
❑ MG-20561 [M]	The Great, Wide World of Quincy Jones	1960	12.50	25.00	50.00
❑ MG-20612 [M]	I Dig Dancers	1960	10.00	20.00	40.00
❑ MG-20614 [M]	Around the World	1961	7.50	15.00	30.00
❑ MG-20653 [M]	Quincy Jones at Newport '61	1961	7.50	15.00	30.00
❑ MG-20751 [M]	Big Band Bossa Nova	1962	7.50	15.00	30.00
❑ MG-20799 [M]	Quincy Jones Plays Hip Hits	1963	7.50	15.00	30.00
❑ MG-20863 [M]	Quincy Jones Explores the Music of Henry Mancini	1964	5.00	10.00	20.00
❑ MG-20938 [M]	Golden Boy	1964	5.00	10.00	20.00
❑ MG-21011 [M]	The Pawnbroker	1964	5.00	10.00	20.00
❑ MG-21025 [M]	Mirage	1965	5.00	10.00	20.00
❑ MG-21050 [M]	Quincy Jones Plays for	1965	5.00	10.00	20.00
❑ MG-21063 [M]	Quincy's Got a Brand New Bag	1965	5.00	10.00	20.00
❑ MG-21070 [M]	Slender Thread	1966	5.00	10.00	20.00
❑ SR-60129 [S]	Birth of a Band	1959	15.00	30.00	60.00
❑ SR-60221 [S]	The Great, Wide World of Quincy Jones	1960	15.00	30.00	60.00
❑ SR-60612 [S]	I Dig Dancers	1960	12.50	25.00	50.00
❑ SR-60614 [S]	Around the World	1961	10.00	20.00	40.00
❑ SR-60653 [S]	Quincy Jones at Newport '61	1961	10.00	20.00	40.00
❑ SR-60751 [S]	Big Band Bossa Nova	1962	10.00	20.00	40.00
❑ SR-60799 [S]	Quincy Jones Plays Hip Hits	1963	10.00	20.00	40.00
❑ SR-60863 [S]	Quincy Jones Explores the Music of Henry Mancini	1964	6.25	12.50	25.00
❑ SR-60938 [S]	Golden Boy	1964	6.25	12.50	25.00
❑ SR-61011 [S]	The Pawnbroker	1964	6.25	12.50	25.00
❑ SR-61025 [S]	Mirage	1965	6.25	12.50	25.00
❑ SR-61050 [S]	Quincy Jones Plays for	1965	6.25	12.50	25.00
❑ SR-61063 [S]	Quincy's Got a Brand New Bag	1965	6.25	12.50	25.00
❑ SR-61070 [S]	Slender Thread	1966	6.25	12.50	25.00

MOBILE FIDELITY
| ❑ 1-078 | You've Got It Bad Girl | 1981 | 6.25 | 12.50 | 25.00 |
| -- Audiophile vinyl | | | | | |

NAUTILUS
| ❑ NR-52 | The Dude | 198? | 10.00 | 20.00 | 40.00 |
| -- Audiophile vinyl | | | | | |

PRESTIGE
| ❑ PRLP-172 [10] | Quincy Jones with the Swedish-American All Stars | 1953 | 50.00 | 100.00 | 200.00 |

QWEST
| ❑ 25356 [(2)] | The Color Purple | 1985 | 5.00 | 10.00 | 20.00 |
| -- Boxed set on purple vinyl | | | | | |

UNITED ARTISTS
| ❑ UAS-5214 | They Call Me Mister Tibbs | 1970 | 6.25 | 12.50 | 25.00 |

JONES, RICKIE LEE
MOBILE FIDELITY
| ❑ 1-089 | Rickie Lee Jones | 1982 | 50.00 | 100.00 | 200.00 |
| -- Audiophile vinyl | | | | | |

JONES, RUFUS
CAMEO
| ❑ C-1076 [M] | Five on Eight | 1964 | 6.25 | 12.50 | 25.00 |
| ❑ SC-1076 [S] | Five on Eight | 1964 | 7.50 | 15.00 | 30.00 |

JONES, SPIKE, AND THE CITY SLICKERS
LIBERTY
❑ LRP-3140 [M]	Omnibust	1959	12.50	25.00	50.00
❑ LRP-3154 [M]	60 Years of Music America Hates Best	1960	12.50	25.00	50.00
❑ LRP-3338 [M]	Washington Square	1963	5.00	10.00	20.00
❑ LRP-3349 [M]	Spike Jones' New Band	1964	7.50	15.00	30.00
❑ LRP-3370 [M]	My Man	1964	5.00	10.00	20.00
❑ LRP-3401 [M]	Spike Jones Plays Hank Williams Hits	1965	5.00	10.00	20.00
❑ LST-7140 [S]	Omnibust	1959	37.50	75.00	150.00
-- Red vinyl					
❑ LST-7140 [S]	Omnibust	1959	18.75	37.50	75.00
-- Black vinyl					
❑ LST-7154 [S]	60 Years of Music America Hates Best	1960	18.75	37.50	75.00
❑ LST-7338 [S]	Washington Square	1963	6.25	12.50	25.00
❑ LST-7349 [S]	Spike Jones' New Band	1964	10.00	20.00	40.00
❑ LST-7370 [S]	My Man	1964	6.25	12.50	25.00
❑ LST-7401 [S]	Spike Jones Plays Hank Williams Hits	1965	6.25	12.50	25.00

RCA RED SEAL
| ❑ LSC-3235 [R] | Spike Jones Is Murdering the Classics! | 1971 | 5.00 | 10.00 | 20.00 |

RCA VICTOR
❑ LPT-18 [10]	Spike Jones Plays the Charleston	1952	50.00	100.00	200.00
❑ LPM-2224 [M]	Thank You Music Lovers	1960	12.50	25.00	50.00
❑ LPM-3054 [10]	Bottoms Up	1952	50.00	100.00	200.00
❑ LPM-3128 [10]	Spike Jones Murders Carmen and Kids the Classics	1953	50.00	100.00	200.00
❑ LPM-3849 [M]	The Best of Spike Jones	1967	6.25	12.50	25.00
❑ LSP-3849 [R]	The Best of Spike Jones	1967	5.00	10.00	20.00

VERVE
❑ MGV-2021 [M]	Let's Sing a Song for Christmas	1956	12.50	25.00	50.00
❑ V-2021 [M]	Let's Sing a Song for Christmas	1961	7.50	15.00	30.00
❑ MGV-4005 [M]	Dinner Music...For People Who Aren't Very Hungry	1957	12.50	25.00	50.00
❑ V-4005 [M]	Dinner Music...For People Who Aren't Very Hungry	1961	6.25	12.50	25.00

WARNER BROS.
| ❑ W 1332 [M] | Spike Jones in Hi-Fi | 1959 | 10.00 | 20.00 | 40.00 |
| ❑ WS 1332 [S] | Spike Jones in Stereo | 1959 | 12.50 | 25.00 | 50.00 |

JONES, STAN
BUENA VISTA
| ❑ BV-3306 [M] | Ghost Riders in the Sky | 1961 | 6.25 | 12.50 | 25.00 |
| -- Reissue of Disneyland WDL-3015 | | | | | |

DISNEYLAND
❑ WDL-1005 [M]	Songs of the National Parks	1958	10.00	20.00	40.00
-- Sold only at national parks					
❑ WDL-3015 [M]	Creakin' Leather	1958	10.00	20.00	40.00
❑ WDL-3033 [M]	This Was the West -- The Story and the Songs	1958	10.00	20.00	40.00

JONES, TOM
PARROT
| ❑ XPAS-1 [DJ] | Special Tom Jones Interview | 1970 | 25.00 | 50.00 | 100.00 |
| -- Promo-only open-end interview with gatefold cover and script | | | | | |

JOPLIN, JANIS
Also see BIG BROTHER AND THE HOLDING COMPANY.
COLUMBIA
❑ AS 1377 [DJ]	A Collection	1982	5.00	10.00	20.00
❑ KCS 9913	I Got Dem Ol' Kozmik Blues Again Mama!	1969	5.00	10.00	20.00
-- "360 Sound Stereo" on label					
❑ CQ 30322 [Q]	Pearl	1974	5.00	10.00	20.00
❑ C2X 31160 [(2)]	Joplin in Concert	1972	5.00	10.00	20.00

COLUMBIA SPECIAL PRODUCTS
| ❑ 2P 13792 [(2)] | The Greatest Hits of Janis Joplin | 1977 | 5.00 | 10.00 | 20.00 |

Number	Title	Yr	VG	VG+	NM

JORDAN, KING
CORAL
| ❏ CRL 57372 [M] | Phantom Guitar | 1962 | 5.00 | 10.00 | 20.00 |
| ❏ CRL 757372 [S] | Phantom Guitar | 1962 | 6.25 | 12.50 | 25.00 |

JORDAN, LOUIS
DECCA
| ❏ DL 5035 [M] | Greatest Hits | 1968 | 7.50 | 15.00 | 30.00 |
| ❏ DL 8551 [M] | Let the Good Times Roll | 1958 | 25.00 | 50.00 | 100.00 |
-- Black label, silver print
MERCURY
| ❏ MG-20242 [M] | Somebody Up There Digs Me | 1957 | 30.00 | 60.00 | 120.00 |
| ❏ MG-20331 [M] | Man, We're Wailin' | 1958 | 30.00 | 60.00 | 120.00 |
SCORE
| ❏ SLP-4007 [M] | Go Blow Your Horn | 1957 | 50.00 | 100.00 | 200.00 |
TANGERINE
| ❏ 1503 [M] | Hallelujah | 1964 | 5.00 | 10.00 | 20.00 |
| ❏ S-1503 [S] | Hallelujah | 1964 | 6.25 | 12.50 | 25.00 |
WING
| ❏ MGW-12126 [M] | Somebody Up There Digs Me | 1962 | 6.25 | 12.50 | 25.00 |

JORDANAIRES, THE
CAPITOL
❏ T 1011 [M]	Heavenly Spirit	1958	10.00	20.00	40.00
❏ T 1167 [M]	Gloryland	1959	10.00	20.00	40.00
❏ ST 1311 [S]	Land of Jordan	1960	10.00	20.00	40.00
❏ T 1311 [M]	Land of Jordan	1960	7.50	15.00	30.00
❏ ST 1559 [S]	To God Be the Glory	1961	6.25	12.50	25.00
❏ T 1559 [M]	To God Be the Glory	1961	5.00	10.00	20.00
❏ ST 1742 [S]	Spotlight on the Jordanaires	1962	7.50	15.00	30.00
❏ T 1742 [M]	Spotlight on the Jordanaires	1962	6.25	12.50	25.00
COLUMBIA
❏ CL 2214 [M]	This Land	1964	5.00	10.00	20.00
❏ CL 2458 [M]	The Big Country Hits	1966	5.00	10.00	20.00
❏ CS 9014 [S]	This Land	1964	6.25	12.50	25.00
❏ CS 9258 [S]	The Big Country Hits	1966	6.25	12.50	25.00
DECCA
| ❏ DL 8681 [M] | Peace in the Valley | 1957 | 12.50 | 25.00 | 50.00 |
RCA VICTOR
| ❏ LPM-3081 [10] | Beautiful City | 1953 | 25.00 | 50.00 | 100.00 |
SESAC
| ❏ 1401/1402 [M] | Of Rivers and Plains | 195? | 20.00 | 40.00 | 80.00 |

JORGENSON, CHRISTINE
J RECORDS
| ❏ J-1 [M] | Christine Jorgenson Reveals | 1958 | 12.50 | 25.00 | 50.00 |

JOSEFUS
HOOKAH
| ❏ 330 | Dead Man | 1969 | 75.00 | 150.00 | 300.00 |
MAINSTREAM
| ❏ S-6127 | Josefus | 1970 | 25.00 | 50.00 | 100.00 |

JOSEPH
SCEPTER
| ❏ SRS-674 | Stoned Age Man | 1970 | 20.00 | 40.00 | 80.00 |

JOSEPH, MARGIE
VOLT
| ❏ VOS-6012 | Margie Joseph Makes a New Impression | 1971 | 7.50 | 15.00 | 30.00 |
| ❏ VOS-6016 | Phase II | 1971 | 7.50 | 15.00 | 30.00 |

JOSHUA FOX
TETRAGRAMMATON
| ❏ T-125 | Joshua Fox | 1968 | 7.50 | 15.00 | 30.00 |

JOSIE AND THE PUSSYCATS
CAPITOL
| ❏ ST-665 | Josie and the Pussycats | 1970 | 50.00 | 100.00 | 200.00 |

JOURNEY
COLUMBIA
| ❏ HC 44912 | Infinity | 1982 | 7.50 | 15.00 | 30.00 |
-- Half-speed mastered edition
| ❏ HC 46339 | Departure | 1980 | 5.00 | 10.00 | 20.00 |
-- Half-speed mastered edition
| ❏ HC 47408 | Escape | 1982 | 5.00 | 10.00 | 20.00 |
-- Half-speed mastered edition
| ❏ HC 47998 | Dream After Dream | 1982 | 7.50 | 15.00 | 30.00 |
-- Half-speed mastered edition
| ❏ HC 48504 | Frontiers | 1983 | 7.50 | 15.00 | 30.00 |
-- Half-speed mastered edition
MOBILE FIDELITY
| ❏ 1-144 | Escape | 1984 | 50.00 | 100.00 | 200.00 |
-- Audiophile vinyl

JOURNEYMEN, THE
Also see SCOTT McKENZIE.
CAPITOL
❏ ST 1629 [S]	The Journeymen	1961	7.50	15.00	30.00
❏ T 1629 [M]	The Journeymen	1961	6.25	12.50	25.00
❏ ST 1770 [S]	Coming Attraction -- Live!	1962	7.50	51.00	30.00
❏ T 1770 [M]	Coming Attraction -- Live!	1962	6.25	12.50	25.00
❏ ST 1951 [S]	New Directions in Folk Music	1963	7.50	15.00	30.00
❏ T 1951 [M]	New Directions in Folk Music	1963	6.25	12.50	25.00

JOY DIVISION
Also see NEW ORDER.
FACTORY
| ❏ FACT US 1 | Unknown Pleasures | 1979 | 5.00 | 10.00 | 20.00 |
| ❏ FACT US 6 | Closer | 1980 | 6.25 | 12.50 | 25.00 |
-- Red tint vinyl
| ❏ FACT US 6 | Closer | 1980 | 12.50 | 25.00 | 50.00 |
-- Purple tint vinyl

JOY STRINGS, THE
EPIC
| ❏ LN 24321 [M] | Well Seasoned | 1967 | 5.00 | 10.00 | 20.00 |
| ❏ BN 26321 [S] | Well Seasoned | 1967 | 5.00 | 10.00 | 20.00 |

JOY UNLIMITED
BASF
| ❏ 21090 | Butterflies | 1972 | 6.25 | 12.50 | 25.00 |
MERCURY
| ❏ SR-61283 | Joy Unlimited | 1970 | 6.25 | 12.50 | 25.00 |

JOYCE, JIMMY
WARNER BROS.
| ❏ WS 1237 [S] | A Christmas to Remember | 1959 | 5.00 | 10.00 | 20.00 |
| ❏ WS 1566 [S] | This Is Christmas: A Complete Collection of the Alfred S. Burt Carols | 1964 | 5.00 | 10.00 | 20.00 |

JOYOUS NOISE
CAPITOL
| ❏ SMAS-844 | Joyous Noise | 1971 | 5.00 | 10.00 | 20.00 |

JUDAS PRIEST
COLUMBIA
| ❏ AS99 1543 [DJ] | Screaming for Vengeance | 1982 | 5.00 | 10.00 | 20.00 |
-- Promo-only "world tour" picture disc; plays the correct LP
| ❏ AS99 1543 [DJ] | Screaming for Vengeance | 1982 | 7.50 | 15.00 | 30.00 |
-- Promo-only "world tour" picture disc; plays Neil Diamond's "Heartlight" LP in error
| ❏ 9C9 39926 [PD] | Great Vinyl and Concert Hits | 1984 | 15.00 | 30.00 | 60.00 |
JANUS
| ❏ 7019 | Sad Wings of Destiny | 1976 | 6.25 | 12.50 | 25.00 |
VISA
| ❏ IMP-7001 | Rocka Rolla | 1974 | 6.25 | 12.50 | 25.00 |
-- Front cover has a bottle-cap motif (this LP was reissued around 1979 with the same number but a different cover)

JUDD, WYNONNA
MCA
| ❏ 1P-8201 | Wynonna | 1992 | 6.25 | 12.50 | 25.00 |
-- Only released on vinyl through Columbia House; label misspells her name as "Wyonna"!

JULIAN'S TREATMENT
DECCA
| ❏ DL 75224 | A Time Before This | 1970 | 5.00 | 10.00 | 20.00 |

JULLIARD STRING QUARTET
RCA VICTOR RED SEAL
| ❏ LSC-2378 [S] | Schubert: String Quartet No. 14 "Death and the Maiden" | 1960 | 37.50 | 75.00 | 150.00 |
-- Original with "shaded dog" label
| ❏ LSC-2413 [S] | Debussy: String Quartet in G; Ravel: String Quartet in F | 1960 | 15.00 | 30.00 | 60.00 |
-- Original with "shaded dog" label
| ❏ LSC-2481 [S] | Carter: String Quartet No. 2; Schuman: String Quartet No. 3 | 1961 | 10.00 | 20.00 | 40.00 |
-- Original with "shaded dog" label

Number	Title	Yr	VG	VG+	NM
❑ LSC-2524 [S]	Dvorak: String Quartet in C; Wolf: Italian Serenade	1961	10.00	20.00	40.00
-- Originals with "shaded dog" label					
❑ LSC-2531 [S]	Berg: Lyric Suite; Webern: 5 Pieces; Six Bagatelles	1961	12.50	25.00	50.00
-- Originals with "shaded dog" label					
❑ LSC-2616 [S]	Beethoven: String Quartet in C# Minor	1962	10.00	20.00	40.00
-- Original with "shaded dog" label					
❑ LSC-2632 [S]	Beethoven: String Quartet in F, Op. 95; String Quartet in F, Op. 135	1962	12.50	25.00	50.00
-- Original with "shaded dog" label					

JULY
EPIC
Number	Title	Yr	VG	VG+	NM
❑ BN 26416	July	1969	50.00	100.00	200.00

JUNIOR'S EYES
A&M
Number	Title	Yr	VG	VG+	NM
❑ SP-4189	Junior's Eyes	1970	5.00	10.00	20.00

JUST IV
LIBERTY
Number	Title	Yr	VG	VG+	NM
❑ LRP-3340 [M]	First Twelve Sides	1964	5.00	10.00	20.00
❑ LST-7340 [S]	First Twelve Sides	1964	6.25	12.50	25.00

JUST US
KAPP
Number	Title	Yr	VG	VG+	NM
❑ KL-1502 [M]	I Can't Grow Peaches on a Cherry Tree	1966	5.00	10.00	20.00
❑ KS-3502 [S]	I Can't Grow Peaches on a Cherry Tree	1966	6.25	12.50	25.00

JUSTICE, JIMMY
KAPP
Number	Title	Yr	VG	VG+	NM
❑ KL-1308 [M]	Justice for All	1963	6.25	12.50	25.00
❑ KS-3308 [S]	Justice for All	1963	10.00	20.00	40.00

JUSTIS, BILL
PHILLIPS INTERNATIONAL
Number	Title	Yr	VG	VG+	NM
❑ PLP-1950 [M]	Cloud Nine	1959	100.00	200.00	400.00

SMASH
Number	Title	Yr	VG	VG+	NM
❑ SRS-67021 [S]	Bill Justis Plays 12 Big Instrumental Hits (Alley Cat/Green Onions)	1962	5.00	10.00	20.00
❑ SRS-67030 [S]	Bill Justis Plays 12 More Big Instrumental Hits (Telstar/The Lonely Bull)	1963	5.00	10.00	20.00
❑ SRS-67031 [S]	Bill Justis Plays 12 Smash Instrumental Hits	1963	5.00	10.00	20.00
❑ SRS-67036 [S]	Bill Justis Plays 12 Top Tunes	1963	5.00	10.00	20.00
❑ SRS-67043 [S]	Bill Justis Plays 12 Other Instrumental Hits	1964	5.00	10.00	20.00
❑ SRS-67047 [S]	Dixieland Folk Style	1964	5.00	10.00	20.00
❑ SRS-67065 [S]	More Instrumental Hits	1965	5.00	10.00	20.00
❑ SRS-67077 [S]	Taste of Honey/The "In" Crowd	1966	5.00	10.00	20.00

K

K-DOE, ERNIE
JANUS
Number	Title	Yr	VG	VG+	NM
❑ JLS-3030	Ernie K-Doe	1971	6.25	12.50	25.00
MINIT
❑ LP-0002 [M]	Mother-in-Law	1961	50.00	100.00	200.00
-- Orange label					
❑ LP-24002 [R]	Mother-in-Law	196?	37.50	75.00	150.00
-- Black label, not issued until after Imperial bought Minit					

KAEMPFERT, BERT
DECCA
Number	Title	Yr	VG	VG+	NM
❑ DL 4925 [M]	The World We Knew	1967	5.00	10.00	20.00
❑ DL 4986 [M]	Love That	1968	5.00	10.00	20.00
❑ DXS 7200 [(2)]	The Best of Bert Kaempfert	197?	5.00	10.00	20.00
❑ DL 34485	The Best of Bert Kaempfert	197?	5.00	10.00	20.00
-- Special Decca Custom Division edition					
❑ DL 74101 [S]	Wonderland by Night	1960	5.00	10.00	20.00
❑ DL 74117 [S]	The Wonderland of Bert Kaempfert	1961	5.00	10.00	20.00
❑ DL 74161 [S]	Dancing in Wonderland	1961	5.00	10.00	20.00
❑ DL 78881 [S]	April in Portugal	1959	5.00	10.00	20.00

KAK
EPIC
Number	Title	Yr	VG	VG+	NM
❑ BN 26429	Kak	1969	62.50	125.00	250.00

KALABASH CORP., THE
UNCLE BILL
Number	Title	Yr	VG	VG+	NM
❑ KB-3114	The Kalabash Corp.	1970	20.00	40.00	80.00

KALEIDOSCOPE, THE
EPIC
Number	Title	Yr	VG	VG+	NM
❑ LN 24304 [M]	Side Trips	1967	7.50	15.00	30.00
❑ LN 24333 [M]	Beacon from Mars	1967	15.00	30.00	60.00
❑ BN 26304 [S]	Side Trips	1967	10.00	20.00	40.00
❑ BN 26333 [S]	Beacon from Mars	1967	25.00	50.00	100.00
❑ BN 26467	Incredible Kaleidoscope	1969	7.50	15.00	30.00
❑ BN 26508	Bernice	1970	7.50	15.00	30.00

KALIN TWINS, THE
DECCA
Number	Title	Yr	VG	VG+	NM
❑ DL 8812 [M]	The Kalin Twins	1959	25.00	50.00	100.00

KALLEN, KITTY
COLUMBIA
Number	Title	Yr	VG	VG+	NM
❑ CL 1404 [M]	If I Give My Heart to You	1960	5.00	10.00	20.00
❑ CL 1662 [M]	Honky Tonk Angel	1961	5.00	10.00	20.00
❑ CS 8204 [S]	If I Give My Heart to You	1960	6.25	12.50	25.00
❑ CS 8462 [S]	Honky Tonk Angel	1961	6.25	12.50	25.00
DECCA
| ❑ DL 8397 [M] | It's a Lonesome Old Town | 1958 | 10.00 | 20.00 | 40.00 |
MERCURY
| ❑ MG 25206 [10] | Pretty Kitty Kallen Sings | 1955 | 12.50 | 25.00 | 50.00 |
RCA VICTOR
| ❑ LPM-2640 [M] | My Coloring Book | 1963 | 5.00 | 10.00 | 20.00 |
| ❑ LSP-2640 [S] | My Coloring Book | 1963 | 6.25 | 12.50 | 25.00 |
VOCALION
| ❑ VL 3679 [M] | Little Things Mean a Lot | 1959 | 6.25 | 12.50 | 25.00 |

KALLMAN, DICK
RCA VICTOR
Number	Title	Yr	VG	VG+	NM
❑ LPM-3485 [M]	Dick Kallman Drops In as Hank	1966	5.00	10.00	20.00
❑ LSP-3485 [S]	Dick Kallman Drops In as Hank	1966	6.25	12.50	25.00

KANE'S COUSINS
SHOVE LOVE
Number	Title	Yr	VG	VG+	NM
❑ 9827	Undergum Bubbleground	1969	10.00	20.00	40.00

KANGAROO
MGM
Number	Title	Yr	VG	VG+	NM
❑ SE-4586	Kangaroo	1968	6.25	12.50	25.00

KANNIBAL KOMIX
COLOSSUS
Number	Title	Yr	VG	VG+	NM
❑ 1004	Kannibal Komix	1970	5.00	10.00	20.00

Number	Title	Yr	VG	VG+	NM

KANSAS
KIRSHNER
❏ AS 555 [DJ]	Two for the Show (Sampler)	1978	5.00	10.00	20.00
-- Promo-only single disc of selections from two-record set of the same name					
❏ HZ 44224	Leftoverture	1982	10.00	20.00	40.00
-- Half-speed mastered edition					
❏ HZ 44929	Point of Know Return	1982	10.00	20.00	40.00
-- Half-speed mastered edition					
❏ HZ 46008	Monolith	1982	12.50	25.00	50.00
-- Half-speed mastered edition					
❏ HZ 48002	Vinyl Confessions	1982	25.00	50.00	100.00
-- Half-speed mastered edition					

KANTNER, PAUL/JEFFERSON STARSHIP
Also see JEFFERSON STARSHIP.
RCA VICTOR
❏ LSP-4448 [DJ]	Blows Against the Empire	1970	37.50	75.00	150.00
-- Clear vinyl promo					

KARLOFF, BORIS
CAEDMON
❏ TC-1038 [M]	Just So Stories and Other Tales	195?	6.25	12.50	25.00
❏ TC-1074 [M]	The Reluctant Dragon	196?	6.25	12.50	25.00
❏ TC-1075 [M]	The Pied Piper; The Hunting of the Snarks	196?	6.25	12.50	25.00
❏ TC-1088 [M]	More of Kipling's Just So Stories	196?	6.25	12.50	25.00
❏ TC-1100 [M]	Kipling's Jungle Books: How Fear Came	196?	6.25	12.50	25.00
❏ TC-1109 [M]	The Ugly Duckling and Other Tales	196?	6.25	12.50	25.00
❏ TC-1117 [M]	The Little Match Girl and Other Tales	196?	6.25	12.50	25.00
❏ TC-1129 [M]	The Three Bears, Henny Penny and Other Fairy Tales	1962	6.25	12.50	25.00
❏ TC-1139 [M]	The Cat That Walked By Herself	196?	6.25	12.50	25.00
❏ TC-1176 [M]	Kipling's Jungle Books: Toomai of the Elephants	196?	6.25	12.50	25.00
❏ TC-1221 [M]	Aesop's Fables	1967	5.00	10.00	20.00
DECCA
❏ DL 4833 [M]	An Evening with Boris Karloff and His Friends	1967	5.00	10.00	20.00
❏ DL 74833 [S]	An Evening with Boris Karloff and His Friends	1967	6.25	12.50	25.00
MERCURY
❏ MG-20815 [M]	Tales of the Frightened, Volume 1	1963	10.00	20.00	40.00
❏ MG-20816 [M]	Tales of the Frightened, Volume 2	1963	10.00	20.00	40.00
❏ SR-60815 [S]	Tales of the Frightened, Volume 1	1963	12.50	25.00	50.00
❏ SR-60816 [S]	Tales of the Frightened, Volume 2	1963	12.50	25.00	50.00

KATMANDU
MAINSTREAM
❏ S-6131	Katmandu	1971	10.00	20.00	40.00

KATZ, MICKEY
CAPITOL
❏ H 298 [10]	Mickey Katz: The Star of Broadway's Borschtcapades	195?	10.00	20.00	40.00
❏ T 298 [M]	The Very Best of Mickey Katz	195?	7.50	15.00	30.00
-- Turquoise or gray label					
❏ H 457 [10]	The Family Danced	195?	10.00	20.00	40.00
❏ T 799 [M]	Mish Mosh	1957	7.50	15.00	30.00
-- Turquoise or gray label					
❏ T 934 [M]	Katz Puts On the Dog	1958	7.50	15.00	30.00
-- Turquoise or gray label					
❏ T 1021 [M]	Katz Plays Music for Weddings, Bar Mitzvahs and Brisses	1958	7.50	15.00	30.00
-- Turquoise or gray label					
❏ T 1102 [M]	The Most Mishige	1959	6.25	12.50	25.00
-- Black colorband label, logo at left					
❏ W 1257 [M]	Katz Pajamas	1959	6.25	12.50	25.00
-- Black colorband label, logo at left					
❏ W 1307 [M]	Comin' Round the Katzkills	1959	6.25	12.50	25.00
-- Black colorband label, logo at left					
❏ ST 1445 [S]	The Borscht Jester	1960	6.25	12.50	25.00
-- Black colorband label, logo at left					
❏ T 1445 [M]	The Borscht Jester	1960	5.00	10.00	20.00
-- Black colorband label, logo at left					
❏ ST 1603 [S]	At the U.N.	1961	6.25	12.50	25.00
-- Black colorband label, logo at left					
❏ T 1603 [M]	At the U.N.	1961	5.00	10.00	20.00
-- Black colorband label, logo at left					
❏ ST 1744 [S]	Sing Along with Mickele	1962	6.25	12.50	25.00
❏ T 1744 [M]	Sing Along with Mickele	1962	5.00	10.00	20.00
RCA VICTOR
❏ LPM-3193 [10]	Borscht	1954	10.00	20.00	40.00

KAUFMANN, BOB
LHI
❏ 12002	Trip Through a Blown Mind	1967	15.00	30.00	60.00

KAY, JOHN, AND SPARROW -- See SPARROW.

KAY, JOHN, AND STEPPENWOLF -- See STEPPENWOLF.

KAYAK
JANUS
❏ (no #) [PD]	Phantom of the Night	1979	6.25	12.50	25.00
-- Numbered limited edition of 3,000					

KAYE, DANNY
CAPITOL
❏ T 937 [M]	Mommy Gimme a Drinka Water	1958	10.00	20.00	40.00
COLUMBIA
❏ CL 6023 [10]	Danny Kaye	1949	12.50	25.00	50.00
❏ CL 6249 [10]	Danny Kaye Entertains	195?	12.50	25.00	50.00
DECCA
❏ DXB 175 [(2) M]	The Best of Danny Kaye	1965	6.25	12.50	25.00
❏ DLP 5033 [10]	Danny Kaye	1950	12.50	25.00	50.00
❏ DL 5094 [10]	Gilbert and Sullivan and Danny Kaye	1950	12.50	25.00	50.00
❏ DL 8212 [M]	The Court Jester	1955	12.50	25.00	50.00
-- Black label, silver print					
❏ DL 8461 [M]	Danny at the Palace	1957	12.50	25.00	50.00
-- Black label, silver print					
❏ DL 8461 [M]	Danny at the Palace	1960	6.25	12.50	25.00
-- Black label with color bars					
❏ DL 8726 [M]	Danny Kaye for Children	1959	7.50	15.00	30.00
-- Black label, silver print					
❏ DL 8726 [M]	Danny Kaye for Children	1960	6.25	12.50	25.00
-- Black label with color bars					

KAYE, MARY
DECCA
❏ DL 8238 [M]	The Mary Kaye Trio	1956	7.50	15.00	30.00
❏ DL 8434 [M]	Music on a Silver Platter	1957	7.50	15.00	30.00
❏ DL 8650 [M]	You Don't Know What Love Is	1958	7.50	15.00	30.00
VERVE
❏ MGV-2142 [M]	Up Front!	1960	10.00	20.00	40.00
❏ V-8446 [M]	For the Record	1962	5.00	10.00	20.00
❏ V6-8446 [S]	For the Record	1962	6.25	12.50	25.00
WARNER BROS.
❏ W 1263 [M]	Jackpot	1959	5.00	10.00	20.00
❏ W 1342 [M]	The Mary Kaye Trio on Sunset Strip	1959	5.00	10.00	20.00
❏ WS 1263 [S]	Jackpot	1959	6.25	12.50	25.00
❏ WS 1342 [S]	The Mary Kaye Trio on Sunset Strip	1959	6.25	12.50	25.00

KAYE, SAMMY
COLUMBIA
❏ CL 561 [M]	Swing and Sway with Sammy Kaye	195?	7.50	15.00	30.00
❏ CL 668 [M]	Music, Maestro, Please!	195?	7.50	15.00	30.00
❏ CL 885 [M]	My Fair Lady (For Dancing)	1956	5.00	10.00	20.00
❏ CL 891 [M]	What Makes Sammy Swing and Sway	1956	5.00	10.00	20.00
❏ CL 964 [M]	Sunday Serenade	1957	5.00	10.00	20.00
❏ CL 1018 [M]	Popular American Waltzes	1957	5.00	10.00	20.00
❏ CL 2541 [10]	Christmas Serenade	1955	10.00	20.00	40.00
-- "House Party Series" issue					
❏ CL 6155 [10]	Sunday Serenade	1953	10.00	20.00	40.00
RCA CAMDEN
❏ CAL-355 [M]	Swing and Sway with Sammy	1957	5.00	10.00	20.00
RCA VICTOR
❏ LPM-3966 [M]	The Best of Sammy Kaye	1967	5.00	10.00	20.00

KAZAN, LAINIE
MGM
❏ E-4340 [M]	Right Now	1966	5.00	10.00	20.00
❏ SE-4340 [S]	Right Now	1966	6.25	12.50	25.00
❏ E-4385 [M]	Lainie Kazan	1966	5.00	10.00	20.00
❏ SE-4385 [S]	Lainie Kazan	1966	6.25	12.50	25.00
❏ E-4451 [M]	The Love Album	1967	6.25	12.50	25.00
❏ SE-4451 [S]	The Love Album	1967	5.00	10.00	20.00
❏ SE-4496	Love Is	1968	5.00	10.00	20.00
❏ SE-4631	The Best of Lainie Kazan	1969	5.00	10.00	20.00

KEITH
MERCURY
❏ SR-61102 [S]	98.6/Ain't Gonna Lie	1967	5.00	10.00	20.00
❏ SR-61129 [S]	Out of Crank	1967	5.00	10.00	20.00

Number	Title	Yr	VG	VG+	NM
RCA VICTOR					
❏ LSP-4143	The Adventures of Keith	1969	5.00	10.00	20.00
KEITH AND DONNA					
Also see THE GRATEFUL DEAD.					
ROUND					
❏ RX-104	Keith and Donna	1975	7.50	15.00	30.00
KELLER, JERRY					
KAPP					
❏ KL-1178 [M]	Here Comes Jerry Keller	1959	10.00	20.00	40.00
❏ KS-3178 [S]	Here Comes Jerry Keller	1959	12.50	25.00	50.00
KELLERMAN, SALLY					
DECCA					
❏ DL 75359	Roll with the Feelin'	1972	5.00	10.00	20.00
KELLIN, MIKE					
VERVE FORECAST					
❏ FT-3028 [M]	Mike Kellin	1967	6.25	12.50	25.00
❏ FTS-3028 [S]	Mike Kellin	1967	6.25	12.50	25.00
KELLY BROTHERS, THE					
EXCELLO					
❏ LPS-8007	Sweet Soul	1968	12.50	25.00	50.00
KING					
❏ 810 [M]	The Kelly Brothers Sing a Page of Songs from the Good Book	1962	25.00	50.00	100.00
KELLY, EMMETT					
ROULETTE					
❏ R-25130 [M]	Sing Along with Emmett Kelly	1962	6.25	12.50	25.00
❏ SR-25130 [S]	Sing Along with Emmett Kelly	1962	7.50	15.00	30.00
KELLY, MONTY					
CARLTON					
❏ LP 12-111 [M]	Porgy and Bess	1959	5.00	10.00	20.00
❏ STLP 12-111 [S]	Porgy and Bess	1959	6.25	12.50	25.00
❏ LP 12-123 [M]	Summer Set	1960	5.00	10.00	20.00
❏ STLP 12-123 [S]	Summer Set	1960	6.25	12.50	25.00
KENDALLS, THE					
STOP					
❏ 1020	Meet the Kendalls	1970	5.00	10.00	20.00
KENNEDY, DAVE					
COULEE					
❏ 1001 [M]	Breaking Up Is Hard to Do	1964	12.50	25.00	50.00
KENNEDY, JERRY					
Also see TOM & JERRY.					
SMASH					
❏ MGS-27004 [M]	Dancing Guitars Rock Elvis' Hits	1962	7.50	15.00	30.00
❏ MGS-27024 [M]	Jerry Kennedy's Guitars and Strings Play the Golden Standards	1963	5.00	10.00	20.00
❏ MGS-27066 [M]	From Nashville to Soulville	1965	5.00	10.00	20.00
❏ SRS-67004 [S]	Dancing Guitars Rock Elvis' Hits	1962	10.00	20.00	40.00
❏ SRS-67024 [S]	Jerry Kennedy's Guitars and Strings Play the Golden Standards	1963	6.25	12.50	25.00
❏ SRS-67066 [S]	From Nashville to Soulville	1965	6.25	12.50	25.00
KENNEDY, JOHN FITZGERALD					
All the below are tribute albums released in the wake of his assassination.					
CAEDMON					
❏ TC-2021 [(2)]	Self-Portrait	196?	5.00	10.00	20.00
CAPITOL					
❏ ST 2486 [S]	Years of Lightning, Day of Drums	1966	7.50	15.00	30.00
❏ T 2486 [M]	Years of Lightning, Day of Drums	1966	5.00	10.00	20.00
-- Narrated by Gregory Peck; U.S. Information Agency movie soundtrack					
COLPIX					
❏ CP 2500 [M]	Four Days That Shocked the World	1964	12.50	25.00	50.00
-- Narrated by Reid Collins; covers Nov. 22-25, 1963					
DECCA					
❏ DL 9116 [M]	That Was The Week That Was	1963	5.00	10.00	20.00
-- BBC show's tribute to JFK, broadcast Nov. 23, 1963					
DOCUMENTARIES UNLIMITED					
❏ (no #) [M]	JFK The Man, The President	1963	5.00	10.00	20.00
-- Narrated by Barry Gray					

Number	Title	Yr	VG	VG+	NM
HARMONICA					
❏ HLP-3005 [M]	Kennedy Speaks	1963	5.00	10.00	20.00
LEGACY					
❏ L2L 1017 [(2) M]	John Fitzgerald Kennedy...As We Remember Him	1965	6.25	12.50	25.00
-- Narrated by Charles Kuralt; with 240-page book					
PREMIER					
❏ 2099 [M]	A Memorial Album	1963	5.00	10.00	20.00
-- From WMCA Radio, New York, Nov. 22, 1963					
20TH CENTURY					
❏ TCF 3127 [M]	The Presidential Years 1960-1963	1963	5.00	10.00	20.00
-- Narrated by David Teig					
KENNEDY, ROBERT FRANCIS					
The below is a tribute album.					
COLUMBIA					
❏ C2S 792 [(2)]	A Memorial	1968	5.00	10.00	20.00
KENNER, CHRIS					
ATLANTIC					
❏ 8117 [M]	Land of 1,000 Dances	1965	20.00	40.00	80.00
KENNY AND THE KASUALS					
MARK					
❏ 5000 [M]	The Impact Sound of Kenny and the Kasuals Live at the Studio Club	1966	250.00	500.00	1,000.
❏ 5000 [M]	The Impact Sound of Kenny and the Kasuals Live at the Studio Club	1977	6.25	12.50	25.00
-- "Reissue, 1977" appears on cover					
❏ 6000 [M]	Teen Dreams	1978	62.50	125.00	250.00
-- Red vinyl; numbered, signed limited edition					
❏ 7000 [S]	Garage Kings	1979	6.25	12.50	25.00
KENNY, BILL					
WARWICK					
❏ W-2021 [M]	Mr. Ink Spot	1960	6.25	12.50	25.00
KENSINGTON MARKET					
WARNER BROS.					
❏ WS 1754	Avenue Road	1968	5.00	10.00	20.00
❏ WS 1780	Aardvark	1969	5.00	10.00	20.00
KENTON, STAN					
CAPITOL					
❏ H 155 [10]	Encores	1950	15.00	30.00	60.00
❏ T 155 [M]	Encores	195?	10.00	20.00	40.00
-- Turquoise label					
❏ H 167 [10]	Artistry in Rhythm	1950	15.00	30.00	60.00
❏ T 167 [M]	Artistry in Rhythm	195?	10.00	20.00	40.00
-- Turquoise label					
❏ H 172 [10]	A Presentation of Progressive Jazz	1950	15.00	30.00	60.00
❏ T 172 [M]	A Presentation of Progressive Jazz	195?	10.00	20.00	40.00
❏ P 189 [10]	Innovations in Modern Music	1950	15.00	30.00	60.00
❏ H 190 [10]	Milestones	1950	15.00	30.00	60.00
❏ T 190 [M]	Milestones	195?	10.00	20.00	40.00
-- Turquoise label					
❏ L 248 [10]	Stan Kenton Presents	1951	15.00	30.00	60.00
❏ T 248 [M]	Stan Kenton Presents	195?	10.00	20.00	40.00
-- Turquoise label					
❏ H 353 [10]	City of Glass	1952	15.00	30.00	60.00
❏ H 358 [10]	Classics	1952	15.00	30.00	60.00
❏ T 358 [M]	Classics	195?	10.00	20.00	40.00
-- Turquoise label					
❏ H 383 [10]	New Concepts of Artistry in	1953	15.00	30.00	60.00
❏ T 383 [M]	New Concepts of Artistry in	195?	10.00	20.00	40.00
-- Turquoise label					
❏ H 386 [10]	Prologue: This Is an Orchestra	1953	15.00	30.00	60.00
❏ H 421 [10]	Popular Favorites	1953	15.00	30.00	60.00
❏ T 421 [M]	Popular Favorites	195?	10.00	20.00	40.00
-- Turquoise label					
❏ H 426 [10]	Sketches on Standards	1953	15.00	30.00	60.00
❏ T 426 [M]	Sketches on Standards	195?	10.00	20.00	40.00
-- Turquoise label					
❏ H 460 [10]	This Modern World	1953	15.00	30.00	60.00
❏ H 462 [10]	Portraits on Standards	1953	15.00	30.00	60.00
❏ T 462 [M]	Portraits on Standards	195?	10.00	20.00	40.00
-- Turquoise label					
❏ W 524 [M]	Kenton Showcase	1954	10.00	20.00	40.00
❏ H 525 [10]	Kenton Showcase -- The Music of Bill Russo	1954	15.00	30.00	60.00
❏ H 526 [10]	Kenton Showcase -- The Music of Bill Holman	1954	15.00	30.00	60.00
❏ TDB 569 [(4) M]	The Kenton Era	1955	25.00	50.00	100.00
-- Box set with 44-page book					

(Top left) This album, which came out on the 20th Century Fox label in 1968, was one of several posthumous tribute albums to Martin Luther King. There were nowhere near as many of these tributes as there were to John F. Kennedy, and those that did come out are much harder to find than the JFK albums. (Top right) In the beginning, there was the mighty riff of "You Really Got Me." It was actually the third Kinks single, but it was the first hit. Reprise answered with this pretty good collection as a debut album. (Bottom left) Another rare Capitol Record Club pressing, this one is of the Kinks' *Arthur* album. (Bottom right) Billy J. Kramer and the Dakotas were teamed by Brian Epstein, and thanks to a wonderful double-sided hit single, the Lennon-McCartney "Bad to Me" and the title song of the above album, became another group to have success in the States on the waves of the British Invasion of 1964.

Number	Title	Yr	VG	VG+	NM
❑ T 656 [M]	Duet	1955	10.00	20.00	40.00
-- With June Christy; turquoise label					
❑ T 666 [M]	Contemporary Concepts	1955	10.00	20.00	40.00
-- Turquoise label					
❑ W 724 [M]	Kenton in Hi-Fi	1956	10.00	20.00	40.00
-- Turquoise label					
❑ T 731 [M]	Cuban Fire!	1956	10.00	20.00	40.00
-- Turquoise label					
❑ T 731 [M]	Cuban Fire!	1959	5.00	10.00	20.00
-- Black label with colorband, Capitol logo at left					
❑ T 736 [M]	City of Glass/This Modern World	1956	10.00	20.00	40.00
-- Combination of 353 and 460 onto one 12-inch LP, turquoise label					
❑ T 810 [M]	Kenton with Voices	1957	10.00	20.00	40.00
-- Turquoise label					
❑ T 932 [M]	Rendezvous with Kenton	1957	10.00	20.00	40.00
-- Turquoise label					
❑ T 995 [M]	Back to Balboa	1958	10.00	20.00	40.00
-- Turquoise label					
❑ ST 1068 [S]	The Ballad Style of Stan Kenton	1959	5.00	10.00	20.00
-- Black label with colorband, Capitol logo at left					
❑ T 1068 [M]	The Ballad Style of Stan Kenton	1959	6.25	12.50	25.00
-- Black label with colorband, Capitol logo at left					
❑ ST 1130 [S]	Lush Interlude	1959	5.00	10.00	20.00
-- Black label with colorband, Capitol logo at left					
❑ T 1130 [M]	Lush Interlude	1959	6.25	12.50	25.00
-- Black label with colorband, Capitol logo at left					
❑ ST 1166 [S]	The Stage Door Swings	1959	5.00	10.00	20.00
-- Black label with colorband, Capitol logo at left					
❑ T 1166 [M]	The Stage Door Swings	1959	6.25	12.50	25.00
-- Black label with colorband, Capitol logo at left					
❑ ST 1276 [S]	The Kenton Touch	1960	5.00	10.00	20.00
-- Black label with colorband, Capitol logo at left					
❑ T 1276 [M]	The Kenton Touch	1960	6.25	12.50	25.00
-- Black label with colorband, Capitol logo at left					
❑ SW 1305 [S]	Viva Kenton!	1960	5.00	10.00	20.00
-- Black label with colorband, Capitol logo at left					
❑ W 1305 [M]	Viva Kenton!	1960	6.25	12.50	25.00
-- Black label with colorband, Capitol logo at left					
❑ STBO 1327 [(2) S]	Road Show	1960	7.50	15.00	30.00
-- Black label with colorband, Capitol logo at left					
❑ TBO 1327 [(2) M]	Road Show	1960	10.00	20.00	40.00
-- Black label with colorband, Capitol logo at left					
❑ TBO 1327 [(2) M]	Road Show	1962	5.00	10.00	20.00
-- Black label with colorband, Capitol logo at top					
❑ ST 1394 [S]	Standards in Silhouette	1960	5.00	10.00	20.00
-- Black label with colorband, Capitol logo at left					
❑ T 1394 [M]	Standards in Silhouette	1960	6.25	12.50	25.00
-- Black label with colorband, Capitol logo at left					
❑ ST 1460 [S]	Kenton at the Las Vegas Tropicana	1961	5.00	10.00	20.00
-- Black label with colorband, Capitol logo at left					
❑ T 1460 [M]	Kenton at the Las Vegas Tropicana	1961	6.25	12.50	25.00
-- Black label with colorband, Capitol logo at left					
❑ ST 1533 [S]	The Romantic Approach	1961	5.00	10.00	20.00
-- Black label with colorband, Capitol logo at left					
❑ T 1533 [M]	The Romantic Approach	1961	6.25	12.50	25.00
-- Black label with colorband, Capitol logo at left					
❑ ST 1609 [S]	Kenton's West Side Story	1961	5.00	10.00	20.00
-- Black label with colorband, Capitol logo at left					
❑ T 1609 [M]	Kenton's West Side Story	1961	6.25	12.50	25.00
-- Black label with colorband, Capitol logo at left					
CREATIVE WORLD					
❑ ST 1030 [(4) R]	The Kenton Era	197?	5.00	10.00	20.00
-- Reissue of Capitol TDB 569					
❑ ST 1058 [(2) Q]	Live at Butler University	1972	5.00	10.00	20.00
❑ ST 1059 [(2) Q]	Stan Kenton with the Four Freshmen at Butler University	1972	5.00	10.00	20.00
❑ ST 1060 [(2) Q]	National Anthems of the World	1972	5.00	10.00	20.00
DECCA					
❑ DL 8259 [M]	Stan Kenton -- Formative Years	195?	6.25	12.50	25.00
-- All-black label with silver print					
MOBILE FIDELITY					
❑ 1-091	Kenton Plays Wagner	1982	6.25	12.50	25.00
-- Audiophile vinyl					

KENTON, STAN, AND TEX RITTER
Also see each artist's individual listings.
CAPITOL

Number	Title	Yr	VG	VG+	NM
❑ ST 1757 [S]	Stan Kenton/Tex Ritter	1962	20.00	40.00	80.00
❑ T 1757 [M]	Stan Kenton/Tex Ritter	1962	15.00	30.00	60.00

KENTUCKY COLONELS, THE
BRIAR

Number	Title	Yr	VG	VG+	NM
❑ 109	The New Sounds of Bluegrass America	1976	10.00	20.00	40.00
❑ BT-7202	Livin' in the Past	1975	7.50	15.00	30.00
WORLD PACIFIC					
❑ ST 1821 [S]	Appalachian Swing	1964	15.00	30.00	60.00
❑ T 1821 [M]	Appalachian Swing	1964	12.50	25.00	50.00

KEROUAC, JACK
DOT

Number	Title	Yr	VG	VG+	NM
❑ DLP-3154 [M]	Poetry for the Beat Generation	1959	250.00	500.00	1,000.
-- Acknowledged to be extremely rare; the same performance is on Hanover 5000					
HANOVER					
❑ HML-5000 [M]	Poetry for the Beat Generation	1959	62.50	125.00	250.00
-- STEVE ALLEN plays piano behind Kerouac on this album					
❑ HML-5006 [M]	Blues and Haikus	1959	62.50	125.00	250.00
RHINO					
❑ R1-70939 [(4)]	The Jack Kerouac Collection	1990	15.00	30.00	60.00
-- Box set compiling the Hanover and Verve LPs plus an LP of unreleased material					
VERVE					
❑ MGV-15005 [M]	Readings on the Beat Generation	1960	62.50	125.00	250.00

KERR, ANITA, SINGERS
DECCA

Number	Title	Yr	VG	VG+	NM
❑ DL 74061 [S]	For You, For Me, Forevermore	1960	5.00	10.00	20.00

KERSHAW, RUSTY AND DOUG
HICKORY

Number	Title	Yr	VG	VG+	NM
❑ LPM-103 [M]	Rusty and Doug Sing Louisiana Man	1960	30.00	60.00	120.00
HICKORY/MGM					
❑ H3G-4506	Louisiana Man	1974	5.00	10.00	20.00

KESEY, KEN
SOUND CITY

Number	Title	Yr	VG	VG+	NM
❑ 27690 [M]	The Acid Test	1967	75.00	150.00	300.00
-- THE GRATEFUL DEAD appear on this LP					

KESNER, DICK
BRUNSWICK

Number	Title	Yr	VG	VG+	NM
❑ BL 54044 [M]	Lawrence Welk Presents Dick Kesner	1958	5.00	10.00	20.00
❑ BL 754044 [S]	Lawrence Welk Presents Dick Kesner	1959	6.25	12.50	25.00
❑ BL 754051 [S]	Dick Kesner and His Magic Stradivarius	1959	5.00	10.00	20.00
❑ BL 754054 [S]	Intermezzo	1960	5.00	10.00	20.00

KEYMEN, THE
ABC-PARAMOUNT

Number	Title	Yr	VG	VG+	NM
❑ 258 [M]	Dance with Dick Clark	1958	7.50	15.00	30.00
❑ S-258 [S]	Dance with Dick Clark	1958	12.50	25.00	50.00
❑ 288 [M]	Dance with Dick Clark, Volume 2	1959	7.50	15.00	30.00
❑ S-288 [S]	Dance with Dick Clark, Volume 2	1959	12.50	25.00	50.00
CORAL					
❑ CRL 57112 [M]	Vocal Sounds of the Keymen	1957	7.50	15.00	30.00
GOLDUST					
❑ LPS-153 [M]	The Keymen Live	196?	12.50	25.00	50.00

KHAZAD DOOM
LPL

Number	Title	Yr	VG	VG+	NM
❑ 892	Level 6 1/2	1970	250.00	500.00	1,000.

KICKSTANDS, THE
CAPITOL

Number	Title	Yr	VG	VG+	NM
❑ ST 2078 [S]	Black Boots and Bikes	1964	37.50	75.00	150.00
❑ T 2078 [M]	Black Boots and Bikes	1964	30.00	60.00	120.00
❑ T/ST 2078	Black Boots and Bikes Bonus Fold-Out	1964	12.50	25.00	50.00

KILGORE, MERLE
STARDAY

Number	Title	Yr	VG	VG+	NM
❑ SLP-251 [M]	There's Gold in Them Thar Hills	1963	7.50	15.00	30.00

KILLING FLOOR
SIRE

Number	Title	Yr	VG	VG+	NM
❑ SES-97019	Killing Floor	1970	12.50	25.00	50.00

KINCAID, BRADLEY
VARSITY

Number	Title	Yr	VG	VG+	NM
❑ 34 [M]	Bradley Kincaid Sings American Ballads and Folk Songs	1957	10.00	20.00	40.00
❑ 6988 [10]	American Ballads	1955	15.00	30.00	60.00

KINES, TOM
ELEKTRA

Number	Title	Yr	VG	VG+	NM
❑ EKL-137 [M]	Of Maids and Mistresses	1958	7.50	15.00	30.00

KING CRIMSON

Number	Title	Yr	VG	VG+	NM
ATLANTIC					
❏ SD 7212	Islands	1972	5.00	10.00	20.00
❏ SD 7263	Larks' Tongues in Aspic	1973	5.00	10.00	20.00
❏ SD 7298	Starless and Bible Black	1974	5.00	10.00	20.00
❏ SD 8245	In the Court of the Crimson King -- An Observation by King Crimson	1969	5.00	10.00	20.00
❏ SD 8266	In the Wake of Poseidon	1970	5.00	10.00	20.00
❏ SD 8278	Lizard	1971	5.00	10.00	20.00
MOBILE FIDELITY					
❏ 1-075	In the Court of the Crimson King -- An Observation by King Crimson	1981	20.00	40.00	80.00
-- Audiophile vinyl					
WARNER BROS.					
❏ WBMS-119 [DJ]	The Return of King Crimson	1981	15.00	30.00	60.00
-- Promo-only interview and music show					

KING CURTIS

Number	Title	Yr	VG	VG+	NM
ATCO					
❏ 33-113 [M]	Have Tenor Sax, Will Blow	1959	10.00	20.00	40.00
❏ SD 33-113 [S]	Have Tenor Sax, Will Blow	1959	15.00	30.00	60.00
❏ 33-189 [M]	That Lovin' Feeling	1966	5.00	10.00	20.00
❏ SD 33-189 [S]	That Lovin' Feeling	1966	6.25	12.50	25.00
❏ 33-198 [M]	Live at Small's Paradise	1966	5.00	10.00	20.00
❏ SD 33-198 [S]	Live at Small's Paradise	1966	6.25	12.50	25.00
❏ 33-211 [M]	The Great Memphis Hits	1967	5.00	10.00	20.00
❏ SD 33-211 [S]	The Great Memphis Hits	1967	6.25	12.50	25.00
❏ 33-231 [M]	King Size Soul	1967	6.25	12.50	25.00
❏ SD 33-231 [S]	King Size Soul	1967	5.00	10.00	20.00
❏ 33-247 [M]	Sweet Soul	1968	7.50	15.00	30.00
❏ SD 33-247 [S]	Sweet Soul	1968	5.00	10.00	20.00
❏ SD 33-266	The Best of King Curtis	1968	5.00	10.00	20.00
❏ SD 33-293	Instant Groove	1969	5.00	10.00	20.00
❏ SD 33-338	Get Ready	1970	5.00	10.00	20.00
❏ SD 33-359	Live at Fillmore West	1971	5.00	10.00	20.00
❏ SD 33-385	Everybody's Talkin'	1972	5.00	10.00	20.00
CAPITOL					
❏ ST 1756 [S]	Country Soul	1963	10.00	20.00	40.00
❏ T 1756 [M]	Country Soul	1963	7.50	15.00	30.00
❏ ST 2095 [S]	Soul Serenade	1964	7.50	15.00	30.00
❏ T 2095 [M]	Soul Serenade	1964	6.25	12.50	25.00
❏ ST 2341 [S]	King Curtis Plays the Hits Made Famous by Sam Cooke	1965	7.50	15.00	30.00
❏ T 2341 [M]	King Curtis Plays the Hits Made Famous by Sam Cooke	1965	6.25	12.50	25.00
❏ ST 2858	The Best of King Curtis	1968	6.25	12.50	25.00
CLARION					
❏ 615 [M]	The Great "K" Curtis	1966	5.00	10.00	20.00
❏ SD 615 [S]	The Great "K" Curtis	1966	6.25	12.50	25.00
ENJOY					
❏ ENLP-2001 [M]	Soul Twist	1962	12.50	25.00	50.00
EVEREST					
❏ SDBR-1121 [S]	Azure	1961	18.75	37.50	75.00
❏ LPBR-5121 [M]	Azure	1961	12.50	25.00	50.00
NEW JAZZ					
❏ NJLP-8237 [M]	The New Scene of King Curtis	1960	15.00	30.00	60.00
-- Purple label					
❏ NJLP-8237 [M]	The New Scene of King Curtis	1965	7.50	15.00	30.00
-- Blue label with trident logo on right					
PRESTIGE					
❏ PRLP-7222 [M]	Soul Meeting	1962	12.50	25.00	50.00
❏ PRST-7222 [S]	Soul Meeting	1962	18.75	37.50	75.00
RCA VICTOR					
❏ LPM-2492 [M]	Arthur Murray's Music for Dancing: The Twist!	1962	6.25	12.50	25.00
❏ LSP-2492 [S]	Arthur Murray's Music for Dancing: The Twist!	1962	7.50	15.00	30.00
TRU-SOUND					
❏ TS-15001 [M]	Trouble in Mind	1961	12.50	25.00	50.00
❏ TS-15008 [M]	It's Party Time	1962	12.50	25.00	50.00
❏ TS-15009 [M]	Doin' the Dixie Twist	1962	12.50	25.00	50.00

KING FLOYD

Number	Title	Yr	VG	VG+	NM
PULSAR					
❏ 10602	A Man in Love	1969	5.00	10.00	20.00
V.I.P.					
❏ 407	The Heart of the Matter	1970	10.00	20.00	40.00

KING PINS, THE

Number	Title	Yr	VG	VG+	NM
KING					
❏ 865 [M]	It Won't Be This Way Always	1963	75.00	150.00	300.00

KING PLEASURE

Number	Title	Yr	VG	VG+	NM
HIFI					
❏ R-425 [M]	Golden Days	1960	10.00	20.00	40.00
❏ RS-425 [S]	Golden Days	1960	12.50	25.00	50.00
PRESTIGE					
❏ PRLP-208 [10]	King Pleasure Sings	1955	50.00	100.00	200.00
❏ PRLP-7128 [M]	King Pleasure Sings	1957	25.00	50.00	100.00
-- Reissue of 208, with four added tracks by Annie Ross					
UNITED ARTISTS					
❏ UAJ-14031 [M]	Mr. Jazz	1962	10.00	20.00	40.00
❏ UAJS-15031 [S]	Mr. Jazz	1962	12.50	25.00	50.00

KING SISTERS, THE

Number	Title	Yr	VG	VG+	NM
CAPITOL					
❏ T 808 [M]	Aloha	1957	6.25	12.50	25.00
-- Turquoise or gray label					
❏ T 919 [M]	Imagination	1958	6.25	12.50	25.00
-- Turquoise or gray label					
❏ ST 1205 [S]	Warm and Wonderful	1959	7.50	15.00	30.00
-- Black colorband label, logo at left					
❏ T 1205 [M]	Warm and Wonderful	1959	5.00	10.00	20.00
-- Black colorband label, logo at left					

KING, ALBERT

Number	Title	Yr	VG	VG+	NM
ATLANTIC					
❏ SD 8213	King of the Blues Guitar	1969	6.25	12.50	25.00
KING					
❏ 852 [M]	Big Blues	1963	125.00	250.00	500.00
❏ KS-1060	Travelin' to California	1969	6.25	12.50	25.00
STAX					
❏ ST-723 [M]	Born Under a Bad Sign	1967	20.00	40.00	80.00
❏ STS-723 [S]	Born Under a Bad Sign	1967	30.00	60.00	120.00
❏ STS-2003	Live Wire/Blues Power	1968	12.50	25.00	50.00
❏ STS-2010	Years Gone By	1969	6.25	12.50	25.00
❏ STS-2015	King Does the King's Thing	1969	6.25	12.50	25.00
❏ STS-2040	Lovejoy	1971	5.00	10.00	20.00
❏ STS-3009	I'll Play the Blues for You	1972	5.00	10.00	20.00

KING, ALBERT/OTIS RUSH

Also see each artist's individual listings.

Number	Title	Yr	VG	VG+	NM
CHESS					
❏ LPS 1538	Door to Door	1969	6.25	12.50	25.00

KING, ALBERT/STEVE CROPPER/POP STAPLES

Number	Title	Yr	VG	VG+	NM
STAX					
❏ STS-2020	Jammed Together	1969	6.25	12.50	25.00

KING, ANNA

Number	Title	Yr	VG	VG+	NM
SMASH					
❏ MGS-27059 [M]	Back to Soul	1964	25.00	50.00	100.00
❏ SRS-67059 [S]	Back to Soul	1964	30.00	60.00	120.00

KING, B.B.

Number	Title	Yr	VG	VG+	NM
ABC-PARAMOUNT					
❏ 456 [M]	Mr. Blues	1963	7.50	15.00	30.00
❏ S-456 [S]	Mr. Blues	1963	10.00	20.00	40.00
❏ 509 [M]	Live at the Regal	1965	10.00	20.00	40.00
❏ S-509 [S]	Live at the Regal	1965	12.50	25.00	50.00
❏ 528 [M]	Confessin' the Blues	1965	7.50	15.00	30.00
❏ S-528 [S]	Confessin' the Blues	1965	10.00	20.00	40.00
BLUESWAY					
❏ BL-6001 [M]	Blues Is King	1967	10.00	20.00	40.00
❏ BLS-6001 [S]	Blues Is King	1967	6.25	12.50	25.00
❏ BLS-6011	Blues on Top of Blues	1968	6.25	12.50	25.00
❏ BLS-6016	Lucille	1968	6.25	12.50	25.00
❏ BLS-6022	His Best/The Electric B.B. King	1969	5.00	10.00	20.00
❏ BLS-6031	Live and Well	1969	5.00	10.00	20.00
❏ BLS-6037	Completely Well	1969	5.00	10.00	20.00
❏ BLS-6050	Back in the Alley	1970	5.00	10.00	20.00
CROWN					
❏ CST-147 [R]	B.B. King Wails	1960	25.00	50.00	100.00
-- Red vinyl					
❏ CST-152 [R]	B.B. King Sings Spirituals	1960	25.00	50.00	100.00
-- Red vinyl					
❏ CST-195 [R]	King of the Blues	1961	25.00	50.00	100.00
-- Red vinyl					
❏ CLP-5020 [M]	Singin' the Blues	1957	25.00	50.00	100.00
-- Black label, silver "Crown"					
❏ CLP-5020 [M]	Singin' the Blues	1963	5.00	10.00	20.00
-- Gray label, black "Crown"					
❏ CLP-5063 [M]	The Blues	1958	20.00	40.00	80.00
-- Black label, silver "Crown"					

Number	Title	Yr	VG	VG+	NM
❑ CLP-5063 [M] The Blues		1963	5.00	10.00	20.00
-- Gray label, black "Crown"					
❑ CLP-5115 [M] B.B. King Wails		1959	20.00	40.00	80.00
-- Black label, silver "Crown"					
❑ CLP-5115 [M] B.B. King Wails		1963	5.00	10.00	20.00
-- Gray label, black "Crown"					
❑ CLP-5119 [M] B.B. King Sings Spirituals		1960	15.00	30.00	60.00
-- Gray label, black "Crown"					
❑ CLP-5143 [M] The Great B.B. King		1961	15.00	30.00	60.00
-- Gray label, black "Crown"					
❑ CLP-5167 [M] King of the Blues		1961	15.00	30.00	60.00
-- Gray label, black "Crown"					
❑ CLP-5188 [M] My Kind of Blues		1961	15.00	30.00	60.00
-- Gray label, black "Crown"					
❑ CLP-5230 [M] More B.B. King		1962	15.00	30.00	60.00
-- Gray label, black "Crown"					
❑ CLP-5248 [M] Twist with B.B. King		1962	15.00	30.00	60.00
-- Gray label, black "Crown"					
❑ CLP-5286 [M] Easy Listening Blues		1962	15.00	30.00	60.00
-- Gray label, black "Crown"					
❑ CLP-5309 [M] Blues in My Heart		1963	10.00	20.00	40.00
-- Gray label, black "Crown"					
❑ CLP-5359 [M] B.B. King		1963	10.00	20.00	40.00
-- Gray label, black "Crown"					

CRUSADERS

❑ 16013 Live in London		1982	6.25	12.50	25.00
-- Part of MCA's "Audiophile Series"					

DIRECT DISK

❑ SD-16616 Midnight Believer		1980	12.50	25.00	50.00
-- Audiophile vinyl					

GALAXY

❑ 202 [M] 16 Greatest Hits		1963	15.00	30.00	60.00
❑ 8202 [S] 16 Greatest Hits		1963	20.00	40.00	80.00

KENT

❑ KST-533 [(2)] From the Beginning		1969	5.00	10.00	20.00
❑ KLP-5012 [M] Rock Me Baby		1964	5.00	10.00	20.00
❑ KLP-5013 [M] Let Me Love You		1965	5.00	10.00	20.00
❑ KLP-5015 [M] B.B. King Live on Stage		1965	5.00	10.00	20.00
❑ KLP-5016 [M] The Soul of B.B. King		1966	5.00	10.00	20.00
❑ KLP-5017 [M] Pure Soul		1966	5.00	10.00	20.00
❑ KLP-5021 [M] The Jungle		1967	5.00	10.00	20.00
❑ KLP-5029 [M] Boss of the Blues		1968	5.00	10.00	20.00

MOBILE FIDELITY

❑ 1-235 Lucille		1995	6.25	12.50	25.00
-- Audiophile vinyl					

KING, BEN E.
Also see THE DRIFTERS.

ATCO

❑ 33-133 [M] Spanish Harlem		1961	25.00	50.00	100.00
-- Yellow label with harp					
❑ 33-133 [M] Spanish Harlem		1962	10.00	20.00	40.00
-- Gold and gray label					
❑ SD 33-133 [S] Spanish Harlem		1961	37.50	75.00	150.00
-- Yellow label with harp					
❑ SD 33-133 [S] Spanish Harlem		1962	12.50	25.00	50.00
-- Purple and brown label					
❑ 33-137 [M] Ben E. King Sings for Soulful Lovers		1962	10.00	20.00	40.00
❑ SD 33-137 [S] Ben E. King Sings for Soulful Lovers		1962	15.00	30.00	60.00
❑ 33-142 [M] Don't Play That Song		1962	10.00	20.00	40.00
❑ SD 33-142 [S] Don't Play That Song		1962	15.00	30.00	60.00
❑ 33-165 [M] Ben E. King's Greatest Hits		1964	7.50	15.00	30.00
❑ SD 33-165 [S] Ben E. King's Greatest Hits		1964	10.00	20.00	40.00
-- Purple and brown label					
❑ 33-174 [M] Seven Letters		1965	10.00	20.00	40.00
❑ SD 33-174 [S] Seven Letters		1965	12.50	25.00	50.00

CLARION

❑ 606 [M] Young Boy Blues		1966	6.25	12.50	25.00
❑ SD 606 [S] Young Boy Blues		1966	7.50	15.00	30.00

MANDALA

❑ MLP-3008 [DJ] Audio Biography		1972	7.50	15.00	30.00
-- Promo-only interview by Richard Robinson					

MAXWELL

❑ 88001 Rough Edges		1969	5.00	10.00	20.00

KING, CAROLE
Also see THE CITY.

ODE

❑ HE 44946 Tapestry		1980	12.50	25.00	50.00
-- Half-speed mastered edition					
❑ SQ-88013 [Q] Music		1974	5.00	10.00	20.00

KING, CLAUDE

COLUMBIA

❑ CL 1810 [M] Meet Claude King		1962	6.25	12.50	25.00
-- Six "eye" logos on label					
❑ CL 2415 [M] Tiger Woman		1965	5.00	10.00	20.00
❑ CS 8610 [S] Meet Claude King		1962	10.00	20.00	40.00
-- Six "eye" logos on label					
❑ CS 8610 [S] Meet Claude King		1963	5.00	10.00	20.00
-- "360 Sound Stereo" on red label					
❑ CS 9215 [S] Tiger Woman		1965	6.25	12.50	25.00
-- "360 Sound Stereo" on red label					

KING, FREDDIE

COTILLION

❑ SD 9004 Freddie King Is a Blues Master		1969	6.25	12.50	25.00
❑ SD 9016 My Feeling for the Blues		1970	6.25	12.50	25.00

KING

❑ 762 [M] Freddie King Sings the Blues		1961	62.50	125.00	250.00
❑ 773 [M] Let's Hide Away and Dance Away		1961	62.50	125.00	250.00
❑ 821 [M] Bossa Nova and Blues		1962	37.50	75.00	150.00
❑ 856 [M] Freddie King Goes Surfin'		1963	20.00	40.00	80.00
❑ KS-856 [S] Freddie King Goes Surfin'		1963	30.00	60.00	120.00
❑ 928 [M] A Bonanza of Instrumentals		1965	12.50	25.00	50.00
❑ KS-928 [S] A Bonanza of Instrumentals		1965	15.00	30.00	60.00
❑ 964 [M] 24 Vocals and Instrumentals		1966	6.25	12.50	25.00

KING, FREDDIE/LULA REED/BOBBY THOMPSON

KING

❑ 777 [M] Boy-Girl-Boy		1962	62.50	125.00	250.00

KING, JEAN

HANNA-BARBERA

❑ HLP-8505 [M] Jean King Sings for the In Crowd		1966	5.00	10.00	20.00

KING, JONATHAN

PARROT

❑ PA 61013 [M] Jonathan King Or Then Again....		1967	10.00	20.00	40.00
❑ PAS 71013 [P] Jonathan King Or Then Again....		1967	12.50	25.00	50.00
-- Only "Where the Sun Has Never Shown" is rechanneled.					

U.K.

❑ 53101 Bubble Rock Is Here to Stay		1972	6.25	12.50	25.00
❑ 53104 Pandora's Box		1973	6.25	12.50	25.00

KING, MORGANA

ASCOT

❑ AM 13014 [M] The Winter of My Discontent		1964	6.25	12.50	25.00
❑ AM 13019 [M] The End of a Love Affair		1965	6.25	12.50	25.00
-- Reissue of United Artists 30020					
❑ AM 13020 [M] Everybody Loves Saturday Night		1965	6.25	12.50	25.00
❑ AM 13025 [M] More Morgana		1965	6.25	12.50	25.00
❑ AS 16014 [S] The Winter of My Discontent		1964	7.50	15.00	30.00
❑ AS 16019 [S] The End of a Love Affair		1965	7.50	15.00	30.00
-- Reissue of United Artists 40020					
❑ AS 16020 [S] Everybody Loves Saturday Night		1965	7.50	15.00	30.00
❑ AS 16025 [S] More Morgana		1965	7.50	15.00	30.00

EMARCY

❑ MG-36079 [M] For You, For Me, Forever More		1956	20.00	40.00	80.00

MAINSTREAM

❑ S-6015 [S] With a Taste of Honey		1964	6.25	12.50	25.00
❑ S-6052 [S] Miss Morgana King		1965	6.25	12.50	25.00
❑ 56015 [M] With a Taste of Honey		1964	5.00	10.00	20.00
❑ 56052 [M] Miss Morgana King		1965	5.00	10.00	20.00

MERCURY

❑ MG-20231 [M] Morgana King Sings the Blues		1958	20.00	40.00	80.00

RCA CAMDEN

❑ CAL-543 [M] The Greatest Songs Ever Swung		1959	5.00	10.00	20.00
❑ CAS-543 [S] The Greatest Songs Ever Swung		1959	7.50	15.00	30.00

REPRISE

❑ PS 6257 [S] Gemini Changes		1967	6.25	12.50	25.00
❑ R 6192 [M] It's a Quiet Thing		1966	5.00	10.00	20.00
❑ RS 6192 [S] It's a Quiet Thing		1966	6.25	12.50	25.00
❑ R 6205 [M] Wild Is Love		1966	5.00	10.00	20.00
❑ RS 6205 [S] Wild Is Love		1966	6.25	12.50	25.00
❑ R 6257 [M] Gemini Changes		1967	5.00	10.00	20.00

UNITED ARTISTS

❑ UAL 3028 [M] Folk Songs A La King		1960	10.00	20.00	40.00
❑ UAS 6028 [S] Folk Songs A La King		1960	12.50	25.00	50.00
❑ UAL 30020 [M] Let Me Love You		1960	12.50	25.00	50.00
❑ UAS 40020 [M] Let Me Love You		1960	15.00	30.00	60.00

VERVE

❑ V-5061 [M] I Know How It Feels		1968	6.25	12.50	25.00
❑ V6-5061 [S] I Know How It Feels		1968	6.25	12.50	25.00

WING

❑ SRW-16307 [S] More Morgana King		1965	5.00	10.00	20.00

Number	Title	Yr	VG	VG+	NM

KING, PEE WEE
BRIAR
| ❏ 102 | Golden Olde Tyme Dances | 1975 | 15.00 | 30.00 | 60.00 |
LONGHORN
| ❏ 1236 [M] | The Legendary Pee Wee King | 1967 | 6.25 | 12.50 | 25.00 |
RCA CAMDEN
| ❏ CAL-876 [M] | Country Barn Dance | 1965 | 5.00 | 10.00 | 20.00 |
RCA VICTOR
❏ LPM-1237 [M]	Swing West	1956	10.00	20.00	40.00
❏ LPM-3028 [10]	Pee Wee King	195?	20.00	40.00	80.00
❏ LPM-3071 [10]	Western Hits	195?	20.00	40.00	80.00
❏ LPM-3109 [10]	Waltzes	195?	20.00	40.00	80.00
❏ LPM-3280 [10]	Swing West	195?	20.00	40.00	80.00
STARDAY
| ❏ SLP-284 [M] | Back Again with the Songs That Made Them Famous | 1964 | 7.50 | 15.00 | 30.00 |

KING, PEGGY
COLUMBIA
| ❏ CL 2549 [10] | Wish Upon a Star | 1955 | 12.50 | 25.00 | 50.00 |
IMPERIAL
| ❏ LP-9078 [M] | Lazy Afternoon | 1959 | 5.00 | 10.00 | 20.00 |
| ❏ LP-12026 [S] | Lazy Afternoon | 1959 | 7.50 | 15.00 | 30.00 |

KING, REV. MARTIN LUTHER
BUDDAH
| ❏ BDS-2002 | Man of Love | 1968 | 5.00 | 10.00 | 20.00 |
CREED
| ❏ 3201 [M] | I Have a Dream | 1968 | 5.00 | 10.00 | 20.00 |
DOOTO
| ❏ DTL-831 [M] | Martin Luther King at Zion Hill | 1962 | 7.50 | 15.00 | 30.00 |
| ❏ DTL-841 | The American Dream | 1968 | 5.00 | 10.00 | 20.00 |
GORDY
| ❏ G-906 [M] | The Great March to Freedom | 1963 | 10.00 | 20.00 | 40.00 |
-- "Gordy" in script at top of label
| ❏ G-908 [M] | The Great March on Washington | 1963 | 10.00 | 20.00 | 40.00 |
-- "Gordy" in script at top of label
| ❏ G-929 | ...Free at Last | 1968 | 7.50 | 15.00 | 30.00 |
-- Original with gatefold cover
MERCURY
| ❏ SR-61170 | In Search of Freedom | 1968 | 5.00 | 10.00 | 20.00 |
MR. MAESTRO
| ❏ 1000 [M] | The March on Washington | 1963 | 7.50 | 15.00 | 30.00 |
20TH CENTURY
| ❏ TCF-3110 [M] | Freedom March on Washington | 1963 | 7.50 | 15.00 | 30.00 |
| ❏ S-3201 | The Rev. Dr. Martin Luther King, Jr. | 1968 | 5.00 | 10.00 | 20.00 |
UNART
| ❏ S 21033 | In the Struggle for Freedom and Human Dignity | 1968 | 5.00 | 10.00 | 20.00 |

KING, TEDDI
CORAL
| ❏ CRL 57278 [M] | All the King's Songs | 1959 | 15.00 | 30.00 | 60.00 |
| ❏ CRL 757278 [S] | All the King's Songs | 1959 | 20.00 | 40.00 | 80.00 |
RCA VICTOR
❏ LPM-1147 [M]	Bidin' My Time	1956	20.00	40.00	80.00
❏ LPM-1313 [M]	To You from Teddi King	1957	20.00	40.00	80.00
❏ LPM-1454 [M]	A Girl and Her Songs	1957	20.00	40.00	80.00
STORYVILLE
❏ STLP-302 [10]	'Round Midnight	1954	50.00	100.00	200.00
❏ STLP-314 [10]	Storyville Presents Teddi King	1954	50.00	100.00	200.00
❏ STLP-903 [M]	Now In Vogue	1956	30.00	60.00	120.00

KINGDOM
SPECIALTY
| ❏ SPS-2135 | Kingdom | 1970 | 15.00 | 30.00 | 60.00 |

KINGFISH
With Bob Weir of THE GRATEFUL DEAD.
ROUND
| ❏ RX-108 | Kingfish | 1976 | 6.25 | 12.50 | 25.00 |

KINGS, THE
ELEKTRA
| ❏ 6E-277 | The Kings Are Here | 1980 | 7.50 | 15.00 | 30.00 |

KINGSLEY, GERSHON
Also see PERREY-KINGSLEY.
AUDIO FIDELITY
| ❏ AFSD-6222 | Music to Moog By | 1969 | 10.00 | 20.00 | 40.00 |

KINGSMEN, THE
WAND
❏ WD-657 [M]	The Kingsmen In Person	1964	7.50	15.00	30.00
❏ WDS-657 [P]	The Kingsmen In Person	1964	10.00	20.00	40.00
❏ WD-659 [M]	The Kingsmen, Volume II	1964	7.50	15.00	30.00
-- With "Death of an Angel"
| ❏ WD-659 [M] | The Kingsmen, Volume II | 1964 | 10.00 | 20.00 | 40.00 |
-- Without "Death of an Angel" (replaced by untitled instrumental)
| ❏ WDS-659 [S] | The Kingsmen, Volume II | 1964 | 10.00 | 20.00 | 40.00 |
-- With "Death of an Angel"
| ❏ WDS-659 [S] | The Kingsmen, Volume II | 1964 | 12.50 | 25.00 | 50.00 |
-- Without "Death of an Angel" (replaced by untitled instrumental)
❏ WD-662 [M]	The Kingsmen, Volume 3	1965	6.25	12.50	25.00
❏ WDS-662 [S]	The Kingsmen, Volume 3	1965	7.50	15.00	30.00
❏ WD-670 [M]	The Kingsmen On Campus	1965	6.25	12.50	25.00
❏ WDS-670 [S]	The Kingsmen On Campus	1965	7.50	15.00	30.00
❏ WD-674 [M]	15 Great Hits	1966	5.00	10.00	20.00
❏ WDS-674 [P]	15 Great Hits	1966	6.25	12.50	25.00
❏ WD-675 [M]	Up and Away	1966	5.00	10.00	20.00
❏ WDS-675 [S]	Up and Away	1966	6.25	12.50	25.00
❏ WDS-681 [S]	The Kingsmen's Greatest Hits	1967	5.00	10.00	20.00
❏ ST-91011 [S]	Up and Away	1966	7.50	15.00	30.00
-- Capitol Record Club edition

KINGSTON TRIO, THE
Also see DAVE GUARD AND THE WHISKEYHILL SINGERS; JOHN STEWART.
CAPITOL
| ❏ STBB-513 [(2)] | Tom Dooley/Scarlet Ribbons | 1970 | 5.00 | 10.00 | 20.00 |
| ❏ T 996 [M] | The Kingston Trio | 1958 | 12.50 | 25.00 | 50.00 |
-- Turquoise label
| ❏ T 996 [M] | The Kingston Trio | 1958 | 10.00 | 20.00 | 40.00 |
-- Black label with colorband, Capitol logo at left
| ❏ T 996 [M] | The Kingston Trio | 1962 | 5.00 | 10.00 | 20.00 |
-- Black label with colorband, Capitol logo at top
| ❏ T 1107 [M] | From the Hungry I | 1959 | 10.00 | 20.00 | 40.00 |
-- Black label with colorband, Capitol logo at left
| ❏ T 1107 [M] | From the Hungry I | 1962 | 5.00 | 10.00 | 20.00 |
-- Black label with colorband, Capitol logo at top
| ❏ ST 1183 [S] | Stereo Concert | 1959 | 12.50 | 25.00 | 50.00 |
-- Black label with colorband, Capitol logo at left
| ❏ ST 1183 [S] | Stereo Concert | 1962 | 6.25 | 12.50 | 25.00 |
-- Black label with colorband, Capitol logo at top
| ❏ ST 1199 [S] | The Kingston Trio at Large | 1959 | 10.00 | 20.00 | 40.00 |
-- Black label with colorband, Capitol logo at left
| ❏ ST 1199 [S] | The Kingston Trio at Large | 1962 | 5.00 | 10.00 | 20.00 |
-- Black label with colorband, Capitol logo at top
| ❏ T 1199 [M] | The Kingston Trio at Large | 1959 | 7.50 | 15.00 | 30.00 |
-- Black label with colorband, Capitol logo at left
| ❏ ST 1258 [S] | Here We Go Again! | 1959 | 10.00 | 20.00 | 40.00 |
-- Black label with colorband, Capitol logo at left
| ❏ ST 1258 [S] | Here We Go Again! | 1962 | 5.00 | 10.00 | 20.00 |
-- Black label with colorband, Capitol logo at top
| ❏ T 1258 [M] | Here We Go Again! | 1959 | 7.50 | 15.00 | 30.00 |
-- Black label with colorband, Capitol logo at left
| ❏ ST 1352 [S] | Sold Out | 1960 | 10.00 | 20.00 | 40.00 |
-- Black label with colorband, Capitol logo at left
| ❏ ST 1352 [S] | Sold Out | 1962 | 5.00 | 10.00 | 20.00 |
-- Black label with colorband, Capitol logo at top
| ❏ T 1352 [M] | Sold Out | 1960 | 7.50 | 15.00 | 30.00 |
-- Black label with colorband, Capitol logo at left
| ❏ ST 1407 [S] | String Along | 1960 | 10.00 | 20.00 | 40.00 |
-- Black label with colorband, Capitol logo at left
| ❏ ST 1407 [S] | String Along | 1962 | 5.00 | 10.00 | 20.00 |
-- Black label with colorband, Capitol logo at top
| ❏ T 1407 [M] | String Along | 1960 | 7.50 | 15.00 | 30.00 |
-- Black label with colorband, Capitol logo at left
❏ ST 1446 [S]	The Last Month of the Year	1960	10.00	20.00	40.00
❏ T 1446 [M]	The Last Month of the Year	1960	7.50	15.00	30.00
❏ ST 1474 [S]	Make Way!	1961	10.00	20.00	40.00
-- Black label with colorband, Capitol logo at left
| ❏ ST 1474 [S] | Make Way! | 1962 | 5.00 | 10.00 | 20.00 |
-- Black label with colorband, Capitol logo at top
| ❏ T 1474 [M] | Make Way! | 1961 | 7.50 | 15.00 | 30.00 |
-- Black label with colorband, Capitol logo at left
| ❏ ST 1564 [S] | Goin' Places | 1961 | 10.00 | 20.00 | 40.00 |
-- Black label with colorband, Capitol logo at left
| ❏ ST 1564 [S] | Goin' Places | 1962 | 5.00 | 10.00 | 20.00 |
-- Black label with colorband, Capitol logo at top
| ❏ T 1564 [M] | Goin' Places | 1961 | 7.50 | 15.00 | 30.00 |
-- Black label with colorband, Capitol logo at left
| ❏ DT 1612 [R] | Encores | 1961 | 5.00 | 10.00 | 20.00 |
-- Black label with colorband, Capitol logo at left
| ❏ T 1612 [M] | Encores | 1961 | 7.50 | 15.00 | 30.00 |
-- Black label with colorband, Capitol logo at left
| ❏ ST 1642 [S] | Close-Up | 1961 | 10.00 | 20.00 | 40.00 |
-- Black label with colorband, Capitol logo at left
| ❏ ST 1642 [S] | Close-Up | 1962 | 5.00 | 10.00 | 20.00 |
-- Black label with colorband, Capitol logo at top
| ❏ T 1642 [M] | Close-Up | 1961 | 7.50 | 15.00 | 30.00 |
-- Black label with colorband, Capitol logo at left

Number	Title	Yr	VG	VG+	NM
❑ ST 1658 [S]	College Concert	1962	6.25	12.50	25.00
❑ T 1658 [M]	College Concert	1962	5.00	10.00	20.00
❑ ST 1705 [P]	The Best of the Kingston Trio	1962	5.00	10.00	20.00
❑ T 1705 [M]	The Best of the Kingston Trio	1962	5.00	10.00	20.00
❑ ST 1747 [S]	Something Special	1962	6.25	12.50	25.00
❑ T 1747 [M]	Something Special	1962	5.00	10.00	20.00
❑ ST 1809 [S]	New Frontier	1962	6.25	12.50	25.00
❑ T 1809 [M]	New Frontier	1962	5.00	10.00	20.00
-- Box set with booklet					
❑ ST 1871 [S]	The Kingston Trio #16	1963	6.25	12.50	25.00
❑ T 1871 [M]	The Kingston Trio #16	1963	5.00	10.00	20.00
❑ ST 1935 [S]	Sunny Side!	1963	6.25	12.50	25.00
❑ T 1935 [M]	Sunny Side!	1963	5.00	10.00	20.00
❑ KAO 2005 [M]	Sing a Song with the Kingston Trio	1963	6.25	12.50	25.00
❑ SKAO 2005 [S]	Sing a Song with the Kingston Trio	1963	7.50	15.00	30.00
❑ ST 2011 [S]	Time to Think	1964	5.00	10.00	20.00
❑ ST 2081 [S]	Back in Town	1964	5.00	10.00	20.00
❑ STCL 2180 [(3) S]	The Folk Era	1964	12.50	25.00	50.00
-- Box set with booklet					
❑ TCL 2180 [(3) M]	The Folk Era	1964	10.00	20.00	40.00
❑ ST 2280 [S]	The Best of the Kingston Trio, Volume 2	1965	5.00	10.00	20.00
❑ ST 2614 [S]	The Best of the Kingston Trio, Volume 3	1966	5.00	10.00	20.00

DECCA

Number	Title	Yr	VG	VG+	NM
❑ DL 4613 [M]	The Kingston Trio (Nick-Bob-John)	1965	6.25	12.50	25.00
❑ DL 4656 [M]	Stay Awhile	1965	6.25	12.50	25.00
❑ DL 4694 [M]	Somethin' Else	1965	6.25	12.50	25.00
❑ DL 4758 [M]	Children of the Morning	1966	6.25	12.50	25.00
❑ DL 74613 [S]	The Kingston Trio (Nick-Bob-John)	1965	7.50	15.00	30.00
❑ DL 74656 [S]	Stay Awhile	1965	7.50	15.00	30.00
❑ DL 74694 [S]	Somethin' Else	1965	7.50	15.00	30.00
❑ DL 74758 [S]	Children of the Morning	1966	7.50	15.00	30.00

NAUTILUS

Number	Title	Yr	VG	VG+	NM
❑ NR-2	Aspen Gold	1979	10.00	20.00	40.00
-- Audiophile vinyl					

TETRAGRAMMATON

Number	Title	Yr	VG	VG+	NM
❑ T-5101 [(2)]	Once Upon a Time	1969	6.25	12.50	25.00

KINKS, THE

ARISTA

Number	Title	Yr	VG	VG+	NM
❑ SP-69 [DJ]	Low Budget Radio Interview	1979	10.00	20.00	40.00
-- Promo-only radio show featuring Ray Davies					
❑ SP-85 [EP]	A Fistful of Kinks	1980	6.25	12.50	25.00
-- Promo-only four-song sampler from "One for the Road"					
❑ AL 4106 [DJ]	Sleepwalker	1977	7.50	15.00	30.00
-- White label promo					
❑ AL 4167 [DJ]	Misfits	1978	7.50	15.00	30.00
-- White label promo					

MCA

Number	Title	Yr	VG	VG+	NM
❑ L33-17281 [DJ]	A Look at "Think Visual"	1987	12.50	25.00	50.00
-- Promo only in white jacket					

MOBILE FIDELITY

Number	Title	Yr	VG	VG+	NM
❑ 1-070	Misfits	1981	5.00	10.00	20.00
-- Audiophile vinyl					

RCA VICTOR

Number	Title	Yr	VG	VG+	NM
❑ LSP-4644	Muswell Hillbillies	1971	7.50	15.00	30.00
❑ CPL2-5040 [(2)]	Preservation Act 2	1974	5.00	10.00	20.00
❑ VPS-6065 [(2)]	Everybody's in Showbiz	1972	5.00	10.00	20.00
-- Orange label					

REPRISE

Number	Title	Yr	VG	VG+	NM
❑ PRO 328 [P-DJ]	God Save the Kinks	1969	125.00	250.00	500.00
-- Mail-order box with decal, postcard, bag of grass, two pins, letter, Kinks consumer guide and "Then Now and In Between" LP. Price is for complete package.					
❑ PRO 328 [P-DJ]	Then Now and In Between	1969	12.50	25.00	50.00
-- Album that came with above box is sometimes found by itself without all the other goodies.					
❑ MS-2127	The Great Lost Kinks Album	1973	12.50	25.00	50.00
❑ R-6143 [M]	You Really Got Me	1965	15.00	30.00	60.00
❑ R-6143 [M-DJ]	You Really Got Me	1965	100.00	200.00	400.00
-- White label promo					
❑ RS-6143 [P]	You Really Got Me	1965	20.00	40.00	80.00
-- Pink, gold and green label					
❑ R-6158 [M]	Kinks-Size	1965	12.50	25.00	50.00
❑ R-6158 [M-DJ]	Kinks-Size	1965	50.00	100.00	200.00
-- White label promo					
❑ RS-6158 [R]	Kinks-Size	1965	7.50	15.00	30.00
❑ R-6173 [M]	Kinda Kinks	1965	12.50	25.00	50.00
❑ R-6173 [M-DJ]	Kinda Kinks	1965	50.00	100.00	200.00
-- White label promo					
❑ RS-6173 [R]	Kinda Kinks	1965	7.50	15.00	30.00
❑ R-6184 [M]	Kinks Kinkdom	1965	12.50	25.00	50.00
❑ R-6184 [M-DJ]	Kinks Kinkdom	1965	50.00	100.00	200.00
-- White label promo					
❑ RS-6184 [R]	Kinks Kinkdom	1965	7.50	15.00	30.00
❑ R-6197 [M]	The Kink Kontroversy	1966	12.50	25.00	50.00
❑ R-6197 [M-DJ]	The Kink Kontroversy	1966	50.00	100.00	200.00
-- White label promo					

Number	Title	Yr	VG	VG+	NM
❑ RS-6197 [R]	The Kink Kontroversy	1966	7.50	15.00	30.00
❑ R-6217 [M]	The Kinks Greatest Hits!	1966	10.00	20.00	40.00
❑ RS-6217 [R]	The Kinks Greatest Hits!	1966	6.25	12.50	25.00
-- Pink, gold and green label					
❑ R-6228 [M]	Face to Face	1967	10.00	20.00	40.00
❑ RS-6228 [P]	Face to Face	1967	7.50	15.00	30.00
-- Pink, gold and green label					
❑ R-6260 [M]	The Live Kinks	1967	8.75	17.50	35.00
❑ RS-6260 [S]	The Live Kinks	1967	6.25	12.50	25.00
-- Pink, gold and green label					
❑ R-6272 [M-DJ]	Something Else by the Kinks	1968	75.00	150.00	300.00
-- White label promo; no stock copies were issued in mono					
❑ RS-6272 [S]	Something Else by the Kinks	1968	7.50	15.00	30.00
-- Pink, gold and green label					
❑ RS-6272 [S]	Something Else by the Kinks	1968	5.00	10.00	20.00
-- Two-tone orange label with "r. and "W7" logos with steamboat					
❑ RS-6327	The Kinks Are the Village Green Preservation Society	1969	7.50	15.00	30.00
-- Two-tone orange label with "r. and "W7" logos with steamboat					
❑ RS-6366	Arthur (Or The Decline and Fall of the British Empire)	1969	6.25	12.50	25.00
-- Two-tone orange label with "r. and "W7" logos with steamboat					
❑ SMAS-93034	Arthur (Or The Decline and Fall of the British Empire)	1970	10.00	20.00	40.00
-- Capitol Record Club edition					

KISS

Also see PETER CRISS; ACE FREHLEY; GENE SIMMONS; PAUL STANLEY.

CASABLANCA

Number	Title	Yr	VG	VG+	NM
❑ NBLP 7001	Kiss	1974	7.50	15.00	30.00
-- Renumbered version adds "Kissin' Time"; dark blue label					
❑ NBLP 7006	Hotter Than Hell	1974	7.50	15.00	30.00
-- Dark blue label					
❑ NBLP 7016	Dressed to Kill	1975	7.50	15.00	30.00
-- Dark blue label					
❑ NBLP 7020 [(2)]	Alive!	1975	10.00	20.00	40.00
-- Dark blue labels; with booklet					
❑ NBLP 7020 [(2)]	Alive!	1976	5.00	10.00	20.00
-- Tan labels with desert scene, "Casablanca" label					
❑ NBLP 7025	Destroyer	1976	7.50	15.00	30.00
-- Dark blue label					
❑ NBLP 7032 [(3)]	The Originals	1976	37.50	75.00	150.00
-- Tan label with desert scene, "Casablanca" label; with booklet, four Kiss cards, a Kiss Army sticker					
❑ NBLP 7032 [(3)]	The Originals	1976	25.00	50.00	100.00
-- Tan label with desert scene, "Casablanca" label; without extras					
❑ NBLP 7032 [(3)]	The Originals	1977	18.75	37.50	75.00
-- Tan label with desert scene, "Casablanca Record and FilmWorks" label; with extras listed above					
❑ NBLP 7032 [(3)]	The Originals	1977	6.25	12.50	25.00
-- Tan label with desert scene, "Casablanca Record and FilmWorks" label; without extras					
❑ NBLP 7037	Rock and Roll Over	1976	5.00	10.00	20.00
-- Tan label with desert scene, "Casablanca" label; comes with order form for sheet of stickers					
❑ NBLP 7057	Love Gun	1977	10.00	20.00	40.00
-- With insert (cardboard gun)					
❑ NBLP 7076 [(2)]	Alive II	1977	100.00	200.00	400.00
-- With three tracks, "Take Me," "Hooligan" and "Do You Love Me," that are not on later editions. Perhaps as few as 50 copies were made.					
❑ NBLP 7076 [(2)]	Alive II	1977	25.00	50.00	100.00
-- With 8-page insert of tattoos. LP cover lists three tracks, "Take Me," "Hooligan" and "Do You Love Me," that are not on the record.					
❑ NBLP 7076 [(2)]	Alive II	1977	18.75	37.50	75.00
-- Without 8-page insert of tattoos. LP cover lists three tracks, "Take Me," "Hooligan" and "Do You Love Me," that are not on the record.					
❑ NBLP 7076 [(2)]	Alive II	1977	10.00	20.00	40.00
-- With 8-page insert of tattoos. Without "Take Me," "Hooligan" and "Do You Love Me" listed on cover					
❑ NBLP 7100 [(2)]	Double Platinum	1978	10.00	20.00	40.00
-- Contains cardboard platinum award, or an order form for it					
❑ NBLP 7261	Music from The Elder	1981	7.50	15.00	30.00
❑ NBLP 7270	Creatures of the Night	1982	10.00	20.00	40.00
-- Original version has band with makeup					
❑ NB 9001	Kiss	1974	20.00	40.00	80.00
-- Original Warner Bros.-distributed version does NOT have "Kissin' Time"					
❑ NB 20128 [DJ]	A Taste of Platinum	1978	12.50	25.00	50.00
-- Promo-only sampler from Double Platinum					
❑ NB 20137 [DJ]	Criss, Frehley, Simmons, Stanley	1978	10.00	20.00	40.00
-- Promo-only sampler from the band's solo albums					

MERCURY

Number	Title	Yr	VG	VG+	NM
❑ 792-1 [DJ]	First Kiss, Last Licks	1990	25.00	50.00	100.00
-- Promo-only sampler					
❑ 522 647-1 [(2)]	Alive III	1994	6.25	12.50	25.00
-- Limited edition white vinyl					
❑ 522 647-1 [(2)]	Alive III	1994	6.25	12.50	25.00
-- Limited edition blue vinyl					
❑ 522 647-1 [(2)]	Alive III	1994	6.25	12.50	25.00
-- Limited edition red vinyl					
❑ 522 647-1 [(2)]	Alive III	1994	6.25	12.50	25.00
-- Limited edition black vinyl					
❑ 528 950-1 [(2)]	MTV Unplugged	1996	5.00	10.00	20.00
❑ 532 741-1 [(2)]	You Wanted the Best, You Got the Best!!	1996	5.00	10.00	20.00

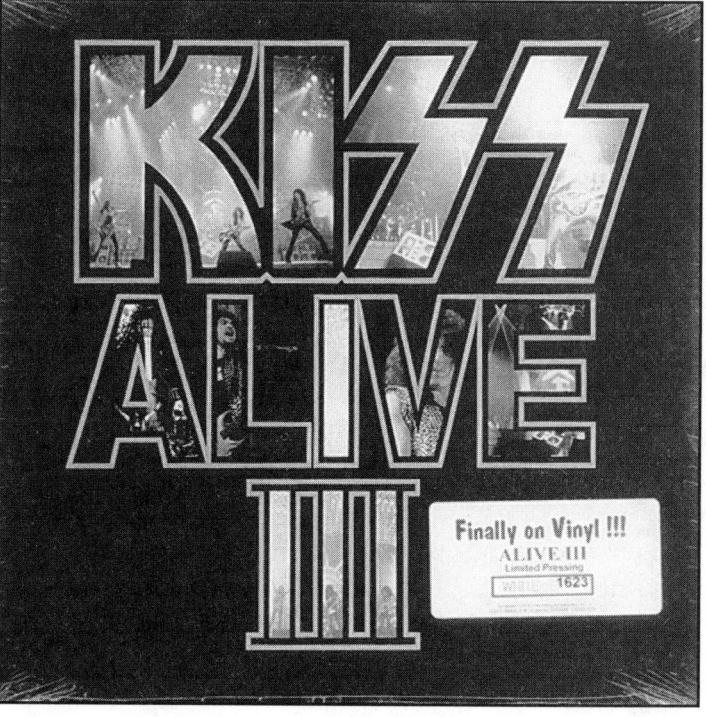

Of all acts that first recorded in the 1970s, among the most collectible, if not atop that list, is Kiss. (Top left) Kiss' debut album, which was originally issued as Casablanca 9001 without the early single "Kissin' Time," was later reissued as Casablanca 7001 with the hit added. (Top right) *Destroyer* was the first Kiss studio album to be a big hit, after the overwhelming success of *Kiss Alive!* The rarest version of *Destroyer* is the initial Casablanca release, which has a dark blue label and was only available for a few months in 1976. (Bottom left) One of the great recent Kiss collectibles is this promo-only vinyl set, *First Kiss Last Licks*. It may be the only cover to feature Kiss in both made-up and non-made-up poses at the same time. (Bottom right) Several of the 1990s Kiss albums were not initially issued on vinyl. By 1994, this was taken care of, as, among others, *Kiss Alive III* was released on red, white and blue vinyl at the same time.

Number	Title	Yr	VG	VG+	NM
❑ 832 903-1 [PD] Crazy Nights		1987	6.25	12.50	25.00
❑ 836 887-1 [PD] Smashes, Thrashes and Hits		1988	6.25	12.50	25.00

KIT KATS, THE
JAMIE

Number	Title	Yr	VG	VG+	NM
❑ LPM-3029 [M]	It's Just a Matter of Time	1966	6.25	12.50	25.00
❑ LPS-3029 [S]	It's Just a Matter of Time	1966	7.50	15.00	30.00
❑ LPM-3032 [M]	The Kit Kats Do Their Thing – Live!	1967	7.50	15.00	30.00
❑ LPS-3032 [S]	The Kit Kats Do Their Thing – Live!	1967	10.00	20.00	40.00

KITCHEN CINQ, THE
LHI

Number	Title	Yr	VG	VG+	NM
❑ E-12000 [M]	Everything But the Kitchen Cinq	1967	7.50	15.00	30.00
❑ E7-12000 [S]	Everything But the Kitchen Cinq	1967	10.00	20.00	40.00

KITT, EARTHA
DECCA

Number	Title	Yr	VG	VG+	NM
❑ DL 4635 [M]	Eartha Kitt Sings in Spanish	1965	7.50	15.00	30.00
❑ DL 74635 [S]	Eartha Kitt Sings in Spanish	1965	10.00	20.00	40.00

KAPP

Number	Title	Yr	VG	VG+	NM
❑ KL-1162 [M]	The Fabulous Eartha Kitt	1959	6.25	12.50	25.00
❑ KL-1192 [M]	Eartha Kitt Revisited	1960	6.25	12.50	25.00
❑ KS-3046 [S]	The Fabulous Eartha Kitt	1959	7.50	15.00	30.00
❑ KS-3192 [S]	Eartha Kitt Revisited	1960	7.50	15.00	30.00

MGM

Number	Title	Yr	VG	VG+	NM
❑ E-4009 [M]	Bad But Beautiful	1962	6.25	12.50	25.00
❑ SE-4009 [S]	Bad But Beautiful	1962	7.50	15.00	30.00

RCA VICTOR

Number	Title	Yr	VG	VG+	NM
❑ LPM-1109 [M]	Down to Eartha	1955	12.50	25.00	50.00
❑ LPM-1153 [M]	That Bad Eartha	1955	12.50	25.00	50.00
❑ LPM-1300 [M]	Thursday's Child	1956	12.50	25.00	50.00
❑ LPM-1661 [M]	St. Louis Blues	1958	10.00	20.00	40.00
❑ LSP-1661 [S]	St. Louis Blues	1958	12.50	25.00	50.00
❑ LPM-3062 [10]	Songs	1953	20.00	40.00	80.00
❑ LPM-3187 [10]	That Bad Eartha	1953	20.00	40.00	80.00

KLARK KENT
Actually Stewart Copeland of THE POLICE.
KRYPTONE/I.R.S.

Number	Title	Yr	VG	VG+	NM
❑ SP 70600 [EP]	Music Madness from the Kinetic Kid	1980	5.00	10.00	20.00
-- Green vinyl 10" in die-cut 12" sleeve					

KLEMMER, JOHN
CADET

Number	Title	Yr	VG	VG+	NM
❑ LP 797 [M]	Involvement	1967	7.50	15.00	30.00
❑ LPS 797 [S]	Involvement	1967	5.00	10.00	20.00
❑ LPS 808	And We Were Lovers	1968	5.00	10.00	20.00

CADET CONCEPT

Number	Title	Yr	VG	VG+	NM
❑ LPS 321	Blowin' Gold	1969	5.00	10.00	20.00
❑ LPS 326	All the Children Cried	1970	5.00	10.00	20.00
❑ LPS 330	Eruptions	1971	5.00	10.00	20.00

MOBILE FIDELITY

Number	Title	Yr	VG	VG+	NM
❑ 1-006	Touch	1979	7.50	15.00	30.00
-- Audiophile vinyl					

NAUTILUS

Number	Title	Yr	VG	VG+	NM
❑ NR-4	Straight from the Heart	1980	20.00	40.00	80.00
-- Audiophile vinyl					
❑ NR-22	Finesse	1981	20.00	40.00	80.00
-- Audiophile vinyl					

KLEMMER, JOHN, AND EDDIE HARRIS
Also see each artist's individual listings.
CRUSADERS

Number	Title	Yr	VG	VG+	NM
❑ 16015	Two Tone	1982	6.25	12.50	25.00
-- Part of MCA's "Audiophile Series"					

KLUGH, EARL
Also see BOB JAMES AND EARL KLUGH.
MOBILE FIDELITY

Number	Title	Yr	VG	VG+	NM
❑ 1-025	Fingerpaintings	1979	7.50	15.00	30.00
-- Audiophile vinyl					
❑ UHQR 1-025	Fingerpaintings	1982	30.00	60.00	120.00
-- "Ultra High Quality" audiophile vinyl in box					
❑ 1-076	Late Night Guitar	1981	12.50	25.00	50.00
-- Audiophile vinyl					

NAUTILUS

Number	Title	Yr	VG	VG+	NM
❑ NR-46	Crazy for You	198?	10.00	20.00	40.00
-- Audiophile vinyl					

KNICKERBOCKERS, THE
CHALLENGE

Number	Title	Yr	VG	VG+	NM
❑ CH-621 [M]	Jerk and Twine Time	1965	100.00	200.00	400.00
❑ CH-622 [M]	Lies	1966	25.00	50.00	100.00
❑ CHS-622 [S]	Lies	1966	50.00	100.00	200.00
❑ LP-12664 [M]	Llyod Thaxton Presents the Knickerbockers	1965	50.00	100.00	200.00

KNIGHT, CHRIS, AND MAUREEN McCORMICK
Of THE BRADY BUNCH.
PARAMOUNT

Number	Title	Yr	VG	VG+	NM
❑ PAS-6062	Chris Knight and Maureen McCormick	1973	30.00	60.00	120.00

KNIGHT, FREDERICK
STAX

Number	Title	Yr	VG	VG+	NM
❑ STS-3011	I've Been Lonely So Long	1973	5.00	10.00	20.00

KNIGHT, GLADYS, AND THE PIPS
BELL

Number	Title	Yr	VG	VG+	NM
❑ 6013	Tastiest Hits	1968	5.00	10.00	20.00

BUDDAH

Number	Title	Yr	VG	VG+	NM
❑ BDS-5602	Claudine	1974	7.50	15.00	30.00

FURY

Number	Title	Yr	VG	VG+	NM
❑ 1003 [M]	Letter Full of Tears	1962	125.00	250.00	500.00

MAXX

Number	Title	Yr	VG	VG+	NM
❑ 3000 [M]	Gladys Knight and the Pips	1964	37.50	75.00	150.00

SOUL

Number	Title	Yr	VG	VG+	NM
❑ S 706 [M]	Everybody Needs Love	1967	5.00	10.00	20.00
❑ SS 706 [S]	Everybody Needs Love	1967	6.25	12.50	25.00
❑ S 707 [M]	Feelin' Bluesy	1968	10.00	20.00	40.00
-- Mono copies are promo only					
❑ SS 707 [S]	Feelin' Bluesy	1968	6.25	12.50	25.00
❑ SS 711	Silk N' Soul	1968	6.25	12.50	25.00
❑ SS 713	Nitty Gritty	1969	6.25	12.50	25.00

SPHERE SOUND

Number	Title	Yr	VG	VG+	NM
❑ SR-7006 [M]	Gladys Knight and the Pips	196?	50.00	100.00	200.00
❑ SSR-7006 [R]	Gladys Knight and the Pips	196?	30.00	60.00	120.00

KNIGHT, JEAN
STAX

Number	Title	Yr	VG	VG+	NM
❑ STS-2045	Mr. Big Stuff	1971	10.00	20.00	40.00

KNIGHT, ROBERT
RISING SONS

Number	Title	Yr	VG	VG+	NM
❑ RSM-7000 [M]	Everlasting Love	1967	7.50	15.00	30.00
❑ RSS-17000 [S]	Everlasting Love	1967	10.00	20.00	40.00

KNIGHT, SONNY
AURA

Number	Title	Yr	VG	VG+	NM
❑ AR-3001 [M]	If You Want This Love	1964	6.25	12.50	25.00
❑ AS-3001 [S]	If You Want This Love	1964	7.50	15.00	30.00

KNIGHT, TED
RANWOOD

Number	Title	Yr	VG	VG+	NM
❑ R-8149	Hi Guys!	1976	5.00	10.00	20.00

KNIGHT, TERRY, AND THE PACK
Predecessor of GRAND FUNK RAILROAD.
ABKCO

Number	Title	Yr	VG	VG+	NM
❑ AB-4217 [(2)]	Mark, Don and Terry 1966-67	1972	5.00	10.00	20.00

CAMEO

Number	Title	Yr	VG	VG+	NM
❑ C 2007 [M]	Reflections	1967	5.00	10.00	20.00
-- Reissue of Lucky Eleven LE-8001					
❑ CS 2007 [S]	Reflections	1967	6.25	12.50	25.00
-- Reissue of Lucky Eleven LES-8001					

LUCKY ELEVEN

Number	Title	Yr	VG	VG+	NM
❑ LE-8000 [M]	Terry Knight and the Pack	1966	10.00	20.00	40.00
❑ LES-8000 [R]	Terry Knight and the Pack	1966	6.25	12.50	25.00
❑ LE-8001 [M]	Reflections	1967	6.25	12.50	25.00
❑ LES-8001 [S]	Reflections	1967	10.00	20.00	40.00

KNIGHTS, THE
At least two, possibly three different groups.
ACE

Number	Title	Yr	VG	VG+	NM
❑ 4763	Cold Days, Hot Knights	196?	100.00	200.00	400.00
❑ 200854	Across the Board	1966	100.00	200.00	400.00
❑ 201302	The Knights 1967	1967	100.00	200.00	400.00

Number	Title	Yr	VG	VG+	NM

CAPITOL
| ❑ DT 2189 [R] | Hot Rod High | 1964 | 100.00 | 200.00 | 400.00 |
| ❑ T 2189 [M] | Hot Rod High | 1964 | 100.00 | 200.00 | 400.00 |

JUSTICE
| ❑ JLP-156 | On the Move | 196? | 75.00 | 150.00 | 300.00 |

KNOCKOUTS, THE
TRIBUTE
| ❑ 1202 [M] | Go Ape with the Knockouts | 1964 | 50.00 | 100.00 | 200.00 |

KNOWBODY ELSE
Members were later in BLACK OAK ARKANSAS.
HIP
| ❑ HIS-7003 | Knowbody Else | 1969 | 10.00 | 20.00 | 40.00 |

KNOX, BUDDY
LIBERTY
| ❑ LRP-3251 [M] | Buddy Knox's Golden Hits | 1962 | 7.50 | 15.00 | 30.00 |
| ❑ LST-7251 [S] | Buddy Knox's Golden Hits | 1962 | 10.00 | 20.00 | 40.00 |

ROULETTE
❑ R 25003 [M]	Buddy Knox	1957	50.00	100.00	200.00
-- Black label, all silver print (original)					
❑ R 25003 [M]	Buddy Knox	1957	37.50	75.00	150.00
-- Black label, red and silver print					
❑ R 25003 [M]	Buddy Knox	1959	25.00	50.00	100.00
-- White label with colored spokes					
❑ R 25048 [M]	Buddy Knox and Jimmy Bowen	1959	50.00	100.00	200.00
-- Black label, red and silver print					
❑ R 25048 [M]	Buddy Knox and Jimmy Bowen	1959	25.00	50.00	100.00
-- White label with colored spokes					

UNITED ARTISTS
| ❑ UAS 6689 | Gypsy Man | 1969 | 6.25 | 12.50 | 25.00 |

KOALA, THE
CAPITOL
| ❑ SKAO-176 | The Koala | 1969 | 15.00 | 30.00 | 60.00 |

KODAKS, THE / THE STARLITES
SPHERE SOUND
| ❑ SSR-7005 [M] | The Kodaks vs. the Starlites | 1965 | 50.00 | 100.00 | 200.00 |

KOERNER, RAY AND GLOVER
AUDIOPHILE
| ❑ AP-78 [M] | Blues, Rags and Hollers | 1963 | 12.50 | 25.00 | 50.00 |
| -- Includes four songs not on the Elektra reissue | | | | | |

ELEKTRA
❑ EKL-240 [M]	Blues, Rags and Hollers	1963	6.25	12.50	25.00
-- Not issued in stereo on Elektra					
❑ EKL-267 [M]	Lots More Blues, Rags and Hollers	1964	5.00	10.00	20.00
❑ EKL-305 [M]	The Return of Koerner, Ray and Glover	1965	5.00	10.00	20.00
❑ EKS-7267 [S]	Lots More Blues, Rags and Hollers	1964	6.25	12.50	25.00
❑ EKS-7305 [S]	The Return of Koerner, Ray and Glover	1965	6.25	12.50	25.00

KOERNER, SPIDER JOHN
ELEKTRA
| ❑ EKL-290 [M] | Spider Blues | 1965 | 5.00 | 10.00 | 20.00 |
| ❑ EKS-7290 [S] | Spider Blues | 1965 | 6.25 | 12.50 | 25.00 |

SWEET JANE
❑ SJL-1074	Some American Folksongs Like They Used To	1974	7.50	15.00	30.00
❑ SJL-5872	Music Is Just a Bunch of Notes	1972	25.00	50.00	100.00
-- With Willie and the Bumblebees and BONNIE RAITT					

KOERNER, SPIDER JOHN, AND WILLIE MURPHY
ELEKTRA
| ❑ EKS-74041 | Running, Jumping, Standing Still | 1969 | 5.00 | 10.00 | 20.00 |

KOFFMAN, MOE
ASCOT
| ❑ AM 13001 [M] | Moe Koffman Plays for the Teens | 1962 | 5.00 | 10.00 | 20.00 |
| ❑ AS 16001 [S] | Moe Koffman Plays for the Teens | 1962 | 6.25 | 12.50 | 25.00 |

JUBILEE
| ❑ JLP-1037 [M] | Cool and Hot Sax | 1957 | 10.00 | 20.00 | 40.00 |
| ❑ JLP-1074 [M] | The Shepherd Swings Again | 1958 | 10.00 | 20.00 | 40.00 |

UNITED ARTISTS
| ❑ UAJ-14029 [M] | Tales of Koffman | 1963 | 6.25 | 12.50 | 25.00 |
| ❑ UAJS-15029 [S] | Tales of Koffman | 1963 | 7.50 | 15.00 | 30.00 |

KOKI, SAM, AND THE PARADISE ISLANDERS
KAPP
| ❑ KS-3321 [S] | Surfin' at Waikiki | 1963 | 5.00 | 10.00 | 20.00 |

KOLE, JERRY, AND THE STRINGERS
CROWN
| ❑ CST-385 [S] | Hot Rod Alley | 1963 | 10.00 | 20.00 | 40.00 |
| ❑ CLP-5385 [M] | Hot Rod Alley | 1963 | 7.50 | 15.00 | 30.00 |

KOLOC, BONNIE
OVATION
❑ OVQD 14-21 [Q]	After All This Time	1971	6.25	12.50	25.00
❑ OVQD 14-26 [Q]	Hold On to Me	1972	6.25	12.50	25.00
❑ OVQD 14-29 [Q]	Bonnie Koloc	1973	6.25	12.50	25.00
❑ OVQD 14-38 [Q]	You're Gonna Love Yourself in the Morning	1974	6.25	12.50	25.00

KOMACK, JAMES
RCA VICTOR
| ❑ LPM-1501 [M] | Inside Me | 1957 | 7.50 | 15.00 | 30.00 |

KOOL AND THE GANG
DE-LITE
| ❑ 2003 | Kool and the Gang | 1969 | 6.25 | 12.50 | 25.00 |

KOOPER, AL
Also see BLOOD, SWEAT AND TEARS; MIKE BLOOMFIELD.
COLUMBIA
| ❑ C2 30031 [(2)] | Easy Does It | 1970 | 5.00 | 10.00 | 20.00 |

KORNER, ALEXIS
MOBILE FIDELITY
| ❑ 1-265 | Blues at the Marquee | 1996 | 5.00 | 10.00 | 20.00 |
| -- Audiophile vinyl | | | | | |

WARNER BROS.
| ❑ 2XS 1966 [(2)] | Bootleg Him | 1972 | 6.25 | 12.50 | 25.00 |

KOSTELANETZ, ANDRE
COLUMBIA
❑ AK 1 [M]	Musical Tour of the World	195?	5.00	10.00	20.00
❑ KZ 1 [M]	Meet Andre Kostelanetz	1955	5.00	10.00	20.00
-- Red and black label with six "eye" logos					
❑ C2L 11 [M]	The Romantic Music of Tchaikovsky	195?	6.25	12.50	25.00
-- Red and black label with six "eye" logos					
❑ CL 720 [M]	Peter and the Wolf; Carnival of the Animals	1956	5.00	10.00	20.00
-- Red and black label with six "eye" logos					
❑ CL 734 [M]	The Music of Victor Youmans	1956	5.00	10.00	20.00
-- Red and black label with six "eye" logos					
❑ CL 765 [M]	The Music of Victor Herbert	1956	5.00	10.00	20.00
-- Red and black label with six "eye" logos					
❑ CL 768 [M]	Music of Irving Berlin	1956	5.00	10.00	20.00
-- Red and black label with six "eye" logos					
❑ CL 780 [M]	Lure of the Tropics	1956	5.00	10.00	20.00
-- Red and black label with six "eye" logos					
❑ CL 781 [M]	Stardust	1956	5.00	10.00	20.00
-- Red and black label with six "eye" logos					
❑ CL 797 [M]	La Boheme for Orchestra	1956	5.00	10.00	20.00
-- Red and black label with six "eye" logos					
❑ CL 806 [M]	Show Boat/South Pacific/ Slaughter on 10th Avenue	1956	5.00	10.00	20.00
-- Red and black label with six "eye" logos					
❑ CL 811 [M]	Calendar Girl	1956	5.00	10.00	20.00
-- Red and black label with six "eye" logos					
❑ CL 843 [M]	The Very Thought of You	1956	5.00	10.00	20.00
-- Red and black label with six "eye" logos					
❑ CL 863 [M]	Café Continental	1956	5.00	10.00	20.00
-- Red and black label with six "eye" logos					
❑ CL 864 [M]	Beautiful Dreamer	1956	5.00	10.00	20.00
-- Red and black label with six "eye" logos					
❑ CS 8328 [S]	Joy to the World: Music for Christmas	1959	5.00	10.00	20.00
-- Red and black label with six "eye" logos					

COLUMBIA MASTERWORKS
❑ ML 2007 [10]	Music of Stephen Foster	195?	6.25	12.50	25.00
❑ ML 2011 [10]	Waltzes of Johann Strauss	195?	6.25	12.50	25.00
❑ ML 2014 [10]	Songs of Cole Porter	195?	7.50	15.00	30.00
❑ ML 2022 [10]	Motion Picture Favorites	195?	6.25	12.50	25.00
❑ ML 2056 [10]	Chopin-Kostelanetz	195?	6.25	12.50	25.00
❑ ML 4065 [M]	Favorites	195?	5.00	10.00	20.00
❑ ML 4066 [M]	Clair de Lune	195?	5.00	10.00	20.00
❑ ML 4082 [M]	Carnival Tropicana	195?	5.00	10.00	20.00
❑ ML 4253 [M]	Music of Fritz Kreisler and Sigmund Romberg	195?	5.00	10.00	20.00

Number	Title	Yr	VG	VG+	NM
❏ ML 4308 [M]	Swan Lake (Highlights)	195?	5.00	10.00	20.00
❏ ML 4409 [M]	Bizet: L'arlesienne Suites 1 & 2	195?	5.00	10.00	20.00
❏ ML 4455 [M]	An American in Paris	195?	5.00	10.00	20.00
❏ ML 4822 [M]	Lure of the Tropics	1956	5.00	10.00	20.00
❏ MS 6106 [S]	Offenbach: Gaite Parisienne; Bizet: Carmen (Highlights)	195?	5.00	10.00	20.00

READER'S DIGEST

Number	Title	Yr	VG	VG+	NM
❏ RD120-A [(8)]	The Best of Andre Kostelanetz	197?	7.50	15.00	30.00

KOTTKE, LEO
OBLIVION

Number	Title	Yr	VG	VG+	NM
❏ S-1	12-String Blues/Live at the Scholar Coffee House	1969	6.25	12.50	25.00

KRAFTWERK
VERTIGO

Number	Title	Yr	VG	VG+	NM
❏ VEL-2003	Autobahn	1974	5.00	10.00	20.00

KRAINIA CONSORT
MERCURY LIVING PRESENCE

Number	Title	Yr	VG	VG+	NM
❏ SR 90397 [S]	Music in Shakespeare's England	196?	15.00	30.00	60.00
-- Maroon label, no "Vendor: Mercury Record Corporation"					
❏ SR 90397 [S]	Music in Shakespeare's England	196?	5.00	10.00	20.00
-- Maroon label, with "Vendor: Mercury Record Corporation"					

KRAINIS, BERNARD
MERCURY LIVING PRESENCE

Number	Title	Yr	VG	VG+	NM
❏ SR 90443 [S]	Concertos for Recorder and Strings	1965	7.50	15.00	30.00
-- Maroon label, with "Vendor: Mercury Record Corporation"					

KRAMER, BILLY J., AND THE DAKOTAS
IMPERIAL

Number	Title	Yr	VG	VG+	NM
❏ LP 9267 [M]	Little Children	1964	12.50	25.00	50.00
-- Black label with stars					
❏ LP 9267 [M]	Little Children	1964	7.50	15.00	30.00
-- Black and pink label					
❏ LP 9273 [M]	I'll Keep You Satisfied/From a Window	1964	7.50	15.00	30.00
❏ LP 9291 [M]	Trains and Boats and Planes	1965	7.50	15.00	30.00
❏ LP 12267 [P]	Little Children	1964	20.00	40.00	80.00
-- Black label with silver print					
❏ LP 12267 [P]	Little Children	1964	10.00	20.00	40.00
-- Black and pink label					
❏ LP 12273 [P]	I'll Keep You Satisfied/From a Window	1964	10.00	20.00	40.00
❏ LP 12921 [R]	Trains and Boats and Planes	1965	6.25	12.50	25.00

KRAVITZ, LENNY
VIRGIN

Number	Title	Yr	VG	VG+	NM
❏ 39169	Are You Gonna Go My Way	1993	6.25	12.50	25.00
-- Clear-vinyl LP plus bonus CD with 8 unreleased tracks					

KRAZY KATS, THE
DAMON

Number	Title	Yr	VG	VG+	NM
❏ 12478 [M]	Movin' Out!! With the Krazy Kats	1964	30.00	60.00	120.00

KREED
VISION OF SOUND

Number	Title	Yr	VG	VG+	NM
❏ 71-56	Kreed	1971	300.00	600.00	1,200.

KRISTOFFERSON, KRIS
MONUMENT

Number	Title	Yr	VG	VG+	NM
❏ SLP-18139	Kristofferson	1970	6.25	12.50	25.00
-- Original label is light green with a yellow ring					
❏ ZQ 30679 [Q]	The Silver Tongued Devil and I	1972	5.00	10.00	20.00
❏ ZQ 31909 [Q]	Jesus Was a Capricorn	1973	5.00	10.00	20.00
❏ PZQ 32914 [Q]	Spooky Lady's Sideshow	1974	5.00	10.00	20.00

KRISTYL
(NO LABEL)

Number	Title	Yr	VG	VG+	NM
❏ (no #)	Kristyl	1975	50.00	100.00	200.00

KUBAN, BOB, AND THE IN-MEN
MUSICLAND U.S.A.

Number	Title	Yr	VG	VG+	NM
❏ LP-3500 [M]	Look Out for the Cheater	1966	7.50	15.00	30.00
❏ SLP-3500 [S]	Look Out for the Cheater	1966	10.00	20.00	40.00

KUSTOM KINGS, THE
SMASH

Number	Title	Yr	VG	VG+	NM
❏ MGS-27051 [M]	Kustom City, U.S.A.	1964	30.00	60.00	120.00
❏ SRS-67051 [S]	Kustom City, U.S.A.	1964	50.00	100.00	200.00

KWESKIN, JIM
REPRISE

Number	Title	Yr	VG	VG+	NM
❏ R 6266 [M]	Garden of Joy	1967	5.00	10.00	20.00

VANGUARD

Number	Title	Yr	VG	VG+	NM
❏ VSD-2158 [S]	Jim Kweskin and the Jug Band	1963	6.25	12.50	25.00
❏ VRS-9139 [M]	Jim Kweskin and the Jug Band	1963	5.00	10.00	20.00
❏ VRS-9163 [M]	Jug Band Music	1965	5.00	10.00	20.00
❏ VRS-9188 [M]	Relax Your Mind	1966	5.00	10.00	20.00
❏ VRS-9234 [M]	See Reverse Side for Title	1967	5.00	10.00	20.00
❏ VRS-9243 [M]	Jump for Joy	1967	5.00	10.00	20.00
❏ VSD-79163 [S]	Jug Band Music	1965	6.25	12.50	25.00
❏ VSD-79188 [S]	Relax Your Mind	1966	6.25	12.50	25.00
❏ VSD-79234 [S]	See Reverse Side for Title	1967	6.25	12.50	25.00
❏ VSD-79243 [S]	Jump for Joy	1967	5.00	10.00	20.00

Number	Title	Yr	VG	VG+	NM

L

L7
EPITAPH
❏ 86401	L7	1988	12.50	25.00	50.00

-- Original press with Donita Sparks' head cut off

SUB POP
❏ 79 [EP]	Smell the Magic	1990	10.00	20.00	40.00

-- First 1,000 on purple vinyl

LA LUPE
ROULETTE
❏ SR-42024	The Queen Does Her Thing	1969	7.50	15.00	30.00

LaBELLE, PATTI, AND THE BLUE BELLES
ATLANTIC
❏ 8119 [M]	Over the Rainbow	1966	7.50	15.00	30.00
❏ SD 8119 [S]	Over the Rainbow	1966	10.00	20.00	40.00
❏ 8147 [M]	Dreamer	1967	7.50	15.00	30.00
❏ SD 8147 [S]	Dreamer	1967	10.00	20.00	40.00

MISTLETOE
❏ MLP-1204	Merry Christmas from LaBelle	1976	5.00	10.00	20.00

NEWTOWN
❏ 631 [M]	Sweethearts of the Apollo	1963	100.00	200.00	400.00
❏ 632 [M]	Sleigh Bells, Jingle Bells and Blue Bells	1963	75.00	150.00	300.00

PARKWAY
❏ P-7043 [M]	The Bluebelles On Stage	1965	37.50	75.00	150.00

-- With bonus single
❏ P-7043 [M]	The Bluebelles On Stage	1965	30.00	60.00	120.00

-- Without bonus single

LACEWING
MAINSTREAM
❏ S-6132	Lacewing	1971	12.50	25.00	50.00

LaFARGE, PETER
COLUMBIA
❏ CL 1795 [M]	Ira Hayes and Other Ballads	1962	5.00	10.00	20.00
❏ CS 8595 [S]	Ira Hayes and Other Ballads	1962	6.25	12.50	25.00

VERVE FOLKWAYS
❏ FV-9004 [M]	Peter LaFarge Sings Women Blues	1965	5.00	10.00	20.00
❏ FVS-9004 [S]	Peter LaFarge Sings Women Blues	1965	6.25	12.50	25.00

LAINE, FRANKIE
ABC
❏ 628 [M]	To Each His Own	1968	5.00	10.00	20.00

COLUMBIA
❏ CL 625 [M]	Command Performance	1954	10.00	20.00	40.00
❏ CL 808 [M]	Jazz Spectacular	1956	7.50	15.00	30.00
❏ CL 975 [M]	Rockin'	1957	7.50	15.00	30.00
❏ CL 1116 [M]	Foreign Affair	1958	7.50	15.00	30.00
❏ CL 1176 [M]	Torchin'	1959	5.00	10.00	20.00
❏ CL 1231 [M]	Frankie Laine's Greatest Hits	1958	6.25	12.50	25.00

-- Red and black label with six "eye" logos
❏ CL 1??? [M]	Reunion in Rhythm	1959	5.00	10.00	20.00
❏ CL 1317 [M]	You Are My Love	1960	5.00	10.00	20.00
❏ CL 1393 [M]	Frankie Laine, Balladeer	1960	5.00	10.00	20.00
❏ CL 1615 [M]	Hell Bent for Leather!	1961	5.00	10.00	20.00

-- Red and black label with six "eye" logos
❏ CL 1696 [M]	Deuces Wild	1962	5.00	10.00	20.00

-- Red and black label with six "eye" logos
❏ CL 2504 [10]	Lover's Laine	1955	10.00	20.00	40.00
❏ CL 2548 [10]	One for My Baby	1955	10.00	20.00	40.00
❏ CL 6200 [10]	One for My Baby	1952	12.50	25.00	50.00
❏ CL 6278 [10]	Mr. Rhythm	1954	12.50	25.00	50.00
❏ CS 8024 [S]	Torchin'	1959	7.50	15.00	30.00
❏ CS 8087 [S]	Reunion in Rhythm	1959	7.50	15.00	30.00
❏ CS 8119 [S]	You Are My Love	1960	6.25	12.50	25.00
❏ CS 8188 [S]	Frankie Laine, Balladeer	1960	6.25	12.50	25.00
❏ CS 8415 [S]	Hell Bent for Leather!	1961	7.50	15.00	30.00

-- Red and black label with six "eye" logos
❏ CS 8415 [S]	Hell Bent for Leather!	1962	5.00	10.00	20.00

-- "360 Sound Stereo" label
❏ CS 8496 [S]	Deuces Wild	1962	6.25	12.50	25.00

-- Red and black label with six "eye" logos
❏ CS 8496 [S]	Deuces Wild	1962	5.00	10.00	20.00

-- "360 Sound Stereo" label
❏ CS 8629 [S]	Call of the Wild	1962	5.00	10.00	20.00
❏ CS 8762 [S]	Wanderlust	1963	5.00	10.00	20.00

MERCURY
❏ MG-20069 [M]	Songs by Frankie Laine	1956	10.00	20.00	40.00
❏ MG-20080 [M]	That's My Desire	1957	10.00	20.00	40.00
❏ MG-20083 [M]	Frankie Laine Sings For Us	1957	10.00	20.00	40.00
❏ MG-20085 [M]	Concert Date	1957	10.00	20.00	40.00
❏ MG-20105 [M]	With All My Heart	1957	10.00	20.00	40.00
❏ MG-20587 [M]	Frankie Laine's Golden Hits	1960	6.25	12.50	25.00
❏ MG-25007 [10]	Favorites	1949	12.50	25.00	50.00
❏ MG-25024 [10]	Songs from the Heart	1950	12.50	25.00	50.00
❏ MG-25025 [10]	Frankie Laine	1950	12.50	25.00	50.00
❏ MG-25026 [10]	Frankie Laine	1950	12.50	25.00	50.00
❏ MG-25027 [10]	Frankie Laine	1950	12.50	25.00	50.00
❏ MG-25082 [10]	Christmas Favorites	1951	12.50	25.00	50.00
❏ MG-25097 [10]	Mr. Rhythm Sings	1951	12.50	25.00	50.00
❏ MG-25124 [10]	Listen to Laine	1952	12.50	25.00	50.00

LAMAS, FERNANDO
ROULETTE
❏ R-25041 [M]	With Love, Fernando Lamas	1958	10.00	20.00	40.00

LAMB
FILLMORE
❏ F 30003	Sign of Change	1970	5.00	10.00	20.00

WARNER BROS.
❏ WS 1920	Cross Between	1971	5.00	10.00	20.00
❏ WS 1952	Bring Out the Sun	1972	5.00	10.00	20.00

LAMEGO, DANNY, AND HIS JUMPIN' JACKS
FORGET-ME-NOT
❏ 105 [M]	The Big Weekend	1964	25.00	50.00	100.00

LAMOUR, DOROTHY
DECCA
❏ DL 5115 [10]	Favorite Hawaiian Songs	1950	20.00	40.00	80.00

LANCE, HERB
CHESS
❏ LP-1506 [M]	The Comeback	1966	6.25	12.50	25.00
❏ LPS-1506 [S]	The Comeback	1966	7.50	15.00	30.00

LANCE, MAJOR
OKEH
❏ OKM-12105 [M]	The Monkey Time	1963	10.00	20.00	40.00
❏ OKM-12106 [M]	Um, Um, Um, Um, Um, Um	1964	10.00	20.00	40.00
❏ OKM-12110 [M]	Major's Greatest Hits	1965	7.50	15.00	30.00
❏ OKS-14105 [S]	The Monkey Time	1963	12.50	25.00	50.00
❏ OKS-14106 [S]	Um, Um, Um, Um, Um, Um	1964	12.50	25.00	50.00
❏ OKS-14110 [S]	Major's Greatest Hits	1965	10.00	20.00	40.00

LANCELOT LINK AND THE EVOLUTION REVOLUTION
ABC
❏ S-715	Lancelot Link and the Evolution Revolution	1970	10.00	20.00	40.00

LANCERS, THE
CORAL
❏ CRL 57100 [M]	Dixieland Ball	1957	6.25	12.50	25.00

IMPERIAL
❏ LP-9075 [M]	Concert in Contrasts	1959	7.50	15.00	30.00
❏ LP-12023 [S]	Concert in Contrasts	1959	10.00	20.00	40.00

TREND
❏ TL-1009 [10]	The Lancers	1954	10.00	20.00	40.00

LANCHESTER, ELSA
HIFI
❏ 405 [M]	Songs for a Smoke-Filled Room	1957	5.00	10.00	20.00
❏ 406 [M]	Songs for a Shuttered Parlor	1958	5.00	10.00	20.00

VERVE
❏ MGV-15015 [M]	Cockney London	1960	7.50	15.00	30.00
❏ MGV-15024 [M]	Herself	1962	7.50	15.00	30.00

LANDSLIDE
CAPITOL
❏ ST-11006	Two-Sided Fantasy	1972	10.00	20.00	40.00

LANE, ABBE
MERCURY
❏ MG-20643 [M]	Abbe Lane with Xavier Cugat and His Orchestra	1961	6.25	12.50	25.00

Number	Title	Yr	VG	VG+	NM
❏ MG-20930 [M]	The Many Sides of Abbe Lane	1964	5.00	10.00	20.00
❏ SR-60643 [S]	Abbe Lane with Xavier Cugat and His Orchestra	1961	7.50	15.00	30.00
❏ SR-60930 [S]	The Many Sides of Abbe Lane	1964	6.25	12.50	25.00

LANEGAN, MARK
Also see SCREAMING TREES.
SUB POP

Number	Title	Yr	VG	VG+	NM
❏ SP 61	The Winding Sheet	1990	6.25	12.50	25.00

-- First 1,000 on red vinyl. Among the backing musicians are Kurt Cobain and Krist Novoselic of NIRVANA.

LANG, K.D.
BUMSTEAD

Number	Title	Yr	VG	VG+	NM
❏ BUM-842	A Truly Western Experience	1984	15.00	30.00	60.00
-- Canadian import					
❏ BUM-862	A Truly Western Experience	1984	5.00	10.00	20.00
-- Canadian import; reissue of Bumstead 842					

SIRE

Number	Title	Yr	VG	VG+	NM
❏ PRO-A-3120 [DJ]	The Making of Shadowland	1988	6.25	12.50	25.00

LANGDON, DORY
VERVE

Number	Title	Yr	VG	VG+	NM
❏ MGV-2101 [M]	Leprechauns Are Upon Me	1957	10.00	20.00	40.00

LANGDON, JIM, TRIO
CUCA

Number	Title	Yr	VG	VG+	NM
❏ 1100 [M]	Jim Langdon Trio	1963	6.25	12.50	25.00

LANGNER SISTERS, THE
STUDIO CITY

Number	Title	Yr	VG	VG+	NM
❏ 9011	The Langner Sisters	1966	7.50	15.00	30.00
❏ 9012	It's the Country Life for Me	1967	7.50	15.00	30.00

LANIN, LESTER
EPIC

Number	Title	Yr	VG	VG+	NM
❏ BSN 146 [(2) S]	The Dance Album	1964	5.00	10.00	20.00
❏ BN 505 [S]	Lester Lanin at the Tiffany Ball	1959	5.00	10.00	20.00
❏ BN 516 [S]	Cocktail Dancing	1959	5.00	10.00	20.00
❏ BN 517 [S]	Have Band, Will Travel	1959	5.00	10.00	20.00
❏ BN 5?? [S]	Lester Lanin Goes to College	1959	5.00	10.00	20.00
❏ BN 5?? [S]	Christmas Dance Party (Volume 9)	1959	5.00	10.00	20.00
❏ BN 556 [S]	Dance to the Lester Lanin Beat	1960	5.00	10.00	20.00

LANZA, MARIO
RCA RED SEAL

Number	Title	Yr	VG	VG+	NM
❏ CRM5-4158 [(5)]	The Mario Lanza Collection	1981	15.00	30.00	60.00
❏ VCS-6192 [(3)]	Mario Lanza's Greatest Hits	1970	6.25	12.50	25.00

RCA VICTOR RED SEAL

Number	Title	Yr	VG	VG+	NM
❏ LM-1127 [M]	The Great Caruso	195?	10.00	20.00	40.00
❏ LM-1188 [M]	Love Songs and a Neapolitan Serenade	195?	10.00	20.00	40.00
❏ LM-1860 [M]	"A Kiss" and Other Love Songs	1955	10.00	20.00	40.00
❏ LM-1927 [M]	The Touch of Your Hand	1955	10.00	20.00	40.00
❏ LM-1943 [M]	Magic Mario	1955	10.00	20.00	40.00
❏ LM-1996 [M]	Serenade	1956	10.00	20.00	40.00
❏ LM-2070 [M]	Lanza on Broadway	1956	7.50	15.00	30.00
❏ LM-2090 [M]	Cavalcade of Show Tunes	1957	7.50	15.00	30.00
❏ LM-2211 [M]	Seven Hills of Rome	1958	7.50	15.00	30.00
❏ LM-2331 [M]	Mario!	1959	5.00	10.00	20.00
❏ LSC-2331 [S]	Mario!	1959	7.50	15.00	30.00
❏ LSC-2333 [S]	Lanza Sings Christmas Carols	1959	5.00	10.00	20.00
❏ LSC-2338 [S]	For the First Time	1959	5.00	10.00	20.00
❏ LSC-2339 [S]	The Student Prince	1959	5.00	10.00	20.00
❏ LSC-2393 [S]	Mario Lanza Sings Caruso Favorites	1960	5.00	10.00	20.00
❏ LM-2422 [M]	Double Feature -- Mario Lanza	1960	5.00	10.00	20.00
❏ LSC-2454 [S]	A Mario Lanza Program	1960	5.00	10.00	20.00
❏ LSC-2509 [S]	The Vagabond King	1961	5.00	10.00	20.00
❏ LM-2607 [M]	I'll Walk with God	1962	5.00	10.00	20.00
❏ LM-2998 [M]	The Best of Mario Lanza, Volume 2	1968	5.00	10.00	20.00

LAREDO, JAIME
RCA VICTOR RED SEAL

Number	Title	Yr	VG	VG+	NM
❏ LSC-2373 [S]	Presenting Jaime Laredo	1960	10.00	20.00	40.00
-- Original with "shaded dog" label					
❏ LSC-2414 [S]	Brahms: Violin Sonata No. 3; Bach: Partita No. 3	1960	15.00	30.00	60.00
-- Original with "shaded dog" label					
❏ LSC-2472 [S]	Bruch: Violin Concerto No. 1; Mozart: Violin Concerto No. 3	1961	12.50	25.00	50.00
-- Original with "shaded dog" label					

LARKIN, BILLY, AND THE DELEGATES
AURA

Number	Title	Yr	VG	VG+	NM
❏ ARS 23003 [S]	Blue Lights	196?	6.25	12.50	25.00
❏ AR 83003 [M]	Blue Lights	196?	5.00	10.00	20.00

WORLD PACIFIC

Number	Title	Yr	VG	VG+	NM
❏ WP-1837 [M]	Hole in the Wall	1966	5.00	10.00	20.00
❏ WP-1843 [M]	Ain't That a Groove	1966	5.00	10.00	20.00
❏ WP-1850 [M]	Hold On	1967	5.00	10.00	20.00
❏ ST-21837 [S]	Hole in the Wall	1966	6.25	12.50	25.00
❏ ST-21843 [S]	Ain't That a Groove	1966	6.25	12.50	25.00
❏ ST-21850 [S]	Hold On	1967	6.25	12.50	25.00

LARKS, THE
MONEY

Number	Title	Yr	VG	VG+	NM
❏ LP-1102 [M]	The Jerk	1965	10.00	20.00	40.00
❏ ST-1102 [S]	The Jerk	1965	12.50	25.00	50.00
❏ LP-1107 [M]	Soul Kaleidoscope	1966	10.00	20.00	40.00
❏ ST-1107 [S]	Soul Kaleidoscope	1966	12.50	25.00	50.00
❏ LP-1110 [M]	Superslick	1967	10.00	20.00	40.00
❏ ST-1110 [S]	Superslick	1967	12.50	25.00	50.00

LaROSA, JULIUS
CADENCE

Number	Title	Yr	VG	VG+	NM
❏ CLP 1007 [M]	Julius LaRosa (Julie's Best)	1955	10.00	20.00	40.00

FORUM

Number	Title	Yr	VG	VG+	NM
❏ FS-16012 [S]	Just Say I Love Her	1960	5.00	10.00	20.00

KAPP

Number	Title	Yr	VG	VG+	NM
❏ KS-3245 [S]	The New Julie LaRosa	1961	5.00	10.00	20.00

RCA VICTOR

Number	Title	Yr	VG	VG+	NM
❏ LPM-1299 [M]	Julius LaRosa	1956	10.00	20.00	40.00

ROULETTE

Number	Title	Yr	VG	VG+	NM
❏ R 25054 [M]	Love Songs A LaRosa	1959	5.00	10.00	20.00
❏ SR 25054 [S]	Love Songs A LaRosa	1959	6.25	12.50	25.00
❏ R 25083 [M]	On the Sunny Side	1960	5.00	10.00	20.00
❏ SR 25083 [S]	On the Sunny Side	1960	6.25	12.50	25.00

LARRY AND HANK
PRESTIGE

Number	Title	Yr	VG	VG+	NM
❏ PRLP-7472 [M]	The Blues/A New Generation	1965	5.00	10.00	20.00
❏ PRST-7472 [S]	The Blues/A New Generation	1965	6.25	12.50	25.00

LARRY AND LENORE
REQUEST

Number	Title	Yr	VG	VG+	NM
❏ 10037 [M]	Traveling Guitars	1959	25.00	50.00	100.00

LAST CALL OF SHILOH, THE
LAST CALL

Number	Title	Yr	VG	VG+	NM
❏ 5136	The Last Call	196?	50.00	100.00	200.00

LAST POETS, THE
BLUE THUMB

Number	Title	Yr	VG	VG+	NM
❏ BT-39	Chastisement	1972	7.50	15.00	30.00
❏ BT-52	At Last	1973	7.50	15.00	30.00

CASABLANCA

Number	Title	Yr	VG	VG+	NM
❏ NBLP 7051	Delights of the Garden	1977	6.25	12.50	25.00

DOUGLAS

Number	Title	Yr	VG	VG+	NM
❏ 3	The Last Poets	1970	12.50	25.00	50.00
❏ Z 30583	This Is Madness	1971	12.50	25.00	50.00
❏ Z 30811	The Last Poets	1971	10.00	20.00	40.00

JUGGERNAUT

Number	Title	Yr	VG	VG+	NM
❏ 8802	Right On!	1971	12.50	25.00	50.00
-- As "The Original Last Poets"					

LATEEF, YUSEF
ARGO

Number	Title	Yr	VG	VG+	NM
❏ LP-634 [M]	Live at Cranbrook	1959	7.50	15.00	30.00

CHARLIE PARKER

Number	Title	Yr	VG	VG+	NM
❏ PLP-814 [M]	Lost in Sound	1962	6.25	12.50	25.00
❏ PLP-814S [S]	Lost in Sound	1962	7.50	15.00	30.00

DELMARK

Number	Title	Yr	VG	VG+	NM
❏ DL-407 [M]	Yusef!	1965	5.00	10.00	20.00
❏ DS-407 [S]	Yusef!	1965	6.25	12.50	25.00

IMPULSE!

Number	Title	Yr	VG	VG+	NM
❏ A-56 [M]	Jazz Around the World	1963	6.25	12.50	25.00
❏ AS-56 [S]	Jazz Around the World	1963	7.50	15.00	30.00
❏ A-69 [M]	Live at Pep's	1964	6.25	12.50	25.00
❏ AS-69 [S]	Live at Pep's	1964	7.50	15.00	30.00
❏ A-84 [M]	1984	1965	6.25	12.50	25.00

Number	Title	Yr	VG	VG+	NM
❑ AS-84 [S]	1984	1965	7.50	15.00	30.00
❑ A-92 [M]	Psychicemotus	1966	6.25	12.50	25.00
❑ AS-92 [S]	Psychicemotus	1966	7.50	15.00	30.00
❑ A-9117 [M]	A Flat, G Flat and C	1966	6.25	12.50	25.00
❑ AS-9117 [S]	A Flat, G Flat and C	1966	7.50	15.00	30.00
❑ A-9125 [M]	The Golden Flute	1966	6.25	12.50	25.00
❑ AS-9125 [S]	The Golden Flute	1966	7.50	15.00	30.00

MOODSVILLE

Number	Title	Yr	VG	VG+	NM
❑ MVLP-22 [M]	Eastern Sounds	1961	10.00	20.00	40.00
-- Green label, silver print					
❑ MVST-22 [S]	Eastern Sounds	1961	12.50	25.00	50.00
-- Green label, silver print					

NEW JAZZ

Number	Title	Yr	VG	VG+	NM
❑ NJLP-8218 [M]	Other Sounds	1959	12.50	25.00	50.00
-- Purple label					
❑ NJLP-8218 [M]	Other Sounds	1965	6.25	12.50	25.00
-- Blue label, trident logo at right					
❑ NJLP-8234 [M]	Cry! Tender	1960	12.50	25.00	50.00
-- Purple label					
❑ NJLP-8234 [M]	Cry! Tender	1965	6.25	12.50	25.00
-- Blue label, trident logo at right					
❑ NJLP-8261 [M]	The Sounds of Yusef	1961	12.50	25.00	50.00
-- Reissue of Prestige 7122; purple label					
❑ NJLP-8261 [M]	The Sounds of Yusef	1965	6.25	12.50	25.00
-- Blue label, trident logo at right					
❑ NJLP-8272 [M]	Into Something	1962	12.50	25.00	50.00
-- Purple label					
❑ NJLP-8272 [M]	Into Something	1965	6.25	12.50	25.00
-- Blue label, trident logo at right					

PRESTIGE

Number	Title	Yr	VG	VG+	NM
❑ PRLP-7122 [M]	The Sounds of Yusef	1957	25.00	50.00	100.00
-- Yellow label					
❑ PRLP-7319 [M]	Eastern Sounds	1964	6.25	12.50	25.00
❑ PRST-7319 [S]	Eastern Sounds	1964	6.25	12.50	25.00
-- Reissue of Moodsville 22					
❑ PRLP-7398 [M]	The Sounds of Yusef Lateef	1966	5.00	10.00	20.00
❑ PRST-7398 [S]	The Sounds of Yusef Lateef	1966	6.25	12.50	25.00
❑ PRLP-7447 [M]	Yusef Lateef Plays for Lovers	1967	6.25	12.50	25.00
❑ PRST-7447 [S]	Yusef Lateef Plays for Lovers	1967	5.00	10.00	20.00

RIVERSIDE

Number	Title	Yr	VG	VG+	NM
❑ RLP-12-325 [M]	Three Faces of Yusef Lateef	1960	10.00	20.00	40.00
❑ RLP-337 [M]	The Centaur and the Phoenix	1960	10.00	20.00	40.00
❑ RLP-1176 [S]	Three Faces of Yusef Lateef	1960	10.00	20.00	40.00
❑ RLP-9337 [S]	The Centaur and the Phoenix	1960	10.00	20.00	40.00

SAVOY

Number	Title	Yr	VG	VG+	NM
❑ MG-12103 [M]	Jazz Mood	1957	12.50	25.00	50.00
❑ MG-12109 [M]	Jazz for the Thinker	1957	12.50	25.00	50.00
❑ MG-12117 [M]	Prayer to the East	1957	12.50	25.00	50.00
❑ MG-12120 [M]	Jazz and the Sounds of Nature	1958	12.50	25.00	50.00
❑ MG-12139 [M]	The Dreamer	1958	12.50	25.00	50.00
❑ MG-12140 [M]	The Fabric of Jazz	1958	12.50	25.00	50.00
❑ SR-13007 [S]	The Dreamer	1959	12.50	25.00	50.00
❑ SR-13008 [S]	The Fabric of Jazz	1959	12.50	25.00	50.00

VERVE

Number	Title	Yr	VG	VG+	NM
❑ MGV-8217 [M]	Before Dawn	1958	25.00	50.00	100.00
❑ V-8217 [M]	Before Dawn	1961	6.25	12.50	25.00

LATIN SOULS, THE
KAPP

Number	Title	Yr	VG	VG+	NM
❑ KL-1524 [M]	Boo-Ga-Loo and Shing-a-Ling	1967	6.25	12.50	25.00
❑ KS-3524 [S]	Boo-Ga-Loo and Shing-a-Ling	1967	5.00	10.00	20.00
❑ KS-3553	Tigar Boo-Ga-Loo	1968	5.00	10.00	20.00

LAUGHTON, CHARLES
CAPITOL

Number	Title	Yr	VG	VG+	NM
❑ STBO 1650 [(2) S]	The Story Teller	1962	7.50	15.00	30.00
❑ TBO 1650 [(2) M]	The Story Teller	1962	6.25	12.50	25.00

DECCA

Number	Title	Yr	VG	VG+	NM
❑ DL 8031 [M]	Readings from the Bible	195?	7.50	15.00	30.00
❑ DLP 8010 [M]	A Christmas Carol/ Mr. Pickwick's Christmas	1955	5.00	10.00	20.00
-- A-side read by Ronald Colman					

MCA

Number	Title	Yr	VG	VG+	NM
❑ 15010	A Christmas Carol/ Mr. Pickwick's Christmas	1973	5.00	10.00	20.00
-- A-side read by Ronald Colman; reissue of Decca LP; black label with rainbow					

LAUPER, CYNDI
Also see BLUE ANGEL.
PORTRAIT

Number	Title	Yr	VG	VG+	NM
❑ 9R9 39610 [PD]	She's So Unusual	1984	7.50	15.00	30.00

LAUREN, ROD
RCA VICTOR

Number	Title	Yr	VG	VG+	NM
❑ LPM-2176 [M]	I'm Rod Lauren	1961	10.00	20.00	40.00
❑ LSP-2176 [S]	I'm Rod Lauren	1961	12.50	25.00	50.00

LAURIE SISTERS, THE
RCA CAMDEN

Number	Title	Yr	VG	VG+	NM
❑ CAL-545 [M]	Hits of the Great Girl Groups	1960	6.25	12.50	25.00
❑ CAS-545 [S]	Hits of the Great Girl Groups	1960	7.50	15.00	30.00

LAURIE, ANNIE
AUDIO LAB

Number	Title	Yr	VG	VG+	NM
❑ AL-1510 [M]	It Hurts to Be in Love	1959	75.00	150.00	300.00

LAWRENCE, BILL
TOPS

Number	Title	Yr	VG	VG+	NM
❑ L-1576 [M]	Bill Lawrence Sings I'm in the Mood for Love	1957	5.00	10.00	20.00

LAWRENCE, CAROL
CAMEO

Number	Title	Yr	VG	VG+	NM
❑ C-1077 [M]	An Evening with Carol Lawrence	1964	5.00	10.00	20.00
❑ SC-1077 [S]	An Evening with Carol Lawrence	1964	6.25	12.50	25.00

CHANCELLOR

Number	Title	Yr	VG	VG+	NM
❑ CHL-5015 [M]	Tonight at 8:30	1960	5.00	10.00	20.00
❑ CHLS-5015 [S]	Tonight at 8:30	1960	7.50	15.00	30.00

LAWRENCE, EDDIE
CORAL

Number	Title	Yr	VG	VG+	NM
❑ CRL 57103 [M]	The Old Philosopher	1956	7.50	15.00	30.00
❑ CRL 57155 [M]	Eddie "The Old Philosopher" Lawrence	1957	7.50	15.00	30.00
❑ CRL 57203 [M]	The Kingdom of Eddie Lawrence	1958	7.50	15.00	30.00
❑ CRL 57371 [M]	The Side Splitting Personality of Eddie Lawrence	1961	7.50	15.00	30.00
❑ CRL 57411 [M]	Seven Characters In Search of Eddie Lawrence	1962	7.50	15.00	30.00
❑ CRL 757411 [S]	Seven Characters In Search of Eddie Lawrence	1962	10.00	20.00	40.00

EPIC

Number	Title	Yr	VG	VG+	NM
❑ LN 24149 [M]	Is That What's Bothering You Bunkie?	1965	7.50	15.00	30.00
❑ BN 26149 [S]	Is That What's Bothering You Bunkie?	1965	10.00	20.00	40.00

SIGNATURE

Number	Title	Yr	VG	VG+	NM
❑ SM-1003 [M]	The Garden of Eddie Lawrence	1960	10.00	20.00	40.00

LAWRENCE, ELLIOT
DECCA

Number	Title	Yr	VG	VG+	NM
❑ DL 5274 [10]	College Prom	1950	12.50	25.00	50.00
❑ DL 5353 [10]	Moonlight on the Campus	1951	12.50	25.00	50.00

FANTASY

Number	Title	Yr	VG	VG+	NM
❑ 3206 [M]	Elliot Lawrence Plays Gerry Mulligan Arrangements	1956	12.50	25.00	50.00
-- Red vinyl					
❑ 3206 [M]	Elliot Lawrence Plays Gerry Mulligan Arrangements	1956	7.50	15.00	30.00
-- Black vinyl, red label, non-flexible vinyl					
❑ 3206 [M]	Elliot Lawrence Plays Gerry Mulligan Arrangements	196?	5.00	10.00	20.00
-- Black vinyl, red label, flexible vinyl					
❑ 3219 [M]	Elliot Lawrence Plays Tiny Kahn and Johnny Mandel Arrangements	1956	12.50	25.00	50.00
-- Red vinyl					
❑ 3219 [M]	Elliot Lawrence Plays Tiny Kahn and Johnny Mandel Arrangements	1956	7.50	15.00	30.00
-- Black vinyl, red label, non-flexible vinyl					
❑ 3219 [M]	Elliot Lawrence Plays Tiny Kahn and Johnny Mandel Arrangements	196?	5.00	10.00	20.00
-- Black vinyl, red label, flexible vinyl					
❑ 3226 [M]	Dream	1956	12.50	25.00	50.00
-- Red vinyl					
❑ 3226 [M]	Dream	1956	7.50	15.00	30.00
-- Black vinyl, red label, non-flexible vinyl					
❑ 3226 [M]	Dream	196?	5.00	10.00	20.00
-- Black vinyl, red label, flexible vinyl					
❑ 3236 [M]	Swinging at the Steel Pier	1956	12.50	25.00	50.00
-- Red vinyl					
❑ 3236 [M]	Swinging at the Steel Pier	1956	7.50	15.00	30.00
-- Black vinyl, red label, non-flexible vinyl					
❑ 3236 [M]	Swinging at the Steel Pier	196?	5.00	10.00	20.00
-- Black vinyl, red label, flexible vinyl					
❑ 3246 [M]	Elliot Lawrence Plays for Swinging Dancers	1957	10.00	20.00	40.00
-- Red vinyl					
❑ 3246 [M]	Elliot Lawrence Plays for Swinging Dancers	1957	6.25	12.50	25.00
-- Black vinyl, red label, non-flexible vinyl					

Number	Title	Yr	VG	VG+	NM
❑ 3261 [M]	Dream On -- Dance On	1958	10.00	20.00	40.00
-- Red vinyl					
❑ 3261 [M]	Dream On -- Dance On	1958	6.25	12.50	25.00
-- Black vinyl, red label, non-flexible vinyl					
❑ 3290 [M]	Big Band Sound	1959	10.00	20.00	40.00
-- Red vinyl					
❑ 3290 [M]	Big Band Sound	1959	6.25	12.50	25.00
-- Black vinyl, red label, non-flexible vinyl					
❑ 8002 [S]	Dream On -- Dance On	196?	7.50	15.00	30.00
-- Blue vinyl					
❑ 8002 [S]	Dream On -- Dance On	196?	5.00	10.00	20.00
-- Black vinyl, blue label, non-flexible vinyl					
❑ 8021 [S]	Elliot Lawrence Plays for Swinging Dancers	196?	7.50	15.00	30.00
-- Blue vinyl					
❑ 8021 [S]	Elliot Lawrence Plays for Swinging Dancers	196?	5.00	10.00	20.00
-- Black vinyl, blue label, non-flexible vinyl					
❑ 8031 [S]	Big Band Sound	196?	7.50	15.00	30.00
-- Blue vinyl					
❑ 8031 [S]	Big Band Sound	196?	5.00	10.00	20.00
-- Black vinyl, blue label, non-flexible vinyl					
JAZZTONE					
❑ J-1279 [M]	Big Band Modern	1958	10.00	20.00	40.00
MOBILE FIDELITY					
❑ 2-229 [(2)]	The Music of Elliot Lawrence	1995	7.50	15.00	30.00
-- Audiophile vinyl					
TOP RANK					
❑ RM-304 [M]	Music for Trapping (Tender, That Is)	1959	10.00	20.00	40.00
VIK					
❑ LX-1113 [M]	Jazz Goes Broadway	1958	10.00	20.00	40.00

LAWRENCE, GERTRUDE
DECCA

Number	Title	Yr	VG	VG+	NM
❑ DL 5418 [10]	Souvenir Album	1952	12.50	25.00	50.00
❑ DL 8673 [M]	A Remembrance	1958	7.50	15.00	30.00
-- Black label, silver print					

LAWRENCE, STEVE
Also see STEVE LAWRENCE AND EYDIE GORME.
ABC-PARAMOUNT

Number	Title	Yr	VG	VG+	NM
❑ 290 [M]	Swing Softly with Me	1959	6.25	12.50	25.00
❑ S-290 [S]	Swing Softly with Me	1959	7.50	15.00	30.00
❑ 392 [M]	The Best of Steve Lawrence	1960	5.00	10.00	20.00
❑ S-392 [S]	The Best of Steve Lawrence	1960	6.25	12.50	25.00
CORAL					
❑ CRL 57050 [M]	About That Girl	1956	10.00	20.00	40.00
❑ CRL 57182 [M]	Songs by Steve Lawrence	1957	10.00	20.00	40.00
❑ CRL 57204 [M]	Here's Steve Lawrence	1958	10.00	20.00	40.00
❑ CRL 57268 [M]	All About Love	1959	7.50	15.00	30.00
❑ CRL 57434 [M]	Songs Everybody Knows	1963	6.25	12.50	25.00
❑ CRL 757268 [S]	All About Love	1959	10.00	20.00	40.00
❑ CRL 757434 [S]	Songs Everybody Knows	1963	7.50	15.00	30.00
KING					
❑ 593 [M]	Steve Lawrence	1959	20.00	40.00	80.00
UNITED ARTISTS					
❑ UAL-3098 [M]	The Steve Lawrence Sound	1960	5.00	10.00	20.00
❑ UAL-3114 [M]	Steve Lawrence Goes Latin	1960	5.00	10.00	20.00
❑ UAL-3150 [M]	Portrait of My Love	1961	5.00	10.00	20.00
❑ UAL-3190 [M]	The Very Best of Steve Lawrence	1962	5.00	10.00	20.00
❑ UAL-3265 [M]	People Will Say We're in Love	1963	5.00	10.00	20.00
❑ UAS-6098 [S]	The Steve Lawrence Sound	1960	6.25	12.50	25.00
❑ UAS-6114 [S]	Steve Lawrence Goes Latin	1960	6.25	12.50	25.00
❑ UAS-6150 [S]	Portrait of My Love	1961	6.25	12.50	25.00
❑ UAS-6190 [S]	The Very Best of Steve Lawrence	1962	6.25	12.50	25.00
❑ UAS-6265 [S]	People Will Say We're in Love	1963	6.25	12.50	25.00
❑ UAS-6368 [S]	Steve Lawrence Conquers Broadway	1964	5.00	10.00	20.00

LAWRENCE, STEVE, AND EYDIE GORME
ABC-PARAMOUNT

Number	Title	Yr	VG	VG+	NM
❑ 300 [M]	We Got Us	1960	5.00	10.00	20.00
❑ S-300 [S]	We Got Us	1960	6.25	12.50	25.00
❑ 311 [M]	Steve and Eydie Sing the Golden Hits	1960	5.00	10.00	20.00
❑ S-311 [S]	Steve and Eydie Sing the Golden Hits	1960	6.25	12.50	25.00
❑ S-469 [S]	Our Best to You	1964	5.00	10.00	20.00
CALENDAR					
❑ KOM-1001 [M]	Golden Rainbow	1968	7.50	15.00	30.00
❑ KOS-1001 [S]	Golden Rainbow	1968	10.00	20.00	40.00

Number	Title	Yr	VG	VG+	NM
CORAL					
❑ CRL 57336 [M]	Steve and Eydie	1962	5.00	10.00	20.00
MATI-MOR					
❑ 8003	It's Us Again	196?	5.00	10.00	20.00
-- Promotional item for Silvirkin shampoo					
UNITED ARTISTS					
❑ UAL-3191 [M]	The Very Best of Eydie and Steve	1962	5.00	10.00	20.00
❑ UAL-3268 [M]	Two on the Aisle	1963	5.00	10.00	20.00
❑ WWL-4509 [M]	Cozy	1961	5.00	10.00	20.00
❑ UAS-6191 [S]	The Very Best of Eydie and Steve	1962	6.25	12.50	25.00
❑ UAS-6268 [S]	Two on the Aisle	1963	6.25	12.50	25.00
❑ WWS-8509 [S]	Cozy	1961	6.25	12.50	25.00

LAWS, HUBERT
CTI

Number	Title	Yr	VG	VG+	NM
❑ 1002	Crying Song	1970	5.00	10.00	20.00

LAWSON, LINDA
CHANCELLOR

Number	Title	Yr	VG	VG+	NM
❑ CHL-5010 [M]	Introducing Linda Lawson	1960	5.00	10.00	20.00

LAY, SAM
BLUE THUMB

Number	Title	Yr	VG	VG+	NM
❑ BTS 14	Sam Lay in Bluesland	1970	6.25	12.50	25.00

LAZARUS
AMAZON

Number	Title	Yr	VG	VG+	NM
❑ 1001	Lazarus	1970	5.00	10.00	20.00

LAZY LESTER
EXCELLO

Number	Title	Yr	VG	VG+	NM
❑ LP-8006 [M]	True Blues	1967	100.00	200.00	400.00
❑ LPS-8006 [M]	True Blues	196?	15.00	30.00	60.00
-- Says "Stereo" but plays mono					

LAZY SMOKE
ONYX

Number	Title	Yr	VG	VG+	NM
❑ 6003	Corridor of Faces	1967	300.00	600.00	1,200.

LEA, TERREA
ABC-PARAMOUNT

Number	Title	Yr	VG	VG+	NM
❑ ABC-141 [M]	Terrea Lea and Her Singing Guitar	1956	7.50	15.00	30.00
HIFI					
❑ R-404 [M]	Folk Songs and Ballads	1957	7.50	15.00	30.00

LEACH, CURTIS
LONGHORN

Number	Title	Yr	VG	VG+	NM
❑ 003	Indescribable	1965	12.50	25.00	50.00

LEADBELLY
ALLEGRO

Number	Title	Yr	VG	VG+	NM
❑ L-4027 [10]	Sinful Songs	195?	62.50	125.00	250.00
CAPITOL					
❑ H 369 [10]	Classics in Jazz	1953	62.50	125.00	250.00
❑ T 1821 [M]	Leadbelly: Huddie Ledbetter's Best	1962	10.00	20.00	40.00
ELEKTRA					
❑ EKL-301/2 [(2)]	The Library of Congress Recordings	1966	6.25	12.50	25.00
FOLKWAYS					
❑ FP-4 [10]	Lead Belly's Legacy, Vol. 1: Take This Hammer	1950	30.00	60.00	120.00
❑ FP-14 [10]	Lead Belly's Legacy, Vol. 2: Rock Island Line	1951	30.00	60.00	120.00
❑ FP-24 [10]	Lead Belly's Legacy, Vol. 3: Early Recordings	1951	30.00	60.00	120.00
❑ FP-34 [10]	Lead Belly's Legacy, Vol. 4: Easy Rider	1951	30.00	60.00	120.00
❑ FP-241 [(2) M]	Leadbelly's Last Sessions, Vol. 1	196?	10.00	20.00	40.00
❑ FP-242 [(2) M]	Leadbelly's Last Sessions, Vol. 2	196?	10.00	20.00	40.00
❑ FA-2004 [10]	Lead Belly's Legacy, Vol. 1: Take This Hammer	195?	12.50	25.00	50.00
-- Reissue of FP-4					
❑ FA-2014 [10]	Lead Belly's Legacy, Vol. 2: Rock Island Line	195?	12.50	25.00	50.00
-- Reissue of FP-14					
❑ FA-2024 [10]	Lead Belly's Legacy, Vol. 3: Early Recordings	195?	12.50	25.00	50.00
-- Reissue of FP-24					
❑ FA-2034 [10]	Lead Belly's Legacy, Vol. 4: Easy Rider	195?	12.50	25.00	50.00
-- Reissue of FP-34					

Number	Title	Yr	VG	VG+	NM
❏ FA-2941 [M]	Leadbelly's Last Sessions, Vol. 3	196?	6.25	12.50	25.00
❏ FA-2942 [M]	Leadbelly's Last Sessions, Vol. 4	196?	6.25	12.50	25.00
❏ FA-3106 [M]	Leadbelly Sings Folk Songs	196?	6.25	12.50	25.00

RCA VICTOR

Number	Title	Yr	VG	VG+	NM
❏ LPV-505 [M]	Midnight Special	1964	10.00	20.00	40.00

ROYALE

Number	Title	Yr	VG	VG+	NM
❏ 18131 [10]	Blues Songs	1954	30.00	60.00	120.00

-- As "The Lonesome Blues Singer"

VERVE FOLKWAYS

Number	Title	Yr	VG	VG+	NM
❏ FT-3019 [M]	From the Last Sessions	1967	6.25	12.50	25.00
❏ FV-9001 [M]	Take This Hammer	1965	6.25	12.50	25.00
❏ FV-9021 [M]	Keep Your Hands Off Her	1965	6.25	12.50	25.00

LEAHY, JOE
TOWER

Number	Title	Yr	VG	VG+	NM
❏ ST 5014 [S]	Tabasco and Trumpets	1966	6.25	12.50	25.00
❏ T 5014 [M]	Tabasco and Trumpets	1966	5.00	10.00	20.00
❏ ST 5057 [S]	A Taste of Trumpets, A Touch of Voices	1967	6.25	12.50	25.00
❏ T 5057 [M]	A Taste of Trumpets, A Touch of Voices	1967	5.00	10.00	20.00

LEAPER, BOB
LONDON

Number	Title	Yr	VG	VG+	NM
❏ SP 4056 [S]	Big Band Beatle Songs	1964	5.00	10.00	20.00

LEAPY LEE
DECCA

Number	Title	Yr	VG	VG+	NM
❏ DL 75076	Little Arrows	1968	5.00	10.00	20.00

LEARY, DR. TIMOTHY
DOUGLAS

Number	Title	Yr	VG	VG+	NM
❏ 1	You Can Be Anyone This Time Around	1969	25.00	50.00	100.00

ESP-DISK'

Number	Title	Yr	VG	VG+	NM
❏ 1027 [M]	Turn On, Tune In, Drop Out	1966	37.50	75.00	150.00

MERCURY

Number	Title	Yr	VG	VG+	NM
❏ MG-21131 [M]	Turn On, Tune In, Drop Out	1967	10.00	20.00	40.00
❏ SR-61131 [S]	Turn On, Tune In, Drop Out	1967	12.50	25.00	50.00

PIXIE

Number	Title	Yr	VG	VG+	NM
❏ CA-1069 [M]	L.S.D.	1966	20.00	40.00	80.00

LEATHERCOATED MINDS, THE
VIVA

Number	Title	Yr	VG	VG+	NM
❏ V-6003 [M]	Trip Down Sunset Strip	1967	15.00	30.00	60.00
❏ V-36003 [S]	Trip Down Sunset Strip	1967	20.00	40.00	80.00

LEAVES, THE
CAPITOL

Number	Title	Yr	VG	VG+	NM
❏ ST 2638 [S]	All the Good That's Happening	1967	7.50	15.00	30.00
❏ T 2638 [M]	All the Good That's Happening	1967	6.25	12.50	25.00

MIRA

Number	Title	Yr	VG	VG+	NM
❏ LP-3005 [M]	Hey Joe	1966	10.00	20.00	40.00
❏ LPS-3005 [S]	Hey Joe	1966	12.50	25.00	50.00

SURREY

Number	Title	Yr	VG	VG+	NM
❏ LPS-3005	Hey Joe	196?	37.50	75.00	150.00

-- Issued in Mira jackets

LED ZEPPELIN
Also see JOHN PAUL JONES; JIMMY PAGE; ROBERT PLANT.
ATLANTIC

Number	Title	Yr	VG	VG+	NM
❏ 7201 [M]	Led Zeppelin III	1970	50.00	100.00	200.00
-- White label promo only					
❏ SD 7201 [DJ]	Led Zeppelin III	1970	50.00	100.00	200.00
-- Stereo white label promo					
❏ 7208 [M]	Led Zeppelin (IV) (Runes)	1971	75.00	150.00	300.00
-- White label promo only					
❏ SD 7208 [DJ]	Led Zeppelin (IV) (Runes)	1971	37.50	75.00	150.00
-- Stereo white label promo					
❏ 7255 [M]	Houses of the Holy	1973	250.00	500.00	1,000.
-- White label promo only					
❏ 8216 [M]	Led Zeppelin	1969	100.00	200.00	400.00
-- White label promo only					
❏ SD 8216 [DJ]	Led Zeppelin	1969	50.00	100.00	200.00
-- Stereo white label promo					
❏ SD 8216 [S]	Led Zeppelin	1969	62.50	125.00	250.00
-- Possible mispress with purple and brown labels					
❏ SD 8216 [S]	Led Zeppelin	1969	5.00	10.00	20.00
-- "1841 Broadway" address on label					
❏ 8236 [M]	Led Zeppelin II	1969	50.00	100.00	200.00
-- White label promo only					
❏ SD 8236 [DJ]	Led Zeppelin II	1969	75.00	150.00	300.00
-- Stereo white label promo					
❏ SD 8236 [S]	Led Zeppelin II	1969	5.00	10.00	20.00
-- "1841 Broadway" address on label					
❏ 82144 [(6)]	Led Zeppelin (Box Set)	1990	25.00	50.00	100.00
❏ SMAS-94019	Led Zeppelin (IV) (Runes)	1972	10.00	20.00	40.00
-- Capitol Record Club edition					

MOBILE FIDELITY

Number	Title	Yr	VG	VG+	NM
❏ 1-065	Led Zeppelin II	1981	20.00	40.00	80.00

-- Audiophile vinyl

LEE, ARTHUR
Also see LOVE.
A&M

Number	Title	Yr	VG	VG+	NM
❏ SP-4356	Vindicator	1972	7.50	15.00	30.00

LEE, BRENDA
DECCA

Number	Title	Yr	VG	VG+	NM
❏ DL 4039 [M]	Brenda Lee	1960	6.25	12.50	25.00
❏ DL 4082 [M]	This Is...Brenda	1960	6.25	12.50	25.00
❏ DL 4104 [M]	Emotions	1961	6.25	12.50	25.00
❏ DL 4176 [M]	All the Way	1961	6.25	12.50	25.00
❏ DL 4216 [M]	Sincerely	1962	6.25	12.50	25.00
❏ DL 4326 [M]	Brenda, That's All	1962	6.25	12.50	25.00
❏ DL 4370 [M]	All Alone Am I	1963	6.25	12.50	25.00
❏ DL 4439 [M]	Let Me Sing	1963	6.25	12.50	25.00
❏ DL 4509 [M]	By Request	1964	5.00	10.00	20.00
❏ DL 4583 [M]	Merry Christmas from Brenda Lee	1964	5.00	10.00	20.00
❏ DL 4626 [M]	Top Teen Hits	1965	5.00	10.00	20.00
❏ DL 4661 [M]	The Versatile Brenda Lee	1965	5.00	10.00	20.00
❏ DL 4684 [M]	Too Many Rivers	1965	5.00	10.00	20.00
❏ DL 4755 [M]	Bye Bye Blues	1966	5.00	10.00	20.00
❏ DL 4757 [M]	10 Golden Years	1966	6.25	12.50	25.00
-- With gatefold cover					
❏ DL 4941 [M]	Reflections in Blue	1967	5.00	10.00	20.00
❏ DL 8873 [M]	Grandma, What Great Songs You Sang	1960	10.00	20.00	40.00
❏ DL 74039 [S]	Brenda Lee	1960	7.50	15.00	30.00
❏ DL 74082 [S]	This Is...Brenda	1960	7.50	15.00	30.00
❏ DL 74104 [S]	Emotions	1961	7.50	15.00	30.00
❏ DL 74176 [S]	All the Way	1961	7.50	15.00	30.00
❏ DL 74216 [S]	Sincerely	1962	7.50	15.00	30.00
❏ DL 74326 [S]	Brenda, That's All	1962	7.50	15.00	30.00
❏ DL 74370 [S]	All Alone Am I	1963	7.50	15.00	30.00
❏ DL 74439 [S]	Let Me Sing	1963	7.50	15.00	30.00
❏ DL 74509 [S]	By Request	1964	6.25	12.50	25.00
❏ DL 74583 [S]	Merry Christmas from Brenda Lee	1964	6.25	12.50	25.00
❏ DL 74626 [S]	Top Teen Hits	1965	6.25	12.50	25.00
❏ DL 74661 [S]	The Versatile Brenda Lee	1965	6.25	12.50	25.00
❏ DL 74684 [S]	Too Many Rivers	1965	6.25	12.50	25.00
❏ DL 74755 [S]	Bye Bye Blues	1966	6.25	12.50	25.00
❏ DL 74757 [S]	10 Golden Years	196?	5.00	10.00	20.00
-- With regular cover					
❏ DL 74757 [S]	10 Golden Years	1966	7.50	15.00	30.00
-- With gatefold cover					
❏ DL 74825 [S]	Coming On Strong	1966	5.00	10.00	20.00
❏ DL 78873 [S]	Grandma, What Great Songs You Sang	1960	12.50	25.00	50.00
❏ ST-92062	Johnny One Time	1969	5.00	10.00	20.00
-- Capitol Record Club edition					
❏ R 103619 [S]	Merry Christmas from Brenda Lee	1971	5.00	10.00	20.00
-- RCA Music Service edition					

MCA

Number	Title	Yr	VG	VG+	NM
❏ 4012 [(2)]	The Brenda Lee Story -- Her Greatest Hits	1973	5.00	10.00	20.00

LEE, BYRON, AND THE DRAGONAIRES
ATCO

Number	Title	Yr	VG	VG+	NM
❏ 33-182 [M]	Jump Up	1966	5.00	10.00	20.00
❏ SD 33-182 [S]	Jump Up	1966	6.25	12.50	25.00

BMN

Number	Title	Yr	VG	VG+	NM
❏ 004	Dance the Ska	196?	5.00	10.00	20.00

JAD

Number	Title	Yr	VG	VG+	NM
❏ JS-1004	Byron Lee and the Dragonaires	1968	5.00	10.00	20.00

TOWERS HALL

Number	Title	Yr	VG	VG+	NM
❏ 006	The Sounds of Jamaica	196?	5.00	10.00	20.00

LEE, DICKEY
SMASH

Number	Title	Yr	VG	VG+	NM
❏ MGS-27020 [M]	The Tale of Patches	1962	7.50	15.00	30.00
❏ SRS-67020 [S]	The Tale of Patches	1962	10.00	20.00	40.00

TCF HALL

Number	Title	Yr	VG	VG+	NM
❏ ST-9001 [S]	"Laurie" and "The Girl from Peyton Place"	1965	6.25	12.50	25.00
❏ T-9001 [M]	"Laurie" and "The Girl from Peyton Place"	1965	5.00	10.00	20.00

Number	Title	Yr	VG	VG+	NM

LEE, JACKIE
MIRWOOD
Number	Title	Yr	VG	VG+	NM
❏ MW-7000 [M]	The Duck	1966	5.00	10.00	20.00
❏ SW-7000 [S]	The Duck	1966	6.25	12.50	25.00

LEE, JULIA
CAPITOL
| ❏ H 228 [10] | Party Time | 1950 | 30.00 | 60.00 | 120.00 |
| ❏ T 228 [M] | Party Time | 195? | 20.00 | 40.00 | 80.00 |

LEE, KATIE
HORIZON
| ❏ WP-1604 [M] | The Best of Katie Lee | 1962 | 5.00 | 10.00 | 20.00 |
| ❏ WP-1604 [S] | The Best of Katie Lee | 1962 | 6.25 | 12.50 | 25.00 |
REPRISE
| ❏ R-6025 [M] | Songs of Coach and Consultation | 1961 | 6.25 | 12.50 | 25.00 |
SPECIALTY
| ❏ SP-5000 [M] | Spicy Songs for Cool Knights | 1959 | 7.50 | 15.00 | 30.00 |

LEE, LAURA
CHESS
| ❏ CH-50031 | Love More Than Pride | 1972 | 5.00 | 10.00 | 20.00 |

LEE, MICHELE
COLUMBIA
| ❏ CS 9286 [S] | A Taste of the Fantastic | 1966 | 5.00 | 10.00 | 20.00 |
| ❏ CS 9682 | L. David Sloane and Other Hits of Today | 1968 | 5.00 | 10.00 | 20.00 |

LEE, PEGGY
CAPITOL
| ❏ ST-105 | Two Shows Nightly | 1969 | 50.00 | 100.00 | 200.00 |

-- Withdrawn immediately after release

| ❏ H 151 [10] | Rendezvous with Peggy Lee | 1952 | 25.00 | 50.00 | 100.00 |
| ❏ T 151 [M] | Rendezvous with Peggy Lee | 1954 | 12.50 | 25.00 | 50.00 |

-- Turquoise or gray label

| ❏ T 151 [M] | Rendezvous with Peggy Lee | 1959 | 6.25 | 12.50 | 25.00 |

-- Black label with colorband, Capitol logo at left

| ❏ H 204 [10] | My Best to You | 1952 | 25.00 | 50.00 | 100.00 |
| ❏ T 204 [M] | My Best to You | 1954 | 12.50 | 25.00 | 50.00 |

-- Turquoise or gray label

| ❏ T 204 [M] | My Best to You | 1959 | 6.25 | 12.50 | 25.00 |

-- Black label with colorband, Capitol logo at left

❏ STCL-576 [(3)]	Peggy Lee	1970	6.25	12.50	25.00
❏ SW 864 [S]	The Man I Love	1959	7.50	15.00	30.00
❏ W 864 [M]	The Man I Love	1957	12.50	25.00	50.00

-- Turquoise or gray label

| ❏ W 864 [M] | The Man I Love | 1959 | 6.25 | 12.50 | 25.00 |

-- Black label with colorband, Capitol logo at left

| ❏ ST 975 [S] | Jump for Joy | 1959 | 7.50 | 15.00 | 30.00 |
| ❏ T 975 [M] | Jump for Joy | 1958 | 10.00 | 20.00 | 40.00 |

-- Turquoise or gray label

| ❏ T 975 [M] | Jump for Joy | 1959 | 6.25 | 12.50 | 25.00 |

-- Black label with colorband, Capitol logo at left

❏ ST 1049 [S]	Things Are Swingin'	1959	7.50	15.00	30.00
❏ T 1049 [M]	Things Are Swingin'	1958	6.25	12.50	25.00
❏ ST 1131 [S]	I Like Men	1959	7.50	15.00	30.00
❏ T 1131 [M]	I Like Men	1959	6.25	12.50	25.00
❏ ST 1213 [S]	Alright, Okay, You Win	1959	7.50	15.00	30.00
❏ T 1213 [M]	Alright, Okay, You Win	1959	6.25	12.50	25.00
❏ ST 1219 [S]	Beauty and the Beast	1959	7.50	15.00	30.00

-- With George Shearing; black label with colorband, Capitol logo at left

| ❏ ST 1219 [S] | Beauty and the Beast | 1962 | 5.00 | 10.00 | 20.00 |

-- With George Shearing; black label with colorband, Capitol logo at top

| ❏ T 1219 [M] | Beauty and the Beast | 1959 | 6.25 | 12.50 | 25.00 |

-- With George Shearing; black label with colorband, Capitol logo at left

| ❏ ST 1290 [S] | Latin Ala Lee! | 1960 | 6.25 | 12.50 | 25.00 |

-- Black label with colorband, Capitol logo at left

| ❏ T 1290 [M] | Latin Ala Lee! | 1960 | 5.00 | 10.00 | 20.00 |

-- Black label with colorband, Capitol logo at left

| ❏ ST 1366 [S] | All Aglow Again | 1960 | 6.25 | 12.50 | 25.00 |

-- Black label with colorband, Capitol logo at left

| ❏ T 1366 [M] | All Aglow Again | 1960 | 5.00 | 10.00 | 20.00 |

-- Black label with colorband, Capitol logo at left

| ❏ ST 1401 [S] | Pretty Eyes | 1960 | 6.25 | 12.50 | 25.00 |

-- Black label with colorband, Capitol logo at left

| ❏ T 1401 [M] | Pretty Eyes | 1960 | 5.00 | 10.00 | 20.00 |

-- Black label with colorband, Capitol logo at left

❏ ST 1423 [S]	Christmas Carousel	1960	6.25	12.50	25.00
❏ T 1423 [M]	Christmas Carousel	1960	5.00	10.00	20.00
❏ ST 1475 [S]	Ole Ala Lee!	1961	6.25	12.50	25.00
❏ T 1475 [M]	Ole Ala Lee!	1961	5.00	10.00	20.00
❏ ST 1520 [S]	Basin Street East	1961	6.25	12.50	25.00

-- Black label with colorband, Capitol logo at left

Number	Title	Yr	VG	VG+	NM
❏ T 1520 [M]	Basin Street East	1961	5.00	10.00	20.00

-- Black label with colorband, Capitol logo at left

❏ ST 1630 [S]	If You Go	1962	6.25	12.50	25.00
❏ T 1630 [M]	If You Go	1962	5.00	10.00	20.00
❏ ST 1671 [S]	Blue Cross Country	1962	6.25	12.50	25.00
❏ T 1671 [M]	Blue Cross Country	1962	5.00	10.00	20.00
❏ T 1743 [M]	Bewitching-Lee!	1962	6.25	12.50	25.00
❏ ST 1772 [S]	Sugar 'n' Spice	1962	6.25	12.50	25.00
❏ T 1772 [M]	Sugar 'n' Spice	1962	5.00	10.00	20.00
❏ ST 1850 [S]	Mink Jazz	1963	6.25	12.50	25.00
❏ T 1850 [M]	Mink Jazz	1963	5.00	10.00	20.00
❏ ST 1857 [S]	I'm a Woman	1963	6.25	12.50	25.00
❏ T 1857 [M]	I'm a Woman	1963	5.00	10.00	20.00
❏ ST 1969 [S]	In Love Again	1963	6.25	12.50	25.00
❏ T 1969 [M]	In Love Again	1963	5.00	10.00	20.00
❏ ST 2096 [S]	In the Name of Love	1964	5.00	10.00	20.00
❏ ST 2320 [S]	Pass Me By	1965	5.00	10.00	20.00
❏ ST 2388 [S]	That Was Then, Now Is Now	1965	5.00	10.00	20.00
❏ ST 2469 [S]	Guitars Ala Lee	1966	5.00	10.00	20.00
❏ ST 2475 [S]	Big $pender	1966	5.00	10.00	20.00
❏ T 2732 [M]	Extra Special	1967	5.00	10.00	20.00

COLUMBIA
| ❏ CL 6033 [10] | Benny Goodman and Peggy Lee | 1949 | 15.00 | 30.00 | 60.00 |

DECCA
❏ DXB 164 [(2) M]	The Best of Peggy Lee	1964	7.50	15.00	30.00
❏ DL 4458 [M]	Lover	1964	6.25	12.50	25.00
❏ DL 4461 [M]	The Fabulous Peggy Lee	1964	6.25	12.50	25.00
❏ DL 5482 [10]	Black Coffee	1953	25.00	50.00	100.00
❏ DL 5539 [10]	Songs in an Intimate Style	1953	20.00	40.00	80.00
❏ DXSB 7164 [(2) R]	The Best of Peggy Lee	1964	5.00	10.00	20.00
❏ DL 8358 [M]	Black Coffee	1956	15.00	30.00	60.00
❏ DL 8411 [M]	Dream Street	1957	15.00	30.00	60.00
❏ DL 8591 [M]	Sea Shells	1958	15.00	30.00	60.00
❏ DL 8816 [M]	Miss Wonderful	1959	15.00	30.00	60.00

HARMONY
| ❏ HL 7005 [M] | Peggy Lee Sings with Benny Goodman | 195? | 6.25 | 12.50 | 25.00 |

LEE, PINKY
DECCA
| ❏ DL 8421 [M] | The Surprise Party | 1957 | 10.00 | 20.00 | 40.00 |

LEE, ROBIN
DOT
| ❏ DLP-3661 [M] | Robin Lee | 1965 | 6.25 | 12.50 | 25.00 |

LEFEVERE, KAMIEL
MERCURY LIVING PRESENCE
| ❏ SR 90189 [S] | The Magic of the Bells | 196? | 17.50 | 35.00 | 70.00 |

-- Maroon label, no "Vendor: Mercury Record Corporation"

LEFEVRE, RAYMOND
ATLANTIC
| ❏ 8044 [M] | Romantica | 1961 | 5.00 | 10.00 | 20.00 |
| ❏ SD 8044 [S] | Romantica | 1961 | 6.25 | 12.50 | 25.00 |

LEFT BANKE, THE
SMASH
❏ MGS-27088 [M]	Walk Away Renee/Pretty Ballerina	1967	10.00	20.00	40.00
❏ SRS-67088 [S]	Walk Away Renee/Pretty Ballerina	1967	10.00	20.00	40.00
❏ SRS-67113	The Left Banke, Too	1968	12.50	25.00	50.00

LEGEND
Probably two different groups.
BELL
| ❏ 6027 | Legend | 1969 | 10.00 | 20.00 | 40.00 |
MEGAPHONE
| ❏ 101 | Legend | 1970 | 20.00 | 40.00 | 80.00 |

LEGENDS, THE
CAPITOL
| ❏ ST 1925 [S] | The Legends Let Loose | 1963 | 20.00 | 40.00 | 80.00 |
| ❏ T 1925 [M] | The Legends Let Loose | 1963 | 15.00 | 30.00 | 60.00 |
COLUMBIA
| ❏ CL 1707 [M] | Hit Sounds of Today's Smash Hit Combos | 1961 | 7.50 | 15.00 | 30.00 |
| ❏ CS 8507 [S] | Hit Sounds of Today's Smash Hit Combos | 1961 | 10.00 | 20.00 | 40.00 |
ERMINE
| ❏ LP-101 [M] | The Legends Let Loose | 1963 | 50.00 | 100.00 | 200.00 |

LEGRAND, MICHEL
COLUMBIA

Number	Title	Yr	VG	VG+	NM
❏ CL 555 [M]	I Love Paris	1954	10.00	20.00	40.00
❏ CL 647 [M]	Holiday in Rome	1955	6.25	12.50	25.00
❏ CL 706 [M]	Vienna Holiday	1955	6.25	12.50	25.00
❏ CL 888 [M]	Castles in Spain	1956	6.25	12.50	25.00
❏ CL 1115 [M]	Michel Legrand Plays Cole Porter	1957	6.25	12.50	25.00
❏ CL 1139 [M]	Legrand in Rio	1957	6.25	12.50	25.00
❏ CL 1250 [M]	Legrand Jazz	1958	10.00	20.00	40.00
-- Miles Davis appears on this record					
❏ CL 1437 [M]	I Love Paris	1960	6.25	12.50	25.00
❏ CS 8079 [S]	Legrand Jazz	1959	10.00	20.00	40.00
-- Miles Davis appears on this record					
❏ CS 8237 [S]	I Love Paris	1960	5.00	10.00	20.00

MOBILE FIDELITY

Number	Title	Yr	VG	VG+	NM
❏ 1-504	Jazz Grand	198?	12.50	25.00	50.00
-- Audiophile vinyl					

PHILIPS

Number	Title	Yr	VG	VG+	NM
❏ PHM 200-074 [M]	The Michel Legrand Big Band Plays Richard Rogers	1963	5.00	10.00	20.00
❏ PHM 200-143 [M]	Michel Legrand Sings	1964	6.25	12.50	25.00
❏ PHS 600-074 [S]	The Michel Legrand Big Band Plays Richard Rogers	1963	6.25	12.50	25.00
❏ PHS 600-143 [S]	Michel Legrand Sings	1964	7.50	15.00	30.00

LEGS DIAMOND
CREAM

Number	Title	Yr	VG	VG+	NM
❏ CR 1010	Firepower	1979	6.25	12.50	25.00

MERCURY

Number	Title	Yr	VG	VG+	NM
❏ SRM-1-1136	Legs Diamond	1977	7.50	15.00	30.00
❏ SRM-1-1191	A Diamond Is a Hard Rock	1977	7.50	15.00	30.00

LEHRER, TOM
LEHRER

Number	Title	Yr	VG	VG+	NM
❏ TL-1 [10]	Songs by Tom Lehrer	1952	25.00	50.00	100.00
❏ TL-101 [M]	Songs by Tom Lehrer	1959	10.00	20.00	40.00
❏ TL-102 [M]	More of Tom Lehrer	1958	10.00	20.00	40.00
❏ TL-102S [S]	More of Tom Lehrer	1959	10.00	20.00	40.00
❏ TL-201 [M]	Tom Lehrer Revisited	1959	6.25	12.50	25.00
❏ TL-202 [M]	An Evening Wasted with Tom Lehrer	1959	6.25	12.50	25.00
❏ TL-202S [S]	An Evening Wasted with Tom Lehrer	1959	10.00	20.00	40.00

REPRISE

Number	Title	Yr	VG	VG+	NM
❏ R-6179 [M]	That Was the Year That Was	1965	5.00	10.00	20.00
❏ RS-6179 [S]	That Was the Year That Was	1965	6.25	12.50	25.00
-- Pink, yellow and green label					
❏ R 6199 [M]	An Evening Wasted with Tom Lehrer	1966	5.00	10.00	20.00
-- Reissue of Lehrer 202					
❏ RS 6199 [S]	An Evening Wasted with Tom Lehrer	1966	6.25	12.50	25.00
-- Reissue of Lehrer 202					
❏ R-6216 [M]	Songs of Tom Lehrer	1966	5.00	10.00	20.00
❏ RS-6216 [S]	Songs of Tom Lehrer	1966	6.25	12.50	25.00

LEIBER AND STOLLER BIG BAND, THE
ATLANTIC

Number	Title	Yr	VG	VG+	NM
❏ 8047 [M]	Yakety Yak	1960	10.00	20.00	40.00
-- White "fan" logo on right side of label					
❏ 8047 [M]	Yakety Yak	1962	5.00	10.00	20.00
-- Black "fan" logo on right side of label					
❏ SD 8047 [S]	Yakety Yak	1960	12.50	25.00	50.00
-- White "fan" logo on right side of label					
❏ SD 8047 [S]	Yakety Yak	1962	6.25	12.50	25.00
-- Black "fan" logo on right side of label					

LEIBER, JERRY
KAPP

Number	Title	Yr	VG	VG+	NM
❏ KL-1127 [M]	Scooby-Doo	1959	12.50	25.00	50.00

LEIBERT, DICK
WESTMINSTER

Number	Title	Yr	VG	VG+	NM
❏ WST 15006 [S]	Leibert Takes Broadway	195?	5.00	10.00	20.00
❏ WST 15009 [S]	Leibert Takes Richmond	195?	5.00	10.00	20.00
❏ WST 15020 [S]	A Merry Wurlitzer Christmas	195?	5.00	10.00	20.00
❏ WST 15034 [S]	Leibert Takes a Holiday	195?	5.00	10.00	20.00
❏ WST 15043 [S]	Leibert Takes You Dancing	195?	5.00	10.00	20.00
❏ WST 15050 [S]	Sing a Song with Leibert	195?	5.00	10.00	20.00

LEMMON, JACK
CAPITOL

Number	Title	Yr	VG	VG+	NM
❏ ST 1943 [S]	Jack Lemmon Plays Piano Selections from Irma La Douce	1963	15.00	30.00	60.00
❏ T 1943 [M]	Jack Lemmon Plays Piano Selections from Irma La Douce	1963	12.50	25.00	50.00

EPIC

Number	Title	Yr	VG	VG+	NM
❏ BN 523 [S]	A Twist of Lemmon	1959	12.50	25.00	50.00
❏ BN 528 [S]	Jack Lemmon Sings and Plays Music from Some Like It Hot	1959	12.50	25.00	50.00
❏ LN 3491 [M]	A Twist of Lemmon	1959	10.00	20.00	40.00
❏ LN 3559 [M]	Jack Lemmon Sings and Plays Music from Some Like It Hot	1959	10.00	20.00	40.00

LEMON PIPERS, THE
BUDDAH

Number	Title	Yr	VG	VG+	NM
❏ BD-5009 [M]	Green Tambourine	1968	6.25	12.50	25.00
❏ BDS-5009 [S]	Green Tambourine	1968	6.25	12.50	25.00
❏ BDS-5016	Jungle Marmalade	1968	6.25	12.50	25.00

LEMONHEADS, THE
ATLANTIC

Number	Title	Yr	VG	VG+	NM
❏ 82537	Come On Feel the Lemonheads	1993	5.00	10.00	20.00
-- 5,000 copies pressed, all on green vinyl					

TAANG!

Number	Title	Yr	VG	VG+	NM
❏ 15	Hate Your Friends	1987	5.00	10.00	20.00
-- First pressing: Black vinyl, yellow lettering on sleeve, yellow label					

LENNON SISTERS, THE
BRUNSWICK

Number	Title	Yr	VG	VG+	NM
❏ BL 54031 [M]	Let's Get Acquainted	1957	6.25	12.50	25.00
❏ BL 54039 [M]	Lawrence Welk Presents the Lennon Sisters	1958	6.25	12.50	25.00

DOT

Number	Title	Yr	VG	VG+	NM
❏ DLP 25343 [S]	Christmas with the Lennon Sisters	1961	5.00	10.00	20.00
❏ DLP-25250 [S]	Best-Loved Catholic Hymns	1959	5.00	10.00	20.00
❏ DLP-25292 [S]	The Lennon Sisters Sing 12 Great Hits	1960	5.00	10.00	20.00
❏ DLP-25398 [S]	Sad Movies (Make Me Cry)	1961	5.00	10.00	20.00

LENNON, JOHN
Also see THE BEATLES.
ADAM VIII

Number	Title	Yr	VG	VG+	NM
❏ A-8018	John Lennon Sings the Great Rock & Roll Hits (Roots)	1975	250.00	500.00	1,000.

-- Counterfeits abound. On authentic copies, cover is posterboard (not slicks); labels are normal size (not overly large); printing on cover is sharp, not blurry; the word "Greatest" does NOT appear on the spine. Authentic copies usually have ad sleeve also.

APPLE

Number	Title	Yr	VG	VG+	NM
❏ SMAX-3361	Wedding Album	1969	37.50	75.00	150.00

-- With photo strip, postcard, poster of wedding photos, poster of lithographs, "Bagism" bag, booklet, photo of slice of wedding cake. Missing inserts reduce the value.

Number	Title	Yr	VG	VG+	NM
❏ SW-3362	Live Peace in Toronto 1969	1970	5.00	10.00	20.00

-- By "The Plastic Ono Band"; with calendar. A recent warehouse find of sealed copies has deflated this LP's value

Number	Title	Yr	VG	VG+	NM
❏ SW-3372	John Lennon Plastic Ono Band	1970	5.00	10.00	20.00
❏ SW-3379	Imagine	1971	5.00	10.00	20.00

-- With either of two postcard inserts, lyric sleeve, poster

Number	Title	Yr	VG	VG+	NM
❏ SW-3379	Imagine	1975	5.00	10.00	20.00

-- "All Rights Reserved" label

Number	Title	Yr	VG	VG+	NM
❏ SVBB-3392 [(2)]	Some Time in New York City	1972	7.50	15.00	30.00

-- By John and Yoko; with photo card and petition

Number	Title	Yr	VG	VG+	NM
❏ SVBB-3392 [(2)] DJ	Some Time in New York City	1972	250.00	500.00	1,000.

-- White label promo

Number	Title	Yr	VG	VG+	NM
❏ SW-3414	Mind Games	1973	5.00	10.00	20.00
❏ SW-3416	Walls and Bridges	1974	5.00	10.00	20.00

-- With fold-open segmented front cover

Number	Title	Yr	VG	VG+	NM
❏ SK-3419	Rock 'n' Roll	1975	5.00	10.00	20.00
❏ SW-3421	Shaved Fish	1975	5.00	10.00	20.00
❏ T-5001	Two Virgins -- Unfinished Music No. 1	1968	37.50	75.00	150.00

-- With Yoko Ono; price with brown bag

Number	Title	Yr	VG	VG+	NM
❏ T-5001	Two Virgins -- Unfinished Music No. 1	1968	12.50	25.00	50.00

-- With Yoko Ono; without brown bag

Number	Title	Yr	VG	VG+	NM
❏ T-5001	Two Virgins -- Unfinished Music No. 1	1968	37.50	75.00	150.00

-- With Yoko Ono; with die-cut bag

CAPITOL

Number	Title	Yr	VG	VG+	NM
❏ SW-3372	John Lennon Plastic Ono Band	1982	5.00	10.00	20.00

-- Black label, print in colorband

Number	Title	Yr	VG	VG+	NM
❏ SW-3372	John Lennon Plastic Ono Band	1988	7.50	15.00	30.00

-- Purple label, small Capitol logo

Number	Title	Yr	VG	VG+	NM
❏ SW-3379	Imagine	1986	7.50	15.00	30.00

-- Black label, print in colorband

Number	Title	Yr	VG	VG+	NM
❏ SW-3379	Imagine	1987	6.25	12.50	25.00

-- Black label, print in colorband; "Digitally Re-Mastered" at top of front cover

Number	Title	Yr	VG	VG+	NM
❏ SW-3379	Imagine	1988	7.50	15.00	30.00

-- Purple label, small Capitol logo

Number	Title	Yr	VG	VG+	NM
❏ SVBB-3392 [(2)] Some Time in New York City		197?	25.00	50.00	100.00
-- Both discs in single-pocket gatefold (the other pocket is glued shut)					
❏ SVBB-3392 [(2)] Some Time in New York City		197?	6.25	12.50	25.00
-- By John and Yoko; purple label, large Capitol logo					
❏ SW-3414	Mind Games	1978	10.00	20.00	40.00
-- Purple label, large Capitol logo					
❏ SW-3416	Walls and Bridges	1982	7.50	15.00	30.00
-- Black label, print in colorband					
❏ SW-3416	Walls and Bridges	1989	7.50	15.00	30.00
-- Purple label, small Capitol logo					
❏ SK-3419	Rock 'n' Roll	1978	10.00	20.00	40.00
-- Purple label, large Capitol logo					
❏ SW-3421	Shaved Fish	1978	10.00	20.00	40.00
-- Purple Capitol label with Capitol logo on cover					
❏ SW-3421	Shaved Fish	1983	10.00	20.00	40.00
-- Black Capitol label with Capitol logo on cover					
❏ SW-3421	Shaved Fish	1983	5.00	10.00	20.00
-- Black Capitol label with Apple logo on cover					
❏ SW-3421	Shaved Fish	1989	10.00	20.00	40.00
-- Purple Capitol label (small logo) with Capitol logo on cover					
❏ ST-12239	Live Peace in Toronto 1969	1983	12.50	25.00	50.00
-- By "The Plastic Ono Band"; reissue, black Capitol label					
❏ C1-90803 [(2)] Imagine: Music from the Motion Picture		1988	5.00	10.00	20.00
❏ C1-91425	Double Fantasy	1989	5.00	10.00	20.00
-- Very briefly available reissue					
❏ R 144136	Menlove Ave.	1986	12.50	25.00	50.00
-- RCA Music Service edition					
❏ R 144136	Menlove Ave.	198?	12.50	25.00	50.00
-- BMG Direct Marketing edition					
❏ C1-591425	Double Fantasy	1989	15.00	30.00	60.00
-- Columbia House edition of reissue					
GEFFEN					
❏ GHS 2001	Double Fantasy	1981	18.75	37.50	75.00
-- Columbia House edition (all have corrected back cover) with "CH" on label					
❏ GHS 2001	Double Fantasy	1986	12.50	25.00	50.00
-- Same as above, but with black Geffen label					
❏ GHSP 2023	The John Lennon Collection	1982	5.00	10.00	20.00
❏ GHSP 2023	The John Lennon Collection	1982	12.50	25.00	50.00
-- Promo only on Quiex II audiophile vinyl					
❏ R 104689	Double Fantasy	1981	10.00	20.00	40.00
-- RCA Music Service edition					
MOBILE FIDELITY					
❏ 1-153	Imagine	1984	12.50	25.00	50.00
-- Audiophile vinyl					
NAUTILUS					
❏ NR-47	Double Fantasy	1982	500.00	1,000.	2,000.
-- Half-speed master; alternate experimental cover with yellow and red added to black and white front					
❏ NR-47	Double Fantasy	1982	20.00	40.00	80.00
-- Half-speed master					
PARLOPHONE					
❏ 21954 [(2)]	Lennon Legend	1998	5.00	10.00	20.00
-- "Made in U.S.A." on back cover					
POLYDOR					
❏ 817 160-1	Milk and Honey	1984	37.50	75.00	150.00
-- Yellow or green vinyl; unauthorized "inside jobs"					
SILHOUETTE					
❏ SM-10012 [(2)] Reflections and Poetry		1984	6.25	12.50	25.00
ZAPPLE					
❏ ST-3357	Life with the Lions -- Unfinished Music No. 2	1969	5.00	10.00	20.00
-- With Yoko Ono; a recent warehouse find of sealed copies has deflated this LP's value					

LENNON, JULIAN
ATLANTIC

Number	Title	Yr	VG	VG+	NM
❏ PR 2693 [DJ] Mr. Jordan According to Mr. Lennon		1989	5.00	10.00	20.00
-- Promo-only interview album					

LENOIR, J.B.
CHESS

Number	Title	Yr	VG	VG+	NM
❏ LP-410	Natural Man	1970	10.00	20.00	40.00

LENYA, LOTTE
COLUMBIA MASTERWORKS

Number	Title	Yr	VG	VG+	NM
❏ ML 5056 [M]	Berlin Theater Songs by Kurt Weill	1957	7.50	15.00	30.00
❏ KL 5229 [M]	September Song	1958	7.50	15.00	30.00

LEONARD, HARLAN, AND HIS ROCKETS
RCA VICTOR

Number	Title	Yr	VG	VG+	NM
❏ LPV-531 [M]	Harlan Leonard and His Rockets	1966	5.00	10.00	20.00

LEONARD, JACK E.
VIK

Number	Title	Yr	VG	VG+	NM
❏ LX-1080 [M]	Rock 'n Roll for People Over Sixteen	1957	10.00	20.00	40.00

LEOPARDS, THE
MOON

Number	Title	Yr	VG	VG+	NM
❏ (# unknown)	Kansas City Slickers	1977	6.25	12.50	25.00

LES DJINNS SINGERS
ABC-PARAMOUNT

Number	Title	Yr	VG	VG+	NM
❏ ABCS-397 [S]	Joyeaux Noel	1961	5.00	10.00	20.00

LESTER, KETTY
ERA

Number	Title	Yr	VG	VG+	NM
❏ EL-108 [M]	Love Letters	1962	10.00	20.00	40.00
❏ ES-108 [S]	Love Letters	1962	15.00	30.00	60.00
RCA VICTOR					
❏ LPM-2945 [M]	The Soul of Me	1964	6.25	12.50	25.00
❏ LSP-2945 [S]	The Soul of Me	1964	7.50	15.00	30.00
❏ LPM-3326 [M]	Where Is Love	1965	6.25	12.50	25.00
❏ LSP-3326 [S]	Where Is Love	1965	7.50	15.00	30.00
TOWER					
❏ ST 5029 [S]	When a Woman Loves a Man	1966	6.25	12.50	25.00
❏ T 5029 [M]	When a Woman Loves a Man	1966	6.25	12.50	25.00

LETTERMEN, THE
CAPITOL

Number	Title	Yr	VG	VG+	NM
❏ STCL-577 [(3)] The Lettermen		1970	6.25	12.50	25.00
❏ ST 1669 [S]	A Song for Young Love	1962	5.00	10.00	20.00
❏ ST 1711 [S]	Once Upon a Time	1962	5.00	10.00	20.00
❏ ST 1761 [S]	Jim, Tony and Bob	1962	5.00	10.00	20.00
❏ ST 1829 [S]	College Standards	1963	5.00	10.00	20.00
❏ ST 1936 [S]	The Lettermen In Concert	1963	5.00	10.00	20.00
❏ ST-8-2587 [S]	For Christmas This Year	1966	5.00	10.00	20.00
-- Capitol Record Club edition					
❏ T 2758 [M]	The Lettermen!!!... And "Live!"	1967	5.00	10.00	20.00
LONGINES SYMPHONETTE					
❏ 220 [(5)]	A Time for Us	1972	7.50	15.00	30.00

LEVIATHAN
MACH

Number	Title	Yr	VG	VG+	NM
❏ XMA-12501	Leviathan	1974	10.00	20.00	40.00

LEWD
ICI

Number	Title	Yr	VG	VG+	NM
❏ CF 200	American Wino	1982	10.00	20.00	40.00

LEWIS AND CLARKE EXPEDITION, THE
COLGEMS

Number	Title	Yr	VG	VG+	NM
❏ COM-105 [M]	The Lewis and Clarke Expedition	1967	6.25	12.50	25.00
❏ COS-105 [S]	The Lewis and Clarke Expedition	1967	7.50	15.00	30.00

LEWIS CONNECTION, THE
Minneapolis group; PRINCE is featured on one track.
(NO LABEL)

Number	Title	Yr	VG	VG+	NM
❏ (no #)	The Lewis Connection	1979	100.00	200.00	400.00

LEWIS FAMILY, THE
STARDAY

Number	Title	Yr	VG	VG+	NM
❏ SLP-121 [M]	Singin' Time Down South	1960	7.50	15.00	30.00
❏ SLP-161 [M]	Anniversary Celebration	1962	7.50	15.00	30.00
❏ SLP-193 [M]	Gospel Special	1962	7.50	15.00	30.00
❏ SLP-238 [M]	Sing Me a Gospel Song	1962	7.50	15.00	30.00
❏ SLP-252 [M]	All Night Singing Convention	1963	7.50	15.00	30.00
❏ SLP-289 [M]	Singin' in My Soul	1964	7.50	15.00	30.00
❏ SLP-331 [M]	The First Family of Gospel Music	1965	7.50	15.00	30.00
❏ SLP-364 [M]	The Lewis Family Sings the Gospel with Carl Story	1965	7.50	15.00	30.00
❏ SLP-381 [M]	The Lewis Family Album	1965	7.50	15.00	30.00
❏ SLP-395 [M]	Shall We Gather at the River	1966	6.25	12.50	25.00
❏ SLP-408 [M]	Time Is Moving On	1966	6.25	12.50	25.00
❏ SLP-422	Golden Gospel Banjo	1968	5.00	10.00	20.00
❏ SLP-433	Did You Ever Go Sailing	1969	5.00	10.00	20.00
❏ SLP-450	Golden Gospel of the Lewis	1970	5.00	10.00	20.00

LEWIS, BARBARA
ATLANTIC

Number	Title	Yr	VG	VG+	NM
❏ 8086 [M]	Hello Stranger	1963	10.00	20.00	40.00
❏ SD 8086 [S]	Hello Stranger	1963	12.50	25.00	50.00
❏ 8090 [M]	Snap Your Fingers	1964	10.00	20.00	40.00
❏ SD 8090 [S]	Snap Your Fingers	1964	12.50	25.00	50.00
❏ 8110 [M]	Baby, I'm Yours	1965	10.00	20.00	40.00
❏ SD 8110 [S]	Baby, I'm Yours	1965	12.50	25.00	50.00
❏ 8118 [M]	It's Magic	1966	7.50	15.00	30.00

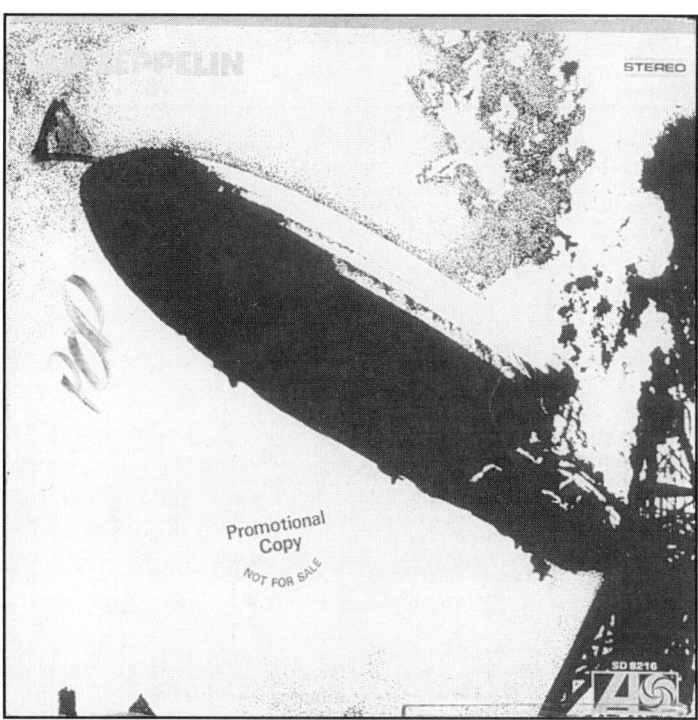

(Top left) Even from her debut album, the Canada-only release *A Truly Western Experience,* the soon-to-be-famous singer was listed in all small letters as "k.d. lang." (Top right) The original edition of Led Zeppelin's debut album isn't as easy to find as it once was. Promotional copies such as this one never were easy to find, and the price on them reflects that. (Bottom left) Released in 1964, Brenda Lee's *Merry Christmas* became an enduring part of the holiday season and was in print for over 20 years on vinyl. Original pressings on Decca are the most sought-after. (Bottom right) While the most collectible Jerry Lee Lewis albums are from the early Sun label (1200 series), many of his Smash albums are tough to find. Here is an album of duets he did in 1968 with his sister, Linda Gail Lewis.

Number	Title	Yr	VG	VG+	NM
❑ SD 8118 [S]	It's Magic	1966	10.00	20.00	40.00
❑ SD 8173	Workin' on a Groovy Thing	1968	6.25	12.50	25.00
❑ SD 8286	The Best of Barbara Lewis	1971	5.00	10.00	20.00

ENTERPRISE

Number	Title	Yr	VG	VG+	NM
❑ ENS-1006	The Many Grooves of Barbara Lewis	1970	6.25	12.50	25.00

LEWIS, BOBBY (I)
R&B artist.
BELTONE

Number	Title	Yr	VG	VG+	NM
❑ 4000 [M]	Tossin' and Turnin'	1961	50.00	100.00	200.00

LEWIS, BOBBY (II)
Country artist.
UNITED ARTISTS

Number	Title	Yr	VG	VG+	NM
❑ UAL-3582 [M]	How Long Has It Been	1967	6.25	12.50	25.00
❑ UAS-6582 [S]	How Long Has It Been	1967	6.25	12.50	25.00
❑ UAS-6616	A World of Love from Bobby	1967	5.00	10.00	20.00
❑ UAS-6629	An Ordinary Miracle	1968	5.00	10.00	20.00
❑ UAS-6673	From Heaven to Heartache	1968	5.00	10.00	20.00
❑ UAS-6717	Thanks for You and I	1969	5.00	10.00	20.00

LEWIS, DAVE
A&M

Number	Title	Yr	VG	VG+	NM
❑ LP-105 [M]	Little Green Thing	1964	5.00	10.00	20.00
❑ SP-4105 [S]	Little Green Thing	1964	6.25	12.50	25.00

JERDEN

Number	Title	Yr	VG	VG+	NM
❑ JRL-7006 [M]	Dave Lewis Plays Herb Alpert and the Tijuana Brass	1966	5.00	10.00	20.00
❑ JRLS-7006 [S]	Dave Lewis Plays Herb Alpert and the Tijuana Brass	1966	6.25	12.50	25.00

LEWIS, FURRY
AMPEX

Number	Title	Yr	VG	VG+	NM
❑ A-10140	Live at the Gaslight	1971	6.25	12.50	25.00

BLUESVILLE

Number	Title	Yr	VG	VG+	NM
❑ BVLP-1036 [M]	Back on My Feet Again	1961	25.00	50.00	100.00
-- Blue label, silver print					
❑ BVLP-1036 [M]	Back on My Feet Again	1964	7.50	15.00	30.00
-- Blue label, trident logo at right					
❑ BVLP-1037 [M]	Done Changed My Mind	1961	25.00	50.00	100.00
-- Blue label, silver print					
❑ BVLP-1037 [M]	Done Changed My Mind	1964	7.50	15.00	30.00
-- Blue label, trident logo at right					

LEWIS, GARY, AND THE PLAYBOYS
LIBERTY

Number	Title	Yr	VG	VG+	NM
❑ LRP-3408 [M]	This Diamond Ring	1965	5.00	10.00	20.00
❑ LRP-3419 [M]	A Session with Gary Lewis and the Playboys	1965	5.00	10.00	20.00
❑ LRP-3428 [M]	Everybody Loves a Clown	1965	5.00	10.00	20.00
❑ LRP-3487 [M]	(You Don't Have to) Paint Me a Picture	1967	5.00	10.00	20.00
-- Side 1, Song 4 claims to be "Tina" but plays "Ice Melts in the Sun"					
❑ LST-7408 [S]	This Diamond Ring	1965	6.25	12.50	25.00
❑ LST-7419 [S]	A Session with Gary Lewis and the Playboys	1965	6.25	12.50	25.00
❑ LST-7428 [S]	Everybody Loves a Clown	1965	6.25	12.50	25.00
❑ LST-7435 [S]	She's Just My Style	1966	5.00	10.00	20.00
❑ LST-7452 [S]	Hits Again!	1966	5.00	10.00	20.00
❑ LST-7468 [S]	Golden Greats	1966	7.50	15.00	30.00
-- Side 2, Song 2 claims to be "I Won't Make That Mistake Again" but it plays "You've Got to Hide Your Love Away"					
❑ LST-7468 [S]	Golden Greats	1966	5.00	10.00	20.00
-- Side 2 plays as listed					
❑ LST-7487 [S]	(You Don't Have to) Paint Me a Picture	1967	5.00	10.00	20.00
-- Side 1 plays as listed					
❑ LST-7487 [S]	(You Don't Have to) Paint Me a Picture	1967	6.25	12.50	25.00
-- Side 1, Song 4 claims to be "Tina" but plays "Ice Melts in the Sun"					

LEWIS, HUEY, AND THE NEWS
MOBILE FIDELITY

Number	Title	Yr	VG	VG+	NM
❑ 1-181	Sports	1985	6.25	12.50	25.00
-- Audiophile vinyl					

LEWIS, HUGH X.
KAPP

Number	Title	Yr	VG	VG+	NM
❑ KL-1462 [M]	The Hugh X. Lewis Album	1966	5.00	10.00	20.00
❑ KL-1494 [M]	Just Before Dawn	1966	5.00	10.00	20.00
❑ KL-1522 [M]	My Kind of Country	1967	7.50	15.00	30.00
❑ KS-3462 [S]	The Hugh X. Lewis Album	1966	6.25	12.50	25.00

Number	Title	Yr	VG	VG+	NM
❑ KS-3494 [S]	Just Before Dawn	1966	6.25	12.50	25.00
❑ KS-3522 [S]	My Kind of Country	1967	6.25	12.50	25.00
❑ KS-3545	Just a Prayer Away	1968	6.25	12.50	25.00
❑ KS-3563	Country Fever	1968	6.25	12.50	25.00

LEWIS, JERRY
DECCA

Number	Title	Yr	VG	VG+	NM
❑ DL 8410 [M]	Jerry Lewis Just Sings	1956	15.00	30.00	60.00
❑ DL 8595 [M]	More Jerry Lewis	1957	15.00	30.00	60.00
❑ DL 8936 [M]	Big Songs for Little People	1959	12.50	25.00	50.00
❑ DL 78936 [S]	Big Songs for Little People	1959	15.00	30.00	60.00

DOT

Number	Title	Yr	VG	VG+	NM
❑ DLP 25664 [S]	The Jerry Lewis Singers	1964	5.00	10.00	20.00

LEWIS, JERRY LEE
DESIGN

Number	Title	Yr	VG	VG+	NM
❑ DLP-165 [M]	Rockin' with Jerry Lee Lewis	1963	6.25	12.50	25.00
❑ DST-165 [R]	Rockin' with Jerry Lee Lewis	1963	5.00	10.00	20.00

MERCURY

Number	Title	Yr	VG	VG+	NM
❑ 690 [DJ]	A Jerry Lee Lewis Radio Special	1973	12.50	25.00	50.00
❑ SRM-2-803 [(2)]	The Session	1973	5.00	10.00	20.00
❑ SR-61318	In Loving Memories	1970	7.50	15.00	30.00
❑ SR-61343	Touching Home	1971	5.00	10.00	20.00
-- With drawing on cover and small photo of Jerry Lee					

SEARS

Number	Title	Yr	VG	VG+	NM
❑ SPS-610	Hound Dog	1970	6.25	12.50	25.00

SMASH

Number	Title	Yr	VG	VG+	NM
❑ MGS-27040 [M]	The Golden Hits of Jerry Lee Lewis	1964	6.25	12.50	25.00
❑ MGS-27056 [M]	The Greatest Live Show on Earth	1964	25.00	50.00	100.00
❑ MGS-27063 [M]	The Return of Rock	1965	7.50	15.00	30.00
❑ MGS-27071 [M]	Country Songs for City Folks	1965	6.25	12.50	25.00
❑ MGS-27079 [M]	Memphis Beat	1966	6.25	12.50	25.00
❑ MGS-27086 [M]	By Request -- More of the Greatest Live Show on Earth	1966	7.50	15.00	30.00
❑ MGS-27097 [M]	Soul My Way	1967	7.50	15.00	30.00
❑ SRS-67040 [S]	The Golden Hits of Jerry Lee Lewis	1964	7.50	15.00	30.00
❑ SRS-67056 [S]	The Greatest Live Show on Earth	1964	37.50	75.00	150.00
❑ SRS-67063 [S]	The Return of Rock	1965	10.00	20.00	40.00
❑ SRS-67071 [S]	Country Songs for City Folks	1965	7.50	15.00	30.00
❑ SRS-67079 [S]	Memphis Beat	1966	7.50	15.00	30.00
❑ SRS-67086 [S]	By Request -- More of the Greatest Live Show on Earth	1966	10.00	20.00	40.00
❑ SRS-67097 [S]	Soul My Way	1967	10.00	20.00	40.00
❑ SRS-67104	Another Place Another Time	1968	5.00	10.00	20.00
❑ SRS-67112	She Still Comes Around (To Love What's Left of Me)	1969	5.00	10.00	20.00
❑ SRS-67117	Jerry Lee Lewis Sings the Country Music Hall of Fame Hits, Vol. 1	1969	5.00	10.00	20.00
❑ SRS-67118	Jerry Lee Lewis Sings the Country Music Hall of Fame Hits, Vol. 2	1969	5.00	10.00	20.00
❑ SRS-67126	Together	1969	5.00	10.00	20.00
-- With Linda Gail Lewis					
❑ SRS-67128	She Even Woke Me Up to Say Goodbye	1970	5.00	10.00	20.00
❑ SRS-67131	The Best of Jerry Lee Lewis	1970	5.00	10.00	20.00

SUN

Number	Title	Yr	VG	VG+	NM
❑ SLP-1230 [M]	Jerry Lee Lewis	1958	50.00	100.00	200.00
❑ SLP-1265 [M]	Jerry Lee's Greatest	1961	62.50	125.00	250.00
❑ SLP-1265 [M-DJ]	Jerry Lee's Greatest	1961	200.00	400.00	800.00
-- White label promo					

WING

Number	Title	Yr	VG	VG+	NM
❑ PKW2-125 [(2)]	The Legend of Jerry Lee Lewis	1969	6.25	12.50	25.00

LEWIS, KATHERINE HANDY
FOLKWAYS

Number	Title	Yr	VG	VG+	NM
❑ FG-3540 [M]	W.C. Handy Blues	196?	5.00	10.00	20.00

LEWIS, LINDA GAIL
SMASH

Number	Title	Yr	VG	VG+	NM
❑ SRS-67119	Two Sides of Linda Gail Lewis	1969	6.25	12.50	25.00

LEWIS, RAMSEY
ARGO

Number	Title	Yr	VG	VG+	NM
❑ 611 [M]	Gentleman of Swing	1958	12.50	25.00	50.00
❑ 611S [S]	Gentleman of Swing	1959	15.00	30.00	60.00
❑ 627 [M]	Gentleman of Jazz	1958	12.50	25.00	50.00
❑ 627S [S]	Gentleman of Jazz	1959	15.00	30.00	60.00
❑ 642 [M]	The Ramsey Lewis Trio with Lee Winchester	1959	10.00	20.00	40.00
❑ 642S [S]	The Ramsey Lewis Trio with Lee Winchester	1959	12.50	25.00	50.00

Number	Title	Yr	VG	VG+	NM
❑ 645 [M]	An Hour with the Ramsey Lewis Trio	1959	10.00	20.00	40.00
❑ 645S [S]	An Hour with the Ramsey Lewis Trio	1959	12.50	25.00	50.00
❑ 665 [M]	Stretching Out	1960	10.00	20.00	40.00
❑ 665S [S]	Stretching Out	1960	12.50	25.00	50.00
❑ 671 [M]	The Ramsey Lewis Trio in Chicago	1961	10.00	20.00	40.00
❑ 671S [S]	The Ramsey Lewis Trio in Chicago	1961	12.50	25.00	50.00
❑ 680 [M]	More Music from the Soil	1961	10.00	20.00	40.00
❑ 680S [S]	More Music from the Soil	1961	12.50	25.00	50.00
❑ 687 [M]	Sound of Christmas	1961	10.00	20.00	40.00
❑ 687-S [S]	Sound of Christmas	1961	12.50	25.00	50.00
❑ 693 [M]	The Sound of Spring	1962	6.25	12.50	25.00
❑ 693S [S]	The Sound of Spring	1962	7.50	15.00	30.00
❑ 701 [M]	Country Meets the Blues	1962	6.25	12.50	25.00
❑ 701S [S]	Country Meets the Blues	1962	7.50	15.00	30.00
❑ 705 [M]	Bossa Nova	1962	6.25	12.50	25.00
❑ 705S [S]	Bossa Nova	1962	7.50	15.00	30.00
❑ 715 [M]	Pot Luck	1963	6.25	12.50	25.00
❑ 715S [S]	Pot Luck	1963	7.50	15.00	30.00
❑ 723 [M]	Barefoot Sunday Blues	1963	6.25	12.50	25.00
❑ 723S [S]	Barefoot Sunday Blues	1963	7.50	15.00	30.00
❑ 732 [M]	Bach to the Blues	1964	6.25	12.50	25.00
❑ 732S [S]	Bach to the Blues	1964	7.50	15.00	30.00
❑ 741 [M]	The Ramsey Lewis Trio at the Bohemian Caverns	1964	6.25	12.50	25.00
❑ 741S [S]	The Ramsey Lewis Trio at the Bohemian Caverns	1964	7.50	15.00	30.00
❑ 745 [M]	More Sounds of Christmas	1964	6.25	12.50	25.00
❑ 745-S [S]	More Sounds of Christmas	1964	7.50	15.00	30.00
❑ 750 [M]	You Better Believe It	1965	6.25	12.50	25.00
❑ 750S [S]	You Better Believe It	1965	7.50	15.00	30.00
❑ 757 [M]	The In Crowd	1965	6.25	12.50	25.00
❑ 757S [S]	The In Crowd	1965	7.50	15.00	30.00

CADET

Number	Title	Yr	VG	VG+	NM
❑ 687X [M]	Sound of Christmas	1966	5.00	10.00	20.00
-- Reissue of Argo 687					
❑ 687X-S [S]	Sound of Christmas	1966	5.00	10.00	20.00
-- Reissue of Argo 687-S					
❑ 745-S [S]	More Sounds of Christmas	1964	5.00	10.00	20.00
❑ LPS-755 [S]	Choice! The Best of the Ramsey Lewis Trio	1965	5.00	10.00	20.00
❑ LPS-761 [S]	Hang On Ramsey!	1966	5.00	10.00	20.00
❑ LPS-771 [S]	Swingin'	1966	5.00	10.00	20.00
❑ LPS-774 [S]	Wade in the Water	1966	5.00	10.00	20.00
❑ LP-782 [M]	The Movie Album	1967	5.00	10.00	20.00
❑ LP-790 [M]	Goin' Latin	1967	5.00	10.00	20.00
❑ LP-794 [M]	Dancing in the Street	1967	5.00	10.00	20.00

COLUMBIA

Number	Title	Yr	VG	VG+	NM
❑ HC 43194	Sun Goddess	1982	12.50	25.00	50.00
-- Half-speed mastered edition					
❑ HC 47687	Live at the Savoy	1982	20.00	40.00	80.00
-- Half-speed mastered edition					

EMARCY

Number	Title	Yr	VG	VG+	NM
❑ MG-36150 [M]	Down to Earth	1958	10.00	20.00	40.00
❑ SR-80029 [S]	Down to Earth	1958	12.50	25.00	50.00

MERCURY

Number	Title	Yr	VG	VG+	NM
❑ MG-20536 [M]	Down to Earth	1965	5.00	10.00	20.00
❑ SR-60536 [S]	Down to Earth	1965	6.25	12.50	25.00

LEWIS, ROBERT Q.
ATCO

Number	Title	Yr	VG	VG+	NM
❑ 33-212 [M]	I'm Just Wild About Vaudeville	1963	6.25	12.50	25.00
❑ SD 33-212 [S]	I'm Just Wild About Vaudeville	1963	7.50	15.00	30.00

"X"

Number	Title	Yr	VG	VG+	NM
❑ LXA-1033 [M]	Robert Q. Lewis and His Gang	1956	12.50	25.00	50.00

LEWIS, SHARI
RCA CAMDEN

Number	Title	Yr	VG	VG+	NM
❑ CAL-1052 [M]	Jack and the Beanstalk and Other Stories	1964	7.50	15.00	30.00
❑ CAS-1052 [S]	Jack and the Beanstalk and Other Stories	1964	7.50	15.00	30.00

RCA VICTOR

Number	Title	Yr	VG	VG+	NM
❑ LBY-1006 [M]	Fun in Shariland	1954	20.00	40.00	80.00

LEWIS, SMILEY
IMPERIAL

Number	Title	Yr	VG	VG+	NM
❑ LP-9141 [M]	I Hear You Knocking	1961	150.00	300.00	600.00
-- Black vinyl					
❑ LP-9141 [M]	I Hear You Knocking	1961	1,500.	3,000.	6,000.
-- Green vinyl (one copy known)					

LIBERACE
COLUMBIA

Number	Title	Yr	VG	VG+	NM
❑ CL 575 [M]	Liberace at the Piano	1954	10.00	20.00	40.00
-- Maroon label, gold print					
❑ CL 589 [M]	Christmas at Liberace's	1954	12.50	25.00	50.00
-- Maroon label, gold print					
❑ CL 600 [M]	Liberace at the Hollywood Bowl	1955	10.00	20.00	40.00
❑ CL 645 [M]	Hollywood Bowl Encore	1955	10.00	20.00	40.00
❑ CL 661 [M]	Liberace by Candlelight	1955	10.00	20.00	40.00
❑ CL 800 [M]	Sincerely Yours	1956	12.50	25.00	50.00
❑ CL 896 [M]	Liberace at Home	1956	12.50	25.00	50.00
❑ CL 2516 [10]	Piano Reverie	1955	15.00	30.00	60.00
❑ CL 2592 [10]	Kiddin' on the Keys	1955	15.00	30.00	60.00
❑ CL 6217 [10]	Liberace at the Piano	1952	20.00	40.00	80.00
❑ CL 6239 [10]	An Evening with Liberace	1953	20.00	40.00	80.00
❑ CL 6251 [10]	Liberace by Candlelight	1953	20.00	40.00	80.00
❑ CL 6269 [10]	Concertos for You	1953	20.00	40.00	80.00
❑ CL 6283 [10]	Concertos for You, Volume 2	1953	20.00	40.00	80.00
❑ CL 6327 [10]	Liberace Plays Chopin	1954	20.00	40.00	80.00
❑ CL 6328 [10]	Liberace Plays Chopin, Volume 2	1954	20.00	40.00	80.00

CORAL

Number	Title	Yr	VG	VG+	NM
❑ 7CXB 9 [(2) S]	The Best of Liberace	1965	5.00	10.00	20.00
❑ CRL 757292 [S]	Piano Song Book -- Movie Themes	1959	5.00	10.00	20.00
❑ CRL 757305 [S]	The Magic Pianos of Liberace	1960	5.00	10.00	20.00

LIBERACE, GEORGE
COLUMBIA

Number	Title	Yr	VG	VG+	NM
❑ CL 587 [M]	A Musical Journey with George Liberace	1954	10.00	20.00	40.00
-- Maroon label, gold print					

IMPERIAL

Number	Title	Yr	VG	VG+	NM
❑ LP-9039 [M]	George Liberace Goes Teenage	1957	12.50	25.00	50.00

LIBERMAN, JEFFERY
LIBRAH

Number	Title	Yr	VG	VG+	NM
❑ 1545	Jeffery Liberman	1975	20.00	40.00	80.00
❑ 6969	Solitude Within	1975	30.00	60.00	120.00
❑ 12157	Synergy	1976	30.00	60.00	120.00

LIGGINS, JOE
MERCURY

Number	Title	Yr	VG	VG+	NM
❑ MG-20731 [M]	Honeydripper	1962	20.00	40.00	80.00
❑ SR-60731 [S]	Honeydripper	1962	25.00	50.00	100.00

LIGHT CRUST DOUGHBOYS, THE
AUDIO LAB

Number	Title	Yr	VG	VG+	NM
❑ AL-1525 [M]	The Light Crust Doughboys	1959	37.50	75.00	150.00

LIGHT, ENOCH
GRAND AWARD

Number	Title	Yr	VG	VG+	NM
❑ GA-201 SD [S]	The Roaring Twenties	1958	6.25	12.50	25.00
❑ GA-202 SD [S]	The Flirty Thirties	1958	6.25	12.50	25.00
❑ GA-203 SD [S]	Waltzes for Dancing	1958	6.25	12.50	25.00
❑ GA-206 SD [S]	Tommy Dorsey's Song Hits	1958	6.25	12.50	25.00
❑ GA-207 SD [S]	Glenn Miller's Song Hits	1958	6.25	12.50	25.00
❑ GA-211 SD [S]	The Roaring Twenties, Volume 2	1958	6.25	12.50	25.00
❑ GA-214 SD [S]	Around the World in 80 Days	1958	6.25	12.50	25.00
❑ GA-215 SD [S]	Gigi	1958	6.25	12.50	25.00
❑ GA-216 SD [S]	My Fair Lady	1958	6.25	12.50	25.00
❑ GA-217 SD [S]	Oklahoma/South Pacific	1958	6.25	12.50	25.00
❑ GA-220 SD [S]	The Torchy Thirties	1958	6.25	12.50	25.00
❑ GA-222 SD [S]	I Want to Be Happy Cha Cha's	1959	6.25	12.50	25.00
❑ GA-224 SD [S]	New World Symphony	1958	6.25	12.50	25.00
❑ GA-225 SD [S]	The Great Themes of America's Great Bands	1958	6.25	12.50	25.00
❑ GA-227 SD [S]	Happy Cha Cha's, Vol. 2	1959	6.25	12.50	25.00
❑ GA-228 SD [S]	Show Spectacular	1959	6.25	12.50	25.00
❑ GA-229 SD [S]	The Roaring Twenties, Volume 3	1959	6.25	12.50	25.00
❑ GA-236 SD [S]	All the Things You Are	1959	6.25	12.50	25.00
❑ GA-237 SD [S]	Come to Hawaii	1959	6.25	12.50	25.00
❑ GA-238 SD [S]	With My Eyes Wide Open I'm Dreaming	1959	6.25	12.50	25.00
❑ GA-242 SD [S]	Something to Remember You By	1959	6.25	12.50	25.00
❑ GA-246 SD [S]	Just for Kicks	1959	6.25	12.50	25.00
❑ GA-251 SD [S]	Sing Along with the Original Roaring 20's	1959	6.25	12.50	25.00
❑ GA 33-327 [M]	The Roaring Twenties	1958	5.00	10.00	20.00
❑ GA 33-353 [M]	The Roaring Twenties, Volume 3	1959	5.00	10.00	20.00
❑ GA 33-371 [M]	The Flirty Thirties	1958	5.00	10.00	20.00
❑ GA 33-372 [M]	Waltzes for Dancing	1958	5.00	10.00	20.00
❑ GA 33-380 [M]	Paris Spectacular	1958	5.00	10.00	20.00
❑ GA 33-381 [M]	Glenn Miller's Song Hits	1958	5.00	10.00	20.00

Number	Title	Yr	VG	VG+	NM
❑ GA 33-382 [M]	Tommy Dorsey's Song Hits	1958	5.00	10.00	20.00
❑ GA 33-388 [M]	I Want to Be Happy Cha Cha's	1959	5.00	10.00	20.00
❑ GA 33-391 [M]	Happy Cha Cha's, Vol. 2	1959	5.00	10.00	20.00
❑ GA 33-392 [M]	The Great Themes of America's Great Bands	1958	5.00	10.00	20.00
❑ GA 33-399 [M]	All the Things You Are	1959	5.00	10.00	20.00
❑ GA 33-405 [M]	Come to Hawaii	1959	5.00	10.00	20.00
❑ GA 33-406 [M]	With My Eyes Wide Open I'm Dreaming	1959	5.00	10.00	20.00
❑ GA 33-410 [M]	Something to Remember You By	1959	5.00	10.00	20.00
❑ GA 33-419 [M]	Sing Along with the Original Roaring 20's	1959	5.00	10.00	20.00

PROJECT 3

Number	Title	Yr	VG	VG+	NM
❑ PR4C-6003/4 [(2) Q]	Big Hits of the Seventies	1974	5.00	10.00	20.00
❑ PR4C-6005/6 [(2) Q]	Big Band Hits of the 30's, 40's & 50's	1974	5.00	10.00	20.00
❑ PR4C-6013/14 [(2) Q]	Big Band Hits of the 30's and 40's	197?	5.00	10.00	20.00

LIGHTFOOT, GORDON
MOBILE FIDELITY

Number	Title	Yr	VG	VG+	NM
❑ 1-018	Sundown	1979	10.00	20.00	40.00
-- Audiophile vinyl					

REPRISE

Number	Title	Yr	VG	VG+	NM
❑ ST-93228	Sit Down Young Stranger	1970	5.00	10.00	20.00
-- Capitol Record Club edition					

UNITED ARTISTS

Number	Title	Yr	VG	VG+	NM
❑ UAL-3487 [M]	Lightfoot	1966	5.00	10.00	20.00
❑ UAL-3587 [M]	The Way I Feel	1967	5.00	10.00	20.00
❑ UAS-6487 [S]	Lightfoot	1966	6.25	12.50	25.00
❑ UAS-6587 [S]	The Way I Feel	1967	6.25	12.50	25.00
❑ UAS-6649	Did She Mention My Name	1968	5.00	10.00	20.00
❑ UAS-6672	Back Here on Earth	1969	5.00	10.00	20.00

LIGHTHOUSE
EVOLUTION

Number	Title	Yr	VG	VG+	NM
❑ 3014 [(2)]	Lighthouse Live!	1972	5.00	10.00	20.00

LIGHTNIN' SLIM
EXCELLO

Number	Title	Yr	VG	VG+	NM
❑ LP 8000 [M]	Rooster Blues	1960	150.00	300.00	600.00
❑ LPS 8000 [S]	Rooster Blues	196?	12.50	25.00	50.00
-- Though labeled "Electronic Stereo," this record is mono					
❑ LP 8004 [M]	Lightnin' Slim's Bell Ringer	1965	75.00	150.00	300.00
❑ LPS 8004 [M]	Lightnin' Slim's Bell Ringer	196?	12.50	25.00	50.00
-- Though labeled "Electronic Stereo," this record is mono					

LIGHTNING
P.I.P.

Number	Title	Yr	VG	VG+	NM
❑ 6807	Lightning	1971	7.50	15.00	30.00

LILLIE, BEATRICE
DECCA

Number	Title	Yr	VG	VG+	NM
❑ DL 5453 [10]	Souvenir Album	1954	12.50	25.00	50.00

LIBERTY MUSIC SHOP

Number	Title	Yr	VG	VG+	NM
❑ 1002 [10]	Thirty Minutes with Bea Lillie	1954	12.50	25.00	50.00

LONDON

Number	Title	Yr	VG	VG+	NM
❑ LL 1373 [M]	An Evening with Bea Little	1956	7.50	15.00	30.00
❑ 5471 [M]	Auntie Bea	1959	7.50	15.00	30.00

LILLY BROTHERS, THE
FOLKLORE

Number	Title	Yr	VG	VG+	NM
❑ FL-14010 [M]	Bluegrass Breakdown	1963	5.00	10.00	20.00
❑ FLS-14010 [S]	Bluegrass Breakdown	1963	6.25	12.50	25.00
❑ FL-14035 [M]	Country Songs	1964	5.00	10.00	20.00
❑ FLS-14035 [S]	Country Songs	1964	6.25	12.50	25.00

FOLKWAYS

Number	Title	Yr	VG	VG+	NM
❑ FA-2433 [M]	Folk Songs from the Southern Mountains	196?	5.00	10.00	20.00

LIMELITERS, THE
Also see GLENN YARBROUGH.
ELEKTRA

Number	Title	Yr	VG	VG+	NM
❑ EKM-180 [M]	The Limeliters	1960	5.00	10.00	20.00
❑ EKS-7180 [S]	The Limeliters	1960	6.25	12.50	25.00

RCA VICTOR

Number	Title	Yr	VG	VG+	NM
❑ LPM-2272 [M]	Tonight: In Person	1961	5.00	10.00	20.00
❑ LSP-2272 [S]	Tonight: In Person	1961	6.25	12.50	25.00
❑ LPM-2393 [M]	The Slightly Fabulous Limeliters	1961	5.00	10.00	20.00
❑ LSP-2393 [S]	The Slightly Fabulous Limeliters	1961	6.25	12.50	25.00
❑ LPM-2445 [M]	Sing Out!	1962	5.00	10.00	20.00
❑ LSP-2445 [S]	Sing Out!	1962	6.25	12.50	25.00
❑ LPM-2512 [M]	Through Children's Eyes	1962	5.00	10.00	20.00
❑ LSP-2512 [S]	Through Children's Eyes	1962	6.25	12.50	25.00
❑ LPM-2547 [M]	Folk Matinee	1962	5.00	10.00	20.00
❑ LSP-2547 [S]	Folk Matinee	1962	6.25	12.50	25.00
❑ LPM-2588 [M]	Makin' a Joyful Noise	1963	5.00	10.00	20.00
❑ LSP-2588 [S]	Makin' a Joyful Noise	1963	6.25	12.50	25.00
❑ LPM-2609 [M]	Our Men in San Francisco	1963	5.00	10.00	20.00
❑ LSP-2609 [S]	Our Men in San Francisco	1963	6.25	12.50	25.00
❑ LPM-2671 [M]	Fourteen 14K Folk Songs	1963	5.00	10.00	20.00
❑ LSP-2671 [S]	Fourteen 14K Folk Songs	1963	6.25	12.50	25.00
❑ LSP-2844 [S]	More of Everything!	1964	5.00	10.00	20.00
❑ LSP-2889 [S]	The Best of the Limeliters	1964	5.00	10.00	20.00
❑ LSP-2907 [S]	London Concert	1964	5.00	10.00	20.00
❑ LSP-3385 [S]	The Limeliters Look at Love... In Depth	1965	5.00	10.00	20.00

LIMOUSINE
GSF

Number	Title	Yr	VG	VG+	NM
❑ 1002	Limousine	1972	5.00	10.00	20.00

LINCOLN STREET EXIT
MAINSTREAM

Number	Title	Yr	VG	VG+	NM
❑ S-6126	Drive It	1970	25.00	50.00	100.00

LINCOLN, PHILAMORE
EPIC

Number	Title	Yr	VG	VG+	NM
❑ BN 26497	North Wind Blew South	1970	6.25	12.50	25.00

LIND, BOB
VERVE FOLKWAYS

Number	Title	Yr	VG	VG+	NM
❑ FT-3005 [M]	The Elusive Bob Lind	1966	6.25	12.50	25.00
❑ FTS-3005 [S]	The Elusive Bob Lind	1966	7.50	15.00	30.00

WORLD PACIFIC

Number	Title	Yr	VG	VG+	NM
❑ WP-1841 [M]	Don't Be Concerned	1966	5.00	10.00	20.00
❑ WP-1851 [M]	Photographs of Feeling	1966	5.00	10.00	20.00
❑ ST-21841 [S]	Don't Be Concerned	1966	6.25	12.50	25.00
❑ ST-21851 [S]	Photographs of Feeling	1966	6.25	12.50	25.00

LINDE, DENNIS
INTREPID

Number	Title	Yr	VG	VG+	NM
❑ 4004 [M]	Linde Manor	1966	5.00	10.00	20.00
❑ 74004 [S]	Linde Manor	1966	6.25	12.50	25.00

LINDEN, KATHY
FELSTED

Number	Title	Yr	VG	VG+	NM
❑ 7501 [M]	That Certain Boy	1959	15.00	30.00	60.00

LINDSEY, GEORGE
CAPITOL

Number	Title	Yr	VG	VG+	NM
❑ ST-230	96 Miles to Bakersfield	1969	6.25	12.50	25.00
❑ ST 2965	Goober Sings!	1968	6.25	12.50	25.00

LINKLETTER, ART
COLUMBIA

Number	Title	Yr	VG	VG+	NM
❑ CL 703 [M]	Howlers, Boners and Shockers	1956	10.00	20.00	40.00

LINN COUNTY
MERCURY

Number	Title	Yr	VG	VG+	NM
❑ SR-61181	Proud Flesh Soothseer	1968	5.00	10.00	20.00
❑ SR-61218	Fever Shot	1969	5.00	10.00	20.00

LINTON, SHERWIN
BLACK GOLD

Number	Title	Yr	VG	VG+	NM
❑ 7116	I'm Not Johnny Cash	1972	6.25	12.50	25.00

RE-CAR

Number	Title	Yr	VG	VG+	NM
❑ 2108	Sherwin Linton and the Cotton Kings	1968	15.00	30.00	60.00

LIPSCOMB, MANCE
ARHOOLIE

Number	Title	Yr	VG	VG+	NM
❑ 1001 [M]	Texas Sharecropper and Songster	1960	12.50	25.00	50.00
❑ 1023 [M]	Texas Songster, Vol. 2	1963	10.00	20.00	40.00
❑ 1026 [M]	Texas Songster, Vol. 3	1965	10.00	20.00	40.00
❑ 1033 [M]	Mance Lipscomb, Vol. 4	1966	10.00	20.00	40.00
❑ 1049	Mance Lipscomb, Vol. 5	1970	6.25	12.50	25.00
❑ 1069	Mance Lipscomb, Vol. 6	1975	6.25	12.50	25.00

REPRISE

Number	Title	Yr	VG	VG+	NM
❑ R-2012 [M]	Trouble in Mind	1961	25.00	50.00	100.00
❑ R9-2012 [S]	Trouble in Mind	1961	37.50	75.00	150.00
❑ RS-6404	Trouble in Mind	1969	7.50	15.00	30.00

Number	Title	Yr	VG	VG+	NM

LIPSTIQUE
SALSOUL
❑ 4500	At the Discotheque	1978	5.00	10.00	20.00

LIPTON, PEGGY
ODE
| ❑ Z12 44006 | Peggy Lipton | 1968 | 6.25 | 12.50 | 25.00 |

LIQUID SMOKE
AVCO EMBASSY
| ❑ AVE-33005 | Liquid Smoke | 1970 | 6.25 | 12.50 | 25.00 |

LIST, EUGENE
MERCURY LIVING PRESENCE
| ❑ SR 90290 [S] | Gershwin Favorites | 196? | 7.50 | 15.00 | 30.00 |
| -- Maroon label, no "Vendor: Mercury Record Corporation" | | | | | |

LISTENING
VANGUARD
| ❑ VSD-6504 | Listening | 1968 | 15.00 | 30.00 | 60.00 |

LITE STORM, THE
BEVERLY HILLS
| ❑ 1135 | Lite Storm Warning | 1973 | 15.00 | 30.00 | 60.00 |

LITTER
HEXAGON
| ❑ 681 | $100 Fine | 1968 | 100.00 | 200.00 | 400.00 |
PROBE
| ❑ 4504 | Emerge | 1969 | 12.50 | 25.00 | 50.00 |
WARICK
| ❑ 671 | Distortions | 1967 | 125.00 | 250.00 | 500.00 |

LITTLE ANTHONY AND THE IMPERIALS
AVCO
| ❑ AV-11012 | On a New Street | 1973 | 5.00 | 10.00 | 20.00 |
DCP
❑ DCL-3801 [M]	I'm On the Outside Looking In	1964	6.25	12.50	25.00
❑ DCL-3808 [M]	Goin' Out of My Head	1965	6.25	12.50	25.00
❑ DCL-3809 [M]	The Best of Little Anthony and the Imperials	1965	5.00	10.00	20.00
❑ DCS-6801 [S]	I'm On the Outside Looking In	1964	7.50	15.00	30.00
❑ DCS-6808 [S]	Goin' Out of My Head	1965	7.50	15.00	30.00
❑ DCS-6809 [S]	The Best of Little Anthony and the Imperials	1965	6.25	12.50	25.00
END
| ❑ LP 303 [M] | We Are The Imperials Featuring Little Anthony | 1959 | 62.50 | 125.00 | 250.00 |
| ❑ LP 311 [M] | Shades of the 40's | 1960 | 50.00 | 100.00 | 200.00 |
ROULETTE
| ❑ R-25294 [M] | Little Anthony and the Imperials' Greatest Hits | 1965 | 6.25 | 12.50 | 25.00 |
| ❑ SR-25294 [R] | Little Anthony and the Imperials' Greatest Hits | 1965 | 5.00 | 10.00 | 20.00 |
UNITED ARTISTS
| ❑ UA-LA026-G [(2)] | Legendary Masters Series | 1972 | 6.25 | 12.50 | 25.00 |
| ❑ UAS 6720 | Out of Sight, Out of Mind | 1969 | 5.00 | 10.00 | 20.00 |
VEEP
❑ VPS 16510 [S]	I'm On the Outside Looking In	1966	5.00	10.00	20.00
❑ VPS 16511 [S]	Goin' Out of My Head	1966	5.00	10.00	20.00
❑ VPS 16512 [S]	The Best of Little Anthony and the Imperials	1966	5.00	10.00	20.00
❑ VPS 16513 [S]	Payin' Our Dues	1966	5.00	10.00	20.00
❑ VPS 16514 [S]	Reflections	1967	5.00	10.00	20.00
❑ VPS 16516 [S]	Movie Grabbers	1967	5.00	10.00	20.00

LITTLE BILL AND THE BLUENOTES
CAMELOT
| ❑ 102 [M] | The Fiesta Club Presents Little Bill and the Bluenotes | 1960 | 100.00 | 200.00 | 400.00 |

LITTLE BOY BLUES
FONTANA
| ❑ SRF-67578 | In the Woodland of Weir | 1968 | 75.00 | 15.00 | 30.00 |

LITTLE CAESAR AND THE ROMANS
DEL-FI
| ❑ DFLP-1218 [M] | Memories of Those Oldies But Goodies | 1961 | 75.00 | 150.00 | 300.00 |

LITTLE ESTHER -- See ESTHER PHILLIPS.

LITTLE EVA
DIMENSION
❑ DLP-6000 [M]	LLLLLoco-Motion	1962	37.50	75.00	150.00
-- Without "Keep Your Hands Off My Baby"					
❑ DLP-6000 [M]	LLLLLoco-Motion	1962	50.00	100.00	200.00
-- With "Keep Your Hands Off My Baby"					
❑ DLPS-6000 [R]	LLLLLoco-Motion	1962	37.50	75.00	150.00
-- Without "Keep Your Hands Off My Baby"					
❑ DLPS-6000 [R]	LLLLLoco-Motion	1962	50.00	100.00	200.00
-- With "Keep Your Hands Off My Baby"					

LITTLE FEAT
MOBILE FIDELITY
| ❑ 1-013 [(2)] | Waiting for Columbus | 1979 | 20.00 | 40.00 | 80.00 |
| -- Audiophile vinyl | | | | | |
NAUTILUS
| ❑ NR-24 | Time Loves a Hero | 198? | 12.50 | 25.00 | 50.00 |
| -- Audiophile vinyl | | | | | |
WARNER BROS.
❑ PRO-A-984 [DJ]	Hoy-Hoy!	1981	5.00	10.00	20.00
-- Single-album sampler of 2-LP set					
❑ WS 1890	Little Feat	1971	5.00	10.00	20.00
-- Green "WB" label; with photo on back cover					
ZOO/CLASSIC
| ❑ 11097 [(2)] | Ain't Had Enough Fun | 1995 | 5.00 | 10.00 | 20.00 |
| -- 180-gram vinyl | | | | | |

LITTLE JOE
BRUNSWICK
| ❑ BL 754135 | Little Joe (Sure Can Sing) | 1968 | 5.00 | 10.00 | 20.00 |

LITTLE MILTON
CHECKER
❑ LP-2995 [M]	We're Gonna Make It	196?	6.25	12.50	25.00
-- Blue, fading to white, label					
❑ LP-2995 [M]	We're Gonna Make It	1965	25.00	50.00	100.00
-- Black label					
❑ LP-2995 [M]	We're Gonna Make It	1966	17.50	35.00	70.00
-- Blue label with red and black checkers					
❑ LP-3002 [M]	Little Milton Sings Big Blues	1966	12.50	25.00	50.00
❑ LP-3011	Grits Ain't Groceries	1969	6.25	12.50	25.00
❑ LP-3012	If Walls Could Talk	1970	6.25	12.50	25.00
STAX
| ❑ STS-3012 | Waiting for Little Milton | 1973 | 5.00 | 10.00 | 20.00 |
| ❑ 5514 | Blues 'n' Soul | 1974 | 5.00 | 10.00 | 20.00 |

LITTLE MISS CORNSHUCKS
CHESS
| ❑ LP-1453 [M] | The Loneliest Gal in Town | 1961 | 50.00 | 100.00 | 200.00 |

LITTLE RICHARD
20TH FOX
| ❑ FXG-5010 [M] | Little Richard Sings Gospel | 1959 | 25.00 | 50.00 | 100.00 |
| ❑ SGM-5010 [S] | Little Richard Sings Gospel | 1959 | 37.50 | 75.00 | 150.00 |
AUDIO ENCORES
| ❑ 1002 | Little Richard | 1980 | 6.25 | 12.50 | 25.00 |
BUDDAH
| ❑ BDS-7501 | Little Richard | 1969 | 7.50 | 15.00 | 30.00 |
CORAL
| ❑ CRL 57446 [M] | Coming Home | 1963 | 10.00 | 20.00 | 40.00 |
| ❑ CRL 757446 [S] | Coming Home | 1963 | 12.50 | 25.00 | 50.00 |
CROWN
| ❑ CLP-5362 [M] | Little Richard Sings Freedom Songs | 1963 | 5.00 | 10.00 | 20.00 |
EPIC
| ❑ EG 30428 [(2)] | Cast a Long Shadow | 1971 | 5.00 | 10.00 | 20.00 |
KAMA SUTRA
| ❑ KSBS-2023 | Little Richard | 1970 | 6.25 | 12.50 | 25.00 |
MERCURY
| ❑ MG-20656 [M] | It's Real | 1961 | 12.50 | 25.00 | 50.00 |
| ❑ SR-60656 [S] | It's Real | 1961 | 15.00 | 30.00 | 60.00 |
MODERN
❑ 100 [M]	His Greatest Hits/Recorded Live	1966	5.00	10.00	20.00
❑ 103 [M]	The Explosive Little Richard	1966	5.00	10.00	20.00
❑ 1000 [S]	His Greatest Hits/Recorded Live	1966	6.25	12.50	25.00
❑ 1003 [S]	The Explosive Little Richard	1966	6.25	12.50	25.00
OKEH
| ❑ OKM 12117 [M] | The Explosive Little Richard | 1967 | 6.25 | 12.50 | 25.00 |
| ❑ OKM 12121 [M] | Little Richard's Greatest Hits | 1967 | 6.25 | 12.50 | 25.00 |

Number	Title	Yr	VG	VG+	NM
❏ OKS 14117 [S] The Explosive Little Richard		1967	5.00	10.00	20.00
❏ OKS 14121 [S] Little Richard's Greatest Hits		1967	5.00	10.00	20.00
RCA CAMDEN					
❏ CAL-420 [M]	Little Richard	1956	50.00	100.00	200.00
REPRISE					
❏ MS 2107	The Second Coming	1973	5.00	10.00	20.00
❏ RS 6406	The Rill Thing	1971	5.00	10.00	20.00
❏ RS 6462	King of Rock and Roll	1972	5.00	10.00	20.00
SPECIALTY					
❏ 100 [M]	Here's Little Richard	1957	175.00	350.00	700.00
❏ SP-2100 [M]	Here's Little Richard	1957	50.00	100.00	200.00
-- Thick vinyl					
❏ SP-2103 [M]	Little Richard	1958	37.50	75.00	150.00
-- Front cover photo occupies the entire cover					
❏ SP-2103 [M]	Little Richard	196?	25.00	50.00	100.00
-- Front cover photo partially obscured by a black triangle at upper right; thick vinyl					
❏ SP-2103 [M]	Little Richard	197?	5.00	10.00	20.00
-- Reissue with thinner vinyl					
❏ SP-2104 [M]	The Fabulous Little Richard	1958	37.50	75.00	150.00
-- Thick vinyl					
❏ SP-2104 [M]	The Fabulous Little Richard	197?	5.00	10.00	20.00
-- Reissue with thinner vinyl					
❏ SP-2111	Little Richard -- His Biggest Hits	1963	12.50	25.00	50.00
-- Thick vinyl					
❏ SP-2111 [M]	Little Richard -- His Biggest Hits	197?	5.00	10.00	20.00
-- Reissue with thinner vinyl					
❏ SP-2113	Little Richard's Grooviest 17 Original Hits	1968	6.25	12.50	25.00
-- Thick vinyl					
❏ SP-2136	Well Alright!	1970	5.00	10.00	20.00
❏ SP-8508 [(5)]	The Specialty Sessions	1989	10.00	20.00	40.00
VEE JAY					
❏ LP-1107 [M]	Little Richard Is Back!	1964	12.50	25.00	50.00
❏ LPS-1107 [S]	Little Richard Is Back!	1964	17.50	35.00	70.00
❏ LP-1124 [M]	Little Richard's Greatest Hits	1965	6.25	12.50	25.00
❏ LPS-1124 [S]	Little Richard's Greatest Hits	1965	10.00	20.00	40.00
WING					
❏ SRW-16288 [S]	King of the Gospel Singers	1964	5.00	10.00	20.00

LITTLE RIVER BAND
MOBILE FIDELITY

Number	Title	Yr	VG	VG+	NM
❏ 1-036	First Under the Wire	1980	6.25	12.50	25.00
-- Audiophile vinyl					

LITTLE SISTERS, THE
MGM

Number	Title	Yr	VG	VG+	NM
❏ E-4116 [M]	The Joys of Love	1963	6.25	12.50	25.00
❏ SE-4116 [S]	The Joys of Love	1963	7.50	15.00	30.00

LITTLE SONNY
ENTERPRISE

Number	Title	Yr	VG	VG+	NM
❏ ENS-1005	New King of the Blues Harmonica	1970	10.00	20.00	40.00
❏ ENS-1018	Black and Blue	1971	10.00	20.00	40.00
❏ ENS-1036	Hard Goin' Up	1973	10.00	20.00	40.00

LITTLE WALTER
CHECKER

Number	Title	Yr	VG	VG+	NM
❏ LP-1428 [M]	The Best of Little Walter	1957	125.00	250.00	500.00
-- Black or maroon label					
❏ LP-3004 [M]	The Best of Little Walter	1967	12.50	25.00	50.00
-- Reissue of 1428					
CHESS					
❏ 2ACMB-202 [(2)] Little Walter		1976	5.00	10.00	20.00
-- Reissue of 60014					
❏ LP-1535 [M]	Hate to See You Go	1969	6.25	12.50	25.00
❏ 2CH-60014 [(2)] Boss Blues Harmonica		1972	5.00	10.00	20.00

LIVE
RADIOACTIVE

Number	Title	Yr	VG	VG+	NM
❏ 10997	Throwing Copper	1994	5.00	10.00	20.00
-- Issued on clear vinyl					

LIVELY ONES, THE
DEL-FI

Number	Title	Yr	VG	VG+	NM
❏ DFLP-1226 [M] Surf Rider		1963	25.00	50.00	100.00
❏ DFST-1226 [S] Surf Rider		1963	37.50	75.00	150.00
❏ DFLP-1231 [M] Surf Drums		1963	12.50	25.00	50.00
❏ DFST-1231 [S] Surf Drums		1963	17.50	35.00	70.00
❏ DFLP-1237 [M] Surf City		1963	10.00	20.00	40.00
❏ DFST-1237 [S] Surf City		1963	12.50	25.00	50.00
❏ DFLP-1240 [M] Surfin' South of the Border		1964	10.00	20.00	40.00
❏ DFST-1240 [S] Surfin' South of the Border		1964	12.50	25.00	50.00

MGM

Number	Title	Yr	VG	VG+	NM
❏ E-4449 [M]	Bugalu Party	1967	5.00	10.00	20.00
❏ SE-4449 [S]	Bugalu Party	1967	6.25	12.50	25.00

LIVERPOOL BEATS, THE
RONDO

Number	Title	Yr	VG	VG+	NM
❏ 2026 [M]	The New Merseyside Sound	1964	7.50	15.00	30.00

LIVERPOOL FIVE, THE
RCA VICTOR

Number	Title	Yr	VG	VG+	NM
❏ LPM-3583 [M]	The Liverpool Five Arrive	1966	6.25	12.50	25.00
❏ LSP-3583 [S]	The Liverpool Five Arrive	1966	7.50	15.00	30.00
❏ LPM-3682 [M]	Out of Sight	1967	6.25	12.50	25.00
❏ LSP-3682 [S]	Out of Sight	1967	7.50	15.00	30.00

LIVERPOOL SCENE, THE
EPIC

Number	Title	Yr	VG	VG+	NM
❏ LN 24336 [M]	The Incredible New Liverpool Scene	1967	6.25	12.50	25.00
❏ BN 26336 [S]	The Incredible New Liverpool Scene	1967	7.50	15.00	30.00

LIVERPOOLS, THE
WYNCOTE

Number	Title	Yr	VG	VG+	NM
❏ SW-9001 [S]	Beatle Mania! In the U.S.A.	1964	6.25	12.50	25.00
❏ W-9001 [M]	Beatle Mania! In the U.S.A.	1964	5.00	10.00	20.00
❏ SW-9061 [S]	The Hit Sounds from England	1964	5.00	10.00	20.00

LIVIN' BLUES
DWARF

Number	Title	Yr	VG	VG+	NM
❏ 2003	Dutch Treat	1971	7.50	15.00	30.00

LIVING COLOUR
EPIC

Number	Title	Yr	VG	VG+	NM
❏ E 46202	Time's Up	1990	5.00	10.00	20.00
-- Yellow vinyl					

LLOYD, CHARLES
ATLANTIC

Number	Title	Yr	VG	VG+	NM
❏ SD 1459 [S]	Dream Weaver	1966	5.00	10.00	20.00
❏ SD 1473 [S]	Forest Flower	1967	5.00	10.00	20.00
❏ 1481 [M]	Love-In	1967	5.00	10.00	20.00
COLUMBIA					
❏ CL 2267 [M]	Discovery!	1965	6.25	12.50	25.00
❏ CL 2412 [M]	Of Course, Of Course	1966	6.25	12.50	25.00
❏ CS 9067 [S]	Discovery!	1965	7.50	15.00	30.00
❏ CS 9212 [S]	Of Course, Of Course	1966	7.50	15.00	30.00
❏ CS 9609	Nirvana	1968	6.25	12.50	25.00

LLOYD, DAVID
EPIC

Number	Title	Yr	VG	VG+	NM
❏ BN 26151 [S]	Confidential (Sounds for a Secret Agent)	1965	6.25	12.50	25.00
❏ LN 24151 [M]	Confidential (Sounds for a Secret Agent)	1965	5.00	10.00	20.00

LLOYD, HAROLD, JR.
CORAL

Number	Title	Yr	VG	VG+	NM
❏ CRL 757471 [S] The Intimate Style of Harold Lloyd, Jr.		1963	5.00	10.00	20.00

LOADING ZONE, THE
RCA VICTOR

Number	Title	Yr	VG	VG+	NM
❏ LSP-3959	The Loading Zone	1968	6.25	12.50	25.00
UMBRELLA					
❏ US-101	One for All	1967	20.00	40.00	80.00

LOCKLIN, HANK
KING

Number	Title	Yr	VG	VG+	NM
❏ 672 [M]	The Best of Hank Locklin	1961	15.00	30.00	60.00
❏ 738 [M]	Encores	1961	15.00	30.00	60.00
RCA VICTOR					
❏ LPM-1673 [M]	Foreign Love	1958	15.00	30.00	60.00
❏ LPM-2291 [M]	Please Help Me, I'm Falling	1960	7.50	15.00	30.00
❏ LSP-2291 [S]	Please Help Me, I'm Falling	1960	10.00	20.00	40.00
❏ LPM-2464 [M]	Happy Journey	1962	6.25	12.50	25.00
❏ LSP-2464 [S]	Happy Journey	1962	7.50	15.00	30.00
❏ LPM-2597 [M]	A Tribute to Roy Acuff, the King of Country Music	1962	6.25	12.50	25.00

(Top left) The third Specialty album of Little Richard material, *The Fabulous Little Richard,* can bring in the $200 range on its original thick vinyl pressing on the gold and black label. (Top right) The debut album by the Lovin' Spoonful, who sold a lot of albums from 1965 through 1967. (Bottom left) Into the early 1970s, both the Atlantic and Atco labels made special mono editions of selected albums for AM radio use only. Finding these today is not easy, and new titles are being discovered all the time. The mono edition of Lulu's *Melody Fair,* though probably known before then, was not listed in a price guide until 1997. (Bottom right) The original front cover of Lynyrd Skynyrd's *Street Survivors* featured the band in flames. Shortly after the LP's release, three members of the group died in a fiery plane crash. Once the original pressing was sold out, the front cover was replaced with an enlarged version of the original back-cover photo. There seem to be plenty of copies of the "flames" cover to meet the demand; its value hasn't gone up in 20 years.

Number	Title	Yr	VG	VG+	NM
❑ LSP-2597 [S]	A Tribute to Roy Acuff, the King of Country Music	1962	7.50	15.00	30.00
❑ LPM-2680 [M]	The Ways of Love	1963	6.25	12.50	25.00
❑ LSP-2680 [S]	The Ways of Love	1963	7.50	15.00	30.00
❑ LPM-2801 [M]	Irish Songs, Country Style	1964	5.00	10.00	20.00
❑ LSP-2801 [S]	Irish Songs, Country Style	1964	6.25	12.50	25.00
❑ LPM-2997 [M]	Hank Locklin Sings Hank Williams	1964	5.00	10.00	20.00
❑ LSP-2997 [S]	Hank Locklin Sings Hank Williams	1964	6.25	12.50	25.00
❑ LPM-3391 [M]	Hank Locklin Sings Eddy Arnold	1965	5.00	10.00	20.00
❑ LSP-3391 [S]	Hank Locklin Sings Eddy Arnold	1965	6.25	12.50	25.00
❑ LPM-3465 [M]	Once Over Lightly	1965	5.00	10.00	20.00
❑ LSP-3465 [S]	Once Over Lightly	1965	6.25	12.50	25.00
❑ LPM-3559 [M]	The Best of Hank Locklin	1966	5.00	10.00	20.00
❑ LSP-3559 [S]	The Best of Hank Locklin	1966	6.25	12.50	25.00
❑ LPM-3588 [M]	The Girls Get Prettier	1966	5.00	10.00	20.00
❑ LSP-3588 [S]	The Girls Get Prettier	1966	6.25	12.50	25.00
❑ LPM-3656 [M]	The Gloryland Way	1966	5.00	10.00	20.00
❑ LSP-3656 [S]	The Gloryland Way	1966	6.25	12.50	25.00
❑ LPM-3770 [M]	Send Me the Pillow You Dream On	1967	6.25	12.50	25.00
❑ LSP-3770 [S]	Send Me the Pillow You Dream On	1967	5.00	10.00	20.00
❑ LPM-3841 [M]	Nashville Women	1967	6.25	12.50	25.00
❑ LSP-3841 [S]	Nashville Women	1967	5.00	10.00	20.00
❑ LPM-3946 [M]	Country Hall of Fame	1968	25.00	50.00	100.00
❑ LSP-3946 [S]	Country Hall of Fame	1968	5.00	10.00	20.00
❑ LSP-4030	My Love Song for You	1968	5.00	10.00	20.00
❑ LSP-4113	Softly	1969	5.00	10.00	20.00

SEARS

Number	Title	Yr	VG	VG+	NM
❑ SPS-104	Send Me the Pillow You Dream On	196?	6.25	12.50	25.00

WRANGLER

Number	Title	Yr	VG	VG+	NM
❑ 1004 [M]	Hank Locklin	1962	6.25	12.50	25.00

LOCKWOOD, ROBERT, JR.
TRIX

Number	Title	Yr	VG	VG+	NM
❑ 3307	Contrasts	197?	5.00	10.00	20.00

LOCO, JOE
FANTASY

Number	Title	Yr	VG	VG+	NM
❑ 3215 [M]	Invitation to the Mambo	1956	7.50	15.00	30.00
-- Red vinyl					
❑ 3215 [M]	Invitation to the Mambo	1956	5.00	10.00	20.00
-- Black vinyl, red label, non-flexible vinyl					
❑ 3277 [M]	Cha-Cha-Cha	1958	7.50	15.00	30.00
-- Red vinyl					
❑ 3277 [M]	Cha-Cha-Cha	1958	5.00	10.00	20.00
-- Black vinyl, red label, non-flexible vinyl					
❑ 3280 [M]	Going Loco	1958	7.50	15.00	30.00
-- Red vinyl					
❑ 3280 [M]	Going Loco	1958	5.00	10.00	20.00
-- Black vinyl, red label, non-flexible vinyl					
❑ 3285 [M]	Ole, Ole, Ole	1959	7.50	15.00	30.00
-- Red vinyl					
❑ 3285 [M]	Ole, Ole, Ole	1959	5.00	10.00	20.00
-- Black vinyl, red label, non-flexible vinyl					
❑ 3294 [M]	Latin Jewels	1959	7.50	15.00	30.00
-- Red vinyl					
❑ 3294 [M]	Latin Jewels	1959	5.00	10.00	20.00
-- Black vinyl, red label, non-flexible vinyl					
❑ 3303 [M]	The Best of Joe Loco	1960	7.50	15.00	30.00
-- Red vinyl					
❑ 3303 [M]	The Best of Joe Loco	1960	5.00	10.00	20.00
-- Black vinyl, red label, non-flexible vinyl					
❑ 3321 [M]	Pachanga with Joe Loco	1961	7.50	15.00	30.00
-- Red vinyl					
❑ 3321 [M]	Pachanga with Joe Loco	1961	5.00	10.00	20.00
-- Black vinyl, red label, non-flexible vinyl					
❑ 8022 [S]	Cha-Cha-Cha	1962	7.50	15.00	30.00
-- Blue vinyl					
❑ 8022 [S]	Cha-Cha-Cha	1962	5.00	10.00	20.00
-- Black vinyl, blue label, non-flexible vinyl					
❑ 8028 [S]	Ole, Ole, Ole	1962	7.50	15.00	30.00
-- Blue vinyl					
❑ 8028 [S]	Ole, Ole, Ole	1962	5.00	10.00	20.00
-- Black vinyl, blue label, non-flexible vinyl					
❑ 8041 [S]	Latin Jewels	1962	7.50	15.00	30.00
-- Blue vinyl					
❑ 8041 [S]	Latin Jewels	1962	5.00	10.00	20.00
-- Black vinyl, blue label, non-flexible vinyl					
❑ 8042 [S]	Going Loco	1962	7.50	15.00	30.00
-- Blue vinyl					
❑ 8042 [S]	Going Loco	1962	5.00	10.00	20.00
-- Black vinyl, blue label, non-flexible vinyl					
❑ 8048 [S]	The Best of Joe Loco	1962	7.50	15.00	30.00
-- Blue vinyl					
❑ 8048 [S]	The Best of Joe Loco	1962	5.00	10.00	20.00
-- Black vinyl, blue label, non-flexible vinyl					
❑ 8064 [S]	Pachanga with Joe Loco	1962	7.50	15.00	30.00
-- Blue vinyl					

Number	Title	Yr	VG	VG+	NM
❑ 8064 [S]	Pachanga with Joe Loco	1962	5.00	10.00	20.00
-- Black vinyl, blue label, non-flexible vinyl					

IMPERIAL

Number	Title	Yr	VG	VG+	NM
❑ LP-9070 [M]	Let's Go Loco	1959	5.00	10.00	20.00
❑ LP-9073 [M]	Happy Go Loco	1959	5.00	10.00	20.00
❑ LP-9166 [M]	Pachanga Twist	1962	5.00	10.00	20.00
❑ LP-12014 [S]	Let's Go Loco	1959	6.25	12.50	25.00
❑ LP-12019 [S]	Happy Go Loco	1959	6.25	12.50	25.00
❑ LP-12079 [S]	Pachanga Twist	1962	6.25	12.50	25.00

TICO

Number	Title	Yr	VG	VG+	NM
❑ LP-109 [10]	Mambos, Vol. 1	195?	10.00	20.00	40.00
❑ LP-121 [10]	Mambos, Vol. 2	195?	10.00	20.00	40.00
❑ LP-121 [10]	Mambos, Vol. 3	195?	10.00	20.00	40.00
❑ LP-122 [10]	Mambos, Vol. 4	195?	10.00	20.00	40.00
❑ LP-123 [10]	Mambo Dance Favorites, Vol. 5	195?	10.00	20.00	40.00
❑ LP-129 [10]	Mambo U.S.A.	1954	10.00	20.00	40.00
❑ LP-132 [10]	Instrumental Mambos (Vol. 7)	1955	10.00	20.00	40.00
❑ LP-1006 [M]	Mambo Moods	1955	7.50	15.00	30.00
❑ LP-1008 [M]	Make Mine Mambo	1955	7.50	15.00	30.00
❑ LP-1012 [M]	Mambo Fantasy	1956	7.50	15.00	30.00
❑ LP-1013 [M]	Viva Mambo!	1956	7.50	15.00	30.00

LODI
MOWEST

Number	Title	Yr	VG	VG+	NM
❑ MW 101L	Happiness	1972	6.25	12.50	25.00

LOFGREN, NILS
A&M

Number	Title	Yr	VG	VG+	NM
❑ SP-8362 [DJ]	Authorized Bootleg	1976	6.25	12.50	25.00

LOGGINS AND MESSINA
Also see KENNY LOGGINS; JIM MESSINA.
COLUMBIA

Number	Title	Yr	VG	VG+	NM
❑ HC 44388	The Best of Friends	1982	12.50	25.00	50.00
-- Half-speed mastered edition					

DIRECT DISC

Number	Title	Yr	VG	VG+	NM
❑ SD 16606	Full Sail	198?	7.50	15.00	30.00
-- Audiophile vinyl					

EPIC

Number	Title	Yr	VG	VG+	NM
❑ PC 34388	The Best of Friends	1976	5.00	10.00	20.00
-- Mispressing with wrong label					

LOGGINS, KENNY
Also see LOGGINS AND MESSINA.
COLUMBIA

Number	Title	Yr	VG	VG+	NM
❑ HC 45837	Nightwatch	198?	17.50	35.00	70.00
-- Half-speed mastered edition					

LOGSDON, JIMMIE
KING

Number	Title	Yr	VG	VG+	NM
❑ 843 [M]	Howdy Neighbors	1963	15.00	30.00	60.00

LOLITA
KAPP

Number	Title	Yr	VG	VG+	NM
❑ KL-1219 [M]	Sailor	1961	6.25	12.50	25.00
❑ KL-1229 [M]	Songs You Will Never Forget	1961	6.25	12.50	25.00
❑ KS-3219 [S]	Sailor	1961	7.50	15.00	30.00
❑ KS-3229 [S]	Songs You Will Never Forget	1961	7.50	15.00	30.00

LOLLIPOP SHOPPE, THE
UNI

Number	Title	Yr	VG	VG+	NM
❑ 73019	The Lollipop Shoppe	1968	20.00	40.00	80.00

LOMAX. JACKIE
APPLE

Number	Title	Yr	VG	VG+	NM
❑ ST-3354	Is This What You Want?	1969	6.25	12.50	25.00

WARNER BROS.

Number	Title	Yr	VG	VG+	NM
❑ PRO 520 [DJ]	An Interview with Jackie Lomax	1972	10.00	20.00	40.00

LOMBARDO, GUY
CAPITOL

Number	Title	Yr	VG	VG+	NM
❑ W 738 [M]	Lombardo in Hi-Fi	1956	5.00	10.00	20.00
-- Turquoise or gray label					
❑ T 739 [M]	Your Guy Lombardo Medley	1956	5.00	10.00	20.00
-- Turquoise or gray label					
❑ T 788 [M]	A Decade on Broadway 1946-56	1956	5.00	10.00	20.00
-- Turquoise or gray label					
❑ T 892 [M]	Lively Guy	1957	5.00	10.00	20.00
-- Turquoise or gray label					

Number	Title	Yr	VG	VG+	NM
❏ T 916 [M]	A Decade on Broadway 1935-45	1958	5.00	10.00	20.00
-- Turquoise or gray label					
❏ ST 1019 [S]	Berlin by Lombardo	1959	6.25	12.50	25.00
-- Black colorband label, logo at left					
❏ T 1019 [M]	Berlin by Lombardo	1958	5.00	10.00	20.00
-- Turquoise or gray label					
❏ ST 1121 [S]	Dancing Room Only	1959	5.00	10.00	20.00
-- Black colorband label, logo at left					
❏ ST 1244 [S]	Your Guy Lombardo Medley, Vol. 2	1960	5.00	10.00	20.00
-- Black colorband label, logo at left					
❏ ST 1306 [S]	The Sweetest Waltzes This Side of Heaven	1960	5.00	10.00	20.00
-- Black colorband label, logo at left					
❏ SKAO 1443 [S]	Sing the Songs of Christmas	1960	5.00	10.00	20.00
-- Black colorband label, logo at left					
❏ T 1461 [M]	The Best of Guy Lombardo	1961	5.00	10.00	20.00
-- Black colorband label, logo at left					
❏ ST 1593 [S]	Drifting and Dreaming	1961	5.00	10.00	20.00
-- Black colorband label, logo at left					
❏ ST 1598 [S]	Your Guy Lombardo Medley, Vol. 3	1961	5.00	10.00	20.00
-- Black colorband label, logo at left					
❏ STDL 2181 [(4) S]	The Lombardo Years	1964	7.50	15.00	30.00
❏ TDL 2181 [(4) M]	The Lombardo Years	1964	6.25	12.50	25.00

DECCA

Number	Title	Yr	VG	VG+	NM
❏ DXB 185 [(2) M]	The Best of Guy Lombardo	1964	5.00	10.00	20.00
❏ DL 5127 [10]	Latin Rhythms	195?	7.50	15.00	30.00
❏ DL 8070 [M]	A Night at the Roosevelt	195?	5.00	10.00	20.00
-- Black label, silver print					
❏ DL 8097 [M]	Lombardoland, U.S.A.	195?	5.00	10.00	20.00
-- Black label, silver print					
❏ DL 8119 [M]	Twin Pianos	195?	5.00	10.00	20.00
-- Black label, silver print					
❏ DL 8135 [M]	Soft and Sweet	1955	5.00	10.00	20.00
-- Black label, silver print					
❏ DL 8136 [M]	Enjoy Yourself	1955	5.00	10.00	20.00
-- Black label, silver print					
❏ DL 8205 [M]	Waltz Time	1955	5.00	10.00	20.00
-- Black label, silver print					
❏ DL 8208 [M]	The Band Played On	195?	5.00	10.00	20.00
-- Black label, silver print					
❏ DL 8249 [M]	Lombardoland	1956	5.00	10.00	20.00
-- Black label, silver print					
❏ DL 8251 [M]	Twin Piano Magic	1956	5.00	10.00	20.00
-- Black label, silver print					
❏ DL 8254 [M]	Everybody Dance	1956	5.00	10.00	20.00
-- Black label, silver print					
❏ DL 8255 [M]	Oh! How We Danced	1956	5.00	10.00	20.00
-- Black label, silver print					
❏ DL 8256 [M]	Waltzland	1956	5.00	10.00	20.00
-- Black label, silver print					
❏ DL 8333 [M]	Silver Jubilee	1956	5.00	10.00	20.00
-- Black label, silver print					
❏ DL 8354 [M]	Jingle Bells	1956	5.00	10.00	20.00
-- Black label, silver print					
❏ DL 8843 [M]	Instrumentally Yours	1959	5.00	10.00	20.00
-- Black label, silver print					
❏ DL 8894 [M]	The Sidewalks of New York	1959	5.00	10.00	20.00
-- Black label, silver print					

LONDON POPS ORCHESTRA (FREDERICK FENNELL, COND.)
MERCURY LIVING PRESENCE

Number	Title	Yr	VG	VG+	NM
❏ SR 90439 [S]	Coates: Three Elizabeths; London Suite; Four Ways Suite	1965	6.25	12.50	25.00
-- Maroon label, with "Vendor: Mercury Record Corporation"					

LONDON PROMS SYMPHONY ORCHESTRA (RAYMOND AGOULT, CONDUCTOR)
RCA VICTOR RED SEAL

Number	Title	Yr	VG	VG+	NM
❏ LSC-2326 [S]	Clair de Lune	1960	37.50	75.00	150.00
-- Original with "shaded dog" label					
❏ LSC-2326 [S]	Clair de Lune	199?	6.25	12.50	25.00
-- Classic Records reissue					

LONDON PROMS SYMPHONY ORCHESTRA (CHARLES MACKERRAS, CONDUCTOR)
RCA VICTOR RED SEAL

Number	Title	Yr	VG	VG+	NM
❏ LSC-2336 [S]	Sibelius: Finlandia	1960	17.50	35.00	70.00
-- Original with "shaded dog" label					
❏ LSC-2336 [S]	Sibelius: Finlandia	199?	6.25	12.50	25.00
-- Classic Records reissue					

LONDON PROMS SYMPHONY ORCHESTRA (ROBERT SHARPLES, CONDUCTOR)
RCA VICTOR RED SEAL

Number	Title	Yr	VG	VG+	NM
❏ LSC-2299 [S]	Lehar: Waltzes	1959	5.00	10.00	20.00
-- Original with "shaded dog" label					

LONDON SOUND 70 ORCHESTRA AND CHORUS
DECCA

Number	Title	Yr	VG	VG+	NM
❏ DEB 7-7 [(3)]	The Sounds of Christmas	1970	6.25	12.50	25.00

LONDON SYMPHONY ORCHESTRA (ARTHUR BLISS, COND.)
RCA VICTOR RED SEAL

Number	Title	Yr	VG	VG+	NM
❏ LSC-2257 [S]	Elgar: Pomp and Circumstance Marches 1-5	1959	30.00	60.00	120.00
-- Original with "shaded dog" label					

LONDON SYMPHONY ORCHESTRA (ANTAL DORATI, COND.)
MERCURY LIVING PRESENCE

Number	Title	Yr	VG	VG+	NM
❏ SR 90006 [S]	Prokofiev: Love for Three Oranges Suite; Scythian Suite	195?	75.00	150.00	300.00
❏ SR 90006 [S]	Prokofiev: Love for Three Oranges Suite; Scythian Suite	199?	6.25	12.50	25.00
-- Classic Records reissue					
❏ SR 90122 [S]	Borodin: Polovetsian Dances; Rimsky-Korsakov: Coq d-Or	1960	10.00	20.00	40.00
-- Maroon label, no "Vendor: Mercury Record Corporation"					
❏ SR 90123 [S]	Mendelssohn: Symphony No. 3; Fingel's Cave Overture	1960	12.50	25.00	50.00
-- Maroon label, no "Vendor: Mercury Record Corporation"					
❏ SR 90153 [S]	Respighi: The Birds; Brazilian Impressions	196?	20.00	40.00	80.00
-- Maroon label, with "Vendor: Mercury Record Corporation"					
❏ SR 90153 [S]	Respighi: The Birds; Brazilian Impressions	196?	45.00	90.00	180.00
-- Maroon label, no "Vendor: Mercury Record Corporation"					
❏ SR 90154 [S]	Brahms: Haydn Variations; Hungarian Dances	196?	7.50	15.00	30.00
-- Maroon label, no "Vendor: Mercury Record Corporation"					
❏ SR 90155 [S]	Haydn: Symphonies 100 and 101	196?	10.00	20.00	40.00
-- Maroon label, with "Vendor: Mercury Record Corporation"					
❏ SR 90156 [S]	Verdi: Overtures	196?	5.00	10.00	20.00
-- Maroon label, no "Vendor: Mercury Record Corporation"					
❏ SR 90158 [S]	Handel-Harty: Water Music Suite; Royal Fireworks Music	196?	7.50	15.00	30.00
-- Maroon label, no "Vendor: Mercury Record Corporation"					
❏ SR 90209 [S]	Khachaturian: Gayne Ballet Suite; Tchaikovsky: Romeo and Juliet	196?	15.00	30.00	60.00
-- Maroon label, no "Vendor: Mercury Record Corporation"					
❏ SR 90209 [S]	Khachaturian: Gayne Ballet Suite; Tchaikovsky: Romeo and Juliet	196?	7.50	15.00	30.00
-- Maroon label, with "Vendor: Mercury Record Corporation"					
❏ SR 90214 [S]	Lizst: Les Preludes; Smetana: The Moldau; Mussorgsky: Night on Bald Mountain; Sibelius: Valse Triste	196?	10.00	20.00	40.00
-- Maroon label, no "Vendor: Mercury Record Corporation"					
❏ SR 90226 [S]	Stravinsky: The Firebird	196?	7.50	15.00	30.00
-- Third edition: Dark red (not maroon) label					
❏ SR 90226 [S]	Stravinsky: The Firebird	196?	17.50	35.00	70.00
-- Maroon label, with "Vendor: Mercury Record Corporation"					
❏ SR 90226 [S]	Stravinsky: The Firebird	196?	30.00	60.00	120.00
-- Maroon label, no "Vendor: Mercury Record Corporation"					
❏ SR 90226 [S]	Stravinsky: The Firebird	199?	6.25	12.50	25.00
-- Classic Records reissue					
❏ SR 90234 [S]	Wagner: Tristan und Isolde Prelude and Liebestod; Tannhauser Overture; Lohengrin Prelude	196?	10.00	20.00	40.00
-- Maroon label, no "Vendor: Mercury Record Corporation"					
❏ SR 90235 [S]	Liszt: Hungarian Rhapsodies No. 2 and 3; Enescu: Rumanian Rhapsodies No. 1 and 2	196?	6.25	12.50	25.00
-- Maroon label, no "Vendor: Mercury Record Corporation"					
❏ SR 90235 [S]	Liszt: Hungarian Rhapsodies No. 2 and 3; Enescu: Rumanian Rhapsodies No. 1 and 2	196?	15.00	30.00	60.00
-- Maroon label, with "Vendor: Mercury Record Corporation" (second edition is more sought after than the first)					
❏ SR 90235 [S]	Liszt: Hungarian Rhapsodies No. 2 and 3; Enescu: Rumanian Rhapsodies No. 1 and 2	196?	5.00	10.00	20.00
-- Third edition: Dark red (not maroon) label					
❏ SR 90236 [S]	Dvorak: Symphony No. 4 (8) in G; Carnaval Overture	196?	10.00	20.00	40.00
-- Maroon label, no "Vendor: Mercury Record Corporation"					
❏ SR 90246 [S]	Copland: Appalachian Spring; Billy the Kid	196?	15.00	30.00	60.00
-- Maroon label, no "Vendor: Mercury Record Corporation"					
❏ SR 90246 [S]	Copland: Appalachian Spring; Billy the Kid	196?	20.00	40.00	80.00
-- Maroon label, with "Vendor: Mercury Record Corporation" (second edition is more sought after than the first)					
❏ SR 90246 [S]	Copland: Appalachian Spring; Billy the Kid	196?	5.00	10.00	20.00
-- Third edition: Dark red (not maroon) label					
❏ SR 90255 [S]	Tchaikovsky: Symphony No. 5	196?	15.00	30.00	60.00
-- Maroon label, no "Vendor: Mercury Record Corporation"					
❏ SR 90265 [S]	Rimsky-Korsakov: Capriccio Espagnol; Russian Easter Overture; Borodin: Prince Igor Overture	196?	12.50	25.00	50.00
-- Maroon label, no "Vendor: Mercury Record Corporation"					
❏ SR 90268 [S]	Brahms: Symphony No. 1	196?	17.50	35.00	70.00
-- Maroon label, no "Vendor: Mercury Record Corporation"					

Number	Title	Yr	VG	VG+	NM
❏ SR 90278 [S]	Berg: Suites from Lulu and Wozzeck	196?	20.00	40.00	80.00
-- Maroon label, no "Vendor: Mercury Record Corporation"					
❏ SR 90278 [S]	Berg: Suites from Lulu and Wozzeck	196?	6.25	12.50	25.00
-- Maroon label, with "Vendor: Mercury Record Corporation"					
❏ SR 90280 [S]	Mozart: Symphony No. 40; Haydn: Symphony No. 45	196?	10.00	20.00	40.00
-- Maroon label, no "Vendor: Mercury Record Corporation"					
❏ SR 90287 [S]	Wagner: Mesitersinger Prelude; Tannhauser Overture; Parsifal; Lohengrin Selections	196?	7.50	15.00	30.00
-- Maroon label, no "Vendor: Mercury Record Corporation"					
❏ SR 90287 [S]	Wagner: Mesitersinger Prelude; Tannhauser Overture; Parsifal; Lohengrin Selections	196?	5.00	10.00	20.00
-- Maroon label, with "Vendor: Mercury Record Corporation"					
❏ SR 90311 [S]	Bartok: Bluebeard's Castle	196?	6.25	12.50	25.00
-- Maroon label, with "Vendor: Mercury Record Corporation"					
❏ SR 90312 [S]	Tchakovsky: Symphony No. 6	196?	10.00	20.00	40.00
-- Maroon label, no "Vendor: Mercury Record Corporation"					
❏ SR 90312 [S]	Tchakovsky: Symphony No. 6	196?	7.50	15.00	30.00
-- Maroon label, with "Vendor: Mercury Record Corporation"					
❏ SR 90316 [S]	Vienna 1908-1914	196?	37.50	75.00	150.00
-- Maroon label, no "Vendor: Mercury Record Corporation"					
❏ SR 90316 [S]	Vienna 1908-1914	196?	30.00	60.00	120.00
-- Maroon label, with "Vendor: Mercury Record Corporation"					
❏ SR 90317 [S]	Beethoven: Symphony No. 5; Egmont Overture; Consecration of the House Overture	196?	6.25	12.50	25.00
-- Maroon label, with "Vendor: Mercury Record Corporation"					
❏ SR 90317 [S]	Beethoven: Symphony No. 5; Egmont Overture; Consecration of the House Overture	196?	12.50	25.00	50.00
-- Maroon label, no "Vendor: Mercury Record Corporation"					
❏ SR 90371 [S]	Liszt: Hungarian Rhapsodies Nos. 1, 4, 5 and 6	196?	100.00	200.00	400.00
-- Maroon label, no "Vendor: Mercury Record Corporation"					
❏ SR 90371 [S]	Liszt: Hungarian Rhapsodies Nos. 1, 4, 5 and 6	196?	15.00	30.00	60.00
-- Maroon label, with "Vendor: Mercury Record Corporation"					
❏ SR 90371 [S]	Liszt: Hungarian Rhapsodies Nos. 1, 4, 5 and 6	196?	7.50	15.00	30.00
-- Third edition: Dark red (not maroon) label					
❏ SR 90378 [S]	Bartok: Concerto for Orchestra	196?	12.50	25.00	50.00
-- Maroon label, no "Vendor: Mercury Record Corporation"					
❏ SR 90387 [S]	Stravnisky: Song of the Nightingale; Fireworks; Scherzo; Four Etudes	196?	12.50	25.00	50.00
-- Maroon label, with "Vendor: Mercury Record Corporation"					
❏ SR 90387 [S]	Stravnisky: Song of the Nightingale; Fireworks; Scherzo; Four Etudes	196?	25.00	50.00	100.00
-- Maroon label, no "Vendor: Mercury Record Corporation"					
❏ SR 90409 [S]	Tchaikovsky: Rococo Variations; Saint-Saens: Cello Concerto No. 1	196?	15.00	30.00	60.00
-- Maroon label, no "Vendor: Mercury Record Corporation"					
❏ SR 90409 [S]	Tchaikovsky: Rococo Variations; Saint-Saens: Cello Concerto No. 1	196?	12.50	25.00	50.00
-- Maroon label, with "Vendor: Mercury Record Corporation"					
❏ SR 90415 [S]	Haydn: Symphony No. 100 in G; Beethoven: Symphony No. 6 in F	196?	5.00	10.00	20.00
-- Maroon label, no "Vendor: Mercury Record Corporation"					
❏ SR 90426 [S]	Bartok: The Wooden Prince	196?	10.00	20.00	40.00
-- Maroon label, no "Vendor: Mercury Record Corporation"					
❏ SR 90426 [S]	Bartok: The Wooden Prince	196?	7.50	15.00	30.00
-- Maroon label, with "Vendor: Mercury Record Corporation"					
❏ SR 90435 [S]	Paris 1917-1938	1965	37.50	75.00	150.00
-- Maroon label, with "Vendor: Mercury Record Corporation"					
❏ SR 90435 [S]	Paris 1917-1938	196?	7.50	15.00	30.00
-- Maroon label, oval "Mercury" logo					
❏ SR 90437 [S]	Brahms: 16 Hungarian Dances	1965	10.00	20.00	40.00
-- Maroon label, with "Vendor: Mercury Record Corporation"					

LONDON SYMPHONY ORCHESTRA (ALEXANDER GIBSON, CONDUCTOR)
RCA VICTOR RED SEAL

Number	Title	Yr	VG	VG+	NM
❏ LSC-2405 [S]	Sibelius: Symphony No. 5	1960	37.50	75.00	150.00
-- Original with "shaded dog" label					
❏ LSC-2405 [S]	Sibelius: Symphony No. 5	199?	6.25	12.50	25.00
-- Classic Records reissue					

LONDON SYMPHONY ORCHESTRA (JEAN MARTINON, CONDUCTOR)
RCA VICTOR RED SEAL

Number	Title	Yr	VG	VG+	NM
❏ LSC-2298 [S]	Borodin: Symphony No. 2; Rimsky-Korsakov: Capriccio Espagnole	1960	50.00	100.00	200.00
-- Original with "shaded dog" label					
❏ LSC-2298 [S]	Borodin: Symphony No. 2; Rimsky-Korsakov: Capriccio Espagnole	199?	6.25	12.50	25.00
-- Classic Records reissue					
❏ LSC-2322 [S]	Shostakovich: Symphony No. 1	1960	25.00	50.00	100.00
-- Original with "shaded dog" label					

Number	Title	Yr	VG	VG+	NM
❏ LSC-2322 [S]	Shostakovich: Symphony No. 1	199?	6.25	12.50	25.00
-- Classic Records reissue					
❏ LSC-2419 [S]	Dvorak: Slavonic Dances	1960	50.00	100.00	200.00
-- Original with "shaded dog" label					
❏ LSC-2419 [S]	Dvorak: Slavonic Dances	199?	6.25	12.50	25.00
-- Classic Records reissue					

LONDON SYMPHONY ORCHESTRA (PIERRE MONTEUX, CONDUCTOR)
RCA VICTOR RED SEAL

Number	Title	Yr	VG	VG+	NM
❏ LSC-2177 [S]	Tchaikovsky: Sleeping Beauty (Excerpts)	1959	7.50	15.00	30.00
-- Original with "shaded dog" label					
❏ LSC-2209 [S]	Rimsky-Korsakov: Scheherazade	1959	5.00	10.00	20.00
-- Original with "shaded dog" label					
❏ LSC-2342 [S]	Sibelius: Symphony No. 2	1960	6.25	12.50	25.00
-- Original with "shaded dog" label					
❏ LSC-2342 [S]	Sibelius: Symphony No. 2	199?	6.25	12.50	25.00
-- Classic Records reissue					
❏ LSC-2418 [S]	Elgar: Enigma Variations	1960	30.00	60.00	120.00
-- Original with "shaded dog" label					
❏ LSC-2418 [S]	Elgar: Enigma Variations	199?	6.25	12.50	25.00
-- Classic Records reissue					
❏ LSC-2489 [S]	Dvorak: Symphony No. 2	196?	6.25	12.50	25.00
-- Original with "shaded dog" label					
❏ LSC-2489 [S]	Dvorak: Symphony No. 2	199?	6.25	12.50	25.00
-- Classic Records reissue					

LONDON SYMPHONY ORCHESTRA (HANS SCHMIDT-ISSERSTEDT, CONDUCTOR)
MERCURY LIVING PRESENCE

Number	Title	Yr	VG	VG+	NM
❏ SR 90184 [S]	Mozart: Symphonies No. 39 and 41	196?	50.00	100.00	200.00
-- Maroon label, no "Vendor: Mercury Record Corporation"					
❏ SR 90184 [S]	Mozart: Symphonies No. 39 and 41	196?	5.00	10.00	20.00
-- Maroon label, with "Vendor: Mercury Record Corporation"					

LONDON SYMPHONY ORCHESTRA (WALTER SUSSKIND, HANS SCHMIDT-ISSERSTEDT, CONDUCTORS)
MERCURY LIVING PRESENCE

Number	Title	Yr	VG	VG+	NM
❏ SR 90196 [S]	Schubert: Symphonies No. 4 and 6	196?	10.00	20.00	40.00
-- Maroon label, no "Vendor: Mercury Record Corporation"					

LONDON, JULIE
LIBERTY

Number	Title	Yr	VG	VG+	NM
❏ LRP-3006 [M]	Julie Is Her Name	1956	12.50	25.00	50.00
-- Green label					
❏ LRP-3006 [M]	Julie Is Her Name	1960	5.00	10.00	20.00
-- Black label, colorband and logo at left					
❏ LRP-3012 [M]	Lonely Girl	1956	12.50	25.00	50.00
-- Green label					
❏ LRP-3012 [M]	Lonely Girl	1960	5.00	10.00	20.00
-- Black label, colorband and logo at left					
❏ LRP-3043 [M]	About the Blues	1957	10.00	20.00	40.00
-- Green label					
❏ LRP-3043 [M]	About the Blues	1960	5.00	10.00	20.00
-- Black label, colorband and logo at left					
❏ LRP-3060 [M]	Make Love to Me	1957	10.00	20.00	40.00
-- Green label					
❏ LRP-3060 [M]	Make Love to Me	1960	5.00	10.00	20.00
-- Black label, colorband and logo at left					
❏ LRP-3096 [M]	Julie	1957	10.00	20.00	40.00
-- Green label					
❏ LRP-3100 [M]	Julie Is Her Name, Volume 2	1958	10.00	20.00	40.00
-- Green label					
❏ LRP-3100 [M]	Julie Is Her Name, Volume 2	1960	5.00	10.00	20.00
-- Black label, colorband and logo at left					
❏ LRP-3105 [M]	London By Night	1958	7.50	15.00	30.00
❏ LRP-3119 [M]	Swing Me an Old Song	1959	7.50	15.00	30.00
-- Green label					
❏ LRP-3130 [M]	Your Number Please	1959	7.50	15.00	30.00
-- Green label					
❏ LRP-3130 [M]	Your Number Please	1960	5.00	10.00	20.00
-- Black label, colorband and logo at left					
❏ LRP-3152 [M]	Julie...At Home	1960	7.50	15.00	30.00
❏ LRP-3164 [M]	Around Midnight	1960	7.50	15.00	30.00
❏ LRP-3171 [M]	Send for Me	1961	7.50	15.00	30.00
❏ LRP-3192 [M]	Whatever Julie Wants	1961	7.50	15.00	30.00
❏ LRP-3203 [M]	Sophisticated Lady	1962	6.25	12.50	25.00
❏ LRP-3231 [M]	Love Letters	1962	6.25	12.50	25.00
❏ LRP-3249 [M]	Love on the Rocks	1963	6.25	12.50	25.00
❏ LRP-3278 [M]	Latin in a Satin Mood	1963	6.25	12.50	25.00

Number	Title	Yr	VG	VG+	NM
❏ LRP-3291 [M]	Julie's Golden Hits	1963	6.25	12.50	25.00
-- Black cover					
❏ LRP-3291 [M]	Julie's Golden Hits	1963	6.25	12.50	25.00
-- White cover					
❏ LRP-3300 [M]	The End of the World	1963	6.25	12.50	25.00
❏ LRP-3324 [M]	The Wonderful World of Julie London	1963	6.25	12.50	25.00
❏ LRP-3342 [M]	Julie London	1964	6.25	12.50	25.00
❏ LRP-3375 [M]	Julie London In Person at the Americana	1964	6.25	12.50	25.00
❏ LRP-3392 [M]	Our Fair Lady	1965	6.25	12.50	25.00
❏ LRP-3416 [M]	Feeling Good	1965	6.25	12.50	25.00
❏ LRP-3434 [M]	All Through the Night	1965	6.25	12.50	25.00
❏ LRP-3478 [M]	For the Night People	1966	6.25	12.50	25.00
❏ LRP-3493 [M]	Nice Girls Don't Stay for Breakfast	1967	6.25	12.50	25.00
❏ LRP-3514 [M]	With Body and Soul	1967	7.50	15.00	30.00
❏ LRP-5501 [M]	The Best of Julie London	1962	7.50	15.00	30.00
❏ LST-6501 [S]	The Best of Julie London	1962	10.00	20.00	40.00
❏ LST-7004 [S]	Julie	1958	17.50	35.00	70.00
-- Black label, silver print					
❏ LST-7012 [S]	About the Blues	1958	17.50	35.00	70.00
-- Black label, silver print					
❏ LST-7012 [S]	About the Blues	1960	6.25	12.50	25.00
-- Black label, colorband and logo at left					
❏ LST-7027 [S]	Julie Is Her Name	1958	25.00	50.00	100.00
-- Blue vinyl					
❏ LST-7027 [S]	Julie Is Her Name	1958	10.00	20.00	40.00
-- Black label, silver print					
❏ LST-7027 [S]	Julie Is Her Name	1958	25.00	50.00	100.00
-- Red vinyl					
❏ LST-7027 [S]	Julie Is Her Name	1960	6.25	12.50	25.00
-- Black label, colorband and logo at left					
❏ LST-7029 [S]	Lonely Girl	1958	10.00	20.00	40.00
-- Black label, silver print					
❏ LST-7029 [S]	Lonely Girl	1960	6.25	12.50	25.00
-- Black label, colorband and logo at left					
❏ LST-7060 [S]	Make Love to Me	1958	10.00	20.00	40.00
-- Black label, silver print					
❏ LST-7060 [S]	Make Love to Me	1960	6.25	12.50	25.00
-- Black label, colorband and logo at left					
❏ LST-7100 [S]	Julie Is Her Name, Volume 2	1958	10.00	20.00	40.00
-- Black label, silver print					
❏ LST-7100 [S]	Julie Is Her Name, Volume 2	1960	6.25	12.50	25.00
-- Black label, colorband and logo at left					
❏ LST-7105 [S]	London By Night	1958	10.00	20.00	40.00
-- Black label, silver print					
❏ LST-7119 [S]	Swing Me an Old Song	1959	10.00	20.00	40.00
-- Black label, silver print					
❏ LST-7130 [S]	Your Number Please	1959	10.00	20.00	40.00
-- Black label, silver print					
❏ LST-7130 [S]	Your Number Please	1960	6.25	12.50	25.00
-- Black label, colorband and logo at left					
❏ LST-7152 [S]	Julie...At Home	1960	25.00	50.00	100.00
-- Blue vinyl					
❏ LST-7152 [S]	Julie...At Home	1960	10.00	20.00	40.00
-- Black vinyl					
❏ LST-7164 [S]	Around Midnight	1960	10.00	20.00	40.00
❏ LST-7171 [S]	Send for Me	1961	10.00	20.00	40.00
❏ LST-7192 [S]	Whatever Julie Wants	1961	10.00	20.00	40.00
❏ LST-7203 [S]	Sophisticated Lady	1962	7.50	15.00	30.00
❏ LST-7231 [S]	Love Letters	1962	7.50	15.00	30.00
❏ LST-7249 [S]	Love on the Rocks	1963	7.50	15.00	30.00
❏ LST-7278 [S]	Latin in a Satin Mood	1963	7.50	15.00	30.00
❏ LST-7291 [S]	Julie's Golden Hits	1963	7.50	15.00	30.00
-- Black cover					
❏ LST-7291 [S]	Julie's Golden Hits	1963	7.50	15.00	30.00
-- White cover					
❏ LST-7300 [S]	The End of the World	1963	7.50	15.00	30.00
❏ LST-7324 [S]	The Wonderful World of Julie London	1963	7.50	15.00	30.00
❏ LST-7342 [S]	Julie London	1964	7.50	15.00	30.00
❏ LST-7375 [S]	Julie London In Person at the Americana	1964	7.50	15.00	30.00
❏ LST-7392 [S]	Our Fair Lady	1965	7.50	15.00	30.00
❏ LST-7416 [S]	Feeling Good	1965	7.50	15.00	30.00
❏ LST-7434 [S]	All Through the Night	1965	7.50	15.00	30.00
❏ LST-7478 [S]	For the Night People	1966	7.50	15.00	30.00
❏ LST-7493 [S]	Nice Girls Don't Stay for Breakfast	1967	6.25	12.50	25.00
❏ LST-7514 [S]	With Body and Soul	1967	6.25	12.50	25.00
❏ LST-7546	Easy Does It	1968	5.00	10.00	20.00
❏ LST-7609	Yummy, Yummy, Yummy	1969	5.00	10.00	20.00
❏ SL-9002 [M]	Calendar Girl	1956	25.00	50.00	100.00

LONDON, LAURIE
CAPITOL
Number	Title	Yr	VG	VG+	NM
❏ T 1016 [M]	Laurie London	1958	12.50	25.00	50.00

LONE STAR RAMBLERS, THE
LONGHORN
Number	Title	Yr	VG	VG+	NM
❏ LP-600 [M]	Texas Square Dancing with Red at the 60 Club	196?	6.25	12.50	25.00

LONESOME BLUES SINGER, THE -- See LEADBELLY.

LONESOME PINE FIDDLERS, THE
STARDAY
Number	Title	Yr	VG	VG+	NM
❏ SLP-155 [M]	14 Mountain Songs Featuring 5-String Banjo	1961	10.00	20.00	40.00
❏ SLP-194 [M]	Bluegrass	1962	10.00	20.00	40.00
❏ SLP-222 [M]	More Bluegrass	1963	10.00	20.00	40.00

LONESOME RHODES
RCA VICTOR
Number	Title	Yr	VG	VG+	NM
❏ LPM-3759 [M]	Lonesome Rhodes	1967	7.50	15.00	30.00
❏ LSP-3759 [S]	Lonesome Rhodes	1967	5.00	10.00	20.00

LONESOME SUNDOWN
EXCELLO
Number	Title	Yr	VG	VG+	NM
❏ LPS-8012	Lonesome Lonely Blues	1970	6.25	12.50	25.00

LONG, BARBARA
SAVOY
Number	Title	Yr	VG	VG+	NM
❏ MG-12161 [M]	Soul	1961	7.50	15.00	30.00

LONG, SHORTY
FORD
Number	Title	Yr	VG	VG+	NM
❏ FXM-712 [M]	Country Jamboree	1963	5.00	10.00	20.00
SOUL
| ❏ SS-709 | Here Comes the Judge | 1968 | 5.00 | 10.00 | 20.00 |

LONGBRANCH PENNYWHISTLE
AMOS
Number	Title	Yr	VG	VG+	NM
❏ AAS-7007	Longbranch Pennywhistle	1969	12.50	25.00	50.00

LONZO & OSCAR
COLUMBIA
Number	Title	Yr	VG	VG+	NM
❏ CS 9587	Mountain Dew	1968	5.00	10.00	20.00
DECCA
| ❏ DL 4363 [M] | Country Comedy Time | 1963 | 5.00 | 10.00 | 20.00 |
STARDAY
| ❏ SLP-119 [M] | America's Greatest Country Comedians | 1960 | 10.00 | 20.00 | 40.00 |
| ❏ SLP-244 [M] | Country Music Time | 1963 | 10.00 | 20.00 | 40.00 |

LOOSE
NOCTURNE
Number	Title	Yr	VG	VG+	NM
❏ 906	Freaky Billie, The Wheelie King	1970	7.50	15.00	30.00

LOPEZ, TRINI
GUEST STAR
Number	Title	Yr	VG	VG+	NM
❏ GS-1499 [M]	Trini Lopez and Scott Gregory	1964	12.50	25.00	50.00
-- "Scott Gregory" is said to be a pseudonym for BILL HALEY.					
KING
❏ 863 [M]	Teenage Love Songs	1963	15.00	30.00	60.00
❏ 877 [M]	More of Trini Lopez	1964	15.00	30.00	60.00
❏ 962 [M]	24 Songs by the Great Trini Lopez	1966	7.50	15.00	30.00

LORD SITAR
Not GEORGE HARRISON in disguise, though sometimes thought to be.
CAPITOL
Number	Title	Yr	VG	VG+	NM
❏ ST 2916	Lord Sitar	1968	7.50	15.00	30.00

LORD, BOBBY
HARMONY
Number	Title	Yr	VG	VG+	NM
❏ HL 7322 [M]	Bobby Lord's Best	1964	6.25	12.50	25.00
HICKORY
| ❏ LP-126 [M] | The Bobby Lord Show | 1965 | 5.00 | 10.00 | 20.00 |

LOREN, DONNA
CAPITOL
Number	Title	Yr	VG	VG+	NM
❏ ST 2323 [S]	Beach Blanket Bingo	1965	12.50	25.00	50.00
❏ T 2323 [M]	Beach Blanket Bingo	1965	10.00	20.00	40.00

Number	Title	Yr	VG	VG+	NM

LORING, GLORIA
MGM

Number	Title	Yr	VG	VG+	NM
❏ SE-4499	Today	1968	5.00	10.00	20.00

LOS ANGELES JAZZ CHOIR, THE
MOBILE FIDELITY

❏ 1-096	Listen	1982	20.00	40.00	80.00
-- Audiophile vinyl					

LOS ANGELES PHILHARMONIC (ZUBIN MEHTA, COND.)
MOBILE FIDELITY

❏ 1-008	Suites from "Star Wars" and "Close Encounters of the Third Kind"	1979	12.50	25.00	50.00
-- Audiophile vinyl					

LOS BRAVOS
PARROT

❏ PAS 71021	Bring a Little Lovin'	1968	20.00	40.00	80.00
-- Among the other tracks, "Black Is Black" in in true stereo.					

PRESS

❏ PR 73003 [M]	Black Is Black	1966	12.50	25.00	50.00
❏ PRS 83003 [R]	Black Is Black	1966	7.50	15.00	30.00

LOS INDIOS TABAJARAS
RCA VICTOR

❏ LPM-1788 [M]	Sweet and Savage	1958	10.00	20.00	40.00
❏ LSP-1788 [S]	Sweet and Savage	1958	12.50	25.00	50.00
❏ LPM-2822 [M]	Maria Elena	1963	5.00	10.00	20.00
-- Reissue of LPM-1788					
❏ LSP-2822 [S]	Maria Elena	1963	6.25	12.50	25.00
-- Reissue of LSP-1788					
❏ LSP-2912 [S]	Always in My Heart	1964	5.00	10.00	20.00
❏ LSP-2959 [S]	Twin Guitar Moods	1964	5.00	10.00	20.00
❏ LSP-3413 [S]	Many-Splendored Guitars	1965	5.00	10.00	20.00
❏ LSP-3505 [S]	Casually Classical	1966	5.00	10.00	20.00
❏ LSP-3611 [S]	Twin Guitars -- In a Mood for Lovers	1966	5.00	10.00	20.00
❏ LSP-3723 [S]	Their Very Special Touch	1967	5.00	10.00	20.00
❏ LPM-3909 [M]	Fascinating Rhythms of Their Brazil	1968	5.00	10.00	20.00

LOS LOBOS
NEW VISTAS

❏ 1001	Just Another Band from East L.A.	1978	50.00	100.00	200.00

LOS LOCOS DEL RITMO
DIMSA

❏ 8178	Rock!	196?	25.00	50.00	100.00

LOS SEVEN DAYS
ECO

❏ 314	Sha-La-La	196?	12.50	25.00	50.00

LOST & FOUND
INTERNATIONAL ARTISTS

❏ IA-3	Everybody's Here	1968	25.00	50.00	100.00
-- Original pressing, no "Masterfonics" in dead wax					

LOST NATION, THE
RARE EARTH

❏ RS-518	Paradise Lost	1970	5.00	10.00	20.00

LOTHAR AND THE HAND PEOPLE
CAPITOL

❏ ST-247	Space Hymn	1969	10.00	20.00	40.00
❏ ST 2997	Presenting Lothar and the Hand People	1968	10.00	20.00	40.00

LOUDERMILK, JOHN D.
RCA VICTOR

❏ LPM-2434 [M]	Language of Love	1961	6.25	12.50	25.00
❏ LSP-2434 [S]	Language of Love	1961	7.50	15.00	30.00
❏ LPM-2539 [M]	Twelve Sides of Loudermilk	1962	5.00	10.00	20.00
❏ LSP-2539 [S]	Twelve Sides of Loudermilk	1962	6.25	12.50	25.00
❏ LPM-3497 [M]	A Bizarre Collection of the Most Unusual Songs	1965	5.00	10.00	20.00
❏ LSP-3497 [S]	A Bizarre Collection of the Most Unusual Songs	1965	6.25	12.50	25.00
❏ LPM-3807 [M]	Suburban Attitudes in Country Music	1967	6.25	12.50	25.00
❏ LSP-3807 [S]	Suburban Attitudes in Country Music	1967	5.00	10.00	20.00
❏ LSP-4040	Country Love Songs	1968	5.00	10.00	20.00
❏ LSP-4097	The Open Mind of John D. Loudermilk	1968	5.00	10.00	20.00

LOUDON, DOROTHY
CORAL

❏ CRL 57265 [M]	At the Blue Angel	1959	5.00	10.00	20.00
❏ CRL 757265 [S]	At the Blue Angel	1959	6.25	12.50	25.00

LOUIE AND THE LOVERS
EPIC

❏ E 30026	Rise	1970	5.00	10.00	20.00

LOUISE, TINA
CONCERT HALL

❏ H-1503 [M]	Her Portrait in Hi-Fi	1958	12.50	25.00	50.00
❏ H-1521 [M]	It's Time for Tina	1958	50.00	100.00	200.00

URANIA

❏ ULM-2005 [M]	It's Time for Tina	1959	50.00	100.00	200.00
❏ USD-2005 [S]	It's Time for Tina	1959	75.00	150.00	300.00

LOUISIANA HONEY DRIPPERS, THE
PRESTIGE

❏ PR-13035 [M]	Bluegrass	1961	6.25	12.50	25.00

LOUISIANA RED
ROULETTE

❏ R-25200 [M]	The Lowdown Back Porch Blues	1963	10.00	20.00	40.00

LOUVIN BROTHERS, THE
Also see CHARLES LOUVIN; IRA LOUVIN.
CAPITOL

❏ DT 769 [R]	Tragic Songs of Life	196?	5.00	10.00	20.00
❏ T 769 [M]	Tragic Songs of Life	1956	25.00	50.00	100.00
-- Turquoise label					
❏ T 769 [M]	Tragic Songs of Life	1959	10.00	20.00	40.00
-- Black colorband label, logo at left					
❏ T 769 [M]	Tragic Songs of Life	1962	6.25	12.50	25.00
-- Black colorband label, logo at top					
❏ T 825 [M]	Nearer My God to Thee	1957	25.00	50.00	100.00
-- Turquoise label					
❏ T 825 [M]	Nearer My God to Thee	1959	10.00	20.00	40.00
-- Black colorband label, logo at left					
❏ T 825 [M]	Nearer My God to Thee	1962	6.25	12.50	25.00
-- Black colorband label, logo at top					
❏ T 910 [M]	Ira and Charlie	1958	25.00	50.00	100.00
-- Turquoise label					
❏ T 910 [M]	Ira and Charlie	1959	10.00	20.00	40.00
-- Black colorband label, logo at left					
❏ T 910 [M]	Ira and Charlie	1962	6.25	12.50	25.00
-- Black colorband label, logo at top					
❏ DT 1061 [R]	The Family Who Prays	196?	5.00	10.00	20.00
❏ T 1061 [M]	The Family Who Prays	1958	20.00	40.00	80.00
-- Black colorband label, logo at left					
❏ T 1061 [M]	The Family Who Prays	1962	6.25	12.50	25.00
-- Black colorband label, logo at top					
❏ T 1106 [M]	Country Love Ballads	1959	20.00	40.00	80.00
-- Black colorband label, logo at left					
❏ T 1106 [M]	Country Love Ballads	1962	6.25	12.50	25.00
-- Black colorband label, logo at top					
❏ T 1277 [M]	Satan Is Real	1960	20.00	40.00	80.00
-- Black colorband label, logo at left					
❏ T 1277 [M]	Satan Is Real	1962	6.25	12.50	25.00
-- Black colorband label, logo at top					
❏ T 1385 [M]	My Baby's Gone	1960	20.00	40.00	80.00
-- Black colorband label, logo at left					
❏ T 1385 [M]	My Baby's Gone	1962	6.25	12.50	25.00
-- Black colorband label, logo at top					
❏ T 1449 [M]	A Tribute to the Delmore Brothers	1960	20.00	40.00	80.00
-- Black colorband label, logo at left					
❏ T 1449 [M]	A Tribute to the Delmore Brothers	1962	6.25	12.50	25.00
-- Black colorband label, logo at top					
❏ T 1547 [M]	Encore	1961	20.00	40.00	80.00
-- Black colorband label, logo at left					
❏ T 1547 [M]	Encore	1962	6.25	12.50	25.00
-- Black colorband label, logo at top					
❏ ST 1616 [S]	Country Christmas	1961	20.00	40.00	80.00
-- Black rainbow label with "Capitol" at left					
❏ ST 1616 [S]	Country Christmas	1962	6.25	12.50	25.00
-- Black rainbow label with "Capitol" at top					
❏ T 1616 [M]	Country Christmas	1961	12.50	25.00	50.00
-- Black rainbow label with "Capitol" at left					

Number	Title	Yr	VG	VG+	NM
❑ T 1616 [M]	Country Christmas	1962	5.00	10.00	20.00
-- Black rainbow label with "Capitol" at top					
❑ ST 1721 [S]	Weapon of Prayer	1962	12.50	25.00	50.00
❑ T 1721 [M]	Weapon of Prayer	1962	10.00	20.00	40.00
❑ ST 1834 [S]	Keep Your Eyes on Jesus	1963	12.50	25.00	50.00
❑ T 1834 [M]	Keep Your Eyes on Jesus	1963	10.00	20.00	40.00
❑ ST 2091 [S]	The Louvin Brothers Sing and Play Their Current Hits	1964	7.50	15.00	30.00
❑ T 2091 [M]	The Louvin Brothers Sing and Play Their Current Hits	1964	6.25	12.50	25.00
❑ ST 2331 [S]	Thank God for My Christian Home	1965	7.50	15.00	30.00
❑ T 2331 [M]	Thank God for My Christian Home	1965	6.25	12.50	25.00
❑ ST 2827 [S]	The Great Roy Acuff Songs	1967	7.50	15.00	30.00
❑ T 2827 [M]	The Great Roy Acuff Songs	1967	10.00	20.00	40.00

METRO

Number	Title	Yr	VG	VG+	NM
❑ M-598 [M]	The Louvin Brothers	1966	6.25	12.50	25.00
❑ MS-598 [R]	The Louvin Brothers	1966	5.00	10.00	20.00

MGM

Number	Title	Yr	VG	VG+	NM
❑ E-3426 [M]	The Louvin Brothers	1957	50.00	100.00	200.00

TOWER

Number	Title	Yr	VG	VG+	NM
❑ DT 5038 [R]	Two Different Worlds	1966	5.00	10.00	20.00
❑ DT 5122	Country Heart and Soul	1968	5.00	10.00	20.00
❑ T 5038 [M]	Two Different Worlds	1966	7.50	15.00	30.00

LOUVIN, CHARLIE
Also see THE LOUVIN BROTHERS.
CAPITOL

Number	Title	Yr	VG	VG+	NM
❑ ST-142	Hey Daddy	1969	5.00	10.00	20.00
❑ ST-248	The Kind of Man I Am	1969	5.00	10.00	20.00
❑ ST-416	Here's a Toast to Mama	1970	5.00	10.00	20.00
❑ ST-555	Ten Times	1970	5.00	10.00	20.00
❑ ST 2208 [S]	Less and Less and I Don't Love You Anymore	1965	6.25	12.50	25.00
❑ T 2208 [M]	Less and Less and I Don't Love You Anymore	1965	5.00	10.00	20.00
❑ ST 2437 [S]	The Many Moods of Charlie Louvin	1966	6.25	12.50	25.00
❑ T 2437 [M]	The Many Moods of Charlie Louvin	1966	5.00	10.00	20.00
❑ ST 2482 [S]	Lonesome Is Me	1966	6.25	12.50	25.00
❑ T 2482 [M]	Lonesome Is Me	1966	5.00	10.00	20.00
❑ ST 2689 [S]	I'll Remember Always	1967	5.00	10.00	20.00
❑ T 2689 [M]	I'll Remember Always	1967	6.25	12.50	25.00
❑ ST 2787 [S]	I Forgot to Cry	1967	5.00	10.00	20.00
❑ T 2787 [M]	I Forgot to Cry	1967	6.25	12.50	25.00
❑ ST 2958	Will You Visit Me on Sundays	1968	5.00	10.00	20.00

LOUVIN, CHARLIE, AND MELBA MONTGOMERY
CAPITOL

Number	Title	Yr	VG	VG+	NM
❑ ST-686	Somethin' to Brag About	1971	5.00	10.00	20.00
❑ ST-808	Baby, You've Got What It Takes	1971	5.00	10.00	20.00

LOUVIN, IRA
Also see THE LOUVIN BROTHERS.
CAPITOL

Number	Title	Yr	VG	VG+	NM
❑ ST 2413 [S]	The Unforgettable Ira Louvin	1965	7.50	15.00	30.00
❑ T 2413 [M]	The Unforgettable Ira Louvin	1965	6.25	12.50	25.00

LOVE
Also see ARTHUR LEE.
BLUE THUMB

Number	Title	Yr	VG	VG+	NM
❑ BTS-8822	False Start	1970	5.00	10.00	20.00
❑ BTS-9000 [(2)]	Out Here	1969	6.25	12.50	25.00

ELEKTRA

Number	Title	Yr	VG	VG+	NM
❑ EKL-4001 [M]	Love	1966	25.00	50.00	100.00
❑ EKL-4001 [M-DJ]	Love	1966	75.00	150.00	300.00
-- White label promo					
❑ EKL-4005 [M]	Da Capo	1967	25.00	50.00	100.00
❑ EKL-4013 [M]	Forever Changes	1967	12.50	25.00	50.00
❑ EKL-4013 [M-DJ]	Forever Changes	1967	37.50	75.00	150.00
-- White label promo					
❑ EKS-74001 [S]	Love	1966	12.50	25.00	50.00
-- Brown label					
❑ EKS-74005 [S]	Da Capo	1967	10.00	20.00	40.00
-- Brown label					
❑ EKS-74013 [S]	Forever Changes	1967	7.50	15.00	30.00
-- Brown label					
❑ EKS-74049	Four Sail	1969	6.25	12.50	25.00
-- Red label with large stylized "E"					
❑ EKS-74049 [DJ]	Four Sail	1969	20.00	40.00	80.00
-- White label promo					
❑ EKS-74058	Revisited	1970	6.25	12.50	25.00
-- Red label with large stylized "E"					

LOVE EXCHANGE, THE
TOWER

Number	Title	Yr	VG	VG+	NM
❑ ST 5115	The Love Exchange	1968	6.25	12.50	25.00

LOVE GENERATION, THE
IMPERIAL

Number	Title	Yr	VG	VG+	NM
❑ LP-9351 [M]	The Love Generation	1967	5.00	10.00	20.00
❑ LP-12351 [S]	The Love Generation	1967	5.00	10.00	20.00
❑ LP-12364	A Generation of Love	1968	5.00	10.00	20.00
❑ LP-12408	Montage	1968	5.00	10.00	20.00

LOVE SCULPTURE
Also see DAVE EDMUNDS.
PARROT

Number	Title	Yr	VG	VG+	NM
❑ PAS 71035	Forms and Feelings	1970	6.25	12.50	25.00

RARE EARTH

Number	Title	Yr	VG	VG+	NM
❑ RS-505	Blues Helping	1969	10.00	20.00	40.00

LOVE, HOLLY
ACE

Number	Title	Yr	VG	VG+	NM
❑ LP-1022 [M]	My Love Confessions	1962	7.50	15.00	30.00

LOVE, PRESTON
KENT

Number	Title	Yr	VG	VG+	NM
❑ KST-540	Omaha Bar-B-Q	1968	5.00	10.00	20.00

LOVECRAFT -- See H.P. LOVECRAFT.

LOVELITES, THE
UNI

Number	Title	Yr	VG	VG+	NM
❑ 73081	The Lovelites	1970	6.25	12.50	25.00

LOVICH, LENE
STIFF/EPIC

Number	Title	Yr	VG	VG+	NM
❑ JE 36102	Stateless	1979	5.00	10.00	20.00
-- Red vinyl					

LOVIN' SPOONFUL, THE
Also see JOHN SEBASTIAN; ZALMAN YANOVSKY.
KAMA SUTRA

Number	Title	Yr	VG	VG+	NM
❑ KOPS-750 [(2)]	24 Karat Hits	1968	5.00	10.00	20.00
❑ KSBS-2608 [(2)]	The Best...Lovin' Spoonful	1976	5.00	10.00	20.00
❑ KLP-8050 [M]	Do You Believe in Magic	1965	5.00	10.00	20.00
❑ KLPS-8050 [S]	Do You Believe in Magic	1965	7.50	15.00	30.00
❑ KLP-8051 [M]	Daydream	1966	5.00	10.00	20.00
❑ KLPS-8051 [S]	Daydream	1966	7.50	15.00	30.00
❑ KLP-8053 [M]	What's Up, Tiger Lily?	1966	5.00	10.00	20.00
❑ KLPS-8053 [S]	What's Up, Tiger Lily?	1966	7.50	15.00	30.00
❑ KLP-8054 [M]	Hums of the Lovin' Spoonful	1966	5.00	10.00	20.00
❑ KLPS-8054 [S]	Hums of the Lovin' Spoonful	1966	7.50	15.00	30.00
❑ KLP-8058 [M]	You're a Big Boy Now	1967	5.00	10.00	20.00
❑ KLPS-8058 [S]	You're a Big Boy Now	1967	5.00	10.00	20.00
❑ KLPS-8061	Everything Playing	1968	5.00	10.00	20.00
❑ KLPS-8064	The Best of the Lovin' Spoonful, Volume 2	1968	5.00	10.00	20.00
❑ KLPS-8073	Revelation: Revolution '69	1969	6.25	12.50	25.00
❑ ST-90597 [S]	Do You Believe in Magic	1965	10.00	20.00	40.00
-- Capitol Record Club edition					
❑ T-90597 [M]	Do You Believe in Magic	1965	7.50	15.00	30.00
-- Capitol Record Club edition					
❑ ST-91102 [S]	The Best of the Lovin' Spoonful	1967	5.00	10.00	20.00
-- Capitol Record Club edition					

LOWE, BERNIE, ORCHESTRA
CAMEO

Number	Title	Yr	VG	VG+	NM
❑ C-1057 [M]	Encore	1963	5.00	10.00	20.00
❑ C-4005 [M]	If the Big Bands Were Here Today	1962	5.00	10.00	20.00
❑ SC-4005 [S]	If the Big Bands Were Here Today	1962	6.25	12.50	25.00
❑ C-4007 [M]	If the Big Bands Were Here Today, Vol. 2	1962	5.00	10.00	20.00
❑ SC-4007 [S]	If the Big Bands Were Here Today, Vol. 2	1962	6.25	12.50	25.00

LOWE, JIM
DOT

Number	Title	Yr	VG	VG+	NM
❑ DLP-3051 [M]	The Green Door	1956	37.50	75.00	150.00
❑ DLP-3114 [M]	Wicked Women	1958	25.00	50.00	100.00
❑ DLP-3681 [M]	Songs They Sing Behind the Green Door	1965	6.25	12.50	25.00
❑ DLP-25881 [S]	Songs They Sing Behind the Green Door	1965	7.50	15.00	30.00

MERCURY

Number	Title	Yr	VG	VG+	NM
❑ MG-20246 [M]	The Door of Fame	1957	37.50	75.00	150.00

Number	Title	Yr	VG	VG+	NM

LOWE, NICK
COLUMBIA
❑ AS 1400 [DJ]   An Interrogation of Nick Lowe   1990   6.25   12.50   25.00
-- Promo-only interview album
❑ JC 35529   Pure Pop for Now People   1978   5.00   10.00   20.00

LOWE, SAMMY
RCA VICTOR
❑ LPM-2770 [M]   Hitsville U.S.A.   1963   5.00   10.00   20.00
❑ LSP-2770 [S]   Hitsville U.S.A.   1963   6.25   12.50   25.00

LRY
CONGRESS OF THE CROW
❑ 8031002   The LRY Record   1968   50.00   100.00   200.00

LUBOFF, NORMAN, CHOIR
COLUMBIA
❑ CL 545 [M]   Easy to Remember   1954   5.00   10.00   20.00
-- Maroon label, gold print
❑ CL 2545 [10]   Carols for Christmas   1955   7.50   15.00   30.00
-- "House Party Series"
❑ CL 6272 [10]   Christmas Carols   1953   10.00   20.00   40.00

LUCAS, BUDDY
UNITED ARTISTS
❑ UAL-3482 [M]   Fifty Fabulous Harmonica Favorites   1966   5.00   10.00   20.00
❑ UAS-6482 [S]   Fifty Fabulous Harmonica Favorites   1966   6.25   12.50   25.00

LUCAS, NICK
DECCA
❑ DL 8653 [M]   Painting the Clouds with Sunshine   1957   10.00   20.00   40.00

LUCEY, CHRIS
SURREY
❑ SS-1027 [M]   Songs of Protest and Anti-Protest   197?   10.00   20.00   40.00

LUDDEN, ALLEN
RCA VICTOR
❑ LPM-2934 [M]   Allen Ludden Sings His Favorite Songs   1964   5.00   10.00   20.00
❑ LSP-2934 [S]   Allen Ludden Sings His Favorite Songs   1964   6.25   12.50   25.00

LULU
ATCO
❑ 33-310 [M-DJ]   New Routes   1970   7.50   15.00   30.00
-- White label promo; no stock copies were issued in mono
❑ 33-330 [M-DJ]   Melody Fair   1970   7.50   15.00   30.00
-- White label promo; no stock copies were issued in mono
CHELSEA
❑ CHL-518   Heaven and Earth and the Stars   1976   5.00   10.00   20.00
EPIC
❑ LN 24339 [M]   To Sir with Love   1967   6.25   12.50   25.00
❑ BN 26339 [P]   To Sir with Love   1967   7.50   15.00   30.00
HARMONY
❑ H 30249   To Love Somebody   1970   5.00   10.00   20.00
PARROT
❑ PA 61016 [M]   From Lulu with Love   1967   15.00   30.00   60.00
❑ PAS 71016 [S]   From Lulu with Love   1967   20.00   40.00   80.00

LULU BELLE AND SCOTTY
STARDAY
❑ SLP-206 [M]   The Sweethearts of Country Music   1963   10.00   20.00   40.00
❑ SLP-285 [M]   Down Memory Lane   1964   10.00   20.00   40.00
❑ SLP-351 [M]   Lulu Belle & Scotty   1965   10.00   20.00   40.00
SUPER
❑ 6201 [M]   Lule Belle & Scotty   1963   12.50   25.00   50.00

LUMAN, BOB
EPIC
❑ BN 26393   Ain't Got Time to Be Unhappy   1968   5.00   10.00   20.00
❑ BN 26463   Come On Home and Sing the Blues   1969   5.00   10.00   20.00
❑ BN 26541   Gettin' Back   1970   5.00   10.00   20.00
❑ E 30617   Is It Any Wonder   1971   5.00   10.00   20.00
❑ E 30923   Chain Don't Take to Me   1972   5.00   10.00   20.00
❑ KE 31375   When You Say Love   1972   5.00   10.00   20.00
❑ KE 31746   Lonely Women Make Good Lovers   1972   5.00   10.00   20.00

HICKORY
❑ LPM-124 [M]   Livin' Lovin' Sounds   1965   6.25   12.50   25.00
❑ LPS-124 [S]   Livin' Lovin' Sounds   1965   7.50   15.00   30.00
WARNER BROS.
❑ W 1396 [M]   Let's Think About Livin'   1960   12.50   25.00   50.00
❑ WS 1396 [S]   Let's Think About Livin'   1960   17.50   35.00   70.00

LUMLEY, RUFUS
RCA VICTOR
❑ LPM-3898 [M]   Rufus Lumley   1967   12.50   25.00   50.00
❑ LSP-3898 [S]   Rufus Lumley   1967   10.00   20.00   40.00

LUNCH, LYDIA
RUBY
❑ JRR 806   13.13   1982   7.50   15.00   30.00
ZE/BUDDAH
❑ 33006   Queen of Siam   1980   7.50   15.00   30.00

LUND, GARRETT
(NO LABEL)
❑ (no #)   Almost Grown   1975   75.00   150.00   300.00

LUNDY, PAT
COLUMBIA
❑ CS 9588   Soul Ain't Nothin' But the Blues   1968   5.00   10.00   20.00

LUNN, ROBERT
STARDAY
❑ SLP-228 [M]   The Original Talking Blues Man   1962   7.50   15.00   30.00

LUTCHER, NELLIE
CAPITOL
❑ H 232 [10]   Real Gone   1950   15.00   30.00   60.00
❑ T 232 [M]   Real Gone   1955   10.00   20.00   40.00
EPIC
❑ LN 1108 [10]   Whee! Nellie   1955   12.50   25.00   50.00
LIBERTY
❑ LRP-3014 [M]   Our New Nellie   1956   10.00   20.00   40.00

LYMAN, ARTHUR
GNP CRESCENDO
❑ GNPS-605 [S]   Exotic Sounds   1963   5.00   10.00   20.00
❑ GNPS-606 [S]   Paradise   1964   5.00   10.00   20.00
❑ GNPS-607 [S]   Cast Your Fate to the Wind   1965   5.00   10.00   20.00
HIFI
❑ R-607 [M]   Leis of Jazz   1958   5.00   10.00   20.00
❑ SR-607 [S]   Leis of Jazz   1958   7.50   15.00   30.00
❑ R-806 [M]   Taboo   1958   5.00   10.00   20.00
❑ SR-806 [S]   Taboo   1958   7.50   15.00   30.00
❑ R-807 [M]   Hawaiian Sunset   1959   5.00   10.00   20.00
❑ SR-807 [S]   Hawaiian Sunset   1959   7.50   15.00   30.00
❑ R-808 [M]   Bwan-A   1959   5.00   10.00   20.00
❑ SR-808 [S]   Bwan-A   1959   7.50   15.00   30.00
❑ R-813 [M]   The Legend of Pele   1959   5.00   10.00   20.00
❑ SR-813 [S]   The Legend of Pele   1959   7.50   15.00   30.00
❑ R-815 [M]   Bahia   1959   5.00   10.00   20.00
❑ SR-815 [S]   Bahia   1959   7.50   15.00   30.00
❑ R-818 [M]   Arthur Lyman On Broadway   1960   5.00   10.00   20.00
❑ SR-818 [S]   Arthur Lyman On Broadway   1960   7.50   15.00   30.00
❑ R-822 [M]   Taboo (Volume 2)   1960   5.00   10.00   20.00
❑ SR-822 [S]   Taboo (Volume 2)   1960   7.50   15.00   30.00
LIFE
❑ L 1004 [M]   Percussion Spectacular   1961   7.50   15.00   30.00
❑ SL 1004 [S]   Percussion Spectacular   1961   10.00   20.00   40.00
❑ L 1004 [M]   Yellow Bird   1961   5.00   10.00   20.00
-- Reissue with new title reflecting the hit single
❑ SL 1004 [S]   Yellow Bird   1961   6.25   12.50   25.00
-- Reissue with new title reflecting the hit single
❑ L 1005 [M]   The Colorful Percussions of Arthur Lyman   1962   5.00   10.00   20.00
❑ SL 1005 [S]   The Colorful Percussions of Arthur Lyman   1962   6.25   12.50   25.00
❑ L 1007 [M]   The Many Moods of Arthur Lyman   1962   5.00   10.00   20.00
❑ SL 1007 [S]   The Many Moods of Arthur Lyman   1962   6.25   12.50   25.00
❑ L 1009 [M]   Love for Sale!   1963   6.25   12.50   25.00
-- Alternate title
❑ SL 1009 [S]   Love for Sale!   1963   7.50   15.00   30.00
-- Alternate title
❑ L 1009 [M]   I Wish You Love   1963   5.00   10.00   20.00
❑ SL 1009 [S]   I Wish You Love   1963   6.25   12.50   25.00
❑ L 1010 [M]   Cotton Fields   1963   5.00   10.00   20.00
❑ SL 1010 [S]   Cotton Fields   1963   6.25   12.50   25.00

Number	Title	Yr	VG	VG+	NM
❑ L 1014 [M]	Blowin' in the Wind	1963	5.00	10.00	20.00
❑ SL 1014 [S]	Blowin' in the Wind	1963	6.25	12.50	25.00
❑ L 1018 [M]	Mele Kalikimaka (Merry Christmas)	1963	5.00	10.00	20.00
❑ SL 1018 [S]	Mele Kalikimaka (Merry Christmas)	1963	6.25	12.50	25.00
❑ L 1023 [M]	Isle of Enchantment	1964	5.00	10.00	20.00
❑ SL 1023 [S]	Isle of Enchantment	1964	6.25	12.50	25.00
❑ L 1024 [M]	Call of the Midnight Sun	1964	5.00	10.00	20.00
❑ SL 1024 [S]	Call of the Midnight Sun	1964	6.25	12.50	25.00
❑ SL 1025 [S]	Hawaiian Sunset, Volume 2	1965	5.00	10.00	20.00
❑ SL 1027 [S]	Polynesia	1965	5.00	10.00	20.00
❑ SL 1031 [S]	Lyman '66	1965	5.00	10.00	20.00
❑ SL 1033 [S]	The Shadow of Your Smile	1966	5.00	10.00	20.00
❑ SL 1034 [S]	Aloha, Amigo	1966	5.00	10.00	20.00
❑ SL 1035 [S]	Ilikai	1967	5.00	10.00	20.00
❑ SL 1036 [S]	Arthur Lyman at the Port of L.A.	1967	5.00	10.00	20.00

LYMON, FRANKIE
GUEST STAR

Number	Title	Yr	VG	VG+	NM
❑ GS-1406 [M]	Teen Time Tunes Starring Frankie Lymon	1959	10.00	20.00	40.00
-- Various-artists compilation; color cover					
❑ GS-1406 [M]	Rock & Roll Party Starring Frankie Lymon	196?	6.25	12.50	25.00
-- Various-artists compilation; retitled, black and white cover					

ROULETTE

Number	Title	Yr	VG	VG+	NM
❑ R-25013 [M]	Frankie Lymon at the London Palladium	1958	75.00	150.00	300.00
❑ R-25036 [M]	Rock 'n' Roll	1958	75.00	150.00	300.00
❑ R-25250 [M]	Frankie Lymon's Greatest	1964	7.50	15.00	30.00
❑ SR-25250 [R]	Frankie Lymon's Greatest	1964	6.25	12.50	25.00

LYMON, FRANKIE, AND THE TEENAGERS
GEE

Number	Title	Yr	VG	VG+	NM
❑ GLP-701 [M]	The Teenagers Featuring Frankie Lymon	1956	125.00	250.00	500.00
-- Red label					
❑ GLP-701 [M]	The Teenagers Featuring Frankie Lymon	1961	37.50	75.00	150.00
-- Gray label					

MURRAY HILL

Number	Title	Yr	VG	VG+	NM
❑ 148 [(5)]	Frankie Lymon and the Teenagers	198?	17.50	35.00	70.00

LYNN, BARBARA
ATLANTIC

Number	Title	Yr	VG	VG+	NM
❑ 8171 [M]	Here Is Barbara Lynn	1968	12.50	25.00	50.00
❑ SD 8171 [S]	Here Is Barbara Lynn	1968	10.00	20.00	40.00

JAMIE

Number	Title	Yr	VG	VG+	NM
❑ JLP-3023 [M]	You'll Lose a Good Thing	1962	12.50	25.00	50.00
❑ JLPS-3023 [R]	You'll Lose a Good Thing	1962	12.50	25.00	50.00

LYNN, DIANA
CAPITOL

Number	Title	Yr	VG	VG+	NM
❑ H 180 [10]	Piano Moods	1950	15.00	30.00	60.00

LYNN, DONNA
CAPITOL

Number	Title	Yr	VG	VG+	NM
❑ ST 2085 [S]	Java Jones/My Boyfriend Got a Beatle Haircut	1964	7.50	15.00	30.00
❑ T 2085 [M]	Java Jones/My Boyfriend Got a Beatle Haircut	1964	5.00	10.00	20.00

LYNN, JUDY
UNITED ARTISTS

Number	Title	Yr	VG	VG+	NM
❑ UAL-3226 [M]	Judy Lynn Sings at the Golden Nugget	1962	5.00	10.00	20.00
❑ UAS-6226 [S]	Judy Lynn Sings at the Golden Nugget	1962	6.25	12.50	25.00
❑ UAS-6288 [S]	Here Is Our Gal, Judy Lynn	1963	5.00	10.00	20.00
❑ UAS-6342 [S]	Country and Western Girl Singer	1964	5.00	10.00	20.00
❑ UAS-6390 [S]	The Judy Lynn Show	1964	5.00	10.00	20.00
❑ UAS-6443 [S]	The Judy Lynn Show Act 2	1965	5.00	10.00	20.00

LYNN, LORETTA
Also see CONWAY TWITTY AND LORETTA LYNN.
DECCA

Number	Title	Yr	VG	VG+	NM
❑ DL 4457 [M]	Loretta Lynn Sings	1963	15.00	30.00	60.00
❑ DL 4541 [M]	Before I'm Over You	1964	7.50	15.00	30.00
❑ DL 4620 [M]	Songs from My Heart	1965	7.50	15.00	30.00
❑ DL 4665 [M]	Blue Kentucky Girl	1965	7.50	15.00	30.00
❑ DL 4695 [M]	Hymns	1965	7.50	15.00	30.00
❑ DL 4744 [M]	I Like 'Em Country	1966	6.25	12.50	25.00
❑ DL 4783 [M]	You Ain't Woman Enough	1966	6.25	12.50	25.00

Number	Title	Yr	VG	VG+	NM
❑ DL 4817 [M]	Country Christmas	1966	6.25	12.50	25.00
❑ DL 4842 [M]	Don't Come Home a-Drinkin' (With Lovin' on Your Mind)	1967	7.50	15.00	30.00
❑ DL 4928 [M]	Who Says God Is Dead!	1967	10.00	20.00	40.00
❑ DL 4930 [M]	Singin' with Feelin'	1967	7.50	15.00	30.00
❑ DL 74457 [S]	Loretta Lynn Sings	1963	20.00	40.00	80.00
❑ DL 74541 [S]	Before I'm Over You	1964	10.00	20.00	40.00
❑ DL 74620 [S]	Songs from My Heart	1965	10.00	20.00	40.00
❑ DL 74665 [S]	Blue Kentucky Girl	1965	10.00	20.00	40.00
❑ DL 74695 [S]	Hymns	1965	10.00	20.00	40.00
❑ DL 74744 [S]	I Like 'Em Country	1966	7.50	15.00	30.00
❑ DL 74783 [S]	You Ain't Woman Enough	1966	7.50	15.00	30.00
❑ DL 74817 [S]	Country Christmas	1966	7.50	15.00	30.00
❑ DL 74842 [S]	Don't Come Home a-Drinkin' (With Lovin' on Your Mind)	1967	6.25	12.50	25.00
❑ DL 74928 [S]	Who Says God Is Dead!	1967	6.25	12.50	25.00
❑ DL 74930 [S]	Singin' with Feelin'	1967	6.25	12.50	25.00
❑ DL 74997	Fist City	1968	6.25	12.50	25.00
❑ DL 75000	Loretta Lynn's Greatest Hits	1968	6.25	12.50	25.00
❑ DL 75084	Your Squaw Is On the Warpath	1969	10.00	20.00	40.00
-- First editions had a track called "Barney"					
❑ DL 75084	Your Squaw Is On the Warpath	1969	6.25	12.50	25.00
-- Later editions delete the track "Barney"					
❑ DL 75113	Woman of the World/To Make a Man	1969	6.25	12.50	25.00
❑ DL 75163	Wings Upon Your Horns	1970	6.25	12.50	25.00
❑ DL 75198	Loretta Lynn Writes 'Em and Sings 'Em	1970	6.25	12.50	25.00
❑ DL 75253	Coal Miner's Daughter	1971	5.00	10.00	20.00
❑ DL 75282	I Wanna Be Free	1971	5.00	10.00	20.00
❑ DL 75310	You're Lookin' at Country	1971	5.00	10.00	20.00
❑ DL 75334	One's On the Way	1972	5.00	10.00	20.00
❑ DL 75351	God Bless America Again	1972	5.00	10.00	20.00
❑ DL 75381	Here I Am Again	1972	5.00	10.00	20.00

MCA

Number	Title	Yr	VG	VG+	NM
❑ L33-1934 [DJ]	Loretta Lynn	1974	10.00	20.00	40.00
-- Promo-only compilation					
❑ 35013	Allis-Chalmers Presents Loretta Lynn	1978	10.00	20.00	40.00
-- Special products compilation					
❑ 35018	Crisco Presents Loretta Lynn's Country Classics	1979	10.00	20.00	40.00
-- Special products compilation					

LYNN, LORETTA, AND CONWAY TWITTY -- See CONWAY TWITTY AND LORETTA LYNN.

LYNN, LORETTA, AND ERNEST TUBB
Also see each artist's individual listings.
DECCA

Number	Title	Yr	VG	VG+	NM
❑ DL 4639 [M]	Mr. and Mrs. Used to Be	1965	7.50	15.00	30.00
❑ DL 4872 [M]	Singin' Again	1967	7.50	15.00	30.00
❑ DL 74639 [S]	Mr. and Mrs. Used to Be	1965	10.00	20.00	40.00
❑ DL 74872 [S]	Singin' Again	1967	6.25	12.50	25.00
❑ DL 75115	If We Put Our Heads Together	1969	6.25	12.50	25.00

LYNN, VERA
LONDON

Number	Title	Yr	VG	VG+	NM
❑ LL 1306 [M]	Vera Lynn Concert	195?	5.00	10.00	20.00
❑ LL 1510 [M]	If I Am Dreaming	195?	5.00	10.00	20.00

LYNNE, GLORIA
EVEREST

Number	Title	Yr	VG	VG+	NM
❑ ES-1001 [S]	Gloria Lynne Live! Take 1	1959	10.00	20.00	40.00
❑ SDBR-1022 [S]	Miss Gloria Lynne	1959	7.50	15.00	30.00
❑ SDBR-1063 [S]	Lonely and Sentimental	1960	7.50	15.00	30.00
❑ SDBR-1090 [S]	Try a Little Tenderness	1960	7.50	15.00	30.00
❑ SDBR-1101 [S]	Day In, Day Out	1961	7.50	15.00	30.00
❑ SDBR-1126 [S]	I'm Glad There Is You	1961	7.50	15.00	30.00
❑ SDBR-1128 [S]	He Needs Me	1961	7.50	15.00	30.00
❑ SDBR-1131 [S]	This Little Boy of Mine	1961	7.50	15.00	30.00
❑ SDBR-1132 [S]	Gloria Lynne at Basin Street East	1962	7.50	15.00	30.00
❑ SDBR-1203 [S]	Gloria Blue	1962	7.50	15.00	30.00
❑ SDBR-1208 [S]	Gloria Lynne at the Las Vegas Thunderbird	1963	7.50	15.00	30.00
❑ EV-1220 [S]	Gloria, Marty & Strings	1963	7.50	15.00	30.00
❑ EV-1226 [S]	I Wish You Love	1964	6.25	12.50	25.00
❑ EV-1228 [S]	Glorious Gloria Lynne	1964	6.25	12.50	25.00
❑ EV-1230 [S]	After Hours	1965	6.25	12.50	25.00
❑ EV-1231 [S]	The Best of Gloria Lynne	1965	5.00	10.00	20.00
❑ EV-1237 [S]	Go, Go, Go	1965	5.00	10.00	20.00
❑ EV-1238 [S]	Gloria Lynne '66	1966	5.00	10.00	20.00
❑ E-5001 [M]	Gloria Lynne Live! Take 1	1959	7.50	15.00	30.00
❑ LPBR-5022 [M]	Miss Gloria Lynne	1959	5.00	10.00	20.00
❑ LPBR-5063 [M]	Lonely and Sentimental	1960	5.00	10.00	20.00

Number	Title	Yr	VG	VG+	NM
❑ LPBR-5090 [M]	Try a Little Tenderness	1960	5.00	10.00	20.00
❑ LPBR-5101 [M]	Day In, Day Out	1961	5.00	10.00	20.00
❑ LPBR-5126 [M]	I'm Glad There Is You	1961	5.00	10.00	20.00
❑ LPBR-5128 [M]	He Needs Me	1961	5.00	10.00	20.00
❑ LPBR-5131 [M]	This Little Boy of Mine	1961	5.00	10.00	20.00
❑ LPBR-5132 [M]	Gloria Lynne at Basin Street East	1962	5.00	10.00	20.00
❑ LPBR-5203 [M]	Gloria Blue	1962	5.00	10.00	20.00
❑ LPBR-5208 [M]	Gloria Lynne at the Las Vegas Thunderbird	1963	5.00	10.00	20.00
❑ EV-5220 [M]	Gloria, Marty & Strings	1963	5.00	10.00	20.00
❑ EV-5226 [M]	I Wish You Love	1964	5.00	10.00	20.00
❑ EV-5228 [M]	Glorious Gloria Lynne	1964	5.00	10.00	20.00
❑ EV-5230 [M]	After Hours	1965	5.00	10.00	20.00

FONTANA

Number	Title	Yr	VG	VG+	NM
❑ MGF-27571 [M]	The Other Side of Gloria Lynne	1967	5.00	10.00	20.00
❑ SRF-67528 [S]	Intimate Moments	1964	5.00	10.00	20.00
❑ SRF-67541 [S]	Soul Serenade	1965	5.00	10.00	20.00
❑ SRF-67546 [S]	Love and a Woman	1965	5.00	10.00	20.00
❑ SRF-67555 [S]	Where It's At	1966	5.00	10.00	20.00
❑ SRF-67561 [S]	Gloria	1966	5.00	10.00	20.00

HIFI

Number	Title	Yr	VG	VG+	NM
❑ SR-440 [S]	Gloria Lynne	1966	5.00	10.00	20.00

LYNYRD SKYNYRD
ATLANTIC

Number	Title	Yr	VG	VG+	NM
❑ A1-82258	Lynyrd Skynyrd 1991	1991	5.00	10.00	20.00

-- *The only U.S. vinyl version was released through Columbia House*

MCA

Number	Title	Yr	VG	VG+	NM
❑ L33-1946 [(2) DJ]	One More From the Road	1976	12.50	25.00	50.00

-- *Promo on blue, gold, purple or red vinyl (each has the same value)*

Number	Title	Yr	VG	VG+	NM
❑ L33-1946 [(2) DJ]	One More From the Road	1976	6.25	12.50	25.00

-- *Promo only on black vinyl*

Number	Title	Yr	VG	VG+	NM
❑ L33-1988 [DJ]	Skynyrd's First and...Last	1978	6.25	12.50	25.00

-- *Promo sampler*

Number	Title	Yr	VG	VG+	NM
❑ 3029	Street Survivors	1977	6.25	12.50	25.00

-- *Originals with the band in flames on the front cover and a smaller band photo on the back cover*

SOUNDS OF THE SOUTH

Number	Title	Yr	VG	VG+	NM
❑ 363	(pronounced leh-nerd skin-nerd)	1973	5.00	10.00	20.00
❑ 413	Second Helping	1974	5.00	10.00	20.00

-- *Both of the above are original pressings with yellow labels*

LYONS, MARIE
DELUXE

Number	Title	Yr	VG	VG+	NM
❑ 12001	Soul Fever	1970	6.25	12.50	25.00

M

MABLEY, MOMS
CHESS

Number	Title	Yr	VG	VG+	NM
❑ LP-1447 [M]	Moms Mabley, Funniest Woman in the World, Onstage	1961	6.25	12.50	25.00
❑ LP-1452 [M]	Moms Mabley at the "UN"	1961	6.25	12.50	25.00
❑ LP-1460 [M]	Moms Mabley at the Playboy Club	1961	6.25	12.50	25.00
❑ LP-1463 [M]	Moms Mabley at Geneva Conference	1962	6.25	12.50	25.00
❑ LP-1472 [M]	Moms Mabley Breaks It Up	1962	6.25	12.50	25.00
❑ LP-1477 [M]	Young Men, Si -- Old Men, No	1962	6.25	12.50	25.00
❑ LP-1479 [M]	I Got Somethin' to Tell You!	1963	6.25	12.50	25.00
❑ LP-1482 [M]	The Funny Sides of Moms Mabley	1963	6.25	12.50	25.00
❑ LP-1486 [M]	Moms Wows	1964	6.25	12.50	25.00
❑ LP-1487 [M]	The Best of Moms	1964	6.25	12.50	25.00
❑ LP-1497 [M]	The Man in My Life	1965	5.00	10.00	20.00
❑ LPS-1525	Moms Mabley Breaks Up the Network	1968	5.00	10.00	20.00
❑ LPS-1530	Moms Mabley Sings	1969	5.00	10.00	20.00

MERCURY

Number	Title	Yr	VG	VG+	NM
❑ MG-21139 [M]	The Best of Moms Mabley	1967	6.25	12.50	25.00
❑ SR-60889 [S]	Out on a Limb	1964	5.00	10.00	20.00
❑ SR-60907 [S]	Moms the Word	1964	5.00	10.00	20.00
❑ SR-61012 [S]	Now Hear This	1965	5.00	10.00	20.00
❑ SR-61090 [S]	Moms Mabley at the White House	1966	5.00	10.00	20.00

MABON, WILLIE
CHESS

Number	Title	Yr	VG	VG+	NM
❑ LP-1439 [M]	Willie Mabon	1958	100.00	200.00	400.00

-- *Black label*

MacARTHUR, DOUGLAS
ATLANTIC

Number	Title	Yr	VG	VG+	NM
❑ 8095 [M]	The Life of General MacArthur	1964	10.00	20.00	40.00

MacDONALD, JEANETTE, AND NELSON EDDY
RCA VICTOR

Number	Title	Yr	VG	VG+	NM
❑ LPT-16 [10]	Rose Marie	1952	15.00	30.00	60.00
❑ LPV-526 [M]	Rose Marie	1965	6.25	12.50	25.00
❑ LPM-1738 [M]	Favorites in Hi-Fi	1958	10.00	20.00	40.00

MACEO AND ALL THE KING'S MEN
EXCELLO

Number	Title	Yr	VG	VG+	NM
❑ LPS-8022	Funky Music Machine	1972	7.50	15.00	30.00

HOUSE OF FOX

Number	Title	Yr	VG	VG+	NM
❑ LP-1	Doing Their Own Thing	1971	7.50	15.00	30.00

MACEO AND THE MACKS
PEOPLE

Number	Title	Yr	VG	VG+	NM
❑ PE-6601	Us	1973	7.50	15.00	30.00

MACK, LONNIE
ELEKTRA

Number	Title	Yr	VG	VG+	NM
❑ EKS-74040	Glad I'm In the Band	1969	6.25	12.50	25.00
❑ EKS-74050	Whatever's Right	1969	6.25	12.50	25.00
❑ EKS-74077	For Collectors Only	1970	6.25	12.50	25.00
❑ EKS-74102	The Hills of Indiana	1971	6.25	12.50	25.00

FRATERNITY

Number	Title	Yr	VG	VG+	NM
❑ SF-1014 [M]	The Wham of That Memphis Man	1963	30.00	60.00	120.00
❑ SSF-1014 [S]	The Wham of That Memphis Man	1963	75.00	150.00	300.00

MACK, WARNER
DECCA

Number	Title	Yr	VG	VG+	NM
❑ DL 4692 [M]	The Bridge Washed Out	1965	5.00	10.00	20.00
❑ DL 4766 [M]	The Country Touch	1966	5.00	10.00	20.00
❑ DL 4883 [M]	Drifting Apart	1967	6.25	12.50	25.00
❑ DL 4912 [M]	Songs We Sang in Church and Home	1967	6.25	12.50	25.00
❑ DL 74692 [S]	The Bridge Washed Out	1965	6.25	12.50	25.00
❑ DL 74766 [S]	The Country Touch	1966	6.25	12.50	25.00
❑ DL 74883 [S]	Drifting Apart	1967	5.00	10.00	20.00
❑ DL 74912 [S]	Songs We Sang in Church and Home	1967	5.00	10.00	20.00
❑ DL 74995	The Many Country Moods of Warner Mack	1968	5.00	10.00	20.00
❑ DL 75092	The Country Beat of Warner Mack	1969	5.00	10.00	20.00
❑ DL 75165	I'll Still Be Missing You	1969	5.00	10.00	20.00

Number	Title	Yr	VG	VG+	NM

KAPP
❑ KL-1255 [M]	Golden Country Hits	1961	5.00	10.00	20.00
❑ KL-1279 [M]	Golden Country Hits, Vol. 2	1962	5.00	10.00	20.00
❑ KS-3255 [S]	Golden Country Hits	1961	6.25	12.50	25.00
❑ KS-3279 [S]	Golden Country Hits, Vol. 2	1962	6.25	12.50	25.00
❑ KS-3461 [S]	Everybody's Country Favorites	196?	5.00	10.00	20.00

MacKENZIE, GISELE
EVEREST
| ❑ SDBR-1069 [S] | In Person at the Empire Room | 1959 | 7.50 | 15.00 | 30.00 |
| ❑ LPBR-5069 [M] | In Person at the Empire Room | 1959 | 6.25 | 12.50 | 25.00 |
RCA VICTOR
❑ LPM-1790 [M]	Gisele	1958	7.50	15.00	30.00
❑ LSP-1790 [S]	Gisele	1958	10.00	20.00	40.00
❑ LPM-2006 [M]	Christmas with Gisele	1959	7.50	15.00	30.00
❑ LSP-2006 [S]	Christmas with Gisele	1959	10.00	20.00	40.00
VIK
❑ LX-1055 [M]	Gisele MacKenzie	1956	10.00	20.00	40.00
❑ LX-1075 [M]	Mam'selle MacKenzie	1956	10.00	20.00	40.00
❑ LX-1099 [M]	Christmas with Gisele	1957	10.00	20.00	40.00

MACON, UNCLE DAVE
DECCA
| ❑ DL 4760 [M] | Uncle Dave Macon | 1966 | 7.50 | 15.00 | 30.00 |

MacRAE, GORDON
CAPITOL
❑ H 231 [10]	Songs	1950	10.00	20.00	40.00
❑ ST 980 [S]	Gordon MacRae in Concert	1959	10.00	20.00	40.00
-- Black colorband label, logo at left					
❑ T 1050 [M]	This Is Gordon MacRae	1958	7.50	15.00	30.00
-- Turquoise or gray label					
❑ T 537 [M]	Romantic Ballads	1955	7.50	15.00	30.00
-- Turquoise or gray label					
❑ T 681 [M]	Operetta Favorites	1956	7.50	15.00	30.00
-- Turquoise or gray label					
❑ T 765 [M]	The Best Things in Life Are Free	1956	7.50	15.00	30.00
-- Turquoise or gray label					
❑ T 834 [M]	Cowboy's Lament	1957	7.50	15.00	30.00
-- Turquoise or gray label					
❑ T 875 [M]	Motion Picture Soundstage	1957	7.50	15.00	30.00
-- Turquoise or gray label					
❑ T 980 [M]	Gordon MacRae in Concert	1957	7.50	15.00	30.00
-- Turquoise or gray label					

MacRAE, GORDON, AND JO STAFFORD -- See JO STAFFORD AND GORDON MacRAE.

MacRAE, SHEILA
ABC
| ❑ ABCS-611 | How Sweet She Is | 1968 | 6.25 | 12.50 | 25.00 |

MAD LADS, THE
VOLT
❑ 414 [M]	The Mad Lads In Action	1966	7.50	15.00	30.00
❑ S-414 [S]	The Mad Lads In Action	1966	10.00	20.00	40.00
❑ VOS-6005	The Mad, Mad, Mad, Mad, Mad Lads	1969	7.50	15.00	30.00
❑ VOS-6020	A New Beginning	1973	5.00	10.00	20.00

MAD RIVER
CAPITOL
| ❑ ST-185 | Paradise Bar and Grill | 1969 | 10.00 | 20.00 | 40.00 |
| ❑ ST 2985 | Mad River | 1968 | 12.50 | 25.00 | 50.00 |

MADDOX BROTHERS AND ROSE, THE
Also see ROSE MADDOX.
KING
❑ 669 [M]	A Collection of Standard Sacred Songs	1959	37.50	75.00	150.00
❑ 677 [M]	The Maddox Brothers and Rose	1960	30.00	60.00	120.00
❑ 752 [M]	I'll Write Your Name in the Sand	1961	30.00	60.00	120.00
WRANGLER
❑ W-1003 [M]	The Maddox Brothers and Rose	1962	7.50	15.00	30.00
❑ WS-1003 [S]	The Maddox Brothers and Rose	1962	10.00	20.00	40.00

MADDOX, JOHNNY
DOT
❑ DLP-102 [10]	Authentic Ragtime	1952	10.00	20.00	40.00
❑ DLP-3005 [M]	Johnny Maddox Plays	1955	6.25	12.50	25.00
❑ DLP-3008 [M]	Tap Dance Rhythms	1955	6.25	12.50	25.00

Number	Title	Yr	VG	VG+	NM
❑ DLP-3044 [M]	King of Ragtime	1957	5.00	10.00	20.00
❑ DLP-3063 [M]	The Thirties in Ragtime	1957	5.00	10.00	20.00
❑ DLP-3067 [M]	My Old Flames	1957	5.00	10.00	20.00

MADDOX, LESTER
LEFEVRE
| ❑ MLSP-3485 | God, Family and Country | 197? | 10.00 | 20.00 | 40.00 |

MADDOX, ROSE
Also see THE MADDOX BROTHERS AND ROSE.
CAPITOL
❑ ST 1312 [S]	The One Rose	1960	10.00	20.00	40.00
❑ T 1312 [M]	The One Rose	1960	7.50	15.00	30.00
❑ ST 1437 [S]	Glorybound Train	1960	10.00	20.00	40.00
❑ T 1437 [M]	Glorybound Train	1960	7.50	15.00	30.00
❑ ST 1548 [S]	A Big Bouquet of Roses	1961	10.00	20.00	40.00
❑ T 1548 [M]	A Big Bouquet of Roses	1961	7.50	15.00	30.00
❑ ST 1799 [S]	Rose Maddox Sings Bluegrass	1962	12.50	25.00	50.00
❑ T 1799 [M]	Rose Maddox Sings Bluegrass	1962	10.00	20.00	40.00
❑ ST 1993 [S]	Alone with You	1963	10.00	20.00	40.00
❑ T 1993 [M]	Alone with You	1963	7.50	15.00	30.00
COLUMBIA
❑ CL 1159 [M]	Precious Memories	1958	10.00	20.00	40.00

MADIGAN, BETTY
MGM
| ❑ E-3448 [M] | Am I Blue? | 1956 | 10.00 | 20.00 | 40.00 |

MADONNA
MAVERICK
❑ PRO-A-5904 [(2) DJ]	Erotica	1992	12.50	25.00	50.00
-- Vinyl is promo only					
❑ PRO-A-7311 [(2)DJ]	Bedtime Stories	1994	12.50	25.00	50.00
-- Promo only on pink vinyl					
❑ PRO-A-9378 [(2)DJ]	Ray of Light	1998	12.50	25.00	50.00
-- Vinyl is promo only; generic cover with sticker					
SIRE
❑ PRO-A-2892	You Can Dance	1987	7.50	15.00	30.00
-- Promo-only; contains single edits of the seven songs on the stock editions					
❑ 23867	Madonna	1983	5.00	10.00	20.00
-- First pressing with 4:48 version of "Burning Up"					
❑ 25157	Like a Virgin	1984	15.00	30.00	60.00
-- White vinyl with silver colored spine					
❑ 25157	Like a Virgin	1984	12.50	25.00	50.00
-- White vinyl with cream colored spine					
❑ W1-26440 [(2)]	The Immaculate Collection	1990	5.00	10.00	20.00
-- Columbia House edition					
❑ R 254164 [(2)]	The Immaculate Collection	1990	5.00	10.00	20.00
-- BMG Direct Marketing edition					

MADRIGAL
SSS INTERNATIONAL
| ❑ 18 | Madrigal | 1971 | 7.50 | 15.00 | 30.00 |

MADURA
COLUMBIA
| ❑ G 30794 [(2)] | Madura | 1971 | 5.00 | 10.00 | 20.00 |

MAESTRO, JOHNNY
Also see THE CRESTS.
BUDDAH
| ❑ BDS-5091 | The Johnny Maestro Story | 1971 | 10.00 | 20.00 | 40.00 |
| -- With inserts; deduct 40% if missing | | | | | |

MAGI, THE
UNCLE DIRTY
| ❑ 6102-N13 | Win or Lose | 1975 | 75.00 | 150.00 | 300.00 |

MAGIC
May be two different groups.
ARMADILLO
| ❑ 8031 | Enclosed | 1970 | 100.00 | 200.00 | 400.00 |
RARE EARTH
| ❑ RS-527 | Magic | 1971 | 6.25 | 12.50 | 25.00 |

MAGIC FERN, THE
PANORAMA
| ❑ 108 | The Magic Fern | 1980 | 37.50 | 75.00 | 150.00 |

MAGIC LANTERNS
ATLANTIC
| ❑ SD 8217 | Shame, Shame | 1969 | 5.00 | 10.00 | 20.00 |

Number	Title	Yr	VG	VG+	NM

MAGIC SAM
DELMARK
❑ DL-615	West Side Soul	1968	12.50	25.00	50.00
❑ DL-620	Black Magic	1969	12.50	25.00	50.00

MAGIC SAND
UNI
❑ 73094	Magic Sand	1971	6.25	12.50	25.00

MAGNIFICENT MEN, THE
CAPITOL
❑ T 2678 [M]	The Magnificent Men	1967	5.00	10.00	20.00
❑ T 2775 [M]	The Magnificent Men "Live!"	1967	5.00	10.00	20.00
❑ T 2846 [M]	World of Soul	1968	5.00	10.00	20.00

MAHAL, TAJ
COLUMBIA
❑ GP 18 [(2)]	Giant Step/De Old Folks at Home	1969	5.00	10.00	20.00
-- Red "360 Sound" label					
❑ CL 2779 [M]	Taj Mahal	1967	7.50	15.00	30.00
❑ G 30619 [(2)]	The Real Thing	1971	5.00	10.00	20.00
CRYSTAL CLEAR
❑ 5011	Live and Direct	1980	6.25	12.50	25.00
-- Direct-to-disc recording					

MAHAN, LARRY
WARNER BROS.
❑ BS 2959	King of the Rodeo	1976	5.00	10.00	20.00

MAHAVISHNU ORCHESTRA
COLUMBIA
❑ CQ 31996 [Q]	Birds of Fire	1973	5.00	10.00	20.00
❑ CQ 32766 [Q]	Between Nothingness and Eternity	1973	5.00	10.00	20.00

MAHOGANY RUSH
20TH CENTURY
❑ T-451	Child of the Novelty	1974	6.25	12.50	25.00
❑ T-463	Maxoom	1975	6.25	12.50	25.00
❑ T-482	Strange Universe	1975	5.00	10.00	20.00

MAIDEN, SIDNEY
BLUESVILLE
❑ BVLP-1035 [M]	Trouble An' Blues	1961	20.00	40.00	80.00
-- Blue label, silver print					
❑ BVLP-1035 [M]	Trouble An' Blues	1964	5.00	10.00	20.00
-- Blue label, trident logo at right					

MAIN ATTRACTION, THE
TOWER
❑ ST-5177	And Now...The Main Attraction	1968	6.25	12.50	25.00

MAINER, J.E.
KING
❑ 666 [M]	Good Ole Mountain Music	1960	20.00	40.00	80.00
❑ 765 [M]	Variety Album	1961	20.00	40.00	80.00

MAINER, WADE, AND THE MOUNTAINEERS
KING
❑ 666 [M]	Good Ole Mountain Music	1959	25.00	50.00	100.00
❑ 765 [M]	Variety Album	1961	25.00	50.00	100.00
❑ 769 [M]	Soulful Sacred Songs	1961	25.00	50.00	100.00

MAIZE, JOE
DECCA
❑ DL 4555 [M]	Isle of Dreams	1965	5.00	10.00	20.00
❑ DL 8590 [M]	Presenting Joe Maize and His Cordsmen	1958	7.50	15.00	30.00
❑ DL 8817 [M]	Hawaiian Dreams	1959	5.00	10.00	20.00
❑ DL 74555 [S]	Isle of Dreams	1965	6.25	12.50	25.00
❑ DL 78817 [S]	Hawaiian Dreams	1959	6.25	12.50	25.00

MAJIC SHIP, THE
BEL AMI
❑ BA-711	The Majic Ship	1968	125.00	250.00	500.00

MAJORS, THE
IMPERIAL
❑ LP-9222 [M]	Meet the Majors	1963	37.50	75.00	150.00
❑ LP-12222 [S]	Meet the Majors	1963	75.00	150.00	300.00

MAKEBA, MIRIAM
KAPP
❑ KL-1274 [M]	The Many Voices of Miriam Makeba	1962	5.00	10.00	20.00
❑ KS-3274 [S]	The Many Voices of Miriam Makeba	1962	6.25	12.50	25.00
RCA VICTOR
❑ LPM-2267 [M]	Miriam Makeba	1960	5.00	10.00	20.00
❑ LSP-2267 [S]	Miriam Makeba	1960	6.25	12.50	25.00
❑ LSP-2750 [S]	The World of Miriam Makeba	1963	5.00	10.00	20.00
❑ LSP-2845 [S]	The Voice of Africa	1964	5.00	10.00	20.00
❑ LSP-3321 [S]	Makeba Sings	1965	5.00	10.00	20.00
❑ LSP-3512 [S]	The Magic of Makeba	1966	5.00	10.00	20.00
❑ LPM-3982 [M]	The Best of Miriam Makeba	1968	6.25	12.50	25.00

MAKEM, TOMMY
TRADITION
❑ TLP-1044 [M]	Songs of Tommy Makem	1961	7.50	15.00	30.00
❑ TLPS-1044 [S]	Songs of Tommy Makem	1961	10.00	20.00	40.00

MALACHI
VERVE
❑ V-5024 [M]	Holy Music	1967	7.50	15.00	30.00
❑ V6-5024 [S]	Holy Music	1967	10.00	20.00	40.00

MALCOLM X
DOUGLAS
❑ SD 795 [M]	Malcolm X Talks to Young People	1968	7.50	15.00	30.00
❑ Z 30743 [M]	By Any Means Necessary	1971	7.50	15.00	30.00

MALTBY, RICHARD
COLUMBIA
❑ CL 1??? [M]	Swingin' Down the Lane	1959	5.00	10.00	20.00
❑ CL 1??? [M]	Hello Young Lovers	1959	5.00	10.00	20.00
❑ CS 8083 [S]	Swingin' Down the Lane	1959	6.25	12.50	25.00
❑ CS 8151 [S]	Hello Young Lovers	1959	6.25	12.50	25.00
RCA CAMDEN
❑ CAL-526 [M]	A Bow to the Big Name Bands	1959	5.00	10.00	20.00
❑ CAL-600 [M]	Music from Mr. Lucky	1960	5.00	10.00	20.00
❑ CAL-711 [M]	Most Requested	1961	5.00	10.00	20.00
ROULETTE
❑ R-25129 [M]	Richard Maltby Swings for Dancers	1960	5.00	10.00	20.00
❑ R-25148 [M]	Swing Folksongs	1961	5.00	10.00	20.00
❑ R-25178 [M]	Brilliant Big Band Ballads and Blues	1962	5.00	10.00	20.00
❑ SR-25148 [S]	Swing Folksongs	1961	6.25	12.50	25.00
❑ SR-25178 [S]	Brilliant Big Band Ballads and Blues	1962	6.25	12.50	25.00
VIK
❑ LX-1051 [M]	Hue-Fi Moods by Maltby	1957	7.50	15.00	30.00
❑ LX-1068 [M]	Manhattan Bandstand	1957	7.50	15.00	30.00
❑ LX-1071 [M]	Maltby with Strings Attached	1958	7.50	15.00	30.00
"X"
❑ LX-1038 [M]	Make Mine Maltby	1956	7.50	15.00	30.00

MALVIN, ARTIE
WALDORF MUSIC HALL
❑ 33-149 [10]	Rock and Roll	1955	30.00	60.00	120.00

MAMA CASS -- See CASS ELLIOT.

MAMA LION
FAMILY PRODUCTIONS
❑ FPS-2702	Mama Lion	1972	5.00	10.00	20.00
❑ FPS-2713	Give It Everything I've Got	1973	5.00	10.00	20.00

MAMAS AND THE PAPAS, THE
Also see CASS ELLIOT.
ABC DUNHILL
❑ DS-50036	Golden Era, Volume 2	1968	5.00	10.00	20.00
❑ DS-50073 [(2)]	A Gathering of Flowers	1970	6.25	12.50	25.00
❑ DSX-50145 [(2)]	20 Golden Hits	1973	5.00	10.00	20.00
DUNHILL
❑ D-50006 [M]	If You Can Believe Your Eyes and Ears	1966	20.00	40.00	80.00
-- With toilet completely visible in lower right					
❑ D-50006 [M]	If You Can Believe Your Eyes and Ears	1966	5.00	10.00	20.00
-- With scroll over toilet					
❑ DS-50006 [S]	If You Can Believe Your Eyes and Ears	1966	25.00	50.00	100.00
-- With toilet completely visible in lower right					

Number	Title	Yr	VG	VG+	NM
❏ DS-50006 [S]	If You Can Believe Your Eyes and Ears	1966	6.25	12.50	25.00
-- With scroll over toilet proclaiming "Includes California Dreamin' "					
❏ DS-50006 [S]	If You Can Believe Your Eyes and Ears	1966	6.25	12.50	25.00
-- With scroll over toilet proclaiming "Includes California Dreamin'...Monday Monday...I Call Your Name"					
❏ DS-50006 [S]	If You Can Believe Your Eyes and Ears	1966	12.50	25.00	50.00
-- Black cover with photo cropped to render toilet invisible					
❏ D-50010 [M]	The Mamas and the Papas	1966	5.00	10.00	20.00
❏ DS-50010 [S]	The Mamas and the Papas	1966	6.25	12.50	25.00
❏ D-50014 [M]	The Mamas and the Papas Deliver	1967	5.00	10.00	20.00
❏ DS-50014 [S]	The Mamas and the Papas Deliver	1967	6.25	12.50	25.00
❏ D-50025 [M]	Farewell to the First Golden Era	1967	5.00	10.00	20.00
❏ DS-50025 [S]	Farewell to the First Golden Era	1967	5.00	10.00	20.00
❏ DS-50031	The Papas and the Mamas	1968	6.25	12.50	25.00
❏ ST-90797 [S]	If You Can Believe Your Eyes and Ears	1966	12.50	25.00	50.00
-- Capitol Record Club edition; known copies have scroll proclaiming "Includes California Dreamin'."					

MAN
PHILIPS

Number	Title	Yr	VG	VG+	NM
❏ PHS 600-313	Revelation	1969	5.00	10.00	20.00
-- As "Manpower"					

MANCHESTER, MELISSA
MOBILE FIDELITY

Number	Title	Yr	VG	VG+	NM
❏ 1-028	Melissa	1980	5.00	10.00	20.00
-- Audiophile vinyl					

NAUTILUS

Number	Title	Yr	VG	VG+	NM
❏ NR-33	Don't Cry Out Loud	198?	10.00	20.00	40.00
-- Audiophile vinyl					

MANCHESTERS, THE
DIPLOMAT

Number	Title	Yr	VG	VG+	NM
❏ DS-2307 [S]	Beatlerama	1964	5.00	10.00	20.00
-- No artist credited on label or cover					
❏ DS-2307 [S]	Beatlerama	1964	5.00	10.00	20.00
-- With artist credited					

GUEST STAR

Number	Title	Yr	VG	VG+	NM
❏ GS-2307 [S]	Beatlerama	1964	5.00	10.00	20.00

MANCINI, HENRY
Also includes many of his soundtracks for TV and films.
LIBERTY

Number	Title	Yr	VG	VG+	NM
❏ LRP-3121 [M]	The Versatile Henry Mancini	1959	5.00	10.00	20.00
❏ LST-7121 [S]	The Versatile Henry Mancini	1959	7.50	15.00	30.00

PARAMOUNT

Number	Title	Yr	VG	VG+	NM
❏ PAS-6000	The Molly Maguires	1970	5.00	10.00	20.00

RCA VICTOR

Number	Title	Yr	VG	VG+	NM
❏ PRS-175 [S]	Academy Award Songs, Volume Two	1965	5.00	10.00	20.00
-- Made for the B.F. Goodrich tire company					
❏ LPM-1956 [M]	The Music from Peter Gunn	1959	10.00	20.00	40.00
-- Original cover is a "block" design with "Peter Gunn" at top					
❏ LPM-1956 [M]	The Music from Peter Gunn	1959	5.00	10.00	20.00
-- Reissue cover is green/blue with huge "Peter Gunn" in center					
❏ LSP-1956 [S]	The Music from Peter Gunn	1959	12.50	25.00	50.00
-- Original cover is a "block" design with "Peter Gunn" at top					
❏ LSP-1956 [S]	The Music from Peter Gunn	1959	6.25	12.50	25.00
-- Reissue cover is green/blue with huge "Peter Gunn" in center					
❏ LPM-2040 [M]	More Music from Peter Gunn	1959	5.00	10.00	20.00
❏ LSP-2040 [S]	More Music from Peter Gunn	1959	6.25	12.50	25.00
❏ LPM-2101 [M]	The Mancini Touch	1959	5.00	10.00	20.00
❏ LSP-2101 [S]	The Mancini Touch	1959	6.25	12.50	25.00
❏ LPM-2147 [M]	The Blues and the Beat	1960	6.25	12.50	25.00
❏ LSP-2147 [S]	The Blues and the Beat	1960	7.50	15.00	30.00
❏ LPM-2198 [M]	Music from Mr. Lucky	1960	5.00	10.00	20.00
❏ LSP-2198 [S]	Music from Mr. Lucky	1960	6.25	12.50	25.00
❏ LPM-2258 [M]	Combo!	1960	5.00	10.00	20.00
❏ LSP-2258 [S]	Combo!	1960	6.25	12.50	25.00
❏ LPM-2360 [M]	Mr. Lucky Goes Latin	1961	5.00	10.00	20.00
❏ LSP-2360 [S]	Mr. Lucky Goes Latin	1961	6.25	12.50	25.00
❏ LPM-2362 [M]	Breakfast at Tiffany's	1961	5.00	10.00	20.00
❏ LSP-2362 [S]	Breakfast at Tiffany's	1961	6.25	12.50	25.00
❏ LPM-2442 [M]	Experiment in Terror	1962	6.25	12.50	25.00
-- Original cover has Lee Remick under attack					
❏ LPM-2442 [M]	Experiment in Terror	1962	5.00	10.00	20.00
-- Reissue cover has two mannequins					
❏ LSP-2442 [S]	Experiment in Terror	1962	10.00	20.00	40.00
-- Original cover has Lee Remick under attack					
❏ LSP-2442 [S]	Experiment in Terror	1962	6.25	12.50	25.00
-- Reissue cover has two mannequins					
❏ LPM-2559 [M]	Hatari!	1962	5.00	10.00	20.00

Number	Title	Yr	VG	VG+	NM
❏ LSP-2559 [S]	Hatari!	1962	6.25	12.50	25.00
❏ LSP-2604 [S]	Our Man in Hollywood	1963	5.00	10.00	20.00
❏ LSP-2692 [S]	Uniquely Mancini	1963	5.00	10.00	20.00
❏ LSP-2755 [S]	Charade	1963	5.00	10.00	20.00
❏ LSP-2795 [S]	The Pink Panther	1964	5.00	10.00	20.00
❏ LPM-3802 [M]	Two for the Road	1967	5.00	10.00	20.00
❏ LPM-3840 [M]	Gunn	1967	5.00	10.00	20.00
❏ LSP-3840 [S]	Gunn	1967	7.50	15.00	30.00
❏ LPM-3887 [M]	Encore! More of the Concert Sound of Henry Mancini	1967	5.00	10.00	20.00
❏ LPM-3997 [M]	Party	1968	6.25	12.50	25.00
❏ LSP-6013 [(2) S]	The Academy Award Songs	1966	5.00	10.00	20.00
❏ VPS-6029 [(2)]	This Is Henry Mancini	1970	5.00	10.00	20.00
❏ VPS-6053 [(2)]	This Is Henry Mancini, Volume 2	1972	5.00	10.00	20.00

UNITED ARTISTS

Number	Title	Yr	VG	VG+	NM
❏ SW-93297	The Hawaiians	1970	5.00	10.00	20.00
-- Capitol Record Club edition					

WARNER BROS.

Number	Title	Yr	VG	VG+	NM
❏ W 1312 [M]	March Step in Hi-Fi	1959	5.00	10.00	20.00
❏ WS 1312 [S]	March Step in Stereo	1959	7.50	15.00	30.00
❏ WS 1465 [S]	Sousa's Greatest Marches	1962	5.00	10.00	20.00
❏ WS 1491 [S]	Marches	1963	5.00	10.00	20.00

MANDEL, HARVEY
PHILIPS

Number	Title	Yr	VG	VG+	NM
❏ PHS 600-281	Cristo Redentor	1969	6.25	12.50	25.00
❏ PHS 600-306	Righteous	1969	6.25	12.50	25.00
❏ PHS 600-325	Games Guitars Play	1970	6.25	12.50	25.00

MANDO AND THE CHILI PEPPERS
GOLDEN CREST

Number	Title	Yr	VG	VG+	NM
❏ CR-3023 [M]	On the Road with Rock and Roll	1957	125.00	250.00	500.00

MANDRAKE MEMORIAL
POPPY

Number	Title	Yr	VG	VG+	NM
❏ PYS 40,002	Mandrake Memorial	1968	10.00	20.00	40.00
❏ PYS 40,003	Medium	1969	10.00	20.00	40.00
❏ PYS 40,006	Puzzle	1970	10.00	20.00	40.00

MANDRELL, BARBARA
COLUMBIA

Number	Title	Yr	VG	VG+	NM
❏ C 30967	Treat Him Right	1971	5.00	10.00	20.00

MANGIONE, CHUCK
JAZZLAND

Number	Title	Yr	VG	VG+	NM
❏ JLP-84 [M]	Recuerdo	1962	10.00	20.00	40.00
❏ JLP-984 [S]	Recuerdo	1962	12.50	25.00	50.00

MOBILE FIDELITY

Number	Title	Yr	VG	VG+	NM
❏ 1-068	Feels So Good	1981	6.25	12.50	25.00
-- Audiophile vinyl					

MANHATTAN TRANSFER
MOBILE FIDELITY

Number	Title	Yr	VG	VG+	NM
❏ 1-022	Manhattan Transfer Live	1979	5.00	10.00	20.00
-- Audiophile vinyl					
❏ 1-199	Extensions	1994	6.25	12.50	25.00
-- Audiophile vinyl					

MANHATTANS, THE
CARNIVAL

Number	Title	Yr	VG	VG+	NM
❏ CMLP-201 [M]	Dedicated to You	1966	62.50	125.00	250.00
❏ CSLP-201 [S]	Dedicated to You	1966	125.00	250.00	500.00
❏ CMLP-202 [M]	For You and Yours	1967	37.50	75.00	150.00
❏ CSLP-202 [S]	For You and Yours	1967	75.00	150.00	300.00

COLUMBIA

Number	Title	Yr	VG	VG+	NM
❏ PCQ 34450 [Q]	It Feels So Good	1977	5.00	10.00	20.00

DELUXE

Number	Title	Yr	VG	VG+	NM
❏ 12000	With These Hands	1971	6.25	12.50	25.00
❏ 12004	A Million to One	1972	6.25	12.50	25.00

MANILLA ROAD
ROADSTER

Number	Title	Yr	VG	VG+	NM
❏ MR 1001	Invasion	1980	25.00	50.00	100.00
❏ MR 1002	Metal	1982	25.00	50.00	100.00
❏ MR 1003	Crystal Logic	1983	12.50	25.00	50.00

MANILOW, BARRY
ARISTA

Number	Title	Yr	VG	VG+	NM
❏ AB 2500 [EP]	Oh, Julie!	1982	5.00	10.00	20.00
❏ A2L 8601 [(2) PD]	Greatest Hits	1979	10.00	20.00	40.00
-- Entire contents on two picture discs (yes, it has the same number as the regular issue)					
❏ AL-8638 [(2)]	Live on Broadway	1990	5.00	10.00	20.00

Number	Title	Yr	VG	VG+	NM
BELL					
❏ 1129	Barry Manilow	1973	6.25	12.50	25.00
MOBILE FIDELITY					
❏ 1-097	Barry Manilow I	1981	5.00	10.00	20.00
-- Audiophile vinyl					
MANN, BARRY					
ABC-PARAMOUNT					
❏ 399 [M]	Who Put the Bomp	1963	30.00	60.00	120.00
❏ S-399 [S]	Who Put the Bomp	1963	75.00	150.00	300.00
RCA VICTOR					
❏ DJL1-1162 [DJ]	Flo and Eddie Interview Barry Mann	1975	12.50	25.00	50.00
MANN, CARL					
PHILLIPS INT'L.					
❏ PLP-1960 [M]	Like Mann	1960	150.00	300.00	600.00
MANN, HERBIE					
A&M					
❏ 3003 [M]	Glory of Love	1967	5.00	10.00	20.00
ATLANTIC					
❏ SD 1343 [S]	The Common Ground	1960	5.00	10.00	20.00
❏ SD 1371 [S]	The Family of Mann	1961	5.00	10.00	20.00
❏ SD 1380 [S]	Herbie Mann at the Village Gate	1962	5.00	10.00	20.00
❏ SD 1384 [S]	Right Now	1962	5.00	10.00	20.00
❏ SD 1397 [S]	Do the Bossa Nova with Herbie Mann	1962	5.00	10.00	20.00
❏ SD 1407 [S]	Herbie Mann Returns to the Village Gate	1963	5.00	10.00	20.00
❏ SD 1413 [S]	Herbie Mann Live at Newport	1963	5.00	10.00	20.00
❏ SD 1422 [S]	Latin Fever	1964	5.00	10.00	20.00
❏ SD 1426 [S]	Nirvana	1964	5.00	10.00	20.00
❏ SD 1433 [S]	My Kinda Groove	1965	5.00	10.00	20.00
❏ SD 1437 [S]	The Roar of the Greasepaint, The Smell of the Crowd	1965	5.00	10.00	20.00
❏ SD 1445 [S]	Standing Ovation at Newport	1965	5.00	10.00	20.00
❏ SD 1454 [S]	Herbie Mann Today	1966	5.00	10.00	20.00
❏ SD 1462 [S]	Monday Night at the Village Gate	1966	5.00	10.00	20.00
❏ SD 1464 [S]	Our Mann Flute	1966	5.00	10.00	20.00
❏ 1471 [M]	New Mann at Newport	1967	5.00	10.00	20.00
❏ 1475 [M]	Impressions of the Middle East	1967	5.00	10.00	20.00
❏ 1483 [M]	The Beat Goes On	1967	5.00	10.00	20.00
❏ 1490 [M]	The Herbie Mann String Album	1968	6.25	12.50	25.00
❏ QD 1632 [Q]	Hold On, I'm Comin'	1973	5.00	10.00	20.00
❏ SD 8105 [S]	Herbie Mann and Joao Gilberto with Antonio Carlos Jobim	1965	5.00	10.00	20.00
❏ 8141 [M]	Mann and a Woman	1967	5.00	10.00	20.00
BETHLEHEM					
❏ BCP-24 [M]	Flamingo, My Goodness -- Four Flutes, Vol. 2	1955	12.50	25.00	50.00
❏ BCP-40 [M]	The Herbie Mann-Sam Most Quintet	1956	12.50	25.00	50.00
❏ BCP-58 [M]	Herbie Mann Plays	1956	12.50	25.00	50.00
❏ BCP-63 [M]	Love and the Weather	1956	12.50	25.00	50.00
❏ BCP-1018 [10]	East Coast Jazz 4	1954	25.00	50.00	100.00
❏ BCP-6020 [M]	The Mann with the Most	1960	10.00	20.00	40.00
❏ BCP-6067 [M]	The Epitome of Jazz	1963	7.50	15.00	30.00
COLUMBIA					
❏ CS 9188 [S]	Latin Mann	1965	5.00	10.00	20.00
EPIC					
❏ LN 3395 [M]	Salute to the Flute	1957	15.00	30.00	60.00
❏ LN 3499 [M]	Herbie Mann with the Ilcken Trio	1958	15.00	30.00	60.00
INTERLUDE					
❏ MO-503 [M]	Flute Fraternity	1959	10.00	20.00	40.00
-- Reissue of Mode 114					
❏ ST-1103 [S]	Flute Fraternity	1959	7.50	15.00	30.00
JAZZLAND					
❏ JLP-5 [M]	Herbie Mann Quintet	1960	7.50	15.00	30.00
-- Reissue of Riverside 245					
MODE					
❏ LP-114 [M]	Flute Fraternity	1957	17.50	35.00	70.00
NEW JAZZ					
❏ NJLP-8211 [M]	Just Walkin'	1958	12.50	25.00	50.00
-- Purple label					
❏ NJLP-8211 [M]	Just Walkin'	1964	6.25	12.50	25.00
-- Blue label with trident logo					
PRESTIGE					
❏ PRLP-7101 [M]	Flute Souffle	1957	20.00	40.00	80.00
❏ PRLP-7124 [M]	Flute Flight	1957	20.00	40.00	80.00
❏ PRLP-7136 [M]	Mann in the Morning	1958	20.00	40.00	80.00

Number	Title	Yr	VG	VG+	NM
RIVERSIDE					
❏ RLP-12-234 [M]	Sultry Serenade	1957	15.00	30.00	60.00
-- Blue on white label					
❏ RLP-12-234 [M]	Sultry Serenade	1958	10.00	20.00	40.00
-- Blue label with reel and microphone logo					
❏ RLP-12-245 [M]	Great Ideas of Western Mann	1957	10.00	20.00	40.00
ROULETTE					
❏ SR-52122 [S]	Afro-Jazziac	1963	5.00	10.00	20.00
SAVOY					
❏ MG-12102 [M]	Flute Suite	1957	12.50	25.00	50.00
❏ MG-12107 [M]	Mann Alone	1957	12.50	25.00	50.00
❏ MG-12108 [M]	Yardbird Suite	1957	12.50	25.00	50.00
SURREY					
❏ SS-1015 [S]	Big Band	1965	5.00	10.00	20.00
UNITED ARTISTS					
❏ UAL-4042 [M]	African Suite	1959	7.50	15.00	30.00
❏ UAS-5042 [S]	African Suite	1959	10.00	20.00	40.00
❏ UAJ-14009 [M]	Brasil, Bossa Nova and Blue	1962	7.50	15.00	30.00
❏ UAJ-14022 [M]	St. Thomas	1962	7.50	15.00	30.00
❏ UAJS-15009 [S]	Brasil, Bossa Nova and Blue	1962	10.00	20.00	40.00
❏ UAJS-15022 [S]	St. Thomas	1962	10.00	20.00	40.00
VERVE					
❏ MGVS-6074 [S]	Flautista! -- Herbie Mann Plays Afro-Cuban Jazz	1960	7.50	15.00	30.00
❏ MGV-8247 [M]	The Magic Flute of Herbie Mann	1958	10.00	20.00	40.00
❏ V-8247 [M]	The Magic Flute of Herbie Mann	1961	5.00	10.00	20.00
❏ MGV-8336 [M]	Flautista! -- Herbie Mann Plays Afro-Cuban Jazz	1959	10.00	20.00	40.00
❏ V-8336 [M]	Flautista! -- Herbie Mann Plays Afro-Cuban Jazz	1961	5.00	10.00	20.00
❏ MGV-8392 [M]	Flute, Brass, Vibes and	1960	7.50	15.00	30.00
❏ V-8392 [M]	Flute, Brass, Vibes and	1961	5.00	10.00	20.00
❏ V-8527 [M]	The Sound of Mann	1963	5.00	10.00	20.00
MANN, JOHNNY, SINGERS					
LIBERTY					
❏ LST-7134 [S]	Alma Mater	1959	5.00	10.00	20.00
❏ LST-7149 [S]	Roar Along with the Singing Twenties	1960	5.00	10.00	20.00
❏ LST-7156 [S]	Swing Along with the Singing Thirties	1960	5.00	10.00	20.00
❏ LST-7198 [S]	Ballads of the King	1961	5.00	10.00	20.00
❏ LST-7217 [S]	Ballads of the King, Volume 2	1961	5.00	10.00	20.00
❏ LST-7391 [S]	The Ballad Sound (Beatle Songs)	1964	5.00	10.00	20.00
❏ LSS-14017 [S]	The Great Bands with Great Voices Swing the Great Voices of the Great Bands	1962	5.00	10.00	20.00
MANN, MANFRED					
Also see PAUL JONES.					
ASCOT					
❏ AM-13015 [M]	The Manfred Mann Album	1964	10.00	20.00	40.00
❏ AM-13018 [M]	The Five Faces of Manfred Mann	1965	10.00	20.00	40.00
❏ AM-13021 [M]	My Little Red Book of Winners	1965	10.00	20.00	40.00
❏ AM-13024 [M]	Mann Made	1966	10.00	20.00	40.00
❏ AS-16015 [P]	The Manfred Mann Album	1964	12.50	25.00	50.00
❏ AS-16018 [P]	The Five Faces of Manfred Mann	1965	12.50	25.00	50.00
❏ AS-16021 [S]	My Little Red Book of Winners	1965	12.50	25.00	50.00
❏ AS-16024 [S]	Mann Made	1966	12.50	25.00	50.00
MERCURY					
❏ SR-61168	The Mighty Quinn	1968	6.25	12.50	25.00
UNITED ARTISTS					
❏ 94 [DJ]	Manfred Mann Interview	1966	50.00	100.00	200.00
-- Promotional album in plain white jacket					
❏ UAL 3549 [M]	Pretty Flamingo	1966	7.50	15.00	30.00
❏ UAL 3551 [M]	Manfred Mann's Greatest Hits	1966	7.50	15.00	30.00
❏ UAS 6549 [S]	Pretty Flamingo	1966	10.00	20.00	40.00
❏ UAS 6551 [P]	Manfred Mann's Greatest Hits	1966	10.00	20.00	40.00
-- "Do Wah Diddy Diddy," "Sha La La," "I Got You Babe" and "Satisfaction" are rechanneled.					
MANN, REV. COLUMBUS					
TAMLA					
❏ T-227 [M]	They Shall Be Mine	1962	2,000.	3,000.	4,000.
WINGATE					
❏ 701 [M]	He Satisfies Me	196?	300.00	600.00	900.00
MANN, SHADOW					
TOMORROW					
❏ TPS-69001	Come Live with Me	1974	15.00	30.00	60.00
MANNA, CHARLIE					
DECCA					
❏ DL 4159 [M]	Manna Overboard!!	1961	6.25	12.50	25.00
❏ DL 4213 [M]	Manna Live!!	1962	6.25	12.50	25.00

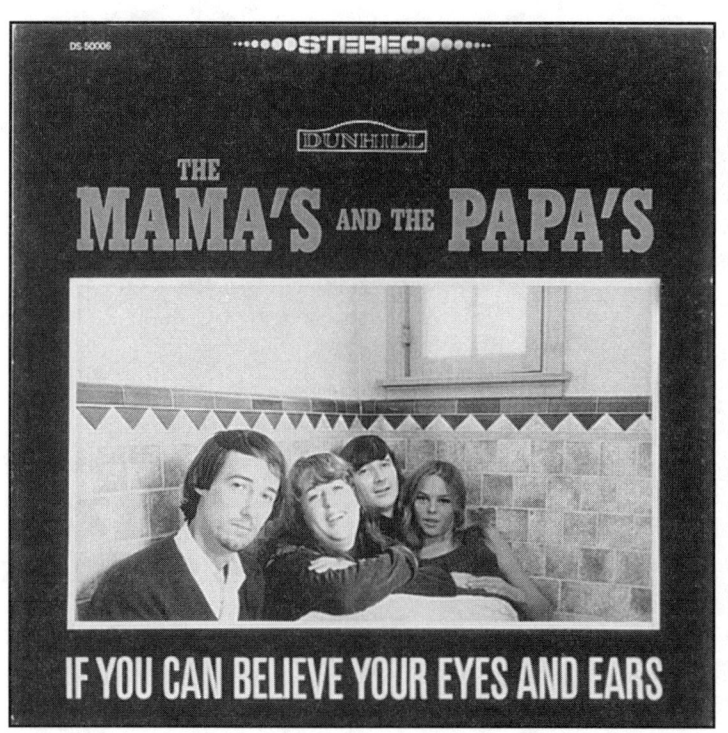

(Top left) The most unusual of the several cover variations of *If You Can Believe Your Eyes And Ears,* the debut album by the Mamas and the Papas, is this version that put a huge black border around the outside of a cropped version of the original cover photo, thus completely obscuring the "offensive" toilet. The exact origin of this version remains obscure, though it was not a record club edition, as has been suggested. (Top right) One of the toughest Mamas and the Papas albums to find is this two-record box from 1970, *A Gathering of Flowers,* on which John Phillips and Cass Elliot talk about the group and their songs as some of their greatest hits play. (Bottom left) When *Barry Manilow,* his debut album, came out in 1973, he was best known as Bette Midler's musical director. By the time this scarce Bell release was reissued on Arista in 1975, it had a different cover, several tracks were remixed, and Manilow was a star on his own. (Bottom right) *The Manfred Mann Album* was the group's debut on Ascot in 1964. This album may be why, most of the time, Manfred Mann is filed under "Manfred" rather than "Mann." Even though there was a group member named Manfred Mann, the album said that Manfred Mann was a group.

Number	Title	Yr	VG	VG+	NM

MANNING, TERRY
ENTERPRISE
❏ ENS-1008	Home Sweet Home	1969	10.00	20.00	40.00

MANONE, WINGY
DECCA
❏ DL 8473 [M]	Trumpet on the Wing	1957	10.00	20.00	40.00

"X"
❏ LVA-3014 [10]	Wingy Manone, Vol. 1	1954	12.50	25.00	50.00

MANPOWER -- See MAN.

MANSFIELD, JAYNE
MGM
❏ E-4202 [M]	Shakespeare, Tchaikovsky and Me	1964	10.00	20.00	40.00
❏ SE-4202 [S]	Shakespeare, Tchaikovsky and Me	1964	15.00	30.00	60.00

20TH CENTURY
❏ FOX-3049 [M]	Jayne Mansfield Busts Up Las Vegas	1961	50.00	100.00	200.00

MANSON, CHARLES
AWARENESS
❏ LP-2144	Lie: The Love and Terror Cult	197?	10.00	20.00	40.00
❏ 08903-1056	Lie: The Love and Terror Cult	1987	5.00	10.00	20.00

ESP-DISK'
❏ 2003	Lie: The Love and Terror Cult	1970	50.00	100.00	200.00

MANTLE, MICKEY
RCA VICTOR
❏ LPM-1704 [M]	My Favorite Hits	1958	100.00	200.00	400.00

MANTOVANI
LONDON
❏ SS 1 [S]	Mantovani Stereo Showcase	1959	5.00	10.00	20.00
❏ PS 106 [S]	Gems Forever	1959	5.00	10.00	20.00
❏ PS 118 [S]	Strauss Waltzes	1959	5.00	10.00	20.00
❏ PS 119 [S]	Waltz Encores	1959	5.00	10.00	20.00
❏ PS 133 [S]	Concert Encores	1959	5.00	10.00	20.00
❏ PS 142 [S]	Christmas Carols	1959	5.00	10.00	20.00
❏ PS 147 [S]	Continental Encores	1959	5.00	10.00	20.00
❏ PS 164 [S]	Film Encores, Vol. 2	1959	5.00	10.00	20.00
❏ PS 165 [S]	The Music of Victor Herbert and Sigmund Romberg	1959	5.00	10.00	20.00
❏ PS 165/6 [(2) S]	All-American Showcase	1959	6.25	12.50	25.00
❏ PS 166 [S]	The Music of Irving Berlin and Rudolf Friml	1959	5.00	10.00	20.00

-- Originals of all the above PS series have blue back covers, "Stereophonic" on upper left front cover and dark blue "FFSS" labels

❏ LL 570 [M]	Greensleeves (A Selection of Favorite Waltzes)	1952	5.00	10.00	20.00
❏ LL 685 [M]	Strauss Waltzes	1953	5.00	10.00	20.00
❏ LL 766 [M]	An Enchanted Evening with Mantovani	1953	5.00	10.00	20.00
❏ LL 768 [M]	Mantovani Plays Tangos	1953	5.00	10.00	20.00
❏ LL 979 [M]	Romantic Melodies	1954	5.00	10.00	20.00
❏ LL 1094 [M]	Waltz Time	1954	5.00	10.00	20.00
❏ LL 1150 [M]	The Music of Rudolf Friml	1955	5.00	10.00	20.00
❏ LL 1219 [M]	Song Hits from Theatreland	1955	5.00	10.00	20.00
❏ LL 1259 [M]	Lonely Ballerina (Musical Modes)	1956	5.00	10.00	20.00
❏ LL 1262 [M]	Gershwin: Rhapsody in Blue	1955	5.00	10.00	20.00
❏ LL 1262 [M]	Gershwin: Concerto	1955	5.00	10.00	20.00
❏ LL 1331 [M]	Operatic Arias	1955	5.00	10.00	20.00
❏ LL 1452 [M]	Waltzes of Irving Berlin	1956	5.00	10.00	20.00
❏ LL 1513 [M]	Music from the Films	1956	5.00	10.00	20.00
❏ LL 1525 [M]	Music from the Ballet	1956	5.00	10.00	20.00
❏ LL 1700 [M]	Film Encores	1957	5.00	10.00	20.00
❏ LL 1748 [M]	The World's Favorite Love Songs	1957	5.00	10.00	20.00
❏ LL 3122/3 [(2) M]	All-American Showcase	1959	5.00	10.00	20.00

MAPHIS, JOE
COLUMBIA
❏ CL 1005 [M]	Fire on the Strings	1957	25.00	50.00	100.00

HARMONY
❏ HL 7180 [M]	Hi-Fi Holiday for Banjo	1959	6.25	12.50	25.00
❏ HS 11032 [S]	Hi-Fi Holiday for Banjo	1959	7.50	15.00	30.00

KAPP
❏ KL-1347 [M]	Hootenanny Star	1964	5.00	10.00	20.00
❏ KS-3347 [S]	Hootenanny Star	1964	6.25	12.50	25.00

MACGREGOR
❏ MGR-1205 [M]	King of the Strings	196?	20.00	40.00	80.00

MOSRITE
❏ MA-400 [M]	The New Sound of Joe Maphis	1967	7.50	15.00	30.00
❏ MS-400 [S]	The New Sound of Joe Maphis	1967	7.50	15.00	30.00

STARDAY
❏ SLP-316 [M]	King of the Strings	1966	12.50	25.00	50.00
❏ SLP-373 [M]	Country Guitar Goes to the Jimmy Dean Show	1966	15.00	30.00	60.00

-- Deduct 1/3 if instruction book is missing

MAPHIS, JOE AND ROSE LEE
CAPITOL
❏ ST 1778 [S]	Rose Lee and Joe Maphis	1962	10.00	20.00	40.00
❏ T 1778 [M]	Rose Lee and Joe Maphis	1962	7.50	15.00	30.00

STARDAY
❏ SLP-286 [M]	Mr. and Mrs. Country Music	1964	7.50	15.00	30.00
❏ SLP-322 [M]	Golden Gospel	1966	7.50	15.00	30.00

MAPHIS, ROSE LEE
COLUMBIA
❏ CL 1598 [M]	Rose Lee Maphis	1961	7.50	15.00	30.00
❏ CS 8398 [S]	Rose Lee Maphis	1961	10.00	20.00	40.00

MAR-KEYS
ATLANTIC
❏ 8055 [M]	Last Night	1961	25.00	50.00	100.00
-- White "fan" logo on right					
❏ 8055 [M]	Last Night	1962	12.50	25.00	50.00
-- Black "fan" logo on right					
❏ SD 8055 [R]	Last Night	1966	10.00	20.00	40.00
❏ 8062 [M]	Do the Pop-Eye with the Mar-Keys	1962	12.50	25.00	50.00
❏ SD 8062 [R]	Do the Pop-Eye with the Mar-Keys	1966	10.00	20.00	40.00

STAX
❏ ST-707 [M]	The Great Memphis Sound	1966	12.50	25.00	50.00
❏ STS-707 [R]	The Great Memphis Sound	1966	10.00	20.00	40.00
❏ STS-2025	Damifiknew	1969	5.00	10.00	20.00
❏ STS-2036	Memphis Experience	1971	5.00	10.00	20.00

MAR-KEYS/BOOKER T. AND THE MG'S
Also see each artist's individual listings.
STAX
❏ ST-720 [M]	Back to Back	1967	5.00	10.00	20.00
❏ STS-720 [S]	Back to Back	1967	6.25	12.50	25.00

MARAIS, JOSEPH
DECCA
❏ DL 5014 [10]	South African Veld	1949	12.50	25.00	50.00
❏ DL 5083 [10]	Songs from the Veld, Vol. 2	1950	12.50	25.00	50.00
❏ DL 5106 [10]	Songs of Many Lands	1950	12.50	25.00	50.00

MARAIS, JOSEPH, AND MIRANDA
DECCA
❏ DL 5268 [10]	Ballads of Many Lands	1950	12.50	25.00	50.00
❏ DL 8711 [M]	Sundown Songs	1957	6.25	12.50	25.00
❏ DL 9026 [M]	Marais and Miranda In Person, Vol. 1	1955	7.50	15.00	30.00
❏ DL 9027 [M]	Marais and Miranda In Person, Vol. 2	1955	7.50	15.00	30.00
❏ DL 9030 [M]	Christmas with Joseph and Miranda	1955	7.50	15.00	30.00
❏ DL 9047 [M]	Africana Suite and Songs of Spirit and Humor	1956	7.50	15.00	30.00

MARATHONS, THE
ARVEE
❏ A-428 [M]	Peanut Butter	1961	45.00	90.00	180.00

MARBLE PHROGG, THE
DERRICK
❏ 8868	The Marble Phrogg	1968	250.00	500.00	1,000.

MARCEAU, MARCEL
GONE
❏ LP 1F	The Best of Marcel Marceau	196?	12.50	25.00	50.00

MGM
❏ SE-4	The Best of Marcel Marceau	196?	10.00	20.00	40.00

-- The above records are identical: 38 minutes of silence and 2 minutes of applause!

MARCELS, THE
COLPIX
❏ CP-416 [M]	Blue Moon	1961	87.50	175.00	350.00
-- Gold label					
❏ CP-416 [M]	Blue Moon	1963	30.00	60.00	120.00
-- Blue label					

Number	Title	Yr	VG	VG+	NM

MARCH, HAL
DOT
- DLP-3092 [M] The Moods of March — 1958 — 7.50 — 15.00 — 30.00
- DLP-25092 [S] The Moods of March — 1958 — 10.00 — 20.00 — 40.00

HAMILTON
- HLP-12101 [S] Hal March Conducts — 1960 — 5.00 — 10.00 — 20.00
-- *Reissue of Dot LP*

MARCH, LITTLE PEGGY
RCA VICTOR
- LPM-2732 [M] I Will Follow Him — 1963 — 15.00 — 30.00 — 60.00
- LSP-2732 [S] I Will Follow Him — 1963 — 20.00 — 40.00 — 80.00
- LPM-3883 [M] No Foolin' — 1968 — 10.00 — 20.00 — 40.00
- LSP-3883 [S] No Foolin' — 1968 — 6.25 — 12.50 — 25.00

MARCH, LITTLE PEGGY/BENNIE THOMAS
RCA VICTOR
- LPM-3408 [M] In Our Fashion — 1965 — 10.00 — 20.00 — 40.00
- LSP-3408 [S] In Our Fashion — 1965 — 12.50 — 25.00 — 50.00

MARCHAN, BOBBY
SPHERE SOUND
- SR-7004 [M] There's Something on Your Mind — 1964 — 50.00 — 100.00 — 200.00
- SSR-7004 [S] There's Something on Your Mind — 1964 — 75.00 — 150.00 — 300.00

MARESCA, ERNIE
SEVILLE
- SV 77001 [M] Shout! Shout! Knock Yourself Out — 1962 — 30.00 — 60.00 — 120.00
- SV 87001 [S] Shout! Shout! Knock Yourself Out — 1962 — 50.00 — 100.00 — 200.00

MARGOLIN, STUART
WARNER BROS.
- BSK 3439 And the Angel Sings — 1980 — 5.00 — 10.00 — 20.00

MARGULIS, CHARLIE
CARLTON
- LP 12-103 [M] Marvelous Margulis — 1958 — 6.25 — 12.50 — 25.00
- STLP 12-103 [S] Marvelous Margulis — 1959 — 7.50 — 15.00 — 30.00

MARIANI
SONOBEAT
- 1001 Perpetuum Mobile — 197? — 1,000. — 1,750. — 2,500.
-- *Not issued with a cover*

MARINERS, THE
CADENCE
- CLP-1008 [M] The Mariners Sing Spirituals — 1956 — 10.00 — 20.00 — 40.00

COLUMBIA
- CL 609 [M] Hymns — 1955 — 10.00 — 20.00 — 40.00

MARINO, FRANK, AND MAHOGANY RUSH -- See MAHOGANY RUSH.

MARKETTS, THE
LIBERTY
- LRP-3226 [M] Surfer's Stomp — 1962 — 10.00 — 20.00 — 40.00
-- *Add 20% if "Surfer's Stomp" instruction sheet is enclosed*
- LRP-3226 [M] The Surfing Scene — 196? — 7.50 — 15.00 — 30.00
-- *Retitled version of above*
- LST-7226 [S] Surfer's Stomp — 1962 — 12.50 — 25.00 — 50.00
-- *Add 20% if "Surfer's Stomp" instruction sheet is enclosed*
- LST-7226 [S] The Surfing Scene — 196? — 10.00 — 20.00 — 40.00
-- *Retitled version of above*

WARNER BROS.
- W 1509 [M] The Marketts Take to Wheels — 1963 — 10.00 — 20.00 — 40.00
- WS 1509 [S] The Marketts Take to Wheels — 1963 — 12.50 — 25.00 — 50.00
- W 1537 [M] Out of Limits! — 1964 — 7.50 — 15.00 — 30.00
- WS 1537 [S] Out of Limits! — 1964 — 10.00 — 20.00 — 40.00
- W 1642 [M] The Batman Theme — 1966 — 10.00 — 20.00 — 40.00
- WS 1642 [S] The Batman Theme — 1966 — 12.50 — 25.00 — 50.00

WORLD PACIFIC
- WP-1870 [M] Sun Power — 1967 — 6.25 — 12.50 — 25.00
- WPS-21870 [S] Sun Power — 1967 — 5.00 — 10.00 — 20.00

MARKHAM, PIGMEAT
CHESS
- LP-1451 [M] The Trial — 1961 — 6.25 — 12.50 — 25.00
- LP-1462 [M] Pigmeat Markham At the Party — 1962 — 6.25 — 12.50 — 25.00
- LP-1467 [M] Anything Goes — 1962 — 6.25 — 12.50 — 25.00
- LP-1475 [M] The World's Greatest Clown — 1963 — 6.25 — 12.50 — 25.00
- LP-1484 [M] Open the Door, Richard — 1964 — 6.25 — 12.50 — 25.00
- LP-1493 [M] Mr. Funny Man — 1965 — 6.25 — 12.50 — 25.00
- LP-1500 [M] This'll Kill Ya — 1965 — 6.25 — 12.50 — 25.00
- LPS-1505 [S] If You Can't Be Good, Be Careful — 1966 — 5.00 — 10.00 — 20.00
- LPS-1515 [S] Mr. Vaudeville — 1967 — 5.00 — 10.00 — 20.00
- LP-1517 [M] Save Your Soul, Baby — 1967 — 5.00 — 10.00 — 20.00
- LPS-1517 [S] Save Your Soul, Baby — 1967 — 5.00 — 10.00 — 20.00
- LP-1521 [M] Backstage — 1968 — 5.00 — 10.00 — 20.00
- LPS-1521 [S] Backstage — 1968 — 5.00 — 10.00 — 20.00
- LPS-1525 Here Comes the Judge — 1968 — 5.00 — 10.00 — 20.00

MARKLEY
FORWARD
- 1007 A Group — 1969 — 7.50 — 15.00 — 30.00

MARKS, GUY
ABC
- S-648 Loving You Has Made Me Bananas — 1968 — 5.00 — 10.00 — 20.00

MARKS, J., AND SHIPEN LEBZELTER
COLUMBIA MASTERWORKS
- MS 7193 Rock and Other Four-Letter Words — 1969 — 7.50 — 15.00 — 30.00
- M 30006 First National Nothing — 1970 — 5.00 — 10.00 — 20.00

MARLEY, BOB, AND THE WAILERS
ISLAND
- SW-9241 Catch a Fire — 1973 — 12.50 — 25.00 — 50.00
-- *"Cigarette lighter" cover with flip-open top; Capitol distribution*
- SW-9256 Burnin' — 1973 — 5.00 — 10.00 — 20.00
-- *Capitol distribution*
- ILPS 9383 [DJ] Rastaman Vibration — 1976 — 25.00 — 50.00 — 100.00
-- *Promotional package with burlap box and press kit*

MOBILE FIDELITY
- 1-221 Exodus — 1995 — 6.25 — 12.50 — 25.00
-- *Audiophile vinyl*
- 1-236 Catch a Fire — 1995 — 6.25 — 12.50 — 25.00
-- *Audiophile vinyl*

MARLO, MICKI
ABC-PARAMOUNT
- 295 [M] Married I Can Always Get — 1959 — 5.00 — 10.00 — 20.00
- S-295 [S] Married I Can Always Get — 1959 — 6.25 — 12.50 — 25.00

MARLOWE, MARION, AND FRANK PARKER
COLUMBIA
- CL 576 [M] Arthur Godfrey's TV Sweethearts — 1954 — 7.50 — 15.00 — 30.00
-- *Maroon label, gold print*

MARLOWE, MEXIE
KING
- 799 [M] Meet Mexie Marlowe — 1962 — 25.00 — 50.00 — 100.00

MARMALADE, THE
EPIC
- BN 26553 The Best of the Marmalade — 1970 — 5.00 — 10.00 — 20.00

LONDON
- PS 575 Reflections of My Life — 1970 — 5.00 — 10.00 — 20.00

MARR, HANK
KING
- 829 [M] Teentime Dance Steps — 1963 — 7.50 — 15.00 — 30.00
- 899 [M] Live at Club 502 — 1964 — 10.00 — 20.00 — 40.00
- 933 [M] On and Off Stage — 1965 — 7.50 — 15.00 — 30.00
- 1011 [M] Hank Marr Plays 24 Originals — 1966 — 5.00 — 10.00 — 20.00
- 1025 [M] Sounds from the Marr-Ket Place — 1968 — 5.00 — 10.00 — 20.00
- KSD-1061 Greasy Spoon — 1969 — 5.00 — 10.00 — 20.00

MARS, CHRIS
Also see THE REPLACEMENTS.
SMASH
- 513 198-1 [DJ] Horseshoes and Hand Grenades — 1992 — 5.00 — 10.00 — 20.00
-- *Vinyl is promo-only*

MARS, SYLVIA
LYRIC
- 124 Blues Walk Right In — 196? — 15.00 — 30.00 — 60.00

MARSALIS, WYNTON
COLUMBIA
- HC 47574 Wynton Marsalis — 198? — 7.50 — 15.00 — 30.00
-- *Half-speed mastered edition*

MARSHALL, CHUCK
DECCA

Number	Title	Yr	VG	VG+	NM
❏ DL 74267 [S]	Twist to Songs Everybody Knows	1962	5.00	10.00	20.00

MARSHALL, JACK
CAPITOL

Number	Title	Yr	VG	VG+	NM
❏ ST 1108 [S]	18th Century Jazz	1959	6.25	12.50	25.00
❏ T 1108 [M]	18th Century Jazz	1959	5.00	10.00	20.00
❏ ST 1194 [S]	Soundsville!	1959	6.25	12.50	25.00
❏ T 1194 [M]	Soundsville!	1959	5.00	10.00	20.00
❏ ST 1351 [S]	Jack Marshall Swings	1960	6.25	12.50	25.00
❏ T 1351 [M]	Jack Marshall Swings	1960	5.00	10.00	20.00
❏ ST 1601 [S]	Songs Without Words	1961	6.25	12.50	25.00
❏ T 1601 [M]	Songs Without Words	1961	5.00	10.00	20.00
❏ ST 1727 [S]	The Twangy, Shoutin', Fantastic Big-Band Sounds of Tuff Jack	1962	10.00	20.00	40.00
❏ T 1727 [M]	The Twangy, Shoutin', Fantastic Big-Band Sounds of Tuff Jack	1962	7.50	15.00	30.00
❏ ST 1939 [S]	My Son the Surf Nut	1963	10.00	20.00	40.00
❏ T 1939 [M]	My Son the Surf Nut	1963	7.50	15.00	30.00

MARSHALL, PENNY, AND CINDY WILLIAMS
ATLANTIC

Number	Title	Yr	VG	VG+	NM
❏ SD 18203	Laverne and Shirley Sing	1979	6.25	12.50	25.00

MARSHALL, PETER
DOT

Number	Title	Yr	VG	VG+	NM
❏ DLP-25930	For the Love of Pete	1969	6.25	12.50	25.00

MARSHMALLOW WAY
UNITED ARTISTS

Number	Title	Yr	VG	VG+	NM
❏ UAS-6708	Marshmallow Way	1969	5.00	10.00	20.00

MARTHA AND THE VANDELLAS
GORDY

Number	Title	Yr	VG	VG+	NM
❏ G-902 [M]	Come and Get These Memories	1963	100.00	200.00	400.00
❏ GS-902 [S]	Come and Get These Memories	1963	200.00	400.00	800.00
❏ G-907 [M]	Heat Wave	1963	37.50	75.00	150.00
❏ GS-907 [S]	Heat Wave	1963	100.00	200.00	400.00
-- Mono cover with "Stereo" sticker					
❏ GS-907 [R]	Heat Wave	1963	37.50	75.00	150.00
-- "Stereo" banner pre-printed on cover					
❏ G-915 [M]	Dance Party	1965	10.00	20.00	40.00
❏ GS-915 [S]	Dance Party	1965	15.00	30.00	60.00
❏ G-917 [M]	Greatest Hits	1966	6.25	12.50	25.00
❏ GS-917 [S]	Greatest Hits	1966	7.50	15.00	30.00
❏ G-920 [M]	Watchout!	1966	6.25	12.50	25.00
❏ GS-920 [S]	Watchout!	1966	7.50	15.00	30.00
❏ G-925 [M]	Martha and the Vandellas Live!	1967	7.50	15.00	30.00
❏ GS-925 [S]	Martha and the Vandellas Live!	1967	6.25	12.50	25.00
❏ G-926 [M]	Ridin' High	1968	10.00	20.00	40.00
-- Mono is promo only					
❏ GS-926 [S]	Ridin' High	1968	5.00	10.00	20.00
❏ GS-944	Sugar 'N Spice	1969	5.00	10.00	20.00
❏ GS-952	Natural Resources	1970	5.00	10.00	20.00
❏ GS-958	Black Magic	1972	5.00	10.00	20.00

MARTIN, BENNY
STARDAY

Number	Title	Yr	VG	VG+	NM
❏ SLP-131 [M]	Country Music's Sensational Entertainer	1961	12.50	25.00	50.00

MARTIN, BOBBI
CORAL

Number	Title	Yr	VG	VG+	NM
❏ CRL 757472 [S]	Don't Forget I Still Love You	1965	5.00	10.00	20.00
❏ CRL 757478 [S]	I Love You So	1965	5.00	10.00	20.00

MARTIN, DEAN
CAPITOL

Number	Title	Yr	VG	VG+	NM
❏ H 401 [10]	Dean Martin Sings	1953	25.00	50.00	100.00
❏ T 401 [M]	Dean Martin Sings	1953	12.50	25.00	50.00
❏ STBB-523 [(2)]	You're Nobody 'Til Somebody Loves You/Return to Me	1970	5.00	10.00	20.00
❏ T 576 [M]	Swingin' Down Yonder	1955	7.50	15.00	30.00
❏ T 849 [M]	Pretty Baby	1957	7.50	15.00	30.00
❏ T 1047 [M]	This Is Dean Martin	1958	7.50	15.00	30.00
❏ ST 1150 [S]	Sleep Warm	1959	7.50	15.00	30.00
❏ T 1150 [M]	Sleep Warm	1959	6.25	12.50	25.00
❏ ST 1285 [S]	A Winter Romance	1959	7.50	15.00	30.00
❏ T 1285 [M]	A Winter Romance	1959	5.00	10.00	20.00
❏ ST 1442 [S]	This Time I'm Swingin'	1961	7.50	15.00	30.00
❏ T 1442 [M]	This Time I'm Swingin'	1961	5.00	10.00	20.00
❏ SW 1580 [S]	Dean Martin	1961	7.50	15.00	30.00
❏ W 1580 [M]	Dean Martin	1961	5.00	10.00	20.00
❏ ST 1659 [S]	Dino -- Italian Love Songs	1962	7.50	15.00	30.00
❏ T 1659 [M]	Dino -- Italian Love Songs	1962	5.00	10.00	20.00
❏ ST 1702 [S]	Cha Cha De Amor	1962	7.50	15.00	30.00
❏ T 1702 [M]	Cha Cha De Amor	1962	5.00	10.00	20.00
❏ T 2212 [M]	Hey Brother Pour the Wine	1964	5.00	10.00	20.00
❏ ST 2297 [S]	Dean Martin Sings -- Sinatra Conducts	1965	5.00	10.00	20.00
❏ STT 2343 [S]	Holiday Cheer	1965	5.00	10.00	20.00
-- Some copies of this LP have labels that state the title as "Baby, It's Cold Outside."					
❏ DTCL 2815 [(3) R]	The Dean Martin Deluxe Set	1967	10.00	20.00	40.00
❏ TCL 2815 [(3) M]	The Dean Martin Deluxe Set	1967	7.50	15.00	30.00
REPRISE					
❏ R9-6021 [S]	French Style	1962	5.00	10.00	20.00
❏ R9-6054 [S]	Dino Latino	1962	5.00	10.00	20.00
❏ R9-6061 [S]	Country Style	1963	5.00	10.00	20.00
❏ R9-6085 [S]	Dean "Tex" Martin Rides Again	1963	5.00	10.00	20.00
❏ R-6211 [M]	The Silencers	1966	5.00	10.00	20.00
❏ RS-6211 [S]	The Silencers	1966	6.25	12.50	25.00
❏ RS 6222 [S]	The Dean Martin Christmas Album	1966	5.00	10.00	20.00
TOWER					
❏ T 5006 [M]	The Lush Years	1965	5.00	10.00	20.00
❏ T 5018 [M]	Relaxin'	1966	5.00	10.00	20.00
❏ ST 5036 [S]	Happy in Love	1966	5.00	10.00	20.00

MARTIN, DEWEY, AND MEDICINE BALL
UNI

Number	Title	Yr	VG	VG+	NM
❏ 73088	Dewey Martin and Medicine Ball	1970	6.25	12.50	25.00

MARTIN, GEORGE
UNITED ARTISTS

Number	Title	Yr	VG	VG+	NM
❏ UAL 3377 [M]	Off the Beatle Track	1964	20.00	40.00	80.00
❏ UAL 3383 [M]	A Hard Day's Night	1964	10.00	20.00	40.00
❏ UAL 3420 [M]	George Martin	1965	10.00	20.00	40.00
❏ UAL 3448 [M]	George Martin Plays "Help"	1965	12.50	25.00	50.00
❏ UAL 3539 [M]	George Martin Salutes the Beatle Girls	1966	12.50	25.00	50.00
❏ UAL 3647 [M]	London by George	1967	7.50	15.00	30.00
❏ UAS 6377 [S]	Off the Beatle Track	1964	25.00	50.00	100.00
❏ UAS 6383 [S]	A Hard Day's Night	1964	12.50	25.00	50.00
❏ UAS 6420 [S]	George Martin	1965	12.50	25.00	50.00
❏ UAS 6448 [S]	George Martin Plays "Help"	1965	20.00	40.00	80.00
❏ UAS 6539 [S]	George Martin Salutes the Beatle Girls	1966	20.00	40.00	80.00
❏ UAS 6647 [S]	London by George	1967	10.00	20.00	40.00

MARTIN, GRADY
DECCA

Number	Title	Yr	VG	VG+	NM
❏ DL 4072 [M]	Big City Lights	1960	5.00	10.00	20.00
❏ DL 5566 [10]	Dance-O-Rama	1955	50.00	100.00	200.00
❏ DL 8181 [M]	Powerhouse Dance Party	1955	7.50	15.00	30.00
❏ DL 8292 [M]	Juke Box Jamboree	1956	7.50	15.00	30.00
❏ DL 8648 [M]	The Roaring Twenties	1957	7.50	15.00	30.00
❏ DL 8883 [M]	Hot Time Tonight	1959	5.00	10.00	20.00
❏ DL 74072 [S]	Big City Lights	1960	6.25	12.50	25.00
❏ DL 74286 [S]	Swingin' Down the River	1962	5.00	10.00	20.00
❏ DL 74476 [S]	Songs Everybody Knows	1963	5.00	10.00	20.00
❏ DL 78883 [S]	Hot Time Tonight	1959	6.25	12.50	25.00

MARTIN, JIMMY
DECCA

Number	Title	Yr	VG	VG+	NM
❏ DL 4016 [M]	Good 'n Country	1960	6.25	12.50	25.00
❏ DL 4285 [M]	Country Music Time	1962	6.25	12.50	25.00
❏ DL 4360 [M]	This World Is Not My Home	1963	6.25	12.50	25.00
❏ DL 4536 [M]	Widow Maker	1964	5.00	10.00	20.00
❏ DL 4643 [M]	Sunny Side of the Mountain	1965	5.00	10.00	20.00
❏ DL 4769 [M]	Mr. Good 'n Country Music	1966	5.00	10.00	20.00
❏ DL 4891 [M]	Big and Country Instrumentals	1967	5.00	10.00	20.00
❏ DL 74016 [S]	Good 'n Country	1960	7.50	15.00	30.00
❏ DL 74285 [S]	Country Music Time	1962	7.50	15.00	30.00
❏ DL 74360 [S]	This World Is Not My Home	1963	7.50	15.00	30.00
❏ DL 74536 [S]	Widow Maker	1964	6.25	12.50	25.00
❏ DL 74643 [S]	Sunny Side of the Mountain	1965	6.25	12.50	25.00
❏ DL 74769 [S]	Mr. Good 'n Country Music	1966	6.25	12.50	25.00
❏ DL 74891 [S]	Big and Country Instrumentals	1967	5.00	10.00	20.00
❏ DL 74996	Tennessee	1968	5.00	10.00	20.00

MARTIN, MARTY -- See BOXCAR WILLIE.

MARTIN, MARY
COLUMBIA MASTERWORKS

Number	Title	Yr	VG	VG+	NM
❏ ML 2061 [10]	Mary Martin Sings for You	1949	12.50	25.00	50.00

Number	Title	Yr	VG	VG+	NM

DISNEYLAND

Number	Title	Yr	VG	VG+	NM
❑ WDL-1038 [M]	Hi-Ho -- Mary Martin Sings and Swings Walt Disney Favorites	1958	5.00	10.00	20.00
❑ STER-1296 [S]	Mary Martin Songs from Rodgers and Hammerstein's The Sound of Music	1966	5.00	10.00	20.00
❑ ST-2002 [M]	The Little Lame Lamb	1958	12.50	25.00	50.00
❑ STER-3031 [S]	Mary Martin Sings a Musical Love Story	1959	6.25	12.50	25.00
❑ WD-3031 [M]	Mary Martin Sings a Musical Love Story	1958	5.00	10.00	20.00
❑ STER-3038 [S]	Hi-Ho!	1959	6.25	12.50	25.00
❑ WD-3038 [M]	Hi-Ho!	1958	5.00	10.00	20.00
❑ ST-3911 [M]	The Story of Sleeping Beauty	1958	7.50	15.00	30.00
-- *Back cover art features Sleeping Beauty and prince*					
❑ ST-3911 [M]	The Story of Sleeping Beauty	1969	5.00	10.00	20.00
-- *Back cover art features pictures from the booklet*					
❑ STER-3936 [S]	Mary Martin Songs from Rodgers and Hammerstein's The Sound of Music	1966	5.00	10.00	20.00
❑ STER-4016 [S]	Hi-Ho!	1959	7.50	15.00	30.00
❑ WDL-4016 [M]	Hi-Ho!	1958	5.00	10.00	20.00

MARTIN, TONY
DECCA

Number	Title	Yr	VG	VG+	NM
❑ DL 8287 [M]	Our Love Affair	195?	6.25	12.50	25.00
-- *Black label, silver print*					
❑ DL 8366 [M]	In the Spotlight	195?	6.25	12.50	25.00
-- *Black label, silver print*					

RCA VICTOR

Number	Title	Yr	VG	VG+	NM
❑ LPM-2146 [M]	Tony Martin at the Desert Inn	1960	5.00	10.00	20.00
❑ LSP-2146 [S]	Tony Martin at the Desert Inn	1960	6.25	12.50	25.00

MARTIN, VINCE, AND FRED NEIL
ELEKTRA

Number	Title	Yr	VG	VG+	NM
❑ EKL-248 [M]	Tear Down the Walls	1964	12.50	25.00	50.00
❑ EKS-7248 [S]	Tear Down the Walls	1964	15.00	30.00	60.00

MARTINDALE, WINK
DOT

Number	Title	Yr	VG	VG+	NM
❑ DLP-3245 [M]	Deck of Cards	1960	5.00	10.00	20.00
❑ DLP-25245 [S]	Deck of Cards	1960	6.25	12.50	25.00
❑ DLP-25293 [S]	The Bible Story	1960	5.00	10.00	20.00
❑ DLP-25403 [S]	Big Bad John	1962	5.00	10.00	20.00
❑ DLP-25571 [S]	My True Love	1964	5.00	10.00	20.00
❑ DLP-25692 [S]	Giddyup Go	1966	5.00	10.00	20.00

MARTINEZ, TONY
DEL-FI

Number	Title	Yr	VG	VG+	NM
❑ DFLP-1205 [M]	The Many Sides of Pepino	1959	7.50	15.00	30.00
❑ DFLP-1205S [S]	The Many Sides of Pepino	1959	10.00	20.00	40.00

MARTINO, AL
CAPITOL

Number	Title	Yr	VG	VG+	NM
❑ STCL-572 [(3)]	Al Martino	1971	6.25	12.50	25.00
❑ ST 1774 [S]	The Exciting Voice of Al Martino	1962	5.00	10.00	20.00
❑ ST 1907 [S]	The Italian Voice of Al Martino	1963	5.00	10.00	20.00

MOVIETONE

Number	Title	Yr	VG	VG+	NM
❑ MTM 2015 [M]	All of Me	1967	5.00	10.00	20.00
❑ MTS 72002 [S]	That Old Feeling	196?	5.00	10.00	20.00

20TH CENTURY FOX

Number	Title	Yr	VG	VG+	NM
❑ SF-3025 [M]	Al Martino	1959	6.25	12.50	25.00
❑ SFX-3025 [S]	Al Martino	1959	7.50	15.00	30.00
❑ SF-3032 [M]	Sing Along with Al Martino	1959	6.25	12.50	25.00
❑ SFX-3032 [S]	Sing Along with Al Martino	1959	7.50	15.00	30.00
❑ TF-4168 [M]	Al Martino Sings	196?	5.00	10.00	20.00
❑ TFS-4168 [S]	Al Martino Sings	196?	6.25	12.50	25.00
❑ TF-5009 [M]	Love Notes	196?	5.00	10.00	20.00
❑ TFS-5009 [S]	Love Notes	196?	6.25	12.50	25.00

MARVELETTES, THE
TAMLA

Number	Title	Yr	VG	VG+	NM
❑ T-228 [M]	Please Mr. Postman	1961	150.00	300.00	600.00
-- *White label*					
❑ T-228 [M]	Please Mr. Postman	1963	75.00	150.00	300.00
-- *Yellow label with globes logo*					
❑ T-229 [M]	Smash Hits of 62'	1962	600.00	900.00	1,200.
-- *Title as listed on front cover; large black "M" with song titles in circles*					
❑ T-229 [M]	The Marveletts Sing	1962	125.00	250.00	500.00
-- *Title as listed on front cover (misspelled); all-black cover with white circles*					
❑ T-229 [M]	The Marvelets Sing	1963	62.50	125.00	250.00
-- *Yellow label with side-by-side globes logo*					
❑ T-231 [M]	Playboy	1962	125.00	250.00	500.00
-- *Yellow label with overlapping record and globe logo*					
❑ T-231 [M]	Playboy	1962	150.00	300.00	600.00
-- *White label*					
❑ T-231 [M]	Playboy	1963	62.50	125.00	250.00
-- *Yellow label with side-by-side globes logo*					
❑ T-237 [M]	The Marvelous Marvelettes	1963	37.50	75.00	150.00
❑ T-243 [M]	Recorded Live On Stage	1963	20.00	40.00	80.00
❑ T-253 [M]	Greatest Hits	1966	7.50	15.00	30.00
-- *Yellow cover*					
❑ T-253 [M]	Greatest Hits	1967	6.25	12.50	25.00
-- *Green cover*					
❑ TS-253 [S]	Greatest Hits	1966	10.00	20.00	40.00
-- *Yellow cover*					
❑ TS-253 [S]	Greatest Hits	1967	5.00	10.00	20.00
-- *Green cover*					
❑ T-274 [M]	The Marvelettes	1967	7.50	15.00	30.00
❑ TS-274 [S]	The Marvelettes	1967	5.00	10.00	20.00
❑ T-286 [M]	Sophisticated Soul	1968	10.00	20.00	40.00
❑ TS-286 [S]	Sophisticated Soul	1968	5.00	10.00	20.00

MARVELOWS, THE
ABC

Number	Title	Yr	VG	VG+	NM
❑ S-643	The Mighty Marvelows	1968	7.50	15.00	30.00

MARVIN AND JOHNNY
CROWN

Number	Title	Yr	VG	VG+	NM
❑ CLP-5381 [M]	Marvin and Johnny	1963	12.50	25.00	50.00

MARX, GROUCHO
DECCA

Number	Title	Yr	VG	VG+	NM
❑ DL 5405 [10]	Hooray for Captain Spaulding	1954	62.50	125.00	250.00

MARX, HARPO
MERCURY

Number	Title	Yr	VG	VG+	NM
❑ MG-20232 [M]	Harpo in Hi-Fi	1957	12.50	25.00	50.00
❑ MG-20363 [M]	Harpo at Work!	1959	12.50	25.00	50.00
❑ SR-60016 [S]	Harpo at Work!	1959	20.00	40.00	80.00

RCA VICTOR

Number	Title	Yr	VG	VG+	NM
❑ LPM-27 [10]	Harp by Harpo	1952	37.50	75.00	150.00

WING

Number	Title	Yr	VG	VG+	NM
❑ MGW-12164 [M]	Harpo	1960	6.25	12.50	25.00

MARY BUTTERWORTH
CUSTOM FIDELITY

Number	Title	Yr	VG	VG+	NM
❑ 2092	Mary Butterworth	1969	75.00	150.00	300.00

MASEKELA, HUGH
MERCURY

Number	Title	Yr	VG	VG+	NM
❑ SR-60797 [S]	The Trumpet of Hugh Masekela	1963	5.00	10.00	20.00

UNI

Number	Title	Yr	VG	VG+	NM
❑ 3015 [M]	Hugh Masekela Is Alive and Well at the Whisky	1967	5.00	10.00	20.00

MASKED MARAUDERS, THE
Also see THE CLEANLINESS AND GODLINESS SKIFFLE BAND.
DEITY

Number	Title	Yr	VG	VG+	NM
❑ RS 6378	The Masked Marauders	1969	5.00	10.00	20.00

MASON, BARBARA
ARCTIC

Number	Title	Yr	VG	VG+	NM
❑ ALP-1000 [M]	Yes, I'm Ready	1965	7.50	15.00	30.00
❑ ALPS-1000 [P]	Yes, I'm Ready	1965	12.50	25.00	50.00
❑ ALPS-1004	Oh, How It Hurts	1968	7.50	15.00	30.00

NATIONAL GENERAL

Number	Title	Yr	VG	VG+	NM
❑ 2001	If You Knew Him Like I Do	1970	7.50	15.00	30.00

MASON, DAVE
BLUE THUMB

Number	Title	Yr	VG	VG+	NM
❑ BTS-19	All Together	1970	50.00	100.00	200.00
-- *Erroneous pressing of "Alone Together"*					
❑ BTS-19	Alone Together	1970	5.00	10.00	20.00
-- *Originals on multicolored vinyl*					
❑ BTS-8819	Alone Together	1971	12.50	25.00	50.00
-- *Capitol-distributed black vinyl reissue*					

MCA

Number	Title	Yr	VG	VG+	NM
❑ 11319	Alone Together	1995	5.00	10.00	20.00
-- *"Heavy Vinyl" gatefold reissue*					

MASON, DAVE, AND CASS ELLIOT
Also see each artist's individual listings.
BLUE THUMB

Number	Title	Yr	VG	VG+	NM
❑ BTS-8825	Dave Mason and Cass Elliot	1971	5.00	10.00	20.00

Number	Title	Yr	VG	VG+	NM

MASON, JACKIE
VERVE
❏ V-15033 [M]	I'm the Greatest Comedian in the World Only Nobody Knows It Yet	1962	5.00	10.00	20.00
❏ V-15034 [M]	I Want to Leave You with the Words of a Great Comedian	1963	5.00	10.00	20.00
❏ V-15045 [M]	Great Moments in Comedy	1964	5.00	10.00	20.00

MATHIS, COUNTRY JOHNNY
Not the same person as the famous balladeer, below.
HILLTOP
| ❏ 7004 | Hilltop Gospel | 1965 | 6.25 | 12.50 | 25.00 |
LITTLE DARLIN'
| ❏ 8007 | He Keeps Me Singin' | 1967 | 5.00 | 10.00 | 20.00 |

MATHIS, JOHNNY
Not to be confused with COUNTRY JOHNNY MATHIS, above.
COLUMBIA
❏ C2L 17 [(2) M]	The Rhythms and Ballads of Broadway	1960	6.25	12.50	25.00
-- Red and black label with six "eye" logos					
❏ C2L 17 [(2) M]	The Rhythms and Ballads of Broadway	1962	5.00	10.00	20.00
-- Red label with either "Guaranteed High Fidelity" or "360 Sound Mono"					
❏ C2S 803 [(2) S]	The Rhythms and Ballads of Broadway	1960	7.50	15.00	30.00
-- Red and black label with six "eye" logos					
❏ C2S 803 [(2) S]	The Rhythms and Ballads of Broadway	1962	6.25	12.50	25.00
-- Red "360 Sound" label					
❏ C2S 834 [(2) S]	The Great Years	1964	5.00	10.00	20.00
-- Red "360 Sound" label					
❏ CL 887 [M]	Johnny Mathis	1957	12.50	25.00	50.00
❏ CL 1028 [M]	Wonderful Wonderful	1957	7.50	15.00	30.00
-- Red and black label with six "eye" logos					
❏ CL 1078 [M]	Warm	1957	7.50	15.00	30.00
-- Red and black label with six "eye" logos					
❏ CL 1119 [M]	Good Night, Dear Lord	1958	7.50	15.00	30.00
-- Red and black label with six "eye" logos					
❏ CL 1133 [M]	Johnny's Greatest Hits	1958	7.50	15.00	30.00
-- Red and black label with six "eye" logos					
❏ CL 1165 [M]	Swing Softly	1958	7.50	15.00	30.00
-- Red and black label with six "eye" logos					
❏ CL 1195 [M]	Merry Christmas	1958	10.00	20.00	40.00
-- Original cover has Johnny standing, holding skis and poles					
❏ CL 1195 [M]	Merry Christmas	196?	7.50	15.00	30.00
-- Second cover has Johnny sitting, with skis and poles in snow					
❏ CL 1270 [M]	Open Fire, Two Guitars	1959	7.50	15.00	30.00
-- Red and black label with six "eye" logos					
❏ CL 1344 [M]	More Johnny's Greatest Hits	1959	6.25	12.50	25.00
-- Red and black label with six "eye" logos					
❏ CL 1351 [M]	Heavenly	1959	5.00	10.00	20.00
-- Red and black label with six "eye" logos					
❏ CL 1422 [M]	Faithfully	1959	5.00	10.00	20.00
-- Red and black label with six "eye" logos					
❏ CL 1526 [M]	Johnny's Mood	1960	5.00	10.00	20.00
-- Red and black label with six "eye" logos					
❏ CS 8012 [S]	Good Night, Dear Lord	1958	10.00	20.00	40.00
❏ CS 8012 [S]	Good Night, Dear Lord	1962	5.00	10.00	20.00
-- Red "360 Sound" label					
❏ CS 8021 [S]	Merry Christmas	1959	6.25	12.50	25.00
-- Original cover has Johnny standing, holding skis and poles					
❏ CS 8021 [S]	Merry Christmas	196?	5.00	10.00	20.00
-- Second cover has Johnny sitting, with skis and poles in snow					
❏ CS 8039 [S]	Warm	1958	10.00	20.00	40.00
-- Red and black label with six "eye" logos					
❏ CS 8039 [S]	Warm	1962	5.00	10.00	20.00
-- Red "360 Sound" label					
❏ CS 8056 [S]	Open Fire, Two Guitars	1959	10.00	20.00	40.00
-- Red and black label with six "eye" logos					
❏ CS 8056 [S]	Open Fire, Two Guitars	1962	5.00	10.00	20.00
-- Red "360 Sound" label					
❏ CS 8150 [S]	More Johnny's Greatest Hits	1959	7.50	15.00	30.00
-- Red and black label with six "eye" logos					
❏ CS 8150 [S]	More Johnny's Greatest Hits	1962	5.00	10.00	20.00
-- Red "360 Sound" label					
❏ CS 8152 [S]	Heavenly	1959	7.50	15.00	30.00
-- Red and black label with six "eye" logos					
❏ CS 8152 [S]	Heavenly	1962	5.00	10.00	20.00
-- Red "360 Sound" label					
❏ CS 8219 [S]	Faithfully	1959	6.25	12.50	25.00
-- Red and black label with six "eye" logos					
❏ CS 8219 [S]	Faithfully	1962	5.00	10.00	20.00
-- Red "360 Sound" label					
❏ CS 8326 [S]	Johnny's Mood	1960	6.25	12.50	25.00
-- Red and black label with six "eye" logos					
❏ CS 8326 [S]	Johnny's Mood	1962	5.00	10.00	20.00
-- Red "360 Sound" label					
❏ CS 8423 [S]	I'll Buy You a Star	1961	5.00	10.00	20.00
-- Red and black label with six "eye" logos					
❏ CS 8444 [S]	Portrait of Johnny	1961	5.00	10.00	20.00
-- Red and black label with six "eye" logos; add 1/3 if portrait is there					
❏ CS 8511 [S]	Live It Up!	1962	5.00	10.00	20.00
-- Red and black label with six "eye" logos					
❏ CQ 30740 [Q]	You've Got a Friend	1972	5.00	10.00	20.00
❏ 2CQ 30979 [(2) Q]	Johnny Mathis in Person	1972	6.25	12.50	25.00
❏ CQ 31342 [Q]	The First Time Ever (I Saw Your Face)	1972	5.00	10.00	20.00
❏ CQ 31626 [Q]	Song Sung Blue	1972	5.00	10.00	20.00
COLUMBIA MUSICAL TREASURY
| ❏ 6P 6030 [(6)] | The Johnny Mathis Treasury | 197? | 7.50 | 15.00 | 30.00 |
COLUMBIA SPECIAL PRODUCTS
❏ P3 11837 [(3)]	Romantically, Johnny Mathis	197?	6.25	12.50	25.00
❏ P6 14628 [(6)]	Misty Memories: The Complete Johnny Mathis Treasury	197?	7.50	15.00	30.00
-- Manufactured for Candelite Music					
❏ P 14658	Holidays at the Fireside	197?	5.00	10.00	20.00
-- Bonus album with box set 14628					
❏ P4 14971 [(4)]	Johnny	197?	6.25	12.50	25.00
MOBILE FIDELITY
| ❏ 1-171 | Heavenly | 1985 | 6.25 | 12.50 | 25.00 |
| -- Audiophile vinyl | | | | | |
READER'S DIGEST
| ❏ RB4-097 [(6)] | His Greatest Hits and Finest Performances | 198? | 6.25 | 12.50 | 25.00 |

MATTEA, KATHY
MERCURY
| ❏ R 110791 | A Collection of Hits | 1990 | 5.00 | 10.00 | 20.00 |
| -- Only released on vinyl by BMG Direct Marketing | | | | | |

MAUDS, THE
MERCURY
| ❏ MG-21135 [M] | The Mauds Hold On | 1967 | 5.00 | 10.00 | 20.00 |
| ❏ SR-61135 [S] | The Mauds Hold On | 1967 | 6.25 | 12.50 | 25.00 |

MAURIAT, PAUL
PHILIPS
| ❏ PHM 200-248 [M] | Blooming Hits | 1967 | 5.00 | 10.00 | 20.00 |
| ❏ PHM 200-255 [M] | The Christmas Album | 1967 | 5.00 | 10.00 | 20.00 |

MAXIMILLIAN
ABC
| ❏ S-696 | Maximillian | 1969 | 10.00 | 20.00 | 40.00 |

MAXWELL, DIANE
CHALLENGE
| ❏ CHL-607 [M] | Almost Seventeen | 1959 | 10.00 | 20.00 | 40.00 |
| ❏ CHS-2501 [S] | Almost Seventeen | 1959 | 12.50 | 25.00 | 50.00 |

MAY BLITZ
PARAMOUNT
| ❏ PAS-5020 | May Blitz | 1970 | 5.00 | 10.00 | 20.00 |

MAYALL, JOHN
LONDON
❏ PS 492 [S]	Blues Breakers with Eric Clapton	1966	10.00	20.00	40.00
❏ PS 502 [S]	A Hard Road	1967	5.00	10.00	20.00
❏ PS 529 [S]	Crusade	1967	5.00	10.00	20.00
❏ LL 3492 [M]	Blues Breakers with Eric Clapton	1966	7.50	15.00	30.00
❏ LL 3502 [M]	A Hard Road	1967	5.00	10.00	20.00
❏ LL 3529 [M]	Crusade	1967	5.00	10.00	20.00
MOBILE FIDELITY
❏ 1-183	Blues Breakers with Eric Clapton	1985	10.00	20.00	40.00
-- Audiophile vinyl					
❏ 1-246	The Blues Alone	1996	7.50	15.00	30.00
-- Audiophile vinyl					

MAYER, NATHANIEL
FORTUNE
❏ 8014 [M]	Goin' Back to the Village of Love	1964	75.00	150.00	300.00
-- Light blue label					
❏ 8014 [M]	Goin' Back to the Village of Love	196?	37.50	75.00	150.00
-- Purple label					
❏ 8014 [M]	Goin' Back to the Village of Love	196?	15.00	30.00	60.00
-- Yellow label					

MAYFIELD, CURTIS
Also see THE IMPRESSIONS.
CURTOM
| ❏ CRS-8008 [(2)] | Curtis/Live! | 1971 | 5.00 | 10.00 | 20.00 |
| ❏ CRS-8014 | Superfly | 1972 | 5.00 | 10.00 | 20.00 |

(Top left) Mickey Mantle doesn't sing a word on this album, unlike on Teresa Brewer's "I Love Mickey" single. This is a various-artists collection of songs the New York Yankee claimed were among his favorites. Today, it's a major rarity sought by both record and sports collectors. (Top right) Martin & Neil were Vince Martin, of "Cindy, Oh Cindy" fame, and Fred Neil, who wrote "Everybody's Talkin'," the future Nilsson hit. This Elektra album features the two folk singers together. (Bottom left) One of the most unlikely duet albums of all time features a former member of Traffic with a former member of the Mamas and the Papas. It actually kinda works, too. (Bottom right) In 1990, members of the Columbia House record club got a surprise: *Tripping the Live Fantastic…Highlights!,* which was only issued on cassette and CD to the general public, was issued on vinyl for club members. Better yet, the vinyl version featured a track ("All My Trials") that does not appear on the CD or cassette! Little-known to collectors is that as many as 100 albums that were otherwise not available on vinyl in the U.S. *were* issued on vinyl through either Columbia House or the BMG Music Service from 1990 through 1992.

Number	Title	Yr	VG	VG+	NM

MAYFIELD, PERCY
BRUNSWICK
❑ BL 754145	Walking on a Tightrope	1968	5.00	10.00	20.00

SPECIALTY
❑ SPS-2126	The Best of Percy Mayfield	1970	5.00	10.00	20.00

TANGERINE
❑ TRC-1505 [M]	My Jug and I	1966	5.00	10.00	20.00
❑ TRCS-1505 [S]	My Jug and I	1966	6.25	12.50	25.00
❑ TRC-1510 [M]	Bought Blues	1967	5.00	10.00	20.00
❑ TRCS-1510 [S]	Bought Blues	1967	6.25	12.50	25.00

MAYPOLE
COLOSSUS
❑ CS-1007	Maypole	1971	15.00	30.00	60.00

MAZE
MTA
❑ 5012	Armageddon	1969	25.00	50.00	100.00

MC5
ATLANTIC
❑ SD 8247	Back in the U.S.A.	1970	12.50	25.00	50.00
❑ SD 8285	High Time	1971	12.50	25.00	50.00

ELEKTRA
❑ EKS-74042	Kick Out the Jams	1969	12.50	25.00	50.00
-- Gatefold cover with John Sinclair liner notes in center spread; brownish label					
❑ EKS-74042	Kick Out the Jams	1969	5.00	10.00	20.00
-- All other editions					

McAULIFF, LEON
ABC-PARAMOUNT
❑ ABC-394 [M]	Cozy Inn	1961	10.00	20.00	40.00
❑ ABCS-394 [S]	Cozy Inn	1961	15.00	30.00	60.00

CAPITOL
❑ ST 2016 [S]	The Dancin'est Band Around	1964	10.00	20.00	40.00
❑ T 2016 [M]	The Dancin'est Band Around	1964	7.50	15.00	30.00
❑ ST 2148 [S]	Everybody Dance! Everybody Swing!	1964	10.00	20.00	40.00
❑ T 2148 [M]	Everybody Dance! Everybody Swing!	1964	7.50	15.00	30.00

CIMARRON
❑ CLP-2002 [M]	The Swingin' Western Strings of Leon McAuliff	1960	12.50	25.00	50.00

DOT
❑ DLP-3139 [M]	Take Off	1958	15.00	30.00	60.00
❑ DLP-3689 [M]	Golden Country Hits	1966	10.00	20.00	40.00
❑ DLP-25689 [R]	Golden Country Hits	1966	6.25	12.50	25.00

SESAC
❑ (# unknown) [M]	Just a Minute	1957	25.00	50.00	100.00
❑ 1601 [M]	Points West	1957	25.00	50.00	100.00

STARDAY
❑ SLP-171 [M]	Mr. Western Swing	1962	12.50	25.00	50.00
❑ SLP-280 [M]	The Swingin' West with Leon McAuliff	1964	10.00	20.00	40.00
❑ SLP-309 [M]	The Swingin' Western Strings of Leon McAuliff	1964	10.00	20.00	40.00

McCALL, TOUSSAINT
RONN
❑ 7527 [M]	Nothing Can Take the Place of You	1967	7.50	15.00	30.00
❑ 7527S [S]	Nothing Can Take the Place of You	1967	10.00	20.00	40.00

McCANN, LES
LIMELIGHT
❑ LM-82043 [M]	Bucket O' Grease	1967	5.00	10.00	20.00
❑ LM-82046 [M]	Live at the Bohemian Caverns, Washington, D.C.	1967	5.00	10.00	20.00
❑ LS-86016 [S]	But Not Really	1965	5.00	10.00	20.00
❑ LS-86025 [S]	Poo Boo	1965	5.00	10.00	20.00
❑ LS-86031 [S]	Beaux J. Pooboo	1966	5.00	10.00	20.00
❑ LS-86036 [S]	Live at Shelly's Manne-Hole	1966	5.00	10.00	20.00
❑ LS-86041 [S]	Les McCann Plays the Hits	1966	5.00	10.00	20.00

PACIFIC JAZZ
❑ PJ-2 [M]	The Truth	1960	6.25	12.50	25.00
❑ ST-2 [S]	The Truth	1960	7.50	15.00	30.00
❑ PJ-7 [M]	The Shout	1960	6.25	12.50	25.00
❑ ST-7 [S]	The Shout	1960	7.50	15.00	30.00
❑ PJ-16 [M]	Les McCann in San Francisco	1961	6.25	12.50	25.00
❑ ST-16 [S]	Les McCann in San Francisco	1961	7.50	15.00	30.00
❑ PJ-25 [M]	Pretty Lady	1961	5.00	10.00	20.00
❑ ST-25 [S]	Pretty Lady	1961	6.25	12.50	25.00
❑ PJ-31 [M]	Les McCann Sings	1961	5.00	10.00	20.00
❑ ST-31 [S]	Les McCann Sings	1961	6.25	12.50	25.00
❑ PJ-45 [M]	Les McCann in New York	1962	5.00	10.00	20.00
❑ ST-45 [S]	Les McCann in New York	1962	6.25	12.50	25.00
❑ PJ-56 [M]	On Time	1962	10.00	20.00	40.00
-- Yellow vinyl					
❑ PJ-56 [M]	On Time	1962	5.00	10.00	20.00
-- Black vinyl					
❑ ST-56 [S]	On Time	1962	12.50	25.00	50.00
-- Yellow vinyl					
❑ ST-56 [S]	On Time	1962	6.25	12.50	25.00
-- Black vinyl					
❑ ST-63 [S]	Shampoo	1962	5.00	10.00	20.00
❑ ST-69 [S]	The Gospel Truth	1963	5.00	10.00	20.00
❑ ST-78 [S]	Soul Hits	1963	5.00	10.00	20.00
❑ ST-81 [S]	Jazz Waltz	1964	5.00	10.00	20.00
❑ ST-84 [S]	McCanna	1964	5.00	10.00	20.00
❑ ST-91 [S]	McCann/Wilson	1965	5.00	10.00	20.00
-- With Gerald Wilson					
❑ ST-20097 [S]	Spanish Onions	1966	5.00	10.00	20.00
❑ ST-20107 [S]	A Bag of Gold	1966	5.00	10.00	20.00

McCARTNEY, PAUL
Includes Thrillington and Wings. Also see THE BEATLES.
APPLE
❑ SMAS-3363	McCartney	197?	5.00	10.00	20.00
-- New prefix on label					
❑ SMAS-3363	McCartney	1975	25.00	50.00	100.00
-- With "All Rights Reserved" on label					
❑ STAO-3363	McCartney	1970	20.00	40.00	80.00
-- Apple label with small Capitol logo on B-side					
❑ STAO-3363	McCartney	1970	7.50	15.00	30.00
-- "McCartney" and "Paul McCartney" on separate lines on label; California address on back cover					
❑ STAO-3363	McCartney	1970	6.25	12.50	25.00
-- "McCartney" and "Paul McCartney" on separate lines on label; New York address on back cover					
❑ STAO-3363	McCartney	1970	6.25	12.50	25.00
-- Only "McCartney" on label; back cover says "An Abkco managed company"					
❑ STAO-3363	McCartney	1970	5.00	10.00	20.00
-- Only "McCartney" on label; back cover does NOT say "An Abkco managed company"					
❑ MAS-3375 [M]	Ram	1971	1,000.	2,000.	4,000.
-- Credited to "Paul and Linda McCartney"; mono record in stereo cover for radio station use only					
❑ SMAS-3375	Ram	1971	12.50	25.00	50.00
-- Credited to "Paul and Linda McCartney"; Apple label with small Capitol logo on B-side					
❑ SMAS-3375	Ram	1971	7.50	15.00	30.00
-- Credited to "Paul and Linda McCartney"; unsliced apple on both labels					
❑ SMAS-3375	Ram	1975	25.00	50.00	100.00
-- Credited to "Paul and Linda McCartney"; with "All Rights Reserved" on label					
❑ SMAL-3409	Red Rose Speedway	1973	5.00	10.00	20.00
-- Credited to "Paul McCartney and Wings"; with bound-in booklet					
❑ SO-3415	Band on the Run	1973	5.00	10.00	20.00
-- Credited to "Paul McCartney and Wings"; with photo innersleeve and poster					
❑ SPRO-6210	Brung to Ewe By	1971	100.00	200.00	400.00
-- Promo-only radio spots for "Ram"; counterfeits have uneven spacing between tracks					

CAPITOL
❑ SMAS-3363	McCartney	1976	6.25	12.50	25.00
-- Black label, "Manufactured by McCartney Music Inc" at top					
❑ SMAS-3363	McCartney	1976	5.00	10.00	20.00
-- Black label, "Manufactured by MPL Communications Inc" at top					
❑ SMAS-3375	Ram	1976	7.50	15.00	30.00
-- Credited to "Paul and Linda McCartney"; black label, "Manufactured by McCartney Music Inc" at top					
❑ SMAS-3375	Ram	197?	5.00	10.00	20.00
-- Credited to "Paul and Linda McCartney"; black label, "Manufactured by MPL Communications Inc" at top					
❑ SMAS-3375	Ram	197?	10.00	20.00	40.00
-- Credited to "Paul and Linda McCartney"; black label, "Manufactured by Capitol Records..." on label					
❑ SW-3386	Wild Life	1976	7.50	15.00	30.00
-- Credited to "Wings"; black label, "Manufactured by McCartney Music Inc" at top					
❑ SW-3386	Wild Life	197?	5.00	10.00	20.00
-- Credited to "Wings"; black label, "Manufactured by MPL Communications Inc" at top					
❑ SMAL-3409	Red Rose Speedway	1976	7.50	15.00	30.00
-- Credited to "Paul McCartney and Wings"; black label, "Manufactured by McCartney Music Inc" at top					
❑ SMAL-3409	Red Rose Speedway	197?	6.25	12.50	25.00
-- Credited to "Paul McCartney and Wings"; black label, "Manufactured by MPL Communications Inc" at top					
❑ SO-3415	Band on the Run	1975	5.00	10.00	20.00
-- Credited to "Paul McCartney and Wings"; custom label with MPL logo					
❑ SO-3415	Band on the Run	197?	12.50	25.00	50.00
-- Credited to "Paul McCartney and Wings"; black label, "Manufactured by Capitol Records..."					
❑ SO-3415	Band on the Run	197?	5.00	10.00	20.00
-- Credited to "Paul McCartney and Wings"; black label, "Maunfactured by MPL Communications Inc." at top					
❑ SW-11525 [DJ]	Wings at the Speed of Sound	1976	75.00	150.00	300.00
-- Credited to "Wings"; white label advance promo					
❑ SWCO-11593 [(3)]	Wings Over America	1976	6.25	12.50	25.00
-- Credited to "Wings"; custom labels with poster					
❑ ST-11642	Thrillington	1977	25.00	50.00	100.00
-- Credited to "Percy 'Thrills' Thrillington"; instrumental versions of songs from Ram LP					

Number	Title	Yr	VG	VG+	NM
❏ SEAX-11901[PD] Band on the Run		1978	10.00	20.00	40.00
-- Credited to "Paul McCartney and Wings"; picture disc					
❏ SOO-11905 [DJ] Wings Greatest		1978	100.00	200.00	400.00
-- Credited to "Wings"; white label advance promo/test pressing					
❏ CLW-48287 [(2)] All the Best!		1987	5.00	10.00	20.00
❏ C1-91653 Flowers in the Dirt		1989	5.00	10.00	20.00
❏ C1-94778 [(3)] Tripping the Live Fantastic		1990	15.00	30.00	60.00
❏ C1-595379 Tripping the Live Fantastic -- Highlights!		1990	6.25	12.50	25.00
-- Released on vinyl only through Columbia House; with U.S. address on back cover					
❏ C1-595379 Tripping the Live Fantastic -- Highlights!		1990	6.25	12.50	25.00
-- Released on vinyl only through Columbia House; with Canada address on back cover, this was sold in the U.S. by Columbia House					
COLUMBIA					
❏ A2S 821 [(2)] The McCartney Interview		1980	10.00	20.00	40.00
-- Promo-only set; one LP is the entire interview, the other is banded for airplay; white labels with black print; counterfeits have blank white labels					
❏ FC 36057 [DJ] Back to the Egg		1979	10.00	20.00	40.00
-- Credited to "Wings"; "Demonstration -- Not for Sale" on custom label					
❏ PC 36057 Back to the Egg		1984	7.50	15.00	30.00
-- Credited to "Wings"; "PC" cover with "FC" label					
❏ PC 36057 Back to the Egg		1984	10.00	20.00	40.00
-- Credited to "Wings"; "PC" cover with "PC" label					
❏ JC 36482 Band on the Run		198?	25.00	50.00	100.00
-- Credited to "Paul McCartney and Wings"; white "MPL" logo on lower left front cover					
❏ PC 36482 Band on the Run		198?	5.00	10.00	20.00
-- Credited to "Paul McCartney and Wings"; "PC" cover with "JC" label					
❏ PC 36482 Band on the Run		198?	7.50	15.00	30.00
-- Credited to "Paul McCartney and Wings"; "PC" cover with "PC" label					
❏ FC 36511 [DJ] McCartney II		1980	7.50	15.00	30.00
-- White label promo					
❏ PC 36511 McCartney II		1984	6.25	12.50	25.00
-- "PC" cover with "FC" label					
❏ PC 36511 McCartney II		1984	25.00	50.00	100.00
-- "PC" cover with "PC" label					
❏ PC 37462 Tug of War		1984	7.50	15.00	30.00
-- Custom label; "PC" cover with "TC" label					
❏ PC 37462 Tug of War		1984	25.00	50.00	100.00
-- Regular Columbia label; "PC" cover with "PC" label					
❏ C3X 37990 [(3)]Wings Over America		1982	12.50	25.00	50.00
-- Credited to "Wings"; custom labels, no poster					
❏ HC 46382 Band on the Run		1981	12.50	25.00	50.00
-- Credited to "Paul McCartney and Wings"; half-speed mastered edition					
MPL/PARLOPHONE					
❏ 96413 Unplugged (The Official Bootleg)		1991	18.75	37.50	75.00
-- No U.S. pressings; "American" copies were U.K. imports with liner notes in Spanish!					
NATIONAL FEATURES CORP.					
❏ 2955/6 Band on the Run Radio Interview Special		1973	375.00	750.00	1,500.
-- Promo-only interview disc					

McCLINTON, DELBERT
ABC

Number	Title	Yr	VG	VG+	NM
❏ ABCD-907	Victim of Life's Circumstances	1975	5.00	10.00	20.00
❏ ABCD-959	Genuine Cowhide	1976	5.00	10.00	20.00
❏ ABCD-991	Love Rustler	1977	5.00	10.00	20.00
CAPRICORN					
❏ CPN-0201	Second Wind	1978	5.00	10.00	20.00

McCLINTON, O.B.
ENTERPRISE

Number	Title	Yr	VG	VG+	NM
❏ ENS-1023	Country	1972	7.50	15.00	30.00
❏ ENS-1029	Obie from Senatobie	1973	7.50	15.00	30.00
❏ ENS-1037	Live at Randy's Rodeo	1973	7.50	15.00	30.00
❏ ENS-7506	If You Loved Her That Way	1974	6.25	12.50	25.00

McCORMICK BROTHERS, THE
HICKORY

Number	Title	Yr	VG	VG+	NM
❏ LP-102 [M]	Songs for Home Folks	1961	20.00	40.00	80.00
❏ LP-108 [M]	Authentic Bluegrass Hits	1962	15.00	30.00	60.00
METROMEDIA					
❏ MM-1019	Grass Meets Brass	1969	5.00	10.00	20.00

McCOY, VAN
COLUMBIA

Number	Title	Yr	VG	VG+	NM
❏ CL 2497 [M]	Night Time Is the Lonely Time	1966	5.00	10.00	20.00
❏ CS 9297 [S]	Night Time Is the Lonely Time	1966	6.25	12.50	25.00

McCOYS, THE
Also see RICK DERRINGER.
BANG

Number	Title	Yr	VG	VG+	NM
❏ BLP-212 [M]	Hang On Sloopy	1965	7.50	15.00	30.00
❏ BLPS-212 [S]	Hang On Sloopy	1965	10.00	20.00	40.00
❏ BLP-213 [M]	You Make Me Feel So Good	1966	7.50	15.00	30.00
❏ BLPS-213 [S]	You Make Me Feel So Good	1966	10.00	20.00	40.00
MERCURY					
❏ SR-61163	Infinite McCoys	1968	6.25	12.50	25.00
❏ SR-61207	Human Ball	1969	6.25	12.50	25.00

McCRACKLIN, JIMMY
CHESS

Number	Title	Yr	VG	VG+	NM
❏ LP-1464 [M]	Jimmy McCracklin Sings	1961	30.00	60.00	120.00
CROWN					
❏ CLP-5244 [M]	Twist with Jimmy McCracklin	1962	12.50	25.00	50.00
-- Black label, silver "Crown"					
❏ CLP-5244 [M]	Twist with Jimmy McCracklin	1962	6.25	12.50	25.00
-- Gray label					
IMPERIAL					
❏ LP-9219 [M]	I Just Gotta Know	1964	6.25	12.50	25.00
❏ LP-9285 [M]	Every Night, Every Day	1965	6.25	12.50	25.00
❏ LP-9297 [M]	Think	1965	6.25	12.50	25.00
❏ LP-9306 [M]	My Answer	1966	6.25	12.50	25.00
❏ LP-9316 [M]	The New Soul of Jimmy	1966	6.25	12.50	25.00
❏ LP-12219 [S]	I Just Gotta Know	1964	7.50	15.00	30.00
❏ LP-12285 [S]	Every Night, Every Day	1965	7.50	15.00	30.00
❏ LP-12297 [S]	Think	1965	7.50	15.00	30.00
❏ LP-12306 [S]	My Answer	1966	7.50	15.00	30.00
❏ LP-12316 [S]	The New Soul of Jimmy	1966	7.50	15.00	30.00
MINIT					
❏ LP-4009 [M]	The Best of Jimmy McCracklin	1967	7.50	15.00	30.00
❏ LP-24009 [S]	The Best of Jimmy McCracklin	1967	6.25	12.50	25.00
❏ LP-24011	Let's Get Together	1968	6.25	12.50	25.00
❏ LP-24017	Stinger Man	1969	6.25	12.50	25.00
STAX					
❏ STS-2047	Yesterday Is Gone	1972	5.00	10.00	20.00

McCULLOCH, DANNY
CAPITOL

Number	Title	Yr	VG	VG+	NM
❏ ST-174	Wings of a Man	1969	5.00	10.00	20.00

McCURDY, ED
DAWN

Number	Title	Yr	VG	VG+	NM
❏ DLP-1127 [M]	The Folk Singer	195?	7.50	15.00	30.00
ELEKTRA					
❏ EKL-24 [10]	Sin Songs -- Pro and Con	1955	10.00	20.00	40.00
❏ EKL-108 [M]	Blood Booze 'n' Bones	1956	7.50	15.00	30.00
❏ EKL-110 [M]	When Dalliance Was In Flower 1	1956	7.50	15.00	30.00
❏ EKL-112 [M]	Songs of the Old West	1956	7.50	15.00	30.00
❏ EKL-124 [M]	Sin Songs -- Pro and Con	1957	7.50	15.00	30.00
-- Reissue of EKL-24 with extra tracks					
❏ EKL-140 [M]	When Dalliance Was In Flower 2	1958	7.50	15.00	30.00
❏ EKL-160 [M]	When Dalliance Was In Flower 3	1959	7.50	15.00	30.00
❏ EKL-170 [M]	Son of Dalliance	1959	7.50	15.00	30.00
❏ EKL-205 [M]	A Treasure Chest of American Folk Song	1961	6.25	12.50	25.00
❏ EKL-213 [(2) M]	The Best of Dalliance	1961	7.50	15.00	30.00
❏ EKS-7160 [S]	When Dalliance Was In Flower 3	1959	10.00	20.00	40.00
RIVERSIDE					
❏ RLP 12-601 [M]	The Ballad Record	195?	7.50	15.00	30.00
TRADITION					
❏ TLP-1003 [M]	A Ballad Singer's Choice	195?	7.50	15.00	30.00
❏ TLP-1027 [M]	Children's Songs	195?	7.50	15.00	30.00
❏ TLP-2061 [M]	Songs of the West	196?	5.00	10.00	20.00

McCURDY, ED; JACK ELLIOTT; OSCAR BRAND
Also see each artist's individual listings.
ELEKTRA

Number	Title	Yr	VG	VG+	NM
❏ EKL-14 [10]	Badmen and Heroes	1955	12.50	25.00	50.00

McCURDY, ED; JACK ELLIOTT; OSCAR BRAND; DICK WILDER
Also see each artist's individual listings.
ELEKTRA

Number	Title	Yr	VG	VG+	NM
❏ EKL-129 [M]	Badmen, Heroes and Pirate Songs	1957	7.50	15.00	30.00

McCURN, GEORGE
A&M

Number	Title	Yr	VG	VG+	NM
❏ LP-102 [M]	The Country Boy Comes to Town	1963	6.25	12.50	25.00

McDANIEL, WILLARD
CROWN

Number	Title	Yr	VG	VG+	NM
❏ CLP-5024 [M]	88 A La Carte	1958	25.00	50.00	100.00

Number	Title	Yr	VG	VG+	NM

McDANIELS, GENE
LIBERTY

Number	Title	Yr	VG	VG+	NM
❏ LRP-3146 [M]	In Times Like These	1960	7.50	15.00	30.00
❏ LRP-3175 [M]	Sometimes I'm Happy, Sometimes I'm Blue	1960	7.50	15.00	30.00
❏ LRP-3191 [M]	100 Lbs. of Clay!	1961	7.50	15.00	30.00
❏ LRP-3204 [M]	Gene McDaniels Sings Movie Memories	1962	7.50	15.00	30.00
❏ LRP-3215 [M]	Tower of Strength	1962	7.50	15.00	30.00
❏ LRP-3258 [M]	Hit After Hit	1962	7.50	15.00	30.00
❏ LRP-3275 [M]	Spanish Lace	1963	6.25	12.50	25.00
❏ LRP-3311 [M]	The Wonderful World of Gene McDaniels	1963	6.25	12.50	25.00
❏ LST-7146 [S]	In Times Like These	1960	50.00	100.00	200.00
-- *Blue vinyl*					
❏ LST-7146 [S]	In Times Like These	1960	10.00	20.00	40.00
-- *Black vinyl*					
❏ LST-7175 [S]	Sometimes I'm Happy, Sometimes I'm Blue	1960	10.00	20.00	40.00
❏ LST-7191 [S]	100 Lbs. of Clay!	1961	10.00	20.00	40.00
❏ LST-7204 [S]	Gene McDaniels Sings Movie Memories	1962	10.00	20.00	40.00
❏ LST-7215 [S]	Tower of Strength	1962	10.00	20.00	40.00
❏ LST-7258 [S]	Hit After Hit	1962	10.00	20.00	40.00
❏ LST-7275 [S]	Spanish Lace	1963	7.50	15.00	30.00
❏ LST-7311 [S]	The Wonderful World of Gene McDaniels	1963	7.50	15.00	30.00

McDONALD, COUNTRY JOE -- See COUNTRY JOE AND THE FISH.

McDONALD, KATHI
CAPITOL

Number	Title	Yr	VG	VG+	NM
❏ ST-11224	Insane Asylum	1974	7.50	15.00	30.00

McDONALD, MARIE
RCA VICTOR

Number	Title	Yr	VG	VG+	NM
❏ LPM-1585 [M]	"The Body" Sings!	1957	12.50	25.00	50.00

McDONALD, MICHAEL
Also see THE DOOBIE BROTHERS.
MOBILE FIDELITY

Number	Title	Yr	VG	VG+	NM
❏ 1-149	If That's What It Takes	1985	5.00	10.00	20.00
-- *Audiophile vinyl*					

McDONALD, SKEETS
CAPITOL

Number	Title	Yr	VG	VG+	NM
❏ T 1040 [M]	Goin' Steady with the Blues	1958	20.00	40.00	80.00
❏ T 1179 [M]	The Country's Best	1959	12.50	25.00	50.00
COLUMBIA					
❏ CL 2170 [M]	Call Me Skeets	1964	6.25	12.50	25.00
❏ CS 8970 [S]	Call Me Skeets	1964	7.50	15.00	30.00
FORTUNE					
❏ 3001	The Tattooed Lady and Other Songs	1969	12.50	25.00	50.00
SEARS					
❏ SPS-116 [R]	Skeets	196?	6.25	12.50	25.00

McDOWELL, MISSISSIPPI FRED
ARHOOLIE

Number	Title	Yr	VG	VG+	NM
❏ F-1021 [M]	Delta Blues	1964	12.50	25.00	50.00
❏ F-1027 [M]	Delta Blues, Volume 2	1966	12.50	25.00	50.00
❏ F-1046	Mississippi Fred McDowell and His Blues Boys	1970	7.50	15.00	30.00
❏ F-1068	Keep Your Lamp Trimmed and Burning	1973	5.00	10.00	20.00
CAPITOL					
❏ ST-403	I Do Not Play No Rock and Roll	1970	6.25	12.50	25.00
MILESTONE					
❏ MLP-3003 [M]	Long Way from Home	1966	7.50	15.00	30.00
❏ MLS-93003 [S]	Long Way from Home	1966	10.00	20.00	40.00
SIRE					
❏ SES-97018	Mississippi Fred McDowell in London	1970	7.50	15.00	30.00

McDOWELL, RONNIE
SCORPION

Number	Title	Yr	VG	VG+	NM
❏ 8021	The King Is Gone	1977	5.00	10.00	20.00

McDUFF, JACK
ATLANTIC

Number	Title	Yr	VG	VG+	NM
❏ 1472 [M]	Tobacco Road	1967	5.00	10.00	20.00
❏ SD 1463 [S]	A Change Is Gonna Come	1966	5.00	10.00	20.00

PRESTIGE

Number	Title	Yr	VG	VG+	NM
❏ PRLP-7174 [M]	Brother Jack	1960	12.50	25.00	50.00
❏ PRLP-7185 [M]	Tough 'Duff	1960	12.50	25.00	50.00
❏ PRLP-7199 [M]	The Honeydripper	1961	12.50	25.00	50.00
❏ PRLP-7220 [M]	Goodnight, It's Time to Go	1961	10.00	20.00	40.00
❏ PRST-7220 [S]	Goodnight, It's Time to Go	1961	10.00	20.00	40.00
❏ PRLP-7228 [M]	Mellow Gravy -- Brother Jack Meets the Boss	1962	10.00	20.00	40.00
❏ PRST-7228 [S]	Mellow Gravy -- Brother Jack Meets the Boss	1962	10.00	20.00	40.00
❏ PRLP-7259 [M]	Screamin'	1963	10.00	20.00	40.00
❏ PRST-7259 [S]	Screamin'	1963	10.00	20.00	40.00
❏ PRLP-7265 [M]	Somethin' Slick!	1963	10.00	20.00	40.00
❏ PRST-7265 [S]	Somethin' Slick!	1963	10.00	20.00	40.00
❏ PRLP-7274 [M]	Live!	1963	10.00	20.00	40.00
❏ PRST-7274 [S]	Live!	1963	10.00	20.00	40.00
❏ PRLP-7286 [M]	Live! At the Jazz Workshop	1964	10.00	20.00	40.00
❏ PRST-7286 [S]	Live! At the Jazz Workshop	1964	10.00	20.00	40.00
❏ PRLP-7323 [M]	Dynamic!	1964	10.00	20.00	40.00
❏ PRST-7323 [S]	Dynamic!	1964	10.00	20.00	40.00
❏ PRLP-7333 [M]	Prelude	1964	6.25	12.50	25.00
❏ PRST-7333 [S]	Prelude	1964	7.50	15.00	30.00
❏ PRLP-7362 [M]	The Concert McDuff Recorded Live!	1965	6.25	12.50	25.00
❏ PRST-7362 [S]	The Concert McDuff Recorded Live!	1965	7.50	15.00	30.00
❏ PRLP-7404 [M]	Silk and Soul	1965	6.25	12.50	25.00
❏ PRST-7404 [S]	Silk and Soul	1965	7.50	15.00	30.00
❏ PRLP-7422 [M]	Hot Barbeque	1966	5.00	10.00	20.00
❏ PRST-7422 [S]	Hot Barbeque	1966	6.25	12.50	25.00
❏ PRLP-7476 [M]	Walk On By	1967	6.25	12.50	25.00
❏ PRST-7476 [S]	Walk On By	1967	5.00	10.00	20.00
❏ PRLP-7481 [M]	Brother Jack McDuff's Greatest Hits	1967	6.25	12.50	25.00
❏ PRST-7481 [S]	Brother Jack McDuff's Greatest Hits	1967	5.00	10.00	20.00
❏ PRLP-7492 [M]	Hallelujah Time!	1967	6.25	12.50	25.00
❏ PRST-7492 [S]	Hallelujah Time!	1967	5.00	10.00	20.00
❏ PRST-7529	The Midnight Sun	1968	5.00	10.00	20.00
❏ PRST-7567	Soul Circle	1968	5.00	10.00	20.00
❏ PRST-7596	Jack McDuff Plays for Beautiful People	1969	5.00	10.00	20.00
❏ PRST-7642	I Got a Woman	1969	5.00	10.00	20.00
❏ PRST-7666	Steppin' Out	1969	5.00	10.00	20.00
❏ PRST-7703	Live! The Best of Brother Jack McDuff	1969	5.00	10.00	20.00

McENTIRE, REBA
MCA

Number	Title	Yr	VG	VG+	NM
❏ 1P-8162	For My Broken Heart	1991	6.25	12.50	25.00
-- *Only released on vinyl through Columbia House*					
❏ 10016	Rumor Has It	1990	5.00	10.00	20.00
❏ R 244602 [(2)]	Reba Live	1989	6.25	12.50	25.00
-- *Only released on vinyl through BMG Direct Marketing*					
MERCURY					
❏ SRM-1-1177	Reba McEntire	1977	25.00	50.00	100.00
❏ SRM-1-4047	Unlimited	1982	6.25	12.50	25.00
❏ SRM-1-5002	Reba McEntire	1977	10.00	20.00	40.00
-- *Reissue of 1177*					
❏ SRM-1-5017	Out of a Dream	1979	10.00	20.00	40.00
❏ SRM-1-5029	Feel the Fire	1980	7.50	15.00	30.00
❏ SRM-1-6003	Heart to Heart	1981	7.50	15.00	30.00
❏ 812 781-1	Behind the Scene	1983	5.00	10.00	20.00

McFADDEN, BOB
BRUNSWICK

Number	Title	Yr	VG	VG+	NM
❏ BL 54056 [M]	Songs Our Mummy Taught Us	1959	50.00	100.00	200.00
❏ BL 754056 [S]	Songs Our Mummy Taught Us	1959	75.00	150.00	300.00

McFARLAND, GARY
IMPULSE!

Number	Title	Yr	VG	VG+	NM
❏ A-46 [M]	Points of Departure	1963	5.00	10.00	20.00
❏ AS-46 [S]	Points of Departure	1963	6.25	12.50	25.00
❏ A-9104 [M]	Tijuana Jazz	1966	5.00	10.00	20.00
❏ AS-9104 [S]	Tijuana Jazz	1966	6.25	12.50	25.00
❏ A-9112 [M]	Profiles	1966	5.00	10.00	20.00
❏ AS-9112 [S]	Profiles	1966	6.25	12.50	25.00
❏ A-9122 [M]	Simpatico	1966	5.00	10.00	20.00
❏ AS-9122 [S]	Simpatico	1966	6.25	12.50	25.00
VERVE					
❏ V6-8443 [S]	How to Succeed in Business Without Really Trying	1962	5.00	10.00	20.00
❏ V6-8518 [S]	The Gary McFarland Orchestra with Special Guest Soloist Bill Evans	1963	5.00	10.00	20.00
❏ V6-8603 [S]	Soft Samba	1964	5.00	10.00	20.00
❏ V6-8632 [S]	The "In" Sound	1965	5.00	10.00	20.00
❏ V6-8682 [S]	Soft Samba Strings	1966	5.00	10.00	20.00
❏ V-8738 [M]	Scorpio and Other Signs	1967	5.00	10.00	20.00

McGEE, SAM AND KIRK, AND THE CROOK BROTHERS
STARDAY

Number	Title	Yr	VG	VG+	NM
❏ SLP-182 [M]	Opry Old Timers	1962	10.00	20.00	40.00

Number	Title	Yr	VG	VG+	NM

McGHEE, BROWNIE
BLUESVILLE
❏ BVLP-1042 [M]	Brownie's Blues	1962	20.00	40.00	80.00
	-- Blue label, silver print				
❏ BVLP-1042 [M]	Brownie's Blues	1964	6.25	12.50	25.00
	-- Blue label, trident logo at right				
FOLKWAYS
| ❏ FP-30 [10] | Brownie McGhee Blues | 1951 | 30.00 | 60.00 | 120.00 |
| ❏ FA-2030 [10] | Brownie McGhee Blues | 1951 | 25.00 | 50.00 | 100.00 |

McGHEE, BROWNIE, AND SONNY TERRY – See SONNY TERRY AND BROWNIE McGHEE.

McGHEE, STICK, AND JOHN LEE HOOKER
Also see JOHN LEE HOOKER.
AUDIO LAB
| ❏ AL-1520 [M] | Highway of Blues | 1959 | 87.50 | 175.00 | 350.00 |

McGRIFF, JIMMY
SOLID STATE
❏ SM-17006 [M]	Cherry	1967	5.00	10.00	20.00
❏ SS-18001 [S]	The Big Band of Jimmy McGriff	1966	5.00	10.00	20.00
❏ SS-18002 [S]	A Bag Full of Soul	1966	5.00	10.00	20.00
❏ SS-18006 [S]	Cherry	1967	5.00	10.00	20.00
❏ SS-18017	A Bag Full of Blues	1968	5.00	10.00	20.00
❏ SS-18030	I've Got a New Woman	1968	5.00	10.00	20.00
❏ SS-18036	Honey	1968	5.00	10.00	20.00
❏ SS-18045	The Worm	1968	5.00	10.00	20.00
❏ SS-18053	Step I	1969	5.00	10.00	20.00
❏ SS-18060	A Thing to Come By	1969	5.00	10.00	20.00
❏ SS-18063	The Way You Look Tonight	1970	5.00	10.00	20.00
SUE
❏ LP-1012 [M]	I've Got a Woman	1962	7.50	15.00	30.00
❏ SLP-1012 [S]	I've Got a Woman	1962	10.00	20.00	40.00
❏ LP-1017 [M]	Jimmy McGriff at the Apollo	1963	7.50	15.00	30.00
❏ SLP-1017 [S]	Jimmy McGriff at the Apollo	1963	10.00	20.00	40.00
❏ LP-1020 [M]	Jimmy McGriff at the Organ	1963	7.50	15.00	30.00
❏ SLP-1020 [S]	Jimmy McGriff at the Organ	1963	10.00	20.00	40.00
❏ LP-1033 [M]	Topkapi	1964	7.50	15.00	30.00
❏ SLP-1033 [S]	Topkapi	1964	10.00	20.00	40.00
❏ LP-1039 [M]	Blues for Mister Jimmy	1965	7.50	15.00	30.00
❏ SLP-1039 [S]	Blues for Mister Jimmy	1965	10.00	20.00	40.00

McGUINN, ROGER
Also see THE BYRDS.
COLUMBIA
| ❏ AS 353 [DJ] | The Roger McGuinn Airplay Anthology | 1977 | 7.50 | 15.00 | 30.00 |
| | *-- Promo only; also includes Byrds tracks* | | | | |

McGUIRE SISTERS, THE
Also see PHYLLIS McGUIRE.
ABC-PARAMOUNT
| ❏ S-530 [S] | The McGuire Sisters Today | 1966 | 5.00 | 10.00 | 20.00 |
CORAL
❏ CXB 6 [(2) M]	The Best of the McGuire Sisters	1965	6.25	12.50	25.00
❏ 7CXB 6 [(2) P]	The Best of the McGuire Sisters	1965	6.25	12.50	25.00
❏ CRL 56123 [10]	By Request	1955	12.50	25.00	50.00
❏ CRL 57026 [M]	Do You Remember When	1956	10.00	20.00	40.00
❏ CRL 57028 [M]	'S Wonderful	1956	10.00	20.00	40.00
❏ CRL 57033 [M]	He	1956	10.00	20.00	40.00
❏ CRL 57052 [M]	Sincerely	1956	10.00	20.00	40.00
❏ CRL 57097 [M]	Children's Holiday	1956	10.00	20.00	40.00
❏ CRL 57134 [M]	Teenage Party	1957	7.50	15.00	30.00
❏ CRL 57145 [M]	While the Lights Are Low	1957	7.50	15.00	30.00
❏ CRL 57180 [M]	Musical Magic	1957	7.50	15.00	30.00
❏ CRL 57217 [M]	Sugartime	1958	7.50	15.00	30.00
❏ CRL 57225 [M]	Greetings from the McGuire	1958	7.50	15.00	30.00
❏ CRL 57296 [M]	May You Always	1959	5.00	10.00	20.00
❏ CRL 57303 [M]	In Harmony with Him	1959	6.25	12.50	25.00
❏ CRL 57337 [M]	His and Hers	1960	5.00	10.00	20.00
❏ CRL 57349 [M]	Our Golden Favorites	1961	5.00	10.00	20.00
❏ CRL 57385 [M]	Just for Old Times' Sake	1961	5.00	10.00	20.00
❏ CRL 57443 [M]	Showcase	196?	5.00	10.00	20.00
❏ CRL 757296 [S]	May You Always	1959	7.50	15.00	30.00
❏ CRL 757303 [S]	In Harmony with Him	1959	10.00	20.00	40.00
❏ CRL 757337 [S]	His and Hers	1960	7.50	15.00	30.00
❏ CRL 757385 [S]	Just for Old Times' Sake	1961	7.50	15.00	30.00
❏ CRL 757398 [S]	Subways Are for Sleeping	1961	5.00	10.00	20.00
❏ CRL 757415 [S]	Songs Everybody Knows	1962	5.00	10.00	20.00
VOCALION
| ❏ VL 3685 [M] | Children's Holiday | 1960 | 5.00 | 10.00 | 20.00 |

McGUIRE, BARRY
Also see THE NEW CHRISTY MINSTRELS.
ABC DUNHILL
| ❏ DS-50033 | The World's Last Private Citizen | 1968 | 6.25 | 12.50 | 25.00 |
DUNHILL
❏ D-50003 [M]	Eve of Destruction	1965	7.50	15.00	30.00
❏ DS-50003 [S]	Eve of Destruction	1965	10.00	20.00	40.00
❏ D-50005 [M]	This Precious Time	1966	6.25	12.50	25.00
❏ DS-50005 [S]	This Precious Time	1966	7.50	15.00	30.00
HORIZON
| ❏ ST-1636 [S] | The Barry McGuire Album | 1963 | 10.00 | 20.00 | 40.00 |
| ❏ WP-1636 [M] | The Barry McGuire Album | 1963 | 7.50 | 15.00 | 30.00 |
MIRA
❏ LP-3000 [M]	The Barry McGuire Album	1965	5.00	10.00	20.00
	-- Reissue of Horizon LP				
❏ LPS-3000 [S]	The Barry McGuire Album	1965	6.25	12.50	25.00
	-- Reissue of Horizon LP				

McGUIRE, BARRY, AND BARRY KANE
HORIZON
| ❏ SWP-1608 [S] | Barry and Barry: Here and Now! | 1962 | 7.50 | 15.00 | 30.00 |
| ❏ WP-1608 [M] | Barry and Barry: Here and Now! | 1962 | 6.25 | 12.50 | 25.00 |

McGUIRE, PHYLLIS
Also see THE McGUIRE SISTERS.
ABC-PARAMOUNT
| ❏ S-552 [S] | Phyllis McGuire Sings | 1966 | 5.00 | 10.00 | 20.00 |

McKAY, SCOTTY
ACE
| ❏ LP-1017 [M] | Tonight In Person | 1961 | 20.00 | 40.00 | 80.00 |

McKENZIE, SCOTT
ODE
| ❏ Z12 44002 [S] | The Voice of Scott McKenzie | 1967 | 6.25 | 12.50 | 25.00 |

McKUEN, ROD
CAPITOL
| ❏ ST 2079 [S] | Rod McKuen Sings Rod McKuen | 1964 | 5.00 | 10.00 | 20.00 |
DECCA
❏ DL 4969 [M]	Very Warm	1968	5.00	10.00	20.00
❏ DL 8882 [M]	Anywhere I Wander	1958	5.00	10.00	20.00
❏ DL 8946 [M]	Alone After Dark	1959	5.00	10.00	20.00
❏ DL 78882 [S]	Anywhere I Wander	1958	7.50	15.00	30.00
❏ DL 78946 [S]	Alone After Dark	1959	7.50	15.00	30.00
HIFI
❏ R 407 [M]	Time of Desire	1958	5.00	10.00	20.00
❏ SR 407 [S]	Time of Desire	1958	6.25	12.50	25.00
❏ R 419 [M]	Beatsville	1960	5.00	10.00	20.00
❏ SR 419 [S]	Beatsville	1960	6.25	12.50	25.00
HORIZON
| ❏ ST-1612 [S] | New Sounds in Folk Music | 1963 | 6.25 | 12.50 | 25.00 |
| ❏ WP-1612 [M] | New Sounds in Folk Music | 1963 | 5.00 | 10.00 | 20.00 |
IN
| ❏ 1003 [M] | Seasons in the Sun | 1964 | 5.00 | 10.00 | 20.00 |
| ❏ S-1003 [S] | Seasons in the Sun | 1964 | 6.25 | 12.50 | 25.00 |
JUBILEE
| ❏ J-5013 [M] | Mr. Oliver Twist | 1962 | 5.00 | 10.00 | 20.00 |
| ❏ SJ-5013 [S] | Mr. Oliver Twist | 1962 | 6.25 | 12.50 | 25.00 |
KAPP
| ❏ KL-1538 [M] | In a Lonely Place | 1967 | 5.00 | 10.00 | 20.00 |
LIBERTY
| ❏ LRP-3011 [M] | Lazy Afternoon | 1956 | 10.00 | 20.00 | 40.00 |
RCA VICTOR
❏ LSP-3424 [S]	Rod McKuen Sings His Own	1965	5.00	10.00	20.00
❏ LSP-3508 [S]	The Loner	1966	5.00	10.00	20.00
❏ LSP-3635 [S]	Other Kinds of Songs	1966	5.00	10.00	20.00
❏ LPM-3786 [M]	Through European Windows	1967	5.00	10.00	20.00
❏ LPM-3863 [M]	Listen to the Warm	1967	5.00	10.00	20.00
TRADITION
| ❏ 2063 [M] | A San Francisco Hippie Trip | 1967 | 6.25 | 12.50 | 25.00 |
WARNER BROS.
| ❏ 2WS 1794 [(2)] | Rod McKuen at Carnegie Hall | 1969 | 5.00 | 10.00 | 20.00 |

McKUEN, ROD; TAK SHINDO; JULIE MEREDITH
IMPERIAL
| ❏ LP-9092 [M] | The Yellow Unicorn | 1960 | 10.00 | 20.00 | 40.00 |
| ❏ LP-12036 [S] | The Yellow Unicorn | 1960 | 12.50 | 25.00 | 50.00 |

Number	Title	Yr	VG	VG+	NM

McLACHLAN, SARAH
ARISTA
| ❑ AL 8594 | Touch | 1989 | 5.00 | 10.00 | 20.00 |

ARISTA/CLASSIC
| ❑ RTH-2000 [(2)] | Fumbling Toward Ecstasy and The Freedom Sessions | 1997 | 10.00 | 20.00 | 40.00 |

-- *Audiophile vinyl issue of both CDs on 2-LP set*

McLAIN, DENNY
CAPITOL
| ❑ ST-204 | Denny McLain In Las Vegas | 1969 | 6.25 | 12.50 | 25.00 |
| ❑ ST 2881 | Denny McLain at the Organ | 1968 | 6.25 | 12.50 | 25.00 |

McLAUGHLIN, JOHN
RYKO ANALOGUE
| ❑ RALP-0051 | My Goals Beyond | 1987 | 5.00 | 10.00 | 20.00 |

-- *Clear vinyl reissue*

McLEAN, DON
MEDIARTS
| ❑ 41-4 | Tapestry | 1970 | 5.00 | 10.00 | 20.00 |

McLOLLIE, OSCAR
CROWN
| ❑ CLP-5016 [M] | Oscar McLollie and His Honey Jumpers | 1956 | 100.00 | 200.00 | 400.00 |

-- *Opinions differ as to whether this LP actually exists. Value is probably conservative.*

McLUHAN
BRUNSWICK
| ❑ BL 754177 | Anomaly | 1972 | 5.00 | 10.00 | 20.00 |

McLUHAN, MARSHALL
COLUMBIA
| ❑ CL 2701 [M] | The Medium Is the Message | 1967 | 6.25 | 12.50 | 25.00 |
| ❑ CS 9501 [S] | The Medium Is the Message | 1967 | 6.25 | 12.50 | 25.00 |

McMAHON, ED
CAMEO
| ❑ C-2009 [M] | And Me...I'm Ed McMahon | 1964 | 6.25 | 12.50 | 25.00 |

RCA CAMDEN
| ❑ CAL-1083 [M] | What Do You Want to Be When You Grow Up? | 1965 | 5.00 | 10.00 | 20.00 |
| ❑ CAS-1083 [S] | What Do You Want to Be When You Grow Up? | 1965 | 6.25 | 12.50 | 25.00 |

McNAIR, BARBARA
AUDIO FIDELITY
| ❑ AFSD-6222 | More Today Than Yesterday | 1969 | 5.00 | 10.00 | 20.00 |

MOTOWN
❑ 644 [M]	Where I Am	1966	12.50	25.00	50.00
❑ S-644 [S]	Where I Am	1966	15.00	30.00	60.00
❑ S-680	The Real Barbara McNair	1969	7.50	15.00	30.00

SIGNATURE
| ❑ SM 1042 [M] | Love Talk | 1960 | 10.00 | 20.00 | 40.00 |
| ❑ SS 1042 [S] | Love Talk | 1960 | 12.50 | 25.00 | 50.00 |

WARNER BROS.
❑ W 1541 [M]	I Enjoy Being a Girl	1964	6.25	12.50	25.00
❑ WS 1541 [S]	I Enjoy Being a Girl	1964	7.50	15.00	30.00
❑ W 1570 [M]	The Livin' End	1964	6.25	12.50	25.00
❑ WS 1570 [S]	The Livin' End	1964	7.50	15.00	30.00

McNEELY, BIG JAY
FEDERAL
| ❑ 295-96 [10] | Big Jay McNeely | 1954 | 750.00 | 1,500. | 3,000. |
| ❑ 395-530 [M] | Big Jay McNeely in 3-D | 1956 | 200.00 | 400.00 | 800.00 |

KING
| ❑ 650 [M] | Big Jay McNeely in 3-D | 1959 | 125.00 | 250.00 | 500.00 |

SAVOY
| ❑ MG-15045 [10] | A Rhythm and Blues Concert | 1955 | 1,000. | 1,500. | 2,000. |

WARNER BROS.
| ❑ W 1533 [M] | Big Jay McNeely | 1963 | 20.00 | 40.00 | 80.00 |
| ❑ WS 1533 [S] | Big Jay McNeely | 1963 | 25.00 | 50.00 | 100.00 |

McNEILL, DON
CORAL
| ❑ CRL 57288 [M] | Book, Candle, Prayer | 1958 | 7.50 | 15.00 | 30.00 |
| ❑ CRL 57291 [M] | March Around the Breakfast Table | 1958 | 7.50 | 15.00 | 30.00 |

McNICHOL, KRISTY AND JIMMY
RCA VICTOR
| ❑ AFL1-2875 | Kristy and Jimmy McNichol | 1978 | 5.00 | 10.00 | 20.00 |

McPEAK, CURTIS
ABC-PARAMOUNT
| ❑ ABC-446 [M] | Bluegrass Hillbillies | 1963 | 5.00 | 10.00 | 20.00 |
| ❑ ABCS-446 [S] | Bluegrass Hillbillies | 1963 | 6.25 | 12.50 | 25.00 |

McPHATTER, CLYDE
Also see THE DRIFTERS.
ATLANTIC
| ❑ 8024 [M] | Love Ballads | 1958 | 125.00 | 250.00 | 500.00 |

-- *Black label*
| ❑ 8024 [M] | Love Ballads | 1960 | 50.00 | 100.00 | 200.00 |

-- *Brown and purple label*
| ❑ 8031 [M] | Clyde | 1959 | 125.00 | 250.00 | 500.00 |

-- *Black label*
| ❑ 8031 [M] | Clyde | 1960 | 50.00 | 100.00 | 200.00 |

-- *Brown and purple label*
| ❑ 8031 [M] | Clyde | 1960 | 100.00 | 200.00 | 400.00 |

-- *White "bullseye" label*
| ❑ 8077 [M] | The Best of Clyde McPhatter | 1963 | 50.00 | 100.00 | 200.00 |

DECCA
| ❑ DL 75231 | Welcome Home | 1970 | 6.25 | 12.50 | 25.00 |

MERCURY
❑ MG-20597 [M]	Ta Ta	1960	12.50	25.00	50.00
❑ MG-20655 [M]	Golden Blues Hits	1961	12.50	25.00	50.00
❑ MG-20711 [M]	Lover Please	1962	12.50	25.00	50.00
❑ MG-20750 [M]	Rhythm and Soul	1962	12.50	25.00	50.00
❑ MG-20783 [M]	Clyde McPhatter's Greatest Hits	1963	7.50	15.00	30.00
❑ MG-20902 [M]	Songs of the Big City	1964	7.50	15.00	30.00
❑ MG-20915 [M]	Live at the Apollo	1964	7.50	15.00	30.00
❑ SR-60262 [S]	Ta Ta	1960	17.50	35.00	70.00
❑ SR-60655 [S]	Golden Blues Hits	1961	17.50	35.00	70.00
❑ SR-60711 [S]	Lover Please	1962	17.50	35.00	70.00
❑ SR-60750 [S]	Rhythm and Soul	1962	17.50	35.00	70.00
❑ SR-60783 [S]	Clyde McPhatter's Greatest Hits	1963	10.00	20.00	40.00
❑ SR-60902 [S]	Songs of the Big City	1964	10.00	20.00	40.00
❑ SR-60915 [S]	Live at the Apollo	1964	10.00	20.00	40.00

MGM
❑ E-3775 [M]	Let's Start Over Again	1959	37.50	75.00	150.00
❑ SE-3775 [S]	Let's Start Over Again	1959	50.00	100.00	200.00
❑ E-3866 [M]	Clyde McPhatter's Greatest Hits	1960	17.50	35.00	70.00
❑ SE-3866 [S]	Clyde McPhatter's Greatest Hits	1960	20.00	40.00	80.00

WING
| ❑ MGW-12224 [M] | May I Sing for You? | 1962 | 6.25 | 12.50 | 25.00 |
| ❑ SRW-16224 [S] | May I Sing for You? | 1962 | 7.50 | 15.00 | 30.00 |

McRAE, CARMEN
ATLANTIC
| ❑ SD 2-904 [(2)] | The Great American Songbook | 1971 | 5.00 | 10.00 | 20.00 |
| ❑ 8143 [M] | For Once in My Life | 1967 | 5.00 | 10.00 | 20.00 |

BETHLEHEM
| ❑ BCP-1023 [10] | Carmen McRae | 1955 | 25.00 | 50.00 | 100.00 |

COLUMBIA
❑ CL 1730 [M]	Lover Man	1962	5.00	10.00	20.00
❑ CL 1943 [M]	Something Wonderful	1962	5.00	10.00	20.00
❑ CS 8530 [S]	Lover Man	1962	6.25	12.50	25.00
❑ CS 8743 [S]	Something Wonderful	1962	6.25	12.50	25.00

DECCA
| ❑ DL 8173 [M] | By Special Request | 1955 | 12.50 | 25.00 | 50.00 |

-- *Black label, silver print*
| ❑ DL 8173 [M] | By Special Request | 1960 | 5.00 | 10.00 | 20.00 |

-- *Black label with color bars*
| ❑ DL 8267 [M] | Torchy! | 1956 | 12.50 | 25.00 | 50.00 |

-- *Black label, silver print*
| ❑ DL 8267 [M] | Torchy! | 1960 | 5.00 | 10.00 | 20.00 |

-- *Black label with color bars*
| ❑ DL 8347 [M] | Blue Moon | 1957 | 12.50 | 25.00 | 50.00 |

-- *Black label, silver print*
| ❑ DL 8347 [M] | Blue Moon | 1960 | 5.00 | 10.00 | 20.00 |

-- *Black label with color bars*
| ❑ DL 8583 [M] | After Glow | 1957 | 12.50 | 25.00 | 50.00 |

-- *Black label, silver print*
| ❑ DL 8583 [M] | After Glow | 1960 | 5.00 | 10.00 | 20.00 |

-- *Black label with color bars*
| ❑ DL 8662 [M] | Mad About the Man | 1958 | 12.50 | 25.00 | 50.00 |

-- *Black label, silver print*
| ❑ DL 8662 [M] | Mad About the Man | 1960 | 5.00 | 10.00 | 20.00 |

-- *Black label with color bars*
| ❑ DL 8738 [M] | Carmen for Cool Ones | 1958 | 12.50 | 25.00 | 50.00 |

-- *Black label, silver print*
| ❑ DL 8738 [M] | Carmen for Cool Ones | 1960 | 5.00 | 10.00 | 20.00 |

-- *Black label with color bars*

Number	Title	Yr	VG	VG+	NM
❏ DL 8815 [M]	Birds of a Feather	1959	12.50	25.00	50.00
-- Black label, silver print					
❏ DL 8815 [M]	Birds of a Feather	1960	5.00	10.00	20.00
-- Black label with color bars					
FOCUS					
❏ FS-334 [S]	Bittersweet	1964	5.00	10.00	20.00
HARMONY					
❏ HL 7452 [M]	Yesterdays	1968	5.00	10.00	20.00
KAPP					
❏ KL-1117 [M]	Book of Ballads	1958	6.25	12.50	25.00
❏ KL-1135 [M]	When You're Away	1959	6.25	12.50	25.00
❏ KL-1169 [M]	Something to Swing About	1960	6.25	12.50	25.00
❏ KL-1541 [M]	This Is Carmen McRae	1967	5.00	10.00	20.00
❏ KS-3000 [S]	Book of Ballads	1958	7.50	15.00	30.00
❏ KS-3018 [S]	When You're Away	1959	7.50	15.00	30.00
❏ KS-3053 [S]	Something to Swing About	1960	7.50	15.00	30.00
MAINSTREAM					
❏ S-6028 [S]	Second to None	1965	5.00	10.00	20.00
❏ S-6044 [S]	Haven't We Met?	1965	5.00	10.00	20.00
❏ S-6065 [S]	Woman Talk	1966	5.00	10.00	20.00
❏ S-6084 [S]	Alfie	1966	5.00	10.00	20.00
❏ 56091 [M]	In Person/San Francisco	1967	5.00	10.00	20.00
TIME					
❏ S-2104 [S]	Live at Sugar Hill	1960	6.25	12.50	25.00
❏ 52104 [M]	Live at Sugar Hill	1960	5.00	10.00	20.00

McSHANN, JAY
CAPITOL

Number	Title	Yr	VG	VG+	NM
❏ ST 2645 [S]	McShann's Piano	1967	5.00	10.00	20.00
❏ T 2645 [M]	McShann's Piano	1967	5.00	10.00	20.00
DECCA					
❏ DL 5503 [10]	Kansas City Memories	1954	125.00	250.00	500.00
-- CHARLIE PARKER appears on this LP					
❏ DL 9236 [M]	Kansas City Memories	1958	50.00	100.00	200.00

McTELL, BLIND WILLIE
BLUESVILLE

Number	Title	Yr	VG	VG+	NM
❏ BVLP-1040 [M]	Last Session	1962	30.00	60.00	120.00
-- Blue label, silver print					
❏ BVLP-1040 [M]	Last Session	1964	7.50	15.00	30.00
-- Blue label, trident logo at right					
MELODEON					
❏ 7323 [M]	1940	1956	37.50	75.00	150.00

McTELL, RALPH
CAPITOL

Number	Title	Yr	VG	VG+	NM
❏ ST-240	Eight Frames a Second	1969	5.00	10.00	20.00

McWILLIAMS, DAVID
KAPP

Number	Title	Yr	VG	VG+	NM
❏ KS-3547	Days of Pearly Spencer	1967	6.25	12.50	25.00

MEADER, VAUGHN
CADENCE

Number	Title	Yr	VG	VG+	NM
❏ CLP 3065 [M]	The First Family, Volume Two	1963	5.00	10.00	20.00
❏ CLP 25065 [S]	The First Family, Volume Two	1963	7.50	15.00	30.00
VERVE					
❏ V6-15042 [S]	Have Some Nuts	1964	5.00	10.00	20.00

MEADOW
Supposedly, Laura Branigan was in this group.
PARAMOUNT

Number	Title	Yr	VG	VG+	NM
❏ PAS-6066	The Friend Ship	1973	5.00	10.00	20.00

MEAT LOAF
Also see STONEY AND MEATLOAF.
EPIC

Number	Title	Yr	VG	VG+	NM
❏ E99 34974 [PD]	Bat Out of Hell	1978	5.00	10.00	20.00
❏ HE 44974	Bat Out of Hell	1981	10.00	20.00	40.00
-- Half-speed mastered edition					

MEAT PUPPETS
LONDON

Number	Title	Yr	VG	VG+	NM
❏ 1109 [10]	Raw Meat	199?	5.00	10.00	20.00
-- Promo-only five-song 10-inch EP					

MECKI MARK MEN, THE
LIMELIGHT

Number	Title	Yr	VG	VG+	NM
❏ LS-86054	The Mecki Mark Men	1968	6.25	12.50	25.00
❏ LS-86068	Running in the Summer Night	1969	6.25	12.50	25.00

MEDIUM
GAMMA

Number	Title	Yr	VG	VG+	NM
❏ GS-503	Medium	196?	25.00	50.00	100.00

MEDLEY, BILL
Also see THE RIGHTEOUS BROTHERS.
MGM

Number	Title	Yr	VG	VG+	NM
❏ SE-4583	Bill Medley 100%	1968	5.00	10.00	20.00
❏ SE-4603	Soft and Soulful	1969	5.00	10.00	20.00
❏ SE-4640	Someone Is Standing Outside	1969	5.00	10.00	20.00

MEEUWSEN, TERRY ANN
SANDY

Number	Title	Yr	VG	VG+	NM
❏ SRS-9003	Meet Terry	1976	7.50	15.00	30.00

MEL AND TIM
BAMBOO

Number	Title	Yr	VG	VG+	NM
❏ BMS-8001	Good Guys Only Win in the Movies	1970	6.25	12.50	25.00
STAX					
❏ STS-3007	Starting All Over Again	1972	5.00	10.00	20.00
❏ STS-5501	Mel and Tim	1974	5.00	10.00	20.00

MELACHRINO, GEORGE
RCA VICTOR

Number	Title	Yr	VG	VG+	NM
❏ LPM-1000 [M]	Music for Dining	195?	6.25	12.50	25.00
❏ LPM-1001 [M]	Music for Relaxation	195?	6.25	12.50	25.00
❏ LPM-1002 [M]	Music for Reading	195?	6.25	12.50	25.00
❏ LPM-1005 [M]	Music for Courage and Confidence	195?	6.25	12.50	25.00
❏ LPM-1006 [M]	Music to Help You Sleep	195?	6.25	12.50	25.00
❏ LPM-1008 [M]	Show Tunes	195?	6.25	12.50	25.00
❏ LPM-1027 [M]	Music for Two People Alone	195?	6.25	12.50	25.00
❏ LPM-1028 [M]	Music for Daydreaming	195?	6.25	12.50	25.00
❏ LPM-1029 [M]	Music to Work or Study By	195?	6.25	12.50	25.00
❏ LPM-1045 [M]	Christmas in High Fidelity	1954	6.25	12.50	25.00
❏ LPM-1110 [M]	Immortal Ladies	1955	5.00	10.00	20.00
❏ LPM-1184 [M]	Masquerade	1955	5.00	10.00	20.00
❏ LPM-1261 [M]	Sounds of Paris	1956	5.00	10.00	20.00
❏ LPM-1307 [M]	Melachrino on Broadway	1956	5.00	10.00	20.00
❏ LPM-1329 [M]	I'll Walk Beside You	1956	5.00	10.00	20.00
❏ LPM-1330 [M]	Those Beautiful Strings	1956	5.00	10.00	20.00
❏ LSP-1757 [S]	Strauss Waltzes	1958	5.00	10.00	20.00
❏ LSP-1762 [S]	Lisbon at Twilight	1958	5.00	10.00	20.00

MELLENCAMP, JOHN
MCA

Number	Title	Yr	VG	VG+	NM
❏ 2225	Chestnut Street Incident	1977	6.25	12.50	25.00
-- As "Johnny Cougar"					
MOBILE FIDELITY					
❏ 1-222	The Lonesome Jubilee	1995	5.00	10.00	20.00
-- Audiophile vinyl					

MELLO-KINGS, THE
HERALD

Number	Title	Yr	VG	VG+	NM
❏ H-1013 [M]	Tonight-Tonight	1960	125.00	250.00	500.00
-- Yellow label					
❏ H-1013 [M]	Tonight-Tonight	196?	62.50	125.00	250.00
-- Multi-color label					

MELLO-LARKS, THE
RCA CAMDEN

Number	Title	Yr	VG	VG+	NM
❏ CAL-530 [M]	Just for a Lark	1959	10.00	20.00	40.00

MELTZER, DAVID AND TINA
VANGUARD

Number	Title	Yr	VG	VG+	NM
❏ VSD-6619	Poet Song	1969	6.25	12.50	25.00

MELVIN, HAROLD, AND THE BLUE NOTES
Also see TEDDY PENDERGRASS.
PHILADELPHIA INT'L.

Number	Title	Yr	VG	VG+	NM
❏ ZQ 32407 [Q]	Black & Blue	1973	5.00	10.00	20.00
❏ PZQ 33808 [Q]	Wake Up Everybody	1975	5.00	10.00	20.00

MEMPHIS SLIM
BATTLE

Number	Title	Yr	VG	VG+	NM
❏ BM-6118 [M]	Alone with My Friends	1963	12.50	25.00	50.00
❏ BM-6122 [M]	Baby Please Come Home	1963	12.50	25.00	50.00
BLUESVILLE					
❏ BVLP-1018 [M]	Just Blues	1961	30.00	60.00	120.00
-- Blue label, silver print					

Number	Title	Yr	VG	VG+	NM
❏ BVLP-1018 [M] Just Blues		1964	7.50	15.00	30.00
-- Blue label, trident logo at right					
❏ BVLP-1031 [M] No Strain		1961	30.00	60.00	120.00
-- Blue label, silver print					
❏ BVLP-1031 [M] No Strain		1964	7.50	15.00	30.00
-- Blue label, trident logo at right					
❏ BVLP-1053 [M] All Kinds of Blues		1962	25.00	50.00	100.00
-- Blue label, silver print					
❏ BVLP-1053 [M] All Kinds of Blues		1964	7.50	15.00	30.00
-- Blue label, trident logo at right					
❏ BVLP-1075 [M] Steady Rollin' Blues		1963	25.00	50.00	100.00
-- Blue label, silver print					
❏ BVLP-1075 [M] Steady Rollin' Blues		1964	7.50	15.00	30.00
-- Blue label, trident logo at right					

BUDDAH

Number	Title	Yr	VG	VG+	NM
❏ BDS-7505	Mother Earth	1969	5.00	10.00	20.00

CANDID

❏ CM-8023 [M]	Slim's Tribute to Big Bill Broonzy	1961	15.00	30.00	60.00
❏ CM-8024 [M]	Memphis Slim U.S.A.	1962	15.00	30.00	60.00
❏ CS-9023 [S]	Slim's Tribute to Big Bill Broonzy	1961	20.00	40.00	80.00
❏ CS-9024 [S]	Memphis Slim U.S.A.	1962	20.00	40.00	80.00

CHESS

❏ LP-1455 [M]	Memphis Slim	1961	37.50	75.00	150.00
-- Black label					
❏ LP-1510 [M]	The Real Folk Blues	1966	20.00	40.00	80.00

DISC

❏ D-105 [M]	If the Rabbit Had a Gun	1964	10.00	20.00	40.00

FOLKWAYS

❏ FG-3524 [M]	The Real Boogie Woogie	1959	25.00	50.00	100.00
❏ FG-3535 [M]	Memphis Slim...And the Real Honky Tonk	1960	25.00	50.00	100.00
❏ FG-3536 [M]	Chicago Blues	1961	25.00	50.00	100.00

JUBILEE

❏ JGM-8003 [M]	Legend of the Blues	1967	6.25	12.50	25.00
❏ JGS-8003 [S]	Legend of the Blues	1967	6.25	12.50	25.00

KING

❏ 885 [M]	Memphis Slim Sings Folk Blues	1964	12.50	25.00	50.00

SCEPTER

❏ SM-535 [M]	Self Portrait	1966	5.00	10.00	20.00
❏ SMS-535 [S]	Self Portrait	1966	6.25	12.50	25.00

SPIN-O-RAMA

❏ 149 [M]	Lonesome Blues	196?	5.00	10.00	20.00

STRAND

❏ SL-1046 [M]	The World's Foremost Blues	1962	10.00	20.00	40.00
❏ SLS-1046 [S]	The World's Foremost Blues	1962	12.50	25.00	50.00

UNITED ARTISTS

❏ UAL-3137 [M]	Broken Soul Blues	1961	15.00	30.00	60.00
❏ UAS-6137 [S]	Broken Soul Blues	1961	20.00	40.00	80.00

VEE JAY

❏ LP-1012 [M]	Memphis Slim at the Gate of the Horn	1959	50.00	100.00	200.00
-- Maroon label					
❏ LP-1012 [M]	Memphis Slim at the Gate of the Horn	1961	30.00	60.00	120.00
-- Black rainbow label, oval logo					

MEMPHIS WILLIE B
BLUESVILLE

❏ BVLP-1034 [M] Introducing Memphis Willie B		1961	25.00	50.00	100.00
-- Blue label, silver print					
❏ BVLP-1034 [M] Introducing Memphis Willie B		1964	7.50	15.00	30.00
-- Blue label, trident logo at right					
❏ BVLP-1048 [M] Hard Working Man Blues		1962	25.00	50.00	100.00
-- Blue label, silver print					
❏ BVLP-1048 [M] Hard Working Man Blues		1964	7.50	15.00	30.00
-- Blue label, trident logo at right					

MEN AT WORK
COLUMBIA

❏ HC 47978	Business as Usual	1983	6.25	12.50	25.00
-- Half-speed mastered edition					
❏ HC 48660	Cargo	1983	6.25	12.50	25.00
-- Half-speed mastered edition					

MEN WITHOUT HATS
STIFF

❏ TEES-12-01 [EP] Folk of the 80's		1981	7.50	15.00	30.00
-- Reissue of Trend 10-inch EP					

TREND

❏ HATS-001 [10] Folk of the 80's		1981	10.00	20.00	40.00
-- 10-inch four-song EP; possibly released only in Canada					

MEN, THE
Also recorded as The Mentally Ill.
SNAT-5

Number	Title	Yr	VG	VG+	NM
❏ 2001	Hermeneutics	1981	6.25	12.50	25.00

MENDES, SERGIO
ATLANTIC

❏ SD 1434 [S]	The Swinger from Rio	1965	5.00	10.00	20.00
❏ SD 1466 [S]	Great Arrival	1966	5.00	10.00	20.00
❏ 1480 [M]	The Beat of Brazil	1967	5.00	10.00	20.00
❏ 8112 [M]	Sergio Mendes In Person at the El Matador	1967	5.00	10.00	20.00
❏ SD 8177	Sergio Mendes' Favorite Things	1968	5.00	10.00	20.00

CAPITOL

❏ ST 2294 [S]	In a Brazilan Bag	1965	15.00	30.00	60.00
❏ T 2294 [M]	In a Brazilan Bag	1965	12.50	25.00	50.00

MOBILE FIDELITY

❏ 1-118	Sergio Mendes and Brasil '66	1984	12.50	25.00	50.00
-- Audiophile vinyl					

PHILIPS

❏ PHM 200-263 [M] Quiet Nights		1968	5.00	10.00	20.00

TOWER

❏ ST 5052 [S]	In a Brazilan Bag	1966	12.50	25.00	50.00
-- Reissue of Capitol 2294					
❏ T 5052 [M]	In a Brazilan Bag	1966	10.00	20.00	40.00
-- Reissue of Capitol 2294					

MENUHIN, YEHUDI
MERCURY LIVING PRESENCE

❏ SR 90003 [S]	Bartok: Violin Concerto No. 2	1959	12.50	25.00	50.00
-- With Antal Dorati/Minneapolis Symphony Orch.; maroon label, no "Vendor: Mercury Record Corporation"					
❏ SR 90003 [S]	Bartok: Violin Concerto No. 2	196?	7.50	15.00	30.00
-- With Antal Dorati/Minneapolis Symphony Orch.; maroon label, with "Vendor: Mercury Record Corporation"					

MEPHISTOPHELES
REPRISE

❏ RS 6355	In Frustration I Hear Singing	1969	10.00	20.00	40.00

MERCER, JOHNNY
CAPITOL

❏ H 210 [10]	Music of Jerome Kern	1950	20.00	40.00	80.00
❏ H 214 [10]	Johnny Mercer Sings	1950	20.00	40.00	80.00
❏ T 907 [M]	Ac-Cent-Tchu-Ate the Positive	1957	12.50	25.00	50.00

JUPITER

❏ 1001 [M]	Just for Fun	1956	12.50	25.00	50.00

MERCER, MABEL
ATLANTIC

❏ ALS-402 [10]	Songs by Mabel Mercer, Volume 1	1954	20.00	40.00	80.00
❏ ALS-403 [10]	Songs by Mabel Mercer, Volume 2	1954	20.00	40.00	80.00
❏ 2-602 [(2) M]	The Art of Mabel Mercer	1959	15.00	30.00	60.00
-- Black labels					
❏ 1213 [M]	Mabel Mercer Sings Cole Porter	1955	10.00	20.00	40.00
-- Black label					
❏ 1244 [M]	Midnight at Mabel Mercer's	1956	10.00	20.00	40.00
-- Black label					
❏ 1301 [M]	Once in a Blue Moon	1959	10.00	20.00	40.00
-- Black label					
❏ SD 1301 [S]	Once in a Blue Moon	1959	12.50	25.00	50.00
-- Green label					
❏ 1322 [M]	Merely Marvelous Mabel Mercer	1960	10.00	20.00	40.00
-- Black label					
❏ SD 1322 [S]	Merely Marvelous Mabel Mercer	1960	12.50	25.00	50.00
-- Green label					

MERCHANTS OF DREAM, THE
A&M

❏ SP-4199	Strange Night Voyage	1969	6.25	12.50	25.00

MERCY
SUNDI

❏ SRLP-803	The Mercy & Love (Can Make You Happy)	1969	5.00	10.00	20.00
-- Has the original version of the title song plus filler instrumentals					

MERCY DEE
ARHOOLIE

❏ F-1007 [M]	Mercy Dee	1961	15.00	30.00	60.00

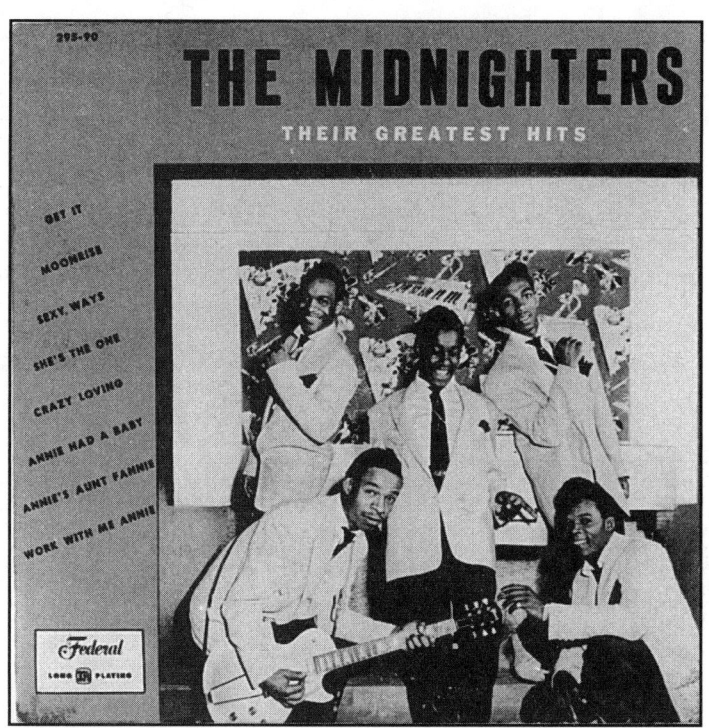

(Top left) After the small Sundi label had a hit with Mercy's "Love (Can Make You Happy)," Mercy jumped to Warner Bros. for their full-length album, which has a re-recorded version of the hit. Sundi's own album had the original hit version surrounded by filler instrumentals. (Top right) The 10-inch version of *The Midnighters: Their Greatest Hits* on Federal has dropped in value recently. It's still not exactly a bargain-bin item at $8,000 for a near-mint copy, though. (Bottom left) Most Glenn Miller music is more valuable on LP reissues than it is on the original 78s, because the supply far exceeds the demand for the 78s. One of the more interesting LP reissues is this one, done for Salada Foods, that features six-minute versions of both "Chattanooga Choo Choo" and "(I've Got a Gal in) Kalamazoo." (Bottom right) The Steve Miller Band's *Brave New World,* their third album, has a $20 near-mint price tag if it has the original black colorband label, which was at the tail end of its usage in 1969.

Number	Title	Yr	VG	VG+	NM
BLUESVILLE					
❏ BVLP-1039 [M] A Pity and a Shame		1962	20.00	40.00	80.00
-- Blue label, silver print					
❏ BVLP-1039 [M] A Pity and a Shame		1964	6.25	12.50	25.00
-- Blue label, trident logo at right					
MEREDITH, BUDDY					
STARDAY					
❏ SLP-225 [M]	Sing Me a Heart Song	1963	7.50	15.00	30.00
MEREDITH, BURGESS					
COLPIX					
❏ CP-452 [M]	Burgess Meredith Sings Songs from "How the West Was Won"	1964	5.00	10.00	20.00
❏ SCP-452 [S]	Burgess Meredith Sings Songs from "How the West Was Won"	1964	6.25	12.50	25.00
EPIC					
❏ BN 590 [S]	Songs and Stories of the Gold Rush	1961	7.50	15.00	30.00
❏ LN 3656 [M]	Songs and Stories of the Gold Rush	1961	6.25	12.50	25.00
MERKIN					
WINDI					
❏ 1004/5	Music from Merkin	1972	100.00	200.00	400.00
MERMAIDS, THE -- See THE MURMAIDS.					
MERMAN, ETHEL					
DECCA					
❏ DXA 153 [(2) M] A Musical Autobiography		195?	10.00	20.00	40.00
❏ DL 5053 [10]	Songs She Made Famous	1950	15.00	30.00	60.00
❏ DL 8178 [M]	A Musical Autobiography, Volume 1	195?	6.25	12.50	25.00
-- Black label, silver print					
❏ DL 8179 [M]	A Musical Autobiography, Volume 2	195?	6.25	12.50	25.00
-- Black label, silver print					
❏ DL 9028 [M]	Memories	1955	10.00	20.00	40.00
-- Black label, silver print					
MERRILL, TONI					
RAMA					
❏ RLP-5004 [M]	Songs from the Heart	1957	20.00	40.00	80.00
MERRIWETHER, ROY, TRIO					
CAPITOL					
❏ ST-102	Soul Knight	1968	6.25	12.50	25.00
MERRY-GO-ROUND, THE					
A&M					
❏ LP-132 [M]	The Merry-Go-Round	1967	10.00	20.00	40.00
❏ SP-4132 [S]	The Merry-Go-Round	1967	7.50	15.00	30.00
MERRYWEATHER, NEIL					
CAPITOL					
❏ STBB-278 [(2)]	Word of Mouth	1969	5.00	10.00	20.00
MERSEYBEATS, THE					
ARC INTERNATIONAL					
❏ 834 [M]	England's Best Sellers	1964	10.00	20.00	40.00
MERSEYBOYS, THE					
VEE JAY					
❏ VJ-1101 [M]	15 Greatest Songs of the Beatles	1964	25.00	50.00	100.00
❏ VJS-1101 [S]	15 Greatest Songs of the Beatles	1964	37.50	75.00	150.00
MESHEL, BILLY					
PROBE					
❏ CPLP-4502	The Love Songs of A. Wilbur Meshel	1969	5.00	10.00	20.00
MESMERIZING EYE, THE					
SMASH					
❏ MGS-27090 [M] Psychedelia -- A Musical Light Show		1967	12.50	25.00	50.00
❏ SRS-67090 [S] Psychedelia -- A Musical Light Show		1967	15.00	30.00	60.00
MESSENGERS, THE					
RARE EARTH					
❏ RS-509	The Messengers	1969	5.00	10.00	20.00

Number	Title	Yr	VG	VG+	NM
MESSINA, JIM					
Also see LOGGINS AND MESSINA.					
AUDIO FIDELITY					
❏ DFM-3037 [M]	The Dragsters	1964	20.00	40.00	80.00
❏ DFS-7037 [S]	The Dragsters	1964	25.00	50.00	100.00
WARNER BROS.					
❏ BSK 3559 [DJ]	Messina	1981	5.00	10.00	20.00
-- Promo-only version on Quiex II vinyl					
METALLICA					
ELEKTRA					
❏ 60757 [EP]	Garage Days Re-Revisited	1987	10.00	20.00	40.00
❏ 60812 [(2)]	...And Justice for All	1988	5.00	10.00	20.00
❏ 61113 [(2)]	Metallica	1991	10.00	20.00	40.00
❏ 62299 [(3)]	Garage Inc.	1998	5.00	10.00	20.00
MEGAFORCE					
❏ MRI 069	Kill 'Em All	1983	7.50	15.00	30.00
❏ MRI 069 [PD]	Kill 'Em All	1983	20.00	40.00	80.00
-- Numbered limited edition version					
❏ MRI 069 [PD]	Kill 'Em All	1983	10.00	20.00	40.00
-- Un-numbered version					
❏ MRI 769	Ride the Lightning	1984	7.50	15.00	30.00
METERS, THE					
JOSIE					
❏ JOS-4010	The Meters	1969	17.50	35.00	70.00
❏ JOS-4011	Look-Ka Py Py	1970	17.50	35.00	70.00
❏ JOS-4012	Struttin'	1970	17.50	35.00	70.00
REPRISE					
❏ MS 2076	Cabbage Alley	1972	17.50	35.00	70.00
❏ MS 2200	Rejuvenation	1974	12.50	25.00	50.00
❏ MS 2228	Fire on the Bayou	1975	12.50	25.00	50.00
❏ MS 2252	Trick Bag	1976	12.50	25.00	50.00
ROUNDER					
❏ 2103	Look-Ka Py Py	1990	5.00	10.00	20.00
-- Reissue of Josie 4011					
❏ 2104	Good Old Funky Music	1990	5.00	10.00	20.00
VIRGO					
❏ 12002	The Best of the Meters	1972	12.50	25.00	50.00
WARNER BROS.					
❏ BS 3042	New Directions	1977	12.50	25.00	50.00
METRONOMES, THE					
STRAND					
❏ SL-1057 [M]	The Fabulous Metronomes Sing the Standard Hits	1962	7.50	15.00	30.00
❏ SLS-1057 [S]	The Fabulous Metronomes Sing the Standard Hits	1962	10.00	20.00	40.00
WYNNE					
❏ 106 [M]	And Now... The Metronomes	1960	30.00	60.00	120.00
METROS, THE					
RCA VICTOR					
❏ LPM-3776 [M] Sweetest One		1967	20.00	40.00	80.00
❏ LSP-3776 [S] Sweetest One		1967	25.00	50.00	100.00
METROTONES, THE					
COLUMBIA					
❏ CL 6341 [10]	Tops in Rock and Roll	1955	62.50	125.00	250.00
MEYER, AUGIE					
PARAMOUNT					
❏ PAS-6065	California Blues	1973	5.00	10.00	20.00
POLYDOR					
❏ 24-4069	Western Head Music Co.	1971	5.00	10.00	20.00
MIAMI SOUND MACHINE					
AUDIOFON					
❏ AUS 5426	Live Again -- Renacer	1977	50.00	100.00	200.00
-- First 600 have a cover where the backdrop is clearly visible					
❏ AUS 5426	Live Again -- Renacer	1977	25.00	50.00	100.00
-- The rest have a cover with a blue and yellow "tropical" background					
❏ AUS 5427	Miami Sound Machine	1978	25.00	50.00	100.00
-- Spanish-language version					
CBS INTERNATIONAL					
❏ DML 10306	Imported	1980	10.00	20.00	40.00
-- Reissue of 10455					
❏ DHL 10311	Miami Sound Machine	1980	12.50	25.00	50.00
❏ DIL 10320	Otra Vez	1981	12.50	25.00	50.00
❏ DIL 10330	Rio	1982	12.50	25.00	50.00

Number	Title	Yr	VG	VG+	NM
❑ DSL 10335	7Up Presenta Los Hits de Miami Sound Machine	1983	25.00	50.00	100.00
-- Only available in the Miami area from 7Up dealers					
❑ DIL 10349	A Toda Maquina	1984	10.00	20.00	40.00
-- Spanish-language version of "Eyes of Innocence," their first all-English LP					
❑ DKL 10455	Imported	1979	12.50	25.00	50.00
-- Reissue of MSM album					
ELECTRIC CAT					
❑ ECS 226	Miami Sound Machine	1978	25.00	50.00	100.00
-- Partially English-language version					
MSM					
❑ ERK 0714	Imported	1979	25.00	50.00	100.00
TOP HITS					
❑ TH-AM 2185	Live Again -- Renacer	1982	12.50	25.00	50.00
-- Reissue of Audiofon LP of the same name					
❑ TH-AM 2187	Miami Sound Machine	1982	12.50	25.00	50.00
-- Reissue of Audiofon LP of the same name					
❑ TH-AM 2228	Lo Mejor De Miami Sound Machine -- A Portrait of the Originals	1983	12.50	25.00	50.00
-- Compilation from first two Spanish-language LPs					

MICHAELS, LEE
A&M
Number	Title	Yr	VG	VG+	NM
❑ SP-4140	Carnival of Life	1968	10.00	20.00	40.00
❑ SP-4152	Recital	1968	5.00	10.00	20.00
COLUMBIA					
❑ CQ 32275 [Q]	Nice Day for Something	1973	5.00	10.00	20.00

MICKELSON, PAUL
RCA VICTOR
Number	Title	Yr	VG	VG+	NM
❑ LPM-1115 [M]	Christmas Bells	1955	5.00	10.00	20.00
❑ LPM-1517 [M]	The Best of Christmas	1957	5.00	10.00	20.00

MICKEY AND SYLVIA
RCA CAMDEN
Number	Title	Yr	VG	VG+	NM
❑ CAL-863 [M]	Love Is Strange	1965	12.50	25.00	50.00
❑ CAS-863(e) [R]	Love Is Strange	1965	7.50	15.00	30.00
VIK					
❑ LX-1102 [M]	New Sounds	1957	100.00	200.00	400.00

MIDNIGHTERS, THE
FEDERAL
Number	Title	Yr	VG	VG+	NM
❑ 295-90 [10]	Their Greatest Hits	1954	4,000.	6,000.	8,000.
❑ 395-541 [M]	Their Greatest Hits	1955	375.00	750.00	1,500.
-- Red cover					
❑ 395-541 [M]	Their Greatest Hits	1955	250.00	500.00	1,000.
-- Yellow cover					
❑ 395-581 [M]	The Midnighters, Volume 2	1955	300.00	600.00	1,200.
KING					
❑ 541 [M]	Their Greatest Jukebox Hits	1958	100.00	200.00	400.00
-- Crownless black label, "King" is two inches wide on label					
❑ 541 [M]	Their Greatest Jukebox Hits	196?	75.00	150.00	300.00
-- Crownless black label, "King" is three inches wide on label. Above two have a girl on the cover.					
❑ 541 [M]	Their Greatest Jukebox Hits	196?	50.00	100.00	200.00
-- Reissue with Hank Ballard on cover					
❑ 581 [M]	The Midnighters, Volume 2	1958	75.00	150.00	300.00
-- Crownless black label, "King" is two inches wide on label					
❑ 581 [M]	The Midnighters, Volume 2	196?	50.00	100.00	200.00
-- Crownless black label, "King" is three inches wide on label					

MIGHTY BABY
HEAD
Number	Title	Yr	VG	VG+	NM
❑ LPS-025	Mighty Baby	1969	15.00	30.00	60.00

MIGHTY CLOUDS OF JOY
PEACOCK
Number	Title	Yr	VG	VG+	NM
❑ 114	Family Circle	196?	5.00	10.00	20.00
❑ 121	The Bright Side	196?	5.00	10.00	20.00
❑ 134	Mighty Clouds of Joy At the Music Hall	196?	5.00	10.00	20.00
❑ 136	The Best of Mighty Clouds of Joy	196?	5.00	10.00	20.00
❑ 151	The Untouchables	196?	5.00	10.00	20.00
❑ 161	Out Talking to Yourself	196?	5.00	10.00	20.00
❑ 163	Songs of Rev. Julius Cheeks and the Nightingales	196?	5.00	10.00	20.00

MIGHTY FAITH INCREASERS, THE
KING
Number	Title	Yr	VG	VG+	NM
❑ 806 [M]	The Mighty Faith Increasers with Willa Dorsey	1962	37.50	75.00	150.00
❑ 814 [M]	A Festival of Spiritual Songs	1962	37.50	75.00	150.00

MILANOV, ZINKA
RCA VICTOR RED SEAL
Number	Title	Yr	VG	VG+	NM
❑ LSC-2303 [S]	Operatic Arias by Puccini	1959	6.25	12.50	25.00
-- Originals on "shaded dog" label					

MILBURN, AMOS
ALADDIN
Number	Title	Yr	VG	VG+	NM
❑ LP-704 [10]	Rockin' the Boogie	1955	2,000.	4,000.	8,000.
-- Red vinyl, blue cover					
❑ LP-704 [10]	Rockin' the Boogie	1955	1,000.	2,000.	4,000.
-- Black vinyl					
IMPERIAL					
❑ LP-9176 [M]	Million Sellers	1962	125.00	250.00	500.00
MOTOWN					
❑ 608 [M]	The Return of Amos Milburn, "The" Blues Boss	1963	225.00	450.00	900.00
SCORE					
❑ LP-4012 [M]	Let's Have a Party	1957	200.00	400.00	800.00

MILBURN, AMOS/WYNONIE HARRIS/ETC.
ALADDIN
Number	Title	Yr	VG	VG+	NM
❑ LP-703 [10]	Party After Hours	1955	2,000.	4,000.	8,000.
-- Red vinyl, blue cover					
❑ LP-703 [10]	Party After Hours	1955	1,000.	2,000.	4,000.
-- Black vinyl					

MILES, BUDDY
COLUMBIA
Number	Title	Yr	VG	VG+	NM
❑ CQ 32048 [Q]	Chapter VII	1973	5.00	10.00	20.00
❑ CQ 32694 [Q]	Booger Bear	1973	5.00	10.00	20.00
MERCURY					
❑ SR-61196	Expressway to Your Skull	1968	5.00	10.00	20.00
❑ SR-61222	Electric Church	1969	5.00	10.00	20.00

MILES, LIZZY
COOK
Number	Title	Yr	VG	VG+	NM
❑ 1181 [10]	Queen Mother of the Rue Royale	1955	15.00	30.00	60.00
❑ 1182 [M]	Moans and Blues	195?	12.50	25.00	50.00
❑ 1183 [M]	Hot Songs My Mother Taught Me	195?	12.50	25.00	50.00
❑ 1184 [M]	Torchy Lullabies My Mother Taught Me	195?	12.50	25.00	50.00

MILES, LUKE "LONG GONE"
WORLD PACIFIC
Number	Title	Yr	VG	VG+	NM
❑ ST-1820 [S]	Country Born	1964	7.50	15.00	30.00
❑ WP-1820 [M]	Country Born	1964	6.25	12.50	25.00

MILKWOOD
Two different groups.
A&M
Number	Title	Yr	VG	VG+	NM
❑ SP-4226	Under Milkwood	1969	75.00	150.00	300.00
PARAMOUNT					
❑ PAS-6046	How's the Weather?	1973	10.00	20.00	40.00

MILKWOOD TAPESTRY
METROMEDIA
Number	Title	Yr	VG	VG+	NM
❑ MD-1007	Milkwood Tapestry	1969	12.50	25.00	50.00

MILLARD & DYCE
KAYMAR
Number	Title	Yr	VG	VG+	NM
❑ KS-7-265	Open	1973	15.00	30.00	60.00

MILLENNIUM
COLUMBIA
Number	Title	Yr	VG	VG+	NM
❑ CS 9663	Begin	1968	7.50	15.00	30.00

MILLER, CHUCK
MERCURY
Number	Title	Yr	VG	VG+	NM
❑ MG-20195 [M]	After Hours	1956	20.00	40.00	80.00

MILLER, CLARENCE "BIG"
COLUMBIA
Number	Title	Yr	VG	VG+	NM
❑ CL 1611 [M]	Revelation and the Blues	1961	6.25	12.50	25.00
❑ CL 1808 [M]	Big Miller Sings, Twists, Shouts	1962	6.25	12.50	25.00
❑ CS 8411 [S]	Revelation and the Blues	1961	7.50	15.00	30.00
❑ CS 8608 [S]	Big Miller Sings, Twists, Shouts and Preaches	1962	7.50	15.00	30.00

Number	Title	Yr	VG	VG+	NM

UNITED ARTISTS
| ❏ UAL-3047 [M] | Did You Ever Hear the Blues? | 1959 | 10.00 | 20.00 | 40.00 |
| ❏ UAS-6047 [S] | Did You Ever Hear the Blues? | 1959 | 15.00 | 30.00 | 60.00 |

MILLER, FRANKIE
AUDIO LAB
| ❏ AL-1562 [M] | The Fine Country Singing of Frankie Miller | 1963 | 37.50 | 75.00 | 150.00 |

STARDAY
❏ SLP-134 [M]	Country Music's Great New Star	1961	25.00	50.00	100.00
❏ SLP-199 [M]	The True Country Style of Frankie Miller	1962	25.00	50.00	100.00
❏ SLP-339 [M]	Blackland Farmer	1965	15.00	30.00	60.00

MILLER, GLENN
Reissues of original 1930s and 1940s recordings.
BLUEBIRD
| ❏ 9785-1-RB [(4)] | The Popular Recordings 1938-1942 | 1989 | 6.25 | 12.50 | 25.00 |

EPIC
| ❏ LA 16002 [M] | Glenn Miller | 1960 | 5.00 | 10.00 | 20.00 |

RCA VICTOR
❏ LPT-16 [10]	Glenn Miller Concert -- Volume 1	1951	15.00	30.00	60.00
❏ LPT-30 [10]	Glenn Miller Concert -- Volume 2	1951	15.00	30.00	60.00
❏ LPT-31 [10]	Glenn Miller	1951	15.00	30.00	60.00
❏ PR-114 [M]	Glenn Miller Originals	1962	5.00	10.00	20.00
-- Promotional item for Salada Foods Inc.					
❏ LOP-1005 [M]	The Marvelous Miller Medleys	1955	10.00	20.00	40.00
❏ LPT-1016 [M]	Juke Box Saturday Night	1955	10.00	20.00	40.00
❏ LPT-1031 [M]	The Nearness of You	1955	10.00	20.00	40.00
❏ LPM-1189 [M]	The Sound of Glenn Miller	1956	10.00	20.00	40.00
❏ LPM-1190 [M]	This Is Glenn Miller	1956	10.00	20.00	40.00
❏ LPM-1192 [M]	Selections from "The Glenn Miller Story" and Other Hits	1956	10.00	20.00	40.00
❏ LPM-1193 [M]	Glenn Miller Concert	1956	10.00	20.00	40.00
❏ LPM-1494 [M]	Marvelous Miller Moods	1957	10.00	20.00	40.00
❏ LPM-1506 [M]	The Glenn Miller Carnegie Hall Concert	1957	10.00	20.00	40.00
❏ LPM-1973 [M]	The Marvelous Miller Medleys	1959	7.50	15.00	30.00
❏ LPT-3001 [10]	Glenn Miller Concert -- Volume 3	195?	15.00	30.00	60.00
❏ LPT-3002 [10]	This Is Glenn Miller	195?	15.00	30.00	60.00
❏ LPT-3036 [10]	This Is Glenn Miller -- Volume 2	195?	15.00	30.00	60.00
❏ LPT-3057 [10]	Selections from the Film "The Glenn Miller Story"	1954	15.00	30.00	60.00
❏ LPT-3067 [10]	Sunrise Serenade	1954	15.00	30.00	60.00
❏ LPM-6100 [(3) M]	For the Very First Time...	195?	12.50	25.00	50.00
-- Black "Long Play" labels in leatherette spiral-bound binder					
❏ LPM-6101 [(3) M]	Glenn Miller On the Air	1963	10.00	20.00	40.00
❏ LSP-6101 [(3) R]	Glenn Miller On the Air	1963	6.25	12.50	25.00
❏ LPT-6700 [(5) M]	Glenn Miller and His Orchestra Limited Edition	1953	37.50	75.00	150.00
-- Silver labels with red print in leatherette spiral-bound binder					
❏ LPT-6700 [(5) M]	Glenn Miller and His Orchestra Limited Edition -- Second Pressing	195?	15.00	30.00	60.00
-- Black "Long Play" labels in leatherette spiral-bound binder					
❏ LPT-6701 [(5) M]	Glenn Miller and His Orchestra Limited Edition Volume Two	1954	30.00	60.00	120.00
-- Black "Long Play" labels in leatherette spiral-bound binder					
❏ LPT-6701 [(5) M]	Glenn Miller and His Orchestra Limited Edition Volume Two -- Second Pressing	195?	15.00	30.00	60.00
-- Black "Long Play" labels in leatherette spiral-bound binder; identified as "Second Pressing" throughout					
❏ LPT-6702 [(4) M]	Glenn Miller Army Air Force Band	1955	30.00	60.00	120.00
-- Black "Long Play" labels in leatherette spiral-bound binder					
❏ LPT-6702 [(4) M]	Glenn Miller Army Air Force Band	195?	15.00	30.00	60.00
-- Same as above, but in box rather than in binder					

20TH FOX
| ❏ TCF-100-2 [(2) M] | Glenn Miller and His Orchestra Original Film Sound Tracks | 1958 | 7.50 | 15.00 | 30.00 |
| ❏ TCF-100-2S [(2) R] | Glenn Miller and His Orchestra Original Film Sound Tracks | 1961 | 5.00 | 10.00 | 20.00 |

MILLER, JODY
CAPITOL
❏ ST 1913 [S]	Wednesday's Child Is Full of Woe	1963	10.00	20.00	40.00
❏ T 1913 [M]	Wednesday's Child Is Full of Woe	1963	7.50	15.00	30.00
❏ ST 2349 [S]	Queen of the House	1965	5.00	10.00	20.00
❏ ST 2412 [S]	Home of the Brave	1965	5.00	10.00	20.00
❏ ST 2446 [S]	Jody Miller Sings the Great Hits of Buck Owens	1966	5.00	10.00	20.00

MILLER, MICKEY
FOLKWAYS
| ❏ FA-2393 [M] | American Folk Songs | 1959 | 7.50 | 15.00 | 30.00 |

MILLER, MITCH
COLUMBIA
❏ CL 601 [M]	Mmmmitch!	1954	5.00	10.00	20.00
-- Maroon label, gold print					
❏ CL 779 [M]	It's So Peaceful in the Country	1956	5.00	10.00	20.00
-- Red and black label with six "eye" logos					
❏ CS 8004 [S]	Sing Along with Mitch	1959	5.00	10.00	20.00
-- Red and black label with six "eye" logos					
❏ CS 8027 [S]	Christmas Sing Along with Mitch	1959	5.00	10.00	20.00
-- Originals have gatefold cover with eight detachable lyric sheets inside					
❏ CS 8043 [S]	More Sing Along with Mitch	1959	5.00	10.00	20.00
❏ CS 8099 [S]	Still More! Sing Along with Mitch	1959	5.00	10.00	20.00
❏ CS 8118 [S]	Folk Songs Sing Along with Mitch	1959	5.00	10.00	20.00
❏ CS 8138 [S]	Party Sing Along with Mitch	1959	5.00	10.00	20.00
❏ CS 8184 [S]	Fireside Sing Along with Mitch	1959	5.00	10.00	20.00

MILLER, MRS.
AMARET
| ❏ 5000 | Mrs. Miller Does Her Thing | 1969 | 5.00 | 10.00 | 20.00 |
CAPITOL
❏ ST 2494 [S]	Mrs. Miller's Greatest Hits	1966	7.50	15.00	30.00
❏ T 2494 [M]	Mrs. Miller's Greatest Hits	1966	6.25	12.50	25.00
❏ ST 2579 [S]	Will Success Spoil Mrs. Miller?	1966	7.50	15.00	30.00
❏ T 2579 [M]	Will Success Spoil Mrs. Miller?	1966	6.25	12.50	25.00
❏ ST 2734 [S]	The Country Soul of Mrs. Miller	1967	6.25	12.50	25.00
❏ T 2734 [M]	The Country Soul of Mrs. Miller	1967	6.25	12.50	25.00

MILLER, NED
CAPITOL
❏ ST 2330 [S]	Ned Miller Sings the Songs of Ned Miller	1965	6.25	12.50	25.00
❏ T 2330 [M]	Ned Miller Sings the Songs of Ned Miller	1965	5.00	10.00	20.00
❏ ST 2414 [S]	The Best of Ned Miller	1966	5.00	10.00	20.00
❏ ST 2586 [S]	Teardrop Lane	1967	5.00	10.00	20.00
❏ T 2586 [M]	Teardrop Lane	1967	5.00	10.00	20.00
FABOR
❏ FLP-1001 [M]	From a Jack to a King	1963	25.00	50.00	100.00
-- Colored vinyl					
❏ FLP-1001 [M]	From a Jack to a King	1963	10.00	20.00	40.00
-- Black vinyl					

MILLER, ROGER
SMASH
❏ MGS-27092 [M]	Walkin' in the Sunshine	1967	5.00	10.00	20.00
❏ MGS-27096 [M]	Waterhole #3	1967	6.25	12.50	25.00
❏ SRS-67049 [S]	Roger and Out	1964	5.00	10.00	20.00
❏ SRS-67061 [S]	The Return of Roger Miller	1965	5.00	10.00	20.00
❏ SRS-67068 [S]	The 3rd Time Around	1965	5.00	10.00	20.00
❏ SRS-67073 [S]	Golden Hits	1965	5.00	10.00	20.00
❏ SRS-67075 [S]	Words and Music	1966	5.00	10.00	20.00
❏ SRS-67092 [S]	Walkin' in the Sunshine	1967	5.00	10.00	20.00
❏ SRS-67096 [S]	Waterhole #3	1967	5.00	10.00	20.00
❏ SRS-67103	A Tender Look at Love	1968	5.00	10.00	20.00
❏ SRS-67123	Roger Miller	1969	5.00	10.00	20.00
❏ SRS-67129	Roger Miller 1970	1970	5.00	10.00	20.00
STARDAY
❏ SLP-318 [M]	Wild Child Roger Miller	1965	7.50	15.00	30.00
❏ SLP-318 [M]	The Country Side of Roger Miller	196?	6.25	12.50	25.00
-- Retitled version of "Wild Child"					

MILLER, STEVE, BAND
CAPITOL
❏ ST-184	Brave New World	1969	5.00	10.00	20.00
-- Black label with colorband					
❏ SKAO 2920	Children of the Future	1968	6.25	12.50	25.00
-- Black label with colorband					
❏ ST 2984	Sailor	1968	6.25	12.50	25.00
-- Black label with colorband					
❏ SOO-11872 [DJ]	Greatest Hits 1974-1978	1978	7.50	15.00	30.00
-- Promo only on blue vinyl					
MOBILE FIDELITY
| ❏ 1-021 | Fly Like an Eagle | 1979 | 10.00 | 20.00 | 40.00 |
| -- Audiophile vinyl | | | | | |

MILLER, STEVE, BAND/QUICKSILVER MESSENGER SERVICE/THE BAND
Also see each artist's individual listings.
CAPITOL
| ❏ STCR-288 [(3)] | Sailor/Quicksilver Messenger Service/Music from Big Pink | 1969 | 10.00 | 20.00 | 40.00 |
| -- Special 3-LP box set combining these three LPs, also listed separately in each group's listing, in one package | | | | | |

Number	Title	Yr	VG	VG+	NM

MILLS BROTHERS, THE
DECCA

Number	Title	Yr	VG	VG+	NM
☐ DXB 193 [(2) M]	The Best of the Mills Brothers	1965	5.00	10.00	20.00
☐ DL 4084 [M]	Our Golden Favorites	1960	5.00	10.00	20.00
☐ DL 5050 [10]	Barber Shop Ballads	1950	12.50	25.00	50.00
☐ DL 5051 [10]	Barber Shop Ballads	1950	12.50	25.00	50.00
☐ DL 5102 [10]	Souvenir Album	1950	12.50	25.00	50.00
☐ DL 5337 [10]	Wonderful Words	1951	12.50	25.00	50.00
☐ DL 5506 [10]	Meet the Mills Brothers	1954	12.50	25.00	50.00
☐ DL 5516 [10]	Four Boys and a Guitar	1954	12.50	25.00	50.00
☐ DL 8148 [M]	Souvenir Album	1955	7.50	15.00	30.00
☐ DL 8209 [M]	Singin' and Swingin'	1956	7.50	15.00	30.00
☐ DL 8219 [M]	Memory Lane	1956	7.50	15.00	30.00
☐ DL 8491 [M]	One Dozen Roses	1957	7.50	15.00	30.00
☐ DL 8664 [M]	The Mills Brothers in Hi-Fi	1958	7.50	15.00	30.00
☐ DL 8827 [M]	Glow with the Mills Brothers	1958	7.50	15.00	30.00
☐ DL 8890 [M]	Barber Shop Harmony	1959	7.50	15.00	30.00
☐ DL 8892 [M]	Harmonizin' with the Mills Brothers	1959	7.50	15.00	30.00

DOT

Number	Title	Yr	VG	VG+	NM
☐ DLP-3103 [M]	Mmmm, The Mills Brothers	1958	5.00	10.00	20.00
☐ DLP-3157 [M]	The Mills Brothers' Great Hits	1958	5.00	10.00	20.00
☐ DLP-3208 [M]	Great Barbershop Hits	1959	5.00	10.00	20.00
☐ DLP-3232 [M]	Merry Christmas	1959	5.00	10.00	20.00
☐ DLP-3237 [M]	The Mills Brothers Sing	1960	5.00	10.00	20.00
☐ DLP-25103 [S]	Mmmm, The Mills Brothers	1958	7.50	15.00	30.00
☐ DLP-25157 [S]	The Mills Brothers' Great Hits	195?	15.00	30.00	60.00
-- Blue vinyl					
☐ DLP-25157 [S]	The Mills Brothers' Great Hits	1958	7.50	15.00	30.00
-- Black vinyl					
☐ DLP-25208 [S]	Great Barbershop Hits	1959	7.50	15.00	30.00
☐ DLP-25232 [S]	Merry Christmas	1959	7.50	15.00	30.00
☐ DLP-25237 [S]	The Mills Brothers Sing	1960	7.50	15.00	30.00
☐ DLP-25308 [S]	The Mills Brothers' Great Hits, Volume 2	1960	5.00	10.00	20.00
☐ DLP-25338 [S]	Yellow Bird	1960	5.00	10.00	20.00
☐ DLP-25363 [S]	San Antonio Rose	1961	5.00	10.00	20.00
☐ DLP-25368 [S]	Great Hawaiian Hits	1961	5.00	10.00	20.00

MILLS, ALAN
FOLKWAYS

Number	Title	Yr	VG	VG+	NM
☐ FP-29 [10]	Folk Songs of French Canada	1952	12.50	25.00	50.00
☐ FP-831 [10]	Folk Songs of Newfoundland	1953	12.50	25.00	50.00
☐ FA-2313 [M]	Songs of the Sea	1957	7.50	15.00	30.00
☐ FW-3000 [(2) M]	Canada's Story in Song	1960	10.00	20.00	40.00
☐ FW-3001 [M]	O Canada: A History in Song	1956	7.50	15.00	30.00
☐ FW-6831 [M]	Folk Songs of Newfoundland	195?	7.50	15.00	30.00
☐ FW-6929 [M]	Folk Songs of French Canada	195?	7.50	15.00	30.00
☐ FC-7018 [M]	French Folk Songs for Children in English	1957	7.50	15.00	30.00
☐ FC-7208 [M]	French Folk Songs for Children	1957	7.50	15.00	30.00
☐ FC-7642 [M]	More Animals, Vol. 2	1956	7.50	15.00	30.00
☐ FC-7677 [M]	Animals, Vol. 1	1956	7.50	15.00	30.00
☐ FC-7750 [M]	Christmas Songs from Many	1956	7.50	15.00	30.00
☐ FW-8771 [M]	We'll Rant and We'll Roar: Songs of Newfoundland	1958	7.50	15.00	30.00

MILLS, HAYLEY
BUENA VISTA

Number	Title	Yr	VG	VG+	NM
☐ BV-3311 [M]	Let's Get Together	1962	6.25	12.50	25.00
☐ STER-3311 [S]	Let's Get Together	1962	10.00	20.00	40.00

MILSAP, RONNIE
RCA

Number	Title	Yr	VG	VG+	NM
☐ R 183710	Back to the Grindstone	1991	5.00	10.00	20.00
-- Only released on vinyl through BMG Direct Marketing					

RCA VICTOR

Number	Title	Yr	VG	VG+	NM
☐ APL1-0338	Where My Heart Is	1973	5.00	10.00	20.00
☐ APD1-0500 [Q]	Pure Love	1974	5.00	10.00	20.00
☐ APD1-0846 [Q]	A Legend in My Time	1975	5.00	10.00	20.00

WARNER BROS.

Number	Title	Yr	VG	VG+	NM
☐ WS 1934	Ronnie Milsap	1971	5.00	10.00	20.00

MILTON, ROY
KENT

Number	Title	Yr	VG	VG+	NM
☐ KST-554 [R]	The Great Roy Milton	196?	7.50	15.00	30.00
☐ KLP-5054 [M]	The Great Roy Milton	1963	12.50	25.00	50.00

MIMMS, GARNET, AND THE ENCHANTERS
UNITED ARTISTS

Number	Title	Yr	VG	VG+	NM
☐ UAL 3305 [M]	Cry Baby and 11 Other Hits	1963	20.00	40.00	80.00
☐ UAL 3396 [M]	As Long As I Have You	1964	12.50	25.00	50.00
☐ UAL 3498 [M]	I'll Take Good Care of You	1966	12.50	25.00	50.00
☐ UAS 6305 [S]	Cry Baby and 11 Other Hits	1963	25.00	50.00	100.00
☐ UAS 6396 [S]	As Long As I Have You	1964	17.50	35.00	70.00
☐ UAS 6498 [S]	I'll Take Good Care of You	1966	17.50	35.00	70.00

MIND EXPANDERS, THE
DOT

Number	Title	Yr	VG	VG+	NM
☐ DLP-3773 [M]	What's Happening	1967	25.00	50.00	100.00
☐ DLP-25773 [S]	What's Happening	1967	20.00	40.00	80.00

MIND GARAGE, THE
RCA VICTOR

Number	Title	Yr	VG	VG+	NM
☐ LSP-4218	The Mind Garage	1969	5.00	10.00	20.00
☐ LSP-4319	The Mind Garage Again!	1970	5.00	10.00	20.00

MINDBENDERS, THE
Also see WAYNE FONTANA AND THE MINDBENDERS.
FONTANA

Number	Title	Yr	VG	VG+	NM
☐ MGF-27554 [M]	A Groovy Kind of Love	1966	7.50	15.00	30.00
-- With "Don't Cry No More"					
☐ MGF-27554 [M]	A Groovy Kind of Love	1966	6.25	12.50	25.00
-- With "Ashes to Ashes"					
☐ SRF-67554 [R]	A Groovy Kind of Love	1966	6.25	12.50	25.00
-- With "Don't Cry No More"					
☐ SRF-67554 [R]	A Groovy Kind of Love	1966	5.00	10.00	20.00
-- With "Ashes to Ashes"					

MINEO, SAL
EPIC

Number	Title	Yr	VG	VG+	NM
☐ LN 3405 [M]	Sal	1958	37.50	75.00	150.00

MINNEAPOLIS SYMPHONY ORCHESTRA (ANTAL DORATI, CONDUCTOR)
MERCURY LIVING PRESENCE

Number	Title	Yr	VG	VG+	NM
☐ SR 90007 [S]	Albeniz-Artos: Iberia; Falla: Interlude and Dance	1959	12.50	25.00	50.00
-- Maroon label, no "Vendor: Mercury Record Corporation"					
☐ SR 90011 [S]	Beethoven: Symphony No. 3	1959	7.50	15.00	30.00
-- Maroon label, no "Vendor: Mercury Record Corporation"					
☐ SR 90016 [S]	Offenbach: Gaite Parisienne; Strauss, Johann: Graduation Ball	1959	5.00	10.00	20.00
-- Maroon label, no "Vendor: Mercury Record Corporation"					
☐ SR 90098 [S]	Bartok: Suite No. 2	1959	20.00	40.00	80.00
-- Maroon label, no "Vendor: Mercury Record Corporation"					
☐ SR 90132 [S]	Kodaly: Hary Janos Suite; Bartok: Hungarian Sketches; Rumanian Dances	1960	30.00	60.00	120.00
-- Maroon label, no "Vendor: Mercury Record Corporation"					
☐ SR 90132 [S]	Kodaly: Hary Janos Suite; Bartok: Hungarian Sketches; Rumanian Dances	196?	12.50	25.00	50.00
-- Maroon label, with "Vendor: Mercury Record Corporation"					
☐ SR 90139 [S]	Rossini: Overtures	196?	20.00	40.00	80.00
-- Maroon label, no "Vendor: Mercury Record Corporation"					
☐ SR 90139 [S]	Rossini: Overtures	196?	10.00	20.00	40.00
-- Maroon label, with "Vendor: Mercury Record Corporation"					
☐ SR 90171 [S]	Brahms: Symphony No. 2	196?	10.00	20.00	40.00
-- Maroon label, no "Vendor: Mercury Record Corporation"					
☐ SR 90172 [S]	Copland: Rodeo; El Salon Mexico; Danzon Cubano	196?	12.50	25.00	50.00
-- Maroon label, with "Vendor: Mercury Record Corporation"					
☐ SR 90172 [S]	Copland: Rodeo; El Salon Mexico; Danzon Cubano	196?	37.50	75.00	150.00
-- Maroon label, no "Vendor: Mercury Record Corporation"					
☐ SR 90178 [S]	The Strauss Family Album	196?	5.00	10.00	20.00
-- Maroon label, no "Vendor: Mercury Record Corporation"					
☐ SR 90195 [S]	Rimsky-Korsakov: Scheherazade	196?	7.50	15.00	30.00
-- Maroon label, no "Vendor: Mercury Record Corporation"					
☐ SR 90201 [S]	Tchaikovsky: March Slave; Polonaise and Waltz; Francesca da Rimini	196?	12.50	25.00	50.00
-- Maroon label, no "Vendor: Mercury Record Corporation"					
☐ SR 90201 [S]	Tchaikovsky: March Slave; Polonaise and Waltz; Francesca da Rimini	196?	7.50	15.00	30.00
-- Maroon label, with "Vendor: Mercury Record Corporation"					
☐ SR 90202 [S]	Strauss, Richard: Don Juan; Death and Transfiguration	196?	20.00	40.00	80.00
-- Maroon label, no "Vendor: Mercury Record Corporation"					
☐ SR 90216 [S]	Stravinsky: Petrouchka	196?	20.00	40.00	80.00
-- Maroon label, no "Vendor: Mercury Record Corporation"					
☐ SR 90216 [S]	Stravinsky: Petrouchka	196?	15.00	30.00	60.00
-- Maroon label, with "Vendor: Mercury Record Corporation"					
☐ SR 90217 [S]	Mussorgsky: Pictures at an Exhibition	196?	30.00	60.00	120.00
-- Maroon label, no "Vendor: Mercury Record Corporation"					
☐ SR 90217 [S]	Mussorgsky: Pictures at an Exhibition	196?	5.00	10.00	20.00
-- Maroon label, with "Vendor: Mercury Record Corporation"					
☐ SR 90248 [S]	Dorati: Symphony; Nocturne; Capriccio	196?	45.00	90.00	180.00
-- Maroon label, no "Vendor: Mercury Record Corporation"					
☐ SR 90253 [S]	Stravinsky: Le Sacre du Printemps (The Rite of Spring)	196?	10.00	20.00	40.00
-- Maroon label, no "Vendor: Mercury Record Corporation"					

Number	Title	Yr	VG	VG+	NM
❑ SR 90253 [S]	Stravinsky: Le Sacre du Printemps (The Rite of Spring)	196?	5.00	10.00	20.00

-- Maroon label, with "Vendor: Mercury Record Corporation"

❑ SR 90282 [S]	Schuller: Seven Studies on Themes of Paul Klee; Fetler: Contrasts for Orchestra	196?	17.50	35.00	70.00

-- Maroon label, no "Vendor: Mercury Record Corporation"

❑ SR 90282 [S]	Schuller: Seven Studies on Themes of Paul Klee; Fetler: Contrasts for Orchestra	196?	15.00	30.00	60.00

-- Maroon label, with "Vendor: Mercury Record Corporation"

❑ SR 90288 [S]	Bloch: Sinfonia Brave; Peterson, Wayne: Free Variations for Orchestra	196?	37.50	75.00	150.00

-- Maroon label, no "Vendor: Mercury Record Corporation"

❑ SR 90298 [S]	Respighi: Pines and Fountains of Rome	196?	12.50	25.00	50.00

-- Maroon label, no "Vendor: Mercury Record Corporation"

❑ SR 90298 [S]	Respighi: Pines and Fountains of Rome	196?	7.50	15.00	30.00

-- Maroon label, with "Vendor: Mercury Record Corporation"

❑ SR 90431 [S]	Offenbach: Gaite Parisienne; Gershwin: An American in Paris	1965	5.00	10.00	20.00

-- Maroon label, with "Vendor: Mercury Record Corporation"

❑ SR 90499 [S]	Dorati: Symphony; Nocturne and Capriccio	196?	5.00	10.00	20.00

-- Maroon label, with "Vendor: Mercury Record Corporation"

MINNEAPOLIS SYMPHONY ORCHESTRA (STANISLAW SKROWACZEWSKI, CONDUCTOR)
MERCURY LIVING PRESENCE

❑ SR 90060 [S]	Khachatourian: Gayne Ballet; Shostakovich: Symphony No. 5	1960	50.00	100.00	200.00

-- Maroon label, no "Vendor: Mercury Record Corporation"

❑ SR 90218 [S]	Schubert: Symphony in B "Unfinished"	196?	12.50	25.00	50.00

-- Maroon label, "Vendor: Mercury Record Corporation"

❑ SR 90218 [S]	Schubert: Symphony in B "Unfinished"	196?	6.25	12.50	25.00

-- Maroon label, with "Vendor: Mercury Record Corporation"

❑ SR 90272 [S]	Schubert: Symphony No. 7 (9) in C	196?	10.00	20.00	40.00

-- Maroon label, no "Vendor: Mercury Record Corporation"

❑ SR 90315 [S]	Prokofiev: Romeo and Juliet Ballet Suites 1 and 2	196?	15.00	30.00	60.00

-- Maroon label, no "Vendor: Mercury Record Corporation"

❑ SR 90315 [S]	Prokofiev: Romeo and Juliet Ballet Suites 1 and 2	196?	5.00	10.00	20.00

-- Maroon label, with "Vendor: Mercury Record Corporation"

❑ SR 90356 [S]	Mendelssohn: Symphony No. 4; Schubert: Symphony No. 5	196?	5.00	10.00	20.00

-- Maroon label, no "Vendor: Mercury Record Corporation"

MINNELLI, LIZA
Also see JUDY GARLAND AND LIZA MINNELLI.
CAPITOL

❑ ST 2174 [S]	Liza! Liza!	1964	6.25	12.50	25.00
❑ T 2174 [M]	Liza! Liza!	1964	5.00	10.00	20.00
❑ ST 2271 [S]	It Amazes Me	1965	6.25	12.50	25.00
❑ T 2271 [M]	It Amazes Me	1965	5.00	10.00	20.00
❑ ST 2448 [S]	There Is a Time	1966	6.25	12.50	25.00
❑ T 2448 [M]	There Is a Time	1966	5.00	10.00	20.00

COLUMBIA

❑ CQ 32149 [Q]	Liza Minnelli The Singer	1973	5.00	10.00	20.00

MINNIE PEARL
STARDAY

❑ SLP-224 [M]	Howdee!	1963	10.00	20.00	40.00
❑ SLP-380 [M]	America's Beloved Minnie Pearl	1965	10.00	20.00	40.00
❑ SLP-397 [M]	The Country Music Story	1966	7.50	15.00	30.00

MINOR THREAT
DISCHORD

❑ 10	Out of Step	1983	12.50	25.00	50.00

-- First stock pressing, black back cover with lyrics

❑ 10	Out of Step	1983	5.00	10.00	20.00

-- Second stock pressing, gray back cover with photos

❑ 10 [DJ]	Out of Step	1983	125.00	250.00	500.00

-- Test pressing of 50; black silkscreen cover with sheep logo; paste-on back cover; blank labels; plain innersleeve with rubber stamp

MINT TATTOO
DOT

❑ DLP-25918	Mint Tattoo	1969	7.50	15.00	30.00

MINUTEMEN
SST

❑ 004	The Punch Line	1981	5.00	10.00	20.00

-- Original copies have white labels

Number	Title	Yr	VG	VG+	NM
❑ PSST E28 [DJ]	Excerpts from Double Nickels on the Dime	1984	6.25	12.50	25.00

-- One-sided promo LP with etched B-side and sticker on blank cover

MIRACLES, THE
Includes records released as "Smokey Robinson and the Miracles."
COLUMBIA

❑ PCQ 34460 [Q]	Love Crazy	1977	5.00	10.00	20.00

MOTOWN

❑ 793 [(3)]	Smokey Robinson and the Miracles Anthology	1974	5.00	10.00	20.00

TAMLA

❑ T 220 [M]	Hi We're the Miracles	1961	150.00	300.00	600.00

-- White label

❑ T 223 [M]	Cookin' with the Miracles	1962	200.00	400.00	800.00

-- White label

❑ T 230 [M]	I'll Try Something New	1962	150.00	300.00	600.00

-- White label

❑ T 236 [M]	Christmas with the Miracles	1963	75.00	150.00	300.00

-- Originals have two globes on the top of the label

❑ T 238 [M]	The Fabulous Miracles	1963	75.00	150.00	300.00
❑ T 238 [M]	You've Really Got a Hold on Me	1963	50.00	100.00	200.00

-- Retitled version of "The Fabulous Miracles"

❑ T 241 [M]	The Miracles On Stage	1963	50.00	100.00	200.00
❑ T 245 [M]	Doin' Mickey's Monkey	1963	50.00	100.00	200.00
❑ TS 245 [S]	Doin' Mickey's Monkey	1963	75.00	150.00	300.00
❑ T 254 [(2) M]	Greatest Hits from the Beginning	1965	12.50	25.00	50.00
❑ TS 254 [(2) P]	Greatest Hits from the Beginning	1965	10.00	20.00	40.00
❑ T 267 [M]	Going to a Go-Go	1966	7.50	15.00	30.00
❑ TS 267 [S]	Going to a Go-Go	1966	10.00	20.00	40.00
❑ T 271 [M]	Away We a Go-Go	1966	6.25	12.50	25.00
❑ TS 271 [S]	Away We a Go-Go	1966	7.50	15.00	30.00
❑ T 276 [M]	Make It Happen	1967	6.25	12.50	25.00
❑ TS 276 [S]	Make It Happen	1967	7.50	15.00	30.00
❑ TS 280	Greatest Hits, Vol. 2	1968	6.25	12.50	25.00
❑ TS 289	Live!	1969	5.00	10.00	20.00
❑ TS 290	Special Occasion	1968	5.00	10.00	20.00
❑ TS 295	Time Out for Smokey Robinson & the Miracles	1969	5.00	10.00	20.00
❑ TS 297	Four in Blue	1969	5.00	10.00	20.00
❑ TS 320 [(2)]	1957-1972	1972	5.00	10.00	20.00

MISFITS, THE
CAROLINE

❑ 7515	Collection II	1995	25.00	50.00	100.00

-- Clear vinyl (500 made); sealed copies have bar code at upper right or not at all

❑ 7515	Collection II	1995	7.50	15.00	30.00

-- Green vinyl (3,500 made); sealed copies have bar code roughly 1/4 to 1/2 inch from bottom of back cover

❑ 7515	Collection II	1995	10.00	20.00	40.00

-- Red vinyl (6,000 made); sealed copies have bar code roughly 1 inch from the bottom of back cover

❑ 7520	Static Age	1997	25.00	50.00	100.00

-- Purple vinyl (500 made)

❑ 7520	Static Age	1997	7.50	15.00	30.00

-- Yellow vinyl (1,000 made)

❑ 7520	Static Age	1997	10.00	20.00	40.00

-- Red vinyl (2,000 made)

PLAN 9

❑ PL9-02	Earth A.D.	1983	100.00	200.00	400.00

-- 100 on green vinyl

❑ PL9-02	Earth A.D.	1983	62.50	125.00	250.00

-- 200 on dark purple vinyl

❑ PL9-02	Earth A.D.	1983	62.50	125.00	250.00

-- 200 on clear vinyl with red and blue swirls

❑ PL9-02	Earth A.D.	1983	62.50	125.00	250.00

-- 500 on yellow vinyl

❑ PL9-03 [EP]	Die, Die My Darling	1984	30.00	60.00	120.00

-- 500 on white vinyl (distributed by Caroline)

❑ PL9-03 [EP]	Die, Die My Darling	1984	37.50	75.00	150.00

-- 500 on purple vinyl

❑ PL9-06	Legacy of Brutality	1986	500.00	1,000.	2,000.

-- 16 (!!) on pink vinyl

❑ PL9-06	Legacy of Brutality	1986	50.00	100.00	200.00

-- 500 on white vinyl

❑ PL9-06	Legacy of Brutality	1986	37.50	75.00	150.00

-- 500 on red vinyl

❑ PL9-06	Legacy of Brutality	1986	5.00	10.00	20.00

-- Black vinyl (distributed by Caroline)

❑ PL9-08 [EP]	Evilive	1987	15.00	30.00	60.00

-- 2,000 on green vinyl (distributed by Caroline)

❑ PL9-08 [EP]	Evilive	1987	5.00	10.00	20.00

-- Black vinyl (distributed by Caroline)

RUBY/SLASH

❑ JRR 804	Walk Among Us	1982	25.00	50.00	100.00

-- Original red cover; has custom innersleeve and insert

❑ JRR 804	Walk Among Us	1982	12.50	25.00	50.00

-- Purple cover with innersleeve and insert

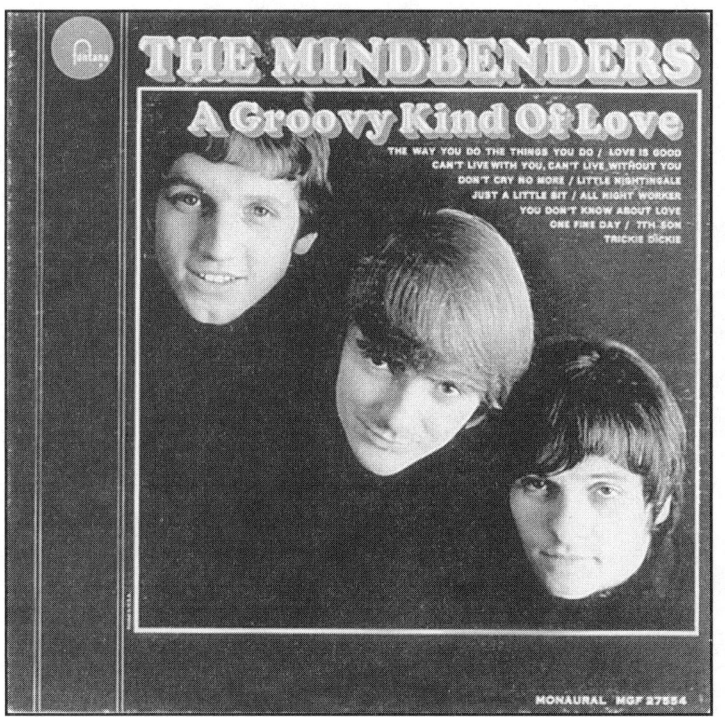

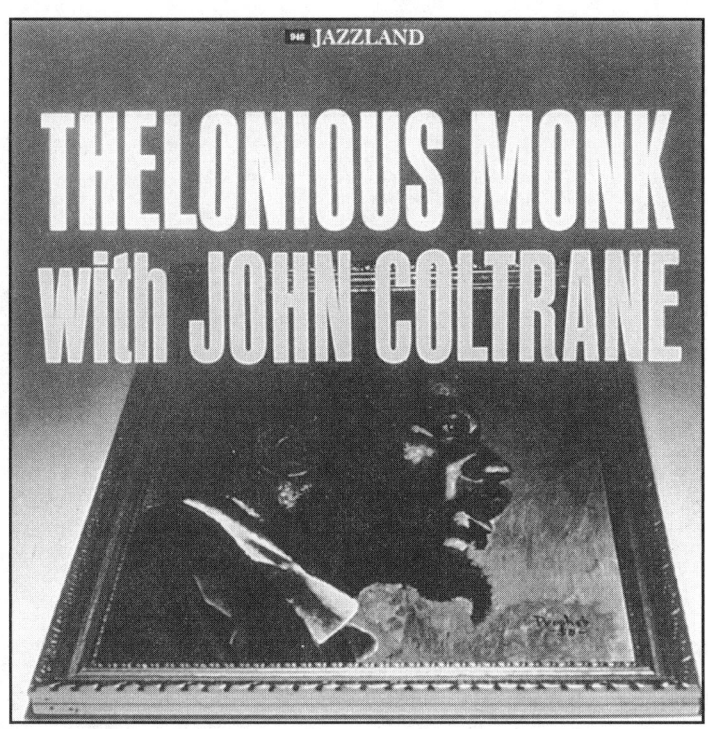

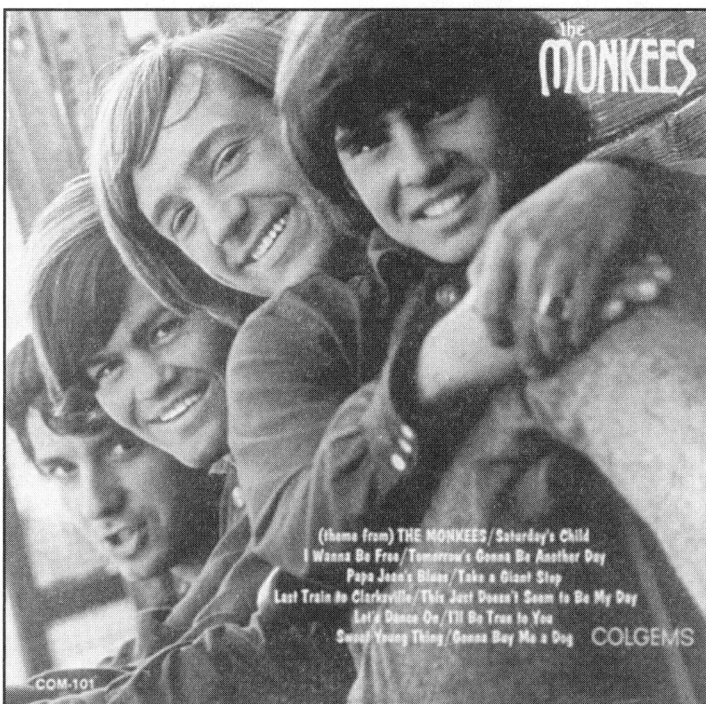

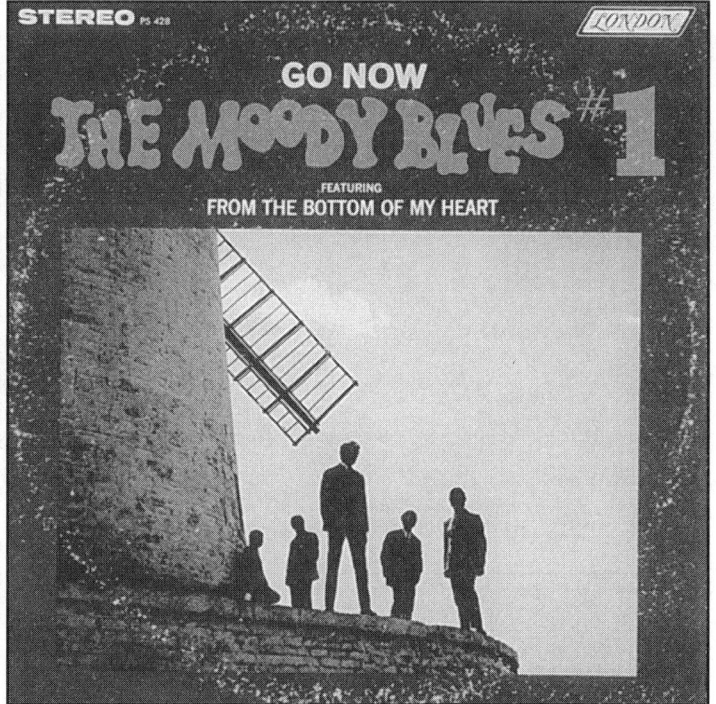

(Top left) After the departure of Wayne Fontana for a solo career, the rest of the Mindbenders carried on and had one more big hit, the title song of the above album. (Top right) This Jazzland album from 1961 paired two of the top jazzmen of the era, Thelonious Monk and John Coltrane. It has since been reissued at least twice, on both Milestone and the Fantasy Original Jazz Classics series. (Bottom left) Most of the early Monkees albums are pretty common in mediocre to bad condition, though they can be tough to find in near-mint. This one is an exception. The first pressing of *The Monkees,* both mono and stereo versions, called the fifth song on Side 1 "Papa Jean's Blues" on the front and back cover and on the label. This was promptly changed to "Papa Gene's Blues," and an "RE" was added to the numbers on the upper right of the back cover. (Bottom right) The mono version is more sought-after, but even the rechanneled stereo version of *The Moody Blues #1* is a tough find these days.

Number	Title	Yr	VG	VG+	NM

SLASH
| ❏ 25756 | Walk Among Us | 1988 | 5.00 | 10.00 | 20.00 |

-- Reissue of JRR 804; some copies came with a Halloween bag, which can double or even triple the value!

MISSOURI
PANAMA
| ❏ 1022 | Missouri | 1977 | 7.50 | 15.00 | 30.00 |

MISTAKEN, THE -- See ANGRY SAMOANS.

MR. GASSER AND THE WEIRDOS
CAPITOL
❏ ST 2010 [S]	Hot Rod Hootenanny	1963	30.00	60.00	120.00
❏ T 2010 [M]	Hot Rod Hootenanny	1963	25.00	50.00	100.00
❏ ST 2057 [S]	Rods n' Ratfinks	1963	30.00	60.00	120.00

-- Add 25% if ratfink decal is enclosed
| ❏ T 2057 [M] | Rods n' Ratfinks | 1963 | 25.00 | 50.00 | 100.00 |

-- Add 25% if ratfink decal is enclosed
| ❏ ST 2114 [S] | Surfink! | 1964 | 50.00 | 100.00 | 200.00 |

-- With bonus single in pocket on cover: "Santa Barbara"/"Midnight Run" by the Super Stocks
| ❏ ST 2114 [S] | Surfink! | 1964 | 37.50 | 75.00 | 150.00 |

-- Without bonus single
| ❏ T 2114 [M] | Surfink! | 1964 | 37.50 | 75.00 | 150.00 |

-- With bonus single in pocket on cover: "Santa Barbara"/"Midnight Run" by the Super Stocks
| ❏ T 2114 [M] | Surfink! | 1964 | 25.00 | 50.00 | 100.00 |

-- Without bonus single

MR. SHORT STUFF
SPIVEY
| ❏ 1005 | Mr. Short Stuff | 196? | 5.00 | 10.00 | 20.00 |

MITCHELL TRIO, THE
Also see JOHN DENVER.
MERCURY
❏ SR-60944 [S]	The Slightly Irreverent Mitchell Trio	1964	5.00	10.00	20.00
❏ SR-60992 [S]	Typical American Boys	1965	5.00	10.00	20.00
❏ SR-61049 [S]	That's the Way It's Gonna Be	1965	5.00	10.00	20.00
❏ SR-61067 [S]	Violets of Dawn	1966	5.00	10.00	20.00
REPRISE
| ❏ R-6258 [M] | Alive | 1967 | 5.00 | 10.00 | 20.00 |

MITCHELL, CHAD
WARNER BROS.
| ❏ WS 1667 [S] | Chad Mitchell Himself | 1966 | 5.00 | 10.00 | 20.00 |
| ❏ W 1706 [M] | A Feeling of Love | 1967 | 5.00 | 10.00 | 20.00 |

MITCHELL, CHAD, TRIO
COLPIX
❏ CP-411 [M]	The Chad Mitchell Trio	1961	5.00	10.00	20.00
❏ SCP-411 [S]	The Chad Mitchell Trio	1961	7.50	15.00	30.00
❏ CP-463 [M]	Everybody's Listening	1964	5.00	10.00	20.00
❏ SCP-463 [S]	Everybody's Listening	1964	7.50	15.00	30.00
KAPP
❏ KL-1262 [M]	Mighty Day on Campus	1962	5.00	10.00	20.00
❏ KL-1281 [M]	The Chad Mitchell Trio at the Bitter End	1962	5.00	10.00	20.00
❏ KL-1313 [M]	Blowin' in the Wind	1963	5.00	10.00	20.00
❏ KL-1334 [M]	The Best of Chad Mitchell Trio	1963	5.00	10.00	20.00
❏ KS-3262 [S]	Mighty Day on Campus	1962	6.25	12.50	25.00
❏ KS-3281 [S]	The Chad Mitchell Trio at the Bitter End	1962	6.25	12.50	25.00
❏ KS-3313 [S]	Blowin' in the Wind	1963	6.25	12.50	25.00
❏ KS-3334 [S]	The Best of Chad Mitchell Trio	1963	6.25	12.50	25.00
MERCURY
| ❏ SR-60838 [S] | Singin' Our Mind | 1963 | 5.00 | 10.00 | 20.00 |
| ❏ SR-60891 [S] | Reflecting | 1964 | 5.00 | 10.00 | 20.00 |

MITCHELL, FREDDIE
ALLEGRO ROYALE
| ❏ 1600 [M] | That Boogie Beat | 195? | 15.00 | 30.00 | 60.00 |

MITCHELL, GUY
COLUMBIA
| ❏ CL 1211 [M] | Guy in Love | 1958 | 10.00 | 20.00 | 40.00 |
| ❏ CL 1226 [M] | Guy's Greatest Hits | 1959 | 12.50 | 25.00 | 50.00 |

-- Red and black label with six "eye" logos
| ❏ CL 1226 [M] | Guy's Greatest Hits | 1962 | 7.50 | 15.00 | 30.00 |

-- "Guaranteed High Fidelity" on red label
| ❏ CL 1226 [M] | Guy's Greatest Hits | 1965 | 5.00 | 10.00 | 20.00 |

-- "360 Sound Mono" on red label

❏ CL 1552 [M]	Sunshine Guitar	1960	7.50	15.00	30.00
❏ CL 6231 [10]	Open Spaces	1953	17.50	35.00	70.00
❏ CS 8011 [S]	Guy in Love	1959	12.50	25.00	50.00
❏ CS 8352 [S]	Sunshine Guitar	1960	10.00	20.00	40.00
KING
| ❏ 644 [M] | Sincerely Yours | 1959 | 75.00 | 150.00 | 300.00 |
STARDAY
| ❏ 412 | Traveling Shoes | 1968 | 5.00 | 10.00 | 20.00 |
| ❏ 432 | Singin' Up a Storm | 1969 | 5.00 | 10.00 | 20.00 |

MITCHELL, JONI
ASYLUM
| ❏ EQ-1001 [Q] | Court and Spark | 1974 | 5.00 | 10.00 | 20.00 |
| ❏ EQ-1051 [Q] | The Hissing of Summer Lawns | 1975 | 5.00 | 10.00 | 20.00 |
DCC COMPACT CLASSICS
| ❏ LPZ-2044 | Court and Spark | 1997 | 6.25 | 12.50 | 25.00 |

-- Audiophile vinyl
| ❏ LPZ-2069 | Blue | 1999 | 6.25 | 12.50 | 25.00 |

-- Audiophile vinyl
NAUTILUS
| ❏ NR-11 | Court and Spark | 1980 | 12.50 | 25.00 | 50.00 |

-- Audiophile vinyl
REPRISE
| ❏ RS 6293 | Joni Mitchell | 1968 | 5.00 | 10.00 | 20.00 |

-- With "W7" and "r:" logos on two-tone orange label
| ❏ RS 6341 | Clouds | 1969 | 5.00 | 10.00 | 20.00 |

-- With "W7" and "r:" logos on two-tone orange label
| ❏ RS 6376 | Ladies of the Canyon | 1970 | 5.00 | 10.00 | 20.00 |

-- With "W7" and "r:" logos on two-tone orange label

MITCHELL, WILLIE
HI
❏ HL-32010 [M]	Sunrise Serenade	1963	10.00	20.00	40.00
❏ SHL-32010 [S]	Sunrise Serenade	1963	6.25	12.50	25.00
❏ HL-32021 [M]	Hold It	1964	6.25	12.50	25.00
❏ SHL-32021 [S]	Hold It	1964	7.50	15.00	30.00
❏ HL-32026 [M]	It's Dance Time	1965	6.25	12.50	25.00
❏ SHL-32026 [S]	It's Dance Time	1965	7.50	15.00	30.00
❏ HL-32029 [M]	Driving Beat	1966	6.25	12.50	25.00
❏ SHL-32029 [S]	Driving Beat	1966	7.50	15.00	30.00
❏ HL-32034 [M]	The Hit Sound of Willie Mitchell	1967	7.50	15.00	30.00
❏ SHL-32034 [S]	The Hit Sound of Willie Mitchell	1967	6.25	12.50	25.00
❏ HL-32039 [M]	Ooh Baby, You Turn Me On	1967	7.50	15.00	30.00
❏ SHL-32039 [S]	Ooh Baby, You Turn Me On	1967	6.25	12.50	25.00
❏ SHL-32042	Willie Mitchell Live	1968	6.25	12.50	25.00
❏ SHL-32045	Solid Soul	1968	6.25	12.50	25.00
❏ SHL-32048	On Top	1969	6.25	12.50	25.00
❏ SHL-32050	Soul Bag	1969	6.25	12.50	25.00
❏ SHL-32056	The Many Moods of Willie Mitchell	1970	6.25	12.50	25.00
❏ SHL-32058	Robin's Nest	1970	6.25	12.50	25.00
❏ SHL-32068/9 [(2)]	The Best of Willie Mitchell	1971	7.50	15.00	30.00

MITCHUM, ROBERT
CAPITOL
| ❏ T 853 [M] | Calypso -- Is Like So... | 1957 | 25.00 | 50.00 | 100.00 |
MONUMENT
| ❏ MLP-8066 [M] | That Man, Robert Mitchum, Sings | 1967 | 6.25 | 12.50 | 25.00 |
| ❏ SLP-18066 [S] | That Man, Robert Mitchum, Sings | 1967 | 6.25 | 12.50 | 25.00 |

MIXTURES, THE
LINDA
| ❏ 3301 [M] | Stompin' at the Rainbow | 1962 | 25.00 | 50.00 | 100.00 |

MIZE, BILLY
IMPERIAL
| ❏ LP-12441 | This Time and Place | 1969 | 5.00 | 10.00 | 20.00 |

MOB, THE
COLOSSUS
| ❏ CS-1006 | The Mob | 1971 | 5.00 | 10.00 | 20.00 |

MOBY GRAPE
COLUMBIA
| ❏ MGS 1 | Grape Jam | 1968 | 5.00 | 10.00 | 20.00 |
| ❏ CXS 3 [(2)] | Wow/Grape Jam | 1968 | 7.50 | 15.00 | 30.00 |

-- Joint release of the two albums under one cover
| ❏ CL 2698 [M] | Moby Grape | 1967 | 10.00 | 20.00 | 40.00 |

-- Cover has Don Stephenson "giving the finger" on his washboard
| ❏ CL 2698 [M] | Moby Grape | 1967 | 5.00 | 10.00 | 20.00 |

-- Cover has offending finger airbrushed out
| ❏ CS 9498 [S] | Moby Grape | 1967 | 5.00 | 10.00 | 20.00 |

-- Cover has offending finger airbrushed out

Number	Title	Yr	VG	VG+	NM
❑ CS 9498 [S]	Moby Grape	1967	10.00	20.00	40.00
-- Cover has Don Stephenson "giving the finger" on his washboard					
❑ CS 9613	Wow	1968	5.00	10.00	20.00
❑ CS 9696	Moby Grape '69	1969	5.00	10.00	20.00
❑ CS 9912	Truly Fine Citizen	1969	5.00	10.00	20.00
REPRISE					
❑ RS 6460	20 Granite Creek	1971	5.00	10.00	20.00

MOD AND THE ROCKERS
JUSTICE

Number	Title	Yr	VG	VG+	NM
❑ JLP-153	Mod and the Rockers Now!	1967	100.00	200.00	400.00

MODERN FOLK QUARTET, THE
WARNER BROS.

Number	Title	Yr	VG	VG+	NM
❑ W 1511 [M]	The Modern Folk Quartet	1963	6.25	12.50	25.00
❑ WS 1511 [S]	The Modern Folk Quartet	1963	7.50	15.00	30.00
❑ W 1546 [M]	Changes	1964	6.25	12.50	25.00
❑ WS 1546 [S]	Changes	1964	7.50	15.00	30.00

MODERN JAZZ QUARTET, THE
APPLE

Number	Title	Yr	VG	VG+	NM
❑ ST-3353	Under the Jasmine Tree	1969	6.25	12.50	25.00
❑ ST-5-3353	Under the Jasmine Tree	1969	10.00	20.00	40.00
-- Capitol Record Club edition					
❑ STAO-3360	Space	1970	6.25	12.50	25.00
❑ STAO-5-3360	Space	1970	10.00	20.00	40.00
-- Capitol Record Club edition					

ATLANTIC

Number	Title	Yr	VG	VG+	NM
❑ 2-603 [(2) M]	The European Concert	1961	7.50	15.00	30.00
-- Multicolor labels, white "fan" logo at right					
❑ 2-603 [(2) M]	The European Concert	1963	5.00	10.00	20.00
❑ SD 2-603 [(2) S]	The European Concert	1961	10.00	20.00	40.00
-- Multicolor labels, white "fan" logo at right					
❑ SD 2-603 [(2) S]	The European Concert	1963	6.25	12.50	25.00
-- Multicolor labels, black "fan" logo at right					
-- Multicolor labels, black "fan" logo at right					
❑ 1231 [M]	Fontessa	1956	10.00	20.00	40.00
-- Black label					
❑ 1231 [M]	Fontessa	1960	5.00	10.00	20.00
-- Multicolor label, white "fan" logo at right					
❑ SD 1231 [S]	Fontessa	1958	7.50	15.00	30.00
-- Green label					
❑ 1247 [M]	The Modern Jazz Quartet at the Music Inn	1956	10.00	20.00	40.00
-- Black label					
❑ 1247 [M]	The Modern Jazz Quartet at the Music Inn	1960	5.00	10.00	20.00
-- Multicolor label, white "fan" logo at right					
❑ 1265 [M]	The Modern Jazz Quartet	1957	10.00	20.00	40.00
-- Black label					
❑ 1265 [M]	The Modern Jazz Quartet	1960	5.00	10.00	20.00
-- Multicolor label, white "fan" logo at right					
❑ 1284 [M]	No Sun in Venice	1958	10.00	20.00	40.00
-- Black label					
❑ 1284 [M]	No Sun in Venice	1960	5.00	10.00	20.00
-- Multicolor label, white "fan" logo at right					
❑ SD 1284 [S]	No Sun in Venice	1958	7.50	15.00	30.00
-- Green label					
❑ 1299 [M]	The Modern Jazz Quartet at the Music Inn, Volume 2	1958	10.00	20.00	40.00
-- Black label					
❑ 1299 [M]	The Modern Jazz Quartet at the Music Inn, Volume 2	1960	5.00	10.00	20.00
-- Multicolor label, white "fan" logo at right					
❑ SD 1299 [S]	The Modern Jazz Quartet at the Music Inn, Volume 2	1958	7.50	15.00	30.00
-- Green label					
❑ 1325 [M]	Pyramid	1960	10.00	20.00	40.00
-- Black label					
❑ 1325 [M]	Pyramid	1961	5.00	10.00	20.00
-- Multicolor label, white "fan" logo at right					
❑ SD 1325 [S]	Pyramid	1960	7.50	15.00	30.00
-- Green label					
❑ 1345 [M]	Third Stream Music	1960	5.00	10.00	20.00
-- Multicolor label, white "fan" logo at right					
❑ SD 1345 [S]	Third Stream Music	1960	6.25	12.50	25.00
-- Multicolor label, white "fan" logo at right					
❑ 1359 [M]	The Modern Jazz Quartet and Orchestra	1961	5.00	10.00	20.00
-- Multicolor label, white "fan" logo at right					
❑ SD 1359 [S]	The Modern Jazz Quartet and Orchestra	1961	6.25	12.50	25.00
-- Multicolor label, white "fan" logo at right					
❑ SD 1381 [S]	Lonely Woman	1962	5.00	10.00	20.00
-- Multicolor label, black "fan" logo at right					
❑ SD 1385 [S]	The European Concert, Volume 1	1962	5.00	10.00	20.00
-- Multicolor label, black "fan" logo at right					
❑ SD 1386 [S]	The European Concert, Volume 2	1962	5.00	10.00	20.00
-- Multicolor label, black "fan" logo at right					

Number	Title	Yr	VG	VG+	NM
❑ SD 1390 [S]	The Comedy	1963	5.00	10.00	20.00
-- Multicolor label, black "fan" logo at right					
❑ SD 1414 [S]	The Sheriff	1964	5.00	10.00	20.00
-- Multicolor label, black "fan" logo at right					
❑ SD 1420 [S]	A Quartet Is a Quartet Is a Quartet	1964	5.00	10.00	20.00
-- Multicolor label, black "fan" logo at right					
MOBILE FIDELITY					
❑ 1-090	Live at the Lighthouse	1982	12.50	25.00	50.00
-- Audiophile vinyl					
❑ 1-205	The Modern Jazz Quartet	1994	7.50	15.00	30.00
-- Audiophile vinyl					
❑ 1-206	Blues at Carnegie Hall	1994	7.50	15.00	30.00
-- Audiophile vinyl					
❑ 1-228	The Modern Jazz Quartet at the Music Inn, Volume 2	1995	15.00	30.00	60.00
-- Audiophile vinyl					
PRESTIGE					
❑ PRLP-160 [10]	The Modern Jazz Quartet with Milt Jackson	1953	30.00	60.00	120.00
❑ PRLP-170 [10]	The Modern Jazz Quartet, Volume 2	1953	30.00	60.00	120.00
❑ PRLP-7005 [M]	Concorde	1955	17.50	35.00	70.00
-- Yellow label originals					
❑ PRLP-7057 [M]	Django	1956	17.50	35.00	70.00
❑ PRLP-7059 [M]	Modern Jazz Quartet/ Milt Jackson Quintet	1956	17.50	35.00	70.00
-- Yellow label originals					
SAVOY					
❑ MG-12046 [M]	Modern Jazz Quartet	1955	12.50	25.00	50.00
UNITED ARTISTS					
❑ UAL-4072 [M]	Patterns	1960	6.25	12.50	25.00
❑ UAS-5072 [S]	Patterns	1960	7.50	15.00	30.00

MODERN LOVERS, THE -- See JONATHAN RICHMAN AND THE MODERN LOVERS.

MODUGNO, DOMENICO
DECCA

Number	Title	Yr	VG	VG+	NM
❑ DL 4133 [M]	Viva Italia	1961	7.50	15.00	30.00
❑ DL 8808 [M]	Nel Blu Dipinto Di Blu (Volare) and Other Italian Favorites	1958	12.50	25.00	50.00
❑ DL 8853 [M]	Encore	1959	10.00	20.00	40.00

MOJO MEN, THE
GRT

Number	Title	Yr	VG	VG+	NM
❑ 10003	Mojo Magic	1969	6.25	12.50	25.00

MOLLY HATCHET
EPIC

Number	Title	Yr	VG	VG+	NM
❑ AS99 694 [DJ]	Flirtin' with Disaster	1979	10.00	20.00	40.00
-- Promo-only picture disc					
❑ AS99 844 [DJ]	Beatin' the Odds	1980	10.00	20.00	40.00
-- Promo-only picture disc					
❑ AS99 1320 [DJ]	Take No Prisoners	1981	6.25	12.50	25.00
-- Promo-only picture disc					

MOLOCH
ENTERPRISE

Number	Title	Yr	VG	VG+	NM
❑ ENS-1002	Moloch	1969	5.00	10.00	20.00

MOM'S APPLE PIE
BROWN BAG

Number	Title	Yr	VG	VG+	NM
❑ 14200	Mom's Apple Pie	1972	5.00	10.00	20.00
-- With vulva showing in the apple pie					
❑ 14200	Mom's Apple Pie	1972	5.00	10.00	20.00
-- With barbed wire wall covering the former opening. This is much rarer than the first version, though less sought-after					

MOMENTS, THE
STANG

Number	Title	Yr	VG	VG+	NM
❑ ST-1000	Not On the Outside, But On the Inside Strong	1969	7.50	15.00	30.00
❑ ST-1002	The Moments On Top	1970	7.50	15.00	30.00
❑ ST-1003	A Moment with the Moments	1970	7.50	15.00	30.00
❑ ST-1004	Moments Greatest Hits	1971	5.00	10.00	20.00
❑ ST-1006	The Moments Live at the New York State Womans Prison	1971	6.25	12.50	25.00
❑ ST-1009	The Other Side of the Moments	1972	6.25	12.50	25.00
❑ ST-1015	Live at the Miss Black America Pageant	1972	5.00	10.00	20.00
❑ 2ST-1033 [(2)]	Greatest Hits	1977	5.00	10.00	20.00

Number	Title	Yr	VG	VG+	NM

MONDAY BLUES
VAULT
| ❏ 133 | The Phil Spector Song Book | 1970 | 5.00 | 10.00 | 20.00 |

MONEY, ZOOT
EPIC
| ❏ LN 24241 [M] | All Happening Zoot Money's Big Roll Band at Klooks Kleek | 1966 | 5.00 | 10.00 | 20.00 |

MONICA, CORBETT
DOT
| ❏ DLP-3303 [M] | For Laughs | 1960 | 7.50 | 15.00 | 30.00 |

MONITORS, THE
SOUL
| ❏ SS-714 | Greetings, We're the Monitors | 1969 | 15.00 | 30.00 | 60.00 |

MONK, THELONIOUS
BLUE NOTE
❏ BLP-1510 [M]	Genius of Modern Music, Vol. 1	1956	50.00	100.00	200.00
-- "Deep groove" version (deep indentation under label on both sides)					
❏ BLP-1510 [M]	Genius of Modern Music, Vol. 1	1956	37.50	75.00	150.00
-- Regular edition, Lexington Ave. address on label					
❏ BLP-1510 [M]	Genius of Modern Music, Vol. 1	1963	6.25	12.50	25.00
-- "New York, USA" address on label					
❏ BLP-1511 [M]	Genius of Modern Music, Vol. 2	1956	50.00	100.00	200.00
-- "Deep groove" version (deep indentation under label on both sides)					
❏ BLP-1511 [M]	Genius of Modern Music, Vol. 2	1956	37.50	75.00	150.00
-- Regular edition, Lexington Ave. address on label					
❏ BLP-1511 [M]	Genius of Modern Music, Vol. 2	1963	6.25	12.50	25.00
-- "New York, USA" address on label					
❏ BLP-5002 [10]	Genius of Modern Music, Vol. 1	1952	100.00	200.00	400.00
❏ BLP-5009 [10]	Genius of Modern Music, Vol. 2	1952	100.00	200.00	400.00

COLUMBIA
❏ CL 1965 [M]	Monk's Dream	1963	5.00	10.00	20.00
❏ CL 2038 [M]	Criss-Cross	1963	5.00	10.00	20.00
❏ CL 2164 [M]	Monk Big Band and Quartet In Concert	1964	5.00	10.00	20.00
❏ CL 2184 [M]	It's Monk's Time	1964	5.00	10.00	20.00
❏ CL 2291 [M]	Monk	1965	5.00	10.00	20.00
❏ CL 2349 [M]	Solo Monk	1965	5.00	10.00	20.00
❏ CL 2416 [M]	Misterioso	1966	5.00	10.00	20.00
❏ CL 2651 [M]	Straight No Chaser	1967	7.50	15.00	50.00
❏ CS 8765 [S]	Monk's Dream	1963	6.25	12.50	25.00
❏ CS 8838 [S]	Criss-Cross	1963	6.25	12.50	25.00
❏ CS 8964 [S]	Monk Big Band and Quartet In Concert	1964	6.25	12.50	25.00
❏ CS 8984 [S]	It's Monk's Time	1964	6.25	12.50	25.00
❏ CS 9091 [S]	Monk	1965	6.25	12.50	25.00
❏ CS 9149 [S]	Solo Monk	1965	6.25	12.50	25.00
-- Red "360 Sound" label					
❏ CS 9216 [S]	Misterioso	1966	6.25	12.50	25.00
❏ CS 9451 [S]	Straight No Chaser	1967	5.00	10.00	20.00
-- Red "360 Sound" label					
❏ CS 9632	Underground	1968	5.00	10.00	20.00
-- Red "360 Sound" label					
❏ CS 9806	Monk's Blues	1969	5.00	10.00	20.00
-- Red "360 Sound" label					

COLUMBIA MUSICAL TREASURY
| ❏ DS 338 | Monk's Miracles | 1967 | 6.25 | 12.50 | 25.00 |
| -- Columbia Record Club exclusive | | | | | |

MOSAIC
| ❏ MR4-112 [(4)] | The Complete Black Lion and Vogue Recordings | 199? | 15.00 | 30.00 | 60.00 |

PRESTIGE
❏ PRLP-142 [10]	Thelonious Monk Trio	1953	50.00	100.00	200.00
❏ PRLP-166 [10]	Thelonious Monk Quintet with Sonny Rollins and Julius Watkins	1953	50.00	100.00	200.00
❏ PRLP-180 [10]	Thelonious Monk Quintet	1954	50.00	100.00	200.00
❏ PRLP-189 [10]	Thelonious Monk Trio	1954	50.00	100.00	200.00
❏ PRLP-7027 [M]	Thelonious Monk	1956	25.00	50.00	100.00
-- Reissue of 142 and 189 on one 12-inch record					
❏ PRLP-7053 [M]	Monk	1956	25.00	50.00	100.00
-- Reissue of 150					
❏ PRLP-7075 [M]	Thelonious Monk/Sonny Rollins	1957	25.00	50.00	100.00
-- Reissue of 166					
❏ PRLP-7159 [M]	Monk's Moods	1959	18.75	37.50	75.00
-- Reissue of 7027					
❏ PRLP-7169 [M]	Work	1959	18.75	37.50	75.00
-- Reissue of 7075					
❏ PRLP-7245 [M]	We See	1962	18.75	37.50	75.00
-- Reissue of 7053					
❏ PRLP-7363 [M]	The Golden Monk	1965	7.50	15.00	30.00
-- Reissue of 7245					
❏ PRLP-7508 [M]	The High Priest	1967	7.50	15.00	30.00
-- Reissue of 7159					

RIVERSIDE
❏ R-022 [(22)]	The Complete Riverside Recordings	1987	100.00	200.00	400.00
❏ RLP 12-201 [M]	Thelonious Monk Plays Duke Ellington	1955	100.00	200.00	400.00
-- White label with blue print					
❏ RLP 12-201 [M]	Thelonious Monk Plays Duke Ellington	1958	10.00	20.00	40.00
-- Blue label with reel and microphone logo					
❏ RLP 12-209 [M]	The Unique Thelonious Monk	1956	25.00	50.00	100.00
-- White label with blue print					
❏ RLP 12-209 [M]	The Unique Thelonious Monk	1958	10.00	20.00	40.00
-- Blue label with reel and microphone logo					
❏ RLP 12-226 [M]	Brilliant Corners	1957	25.00	50.00	100.00
-- White label with blue print					
❏ RLP 12-226 [M]	Brilliant Corners	1958	10.00	20.00	40.00
-- Blue label with reel and microphone logo					
❏ RLP 12-235 [M]	Thelonious Himself	1957	25.00	50.00	100.00
-- White label with blue print					
❏ RLP 12-235 [M]	Thelonious Himself	1958	10.00	20.00	40.00
-- Blue label with reel and microphone logo					
❏ RLP 12-242 [M]	Monk's Music	1957	25.00	50.00	100.00
-- White label with blue print					
❏ RLP 12-242 [M]	Monk's Music	1958	10.00	20.00	40.00
-- Blue label with reel and microphone logo					
❏ RLP 12-247 [M]	Mulligan Meets Monk	1957	25.00	50.00	100.00
-- White label with blue print					
❏ RLP 12-247 [M]	Mulligan Meets Monk	1958	10.00	20.00	40.00
-- Blue label with reel and microphone logo					
❏ RLP 12-262 [M]	Thelonious in Action Recorded at the Five Spot Café, New York, With Johnny Griffin	1958	10.00	20.00	40.00
❏ RLP 12-279 [M]	Misterioso	1958	10.00	20.00	40.00
❏ RLP 12-300 [M]	The Thelonious Monk Orchestra at Town Hall	1959	10.00	20.00	40.00
❏ RLP 12-305 [M]	5 By Monk By 5	1959	10.00	20.00	40.00
❏ RLP 12-312 [M]	Thelonious Alone in San Francisco	1959	10.00	20.00	40.00
❏ RLP 12-323 [M]	Thelonious Monk Quartet Plus Two at the Blackhawk	1960	10.00	20.00	40.00
❏ RLP-421 [M]	Thelonious Monk's Greatest Hits	1962	5.00	10.00	20.00
❏ RLP-443 [M]	Monk in Italy	1963	5.00	10.00	20.00
❏ RLP-460/1 [(2) M]	April in Paris	1963	10.00	20.00	40.00
❏ RLP-483 [M]	The Thelonious Monk Story, Volume 1	1965	5.00	10.00	20.00
❏ RLP-484 [M]	The Thelonious Monk Story, Volume 2	1965	5.00	10.00	20.00
❏ RLP-491 [M]	Monk in France	1965	5.00	10.00	20.00
❏ RLP 1101 [S]	Monk's Music	1959	10.00	20.00	40.00
-- Black label with reel and microphone logo					
❏ RLP 1106 [S]	Mulligan Meets Monk	1959	10.00	20.00	40.00
-- Black label with reel and microphone logo					
❏ RLP 1133 [S]	Misterioso	1958	12.50	25.00	50.00
❏ RLP 1138 [S]	The Thelonious Monk Orchestra at Town Hall	1959	12.50	25.00	50.00
❏ RLP 1150 [S]	5 By Monk By 5	1959	12.50	25.00	50.00
❏ RLP 1158 [S]	Thelonious Alone in San Francisco	1959	12.50	25.00	50.00
❏ RLP 1171 [S]	Thelonious Monk Quartet Plus Two at the Blackhawk	1960	12.50	25.00	50.00
❏ RLP 1190 [S]	Thelonious in Action Recorded at the Five Spot Café, New York, With Johnny Griffin	1960	12.50	25.00	50.00
❏ RM-3000 [M]	Mighty Monk	1967	5.00	10.00	20.00
❏ RM-3004 [M]	Monk's Music	1967	5.00	10.00	20.00
❏ RS-9421 [S]	Thelonious Monk's Greatest Hits	1962	6.25	12.50	25.00
❏ RS-9443 [S]	Monk in Italy	1963	6.25	12.50	25.00
❏ RS-9460/1 [(2) S]	April in Paris	1963	12.50	25.00	50.00
❏ RS-9483 [S]	The Thelonious Monk Story, Volume 1	1965	6.25	12.50	25.00
❏ RS-9484 [S]	The Thelonious Monk Story, Volume 2	1965	6.25	12.50	25.00
❏ RS-9491 [S]	Monk in France	1965	6.25	12.50	25.00

MONK, THELONIOUS, AND JOHN COLTRANE
Also see each artist's individual listings.
JAZZLAND
| ❏ JLP-46 [M] | Thelonious Monk with John Coltrane | 1961 | 10.00 | 20.00 | 40.00 |
| ❏ JLP-946 [S] | Thelonious Monk with John Coltrane | 1961 | 12.50 | 25.00 | 50.00 |

RIVERSIDE
❏ RLP-490 [M]	Thelonious Monk with John Coltrane	1965	6.25	12.50	25.00
-- Reissue of Jazzland 46					
❏ RS-9490 [S]	Thelonious Monk with John Coltrane	1965	7.50	15.00	30.00
-- Reissue of Jazzland 946					

MONKEES, THE
Also see DAVY JONES; MICHAEL NESMITH.
BELL
| ❏ 6081 | Re-Focus | 1972 | 7.50 | 15.00 | 30.00 |

Number	Title	Yr	VG	VG+	NM

COLGEMS

Number	Title	Yr	VG	VG+	NM
❑ COM-101 [M]	The Monkees	1966	6.25	12.50	25.00
-- First pressing: Side 1, Song 5 listed as "Papa Jean's Blues"					
❑ COM-101 [M]	The Monkees	1966	5.00	10.00	20.00
-- Second pressing: Side 1, Song 5 listed as "Papa Gene's Blues" (RE after number on upper right back cover)					
❑ COS-101 [S]	The Monkees	1966	6.25	12.50	25.00
-- First pressing: Side 1, Song 5 listed as "Papa Jean's Blues"					
❑ COS-101 [S]	The Monkees	1966	5.00	10.00	20.00
-- Second pressing: Side 1, Song 5 listed as "Papa Gene's Blues" (RE after number on upper right back cover)					
❑ COM-102 [M]	More of the Monkees	1966	5.00	10.00	20.00
❑ COS-102 [S]	More of the Monkees	1966	5.00	10.00	20.00
❑ COM-103 [M]	The Monkees' Headquarters	1967	5.00	10.00	20.00
-- First pressing: Back cover, center bottom photo is of two of the LP's producers					
❑ COM-103 [M]	The Monkees' Headquarters	1967	7.50	15.00	30.00
-- Second pressing: Back cover, center bottom photo is of producers plus the Monkees with beards; "RE" on upper right back cover					
❑ COS-103 [S]	The Monkees' Headquarters	1967	5.00	10.00	20.00
-- First pressing: Back cover, center bottom photo is of two of the LP's producers					
❑ COS-103 [S]	The Monkees' Headquarters	1967	7.50	15.00	30.00
-- Second pressing: Back cover, center bottom photo is of producers plus the Monkees with beards; "RE" on upper right back cover					
❑ COM-104 [M]	Pisces, Aquarius, Capricorn & Jones Ltd.	1967	10.00	20.00	40.00
❑ COS-104 [S]	Pisces, Aquarius, Capricorn & Jones Ltd.	1967	5.00	10.00	20.00
❑ COM-109 [M]	The Birds, the Bees & the Monkees	1968	25.00	50.00	100.00
❑ COS-109 [S]	The Birds, the Bees & the Monkees	1968	5.00	10.00	20.00
❑ COS-113	Instant Replay	1969	10.00	20.00	40.00
❑ COS-115	The Monkees Greatest Hits	1969	10.00	20.00	40.00
❑ COS-117	The Monkees Present	1969	12.50	25.00	50.00
❑ COS-119	Changes	1970	20.00	40.00	80.00
❑ PRS-329	The Monkees' Golden Hits	1971	25.00	50.00	100.00
-- RCA Special Products edition					
❑ SCOS-1001 [(2)]	A Barrel Full of Monkees	1971	18.75	37.50	75.00
❑ COSO-5008	Head	1968	12.50	25.00	50.00

FSH

Number	Title	Yr	VG	VG+	NM
❑ 71110	Live, 20th Anniversary Tour	1987	5.00	10.00	20.00
-- Live album sold at tour stops					

LAURIE HOUSE

Number	Title	Yr	VG	VG+	NM
❑ LH-8009	The Monkees	1974	5.00	10.00	20.00
-- TV mail-order offer					

PAIR

Number	Title	Yr	VG	VG+	NM
❑ ARPDL2-1109 [(2)]	Hit Factory	1986	5.00	10.00	20.00

RCA SPECIAL PRODUCTS

Number	Title	Yr	VG	VG+	NM
❑ DPL2-0188 [(2)]	The Monkees	1976	6.25	12.50	25.00
-- TV mail-order offer					

MONRO, MATT

LIBERTY

Number	Title	Yr	VG	VG+	NM
❑ LST-7240 [S]	Matt Monro	1962	5.00	10.00	20.00
❑ LST-7256 [S]	From Hollywood With Love	1962	5.00	10.00	20.00

LONDON

Number	Title	Yr	VG	VG+	NM
❑ LL 1611 [M]	Blue and Sentimental	1957	7.50	15.00	30.00

WARWICK

Number	Title	Yr	VG	VG+	NM
❑ W 2045 [M]	My Kind of Girl	1961	7.50	15.00	30.00
❑ WST 2045 [S]	My Kind of Girl	1961	12.50	25.00	50.00

MONROE, BILL

DECCA

Number	Title	Yr	VG	VG+	NM
❑ DL 4080 [M]	Mr. Bluegrass	1960	7.50	15.00	30.00
❑ DL 4266 [M]	Bluegrass Ramble	1962	7.50	15.00	30.00
❑ DL 4327 [M]	My All Time Country Favorites	1962	6.25	12.50	25.00
❑ DL 4382 [M]	Bluegrass Special	1963	6.25	12.50	25.00
❑ DL 4537 [M]	I'll Meet You in Church Sunday Morning	1964	6.25	12.50	25.00
❑ DL 4601 [M]	Bluegrass Instrumentals	1965	5.00	10.00	20.00
❑ DL 4780 [M]	The High Lonesome Sound of Bill Monroe	1966	5.00	10.00	20.00
❑ DL 4896 [M]	Bluegrass Time	1967	7.50	15.00	30.00
❑ DL 8731 [M]	Knee Deep in Bluegrass	1958	12.50	25.00	50.00
❑ DL 8769 [M]	I Saw the Light	1959	12.50	25.00	50.00
❑ DL 74080 [S]	Mr. Bluegrass	1960	10.00	20.00	40.00
❑ DL 74266 [S]	Bluegrass Ramble	1962	10.00	20.00	40.00
❑ DL 74327 [S]	My All Time Country Favorites	1962	7.50	15.00	30.00
❑ DL 74382 [S]	Bluegrass Special	1963	7.50	15.00	30.00
❑ DL 74537 [S]	I'll Meet You in Church Sunday Morning	1964	7.50	15.00	30.00
❑ DL 74601 [S]	Bluegrass Instrumentals	1965	6.25	12.50	25.00
❑ DL 74780 [S]	The High Lonesome Sound of Bill Monroe	1966	6.25	12.50	25.00
❑ DL 74896 [S]	Bluegrass Time	1967	5.00	10.00	20.00
❑ DL 75010	Bill Monroe's Greatest Hits	1968	5.00	10.00	20.00
❑ DL 75135	A Voice from On High	1969	5.00	10.00	20.00
❑ DL 75213	Kentucky Bluegrass	1970	5.00	10.00	20.00
❑ DL 75281	Country Music Hall of Fame	1972	5.00	10.00	20.00
❑ DL 78731 [S]	Knee Deep in Bluegrass	1958	17.50	35.00	70.00
❑ DL 78769 [S]	I Saw the Light	1959	17.50	35.00	70.00

HARMONY

Number	Title	Yr	VG	VG+	NM
❑ HL 7290 [M]	The Great Bill Monroe and His Bluegrass Boys	1961	6.25	12.50	25.00
❑ HL 7315 [M]	Bill Monroe's Best	1964	5.00	10.00	20.00
❑ HL 7338 [M]	The Original Bluegrass Sound	1965	5.00	10.00	20.00

MCA

Number	Title	Yr	VG	VG+	NM
❑ 8002 [(2)]	Bean Blossom	1973	5.00	10.00	20.00

RCA CAMDEN

Number	Title	Yr	VG	VG+	NM
❑ CAL-719 [M]	Father of Bluegrass Music	1962	6.25	12.50	25.00

MONROE, CHARLIE

STARDAY

Number	Title	Yr	VG	VG+	NM
❑ SLP-361 [M]	Lord, Build Me a Cabin	1965	6.25	12.50	25.00
❑ SLP-372 [M]	Charlie Monroe Sings Again	1966	6.25	12.50	25.00

MONROE, MARILYN

ASCOT

Number	Title	Yr	VG	VG+	NM
❑ AM-13008 [M]	Marilyn Monroe	1963	10.00	20.00	40.00
❑ AS-16008 [S]	Marilyn Monroe	1963	12.50	25.00	50.00

MOVIETONE

Number	Title	Yr	VG	VG+	NM
❑ 1016 [M]	The Unforgettable Marilyn Monroe	1967	6.25	12.50	25.00
❑ 72016 [R]	The Unforgettable Marilyn Monroe	1967	5.00	10.00	20.00

SANDY HOOK

Number	Title	Yr	VG	VG+	NM
❑ SH-2013 [PD]	Rare Recordings 1948-1962	1980	6.25	12.50	25.00

20TH CENTURY

Number	Title	Yr	VG	VG+	NM
❑ T-901	Remember Marilyn	1973	6.25	12.50	25.00

20TH FOX

Number	Title	Yr	VG	VG+	NM
❑ FXG-5000 [M]	Marilyn	1962	37.50	75.00	150.00
❑ SXG-5000 [R]	Marilyn	1962	25.00	50.00	100.00
❑ F/SXG-5000	Marilyn Bonus Photo	1962	12.50	25.00	50.00

MONROE, VAUGHN

DOT

Number	Title	Yr	VG	VG+	NM
❑ DLP-3419 [M]	Surfer's Stomp	1962	7.50	15.00	30.00
❑ DLP-25419 [S]	Surfer's Stomp	1962	10.00	20.00	40.00

RCA VICTOR

Number	Title	Yr	VG	VG+	NM
❑ LPM-1799 [M]	There I Sing, Swing It Again	1958	5.00	10.00	20.00
❑ LSP-1799 [S]	There I Sing, Swing It Again	1958	7.50	15.00	30.00
❑ LPM-3048 [10]	Vaughn Monroe's Caravan	1952	10.00	20.00	40.00

MONROES, THE

ALFA

Number	Title	Yr	VG	VG+	NM
❑ AAE-15015 [EP]	The Monroes	1982	5.00	10.00	20.00

MONTAGE

LAURIE

Number	Title	Yr	VG	VG+	NM
❑ SLP-2049	Montage	1969	5.00	10.00	20.00

MONTANA SLIM (WILF CARTER)

DECCA

Number	Title	Yr	VG	VG+	NM
❑ DL 4092 [M]	The Dynamite Trail	1960	12.50	25.00	50.00
❑ DL 8917 [M]	I'm Ragged But I'm Right	1959	15.00	30.00	60.00
❑ DL 74092 [S]	The Dynamite Trail	1960	15.00	30.00	60.00

RCA CAMDEN

Number	Title	Yr	VG	VG+	NM
❑ CAL-527 [M]	Wilf Carter/Montana Slim	1958	10.00	20.00	40.00
❑ CAL-668 [M]	Reminiscin' with Montana Slim	1962	6.25	12.50	25.00
❑ CAL-846 [M]	32 Wonderful Years	1965	5.00	10.00	20.00

STARDAY

Number	Title	Yr	VG	VG+	NM
❑ SLP-300 [M]	Wilf Carter As Montana Slim	1964	7.50	15.00	30.00
❑ SLP-389 [M]	Wilf Carter	1966	7.50	15.00	30.00

MONTANA, PATSY

SIMS

Number	Title	Yr	VG	VG+	NM
❑ 122 [M]	The New Sound of Patsy Montana	1964	12.50	25.00	50.00

MONTE, LOU

RCA VICTOR

Number	Title	Yr	VG	VG+	NM
❑ LPM-1651 [M]	Lou Monte Sings for You	1957	6.25	12.50	25.00
❑ LPM-1877 [M]	Songs for Pizza Lovers	1958	6.25	12.50	25.00
❑ LPM-1976 [M]	Italian House Party	1959	5.00	10.00	20.00
❑ LSP-1976 [S]	Italian House Party	1959	6.25	12.50	25.00

REPRISE

Number	Title	Yr	VG	VG+	NM
❑ R-6005 [M]	Great Italian-American Hits	1961	5.00	10.00	20.00
❑ R9-6005 [S]	Great Italian-American Hits	1961	6.25	12.50	25.00

Number	Title	Yr	VG	VG+	NM
❏ R-6014 [M]	Live in Person	1961	5.00	10.00	20.00
❏ R9-6014 [S]	Live in Person	1961	6.25	12.50	25.00
❏ R-6058 [M]	Pepino The Italian Mouse & Other Italian Fun Songs	1962	5.00	10.00	20.00
❏ R9-6058 [S]	Pepino The Italian Mouse & Other Italian Fun Songs	1962	6.25	12.50	25.00
❏ R-6099 [M]	More Italian Fun Songs	1963	5.00	10.00	20.00
❏ R9-6099 [S]	More Italian Fun Songs	1963	6.25	12.50	25.00
❏ RS-6118 [S]	The Golden Hits of Lou Monte	1964	5.00	10.00	20.00

ROULETTE

Number	Title	Yr	VG	VG+	NM
❏ R-25126 [M]	Italiano U.S.A.	1960	5.00	10.00	20.00
❏ SR-25126 [S]	Italiano U.S.A.	1960	6.25	12.50	25.00
❏ SR-25257 [S]	The Magic World of Italy	1963	5.00	10.00	20.00

MONTENEGRO, HUGO

Includes some of his soundtracks; others are in the "Soundtracks" and "Television Albums" sections.

RCA VICTOR

Number	Title	Yr	VG	VG+	NM
❏ APD1-0025 [Q]	Scenes and Themes	1973	5.00	10.00	20.00
❏ APD1-1024 [Q]	Rocket Man	1975	5.00	10.00	20.00
❏ LPM-3927 [M]	Music from A Fistful of Dollars & For a Few Dollars More & The Good, The Bad and The Ugly	1968	5.00	10.00	20.00
❏ LSP-4170	Moog Power	1969	5.00	10.00	20.00

TIME

Number	Title	Yr	VG	VG+	NM
❏ S-2018 [S]	Cha Chas for Dancing	196?	5.00	10.00	20.00
❏ S-2020 [S]	Boogie Woogie and Bongos	196?	5.00	10.00	20.00
❏ S-2030 [S]	Arriba	196?	5.00	10.00	20.00

20TH CENTURY FOX

Number	Title	Yr	VG	VG+	NM
❏ S-4204	Lady in Cement	1968	5.00	10.00	20.00

20TH FOX

Number	Title	Yr	VG	VG+	NM
❏ 3018 [M]	The 20th Century Strings, Volume 1	1959	5.00	10.00	20.00

VIK

Number	Title	Yr	VG	VG+	NM
❏ LX-1089 [M]	Loves of My Life	1957	6.25	12.50	25.00
❏ LX-1106 [M]	Ellington Fantasy	1957	6.25	12.50	25.00

MONTEZ, CHRIS

A&M

Number	Title	Yr	VG	VG+	NM
❏ LP-115 [M]	The More I See You/Call Me	1966	5.00	10.00	20.00
❏ SP-4115 [S]	The More I See You/Call Me	1966	6.25	12.50	25.00
❏ SP-4120 [S]	Time After Time	1966	5.00	10.00	20.00
❏ SP-4128 [S]	Foolin' Around	1967	5.00	10.00	20.00
❏ SP-4157 [S]	Watch What Happens	1967	5.00	10.00	20.00

MONOGRAM

Number	Title	Yr	VG	VG+	NM
❏ M-100 [M]	Let's Dance and Have Some Kinda' Fun!!!	1963	100.00	200.00	400.00

MONTGOMERY, LITTLE BROTHER

BLUESVILLE

Number	Title	Yr	VG	VG+	NM
❏ BVLP-1012 [M]	Tasty Blues	1961	20.00	40.00	80.00
-- Blue label, silver print					
❏ BVLP-1012 [M]	Tasty Blues	1964	7.50	15.00	30.00
-- Blue label with trident logo at right					

RIVERSIDE

Number	Title	Yr	VG	VG+	NM
❏ RLP-410 [M]	Little Brother Montgomery, Chicago Living Legend	1962	7.50	15.00	30.00
❏ RS-9410 [S]	Little Brother Montgomery, Chicago Living Legend	1962	10.00	20.00	40.00

MONTGOMERY, MELBA

Also see GEORGE JONES AND MELBA MONTGOMERY.

MUSICOR

Number	Title	Yr	VG	VG+	NM
❏ MM-2113 [M]	Melba Toast	1967	5.00	10.00	20.00
❏ MM-2114 [M]	Don't Keep Me Lonely Too Long	1967	5.00	10.00	20.00
❏ MS-3074 [S]	Country Girl	1966	5.00	10.00	20.00
❏ MS-3097 [S]	The Hallelujah Road	1966	5.00	10.00	20.00
❏ MS-3113 [S]	Melba Toast	1967	5.00	10.00	20.00
❏ MS-3114 [S]	Don't Keep Me Lonely Too Long	1967	5.00	10.00	20.00

STARDAY

Number	Title	Yr	VG	VG+	NM
❏ SLP-352 [M]	Queen of Country Music	1965	6.25	12.50	25.00

UNITED ARTISTS

Number	Title	Yr	VG	VG+	NM
❏ UAL-3341 [M]	America's Number One Country & Western Singer	1964	5.00	10.00	20.00
❏ UAL-3369 [M]	Down Home	1964	5.00	10.00	20.00
❏ UAL-3391 [M]	I Can't Get Used to Being Lonely	1965	5.00	10.00	20.00
❏ UAS-6341 [S]	America's Number One Country & Western Singer	1964	6.25	12.50	25.00
❏ UAS-6369 [S]	Down Home	1964	6.25	12.50	25.00
❏ UAS-6391 [S]	I Can't Get Used to Being Lonely	1965	6.25	12.50	25.00

MONTGOMERY, WES

A&M

Number	Title	Yr	VG	VG+	NM
❏ LP-2001 [M]	A Day in the Life	1967	5.00	10.00	20.00

DCC COMPACT CLASSICS

Number	Title	Yr	VG	VG+	NM
❏ LPZ-2014	Goin' Out of My Head	1996	6.25	12.50	25.00
-- Audiophile vinyl					

MOBILE FIDELITY

Number	Title	Yr	VG	VG+	NM
❏ MFSL-508	Bumpin'	198?	7.50	15.00	30.00
-- Audiophile vinyl					

PACIFIC JAZZ

Number	Title	Yr	VG	VG+	NM
❏ PJ-5 [M]	Montgomeryland	1960	7.50	15.00	30.00
❏ ST-5 [S]	Montgomeryland	1960	10.00	20.00	40.00
❏ PJ-10130 [M]	Kismet	1967	5.00	10.00	20.00
❏ ST-20104 [S]	Easy Groove	1966	5.00	10.00	20.00

RIVERSIDE

Number	Title	Yr	VG	VG+	NM
❏ RLP 12-310 [M]	New Concepts in Jazz Guitar	1959	7.50	15.00	30.00
❏ RLP 12-320 [M]	The Incredible Jazz Guitar of Wes Montgomery	1960	7.50	15.00	30.00
❏ RLP-342 [M]	Movin' Along	1960	6.25	12.50	25.00
❏ RLP-382 [M]	So Much Guitar!	1961	6.25	12.50	25.00
❏ RLP-434 [M]	Full House	1962	7.50	15.00	30.00
❏ RLP-459 [M]	Boss Guitar	1963	5.00	10.00	20.00
❏ RLP-472 [M]	Fusion! Wes Montgomery with Strings	1964	5.00	10.00	20.00
❏ RLP 1156 [S]	New Concepts in Jazz Guitar	1959	7.50	15.00	30.00
❏ RLP 1169 [S]	The Incredible Jazz Guitar of Wes Montgomery	1960	7.50	15.00	30.00
❏ RS-9342 [S]	Movin' Along	1960	6.25	12.50	25.00
❏ RS-9382 [S]	So Much Guitar!	1961	6.25	12.50	25.00
❏ RS-9434 [S]	Full House	1962	7.50	15.00	30.00
❏ RS-9459 [S]	Boss Guitar	1963	6.25	12.50	25.00
❏ RS-9472 [S]	Fusion! Wes Montgomery with Strings	1964	6.25	12.50	25.00
❏ RS-9492 [S]	Portrait of Wes	1965	5.00	10.00	20.00
❏ RS-9494 [S]	Guitar on the Go	1965	5.00	10.00	20.00

VERVE

Number	Title	Yr	VG	VG+	NM
❏ V6-8610 [S]	Movin' Wes	1965	5.00	10.00	20.00
❏ V6-8625 [S]	Bumpin'	1965	5.00	10.00	20.00
❏ V6-8642 [S]	Goin' Out of My Head	1966	5.00	10.00	20.00
❏ V6-8653 [S]	Tequila	1966	5.00	10.00	20.00
❏ V-8672 [M]	California Dreaming	1967	5.00	10.00	20.00
❏ V-8714 [M]	The Best of Wes Montgomery	1967	5.00	10.00	20.00

MONTY PYTHON

ARISTA

Number	Title	Yr	VG	VG+	NM
❏ SP-101 [DJ]	Monty Python's Contractual Obligation Sampler	1980	7.50	15.00	30.00
-- One side is censored, the other is uncensored					
❏ AL 4039	Matching Tie & Handkerchief	1975	5.00	10.00	20.00
-- Side 2 is "trick tracked," with two different routines depending on where you place the needle at the start					
❏ AL 4050	The Album of the Soundtrack of the Trailer of the Film of "Monty Python and the Holy Grail"	1975	5.00	10.00	20.00
❏ AL 4073	Monty Python Live! At City	1976	5.00	10.00	20.00
❏ AB 9536	Monty Python's Contractual Obligation Album	1980	5.00	10.00	20.00

BUDDAH

Number	Title	Yr	VG	VG+	NM
❏ BDS 5656 [(2)]	The Worst of Monty Python	1976	5.00	10.00	20.00
-- Repackage of the two Charisma LPs					

CHARISMA

Number	Title	Yr	VG	VG+	NM
❏ CAS 1049	Another Monty Python Record	1972	6.25	12.50	25.00
❏ CAS 1063	Monty Python's Previous Record	1972	6.25	12.50	25.00

PYE

Number	Title	Yr	VG	VG+	NM
❏ 12116	Monty Python's Flying Circus	1975	5.00	10.00	20.00

VIRGIN

Number	Title	Yr	VG	VG+	NM
❏ 90865 [(2)]	The Final Rip Off	1988	5.00	10.00	20.00

MOODY BLUES, THE

Also see JUSTIN HAYWARD AND JOHN LODGE; RAY THOMAS.

DERAM

Number	Title	Yr	VG	VG+	NM
❏ DE 16012 [M]	Days of Future Passed	1968	62.50	125.00	250.00
❏ DES 18012 [S]	Days of Future Passed	1968	5.00	10.00	20.00
❏ DES 18017	In Search of the Lost Chord	1968	5.00	10.00	20.00
-- Originals have gatefold covers					
❏ DES 18025	On the Threshold of a Dream	1969	5.00	10.00	20.00
-- Originals have gatefold covers and lyric booklet					
❏ DES 18051 [R]	In the Beginning	1971	5.00	10.00	20.00

LONDON

Number	Title	Yr	VG	VG+	NM
❏ PS 428 [R]	Go Now -- The Moody Blues #1	1965	10.00	20.00	40.00
❏ PS 708 [DJ]	Octave	1978	7.50	15.00	30.00
-- Promo only on blue vinyl					
❏ LL 3428 [M]	Go Now -- The Moody Blues #1	1965	12.50	25.00	50.00

MOBILE FIDELITY

Number	Title	Yr	VG	VG+	NM
❏ 1-042	Days of Future Passed	1980	15.00	30.00	60.00
-- Audiophile vinyl					
❏ 1-151	Seventh Sojourn	1984	17.50	35.00	70.00
-- Audiophile vinyl					
❏ 1-215	On the Threshold of a Dream	1994	6.25	12.50	25.00
-- Audiophile vinyl					

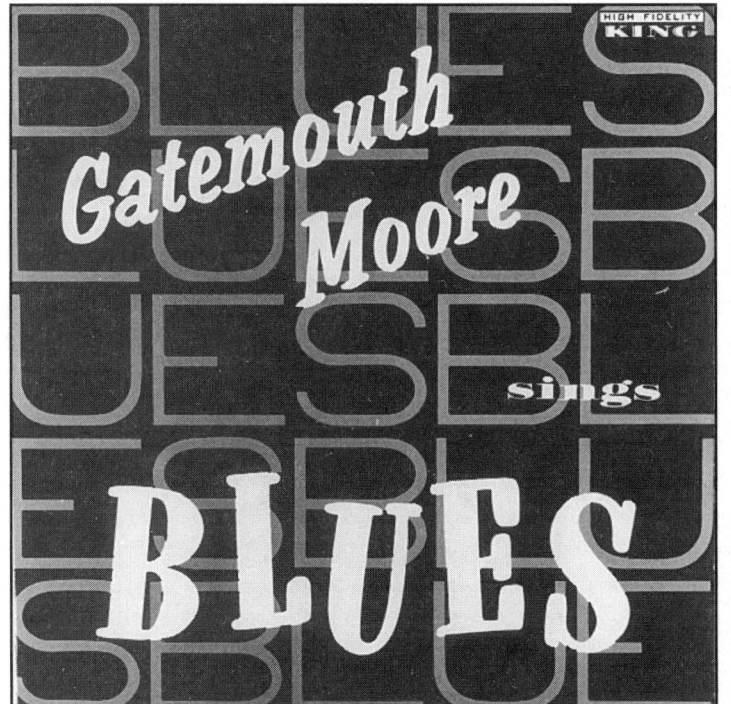

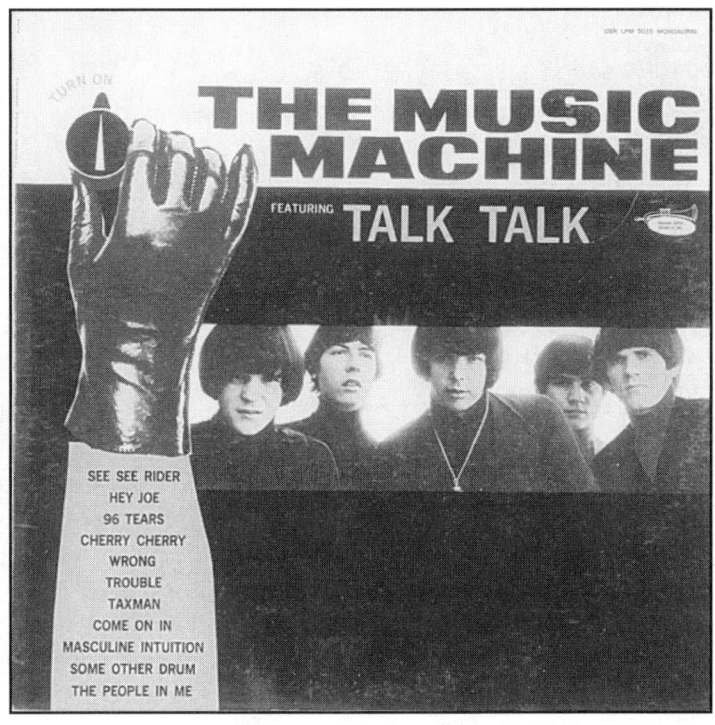

(Top left) One of the most sought-after of all blues albums is the King issue of *Gatemouth Moore Sings Blues.* Its near-mint value is approximately $5,000. (Top right) *Living with the Animals* was the debut album by Mother Earth, the group that gave us Tracy Nelson. (Bottom left) Even though often believed to be a manufactured group, the Music Explosion was a real group from Mansfield, Ohio. This was their one and only album, based around the big hit "Little Bit o' Soul." (Bottom right) The Music Machine's biggest hit was one minute and 56 seconds of pure angst, "Talk Talk." The result was the sought-after album *Turn On The Music Machine,* which is especially hard to find in stereo.

Number	Title	Yr	VG	VG+	NM
❑ 1-232	Every Good Boy Deserves	1995	6.25	12.50	25.00
-- Audiophile vinyl					
❑ 1-253	To Our Children's Children's Children	1996	15.00	30.00	60.00
-- Audiophile vinyl					
NAUTILUS					
❑ NR-21	On the Threshold of a Dream	1981	15.00	30.00	60.00
-- Audiophile vinyl					
❑ NR-21	On the Threshold of a Dream	1981	12.50	25.00	50.00
-- Audiophile vinyl; DBX-encoded version					
THRESHOLD					
❑ THX-100 [DJ]	Special Interview Kit	1971	37.50	75.00	150.00
-- Includes script					
❑ SMAS-93329	A Question of Balance	1971	5.00	10.00	20.00
-- Capitol Record Club edition					

MOODY, CLYDE
KING

Number	Title	Yr	VG	VG+	NM
❑ 891 [M]	The Best of Clyde Moody	1964	20.00	40.00	80.00

MOOG MACHINE, THE
COLUMBIA

Number	Title	Yr	VG	VG+	NM
❑ CS 9921	Switched-On Rock	1969	5.00	10.00	20.00
❑ CS 9959	Christmas Becomes Electric	1969	5.00	10.00	20.00

MOON, KEITH
Also see THE WHO.
TRACK/MCA

Number	Title	Yr	VG	VG+	NM
❑ 2136	Two Sides of the Moon	1975	10.00	20.00	40.00

MOON, THE
IMPERIAL

Number	Title	Yr	VG	VG+	NM
❑ LP-12381	Without Earth	1968	10.00	20.00	40.00
❑ LP-12444	The Moon	1969	10.00	20.00	40.00

MOONDOG
COLUMBIA

Number	Title	Yr	VG	VG+	NM
❑ KC 30897	Moondog II	1971	6.25	12.50	25.00

COLUMBIA MASTERWORKS

Number	Title	Yr	VG	VG+	NM
❑ MS 7335	Moondog	1969	6.25	12.50	25.00

EPIC

Number	Title	Yr	VG	VG+	NM
❑ LG 1002 [10]	Moondog and His Friends	1954	50.00	100.00	200.00

MUSICAL HERITAGE SOCIETY

Number	Title	Yr	VG	VG+	NM
❑ 3803	Moondog	198?	7.50	15.00	30.00

PRESTIGE

Number	Title	Yr	VG	VG+	NM
❑ PRLP-7042 [M]	Moondog	1956	25.00	50.00	100.00
❑ PRLP-7069 [M]	More Moondog	1957	25.00	50.00	100.00
❑ PRLP-7099 [M]	The Story of Moondog	1957	25.00	50.00	100.00

MOONGLOWS, THE
CHESS

Number	Title	Yr	VG	VG+	NM
❑ LP 1430 [M]	Look! It's the Moonglows	1959	125.00	250.00	500.00
❑ LP 1471 [M]	The Best of Bobby Lester & the Moonglows	1962	75.00	150.00	300.00
-- Black label					
❑ LP 1471 [M]	The Best of Bobby Lester & the Moonglows	1966	12.50	25.00	50.00
-- Blue, fading to white label					

CONSTELLATION

Number	Title	Yr	VG	VG+	NM
❑ C-2 [M]	Collectors Showcase -- The Moonglows	1964	12.50	25.00	50.00
-- Dark blue lettering					
❑ C-2 [M]	Collectors Showcase -- The Moonglows	1964	25.00	50.00	100.00
-- Light blue lettering					

MOONLIGHTERS, THE
CENTURY

Number	Title	Yr	VG	VG+	NM
❑ 29132	An Evening with the Moonlighters	197?	5.00	10.00	20.00

MOONRAKERS, THE
SHAMLEY

Number	Title	Yr	VG	VG+	NM
❑ 704	Together	1968	10.00	20.00	40.00

MOONSHINERS, THE
VILLAGE GATE

Number	Title	Yr	VG	VG+	NM
❑ 2002 [M]	Breakout!	1964	5.00	10.00	20.00

MOOR, DET
Actually producer and composer Robert Mersey.
GALLANT

Number	Title	Yr	VG	VG+	NM
❑ GT 4001 [M]	Great Jazz from Great TV	1962	10.00	20.00	40.00

MOORE, ADA
DEBUT

Number	Title	Yr	VG	VG+	NM
❑ DLP-15 [10]	Jazz Workshop	1955	50.00	100.00	200.00

MOORE, BOB
HICKORY

Number	Title	Yr	VG	VG+	NM
❑ LPS-131 [S]	Viva Bob Moore	1965	5.00	10.00	20.00

MONUMENT

Number	Title	Yr	VG	VG+	NM
❑ MLP-4005 [M]	Mexico and Other Great Hits!	1961	5.00	10.00	20.00
❑ SLP-4005 [S]	Mexico and Other Great Hits!	1961	6.25	12.50	25.00

MOORE, BOBBY, AND THE RHYTHM ACES
CHECKER

Number	Title	Yr	VG	VG+	NM
❑ LP-3000 [M]	Searching for My Love	1966	7.50	15.00	30.00
❑ LPS-3000 [R]	Searching for My Love	1966	5.00	10.00	20.00

MOORE, CHARLIE, AND BILL NAPIER
KING

Number	Title	Yr	VG	VG+	NM
❑ 828 [M]	Folk 'n' Hill	1963	12.50	25.00	50.00
❑ 880 [M]	The Best of Charlie Moore and Bill Napier	1964	12.50	25.00	50.00
❑ 917 [M]	Country Hymnal	1964	10.00	20.00	40.00
❑ 936 [M]	Songs of the Lonesome Truck Drivers	1965	7.50	15.00	30.00
❑ KS-936 [S]	Songs of the Lonesome Truck Drivers	1965	10.00	20.00	40.00
❑ 982 [M]	Country Music Goes to Viet Nam	1966	7.50	15.00	30.00
❑ KS-982 [S]	Country Music Goes to Viet Nam	1966	10.00	20.00	40.00
❑ 992 [M]	City Folks Back on the Farm	1966	7.50	15.00	30.00
❑ KS-992 [S]	City Folks Back on the Farm	1966	10.00	20.00	40.00
❑ 1014 [M]	Spectacular Instrumentals	1967	6.25	12.50	25.00
❑ KS-1014 [S]	Spectacular Instrumentals	1967	5.00	10.00	20.00
❑ 1017 [M]	Gospel and Sacred Songs	1967	6.25	12.50	25.00
❑ KS-1017 [S]	Gospel and Sacred Songs	1967	5.00	10.00	20.00
❑ 1021 [M]	Brand New Country & Western Songs	1967	6.25	12.50	25.00
❑ KS-1021 [S]	Brand New Country & Western Songs	1967	5.00	10.00	20.00

MOORE, DANNY
EVEREST

Number	Title	Yr	VG	VG+	NM
❑ SDBR-1211 [S]	Folk Songs from Here and There	1963	6.25	12.50	25.00
❑ LPBR-5211 [M]	Folk Songs from Here and There	1963	5.00	10.00	20.00

MOORE, DEBBY
TOP RANK

Number	Title	Yr	VG	VG+	NM
❑ RM-12-301 [M]	My Kind of Blues	1959	10.00	20.00	40.00

MOORE, DUDLEY
ATLANTIC

Number	Title	Yr	VG	VG+	NM
❑ 1403 [M]	Beyond the Fringe and All That Jazz	1963	6.25	12.50	25.00
❑ SD 1403 [S]	Beyond the Fringe and All That Jazz	1963	7.50	15.00	30.00

LONDON

Number	Title	Yr	VG	VG+	NM
❑ PS 558	Dudley Moore Trio	1969	6.25	12.50	25.00

MOORE, GATEMOUTH
AUDIO FIDELITY

Number	Title	Yr	VG	VG+	NM
❑ AFLP-1921 [M]	Revival!	196?	15.00	30.00	60.00
❑ AFSD-5921 [S]	Revival!	196?	20.00	40.00	80.00

KING

Number	Title	Yr	VG	VG+	NM
❑ 684 [M]	Gatemouth Moore Sings Blues	1960	1,250.	2,500.	5,000.

MOORE, LATTIE
AUDIO LAB

Number	Title	Yr	VG	VG+	NM
❑ AL-1555 [M]	The Best of Lattie Moore	1960	50.00	100.00	200.00
❑ AL-1573 [M]	Country Side	1962	37.50	75.00	150.00

DERBYTOWN

Number	Title	Yr	VG	VG+	NM
❑ 102 [M]	Lattie Moore	196?	10.00	20.00	40.00

MOORE, SCOTTY
ELVIS PRESLEY's guitarist in the early days.
EPIC

Number	Title	Yr	VG	VG+	NM
❑ LN 24103 [M]	The Guitar That Changed the World	1964	20.00	40.00	80.00
❑ BN 26103 [S]	The Guitar That Changed the World	1964	25.00	50.00	100.00

MOORE, SHELLY
ARGO

Number	Title	Yr	VG	VG+	NM
❑ LP-4016 [M]	For the First Time	1962	7.50	15.00	30.00
❑ LPS-4016 [S]	For the First Time	1962	10.00	20.00	40.00

Number	Title	Yr	VG	VG+	NM

MOORE, TIM
A SMALL RECORD COMPANY

Number	Title	Yr	VG	VG+	NM
❏ SRS-10001	Tim Moore	1974	7.50	15.00	30.00

MOREL, TERRY
BETHLEHEM

❏ BLP-47 [M]	Songs of a Woman in Love	1956	7.50	15.00	30.00

MORENO, RITA
STRAND

❏ L-1039 [M]	Rita Moreno Sings	1962	7.50	15.00	30.00
❏ SL-1039 [S]	Rita Moreno Sings	1962	10.00	20.00	40.00

WYNNE

❏ WLP-103 [M]	Warm, Wild, Wonderful	1964	5.00	10.00	20.00
❏ WLP-703 [S]	Warm, Wild, Wonderful	1964	6.25	12.50	25.00

MOREY STORE BAND, THE
SOUND MACHINE

❏ 49007	Cry for the Dreamer	197?	25.00	50.00	100.00

MORGAN, GEORGE
COLUMBIA

❏ CL 1044 [M]	Morgan, By George	1957	12.50	25.00	50.00
❏ CL 1631 [M]	Golden Memories	1961	6.25	12.50	25.00
❏ CL 2111 [M]	Tender Lovin' Care	1964	5.00	10.00	20.00
❏ CL 2333 [M]	Red Roses for a Blue Lady	1965	5.00	10.00	20.00
❏ CS 8431 [S]	Golden Memories	1961	7.50	15.00	30.00
❏ CS 8911 [S]	Tender Lovin' Care	1964	6.25	12.50	25.00
❏ CS 9133 [S]	Red Roses for a Blue Lady	1965	6.25	12.50	25.00

STARDAY

❏ SLP-400	Candy Kisses	1967	6.25	12.50	25.00
❏ SLP-410	Country Hits by Candlelight	1967	6.25	12.50	25.00
❏ SLP-413	Steal Away	1968	5.00	10.00	20.00
❏ SLP-417	Barbara	1969	5.00	10.00	20.00

MORGAN, GEORGE, AND MARION WORTH
COLUMBIA

❏ CL 2197 [M]	Slippin' Around	1964	5.00	10.00	20.00
❏ CS 8997 [S]	Slippin' Around	1964	6.25	12.50	25.00

MORGAN, JANE
COLPIX

❏ SCP 497 [S]	The Jane Morgan Album	1966	5.00	10.00	20.00

KAPP

❏ KL-1023 [M]	Jane Morgan	1956	7.50	15.00	30.00
❏ KL-1066 [M]	Fascination	1957	7.50	15.00	30.00
❏ KL-1080 [M]	All the Way	1958	7.50	15.00	30.00
❏ KL-1089 [M]	Something Old, New, Borrowed, Blue	1958	7.50	15.00	30.00
❏ KL-1089S [S]	Something Old, New, Borrowed, Blue	1958	10.00	20.00	40.00
❏ KL-1093 [M]	Jane Morgan	1958	7.50	15.00	30.00
❏ KL-1105 [M]	The Day the Rains Came	1958	7.50	15.00	30.00
❏ KL-1105S [S]	The Day the Rains Came	1958	10.00	20.00	40.00
❏ KL-1129 [M]	Jane in Spain	1959	6.25	12.50	25.00
❏ KL-1170 [M]	Jane Morgan Time	1959	5.00	10.00	20.00
❏ KS-3001 [S]	Broadway in Stereo	1959	7.50	15.00	30.00
❏ KS-3014 [S]	Jane in Spain	1959	7.50	15.00	30.00
❏ KS-3017 [S]	Fascination	1959	7.50	15.00	30.00
❏ KS-3054 [S]	Jane Morgan Time	1959	6.25	12.50	25.00
❏ KS-3066 [S]	Fascination	1962	5.00	10.00	20.00
❏ KS-3191 [S]	Ballads of Lady Jane	1960	5.00	10.00	20.00
❏ KS-3239 [S]	Second Time Around	1961	5.00	10.00	20.00
❏ KS-3246 [S]	The Great Golden Hits	1961	5.00	10.00	20.00
❏ KS-3247 [S]	Big Hits from Broadway	1961	5.00	10.00	20.00
❏ KS-3250 [S]	Love Makes the World Go 'Round	1961	5.00	10.00	20.00
❏ KS-3268 [S]	Jane Morgan at the Cocoanut Grove	1962	5.00	10.00	20.00
❏ KS-3275 [S]	More Golden Hits	1962	5.00	10.00	20.00
❏ KS-3296 [S]	What Now My Love	1962	5.00	10.00	20.00
❏ UXL-5006 [(2) M]	Great Songs from the Great Shows of the Century	195?	10.00	20.00	40.00

MORGAN, JAYE P.
MGM

❏ E-3774 [M]	Slow and Easy	1959	6.25	12.50	25.00
❏ SE-3774 [S]	Slow and Easy	1959	7.50	15.00	30.00
❏ E-3830 [M]	Up North	1960	6.25	12.50	25.00
❏ SE-3830 [S]	Up North	1960	7.50	15.00	30.00
❏ E-3867 [M]	Down South	1960	6.25	12.50	25.00
❏ SE-3867 [S]	Down South	1960	7.50	15.00	30.00
❏ E-3940 [M]	That Country Sound	1961	6.25	12.50	25.00
❏ SE-3940 [S]	That Country Sound	1961	7.50	15.00	30.00

RCA VICTOR

❏ LPM-1155 [M]	Jaye P. Morgan	1955	12.50	25.00	50.00

RONDO-LETTE

❏ A-13 [M]	Jaye P. Morgan Sings	1958	6.25	12.50	25.00

MORGAN, LEE
BLUE NOTE

❏ BLP-1538 [M]	Lee Morgan Indeed!	1957	62.50	125.00	250.00
-- "Deep groove" version (deep indentation under label on both sides)					
❏ BLP-1538 [M]	Lee Morgan Indeed!	1957	50.00	100.00	200.00
-- Regular edition, Lexington Ave. address on label					
❏ BLP-1538 [M]	Lee Morgan Indeed!	1963	6.25	12.50	25.00
-- "New York, USA" address on label					
❏ BLP-1541 [M]	Lee Morgan, Volume 2	1957	62.50	125.00	250.00
-- "Deep groove" version (deep indentation under label on both sides)					
❏ BLP-1541 [M]	Lee Morgan, Volume 2	1957	50.00	100.00	200.00
-- Regular edition, Lexington Ave. address on label					
❏ BLP-1541 [M]	Lee Morgan, Volume 2	1963	6.25	12.50	25.00
-- "New York, USA" address on label					
❏ BLP-1557 [M]	Lee Morgan, Volume 3	1957	37.50	75.00	150.00
-- "Deep groove" version (deep indentation under label on both sides)					
❏ BLP-1557 [M]	Lee Morgan, Volume 3	1957	25.00	50.00	100.00
-- Regular edition, W. 63rd St. address on label					
❏ BLP-1557 [M]	Lee Morgan, Volume 3	1963	6.25	12.50	25.00
-- "New York, USA" address on label					
❏ BLP-1575 [M]	City Lights	1958	37.50	75.00	150.00
-- "Deep groove" version (deep indentation under label on both sides)					
❏ BLP-1575 [M]	City Lights	1958	25.00	50.00	100.00
-- Regular edition, W. 63rd St. address on label					
❏ BLP-1575 [M]	City Lights	1963	6.25	12.50	25.00
-- "New York, USA" address on label					
❏ BST-1575 [S]	City Lights	1959	25.00	50.00	100.00
-- "Deep groove" version (deep indentation under label on both sides)					
❏ BST-1575 [S]	City Lights	1959	20.00	40.00	80.00
-- Regular edition, W. 63rd St. address on label					
❏ BST-1575 [S]	City Lights	1963	5.00	10.00	20.00
-- "New York, USA" address on label					
❏ BLP-1578 [M]	The Cooker	1958	37.50	75.00	150.00
-- "Deep groove" version (deep indentation under label on both sides)					
❏ BLP-1578 [M]	The Cooker	1958	25.00	50.00	100.00
-- Regular edition, W. 63rd St. address on label					
❏ BLP-1578 [M]	The Cooker	1963	6.25	12.50	25.00
-- "New York, USA" address on label					
❏ BST-1578 [S]	The Cooker	1959	25.00	50.00	100.00
-- "Deep groove" version (deep indentation under label on both sides)					
❏ BST-1578 [S]	The Cooker	1959	20.00	40.00	80.00
-- Regular edition, W. 63rd St. address on label					
❏ BST-1578 [S]	The Cooker	1963	5.00	10.00	20.00
-- "New York, USA" address on label					
❏ BLP-1590 [M]	Candy	1958	37.50	75.00	150.00
-- "Deep groove" version (deep indentation under label on both sides)					
❏ BLP-1590 [M]	Candy	1958	25.00	50.00	100.00
-- Regular edition, W. 63rd St. address on label					
❏ BLP-1590 [M]	Candy	1963	6.25	12.50	25.00
-- "New York, USA" address on label					
❏ BST-1590 [S]	Candy	1959	25.00	50.00	100.00
-- "Deep groove" version (deep indentation under label on both sides)					
❏ BST-1590 [S]	Candy	1959	20.00	40.00	80.00
-- Regular edition, W. 63rd St. address on label					
❏ BST-1590 [S]	Candy	1963	5.00	10.00	20.00
-- "New York, USA" address on label					
❏ BLP-4034 [M]	Lee-Way	1960	30.00	60.00	120.00
-- "Deep groove" version (deep indentation under label on both sides)					
❏ BLP-4034 [M]	Lee-Way	1960	20.00	40.00	80.00
-- Regular edition, W. 63rd St. address on label					
❏ BLP-4034 [M]	Lee-Way	1963	6.25	12.50	25.00
-- "New York, USA" address on label					
❏ BLP-4157 [M]	The Sidewinder	1964	7.50	15.00	30.00
❏ BLP-4169 [M]	Search for the New Land	1965	7.50	15.00	30.00
❏ BLP-4199 [M]	The Rumproller	1966	7.50	15.00	30.00
❏ BLP-4212 [M]	The Gigolo	1966	7.50	15.00	30.00
❏ BLP-4222 [M]	Cornbread	1967	7.50	15.00	30.00
❏ BLP-4243 [M]	Delightfulee Morgan	1967	10.00	20.00	40.00
❏ BST-84034 [S]	Lee-Way	1960	12.50	25.00	50.00
-- Regular edition, W. 63rd St. address on label					
❏ BST-84034 [S]	Lee-Way	1963	5.00	10.00	20.00
-- "New York, USA" address on label					
❏ BST-84157 [S]	The Sidewinder	1964	10.00	20.00	40.00
-- "New York, USA" address on label					
❏ BST-84169 [S]	Search for the New Land	1965	10.00	20.00	40.00
-- "New York, USA" address on label					
❏ BST-84199 [S]	The Rumproller	1966	10.00	20.00	40.00
-- "New York, USA" address on label					
❏ BST-84212 [S]	The Gigolo	1966	10.00	20.00	40.00
-- "New York, USA" address on label					
❏ BST-84222 [S]	Cornbread	1967	10.00	20.00	40.00
-- "New York, USA" address on label					

Number	Title	Yr	VG	VG+	NM
❏ BST-84243 [S] Delightfulee Morgan		1967	7.50	15.00	30.00
-- "New York, USA" address on label					
❏ BST-84289	Caramba!	1969	6.25	12.50	25.00
❏ BST-84312	Charisma	1969	6.25	12.50	25.00
❏ BST-84335	The Sixth Sense	1969	6.25	12.50	25.00
❏ BST-84901 [(2)] Lee Morgan		1972	5.00	10.00	20.00
❏ BST-89906 [(2)] Lee Morgan at the Lighthouse		1970	6.25	12.50	25.00

GNP CRESCENDO

Number	Title	Yr	VG	VG+	NM
❏ GNP-2079 [(2)] Lee Morgan		1973	5.00	10.00	20.00

JAZZLAND

Number	Title	Yr	VG	VG+	NM
❏ JLP-80 [M]	Take Twelve	1962	7.50	15.00	30.00
❏ JLP-980 [S]	Take Twelve	1962	10.00	20.00	40.00

MOSAIC

Number	Title	Yr	VG	VG+	NM
❏ MQ6-162 [(6)] The Complete Blue Note Lee Morgan Fifties Sessions		199?	25.00	50.00	100.00

SAVOY

Number	Title	Yr	VG	VG+	NM
❏ MG-12091 [M] Introducing Lee Morgan		1956	50.00	100.00	200.00

VEE JAY

Number	Title	Yr	VG	VG+	NM
❏ LP-2508 [M]	Lee Morgan Quintet	1965	7.50	15.00	30.00
❏ LPS-2508 [S]	Lee Morgan Quintet	1965	10.00	20.00	40.00
❏ LP-3007 [M]	Here's Lee Morgan	1960	7.50	15.00	30.00
❏ SR-3007 [S]	Here's Lee Morgan	1960	10.00	20.00	40.00
❏ LP-3015 [M]	Expoobident	1960	7.50	15.00	30.00
❏ SR-3015 [S]	Expoobident	1960	10.00	20.00	40.00

MORGAN, LORRIE
RCA

Number	Title	Yr	VG	VG+	NM
❏ R 183848	Something in Red	1991	5.00	10.00	20.00
-- Only available on vinyl through BMG Direct Marketing					

MORGAN, RUSS
DECCA

Number	Title	Yr	VG	VG+	NM
❏ DL 5098 [10]	Music in the Morgan Manner	1950	7.50	15.00	30.00
❏ DL 5278 [10]	College Marching Songs	195?	7.50	15.00	30.00

MORGEN
PROBE

Number	Title	Yr	VG	VG+	NM
❏ CPLP-4507	Morgen	1969	37.50	75.00	150.00

MORLY GREY
STARSHINE

Number	Title	Yr	VG	VG+	NM
❏ 69000	The Only Truth	1969	50.00	100.00	200.00

MORMON TABERNACLE CHOIR
BOOK-OF-THE-MONTH

Number	Title	Yr	VG	VG+	NM
❏ 71-6406 [(3)] Christmas Celebration		1980	6.25	12.50	25.00
-- Contains 20-page lyric booklet					

COLUMBIA HOUSE

Number	Title	Yr	VG	VG+	NM
❏ 6P 6007 [(6)] The Mormon Tabernacle Choir		1973	7.50	15.00	30.00

COLUMBIA MASTERWORKS

Number	Title	Yr	VG	VG+	NM
❏ M2L 263 [(2) M] Handel: Messiah		1959	5.00	10.00	20.00
-- Gray and black labels with six "eye" logos					
❏ M2S 607 [(2) S] Handel: Messiah		1959	6.25	12.50	25.00
-- Gray and black labels with six "eye" logos					
❏ M2S 686 [(2) S] Brahms: A German Requiem Sung in English		1963	5.00	10.00	20.00
-- Gray label, "360 Sound Stereo" in black					
❏ M2S 703 [(2) S] This Is My Country		1963	5.00	10.00	20.00
-- Gray label, "360 Sound Stereo" in black; not to be confused with the single-record LP of the same name					
❏ ML 2077 [10] The Mormon Tabernacle Choir of Salt Lake City		1949	10.00	20.00	40.00
-- Their first album					
❏ ML 2098 [10] The Mormon Tabernacle Choir of Salt Lake City Volume II		1950	7.50	15.00	30.00
❏ ML 4789 [M] The Mormon Tabernacle Choir of Salt Lake City		195?	6.25	12.50	25.00
-- Reissue of two 10-inch LPs onto one 12-inch LP					
❏ ML 5048 [M] Concert of Sacred Music		1955	5.00	10.00	20.00
❏ ML 5203 [M] Songs of Faith and Devotion		1957	5.00	10.00	20.00
❏ ML 5222 [M] The Mormon Tabernacle Choir Sings Christmas Carols		1957	5.00	10.00	20.00
❏ ML 6019 [M] The Mormon Tabernacle Choir at the World's Fair		1964	5.00	10.00	20.00
❏ MS 6019 [S] The Lord Is My Shepherd		1958	5.00	10.00	20.00
-- Gray and black label with six "eye" logos					
❏ MS 6058 [S] The Beloved Choruses		1958	5.00	10.00	20.00
-- Gray and black label with six "eye" logos					
❏ MS 6068 [S] The Lord's Prayer		1959	5.00	10.00	20.00
-- Gray and black label with six "eye" logos					
❏ MS 6619 [S] The Mormon Tabernacle Choir at the World's Fair		1964	6.25	12.50	25.00

COLUMBIA SPECIAL PRODUCTS

Number	Title	Yr	VG	VG+	NM
❏ CSS 1667	The Mormon Tabernacle Choir in South Carolina -- Tricentennial Concert	1970	5.00	10.00	20.00

FRANKLIN MINT

Number	Title	Yr	VG	VG+	NM
❏ (no #) [(2)] The Greatest Songs of Christmas		1980	6.25	12.50	25.00
-- Maroon vinyl; the choir's first digital recording					

READER'S DIGEST

Number	Title	Yr	VG	VG+	NM
❏ RD4-093 [(5)] The Mormon Tabernacle Choir Sings		1973	6.25	12.50	25.00
❏ RBA-128/A [(4)] Climb Ev'ry Mountain: The Mormon Tabernacle Choir Sings Great Songs of Inspiration		1988	6.25	12.50	25.00
❏ P2 15176/7 [(2)] 50th Anniversary Album		1980	5.00	10.00	20.00

TIME-LIFE

Number	Title	Yr	VG	VG+	NM
❏ SMT 104 [(3)] Christmas Celebration		1987	5.00	10.00	20.00
-- Same contents as Book-of-the-Month LP. Side 1, 2 and 6 are identical; Side 3 is BOTM's Side 5, Side 4 is BOTM's Side 3, and Side 5 is BOTM's Side 4.					

MORNING DEW, THE
ROULETTE

Number	Title	Yr	VG	VG+	NM
❏ SR-42049	The Morning Dew	1970	37.50	75.00	150.00

MORNING GLORY
FONTANA

Number	Title	Yr	VG	VG+	NM
❏ SRF-67573	Two Suns Worth	1968	6.25	12.50	25.00

MORNINGLORY
TOYA

Number	Title	Yr	VG	VG+	NM
❏ STLP-003	Growing	1972	10.00	20.00	40.00

MORRIS, GREG
DOT

Number	Title	Yr	VG	VG+	NM
❏ DLP-25881	For You	1968	5.00	10.00	20.00

MORRISON, HAROLD
DECCA

Number	Title	Yr	VG	VG+	NM
❏ DL 74680 [S]	Hoss, He's the Boss	1965	5.00	10.00	20.00

MORRISON, VAN
BANG

Number	Title	Yr	VG	VG+	NM
❏ BLB-218 [M]	Blowin' Your Mind	1968	12.50	25.00	50.00
-- With the censored "Brown Eyed Girl" lyric, "Laughin' and a-runnin', hey hey, behind the stadium with you," part of which was spliced in from another part of the song. This has been confirmed to exist in mono.					
❏ BLP-218 [M]	Blowin' Your Mind	1967	7.50	15.00	30.00
-- With the true "Brown Eyed Girl" lyric, "Makin' love in the green grass behind the stadium with you."					
❏ BLBS-218 [S]	Blowin' Your Mind	1968	5.00	10.00	20.00
-- With the censored "Brown Eyed Girl" lyric, "Laughin' and a-runnin', hey hey, behind the stadium with you," part of which was spliced in from another part of the song!					
❏ BLPS-218 [S]	Blowin' Your Mind	1967	10.00	20.00	40.00
-- With the true "Brown Eyed Girl" lyric, "Makin' love in the green grass behind the stadium with you."					
❏ BLPS-400	T.B. Sheets	1973	5.00	10.00	20.00

DIRECT DISK

Number	Title	Yr	VG	VG+	NM
❏ SD-16604	Moondance	1981	25.00	50.00	100.00
-- Audiophile vinyl					

WARNER BROS.

Number	Title	Yr	VG	VG+	NM
❏ WBMS-102 [DJ] Live at the Roxy		1978	12.50	25.00	50.00
❏ WS 1768	Astral Weeks	1968	6.25	12.50	25.00
-- With "W7" logo on green label					
❏ WS 1835	Moondance	1969	5.00	10.00	20.00
-- With "W7" logo on green label					

MORRISSEY, PAT
MERCURY

Number	Title	Yr	VG	VG+	NM
❏ MG-20197 [M] I'm Pat Morrissey, I Sing		1957	25.00	50.00	100.00

MORROW, BUDDY
EPIC

Number	Title	Yr	VG	VG+	NM
❏ LN 24095 [M]	Big Band Beatlemania	1964	6.25	12.50	25.00
❏ BN 26095 [S]	Big Band Beatlemania	1964	7.50	15.00	30.00

MERCURY

Number	Title	Yr	VG	VG+	NM
❏ MG-20062 [M] Shall We Dance?		195?	7.50	15.00	30.00
❏ MG-20204 [M] A Salute to the Fabulous Dorseys		1957	7.50	15.00	30.00
❏ MG-20221 [M] Golden Trombone		1956	7.50	15.00	30.00
❏ MG-20290 [M] Tribute to Tommy Dorsey		1957	7.50	15.00	30.00
❏ MG-20372 [M] Just We Two		195?	7.50	15.00	30.00
❏ MG-20396 [M] Night Train		195?	7.50	15.00	30.00
❏ MG-20702 [M] Night Train Goes to Hollywood		1962	6.25	12.50	25.00
❏ SR-60009 [S] Night Train		1958	10.00	20.00	40.00
❏ SR-60018 [S] Just We Two		1958	10.00	20.00	40.00
❏ SR-60702 [S] Night Train Goes to Hollywood		1962	7.50	15.00	30.00

Number	Title	Yr	VG	VG+	NM
RCA VICTOR					
❏ LPM-1427 [M]	Night Train	1956	10.00	20.00	40.00
❏ LPM-1925 [M]	Dancing Tonight To Morrow	1958	7.50	15.00	30.00
❏ LSP-1925 [S]	Dancing Tonight To Morrow	1958	10.00	20.00	40.00
❏ LPM-2018 [M]	Big Band Guitar	1959	7.50	15.00	30.00
❏ LSP-2018 [S]	Big Band Guitar	1959	10.00	20.00	40.00
❏ LPM-2042 [M]	Impact	1959	7.50	15.00	30.00
❏ LSP-2042 [S]	Impact	1959	10.00	20.00	40.00
❏ LPM-2180 [M]	Double Impact	1960	7.50	15.00	30.00
❏ LSP-2180 [S]	Double Impact	1960	10.00	20.00	40.00
❏ LPM-2208 [M]	Poe for Moderns	1960	7.50	15.00	30.00
❏ LSP-2208 [S]	Poe for Moderns	1960	10.00	20.00	40.00

MORSE, ELLA MAE

Number	Title	Yr	VG	VG+	NM
CAPITOL					
❏ H 513 [10]	Barrelhouse Boogie and the Blues	1954	100.00	200.00	400.00
❏ T 513 [M]	Barrelhouse Boogie and the Blues	1955	62.50	125.00	250.00
❏ T 898 [M]	Morse Code	1957	25.00	50.00	100.00
❏ ST 1802 [S]	Hits of Ella Mae Morse and Freddie Slack	1962	12.50	25.00	50.00
❏ T 1802 [M]	Hits of Ella Mae Morse and Freddie Slack	1962	10.00	20.00	40.00

MORSE, ROBERT, AND CHARLES NELSON REILLY

Number	Title	Yr	VG	VG+	NM
CAPITOL					
❏ ST 1862 [S]	A Jolly Theatrical Christmas	1963	6.25	12.50	25.00
❏ T 1862 [M]	A Jolly Theatrical Christmas	1963	5.00	10.00	20.00

MORTIMER

Number	Title	Yr	VG	VG+	NM
PHILIPS					
❏ PHS 600-267	Mortimer	1969	6.25	12.50	25.00

MOSBY, JOHNNY AND JONIE

Number	Title	Yr	VG	VG+	NM
COLUMBIA					
❏ CS 9097 [S]	Mr. & Mrs. Country Music	1965	5.00	10.00	20.00
STARDAY					
❏ 328 [M]	The New Sweethearts of Country Music	1965	7.50	15.00	30.00

MOSLEY, BOB

Number	Title	Yr	VG	VG+	NM
REPRISE					
❏ RS 2068	Bob Mosley	1972	5.00	10.00	20.00

MOSS, GENE

Number	Title	Yr	VG	VG+	NM
RCA VICTOR					
❏ LPM-2977 [M]	Dracula's Greatest Hits	1964	7.50	15.00	30.00
❏ LSP-2977 [S]	Dracula's Greatest Hits	1964	10.00	20.00	40.00

MOTELS, THE

Number	Title	Yr	VG	VG+	NM
CAPITOL					
❏ ST-12177 [DJ]	All Four One	1982	5.00	10.00	20.00
-- Promo-only high-grade vinyl pressing (different front cover)					

MOTHER EARTH

Number	Title	Yr	VG	VG+	NM
MERCURY					
❏ SR-61194	Living with the Animals	1968	6.25	12.50	25.00
❏ SR-61226	Make a Joyful Noise	1969	5.00	10.00	20.00
❏ SR-61230	Tracy Nelson Country	1969	5.00	10.00	20.00
❏ SR-61270	Satisfied	1970	5.00	10.00	20.00

MOTHER LOVE BONE

Number	Title	Yr	VG	VG+	NM
POLYDOR					
❏ 843 191-1	Apple	1990	12.50	25.00	50.00
STARDOG					
❏ 839 011-1 [EP]	Shine	1989	12.50	25.00	50.00
-- Four songs on side one, the same four songs on side two					

MOTHERS OF INVENTION, THE -- See FRANK ZAPPA.

MOTIONS, THE

Number	Title	Yr	VG	VG+	NM
PHILIPS					
❏ PHS 600-317	Electric Baby	1969	5.00	10.00	20.00

MOTLEY CRUE

Number	Title	Yr	VG	VG+	NM
LEATHUR					
❏ LR-1281	Too Fast for Love	1981	75.00	150.00	300.00
-- First pressing with white lettering on cover					
❏ LR-1281	Too Fast for Love	1981	37.50	75.00	150.00
-- Second pressing with red lettering on cover. Both Leathur pressings contain "Stick to Your Guns," which was not on the Elektra reissue					

MOTT THE HOOPLE

Number	Title	Yr	VG	VG+	NM
ATLANTIC					
❏ SD 7297	Rock and Roll Queen	1974	5.00	10.00	20.00
❏ SD 8258	Mott the Hoople	1970	5.00	10.00	20.00
-- With "1841 Broadway" address and no mention of Warner Communications on label					
❏ SD 8272	Mad Shadows	1970	5.00	10.00	20.00
❏ SD 8284	Wildlife	1971	5.00	10.00	20.00
❏ SD 8304	Brain Capers	1972	5.00	10.00	20.00
COLUMBIA					
❏ PCQ 32871 [Q]	The Hoople	1974	6.25	12.50	25.00

MOTTOLA, TONY

Number	Title	Yr	VG	VG+	NM
COMMAND					
❏ QD-40001 [Q]	Guitar -- Paris	1972	5.00	10.00	20.00

MOUNT ALVERNIA SEMINARY CHOIR

Number	Title	Yr	VG	VG+	NM
ABC-PARAMOUNT					
❏ 211 [M]	Christmas in a Monastery: The Sons of St. Francis Sing	1957	5.00	10.00	20.00

MOUNT RUSHMORE

Number	Title	Yr	VG	VG+	NM
DOT					
❏ DLP-25898	High on Mount Rushmore	1968	5.00	10.00	20.00
❏ DLP-25934	Mount Rushmore '69	1969	5.00	10.00	20.00

MOUNTAIN

Number	Title	Yr	VG	VG+	NM
COLUMBIA					
❏ CQ 32079 [Q]	The Best of Mountain	1973	5.00	10.00	20.00
❏ CQ 33008 [Q]	Avalanche	1974	5.00	10.00	20.00

MOUNTAIN BUS

Number	Title	Yr	VG	VG+	NM
GOOD					
❏ 101	Sundance	1971	37.50	75.00	150.00

MOUNTAIN RAMBLERS, THE

Number	Title	Yr	VG	VG+	NM
ATLANTIC					
❏ 1347 [M]	Blue Ridge Mountain Music	1962	6.25	12.50	25.00
❏ SD 1347 [S]	Blue Ridge Mountain Music	1962	7.50	15.00	30.00

MOVE, THE

Also see ROY WOOD.

Number	Title	Yr	VG	VG+	NM
A&M					
❏ SP-4259	Shazam	1969	7.50	15.00	30.00
CAPITOL					
❏ ST-658	Looking On	1971	5.00	10.00	20.00
❏ ST-811	Message from the Country	1971	5.00	10.00	20.00

MOVING SIDEWALKS, THE

Billy Gibbons of ZZ TOP was in this group.

Number	Title	Yr	VG	VG+	NM
TANTARA					
❏ 6919	Flash	1968	75.00	150.00	300.00

MU

Also see MERRILL FANKHAUSER.

Number	Title	Yr	VG	VG+	NM
CAS					
❏ 300	Mu	1971	75.00	150.00	300.00

MUDHONEY

Number	Title	Yr	VG	VG+	NM
SUB POP					
❏ 21 [EP]	Superfuzz Bigmuff	1988	5.00	10.00	20.00
-- Without poster					
❏ 21 [EP]	Superfuzz Bigmuff	1988	7.50	15.00	30.00
-- With poster					
❏ 44	Mudhoney	1989	5.00	10.00	20.00
-- Without gatefold and poster					
❏ 44	Mudhoney	1989	7.50	15.00	30.00
-- First 3,000 have gatefold sleeve and poster					
❏ 105 PD [PD]	Every Good Boy Deserves Fudge	1991	7.50	15.00	30.00
-- Picture disc -- limited edition of 2,500					

MUGWUMPS, THE

Also see CASS ELLIOT.

Number	Title	Yr	VG	VG+	NM
WARNER BROS.					
❏ W 1697 [M]	The Mugwumps	1967	6.25	12.50	25.00
❏ WS 1697 [S]	The Mugwumps	1967	7.50	15.00	30.00

MULCAY, JIMMY AND MILDRED

Number	Title	Yr	VG	VG+	NM
JUBILEE					
❏ JGM-5017 [M]	Magic Millions	1962	7.50	15.00	30.00

Number	Title	Yr	VG	VG+	NM

MULDAUR, GEOFF
FOLKLORE
❏ FRLP-14004 [M] Sleepy Man Blues		1964	7.50	15.00	30.00
❏ FRST-14004 [S] Sleepy Man Blues		1964	10.00	20.00	40.00

PRESTIGE
❏ PRST-7727	Sleepy Man Blues	1969	5.00	10.00	20.00
-- Reissue of Folklore LP					

MULLER, WERNER
DECCA
❏ DL 8388 [M]	O, Tannenbaum (Christmas on the Rhine)	1956	5.00	10.00	20.00
-- Black label, silver print					

MULLICAN, MOON
AUDIO LAB
❏ AL-1568 [M]	Instrumentals	1962	37.50	75.00	150.00

CORAL
❏ CRL 57235 [M] Moon Over Mullican		1958	125.00	250.00	500.00

HILLTOP
❏ JS-6033	Good Times Gonna Roll Again	1966	6.25	12.50	25.00

KAPP
❏ KS-3600	Showcase	1968	7.50	15.00	30.00

KING
❏ 555 [M]	Moon Mullican Sings His All-Time Greatest Hits	1958	50.00	100.00	200.00
❏ 628 [M]	Moon Mullican Plays and Sings 16 of His Favorite Tunes	1959	37.50	75.00	150.00
❏ 681 [M]	The Many Moods of Moon Mullican	1960	37.50	75.00	150.00
❏ 937 [M]	Moon Mullican Sings 24 of His Favorite Tunes	1965	12.50	25.00	50.00

NASHVILLE
❏ 2080	I'll Sail My Ship Alone	1970	5.00	10.00	20.00

SPAR
❏ SP-3005 [M]	Mister Honky Tonk Man	1965	25.00	50.00	100.00

STARDAY
❏ SLP-135 [M]	Playin' and Singin'	1963	25.00	50.00	100.00
❏ SLP-267 [M]	Mister Piano Man	1964	12.50	25.00	50.00
❏ SLP-398 [M]	The Unforgettable Moon Mullican	1967	10.00	20.00	40.00

STERLING
❏ ST-601 [M]	I'll Sail My Ship Alone	1958	50.00	100.00	200.00

MULLIGAN, GERRY
CAPITOL
❏ H 439 [10]	Gerry Mulligan and His Ten-Tette	1953	62.50	125.00	250.00

COLUMBIA
❏ CL 1307 [M]	What Is There to Say?	1959	10.00	20.00	40.00
-- Red and black label with six "eye" logos					
❏ CL 1932 [M]	Jeru	1963	7.50	15.00	30.00
❏ CS 8116 [S]	What Is There to Say?	1959	10.00	20.00	40.00
-- Red and black label with six "eye" logos					
❏ CS 8732 [S]	Jeru	1963	7.50	15.00	30.00

EMARCY
❏ MG-36056 [M]	Presenting the Gerry Mulligan Sextet	1955	37.50	75.00	150.00
❏ MG-36101 [M]	Mainstream of Jazz	1956	37.50	75.00	150.00

FANTASY
❏ 3-6 [10]	Gerry Mulligan Quartet	1953	50.00	100.00	200.00

GENE NORMAN PRESENTS
❏ GNP-3 [10]	Gerry Mulligan Quartet	1952	62.50	125.00	250.00

JAZZTONE
❏ J-1253 [M]	Gerry Mulligan and Chet Baker	195?	10.00	20.00	40.00

LIMELIGHT
❏ LM-82004 [M]	Butterfly with Hiccups	1964	6.25	12.50	25.00
❏ LM-82021 [M]	If You Can't Beat 'Em, Join 'Em	1965	6.25	12.50	25.00
❏ LM-82030 [M]	Feelin' Good	1965	6.25	12.50	25.00
❏ LM-82040 [M]	Something Borrowed, Something Blue	1966	5.00	10.00	20.00
❏ LS-82030 [S]	Feelin' Good	1965	7.50	15.00	30.00
❏ LS-86004 [S]	Butterfly with Hiccups	1964	7.50	15.00	30.00
❏ LS-86021 [S]	If You Can't Beat 'Em, Join 'Em	1965	7.50	15.00	30.00
❏ LS-86040 [S]	Something Borrowed, Something Blue	1966	6.25	12.50	25.00

MERCURY
❏ MG-20453 [M]	A Profile of Gerry Mulligan	1959	15.00	30.00	60.00

MOBILE FIDELITY
❏ 1-179	At the Village Vanguard	1985	10.00	20.00	40.00
-- Audiophile vinyl					
❏ 1-234	Gerry Mulligan Meets Ben Webster	1995	10.00	20.00	40.00
-- Audiophile vinyl					
❏ 1-241	Blues in Time	1996	7.50	15.00	30.00
-- Audiophile vinyl					

PACIFIC JAZZ
❏ PJLP-1 [10]	Gerry Mulligan Quartet	1953	75.00	150.00	300.00
❏ PJLP-2 [10]	Lee Konitz Plays with the Gerry Mulligan Quartet	1953	75.00	150.00	300.00
❏ PJLP-5 [10]	Gerry Mulligan Quartet	1953	75.00	150.00	300.00
❏ PJ-8 [M]	The Genius of Gerry Mulligan	1960	10.00	20.00	40.00
❏ PJLP-10 [10]	Lee Konitz and the Gerry Mulligan Quartet	1954	62.50	125.00	250.00
❏ PJ-38 [M]	Konitz Meets Mulligan	1962	7.50	15.00	30.00
❏ PJ-47 [M]	Reunion with Chet Baker	1962	7.50	15.00	30.00
❏ ST-47 [S]	Reunion with Chet Baker	1962	7.50	15.00	30.00
❏ PJ-50 [M]	California Concerts	1962	7.50	15.00	30.00
❏ PJ-75 [M]	Timeless	1963	7.50	15.00	30.00
❏ PJM-406 [M]	Lee Konitz with the Gerry Mulligan Quartet	1956	37.50	75.00	150.00
❏ PJ-1201 [M]	California Concerts	1955	37.50	75.00	150.00
❏ PJ-1207 [M]	The Original Mulligan Quartet	1955	37.50	75.00	150.00
❏ PJ-1210 [M]	Paris Concert	1956	37.50	75.00	150.00
❏ PJ-1228 [M]	Gerry Mulligan at Storyville	1957	37.50	75.00	150.00
❏ PJ-10102 [M]	Paris Concert	1966	5.00	10.00	20.00
❏ ST-20102 [S]	Paris Concert	1966	5.00	10.00	20.00

PHILIPS
❏ PHM 200-077 [M] Spring Is Sprung		1963	5.00	10.00	20.00
❏ PHM 200-108 [M] Night Lights		1963	5.00	10.00	20.00
❏ PHS 600-077 [S] Spring Is Sprung		1963	6.25	12.50	25.00
❏ PHS 600-108 [S] Night Lights		1963	6.25	12.50	25.00

PRESTIGE
❏ PRLP-120 [10] Gerry Mulligan Blows		1952	75.00	150.00	300.00
❏ PRLP-141 [10] Mulligan Too Blows		1953	75.00	150.00	300.00
❏ PRLP-7006 [M] Mulligan Plays Mulligan		1956	25.00	50.00	100.00
-- Yellow label					
❏ PRLP-7251 [M] Historically Speaking		1963	10.00	20.00	40.00
-- Yellow label					

VERVE
❏ MGVS-6003 [S] Getz Meets Mulligan in Hi-Fi		1960	10.00	20.00	40.00
❏ MGVS-6104 [S] Gerry Mulligan Meets Ben Webster		1960	10.00	20.00	40.00
❏ MGV-8246 [M]	The Gerry Mulligan-Paul Desmond Quartet	1958	12.50	25.00	50.00
❏ MGV-8249 [M] Getz Meets Mulligan in Hi-Fi		1958	10.00	20.00	40.00
❏ MGV-8343 [M]	Gerry Mulligan Meets Ben Webster	1959	10.00	20.00	40.00
❏ MGV-8367 [M]	Gerry Mulligan Meets Johnny Hodge	1960	10.00	20.00	40.00
❏ V6-8367 [S]	Gerry Mulligan Meets Johnny Hodges	1961	6.25	12.50	25.00
❏ MGV-8388 [M]	Gerry Mulligan and the Concert Jazz Band	1960	10.00	20.00	40.00
❏ V6-8388 [S]	Gerry Mulligan and the Concert Jazz Band	1961	6.25	12.50	25.00
❏ MGV-8396 [M]	Gerry Mulligan and the Concert Jazz Band at the Village Vanguard	1960	10.00	20.00	40.00
❏ V6-8396 [S]	Gerry Mulligan and the Concert Jazz Band at the Village Vanguard	1961	6.25	12.50	25.00
❏ V-8415 [M]	Gerry Mulligan and the Concert Jazz Band Presents a Concert in Jazz	1961	6.25	12.50	25.00
❏ V6-8415 [S]	Gerry Mulligan and the Concert Jazz Band Presents a Concert in Jazz	1961	7.50	15.00	30.00
❏ V-8438 [M]	The Gerry Mulligan Concert Jazz Band On Tour with Guest Soloist Zoot Sims	1962	6.25	12.50	25.00
❏ V6-8438 [S]	The Gerry Mulligan Concert Jazz Band On Tour with Guest Soloist Zoot Sims	1962	7.50	15.00	30.00
❏ V-8466 [M]	The Gerry Mulligan Quartet	1962	6.25	12.50	25.00
❏ V6-8466 [S]	The Gerry Mulligan Quartet	1962	7.50	15.00	30.00
❏ V-8478 [M]	Blues in Time	1962	5.00	10.00	20.00
❏ V6-8478 [S]	Blues in Time	1962	6.25	12.50	25.00
❏ V-8515 [M]	Gerry Mulligan '63 -- The Concert Jazz Band	1963	5.00	10.00	20.00
❏ V6-8515 [S]	Gerry Mulligan '63 -- The Concert Jazz Band	1963	6.25	12.50	25.00

WORLD PACIFIC
❏ PJM-406 [M]	Lee Konitz with the Gerry Mulligan Quartet	1958	20.00	40.00	80.00
❏ ST-1001 [S]	The Gerry Mulligan Songbook	1958	25.00	50.00	100.00
❏ ST-1006 [S]	Gerry Mulligan at Storyville	1958	25.00	50.00	100.00
❏ ST-1007 [S]	Reunion with Chet Baker	1958	20.00	40.00	80.00
❏ WP-1201 [M]	California Concerts	1958	20.00	40.00	80.00
❏ WP-1207 [M]	The Original Mulligan Quartet	1958	20.00	40.00	80.00
❏ WP-1210 [M]	Paris Concert	1958	20.00	40.00	80.00
❏ WP-1228 [M]	Gerry Mulligan at Storyville	1958	20.00	40.00	80.00
❏ PJ-1237 [M]	The Gerry Mulligan Songbook	1957	30.00	60.00	120.00
❏ WP-1237 [M]	The Gerry Mulligan Songbook	1958	20.00	40.00	80.00
❏ PJ-1241 [M]	Reunion with Chet Baker	1957	30.00	60.00	120.00
❏ WP-1241 [M]	Reunion with Chet Baker	1958	20.00	40.00	80.00
❏ WP-1273 [M]	Lee Konitz Plays with the Gerry Mulligan Quartet	1959	20.00	40.00	80.00
-- Reissue of 406					

Number	Title	Yr	VG	VG+	NM

MULLIGAN, GERRY / BUDDY DeFRANCO
GENE NORMAN PRESENTS

❏ GNP-26 [M]	The Gerry Mulligan Quartet with Chet Baker/Buddy DeFranco Quartet	1957	20.00	40.00	80.00
-- Combined reissue of two 10-inch LPs					
❏ GNP-56 [M]	The Gerry Mulligan Quartet with Chet Baker/Buddy DeFranco Quartet	196?	10.00	20.00	40.00
-- Reissue of 26					

MULLIGAN, GERRY / PAUL DESMOND
Also see each artist's individual listings.
FANTASY

❏ 3220 [M]	Gerry Mulligan Quartet/ Paul Desmond Quintet	1956	20.00	40.00	80.00
-- Red vinyl; combined reissue of two 10-inch LPs					
❏ 3220 [M]	Gerry Mulligan Quartet/ Paul Desmond Quintet	1956	10.00	20.00	40.00
-- Black vinyl					

MULTIPLICATION ROCK (SOUNDTRACK)
CAPITOL

| ❏ SJA-11174 | Multiplication Rock | 1973 | 10.00 | 20.00 | 40.00 |

MUMY, BILL
BB

| ❏ 103 | Bill Mumy | 1980 | 6.25 | 12.50 | 25.00 |

MUNSTERS, THE
DECCA

| ❏ DL 4588 [M] | The Munsters | 1964 | 25.00 | 50.00 | 100.00 |
| ❏ DL 74588 [S] | The Munsters | 1964 | 37.50 | 75.00 | 150.00 |

MURE, BILLY
EVEREST

❏ SDBR-1067 [S]	A String of Trumpets	1960	7.50	15.00	30.00
❏ SDBR-1072 [S]	Songs of Hank Williams	1960	7.50	15.00	30.00
❏ SDBR-1120 [S]	Strictly Cha-Cha-Cha	1961	7.50	15.00	30.00
❏ LPBR-5067 [M]	A String of Trumpets	1960	5.00	10.00	20.00
❏ LPBR-5072 [M]	Songs of Hank Williams	1960	5.00	10.00	20.00
❏ LPBR-5120 [M]	Strictly Cha-Cha-Cha	1961	5.00	10.00	20.00
KAPP					
❏ KL-1253 [M]	Tough Strings	1961	5.00	10.00	20.00
❏ KS-3253 [S]	Tough Strings	1961	7.50	15.00	30.00
MGM					
❏ E-3780 [M]	Supersonic Guitars	1959	7.50	15.00	30.00
❏ SE-3780 [S]	Supersonic Guitars	1959	12.50	25.00	50.00
❏ E-3807 [M]	Supersonic Guitars, Vol. 2	1959	7.50	15.00	30.00
❏ SE-3807 [S]	Supersonic Guitars, Vol. 2	1959	12.50	25.00	50.00
❏ E-4131 [M]	Teen Bossa Nova	1963	5.00	10.00	20.00
❏ SE-4131 [S]	Teen Bossa Nova	1963	7.50	15.00	30.00
❏ E-4189 [M]	Maria Elena and Other Great Songs	1964	5.00	10.00	20.00
❏ SE-4189 [S]	Maria Elena and Other Great Songs	1964	7.50	15.00	30.00
❏ E-4406 [M]	Happy Guitars	1966	5.00	10.00	20.00
❏ SE-4406 [S]	Happy Guitars	1966	6.25	12.50	25.00
RCA VICTOR					
❏ LPM-1536 [M]	Supersonic Guitars in Hi-Fi	1957	10.00	20.00	40.00
❏ LPM-1694 [M]	Fireworks	1958	7.50	15.00	30.00
❏ LSP-1694 [S]	Fireworks	1958	10.00	20.00	40.00
❏ LPM-1869 [M]	Supersonic in Flight	1959	7.50	15.00	30.00
❏ LSP-1869 [S]	Supersonic in Flight	1959	12.50	25.00	50.00
STRAND					
❏ SL-1010 [M]	Hawaiian Percussion	1961	6.25	12.50	25.00
❏ SL-1021 [M]	'Round the World in Percussion	1961	6.25	12.50	25.00
❏ SL-1070 [M]	Pink Hawaii	1962	5.00	10.00	20.00
❏ SLS-1010 [S]	Hawaiian Percussion	1961	10.00	20.00	40.00
❏ SLS-1021 [S]	'Round the World in Percussion	1961	10.00	20.00	40.00
❏ SLS-1070 [S]	Pink Hawaii	1962	7.50	15.00	30.00
UNITED ARTISTS					
❏ UAL-3031 [M]	Bandstand Record Hop	1959	10.00	20.00	40.00
❏ UAS-6031 [S]	Bandstand Record Hop	1959	15.00	30.00	60.00

MURMAIDS, THE
CHATTAHOOCHEE

| ❏ CHLP-628 [M] | The Mermaids Resurface! | 1981 | 7.50 | 15.00 | 30.00 |

MURPHY, ELLIOTT
POLYDOR

❏ PD-5061	Aquashow	1973	5.00	10.00	20.00
-- First edition with "Like a Great Gatsby" listed as a song title					
RCA VICTOR					
❏ APL1-0916	Lost Generation	1975	5.00	10.00	20.00
-- Orange or tan labels					
❏ APL1-1318	Night Lights	1976	5.00	10.00	20.00
-- Orange or tan labels					

MURRAY THE K -- See VARIOUS ARTISTS COLLECTIONS in back.

MURRAY, ANNE
CAPITOL NASHVILLE

| ❏ R 173232 | You Will | 1990 | 5.00 | 10.00 | 20.00 |
| -- Only released on vinyl through BMG Direct Marketing | | | | | |

MUSCLE SHOALS HORNS, THE
BANG

| ❏ BLP-403 | Born to Get Down | 1975 | 5.00 | 10.00 | 20.00 |

MUSIC ASYLUM, THE
UNITED ARTISTS

| ❏ UAS-6778 | Commit Thyself | 1970 | 5.00 | 10.00 | 20.00 |

MUSIC COMPANY, THE
CRESTVIEW

❏ CRS-3057	Hard and Heavy	196?	6.25	12.50	25.00
MIRWOOD					
❏ M-7002 [M]	Rubber Soul Jazz	1966	5.00	10.00	20.00
❏ MS-7002 [S]	Rubber Soul Jazz	1966	6.25	12.50	25.00

MUSIC EMPORIUM, THE
SENTINEL

| ❏ 69001 | The Music Emporium | 1969 | 500.00 | 1,000. | 2,000. |

MUSIC EXPLOSION, THE
LAURIE

| ❏ LLP-2040 [M] | Little Bit O'Soul | 1967 | 5.00 | 10.00 | 20.00 |
| ❏ SLLP-2040 [S] | Little Bit O'Soul | 1967 | 6.25 | 12.50 | 25.00 |

MUSIC MACHINE, THE
ORIGINAL SOUND

❏ 5015 [M]	(Turn On) The Music Machine	1966	10.00	20.00	40.00
❏ 8875 [S]	(Turn On) The Music Machine	1966	12.50	25.00	50.00
WARNER BROS.					
❏ W 1732 [M]	Bonniwell's Music Machine	1967	6.25	12.50	25.00
❏ WS 1732 [S]	Bonniwell's Music Machine	1967	10.00	20.00	40.00

MUSSELWHITE, CHARLIE
VANGUARD

❏ VSD-6258	Tennessee Woman	1969	5.00	10.00	20.00
❏ VRS-9232 [M]	Stand Back! Here Comes Charlie Musselwhite's South Side Band	1966	5.00	10.00	20.00
❏ VSD-79232 [S]	Stand Back! Here Comes Charlie Musselwhite's South Side Band	1966	6.25	12.50	25.00
❏ VSD-79287	Charlie Musselwhite	1968	5.00	10.00	20.00

MUSSO, VIDO
CROWN

❏ CLP-5007 [M]	The Swingin'st	1957	12.50	25.00	50.00
-- Reissue of Modern LP					
❏ CLP-5029 [M]	Teenage Dance Party	1957	12.50	25.00	50.00
MODERN					
❏ MLP-1207 [M]	The Swingin'st	1956	25.00	50.00	100.00

MUSTANGS, THE
PROVIDENCE

| ❏ PLP-001 [M] | Dartell Stomp | 1964 | 12.50 | 25.00 | 50.00 |

MUTZIE
SUSSEX

| ❏ SUX-7001 | Light of Your Shadow | 1970 | 6.25 | 12.50 | 25.00 |

MY BLOODY VALENTINE
CREATION/RELATIVITY

| ❏ 1006 | Isn't Anything | 1989 | 5.00 | 10.00 | 20.00 |

MYERS, DAVE
CAROLE

❏ 8002 [M]	Greatest Racing Themes	1967	12.50	25.00	50.00
DEL-FI					
❏ DFLP-1239 [M]	Hangin' Twenty	1963	20.00	40.00	80.00
❏ DFST-1239 [S]	Hangin' Twenty	1963	45.00	90.00	180.00

MYERSON, BESS
MGM

| ❏ E-3785 [M] | Fashions in Music | 1959 | 7.50 | 15.00 | 30.00 |
| ❏ SE-3785 [S] | Fashions in Music | 1959 | 10.00 | 20.00 | 40.00 |

Number	Title	Yr	VG	VG+	NM
MYRICK, GARY, AND THE FIGURES					
EPIC					
❏ AS 912 [DJ]	Talks in Stereo	1981	10.00	20.00	40.00
-- Side one has studio tracks, side two has live versions of songs on side one					
MYSTIC ASTROLOGICAL CRYSTAL BAND, THE					
CAROLE					
❏ 8001 [M]	Mystic Astrological Crystal Band	1967	6.25	12.50	25.00
❏ S-8001 [S]	Mystic Astrological Crystal Band	1967	7.50	15.00	30.00
❏ S-8003	Clip Out, Put On Book	1968	7.50	15.00	30.00
MYSTIC MOODS ORCHESTRA, THE					
MOBILE FIDELITY					
❏ 1-001	Emotions	1979	6.25	12.50	25.00
-- Audiophile vinyl					
❏ 1-002	Cosmic Forces	1979	6.25	12.50	25.00
-- Audiophile vinyl					
❏ 1-003	Stormy Weekend	1979	6.25	12.50	25.00
-- Audiophile vinyl					
MYSTIC NUMBER NATIONAL BANK, THE					
PROBE					
❏ CPLP-4501	The Mystic Number National Bank	1969	5.00	10.00	20.00
MYSTIC SIVA					
VO					
❏ 19713	Mystic Siva	1971	250.00	500.00	1,000.

Number	Title	Yr	VG	VG+	NM
N					
N.W.A.					
PRIORITY					
❏ 30080 [DJ]	Greatest Hits/In-Store Play	1996	5.00	10.00	20.00
-- Promo-only "clean" versions for retailer use					
NABORS, JIM					
COLUMBIA					
❏ CL 2368 [M]	Shazam! (Gomer Pyle, U.S.M.C.)	1965	5.00	10.00	20.00
❏ CS 9168 [S]	Shazam! (Gomer Pyle, U.S.M.C.)	1965	6.25	12.50	25.00
NAGLE, RON					
WARNER BROS.					
❏ WS 1902	Bad Rice	1970	5.00	10.00	20.00
NAKED RAYGUN					
CAROLINE					
❏ 1348	Jettison	1988	5.00	10.00	20.00
❏ 1371	Understand?	1989	5.00	10.00	20.00
❏ 1642	Raygun...Naked Raygun	1990	5.00	10.00	20.00
HOMESTEAD					
❏ HMS 008	Throb Throb	1984	7.50	15.00	30.00
-- First edition has lyric sheet					
❏ HMS 008	Throb Throb	1984	5.00	10.00	20.00
-- Second edition has lyric innersleeve					
❏ HMS 045	All Rise	1985	7.50	15.00	30.00
RUTHLESS					
❏ 03 [EP]	Basement Screams	1983	20.00	40.00	80.00
NAPOLEON XIV					
WARNER BROS.					
❏ W 1661 [M]	They're Coming to Take Me Away, Ha-Haaa!	1966	15.00	30.00	60.00
❏ WS 1661 [S]	They're Coming to Take Me Away, Ha-Haaa!	1966	25.00	50.00	100.00
NARZ, JACK					
DOT					
❏ DLP-3244 [M]	Sing the Folk Hits with Jack Narz	1960	6.25	12.50	25.00
❏ DLP-25244 [S]	Sing the Folk Hits with Jack Narz	1960	7.50	15.00	30.00
NASH, JOHNNY					
ABC-PARAMOUNT					
❏ 244 [M]	Johnny Nash	1958	7.50	15.00	30.00
❏ S-244 [S]	Johnny Nash	1959	10.00	20.00	40.00
❏ 276 [M]	Quiet Hour	1959	7.50	15.00	30.00
❏ S-276 [S]	Quiet Hour	1959	10.00	20.00	40.00
❏ 299 [M]	I Got Rhythm	1959	7.50	15.00	30.00
❏ S-299 [S]	I Got Rhythm	1959	10.00	20.00	40.00
❏ 344 [M]	Let's Get Lost	1960	7.50	15.00	30.00
❏ S-344 [S]	Let's Get Lost	1960	10.00	20.00	40.00
❏ 383 [M]	Studio Time	1961	7.50	15.00	30.00
❏ S-383 [S]	Studio Time	1961	10.00	20.00	40.00
ARGO					
❏ LP-4038 [M]	Composer's Choice	1964	5.00	10.00	20.00
❏ LPS-4038 [S]	Composer's Choice	1964	6.25	12.50	25.00
JAD					
❏ JS-1001	Prince of Peace	1969	6.25	12.50	25.00
❏ JS-1006	Folk Soul	1970	6.25	12.50	25.00
❏ JS-1207	Hold Me Tight	1968	7.50	15.00	30.00
NASHVILLE ALL STARS, THE					
RCA VICTOR					
❏ LPM-2302 [M]	After the Riot at Newport	1960	10.00	20.00	40.00
❏ LSP-2302 [S]	After the Riot at Newport	1960	12.50	25.00	50.00
NASHVILLE GUITARS, THE					
MONUMENT					
❏ SLP-18058 [S]	The Nashville Guitars	1966	5.00	10.00	20.00
NASHVILLE TEENS, THE					
LONDON					
❏ PS 407 [R]	Tobacco Road	1964	20.00	40.00	80.00
❏ LL 3407 [M]	Tobacco Road	1964	25.00	50.00	100.00

Number	Title	Yr	VG	VG+	NM

NASTOS, NICK
STRAND
| ❑ SL-1097 [M] | Guitars on Fire | 1962 | 5.00 | 10.00 | 20.00 |
| ❑ SLS-1097 [S] | Guitars on Fire | 1962 | 6.25 | 12.50 | 25.00 |

NATIONAL GALLERY, THE
PHILIPS
| ❑ PHS 600-266 | The National Gallery (Performing Musical Interpretations of the Paintings of Paul Klee) | 1968 | 7.50 | 15.00 | 30.00 |

NATIONAL LAMPOON
LABEL 21
| ❑ PIC-2001 [PD] | That's Not Funny, That's Sick! | 1978 | 5.00 | 10.00 | 20.00 |

NATIONAL SYMPHONY ORCHESTRA (HOWARD MITCHELL, CONDUCTOR)
RCA VICTOR RED SEAL
| ❑ LSC-2261 [S] | Shostakovich: Symphony No. 5 | 1959 | 10.00 | 20.00 | 40.00 |
| -- Original with "shaded dog" label | | | | | |

NATURAL FOUR, THE
CURTOM
| ❑ CU 5004 | Heaven Right Here on Earth | 1975 | 5.00 | 10.00 | 20.00 |
| ❑ CRT-8600 | The Natural Four | 1974 | 5.00 | 10.00 | 20.00 |

NAVARRO, TOMMY, AND THE SUNDIALERS
URANIA
| ❑ UR-900 [M] | Twist Around the Town | 1961 | 25.00 | 50.00 | 100.00 |
| ❑ US-5900 [S] | Twist Around the Town | 1961 | 37.50 | 75.00 | 150.00 |

NAZARETH
WARNER BROS.
| ❑ BS 2615 | Nazareth | 1972 | 5.00 | 10.00 | 20.00 |
| ❑ BS 2639 | Exercises | 1972 | 5.00 | 10.00 | 20.00 |

NAZZ
Also see TODD RUNDGREN.
SGC
❑ SD 5001	Nazz	1968	10.00	20.00	40.00
❑ 5002 [DJ]	Nazz Nazz	1969	20.00	40.00	80.00
-- Promo-only mono pressing on red vinyl					
❑ SD 5002	Nazz Nazz	1969	20.00	40.00	80.00
-- Black vinyl					
❑ SD 5002	Nazz Nazz	1969	10.00	20.00	40.00
-- Red vinyl					
❑ SD 5004	Nazz III	1970	10.00	20.00	40.00

NBC SYMPHONY ORCHESTRA (LEOPOLD STOKOWSKI, CONDUCTOR)
RCA VICTOR RED SEAL
| ❑ LSC-2555 [S] | The Sound of Stokowski and Wagner | 1961 | 7.50 | 15.00 | 30.00 |
| -- "Shaded dog" or "white dog" version | | | | | |

NDEGEOCELLO, ME'SHELL
MAVERICK
| ❑ PRO-A-6622 [(2)DJ] | Plantation Lullabies | 1993 | 5.00 | 10.00 | 20.00 |
| -- Promo-only U.S. vinyl release | | | | | |

NECROS
TOUCH & GO
| ❑ 2 | Conquest for Death | 1983 | 17.50 | 35.00 | 70.00 |

NEFF, HILDEGARDE
LONDON
| ❑ PS 596 | From Here On It Gets Rough | 1971 | 5.00 | 10.00 | 20.00 |

NEGATIVLAND
SST
| ❑ 272 [EP] | U2 | 1990 | 25.00 | 50.00 | 100.00 |
| -- Withdrawn thanks to pressure from the record company of U2 (the band) | | | | | |

NEIGHB'RHOOD CHILDREN
ACTA
| ❑ 8005 [M] | The Neighb'rhood Children | 1968 | 20.00 | 40.00 | 80.00 |
| ❑ 38005 [S] | The Neighb'rhood Children | 1968 | 25.00 | 50.00 | 100.00 |

NEIL, FRED
Also see VINCE MARTIN AND FRED NEIL.
CAPITOL
❑ ST-294	Everybody's Talkin'	1969	6.25	12.50	25.00
❑ ST 2665 [S]	Fred Neil	1966	10.00	20.00	40.00
-- With color photo on back					
❑ ST 2665 [S]	Fred Neil	1967	7.50	15.00	30.00
-- With black & white photo on back					
❑ T 2665 [M]	Fred Neil	1966	7.50	15.00	30.00
❑ ST 2862 [S]	Fred Neil Sessions	1968	7.50	15.00	30.00
❑ T 2862 [M]	Fred Neil Sessions	1968	10.00	20.00	40.00
ELEKTRA
❑ EKL-293 [M]	Bleecker and MacDougal	1965	7.50	15.00	30.00
❑ EKS-7293 [S]	Bleecker and MacDougal	1965	10.00	20.00	40.00
❑ EKS-74073	Little Bit of Rain	1970	5.00	10.00	20.00
-- Reissue of 7293					

NELSON, RICKY
Also includes later releases as "Rick Nelson."
DECCA
❑ DL 4419 [M]	For Your Sweet Love	1963	7.50	15.00	30.00
❑ DL 4479 [M]	Rick Nelson Sings "For You"	1963	7.50	15.00	30.00
❑ DL 4559 [M]	The Very Thought of You	1964	7.50	15.00	30.00
❑ DL 4608 [M]	Spotlight on Rick	1964	7.50	15.00	30.00
❑ DL 4660 [M]	Best Always	1965	7.50	15.00	30.00
❑ DL 4678 [M]	Love and Kisses	1965	7.50	15.00	30.00
❑ DL 4779 [M]	Bright Lights and Country Music	1966	6.25	12.50	25.00
❑ DL 4827 [M]	Country Fever	1967	6.25	12.50	25.00
❑ DL 4944 [M]	Another Side of Rick	1967	6.25	12.50	25.00
❑ DL 5014 [M]	Perspective	1968	12.50	25.00	50.00
-- Mono copies are promo only					
❑ DL 74419 [S]	For Your Sweet Love	1963	10.00	20.00	40.00
❑ DL 74479 [S]	Rick Nelson Sings "For You"	1963	10.00	20.00	40.00
❑ DL 74559 [S]	The Very Thought of You	1964	10.00	20.00	40.00
❑ DL 74608 [S]	Spotlight on Rick	1964	10.00	20.00	40.00
❑ DL 74660 [S]	Best Always	1965	10.00	20.00	40.00
❑ DL 74678 [S]	Love and Kisses	1965	10.00	20.00	40.00
❑ DL 74779 [S]	Bright Lights and Country Music	1966	7.50	15.00	30.00
❑ DL 74827 [S]	Country Fever	1967	7.50	15.00	30.00
❑ DL 74944 [S]	Another Side of Rick	1967	7.50	15.00	30.00
❑ DL 75014 [S]	Perspective	1968	7.50	15.00	30.00
❑ DL 75162	Rick Nelson In Concert	1970	6.25	12.50	25.00
❑ DL 75236	Rick Sings Nelson	1970	6.25	12.50	25.00
-- Deduct 20 percent if poster is missing					
❑ DL 75297	Rudy the Fifth	1971	6.25	12.50	25.00
❑ DL 75391	Garden Party	1972	6.25	12.50	25.00
IMPERIAL
❑ LP 9048 [M]	Ricky	1957	25.00	50.00	100.00
-- Black label with stars					
❑ LP 9048 [M]	Ricky	1964	6.25	12.50	25.00
-- Black label with pink and white at left					
❑ LP 9048 [M]	Ricky	1966	5.00	10.00	20.00
-- Black label with green and white at left					
❑ LP 9050 [M]	Ricky Nelson	1958	25.00	50.00	100.00
-- Black label with stars					
❑ LP 9050 [M]	Ricky Nelson	1964	6.25	12.50	25.00
-- Black label with pink and white at left					
❑ LP 9050 [M]	Ricky Nelson	1966	5.00	10.00	20.00
-- Black label with green and white at left					
❑ LP 9061 [M]	Ricky Sings Again	1959	25.00	50.00	100.00
-- Black label with stars					
❑ LP 9061 [M]	Ricky Sings Again	1964	6.25	12.50	25.00
-- Black label with pink and white at left					
❑ LP 9061 [M]	Ricky Sings Again	1966	5.00	10.00	20.00
-- Black label with green and white at left					
❑ LP 9082 [M]	Songs by Ricky	1959	18.75	37.50	75.00
-- Black label with stars					
❑ LP 9082 [M]	Songs by Ricky	1964	6.25	12.50	25.00
-- Black label with pink and white at left					
❑ LP 9082 [M]	Songs by Ricky	1966	5.00	10.00	20.00
-- Black label with green and white at left					
❑ LP 9122 [M]	More Songs by Ricky	1960	18.75	37.50	75.00
-- Black label with stars					
❑ LP 9122 [M]	More Songs by Ricky	1964	6.25	12.50	25.00
-- Black label with pink and white at left					
❑ LP 9122 [M]	More Songs by Ricky	1966	5.00	10.00	20.00
-- Black label with green and white at left					
❑ LP 9152 [M]	Rick Is 21	1961	10.00	20.00	40.00
-- Black label with stars					
❑ LP 9152 [M]	Rick Is 21	1964	6.25	12.50	25.00
-- Black label with pink and white at left					
❑ LP 9152 [M]	Rick Is 21	1966	5.00	10.00	20.00
-- Black label with green and white at left					
❑ LP 9167 [M]	Album Seven by Rick	1962	10.00	20.00	40.00
-- Black label with stars					
❑ LP 9167 [M]	Album Seven by Rick	1964	6.25	12.50	25.00
-- Black label with pink and white at left					
❑ LP 9167 [M]	Album Seven by Rick	1966	5.00	10.00	20.00
-- Black label with green and white at left					

Number	Title	Yr	VG	VG+	NM
❏ LP 9218 [M]	Best Sellers by Rick Nelson	1963	10.00	20.00	40.00
-- Black label with stars					
❏ LP 9218 [M]	Best Sellers by Rick Nelson	1964	6.25	12.50	25.00
-- Black label with pink and white at left					
❏ LP 9218 [M]	Best Sellers by Rick Nelson	1966	5.00	10.00	20.00
-- Black label with green and white at left					
❏ LP 9223 [M]	It's Up to You	1963	10.00	20.00	40.00
-- Black label with stars					
❏ LP 9223 [M]	It's Up to You	1964	6.25	12.50	25.00
-- Black label with pink and white at left					
❏ LP 9223 [M]	It's Up to You	1966	5.00	10.00	20.00
-- Black label with green and white at left					
❏ LP 9232 [M]	Million Sellers	1963	10.00	20.00	40.00
-- Black label with stars					
❏ LP 9232 [M]	Million Sellers	1964	6.25	12.50	25.00
-- Black label with pink and white at left					
❏ LP 9232 [M]	Million Sellers	1966	5.00	10.00	20.00
-- Black label with green and white at left					
❏ LP 9244 [M]	A Long Vacation	1963	10.00	20.00	40.00
-- Black label with stars					
❏ LP 9244 [M]	A Long Vacation	1964	6.25	12.50	25.00
-- Black label with pink and white at left					
❏ LP 9244 [M]	A Long Vacation	1966	5.00	10.00	20.00
-- Black label with green and white at left					
❏ LP 9251 [M]	Rick Nelson Sings for You	1964	10.00	20.00	40.00
-- Black label with stars					
❏ LP 9251 [M]	Rick Nelson Sings for You	1964	6.25	12.50	25.00
-- Black label with pink and white at left					
❏ LP 9251 [M]	Rick Nelson Sings for You	1966	5.00	10.00	20.00
-- Black label with green and white at left					
❏ LP 12030 [S]	Songs by Ricky	1959	50.00	100.00	200.00
-- Black label with silver print					
❏ LP 12030 [S]	Songs by Ricky	1964	10.00	20.00	40.00
-- Black label with pink and white at left					
❏ LP 12030 [S]	Songs by Ricky	1966	6.25	12.50	25.00
-- Black label with green and white at left					
❏ LP 12059 [DJ]	More Songs by Ricky	1960	250.00	500.00	1,000.
-- Promo copy on blue vinyl. Add 20 percent for enclosed poster.					
❏ LP 12059 [S]	More Songs by Ricky	1960	25.00	50.00	100.00
-- Black label with silver print					
❏ LP 12059 [S]	More Songs by Ricky	1964	10.00	20.00	40.00
-- Black label with pink and white at left					
❏ LP 12059 [S]	More Songs by Ricky	1966	6.25	12.50	25.00
-- Black label with green and white at left					
❏ LP 12071 [S]	Rick Is 21	1961	25.00	50.00	100.00
-- Black label with silver print					
❏ LP 12071 [S]	Rick Is 21	1964	10.00	20.00	40.00
-- Black label with pink and white at left					
❏ LP 12071 [S]	Rick Is 21	1966	6.25	12.50	25.00
-- Black label with green and white at left					
❏ LP 12082 [S]	Album Seven by Rick	1962	25.00	50.00	100.00
-- Black label with silver print					
❏ LP 12082 [S]	Album Seven by Rick	1964	10.00	20.00	40.00
-- Black label with pink and white at left					
❏ LP 12082 [S]	Album Seven by Rick	1966	6.25	12.50	25.00
-- Black label with green and white at left					
❏ LP 12090 [S]	Ricky Sings Again	1962	37.50	75.00	150.00
-- Black label with silver print					
❏ LP 12090 [S]	Ricky Sings Again	1964	10.00	20.00	40.00
-- Black label with pink and white at left					
❏ LP 12090 [S]	Ricky Sings Again	1966	6.25	12.50	25.00
-- Black label with green and white at left					
❏ LP 12218 [R]	Best Sellers	1964	5.00	10.00	20.00
-- Black label with pink and white at left					
❏ LP 12232 [R]	Million Sellers	1964	5.00	10.00	20.00
-- Black label with pink and white at left					
❏ LP 12244 [R]	A Long Vacation	1964	5.00	10.00	20.00
-- Black label with pink and white at left					
❏ LP 12251 [R]	Rick Nelson Sings for You	1964	6.25	12.50	25.00
-- Black label with silver print					
❏ LP 12251 [R]	Rick Nelson Sings for You	1964	5.00	10.00	20.00
-- Black label with pink and white at left					

SUNSET

Number	Title	Yr	VG	VG+	NM
❏ SUS-5118 [P]	Ricky Nelson	1966	5.00	10.00	20.00

UNITED ARTISTS

Number	Title	Yr	VG	VG+	NM
❏ UAS-9960 [(2)]	Legendary Masters	1971	6.25	12.50	25.00

VERVE

Number	Title	Yr	VG	VG+	NM
❏ V 2083 [M]	Teen Time	1957	125.00	250.00	500.00
-- Has three Ricky Nelson songs plus tracks by four others; usually treated as Rick's LP because of his prominence on the cover					

NELSON, SANDY

IMPERIAL

Number	Title	Yr	VG	VG+	NM
❏ LP 9105 [M]	Sandy Nelson Plays Teen Beat	1960	7.50	15.00	30.00
❏ LP 9136 [M]	He's a Drummer Boy	1961	7.50	15.00	30.00
❏ LP 9159 [M]	Let There Be Drums	1962	7.50	15.00	30.00
❏ LP 9168 [M]	Drums Are My Beat!	1962	5.00	10.00	20.00
❏ LP 9189 [M]	Drummin' Up a Storm	1962	5.00	10.00	20.00
❏ LP 9202 [M]	Golden Hits	1962	5.00	10.00	20.00

Number	Title	Yr	VG	VG+	NM
❏ LP 9203 [M]	Country Style	1962	5.00	10.00	20.00
❏ LP 9204 [M]	Compelling Percussion	1962	5.00	10.00	20.00
❏ LP 9215 [M]	Teenage House Party	1963	5.00	10.00	20.00
❏ LP 9272 [M]	Live! In Las Vegas	1964	5.00	10.00	20.00
❏ LP 12044 [S]	Sandy Nelson Plays Teen Beat	1960	10.00	20.00	40.00
❏ LP 12080 [R]	Let There Be Drums	1962	6.25	12.50	25.00
❏ LP 12083 [S]	Drums Are My Beat!	1962	6.25	12.50	25.00
❏ LP 12089 [R]	He's a Drummer Boy	1962	6.25	12.50	25.00
❏ LP 12189 [R]	Drummin' Up a Storm	1962	6.25	12.50	25.00
❏ LP 12202 [P]	Golden Hits	1962	6.25	12.50	25.00
❏ LP 12203 [S]	Country Style	1962	6.25	12.50	25.00
❏ LP 12203 [S]	On the Wild Side	1966	5.00	10.00	20.00
-- Same LP as above, but new title on cover					
❏ LP 12204 [S]	Compelling Percussion	1962	6.25	12.50	25.00
❏ LP 12215 [S]	Teenage House Party	1963	6.25	12.50	25.00
❏ LP 12224 [S]	The Best of the Beats	1963	5.00	10.00	20.00
❏ LP 12237 [S]	Beat That Drum	1963	5.00	10.00	20.00
❏ LP 12249 [S]	Sandy Nelson Plays	1963	5.00	10.00	20.00
❏ LP 12258 [S]	Be True to Your School	1964	5.00	10.00	20.00
❏ LP 12278 [S]	Teen Beat '65	1965	5.00	10.00	20.00
❏ LP 12283 [S]	Drum Discotheque	1965	5.00	10.00	20.00
❏ LP 12287 [S]	Drums A Go-Go	1965	5.00	10.00	20.00
❏ LP 12298 [S]	Boss Beat	1965	5.00	10.00	20.00
❏ LP 12305 [S]	"In" Beat	1966	5.00	10.00	20.00
❏ LP 12314 [S]	Super Drums	1966	5.00	10.00	20.00

NELSON, TRACY

PRESTIGE

Number	Title	Yr	VG	VG+	NM
❏ PRLP 7393 [M]	Deep Are the Roots	1965	6.25	12.50	25.00
❏ PRST 7393 [S]	Deep Are the Roots	1965	7.50	15.00	30.00

NELSON, WILLIE

ATLANTIC

Number	Title	Yr	VG	VG+	NM
❏ SD 7262	Shotgun Willie	1973	5.00	10.00	20.00
❏ SD 7291	Phases and Stages	1974	5.00	10.00	20.00

COLUMBIA

Number	Title	Yr	VG	VG+	NM
❏ CX 38250 [(10)]	Willie Nelson	1983	30.00	60.00	120.00
❏ 9C9 39943 [PD]	Always on My Mind	1985	5.00	10.00	20.00
❏ HC 43482	Red Headed Stranger	1982	10.00	20.00	40.00
-- Half-speed mastered edition					
❏ HC 45305	Stardust	1981	17.50	35.00	70.00
-- Half-speed mastered edition					
❏ HC 47951	Always on My Mind	1982	12.50	25.00	50.00
-- Half-speed mastered edition					
❏ HC 48248	Tougher Than Leather	1983	12.50	25.00	50.00
-- Half-speed mastered edition					

LIBERTY

Number	Title	Yr	VG	VG+	NM
❏ LRP-3239 [M]	...And Then I Wrote	1962	10.00	20.00	40.00
❏ LRP-3308 [M]	Here's Willie Nelson	1963	10.00	20.00	40.00
❏ LST-7239 [S]	...And Then I Wrote	1962	12.50	25.00	50.00
❏ LST-7308 [S]	Here's Willie Nelson	1963	12.50	25.00	50.00

RCA VICTOR

Number	Title	Yr	VG	VG+	NM
❏ LPM-3418 [M]	Country Willie -- His Own Songs	1965	5.00	10.00	20.00
❏ LSP-3418 [S]	Country Willie -- His Own Songs	1965	6.25	12.50	25.00
❏ LPM-3528 [M]	Country Favorites, Willie Nelson Style	1966	5.00	10.00	20.00
❏ LSP-3528 [S]	Country Favorites, Willie Nelson Style	1966	6.25	12.50	25.00
❏ LPM-3659 [M]	Country Music Concert	1966	5.00	10.00	20.00
❏ LSP-3659 [S]	Country Music Concert	1966	6.25	12.50	25.00
❏ LPM-3748 [M]	Make Way for Willie Nelson	1967	5.00	10.00	20.00
❏ LSP-3748 [S]	Make Way for Willie Nelson	1967	6.25	12.50	25.00
❏ LPM-3858 [M]	The Party's Over and Other Great Willie Nelson Songs	1967	6.25	12.50	25.00
❏ LSP-3858 [S]	The Party's Over and Other Great Willie Nelson Songs	1967	5.00	10.00	20.00
❏ LPM-3937 [M]	Texas in My Soul	1968	25.00	50.00	100.00
❏ LSP-3937 [S]	Texas in My Soul	1968	5.00	10.00	20.00
❏ LSP-4057	Good Times	1968	5.00	10.00	20.00
❏ LSP-4111	My Own Peculiar Way	1969	5.00	10.00	20.00
❏ LSP-4294	Both Sides Now	1970	5.00	10.00	20.00
❏ LSP-4404	Laying My Burdens Down	1970	5.00	10.00	20.00
❏ LSP-4489	Willie Nelson & Family	1971	5.00	10.00	20.00
❏ LSP-4568	Yesterday's Wine	1971	5.00	10.00	20.00
❏ LSP-4653	The Picture	1972	5.00	10.00	20.00
❏ LSP-4760	The Willie Way	1972	5.00	10.00	20.00

SUNSET

Number	Title	Yr	VG	VG+	NM
❏ SUS-5138 [S]	Hello Walls	1966	5.00	10.00	20.00

TIME-LIFE

Number	Title	Yr	VG	VG+	NM
❏ P 16946 [(3)]	Country and Western Classics	1983	5.00	10.00	20.00

NEON PHILHARMONIC, THE

WARNER BROS.

Number	Title	Yr	VG	VG+	NM
❏ WS 1769	The Moth Confesses	1968	6.25	12.50	25.00

(Top left) We had to include a photo of at least one rare classical album, seeing as we've put some of that material in this book. *Overture! Overture!* by the New Symphony Orchestra of London conducted by Raymond Agoult is rare enough that it was part of the mid-1990s Classic Records reissue series. It also has two different covers, and the Classic Records version used the other one! (Top right) A prophetic album title for the New York Dolls: Soon after the release of the 1974 *In Too Much Too Soon,* they broke up. (Bottom left) Most of Olivia Newton-John's albums are common. But her American debut, *If Not for You,* was only available for a short time and was never reissued. In fact, some of the tracks ended up on her next album, *Let Me Be There.* (Bottom right) A nice relic from the age of bubblegum, this is the debut album by 1910 Fruitgum Company.

Number	Title	Yr	VG	VG+	NM

NEP-TUNES, THE
FAMILY
| ❏ FLP-152 [M] | Surfer's Holiday | 1963 | 50.00 | 100.00 | 200.00 |
| ❏ SFLP-152 [S] | Surfer's Holiday | 1963 | 75.00 | 150.00 | 300.00 |

NERO, PETER
CRYSTAL CLEAR
| ❏ 6001 | The Wiz | 198? | 5.00 | 10.00 | 20.00 |
| -- Direct-to-disc recording | | | | | |
RCA VICTOR
❏ PRS-241 [S]	Tender Is the Night	1967	5.00	10.00	20.00
-- Special-products release					
❏ LSP-2334 [S]	Piano Forte	1961	5.00	10.00	20.00
❏ LSP-2383 [S]	New Piano in Town	1961	5.00	10.00	20.00
❏ LSP-2484 [S]	Young and Warm and Wonderful	1962	5.00	10.00	20.00
❏ LSP-2536 [S]	For the Nero-Minded	1962	5.00	10.00	20.00
❏ LSP-2618 [S]	The Colorful Peter Nero	1963	5.00	10.00	20.00
❏ LSP-2638 [S]	Hail the Conquering Nero	1963	5.00	10.00	20.00
❏ LSP-2710 [S]	Peter Nero in Person	1963	5.00	10.00	20.00
❏ LSP-2827 [S]	Sunday in New York	1964	5.00	10.00	20.00
❏ LSP-2853 [S]	Reflections	1964	5.00	10.00	20.00
❏ LSP-2935 [S]	Songs You Won't Forget	1964	5.00	10.00	20.00
❏ LSP-2978 [S]	The Best of Peter Nero	1965	5.00	10.00	20.00
❏ LSP-3313 [S]	Career Girls	1965	5.00	10.00	20.00

NESBITT, JIM
CHART
❏ CHM-1005 [M]	Truck Drivin' Cat with Nine Wives	1968	7.50	15.00	30.00
❏ CHS-1005 [S]	Truck Drivin' Cat with Nine Wives	1968	5.00	10.00	20.00
❏ CHS-1031	Runnin' Bare	1970	5.00	10.00	20.00

NESMITH, MICHAEL
Also see THE MONKEES.
PACIFIC ARTS
❏ (no #) [DJ]	The Michael Nesmith Radio Special	1979	10.00	20.00	40.00
❏ 7-101	The Prison	197?	5.00	10.00	20.00
-- Standard cover					
❏ 11-101A	The Prison	1975	12.50	25.00	50.00
-- Boxed set with booklet					
❏ 7-106	Compilation	1976	5.00	10.00	20.00
❏ 7-107	From a Radio Engine to the Photon Wing	1977	5.00	10.00	20.00
❏ 7-116	And the Hits Just Keep On Comin'	1978	5.00	10.00	20.00
-- Reissue of RCA 4695					
❏ 7-117	Pretty Much Your Standard Ranch Stash	1978	5.00	10.00	20.00
-- Reissue of RCA APL1-0164					
❏ 7-118	Live at the Palais	1978	5.00	10.00	20.00
❏ 7-130	Infinite Rider on the Big Dogma	1979	5.00	10.00	20.00
RCA VICTOR
❏ APL1-0164	Pretty Much Your Standard Ranch Stash	1973	6.25	12.50	25.00
❏ LSP-4371	Magnetic South	1970	7.50	15.00	30.00
❏ LSP-4415	Loose Salute	1970	7.50	15.00	30.00
❏ LSP-4497	Nevada Fighter	1971	6.25	12.50	25.00
❏ LSP-4563	Tantamount to Treason	1971	6.25	12.50	25.00
❏ LSP-4695	And the Hits Just Keep On Comin'	1972	6.25	12.50	25.00

NETHERWORLD
R.E.M.
| ❏ 4441 | Netherworld | 196? | 15.00 | 30.00 | 60.00 |

NEVILLE BROTHERS, THE
Also see AARON NEVILLE.
CAPITOL
| ❏ ST-11865 | The Neville Brothers | 1978 | 7.50 | 15.00 | 30.00 |

NEVILLE, AARON
MINIT
| ❏ LP 24007 [R] | Like It 'Tis | 1967 | 7.50 | 15.00 | 30.00 |
| ❏ LP 40007 [M] | Like It 'Tis | 1967 | 10.00 | 20.00 | 40.00 |
PAR-LO
| ❏ 1 [M] | Tell It Like It Is | 1967 | 20.00 | 40.00 | 80.00 |
| ❏ 1 [S] | Tell It Like It Is | 1967 | 50.00 | 100.00 | 200.00 |

NEW APOCALYPSE, THE
M.T.A.
| ❏ S-5017 | Stainless Soul | 1970 | 5.00 | 10.00 | 20.00 |

NEW BIRTH, THE
RCA VICTOR
| ❏ APD1-0285 [Q] | It's Been a Long Time | 1974 | 5.00 | 10.00 | 20.00 |

NEW CHRISTY MINSTRELS, THE
At one time or another, KIM CARNES, Gene Clark of THE BYRDS, BARRY McGUIRE, KENNY ROGERS and RANDY SPARKS were members, as were most of the original FIRST EDITION.
COLUMBIA
❏ CL 1872 [M]	The New Christy Minstrels	1962	5.00	10.00	20.00
❏ CL 1941 [M]	The New Christy Minstrels In Person	1963	5.00	10.00	20.00
❏ CL 2017 [M]	Tall Tales! Legends & Nonsense	1963	5.00	10.00	20.00
❏ CL 2055 [M]	Ramblin' Featuring Green, Green	1963	5.00	10.00	20.00
❏ CL 2096 [M]	Merry Christmas	1963	5.00	10.00	20.00
❏ CL 2159 [M]	Today	1964	5.00	10.00	20.00
❏ CL 2187 [M]	Land of Giants	1964	5.00	10.00	20.00
❏ CL 2280 [M]	The Quiet Sides of the New Christy Minstrels	1965	5.00	10.00	20.00
❏ CL 2303 [M]	Cowboys and Indians	1965	5.00	10.00	20.00
❏ CL 2369 [M]	Chim Chim Cher-ee	1965	5.00	10.00	20.00
❏ CL 2384 [M]	The Wandering Minstrels	1965	5.00	10.00	20.00
❏ CL 2479 [M]	Greatest Hits	1966	5.00	10.00	20.00
❏ CL 2531 [M]	In Italy...In Italian	1966	5.00	10.00	20.00
❏ CL 2542 [M]	New Kick	1967	5.00	10.00	20.00
❏ CL 2556 [M]	Christmas with the Christies	1966	5.00	10.00	20.00
❏ CS 8672 [S]	The New Christy Minstrels	1962	6.25	12.50	25.00
❏ CS 8741 [S]	The New Christy Minstrels In Person	1963	6.25	12.50	25.00
❏ CS 8817 [S]	Tall Tales! Legends & Nonsense	1963	6.25	12.50	25.00
❏ CS 8855 [S]	Ramblin' Featuring Green, Green	1963	6.25	12.50	25.00
❏ CS 8896 [S]	Merry Christmas	1963	6.25	12.50	25.00
❏ CS 8959 [S]	Today	1964	6.25	12.50	25.00
❏ CS 8987 [S]	Land of Giants	1964	6.25	12.50	25.00
❏ CS 9080 [S]	The Quiet Sides of the New Christy Minstrels	1965	6.25	12.50	25.00
❏ CS 9103 [S]	Cowboys and Indians	1965	6.25	12.50	25.00
❏ CS 9169 [S]	Chim Chim Cher-ee	1965	6.25	12.50	25.00
❏ CS 9184 [S]	The Wandering Minstrels	1965	6.25	12.50	25.00
❏ CS 9279 [S]	Greatest Hits	1966	6.25	12.50	25.00
❏ CS 9331 [S]	In Italy...In Italian	1966	6.25	12.50	25.00
❏ CS 9342 [S]	New Kick	1967	6.25	12.50	25.00
❏ CS 9356 [S]	Christmas with the Christies	1966	6.25	12.50	25.00
❏ CS 9616	On Tour Through Motortown	1968	5.00	10.00	20.00
❏ CS 9709	Chitty Chitty Bang Bang	1969	5.00	10.00	20.00

NEW COLONY SIX, THE
MERCURY
| ❏ SR-61165 | Revelations | 1968 | 7.50 | 15.00 | 30.00 |
| ❏ SR-61228 | Attacking a Straw Man | 1969 | 7.50 | 15.00 | 30.00 |
SENTAR
❏ LP-101 [M]	Breakthrough	1966	125.00	250.00	500.00
❏ SST-3001 [S]	Colonization	1967	15.00	30.00	60.00
❏ ST-3001 [M]	Colonization	1967	12.50	25.00	50.00

NEW DAWN, THE
HOOT
| ❏ GR 70-4569 | There's a New Dawn | 1970 | 250.00 | 500.00 | 1,000. |

NEW DIMENSIONS, THE
SUTTON
❏ SSU-331 [S]	Deuces and Eights	1963	25.00	50.00	100.00
❏ SU-331 [M]	Deuces and Eights	1963	20.00	40.00	80.00
❏ SSU-332 [S]	Surf 'N' Bongos	1963	12.50	25.00	50.00
❏ SU-332 [M]	Surf 'N' Bongos	1963	10.00	20.00	40.00
❏ SSU-336 [S]	Soul Surf	1964	12.50	25.00	50.00
❏ SU-336 [M]	Soul Surf	1964	10.00	20.00	40.00

NEW HOPE
Also see THE KIT KATS.
JAMIE
| ❏ JLPS-3034 | To Understand Is to Love | 1970 | 7.50 | 15.00 | 30.00 |

NEW LEGION ROCK SPECTACULAR, THE
SPECTACULAR
| ❏ 7777 | Wild Ones! | 1975 | 15.00 | 30.00 | 60.00 |

NEW MIX, THE
UNITED ARTISTS
| ❏ UAS-6678 | The New Mix | 1968 | 5.00 | 10.00 | 20.00 |

NEW ORDER
Also see JOY DIVISION.
FACTORY
| ❏ FACTUS 8 [EP] | 1981-1982 | 1983 | 5.00 | 10.00 | 20.00 |
| ❏ FACTUS 12 | Power, Corruption and Lies | 1983 | 5.00 | 10.00 | 20.00 |

Number	Title	Yr	VG	VG+	NM
❑ FACTUS 50	Movement	1981	5.00	10.00	20.00
-- Originals have no bar code					
❑ FACTUS 50	Movement	1981	12.50	25.00	50.00
-- Purple vinyl (looks more black, but will appear purple when held to a light)					

NEW RENAISSANCE SOCIETY, THE
HANNA-BARBERA
| ❑ HLP-9504 [M] | Baroque n' Stones | 1966 | 5.00 | 10.00 | 20.00 |
| ❑ HST-9504 [S] | Baroque n' Stones | 1966 | 6.25 | 12.50 | 25.00 |

NEW RIDERS OF THE PURPLE SAGE
COLUMBIA
| ❑ CQ 32450 [Q] | The Adventures of Panama Red | 1974 | 5.00 | 10.00 | 20.00 |

NEW SEEKERS, THE
ELEKTRA
| ❑ EQ-5051 [Q] | The Best of the New Seekers | 1973 | 5.00 | 10.00 | 20.00 |

NEW STRANGERS, THE
FOLKLORE
| ❑ FRLP-14027 [M] Meet the New Strangers | | 1964 | 5.00 | 10.00 | 20.00 |
| ❑ FRST-14027 [S] Meet the New Strangers | | 1964 | 6.25 | 12.50 | 25.00 |

NEW SYMPHONY ORCHESTRA OF LONDON (RAYMOND AGOULT, CONDUCTOR)
RCA VICTOR RED SEAL
❑ LSC-2134 [S]	Overture! Overture!	1959	25.00	50.00	100.00
-- Original with "shaded dog" label; issued with two different covers					
❑ LSC-2134 [S]	Overture! Overture!	199?	6.25	12.50	25.00
-- Classic Records reissue					

NEW SYMPHONY ORCHESTRA OF LONDON (RONALD BINGE, CONDUCTOR)
RCA VICTOR RED SEAL
| ❑ LSC-2399 [S] | Mendelssohniana | 1960 | 10.00 | 20.00 | 40.00 |
| -- Originals with "shaded dog" label | | | | | |

NEW SYMPHONY ORCHESTRA OF LONDON (ALEXANDER GIBSON, CONDUCTOR)
RCA VICTOR RED SEAL
❑ LSC-2225 [S]	Witches' Brew	1959	50.00	100.00	200.00
-- Original with "shaded dog" label					
❑ LSC-2225 [S]	Witches' Brew	199?	6.25	12.50	25.00
-- Classic Records reissue					

NEW TWEEDY BROTHERS, THE
RIDON
❑ 234	The New Tweedy Brothers	1968	500.00	1,000.	2,000.
-- With oversized hexagonal cover designed to look like a sugar cube					
❑ 234	The New Tweedy Brothers	1968	100.00	200.00	400.00
-- With plain white cover					

NEW WAVE, THE
CANTERBURY
| ❑ CLPS-1501 | The New Wave | 1967 | 6.25 | 12.50 | 25.00 |

NEW YORK DOLLS
Also see DAVID JOHANSEN.
MERCURY
| ❑ SRM-1-675 | New York Dolls | 1973 | 10.00 | 20.00 | 40.00 |
| ❑ SRM-1-1001 | In Too Much Too Soon | 1974 | 10.00 | 20.00 | 40.00 |

NEW YORK PHILHARMONIC ORCHESTRA (BRUNO WALTER, CONDUCTOR)
COLUMBIA MASTERWORKS
❑ ML 4001 [M]	Mendelssohn: Violin Concerto	1948	10.00	20.00	40.00
-- Violinist: Nathan Milstein; the very first microgroove LP!					
❑ ML 4001 [M]	Mendelssohn: Violin Concerto	1999	6.25	12.50	25.00
-- Violinist: Nathan Milstein; Classic Records commemorative reissue					

NEW YORK PRO MUSICA ANTIQUA
COUNTERPOINT/ESOTERIC
| ❑ CPT 521 [M] | English Medieval Christmas Carols | 196? | 5.00 | 10.00 | 20.00 |

NEWBEATS, THE
HICKORY
❑ LPM 120 [M]	Bread and Butter	1964	12.50	25.00	50.00
❑ LPS 120 [S]	Bread and Butter	1964	37.50	75.00	150.00
❑ LPM 122 [M]	Big Beat Sounds by the Newbeats	1965	12.50	25.00	50.00
❑ LPS 122 [S]	Big Beat Sounds by the Newbeats	1965	25.00	50.00	100.00
❑ LPM 128 [M]	Run Baby Run	1965	12.50	25.00	50.00
❑ LPS 128 [S]	Run Baby Run	1965	25.00	50.00	100.00
❑ DT 90701 [R]	Bread and Butter	1965	37.50	75.00	150.00
-- Capitol Record Club edition					
❑ ST 90701 [S]	Bread and Butter	1965	50.00	100.00	200.00
-- Capitol Record Club edition					
❑ T 90701 [M]	Bread and Butter	1965	37.50	75.00	150.00
-- Capitol Record Club edition					

NEWBURY, MICKEY
ELEKTRA
| ❑ EQ-4107 [Q] | 'Frisco Mabel Joy | 1974 | 5.00 | 10.00 | 20.00 |

NEWHART, BOB
MURRAY HILL
| ❑ OP 2529 [(2)] | The Best of the Button-Down Mind | 197? | 5.00 | 10.00 | 20.00 |
WARNER BROS.
❑ W 1379 [M]	The Button-Down Mind of Bob Newhart	1960	7.50	15.00	30.00
❑ WS 1379 [S]	The Button-Down Mind of Bob Newhart	1960	6.25	12.50	25.00
❑ W 1393 [M]	The Button-Down Mind Strikes Back!	1960	7.50	15.00	30.00
❑ WS 1393 [S]	The Button-Down Mind Strikes Back!	1960	6.25	12.50	25.00
❑ 2N 1399 [(2) M]	The Bob Newhart Deluxe Edition	1961	12.50	25.00	50.00
❑ 2NS 1399 [(2) S]	The Bob Newhart Deluxe Edition	1961	10.00	20.00	40.00
❑ W 1417 [M]	Behind the Button-Down Mind of Bob Newhart	1961	6.25	12.50	25.00
❑ WS 1417 [S]	Behind the Button-Down Mind of Bob Newhart	1961	5.00	10.00	20.00
❑ W 1467 [M]	The Button-Down Mind on TV	1962	6.25	12.50	25.00
❑ WS 1467 [S]	The Button-Down Mind on TV	1962	5.00	10.00	20.00
❑ W 1517 [M]	Bob Newhart Faces Bob Newhart (Faces Bob Newhart)	1964	6.25	12.50	25.00
❑ W 1588 [M]	The Windmills Are Weakening	1965	7.50	15.00	30.00
❑ W 1672 [M]	The Best of Bob Newhart	1966	7.50	15.00	30.00
❑ WS 1672 [S]	The Best of Bob Newhart	1966	6.25	12.50	25.00
-- Gold label					
❑ WS 1672 [S]	The Best of Bob Newhart	1968	5.00	10.00	20.00
-- Green "W7" label					
❑ W 1717 [M]	This Is It	1967	7.50	15.00	30.00

NEWLEY, ANTHONY
LONDON
| ❑ PS 244 [S] | Tony | 1962 | 6.25 | 12.50 | 25.00 |
| ❑ LL 3156 [M] | Love Is a Now and Then Thing | 1960 | 5.00 | 10.00 | 20.00 |
RCA VICTOR
| ❑ LSP-2925 [S] | In My Solitude | 1964 | 5.00 | 10.00 | 20.00 |

NEWMAN, BOB
AUDIO LAB
| ❑ AL-1536 [M] | The Kentucky Colonel | 1959 | 50.00 | 100.00 | 200.00 |

NEWMAN, DAVID "FATHEAD"
ATLANTIC
❑ 1304 [M]	Ray Charles Presents David "Fathead" Newman	1959	10.00	20.00	40.00
-- Black label					
❑ SD 1304 [S]	Ray Charles Presents David "Fathead" Newman	1959	12.50	25.00	50.00
-- Green label					
❑ SD 1304 [S]	Ray Charles Presents David "Fathead" Newman	1961	5.00	10.00	20.00
-- Multicolor label with white "fan" logo					
❑ 1366 [M]	Straight Ahead	1961	7.50	15.00	30.00
-- Multicolor label with white "fan" logo					
❑ SD 1366 [S]	Straight Ahead	1961	10.00	20.00	40.00
-- Multicolor label with white "fan" logo					
❑ 1399 [M]	Fathead Comes On	1962	7.50	15.00	30.00
❑ SD 1399 [S]	Fathead Comes On	1962	10.00	20.00	40.00
❑ SD 1489	House of David	1968	5.00	10.00	20.00
❑ SD 1505	Bigger and Better	1968	5.00	10.00	20.00

NEWMAN, JIMMY
DECCA
❑ DL 4221 [M]	Jimmy Newman	1962	6.25	12.50	25.00
❑ DL 4398 [M]	Folk Songs of the Bayou Country	1963	10.00	20.00	40.00
❑ DL 4748 [M]	Artificial Rose	1966	5.00	10.00	20.00
❑ DL 4781 [M]	Jimmy Newman Sings Country Songs	1966	5.00	10.00	20.00

Number	Title	Yr	VG	VG+	NM
❑ DL 4885 [M]	The World of Country Music	1967	6.25	12.50	25.00
❑ DL 4960 [M]	The Jimmy Newman Way	1967	6.25	12.50	25.00
❑ DL 74221 [S]	Jimmy Newman	1962	7.50	15.00	30.00
❑ DL 74398 [S]	Folk Songs of the Bayou Country	1963	12.50	25.00	50.00
❑ DL 74748 [S]	Artificial Rose	1966	6.25	12.50	25.00
❑ DL 74781 [S]	Jimmy Newman Sings Country Songs	1966	6.25	12.50	25.00
❑ DL 74885 [S]	The World of Country Music	1967	5.00	10.00	20.00
❑ DL 74960 [S]	The Jimmy Newman Way	1967	5.00	10.00	20.00
❑ DL 75065	Born to Love You	1968	5.00	10.00	20.00

DOT

Number	Title	Yr	VG	VG+	NM
❑ DLP-3690 [M]	A Fallen Star	1965	7.50	15.00	30.00
❑ DLP-3736 [M]	Country Crossroads	1966	7.50	15.00	30.00
❑ DLP-25736 [R]	Country Crossroads	1966	5.00	10.00	20.00

MGM

Number	Title	Yr	VG	VG+	NM
❑ E-3777 [M]	This Is Jimmy Newman	1959	6.25	12.50	25.00
❑ SE-3777 [S]	This Is Jimmy Newman	1959	7.50	15.00	30.00
❑ E-4045 [M]	Songs by Jimmy Newman	1962	6.25	12.50	25.00
❑ SE-4045 [S]	Songs by Jimmy Newman	1962	7.50	15.00	30.00

NEWMAN, RANDY
REPRISE

Number	Title	Yr	VG	VG+	NM
❑ RS 6286	Randy Newman	1968	5.00	10.00	20.00

-- Cover with Randy standing in the clouds

NEWTON, JUICE
RCA VICTOR

Number	Title	Yr	VG	VG+	NM
❑ APL1-1004	Juice Newton and Silver Spur	1975	5.00	10.00	20.00

NEWTON, WAYNE
CAPITOL

Number	Title	Yr	VG	VG+	NM
❑ ST 1973 [S]	Danke Schoen	1963	5.00	10.00	20.00
❑ ST 2029 [S]	Wayne Newton In Person	1964	5.00	10.00	20.00
❑ ST 2130 [S]	Wayne Newton Sings Hit Songs	1964	5.00	10.00	20.00
❑ ST 2335 [S]	Red Roses for a Blue Lady	1965	5.00	10.00	20.00
❑ ST 2389 [S]	Summer Wind	1965	5.00	10.00	20.00
❑ ST 2445 [S]	Wayne Newton -- Now!	1966	5.00	10.00	20.00
❑ ST 2563 [S]	The Old Rugged Cross	1966	5.00	10.00	20.00
❑ ST 2635 [S]	It's Only the Good Times	1967	5.00	10.00	20.00
❑ T 2714 [M]	Song of the Year... Wayne Newton Style	1967	5.00	10.00	20.00
❑ T 2797 [M]	The Best of Wayne Newton	1967	5.00	10.00	20.00
❑ T 2832 [M]	God Is Alive	1968	5.00	10.00	20.00
❑ T 2847 [M]	Wayne Newton -- The Greatest	1968	5.00	10.00	20.00

MGM

Number	Title	Yr	VG	VG+	NM
❑ E-4523 [M]	Walking on New Grass	1968	5.00	10.00	20.00
❑ E-4549 [M]	One More Time	1968	5.00	10.00	20.00

NEWTON-JOHN, OLIVIA
MCA

Number	Title	Yr	VG	VG+	NM
❑ 16011	Physical	1982	6.25	12.50	25.00

-- Audiophile edition

MOBILE FIDELITY

Number	Title	Yr	VG	VG+	NM
❑ 1-040	Totally Hot	1980	5.00	15.00	20.00

-- Audiophile vinyl

UNI

Number	Title	Yr	VG	VG+	NM
❑ 73117	If Not for You	1971	20.00	40.00	80.00

NEXT MORNING, THE
CALLA

Number	Title	Yr	VG	VG+	NM
❑ SC-2002	The Next Morning	1972	25.00	50.00	100.00

NICE, THE
Keith Emerson of EMERSON, LAKE AND PALMER was in this group.
IMMEDIATE

Number	Title	Yr	VG	VG+	NM
❑ Z12 52004	Thoughts of Emerlist Davjack	1968	5.00	10.00	20.00
❑ Z12-52020	Ars Longa Vita Brevis	1969	5.00	10.00	20.00

NICHOLAS BROTHERS, THE
MERCURY

Number	Title	Yr	VG	VG+	NM
❑ MG-20355 [M]	We Do Sing, Too	1958	7.50	15.00	30.00

NICHOLS, MIKE, AND ELAINE MAY
MERCURY

Number	Title	Yr	VG	VG+	NM
❑ SRM-2-628 [(2)]	Retrospect	1972	5.00	10.00	20.00
❑ OCM 2200 [M]	An Evening with Mike Nichols and Elaine May	1961	7.50	15.00	30.00
❑ OCS 6200 [S]	An Evening with Mike Nichols and Elaine May	1961	10.00	20.00	40.00
❑ MG 20376 [M]	Improvisations to Music	1959	7.50	15.00	30.00

Number	Title	Yr	VG	VG+	NM
❑ MG 20680 [M]	Nichols and May Examine Doctors	1962	6.25	12.50	25.00
❑ MG 20997 [M]	The Best of Nichols and May	1965	5.00	10.00	20.00
❑ SR 60040 [S]	Improvisations to Music	1959	10.00	20.00	40.00
❑ SR 60680 [S]	Nichols and May Examine Doctors	1962	7.50	15.00	30.00
❑ SR 60997 [S]	The Best of Nichols and May	1965	6.25	12.50	25.00

NICHOLS, NICHELLE
EPIC

Number	Title	Yr	VG	VG+	NM
❑ BN 26351	Down to Earth	1968	10.00	20.00	40.00

NICHOLS, RED, AND THE FIVE PENNIES
AUDIOPHILE

Number	Title	Yr	VG	VG+	NM
❑ AP-1 [M]	Red Nichols and Band	195?	12.50	25.00	50.00
❑ AP-7 [M]	Syncopated Chamber Music, Volume 1	195?	12.50	25.00	50.00
❑ AP-8 [M]	Syncopated Chamber Music, Volume 2	195?	12.50	25.00	50.00

BRUNSWICK

Number	Title	Yr	VG	VG+	NM
❑ BL 54008 [M]	For Collectors Only	1954	12.50	25.00	50.00
❑ BL 54047 [M]	The Red Nichols Story	1959	12.50	25.00	50.00
❑ BL 58008 [10]	Classics, Volume 1	1950	20.00	40.00	80.00
❑ BL 58009 [10]	Classics, Volume 2	1950	20.00	40.00	80.00
❑ BL 58027 [10]	Volume 3	1951	20.00	40.00	80.00

CAPITOL

Number	Title	Yr	VG	VG+	NM
❑ H 215 [10]	Jazz Time	1950	20.00	40.00	80.00
❑ T 775 [M]	Hot Pennies	1956	12.50	25.00	50.00
❑ ST 1051 [S]	Parade of the Pennies	1958	7.50	15.00	30.00
❑ T 1051 [M]	Parade of the Pennies	1958	5.00	10.00	20.00
❑ ST 1297 [S]	Dixieland Dinner Dance	1960	5.00	10.00	20.00
❑ ST 1803 [S]	The All-Time Hits of Red Nichols	1962	5.00	10.00	20.00
❑ ST 2065 [S]	Blues and Old-Time Rags	1963	5.00	10.00	20.00

MOBILE FIDELITY

Number	Title	Yr	VG	VG+	NM
❑ 1-093	Red Nichols and the Five Pennies at Marineland	1982	5.00	10.00	20.00

-- Audiophile vinyl

NICKEL BAG, THE
KAMA SUTRA

Number	Title	Yr	VG	VG+	NM
❑ KLPS-8066	Doing Their Love Thing	1968	6.25	12.50	25.00

NICKS, STEVIE
Also see BUCKINGHAM NICKS; FLEETWOOD MAC.
ATLANTIC

Number	Title	Yr	VG	VG+	NM
❑ 1P-8160	TimeSpace -- The Best of Stevie Nicks	1991	5.00	10.00	20.00

-- Columbia House edition; only US vinyl version

MOBILE FIDELITY

Number	Title	Yr	VG	VG+	NM
❑ 1-121	Bella Donna	1984	12.50	25.00	50.00

-- Audiophile vinyl

MODERN

Number	Title	Yr	VG	VG+	NM
❑ PR-2881 [DJ]	Reflections from the Other Side of the Mirror	1989	10.00	20.00	40.00

-- Promo-only interview album with script

NICO
ELEKTRA

Number	Title	Yr	VG	VG+	NM
❑ EKS-74029	The Marble Index	1968	6.25	12.50	25.00

REPRISE

Number	Title	Yr	VG	VG+	NM
❑ RS 6424	Desert Shore	1970	5.00	10.00	20.00

VERVE

Number	Title	Yr	VG	VG+	NM
❑ V-5032 [M]	Chelsea Girl	1967	7.50	15.00	30.00
❑ V6-5032 [S]	Chelsea Girl	1967	10.00	20.00	40.00

NIELSEN, GERTRUDE
DECCA

Number	Title	Yr	VG	VG+	NM
❑ DL 5138 [10]	Gertrude Nielsen	1951	12.50	25.00	50.00

NIGHT OWLS, THE
VALMOR

Number	Title	Yr	VG	VG+	NM
❑ 79 [M]	Twisting the Oldies	1962	25.00	50.00	100.00

NIGHT SHADOWS, THE
HOTTRAX

Number	Title	Yr	VG	VG+	NM
❑ 1414	The Square Root of Two	1979	12.50	25.00	50.00

-- Reissue of Spectrum LP

Number	Title	Yr	VG	VG+	NM
❑ 1430	Live at the Spot	1981	6.25	12.50	25.00
❑ 1450	Invasion of the Acid Eaters	1982	6.25	12.50	25.00

SPECTRUM

Number	Title	Yr	VG	VG+	NM
❑ 2001	The Square Root of Two	1968	250.00	500.00	1,000.

-- With neither bonus 45 nor psychedelic poster

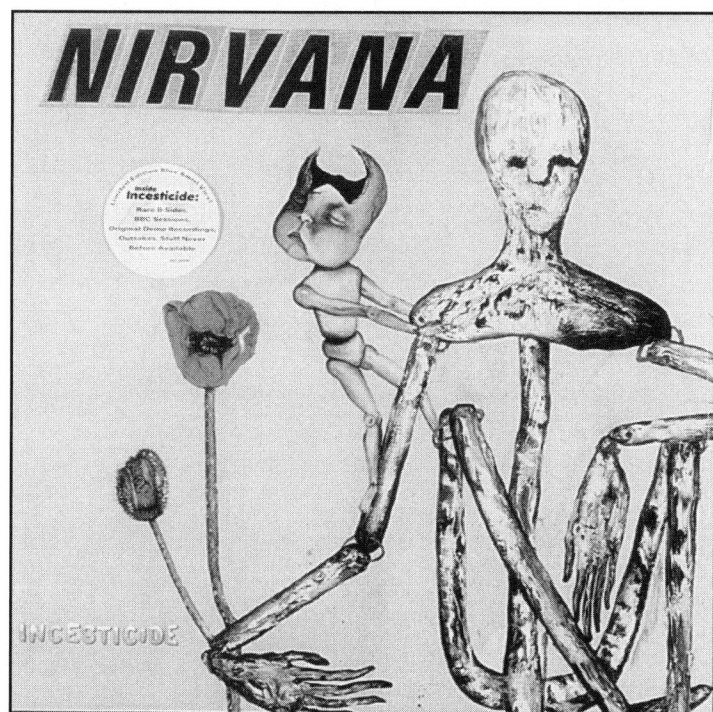

Time will tell what the rock history books will say about Nirvana, but the Seattle band is right up there among the most collectible acts of the 1990s. (Top left) Their debut album, *Bleach,* came out on six different colors (or color combinations) of vinyl over a three-year period before the vinyl version was deleted in 1992. The most collectible versions are on white, red and white swirl, and black vinyl with an added poster not in any of the other colored versions. (Top right) Nirvana's breakthrough album, *Nevermind,* is common on compact disc, but on vinyl, especially the American pressing, it's tough. Even rarer is the Mobile Fidelity audiophile vinyl version, which is one of the most sought-after from the second wave of MoFi vinyl issues. (Bottom left) *Incesticide* was a stopgap album, a collection of old singles and other rarities. The U.S. vinyl copies were pressed on a blue swirl vinyl, and those, too, are now sought after; they've been known to fetch $30 or more. (Bottom right) The first Nirvana LP after the death of Kurt Cobain was *MTV Unplugged in New York*. Again the vinyl version is collectible; the U.S. version was pressed on white wax.

Number	Title	Yr	VG	VG+	NM
❑ 2001	The Square Root of Two	1968	275.00	550.00	1,100.
-- With bonus 45, but no poster					
❑ 2001	The Square Root of Two	1968	300.00	600.00	1,200.
-- With poster, but no 45					
❑ 2001	The Square Root of Two	1968	375.00	750.00	1,500.
-- With both 45 and poster					

NIGHTCAPS, THE
VANDAN

Number	Title	Yr	VG	VG+	NM
❑ VRLP-8124	Wine, Wine, Wine	196?	37.50	75.00	150.00

NIGHTCRAWLERS, THE
KAPP

Number	Title	Yr	VG	VG+	NM
❑ KL-1520 [M]	The Little Black Egg	1967	15.00	30.00	60.00
❑ KS-3520 [S]	The Little Black Egg	1967	10.00	20.00	40.00

NIGHTHAWKS, THE
ALADDIN

Number	Title	Yr	VG	VG+	NM
❑ LP-101	Rock and Roll	197?	50.00	100.00	200.00

NILES, JOHN JACOB
BOONE-TOLLIVER

Number	Title	Yr	VG	VG+	NM
❑ BTR-22 [10]	American Folk Songs to Dulcimer Accompaniment	195?	12.50	25.00	50.00
❑ BTR-23 [10]	Ballads	195?	12.50	25.00	50.00

RCA CAMDEN

Number	Title	Yr	VG	VG+	NM
❑ CAL-219 [M]	American Folk and Gambling Songs	195?	6.25	12.50	25.00
❑ CAL-245 [M]	American Folk Songs	195?	6.25	12.50	25.00
❑ CAL-330 [M]	50th Anniversary Album	195?	6.25	12.50	25.00

TRADITION

Number	Title	Yr	VG	VG+	NM
❑ TLP-1023 [M]	I Wonder As I Wander	1957	7.50	15.00	30.00
❑ TLP-1036 [M]	An Evening with John Jacob Niles	195?	7.50	15.00	30.00

NILSSON
RCA VICTOR

Number	Title	Yr	VG	VG+	NM
❑ (no #) [M]	The True One	1967	50.00	100.00	200.00
-- Boxed set with mono copy of RCA Victor 3874, two photos, button, poster, sticker, bios					
❑ APD1-0319 [Q]	Nilsson Schmilsson	1974	5.00	10.00	20.00
❑ SPS-33-567 [DJ]	Scatalogue	197?	25.00	50.00	100.00
❑ APD1-0570 [Q]	Pussy Cats	1974	7.50	15.00	30.00
❑ CPL1-0570	Pussy Cats	1974	5.00	10.00	20.00
❑ APD1-0817 [Q]	Duit On Mon Dei	1975	5.00	10.00	20.00
❑ APD1-1031 [Q]	Sandman	1976	5.00	10.00	20.00
❑ LPM-3874 [M]	Pandemonium Shadow Show	1967	10.00	20.00	40.00
❑ LSP-3874 [S]	Pandemonium Shadow Show	1967	5.00	10.00	20.00
-- "Stereo" on black label					
❑ LPM-3956 [M]	Aerial Ballet	1968	12.50	25.00	50.00
❑ LSP-3956 [S]	Aerial Ballet	1968	5.00	10.00	20.00
-- "Stereo" on black label					

TOWER

Number	Title	Yr	VG	VG+	NM
❑ ST 5095 [S]	Spotlight on Nilsson	1967	5.00	10.00	20.00
❑ T 5095 [M]	Spotlight on Nilsson	1967	5.00	10.00	20.00

NIMOY, LEONARD
CAEDMON

Number	Title	Yr	VG	VG+	NM
❑ TC-1466	The Martian Chronicles	1976	7.50	15.00	30.00
❑ TC-1479	The Illustrated Man	1976	7.50	15.00	30.00
❑ TC-1520	War of the Worlds	1977	7.50	15.00	30.00
❑ TC-1526	Green Hills of Earth	1977	7.50	15.00	30.00

DOT

Number	Title	Yr	VG	VG+	NM
❑ DLP 3794 [M]	Mr. Spock's Music from Outer Space	1967	12.50	25.00	50.00
❑ DLP 3835 [M]	Two Sides of Leonard Nimoy	1968	12.50	25.00	50.00
❑ DLP 25794 [S]	Mr. Spock's Music from Outer Space	1967	20.00	40.00	80.00
❑ DLP 25835 [S]	Two Sides of Leonard Nimoy	1968	20.00	40.00	80.00
❑ DLP 25883	The Way I Feel	1968	15.00	30.00	60.00
❑ DLP 25910	The Touch of Leonard Nimoy	1969	15.00	30.00	60.00
❑ DLP 25966	The New World of Leonard Nimoy	1969	15.00	30.00	60.00

JRT

Number	Title	Yr	VG	VG+	NM
❑ (# unknown)	The Mysterious Golem	1982	10.00	20.00	40.00

PARAMOUNT

Number	Title	Yr	VG	VG+	NM
❑ PAS-1030 [(2)]	Outer Space/Inner Mind	1970	12.50	25.00	50.00

PICKWICK

Number	Title	Yr	VG	VG+	NM
❑ SPC-3199	Space Odyssey	197?	12.50	25.00	50.00

SEARS

Number	Title	Yr	VG	VG+	NM
❑ SPS-491	Leonard Nimoy	196?	20.00	40.00	80.00

NINE INCH NAILS
NOTHING/TVT/INTERSCOPE

Number	Title	Yr	VG	VG+	NM
❑ PR 5509 [(2)]	The Downward Spiral	1994	6.25	12.50	25.00
-- Promo-only U.S. vinyl					

94 EAST
HOT PINK

Number	Title	Yr	VG	VG+	NM
❑ HLP 3223	Minneapolis Genius -- 94 East	1977	10.00	20.00	40.00
-- Early recordings by PRINCE; deduct 25% for cut-outs					

1910 FRUITGUM COMPANY
BUDDAH

Number	Title	Yr	VG	VG+	NM
❑ BDS-5010	Simon Says	1968	6.25	12.50	25.00
❑ BDS-5022	1,2,3 Red Light	1968	6.25	12.50	25.00
❑ BDS-5027	Goody, Goody Gumdrops	1969	6.25	12.50	25.00
❑ BDS-5036	Indian Giver	1969	6.25	12.50	25.00
❑ BDS-5043	Hard Ride	1969	6.25	12.50	25.00
❑ BDS-5057	Juiciest Fruitgum	1970	6.25	12.50	25.00

NIRVANA
The late 60s psychedelic group.
BELL

Number	Title	Yr	VG	VG+	NM
❑ 6015	The Story of Simon Simopath	1968	6.25	12.50	25.00
❑ 6024	All of Us	1969	6.25	12.50	25.00

METROMEDIA

Number	Title	Yr	VG	VG+	NM
❑ MD-1018	Nirvana	1970	6.25	12.50	25.00

NIRVANA
The early 90s grunge group.
DGC

Number	Title	Yr	VG	VG+	NM
❑ 24425	Nevermind	1991	5.00	10.00	20.00
-- All copies on black vinyl					
❑ 24504	Incesticide	1992	7.50	15.00	30.00
-- All copies on blue swirl vinyl					
❑ 24607	In Utero	1993	7.50	15.00	30.00
-- All copies on clear vinyl					
❑ 24727	MTV Unplugged in New York	1994	5.00	10.00	20.00
-- All copies on white vinyl					

MOBILE FIDELITY

Number	Title	Yr	VG	VG+	NM
❑ 1-258	Nevermind	1996	25.00	50.00	100.00
-- Audiophile vinyl					

SUB POP

Number	Title	Yr	VG	VG+	NM
❑ SP 34	Bleach	1989	50.00	100.00	200.00
-- First 1,000 were pressed on white vinyl					
❑ SP 34	Bleach	1989	50.00	100.00	200.00
-- Second 1,000 were pressed on black vinyl and include a poster					
❑ SP 34	Bleach	1989	37.50	75.00	150.00
-- Red and white swirl vinyl					
❑ SP 34	Bleach	1989	15.00	30.00	60.00
-- Pink vinyl					
❑ SP 34	Bleach	1989	15.00	30.00	60.00
-- Purple vinyl					
❑ SP 34	Bleach	1989	5.00	10.00	20.00
-- Red vinyl					

NITTY GRITTY DIRT BAND
LIBERTY

Number	Title	Yr	VG	VG+	NM
❑ LRP-3501 [M]	The Nitty Gritty Dirt Band	1967	6.25	12.50	25.00
❑ LRP-3516 [M]	Ricochet	1967	6.25	12.50	25.00
❑ LST-7501 [S]	The Nitty Gritty Dirt Band	1967	7.50	15.00	30.00
❑ LST-7516 [S]	Ricochet	1967	7.50	15.00	30.00
❑ LST-7540	Rare Junk	1968	6.25	12.50	25.00
❑ LST-7611	Alive	1969	6.25	12.50	25.00
❑ LST-7642	Uncle Charlie and His Dog Teddy	1970	6.25	12.50	25.00
-- Standard issue of LP					
❑ LST-7642 [DJ]	Uncle Charlie and His Dog Teddy	1970	30.00	60.00	120.00
-- Leatherette promo pack with LP, two other discs, photos, booklet					

UNITED ARTISTS

Number	Title	Yr	VG	VG+	NM
❑ UA-LA670-L3 [(3)]	Dirt, Silver and Gold	1976	5.00	10.00	20.00
❑ UAS-9801 [(3)]	Will the Circle Be Unbroken	1972	7.50	15.00	30.00

UNIVERSAL

Number	Title	Yr	VG	VG+	NM
❑ UVL2-12500 [(2)]	Will the Circle Be Unbroken, Volume Two	1989	5.00	10.00	20.00

NITZSCHE, JACK
REPRISE

Number	Title	Yr	VG	VG+	NM
❑ MS 2092	St. Giles Cripplegate	1972	5.00	10.00	20.00
❑ R 6101 [M]	The Lonely Surfer	1963	25.00	50.00	100.00
❑ RS 6101 [S]	The Lonely Surfer	1963	50.00	100.00	200.00
-- Pink, gold and green label					
❑ RS 6101 [S]	The Lonely Surfer	197?	5.00	10.00	20.00
-- With only "r" logo on all-orange (tan) label					
❑ R 6115 [M]	Dance to the Hits of the Beatles	1964	12.50	25.00	50.00
❑ RS 6115 [S]	Dance to the Hits of the Beatles	1964	15.00	30.00	60.00
❑ R 6200 [M]	Chopin '66	1966	6.25	12.50	25.00
❑ RS 6200 [S]	Chopin '66	1966	7.50	15.00	30.00

NKRUMAH, KWAME
COLUMBIA

Number	Title	Yr	VG	VG+	NM
❑ CS 9863	Ninth Son	1969	6.25	12.50	25.00

Number	Title	Yr	VG	VG+	NM
NOBLES, CLIFF					
MOON SHOT					
❏ 601	Pony the Horse	1969	10.00	20.00	40.00
PHIL-L.A. OF SOUL					
❏ 4001	The Horse	1968	15.00	30.00	60.00
NOGUEZ, JACKY					
JAMIE					
❏ JLP-3007 [M]	Chow Chow Bambina	1959	5.00	10.00	20.00
❏ JLPS-3007 [S]	Chow Chow Bambina	1959	7.50	15.00	30.00
❏ JLP-3012 [M]	Jacky Noguez	1960	5.00	10.00	20.00
❏ JLPS-3012 [S]	Jacky Noguez	1960	7.50	15.00	30.00
❏ JLP-3013 [M]	Dance Along with Jacky Noguez	1960	5.00	10.00	20.00
❏ JLPS-3013 [S]	Dance Along with Jacky Noguez	1960	7.50	15.00	30.00
NOLAND, TERRY					
BRUNSWICK					
❏ BL 54041 [M]	Terry Noland	1958	150.00	300.00	600.00
-- BUDDY HOLLY plays guitar					
NORDINE, KEN					
BLUE THUMB					
❏ BTS-33 [(2)]	How Are Things in Your Town?	1971	6.25	12.50	25.00
❏ BTS-35 [(2)]	Ken Nordine	1972	6.25	12.50	25.00
DECCA					
❏ DL 8550 [M]	Concert in the Sky	1957	15.00	30.00	60.00
DOT					
❏ DLP-3075 [M]	Word Jazz	1958	10.00	20.00	40.00
❏ DLP-3096 [M]	Son of Word Jazz	1958	10.00	20.00	40.00
❏ DLP-3115 [M]	Love Words	1958	10.00	20.00	40.00
❏ DLP-3142 [M]	My Baby	1959	10.00	20.00	40.00
❏ DLP-3196 [M]	Next!	1959	10.00	20.00	40.00
❏ DLP-3301 [M]	Word Jazz, Vol. 2	1960	10.00	20.00	40.00
❏ DLP-25075 [S]	Word Jazz	1959	12.50	25.00	50.00
❏ DLP-25096 [S]	Son of Word Jazz	1959	12.50	25.00	50.00
❏ DLP-25115 [S]	Love Words	1959	12.50	25.00	50.00
❏ DLP-25142 [S]	My Baby	1959	12.50	25.00	50.00
❏ DLP-25196 [S]	Next!	1959	12.50	25.00	50.00
❏ DLP-25301 [S]	Word Jazz, Vol. 2	1960	12.50	25.00	50.00
❏ DLP-25880	The Best of Word Jazz	1968	5.00	10.00	20.00
HAMILTON					
❏ HL-102 [M]	The Voice of Love	1964	5.00	10.00	20.00
❏ HL-12102 [S]	The Voice of Love	1964	6.25	12.50	25.00
PHILIPS					
❏ PHM 200-224 [M]	Colors	1966	5.00	10.00	20.00
❏ PHM 200-258 [M]	Twink	1967	5.00	10.00	20.00
❏ PHS 600-224 [S]	Colors	1966	6.25	12.50	25.00
❏ PHS 600-258 [S]	Twink	1967	6.25	12.50	25.00
SNAIL					
❏ SR-1003	Grandson of Word Jazz	1987	5.00	10.00	20.00
NORMA JEAN					
HARMONY					
❏ HL 7363 [M]	Country's Favorite	1966	5.00	10.00	20.00
RCA VICTOR					
❏ LPM-2961 [M]	Let's Go All the Way	1964	6.25	12.50	25.00
❏ LSP-2961 [S]	Let's Go All the Way	1964	7.50	15.00	30.00
❏ LPM-3449 [M]	Pretty Miss Norma Jean	1965	6.25	12.50	25.00
❏ LSP-3449 [S]	Pretty Miss Norma Jean	1965	7.50	15.00	30.00
❏ LPM-3541 [M]	Please Don't Hurt Me	1966	6.25	12.50	25.00
❏ LSP-3541 [S]	Please Don't Hurt Me	1966	7.50	15.00	30.00
❏ LPM-3664 [M]	Norma Jean Sings a Tribute to Kitty Wells	1966	6.25	12.50	25.00
❏ LSP-3664 [S]	Norma Jean Sings a Tribute to Kitty Wells	1966	7.50	15.00	30.00
❏ LPM-3700 [M]	Norma Jean Sings Porter Wagoner	1967	7.50	15.00	30.00
❏ LSP-3700 [S]	Norma Jean Sings Porter Wagoner	1967	6.25	12.50	25.00
❏ LPM-3836 [M]	Jackson Ain't a Very Big Town	1967	7.50	15.00	30.00
❏ LSP-3836 [S]	Jackson Ain't a Very Big Town	1967	6.25	12.50	25.00
❏ LPM-3910 [M]	Heaven's Just a Prayer Away	1967	12.50	25.00	50.00
❏ LSP-3910 [S]	Heaven's Just a Prayer Away	1967	6.25	12.50	25.00
❏ LSP-3977	Body and Mind	1968	6.25	12.50	25.00
❏ LSP-4080	Love's a Woman's Job	1968	6.25	12.50	25.00
❏ LSP-4146	Country Giants	1969	6.25	12.50	25.00
❏ LSP-4227	The Best of Norma Jean	1969	6.25	12.50	25.00
❏ LSP-4446	It's Time for Norma Jean	1969	6.25	12.50	25.00
NORMAN, LARRY					
Also see PEOPLE.					
AB					
❏ 777	Streams of White Light Into Darkened Corners	1977	6.25	12.50	25.00

Number	Title	Yr	VG	VG+	NM
CAPITOL					
❏ ST-446	Upon This Rock	1970	7.50	15.00	30.00
IMPACT					
❏ 3121	Upon This Rock	197?	5.00	10.00	20.00
MGM					
❏ SE-4942	So Long Ago the Garden	1974	10.00	20.00	40.00
ONE WAY					
❏ 900	Bootleg	1972	7.50	15.00	30.00
-- Regular cover					
❏ 4847	Bootleg	1972	10.00	20.00	40.00
-- Gatefold cover					
❏ 7397	Street Level	1971	7.50	15.00	30.00
VERVE					
❏ V6-5092	Only Visiting This Planet	1973	10.00	20.00	40.00
-- Gatefold cover					
❏ V6-5092	Only Visiting This Planet	1973	7.50	15.00	30.00
-- Tri-fold cover					
NORTH, JAY					
KEM					
❏ 27	Look Who's Singing!	1960	25.00	50.00	100.00
NORTHCOTT, TOM					
UNI					
❏ 73108	Upside Downside	1971	5.00	10.00	20.00
NORTHERN FRONT					
KADER					
❏ (# unknown)	Furniture Store	1975	25.00	50.00	100.00
NOSY PARKER					
(NO LABEL)					
❏ (no #)	Nosy Parker	1975	62.50	125.00	250.00
NOTES FROM THE UNDERGROUND					
VANGUARD					
❏ VSD-6502	Notes from the Underground	1970	20.00	40.00	80.00
NOVA LOCAL, THE					
DECCA					
❏ DL 74977	Nova 1	1968	12.50	25.00	50.00
NOVELLS, THE					
MOTHER'S					
❏ MLPS-73	A Happening	1968	12.50	25.00	50.00
NRBQ					
ANNUIT COEPTIS					
❏ 1001/2 [(2)]	Scraps/Workshop	1976	5.00	10.00	20.00
-- Reissue of Kama Sutra LPs					
COLUMBIA					
❏ CS 9858	NRBQ	1969	6.25	12.50	25.00
-- "360 Sound Stereo" label					
KAMA SUTRA					
❏ KSBS-2045	Scraps	1972	7.50	15.00	30.00
❏ KSBS-2065	Workshop	1973	10.00	20.00	40.00
NUCLEUS					
MAINSTREAM					
❏ S-6120	Nucleus	1969	12.50	25.00	50.00
NUDIE					
NUDIE					
❏ 3203	Nudie and His Mandolin	196?	10.00	20.00	40.00
NUGENT, TED					
Also see THE AMBOY DUKES.					
EPIC					
❏ AS-99-607 [PD]	State of Shock	1979	10.00	20.00	40.00
-- Promo-only picture disc					
❏ PEQ 34121 [Q]	Free-for-All	1976	5.00	10.00	20.00
NUTTY SQUIRRELS, THE					
COLUMBIA					
❏ CL 1589 [M]	Bird Watching	1961	7.50	15.00	30.00
❏ CS 8389 [S]	Bird Watching	1961	10.00	20.00	40.00
HANOVER					
❏ HML-8014 [M]	The Nutty Squirrels	1960	12.50	25.00	50.00

Number	Title	Yr	VG	VG+	NM
MGM					
❑ E-4272 [M]	A Hard Day's Night	1964	6.25	12.50	25.00
❑ SE-4272 [S]	A Hard Day's Night	1964	7.50	15.00	30.00

NYE, LOUIS
RIVERSIDE

Number	Title	Yr	VG	VG+	NM
❑ RLP-842 [M]	Heigh-Ho, Madison Avenue	1960	6.25	12.50	25.00

NYRO, LAURA
COLUMBIA

Number	Title	Yr	VG	VG+	NM
❑ CL 2826 [M]	Eli and the Thirteenth Confession	1968	10.00	20.00	40.00
❑ PC2 34331 [(2) DJ]	Season of Lights...Laura Nyro in Concert	1977	12.50	25.00	50.00

-- *Promo only in plain cardboard jacket; this LP was edited to one LP for official release*

VERVE FOLKWAYS

Number	Title	Yr	VG	VG+	NM
❑ FT-3020 [M]	Laura Nyro -- More Than a New Discovery	1967	7.50	15.00	30.00
❑ FTS-3020 [S]	Laura Nyro -- More Than a New Discovery	1967	7.50	15.00	30.00

VERVE FORECAST

Number	Title	Yr	VG	VG+	NM
❑ FTS-3020 [S]	Laura Nyro -- More Than a New Discovery	1967	5.00	10.00	20.00
❑ ST 93036	Laura Nyro -- More Than a New Discovery	1968	6.25	12.50	25.00

-- *Capitol Record Club edition*

O

O'BRIAN, HUGH
ABC-PARAMOUNT

Number	Title	Yr	VG	VG+	NM
❑ ABC-203 [M]	TV's Wyatt Earp Sings	1957	15.00	30.00	60.00

O'BRYANT, JOAN
FOLKWAYS

Number	Title	Yr	VG	VG+	NM
❑ FA-2134 [M]	Folksongs and Ballads of Kansas	1957	7.50	15.00	30.00
❑ FA-2338 [M]	American Ballads and Folksongs	1958	7.50	15.00	30.00

O'CONNELL, HELEN
VIK

Number	Title	Yr	VG	VG+	NM
❑ LX-1093 [M]	Green Eyes	1957	10.00	20.00	40.00

O'CONNOR, CARROLL
A&M

Number	Title	Yr	VG	VG+	NM
❑ SP-4340	Remembering You	1972	6.25	12.50	25.00
AUDIO FIDELITY					
❑ AFSD-6727	Carroll O'Connor Sings for Old P.F.A.R.T.S.	1976	6.25	12.50	25.00

O'DAY, MOLLY
AUDIO LAB

Number	Title	Yr	VG	VG+	NM
❑ AL-1544 [M]	Music for the Country Folks	1960	7.50	15.00	30.00
HARMONY					
❑ HL 7299 [M]	The Unforgettable Molly O'Day	1963	5.00	10.00	20.00
STARDAY					
❑ SLP-367	The Living Legend of Country Music	1966	6.25	12.50	25.00

O'DELL, DOYE
ERA

Number	Title	Yr	VG	VG+	NM
❑ EL-20004 [M]	Doye	1956	12.50	25.00	50.00
-- *Red vinyl*					
❑ EL-20004 [M]	Doye	1956	7.50	15.00	30.00
-- *Black vinyl*					
SAGE					
❑ C-36 [M]	Crossroads	195?	7.50	15.00	30.00

O'DELL, KENNY
VEGAS

Number	Title	Yr	VG	VG+	NM
❑ 401	Beautiful People	1968	6.25	12.50	25.00

O'GWYNN, JAMES
MERCURY

Number	Title	Yr	VG	VG+	NM
❑ MG-20727 [M]	The Best of James O'Gwynn	1962	7.50	15.00	30.00
❑ SR-60727 [S]	The Best of James O'Gwynn	1962	10.00	20.00	40.00
WING					
❑ MGW-12290 [M]	Heartaches and Memories	1964	5.00	10.00	20.00
❑ SRW-16290 [S]	Heartaches and Memories	1964	6.25	12.50	25.00

O'HARA, MAUREEN
COLUMBIA

Number	Title	Yr	VG	VG+	NM
❑ CL 1750 [M]	Maureen O'Hara Sings Her Favorite Irish Songs	1962	10.00	20.00	40.00
❑ CS 8550 [S]	Maureen O'Hara Sings Her Favorite Irish Songs	1962	12.50	25.00	50.00
RCA VICTOR					
❑ LPM-1953 [M]	Love Letters	1959	12.50	25.00	50.00
❑ LSP-1953 [S]	Love Letters	1959	15.00	30.00	60.00

O'JAYS, THE
BELL

Number	Title	Yr	VG	VG+	NM
❑ 6014	Back on Top	1968	5.00	10.00	20.00
IMPERIAL					
❑ LP 12290 [S]	Comin' Through	1965	12.50	25.00	50.00
❑ LP 9290 [M]	Comin' Through	1965	10.00	20.00	40.00
MINIT					
❑ LP-24008 [S]	Soul Sounds	1967	12.50	25.00	50.00
❑ LP-40008 [M]	Soul Sounds	1967	10.00	20.00	40.00
NEPTUNE					
❑ 202	The O'Jays in Philadelphia	1969	7.50	15.00	30.00

O'KAYSIONS, THE
ABC

Number	Title	Yr	VG	VG+	NM
❑ S-664	Girl Watcher	1968	10.00	20.00	40.00

Number	Title	Yr	VG	VG+	NM
O'KEEFE, DANNY					
PANORAMA					
❏ 105	Introducing Danny O'Keefe	1966	10.00	20.00	40.00
O'SHEA, MILO					
COLUMBIA					
❏ CS 9647	An Evening in Dublin	1969	5.00	10.00	20.00
OAK RIDGE BOYS, THE					
CADENCE					
❏ CLP-3019 [M]	The Oak Ridge Quartet	1958	15.00	30.00	60.00
CANAAN					
❏ 9625	Together	1966	5.00	10.00	20.00
-- With the Harvesters					
MCA					
❏ L33-2-1276 [(2) DJ]	"Step On Out" World Premiere	1985	6.25	12.50	25.00
-- Promo-only interview and music LP with no script or cover					
SKYLITE					
❏ RLP-6020 [M]	The Oak Ridge Boys Sing for You	1964	5.00	10.00	20.00
❏ SRLP-6020 [S]	The Oak Ridge Boys Sing for You	1964	6.25	12.50	25.00
❏ RLP-6030 [M]	I Wouldn't Take Nothing for My Journey Now	1965	5.00	10.00	20.00
❏ SRLP-6030 [S]	I Wouldn't Take Nothing for My Journey Now	1965	6.25	12.50	25.00
❏ RLP-6040 [M]	The Solid Gospel Sound of the Oak Ridge Boys	1966	5.00	10.00	20.00
❏ SRLP-6040 [S]	The Solid Gospel Sound of the Oak Ridge Boys	1966	6.25	12.50	25.00
❏ RLP-6045 [M]	River of Love	1967	5.00	10.00	20.00
❏ SRLP-6045 [S]	River of Love	1967	6.25	12.50	25.00
STARDAY					
❏ SLP-356 [M]	The Sensational Oak Ridge Boys	1965	6.25	12.50	25.00
UNITED ARTISTS					
❏ UAL 3554 [M]	The Oak Ridge Boys at Their Best	1966	5.00	10.00	20.00
❏ UAS 6554 [S]	The Oak Ridge Boys at Their Best	1966	6.25	12.50	25.00
WARNER BROS.					
❏ W 1497 [M]	With Sounds of Nashville	1963	5.00	10.00	20.00
❏ WS 1497 [S]	With Sounds of Nashville	1963	6.25	12.50	25.00
❏ W 1521 [M]	Folk-Minded Spirituals for Spiritual-Minded Folks	1963	5.00	10.00	20.00
❏ WS 1521 [S]	Folk-Minded Spirituals for Spiritual-Minded Folks	1963	6.25	12.50	25.00
OBERNKIRCHEN CHILDREN'S CHOIR					
ANGEL					
❏ ANG.65021 [M]	Christmas Songs	1955	5.00	10.00	20.00
OBOLER, ARCH					
CAPITOL					
❏ ST 1763 [S]	Drop Dead! An Exercise in Horror	1962	7.50	15.00	30.00
❏ T 1763 [M]	Drop Dead! An Exercise in Horror	1962	6.25	12.50	25.00
OCHS, PHIL					
A&M					
❏ LP-133 [M]	Pleasures of the Harbor	1967	6.25	12.50	25.00
❏ SP-4133 [S]	Pleasures of the Harbor	1967	5.00	10.00	20.00
❏ SP-4148	Tape from California	1968	5.00	10.00	20.00
❏ SP-4181	Rehearsals for Retirement	1969	5.00	10.00	20.00
❏ SP-4253	Phil Ochs Greatest Hits	1970	5.00	10.00	20.00
❏ SP-4???	Gunfight at Carnegie Hall	197?	5.00	10.00	20.00
❏ SP-6511 [(2)]	Chords of Fame	1976	5.00	10.00	20.00
ELEKTRA					
❏ EKL-269 [M]	All the News That's Fit to Sing	1964	7.50	15.00	30.00
-- Gold label with "guitar player" logo					
❏ EKL-269 [M]	All the News That's Fit to Sing	1966	5.00	10.00	20.00
-- Gold label with stylized "E" logo					
❏ EKL-287 [M]	I Ain't Marching Anymore	1965	7.50	15.00	30.00
-- Gold label with "guitar player" logo					
❏ EKL-287 [M]	I Ain't Marching Anymore	1966	5.00	10.00	20.00
-- Gold label with stylized "E" logo					
❏ EKL-310 [M]	Phil Ochs in Concert	1966	5.00	10.00	20.00
❏ EKS-7269 [S]	All the News That's Fit to Sing	1964	10.00	20.00	40.00
-- Gold label with "guitar player" logo					
❏ EKS-7269 [S]	All the News That's Fit to Sing	1966	6.25	12.50	25.00
-- Gold label with stylized "E" logo					
❏ EKS-7287 [S]	I Ain't Marching Anymore	1965	10.00	20.00	40.00
-- Gold label with "guitar player" logo					
❏ EKS-7287 [S]	I Ain't Marching Anymore	1966	6.25	12.50	25.00
-- Gold label with stylized "E" logo					
❏ EKS-7310 [S]	Phil Ochs in Concert	1966	6.25	12.50	25.00

Number	Title	Yr	VG	VG+	NM
OCTOBER COUNTRY					
EPIC					
❏ BN 26381	October Country	1968	5.00	10.00	20.00
ODA					
LOUD					
❏ A 0011	Oda	1973	50.00	100.00	200.00
ODETTA					
FANTASY					
❏ 3-15 [10]	Odetta and Larry	1955	12.50	25.00	50.00
❏ F-3252 [M]	Odetta and Larry	1957	12.50	25.00	50.00
-- Dark red vinyl					
❏ F-3252 [M]	Odetta and Larry	1958	7.50	15.00	30.00
RCA VICTOR					
❏ LPM-2573 [M]	Sometimes I Feel Like Crying	1962	5.00	10.00	20.00
❏ LSP-2573 [S]	Sometimes I Feel Like Crying	1962	6.25	12.50	25.00
❏ LPM-2643 [M]	Odetta Sings Folk Songs	1963	5.00	10.00	20.00
❏ LSP-2643 [S]	Odetta Sings Folk Songs	1963	6.25	12.50	25.00
❏ LSP-2792 [S]	It's a Mighty World	1964	5.00	10.00	20.00
❏ LSP-3324 [S]	Odetta Sings Dylan	1965	5.00	10.00	20.00
❏ LSP-3457 [S]	Odetta in Japan	1965	5.00	10.00	20.00
RIVERSIDE					
❏ RLP-417 [M]	Odetta and the Blues	1962	6.25	12.50	25.00
❏ RS-9417 [S]	Odetta and the Blues	1962	7.50	15.00	30.00
TRADITION					
❏ TRP-1010 [M]	Odetta Sings Ballads and Blues	1957	7.50	15.00	30.00
❏ TRP-1025 [M]	Odetta at the Gate of Horn	1958	7.50	15.00	30.00
❏ TRP-1052 [M]	The Best of Odetta	1967	5.00	10.00	20.00
VANGUARD					
❏ VSD-2046 [S]	My Eyes Have Seen	1960	6.25	12.50	25.00
❏ VSD-2057 [S]	Ballads for Americans	1960	6.25	12.50	25.00
❏ VSD-2072 [S]	Odetta at Carnegie Hall	1961	6.25	12.50	25.00
❏ VSD-2079 [S]	Christmas Spirituals	1961	6.25	12.50	25.00
❏ VSD-2109 [S]	Odetta at Town Hall	1962	6.25	12.50	25.00
❏ VSD-2153 [S]	One Grain of Sand	1963	6.25	12.50	25.00
❏ VRS-9059 [M]	My Eyes Have Seen	1960	5.00	10.00	20.00
❏ VRS-9066 [M]	Ballads for Americans	1960	5.00	10.00	20.00
❏ VRS-9076 [M]	Odetta at Carnegie Hall	1961	5.00	10.00	20.00
❏ VRS-9079 [M]	Christmas Spirituals	1961	5.00	10.00	20.00
❏ VRS-9103 [M]	Odetta at Town Hall	1962	5.00	10.00	20.00
❏ VRS-9137 [M]	One Grain of Sand	1963	5.00	10.00	20.00
❏ VSD-73003 [S]	Odetta at Carnegie Hall	1967	5.00	10.00	20.00
OFF BROADWAY USA					
ATLANTIC					
❏ SD 19263	On	1980	5.00	10.00	20.00
OFFSPRING, THE					
NEMESIS					
❏ 6	The Offspring	1989	25.00	50.00	100.00
-- Original issue, 5,000 copies pressed; reissued on Nitro in 1995 with different cover ($10 NM)					
OHIO EXPRESS, THE					
BUDDAH					
❏ BDS 5018	The Ohio Express	1968	5.00	10.00	20.00
❏ BDS 5026	Chewy, Chewy	1969	5.00	10.00	20.00
❏ BDS 5037	Mercy	1969	5.00	10.00	20.00
❏ BDS 5058	The Very Best of the Ohio	1970	5.00	10.00	20.00
CAMEO					
❏ C 20,000 [M]	Beg, Borrow and Steal	1967	7.50	15.00	30.00
❏ CS 20,000 [S]	Beg, Borrow and Steal	1967	10.00	20.00	40.00
OHIO PLAYERS, THE					
CAPITOL					
❏ ST-192	Observations in Time	1969	12.50	25.00	50.00
WESTBOUND					
❏ 2015	Pain	1972	5.00	10.00	20.00
❏ 2017	Pleasure	1973	5.00	10.00	20.00
❏ 2021	Ecstasy	1973	5.00	10.00	20.00
OINGO BOINGO					
MCA					
❏ L33-18137 [PD]	Dark at the End of the Tunnel	1990	10.00	20.00	40.00
-- Promo-only picture disc					
OLA AND THE JANGLERS					
GNP CRESCENDO					
❏ GNPS-2050	Let's Dance/What a Way to Die	1969	5.00	10.00	20.00

Number	Title	Yr	VG	VG+	NM

OLD & IN THE WAY
JERRY GARCIA heads a bluegrass band!
ROUND
| ❑ RX-103 | Old & In the Way | 1975 | 6.25 | 12.50 | 25.00 |

OLDFIELD, MIKE
VIRGIN
❑ QR 13-105 [Q]	Tubular Bells	1974	6.25	12.50	25.00
❑ VR 13-109 [DJ]	Hergest Ridge	1974	5.00	10.00	20.00
-- Banded for airplay					
❑ PZQ 33913 [Q]	Ommadawn	1975	6.25	12.50	25.00
VIRGIN/EPIC
❑ HE 44116	Tubular Bells	1982	7.50	15.00	30.00
-- Half-speed mastered edition					

OLDHAM, ANDREW
LONDON
| ❑ PS 457 [S] | The Rolling Stones Songbook | 1965 | 37.50 | 75.00 | 150.00 |
| ❑ LL 3457 [M] | The Rolling Stones Songbook | 1965 | 25.00 | 50.00 | 100.00 |
PARROT
| ❑ PA 61003 [M] | East Meets West | 1965 | 20.00 | 40.00 | 80.00 |
| ❑ PAS 71003 [S] | East Meets West | 1965 | 25.00 | 50.00 | 100.00 |

OLENN, JOHNNY
LIBERTY
| ❑ LRP-3029 [M] | Just Rollin' with Johnny Olenn | 1956 | 75.00 | 150.00 | 300.00 |

OLIVA, TONY
KUBANY
| ❑ SD-600 | My Favorite Music | 1966 | 7.50 | 15.00 | 30.00 |

OLIVER AND THE TWISTERS
COLPIX
| ❑ CP-423 [M] | Look Who's Twistin' Everybody | 1961 | 10.00 | 20.00 | 40.00 |

OLIVER, JIMMY
SUE
| ❑ LP-1041 [M] | Hits A-Go-Go | 1966 | 5.00 | 10.00 | 20.00 |
| ❑ STLP-1041 [S] | Hits A-Go-Go | 1966 | 6.25 | 12.50 | 25.00 |

OLIVER, SY
MOBILE FIDELITY
| ❑ 1-242 [(2)] | Oliver's Twist/Easy Walkin' | 1996 | 7.50 | 15.00 | 30.00 |
| -- Audiophile vinyl | | | | | |

OLLIE AND THE NIGHTINGALES
STAX
| ❑ STS-2021 | Ollie and the Nightingales | 1969 | 12.50 | 25.00 | 50.00 |

OLSEN, DOROTHY
RCA VICTOR
| ❑ LPM-1606 [M] | I Know Where I'm Going | 1957 | 7.50 | 15.00 | 30.00 |

OLSSON, NIGEL
ROCKET
| ❑ L33-1962 [DJ] | Drummers Can Sing Too! | 1975 | 5.00 | 10.00 | 20.00 |
| -- Promo-only interview album | | | | | |

OLYMPICS, THE
ARVEE
❑ A-423 [M]	Doin' the Hully Gully	1960	40.00	80.00	160.00
❑ A-424 [M]	Dance by the Light of the Moon	1961	30.00	60.00	120.00
❑ A-429 [M]	Party Time	1961	30.00	60.00	120.00
MIRWOOD
❑ M-7003 [M]	Something Old, Something New	1966	10.00	20.00	40.00
❑ MS-7003 [S]	Something Old, Something New	1966	12.50	25.00	50.00
POST
❑ 8000	The Olympics Sing	196?	6.25	12.50	25.00
TRI-DISC
❑ 1001 [M]	Do the Bounce	1963	20.00	40.00	80.00

OMNIBUS
UNITED ARTISTS
| ❑ UAS-6743 | Omnibus | 1970 | 10.00 | 20.00 | 40.00 |

ONE
VILLAGE
| ❑ (# unknown) | Creation Earth | 1977 | 12.50 | 25.00 | 50.00 |
| -- Includes posters | | | | | |

ONO, YOKO
Also see JOHN LENNON.
APPLE
❑ SVBB-3380 [(2)]	Fly	1971	6.50	12.50	25.00
❑ SVBB-3399 [(2)]	Approximately Infinite Universe	1973	6.25	12.50	25.00
❑ SW-3373	Yoko Ono Plastic Ono Band	1970	5.00	10.00	20.00
❑ SW-3412	Feeling the Space	1973	5.00	10.00	20.00

ORANG UTAN
BELL
| ❑ 6054 | Orang Utan | 1971 | 10.00 | 20.00 | 40.00 |

ORANGE COLORED SKY
UNI
| ❑ 73031 | Orange Colored Sky | 1968 | 12.50 | 25.00 | 50.00 |

ORANGE WEDGE
(NO LABEL)
| ❑ (no #) | No One Left But Me | 1975 | 75.00 | 150.00 | 300.00 |
| ❑ (no #) | Wedge | 1975 | 75.00 | 150.00 | 300.00 |

ORBACH, JERRY
MGM
| ❑ E-4056 [M] | Jerry Orbach Off Broadway | 1963 | 5.00 | 10.00 | 20.00 |
| ❑ SE-4056 [S] | Jerry Orbach Off Broadway | 1963 | 6.25 | 12.50 | 25.00 |

ORBISON, ROY
MGM
❑ E-4308 [M]	There Is Only One Roy Orbison	1965	6.25	12.50	25.00
❑ SE-4308 [S]	There Is Only One Roy Orbison	1965	8.75	17.50	35.00
❑ E-4322 [M]	The Orbison Way	1965	6.25	12.50	25.00
❑ SE-4322 [S]	The Orbison Way	1965	8.75	17.50	35.00
❑ E-4379 [M]	The Classic Roy Orbison	1966	6.25	12.50	25.00
❑ SE-4379 [S]	The Classic Roy Orbison	1966	8.75	17.50	35.00
❑ E-4424 [M]	Roy Orbison Sings Don Gibson	1967	6.25	12.50	25.00
❑ SE-4424 [S]	Roy Orbison Sings Don Gibson	1967	8.75	17.50	35.00
❑ E-4514 [M]	Cry Softly, Lonely One	1967	6.25	12.50	25.00
❑ SE-4514 [S]	Cry Softly, Lonely One	1967	8.75	17.50	35.00
❑ SE-4636	The Many Moods of Roy Orbison	1969	6.25	12.50	25.00
❑ SE-4659	The Great Songs of Roy Orbison	1970	6.25	12.50	25.00
❑ SE-4683	Hank Williams the Roy Orbison Way	1970	6.25	12.50	25.00
❑ ST 90454 [S]	There Is Only One Roy Orbison	1965	10.00	20.00	40.00
-- Capitol Record Club edition					
❑ T 90454 [M]	There Is Only One Roy Orbison	1965	10.00	20.00	40.00
-- Capitol Record Club edition					
❑ ST-90631 [S]	The Orbison Way	1965	8.75	17.50	35.00
-- Capitol Record Club edition					
❑ T-90631 [M]	The Orbison Way	1965	8.75	17.50	35.00
-- Capitol Record Club edition					
❑ ST-90928 [S]	The Classic Roy Orbison	1966	8.75	17.50	35.00
-- Capitol Record Club edition					
❑ T-90928 [M]	The Classic Roy Orbison	1966	8.75	17.50	35.00
-- Capitol Record Club edition					
❑ ST-91173 [S]	Roy Orbison Sings Don Gibson	1967	8.75	17.50	35.00
-- Capitol Record Club edition					
❑ T-91173 [M]	Roy Orbison Sings Don Gibson	1967	8.75	17.50	35.00
-- Capitol Record Club edition					
MONUMENT
❑ M-4002 [M]	Lonely and Blue	1961	37.50	75.00	150.00
❑ M-4007 [M]	Crying	1962	30.00	60.00	120.00
❑ M-4009 [M]	Roy Orbison's Greatest Hits	1962	12.50	25.00	50.00
❑ MLP-8000 [M]	Roy Orbison's Greatest Hits	1963	7.50	15.00	30.00
❑ MLP-8003 [M]	In Dreams	1963	12.50	25.00	50.00
-- White and rainbow label					
❑ MLP-8003 [M]	In Dreams	1964	7.50	15.00	30.00
-- Green and gold label					
❑ MLP-8023 [M]	Early Orbison	1964	7.50	15.00	30.00
❑ MLP-8024 [M]	More of Roy Orbison's Greatest Hits	1964	7.50	15.00	30.00
❑ MLP-8035 [M]	Orbisongs	1965	6.25	12.50	25.00
❑ MLP-8045 [M]	The Very Best of Roy Orbison	1966	6.25	12.50	25.00
❑ SM-14002 [S]	Lonely and Blue	1961	150.00	300.00	600.00
❑ SM-14007 [S]	Crying	1962	150.00	300.00	600.00
❑ SM-14009 [S]	Roy Orbison's Greatest Hits	1962	20.00	40.00	80.00
❑ SLP-18000 [S]	Roy Orbison's Greatest Hits	1963	10.00	20.00	40.00
❑ SLP-18003 [S]	In Dreams	1963	25.00	50.00	100.00
-- White and rainbow label					
❑ SLP-18003 [S]	In Dreams	1964	12.50	25.00	50.00
-- Green and gold label					
❑ SLP-18023 [S]	Early Orbison	1964	12.50	25.00	50.00
❑ SLP-18024 [S]	More of Roy Orbison's Greatest Hits	1964	10.00	20.00	40.00
❑ SLP-18035 [S]	Orbisongs	1965	8.75	17.50	35.00
❑ SLP-18045 [P]	The Very Best of Roy Orbison	1966	8.75	17.50	35.00
-- "It's Over" is rechanneled					

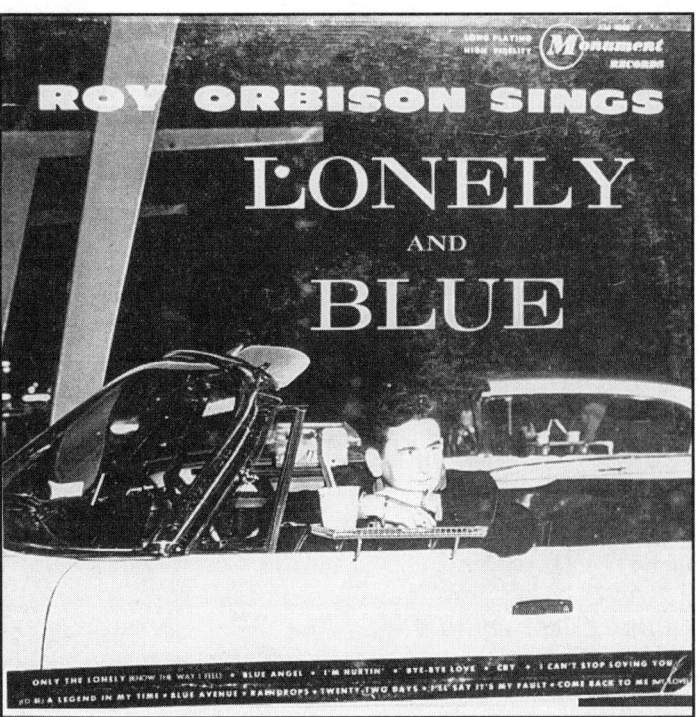

(Top left) A fine, underrated power pop album from 1980, Off Broadway USA's *On* has become a sought-after item in recent years. It contains the mid-level chart hit "Stay In Time." (Top right) Roy Orbison's first album, *Lonely and Blue,* is a three-figure album in near-mint condition in either mono or stereo. But the stereo version is especially well-recorded for early stereo rock and is highly sought after for that reason. It's also a great album! (Bottom left) In recent years, psychedelic and garage-type bands on the Mainstream label have become highly collectible. One of them is the Orient Express. (Bottom right) Most of Buck Owens' albums, especially from the 1960s, are hard to find. They also went out of print on vinyl in the 1970s when Buck Owens bought the rights to his Capitol masters. *Your Tender Loving Care* was based around a 1967 hit single.

Number	Title	Yr	VG	VG+	NM
❑ KZG 31484 [(2)]	The All-Time Greatest Hits of Roy Orbison	1972	6.25	12.50	25.00
SUN					
❑ SLP-1260 [M]	Roy Orbison at the Rockhouse	1961	150.00	300.00	600.00
TIME-LIFE					
❑ SRNR 34 [(2)]	Roy Orbison 1960-1965	1990	5.00	10.00	20.00
-- Box set in "The Rock 'n' Roll Era" series					

ORCHIDS, THE
ROULETTE

Number	Title	Yr	VG	VG+	NM
❑ R-25169 [M]	Twistin' at the Roundtable	1962	5.00	10.00	20.00
❑ SR-25169 [S]	Twistin' at the Roundtable	1962	6.25	12.50	25.00

ORGAN GRINDERS, THE
MERCURY

❑ SR-61282	Out of the Egg	1970	7.50	15.00	30.00

ORIENT EXPRESS, THE
MAINSTREAM

❑ S-6117	The Orient Express	1969	20.00	40.00	80.00

ORIGINAL LAST POETS, THE -- See THE LAST POETS.

ORIGINAL SURFARIS, THE
DIPLOMAT

❑ D-2309 [M]	Wheels-Shorts-Hot Rods	1963	6.25	12.50	25.00
❑ DS-2309 [S]	Wheels-Shorts-Hot Rods	1963	7.50	15.00	30.00

ORIGINAL TWISTERS, THE
WING

❑ MGW-12217 [M]	Come On and Twist	1962	5.00	10.00	20.00
❑ SRW-16217 [S]	Come On and Twist	1962	6.25	12.50	25.00

ORIGINAL WASHBOARD BAND, THE
RCA VICTOR

❑ LPM-1958 [M]	Scrubbin' and Pickin'	1959	5.00	10.00	20.00
❑ LSP-1958 [S]	Scrubbin' and Pickin'	1959	6.25	12.50	25.00

ORIGINALS, THE
SOUL

❑ SS-716	Baby I'm for Real	1969	10.00	20.00	40.00
❑ SS-724	Portrait of the Originals	1970	6.25	12.50	25.00
❑ SS-729	Naturally Together	1971	6.25	12.50	25.00
❑ SS-734	Definitions	1971	5.00	10.00	20.00

ORIOLES, THE
BIG A

❑ LP-2001	The Orioles' Greatest All-Time Hits	1969	7.50	15.00	30.00
CHARLIE PARKER					
❑ PLP-816 [M]	Modern Sounds of the Orioles	1962	20.00	40.00	80.00
❑ PLP-816S [S]	Modern Sounds of the Orioles	1962	25.00	50.00	100.00
MURRAY HILL					
❑ M 61234 [(5)]	For Collectors Only	1983	10.00	20.00	40.00

ORION
Also see JIMMY ELLIS.
SUN

❑ 1012	Orion Reborn	1978	7.50	15.00	30.00
-- White cover, also known as the "coffin cover"					

ORION THE HUNTER
With Barry Goudreau, formerly of BOSTON.
PORTRAIT

❑ BFR 39239	Orion the Hunter	1984	5.00	10.00	20.00

ORION, P.J., AND THE MAGNATES
MAGNATE

❑ 122459	P.J. Orion and the Magnates	196?	37.50	75.00	150.00

ORLANDO, TONY
EPIC

❑ BN 611 [S]	Bless You and 11 Other Great Hits	1961	10.00	20.00	40.00
❑ LN 3808 [M]	Bless You and 11 Other Great Hits	1961	7.50	15.00	30.00

ORLONS, THE
CAMEO

❑ C 1020 [M]	The Wah-Watusi	1962	15.00	30.00	60.00
❑ C 1033 [M]	All the Hits by the Orlons	1962	15.00	30.00	60.00
❑ C 1041 [M]	South Street	1963	15.00	30.00	60.00
❑ C 1054 [M]	Not Me	1963	12.50	25.00	50.00
❑ C 1061 [M]	The Orlons' Biggest Hits	1964	12.50	25.00	50.00
❑ C 1073 [M]	Down Memory Lane with the Orlons	1964	12.50	25.00	50.00

ORLONS, THE / THE DOVELLS
Also see each artist's individual listings.
CAMEO

❑ C 1067 [M]	Golden Hits of the Orlons and the Dovells	1964	12.50	25.00	50.00

ORPHAN EGG
CAROLE

❑ CARS-8004	Orphan Egg	1968	10.00	20.00	40.00

ORPHANN
O.M.I.

❑ 70021	Up for Adoption	1977	25.00	50.00	100.00

ORPHEUS
MGM

❑ E-4524 [M]	Orpheus	1968	6.25	12.50	25.00
❑ SE-4524 [S]	Orpheus	1968	5.00	10.00	20.00
❑ SE-4569	Ascending	1968	5.00	10.00	20.00
❑ SE-4599	Joyful	1969	5.00	10.00	20.00

ORTEGA, FRANKIE
JUBILEE

❑ JLP-1051 [M]	Twinkling Pinkies	1958	6.25	12.50	25.00
❑ JLP-1080 [M]	Swingin' Abroad	1958	5.00	10.00	20.00
❑ SDJLP-1080 [S]	Swingin' Abroad	1958	6.25	12.50	25.00
❑ JLP-1106 [M]	77 Sunset Strip	1959	6.25	12.50	25.00
❑ JGS-1106 [S]	77 Sunset Strip	1959	10.00	20.00	40.00
❑ JGM-1112 [M]	Frankie Ortega at the Embers	1960	5.00	10.00	20.00
❑ JGS-1112 [S]	Frankie Ortega at the Embers	1960	6.25	12.50	25.00

OSBORNE BROTHERS, THE
DECCA

❑ DL 4993 [M]	Yesterday, Today and The Osborne Brothers	1968	6.25	12.50	25.00
❑ DL 74602 [S]	Voices in the Bluegrass	1965	5.00	10.00	20.00
❑ DL 74767 [S]	Up This Hill and Down	1966	5.00	10.00	20.00
❑ DL 74903 [S]	Modern Sounds of Bluegrass	1967	5.00	10.00	20.00
❑ DL 74993 [S]	Yesterday, Today and The Osborne Brothers	1968	5.00	10.00	20.00
❑ DL 75079	Favorite Hymns by the Osborne Brothers	1969	5.00	10.00	20.00
❑ DL 75128	Up to Date and Down to Earth	1969	5.00	10.00	20.00
❑ DL 75204	Ru-Beeeee	1970	5.00	10.00	20.00
MGM					
❑ GAS 140	The Osborne Brothers (Golden Archive Series)	1970	5.00	10.00	20.00
❑ E-3734 [M]	Country Pickin' and Hillside Singin'	1959	12.50	25.00	50.00
❑ E-4018 [M]	Bluegrass Music	1962	6.25	12.50	25.00
❑ SE-4018 [S]	Bluegrass Music	1962	7.50	15.00	30.00
❑ E-4090 [M]	Bluegrass Instrumentals	1962	6.25	12.50	25.00
❑ SE-4090 [S]	Bluegrass Instrumentals	1962	7.50	15.00	30.00
❑ E-4149 [M]	Cuttin' Grass	1963	6.25	12.50	25.00
❑ SE-4149 [S]	Cuttin' Grass	1963	7.50	15.00	30.00

OSBORNE, JIMMY
AUDIO LAB

❑ AL-1527 [M]	Singing Songs He Wrote	1959	25.00	50.00	100.00
KING					
❑ 730 [M]	The Legendary Jimmy Osborne	1961	12.50	25.00	50.00
❑ 782 [M]	Golden Harvest	1963	12.50	25.00	50.00
❑ 892 [M]	The Very Best of Jimmy Osborne	1964	10.00	20.00	40.00
❑ 941 [M]	Jimmy Osborne's Golden Harvest	1965	10.00	20.00	40.00

OSBORNE, MARY
WARWICK

❑ W-2004 [M]	A Girl and Her Guitar	1960	25.00	50.00	100.00

OSBOURNE, OZZY
Also see BLACK SABBATH.
CBS ASSOCIATED

❑ AS 1828 [DJ]	Interview with Ozzy	1984	7.50	15.00	30.00
❑ 9Z9 40543 [EP]	The Ultimate Live Ozzy	1986	10.00	20.00	40.00
-- Picture disc with live material					
❑ Z 46795	No More Tears	1991	5.00	10.00	20.00

Number	Title	Yr	VG	VG+	NM
JET					
❑ AS99 1372 [PD] Diary of a Madman		1981	10.00	20.00	40.00
-- Promo-only picture disc					
❑ 8Z8 37640 [EP] Mr. Crowley		1982	7.50	15.00	30.00
-- Three-song picture disc with live material					
OSIBISA					
BUDDAH					
❑ BDS-5136	Super Fly T.N.T.	1973	7.50	15.00	30.00
OSIPOV STATE RUSSIAN FOLK ORCHESTRA (VITALY GNUTOV, CONDUCTOR)					
MERCURY LIVING PRESENCE					
❑ SR 90310 [S]	Balalaika Favorites	196?	25.00	50.00	100.00
-- Maroon label, no "Vendor: Mercury Record Corporation"					
❑ SR 90310 [S]	Balalaika Favorites	196?	10.00	20.00	40.00
-- Maroon label, with "Vendor: Mercury Record Corporation"					
❑ SR 90310 [S]	Balalaika Favorites	196?	10.00	20.00	40.00
-- Third edition: Dark red (not maroon) label					
❑ SR 90310 [S]	Balalaika Favorites	1998	6.25	12.50	25.00
-- Classic Records reissue					
OSMONDS, THE					
All of the below are from the era when they were known as "The Osmond Brothers."					
METRO					
❑ MS 543 [S]	We Sing You a Merry Christmas	1965	5.00	10.00	20.00
MGM					
❑ PM-7 [M]	The Travels of Jaimie McPheeters	1963	12.50	25.00	50.00
-- Side 1: Dialogue from TV show; Side 2: Osmond Brothers tracks. AC Spark Plugs promo.					
❑ E-4146 [M]	Songs We Sang on the Andy Williams Show	1963	6.25	12.50	25.00
❑ SE-4146 [S]	Songs We Sang on the Andy Williams Show	1963	7.50	15.00	30.00
❑ E-4187 [M]	We Sing You a Merry Christmas	1963	6.25	12.50	25.00
❑ SE-4187 [S]	We Sing You a Merry Christmas	1963	7.50	15.00	30.00
❑ E-4235 [M]	The Osmond Brothers Sing the All-Time Hymn Favorites	1964	5.00	10.00	20.00
❑ SE-4235 [S]	The Osmond Brothers Sing the All-Time Hymn Favorites	1964	6.25	12.50	25.00
❑ E-4291 [M]	The New Sound of the Osmond Brothers	1965	5.00	10.00	20.00
❑ SE-4291 [S]	The New Sound of the Osmond Brothers	1965	6.25	12.50	25.00
❑ ST 90403 [S]	The New Sound of the Osmond Brothers	1965	10.00	20.00	40.00
-- Capitol Record Club edition					
❑ T 90403 [M]	The New Sound of the Osmond Brothers	1965	10.00	20.00	40.00
-- Capitol Record Club edition					
OSWALD, LEE HARVEY					
The below are documentary records, all based on the same radio interview.					
EYEWITNESS					
❑ 1002	Lee Harvey Oswald Speaks	1967	20.00	40.00	80.00
INCA					
❑ 1001	Oswald: Self Portrait in Red	1965	25.00	50.00	100.00
KEY					
❑ 880	The President's Assassin Speaks	1964	25.00	50.00	100.00
OTHER HALF, THE					
Two different groups.					
ACTA					
❑ 38004	The Other Half	1968	25.00	50.00	100.00
7/2					
❑ (no #)	The Other Half	1966	375.00	750.00	1,500.
-- Album has been counterfeited, but those records are translucent when held to a light, originals are not					
OTIS AND CARLA					
Also see OTIS REDDING; CARLA THOMAS.					
STAX					
❑ ST-716 [M]	King and Queen	1967	8.75	17.50	35.00
❑ STS-716 [S]	King and Queen	1967	12.50	25.00	50.00
OTIS, JOHNNY					
CAPITOL					
❑ T 940 [M]	The Johnny Otis Show	1958	62.50	125.00	250.00
DIG					
❑ 104 [M]	Rock and Roll Hit Parade, Volume 1	1957	300.00	600.00	900.00
-- Gold cover with thick cardboard and thick vinyl records. Counterfeits have noticeably thinner vinyl.					

Number	Title	Yr	VG	VG+	NM
❑ 104 [M]	Rock and Roll Hit Parade, Volume 1	1958	150.00	300.00	600.00
-- Yellow cover with thick cardboard and thick vinyl records. Counterfeits have noticeably thinner vinyl.					
EPIC					
❑ BN 26524	Cuttin' Up	1970	6.25	12.50	25.00
❑ EG 30473 [(2)]	The Johnny Otis Show Live at Monterey	1971	7.50	15.00	30.00
KENT					
❑ KST-534	Cold Shot	1968	6.25	12.50	25.00
OUTLAW BLUES BAND, THE					
BLUESWAY					
❑ BLS-6020	Breakin' In	1969	6.25	12.50	25.00
❑ BLS-6021	The Outlaw Blues Band	1968	6.25	12.50	25.00
OUTLAWS					
DIRECT DISC					
❑ SD 16617	Outlaws	198?	12.50	25.00	50.00
-- Audiophile vinyl					
OUTSIDERS, THE					
CAPITOL					
❑ ST 2501 [S]	Time Won't Lert Me	1966	7.50	15.00	30.00
❑ T 2501 [M]	Time Won't Lert Me	1966	6.25	12.50	25.00
❑ ST 2568 [S]	The Outsiders Album #2	1966	7.50	15.00	30.00
❑ T 2568 [M]	The Outsiders Album #2	1966	6.25	12.50	25.00
❑ ST 2636 [S]	In	1967	6.25	12.50	25.00
❑ T 2636 [M]	In	1967	7.50	15.00	30.00
❑ ST 2745 [S]	Happening "Live!"	1967	6.25	12.50	25.00
❑ T 2745 [M]	Happening "Live!"	1967	7.50	15.00	30.00
OVATIONS, THE					
SOUNDS OF MEMPHIS					
❑ 7001	Hooked on a Feeling	1972	5.00	10.00	20.00
OVERSTREET, TOMMY					
DOT					
❑ DLP-25992	Gwen (Congratulations)	1971	5.00	10.00	20.00
❑ DLP-25994	This Is Tommy Overstreet	1972	5.00	10.00	20.00
❑ DLP-26003	Heaven Is My Woman's Love	1972	5.00	10.00	20.00
❑ DLP-26010	My Friends Call Me T.O.	1973	5.00	10.00	20.00
❑ DLP-26021	Woman, Your Name Is My Song	1974	5.00	10.00	20.00
OWEN, JIM, AND THE DRIFTING COWBOYS					
EPIC					
❑ PEG 34852 [(2)] A Song for Us All: A Salute to Hank Williams		1977	5.00	10.00	20.00
OWEN, REG					
DECCA					
❑ DL 8859 [M]	Under Paris Skies	1959	5.00	10.00	20.00
❑ DL 78859 [S]	Under Paris Skies	1959	6.25	12.50	25.00
PALETTE					
❑ 1001 [M]	Manhattan Spiritual	1959	7.50	15.00	30.00
❑ S-1001 [S]	Manhattan Spiritual	1959	10.00	20.00	40.00
❑ PZ-1004 [M]	Get Happy	1960	5.00	10.00	20.00
❑ PZ-1018 [M]	Fiorello!	1960	5.00	10.00	20.00
❑ SPZ-31004 [S]	Get Happy	1960	6.25	12.50	25.00
❑ SPZ-31018 [S]	Fiorello!	1960	6.25	12.50	25.00
RCA VICTOR					
❑ LPM-1542 [M]	The Best of Irving Berlin	1957	6.25	12.50	25.00
❑ LPM-1580 [M]	Dreaming	1958	6.25	12.50	25.00
❑ LPM-1582 [M]	Coffee Break	1958	5.00	10.00	20.00
❑ LSP-1582 [S]	Coffee Break	1958	6.25	12.50	25.00
❑ LPM-1597 [M]	Holiday Abroad in Dublin	1958	5.00	10.00	20.00
❑ LSP-1597 [S]	Holiday Abroad in Dublin	1958	6.25	12.50	25.00
❑ LPM-1599 [M]	Holiday Abroad in London	1958	5.00	10.00	20.00
❑ LSP-1599 [S]	Holiday Abroad in London	1958	6.25	12.50	25.00
❑ LPM-1675 [M]	The British Isles	1958	5.00	10.00	20.00
❑ LSP-1675 [S]	The British Isles	1958	6.25	12.50	25.00
❑ LPM-1906 [M]	I'll Sing You 1,000 Love Songs	1959	5.00	10.00	20.00
❑ LSP-1906 [S]	I'll Sing You 1,000 Love Songs	1959	6.25	12.50	25.00
❑ LPM-1907 [M]	Deep in a Dream	1959	5.00	10.00	20.00
❑ LPM-1908 [M]	Girls Were Made to Take Care of Boys	1959	5.00	10.00	20.00
❑ LSP-1908 [S]	Girls Were Made to Take Care of Boys	1959	6.25	12.50	25.00
❑ LPM-1914 [M]	Cuddle Up a Little Closer	1959	5.00	10.00	20.00
❑ LSP-1914 [S]	Cuddle Up a Little Closer	1959	6.25	12.50	25.00
❑ LPM-1915 [M]	You Don't Know Paree	1959	6.25	12.50	25.00

Number	Title	Yr	VG	VG+	NM
OWEN-B					
MUS-I-COL					
❏ 101209	Owen-B	1970	15.00	30.00	60.00
OWENS, BONNIE					
Also see MERLE HAGGARD AND BONNIE OWENS.					
CAPITOL					
❏ ST-195	Lead Me On	1969	6.25	12.50	25.00
❏ ST-341	Hi-Fi to Cry By	1969	6.25	12.50	25.00
❏ ST-557	Mother's Favorite Hymns	1970	6.25	12.50	25.00
❏ ST 2403 [S]	Don't Take Advantage of Me	1965	6.25	12.50	25.00
❏ T 2403 [M]	Don't Take Advantage of Me	1965	5.00	10.00	20.00
❏ ST 2600 [S]	All of Me Belongs to You	1967	6.25	12.50	25.00
❏ T 2600 [M]	All of Me Belongs to You	1967	6.25	12.50	25.00
❏ ST 2861	Somewhere Between	1968	6.25	12.50	25.00
OWENS, BUCK					
Also see THE BUCKAROOS.					
CAPITOL					
❏ ST-131	I've Got You on My Mind Again	1969	5.00	10.00	20.00
❏ SKAO-145	The Best of Buck Owens, Volume 3	1969	5.00	10.00	20.00
❏ ST-194	Anywhere U.S.A.	1969	5.00	10.00	20.00
❏ ST-212	Tall Dark Stranger	1969	5.00	10.00	20.00
❏ ST-232	Buck Owens in London	1969	5.00	10.00	20.00
❏ SWBB-257 [(2)]	Close-Up	1969	5.00	10.00	20.00
-- Reissue of "Together Again" and "No One But You"					
❏ ST-439	Your Mother's Prayer	1970	5.00	10.00	20.00
❏ ST-476	The Kansas City Song	1970	5.00	10.00	20.00
❏ STBB-486 [(2)]	A Merry "Hee Haw" Christmas	1970	6.25	12.50	25.00
❏ STCL-574 [(3)]	Buck Owens	1970	10.00	20.00	40.00
❏ ST-628	I Wouldn't Live in New York City	1970	5.00	10.00	20.00
❏ ST 1482 [S]	Buck Owens Sings Harlan Howard	1961	12.50	25.00	50.00
❏ T 1482 [M]	Buck Owens Sings Harlan Howard	1961	10.00	20.00	40.00
❏ DT 1489 [R]	Under Your Spell Again	1968	6.25	12.50	25.00
❏ T 1489 [M]	Under Your Spell Again	1961	10.00	20.00	40.00
❏ ST 1777 [S]	You're for Me	1962	12.50	25.00	50.00
❏ T 1777 [M]	You're for Me	1962	10.00	20.00	40.00
❏ ST 1879 [S]	On the Bandstand	1963	12.50	25.00	50.00
❏ T 1879 [M]	On the Bandstand	1963	10.00	20.00	40.00
❏ ST 1989 [S]	Buck Owens Sings Tommy Collins	1963	12.50	25.00	50.00
❏ T 1989 [M]	Buck Owens Sings Tommy Collins	1963	10.00	20.00	40.00
❏ ST 2105 [S]	The Best of Buck Owens	1964	7.50	15.00	30.00
❏ T 2105 [M]	The Best of Buck Owens	1964	6.25	12.50	25.00
❏ ST 2135 [S]	Together Again/My Heart Skips a Beat	1964	7.50	15.00	30.00
❏ T 2135 [M]	Together Again/My Heart Skips a Beat	1964	6.25	12.50	25.00
❏ ST 2186 [S]	I Don't Care	1964	7.50	15.00	30.00
❏ T 2186 [M]	I Don't Care	1964	6.25	12.50	25.00
❏ ST 2283 [S]	I've Got a Tiger by the Tail	1965	7.50	15.00	30.00
❏ T 2283 [M]	I've Got a Tiger by the Tail	1965	6.25	12.50	25.00
❏ ST 2353 [S]	Before You Go	1965	7.50	15.00	30.00
❏ T 2353 [M]	Before You Go	1965	6.25	12.50	25.00
❏ ST 2367 [S]	The Instrumental Hits of Buck Owens & the Buckaroos	1965	7.50	15.00	30.00
❏ T 2367 [M]	The Instrumental Hits of Buck Owens & the Buckaroos	1965	6.25	12.50	25.00
❏ ST 2396 [S]	Christmas with Buck Owens and His Buckaroos	1965	7.50	15.00	30.00
❏ T 2396 [M]	Christmas with Buck Owens and His Buckaroos	1965	5.00	10.00	20.00
❏ ST 2443 [S]	Roll Out the Red Carpet for Buck Owens & The Buckaroos	1966	6.25	12.50	25.00
❏ T 2443 [M]	Roll Out the Red Carpet for Buck Owens & The Buckaroos	1966	5.00	10.00	20.00
❏ ST 2497 [S]	Dust on Mother's Bible	1966	6.25	12.50	25.00
❏ T 2497 [M]	Dust on Mother's Bible	1966	5.00	10.00	20.00
❏ ST 2556 [S]	Carnegie Hall Concert	1966	6.25	12.50	25.00
❏ T 2556 [M]	Carnegie Hall Concert	1966	5.00	10.00	20.00
❏ ST 2640 [S]	Open Up Your Heart	1967	6.25	12.50	25.00
❏ T 2640 [M]	Open Up Your Heart	1967	5.00	10.00	20.00
❏ ST 2715 [S]	Buck Owens and His Buckaroos in Japan	1967	6.25	12.50	25.00
❏ T 2715 [M]	Buck Owens and His Buckaroos in Japan	1967	5.00	10.00	20.00
❏ ST 2760 [S]	Your Tender Loving Care	1967	6.25	12.50	25.00
❏ T 2760 [M]	Your Tender Loving Care	1967	6.25	12.50	25.00
❏ ST 2841	It Takes People Like You to Make People Like Me	1968	6.25	12.50	25.00
❏ ST 2897	The Best of Buck Owens, Vol. 2	1968	6.25	12.50	25.00
❏ ST 2902	A Night on the Town	1968	6.25	12.50	25.00
❏ ST 2962	Sweet Rosie Jones	1968	6.25	12.50	25.00
❏ ST 2977	Christmas Shopping	1968	6.25	12.50	25.00
❏ SPRO 2980/1 [DJ]	Minute Masters	1966	12.50	25.00	50.00
-- Promo-only excerpts of 24 songs					
❏ ST 2994	Buck Owens, The Guitar Player	1968	6.25	12.50	25.00

Number	Title	Yr	VG	VG+	NM
LABREA					
❏ 1017 [M]	Buck Owens	1961	25.00	50.00	100.00
❏ 8017 [S]	Buck Owens	1961	37.50	75.00	150.00
STARDAY					
❏ SLP-172	The Fabulous Country Music Sound of Buck Owens	1962	12.50	25.00	50.00
❏ SLP-324	Country Hit Maker #1	1964	6.25	12.50	25.00
OWENS, BUCK, AND SUSAN RAYE					
CAPITOL					
❏ ST-448	We're Gonna Get Together	1970	5.00	10.00	20.00
OXFORD, VERNON					
RCA VICTOR					
❏ LPM-3704 [M]	Woman, Let Me Sing You a Song	1967	10.00	20.00	40.00
❏ LSP-3704 [S]	Woman, Let Me Sing You a Song	1967	7.50	15.00	30.00
OZ KNOZZ					
OZONE					
❏ O2-1000	Ruff Mix	1975	125.00	250.00	500.00

Number	Title	Yr	VG	VG+	NM

P

P.H. PHACTOR
PICCADILLY
| ❏ PIC-3343 | Merryjuana | 1980 | 25.00 | 50.00 | 100.00 |

-- Cover spells the group's name "Factor" but the label has it "Phactor"

PABLO CRUISE
MOBILE FIDELITY
| ❏ 1-029 | A Place in the Sun | 1979 | 5.00 | 10.00 | 20.00 |

-- Audiophile vinyl

NAUTILUS
| ❏ NR-6 | Lifeline | 1980 | 5.00 | 10.00 | 20.00 |

-- Audiophile vinyl

| ❏ NR-28 | Worlds Away | 1981 | 5.00 | 10.00 | 20.00 |

-- Audiophile vinyl

PACERS, THE
RAZORBACK
| ❏ 121 [M] | You Asked For It | 1965 | 25.00 | 50.00 | 100.00 |

PACIFIC DRIFT
DERAM
| ❏ DES 18040 | Feelin' Free | 1970 | 5.00 | 10.00 | 20.00 |

PACIFIC GAS & ELECTRIC
BRIGHT ORANGE
| ❏ 701 | Get It On | 1968 | 10.00 | 20.00 | 40.00 |

POWER
| ❏ 701 | Get It On | 1969 | 6.25 | 12.50 | 25.00 |

PACIFIC OCEAN
V.M.C.
| ❏ 135 | Pacific Ocean | 1969 | 5.00 | 10.00 | 20.00 |

PACK, MARSHALL
STARDAY
| ❏ SLP-120 [M] | Marshall Pack | 1960 | 10.00 | 20.00 | 40.00 |

PACKERS, THE
PURE SOUL MUSIC
| ❏ 1001 [S] | Hole in the Wall | 1966 | 5.00 | 10.00 | 20.00 |

PAGE, JIMMY
Also see LED ZEPPELIN; THE YARDBIRDS.
SPRINGBOARD
| ❏ SPB-4038 | Special Early Works | 1972 | 6.25 | 12.50 | 25.00 |

PAGE, PATTI
COLUMBIA
❏ CL 2761 [M]	Today My Way	1967	5.00	10.00	20.00
❏ CS 8849 [S]	Say Wonderful Things	1963	5.00	10.00	20.00
❏ CS 8932 [S]	Love After Midnight	1964	5.00	10.00	20.00
❏ CS 9153 [S]	Hush, Hush, Sweet Charlotte	1965	5.00	10.00	20.00

EMARCY
❏ MG-36074 [M]	In the Land of Hi-Fi	1956	12.50	25.00	50.00
❏ MG-36116 [M]	The East Side	1957	12.50	25.00	50.00
❏ MG-36136 [M]	The West Side	1957	12.50	25.00	50.00
❏ SR-60013 [S]	The West Side	1959	12.50	25.00	50.00
❏ SR-60014 [S]	The East Side	1959	12.50	25.00	50.00
❏ SR-80000 [S]	In the Land of Hi-Fi	1959	12.50	25.00	50.00

MERCURY
❏ MG 20093 [M]	Christmas with Patti Page	1956	7.50	15.00	30.00
❏ MG-20076 [M]	Romance on the Range	1955	7.50	15.00	30.00
❏ MG-20095 [M]	Page I	1955	7.50	15.00	30.00
❏ MG-20096 [M]	Page II	1955	7.50	15.00	30.00
❏ MG-20097 [M]	Page III	1955	7.50	15.00	30.00
❏ MG-20098 [M]	You Go to My Head	1955	7.50	15.00	30.00
❏ MG-20099 [M]	Music for Two in Love	1955	7.50	15.00	30.00
❏ MG-20100 [M]	The Voice of Patti Page	1955	7.50	15.00	30.00
❏ MG-20101 [M]	Page IV	1955	7.50	15.00	30.00
❏ MG-20102 [M]	This Is My Song	1955	7.50	15.00	30.00
❏ MG-20226 [M]	Manhattan Tower	1956	7.50	15.00	30.00
❏ MG-20318 [M]	The Waltz Queen	1957	7.50	15.00	30.00
❏ MG-20387 [M]	Let's Get Away From it All	1957	7.50	15.00	30.00
❏ MG-20388 [M]	I've Heard That Song Before	1957	7.50	15.00	30.00
❏ MG-20398 [M]	Patti Page On Camera	1958	7.50	15.00	30.00
❏ MG-20405 [M]	Indiscretion	1959	7.50	15.00	30.00

❏ MG-20406 [M]	I'll Remember April	1959	7.50	15.00	30.00
❏ MG-20417 [M]	Three Little Words	1960	7.50	15.00	30.00
❏ MG-20495 [M]	Patti Page's Golden Hits	1960	7.50	15.00	30.00
❏ MG-20573 [M]	Just a Closer Walk with Thee	1960	7.50	15.00	30.00
❏ MG-20599 [M]	Patti Page Sings and Stars In "Elmer Gantry"	1960	6.25	12.50	25.00
❏ MG-20615 [M]	Country & Western Golden Hits	1961	5.00	10.00	20.00
❏ MG-20689 [M]	Go On Home	1962	5.00	10.00	20.00
❏ MG-20712 [M]	Golden Hits of the Boys	1962	5.00	10.00	20.00
❏ MG-20758 [M]	Patti Page On Stage	1963	5.00	10.00	20.00
❏ MG-20794 [M]	Patti Page's Golden Hits, Volume 2	1963	5.00	10.00	20.00
❏ MG-20819 [M]	The Singing Rage	1963	5.00	10.00	20.00
❏ MG-20909 [M]	Blue Dream Street	1964	5.00	10.00	20.00
❏ MG-25059 [10]	Songs	1950	10.00	20.00	40.00
❏ MG-25101 [10]	Folksong Favorites	1951	10.00	20.00	40.00
❏ MG-25109 [10]	Christmas	1951	10.00	20.00	40.00
❏ MG-25154 [10]	Tennessee Waltz	1952	10.00	20.00	40.00
❏ MG-25185 [10]	Patti Sings for Romance	1954	10.00	20.00	40.00
❏ MG-25187 [10]	Song Souvenirs	1954	10.00	20.00	40.00
❏ MG-25196 [10]	Just Patti	1954	10.00	20.00	40.00
❏ MG-25197 [10]	Patti's Songs	1954	10.00	20.00	40.00
❏ MG-25209 [10]	And I Thought About You	1954	10.00	20.00	40.00
❏ MG-25210 [10]	So Many Memories	1954	10.00	20.00	40.00
❏ SR-60010 [S]	Let's Get Away From it All	1959	10.00	20.00	40.00
❏ SR-60011 [S]	I've Heard That Song Before	1959	10.00	20.00	40.00
❏ SR-60025 [S]	Patti Page On Camera	1959	10.00	20.00	40.00
❏ SR-60037 [S]	Three Little Words	1960	10.00	20.00	40.00
❏ SR-60049 [S]	The Waltz Queen	1959	10.00	20.00	40.00
❏ SR-60059 [S]	Indiscretion	1959	10.00	20.00	40.00
❏ SR-60081 [S]	I'll Remember April	1959	10.00	20.00	40.00
❏ SR-60233 [S]	Just a Closer Walk with Thee	1960	10.00	20.00	40.00
❏ SR-60260 [S]	Patti Page Sings and Stars In "Elmer Gantry"	1960	7.50	15.00	30.00
❏ SR-60495 [S]	Patti Page's Golden Hits	196?	6.25	12.50	25.00
❏ SR-60615 [S]	Country & Western Golden Hits	1961	6.25	12.50	25.00
❏ SR-60689 [S]	Go On Home	1962	6.25	12.50	25.00
❏ SR-60712 [S]	Golden Hits of the Boys	1962	6.25	12.50	25.00
❏ SR-60758 [S]	Patti Page On Stage	1963	6.25	12.50	25.00
❏ SR-60794 [S]	Patti Page's Golden Hits, Volume 2	1963	6.25	12.50	25.00
❏ SR-60819 [S]	The Singing Rage	1963	6.25	12.50	25.00
❏ SR-60909 [S]	Blue Dream Street	1964	6.25	12.50	25.00
❏ SR-60952 [S]	The Nearness of You	1965	5.00	10.00	20.00

WING
| ❏ MGW 12174 [M] | Christmas with Patti Page | 196? | 5.00 | 10.00 | 20.00 |

-- Same contents and order as Mercury 20093

PAIGE, JANIS
BALLY
| ❏ BAL-12008 [M] | Let's Fall in Love | 1957 | 10.00 | 20.00 | 40.00 |

PAIR, THE
LIBERTY
❏ LRP-3410 [M]	The Pair Live! At the Ice House	1965	5.00	10.00	20.00
❏ LST-7410 [S]	The Pair Live! At the Ice House	1965	6.25	12.50	25.00
❏ LST-7440 [S]	The Pair Extraordinaire	1966	5.00	10.00	20.00
❏ LST-7461 [S]	"In"-Citement	1966	5.00	10.00	20.00
❏ LST-7504 [S]	It's a Wonderful World	1967	5.00	10.00	20.00

PAISLEYS, THE
AUDIO CITY
| ❏ 70 | Cosmic Mind at Play | 1970 | 50.00 | 100.00 | 200.00 |

PALANCE, JACK
WARNER BROS.
| ❏ WS 1865 | Palance | 1970 | 7.50 | 15.00 | 30.00 |

PALEY, TOM
ELEKTRA
| ❏ EKL-12 [M] | Folk Songs from the Southern Appalachians | 195? | 10.00 | 20.00 | 40.00 |

PALMER, BRUCE
VERVE FORECAST
| ❏ FTS-3086 | The Cycle Is Complete | 1970 | 5.00 | 10.00 | 20.00 |

PALMER, EARL
LIBERTY
❏ LRP-3201 [M]	Drumsville	1961	7.50	15.00	30.00
❏ LRP-3227 [M]	Percolator Twist	1962	7.50	15.00	30.00
❏ LST-7201 [S]	Drumsville	1961	10.00	20.00	40.00
❏ LST-7227 [S]	Percolator Twist	1962	10.00	20.00	40.00

Number	Title	Yr	VG	VG+	NM

PALMER, ROBERT
ISLAND
Number	Title	Yr	VG	VG+	NM
❏ PRO-819 [DJ]	Secrets	1979	7.50	15.00	30.00
-- Promo-only picture disc					

WARNER BROS.
| ❏ WBMS-111 [DJ] | Live in Boston | 1979 | 7.50 | 15.00 | 30.00 |
| -- Part of "The Warner Bros. Music Show" | | | | | |

PANDIT, KORLA
FANTASY
Number	Title	Yr	VG	VG+	NM
❏ 3272 [M]	Music of the Exotic East	1958	10.00	20.00	40.00
-- Red vinyl					
❏ 3272 [M]	Music of the Exotic East	1958	6.25	12.50	25.00
-- Black vinyl					
❏ 3284 [M]	Latin Holiday	1959	10.00	20.00	40.00
-- Red vinyl					
❏ 3284 [M]	Latin Holiday	1959	6.25	12.50	25.00
-- Black vinyl					
❏ 3286 [M]	Korla Pandit at the Pipe Organ	1959	10.00	20.00	40.00
-- Red vinyl					
❏ 3286 [M]	Korla Pandit at the Pipe Organ	1959	6.25	12.50	25.00
-- Black vinyl					
❏ 3288 [M]	Tropical Magic	1959	10.00	20.00	40.00
-- Red vinyl					
❏ 3288 [M]	Tropical Magic	1959	6.25	12.50	25.00
-- Black vinyl					
❏ 3293 [M]	Speak to Me of Love	1959	10.00	20.00	40.00
-- Red vinyl					
❏ 3293 [M]	Speak to Me of Love	1959	6.25	12.50	25.00
-- Black vinyl					
❏ 33?? [M]	Christmas with Korla Pandit	196?	10.00	20.00	40.00
-- Red vinyl					
❏ 33?? [M]	Christmas with Korla Pandit	196?	6.25	12.00	25.00
-- Black vinyl					
❏ 3304 [M]	Korla Pandit in Concert	1960	10.00	20.00	40.00
-- Red vinyl					
❏ 3304 [M]	Korla Pandit in Concert	1960	6.25	12.50	25.00
-- Black vinyl					
❏ 3320 [M]	Music of Mystery and Romance	1961	10.00	20.00	40.00
-- Red vinyl					
❏ 3320 [M]	Music of Mystery and Romance	1961	6.25	12.50	25.00
-- Black vinyl					
❏ 3327 [M]	Love Letters	1961	10.00	20.00	40.00
-- Red vinyl					
❏ 3327 [M]	Love Letters	1961	6.25	12.50	25.00
-- Black vinyl					
❏ 3329 [M]	Hypnotique	1961	10.00	20.00	40.00
-- Red vinyl					
❏ 3329 [M]	Hypnotique	1961	6.25	12.50	25.00
-- Black vinyl					
❏ 3334 [M]	Music of Hollywood	1962	10.00	20.00	40.00
-- Red vinyl					
❏ 3334 [M]	Music of Hollywood	1962	6.25	12.50	25.00
-- Black vinyl					
❏ 3342 [M]	Music for Meditation	1962	10.00	20.00	40.00
-- Red vinyl					
❏ 3342 [M]	Music for Meditation	1962	6.25	12.50	25.00
-- Black vinyl					
❏ 3347 [M]	Korla Pandit in Paris	1962	6.25	12.50	25.00
❏ 80?? [S]	Christmas with Korla Pandit	196?	12.50	25.00	50.00
-- Blue vinyl					
❏ 80?? [S]	Christmas with Korla Pandit	196?	7.50	15.00	30.00
-- Black vinyl					
❏ 8013 [S]	Music of the Exotic East	1960	12.50	25.00	50.00
-- Blue vinyl					
❏ 8013 [S]	Music of the Exotic East	1960	7.50	15.00	30.00
-- Black vinyl					
❏ 8018 [S]	Korla Pandit at the Pipe Organ	1960	12.50	25.00	50.00
-- Blue vinyl					
❏ 8018 [S]	Korla Pandit at the Pipe Organ	1960	7.50	15.00	30.00
-- Black vinyl					
❏ 8027 [S]	Latin Holiday	1960	12.50	25.00	50.00
-- Blue vinyl					
❏ 8027 [S]	Latin Holiday	1960	7.50	15.00	30.00
-- Black vinyl					
❏ 8034 [S]	Tropical Magic	1960	12.50	25.00	50.00
-- Blue vinyl					
❏ 8034 [S]	Tropical Magic	1960	7.50	15.00	30.00
-- Black vinyl					
❏ 8039 [S]	Speak to Me of Love	1960	12.50	25.00	50.00
-- Blue vinyl					
❏ 8039 [S]	Speak to Me of Love	1960	7.50	15.00	30.00
-- Black vinyl					
❏ 8049 [S]	Korla Pandit in Concert	1960	12.50	25.00	50.00
-- Blue vinyl					
❏ 8049 [S]	Korla Pandit in Concert	1960	7.50	15.00	30.00
-- Black vinyl					
❏ 8061 [S]	Music of Mystery and Romance	1961	12.50	25.00	50.00
-- Blue vinyl					
❏ 8061 [S]	Music of Mystery and Romance	1961	7.50	15.00	30.00
-- Black vinyl					
❏ 8070 [S]	Love Letters	1961	12.50	25.00	50.00
-- Blue vinyl					
❏ 8070 [S]	Love Letters	1961	7.50	15.00	30.00
-- Black vinyl					
❏ 8075 [S]	Hypnotique	1961	12.50	25.00	50.00
-- Blue vinyl					
❏ 8075 [S]	Hypnotique	1961	7.50	15.00	30.00
-- Black vinyl					
❏ 8086 [S]	Music of Hollywood	1962	12.50	25.00	50.00
-- Blue vinyl					
❏ 8086 [S]	Music of Hollywood	1962	7.50	15.00	30.00
-- Black vinyl					
❏ 8342 [S]	Music for Meditation	1962	12.50	25.00	50.00
-- Blue vinyl					
❏ 8342 [S]	Music for Meditation	1962	7.50	15.00	30.00
-- Black vinyl					
❏ 8347 [S]	Korla Pandit in Paris	1962	7.50	15.00	30.00

VITA
| ❏ VLP-14 [10] | Rememb'ring with Korla Pandit | 195? | 20.00 | 40.00 | 80.00 |

PANICS, THE
CHANCELLOR
| ❏ CHL-5026 [M] | Panicsville | 1962 | 7.50 | 15.00 | 30.00 |
| ❏ CHLS-5026 [S] | Panicsville | 1962 | 10.00 | 20.00 | 40.00 |
PHILIPS
| ❏ PHS 600-159 [S] | Discotheque Dance Party | 1964 | 5.00 | 10.00 | 20.00 |

PANTERA
METAL MAGIC
❏ MMR 1283	Metal Magic	1983	25.00	50.00	100.00
❏ MMR 1984	Projects in the Jungle	1984	15.00	30.00	60.00
❏ MMR 1985	I Am the Night	1985	15.00	30.00	60.00
❏ MMR 1988	Power Metal	1988	10.00	20.00	40.00

PAPER GARDEN, THE
MUSICOR
| ❏ MS-31?? | The Paper Garden | 1968 | 10.00 | 20.00 | 40.00 |

PARAGONS, THE & THE HARPTONES
MUSICTONE
| ❏ M-8001 [M] | The Paragons vs. the Harptones | 1964 | 10.00 | 20.00 | 40.00 |

PARAGONS, THE & THE JESTERS
JOSIE
| ❏ 4008 [M] | The Paragons Meet the Jesters | 1962 | 50.00 | 100.00 | 200.00 |
JUBILEE
❏ JLP-1098 [M]	The Paragons Meet the Jesters	1959	750.00	1,125.	1,500.
-- Multi-color splash vinyl					
❏ JLP-1098 [M]	The Paragons Meet the Jesters	1959	75.00	150.00	300.00
-- Blue label, black vinyl					
❏ JLP-1098 [M]	The Paragons Meet the Jesters	196?	37.50	75.00	150.00
-- Flat black label					
❏ JLP-1098 [M]	The Paragons Meet the Jesters	196?	15.00	30.00	60.00
-- Black label with multi-color logo					
WINLEY
| ❏ LP-6003 [M] | War! The Jesters vs. the Paragons | 195? | 125.00 | 250.00 | 500.00 |

PARIS CONSERVATOIRE ORCHESTRE (ANATOLE FISTOULARI, CONDUCTOR)
RCA VICTOR RED SEAL
❏ LSC-2400 [S]	Ballet Music from the Opera	1960	100.00	200.00	400.00
-- Original with "shaded dog" label					
❏ LSC-2400 [S]	Ballet Music from the Opera	199?	6.25	12.50	25.00
-- Classic Records reissue					

PARIS CONSERVATOIRE ORCHESTRE (JEAN MARTINON, CONDUCTOR)
RCA VICTOR RED SEAL
❏ LSC-2272 [S]	Prokofiev: Symphony No. 5	1959	62.50	125.00	250.00
-- Original with "shaded dog" label					
❏ LSC-2288 [S]	Prokofiev: Symphony No. 7	1959	37.50	75.00	150.00
-- Original with "shaded dog" label					
❏ LSC-2288 [S]	Prokofiev: Symphony No. 7	199?	6.25	12.50	25.00
-- Classic Records reissue					

PARIS CONSERVATOIRE ORCHESTRE (PIERRE MONTEUX, CONDUCTOR)
RCA VICTOR RED SEAL
| ❏ LSC-2085 [S] | Stravinsky: The Rite of Spring | 1958 | 7.50 | 15.00 | 30.00 |
| -- Original with "shaded dog" label | | | | | |

Number	Title	Yr	VG	VG+	NM
❏ LSC-2085 [S]	Stravinsky: The Rite of Spring	1964	10.00	20.00	40.00
-- Second issue with "white dog" label					

PARIS CONSERVATOIRE ORCHESTRE (JEAN-PAUL MOREL, CONDUCTOR)
RCA VICTOR RED SEAL

Number	Title	Yr	VG	VG+	NM
❏ LSC-6094 [(2)]	Albaniz: Iberia; Ravel: Rapsodie Espagnole	196?	100.00	200.00	400.00
-- Original with "shaded dog" label					

PARIS CONSERVATOIRE ORCHESTRE (HUGH RIGNOLD, CONDUCTOR)
RCA VICTOR RED SEAL

Number	Title	Yr	VG	VG+	NM
❏ LSC-2485 [S]	Delibes: Sylvia and Coppelia Ballet Suites	1961	20.00	40.00	80.00
-- Original with "shaded dog" label					

PARIS CONSERVATOIRE ORCHESTRE (ALBERT WOLFF, CONDUCTOR)
RCA VICTOR RED SEAL

Number	Title	Yr	VG	VG+	NM
❏ LSC-2301 [S]	Adam: Giselle	1959	17.50	35.00	70.00
-- Original with "shaded dog" label					

PARIS PILOT
HIP

Number	Title	Yr	VG	VG+	NM
❏ 7004	Paris Pilot	1970	6.25	12.50	25.00

PARIS SISTERS, THE
Also see PRISCILLA PARIS.
REPRISE

Number	Title	Yr	VG	VG+	NM
❏ R-6259 [M]	Everything Under the Sun	1967	10.00	20.00	40.00
❏ RS-6359 [S]	Everything Under the Sun	1967	15.00	30.00	60.00
SIDEWALK					
❏ DT 5906 [R]	Golden Hits of the Paris Sisters	1967	7.50	15.00	30.00
❏ T 5906 [M]	Golden Hits of the Paris Sisters	1967	12.50	25.00	50.00
UNIFILMS					
❏ 505 [M]	The Paris Sisters Sing Songs from Glass House	1966	10.00	20.00	40.00
❏ S-505 [S]	The Paris Sisters Sing Songs from Glass House	1966	12.50	25.00	50.00

PARIS, FREDDIE
RCA VICTOR

Number	Title	Yr	VG	VG+	NM
❏ LSP-4064	Lovin' Mood	1968	5.00	10.00	20.00

PARIS, PRISCILLA
Also see THE PARIS SISTERS.
HAPPY TIGER

Number	Title	Yr	VG	VG+	NM
❏ HT-1002	Priscilla Loves Billy	1968	10.00	20.00	40.00
YORK					
❏ 4005 [M]	Priscilla Sings Herself	1967	7.50	15.00	30.00
❏ 4005-S [S]	Priscilla Sings Herself	1967	10.00	20.00	40.00

PARISH HALL
FANTASY

Number	Title	Yr	VG	VG+	NM
❏ 8398	Parish Hall	1969	5.00	10.00	20.00

PARKER FAMILY, THE
AUDIO LAB

Number	Title	Yr	VG	VG+	NM
❏ AL-1548 [M]	Songs for Salvation	196?	37.50	75.00	150.00
❏ AL-1574 [M]	Songs for Salvation, Vol. 2	196?	37.50	75.00	150.00
KING					
❏ 932 [M]	Just a Real Nice Family	1965	10.00	20.00	40.00

PARKER, CHARLIE
BARONET

Number	Title	Yr	VG	VG+	NM
❏ B-105 [M]	A Handful of Modern Jazz	1962	5.00	10.00	20.00
❏ B-107 [M]	The Early Bird	1962	5.00	10.00	20.00
BIRDLAND					
❏ 425 [10]	A Night at Carnegie Hall	1956	75.00	150.00	300.00
BLUE RIBBON					
❏ 8011 [M]	The Early Bird	1962	5.00	10.00	20.00
CHARLIE PARKER					
❏ PLP-401 [M]	Bird Is Free	1961	10.00	20.00	40.00
❏ PLP-404 [M]	The Happy Bird	1961	10.00	20.00	40.00
❏ PLP-406 [M]	Charlie Parker	1961	10.00	20.00	40.00
❏ PLP-407 [M]	Bird Symbols	1961	10.00	20.00	40.00
❏ PLP-408 [M]	Once There Was Bird	1961	10.00	20.00	40.00

Number	Title	Yr	VG	VG+	NM
❏ CP-2-502 [(2) M]	Live at Rockland Palace, September 26, 1952	1961	12.50	25.00	50.00
❏ CP-513 [M]	Charlie Parker Plus Strings	196?	10.00	20.00	40.00
❏ PLP-701 [(3)]	Historical Masterpieces	196?	15.00	30.00	60.00
CLEF					
❏ MGC-157 [10]	Charlie Parker	1954	100.00	200.00	400.00
❏ MGC-501 [10]	Charlie Parker with Strings	1954	100.00	200.00	400.00
-- Reissue of Mercury 501					
❏ MGC-509 [10]	Charlie Parker with Strings, Volume 2	1954	100.00	200.00	400.00
-- Reissue of Mercury 509					
❏ MGC-512 [10]	Bird and Diz	1954	100.00	200.00	400.00
-- Reissue of Mercury 512					
❏ MGC-513 [10]	South of the Border	1954	100.00	200.00	400.00
-- Reissue of Mercury 513					
❏ MGC-609 [M]	Charlie Parker Big Band	1954	100.00	200.00	400.00
❏ MGC-646 [M]	The Magnificent Charlie Parker	1955	100.00	200.00	400.00
❏ MGC-675 [M]	Charlie Parker with Strings	1955	100.00	200.00	400.00
❏ MGC-725 [M]	Night and Day	1956	30.00	60.00	120.00
CONCERT HALL JAZZ					
❏ 1004 [10]	The Fabulous Bird	1955	15.00	30.00	60.00
❏ 1017 [10]	The Art of Charlie Parker, Vol. 2	1955	15.00	30.00	60.00
CONTINENTAL					
❏ 16004 [M]	Bird Lives	1962	10.00	20.00	40.00
DEBUT					
❏ DEB-611 [M]	Bird on 52nd Street	196?	12.50	25.00	50.00
DIAL					
❏ LP-1 [M]	The Bird Blows the Blues	1949	1,000.	2,000.	4,000.
-- Mail-order offer					
❏ LP-201 [10]	Charlie Parker Quintet	1949	200.00	400.00	800.00
❏ LP-202 [10]	Charlie Parker Quintet	1949	200.00	400.00	800.00
❏ LP-203 [10]	Charlie Parker	1949	200.00	400.00	800.00
❏ LP-207 [10]	Charlie Parker Sextet	1949	200.00	400.00	800.00
❏ LP-901 [M]	The Bird Blows the Blues	1950	150.00	300.00	600.00
❏ LP-904 [M]	Alternate Masters	1951	150.00	300.00	600.00
❏ LP-905 [M]	Alternate Masters	1951	150.00	300.00	600.00
FANTASY					
❏ 6011 [M]	Bird on 52nd St.	1964	7.50	15.00	30.00
❏ 6012 [M]	Bird at St. Nick's	1964	7.50	15.00	30.00
JAZZ WORKSHOP					
❏ JWS-500 [M]	Bird at St. Nick's	1958	30.00	60.00	120.00
❏ JWS-501 [M]	Bird on 52nd Street	1958	30.00	60.00	120.00
JAZZTONE					
❏ J-1204 [M]	Giants of Modern Jazz	1955	12.50	25.00	50.00
❏ J-1214 [M]	The Fabulous Bird	1955	12.50	25.00	50.00
❏ J-1240 [M]	The Saxes of Stan Getz and Charlie Parker	1957	12.50	25.00	50.00
LES JAZZ COOL					
❏ 101 [M]	Les Jazz Cool, Volume 1	1960	12.50	25.00	50.00
❏ 102 [M]	Les Jazz Cool, Volume 2	1960	12.50	25.00	50.00
❏ 103 [M]	Les Jazz Cool, Volume 3	1960	12.50	25.00	50.00
MERCURY					
❏ MGC-101 [10]	Charlie Parker with Strings	1950	125.00	250.00	500.00
-- Reissue of 35010					
❏ MGC-109 [10]	Charlie Parker with Strings, Volume 2	1950	125.00	250.00	500.00
❏ MGC-501 [10]	Charlie Parker with Strings	1951	125.00	250.00	500.00
-- Reissue of 101 with new number					
❏ MGC-509 [10]	Charlie Parker with Strings, Volume 2	1952	125.00	250.00	500.00
-- Reissue of 109 with new number					
❏ MGC-512 [10]	Bird and Diz	1952	125.00	250.00	500.00
❏ MGC-513 [10]	South of the Border	1952	125.00	250.00	500.00
❏ MG-35010 [10]	Charlie Parker with Strings	1950	150.00	300.00	600.00
MOSAIC					
❏ 129 [(10)]	The Complete Dean Benedetti Recordings of Charlie Parker	199?	25.00	50.00	100.00
ROOST					
❏ LP-2210 [M]	All Star Sextet	1958	30.00	60.00	120.00
❏ LP-2257 [M]	The World of Charlie Parker	1963	10.00	20.00	40.00
SAVOY					
❏ MG-9000 [10]	Charlie Parker	1950	125.00	250.00	500.00
❏ MG-9001 [10]	Charlie Parker, Volume 2	1951	125.00	250.00	500.00
❏ MG-9010 [10]	Charlie Parker, Volume 3	1952	125.00	250.00	500.00
❏ MG-9011 [10]	Charlie Parker, Volume 4	1952	125.00	250.00	500.00
❏ MG-12000 [M]	Charlie Parker Memorial	1955	25.00	50.00	100.00
❏ MG-12001 [M]	The Immortal Charlie Parker	1955	25.00	50.00	100.00
❏ MG-12009 [M]	The Genius of Charlie Parker, Volume 1	1955	25.00	50.00	100.00
❏ MG-12014 [M]	The Genius of Charlie Parker, Volume 2	1955	25.00	50.00	100.00
❏ MG-12079 [M]	The Charlie Parker Story	1956	25.00	50.00	100.00
❏ MG-12138 [M]	Bird's Night	1960	10.00	20.00	40.00
❏ MG-12152 [M]	An Evening at Home with the Bird	196?	10.00	20.00	40.00

Number	Title	Yr	VG	VG+	NM
❑ MG-12179 [M]	The "Bird" Returns	196?	7.50	15.00	30.00
❑ MG-12186 [M]	Newly Discovered Sides by the Immortal Charlie Parker	1966	7.50	15.00	30.00

SAVOY JAZZ

Number	Title	Yr	VG	VG+	NM
❑ SJL-5500 [(5)]	The Complete Savoy Studio Sessions	197?	7.50	15.00	30.00

VERVE

Number	Title	Yr	VG	VG+	NM
❑ VSP-23 [M]	Bird Wings	1966	5.00	10.00	20.00
❑ MGV-8000 [M]	The Charlie Parker Story, Volume 1	1957	20.00	40.00	80.00
❑ V-8000 [M]	The Charlie Parker Story, Volume 1	1961	6.25	12.50	25.00
❑ MGV-8001 [M]	The Charlie Parker Story, Volume 2	1957	20.00	40.00	80.00
❑ V-8001 [M]	The Charlie Parker Story, Volume 2	1961	6.25	12.50	25.00
❑ MGV-8002 [M]	The Charlie Parker Story, Volume 3	1957	20.00	40.00	80.00
❑ V-8002 [M]	The Charlie Parker Story, Volume 3	1961	6.25	12.50	25.00
❑ MGV-8003 [M]	Night and Day (The Genius of Charlie Parker #1)	1957	20.00	40.00	80.00
❑ V-8003 [M]	Night and Day (The Genius of Charlie Parker #1)	1961	6.25	12.50	25.00
❑ MGV-8004 [M]	April in Paris (The Genius of Charlie Parker #2)	1957	20.00	40.00	80.00
❑ V-8004 [M]	April in Paris (The Genius of Charlie Parker #2)	1961	6.25	12.50	25.00
❑ MGV-8005 [M]	Now's the Time (The Genius of Charlie Parker #3)	1957	20.00	40.00	80.00
❑ V-8005 [M]	Now's the Time (The Genius of Charlie Parker #3)	1961	6.25	12.50	25.00
❑ MGV-8006 [M]	Bird and Diz (The Genius of Charlie Parker #4)	1957	20.00	40.00	80.00
❑ V-8006 [M]	Bird and Diz (The Genius of Charlie Parker #4)	1961	6.25	12.50	25.00
❑ MGV-8007 [M]	Charlie Parker Plays Cole Porter (The Genius of Charlie Parker #5)	1957	20.00	40.00	80.00
❑ V-8007 [M]	Charlie Parker Plays Cole Porter (The Genius of Charlie Parker #5)	1961	6.25	12.50	25.00
❑ MGV-8008 [M]	Fiesta (The Genius of Charlie Parker #6)	1957	20.00	40.00	80.00
❑ V-8008 [M]	Fiesta (The Genius of Charlie Parker #6)	1961	6.25	12.50	25.00
❑ MGV-8009 [M]	Jazz Perennial (The Genius of Charlie Parker #7)	1957	20.00	40.00	80.00
❑ V-8009 [M]	Jazz Perennial (The Genius of Charlie Parker #7)	1961	6.25	12.50	25.00
❑ MGV-8010 [M]	Swedish Schnapps (The Genius of Charlie Parker #8)	1957	20.00	40.00	80.00
❑ V-8010 [M]	Swedish Schnapps (The Genius of Charlie Parker #8)	1961	6.25	12.50	25.00
❑ MGV-8100-3 [(3) M]	The Charlie Parker Story	1957	37.50	75.00	150.00
-- Combines 8000, 8001 and 8002 in a box set					
❑ V-8100-3 [(3) M]	The Charlie Parker Story	1961	15.00	30.00	60.00
-- Combines 8000, 8001 and 8002 in a box set					
❑ V-8409 [M]	The Essential Charlie Parker	1961	6.25	12.50	25.00

VOGUE

Number	Title	Yr	VG	VG+	NM
❑ LAE-12002 [M]	Memorial Album	1955	37.50	75.00	150.00

WARNER BROS.

Number	Title	Yr	VG	VG+	NM
❑ 6BS 3159 [(6)]	The Complete Dial Recordings	1977	20.00	40.00	80.00
-- Limited edition of 4,000 box sets					

PARKER, FESS
COLUMBIA

Number	Title	Yr	VG	VG+	NM
❑ CL 666 [M]	Walt Disney's Davy Crockett, King of the Wild Frontier	1955	25.00	50.00	100.00

DISNEYLAND

Number	Title	Yr	VG	VG+	NM
❑ WDL-1007 [M]	Yarns and Songs of the West	1959	7.50	15.00	30.00
-- Reissue of 3006					
❑ DQ-1269 [M]	Pecos Bill and Other Stories in Song	1965	7.50	15.00	30.00
❑ DQ-1315 [M]	Three Adventures of Davy Crockett	1968	6.25	12.50	25.00
-- Another reissue, this time of 1926					
❑ DQ-1336	Cowboy and Indian Songs	1969	7.50	15.00	30.00
❑ ST-1926 [M]	Three Adventures of Davy Crockett	1963	7.50	15.00	30.00
-- Reissue of 3602					
❑ WDL-3006 [M]	Yarns and Songs	1957	10.00	20.00	40.00
❑ WDL-3041 [M]	Westward Ho the Wagons	1959	7.50	15.00	30.00
-- Reissue of 4008					
❑ WDA-3602 [M]	Three Adventures of Davy Crockett	1958	12.50	25.00	50.00
-- Reissue of Columbia 666					
❑ WDL-4006 [M]	Westward Ho the Wagons	1956	20.00	40.00	80.00

RCA VICTOR

Number	Title	Yr	VG	VG+	NM
❑ LPM-2973 [M]	Fess Parker Sings About Daniel Boone, Davy Crockett and Abe Lincoln	1964	6.25	12.50	25.00
❑ LSP-2973 [S]	Fess Parker Sings About Daniel Boone, Davy Crockett and Abe Lincoln	1964	7.50	15.00	30.00

PARKER, GRAHAM
ARISTA

Number	Title	Yr	VG	VG+	NM
❑ SP-63 [DJ]	Live Sparks	1979	7.50	15.00	30.00

PARKER, JUNIOR
DUKE

Number	Title	Yr	VG	VG+	NM
❑ DLP-76 [M]	Driving Wheel	196?	25.00	50.00	100.00
-- With Wagon Wheel on front cover					
❑ DLP-76 [M]	Driving Wheel	1962	37.50	75.00	150.00
-- With Cadillac on front cover					
❑ DLP-83 [M]	The Best of Junior Parker	1967	12.50	25.00	50.00
❑ DLPS-83 [P]	The Best of Junior Parker	1967	10.00	20.00	40.00

MERCURY

Number	Title	Yr	VG	VG+	NM
❑ MG-21101 [M]	Like It Is	1967	7.50	15.00	30.00
❑ SR-61101 [S]	Like It Is	1967	6.25	12.50	25.00

MINIT

Number	Title	Yr	VG	VG+	NM
❑ 24024	Blues Man	1969	6.25	12.50	25.00

PARKER, JUNIOR, AND BOBBY BLAND
Also see each artist's individual listings.
DUKE

Number	Title	Yr	VG	VG+	NM
❑ DLP-72 [M]	Blues Consolidated	1961	37.50	75.00	150.00

PARKER, ROBERT
NOLA

Number	Title	Yr	VG	VG+	NM
❑ LP-1001 [M]	Barefootin'	1966	7.50	15.00	30.00

PARKS, ANDY
CAPITOL

Number	Title	Yr	VG	VG+	NM
❑ ST 2799 [S]	Sex, School...And Like Other Pressures	1967	5.00	10.00	20.00
❑ T 2799 [M]	Sex, School...And Like Other Pressures	1967	5.00	10.00	20.00

PARKS, VAN DYKE
WARNER BROS.

Number	Title	Yr	VG	VG+	NM
❑ WS 1727	Song Cycle	1968	6.25	12.50	25.00
-- Gold label					

PARLIAMENT
Also see FUNKADELIC.
CASABLANCA

Number	Title	Yr	VG	VG+	NM
❑ NBLP 7002	Up for the Down Stroke	1974	10.00	20.00	40.00
❑ NBLP 7014	Chocolate City	1975	10.00	20.00	40.00
❑ NBLP 7022	Mothership Connection	1976	7.50	15.00	30.00
❑ NBLP 7034	The Clones of Dr. Funkenstein	1976	7.50	15.00	30.00
❑ NBLP 7053 [(2)]	Parliament Live/P. Funk Earth Tour	1977	10.00	20.00	40.00
❑ NBLP 7084	Funkentelechy vs. the Placebo Syndrome	1977	7.50	15.00	30.00
❑ NBLP 7125	Motor-Booty Affair	1978	7.50	15.00	30.00
❑ NBPIX 7125 [PD]	Motor-Booty Affair	1978	10.00	20.00	40.00
❑ NBLP 7195	Gloryhallastoopid (Or Pin the Tale on the Funky)	1979	7.50	15.00	30.00
❑ NBLP 7249	Trombipulation	1980	7.50	15.00	30.00
❑ NBLP 9003	Up for the Down Stroke	1974	12.50	25.00	50.00
-- Original pressing, distributed by Warner Bros.					

INVICTUS

Number	Title	Yr	VG	VG+	NM
❑ ST-7302	Osmium	1970	25.00	50.00	100.00

PARSONS, ALAN, PROJECT
ARISTA

Number	Title	Yr	VG	VG+	NM
❑ SP-68 [(6) DJ]	Audio Guide to the Alan Parsons Project	1979	12.50	25.00	50.00
-- Contains first four APP LPs plus a two-record set of other Parsons work					
❑ SP-140 [(8) DJ]	Complete Audio Guide to the Alan Parsons Project	1982	20.00	40.00	80.00
-- Contains first six APP LPs plus a two-record set of other Parsons work					
❑ ALPD 8263 [DJ]	Vulture Culture	1985	6.25	12.50	25.00
-- Promo-only picture disc					

MOBILE FIDELITY

Number	Title	Yr	VG	VG+	NM
❑ 1-084	I Robot	1982	10.00	20.00	40.00
-- Audiophile vinyl					
❑ MFQR 1-084	I Robot	1982	20.00	40.00	80.00
-- Audiophile vinyl; Ultra High Quality pressing in box					
❑ 1-204	Tales of Mystery and Imagination - Edgar Allan Poe	1994	5.00	10.00	20.00
-- Audiophile vinyl					

PARTON, DOLLY
Also see PORTER WAGONER AND DOLLY PARTON.
COLUMBIA

Number	Title	Yr	VG	VG+	NM
❑ C 46882	Eagle When She Flies	1991	5.00	10.00	20.00
-- Available on vinyl only through Columbia House					

MONUMENT

Number	Title	Yr	VG	VG+	NM
❑ MLP-8085 [M]	Hello, I'm Dolly	1967	7.50	15.00	30.00

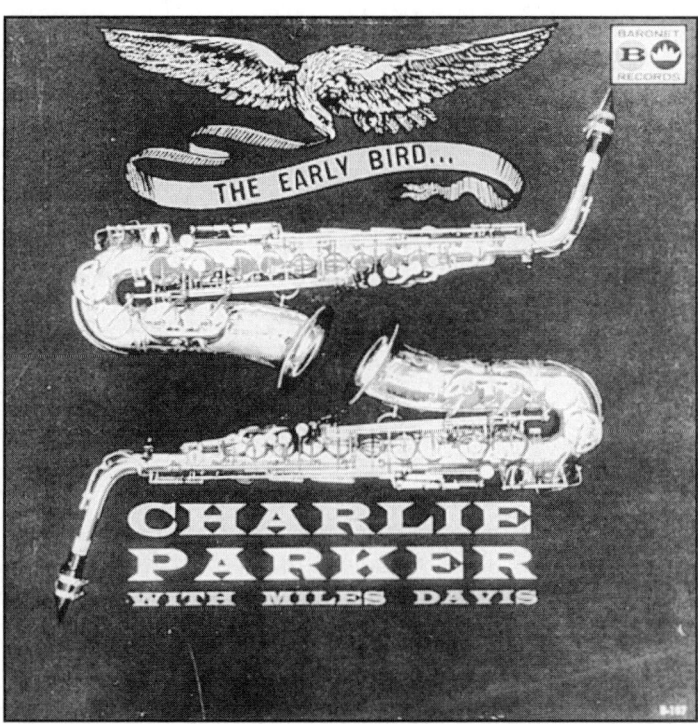

(Top left) The title song of this Patti Page 10-inch album, "Tennessee Waltz," was her biggest hit. The LP that revolves around the hit is much harder to find. (Top right) Charlie Parker's early material was packaged and re-packaged in seemingly endless ways. *The Early Bird* was a collection that appeared on Baronet, a budget label of the 1960s. (Bottom left) Peter, Paul and Mary sold a lot of albums in the 1960s, which is one reason why their records are not that valuable. Having some nominal value, enough to make this book, are the original gold-label pressings of their early work, including their self-titled debut. (Bottom right) Pink Floyd's American debut, *The Piper at the Gates of Dawn*, a title that only appears on the back cover by the way, is different from the U.K. version of the same album, most notably in the subtraction of some album tracks and the addition of the single "See Emily Play."

Number	Title	Yr	VG	VG+	NM
❏ SLP-18085 [S]	Hello, I'm Dolly	1967	10.00	20.00	40.00
❏ SLP-18136	As Long As I Love	1970	5.00	10.00	20.00
❏ KZG 31913 [(2)]	The World of Dolly	1972	5.00	10.00	20.00
❏ KZG 33876 [(2)]	Hello, I'm Dolly	1975	5.00	10.00	20.00

RCA VICTOR

Number	Title	Yr	VG	VG+	NM
❏ APD1-0033 [Q]	My Tennessee Mountain Home	1973	5.00	10.00	20.00
❏ LPM-3949 [M]	Just Because I'm a Woman	1968	25.00	50.00	100.00
❏ LSP-3949 [S]	Just Because I'm a Woman	1968	7.50	15.00	30.00
-- "Stereo" on black label					
❏ LSP-3949 [S]	Just Because I'm a Woman	1968	5.00	10.00	20.00
-- Orange label					
❏ LSP-4099	In the Good Old Days	1969	5.00	10.00	20.00
❏ LSP-4188	My Blue Ridge Mountain Boy	1969	5.00	10.00	20.00
❏ LSP-4288	The Fairest of Them All	1970	5.00	10.00	20.00
❏ LSP-4387	A Real Live Dolly	1970	6.25	12.50	25.00
-- Four songs feature Porter Wagoner					
❏ LSP-4398	Golden Streets of Glory	1971	5.00	10.00	20.00
❏ LSP-4449	The Best of Dolly Parton	1970	5.00	10.00	20.00
❏ LSP-4507	Joshua	1971	5.00	10.00	20.00
❏ LSP-4603	Coat of Many Colors	1971	5.00	10.00	20.00
❏ LSP-4686	Touch Your Woman	1972	5.00	10.00	20.00
❏ LSP-4752	My Favorite Song Writer: Porter Wagoner	1972	5.00	10.00	20.00

PARTON, DOLLY/GEORGE JONES
Also see each artist's individual listings.
STARDAY

Number	Title	Yr	VG	VG+	NM
❏ LP 429 [P]	Dolly Parton and George Jones	1968	10.00	20.00	40.00
-- One side of Dolly in stereo, one side of "Possum" in rechanneled stereo					

PARTON, DOLLY/FAYE TUCKER
SOMERSET

Number	Title	Yr	VG	VG+	NM
❏ S-9700 [M]	Hits Made Famous by Country Queens	1963	6.25	12.50	25.00
❏ SF-19700 [S]	Hits Made Famous by Country Queens	1963	7.50	15.00	30.00
-- Dolly Parton sings songs made famous by Kitty Wells					

TIME

Number	Title	Yr	VG	VG+	NM
❏ 2108	Country & Western Soul	1963	10.00	20.00	40.00

PARTON, STELLA
SOUL COUNTRY & BLUES

Number	Title	Yr	VG	VG+	NM
❏ 6006	I Want to Hold You in My Dreams Tonight	1975	5.00	10.00	20.00

PARTRIDGE FAMILY, THE
Also see DAVID CASSIDY.
BELL

Number	Title	Yr	VG	VG+	NM
❏ 1107	The Partridge Family At Home with Their Greatest Hits	1972	5.00	10.00	20.00
❏ 1111	The Partridge Family Notebook	1972	6.25	12.50	25.00
❏ 1122	Crossword Puzzle	1973	7.50	15.00	30.00
❏ 1137	Bulletin Board	1973	12.50	25.00	50.00
❏ 1319 [(2)]	The World of the Partridge Family	1974	10.00	20.00	40.00
❏ 6050	The Partridge Family Album	1970	5.00	10.00	20.00
❏ 6050	The Partridge Family Album Bonus Photo	1970	2.50	5.00	10.00
❏ 6059	Up to Date	1971	5.00	10.00	20.00
❏ 6059	Up to Date Book Cover	1971	2.50	5.00	10.00
❏ 6064	The Partridge Family Sound Magazine	1971	5.00	10.00	20.00
❏ 6066	A Partridge Family Christmas	1971	10.00	20.00	40.00
-- With Christmas card printed on the cover (later pressing)					
❏ 6066	A Partridge Family Christmas	1971	6.25	12.50	25.00
-- With attached Christmas card					
❏ 6072	The Partridge Family Shopping Bag	1972	5.00	10.00	20.00
❏ 6072	The Partridge Family Shopping Bag Bonus Shopping Bag	1972	2.50	5.00	10.00

LAURIE HOUSE

Number	Title	Yr	VG	VG+	NM
❏ H-8014 [(2)]	The Partridge Family	197?	12.50	25.00	50.00

PASTEL SIX, THE
ZEN

Number	Title	Yr	VG	VG+	NM
❏ 1001 [M]	The Cinnamon Cinder	1963	25.00	50.00	100.00

PATCHEN, KENNETH, WITH THE CHAMBER JAZZ SEXTET
CADENCE

Number	Title	Yr	VG	VG+	NM
❏ CLP-3004 [M]	Kenneth Patchen Reads His Poetry	1957	75.00	150.00	300.00

PATRON SAINTS, THE
(NO LABEL)

Number	Title	Yr	VG	VG+	NM
❏ JT-1001	Fohhob Bohob	1969	1,000.	2,000.	3,000.
-- 100 copies were pressed					

PATRON SAINT

Number	Title	Yr	VG	VG+	NM
❏ JT-1001	Fohhob Bohob	1997	6.25	12.50	25.00
-- Authorized reissue with bonus 7-inch single; numbered edition of 500					

PATTERSON SINGERS, THE
ATCO

Number	Title	Yr	VG	VG+	NM
❏ SD 33-380	The Patterson Singers	1972	5.00	10.00	20.00

KING

Number	Title	Yr	VG	VG+	NM
❏ 763 [M]	Gospel Songs by the Patterson Singers	1962	12.50	25.00	50.00
❏ KS-1129	Jesus Knows	1971	5.00	10.00	20.00

MINIT

Number	Title	Yr	VG	VG+	NM
❏ LP-40021	The Soul of Gospel	1969	5.00	10.00	20.00

VEE JAY

Number	Title	Yr	VG	VG+	NM
❏ LP-5017 [M]	My Prayer	1962	6.25	12.50	25.00
❏ LP-5032 [M]	The Lord's Prayer	1963	6.25	12.50	25.00
❏ LP-5046 [M]	Songs of Faith	1963	5.00	10.00	20.00
❏ SR-5046 [S]	Songs of Faith	1963	7.50	15.00	30.00
❏ LP-5060 [M]	The Soul of the Patterson Singers	1964	5.00	10.00	20.00

PATTERSON, DON
PRESTIGE

Number	Title	Yr	VG	VG+	NM
❏ PR-7331 [M]	The Exciting New Organ of Don Patterson	1964	6.25	12.50	25.00
❏ PRST-7331 [S]	The Exciting New Organ of Don Patterson	1964	7.50	15.00	30.00
❏ PR-7349 [M]	Hip Cake Walk	1965	6.25	12.50	25.00
❏ PRST-7349 [S]	Hip Cake Walk	1965	7.50	15.00	30.00
❏ PR-7381 [M]	Patterson's People	1965	6.25	12.50	25.00
❏ PRST-7381 [S]	Patterson's People	1965	7.50	15.00	30.00
❏ PR 7415 [M]	Holiday Soul	1965	6.25	12.50	25.00
❏ PRST 7415 [S]	Holiday Soul	1965	7.50	15.00	30.00
❏ PR-7430 [M]	Satisfaction	1966	6.25	12.50	25.00
❏ PRST-7430 [S]	Satisfaction	1966	7.50	15.00	30.00
❏ PR-7466 [M]	The Boss Men	1967	7.50	15.00	30.00
❏ PRST-7466 [S]	The Boss Men	1967	6.25	12.50	25.00
❏ PR-7484 [M]	Soul Happening!	1967	6.25	12.50	25.00
❏ PRST-7484 [S]	Soul Happening!	1967	5.00	10.00	20.00
❏ PR-7510 [M]	Mellow Soul	1967	6.25	12.50	25.00
❏ PRST-7510 [S]	Mellow Soul	1967	5.00	10.00	20.00
❏ PR-7533 [M]	Four Dimensions	1967	6.25	12.50	25.00
❏ PRST-7533 [S]	Four Dimensions	1967	5.00	10.00	20.00

PATTO
Also see SPOOKY TOOTH.
ISLAND

Number	Title	Yr	VG	VG+	NM
❏ SW-9322	Roll 'Em, Smoke 'Em, Put Another Line Out	1972	7.50	15.00	30.00

PATTON, CHARLEY
ORIGIN JAZZ LIBRARY

Number	Title	Yr	VG	VG+	NM
❏ OJL-1 [M]	The Immortal Charley Patton No. 1	1962	6.25	12.50	25.00
❏ OJL-7 [M]	The Immortal Charley Patton No. 2	1962	6.25	12.50	25.00

YAZOO

Number	Title	Yr	VG	VG+	NM
❏ 2001 [(2)]	King of the Delta Blues	197?	7.50	15.00	30.00
❏ 2010 [(2)]	Founder of the Delta Blues	197?	7.50	15.00	30.00

PATTON, JIMMY
MOON

Number	Title	Yr	VG	VG+	NM
❏ 101 [M]	Make Room for the Blues	1966	10.00	20.00	40.00

SIMS

Number	Title	Yr	VG	VG+	NM
❏ 127 [M]	Blue Darlin'	1965	7.50	15.00	30.00

SOURDOUGH

Number	Title	Yr	VG	VG+	NM
❏ 127 [M]	Blue Darlin'	1965	12.50	25.00	50.00

STEREOPHONIC

Number	Title	Yr	VG	VG+	NM
❏ LP-1002 [S]	Take 30 Minutes with Jimmy	196?	30.00	60.00	120.00

PAUL AND PAULA
PHILIPS

Number	Title	Yr	VG	VG+	NM
❏ PHM 200-078 [M]	Paul and Paula Sing for Young Lovers	1963	7.50	15.00	30.00
❏ PHM 200-089 [M]	We Go Together	1963	7.50	15.00	30.00
❏ PHM 200-101 [M]	Holiday for Teens	1963	7.50	15.00	30.00
❏ PHS 600-078 [S]	Paul and Paula Sing for Young Lovers	1963	10.00	20.00	40.00
❏ PHS 600-089 [S]	We Go Together	1963	10.00	20.00	40.00
❏ PHS 600-101 [S]	Holiday for Teens	1963	10.00	20.00	40.00

PAUL, BILLY
GAMBLE

Number	Title	Yr	VG	VG+	NM
❏ SG-5002	Feeling Good at the Cadillac Club	1968	7.50	15.00	30.00

Number	Title	Yr	VG	VG+	NM
NEPTUNE					
❏ 201	Ebony Woman	1970	5.00	10.00	20.00
PHILADELPHIA INT'L.					
❏ ZQ 31793 [Q]	360 Degrees of Billy Paul	1972	5.00	10.00	20.00
❏ ZQ 32409 [Q]	War of the Gods	1973	5.00	10.00	20.00
❏ ZQ 32952 [Q]	Live in Europe	1974	5.00	10.00	20.00

PAUL, LES
DECCA

Number	Title	Yr	VG	VG+	NM
❏ DL-5018 [10]	Hawaiian Paradise	1949	25.00	50.00	100.00
❏ DL-5376 [10]	Galloping Guitars	1952	25.00	50.00	100.00
❏ DL 8589 [M]	More of Les	1957	10.00	20.00	40.00

PAUL, LES, AND MARY FORD
Also see each artist's individual listings.
CAPITOL

Number	Title	Yr	VG	VG+	NM
❏ H 226 [10]	The New Sound, Volume 1	1950	20.00	40.00	80.00
❏ T 226 [M]	The New Sound, Volume 1	1955	12.50	25.00	50.00
❏ H 286 [10]	The New Sound, Volume 2	1951	20.00	40.00	80.00
❏ T 286 [M]	The New Sound, Volume 2	1955	12.50	25.00	50.00
❏ H 356 [10]	Bye Bye Blues	1952	20.00	40.00	80.00
❏ T 356 [M]	Bye Bye Blues	1955	12.50	25.00	50.00
❏ H 416 [10]	The Hit Makers	1953	20.00	40.00	80.00
❏ T 416 [M]	The Hit Makers	1955	12.50	25.00	50.00
❏ H 577 [10]	Les and Mary	1955	20.00	40.00	80.00
❏ W 577 [M]	Les and Mary	1955	12.50	25.00	50.00
❏ T 802 [M]	Time to Dream	1956	12.50	25.00	50.00
❏ DT 1476 [R]	The Hits of Les and Mary	1960	5.00	10.00	20.00
❏ T 1476 [M]	The Hits of Les and Mary	1960	6.25	12.50	25.00
COLUMBIA					
❏ CL 1276 [M]	Lover's Luau	1959	5.00	10.00	20.00
❏ CL 1688 [M]	Warm and Wonderful	1962	5.00	10.00	20.00
❏ CL 1821 [M]	Bouquet of Roses	1962	5.00	10.00	20.00
❏ CS 8488 [S]	Warm and Wonderful	1962	6.25	12.50	25.00
❏ CS 8621 [S]	Bouquet of Roses	1962	6.25	12.50	25.00
❏ CS 8728 [S]	Swingin' South	1963	5.00	10.00	20.00

PAULSON, PAT
RUBICON/MERCURY

Number	Title	Yr	VG	VG+	NM
❏ SR 61179	Pat Paulson for President	1968	5.00	10.00	20.00

PAUPERS, THE
VERVE FORECAST

Number	Title	Yr	VG	VG+	NM
❏ FT-3026 [M]	Magic People	1967	5.00	10.00	20.00
❏ FTS-3026 [S]	Magic People	1967	5.00	10.00	20.00

PAVLOV'S DOG
ABC

Number	Title	Yr	VG	VG+	NM
❏ D-866	Pampered Menial	1975	6.25	12.50	25.00

PAVONE, RITA
RCA VICTOR

Number	Title	Yr	VG	VG+	NM
❏ LSP-2900 [S]	Rita Pavone	1964	5.00	10.00	20.00
❏ LSP-2996 [S]	Small Wonder	1965	5.00	10.00	20.00

PAXTON, TOM
ELEKTRA

Number	Title	Yr	VG	VG+	NM
❏ EKL-277 [M]	Ramblin' Boy	1964	5.00	10.00	20.00
❏ EKL-298 [M]	Ain't That News	1965	5.00	10.00	20.00
❏ EKL-317 [M]	Outward Bound	1966	5.00	10.00	20.00
❏ 7E-2003 [(2)]	The Compleat Tom Paxton	1971	5.00	10.00	20.00
❏ EKS-7277 [S]	Ramblin' Boy	1964	6.25	12.50	25.00
❏ EKS-7298 [S]	Ain't That News	1965	6.25	12.50	25.00
❏ EKS-7317 [S]	Outward Bound	1966	6.25	12.50	25.00
❏ EKS-74019	Morning Again	1968	5.00	10.00	20.00
GASLIGHT					
❏ GV-116 [M]	I'm the Man Who Built the Bridges	1962	20.00	40.00	80.00

PAYCHECK, JOHNNY
LITTLE DARLIN'

Number	Title	Yr	VG	VG+	NM
❏ LD-4001 [M]	Johnny Paycheck at Carnegie Hall	1966	5.00	10.00	20.00
❏ LD-4003 [M]	The Lovin' Machine	1966	5.00	10.00	20.00
❏ LD-4004 [M]	Gospeltime in My Fashion	1967	5.00	10.00	20.00
❏ LD-4006 [M]	Johnny Paycheck Sings Jukebox Charlie	1967	6.25	12.50	25.00
❏ SLD-8001 [S]	Johnny Paycheck at Carnegie Hall	1966	6.25	12.50	25.00
❏ SLD-8003 [S]	The Lovin' Machine	1966	6.25	12.50	25.00
❏ SLD-8004 [S]	Gospeltime in My Fashion	1967	6.25	12.50	25.00
❏ SLD-8006 [S]	Johnny Paycheck Sings Jukebox Charlie	1967	6.25	12.50	25.00
❏ SLD-8010	Country Soul	1968	6.25	12.50	25.00
❏ SLD-8012	Johnny Paycheck's Greatest Hits	1968	6.25	12.50	25.00
❏ SLD-8023	Wherever You Are	1969	6.25	12.50	25.00

PAYNE, DENNIS, AND THE RENEGADES
RED MAN

Number	Title	Yr	VG	VG+	NM
❏ 1492	We're Indian	1969	37.50	75.00	150.00

PAYNE, FREDA
IMPULSE!

Number	Title	Yr	VG	VG+	NM
❏ A-53 [M]	After the Lights Go Down Low…And Much More	1964	7.50	15.00	30.00
❏ AS-53 [S]	After the Lights Go Down Low…And Much More	1964	10.00	20.00	40.00
MGM					
❏ E-4370 [M]	How Do You Say I Don't Love You Anymore	1966	5.00	10.00	20.00
❏ SE-4370 [S]	How Do You Say I Don't Love You Anymore	1966	6.25	12.50	25.00

PAYNE, JIMMY
EPIC

Number	Title	Yr	VG	VG+	NM
❏ BN 26372	Woman	1968	5.00	10.00	20.00

PAYNE, LEON
STARDAY

Number	Title	Yr	VG	VG+	NM
❏ SLP-231 [M]	Leon Payne: A Living Legend of Country Music	1963	20.00	40.00	80.00
❏ SLP-236 [M]	Americana	1963	12.50	25.00	50.00

PEACE, JOE
RITE

Number	Title	Yr	VG	VG+	NM
❏ 29917	Finding Peace	1972	50.00	100.00	200.00

PEACHES AND HERB
DATE

Number	Title	Yr	VG	VG+	NM
❏ TEM 3004 [M]	Let's Fall in Love	1967	5.00	10.00	20.00
❏ TEM 3005 [M]	For Your Love	1967	6.25	12.50	25.00
❏ TEM 3007 [M]	Golden Duets	1968	7.50	15.00	30.00
❏ TES 4004 [S]	Let's Fall in Love	1967	6.25	12.50	25.00
❏ TES 4005 [S]	For Your Love	1967	5.00	10.00	20.00
❏ TES 4007 [S]	Golden Duets	1968	5.00	10.00	20.00
❏ TES 4012	Peaches and Herb's Greatest Hits	1968	5.00	10.00	20.00

PEANUT BUTTER CONSPIRACY, THE
CHALLENGE

Number	Title	Yr	VG	VG+	NM
❏ 2000	For Children of All Ages	1969	7.50	15.00	30.00
COLUMBIA					
❏ CL 2654 [M]	The Peanut Butter Conspiracy Is Spreading	1967	7.50	15.00	30.00
❏ CL 2790 [M]	The Great Conspiracy	1968	10.00	20.00	40.00
❏ CS 9454 [S]	The Peanut Butter Conspiracy Is Spreading	1967	7.50	15.00	30.00
❏ CS 9590 [S]	The Great Conspiracy	1968	7.50	15.00	30.00

PEARLS BEFORE SWINE
ESP-DISK

Number	Title	Yr	VG	VG+	NM
❏ 1054 [M]	One Nation Under Ground	1967	12.50	25.00	50.00
❏ 1054 [S]	One Nation Under Ground	1967	12.50	25.00	50.00
-- Sepia-tone cover with white border					
❏ 1054 [S]	One Nation Under Ground	1967	12.50	25.00	50.00
-- Sepia-tone cover with no border					
❏ 1054 [S]	One Nation Under Ground	1967	12.50	25.00	50.00
-- Black and white cover					
❏ 1054 [S]	One Nation Under Ground	1968	7.50	15.00	30.00
-- Full-color cover					
❏ 1054	One Nation Under Ground Bonus Poster	1967	6.25	12.50	25.00
❏ 1075	Balaklava	1968	10.00	20.00	40.00
REPRISE					
❏ RS 6364	These Things Too	1969	7.50	15.00	30.00
❏ RS 6405	The Use of Ashes	1970	7.50	15.00	30.00
❏ RS 6442	City of Gold	1971	10.00	20.00	40.00
❏ RS 6467	Beautiful Lies You Could Live In	1971	10.00	20.00	40.00

PEARSON, ALBIE
VIBRANT

Number	Title	Yr	VG	VG+	NM
❏ 1501	Albie Pearson	1973	6.25	12.50	25.00

PEARSON, DUKE
BLUE NOTE

Number	Title	Yr	VG	VG+	NM
❏ BLP-4022 [M]	Profile -- Duke Pearson	1959	30.00	60.00	120.00
-- "Deep groove" version (deep indentation under label on both sides)					

Number	Title	Yr	VG	VG+	NM
❑ BLP-4022 [M]	Profile -- Duke Pearson	1959	20.00	40.00	80.00
-- Regular version with W. 63rd St. address on label					
❑ BLP-4022 [M]	Profile -- Duke Pearson	1963	6.25	12.50	25.00
-- With New York, USA address on label					
❑ BLP-4035 [M]	Tender Feelin's	1960	30.00	60.00	120.00
-- "Deep groove" version (deep indentation under label on both sides)					
❑ BLP-4035 [M]	Tender Feelin's	1960	20.00	40.00	80.00
-- Regular version with W. 63rd St. address on label					
❑ BLP-4035 [M]	Tender Feelin's	1963	6.25	12.50	25.00
-- With New York, USA address on label					
❑ BLP-4191 [M]	Wahoo!	1965	7.50	15.00	30.00
❑ BLP-4252 [M]	Sweet Honey Bee	1966	7.50	15.00	30.00
❑ BLP-84022 [S]	Profile -- Duke Pearson	1959	15.00	30.00	60.00
-- With W. 63rd St. address on label					
❑ BLP-84022 [S]	Profile -- Duke Pearson	1963	5.00	10.00	20.00
-- With New York, USA address on label					
❑ BLP-84035 [S]	Tender Feelin's	1960	15.00	30.00	60.00
-- With W. 63rd St. address on label					
❑ BLP-84035 [S]	Tender Feelin's	1963	5.00	10.00	20.00
-- With New York, USA address on label					
❑ BLP-84191 [S]	Wahoo!	1965	7.50	15.00	30.00
-- With New York, USA address on label					
❑ BLP-84252 [S]	Sweet Honey Bee	1966	7.50	15.00	30.00
-- With New York, USA address on label					
❑ BLP-84267	The Right Touch	1968	6.25	12.50	25.00
❑ BLP-84276	Introducing Duke Pearson's Big Band	1968	6.25	12.50	25.00
❑ BLP-84293	The Phantom	1969	6.25	12.50	25.00
❑ BLP-84308	Now Hear This	1969	6.25	12.50	25.00
❑ BLP-84323	Merry Ole Soul	1970	5.00	10.00	20.00
❑ BLP-84344	How Insensitive	1970	5.00	10.00	20.00

PEBBLES AND BAMM-BAMM
HANNA-BARBERA

❑ HLP-2033 [M]	Pebbles and Bamm-Bamm Sing Songs of Christmas	1965	30.00	60.00	120.00
❑ HLP-2040 [M]	On the Good Ship Lollipop	1966	25.00	50.00	100.00

PEDICIN, MIKE
APOLLO

❑ LP-484 [M]	Musical Medicine	1957	37.50	75.00	150.00

PEEBLES, ANN
HI

❑ SHL-32059	Part Time Love	1971	5.00	10.00	20.00
❑ SHL-32065	Straight from the Heart	1972	5.00	10.00	20.00
❑ XSHL-32079	I Can't Stand the Rain	1974	5.00	10.00	20.00
❑ SHL-32091	Tellin' It	1975	5.00	10.00	20.00

PEEL, DAVID
APPLE

❑ SW-3391	The Pope Smokes Dope	1972	18.75	37.50	75.00

ELEKTRA

❑ EKS-74032	Have a Marijuana	1968	10.00	20.00	40.00
❑ EKS-74069	The American Revolution	1970	7.50	15.00	30.00

PEELS, THE
KARATE

❑ 5402 [M]	Juanita Banana	1966	20.00	40.00	80.00

PEGGY SUE
DECCA

❑ DL 75153	Dynamite!	1969	6.25	12.50	25.00
❑ DL 75215	All American Husband	1970	6.25	12.50	25.00

PENDERGRASS, TEDDY
Also see HAROLD MELVIN AND THE BLUE NOTES.
PHILADELPHIA INT'L.

❑ HZ 47491	Time for Love	198?	10.00	20.00	40.00
-- Half-speed mastered edition					

PENGUINS, THE
DOOTO

❑ DTL-204 [M]	The Best Vocal Groups... Rhythm and Blues	1959	50.00	100.00	200.00
-- Reissue of Dootone 204; blue and yellow label					
❑ DTL-204 [M]	The Best Vocal Groups... Rhythm and Blues	196?	25.00	50.00	100.00
-- Black label with gold/orange/blue ring. This is NOT a counterfeit.					
❑ DTL-242 [M]	The Cool, Cool Penguins	1959	175.00	350.00	700.00
-- Red and yellow label					
❑ DTL-242 [M]	The Cool, Cool Penguins	1959	175.00	350.00	700.00
-- Blue and yellow label					

Number	Title	Yr	VG	VG+	NM
❑ DTL-242 [M]	The Cool, Cool Penguins	196?	50.00	100.00	200.00
-- Black label with gold/orange/blue ring. This is NOT a counterfeit.					

DOOTONE

❑ DTL-204 [M]	The Best Vocal Groups... Rhythm and Blues	1957	375.00	750.00	1,500.
-- Also includes tracks by the Medallions, Don Julian and the Meadowlarks, and the Dootones. Flat maroon label.					
❑ DTL-204 [M]	The Best Vocal Groups... Rhythm and Blues	195?	125.00	250.00	500.00
-- As above; glossy maroon label					

PENNY AND JEAN
RCA VICTOR

❑ LPM-2244 [M]	Two for the Road	1961	5.00	10.00	20.00
❑ LSP-2244 [S]	Two for the Road	1961	6.25	12.50	25.00

PENNY, HANK
AUDIO LAB

❑ AL-1508 [M]	Hank Penny Sings	1959	50.00	100.00	200.00

PENTANGLE, THE
REPRISE

❑ RS 6315	The Pentangle	1968	5.00	10.00	20.00
-- With "W7" and "r:" logos on two-tone orange label					
❑ 2RS 6334 [(2)]	Sweet Child	1969	6.25	12.50	25.00
-- With "W7" and "r:" logos on two-tone orange label					
❑ RS 6372	Basket of Light	1969	5.00	10.00	20.00
-- With "W7" and "r:" logos on two-tone orange label					

PEOPLE
Also see LARRY NORMAN.
CAPITOL

❑ ST-151	Both Sides of People	1969	10.00	20.00	40.00
❑ ST 2924	I Love You	1968	10.00	20.00	40.00

PARAMOUNT

❑ PAS-5013	There Are People	1970	5.00	10.00	20.00

PEPPER, JIM
EMBRYO

❑ SD-731 [(2)]	Pepper's Powwow	196?	10.00	20.00	40.00

PEPPERMINT RAINBOW, THE
DECCA

❑ DL 75129	Will You Be Staying After Sunday	1969	5.00	10.00	20.00

PEPPERMINT TROLLEY COMPANY, THE
ACTA

❑ 38007	The Peppermint Trolley Company	1968	6.25	12.50	25.00

PEPPERMINT, DANNY
CARLTON

❑ LP-20,001 [M]	Twist with Danny Peppermint	1962	10.00	20.00	40.00
❑ STLP-20,001 [S]	Twist with Danny Peppermint	1962	12.50	25.00	50.00

PERE UBU
BLANK

❑ 001	The Modern Dance	1978	10.00	20.00	40.00

CHRYSALIS

❑ CHR 1207	Dub Housing	1979	6.25	12.50	25.00

ROUGH TRADE

❑ ROUGH US 4	The Art of Walking	1980	10.00	20.00	40.00
-- First 1,800 were incorrectly mastered					
❑ ROUGH US 4	The Art of Walking	1980	5.00	10.00	20.00
-- Revised version: Vocal added on "Arabia"; "Miles" is shortened					
❑ ROUGH US 7	The Modern Dance	1981	5.00	10.00	20.00
-- Reissue of Blank 001					
❑ ROUGH US 10	390 Degrees of Simulated Stereo	1981	5.00	10.00	20.00
❑ ROUGH US 21	The Song of the Bailing Man	1982	5.00	10.00	20.00

PERHACS, LINDA
KAPP

❑ KS-3636	Parallelograms	1970	50.00	100.00	200.00

PERKINS, CARL
COLUMBIA

❑ CL 1234 [DJ]	Whole Lotta Shakin'	1958	200.00	400.00	800.00
-- White label promo					
❑ CL 1234 [M]	Whole Lotta Shakin'	1958	100.00	200.00	400.00
❑ CS 9833	Carl Perkins' Greatest Hits	1969	6.25	12.50	25.00
-- Red "360 Sound Stereo" label					

Number	Title	Yr	VG	VG+	NM
❑ CS 9931	Carl Perkins On Top	1969	6.25	12.50	25.00
-- Red "360 Sound Stereo" label					
❑ CS 9981	Boppin' the Blues	1970	6.25	12.50	25.00
-- Red "360 Sound Stereo" label					
DESIGN					
❑ DLP-611 [M]	Tennessee	1963	7.50	15.00	30.00
❑ SDLP-611 [R]	Tennessee	1963	5.00	10.00	20.00
DOLLIE					
❑ 4001	Country Boy's Dream	1967	7.50	15.00	30.00
❑ ST-91428	Country Boy's Dream	1967	10.00	20.00	40.00
-- Capitol Record Club edition					
SUN					
❑ SLP-1225 [M]	The Dance Album of Carl Perkins	1957	300.00	600.00	1,200.
❑ SLP-1225 [M]	Teen Beat -- The Best of Carl Perkins	1961	125.00	250.00	500.00
-- Reissue with new title					

PERKINS, TONY

Number	Title	Yr	VG	VG+	NM
EPIC					
❑ LN 3394 [M]	Tony Perkins	1957	12.50	25.00	50.00
RCA VICTOR					
❑ LPM-1679 [M]	From My Heart	1958	10.00	20.00	40.00
❑ LSP-1679 [S]	From My Heart	1958	15.00	30.00	60.00
❑ LPM-1853 [M]	On a Rainy Afternoon	1958	10.00	20.00	40.00
❑ LSP-1853 [S]	On a Rainy Afternoon	1958	15.00	30.00	60.00

PERREY, JEAN-JACQUES

Number	Title	Yr	VG	VG+	NM
PICKWICK					
❑ PC-3160 [M]	The Happy Moog	196?	5.00	10.00	20.00
❑ SPC-3160 [S]	The Happy Moog	196?	6.25	12.50	25.00
-- Silver label					
VANGUARD					
❑ VSD-6549	Moog Indigo	1969	10.00	20.00	40.00
❑ VSD-79286	The Amazing New Electronic Pop Sound of Jean-Jacques Perrey	1968	10.00	20.00	40.00

PERREY-KINGSLEY

Also see GERSHON KINGSLEY; JEAN-JACQUES PERREY.

Number	Title	Yr	VG	VG+	NM
VANGUARD					
❑ VSD-71/72 [(2)]	The Essential Perrey & Kingsley	197?	7.50	15.00	30.00
❑ VSD-6525	Kaleidoscopic Vibrations	1969	7.50	15.00	30.00
❑ VRS-9222 [M]	The In Sound from Way Out!	1966	7.50	15.00	30.00
❑ VSD-79222 [S]	The In Sound from Way Out!	1966	10.00	20.00	40.00

PERRINE, PEP

Number	Title	Yr	VG	VG+	NM
HIDEOUT					
❑ 1003 [M]	Pep Perrine Live and In Person	196?	30.00	60.00	120.00

PERSUADERS, THE

Soul group.

Number	Title	Yr	VG	VG+	NM
ATCO					
❑ SD 7021	The Persuaders	1973	5.00	10.00	20.00
❑ SD 7046	Best Thing That Ever Happened to Me	1974	5.00	10.00	20.00
WIN OR LOSE					
❑ SD 33-387	Thin Line Between Love and Hate	1972	6.25	12.50	25.00

PERSUADERS, THE

Surf group.

Number	Title	Yr	VG	VG+	NM
SATURN					
❑ SAT-5000 [M]	Surfer's Nightmare	1963	75.00	150.00	300.00
❑ SATS-5000 [S]	Surfer's Nightmare	1963	100.00	200.00	400.00

PERSUASIONS, THE

Number	Title	Yr	VG	VG+	NM
CAPITOL					
❑ ST-791	We Came to Play	1971	6.25	12.50	25.00
❑ ST-872	Street Corner Symphony	1972	6.25	12.50	25.00
❑ ST-11101	Spread the Word	1972	6.25	12.50	25.00
CATAMOUNT					
❑ 905	Stardust	197?	10.00	20.00	40.00
REPRISE					
❑ RS 6394	Acapella	1970	7.50	15.00	30.00

PET SHOP BOYS

Number	Title	Yr	VG	VG+	NM
EMI					
❑ E1-34023 [(3)]	Alternative	1995	10.00	20.00	40.00
-- Box set pressed in UK for import into the US (regular UK pressings have gatefold sleeves)					
EMI MANHATTAN					
❑ SPRO 04233 [(3) DJ]	Special Limited Edition: Introspective Club Mixes	1988	10.00	20.00	40.00
-- Promo-only set of three 12" records of remixes					

Number	Title	Yr	VG	VG+	NM
❑ E1-90263 [(2)]	Actually	1988	5.00	10.00	20.00
-- Limited double-LP set with extra record of remixes					

PETER AND GORDON

Number	Title	Yr	VG	VG+	NM
CAPITOL					
❑ ST 2115 [S]	A World Without Love	1964	6.25	12.50	25.00
❑ T 2115 [M]	A World Without Love	1964	5.00	10.00	20.00
❑ ST 2220 [S]	I Don't Want to See You Again	1964	6.25	12.50	25.00
❑ T 2220 [M]	I Don't Want to See You Again	1964	5.00	10.00	20.00
❑ ST 2324 [S]	I Go to Pieces	1965	6.25	12.50	25.00
❑ T 2324 [M]	I Go to Pieces	1965	5.00	10.00	20.00
❑ ST 2368 [S]	True Love Ways	1965	6.25	12.50	25.00
❑ T 2368 [M]	True Love Ways	1965	5.00	10.00	20.00
❑ ST 2430 [S]	Peter and Gordon Sing the Hits of Nashville	1966	6.25	12.50	25.00
❑ T 2430 [M]	Peter and Gordon Sing the Hits of Nashville	1966	5.00	10.00	20.00
❑ ST 2477 [P]	Woman	1966	6.25	12.50	25.00
-- "Woman" is rechanneled					
❑ T 2477 [M]	Woman	1966	5.00	10.00	20.00
❑ ST 2664 [S]	Lady Godiva	1967	5.00	10.00	20.00
❑ ST 2729 [S]	Knight in Rusty Armour	1967	5.00	10.00	20.00
❑ ST 2747 [S]	In London for Tea	1967	5.00	10.00	20.00
❑ ST 2882 [S]	Hot, Cold and Custard	1968	6.25	12.50	25.00

PETER, PAUL AND MARY

Number	Title	Yr	VG	VG+	NM
WARNER BROS.					
❑ W 1449 [M]	Peter, Paul and Mary	1962	5.00	10.00	20.00
❑ WS 1449 [S]	Peter, Paul and Mary	1962	6.25	12.50	25.00
-- Gold label					
❑ W 1473 [M]	(Moving)	1963	5.00	10.00	20.00
❑ WS 1473 [S]	(Moving)	1963	6.25	12.50	25.00
-- Gold label					
❑ W 1507 [M]	In the Wind	1963	5.00	10.00	20.00
❑ WS 1507 [S]	In the Wind	1963	6.25	12.50	25.00
❑ 2W 1555 [(2) M]	Peter, Paul and Mary In Concert	1964	6.25	12.50	25.00
❑ 2WS 1555 [(2) S]	Peter, Paul and Mary In Concert	1964	7.50	15.00	30.00
-- Gold labels					
❑ W 1589 [M]	A Song Will Rise	1965	5.00	10.00	20.00
❑ WS 1589 [S]	A Song Will Rise	1965	6.25	12.50	25.00
-- Gold label					
❑ W 1615 [M]	See What Tomorrow Brings	1965	5.00	10.00	20.00
❑ WS 1615 [S]	See What Tomorrow Brings	1965	6.25	12.50	25.00
-- Gold label					
❑ W 1648 [M]	Peter, Paul and Mary Album	1966	5.00	10.00	20.00
❑ WS 1648 [S]	Peter, Paul and Mary Album	1966	6.25	12.50	25.00
-- Gold label					
❑ W 1700 [M]	Album 1700	1967	6.25	12.50	25.00
-- Gold label					
❑ WS 1700 [S]	Album 1700	1967	6.25	12.50	25.00
-- Gold label					

PETERS, BROCK

Number	Title	Yr	VG	VG+	NM
UNITED ARTISTS					
❑ UAL-3041 [M]	Sing'a Man	1960	7.50	15.00	30.00
❑ UAL-3062 [M]	Brock Peters at the Village Gate	1961	6.25	12.50	25.00
❑ UAL-3127 [M]	Brock Peters	1963	5.00	10.00	20.00
❑ UAS-6041 [S]	Sing'a Man	1960	10.00	20.00	40.00
❑ UAS-6062 [S]	Brock Peters at the Village Gate	1961	7.50	15.00	30.00
❑ UAS-6127 [S]	Brock Peters	1963	6.25	12.50	25.00

PETERS, ROBERTA

Number	Title	Yr	VG	VG+	NM
RCA VICTOR RED SEAL					
❑ LSC-2379 [S]	Roberta Peters in Recital	1960	5.00	10.00	20.00
-- Original with "shaded dog" label					

PETERSEN, PAUL

Number	Title	Yr	VG	VG+	NM
COLPIX					
❑ CP-429 [M]	Lollipops and Roses	1962	12.50	25.00	50.00
❑ SCP-429 [S]	Lollipops and Roses	1962	15.00	30.00	60.00
❑ CP-442 [M]	My Dad	1963	12.50	25.00	50.00
❑ SCP-442 [S]	My Dad	1963	15.00	30.00	60.00

PETERSON, OSCAR

Number	Title	Yr	VG	VG+	NM
CLEF					
❑ MGC-106 [10]	Oscar Peterson Piano Solos	1951	25.00	50.00	100.00
-- Reissue of Mercury 25024					
❑ MGC-107 [10]	Oscar Peterson at Carnegie Hall	1951	25.00	50.00	100.00
❑ MGC-110 [10]	Oscar Peterson Collates	1952	25.00	50.00	100.00
❑ MGC-116 [10]	The Oscar Peterson Quartet	1952	25.00	50.00	100.00
❑ MGC-119 [10]	Oscar Peterson Plays Pretty	1952	25.00	50.00	100.00
❑ MGC-127 [10]	Oscar Peterson Collates No. 2	1953	20.00	40.00	80.00
❑ MGC-145 [10]	Oscar Peterson Sings	1954	20.00	40.00	80.00
❑ MGC-155 [10]	Oscar Peterson Plays Pretty No. 2	1954	20.00	40.00	80.00

Number	Title	Yr	VG	VG+	NM
❏ MGC-168 [10]	The Oscar Peterson Quartet No. 2	1954	20.00	40.00	80.00
❏ MGC-603 [M]	Oscar Peterson Plays Cole Porter	1953	15.00	30.00	60.00
❏ MGC-604 [M]	Oscar Peterson Plays Irving Berlin	1953	15.00	30.00	60.00
❏ MGC-605 [M]	Oscar Peterson Plays George Gershwin	1953	15.00	30.00	60.00
❏ MGC-606 [M]	Oscar Peterson Plays Duke Ellington	1953	15.00	30.00	60.00
❏ MGC-623 [M]	Oscar Peterson Plays Jerome Kern	1954	12.50	25.00	50.00
❏ MGC-624 [M]	Oscar Peterson Plays Richard Rodgers	1954	12.50	25.00	50.00
❏ MGC-625 [M]	Oscar Peterson Plays Vincent Youmans	1954	12.50	25.00	50.00
❏ MGC-648 [M]	Oscar Peterson Plays Harry Warren	1955	12.50	25.00	50.00
❏ MGC-649 [M]	Oscar Peterson Plays Harold Arlen	1955	12.50	25.00	50.00
❏ MGC-650 [M]	Oscar Peterson Plays Jimmy McHugh	1955	12.50	25.00	50.00
❏ MGC-688 [M]	The Oscar Peterson Quartet	1956	12.50	25.00	50.00
-- Reissue of 116					
❏ MGC-694 [M]	Recital by Oscar Peterson	1956	12.50	25.00	50.00
❏ MGC-695 [M]	Nostalgic Memories by Oscar Peterson	1956	12.50	25.00	50.00
❏ MGC-696 [M]	Tenderly -- Music by Oscar Peterson	1956	12.50	25.00	50.00
❏ MGC-697 [M]	Keyboard Music by Oscar Peterson	1956	12.50	25.00	50.00
❏ MGC-698 [M]	An Evening with the Oscar Peterson Duo/Quartet	1956	12.50	25.00	50.00
❏ MGC-708 [M]	Oscar Peterson Plays Count Basie	1956	12.50	25.00	50.00

DCC COMPACT CLASSICS

Number	Title	Yr	VG	VG+	NM
❏ LPZ-2021	West Side Story	1996	6.25	12.50	25.00
-- Audiophile vinyl					

LIMELIGHT

Number	Title	Yr	VG	VG+	NM
❏ LM-82044 [M]	Soul Español	1967	5.00	10.00	20.00
❏ LS-86010 [S]	Canadiana Suite	1965	5.00	10.00	20.00
❏ LS-86023 [S]	Eloquence	1965	5.00	10.00	20.00
❏ LS-86029 [S]	With Respect to Nat	1966	5.00	10.00	20.00

MERCURY

Number	Title	Yr	VG	VG+	NM
❏ MG-20975 [M]	Oscar Peterson Trio + One	1964	6.25	12.50	25.00
❏ MG-25024 [10]	Oscar Peterson Piano Solos	1950	37.50	75.00	150.00
❏ SR-60975 [S]	Oscar Peterson Trio + One	1964	7.50	15.00	30.00

MOBILE FIDELITY

Number	Title	Yr	VG	VG+	NM
❏ 1-243	Very Tall	1995	5.00	10.00	20.00
-- Audiophile vinyl					

RCA VICTOR

Number	Title	Yr	VG	VG+	NM
❏ LPT-3006 [10]	This Is Oscar Peterson	1952	30.00	60.00	120.00

VERVE

Number	Title	Yr	VG	VG+	NM
❏ MGV-2002 [M]	In a Romantic Mood -- Oscar Peterson with Strings	1956	10.00	20.00	40.00
❏ V-2002 [M]	In a Romantic Mood -- Oscar Peterson with Strings	1961	5.00	10.00	20.00
❏ MGV-2004 [M]	Pastel Moods by Oscar Peterson	1956	10.00	20.00	40.00
❏ V-2004 [M]	Pastel Moods by Oscar Peterson	1961	5.00	10.00	20.00
❏ MGV-2012 [M]	Romance -- The Vocal Styling of Oscar Peterson	1956	10.00	20.00	40.00
-- Reissue of Clef 145					
❏ V-2012 [M]	Romance -- The Vocal Styling of Oscar Peterson	1961	5.00	10.00	20.00
❏ MGV-2044 [M]	Recital by Oscar Peterson	1957	10.00	20.00	40.00
-- Reissue of Clef 694					
❏ V-2044 [M]	Recital by Oscar Peterson	1961	5.00	10.00	20.00
❏ MGV-2045 [M]	Nostalgic Memories by Oscar Peterson	1957	10.00	20.00	40.00
-- Reissue of Clef 695					
❏ V-2045 [M]	Nostalgic Memories by Oscar Peterson	1961	5.00	10.00	20.00
❏ MGV-2046 [M]	Tenderly -- Music by Oscar Peterson	1957	10.00	20.00	40.00
-- Reissue of Clef 696					
❏ V-2046 [M]	Tenderly -- Music by Oscar Peterson	1961	5.00	10.00	20.00
❏ MGV-2047 [M]	Keyboard Music by Oscar Peterson	1957	10.00	20.00	40.00
-- Reissue of Clef 697					
❏ V-2047 [M]	Keyboard Music by Oscar	1961	5.00	10.00	20.00
❏ MGV-2048 [M]	An Evening with Oscar Peterson	1957	10.00	20.00	40.00
-- Reissue of Clef 698					
❏ V-2048 [M]	An Evening with Oscar Peterson	1961	5.00	10.00	20.00
❏ MGV-2052 [M]	Oscar Peterson Plays The Cole Porter Songbook	1957	10.00	20.00	40.00
-- Reissue of Clef 603					
❏ V-2052 [M]	Oscar Peterson Plays The Cole Porter Songbook	1961	5.00	10.00	20.00
❏ MGV-2053 [M]	Oscar Peterson Plays The Irving Berlin Songbook	1957	10.00	20.00	40.00
-- Reissue of Clef 604					
❏ V-2053 [M]	Oscar Peterson Plays The Irving Berlin Songbook	1961	5.00	10.00	20.00
❏ MGV-2054 [M]	Oscar Peterson Plays The George Gershwin Songbook	1957	10.00	20.00	40.00
-- Reissue of Clef 605					
❏ V-2054 [M]	Oscar Peterson Plays The George Gershwin Songbook	1961	5.00	10.00	20.00
❏ MGV-2055 [M]	Oscar Peterson Plays The Duke Ellington Songbook	1957	10.00	20.00	40.00
-- Reissue of Clef 606					
❏ V-2055 [M]	Oscar Peterson Plays The Duke Ellington Songbook	1961	5.00	10.00	20.00
❏ MGV-2056 [M]	Oscar Peterson Plays The Jerome Kern Songbook	1957	10.00	20.00	40.00
-- Reissue of Clef 623					
❏ V-2056 [M]	Oscar Peterson Plays The Jerome Kern Songbook	1961	5.00	10.00	20.00
❏ MGV-2057 [M]	Oscar Peterson Plays The Richard Rodgers Songbook	1957	10.00	20.00	40.00
-- Reissue of Clef 624					
❏ V-2057 [M]	Oscar Peterson Plays The Richard Rodgers Songbook	1961	5.00	10.00	20.00
❏ V-2058 [M]	Oscar Peterson Plays The Vincent Youmans Songbook	1961	5.00	10.00	20.00
❏ MGV-2059 [M]	Oscar Peterson Plays The Harry Warren Songbook	1957	10.00	20.00	40.00
-- Reissue of Clef 648					
❏ V-2059 [M]	Oscar Peterson Plays The Harry Warren Songbook	1961	5.00	10.00	20.00
❏ MGV-2060 [M]	Oscar Peterson Plays The Harold Arlen Songbook	1957	10.00	20.00	40.00
-- Reissue of Clef 649					
❏ V-2060 [M]	Oscar Peterson Plays The Harold Arlen Songbook	1961	5.00	10.00	20.00
❏ MGV-2061 [M]	Oscar Peterson Plays The Jimmy McHugh Songbook	1957	10.00	20.00	40.00
-- Reissue of Clef 650					
❏ V-2061 [M]	Oscar Peterson Plays The Jimmy McHugh Songbook	1961	5.00	10.00	20.00
❏ MGV-2079 [M]	Soft Sands	1957	10.00	20.00	40.00
❏ V-2079 [M]	Soft Sands	1961	5.00	10.00	20.00
❏ MGV-2119 [M]	Oscar Peterson Plays "My Fair Lady"	1958	10.00	20.00	40.00
❏ V-2119 [M]	Oscar Peterson Plays "My Fair Lady"	1961	5.00	10.00	20.00
❏ MGVS-6060 [S]	Oscar Peterson Plays "My Fair Lady"	1960	7.50	15.00	30.00
❏ MGVS-6069 [S]	The Oscar Peterson Trio with the Modern Jazz Quartet at the Opera House	1960	7.50	15.00	30.00
❏ MGVS-6071 [S]	Songs for a Swingin' Affair -- A Jazz Portrait of Sinatra	1960	10.00	20.00	40.00
❏ MGVS-6083 [S]	Oscar Peterson Plays The Cole Porter Songbook	1960	7.50	15.00	30.00
❏ MGVS-6084 [S]	Oscar Peterson Plays The Irving Berlin Songbook	1960	7.50	15.00	30.00
❏ MGVS-6085 [S]	Oscar Peterson Plays The George Gershwin Songbook	1960	7.50	15.00	30.00
❏ MGVS-6086 [S]	Oscar Peterson Plays The Duke Ellington Songbook	1960	7.50	15.00	30.00
❏ MGVS-6087 [S]	Oscar Peterson Plays The Jerome Kern Songbook	1960	7.50	15.00	30.00
❏ MGVS-6088 [S]	Oscar Peterson Plays The Richard Rodgers Songbook	1960	7.50	15.00	30.00
❏ MGVS-6090 [S]	Oscar Peterson Plays The Harry Warren Songbook	1960	7.50	15.00	30.00
❏ MGVS-6091 [S]	Oscar Peterson Plays The Harold Arlen Songbook	1960	7.50	15.00	30.00
❏ MGVS-6092 [S]	Oscar Peterson Plays The Jimmy McHugh Songbook	1960	7.50	15.00	30.00
❏ MGVS-6119 [S]	Swinging Brass with the Oscar Peterson Trio	1960	7.50	15.00	30.00
❏ MGV-8024 [M]	The Oscar Peterson Trio at the Stratford Shakespearean Festival	1957	10.00	20.00	40.00
❏ V-8024 [M]	The Oscar Peterson Trio at the Stratford Shakespearean Festival	1961	5.00	10.00	20.00
❏ MGV-8072 [M]	The Oscar Peterson Quartet No. 1	1957	10.00	20.00	40.00
❏ V-8072 [M]	The Oscar Peterson Quartet No. 1	1961	5.00	10.00	20.00
❏ MGV-8092 [M]	Oscar Peterson Plays Count Basie	1957	10.00	20.00	40.00
-- Reissue of Clef 708					
❏ V-8092 [M]	Oscar Peterson Plays Count Basie	1961	5.00	10.00	20.00
❏ MGV-8239 [M]	The Oscar Peterson Trio with Sonny Stitt, Roy Eldredge and Jo Jones at Newport	1958	10.00	20.00	40.00
❏ V-8239 [M]	The Oscar Peterson Trio with Sonny Stitt, Roy Eldredge and Jo Jones at Newport	1961	5.00	10.00	20.00
❏ MGV-8268 [M]	The Oscar Peterson Trio at the Concertgebouw	1958	10.00	20.00	40.00
❏ V-8268 [M]	The Oscar Peterson Trio at the Concertgebouw	1961	5.00	10.00	20.00
❏ MGV-8269 [M]	The Oscar Peterson Trio with the Modern Jazz Quartet at the Opera House	1958	10.00	20.00	40.00
❏ V-8269 [M]	The Oscar Peterson Trio with the Modern Jazz Quartet at the Opera House	1961	5.00	10.00	20.00
❏ MGV-8287 [M]	A Night on the Town	1958	10.00	20.00	40.00

Number	Title	Yr	VG	VG+	NM
❑ V-8287 [M]	A Night on the Town	1961	5.00	10.00	20.00
❑ MGV-8334 [M]	Songs for a Swingin' Affair -- A Jazz Portrait of Sinatra	1959	12.50	25.00	50.00
❑ V-8334 [M]	Songs for a Swingin' Affair -- A Jazz Portrait of Sinatra	1961	5.00	10.00	20.00
❑ MGV-8340 [M]	Porgy and Bess	1959	10.00	20.00	40.00
❑ V-8340 [M]	Porgy and Bess	1961	5.00	10.00	20.00
❑ MGV-8351 [M]	The Jazz Soul of Oscar Peterson	1959	10.00	20.00	40.00
❑ V-8351 [M]	The Jazz Soul of Oscar Peterson	1961	5.00	10.00	20.00
❑ MGV-8364 [M]	Swinging Brass with the Oscar Peterson Trio	1959	10.00	20.00	40.00
❑ V-8364 [M]	Swinging Brass with the Oscar Peterson Trio	1961	5.00	10.00	20.00
❑ MGV-8366 [M]	The Music from "Fiorello!"	1960	10.00	20.00	40.00
❑ V-8366 [M]	The Music from "Fiorello!"	1961	5.00	10.00	20.00
❑ MGV-8368 [M]	The Oscar Peterson Trio at J.A.T.P.	1960	10.00	20.00	40.00
❑ V-8368 [M]	The Oscar Peterson Trio at J.A.T.P.	1961	5.00	10.00	20.00
❑ V-8420 [M]	The Trio -- Live from Chicago	1961	6.25	12.50	25.00
❑ V6-8420 [S]	The Trio -- Live from Chicago	1961	7.50	15.00	30.00
❑ V-8429 [M]	Very Tall	1962	6.25	12.50	25.00
❑ V6-8429 [S]	Very Tall	1962	7.50	15.00	30.00
❑ V-8454 [M]	West Side Story	1962	6.25	12.50	25.00
❑ V6-8454 [S]	West Side Story	1962	7.50	15.00	30.00
❑ V-8476 [M]	Bursting Out with the All Star Big Band!	1962	6.25	12.50	25.00
❑ V6-8476 [S]	Bursting Out with the All Star Big Band!	1962	7.50	15.00	30.00
❑ V-8490 [M]	The Sound of the Trio	1962	6.25	12.50	25.00
❑ V6-8490 [S]	The Sound of the Trio	1962	7.50	15.00	30.00
❑ V-8492 [M]	The Modern Jazz Quartet and the Oscar Peterson Trio at the Opera House	1962	5.00	10.00	20.00
-- Reissue of 8269					
❑ V6-8492 [S]	The Modern Jazz Quartet and the Oscar Peterson Trio at the Opera House	1962	5.00	10.00	20.00
-- Reissue of 8269					
❑ V-8516 [M]	Affinity	1963	6.25	12.50	25.00
❑ V6-8516 [S]	Affinity	1963	7.50	15.00	30.00
❑ V-8538 [M]	Night Train	1963	6.25	12.50	25.00
❑ V6-8538 [S]	Night Train	1963	7.50	15.00	30.00
❑ V-8562 [M]	The Oscar Peterson Trio with Nelson Riddle	1963	6.25	12.50	25.00
❑ V6-8562 [S]	The Oscar Peterson Trio with Nelson Riddle	1963	7.50	15.00	30.00
❑ V6-8581 [S]	Oscar Peterson Plays "My Fair Lady"	1964	5.00	10.00	20.00
❑ V6-8591 [S]	The Oscar Peterson Trio Plays	1964	5.00	10.00	20.00
❑ V6-8606 [S]	We Get Requests	1965	5.00	10.00	20.00
❑ V6-8660 [S]	Put On a Happy Face	1966	5.00	10.00	20.00
❑ V6-8681 [S]	Something Warm	1966	5.00	10.00	20.00
❑ V-8740 [M]	Night Train, Volume 2	1967	5.00	10.00	20.00

PETERSON, RAY
DECCA

Number	Title	Yr	VG	VG+	NM
❑ DL 75307	Ray Peterson Country	1971	5.00	10.00	20.00

MGM

Number	Title	Yr	VG	VG+	NM
❑ E-4250 [M]	The Very Best of Ray Peterson	1964	6.25	12.50	25.00
❑ SE-4250 [S]	The Very Best of Ray Peterson	1964	7.50	15.00	30.00
❑ E-4277 [M]	The Other Side of Ray Peterson	1965	6.25	12.50	25.00
❑ SE-4277 [S]	The Other Side of Ray Peterson	1965	7.50	15.00	30.00

RCA VICTOR

Number	Title	Yr	VG	VG+	NM
❑ LPM-2297 [M]	Tell Laura I Love Her	1960	25.00	50.00	100.00
❑ LSP-2297 [S]	Tell Laura I Love Her	1960	37.50	75.00	150.00

UNI

Number	Title	Yr	VG	VG+	NM
❑ 73078	The Best of Ray Peterson	1969	5.00	10.00	20.00

PETTY, NORMAN, TRIO
COLUMBIA

Number	Title	Yr	VG	VG+	NM
❑ CL 1092 [M]	Moondreams	1958	37.50	75.00	150.00

TOP RANK

Number	Title	Yr	VG	VG+	NM
❑ R-639 [M]	Petty for Your Thoughts	1960	7.50	15.00	30.00
❑ RS-639 [S]	Petty for Your Thoughts	1960	10.00	20.00	40.00

VIK

Number	Title	Yr	VG	VG+	NM
❑ LX-1073 [M]	Corsage	1957	17.50	35.00	70.00

PETTY, TOM, AND THE HEARTBREAKERS
SHELTER

Number	Title	Yr	VG	VG+	NM
❑ TP-12677 [DJ]	Official Live 'Leg	1977	10.00	20.00	40.00
-- Promo-only live album with letter to radio (has been counterfeited)					
❑ DA-52029 [DJ]	You're Gonna Get It!	1978	6.25	12.50	25.00
-- Promo only on red vinyl					

WARNER BROS.

Number	Title	Yr	VG	VG+	NM
❑ 45759 [(2)]	Wildflowers	1994	5.00	10.00	20.00
❑ 47294 [(2)]	Echo	1999	5.00	10.00	20.00

PHANTOM, THE
CAPITOL

Number	Title	Yr	VG	VG+	NM
❑ ST-11313	The Phantom's Divine Comedy, Part One	1974	15.00	30.00	60.00

PHAPHNER
DRAGON

Number	Title	Yr	VG	VG+	NM
❑ LP-101	Overdrive	1971	1,000.	2,000.	3,000.

PHILBIN, REGIS
MERCURY

Number	Title	Yr	VG	VG+	NM
❑ SR-61169	It's Time for Regis!	1968	6.25	12.50	25.00

PHILHARMONIA HUNGARICA (ANTAL DORATI, COND.)
MERCURY LIVING PRESENCE

Number	Title	Yr	VG	VG+	NM
❑ SR 90179 [S]	Kodaly: Dances of Galanta; Marosszek Dances; Bartok-Weiner: Two Romanian Dances	196?	15.00	30.00	60.00
-- Maroon label, no "Vendor: Mercury Record Corporation"					
❑ SR 90183 [S]	Bartok: Dance Suite; Deux Portraits; Mikrokosmos	196?	37.50	75.00	150.00
-- Maroon label, no "Vendor: Mercury Record Corporation"					
❑ SR 90190 [S]	Wienerwalzer Paprika	196?	5.00	10.00	20.00
-- Maroon label, no "Vendor: Mercury Record Corporation"					
❑ SR 90199 [S]	Respighi: Ancient Airs and Dances, Suites 1-3	196?	12.50	25.00	50.00
-- Maroon label, no "Vendor: Mercury Record Corporation"					
❑ SR 90199 [S]	Respighi: Ancient Airs and Dances, Suites 1-3	196?	12.50	25.00	50.00
-- Maroon label, with "Vendor: Mercury Record Corporation"					
❑ SR 90199 [S]	Respighi: Ancient Airs and Dances, Suites 1-3	196?	10.00	20.00	40.00
-- Third edition: Dark red (not maroon) label					
❑ SR 90200 [S]	Tchaikovsky: Serenade in C; Arensky: Tchaikovsky Variations	196?	12.50	25.00	50.00
-- Maroon label, no "Vendor: Mercury Record Corporation"					
❑ SR 90208 [S]	Haydn: Symphonies 94 and 103	196?	10.00	20.00	40.00
-- Maroon label, no "Vendor: Mercury Record Corporation"					

PHILLIPS, BILL
DECCA

Number	Title	Yr	VG	VG+	NM
❑ DL 4792 [M]	Put It Off Until Tomorrow	1966	7.50	15.00	30.00
❑ DL 4897 [M]	Bill Phillips' Style	1967	7.50	15.00	30.00
❑ DL 74792 [M]	Put It Off Until Tomorrow	1966	10.00	20.00	40.00
❑ DL 74897 [S]	Bill Phillips' Style	1967	6.25	12.50	25.00
❑ DL 75022	Country Action	1968	5.00	10.00	20.00
❑ DL 75182	Little Boy Sad	1970	5.00	10.00	20.00

HARMONY

Number	Title	Yr	VG	VG+	NM
❑ HL 7309 [M]	Bill Phillips' Best	1964	5.00	10.00	20.00

PHILLIPS, ESTHER
ATLANTIC

Number	Title	Yr	VG	VG+	NM
❑ SD 1565	Burnin'	1970	6.25	12.50	25.00
❑ 8102 [M]	And I Love Him	1965	12.50	25.00	50.00
-- Cover has a pink Cupid on it					
❑ SD 8102 [S]	And I Love Him	1965	20.00	40.00	80.00
-- Cover has a pink Cupid on it					
❑ 8102 [M]	And I Love Him	1966	7.50	15.00	30.00
-- Cover has a black photo on it					
❑ SD 8102 [S]	And I Love Him	1966	10.00	20.00	40.00
-- Cover has a black photo on it					
❑ 8122 [M]	Esther	1966	7.50	15.00	30.00
❑ SD 8122 [S]	Esther	1966	10.00	20.00	40.00
❑ 8130 [M]	The Country Side of Esther Phillips	1966	7.50	15.00	30.00
❑ SD 8130 [S]	The Country Side of Esther Phillips	1966	10.00	20.00	40.00

KING

Number	Title	Yr	VG	VG+	NM
❑ 622 [M]	Memory Lane	1959	1,000.	2,000.	4,000.

LENOX

Number	Title	Yr	VG	VG+	NM
❑ 227 [M]	Release Me	1962	25.00	50.00	100.00
❑ S-227 [S]	Release Me	1962	50.00	100.00	200.00

PHILLIPS, GENE
CROWN

Number	Title	Yr	VG	VG+	NM
❑ CLP-5375 [M]	Gene Phillips and the Rockers	1963	7.50	15.00	30.00

PHILLIPS, STU
CAPITOL

Number	Title	Yr	VG	VG+	NM
❑ ST 2356 [S]	Feels Like Lovin'	1965	7.50	15.00	30.00
❑ T 2356 [M]	Feels Like Lovin'	1965	6.25	12.50	25.00

RCA VICTOR

Number	Title	Yr	VG	VG+	NM
❑ LPM-3619 [M]	Singin' Stu Phillips	1966	5.00	10.00	20.00
❑ LSP-3619 [S]	Singin' Stu Phillips	1966	6.25	12.50	25.00

Number	Title	Yr	VG	VG+	NM
❏ LPM-3717 [M]	Grassroots Country	1967	7.50	15.00	30.00
❏ LSP-3717 [S]	Grassroots Country	1967	6.25	12.50	25.00
❏ LSP-4012	Our Last Rendezvous	1968	6.25	12.50	25.00

PHILLIPS, WARREN, AND THE ROCKETS
PARROT
❏ PAS 71044	Rocked Out	1970	7.50	15.00	30.00

PHILOSOPHERS, THE
PHILO
❏ 1001	After Sundown	1969	37.50	75.00	150.00

PHIPPS FAMILY, THE
STARDAY
❏ SLP-139 [M]	The Phipps Family Sings the Most Requested Sacred Songs of the Carter Family	1961	10.00	20.00	40.00
❏ SLP-195 [M]	Old Time Pickin' and Singin'	1962	7.50	15.00	30.00
❏ SLP-248 [M]	Echoes of the Carter Family	1963	7.50	15.00	30.00

PHLUPH
VERVE
❏ V6-5054	Phluph	1968	7.50	15.00	30.00

PIAF, EDITH
CAPITOL
❏ DTCL 2953 [(3)]	The Edith Piaf Deluxe Set	1968	7.50	15.00	30.00
❏ T 10210 [M]	Piaf	1959	6.25	12.50	25.00
❏ ST 10283 [S]	Piaf of Paris	1961	5.00	10.00	20.00
❏ ST 10295 [S]	Potpourri Par Piaf	1962	5.00	10.00	20.00
❏ ST 10348 [S]	Piaf and Sarapo at the Bobido	1963	5.00	10.00	20.00
❏ ST 10368 [S]	Piaf at the Olympia	1964	5.00	10.00	20.00

COLUMBIA
❏ CL 898 [M]	La Vie En Rose	1956	10.00	20.00	40.00
❏ CL 6223 [10]	Encore Parisiennes	1952	12.50	25.00	50.00

DECCA
❏ DL 6004 [10]	Chansons de Cafes du Paris	1951	15.00	30.00	60.00

PHILIPS
❏ PCC 208 [M]	Adieu, Edith Piaf, Little Sparrow	1964	5.00	10.00	20.00

PIANO RED
GROOVE
❏ LG-1002 [M]	Piano Red In Concert	1956	150.00	300.00	600.00

KING
❏ KS-1117	Happiness Is Piano Red	1970	5.00	10.00	20.00

PIATIGORSKI, GREGOR
RCA VICTOR RED SEAL
❏ LSC-2490 [S]	Dvorak: Cello Concerto	1961	7.50	15.00	30.00
-- With Charles Munch/Boston Symphony Orch.; original with "shaded dog" label					
❏ LSC-2490 [S]	Dvorak: Cello Concerto	199?	6.25	12.50	25.00
-- With Charles Munch/Boston Symphony Orch.; Classic Records reissue					

PICHON, WALTER "FATS"
DECCA
❏ DL 8390 [M]	Appearing Nightly	1956	10.00	20.00	40.00

PICKETT, BOBBY "BORIS"
GARPAX
❏ GPX 67001 [M]	The Original Monster Mash	1962	37.50	75.00	150.00
❏ SGP 67001 [S]	The Original Monster Mash	1962	62.50	125.00	250.00

PARROT
❏ XPAS 71063	The Original Monster Mash	1973	6.25	12.50	25.00
-- Reissue of Garpax LP with four tracks deleted and one added					

PICKETT, WILSON
ATLANTIC
❏ SD 2-501 [(2)]	Wilson Pickett's Greatest Hits	1973	5.00	10.00	20.00
❏ 8114 [M]	In the Midnight Hour	1965	10.00	20.00	40.00
❏ SD 8114 [R]	In the Midnight Hour	1965	7.50	15.00	30.00
❏ 8129 [M]	The Exciting Wilson Pickett	1966	10.00	20.00	40.00
❏ SD 8129 [R]	The Exciting Wilson Pickett	1966	7.50	15.00	30.00
❏ 8136 [M]	The Wicked Pickett	1967	10.00	20.00	40.00
❏ SD 8136 [R]	The Wicked Pickett	1967	7.50	15.00	30.00
❏ 8145 [M]	The Sound of Wilson Pickett	1967	10.00	20.00	40.00
❏ SD 8145 [P]	The Sound of Wilson Pickett	1967	10.00	20.00	40.00
❏ 8151 [M]	The Best of Wilson Pickett	1967	10.00	20.00	40.00
❏ SD 8151 [R]	The Best of Wilson Pickett	1967	5.00	10.00	20.00
❏ SD 8175	I'm in Love	1968	6.25	12.50	25.00
❏ SD 8183	The Midnight Mover	1968	6.25	12.50	25.00

Number	Title	Yr	VG	VG+	NM
❏ SD 8215	Hey Jude	1969	5.00	10.00	20.00
❏ SD 8250	Right On	1970	5.00	10.00	20.00
❏ SD 8270	Wilson Pickett in Philadelphia	1970	5.00	10.00	20.00

DOUBLE-L
❏ DL-2300 [M]	It's Too Late	1963	12.50	25.00	50.00
❏ SDL-8300 [S]	It's Too Late	1963	17.50	35.00	70.00

WAND
❏ WD-672 [M]	Great Wilson Pickett Hits	1966	7.50	15.00	30.00
❏ WDS-672 [R]	Great Wilson Pickett Hits	1966	5.00	10.00	20.00

WICKED
❏ 9001	Chocolate Mountain	1976	6.25	12.50	25.00

PIERCE, WEBB
DECCA
❏ DXB 181 [(2) M]	The Webb Pierce Story	1964	7.50	15.00	30.00
-- Deduct 25% if booklet is missing					
❏ DL 4015 [M]	Webb with a Beat	1960	7.50	15.00	30.00
❏ DL 4079 [M]	Walking the Streets	1960	7.50	15.00	30.00
❏ DL 4110 [M]	Golden Favorites	1961	7.50	15.00	30.00
❏ DL 4144 [M]	Fallen Angel	1961	7.50	15.00	30.00
❏ DL 4218 [M]	Hideaway Heart	1962	7.50	15.00	30.00
❏ DL 4294 [M]	Cross Country	1962	7.50	15.00	30.00
❏ DL 4358 [M]	I've Got a New Heartache	1963	6.25	12.50	25.00
❏ DL 4384 [M]	Bow Thy Head	1963	6.25	12.50	25.00
❏ DL 4486 [M]	Sands of Gold	1964	6.25	12.50	25.00
❏ DL 4604 [M]	Memory #1	1965	6.25	12.50	25.00
❏ DL 4659 [M]	Country Music Time	1965	6.25	12.50	25.00
❏ DL 4739 [M]	Sweet Memories	1966	6.25	12.50	25.00
❏ DL 4782 [M]	Webb's Choice	1966	6.25	12.50	25.00
❏ DL 4844 [M]	Where'd Ya Stay Last Night	1967	7.50	15.00	30.00
❏ DL 4964 [M]	Fool, Fool, Fool	1968	12.50	25.00	50.00
❏ DL 5536 [10]	That Wondering Boy	1954	30.00	60.00	120.00
❏ DXSB 7181 [(2) S]	The Webb Pierce Story	1964	10.00	20.00	40.00
-- Deduct 25% if booklet is missing					
❏ DL 8129 [M]	Webb Pierce	1955	15.00	30.00	60.00
-- Black label, silver print					
❏ DL 8129 [M]	Webb Pierce	196?	7.50	15.00	30.00
-- Black label with color bar					
❏ DL 8295 [M]	That Wondering Boy	1956	15.00	30.00	60.00
-- Black label, silver print					
❏ DL 8295 [M]	That Wondering Boy	196?	7.50	15.00	30.00
-- Black label with color bar					
❏ DL 8728 [M]	Just Imagination	1957	12.50	25.00	50.00
-- Black label, silver print					
❏ DL 8728 [M]	Just Imagination	196?	7.50	15.00	30.00
-- Black label with color bar					
❏ DL 8889 [M]	Bound for the Kingdom	1959	10.00	20.00	40.00
-- Black label, silver print					
❏ DL 8889 [M]	Bound for the Kingdom	196?	6.25	12.50	25.00
-- Black label with color bar					
❏ DL 8899 [M]	Webb!	1959	10.00	20.00	40.00
-- Black label, silver print					
❏ DL 8899 [M]	Webb!	196?	6.25	12.50	25.00
-- Black label with color bar					
❏ DL 74015 [S]	Webb with a Beat	1960	10.00	20.00	40.00
❏ DL 74079 [S]	Walking the Streets	1960	10.00	20.00	40.00
❏ DL 74110 [S]	Golden Favorites	1961	10.00	20.00	40.00
❏ DL 74144 [S]	Fallen Angel	1961	10.00	20.00	40.00
❏ DL 74218 [S]	Hideaway Heart	1962	10.00	20.00	40.00
❏ DL 74294 [S]	Cross Country	1962	10.00	20.00	40.00
❏ DL 74358 [S]	I've Got a New Heartache	1963	7.50	15.00	30.00
❏ DL 74384 [S]	Bow Thy Head	1963	7.50	15.00	30.00
❏ DL 74486 [S]	Sands of Gold	1964	7.50	15.00	30.00
❏ DL 74604 [S]	Memory #1	1965	7.50	15.00	30.00
❏ DL 74659 [S]	Country Music Time	1965	7.50	15.00	30.00
❏ DL 74739 [S]	Sweet Memories	1966	7.50	15.00	30.00
❏ DL 74782 [S]	Webb's Choice	1966	7.50	15.00	30.00
❏ DL 74844 [S]	Where'd Ya Stay Last Night	1967	6.25	12.50	25.00
❏ DL 74964 [S]	Fool, Fool, Fool	1968	6.25	12.50	25.00
❏ DL 74999	Webb Pierce's Greatest Hits	1968	6.25	12.50	25.00
❏ DL 75071	Saturday Night	1969	6.25	12.50	25.00
❏ DL 75132	Webb Pierce Sings This Thing	1969	6.25	12.50	25.00
❏ DL 75168	Love Ain't Never Gonna Be No Better	1970	6.25	12.50	25.00
❏ DL 75210	Merry-Go-Round World	1970	5.00	10.00	20.00
❏ DL 75280	The Webb Pierce Road Show	1971	5.00	10.00	20.00
❏ DL 75393	I'm Gonna Be a Swinger	1972	5.00	10.00	20.00
❏ DL 78889 [S]	Bound for the Kingdom	1959	12.50	25.00	50.00
-- Black label, silver print					
❏ DL 78889 [S]	Bound for the Kingdom	196?	7.50	15.00	30.00
-- Black label with color bar					
❏ DL 78899 [S]	Webb!	1959	12.50	25.00	50.00
-- Black label, silver print					
❏ DL 78899 [M]	Webb!	196?	7.50	15.00	30.00
-- Black label with color bar					

KING
❏ 648 [M]	The One and Only Webb Pierce	1959	17.50	35.00	70.00

Number	Title	Yr	VG	VG+	NM
PIERCE, WEBB; MARVIN RAINWATER; STUART HAMBLEN					
AUDIO LAB					
❏ AL-1563 [M]	Sing for You	1960	50.00	100.00	200.00
PIKE, PETE					
AUDIO LAB					
❏ AL-1559 [M]	Pete Pike	1960	25.00	50.00	100.00
PILOT					
RCA VICTOR					
❏ LSP-4825	Point of View	1973	5.00	10.00	20.00
PINETOPPERS, THE					
CORAL					
❏ CRL 56200 [10]	Square Dances	195?	10.00	20.00	40.00
❏ CRL 57048 [M]	The Pinetoppers	195?	7.50	15.00	30.00
DECCA					
❏ DL 8348 [M]	Saturday Night Barn Dance	1956	7.50	15.00	30.00
PINK FLOYD					
Also see SYD BARRETT.					
CAPITOL					
❏ SPRO-8116/7 [DJ]	Pink Floyd Tour '75	1975	20.00	40.00	80.00
❏ SEAX-11902 [PD]	The Dark Side of the Moon	1978	7.50	15.00	30.00
COLUMBIA					
❏ AP-1 [DJ]	Animals	1977	37.50	75.00	150.00
-- White cover, with the song "Pigs" edited for airplay					
❏ AS 736 [DJ]	Off the Wall	1979	37.50	75.00	150.00
-- Sampler from 2-LP set					
❏ AS 1636 [DJ]	The Final Cut	1983	6.25	12.50	25.00
-- White label, record banded for airplay					
❏ HC 33453	Wish You Were Here	1981	15.00	30.00	60.00
-- First version of the half-speed mastered edition					
❏ PC 33453 [DJ]	Wish You Were Here	1975	62.50	125.00	250.00
-- White cover, "Special DJ Copy"; banded for airplay					
❏ PC 33453 [DJ]	Wish You Were Here	1975	75.00	150.00	300.00
-- Blue cover with photo and title on jacket; unbanded record					
❏ PC 33453	Wish You Were Here	1975	6.25	12.50	25.00
-- Original copies had a blue wraparound with title/artist sticker, which comprises roughly 50% of the above value. Most buyers threw this out upon opening the LP!					
❏ PCQ 33453 [Q]	Wish You Were Here	1975	50.00	100.00	200.00
❏ JC 33474 [DJ]	Animals	1977	25.00	50.00	100.00
-- "Demonstration Not for Sale" on label; also has insert					
❏ HC 43453	Wish You Were Here	1982	10.00	20.00	40.00
-- Half-speed mastered edition (reissue)					
❏ PC2 44484 [(2)]	Delicate Sound of Thunder	1988	5.00	10.00	20.00
❏ HC2 46183 [(2)]	The Wall	1983	62.50	125.00	250.00
-- Half-speed mastered edition					
❏ HC 47680	A Collection of Great Dance Songs	1982	12.50	25.00	50.00
-- Half-speed mastered edition					
❏ C 64200	The Division Bell	1994	5.00	10.00	20.00
-- U.S. pressings on blue vinyl					
EMI/COLUMBIA					
❏ 32700 [(4)]	Pulse	1995	15.00	30.00	60.00
-- Pressed in U.K. for U.S. release; box set with 12x12 hardback book; identical to British pressings except for American bar code (67065) on shrink wrap					
HARVEST					
❏ SKAO-382	Atom Heart Mother	1970	6.25	12.50	25.00
-- Without title on front cover					
❏ STBB-388 [(2)]	Ummagumma	1969	10.00	20.00	40.00
-- With the soundtrack LP from "Gigi" leaning against wall on front cover					
❏ STBB-388 [(2)]	Ummagumma	1970	5.00	10.00	20.00
-- With white LP cover leaning against wall on front cover					
❏ SMAS-11163	The Dark Side of the Moon	1973	6.25	12.50	25.00
-- With poster and two stickers					
MOBILE FIDELITY					
❏ 1-017	The Dark Side of the Moon	1980	12.50	25.00	50.00
-- Audiophile vinyl					
❏ MFQR-017	The Dark Side of the Moon	1982	75.00	150.00	300.00
-- Audiophile vinyl; "Ultra High Quality Recording" in box					
❏ 1-190	Meddle	1987	12.50	25.00	50.00
-- Audiophile vinyl					
❏ 1-202	Atom Heart Mother	1994	7.50	15.00	30.00
-- Audiophile vinyl					
TOWER					
❏ ST 5093 [S]	Pink Floyd (The Piper at the Gates of Dawn)	1967	20.00	40.00	80.00
-- Orange label					
❏ ST 5093 [S]	Pink Floyd (The Piper at the Gates of Dawn)	1968	10.00	20.00	40.00
-- Multi-color striped label					
❏ T 5093 [M]	Pink Floyd (The Piper at the Gates of Dawn)	1967	62.50	125.00	250.00
❏ ST 5131	A Saucerful of Secrets	1968	20.00	40.00	80.00
-- Orange label					

Number	Title	Yr	VG	VG+	NM
❏ ST 5131	A Saucerful of Secrets	1968	10.00	20.00	40.00
-- Multi-color striped label					
❏ ST 5169	More	1968	12.50	25.00	50.00
PIPKINS, THE					
CAPITOL					
❏ ST-483	Gimme Dat Ding	1970	6.25	12.50	25.00
PIRANHAS, THE					
CUSTOM FIDELITY					
❏ 1452	Somethin' Fishy	1969	37.50	75.00	150.00
PITNEY, GENE					
Also see GEORGE JONES/MELBA MONTGOMERY/GENE PITNEY.					
MUSICOR					
❏ MM-2001 [M]	The Many Sides of Gene Pitney	1962	12.50	25.00	50.00
-- Brown label					
❏ MM-2001 [M]	The Many Sides of Gene Pitney	1963	6.25	12.50	25.00
-- Black label					
❏ MM-2003 [M]	Only Love Can Break a Heart	1962	10.00	20.00	40.00
-- Brown label					
❏ MM-2003 [M]	Only Love Can Break a Heart	1963	6.25	12.50	25.00
-- Black label					
❏ MM-2004 [M]	Gene Pitney Sings Just for You	1963	7.50	15.00	30.00
❏ MM-2005 [M]	World-Wide Winners	1963	7.50	15.00	30.00
❏ MM-2006 [M]	Blue Gene	1963	7.50	15.00	30.00
❏ MM-2007 [M]	The Fair Young Ladies of Folkland	1964	7.50	15.00	30.00
❏ MM-2008 [M]	Gene Pitney's Big Sixteen	1964	7.50	15.00	30.00
❏ MM-2015 [M]	Gene Italiano	1964	6.25	12.50	25.00
❏ MM-2019 [M]	It Hurts to Be in Love	1964	6.25	12.50	25.00
❏ MM-2043 [M]	Gene Pitney's More Big Sixteen	1965	6.25	12.50	25.00
❏ MM-2056 [M]	I Must Be Seeing Things	1965	6.25	12.50	25.00
❏ MM-2069 [M]	Looking Through the Eyes of Love	1965	6.25	12.50	25.00
❏ MM-2072 [M]	Gene Pitney En Español	1965	6.25	12.50	25.00
❏ MM-2085 [M]	Big Sixteen, Vol. 3	1966	5.00	10.00	20.00
❏ MM-2095 [M]	Backstage I'm Lonely	1966	5.00	10.00	20.00
❏ MM-2100 [M]	Messumo Mi Puo Giudicare	1966	5.00	10.00	20.00
❏ MM-2101 [M]	The Gene Pitney Show	1966	5.00	10.00	20.00
❏ MM-2102 [M]	Greatest Hits of All Times	1966	5.00	10.00	20.00
❏ MM-2104 [M]	The Country Side of Gene Pitney	1967	5.00	10.00	20.00
❏ MM-2108 [M]	Young and Warm and Wonderful	1967	5.00	10.00	20.00
❏ MM-2117 [M]	Just One Smile	1967	5.00	10.00	20.00
❏ MM-2134 [M]	Golden Greats	1967	6.25	12.50	25.00
❏ MS-2043 [P]	Gene Pitney's More Big Sixteen	1965	7.50	15.00	30.00
❏ MS-3001 [R]	The Many Sides of Gene Pitney	1962	7.50	15.00	30.00
-- Brown label					
❏ MS-3001 [R]	The Many Sides of Gene Pitney	1963	5.00	10.00	20.00
-- Black label					
❏ MS-3003 [S]	Only Love Can Break a Heart	1962	12.50	25.00	50.00
-- Brown label					
❏ MS-3003 [S]	Only Love Can Break a Heart	1963	7.50	15.00	30.00
-- Black label					
❏ MS-3004 [S]	Gene Pitney Sings Just for You	1963	10.00	20.00	40.00
❏ MS-3005 [P]	World-Wide Winners	1963	10.00	20.00	40.00
❏ MS-3006 [S]	Blue Gene	1963	10.00	20.00	40.00
❏ MS-3007 [S]	The Fair Young Ladies of Folkland	1964	10.00	20.00	40.00
❏ MS-3008 [P]	Gene Pitney's Big Sixteen	1964	10.00	20.00	40.00
❏ MS-3015 [S]	Gene Italiano	1964	7.50	15.00	30.00
❏ MS-3019 [S]	It Hurts to Be in Love	1964	7.50	15.00	30.00
❏ MS-3056 [S]	I Must Be Seeing Things	1965	7.50	15.00	30.00
❏ MS-3069 [S]	Looking Through the Eyes of Love	1965	7.50	15.00	30.00
❏ MS-3072 [S]	Gene Pitney En Español	1965	7.50	15.00	30.00
❏ MS-3085 [S]	Big Sixteen, Vol. 3	1966	6.25	12.50	25.00
❏ MS-3095 [S]	Backstage I'm Lonely	1966	6.25	12.50	25.00
❏ MS-3100 [S]	Messumo Mi Puo Giudicare	1966	6.25	12.50	25.00
❏ MS-3101 [S]	The Gene Pitney Show	1966	6.25	12.50	25.00
❏ MS-3102 [P]	Greatest Hits of All Times	1966	6.25	12.50	25.00
❏ MS-3104 [S]	The Country Side of Gene Pitney	1967	6.25	12.50	25.00
❏ MS-3108 [S]	Young and Warm and Wonderful	1967	6.25	12.50	25.00
❏ MS-3117 [S]	Just One Smile	1967	6.25	12.50	25.00
❏ MS-3134 [S]	Golden Greats	1967	5.00	10.00	20.00
❏ M2-3148 [(2) M]	The Gene Pitney Story	1968	10.00	20.00	40.00
-- Mono is promo only					
❏ M2S-3148 [(2) S]	The Gene Pitney Story	1968	6.25	12.50	25.00
-- Add 40% if bonus photo is enclosed					
❏ MS-3161	Gene Pitney Sings Burt Bacharach	1968	5.00	10.00	20.00
❏ MS-3164	She's a Heartbreaker	1968	5.00	10.00	20.00
❏ MS-3174	The Greatest Hits of Gene Pitney	1969	5.00	10.00	20.00
PITNEY, GENE, AND GEORGE JONES					
Also see each artist's individual listings.					
MUSICOR					
❏ MM-2044 [M]	For the First Time! Two Great Singers Together: George Jones and Gene Pitney	1965	6.25	12.50	25.00
❏ MM-2065 [M]	It's Country Time Again	1965	6.25	12.50	25.00

Number	Title	Yr	VG	VG+	NM
❏ MS-3044 [S]	For the First Time! Two Great Singers Together: George Jones and Gene Pitney	1965	7.50	15.00	30.00
❏ MS-3065 [S]	It's Country Time Again	1965	7.50	15.00	30.00

PITNEY, GENE, AND MELBA MONTGOMERY
Also see each artist's individual listings.
MUSICOR

Number	Title	Yr	VG	VG+	NM
❏ MM-2077 [M]	Being Together	1966	6.25	12.50	25.00
❏ MS-3077 [S]	Being Together	1966	7.50	15.00	30.00

PIXIES
ELEKTRA

Number	Title	Yr	VG	VG+	NM
❏ PR-8127 [DJ]	Live	1989	12.50	25.00	50.00

-- Promo-only seven-song live collection of mostly songs from their pre-Elektra days
ROUGH TRADE

Number	Title	Yr	VG	VG+	NM
❏ ROUGH US 38	Surfer Rosa	1988	5.00	10.00	20.00

PIXIES THREE, THE
MERCURY

Number	Title	Yr	VG	VG+	NM
❏ MG-20912 [M]	Party with the Pixies Three	1964	37.50	75.00	150.00
❏ SR-60912 [S]	Party with the Pixies Three	1964	50.00	100.00	200.00

PLAIN JANE
HOBBIT

Number	Title	Yr	VG	VG+	NM
❏ 5000	Plain Jane	1969	6.25	12.50	25.00

PLANET P
MCA

Number	Title	Yr	VG	VG+	NM
❏ 8019 [(2)]	Pink World	1984	5.00	10.00	20.00

-- As "Planet P Project"; pink vinyl

PLANT & SEE
WHITE WHALE

Number	Title	Yr	VG	VG+	NM
❏ WWS-7120	Plant & See	1969	6.25	12.50	25.00

PLANT, ROBERT
Also see LED ZEPPELIN.
ES PARANZA

Number	Title	Yr	VG	VG+	NM
❏ PR 2244 [(2)]	Non-Stop Go	1988	12.50	25.00	50.00

-- Promo-only interview album

PLASMATICS
STIFF

Number	Title	Yr	VG	VG+	NM
❏ USE-9	New Hope for the Wretched	1980	6.25	12.50	25.00
❏ USE-11	Beyond the Valley of 1984	1981	6.25	12.50	25.00
❏ WOW-666 [EP]	Metal Priestess	1981	6.25	12.50	25.00

VICE SQUAD

Number	Title	Yr	VG	VG+	NM
❏ VS 105/106 [EP]	Meet the Plasmatics	1979	12.50	25.00	50.00

PLASTER CASTERS, THE
BLUESTIME

Number	Title	Yr	VG	VG+	NM
❏ BTS-9001	The Plaster Casters Blues Band	1969	12.50	25.00	50.00

PLASTIC COW, THE
DOT

Number	Title	Yr	VG	VG+	NM
❏ DLP 25961	The Plastic Cow Goes Mooooooog	1969	5.00	10.00	20.00

PLASTIC ONO BAND -- See JOHN LENNON; YOKO ONO.

PLATTERS, THE
Also see TONY WILLIAMS.
FEDERAL

Number	Title	Yr	VG	VG+	NM
❏ 549 [M]	The Platters	1957	400.00	800.00	1,600.

KING

Number	Title	Yr	VG	VG+	NM
❏ 651 [M]	The Platters	1959	200.00	400.00	800.00

MERCURY

Number	Title	Yr	VG	VG+	NM
❏ MG-20146 [M]	The Platters	1956	25.00	50.00	100.00
❏ MG-20216 [M]	The Platters, Volume Two	1956	25.00	50.00	100.00
❏ MG-20298 [M]	The Flying Platters	1957	25.00	50.00	100.00
❏ MG-20366 [M]	The Flying Platters Around the World	1958	7.50	15.00	30.00
❏ MG-20410 [M]	Remember When?	1959	7.50	15.00	30.00
❏ MG-20472 [M]	Encore of Golden Hits	1960	7.50	15.00	30.00
❏ MG-20481 [M]	Reflections	1960	6.25	12.50	25.00
❏ MG-20589 [M]	Life Is Just a Bowl of Cherries	1960	6.25	12.50	25.00
❏ MG-20591 [M]	More Encore of Golden Hits	1960	6.25	12.50	25.00
❏ MG-20613 [M]	Encore of Broadway Golden Hits	1961	5.00	10.00	20.00
❏ MG-20669 [M]	Song for the Lonely	1962	5.00	10.00	20.00
❏ MG-20759 [M]	Moonlight Memories	1963	5.00	10.00	20.00

Number	Title	Yr	VG	VG+	NM
❏ MG-20782 [M]	The Platters Present All-Time Movie Hits	1963	5.00	10.00	20.00
❏ MG-20808 [M]	The Platters Sing Latino	1963	5.00	10.00	20.00
❏ MG-20841 [M]	Christmas with the Platters	1963	7.50	15.00	30.00
❏ MG-20893 [M]	Encore of Golden Hits of the Groups	1964	5.00	10.00	20.00
❏ MG-20933 [M]	10th Anniversary Album	1964	5.00	10.00	20.00
❏ SR-60043 [S]	The Flying Platters Around the World	1959	12.50	25.00	50.00
❏ SR-60087 [S]	Remember When?	1959	12.50	25.00	50.00
❏ SR-60160 [S]	Reflections	1960	7.50	15.00	30.00
❏ SR-60243 [P]	Encore of Golden Hits	1960	10.00	20.00	40.00
❏ SR-60245 [S]	Life Is Just a Bowl of Cherries	1960	7.50	15.00	30.00
❏ SR-60252 [S]	More Encore of Golden Hits	1960	7.50	15.00	30.00
❏ SR-60613 [S]	Encore of Broadway Golden Hits	1961	6.25	12.50	25.00
❏ SR-60669 [S]	Song for the Lonely	1962	6.25	12.50	25.00
❏ SR-60759 [S]	Moonlight Memories	1963	6.25	12.50	25.00
❏ SR-60782 [S]	The Platters Present All-Time Movie Hits	1963	6.25	12.50	25.00
❏ SR-60808 [S]	The Platters Sing Latino	1963	6.25	12.50	25.00
❏ SR-60841 [S]	Christmas with the Platters	1963	10.00	20.00	40.00
❏ SR-60893 [S]	Encore of Golden Hits of the Groups	1964	6.25	12.50	25.00
❏ SR-60933 [S]	10th Anniversary Album	1964	6.25	12.50	25.00
❏ SR-60983 [S]	The New Soul of the Platters	1965	5.00	10.00	20.00

MUSICOR

Number	Title	Yr	VG	VG+	NM
❏ MM-2141 [M]	New Golden Hits of the Platters	1967	5.00	10.00	20.00
❏ MS-3091 [S]	I Love You 1,000 Times	1966	5.00	10.00	20.00
❏ MS-3111 [S]	The Platters Have the Magic	1966	5.00	10.00	20.00

WING

Number	Title	Yr	VG	VG+	NM
❏ MGW-12112 [M]	Encores!	1959	7.50	15.00	30.00

-- With liner notes on back cover

PLAYERS, THE
MINIT

Number	Title	Yr	VG	VG+	NM
❏ LP-24006 [S]	He'll Be Back	1966	7.50	15.00	30.00
❏ LP-40006 [M]	He'll Be Back	1966	6.25	12.50	25.00

PLAYMATES, THE
FORUM

Number	Title	Yr	VG	VG+	NM
❏ SF-16001 [S]	The Playmates Visit West of the Indies	1960	5.00	10.00	20.00

ROULETTE

Number	Title	Yr	VG	VG+	NM
❏ R-25001 [M]	Calypso	1957	6.25	12.50	25.00
❏ R-25043 [M]	At Play with the Playmates	1958	6.25	12.50	25.00
❏ SR-25043 [S]	At Play with the Playmates	1958	7.50	15.00	30.00
❏ R-25059 [M]	Rock and Roll Record Hop	1959	5.00	10.00	20.00
❏ SR-25059 [S]	Rock and Roll Record Hop	1959	6.25	12.50	25.00
❏ R-25068 [M]	Cuttin' Capers	1960	5.00	10.00	20.00
❏ SR-25068 [S]	Cuttin' Capers	1960	6.25	12.50	25.00
❏ R-25084 [M]	Broadway Show Stoppers	1961	5.00	10.00	20.00
❏ SR-25084 [S]	Broadway Show Stoppers	1961	6.25	12.50	25.00

PLEASURE FAIR, THE
Robb Royer, later of BREAD, was in this group.
UNI

Number	Title	Yr	VG	VG+	NM
❏ 3008 [M]	The Pleasure Fair	1967	5.00	10.00	20.00
❏ 73008 [S]	The Pleasure Fair	1967	5.00	10.00	20.00

PLIMSOULS, THE
BEAT

Number	Title	Yr	VG	VG+	NM
❏ BE-1001 [EP]	Zero Hour	1980	6.25	12.50	25.00

PLANET

Number	Title	Yr	VG	VG+	NM
❏ 13	The Plimsouls	1981	5.00	10.00	20.00

PLUGZ
FATIMA

Number	Title	Yr	VG	VG+	NM
❏ 80	Better Luck	1981	6.25	12.50	25.00

PLUG/REAL LIFE

Number	Title	Yr	VG	VG+	NM
❏ 001	Electrify Me	1979	15.00	30.00	60.00

PLUM NELLY
CAPITOL

Number	Title	Yr	VG	VG+	NM
❏ ST-692	Deceptive Lines	1971	5.00	10.00	20.00

PM DAWN
GEE STREET

Number	Title	Yr	VG	VG+	NM
❏ 6768 [(2) DJ]	The Bliss Album	1993	5.00	10.00	20.00

-- Promo-only vinyl edition

POCO
EPIC

Number	Title	Yr	VG	VG+	NM
❏ CQ 30209 [Q]	Deliverin'	1972	5.00	10.00	20.00
❏ CQ 32895 [Q]	Seven	1974	5.00	10.00	20.00
❏ PCQ 33192 [Q]	Cantamos	1974	5.00	10.00	20.00

(Top left) By far the most sought-after album by Robert Plant as a solo artist is *Non-Stop Go!,* a two-record set of interviews and music tied in to the release of the album *Now and Zen.* (Top right) If you're going to randomly find an album by the early Platters, this is the one most likely to pop up. *Encore of Golden Hits* was released in 1960 and spent over three years on the *Billboard* charts. (Bottom left) A few years before their biggest hit, "Catch Me (I'm Falling)," Pretty Poison released this four-song 12-inch EP on their own Svengali Records. It's tough to find outside the Philadelphia area. (Bottom right) During the 1990s, every once in a while a record company would release an album on vinyl as a promotional item, but not to the general public. Such was the case with Prince's *The Gold Experience,* which came out as a numbered, two-record set on gold vinyl – but only as a promo.

Number	Title	Yr	VG	VG+	NM

MOBILE FIDELITY
| ❏ 1-020 | Legend | 1979 | 5.00 | 10.00 | 20.00 |
-- *Audiophile vinyl*

POGUES, THE
ENIGMA
| ❏ ST-73225 | Red Roses for Me | 1986 | 6.25 | 12.50 | 25.00 |
STIFF/MCA
| ❏ 5744 | Rum, Sodomy and the Lash | 1985 | 5.00 | 10.00 | 20.00 |
| ❏ 36015 [EP] | Poguetry in Motion | 1986 | 5.00 | 10.00 | 20.00 |

POI DOG PONDERING
COLUMBIA
| ❏ CAS 1856 [DJ] | Interchords | 1989 | 5.00 | 10.00 | 20.00 |
-- *Promo-only interview and music*

POISON
CAPITOL
| ❏ SPRO 79319/20 | Open Up and Say Ahhh! | 1988 | 6.25 | 12.50 | 25.00 |
| [(2)] | World Premiere Weekend | | | | |
-- *Special radio-only version to promote the LP's release*

POITIER, SIDNEY
WARNER BROS.
| ❏ W 1561 [M] | Poitier Meets Plato | 1965 | 6.25 | 12.50 | 25.00 |
| ❏ WS 1561 [S] | Poitier Meets Plato | 1965 | 7.50 | 15.00 | 30.00 |

POLICE, THE
Also see KLARK KENT; STING.
A&M
| ❏ SP-3713 [10 (2)] | Reggatta da Blanc | 1979 | 10.00 | 20.00 | 40.00 |
-- *Two 10" records with poster*
| ❏ SP-3730 [DJ] | Ghost in the Machine | 1981 | 250.00 | 500.00 | 1,000. |
-- *Special prototype picture disc that lights up when placed on a turntable*
| ❏ SP-3735 | Synchronicity | 1983 | 20.00 | 40.00 | 80.00 |
-- *Black & white cover*
| ❏ SP-3735 | Synchronicity | 1983 | 10.00 | 20.00 | 40.00 |
-- *With gold, silver and bronze color bands on cover; used on audiophile pressings*
NAUTILUS
| ❏ NR-19 | Zenyatta Mondatta | 1981 | 10.00 | 20.00 | 40.00 |
-- *Audiophile vinyl*
| ❏ NR-40 | Ghost in the Machine | 1982 | 10.00 | 20.00 | 40.00 |
-- *Audiophile vinyl*

POLLUTION
CAPITOL
| ❏ ST-205 | Heir: Pollution | 1969 | 5.00 | 10.00 | 20.00 |
PROPHECY
| ❏ SD 6051 | Pollution | 1971 | 5.00 | 10.00 | 20.00 |
| ❏ SD 6067 | Pollution II | 1972 | 5.00 | 10.00 | 20.00 |

PONCE, PONCIE
WARNER BROS.
| ❏ W 1453 [M] | Poncie Ponce Sings | 1962 | 5.00 | 10.00 | 20.00 |
| ❏ WS 1453 [S] | Poncie Ponce Sings | 1962 | 6.25 | 12.50 | 25.00 |

PONTY, JEAN-LUC
DIRECT DISC
| ❏ SD-16603 | Cosmic Messenger | 1980 | 7.50 | 15.00 | 30.00 |
-- *Audiophile vinyl*
PACIFIC JAZZ
| ❏ ST-20172 | King Kong -- Jean-Luc Ponty Plays the Music of Frank Zappa | 1970 | 6.25 | 12.50 | 25.00 |

POOBAH
A.E.I.
| ❏ A-LP-1 | U.S. Rock | 1976 | 62.50 | 125.00 | 250.00 |
PEPPERMINT
| ❏ PP-1180 | Steamroller | 1979 | 37.50 | 75.00 | 150.00 |
RITE
| ❏ (no #) | Let Me In | 1972 | 150.00 | 300.00 | 600.00 |

POOLE, BRIAN, AND THE TREMELOES
Also see THE TREMELOES.
AUDIO FIDELITY
❏ AFLP 2151 [M]	Brian Poole Is Here	1966	12.50	25.00	50.00
❏ AFSD 2151 [R]	Brian Poole Is Here	1966	10.00	20.00	40.00
❏ AFLP 2177 [M]	The Tremeloes Are Here	1967	10.00	20.00	40.00
-- *Reissue of above album with new title*
| ❏ AFSD 2177 [R] | The Tremeloes Are Here | 1967 | 7.50 | 15.00 | 30.00 |
-- *Reissue of above album with new title*

Number	Title	Yr	VG	VG+	NM

POP WILL EAT ITSELF
RCA
| ❏ 9742-1-R | This Is the Day...This Is the Hour... This Is This! | 1989 | 6.25 | 12.50 | 25.00 |
ROUGH TRADE
| ❏ ROUGH US 22 | Now for a Feast | 198? | 6.25 | 12.50 | 25.00 |
| ❏ ROUGH US 33 | Box Frenzy! | 1988 | 6.25 | 12.50 | 25.00 |

POPCORN BLIZZARD, THE
DE-LITE
| ❏ DE-2004 | Explode! | 1969 | 10.00 | 20.00 | 40.00 |

POPPIES, THE
EPIC
| ❏ LN 24200 [M] | Lullaby of Love | 1966 | 10.00 | 20.00 | 40.00 |
| ❏ BN 26200 [S] | Lullaby of Love | 1966 | 12.50 | 25.00 | 50.00 |

PORCELAIN BEARMEAT
DILL PICKLE
| ❏ 3468 | Free Love, Free Sex, Free Music | 1971 | 5.00 | 10.00 | 20.00 |

PORTER, DAVID
ENTERPRISE
❏ ENS-1009	Gritty, Groovy, & Gettin' It	1970	5.00	10.00	20.00
❏ ENS-1012	David Porter...Into a Real Thing	1971	5.00	10.00	20.00
❏ ENS-1019	Victim of the Joke?	1972	5.00	10.00	20.00
❏ ENS-1026	Sweat and Love	1973	5.00	10.00	20.00

PORTER, JERRY
MIRROR
| ❏ SWB-123 [M] | Don't Bother Me! | 1966 | 25.00 | 50.00 | 100.00 |

PORTER, PEPPER
FIRST AMERICAN
| ❏ FA-7756 | Invasion | 1980 | 6.25 | 12.50 | 25.00 |

POSEY, SANDY
MGM
❏ SE-4418 [S]	Born a Woman	1966	5.00	10.00	20.00
❏ E-4455 [M]	Single Girl	1967	5.00	10.00	20.00
❏ SE-4455 [S]	Single Girl	1967	5.00	10.00	20.00
❏ E-4480 [M]	I Take It Back	1967	5.00	10.00	20.00
❏ SE-4480 [S]	I Take It Back	1967	5.00	10.00	20.00
❏ E-4509 [M]	The Best of Sandy Posey	1967	6.25	12.50	25.00
❏ SE-4509 [S]	The Best of Sandy Posey	1967	5.00	10.00	20.00
❏ E-4525 [M]	Looking at You	1968	6.25	12.50	25.00
❏ ST-91110	Single Girl	1967	6.25	12.50	25.00
-- *Capitol Record Club issue*

POSSUM HUNTERS, THE
TAKOMA
| ❏ C-1010 | Death on Lee Highway | 1970 | 5.00 | 10.00 | 20.00 |

POTTER, CURTIS
DOT
| ❏ DLP-25988 | Here Comes Curtis Potter | 1971 | 5.00 | 10.00 | 20.00 |

POWELL, ANDREW, AND THE PHILHARMONIA ORCHESTRA
MOBILE FIDELITY
| ❏ 1-175 | The Best of the Alan Parsons Project | 1986 | 6.25 | 12.50 | 25.00 |
-- *Audiophile vinyl*

POWELL, DICK
DECCA
| ❏ DL 8837 [M] | Song Book | 1959 | 10.00 | 20.00 | 40.00 |
RPC
| ❏ 105 [M] | The Wonderful Teens | 1962 | 6.25 | 12.50 | 25.00 |

POWELL, JANE
COLUMBIA MASTERWORKS
| ❏ ML 2034 [10] | Romance | 1949 | 20.00 | 40.00 | 80.00 |
| ❏ ML 2045 [10] | A Date with Jane Powell | 1949 | 20.00 | 40.00 | 80.00 |
LION
| ❏ L-70111 [M] | Jane Powell Sings | 1960 | 5.00 | 10.00 | 20.00 |
MGM
| ❏ E-3451 [M] | Something Wonderful | 1957 | 10.00 | 20.00 | 40.00 |

Number	Title	Yr	VG	VG+	NM
VERVE					
❏ MGV-2023 [M] Can't We Be Friends?		1957	10.00	20.00	40.00
POWERS OF BLUE, THE					
MTA					
❏ 1002 [M]	Flipout	1967	7.50	15.00	30.00
❏ 5002 [S]	Flipout	1967	7.50	15.00	30.00
POWERS, JOEY					
AMY					
❏ 8001 [M]	Midnight Mary	1964	7.50	15.00	30.00
POZO-SECO SINGERS, THE					
Also see DON WILLIAMS.					
COLUMBIA					
❏ CL 2600 [M]	I Can Make It with You	1967	5.00	10.00	20.00
❏ CS 9315 [S]	Time/I'll Be Gone	1966	5.00	10.00	20.00
PRADO, PEREZ					
RCA CAMDEN					
❏ CAL-409 [M]	Mambo Happy!	1957	5.00	10.00	20.00
❏ CAL-547 [M]	Latino!	1960	5.00	10.00	20.00
RCA VICTOR					
❏ LPM-21 [10]	Perez Prado Plays Mucho Mambo for Dancing	1951	15.00	30.00	60.00
❏ LPM-1075 [M]	Mambo Mania	1955	10.00	20.00	40.00
❏ LPM-1101 [M]	Voodoo Suite (and Six All-Time Greats)	1955	10.00	20.00	40.00
❏ LPM-1196 [M]	Mambo by the King	1956	10.00	20.00	40.00
❏ LPM-1257 [M]	Havana 3 A.M.	1956	10.00	20.00	40.00
❏ LPM-1459 [M]	Latin Satin	1957	10.00	20.00	40.00
❏ LPM-1556 [M]	"Prez"	1958	7.50	15.00	30.00
❏ LSP-1556 [S]	"Prez"	1959	10.00	20.00	40.00
❏ LPM-1883 [M]	Dilo (Ugh!)	1958	7.50	15.00	30.00
❏ LSP-1883 [S]	Dilo (Ugh!)	1959	10.00	20.00	40.00
❏ LPM-2028 [M]	Pops and Prado	1959	7.50	15.00	30.00
❏ LSP-2028 [S]	Pops and Prado	1959	10.00	20.00	40.00
❏ LPM-2104 [M]	Big Hits by Prado	1959	7.50	15.00	30.00
❏ LSP-2104 [S]	Big Hits by Prado	1959	10.00	20.00	40.00
❏ LPM-2133 [M]	A Touch of Tabasco	1960	5.00	10.00	20.00
❏ LSP-2133 [S]	A Touch of Tabasco	1960	7.50	15.00	30.00
❏ LPM-2308 [M]	Rockambo	1961	5.00	10.00	20.00
❏ LSP-2308 [S]	Rockambo	1961	7.50	15.00	30.00
❏ LPM-2379 [M]	The New Dance La Chunga	1961	5.00	10.00	20.00
❏ LSP-2379 [S]	The New Dance La Chunga	1961	7.50	15.00	30.00
❏ LPM-2524 [M]	The Twist Goes Latin	1962	5.00	10.00	20.00
❏ LSP-2524 [S]	The Twist Goes Latin	1962	7.50	15.00	30.00
❏ LPM-2571 [M]	Exotic Suite	1962	5.00	10.00	20.00
❏ LSP-2571 [S]	Exotic Suite	1962	7.50	15.00	30.00
❏ LPM-2610 [M]	Our Man in Latin America	1963	5.00	10.00	20.00
❏ LSP-2610 [S]	Our Man in Latin America	1963	7.50	15.00	30.00
❏ LPM-3108 [10]	Mambo by the King	1953	15.00	30.00	60.00
❏ LSP-3330 [S]	Dance Latino	1965	5.00	10.00	20.00
❏ LPM-3732 [M]	The Best of Perez Prado	1967	5.00	10.00	20.00
PREMIERS, THE					
WARNER BROS.					
❏ W 1565 [M]	Farmer John	1964	10.00	20.00	40.00
❏ WS 1565 [S]	Farmer John	1964	12.50	25.00	50.00
PRESIDENTS, THE					
SUSSEX					
❏ SXBX-7005	5-10-15-20 (25-30 Years of Love)	1970	6.25	12.50	25.00
PRESLEY, ELVIS					
BOXCAR					
❏ (no #)	Having Fun with Elvis on Stage	1974	37.50	75.00	150.00
-- All-talking record sold at Elvis concerts in 1974					
DCC COMPACT CLASSICS					
❏ LPZ-2037 [S]	Elvis Is Back!	1997	6.25	12.50	25.00
-- Audiophile vinyl					
❏ LPZ-2040 [(2)]	24 Karat Hits!	1997	7.50	15.00	30.00
-- Audiophile vinyl					
FOTOPLAY					
❏ FSP-1001 [PD]	To Elvis: Love Still Burning	1978	6.25	12.50	25.00
-- Tribute-song picture disc of Elvis; in plastic bag with 11x11 insert					
❏ FSP-1001 [PD]	To Elvis: Love Still Burning	1978	7.50	15.00	30.00
-- In white cardboard cover with black printing					
GOLDEN EDITIONS					
❏ GEL-101	The First Year (Elvis, Scotty and Bill)	1979	5.00	10.00	20.00

Number	Title	Yr	VG	VG+	NM
GREEN VALLEY					
❏ GV-2001	Elvis Exclusive Live Press Conference (Memphis, Tennessee, February 1961)	1977	10.00	20.00	40.00
-- Issued with two slightly different covers					
❏ GV-2001/3 [(2)]	Elvis (Speaks to You)	1978	7.50	15.00	30.00
-- Elvis interviews plus tracks by the Jordanaires					
HALW					
❏ HALW-0001	The First Years	1978	7.50	15.00	30.00
-- With stamped, limited edition number					
❏ HALW-0001	The First Years	1978	5.00	10.00	20.00
-- Without limited edition number					
K-TEL					
❏ NU 9900	Love Songs	1981	5.00	10.00	20.00
LOUISIANA HAYRIDE					
❏ LH-3061	Beginning Years	1984	5.00	10.00	20.00
-- With booklet and facsimile contract					
MOBILE FIDELITY					
❏ 1-059	From Elvis in Memphis	1982	12.50	25.00	50.00
-- Audiophile vinyl					
OAK					
❏ 1003	Vintage 1955 Elvis	1990	15.00	30.00	60.00
PAIR					
❏ PDL2-1010 [(2)]	Double Dynamite	1982	5.00	10.00	20.00
❏ PDL2-1037 [(2)]	Remembering	1983	7.50	15.00	30.00
❏ PDL2-1185 [(2)]	Elvis Aron Presley Forever	1988	5.00	10.00	20.00
PICKWICK					
❏ (no #) [(7)]	The Pickwick Pack (unofficial title)	1978	15.00	30.00	60.00
-- Seven Pickwick albums in special package and cardboard wrapper; one of the LPs is Elvis' Christmas Album					
❏ (no #) [(7)]	The Pickwick Pack (unofficial title)	1979	15.00	30.00	60.00
-- Seven Pickwick albums in special package and cardboard wrapper; one of the LPs is Frankie and Johnny					
❏ DL2-5001 [(2)]	Double Dynamite	1975	6.25	12.50	25.00
❏ ACL-7064	Mahalo from Elvis	1978	5.00	10.00	20.00
PREMORE					
❏ PL-589	Early Elvis (1954-1956 Live at the Louisiana Hayride)	1989	7.50	15.00	30.00
RCA					
❏ 2227-1-R	The Great Performances	1990	10.00	20.00	40.00
❏ 5600-1-R	Return of the Rocker	1986	5.00	10.00	20.00
❏ 6221-1-R [(2)]	The Memphis Record	1987	7.50	15.00	30.00
❏ 6313-1-R	Elvis Talks!	1987	7.50	15.00	30.00
❏ 6382-1-R	The Number One Hits	1987	7.50	15.00	30.00
❏ 6383-1-R [(2)]	The Top Ten Hits	1987	7.50	15.00	30.00
❏ 6414-1-R [(2)]	The Complete Sun Sessions	1987	7.50	15.00	30.00
❏ 6738-1-R	Essential Elvis: The First Movies	1988	6.25	12.50	25.00
❏ 6985-1-R	The Alternate Aloha	1988	5.00	10.00	20.00
❏ 8468-1-R	Elvis in Nashville (1956-1971)	1988	10.00	20.00	40.00
❏ 9586-1-R	Elvis Gospel 1957-1971 (Known Only to Him)	1989	10.00	20.00	40.00
❏ 9589-1-R	Essential Elvis, Vol. 2 (Stereo '57)	1989	6.25	12.50	25.00
❏ 07863-67642-1	Elvis' Golden Records	1997	7.50	15.00	30.00
-- Reissue for the Tower Records chain with 6 bonus tracks					
❏ 07863-67643-1	Elvis' Gold Records Volume 2 -- 50,000,000 Elvis Fans Can't Be Wrong	1997	7.50	15.00	30.00
-- Reissue for the Tower Records chain with 10 bonus tracks					
RCA CAMDEN					
❏ CAS-2304	Elvis Sings Flaming Star	1969	7.50	15.00	30.00
❏ CAS-2408	Let's Be Friends	1970	7.50	15.00	30.00
❏ CAL-2428 [M]	Elvis' Christmas Album	1970	7.50	15.00	30.00
-- Blue label, non-flexible vinyl					
❏ CAS-2440	Almost in Love	1970	10.00	20.00	40.00
-- Last song on Side 2 is "Stay Away, Joe"					
❏ CAS-2440	Almost in Love	1973	6.25	12.50	25.00
-- Last song on Side 2 is "Stay Away"					
❏ CAL-2472	You'll Never Walk Alone	1974	7.50	15.00	30.00
❏ CAL-2518	C'mon Everybody	1971	5.00	10.00	20.00
❏ CAL-2533	I Got Lucky	1971	6.25	12.50	25.00
❏ CAS-2567	Elvis Sings Hits from His Movies, Volume 1	1972	5.00	10.00	20.00
❏ CAS-2595	Burning Love And Hits from His Movies, Vol. 2	1972	6.25	12.50	25.00
-- With star on front cover advertising a bonus photo, the presence of which doubles the value of this LP					
❏ CAS-2611	Separate Ways	1973	7.50	15.00	30.00
RCA SPECIAL PRODUCTS					
❏ DPL2-0056(e) [(2)]	Elvis	1973	12.50	25.00	50.00
-- Mustard labels					
❏ DPL2-0056(e) [(2)]	Elvis	1973	6.25	12.50	25.00
-- Blue labels					
❏ DPL2-0056(e) [(2)]	Elvis Commemorative Album	1978	20.00	40.00	80.00
-- Reissue of "Elvis" (same number) with new title and gold vinyl					
❏ DPL2-0168 [(2)]	Elvis in Hollywood	1976	15.00	30.00	60.00
-- Blue labels; with 20-page booklet					

Number	Title	Yr	VG	VG+	NM
❏ DML5-0263 [(5)] The Elvis Story		1977	15.00	30.00	60.00
-- Available through Candelite Music via mail order					
❏ DPL5-0347 [(5)] Memories of Elvis		1978	20.00	40.00	80.00
(A Lasting Tribute to the King of Rock 'N' Roll)					
❏ DML6-0412 [(6)] The Legendary Recordings of Elvis Presley		1979	25.00	50.00	100.00
❏ DML3-0632 [(3)] The Elvis Presley Collection		1984	20.00	40.00	80.00
-- Available through Candelite Music via mail order					
❏ DPL1-0647	Elvis Country	1984	7.50	15.00	30.00
❏ DVM1-0704	Elvis (One Night with You)	1984	15.00	30.00	60.00
-- With poster (deduct 25% if missing)					
❏ SVL3-0710 [(3)] 50 Years -- 50 Hits		1985	7.50	15.00	30.00
❏ DVL2-0728 [(2)] His Songs of Faith and Inspiration		1986	12.50	25.00	50.00
❏ SVL2-0824 [(2)] Good Rockin' Tonight		1988	5.00	10.00	20.00
❏ CAL-2428 [M]	Elvis' Christmas Album	1986	7.50	15.00	30.00
-- Reissue for The Special Music Company					

RCA VICTOR

Number	Title	Yr	VG	VG+	NM
❏ (no #)	International Hotel, Las Vegas Nevada, Presents Elvis, 1969	1969	1,250.	1,875.	2,500.
-- Gift box to guests at Elvis' July 31-Aug, 1, 1969 shows. Includes LPM-4088 and LSP-4155; press release; 1969 catalog; three photos; and thank-you note from Elvis and the Colonel. Most of the value is for the box.					
❏ (no #)	International Hotel, Las Vegas Nevada, Presents Elvis, 1970	1970	1,250.	1,875.	2,500.
-- Gift box to guests at Elvis' Jan. 28, 1970 show. Includes LSP-6020 and 47-9791; press release; 1970 catalog; photo; booklet; and dinner menu. Most of the value is for the box.					
❏ PRS-279	Singer Presents Elvis Singing Flaming Star and Others	1968	25.00	50.00	100.00
-- Sold only at Singer sewing machine dealers; reissued on RCA Camden 2304					
❏ APL1-0283	Elvis	1973	12.50	25.00	50.00
❏ CPL1-0341	A Legendary Performer, Volume 1	1974	6.25	12.50	25.00
-- Includes booklet (deduct 40% if missing); with die-cut hole in front cover					
❏ APL1-0388	Raised on Rock/For Ol' Times Sake	1973	7.50	15.00	30.00
-- Orange label					
❏ APL1-0388	Raised on Rock/For Ol' Times Sake	1975	7.50	15.00	30.00
-- Tan label					
❏ SP-33-461 [DJ] Special Palm Sunday Programming		1967	175.00	350.00	700.00
-- White label promo. Add 25% for cue sheet.					
❏ CPL1-0475	Good Times	1974	12.50	25.00	50.00
-- Orange label					
❏ SPS-33-571[DJ] Elvis As Recorded at Madison Square Garden		1972	75.00	150.00	300.00
-- "Radio Station Banded Special Version"; came in plain white cover with stickers					
❏ APD1-0606 [Q] Elvis Recorded Live on Stage in Memphis		1974	50.00	100.00	200.00
-- "RCA QuadraDisc" labels					
❏ CPL1-0606	Elvis Recorded Live on Stage in Memphis	1974	6.25	12.50	25.00
-- Orange label					
❏ CPL1-0606	Elvis Recorded Live on Stage in Memphis	1975	6.25	12.50	25.00
-- Tan label					
❏ DJL1-0606 [DJ] Elvis Recorded Live on Stage in Memphis		1974	75.00	150.00	300.00
-- Special banded version for radio airplay					
❏ AFM1-0818	Having Fun with Elvis on Stage	1977	6.25	12.50	25.00
-- Black label, dog near top					
❏ CPM1-0818	Having Fun with Elvis on Stage	1974	7.50	15.00	30.00
-- Commercial issue of Boxcar LP; orange label					
❏ CPM1-0818	Having Fun with Elvis on Stage	1975	5.00	10.00	20.00
-- Tan label					
❏ DJM1-0835 [DJ] Elvis Presley Interview Record: An Audio Self-Portrait		1984	20.00	40.00	80.00
-- Promotional item for "50th Anniversary" series; later issued as RCA 6313-1-R					
❏ APD1-0873 [Q] Promised Land		1975	50.00	100.00	200.00
-- "RCA QuadraDisc" label					
❏ APD1-0873 [Q] Promised Land		1977	30.00	60.00	120.00
-- Black label, dog near top; quadraphonic reissue					
❏ APL1-0873	Promised Land	1975	5.00	10.00	20.00
-- Tan label					
❏ APL1-0873	Promised Land	1975	15.00	30.00	60.00
-- Orange label					
❏ LOC-1035 [M]	Elvis' Christmas Album	1957	7,500.	11,250.	15,000.
-- Red vinyl; unique					
❏ LOC-1035 [M]	Elvis' Christmas Album	1957	125.00	250.00	500.00
-- Gatefold cover; title printed in gold on LP spine; includes bound-in booklet but not sticker					
❏ LOC-1035 [M]	Elvis' Christmas Album	1957	125.00	250.00	500.00
-- Gatefold cover; title printed in silver on LP spine; includes bound-in booklet but not sticker					
❏ LOC-1035 [M]	Elvis' Christmas Album Sticker	1957	37.50	75.00	150.00
-- Gold sticker with "To_____" and "From_____" blanks					
❏ APD1-1039 [Q] Elvis Today		1975	50.00	100.00	200.00
-- "RCA QuadraDisc" labels					
❏ APD1-1039 [Q] Elvis Today		1977	37.50	75.00	150.00
-- Black label, dog near top; quadraphonic reissue					
❏ APL1-1039	Elvis Today	1975	15.00	30.00	60.00
-- Orange label					
❏ APL1-1039	Elvis Today	1975	7.50	15.00	30.00
-- Tan label					
❏ LPM-1254 [M]	Elvis Presley	1956	125.00	250.00	500.00
-- Version 1: "Long Play" on label; "Elvis" in pale pink, "Presley" in pale green on cover; pale green logo box in upper right front cover					
❏ LPM-1254 [M]	Elvis Presley	1956	100.00	200.00	400.00
-- Version 2: "Long Play" on label; "Elvis" in pale pink, "Presley" in neon green on cover; neon green logo box in upper right front cover					
❏ LPM-1254 [M]	Elvis Presley	1956	62.50	125.00	250.00
-- Version 3: "Long Play" on label; "Elvis" in pale pink, "Presley" in neon green on cover; black logo box in upper right front cover					
❏ LPM-1254 [M]	Elvis Presley	1958	50.00	100.00	200.00
-- Version 4: "Long Play" on label; "Elvis" in neon pink, almost red, "Presley" in neon green on cover; black logo box in upper right front cover					
❏ LPM-1254 [M]	Elvis Presley	1963	30.00	60.00	120.00
-- "Mono" on label; cover photo is slightly left of center, otherwise same as Version 4 above					
❏ LPM-1254 [M]	Elvis Presley	1964	15.00	30.00	60.00
-- "Monaural" on label					
❏ LSP-1254(e) [R] Elvis Presley		1962	50.00	100.00	200.00
-- "Stereo Electronically Reprocessed" and silver "RCA Victor" on label					
❏ LSP-1254(e) [R] Elvis Presley		1965	10.00	20.00	40.00
-- "Stereo Electronically Reprocessed" and white "RCA Victor" on label					
❏ LSP-1254(e) [R] Elvis Presley		1968	7.50	15.00	30.00
-- Orange label, non-flexible vinyl					
❏ CPL1-1349	A Legendary Performer, Volume 2	1976	15.00	30.00	60.00
-- Without false starts and outtakes of "Such a Night" and "Cane and a High Starched Collar," which are supposed to be there. End of matrix number may be "31."					
❏ CPL1-1349	A Legendary Performer, Volume 2	1976	7.50	15.00	30.00
-- Includes booklet (deduct 40% if missing); with die-cut hole in front cover					
❏ LPM-1382 [M]	Elvis	1956	200.00	400.00	800.00
-- With alternate take of "Old Shep" on side 2. Matrix number ends in "15S," "17S" or "19S," but should be played for positive ID. On alternate take, Elvis sings "he grew old AND his eyes were growing dim" (no AND on standard press)					
❏ LPM-1382 [M]	Elvis	1956	100.00	200.00	400.00
-- With tracks listed on labels as "Band 1" through "Band 6"					
❏ LPM-1382 [M]	Elvis	1956	75.00	150.00	300.00
-- Back cover has ads for other albums. At least 11 different variations of this are known, all of equal value.					
❏ LPM-1382 [M]	Elvis	1956	75.00	150.00	300.00
-- Back cover has no ads for other albums. "Long Play" on label.					
❏ LPM-1382 [M]	Elvis	1963	20.00	40.00	80.00
-- "Mono" on label					
❏ LPM-1382 [M]	Elvis	1965	15.00	30.00	60.00
-- "Monaural" on label					
❏ LSP-1382(e) [R] Elvis		1962	50.00	100.00	200.00
-- "Stereo Electronically Reprocessed" and silver "RCA Victor" on label					
❏ LSP-1382(e) [R] Elvis		1964	12.50	25.00	50.00
-- "Stereo Electronically Reprocessed" and white "RCA Victor" on label					
❏ LSP-1382(e) [R] Elvis		1968	7.50	15.00	30.00
-- Orange label, non-flexible vinyl					
❏ LSP-1382(e) [R] Elvis		1971	5.00	10.00	20.00
-- Orange label, flexible vinyl					
❏ APL1-1506	From Elvis Presley Boulevard, Memphis, Tennessee	1976	7.50	15.00	30.00
-- Tan label					
❏ LPM-1515 [M]	Loving You	1957	75.00	150.00	300.00
-- "Long Play" on label					
❏ LPM-1515 [M]	Loving You	1963	25.00	50.00	100.00
-- "Mono" on label					
❏ LPM-1515 [M]	Loving You	1964	12.50	25.00	50.00
-- "Monaural" on label					
❏ LSP-1515(e) [R] Loving You		1962	37.50	75.00	150.00
-- "Stereo Electronically Reprocessed" and silver "RCA Victor" on label					
❏ LSP-1515(e) [R] Loving You		1964	12.50	25.00	50.00
-- "Stereo Electronically Reprocessed" and white "RCA Victor" on label					
❏ LSP-1515(e) [R] Loving You		1968	10.00	20.00	40.00
-- Orange label, non-flexible vinyl					
❏ LSP-1515(e) [R] Loving You		1971	5.00	10.00	20.00
-- Orange label, flexible vinyl					
❏ LSP-1515(e) [R] Loving You		1975	5.00	10.00	20.00
-- Tan label					
❏ APM1-1675	The Sun Sessions	1976	5.00	10.00	20.00
-- Tan label					
❏ LPM-1707 [M]	Elvis' Golden Records	1958	62.50	125.00	250.00
-- Title on cover in light blue letters; no song titles listed on front cover					
❏ LPM-1707 [M]	Elvis' Golden Records	1958	37.50	75.00	150.00
-- Title on cover in light blue letters; no song titles listed on front cover; "RE" on back cover					
❏ LPM-1707 [M]	Elvis' Golden Records	1963	15.00	30.00	60.00
-- "Mono" on label; title on cover in white letters; song titles added to front cover					
❏ LPM-1707 [M]	Elvis' Golden Records	1964	10.00	20.00	40.00
-- "Monaural" on label; "RE2" on back cover					
❏ LSP-1707(e) [R] Elvis' Golden Records		1962	50.00	100.00	200.00
-- "Stereo Electronically Reprocessed" and silver "RCA Victor" on label					
❏ LSP-1707(e) [R] Elvis' Golden Records		1964	12.50	25.00	50.00
-- "Stereo Electronically Reprocessed" and white "RCA Victor" on label					
❏ LSP-1707(e) [R] Elvis' Golden Records		1968	7.50	15.00	30.00
-- Orange label, non-flexible vinyl					
❏ LSP-1707(e) [R] Elvis' Golden Records		1971	5.00	10.00	20.00
-- Orange label, flexible vinyl					
❏ LSP-1707(e) [R] Elvis' Golden Records		1975	5.00	10.00	20.00
-- Tan label					
❏ LPM-1884 [M]	King Creole	1958	50.00	100.00	200.00
-- "Long Play" on label; contrary to some other sources, this was NOT issued with a bonus photo					

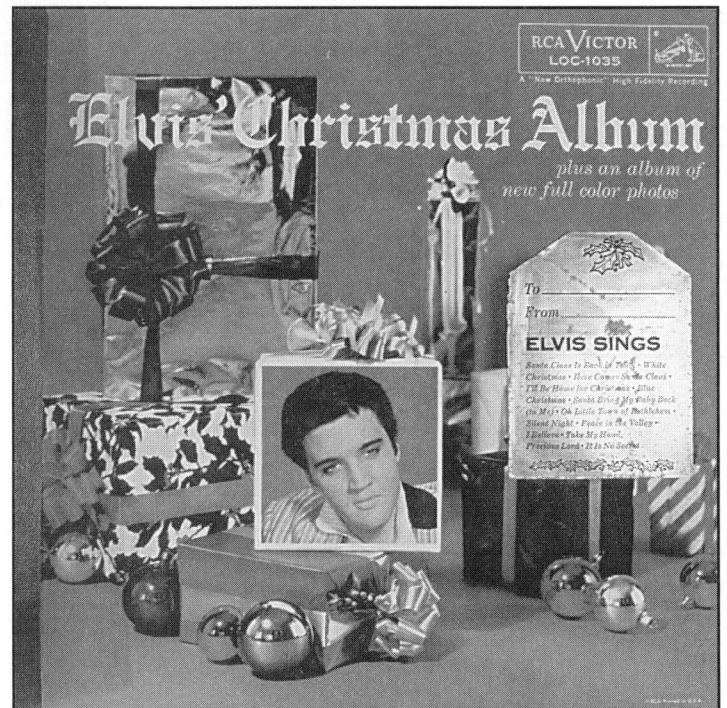

They may all look the same, but the above are three different issues of *Elvis' Christmas Album*. (Top left) The original edition, LOC-1035, came out in 1957 and was available for less than two years, one of the shortest lifespans for any RCA Victor Elvis album. It had a booklet of photos, and some copies (as illustrated) came with a tag. (Top right) In 1985, RCA reissued the original version, complete with photo book, after other variations called *Elvis' Christmas Album* had been available since 1959. There are two obvious differences between this album and the original; the number is different (AFM1-5486), and many (though not all) of the records were pressed on green vinyl. (Bottom) Look closely at this photo near where the bottom of the record overlaps the cover. You can see that the top record is translucent. Yes, this is a photo of the legendary red vinyl *Elvis' Christmas Album,* pressed by an RCA employee in 1957 and found in his collection in 1994. It sold at auction in 1997 for over $15,000.

Number	Title	Yr	VG	VG+	NM
❑ LPM-1884 [M] King Creole		1963	20.00	40.00	80.00
-- "Mono" on label					
❑ LPM-1884 [M] King Creole		1964	15.00	30.00	60.00
-- "Monaural" on label					
❑ LSP-1884(e) [R] King Creole		1962	37.50	75.00	150.00
-- "Stereo Electronically Reprocessed" and silver "RCA Victor" on label					
❑ LSP-1884(e) [R] King Creole		1964	15.00	30.00	60.00
-- "Stereo Electronically Reprocessed" and white "RCA Victor" on label					
❑ LSP-1884(e) [R] King Creole		1968	10.00	20.00	40.00
-- Orange label, non-flexible vinyl					
❑ LSP-1884(e) [R] King Creole		1971	5.00	10.00	20.00
-- Orange label, flexible vinyl					
❑ LSP-1884(e) [R] King Creole		1975	5.00	10.00	20.00
-- Tan label					
❑ LPM-1951 [M] Elvis' Christmas Album		1958	37.50	75.00	150.00
-- Same contents as LOC-1035, but with non-gatefold blue cover; "Long Play" at bottom of label					
❑ LPM-1951 [M] Elvis' Christmas Album		1963	17.50	35.00	70.00
-- "Mono" at bottom of label: "RE" on lower left front cover (photos on back were altered)					
❑ LPM-1951 [M] Elvis' Christmas Album		1964	10.00	20.00	40.00
-- "Monaural" at bottom of label; "RE" on lower left front cover					
❑ LSP-1951(e) [R] Elvis' Christmas Album		1964	12.50	25.00	50.00
-- Black label, dog on top; "Stereo Electronically Reprocessed" at bottom of label					
❑ LSP-1951(e) [R] Elvis' Christmas Album		1968	15.00	30.00	60.00
-- Orange label, non-flexible vinyl					
❑ LPM-1990 [M] For LP Fans Only		1959	62.50	125.00	250.00
-- "Long Play" on label					
❑ LPM-1990 [M] For LP Fans Only		1963	20.00	40.00	80.00
-- "Mono" on label					
❑ LPM-1990 [M] For LP Fans Only		1964	12.50	25.00	50.00
-- "Monaural" on label					
❑ LSP-1990(e) [R] For LP Fans Only		1965	75.00	150.00	300.00
-- "Stereo Electronically Reprocessed" on label; error cover with same photo on both front and back					
❑ LSP-1990(e) [R] For LP Fans Only		1965	12.50	25.00	50.00
-- "Stereo Electronically Reprocessed" on label; normal cover with different front and back cover photos					
❑ LSP-1990(e) [R] For LP Fans Only		1968	7.50	15.00	30.00
-- Orange label, non-flexible vinyl					
❑ LSP-1990(e) [R] For LP Fans Only		1975	5.00	10.00	20.00
-- Tan label					
❑ LPM-2011 [M] A Date with Elvis		1959	125.00	250.00	500.00
-- "Long Play" on label; gatefold cover, with sticker on cover					
❑ LPM-2011 [M] A Date with Elvis		1959	100.00	200.00	400.00
-- "Long Play" on label; gatefold cover, no sticker on cover					
❑ LPM-2011 [M] A Date with Elvis		1963	25.00	50.00	100.00
-- "Mono" on label; no gatefold cover					
❑ LPM-2011 [M] A Date with Elvis		1965	12.50	25.00	50.00
-- "Monaural" on label					
❑ LSP-2011(e) [R] A Date with Elvis		1965	12.50	25.00	50.00
-- Black label, "Stereo Electronically Reprocessed" on label					
❑ LSP-2011(e) [R] A Date with Elvis		1968	7.50	15.00	30.00
-- Orange label, non-flexible vinyl					
❑ LSP-2011(e) [R] A Date with Elvis		1971	5.00	10.00	20.00
-- Orange label, flexible vinyl					
❑ LSP-2011(e) [R] A Date with Elvis		1975	5.00	10.00	20.00
-- Tan label					
❑ LPM-2075 [M] Elvis' Gold Records Volume 2 -- 50,000,000 Elvis Fans Can't Be Wrong		1960	50.00	100.00	200.00
-- "Long Play" on label; "Magic Millions" on upper right front cover with RCA Victor logo					
❑ LPM-2075 [M] Elvis' Gold Records Volume 2 -- 50,000,000 Elvis Fans Can't Be Wrong		1963	20.00	40.00	80.00
-- "Mono" on label; "RE" on lower right front cover					
❑ LPM-2075 [M] Elvis' Gold Records Volume 2 -- 50,000,000 Elvis Fans Can't Be Wrong		1964	12.50	25.00	50.00
-- "Monaural" on label; label only has "Elvis' Gold Records - Vol. 2"					
❑ LPM-2075 [M] Elvis' Gold Records Volume 2 -- 50,000,000 Elvis Fans Can't Be Wrong		1964	12.50	25.00	50.00
-- "Monaural" on label; label has words "50,000,000 Elvis Presley Fans Can't Be Wrong"					
❑ LSP-2075(e) [R] Elvis' Gold Records Volume 2 -- 50,000,000 Elvis Fans Can't Be Wrong		1962	37.50	75.00	150.00
-- "Stereo Electronically Reprocessed" on label; label has words "50,000,000 Elvis Presley Fans Can't Be Wrong"					
❑ LSP-2075(e) [R] Elvis' Gold Records Volume 2 -- 50,000,000 Elvis Fans Can't Be Wrong		1964	12.50	25.00	50.00
-- "Stereo Electronically Reprocessed" and white "RCA Victor" on label					
❑ LSP-2075(e) [R] Elvis' Gold Records Volume 2 -- 50,000,000 Elvis Fans Can't Be Wrong		1968	7.50	15.00	30.00
-- Orange label, non-flexible vinyl					
❑ LSP-2075(e) [R] Elvis' Gold Records Volume 2 -- 50,000,000 Elvis Fans Can't Be Wrong		1971	5.00	10.00	20.00
-- Orange label, flexible vinyl					
❑ LSP-2075(e) [R] Elvis' Gold Records Volume 2 -- 50,000,000 Elvis Fans Can't Be Wrong		1975	5.00	10.00	20.00
-- Tan label					
❑ LPM-2231 [M] Elvis Is Back!		1960	50.00	100.00	200.00
-- With no sticker attached to front cover. Side 2, Song 4 is listed as "The Girl Next Door Went a-Walking."					
❑ LPM-2231 [M] Elvis Is Back!		1960	37.50	75.00	150.00
-- With sticker attached to front cover. Side 2, Song 4 is listed as "The Girl Next Door Went a-Walking."					
❑ LPM-2231 [M] Elvis Is Back!		1960	50.00	100.00	200.00
-- With no sticker attached to front cover. Side 2, Song 4 is listed as "The Girl Next Door."					
❑ LPM-2231 [M] Elvis Is Back!		1960	37.50	75.00	150.00
-- With sticker attached to front cover. Side 2, Song 4 is listed as "The Girl Next Door."					
❑ LPM-2231 [M] Elvis Is Back!		1963	15.00	30.00	60.00
-- "Mono" on label; song titles printed on front cover					
❑ LPM-2231 [M] Elvis Is Back!		1964	15.00	30.00	60.00
-- "Monaural" on label					
❑ LSP-2231 [S] Elvis Is Back!		1960	75.00	150.00	300.00
-- "Living Stereo" on label; with no sticker attached to front cover. Side 2, Song 4 is listed as "The Girl Next Door Went a-Walking."					
❑ LSP-2231 [S] Elvis Is Back!		1960	75.00	150.00	300.00
-- "Living Stereo" on label; with sticker attached to front cover. Side 2, Song 4 is listed as "The Girl Next Door Went a-Walking."					
❑ LSP-2231 [S] Elvis Is Back!		1960	75.00	150.00	300.00
-- "Living Stereo" on label; with no sticker attached to front cover. Side 2, Song 4 is listed as "The Girl Next Door."					
❑ LSP-2231 [S] Elvis Is Back!		1960	75.00	150.00	300.00
-- "Living Stereo" on label; with sticker attached to front cover. Side 2, Song 4 is listed as "The Girl Next Door."					
❑ LSP-2231 [S] Elvis Is Back!		1964	15.00	30.00	60.00
-- "Stereo" on label; song titles printed on front cover					
❑ LSP-2231 [S] Elvis Is Back!		1968	10.00	20.00	40.00
-- Orange label, non-flexible vinyl					
❑ LSP-2231 [S] Elvis Is Back!		1975	5.00	10.00	20.00
-- Tan label					
❑ LPM-2256 [M] G.I. Blues		1960	125.00	250.00	500.00
-- "Long Play" on label; with sticker on front cover advertising the presence of "Wooden Heart"					
❑ LPM-2256 [M] G.I. Blues		1960	30.00	60.00	120.00
-- "Long Play" on label; with no sticker on front cover					
❑ LPM-2256 [M] G.I. Blues		1963	25.00	50.00	100.00
-- "Mono" on label					
❑ LPM-2256 [M] G.I. Blues		1964	12.50	25.00	50.00
-- "Monaural" on label					
❑ LSP-2256 [S] G.I. Blues		1960	150.00	300.00	600.00
-- "Living Stereo" on label; with sticker on front cover advertising the presence of "Wooden Heart"					
❑ LSP-2256 [S] G.I. Blues		1960	25.00	50.00	100.00
-- "Living Stereo" on label; with no sticker on front cover					
❑ LSP-2256 [S] G.I. Blues		1964	12.50	25.00	50.00
-- "Stereo" on black label					
❑ LSP-2256 [S] G.I. Blues		1968	10.00	20.00	40.00
-- Orange label, non-flexible vinyl					
❑ LSP-2256 [S] G.I. Blues		1971	5.00	10.00	20.00
-- Orange label, flexible vinyl					
❑ LSP-2256 [S] G.I. Blues		1975	6.25	12.50	25.00
-- Tan label					
❑ APL1-2274 Welcome to My World		1977	5.00	10.00	20.00
-- Black label, dog near top					
❑ LPM-2328 [M] His Hand in Mine		1960	30.00	60.00	120.00
-- "Long Play" on label					
❑ LPM-2328 [M] His Hand in Mine		1963	15.00	30.00	60.00
-- "Mono" on label					
❑ LPM-2328 [M] His Hand in Mine		1964	12.50	25.00	50.00
-- "Monaural" on label					
❑ LSP-2328 [S] His Hand in Mine		1960	50.00	100.00	200.00
-- "Living Stereo" on label					
❑ LSP-2328 [S] His Hand in Mine		1964	150.00	300.00	600.00
-- "Stereo" and silver "RCA Victor" on black label					
❑ LSP-2328 [S] His Hand in Mine		1964	25.00	50.00	100.00
-- "Stereo" and white "RCA Victor" on black label					
❑ LSP-2328 [S] His Hand in Mine		1968	12.50	25.00	50.00
-- Orange label, non-flexible vinyl					
❑ LSP-2328 [S] His Hand in Mine		197?	5.00	10.00	20.00
-- Orange label, flexible vinyl					
❑ LSP-2328 [S] His Hand in Mine		1975	5.00	10.00	20.00
-- Tan label					
❑ AHL1-2347 Greatest Hits, Volume One		1981	6.25	12.50	25.00
-- With embossed cover					
❑ LPM-2370 [M] Something for Everybody		1961	30.00	60.00	120.00
-- "Long Play" on label; back cover advertises RCA Compact 33 singles and doubles					
❑ LPM-2370 [M] Something for Everybody		1963	20.00	40.00	80.00
-- "Mono" on label; back cover advertises "Viva Las Vegas" EP					
❑ LPM-2370 [M] Something for Everybody		1964	12.50	25.00	50.00
-- "Monaural" on label; back cover advertises "Viva Las Vegas" EP					
❑ LSP-2370 [S] Something for Everybody		1961	50.00	100.00	200.00
-- "Living Stereo" on label; back cover advertises RCA Compact 33 singles and doubles					
❑ LSP-2370 [S] Something for Everybody		1964	25.00	50.00	100.00
-- "Stereo" and silver "RCA Victor" on black label; back cover advertises Elvis' Christmas Album and His Hand in Mine LPs and "Viva Las Vegas" EP					
❑ LSP-2370 [S] Something for Everybody		1964	12.50	25.00	50.00
-- "Stereo" and white "RCA Victor" on black label; back cover advertises "Viva Las Vegas" EP					
❑ LSP-2370 [S] Something for Everybody		1968	10.00	20.00	40.00
-- Orange label, non-flexible vinyl; final back cover change advertises Elvis (NBC-TV Special), Elvis' Christmas Album and His Hand in Mine LPs					
❑ LSP-2370 [S] Something for Everybody		1971	5.00	10.00	20.00
-- Orange label, flexible vinyl					
❑ LSP-2370 [S] Something for Everybody		1975	5.00	10.00	20.00
-- Tan label					
❑ LPM-2426 [M] Blue Hawaii		1961	25.00	50.00	100.00
-- "Long Play" on label; with sticker on cover advertising the presence of "Can't Help Falling in Love" and "Rock-a-Hula Baby"					
❑ LPM-2426 [M] Blue Hawaii		1962	15.00	30.00	60.00
-- "Long Play" on label; no sticker on front cover					

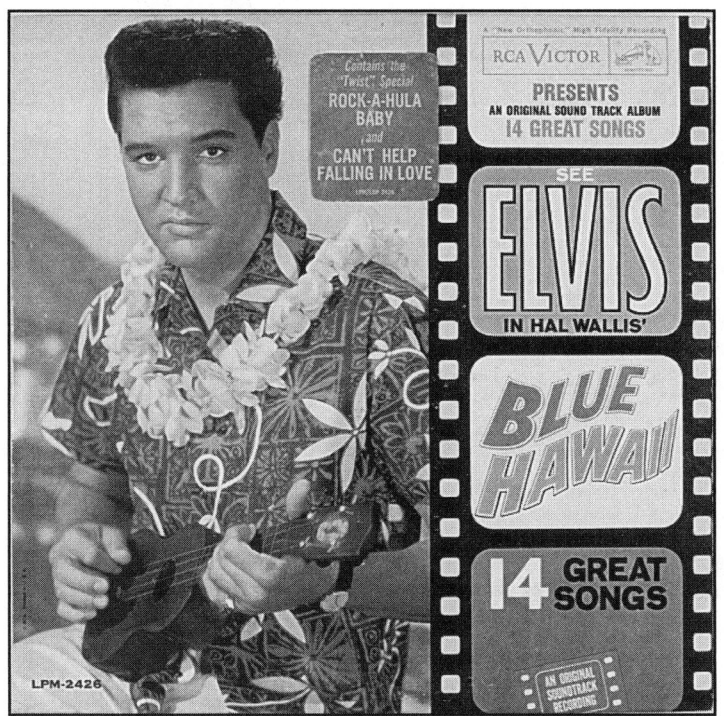

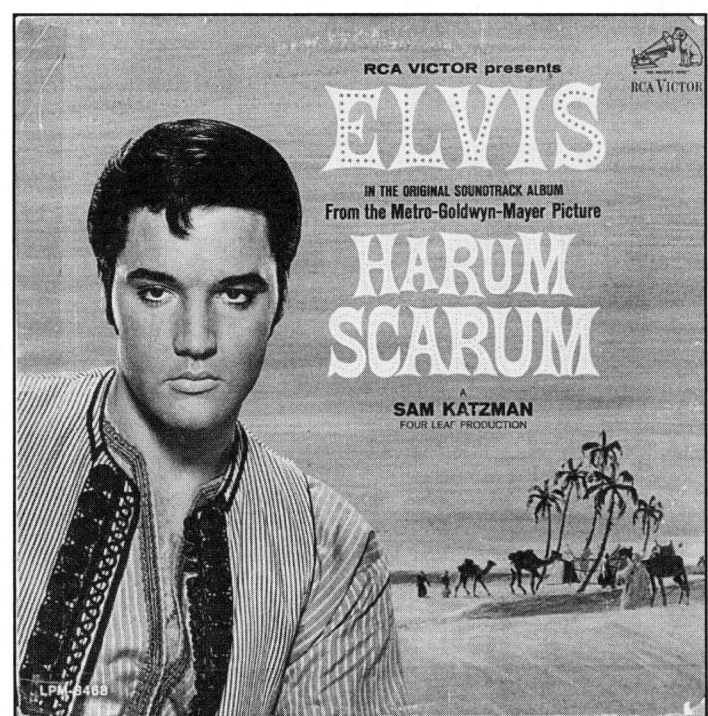

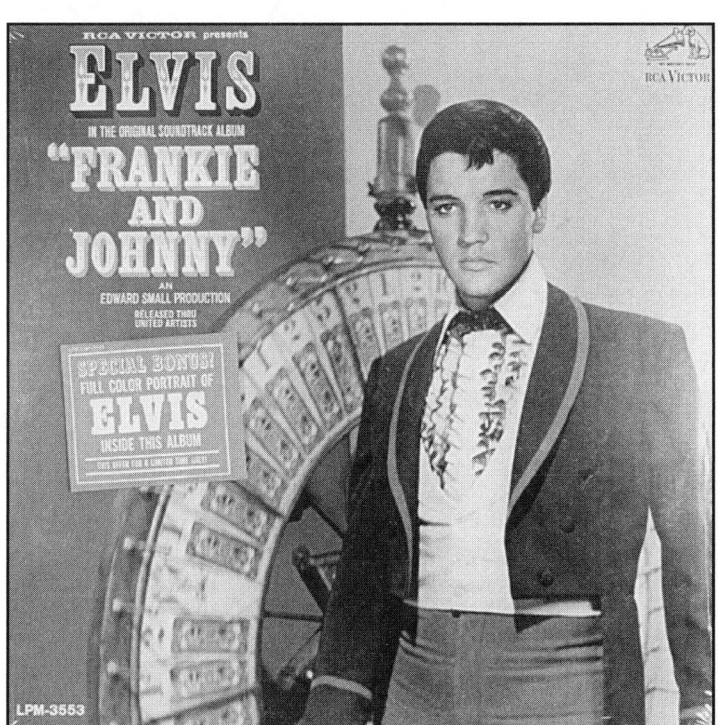

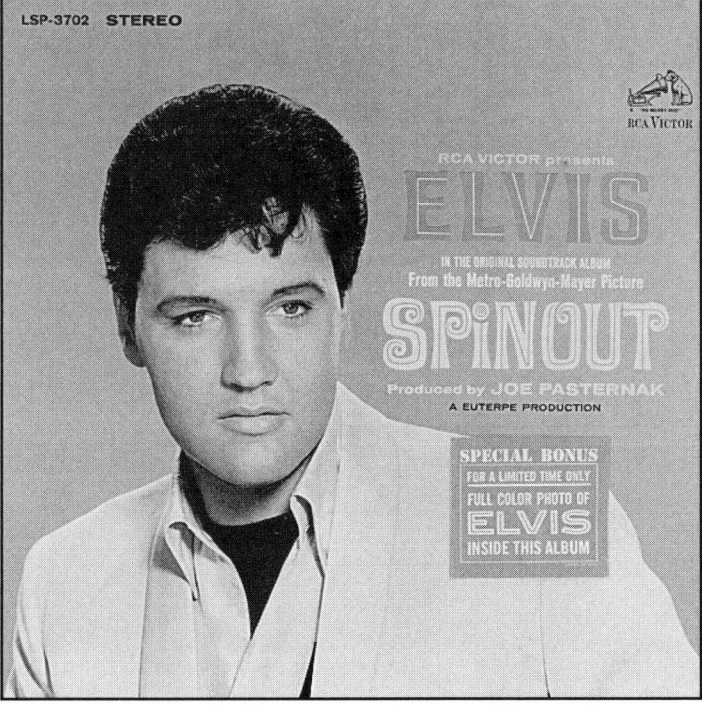

Most of Elvis' 1960s albums were movie soundtracks. Some were good, some were OK, others were dreadful. Here are four of them. (Top left) *Blue Hawaii,* which features "Can't Help Falling in Love." Early copies of the album had a sticker affixed directly on the cover advertising the presence of both this song and "Rock-a-Hula Baby"; that adds significantly to the value. (Top right) A mono copy of *Harum Scarum,* one of a very few number of Elvis albums that was deleted in the 1960s – it was never issued on the orange label. (Bottom left) The next soundtrack after that, *Frankie and Johnny,* also never got out of the 1960s on RCA. This copy still has the sticker advertising the bonus photo inside, which goes for as much as the LP does! (Bottom right) Yet another soundtrack that was out of print before the end of the 1960s, *Spinout* also had a bonus photo, as advertised on this copy.

Number	Title	Yr	VG	VG+	NM
❏ LPM-2426 [M] Blue Hawaii		1963	12.50	25.00	50.00
-- "Mono" on label					
❏ LPM-2426 [M] Blue Hawaii		1964	10.00	20.00	40.00
-- "Monaural" on label					
❏ LSP-2426 [S] Blue Hawaii		1961	37.50	75.00	150.00
-- "Living Stereo" on label and upper right front cover; with sticker on cover advertising the presence of "Can't Help Falling in Love" and "Rock-a-Hula Baby"					
❏ LSP-2426 [S] Blue Hawaii		1962	20.00	40.00	80.00
-- "Living Stereo" on label and upper right front cover; no sticker on front cover					
❏ LSP-2426 [S] Blue Hawaii		1964	12.50	25.00	50.00
-- "Stereo" on label; "Victor Stereo" on upper right front cover					
❏ LSP-2426 [S] Blue Hawaii		1968	10.00	20.00	40.00
-- Orange label, non-flexible vinyl					
❏ LSP-2426 [S] Blue Hawaii		1971	5.00	10.00	20.00
-- Orange label, flexible vinyl					
❏ LSP-2426 [S] Blue Hawaii		1975	5.00	10.00	20.00
-- Tan label					
❏ LSP-2426 [S] Blue Hawaii		197?	250.00	500.00	1,000.
-- One-of-a-kind blue vinyl pressing with black label, dog near top					
❏ AFK1-2428 Moody Blue		1977	1,500.	2,250.	3,000.
-- Alternate cover slick (never put on an actual cover), with the words "Moody Blue" inside the large word "Elvis." See any late-1970s Elvis inner sleeve for a black and white photo of the scrapped cover.					
❏ AFL1-2428 Moody Blue		1977	50.00	100.00	200.00
-- Black vinyl (pressings on blue vinyl are worth, at most, $10 NM)					
❏ AFL1-2428 [DJ] Moody Blue		1977	500.00	1,000.	2,000.
-- Experimental colored vinyl pressings (with no cover), any color or combination except blue or black					
❏ AQL1-2428 Moody Blue		1979	6.25	12.50	25.00
-- Reissue with new prefix					
❏ LPM-2523 [M] Pot Luck with Elvis		1962	25.00	50.00	100.00
-- "Long Play" on label					
❏ LPM-2523 [M] Pot Luck with Elvis		1964	30.00	60.00	120.00
-- "Monaural" on label					
❏ LSP-2523 [S] Pot Luck with Elvis		1962	37.50	75.00	150.00
-- "Living Stereo" on label					
❏ LSP-2523 [S] Pot Luck with Elvis		1964	15.00	30.00	60.00
-- "Stereo" on black label					
❏ LSP-2523 [S] Pot Luck with Elvis		1968	10.00	20.00	40.00
-- Orange label, non-flexible vinyl					
❏ LSP-2523 [S] Pot Luck with Elvis		1975	5.00	10.00	20.00
-- Tan label					
❏ APL2-2587 [(2)] Elvis in Concert		1977	6.25	12.50	25.00
❏ CPL2-2587 [(2)] Elvis in Concert		1982	10.00	20.00	40.00
❏ LPM-2621 [M] Girls! Girls! Girls!		1962	20.00	40.00	80.00
-- "Long Play" on label					
❏ LPM-2621 [M] Girls! Girls! Girls!		1963	15.00	30.00	60.00
-- "Mono" on label					
❏ LPM-2621 [M] Girls! Girls! Girls!		1964	10.00	20.00	40.00
-- "Monaural" on label					
❏ LSP-2621 [S] Girls! Girls! Girls!		1962	37.50	75.00	150.00
-- "Living Stereo" on label					
❏ LSP-2621 [S] Girls! Girls! Girls!		1964	15.00	30.00	60.00
-- "Stereo" on black label					
❏ LSP-2621 [S] Girls! Girls! Girls!		1968	10.00	20.00	40.00
-- Orange label, non-flexible vinyl					
❏ LSP-2621 [S] Girls! Girls! Girls!		1971	5.00	10.00	20.00
-- Orange label, flexible vinyl					
❏ LSP-2621 [S] Girls! Girls! Girls!		1975	6.25	12.50	25.00
-- Tan label					
❏ LPM/LSP-2621 Girls! Girls! Girls! Bonus 1963 Calendar		1962	37.50	75.00	150.00
-- With listing of other Elvis records on back					
❏ CPD2-2642 [(2) Q] Aloha from Hawaii Via Satellite		1975	7.50	15.00	30.00
-- Orange labels					
❏ CPD2-2642 [(2) Q] Aloha from Hawaii Via Satellite		1977	20.00	40.00	80.00
-- Black labels, dog near top					
❏ LPM-2697 [M] It Happened at the World's Fair		1963	30.00	60.00	120.00
❏ LPM/LSP-2697 It Happened at the World's Fair Photo		1963	62.50	125.00	250.00
❏ LSP-2697 [S] It Happened at the World's Fair		1963	50.00	100.00	200.00
-- "Stereo" and silver "RCA Victor" on black label					
❏ LSP-2697 [S] It Happened at the World's Fair		1964	20.00	40.00	80.00
-- "Stereo" and white "RCA Victor" on black label					
❏ LPM-2756 [M] Fun in Acapulco		1963	20.00	40.00	80.00
-- "Mono" on label					
❏ LPM-2756 [M] Fun in Acapulco		1964	12.50	25.00	50.00
-- "Monaural" on label					
❏ LSP-2756 [S] Fun in Acapulco		1963	25.00	50.00	100.00
-- "Stereo" and silver "RCA Victor" on black label					
❏ LSP-2756 [S] Fun in Acapulco		1964	15.00	30.00	60.00
-- "Stereo" and white "RCA Victor" on black label					
❏ LSP-2756 [S] Fun in Acapulco		1968	10.00	20.00	40.00
-- Orange label, non-flexible vinyl					
❏ LSP-2756 [S] Fun in Acapulco		1975	6.25	12.50	25.00
-- Tan label					
❏ LPM-2765 [M] Elvis' Golden Records, Volume 3		1963	25.00	50.00	100.00
-- "Mono" on label					
❏ LPM-2765 [M] Elvis' Golden Records, Volume 3		1964	15.00	30.00	60.00
-- "Monaural" on label					
❏ LSP-2765 [S] Elvis' Golden Records, Volume 3		1963	37.50	75.00	150.00
-- "Stereo" and silver "RCA Victor" on black label					
❏ LSP-2765 [S] Elvis' Golden Records, Volume 3		1964	12.50	25.00	50.00
-- "Stereo" and white "RCA Victor" on black label					
❏ LSP-2765 [S] Elvis' Golden Records, Volume 3		1968	10.00	20.00	40.00
-- Orange label, non-flexible vinyl					
❏ LSP-2765 [S] Elvis' Golden Records, Volume 3		1975	5.00	10.00	20.00
-- Tan label					
❏ AFL1-2772 He Walks Beside Me		1978	6.25	12.50	25.00
-- Includes 20-page photo booklet					
❏ LPM-2894 [M] Kissin' Cousins		1964	50.00	100.00	200.00
-- "Monaural" on label; front cover does NOT have black and white photo in lower right					
❏ LPM-2894 [M] Kissin' Cousins		1964	50.00	100.00	200.00
-- "Mono" on label; front cover does NOT have black and white photo in lower right					
❏ LPM-2894 [M] Kissin' Cousins		1964	25.00	50.00	100.00
-- "Monaural" on label; front cover has a small black and white photo of six cast members in lower right					
❏ LPM-2894 [M] Kissin' Cousins		1964	20.00	40.00	80.00
-- "Mono" on label; front cover has a small black and white photo of six cast members in lower right					
❏ LSP-2894 [S] Kissin' Cousins		1964	50.00	100.00	200.00
-- "Stereo" and silver "RCA Victor" on black label; front cover does NOT have black and white photo in lower right					
❏ LSP-2894 [S] Kissin' Cousins		1964	30.00	60.00	120.00
-- "Stereo" and silver "RCA Victor" on black label; front cover has a small black and white photo of six cast members in lower right					
❏ LSP-2894 [S] Kissin' Cousins		1964	15.00	30.00	60.00
-- "Stereo" and white "RCA Victor" on black label; all front covers have the cast photo in lower right					
❏ LSP-2894 [S] Kissin' Cousins		1968	10.00	20.00	40.00
-- Orange label, non-flexible vinyl					
❏ LSP-2894 [S] Kissin' Cousins		1971	5.00	10.00	20.00
-- Orange label, flexible vinyl					
❏ LSP-2894 [S] Kissin' Cousins		1975	6.25	12.50	25.00
-- Tan label					
❏ LSP-2894 [S] Kissin' Cousins		1976	375.00	750.00	1,500.
-- Black label, dog near top; blue vinyl					
❏ CPL1-2901 Elvis Sings for Children and Grownups Too!		1978	5.00	10.00	20.00
-- With two slits for removable greeting card on back cover (card should be with package)					
❏ LPM-2999 [M] Roustabout		1964	25.00	50.00	100.00
-- "Mono" on label					
❏ LPM-2999 [M] Roustabout		1965	15.00	30.00	60.00
-- "Monaural" on label					
❏ LSP-2999 [S] Roustabout		1964	150.00	300.00	600.00
-- "Stereo" and silver "RCA Victor" on black label					
❏ LSP-2999 [S] Roustabout		1964	15.00	30.00	60.00
-- "Stereo" and white "RCA Victor" on black label					
❏ LSP-2999 [S] Roustabout		1968	10.00	20.00	40.00
-- Orange label, non-flexible vinyl					
❏ LSP-2999 [S] Roustabout		1971	5.00	10.00	20.00
-- Orange label, flexible vinyl					
❏ LSP-2999 [S] Roustabout		1975	5.00	10.00	20.00
-- Tan label					
❏ CPL1-3078 [PD] A Legendary Performer, Volume 3		1978	6.25	12.50	25.00
-- Picture disc applied to blue or black vinyl LP; with booklet (deduct 40% if missing)					
❏ CPL1-3082 A Legendary Performer, Volume 3		1978	6.25	12.50	25.00
-- Includes booklet (deduct 40% if missing); with die-cut hole in front cover					
❏ AQL1-3279 Our Memories of Elvis		1979	5.00	10.00	20.00
❏ LPM-3338 [M] Girl Happy		1965	15.00	30.00	60.00
❏ LSP-3338 [S] Girl Happy		1965	15.00	30.00	60.00
-- "Stereo" on black label					
❏ LSP-3338 [S] Girl Happy		1968	10.00	20.00	40.00
-- Orange label, non-flexible vinyl					
❏ LSP-3338 [S] Girl Happy		1971	5.00	10.00	20.00
-- Orange label, flexible vinyl					
❏ LSP-3338 [S] Girl Happy		1975	6.25	12.50	25.00
-- Tan label					
❏ AQL1-3448 Our Memories of Elvis, Volume 2		1979	5.00	10.00	20.00
❏ LPM-3450 [M] Elvis for Everyone		1965	15.00	30.00	60.00
❏ LSP-3450 [P] Elvis for Everyone		1965	15.00	30.00	60.00
-- Black label, "Stereo" on label					
❏ LSP-3450 [P] Elvis for Everyone		1968	10.00	20.00	40.00
-- Orange label, non-flexible vinyl					
❏ LSP-3450 [P] Elvis for Everyone		1971	5.00	10.00	20.00
-- Orange label, flexible vinyl					
❏ LSP-3450 [P] Elvis for Everyone		1975	5.00	10.00	20.00
-- Tan label					
❏ DJL1-3455 [DJ] Pure Elvis		1979	150.00	300.00	600.00
-- Promo-only item for Our Memories of Elvis, Volume 2; contains original version of five songs on one side, "unsweetened" versions of same songs on the other					
❏ LPM-3468 [M] Harum Scarum		1965	15.00	30.00	60.00
❏ LPM/LSP-3468 Harum Scarum Bonus Photo		1965	15.00	30.00	60.00
❏ LSP-3468 [S] Harum Scarum		1965	15.00	30.00	60.00
-- "Stereo" on black label					
❏ LPM-3553 [M] Frankie and Johnny		1966	15.00	30.00	60.00
❏ LPM/LSP-3553 Frankie and Johnny Bonus Print		1966	15.00	30.00	60.00
❏ LSP-3553 [S] Frankie and Johnny		1966	15.00	30.00	60.00
-- "Stereo" on black label					
❏ LPM-3643 [M] Paradise, Hawaiian Style		1966	15.00	30.00	60.00
❏ LSP-3643 [S] Paradise, Hawaiian Style		1966	15.00	30.00	60.00
-- "Stereo" on black label					
❏ LSP-3643 [S] Paradise, Hawaiian Style		1968	10.00	20.00	40.00
-- Orange label, non-flexible vinyl					
❏ LSP-3643 [S] Paradise, Hawaiian Style		1971	5.00	10.00	20.00
-- Orange label, flexible vinyl					

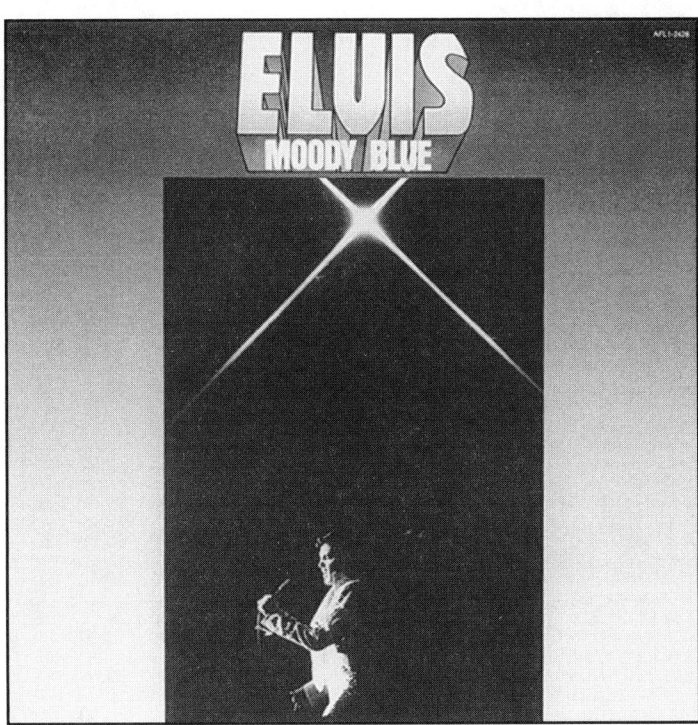

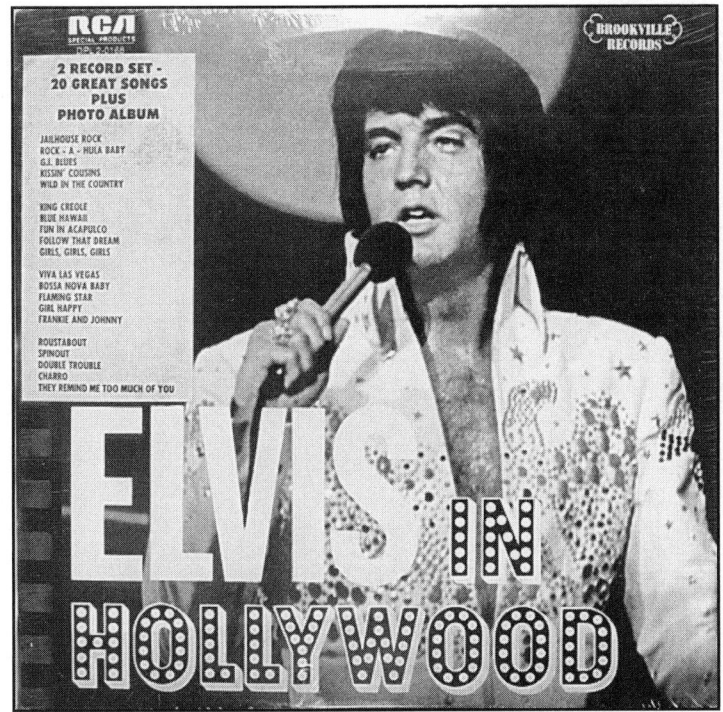

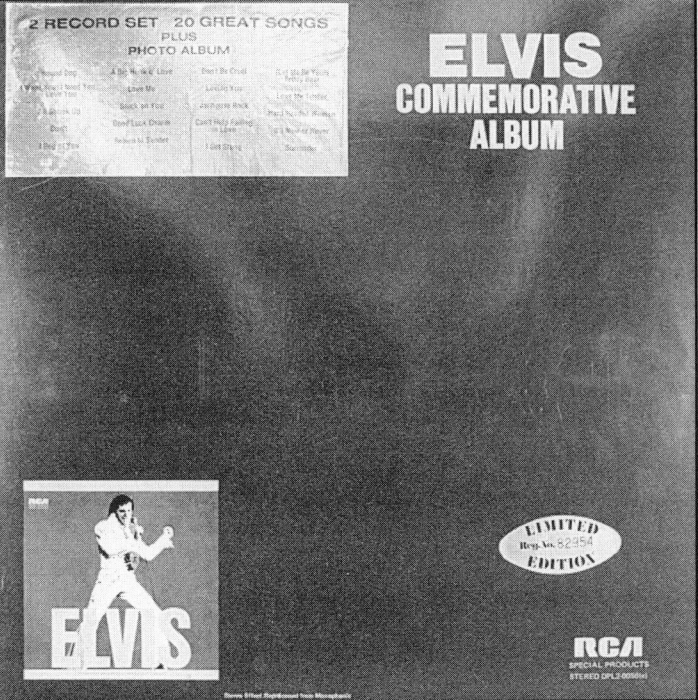

In the 1970s, Elvis' older music began to be marketed on television. Also, the quality of the new material began a rapid downturn after about 1972, though some collectibles still resulted. (Top left) *Elvis Today,* which was issued in 1975, was also available as a quadraphonic issue, which can bring three figures in near-mint condition. (Top right) The *Moody Blue* album. Versions on black vinyl or colors *other* than blue are worth money; blue vinyl versions are nearly worthless. See more on this album at the beginning of the book. (Bottom left) *Elvis in Hollywood* was a mail-order collection of songs from his movies and came with a 20-page booklet; it's a $60 item in near-mint today. (Bottom right) The *Elvis Commemorative Album* was a reissue of the popular TV-offered *Elvis.* Even its catalog number is the same as its predecessor; the only differences are in the title and in the limited-edition number on the front.

Number	Title	Yr	VG	VG+	NM
❏ CPL8-3699 [(8)] Elvis Aron Presley		1980	25.00	50.00	100.00
-- Box set; regular issue with booklet					
❏ CPL8-3699 [(8)] Elvis Aron Presley		1980	62.50	125.00	250.00
-- Box set; "Reviewer Series" edition (will be identified as such on the cover)					
❏ LPM-3702 [M] Spinout		1966	15.00	30.00	60.00
❏ LPM/LSP-3702 Spinout Bonus Photo		1966	15.00	30.00	60.00
❏ LSP-3702 [S] Spinout		1966	15.00	30.00	60.00
-- "Stereo" on black label					
❏ DJL1-3729 [DJ] Elvis Aron Presley (Excerpts)		1980	30.00	60.00	120.00
-- Promo-only excerpts of songs from box set					
❏ LPM-3758 [M] How Great Thou Art		1967	15.00	30.00	60.00
-- "Mono Dynagroove" on label					
❏ LSP-3758 [S] How Great Thou Art		1967	15.00	30.00	60.00
-- "Stereo Dynagroove" on black label					
❏ LSP-3758 [S] How Great Thou Art		1968	10.00	20.00	40.00
-- Orange label, non-flexible vinyl					
❏ LSP-3758 [S] How Great Thou Art		1971	6.25	12.50	25.00
-- Orange label, flexible vinyl					
❏ LSP-3758 [S] How Great Thou Art		1975	5.00	10.00	20.00
-- Tan label					
❏ DJL1-3781 [DJ] Elvis Aron Presley (Selections)		1980	30.00	60.00	120.00
-- Promo-only complete versions of songs from box set					
❏ LPM-3787 [M] Double Trouble		1967	15.00	30.00	60.00
-- With bonus photo announcement on cover					
❏ LPM/LSP-3787 Double Trouble Bonus Photo		1967	12.50	25.00	50.00
❏ LPM-3787 [M] Double Trouble		1967	20.00	40.00	80.00
-- With no bonus photo announcement on cover					
❏ LSP-3787 [S] Double Trouble		1967	15.00	30.00	60.00
-- With bonus photo announcement on cover					
❏ LSP-3787 [S] Double Trouble		1967	17.50	35.00	70.00
-- With no bonus photo announcement on cover; black label "Stereo"					
❏ LSP-3787 [S] Double Trouble		1968	10.00	20.00	40.00
-- Orange label, non-flexible vinyl					
❏ LSP-3787 [S] Double Trouble		1975	5.00	10.00	20.00
-- Tan label					
❏ LPM-3893 [M] Clambake		1967	62.50	125.00	250.00
❏ LPM/LSP-3893 Clambake Bonus Photo		1967	12.50	25.00	50.00
❏ LSP-3893 [S] Clambake		1967	15.00	30.00	60.00
❏ AAL1-3917 Guitar Man		1981	7.50	15.00	30.00
❏ LPM-3921 [M] Elvis' Gold Records, Volume 4		1968	500.00	1,000.	2,000.
-- "Monaural" on label					
❏ LSP-3921 [P] Elvis' Gold Records, Volume 4		1968	10.00	20.00	40.00
-- Orange label, non-flexible vinyl					
❏ LSP-3921 [P] Elvis' Gold Records, Volume 4		1968	12.50	25.00	50.00
-- "Stereo" and white "RCA Victor" on black label					
❏ LSP-3921 [P] Elvis' Gold Records, Volume 4		197?	5.00	10.00	20.00
-- Orange label, flexible vinyl					
❏ LSP-3921 [P] Elvis' Gold Records, Volume 4		1975	6.25	12.50	25.00
-- Tan label					
❏ LPM-3989 [M] Speedway		1968	500.00	1,000.	2,000.
❏ LPM/LSP-3989 Speedway Bonus Photo		1968	12.50	25.00	50.00
❏ LSP-3989 [S] Speedway		1968	15.00	30.00	60.00
-- "Stereo" on black label					
❏ LSP-3989 [S] Speedway		1968	10.00	20.00	40.00
-- Orange label, non-flexible vinyl					
❏ LSP-3989 [S] Speedway		1971	5.00	10.00	20.00
-- Orange label, flexible vinyl					
❏ LSP-3989 [S] Speedway		1975	5.00	10.00	20.00
-- Tan label					
❏ LPM-4088 Elvis (NBC-TV Special)		1968	10.00	20.00	40.00
-- Orange label, non-flexible vinyl					
❏ LPM-4088 Elvis (NBC-TV Special)		1971	7.50	15.00	30.00
-- Orange label, flexible vinyl					
❏ LPM-4088 Elvis (NBC-TV Special)		1975	5.00	10.00	20.00
-- Tan label					
❏ LSP-4155 From Elvis in Memphis		1969	10.00	20.00	40.00
-- Orange label, non-flexible vinyl					
❏ LSP-4155 From Elvis in Memphis Bonus Photo		1969	10.00	20.00	40.00
❏ LSP-4155 From Elvis in Memphis		1971	7.50	15.00	30.00
-- Orange label, flexible vinyl					
❏ LSP-4155 From Elvis in Memphis		1975	6.25	12.50	25.00
-- Tan label					
❏ LSP-4362 On Stage February, 1970		1970	10.00	20.00	40.00
-- Orange label, non-flexible vinyl					
❏ LSP-4362 On Stage February, 1970		1971	6.25	12.50	25.00
-- Orange label, flexible vinyl					
❏ LSP-4362 On Stage February, 1970		1975	6.25	12.50	25.00
-- Tan label					
❏ LSP-4362 On Stage February, 1970		1976	7.50	15.00	30.00
-- Black label, dog near top					
❏ LSP-4428 Elvis in Person at the International Hotel, Las Vegas, Nevada		1970	12.50	25.00	50.00
-- Orange label, non-flexible vinyl					
❏ LSP-4428 Elvis in Person at the International Hotel, Las Vegas, Nevada		1971	10.00	20.00	40.00
-- Orange label, flexible vinyl					
❏ LSP-4428 Elvis in Person at the International Hotel, Las Vegas, Nevada		1975	6.25	12.50	25.00
-- Tan label					

Number	Title	Yr	VG	VG+	NM
❏ LSP-4429 Back in Memphis		1970	10.00	20.00	40.00
-- Orange label, non-flexible vinyl					
❏ LSP-4429 Back in Memphis		1971	7.50	15.00	30.00
-- Orange label, flexible vinyl					
❏ LSP-4429 Back in Memphis		1975	6.25	12.50	25.00
-- Tan label					
❏ LSP-4445 That's the Way It Is		1970	20.00	40.00	80.00
-- Orange label, non-flexible vinyl					
❏ LSP-4445 That's the Way It Is		1971	6.25	12.50	25.00
-- Orange label, flexible vinyl					
❏ LSP-4445 That's the Way It Is		1975	5.00	10.00	20.00
-- Tan label					
❏ LSP-4460 Elvis Country ("I'm 10,000 Years Old")		1971	10.00	20.00	40.00
-- Orange label, non-flexible vinyl					
❏ LSP-4460 Elvis Country ("I'm 10,000 Years Old")		1971	6.25	12.50	25.00
-- Orange label, flexible vinyl					
❏ LSP-4460 Elvis Country ("I'm 10,000 Years Old") Bonus Photo		1971	3.75	7.50	15.00
-- Available in either orange-label pressing					
❏ LSP-4460 Elvis Country ("I'm 10,000 Years Old")		1975	6.25	12.50	25.00
-- Tan label					
❏ LSP-4460 Elvis Country ("I'm 10,000 Years Old")		197?	500.00	1,000.	2,000.
-- Green vinyl; black label, dog near top					
❏ LSP-4530 Love Letters from Elvis		1971	7.50	15.00	30.00
-- Orange label; "Love Letters" on one line of cover; "from" on a second line, "Elvis" on a third line					
❏ LSP-4530 Love Letters from Elvis		1971	10.00	20.00	40.00
-- Orange label; "Love Letters from" on one line of cover, "Elvis" on a second line					
❏ LSP-4530 Love Letters from Elvis		1975	6.25	12.50	25.00
-- Tan label; "Love Letters" on one line of cover; "from" on a second line, "Elvis" on a third line					
❏ LSP-4530 Love Letters from Elvis		1975	7.50	15.00	30.00
-- Tan label; "Love Letters from" on one line of cover, "Elvis" on a second line					
❏ LSP-4530 Love Letters from Elvis		1976	5.00	10.00	20.00
-- Black label, dog near top					
❏ LSP-4579 Elvis Sings the Wonderful World of Christmas		1971	7.50	15.00	30.00
-- Orange label; bonus postcard is priced separately					
❏ LSP-4579 Elvis Sings the Wonderful World of Christmas Postcard		1971	5.00	10.00	20.00
❏ LSP-4671 Elvis Now		1972	7.50	15.00	30.00
-- Orange label					
❏ LSP-4671 [DJ] Elvis Now		1972	25.00	50.00	100.00
-- Orange label; with white timing sticker on front cover					
❏ LSP-4671 Elvis Now		1975	6.25	12.50	25.00
-- Tan label					
❏ LSP-4690 He Touched Me		1972	10.00	20.00	40.00
-- Orange label					
❏ LSP-4690 [DJ] He Touched Me		1972	25.00	50.00	100.00
-- Orange label; with white timing sticker on front cover					
❏ LSP-4690 He Touched Me		1975	5.00	10.00	20.00
-- Tan label					
❏ LSP-4776 Elvis As Recorded at Madison Square Garden		1972	7.50	15.00	30.00
-- Orange label					
❏ LSP-4776 [DJ] Elvis As Recorded at Madison Square Garden		1972	25.00	50.00	100.00
-- Orange label; with white timing sticker on front cover					
❏ LSP-4776 Elvis As Recorded at Madison Square Garden		1975	5.00	10.00	20.00
-- Tan label					
❏ CPL1-4848 A Legendary Performer, Volume 4		1983	7.50	15.00	30.00
-- Includes booklet (deduct 40% if missing); with die-cut hole in front cover					
❏ CPL1-4848 A Legendary Performer, Volume 4		1986	5.00	10.00	20.00
-- No die-cut hole in cover					
❏ CPM6-5172 [(6)] A Golden Celebration		1984	25.00	50.00	100.00
❏ AFM1-5182 Rocker		1984	5.00	10.00	20.00
❏ AFM1-5196 [M] Elvis' Golden Records		1984	5.00	10.00	20.00
-- 50th Anniversary reissue in mono with banner					
❏ AFM1-5197 [M] Elvis' Gold Records Volume 2 -- 50,000,000 Elvis Fans Can't Be Wrong		1984	5.00	10.00	20.00
-- 50th Anniversary reissue in mono with banner					
❏ AFM1-5198 [M] Elvis Presley		1984	5.00	10.00	20.00
-- 50th Anniversary reissue in mono with banner					
❏ AFM1-5199 [M] Elvis		1984	5.00	10.00	20.00
-- 50th Anniversary reissue in mono with banner					
❏ AFL1-5353 A Valentine Gift for You		1985	5.00	10.00	20.00
-- Red vinyl					
❏ AFL1-5418 Reconsider Baby		1985	5.00	10.00	20.00
-- All copies on blue vinyl					
❏ AFL1-5430 Always on My Mind		1985	5.00	10.00	20.00
-- All copies on purple vinyl					
❏ AFM1-5486 [M] Elvis' Christmas Album		1985	5.00	10.00	20.00
-- Same as LOC-1035; green vinyl with booklet					
❏ UNRM-5697/8 [DJ] Special Christmas Programming		1967	300.00	600.00	1,200.
-- White label promo. Add 25% for script.					

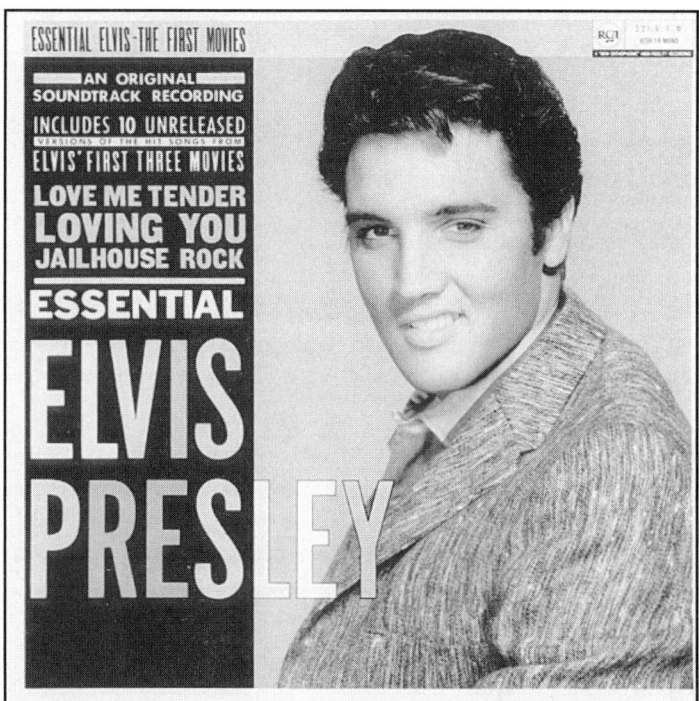

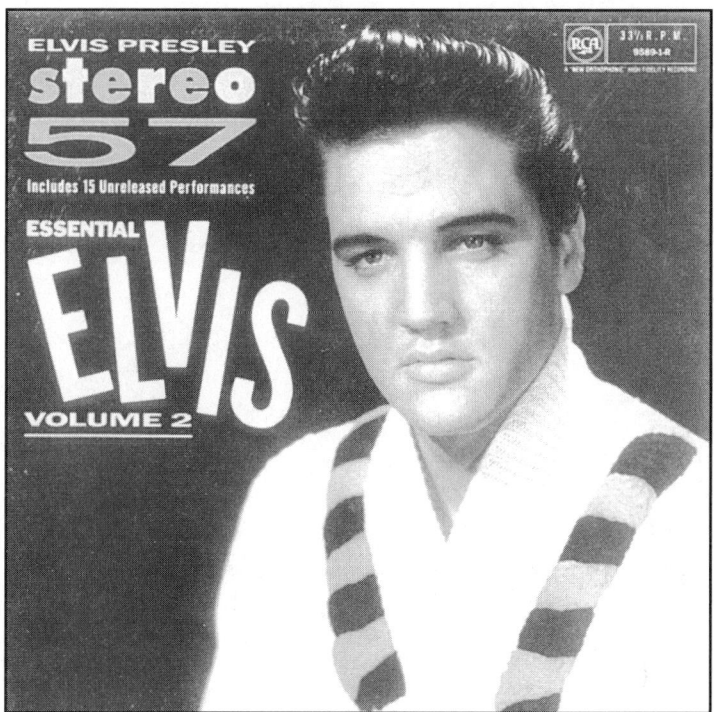

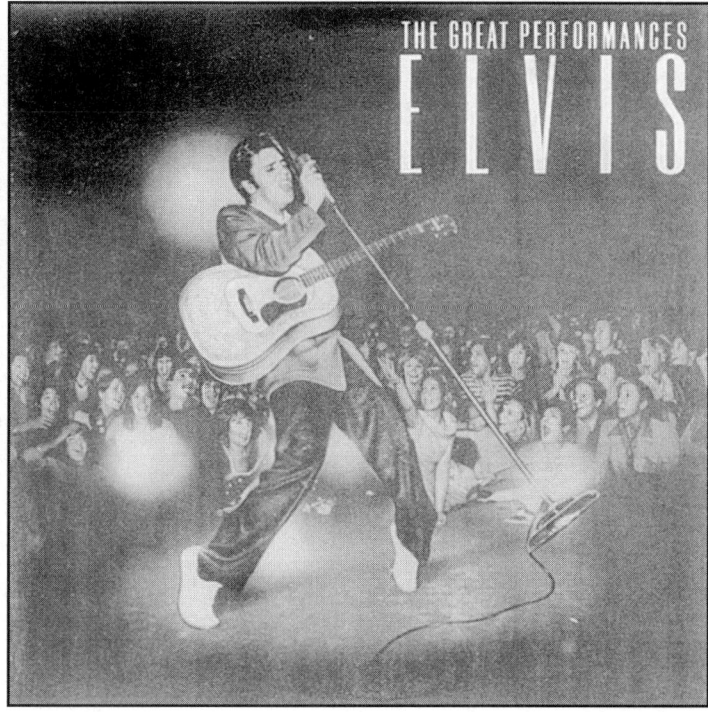

By 1987, 10 years after his death, the quality of Elvis reissues was improving, but most of the sales were taking place on compact disc, thus making the vinyl versions, in some cases, very hard to find. (Top left) *The Complete Sun Sessions*, in fact, was more nearly complete in its two-record vinyl version. The CD version was only one disc, and it deleted many of the alternate takes that can be found on the records. (Top right) Originally issued overseas before it saw U.S. release, the first of the *Essential Elvis* series was a collection of outtakes and alternate takes from his 1950s movies. (Bottom left) The second *Essential Elvis* album was a revelation: Subtitled *Stereo '57,* it featured binaural safety recordings of many of the sacred songs he recorded that later appeared on his first Christmas album. The tape boxes said they were supposed to be destroyed, but they never were. (Bottom right) One of the last Elvis albums issued on vinyl, *The Great Performances*, from 1990, featured "My Happiness," one of the two songs he recorded on an acetate in 1953 that were his first recordings.

Number	Title	Yr	VG	VG+	NM
❑ LSP-6020 [(2)]	From Memphis to Vegas/From Vegas to Memphis	1969	37.50	75.00	150.00

-- Orange labels, non-flexible vinyl; with composers of "Words" incorrectly listed as Tommy Boyce and Bobby Hart

❑ LSP-6020 [(2)]	From Memphis to Vegas/From Vegas to Memphis	1969	25.00	50.00	100.00

-- Orange labels, non-flexible vinyl; with composers of "Words" correctly listed as Barry, Robin and Maurice Gibb

❑ LSP-6020	From Memphis to Vegas/From Memphis Bonus Photos	1969	12.50	25.00	50.00

-- Four different photos came with LP, but no more than two per set. Value is for any two different of the four photos.

❑ LSP-6020 [(2)]	From Memphis to Vegas/From Vegas to Memphis	1971	10.00	20.00	40.00

-- Orange labels, flexible vinyl

❑ LSP-6020 [(2)]	From Memphis to Vegas/From Vegas to Memphis	1975	7.50	15.00	30.00

-- Tan labels

❑ LSP-6020 [(2)]	From Memphis to Vegas/From Vegas to Memphis	1976	5.00	10.00	20.00

-- Black label, dog near top

❑ VPSX-6089 [(2) DJ]	Aloha from Hawaii Via Satellite	1973	500.00	1,000.	2,000.

-- Orange or dark orange label; with white timing sticker on front cover

❑ VPSX-6089 [(2) Q]	Aloha from Hawaii Via Satellite	1973	2,500.	3,750.	5,000.

-- Stokely-Van Camp employee version with Saturn-shaped sticker on front cover with "Chicken of the Sea" and mermaid

❑ VPSX-6089 [(2) Q]	Aloha from Hawaii Via Satellite	1973	25.00	50.00	100.00

-- Dark orange labels, "QuadraDisc" on top, "RCA" on bottom

❑ VPSX-6089 [(2) Q]	Aloha from Hawaii Via Satellite	1973	10.00	20.00	40.00

-- Lighter orange labels, "RCA" on side

❑ VPSX-6089 [(2) Q]	Aloha from Hawaii Via Satellite	1975	7.50	15.00	30.00

-- Tan labels

❑ LPM-6401 [(4)]	Worldwide 50 Gold Award Hits, Vol. 1	1970	20.00	40.00	80.00

-- Orange labels, non-flexible vinyl; with blurb for photo book on cover

❑ LPM-6401 [(4)]	Worldwide 50 Gold Award Hits, Vol. 1	1970	20.00	40.00	80.00

-- Orange labels, flexible vinyl; with blurb for photo book on cover

❑ LPM-6401	Worldwide 50 Gold Award Hits, Vol. 1 Photo Book	1970	10.00	20.00	40.00

-- Two different books have been found in this LP box; price is for either

❑ LPM-6401 [(4)]	Worldwide 50 Gold Award Hits, Vol. 1	1975	10.00	20.00	40.00

-- Tan labels

❑ LPM-6401 [(4)]	Worldwide 50 Gold Award Hits, Vol. 1	1977	7.50	15.00	30.00

-- Black labels, dog near top

❑ LPM-6402 [(4)]	The Other Sides: Worldwide 50 Gold Award Hits, Vol. 2	1971	17.50	35.00	70.00

-- Orange labels, flexible vinyl; with blurb for inserts on cover

❑ LPM-6402	The Other Sides: Worldwide 50 Gold Award Hits, Vol. 2 Swatch and Envelope	1971	6.25	12.50	25.00
❑ LPM-6402	The Other Sides: Worldwide 50 Gold Award Hits, Vol. 2 Poster	1971	6.25	12.50	25.00
❑ LPM-6402 [(4)]	The Other Sides: Worldwide 50 Gold Award Hits, Vol. 2	1975	7.50	15.00	30.00

-- Tan labels

❑ LPM-6402 [(4)]	The Other Sides: Worldwide 50 Gold Award Hits, Vol. 2	1977	5.00	10.00	20.00

-- Black labels, dog near top

❑ KKL1-7065	A Canadian Tribute	1978	5.00	10.00	20.00

-- Gold vinyl, embossed cover

❑ R 213690 [(2)]	Worldwide Gold Award Hits, Parts 1 & 2	1974	30.00	60.00	120.00

-- RCA Record Club version; one label is orange, the other is tan (orange label on both records is unknown)

❑ R 213690 [(2)]	Worldwide Gold Award Hits, Parts 1 & 2	1974	10.00	20.00	40.00

-- RCA Record Club version; tan labels

❑ R 213690 [(2)]	Worldwide Gold Award Hits, Parts 1 & 2	1977	6.25	12.50	25.00

-- RCA Record Club version; black labels, dog near top

❑ R 213736 [(2) S]	Aloha from Hawaii Via Satellite	1973	17.50	35.00	70.00

-- RCA Record Club edition in stereo instead of quadraphonic; orange labels

❑ R 213736 [(2) S]	Aloha from Hawaii Via Satellite	1975	15.00	30.00	60.00

-- RCA Record Club edition in stereo instead of quadraphonic; tan labels

❑ R 213736 [(2) S]	Aloha from Hawaii Via Satellite	1977	7.50	5.00	30.00

-- RCA Record Club edition in stereo instead of quadraphonic; black labels, dog near top

❑ R 214657 [(2)]	Worldwide Gold Award Hits, Parts 3 & 4	1978	5.00	10.00	20.00

-- RCA Record Club version; black labels, dog near top

❑ R 233299(e) [(2)]	Country Classics	1980	10.00	20.00	40.00

-- RCA Music Service exclusive

❑ R 234340 [(2)]	From Elvis with Love	1978	10.00	20.00	40.00

-- RCA Music Service exclusive

❑ R 244047 [(2)]	The Legendary Concert Performances	1978	10.00	20.00	40.00

-- RCA Music Service exclusive

❑ R 244069 [(2)]	Country Memories	1978	10.00	20.00	40.00

-- RCA Music Service exclusive

Number	Title	Yr	VG	VG+	NM
READER'S DIGEST					
❑ RD10/A [(8)]	His Greatest Hits	1979	100.00	200.00	400.00

-- White box

❑ 010/A [(7)]	His Greatest Hits	1983	15.00	30.00	60.00

-- Yellow box

❑ 010/A [(7)]	His Greatest Hits	1990	10.00	20.00	40.00

-- White box

❑ RBA-072/D	Great Hits of 1956-57	1987	5.00	10.00	20.00
❑ RD4A-181/D	Elvis Sings Inspirational Favorites	1983	5.00	10.00	20.00
❑ RB4-191/A [(7)]	The Legend Lives On	1986	15.00	30.00	60.00
❑ RDA-242/D	Elvis Sings Country Favorites	1984	15.00	30.00	60.00
SHOW-LAND					
❑ LP-2001	The First of Elvis	1979	25.00	50.00	100.00
SILHOUETTE					
❑ 10001/2 [(2)]	Personally Elvis	1979	7.50	15.00	30.00

-- Interview records; no music

STARDAY					
❑ SD-995	Interviews with Elvis (Canada 1957)	1978	10.00	20.00	40.00

-- Reissue of Great Northwest album

SUN					
❑ 1001	The Sun Years -- Interviews and Memories	1977	6.25	12.50	25.00

-- With "Memphis, Tennessee" on label

TIME-LIFE					
❑ STL-106 [(2)]	Elvis Presley: 1954-1961	1986	7.50	15.00	30.00
❑ STW-106	Country Music	1981	5.00	10.00	20.00
❑ STL-126 [(2)]	Elvis the King: 1954-1965	1989	20.00	40.00	80.00

PRESNELL, HARVE
MGM

Number	Title	Yr	VG	VG+	NM
❑ E-4194 [M]	The World's Greatest Love Songs	1964	5.00	10.00	20.00
❑ SE-4194 [S]	The World's Greatest Love Songs	1964	6.25	12.50	25.00
❑ E-4266 [M]	New Echoes of the Old West	1965	5.00	10.00	20.00
❑ SE-4266 [S]	New Echoes of the Old West	1965	6.25	12.50	25.00

PRESTI, IDA, AND ALEXANDRE LAGOYA
MERCURY LIVING PRESENCE

Number	Title	Yr	VG	VG+	NM
❑ SR 90380 [S]	Four Concertos for Two Guitars by Vivaldi	196?	6.25	12.50	25.00

-- Maroon label, no "Vendor: Mercury Record Corporation"

❑ SR 90427 [S]	Spanish Music for Two Guitars	196?	10.00	20.00	40.00

-- Maroon label, no "Vendor: Mercury Record Corporation"

❑ SR 90457 [S]	Baroque Music for Two Guitars	196?	12.50	25.00	50.00

-- Maroon label, with "Vendor: Mercury Record Corporation"

PRESTON, BILLY
APPLE

Number	Title	Yr	VG	VG+	NM
❑ ST-3359	That's the Way God Planned It	1969	12.50	25.00	50.00

-- Cover has close-up of Billy Preston

❑ ST-3359	That's the Way God Planned It	1972	5.00	10.00	20.00

-- Cover has multiple images of Billy Preston

❑ ST-3370	Encouraging Words	1970	5.00	10.00	20.00
CAPITOL					
❑ ST 2532 [S]	Wildest Organ in Town!	1966	10.00	20.00	40.00
❑ T 2532 [M]	Wildest Organ in Town!	1966	7.50	15.00	30.00
❑ DT 2607 [R]	Club Meetin'	1967	5.00	10.00	20.00
❑ T 2607 [M]	Club Meetin'	1967	7.50	15.00	30.00
DERBY					
❑ LPM-701 [M]	16 Year Old Soul	1963	62.50	125.00	250.00
EXODUS					
❑ 304 [M]	Early Hits of 1965	1965	6.25	12.50	25.00
VEE JAY					
❑ LP-1123 [M]	The Most Exciting Organ Ever	1965	7.50	15.00	30.00
❑ LPS-1123 [S]	The Most Exciting Organ Ever	1965	12.50	25.00	50.00
❑ LP-1142 [M]	Greatest Hits	1966	7.50	15.00	30.00
❑ LPS-1142 [S]	Greatest Hits	1966	12.50	25.00	50.00

PRESTON, JOHNNY
MERCURY

Number	Title	Yr	VG	VG+	NM
❑ MG-20592 [M]	Running Bear	1960	25.00	50.00	100.00
❑ MG-20609 [M]	Come Rock with Me	1960	25.00	50.00	100.00
❑ SR-60250 [S]	Running Bear	1960	37.50	75.00	150.00

-- Black label

❑ SR-60609 [S]	Come Rock with Me	1960	37.50	75.00	150.00
WING					
❑ MGW-12246 [M]	Running Bear	1963	5.00	10.00	20.00
❑ SRW-16246 [S]	Running Bear	1963	6.25	12.50	25.00

Number	Title	Yr	VG	VG+	NM

PRETENDERS
NAUTILUS
| ❑ NR-38 | Pretenders | 1982 | 7.50 | 15.00 | 30.00 |

-- *Audiophile vinyl*

WARNER BROS.
| ❑ WBMS-114 [DJ] | Pretenders Live | 1980 | 10.00 | 20.00 | 40.00 |

-- *Part of "The Warner Bros. Music Show" series; comes in red die-cut cover*

| ❑ WBMS-121 [DJ] | Pretenders Live (Star Fleet) | 1982 | 10.00 | 20.00 | 40.00 |

-- *Part of "The Warner Bros. Music Show" series; comes in black cover with white sticker*

| ❑ WBMS-142 [DJ] | Get Close Interview | 1987 | 5.00 | 10.00 | 20.00 |

-- *Part of "The Warner Bros. Music Show" series*

PRETTY POISON
SVENGALI
| ❑ SRPP-1 [EP] | Laced | 1984 | 5.00 | 10.00 | 20.00 |

PRETTY THINGS, THE
FONTANA
| ❑ MGF-27544 [M] | The Pretty Things | 1965 | 20.00 | 40.00 | 80.00 |
| ❑ SRF-67544 [P] | The Pretty Things | 1965 | 20.00 | 40.00 | 80.00 |

RARE EARTH
| ❑ RS 506 | S.F. Sorrow | 1969 | 12.50 | 25.00 | 50.00 |

-- *Original covers are rounded at top*

| ❑ RS 506 | S.F. Sorrow | 1969 | 5.00 | 10.00 | 20.00 |

-- *Later copies are standard in shape*

| ❑ RS 515 | Parachute | 1970 | 5.00 | 10.00 | 20.00 |

PREVIN, ANDRE
COLUMBIA
❑ CL 1530 [M]	Give My Regards to Broadway	1960	5.00	10.00	20.00
❑ CL 1569 [M]	Camelot	1961	5.00	10.00	20.00
❑ CL 1595 [M]	Thinking of You	1961	5.00	10.00	20.00
❑ CL 1649 [M]	A Touch of Elegance	1961	5.00	10.00	20.00
❑ CL 1741 [M]	Mack the Knife and Other Kurt Weill Music	1962	5.00	10.00	20.00
❑ CL 1786 [M]	Faraway Part of Town	1962	5.00	10.00	20.00
❑ CL 1888 [M]	The Light Fantastic	1962	5.00	10.00	20.00
❑ CS 8233 [S]	Like Love	1960	5.00	10.00	20.00
❑ CS 8286 [S]	Rhapsody in Blue	1960	5.00	10.00	20.00
❑ CS 8330 [S]	Give My Regards to Broadway	1960	6.25	12.50	25.00
❑ CS 8369 [S]	Camelot	1961	6.25	12.50	25.00
❑ CS 8395 [S]	Thinking of You	1961	6.25	12.50	25.00
❑ CS 8541 [S]	Mack the Knife and Other Kurt Weill Music	1962	6.25	12.50	25.00
❑ CS 8586 [S]	Faraway Part of Town	1962	6.25	12.50	25.00
❑ CS 8649 [S]	A Touch of Elegance	1961	6.25	12.50	25.00
❑ CS 8688 [S]	The Light Fantastic	1962	6.25	12.50	25.00
❑ CS 8834 [S]	Andre Previn in Hollywood	1963	5.00	10.00	20.00
❑ CS 8914 [S]	The Soft and Swinging Music of Jimmy McHugh	1964	5.00	10.00	20.00
❑ CS 8995 [S]	My Fair Lady	1964	5.00	10.00	20.00
❑ CS 9094 [S]	Popular Previn	1965	5.00	10.00	20.00

CONTEMPORARY
❑ C-3525 [M]	Andre Previn with Shelly Manne	1956	12.50	25.00	50.00
❑ C-3537 [M]	Double Play!	1957	12.50	25.00	50.00
❑ C-3543 [M]	Pal Joey	1957	12.50	25.00	50.00
❑ C-3548 [M]	Gigi	1958	12.50	25.00	50.00
❑ M-3558 [M]	Andre Previn Plays Vernon Duke	1959	12.50	25.00	50.00
❑ M-3567 [M]	Andre Previn Plays Jerome Kern	1959	12.50	25.00	50.00
❑ M-3570 [M]	Jazz Trio, King Size	1959	12.50	25.00	50.00
❑ M-3572 [M]	West Side Story	1960	10.00	20.00	40.00
❑ M-3575 [M]	Like Previn	1960	10.00	20.00	40.00
❑ M-3586 [M]	Andre Previn Plays Harold Arlen	1960	10.00	20.00	40.00
❑ S-7011 [S]	Double Play!	1959	10.00	20.00	40.00
❑ S-7543 [S]	Pal Joey	1959	10.00	20.00	40.00
❑ S-7548 [S]	Gigi	1959	10.00	20.00	40.00
❑ S-7558 [S]	Andre Previn Plays Vernon Duke	1959	10.00	20.00	40.00
❑ S-7567 [S]	Andre Previn Plays Jerome Kern	1959	10.00	20.00	40.00
❑ S-7570 [S]	Jazz Trio, King Size	1959	10.00	20.00	40.00
❑ S-7572 [S]	West Side Story	1960	7.50	15.00	30.00
❑ S-7575 [S]	Like Previn	1960	7.50	15.00	30.00
❑ S-7586 [S]	Andre Previn Plays Harold Arlen	1960	7.50	15.00	30.00

DECCA
| ❑ DL 8131 [M] | Let's Get Away From It All | 1955 | 10.00 | 20.00 | 40.00 |
| ❑ DL 8341 [M] | Hollywood at Midnight | 1957 | 10.00 | 20.00 | 40.00 |

MGM
❑ E-3716 [M]	Secret Songs for Young Lovers	1959	5.00	10.00	20.00
❑ SE-3716 [S]	Secret Songs for Young Lovers	1959	6.25	12.50	25.00
❑ E-3811 [M]	Like Blue	1960	5.00	10.00	20.00
❑ SE-3811 [S]	Like Blue	1960	6.25	12.50	25.00
❑ SE-4186 [S]	Andre Previn -- Composer, Conductor, Arranger, Pianist	1964	5.00	10.00	20.00

MOBILE FIDELITY
| ❑ 1-095 | West Side Story | 1982 | 6.25 | 12.50 | 25.00 |

-- *Audiophile vinyl*

MONARCH
| ❑ 203 [10] | All Star Jazz | 1952 | 20.00 | 40.00 | 80.00 |
| ❑ 204 [10] | Andre Previn Plays Duke | 1952 | 20.00 | 40.00 | 80.00 |

RCA VICTOR
❑ LPM-1011 [M]	Gershwin	1955	10.00	20.00	40.00
❑ LPM-1356 [M]	Three Little Words	1957	10.00	20.00	40.00
❑ LPT-3002 [10]	Andre Previn Plays Harry Warren	1952	20.00	40.00	80.00

STEREO RECORDS
❑ S-7004 [S]	Pal Joey	1958	12.50	25.00	50.00
❑ S-7011 [S]	Double Play!	1958	12.50	25.00	50.00
❑ S-7020 [S]	Gigi	1958	12.50	25.00	50.00

PRICE, ALAN
Also see THE ANIMALS.
PARROT
| ❑ PAS 71018 [P] | The Price Is Right | 1968 | 7.50 | 15.00 | 30.00 |

PRICE, KENNY
BOONE
| ❑ 1211 | One Hit Follows Another | 1967 | 6.25 | 12.50 | 25.00 |
| ❑ 1214 | Southern Bound | 1968 | 6.25 | 12.50 | 25.00 |

RCA VICTOR
❑ LSP-4224	Happy Tracks	1969	5.00	10.00	20.00
❑ LSP-4292	The Heavyweight	1970	5.00	10.00	20.00
❑ LSP-4373	Northeast Arkansas Mississippi County Bootlegger	1970	5.00	10.00	20.00
❑ LSP-4469	The Red Foley Songbook	1971	5.00	10.00	20.00
❑ LSP-4527	The Sheriff of Boone County	1971	5.00	10.00	20.00
❑ LSP-4605	Charlotte Fever	1971	5.00	10.00	20.00
❑ LSP-4681	Supersideman	1972	5.00	10.00	20.00
❑ LSP-4763	You Almost Slipped My Mind	1972	5.00	10.00	20.00
❑ LSP-4839	Sea of Heartbreak	1973	5.00	10.00	20.00

PRICE, LEONTYNE
LONDON
| ❑ 5644 [M] | A Christmas Offering | 1961 | 5.00 | 10.00 | 20.00 |
| ❑ OS 25280 [S] | A Christmas Offering | 1961 | 6.25 | 12.50 | 25.00 |

RCA VICTOR RED SEAL
| ❑ LSC-2279 [S] | A Program of Song | 1959 | 5.00 | 10.00 | 20.00 |

-- *Original with "shaded dog" label*

| ❑ LSC-2600 [S] | Swing Low, Sweet Chariot | 1962 | 6.25 | 12.50 | 25.00 |

-- *Original with "shaded dog" label*

PRICE, LLOYD
ABC-PARAMOUNT
❑ 277 [M]	The Exciting Lloyd Price	1959	10.00	20.00	40.00
❑ S-277 [S]	The Exciting Lloyd Price	1959	20.00	40.00	80.00
❑ 297 [M]	Mr. Personality	1959	10.00	20.00	40.00
❑ S-297 [S]	Mr. Personality	1959	20.00	40.00	80.00
❑ 315 [M]	Mr. Personality Sings the Blues	1960	10.00	20.00	40.00
❑ S-315 [S]	Mr. Personality Sings the Blues	1960	20.00	40.00	80.00
❑ 324 [M]	Mr. Personality's Big 15	1960	10.00	20.00	40.00
❑ 346 [M]	The Fantastic Lloyd Price	1960	10.00	20.00	40.00
❑ S-346 [R]	The Fantastic Lloyd Price	196?	6.25	12.50	25.00
❑ 366 [M]	Lloyd Price Sings the Million Sellers	1961	10.00	20.00	40.00
❑ S-366 [S]	Lloyd Price Sings the Million Sellers	1961	12.50	25.00	50.00
❑ 382 [M]	Cookin' with Lloyd Price	1961	10.00	20.00	40.00
❑ S-382 [S]	Cookin' with Lloyd Price	1961	12.50	25.00	50.00

DOUBLE-L
❑ DL-2301 [M]	The Lloyd Price Orchestra	1963	6.25	12.50	25.00
❑ DL-2303 [M]	Misty	1963	6.25	12.50	25.00
❑ SDL-8301 [S]	The Lloyd Price Orchestra	1963	10.00	20.00	40.00
❑ SDL-8303 [S]	Misty	1963	10.00	20.00	40.00

JAD
| ❑ 1002 | Lloyd Price Now | 1969 | 6.25 | 12.50 | 25.00 |

MONUMENT
| ❑ MLP-8032 [M] | Lloyd Swings for Sammy | 1965 | 6.25 | 12.50 | 25.00 |
| ❑ SLP-18032 [S] | Lloyd Swings for Sammy | 1965 | 10.00 | 20.00 | 40.00 |

SPECIALTY
| ❑ SP-2105 [M] | Lloyd Price | 1959 | 45.00 | 90.00 | 180.00 |

PRICE, RAY
COLUMBIA
❑ CL 1015 [M]	Ray Price Sings Heart Songs	1957	12.50	25.00	50.00
❑ CL 1148 [M]	Talk to Your Heart	1958	10.00	20.00	40.00
❑ CL 1494 [M]	Faith	1960	7.50	15.00	30.00
❑ CL 1566 [M]	Ray Price's Greatest Hits	1961	7.50	15.00	30.00
❑ CL 1756 [M]	San Antonio Rose	1962	5.00	10.00	20.00
❑ CL 2339 [M]	Western Strings	1965	5.00	10.00	20.00
❑ CL 2606 [M]	Touch My Heart	1967	5.00	10.00	20.00

Number	Title	Yr	VG	VG+	NM
❑ CL 2670 [M]	Ray Price's Greatest Hits, Volume 2	1967	5.00	10.00	20.00
❑ CL 2677 [M]	Danny Boy	1967	5.00	10.00	20.00
❑ CL 2806 [M]	Take Me As I Am	1968	7.50	15.00	30.00
❑ CS 8285 [S]	Faith	1960	10.00	20.00	40.00
❑ CS 8556 [S]	San Antonio Rose	1962	7.50	15.00	30.00
❑ CS 8771 [S]	Night Life	1963	5.00	10.00	20.00
❑ CS 8989 [S]	Love Life	1964	5.00	10.00	20.00
❑ CS 9089 [S]	Burning Memories	1965	5.00	10.00	20.00
❑ CS 9139 [S]	Western Strings	1965	6.25	12.50	25.00
❑ CS 9182 [S]	The Other Woman	1965	5.00	10.00	20.00
❑ CS 9328 [S]	Another Bridge to Burn	1966	5.00	10.00	20.00
❑ CQ 30106 [Q]	For the Good Times	1972	5.00	10.00	20.00

PRICE, RUTH
AVA

Number	Title	Yr	VG	VG+	NM
❑ A-54 [M]	Live and Beautiful	1963	10.00	20.00	40.00
❑ AS-54 [S]	Live and Beautiful	1963	12.50	25.00	50.00

CONTEMPORARY

Number	Title	Yr	VG	VG+	NM
❑ M-3590 [M]	Ruth Price with Shelly Manne at the Manne-Hole	1961	12.50	25.00	50.00
❑ S-7590 [S]	Ruth Price with Shelly Manne at the Manne-Hole	1961	15.00	30.00	60.00

KAPP

Number	Title	Yr	VG	VG+	NM
❑ KL-1006 [M]	My Name Is Ruth Price. I Sing.	1955	25.00	50.00	100.00
❑ KL-1054 [M]	The Party's Over	1957	25.00	50.00	100.00

ROOST

Number	Title	Yr	VG	VG+	NM
❑ LP-2217 [M]	Ruth Price Sings!	195?	25.00	50.00	100.00

PRICE, VINCENT
CAEDMON

Number	Title	Yr	VG	VG+	NM
❑ TC-1059 [M]	Vincent Price Reads Poems of Shelley	196?	7.50	15.00	30.00

CAPITOL

Number	Title	Yr	VG	VG+	NM
❑ SWBB-342 [(2)]	Witchcraft/Magic	1969	7.50	15.00	30.00

CAPITOL CUSTOM

Number	Title	Yr	VG	VG+	NM
❑ SGP-6256/7 [S]	The World Tomorrow	1965	10.00	20.00	40.00
-- Blue vinyl					
❑ SGP-6258/9 [S]	The World of the 21st Century	1965	10.00	20.00	40.00
-- Blue vinyl					

COLUMBIA MASTERWORKS

Number	Title	Yr	VG	VG+	NM
❑ ML 5668 [M]	America the Beautiful	1961	7.50	15.00	30.00

DOT

Number	Title	Yr	VG	VG+	NM
❑ DLP-3195 [M]	Gallery	1962	6.25	12.50	25.00
❑ DLP-25195 [S]	Gallery	1962	7.50	15.00	30.00

NELSON INDUSTRIES

Number	Title	Yr	VG	VG+	NM
❑ (# unknown)	International Cooking Course	1977	10.00	20.00	40.00

PRIDE
WARNER BROS.

Number	Title	Yr	VG	VG+	NM
❑ WS 1848	Pride	1970	6.25	12.50	25.00

PRIDE, CHARLEY
RCA VICTOR

Number	Title	Yr	VG	VG+	NM
❑ APD1-0217 [Q]	Sweet Country	1973	6.25	12.50	25.00
❑ APD1-0397 [Q]	Amazing Love	1974	6.25	12.50	25.00
❑ APD1-0757 [Q]	Pride of America	1974	6.25	12.50	25.00
❑ APD1-1038 [Q]	Charley	1975	6.25	12.50	25.00
❑ APD1-1241 [Q]	The Happiness of Having You	1975	6.25	12.50	25.00
❑ APD1-1359 [Q]	Sunday Morning with Charley Pride	1976	6.25	12.50	25.00
❑ LPM-3645 [M]	Country Charley Pride	1966	6.25	12.50	25.00
❑ LSP-3645 [S]	Country Charley Pride	1966	7.50	15.00	30.00
❑ LPM-3775 [M]	The Pride of Country Music	1967	6.25	12.50	25.00
❑ LSP-3775 [S]	The Pride of Country Music	1967	5.00	10.00	20.00
❑ LPM-3895 [M]	The Country Way	1967	6.25	12.50	25.00
❑ LSP-3895 [S]	The Country Way	1967	5.00	10.00	20.00
❑ LPM-3952 [M]	Make Mine Country	1968	15.00	30.00	60.00
❑ LSP-3952 [S]	Make Mine Country	1968	5.00	10.00	20.00
❑ LSP-4041	Songs of Pride -- Charley, That Is	1968	5.00	10.00	20.00
❑ LSP-4094	Charley Pride -- In Person	1969	5.00	10.00	20.00
❑ LSP-4153	The Sensational Charley Pride	1969	5.00	10.00	20.00
❑ LSP-4223	The Best of Charley Pride	1969	5.00	10.00	20.00
❑ LSP-4290	Just Plain Charley	1970	5.00	10.00	20.00
❑ LSP-4367	Charley Pride's 10th Album	1970	5.00	10.00	20.00
❑ LSP-4406	Christmas in My Home Town	1970	5.00	10.00	20.00
❑ LSP-4468	From Me to You	1971	5.00	10.00	20.00
❑ LSP-4513	Did You Think to Pray	1971	5.00	10.00	20.00
❑ LSP-4560	I'm Just Me	1971	5.00	10.00	20.00
❑ LSP-4617	Charley Pride Sings Heart Songs	1971	5.00	10.00	20.00
❑ LSP-4682	The Best of Charley Pride, Volume 2	1972	5.00	10.00	20.00
❑ LSP-4742	A Sunshiny Day with Charley Pride	1972	5.00	10.00	20.00

READER'S DIGEST

Number	Title	Yr	VG	VG+	NM
❑ (# unknown) [(6)]	Charley Pride's Country	1979	10.00	20.00	40.00

PRIMA, LOUIS
CAPITOL

Number	Title	Yr	VG	VG+	NM
❑ T 755 [M]	The Wildest	1956	12.50	25.00	50.00
❑ T 836 [M]	Call of the Wildest	1957	12.50	25.00	50.00
❑ T 908 [M]	The Wildest Show at Tahoe	1957	12.50	25.00	50.00
❑ T 1010 [M]	Las Vegas Prima Style	1958	12.50	25.00	50.00
❑ T 1132 [M]	Strictly Prima	1959	7.50	15.00	30.00
❑ ST 1723 [S]	The Wildest Comes Home	1962	7.50	15.00	30.00
❑ T 1723 [M]	The Wildest Comes Home	1962	6.25	12.50	25.00
❑ ST 1797 [S]	Lake Tahoe Prima Style	1962	7.50	15.00	30.00
❑ T 1797 [M]	Lake Tahoe Prima Style	1962	6.25	12.50	25.00

COLUMBIA

Number	Title	Yr	VG	VG+	NM
❑ CL 1206 [M]	Breakin' It Up	1959	10.00	20.00	40.00

DOT

Number	Title	Yr	VG	VG+	NM
❑ DLP-3262 [M]	His Greatest Hits	1960	6.25	12.50	25.00
❑ DLP-3264 [M]	Pretty Music Prima Style	1960	6.25	12.50	25.00
❑ DLP-3352 [M]	Wonderland by Night	1960	6.25	12.50	25.00
❑ DLP-3385 [M]	Blue Moon	1961	6.25	12.50	25.00
❑ DLP-3392 [M]	Return of the Wildest!	1961	6.25	12.50	25.00
❑ DLP-3410 [M]	Doin' the Twist	1961	6.25	12.50	25.00
❑ DLP-25262 [S]	His Greatest Hits	1960	7.50	15.00	30.00
❑ DLP-25264 [S]	Pretty Music Prima Style	1960	7.50	15.00	30.00
❑ DLP-25352 [S]	Wonderland by Night	1960	7.50	15.00	30.00
❑ DLP-25385 [S]	Blue Moon	1961	7.50	15.00	30.00
❑ DLP-25392 [S]	Return of the Wildest!	1961	7.50	15.00	30.00
❑ DLP-25410 [S]	Doin' the Twist	1961	7.50	15.00	30.00

MERCURY

Number	Title	Yr	VG	VG+	NM
❑ MG-25142 [10]	Louis Prima Plays	1953	20.00	40.00	80.00

RONDO-LETTE

Number	Title	Yr	VG	VG+	NM
❑ 9 [M]	Louis Prima in All His Moods	1959	7.50	15.00	30.00

PRIMA, LOUIS, AND KEELY SMITH
CAPITOL

Number	Title	Yr	VG	VG+	NM
❑ T 1160 [M]	Hey Boy! Hey Girl!	1959	12.50	25.00	50.00
❑ ST 1531 [S]	The Hits of Louis and Keely	1961	7.50	15.00	30.00
❑ T 1531 [M]	The Hits of Louis and Keely	1961	6.25	12.50	25.00

DOT

Number	Title	Yr	VG	VG+	NM
❑ DLP-3210 [M]	Louis and Keely!	1959	7.50	15.00	30.00
❑ DLP-3263 [M]	Together	1960	6.25	12.50	25.00
❑ DLP-3266 [M]	Louis and Keely on Stage	1960	6.25	12.50	25.00
❑ DLP-25210 [S]	Louis and Keely!	1959	10.00	20.00	40.00
❑ DLP-25263 [S]	Together	1960	7.50	15.00	30.00
❑ DLP-25266 [S]	Louis and Keely on Stage	1960	7.50	15.00	30.00

PRINCE
Also see THE LEWIS CONNECTION; 94 EAST.
NPG/BELLMARK

Number	Title	Yr	VG	VG+	NM
❑ 71003 [EP]	The Beautiful Experience	1994	5.00	10.00	20.00

PAISLEY PARK

Number	Title	Yr	VG	VG+	NM
❑ 25677	The Black Album	1987	500.00	1,000.	2,000.
-- Withdrawn prior to release, though a few copies escaped. Numerous counterfeits exist on other labels and colored vinyl.					
❑ 25677DJ [(2)]	The Black Album	1987	750.00	1,500.	3,000.
-- Entire album on two 12-inch records that play at 45 RPM					
❑ 25720DJ [DJ]	Lovesexy	1988	5.00	10.00	20.00
-- Gold stamped and stickered cover (no UPC) with promo labels; tracks are banded					

WARNER BROS.

Number	Title	Yr	VG	VG+	NM
❑ BSK 3150	For You	1978	5.00	10.00	20.00
-- First edition on Burbank "palm trees" label					
❑ PRO-A-7270 [(2)DJ]	Come	1994	7.50	15.00	30.00
-- Promo-only vinyl					
❑ PRO-A-7330 [DJ]	The Black Album	1994	12.50	25.00	50.00
-- Promo-only vinyl					
❑ PRO-A-7835 [(2)DJ]	The Gold Experience	1995	20.00	40.00	80.00
-- Promo-only gold vinyl with numbered gold foil jacket					
❑ 25110	Purple Rain	1984	12.50	25.00	50.00
-- Purple vinyl; comes with poster					
❑ 45793 [DJ]	The Black Album	1994	100.00	200.00	400.00
-- Black and white vinyl; 50 copies					
❑ 45793 [DJ]	The Black Album	1994	50.00	100.00	200.00
-- White vinyl; 300 copies, numbered in gold on the label					
❑ 45793 [DJ]	The Black Album	1994	30.00	60.00	120.00
-- Peach vinyl; 1,000 copies					

PRINCE BUSTER
RCA VICTOR

Number	Title	Yr	VG	VG+	NM
❑ LPM-3792 [M]	Ten Commandments	1967	6.25	12.50	25.00
❑ LSP-3792 [S]	Ten Commandments	1967	7.50	15.00	30.00

PRINZ, ROSEMARY
PHAROS

Number	Title	Yr	VG	VG+	NM
❑ MN-10001 [M]	TV's Penny Sings	1966	5.00	10.00	20.00
❑ SN-30001 [S]	TV's Penny Sings	1966	6.25	12.50	25.00

Number	Title	Yr	VG	VG+	NM

PROBY, P.J.
LIBERTY
Number	Title	Yr	VG	VG+	NM
❏ LRP-3406 [M]	Somewhere/Go Go P.J. Proby	1965	5.00	10.00	20.00
❏ LRP-3421 [M]	P.J. Proby	1965	5.00	10.00	20.00
❏ LRP-3497 [M]	Enigma	1967	5.00	10.00	20.00
❏ LRP-3515 [M]	Phenomenon	1967	5.00	10.00	20.00
❏ LST-7406 [S]	Somewhere/Go Go P.J. Proby	1965	6.25	12.50	25.00
❏ LST-7421 [S]	P.J. Proby	1965	6.25	12.50	25.00
❏ LST-7497 [S]	Enigma	1967	6.25	12.50	25.00
❏ LST-7515 [S]	Phenomenon	1967	6.25	12.50	25.00
❏ LST-7561	What's Wrong with My World?	1968	6.25	12.50	25.00

PROCESSION
SMASH
❏ SRS-67122	Procession	1969	5.00	10.00	20.00

PROCOL HARUM
A&M
❏ SP-4151	Shine On Brightly	1968	6.25	12.50	25.00
❏ SP-8503 [DJ]	Procol Harum Lives	197?	12.50	25.00	50.00
-- Interview LP alone					
❏ SP-8503 [DJ]	Procol Harum Lives	197?	75.00	150.00	300.00
-- Promo-only box set with press kit, photos, keychain and interview LP					

DERAM
❏ DE 16008 [M]	Procol Harum	1967	20.00	40.00	80.00
❏ DE/S 16/18008	Procol Harum Bonus Poster	1967	6.25	12.50	25.00
❏ DES 18008 [R]	Procol Harum	1967	10.00	20.00	40.00

PRODIGY
MAVERICK
❏ PRO-A-8929 [(2)DJ]	The Fat of the Land	1997	6.25	12.50	25.00
-- Promo-only U.S. vinyl in generic white sleeve					

PROFESSOR LONGHAIR
ATLANTIC
❏ SD 7225	New Orleans Piano	1972	6.25	12.50	25.00

PROVINE, DOROTHY
WARNER BROS.
❏ W 1394 [M]	The Roaring 20's	1961	5.00	10.00	20.00
❏ WS 1394 [S]	The Roaring 20's	1961	6.25	12.50	25.00
❏ W 1419 [M]	The Vamp of the Roaring 20's	1961	5.00	10.00	20.00
❏ WS 1419 [S]	The Vamp of the Roaring 20's	1961	6.25	12.50	25.00

PRYOR, RICHARD
DOVE
❏ RS 6325	Richard Pryor	1968	5.00	10.00	20.00

PRYSOCK, ARTHUR
DECCA
❏ DL 74581 [S]	Strictly Sentimental	1965	5.00	10.00	20.00
❏ DL 74628 [S]	Showcase	1965	5.00	10.00	20.00

OLD TOWN
❏ LP-102 [M]	I Worry About You	1962	12.50	25.00	50.00
❏ LP-2004 [M]	Arthur Prysock Sings Only for You	1962	12.50	25.00	50.00
❏ LP-2005 [M]	Coast to Coast	1963	10.00	20.00	40.00
❏ LP-2006 [M]	A Portrait of Arthur Prysock	1963	10.00	20.00	40.00
❏ LP-2007 [M]	Everlasting Songs for Everlasting Lovers	1964	10.00	20.00	40.00
❏ LP-2008 [M]	Intimately Yours	1964	10.00	20.00	40.00
❏ LP-2009 [M]	A Double Header with Arthur Prysock	1965	10.00	20.00	40.00
❏ LP-2010 [M]	In a Mood	1965	10.00	20.00	40.00
❏ T-90604 [M]	A Portrait of Arthur Prysock	1965	10.00	20.00	40.00
-- Capitol Record Club edition					

PRYSOCK, ARTHUR/COUNT BASIE
Also see each artist's individual listings.
VERVE
❏ V6-8646 [S]	Arthur Prysock/Count Basie	1966	5.00	10.00	20.00

PRYSOCK, RED
MERCURY
❏ MG-20088 [M]	Rock 'n Roll	1955	50.00	100.00	200.00
❏ MG-20211 [M]	Fruit Boots	1957	30.00	60.00	120.00
❏ MG-20307 [M]	The Beat	1957	20.00	40.00	80.00
❏ MG-20512 [M]	Swing Softly Red	1958	12.50	25.00	50.00
❏ SR-60188 [S]	Swing Softly Red	1959	20.00	40.00	80.00

WING
❏ MGW-12007 [M]	Fruit Boots	1959	10.00	20.00	40.00
-- Originals have liner notes on back cover					
❏ MGW-12007 [M]	Fruit Boots	196?	5.00	10.00	20.00
-- Reissues have other LPs listed on back cover					

PSYCHEDELIC FURS
COLUMBIA
❏ AS 1296 [DJ]	Interchords	1981	6.25	12.50	25.00
❏ CAS 01310 [DJ]	Interchords with Richard Butler	1988	5.00	10.00	20.00

PSYCHOTIC PINEAPPLE, THE
RICHMOND
❏ 6026	Where's the Party	1980	6.25	12.50	25.00

PUCKETT, GARY, AND THE UNION GAP
COLUMBIA
❏ CS 1042	Gary Puckett and the Union Gap's Greatest Hits	1970	5.00	10.00	20.00
❏ CS 9612	Woman, Woman	1968	5.00	10.00	20.00
-- As "The Union Gap Featuring Gary Puckett"					
❏ CS 9664	Young Girl	1968	5.00	10.00	20.00
❏ CS 9715	Incredible	1968	5.00	10.00	20.00
❏ CS 9935	The New Gary Puckett and the Union Gap Album	1969	5.00	10.00	20.00

PUGSLEY MUNION
J&S
❏ SLP-001	Just Like You	1969	25.00	50.00	100.00

PULLEN, WHITEY
CROWN
❏ CLP-5332 [M]	Whitey Pullen	1963	10.00	20.00	40.00

PULLINS, LEROY
KAPP
❏ KL-1488 [M]	I'm a Nut	1966	6.25	12.50	25.00
❏ KS-3488 [S]	I'm a Nut	1966	7.50	15.00	30.00
❏ KS-3557	Funny Bones and Hearts	1968	6.25	12.50	25.00

PULSE
POISON RING
❏ 2237	Pulse	1969	6.25	12.50	25.00

PURDIE, BERNARD "PRETTY"
DATE
❏ TEM 3006 [M]	Soul Drums	1967	5.00	10.00	20.00
❏ TES 4006 [S]	Soul Drums	1967	5.00	10.00	20.00

PURE PRAIRIE LEAGUE
RCA VICTOR
❏ APD1-0933 [Q]	Two Lane Highway	1975	5.00	10.00	20.00
❏ APD1-1247 [Q]	If The Shoe Fits	1976	5.00	10.00	20.00

PURIFY, JAMES AND BOBBY
BELL
❏ 6003 [M]	James and Bobby Purify	1966	6.25	12.50	25.00
❏ S-6003 [S]	James and Bobby Purify	1966	7.50	15.00	30.00
❏ 6010 [M]	The Pure Sound of the Purifys	1967	6.25	12.50	25.00
❏ S-6010 [S]	The Pure Sound of the Purifys	1967	7.50	15.00	30.00

PURPLE GANG, THE
SIRE
❏ SES 97006	The Purple Gang Strikes	1969	5.00	10.00	20.00

PURPLE IMAGE
MAP CITY
❏ 3015	Purple Image	1971	12.50	25.00	50.00

PURSELL, BILL
COLUMBIA
❏ CS 8792 [S]	Our Winter Love	1963	5.00	10.00	20.00
❏ CS 8877 [S]	Chasing a Dream	1964	5.00	10.00	20.00
❏ CS 9221 [S]	Remembered Love	1965	5.00	10.00	20.00

PUSSY GALORE
BUY OUR RECORDS
❏ 10 [EP]	Pussy Gold 5000	1986	12.50	25.00	50.00

CAROLINE
❏ CAROL 1337	Right Now!	1987	6.25	12.50	25.00
❏ CAROL 1369	Dial "M" for Motherfucker	1989	6.25	12.50	25.00

Number	Title	Yr	VG	VG+	NM
SHOVE					
❑ 2	Groovy Hate Fuck	1986	12.50	25.00	50.00
PUYANA, RAFAEL					
MERCURY LIVING PRESENCE					
❑ SR 90259 [S]	Picchi: Belli d'Arpsichordo; Frescobaldi: Music for Harpsichord	196?	7.50	15.00	30.00
-- Maroon label, no "Vendor: Mercury Record Corporation"					
❑ SR 90304 [S]	The Golden Age of Harpsichord Music	196?	6.25	12.50	25.00
-- Maroon label, no "Vendor: Mercury Record Corporation"					
❑ SR 90322 [S]	Bachs: Harpsichord Music	196?	10.00	20.00	40.00
-- Maroon label, no "Vendor: Mercury Record Corporation"					
❑ SR 90369 [S]	Bach for Harpsichord	196?	7.50	15.00	30.00
-- Maroon label, no "Vendor: Mercury Record Corporation"					
❑ SR 90369 [S]	Bach for Harpsichord	196?	6.25	12.50	25.00
-- Maroon label, with "Vendor: Mercury Record Corporation"					
❑ SR 90411 [S]	Baroque Masterpieces for the Harpsichord	196?	7.50	15.00	30.00
-- Maroon label, no "Vendor: Mercury Record Corporation"					
❑ SR 90459 [S]	Soler: Harpsichord Music	196?	7.50	15.00	30.00
-- Maroon label, with "Vendor: Mercury Record Corporation"					
PUZZLE					
ABC					
❑ ABCS-671	Puzzle	1969	5.00	10.00	20.00
PYLE, JACK					
CAMEO					
❑ C-1017 [M]	Listen Son...And Other Readings by Jack Pyle	1963	5.00	10.00	20.00
PYRAMIDS, THE					
BEST					
❑ LPM-1001 [M]	The Original Penetration! And Other Favorites	1964	62.50	125.00	250.00
-- Original issue with "Walkin' the Dog"					
❑ BR 16501 [M]	The Original Penetration! And Other Favorites	1964	50.00	100.00	200.00
-- Reissue with "Road Runnah"					
❑ BS 36501 [R]	The Original Penetration! And Other Favorites	1964	30.00	60.00	120.00

Number	Title	Yr	VG	VG+	NM
Q					
QUARTERMASS					
HARVEST					
❑ SKAO-314	Quartermass	1970	7.50	15.00	30.00
QUARTETTE TRES BIEN					
GNP					
❑ GNP-102 [M]	Quartette Tres Bien	1962	5.00	10.00	20.00
❑ GNPS-102 [S]	Quartette Tres Bien	1962	6.25	12.50	25.00
❑ GNP-107 [M]	Kilimanjaro	1963	5.00	10.00	20.00
❑ GNPS-107 [S]	Kilimanjaro	1963	6.25	12.50	25.00
QUATTLEBAUM, DOUG					
BLUESVILLE					
❑ BVLP-1065 [M]	Softee Man Blues	1963	15.00	30.00	60.00
-- Blue label, silver print					
❑ BVLP-1065 [M]	Softee Man Blues	1964	5.00	10.00	20.00
-- Blue label, trident logo at right					
QUEEN					
ELEKTRA					
❑ 6E-112 [DJ]	News of the World	1977	37.50	75.00	150.00
-- White label promo with oversize cover and press kit					
❑ 7E-1026 [DJ]	Sheer Heart Attack	1974	12.50	25.00	50.00
-- White label promo					
❑ EQ-5064 [Q]	Queen	1973	10.00	20.00	40.00
❑ EKS-75064	Queen	1973	7.50	15.00	30.00
-- With "Queen" gold-embossed on the cover					
❑ EKS-75064 [DJ]	Queen	1973	12.50	25.00	50.00
-- White label promo					
❑ EKS-75082 [DJ]	Queen II	1974	12.50	25.00	50.00
-- White label promo					
HOLLYWOOD					
❑ ED-62005 [PD]	Queen at the BBC	1995	25.00	50.00	100.00
-- Promo-only picture disc (no U.S. stock vinyl)					
❑ 62017	Made in Heaven	1996	5.00	10.00	20.00
-- Imported from Europe; the only distinguishing mark to make this a U.S. version is the Hollywood bar code, which was stuck to the shrink wrap					
MOBILE FIDELITY					
❑ 1-067	A Night at the Opera	1980	20.00	40.00	80.00
-- Audiophile vinyl					
❑ 1-211	The Game	1995	7.50	15.00	30.00
-- Audiophile vinyl					
❑ 1-256	A Day at the Races	1996	12.50	25.00	50.00
-- Audiophile vinyl					
QUEEN'S NECTARINE MACHINE, THE					
ABC					
❑ S-666	The Mystical Powers of Roving Tarot Gamble	1969	10.00	20.00	40.00
QUEENSRYCHE					
EMI AMERICA					
❑ ST-17134 [DJ]	The Warning	1984	10.00	20.00	40.00
-- Promo-only "High Quality Vinyl" pressing					
❑ SPRO-19006 [DJ]	Queensryche	1983	10.00	20.00	40.00
-- White label version in a film can					
EMI MANHATTAN					
❑ SPRO-04136/7 [PD]	Operation: Mindcrime	1988	20.00	40.00	80.00
-- Promo-only picture disc					
❑ SPRO-04194 [DJ]	Speak the Word	1988	7.50	15.00	30.00
-- Promo-only interview album					
206 RECORDS					
❑ R-101 [EP]	Queensryche	1983	25.00	50.00	100.00
QUEERS, THE					
SHAKIN' STREET					
❑ 010	Grow Up	1990	50.00	100.00	200.00
-- Only 100-150 copies exist of a planned pressing of 500 (others were destroyed at the plant)					
? (QUESTION MARK) AND THE MYSTERIANS					
CAMEO					
❑ C-2004 [M]	96 Tears	1966	25.00	50.00	100.00
❑ CS-2004 [R]	96 Tears	1966	17.50	35.00	70.00
❑ C-2006 [M]	Action	1967	37.50	75.00	150.00
❑ CS-2006 [R]	Action	1967	25.00	50.00	100.00
QUICKSILVER MESSENGER SERVICE					
CAPITOL					
❑ ST-120	Happy Trails	1969	7.50	15.00	30.00
-- Black label with colorband					

Number	Title	Yr	VG	VG+	NM
❑ SKAO-391	Shady Grove	1969	6.25	12.50	25.00
-- Lime green label					
❑ SMAS-498	Just for Love	1970	6.25	12.50	25.00
-- Lime green label					
❑ SMAS-630	What About Me	1970	6.25	12.50	25.00
-- Lime green label					
❑ SW-819	Quicksilver	1971	6.25	12.50	25.00
-- Red label with stylized "C" at top					
❑ ST 2904	Quicksilver Messenger Service	1968	10.00	20.00	40.00
-- Black label with colorband; glossy black cover with red and silver foil-like printing					
❑ ST-2904	Quicksilver Messenger Service	1969	5.00	10.00	20.00
-- Lime green or red label					
❑ SVBB-11165 [(2)]	Anthology	1973	5.00	10.00	20.00

QUILL
COTILLION

Number	Title	Yr	VG	VG+	NM
❑ SD 9017	Quill	1970	5.00	10.00	20.00

QUINN, ANTHONY
CAPITOL

Number	Title	Yr	VG	VG+	NM
❑ ST-116	In My Own Way... I Love You	1969	7.50	15.00	30.00

QUINN, CARMEL
COLUMBIA

Number	Title	Yr	VG	VG+	NM
❑ CL 629 [M]	Arthur Godfrey Presents Carmel Quinn	1955	7.50	15.00	30.00

QUINTESSENCE
ISLAND

Number	Title	Yr	VG	VG+	NM
❑ SMAS-9301	Quintessence	1971	6.25	12.50	25.00
❑ SW-9305	Dive Deep	1971	6.25	12.50	25.00

R

R.E.M.
MOBILE FIDELITY

Number	Title	Yr	VG	VG+	NM
❑ 1-231	Murmur	1995	5.00	10.00	20.00
-- Audiophile vinyl					
❑ 1-261	Reckoning	1996	20.00	40.00	80.00
-- Audiophile vinyl					

WARNER BROS.

Number	Title	Yr	VG	VG+	NM
❑ PRO-A-3377 [(2)] DJ	Should We Talk About the Weather?	1988	10.00	20.00	40.00
-- Promo-only interviews and music					

R.P.S.
MARS

Number	Title	Yr	VG	VG+	NM
❑ (# unknown)	R.P.S.	197?	20.00	40.00	80.00

RABBLE, THE
ROULETTE

Number	Title	Yr	VG	VG+	NM
❑ SR-42010	The Rabble	1968	37.50	75.00	150.00

RACKET SQUAD, THE
JUBILEE

Number	Title	Yr	VG	VG+	NM
❑ JGS-8015	The Racket Squad	1968	10.00	20.00	40.00
❑ JGS-8026	Corners of Your Mind	1969	10.00	20.00	40.00

RADHA KRISHNA TEMPLE
APPLE

Number	Title	Yr	VG	VG+	NM
❑ SKAO-3376	The Radha Krishna Temple	1971	5.00	10.00	20.00

RADIO BIRDMAN
SIRE

Number	Title	Yr	VG	VG+	NM
❑ SRK 6050	Radio Appears	1978	10.00	20.00	40.00

RADIO CITY MUSIC HALL ORCHESTRA
RCA VICTOR

Number	Title	Yr	VG	VG+	NM
❑ LOP-1010 [M]	Christmas Holidays at Radio City Music Hall	1958	5.00	10.00	20.00
-- With gatefold and 10-page bound-in booklet with fold-open poster of the Rockettes					
❑ LSO-1010 [S]	Christmas Holidays at Radio City Music Hall	1958	10.00	20.00	40.00
-- "Living Stereo" banner on cover					

RAE, CHARLOTTE
VANGUARD

Number	Title	Yr	VG	VG+	NM
❑ VRS-9004 [M]	Songs I Taught My Mother	1956	10.00	20.00	40.00

RAFFERTY, GERRY
Also see THE HUMBLEBUMS; STEALERS WHEEL.
BLUE THUMB

Number	Title	Yr	VG	VG+	NM
❑ BT-58	Can I Have My Money Back?	1973	5.00	10.00	20.00

MOBILE FIDELITY

Number	Title	Yr	VG	VG+	NM
❑ 1-058	City to City	1980	10.00	20.00	40.00
-- Audiophile vinyl					

RAIDERS, THE
LIBERTY

Number	Title	Yr	VG	VG+	NM
❑ LRP-3225 [M]	Twistin' the Country Classics	1962	6.25	12.50	25.00
❑ LST-7225 [S]	Twistin' the Country Classics	1962	7.50	15.00	30.00

RAIN
Proably two different groups.
PROJECT 3

Number	Title	Yr	VG	VG+	NM
❑ PR 5072 SD	New Rock Group	1972	6.25	12.50	25.00

WHAZOO

Number	Title	Yr	VG	VG+	NM
❑ USR-3049	Live Christmas Night	1969	37.50	75.00	150.00
-- Issued with no cover					

RAINBOW
GNP CRESCENDO

Number	Title	Yr	VG	VG+	NM
❑ GNPS-2049	After the Storm	1969	6.25	12.50	25.00

RAINBOW PRESS, THE
MR. G

Number	Title	Yr	VG	VG+	NM
❑ 9003	There's a War On	1968	7.50	15.00	30.00
❑ 9004	Sunday Funnies	1969	7.50	15.00	30.00

Number	Title	Yr	VG	VG+	NM

RAINBOW PROMISE, THE
NEW WINE
❑ LPS-251-01	The Rainbow Promise	1970	75.00	150.00	300.00

RAINCOATS, THE
ROUGH TRADE
❑ ROUGH US 13	Odyshape	1981	6.25	12.50	25.00

RAINDROPS, THE
Also see ELLIE GREENWICH.
JUBILEE
❑ JGM-5023 [M]	The Raindrops	1963	37.50	75.00	150.00
❑ JGS-5023 [S]	The Raindrops	1963	75.00	150.00	300.00

RAINEY, MA
RIVERSIDE
❑ RLP-12-108 [M]	Ma Rainey	1955	50.00	100.00	200.00
❑ RLP-12-137 [M]	Broken Hearted Blues	1956	25.00	50.00	100.00
❑ RLP-1003 [10]	Ma Rainey, Vol. 1	1953	62.50	125.00	250.00
❑ RLP-1016 [10]	Ma Rainey, Vol. 2	1953	62.50	125.00	250.00
❑ RLP-1045 [10]	Ma Rainey, Vol. 3	1954	62.50	125.00	250.00

RAINWATER, MARVIN
MGM
❑ E-3534 [M]	Songs by Marvin Rainwater	1957	37.50	75.00	150.00
❑ E-3721 [M]	Marvin Rainwater Sings with a Beat	1958	30.00	60.00	120.00
❑ E-4046 [M]	Gonna Find Me a Bluebird	1962	20.00	40.00	80.00
❑ SE-4046 [R]	Gonna Find Me a Bluebird	1962	12.50	25.00	50.00

RAINY DAZE, THE
UNI
❑ 3002 [M]	That Acapulco Gold	1967	5.00	10.00	20.00
❑ 73002 [S]	That Acapulco Gold	1967	6.25	12.50	25.00

RAITT, BONNIE
DCC COMPACT CLASSICS
❑ LPZ-2025	Nick of Time	1996	5.00	10.00	20.00
-- Audiophile vinyl					
❑ LPZ-2031	Luck of the Draw	1997	5.00	10.00	20.00
-- Audiophile vinyl					

RAITT, JOHN
CAPITOL
❑ T 583 [M]	Highlights of Broadway	1955	7.50	15.00	30.00
❑ T 714 [M]	Mediterranean Magic	1956	7.50	15.00	30.00
❑ ST 1058 [S]	Under Open Skies	1958	10.00	20.00	40.00
❑ T 1058 [M]	Under Open Skies	1958	7.50	15.00	30.00

RAM
POLYDOR
❑ 24-5013	Where (In Conclusion)	1972	6.25	12.50	25.00

RAM, BUCK
MERCURY
❑ MG-20392 [M]	The Magic Touch	1960	7.50	15.00	30.00
❑ SR-60067 [S]	The Magic Touch	1960	10.00	20.00	40.00

RAMBEAU, EDDIE
DYNO VOICE
❑ 9001 [M]	Concrete and Clay	1965	5.00	10.00	20.00
❑ DS-9001 [S]	Concrete and Clay	1965	6.25	12.50	25.00

RAMONES, THE
SIRE
❑ PRO-A-605 [DJ]	Rock 'n' Roll High School Radio Sampler	1979	6.25	12.50	25.00
❑ PRO-A-756 [DJ]	Road to Ruin Radio Sampler	1978	6.25	12.50	25.00
❑ PRO-A-996 [DJ]	Pleasant Dreams Radio Sampler	1980	6.25	12.50	25.00
❑ SASD-7520	Ramones	1976	6.25	12.50	25.00
-- First issue, distributed by ABC					
❑ SA-7528	Ramones Leave Home	1977	12.50	25.00	50.00
-- First issue, distributed by ABC, with "Carbona Not Glue"					
❑ SA-7528	Ramones Leave Home	1977	6.25	12.50	25.00
-- Second issue, distributed by ABC, with "Sheena Is a Punk Rocker" replacing "Carbona Not Glue"					

RAMSAY, OBRAY
PRESTIGE
❑ PRLP-13009 [M]	Obray Ramsay Sings Jimmie Rodgers Favorites	1960	7.50	15.00	30.00
❑ PRLP-13020 [M]	Folk Songs from the Three Laurels	1961	7.50	15.00	30.00

RIVERSIDE
❑ RLP-12-649 [M]	Banjo Songs of the Blue Ridge and Great Smokies	196?	7.50	15.00	30.00

RANDALL, TONY
IMPERIAL
❑ LP-9090 [M]	Tony Randall	1958	7.50	15.00	30.00
MERCURY					
❑ MG-21108 [M]	Vo, Vo, De Oh, Doe	1967	5.00	10.00	20.00
❑ MG-21128 [M]	Warm and Wavery	1967	5.00	10.00	20.00
❑ SR-61108 [S]	Vo, Vo, De Oh, Doe	1967	6.25	12.50	25.00
❑ SR-61128 [S]	Warm and Wavery	1967	6.25	12.50	25.00

RANDALL, TONY, AND JACK KLUGMAN
LONDON
❑ XPS 903	The Odd Couple Sings	1973	12.50	25.00	50.00

RANDAZZO, TEDDY
ABC-PARAMOUNT
❑ 352 [M]	Journey to Love	1961	7.50	15.00	30.00
❑ S-352 [S]	Journey to Love	1961	10.00	20.00	40.00
❑ 421 [M]	Teddy Randazzo Twists	1962	7.50	15.00	30.00
❑ S-421 [S]	Teddy Randazzo Twists	1962	10.00	20.00	40.00
COLPIX					
❑ CP-445 [M]	Big Wide World	1963	7.50	15.00	30.00
❑ SCP-445 [S]	Big Wide World	1963	10.00	20.00	40.00
VIK					
❑ LX-1121 [M]	I'm Confessin'	1958	50.00	100.00	200.00

RANDOLPH, BOOTS
MONUMENT
❑ MLP-8002 [M]	Boots Randolph's Yakety Sax	1963	5.00	10.00	20.00
❑ MLP-8079 [M]	Sax-Sational	1967	5.00	10.00	20.00
❑ MLP-8082 [M]	Boots Randolph with the Knightsbridge Strings & Voices	1967	5.00	10.00	20.00
❑ SLP-18002 [S]	Boots Randolph's Yakety Sax	1963	6.25	12.50	25.00
❑ SLP-18015 [S]	Hip Boots	1964	5.00	10.00	20.00
❑ SLP-18029 [S]	12 Monstrous Sax Hits	1965	5.00	10.00	20.00
❑ SLP-18037 [S]	Boots Randolph Plays More Yakety Sax	1965	5.00	10.00	20.00
❑ SLP-18042 [S]	The Fantastic Boots Randolph	1966	5.00	10.00	20.00
❑ SLP-18066 [S]	Boots with Strings	1966	5.00	10.00	20.00
❑ SLP-18092	Sunday Sax	1968	5.00	10.00	20.00
❑ SLP-18099	The Sound of Boots	1968	5.00	10.00	20.00
RCA VICTOR					
❑ LPM-2165 [M]	Yakety Sax	1960	10.00	20.00	40.00
❑ LSP-2165 [S]	Yakety Sax	1960	12.50	25.00	50.00

RANEY, SUE
CAPITOL
❑ ST 1335 [S]	Songs for a Raney Day	1960	6.25	12.50	25.00
❑ T 1335 [M]	Songs for a Raney Day	1960	5.00	10.00	20.00
❑ ST 2032 [S]	All By Myself	1964	5.00	10.00	20.00

RANEY, WAYNE
KING
❑ 588 [M]	Songs from the Hills	1958	25.00	50.00	100.00
STARDAY					
❑ SLP-124 [M]	Wayne Raney and the Raney Family	1960	10.00	20.00	40.00
❑ SLP-279 [M]	Don't Try to Be What You Ain't	1964	10.00	20.00	40.00

RANGER, ANDY
DOT
❑ DLP-3028 [M]	The Song That Never Ends	1956	15.00	30.00	60.00

RARE BIRD
PROBE
❑ 4514	Rare Bird	1970	6.25	12.50	25.00

RARE EARTH
RARE EARTH
❑ RS 507	Get Ready	1969	7.50	15.00	30.00
-- Original cover has a rounded top					
VERVE					
❑ V6-5066	Dreams/Answers	1968	12.50	25.00	50.00

Number	Title	Yr	VG	VG+	NM
RASCALS, THE					
ATLANTIC					
❏ ST-137 [DJ]	Freedom Suite Sampler	1969	12.50	25.00	50.00
❏ SD 2-901 [(2)]	Freedom Suite	1969	5.00	10.00	20.00
❏ 8123 [M]	The Young Rascals	1966	7.50	15.00	30.00
❏ SD 8123 [S]	The Young Rascals	1966	12.50	25.00	50.00
-- Purple and green label					
❏ SD 8123 [S]	The Young Rascals	1966	10.00	20.00	40.00
-- Green and blue label					
❏ 8134 [M]	Collections	1967	6.25	12.50	25.00
❏ SD 8134 [S]	Collections	1967	7.50	15.00	30.00
-- Green and blue label					
❏ 8148 [M]	Groovin'	1967	6.25	12.50	25.00
❏ SD 8148 [S]	Groovin'	1967	7.50	15.00	30.00
-- Green and blue label					
❏ 8169 [M]	Once Upon a Dream	1968	10.00	20.00	40.00
❏ SD 8169 [S]	Once Upon a Dream	1968	6.25	12.50	25.00
-- Green and blue label					
❏ 8190 [M]	Time Peace/The Rascals' Greatest Hits	1968	12.50	25.00	50.00
-- Mono is promo only					
❏ SD 8190 [S]	Time Peace/The Rascals' Greatest Hits	1968	6.25	12.50	25.00
-- Green and blue label					
WARNER SPECIAL PRODUCTS					
❏ SP-2502 [(2)]	24 Greatest Hits	1971	5.00	10.00	20.00
WES FARRELL					
❏ PFT-1002 [DJ]	Songs from the Rascals	197?	6.25	12.50	25.00
-- Promo-only publisher's demo					
RASPBERRIES					
CAPITOL					
❏ SK-11036	Raspberries	1972	7.50	15.00	30.00
-- Originals have red labels and a "scratch 'n' sniff" cover, the smell of which fades over time					
❏ ST-11036	Raspberries	1973	5.00	10.00	20.00
-- Orange label, "Capitol" at bottom					
❏ SMAS-11220	Side 3	1973	5.00	10.00	20.00
-- With cover cut in the shape of a basket of raspberries					
❏ ST-11123	Fresh	1972	5.00	10.00	20.00
❏ ST-11329	Starting Over	1974	5.00	10.00	20.00
RATHBONE, BASIL					
CAEDMON					
❏ TC 1028 [M]	Basil Rathbone Reads Edgar Allan Poe	195?	6.25	12.50	25.00
❏ TC 1044 [M]	The Happy Prince and Other Oscar Wilde Fairy Tales	195?	6.25	12.50	25.00
❏ TC 1115 [M]	Basil Rathbone Reads Edgar Allan Poe, Vol. 2	195?	6.25	12.50	25.00
❏ TC 1120 [M]	Stories of Hawthorne	195?	6.25	12.50	25.00
❏ TC 1172 [M]	Stories of Sherlock Holmes, Vol. 1	1963	6.25	12.50	25.00
❏ TC 1195 [M]	Basil Rathbone Reads Edgar Allan Poe, Vol. 3	196?	6.25	12.50	25.00
❏ TC 1197 [M]	Stories of Hawthorne, Vol. 2	196?	6.25	12.50	25.00
❏ TC 1208 [M]	Stories of Sherlock Holmes, Vol. 2	1966	6.25	12.50	25.00
❏ TC 1220 [M]	Stories of Sherlock Holmes, Vol. 3	1967	6.25	12.50	25.00
❏ TC 1240 [M]	Stories of Sherlock Holmes, Vol. 4	1967	6.25	12.50	25.00
CO-STAR					
❏ C-107 [M]	The Brothers Karamazov	196?	5.00	10.00	20.00
❏ CS-107 [S]	The Brothers Karamazov	196?	6.25	12.50	25.00
COLUMBIA MASTERWORKS					
❏ ML 4038 [10]	Peter and the Wolf; Treasure Island	1949	12.50	25.00	50.00
❏ ML 4081 [10]	A Christmas Carol	1950	12.50	25.00	50.00
DECCA					
❏ DL 9109 [M]	Selections from The Jungle Book	1962	7.50	15.00	30.00
RATIONALS, THE					
CREWE					
❏ CR-1334	The Rationals	1969	10.00	20.00	40.00
RATTLES, THE					
MERCURY					
❏ MG 21127 [M]	The Rattles' Greatest Hits	1967	20.00	40.00	80.00
❏ SR 61127 [R]	The Rattles' Greatest Hits	1967	12.50	25.00	50.00
RAVEN					
Two different groups?					
COLUMBIA					
❏ CS 9903	Raven	1969	5.00	10.00	20.00
DISCOVERY					
❏ 36133	Live at the Inferno	1967	20.00	40.00	80.00
RAVENS, THE					
Also see JIMMY RICKS.					
REGENT					
❏ MG-6062 [M]	Write Me a Letter	195?	37.50	75.00	150.00
-- Red label					
❏ MG-6062 [M]	Write Me a Letter	1957	75.00	150.00	300.00
-- Green label					
RAVENSCROFT, THURL					
DOT					
❏ DLP-3430 [M]	Great Hits	1962	7.50	15.00	30.00
❏ DLP-25430 [S]	Great Hits	1962	10.00	20.00	40.00
RAW					
CORAL					
❏ CRL 757515	Raw Holly	1971	7.50	15.00	30.00
RAW SPITT					
UNITED ARTISTS					
❏ UAS-6795	Maybe You Ain't Black	1971	6.25	12.50	25.00
RAWLS, LOU					
CAPITOL					
❏ SWBB-261 [(2)]	Close-Up	1969	5.00	10.00	20.00
-- Reissue of 1824 and 2042 in one package					
❏ STBB-720 [(2)]	Down Here on the Ground/I'd Rather Drink Muddy Water	1971	5.00	10.00	20.00
❏ ST 1714 [S]	Stormy Monday	1962	6.25	12.50	25.00
❏ T 1714 [M]	Stormy Monday	1962	5.00	10.00	20.00
❏ ST 1824 [S]	Black and Blue	1963	6.25	12.50	25.00
❏ T 1824 [M]	Black and Blue	1963	5.00	10.00	20.00
❏ ST 2042 [S]	Tobacco Road	1964	6.25	12.50	25.00
❏ T 2042 [M]	Tobacco Road	1964	5.00	10.00	20.00
❏ ST 2273 [S]	Nobody But Lou	1965	6.25	12.50	25.00
❏ T 2273 [M]	Nobody But Lou	1965	5.00	10.00	20.00
❏ ST 2401 [S]	Lou Rawls and Strings	1965	6.25	12.50	25.00
❏ T 2401 [M]	Lou Rawls and Strings	1965	5.00	10.00	20.00
❏ ST 2459 [S]	Lou Rawls Live!	1966	5.00	10.00	20.00
❏ ST 2566 [S]	Lou Rawls Soulin'	1966	5.00	10.00	20.00
❏ ST 2632 [S]	Lou Rawls Carryin' On!	1966	5.00	10.00	20.00
❏ T 2713 [M]	Too Much!	1967	5.00	10.00	20.00
❏ T 2756 [M]	That's Lou	1967	5.00	10.00	20.00
❏ T 2864 [M]	Feelin' Good	1968	7.50	15.00	30.00
RAY, DAVE					
ELEKTRA					
❏ EKL-284 [M]	Snaker's Here	1965	5.00	10.00	20.00
❏ EKL-319 [M]	Fine Soft Land	1966	5.00	10.00	20.00
❏ EKS-7284 [S]	Snaker's Here	1965	6.25	12.50	25.00
❏ EKS-7319 [S]	Fine Soft Land	1966	6.25	12.50	25.00
RAY, DIANE					
MERCURY					
❏ MG-20903 [M]	The Exciting Years	1964	20.00	40.00	80.00
❏ SR-60903 [S]	The Exciting Years	1964	25.00	50.00	100.00
RAY, JAMES					
CAPRICE					
❏ LP-1002 [M]	James Ray	1962	20.00	40.00	80.00
❏ SLP-1002 [S]	James Ray	1962	30.00	60.00	120.00
RAY, JOHNNIE					
COLUMBIA					
❏ CL 961 [M]	The Big Beat	1957	12.50	25.00	50.00
❏ CL 1093 [M]	At the Desert Inn in Las Vegas	1957	12.50	25.00	50.00
❏ CL 1225 [M]	'Til Morning	1958	10.00	20.00	40.00
❏ CL 1227 [M]	Johnnie Ray's Greatest Hits	1958	10.00	20.00	40.00
-- Red and black label with 6 "eye" logos					
❏ CL 1227 [M]	Johnnie Ray's Greatest Hits	1962	6.25	12.50	25.00
-- "Guaranteed High Fidelity" on label					
❏ CL 1385 [M]	On the Trail	1959	10.00	20.00	40.00
❏ CL 2510 [10]	I Cry for You	1955	17.50	35.00	70.00
-- "House Party Series" issue					
❏ CL 6199 [10]	Johnnie Ray	1951	20.00	40.00	80.00
❏ CS 8180 [S]	On the Trail	1959	12.50	25.00	50.00
EPIC					
❏ LN 1120 [10]	Johnnie Ray	1955	20.00	40.00	80.00
LIBERTY					
❏ LRP-3221 [M]	Johnnie Ray	1962	5.00	10.00	20.00
❏ LST-7221 [S]	Johnnie Ray	1962	7.50	15.00	30.00

Number	Title	Yr	VG	VG+	NM

RAY, WADE
ABC-PARAMOUNT
❏ ABCS-539 [S] A Ray of Country Sun | 1966 | 5.00 | 10.00 | 20.00

RAYBURN, MARGIE
LIBERTY
❏ LRP-3126 [M] Margie | 1959 | 6.25 | 12.50 | 25.00
❏ LST-7126 [S] Margie | 1959 | 10.00 | 20.00 | 40.00

RAYE, JERRY
DEVILLE
❏ LP-101 [M] The Many Sides of Jerry Raye and Fenwyck | 1967 | 150.00 | 300.00 | 600.00

RAYE, MARTHA
EPIC
❏ LG 3061 [M] Here's Martha Raye | 1954 | 10.00 | 20.00 | 40.00

RAYMOND, LEW
TOPS
❏ L-1583 [M] For Men Only | 1958 | 10.00 | 20.00 | 40.00
-- *Jayne Mansfield is the cover model*
❏ L-1647 [M] Million Sellers | 1960 | 7.50 | 15.00 | 30.00
-- *Mary Tyler Moore is the cover model*

RCA VICTOR SYMPHONY ORCHESTRA (ROBERT RUSSELL BENNETT, CONDUCTOR)
RCA VICTOR RED SEAL
❏ LSC-2238 [S] It's Classic But It's Good | 1959 | 7.50 | 15.00 | 30.00
-- *Original with "shaded dog" label*

RCA VICTOR SYMPHONY ORCHESTRA (KIRIL KONDRASHIN, CONDUCTOR)
RCA VICTOR RED SEAL
❏ LSC-2323 [S] Tchaikovsky: Capriccio Italien; Rimsky-Korsakov: Capriccio Espagnole | 1959 | 12.50 | 25.00 | 50.00
-- *Original with "shaded dog" label*
❏ LSC-2323 [S] Tchaikovsky: Capriccio Italien; Rimsky-Korsakov: Capriccio Espagnole | 199? | 6.25 | 12.50 | 25.00
-- *Classic Records reissue*
❏ LSC-2398 [S] Khachaturian: Masquerade Suite; Kabalevsky: The Comedians | 1960 | 62.50 | 125.00 | 250.00
-- *Original with "shaded dog" label*
❏ LSC-2398 [S] Khachaturian: Masquerade Suite; Kabalevsky: The Comedians | 1964 | 25.00 | 50.00 | 100.00
-- *Second edition with "white dog" label*
❏ LSC-2398 [S] Khachaturian: Masquerade Suite; Kabalevsky: The Comedians | 1969 | 6.25 | 12.50 | 25.00
-- *Third edition with no dog on label*
❏ LSC-2398 [S] Khachaturian: Masquerade Suite; Kabalevsky: The Comedians | 199? | 6.25 | 12.50 | 25.00
-- *Classic Records reissue*

RCA VICTOR SYMPHONY ORCHESTRA (LEOPOLD STOKOWSKI, CONDUCTOR)
RCA VICTOR RED SEAL
❏ LSC-2471 [S] Rhapsodies | 196? | 6.25 | 12.50 | 25.00
-- *Original with "shaded dog" label or second edition with "white dog" label*
❏ LSC-2471 [S] Rhapsodies | 199? | 6.25 | 12.50 | 25.00
-- *Classic Records reissue*
❏ LSC-2612 [S] Handel: Royal Fireworks Music; Water Music | 1962 | 7.50 | 15.00 | 30.00
-- *Original with "shaded dog" label*
❏ LSC-2612 [S] Handel: Royal Fireworks Music; Water Music | 1964 | 5.00 | 10.00 | 20.00
-- *Second edition with "white dog" label*

REAGAN, RONALD
DECCA
❏ DL 4943 [M] Freedom's Finest Hour | 1967 | 6.25 | 12.50 | 25.00
❏ DL 74943 [S] Freedom's Finest Hour | 1967 | 7.50 | 15.00 | 30.00
KEY
❏ 690 [M] Rendezvous with Destiny | 1964 | 6.25 | 12.50 | 25.00
"X"
❏ LVA-3051 [M] Tales from the Great Book | 1956 | 10.00 | 20.00 | 40.00

REALLY RED
C.I.A.
❏ 006 Teaching You the Fear | 1981 | 20.00 | 40.00 | 80.00

REBECCA AND THE SUNNY BROOK FARMERS
MUSICOR
❏ MS-3176 Rebecca and the Sunny Brook Farmers | 1969 | 10.00 | 20.00 | 40.00

REBIRTH
AVANT GARDE
❏ AVS-135 Rebirth | 1971 | 12.50 | 25.00 | 50.00

REBS, THE
FREDLO
❏ 6830 1968 A.D. Break Through | 1968 | 100.00 | 200.00 | 400.00

RED CRAYOLA, THE
INTERNATIONAL ARTISTS
❏ 2 [M] Parable of the Arable Land | 1968 | 25.00 | 50.00 | 100.00
❏ 2 [S] Parable of the Arable Land | 1968 | 15.00 | 30.00 | 60.00
❏ 7 God Bless the Red Crayola | 1968 | 15.00 | 30.00 | 60.00

RED HOT CHILI PEPPERS
WARNER BROS.
❏ PRO-A-5170 Blood Sugar Sex Magik | 1991 | 10.00 | 20.00 | 40.00
[(2) DJ]
-- *"Radio-ready" version of LP, this is the only U.S. vinyl release of this album*
❏ 47386 [(2)] Californication | 1999 | 5.00 | 10.00 | 20.00

RED RIVER DAVE
CONTINENTAL
❏ 1507 [M] Red River Dave Sings | 1962 | 6.25 | 12.50 | 25.00
VARSITY
❏ 6962 [10] Red River Dave | 1951 | 17.50 | 35.00 | 70.00

REDBONE
EPIC
❏ EGP 501 [(2)] Redbone | 1970 | 5.00 | 10.00 | 20.00
❏ EQ 30815 [Q] Message from a Drum | 1973 | 5.00 | 10.00 | 20.00
❏ EQ 33053 [Q] Bearded Dreams Through Turquoise Eyes | 1974 | 5.00 | 10.00 | 20.00
❏ KEG 33456 [(2)] Come & Get Your Redbone | 1975 | 5.00 | 10.00 | 20.00

REDBONE, LEON
WARNER BROS.
❏ BS 2888 On the Track | 1975 | 6.25 | 12.50 | 25.00
❏ BS 2971 Double Time | 1977 | 6.25 | 12.50 | 25.00
❏ BS 3165 Champagne Charlie | 1978 | 6.25 | 12.50 | 25.00

REDD, VI
ATCO
❏ 33-157 [M] Lady Soul | 1963 | 7.50 | 15.00 | 30.00
❏ SD 33-157 [S] Lady Soul | 1963 | 10.00 | 20.00 | 40.00
UNITED ARTISTS
❏ UAJ-14016 [M] Bird Call | 1962 | 10.00 | 20.00 | 40.00
❏ UAJS-15016 [S] Bird Call | 1962 | 12.50 | 25.00 | 50.00

REDDING, OTIS
ATCO
❏ 33-161 [M] Pain in My Heart | 1964 | 62.50 | 125.00 | 250.00
❏ SD 33-161 [R] Pain in My Heart | 1968 | 62.50 | 125.00 | 250.00
❏ 33-252 [M] The Immortal Otis Redding | 1968 | 12.50 | 25.00 | 50.00
-- *Mono is white label promo only*
❏ SD 2-801 [(2)] The Best of Otis Redding | 1972 | 5.00 | 10.00 | 20.00
ATLANTIC
❏ 81762 [(4)] The Otis Redding Story | 1987 | 7.50 | 15.00 | 30.00
VOLT
❏ 411 [M] The Great Otis Redding Sings Soul Ballads | 1965 | 22.50 | 45.00 | 90.00
❏ S-411 [R] The Great Otis Redding Sings Soul Ballads | 1968 | 27.50 | 55.00 | 110.00
❏ 412 [M] Otis Blue/Otis Redding Sings Soul | 1965 | 10.00 | 20.00 | 40.00
❏ S-412 [M] Otis Blue/Otis Redding Sings Soul | 1965 | 12.50 | 25.00 | 50.00
❏ 413 [M] The Soul Album | 1966 | 10.00 | 20.00 | 40.00
❏ S-413 [S] The Soul Album | 1966 | 12.50 | 25.00 | 50.00
❏ 415 [M] Complete & Unbelievable...The Otis Redding Dictionary of Soul | 1966 | 10.00 | 20.00 | 40.00
❏ S-415 [S] Complete & Unbelievable...The Otis Redding Dictionary of Soul | 1966 | 12.50 | 25.00 | 50.00
❏ 416 [M] Otis Redding Live in Europe | 1967 | 7.50 | 15.00 | 30.00
❏ S-416 [S] Otis Redding Live in Europe | 1967 | 10.00 | 20.00 | 40.00
❏ 418 [M] History of Otis Redding | 1967 | 10.00 | 20.00 | 40.00
❏ S-418 [S] History of Otis Redding | 1967 | 7.50 | 15.00 | 30.00
❏ S-419 The Dock of the Bay | 1968 | 7.50 | 15.00 | 30.00

Number	Title	Yr	VG	VG+	NM

REDNOW, EIVETS -- See STEVIE WONDER.

REDPATH, JEAN
ELEKTRA
❑ EKL-214 [M]	Scottish Ballad Book	1962	6.25	12.50	25.00
❑ EKL-224 [M]	Songs of Love, Lilt and Laughter	1963	6.25	12.50	25.00
❑ EKL-274 [M]	Laddie Lie Near Me	1964	5.00	10.00	20.00
❑ EKS-7274 [S]	Laddie Lie Near Me	1964	6.25	12.50	25.00

PRESTIGE
❑ PR-13041 [M]	Skipping Barefoot Through the Heather	1962	7.50	15.00	30.00

REED, JERRY
RCA VICTOR
❑ APD1-0238 [Q]	Lord, Mr. Ford	1973	6.25	12.50	25.00
❑ LPM-3756 [M]	The Unbelievable Guitar and Voice of Jerry Reed	1967	6.25	12.50	25.00
❑ LSP-3756 [S]	The Unbelievable Guitar and Voice of Jerry Reed	1967	5.00	10.00	20.00
❑ LPM-3978 [M]	Nashville Underground	1968	12.50	25.00	50.00
❑ LSP-3978 [S]	Nashville Underground	1968	5.00	10.00	20.00
❑ LSP-4069	Alabama Wild Man	1968	5.00	10.00	20.00
❑ LSP-4147	Better Things in Life	1969	5.00	10.00	20.00
❑ LSP-4204	Jerry Reed Explores Guitar Country	1969	5.00	10.00	20.00
❑ LSP-4293	Cookin'	1970	5.00	10.00	20.00
❑ LSP-4391	Georgia Sunshine	1970	5.00	10.00	20.00

REED, JIMMY
BLUESVILLE
❑ BLS-6073 [(2)]	Jimmy Reed at Carnegie Hall	1973	5.00	10.00	20.00

BLUESWAY
❑ BL-6004 [M]	The New Jimmy Reed Album	1967	5.00	10.00	20.00
❑ BLS-6004 [S]	The New Jimmy Reed Album	1967	5.00	10.00	20.00
❑ BL-6009 [M]	Soulin'	1967	5.00	10.00	20.00
❑ BLS-6009 [S]	Soulin'	1967	5.00	10.00	20.00
❑ BLS-6015	Big Boss Man	1968	5.00	10.00	20.00
❑ BLS-6024	Down in Virginia	1969	5.00	10.00	20.00

VEE JAY
❑ LP-1004 [M]	I'm Jimmy Reed	1958	55.00	110.00	220.00
-- Maroon label					
❑ LP-1004 [M]	I'm Jimmy Reed	1961	20.00	40.00	80.00
-- Black label with colorband					
❑ LP-1008 [M]	Rockin' with Reed	1959	50.00	100.00	200.00
-- Maroon label					
❑ LP-1008 [M]	Rockin' with Reed	1961	20.00	40.00	80.00
-- Black label with colorband					
❑ LP-1022 [M]	Found Love	1959	50.00	100.00	200.00
-- Maroon label					
❑ LP-1022 [M]	Found Love	1961	20.00	40.00	80.00
-- Black label with colorband					
❑ LP-1025 [M]	Now Appearing	1960	20.00	40.00	80.00
❑ 2LP-1035 [(2) M]	Jimmy Reed at Carnegie Hall	1961	12.50	25.00	50.00
❑ 2SR-1035 [(2)]	Jimmy Reed at Carnegie Hall	1961	17.50	35.00	70.00
❑ LP-1039 [M]	The Best of Jimmy Reed	1962	10.00	20.00	40.00
❑ SR-1039 [S]	The Best of Jimmy Reed	1962	15.00	30.00	60.00
❑ LP-1050 [M]	Just Jimmy Reed	1962	10.00	20.00	40.00
❑ SR-1050 [S]	Just Jimmy Reed	1962	15.00	30.00	60.00
❑ LP-1067 [M]	T'Ain't No Big Thing...But He Is Jimmy Reed	1963	10.00	20.00	40.00
❑ SR-1067 [S]	T'Ain't No Big Thing...But He Is Jimmy Reed	1963	15.00	30.00	60.00
❑ LP-1072 [M]	The Best of the Blues	1963	10.00	20.00	40.00
❑ LP-1073 [M]	The 12 String Guitar Blues	1963	10.00	20.00	40.00
❑ SR-1073 [S]	The 12 String Guitar Blues	1963	37.50	7.50	150.00
❑ LP-1080 [M]	More of the Best of Jimmy Reed	1964	10.00	20.00	40.00
❑ SR-1080 [S]	More of the Best of Jimmy Reed	1964	37.50	75.00	150.00
❑ LP-1095 [M]	Jimmy Reed at Soul City	1964	10.00	20.00	40.00
❑ LP-8501 [M]	The Legend, The Man	1965	10.00	20.00	40.00
❑ VJS-8501 [S]	The Legend, The Man	1965	37.50	75.00	150.00

REED, LOU
Also see THE VELVET UNDERGROUND.
DIRECT DISK
❑ (no #) [DJ]	The Blue Mask	1982	37.50	75.00	150.00
-- Only exists on test pressings; no stock copies made					

RCA VICTOR
❑ CPL1-0611	Sally Can't Dance	1974	5.00	10.00	20.00
❑ APD2-1101 [(2) Q]	Metal Machine Music	1975	37.50	75.00	150.00
❑ CPL2-1101 [(2)]	Metal Machine Music	1975	12.50	25.00	50.00
-- Orange or brown label					
❑ DJL1-4266 [DJ]	Special Radio Series, Vol. XVII	1980	6.25	12.50	25.00
-- Promo-only with insert					
❑ DJL1-4267 [DJ]	The Blue Mask Interview Album	1982	10.00	20.00	40.00
❑ LSP-4701	Lou Reed	1972	5.00	10.00	20.00
❑ LSP-4807	Transformer	1972	5.00	10.00	20.00

REED, LULA
KING
❑ 604 [M]	Blue and Moody	1958	500.00	1,000.	2,000.

REESE, DELLA
ABC
❑ 589 [M]	One More Time	1967	5.00	10.00	20.00
❑ S-569 [S]	Della Reese Live	1966	5.00	10.00	20.00
❑ 612 [M]	Della on Strings of Blue	1967	5.00	10.00	20.00

ABC-PARAMOUNT
❑ S-524 [S]	C'mon and Hear Della Reese	1965	5.00	10.00	20.00
❑ S-540 [S]	I Like It Like Dat!	1966	5.00	10.00	20.00

JUBILEE
❑ JLP-1026 [M]	Melancholy Baby	1957	7.50	15.00	30.00
❑ JLP-1071 [M]	A Date with Della Reese at Mr. Kelly's in Chicago	1959	6.25	12.50	25.00
❑ SDJLP-1071 [S]	A Date with Della Reese at Mr. Kelly's in Chicago	1959	7.50	15.00	30.00
❑ JLP-1083 [M]	Amen	1959	6.25	12.50	25.00
❑ SDJLP-1083 [S]	Amen	1959	7.50	15.00	30.00
❑ JLP-1095 [M]	The Story of the Blues	1960	6.25	12.50	25.00
❑ SDJLP-1095 [S]	The Story of the Blues	1960	7.50	15.00	30.00
❑ JLP-1109 [M]	What Do You Know About Love	1960	6.25	12.50	25.00
❑ JLP-1116 [M]	And That Reminds Me	1960	6.25	12.50	25.00
❑ JGS-5002 [S]	The Best of Della Reese	196?	5.00	10.00	20.00

RCA VICTOR
❑ LPM-2157 [M]	Della	1960	5.00	10.00	20.00
❑ LSP-2157 [S]	Della	1960	6.25	12.50	25.00
❑ LPM-2204 [M]	Della by Starlight	1960	5.00	10.00	20.00
❑ LSP-2204 [S]	Della by Starlight	1960	6.25	12.50	25.00
❑ LPM-2280 [M]	Della Della Cha-Cha-Cha	1961	5.00	10.00	20.00
❑ LSP-2280 [S]	Della Della Cha-Cha-Cha	1961	6.25	12.50	25.00
❑ LPM-2391 [M]	Special Delivery	1961	5.00	10.00	20.00
❑ LSP-2391 [S]	Special Delivery	1961	6.25	12.50	25.00
❑ LPM-2419 [M]	The Classic Della	1962	5.00	10.00	20.00
❑ LSP-2419 [S]	The Classic Della	1962	6.25	12.50	25.00
❑ LPM-2568 [M]	Della on Stage	1962	5.00	10.00	20.00
❑ LSP-2568 [S]	Della on Stage	1962	6.25	12.50	25.00
❑ LPM-2711 [M]	Waltz with Me	1963	5.00	10.00	20.00
❑ LSP-2711 [S]	Waltz with Me	1963	6.25	12.50	25.00
❑ LPM-2872 [M]	Della Reese at Basin Street East	1964	5.00	10.00	20.00
❑ LSP-2872 [S]	Della Reese at Basin Street East	1964	6.25	12.50	25.00

REEVES, DEL
UNITED ARTISTS
❑ UAL-3441 [M]	Del Reeves Sings Girl on the Billboard	1965	6.25	12.50	25.00
❑ UAL-3458 [M]	Doodle-Oo-Doo-Doo	1965	5.00	10.00	20.00
❑ UAL-3468 [M]	Del Reeves Sings Jim Reeves	1966	5.00	10.00	20.00
❑ UAL-3488 [M]	Special Delivery	1966	5.00	10.00	20.00
❑ UAL-3528 [M]	Santa's Boy	1966	5.00	10.00	20.00
❑ UAL-3530 [M]	Gettin' Any Feed for Your Chickens?	1966	5.00	10.00	20.00
❑ UAL-3571 [M]	Struttin' My Stuff	1967	6.25	12.50	25.00
❑ UAL-3595 [M]	Six of One, Half a Dozen of the Other	1967	6.25	12.50	25.00
❑ UAL-3612 [M]	The Little Church in the Dell	1967	7.50	15.00	30.00
❑ UAS-6441 [S]	Del Reeves Sings Girl on the Billboard	1965	7.50	15.00	30.00
❑ UAS-6458 [S]	Doodle-Oo-Doo-Doo	1965	6.25	12.50	25.00
❑ UAS-6468 [S]	Del Reeves Sings Jim Reeves	1966	6.25	12.50	25.00
❑ UAS-6488 [S]	Special Delivery	1966	6.25	12.50	25.00
❑ UAS-6528 [S]	Santa's Boy	1966	6.25	12.50	25.00
❑ UAS-6530 [S]	Gettin' Any Feed for Your Chickens?	1966	6.25	12.50	25.00
❑ UAS-6571 [S]	Struttin' My Stuff	1967	5.00	10.00	20.00
❑ UAS-6595 [S]	Six of One, Half a Dozen of the Other	1967	5.00	10.00	20.00
❑ UAS-6612 [S]	The Little Church in the Dell	1967	6.25	12.50	25.00
❑ UAS-6635	The Best of Del Reeves	1968	5.00	10.00	20.00
❑ UAS-6643	Running Wild	1968	5.00	10.00	20.00
❑ UAS-6674	Looking at the World Through a Windshield	1968	5.00	10.00	20.00
❑ UAS-6705	Down at Good Time Charlie's	1969	5.00	10.00	20.00
❑ UAS-6733	Big Daddy Del	1970	5.00	10.00	20.00
❑ UAS-6758	The Best of Del Reeves, Vol. 2	1970	5.00	10.00	20.00
❑ UAS-6789	Friends and Neighbors	1971	5.00	10.00	20.00
❑ UAS-6820	The Del Reeves Album	1971	5.00	10.00	20.00
❑ UAS-6830	Before Goodbye	1972	5.00	10.00	20.00

REEVES, JIM
ABBOTT
❑ LP-5001 [M]	Jim Reeves Sings	1956	1,000.	1,500.	2,000.

Number	Title	Yr	VG	VG+	NM
RCA CAMDEN					
❏ CAL-583 [M]	According to My Heart	1960	5.00	10.00	20.00
❏ CAS-583 [R]	According to My Heart	1960	5.00	10.00	20.00
❏ CAL-686 [M]	The Country Side of Jim Reeves	1962	5.00	10.00	20.00
❏ CAS-686 [S]	The Country Side of Jim Reeves	1962	5.00	10.00	20.00
❏ CAL-784 [M]	Good 'N' Country	1963	5.00	10.00	20.00
❏ CAS-784 [S]	Good 'N' Country	1963	5.00	10.00	20.00
❏ CAL-842 [M]	Have I Told You Lately That I Love You?	1964	5.00	10.00	20.00
❏ CAS-842 [S]	Have I Told You Lately That I Love You?	1964	5.00	10.00	20.00
❏ CAX-9001 [(2)]	Jim Reeves	1972	5.00	10.00	20.00
RCA VICTOR					
❏ APL1-0039	Am I That Easy to Forget	1973	5.00	10.00	20.00
❏ APL1-0330	Great Moments with Jim Reeves	1973	5.00	10.00	20.00
❏ APL1-0537	I'd Fight the World	1974	5.00	10.00	20.00
❏ APL1-0793	The Best of Jim Reeves Sacred Songs	1974	5.00	10.00	20.00
❏ APL1-1037	Songs of Love	1975	5.00	10.00	20.00
❏ APL1-1224	I Love You Because	1976	5.00	10.00	20.00
❏ LPM-1256 [M]	Singing Down the Lane	1956	50.00	100.00	200.00
❏ LPM-1410 [M]	Bimbo	1957	50.00	100.00	200.00
-- Reissue of Abbott LP					
❏ LPM-1576 [M]	Jim Reeves	1957	20.00	40.00	80.00
❏ LPM-1685 [M]	Girls I Have Known	1958	15.00	30.00	60.00
❏ CPL1-1891	A Legendary Performer	1976	5.00	10.00	20.00
❏ LPM-1950 [M]	God Be With You	1958	10.00	20.00	40.00
❏ LSP-1950 [S]	God Be With You	1958	12.50	25.00	50.00
❏ LPM-2001 [M]	Songs to Warm the Heart	1959	10.00	20.00	40.00
❏ LSP-2001 [S]	Songs to Warm the Heart	1959	12.50	25.00	50.00
❏ LPM-2216 [M]	The Intimate Jim Reeves	1960	7.50	15.00	30.00
❏ LSP-2216 [S]	The Intimate Jim Reeves	1960	10.00	20.00	40.00
❏ LPM-2223 [M]	He'll Have to Go	1960	7.50	15.00	30.00
❏ LSP-2223 [S]	He'll Have to Go	1960	10.00	20.00	40.00
❏ LPM-2284 [M]	Tall Tales and Short Tempers	1961	6.25	12.50	25.00
❏ LSP-2284 [S]	Tall Tales and Short Tempers	1961	7.50	15.00	30.00
❏ LPM-2339 [M]	Talkin' to Your Heart	1961	6.25	12.50	25.00
❏ LSP-2339 [S]	Talkin' to Your Heart	1961	7.50	15.00	30.00
❏ LPM-2487 [M]	A Touch of Velvet	1962	6.25	12.50	25.00
❏ LSP-2487 [S]	A Touch of Velvet	1962	7.50	15.00	30.00
❏ LPM-2552 [M]	We Thank Thee	1962	6.25	12.50	25.00
❏ LSP-2552 [S]	We Thank Thee	1962	7.50	15.00	30.00
❏ LPM-2605 [M]	Gentleman Jim	1963	6.25	12.50	25.00
❏ LSP-2605 [S]	Gentleman Jim	1963	7.50	15.00	30.00
❏ LPM-2704 [M]	The International Jim Reeves	1963	6.25	12.50	25.00
❏ LSP-2704 [S]	The International Jim Reeves	1963	7.50	15.00	30.00
❏ LPM-2758 [M]	Twelve Songs of Christmas	1963	6.25	12.50	25.00
❏ LSP-2758 [S]	Twelve Songs of Christmas	1963	7.50	15.00	30.00
❏ LPM-2780 [M]	Kimberley Jim	1964	6.25	12.50	25.00
❏ LSP-2780 [S]	Kimberley Jim	1964	7.50	15.00	30.00
❏ LPM-2854 [M]	Moonlight and Roses	1964	6.25	12.50	25.00
❏ LSP-2854 [S]	Moonlight and Roses	1964	7.50	15.00	30.00
❏ LPM-2890 [M]	The Best of Jim Reeves	1964	5.00	10.00	20.00
❏ LSP-2890 [S]	The Best of Jim Reeves	1964	6.25	12.50	25.00
❏ LPM-2968 [M]	The Jim Reeves Way	1965	5.00	10.00	20.00
❏ LSP-2968 [S]	The Jim Reeves Way	1965	6.25	12.50	25.00
❏ LPM-3427 [M]	Up Through the Years	1965	5.00	10.00	20.00
❏ LSP-3427 [S]	Up Through the Years	1965	6.25	12.50	25.00
❏ LPM-3482 [M]	The Best of Jim Reeves, Vol. II	1966	5.00	10.00	20.00
❏ LSP-3482 [S]	The Best of Jim Reeves, Vol. II	1966	6.25	12.50	25.00
❏ LPM-3542 [M]	Distant Drums	1966	5.00	10.00	20.00
❏ LSP-3542 [S]	Distant Drums	1966	6.25	12.50	25.00
❏ LPM-3709 [M]	Yours Sincerely, Jim Reeves	1966	5.00	10.00	20.00
❏ LSP-3709 [S]	Yours Sincerely, Jim Reeves	1966	6.25	12.50	25.00
❏ LPM-3793 [M]	Blue Side of Lonesome	1967	6.25	12.50	25.00
❏ LSP-3793 [S]	Blue Side of Lonesome	1967	5.00	10.00	20.00
❏ LPM-3903 [M]	My Cathedral	1967	7.50	15.00	30.00
❏ LSP-3903 [S]	My Cathedral	1967	6.25	12.50	25.00
❏ LPM-3987 [M]	A Touch of Sadness	1968	15.00	30.00	60.00
❏ LSP-3987 [S]	A Touch of Sadness	1968	5.00	10.00	20.00
❏ LSP-4062	Jim Reeves On Stage	1968	5.00	10.00	20.00
❏ LSP-4112	Jim Reeves and Some Friends	1969	5.00	10.00	20.00
❏ LSP-4187	The Best of Jim Reeves Volume III	1969	5.00	10.00	20.00
❏ LSP-4475	Jim Reeves Writes You a Record	1971	5.00	10.00	20.00
❏ LSP-4528	Something Special	1971	5.00	10.00	20.00
❏ LSP-4646	My Friend	1972	5.00	10.00	20.00
❏ LSP-4749	Missing You	1972	5.00	10.00	20.00

REFLECTIONS, THE
GOLDEN WORLD

Number	Title	Yr	VG	VG+	NM
❏ 300 [M]	(Just Like) Romeo and Juliet	1964	37.50	75.00	150.00

REGENT CONCERT ORCHESTRA, THE
REGENT

Number	Title	Yr	VG	VG+	NM
❏ 6091 [M]	Amor	1958	12.50	25.00	50.00
-- Cover model is Jayne Mansfield					

REGENTS, THE
CAPITOL

Number	Title	Yr	VG	VG+	NM
❏ KAO 2153 [M]	Live at the AM-PM Discotheque	1964	12.50	25.00	50.00
❏ SKAO 2153 [S]	Live at the AM-PM Discotheque	1964	15.00	30.00	60.00
GEE					
❏ GLP-706 [M]	Barbara Ann	1961	37.50	75.00	150.00
❏ SGLP-706 [S]	Barbara Ann	1961	62.50	125.00	250.00
❏ SGLP-706	Barbara Ann	197?	6.25	12.50	25.00
-- Reissue by Publishers Central Bureau (clearly marked as such on cover)					

REID, CLARENCE
ATCO

Number	Title	Yr	VG	VG+	NM
❏ SD 33-307	Dancin' with Nobody But You	1969	7.50	15.00	30.00

REINER, CARL, AND MEL BROOKS
CAPITOL

Number	Title	Yr	VG	VG+	NM
❏ SW 1529 [S]	2000 Years	1961	5.00	10.00	20.00
❏ SW 1618 [S]	2000 and One Years	1961	5.00	10.00	20.00
❏ SW 1815 [S]	At the Cannes Film Festival	1962	5.00	10.00	20.00
WARNER BROS.					
❏ 3XX 2744 [(3)]	The Incomplete Works of Reiner and Brooks	1973	6.25	12.50	25.00
WORLD PACIFIC					
❏ WP-1401 [M]	2000 Years	1960	7.50	15.00	30.00

REMAINS, THE
EPIC

Number	Title	Yr	VG	VG+	NM
❏ BN 26214 [S]	The Remains	1966	75.00	150.00	300.00
❏ LN 24214 [M]	The Remains	1966	50.00	100.00	200.00

REMINGTON, HERB
UNITED ARTISTS

Number	Title	Yr	VG	VG+	NM
❏ UAL-3167 [M]	Steel Guitar Holiday	1961	6.25	12.50	25.00
❏ UAS-6167 [S]	Steel Guitar Holiday	1961	7.50	15.00	30.00

RENAISSANCE
ELEKTRA

Number	Title	Yr	VG	VG+	NM
❏ EKS-74068	Renaissance	1969	7.50	15.00	30.00
MOBILE FIDELITY					
❏ 1-099	Scheherazade and Other Stories	1982	12.50	25.00	50.00
-- Audiophile vinyl					

RENAY, DIANE
20TH CENTURY FOX

Number	Title	Yr	VG	VG+	NM
❏ TF-3133 [M]	Navy Blue	1964	20.00	40.00	80.00
❏ TFS-3133 [S]	Navy Blue	1964	37.50	75.00	150.00

RENE, GOOGIE
CLASS

Number	Title	Yr	VG	VG+	NM
❏ LP-200 [M]	Flapjacks	1963	5.00	10.00	20.00
❏ LP-5001 [M]	Beautiful Weekend	1957	6.25	12.50	25.00
❏ LP-5003 [M]	Googie Rene Presents Romesville	1959	6.25	12.50	25.00

RENE, HENRI
IMPERIAL

Number	Title	Yr	VG	VG+	NM
❏ LP-9074 [M]	White Heat	1959	5.00	10.00	20.00
❏ LP-9096 [M]	Swingin' 59	1960	5.00	10.00	20.00
❏ LP-12021 [S]	White Heat	1959	7.50	15.00	30.00
❏ LP-12040 [S]	Swingin' 59	1960	7.50	15.00	30.00
RCA VICTOR					
❏ LPM-1033 [M]	Passion in Paint	1955	20.00	40.00	80.00
❏ LPM-1046 [M]	Music for Bachelors	1955	30.00	60.00	120.00
-- Cover model is Jayne Mansfield					
❏ LPM-1583 [M]	Music for the Weaker Sex	1957	6.25	12.50	25.00
❏ LPM-1947 [M]	Compulsion to Swing	1958	5.00	10.00	20.00
❏ LSP-1947 [S]	Compulsion to Swing	1958	7.50	15.00	30.00
❏ LPM-2002 [M]	Riot in Rhythm	1959	5.00	10.00	20.00
❏ LSP-2002 [S]	Riot in Rhythm	1959	7.50	15.00	30.00
❏ LSA-2396 [S]	Dynamic Dimensions	1961	7.50	15.00	30.00
❏ LPM-3049 [10]	Serenade to Love	1953	10.00	20.00	40.00
❏ LPM-3076 [10]	Listen to Rene	1953	10.00	20.00	40.00

RENO AND SMILEY
DOT

Number	Title	Yr	VG	VG+	NM
❏ DLP-3490 [M]	Bluegrass Hits	1963	6.25	12.50	25.00
❏ DLP-25490 [S]	Bluegrass Hits	1963	7.50	15.00	30.00
KING					
❏ 550 [M]	Sacred Songs	1958	30.00	60.00	120.00
❏ 552 [M]	Reno and Smiley Instrumentals	1958	25.00	50.00	100.00

(Top left) Most of the vinyl albums by Queen sold so many copies that the supply still outstrips the demand. This is not true, however, of the three Mobile Fidelity vinyl issues. *A Day at the Races,* from 1996, was one of the last MoFi releases from its second wave, and as such, it's quite scarce. (Top right) *Time Peace/The Rascals' Greatest Hits* was their biggest album; it got to No. 1 on the *Billboard* charts in 1968. Nonetheless, the original pressings on a green and blue label are tough to find in near-mint condition. By 1969, the label had been replaced with a red and green label. (Bottom left) The newest album pictured in this book, *Californication* by Red Hot Chili Peppers came out in June 1999 on vinyl. It was issued as a two-record set on 180-gram vinyl, and had a price tag to match – about $20, sometimes more. (Bottom right) Renaissance, when it issued its debut album, was headed by Keith and Jane Relf. By the time the group's second album, *Prologue,* came out, only the name was the same; no one was left from the original group.

Number	Title	Yr	VG	VG+	NM
❏ 579 [M]	Folk Ballads and Instrumentals	1958	25.00	50.00	100.00
❏ 617 [M]	Someone Will Love Me in Heaven	1959	25.00	50.00	100.00
❏ 621 [M]	Good Old Country Ballads	1959	25.00	50.00	100.00
❏ 646 [M]	A Variety of Country Songs	1959	25.00	50.00	100.00
❏ 693 [M]	Hymns Sacred and Gospel	1959	25.00	50.00	100.00
❏ 701 [M]	Country Songs	1959	25.00	50.00	100.00
❏ 718 [M]	Wanted	1961	25.00	50.00	100.00
❏ 756 [M]	Folk Songs of the Civil War	1961	25.00	50.00	100.00
❏ 776 [M]	Country Singing and Instrumentals	1962	20.00	40.00	80.00
❏ 787 [M]	Banjo Special	1962	20.00	40.00	80.00
❏ 816 [M]	Another Day with Reno and Smiley	1962	20.00	40.00	80.00
❏ 853 [M]	The 15 Greatest Hymns of All	1963	20.00	40.00	80.00
❏ 861 [M]	The World's Best Five String Banjo	1963	20.00	40.00	80.00
❏ 874 [M]	The True Meaning of Christmas	1963	25.00	50.00	100.00
❏ 874 [M]	The True Meaning of Christmas	1963	20.00	40.00	80.00
❏ 911 [M]	On the Road with Reno and Smiley	1964	20.00	40.00	80.00
❏ 914 [M]	A Bluegrass Tribute to Cowboy Copas	1964	20.00	40.00	80.00
❏ KSD-1044	I Know You're Married	1969	6.25	12.50	25.00
❏ KSD-1091	The Best of Reno and Smiley	1970	6.25	12.50	25.00

RENO, DON, AND BILL HARRELL
JALYN

❏ JLP-108 [M]	Bluegrass Favorites	1964	6.25	12.50	25.00
❏ JLP-119 [M]	The Most Requested Songs	1966	6.25	12.50	25.00

KING

❏ KSD-1029	A Variety of New Sacred Gospel Songs	1968	5.00	10.00	20.00
❏ KSD-1033	All the Way to Reno	1968	5.00	10.00	20.00
❏ KSD-1068	I'm Using My Bible for a Roadmap	1969	5.00	10.00	20.00

RENO, JACK
ATCO

❏ SD 33-251	Meet Jack Reno	1968	6.25	12.50	25.00

DERBYTOWN

❏ 101	Yellow Pages	197?	5.00	10.00	20.00

DOT

❏ DLP 25921	I Want One	1968	6.25	12.50	25.00
❏ DLP 25946	I'm a Good Man in a Bad Frame of Mind	1969	6.25	12.50	25.00

TARGET

❏ 1313	Hitchin' a Ride	1972	5.00	10.00	20.00

REO SPEEDWAGON
EPIC

❏ HE 45062	You Can Tune a Piano, But You Can't Tuna Fish	198?	10.00	20.00	40.00
-- Half-speed mastered edition					
❏ HE 46844	Hi Infidelity	1982	7.50	15.00	30.00
-- Half-speed mastered edition					
❏ HE 48100	Good Trouble	1982	7.50	15.00	30.00
-- Half-speed mastered edition					

REPARATA AND THE DELRONS
AVCO EMBASSY

❏ AVE-33008	Rock and Roll Revolution	1970	6.25	12.50	25.00

WORLD ARTISTS

❏ WAM-2006 [M]	Whenever a Teenager Cries	1965	12.50	25.00	50.00
❏ WAS-3006 [S]	Whenever a Teenager Cries	1965	15.00	30.00	60.00

REPLACEMENTS, THE
SIRE

❏ PRO-A-4632 [DJ]	Don't Sell Or Buy...It's Crap	1991	7.50	15.00	30.00
-- Promo-only 5-track sampler					

WARNER BROS.

❏ WBMS-148 [DJ]	The Warner Bros. Music Show: An Interview with Paul Westerberg	1987	10.00	20.00	40.00

REPRISE REPERTORY THEATRE, THE

Artists who were signed to Reprise at the time, such as ROSEMARY CLOONEY, BING CROSBY, SAMMY DAVIS, JR., DEAN MARTIN, FRANK SINATRA, and JO STAFFORD, perform new versions of famous musicals under this collective name.

REPRISE

❏ F-2015 [M]	Finian's Rainbow	1964	7.50	15.00	30.00
-- Gatefold cover					
❏ F-2015 [M]	Finian's Rainbow	196?	5.00	10.00	20.00
-- Standard cover					
❏ FS-2015 [S]	Finian's Rainbow	1964	10.00	20.00	40.00
-- Gatefold cover					
❏ FS-2015 [S]	Finian's Rainbow	196?	6.25	12.50	25.00
-- Standard cover					
❏ F-2016 [M]	Guys and Dolls	1964	7.50	15.00	30.00
-- Gatefold cover					
❏ F-2016 [M]	Guys and Dolls	196?	5.00	10.00	20.00
-- Standard cover					
❏ FS-2016 [S]	Guys and Dolls	1964	10.00	20.00	40.00
-- Gatefold cover					
❏ FS-2016 [S]	Guys and Dolls	196?	6.25	12.50	25.00
-- Standard cover					
❏ F-2017 [M]	Kiss Me, Kate	1964	7.50	15.00	30.00
-- Gatefold cover					
❏ F-2017 [M]	Kiss Me, Kate	196?	5.00	10.00	20.00
-- Standard cover					
❏ FS-2017 [S]	Kiss Me, Kate	1964	10.00	20.00	40.00
-- Gatefold cover					
❏ FS-2017 [S]	Kiss Me, Kate	196?	6.25	12.50	25.00
-- Standard cover					
❏ F-2018 [M]	South Pacific	1964	7.50	15.00	30.00
-- Gatefold cover					
❏ F-2018 [M]	South Pacific	196?	5.00	10.00	20.00
-- Standard cover					
❏ FS-2018 [S]	South Pacific	1964	10.00	20.00	40.00
-- Gatefold cover					
❏ FS-2018 [S]	South Pacific	196?	6.25	12.50	25.00
-- Standard cover					
❏ F-2019 [(4) M]	The Reprise Repertory Theatre	1964	50.00	100.00	200.00
-- Box set of all four of the above LPs in gatefold covers					
❏ FS-2019 [(4) S]	The Reprise Repertory Theatre	1964	75.00	150.00	300.00
-- Box set of all four of the above LPs in gatefold covers					

RESIDENTS, THE
CRYPTIC

❏ S-18335 SP-2	For Elsie	1987	18.75	37.50	75.00
-- Green vinyl one-sided LP					

EPISODE

❏ ED 21	The Census Taker (Soundtrack)	1985	5.00	10.00	20.00
❏ ED 21	The Census Taker (Soundtrack)	1985	6.25	12.50	25.00
-- Red vinyl					

OP

❏ 011 [DJ]	Freak Show	1991	12.50	25.00	50.00
-- Promo-only black vinyl pressing; 400 made					

RALPH

❏ Mole Show 001	The Mole Show (The Roxy)	1983	7.50	15.00	30.00
❏ RR 0274	Meet the Residents	1974	50.00	100.00	200.00
-- First version: "Meet the Beatles" LP parody cover and "First Edition" on back cover					
❏ RR 0677	Meet the Residents	1977	5.00	10.00	20.00
-- Second version: "She Loves You" picture sleeve parody cover, split "a" Ralph logo					
❏ RR 1075	The Third Reich 'N' Roll	1976	12.50	25.00	50.00
-- First version of 1,000: Liner notes inside, orange carrot					
❏ RR 1075	The Third Reich 'N' Roll	1976	375.00	750.00	1,500.
-- Numbered box set on marbled vinyl, silkscreened cover and lithographs inside					
❏ RR 1075	The Third Reich 'N' Roll	1976	12.50	25.00	50.00
-- Censored cover with swastikas obscured, pressed in U.S. for export to Germany					
❏ RR 1174	Not Available	1978	6.25	12.50	25.00
-- Purple label, mis-mastered, "Re-1" in trail-off vinyl					
❏ RR 1276	Fingerprince	1977	20.00	40.00	80.00
-- First version: Dark brown cover, "First Pressing" written on back cover					
❏ RR 1276	Fingerprince	1977	5.00	10.00	20.00
-- Second version: Lighter brown cover					
❏ RZ 7707 [PD]	Meet the Residents	1986	6.25	12.50	25.00
-- Picture disc, with original cover on one side, replacement cover on other					
❏ DJ 7901 [DJ]	Please Do Not Steal It!	1979	6.25	12.50	25.00
-- Promo-only sampler					
❏ ESK 7906	Eskimo	1979	6.25	12.50	25.00
-- First version: White vinyl, gatefold cover					
❏ RZ 7906 [PD]	Eskimo	1979	7.50	15.00	30.00
-- Picture disc					
❏ RZ 8052	The Residents Commercial Album	1980	5.00	10.00	20.00
-- First version: Purple Ralph logo, songs listed in wrong order					
❏ RZ 8152	Mark of the Mole	1981	12.50	25.00	50.00
-- Signed brown vinyl edition with lyrics					
❏ RZ 8402	George & James	1984	7.50	15.00	30.00
-- First edition: Rejected mix with "Re-1" in trail-off					
❏ RZ 8452	Whatever Happened to Vileness Fats?	1984	12.50	25.00	50.00
-- Red vinyl					
❏ RZ 8552	The Big Bubble	1985	12.50	25.00	50.00
-- Pink vinyl					
❏ RZ 8602	The Eyeball Show (The 13th Anniversary Show) Live in Japan	1986	5.00	10.00	20.00
-- White vinyl					
❏ RZ 8652	Stars & Hank Forever	1986	5.00	10.00	20.00
-- Blue vinyl					

RESTIVO, JOHNNY
RCA VICTOR

❏ LPM-2149 [M]	Oh, Johnny!	1959	15.00	30.00	60.00
❏ LSP-2149 [S]	Oh, Johnny!	1959	25.00	50.00	100.00

RESTUM, WILLIE
GONE

❏ LP-5011 [M]	Willie Restum at the Dream	1960	62.50	125.00	250.00

Number	Title	Yr	VG	VG+	NM
ROULETTE					
❑ R-25152 [M]	Dream Bar	1961	15.00	30.00	60.00
REVELLS, THE					
REPRISE					
❑ R-6160 [M]	The Go Sound of the Slots	1965	37.50	75.00	150.00
❑ RS-6160 [S]	The Go Sound of the Slots	1965	50.00	100.00	200.00
REVELS, THE					
IMPACT					
❑ LPM-1 [M]	Revels on a Rampage	1964	125.00	250.00	500.00
REVENGERS, THE					
METRO					
❑ M-565 [M]	Batman and Other Supermen	1966	7.50	15.00	30.00
❑ MS-565 [S]	Batman and Other Supermen	1966	10.00	20.00	40.00
REVERE, PAUL, AND THE RAIDERS					
COLUMBIA					
❑ GP 12 [(2)]	Two All Time Great Selling LPs	1969	6.25	12.50	25.00
-- Combines 9395 and 9521 in one package; red labels					
❑ GP 12 [(2)]	Two All Time Great Selling LPs	1971	5.00	10.00	20.00
-- Combines 9395 and 9521 in one package; orange labels					
❑ CL 2307 [M]	Here They Come!	1965	7.50	15.00	30.00
-- "Guaranteed High Fidelity" on label					
❑ CL 2307 [M]	Here They Come!	1965	5.00	10.00	20.00
-- "360 Sound Mono" on label					
❑ CL 2451 [M]	Just Like Us!	1966	6.25	12.50	25.00
❑ CL 2508 [M]	Midnight Ride	1966	6.25	12.50	25.00
❑ CL 2595 [M]	The Spirit of '67	1966	6.25	12.50	25.00
❑ KCL 2662 [M]	Greatest Hits	1967	7.50	15.00	30.00
-- Add 20% if booklet is included					
❑ CL 2721 [M]	Revolution!	1967	7.50	15.00	30.00
❑ CL 2755 [M]	A Christmas Present...And Past	1967	15.00	30.00	60.00
❑ CL 2805 [M]	Goin' to Memphis	1968	20.00	40.00	80.00
❑ CS 9107 [S]	Here They Come!	1965	6.25	12.50	25.00
-- "360 Sound Stereo" in white on label					
❑ CS 9107 [S]	Here They Come!	1965	10.00	20.00	40.00
-- "360 Sound Stereo" in black on label					
❑ CS 9251 [S]	Just Like Us!	1966	7.50	15.00	30.00
❑ CS 9308 [S]	Midnight Ride	1966	7.50	15.00	30.00
❑ CS 9395 [S]	The Spirit of '67	1966	7.50	15.00	30.00
❑ KCS 9462 [S]	Greatest Hits	1967	6.25	12.50	25.00
-- Add 20% if booklet is included					
❑ CS 9521 [S]	Revolution!	1967	6.25	12.50	25.00
❑ CS 9555 [S]	A Christmas Present...And Past	1967	6.25	12.50	25.00
❑ CS 9605 [S]	Goin' to Memphis	1968	5.00	10.00	20.00
❑ CS 9665	Something Happening	1968	5.00	10.00	20.00
❑ CS 9753	Hard 'N' Heavy (With Marshmallow)	1969	7.50	15.00	30.00
-- Color cover					
❑ CS 9753	Hard 'N' Heavy (With Marshmallow)	1969	5.00	10.00	20.00
-- Black and white cover					
❑ CS 9905	Alias Pink Puzz	1969	5.00	10.00	20.00
❑ CS 9964	Collage	1970	5.00	10.00	20.00
❑ C 30386	Greatest Hits, Volume 2	1971	5.00	10.00	20.00
❑ KG 31464 [(2)]	All-Time Greatest Hits	1972	5.00	10.00	20.00
GARDENA					
❑ LP-G1000 [M]	Like, Long Hair	1961	150.00	300.00	600.00
JERDEN					
❑ JRL-7004 [M]	Paul Revere and the Raiders In the Beginning	1966	15.00	30.00	60.00
❑ JRS-7004 [R]	Paul Revere and the Raiders In the Beginning	1966	7.50	15.00	30.00
❑ DT-90709 [R]	Paul Revere and the Raiders In the Beginning	1966	12.50	25.00	50.00
-- Capitol Record Club edition					
❑ T-90709 [M]	Paul Revere and the Raiders In the Beginning	1966	12.50	25.00	50.00
-- Capitol Record Club edition					
SANDE					
❑ S-1001 [M]	Paul Revere and the Raiders	1963	300.00	600.00	1,200.
-- Original version with "Sande" and no mention of "Etiquette" in trail-off area					
❑ S-1001 [M]	Paul Revere and the Raiders	1979	6.25	12.50	25.00
-- Legitimate reissue with "Sande" and "Etiquette" in trail-off area					
SEARS					
❑ SPS-493	Paul Revere and the Raiders	1969	6.25	12.50	25.00
REXROTH, KENNETH					
FANTASY					
❑ 7008 [M]	Poetry and Jazz at the Blackhawk	1958	50.00	100.00	200.00
-- Red vinyl					
❑ 7008 [M]	Poetry and Jazz at the Blackhawk	1958	25.00	50.00	100.00
-- Black vinyl					

Number	Title	Yr	VG	VG+	NM
REXROTH, KENNETH, AND LAWRENCE FERLINGHETTI					
Also see each artist's individual listings.					
FANTASY					
❑ 7002 [M]	Poetry Readings from the Cellar	1957	50.00	100.00	200.00
-- Red vinyl					
❑ 7002 [M]	Poetry Readings from the Cellar	1957	25.00	50.00	100.00
-- Black vinyl					
REY, ALVINO					
CAPITOL					
❑ T 808 [M]	Aloha	1957	7.50	15.00	30.00
❑ ST 1085 [S]	Swinging Fling	1958	7.50	15.00	30.00
❑ T 1085 [M]	Swinging Fling	1958	6.25	12.50	25.00
❑ ST 1262 [S]	Ping Pong	1959	6.25	12.50	25.00
❑ T 1262 [M]	Ping Pong	1959	5.00	10.00	20.00
❑ ST 1395 [S]	That Lonely Feeling	1960	6.25	12.50	25.00
❑ T 1395 [M]	That Lonely Feeling	1960	5.00	10.00	20.00
REYNOLDS, ART, SINGERS					
THELMA HOUSTON was in this group.					
CAPITOL					
❑ ST-191	It's a Wonderful World	1969	5.00	10.00	20.00
❑ ST 2534 [S]	Tellin' It Like It Is	1966	6.25	12.50	25.00
❑ T 2534 [M]	Tellin' It Like It Is	1966	5.00	10.00	20.00
❑ ST 2811 [S]	Long Dusty Road	1967	5.00	10.00	20.00
❑ T 2811 [M]	Long Dusty Road	1967	6.25	12.50	25.00
❑ ST 2900	Soul-Gospel Sounds	1968	5.00	10.00	20.00
REYNOLDS, BURT					
MERCURY					
❑ MK-4 [DJ]	A Burt Reynolds Radio Special	1973	6.25	12.50	25.00
REYNOLDS, DEBBIE					
DOT					
❑ DLP-3191 [M]	Debbie	1959	7.50	15.00	30.00
❑ DLP-3295 [M]	Am I That Easy to Forget?	1960	7.50	15.00	30.00
❑ DLP-3298 [M]	Fine and Dandy	1960	5.00	10.00	20.00
❑ DLP-3492 [M]	Tammy	1963	5.00	10.00	20.00
❑ DLP-25191 [S]	Debbie	1959	10.00	20.00	40.00
❑ DLP-25295 [S]	Am I That Easy to Forget?	1960	10.00	20.00	40.00
-- Black vinyl					
❑ DLP-25295 [S]	Am I That Easy to Forget?	1960	20.00	40.00	80.00
-- Blue vinyl					
❑ DLP-25298 [S]	Fine and Dandy	1960	6.25	12.50	25.00
❑ DLP-25492 [S]	Tammy	1963	6.25	12.50	25.00
MGM					
❑ E-3806 [M]	From Debbie with Love	1959	10.00	20.00	40.00
REYNOLDS, LAWRENCE					
WARNER BROS.					
❑ WS 1825	Jesus Is a Soul Man	1969	5.00	10.00	20.00
REYNOLDS, TEDDY, AND THE TWISTERS					
CROWN					
❑ CST-247 [S]	The Twist	1962	10.00	20.00	40.00
❑ CLP-5247 [M]	The Twist	1962	7.50	15.00	30.00
RHEIMS, ROBERT					
RHEIMS					
❑ LP-6006 [M]	Merry Christmas Carols	1958	5.00	10.00	20.00
-- Red vinyl with lyric innersleeve					
❑ ST-7706 [S]	Merry Christmas Carols	1958	6.25	12.50	25.00
-- Green vinyl with lyric innersleeve					
RHINOCEROS					
ELEKTRA					
❑ EKS-74030	Rhinoceros	1968	6.25	12.50	25.00
❑ EKS-74056	Satin Chickens	1969	5.00	10.00	20.00
❑ EKS-74075	Better Times Are Coming	1970	5.00	10.00	20.00
RHODES, EMITT					
A&M					
❑ SP-4254	The American Dream	1970	6.25	12.50	25.00
-- Original album contains "You're a Very Lovely Woman" and has Rhodes in front of a paint-covered backdrop on cover					
RHODES, TODD					
KING					
❑ 295-88 [10]	Todd Rhodes Playing His Greatest Hits	1954	375.00	750.00	1,500.
❑ 658 [M]	Dance Music	1960	200.00	400.00	800.00

Number	Title	Yr	VG	VG+	NM

RHYTHM DEVILS, THE
PASSPORT
❏ PB-9844	The Rhythm Devils Play River Music	1980	5.00	10.00	20.00

RHYTHM MASTERS, THE
ACE
| ❏ LP-1010 [M] | Hymns and Spirituals | 1961 | 25.00 | 50.00 | 100.00 |

RHYTHM ROCKERS, THE
CHALLENGE
| ❏ CHL-617 [M] | Soul Surfin' | 1963 | 22.50 | 45.00 | 90.00 |

RICE, BOBBY G.
METROMEDIA
| ❏ BML1-0186 | You Lay So Easy on My Mind | 1973 | 5.00 | 10.00 | 20.00 |
ROYAL AMERICAN
| ❏ 1003 | Hit After Hit | 1972 | 5.00 | 10.00 | 20.00 |

RICH, BUDDY
ARGO
| ❏ LP-676 [M] | Playtime | 1961 | 7.50 | 15.00 | 30.00 |
| ❏ LPS-676 [S] | Playtime | 1961 | 10.00 | 20.00 | 40.00 |
EMARCY
| ❏ 66006 | Driver | 1967 | 5.00 | 10.00 | 20.00 |
GREAT AMERICAN
| ❏ 1030 | Class of '78 | 1978 | 5.00 | 10.00 | 20.00 |
| -- Direct-to-disc version of Gryphon 781 | | | | | |
MERCURY
❏ MG-20448 [M]	Rich Versus Roach	1959	15.00	30.00	60.00
❏ MG-20451 [M]	Richcraft	1959	15.00	30.00	60.00
❏ MG-20461 [M]	The Voice Is Rich	1959	12.50	25.00	50.00
❏ SR-60133 [S]	Rich Versus Roach	1959	17.50	35.00	70.00
❏ SR-60136 [S]	Richcraft	1959	17.50	35.00	70.00
❏ SR-60144 [S]	The Voice Is Rich	1959	15.00	30.00	60.00
NORGRAN
❏ MGN-26 [10]	Buddy Rich Swingin'	1954	30.00	60.00	120.00
❏ MGN-1031 [M]	Sing and Swing with Buddy Rich	1955	20.00	40.00	80.00
❏ MGN-1038 [M]	Buddy Rich and Sweets Edison	1955	20.00	40.00	80.00
❏ MGN-1052 [M]	The Swingin' Buddy Rich	1955	15.00	30.00	60.00
-- Reissue of 26					
❏ MGN-1078 [M]	The Wailing Buddy Rich	1956	15.00	30.00	60.00
❏ MGN-1088 [M]	This One's for Basie	1956	15.00	30.00	60.00
PACIFIC JAZZ
❏ PJ-10113 [M]	Swingin' New Big Band	1966	6.25	12.50	25.00
❏ PJ-10117 [M]	Big Swing Face	1967	6.25	12.50	25.00
❏ ST-20113 [S]	Swingin' New Big Band	1966	5.00	10.00	20.00
❏ ST-20117 [S]	Big Swing Face	1967	5.00	10.00	20.00
❏ ST-20126	A New One	1968	5.00	10.00	20.00
VERVE
❏ MGV-2009 [M]	Buddy Rich Sings Johnny Mercer	1956	15.00	30.00	60.00
❏ V-2009 [M]	Buddy Rich Sings Johnny Mercer	1961	5.00	10.00	20.00
❏ MGV-2075 [M]	Buddy Rich Just Sings	1957	15.00	30.00	60.00
❏ V-2075 [M]	Buddy Rich Just Sings	1961	5.00	10.00	20.00
❏ MGV-8129 [M]	Buddy and Sweets	1957	12.50	25.00	50.00
-- Reissue of Norgran 1038					
❏ V-8129 [M]	Buddy and Sweets	1961	5.00	10.00	20.00
❏ MGV-8142 [M]	The Swingin' Buddy Rich	1957	12.50	25.00	50.00
-- Reissue of Norgran 1052					
❏ V-8142 [M]	The Swingin' Buddy Rich	1961	5.00	10.00	20.00
❏ MGV-8168 [M]	The Wailing Buddy Rich	1957	12.50	25.00	50.00
-- Reissue of Norgran 1078					
❏ V-8168 [M]	The Wailing Buddy Rich	1961	5.00	10.00	20.00
❏ MGV-8176 [M]	This One's for Basie	1957	12.50	25.00	50.00
-- Reissue of Norgran 1086					
❏ V-8176 [M]	This One's for Basie	1961	5.00	10.00	20.00
❏ MGV-8285 [M]	Buddy Rich in Miami	1958	15.00	30.00	60.00
❏ V-8285 [M]	Buddy Rich in Miami	1961	5.00	10.00	20.00
❏ V-8425 [M]	Blues Caravan	1962	6.25	12.50	25.00
❏ V6-8425 [S]	Blues Caravan	1962	7.50	15.00	30.00
❏ V-8471 [M]	Burnin' Beat	1962	6.25	12.50	25.00
❏ V6-8471 [S]	Burnin' Beat	1962	7.50	15.00	30.00
❏ V-8484 [M]	Drum Battle: Gene Krupa vs. Buddy Rich	1962	6.25	12.50	25.00
❏ V6-8484 [S]	Drum Battle: Gene Krupa vs. Buddy Rich	1962	7.50	15.00	30.00
❏ V-8712 [M]	Big Band Shout	1967	5.00	10.00	20.00

RICH, CHARLIE
EPIC
| ❏ AS 50 [DJ] | Charlie Rich | 1973 | 7.50 | 15.00 | 30.00 |
| -- Promo-only compilation | | | | | |

Number	Title	Yr	VG	VG+	NM
❏ AS 139 [DJ]	Everything You Always Wanted to Hear by Charlie Rich But Were Afraid to Ask For	1976	6.25	12.50	25.00
-- Promo-only sampler					
❏ BN 26376	Set Me Free	1968	5.00	10.00	20.00
❏ BN 26516	The Fabulous Charlie Rich	1970	5.00	10.00	20.00
❏ E 30214	Boss Man	1970	5.00	10.00	20.00
❏ CQ 31933 [Q]	The Best of Charlie Rich	1972	5.00	10.00	20.00
❏ CQ 32247 [Q]	Behind Closed Doors	1973	5.00	10.00	20.00
❏ PEQ 32531 [Q]	Very Special Love Songs	1974	5.00	10.00	20.00
❏ PEQ 33250 [Q]	The Silver Fox	1974	5.00	10.00	20.00
❏ PEQ 33455 [Q]	Every Time You Touch Me (I Get High)	1975	5.00	10.00	20.00
GROOVE
| ❏ GM-1000 [M] | Charlie Rich | 1964 | 37.50 | 75.00 | 150.00 |
| ❏ GS-1000 [S] | Charlie Rich | 1964 | 75.00 | 150.00 | 300.00 |
HI
| ❏ HL 12037 [M] | Charlie Rich Sings Country and Western | 1967 | 7.50 | 15.00 | 30.00 |
| ❏ SHL 32037 [S] | Charlie Rich Sings Country and Western | 1967 | 5.00 | 10.00 | 20.00 |
PHILLIPS INTERNATIONAL
| ❏ PLP-1970 [M] | Lonely Weekends | 1960 | 150.00 | 300.00 | 600.00 |
RCA VICTOR
❏ LPM-3352 [M]	That's Rich	1965	10.00	20.00	40.00
❏ LSP-3352 [S]	That's Rich	1965	12.50	25.00	50.00
❏ LPM-3537 [M]	Big Boss Man	1966	10.00	20.00	40.00
❏ LSP-3557 [S]	Big Boss Man	1966	12.50	25.00	50.00
SMASH
❏ MGS-27070 [M]	The Many New Sides of Charlie Rich	1965	7.50	15.00	30.00
❏ MGS-27078 [M]	The Best Years	1966	7.50	15.00	30.00
❏ SRS-67070 [S]	The Many New Sides of Charlie Rich	1965	10.00	20.00	40.00
❏ SRS-67070 [S]	The Best Years	1966	10.00	20.00	40.00

RICH, DAVE
STOP
| ❏ 10007 | Soul Brother | 196? | 7.50 | 15.00 | 30.00 |

RICHARD AND JIM
CAPITOL
❏ ST 2058 [S]	Folk Songs and Country Sounds	1964	6.25	12.50	25.00
❏ T 2058 [M]	Folk Songs and Country Sounds	1964	5.00	10.00	20.00
❏ ST 2287 [S]	Two Boys from Alabama	1965	6.25	12.50	25.00
❏ T 2287 [M]	Two Boys from Alabama	1965	5.00	10.00	20.00

RICHARD, CLIFF
ABC-PARAMOUNT
❏ 321 [M]	Cliff Sings	1960	20.00	40.00	80.00
❏ S-321 [S]	Cliff Sings	1960	25.00	50.00	100.00
❏ 391 [M]	Listen to Cliff	1961	20.00	40.00	80.00
❏ S-391 [S]	Listen to Cliff	1961	25.00	50.00	100.00
EPIC
❏ LN 24063 [M]	Summer Holiday	1963	10.00	20.00	40.00
❏ LN 24089 [M]	It's All in the Game	1964	7.50	15.00	30.00
❏ LN 24115 [M]	Cliff Richard in Spain	1965	7.50	15.00	30.00
❏ BN 26063 [S]	Summer Holiday	1963	12.50	25.00	50.00
❏ BN 26089 [S]	It's All in the Game	1964	10.00	20.00	40.00
❏ BN 26115 [S]	Cliff Richard in Spain	1965	10.00	20.00	40.00

RICHARDS, ANN
ATCO
| ❏ 33-136 [M] | Ann, Man! | 1961 | 10.00 | 20.00 | 40.00 |
| ❏ SD 33-136 [S] | Ann, Man! | 1961 | 15.00 | 30.00 | 60.00 |
CAPITOL
❏ ST 1087 [S]	I'm Shooting High	1959	10.00	20.00	40.00
❏ T 1087 [M]	I'm Shooting High	1959	7.50	15.00	30.00
❏ ST 1406 [S]	The Many Moods of Ann Richards	1960	10.00	20.00	40.00
❏ T 1406 [M]	The Many Moods of Ann Richards	1960	7.50	15.00	30.00
VEE JAY
| ❏ LP-1070 [M] | Live...At the Losers | 1963 | 10.00 | 20.00 | 40.00 |
| ❏ SR-1070 [S] | Live...At the Losers | 1963 | 12.50 | 25.00 | 50.00 |

RICHARDS, TRUDY
CAPITOL
| ❏ T 838 [M] | Crazy in Love | 1957 | 7.50 | 15.00 | 30.00 |

RICHARDSON, JIMMY
STARDAY
| ❏ SLP-126 [M] | Sweet with a Beat | 1960 | 7.50 | 15.00 | 30.00 |

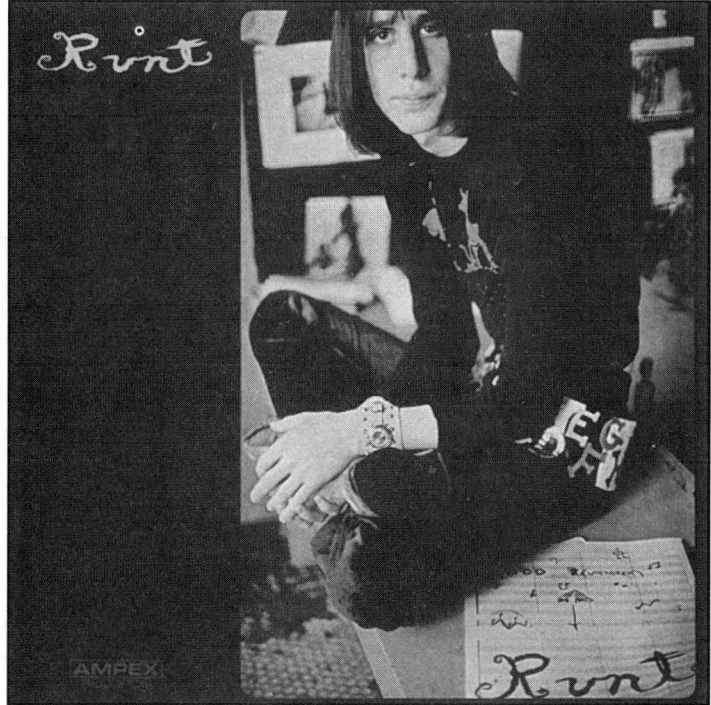

(Top left) Named after their first hit, the only 1960s album for Reparata and the Delrons was on the World Pacific label, *Whenever a Teenager Cries.* In the 1970s, Reparata was one of the singers in Barry Manilow's female backing group, Lady Flash. (Top right) After the success of "Memphis," Johnny Rivers did a series of albums of either live or live-sounding material, mostly consisting of remakes. The big hit on *Meanwhile Back at the Whisky A Go Go* was "Seventh Son." (Bottom left) The Side 1 label of *Presenting the Fabulous Ronettes Featuring Veronica* illustrates that the LP was almost a greatest-hits collection. Any album on Philles is at least worth picking up, and except for the Righteous Brothers' LPs, they are pricey, too. (Bottom right) Before he recorded as Todd Rundgren, he was "Runt." His first solo album exists in three different versions; one has 12 tracks, one has 11 tracks, the "official" version has 10. You actually need to count the tracks to tell the difference.

Number	Title	Yr	VG	VG+	NM

RICHARDSON, WARREN S., JR.
COTILLION
❏ SD 9013	Warren S. Richardson, Jr.	1970	7.50	15.00	30.00

RICHIE, LITTLE JOE -- See LITTLE JOE.

RICHMAN, JONATHAN, AND THE MODERN LOVERS
BESERKLEY
❏ BZ-0048	Jonathan Richman and the Modern Lovers	1976	7.50	15.00	30.00
-- Distributed by GRT					
❏ JBZ 0048	Jonathan Richman and the Modern Lovers	1976	6.25	12.50	25.00
-- Distributed by Playboy/CBS					
❏ BZ-0050	The Modern Lovers	1976	7.50	15.00	30.00
-- Distributed by GRT					
❏ JBZ 0050	The Modern Lovers	1978	6.25	12.50	25.00
-- Distributed by Playboy/CBS					

BOMP!
❏ 4021	The Original Modern Lovers	1981	5.00	10.00	20.00
-- Same album as Mohawk releasse					

HOME OF THE HITS
❏ HH-1910	The Modern Lovers	1975	12.50	25.00	50.00

MOHAWK
❏ SCALP 0002	The Original Modern Lovers	1981	6.25	12.50	25.00

RICKS, JIMMY
Also see THE RAVENS.
JUBILEE
❏ JGS-8021	Tell Her You Love Her	1969	12.50	25.00	50.00

MAINSTREAM
❏ 56050 [M]	Vibrations	1965	12.50	25.00	50.00
❏ S-6050 [S]	Vibrations	1965	15.00	30.00	60.00

SIGNATURE
❏ SM-1032 [M]	Jimmy Ricks	1961	75.00	150.00	300.00
❏ SM-1032 [M-DJ]	Jimmy Ricks	1961	50.00	100.00	200.00

RIDDLE, NELSON
AVON
❏ 10170	Avon Wishes You a Happy Holiday and a Joyous New Year	1970	5.00	10.00	20.00
-- Given to Avon salespeople					

CAPITOL
❏ T 753 [M]	The Tender Touch	1956	6.25	12.50	25.00
❏ T 813 [M]	Hey, Let Yourself Go	1957	6.25	12.50	25.00
❏ T 893 [M]	C'mon, Get Happy	1957	6.25	12.50	25.00
❏ T 915 [M]	Sea of Dreams	1958	6.25	12.50	25.00
❏ ST 1148 [S]	The Joy of Living	1959	6.25	12.50	25.00
❏ T 1148 [M]	The Joy of Living	1959	5.00	10.00	20.00
❏ STAO 1259 [S]	Sing a Song with Riddle	1960	6.25	12.50	25.00
❏ TAO 1259 [M]	Sing a Song with Riddle	1960	5.00	10.00	20.00
❏ ST 1365 [S]	Can-Can	1961	6.25	12.50	25.00
❏ T 1365 [M]	Can-Can	1961	5.00	10.00	20.00
❏ ST 1571 [S]	Love Tide	1961	6.25	12.50	25.00
❏ T 1571 [M]	Love Tide	1961	5.00	10.00	20.00
❏ ST 1670 [S]	Magic Moments from "The Gay Life"	1962	6.25	12.50	25.00
❏ T 1670 [M]	Magic Moments from "The Gay Life"	1962	5.00	10.00	20.00
❏ ST 1771 [S]	Route 66 Theme and Other Great TV Themes	1962	7.50	15.00	30.00
❏ T 1771 [M]	Route 66 Theme and Other Great TV Themes	1962	6.25	12.50	25.00
❏ ST 1817 [S]	Love Is a Game of Poker	1962	6.25	12.50	25.00
❏ T 1817 [M]	Love Is a Game of Poker	1962	5.00	10.00	20.00
❏ ST 1869 [S]	More Hit TV Themes	1963	6.25	12.50	25.00
❏ T 1869 [M]	More Hit TV Themes	1963	5.00	10.00	20.00

RIDERS OF THE PURPLE SAGE, THE -- See FOY WILLING.

RIG
CAPITOL
❏ ST-473	Rig	1970	5.00	10.00	20.00

RIGHTEOUS BROTHERS, THE
Also see BILL MEDLEY.
MOONGLOW
❏ MLP-1001 [M]	Right Now!	1963	10.00	20.00	40.00
❏ MSP-1001 [S]	Right Now!	1963	15.00	30.00	60.00
❏ MLP-1002 [M]	Some Blue-Eyed Soul	1964	10.00	20.00	40.00
❏ MSP-1002 [S]	Some Blue-Eyed Soul	1964	15.00	30.00	60.00
❏ MLP-1003 [M]	This Is New!	1965	10.00	20.00	40.00
❏ MSP-1003 [S]	This Is New!	1965	15.00	30.00	60.00
❏ MLP-1004 [M]	The Best of the Righteous Brothers	1966	6.25	12.50	25.00

Number	Title	Yr	VG	VG+	NM
❏ MSP-1004 [S]	The Best of the Righteous Brothers	1966	7.50	15.00	30.00

PHILLES
❏ PHLP-4007 [M]	You've Lost That Lovin' Feelin'	1964	6.25	12.50	25.00
❏ PHLPS-4007 [S]	You've Lost That Lovin' Feelin'	1964	10.00	20.00	40.00
❏ PHLP-4008 [M]	Just Once in My Life	1965	6.25	12.50	25.00
❏ PHLPS-4008 [S]	Just Once in My Life	1965	10.00	20.00	40.00
❏ PHLP-4009 [M]	Back to Back	1965	6.25	12.50	25.00
❏ PHLPS-4009 [S]	Back to Back	1965	10.00	20.00	40.00
❏ ST-90692 [S]	You've Lost That Lovin' Feelin'	1965	12.50	25.00	50.00
-- Capitol Record Club edition					
❏ T-90692 [M]	You've Lost That Lovin' Feelin'	1965	12.50	25.00	50.00
-- Capitol Record Club edition					

VERVE
❏ V-5001 [M]	Soul and Inspiration	1966	5.00	10.00	20.00
❏ V6-5001 [S]	Soul and Inspiration	1966	6.25	12.50	25.00
❏ V-5004 [M]	Go Ahead and Cry	1966	5.00	10.00	20.00
❏ V6-5004 [S]	Go Ahead and Cry	1966	6.25	12.50	25.00
❏ V-5010 [M]	Sayin' Somethin'	1967	5.00	10.00	20.00
❏ V6-5010 [S]	Sayin' Somethin'	1967	6.25	12.50	25.00
❏ V-5020 [M]	Greatest Hits	1967	6.25	12.50	25.00
❏ V6-5020 [S]	Greatest Hits	1967	5.00	10.00	20.00
❏ V-5031 [M]	Souled Out	1967	7.50	15.00	30.00
❏ V6-5031 [S]	Souled Out	1967	5.00	10.00	20.00
❏ V6-5051	Standards	1968	5.00	10.00	20.00
❏ V6-5058	One for the Road	1968	5.00	10.00	20.00
-- Without The Blossoms credited on the back cover					
❏ V6-5058	One for the Road	1968	7.50	15.00	30.00
-- With The Blossoms credited on the back cover					
❏ V6-5071	Greatest Hits, Vol. 2	1969	5.00	10.00	20.00
❏ V6-5076	Re-Birth	1970	5.00	10.00	20.00
❏ ST-91057 [S]	Sayin' Somethin'	1967	6.25	12.50	25.00
-- Capitol Record Club edition					

RILEY, BILLY LEE
GNP CRESCENDO
❏ GNPS-2020 [S]	Billy Lee Riley	1966	5.00	10.00	20.00

MERCURY
❏ MG-20958 [M]	The Whiskey A-Go-Go Presents Billy Lee Riley	1964	5.00	10.00	20.00
❏ MG-20965 [M]	Big Harmonica Special	1964	5.00	10.00	20.00
❏ MG-20974 [M]	Beatlemania Harmonica	1965	5.00	10.00	20.00
❏ SR-60958 [S]	The Whiskey A-Go-Go Presents Billy Lee Riley	1964	6.25	12.50	25.00
❏ SR-60965 [S]	Big Harmonica Special	1964	6.25	12.50	25.00
❏ SR-60974 [S]	Beatlemania Harmonica	1965	6.25	12.50	25.00

RILEY, JEANNIE C.
PLANTATION
❏ PLP 1	Harper Valley P.T.A.	1968	5.00	10.00	20.00

RINCON SURFSIDE BAND, THE
Another creation of P.F. SLOAN and STEVE BARRI.
DUNHILL
❏ D 50001 [M]	Surfing Songbook	1965	50.00	100.00	200.00
❏ DS 50001 [S]	Surfing Songbook	1965	75.00	150.00	300.00

RIOPELLE, JERRY
CAPITOL
❏ ST-732	Jerry Riopelle	1971	5.00	10.00	20.00
❏ ST-863	Second Album	1971	5.00	10.00	20.00

RIOT
FIRE-SIGN
❏ 87001	Rock City	1977	7.50	15.00	30.00

RIP CHORDS, THE
COLUMBIA
❏ CL 2151 [M]	Hey Little Cobra and Other Hot Rod Hits	1964	10.00	20.00	40.00
❏ CL 2216 [M]	Three Window Coupe	1964	12.50	25.00	50.00
❏ CS 8951 [S]	Hey Little Cobra and Other Hot Rod Hits	1964	12.50	25.00	50.00
❏ CS 9016 [S]	Three Window Coupe	1964	17.50	35.00	70.00

RIPERTON, MINNIE
Also see ROTARY CONNECTION.
EPIC
❏ PEQ 33454 [Q]	Adventures in Paradise	1975	5.00	10.00	20.00

RIPPY, RODNEY ALLEN
BELL
❏ 1311	Take Life a Little Easier	1974	5.00	10.00	20.00

Number	Title	Yr	VG	VG+	NM

RISERS, THE
IMPERIAL
| ❏ LP-9269 [M] | She's a Bad Motorcycle | 1964 | 25.00 | 50.00 | 100.00 |
| ❏ LP-12269 [S] | She's a Bad Motorcycle | 1964 | 37.50 | 75.00 | 150.00 |

RISING STORM, THE
ARF! ARF!
| ❏ 007 | Alive in Anover Again | 1983 | 30.00 | 60.00 | 120.00 |
REMNANT
| ❏ BBA-3571 | Calm Before the Rising Storm | 1968 | 600.00 | 900.00 | 1,200. |
STANTON PARK
| ❏ 001 | Calm Before the Rising Storm | 1991 | 5.00 | 10.00 | 20.00 |
| -- Reissue of Remnant album | | | | | |

RITENOUR, LEE
MOBILE FIDELITY
| ❏ 1-147 | Captain Fingers | 1985 | 6.25 | 12.50 | 25.00 |
| -- Audiophile vinyl | | | | | |
NAUTILUS
| ❏ NR-41 | Rit | 198? | 10.00 | 20.00 | 40.00 |
| -- Audiophile vinyl | | | | | |

RITTER, TEX
CAPITOL
❏ ST-213	Chuck Wagon Days	1969	5.00	10.00	20.00
❏ ST-467	Green Green Valley	1970	5.00	10.00	20.00
❏ T 971 [M]	Songs from the Western Screen	1958	20.00	40.00	80.00
-- Turquoise or gray label					
❏ T 971 [M]	Songs from the Western Screen	1959	10.00	20.00	40.00
-- Black colorband label, logo at left					
❏ T 971 [M]	Songs from the Western Screen	1962	6.25	12.50	25.00
-- Black colorband label, logo at top					
❏ T 1100 [M]	Psalms	1959	12.50	25.00	50.00
❏ ST 1292 [S]	Blood on the Saddle	1960	10.00	20.00	40.00
-- Black colorband label, logo at left					
❏ T 1100 [M]	Psalms	1962	6.25	12.50	25.00
-- Black colorband label, logo at top					
❏ ST 1292 [S]	Blood on the Saddle	1962	6.25	12.50	25.00
-- Black colorband label, logo at left					
❏ T 1292 [M]	Blood on the Saddle	1960	7.50	15.00	30.00
-- Black colorband label, logo at left					
❏ T 1292 [M]	Blood on the Saddle	1962	5.00	10.00	20.00
-- Black colorband label, logo at top					
❏ SW 1562 [S]	The Lincoln Hymns	1961	10.00	20.00	40.00
❏ W 1562 [M]	The Lincoln Hymns	1961	7.50	15.00	30.00
❏ ST 1623 [S]	Hillbilly Heaven	1961	10.00	20.00	40.00
-- Black colorband label, logo at left					
❏ ST 1623 [S]	Hillbilly Heaven	1962	6.25	12.50	25.00
-- Black colorband label, logo at left					
❏ T 1623 [M]	Hillbilly Heaven	1961	7.50	15.00	30.00
-- Black colorband label, logo at left					
❏ T 1623 [M]	Hillbilly Heaven	1962	5.00	10.00	20.00
-- Black colorband label, logo at top					
❏ ST 1910 [S]	Border Affair	1963	6.25	12.50	25.00
❏ T 1910 [M]	Border Affair	1963	5.00	10.00	20.00
❏ ST 2402 [S]	The Friendly Voice of Tex Ritter	1965	6.25	12.50	25.00
❏ T 2402 [M]	The Friendly Voice of Tex Ritter	1965	5.00	10.00	20.00
❏ T 2595 [M]	The Best of Tex Ritter	1966	6.25	12.50	25.00
❏ ST 2743 [S]	Sweet Land of Liberty	1967	6.25	12.50	25.00
❏ T 2743 [M]	Sweet Land of Liberty	1967	7.50	15.00	30.00
❏ ST 2786 [S]	Just Beyond the Moon	1967	6.25	12.50	25.00
❏ T 2786 [M]	Just Beyond the Moon	1967	7.50	15.00	30.00
❏ ST 2890 [S]	Bum Tiddil Dee Bum Bum!	1968	6.25	12.50	25.00
❏ T 2890 [M]	Bum Tiddil Dee Bum Bum!	1968	12.50	25.00	50.00
❏ ST 2974	Tex Ritter's Wild West	1968	6.25	12.50	25.00
❏ H 4004 [10]	Cowboy Favorites	195?	45.00	90.00	180.00
❏ SKC?-11241 [(3)]	An American Legend	1973	7.50	15.00	30.00
-- Black colorband label, logo at left					
LABREA
❏ L-8036 [M]	Jamboree, Nashville Style	196?	5.00	10.00	20.00
❏ LS-8036 [S]	Jamboree, Nashville Style	196?	6.25	12.50	25.00

RIVERA, HECTOR
WING
| ❏ MGW-12197 [M] | Let's Cha Cha Cha | 1960 | 5.00 | 10.00 | 20.00 |

RIVERA, LUIS
IMPERIAL
| ❏ LP-9139 [M] | Filet of Soul | 1961 | 7.50 | 15.00 | 30.00 |

RIVERA, LUIS, AND DOC BAGBY
KING
| ❏ 631 [M] | Battle of the Organs | 1959 | 25.00 | 50.00 | 100.00 |

RIVERS, JERRY
STARDAY
| ❏ SLP-281 [M] | Fantastic Fiddlin' and Tall Tales | 1964 | 7.50 | 15.00 | 30.00 |

RIVERS, JOHNNY
CAPITOL
| ❏ ST 2161 [S] | The Sensational Johnny Rivers | 1964 | 6.25 | 12.50 | 25.00 |
| ❏ T 2161 [M] | The Sensational Johnny Rivers | 1964 | 5.00 | 10.00 | 20.00 |
IMPERIAL
❏ LP-9264 [M]	Johnny Rivers at the Whiskey A-Go-Go	1964	5.00	10.00	20.00
-- Black label with pink and white at left					
❏ LP-9274 [M]	Here We A-Go-Go Again!	1964	5.00	10.00	20.00
-- Black label with pink and white at left					
❏ LP-9280 [M]	Johnny Rivers In Action!	1965	5.00	10.00	20.00
-- Black label with pink and white at left					
❏ LP-9284 [M]	Meanwhile Back at the Whiskey A-Go-Go	1965	5.00	10.00	20.00
-- Black label with pink and white at left					
❏ LP-9293 [M]	Johnny Rivers Rocks the Folk	1965	5.00	10.00	20.00
-- Black label with pink and white at left					
❏ LP-9307 [M]	...And I Know You Wanna Dance	1966	5.00	10.00	20.00
-- Black label with pink and white at left					
❏ LP-9341 [M]	Rewind	1967	5.00	10.00	20.00
❏ LP-12264 [S]	Johnny Rivers at the Whiskey A-Go-Go	1964	6.25	12.50	25.00
-- Black label with pink and white at left					
❏ LP-12274 [S]	Here We A-Go-Go Again!	1964	6.25	12.50	25.00
-- Black label with pink and white at left					
❏ LP-12280 [S]	Johnny Rivers In Action!	1965	6.25	12.50	25.00
-- Black label with pink and white at left					
❏ LP-12284 [S]	Meanwhile Back at the Whiskey A-Go-Go	1965	6.25	12.50	25.00
-- Black label with pink and white at left					
❏ LP-12293 [S]	Johnny Rivers Rocks the Folk	1965	6.25	12.50	25.00
-- Black label with pink and white at left					
❏ LP-12307 [S]	...And I Know You Wanna Dance	1966	6.25	12.50	25.00
-- Black label with pink and white at left					
❏ LP-12324 [S]	Johnny Rivers' Golden Hits	1966	5.00	10.00	20.00
❏ LP-12334 [S]	Changes	1966	5.00	10.00	20.00
❏ LP-12341 [S]	Rewind	1967	5.00	10.00	20.00
❏ LP-12372	Realization	1968	5.00	10.00	20.00
❏ LP-12427	A Touch of Gold	1969	5.00	10.00	20.00
❏ LP-16001	Slim Slo Slider	1970	5.00	10.00	20.00
SEARS
❏ SPS-417	Mr. Teenage	196?	6.25	12.50	25.00
❏ SPS-487	Groovin'	1968	6.25	12.50	25.00
SOUL CITY
❏ SC 1007-1	Greatest Hits	1998	5.00	10.00	20.00
-- 500 copies, each autographed by Johnny Rivers					
UNITED ARTISTS
❏ USX-93 [(2)]	Johnny Rivers Superpak	1971	5.00	10.00	20.00
❏ UAL-3386 [M]	Go, Johnny, Go	1964	5.00	10.00	20.00
❏ UAS-6386 [S]	Go, Johnny, Go	1964	6.25	12.50	25.00
❏ ST-90813 [S]	Go, Johnny, Go	1965	7.50	15.00	30.00
-- Capitol Record Club edition					
❏ T-90813 [M]	Go, Johnny, Go	1965	6.25	12.50	25.00
-- Capitol Record Club edition					

RIVIERAS, THE (1)
Vocal group.
POST
| ❏ 2000 | The Rivieras Sing | 196? | 10.00 | 20.00 | 40.00 |

RIVIERAS, THE (2)
"Surf" band from South Bend, Indiana.
RIVIERA
| ❏ 701 [M] | Campus Party | 1964 | 62.50 | 125.00 | 250.00 |
U.S.A.
| ❏ 102 [M] | Let's Have a Party | 1964 | 37.50 | 75.00 | 150.00 |

RIVINGTONS, THE
LIBERTY
| ❏ LRP-3282 [M] | Doin' the Bird | 1963 | 25.00 | 50.00 | 100.00 |
| ❏ LST-7282 [S] | Doin' the Bird | 1963 | 50.00 | 100.00 | 200.00 |

ROAD RUNNERS, THE
LONDON
| ❏ PS 381 [S] | The New Mustang (And Other Hot Rod Hits) | 1964 | 75.00 | 150.00 | 300.00 |
| ❏ LL 3381 [M] | The New Mustang (And Other Hot Rod Hits) | 1964 | 50.00 | 100.00 | 200.00 |

Number	Title	Yr	VG	VG+	NM

ROAD, THE
KAMA SUTRA
❑ KSBS-2032 [(2)] Cognition		1970	5.00	10.00	20.00
❑ KLPS-8075	The Road	1969	5.00	10.00	20.00

ROBBINS, HARGUS "PIG"
TIME
❑ S-2107 [S]	A Bit of Country Piano	1963	6.25	12.50	25.00
❑ 52107 [M]	A Bit of Country Piano	1963	5.00	10.00	20.00

ROBBINS, MARTY
ARTCO
❑ 110	The Best of Marty Robbins	1973	10.00	20.00	40.00

COLUMBIA
❑ GP 15 [(2)]	Marty's Country	1969	6.25	12.50	25.00
❑ CL 976 [M]	The Song of Robbins	1957	25.00	50.00	100.00
-- Red and black label with six "eye" logos					
❑ CL 976 [M]	The Song of Robbins	1963	5.00	10.00	20.00
-- Red label with "Guaranteed High Fidelity" or "360 Sound Mono"					
❑ CL 1087 [M]	Song of the Islands	1957	30.00	60.00	120.00
-- Red and black label with six "eye" logos					
❑ CL 1087 [M]	Song of the Islands	1963	5.00	10.00	20.00
-- Red label with "Guaranteed High Fidelity" or "360 Sound Mono"					
❑ CL 1189 [M]	Marty Robbins	1958	20.00	40.00	80.00
-- Red and black label with six "eye" logos					
❑ CL 1189 [M]	Marty Robbins	1963	5.00	10.00	20.00
-- Red label with "Guaranteed High Fidelity" or "360 Sound Mono"					
❑ CL 1325 [M]	Marty's Greatest Hits	1959	20.00	40.00	80.00
-- Red and black label with six "eye" logos					
❑ CL 1325 [M]	Marty's Greatest Hits	1963	5.00	10.00	20.00
-- Red label with "Guaranteed High Fidelity" or "360 Sound Mono"					
❑ CL 1349 [M]	Gunfighter Ballads and Trail Songs	1959	7.50	15.00	30.00
❑ CL 1481 [M]	More Gunfighter Ballads and Trail Songs	1960	7.50	15.00	30.00
-- Red and black label with six "eye" logos					
❑ CL 1635 [M]	More Greatest Hits	1961	6.25	12.50	25.00
-- Red and black label with six "eye" logos					
❑ CL 1666 [M]	Just a Little Sentimental	1961	6.25	12.50	25.00
-- Red and black label with six "eye" logos					
❑ CL 1801 [M]	Marty After Midnight	1962	5.00	10.00	20.00
-- Red label with "Guaranteed High Fidelity"					
❑ CL 1801 [M]	Marty After Midnight	1962	12.50	25.00	50.00
-- Red and black label with six "eye" logos					
❑ CL 1855 [M]	Portrait of Marty	1962	10.00	20.00	40.00
❑ CL 1855/CS 8655 Portrait of Marty Bonus Photo		1962	7.50	15.00	30.00
❑ CL 1918 [M]	Devil Woman	1962	6.25	12.50	25.00
-- Red label with "Guaranteed High Fidelity"					
❑ CL 2040 [M]	Hawaii's Calling Me	1963	6.25	12.50	25.00
-- Red label with "Guaranteed High Fidelity"					
❑ CL 2072 [M]	Return of the Gunfighter	1963	5.00	10.00	20.00
-- Red label with "Guaranteed High Fidelity"					
❑ CL 2176 [M]	Island Woman	1964	7.50	15.00	30.00
-- Red label with "Guaranteed High Fidelity"					
❑ CL 2176 [M]	Island Woman	1965	5.00	10.00	20.00
-- Red label with "360 Sound Mono"					
❑ CL 2220 [M]	R.F.D.	1964	5.00	10.00	20.00
-- Red label with "Guaranteed High Fidelity"					
❑ CL 2304 [M]	Turn the Lights Down Low	1965	6.25	12.50	25.00
-- Red label with "Guaranteed High Fidelity"					
❑ CL 2601 [10]	Rock 'N Roll 'N Robbins	1956	250.00	500.00	1,000.
❑ CL 2645 [M]	My Kind of Country	1967	6.25	12.50	25.00
❑ CL 2725 [M]	Tonight Carmen	1967	7.50	15.00	30.00
❑ CL 2735 [M]	Christmas with Marty Robbins	1967	12.50	25.00	50.00
❑ CL 2817 [M]	By the Time I Get to Phoenix	1968	15.00	30.00	60.00
❑ CS 8158 [S]	Gunfighter Ballads and Trail Songs	1959	10.00	20.00	40.00
-- Red and black label with six "eye" logos					
❑ CS 8158 [S]	Gunfighter Ballads and Trail Songs	1963	5.00	10.00	20.00
-- Red label with "360 Sound Stereo"					
❑ CS 8272 [S]	More Gunfighter Ballads and Trail Songs	1960	10.00	20.00	40.00
-- Red and black label with six "eye" logos					
❑ CS 8272 [S]	More Gunfighter Ballads and Trail Songs	1963	5.00	10.00	20.00
-- Red label with "360 Sound Stereo"					
❑ CS 8435 [S]	More Greatest Hits	1961	7.50	15.00	30.00
-- Red and black label with six "eye" logos					
❑ CS 8435 [S]	More Greatest Hits	1963	5.00	10.00	20.00
-- Red label with "360 Sound Stereo"					
❑ CS 8466 [S]	Just a Little Sentimental	1961	7.50	15.00	30.00
-- Red and black label with six "eye" logos					
❑ CS 8466 [S]	Just a Little Sentimental	1963	5.00	10.00	20.00
-- Red label with "360 Sound Stereo"					
❑ CS 8601 [S]	Marty After Midnight	1962	7.50	15.00	30.00
-- Red and black label with "360 Sound Stereo" in black					
❑ CS 8601 [S]	Marty After Midnight	1962	20.00	40.00	80.00
-- Red and black label with six "eye" logos					
❑ CS 8601 [S]	Marty After Midnight	1965	5.00	10.00	20.00
-- Red label with "360 Sound Stereo" in white					

❑ CS 8639 [P]	Marty's Greatest Hits	1962	7.50	15.00	30.00
-- Red label with "360 Sound Stereo" in black					
❑ CS 8639 [P]	Marty's Greatest Hits	1965	5.00	10.00	20.00
-- Red label with "360 Sound Stereo" in white					
❑ CS 8655 [S]	Portrait of Marty	1962	12.50	25.00	50.00
❑ CS 8718 [S]	Devil Woman	1962	7.50	15.00	30.00
-- Red label with "360 Sound Stereo" in black					
❑ CS 8718 [S]	Devil Woman	1965	5.00	10.00	20.00
-- Red label with "360 Sound Stereo" in white					
❑ CS 8840 [S]	Hawaii's Calling Me	1963	7.50	15.00	30.00
-- Red label with "360 Sound Stereo" in black					
❑ CS 8840 [S]	Hawaii's Calling Me	1965	5.00	10.00	20.00
-- Red label with "360 Sound Stereo" in white					
❑ CS 8872 [S]	Return of the Gunfighter	1963	6.25	12.50	25.00
-- Red label with "360 Sound Stereo" in black					
❑ CS 8872 [S]	Return of the Gunfighter	1965	5.00	10.00	20.00
-- Red label with "360 Sound Stereo" in white					
❑ CS 8976 [S]	Island Woman	1964	10.00	20.00	40.00
-- Red label with "360 Sound Stereo" in black					
❑ CS 8976 [S]	Island Woman	1965	7.50	15.00	30.00
-- Red label with "360 Sound Stereo" in white					
❑ CS 9020 [S]	R.F.D.	1964	6.25	12.50	25.00
-- Red label with "360 Sound Stereo" in black					
❑ CS 9020 [S]	R.F.D.	1965	5.00	10.00	20.00
-- Red label with "360 Sound Stereo" in white					
❑ CS 9104 [S]	Turn the Lights Down Low	1965	7.50	15.00	30.00
-- Red label with "360 Sound Stereo" in black					
❑ CS 9104 [S]	Turn the Lights Down Low	1965	5.00	10.00	20.00
-- Red label with "360 Sound Stereo" in white					
❑ CS 9248 [S]	What God Has Done	1966	5.00	10.00	20.00
-- Red "360 Sound" label					
❑ CS 9327 [S]	The Drifter	1966	5.00	10.00	20.00
-- Red "360 Sound" label					
❑ CS 9445 [S]	My Kind of Country	1967	5.00	10.00	20.00
❑ CS 9525 [S]	Tonight Carmen	1967	5.00	10.00	20.00
-- Red "360 Sound" label					
❑ CS 9535 [S]	Christmas with Marty Robbins	1967	7.50	15.00	30.00
❑ CS 9617 [S]	By the Time I Get to Phoenix	1968	5.00	10.00	20.00
❑ CS 9725	I Walk Alone	1968	5.00	10.00	20.00
-- Red "360 Sound" label					
❑ CS 9811	It's a Sin	1969	5.00	10.00	20.00
-- Red "360 Sound" label					
❑ CS 9978	My Woman, My Woman, My Wife	1970	5.00	10.00	20.00
-- Red "360 Sound" label					
❑ G 30881 [(2)] The World of Marty Robbins		1971	5.00	10.00	20.00
❑ KG 31361 [(2)] Marty Robbins' All-Time Greatest Hits		1972	5.00	10.00	20.00

COLUMBIA MUSICAL TREASURY
❑ P5S 5812 [(5)] Marty		1972	10.00	20.00	40.00

COLUMBIA RECORD CLUB
❑ DS 445	Bend in the River	1968	10.00	20.00	40.00

COLUMBIA SPECIAL PRODUCTS
❑ 3P 16578 [(3)] Classics		1983	5.00	10.00	20.00

HARMONY
❑ H 31258	Songs of the Islands	1972	5.00	10.00	20.00

ROBBINS, MARTY, JR.
COLUMBIA
❑ CS 9944	Columbia Records Presents Marty Robbins Jr.	1970	6.25	12.50	25.00

ROBBS, THE
MERCURY
❑ MG-21130 [M]	The Robbs	1967	10.00	20.00	40.00
❑ SR-61130 [S]	The Robbs	1967	7.50	15.00	30.00

ROBERTINO
KAPP
❑ KS-3252 [S]	O Sole Mio	1962	5.00	10.00	20.00
❑ KS-3293 [S]	The Young Italian Singing Sensation	1962	5.00	10.00	20.00
❑ KS-3338 [S]	Italia Mia	1963	5.00	10.00	20.00

ROBERTS, KENNY
STARDAY
❑ SLP-336 [M]	Indian Love Call	1965	10.00	20.00	40.00
❑ SLP-406 [M]	The Incredible Kenny Roberts	1967	7.50	15.00	30.00
❑ SLP-434	Country Music Singing Sensation	1969	5.00	10.00	20.00

ROBERTS, PERNELL
RCA VICTOR
❑ LPM-2662 [M]	Come All Ye Fair and Tender Ladies	1963	7.50	15.00	30.00
❑ LSP-2662 [S]	Come All Ye Fair and Tender Ladies	1963	10.00	20.00	40.00

ROBERTS, ROCKY, AND THE AIREDALES
BRUNSWICK
❑ BL 754133	Rocky Roberts and the Airedales	1968	5.00	10.00	20.00

Number	Title	Yr	VG	VG+	NM

ROBERTSON, DALE
RCA VICTOR

Number	Title	Yr	VG	VG+	NM
❏ LPM-2158 [M]	Dale Robertson Presents His Album of Western Classics	1959	20.00	40.00	80.00
❏ LSP-2158 [S]	Dale Robertson Presents His Album of Western Classics	1959	25.00	50.00	100.00

ROBERTSON, DON
RCA VICTOR

| ❏ LPM-3348 [M] | Heart on My Sleeve | 1965 | 5.00 | 10.00 | 20.00 |
| ❏ LSP-3348 [S] | Heart on My Sleeve | 1965 | 6.25 | 12.50 | 25.00 |

ROBERTSON, ROBBIE
Also see THE BAND.
GEFFEN

| ❏ GEF 24303 | Storyville | 1991 | 6.25 | 12.50 | 25.00 |

ROBERTSON, TEXAS JIM
MASTERSEAL

| ❏ (# unknown) [10] | Eight Top Western Hits | 195? | 15.00 | 30.00 | 60.00 |

STRAND

| ❏ 1016 [M] | Texas Jim Robertson | 1961 | 10.00 | 20.00 | 40.00 |

ROBESON, PAUL
COLUMBIA MASTERWORKS

| ❏ ML 2038 [10] | Swing Low Sweet Chariot | 1949 | 20.00 | 40.00 | 80.00 |
| ❏ ML 4105 [10] | Spirituals | 1949 | 20.00 | 40.00 | 80.00 |

VANGUARD

❏ VRS-9037 [M]	Spirituals and Folksongs	1959	10.00	20.00	40.00
❏ VRS-9051 [M]	Paul Robeson at Carnegie Hall	1960	5.00	10.00	20.00
❏ VRS-9193 [M]	Ballad for Americans: Carnegie Hall Concert, Vol. 2	1965	5.00	10.00	20.00
❏ VSD-57/58 [(2)]	Essential Paul Robeson	197?	5.00	10.00	20.00
❏ VSD-79193 [S]	Ballad for Americans: Carnegie Hall Concert, Vol. 2	1965	5.00	10.00	20.00

ROBINS, THE
WHIPPET

| ❏ WLP-703 [M] | Rock 'n' Roll with the Robins | 1958 | 200.00 | 400.00 | 800.00 |

ROBINSON, FLOYD
RCA VICTOR

| ❏ LPM-2162 [M] | Floyd Robinson | 1960 | 20.00 | 40.00 | 80.00 |
| ❏ LSP-2162 [S] | Floyd Robinson | 1960 | 30.00 | 60.00 | 120.00 |

ROBINSON, JOHNNY
EPIC

| ❏ BN 26528 | Memphis High | 1970 | 5.00 | 10.00 | 20.00 |

ROBINSON, SMOKEY, AND THE MIRACLES -- See THE MIRACLES.

ROBINSON, SUGAR CHILE
CAPITOL

| ❏ T 589 [M] | Boogie Woogie | 1955 | 30.00 | 60.00 | 120.00 |

ROBISON, CARSON
COLUMBIA

| ❏ CL 2551 [10] | Square Dance | 1955 | 20.00 | 40.00 | 80.00 |
| ❏ CL 6029 [10] | Square Dance | 1949 | 20.00 | 40.00 | 80.00 |

MGM

❏ E-13 [10]	Call Your Own Square Dances	195?	15.00	30.00	60.00
❏ E-557 [10]	Square Dances with Calls	1952	15.00	30.00	60.00
❏ E-3258 [M]	Square Dances	1955	7.50	15.00	30.00
❏ E-3594 [M]	Life Gets Tee-Jus, Don't It	1958	12.50	25.00	50.00

RCA VICTOR

| ❏ LPM-1238 [M] | Square Dances | 1956 | 7.50 | 15.00 | 30.00 |
| ❏ LPM-3030 [10] | Square Dances | 1952 | 15.00 | 30.00 | 60.00 |

ROCCA, ANTONIO
MGM

| ❏ E-4183 [M] | In This Corner...The Musical World of Antonio Rocca | 1963 | 5.00 | 10.00 | 20.00 |
| ❏ SE-4183 [S] | In This Corner...The Musical World of Antonio Rocca | 1963 | 6.25 | 12.50 | 25.00 |

ROCHES, THE
MCA

| ❏ 10020 | We Three Kings | 1990 | 5.00 | 10.00 | 20.00 |

ROCK ISLAND
PROJECT 3

Number	Title	Yr	VG	VG+	NM
❏ PR-4005 SD	Rock Island	1970	7.50	15.00	30.00

ROCK-A-TEENS, THE
ROULETTE

| ❏ R-25109 [M] | Woo-Hoo | 1960 | 37.50 | 75.00 | 150.00 |
| ❏ SR-25109 [S] | Woo-Hoo | 1960 | 62.50 | 125.00 | 250.00 |

ROCKATS
ISLAND

| ❏ ILPS 9626 | Live at the Ritz | 1981 | 6.25 | 12.50 | 25.00 |

ROCKETS, THE
WHITE WHALE

| ❏ WWS-7116 | The Rockets | 1968 | 6.25 | 12.50 | 25.00 |

ROCKIN' FOO
HOBBIT

| ❏ HB-5001 | Rockin' Foo | 1969 | 6.25 | 12.50 | 25.00 |

ROCKIN' REBELS, THE
SWAN

| ❏ SLP-509 [M] | Wild Weekend | 1963 | 50.00 | 100.00 | 200.00 |

ROCKY FELLERS, THE
SCEPTER

| ❏ SP-512 [M] | Killer Joe | 1964 | 7.50 | 15.00 | 30.00 |
| ❏ SPS-512 [S] | Killer Joe | 1964 | 10.00 | 20.00 | 40.00 |

RODGERS, JIMMIE (1)
The legendary "Singing Brakeman" of early country-western fame.
RCA VICTOR

| ❏ DPL2-0075 [(2)] | The Legendary Jimmie Rodgers, Vol. 1 | 1974 | 10.00 | 20.00 | 40.00 |

-- Special-products issue for Country Music Magazine

❏ LPM-1232 [M]	Never No Mo' Blues -- A Memorial Album	1955	37.50	75.00	150.00
❏ LPM-1640 [M]	Train Whistle Blues	1957	37.50	75.00	150.00
❏ LPM-2112 [M]	My Rough and Rowdy Ways	1960	20.00	40.00	80.00
❏ LPM-2213 [M]	Jimmie the Kid	1961	20.00	40.00	80.00
❏ LPM-2531 [M]	Country Music Hall of Fame	1962	20.00	40.00	80.00
❏ LPM-2634 [M]	The Short But Brilliant Life of Jimmie Rodgers	1963	20.00	40.00	80.00
❏ LPM-2865 [M]	My Time Ain't Long	1964	12.50	25.00	50.00
❏ LPM-3037 [10]	Jimmie Rodgers Memorial Album, Volume 1	1952	100.00	200.00	400.00
❏ LPM-3038 [10]	Jimmie Rodgers Memorial Album, Volume 2	1952	100.00	200.00	400.00
❏ LPM-3039 [10]	Jimmie Rodgers Memorial Album, Volume 3	1952	100.00	200.00	400.00
❏ LPM-3073 [10]	Travelin' Blues	1952	100.00	200.00	400.00
❏ LPM-3315 [M]	The Best of the Legendary Jimmie Rodgers	1965	10.00	20.00	40.00
❏ LSP-3315 [R]	The Best of the Legendary Jimmie Rodgers	1965	5.00	10.00	20.00
❏ VPS-6091(e) [(2)]	This Is Jimmie Rodgers	1971	5.00	10.00	20.00

RODGERS, JIMMIE (2)
Pop-country-folk singer of the late 1950s and 1960s.
A&M

| ❏ SP-130 [M] | Child of Clay | 1967 | 6.25 | 12.50 | 25.00 |

DOT

❏ DLP-3556 [M]	Town and Country	1964	5.00	10.00	20.00
❏ DLP-3815 [M]	Golden Hits/15 Hits of Jimmie Rodgers	1967	5.00	10.00	20.00
❏ DLP-25453 [S]	No One Will Ever Know	1962	5.00	10.00	20.00
❏ DLP-25496 [S]	Jimmie Rodgers Folk Concert	1963	5.00	10.00	20.00
❏ DLP-25502 [S]	My Favorite Hymns	1963	5.00	10.00	20.00
❏ DLP-25525 [S]	Honeycomb & Kisses Sweeter Than Wine	1963	5.00	10.00	20.00
❏ DLP-25556 [S]	Town and Country	1964	6.25	12.50	25.00
❏ DLP-25556 [S]	The World I Used to Know	1964	5.00	10.00	20.00

-- Retitled version of above

❏ DLP-25579 [S]	12 Great Hits	1964	5.00	10.00	20.00
❏ DLP-25614 [S]	Deep Purple	1965	5.00	10.00	20.00
❏ DLP-25687 [S]	The Nashville Sound	1966	5.00	10.00	20.00
❏ DLP-25710 [S]	Country Music 1966	1966	5.00	10.00	20.00
❏ DLP-25717 [S]	It's Over	1966	5.00	10.00	20.00
❏ DLP-25780 [S]	Love Me, Please Love Me	1967	5.00	10.00	20.00

ROULETTE

Number	Title	Yr	VG	VG+	NM
R-25020 [M]	Jimmie Rodgers	1957	12.50	25.00	50.00
-- Black label					
R-25020 [M]	Jimmie Rodgers	1959	6.25	12.50	25.00
-- White label with colored spokes					
R-25033 [M]	Number One Ballads	1958	12.50	25.00	50.00
-- Black label					
R-25033 [M]	Number One Ballads	1959	6.25	12.50	25.00
-- White label with colored spokes					
R-25042 [M]	Jimmie Rodgers Sings Folk Songs	1958	12.50	25.00	50.00
-- Black label					
R-25042 [M]	Jimmie Rodgers Sings Folk Songs	1959	6.25	12.50	25.00
-- White label with colored spokes					
R-25057 [M]	His Golden Year	1959	6.25	12.50	25.00
R-25071 [M]	TV Favorites	1959	7.50	15.00	30.00
SR-25071 [S]	TV Favorites	1959	12.50	25.00	50.00
R-25081 [M]	Twilight on the Trail	1959	7.50	15.00	30.00
SR-25081 [S]	Twilight on the Trail	1959	12.50	25.00	50.00
R 25095 [M]	It's Christmas Once Again	1959	7.50	15.00	30.00
SR 25095 [S]	It's Christmas Once Again	1959	12.50	25.00	50.00
R-25103 [M]	When the Spirit Moves You	1960	7.50	15.00	30.00
SR-25103 [S]	When the Spirit Moves You	1960	10.00	20.00	40.00
R-25128 [M]	At Home with Jimmie Rodgers: An Evening of Folk Songs	1960	7.50	15.00	30.00
SR-25128 [S]	At Home with Jimmie Rodgers: An Evening of Folk Songs	1960	10.00	20.00	40.00
R-25150 [M]	The Folk Song World of Jimmie Rodgers	1961	7.50	15.00	30.00
SR-25150 [S]	The Folk Song World of Jimmie Rodgers	1961	10.00	20.00	40.00
R-25160 [M]	The Best of Jimmie Rodgers' Folk Tunes	1961	7.50	15.00	30.00
SR-25160 [S]	The Best of Jimmie Rodgers' Folk Tunes	1961	62.50	125.00	250.00
-- Red vinyl					
SR-25160 [S]	The Best of Jimmie Rodgers' Folk Tunes	1961	10.00	20.00	40.00
-- Black vinyl					
R-25179 [M]	15 Million Sellers	1962	6.25	12.50	25.00
SR-25179 [P]	15 Million Sellers	1962	7.50	15.00	30.00
R-25199 [M]	Folk Songs	1963	5.00	10.00	20.00
SR-25199 [S]	Folk Songs	1963	6.25	12.50	25.00

ROE, TOMMY
ABC

Number	Title	Yr	VG	VG+	NM
S-467 [R]	Something for Everybody	1968	12.50	25.00	50.00
-- Issued in rechanneled stereo four years after its original release					
594 [M]	It's Now Winters Day	1967	5.00	10.00	20.00
S-594 [S]	It's Now Winters Day	1967	6.25	12.50	25.00
610 [M]	Phantasy	1967	10.00	20.00	40.00
S-610 [S]	Phantasy	1967	10.00	20.00	40.00
S-683	Dizzy	1969	5.00	10.00	20.00
S-700	12 in a Roe/A Collection of Tommy Roe's Greatest Hits	1969	5.00	10.00	20.00
ST-90883 [S]	Sweet Pea	1966	10.00	20.00	40.00
-- Capitol Record Club issue					
T-90883 [M]	Sweet Pea	1966	10.00	20.00	40.00
-- Capitol Record Club issue					

ABC-PARAMOUNT

Number	Title	Yr	VG	VG+	NM
432 [M]	Sheila	1962	10.00	20.00	40.00
S-432 [S]	Sheila	1962	12.50	25.00	50.00
467 [M]	Something for Everybody	1964	7.50	15.00	30.00
575 [M]	Sweet Pea	1966	7.50	51.00	30.00
S-575 [S]	Sweet Pea	1966	10.00	20.00	40.00

ROGERS, DAVID
ATLANTIC

Number	Title	Yr	VG	VG+	NM
SD 7283	Farewell to the Ryman	1972	5.00	10.00	20.00

ROGERS, JULIE
MERCURY

Number	Title	Yr	VG	VG+	NM
SR-60981 [S]	Julie Rogers	1965	5.00	10.00	20.00

ROGERS, KENNY
Also see THE BOBBY DOYLE THREE; THE FIRST EDITION; THE NEW CHRISTY MINSTRELS.
MOBILE FIDELITY

Number	Title	Yr	VG	VG+	NM
1-044	The Gambler	1981	5.00	10.00	20.00
-- Audiophile vinyl					
1-049	Kenny Rogers' Greatest Hits	1981	5.00	10.00	20.00
-- Audiophile vinyl					

REPRISE

Number	Title	Yr	VG	VG+	NM
R 144593	Love Is Strange	1990	5.00	10.00	20.00
-- Only available on vinyl from BMG Direct Marketing					

ROGERS, KENNY, AND THE FIRST EDITION –
See THE FIRST EDITION.

ROGERS, ROY
CAPITOL

Number	Title	Yr	VG	VG+	NM
ST-594	The Country Side of Roy Rogers	1970	5.00	10.00	20.00
ST-785	A Man from Duck Run	1971	5.00	10.00	20.00

RCA

Number	Title	Yr	VG	VG+	NM
3024-1-RRE [PD]	Roy Rogers Tribute	1991	10.00	20.00	40.00
-- Picture disc; only vinyl edition of this release					

RCA CAMDEN

Number	Title	Yr	VG	VG+	NM
CAL-1054 [M]	Pecos Bill	1964	6.25	12.50	25.00
CAL-1074 [M]	Lore of the West	1966	6.25	12.50	25.00
CAL-1097 [M]	Peter Cottontail and His Friends	1968	6.25	12.50	25.00

RCA VICTOR

Number	Title	Yr	VG	VG+	NM
LBY-1022 [M]	Jesus Loves Me	1959	12.50	25.00	50.00
-- On the "Children's Bluebird Series"					
LPM-3041 [10]	Roy Rogers Souvenir Album	1952	75.00	150.00	300.00
LPM-3168 [10]	Hymns of Faith	1954	50.00	100.00	200.00

ROGERS, ROY, AND DALE EVANS
CAPITOL

Number	Title	Yr	VG	VG+	NM
ST 1745 [S]	The Bible Tells Me So	1962	12.50	25.00	50.00
T 1745 [M]	The Bible Tells Me So	1962	10.00	20.00	40.00
ST 2818 [S]	Christmas Is Always	1967	7.50	15.00	30.00
T 2818 [M]	Christmas Is Always	1967	7.50	15.00	30.00

GOLDEN

Number	Title	Yr	VG	VG+	NM
A198-6 [M]	Roy Rogers' and Dale Evans' Song Wagon	1958	20.00	40.00	80.00
-- Originals have black labels and "198" prefix					
A198-7 [M]	16 Great Songs of the Old West	1958	20.00	40.00	80.00
-- Originals have black labels and "198" prefix					
A298-81 [M]	Peter Cottontail	1962	15.00	30.00	60.00
-- Originals have black labels and "298" prefix					

RCA VICTOR

Number	Title	Yr	VG	VG+	NM
LPM-1439 [M]	Sweet Hour of Prayer	1957	20.00	40.00	80.00

ROGERS, TIMMIE
PHILIPS

Number	Title	Yr	VG	VG+	NM
PHM 200-088 [M]	If I Were President	1963	5.00	10.00	20.00
PHS 600-088 [S]	If I Were President	1963	6.25	12.50	25.00

ROKES, THE
RCA VICTOR INTERNATIONAL

Number	Title	Yr	VG	VG+	NM
FPM-185 [M]	Che Mondo Strano	1967	20.00	40.00	80.00

ROLLING STONES, THE
Also see BRIAN JONES; RON WOOD; BILL WYMAN.
ABKCO

Number	Title	Yr	VG	VG+	NM
MPD-1 [DJ]	Songs of the Rolling Stones	1975	175.00	350.00	700.00
-- "Band in field" cover					
MPD-1 [DJ]	Songs of the Rolling Stones	1975	1,000.	2,000.	3,000.
-- "Rock and Roll Circus" cover					
DVL2-0268 [P (2)]	The Rolling Stones' Greatest Hits	1977	5.00	10.00	20.00
-- RCA Special Products mail-order offer					
1218-1 [(4)]	Singles Collection: The London Years	1989	12.50	25.00	50.00

LONDON

Number	Title	Yr	VG	VG+	NM
NP 1 [M]	Big Hits (High Tide and Green Grass)	1966	2,000.	4,000.	8,000.
-- With two lines of type on the front cover, all in small letters					
NP 1 [M]	Big Hits (High Tide and Green Grass)	1966	10.00	20.00	40.00
-- With five lines of type on the front cover, all in capital letters					
RSD-1 [DJ]	The Rolling Stones -- The Promotional Album	1969	1,000.	2,000.	3,000.
-- Not to be confused with imports of this rare promo					
NP 2 [M]	Their Satanic Majesties Request	1967	62.50	125.00	250.00
NPS 2 [S]	Their Satanic Majesties Request	1967	10.00	20.00	40.00
-- With 3-D cover					
NPS 3 [PD]	Through the Past, Darkly (Big Hits Vol. 2)	1969	3,000.	4,500.	6,000.
-- Prototype picture discs that used the cover art from "Big Hits (High Tide and Green Grass)" either on one or both sides.					
NPS 3 [S]	Through the Past, Darkly (Big Hits Vol. 2)	197?	5.00	10.00	20.00
-- Reissue with regular square cover					
NPS-5	Let It Bleed	1970	5,000.	7,500.	10,000.
-- One-of-a-kind red/yellow/blue/green vinyl (all on the same record!)					
PS 375 [R]	England's Newest Hit Makers -- The Rolling Stones	1964	75.00	150.00	300.00
-- Dark blue label; lower left-hand corner of cover advertises a bonus photo					
PS 375 [R]	England's Newest Hit Makers -- The Rolling Stones	1965	6.25	12.50	25.00
-- Dark blue label with "London" unboxed at top					

Here are three of the rarest of all American Rolling Stones albums, two of which are pictured in a price guide for the first time. (Top left) When first proposed, the hits collection *Big Hits (High Tide and Green Grass)* was going to have its title in two lines, as illustrated, in all lowercase letters and with a much darker blue cover than was eventually released. The regular issue has the title in all capital letters and over five lines rather than two. (Top right) Here's one of those semi-legitimate colored-vinyl albums. (It wasn't authorized by the record company, but it was done on the same presses.) This one is a previously unknown pressing of *Let It Bleed*, and this one has segments of red, blue and green vinyl with the "X" in an almost banana-colored yellow. (Bottom) Rumored to exist for years, here's an American copy of the full *Beggars Banquet* cover with the toilet graffiti that London Records refused to release. A different version of this cover did come out in 1986, but this one has two obvious differences. First, the 1986 copies have lines on the back cover "Digitally Remastered from Original Master Recording" and "100% Virgin Vinyl." Second, the 1986 copies only have the catalog number below the "London" logo on the front. This one also includes the word "Stereo" with the catalog number.

Number	Title	Yr	VG	VG+	NM
❏ PS 402 [R]	12 x 5	1964	6.25	12.50	25.00

-- *Dark blue label with "London" unboxed at top*

❏ PS 420 [R]	The Rolling Stones, Now!	1965	6.25	12.50	25.00

-- *Dark blue label with "London" unboxed at top. Add 20% for complete liner notes (or sticker) on back cover (both columns of type about equal in length).*

❏ PS 429 [R]	Out of Our Heads	1965	6.25	12.50	25.00

-- *Dark blue label with "London" unboxed at top*

❏ PS 451 [R-S]	December's Children (and Everybody's)	1965	6.25	12.50	25.00

-- *Dark blue label with "London" unboxed at top*

❏ PS 539 [S]	Beggars Banquet	1968	2,500.	5,000.	10,000.

-- *Original "toilet graffiti" cover; not to be confused with the 1986 reissue, which says "Digitally Remastered from Original Master Recording" and "100% Virgin Vinyl" on the back cover*

❏ PS 539 [S]	Beggars Banquet	1968	6.25	12.50	25.00

-- *With all songs credited to "Jagger-Richard"*

❏ 2PS 606/7 [P(2)]	Hot Rocks 1964-1971	1971	250.00	500.00	1,000.

-- *With alternate mixes of "Brown Sugar" and "Wild Horses" unavailable elsewhere. The date "11-5-71" is in the Side 4 trail-off area.*

❏ 2PS 606/7 [P (2)]	Hot Rocks 1964-1971	1971	5.00	10.00	20.00

-- *With regular mixes of all tracks. All of Side 1 and "Mothers Little Helper" and "19th Nervous Breakdown" on Side 2 are rechanneled. All of Side 3 and 4 are stereo.*

❏ 2PS 626/7 [P (2)]	More Hot Rocks (Big Hits and Fazed Cookies)	1972	5.00	10.00	20.00

-- *All of Side 4 is rechanneled; stereo content uncertain otherwise*

❏ LL 3375 [DJ]	England's Newest Hit Makers -- The Rolling Stones	1964	750.00	1,500.	3,000.

-- *White label promo*

❏ LL 3375 [M]	England's Newest Hit Makers -- The Rolling Stones	1964	75.00	150.00	300.00

-- *Maroon label with "Full Frequency Range Recording" inside horizontal lines that go through the center hole; lower left-hand corner of cover advertises a bonus photo*

❏ LL 3375	England's Newest Hit Makers -- The Rolling Stones Bonus Photo	1964	50.00	100.00	200.00
❏ LL 3375 [M]	England's Newest Hit Makers -- The Rolling Stones	1965	15.00	30.00	60.00

-- *Maroon label with "London" unboxed at top*

❏ LL 3375 [M]	England's Newest Hit Makers -- The Rolling Stones	1966	10.00	20.00	40.00

-- *Red or maroon label with "London" boxed at top*

❏ LL 3402 [M]	12 x 5	1964	50.00	100.00	200.00

-- *Maroon label with "London/ffrr" in a box at top*

❏ LL 3402 [M]	12 x 5	1964	15.00	30.00	60.00

-- *Maroon label with "London" unboxed at top*

❏ LL 3402 [M]	12 x 5	1964	5,000.	7,500.	10,000.

-- *Maroon label with "London" unboxed at top; possibly unique blue vinyl pressing*

❏ LL 3402 [M]	12 x 5	1965	10.00	20.00	40.00

-- *Red or maroon label with "London" boxed at top*

❏ LL 3420 [M]	The Rolling Stones, Now!	1965	50.00	100.00	200.00

-- *Maroon label with "London/ffrr" in a box at top. Add 20% for complete liner notes (or sticker) on back cover (both columns of type about equal in length).*

❏ LL 3420 [M]	The Rolling Stones, Now!	1965	15.00	30.00	60.00

-- *Maroon label with "London" unboxed at top. Add 20% for complete liner notes (or sticker) on back cover (both columns of type about equal in length).*

❏ LL 3420 [M]	The Rolling Stones, Now!	1966	10.00	20.00	40.00

-- *Red or maroon label with "London" boxed at top and censored liner notes (second column an inch shorter than the first column)*

❏ LL 3429 [M]	Out of Our Heads	1965	50.00	100.00	200.00

-- *Maroon label with "London/ffrr" in a box at top*

❏ LL 3429 [M]	Out of Our Heads	1965	10.00	20.00	40.00

-- *Maroon label with "London" unboxed at top*

❏ LL 3429 [M]	Out of Our Heads	1966	6.25	12.50	25.00

-- *Red or maroon label with "London" boxed at top*

❏ LL 3451 [M]	December's Children (and Everybody's)	1965	10.00	20.00	40.00

-- *Maroon label with "London" unboxed at top*

❏ LL 3451 [M]	December's Children (and Everybody's)	1966	6.25	12.50	25.00

-- *Maroon label with "London" boxed at top*

❏ LL 3476 [M]	Aftermath	1966	10.00	20.00	40.00
❏ LL 3493 [M]	Got Live If You Want It!	1966	10.00	20.00	40.00
❏ LL 3499 [M]	Between the Buttons	1967	10.00	20.00	40.00
❏ LL 3509 [M]	Flowers	1967	12.50	25.00	50.00

MOBILE FIDELITY

❏ RC-1 [(11)]	The Rolling Stones	1984	125.00	250.00	500.00

-- *London LPs pressed on audiophile vinyl in box*

❏ 1-060	Sticky Fingers	1980	12.50	25.00	50.00

-- *Audiophile vinyl*

❏ 1-087	Some Girls	1982	12.50	25.00	50.00

-- *Audiophile vinyl*

RADIO PULSEBEAT NEWS

❏ 4	It's Here Luv!!	1965	45.00	90.00	180.00

-- *Ed Rudy interview album; this has been counterfeited, but originals can be identified thus: Charlie Watts' jacket should be completely black with no white marks; the label is very clear; the vinyl is all black*

ROLLING STONES

❏ PR 164 [DJ]	Interview with Mick Jagger by Tom Donahue	1971	62.50	125.00	250.00

-- *White label*

Number	Title	Yr	VG	VG+	NM
❏ PR 164 [DJ]	Interview with Mick Jagger by Tom Donahue	1971	50.00	100.00	200.00

-- *Yellow label*

❏ COC 39100	Jamming with Edward	1972	43.75	87.50	175.00

-- *White label stereo promo*

❏ COC 39100 [M]	Jamming with Edward	1972	62.50	125.00	250.00

-- *White label mono promo*

❏ COC 39114	Still Life (American Concert 1981)	1982	10.00	20.00	40.00
❏ C 47456	Flashpoint	1991	5.00	10.00	20.00
❏ COC 59100	Sticky Fingers	1971	75.00	150.00	300.00

-- *White label stereo promo*

❏ COC 59100 [M]	Sticky Fingers	1971	125.00	250.00	500.00

-- *White label mono promo*

❏ 90176	Rewind (1971-1984)	1984	6.25	12.50	25.00

VIRGIN

❏ V 2750	Voodoo Lounge	1994	5.00	10.00	20.00
(8 39782 1) [(2)]					

-- *U.S. versions pressed in U.K., but have UPC code paste-over and blue sticker "Marketed by Caroline"*

ROMEO VOID
415 RECORDS

❏ A-0007 [EP]	Never Say Never	1981	6.25	12.50	25.00

ROMEOS, THE
MARK II

❏ 1001	Precious Memories	1967	6.25	12.50	25.00

ROMERO, CELEDONIO
MERCURY LIVING PRESENCE

❏ SR 90296 [S]	Guitar Music from the Courts of Spain	196?	5.00	10.00	20.00

-- *Maroon label, no "Vendor: Mercury Record Corporation"*

ROMERO, CELEDONIO; CELIN; PEPE; AND ANGEL
MERCURY LIVING PRESENCE

❏ SR 90295 [S]	The Royal Family of the Spanish Guitar	196?	10.00	20.00	40.00

-- *Maroon label, no "Vendor: Mercury Record Corporation"*

❏ SR 90295 [S]	The Royal Family of the Spanish Guitar	196?	7.50	15.00	30.00

-- *Maroon label, with "Vendor: Mercury Record Corporation"*

❏ SR 90417 [S]	Spain's Royal Family of the Guitar	196?	6.25	12.50	25.00

-- *Maroon label, no "Vendor: Mercury Record Corporation"*

❏ SR 90434 [S]	An Evening of Flamenco Music	1965	10.00	20.00	40.00

-- *Maroon label, with "Vendor: Mercury Record Corporation"*

ROMERO, CESAR
TOPS

❏ L-1631 [M]	Songs by a Latin Lover	1958	7.50	15.00	30.00

ROMERO, PEPE
MERCURY LIVING PRESENCE

❏ SR 90297 [S]	Flamenco	196?	7.50	15.00	30.00

-- *Maroon label, no "Vendor: Mercury Record Corporation"*

ROMNEY, HUGH
Later known as "Wavy Gravy."
WORLD PACIFIC

❏ ST-1805 [S]	Third Stream Humor	1962	10.00	20.00	40.00
❏ WP-1805 [M]	Third Stream Humor	1962	7.50	15.00	30.00

RONDO, DON
JUBILEE

❏ JLP-1052 [M]	Rondo	195?	5.00	10.00	20.00
❏ JLP-1081 [M]	Have You Met Don Rondo	195?	5.00	10.00	20.00

RONETTES, THE
COLPIX

❏ CLP-486 [M]	The Ronettes Featuring Veronica	1965	50.00	100.00	200.00

-- *Gold label*

❏ CLP-486 [M]	The Ronettes Featuring Veronica	1965	25.00	50.00	100.00

-- *Blue label*

❏ CST-486 [S]	The Ronettes Featuring Veronica	1965	75.00	150.00	300.00

-- *Gold label*

❏ CST-486 [S]	The Ronettes Featuring Veronica	1965	37.50	75.00	150.00

-- *Blue label*

PHILLES

❏ PHLP-4006 [M]	Presenting the Fabulous Ronettes Featuring Veronica	1964	200.00	400.00	800.00

-- *Blue and black label*

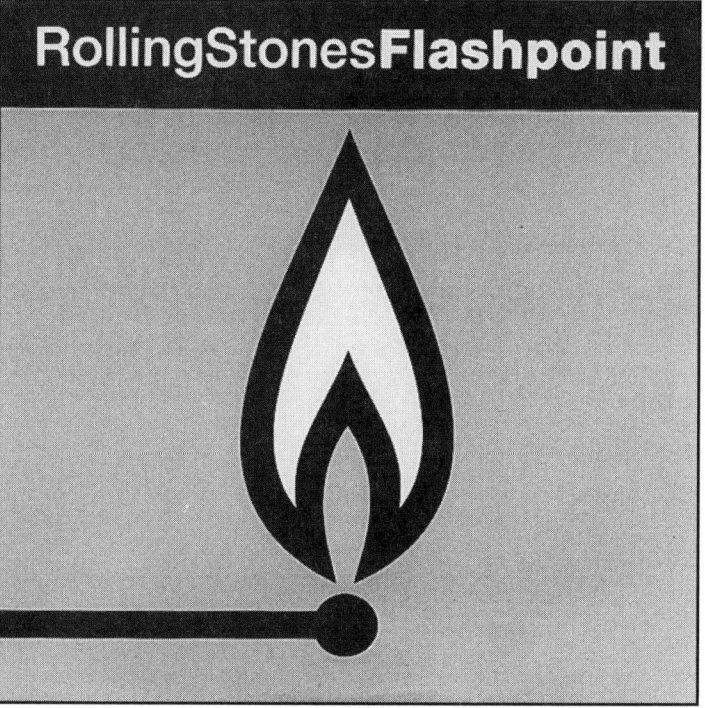

A mix of older and more recent Rolling Stones vinyl collectibles: (Top left) A favorite among collectors is the 3-D hologram-style cover of *Their Satanic Majesties Request,* which was issued at the end of 1967. The mono version of this album is among the more difficult regular Stones albums to find. (Top right) The contractual obligation hits collection *Rewind,* poorly promoted in 1984, became the first regular Stones album not to make at least the top 20 on the *Billboard* album charts. It was also the first Stones album to contain the lyrics to the songs! Today, it's not so easy to find. (Bottom left) The 1989 Abkco box set *Singles Collection: The London Years* is an excellent package, well worth searching out on vinyl. It is the first American LP to contain several early singles, including the legendary "banned" instrumental "Stoned." (Bottom right) *Flashpoint,* a collection of mostly live tracks plus a couple new studio recordings, was spottily distributed on vinyl and can be tough to find in the format.

Number	Title	Yr	VG	VG+	NM
❏ PHLP-4006 [M]	Presenting the Fabulous Ronettes Featuring Veronica	1964	100.00	200.00	400.00
-- Yellow and red label					
❏ PHLP-ST-4006 [S]	Presenting the Fabulous Ronettes Featuring Veronica	1965	150.00	300.00	600.00
❏ ST-90721 [S]	Presenting the Fabulous Ronettes Featuring Veronica	1965	100.00	200.00	400.00
-- Capitol Record Club edition					
❏ T-90721 [M]	Presenting the Fabulous Ronettes Featuring Veronica	1965	62.50	125.00	250.00
-- Capitol Record Club edition					

RONNIE AND THE DEADBEATS
CHECK
❏ 103 [M]	Groovin' with Ronnie and the Deadbeats	197?	5.00	10.00	20.00

RONNIE AND THE POMONA CASUALS
DONNA
❏ 2113 [M]	Everybody Jerk	1965	7.50	15.00	30.00

RONNY AND THE DAYTONAS
MALA
❏ 4001 [M]	G.T.O.	1964	30.00	60.00	120.00
❏ 4002 [M]	Sandy	1966	20.00	40.00	80.00
❏ 4002S [S]	Sandy	1966	25.00	50.00	100.00

RONSTADT, LINDA
Also see STONE PONEYS.
ASYLUM
❏ 60489 [(3)]	'Round Midnight: The Nelson Riddle Sessions	1987	6.25	12.50	25.00

CAPITOL
❏ ST-208	Hand Sown...Home Grown	1969	5.00	10.00	20.00
-- Black label with colorband					
❏ ST-8-0407	Silk Purse	1970	5.00	10.00	20.00
-- Capitol Record Club edition					

MOBILE FIDELITY
❏ 1-158	What's New	1984	12.50	25.00	50.00
-- Audiophile vinyl					

NAUTILUS
❏ NR-26	Simple Dreams	1982	12.50	25.00	50.00
-- Audiophile vinyl					

ROOFTOP SINGERS, THE
VANGUARD
❏ VSD-2136 [S]	Walk Right In	1963	5.00	10.00	20.00
❏ VSD-79134 [S]	Good Time	1964	5.00	10.00	20.00
❏ VSD-79190 [S]	Rainy River	1965	5.00	10.00	20.00

ROOMFUL OF BLUES
ANTILLES
❏ 7071	Let's Have a Party!	1980	5.00	10.00	20.00
BLUE FLAME
❏ 1001	Hot Little Mama	197?	6.25	12.50	25.00
ISLAND
❏ ILPS 9474	Roomful of Blues	1977	6.25	12.50	25.00

ROONEY, MICKEY
RCA VICTOR
❏ LPM-1520 [M]	Mickey Rooney Sings George M. Cohan	1957	20.00	40.00	80.00

ROSE GARDEN, THE
ATCO
❏ SD 33-225	The Rose Garden	1968	6.25	12.50	25.00

ROSE MARIE
KAPP
❏ KFL-4500 [M]	Songs for Single Girls	1964	7.50	15.00	30.00

ROSE, DAVID
KAPP
❏ K-1100-S [S]	Great Waltzes of the Fabulous Century	1958	6.25	12.50	25.00
❏ KL-1100 [M]	Great Waltzes of the Fabulous Century	1958	5.00	10.00	20.00
❏ KS-3010 [S]	Waltzes in Stereo	1959	7.50	15.00	30.00
❏ KS-3205 [S]	Songs of the Fabulous Thirties, Vol. 1	1960	5.00	10.00	20.00

Number	Title	Yr	VG	VG+	NM
❏ KS-3206 [S]	Songs of the Fabulous Thirties, Vol. 2	1960	5.00	10.00	20.00
❏ KX-5004-S [(2) S]	Songs of the Fabulous Thirties	1958	7.50	15.00	30.00
❏ KXL-5004 [(2) M]	Songs of the Fabulous Thirties	1958	6.25	12.50	25.00

MGM
❏ E-196 [10]	Magic Music Box	195?	10.00	20.00	40.00
❏ E-3067 [M]	Beautiful Music to Love By	195?	7.50	15.00	30.00
-- Yellow label					
❏ E-3101 [M]	Let's Fall in Love	195?	7.50	15.00	30.00
-- Yellow label					
❏ E-3108 [M]	Fiddlin' for Fun	195?	7.50	15.00	30.00
-- Yellow label					
❏ E-3123 [M]	Love Walked In -- The Music of George Gershwin	195?	7.50	15.00	30.00
-- Yellow label					
❏ E-3215 [M]	Holiday for Strings	195?	7.50	15.00	30.00
-- Yellow label					
❏ E-3397 [M]	Music from Motion Pictures	195?	7.50	15.00	30.00
-- Yellow label					
❏ E-3469 [M]	A Merry Christmas to You	1956	6.25	12.50	25.00
❏ E-3481 [M]	Hi Fiddles	195?	5.00	10.00	20.00
-- Yellow label					
❏ E-3592 [M]	Autumn Leaves	195?	5.00	10.00	20.00
-- Yellow label					
❏ SE-3592 [S]	Autumn Leaves	195?	7.50	15.00	30.00
-- Yellow label					
❏ E-3716 [M]	Secret Songs for Young Lovers	1959	5.00	10.00	20.00
-- Yellow label					
❏ SE-3716 [S]	Secret Songs for Young Lovers	1959	7.50	15.00	30.00
-- Yellow label					
❏ SE-3950 [S]	Exodus	1961	5.00	10.00	20.00
❏ SE-4004 [S]	21 Channel Sound	1962	5.00	10.00	20.00
❏ SE-4062 [S]	The Stripper and Other Fun Songs for the Family	1962	5.00	10.00	20.00
-- Black label					
❏ SE-4099 [S]	More, More, More, Music of the Stripper	1963	5.00	10.00	20.00
❏ ST 90534 [S]	The Stripper and Other Fun Songs for the Family	1965	5.00	10.00	20.00
-- Capitol Record Club edition					
❏ T 90534 [M]	The Stripper and Other Fun Songs for the Family	1965	5.00	10.00	20.00
-- Capitol Record Club edition					

ROSIE AND THE ORIGINALS
BRUNSWICK
❏ BL 54102 [M]	Lonely Blue Nights with Rosie	1961	37.50	75.00	150.00
❏ BL 754102 [S]	Lonely Blue Nights with Rosie	1961	50.00	100.00	200.00

ROSS, DIANA
Also see THE SUPREMES.
NAUTILUS
❏ NR-37	Diana	1981	10.00	20.00	40.00
-- Audiophile vinyl					

ROSS, DIANA, AND THE SUPREMES -- See THE SUPREMES.

ROSS, JACK
DOT
❏ DLP-3429 [M]	Cinderella	1962	5.00	10.00	20.00
❏ DLP-25429 [S]	Cinderella	1962	6.25	12.50	25.00

ROSS, JACKIE
CHESS
❏ LP-1489 [M]	In Full Bloom	1966	7.50	15.00	30.00
❏ LPS-1489 [S]	In Full Bloom	1966	10.00	20.00	40.00

ROSS, JOE E.
ROULETTE
❏ R-25281 [M]	Love Songs from a Cop	1965	6.25	12.50	25.00
❏ SR-25281 [S]	Love Songs from a Cop	1965	7.50	15.00	30.00

ROSS, SPENCER
COLUMBIA
❏ CL 1525 [M]	Spencer Ross and His Orchestra	1960	5.00	10.00	20.00
❏ CS 8??? [S]	Spencer Ross and His Orchestra	1960	6.25	12.50	25.00

ROSS, STAN
DEL-FI
❏ DFLP-1233 [M]	My Son the Copy Cat	1963	7.50	15.00	30.00
❏ DFST-1233 [S]	My Son the Copy Cat	1963	10.00	20.00	40.00

Number	Title	Yr	VG	VG+	NM

ROTARY CONNECTION
Also see MINNIE RIPERTON.
CADET
| CS-50006 | Hey Love | 1971 | 5.00 | 10.00 | 20.00 |

CADET CONCEPT
LPS 318	Peace	1969	5.00	10.00	20.00
LPS-312	Rotary Connection	1968	6.25	12.50	25.00
LPS-317	Aladdin	1968	6.25	12.50	25.00
LPS-322	Songs	1969	6.25	12.50	25.00
LSP-328	Dinner Music	1970	6.25	12.50	25.00

ROTH, LILLIAN
EPIC
| LN 3206 [M] | I'll Cry Tomorrow | 1957 | 7.50 | 15.00 | 30.00 |

TOPS
| L-1567 [M] | Lillian Roth Sings | 1958 | 6.25 | 12.50 | 25.00 |

ROUND ROBIN
CHALLENGE
| LP-620 [M] | The Land of 1,000 Dances | 1965 | 6.25 | 12.50 | 25.00 |

DOMAIN
| 101 [M] | Greatest Dance Hits Slauson Style | 1964 | 10.00 | 20.00 | 40.00 |

ROUND, JONATHAN
WESTBOUND
| 2009 | Jonathan Round | 1971 | 7.50 | 15.00 | 30.00 |
-- Round cover

ROUTERS, THE
WARNER BROS.
W 1490 [M]	Let's Go! with the Routers	1963	6.25	12.50	25.00
WS 1490 [S]	Let's Go! with the Routers	1963	7.50	15.00	30.00
W 1524 [M]	1963's Great Instrumental Hits	1964	7.50	15.00	30.00
WS 1524 [S]	1963's Great Instrumental Hits	1964	10.00	20.00	40.00
W 1559 [M]	Charge!	1964	6.25	12.50	25.00
WS 1559 [S]	Charge!	1964	7.50	15.00	30.00
W 1595 [M]	Go Go Go with the Chuck Berry Songbook	1965	5.00	10.00	20.00
WS 1595 [S]	Go Go Go with the Chuck Berry Songbook	1965	6.25	12.50	25.00

ROXY MUSIC
ATCO
| SD 36-106 | Country Life | 1975 | 6.25 | 12.50 | 25.00 |
-- Original cover shows two semi-naked women on a grassy background
| SD 38-114 [PD] | Manifesto | 1979 | 7.50 | 15.00 | 30.00 |
-- Picture disc

REPRISE
| MS 2114 | Roxy Music | 1972 | 7.50 | 15.00 | 30.00 |

WARNER BROS.
| BS 2696 | For Your Pleasure | 1973 | 6.25 | 12.50 | 25.00 |

ROYAL CHORAL SOCIETY, THE
RCA VICTOR BLUEBIRD CLASSICS
| LBC-1044 [M] | Yuletide Hymns and Carols | 1954 | 6.25 | 12.50 | 25.00 |

ROYAL GUARDSMEN, THE
LAURIE
LLP-2038 [M]	Snoopy vs. the Red Baron	1967	5.00	10.00	20.00
SLLP-2038 [S]	Snoopy vs. the Red Baron	1967	6.25	12.50	25.00
LLP-2039 [M]	The Return of the Red Baron	1967	5.00	10.00	20.00
SLLP-2039 [S]	The Return of the Red Baron	1967	6.25	12.50	25.00
LLP 2042 [M]	Snoopy and His Friends	1967	6.25	12.50	25.00
-- With "Merry Snoopy's Christmas" poster still attached to back cover
| SLLP 2042 [S] | Snoopy and His Friends | 1967 | 7.50 | 15.00 | 30.00 |
-- With "Merry Snoopy's Christmas" poster still attached to back cover
| SLLP 2042 [S] | Snoopy and His Friends | 1967 | 5.00 | 10.00 | 20.00 |
-- With "Merry Snoopy's Christmas" poster missing
| SLLP-2046 | Snoopy for President | 1968 | 6.25 | 12.50 | 25.00 |

ROYAL MALE CHOIR OF HOLLAND, THE
EPIC
| LC 3074 | Christmas Carols | 195? | 5.00 | 10.00 | 20.00 |

ROYAL OPERA HOUSE ORCHESTRA (ERNEST ANSERMET, CONDUCTOR)
RCA VICTOR RED SEAL
| LDS-6065 [(2) S] | The Royal Ballet Gala Performances | 195? | 500.00 | 1,000. | 2,000. |
-- Original with "shaded dog" labels

Number	Title	Yr	VG	VG+	NM
LDS-6065 [(2) S]	The Royal Ballet Gala Performances	199?	10.00	20.00	40.00
-- Classic Records reissue at 33 1/3 rpm
| LDS-6065 [(9) S] | The Royal Ballet Gala Performances | 199? | 30.00 | 60.00 | 120.00 |
-- Classic Records reissue at 45 rpm

ROYAL OPERA HOUSE ORCHESTRA (ANATOLE FISTOULARI, CONDUCTOR)
RCA VICTOR RED SEAL
| LSC-2285 [S] | Walton: Facade Suite | 1959 | 62.50 | 125.00 | 250.00 |
-- Original with "shaded dog" label
| LSC-2285 [S] | Walton: Facade Suite | 199? | 6.25 | 12.50 | 25.00 |
-- Classic Records reissue

ROYAL OPERA HOUSE ORCHESTRA (ALEXANDER GIBSON, CONDUCTOR)
RCA VICTOR RED SEAL
| LSC-2449 [S] | Gounod: Ballet Music of Faust; Bizet: Carmen | 1960 | 250.00 | 500.00 | 1,000. |
-- Original with "shaded dog" label
| LSC-2449 [S] | Gounod: Ballet Music of Faust; Bizet: Carmen | 199? | 6.25 | 12.50 | 25.00 |
-- Classic Records reissue

ROYAL OPERA HOUSE ORCHESTRA (JEAN MOREL, COND.)
RCA VICTOR RED SEAL
| LSC-2327 [S] | Bizet: L'Arlesienne Suites | 1960 | 20.00 | 40.00 | 80.00 |
-- Original with "shaded dog" label
| LSC-2327 [S] | Bizet: L'Arlesienne Suites | 199? | 6.25 | 12.50 | 25.00 |
-- Classic Records reissue
| LSC-6094 [(2) S] | Albeniz: Iberia (Complete); Ravel: Rapsodie Espagnole | 196? | 100.00 | 200.00 | 400.00 |
-- Original with "shaded dog" labels
| LSC-6094 [(2) S] | Albeniz: Iberia (Complete); Ravel: Rapsodie Espagnole | 199? | 10.00 | 20.00 | 40.00 |
-- Classic Records reissue

ROYAL OPERA HOUSE ORCHESTRA (HUGO RIGNOLD, CONDUCTOR)
RCA VICTOR RED SEAL
| LSC-2135 [S] | Prokofiev: Cinderella | 199? | 6.25 | 12.50 | 25.00 |
-- Classic Records issue. This album is not known to have been issued in stereo before this.
| LSC-2450 [S] | Schumann: Carnaval; Meyerbeer: Les Patineurs | 1960 | 20.00 | 40.00 | 80.00 |
-- Original with "shaded dog" label
| LSC-2450 [S] | Schumann: Carnaval; Meyerbeer: Les Patineurs | 199? | 6.25 | 12.50 | 25.00 |
-- Classic Records reissue

ROYAL OPERA HOUSE ORCHESTRA (SIR GEORGE SOLTI, CONDUCTOR)
RCA VICTOR RED SEAL
| LSC-2313 [S] | Venice | 1959 | 20.00 | 40.00 | 80.00 |
-- Original with "shaded dog" label
| LSC-2313 [S] | Venice | 199? | 6.25 | 12.50 | 25.00 |
-- Classic Records reissue

ROYAL PHILHARMONIC ORCHESTRA (RENE LEIBOWITZ, CONDUCTOR)
RCA VICTOR RED SEAL
| VCS-2659 [S] | The Power of the Orchestra | 1962 | 17.50 | 35.00 | 70.00 |
-- Original with "shaded dog" label

ROYAL PLAYBOYS, THE
WALDORF
| 33-136 [10] | Rock and Roll/New Orleans Blues | 195? | 125.00 | 250.00 | 500.00 |

ROYAL TEENS, THE
MUSICOR
| MS-3186 | Newies But Oldies | 1970 | 5.00 | 10.00 | 20.00 |
TRU-GEMS
| 1001 | Short Shorts & Others | 1975 | 5.00 | 10.00 | 20.00 |

ROYAL, BILLY JOE
COLUMBIA
| CL 2403 [M] | Down in the Boondocks | 1965 | 5.00 | 10.00 | 20.00 |
| CL 2781 [M] | Billy Joe Royal | 1967 | 6.25 | 12.50 | 25.00 |

Number	Title	Yr	VG	VG+	NM
❏ CS 9203 [S]	Down in the Boondocks	1965	6.25	12.50	25.00
❏ CS 9581 [S]	Billy Joe Royal	1967	6.25	12.50	25.00
❏ CS 9974	Cherry Hill Park	1969	6.25	12.50	25.00

ROYALETTES, THE
MGM

Number	Title	Yr	VG	VG+	NM
❏ E-4332 [M]	It's Gonna Take a Miracle	1965	5.00	10.00	20.00
❏ SE-4332 [S]	It's Gonna Take a Miracle	1965	6.25	12.50	25.00
❏ E-4366 [M]	The Elegant Sound of the Royalettes	1966	5.00	10.00	20.00
❏ SE-4366 [S]	The Elegant Sound of the Royalettes	1966	6.25	12.50	25.00

RUBBER BAND, THE
GRT

Number	Title	Yr	VG	VG+	NM
❏ 10000	Cream Songbook	1969	6.25	12.50	25.00
❏ 10007	Hendrix Songbook	1969	6.25	12.50	25.00
❏ 10015	Beatles Songbook	1969	6.25	12.50	25.00

RUBBER CITY REBELS
CAPITOL

Number	Title	Yr	VG	VG+	NM
❏ ST-12100	Rubber City Rebels	1980	10.00	20.00	40.00

RUBBER MEMORY
R.P.C.

Number	Title	Yr	VG	VG+	NM
❏ 69401	Welcome	196?	250.00	500.00	1,000.

RUBENSTEIN, ARTUR
RCA VICTOR RED SEAL

Number	Title	Yr	VG	VG+	NM
❏ LSC-1831 [S]	Brahms: Piano Concerto No. 1	199?	6.25	12.50	25.00
-- With the Chicago Symphony (Fritz Reiner cond.); Classic Records issue. This album is not known to have been issued in stereo before this.					
❏ LSC-2068 [S]	Rachmaninoff: Piano Concerto No. 2; Lizst: Piano Concerto No. 1	1958	15.00	30.00	60.00
-- Original with "shaded dog" label					
❏ LSC-2120 [S]	Beethoven: Piano Concerto No. 1	1959	6.25	12.50	25.00
-- With Josef Krips/NBC "Symphony of the Air" Orchestra; original with "shaded dog" label					
❏ LSC-2121 [S]	Beethoven: Piano Concerto No. 2	1959	6.25	12.50	25.00
-- With Josef Krips/NBC "Symphony of the Air" Orchestra; original with "shaded dog" label					
❏ LSC-2122 [S]	Beethoven: Piano Concerto No. 3	1959	5.00	10.00	20.00
-- With Josef Krips/NBC "Symphony of the Air" Orchestra; original with "shaded dog" label					
❏ LSC-2123 [S]	Beethoven: Piano Concerto No. 4	1959	5.00	10.00	20.00
-- With Josef Krips/NBC "Symphony of the Air" Orchestra; original with "shaded dog" label					
❏ LSC-2124 [S]	Beethoven: Piano Concerto No. 5	1959	5.00	10.00	20.00
-- With Josef Krips/NBC "Symphony of the Air" Orchestra; original with "shaded dog" label					
❏ LSC-2234 [S]	Saint-Saens: Piano Concerto No. 2	1959	10.00	20.00	40.00
-- With the Symphony of the Air Orchestra (Alfred Wallerstein, conductor); original with "shaded dog" label					
❏ LSC-2234 [S]	Saint-Saens: Piano Concerto No. 2	199?	6.25	12.50	25.00
-- With the Symphony of the Air Orchestra (Alfred Wallerstein, conductor); Classic Records reissue					
❏ LSC-2256 [S]	Schubert: Piano Concerto in A	1959	5.00	10.00	20.00
-- With Josef Krips/RCA Victor Symphony Orchestra; original with "shaded dog" label					
❏ LSC-2265 [S]	The Rubenstein Story	1959	7.50	15.00	30.00
-- With Alfred Wallerstein/NBC Symphony Orchestra; original with "shaded dog" label and gatefold cover					
❏ LSC-2296 [S]	Brahms: Piano Concerto No. 2	1959	7.50	15.00	30.00
-- With Josef Krips/RCA Victor Symphony Orchestra; original with "shaded dog" label					
❏ LSC-2368 [S]	Chopin: Scherzos 1-4	1960	5.00	10.00	20.00
-- Original with "shaded dog" label					
❏ LSC-2370 [S]	Chopin: Ballades 1-4	1960	5.00	10.00	20.00
-- Original with "shaded dog" label					
❏ LSC-2429 [S]	Grieg: Piano Concerto in A; Lizst: Piano Concerto No. 1	1960	6.25	12.50	25.00
-- Original with "shaded dog" label					
❏ LSC-2430 [S]	Rachmaninoff: Rhapsody on a Theme of Paganini	1960	17.50	35.00	70.00
-- With Fritz Reiner/Chicago Symphony Orchestra; original with "shaded dog" label					
❏ LSC-2430 [S]	Rachmaninoff: Rhapsody on a Theme of Paganini	199?	6.25	12.50	25.00
-- With Fritz Reiner/Chicago Symphony Orchestra; Classic Records reissue					
❏ LSC-2459 [S]	Brahms: Piano Sonata in F; Intermezzo; Romance	1961	10.00	20.00	40.00
-- Original with "shaded dog" label					
❏ LDS-2554 [S]	Chopin: Piano Sonatas No. 2 and 3	1961	7.50	15.00	30.00
-- Original with "shaded dog" label					
❏ LSC-2566 [S]	Grieg: Piano Concerto	1962	5.00	10.00	20.00
-- Original with "shaded dog" label					
❏ LSC-2605 [S]	Rubenstein at Carnegie Hall	1962	5.00	10.00	20.00
-- Original with "shaded dog" label					
❏ LSC-2636 [S]	Mozart: Piano Concerto No. 17; Schubert: Impromptus	1962	10.00	20.00	40.00
-- Original with "shaded dog" label					

RUBY AND THE ROMANTICS
ABC

Number	Title	Yr	VG	VG+	NM
❏ S-638	More Than Yesterday	1968	5.00	10.00	20.00

KAPP

Number	Title	Yr	VG	VG+	NM
❏ KL-1323 [M]	Our Day Will Come	1963	7.50	15.00	30.00
❏ KL-1341 [M]	Till Then	1963	6.25	12.50	25.00
❏ KL-1458 [M]	The Greatest Hits Album	1966	5.00	10.00	20.00
❏ KL-1526 [M]	Ruby and the Romantics	1967	6.25	12.50	25.00
❏ KS-3323 [S]	Our Day Will Come	1963	10.00	20.00	40.00
❏ KS-3341 [S]	Till Then	1963	7.50	15.00	30.00
❏ KS-3458 [S]	The Greatest Hits Album	1966	6.25	12.50	25.00
❏ KS-3526 [S]	Ruby and the Romantics	1967	6.25	12.50	25.00

RUFFIN, DAVID
Also see THE TEMPTATIONS.
MOTOWN

Number	Title	Yr	VG	VG+	NM
❏ MS-685	My Whole World Ended	1969	5.00	10.00	20.00

RUFFIN, JIMMY
SOUL

Number	Title	Yr	VG	VG+	NM
❏ 704 [M]	Top Ten	1967	12.50	25.00	50.00
-- One-color cover					
❏ 704 [M]	Top Ten	1967	6.25	12.50	25.00
-- Full-color cover					
❏ S-704 [S]	Top Ten	1967	6.25	12.50	25.00
❏ S-708	Ruff'n Ready	1969	6.25	12.50	25.00
❏ SS-727	The Groove Governor	1970	5.00	10.00	20.00

RUFFIN, JIMMY AND DAVID
Also see each artist's individual listings.
SOUL

Number	Title	Yr	VG	VG+	NM
❏ SS-728	I Am My Brother's Keeper	1970	5.00	10.00	20.00

RUFUS (FEATURING CHAKA KHAN)
ABC

Number	Title	Yr	VG	VG+	NM
❏ AA-1049 [PD]	Street Player	1978	6.25	12.50	25.00
-- Promo-only picture disc					
❏ AA-1098 [PD]	Numbers	1979	5.00	10.00	20.00
-- Promo-only picture disc					

COMMAND

Number	Title	Yr	VG	VG+	NM
❏ CQD-40023 [Q]	Rufusized	1974	5.00	10.00	20.00
❏ CQD-40024 [Q]	Rags to Rufus	1974	5.00	10.00	20.00

RUGBYS, THE
AMAZON

Number	Title	Yr	VG	VG+	NM
❏ 1000	Hot Cargo	1970	5.00	10.00	20.00

RUMBLERS, THE
DOT

Number	Title	Yr	VG	VG+	NM
❏ DLP-3509 [M]	Boss!	1963	12.50	25.00	50.00
❏ DLP-25509 [S]	Boss!	1963	15.00	30.00	60.00

DOWNEY

Number	Title	Yr	VG	VG+	NM
❏ DLP-1001 [M]	Boss!	1963	45.00	90.00	180.00
❏ DLPS-1001 [S]	Boss!	1963	62.50	125.00	250.00

RUMPLESTILTSKIN
BELL

Number	Title	Yr	VG	VG+	NM
❏ 6047	Rumplestiltskin	1970	5.00	10.00	20.00

RUNAWAYS, THE
Also see CHERIE AND MARIE CURRIE; LITA FORD; JOAN JETT.
MERCURY

Number	Title	Yr	VG	VG+	NM
❏ SRM-1-1090	The Runaways	1976	6.25	12.50	25.00
❏ SRM-1-1126	Queens of Noise	1977	6.25	12.50	25.00
❏ SRM-1-3705	Waiting for the Night	1977	6.25	12.50	25.00
❏ SRM-1-3740	Live in Japan	1978	12.50	25.00	50.00

RHINO

Number	Title	Yr	VG	VG+	NM
❏ RNDF-250 [PD]	Little Lost Girls	1982	6.25	12.50	25.00

RUNDGREN, TODD
Includes records issued as "Runt." Also see NAZZ.
AMPEX

Number	Title	Yr	VG	VG+	NM
❏ A-10105	Runt	1970	37.50	75.00	150.00
-- LP jacket and label list 10 tracks, but the album has 12					
❏ A-10105	Runt	1970	25.00	50.00	100.00
-- LP jacket and label list 10 tracks, but the album has 11					
❏ A-10105	Runt	1970	12.50	25.00	50.00
-- LP jacket and label list 10 tracks and album actually has 10					

Number	Title	Yr	VG	VG+	NM
BEARSVILLE					
❑ PRO 524 [DJ]	The Todd Rundgren Radio Show	1972	37.50	75.00	150.00
❑ PRO 597 [DJ]	Ikon/Todd Rundgren Interview	1974	30.00	60.00	120.00
❑ PRO-A-788 [DJ]	Todd Rundgren Radio Sampler	1978	12.50	25.00	50.00
-- Highlights of "Back to the Bars" plus interview of Todd by Patti Smith					
❑ 2BX 2066 [(2)]	Something/Anything?	1972	100.00	200.00	400.00
-- White label with one record on red vinyl and the other on blue vinyl					
❑ 2BX 2066 [(2)]	Something/Anything?	1972	6.25	12.50	25.00
-- Regular copy with black vinyl					
❑ A-10105	Runt	1971	6.25	12.50	25.00
-- Reissue with new label					
❑ A-10116	The Ballad of Todd Rundgren	1971	20.00	40.00	80.00
MOBILE FIDELITY					
❑ 2-225	Something/Anything?	1995	10.00	20.00	40.00
-- Audiophile vinyl					
RHINO					
❑ R1-71491	Anthology (1968-1985)	1989	5.00	10.00	20.00
RUSH					
ATLANTIC					
❑ 82040	Presto	1989	5.00	10.00	20.00
MERCURY					
❑ MK-32 [DJ]	Everything Your Listener Ever Wanted to Hear by Rush	1975	25.00	50.00	100.00
❑ MK-185 [DJ]	Rush N Roulette	1981	25.00	50.00	100.00
-- Promo-only six-track EP that has six grooves cut in it; the song it plays is based on where you place the stylus					
❑ SRP-1-1300 [PD]	Hemispheres	1979	10.00	20.00	40.00
❑ SRM-3-9200 [(3)]	Archives	1978	5.00	10.00	20.00
RUSH, MERRILEE					
BELL					
❑ 6020	Angel of the Morning	1968	5.00	10.00	20.00
RUSH, OTIS					
BLUE HORIZON					
❑ BH-4602	Blues Masters, Volume 2	1968	6.25	12.50	25.00
❑ BH-4805	Chicago Blues	1970	6.25	12.50	25.00
COTILLION					
❑ SD 9006	Mourning in the Morning	1969	6.25	12.50	25.00
RUSH, TOM					
FOLKLORE					
❑ FRLP-14003 [M]	Got a Mind to Ramble	1964	5.00	10.00	20.00
❑ FRST-14003 [S]	Got a Mind to Ramble	1964	6.25	12.50	25.00
LY CORNU					
❑ SA-70-2	Tom Rush at the Unicorn	1970	5.00	10.00	20.00
PRESTIGE					
❑ PRLP-7374 [M]	Blues -- Songs -- Ballads	1965	5.00	10.00	20.00
❑ PRST-7374 [S]	Blues -- Songs -- Ballads	1965	6.25	12.50	25.00
RUSHING, JIMMY					
Also see CHAMPION JACK DUPREE AND JIMMY RUSHING.					
BLUESWAY					
❑ BL-3005 [M]	Everyday I Have the Blues	1967	5.00	10.00	20.00
❑ BLS-6005 [S]	Everyday I Have the Blues	1967	5.00	10.00	20.00
❑ BLS-6017	Livin' the Blues	1968	5.00	10.00	20.00
COLPIX					
❑ CP-446 [M]	Five Feet of Soul	1963	10.00	20.00	40.00
COLUMBIA					
❑ CL 963 [M]	The Jazz Odyssey of James Rushing, Esq.	1957	10.00	20.00	40.00
❑ CL 1152 [M]	Little Jimmy Rushing and the Big Brass	1958	10.00	20.00	40.00
❑ CL 1401 [M]	Rushing Lullabies	1959	10.00	20.00	40.00
❑ CL 1605 [M]	Jimmy Rushing and the Smith Girls	1961	7.50	15.00	30.00
❑ CS 8060 [S]	Little Jimmy Rushing and the Big Brass	1958	12.50	25.00	50.00
❑ CS 8196 [S]	Rushing Lullabies	1959	12.50	25.00	50.00
❑ CS 8405 [S]	Jimmy Rushing and the Smith Girls	1961	10.00	20.00	40.00
JAZZTONE					
❑ J-1244 [M]	Listen to the Blues	195?	10.00	20.00	40.00
VANGUARD					
❑ VSD-2008 [S]	If This Ain't the Blues	1958	15.00	30.00	60.00
❑ VRS-8011 [10]	Jimmy Rushing Sings the Blues	1955	25.00	50.00	100.00
❑ VRS-8505 [M]	Listen to the Blues	1955	12.50	25.00	50.00
❑ VRS-8513 [M]	If This Ain't the Blues	1957	12.50	25.00	50.00
❑ VRS-8518 [M]	Going to Chicago	1957	12.50	25.00	50.00

Number	Title	Yr	VG	VG+	NM
RUSHING, JIMMY; ADA MOORE; BUCK CLAYTON					
COLUMBIA					
❑ CL 778 [M]	Cat Meets Chick	1956	15.00	30.00	60.00
RUSKIN-SPEAR, ROGER					
Also see THE BONZO DOG BAND.					
UNITED ARTISTS					
❑ UA-LA097-F	Electric Shocks	1973	6.25	12.50	25.00
RUSSELL, ANNA					
COLUMBIA MASTERWORKS					
❑ ML 4594 [M]	Anna Russell Sings?	1953	6.25	12.50	25.00
❑ ML 4733 [M]	Anna Russell Sings! Again?	1954	6.25	12.50	25.00
❑ ML 4928 [M]	Anna Russell's Guide to Concert Audiences	1955	6.25	12.50	25.00
❑ ML 5036 [M]	A Square Talk on Popular Music	1956	6.25	12.50	25.00
❑ ML 5195 [M]	In Darkest Africa	1957	7.50	15.00	30.00
❑ ML 5295 [M]	A Practical Banana Promotion	1959	12.50	25.00	50.00
❑ MG 31199 [(2)]	The Anna Russell Album?	1972	5.00	10.00	20.00
RUSSELL, BOBBY					
ELF					
❑ 5500	Words, Music, Laughter & Tears	1969	5.00	10.00	20.00
RUSSELL, JANE					
MGM					
❑ E-3715 [M]	Jane Russell	1959	12.50	25.00	50.00
❑ SE-3715 [S]	Jane Russell	1959	25.00	50.00	100.00
RUSSELL, KURT					
CAPITOL					
❑ SKAO-492	Kurt Russell	1970	7.50	15.00	30.00
RUSSELL, LEON					
SHELTER					
❑ SHE-1001	Leon Russell	1968	5.00	10.00	20.00
❑ STCO-8917 [(3)]	Leon Live	1973	5.00	10.00	20.00
RUSSELL, LEON, AND MARC BENNO					
SMASH					
❑ SRS-67107	Look Inside	1968	5.00	10.00	20.00
-- As "Asylum Choir"					
RUSTIX, THE					
RARE EARTH					
❑ RS-508	Bedlam	1969	7.50	15.00	30.00
-- Rounded-top cover					
RUSTY AND DOUG -- See RUSTY AND DOUG KERSHAW.					
RUTLES, THE					
WARNER BROS.					
❑ PRO-A-723 [DJ]	The Rutles	1978	6.25	12.50	25.00
-- Yellow vinyl with five songs and "banana" label					
❑ HS 3151	The Rutles	1978	6.25	12.50	25.00
-- With bound-in booklet					
RYAN, BUCK, AND SMITTY IRWIN					
MONUMENT					
❑ MLP-8031 [M]	Ballads and Bluegrass	1965	5.00	10.00	20.00
❑ SLP-18031 [S]	Ballads and Bluegrass	1965	6.25	12.50	25.00
RYAN, CHARLIE					
HILLTOP					
❑ JM-6006 [M]	Hot Rod Lincoln Drags Again	1964	12.50	25.00	50.00
❑ JS-6006 [R]	Hot Rod Lincoln Drags Again	1964	6.25	12.50	25.00
KING					
❑ 751 [M]	Hot Rod Lincoln	1961	100.00	200.00	400.00
RYDELL, BOBBY					
CAMEO					
❑ C-1006 [M]	We Got Love	1959	15.00	30.00	60.00
❑ C-1007 [M]	Bobby Sings	1960	12.50	25.00	50.00
❑ C-1009 [M]	Bobby's Biggest Hits	1961	20.00	40.00	80.00
-- Original with die-cut cover and textured inner sleeve					
❑ C-1009 [M]	Bobby's Biggest Hits	1961	6.25	12.50	25.00
-- Standard cover					

Number	Title	Yr	VG	VG+	NM
❑ C-1010 [M]	Bobby Rydell Salutes "The Great Ones"	1961	6.25	12.50	25.00
❑ SC-1010 [S]	Bobby Rydell Salutes "The Great Ones"	1961	10.00	20.00	40.00
❑ C-1011 [M]	Rydell at the Copa	1961	6.25	12.50	25.00
❑ SC-1011 [S]	Rydell at the Copa	1961	10.00	20.00	40.00
❑ C-1019 [M]	All the Hits	1962	37.50	75.00	150.00
-- Red vinyl					
❑ C-1019 [M]	All the Hits	1962	6.25	12.50	25.00
-- Black vinyl					
❑ C-1028 [M]	Bobby Rydell's Biggest Hits, Volume 2	1962	6.25	12.50	25.00
❑ C-1040 [M]	All the Hits, Volume 2	1963	6.25	12.50	25.00
❑ SC-1040 [P]	All the Hits, Volume 2	1963	10.00	20.00	40.00
❑ C-1043 [M]	Bye Bye Birdie	1963	6.25	12.50	25.00
❑ C-1055 [M]	Wild (Wood) Days	1963	5.00	10.00	20.00
❑ SC-1055 [S]	Wild (Wood) Days	1963	7.50	15.00	30.00
❑ C-1070 [M]	The Top Hits of 1963	1963	5.00	10.00	20.00
-- Came with bonus single, also numbered 1070					
❑ SC-1070 [S]	The Top Hits of 1963	1963	7.50	15.00	30.00
-- Came with bonus single, also numbered 1070					
❑ C-1080 [M]	Forget Him	1964	5.00	10.00	20.00
❑ SC-1080 [R]	Forget Him	1964	5.00	10.00	20.00
❑ C-2001 [M]	16 Golden Hits	1965	5.00	10.00	20.00
❑ SC-2001 [R]	16 Golden Hits	1965	5.00	10.00	20.00
CAPITOL					
❑ ST 2281 [S]	Somebody Loves You	1965	5.00	10.00	20.00
STRAND					
❑ SL-1120 [M]	Bobby Rydell Sings	196?	6.25	12.50	25.00
❑ SLS-1120 [R]	Bobby Rydell Sings	196?	5.00	10.00	20.00
VENISE					
❑ 10035 [M]	Twistin'	1962	6.25	12.50	25.00
-- Also includes tracks by Barry Norman and Stephen Garrick					

RYDELL, BOBBY/CHUBBY CHECKER
Also see each artist's individual listings.
CAMEO

Number	Title	Yr	VG	VG+	NM
❑ C 1013 [M]	Bobby Rydell/Chubby Checker	1961	7.50	15.00	30.00
❑ C-1063 [M]	Chubby Checker and Bobby Rydell	1963	5.00	10.00	20.00

RYDER, MITCH
Also see MITCH RYDER AND THE DETROIT WHEELS.
DYNO VOICE

Number	Title	Yr	VG	VG+	NM
❑ 1901 [M]	What Now My Love	1967	5.00	10.00	20.00
❑ 31901 [S]	What Now My Love	1967	5.00	10.00	20.00

RYDER, MITCH, AND THE DETROIT WHEELS
Also see MITCH RYDER.
NEW VOICE

Number	Title	Yr	VG	VG+	NM
❑ 2000 [M]	Take a Ride	1966	6.25	12.50	25.00
❑ S-2000 [S]	Take a Ride	1966	7.50	15.00	30.00
❑ 2002 [M]	Breakout…!!!	1966	5.00	10.00	20.00
-- With "Devil with a Blue Dress On/Good Golly Miss Molly"					
❑ 2002 [M]	Breakout…!!!	1966	6.25	12.50	25.00
-- Without "Devil with a Blue Dress On/Good Golly Miss Molly"					
❑ S-2002 [S]	Breakout…!!!	1966	6.25	12.50	25.00
-- With "Devil with a Blue Dress On/Good Golly Miss Molly"					
❑ S-2002 [S]	Breakout…!!!	1966	7.50	15.00	30.00
-- Without "Devil with a Blue Dress On/Good Golly Miss Molly"					
❑ 2003 [M]	Sock It To Me!	1967	6.25	12.50	25.00
❑ S-2003 [S]	Sock It To Me!	1967	7.50	15.00	30.00
❑ 2004 [M]	All Mitch Ryder Hits!	1967	7.50	15.00	30.00
❑ S-2004 [S]	All Mitch Ryder Hits!	1967	5.00	10.00	20.00
❑ S-2005	Mitch Ryder Sings the Hits	1968	5.00	10.00	20.00

RYLES, JOHN WESLEY
COLUMBIA

Number	Title	Yr	VG	VG+	NM
❑ CS 9768	Kay	1969	5.00	10.00	20.00

S

SABRES, THE
RCA VICTOR

Number	Title	Yr	VG	VG+	NM
❑ LPM-1376 [M]	Ridin' High with the Sabres	1956	15.00	30.00	60.00

SACRED MUSHROOM, THE
PARALLAX

Number	Title	Yr	VG	VG+	NM
❑ P-4001	The Sacred Mushroom	1969	37.50	75.00	150.00
-- Members of this group were later in Poco and Pure Prairie League					

SADLER, SSGT. BARRY
RCA VICTOR

Number	Title	Yr	VG	VG+	NM
❑ LSP-3547 [S]	Ballads of the Green Berets	1966	5.00	10.00	20.00
❑ LSP-3605 [S]	The "A" Team	1966	5.00	10.00	20.00

SAGITTARIUS
COLUMBIA

Number	Title	Yr	VG	VG+	NM
❑ CS 9644	Present Tense	1968	7.50	15.00	30.00
TOGETHER					
❑ STT-1002	The Blue Marble	1969	12.50	25.00	50.00
-- With two bonus photos; deduct 25 percent if missing					

SAHL, MORT
FANTASY

Number	Title	Yr	VG	VG+	NM
❑ 7005 [M]	Mort Sahl at Sunset	196?	10.00	20.00	40.00
-- Red vinyl					
❑ 7005 [M]	Mort Sahl at Sunset	196?	7.50	15.00	30.00
-- Black vinyl					
MERCURY					
❑ MG-21112 [M]	Anyway…Onward	1967	5.00	10.00	20.00
❑ SR-61112 [S]	Anyway…Onward	1967	5.00	10.00	20.00
REPRISE					
❑ R-5002 [M]	The New Frontier	1961	5.00	10.00	20.00
❑ R9-5002 [S]	The New Frontier	1961	6.25	12.50	25.00
❑ R-5003 [M]	Mort Sahl On Relationships	1961	10.00	20.00	40.00
❑ R9-5003 [S]	Mort Sahl On Relationships	1961	12.50	25.00	50.00
-- Joan Collins appears on the cover					
VERVE					
❑ MGV-15002 [M]	The Future Lies Ahead	1959	5.00	10.00	20.00
❑ MGV-15004 [M]	1960: Look Forward in Anger	1959	5.00	10.00	20.00
❑ MGV-15006 [M]	A Way of Life	1960	5.00	10.00	20.00
❑ MGV-15012 [M]	Mort Sahl at the Hungry I	1960	5.00	10.00	20.00
❑ MGVS-15012 [S]	Mort Sahl at the Hungry I	1960	6.25	12.50	25.00
❑ V-15021 [M]	The Next President	1961	5.00	10.00	20.00
❑ V6-15021 [S]	The Next President	1961	6.25	12.50	25.00

SAHM, DOUG
Also see SIR DOUGLAS QUINTET.
MERCURY

Number	Title	Yr	VG	VG+	NM
❑ SRM-1-655	Rough Edges	1972	7.50	15.00	30.00
WARNER BROS.					
❑ BS 2810	Groovers Paradise	1974	5.00	10.00	20.00

SAIN, OLIVER
ABAT

Number	Title	Yr	VG	VG+	NM
❑ 404	Main Man	1973	5.00	10.00	20.00
❑ 406	Bus Stop	1974	5.00	10.00	20.00

ST. ANTHONY'S FIRE
ZONK

Number	Title	Yr	VG	VG+	NM
❑ (# unknown)	St. Anthony's Fire	1968	100.00	200.00	400.00

ST. LOUIS JIMMY
BLUESVILLE

Number	Title	Yr	VG	VG+	NM
❑ BVLP-1028 [M]	Goin' Down Blues	1961	30.00	60.00	120.00
-- Blue label, silver print					
❑ BVLP-1028 [M]	Goin' Down Blues	1964	6.25	12.50	25.00
-- Blue label, trident logo at right					

SAINT PETER'S CHOIR
CORAL

Number	Title	Yr	VG	VG+	NM
❑ CRL 56015 [10]	Hark! The Herald Angels Sing	1950	10.00	20.00	40.00

ST. PETERS, CRISPIAN
JAMIE

Number	Title	Yr	VG	VG+	NM
❑ JLPM-3027 [M]	The Pied Piper	1966	12.50	25.00	50.00
❑ JLPS-3027 [R]	The Pied Piper	1966	8.75	17.50	35.00

Number	Title	Yr	VG	VG+	NM

ST. SHAW, MIKE
REPRISE

Number	Title	Yr	VG	VG+	NM
❑ R-6128 [M]	The Mike St. Shaw Trio	1964	5.00	10.00	20.00
❑ RS-6128 [S]	The Mike St. Shaw Trio	1964	6.25	12.50	25.00

SAINT STEVEN
PROBE

❑ CPLP-4506	Over the Hills	1969	15.00	30.00	60.00

SAINTE-MARIE, BUFFY
VANGUARD

❑ VSD 3/4 [(2)]	The Best of Buffy Sainte-Marie	1970	5.00	10.00	20.00
❑ VSD 79142 [S]	It's My Way	1964	5.00	10.00	20.00
❑ VSD 79171 [S]	Many a Mile	1965	5.00	10.00	20.00
❑ VSD 79211 [S]	Little Wheel Spin and Spin	1966	5.00	10.00	20.00
❑ VSD 79250 [S]	Fire & Fire & Candlelight	1967	5.00	10.00	20.00

SAKAMOTO, KYU
CAPITOL

❑ T 10349 [M]	Sukiyaki and Other Japanese Hits	1963	6.25	12.50	25.00

SALEM MASS
SALEM MASS

❑ SM-101	Witch Burning	1972	62.50	125.00	250.00

SALES, SOUPY
ABC-PARAMOUNT

❑ 503 [M]	Spy with a Pie	1965	6.25	12.50	25.00
❑ S-503 [S]	Spy with a Pie	1965	7.50	15.00	30.00
❑ 517 [M]	Soupy Sales Sez Do the Mouse and Other Teen Hits	1965	6.25	12.50	25.00
❑ S-517 [S]	Soupy Sales Sez Do the Mouse and Other Teen Hits	1965	7.50	15.00	30.00

MOTOWN

❑ MS 686	A Bag of Soup	1969	6.25	12.50	25.00

REPRISE

❑ R 6010 [M]	The Soupy Sales Show	1961	7.50	15.00	30.00
❑ R9 6010 [S]	The Soupy Sales Show	1961	10.00	20.00	40.00
❑ R 6052 [M]	Up in the Air	1962	7.50	15.00	30.00
❑ R9 6052 [S]	Up in the Air	1962	10.00	20.00	40.00

SALT WATER TAFFY
BUDDAH

❑ BDS-5021	Finders Keepers	1968	5.00	10.00	20.00

SALVATION
ABC

❑ S-623	Salvation	1968	5.00	10.00	20.00
❑ S-653	Gypsy Carnival Caravan	1968	5.00	10.00	20.00

SAM AND DAVE
ATLANTIC

❑ SD 8205	I Thank You	1968	6.25	12.50	25.00
❑ SD 8218	The Best of Sam and Dave	1969	5.00	10.00	20.00

ROULETTE

❑ R-25323 [M]	Sam and Dave	1966	7.50	15.00	30.00
❑ SR-25323 [S]	Sam and Dave	1966	10.00	20.00	40.00

STAX

❑ ST-708 [M]	Hold On, I'm Comin'	1966	10.00	20.00	40.00
❑ STS-708 [S]	Hold On, I'm Comin'	1966	12.50	25.00	50.00
❑ ST-712 [M]	Double Dynamite	1966	7.50	15.00	30.00
❑ STS-712 [S]	Double Dynamite	1966	10.00	20.00	40.00
❑ ST-725 [M]	Soul Men	1967	7.50	15.00	30.00
❑ STS-725 [S]	Soul Men	1967	10.00	20.00	40.00

SAM THE SHAM AND THE PHARAOHS
MGM

❑ E-4297 [M]	Wooly Bully	1965	7.50	15.00	30.00
❑ SE-4297 [S]	Wooly Bully	1965	10.00	20.00	40.00
❑ E-4317 [M]	Their Second Album	1965	6.25	12.50	25.00
❑ SE-4317 [S]	Their Second Album	1965	7.50	15.00	30.00
❑ E-4347 [M]	On Tour	1966	6.25	12.50	25.00
❑ SE-4347 [S]	On Tour	1966	7.50	15.00	30.00
❑ E-4407 [M]	Lil' Red Riding Hood	1966	6.25	12.50	25.00
❑ SE-4407 [S]	Lil' Red Riding Hood	1966	7.50	15.00	30.00
❑ E-4422 [M]	The Best of Sam the Sham and the Pharaohs	1967	5.00	10.00	20.00
❑ SE-4422 [S]	The Best of Sam the Sham and the Pharaohs	1967	6.25	12.50	25.00

❑ E-4477 [M]	Nefertiti	1967	6.25	12.50	25.00
❑ SE-4477 [S]	Nefertiti	1967	6.25	12.50	25.00
❑ SE-4477	The Sam The Sham Revue	1968	5.00	10.00	20.00
-- Retitled reissue					
❑ SE-4526	Ten of Pentacles	1968	5.00	10.00	20.00
❑ ST 90422 [S]	Wooly Bully	1965	12.50	25.00	50.00
-- Capitol Record Club edition					
❑ T 90422 [M]	Wooly Bully	1965	10.00	20.00	40.00
-- Capitol Record Club edition					

SAMHAIN
Also see MISFITS.
PLAN 9

❑ PL9-04	Initium	1984	100.00	200.00	400.00
-- Pink vinyl "error" pressing					
❑ PL9-04	Initium	1984	75.00	150.00	300.00
-- No more than 100 on marbled black and white vinyl					
❑ PL9-04	Initium	1984	75.00	150.00	300.00
-- 100 on white vinyl					
❑ PL9-04	Initium	1984	25.00	50.00	100.00
-- 500 on red vinyl					
❑ PL9-04	Initium	1984	12.50	25.00	50.00
-- Black vinyl; "8-84" scrawled in trail-off wax					
❑ PL9-05 [EP]	Unholy Passion	1985	20.00	40.00	80.00
-- Black vinyl, tan cover (original)					
❑ PL9-05 [EP]	Unholy Passion	1985	25.00	50.00	100.00
-- Red vinyl, maroon cover					
❑ PL9-05 [EP]	Unholy Passion	1985	25.00	50.00	100.00
-- White vinyl, tan cover					
❑ PL9-07	November Coming Fire	1986	37.50	75.00	150.00
-- 200 on orange vinyl					
❑ PL9-07	November Coming Fire	1986	7.50	15.00	30.00
-- Regular issue on black vinyl					

SAMPLE, JOE
MOBILE FIDELITY

❑ 1-016	Rainbow Seeker	1979	5.00	10.00	20.00
-- Audiophile vinyl					

SAMPLES, JUNIOR
CHART

❑ CHM-1002 [M]	The World of Junior Samples	1967	5.00	10.00	20.00
❑ CHS-1002 [S]	The World of Junior Samples	1967	5.00	10.00	20.00

SAN REMO GOLDEN STRINGS
GORDY

❑ G-923 [M]	Hungry for Love	1967	6.25	12.50	25.00
❑ GS-923 [S]	Hungry for Love	1967	7.50	15.00	30.00
❑ GS-928	Swing	1968	5.00	10.00	20.00

RIC-TIC

❑ 901 [M]	Hungry for Love	1966	12.50	25.00	50.00
❑ S-901 [S]	Hungry for Love	1966	15.00	30.00	60.00

SAN SEBASTIAN STRINGS, THE
WARNER BROS.

❑ 3WS 1730 [(3)]	The Sea, The Earth, The Sky	1968	5.00	10.00	20.00
❑ 3WS 1827 [(3)]	The Complete Sea	1969	5.00	10.00	20.00
❑ 4WS 2754 [(4)]	Seasons	1973	5.00	10.00	20.00

SANDALS, THE
WORLD PACIFIC

❑ ST-1818 [S]	Scrambler	1964	62.50	125.00	250.00
-- As "The Sandells"; red vinyl					
❑ ST-1818 [S]	Scrambler	1964	25.00	50.00	100.00
-- As "The Sandells"; black vinyl					
❑ WP-1818 [M]	Scrambler	1964	20.00	40.00	80.00
-- As "The Sandells"					
❑ ST-1832 [S]	The Endless Summer	1966	7.50	15.00	30.00
❑ WP-1832 [M]	The Endless Summer	1966	6.25	12.50	25.00
❑ ST-21884	The Last of the Ski Bums	1969	6.25	12.50	25.00
-- With skiers' silhouettes on cover					
❑ ST-21884	The Last of the Ski Bums	1969	6.25	12.50	25.00
-- With Volkswagon bus on cover					

SANDBERG, CARL
COLUMBIA MASTERWORKS

❑ ML 5539 [M]	Flat Rock Ballads	1959	5.00	10.00	20.00

DECCA

❑ DL 5135 [10]	The People, Yes	1950	12.50	25.00	50.00
❑ DL 9105 [M]	Cowboy Songs and Negro Spirituals	1964	5.00	10.00	20.00

LYRICHORD

❑ LL-4 [10]	American Songbag	1951	12.50	25.00	50.00
❑ LL-66 [M]	The Great Carl Sandburg	1957	7.50	15.00	30.00

Number	Title	Yr	VG	VG+	NM

SANDERS, ED
REPRISE
| ☐ MS 2105 | Beer Cans on the Moon | 1972 | 6.25 | 12.50 | 25.00 |
| ☐ RS-6374 | Sanders' Truckstop | 1969 | 6.25 | 12.50 | 25.00 |

SANDERS, FELICIA
COLUMBIA
| ☐ CL 654 [M] | Felicia Sanders at the Blue Angel | 1955 | 7.50 | 15.00 | 30.00 |
| ☐ CL 713 [M] | Girl Meets Boy | 1955 | 7.50 | 15.00 | 30.00 |
DECCA
| ☐ DL 8762 [M] | That Certain Feeling | 1958 | 6.25 | 12.50 | 25.00 |
| ☐ DL 78762 [S] | That Certain Feeling | 1959 | 10.00 | 20.00 | 40.00 |

SANDERS, GEORGE
ABC-PARAMOUNT
| ☐ ABC-231 [M] | The George Sanders Touch | 1958 | 7.50 | 15.00 | 30.00 |

SANDERS, PHARAOH
ABC IMPULSE!
☐ A-9138 [M]	Tauhid	1967	7.50	15.00	30.00
☐ AS-9138 [S]	Tauhid	1967	5.00	10.00	20.00
☐ AS-9181	Karma	1969	5.00	10.00	20.00
☐ AS-9190	Jewels of Thought	1970	5.00	10.00	20.00
☐ AS-9199	Summun Bukmun Umyum	1970	5.00	10.00	20.00
☐ AS-9229 [(2)]	The Best of Pharaoh Sanders	1973	5.00	10.00	20.00
ESP-DISK'
| ☐ 1003 [M] | Pharaoh's First | 1965 | 6.25 | 12.50 | 25.00 |
| ☐ S-1003 [S] | Pharaoh's First | 1965 | 7.50 | 15.00 | 30.00 |

SANDS, TOMMY
CAPITOL
☐ T 848 [M]	Steady Date with Tommy Sands	1957	15.00	30.00	60.00
☐ T 929 [M]	Sing Boy Sing	1958	15.00	30.00	60.00
☐ T 1081 [M]	Sands Storm	1959	12.50	25.00	50.00
☐ ST 1123 [S]	This Thing Called Love	1959	10.00	20.00	40.00
☐ T 1123 [M]	This Thing Called Love	1959	7.50	15.00	30.00
☐ ST 1239 [S]	When I'm Thinking of You	1960	10.00	20.00	40.00
☐ T 1239 [M]	When I'm Thinking of You	1960	7.50	15.00	30.00
☐ ST 1364 [S]	Sands at the Sands	1960	10.00	20.00	40.00
☐ T 1364 [M]	Sands at the Sands	1960	7.50	15.00	30.00
☐ ST 1426 [S]	Dream with Me	1961	10.00	20.00	40.00
☐ T 1426 [M]	Dream with Me	1961	7.50	15.00	30.00

SANTA FE
RTV
| ☐ 301 | Good Earth | 197? | 7.50 | 15.00 | 30.00 |

SANTAMARIA, MONGO
BATTLE
| ☐ B-6120 [M] | Watermelon Man! | 1963 | 5.00 | 10.00 | 20.00 |
| ☐ BS-96120 [S] | Watermelon Man! | 1963 | 6.25 | 12.50 | 25.00 |
COLUMBIA
| ☐ CS 9175 [S] | La Bamba | 1965 | 5.00 | 10.00 | 20.00 |
FANTASY
☐ 3267 [M]	Yambu	1959	10.00	20.00	40.00
-- Red vinyl					
☐ 3267 [M]	Yambu	1959	7.50	15.00	30.00
-- Black vinyl					
☐ 3291 [M]	Mongo	1959	10.00	20.00	40.00
-- Red vinyl					
☐ 3291 [M]	Mongo	1959	7.50	15.00	30.00
-- Black vinyl					
☐ 3302 [M]	Our Man in Havana	1960	10.00	20.00	40.00
-- Red vinyl					
☐ 3302 [M]	Our Man in Havana	1960	7.50	15.00	30.00
-- Black vinyl					
☐ 3311 [M]	Mongo in Havana	1960	10.00	20.00	40.00
-- Red vinyl					
☐ 3311 [M]	Mongo in Havana	1960	7.50	15.00	30.00
-- Black vinyl					
☐ 3314 [M]	Sabroso	1960	10.00	20.00	40.00
-- Red vinyl					
☐ 3314 [M]	Sabroso	1960	7.50	15.00	30.00
-- Black vinyl					
☐ 3324 [M]	Arriba!	1961	10.00	20.00	40.00
-- Red vinyl					
☐ 3324 [M]	Arriba!	1961	7.50	15.00	30.00
-- Black vinyl					
☐ 3328 [M]	Mas Sabroso	1962	10.00	20.00	40.00
-- Red vinyl					
☐ 3328 [M]	Mas Sabroso	1962	7.50	15.00	30.00
-- Black vinyl					
☐ 3335 [M]	Viva Mongo!	1962	10.00	20.00	40.00
-- Red vinyl					
☐ 3335 [M]	Viva Mongo!	1962	7.50	15.00	30.00
-- Black vinyl					
☐ 8012 [S]	Yambu	1962	7.50	15.00	30.00
-- Blue vinyl					
☐ 8012 [S]	Yambu	1962	5.00	10.00	20.00
-- Black vinyl					
☐ 8032 [S]	Mongo	1962	7.50	15.00	30.00
-- Blue vinyl					
☐ 8032 [S]	Mongo	1962	5.00	10.00	20.00
-- Blue vinyl					
☐ 8045 [S]	Our Man in Havana	1962	7.50	15.00	30.00
-- Blue vinyl					
☐ 8045 [S]	Our Man in Havana	1962	5.00	10.00	20.00
-- Black vinyl					
☐ 8055 [S]	Mongo in Havana	1962	7.50	15.00	30.00
-- Blue vinyl					
☐ 8055 [S]	Mongo in Havana	1962	5.00	10.00	20.00
-- Black vinyl					
☐ 8058 [S]	Sabroso	1962	7.50	15.00	30.00
-- Blue vinyl					
☐ 8058 [S]	Sabroso	1962	5.00	10.00	20.00
-- Black vinyl					
☐ 8067 [S]	Arriba!	1962	7.50	15.00	30.00
-- Blue vinyl					
☐ 8067 [S]	Arriba!	1962	5.00	10.00	20.00
-- Black vinyl					
☐ 8071 [S]	Mas Sabroso	1962	7.50	15.00	30.00
-- Blue vinyl					
☐ 8071 [S]	Mas Sabroso	1962	5.00	10.00	20.00
-- Black vinyl					
☐ 8087 [S]	Viva Mongo!	1962	7.50	15.00	30.00
-- Blue vinyl					
☐ 8087 [S]	Viva Mongo!	1962	5.00	10.00	20.00
-- Black vinyl					
☐ 8351 [S]	Mighty Mongo	1963	5.00	10.00	20.00
RIVERSIDE
☐ RLP-423 [M]	Go, Mongo	1962	6.25	12.50	25.00
☐ R-3008 [M]	Explosion	1967	6.25	12.50	25.00
☐ RM-3523 [M]	Mongo Introduces La Lupe	1963	5.00	10.00	20.00
☐ RM-3529 [M]	Mongo at the Village Gate	1963	5.00	10.00	20.00
☐ RM-3530 [M]	Mongo Santamaria Explodes!	1964	5.00	10.00	20.00
☐ RS-9423 [S]	Go, Mongo!	1962	7.50	15.00	30.00
☐ RS-93523 [S]	Mongo Introduces La Lupe	1963	6.25	12.50	25.00
☐ RS-93529 [S]	Mongo at the Village Gate	1963	6.25	12.50	25.00
☐ RS-93530 [S]	Mongo Santamaria Explodes!	1964	6.25	12.50	25.00

SANTANA
COLUMBIA
☐ CQ 30130 [Q]	Abraxas	1972	5.00	10.00	20.00
☐ CQ 30595 [Q]	Santana	1972	5.00	10.00	20.00
☐ PCQ 31610 [Q]	Caravanserai	1974	5.00	10.00	20.00
☐ PCQ 32455 [Q]	Welcome	1974	5.00	10.00	20.00
☐ PCQ 33050 [Q]	Santana's Greatest Hits	1974	5.00	10.00	20.00
☐ PCQ 33135 [Q]	Borboletta	1974	5.00	10.00	20.00
☐ PCQ 33576 [Q]	Amigos	1976	5.00	10.00	20.00
☐ JCQ 34423 [Q]	Festival	1977	5.00	10.00	20.00
☐ HC 40130	Abraxas	1981	20.00	40.00	80.00
-- Half-speed mastered edition					
☐ C3X 44344 [(3)]	Viva Santana	1988	5.00	10.00	20.00
☐ HC 47158	Zebop!	1981	10.00	20.00	40.00
-- Half-speed mastered edition					

SANTO AND JOHNNY
CANADIAN AMERICAN
☐ CALP-1001 [M]	Santo & Johnny	1959	15.00	30.00	60.00
☐ SCALP-1001 [S]	Santo & Johnny	1959	20.00	40.00	80.00
☐ CALP-1002 [M]	Encore	1960	10.00	20.00	40.00
☐ SCALP-1002 [S]	Encore	1960	12.50	25.00	50.00
☐ CALP-1004 [M]	Hawaii	1961	10.00	20.00	40.00
☐ SCALP-1004 [S]	Hawaii	1961	12.50	25.00	50.00
☐ CALP-1006 [M]	Come On In	1962	7.50	15.00	30.00
☐ SCALP-1006 [S]	Come On In	1962	10.00	20.00	40.00
☐ CALP-1008 [M]	Around the World with Santo and Johnny	1962	7.50	15.00	30.00
☐ SCALP-1008 [S]	Around the World with Santo and Johnny	1962	10.00	20.00	40.00
☐ CALP-1011 [M]	Off Shore	1963	7.50	15.00	30.00
☐ SCALP-1011 [S]	Off Shore	1963	10.00	20.00	40.00
☐ CALP-1014 [M]	In the Still of the Night	1963	7.50	15.00	30.00
☐ SCALP-1014 [S]	In the Still of the Night	1963	10.00	20.00	40.00
☐ CALP-1016 [M]	Wish You Love	1964	7.50	15.00	30.00
☐ SCALP-1016 [S]	Wish You Love	1964	10.00	20.00	40.00
☐ CALP-1017 [M]	The Beatles' Greatest Hits	1965	10.00	20.00	40.00
☐ SCALP-1017 [S]	The Beatles' Greatest Hits	1965	12.50	25.00	50.00
☐ CALP-1018 [M]	Mucho	1965	7.50	15.00	30.00
☐ SCALP-1018 [S]	Mucho	1965	10.00	20.00	40.00

Number	Title	Yr	VG	VG+	NM
IMPERIAL					
❏ LP-12363 [S]	Brilliant Guitar Sounds	1967	5.00	10.00	20.00
SANTOS, LARRY					
EVOLUTION					
❏ 2002	Just a Man	1969	5.00	10.00	20.00
SAPODILLA PUNCH					
PHILIPS					
❏ PHS 600-312	Sapodilla Punch	1969	5.00	10.00	20.00
SAPPHIRE THINKERS, THE					
HOBBIT					
❏ HB-5003	From Within	1969	7.50	15.00	30.00
SAPPHIRES, THE					
SWAN					
❏ LP-513 [M]	Who Do You Love	1964	75.00	150.00	300.00
SATAN AND THE DISCIPLES					
GOLDBAND					
❏ 7750	Underground	1969	10.00	20.00	40.00
SATAN'S FOUR					
B.T. PUPPY					
❏ BTS-1010	Mixed Soul	1970	37.50	75.00	150.00
-- With the Cinnamon Angels					
SATANS, THE					
(NO LABEL)					
❏ (no #) [M]	Raisin' Hell	1962	75.00	150.00	300.00
SAUNDERS, MERL					
CRYSTAL CLEAR					
❏ 5006	Do I Move You	1980	5.00	10.00	20.00
-- Direct-to-disc recording					
FANTASY					
❏ 9421	Fire Up	1973	5.00	10.00	20.00
-- With Jerry Garcia and Tom Fogerty					
❏ 79002 [(2)]	Live at the Keystone	198?	5.00	10.00	20.00
SAVAGE RESURRECTION					
MERCURY					
❏ SR-61156	Savage Resurrection	1968	25.00	50.00	100.00
SAVAGE ROSE					
POLYDOR					
❏ 24-6001	In the Plain	1969	5.00	10.00	20.00
-- Gatefold cover					
SAVATAGE					
PAR					
❏ PAR-1050	Sirens	1983	100.00	200.00	400.00
-- Blue vinyl					
SAVITT, BUDDY					
PARKWAY					
❏ P-7012 [M]	The Most Heard Sax in the World	1962	12.50	25.00	50.00
❏ SP-7012 [S]	The Most Heard Sax in the World	1962	25.00	50.00	100.00
SAVOY BROWN					
PARROT					
❏ PAS 71024	Getting to the Point	1968	6.25	12.50	25.00
❏ PAS 71027	Blue Matter	1969	6.25	12.50	25.00
SAWBUCK					
FILLMORE					
❏ Z 31248	Sawbuck	1972	5.00	10.00	20.00
SAXON, SKY					
Also see THE SEEDS.					
GNP CRESCENDO					
❏ GNP-2040 [M]	A Full Spoon of Seedy Blues	1967	10.00	20.00	40.00
❏ GNPS-2040 [S]	A Full Spoon of Seedy Blues	1967	7.50	15.00	30.00
SAXONS, THE					
MIRASONIC					
❏ A-1017 [M]	The Saxons	1966	10.00	20.00	40.00
❏ AS-1017 [S]	The Saxons	1966	20.00	40.00	80.00

Number	Title	Yr	VG	VG+	NM
SCAFFOLD, THE					
BELL					
❏ 6018 [M]	Thank U Very Much	1968	12.50	25.00	50.00
-- Mono copies are promo only					
❏ 6018 [S]	Thank U Very Much	1968	12.50	25.00	50.00
SCAGGS, BOZ					
Also see STEVE MILLER BAND.					
COLUMBIA					
❏ A2S 71 [(2) DJ]	KSAN Live Concert	1974	12.50	25.00	50.00
-- Promo-only set released in plain cardboard jacket					
❏ AS 203 [DJ]	The Boz Scaggs Sampler	1976	5.00	10.00	20.00
❏ HC 43920	Silk Degrees	1981	7.50	15.00	30.00
-- Half-speed mastered edition					
SCAMPS, THE					
PROJECT					
❏ 8002 [M]	Teen Dance and Sing Along Party	1962	10.00	20.00	40.00
SCANDAL					
COLUMBIA					
❏ 8C8 39905 [EP]	Scandal featuring Patty Smyth	1985	5.00	10.00	20.00
-- Picture disc EP with four of the group's biggest hits					
SCHAFER, KERMIT					
JUBILEE					
❏ BL-1 [M]	Blooperama	196?	5.00	10.00	20.00
❏ KS-1 [(2) M]	The Best of Bloopers	1959	6.25	12.50	25.00
❏ PMB-1 [M]	Pardon My Blooper! Volume 1	1958	5.00	10.00	20.00
❏ LP-2 [10]	Pardon My Blooper!	1954	10.00	20.00	40.00
❏ PMB-2 [M]	Pardon My Blooper! Volume 2	1958	5.00	10.00	20.00
❏ LP-3 [10]	Pardon My Blooper! Volume 2	1954	10.00	20.00	40.00
❏ PMB-3 [M]	Pardon My Blooper! Volume 3	1958	5.00	10.00	20.00
❏ PMB-4 [M]	Pardon My Blooper! Volume 4	1958	5.00	10.00	20.00
❏ PMB-5 [M]	Pardon My Blooper! Volume 5	1959	5.00	10.00	20.00
❏ PMB-6 [M]	Pardon My Blooper! Volume 6	1959	5.00	10.00	20.00
❏ PMB-7 [M]	Pardon My Blooper! Volume 7	1959	5.00	10.00	20.00
❏ PMB-8 [M]	Pardon My Blooper! Volume 8	1959	5.00	10.00	20.00
❏ SPMB-9 [M]	Pardon My Sports Blooper!	196?	5.00	10.00	20.00
❏ QPMB-10 [M]	Pardon My Quiz Blooper!	196?	5.00	10.00	20.00
❏ WPMB-11 [M]	Pardon My Washington Blooper!	196?	5.00	10.00	20.00
❏ LP-19 [10]	Pardon My Blooper! Volume 3	1955	10.00	20.00	40.00
❏ JLP-1000 [M]	Special Edition: Pardon My Blooper	195?	7.50	15.00	30.00
❏ JGM-2001 [M]	Comedy of Errors	196?	5.00	10.00	20.00
❏ JGM-2002 [M]	Slipped Disks	196?	5.00	10.00	20.00
❏ JGM-2003 [M]	Prize Bloopers	196?	5.00	10.00	20.00
❏ JGM-2004 [M]	Super Bloopers	196?	5.00	10.00	20.00
❏ JGM-2005 [M]	Off the Record	196?	5.00	10.00	20.00
❏ JGM-2006 [M]	Station Breaks	196?	5.00	10.00	20.00
❏ JGM-2007 [M]	Funny Boners	196?	5.00	10.00	20.00
❏ JGM-2008 [M]	Foot 'n Mouth Club	196?	5.00	10.00	20.00
SCHIFRIN, LALO					
Includes some of his soundtrack work.					
AUDIO FIDELITY					
❏ AFLP-1981 [M]	Bossa Nova -- New Brazilian Jazz	1962	5.00	10.00	20.00
❏ AFLP-2117 [M]	Eso Es Latino Jazz	1963	5.00	10.00	20.00
❏ AFSD-5981 [S]	Bossa Nova -- New Brazilian Jazz	1962	6.25	12.50	25.00
❏ AFSD-6117 [S]	Eso Es Latino Jazz	1963	6.25	12.50	25.00
COLGEMS					
❏ COMO-5003 [M]	Murderer's Row	1967	12.50	25.00	50.00
❏ COSO-5003 [S]	Murderer's Row	1967	25.00	50.00	100.00
DOT					
❏ DLP-3831 [M]	Music from Mission: Impossible	1967	7.50	15.00	30.00
❏ DLP-3833 [M]	Cool Hand Luke	1968	12.50	25.00	50.00
❏ DLP-25831 [S]	Music from Mission: Impossible	1967	10.00	20.00	40.00
❏ DLP-25833 [S]	Cool Hand Luke	1968	12.50	25.00	50.00
❏ DLP-25852	There's a Whole Lot of Schifrin Goin' On	1968	5.00	10.00	20.00
ENTR'ACTE					
❏ ERS-6508	Voyage of the Damned	1977	6.25	12.50	25.00
MGM					
❏ SE-4110 [S]	Piano, Strings and Bossa Nova	1963	5.00	10.00	20.00
❏ SE-4156 [S]	Between Broadway and Hollywood	1963	5.00	10.00	20.00
❏ E-4313 [M]	The Cincinnati Kid	1965	5.00	10.00	20.00
❏ SE-4313 [S]	The Cincinnati Kid	1965	6.25	12.50	25.00
❏ E-4413 ST [M]	Liquidator	1966	5.00	10.00	20.00
❏ SE-4413 ST [S]	Liquidator	1966	6.25	12.50	25.00
❏ SE-4742	Medical Center and Other Great Themes	1971	5.00	10.00	20.00
NAUTILUS					
❏ NR-51	Ins and Outs	198?	10.00	20.00	40.00
-- Audiophile vinyl					

Number	Title	Yr	VG	VG+	NM

PARAMOUNT

Number	Title	Yr	VG	VG+	NM
❑ PAS-5002	More Music from Mission: Impossible	1969	10.00	20.00	40.00
❑ PAS-5004	Mannix	1969	7.50	15.00	30.00

ROULETTE

❑ R 52088 [M]	Lalo Brilliance	1962	5.00	10.00	20.00
❑ SR 52088 [S]	Lalo Brilliance	1962	6.25	12.50	25.00

TETRAGRAMMATON

❑ T-5006	Che!	1969	7.50	15.00	30.00

TICO

❑ LP-1070 [M]	Piano Español	1960	6.25	12.50	25.00
❑ LPS-1070 [S]	Piano Español	1960	7.50	15.00	30.00

VERVE

❑ V6-8543 [S]	Samba Paros Dos	1963	5.00	10.00	20.00

-- With Bob Brookmeyer

❑ V6-8601 [S]	New Fantasy	1964	5.00	10.00	20.00
❑ V6-8624 [S]	Once a Thief and Other Themes	1965	5.00	10.00	20.00
❑ V6-8654 [S]	The Dissection and Reconstruction of Music from the Past	1966	5.00	10.00	20.00

WARNER BROS.

❑ WS 1777	Bullitt	1968	12.50	25.00	50.00
❑ BS 2727	Enter the Dragon	1973	12.50	25.00	50.00

SCHILLER, LAWRENCE
CAPITOL

❑ TAO 2574 [M]	LSD	1966	25.00	50.00	100.00
❑ KAO 2630 [M]	Why Did Lenny Bruce Die?	1967	7.50	15.00	30.00
❑ KAO 2652 [M]	Homosexuality in the American Male	1967	7.50	15.00	30.00

SCHLAMME, MARTHA
VANGUARD

❑ VRS 497 [M]	Chansons de Noel	1956	7.50	15.00	30.00
❑ VRS-9011 [M]	Raisins and Almonds and Other Jewish Folk Songs	195?	7.50	15.00	30.00
❑ VRS-9019 [M]	Folk Songs of Many Lands	195?	7.50	15.00	30.00

SCHORY, DICK
CONCERT DISC

❑ SC-21 [M]	Re-Percussion	1957	15.00	30.00	60.00

RCA VICTOR

❑ LPM-1866 [M]	Music for Bang, Barroom and Harp	1958	15.00	30.00	60.00
❑ LSP-1866 [S]	Music for Bang, Barroom and Harp	1958	50.00	100.00	200.00
❑ LPM-2125 [M]	Music to Break Any Mood	1960	7.50	15.00	30.00
❑ LSP-2125 [S]	Music to Break Any Mood	1960	25.00	50.00	100.00
❑ LPM-2289 [M]	Wild Percussion and Horns A-Plenty	1960	7.50	15.00	30.00
❑ LSP-2289 [S]	Wild Percussion and Horns A-Plenty	1960	15.00	30.00	60.00
❑ LSA-2306 [S]	Runnin' Wild	1960	10.00	20.00	40.00
❑ LSA-2382 [S]	Stereo Action Goes Broadway	1961	10.00	20.00	40.00
❑ LPM-2485 [M]	Holiday for Percussion	1962	7.50	15.00	30.00
❑ LSA-2485 [S]	Holiday for Percussion	1962	10.00	20.00	40.00
❑ LSP-2613 [S]	Supercussion	1963	10.00	20.00	40.00
❑ LPM-2738 [M]	Politely Percussive	1963	7.50	15.00	30.00
❑ LSP-2738 [S]	Politely Percussive	1963	10.00	20.00	40.00
❑ LPM-2806 [M]	Dick Schory on Tour	1964	5.00	10.00	20.00
❑ LSP-2806 [S]	Dick Schory on Tour	1964	6.25	12.50	25.00

SCHUMANN, WALTER
CAPITOL

❑ H 297 [10]	The Voices of Walter Schumann	195?	10.00	20.00	40.00
❑ T 297 [M]	The Voices of Walter Schumann	1955	6.25	12.50	25.00
❑ H 9016 [10]	Christmas in the Air!	1951	10.00	20.00	40.00

-- Original issue with purple label

❑ L 9016 [10]	Christmas in the Air!	1952?	8.75	17.50	35.00

-- Reissue with red label and new prefix

RCA VICTOR

❑ LPM-1025 [M]	Exploring the Unknown	1955	12.50	25.00	50.00
❑ LPM-1141 [M]	The Voices of Christmas	1955	5.00	10.00	20.00

-- Original cover has all-yellow lettering on front cover and eight LP/EP covers on back

❑ LPM-1465 [M]	Scrapbook: The Voices of Walter Schumann	1957	5.00	10.00	20.00
❑ LPM-1477 [M]	When We Were Young	1957	5.00	10.00	20.00
❑ LSP-1558 [S]	Walter Schumann Presents the Voices	1958	5.00	10.00	20.00

SCORPION
TOWER

❑ ST 5171	Scorpion	1969	12.50	25.00	50.00

SCORPIONS
BILLINGSGATE

❑ 1004	Lonesome Crow	1974	7.50	15.00	30.00

SCOT, PATRICIA
ABC-PARAMOUNT

❑ 301 [M]	Once Around the Clock	1959	5.00	10.00	20.00
❑ S-301 [S]	Once Around the Clock	1959	6.25	12.50	25.00

SCOTT, CALVIN
STAX

❑ STS-2046	I'm Not Blind... I Just Can't See	1972	20.00	40.00	80.00

SCOTT, CLIFFORD
WORLD PACIFIC

❑ ST-1811 [S]	The Big Ones	1964	7.50	15.00	30.00

-- Black vinyl

❑ ST-1811 [S]	The Big Ones	1964	20.00	40.00	80.00

-- Green vinyl

❑ WP-1811 [M]	The Big Ones	1964	5.00	10.00	20.00

-- Black vinyl

❑ WP-1811 [M]	The Big Ones	1964	15.00	30.00	60.00

-- Green vinyl

❑ ST-1825 [S]	Lavender Sax	1964	10.00	20.00	40.00
❑ WP-1825 [M]	Lavender Sax	1964	7.50	15.00	30.00

SCOTT, FREDDIE
COLPIX

❑ CP-461 [M]	Freddie Scott Sings and Sings and Sings	1964	15.00	30.00	60.00

-- Gold label

❑ CP-461 [M]	Freddie Scott Sings and Sings and Sings	1965	10.00	20.00	40.00

-- Blue label

❑ SCP-461 [S]	Freddie Scott Sings and Sings and Sings	1964	30.00	60.00	120.00

-- Gold label

❑ SCP-461 [R]	Freddie Scott Sings and Sings and Sings	1965	7.50	1.00	30.00

-- Blue label

COLUMBIA

❑ CL 2258 [M]	Everything I Have Is Yours	1964	5.00	10.00	20.00
❑ CL 2660 [M]	Lonely Man	1967	5.00	10.00	20.00
❑ CS 9058 [S]	Everything I Have Is Yours	1964	6.25	12.50	25.00
❑ CS 9460 [S]	Lonely Man	1967	6.25	12.50	25.00

PROBE

❑ CPLP-4517	I Shall Be Released	1970	6.25	12.50	25.00

SHOUT

❑ SLP-501 [M]	Are You Lonely for Me	1967	5.00	10.00	20.00
❑ SLPS-501 [S]	Are You Lonely for Me	1967	6.25	12.50	25.00

SCOTT, JACK
CAPITOL

❑ ST 2035 [S]	Burning Bridges	1964	37.50	75.00	150.00
❑ T 2035 [M]	Burning Bridges	1964	20.00	40.00	80.00
❑ ST-8-2035	Burning Bridges	196?	50.00	100.00	200.00

-- Capitol Record Club edition

CARLTON

❑ LP-12-107 [M]	Jack Scott	1959	37.50	75.00	150.00
❑ STLP-12-107 [S]	Jack Scott	1959	100.00	200.00	400.00

-- With "Stereo" in felt letters vertically along the left of cover

❑ STLP-12-107 [S]	Jack Scott	1959	75.00	150.00	300.00

-- With "Stereo" in felt letters horizontally along the top of cover

❑ STLP-12-107 [S]	Jack Scott	1959	50.00	100.00	200.00

-- With "Stereo" printed across the top

❑ LP-12-122 [M]	What Am I Living For	1959	30.00	60.00	120.00
❑ STLP-12-122 [S]	What Am I Living For	1959	80.00	160.00	320.00

TOP RANK

❑ RM-319 [M]	I Remember Hank Williams	1960	37.50	75.00	150.00
❑ RM-326 [M]	What in the World's Come Over You	1960	37.50	75.00	150.00
❑ RM-348 [M]	The Spirit Moves Me	1961	37.50	75.00	150.00
❑ SM-319 [S]	I Remember Hank Williams	1960	62.50	125.00	250.00
❑ SM-626 [S]	What in the World's Come Over You	1960	62.50	125.00	250.00
❑ SM-648 [S]	The Spirit Moves Me	1961	62.50	125.00	250.00

SCOTT, JIMMY
SAVOY

❑ MG-12027 [M]	Very Truly Yours	1955	15.00	30.00	60.00
❑ MG-12150 [M]	The Fabulous Little Jimmy Scott	195?	10.00	20.00	40.00
❑ MG-12181 [M]	If You Only Knew	195?	10.00	20.00	40.00

TANGERINE

❑ TRCS-1501 [S]	Falling in Love Is Wonderful	1963	5.00	10.00	20.00

SCOTT, LINDA
CANADIAN AMERICAN

❑ CALP-1005 [M]	Starlight, Starbright	1961	25.00	50.00	100.00
❑ SCALP-1005 [S]	Starlight, Starbright	1961	37.50	75.00	150.00

Number	Title	Yr	VG	VG+	NM
❑ CALP-1007 [M] Great Scott!! Her Greatest Hits		1962	25.00	50.00	100.00
❑ SCALP-1007 [S] Great Scott!! Her Greatest Hits		1962	37.50	75.00	150.00
CONGRESS					
❑ CGL-3001 [M]	Linda	1962	10.00	20.00	40.00
❑ CGS-3001 [S]	Linda	1962	12.50	25.00	50.00
KAPP					
❑ KL-1424 [M]	Hey, Look at Me Now	1965	10.00	20.00	40.00
❑ KS-3424 [S]	Hey, Look at Me Now	1965	12.50	25.00	50.00

SCOTT, LIZABETH
VIK

Number	Title	Yr	VG	VG+	NM
❑ LX-1130 [M]	Lizabeth	1958	15.00	30.00	60.00

SCOTT, PEGGY, AND JO JO BENSON
SSS INTERNATIONAL

Number	Title	Yr	VG	VG+	NM
❑ 1	Soulshake	1968	6.25	12.50	25.00
❑ 2	Lover's Heaven	1969	6.25	12.50	25.00

SCOTT, TOM
ABC IMPULSE!

Number	Title	Yr	VG	VG+	NM
❑ A-9163 [M]	Honeysuckle Breeze	1967	10.00	20.00	40.00
❑ AS-9163 [S]	Honeysuckle Breeze	1967	6.25	12.50	25.00
❑ AS-9171	Rural Still Life	1968	6.25	12.50	25.00
FLYING DUTCHMAN					
❑ 106	Hair	1969	5.00	10.00	20.00
❑ 114	Paint Your Wagon	1970	5.00	10.00	20.00

SCOTT, WALTER
Also see BOB KUBAN AND THE IN-MEN.
MUSICLAND U.S.A.

Number	Title	Yr	VG	VG+	NM
❑ LP-3502 [M]	Great Scott	1967	5.00	10.00	20.00
❑ SLP-3502 [S]	Great Scott	1967	6.25	12.50	25.00
WHITE WHALE					
❑ WWS-7131	Walter Scott	1970	5.00	10.00	20.00

SCOTT-HERON, GIL
FLYING DUTCHMAN

Number	Title	Yr	VG	VG+	NM
❑ BLD1-0613	The Revolution Will Not Be Televised	1974	5.00	10.00	20.00
❑ 10143	Pieces of a Man	1971	5.00	10.00	20.00
❑ 10153	Free Will	1972	5.00	10.00	20.00

SCOTTSVILLE SQUIRREL BARKERS, THE
Chris Hillman, later of THE BYRDS, makes his first appearance on record here.
CROWN

Number	Title	Yr	VG	VG+	NM
❑ CST-346 [S]	Bluegrass Favorites	1963	15.00	30.00	60.00
❑ CLP-5346 [M]	Bluegrass Favorites	1963	12.50	25.00	50.00

SCRAMBLERS, THE
CROWN

Number	Title	Yr	VG	VG+	NM
❑ CST-384 [S]	Cycle Psychos	1964	6.25	12.50	25.00
❑ CLP-5384 [M]	Cycle Psychos	1964	5.00	10.00	20.00
DIPLOMAT					
❑ D-2316 [M]	Motorcycle Scramble	1964	5.00	10.00	20.00
❑ DS-2316 [S]	Motorcycle Scramble	1964	6.25	12.50	25.00
WYNCOTE					
❑ SW-9048 [S]	Little Honda	1964	6.25	12.50	25.00
❑ W-9048 [M]	Little Honda	1964	5.00	10.00	20.00

SCREAMING GYPSY BANDITS
BAR-B-Q

Number	Title	Yr	VG	VG+	NM
❑ 004	The Dancer Inside You	1974	20.00	40.00	80.00
❑ 22185	In the Eye	1973	20.00	40.00	80.00

SCREAMING TREES
Also see MARK LANEGAN.
VELVETONE

Number	Title	Yr	VG	VG+	NM
❑ 86002	Clairvoyance	1986	10.00	20.00	40.00

SEA, JOHNNY
PHILIPS

Number	Title	Yr	VG	VG+	NM
❑ PHM 200-139 [M] World of a Country Boy		1964	5.00	10.00	20.00
❑ PHM 200-194 [M] Live at the Bitter End		1965	5.00	10.00	20.00
❑ PHS 600-139 [S] World of a Country Boy		1964	6.25	12.50	25.00
❑ PHS 600-194 [S] Live at the Bitter End		1965	6.25	12.50	25.00
WARNER BROS.					
❑ WS 1659 [S]	Day for Decision	1966	5.00	10.00	20.00

SEALS AND CROFTS
NAUTILUS

Number	Title	Yr	VG	VG+	NM
❑ NR-10	Summer Breeze	1979	7.50	15.00	30.00
-- Audiophile vinyl					
T-A					
❑ 5001	Seals and Crofts	1969	6.25	12.50	25.00
❑ 5004	Down Home	1970	6.25	12.50	25.00
WARNER BROS.					
❑ BS4 2629 [Q]	Summer Breeze	1974	5.00	10.00	20.00
❑ BS4 2699 [Q]	Diamond Girl	1974	5.00	10.00	20.00
❑ BS4 2761 [Q]	Unborn Child	1974	5.00	10.00	20.00
❑ BS4 2848 [Q]	I'll Play for You	1975	5.00	10.00	20.00

SEALS, DAN
CAPITOL

Number	Title	Yr	VG	VG+	NM
❑ 1P 7999	On Arrival	1990	5.00	10.00	20.00
-- Only available on vinyl from Columbia House					

SEARCH PARTY
CENTURY

Number	Title	Yr	VG	VG+	NM
❑ 32013	Montgomery Chapel	1969	500.00	1,000.	2,000.

SEARCHERS, THE
KAPP

Number	Title	Yr	VG	VG+	NM
❑ KL-1363 [M]	Meet the Searchers	1964	10.00	20.00	40.00
-- With black and blue label					
❑ KL-1363 [M]	Meet the Searchers	1964	6.25	12.50	25.00
-- With black label					
❑ KL-1409 [M]	This Is Us	1964	6.25	12.50	25.00
-- Version 1: No sticker on front cover					
❑ KL-1409 [M]	This Is Us	1964	6.25	12.50	25.00
-- Version 2: With sticker on front cover referring to "Love Potion No. 9"					
❑ KL-1412 [M]	The New Searchers LP	1965	6.25	12.50	25.00
❑ KL-1449 [M]	The Searchers No. 4	1965	6.25	12.50	25.00
❑ KL-1477 [M]	Take Me for What I'm Worth	1966	6.25	12.50	25.00
❑ KS-3363 [S]	Meet the Searchers	1964	12.50	25.00	50.00
-- With black and blue label					
❑ KS-3363 [S]	Meet the Searchers	1964	7.50	15.00	30.00
-- With black label					
❑ KS-3409 [S]	This Is Us	1964	7.50	15.00	30.00
-- Version 1: No sticker on front cover					
❑ KS-3409 [S]	This Is Us	1964	7.50	15.00	30.00
-- Version 2: With sticker on front cover referring to "Love Potion No. 9"					
❑ KS-3412 [S]	The New Searchers LP	1965	7.50	15.00	30.00
❑ KS-3419 [S]	The Searchers No. 4	1965	7.50	15.00	30.00
❑ KS-3477 [S]	Take Me for What I'm Worth	1966	7.50	15.00	30.00
MERCURY					
❑ MG-20914 [M] Hear! Hear!		1964	12.50	25.00	50.00
-- Version 1: With only the title on the front cover					
❑ MG-20914 [M] Hear! Hear!		1964	7.50	15.00	30.00
-- Version 3: With "Live from the Star Club" imprinted on cover					
❑ MG-20914 [M] Hear! Hear!		1964	10.00	20.00	40.00
-- Version 2: With sticker "Live from the Star Club" on cover					
❑ MG-20914 [DJ] Hear! Hear!		1964	12.50	25.00	50.00
-- White label promo					
❑ MG-20994 [M] The Searchers Meet the Rattles		1965	18.75	37.50	75.00
❑ SR-60914 [S] Hear! Hear!		1964	10.00	20.00	40.00
-- Version 1: With only the title on the front cover					
❑ SR-60914 [S] Hear! Hear!		1964	7.50	15.00	30.00
-- Version 2: With sticker "Live from the Star Club" on cover					
❑ SR-60914 [S] Hear! Hear!		1964	6.25	12.50	25.00
-- Version 3: With "Live from the Star Club" imprinted on cover					
❑ SR-60994 [S] The Searchers Meet the Rattles		1965	12.50	25.00	50.00

SEBASTIAN, JOHN
Also see THE LOVIN' SPOONFUL.
REPRISE

Number	Title	Yr	VG	VG+	NM
❑ RS 6379	John B. Sebastian	1969	5.00	10.00	20.00
-- Same album as MGM 4654, but a different mix					

SECOND TIME, THE
TOWER

Number	Title	Yr	VG	VG+	NM
❑ ST 5146	Listen to the Music	1968	5.00	10.00	20.00

SECRET OYSTER
PETERS INT'L.

Number	Title	Yr	VG	VG+	NM
❑ 9003	Furtive Pearl	1973	7.50	15.00	30.00
❑ 9009	Sea Son	1974	6.25	12.50	25.00

SEDAKA, NEIL
RCA VICTOR

Number	Title	Yr	VG	VG+	NM
❑ LPM-2065 [M]	Neil Sedaka	1959	15.00	30.00	60.00
❑ LSP-2065 [S]	Neil Sedaka	1959	25.00	50.00	100.00

Number	Title	Yr	VG	VG+	NM
❑ LPM-2317 [M]	Circulate	1960	12.50	25.00	50.00
❑ LSP-2317 [S]	Circulate	1960	15.00	30.00	60.00
❑ LPM-2421 [M]	"Little Devil" and His Other Hits	1961	12.50	25.00	50.00
❑ LSP-2421 [S]	"Little Devil" and His Other Hits	1961	15.00	30.00	60.00
❑ LPM-2627 [M]	Neil Sedaka Sings His Greatest Hits	1962	10.00	20.00	40.00
❑ LSP-2627 [S]	Neil Sedaka Sings His Greatest Hits	1962	12.50	25.00	50.00

SEDAKA, NEIL, AND THE TOKENS / THE COINS
Also see NEIL SEDAKA; THE TOKENS.
CROWN

Number	Title	Yr	VG	VG+	NM
❑ CLP-5366 [M]	Neil Sedaka and the Tokens and the Coins	1963	7.50	15.00	30.00
❑ CST-366 [R]	Neil Sedaka and the Tokens and the Coins	1963	5.00	10.00	20.00

SEEDS, THE
Also see SKY SAXON.
GNP CRESCENDO

Number	Title	Yr	VG	VG+	NM
❑ GNP-2023 [M]	The Seeds	1966	15.00	30.00	60.00
❑ GNPS-2023 [S]	The Seeds	1966	10.00	20.00	40.00
❑ GNP-2033 [M]	A Web of Sound	1967	15.00	30.00	60.00
❑ GNPS-2033 [S]	A Web of Sound	1967	10.00	20.00	40.00
❑ GNP-2038 [M]	Future	1967	10.00	20.00	40.00
-- Deduct 25% if two inserts are missing					
❑ GNPS-2038 [S]	Future	1967	7.50	15.00	30.00
-- Deduct 25% if two inserts are missing					
❑ GNPS-2040	Full Spoon of Seedy Blues	1968	6.25	12.50	25.00
❑ GNPS-2043	Raw and Alive	1968	6.25	12.50	25.00
❑ ST-91224	A Web of Sound	1968	7.50	15.00	30.00
-- Capitol Record Club edition					

SEEGER, PEGGY
FOLK-LYRIC

Number	Title	Yr	VG	VG+	NM
❑ FL 114 [M]	American Folksongs for Banjo	196?	7.50	15.00	30.00
❑ FL 120 [M]	Popular Ballads	196?	7.50	15.00	30.00

FOLKLORE

❑ FRLP-14016 [M]	The Best of Peggy Seeger	196?	6.25	12.50	25.00

FOLKWAYS

❑ FP-49 [10]	Folk Songs of Courting and Complaint	1955	25.00	50.00	100.00
❑ FP-2049 [10]	Folk Songs of Courting and Complaint	195?	20.00	40.00	80.00
❑ FC-7551 [10]	Animal Folksongs for Children	1957	25.00	50.00	100.00

PRESTIGE

❑ PRLP-13005 [M]	The Best of Peggy Seeger	1961	7.50	15.00	30.00
❑ PRLP-13058 [M]	A Song for You and Me	1962	7.50	15.00	30.00

RIVERSIDE

❑ RLP-12-655 [M]	Folksongs and Ballads	1958	10.00	20.00	40.00

TOPIC

❑ 10T-9 [10]	Peggy Seeger	1956	25.00	50.00	100.00

SEEGER, PEGGY, BARBARA AND PENNY
FOLKWAYS

Number	Title	Yr	VG	VG+	NM
❑ FC-7553 [10]	American Folk Songs for Christmas	195?	12.50	25.00	50.00

SCHOLASTIC

❑ SC 7553 [M]	American Folk Songs for Christmas	1966	5.00	10.00	20.00
-- Reissue of Folkways material					

SEEGER, PETE
CAPITOL

Number	Title	Yr	VG	VG+	NM
❑ T 2718 [M]	Freight Train	1967	5.00	10.00	20.00
❑ W 2172 [M]	Folk Songs	1964	5.00	10.00	20.00

COLUMBIA

❑ CL 1668 [M]	Pete Seeger Story Songs	1961	6.25	12.50	25.00
❑ CL 1916 [M]	The Bitter and the Sweet	1962	6.25	12.50	25.00
❑ CL 1947 [M]	Children's Concert at Town Hall	1963	6.25	12.50	25.00
❑ CL 2616 [M]	Pete Seeger's Greatest Hits	1967	5.00	10.00	20.00
❑ CL 2705 [M]	Waist Deep in the Big Muddy	1967	5.00	10.00	20.00
❑ CS 8468 [S]	Pete Seeger Story Songs	1961	7.50	15.00	30.00
❑ CS 8716 [S]	The Bitter and the Sweet	1962	7.50	15.00	30.00
❑ CS 8747 [S]	Children's Concert at Town Hall	1963	7.50	15.00	30.00
❑ CS 8901 [S]	We Shall Overcome	1963	5.00	10.00	20.00
❑ CS 9057 [S]	I Can See a New Day	1965	5.00	10.00	20.00
❑ CS 9134 [S]	Strangers and Cousins	1964	5.00	10.00	20.00
❑ CS 9232 [S]	God Bless the Grass	1966	5.00	10.00	20.00
❑ CS 9303 [S]	Dangerous Songs?	1966	5.00	10.00	20.00

FOLKWAYS

❑ FP-3 [10]	Darling Corey	1950	25.00	50.00	100.00
❑ FP-10 [10]	Lonesome Valley	195?	25.00	50.00	100.00
❑ FP-43 [10]	A Pete Seeger Sampler	195?	25.00	50.00	100.00
❑ FP-45 [10]	Goofing Off Suite	195?	25.00	50.00	100.00
❑ FP-701 [10]	American Folk Songs for Children	195?	25.00	50.00	100.00
❑ FP-710 [10]	Birds, Beasts, Bugs and Little Fishes	1954	25.00	50.00	100.00

Number	Title	Yr	VG	VG+	NM
❑ FP-911 [10]	Folk Songs of Four Continents	195?	25.00	50.00	100.00
❑ FA-2003 [10]	Darling Corey	1950	20.00	40.00	80.00
❑ FA-2010 [10]	Lonesome Valley	195?	20.00	40.00	80.00
❑ FA-2043 [10]	A Pete Seeger Sampler	1954	20.00	40.00	80.00
❑ FA-2045 [10]	Goofing Off Suite	1954	20.00	40.00	80.00
❑ FA-2175 [10]	Frontier Ballads, Volume 1	1954	20.00	40.00	80.00
❑ FA-2176 [10]	Frontier Ballads, Volume 2	1954	20.00	40.00	80.00
❑ FA-2311 [M]	Traditional Christmas Carols	1956	7.50	15.00	30.00
❑ FA-2319 [M]	American Ballads	1957	7.50	15.00	30.00
❑ FA-2320 [M]	American Favorite Ballads, Vol. 1	1957	7.50	15.00	30.00
❑ FA-2321 [M]	American Favorite Ballads, Vol. 2	1957	7.50	15.00	30.00
❑ FA-2322 [M]	American Favorite Ballads, Vol. 3	1957	7.50	15.00	30.00
❑ FA-2323 [M]	American Favorite Ballads, Vol. 4	1961	5.00	10.00	20.00
❑ FA-2412 [M]	Pete Seeger and Sonny Terry	1958	7.50	15.00	30.00
❑ FA-2439 [M]	Nonesuch	196?	5.00	10.00	20.00
❑ FA-2445 [M]	American Favorite Ballads, Vol. 5: Tunes and Songs As Sung by Pete Seeger	1962	5.00	10.00	20.00
❑ FA-2450 [M]	Highlights of Pete Seeger at the Village Gate with Memphis Slim and Willie Dixon	1960	7.50	15.00	30.00
❑ FA-2451 [M]	Pete Seeger at the Village Gate -- Vol. 2	1960	7.50	15.00	30.00
❑ FA-2452 [M]	With Voices Together We Sing	1956	6.25	12.50	25.00
❑ FA-2453 [M]	Love Songs for Friends and Foes	1956	6.25	12.50	25.00
❑ FA-2454 [M]	Rainbow Quest	1960	6.25	12.50	25.00
❑ FA-2455 [M]	Sing Out with Pete!	1961	5.00	10.00	20.00
❑ FA-2456 [M]	Broadsides	1964	5.00	10.00	20.00
❑ FA-2501 [M]	Gazette, Vol. 1	1958	6.25	12.50	25.00
❑ FA-2502 [M]	Gazette, Vol. 2	1962	5.00	10.00	20.00
❑ FN-2511 [M]	Hootenanny Tonight!	195?	6.25	12.50	25.00
❑ FN-2513 [M]	Sing Out! Hootenanny	1963	5.00	10.00	20.00
❑ FS-3851 [M]	Indian Summer	1960	6.25	12.50	25.00
-- With Michael Seeger					
❑ 5003 [(2)]	Frontier Ballads	1954	25.00	50.00	100.00
❑ FH-5210 [M]	Champlain Valley Songs	1960	6.25	12.50	25.00
❑ FH-5233 [M]	Songs of Struggle and Protest 1930-50	1959	6.25	12.50	25.00
❑ FH-5251 [M]	American Industrial Ballads	1956	7.50	15.00	30.00
❑ FH-5302 [M]	Broadside Ballads, Vol. 2	1963	5.00	10.00	20.00
❑ FH-5436 [M]	Songs of the Spanish Civil War, Vol. 1	1961	5.00	10.00	20.00
❑ FH-5485 [M]	Ballads of Sacco and Vanzetti	1963	5.00	10.00	20.00
❑ FH-5595 [M]	WNEW's Story of Selma	1965	5.00	10.00	20.00
❑ FH-5702 [(2)]	Pete Seeger Sings and Answers Questions	1968	6.25	12.50	25.00
❑ FW-6843 [10]	German Folk Songs	1954	20.00	40.00	80.00
❑ FW-6911 [10]	Folk Songs of Four Continents	1955	20.00	40.00	80.00
❑ FW-6912 [10]	Bantu Choral Folk Songs	1955	20.00	40.00	80.00
❑ FC-7020 [10]	Songs to Grow On -- Vol. 2	1951	20.00	40.00	80.00
❑ FC-7027 [10]	Songs to Grow On -- Vol. 3	1951	20.00	40.00	80.00
❑ FC-7601 [10]	American Folk Songs for Children	1953	20.00	40.00	80.00
❑ FC-7610 [10]	Birds, Beasts, Bugs and Little Fishes	1954	20.00	40.00	80.00
❑ FC-7674 [M]	American Game and Activity Songs for Children	1962	5.00	10.00	20.00
❑ FI-8303 [M]	How to Play the Five String Banjo	195?	6.25	12.50	25.00
❑ FI-8354 [M]	Folksinger's Guitar Guide Vol. 1: An Instruction Record	1955	7.50	15.00	30.00
❑ FQ-8354 [M]	The Folksinger's Guitar Guide	1955	6.25	12.50	25.00
❑ FI-8371 [M]	12-String Guitar As Played by Leadbelly	1962	5.00	10.00	20.00

PHILIPS

❑ PHM 2-300 [(2) M]	The Story of the Nativity	1963	5.00	10.00	20.00
❑ PHS 2-300 [(2) S]	The Story of the Nativity	1963	6.25	12.50	25.00

STINSON

❑ SLP-52 [10]	Lincoln Brigade	1953	25.00	50.00	100.00
❑ SLP-57 [10]	A Pete Seeger Concert	1953	25.00	50.00	100.00
❑ SLP-90 [M]	Pete	1963	6.25	12.50	25.00

VERVE FOLKWAYS

❑ FV-9008 [M]	Pete Seeger and Big Bill Broonzy in Concert	1965	5.00	10.00	20.00
❑ FVS-9008 [S]	Pete Seeger and Big Bill Broonzy in Concert	1965	6.25	12.50	25.00
❑ FV-9009 [M]	Pete Seeger On Campus	1965	5.00	10.00	20.00
❑ FVS-9009 [S]	Pete Seeger On Campus	1965	6.25	12.50	25.00
❑ FV-9013 [M]	Folk Music Live at the Village Gate	1965	5.00	10.00	20.00
❑ FVS-9013 [S]	Folk Music Live at the Village Gate	1965	6.25	12.50	25.00
❑ FV-9020 [M]	Little Boxes and Other Broadsides	1965	5.00	10.00	20.00
❑ FVS-9020 [S]	Little Boxes and Other Broadsides	1965	6.25	12.50	25.00

SEEGER, PETE, PENNY AND MICHAEL
PRESTIGE

❑ PRLP-7375 [(2) M]	Pete, Penny and Michael Seeger	1965	5.00	10.00	20.00
❑ PRST-7375 [(2) S]	Pete, Penny and Michael Seeger	1965	6.25	12.50	25.00

Number	Title	Yr	VG	VG+	NM

SEELY, JEANNIE
MONUMENT
☐ MLP-8073 [M]	Thanks, Hank!	1967	6.25	12.50	25.00
☐ SLP-18057 [S]	The Seely Style	1966	5.00	10.00	20.00
☐ SLP-18073 [S]	Thanks, Hank!	1967	5.00	10.00	20.00
☐ SLP-18091	I'll Love You More	1968	5.00	10.00	20.00
☐ SLP-18104	Little Things	1968	5.00	10.00	20.00

SEGAL, GEORGE
PHILIPS
| ☐ PHM 200-242 [M] | The Yama-Yama Man | 1967 | 5.00 | 10.00 | 20.00 |
| ☐ PHS 600-242 [S] | The Yama-Yama Man | 1967 | 5.00 | 10.00 | 20.00 |

SEGALL, RICKY
BELL
| ☐ 1138 | Ricky Segall and the Segalls | 1973 | 5.00 | 10.00 | 20.00 |

SEGER, BOB
CAPITOL
☐ (no #) [PD]	Night Moves	1977	10.00	20.00	40.00
-- Promo-only picture disc					
☐ ST-172	Ramblin' Gamblin' Man	1969	7.50	15.00	30.00
-- Black label with colorband					
☐ ST-236	Noah	1969	20.00	40.00	80.00
☐ SKAO-499	Mongrel	1970	6.25	12.50	25.00
☐ ST-731	Brand New Morning	1971	25.00	50.00	100.00
☐ SPRO-8433	Consensus Cuts Edited for Airplay from "Live Bullet"	1976	6.25	12.50	25.00
☐ SEAX-11904 [PD]	Stranger in Town	1978	6.25	12.50	25.00
MOBILE FIDELITY
☐ 1-034	Night Moves	1980	10.00	20.00	40.00
-- Audiophile vinyl					
☐ 1-127	Against the Wind	1983	10.00	20.00	40.00
-- Audiophile vinyl					
PALLADIUM
| ☐ P-1006 | Smokin' O.P.'s | 1972 | 6.25 | 12.50 | 25.00 |
REPRISE
| ☐ MS 2126 | Back in '72 | 1973 | 15.00 | 30.00 | 60.00 |
| ☐ MS 2184 | Seven | 1974 | 5.00 | 10.00 | 20.00 |

SELAH JUBILEE QUARTET, THE
REMINGTON
| ☐ 1023 [10] | Spirituals | 1951 | 50.00 | 100.00 | 200.00 |

SELENA
CAPITOL/EMI LATIN
☐ H1-42144	Selena Y Los Diños	1989	15.00	30.00	60.00
☐ H1-42299	16 Super Exitos Originales	1990	15.00	30.00	60.00
☐ H1-42359	Ven Conmingo	1990	15.00	30.00	60.00
CBS DISCOS
| ☐ RRL 80323 | Personal Best | 1990 | 15.00 | 30.00 | 60.00 |
GP
☐ LP-1002	Alpha	1986	125.00	250.00	500.00
☐ LP-1005	Menequito De Trapo	1986	75.00	150.00	300.00
☐ LP-1009	And the Winner Is...	1987	50.00	100.00	200.00
RP
| ☐ LP-8801 | Preciosa | 1988 | 37.50 | 75.00 | 150.00 |
| ☐ LP-8803 | Dulce Amor | 1988 | 37.50 | 75.00 | 150.00 |

SELLERS, BROTHER JOHN
VANGUARD
| ☐ VRS-8005 [10] | Brother John Sellers: Folk Songs and Blues | 1954 | 25.00 | 50.00 | 100.00 |
| ☐ VRS-9036 [M] | Blues and Folk Songs | 1957 | 20.00 | 40.00 | 80.00 |

SELLERS, PETER
ACAPELLA
| ☐ 1 | Fool Brittania | 1963 | 6.25 | 12.50 | 25.00 |
| -- With Joan Collins and Anthony Newley | | | | | |
ANGEL
| ☐ 35884 [M] | The Best of Sellers | 1960 | 7.50 | 15.00 | 30.00 |
| ☐ S 35884 [S] | The Best of Sellers | 1960 | 10.00 | 20.00 | 40.00 |
EMI AMERICA
| ☐ SN-16396 | Songs for Swingin' Sellers | 1986 | 5.00 | 10.00 | 20.00 |
| -- First American issue of 1959 U.K. LP | | | | | |

SELLERS, PETER, AND SOPHIA LOREN
ANGEL
| ☐ 35910 [M] | Peter Sellers and Sophia Loren | 1961 | 7.50 | 15.00 | 30.00 |
| ☐ S 35910 [S] | Peter Sellers and Sophia Loren | 1961 | 10.00 | 20.00 | 40.00 |

SENATOR BOBBY
PARKWAY
| ☐ P 7057 [M] | Boston Soul with the Hardly-Worthit Players | 1967 | 5.00 | 10.00 | 20.00 |
| ☐ SP 7057 [S] | Boston Soul with the Hardly-Worthit Players | 1967 | 5.00 | 10.00 | 20.00 |

SENOFSKY, BERL
RCA VICTOR RED SEAL
| ☐ LSC-2488 [S] | Debussy: Violin Sonata; Faure: Violin Sonata No. 1 in A | 1961 | 7.50 | 15.00 | 30.00 |
| -- With Gary Graffman, piano; original with "shaded dog" label | | | | | |

SENSATIONS, THE
ARGO
| ☐ LP-4022 [M] | Let Me In/Music, Music, Music | 1963 | 125.00 | 250.00 | 500.00 |

SENTINALS, THE
DEL-FI
☐ DFLP-1232 [M]	Big Surf!	1963	25.00	50.00	100.00
☐ DFST-1232 [S]	Big Surf!	1963	37.50	75.00	150.00
☐ DFLP-1241 [M]	Surfer Girl	1963	17.50	35.00	70.00
☐ DFST-1241 [S]	Surfer Girl	1963	25.00	50.00	100.00
SUTTON
| ☐ SSU-338 [S] | Vegas Go-Go | 1964 | 12.50 | 25.00 | 50.00 |
| ☐ SU-338 [M] | Vegas Go-Go | 1964 | 10.00 | 20.00 | 40.00 |

SERENDIPITY SINGERS, THE
PHILIPS
☐ PHS 600-115 [S]	The Serendipity Singers	1964	5.00	10.00	20.00
☐ PHS 600-134 [S]	The Many Sides of the Serendipity Singers	1964	5.00	10.00	20.00
☐ PHS 600-151[S]	Take Your Shoes Off with the Serendipity Singers	1964	5.00	10.00	20.00
☐ PHS 600-180 [S]	We Belong Together	1965	5.00	10.00	20.00
☐ PHS 600-190 [S]	Love, Lies and Flying Festoons	1965	5.00	10.00	20.00

SERPENT POWER
VANGUARD
| ☐ VRS-9252 [M] | Serpent Power | 1967 | 30.00 | 60.00 | 120.00 |
| ☐ VSD-79252 [S] | Serpent Power | 1967 | 15.00 | 30.00 | 60.00 |

SETTLE, MIKE
REPRISE
| ☐ R-6149 [M] | The Mike Settle Shindig | 1965 | 5.00 | 10.00 | 20.00 |
| ☐ RS-6149 [S] | The Mike Settle Shindig | 1965 | 6.25 | 12.50 | 25.00 |

SEVEN BLENDS, THE
ROULETTE
| ☐ R-25172 [M] | Twistin' at the Miami Beach Peppermint Lounge | 1962 | 5.00 | 10.00 | 20.00 |
| ☐ SR-25172 [S] | Twistin' at the Miami Beach Peppermint Lounge | 1962 | 6.25 | 12.50 | 25.00 |

SEVENTH SONS, THE
ESP-DISK'
| ☐ 1078 | The Seventh Sons | 1967 | 7.50 | 15.00 | 30.00 |

SEVENTH WAVE, THE
JANUS
| ☐ 7008 | Things to Come | 1974 | 5.00 | 10.00 | 20.00 |
| ☐ 7021 | Psi-Fi | 1975 | 5.00 | 10.00 | 20.00 |

SEVERINSON, DOC
COMMAND
☐ 819 SD [S]	Tempestuous Trumpet	1961	5.00	10.00	20.00
☐ 837 SD [S]	The Big Band's Back in Town	1962	5.00	10.00	20.00
☐ 859 SD [S]	Torch Songs for Trumpet	1963	5.00	10.00	20.00
☐ 883 SD [S]	High, Wide and Wonderful	1965	5.00	10.00	20.00

SEVILLE, DAVID
Also see THE CHIPMUNKS.
LIBERTY
| ☐ LRP-3073 [M] | The Music of David Seville | 1957 | 20.00 | 40.00 | 80.00 |
| ☐ LRP-3092 [M] | The Witch Doctor | 1958 | 25.00 | 50.00 | 100.00 |

SEWARD, ALEC
BLUESVILLE
☐ BVLP-1076 [M]	Creepin' Blues	1963	20.00	40.00	80.00
-- Blue label, silver print					
☐ BVLP-1076 [M]	Creepin' Blues	1964	6.25	12.50	25.00
-- Blue label, trident logo at right					

Number	Title	Yr	VG	VG+	NM

SEX CLARK FIVE
RECORDS TO RUSSIA
❏ RTR-LP 408	Strum & Drum!	1986	30.00	60.00	120.00

-- *Test pressing with 24 tracks*

❏ RTR-LP 408	Strum & Drum!	1987	5.00	10.00	20.00

-- *First pressing: 20 tracks, photos are halftones*

SEX PISTOLS
WARNER BROS.
❏ BSK 3147	Never Mind the Bollocks Here's the Sex Pistols	1978	7.50	15.00	30.00

-- *With sticker "Contains Sub-Mission"*

❏ BSK 3147	Never Mind the Bollocks Here's the Sex Pistols	1978	6.25	12.50	25.00

-- *Any other version with custom label*

SHA NA NA
KAMA SUTRA
❏ KSBS-2073 [(2)]	The Golden Age of Rock 'n' Roll	1973	5.00	10.00	20.00

SHACKLEFORDS, THE
CAPITOL
❏ ST 2450 [S]	The Shacklefords	1966	6.25	12.50	25.00
❏ T 2450 [M]	The Shacklefords	1966	5.00	10.00	20.00
MERCURY
❏ MG-20806 [M]	Until You've Heard the Shacklefords	1963	5.00	10.00	20.00
❏ SR-60806 [S]	Until You've Heard the Shacklefords	1963	6.25	12.50	25.00

SHADES OF BLUE
IMPACT
❏ IM-101 [M]	Happiness Is the Shades of Blue	1966	12.50	25.00	50.00
❏ IM-1001 [S]	Happiness Is the Shades of Blue	1966	15.00	30.00	60.00

SHADES OF JOY
FONTANA
❏ SRF-67592	Shades of Joy	1969	5.00	10.00	20.00

SHADOWS OF KNIGHT, THE
DUNWICH
❏ 666 [M]	Gloria	1966	12.50	25.00	50.00
❏ S-666 [S]	Gloria	1966	20.00	40.00	80.00
❏ 667 [M]	Back Door Men	1966	12.50	25.00	50.00
❏ S-667 [S]	Back Door Men	1966	20.00	40.00	80.00
SUPER K
❏ SKS-6002	The Shadows of Knight	1969	12.50	25.00	50.00

SHADOWS, THE
Also see CLIFF RICHARD.
ATLANTIC
❏ 8084 [M]	Out of the Shadows	1962	37.50	75.00	150.00

-- *Canada-only release?*

❏ 8089 [M]	Surfing with the Shadows	1963	37.50	75.00	150.00
❏ SD 8089 [S]	Surfing with the Shadows	1963	75.00	150.00	300.00
❏ 8097 [M]	The Shadows Know	1964	25.00	50.00	100.00
❏ SD 8097 [S]	The Shadows Know	1964	50.00	100.00	200.00

SHADRACK
IGL
❏ 132	Chameleon	1971	75.00	150.00	300.00

SHAFRAN, DANIEL
RCA VICTOR RED SEAL
❏ LSC-2553 [S]	Shostakovich: Cello Sonata; Schubert: Arpeggione Sonata	1961	15.00	30.00	60.00

-- *Original with "shaded dog" label*

SHAGGS, THE
The group on MCM is not the same as the others.
MCM
❏ 6311	Wink	1967	375.00	750.00	1,500.
ROUNDER
❏ 3032	Philosophy of the World	1980	6.25	12.50	25.00
❏ 3056	Shaggs' Own Thing	1982	6.25	12.50	25.00
THIRD WORLD
❏ 3001	Philosophy of the World	1969	500.00	1,000.	2,000.

SHAKERS, THE
AUDIO FIDELITY
❏ AFLP-2155 [M]	The Shakers Break It All	1966	10.00	20.00	40.00
❏ AFSD-6155 [S]	The Shakers Break It All	1966	12.50	25.00	50.00

SHAKEY JAKE
BLUESVILLE
❏ BVLP-1008 [M]	Good Times	1960	30.00	60.00	120.00

-- *Blue label, silver print*

❏ BVLP-1008 [M]	Good Times	1964	7.50	15.00	30.00

-- *Blue label, trident logo at right*

❏ BVLP-1027 [M]	Mouth Harp Blues	1961	30.00	60.00	120.00

-- *Blue label, silver print*

❏ BVLP-1027 [M]	Mouth Harp Blues	1964	7.50	15.00	30.00

-- *Blue label, trident logo at right*

WORLD PACIFIC
❏ WPS-21886	Blues Makers	196?	7.50	15.00	30.00

SHAKEY VICK
JANUS
❏ JLS-3000	Little Woman, You're So Sweet	1970	5.00	10.00	20.00

SHANGRI-LAS, THE
MERCURY
❏ MG-21099 [M]	The Shangri-Las' Golden Hits	1966	10.00	20.00	40.00
❏ SR-61099 [S]	The Shangri-Las' Golden Hits	1966	12.50	25.00	50.00
POST
❏ 4000	The Shangri-Las Sing	196?	5.00	10.00	20.00
RED BIRD
❏ 20-101 [M]	Leader of the Pack	1965	37.50	75.00	150.00
❏ 20-104 [M]	Shangri-Las '65	1965	37.50	75.00	150.00
❏ 20-104 [M]	I Can Never Go Home Anymore	1966	25.00	50.00	100.00

-- *Retitled version with title song added and "Sophisticated Boom Boom" dropped*

SHANK, BUD
KIMBERLY
❏ 2025 [M]	The Talents of Bud Shank	1963	5.00	10.00	20.00
❏ 11025 [S]	The Talents of Bud Shank	1963	6.25	12.50	25.00
NOCTURNE
❏ NLP-2 [10]	Compositions of Shorty Rogers	1953	50.00	100.00	200.00
PACIFIC JAZZ
❏ PJ-4 [M]	Bud Shank Plays Tenor	1960	6.25	12.50	25.00
❏ ST-4 [S]	Bud Shank Plays Tenor	1960	7.50	15.00	30.00
❏ PJLP-14 [10]	Bud Shank with Three Trombones	1954	30.00	60.00	120.00
❏ PJLP-20 [10]	Bud Shank and Bob Brookmeyer	1954	30.00	60.00	120.00
❏ PJ-21 [M]	New Groove	1961	6.25	12.50	25.00
❏ ST-21 [S]	New Groove	1961	7.50	15.00	30.00
❏ PJ-58 [M]	Bossa Nova Jazz Samba	1962	6.25	12.50	25.00
❏ ST-58 [S]	Bossa Nova Jazz Samba	1962	7.50	15.00	30.00
❏ PJ-64 [M]	Brassamba Bossa Nova	1963	5.00	10.00	20.00
❏ ST-64 [S]	Brassamba Bossa Nova	1963	6.25	12.50	25.00
❏ PJ-89 [M]	Bud Shank and His Brazilian Friends	1965	5.00	10.00	20.00
❏ ST-89 [S]	Bud Shank and His Brazilian Friends	1965	6.25	12.50	25.00
❏ PJM-411 [M]	The Swing's to TV	1957	15.00	30.00	60.00
❏ WPM-411 [M]	The Swing's to TV	1958	10.00	20.00	40.00
❏ PJ-1205 [M]	Bud Shank/Shorty Rogers	1955	20.00	40.00	80.00
❏ PJ-1213 [M]	Strings and Trombones	1956	20.00	40.00	80.00
❏ PJ-1215 [M]	The Bud Shank Quartet	1956	20.00	40.00	80.00
❏ PJ-1219 [M]	Jazz at Cal-Tech	1956	15.00	30.00	60.00
❏ PJ-1226 [M]	Flute 'n Oboe	1957	15.00	30.00	60.00
❏ PJ-1230 [M]	The Bud Shank Quartet	1957	15.00	30.00	60.00
❏ ST-20110 [S]	Bud Shank and the Sax Section	1966	5.00	10.00	20.00
WORLD PACIFIC
❏ ST-1002 [S]	The Swing's to TV	1959	7.50	15.00	30.00
❏ ST-1018 [S]	Holiday in Brazil	1959	7.50	15.00	30.00
❏ WP-1205 [M]	Bud Shank/Shorty Rogers	1958	10.00	20.00	40.00
❏ WP-1215 [M]	The Bud Shank Quartet	1958	10.00	20.00	40.00
❏ WP-1219 [M]	Jazz at Cal-Tech	1958	10.00	20.00	40.00
❏ WP-1226 [M]	Flute 'n Oboe	1958	10.00	20.00	40.00
❏ WP-1230 [M]	The Bud Shank Quartet	1958	10.00	20.00	40.00
❏ WP-1251 [M]	I'll Take Romance	1958	10.00	20.00	40.00
❏ WP-1259 [M]	Holiday in Brazil	1959	10.00	20.00	40.00
❏ ST-1281 [S]	Latin Contrasts	1959	7.50	15.00	30.00
❏ WP-1281 [M]	Latin Contrasts	1959	10.00	20.00	40.00
❏ ST-1286 [S]	Flute 'n Alto	1960	10.00	20.00	40.00
❏ WP-1286 [M]	Flute 'n Alto	1960	7.50	15.00	30.00
❏ ST-1299 [S]	Koto 'n Flute	1960	10.00	20.00	40.00
❏ WP-1299 [M]	Koto 'n Flute	1960	7.50	15.00	30.00
❏ WP-1416 [M]	Improvisations	1961	6.25	12.50	25.00
❏ WP-1424 [M]	Koto 'n Flute	1962	6.25	12.50	25.00
❏ WP-1853 [M]	Girl in Love	1967	5.00	10.00	20.00
❏ WP-1855 [M]	Brazil! Brazil! Brazil!	1967	5.00	10.00	20.00
❏ WP-1864 [M]	Bud Shank Plays Music from Today's Movies	1967	5.00	10.00	20.00
❏ ST-21819 [S]	Folk 'n Flute	1965	5.00	10.00	20.00
❏ ST-21827 [S]	Flute, Oboe and Strings	1965	5.00	10.00	20.00
❏ ST-21840 [S]	Michelle	1966	5.00	10.00	20.00
❏ ST-21845 [S]	California Dreaming	1966	5.00	10.00	20.00

Number	Title	Yr	VG	VG+	NM
SHANKAR, ANANDA					
REPRISE					
❏ RS-6398	Ananda Shankar	1970	5.00	10.00	20.00
SHANKAR, L.					
ZAPPA					
❏ SRZ-1-1602	Touch Me There	1979	5.00	10.00	20.00
SHANKAR, RAVI					
ANGEL					
❏ 35468 [M]	Music of India	196?	6.25	12.50	25.00
❏ 36418 [M]	West Meets East	1967	6.25	12.50	25.00
-- With Yahudi Menuhin					
❏ S 36418 [S]	West Meets East	1967	5.00	10.00	20.00
-- With Yahudi Menuhin					
APPLE					
❏ SVBB-3396 [(2)]	Ravi Shankar In Concert	1973	10.00	20.00	40.00
❏ SWAO-3384	Raga	1971	6.25	12.50	25.00
BLUESVILLE					
❏ BVLP-1078 [M]	The Master Musician of India	1964	6.25	12.50	25.00
CAPITOL					
❏ T 2720 [M]	Three Ragas	1967	5.00	10.00	20.00
❏ ST 10482 [S]	Two Raga Moods	196?	6.25	12.50	25.00
❏ T 10482 [M]	Two Raga Moods	196?	5.00	10.00	20.00
❏ ST 10497 [S]	Exotic Sitar and Sarod	196?	6.25	12.50	25.00
❏ T 10497 [M]	Exotic Sitar and Sarod	196?	5.00	10.00	20.00
COLUMBIA					
❏ WL 119 [M]	The Sounds of India	196?	6.25	12.50	25.00
❏ CL 2760 [M]	The Genius of Ravi Shankar	1967	5.00	10.00	20.00
❏ CS 9296 [S]	Sounds of India	1966	5.00	10.00	20.00
WORLD PACIFIC					
❏ WP-1442 [M]	Ravi Shankar at the Monterey International Pop Festival	1967	5.00	10.00	20.00
❏ ST-21421 [S]	Ravi Shankar In Concert	1965	5.00	10.00	20.00
❏ ST-21422 [S]	India's Master Musician	1965	5.00	10.00	20.00
❏ ST-21430 [S]	Ravi Shankar In London	1966	5.00	10.00	20.00
❏ ST-21431 [S]	Ragas and Talas	1966	5.00	10.00	20.00
❏ ST-21432 [S]	Portrait of Genius	1966	5.00	10.00	20.00
❏ ST-21434 [S]	Sound of the Sitar	1967	5.00	10.00	20.00
❏ ST-21438 [S]	Three Ragas	1967	5.00	10.00	20.00
❏ ST-21441 [S]	Ravi Shankar in New York	1967	5.00	10.00	20.00
❏ ST-21442 [S]	Ravi Shankar at the Monterey International Pop Festival	1967	5.00	10.00	20.00
❏ ST-21449	Ravi Shankar in San Francisco	1968	5.00	10.00	20.00
❏ WPS-26201 [(2)]	His Festival from India	1968	5.00	10.00	20.00
SHANNON, DEL					
AMY					
❏ 8003 [M]	Handy Man	1964	12.50	25.00	50.00
❏ S-8003 [S]	Handy Man	1964	20.00	40.00	80.00
❏ 8004 [M]	Del Shannon Sings Hank Williams	1965	12.50	25.00	50.00
❏ S-8004 [S]	Del Shannon Sings Hank Williams	1965	20.00	40.00	80.00
❏ 8006 [M]	1,661 Seconds with Del Shannon	1965	12.50	25.00	50.00
❏ S-8006 [S]	1,661 Seconds with Del Shannon	1965	20.00	40.00	80.00
BIG TOP					
❏ 12-1303 [M]	Runaway	1961	75.00	150.00	300.00
❏ 12-1303 [S]	Runaway	1961	400.00	800.00	1,600.
❏ 12-1308 [B]	Little Town Flirt	1963	250.00	500.00	1,000.
-- One side is mono, one side is stereo; should be played to identify					
❏ 12-1308 [M]	Little Town Flirt	1963	37.50	75.00	150.00
❏ 12-1308 [S]	Little Town Flirt	1963	375.00	750.00	1,500.
-- Stereo copies are not identified as such on either cover or label; some, but not all, copies have an "S" in the dead wax. Playing is the best way to identify.					
DOT					
❏ DLP 3824 [M]	The Best of Del Shannon	1967	12.50	25.00	50.00
❏ DLP 25824 [R]	The Best of Del Shannon	1967	10.00	20.00	40.00
LIBERTY					
❏ LRP-3453 [M]	This Is My Bag	1966	7.50	15.00	30.00
❏ LRP-3479 [M]	Total Commitment	1966	7.50	15.00	30.00
❏ LRP-3539 [M]	The Further Adventures of Charles Westover	1967	12.50	25.00	50.00
❏ LST-7453 [S]	This Is My Bag	1966	10.00	20.00	40.00
❏ LST-7479 [S]	Total Commitment	1966	10.00	20.00	40.00
❏ LST-7539 [S]	The Further Adventures of Charles Westover	1967	20.00	40.00	80.00
POST					
❏ 9000 [R]	Del Shannon Sings	196?	10.00	20.00	40.00
SIRE					
❏ SASH-3708 [(2) P]	The Vintage Years	1975	6.25	12.50	25.00
UNITED ARTISTS					
❏ UA-LA151-E	Del Shannon Live in England	1973	6.25	12.50	25.00

Number	Title	Yr	VG	VG+	NM
SHANNON, HUGH					
ATLANTIC					
❏ ALS-406 [10]	Hugh Shannon Sings	195?	25.00	50.00	100.00
SHANTY BOYS, THE					
ELEKTRA					
❏ EKL-142 [M]	Off-Beat Folk Songs	1958	7.50	15.00	30.00
SHAPIRO, HELEN					
EPIC					
❏ LN 24075 [M]	A Teenager in Love	1962	6.25	12.50	25.00
❏ BN 26075 [S]	A Teenager in Love	1962	7.50	15.00	30.00
SHARON, RALPH					
ARGO					
❏ LP-635 [M]	2:38 A.M.	1958	10.00	20.00	40.00
BETHLEHEM					
❏ BCP-41 [M]	Ralph Sharon Trio	1956	10.00	20.00	40.00
GORDY					
❏ G-903 [M]	Modern Innovations on Country & Western Themes	1963	50.00	100.00	200.00
LONDON					
❏ LB-733 [10]	Spring Fever	1953	12.50	25.00	50.00
❏ LB-842 [10]	Autumn Leaves	1954	12.50	25.00	50.00
❏ LL 1339 [M]	Spring Fever/Autumn Leaves	1955	10.00	20.00	40.00
❏ LL 1488 [M]	Easy Jazz	1956	10.00	20.00	40.00
RAMA					
❏ RLP-1001 [M]	Jazz Around the World	1957	12.50	25.00	50.00
SHARP, DEE DEE					
CAMEO					
❏ C-1018 [M]	It's Mashed Potato Time	1962	15.00	30.00	60.00
❏ C-1022 [M]	Songs of Faith	1962	10.00	20.00	40.00
❏ SC-1022 [S]	Songs of Faith	1962	12.50	25.00	50.00
❏ C-1027 [M]	All the Hits	1962	10.00	20.00	40.00
❏ SC-1027 [S]	All the Hits	1962	12.50	25.00	50.00
❏ C-1032 [M]	All the Hits, Vol. 2	1963	10.00	20.00	40.00
❏ SC-1032 [S]	All the Hits, Vol. 2	1963	12.50	25.00	50.00
❏ C-1050 [M]	Do the Bird	1963	10.00	20.00	40.00
❏ SC-1050 [S]	Do the Bird	1963	12.50	25.00	50.00
❏ C-1062 [M]	Biggest Hits	1963	10.00	20.00	40.00
❏ C-1074 [M]	Down Memory Lane	1963	10.00	20.00	40.00
❏ C-2002 [M]	18 Golden Hits	1964	10.00	20.00	40.00
❏ SC-2002 [S]	18 Golden Hits	1964	12.50	25.00	50.00
SHARP, DEE DEE, AND CHUBBY CHECKER					
Also see each artist's individual listings.					
CAMEO					
❏ C-1029 [M]	Down to Earth	1962	10.00	20.00	40.00
❏ SC-1029 [S]	Down to Earth	1962	12.50	25.00	50.00
SHARP, RANDY					
NAUTILUS					
❏ NR-1	First in Line	1980	12.50	25.00	50.00
-- Styrofoam cover					
❏ NR-1	First in Line	1980	10.00	20.00	40.00
-- Standard cover					
SHARPE, RAY					
AWARD					
❏ LMP-711 [M]	Welcome Back, Linda Lu	1964	30.00	60.00	120.00
SHATNER, WILLIAM					
DECCA					
❏ DL 75043	The Transformed Man	1969	15.00	30.00	60.00
K-TEL					
❏ NC 494 [(2)]	Captain of the Starship	1978	12.50	25.00	50.00
-- Reissue of Lemli album					
LEMLI					
❏ 9400 [(2)]	William Shatner -- Live!	1977	7.50	15.00	30.00
SHAW, ARTIE					
ALLEGRO					
❏ 1405 [M]	An Hour with Artie Shaw	195?	10.00	20.00	40.00
❏ 1466 [M]	Artie Shaw Hour	195?	10.00	20.00	40.00
CLEF					
❏ MGC-159 [10]	Artie Shaw and His Gramercy Five, Volume 1	1954	15.00	30.00	60.00

Number	Title	Yr	VG	VG+	NM
❑ MGC-160 [10]	Artie Shaw and His Gramercy Five, Volume 2	1954	15.00	30.00	60.00
❑ MGC-630 [M]	Artie Shaw and His Gramercy Five, Volume 3	1954	15.00	30.00	60.00
❑ MGC-645 [M]	Artie Shaw and His Gramercy Five, Volume 4	1955	15.00	30.00	60.00

COLUMBIA MASTERWORKS

Number	Title	Yr	VG	VG+	NM
❑ ML 4260 [M]	Modern Music for Clarinet	1950	12.50	25.00	50.00

DECCA

Number	Title	Yr	VG	VG+	NM
❑ DL 5286 [10]	Artie Shaw Dance Program	195?	12.50	25.00	50.00
❑ DL 5524 [10]	Speak to Me of Love	195?	12.50	25.00	50.00
❑ DL 8309 [M]	Did Someone Say Party?	1956	10.00	20.00	40.00

-- *Black label, silver print*

EPIC

Number	Title	Yr	VG	VG+	NM
❑ LG 1006 [10]	Artie Shaw with Strings	195?	12.50	25.00	50.00
❑ LG 1017 [10]	Non-Stop Flight	195?	12.50	25.00	50.00
❑ LG 1102 [10]	Artie Shaw	195?	12.50	25.00	50.00
❑ LN 3112 [M]	Artie Shaw with Strings	1955	10.00	20.00	40.00
❑ LN 3150 [M]	Artie Shaw and His Orchestra	1955	10.00	20.00	40.00

LION

Number	Title	Yr	VG	VG+	NM
❑ L-70058 [M]	Artie Shaw Plays Irving Berlin and Cole Porter	1958	6.25	12.50	25.00

MGM

Number	Title	Yr	VG	VG+	NM
❑ E-517 [10]	Artie Shaw Plays Cole Porter	1950	12.50	25.00	50.00

RCA CAMDEN

Number	Title	Yr	VG	VG+	NM
❑ CAL-465 [M]	The Great Artie Shaw	195?	5.00	10.00	20.00
❑ CAL-584 [M]	One Night Stand	195?	5.00	10.00	20.00
❑ CAL-908 [M]	September Song and Other Favorites	196?	5.00	10.00	20.00

RCA VICTOR

Number	Title	Yr	VG	VG+	NM
❑ LPT-28 [10]	Artie Shaw Favorites	195?	12.50	25.00	50.00
❑ LPM-30 [10]	Four Star Favorites	195?	12.50	25.00	50.00
❑ LPM-1201 [M]	Both Feet in the Groove	1956	10.00	20.00	40.00
❑ LPM-1217 [M]	Back Bay Shuffle	1956	10.00	20.00	40.00
❑ LPM-1241 [M]	Artie Shaw and His Gramercy Five	1956	10.00	20.00	40.00
❑ LPM-1244 [M]	Moonglow	1956	10.00	20.00	40.00
❑ LPM-1570 [M]	Any Old Time	1957	10.00	20.00	40.00
❑ LPM-1648 [M]	A Man and His Dream	1957	10.00	20.00	40.00
❑ LPT-1020 [M]	My Concerto	195?	10.00	20.00	40.00
❑ LPT-3013 [10]	This Is Artie Shaw	195?	12.50	25.00	50.00
❑ LPT-6000 [(2) M]	In the Blue Room/In the Café Rouge	195?	12.50	25.00	50.00

-- *Originals are in a box; silver labels, red print*

VERVE

Number	Title	Yr	VG	VG+	NM
❑ MGV-2014 [M]	I Can't Get Started	1956	10.00	20.00	40.00
❑ V-2014 [M]	I Can't Get Started	1961	5.00	10.00	20.00
❑ MGV-2015 [M]	Sequence in Music	1956	10.00	20.00	40.00
❑ V-2015 [M]	Sequence in Music	1961	5.00	10.00	20.00

SHAW, MARLENA

CADET

Number	Title	Yr	VG	VG+	NM
❑ LPS-803	Different Bags	1968	5.00	10.00	20.00
❑ LPS-833	Spice of Life	1969	5.00	10.00	20.00

SHAW, ROBERT, CHORALE

RCA VICTOR RED SEAL

Number	Title	Yr	VG	VG+	NM
❑ LM-1112 [M]	Christmas Hymns and Carols	1952	10.00	20.00	40.00

-- *Original has 2" brown border around all four sides of front cover*

| ❑ LM-1112 [M] | Christmas Hymns and Carols, Volume I | 1954 | 7.50 | 15.00 | 30.00 |

-- *Mostly pink front cover with "Enhanced Sound" at top and under dog on label*

| ❑ LM-1711 [M] | Christmas Hymns and Carols Volume II | 1954 | 7.50 | 15.00 | 30.00 |

-- *Original carolers cover; red label with outline of dog*

| ❑ LM-1711 [M] | Christmas Hymns and Carols Vol. 2 | 195? | 6.25 | 12.50 | 25.00 |

-- *Pink "ornaments" cover; maroon label, large dog on top*

| ❑ LM-2139 [M] | Christmas Hymns and Carols, Volume 1 | 1957 | 5.00 | 10.00 | 20.00 |

-- *Original cover has "LM-2139" with "RCA Victor" in box on upper right*

| ❑ LSC-2139 [S] | Christmas Hymns and Carols, Volume 1 | 1958 | 5.00 | 10.00 | 20.00 |

-- *Original with "shaded dog" label*

| ❑ LSC-2199 [S] | A Mighty Fortress | 1959 | 5.00 | 10.00 | 20.00 |

-- *Original with "shaded dog" label*

| ❑ LSC-2231 [S] | On Stage | 1959 | 5.00 | 10.00 | 20.00 |

-- *Original with "shaded dog" label*

| ❑ LSC-2247 [S] | Deep River and Other Spirituals | 1959 | 5.00 | 10.00 | 20.00 |

-- *Original with "shaded dog" label*

| ❑ LSC-2273 [S] | Bach, J.S.: Cantata 4 | 1959 | 5.00 | 10.00 | 20.00 |

-- *Original with "shaded dog" label*

| ❑ LSC-2295 [S] | The Stephen Foster Song Book | 1959 | 5.00 | 10.00 | 20.00 |

-- *Original with "shaded dog" label*

| ❑ LSC-2402 [S] | A Chorus of Love | 1960 | 5.00 | 10.00 | 20.00 |

-- *Original with "shaded dog" label or second edition with "white dog" label*

| ❑ LSC-2403 [S] | What Wondrous Love | 1960 | 5.00 | 10.00 | 20.00 |

-- *Original with "shaded dog" label*

| ❑ LSC-2416 [S] | Operatic Choruses | 1960 | 5.00 | 10.00 | 20.00 |

-- *Original with "shaded dog" label*

| ❑ LSC-2551 [S] | Sea Shanties | 1961 | 7.50 | 15.00 | 30.00 |

-- *Original with "shaded dog" label*

| ❑ LSC-2580 [S] | I'm Goin' to Sing | 1962 | 10.00 | 20.00 | 40.00 |

-- *Original with "shaded dog" label*

| ❑ LSC-2598 [S] | 23 Glee Club Favorites | 1962 | 10.00 | 20.00 | 40.00 |

-- *Original with "shaded dog" label*

SHAW, SANDIE

REPRISE

Number	Title	Yr	VG	VG+	NM
❑ R-6166 [M]	Sandie Shaw	1965	10.00	20.00	40.00
❑ RS-6166 [R]	Sandie Shaw	1965	12.50	25.00	50.00
❑ R-6191 [M]	Me	1966	7.50	15.00	30.00
❑ RS-6191 [S]	Me	1966	10.00	20.00	40.00

SHAW, SERENA

RAMA

Number	Title	Yr	VG	VG+	NM
❑ RLP-5001 [M]	Cry My Love	1956	100.00	200.00	400.00

SHAWN, DICK

20TH CENTURY FOX

Number	Title	Yr	VG	VG+	NM
❑ TFM-3124 [M]	Dick Shawn Sings with His Little People	1964	5.00	10.00	20.00
❑ TFS-4124 [S]	Dick Shawn Sings with His Little People	1964	6.25	12.50	25.00

SHEA, GEORGE BEVERLY

RCA VICTOR

Number	Title	Yr	VG	VG+	NM
❑ LPM-1062 [M]	Evening Vespers	1955	5.00	10.00	20.00
❑ LPM-1187 [M]	Inspirational Songs	1955	5.00	10.00	20.00
❑ LPM-1235 [M]	Sacred Songs	1956	5.00	10.00	20.00
❑ LPM-1349 [M]	Evening Prayer	1956	5.00	10.00	20.00
❑ LPM-1406 [M]	A Billy Graham Crusade in Song	1956	5.00	10.00	20.00
❑ LPM-1564 [M]	George Beverly Shea	1957	5.00	10.00	20.00
❑ LPM-1642 [M]	Through the Years	1957	5.00	10.00	20.00
❑ LSP-1949 [S]	The Love of God	1958	5.00	10.00	20.00
❑ LSP-1967 [S]	Blessed Assurance	1959	5.00	10.00	20.00
❑ LSP-2064 [S]	Christmas Hymns	1959	5.00	10.00	20.00

SHEARING, GEORGE

CAPITOL

Number	Title	Yr	VG	VG+	NM
❑ T 648 [M]	The Shearing Spell	1956	7.50	15.00	30.00

-- *Turquoise label*

| ❑ T 648 [M] | The Shearing Spell | 1959 | 5.00 | 10.00 | 20.00 |

-- *Black label with colorband, logo on left*

| ❑ T 720 [M] | Velvet Carpet | 1956 | 7.50 | 15.00 | 30.00 |

-- *Turquoise label*

| ❑ T 720 [M] | Velvet Carpet | 1959 | 5.00 | 10.00 | 20.00 |

-- *Black label with colorband, logo on left*

| ❑ T 737 [M] | Latin Escapade | 1957 | 7.50 | 15.00 | 30.00 |

-- *Turquoise label*

| ❑ T 737 [M] | Latin Escapade | 1959 | 5.00 | 10.00 | 20.00 |

-- *Black label with colorband, logo on left*

| ❑ ST 858 [S] | Black Satin | 1959 | 5.00 | 10.00 | 20.00 |

-- *Black label with colorband, logo on left*

| ❑ T 858 [M] | Black Satin | 1957 | 7.50 | 15.00 | 30.00 |

-- *Turquoise label*

| ❑ T 858 [M] | Black Satin | 1959 | 5.00 | 10.00 | 20.00 |

-- *Black label with colorband, logo on left*

| ❑ T 909 [M] | Shearing Piano | 1957 | 7.50 | 15.00 | 30.00 |

-- *Turquoise label*

| ❑ T 909 [M] | Shearing Piano | 1959 | 5.00 | 10.00 | 20.00 |

-- *Black label with colorband, logo on left*

| ❑ ST 1038 [S] | Burnished Brass | 1959 | 6.25 | 12.50 | 25.00 |

-- *Black label with colorband, logo on left*

| ❑ ST 1038 [S] | Burnished Brass | 1962 | 5.00 | 10.00 | 20.00 |

-- *Black label with colorband, logo on top*

| ❑ T 1038 [M] | Burnished Brass | 1958 | 5.00 | 10.00 | 20.00 |

-- *Black label with colorband, logo on left*

| ❑ ST 1082 [S] | Latin Lace | 1958 | 6.25 | 12.50 | 25.00 |

-- *Black label with colorband, logo on left*

| ❑ ST 1082 [S] | Latin Lace | 1962 | 5.00 | 10.00 | 20.00 |

-- *Black label with colorband, logo on top*

| ❑ T 1082 [M] | Latin Lace | 1958 | 5.00 | 10.00 | 20.00 |

-- *Black label with colorband, logo on left*

| ❑ ST 1124 [S] | Blue Chiffon | 1959 | 6.25 | 12.50 | 25.00 |

-- *Black label with colorband, logo on left*

| ❑ ST 1124 [S] | Blue Chiffon | 1962 | 5.00 | 10.00 | 20.00 |

-- *Black label with colorband, logo on top*

| ❑ T 1124 [M] | Blue Chiffon | 1959 | 5.00 | 10.00 | 20.00 |

-- *Black label with colorband, logo on left*

| ❑ ST 1187 [S] | George Shearing On Stage | 1959 | 6.25 | 12.50 | 25.00 |

-- *Black label with colorband, logo on left*

(Top left) Not long after "Needles and Pins" became an American hit, Kapp released the first Searchers album, called *Meet the Searchers* in keeping with the Beatles analogy Kapp was already using to promote the group. A picture sleeve for "Needles and Pins" trumpeted how the Searchers knocked the Beatles off the No. 1 spot in England. (Top right) Most albums on the Cameo label are sought after, as much because almost none of the material has ever appeared on compact disc as anything else. One of the collectible Cameo titles is Dee Dee Sharp's debut, *It's Mashed Potato Time*. (Bottom left) Several years before the box-set boom, and several years before Capitol and Reprise issued similar sets (though the Reprise set did not appear on vinyl), Columbia issued a six-LP set of Frank Sinatra's 1943-52 work on the label called *The Voice: The Columbia Years*. As with many boxes, more people bought it on CD than on vinyl. (Bottom right) Almost a novelty album, the first Frank Sinatra *Duets* collection, released in 1993, saw a brief, limited issue on U.S. vinyl at the time.

Number	Title	Yr	VG	VG+	NM
❏ ST 1187 [S]	George Shearing On Stage	1962	5.00	10.00	20.00
-- Black label with colorband, logo on top					
❏ T 1187 [M]	George Shearing On Stage	1959	5.00	10.00	20.00
-- Black label with colorband, logo on left					
❏ ST 1275 [S]	Latin Affair	1960	6.25	12.50	25.00
-- Black label with colorband, logo on left					
❏ ST 1275 [S]	Latin Affair	1962	5.00	10.00	20.00
-- Black label with colorband, logo on top					
❏ T 1275 [M]	Latin Affair	1960	5.00	10.00	20.00
-- Black label with colorband, logo on left					
❏ ST 1334 [S]	White Satin	1960	6.25	12.50	25.00
-- Black label with colorband, logo on left					
❏ ST 1334 [S]	White Satin	1962	5.00	10.00	20.00
-- Black label with colorband, logo on top					
❏ T 1334 [M]	White Satin	1960	5.00	10.00	20.00
-- Black label with colorband, logo on left					
❏ ST 1416 [S]	On the Sunny Side of the Strip	1960	6.25	12.50	25.00
-- Black label with colorband, logo on left					
❏ ST 1416 [S]	On the Sunny Side of the Strip	1962	5.00	10.00	20.00
-- Black label with colorband, logo on top					
❏ T 1416 [M]	On the Sunny Side of the Strip	1960	5.00	10.00	20.00
-- Black label with colorband, logo on left					
❏ ST 1472 [S]	The Shearing Touch	1961	6.25	12.50	25.00
-- Black label with colorband, logo on left					
❏ ST 1472 [S]	The Shearing Touch	1962	5.00	10.00	20.00
-- Black label with colorband, logo on top					
❏ T 1472 [M]	The Shearing Touch	1961	5.00	10.00	20.00
-- Black label with colorband, logo on left					
❏ ST 1567 [S]	Mood Latino	1961	6.25	12.50	25.00
-- Black label with colorband, logo on left					
❏ ST 1567 [S]	Mood Latino	1962	5.00	10.00	20.00
-- Black label with colorband, logo on top					
❏ T 1567 [M]	Mood Latino	1961	5.00	10.00	20.00
-- Black label with colorband, logo on left					
❏ ST 1628 [S]	Satin Affair	1961	6.25	12.50	25.00
-- Black label with colorband, logo on left					
❏ ST 1628 [S]	Satin Affair	1962	5.00	10.00	20.00
-- Black label with colorband, logo on top					
❏ T 1628 [M]	Satin Affair	1961	5.00	10.00	20.00
-- Black label with colorband, logo on left					
❏ ST 1715 [S]	San Francisco Scene	1962	5.00	10.00	20.00
❏ ST 1755 [S]	Concerto for My Love	1962	5.00	10.00	20.00
❏ ST 1827 [S]	Jazz Moments	1963	5.00	10.00	20.00
❏ ST 1873 [S]	Bossa Nova	1963	5.00	10.00	20.00
❏ ST 1874 [S]	Touch Me Softly	1963	5.00	10.00	20.00
❏ ST 1992 [S]	Jazz Concert	1963	5.00	10.00	20.00
DISCOVERY					
❏ DL-3002 [10]	George Shearing Quintet	1950	15.00	30.00	60.00
JAZZLAND					
❏ JLP-55 [M]	Love Walked In	1961	7.50	15.00	30.00
-- Cover has Shearing and the brothers					
❏ JLP-55 [M]	Love Walked In	1962	6.25	12.50	25.00
-- Cover has a woman					
❏ JLP-955 [S]	Love Walked In	1961	10.00	20.00	40.00
-- Cover has Shearing and the brothers					
❏ JLP-955 [S]	Love Walked In	1962	7.50	15.00	30.00
-- Cover has a woman					
LONDON					
❏ LL 295 [10]	Souvenirs	1951	15.00	30.00	60.00
❏ LL 1343 [M]	By Request	1956	7.50	15.00	30.00
MGM					
❏ E-90 [10]	Touch of Genius	1951	12.50	25.00	50.00
❏ E-155 [10]	I Hear Music	1952	12.50	25.00	50.00
❏ E-226 [10]	When Lights Are Low	1953	12.50	25.00	50.00
❏ E-252 [10]	An Evening with George Shearing	1954	12.50	25.00	50.00
❏ E-515 [10]	You're Hearing the George Shearing Quartet	1950	15.00	30.00	60.00
❏ E-3175 [M]	Shearing Caravan	1955	7.50	15.00	30.00
❏ E-3222 [M]	An Evening with George Shearing	1955	7.50	15.00	30.00
❏ E-3264 [M]	When Lights Are Low	1955	7.50	15.00	30.00
❏ E-3265 [M]	Touch of Genius	1955	7.50	15.00	30.00
❏ E-3266 [M]	I Hear Music	1955	7.50	15.00	30.00
❏ E-3293 [M]	Shearing in Hi-Fi	1955	7.50	15.00	30.00
SAVOY					
❏ MG-15003 [10]	Piano Solo	1951	15.00	30.00	60.00

SHELTON, RICKY VAN
COLUMBIA

Number	Title	Yr	VG	VG+	NM
❏ C 46855	Backroads	1990	5.00	10.00	20.00
-- Vinyl available only through Columbia House					

SHELTON, ROSCOE
EXCELLO

Number	Title	Yr	VG	VG+	NM
❏ LP-8002 [M]	Roscoe Shelton Sings	1961	150.00	300.00	600.00

SOUND STAGE 7

Number	Title	Yr	VG	VG+	NM
❏ SSS-5002 [M]	Soul in His Music, Music in His Soul	1966	10.00	20.00	40.00
❏ SSS-15002 [S]	Soul in His Music, Music in His Soul	1966	12.50	25.00	50.00

SHENANDOAH
COLUMBIA

Number	Title	Yr	VG	VG+	NM
❏ C 48885	Greatest Hits	1990	5.00	10.00	20.00
-- Vinyl available only through Columbia House					

SHEP AND THE LIMELITES
HULL

Number	Title	Yr	VG	VG+	NM
❏ 1001 [M]	Our Anniversary	1962	300.00	600.00	1,200.
ROULETTE					
❏ R-25350 [M]	Our Anniversary	1967	20.00	40.00	80.00
❏ SR-25350 [R]	Our Anniversary	1967	12.50	25.00	50.00

SHEPARD, JEAN
CAPITOL

Number	Title	Yr	VG	VG+	NM
❏ T 728 [M]	Songs of a Love Affair	1956	15.00	30.00	60.00
❏ T 1126 [M]	Lonesome Love	1959	10.00	20.00	40.00
❏ T 1253 [M]	This Is Jean Shepard	1959	10.00	20.00	40.00
❏ ST 1525 [S]	Got You on My Mind	1961	7.50	15.00	30.00
❏ T 1525 [M]	Got You on My Mind	1961	6.25	12.50	25.00
❏ ST 1663 [S]	Heartaches and Tears	1962	7.50	15.00	30.00
❏ T 1663 [M]	Heartaches and Tears	1962	6.25	12.50	25.00
❏ T 1922 [M]	The Best of Jean Shepard	1963	6.25	12.50	25.00
❏ ST 2187 [S]	Lighthearted and Blue	1964	5.00	10.00	20.00

SHEPHERD, CYBILL
PARAMOUNT

Number	Title	Yr	VG	VG+	NM
❏ PAS-1018	Cybill Does It...to Cole Porter	1974	5.00	10.00	20.00
-- With poster					

SHEPHERD, JEAN
ELEKTRA

Number	Title	Yr	VG	VG+	NM
❏ EKL-172 [M]	Jean Shepherd and Other Foibles	1959	12.50	25.00	50.00

SHEPPARDS, THE
CONSTELLATION

Number	Title	Yr	VG	VG+	NM
❏ C-4 [M]	Collectors Showcase: The Sheppards	1964	20.00	40.00	80.00
❏ CS-4 [R]	Collectors Showcase: The Sheppards	1964	10.00	20.00	40.00

SHERMAN, ALLAN
JUBLIEE

Number	Title	Yr	VG	VG+	NM
❏ JGM 5019 [M]	More Folk Songs by Allan Sherman	1963	5.00	10.00	20.00
-- Two early Allan Sherman sides plus comedy bits by others					
RCA RED SEAL					
❏ LM-2773 [M]	Peter and the Commissar	1964	5.00	10.00	20.00
❏ LSC-2773 [S]	Peter and the Commissar	1964	6.25	12.50	25.00
-- With Arthur Fiedler and the Boston Pops Orchestra					
WARNER BROS.					
❏ WS 1475 [S]	My Son, the Folk Singer	1962	5.00	10.00	20.00
-- Gold label					
❏ WS 1487 [S]	My Son, the Celebrity	1963	5.00	10.00	20.00
-- Gold label					
❏ WS 1501 [S]	My Son, the Nut	1963	5.00	10.00	20.00
-- Gold label					
❏ WS 1684 [S]	Togetherness	1967	5.00	10.00	20.00
-- Gold label					

SHERRYS, THE
GUYDEN

Number	Title	Yr	VG	VG+	NM
❏ GLP 503 [M]	At the Hop with the Sherrys	1963	62.50	125.00	250.00

SHIGETA, JAMES
CHOREO

Number	Title	Yr	VG	VG+	NM
❏ A-7 [M]	We Speak the Same Language	1962	6.25	12.50	25.00
❏ AS-7 [S]	We Speak the Same Language	1962	7.50	15.00	30.00

SHILOH

Don Henley, later of the EAGLES, was in this group. The LP was produced by KENNY ROGERS.

AMOS

Number	Title	Yr	VG	VG+	NM
❏ AAS-7015	Shiloh	1971	20.00	40.00	80.00

SHIP, THE
ELEKTRA

Number	Title	Yr	VG	VG+	NM
❏ EKS-75036	The Ship	1972	5.00	10.00	20.00

Number	Title	Yr	VG	VG+	NM

SHIRELLES, THE
SCEPTER
Number	Title	Yr	VG	VG+	NM
❏ S-501 [M]	Tonight's the Night	1961	50.00	100.00	200.00
-- "Scepter" in scroll at top of label					
❏ SPM-501 [M]	Tonight's the Night	1962	15.00	30.00	60.00
-- "Scepter Records" at left of label					
❏ SPS-501 [S]	Tonight's the Night	1965	25.00	50.00	100.00
❏ S-502 [M]	The Shirelles Sing to Trumpets and Strings	1961	50.00	100.00	200.00
-- "Scepter" in scroll at top of label					
❏ SPM-502 [M]	The Shirelles Sing to Trumpets and Strings	1962	15.00	30.00	60.00
-- "Scepter Records" at left of label					
❏ SPS-502 [S]	The Shirelles Sing to Trumpets and Strings	1965	25.00	50.00	100.00
❏					
❏ SPM-504 [M]	Baby It's You	1962	25.00	50.00	100.00
❏ SPS-504 [S]	Baby It's You	1965	25.00	50.00	100.00
❏ SPM-505 [M]	A Twist Party	1962	20.00	40.00	80.00
❏ SPS-505 [S]	A Twist Party	1965	25.00	50.00	100.00
❏ SPM-507 [M]	The Shirelles' Greatest Hits	1962	10.00	20.00	40.00
❏ SPS-507 [S]	The Shirelles' Greatest Hits	1965	12.50	25.00	50.00
❏ SPM-511 [M]	Foolish Little Girl	1963	12.50	25.00	50.00
❏ SPS-511 [S]	Foolish Little Girl	1965	20.00	40.00	80.00
❏ SPM-514 [M]	It's a Mad, Mad, Mad, Mad World	1963	10.00	20.00	40.00
❏ SPS-514 [S]	It's a Mad, Mad, Mad, Mad World	1963	12.50	25.00	50.00
❏ SPM-516 [M]	The Shirelles Sing the Golden Oldies	1964	10.00	20.00	40.00
❏ SPS-516 [S]	The Shirelles Sing the Golden Oldies	1964	12.50	25.00	50.00
❏ SPM-560 [M]	The Shirelles' Greatest Hits, Volume 2	1967	5.00	10.00	20.00
❏ SPS-560 [S]	The Shirelles' Greatest Hits, Volume 2	1967	6.25	12.50	25.00
❏ SPM-562 [M]	Spontaneous Combustion	1967	10.00	20.00	40.00
❏ SPS-562 [S]	Spontaneous Combustion	1967	12.50	25.00	50.00
❏ SPS-569	Eternally Soul	1968	7.50	15.00	30.00
❏ SPS-2-599 [(2)]	Remember When	1972	5.00	10.00	20.00

SHIRLEY AND LEE
ALADDIN
❏ 807 [M]	Let the Good Times Roll	1956	375.00	750.00	1,500.
IMPERIAL
| ❏ LP-9179 [M] | Let the Good Times Roll | 1962 | 75.00 | 150.00 | 300.00 |
| -- Reissue of Aladdin LP | | | | | |
SCORE
| ❏ SLP-4023 [M] | Let the Good Times Roll | 1957 | 200.00 | 400.00 | 800.00 |
| -- Reissue of Aladdin LP | | | | | |
WARWICK
| ❏ W-2028 [M] | Let the Good Times Roll | 1961 | 37.50 | 75.00 | 150.00 |
| ❏ W-2028ST [S] | Let the Good Times Roll | 1961 | 75.00 | 150.00 | 300.00 |

SHIRLEY, DON
AUDIO FIDELITY
❏ AFLP-1897 [M]	Don Shirley	1959	5.00	10.00	20.00
❏ AFSD-5897 [S]	Don Shirley	1959	7.50	15.00	30.00
CADENCE
❏ CLP-1001 [M]	Tonal Expressions	1955	10.00	20.00	40.00
❏ CLP-1004 [M]	Piano Perspectives	1955	10.00	20.00	40.00
❏ CLP-1009 [M]	Orpheus in the Underworld	1956	10.00	20.00	40.00
❏ CLP-1015 [M]	Don Shirley Duo	1956	10.00	20.00	40.00
❏ CLP-3007 [M]	Don Shirley Solos	1958	7.50	15.00	30.00
❏ CLP-3008 [M]	Don Shirley with Two Basses	1958	7.50	15.00	30.00
❏ CLP-3032 [M]	Don Shirley Plays Gershwin	1960	6.25	12.50	25.00
❏ CLP-3033 [M]	Don Shirley Plays Standards	1960	6.25	12.50	25.00
❏ CLP-3034 [M]	Don Shirley Plays Love Songs	1960	6.25	12.50	25.00
❏ CLP-3035 [M]	Don Shirley Plays Birdland Lullabies	1960	6.25	12.50	25.00
❏ CLP-3036 [M]	Don Shirley Plays Showtunes	1960	6.25	12.50	25.00
❏ CLP-3037 [M]	Orpheus in the Underworld	1960	6.25	12.50	25.00
-- Reissue of 1009					
❏ CLP-3046 [M]	Trio	1961	5.00	10.00	20.00
❏ CLP-3048 [M]	Pianist Extraordinary	1962	5.00	10.00	20.00
❏ CLP-3049 [M]	Piano Arrangements of Spirituals	1962	5.00	10.00	20.00
❏ CLP-3057 [M]	Drown in My Own Tears	1962	5.00	10.00	20.00
❏ CLP-25046 [S]	Trio	1961	7.50	15.00	30.00
❏ CLP-25048 [S]	Pianist Extraordinary	1962	7.50	15.00	30.00
❏ CLP-25049 [S]	Piano Arrangements of Spirituals	1962	7.50	15.00	30.00
❏ CLP-25057 [S]	Drown in My Own Tears	1962	7.50	15.00	30.00

SHIVA'S HEADBAND
APE
❏ 1001	Psychedelic Yesterday	1981	5.00	10.00	20.00
ARMADILLO
| ❏ (no #) | Coming to a Head | 1969 | 62.50 | 125.00 | 250.00 |

CAPITOL
Number	Title	Yr	VG	VG+	NM
❏ ST-538	Take Me to the Mountains	1970	15.00	30.00	60.00

SHOCKED, MICHELLE
MERCURY
❏ PRO 797 [DJ]	Live	1990	5.00	10.00	20.00
-- Five-song mini-LP for radio stations with custom jacket					

SHOCKING BLUE, THE
COLOSSUS
❏ CS-1000	The Shocking Blue	1970	6.25	12.50	25.00

SHOES
(NO LABEL)
❏ (no #)	One in Versailles	1976	30.00	60.00	120.00
BLACK VINYL
| ❏ 51477 | Black Vinyl Shoes | 1977 | 20.00 | 40.00 | 80.00 |
ELEKTRA
| ❏ AS 11570 [DJ] | Shoes on Ice -- Live | 1982 | 12.50 | 25.00 | 50.00 |
| -- Promo-only 7-song live record; issued in generic jacket | | | | | |
PVC
| ❏ 7904 | Black Vinyl Shoes | 1979 | 5.00 | 10.00 | 20.00 |

SHONDELL, TROY
EVEREST
❏ SDBR-1206 [S]	The Many Sides of Troy Shondell	1963	20.00	40.00	80.00
❏ LPBR-5206 [M]	The Many Sides of Troy Shondell	1963	12.50	25.00	50.00

SHORE, DINAH
CAPITOL
❏ ST 1247 [S]	Dinah, Yes Indeed	1959	6.25	12.50	25.00
❏ T 1247 [M]	Dinah, Yes Indeed	1959	5.00	10.00	20.00
❏ ST 1296 [S]	Somebody Loves Me	1959	6.25	12.50	25.00
❏ T 1296 [M]	Somebody Loves Me	1959	5.00	10.00	20.00
❏ ST 1354 [S]	Dinah Sings Some Blues with Red	1960	7.50	15.00	30.00
❏ T 1354 [M]	Dinah Sings Some Blues with Red	1960	6.25	12.50	25.00
❏ ST 1422 [S]	Dinah Sings/Previn Plays	1960	6.25	12.50	25.00
❏ T 1422 [M]	Dinah Sings/Previn Plays	1960	5.00	10.00	20.00
❏ ST 1655 [S]	Dinah Down Home	1962	6.25	12.50	25.00
❏ T 1655 [M]	Dinah Down Home	1962	5.00	10.00	20.00
❏ ST 1704 [S]	The Fabulous Hits of Dinah Shore	1962	6.25	12.50	25.00
-- Black label with colorband, logo at left					
❏ T 1704 [M]	The Fabulous Hits of Dinah Shore	1962	5.00	10.00	20.00
-- Black label with colorband, logo at left					
COLUMBIA
| ❏ CL 6004 [10] | Dinah Shore Sings | 1949 | 12.50 | 25.00 | 50.00 |
| ❏ CL 6069 [10] | Reminiscing | 1949 | 12.50 | 25.00 | 50.00 |
HARMONY
| ❏ HL 7010 [M] | Dinah Shore Sings Cole Porter and Richard Rodgers | 195? | 5.00 | 10.00 | 20.00 |
RCA VICTOR
❏ LPM-1154 [M]	Holding Hands at Midnight	1955	7.50	15.00	30.00
❏ LPM-1214 [M]	Bouquet of Blues	1956	7.50	15.00	30.00
❏ LPM-1719 [M]	Moments Like These	1958	6.25	12.50	25.00
❏ LPM-3103 [10]	Dinah Shore Sings the Blues	1953	10.00	20.00	40.00
❏ LPM-3214 [10]	The Dinah Shore TV Show	1954	10.00	20.00	40.00

SHORT CROSS
GRIZZLY
❏ S-16013	Arising	1970	62.50	125.00	250.00

SHORT, BOBBY
ATLANTIC
❏ SD 2-606 [(2)]	Bobby Short Loves Cole Porter	1972	5.00	10.00	20.00
❏ SD 2-607 [(2)]	Mad About Noel Coward	1972	5.00	10.00	20.00
❏ 1214 [M]	Songs by Bobby Short	195?	7.50	15.00	30.00
-- Black label					
❏ 1214 [M]	Songs by Bobby Short	1961	5.00	10.00	20.00
-- White "fan" logo at right of label					
❏ 1230 [M]	Bobby Short	195?	7.50	15.00	30.00
-- Black label					
❏ 1230 [M]	Bobby Short	1961	5.00	10.00	20.00
-- White "fan" logo at right of label					
❏ 1262 [M]	Speaking of Love	1958	7.50	15.00	30.00
-- Black label					
❏ 1262 [M]	Speaking of Love	1961	5.00	10.00	20.00
-- White "fan" logo at right of label					
❏ SD 1262 [S]	Speaking of Love	1959	10.00	20.00	40.00
-- Green label					
❏ SD 1262 [S]	Speaking of Love	1961	6.25	12.50	25.00
-- White "fan" logo at right of label					

Number	Title	Yr	VG	VG+	NM
❑ 1285 [M]	Sing Me a Swing Song	1958	7.50	15.00	30.00
-- Black label					
❑ 1285 [M]	Sing Me a Swing Song	1961	5.00	10.00	20.00
-- White "fan" logo at right of label					
❑ 1302 [M]	The Mad Twenties	1959	7.50	15.00	30.00
-- Black label					
❑ 1302 [M]	The Mad Twenties	1961	5.00	10.00	20.00
-- White "fan" logo at right of label					
❑ SD 1302 [S]	The Mad Twenties	1959	10.00	20.00	40.00
-- Green label					
❑ SD 1302 [S]	The Mad Twenties	1961	6.25	12.50	25.00
-- White "fan" logo at right of label					
❑ SD 1302 [S]	The Mad Twenties	1963	5.00	10.00	20.00
-- Black "fan" logo at right of label					
❑ 1321 [M]	On the East Side	1960	7.50	15.00	30.00
-- Black label					
❑ 1321 [M]	On the East Side	1961	5.00	10.00	20.00
-- White "fan" logo at right of label					
❑ SD 1321 [S]	On the East Side	1960	10.00	20.00	40.00
-- Green label					
❑ SD 1321 [S]	On the East Side	1961	6.25	12.50	25.00
-- White "fan" logo at right of label					
❑ SD 1321 [S]	On the East Side	1963	5.00	10.00	20.00
-- Black "fan" logo at right of label					
❑ 81715 [(4)]	50 from Bobby Short	1987	7.50	15.00	30.00

SHORTER, WAYNE
BLUE NOTE

Number	Title	Yr	VG	VG+	NM
❑ BLP-4173 [M]	Night Drreamer	1964	6.25	12.50	25.00
❑ BLP-4182 [M]	Juju	1965	6.25	12.50	25.00
❑ BLP-4194 [M]	Speak No Evil	1966	6.25	12.50	25.00
❑ BLP-4219 [M]	The All Seeing Eye	1966	6.25	12.50	25.00
❑ BST-84173 [S]	Night Drreamer	1964	7.50	15.00	30.00
-- With New York, USA address on label					
❑ BST-84182 [S]	Juju	1965	7.50	15.00	30.00
-- With New York, USA address on label					
❑ BST-84194 [S]	Speak No Evil	1966	7.50	15.00	30.00
-- With New York, USA address on label					
❑ BST-84219 [S]	The All Seeing Eye	1966	7.50	15.00	30.00
-- With New York, USA address on label					
❑ BST-84232	Adam's Apple	1967	5.00	10.00	20.00
❑ BST-84297	Schizophrenia	1969	5.00	10.00	20.00
❑ BST-84332	Super Nova	1970	5.00	10.00	20.00

VEE JAY

Number	Title	Yr	VG	VG+	NM
❑ VJ-3006 [M]	Introducing Wayne Shorter	1960	10.00	20.00	40.00
❑ VJS-3006 [S]	Introducing Wayne Shorter	1960	12.50	25.00	50.00
❑ VJ-3026 [M]	Wayning Moments	1962	7.50	15.00	30.00
❑ VJS-3026 [S]	Wayning Moments	1962	10.00	20.00	40.00
❑ VJ-3057 [M]	Second Genesis	1963	7.50	15.00	30.00
❑ VJS-3057 [S]	Second Genesis	1963	10.00	20.00	40.00

SHOTGUN LTD.
PROPHESY

Number	Title	Yr	VG	VG+	NM
❑ 6050	Shotgun Ltd.	1971	5.00	10.00	20.00

SHRINER, HERB
COLUMBIA

Number	Title	Yr	VG	VG+	NM
❑ CL 774 [M]	Herb Shriner On Stage	1957	7.50	15.00	30.00

DOT

Number	Title	Yr	VG	VG+	NM
❑ DLP-3149 [M]	Polka Dot Party	1959	7.50	15.00	30.00
❑ DLP-25149 [S]	Polka Dot Party	1959	10.00	20.00	40.00

SICKNICKS, THE
AMY

Number	Title	Yr	VG	VG+	NM
❑ 2 [M]	Sick #2	1961	7.50	15.00	30.00

SIDEKICKS, THE
RCA VICTOR

Number	Title	Yr	VG	VG+	NM
❑ LPM-3712 [M]	Fifi the Flea	1966	5.00	10.00	20.00
❑ LSP-3712 [S]	Fifi the Flea	1966	6.25	12.50	25.00

SIDEWINDERS, THE
RCA VICTOR

Number	Title	Yr	VG	VG+	NM
❑ LSP-4694	The Sidewinders	1972	5.00	10.00	20.00

SIEGEL-SCHWALL BAND, THE
VANGUARD

Number	Title	Yr	VG	VG+	NM
❑ VSD-6562	Siegel-Schwall '70	1970	5.00	10.00	20.00
❑ VRS-9235 [M]	The Siegel-Schwall Band	1966	5.00	10.00	20.00
❑ VRS-9249 [M]	Say Siegel-Schwall	1967	6.25	12.50	25.00
❑ VSD-79235 [S]	The Siegel-Schwall Band	1966	6.25	12.50	25.00
❑ VSD-79249 [S]	Say Siegel-Schwall	1967	5.00	10.00	20.00
❑ VSD-79289	Shake!	1968	5.00	10.00	20.00

WOODEN NICKEL

Number	Title	Yr	VG	VG+	NM
❑ BWL1-0121	953 West	1973	5.00	10.00	20.00
❑ BWL1-0288	Last Summer -- Live	1974	5.00	10.00	20.00
❑ BWL1-0554	R.I.P.	1974	5.00	10.00	20.00
❑ WNS-1002	The Siegel-Schwall Band	1971	6.25	12.50	25.00
❑ WNS-1010	Sleepy Hollow	1972	6.25	12.50	25.00

SIGLER, BUNNY
PARKWAY

Number	Title	Yr	VG	VG+	NM
❑ P-50,000 [M]	Let the Good Times Roll	1967	10.00	20.00	40.00
❑ PS-50,000 [S]	Let the Good Times Roll	1967	10.00	20.00	40.00

SIGNATURES, THE
WARNER BROS.

Number	Title	Yr	VG	VG+	NM
❑ W 1250 [M]	The Signatures Sing In	1958	7.50	15.00	30.00
❑ WS 1250 [S]	The Signatures Sing In	1958	10.00	20.00	40.00
❑ W 1353 [M]	Prepare to Flip!	1959	7.50	15.00	30.00
❑ WS 1353 [S]	Prepare to Flip!	1959	10.00	20.00	40.00

WHIPPET

Number	Title	Yr	VG	VG+	NM
❑ WLP-702 [M]	The Signatures -- Their Voices and Instruments	1957	15.00	30.00	60.00

SILHOUETTES, THE
GOODWAY

Number	Title	Yr	VG	VG+	NM
❑ GLP-100	The Silhouettes 1958-1968/ Get a Job	1968	75.00	150.00	300.00

SILK
Also see MICHAEL STANLEY BAND.
ABC

Number	Title	Yr	VG	VG+	NM
❑ S-694	Smooth As Raw Silk	1969	6.25	12.50	25.00

SILKIE, THE
FONTANA

Number	Title	Yr	VG	VG+	NM
❑ MGF 27548 [M]	You've Got to Hide Your Love Away	1965	12.50	25.00	50.00
-- With full-color cover					
❑ MGF 27548 [M]	You've Got to Hide Your Love Away	1965	10.00	20.00	40.00
-- With purplish, black and white cover					
❑ SRF 67548 [R]	You've Got to Hide Your Love Away	1965	10.00	20.00	40.00
-- With full-color cover					
❑ SRF 67548 [R]	You've Got to Hide Your Love Away	1965	7.50	15.00	30.00
-- With purplish, black and white cover					

SILLY SURFERS, THE
MERCURY

Number	Title	Yr	VG	VG+	NM
❑ MG-20977 [M]	The Sounds of the Silly Surfers	1965	20.00	40.00	80.00
❑ SR-60977 [S]	The Sounds of the Silly Surfers	1965	25.00	50.00	100.00

SILLY SURFERS, THE / THE WEIRD-OHS
HAIRY

Number	Title	Yr	VG	VG+	NM
❑ 101 [M]	The Sounds of the Silly Surfers/ The Sounds of the Weird-Ohs	1964	37.50	75.00	150.00

SILVER APPLES
KAPP

Number	Title	Yr	VG	VG+	NM
❑ KS-3562	Silver Apples	1968	7.50	15.00	30.00
-- Add 1/3 if poster is enclosed					
❑ KS-3584	Contact	1969	7.50	15.00	30.00

SILVER, HORACE
BLUE NOTE

Number	Title	Yr	VG	VG+	NM
❑ BN-LA402-H2 [(2)]	Horace Silver	1975	5.00	10.00	20.00
❑ BLP-1518 [M]	Horace Silver and the Jazz Messengers	1956	50.00	100.00	200.00
-- "Deep groove" version (deep indentation under label on both sides)					
❑ BLP-1518 [M]	Horace Silver and the Jazz Messengers	1956	37.50	75.00	150.00
-- Regular edition, Lexington Ave. address on label					
❑ BLP-1518 [M]	Horace Silver and the Jazz Messengers	1963	6.25	12.50	25.00
-- "New York, USA" address on label					
❑ BLP-1520 [M]	Spotlight on Drums	1956	50.00	100.00	200.00
-- "Deep groove" version (deep indentation under label on both sides)					
❑ BLP-1520 [M]	Spotlight on Drums	1956	37.50	75.00	150.00
-- Regular edition, Lexington Ave. address on label					
❑ BLP-1520 [M]	Spotlight on Drums	1963	6.25	12.50	25.00
-- "New York, USA" address on label					
❑ BLP-1539 [M]	Six Pieces of Silver	1957	50.00	100.00	200.00
-- "Deep groove" version (deep indentation under label on both sides)					
❑ BLP-1539 [M]	Six Pieces of Silver	1957	37.50	75.00	150.00
-- Regular edition, Lexington Ave. address on label					

Number	Title	Yr	VG	VG+	NM
❏ BLP-1539 [M] Six Pieces of Silver		1963	6.25	12.50	25.00
-- "New York, USA" address on label					
❏ BLP-1562 [M] The Stylings of Silver		1957	37.50	75.00	150.00
-- "Deep groove" version (deep indentation under label on both sides)					
❏ BLP-1562 [M] The Stylings of Silver		1957	25.00	50.00	100.00
-- Regular edition, W. 63rd St. address on label					
❏ BLP-1562 [M] The Stylings of Silver		1963	6.25	12.50	25.00
-- "New York, USA" address on label					
❏ BST-1562 [S] The Stylings of Silver		1959	25.00	50.00	100.00
-- "Deep groove" version (deep indentation under label on both sides)					
❏ BST-1562 [S] The Stylings of Silver		1959	20.00	40.00	80.00
-- Regular edition, W. 63rd St. address on label					
❏ BST-1562 [S] The Stylings of Silver		1963	5.00	10.00	20.00
-- "New York, USA" address on label					
❏ BLP-1589 [M] Further Explorations		1958	37.50	75.00	150.00
-- "Deep groove" version (deep indentation under label on both sides)					
❏ BLP-1589 [M] Further Explorations		1958	25.00	50.00	100.00
-- Regular edition, W. 63rd St. address on label					
❏ BLP-1589 [M] Further Explorations		1963	6.25	12.50	25.00
-- "New York, USA" address on label					
❏ BST-1589 [S] Further Explorations		1959	25.00	50.00	100.00
-- "Deep groove" version (deep indentation under label on both sides)					
❏ BST-1589 [S] Further Explorations		1959	20.00	40.00	80.00
-- Regular edition, W. 63rd St. address on label					
❏ BST-1589 [S] Further Explorations		1963	5.00	10.00	20.00
-- "New York, USA" address on label					
❏ BLP-4008 [M] Finger Poppin'		1959	37.50	75.00	150.00
-- "Deep groove" version (deep indentation under label on both sides)					
❏ BLP-4008 [M] Finger Poppin'		1959	25.00	50.00	100.00
-- Regular edition, W. 63rd St. address on label					
❏ BLP-4008 [M] Finger Poppin'		1963	6.25	12.50	25.00
-- "New York, USA" address on label					
❏ BST-4008 [S] Finger Poppin'		1959	25.00	50.00	100.00
-- "Deep groove" version (deep indentation under label on both sides)					
❏ BST-4008 [S] Finger Poppin'		1959	20.00	40.00	80.00
-- Regular edition, W. 63rd St. address on label					
❏ BST-4008 [S] Finger Poppin'		1963	5.00	10.00	20.00
-- "New York, USA" address on label					
❏ BLP-4017 [M] Blowin' the Blues Away		1959	30.00	60.00	120.00
-- "Deep groove" version (deep indentation under label on both sides)					
❏ BLP-4017 [M] Blowin' the Blues Away		1959	20.00	40.00	80.00
-- Regular edition, W. 63rd St. address on label					
❏ BLP-4017 [M] Blowin' the Blues Away		1963	6.25	12.50	25.00
-- "New York, USA" address on label					
❏ BLP-4042 [M] Horace-Scope		1960	30.00	60.00	120.00
-- "Deep groove" version (deep indentation under label on both sides)					
❏ BLP-4042 [M] Horace-Scope		1960	20.00	40.00	80.00
-- Regular edition, W. 63rd St. address on label					
❏ BLP-4042 [M] Horace-Scope		1963	6.25	12.50	25.00
-- "New York, USA" address on label					
❏ BLP-4076 [M] Doin' the Thing at the Village Gate		1961	15.00	30.00	60.00
-- 61st St. address on label					
❏ BLP-4076 [M] Doin' the Thing at the Village Gate		1963	5.00	10.00	20.00
-- "New York, USA" address on label					
❏ BLP-4110 [M] The Tokyo Blues		1962	7.50	15.00	30.00
❏ BLP-4131 [M] Silver's Serenade		1963	7.50	15.00	30.00
❏ BLP-4185 [M] Song for My Father (Cantiga Para Meu Pai)		1965	6.25	12.50	25.00
❏ BLP-4220 [M] The Cape Verdean Blues		1965	6.25	12.50	25.00
❏ BLP-4250 [M] The Jody Grind		1966	6.25	12.50	25.00
❏ BLP-5018 [10] New Faces		1953	75.00	150.00	300.00
❏ BLP-5034 [10] Horace Silver Trio, Vol. 2		1954	62.50	125.00	250.00
❏ BLP-5058 [10] Horace Silver Quintet		1955	62.50	125.00	250.00
❏ BLP-5062 [10] Horace Silver Quintet		1955	62.50	125.00	250.00
❏ BST-84017 [S] Blowin' the Blues Away		1959	15.00	30.00	60.00
-- W. 63rd St. address on label					
❏ BST-84017 [S] Blowin' the Blues Away		1963	5.00	10.00	20.00
-- "New York, USA" address on label					
❏ BST-84042 [S] Horace-Scope		1960	15.00	30.00	60.00
-- W. 63rd St. address on label					
❏ BST-84042 [S] Horace-Scope		1963	5.00	10.00	20.00
-- "New York, USA" address on label					
❏ BST-84076 [S] Doin' the Thing at the Village Gate		1961	15.00	30.00	60.00
-- 61st St. address on label					
❏ BST-84076 [S] Doin' the Thing at the Village Gate		1963	5.00	10.00	20.00
-- "New York, USA" address on label					
❏ BST-84110 [S] The Tokyo Blues		1962	10.00	20.00	40.00
-- "New York, USA" address on label					
❏ BST-84131 [S] Silver's Serenade		1963	10.00	20.00	40.00
-- "New York, USA" address on label					
❏ BST-84185 [S] Song for My Father (Cantiga Para Meu Pai)		1965	7.50	15.00	30.00
-- "New York, USA" address on label					
❏ BST-84220 [S] The Cape Verdean Blues		1965	7.50	15.00	30.00
-- "New York, USA" address on label					
❏ BST-84250 [S] The Jody Grind		1966	7.50	15.00	30.00
-- "New York, USA" address on label					
EPIC					
❏ LN 3326 [M] Silver's Blue		1956	20.00	40.00	80.00
❏ LA 16006 [M] Silver's Blue		1959	10.00	20.00	40.00
❏ BA 17006 [R] Silver's Blue		196?	5.00	10.00	20.00

SILVERS, PHIL
COLUMBIA

Number	Title	Yr	VG	VG+	NM
❏ CL 1011 [M]	Phil Silvers and the Swinging Brass	1957	12.50	25.00	50.00

HARMONY

❏ HL 7170 [M]	Bugle Calls for Big Band	196?	6.25	12.50	25.00

SILVERSTEIN, SHEL
ATLANTIC

Number	Title	Yr	VG	VG+	NM
❏ 8072 [M]	Inside Folk Songs	1962	7.50	15.00	30.00
❏ SD 8072 [S]	Inside Folk Songs	1962	10.00	20.00	40.00

CADET

❏ LP 4052 [M]	I'm So Good I Don't Have to Brag!	1965	6.25	12.50	25.00
❏ LPS 4052 [S]	I'm So Good I Don't Have to Brag!	1965	7.50	15.00	30.00
❏ LP 4054 [M]	Drain My Brain	1966	6.25	12.50	25.00
❏ LPS 4054 [S]	Drain My Brain	1966	7.50	15.00	30.00

CRESTVIEW

❏ CRV 804 [M]	Stag Party	1963	6.25	12.50	25.00
❏ CRS 7804 [S]	Stag Party	1963	7.50	15.00	30.00

ELEKTRA

❏ EKL-176 [M]	Hairy Jazz	1961	25.00	50.00	100.00
❏ EKS-7176 [S]	Hairy Jazz	1961	37.50	75.00	150.00

PARACHUTE

❏ 20512 [DJ]	Selected Cuts from Songs and Stories	1978	5.00	10.00	20.00
-- Promo-only EP					

RCA VICTOR

❏ LSP-4192	A Boy Named Sue (And His Other Country Songs)	1969	5.00	10.00	20.00

SIMEONE, HARRY, CHORALE
20TH FOX

Number	Title	Yr	VG	VG+	NM
❏ FOX-3002 [M]	Sing We Now of Christmas	1959	6.25	12.50	25.00
-- With no mention of "The Little Drummer Boy" at bottom of front cover					
❏ FOX-3002 [M]	Sing We Now of Christmas	1959	5.00	10.00	20.00
-- With "The Little Drummer Boy" mentioned at bottom of front cover					
❏ SFX-3002 [S]	Sing We Now of Christmas	1959	5.00	10.00	20.00
-- Sky blue label					

MERCURY

❏ SR 60820 [S]	The Wonderful Songs of Christmas	1963	5.00	10.00	20.00

SIMMONS, GENE
Also see KISS.
CASABLANCA

Number	Title	Yr	VG	VG+	NM
❏ NBLP 7120	Gene Simmons	1978	6.25	12.50	25.00
❏ NBPIX 7120 [PD]	Gene Simmons	1978	15.00	30.00	60.00

SIMMONS, GENE (JUMPIN' GENE)
HI

Number	Title	Yr	VG	VG+	NM
❏ HL 2018 [M]	Jumpin' Gene Simmons	1964	12.50	25.00	50.00
❏ SHL 32018 [S]	Jumpin' Gene Simmons	1964	17.50	35.00	70.00

SIMMONS, JEFF
REPRISE

Number	Title	Yr	VG	VG+	NM
❏ RS-6391	Lucille Has Messed Up My Mind	1969	7.50	15.00	30.00

STRAIGHT

❏ STS-1057	Lucille Has Messed Up My Mind	1969	20.00	40.00	80.00

SIMON AND GARFUNKEL
Also see ART GRAFUNKEL; PAUL SIMON.
COLUMBIA

Number	Title	Yr	VG	VG+	NM
❏ CL 2249 [M]	Wednesday Morning, 3 A.M.	1964	6.25	12.50	25.00
-- "Guaranteed High Fidelity" on label					
❏ CL 2469 [M]	Sounds of Silence	1966	7.50	15.00	30.00
-- With "Simon and Garfunkel" and "Sounds of Silence" in all capital letters on front cover with no list of songs					
❏ CL 2469 [M]	Sounds of Silence	1966	5.00	10.00	20.00
-- With "Simon and Garfunkel" and "Sounds of Silence" in large upper and lowercase letters on front cover with all song titles listed; "Tiger Beat" magazine is pictured twice on back cover					
❏ CL 2563 [M]	Parsley, Sage, Rosemary and Thyme	1966	5.00	10.00	20.00
❏ CS 9049 [S]	Wednesday Morning, 3 A.M.	1964	6.25	12.50	25.00
-- "360 Sound Stereo" in black on label					
❏ CS 9269 [S]	Sounds of Silence	1966	7.50	15.00	30.00
-- With "Simon and Garfunkel" and "Sounds of Silence" in all capital letters on front cover with no list of songs					
❏ CS 9269 [S]	Sounds of Silence	1966	5.00	10.00	20.00
-- With "Simon and Garfunkel" and "Sounds of Silence" in large upper and lowercase letters on front cover with all song titles listed; "Tiger Beat" magazine is pictured twice on back cover					
❏ KCS 9529 [M]	Bookends	1968	7.50	15.00	30.00
-- White label "Special Mono Radio Station Copy"; no stock copies in mono					
❏ CQ 30995 [Q]	Bridge Over Troubled Water	1971	6.25	12.50	25.00

Number	Title	Yr	VG	VG+	NM
❑ C5X 37587 [(5)] Collected Works		1981	10.00	20.00	40.00
❑ HC 41350	Simon and Garfunkel's Greatest Hits	1982	7.50	15.00	30.00
-- Half-speed mastered edition					
❑ HC 49914	Bridge Over Troubled Water	1982	7.50	15.00	30.00
-- Half-speed mastered edition					

MOBILE FIDELITY

Number	Title	Yr	VG	VG+	NM
❑ 1-173	Bridge Over Troubled Water	198?	10.00	20.00	40.00
-- Audiophile vinyl					

PICKWICK

Number	Title	Yr	VG	VG+	NM
❑ PC-3059 [M]	The Hit Sounds of Simon and Garfunkel	1966	15.00	30.00	60.00
❑ SPC-3059 [R]	The Hit Sounds of Simon and Garfunkel	1966	7.50	15.00	30.00

SEARS

Number	Title	Yr	VG	VG+	NM
❑ SP-435	Simon and Garfunkel	196?	7.50	15.00	30.00

SIMON SISTERS, THE
Also see CARLY SIMON.
COLUMBIA

Number	Title	Yr	VG	VG+	NM
❑ CC 24506	The Lobster Quadrille	1969	5.00	10.00	20.00
-- Special edition with booklet					

KAPP

Number	Title	Yr	VG	VG+	NM
❑ KL-1359 [M]	Winkin', Blinkin' and Nod	1964	7.50	15.00	30.00
❑ KL-1397 [M]	Cuddlebug	1964	10.00	20.00	40.00
❑ KS-3359 [S]	Winkin', Blinkin' and Nod	1964	10.00	20.00	40.00
❑ KS-3397 [S]	Cuddlebug	1964	12.50	25.00	50.00

SIMON, CARLY
Also see THE SIMON SISTERS.
DIRECT DISK

Number	Title	Yr	VG	VG+	NM
❑ SD-16608	Boys in the Trees	1980	12.50	25.00	50.00
-- Audiophile vinyl					

ELEKTRA

Number	Title	Yr	VG	VG+	NM
❑ EQ-1002 [Q]	Hotcakes	1974	5.00	10.00	20.00
❑ EQ-1033 [Q]	Playing Possum	1975	5.00	10.00	20.00
❑ EQ-1048 [Q]	The Best of Carly Simon	1975	5.00	10.00	20.00
❑ EQ-1064 [Q]	Another Passenger	1976	5.00	10.00	20.00
❑ EQ-4082 [Q]	Carly Simon	1974	5.00	10.00	20.00
❑ EQ-5049 [Q]	No Secrets	1974	5.00	10.00	20.00

SIMON, FRANK
AUDIO LAB

Number	Title	Yr	VG	VG+	NM
❑ AL-1552 [M]	Four Star Hits	1960	37.50	75.00	150.00

SIMON, JOE
BUDDAH

Number	Title	Yr	VG	VG+	NM
❑ BDS-7512	Joe Simon	1969	6.25	12.50	25.00

SOUND STAGE 7

Number	Title	Yr	VG	VG+	NM
❑ SSM-5003 [M]	Pure Soul	1967	7.50	15.00	30.00
❑ SSS-15003 [S]	Pure Soul	1967	10.00	20.00	40.00
❑ SSS-15004	No Sad Songs	1968	10.00	20.00	40.00
❑ SSS-15005	Simon Sings	1968	10.00	20.00	40.00
❑ SSS-15006	The Chokin' Kind	1969	7.50	15.00	30.00
❑ SSS-15008	Joe Simon...Better Than Ever	1969	7.50	15.00	30.00

SPRING

Number	Title	Yr	VG	VG+	NM
❑ SPR-4701	The Sounds of Simon	1971	6.25	12.50	25.00
❑ SPR-5702	Drowning in the Sea of Love	1972	6.25	12.50	25.00
❑ SPR-5704	The Power of Joe Simon	1973	6.25	12.50	25.00

SIMON, PAUL
Also see SIMON AND GARFUNKEL.
COLUMBIA

Number	Title	Yr	VG	VG+	NM
❑ CQ 30750 [Q]	Paul Simon	1974	5.00	10.00	20.00
❑ CQ 32280 [Q]	There Goes Rhymin' Simon	1974	5.00	10.00	20.00
❑ PCQ 33540 [Q]	Still Crazy After All These Years	1975	5.00	10.00	20.00
❑ C5X 37581 [(5)] Collected Works		1981	10.00	20.00	40.00
-- Contains his first four post-S&G solo albums plus the elusive "Paul Simon Songbook," otherwise unavailable in U.S.					
❑ HC 43540	Still Crazy After All These Years	1981	10.00	20.00	40.00
-- Half-speed mastered edition					
❑ HC 45032	Greatest Hits, Etc.	1981	10.00	20.00	40.00
-- Half-speed mastered edition					

DCC COMPACT CLASSICS

Number	Title	Yr	VG	VG+	NM
❑ LPZ-2060	Paul Simon	1998	6.25	12.50	25.00
-- Audiophile vinyl					
❑ LPZ-2062	There Goes Rhymin' Simon	1998	6.25	12.50	25.00
-- Audiophile vinyl					

WARNER BROS.

Number	Title	Yr	VG	VG+	NM
❑ WBMS-140 [(2) DJ] The Paul Simon Interview Show		1986	12.50	25.00	50.00
-- Promo-only "Graceland"-era program in the "Warner Bros. Music Show" series					
❑ 23942 [DJ]	Hearts and Bones	1983	5.00	10.00	20.00
-- Promo only on Quiex II vinyl					

SIMONE, NINA
BETHLEHEM

Number	Title	Yr	VG	VG+	NM
❑ BCP-6028 [M]	Jazz As Played in an Exclusive Side Street Club	1959	20.00	40.00	80.00
❑ BCP-6028 [M]	The Original Nina Simone	1961	7.50	15.00	30.00
-- Retitled reissue					
❑ SBCP-6028 [S]	Jazz As Played in an Exclusive Side Street Club	1959	25.00	50.00	100.00
❑ SBCP-6028 [S]	The Original Nina Simone	1961	10.00	20.00	40.00
-- Retitled reissue					
❑ BCP-6041 [M]	Nina Simone and Her Friends	1960	10.00	20.00	40.00
❑ SBCP-6041 [S]	Nina Simone and Her Friends	1960	12.50	25.00	50.00
-- With Carmen McRae and Chris Connor					

COLPIX

Number	Title	Yr	VG	VG+	NM
❑ CP-407 [M]	The Amazing Nina Simone	1959	6.25	12.50	25.00
❑ SCP-407 [S]	The Amazing Nina Simone	1959	7.50	15.00	30.00
❑ CP-409 [M]	Nina at Town Hall	1960	6.25	12.50	25.00
❑ SCP-409 [S]	Nina at Town Hall	1960	7.50	15.00	30.00
❑ CP-412 [M]	Nina at Newport	1960	6.25	12.50	25.00
❑ SCP-412 [S]	Nina at Newport	1960	7.50	15.00	30.00
❑ CP-419 [M]	Forbidden Fruit	1961	6.25	12.50	25.00
❑ SCP-419 [S]	Forbidden Fruit	1961	7.50	15.00	30.00
❑ CP-421 [M]	Nina Simone at the Village Gate	1961	6.25	12.50	25.00
❑ SCP-421 [S]	Nina Simone at the Village Gate	1961	7.50	15.00	30.00
❑ CP-425 [M]	Nina Sings Ellington	1962	6.25	12.50	25.00
❑ SCP-425 [S]	Nina Sings Ellington	1962	7.50	15.00	30.00
❑ CP-443 [M]	Nina's Choice	1963	6.25	12.50	25.00
❑ SCP-443 [S]	Nina's Choice	1963	7.50	15.00	30.00
❑ CP-455 [M]	Nina Simone at Carnegie Hall	1963	6.25	12.50	25.00
❑ SCP-455 [S]	Nina Simone at Carnegie Hall	1963	7.50	15.00	30.00
❑ CP-465 [M]	Folksy Nina	1964	6.25	12.50	25.00
❑ SCP-465 [S]	Folksy Nina	1964	7.50	15.00	30.00
❑ CP-496 [M]	Nina with Strings	1966	6.25	12.50	25.00
❑ SCP-496 [S]	Nina with Strings	1966	7.50	15.00	30.00

PHILIPS

Number	Title	Yr	VG	VG+	NM
❑ PHS 600-135 [S]	Nina Simone In Concert	1964	5.00	10.00	20.00
❑ PHS 600-148 [S]	Broadway...Blues...Ballads	1964	5.00	10.00	20.00
❑ PHS 600-172 [S]	I Put a Spell on You	1965	5.00	10.00	20.00
❑ PHS 600-187 [S]	Pastel Blues	1965	5.00	10.00	20.00
❑ PHS 600-202 [S]	Let It All Out	1966	5.00	10.00	20.00
❑ PHS 600-207 [S]	Wild Is the Wind	1966	5.00	10.00	20.00
❑ PHS 600-219 [S]	The High Priestess of Soul	1967	5.00	10.00	20.00
❑ PHS 600-298	The Best of Nina Simone	1969	5.00	10.00	20.00

RCA VICTOR

Number	Title	Yr	VG	VG+	NM
❑ LPM-3789 [M]	Nina Simone Sings the Blues	1967	6.25	12.50	25.00
❑ LPM-3837 [M]	Silk and Soul	1967	6.25	12.50	25.00

SIMPLE MINDS
A&M

Number	Title	Yr	VG	VG+	NM
❑ R 209526 [(2)] Live in the City of Light		1987	5.00	10.00	20.00
-- BMG Direct Marketing edition					

SIMPLY RED
ELEKTRA

Number	Title	Yr	VG	VG+	NM
❑ ED 5236 [DJ]	Simply Red Interview	1989	7.50	15.00	30.00
-- Nelson George interviews Mick Hucknall and Lamont Dozier; promo-only					

SIMPSON, RED
CAPITOL

Number	Title	Yr	VG	VG+	NM
❑ ST 2468 [S]	Roll, Truck, Roll	1966	5.00	10.00	20.00
❑ ST 2569 [S]	The Man Behind the Badge	1966	5.00	10.00	20.00
❑ ST 2691 [S]	Truck Drivin' Fool	1967	5.00	10.00	20.00
❑ T 2691 [M]	Truck Drivin' Fool	1967	5.00	10.00	20.00
❑ ST 2829 [S]	A Bakersfield Dozen	1967	5.00	10.00	20.00
❑ T 2829 [M]	A Bakersfield Dozen	1967	6.25	12.50	25.00

PORTLAND

Number	Title	Yr	VG	VG+	NM
❑ 1005 [M]	Hello, I'm a Truck	1965	20.00	40.00	80.00

SIMPSONS, THE
GEFFEN

Number	Title	Yr	VG	VG+	NM
❑ GHS 24308	The Simpsons Sing the Blues	1990	6.25	12.50	25.00

SIMS, FRANKIE LEE
SPECIALTY

Number	Title	Yr	VG	VG+	NM
❑ SPS-2124	Lucy Mae Blues	1970	10.00	20.00	40.00

SIN SAY SHUNS, THE
VENETT

Number	Title	Yr	VG	VG+	NM
❑ V-940 [M]	I'll Be There	1966	10.00	20.00	40.00
❑ VS-940 [S]	I'll Be There	1966	12.50	25.00	50.00

SINATRA FAMILY, THE -- See VARIOUS ARTISTS COMPILATIONS in back.

Number	Title	Yr	VG	VG+	NM

SINATRA, FRANK

Also see TOMMY DORSEY; HARRY JAMES.

ARTANIS

Number	Title	Yr	VG	VG+	NM
❑ ARZ 101 [(2)]	Sinatra '57 In Concert	1999	7.50	15.00	30.00

-- Audiophile vinyl

BOOK-OF-THE-MONTH

Number	Title	Yr	VG	VG+	NM
❑ (# unknown) [(6)]	Tommy Dorsey/Frank Sinatra: The Complete Sessions	1983	25.00	50.00	100.00

CAPITOL

Number	Title	Yr	VG	VG+	NM
❑ DWBB-254 [(2) R]	Close-Up	1969	5.00	10.00	20.00
-- Reissue in one package of "This Is Sinatra" and "This Is Sinatra, Volume Two"					
❑ H 488 [10]	Songs for Young Lovers	1954	15.00	30.00	60.00
❑ H 528 [10]	Swing Easy	1954	15.00	30.00	60.00
❑ H1-581 [10]	In the Wee Small Hours, Part 1	1955	25.00	50.00	100.00
❑ H2-581 [10]	In the Wee Small Hours, Part 2	1955	25.00	50.00	100.00
❑ W 581 [M]	In the Wee Small Hours	1955	10.00	20.00	40.00
-- Gray label original					
❑ W 581 [M]	In the Wee Small Hours	1959	6.25	12.50	25.00
-- Black label with colorband					
❑ W 587 [M]	Swing Easy/Songs for Young Lovers	1955	10.00	20.00	40.00
-- Gray label original; 12-inch version of two 10-inch LPs					
❑ W 587 [M]	Swing Easy/Songs for Young Lovers	1959	6.25	12.50	25.00
-- Black label with colorband					
❑ W 653 [M]	Songs for Swingin' Lovers!	1956	12.50	25.00	50.00
-- Gray label; cover has Sinatra facing away from the embracing couple					
❑ W 653 [M]	Songs for Swingin' Lovers!	1956	10.00	20.00	40.00
-- Gray label; cover has Sinatra facing toward the embracing couple					
❑ W 653 [M]	Songs for Swingin' Lovers!	1959	6.25	12.50	25.00
-- Black label with colorband					
❑ T 735 [M]	Frank Sinatra Conducts Tone Poems of Color	1956	15.00	30.00	60.00
-- Turquoise label					
❑ T 735 [M]	Frank Sinatra Conducts Tone Poems of Color	1959	10.00	20.00	40.00
-- Black label with colorband					
❑ T 768 [M]	This Is Sinatra!	1956	7.50	15.00	30.00
-- Turquoise label					
❑ T 768 [M]	This Is Sinatra!	196?	5.00	10.00	20.00
-- Black "Starline" label					
❑ W 789 [M]	Close to You	1957	7.50	15.00	30.00
-- Gray label					
❑ W 789 [M]	Close to You	1959	5.00	10.00	20.00
-- Black label with colorband					
❑ W 803 [M]	A Swingin' Affair!	1957	5.00	10.00	20.00
-- Black label with colorband					
❑ W 803 [M]	A Swingin' Affair!	1957	7.50	15.00	30.00
-- Gray label					
❑ SW 855 [S]	Where Are You?	1959	10.00	20.00	40.00
-- Originals do not include "I Cover the Waterfront"					
❑ SW 855 [S]	Where Are You?	196?	7.50	15.00	30.00
-- Later releases restore "I Cover the Waterfront"					
❑ W 855 [M]	Where Are You?	1957	7.50	15.00	30.00
-- Gray label					
❑ W 855 [M]	Where Are You?	1959	5.00	10.00	20.00
-- Black label with colorband					
❑ T 894 [M]	The Sinatra Christmas Album	196?	5.00	10.00	20.00
-- Reissue of A Jolly Christmas with Frank Sinatra with same contents; some copies have this cover and "A Jolly Christmas" labels					
❑ W 894 [M]	A Jolly Christmas from Frank Sinatra	1957	10.00	20.00	40.00
-- Original mono with gray label					
❑ W 894 [M]	A Jolly Christmas from Frank Sinatra	1958	7.50	15.00	30.00
-- Black colorband label, logo at left					
❑ SW 920 [S]	Come Fly with Me	1959	7.50	15.00	30.00
❑ W 920 [M]	Come Fly with Me	1958	10.00	20.00	40.00
-- Gray label					
❑ W 920 [M]	Come Fly with Me	1959	5.00	10.00	20.00
-- Black label with colorband					
❑ W 982 [M]	This Is Sinatra, Volume Two	1958	10.00	20.00	40.00
-- Gray label					
❑ W 982 [M]	This Is Sinatra, Volume Two	1959	5.00	10.00	20.00
-- Black label with colorband					
❑ SW 1053 [S]	Frank Sinatra Sings for Only the Lonely	1959	7.50	15.00	30.00
-- Originals do not include "It's a Lonesome Old Town" and "Spring Is Here"					
❑ SW 1053 [S]	Frank Sinatra Sings for Only the Lonely	196?	6.25	12.50	25.00
-- Later releases restore "It's a Lonesome Old Town" and "Spring Is Here"					
❑ W 1053 [M]	Frank Sinatra Sings for Only the Lonely	1958	10.00	20.00	40.00
-- Gray label					
❑ W 1053 [M]	Frank Sinatra Sings for Only the Lonely	1959	5.00	10.00	20.00
-- Black label with colorband					
❑ SW 1069 [S]	Come Dance with Me!	1959	7.50	15.00	30.00
❑ W 1069 [M]	Come Dance with Me!	1959	5.00	10.00	20.00
❑ W 1164 [M]	Look to Your Heart	1959	7.50	15.00	30.00
❑ SW 1221 [S]	No One Cares	1959	7.50	15.00	30.00
❑ W 1221 [M]	No One Cares	1959	5.00	10.00	20.00
❑ SW 1417 [S]	Nice 'N' Easy	1960	6.25	12.50	25.00

Number	Title	Yr	VG	VG+	NM
❑ W 1417 [M]	Nice 'N' Easy	1960	5.00	10.00	20.00
❑ W 1429 [M]	Swing Easy	1960	5.00	10.00	20.00
❑ W 1432 [M]	Songs for Young Lovers	1960	5.00	10.00	20.00
❑ SW 1491 [S]	Sinatra's Swingin' Session!!!	1961	6.25	12.50	25.00
❑ W 1491 [M]	Sinatra's Swingin' Session!!!	1961	5.00	10.00	20.00
❑ SW 1538 [S]	All the Way	1961	6.25	12.50	25.00
❑ W 1538 [M]	All the Way	1961	5.00	10.00	20.00
❑ SW 1594 [S]	Come Swing with Me!	1961	6.25	12.50	25.00
❑ W 1594 [M]	Come Swing with Me!	1961	5.00	10.00	20.00
❑ SW 1676 [S]	Point of No Return	1962	6.25	12.50	25.00
❑ W 1676 [M]	Point of No Return	1962	5.00	10.00	20.00
❑ SWCO 1726 [(3)P]	Sinatra, The Great Years	1962	10.00	20.00	40.00
❑ WCO 1726 [(3) M]	Sinatra, The Great Years	1962	7.50	15.00	30.00
❑ SW 1729 [P]	Sinatra Sings...Of Love and Things	1962	5.00	10.00	20.00
❑ W 1729 [M]	Sinatra Sings...Of Love and Things	1962	5.00	10.00	20.00
❑ W 1825 [M]	Sinatra Sings Rodgers and Hart	1963	5.00	10.00	20.00
❑ T 1919 [M]	Tell Her You Love Her	1963	5.00	10.00	20.00
❑ W 1994 [M]	Sinatra Sings the Select Johnny Mercer	1963	5.00	10.00	20.00
❑ T 2036 [M]	The Greatest Hits of Frank Sinatra	1964	5.00	10.00	20.00
❑ T 2123 [M]	Sinatra Sings the Select Harold Arlen	1964	25.00	50.00	100.00
-- Only released in Canada, Australia and the UK					
❑ PRO-2163/4/5/6 [(2) DJ]	Selections from Sinatra, The Great Years	1962	10.00	20.00	40.00
❑ W 2301 [M]	Sinatra Sings the Select Cole Porter	1965	5.00	10.00	20.00
❑ T 2602 [M]	Forever Frank	1966	5.00	10.00	20.00
❑ T 2700 [M]	The Movie Songs	1967	5.00	10.00	20.00
❑ STFL 2814 [(6) P]	The Frank Sinatra Deluxe Set	1968	15.00	30.00	60.00
❑ TFL 2814 [(6) M]	The Frank Sinatra Deluxe Set	1968	25.00	50.00	100.00
❑ PRO-2974/5 [DJ]	Frank Sinatra Minute Masters	1965	10.00	20.00	40.00
-- Edited version of 20 songs					
❑ DNFR 7630 [(6) P]	The Sinatra Touch	19??	15.00	30.00	60.00
❑ C1-89611	Duets	1993	5.00	10.00	20.00
❑ W 90986 [M]	Sentimental Journey	1966	6.25	12.50	25.00
-- Capitol Record Club issue					
❑ DQBO 91261 [(2) R]	Songs for the Young at Heart	196?	7.50	15.00	30.00
-- Capitol Record Club issue					
❑ C1-94777 [(5)]	The Capitol Years	1990	25.00	50.00	100.00
-- With book and wraparound banner. Only 5,000 were pressed					
❑ STBB-95191 [(2) R]	Sinatra Sings the Great Ones	1973	5.00	10.00	20.00
-- Longines Symphonette (formerly Capitol) Record Club issue					

COLUMBIA

Number	Title	Yr	VG	VG+	NM
❑ C2L 6 [(2) M]	The Frank Sinatra Story	1958	7.50	15.00	30.00
❑ C3L 42 [(3) M]	The Essential Frank Sinatra	1966	25.00	50.00	100.00
❑ C3S 42 [(3) R]	The Essential Frank Sinatra	1966	12.50	25.00	50.00
❑ CL 606 [M]	Frankie	1955	7.50	15.00	30.00
-- Cover has drawing of Frank Sinatra wearing a hat					
❑ CL 606 [M]	Frankie	1955	6.25	12.50	25.00
-- Cover has Frank with Debbie Reynolds					
❑ CL 743 [M]	The Voice	1956	6.25	12.50	25.00
❑ CL 884 [M]	Frank Sinatra Conducts Music of Alec Wilder	1956	10.00	20.00	40.00
-- Reissue of Columbia Masterworks ML 4271					
❑ CL 902 [M]	That Old Feeling	1956	6.25	12.50	25.00
❑ CL 953 [M]	Adventures of the Heart	1957	6.25	12.50	25.00
❑ CL 1032 [M]	Christmas Dreaming	1957	20.00	40.00	80.00
❑ CL 1136 [M]	Put Your Dreams Away	1958	6.25	12.50	25.00
❑ CL 1241 [M]	Love Is a Kick	1958	6.25	12.50	25.00
❑ CL 1297 [M]	The Broadway Kick	1958	6.25	12.50	25.00
❑ CL 1359 [M]	Come Back to Sorrento	1959	6.25	12.50	25.00
❑ CL 1448 [M]	Reflections	1959	15.00	30.00	60.00
❑ CAS 2475 [DJ]	The Voice: The Columbia Years Sampler	1986	10.00	20.00	40.00
❑ CL 2521 [10]	Get Happy	1955	15.00	30.00	60.00
-- "House Party Series" release					
❑ CL 2539 [10]	I've Got a Crush on You	1955	15.00	30.00	60.00
-- "House Party Series" release; different contents from CL 6290					
❑ CL 2542 [10]	Christmas with Sinatra	1955	15.00	30.00	60.00
-- "House Party Series" release					
❑ CL 2739 [M]	The Essential Frank Sinatra, Volume 1	1967	6.25	12.50	25.00
❑ CL 2740 [M]	The Essential Frank Sinatra, Volume 2	1967	6.25	12.50	25.00
❑ CL 2741 [M]	The Essential Frank Sinatra, Volume 3	1967	6.25	12.50	25.00
❑ CL 2913 [M]	Frank Sinatra in Hollywood	1968	20.00	40.00	80.00
❑ CL 6001 [10]	The Voice of Frank Sinatra	1949	17.50	35.00	70.00
-- Original in pink paper cover					
❑ CL 6001 [10]	The Voice of Frank Sinatra	1950	15.00	30.00	60.00
-- Blue cardboard cover					
❑ CL 6019 [10]	Christmas Songs by Sinatra	1948	25.00	50.00	100.00
-- With "gingerbread man" cover					
❑ CL 6019 [10]	Christmas Songs by Sinatra	1949	20.00	40.00	80.00
-- With green vinylite cover					
❑ CL 6059 [10]	Frankly Sentimental	1951	15.00	30.00	60.00
❑ CL 6087 [10]	Songs by Sinatra, Volume 1	1952	15.00	30.00	60.00
❑ CL 6096 [10]	Dedicated to You	1952	25.00	50.00	100.00
-- Three of the tracks on this LP are alternate takes unavailable on vinyl anywhere else					

Number	Title	Yr	VG	VG+	NM
❑ CL 6143 [10]	Sing and Dance with Frank Sinatra	1953	15.00	30.00	60.00
❑ CL 6290 [10]	I've Got a Crush on You	1954	15.00	30.00	60.00
❑ KG 31358 [(2)]	In the Beginning	1971	10.00	20.00	40.00
❑ PC 40707	Christmas Dreaming	1987	7.50	15.00	30.00
-- Reissue of CL 1032 with an extra track					
❑ C2X 40897 [(2)]	Hello Young Lovers	1988	7.50	15.00	30.00
❑ C6X 40343 [(6)]	The Voice: The Columbia Years 1943-1952	1986	20.00	40.00	80.00
❑ PC 44238 [M]	Sinatra Rarities	1989	10.00	20.00	40.00
COLUMBIA MASTERWORKS					
❑ ML 4271 [M]	Frank Sinatra Conducts Music of Alec Wilder	1955	25.00	50.00	100.00
HARMONY					
❑ HL 7400 [M]	Have Yourself a Merry Little Christmas	1967	7.50	15.00	30.00
❑ HL 7405 [M]	Romantic Scenes from the Early Years	1967	7.50	15.00	30.00
❑ HS 11200 [R]	Have Yourself a Merry Little Christmas	1967	5.00	10.00	20.00
LONGINES SYMPHONETTE					
❑ LS-308A [(10)]	Sinatra: The Works	1972	18.75	37.50	75.00
❑ LS-309A [(6)]	Sinatra: The Works	1973	10.00	20.00	40.00
-- Abridged version of LS-308A					
❑ SYS-5637	Sinatra Like Never Before	1972	6.25	12.50	25.00
-- Bonus LP with purchase of LS-308A					
MOBILE FIDELITY					
❑ SC-1 [(16)]	Sinatra	1983	150.00	300.00	600.00
-- Audiophile vinyl; only two of the 16 records in this box were released individually					
❑ 1-086	Nice 'N' Easy	1981	10.00	20.00	40.00
-- Audiophile vinyl					
❑ 1-135 [M]	A Jolly Christmas from Frank Sinatra	1984	10.00	20.00	40.00
-- Audiophile vinyl using the original title					
RCA VICTOR					
❑ LPV-583 [M]	This Love of Mine	1971	10.00	20.00	40.00
❑ LPM-1569 [M]	Frankie and Tommy	1957	15.00	30.00	60.00
-- First issue of this LP					
❑ LPM-1569 [M]	Tommy Plays, Frankie Sings	1957	10.00	20.00	40.00
-- Second issue with new title					
❑ LPM-1632 [M]	We Three	1958	15.00	30.00	60.00
-- First issue					
❑ LPM-1632 [M]	We Three	1958	10.00	20.00	40.00
-- Second issue, "RE" on cover					
❑ LPT-3063 [10]	Fabulous Frankie	1953	15.00	30.00	60.00
❑ CPL2-4334 [(2)]	The Sinatra/Dorsey Sessions, Vol. 1	1982	6.25	12.50	25.00
❑ CPL2-4335 [(2)]	The Sinatra/Dorsey Sessions, Vol. 2	1982	6.25	12.50	25.00
❑ CPL2-4336 [(2)]	The Sinatra/Dorsey Sessions, Vol. 3	1982	6.25	12.50	25.00
REPRISE					
❑ F 1001 [M]	Ring-a-Ding-Ding!	1961	5.00	10.00	20.00
❑ R9 1001 [S]	Ring-a-Ding-Ding!	1961	6.25	12.50	25.00
❑ F 1002 [M]	Swing Along with Me	1961	10.00	20.00	40.00
-- Original title					
❑ F 1002 [M]	Sinatra Swings	1961	5.00	10.00	20.00
-- Retitled version of "Swing Along with Me"; Capitol threatened legal action because of its "Come Swing With Me!" collection					
❑ R9 1002 [S]	Swing Along with Me	1961	12.50	25.00	50.00
-- Original title					
❑ R9 1002 [S]	Sinatra Swings	1961	6.25	12.50	25.00
-- Retitled version of "Swing Along with Me"; Capitol threatened legal action because of its "Come Swing With Me!" collection					
❑ F 1003 [M]	I Remember Tommy	1961	5.00	10.00	20.00
❑ R9 1003 [S]	I Remember Tommy	1961	6.25	12.50	25.00
❑ R9 1004 [S]	Sinatra & Strings	1962	5.00	10.00	20.00
❑ R9 1005 [S]	Sinatra and Swingin' Brass	1962	5.00	10.00	20.00
❑ F 1006 [M]	Great Songs from Great Britain	1962	20.00	40.00	80.00
-- Only released in the UK					
❑ R9 1006 [S]	Great Songs from Great Britain	1962	25.00	50.00	100.00
-- Only released in the UK					
❑ R9 1007 [S]	All Alone	1962	5.00	10.00	20.00
❑ R9 1008 [S]	Sinatra-Basie	1963	5.00	10.00	20.00
❑ R9 1009 [S]	The Concert Sinatra	1963	6.25	12.50	25.00
-- Original pressings declare this was recorded in "35mm Stereo"					
❑ R9 1009 [S]	The Concert Sinatra	196?	5.00	10.00	20.00
-- Without cover reference to "35mm Stereo"					
❑ R9 1010 [S]	Sinatra's Sinatra	1963	5.00	10.00	20.00
❑ FS 1011 [S]	Days of Wine and Roses, Moon River, and Other Academy Award Winners	1964	5.00	10.00	20.00
❑ FS 1012 [S]	It Might As Well Be Swing	1964	5.00	10.00	20.00
❑ FS 1013 [S]	Softly, As I Leave You	1964	5.00	10.00	20.00
❑ FS 1014 [S]	September of My Years	1965	5.00	10.00	20.00
❑ FS 1015 [S]	My Kind of Broadway	1965	5.00	10.00	20.00
❑ 2F 1016 [(2) M]	A Man and His Music	1965	5.00	10.00	20.00
❑ 2FS 1016 [(2) S]	A Man and His Music	1965	6.25	12.50	25.00
❑ 2F/2FS 1016	A Man and His Music Special Box	1965	50.00	100.00	200.00
-- Blue slipcase with embossed silver front, raised letters, plus 4-page booklet and a signed card (deduct 50% if card missing). Add this to LP value.					

Number	Title	Yr	VG	VG+	NM
❑ FS 1018 [S]	Moonlight Sinatra	1966	5.00	10.00	20.00
❑ 2F 1019 [(2) M]	Sinatra at the Sands	1966	5.00	10.00	20.00
❑ 2FS 1019 [(2) S]	Sinatra at the Sands	1966	6.25	12.50	25.00
❑ FS 1023	The Sinatra Christmas Album	1967	25.00	50.00	100.00
-- Album never released; value is for cover slick					
❑ FS 1024	Francis A. and Edward K.	1968	5.00	10.00	20.00
❑ FS 1028	SinatraJobim	1969	2,000.	3,000.	4,000.
-- Unreleased; test pressings exist (value is for one of these). 8-track tapes also exist and are 10% of this value					
❑ FS4 1029 [Q]	My Way	1974	6.25	12.50	25.00
❑ FS 1030	A Man Alone & Other Songs of Rod McKuen	1969	100.00	200.00	400.00
-- Signed copies with gatefold cover and hardbound book; 400 made					
❑ FS 1031	Watertown	1970	6.25	12.50	25.00
-- With gatefold and poster					
❑ FS4 2155 [Q]	Ol' Blue Eyes Is Back	1974	6.25	12.50	25.00
❑ FS4 2194 [Q]	Some Nice Things I've Missed	1974	6.25	12.50	25.00
❑ 3FS 2300 [(3)]	Trilogy: Past, Present, Future	1980	5.00	10.00	20.00
❑ 5004 [DJ]	A Man and His Music, Part II	1966	75.00	150.00	300.00
-- Promotional album for use by Budweiser					
❑ 5230 [DJ]	Songbook, Vol. 1	1971	12.50	25.00	50.00
❑ 5267 [(2) DJ]	Songbook, Vol. 2	1972	25.00	50.00	100.00
❑ 5409 [DJ]	I Sing the Songs	1976	12.50	25.00	50.00
❑ F 6045 [M]	Sinatra Conducts Music from Pictures and Plays	1962	7.50	15.00	30.00
❑ R9 6045 [S]	Sinatra Conducts Music from Pictures and Plays	1962	10.00	2.00	40.00
❑ RS 6167 [S]	Sinatra '65	1965	5.00	10.00	20.00
TIME-LIFE					
❑ SLGD-02 [(2)]	Legendary Singers	1982	6.25	12.50	25.00

SINATRA, FRANK; DEAN MARTIN; SAMMY DAVIS, JR.
Also see each artist's individual listings.

ARTANIS

❑ ARZ 102 [(2)]	The Summit	1999	7.50	15.00	30.00
-- Audiophile vinyl					

SINATRA, NANCY
RCA VICTOR

❑ LSP-4645	Nancy and Lee Again	1972	7.50	15.00	30.00
-- With Lee Hazlewood					
❑ LSP-4774	Woman	1973	6.25	12.50	25.00
❑ VPS-6078 [(2)]	This Is Nancy Sinatra	1972	12.50	25.00	50.00
REPRISE					
❑ R-6202 [M]	Boots	1966	6.25	12.50	25.00
❑ RS-6202 [S]	Boots	1966	7.50	15.00	30.00
❑ R-6207 [M]	How Does That Grab You?	1966	5.00	10.00	20.00
❑ RS-6207 [S]	How Does That Grab You?	1966	6.25	12.50	25.00
❑ R-6221 [M]	Nancy in London	1966	5.00	10.00	20.00
❑ RS-6221 [S]	Nancy in London	1966	6.25	12.50	25.00
❑ R-6239 [M]	Sugar	1967	6.25	12.50	25.00
❑ RS-6239 [S]	Sugar	1967	5.00	10.00	20.00
❑ R-6251 [M]	Country, My Way	1967	6.25	12.50	25.00
❑ RS-6251 [S]	Country, My Way	1967	5.00	10.00	20.00
❑ RS-6273	Nancy and Lee	1968	5.00	10.00	20.00
-- With Lee Hazlewood					
❑ R-6277 [M]	Movin' with Nancy	1967	6.25	12.50	25.00
❑ RS-6277 [S]	Movin' with Nancy	1967	5.00	10.00	20.00
❑ RS-6333	Nancy	1969	5.00	10.00	20.00
❑ RS-6409	Nancy's Greatest Hits	1970	5.00	10.00	20.00

SING A SONG WITH THE BEATLES
"Instrumental Background Re-Creations of Their Big Hits"; no artist is mentioned.

TOWER

❑ DKAO 5000 [R]	Sing a Song with the Beatles	1965	50.00	100.00	200.00
❑ KAO 5000 [M]	Sing a Song with the Beatles	1965	37.50	75.00	150.00
-- No artist listed on label					

SINGER ORCHESTRA, THE
SINGER

❑ HE-S1 [S]	Favorite Christmas Songs from Singer	1964	5.00	10.00	20.00
-- Cover photo of the cast of "The Donna Reed Show"					

SINGLETON, CHARLIE
RCA CAMDEN

❑ CAL-713 [M]	Big Twist Hits	1962	5.00	10.00	20.00
❑ CAS-713 [S]	Big Twist Hits	1962	6.25	12.50	25.00

SIOUXSIE AND THE BANSHEES
POLYDOR

❑ PD1-6207	The Scream	1978	7.50	15.00	30.00

Number	Title	Yr	VG	VG+	NM
PVC					
❏ 7921	Kaleidoscope	1980	6.25	12.50	25.00
❏ 8903	Ju Ju	1981	6.25	12.50	25.00
-- Original copies include bonus single "Israel"/"Red Over White"					
❏ 8906	Once Upon a Time: The Singles	1981	5.00	10.00	20.00
-- With poster and inner sleeve					
WARNER BROS.					
❏ WBMS-138 [DJ]	The Tinderbox Interview	1986	6.25	12.50	25.00
-- Part of "The Warner Bros. Music Show"					

SIR DOUGLAS QUINTET
Also see DOUG SAHM.

Number	Title	Yr	VG	VG+	NM
PHILIPS					
❏ PHS 600-344	1 + 1 + 1 = 4	1970	6.25	12.50	25.00
❏ PHS 600-353	The Return of Doug Saldana	1971	6.25	12.50	25.00
R&M					
❏ UDL-2343	The Tracker	1981	5.00	10.00	20.00
SMASH					
❏ SRS-67108	Sir Douglas Quintet + 2 = Honkey Blues	1968	7.50	15.00	30.00
❏ SRS-67115	Mendocino	1969	6.25	12.50	25.00
❏ SRS-67130	Together After Five	1970	6.25	12.50	25.00
TRIBE					
❏ TR 37001 [M]	The Best of the Sir Douglas Quintet	1966	17.50	35.00	70.00
❏ TRS 47001 [R]	The Best of the Sir Douglas Quintet	1966	12.50	25.00	50.00

SIR LANCELOT

Number	Title	Yr	VG	VG+	NM
MERCURY					
❏ MG-25159 [10]	Calypso	1952	12.50	25.00	50.00

SIR LORD BALTIMORE

Number	Title	Yr	VG	VG+	NM
MERCURY					
❏ SR-61328	Kingdom Come	1970	6.25	12.50	25.00
❏ SRM-1-613	Sir Lord Baltimore	1971	6.25	12.50	25.00

SIREN

Number	Title	Yr	VG	VG+	NM
ELEKTRA					
❏ EKS-74087	Strange Locomotion	1971	5.00	10.00	20.00

SISTER DOUBLE HAPPINESS

Number	Title	Yr	VG	VG+	NM
REPRISE					
❏ PRO-A-5010 [DJ]	Heart and Mind	1991	10.00	20.00	40.00
-- Vinyl is promo only					

SISTER SLEDGE

Number	Title	Yr	VG	VG+	NM
ATCO					
❏ SD 36-105	Circle of Love	1975	5.00	10.00	20.00

SIZEMORE, ARTHUR

Number	Title	Yr	VG	VG+	NM
DECCA					
❏ DL 4785 [M]	Mountain Ballads and Old Hymns	1966	7.50	15.00	30.00
❏ DL 74785 [S]	Mountain Ballads and Old Hymns	1966	10.00	20.00	40.00

SKELTON, RED

Number	Title	Yr	VG	VG+	NM
LIBERTY					
❏ LRP-3425 [M]	Red Skelton Conducts	1966	5.00	10.00	20.00
❏ LRP-3477 [M]	Music from the Heart	1966	5.00	10.00	20.00
❏ LST-7425 [S]	Red Skelton Conducts	1966	6.25	12.50	25.00
❏ LST-7477 [S]	Music from the Heart	1966	6.25	12.50	25.00

SKID ROW
Two different groups.

Number	Title	Yr	VG	VG+	NM
ATLANTIC					
❏ 1P-8136	Slave to the Grind	1991	5.00	10.00	20.00
-- U.S. vinyl version available only from Columbia House; all copies are the censored version with "Beggars Day"					
EPIC					
❏ E 30404	Skid Row	1971	5.00	10.00	20.00
❏ E 30913	34 Hours	1971	6.25	12.50	25.00

SKIN ALLEY

Number	Title	Yr	VG	VG+	NM
STAX					
❏ STS-3013	Two Quid Deal	1973	5.00	10.00	20.00
-- With poster					

SKINNER, CORNELIA AND OTIS

Number	Title	Yr	VG	VG+	NM
RCA CAMDEN					
❏ CAL-190 [M]	Cornelia Skinner with Otis Skinner	1955	7.50	15.00	30.00

SKINNER, JIMMIE

Number	Title	Yr	VG	VG+	NM
DECCA					
❏ DL 4132 [M]	Country Singer	1961	10.00	20.00	40.00
MERCURY					
❏ MG-20352 [M]	Songs That Make the Jukebox Play	1957	20.00	40.00	80.00
❏ MG-20700 [M]	Jimmie Skinner Sings Jimmie Rodgers	1962	6.25	12.50	25.00
❏ SR-60700 [S]	Jimmie Skinner Sings Jimmie Rodgers	1962	7.50	15.00	30.00
STARDAY					
❏ SLP-240 [M]	Jimmie Skinner	1963	10.00	20.00	40.00
WING					
❏ MGW-12277 [M]	Country Blues	1964	6.25	12.50	25.00

SKIP AND THE CREATIONS

Number	Title	Yr	VG	VG+	NM
JUSTICE					
❏ (# unknown)	Mobam	196?	100.00	200.00	400.00

SKUNKS, THE

Number	Title	Yr	VG	VG+	NM
TEEN TOWN					
❏ TTLP-101	Getting Started	1968	12.50	25.00	50.00

SKYLINERS, THE

Number	Title	Yr	VG	VG+	NM
CALICO					
❏ LP-3000 [M]	The Skyliners	1959	200.00	400.00	600.00
-- Yellow and blue label					
❏ LP-3000 [M]	The Skyliners	196?	50.00	100.00	200.00
-- Blue label					
KAMA SUTRA					
❏ KSBS-2026	Once Upon a Time	1971	6.25	12.50	25.00
ORIGINAL SOUND					
❏ OS-5010 [M]	Since I Don't Have You	1963	12.50	25.00	50.00
❏ OSS-8873 [S]	Since I Don't Have You	1963	17.50	35.00	70.00

SLADE

Number	Title	Yr	VG	VG+	NM
COTILLION					
❏ SD 9035	Play It Loud	1970	5.00	10.00	20.00
FONTANA					
❏ SRF-67598	Ballzy	1969	20.00	40.00	80.00
❏ SRF-67598 [DJ]	Ballzy	1969	12.50	25.00	50.00
-- White label promo					

SLATKIN, FELIX

Number	Title	Yr	VG	VG+	NM
LIBERTY					
❏ LST-7150 [S]	Fantastic Percussion	1960	5.00	10.00	20.00

SLAUGHTER

Number	Title	Yr	VG	VG+	NM
CHRYSALIS					
❏ F1-21911	The Wild Life	1992	5.00	10.00	20.00
-- Vinyl version available only through Columbia House					
❏ R 120666 [EP]	Stick It Live	1990	5.00	10.00	20.00
-- Vinyl version available only through BMG Direct Marketing					

SLAYER

Number	Title	Yr	VG	VG+	NM
DEF AMERICAN					
❏ DFS 24307	Seasons in the Abyss	1990	5.00	10.00	20.00
METAL BLADE					
❏ MBR 1037 [PD]	Live Undead	1984	7.50	15.00	30.00
-- Limited edition picture disc					

SLEDGE, PERCY

Number	Title	Yr	VG	VG+	NM
ATLANTIC					
❏ 8125 [M]	When a Man Loves a Woman	1966	12.50	25.00	50.00
❏ SD 8125 [R]	When a Man Loves a Woman	1966	7.50	15.00	30.00
❏ 8132 [M]	Warm and Tender Soul	1966	12.50	25.00	50.00
❏ SD 8132 [R]	Warm and Tender Soul	1966	7.50	15.00	30.00
❏ 8146 [M]	The Percy Sledge Way	1967	12.50	25.00	50.00
❏ SD 8146 [S]	The Percy Sledge Way	1967	12.50	25.00	50.00
❏ SD 8180	Take Time to Know Her	1968	12.50	25.00	50.00
❏ SD 8210	The Best of Percy Sledge	1969	6.25	12.50	25.00

SLICK, GRACE
Also see THE GREAT SOCIETY; JEFFERSON AIRPLANE; JEFFERSON STARSHIP.

Number	Title	Yr	VG	VG+	NM
RCA VICTOR					
❏ DJL1-3922 [DJ]	Welcome to the Wrecking Ball Interview	1981	5.00	10.00	20.00
❏ DJL1-3923 [DJ]	RCA Special Radio Series	1981	5.00	10.00	20.00

Number	Title	Yr	VG	VG+	NM

SLICKEE BOYS
DACOIT
| ❑ 1001 | Separated Vegetables | 1977 | 20.00 | 40.00 | 80.00 |

-- *Limited edition of 100 copies*

LIMP
| ❑ 1003 | Separated Vegetables | 1980 | 6.25 | 12.50 | 25.00 |

-- *Limited edition of 300 copies; reissue with new cover*

SLIM JIM
SOMA
| ❑ MG 1225 [M] | Slim Jim Sings | 1958 | 10.00 | 20.00 | 40.00 |

SLITS, THE
ANTILLES
| ❑ AN-7077 | Cut | 1979 | 10.00 | 20.00 | 40.00 |

SLOAN, P.F.
ATCO
| ❑ SD 33-268 | Measure of Pleasure | 1968 | 6.25 | 12.50 | 25.00 |
DUNHILL
❑ D-50004 [M]	Songs of Our Times	1965	6.25	12.50	25.00
❑ DS-50004 [S]	Songs of Our Times	1965	7.50	15.00	30.00
❑ D-50007 [M]	Twelve More Times	1966	6.25	12.50	25.00
❑ DS-50007 [S]	Twelve More Times	1966	7.50	15.00	30.00
MUMS
| ❑ KZ 31260 | Raised on Records | 1972 | 5.00 | 10.00 | 20.00 |

SLY AND THE FAMILY STONE
EPIC
| ❑ AS 264 [DJ] | Everything You Always Wanted to Hear by Sly and the Family Stone But Were Afraid to Ask For | 1976 | 6.25 | 12.50 | 25.00 |

-- *Promo-only compilation*

❑ LN 24324 [M]	A Whole New Thing	1967	5.00	10.00	20.00
❑ BN 26324 [S]	A Whole New Thing	1967	5.00	10.00	20.00
❑ EQ 30325 [Q]	Sly and the Family Stone's Greatest Hits	1971	25.00	50.00	100.00

-- *Has alternate mixes of "Hot Fun in the Summertime," "Thank You" and "Everybody Is a Star," which are not rechanneled stereo as they are on other LPs*

| ❑ PEQ 32930 [Q] | Small Talk | 1974 | 6.25 | 12.50 | 25.00 |
| ❑ PEQ 33835 [Q] | High on You | 1975 | 6.25 | 12.50 | 25.00 |

SMACK, THE
AUDIO HOUSE
| ❑ (# unknown) | The Smack | 1967 | 500.00 | 1,000. | 2,000. |

SMALL FACES
IMMEDIATE
| ❑ Z12 52002 [S] | There Are But Four Small Faces | 1967 | 12.50 | 25.00 | 50.00 |

-- *Color cover (counterfeits have either black and white or black and green covers)*

| ❑ Z12 52008 [S] | Ogden's Nut Gone Flake | 1968 | 12.50 | 25.00 | 50.00 |

-- *Originals have a round cover*

SMALL, DANNY
UNITED ARTISTS
| ❑ UAJ-14004 [M] | Woman She Was Born for Sorrow | 1962 | 5.00 | 10.00 | 20.00 |
| ❑ UAJS-15004 [S] | Woman She Was Born for Sorrow | 1962 | 6.25 | 12.50 | 25.00 |

SMALL, MILLIE
SMASH
| ❑ MGS-27055 [M] | My Boy Lollipop | 1964 | 12.50 | 25.00 | 50.00 |
| ❑ SRS-67055 [R] | My Boy Lollipop | 1964 | 10.00 | 20.00 | 40.00 |

SMASHING PUMPKINS
CAROLINE
| ❑ 1705 | Gish | 1991 | 5.00 | 10.00 | 20.00 |

-- *Originals do not have the word "Remastered" under the bar code*

| ❑ 1740 [(2)] | Siamese Dream | 1993 | 6.25 | 12.50 | 25.00 |

-- *Originals have dark red vinyl (in-print version has pink marbled vinyl)*

| ❑ 1767 | Pisces Iscariot | 1994 | 50.00 | 100.00 | 200.00 |

-- *First 2,000 copies, hand-numbered on back cover, came with a bonus 7-inch single*

| ❑ 1767 | Pisces Iscariot | 1994 | 5.00 | 10.00 | 20.00 |

-- *Regular pressing on colored vinyl, not numbered, no bonus 7-inch single*

SMECK, ROY
ABC-PARAMOUNT
❑ ABC-119 [M]	South Seas Serenade	1956	10.00	20.00	40.00
❑ ABC-174 [M]	Melodies with Memories	1957	10.00	20.00	40.00
❑ ABC-234 [M]	Hi-Fi Paradise	1958	10.00	20.00	40.00
❑ ABC-279 [M]	The Magic Ukulele	1959	7.50	15.00	30.00

Number	Title	Yr	VG	VG+	NM
❑ ABCS-279 [S]	The Magic Ukulele	1959	10.00	20.00	40.00
❑ ABC-309 [M]	The Happy Banjo	1959	7.50	15.00	30.00
❑ ABCS-309 [S]	The Happy Banjo	1959	10.00	20.00	40.00
❑ ABC-329 [M]	Adventures in Paradise	1960	6.25	12.50	25.00
❑ ABCS-329 [S]	Adventures in Paradise	1960	7.50	15.00	30.00
❑ ABC-330 [M]	The Haunting Hawaiian Guitar	1960	6.25	12.50	25.00
❑ ABCS-330 [S]	The Haunting Hawaiian Guitar	1960	7.50	15.00	30.00
❑ ABC-358 [M]	Adventures in Paradise, Volume 2	1961	6.25	12.50	25.00
❑ ABCS-358 [S]	Adventures in Paradise, Volume 2	1961	7.50	15.00	30.00
❑ ABC-379 [M]	Roy Smeck, His Singing Guitar and Paradise Serenaders	1961	6.25	12.50	25.00
❑ ABCS-379 [S]	Roy Smeck, His Singing Guitar and Paradise Serenaders	1961	7.50	15.00	30.00
❑ ABC-412 [M]	Stringing Along	1962	6.25	12.50	25.00
❑ ABCS-412 [S]	Stringing Along	1962	7.50	15.00	30.00
❑ ABC-414 [M]	Adventures in Paradise, Volume 3	1962	6.25	12.50	25.00
❑ ABCS-414 [S]	Adventures in Paradise, Volume 3	1962	7.50	15.00	30.00
❑ ABC-452 [M]	The Many Guitar Moods of Roy Smeck	1963	6.25	12.50	25.00
❑ ABCS-452 [S]	The Many Guitar Moods of Roy Smeck	1963	7.50	15.00	30.00
❑ ABC-462 [M]	Adventures in Paradise, Volume 4	1963	6.25	12.50	25.00
❑ ABCS-462 [S]	Adventures in Paradise, Volume 4	1963	7.50	15.00	30.00
❑ ABC-484 [M]	I Love to Hear a Banjo	1964	6.25	12.50	25.00
❑ ABCS-484 [S]	I Love to Hear a Banjo	1964	7.50	15.00	30.00

CORAL
| ❑ CRL 56013 [10] | Drifting and Dreaming | 195? | 30.00 | 60.00 | 120.00 |

DECCA
❑ DL 5458 [10]	Memory Lane	1953	25.00	50.00	100.00
❑ DL 5473 [10]	Songs of the Range	1953	25.00	50.00	100.00
❑ DL 8674 [M]	Memories of You	1958	10.00	20.00	40.00

-- *Black label, silver print*

"X"
| ❑ LPA-3016 [10] | Christmas in Hawaii | 195? | 30.00 | 60.00 | 120.00 |
| ❑ LPX-3012 [10] | South of the Border | 1954 | 30.00 | 60.00 | 120.00 |

SMILE
PICKWICK
| ❑ SPC-3288 | Smile | 1973 | 7.50 | 15.00 | 30.00 |

SMITH, AL
BLUESVILLE
| ❑ BVLP-1001 [M] | Hear My Blues | 1960 | 20.00 | 40.00 | 80.00 |

-- *Blue label, silver print*

| ❑ BVLP-1001 [M] | Hear My Blues | 1964 | 6.25 | 12.50 | 25.00 |

-- *Blue label, trident logo at right*

| ❑ BVLP-1014 [M] | Midnight Special | 1961 | 20.00 | 40.00 | 80.00 |

-- *Blue label, silver print*

| ❑ BVLP-1014 [M] | Midnight Special | 1964 | 6.25 | 12.50 | 25.00 |

-- *Blue label, trident logo at right*

| ❑ BVLP-1069 [M] | Blues Shout | 196? | 5.00 | 10.00 | 20.00 |

SMITH, ARTHUR "GUITAR BOOGIE"
ABC-PARAMOUNT
| ❑ ABC-441 [M] | Arthur "Guitar" Smith and Voices | 1963 | 5.00 | 10.00 | 20.00 |
| ❑ ABCS-441 [S] | Arthur "Guitar" Smith and Voices | 1963 | 6.25 | 12.50 | 25.00 |
DOT
❑ DLP-3600 [M]	Original Guitar Boogie	1964	5.00	10.00	20.00
❑ DLP-3642 [M]	Singing on the Mountain with the Crossroads Quartet	1965	5.00	10.00	20.00
❑ DLP-25600 [S]	Original Guitar Boogie	1964	6.25	12.50	25.00
❑ DLP-25636 [S]	Great Country and Western Hits	1965	5.00	10.00	20.00
❑ DLP-25642 [S]	Singing on the Mountain with the Crossroads Quartet	1965	6.25	12.50	25.00
❑ DLP-25769 [S]	A Tribute to Jim Reeves	1966	5.00	10.00	20.00
MGM
❑ E-236 [10]	Foolish Questions	1954	30.00	60.00	120.00
❑ E-533 [10]	Fingers on Fire	1955	25.00	50.00	100.00
❑ E-3301 [M]	Specials	1955	20.00	40.00	80.00
❑ E-3525 [M]	Fingers on Fire	1957	20.00	40.00	80.00
STARDAY
❑ SLP-173 [M]	Mister Guitar	1962	7.50	15.00	30.00
❑ SLP-186 [M]	Arthur Smith and the Crossroads Quartet	1962	10.00	20.00	40.00
❑ SLP-216 [M]	Arthur "Guitar Boogie" Smith Goes to Town	1963	7.50	15.00	30.00
❑ SLP-241 [M]	In Person	1963	7.50	15.00	30.00
❑ SLP-266 [M]	Down Home	1964	7.50	15.00	30.00

SMITH, BESSIE
COLUMBIA
| ❑ GL 503 [M] | The Bessie Smith Story, Volume 1 | 1951 | 12.50 | 25.00 | 50.00 |

-- *Maroon label, gold print*

Number	Title	Yr	VG	VG+	NM
❑ GL 504 [M]	The Bessie Smith Story, Volume 2	1951	12.50	25.00	50.00
-- Maroon label, gold print					
❑ GL 505 [M]	The Bessie Smith Story, Volume 3	1951	12.50	25.00	50.00
-- Maroon label, gold print					
❑ GL 506 [M]	The Bessie Smith Story, Volume 4	1951	12.50	25.00	50.00
-- Maroon label, gold print					
❑ CL 855 [M]	The Bessie Smith Story, Volume 1	1956	6.25	12.50	25.00
-- Red and black label with six "eye" logos					
❑ CL 856 [M]	The Bessie Smith Story, Volume 2	1956	6.25	12.50	25.00
-- Red and black label with six "eye" logos					
❑ CL 857 [M]	The Bessie Smith Story, Volume 3	1956	6.25	12.50	25.00
-- Red and black label with six "eye" logos					
❑ CL 858 [M]	The Bessie Smith Story, Volume 4	1956	6.25	12.50	25.00
-- Red and black label with six "eye" logos					
❑ C2 47091 [(2)]	The Complete Recordings Volume 1: Empress of the Blues	1991	5.00	10.00	20.00
-- Box set; none of the subsequent volumes came out on vinyl					

COLUMBIA MASTERWORKS

Number	Title	Yr	VG	VG+	NM
❑ ML 4801 [M]	The Bessie Smith Story, Volume 1	1954	7.50	15.00	30.00
❑ ML 4802 [M]	The Bessie Smith Story, Volume 2	1954	7.50	15.00	30.00
❑ ML 4809 [M]	The Bessie Smith Story, Volume 3	1954	7.50	15.00	30.00
❑ ML 4810 [M]	The Bessie Smith Story, Volume 4	1954	7.50	15.00	30.00

SMITH, BOB
KENT

Number	Title	Yr	VG	VG+	NM
❑ KST-551 [(2)]	The Visit	1970	25.00	50.00	100.00
-- Deduct 25 percent if poster is missing					

SMITH, BUSTER
ATLANTIC

Number	Title	Yr	VG	VG+	NM
❑ 1323 [M]	The Legendary Buster Smith	1960	12.50	25.00	50.00
-- Black label					
❑ 1323 [M]	The Legendary Buster Smith	1961	5.00	10.00	20.00
-- Multi-color label, white "fan" logo					
❑ SD 1323 [S]	The Legendary Buster Smith	1960	12.50	25.00	50.00
-- Green label					
❑ SD 1323 [S]	The Legendary Buster Smith	1961	5.00	10.00	20.00
-- Multi-color label, white "fan" logo					

SMITH, CAL
KAPP

Number	Title	Yr	VG	VG+	NM
❑ KL-1504 [M]	All the World Is Lonely Now	1966	6.25	12.50	25.00
❑ KL-1537 [M]	Goin' to Cal's Place	1967	6.25	12.50	25.00
❑ KS-3504 [S]	All the World Is Lonely Now	1966	5.00	10.00	20.00
❑ KS-3537 [S]	Goin' to Cal's Place	1967	5.00	10.00	20.00
❑ KS-3544	Travelin' Man	1968	5.00	10.00	20.00
❑ KS-3608	Drinking Champagne	1968	5.00	10.00	20.00

SMITH, CARL
COLUMBIA

Number	Title	Yr	VG	VG+	NM
❑ GP 31 [(2)]	The Carl Smith Anniversary Album/ 20 Years of Hits	1970	6.25	12.50	25.00
❑ CL 959 [M]	Sunday Down South	1957	12.50	25.00	50.00
❑ CL 1022 [M]	Smith's the Name	1957	12.50	25.00	50.00
❑ CL 1172 [M]	Let's Live a Little	1958	12.50	25.00	50.00
❑ CL 1532 [M]	The Carl Smith Touch	1960	6.25	12.50	25.00
❑ CL 1740 [M]	Easy to Please	1961	6.25	12.50	25.00
❑ CL 1937 [M]	Carl Smith's Greatest Hits	1962	5.00	10.00	20.00
❑ CL 2091 [M]	The Tall, Tall Gentleman	1963	5.00	10.00	20.00
❑ CL 2173 [M]	There Stands the Glass	1964	5.00	10.00	20.00
❑ CL 2293 [M]	I Want to Live and Love	1965	5.00	10.00	20.00
❑ CL 2358 [M]	Kisses Don't Lie	1965	5.00	10.00	20.00
❑ CL 2501 [M]	Man with a Plan	1966	5.00	10.00	20.00
❑ CL 2579 [10]	Carl Smith	1955	25.00	50.00	100.00
❑ CL 2610 [M]	The Country Gentleman	1967	5.00	10.00	20.00
❑ CL 2687 [M]	The Country Gentleman Sings His Favorites	1967	6.25	12.50	25.00
❑ CS 8352 [S]	The Carl Smith Touch	1960	7.50	15.00	30.00
❑ CS 8540 [S]	Easy to Please	1961	7.50	15.00	30.00
❑ CS 8737 [S]	Carl Smith's Greatest Hits	1962	6.25	12.50	25.00
❑ CS 8891 [S]	The Tall, Tall Gentleman	1963	6.25	12.50	25.00
❑ CS 8973 [S]	There Stands the Glass	1964	6.25	12.50	25.00
❑ CL 2822 [M]	Deep Water	1968	7.50	15.00	30.00
❑ CL 9023 [10]	Sentimental Songs	195?	25.00	50.00	100.00
❑ CL 9026 [10]	Softly and Tenderly	195?	20.00	40.00	80.00
❑ CS 9093 [S]	I Want to Live and Love	1965	6.25	12.50	25.00
❑ CS 9158 [S]	Kisses Don't Lie	1965	6.25	12.50	25.00
❑ CS 9301 [S]	Man with a Plan	1966	6.25	12.50	25.00
❑ CS 9410 [S]	The Country Gentleman	1967	6.25	12.50	25.00
❑ CS 9487 [S]	The Country Gentleman Sings His Favorites	1967	5.00	10.00	20.00
❑ CS 9622 [S]	Deep Water	1968	5.00	10.00	20.00
❑ CS 9688	Country on My Mind	1968	5.00	10.00	20.00
❑ CS 9786	Faded Love and Winter Roses	1969	5.00	10.00	20.00
❑ CS 9807	Carl Smith's Greatest Hits, Vol. 2	1969	5.00	10.00	20.00
❑ CS 9870	Carl Smith Sings a Tribute to Roy Acuff	1969	5.00	10.00	20.00
❑ CS 9898	I Love You Because	1970	5.00	10.00	20.00
❑ C 30215	Carl Smith with the Tunesmiths	1970	5.00	10.00	20.00
❑ C 30548	Bluegrass	1971	5.00	10.00	20.00
❑ C 31277	Don't Say You're Mine	1972	5.00	10.00	20.00
❑ KC 31606	If This Is Goodbye	1972	5.00	10.00	20.00

SMITH, CARL; LEFTY FRIZZELL; MARTY ROBBINS
Also see each artist's individual listings.
COLUMBIA

Number	Title	Yr	VG	VG+	NM
❑ CL 2544 [10]	Carl, Lefty and Marty	1955	100.00	200.00	400.00

SMITH, CONNIE
RCA VICTOR

Number	Title	Yr	VG	VG+	NM
❑ LPM-3341 [M]	Connie Smith	1965	5.00	10.00	20.00
❑ LSP-3341 [S]	Connie Smith	1965	6.25	12.50	25.00
❑ LPM-3444 [M]	Cute 'n' Country	1965	5.00	10.00	20.00
❑ LSP-3444 [S]	Cute 'n' Country	1965	6.25	12.50	25.00
❑ LPM-3520 [M]	Miss Smith Goes to Nashville	1966	5.00	10.00	20.00
❑ LSP-3520 [S]	Miss Smith Goes to Nashville	1966	6.25	12.50	25.00
❑ LPM-3589 [M]	Connie Smith Sings Great Sacred Songs	1966	5.00	10.00	20.00
❑ LSP-3589 [S]	Connie Smith Sings Great Sacred Songs	1966	6.25	12.50	25.00
❑ LPM-3628 [M]	Born to Sing	1966	5.00	10.00	20.00
❑ LSP-3628 [S]	Born to Sing	1966	6.25	12.50	25.00
❑ LPM-3725 [M]	Downtown Country	1967	6.25	12.50	25.00
❑ LSP-3725 [S]	Downtown Country	1967	5.00	10.00	20.00
❑ LPM-3768 [M]	Connie Smith Sings Bill Anderson	1967	6.25	12.50	25.00
❑ LSP-3768 [S]	Connie Smith Sings Bill Anderson	1967	5.00	10.00	20.00
❑ LPM-3848 [M]	The Best of Connie Smith	1967	6.25	12.50	25.00
❑ LSP-3848 [S]	The Best of Connie Smith	1967	5.00	10.00	20.00
❑ LPM-3889 [M]	Soul of Country Music	1968	12.50	25.00	50.00
❑ LSP-3889 [S]	Soul of Country Music	1968	5.00	10.00	20.00
❑ LSP-4002	I Love Charley Brown	1968	5.00	10.00	20.00
❑ LSP-4077	Sunshine and Rain	1968	5.00	10.00	20.00
❑ LSP-4132	Connie's Country	1969	5.00	10.00	20.00
❑ LSP-4190	Young Love	1969	5.00	10.00	20.00
-- With Nat Stuckey					
❑ LSP-4229	Back in Baby's Arms	1969	5.00	10.00	20.00
❑ LSP-4324	The Best of Connie Smith Volume II	1970	5.00	10.00	20.00
❑ LSP-4394	I Never Once Stopped Loving You	1970	5.00	10.00	20.00
❑ LSP-4598	Come Along and Walk with Me	1971	5.00	10.00	20.00

SMITH, EFFIE
JUBILEE

Number	Title	Yr	VG	VG+	NM
❑ JGM-2057 [M]	Dial That Telephone	1966	6.25	12.50	25.00

SMITH, ETHEL
DECCA

Number	Title	Yr	VG	VG+	NM
❑ DL 8187 [M]	Christmas Music	1955	5.00	10.00	20.00
-- Black label, silver print					

SMITH, "FIDDLIN' " ARTHUR
STARDAY

Number	Title	Yr	VG	VG+	NM
❑ SLP-202 [M]	Rare Old Time Fiddle Tunes	1962	7.50	15.00	30.00

SMITH, HUEY "PIANO"
ACE

Number	Title	Yr	VG	VG+	NM
❑ LP-1004 [M]	Having a Good Time	1959	100.00	200.00	400.00
❑ LP-1015 [M]	For Dancing	1961	62.50	125.00	250.00
❑ LP-1027 [M]	'Twas the Night Before Christmas	1962	62.50	125.00	250.00
❑ LP-2021	Rock 'n' Roll Revival	197?	7.50	15.00	30.00

GRAND PRIX

Number	Title	Yr	VG	VG+	NM
❑ K-418 [M]	Huey "Piano" Smith	196?	5.00	10.00	20.00

SMITH, JACK
BEL CANTO

Number	Title	Yr	VG	VG+	NM
❑ BCM-37 [M]	You Asked for It: Jack Smith	1959	6.25	12.50	25.00
❑ SR-1015 [S]	You Asked for It: Jack Smith	1959	7.50	15.00	30.00

SMITH, JENNIE
CANADIAN AMERICAN

Number	Title	Yr	VG	VG+	NM
❑ CALP-1010 [M]	Nightly Yours on the Steve Allen Show	1963	6.25	12.50	25.00

COLUMBIA

Number	Title	Yr	VG	VG+	NM
❑ CL 1242 [M]	Love Among the Young	1959	7.50	15.00	30.00
❑ CS 8028 [S]	Love Among the Young	1959	10.00	20.00	40.00

DOT

Number	Title	Yr	VG	VG+	NM
❑ DLP-25586 [S]	Jennie	1964	5.00	10.00	20.00

RCA VICTOR

Number	Title	Yr	VG	VG+	NM
❑ LPM-1523 [M]	Jennie	1957	10.00	20.00	40.00

SMITH, JIMMY

BLUE NOTE

Number	Title	Yr	VG	VG+	NM
❑ BLP-1512 [M]	Jimmy Smith at the Organ, Vol. 1	1956	37.50	75.00	150.00
-- "Deep groove" version (deep indentation under label on both sides)					
❑ BLP-1512 [M]	Jimmy Smith at the Organ, Vol. 1	1956	25.00	50.00	100.00
-- Regular edition, Lexington Ave. address on label					
❑ BLP-1512 [M]	Jimmy Smith at the Organ, Vol. 1	1963	6.25	12.50	25.00
-- With New York, USA address on label					
❑ BLP-1514 [M]	Jimmy Smith at the Organ, Vol. 2	1956	37.50	75.00	150.00
-- "Deep groove" version (deep indentation under label on both sides)					
❑ BLP-1514 [M]	Jimmy Smith at the Organ, Vol. 2	1956	25.00	50.00	100.00
-- Regular edition, Lexington Ave. address on label					
❑ BLP-1514 [M]	Jimmy Smith at the Organ, Vol. 2	1963	6.25	12.50	25.00
-- With New York, USA address on label					
❑ BLP-1525 [M]	The Incredible Jimmy Smith at the Organ, Vol. 3	1956	37.50	75.00	150.00
-- "Deep groove" version (deep indentation under label on both sides)					
❑ BLP-1525 [M]	The Incredible Jimmy Smith at the Organ, Vol. 3	1956	25.00	50.00	100.00
-- Regular edition, Lexington Ave. address on label					
❑ BLP-1525 [M]	The Incredible Jimmy Smith at the Organ, Vol. 3	1963	6.25	12.50	25.00
-- With New York, USA address on label					
❑ BLP-1528 [M]	The Incredible Jimmy Smith at Club Baby Grand, Wilmington, Delaware, Vol. 1	1956	37.50	75.00	150.00
-- "Deep groove" version (deep indentation under label on both sides)					
❑ BLP-1528 [M]	The Incredible Jimmy Smith at Club Baby Grand, Wilmington, Delaware, Vol. 1	1956	25.00	50.00	100.00
-- Regular edition, Lexington Ave. address on label					
❑ BLP-1528 [M]	The Incredible Jimmy Smith at Club Baby Grand, Wilmington, Delaware, Vol. 1	1963	6.25	12.50	25.00
-- With New York, USA address on label					
❑ BLP-1529 [M]	The Incredible Jimmy Smith at Club Baby Grand, Wilmington, Delaware, Vol. 2	1956	37.50	75.00	150.00
-- "Deep groove" version (deep indentation under label on both sides)					
❑ BLP-1529 [M]	The Incredible Jimmy Smith at Club Baby Grand, Wilmington, Delaware, Vol. 2	1956	25.00	50.00	100.00
-- Regular edition, Lexington Ave. address on label					
❑ BLP-1529 [M]	The Incredible Jimmy Smith at Club Baby Grand, Wilmington, Delaware, Vol. 2	1963	6.25	12.50	25.00
-- With New York, USA address on label					
❑ BLP-1547 [M]	A Date with Jimmy Smith, Vol. 1	1957	30.00	60.00	120.00
-- "Deep groove" version (deep indentation under label on both sides)					
❑ BLP-1547 [M]	A Date with Jimmy Smith, Vol. 1	1957	20.00	40.00	80.00
-- Regular edition, W. 63rd St. address on label					
❑ BLP-1547 [M]	A Date with Jimmy Smith, Vol. 1	1963	6.25	12.50	25.00
-- With New York, USA address on label					
❑ BLP-1548 [M]	A Date with Jimmy Smith, Vol. 2	1957	30.00	60.00	120.00
-- "Deep groove" version (deep indentation under label on both sides)					
❑ BLP-1548 [M]	A Date with Jimmy Smith, Vol. 2	1957	20.00	40.00	80.00
-- Regular edition, W. 63rd St. address on label					
❑ BLP-1548 [M]	A Date with Jimmy Smith, Vol. 2	1963	6.25	12.50	25.00
-- With New York, USA address on label					
❑ BLP-1551 [M]	Jimmy Smith at the Organ, Vol. 1	1957	30.00	60.00	120.00
-- "Deep groove" version (deep indentation under label on both sides)					
❑ BLP-1551 [M]	Jimmy Smith at the Organ, Vol. 1	1957	20.00	40.00	80.00
-- Regular edition, W. 63rd St. address on label					
❑ BLP-1551 [M]	Jimmy Smith at the Organ, Vol. 1	1963	6.25	12.50	25.00
-- With New York, USA address on label					
❑ BLP-1552 [M]	Jimmy Smith at the Organ, Vol. 2	1957	30.00	60.00	120.00
-- "Deep groove" version (deep indentation under label on both sides)					
❑ BLP-1552 [M]	Jimmy Smith at the Organ, Vol. 2	1957	20.00	40.00	80.00
-- Regular edition, W. 63rd St. address on label					
❑ BLP-1552 [M]	Jimmy Smith at the Organ, Vol. 2	1963	6.25	12.50	25.00
-- With New York, USA address on label					
❑ BLP-1556 [M]	The Sounds of Jimmy Smith	1957	30.00	60.00	120.00
-- "Deep groove" version (deep indentation under label on both sides)					
❑ BLP-1556 [M]	The Sounds of Jimmy Smith	1957	20.00	40.00	80.00
-- Regular edition, W. 63rd St. address on label					
❑ BLP-1556 [M]	The Sounds of Jimmy Smith	1963	6.25	12.50	25.00
-- With New York, USA address on label					
❑ BLP-1563 [M]	Jimmy Smith Plays Pretty Just for You	1957	30.00	60.00	120.00
-- "Deep groove" version (deep indentation under label on both sides)					
❑ BLP-1563 [M]	Jimmy Smith Plays Pretty Just for You	1957	20.00	40.00	80.00
-- Regular edition, W. 63rd St. address on label					
❑ BLP-1563 [M]	Jimmy Smith Plays Pretty Just for You	1963	6.25	12.50	25.00
-- With New York, USA address on label					
❑ BST-1563 [S]	Jimmy Smith Plays Pretty Just for You	1959	20.00	40.00	80.00
-- "Deep groove" version (deep indentation under label on both sides)					
❑ BST-1563 [S]	Jimmy Smith Plays Pretty Just for You	1959	12.50	25.00	50.00
-- Regular edition, W. 63rd St. address on label					

Number	Title	Yr	VG	VG+	NM
❑ BST-1563 [S]	Jimmy Smith Plays Pretty Just for You	1963	5.00	10.00	20.00
-- With New York, USA address on label					
❑ BLP-1585 [M]	Groovin' at Small's Paradise, Vol. 1	1958	30.00	60.00	120.00
-- "Deep groove" version (deep indentation under label on both sides)					
❑ BLP-1585 [M]	Groovin' at Small's Paradise, Vol. 1	1958	20.00	40.00	80.00
-- Regular edition, W. 63rd St. address on label					
❑ BLP-1585 [M]	Groovin' at Small's Paradise, Vol. 1	1963	6.25	12.50	25.00
-- With New York, USA address on label					
❑ BST-1585 [S]	Groovin' at Small's Paradise, Vol. 1	1959	20.00	40.00	80.00
-- "Deep groove" version (deep indentation under label on both sides)					
❑ BST-1585 [S]	Groovin' at Small's Paradise, Vol. 1	1959	12.50	25.00	50.00
-- Regular edition, W. 63rd St. address on label					
❑ BST-1585 [S]	Groovin' at Small's Paradise, Vol. 1	1963	5.00	10.00	20.00
-- With New York, USA address on label					
❑ BLP-1586 [M]	Groovin' at Small's Paradise, Vol. 2	1958	30.00	60.00	120.00
-- "Deep groove" version (deep indentation under label on both sides)					
❑ BLP-1586 [M]	Groovin' at Small's Paradise, Vol. 2	1958	20.00	40.00	80.00
-- Regular edition, W. 63rd St. address on label					
❑ BLP-1586 [M]	Groovin' at Small's Paradise, Vol. 2	1963	6.25	12.50	25.00
-- With New York, USA address on label					
❑ BST-1586 [S]	Groovin' at Small's Paradise, Vol. 2	1959	20.00	40.00	80.00
-- "Deep groove" version (deep indentation under label on both sides)					
❑ BST-1586 [S]	Groovin' at Small's Paradise, Vol. 2	1959	12.50	25.00	50.00
-- Regular edition, W. 63rd St. address on label					
❑ BST-1586 [S]	Groovin' at Small's Paradise, Vol. 2	1963	5.00	10.00	20.00
-- With New York, USA address on label					
❑ BLP-4002 [M]	House Party	1959	30.00	60.00	120.00
-- "Deep groove" version (deep indentation under label on both sides)					
❑ BLP-4002 [M]	House Party	1959	20.00	40.00	80.00
-- Regular edition, W. 63rd St. address on label					
❑ BLP-4002 [M]	House Party	1963	6.25	12.50	25.00
-- With New York, USA address on label					
❑ BST-4002 [S]	House Party	1959	20.00	40.00	80.00
-- "Deep groove" version (deep indentation under label on both sides)					
❑ BST-4002 [S]	House Party	1959	12.50	25.00	50.00
-- Regular edition, W. 63rd St. address on label					
❑ BST-4002 [S]	House Party	1963	5.00	10.00	20.00
-- With New York, USA address on label					
❑ BLP-4011 [M]	The Sermon	1959	30.00	60.00	120.00
-- "Deep groove" version (deep indentation under label on both sides)					
❑ BLP-4011 [M]	The Sermon	1959	20.00	40.00	80.00
-- Regular edition, W. 63rd St. address on label					
❑ BLP-4011 [M]	The Sermon	1963	6.25	12.50	25.00
-- With New York, USA address on label					
❑ BST-4011 [S]	The Sermon	1959	20.00	40.00	80.00
-- "Deep groove" version (deep indentation under label on both sides)					
❑ BST-4011 [S]	The Sermon	1959	12.50	25.00	50.00
-- Regular edition, W. 63rd St. address on label					
❑ BST-4011 [S]	The Sermon	1963	5.00	10.00	20.00
-- With New York, USA address on label					
❑ BLP-4030 [M]	Crazy Baby	1960	30.00	60.00	120.00
-- "Deep groove" version (deep indentation under label on both sides)					
❑ BLP-4030 [M]	Crazy Baby	1960	20.00	40.00	80.00
-- Regular edition, W. 63rd St. address on label					
❑ BLP-4030 [M]	Crazy Baby	1963	6.25	12.50	25.00
-- With New York, USA address on label					
❑ BLP-4050 [M]	Home Cookin'	1961	12.50	25.00	50.00
-- With W. 63rd St. address on label					
❑ BLP-4050 [M]	Home Cookin'	1963	5.00	10.00	20.00
-- With New York, USA address on label					
❑ BLP-4078 [M]	Midnight Special	1961	12.50	25.00	50.00
-- With 61st St. address on label					
❑ BLP-4078 [M]	Midnight Special	1963	5.00	10.00	20.00
-- With New York, USA address on label					
❑ BLP-4100 [M]	Jimmy Smith Plays Fats Waller	1962	12.50	25.00	50.00
-- With 61st St. address on label					
❑ BLP-4100 [M]	Jimmy Smith Plays Fats Waller	1963	5.00	10.00	20.00
-- With New York, USA address on label					
❑ BLP-4117 [M]	Back at the Chicken Shack	1963	6.25	12.50	25.00
❑ BLP-4141 [M]	Rockin' the Boat	1963	6.25	12.50	25.00
❑ BLP-4164 [M]	Prayer Meetin'	1964	6.25	12.50	25.00
❑ BLP-4200 [M]	Softly as a Summer Breeze	1965	6.25	12.50	25.00
❑ BLP-4235 [M]	Bucket!	1966	6.25	12.50	25.00
❑ BLP-4255 [M]	I'm Movin' On	1967	7.50	15.00	30.00
❑ BST-84030 [S]	Crazy Baby	1960	12.50	25.00	50.00
-- With W. 63rd St. address on label					
❑ BST-84030 [S]	Crazy Baby	1963	5.00	10.00	20.00
-- With New York, USA address on label					
❑ BST-84050 [S]	Home Cookin'	1961	12.50	25.00	50.00
-- With W. 63rd St. address on label					
❑ BST-84050 [S]	Home Cookin'	1963	5.00	10.00	20.00
-- With New York, USA address on label					
❑ BST-84078 [S]	Midnight Special	1961	12.50	25.00	50.00
-- With 61st St. address on label					
❑ BST-84078 [S]	Midnight Special	1963	5.00	10.00	20.00
-- With New York, USA address on label					
❑ BST-84100 [S]	Jimmy Smith Plays Fats Waller	1962	12.50	25.00	50.00
-- With 61st St. address on label					
❑ BST-84100 [S]	Jimmy Smith Plays Fats Waller	1963	5.00	10.00	20.00
-- With New York, USA address on label					

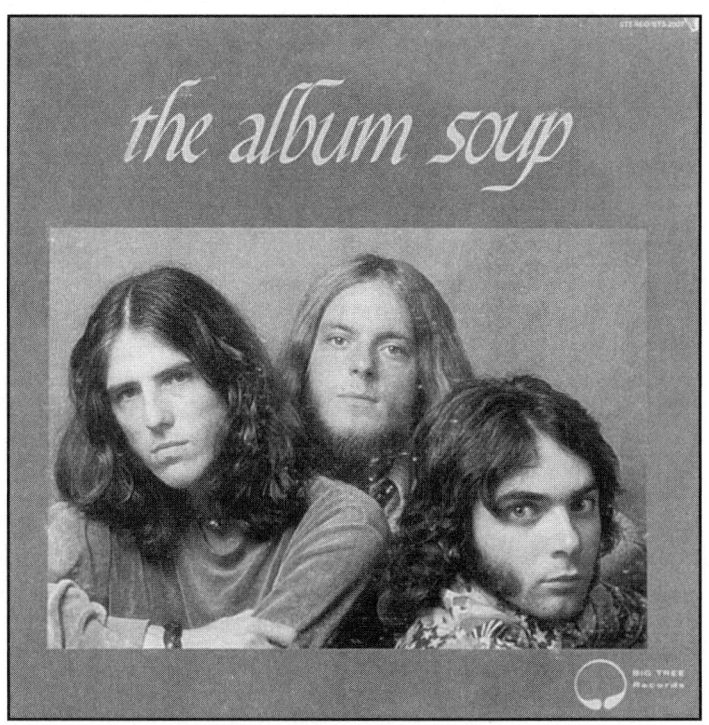

(Top left) One of the Pittsburgh area's finest groups, the Skyliners, parlayed "Since I Don't Have You" and several other hits into a rather rare album on the Calico label. It was issued with two label variations; the yellow and blue label goes for about three times as much as the all-blue label. (Top right) One of dozens, if not hundreds, of local bands to record their own album on a homemade label in the late 1960s, Appleton, Wisconsin's Soup actually went beyond that and did an album on a real label (Big Tree) as well. Both are collectible. (Bottom left) Thanks to publicity surrounding her recent induction into the Rock and Roll Hall of Fame, not to mention her passing early in 1999, many people are re-assessing Dusty Springfield. Her debut American album, the above *Stay Awhile,* also contains her first U.S. hit, "I Only Want to Be with You." (Bottom right) A scarce vinyl issue from 1990 is *Ringo Starr and His All-Starr Band,* which was released on Ryko Analogue, complete with an obi strip, which is not often found on American albums but was standard on late 80s and early 90s Ryko issues.

Number	Title	Yr	VG	VG+	NM
❑ BST-84117 [S]	Back at the Chicken Shack	1963	7.50	15.00	30.00
-- With New York, USA address on label					
❑ BST-84141 [S]	Rockin' the Boat	1963	7.50	15.00	30.00
-- With New York, USA address on label					
❑ BST-84164 [S]	Prayer Meetin'	1964	7.50	15.00	30.00
-- With New York, USA address on label					
❑ BST-84200 [S]	Softly as a Summer Breeze	1965	7.50	15.00	30.00
-- With New York, USA address on label					
❑ BST-84235 [S]	Bucket!	1966	7.50	15.00	30.00
-- With New York, USA address on label					
❑ BST-84255 [S]	I'm Movin' On	1967	5.00	10.00	20.00
❑ BST-84269	Open House	1968	5.00	10.00	20.00
❑ BST-84296	Plain Talk	1969	5.00	10.00	20.00
❑ BST-89901 [(2)]	Jimmy Smith's Greatest Hits!	1969	6.25	12.50	25.00

MOSAIC

Number	Title	Yr	VG	VG+	NM
❑ MQ5-154 [(5)]	The Complete February 1957 Jimmy Smith Blue Note Sessions	199?	20.00	40.00	80.00

VERVE

Number	Title	Yr	VG	VG+	NM
❑ V-8474 [M]	Bashin'	1962	5.00	10.00	20.00
❑ V6-8474 [S]	Bashin'	1962	6.25	12.50	25.00
❑ V-8544 [M]	Hobo Flats	1963	5.00	10.00	20.00
❑ V6-8544 [S]	Hobo Flats	1963	6.25	12.50	25.00
❑ V-8552 [M]	Any Number Can Win	1963	5.00	10.00	20.00
❑ V6-8552 [S]	Any Number Can Win	1963	6.25	12.50	25.00
❑ V-8583 [M]	Who's Afraid of Virginia Woolf?	1964	5.00	10.00	20.00
❑ V6-8583 [S]	Who's Afraid of Virginia Woolf?	1964	6.25	12.50	25.00
❑ V-8587 [M]	The Cat	1964	5.00	10.00	20.00
❑ V6-8587 [S]	The Cat	1964	6.25	12.50	25.00
❑ V-8604 [M]	Christmas '64	1964	5.00	10.00	20.00
❑ V6-8604 [S]	Christmas '64	1964	6.25	12.50	25.00
❑ V-8652 [M]	Peter and the Wolf	1966	5.00	10.00	20.00
❑ V6-8618 [S]	Monster	1965	5.00	10.00	20.00
❑ V-8666 [M]	Christmas Cookin'	1966	5.00	10.00	20.00
❑ V6-8628 [S]	Organ Grinder Swing	1965	5.00	10.00	20.00
❑ V6-8641 [S]	Got My Mojo Workin'	1966	5.00	10.00	20.00
❑ V6-8652 [S]	Peter and the Wolf	1966	6.25	12.50	25.00
❑ V6-8666 [S]	Christmas Cookin'	1966	6.25	12.50	25.00
❑ V6-8667 [S]	Hoochie Coochie Man	1966	5.00	10.00	20.00
❑ V-8705 [M]	Respect	1967	5.00	10.00	20.00
❑ V-8721 [M]	The Best of Jimmy Smith	1967	5.00	10.00	20.00

SMITH, JIMMY, AND WES MONTGOMERY

Also see each artist's individual listings.

VERVE

Number	Title	Yr	VG	VG+	NM
❑ V-8678 [M]	Jimy & Wes, The Dynamic Duo	1967	5.00	10.00	20.00

SMITH, JOHNNY "HAMMOND" -- See JOHNNY HAMMOND.

SMITH, KEELY

Also see LOUIS PRIMA AND KEELY SMITH.

CAPITOL

Number	Title	Yr	VG	VG+	NM
❑ SW 914 [S]	I Wish You Love	1959	7.50	15.00	30.00
-- Black label with colorband, Capitol logo at left					
❑ W 914 [M]	I Wish You Love	1957	12.50	25.00	50.00
-- Turquoise label					
❑ W 914 [M]	I Wish You Love	1959	7.50	15.00	30.00
-- Black label with colorband, Capitol logo at left					
❑ ST 1073 [S]	Politely!	1959	12.50	25.00	50.00
-- Black label with colorband, Capitol logo at left					
❑ ST 1073 [S]	Politely!	1962	5.00	10.00	20.00
-- Black label with colorband, Capitol logo at top					
❑ T 1073 [M]	Politely!	1958	10.00	20.00	40.00
-- Black label with colorband, Capitol logo at left					
❑ ST 1145 [S]	Swingin' Pretty	1959	12.50	25.00	50.00
-- Black label with colorband, Capitol logo at left					
❑ ST 1145 [S]	Swingin' Pretty	1962	5.00	10.00	20.00
-- Black label with colorband, Capitol logo at top					
❑ T 1145 [M]	Swingin' Pretty	1959	10.00	20.00	40.00
-- Black label with colorband, Capitol logo at left					

DOT

Number	Title	Yr	VG	VG+	NM
❑ DLP-3241 [M]	Be My Love	1959	6.25	12.50	25.00
❑ DLP-3265 [M]	Swing, You Lovers	1960	6.25	12.50	25.00
❑ DLP-3287 [M]	Dearly Beloved	1961	6.25	12.50	25.00
❑ DLP-3345 [M]	A Keely Christmas	1961	6.25	12.50	25.00
❑ DLP-3415 [M]	Because You're Mine	1962	6.25	12.50	25.00
❑ DLP-3423 [M]	Twist with Keely Smith	1962	6.25	12.50	25.00
❑ DLP-3460 [M]	Cherokeely Swings	1962	6.25	12.50	25.00
❑ DLP-3461 [M]	What Kind of Fool Am I	1962	6.25	12.50	25.00
❑ DLP-25241 [S]	Be My Love	1959	7.50	15.00	30.00
❑ DLP-25265 [S]	Swing, You Lovers	1960	7.50	15.00	30.00
❑ DLP-25287 [S]	Dearly Beloved	1961	7.50	15.00	30.00
❑ DLP-25345 [S]	A Keely Christmas	1961	7.50	15.00	30.00
❑ DLP-25415 [S]	Because You're Mine	1962	7.50	15.00	30.00
❑ DLP-25423 [S]	Twist with Keely Smith	1962	7.50	15.00	30.00
❑ DLP-25460 [S]	Cherokeely Swings	1962	7.50	15.00	30.00
❑ DLP-25461 [S]	What Kind of Fool Am I	1962	7.50	15.00	30.00

REPRISE

Number	Title	Yr	VG	VG+	NM
❑ R-6086 [M]	Little Girl Blue, Little Girl New	1963	5.00	10.00	20.00
❑ R9-6086 [S]	Little Girl Blue, Little Girl New	1963	6.25	12.50	25.00
❑ R-6132 [M]	The Intimate Keely Smith	1964	5.00	10.00	20.00
❑ RS-6132 [S]	The Intimate Keely Smith	1964	6.25	12.50	25.00
❑ R-6142 [M]	Keely Smith Sings the John Lennon/Paul McCartney Songbook	1964	6.25	12.50	25.00
❑ RS-6142 [S]	Keely Smith Sings the John Lennon/Paul McCartney Songbook	1964	7.50	15.00	30.00
❑ R-6175 [M]	That Old Black Magic	1965	5.00	10.00	20.00
❑ RS-6175 [S]	That Old Black Magic	1965	6.25	12.50	25.00

SMITH, LONNIE

BLUE NOTE

Number	Title	Yr	VG	VG+	NM
❑ BST-84290	Think!	1968	5.00	10.00	20.00
❑ BST-84313	Turning Point	1969	5.00	10.00	20.00

COLUMBIA

Number	Title	Yr	VG	VG+	NM
❑ CL 2696 [M]	Finger-Lickin' Good Soul Organ	1967	6.25	12.50	25.00
❑ CS 9496 [S]	Finger-Lickin' Good Soul Organ	1967	5.00	10.00	20.00

SMITH, O.C.

COLUMBIA

Number	Title	Yr	VG	VG+	NM
❑ CL 2714 [M]	The Dynamic O.C. Smith	1967	5.00	10.00	20.00

SMITH, RAY

COLUMBIA

Number	Title	Yr	VG	VG+	NM
❑ CL 1937 [M]	Ray Smith's Greatest Hits	1963	6.25	12.50	25.00
❑ CS 8737 [S]	Ray Smith's Greatest Hits	1963	7.50	15.00	30.00

JUDD

Number	Title	Yr	VG	VG+	NM
❑ JLPA-701 [M]	Travelin' with Ray	1960	175.00	350.00	700.00

"T"

Number	Title	Yr	VG	VG+	NM
❑ 56062 [M]	The Best of Ray Smith	196?	25.00	50.00	100.00

SMITH, ROBERT CURTIS

BLUESVILLE

Number	Title	Yr	VG	VG+	NM
❑ BVLP-1064 [M]	Clarksdale Blues	1963	20.00	40.00	80.00
-- Blue label, silver print					
❑ BVLP-1064 [M]	Clarksdale Blues	1964	6.25	12.50	25.00
-- Blue label, trident logo at right					

SMITH, ROGER

WARNER BROS.

Number	Title	Yr	VG	VG+	NM
❑ W 1305 [M]	Beach Romance	1960	10.00	20.00	40.00
❑ WS 1305 [S]	Beach Romance	1960	12.50	25.00	50.00

SMITH, SOMETHIN', AND THE REDHEADS

EPIC

Number	Title	Yr	VG	VG+	NM
❑ LN 3138 [M]	Somethin' Smith and the Redheads	1959	7.50	15.00	30.00

MGM

Number	Title	Yr	VG	VG+	NM
❑ E-3941 [M]	Ain't We Got Fun Kinda Songs	1961	5.00	10.00	20.00
❑ SE-3941 [S]	Ain't We Got Fun Kinda Songs	1961	6.25	12.50	25.00

SMITH, TAB

CHECKER

Number	Title	Yr	VG	VG+	NM
❑ LP-2971 [M]	Tab Smith	1960	150.00	300.00	600.00
-- White label promo with multi-color vinyl					
❑ LP-2971 [M]	Tab Smith	1960	25.00	50.00	100.00
-- Regular issue					

UNITED

Number	Title	Yr	VG	VG+	NM
❑ LP-001 [10]	Music Styled by Tab Smith	1955	50.00	100.00	200.00
❑ LP-003 [10]	Red, Hot and Cool Blues	1955	50.00	100.00	200.00

SMITH, VERDELLE

CAPITOL

Number	Title	Yr	VG	VG+	NM
❑ ST 2476 [S]	In My Room	1966	62.50	125.00	250.00
❑ T 2476 [M]	In My Room	1966	50.00	100.00	200.00

SMITH, WARREN

LIBERTY

Number	Title	Yr	VG	VG+	NM
❑ LRP-3199 [M]	The First Country Collection of Warren Smith	1961	12.50	25.00	50.00
❑ LST-7199 [S]	The First Country Collection of Warren Smith	1961	17.50	35.00	70.00

SMITHEREENS, THE

ENIGMA

Number	Title	Yr	VG	VG+	NM
❑ (no #) [DJ]	Live at the Roxy -- Special Forces Radio Concert	1986	10.00	20.00	40.00
❑ SEAX-73258 [PD]	Especially for You	1986	5.00	10.00	20.00
-- Picture disc in plastic sleeve, sticker on sleeve					

Number	Title	Yr	VG	VG+	NM
LITTLE RICKY					
❏ 103 [EP]	Beauty and Sadness	1983	10.00	20.00	40.00
SMITHS, THE					
WARNER BROS.					
❏ WBMS-130 [DJ]	The Warner Bros. Music Show	1985	5.00	10.00	20.00
-- One side: The Smiths; the other side: The Blasters					
SMOKE RISE, THE					
PARAMOUNT					
❏ PAS-9000 [(2)]	The Survival of St. Joan	1971	5.00	10.00	20.00
-- With booklet					
SMOKE, THE					
SIDEWALK					
❏ ST 5912	The Smoke	1968	10.00	20.00	40.00
UNI					
❏ 73052	The Smoke	1969	6.25	12.50	25.00
❏ 73065	The Smoke at George's Coffee Shop	1970	6.25	12.50	25.00
SMOKESTACK LIGHTNIN'					
BELL					
❏ 6026	Off the Wall	1969	5.00	10.00	20.00
SMOKEY BABE					
BLUESVILLE					
❏ BVLP-1063 [M]	Hottest Brand Going	1963	20.00	40.00	80.00
-- Blue label, silver print					
❏ BVLP-1063 [M]	Hottest Brand Going	1964	6.25	12.50	25.00
-- Blue label, trident logo at right					
FOLK-LYRIC					
❏ FL-108 [M]	Smokey Babe	196?	6.25	12.50	25.00
SMOTHERS BROTHERS, THE					
MERCURY					
❏ MGDJ-20 [DJ]	Best of the Smothers Brothers	1964	10.00	20.00	40.00
❏ MGDJ-25 [DJ]	It's Brothers Smothers Month	1964	10.00	20.00	40.00
❏ SR-60611 [S]	The Songs and Comedy of the Smothers Brothers!	1962	5.00	10.00	20.00
❏ SR-60675 [S]	The Two Sides of the Smothers Brothers	1962	5.00	10.00	20.00
❏ SR-60777 [S]	(Think Ethnic!)	1963	5.00	10.00	20.00
❏ SR-60862 [S]	Curb Your Tongue, Knave!	1963	5.00	10.00	20.00
❏ SR-60904 [S]	It Must Have Been Something I Said!	1964	5.00	10.00	20.00
❏ SR-60948 [S]	Tour De Farce American History and Other Unrelated Subjects	1964	5.00	10.00	20.00
❏ SR-60989 [S]	Aesop's Fables the Smothers Brothers Way	1965	5.00	10.00	20.00
❏ SR-61051 [S]	Mom Always Liked You Best!	1965	5.00	10.00	20.00
❏ SR-61064 [S]	The Smothers Brothers Play It Straight	1966	5.00	10.00	20.00
❏ SR-61089 [S]	Golden Hits of the Smothers Brothers, Vol. 2	1966	5.00	10.00	20.00
❏ SR-61193	Smothers Comedy Brothers Hour	1968	5.00	10.00	20.00
SMOTHERS, SMOKEY					
KING					
❏ 779 [M]	The Backporch Blues	1962	250.00	500.00	1,000.
SNEAKY PETE					
SHILO					
❏ 4086	Sneaky Pete	1979	7.50	15.00	30.00
SNELL, TONY					
ESP-DISK'					
❏ 3004	Medieval and Latter Day Lays	197?	5.00	10.00	20.00
SNOW					
EPIC					
❏ BN 26435	Snow	1969	5.00	10.00	20.00
SNOW, HANK					
RCA CAMDEN					
❏ CAL-514 [M]	The Singing Ranger	1959	5.00	10.00	20.00
❏ CAL-680 [M]	The Southern Cannonball	1961	5.00	10.00	20.00

Number	Title	Yr	VG	VG+	NM
❏ CAL-722 [M]	The One and Only Hank Snow	1962	5.00	10.00	20.00
❏ CAL-782 [M]	The Last Ride	1963	5.00	10.00	20.00
RCA VICTOR					
❏ DPL2-0134 [(2)]	The Living Legend	197?	25.00	50.00	100.00
-- RCA Special Products release					
❏ LPM-1113 [M]	Just Keep a-Movin'	1955	25.00	50.00	100.00
❏ LPM-1156 [M]	Old Doc Brown and Other Narrations	1955	25.00	50.00	100.00
❏ LPM-1233 [M]	Country Classics	1956	20.00	40.00	80.00
❏ LPM-1419 [M]	Country and Western Jamboree	1957	20.00	40.00	80.00
❏ LPM-1435 [M]	Hank Snow's Country Guitar	1957	20.00	40.00	80.00
❏ LPM-1638 [M]	Hank Snow Sings Sacred Songs	1958	15.00	30.00	60.00
❏ LPM-2043 [M]	Hank Snow Sings Jimmie Rodgers Songs	1959	12.50	25.00	50.00
❏ LSP-2043 [S]	Hank Snow Sings Jimmie Rodgers Songs	1959	20.00	40.00	80.00
❏ LPM-2285 [M]	Hank Snow Souvenirs	1961	7.50	15.00	30.00
❏ LSP-2285 [S]	Hank Snow Souvenirs	1961	10.00	20.00	40.00
❏ LPM-2458 [M]	Big Country Hits	1961	7.50	15.00	30.00
❏ LSP-2458 [S]	Big Country Hits	1961	10.00	20.00	40.00
❏ LPM-2675 [M]	I've Been Everywhere	1963	7.50	15.00	30.00
❏ LSP-2675 [S]	I've Been Everywhere	1963	10.00	20.00	40.00
❏ LPM-2705 [M]	Railroad Man	1963	7.50	15.00	30.00
❏ LSP-2705 [S]	Railroad Man	1963	10.00	20.00	40.00
❏ LPM-2812 [M]	More Hank Snow Souvenirs	1964	6.25	12.50	25.00
❏ LSP-2812 [S]	More Hank Snow Souvenirs	1964	7.50	15.00	30.00
❏ LPM-2901 [M]	Songs of Tragedy	1964	6.25	12.50	25.00
❏ LSP-2901 [S]	Songs of Tragedy	1964	7.50	15.00	30.00
❏ LPM-3026 [10]	Country Classics	1952	50.00	100.00	200.00
❏ LPM-3070 [10]	Hank Snow Sings	1952	45.00	90.00	180.00
❏ LPM-3131 [10]	Hank Snow Salutes Jimmie Rodgers	1953	45.00	90.00	180.00
❏ LPM-3267 [10]	Hank Snow's Country Guitar	1954	45.00	90.00	180.00
❏ LPM-3317 [M]	Your Favorite Country Hits	1965	6.25	12.50	25.00
❏ LSP-3317 [S]	Your Favorite Country Hits	1965	7.50	15.00	30.00
❏ LPM-3378 [M]	Gloryland March	1965	6.25	12.50	25.00
❏ LSP-3378 [S]	Gloryland March	1965	7.50	15.00	30.00
❏ LPM-3471 [M]	Heartbreak Trail - A Tribute to the Sons of the Pioneers	1966	6.25	12.50	25.00
❏ LSP-3471 [S]	Heartbreak Trail - A Tribute to the Sons of the Pioneers	1966	7.50	15.00	30.00
❏ LPM-3478 [M]	The Best of Hank Snow	1966	5.00	10.00	20.00
❏ LSP-3478 [S]	The Best of Hank Snow	1966	6.25	12.50	25.00
❏ LPM-3548 [M]	Guitar Stylings of Hank Snow	1966	6.25	12.50	25.00
❏ LSP-3548 [S]	Guitar Stylings of Hank Snow	1966	7.50	15.00	30.00
❏ LPM-3595 [M]	Gospel Train	1966	7.50	15.00	30.00
❏ LSP-3595 [S]	Gospel Train	1966	10.00	20.00	40.00
❏ LPM-3737 [M]	Snow in Hawaii	1967	7.50	15.00	30.00
❏ LSP-3737 [S]	Snow in Hawaii	1967	6.25	12.50	25.00
❏ LPM-3826 [M]	Christmas with Hank Snow	1967	7.50	15.00	30.00
❏ LSP-3826 [S]	Christmas with Hank Snow	1967	6.25	12.50	25.00
❏ LPM-3857 [M]	Spanish Fire Ball and Other Great Hank Snow Stylings	1967	7.50	15.00	30.00
❏ LPM-3965 [M]	Hits, Hits and More Hits	1968	25.00	50.00	100.00
❏ LSP-3857 [S]	Spanish Fire Ball and Other Great Hank Snow Stylings	1967	6.25	12.50	25.00
❏ LSP-3965 [S]	Hits, Hits and More Hits	1968	6.25	12.50	25.00
❏ LSP-4032	Tales of the Yukon	1968	6.25	12.50	25.00
❏ LSP-4122	Snow in All Seasons	1969	6.25	12.50	25.00
❏ LSP-4306	Hank Snow Sings in Memory of Jimmie Rodgers	1970	5.00	10.00	20.00
❏ LSP-4379	Cure for the Blues	1970	5.00	10.00	20.00
❏ LSP-4501	Tracks and Trains	1971	5.00	10.00	20.00
❏ LSP-4601	Award Winners	1971	5.00	10.00	20.00
❏ LPM-6014 [(2) M]	This Is My Story	1966	10.00	20.00	40.00
❏ LSP-6014 [(2) S]	This Is My Story	1966	12.50	25.00	50.00
READER'S DIGEST					
❏ RDA-216 [(6)]	I'm Movin' On	197?	30.00	60.00	120.00
SCHOOL OF MUSIC					
❏ 1149 [M]	The Guitar	1958	62.50	125.00	250.00
-- Deduct 20 percent if instruction book is missing					

SNOW, HANK, AND CHET ATKINS
Also see each artist's individual listings.

Number	Title	Yr	VG	VG+	NM
RCA VICTOR					
❏ LPM-2952 [M]	Reminiscing	1964	6.25	12.50	25.00
❏ LSP-2952 [S]	Reminiscing	1964	7.50	15.00	30.00
❏ LSP-4254	By Special Request - C.B. Atkins and C.E. Snow	1970	5.00	10.00	20.00

SNOW, HANK, AND ANITA CARTER
Also see each artist's individual listings.

Number	Title	Yr	VG	VG+	NM
RCA VICTOR					
❏ LPM-2580 [M]	Together Again	1962	7.50	15.00	30.00
❏ LSP-2580 [S]	Together Again	1962	10.00	20.00	40.00

Number	Title	Yr	VG	VG+	NM

SNOW, HANK; PORTER WAGONER; HANK LOCKLIN
Also see each artist's individual listings.
RCA VICTOR
Number	Title	Yr	VG	VG+	NM
❑ LPM-2723 [M]	Three Country Gentlemen	1963	7.50	15.00	30.00
❑ LSP-2723 [S]	Three Country Gentlemen	1963	10.00	20.00	40.00

SNOW, PHOEBE
DCC COMPACT CLASSICS
❑ LPZ-2027	Phoebe Snow	1996	6.25	12.50	25.00
-- Audiophile vinyl					

SNYDER, TERRY, AND THE ALL-STARS -- See ENOCH LIGHT.

SOCIAL DISTORTION
13TH FLOOR
❑ SD 1301	Mommy's Little Monster	1983	15.00	30.00	60.00
-- Gatefold cover					
❑ SD 1301	Mommy's Little Monster	1983	10.00	20.00	40.00
-- Standard cover with lyric sheet					
EPIC
| ❑ E 46055 | Social Distortion | 1990 | 5.00 | 10.00 | 20.00 |
| ❑ E 47948 | Somewhere Between Heaven and Hell | 1992 | 5.00 | 10.00 | 20.00 |
RESTLESS
| ❑ 72251 | Prison Bound | 1988 | 5.00 | 10.00 | 20.00 |
TRIPLE X
| ❑ 51019 | Mommy's Little Monster | 1989 | 5.00 | 10.00 | 20.00 |
| -- Clear vinyl | | | | | |

SOCIAL UNREST
LIBERTINE
❑ LSU 1 [EP]	Rat in a Maze	1982	6.25	12.50	25.00
❑ LSU 2461	SU-2000	1985	5.00	10.00	20.00

SOCIETY OF SEVEN
SILVER SWORD
❑ 7012	How Has Your Love Life Been?	1970	5.00	10.00	20.00

SOFT MACHINE, THE
PROBE
❑ CPLP-4500	The Soft Machine	1968	10.00	20.00	40.00
-- Cover with moving parts					
❑ CPLP-4500	The Soft Machine	1969	5.00	10.00	20.00
-- Regular cover					
❑ CPLP-4505	The Soft Machine, Vol. 2	1969	6.25	12.50	25.00

SOMERSET STRINGS, THE
EPIC
❑ LN 3159 [M]	Music for Christmas at Home	1955	5.00	10.00	20.00

SOMMER, ELKE
MGM
❑ E-4321 [M]	Love in Any Language	1965	6.25	12.50	25.00
❑ SE-4321 [S]	Love in Any Language	1965	7.50	15.00	30.00

SOMMERS, JOANIE
COLUMBIA
❑ CL 2495 [M]	Come Alive	1966	5.00	10.00	20.00
❑ CS 9295 [S]	Come Alive	1966	6.25	12.50	25.00
WARNER BROS.
❑ W 1346 [M]	Positively the Most	1960	7.50	15.00	30.00
❑ WS 1346 [S]	Positively the Most	1960	10.00	20.00	40.00
❑ B 1348 [M]	Behind Closed Doors at a Recording Session	1960	37.50	75.00	150.00
-- Record comes in a box with a booklet included					
❑ W 1412 [M]	Joanie Sommers	1961	7.50	15.00	30.00
❑ WS 1412 [S]	Joanie Sommers	1961	10.00	20.00	40.00
❑ W 1436 [M]	For Those Who Think Young	1962	7.50	15.00	30.00
❑ WS 1436 [S]	For Those Who Think Young	1962	10.00	20.00	40.00
❑ W 1470 [M]	Johnny Get Angry	1962	10.00	20.00	40.00
❑ WS 1470 [S]	Johnny Get Angry	1962	12.50	25.00	50.00
❑ W 1474 [M]	Let's Talk About Love	1962	7.50	15.00	30.00
❑ WS 1474 [S]	Let's Talk About Love	1962	10.00	20.00	40.00
❑ W 1504 [M]	Sommers' Seasons	1963	6.25	12.50	25.00
❑ WS 1504 [S]	Sommers' Seasons	1963	7.50	15.00	30.00
❑ W 1575 [M]	Softly, The Brazilian Sound	1964	6.25	12.50	25.00
❑ WS 1575 [S]	Softly, The Brazilian Sound	1964	7.50	15.00	30.00

SONIC YOUTH
DGC
❑ 24297	Goo	1990	7.50	15.00	30.00
❑ 24485	Dirty	1992	5.00	10.00	20.00
❑ 24632	Experimental Jet Set, Trash and No Star	1994	5.00	10.00	20.00
❑ 24825 [(2)]	Washing Machine	1995	5.00	10.00	20.00
ENIGMA
| ❑ 75403 [(2)] | Daydream Nation | 1988 | 5.00 | 10.00 | 20.00 |
HOMESTEAD
❑ HMS 016	Bad Moon Rising	1985	5.00	10.00	20.00
❑ HMS 021 [EP]	Death Valley '69	1985	5.00	10.00	20.00
-- With Lydia Lunch					
MOBILE FIDELITY
| ❑ 1-257 | Goo | 1996 | 10.00 | 20.00 | 40.00 |
| -- Audiophile vinyl | | | | | |
NEUTRAL
❑ N-1 [EP]	Sonic Youth	1982	12.50	25.00	50.00
❑ 001 [EP]	Sonic Youth	1982	12.50	25.00	50.00
❑ 9	Confusion Is Sex	1983	10.00	20.00	40.00
SST
❑ 059	Evol	1986	5.00	10.00	20.00
❑ 096	Confusion Is Sex	1987	5.00	10.00	20.00
-- Reissue of Neutral 9					
❑ 134	Sister	1987	5.00	10.00	20.00

SONICS, THE
BUCKSHOT
❑ 001	Explosives	1973	50.00	100.00	200.00
ETIQUETTE
❑ ETALB-024 [M]	Here Are the Sonics!!!	1965	62.50	125.00	250.00
-- Red label					
❑ ETALB-024 [M]	Here Are the Sonics!!!	1965	50.00	100.00	200.00
-- Purple label					
❑ ETLPS-024 [S]	Here Are the Sonics!!!	1965	100.00	200.00	400.00
-- Red label					
❑ ETLPS-024 [S]	Here Are the Sonics!!!	1965	75.00	150.00	300.00
-- Purple label					
❑ ETALB-027 [M]	The Sonics Boom	1966	75.00	150.00	300.00
❑ ETLPS-027 [R]	The Sonics Boom	1966	50.00	100.00	200.00
FIRST AMERICAN
❑ FA-7715	Original Northwest Punk	1978	5.00	10.00	20.00
❑ FA-7719	Unreleased	1980	5.00	10.00	20.00
❑ FA-7779	Fire and Ice	1983	5.00	10.00	20.00
JERDEN
| ❑ JRL-7007 [M] | Introducing the Sonics | 1967 | 50.00 | 100.00 | 200.00 |
| ❑ JRS-7007 [R] | Introducing the Sonics | 1967 | 37.50 | 75.00 | 150.00 |

SONICS, THE; THE WAILERS; THE GALAXIES
Also see each artist's individual listings.
ETIQUETTE
❑ ETALB-025 [M]	Merry Christmas	1965	125.00	250.00	500.00

SONNY
Also see SONNY AND CHER.
ATCO
❑ 33-229 [M]	Inner Views	1967	5.00	10.00	20.00
❑ SD 33-229 [S]	Inner Views	1967	5.00	10.00	20.00

SONNY AND CHER
Also see CHER; SONNY.
ATCO
❑ 33-177 [M]	Look At Us	1965	5.00	10.00	20.00
❑ SD 33-177 [S]	Look At Us	1965	6.25	12.50	25.00
❑ SD 33-183 [S]	The Wondrous World of Sonny and Cher	1966	5.00	10.00	20.00
❑ SD 33-203 [S]	In Case You're in Love	1967	5.00	10.00	20.00
❑ SD 33-214 [S]	Good Times	1967	5.00	10.00	20.00
❑ SD 33-219 [S]	The Best of Sonny and Cher	1967	5.00	10.00	20.00
❑ SD 2-804 [(2)]	The Two of Us	1972	5.00	10.00	20.00
-- Combines "Look at Us" and "In Case You're in Love"					
❑ A2M 5177 [(2) M]	Sonny & Cher's Greatest Hits	1967	7.50	15.00	30.00
-- Columbia Record Club exclusive					
❑ A2S 5178 [(2) S]	Sonny & Cher's Greatest Hits	1967	7.50	15.00	30.00
-- Columbia Record Club exclusive					
REPRISE
❑ R 6177 [M]	Baby Don't Go	1965	7.50	15.00	30.00
❑ RS 6177 [P]	Baby Don't Go	1965	7.50	15.00	30.00
-- By "Sonny & Cher & Friends" (also includes The Lettermen, Bill Medley and The Blendells)					

SONNY AND THE DEMONS
UNITED ARTISTS
❑ UAL-3316 [M]	Drag Kings	1964	12.50	25.00	50.00
❑ UAS-6316 [S]	Drag Kings	1964	15.00	30.00	60.00

Number	Title	Yr	VG	VG+	NM

SONS OF CHAMPLIN, THE
CAPITOL
❑ SWBB-200 [(2)] Loosen Up Naturally		1969	12.50	25.00	50.00
-- With the F-word clearly visible as part of the cover artwork					
❑ SWBB-200 [(2)] Loosen Up Naturally		1969	6.25	12.50	25.00
-- With the F-word scratched off the cover artwork					
❑ SWBB-200 [(2)] Loosen Up Naturally		1969	5.00	10.00	20.00
-- With the F-word airbrushed off the cover artwork					
❑ SKAO-322	The Sons	1969	6.25	12.50	25.00
❑ ST-675	Follow Your Heart	1971	5.00	10.00	20.00

GOLDMINE
❑ GM 94930	The Sons of Champlin	1975	5.00	10.00	20.00

SONS OF CHAMPLIN
❑ (no #)	Minus Seeds and Stems	1969	125.00	250.00	500.00

SONS OF HEROES
MCA
❑ 39010	Sons of Heroes	1983	5.00	10.00	20.00

SONS OF THE PIONEERS
RCA CAMDEN
❑ CAL-413 [M]	Wagons West	1958	5.00	10.00	20.00
❑ CAL-587 [M]	Room Full of Roses	1960	5.00	10.00	20.00

RCA VICTOR
❑ PRM-104 [M]	Westward Ho!	1961	6.25	12.50	25.00
-- Special-products issue					
❑ LPM-1130 [M]	Favorite Cowboy Songs	1955	12.50	25.00	50.00
❑ LPM-1431 [M]	How Great Thou Art	1957	12.50	25.00	50.00
❑ LPM-1483 [M]	One Man's Songs	1957	12.50	25.00	50.00
❑ LPM-2118 [M]	Cool Water	1960	6.25	12.50	25.00
❑ LSP-2118 [S]	Cool Water	1960	7.50	15.00	30.00
❑ LPM-2356 [M]	Lure of the West	1961	6.25	12.50	25.00
❑ LSP-2356 [S]	Lure of the West	1961	7.50	15.00	30.00
❑ LPM-2456 [M]	Tumbleweed Trails	1962	6.25	12.50	25.00
❑ LSP-2456 [S]	Tumbleweed Trails	1962	7.50	15.00	30.00
❑ LPM-2603 [M]	Our Men Out West	1963	5.00	10.00	20.00
❑ LSP-2603 [S]	Our Men Out West	1963	6.25	12.50	25.00
❑ LPM-2652 [M]	Hymns of the Cowboy	1963	5.00	10.00	20.00
❑ LSP-2652 [S]	Hymns of the Cowboy	1963	6.25	12.50	25.00
❑ LPM-2737 [M]	Trail Dust	1963	5.00	10.00	20.00
❑ LSP-2737 [S]	Trail Dust	1963	6.25	12.50	25.00
❑ LPM-2855 [M]	Country Fare	1964	5.00	10.00	20.00
❑ LSP-2855 [S]	Country Fare	1964	6.25	12.50	25.00
❑ LPM-2957 [M]	Down Memory Trail	1964	5.00	10.00	20.00
❑ LSP-2957 [S]	Down Memory Trail	1964	6.25	12.50	25.00
❑ LPM-3032 [10]	Cowboy Classics	1952	25.00	50.00	100.00
❑ LPM-3095 [10]	Cowboy Hymns and Spirituals	1952	25.00	50.00	100.00
❑ LPM-3162 [10]	Western Classics	1953	25.00	50.00	100.00
❑ LSP-3351 [S]	Legends of the West	1965	5.00	10.00	20.00
❑ LSP-3476 [S]	The Best of Sons of the Pioneers	1966	5.00	10.00	20.00
❑ LSP-3554 [S]	The Songs of Bob Nolan	1966	5.00	10.00	20.00
❑ LPM-3714 [M]	Campfire Favorites	1967	6.25	12.50	25.00
❑ LSP-3714 [S]	Campfire Favorites	1967	5.00	10.00	20.00
❑ LPM-3964 [M]	South of the Border	1968	20.00	40.00	80.00
❑ LSP-3964 [S]	South of the Border	1968	5.00	10.00	20.00

SONS OF THE PURPLE SAGE
TOPS
❑ L-1588 [M]	Western Favorites	1959	5.00	10.00	20.00

WALDORF
❑ 143 [10]	Songs of the Golden West	1955	12.50	25.00	50.00

SOPHOMORES, THE
SEECO
❑ CELP-451 [M]	The Sophomores	1958	50.00	100.00	200.00

SOPWITH "CAMEL", THE
KAMA SUTRA
❑ KSBS-2063	Hello Hello	1973	5.00	10.00	20.00
❑ KLP-8060 [M]	The Sopwith Camel	1967	7.50	15.00	30.00
❑ KLPS-8060 [S]	The Sopwith Camel	1967	7.50	15.00	30.00

REPRISE
❑ MS 2108	The Miraculous Hump Returns	1973	6.25	12.50	25.00

SOTHERN, ANN
CRAFTSMAN
❑ C-8061 [M]	It's Ann Sothern Time	1961	5.00	10.00	20.00

TOPS
❑ L-1611 [M]	Sothern Exposure	1959	6.25	12.50	25.00

SOUL CHILDREN, THE
STAX
❑ STS-2018	Soul Children	1969	7.50	15.00	30.00
❑ STS-2043	The Best of Two Worlds	1971	7.50	15.00	30.00
❑ STS-3003	Genesis	1972	7.50	15.00	30.00
❑ STS-5507	Friction	1974	7.50	15.00	30.00

SOUL FINDERS, THE
RCA CAMDEN
❑ CAL-2170 [M]	Sweet Soul Music	1967	7.50	15.00	30.00
❑ CAS-2170 [S]	Sweet Soul Music	1967	7.50	15.00	30.00
❑ CAL-2239 [M]	An Explosive Album of Soul	1968	7.50	15.00	30.00
❑ CAS-2239 [S]	An Explosive Album of Soul	1968	7.50	15.00	30.00

SOUL GENERATION, THE
EBONY SOUNDS
❑ 2000	Beyond Body and Soul	1972	5.00	10.00	20.00

SOUL SET, THE
JOHNSON
❑ 1001	The Soul Set	196?	6.25	12.50	25.00

SOUL SISTERS, THE
SUE
❑ LP-1022 [M]	I Can't Stand It	1964	50.00	100.00	200.00
❑ STLP-1022 [S]	I Can't Stand It	1964	100.00	200.00	400.00

SOUL SOCIETY, THE
DOT
❑ DLP-25842	Satisfaction	1969	6.25	12.50	25.00

SOUL STIRRERS, THE
Also see SAM COOKE.
SPECIALTY
❑ SP-2106 [M]	The Soul Stirrers Featuring Sam Cooke	1959	12.50	25.00	50.00

SOUL SURVIVORS
ATCO
❑ SD 33-277	Take Another Look	1969	6.25	12.50	25.00

CRIMSON
❑ CR-502 [M]	When the Whistle Blows Anything Goes	1967	12.50	25.00	50.00
❑ CR-502 S [S]	When the Whistle Blows Anything Goes	1967	7.50	15.00	30.00

SOUL, JIMMY
SPQR
❑ E 16001	If You Wanna Be Happy	1963	37.50	75.00	150.00

SOUND FOUNDATION
SMOBRO
❑ 9001	Sound Foundation	1971	6.25	12.50	25.00

SOUND SYMPOSIUM, THE
DOT
❑ DLP-25952	Bob Dylan Interpreted	1969	5.00	10.00	20.00

SOUNDGARDEN
A&M
❑ SP-5252	Louder Than Love	1989	12.50	25.00	60.00
-- Green vinyl					
❑ SP-5252	Louder Than Love	1989	10.00	20.00	40.00
-- Red vinyl					
❑ SP-5252	Louder Than Love	1989	5.00	10.00	20.00
-- Black vinyl					
❑ SP-17951 [DJ]	Louder Than Live	1990	12.50	25.00	50.00
-- Promo-only live album on blue vinyl					
❑ 31454 0198 1 [(2)] Superunknown		1994	5.00	10.00	20.00
-- Blue vinyl					
❑ 31454 0198 1 [(2)] Superunknown		1994	5.00	10.00	20.00
-- Gold vinyl					
❑ 31454 0198 1 [(2)] Superunknown		1994	5.00	10.00	20.00
-- Clear vinyl					
❑ 75021 5374 1	Badmotorfinger	1991	6.25	12.50	25.00
-- Limited edition on yellow vinyl					

SUB POP
❑ 12 [EP]	Screaming Life	1987	37.50	75.00	150.00
-- First 500 copies on orange vinyl					

Number	Title	Yr	VG	VG+	NM
❏ 12 [EP]	Screaming Life	1987	10.00	20.00	40.00
-- Black vinyl					
❏ 12 [EP]	Screaming Life	1987	5.00	10.00	20.00
-- Reissues on any color vinyl except black or orange					
❏ 17 [EP]	Fopp	1988	12.50	25.00	50.00

SOUNDS ORCHESTRAL
PARKWAY

❏ SP 7046 [S]	Cast Your Fate to the Wind	1965	5.00	10.00	20.00
❏ P 7050 [M]	Impressions of James Bond	1966	5.00	10.00	20.00
❏ SP 7050 [S]	Impressions of James Bond	1966	7.50	15.00	30.00

SOUP
ARF ARM

❏ 1	Soup	1970	30.00	60.00	120.00

BIG TREE

❏ BTS 2007	The Album Soup	1971	6.25	12.50	25.00

SOUTH 40
METROBEAT

❏ MBS-1000	Live at the Someplace Else	1968	6.25	12.50	25.00

SOUTH CENTRAL AVENUE MUNICIPAL BLUES BAND
BLUESWAY

❏ BL-6018	The Soul of Bonnie and Clyde	1968	6.25	12.50	25.00

SOUTH, JOE
CAPITOL

❏ ST-108	Introspect	1968	5.00	10.00	20.00

SOUTHERN CULTURE ON THE SKIDS
LLOYD STREET

❏ SP 002	Southern Culture on the Skids	1985	6.25	12.50	25.00

SAFEHOUSE

❏ SH-2114 [PD]	Ditch Diggin'	1994	5.00	10.00	20.00

SOUTHERN, HAL
SAGE & SAND

❏ 46	You Got a Man on Your Hands	1967	6.25	12.50	25.00

SOUTHSIDE JOHNNY AND THE ASBURY JUKES
EPIC

❏ AS 275 [DJ]	Jukes Live at the Bottom Line	1976	7.50	15.00	30.00

SOUTHWEST F.O.B.
Also see DAN SEALS.
HIP

❏ 7001	Smell of Incense	1969	7.50	15.00	30.00

SOVINE, RED
DECCA

❏ DL 4445 [M]	Red Sovine	1963	7.50	15.00	30.00
❏ DL 4736 [M]	Country Music Time	1966	7.50	15.00	30.00
❏ DL 74445 [R]	Red Sovine	1963	5.00	10.00	20.00
❏ DL 74736 [R]	Country Music Time	1966	5.00	10.00	20.00

MGM

❏ E-3465 [M]	Red Sovine	1957	15.00	30.00	60.00

STARDAY

❏ SLP-132 [M]	The One and Only Red Sovine	1961	10.00	20.00	40.00
❏ SLP-197 [M]	Golden Country Ballads of the 1960s	1962	10.00	20.00	40.00
❏ SLP-341 [M]	Little Rosa	1965	6.25	12.50	25.00
❏ SLP-357	That's Truckdrivin'	196?	5.00	10.00	20.00
❏ SLP-363 [M]	Giddy-Up Go	1966	5.00	10.00	20.00
❏ SLP-383 [M]	Town and Country Action	1966	5.00	10.00	20.00
❏ SLP-396 [M]	The Nashville Sound of Red	1967	5.00	10.00	20.00
❏ SLP-405 [M]	I Didn't Jump the Fence	1967	5.00	10.00	20.00
❏ SLP-414 [M]	Phantom 309	1967	5.00	10.00	20.00
❏ SLP-420	Tell Maude I Slipped	1968	5.00	10.00	20.00
❏ SLP-427	Sunday with Sovine	1968	5.00	10.00	20.00
❏ SLP-436	Classic Narrations	1968	5.00	10.00	20.00
❏ SLP-441	Closing Time 'Til Dawn	1969	5.00	10.00	20.00
❏ SLP-445	Who Am I	1969	5.00	10.00	20.00
❏ SLP-459	I Know You're Married But I Love You Still	1970	5.00	10.00	20.00

SPACE
HAND

❏ 5167	Space	1969	6.25	12.50	25.00

SPACEMEN, THE
ROULETTE

Number	Title	Yr	VG	VG+	NM
❏ R-25275 [M]	Rockin' in the 25th Century	1964	7.50	15.00	30.00
❏ SR-25275 [S]	Rockin' in the 25th Century	1964	10.00	20.00	40.00
❏ R-25322 [M]	Music for Batman and Robin	1966	10.00	20.00	40.00
❏ SR-25322 [S]	Music for Batman and Robin	1966	12.50	25.00	50.00

SPANDAU BALLET
MOBILE FIDELITY

❏ 1-152	True	1984	5.00	10.00	20.00
-- Audiophile vinyl					

SPANIELS, THE
VEE JAY

❏ LP-1002 [M]	Goodnite, It's Time to Go	1958	150.00	300.00	600.00
-- Maroon label; group pictured on cover					
❏ LP-1002 [M]	Goodnite, It's Time to Go	1961	50.00	100.00	200.00
-- Black label; dogs on cover					
❏ LP-1024 [M]	The Spaniels	1960	75.00	150.00	300.00

SPANKY AND OUR GANG
MERCURY

❏ MG-21124 [M]	Spanky and Our Gang	1967	7.50	15.00	30.00
❏ SR-61124 [S]	Spanky and Our Gang	1967	5.00	10.00	20.00
❏ SR-61161	Like to Get to Know You	1968	5.00	10.00	20.00
❏ SR-61183	Anything You Choose/ Without Rhyme or Reason	1969	5.00	10.00	20.00
❏ SR-61227	Spanky's Greatest Hit(s)	1969	5.00	10.00	20.00

SPANN, LUCILLE
BLUESWAY

❏ BLS-6070	Cry Before I Go	1974	6.25	12.50	25.00

SPANN, OTIS
BARNABY

❏ Z 30246	Otis Spann Is the Blues	1970	5.00	10.00	20.00
❏ KZ 31290	Walking the Blues	1972	5.00	10.00	20.00

BLUES TIME

❏ 9006	Sweet Giant of the Blues	1970	5.00	10.00	20.00

BLUESWAY

❏ BL-6003 [M]	The Blues Is Where It's At	1967	6.25	12.50	25.00
❏ BLS-6003 [S]	The Blues Is Where It's At	1967	6.25	12.50	25.00
❏ BLS-6013	The Bottom of the Blues	1968	6.25	12.50	25.00
❏ BLS-6063	Heart Loaded with Trouble	1973	5.00	10.00	20.00

CANDID

❏ CM-8001 [M]	Otis Spann Is the Blues	1966	37.50	75.00	150.00
❏ CS-9001 [S]	Otis Spann Is the Blues	1966	50.00	100.00	200.00

LONDON

❏ PS 543	Raw Blues	1968	7.50	15.00	30.00
❏ PS 551	Cracked Spanner Head	1969	7.50	15.00	30.00

PRESTIGE

❏ PRST-7719	The Blues Will Never Die	1969	5.00	10.00	20.00

VANGUARD

❏ VSD-6514	Cryin' Time	1970	5.00	10.00	20.00

SPARKS
BEARSVILLE

❏ BV 2048	Halfnelson	1971	6.25	12.50	25.00
-- Original issue of "Sparks" as "Halfnelson"					

SPARKS, RANDY
Also see THE NEW CHRISTY MINSTRELS.
VERVE

❏ MGV-2103 [M]	Randy Sparks	1959	7.50	15.00	30.00
❏ MGV-2126 [M]	Walkin' the Low Road	1960	7.50	15.00	30.00
❏ MGV-2143 [M]	Randy Sparks Three	1960	7.50	15.00	30.00

SPARROW
Also see STEPPENWOLF.
COLUMBIA

❏ CS 9758	John Kay and Sparrow	1969	10.00	20.00	40.00
-- Red "360 Sound" label					

SPARROWS, THE
ELKAY

❏ 3009 [M]	That Mersey Sound	1964	10.00	20.00	40.00

SPATS, THE
ABC-PARAMOUNT

❏ 502 [M]	Cookin' with the Spats	1965	5.00	10.00	20.00
❏ S-502 [S]	Cookin' with the Spats	1965	7.50	15.00	30.00

Number	Title	Yr	VG	VG+	NM

SPEARS, BILLIE JO
CAPITOL
| ❏ ST-114 | The Voice of Billie Jo Spears | 1969 | 5.00 | 10.00 | 20.00 |

SPELLBINDERS, THE
COLUMBIA
| ❏ CL 2514 [M] | The Magic of the Spellbinders | 1966 | 5.00 | 10.00 | 20.00 |
| ❏ CS 9314 [S] | The Magic of the Spellbinders | 1966 | 6.25 | 12.50 | 25.00 |

SPENCE, ALEXANDER "SKIP"
Also see MOBY GRAPE.
COLUMBIA
| ❏ CS 9831 | Oar | 1969 | 15.00 | 30.00 | 60.00 |

SPENCER, JON, BLUES EXPLOSION
MATADOR
| ❏ (# unknown) [DJ] | Controversial Negro | 1997 | 5.00 | 10.00 | 20.00 |
| -- Promo-only vinyl issue of a Japanese live CD | | | | | |

SPIDER-MAN
LIFESONG
| ❏ LS 6001 | Rock Reflections of a Superhero | 1976 | 6.25 | 12.50 | 25.00 |

SPIDERS, THE
IMPERIAL
| ❏ LP-9142 [M] | I Didn't Wanna Do It | 1961 | 150.00 | 300.00 | 600.00 |

SPINNERS
ATLANTIC
| ❏ QD 7256 [Q] | Spinners | 1974 | 5.00 | 10.00 | 20.00 |
| ❏ QD 18118 [Q] | New and Improved | 1974 | 5.00 | 10.00 | 20.00 |
MOTOWN
| ❏ M 639 [M] | The Original Spinners | 1967 | 6.25 | 12.50 | 25.00 |
| ❏ MS 639 [P] | The Original Spinners | 1967 | 7.50 | 15.00 | 30.00 |
V.I.P.
| ❏ 405 | 2nd Time Around | 1970 | 10.00 | 20.00 | 40.00 |

SPINNERS, THE
TIME
| ❏ S-2092 [S] | Party -- My Pad After Surfin' | 1963 | 7.50 | 15.00 | 30.00 |
| ❏ 52092 [M] | Party -- My Pad After Surfin' | 1963 | 6.25 | 12.50 | 25.00 |

SPIRAL STARECASE
COLUMBIA
| ❏ CS 9852 | More Today Than Yesterday | 1969 | 6.25 | 12.50 | 25.00 |
| -- "360 Sound" label | | | | | |

SPIRIT
EPIC
❏ E 30267	Twelve Dreams of Dr. Sardonicus	1970	5.00	10.00	20.00
-- Yellow label					
❏ KE 31175	Feedback	1972	5.00	10.00	20.00
-- Yellow label					
ODE
❏ Z12 44004	Spirit	1968	6.25	12.50	25.00
❏ Z12 44014	The Family That Plays Together	1968	6.25	12.50	25.00
❏ Z12 44016	Clear Spirit	1969	6.25	12.50	25.00

SPIRITS AND WORM
A&M
| ❏ SP-4229 | Spirits and Worm | 1969 | 200.00 | 400.00 | 800.00 |

SPIVEY, VICTORIA
SPIVEY
❏ LP-1001 [M]	Basket of Blues	1962	6.25	12.50	25.00
❏ LP-1002 [M]	Victoria and Her Blues	1963	6.25	12.50	25.00
❏ LP-1004 [M]	Three Kings and a Queen	1964	12.50	25.00	50.00
-- Bob Dylan plays on this LP; no blurb on cover					
❏ LP-1004 [M]	Three Kings and a Queen	196?	7.50	15.00	30.00
-- "Historic Tracks, Bob Dylan Appears with Big Joe Williams" blurb on cover					
❏ LP-1006 [M]	The Queen and Her Knights	1964	6.25	12.50	25.00
❏ LP-1008 [M]	The Bluesmen of the Muddy Waters Band	1964	6.25	12.50	25.00
❏ LP-1009 [M]	Encore for the Chicago Blues	1964	6.25	12.50	25.00
❏ LP-1010 [M]	The Bluesmen of the Muddy Waters Band, Volume Two	1964	6.25	12.50	25.00
❏ LP-1012 [M]	Spivey's Blues Parade	196?	6.25	12.50	25.00
❏ LP-1014 [M]	Three Kings and a Queen, Volume Two	196?	6.25	12.50	25.00
❏ LP-1015 [M]	Spivey's Blues Cavalcade	196?	6.25	12.50	25.00
❏ LP-1017 [M]	Spivey's Blues Showcase	196?	6.25	12.50	25.00
❏ LP-2001 [M]	Recorded Legacy of the Blues	196?	6.25	12.50	25.00

SPOELSTRA, MARK
ELEKTRA
❏ EKL-283 [M]	Five and Twenty Questions	1965	5.00	10.00	20.00
❏ EKL-307 [M]	State of Mind	1966	5.00	10.00	20.00
❏ EKS-7283 [S]	Five and Twenty Questions	1965	6.25	12.50	25.00
❏ EKS-7307 [S]	State of Mind	1966	6.25	12.50	25.00
VERVE FOLKWAYS
| ❏ FV-9018 [M] | The Times I've Had | 196? | 5.00 | 10.00 | 20.00 |
| ❏ FVS-9018 [S] | The Times I've Had | 196? | 6.25 | 12.50 | 25.00 |

SPOKESMEN, THE
DECCA
| ❏ DL 4712 [M] | The Dawn of Correction | 1965 | 6.25 | 12.50 | 25.00 |
| ❏ DL 74712 [S] | The Dawn of Correction | 1965 | 7.50 | 15.00 | 30.00 |

SPONTANEOUS COMBUSTION
CAPITOL
| ❏ ST-11021 | Spontaneous Combustion | 1972 | 5.00 | 10.00 | 20.00 |
FLYING DUTCHMAN
| ❏ 102 | Spontaneous Combustion | 1969 | 6.25 | 12.50 | 25.00 |
HARVEST
| ❏ SW-11095 | Triad | 1972 | 5.00 | 10.00 | 20.00 |

SPOOKY TOOTH
BELL
| ❏ 6019 | Spooky Tooth | 1968 | 6.25 | 12.50 | 25.00 |

SPRING
UNITED ARTISTS
❏ UAS-5571	Spring	1972	6.25	12.50	25.00
❏ UAS-5571 [DJ]	Spring	1972	25.00	50.00	100.00
-- Special promo package in 12x12 folder; includes LP, press kit and a packet of seeds					

SPRINGFIELD RIFLE, THE
BURDETTE
| ❏ ST-5159 | The Springfield Rifle | 1969 | 6.25 | 12.50 | 25.00 |

SPRINGFIELD, DUSTY
Also see THE SPRINGFIELDS.
ATLANTIC
| ❏ SD 8214 | Dusty in Memphis | 1969 | 7.50 | 15.00 | 30.00 |
| -- Originals have purple and brown labels | | | | | |
PHILIPS
❏ PHM-200-133 [M]	Stay Awhile	1964	7.50	15.00	30.00
❏ PHM-200-156 [M]	Dusty	1964	7.50	15.00	30.00
❏ PHM-200-174 [M]	Ooooo Weeeee!	1965	10.00	20.00	40.00
❏ PHM-200-210 [M]	You Don't Have to Say You Love Me	1966	7.50	15.00	30.00
❏ PHM-200-220 [M]	Dusty Springfield's Golden Hits	1966	6.25	12.50	25.00
-- With "Goin' Back"					
❏ PHM-200-220 [M]	Dusty Springfield's Golden Hits	1967	5.00	10.00	20.00
-- Without "Goin' Back"					
❏ PHM-200-256 [M]	The Look of Love	1967	6.25	12.50	25.00
❏ PHM-200-303 [M]	Everything's Coming Up Dusty	1967	6.25	12.50	25.00
❏ PHS-600-156 [P]	Dusty	1964	10.00	20.00	40.00
❏ PHS-600-133 [P]	Stay Awhile	1964	10.00	20.00	40.00
❏ PHS-600-174 [S]	Ooooo Weeeee!	1965	12.50	25.00	50.00
❏ PHS-600-210 [S]	You Don't Have to Say You Love Me	1966	10.00	20.00	40.00
❏ PHS-600-220 [P]	Dusty Springfield's Golden Hits	1966	8.75	17.50	35.00
-- With "Goin' Back"					
❏ PHS-600-220 [P]	Dusty Springfield's Golden Hits	1967	6.25	12.50	25.00
-- Without "Goin' Back"					
❏ PHS-600-256 [S]	The Look of Love	1967	7.50	15.00	30.00
❏ PHS-600-303 [S]	Everything's Coming Up Dusty	1967	7.50	15.00	30.00
WING
| ❏ PKW-2-120 [(2)] | Something Special | 196? | 5.00 | 10.00 | 20.00 |

SPRINGFIELD, RICK
CAPITOL
❏ SMAS-11047	Beginnings	1972	5.00	10.00	20.00
❏ SMAS-11206	Comic Book Heroes	1973	10.00	20.00	40.00
-- Withdrawn and reissued on Columbia					

SPRINGFIELDS, THE
Also see DUSTY SPRINGFIELD.
PHILIPS
| ❏ PHM 200-052 [M] | Silver Threads and Golden Needles | 1962 | 7.50 | 15.00 | 30.00 |

Number	Title	Yr	VG	VG+	NM
❑ PHM 200-076 [M] Folksongs from the Hills		1963	7.50	15.00	30.00
❑ PHS 600-052 [S] Silver Threads and Golden Needles		1962	10.00	20.00	40.00
❑ PHS 600-076 [S] Folksongs from the Hills		1963	10.00	20.00	40.00

SPRINGSTEEN, BRUCE
COLUMBIA

Number	Title	Yr	VG	VG+	NM
❑ (# unknown) [PD] Darkness on the Edge of Town		1978	37.50	75.00	150.00
-- Promo-only picture disc					
❑ AS 978 [DJ]	As Requested Around the World	1981	12.50	25.00	50.00
❑ AS 1957 [DJ]	Bruce Springsteen	1985	7.50	15.00	30.00
-- Five-song mini-LP with five B-sides of singles from Born in the U.S.A.					
❑ AS 1957 [DJ]	Bruce Springsteen	1987	5.00	10.00	20.00
-- Five-song mini-LP with five B-sides of singles from Born in the U.S.A.; second pressings say so on the label					
❑ AS 2543 [DJ]	Bruce Springsteen and the E Street Band: Live 1975-1985	1986	7.50	15.00	30.00
-- Sampler from 5-LP live set					
❑ KC 31903	Greetings from Asbury Park, N.J.	1973	5.00	10.00	20.00
❑ KC 31903 [DJ]	Greetings from Asbury Park, N.J.	1973	50.00	100.00	200.00
-- Promotional copy with timing strip and "Bruce Springsteen Fact Sheet" attached to back cover. Authentic fact sheets are on glossy stock					
❑ KC 32432	The Wild, the Innocent & the E Street Shuffle	1973	5.00	10.00	20.00
❑ HC 33795	Born to Run	1981	12.50	25.00	50.00
-- Half-speed mastered edition (original)					
❑ PC 33795 [DJ]	Born to Run	1975	400.00	800.00	1,200.
-- Test pressing with "Bruce Springsteen -- Born to Run" in script print. Also includes mailing envelope, letter from CBS and orange patch					
❑ PC 33795	Born to Run	1975	6.25	12.50	25.00
-- Jon Landau's name is misspelled "John" on the back cover					
❑ PC 33795	Born to Run	1975	25.00	50.00	100.00
-- White label promo					
❑ JC 35318 [DJ]	Darkness on the Edge of Town	1978	25.00	50.00	100.00
-- White label promo					
❑ PC2 36854 [(2) DJ]	The River	1980	18.75	37.50	75.00
-- White label promo, with photocopied letter from CBS					
❑ PC2 36854 [(2) DJ]	The River	1980	10.00	20.00	40.00
-- White label promo, without letter					
❑ C5X 40558 [(5)]	Bruce Springsteen and the E Street Band: Live 1975-1985	1986	10.00	20.00	40.00
❑ HC 43795	Born to Run	1982	10.00	20.00	40.00
-- Half-speed mastered edition (reissue)					
❑ HC 45318	Darkness on the Edge of Town	1981	10.00	20.00	40.00
-- Half-speed mastered edition					

COLUMBIA/CLASSIC

Number	Title	Yr	VG	VG+	NM
❑ PC 33795	Born to Run	1999	7.50	15.00	30.00
-- Classic Records reissue, identified as such on back cover; "error" first pressing with no gatefold					
❑ PC 33795	Born to Run	1999	6.25	12.50	25.00
-- Classic Records reissue, identified as such on back cover; corrected pressing with gatefold					

SPUR
CINEMA

Number	Title	Yr	VG	VG+	NM
❑ CSLP-1500	Spur of the Moment	196?	20.00	40.00	80.00

SPYRO GYRA
MCA

Number	Title	Yr	VG	VG+	NM
❑ 16010	Catching the Sun	1982	10.00	20.00	40.00
-- Audiophile vinyl					

NAUTILUS

Number	Title	Yr	VG	VG+	NM
❑ NR-9	Morning Dance	1979	10.00	20.00	40.00
-- Audiophile vinyl					

SQUEEZE
A&M

Number	Title	Yr	VG	VG+	NM
❑ SP-4687	U.K. Squeeze	1978	5.00	10.00	20.00
-- First pressing on red vinyl					

SRC
CAPITOL

Number	Title	Yr	VG	VG+	NM
❑ ST-134	Milestones	1969	10.00	20.00	40.00
❑ SKAO-273	Travellers Tale	1970	10.00	20.00	40.00
❑ ST 2991	SRC	1968	15.00	30.00	60.00

STACKRIDGE
DECCA

Number	Title	Yr	VG	VG+	NM
❑ DL 75317	Stackridge	1971	6.25	12.50	25.00

STAFFORD, JO
CAPITOL

Number	Title	Yr	VG	VG+	NM
❑ H 75 [10]	American Folk Songs	1950	15.00	30.00	60.00
❑ H 197 [10]	Autumn in New York	195?	15.00	30.00	60.00
❑ T 197 [M]	Autumn in New York	1955	12.50	25.00	50.00
❑ H 247 [10]	Songs for Sunday Evening	195?	15.00	30.00	60.00
❑ T 435 [M]	Starring Jo Stafford	1955	12.50	25.00	50.00
❑ H 435 [10]	Starring Jo Stafford	1953	15.00	30.00	60.00
❑ ST 1653 [S]	American Folk Songs	1962	6.25	12.50	25.00
❑ T 1653 [M]	American Folk Songs	1962	5.00	10.00	20.00
❑ ST 1921 [S]	The Hits of Jo Stafford	1963	6.25	12.50	25.00
❑ T 1921 [M]	The Hits of Jo Stafford	1963	5.00	10.00	20.00
❑ ST 2069 [S]	Sweet Hour of Prayer	1964	6.25	12.50	25.00
❑ T 2069 [M]	Sweet Hour of Prayer	1964	5.00	10.00	20.00
❑ ST 2166 [S]	The Joyful Season	1964	6.25	12.50	25.00
❑ T 2166 [M]	The Joyful Season	1964	5.00	10.00	20.00
❑ H 9014 [10]	Songs of Faith	1950	15.00	30.00	60.00

COLUMBIA

Number	Title	Yr	VG	VG+	NM
❑ CL 578 [M]	New Orleans	1954	10.00	20.00	40.00
-- Maroon label, gold print					
❑ CL 578 [M]	New Orleans	1955	7.50	15.00	30.00
-- Red and black label with six "eye" logos					
❑ CL 584 [M]	Jo Stafford Sings Broadway's Best	1954	10.00	20.00	40.00
-- Maroon label, gold print					
❑ CL 584 [M]	Jo Stafford Sings Broadway's Best	1955	7.50	15.00	30.00
-- Red and black label with six "eye" logos					
❑ CL 691 [M]	Happy Holiday	1955	15.00	30.00	60.00
❑ CL 910 [M]	Ski Trails	1956	10.00	20.00	40.00
❑ CL 968 [M]	Once Over Lightly	1957	10.00	20.00	40.00
❑ CL 1043 [M]	Songs of Scotland	1957	10.00	20.00	40.00
❑ CL 1124 [M]	Swingin' Down Broadway	1958	10.00	20.00	40.00
❑ CL 1228 [M]	Jo Stafford's Greatest Hits	1958	10.00	20.00	40.00
-- Red and black label with six "eye" logos					
❑ CL 1228 [M]	Jo Stafford's Greatest Hits	1963	5.00	10.00	20.00
-- Red label with "Guaranteed High Fidelity" in black					
❑ CL 1262 [M]	I'll Be Seeing You	1959	7.50	15.00	30.00
❑ CL 1339 [M]	Ballad of the Blues	1959	7.50	15.00	30.00
❑ CL 1561 [M]	Jo + Jazz	1960	10.00	20.00	40.00
❑ CL 2501 [10]	Soft and Sentimental	1955	10.00	20.00	40.00
❑ CL 2591 [10]	A Gal Named Jo	1955	10.00	20.00	40.00
❑ CL 6210 [10]	As You Desire Me	1952	12.50	25.00	50.00
❑ CL 6238 [10]	Jo Stafford Sings Broadway's Best	1953	12.50	25.00	50.00
❑ CL 6268 [10]	New Orleans	1954	12.50	25.00	50.00
❑ CL 6268 [10]	My Heart's in the Highland	1954	12.50	25.00	50.00
❑ CL 6286 [10]	Garden of Prayer	1954	12.50	25.00	50.00
❑ CS 8080 [S]	I'll Be Seeing You	1959	10.00	20.00	40.00
❑ CS 8139 [S]	Ballad of the Blues	1959	10.00	20.00	40.00
❑ CS 8361 [S]	Jo + Jazz	1960	15.00	30.00	60.00

DOT

Number	Title	Yr	VG	VG+	NM
❑ DLP-25673 [S] Do I Hear a Waltz?		1966	5.00	10.00	20.00
❑ DLP-25745 [S] This Is Jo Stafford		1967	5.00	10.00	20.00

REPRISE

Number	Title	Yr	VG	VG+	NM
❑ R-6090 [M]	Getting Sentimental Over Tommy Dorsey	1963	5.00	10.00	20.00
❑ R9-6090 [S]	Getting Sentimental Over Tommy Dorsey	1963	6.25	12.50	25.00

STAFFORD, JO, AND GORDON MacRAE
Also see each artist's individual listings.
CAPITOL

Number	Title	Yr	VG	VG+	NM
❑ T 423 [M]	Memory Songs	1955	12.50	25.00	50.00
❑ ST 1696 [S]	Whispering Hope	1962	6.25	12.50	25.00
❑ T 1696 [M]	Whispering Hope	1962	5.00	10.00	20.00
❑ ST 1916 [S]	Peace in the Valley	1963	6.25	12.50	25.00
❑ T 1916 [M]	Peace in the Valley	1963	5.00	10.00	20.00

STAFFORD, TERRY
CRUSADER

Number	Title	Yr	VG	VG+	NM
❑ CLP-1001 [M]	Suspicion!	1964	10.00	20.00	40.00
❑ CLP-1001S [S]	Suspicion!	1964	15.00	30.00	60.00

STAINED GLASS
CAPITOL

Number	Title	Yr	VG	VG+	NM
❑ ST-154	Crazy Horse Roads	1969	7.50	15.00	30.00
❑ ST-242	Aurora	1969	7.50	15.00	30.00

STANDELLS, THE
LIBERTY

Number	Title	Yr	VG	VG+	NM
❑ LRP-3384 [M]	The Standells In Person at P.J.'s	1964	20.00	40.00	80.00
❑ LST-7384 [S]	The Standells In Person at P.J.'s	1964	25.00	50.00	100.00

SUNSET

Number	Title	Yr	VG	VG+	NM
❑ SUM-1136 [M]	Live and Out of Sight	1966	6.25	12.50	25.00
❑ SUS-5136 [S]	Live and Out of Sight	1966	7.50	15.00	30.00

TOWER

Number	Title	Yr	VG	VG+	NM
❑ ST 5027 [S]	Dirty Water	1966	20.00	40.00	80.00
❑ T 5027 [M]	Dirty Water	1966	15.00	30.00	60.00
❑ ST 5044 [S]	Why Pick on Me	1966	15.00	30.00	60.00
❑ T 5044 [M]	Why Pick on Me	1966	12.50	25.00	50.00
❑ ST 5049 [S]	The Hot Ones	1966	15.00	30.00	60.00
❑ T 5049 [M]	The Hot Ones	1966	12.50	25.00	50.00

Number	Title	Yr	VG	VG+	NM
❏ ST 5098 [S]	Try It	1967	15.00	30.00	60.00
❏ T 5098 [M]	Try It	1967	12.50	25.00	50.00

STANLEY BROTHERS, THE
CABIN CREEK

Number	Title	Yr	VG	VG+	NM
❏ LP-203 [M]	Bluegrass Gospel Favorites	1966	15.00	30.00	60.00

HARMONY

Number	Title	Yr	VG	VG+	NM
❏ HL 7291 [M]	The Stanley Brothers	1961	6.25	12.50	25.00

KING

Number	Title	Yr	VG	VG+	NM
❏ 615 [M]	The Stanley Brothers	1959	25.00	50.00	100.00
❏ 645 [M]	Hymns and Sacred Songs	1960	20.00	40.00	80.00
❏ 690 [M]	Everybody's Country Favorites	1961	20.00	40.00	80.00
❏ KS-690 [S]	Everybody's Country Favorites	1961	25.00	50.00	100.00
❏ 698 [M]	For the Good People	1961	20.00	40.00	80.00
❏ 719 [M]	The Stanleys In Person	1961	20.00	40.00	80.00
❏ KS-719 [S]	The Stanleys In Person	1961	25.00	50.00	100.00
❏ 750 [M]	Old Time Camp Meeting	1962	20.00	40.00	80.00
❏ 772 [M]	The Stanley Brothers and the Clinch Mountain Boys Sing the Songs They Like Best	1962	20.00	40.00	80.00
❏ 791 [M]	Award Winners	1962	20.00	40.00	80.00
❏ KS-791 [S]	Award Winners	1962	25.00	50.00	100.00
❏ 805 [M]	Good Old Camp Meeting Songs	1963	20.00	40.00	80.00
❏ KS-805 [S]	Good Old Camp Meeting Songs	1963	25.00	50.00	100.00
❏ 834 [M]	Just Because	1964	12.50	25.00	50.00
❏ 864 [M]	Country Folk Music Spotlight	1964	12.50	25.00	50.00
❏ 872 [M]	Five String Banjo Hootenanny	1964	12.50	25.00	50.00
❏ 918 [M]	Hymns of the Cross	1964	12.50	25.00	50.00
❏ 924 [M]	The Remarkable Stanley Brothers Play and Sing Bluegrass Songs for You	1965	12.50	25.00	50.00
❏ 953 [M]	The Best of the Stanley Brothers	1966	6.25	12.50	25.00
❏ 963 [M]	A Collection of Gospel and Sacred Songs	1966	6.25	12.50	25.00
❏ 1013 [M]	The Stanley Brothers Sing the Best-Loved Sacred Songs of the Carter Family	1967	6.25	12.50	25.00
❏ KS-1013 [S]	The Stanley Brothers Sing the Best-Loved Sacred Songs of the Carter Family	1967	7.50	15.00	30.00

MERCURY

Number	Title	Yr	VG	VG+	NM
❏ MG-20349 [M]	Country Pickin' and Singin'	1958	20.00	40.00	80.00
❏ MG-20884 [M]	Hard Times	1963	6.25	12.50	25.00
❏ SR-60884 [S]	Hard Times	1963	7.50	15.00	30.00

STARDAY

Number	Title	Yr	VG	VG+	NM
❏ SLP-106 [M]	Mountain Song Favorites	1959	12.50	25.00	50.00
❏ SLP-122 [M]	Sacred Songs from the Hills	1960	12.50	25.00	50.00
❏ SLP-201 [M]	The Mountain Music Sound of the Stanley Brothers	1962	10.00	20.00	40.00
❏ SLP-384 [M]	Jacob's Vision	1966	7.50	15.00	30.00

VINTAGE

Number	Title	Yr	VG	VG+	NM
❏ ZK-002 [M]	The Stanley Brothers Live at Antioch College	1961	17.50	35.00	70.00

STANLEY, MICHAEL, BAND
Also see SILK.
TUMBLEWEED

Number	Title	Yr	VG	VG+	NM
❏ TWS 106	Michael Stanley	1972	5.00	10.00	20.00
-- Blue textured cover					

STANLEY, PAUL
Also see KISS.
CASABLANCA

Number	Title	Yr	VG	VG+	NM
❏ NBLP-7123	Paul Stanley	1978	6.25	12.50	25.00
❏ NBPIX-7123 [PD]	Paul Stanley	1978	15.00	30.00	60.00

STANLEY, RALPH
JALYN

Number	Title	Yr	VG	VG+	NM
❏ JLP-118 [M]	Old Time Music	1966	6.25	12.50	25.00
❏ JLP-120 [M]	The Bluegrass Sound of Ralph Stanley	1966	6.25	12.50	25.00
❏ JLP-129 [M]	Ralph Stanley and the Clinch Mountain Boys	196?	6.25	12.50	25.00

KING

Number	Title	Yr	VG	VG+	NM
❏ KSD-1028	Brand New Country Songs by Ralph Stanley	1968	5.00	10.00	20.00
❏ KSD-1032	Over the Sunset Hill	1968	5.00	10.00	20.00
❏ KSD-1046	How Far to Little Rock?	1969	5.00	10.00	20.00
❏ KSD-1069	The Hills of Home	1969	5.00	10.00	20.00

STAPLE SINGERS, THE
Also see MAVIS STAPLES.
BUDDAH

Number	Title	Yr	VG	VG+	NM
❏ BDS-2009	The Best of the Staple Singers	1969	5.00	10.00	20.00
❏ BDS-7508	Will the Circle Be Unbroken	1969	5.00	10.00	20.00

EPIC

Number	Title	Yr	VG	VG+	NM
❏ LN 24132 [M]	Amen	1965	5.00	10.00	20.00
❏ LN 24163 [M]	Freedom Highway	1965	5.00	10.00	20.00
❏ LN 24196 [M]	Why	1966	5.00	10.00	20.00
❏ LN 24237 [M]	Pray On	1967	6.25	12.50	25.00
❏ LN 24332 [M]	For What It's Worth	1967	6.25	12.50	25.00
❏ BN 26132 [S]	Amen	1965	6.25	12.50	25.00
❏ BN 26163 [S]	Freedom Highway	1965	6.25	12.50	25.00
❏ BN 26196 [S]	Why	1966	6.25	12.50	25.00
❏ BN 26237 [S]	Pray On	1967	5.00	10.00	20.00
❏ BN 26332 [S]	For What It's Worth	1967	5.00	10.00	20.00
❏ BN 26373	What the World Needs Now Is Love	1968	5.00	10.00	20.00
❏ EG 30635 [(2)]	The Staple Singers Make You Happy	1971	5.00	10.00	20.00

STAX

Number	Title	Yr	VG	VG+	NM
❏ STS-2004	Soul Folk in Action	1968	6.25	12.50	25.00
❏ STS-2016	We'll Get Over	1969	5.00	10.00	20.00
❏ STS-2034	The Staple Swingers	1971	5.00	10.00	20.00

VEE JAY

Number	Title	Yr	VG	VG+	NM
❏ LP-5000 [M]	Uncloudy Day	1959	7.50	15.00	30.00
❏ LP-5008 [M]	Will the Circle Be Unbroken	1960	7.50	15.00	30.00
❏ LP-5014 [M]	Swing Low	1961	7.50	15.00	30.00
❏ LP-5019 [M]	Best of the Staple Singers	1962	7.50	15.00	30.00
❏ LP-5030 [M]	Swing Low Sweet Chariot	1963	7.50	15.00	30.00

STAPLES, MAVIS
Also see THE STAPLE SINGERS.
VOLT

Number	Title	Yr	VG	VG+	NM
❏ VOS-6007	Mavis Staples	1969	5.00	10.00	20.00
❏ VOS-6010	Only for the Lonely	1970	5.00	10.00	20.00

STARCASTLE
EPIC

Number	Title	Yr	VG	VG+	NM
❏ (# unknown) [PD]	Citadel	1978	12.50	25.00	50.00
-- Picture disc, possibly promo only					

STARCHER, BUDDY
DECCA

Number	Title	Yr	VG	VG+	NM
❏ DL 4796 [M]	History Repeats Itself	1966	5.00	10.00	20.00
❏ DL 74796 [S]	History Repeats Itself	1966	6.25	12.50	25.00

STARDAY

Number	Title	Yr	VG	VG+	NM
❏ SLP-211 [M]	Buddy Starcher and His Mountain Guitar	1962	7.50	15.00	30.00
❏ SLP-382 [M]	History Repeats Itself	1966	7.50	15.00	30.00

STARFIRES, THE
LABREA

Number	Title	Yr	VG	VG+	NM
❏ LS-8018 [M]	Teenbeat A-Go-Go	1965	12.50	25.00	50.00

OHIO RECORDING SERVICE

Number	Title	Yr	VG	VG+	NM
❏ 34 [M]	The Starfires Play	1964	12.50	25.00	50.00

STARK NAKED
RCA VICTOR

Number	Title	Yr	VG	VG+	NM
❏ LSP-4592	Stark Naked	1971	6.25	12.50	25.00

STARKER, JANOS
MERCURY LIVING PRESENCE

Number	Title	Yr	VG	VG+	NM
❏ SR 90303 [S]	Dvorak: Cello Concerto; Bruch: Kol Nidre	196?	25.00	50.00	100.00
-- With Antal Dorati/London Symphony Orchestra; maroon label, no "Vendor: Mercury Record Corporation"					
❏ SR 90303 [S]	Dvorak: Cello Concerto; Bruch: Kol Nidre	196?	15.00	30.00	60.00
-- With Antal Dorati/London Symphony Orchestra; maroon label, with "Vendor: Mercury Record Corporation"					
❏ SR 90303 [S]	Dvorak: Cello Concerto; Bruch: Kol Nidre	196?	10.00	20.00	40.00
-- With Antal Dorati/London Symphony Orchestra; third edition (dark red, not maroon label)					
❏ SR 90320 [S]	Mendelssohn: Cello Sonata; Chopin: Cello Sonata in G	196?	15.00	30.00	60.00
-- Maroon label, with "Vendor: Mercury Record Corporation"					
❏ SR 90320 [S]	Mendelssohn: Cello Sonata; Chopin: Cello Sonata in G	196?	30.00	60.00	120.00
-- Maroon label, no "Vendor: Mercury Record Corporation"					
❏ SR 90347 [S]	Schumann: Cello Concerto; Lalo: Cello Concerto	196?	30.00	60.00	120.00
-- With Stanislaw Skrowaczewski/London Symphony Orchestra; maroon label, no "Vendor: Mercury Record Corporation"					
❏ SR 90347 [S]	Schumann: Cello Concerto; Lalo: Cello Concerto	196?	10.00	20.00	40.00
-- With Stanislaw Skrowaczewski/London Symphony Orchestra; maroon label, with "Vendor: Mercury Record Corporation"					

Number	Title	Yr	VG	VG+	NM
❑ SR 90370 [S]	Bach: Suites 2 and 5 for Solo Violin	196?	20.00	40.00	80.00
-- Maroon label, no "Vendor: Mercury Record Corporation"					
❑ SR 90370 [S]	Bach: Suites 2 and 5 for Solo Violin	196?	12.50	25.00	50.00
-- Maroon label, with "Vendor: Mercury Record Corporation"					
❑ SR 90370 [S]	Bach: Suites 2 and 5 for Solo Violin	196?	10.00	20.00	40.00
-- Third edition: Dark red (not maroon) label					
❑ SR 90392 [S]	Brahms: Cello Sonatas No. 1 and	196?	37.50	75.00	150.00
-- Maroon label, no "Vendor: Mercury Record Corporation"					
❑ SR 90392 [S]	Brahms: Cello Sonatas No. 1 and	196?	12.50	25.00	50.00
-- Maroon label, with "Vendor: Mercury Record Corporation"					
❑ SR 90405 [S]	Bartok: First Rhapsody; Mendelssohn: Various Concertantes; Martinu: Rossini Variations	196?	25.00	50.00	100.00
-- Maroon label, no "Vendor: Mercury Record Corporation"					
❑ SR 90405 [S]	Bartok: First Rhapsody; Mendelssohn: Various Concertantes; Martinu: Rossini Variations	196?	10.00	20.00	40.00
-- Maroon label, with "Vendor: Mercury Record Corporation"					
❑ SR 90405 [S]	Bartok: First Rhapsody; Mendelssohn: Various Concertantes; Martinu: Rossini Variations	196?	7.50	15.00	30.00
-- Third edition: Dark red (not maroon) label					
❑ SR 90480 [S]	Bach, J.S.: Three Sonatas	196?	50.00	100.00	200.00
-- Maroon label, with "Vendor: Mercury Record Corporation"					

STARR, EDWIN
GORDY

Number	Title	Yr	VG	VG+	NM
❑ GS-931	Soul Master	1968	6.25	12.50	25.00
❑ GS-940	25 Miles	1969	6.25	12.50	25.00
❑ GS-945	Just We Two	1969	5.00	10.00	20.00
-- With Blinky					
❑ GS-948	War & Peace	1970	5.00	10.00	20.00
❑ GS-956	Involved	1971	5.00	10.00	20.00

STARR, KAY
CAPITOL

Number	Title	Yr	VG	VG+	NM
❑ H 211 [10]	Songs by Starr	1950	17.50	35.00	70.00
❑ T 211 [M]	Songs by Starr	1955	12.50	25.00	50.00
❑ H 363 [10]	Kay Starr Style	1953	17.50	35.00	70.00
❑ T 363 [M]	Kay Starr Style	1955	12.50	25.00	50.00
❑ H 415 [10]	The Hits of Kay Starr	1953	17.50	35.00	70.00
❑ T 415 [M]	The Hits of Kay Starr	1955	12.50	25.00	50.00
-- Turquoise or gray label					
❑ T 415 [M]	The Hits of Kay Starr	1958	7.50	15.00	30.00
-- Black label with colorband, Capitol logo at left					
❑ T 415 [M]	The Hits of Kay Starr	1962	5.00	10.00	20.00
-- Black label with colorband, Capitol logo at top					
❑ T 580 [M]	In a Blue Mood	1955	12.50	25.00	50.00
❑ ST 1254 [S]	Movin'	1959	7.50	15.00	30.00
❑ T 1254 [M]	Movin'	1959	6.25	12.50	25.00
❑ ST 1303 [S]	Losers Weepers	1960	7.50	15.00	30.00
❑ T 1303 [M]	Losers Weepers	1960	6.25	12.50	25.00
❑ ST 1358 [S]	One More Time	1960	7.50	15.00	30.00
❑ T 1358 [M]	One More Time	1960	6.25	12.50	25.00
❑ ST 1374 [S]	Movin' on Broadway	1960	7.50	15.00	30.00
❑ T 1374 [M]	Movin' on Broadway	1960	6.25	12.50	25.00
❑ ST 1438 [S]	Kay Starr, Jazz Singer	1960	10.00	20.00	40.00
❑ T 1438 [M]	Kay Starr, Jazz Singer	1960	7.50	15.00	30.00
❑ ST 1468 [S]	All Starr Hits	1961	7.50	15.00	30.00
❑ T 1468 [M]	All Starr Hits	1961	6.25	12.50	25.00
❑ ST 1681 [S]	I Cry by Night	1962	6.25	12.50	25.00
❑ T 1681 [M]	I Cry by Night	1962	5.00	10.00	20.00
❑ ST 1795 [S]	Just Plain Country	1962	6.25	12.50	25.00
❑ T 1795 [M]	Just Plain Country	1962	5.00	10.00	20.00
❑ ST-8-1795 [S]	Just Plain Country	196?	7.50	15.00	30.00
-- Capitol Record Club edition					

LIBERTY

Number	Title	Yr	VG	VG+	NM
❑ LRP-3280 [M]	Swingin' with the Starr	1963	6.25	12.50	25.00
-- Reissue of 9001					
❑ LRP-9001 [M]	Swingin' with the Starr	1956	12.50	25.00	50.00

RCA VICTOR

Number	Title	Yr	VG	VG+	NM
❑ LPM-1149 [M]	The One and Only Kay Starr	1955	7.50	15.00	30.00
❑ LPM-1549 [M]	Blue Starr	1957	7.50	15.00	30.00
❑ LPM-1720 [M]	Rockin' with Kay	1958	12.50	25.00	50.00
❑ LPM-2055 [M]	I Hear the Word	1959	6.25	12.50	25.00
❑ LSP-2055 [S]	I Hear the Word	1959	7.50	15.00	30.00

RONDO-LETTE

Number	Title	Yr	VG	VG+	NM
❑ A-3 [M]	Them There Eyes	1958	6.25	12.50	25.00

STARR, LUCILLE
A&M

Number	Title	Yr	VG	VG+	NM
❑ LP-107 [M]	French Song	1966	7.50	15.00	30.00

EPIC

Number	Title	Yr	VG	VG+	NM
❑ BN 26436	Lonely Street	1969	7.50	15.00	30.00

STARR, RINGO
Also see THE BEATLES.
APPLE

Number	Title	Yr	VG	VG+	NM
❑ SW-3365	Sentimental Journey	1970	5.00	10.00	20.00
❑ SMAS-3368	Beaucoups of Blues	1970	5.00	10.00	20.00
❑ SWAL-3413	Ringo	1973	100.00	200.00	400.00
-- With a 5:26 version of "Six O'Clock." On later copies, the song is shortened to 4:05 though the label still says 5:26. All known copies have a promo punch-hole in top corner of jacket; on Side 2 record, "Six O'Clock" will be the widest track.					
❑ SWAL-3413	Ringo	1973	5.00	10.00	20.00
-- Standard issue with booklet; Side 1, Song 2 identified on cover as "Hold On"					
❑ SWAL-3413	Ringo	1974	6.25	12.50	25.00
-- Later issue with booklet; Side 1, Song 2 identified on cover as "Have You Seen My Baby"					

ATLANTIC

Number	Title	Yr	VG	VG+	NM
❑ SD 18193 [DJ]	Ringo's Rotogravure	1976	7.50	15.00	30.00
-- With "DJ Only" scrawled into trail-off area					
❑ SD 19108 [DJ]	Ringo the 4th	1977	7.50	15.00	30.00
-- With "DJ Only" scrawled into trail-off area					

CAPITOL

Number	Title	Yr	VG	VG+	NM
❑ SW-3365	Sentimental Journey	197?	10.00	20.00	40.00
-- Purple label, large Capitol logo					
❑ SN-16218	Sentimental Journey	198?	6.25	12.50	25.00
-- Green label budget-line reissue					
❑ SN-16218	Goodnight Vienna	198?	6.25	12.50	25.00
-- Green label budget-line reissue					
❑ SN-16235	Beaucoups of Blues	198?	5.00	10.00	20.00
-- Green label budget-line reissue					

PORTRAIT

Number	Title	Yr	VG	VG+	NM
❑ JR 35378 [DJ]	Bad Boy	1978	25.00	50.00	100.00
-- White label promo with "Advance Promotion" on label; in plain white cover					
❑ JR 35378 [DJ]	Bad Boy	1978	7.50	15.00	30.00
-- Regular white-label promo in standard jacket					

RHINO

Number	Title	Yr	VG	VG+	NM
❑ R1 70199	Starr Struck: Ringo's Best 1976-1983	1989	6.25	12.50	25.00

RYKODISC

Number	Title	Yr	VG	VG+	NM
❑ RALP 0190	Ringo Starr and His All-Starr Band	1990	7.50	15.00	30.00
-- With limited, numbered obi (deduct $5 if missing)					

STARR, SALLY
Backed by BILL HALEY AND HIS COMETS.
ARCADE

Number	Title	Yr	VG	VG+	NM
❑ 1001 [M]	Our Gal Sal	1960	20.00	40.00	80.00

CLYMAX

Number	Title	Yr	VG	VG+	NM
❑ 1001 [M]	Our Gal Sal	1959	50.00	100.00	200.00

STARZ
CAPITOL

Number	Title	Yr	VG	VG+	NM
❑ SPRO-8657/8 [DJ]	Live at Municipal Auditorium, Louisville, March 30, 1978	1978	7.50	15.00	30.00
-- Promo-only "Superstars Radio Network Presents" album					
❑ SW-11617	Violation	1977	5.00	10.00	20.00
-- Gold vinyl					

STATLER BROTHERS, THE
COLUMBIA

Number	Title	Yr	VG	VG+	NM
❑ CL 2449 [M]	Flowers on the Wall	1966	6.25	12.50	25.00
❑ CL 2719 [M]	The Big Hits	1967	7.50	15.00	30.00
❑ CS 9249 [S]	Flowers on the Wall	1966	7.50	15.00	30.00
❑ CS 9519 [S]	The Big Hits	1967	6.25	12.50	25.00
❑ CS 9878	Oh Happy Day	1969	6.25	12.50	25.00
❑ KG 31557 [(2)]	The World of the Statler Brothers	1972	5.00	10.00	20.00

MERCURY

Number	Title	Yr	VG	VG+	NM
❑ SRM-2-101 [(2)]	Holy Bible/The Old and New Testaments	1978	5.00	10.00	20.00

STATON, CANDI
FAME

Number	Title	Yr	VG	VG+	NM
❑ 1800	Candi Staton	1972	5.00	10.00	20.00
❑ ST-4201	I'm a Prisoner	1970	5.00	10.00	20.00
❑ ST-4202	Stand By Your Man	1971	5.00	10.00	20.00

STATON, DAKOTA
CAPITOL

Number	Title	Yr	VG	VG+	NM
❑ T 876 [M]	The Late, Late Show	1957	12.50	25.00	50.00
-- Turquoise or gray label					
❑ T 876 [M]	The Late, Late Show	1959	7.50	15.00	30.00
-- Black label with colorband, Capitol logo at left					
❑ T 1003 [M]	In the Night	1958	12.50	25.00	50.00
-- Turquoise or gray label					
❑ T 1003 [M]	In the Night	1959	7.50	15.00	30.00
-- Black label with colorband, Capitol logo at left					

Number	Title	Yr	VG	VG+	NM
❑ ST 1054 [S]	Dynamic!	1959	10.00	20.00	40.00
-- Black label with colorband, Capitol logo at left					
❑ ST 1054 [S]	Dynamic!	1962	5.00	10.00	20.00
-- Black label with colorband, Capitol logo at top					
❑ T 1054 [M]	Dynamic!	1958	7.50	15.00	30.00
-- Black label with colorband, Capitol logo at left					
❑ ST 1170 [S]	Crazy He Calls Me	1959	10.00	20.00	40.00
-- Black label with colorband, Capitol logo at left					
❑ ST 1170 [S]	Crazy He Calls Me	1962	5.00	10.00	20.00
-- Black label with colorband, Capitol logo at top					
❑ T 1170 [M]	Crazy He Calls Me	1959	7.50	15.00	30.00
-- Black label with colorband, Capitol logo at left					
❑ ST 1241 [S]	Time to Swing	1959	10.00	20.00	40.00
-- Black label with colorband, Capitol logo at left					
❑ ST 1241 [S]	Time to Swing	1962	5.00	10.00	20.00
-- Black label with colorband, Capitol logo at left					
❑ T 1241 [M]	Time to Swing	1959	7.50	15.00	30.00
-- Black label with colorband, Capitol logo at left					
❑ ST 1325 [S]	More Than the Most	1960	10.00	20.00	40.00
-- Black label with colorband, Capitol logo at left					
❑ ST 1325 [S]	More Than the Most	1962	5.00	10.00	20.00
-- Black label with colorband, Capitol logo at top					
❑ T 1325 [M]	More Than the Most	1960	7.50	15.00	30.00
-- Black label with colorband, Capitol logo at left					
❑ ST 1387 [S]	Ballads and the Blues	1960	10.00	20.00	40.00
-- Black label with colorband, Capitol logo at left					
❑ ST 1387 [S]	Ballads and the Blues	1962	5.00	10.00	20.00
-- Black label with colorband, Capitol logo at top					
❑ T 1387 [M]	Ballads and the Blues	1960	7.50	15.00	30.00
-- Black label with colorband, Capitol logo at left					
❑ ST 1427 [S]	Softly	1961	10.00	20.00	40.00
-- Black label with colorband, Capitol logo at left					
❑ ST 1427 [S]	Softly	1962	5.00	10.00	20.00
-- Black label with colorband, Capitol logo at top					
❑ T 1427 [M]	Softly	1961	7.50	15.00	30.00
-- Black label with colorband, Capitol logo at left					
❑ ST 1490 [S]	Dakota	1961	10.00	20.00	40.00
-- Black label with colorband, Capitol logo at left					
❑ ST 1490 [S]	Dakota	1962	5.00	10.00	20.00
-- Black label with colorband, Capitol logo at top					
❑ T 1490 [M]	Dakota	1961	7.50	15.00	30.00
-- Black label with colorband, Capitol logo at left					
❑ ST 1597 [S]	'Round Midnight	1961	10.00	20.00	40.00
-- Black label with colorband, Capitol logo at left					
❑ ST 1597 [S]	'Round Midnight	1962	5.00	10.00	20.00
-- Black label with colorband, Capitol logo at top					
❑ T 1597 [M]	'Round Midnight	1961	7.50	15.00	30.00
-- Black label with colorband, Capitol logo at left					
❑ ST 1649 [S]	Dakota at Storyville	1962	6.25	12.50	25.00
❑ T 1649 [M]	Dakota at Storyville	1962	5.00	10.00	20.00

LONDON

Number	Title	Yr	VG	VG+	NM
❑ LL 3495 [M]	Dakota '67	1967	5.00	10.00	20.00

UNITED ARTISTS

Number	Title	Yr	VG	VG+	NM
❑ UAL-3292 [M]	From Dakota with Love	1963	5.00	10.00	20.00
❑ UAL-3312 [M]	Live and Swinging	1963	5.00	10.00	20.00
❑ UAL-3355 [M]	Dakota Staton with Strings	1964	5.00	10.00	20.00
❑ UAS-6292 [S]	From Dakota with Love	1963	6.25	12.50	25.00
❑ UAS-6316 [S]	Live and Swinging	1963	6.25	12.50	25.00
❑ UAS-6355 [S]	Dakota Staton with Strings	1964	6.25	12.50	25.00

STATUS QUO
CADET CONCEPT

Number	Title	Yr	VG	VG+	NM
❑ LPS-315	Messages from the Status Quo	1968	12.50	25.00	50.00

STEAGALL, RED
CAPITOL

Number	Title	Yr	VG	VG+	NM
❑ ST-11056	Party Dolls and Wine	1972	5.00	10.00	20.00

STEAM
MERCURY

Number	Title	Yr	VG	VG+	NM
❑ SR 61254	Steam	1969	5.00	10.00	20.00

STEAMHAMMER
EPIC

Number	Title	Yr	VG	VG+	NM
❑ BN 26490	Reflection	1969	7.50	15.00	30.00
❑ BN 26552	Steamhammer	1970	7.50	15.00	30.00

STEARNS, JUNE
COLUMBIA

Number	Title	Yr	VG	VG+	NM
❑ CS 9783	River of Regret	1969	5.00	10.00	20.00

STEEL
EPIC

Number	Title	Yr	VG	VG+	NM
❑ E 30875	Steel	1971	5.00	10.00	20.00

STEELE, TOMMY
LIBERTY

Number	Title	Yr	VG	VG+	NM
❑ LRP-3426 [M]	Everything's Coming Up	1965	5.00	10.00	20.00
❑ LST-7426 [S]	Everything's Coming Up	1965	6.25	12.50	25.00

LONDON

Number	Title	Yr	VG	VG+	NM
❑ LL 1770 [M]	Rock Around the World	195?	12.50	25.00	50.00

STEELEYE SPAN
BIG TREE

Number	Title	Yr	VG	VG+	NM
❑ BTS-2004	Please to See the King	1971	7.50	15.00	30.00

MOBILE FIDELITY

Number	Title	Yr	VG	VG+	NM
❑ 1-027	All Around My Hat	1980	6.25	12.50	25.00
-- Audiophile vinyl					

SHANACHIE

Number	Title	Yr	VG	VG+	NM
❑ 79071/2 [(2)]	Portfolio	1990	5.00	10.00	20.00

STEELY DAN
ABC

Number	Title	Yr	VG	VG+	NM
❑ 2022-1107 [(2)]	Greatest Hits	1978	5.00	10.00	20.00
-- Canadian import on gold vinyl, widely available in U.S.					

ABC DUNHILL

Number	Title	Yr	VG	VG+	NM
❑ SMAS-94976	Can't Buy a Thrill	1973	6.25	12.50	25.00
-- Capitol Record Club edition pressed on the wrong label					

COMMAND

Number	Title	Yr	VG	VG+	NM
❑ QD-40009 [Q]	Can't Buy a Thrill	1974	5.00	10.00	20.00
❑ QD-40010 [Q]	Countdown to Ecstasy	1974	5.00	10.00	20.00
❑ QD-40015 [Q]	Pretzel Logic	1974	5.00	10.00	20.00

MCA

Number	Title	Yr	VG	VG+	NM
❑ 16009	Gaucho	1981	12.50	25.00	50.00
-- Audiophile pressing					
❑ 16016	Gold	1982	12.50	25.00	50.00
-- Audiophile pressing					

MOBILE FIDELITY

Number	Title	Yr	VG	VG+	NM
❑ 1-007	Katy Lied	1979	20.00	40.00	80.00
-- Audiophile vinyl					
❑ 1-033	Aja	1980	12.50	25.00	50.00
-- Audiophile vinyl					

STEPHENS, LEIGH
PHILIPS

Number	Title	Yr	VG	VG+	NM
❑ PHS 600-294	Red Weather	1969	20.00	40.00	80.00

STEPPENWOLF
Also see THE SPARROW.
ABC DUNHILL

Number	Title	Yr	VG	VG+	NM
❑ DS-50029 [S]	Steppenwolf	1968	5.00	10.00	20.00
❑ DS-50037	The Second	1968	7.50	15.00	30.00
-- With white border on cover					
❑ DS-50037	The Second	1968	6.25	12.50	25.00
-- With chrome border on cover					
❑ DSX-50053	At Your Birthday Party	1969	5.00	10.00	20.00
❑ DSX-50060	Early Steppenwolf	1969	5.00	10.00	20.00
-- Actually a 1967 concert by Sparrow (pre-Steppenwolf)					
❑ DSX-50066	Monster	1969	5.00	10.00	20.00
❑ DSD-50075 [(2)]	Steppenwolf 'Live'	1970	6.25	12.50	25.00
❑ DSX-50090	Steppenwolf 7	1970	5.00	10.00	20.00
❑ DSX-50099	Steppenwolf Gold/Their Great Hits	1971	5.00	10.00	20.00
❑ DSX-50101	For Ladies Only	1971	5.00	10.00	20.00
❑ DSX-50124	Rest in Peace	1972	5.00	10.00	20.00
❑ DSX-50135	16 Greatest Hits	1973	5.00	10.00	20.00

DUNHILL

Number	Title	Yr	VG	VG+	NM
❑ D-50029 [M]	Steppenwolf	1968	37.50	75.00	150.00
❑ DS-50029 [S]	Steppenwolf	1968	10.00	20.00	40.00

NAUTILUS

Number	Title	Yr	VG	VG+	NM
❑ NR-53	Wolftracks	198?	12.50	25.00	50.00
-- As "John Kay and Steppenwolf"; audiophile vinyl					

STEVENS, APRIL
Also see NINO TEMPO AND APRIL STEVENS.
AUDIO LAB

Number	Title	Yr	VG	VG+	NM
❑ AL-1534 [M]	Torrid Tunes	1959	50.00	100.00	200.00

IMPERIAL

Number	Title	Yr	VG	VG+	NM
❑ LP-9118 [M]	Teach Me Tiger	1960	15.00	30.00	60.00
❑ LP-12055 [S]	Teach Me Tiger	1960	25.00	50.00	100.00

STEVENS, CAT
A&M

Number	Title	Yr	VG	VG+	NM
❑ QU-53623 [Q]	Buddha and the Chocolate Box	1974	5.00	10.00	20.00
❑ QU-54280 [Q]	Tea for the Tillerman	1974	5.00	10.00	20.00
❑ QU-54313 [Q]	Teaser and the Firecat	1974	5.00	10.00	20.00
❑ QU-54365 [Q]	Catch Bull at Four	1974	5.00	10.00	20.00

Number	Title	Yr	VG	VG+	NM
❏ QU-54391 [Q]	Foreigner	1974	5.00	10.00	20.00
❏ QU-54519 [Q]	Greatest Hits	1975	5.00	10.00	20.00
DERAM					
❏ DE 16005 [M]	Matthew and Son	1967	5.00	10.00	20.00
MOBILE FIDELITY					
❏ 1-035	Tea for the Tillerman	1979	10.00	20.00	40.00
-- Audiophile vinyl					
❏ MFQR-035	Tea for the Tillerman	1984	30.00	60.00	120.00
-- Ultra High Quality Recording in a box					
❏ 1-244	Teaser and the Firecat	1996	10.00	20.00	40.00
-- Audiophile vinyl					
❏ 1-254	Izitso	1996	6.25	12.50	25.00
-- Audiophile vinyl					

STEVENS, CONNIE
WARNER BROS.

Number	Title	Yr	VG	VG+	NM
❏ W 1208 [M]	Conchetta	1958	12.50	25.00	50.00
❏ WS 1208 [S]	Conchetta	1958	15.00	30.00	60.00
❏ W 1382 [M]	Connie Stevens from "Hawaiian Eye"	1960	7.50	15.00	30.00
❏ WS 1382 [S]	Connie Stevens from "Hawaiian Eye"	1960	10.00	20.00	40.00
❏ W 1431 [M]	From Me to You	1962	7.50	15.00	30.00
❏ WS 1431 [S]	From Me to You	1962	10.00	20.00	40.00
❏ W 1432 [M]	Connie	1962	7.50	15.00	30.00
❏ WS 1432 [S]	Connie	1962	10.00	20.00	40.00
❏ W 1460 [M]	The Hank Williams Songbook	1962	7.50	15.00	30.00
❏ WS 1460 [S]	The Hank Williams Songbook	1962	10.00	20.00	40.00

STEVENS, DODIE
DOT

Number	Title	Yr	VG	VG+	NM
❏ DLP-3212 [M]	Dodie Stevens	1960	7.50	15.00	30.00
❏ DLP-3323 [M]	Over the Rainbow	1960	7.50	15.00	30.00
❏ DLP-3371 [M]	Pink Shoelaces	1961	7.50	15.00	30.00
❏ DLP-25212 [S]	Dodie Stevens	1960	10.00	20.00	40.00
❏ DLP-25323 [S]	Over the Rainbow	1960	10.00	20.00	40.00
❏ DLP-25371 [S]	Pink Shoelaces	1961	10.00	20.00	40.00

STEVENS, RAY
MERCURY

Number	Title	Yr	VG	VG+	NM
❏ MG-20732 [M]	1,837 Seconds of Humor	1962	10.00	20.00	40.00
❏ MG-20828 [M]	This Is Ray Stevens	1963	6.25	12.50	25.00
❏ SR-60732 [S]	1,837 Seconds of Humor	1962	12.50	25.00	50.00
❏ SR-60828 [S]	This Is Ray Stevens	1963	7.50	15.00	30.00

STEVENS, TERRI
EVEREST

Number	Title	Yr	VG	VG+	NM
❏ SDBR-1088 [S]	It's Been a Long, Long Time	1960	6.25	12.50	25.00
❏ LPBR-5088 [M]	It's Been a Long, Long Time	1960	5.00	10.00	20.00

STEWARD, ALEC
BLUESVILLE

Number	Title	Yr	VG	VG+	NM
❏ BVLP-1076 [M]	Creepin' Blues	1963	20.00	40.00	80.00
-- Blue label, silver print					
❏ BVLP-1076 [M]	Creepin' Blues	1964	6.25	12.50	25.00
-- Blue label, trident logo at right					

STEWART FAMILY, THE
KING

Number	Title	Yr	VG	VG+	NM
❏ 687 [M]	Country Sacred Songs	1960	7.50	15.00	30.00
❏ 695 [M]	Golden Country Favorites	1960	7.50	15.00	30.00

STEWART, AL
EPIC

Number	Title	Yr	VG	VG+	NM
❏ BN 26564	Love Chronicles	1970	5.00	10.00	20.00
JANUS					
❏ 7026 [DJ]	The Early Years	1977	7.50	15.00	30.00
-- Promo-only condensation of 2-LP set with rubber-stamp cover					
MOBILE FIDELITY					
❏ 1-009	Year of the Cat	1979	10.00	20.00	40.00
-- Audiophile vinyl					
❏ 1-082	Time Passages	1981	7.50	15.00	30.00
-- Audiophile vinyl					
NAUTILUS					
❏ NR-34	24 Carrots	198?	7.50	15.00	30.00
-- Audiophile vinyl					

STEWART, ANDY
CAPITOL

Number	Title	Yr	VG	VG+	NM
❏ ST 10320 [S]	Andy Stewart's Scotland	196?	5.00	10.00	20.00

WARWICK

Number	Title	Yr	VG	VG+	NM
❏ W 3043 [M]	A Scottish Soldier	1961	5.00	10.00	20.00
❏ WST 3043 [S]	A Scottish Soldier	1961	7.50	15.00	30.00

STEWART, BILLY
CHESS

Number	Title	Yr	VG	VG+	NM
❏ LP-1496 [M]	I Do Love You	196?	7.50	15.00	30.00
-- Green "woman" cover					
❏ LP-1496 [M]	I Do Love You	1965	20.00	40.00	80.00
-- Red cover, black "wheel"					
❏ LPS-1496 [S]	I Do Love You	196?	10.00	20.00	40.00
-- Green "woman" cover					
❏ LPS-1496 [S]	I Do Love You	1965	25.00	50.00	100.00
-- Red cover, black "wheel"					
❏ LP-1499 [M]	Unbelievable	1966	7.50	15.00	30.00
❏ LPS-1499 [S]	Unbelievable	1966	10.00	20.00	40.00
❏ LP-1513 [M]	Billy Stewart Teaches Old Standards New Tricks	1967	7.50	15.00	30.00
❏ LPS-1513 [S]	Billy Stewart Teaches Old Standards New Tricks	1967	10.00	20.00	40.00
❏ LPS-1547	Billy Stewart Remembered	1970	6.25	12.50	25.00

STEWART, JOHN
Also see THE KINGSTON TRIO.
CAPITOL

Number	Title	Yr	VG	VG+	NM
❏ ST 2975	Signals Through the Glass	1968	5.00	10.00	20.00

STEWART, REDD
AUDIO LAB

Number	Title	Yr	VG	VG+	NM
❏ AL-1528 [M]	Redd Stewart Sings Favorite Old Time Tunes	1959	50.00	100.00	200.00

STEWART, ROD
Also see FACES.
DCC COMPACT CLASSICS

Number	Title	Yr	VG	VG+	NM
❏ LPZ-2010	Never a Dull Moment	1995	5.00	10.00	20.00
-- Audiophile vinyl					
MERCURY					
❏ SR-61237	The Rod Stewart Album	1969	6.25	12.50	25.00
-- Cover is yellow with no black border					
❏ SR-61264	Gasoline Alley	1970	5.00	10.00	20.00
-- Cover is textured, most noticeably on the pebbles					
MOBILE FIDELITY					
❏ 1-054	Blondes Have More Fun	1980	6.25	12.50	25.00
-- Audiophile vinyl					
UNITED DISTRIBUTORS					
❏ UDL-2391	The Day Will Come	1981	5.00	10.00	20.00
WARNER BROS.					
❏ BSP 3276 [PD]	Blondes Have More Fun	1978	5.00	10.00	20.00
❏ 23743 [(2) DJ]	Absolutely Live	1982	6.25	12.50	25.00
-- Promo only on Quiex II vinyl					

STEWART, SANDY
COLPIX

Number	Title	Yr	VG	VG+	NM
❏ CP-441 [M]	My Coloring Book	1963	6.25	12.50	25.00
❏ SCP-441 [S]	My Coloring Book	1963	7.50	15.00	30.00

STEWART, WYNN
CAPITOL

Number	Title	Yr	VG	VG+	NM
❏ ST-113	In Love	1969	5.00	10.00	20.00
❏ ST-214	Let the Whole World Sing It with Me	1969	5.00	10.00	20.00
❏ ST-324	Yours Forever	1969	5.00	10.00	20.00
❏ ST 2332 [S]	The Songs of Wynn Stewart	1965	6.25	12.50	25.00
❏ T 2332 [M]	The Songs of Wynn Stewart	1965	5.00	10.00	20.00
❏ ST 2737 [S]	It's Such a Pretty World Today	1967	6.25	12.50	25.00
❏ T 2737 [M]	It's Such a Pretty World Today	1967	5.00	10.00	20.00
❏ ST 2849 [S]	Love's Gonna Happen to Me	1968	5.00	10.00	20.00
❏ T 2849 [M]	Love's Gonna Happen to Me	1968	7.50	15.00	30.00
❏ ST 2921	Something Pretty	1968	5.00	10.00	20.00
WRANGLER					
❏ W-1006 [M]	Wynn Stewart	1962	7.50	15.00	30.00
❏ W-31006 [S]	Wynn Stewart	1962	10.00	20.00	40.00

STEWART, WYNN, AND JAN HOWARD
Also see each artist's individual listings.
CHALLENGE

Number	Title	Yr	VG	VG+	NM
❏ CHL-611 [M]	Sweethearts of Country Music	1961	12.50	25.00	50.00
STARDAY					
❏ SLP-421	Wynn Stewart and Jan Howard Sing Their Hits	1968	6.25	12.50	25.00

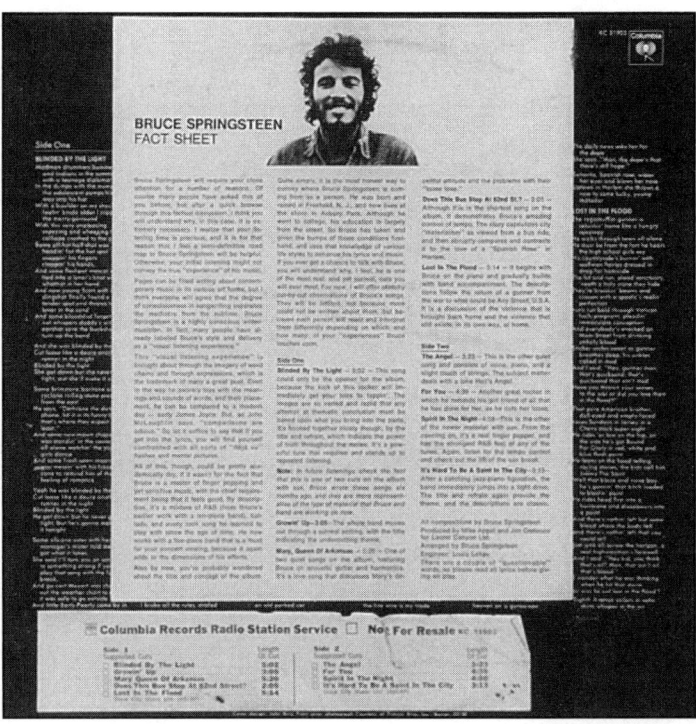

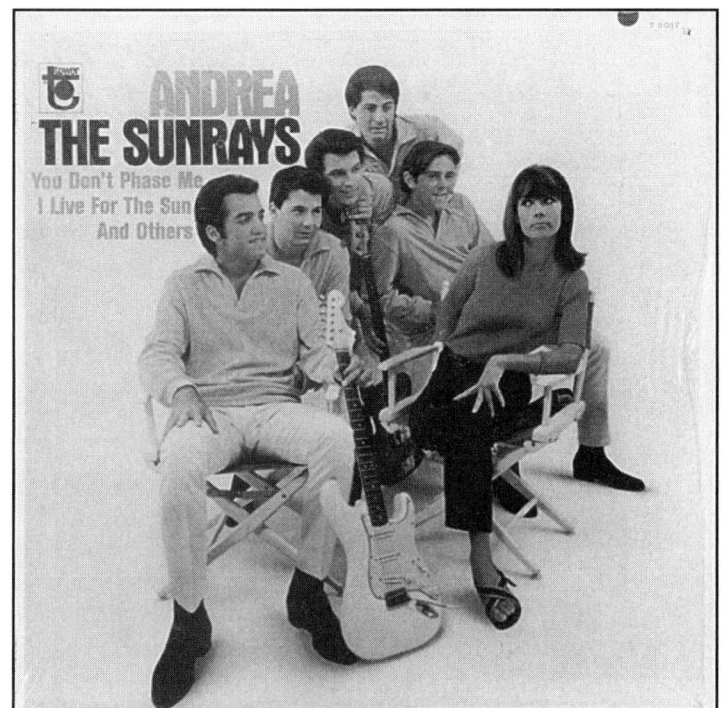

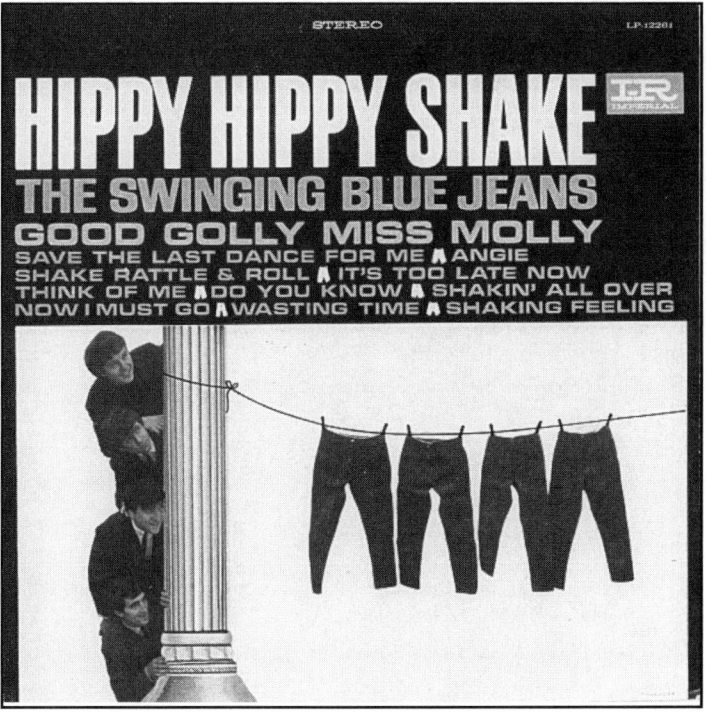

(Top left) All of Bruce Springsteen's regular albums are pretty common, including most pressings of his debut, *Greetings from Asbury Park, N.J.* But this isn't just any copy. For starters, it's the original 1973 issue with a "KC" prefix. By the time the album charted in 1975, the prefix had changed to "PC." (Top right) Not only that, but this copy is one of the rare radio promos. Not only does it have a small Columbia timing strip at the bottom, it also has a glossy-stock "Bruce Springsteen Fact Sheet" attached. The label of this record is the standard orange Columbia label; no white label versions of this were made. (Bottom left) Murry Wilson, father of the Wilson brothers of Beach Boys fame, thought somehow that he was the brains behind his sons' success. After a mid-1960s estrangement, he went into artist management himself and picked up the Sunrays, a decent, though certainly not Beach Boys quality, California band. This was their album, *Andrea.* (Bottom right) One can argue about which version of the song "Hippy Hippy Shake" is best. But the biggest? The British group called The Swinging Blue Jeans earn that honor. Their only American album, named after the hit, is a sought-after British Invasion relic.

Number	Title	Yr	VG	VG+	NM

STIDHAM, ARBEE
BLUESVILLE
❏ BVLP-1021 [M] Tired of Wandering		1961	25.00	50.00	100.00
-- *Blue label, silver print*					
❏ BVLP-1021 [M] Tired of Wandering		1964	6.25	12.50	25.00
-- *Blue label, trident logo at right*					

FOLKWAYS
❏ F-31033	There's Always Tomorrow	1973	5.00	10.00	20.00

STIFF LITTLE FINGERS
CHRYSALIS
❏ CHR 1270	Nobody's Heroes	1980	5.00	10.00	20.00
❏ CHR 1300	Hanx	1980	5.00	10.00	20.00
❏ CHR 1339	Go For It	1981	5.00	10.00	20.00

ROUGH TRADE
❏ ROUGH US 5	Inflammable Material	1980	6.25	12.50	25.00

STILLS, STEPHEN
Also see BUFFALO SPRINGFIELD; CROSBY, STILLS AND NASH; CROSBY, STILLS, NASH AND YOUNG.
COLUMBIA
❏ PCQ 33575 [Q] Stills		1975	5.00	10.00	20.00

STING
Also see THE POLICE.
A&M
❏ SP-3295 [EP]	...Nada Como El Sol	1988	5.00	10.00	20.00
-- *Spanish versions of songs from "...Nothing Like the Sun"*					

MOBILE FIDELITY
❏ 1-185	The Dream of the Blue Turtles	1985	5.00	10.00	20.00
-- *Audiophile vinyl*					

STINGERS, THE
CROWN
❏ CST-476 [S]	Guitars A Go Go	196?	10.00	20.00	40.00
❏ CLP-5476 [M]	Guitars A Go Go	196?	7.50	15.00	30.00

STINSON BROTHERS, THE
CANADIAN AMERICAN
❏ CALP-1012 [M] The Stinson Brothers in Las Vegas		196?	5.00	10.00	20.00
❏ SCALP-1012 [S] The Stinson Brothers in Las Vegas		196?	6.25	12.50	25.00

STITES, GARY
CARLTON
❏ LP-120 [M]	Lonely for You	1960	20.00	40.00	80.00
❏ STLP-120 [S]	Lonely for You	1960	30.00	60.00	120.00

STITT, SONNY
ARGO
❏ LP-629 [M]	Sonny Stitt	1958	10.00	20.00	40.00
❏ LP-661 [M]	Burnin'	1960	6.25	12.50	25.00
❏ LPS-661 [S]	Burnin'	1960	7.50	15.00	30.00
❏ LP-683 [M]	Sonny Stitt at the D.J. Lounge	1961	6.25	12.50	25.00
❏ LPS-683 [S]	Sonny Stitt at the D.J. Lounge	1961	7.50	15.00	30.00
❏ LP-709 [M]	Rearin' Back	1962	6.25	12.50	25.00
❏ LPS-709 [S]	Rearin' Back	1962	7.50	15.00	30.00
❏ LP-730 [M]	Move On Over	1964	6.25	12.50	25.00
❏ LPS-730 [S]	Move On Over	1964	7.50	15.00	30.00
❏ LP-744 [M]	My Main Man	1965	6.25	12.50	25.00
❏ LPS-744 [S]	My Main Man	1965	7.50	15.00	30.00

ATLANTIC
❏ 1395 [M]	Sonny Stitt and the Top Brass	1962	6.25	12.50	25.00
❏ SD 1395 [S]	Sonny Stitt and the Top Brass	1962	7.50	15.00	30.00
❏ 1418 [M]	Stitt Plays Bird	1964	7.50	15.00	30.00
❏ SD 1418 [S]	Stitt Plays Bird	1964	10.00	20.00	40.00

CADET
❏ LPS-760 [S]	Inter-Action	1966	5.00	10.00	20.00
❏ LPS-770 [S]	Soul in the Night	1966	5.00	10.00	20.00

COLPIX
❏ CP-499 [M]	Broadway Soul	1964	7.50	15.00	30.00
❏ SCP-499 [S]	Broadway Soul	1964	7.50	15.00	30.00

IMPULSE!
❏ A-43 [M]	Sonny Stitt Now!	1963	6.25	12.50	25.00
❏ AS-43 [S]	Sonny Stitt Now!	1963	7.50	15.00	30.00
❏ A-52 [M]	Salt and Pepper	1964	6.25	12.50	25.00
❏ AS-52 [S]	Salt and Pepper	1964	7.50	15.00	30.00
-- *With Paul Gonsalves*					

JAZZLAND
❏ JLP-71 [M]	Low Flame	1962	6.25	12.50	25.00
❏ JLP-971 [S]	Low Flame	1962	7.50	15.00	30.00

JAZZTONE
❏ J-1231 [M]	Early Modern	1956	12.50	25.00	50.00
❏ J-1263 [M]	Early Modern	1957	10.00	20.00	40.00

PACIFIC JAZZ
❏ PJ-71 [M]	My Mother's Eyes	1963	5.00	10.00	20.00
❏ ST-71 [S]	My Mother's Eyes	1963	6.25	12.50	25.00

PRESTIGE
❏ PRLP-103 [10] Sonny Stitt Plays		1951	50.00	100.00	200.00
❏ PRLP-111 [10] Mr. Saxophone		1951	50.00	100.00	200.00
❏ PRLP-126 [10] Favorites, Volume 1		1952	50.00	100.00	200.00
❏ PRLP-148 [10] Favorites, Volume 2		1953	50.00	100.00	200.00
❏ PRLP-7024 [M] Sonny Stitt with Bud Powell and J.J. Johnson		1956	25.00	50.00	100.00
❏ PRLP-7077 [M] Kaleidoscope		1957	25.00	50.00	100.00
❏ PRLP-7133 [M] Stitt's Bits		1958	25.00	50.00	100.00
❏ PRLP-7244 [M] Stitt Meets Brother Jack		1962	12.50	25.00	50.00
-- *Yellow label*					
❏ PRLP-7244 [M] Stitt Meets Brother Jack		1964	6.25	12.50	25.00
-- *Blue label*					
❏ PRLP-7248 [M] All God's Chillun Got Rhythm		1962	12.50	25.00	50.00
-- *Yellow label*					
❏ PRLP-7248 [M] All God's Chillun Got Rhythm		1964	6.25	12.50	25.00
-- *Blue label with trident logo*					
❏ PRLP-7297 [M] Soul Shack		1964	12.50	25.00	50.00
-- *Yellow label*					
❏ PRLP-7297 [M] Soul Shack		1965	6.25	12.50	25.00
-- *Blue label with trident logo*					
❏ PRST-7297 [S] Soul Shack		1964	12.50	25.00	50.00
-- *Silver label*					
❏ PRST-7297 [S] Soul Shack		1965	6.25	12.50	25.00
-- *Blue label with trident logo*					
❏ PRLP-7302 [M] Primitive Soul!		1964	10.00	20.00	40.00
-- *Yellow label*					
❏ PRLP-7302 [M] Primitive Soul!		1965	6.25	12.50	25.00
-- *Blue label with trident logo*					
❏ PRST-7302 [S] Primitive Soul!		1964	10.00	20.00	40.00
-- *Silver label*					
❏ PRST-7302 [S] Primitive Soul!		1965	6.25	12.50	25.00
-- *Blue label with trident logo*					
❏ PRLP-7332 [M] Shangri-La		1964	5.00	10.00	20.00
❏ PRST-7332 [S] Shangri-La		1964	6.25	12.50	25.00
❏ PRLP-7372 [M] Soul People		1965	5.00	10.00	20.00
❏ PRST-7372 [S] Soul People		1965	6.25	12.50	25.00
❏ PRLP-7436 [M] Night Crawler		1966	5.00	10.00	20.00
❏ PRST-7436 [S] Night Crawler		1966	6.25	12.50	25.00
❏ PRLP-7452 [M] 'Nuther Fu'ther		1966	5.00	10.00	20.00
❏ PRST-7452 [S] 'Nuther Fu'ther		1966	6.25	12.50	25.00
❏ PRLP-7459 [M] Pow!		1967	6.25	12.50	25.00
❏ PRST-7459 [S] Pow!		1967	5.00	10.00	20.00

ROOST
❏ LP-415 [10]	Sonny Stitt Plays Arrangements from the Pen of Johnny Richards	1952	75.00	150.00	300.00
❏ LP-418 [10]	Jazz at the Hi-Hat	1954	75.00	150.00	300.00
❏ LP-1203 [M]	Battle of Birdland	1955	20.00	40.00	80.00
❏ LP-1208 [M]	Sonny Stitt	1956	20.00	40.00	80.00
❏ LP-2204 [M]	Sonny Stitt Plays Arrangements of Quincy Jones	1957	12.50	25.00	50.00
❏ LP-2208 [M]	Sonny Stitt	1957	12.50	25.00	50.00
❏ LP-2219 [M]	37 Minutes and 48 Seconds of Sonny Stitt	1957	12.50	25.00	50.00
❏ LP-2226 [M]	Sonny Stitt with the New Yorkers	1958	12.50	25.00	50.00
❏ LP-2230 [M]	The Saxophone of Sonny Stitt	1959	10.00	20.00	40.00
❏ SLP-2230 [S]	The Saxophone of Sonny Stitt	1959	7.50	15.00	30.00
❏ LP-2235 [M]	A Little Bit of Stitt	1959	10.00	20.00	40.00
❏ SLP-2235 [S]	A Little Bit of Stitt	1959	7.50	15.00	30.00
❏ LP-2240 [M]	The Sonny Side of Stitt	1960	10.00	20.00	40.00
❏ SLP-2240 [S]	The Sonny Side of Stitt	1960	7.50	15.00	30.00
❏ LP-2244 [M]	Stittsville	1960	10.00	20.00	40.00
❏ SLP-2244 [S]	Stittsville	1960	7.50	15.00	30.00
❏ LP-2245 [M]	Sonny Side Up	196?	6.25	12.50	25.00
❏ SLP-2245 [S]	Sonny Side Up	196?	6.25	12.50	25.00
❏ LP-2247 [M]	Feelin's	196?	6.25	12.50	25.00
❏ SLP-2247 [S]	Feelin's	196?	6.25	12.50	25.00
❏ LP-2252 [M]	Sonny Stitt in Orbit	196?	6.25	12.50	25.00
❏ SLP-2252 [S]	Sonny Stitt in Orbit	196?	6.25	12.50	25.00
❏ LP-2253 [M]	Sonny Stitt Goes Latin	196?	6.25	12.50	25.00
❏ SLP-2253 [S]	Sonny Stitt Goes Latin	196?	6.25	12.50	25.00

ROULETTE
❏ R-25339 [M]	The Matadors Meet the Bull	1965	5.00	10.00	20.00
❏ SR-25339 [S]	The Matadors Meet the Bull	1965	6.25	12.50	25.00
❏ R-25343 [M]	What's New?	1966	5.00	10.00	20.00
❏ SR-25343 [S]	What's New?	1966	6.25	12.50	25.00
❏ R-25348 [M]	I Keep Comin' Back	1967	6.25	12.50	25.00
❏ SR-25348 [S]	I Keep Comin' Back	1967	5.00	10.00	20.00

SAVOY
❏ MG-9006 [10]	All Star Series: Sonny Stitt	1953	50.00	100.00	200.00

Number	Title	Yr	VG	VG+	NM
❑ MG-9012 [10]	New Sounds in Modern Music	1953	50.00	100.00	200.00
❑ MG-9014 [10]	New Trends of Jazz	1953	50.00	100.00	200.00

VERVE

Number	Title	Yr	VG	VG+	NM
❑ MGVS-6038 [S]	The Hard Swing	1960	10.00	20.00	40.00
❑ MGVS-6041 [S]	Sonny Stitt Plays Jimmy Giuffre Arrangements	1960	10.00	20.00	40.00
❑ MGVS-6108 [S]	Sonny Stitt Sits In with the Oscar Peterson Trio	1960	10.00	20.00	40.00
❑ MGVS-6149 [S]	Sonny Stitt Blows the Blues	1960	10.00	20.00	40.00
❑ MGV-8219 [M]	New York Jazz	1957	12.50	25.00	50.00
❑ V-8219 [M]	New York Jazz	1961	6.25	12.50	25.00
❑ MGV-8250 [M]	Only the Blues	1958	12.50	25.00	50.00
❑ V-8250 [M]	Only the Blues	1961	6.25	12.50	25.00
❑ MGV-8262 [M]	Sonny Side Up	1958	15.00	30.00	60.00
❑ V-8262 [M]	Sonny Side Up	1961	7.50	15.00	30.00
❑ MGV-8306 [M]	The Hard Swing	1959	12.50	25.00	50.00
❑ V-8306 [M]	The Hard Swing	1961	6.25	12.50	25.00
❑ V6-8306 [S]	The Hard Swing	1961	5.00	10.00	20.00
❑ MGV-8309 [M]	Sonny Stitt Plays Jimmy Giuffre Arrangements	1959	12.50	25.00	50.00
❑ V-8309 [M]	Sonny Stitt Plays Jimmy Giuffre Arrangements	1961	6.25	12.50	25.00
❑ V6-8309 [S]	Sonny Stitt Plays Jimmy Giuffre Arrangements	1961	5.00	10.00	20.00
❑ MGV-8324 [M]	Personal Appearance	1959	12.50	25.00	50.00
❑ V-8324 [M]	Personal Appearance	1961	6.25	12.50	25.00
❑ MGV-8344 [M]	Sonny Stitt Sits In with the Oscar Peterson Trio	1959	12.50	25.00	50.00
❑ V-8344 [M]	Sonny Stitt Sits In with the Oscar Peterson Trio	1961	6.25	12.50	25.00
❑ V6-8344 [S]	Sonny Stitt Sits In with the Oscar Peterson Trio	1961	5.00	10.00	20.00
❑ MGV-8374 [M]	Sonny Stitt Blows the Blues	1960	12.50	25.00	50.00
❑ V-8374 [M]	Sonny Stitt Blows the Blues	1961	6.25	12.50	25.00
❑ V6-8374 [S]	Sonny Stitt Blows the Blues	1961	5.00	10.00	20.00
❑ MGV-8377 [M]	Saxophone Supremacy	1960	12.50	25.00	50.00
❑ V-8377 [M]	Saxophone Supremacy	1961	6.25	12.50	25.00
❑ MGV-8380 [M]	Sonny Stitt Swings the Most	1960	12.50	25.00	50.00
❑ V-8380 [M]	Sommy Stitt Swings the Most	1961	6.25	12.50	25.00
❑ V-8451 [M]	The Sensual Sound of Sonny Stitt	1962	5.00	10.00	20.00
❑ V6-8451 [S]	The Sensual Sound of Sonny Stitt	1962	6.25	12.50	25.00

VERVE/CLASSIC

Number	Title	Yr	VG	VG+	NM
❑ MGVS-6149	Sonny Stitt Blows the Blues	1996	10.00	20.00	40.00

-- Audiophile reissue

STOECKLEIN, VAL
DOT

Number	Title	Yr	VG	VG+	NM
❑ DLP-25904	Grey Life	1968	10.00	20.00	40.00

STOKOWSKI, LEOPOLD
RCA VICTOR RED SEAL

Number	Title	Yr	VG	VG+	NM
❑ LSC-2593 [S]	Inspiration	1962	7.50	15.00	30.00

-- Original with "shaded dog" label

STOLOFF, MORRIS
DECCA

Number	Title	Yr	VG	VG+	NM
❑ DL 8574 [M]	This Is Kim	1957	15.00	30.00	60.00

-- Black label, silver print; Kim Novak is the cover model

STONE CIRCUS, THE
MAINSTREAM

Number	Title	Yr	VG	VG+	NM
❑ S-6119	The Stone Circus	1969	20.00	40.00	80.00

STONE COUNTRY
RCA VICTOR

Number	Title	Yr	VG	VG+	NM
❑ LSP-3958	Stone Country	1968	5.00	10.00	20.00

STONE HARBOUR
STONE HARBOUR

Number	Title	Yr	VG	VG+	NM
❑ 398	Stone Harbour Emerges	197?	125.00	250.00	500.00

STONE PONEYS
Also see LINDA RONSTADT.
CAPITOL

Number	Title	Yr	VG	VG+	NM
❑ ST 2666 [S]	The Stone Poneys	1967	7.50	15.00	30.00
❑ T 2666 [M]	The Stone Poneys	1967	6.25	12.50	25.00
❑ ST 2763 [S]	Evergreen, Vol. 2	1967	7.50	15.00	30.00
❑ T 2763 [M]	Evergreen, Vol. 2	1967	10.00	20.00	40.00
❑ ST 2863	Linda Ronstadt/Stone Poneys and Friends Vol. III	1968	12.50	25.00	50.00

STONE THE CROWS
POLYDOR

Number	Title	Yr	VG	VG+	NM
❑ 24-4019	Stone the Crows	1970	5.00	10.00	20.00
❑ PD-5020	Teenage Licks	1972	5.00	10.00	20.00
❑ PD-5037	Continuous Performance	1972	5.00	10.00	20.00

STONE, CLIFFIE
CAPITOL

Number	Title	Yr	VG	VG+	NM
❑ T 1080 [M]	The Party's on Me	1958	10.00	20.00	40.00
❑ ST 1230 [S]	Cool Cowboy	1959	10.00	20.00	40.00
❑ T 1230 [M]	Cool Cowboy	1959	7.50	15.00	30.00
❑ ST 1286 [S]	Square Dance Promenade	1960	10.00	20.00	40.00
❑ T 1286 [M]	Square Dance Promenade	1960	7.50	15.00	30.00
❑ KAO 1555 [M]	Original Cowboy Sing-A-Long	1961	7.50	15.00	30.00
❑ SKAO 1555 [S]	Original Cowboy Sing-A-Long	1961	10.00	20.00	40.00
❑ ST 1685 [S]	It's Fun to Square Dance	1962	6.25	12.50	25.00
❑ T 1685 [M]	It's Fun to Square Dance	1962	5.00	10.00	20.00
❑ H 4009 [10]	Square Dances	195?	15.00	30.00	60.00

TOWER

Number	Title	Yr	VG	VG+	NM
❑ ST 5073 [S]	Together Again	1967	7.50	15.00	30.00
❑ T 5073 [M]	Together Again	1967	6.25	12.50	25.00

STONE, KIRBY, FOUR
CADENCE

Number	Title	Yr	VG	VG+	NM
❑ CLP 1023 [M]	Man I Flipped	1958	6.25	12.50	25.00

COLUMBIA

Number	Title	Yr	VG	VG+	NM
❑ CL 1211 [M]	Baubles, Bangles and Beads	1959	5.00	10.00	20.00
❑ CL 1290 [M]	The "Go" Sound of the Kirby Stone Four	1959	5.00	10.00	20.00
❑ CL 1356 [M]	The Kirby Stone Touch	1959	5.00	10.00	20.00
❑ CL 1646 [M]	The Kirby Stone Four at the Playboy Club	1960	5.00	10.00	20.00
❑ CL 1714 [M]	Guys and Dolls	1961	5.00	10.00	20.00
❑ CS 8014 [S]	Baubles, Bangles and Beads	1959	6.25	12.50	25.00
❑ CS 8130 [S]	The "Go" Sound of the Kirby Stone Four	1959	6.25	12.50	25.00
❑ CS 8164 [S]	The Kirby Stone Touch	1959	6.25	12.50	25.00
❑ CS 8446 [S]	The Kirby Stone Four at the Playboy Club	1960	6.25	12.50	25.00
❑ CS 8514 [S]	Guys and Dolls	1961	6.25	12.50	25.00

TOPS

Number	Title	Yr	VG	VG+	NM
❑ L-1582 [M]	The Kirby Stone Four	1957	7.50	15.00	30.00

STONE, ROLAND
ACE

Number	Title	Yr	VG	VG+	NM
❑ LP-1018 [M]	Just a Moment	1961	37.50	75.00	150.00

STONEGROUND
WARNER BROS.

Number	Title	Yr	VG	VG+	NM
❑ 2WS 1956 [(2)]	Family Album	1971	5.00	10.00	20.00

STONEHILL, RANDY
ONE WAY

Number	Title	Yr	VG	VG+	NM
❑ JC-31252	Born Twice	1972	15.00	30.00	60.00

STONEMANS, THE
MGM

Number	Title	Yr	VG	VG+	NM
❑ E-4363 [M]	Those Singin' Swingin' Stompin' Sensational Stonemans	1966	5.00	10.00	20.00
❑ SE-4363 [S]	Those Singin' Swingin' Stompin' Sensational Stonemans	1966	6.25	12.50	25.00
❑ E-4453 [M]	Stoneman's Country	1967	5.00	10.00	20.00
❑ SE-4453 [S]	Stoneman's Country	1967	6.25	12.50	25.00
❑ E-4511 [M]	All in the Family	1968	6.25	12.50	25.00
❑ SE-4511 [S]	All in the Family	1968	5.00	10.00	20.00
❑ SE-4578	The Great Stonemans	1968	5.00	10.00	20.00
❑ SE-4613	A Stoneman Christmas	1968	5.00	10.00	20.00

STARDAY

Number	Title	Yr	VG	VG+	NM
❑ SLP-393 [M]	White Lightning	1965	10.00	20.00	40.00

WORLD PACIFIC

Number	Title	Yr	VG	VG+	NM
❑ ST-1828 [S]	Big Ball in Monterey	1964	10.00	20.00	40.00
❑ WP-1828 [M]	Big Ball in Monterey	1964	7.50	15.00	30.00

STONEY AND MEATLOAF
Also see MEAT LOAF.
RARE EARTH

Number	Title	Yr	VG	VG+	NM
❑ R 528	Stoney and Meatloaf	1971	5.00	10.00	20.00

STOOGES, THE -- See IGGY AND THE STOOGES.

STORIES
KAMA SUTRA

Number	Title	Yr	VG	VG+	NM
❑ KSBS-2068	About Us	1973	7.50	15.00	30.00

-- Gatefold; does NOT contain "Brother Louie"

Number	Title	Yr	VG	VG+	NM

STORM, BILLY
BUENA VISTA
| ❏ BV-3315 [M] | Billy Storm | 1963 | 25.00 | 50.00 | 100.00 |
| ❏ STER-3315 [S] | Billy Storm | 1963 | 30.00 | 60.00 | 120.00 |

FAMOUS
| ❏ F-504 | This Is the Night | 1969 | 25.00 | 50.00 | 100.00 |

STORM, GALE
DOT
❏ DLP-3011 [M]	Gale Storm	1956	12.50	25.00	50.00
❏ DLP-3017 [M]	Sentimental Me	1956	12.50	25.00	50.00
❏ DLP-3098 [M]	Gale Storm Hits	1958	10.00	20.00	40.00
❏ DLP-3197 [M]	Softly and Tenderly	1959	7.50	15.00	30.00
❏ DLP-3209 [M]	Gale Storm Sings	1959	7.50	15.00	30.00
❏ DLP-25197 [S]	Softly and Tenderly	1959	10.00	20.00	40.00
❏ DLP-25209 [S]	Gale Storm Sings	1959	10.00	20.00	40.00

STORY, CARL
MERCURY
❏ MG-20323 [M]	Gospel Quartet Favorites	1958	10.00	20.00	40.00
❏ MG-20584 [M]	More Gospel Quartet Favorites	1961	7.50	15.00	30.00
❏ SR-60584 [S]	More Gospel Quartet Favorites	1961	10.00	20.00	40.00

STARDAY
❏ SLP-107 [M]	America's Favorite Country Gospel Artist	1959	12.50	25.00	50.00
❏ SLP-127 [M]	Gospel Revival	1961	10.00	20.00	40.00
❏ SLP-137 [M]	All Day Singing with Dinner on the Ground	1961	10.00	20.00	40.00
❏ SLP-152 [M]	Get Religion	1962	10.00	20.00	40.00
❏ SLP-219 [M]	Mighty Close to Heaven	1963	10.00	20.00	40.00
❏ SLP-278 [M]	All Day Sacred Singing	1964	10.00	20.00	40.00
❏ SLP-315 [M]	Sacred Songs of Life and the Hereafter	1965	10.00	20.00	40.00
❏ SLP-348 [M]	There's Nothing on Earth (That Heaven Can't Cure)	1965	10.00	20.00	40.00
❏ SLP-411 [M]	My Lord Keeps a Record	1968	7.50	15.00	30.00

STOWAWAYS, THE
JUSTICE
| ❏ JLP-148 | The Stowaways | 1968 | 125.00 | 250.00 | 500.00 |

STRADIVARI STRINGS, THE
SPIN-O-RAMA
| ❏ 590 [M] | String Along with Me | 196? | 7.50 | 15.00 | 30.00 |
| ❏ S-590 [S] | String Along with Me | 196? | 10.00 | 20.00 | 40.00 |
-- Cover model on the above LP is Jayne Mansfield

STRAIT, GEORGE
MCA
| ❏ 10450 | Ten Strait Hits | 1992 | 5.00 | 10.00 | 20.00 |
-- Only available on vinyl through Columbia House
| ❏ 10532 | Holding My Own | 1992 | 5.00 | 10.00 | 20.00 |
-- Only available on vinyl through Columbia House
| ❏ R 153641 | Chill of an Early Fall | 1991 | 5.00 | 10.00 | 20.00 |
-- Only released on vinyl through BMG Direct Marketing

STRANGE
OUTER GALAXIE
| ❏ 1000 | Translucent World | 1973 | 25.00 | 50.00 | 100.00 |
| ❏ 1001 | Raw Power | 1976 | 25.00 | 50.00 | 100.00 |

STRANGE, BILLY
COLISEUM
| ❏ CM-1001 [M] | Limbo Rock | 1962 | 10.00 | 20.00 | 40.00 |
GNP CRESCENDO
| ❏ GNPS-2030 [S] | Billy Strange with the Challengers | 1966 | 5.00 | 10.00 | 20.00 |

STRANGELOVES, THE
BANG
| ❏ BLP-211 [M] | I Want Candy | 1965 | 20.00 | 40.00 | 80.00 |
| ❏ BLPS-211 [S] | I Want Candy | 1965 | 25.00 | 50.00 | 100.00 |

STRANGERS, THE
Also see MERLE HAGGARD.
CAPITOL
❏ ST-169	Instrumental Sounds of Merle Haggard's Strangers	1969	5.00	10.00	20.00
❏ ST-445	Introducing My Friends the Strangers	1970	5.00	10.00	20.00
❏ ST-590	Getting to Know Merle Haggard's Strangers	1970	5.00	10.00	20.00
❏ ST-796	Honky Tonkin'	1971	5.00	10.00	20.00

STRAWBERRY ALARM CLOCK
UNI
❏ 3014 [M]	Incense and Peppermints	1967	12.50	25.00	50.00
❏ 73014 [S]	Incense and Peppermints	1967	10.00	20.00	40.00
❏ 73025	Wake Up It's Tomorrow	1968	10.00	20.00	40.00
❏ 73035	The World in a Sea Shell	1968	10.00	20.00	40.00
❏ 73054	Good Morning Starshine	1969	10.00	20.00	40.00
❏ 73074	The Best of the Strawberry Alarm Clock	1970	10.00	20.00	40.00

VOCALION
| ❏ VL 73915 | Changes | 1971 | 12.50 | 25.00 | 50.00 |

STREET NOISE
EVOLUTION
| ❏ 2010 | Street Noise | 1970 | 5.00 | 10.00 | 20.00 |

STREET PEOPLE
MUSICOR
| ❏ MS-3189 | Jennifer Tomkins | 1970 | 5.00 | 10.00 | 20.00 |

STREISAND, BARBRA
COLUMBIA
| ❏ AS 1779 [DJ] | The Legend of Barbra Streisand | 1983 | 10.00 | 20.00 | 40.00 |
-- Promo-only interview LP for "Yentl"
| ❏ CL 2007 [M] | The Barbra Streisand Album | 1963 | 5.00 | 10.00 | 20.00 |
-- "Guaranteed High Fidelity" on label
| ❏ CL 2054 [M] | The Second Barbra Streisand Album | 1963 | 5.00 | 10.00 | 20.00 |
-- "Guaranteed High Fidelity" on label
| ❏ CL 2054 [M-DJ] | The Second Barbra Streisand Album | 1963 | 50.00 | 100.00 | 200.00 |
-- Promo only on blue vinyl (white label)
| ❏ CL 2154 [M] | The Third Album | 1964 | 5.00 | 10.00 | 20.00 |
-- "Guaranteed High Fidelity" on label
| ❏ CL 2215 [M] | People | 1964 | 5.00 | 10.00 | 20.00 |
-- "Guaranteed High Fidelity" on label
| ❏ CL 2336 [M] | Color Me Barbra | 1966 | 50.00 | 100.00 | 200.00 |
-- Promo only on red vinyl (white label)
❏ CL 2682 [M]	Simply Streisand	1967	7.50	15.00	30.00
❏ CL 2757 [M]	A Christmas Album	1967	6.25	12.50	25.00
❏ CS 8807 [S]	The Barbra Streisand Album	1963	6.25	12.50	25.00
-- "360 Sound Stereo" in black on label
| ❏ CS 8854 [S] | The Second Barbra Streisand Album | 1963 | 6.25 | 12.50 | 25.00 |
-- "360 Sound Stereo" in black on label
| ❏ CS 8854 [S-DJ] | The Second Barbra Streisand Album | 1963 | 50.00 | 100.00 | 200.00 |
-- Promo only on blue vinyl (white label)
| ❏ CS 8954 [S] | The Third Album | 1964 | 6.25 | 12.50 | 25.00 |
-- "360 Sound Stereo" in black on label
| ❏ CS 9015 [S] | People | 1964 | 6.25 | 12.50 | 25.00 |
-- "360 Sound Stereo" in black on label
| ❏ CS 9136 [S] | My Name Is Barbra | 1965 | 6.25 | 12.50 | 25.00 |
-- "360 Sound Stereo" in black on label
| ❏ CS 9209 [S] | My Name Is Barbra, Two | 1965 | 5.00 | 10.00 | 20.00 |
-- Red "360 Sound Stereo" label
| ❏ CS 9278 [S] | Color Me Barbra | 1966 | 5.00 | 10.00 | 20.00 |
-- Red "360 Sound Stereo" label
| ❏ CS 9278 [S-DJ] | Color Me Barbra | 1966 | 50.00 | 100.00 | 200.00 |
-- Promo only on red vinyl (white label)
| ❏ CS 9347 [S] | Je M'Appelle Barbra | 1966 | 5.00 | 10.00 | 20.00 |
-- Red "360 Sound Stereo" label
| ❏ CS 9482 [S] | Simply Streisand | 1967 | 5.00 | 10.00 | 20.00 |
-- Red "360 Sound Stereo" label
| ❏ CS 9557 [S] | A Christmas Album | 1967 | 5.00 | 10.00 | 20.00 |
-- Red "360 Sound Stereo" label
❏ CQ 30378 [Q]	Stoney End	1972	6.25	12.50	25.00
❏ CQ 30792 [Q]	Barbra Joan Streisand	1972	6.25	12.50	25.00
❏ CQ 31760 [Q]	Live Concert at the Forum	1972	6.25	12.50	25.00
❏ PC 32801	Barbra Streisand Featuring The Way We Were and All In Love Is Fair	1974	5.00	10.00	20.00
-- Original version with this title on spine and label, and no title on front cover
❏ PCQ 32801 [Q]	The Way We Were	1974	6.25	12.50	25.00
❏ PCQ 33815 [Q]	Lazy Afternoon	1975	6.25	12.50	25.00
❏ HC 42801	The Way We Were	1982	7.50	5.00	30.00
-- Half-speed mastered edition
| ❏ HC 45679 | Barbra Streisand's Greatest Hits, Volume 2 | 1980 | 7.50 | 15.00 | 30.00 |
-- Half-speed mastered edition
| ❏ HC 46750 | Guilty | 1982 | 7.50 | 15.00 | 30.00 |
-- Half-speed mastered edition
| ❏ HC 47678 | Memories | 1982 | 7.50 | 15.00 | 30.00 |
-- Half-speed mastered edition

Number	Title	Yr	VG	VG+	NM

STRENGTH, TEXAS BILL
RE-CAR
| ❏ 2022 | Greatest Hits | 1967 | 6.25 | 12.50 | 25.00 |

STRIDER
WARNER BROS.
| ❏ BS 2722 | Exposed | 1973 | 5.00 | 10.00 | 20.00 |

STRING CHEESE
WOODEN NICKEL
| ❏ WNS-1001 | String Cheese | 1971 | 5.00 | 10.00 | 20.00 |

STRING-A-LONGS, THE
ATCO
| ❏ SD 33-241 | Wide World Hits | 1969 | 6.25 | 12.50 | 25.00 |
DOT
❏ DLP-3463 [M]	Matilda	1962	6.25	12.50	25.00
❏ DLP-3723 [M]	Great Instrumental Hits	1966	5.00	10.00	20.00
❏ DLP-25463 [S]	Matilda	1962	7.50	15.00	30.00
❏ DLP-25723 [S]	Great Instrumental Hits	1966	6.25	12.50	25.00
WARWICK
| ❏ W-2036 [M] | Pick-A-Hit Featuring "Wheels" | 1961 | 12.50 | 25.00 | 50.00 |
| ❏ W-2036ST [S] | Pick-A-Hit Featuring "Wheels" | 1961 | 20.00 | 40.00 | 80.00 |

STRINGBEAN
STARDAY
❏ SLP-142 [M]	Old Time Pickin' and Singin' with Stringbean	1961	15.00	30.00	60.00
❏ SLP-179 [M]	Stringbean	1962	12.50	25.00	50.00
❏ SLP-215 [M]	A Salute to Uncle Dave Macon	1963	12.50	25.00	50.00
❏ SLP-260 [M]	Way Back in the Hills of Old Kentucky	1964	12.50	25.00	50.00

STRONG, NOLAN, AND THE DIABLOS
FORTUNE
❏ LP-8010 [M]	Fortune of Hits	1961	55.00	110.00	220.00
-- Purple label, thick vinyl					
❏ LP-8010 [M]	Fortune of Hits	196?	12.50	25.00	50.00
-- Yellow label					
❏ LP-8012 [M]	Fortune of Hits, Vol. 2	1962	55.00	110.00	220.00
-- Purple label, thick vinyl					
❏ LP-8012 [M]	Fortune of Hits, Vol. 2	196?	12.50	25.00	50.00
-- Yellow label					
❏ LP-8015 [M]	Mind Over Matter	1963	62.50	125.00	250.00
-- Purple label, thick vinyl					
❏ LP-8015 [M]	Mind Over Matter	196?	15.00	30.00	60.00
-- Yellow label					
❏ LP-8015 [M]	Mind Over Matter	197?	5.00	10.00	20.00
-- Purple label, thinner, more flexible vinyl					

STRYPER
ENIGMA
❏ E-1064	The Yellow and Black Attack	1984	10.00	20.00	40.00
-- Original with six tracks; yellow vinyl					
❏ 71064	The Yellow and Black Attack	1984	5.00	10.00	20.00
-- Original with six tracks; black vinyl					
❏ 72077	Soldiers Under Command	1985	5.00	10.00	20.00
-- White vinyl					
❏ ST-73207	The Yellow and Black Attack	1985	5.00	10.00	20.00
-- Reissue with eight tracks; blue vinyl, round sleeve					
❏ PJAS-73237	To Hell with the Devil	1986	5.00	10.00	20.00
-- Cover has band as winged angels in battle					
❏ SEAX-73277	To Hell with the Devil	1986	6.25	12.50	25.00
-- Picture disc in plastic sleeve					

STUART, MARTY
COLUMBIA
| ❏ B6C 40302 | Marty Stuart | 1986 | 7.50 | 15.00 | 30.00 |
MCA
| ❏ R 170076 | Tempted | 1990 | 6.25 | 12.50 | 25.00 |
| -- Vinyl version available only through BMG Direct Marketing | | | | | |
RIDGE RUNNER
| ❏ RRR 0013 | Marty | 1978 | 7.50 | 15.00 | 30.00 |
SUGAR HILL
| ❏ 3726 | Busy Bee Café | 1981 | 7.50 | 15.00 | 30.00 |

STUART, MARY
BELL
| ❏ 1133 | Mary Stuart | 1973 | 5.00 | 10.00 | 20.00 |
COLUMBIA
| ❏ CL 6333 [10] | Joanne Sings | 1954 | 10.00 | 20.00 | 40.00 |

STUCKEY, NAT
PAULA
❏ LP-2192 [M]	Nat Stuckey Sings	1966	5.00	10.00	20.00
❏ LPS-2192 [S]	Nat Stuckey Sings	1966	6.25	12.50	25.00
❏ LP-2196 [M]	All My Tomorrows	1967	5.00	10.00	20.00
❏ LPS-2196 [S]	All My Tomorrows	1967	6.25	12.50	25.00
❏ LPS-2203	Country Favorites	1968	6.25	12.50	25.00
RCA VICTOR
❏ LSP-4090	Nat Stuckey Sings	1968	5.00	10.00	20.00
❏ LSP-4123	Keep 'Em Country	1969	5.00	10.00	20.00
❏ LSP-4226	New Country Roads	1969	5.00	10.00	20.00

STUFFY AND HIS FROZEN PARACHUTE BAND
PARAMOUNT
| ❏ PAS-6070 | Stuffy and His Frozen Parachute Band | 1974 | 6.25 | 12.50 | 25.00 |

STUTTGART BAROQUE ENSEMBLE (MARCEL COURAND, CONDUCTOR)
MERCURY LIVING PRESENCE
| ❏ SR 90402 [S] | Couperin: Les Nations (selections); Rameau: Concerts en Sextuor Nos. 1, 4, 5 and 6 | 196? | 10.00 | 20.00 | 40.00 |
| -- Maroon label, no "Vendor: Mercury Record Corporation" | | | | | |

STYLISTICS, THE
AVCO
❏ 11006	Round 2: The Stylistics	1972	5.00	10.00	20.00
❏ 11010	Rockin' Roll Baby	1973	5.00	10.00	20.00
❏ 33023	The Stylistics	1971	5.00	10.00	20.00

STYX
A&M
❏ SP-3711	Cornerstone	1979	7.50	15.00	30.00
-- Silver vinyl pressing, reportedly for fan club members					
❏ PR-4724 [PD]	Pieces of Eight	1978	6.25	12.50	25.00
❏ SP-8431 [(2)]	The Styx Radio Special	1977	6.25	12.50	25.00
-- Promo only; green cover					
❏ SP-17053 [(3) DJ]	Styx Radio Special	1978	10.00	20.00	40.00
-- Promo-only box set					
❏ SP-17222 [(2) DJ]	Radio Sampler and Interview Album	1983	6.25	12.50	25.00
-- Promo only; with "Kilroy Was Here" album graphic on cover					
MOBILE FIDELITY
| ❏ 1-026 | The Grand Illusion | 1979 | 7.50 | 15.00 | 30.00 |
| -- Audiophile vinyl | | | | | |
NAUTILUS
❏ NR-15	Pieces of Eight	1981	6.25	12.50	25.00
-- Audiophile vinyl					
❏ NR-27	Cornerstone	1982	5.00	10.00	20.00
-- Audiophile vinyl					
❏ NR-45	Paradise Theater	198?	7.50	15.00	30.00
-- Audiophile vinyl					
WOODEN NICKEL
❏ BWL1-0287	The Serpent Is Rising	1974	5.00	10.00	20.00
❏ BWL1-0638	Man of Miracles	1974	7.50	15.00	30.00
-- Original version contains "Lies"					
❏ BWL1-0638	Man of Miracles	1974	5.00	10.00	20.00
-- Second version contains "Best Thing"					
❏ WNS-1008	Styx	1972	5.00	10.00	20.00
❏ WNS-1012	Styx II	1973	5.00	10.00	20.00
-- With die-cut cover					

SUB-ZERO BAND, THE
SUB-ZERO
| ❏ 1172 | The Sub-Zero Band | 197? | 50.00 | 100.00 | 200.00 |

SUGAR BEARS. THE
KIM CARNES was in this group.
BIG TREE
| ❏ BTS-2009 | Introducing the Sugar Bears | 1972 | 5.00 | 10.00 | 20.00 |

SUGAR CREEK
METROMEDIA
| ❏ MD 1020 | Please Tell a Friend | 1969 | 15.00 | 30.00 | 60.00 |

SUGARLOAF
LIBERTY
| ❏ LST-7640 | Sugarloaf | 1970 | 5.00 | 10.00 | 20.00 |
| ❏ LST-11010 | Spaceship Earth | 1971 | 5.00 | 10.00 | 20.00 |

SUICIDE COMMANDOS
BLANK
| ❏ 002 | The Suicide Commandos Make a Record | 1977 | 6.25 | 12.50 | 25.00 |

Number	Title	Yr	VG	VG+	NM
TWIN/TONE					
❑ TTR 7906	The Commandos Commit Suicide Dance Concert	1979	18.75	37.50	75.00
-- Limited edition of 1,000 copies					
SUKMAN, HARRY					
LIBERTY					
❑ LRP-3005 [M]	Nightfall	1955	5.00	10.00	20.00
❑ LRP-3135 [M]	Command Performance	1959	5.00	10.00	20.00
❑ LRP-3151 [M]	The Franz Liszt Story	1960	5.00	10.00	20.00
❑ LST-7135 [S]	Command Performance	1959	6.25	12.50	25.00
❑ LST-7151 [S]	The Franz Liszt Story	1960	6.25	12.50	25.00
SULLIVAN, JIM					
MERCURY					
❑ MG-21137 [M]	Sitar Beat	1967	5.00	10.00	20.00
❑ SR-61137 [S]	Sitar Beat	1967	5.00	10.00	20.00
SUMAC, YMA					
CAPITOL					
❑ H 244 [10]	Voice of the Xtabay	1952	25.00	50.00	100.00
❑ L 299 [10]	Legend of the Sun Virgin	1952	30.00	60.00	120.00
❑ T 299 [M]	Legend of the Sun Virgin	1955	12.50	25.00	50.00
❑ L 423 [10]	Inca Taqui	1953	25.00	50.00	100.00
❑ H 564 [10]	Mambo!	1954	25.00	50.00	100.00
❑ T 564 [M]	Mambo!	1955	12.50	25.00	50.00
❑ W 684 [M]	Voice of the Xtabay and Inca	1955	12.50	25.00	50.00
❑ T 770 [M]	Legend of the Jivaro	1956	12.50	25.00	50.00
❑ ST 1169 [S]	Fuego del Andes	1959	12.50	25.00	50.00
❑ T 1169 [M]	Fuego del Andes	1959	10.00	20.00	40.00
CORAL					
❑ CRL 56058 [10]	Presenting Yma Sumac	1952	30.00	60.00	120.00
LONDON					
❑ XPS 608	Miracles	1972	5.00	10.00	20.00
SUMMER SOUNDS, THE					
LAUREL					
❑ 90973	Up Down	196?	250.00	500.00	1,000.
SUMMER, DONNA					
CASABLANCA					
❑ NBPIX 7119 [PD]	The Best of Live and More	1979	5.00	10.00	20.00
SUMMERHILL					
TETRAGRAMMATON					
❑ T-114	Summerhill	1969	7.50	15.00	30.00
SUMMERS, ANDREW ROWAN					
FOLKWAYS					
❑ FP-21 [10]	Seeds of Love	1951	12.50	25.00	50.00
❑ FP-41 [10]	The Lady Gay	1954	12.50	25.00	50.00
❑ FP-44 [10]	The Faulse Lady	1954	12.50	25.00	50.00
❑ FA-2002 [10]	Christmas Carols	195?	12.50	25.00	50.00
❑ FA-2021 [10]	Seeds of Love	1951	12.50	25.00	50.00
❑ FA-2041 [10]	The Lady Gay	1954	12.50	25.00	50.00
❑ FA-2044 [10]	The Faulse Lady	1954	12.50	25.00	50.00
❑ FA-2348 [M]	Andrew Rowan Summers	1957	7.50	15.00	30.00
❑ FA-2361 [M]	Hymns and Carols	195?	7.50	15.00	30.00
❑ FA-2364 [M]	The Unquiet Grave and Other American Tragic Ballads	195?	7.50	15.00	30.00
SUMMERS, ANDY, AND ROBERT FRIPP					
Andy Summers was in THE POLICE.					
A&M					
❑ SP-17299 [DJ]	Speak Out Interview	1982	6.25	12.50	25.00
-- Issued in generic cover with sticker					
SUNDOWNERS, THE					
LIBERTY					
❑ LRP-3269 [M]	Folk Songs for the Rich	1962	5.00	10.00	20.00
❑ LST-7269 [S]	Folk Songs for the Rich	1962	6.25	12.50	25.00
SUNGLOWS, THE -- See SUNNY AND THE SUNLINERS.					
SUNNY AND THE SUNLINERS					
KEY-LOC					
❑ 3001 [M]	Smile Now, Cry Later	196?	6.25	12.50	25.00
❑ 3002 [M]	No Te Chifles	196?	6.25	12.50	25.00
❑ 3003 [M]	Sunny and the Sunliners Live in Hollywood	196?	6.25	12.50	25.00
❑ 3004 [M]	Canta Sunny	196?	6.25	12.50	25.00

Number	Title	Yr	VG	VG+	NM
❑ 3005 [M]	A Little Brown-Eyed Soul	196?	6.25	12.50	25.00
❑ 3006 [M]	This Is My Band	196?	6.25	12.50	25.00
❑ 3007 [M]	Versatile	196?	6.25	12.50	25.00
❑ 3008 [M]	Adelante	196?	6.25	12.50	25.00
❑ 3009 [M]	Sky High	196?	6.25	12.50	25.00
❑ 3010 [M]	The Missing Link	196?	6.25	12.50	25.00
SUNGLOW					
❑ SLP-101 [M]	Sunny Ozuna and the Sunglows	1963	25.00	50.00	100.00
-- As "The Sunglows"					
❑ SLP-102 [M]	The Fabulous Sunglows	1964	25.00	50.00	100.00
-- As "The Sunglows"					
❑ SLP-103 [M]	The Original Peanuts	1965	20.00	40.00	80.00
-- As "The Sunglows"					
❑ SLP-103S [S]	The Original Peanuts	1965	25.00	50.00	100.00
-- As "The Sunglows"					
TEAR DROP					
❑ LPM-2000 [M]	Talk to Me	1963	25.00	50.00	100.00
❑ LPM-2001 [M]	Las Vegas Welcomes Sunny and the Sunliners	1964	10.00	20.00	40.00
❑ LPM-2008 [M]	Teardrop Presents Sunny and the Sunliners	196?	10.00	20.00	40.00
SUNNYLAND SLIM					
BLUESVILLE					
❑ BVLP-1016 [M]	Slim's Shout	1961	30.00	60.00	120.00
-- Blue label, silver print					
❑ BVLP-1016 [M]	Slim's Shout	1964	7.50	5.00	30.00
-- Blue label, trident logo at right					
PRESTIGE					
❑ PRST-7723	Slim's Shout	1969	5.00	10.00	20.00
WORLD PACIFIC					
❑ WPS-21890	Slim's Got His Thing Goin' On	1969	5.00	10.00	20.00
SUNRAYS, THE					
TOWER					
❑ ST 5017 [S]	Andrea	1966	15.00	30.00	60.00
❑ T 5017 [M]	Andrea	1966	12.50	25.00	50.00
SUNSET DRAGSTERS, THE					
PALACE					
❑ M-775 [M]	Hot Rod Rally	196?	15.00	30.00	60.00
❑ PST-775 [S]	Hot Rod Rally	196?	20.00	40.00	80.00
SUNSETS, THE					
PALACE					
❑ M-752 [M]	Surfing with the Sunsets	1963	10.00	20.00	40.00
❑ PST-752 [S]	Surfing with the Sunsets	1963	12.50	25.00	50.00
SUNSHINE BOYS, THE					
DOT					
❑ DLP-3189 [M]	Sing Unto Him	1959	7.50	15.00	30.00
❑ DLP-25189 [S]	Sing Unto Him	1959	10.00	20.00	40.00
STARDAY					
❑ SLP-113 [M]	America's Number One Gospel Group	1960	10.00	20.00	40.00
❑ SLP-166 [M]	More Country Music Sing-Along	1962	7.50	15.00	30.00
❑ SLP-349 [M]	A Happy Home Up There	1965	7.50	15.00	30.00
SUNSHINE COMPANY, THE					
IMPERIAL					
❑ LP-9359 [M]	Happy Is the Sunshine Company	1967	5.00	10.00	20.00
❑ LP-9368 [M]	The Sunshine Company	1968	6.25	12.50	25.00
-- Mono copies are promo only					
❑ LP-12359 [S]	Happy Is the Sunshine Company	1967	5.00	10.00	20.00
❑ LP-12368 [S]	The Sunshine Company	1968	5.00	10.00	20.00
❑ LP-12399	Sunshine and Shadows	1969	5.00	10.00	20.00
SUPER STOCKS, THE					
CAPITOL					
❑ ST 1997 [S]	Hot Rod Rally	1963	17.50	35.00	70.00
❑ T 1997 [M]	Hot Rod Rally	1963	12.50	25.00	50.00
❑ ST 2060 [S]	Thunder Road	1964	31.25	62.50	125.00
❑ T 2060 [M]	Thunder Road	1964	25.00	50.00	100.00
❑ (S)T 2060	Thunder Road Bonus Poster	1964	12.50	25.00	50.00
❑ ST 2113 [S]	Surf Route 101	1964	37.50	75.00	150.00
-- With bonus single, "Doin' the Surfink"/"Finksville, U.S.A." by Mr. Gasser and the Weirdos, in special pocket on front cover					
❑ ST 2113 [S]	Surf Route 101	1964	31.25	62.50	125.00
-- Without bonus single					
❑ T 2113 [M]	Surf Route 101	1964	31.25	62.50	125.00
-- With bonus single, "Doin' the Surfink"/"Finksville, U.S.A." by Mr. Gasser and the Weirdos, in special pocket on front cover					

Number	Title	Yr	VG	VG+	NM
❑ T 2113 [M]	Surf Route 101	1964	25.00	50.00	100.00
-- Without bonus single					
❑ ST 2190 [S]	School Is a Drag	1964	30.00	60.00	120.00
❑ T 2190 [M]	School Is a Drag	1964	25.00	50.00	100.00

SUPERFINE DANDELION, THE
MAINSTREAM

Number	Title	Yr	VG	VG+	NM
❑ S-6102 [S]	The Superfine Dandelion	1967	10.00	20.00	40.00
❑ 56102 [M]	The Superfine Dandelion	1967	10.00	20.00	40.00

SUPERSAX
MOBILE FIDELITY

Number	Title	Yr	VG	VG+	NM
❑ 1-511	Supersax Plays Bird	1981	10.00	20.00	40.00
-- Audiophile vinyl					

SUPERSISTER
DWARF

Number	Title	Yr	VG	VG+	NM
❑ PDLP-2001	Supersister	197?	7.50	15.00	30.00

SUPERTRAMP
A&M

Number	Title	Yr	VG	VG+	NM
❑ SP-3730 [PD]	Breakfast in America	1979	125.00	250.00	500.00
-- In-house picture discs featuring A&M staff members posing with the cover model					
❑ SP-4274	Supertramp	1970	5.00	10.00	20.00
-- First edition with brown label					
❑ SP-4311	Indelibly Stamped	1971	5.00	10.00	20.00
-- First edition with brown label					

MOBILE FIDELITY

Number	Title	Yr	VG	VG+	NM
❑ 1-005	Crime of the Century	1979	10.00	20.00	40.00
-- Audiophile vinyl					
❑ MFQR-005	Crime of the Century	1983	30.00	60.00	120.00
-- Ultra High Quality Recording; in box					
❑ 1-045	Breakfast in America	1980	12.50	25.00	50.00
-- Audiophile vinyl					

SWEET THUNDER

Number	Title	Yr	VG	VG+	NM
❑ 5	Even in the Quietest Moments…	198?	10.00	20.00	40.00
-- Audiophile vinyl					

SUPREMES, THE
Also see DIANA ROSS.
DORAL

Number	Title	Yr	VG	VG+	NM
❑ (# unknown)	Doral Presents Diana Ross and the Supremes	1971	12.50	25.00	50.00
-- Available through Doral cigarettes					

MOTOWN

Number	Title	Yr	VG	VG+	NM
❑ PR-102 [DJ]	Touch Interview	1971	6.25	12.50	25.00
❑ M 606 [M]	Meet the Supremes	1963	225.00	450.00	900.00
-- With group sitting on stools					
❑ M 606 [M]	Meet the Supremes	1963	7.50	15.00	30.00
-- With close-up of group's faces					
❑ MS 606 [S]	Meet the Supremes	1964	10.00	20.00	40.00
-- With close-up of group's faces					
❑ M 621 [M]	Where Did Our Love Go	1964	7.50	15.00	30.00
❑ MS 621 [S]	Where Did Our Love Go	1964	10.00	20.00	40.00
❑ M 623 [M]	A Bit of Liverpool	1964	10.00	20.00	40.00
❑ MS 623 [S]	A Bit of Liverpool	1964	12.50	25.00	50.00
❑ M 625 [M]	The Supremes Sing Country Western & Pop	1965	6.25	12.50	25.00
❑ MS 625 [S]	The Supremes Sing Country Western & Pop	1965	7.50	15.00	30.00
❑ M 627 [M]	More Hits by the Supremes	1965	6.25	12.50	25.00
❑ MS 627 [S]	More Hits by the Supremes	1965	7.50	15.00	30.00
❑ M 629 [M]	We Remember Sam Cooke	1965	6.25	12.50	25.00
❑ MS 629 [S]	We Remember Sam Cooke	1965	7.50	15.00	30.00
-- The above LP came out before Motown 627					
❑ M 636 [M]	The Supremes at the Copa	1965	6.25	12.50	25.00
❑ MS 636 [S]	The Supremes at the Copa	1965	7.50	15.00	30.00
❑ MT 638 [M]	Merry Christmas	1965	7.50	15.00	30.00
❑ MS 638 [S]	Merry Christmas	1965	10.00	20.00	40.00
❑ M 643 [M]	I Hear a Symphony	1966	6.25	12.50	25.00
❑ MS 643 [S]	I Hear a Symphony	1966	7.50	15.00	30.00
❑ M 649 [M]	The Supremes A' Go-Go	1966	6.25	12.50	25.00
❑ MS 649 [S]	The Supremes A' Go-Go	1966	7.50	15.00	30.00
❑ M 650 [M]	The Supremes Sing Holland-Dozier-Holland	1967	6.25	12.50	25.00
❑ MS 650 [S]	The Supremes Sing Holland-Dozier-Holland	1967	7.50	15.00	30.00
❑ M 659 [M]	The Supremes Sing Rodgers & Hart	1967	6.25	12.50	25.00
❑ MS 659 [S]	The Supremes Sing Rodgers & Hart	1967	7.50	15.00	30.00
❑ M 663 [(2) M]	Diana Ross and the Supremes Greatest Hits	1967	7.50	15.00	30.00
❑ MS 663 [(2) S]	Diana Ross and the Supremes Greatest Hits	1967	10.00	20.00	40.00
❑ M 665 [M]	Reflections	1968	7.50	15.00	30.00
❑ MS 665 [S]	Reflections	1968	5.00	10.00	20.00

Number	Title	Yr	VG	VG+	NM
❑ MS 670	Love Child	1968	5.00	10.00	20.00
❑ M 672 [M]	Funny Girl	1968	7.50	15.00	30.00
-- Mono appears to be promo only					
❑ MS 672 [S]	Funny Girl	1968	5.00	10.00	20.00
-- The above LP came out before Motown 670					
❑ M 676 [M]	Live at London's Talk of the Town	1968	7.50	51.00	30.00
-- Mono is promo only					
❑ MS 676 [S]	Live at London's Talk of the Town	1968	5.00	10.00	20.00
-- The above LP came out before Motown 670 and 672					
❑ MS 689	Let the Sunshine In	1969	5.00	10.00	20.00
❑ MS 694	Cream of the Crop	1969	5.00	10.00	20.00
❑ MS 702	Diana Ross and the Supremes Greatest Hits, Volume 3	1970	5.00	10.00	20.00
❑ MS 708 [(2)]	Farewell	1970	6.25	12.50	25.00
-- By "Diana Ross and the Supremes"					
❑ M9-794L3 [(3)]	Anthology (1962-1969)	1974	6.25	12.50	25.00
-- By "Diana Ross and the Supremes"					
❑ 5381 ML [(3)]	25th Anniversary	1986	5.00	10.00	20.00
-- By "Diana Ross and the Supremes"					

SUPREMES, THE, DIANA ROSS AND, AND THE TEMPTATIONS
Also see THE SUPREMES; THE TEMPTATIONS.
MOTOWN

Number	Title	Yr	VG	VG+	NM
❑ M 679 [M]	Diana Ross and the Supremes Join the Temptations	1968	7.50	15.00	30.00
❑ MS 679 [S]	Diana Ross and the Supremes Join the Temptations	1968	5.00	10.00	20.00
❑ MS 682	TCB	1968	5.00	10.00	20.00
❑ MS 692	Together	1969	5.00	10.00	20.00
❑ MS 699	On Broadway	1969	5.00	10.00	20.00

SURF STOMPERS, THE
DEL-FI

Number	Title	Yr	VG	VG+	NM
❑ DFLP-1236 [M]	The Original Surfer Stomp	1963	15.00	30.00	60.00
❑ DFST-1236 [S]	The Original Surfer Stomp	1963	20.00	40.00	80.00

SURF TEENS, THE
SUTTON

Number	Title	Yr	VG	VG+	NM
❑ SSU-339 [S]	Surf Mania	1963	15.00	30.00	60.00
❑ SU-339 [M]	Surf Mania	1963	12.50	25.00	50.00

SURFARIS, THE
DECCA

Number	Title	Yr	VG	VG+	NM
❑ DL 4470 [M]	The Surfaris Play Wipe Out	1963	6.25	12.50	25.00
❑ DL 4487 [M]	Hit City '64	1964	10.00	20.00	40.00
❑ DL 4560 [M]	Fun City, U.S.A.	1964	10.00	20.00	40.00
❑ DL 4614 [M]	Hit City '65	1965	10.00	20.00	40.00
❑ DL 4663 [M]	It Ain't Me, Babe	1965	10.00	20.00	40.00
❑ DL 74470 [S]	The Surfaris Play Wipe Out	1963	7.50	15.00	30.00
❑ DL 74487 [S]	Hit City '64	1964	12.50	25.00	50.00
❑ DL 74560 [S]	Fun City, U.S.A.	1964	12.50	25.00	50.00
❑ DL 74614 [S]	Hit City '65	1965	12.50	25.00	50.00
❑ DL 74663 [S]	It Ain't Me, Babe	1965	12.50	25.00	50.00

DOT

Number	Title	Yr	VG	VG+	NM
❑ DLP-3535 [M]	Wipe Out	1963	12.50	25.00	50.00
-- With back cover photo featuring five Surfaris					
❑ DLP-3535 [M]	Wipe Out	1963	10.00	20.00	40.00
-- With back cover photo featuring four Surfaris					
❑ DLP-3535 [M]	Wipe Out	1963	7.50	15.00	30.00
-- With no back cover photo of the Surfaris					
❑ DLP-25535 [S]	Wipe Out	1963	20.00	40.00	80.00
-- With back cover photo featuring five Surfaris					
❑ DLP-25535 [S]	Wipe Out	1963	12.50	25.00	50.00
-- With back cover photo featuring four Surfaris					
❑ DLP-25535 [S]	Wipe Out	1963	10.00	20.00	40.00
-- With no back cover photo of the Surfaris					

SURFERS, THE
HIFI

Number	Title	Yr	VG	VG+	NM
❑ R-408 [M]	On the Rocks	1959	30.00	60.00	120.00
❑ SR-408 [S]	On the Rocks	1959	37.50	75.00	150.00

SURFRIDERS, THE
VAULT

Number	Title	Yr	VG	VG+	NM
❑ LP-105 [M]	Surfbeat, Volume 2	1963	7.50	15.00	30.00
❑ VS-105 [S]	Surfbeat, Volume 2	1963	10.00	20.00	40.00

SURFSIDERS, THE
DESIGN

Number	Title	Yr	VG	VG+	NM
❑ DLPS-208 [S]	The Beach Boys Songbook	1965	5.00	10.00	20.00

SURPRISE PACKAGE
LHI

Number	Title	Yr	VG	VG+	NM
❑ S-12005	Free Up	1968	10.00	20.00	40.00

Number	Title	Yr	VG	VG+	NM
SURRATT, CECIL, AND SMITTY SMITH					
AUDIO LAB					
❑ AL-1565 [M]	Songs Everybody Knows	1961	25.00	50.00	100.00
KING					
❑ 860 [M]	Country Music from the Heart of the Country	1963	12.50	25.00	50.00
❑ 966 [M]	Good Country Singin' and Pickin'	1966	10.00	20.00	40.00
SUTCH, SCREAMING LORD					
COTILLION					
❑ SD 9015	Lord Sutch and Heavy Friends	1970	7.50	15.00	30.00
-- With Jimmy Page, John Bonham and Jeff Beck					
❑ SD 9049	Hands of Jack the Ripper	1972	7.50	15.00	30.00
SUZUKI, PAT					
RCA VICTOR					
❑ LPM-1965 [M]	Broadway '59	1959	5.00	10.00	20.00
❑ LSP-1965 [S]	Broadway '59	1959	6.25	12.50	25.00
❑ LPM-2030 [M]	Pat Suzuki	1959	5.00	10.00	20.00
❑ LSP-2030 [S]	Pat Suzuki	1959	6.25	12.50	25.00
❑ LPM-2186 [M]	Looking at You	1960	5.00	10.00	20.00
❑ LSP-2186 [S]	Looking at You	1960	6.25	12.50	25.00
VIK					
❑ LX-1127 [M]	The Many Sides of Pat Suzuki	1958	7.50	15.00	30.00
❑ LX-1147 [M]	Pat Suzuki	1958	7.50	15.00	30.00
SWAGGART, JIMMY					
JIM					
❑ 24-141 [(2)]	Silver Jubilee Album: The Very Best of Jimmy Swaggart	1981	5.00	10.00	20.00
-- One of the two records is a picture disc					
SWAGMEN, THE					
PARKWAY					
❑ P-7015 [M]	Meet the Swagmen	1962	12.50	25.00	50.00
SWAMP DOGG					
CANYON					
❑ LP-7706	Total Destruction to Your Mind	1970	7.50	15.00	30.00
ELEKTRA					
❑ EKS-74089	Rat On	1971	5.00	10.00	20.00
SWAN SILVERTONES, THE					
SPECIALTY					
❑ SPS-2122	Love Lifted Me	1970	5.00	10.00	20.00
❑ SPS-2148	My Rock	1971	5.00	10.00	20.00
UPFRONT					
❑ UPF-112	The Lord's Prayer	1968	5.00	10.00	20.00
VEE JAY					
❑ LP-5003 [M]	The Swan Silvertones	1959	10.00	20.00	40.00
❑ LP-5006 [M]	Singing in My Soul	1960	7.50	15.00	30.00
❑ LP-5013 [M]	Savior Pass Me Not	1962	7.50	15.00	30.00
❑ LP-5034 [M]	Blessed Assurance	1963	7.50	15.00	30.00
❑ LP-5052 [M]	The Best of the Swan Silvertones	1963	7.50	15.00	30.00
❑ LP-5059 [M]	Let's Go to Church Together	1964	6.25	12.50	25.00
❑ SR-5059 [S]	Let's Go to Church Together	1964	7.50	15.00	30.00
❑ VJS-18008	Pray for Me	1975	5.00	10.00	20.00
SWANN, BETTYE					
MONEY					
❑ 1103 [M]	Make Me Yours	1967	6.25	12.50	25.00
❑ S-1103 [S]	Make Me Yours	1967	6.25	12.50	25.00
SWEENEY TODD					
LONDON					
❑ PS 694	If Wishes Were Horses	1977	15.00	30.00	60.00
-- Possibly a Canadian import only					
SWEET, THE					
BELL					
❑ 1125	The Sweet	1973	6.25	12.50	25.00
CAPITOL					
❑ SPRO-8371/2 [DJ]	For A.O.R. Radio Only	1976	6.25	12.50	25.00
❑ SPRO-8849 [DJ]	Short and Sweet	1978	7.50	15.00	30.00
❑ PRO-11929 [DJ]	Cut Above the Rest	1979	12.50	25.00	50.00
-- Special promo box contains record, cassette, 8-track, photo, bio					

Number	Title	Yr	VG	VG+	NM
SWEET INSPIRATIONS, THE					
ATLANTIC					
❑ SD 8155	The Sweet Inspirations	1968	5.00	10.00	20.00
❑ SD 8182	Songs of Faith and Inspiration	1968	5.00	10.00	20.00
❑ SD 8201	What the World Needs Now Is	1969	5.00	10.00	20.00
❑ SD 8225	Sweets for My Sweet	1969	5.00	10.00	20.00
❑ SD 8253	Sweet, Sweet Soul	1970	5.00	10.00	20.00
STAX					
❑ STS-3017	Estelle, Myrna and Sylvia	1973	5.00	10.00	20.00
SWEET PANTS					
BARKLEY					
❑ 1141	Fat Peter Presents Sweet Pants	1969	50.00	100.00	200.00
SWEET THURSDAY					
TETRAGRAMMATON					
❑ T-112	Sweet Thursday	1969	5.00	10.00	20.00
SWEET TOOTHE					
DOMINION					
❑ NR-7360	Testing	1974	75.00	150.00	300.00
SWENSON, INGA					
LIBERTY					
❑ LRP-3379 [M]	I'm Old Fashioned	1964	6.25	12.50	25.00
❑ LST-7379 [S]	I'm Old Fashioned	1964	7.50	15.00	30.00
SWIFT RAIN					
HI					
❑ SHL-32064	Coming Down	1971	6.25	12.50	25.00
SWINGIN' MEDALLIONS					
SMASH					
❑ MGS-27083 [M]	Double Shot (Of My Baby's Love)	1966	10.00	20.00	40.00
-- First pressing contains the original 45 version of the title song					
❑ MGS-27083 [M]	Double Shot (Of My Baby's Love)	1966	7.50	15.00	30.00
-- Later pressings contain a "censored" version of the title song					
❑ SRS-67083 [S]	Double Shot (Of My Baby's Love)	1966	12.50	25.00	50.00
-- First pressing contains the original 45 version of the title song					
❑ SRS-67083 [S]	Double Shot (Of My Baby's Love)	1966	10.00	20.00	40.00
-- Later pressings contain a "censored" version of the title song					
SWINGING BLUE JEANS, THE					
IMPERIAL					
❑ LP-9261 [M]	Hippy Hippy Shake	1964	20.00	40.00	80.00
❑ LP-12261 [R]	Hippy Hippy Shake	1964	20.00	40.00	80.00
SWITTEL, JIMMY					
DECCA					
❑ DL 8618 [M]	Hymns to the Blessed Virgin Mary	1957	5.00	10.00	20.00
SYKES, ROOSEVELT					
BLUESVILLE					
❑ BVLP-1006 [M]	The Return of Roosevelt Sykes	1960	25.00	50.00	100.00
-- Blue label, silver print					
❑ BVLP-1006 [M]	The Return of Roosevelt Sykes	1964	7.50	15.00	30.00
-- Blue label, trident logo at right					
❑ BVLP-1014 [M]	The Honeydripper	1961	25.00	50.00	100.00
-- Blue label, silver print					
❑ BVLP-1014 [M]	The Honeydripper	1964	7.50	15.00	30.00
-- Blue label, trident logo at right					
CROWN					
❑ CST-287 [S]	Roosevelt Sykes Sings the Blues	1962	12.50	25.00	50.00
❑ CLP-5287 [M]	Roosevelt Sykes Sings the Blues	1962	12.50	25.00	50.00
DELMARK					
❑ DL-607	The Hard Driving Blues of Roosevelt Sykes	1963	12.50	25.00	50.00
SYLVAIN SYLVAIN					
RCA VICTOR					
❑ DJL1-4062 [DJ]	RCA Special Radio Series XII	1981	5.00	10.00	20.00
-- Promo-only interviews and music					
SYLVERN, HANK					
ABC-PARAMOUNT					
❑ 146 [M]	Christmas in Hi-Fi	1956	6.25	12.50	25.00

Number	Title	Yr	VG	VG+	NM

SYLVIA
Also see MICKEY AND SYLVIA.
STANG

| ❏ 1010 | Sylvia | 197? | 5.00 | 10.00 | 20.00 |

SYLVIAN, DAVID
VIRGIN

| ❏ 2167 [DJ] | Ink in the Well -- A Conversation | 1987 | 5.00 | 10.00 | 20.00 |

-- Promo-only interview album

SYMS, SYLVIA
20TH CENTURY FOX

| ❏ TFM-4123 [M] | The Fabulous Sylvia Syms | 1963 | 6.25 | 12.50 | 25.00 |
| ❏ TFS-4123 [S] | The Fabulous Sylvia Syms | 1963 | 7.50 | 15.00 | 30.00 |

ATLANTIC

| ❏ ALS-137 [10] | Songs by Sylvia Syms | 1952 | 25.00 | 50.00 | 100.00 |
| ❏ 1243 [M] | Songs by Sylvia Syms | 1956 | 12.50 | 25.00 | 50.00 |

-- Black label

| ❏ 1243 [M] | Songs by Sylvia Syms | 1960 | 6.25 | 12.50 | 25.00 |

-- Multicolor label, white "fan" logo at right
COLUMBIA

| ❏ CL 1447 [M] | Torch Song | 1960 | 7.50 | 15.00 | 30.00 |

-- Red and black label with six "eye" logos

| ❏ CS 8243 [S] | Torch Song | 1960 | 10.00 | 20.00 | 40.00 |

-- Red and black label with six "eye" logos
DECCA

| ❏ DL 8188 [M] | Sylvia Syms Sings | 1955 | 12.50 | 25.00 | 50.00 |

-- Black label, silver print

| ❏ DL 8639 [M] | Songs of Love | 1958 | 10.00 | 20.00 | 40.00 |

-- Black label, silver print
KAPP

| ❏ KL-1236 [M] | That Man -- Love Songs to Frank Sinatra | 1961 | 7.50 | 15.00 | 30.00 |
| ❏ KS-3236 [S] | That Man -- Love Songs to Frank Sinatra | 1961 | 10.00 | 20.00 | 40.00 |

PRESTIGE

❏ PRLP-7439 [M]	Sylvia Is!	1965	5.00	10.00	20.00
❏ PRST-7439 [S]	Sylvia Is!	1965	6.25	12.50	25.00
❏ PRLP-7489 [M]	For Once in My Life	1967	6.25	12.50	25.00
❏ PRST-7489 [S]	For Once in My Life	1967	5.00	10.00	20.00

VERSION

| ❏ VLP-103 [10] | After Dark | 1954 | 20.00 | 40.00 | 80.00 |

SYNDICATE OF SOUND
BELL

| ❏ 6001 [M] | Little Girl | 1966 | 12.50 | 25.00 | 50.00 |
| ❏ S-6001 [S] | Little Girl | 1966 | 20.00 | 40.00 | 80.00 |

SZABO, GABOR
IMPULSE!

❏ A-9105 [M]	Gypsy 66	1966	5.00	10.00	20.00
❏ AS-9105 [S]	Gypsy 66	1966	6.25	12.50	25.00
❏ A-9123 [M]	Spellbinder	1966	5.00	10.00	20.00
❏ AS-9123 [S]	Spellbinder	1966	6.25	12.50	25.00
❏ A-9128 [M]	Jazz Raga	1967	6.25	12.50	25.00
❏ AS-9128 [S]	Jazz Raga	1967	5.00	10.00	20.00
❏ A-9146 [M]	The Sorcerer	1967	6.25	12.50	25.00
❏ AS-9146 [S]	The Sorcerer	1967	5.00	10.00	20.00

SZERYNG, HENRYK
MERCURY LIVING PRESENCE

| ❏ SR 90308 [S] | Brahms: Violin Concerto in D | 196? | 15.00 | 30.00 | 60.00 |

-- With Antal Dorati/London Symphony Orchestra; maroon label, no "Vendor: Mercury Record Corporation"

| ❏ SR 90308 [S] | Brahms: Violin Concerto in D | 196? | 6.25 | 12.50 | 25.00 |

-- With Antal Dorati/London Symphony Orchestra; maroon label, with "Vendor: Mercury Record Corporation"

| ❏ SR 90348 [S] | Kreisler: Caprice Viennois and 12 Others | 196? | 7.50 | 15.00 | 30.00 |

-- Maroon label, no "Vendor: Mercury Record Corporation"

| ❏ SR 90367 [S] | Treasures | 196? | 5.00 | 10.00 | 20.00 |

-- Maroon label, no "Vendor: Mercury Record Corporation"

| ❏ SR 90393 [S] | Khachaturian: Violin Concerto | 196? | 12.50 | 25.00 | 50.00 |

-- With Antal Dorati/London Symphony Orchestra; maroon label, no "Vendor: Mercury Record Corporation"

| ❏ SR 90393 [S] | Khachaturian: Violin Concerto | 196? | 10.00 | 20.00 | 40.00 |

-- With Antal Dorati/London Symphony Orchestra; maroon label, with "Vendor: Mercury Record Corporation"

| ❏ SR 90393 [S] | Khachaturian: Violin Concerto | 196? | 7.50 | 15.00 | 30.00 |

-- With Antal Dorati/London Symphony Orchestra; third edition (dark red, not maroon, label)

| ❏ SR 90406 [S] | Mendelssohn: Violin Concerto in E; Schumann: Violin Concerto in D | 196? | 5.00 | 10.00 | 20.00 |

-- With Antal Dorati/London Symphony Orchestra; maroon label, no "Vendor: Mercury Record Corporation"

| ❏ SR 90466 [S] | Bach: Violin Concertos in A and E; Double Concerto in D | 196? | 17.50 | 35.00 | 70.00 |

-- Maroon label, with "Vendor: Mercury Record Corporation"
RCA VICTOR RED SEAL

| ❏ LSC-2281 [S] | Brahms: Violin Concerto | 1959 | 15.00 | 30.00 | 60.00 |

-- With Pierre Monteux/London Symphony Orchestra; original with "shaded dog" label

| ❏ LSC-2363 [S] | Tchaikovsky: Violin Concerto in D | 1960 | 12.50 | 25.00 | 50.00 |

-- With Charles Munch/Boston Symphony Orchestra; original with "shaded dog" label

| ❏ LSC-2421 [S] | In Recital | 1960 | 12.50 | 25.00 | 50.00 |

-- Original with "shaded dog" label

| ❏ LSC-2456 [S] | Lalo: Symphonie Espagnole | 1961 | 50.00 | 100.00 | 200.00 |

-- With Walter Hendl/Chicago Symphony Orch.; original with "shaded dog" label

SZERYNG, HENRYK / ARTUR RUBENSTEIN
Also see each artist's individual listings.
RCA VICTOR RED SEAL

| ❏ LSC-2377 [S] | Beethoven: Kreutzer and Spring Sonatas | 1960 | 6.25 | 12.50 | 25.00 |

-- Original with "shaded dog" label

| ❏ LSC-2619 [S] | Brahms: Violin Concertos 2 and 3 | 1962 | 6.25 | 12.50 | 25.00 |

-- Original with "shaded dog" label

| ❏ LSC-2620 [S] | Beethoven: Violin Sonata No. 8; Brahms: Violin Sonata No. 1 | 1962 | 5.00 | 10.00 | 20.00 |

-- Original with "shaded dog" label

SZIGETI, JOSEF
MERCURY LIVING PRESENCE

| ❏ SR 90225 [S] | Brahms: Violin Concerto in D | 196? | 25.00 | 50.00 | 100.00 |

-- Maroon label, no "Vendor: Mercury Record Corporation"

| ❏ SR 90319 [S] | Prokofiev: Violin Sonatas No. 1 and 2 | 196? | 37.50 | 75.00 | 150.00 |

-- Maroon label, no "Vendor: Mercury Record Corporation"

| ❏ SR 90358 [S] | Beethoven: Violin Concerto in D | 196? | 12.50 | 25.00 | 50.00 |

-- With Antal Dorati/London Symphony Orchestra; maroon label, no "Vendor: Mercury Record Corporation"

| ❏ SR 90419 [S] | Prokofiev: Violin Concerto No. 1; Stravinsky: Duo Concertante | 196? | 7.50 | 15.00 | 30.00 |

-- Maroon label, no "Vendor: Mercury Record Corporation"

| ❏ SR 90419 [S] | Prokofiev: Violin Concerto No. 1; Stravinsky: Duo Concertante | 196? | 15.00 | 30.00 | 60.00 |

-- Maroon label, with "Vendor: Mercury Record Corporation" (second edition is more sought after than the first)

| ❏ SR 90442 [S] | Violin Sonatas | 1965 | 12.50 | 25.00 | 50.00 |

-- Maroon label, with "Vendor: Mercury Record Corporation"

SZIGETI, JOSEF; MIECZYSLAW HORSZOWSKI; JOHN BARROWS
MERCURY LIVING PRESENCE

| ❏ SR 90210 [S] | Brahms: Horn Trio; Violin Sonata No. 2 | 196? | 12.50 | 25.00 | 50.00 |

-- Maroon label, with "Vendor: Mercury Record Corporation"

| ❏ SR 90210 [S] | Brahms: Horn Trio; Violin Sonata No. 2 | 196? | 30.00 | 60.00 | 120.00 |

-- Maroon label, no "Vendor: Mercury Record Corporation"

Number	Title	Yr	VG	VG+	NM

T

T-BONES, THE
LIBERTY
Number	Title	Yr	VG	VG+	NM
❑ LRP-3346 [M]	Boss Drag	1963	15.00	30.00	60.00
❑ LRP-3363 [M]	Boss Drag at the Beach	1964	15.00	30.00	60.00
❑ LRP-3404 [M]	Doin' the Jerk	1965	10.00	20.00	40.00
❑ LRP-3439 [M]	No Matter What Shape (Your Stomach's In)	1966	5.00	10.00	20.00
❑ LRP-3446 [M]	Sippin' and Chippin'	1966	5.00	10.00	20.00
❑ LRP-3471 [M]	Everyone's Gone to the Moon	1966	5.00	10.00	20.00
❑ LST-7346 [S]	Boss Drag	1963	25.00	50.00	100.00
❑ LST-7363 [S]	Boss Drag at the Beach	1964	25.00	50.00	100.00
❑ LST-7404 [S]	Doin' the Jerk	1965	15.00	30.00	60.00
❑ LST-7439 [S]	No Matter What Shape (Your Stomach's In)	1966	6.25	12.50	25.00
❑ LST-7446 [S]	Sippin' and Chippin'	1966	6.25	12.50	25.00
❑ LST-7471 [S]	Everyone's Gone to the Moon	1966	6.25	12.50	25.00

T. REX
BLUE THUMB
Number	Title	Yr	VG	VG+	NM
❑ BTS 7	Unicorn	1969	5.00	10.00	20.00
❑ BTS 18	A Beard of Stars	1970	5.00	10.00	20.00

-- Add $5 for bonus single SP-6115/6, "Ride a White Swan"/"Is It Love." For reasons unknown, the single seems to be much more readily available than the LP

REPRISE
Number	Title	Yr	VG	VG+	NM
❑ PRO 511 [DJ]	An Interview with Marc Bolan	1971	25.00	50.00	100.00

T.C. ATLANTIC
DOVE
Number	Title	Yr	VG	VG+	NM
❑ LP-4459	T.C. Atlantic	1966	25.00	50.00	100.00

T.I.M.E.
LIBERTY
Number	Title	Yr	VG	VG+	NM
❑ LST-7558	T.I.M.E.	1968	6.25	12.50	25.00
❑ LST-7605	Smooth Ball	1969	6.25	12.50	25.00

T.V. AND THE TRIBESMEN
HANNA-BARBERA
Number	Title	Yr	VG	VG+	NM
❑ HLP-9507 [S]	Barefootin'	1966	6.25	12.50	25.00

T2
LONDON
Number	Title	Yr	VG	VG+	NM
❑ PS 583	It'll All Work Out in Boomland	1971	20.00	40.00	80.00

TAD
SUB POP
Number	Title	Yr	VG	VG+	NM
❑ 27	God's Balls	1989	5.00	10.00	20.00

-- First 2,000 with gatefold cover

TALISMEN, THE
BLUE STAR
Number	Title	Yr	VG	VG+	NM
❑ M-6323 [M]	Treasury of American Railroad Songs and Ballads	1964	5.00	10.00	20.00
❑ MS-6323 [S]	Treasury of American Railroad Songs and Ballads	1964	6.25	12.50	25.00

PRESTIGE
Number	Title	Yr	VG	VG+	NM
❑ PRLP-7406 [M]	Folk Swingers Extraordinaire	1965	5.00	10.00	20.00
❑ PRST-7406 [S]	Folk Swingers Extraordinaire	1965	6.25	12.50	25.00

TALKING HEADS
SIRE
Number	Title	Yr	VG	VG+	NM
❑ 2SR 3590 [(2)]	The Name of This Band Is Talking Heads	1982	5.00	10.00	20.00
❑ 23771	Speaking in Tongues	1983	5.00	10.00	20.00

-- Clear vinyl in oversize plastic container with Robert Rauschenberg artwork

WARNER BROS.
Number	Title	Yr	VG	VG+	NM
❑ WBMS-104 [DJ]	Talking Heads Live on Tour	1979	6.25	12.50	25.00

-- Part of "The Warner Bros. Music Show" series (has been counterfeited)

TAMPA RED
BLUESVILLE
Number	Title	Yr	VG	VG+	NM
❑ BVLP-1030 [M]	Don't Tampa with the Blues	1961	30.00	60.00	120.00
-- Blue label, silver print					
❑ BVLP-1030 [M]	Don't Tampa with the Blues	1963	7.50	15.00	30.00
-- Blue label, trident logo at right					
❑ BVLP-1043 [M]	Don't Jive Me	1962	30.00	60.00	120.00
-- Blue label, silver print					
❑ BVLP-1043 [M]	Don't Jive Me	1963	7.50	15.00	30.00
-- Blue label, trident logo at right					

TAMS, THE
ABC
Number	Title	Yr	VG	VG+	NM
❑ 596 [M]	Time for the Tams	1967	7.50	15.00	30.00
❑ S-596 [S]	Time for the Tams	1967	7.50	15.00	30.00
❑ S-627	A Little More Soul	1968	6.25	12.50	25.00
❑ S-673	A Portrait of the Tams	1969	6.25	12.50	25.00

ABC-PARAMOUNT
Number	Title	Yr	VG	VG+	NM
❑ 481 [M]	Presenting the Tams	1964	12.50	25.00	50.00
❑ S-481 [R]	Presenting the Tams	1964	7.50	15.00	30.00
❑ 499 [M]	Hey Girl, Don't Bother Me	1964	7.50	15.00	30.00
❑ S-499 [S]	Hey Girl, Don't Bother Me	1964	10.00	20.00	40.00

1-2-3
Number	Title	Yr	VG	VG+	NM
❑ 567	The Best of the Tams	1970	5.00	10.00	20.00

TANEGA, NORMA
NEW VOICE
Number	Title	Yr	VG	VG+	NM
❑ NV-2001 [M]	Walkin' My Cat Named Dog	1966	10.00	20.00	40.00
❑ NVS-2001 [S]	Walkin' My Cat Named Dog	1966	20.00	40.00	80.00

TANGERINE DREAM
VIRGIN
Number	Title	Yr	VG	VG+	NM
❑ PZG 35014 [(2)]	Encore	1977	5.00	10.00	20.00

TANGERINE ZOO, THE
MAINSTREAM
Number	Title	Yr	VG	VG+	NM
❑ S-6107	Tangerine Zoo	1968	12.50	25.00	50.00
❑ S-6118	Outside Looking In	1969	17.50	35.00	70.00

TARANTULA
A&M
Number	Title	Yr	VG	VG+	NM
❑ SP-4202	Tarantula	1969	5.00	10.00	20.00

TARRIERS, THE
ATLANTIC
Number	Title	Yr	VG	VG+	NM
❑ 8042 [M]	Tell the World	1960	7.50	15.00	30.00
❑ SD 8042 [S]	Tell the World	1960	10.00	20.00	40.00

DECCA
Number	Title	Yr	VG	VG+	NM
❑ DL 4342 [M]	The Tarriers	1962	6.25	12.50	25.00
❑ DL 4538 [M]	Gather 'Round	1964	6.25	12.50	25.00
❑ DL 74342 [S]	The Tarriers	1962	7.50	15.00	30.00
❑ DL 74538 [S]	Gather 'Round	1964	7.50	15.00	30.00

GLORY
Number	Title	Yr	VG	VG+	NM
❑ PG-1200 [M]	The Tarriers	1958	15.00	30.00	60.00

KAPP
Number	Title	Yr	VG	VG+	NM
❑ KL 1349 [M]	The Original Tarriers	1963	6.25	12.50	25.00
❑ KS 3349 [S]	The Original Tarriers	1963	7.50	15.00	30.00

UNITED ARTISTS
Number	Title	Yr	VG	VG+	NM
❑ UAL-4033 [M]	Hard Travelin'	1959	7.50	15.00	30.00
❑ UAS-5033 [S]	Hard Travelin'	1959	10.00	20.00	40.00

TASTE
RORY GALLAGHER was in this group.
ATCO
Number	Title	Yr	VG	VG+	NM
❑ SD 33-296	Taste	1969	6.25	12.50	25.00
❑ SD 33-322	On the Boards	1970	6.25	12.50	25.00

TATE, BABY
BLUESVILLE
Number	Title	Yr	VG	VG+	NM
❑ BVLP-1072 [M]	What You Done	1963	20.00	40.00	80.00
-- Blue label, silver print					
❑ BVLP-1072 [M]	What You Done	1963	6.25	12.50	25.00
-- Blue label, trident logo at right					

TATE, HOWARD
ATLANTIC
Number	Title	Yr	VG	VG+	NM
❑ SD 8303	Howard Tate	1971	5.00	10.00	20.00

TURNTABLE
Number	Title	Yr	VG	VG+	NM
❑ 5002	Reaction	1969	5.00	10.00	20.00

VERVE
Number	Title	Yr	VG	VG+	NM
❑ V-5022 [M]	Get It While You Can	1967	5.00	10.00	20.00
❑ V6-5022 [S]	Get It While You Can	1967	6.25	12.50	25.00

TAUPIN, BERNIE
RCA
Number	Title	Yr	VG	VG+	NM
❑ 6420-1-RAB [(2) DJ]	Interview Album	1987	5.00	10.00	20.00

TAVENER, JOHN
APPLE
Number	Title	Yr	VG	VG+	NM
❑ SMAS-3369	The Whale	1972	5.00	10.00	20.00

Number	Title	Yr	VG	VG+	NM
TAX FREE					
POLYDOR					
❏ 24-4053	Tax Free	1971	5.00	10.00	20.00
TAXXI					
FANTASY					
❏ F-9617	States of Emergency	1982	7.50	15.00	30.00
TAYLES, THE					
CINEVISTA					
❏ US 1001	Who Are These Guys -- Live at the Nitty Gritty	1972	20.00	40.00	80.00
TAYLOR, BOBBY, AND THE VANCOUVERS					
GORDY					
❏ G-930 [M]	Bobby Taylor and the Vancouvers	1968	20.00	40.00	80.00
-- Mono is promo only					
❏ GS-930 [S]	Bobby Taylor and the Vancouvers	1968	15.00	30.00	60.00
❏ GS-942	Taylor Made Soul	1969	15.00	30.00	60.00
TAYLOR, BUCK					
JPL					
❏ 14098	That Man from Gunsmoke	197?	10.00	20.00	40.00
TAYLOR, CATHIE					
CAPITOL					
❏ ST 1359 [S]	A Little Bit of Sweetness	1960	6.25	12.50	25.00
❏ T 1359 [M]	A Little Bit of Sweetness	1960	5.00	10.00	20.00
❏ ST 1448 [S]	The Tree Near My House	1961	6.25	12.50	25.00
❏ T 1448 [M]	The Tree Near My House	1961	5.00	10.00	20.00
TAYLOR, CREED					
ABC-PARAMOUNT					
❏ ABC-259 [M]	Shock Music in Hi-Fi	1958	10.00	20.00	40.00
❏ ABCS-259 [S]	Shock Music in Hi-Fi	1958	15.00	30.00	60.00
❏ ABC-308 [M]	Lonelyville "The Nervous Beat"	1960	6.25	12.50	25.00
❏ ABCS-308 [S]	Lonelyville "The Nervous Beat"	1960	7.50	15.00	30.00
❏ ABC-317 [M]	The Best of the Barracks Ballads	1960	6.25	12.50	25.00
❏ ABCS-317 [S]	The Best of the Barracks Ballads	1960	7.50	15.00	30.00
TAYLOR, EARL					
CAPITOL					
❏ ST 2090 [S]	Bluegrass Taylor-Made	1963	12.50	25.00	50.00
❏ T 2090 [M]	Bluegrass Taylor-Made	1963	10.00	20.00	40.00
UNITED ARTISTS					
❏ UAL-3049 [M]	Folk Songs from the Bluegrass	1960	6.25	12.50	25.00
❏ UAS-6049 [S]	Folk Songs from the Bluegrass	1960	7.50	15.00	30.00
TAYLOR, HOUND DOG					
ALLIGATOR					
❏ 4701	Hound Dog Taylor	1971	6.25	12.50	25.00
❏ 4704	Natural Boogie	1974	5.00	10.00	20.00
TAYLOR, JAMES					
APPLE					
❏ SKAO 3352	James Taylor	1969	6.25	12.50	25.00
-- With title in black print					
❏ SKAO 3352	James Taylor	1970	5.00	10.00	20.00
-- With title in orange print					
COLUMBIA					
❏ HC 47009	Dad Loves His Work	1983	10.00	20.00	40.00
-- Half-speed mastered edition					
NAUTILUS					
❏ NR-29	Gorilla	1981	10.00	20.00	40.00
-- Audiophile pressing					
WARNER BROS.					
❏ WS 1843	Sweet Baby James	1970	6.25	12.50	25.00
-- Very early pressings have green label with "W7" logo					
❏ ST-93138	Sweet Baby James	1970	5.00	10.00	20.00
-- Capitol Record Club edition					
TAYLOR, JOHNNIE					
COLUMBIA					
❏ PCQ 33951 [Q]	Eargasm	1976	5.00	10.00	20.00
❏ PCQ 34401 [Q]	Rated Extraordinaire	1977	5.00	10.00	20.00
STAX					
❏ ST-715 [M]	Wanted: One Soul Singer	1967	12.50	25.00	50.00
❏ STS-715 [S]	Wanted: One Soul Singer	1967	15.00	30.00	60.00
❏ STS-2005	Who's Making Love	1968	10.00	20.00	40.00
❏ STS-2008	Raw Blues	1969	6.25	12.50	25.00
❏ STS-2012	Rare Stamps	1969	6.25	12.50	25.00
❏ STS-2023	The Johnnie Taylor Philosophy Continues	1969	6.25	12.50	25.00
❏ STS-2030	One Step Beyond	1971	6.25	12.50	25.00
❏ STS-2032	Johnnie Taylor's Greatest Hits	1970	6.25	12.50	25.00
❏ STS-3014	Taylored in Silk	1973	5.00	10.00	20.00
❏ STS-5509	Super Taylor	1974	5.00	10.00	20.00
❏ STS-5521	The Best of Johnnie Taylor	1975	5.00	10.00	20.00
❏ 88001 [(2)]	Chronicle	1977	5.00	10.00	20.00
TAYLOR, KINGSIZE, AND THE DOMINOES					
MIDNIGHT					
❏ HLP-2101 [M]	Real Gonk Man	1965	12.50	25.00	50.00
❏ HST-2101 [S]	Real Gonk Man	1965	25.00	50.00	100.00
TAYLOR, KOKO					
CHESS					
❏ LPS-1532	Koko Taylor	1969	7.50	15.00	30.00
❏ CH-50018	Basic Soul	1972	6.25	12.50	25.00
TAYLOR, LITTLE JOHNNY					
GALAXY					
❏ 203 [M]	Little Johnny Taylor	1963	25.00	50.00	100.00
❏ 207 [M]	Little Johnny Taylor's Greatest Hits	1964	25.00	50.00	100.00
❏ 8203 [S]	Little Johnny Taylor	1963	37.50	75.00	150.00
❏ 8207 [S]	Little Johnny Taylor's Greatest Hits	1964	37.50	75.00	150.00
RONN					
❏ LPS-7530	Everybody Knows About My Good Thing	1972	6.25	12.50	25.00
❏ LSP-7532	Open House at My House	1973	6.25	12.50	25.00
❏ LSP-7535	L.J.T.	1975	5.00	10.00	20.00
TAYLOR, LITTLE JOHNNY, AND TED TAYLOR					
Also see each artist's individual listings.					
RONN					
❏ LSP-7533	The Super Taylors	1973	5.00	10.00	20.00
TAYLOR, MEL					
WARNER BROS.					
❏ W 1624 [M]	Mel Taylor in Action	1966	7.50	15.00	30.00
❏ WS 1624 [S]	Mel Taylor in Action	1966	10.00	20.00	40.00
TAYLOR, SAM "THE MAN"					
MGM					
❏ E-293 [10]	Music with the Big Beat	195?	25.00	50.00	100.00
❏ E-3292 [M]	Blue Mist	1955	15.00	30.00	60.00
-- Yellow label					
❏ E-3380 [M]	Out of This World	1956	15.00	30.00	60.00
-- Yellow label					
❏ E-3473 [M]	Music with the Big Beat	1956	20.00	40.00	80.00
-- Yellow label					
❏ E-3482 [M]	Music for Melancholy Babies	1957	15.00	30.00	60.00
-- Yellow label					
❏ E-3553 [M]	Rockin' Sax and Rollin' Organ	1957	15.00	30.00	60.00
-- Yellow label					
❏ E-3573 [M]	Prelude to Blues	1957	15.00	30.00	60.00
-- Yellow label					
❏ E-3783 [M]	More Blue Mist	1959	7.50	15.00	30.00
❏ SE-3783 [S]	More Blue Mist	1959	10.00	20.00	40.00
TAYLOR, TED					
Also see LITTLE JOHNNY TAYLOR AND TED TAYLOR.					
OKEH					
❏ OKM-12104 [M]	Be Ever Wonderful	1963	7.50	15.00	30.00
❏ OKM-12109 [M]	Blues and Soul	1965	7.50	15.00	30.00
❏ OKM-12113 [M]	Ted Taylor's Greatest Hits	1966	6.25	12.50	25.00
❏ OKS-14104 [S]	Be Ever Wonderful	1963	10.00	20.00	40.00
❏ OKS-14109 [S]	Blues and Soul	1965	10.00	20.00	40.00
❏ OKS-14113 [S]	Ted Taylor's Greatest Hits	1966	7.50	15.00	30.00
TAYLOR, TUT					
WORLD PACIFIC					
❏ ST-1816 [S]	12 String Dobro	1964	20.00	40.00	80.00
-- Red vinyl					
❏ ST-1816 [S]	12 String Dobro	1964	7.50	15.00	30.00
-- Black vinyl					
❏ WP-1816 [M]	12 String Dobro	1964	6.25	12.50	25.00
❏ ST-1829 [S]	Dobro Country	1964	7.50	15.00	30.00
❏ WP-1829 [M]	Dobro Country	1964	6.25	12.50	25.00

Number	Title	Yr	VG	VG+	NM

TCHAIKOVSKY, ANDRE
RCA VICTOR RED SEAL
❏ LSC-2287 [S]	Mozart: Piano Concerto No. 25	1959	18.75	37.50	75.00
-- With Fritz Reiner/Chicago Symphony Orchestra; original with "shaded dog" label					
❏ LSC-2354 [S]	Mozart: Fantasia in C; Sonata in C, K. 457; Sonata in C, K. 330	1960	25.00	50.00	100.00
-- Original with "shaded dog" label					
❏ LSC-2360 [S]	Chopin: Preludes; Barcarolle: Mazurkas, Etudes, Ballade 3	1960	17.50	35.00	70.00
-- Original with "shaded dog" label					

TEA COMPANY, THE
SMASH
❏ SRS-67105	Come and Have Some Tea	1968	12.50	25.00	50.00

TEARDROPS, THE
20TH CENTURY FOX
❏ FXG-5011 [M]	The Teardrops at Trinchi's	1963	6.25	12.50	25.00

TEDDY AND THE PANDAS
TOWER
❏ ST-5125	Basic Magnetism	1968	6.25	12.50	25.00

TEDDY BEARS, THE
IMPERIAL
❏ LP-9067 [M]	The Teddy Bears Sing!	1959	75.00	150.00	300.00
❏ LP-12010 [S]	The Teddy Bears Sing!	1959	300.00	600.00	1,200.

TEDESCO, TOMMY
IMPERIAL
❏ LP-12263 [S]	The Electric 12 String Guitar of Tommy Tedesco	1964	5.00	10.00	20.00
❏ LP-12295 [S]	Guitars	1965	5.00	10.00	20.00
❏ LP-12321 [S]	Calypso Soul	1966	5.00	10.00	20.00

TEEMATES, THE
AUDIO FIDELITY
❏ AFLP-3042 [M]	Jet Set Dance Discotheque	1964	10.00	20.00	40.00
❏ AFSD-7042 [S]	Jet Set Dance Discotheque	1964	12.50	25.00	50.00

TEEN QUEENS, THE
CROWN
❏ CST-373 [R]	The Teen Queens	1963	7.50	15.00	30.00
❏ CLP-5022 [M]	Eddie My Love	1956	62.50	125.00	250.00
❏ CLP-5373 [M]	The Teen Queens	1963	12.50	25.00	50.00

TEENAGE JESUS AND THE JERKS
MIGRANE/LUST UNLUST
❏ CC-336 [EP]	Teenage Jesus and the Jerks	1979	7.50	15.00	30.00
-- Black vinyl					
❏ CC-336 [EP]	Teenage Jesus and the Jerks	1979	10.00	20.00	40.00
-- Pink vinyl					

TEENAGERS, THE -- See FRANKIE LYMON AND THE TEENAGERS.

TELEVISION
CAPITOL
❏ SPRO-79456 [DJ]	Television	1992	5.00	10.00	20.00
-- Vinyl is promo only					

TEMPEST
WARNER BROS.
❏ BS 2682	Tempest	1973	6.25	12.50	25.00

TEMPESTS, THE
SMASH
❏ MGS-27098 [M]	Would You Believe?	1966	6.25	12.50	25.00
❏ SRS-67098 [S]	Would You Believe?	1966	7.50	15.00	30.00

TEMPLE, PICK
PRESTIGE INT'L.
❏ PRLP-13008 [M]	Pick of the Crop	196?	7.50	15.00	30.00
"X"
❏ LXA-3022 [10]	Folk Songs of the People	1954	12.50	25.00	50.00

TEMPLE, SHIRLEY
20TH CENTURY FOX
❏ TFM-3102 [M]	The Best of Shirley Temple	1963	6.25	12.50	25.00
❏ TFM-3172 [M]	The Best of Shirley Temple, Vol. 2	1965	6.25	12.50	25.00
20TH FOX
❏ TCF-103 [(2) M]	The Shirley Temple Songbook	1961	12.50	25.00	50.00
❏ FOX-3006 [M]	Little Miss Wonderful	1959	10.00	20.00	40.00
-- Shirley Temple pictured as an adult on cover					
❏ FOX-3006 [M]	Little Miss Wonderful	196?	10.00	20.00	40.00
-- Shirley Temple pictured as a child on cover					
❏ FOX-3045 [M]	More Little Miss Wonderful	1961	10.00	20.00	40.00
MOVIETONE
❏ MTM-71001 [M]	On the Good Ship Lollipop	1966	5.00	10.00	20.00
❏ MTM-71012 [M]	Curtain Call	1966	5.00	10.00	20.00

TEMPO, NINO
LIBERTY
❏ LRP-3023 [M]	Rock 'n' Roll Beach Party	1958	30.00	60.00	120.00

TEMPO, NINO, AND APRIL STEVENS
Also see each artist's individual listings.
ATCO
❏ 33-156 [M]	Deep Purple	1963	10.00	20.00	40.00
❏ SD 33-156 [S]	Deep Purple	1963	12.50	25.00	50.00
❏ 33-162 [M]	Nino Tempo and April Stevens Sing the Great Songs	1964	7.50	15.00	30.00
❏ SD 33-162 [S]	Nino Tempo and April Stevens Sing the Great Songs	1964	10.00	20.00	40.00
❏ 33-180 [M]	Hey Baby	1966	7.50	15.00	30.00
❏ SD 33-180 [S]	Hey Baby	1966	10.00	20.00	40.00
WHITE WHALE
❏ WW-113 [M]	All Strung Out	1967	5.00	10.00	20.00
❏ WWS-7113 [S]	All Strung Out	1967	6.25	12.50	25.00

TEMPOS, THE
JUSTICE
❏ JLP-104	Speaking of the Tempos	1966	125.00	250.00	500.00

TEMPREES
WE PRODUCE
❏ 1901	Love Men	1972	15.00	30.00	60.00
❏ 1903	Love Maze	1973	15.00	30.00	60.00
❏ 1905	Temprees 3	1974	15.00	30.00	60.00

TEMPTATIONS, THE
GORDY
❏ G 911 [M]	Meet the Temptations	1964	7.50	15.00	30.00
❏ GS 911 [S]	Meet the Temptations	1964	10.00	20.00	40.00
-- Script "Gordy" at top of label					
❏ GS 911 [S]	Meet the Temptations	1967	5.00	10.00	20.00
-- Block "GORDY" inside "G" on left of label					
❏ G 912 [M]	The Temptations Sing Smokey	1965	7.50	15.00	30.00
❏ GS 912 [S]	The Temptations Sing Smokey	1965	10.00	20.00	40.00
-- Script "Gordy" at top of label					
❏ GS 912 [S]	The Temptations Sing Smokey	1967	5.00	10.00	20.00
-- Block "GORDY" inside "G" on left of label					
❏ G 914 [M]	Temptin' Temptations	1965	6.25	12.50	25.00
❏ GS 914 [S]	Temptin' Temptations	1965	7.50	15.00	30.00
-- Script "Gordy" at top of label					
❏ GS 914 [S]	Temptin' Temptations	1967	5.00	10.00	20.00
-- Block "GORDY" inside "G" on left of label					
❏ G 918 [M]	Gettin' Ready	1966	6.25	12.50	25.00
❏ GS 918 [S]	Gettin' Ready	1966	7.50	15.00	30.00
-- Script "Gordy" at top of label					
❏ GS 918 [S]	Gettin' Ready	1967	5.00	10.00	20.00
-- Block "GORDY" inside "G" on left of label					
❏ G 919 [M]	The Temptations' Greatest Hits	1966	6.25	12.50	25.00
❏ GS 919 [S]	The Temptations' Greatest Hits	1966	7.50	15.00	30.00
-- Script "Gordy" at top of label					
❏ GS 919 [S]	The Temptations' Greatest Hits	1967	5.00	10.00	20.00
-- Block "GORDY" inside "G" on left of label					
❏ G 921 [M]	Temptations Live!	1967	6.25	12.50	25.00
❏ GS 921 [S]	Temptations Live!	1967	7.50	15.00	30.00
-- Script "Gordy" at top of label					
❏ GS 921 [S]	Temptations Live!	1967	5.00	10.00	20.00
-- Block "GORDY" inside "G" on left of label					
❏ G 922 [M]	With a Lot o' Soul	1967	6.25	12.50	25.00
❏ GS 922 [S]	With a Lot o' Soul	1967	5.00	10.00	20.00
-- Block "GORDY" inside "G" on left of label					
❏ GS 922 [S]	With a Lot o' Soul	1967	6.25	12.50	25.00
-- Script "Gordy" at top of label					
❏ G 924 [M]	The Temptations in a Mellow Mood	1967	6.25	12.50	25.00
❏ GS 924 [S]	The Temptations in a Mellow Mood	1967	6.25	12.50	25.00

Number	Title	Yr	VG	VG+	NM
❑ G 927 [M]	The Temptations Wish It Would Rain	1968	10.00	20.00	40.00
-- Mono is white-label promo only					
❑ GS 927 [S]	The Temptations Wish It Would Rain	1968	5.00	10.00	20.00
❑ GS 933	The Temptations Show	1969	5.00	10.00	20.00
❑ GS 938	Live at the Copa	1968	5.00	10.00	20.00
❑ GS 939	Cloud Nine	1969	5.00	10.00	20.00
❑ GS 947	Psychedelic Shack	1970	5.00	10.00	20.00
❑ GS 949	Puzzle People	1969	5.00	10.00	20.00
❑ GS 951	The Temptations' Christmas Card	1969	6.25	12.50	25.00
❑ GS 953	Live at London's Talk of the Town	1970	5.00	10.00	20.00
❑ GS 954	Temptations Greatest Hits II	1970	5.00	10.00	20.00
❑ GS 957	Sky's the Limit	1971	5.00	10.00	20.00
❑ GS 961	Solid Rock	1972	5.00	10.00	20.00
❑ G 962L	All Directions	1972	5.00	10.00	20.00
❑ G 965L	Masterpiece	1973	5.00	10.00	20.00
MOTOWN					
❑ M 782 [(3)]	Anthology	1973	6.25	12.50	25.00

TEN YEARS AFTER
DERAM

Number	Title	Yr	VG	VG+	NM
❑ DE 16009 [M]	Ten Years After	1968	12.50	25.00	50.00
❑ DES 18009 [S]	Ten Years After	1968	5.00	10.00	20.00

10,000 MANIACS
CHRISTIAN BURIAL

Number	Title	Yr	VG	VG+	NM
❑ P-2010 [EP]	Human Conflict #5	1983	20.00	40.00	80.00
❑ P-3001	Secrets of the I Ching	1984	30.00	60.00	120.00
ELEKTRA					
❑ ED 5270 [DJ]	Interview	1987	7.50	15.00	30.00
-- Lenny Kaye interviews Natalie Merchant; promo only					

TERRACE, RAY
TOWER

Number	Title	Yr	VG	VG+	NM
❑ ST-5105	The Home of Boogaloo	1968	5.00	10.00	20.00

TERRELL, TAMMI
Also see MARVIN GAYE AND TAMMI TERRELL.
MOTOWN

Number	Title	Yr	VG	VG+	NM
❑ MS-652	Irresistible Tammi	1969	12.50	25.00	50.00

TERRY, DON
COLUMBIA

Number	Title	Yr	VG	VG+	NM
❑ CL 6288 [10]	Teen-Age Dance Session	1955	12.50	25.00	50.00

TERRY, GORDON
LIBERTY

Number	Title	Yr	VG	VG+	NM
❑ LRP-3218 [M]	Liberty Square Dance Club	1962	5.00	10.00	20.00
-- With calls					
❑ LRP-3219 [M]	Liberty Square Dance Club	1962	5.00	10.00	20.00
-- Without calls					

TERRY, RON
WING

Number	Title	Yr	VG	VG+	NM
❑ SRW-16108 [S]	Polkas and Waltzes	1959	5.00	10.00	20.00

TERRY, SONNY
BLUESVILLE

Number	Title	Yr	VG	VG+	NM
❑ BVLP-1025 [M]	Sonny's Story	1961	20.00	40.00	80.00
-- Bright blue label, no trident logo					
❑ BVLP-1025 [M]	Sonny's Story	1964	6.25	12.50	25.00
-- Blue label with trident logo on right					
❑ BVLP-1069 [M]	Sonny Is King	1963	20.00	40.00	80.00
-- Bright blue label, no trident logo					
❑ BVLP-1069 [M]	Sonny Is King	1964	6.25	12.50	25.00
-- Blue label with trident logo on right					
ELEKTRA					
❑ EKL-14 [10]	Folk Blues	1954	37.50	75.00	150.00
❑ EKL-15 [10]	City Blues	1954	37.50	75.00	150.00
-- With Alec Stewart					
FOLKWAYS					
❑ FP-35 [10]	Harmonica and Vocal Solos	1952	37.50	75.00	150.00
❑ FA-2006 [10]	Sonny Terry's Washboard Band	195?	25.00	50.00	100.00
-- Black and white cover (reissue)					
❑ FA-2035 [10]	Harmonica and Vocal Solos	1952	25.00	50.00	100.00
❑ FP-2006 [10]	Sonny Terry's Washboard Band	1950	37.50	75.00	150.00
-- Blue and white cover					
RIVERSIDE					
❑ RLP-644 [M]	Sonny Terry and His Mouth Harp	195?	20.00	40.00	80.00

STINSON

Number	Title	Yr	VG	VG+	NM
❑ SLP-55 [10]	Sonny Terry and His Mouth Harp	1950	37.50	75.00	150.00

TERRY, SONNY, AND BROWNIE McGHEE
BLUESVILLE

Number	Title	Yr	VG	VG+	NM
❑ BVLP-1002 [M]	Down Home Blues	1960	20.00	40.00	80.00
-- Bright blue label, no trident logo					
❑ BVLP-1002 [M]	Down Home Blues	1964	6.25	12.50	25.00
-- Blue label with trident logo on right					
❑ BVLP-1005 [M]	Blues and Folk	1960	20.00	40.00	80.00
-- Bright blue label, no trident logo					
❑ BVLP-1005 [M]	Blues and Folk	1964	6.25	12.50	25.00
-- Blue label with trident logo on right					
❑ BVLP-1020 [M]	Blues All Around My Head	1961	20.00	40.00	80.00
-- Bright blue label, no trident logo					
❑ BVLP-1020 [M]	Blues All Around My Head	1964	6.25	12.50	25.00
-- Blue label with trident logo on right					
❑ BVLP-1033 [M]	Blues in My Soul	1961	20.00	40.00	80.00
-- Bright blue label, no trident logo					
❑ BVLP-1033 [M]	Blues in My Soul	1964	6.25	12.50	25.00
-- Blue label with trident logo on right					
❑ BVLP-1058 [M]	Live at the Second Fret	1962	20.00	40.00	80.00
-- Bright blue label, no trident logo					
❑ BVLP-1058 [M]	Live at the Second Fret	1964	6.25	12.50	25.00
-- Blue label with trident logo on right					
EVEREST					
❑ 206	Sonny Terry	1968	6.25	12.50	25.00
❑ 242	Brownie McGhee and Sonny Terry	1969	6.25	12.50	25.00
FANTASY					
❑ F-3254 [M]	Sonny Terry & Brownie McGhee	1961	37.50	75.00	150.00
-- Red vinyl					
❑ F-3254 [M]	Sonny Terry & Brownie McGhee	1961	10.00	20.00	40.00
-- Black vinyl					
❑ F-3296 [M]	Just a Closer Walk with Thee	1962	37.50	75.00	150.00
-- Red vinyl					
❑ F-3296 [M]	Just a Closer Walk with Thee	1962	10.00	20.00	40.00
-- Black vinyl					
❑ F-3317 [M]	Blues and Shouts	1962	37.50	75.00	150.00
-- Red vinyl					
❑ F-3317 [M]	Blues and Shouts	1962	10.00	20.00	40.00
-- Black vinyl					
❑ F-3340 [M]	Sonny and Brownie at Sugar Hill	1962	37.50	75.00	150.00
-- Red vinyl					
❑ F-3340 [M]	Sonny and Brownie at Sugar Hill	1962	10.00	20.00	40.00
-- Black vinyl					
❑ FS-8091 [S]	Sonny and Brownie at Sugar Hill	1962	37.50	75.00	150.00
-- Blue vinyl					
❑ FS-8091 [S]	Sonny and Brownie at Sugar Hill	1962	10.00	20.00	40.00
-- Black vinyl					
FOLKLORE					
❑ FRLP-14013 [M]	Down Home Blues	1964	10.00	20.00	40.00
❑ FRST-14013 [S]	Down Home Blues	1964	12.50	25.00	50.00
FOLKWAYS					
❑ FA-2327 [M]	Blues and Folk Songs	1960	7.50	15.00	30.00
❑ F-2421 [M]	Traditional Blues, Volume 1	1961	7.50	15.00	30.00
❑ FS-2421 [S]	Traditional Blues, Volume 1	1961	10.00	20.00	40.00
❑ F-2422 [M]	Traditional Blues, Volume 2	1961	7.50	15.00	30.00
❑ FS-2422 [S]	Traditional Blues, Volume 2	1961	10.00	20.00	40.00
FONTANA					
❑ SGF-67599	Where the Blues Begin	1969	6.25	12.50	25.00
KIMBERLEY					
❑ 2017 [M]	Southern Meetin'	1963	5.00	10.00	20.00
❑ 11017 [S]	Southern Meetin'	1963	6.25	12.50	25.00
MAINSTREAM					
❑ S-6049 [S]	Hometown Blues	1966	6.25	12.50	25.00
❑ 56049 [M]	Hometown Blues	1966	5.00	10.00	20.00
MOBILE FIDELITY					
❑ 1-233	Sonny and Brownie	1996	5.00	10.00	20.00
-- Audiophile vinyl					
ROULETTE					
❑ R-25074 [M]	The Folk Songs of Sonny & Brownie	1959	12.50	25.00	50.00
❑ RS-25074 [S]	The Folk Songs of Sonny & Brownie	1959	20.00	40.00	80.00
SHARP					
❑ 2003 [M]	Down Home Blues	195?	37.50	75.00	150.00
SMASH					
❑ MGS-27067 [M]	Brownie McGhee at the Bunkhouse	1965	7.50	15.00	30.00
❑ SRS-67067 [S]	Brownie McGhee at the Bunkhouse	1965	10.00	20.00	40.00
TOPIC					
❑ T-29 [M]	Songs	1958	12.50	25.00	50.00
VERVE					
❑ MGV 3008 [M]	Blues Is My Companion	1961	20.00	40.00	80.00
VERVE FOLKWAYS					
❑ FV 9010 [M]	Get Together	1965	6.25	12.50	25.00

Number	Title	Yr	VG	VG+	NM
❏ FVS 9010 [S]	Get Together	1965	7.50	15.00	30.00
❏ FV 9019 [M]	Guitar Highway	1965	6.25	12.50	25.00
❏ FVS 9019 [S]	Guitar Highway	1965	7.50	15.00	30.00

WASHINGTON

Number	Title	Yr	VG	VG+	NM
❏ W-702 [M]	Talkin' 'Bout the Blues	1961	12.50	25.00	50.00

WORLD PACIFIC

Number	Title	Yr	VG	VG+	NM
❏ ST-1294 [S]	Blues Is a Story	1960	20.00	40.00	80.00
❏ WP-1294 [M]	Blues Is a Story	1960	12.50	25.00	50.00
❏ ST-1296 [S]	Down South Summit Meetin'	1960	20.00	40.00	80.00
❏ WP-1296 [M]	Down South Summit Meetin'	1960	12.50	25.00	50.00

TEX, JOE
ATLANTIC

Number	Title	Yr	VG	VG+	NM
❏ 8106 [M]	Hold What You've Got	1965	10.00	20.00	40.00
❏ SD 8106 [P]	Hold What You've Got	1965	12.50	25.00	50.00
❏ 8115 [M]	The New Boss	1965	10.00	20.00	40.00
❏ SD 8115 [S]	The New Boss	1965	12.50	25.00	50.00
❏ 8124 [M]	The Love You Save	1966	10.00	20.00	40.00
❏ SD 8124 [S]	The Love You Save	1966	12.50	25.00	50.00
❏ 8133 [M]	I've Got to Do a Little Better	1966	10.00	20.00	40.00
❏ SD 8133 [S]	I've Got to Do a Little Better	1966	12.50	25.00	50.00
❏ 8144 [M]	The Best of Joe Tex	1967	5.00	10.00	20.00
❏ SD 8144 [P]	The Best of Joe Tex	1967	6.25	12.50	25.00
❏ SD 8156	Live and Lively	1968	5.00	10.00	20.00
❏ SD 8187	Soul Country	1968	5.00	10.00	20.00
❏ SD 8211	Happy Soul	1969	5.00	10.00	20.00
❏ SD 8231	Buying a Book	1969	5.00	10.00	20.00

CHECKER

Number	Title	Yr	VG	VG+	NM
❏ LP-2993 [M]	Hold On	1965	37.50	75.00	150.00

KING

Number	Title	Yr	VG	VG+	NM
❏ 935 [M]	The Best of Joe Tex	1965	25.00	50.00	100.00
❏ KS-935 [R]	The Best of Joe Tex	1965	18.75	37.50	75.00

PARROT

Number	Title	Yr	VG	VG+	NM
❏ PA 61002 [M]	The Best of Joe Tex	1965	12.50	25.00	50.00
❏ PAS 71002 [R]	The Best of Joe Tex	1965	7.50	15.00	30.00

TEXAS RANGERS, THE
CUMBERLAND

Number	Title	Yr	VG	VG+	NM
❏ MGC-29507 [M]	The Best of Western Swing	1963	5.00	10.00	20.00
❏ SRC-69505 [S]	The Best of Western Swing	1963	6.25	12.50	25.00

TEXAS RUBY
KING

Number	Title	Yr	VG	VG+	NM
❏ 840 [M]	Texas Ruby Sings His Favorite Songs	1963	12.50	25.00	50.00

TEXAS TROUBADOURS, THE
Backing group for ERNEST TUBB.
DECCA

Number	Title	Yr	VG	VG+	NM
❏ DL 4459 [M]	The Texas Troubadours	1964	6.25	12.50	25.00
❏ DL 4644 [M]	Country Dance Time	1965	5.00	10.00	20.00
❏ DL 4745 [M]	Ernest Tubb's Fabulous Texas Troubadours	1966	5.00	10.00	20.00
❏ DL 74459 [S]	The Texas Troubadours	1964	7.50	15.00	30.00
❏ DL 74644 [S]	Country Dance Time	1965	6.25	12.50	25.00
❏ DL 74745 [S]	Ernest Tubb's Fabulous Texas Troubadours	1966	6.25	12.50	25.00
❏ DL 75017	The Terrific Texas Troubadours and Guests	1968	5.00	10.00	20.00

THAXTON, LLOYD
DECCA

Number	Title	Yr	VG	VG+	NM
❏ DL 4594 [M]	Lloyd Thaxton Presents	1964	5.00	10.00	20.00
❏ DL 74594 [S]	Lloyd Thaxton Presents	1964	6.25	12.50	25.00

THEE MIDNITERS
CHATTAHOOCHIE

Number	Title	Yr	VG	VG+	NM
❏ C-1001 [M]	Thee Midniters	1965	15.00	30.00	60.00
❏ CS-1001 [S]	Thee Midniters	1965	20.00	40.00	80.00

WHITTIER

Number	Title	Yr	VG	VG+	NM
❏ W-5000 [M]	Bring You Love Special Delivery	1966	10.00	20.00	40.00
❏ WS-5000 [S]	Bring You Love Special Delivery	1966	12.50	25.00	50.00
❏ W-5001 [M]	Unlimited	1966	10.00	20.00	40.00
❏ WS-5001 [S]	Unlimited	1966	12.50	25.00	50.00
❏ W-5002 [M]	Giants	1967	10.00	20.00	40.00
❏ WS-5002 [S]	Giants	1967	12.50	25.00	50.00

THEE MUFFINS
(NO LABEL)

Number	Title	Yr	VG	VG+	NM
❏ (no #)	Thee Muffins Pop Up!	1967	50.00	100.00	200.00

THEE PROPHETS
KAPP

Number	Title	Yr	VG	VG+	NM
❏ KS-3596	Playgirl	1969	5.00	10.00	20.00

THEM
Also see VAN MORRISON.
HAPPY TIGER

Number	Title	Yr	VG	VG+	NM
❏ HT-1004	Them	1969	12.50	25.00	50.00
❏ HT-1012	Them In Reality	1971	30.00	60.00	120.00

PARROT

Number	Title	Yr	VG	VG+	NM
❏ PA 61005 [M]	Them Featuring "Here Comes the Night"	1965	20.00	40.00	80.00
❏ PA 61005 [M]	Them Featuring "Gloria"	1966	12.50	25.00	50.00
-- Same album as above, but with slightly different title					
❏ PA 61008 [M]	Them Again	1966	20.00	40.00	80.00
❏ PAS 71005 [R]	Them Featuring "Here Comes the Night"	1965	17.50	35.00	70.00
❏ PAS 71005 [R]	Them Featuring "Gloria"	1966	10.00	20.00	40.00
-- Same album as above, but with slightly different title					
❏ PAS 71008 [R]	Them Again	1966	12.50	25.00	50.00

TOWER

Number	Title	Yr	VG	VG+	NM
❏ ST 5104 [S]	Now and Them	1967	20.00	40.00	80.00
❏ T 5104 [M]	Now and Them	1967	12.50	25.00	50.00
❏ ST 5116 [S]	Time Out! Time In for Them	1968	25.00	50.00	100.00

THEODORE
CORAL

Number	Title	Yr	VG	VG+	NM
❏ CRL 757322 [S]	Coral Records Presents Theodore in Stereo	1959	25.00	50.00	100.00

THESE TRAILS
SINERGIA

Number	Title	Yr	VG	VG+	NM
❏ (# unknown)	These Trails	1973	30.00	60.00	120.00

THIN LIZZY
LONDON

Number	Title	Yr	VG	VG+	NM
❏ PS 594	Thin Lizzy	1971	10.00	20.00	40.00
❏ PS 636	Vagabonds of the Western World	1973	7.50	15.00	30.00

THIRD ESTATE, THE
THIRD ESTATE

Number	Title	Yr	VG	VG+	NM
❏ LP-1000	Years Before the Wine	1976	50.00	100.00	200.00

THIRD POWER
VANGUARD

Number	Title	Yr	VG	VG+	NM
❏ VSD-6554	Believe	1970	7.50	15.00	30.00

THIRD RAIL, THE
EPIC

Number	Title	Yr	VG	VG+	NM
❏ LN 24327 [M]	Id Music	1967	7.50	15.00	30.00
❏ BN 26327 [S]	Id Music	1967	10.00	20.00	40.00

THIRTEENTH FLOOR ELEVATORS, THE
INTERNATIONAL ARTISTS

Number	Title	Yr	VG	VG+	NM
❏ 1 [M]	Psychedelic Sounds	1967	62.50	125.00	250.00
-- Green and yellow label					
❏ 1 [M]	Psychedelic Sounds	1968	37.50	75.00	150.00
-- All-yellow label					
❏ 1 [S]	Psychedelic Sounds	1968	37.50	75.00	150.00
-- All-yellow label					
❏ 1 [S]	Psychedelic Sounds	1979	7.50	15.00	30.00
-- Repressing with "Masterfonics" in dead wax					
❏ 5 [M]	Easter Everywhere	1968	100.00	200.00	400.00
-- Mono is promo only					
❏ 5 [S]	Easter Everywhere	1968	37.50	75.00	150.00
-- With custom inner sleeve					
❏ 5 [S]	Easter Everywhere	1968	37.50	75.00	150.00
-- Without custom inner sleeve					
❏ 5 [S]	Easter Everywhere	1979	7.50	15.00	30.00
-- Repressing with "Masterfonics" in dead wax					
❏ 8	13th Floor Elevators Live	1968	25.00	50.00	100.00
❏ 8	13th Floor Elevators Live	1979	6.25	12.50	25.00
-- Repressing with "Masterfonics" in dead wax					
❏ 9	Bull of the Woods	1968	20.00	40.00	80.00
❏ 9	Bull of the Woods	1979	6.25	12.50	25.00
-- Repressing with "Masterfonics" in dead wax					

31 FLAVORS, THE
CROWN

Number	Title	Yr	VG	VG+	NM
❏ CST-592	Hair	1968	12.50	25.00	50.00

Number	Title	Yr	VG	VG+	NM

31ST OF FEBRUARY, THE
VANGUARD
| ❏ VSD-6503 | The 31st of February | 1969 | 10.00 | 20.00 | 40.00 |

THOMAS, B.J.
DORAL
| ❏ (# unknown) | Doral Presents B.J. Thomas | 1971 | 5.00 | 10.00 | 20.00 |

-- *Mail-order promotion from Doral cigarettes*

HICKORY
❏ LPM-133 [M]	The Very Best of B.J. Thomas	1966	5.00	10.00	20.00
❏ LPS-133 [S]	The Very Best of B.J. Thomas	1966	6.25	12.50	25.00
❏ ST 90956 [S]	The Very Best of B.J. Thomas	1966	7.50	15.00	30.00

-- *Capitol Record Club edition*

| ❏ T 90956 [M] | The Very Best of B.J. Thomas | 1966 | 6.25 | 12.50 | 25.00 |

-- *Capitol Record Club edition*

PACEMAKER
| ❏ PLP-3001 [M] | B.J. Thomas and the Triumphs | 1965 | 50.00 | 100.00 | 200.00 |

SCEPTER
❏ SPS-535 [S]	I'm So Lonesome I Could Cry	1966	6.25	12.50	25.00
❏ SRM-535 [M]	I'm So Lonesome I Could Cry	1966	5.00	10.00	20.00
❏ SPS-556 [S]	Tomorrow Never Comes	1966	5.00	10.00	20.00
❏ SRM-561 [M]	For Lovers and Losers	1967	5.00	10.00	20.00

THOMAS, CARLA
Also see OTIS AND CARLA; RUFUS AND CARLA.
ATLANTIC
| ❏ 8057 [M] | Gee Whiz | 1961 | 25.00 | 50.00 | 100.00 |

-- *With white "fan" logo*

| ❏ 8057 [M] | Gee Whiz | 1963 | 10.00 | 20.00 | 40.00 |

-- *With black "fan" logo*

| ❏ SD 8057 [S] | Gee Whiz | 1961 | 37.50 | 75.00 | 150.00 |

-- *With white "fan" logo*

| ❏ SD 8057 [S] | Gee Whiz | 1963 | 12.50 | 25.00 | 50.00 |

-- *With black "fan" logo*

| ❏ SD 8232 | The Best of Carla Thomas | 1969 | 6.25 | 12.50 | 25.00 |

STAX
❏ ST-706 [M]	Comfort Me	1966	8.75	17.50	35.00
❏ STS-706 [P]	Comfort Me	1966	12.50	25.00	50.00
❏ ST-709 [M]	Carla	1966	8.75	17.50	35.00
❏ STS-709 [S]	Carla	1966	12.50	25.00	50.00
❏ ST-718 [M]	The Queen Alone	1967	8.75	17.50	35.00
❏ STS-718 [S]	The Queen Alone	1967	12.50	25.00	50.00
❏ STS-2019	Memphis Queen	1969	8.75	17.50	35.00
❏ STS-2044	Love Means Carla Thomas	1971	8.75	17.50	35.00

THOMAS, CARLA, AND RUFUS THOMAS -- See RUFUS AND CARLA.

THOMAS, DANNY
MGM
| ❏ E-201 [10] | An Evening with Danny Thomas | 1954 | 25.00 | 50.00 | 100.00 |

THOMAS, DYLAN
CAEDMON
| ❏ TC 1002 [M] | A Child's Christmas in Wales and Five Poems (Dylan Thomas, Volume 1) | 1957 | 5.00 | 10.00 | 20.00 |

-- *Number stamped into dead wax; "New York, 1, New York" address on label and cover*

THOMAS, IRMA
BANDY
| ❏ 70003 | Irma Thomas Sings | 197? | 7.50 | 15.00 | 30.00 |

FUNGUS
| ❏ FB-25150 | In Between Tears | 1973 | 10.00 | 20.00 | 40.00 |

IMPERIAL
❏ LP-9266 [M]	Wish Someone Would Care	1964	12.50	25.00	50.00
❏ LP-9302 [M]	Take a Look	1966	12.50	25.00	50.00
❏ LP-12266 [S]	Wish Someone Would Care	1964	15.00	30.00	60.00
❏ LP-12302 [S]	Take a Look	1966	15.00	30.00	60.00

RCS
| ❏ 1004 | Safe with Me | 1980 | 7.50 | 15.00 | 30.00 |

THOMAS, JOE, AND BILL ELLIOTT
SUE
| ❏ LP-1025 [M] | Speak Your Piece | 1964 | 12.50 | 25.00 | 50.00 |

THOMAS, JON
ABC-PARAMOUNT
| ❏ 351 [M] | Heartbreak | 1960 | 7.50 | 15.00 | 30.00 |
| ❏ S-351 [S] | Heartbreak | 1960 | 10.00 | 20.00 | 40.00 |

WING
| ❏ MGW-12258 [M] | The Big Beat on the Organ | 1963 | 5.00 | 10.00 | 20.00 |

THOMAS, PAT
STRAND
| ❏ SL-1015 [M] | Jazz Patterns | 1961 | 10.00 | 20.00 | 40.00 |
| ❏ SLS-1015 [S] | Jazz Patterns | 1961 | 12.50 | 25.00 | 50.00 |

THOMAS, RAY
Also see THE MOODY BLUES.
THRESHOLD
| ❏ THSX-102 [DJ] | Ray Thomas Discusses The Recording of His First Solo Album From Mighty Oaks | 1975 | 12.50 | 25.00 | 50.00 |

THOMAS, RUFUS
Also see RUFUS AND CARLA.
STAX
❏ ST-704 [M]	Walking the Dog	1963	37.50	75.00	150.00
❏ STS-2028	Do the Funky Chicken	1970	6.25	12.50	25.00
❏ STS-2039	Rufus Thomas Live/Doing the Push and Pull at P.J.'s	1971	6.25	12.50	25.00
❏ STS-3004	Did You Hear Me	1972	6.25	12.50	25.00
❏ STS-3008	Crown Prince of Dance	1973	6.25	12.50	25.00

THOMPSON TWINS
ARISTA
| ❏ ADP 9586 [DJ] | Interview Sampler | 1987 | 5.00 | 10.00 | 20.00 |

-- *One side of interviews, the other of music; promo only*

THOMPSON, HANK
CAPITOL
| ❏ H 418 [10] | Songs of the Brazos Valley | 1953 | 30.00 | 60.00 | 120.00 |
| ❏ T 418 [M] | Songs of the Brazos Valley | 1956 | 20.00 | 40.00 | 80.00 |

-- *Turquoise or gray label*

| ❏ T 418 [M] | Songs of the Brazos Valley | 1959 | 7.50 | 15.00 | 30.00 |

-- *Black colorband label, logo at left*

| ❏ T 418 [M] | Songs of the Brazos Valley | 1962 | 5.00 | 10.00 | 20.00 |

-- *Black colorband label, logo at top*

| ❏ H 618 [10] | North of the Rio Grande | 1953 | 30.00 | 60.00 | 120.00 |
| ❏ T 618 [M] | North of the Rio Grande | 1956 | 20.00 | 40.00 | 80.00 |

-- *Turquoise or gray label*

| ❏ H 729 [10] | New Recordings of Hank's All-Time Hits | 195? | 30.00 | 60.00 | 120.00 |
| ❏ T 729 [M] | New Recordings of Hank's All-Time Hits | 1956 | 20.00 | 40.00 | 80.00 |

-- *Turquoise or gray label*

| ❏ T 729 [M] | New Recordings of Hank's All-Time Hits | 1959 | 7.50 | 15.00 | 30.00 |

-- *Black colorband label, logo at left*

| ❏ T 729 [M] | New Recordings of Hank's All-Time Hits | 1962 | 5.00 | 10.00 | 20.00 |

-- *Black colorband label, logo at top*

| ❏ T 826 [M] | Hank! | 1957 | 20.00 | 40.00 | 80.00 |

-- *Turquoise or gray label*

| ❏ T 826 [M] | Hank! | 1959 | 7.50 | 15.00 | 30.00 |

-- *Black colorband label, logo at left*

| ❏ T 826 [M] | Hank! | 1962 | 5.00 | 10.00 | 20.00 |

-- *Black colorband label, logo at top*

| ❏ T 911 [M] | Hank Thompson Favorites | 1957 | 20.00 | 40.00 | 80.00 |

-- *Turquoise or gray label*

| ❏ T 975 [M] | Hank Thompson's Dance Ranch | 1958 | 20.00 | 40.00 | 80.00 |

-- *Turquoise or gray label*

| ❏ T 975 [M] | Hank Thompson's Dance Ranch | 1959 | 7.50 | 15.00 | 30.00 |

-- *Black colorband label, logo at left*

| ❏ T 975 [M] | Hank Thompson's Dance Ranch | 1962 | 5.00 | 10.00 | 20.00 |

-- *Black colorband label, logo at top*

| ❏ T 1111 [M] | Favorite Waltzes | 1959 | 20.00 | 40.00 | 80.00 |

-- *Black colorband label, logo at left*

| ❏ T 1111 [M] | Favorite Waltzes | 1962 | 5.00 | 10.00 | 20.00 |

-- *Black colorband label, logo at top*

❏ T 1246 [M]	Songs for Rounders	1959	7.50	15.00	30.00
❏ ST 1246 [S]	Songs for Rounders	1959	10.00	20.00	40.00
❏ ST 1360 [S]	Most of All	1960	10.00	20.00	40.00

-- *Black colorband label, logo at left*

| ❏ ST 1360 [S] | Most of All | 1962 | 6.25 | 12.50 | 25.00 |

-- *Black colorband label, logo at top*

| ❏ T 1360 [M] | Most of All | 1960 | 7.50 | 15.00 | 30.00 |

-- *Black colorband label, logo at left*

| ❏ T 1360 [M] | Most of All | 1962 | 5.00 | 10.00 | 20.00 |

-- *Black colorband label, logo at top*

| ❏ ST 1469 [S] | This Broken Heart of Mine | 1960 | 10.00 | 20.00 | 40.00 |

-- *Black colorband label, logo at left*

| ❏ ST 1469 [S] | This Broken Heart of Mine | 1962 | 6.25 | 12.50 | 25.00 |

-- *Black colorband label, logo at top*

| ❏ T 1469 [M] | This Broken Heart of Mine | 1960 | 7.50 | 15.00 | 30.00 |

-- *Black colorband label, logo at left*

| ❏ T 1469 [M] | This Broken Heart of Mine | 1962 | 5.00 | 10.00 | 20.00 |

-- *Black colorband label, logo at top*

| ❏ ST 1544 [S] | An Old Love Affair | 1961 | 7.50 | 15.00 | 30.00 |

-- *Black colorband label, logo at left*

| ❏ ST 1544 [S] | An Old Love Affair | 1962 | 5.00 | 10.00 | 20.00 |

-- *Black colorband label, logo at top*

Number	Title	Yr	VG	VG+	NM
❑ T 1544 [M]	An Old Love Affair	1961	6.25	12.50	25.00
-- Black colorband label, logo at left					
❑ ST 1632 [S]	Hank Thompson at the Golden Nugget	1961	7.50	15.00	30.00
-- Black colorband label, logo at left					
❑ ST 1632 [S]	Hank Thompson at the Golden Nugget	1962	5.00	10.00	20.00
-- Black colorband label, logo at top					
❑ T 1632 [M]	Hank Thompson at the Golden Nugget	1961	6.25	12.50	25.00
-- Black colorband label, logo at left					
❑ DT 1741 [R]	The #1 Country and Western Band	1962	5.00	10.00	20.00
-- Black colorband label, logo at left					
❑ T 1741 [M]	The #1 Country and Western Band	1962	7.50	15.00	30.00
-- Black colorband label, logo at left					
❑ T 1741 [M]	The #1 Country and Western Band	1962	5.00	10.00	20.00
-- Black colorband label, logo at top					
❑ ST 1775 [S]	Cheyenne Frontier Days	1962	6.25	12.50	25.00
❑ T 1775 [M]	Cheyenne Frontier Days	1962	5.00	10.00	20.00
❑ ST 1878 [S]	The Best of Hank Thompson	1963	6.25	12.50	25.00
❑ T 1878 [M]	The Best of Hank Thompson	1963	5.00	10.00	20.00
❑ ST 1955 [S]	Hank Thompson at the State Fair of Texas	1963	6.25	12.50	25.00
❑ T 1955 [M]	Hank Thompson at the State Fair of Texas	1963	5.00	10.00	20.00
❑ ST 2089 [S]	Golden Country Hits	1964	6.25	12.50	25.00
❑ T 2089 [M]	Golden Country Hits	1964	5.00	10.00	20.00
❑ ST 2154 [S]	It's Christmas Time	1963	6.25	12.50	25.00
❑ T 2154 [M]	It's Christmas Time	1963	5.00	10.00	20.00
❑ ST 2274 [S]	Breakin' In Another Heart	1965	6.25	12.50	25.00
❑ T 2274 [M]	Breakin' In Another Heart	1965	5.00	10.00	20.00
❑ ST 2342 [S]	Luckiest Heartache in Town	1965	6.25	12.50	25.00
❑ T 2342 [M]	Luckiest Heartache in Town	1965	5.00	10.00	20.00
❑ ST 2460 [S]	A Six Pack to Go	1966	6.25	12.50	25.00
❑ T 2460 [M]	A Six Pack to Go	1966	5.00	10.00	20.00
❑ ST 2575 [S]	Breakin' the Rules	1966	6.25	12.50	25.00
❑ T 2575 [M]	Breakin' the Rules	1966	5.00	10.00	20.00
❑ ST 2661 [S]	The Best of Hank Thompson Vol. 2	1967	5.00	10.00	20.00
❑ T 2661 [M]	The Best of Hank Thompson Vol. 2	1967	6.25	12.50	25.00
❑ ST 2826 [S]	Just an Old Flame	1967	5.00	10.00	20.00
❑ T 2826 [M]	Just an Old Flame	1967	6.25	12.50	25.00
DOT					
❑ 2000 [(2)]	Hank Thompson's 25th Anniversary Album	1971	5.00	10.00	20.00
WARNER BROS.					
❑ WS 1664 [S]	Where Is the Circus and Other Heart Breakin' Hits	1966	5.00	10.00	20.00
❑ WS 1679 [S]	The Countrypolitan Sound of Hank Thompson	1967	5.00	10.00	20.00
❑ WS 1686 [S]	The Gold Standard Collection of Hank Thompson	1967	5.00	10.00	20.00

THOMPSON, HAYDEN
KAPP
Number	Title	Yr	VG	VG+	NM
❑ KL-1507 [M]	Here's Hayden Thompson	1966	7.50	15.00	30.00
❑ KS-3507 [S]	Here's Hayden Thompson	1966	10.00	20.00	40.00

THOMPSON, KAY
MGM
❑ E-3146 [M]	Kay Thompson Sings	1955	7.50	15.00	30.00
SIGNATURE					
❑ SM-1017 [M]	Let's Talk About Russia	1959	6.25	12.50	25.00

THOMPSON, MAYO
TEXAS REVOLUTION
❑ 2270	Corky's Debt to His Father	1969	20.00	40.00	80.00

THOMPSON, RICHARD
REPRISE
❑ MS 2112	Henry the Human Fly	1972	5.00	10.00	20.00

THOMPSON, RICHARD AND LINDA
ISLAND
❑ ISLA 9421 [(2)]	Bright Lights and Live! More or Less	1977	5.00	10.00	20.00
-- First U.S. issue of "I Want to See the Bright Lights Tonight" plus an LP of unreleased material					

THOMPSON, SONNY
KING
❑ 568 [M]	Moody Blues	1956	125.00	250.00	500.00
❑ 655 [M]	Mellow Blues	1959	62.50	125.00	250.00

THOMPSON, SUE
HICKORY
❑ LPM-104 [M]	Meet Sue Thompson	1962	12.50	25.00	50.00
❑ LPS-104 [S]	Meet Sue Thompson	1962	20.00	40.00	80.00

Number	Title	Yr	VG	VG+	NM
❑ LPM-107 [M]	Two of a Kind	1962	7.50	15.00	30.00
❑ LPS-107 [S]	Two of a Kind	1962	10.00	20.00	40.00
❑ LPM-111 [M]	Sue Thompson's Golden Hits	1963	7.50	15.00	30.00
❑ LPS-111 [S]	Sue Thompson's Golden Hits	1963	10.00	20.00	40.00
❑ LPM-121 [M]	Paper Tiger	1965	7.50	15.00	30.00
❑ LPS-121 [S]	Paper Tiger	1965	10.00	20.00	40.00
❑ LPM-130 [M]	Sue Thompson with Strings Attached	1966	7.50	15.00	30.00
❑ LPS-130 [S]	Sue Thompson with Strings Attached	1966	10.00	20.00	40.00
❑ LPS-148	This Is Sue Thompson Country	1969	5.00	10.00	20.00
WING					
❑ MGW-12317 [M]	The Country Side of Sue Thompson	1965	5.00	10.00	20.00

THORINSHIELD
PHILIPS
❑ PHS 600-251	Thorinshield	1968	5.00	10.00	20.00

THORNTON, BIG MAMA
ARHOOLIE
❑ F-1028 [M]	Big Mama Thornton in Europe	1966	7.50	15.00	30.00
❑ F-1032 [M]	Chicago Blues: The Queen at Monterey	1967	7.50	15.00	30.00
❑ F-1039 [M]	Ball and Chain	1968	7.50	15.00	30.00
BACK BEAT					
❑ BLP-68	She's Back	1970	6.25	12.50	25.00
MERCURY					
❑ SR-61225	Stronger Than Dirt	1969	6.25	12.50	25.00
❑ SR-61249	The Way It Is	1970	6.25	12.50	25.00
PENTAGRAM					
❑ PE-10,005	Saved	1971	5.00	10.00	20.00

THORPE, BILLY
CAPRICORN
❑ CPN 0221	Children of the Sun	1979	5.00	10.00	20.00

THREE CHUCKLES, THE
VIK
❑ LX-1067 [M]	The Three Chuckles	1956	62.50	125.00	250.00

THREE D'S, THE
CAPITOL
❑ ST 2171 [S]	New Dimensions in Folk Songs	1964	6.25	12.50	25.00
❑ T 2171 [M]	New Dimensions in Folk Songs	1964	5.00	10.00	20.00
❑ ST 2314 [S]	I Won't Be Worried Long	1965	6.25	12.50	25.00
❑ T 2314 [M]	I Won't Be Worried Long	1965	5.00	10.00	20.00

THREE DEGREES, THE
ROULETTE
❑ SR-42050	Maybe	1970	10.00	20.00	40.00

THREE DOG NIGHT
ABC DUNHILL
❑ DS-50078	It Ain't Easy	1970	25.00	50.00	100.00
-- Original cover with band members in the nude					
❑ DSD-50168	Hard Labor	1974	7.50	15.00	30.00
-- With uncensored "childbirth" front cover					
AT EASE					
❑ MD 11109	Three Dog Night: Their Greatest Recordings	1978	5.00	10.00	20.00
-- "This Album Compiled Exclusively for Military Personnel" by ABC					
COMMAND					
❑ QD-40014 [Q]	Hard Labor	1974	5.00	10.00	20.00
❑ QD-40018 [Q]	Coming Down Your Way	1975	5.00	10.00	20.00

THREE FACES WEST
OUTPOST
❑ 1000	Three Faces West	197?	5.00	10.00	20.00

THREE FLAMES, THE
MERCURY
❑ MG-20239 [M]	At the Ben Soir	1957	12.50	25.00	50.00

THREE MAN ARMY, THE
KAMA SUTRA
❑ KSBS-2044	A Third of a Lifetime	1971	7.50	15.00	30.00
-- Pink label, gatefold cover					
REPRISE					
❑ MS 2150	Three Man Army	1973	5.00	10.00	20.00
❑ MS 2182	Three Man Army Two	1974	5.00	10.00	20.00

Number	Title	Yr	VG	VG+	NM

THREE SOULS, THE
ARGO
Number	Title	Yr	VG	VG+	NM
❏ LP-4036 [M]	Dangerous Dan Express	1964	5.00	10.00	20.00
❏ LPS-4036 [S]	Dangerous Dan Express	1964	6.25	12.50	25.00
❏ LP-4044 [M]	Soul Sounds	1965	5.00	10.00	20.00
❏ LPS-4044 [S]	Soul Sounds	1965	6.25	12.50	25.00

THREE STOOGES, THE
CORAL
Number	Title	Yr	VG	VG+	NM
❏ CRL 57289 [M]	Nonsense Song Book	1959	20.00	40.00	80.00
❏ CRL 757289 [S]	Nonsense Song Book	1959	25.00	50.00	100.00
GOLDEN
| ❏ GLP-43 [M] | Madcap Musical Nonsense | 1962 | 20.00 | 40.00 | 80.00 |
PETER PAN
| ❏ 8098 | The Three Stooges | 1970 | 6.25 | 12.50 | 25.00 |
VOCALION
| ❏ VL 3823 [M] | The Three Stooges Sing for Kids | 196? | 5.00 | 10.00 | 20.00 |
| ❏ VL 73823 [S] | The Three Stooges Sing for Kids | 196? | 6.25 | 12.50 | 25.00 |

THREE SUNS, THE
RCA VICTOR
Number	Title	Yr	VG	VG+	NM
❏ LPM-3 [10]	Three-Quarter Time	1951	12.50	25.00	50.00
❏ LPM-28 [10]	Hands Across the Table	1951	12.50	25.00	50.00
❏ LPM-52 [10]	Christmas Favorites	1951	12.50	25.00	50.00
❏ LPM-1041 [M]	Soft and Sweet	1955	7.50	15.00	30.00
❏ LPM-1132 [M]	Sounds of Christmas	1955	7.50	15.00	30.00
❏ LPM-1171 [M]	Twilight Time	1956	7.50	15.00	30.00
❏ LPM-1173 [M]	My Reverie	1956	7.50	15.00	30.00
❏ LPM-1219 [M]	Slumber Time	1956	7.50	15.00	30.00
❏ LPM-1220 [M]	Malaguena	1956	7.50	15.00	30.00
❏ LPM-1249 [M]	High Fi and Wide	1956	7.50	15.00	30.00
❏ LPM-1316 [M]	Easy Listening	1956	7.50	15.00	30.00
❏ LPM-1333 [M]	Midnight for Two	1957	7.50	15.00	30.00
❏ LPM-1543 [M]	The Things in Love in Hi-Fi	1958	5.00	10.00	20.00
❏ LSP-1543 [S]	The Things in Love in Hi-Fi	1958	7.50	15.00	30.00
❏ LPM-1578 [M]	Let's Dance with the Three Suns	1958	5.00	10.00	20.00
❏ LSP-1578 [S]	Let's Dance with the Three Suns	1958	7.50	15.00	30.00
❏ LPM-1669 [M]	Love in the Afternoon	1959	5.00	10.00	20.00
❏ LSP-1669 [S]	Love in the Afternoon	1959	7.50	15.00	30.00
❏ LPM-1734 [M]	Having a Ball with the Three Suns	1959	5.00	10.00	20.00
❏ LSP-1734 [S]	Having a Ball with the Three Suns	1959	7.50	15.00	30.00
❏ LPM-1964 [M]	Swingin' on a Star	1959	5.00	10.00	20.00
❏ LSP-1964 [S]	Swingin' on a Star	1959	7.50	15.00	30.00
❏ LPM-2054 [M]	A Ding Dong Dandy Christmas!	1959	5.00	10.00	20.00
❏ LSP-2054 [S]	A Ding Dong Dandy Christmas!	1959	7.50	15.00	30.00
❏ LPM-2120 [M]	Twilight Memories	1960	5.00	10.00	20.00
❏ LSP-2120 [S]	Twilight Memories	1960	6.25	12.50	25.00
❏ LPM-2235 [M]	On a Magic Carpet	1960	5.00	10.00	20.00
❏ LSP-2235 [S]	On a Magic Carpet	1960	6.25	12.50	25.00
❏ LPM-2307 [M]	Dancing on a Cloud	1961	5.00	10.00	20.00
❏ LSP-2307 [S]	Dancing on a Cloud	1961	6.25	12.50	25.00
❏ LPM-2310 [M]	Fever and Smoke	1961	5.00	10.00	20.00
❏ LSP-2310 [S]	Fever and Smoke	1961	6.25	12.50	25.00
❏ LPM-2437 [M]	Fun in the Sun	1961	5.00	10.00	20.00
❏ LSP-2437 [S]	Fun in the Sun	1961	6.25	12.50	25.00
❏ LPM-2532 [M]	Movin' 'N' Groovin'	1962	5.00	10.00	20.00
❏ LSP-2532 [S]	Movin' 'N' Groovin'	1962	6.25	12.50	25.00
❏ LPM-2617 [M]	Warm and Tender	1962	5.00	10.00	20.00
❏ LSP-2617 [S]	Warm and Tender	1962	6.25	12.50	25.00
❏ LSP-2717 [S]	Everything Under the Sun	1963	5.00	10.00	20.00
❏ LSP-2904 [S]	One Enchanted Evening	1964	5.00	10.00	20.00
❏ LSP-2963 [S]	A Swingin' Thing	1964	5.00	10.00	20.00
❏ LPM-3012 [10]	Twilight Moods	1952	12.50	25.00	50.00
❏ LPM-3034 [10]	The Three Suns Present	1952	12.50	25.00	50.00
❏ LPM-3040 [10]	Busy Fingers	1952	12.50	25.00	50.00
❏ LPM-3056 [10]	Christmas Party	1952	12.50	25.00	50.00
❏ LPM-3075 [10]	Slumbertime	1953	12.50	25.00	50.00
❏ LPM-3113 [10]	Pops Concert Favorites	1953	12.50	25.00	50.00
❏ LPM-3125 [10]	Mods	1953	12.50	25.00	50.00
❏ LPM-3130 [10]	Top Pops	1953	12.50	25.00	50.00
❏ LPM-3146 [10]	Polka Time	1954	12.50	25.00	50.00
❏ LPM-3174 [10]	Sacred Hymns	1954	12.50	25.00	50.00
❏ LSP-3354 [S]	Country Music Shindig	1965	5.00	10.00	20.00
❏ LSP-3447 [S]	The Best of the Three Suns	1965	5.00	10.00	20.00
ROYALE
| ❏ 1 [10] | Twilight Time | 1951 | 12.50 | 25.00 | 50.00 |
| ❏ 29 [10] | Midnight Time | 1951 | 12.50 | 25.00 | 50.00 |
VARSITY
| ❏ VLP-6001 [10] | Twilight Time | 1950 | 12.50 | 25.00 | 50.00 |
| ❏ VLP-6048 [10] | Midnight Time | 1950 | 12.50 | 25.00 | 50.00 |

THRILLINGTON, PERCY "THRILLS" -- See PAUL McCARTNEY.

THUDPUCKER, JIMMY
WINDSONG
Number	Title	Yr	VG	VG+	NM
❏ BXL1-2589	Greatest Hits	1977	5.00	10.00	20.00

THUNDER & ROSES
UNITED ARTISTS
Number	Title	Yr	VG	VG+	NM
❏ UAS-6709	King of the Black Sunrise	1969	7.50	15.00	30.00

THUNDER, JOHNNY
DIAMOND
| ❏ D-5001 [M] | Loop De Loop | 1963 | 25.00 | 50.00 | 100.00 |
| ❏ DS-5001 [S] | Loop De Loop | 1963 | 37.50 | 75.00 | 150.00 |

THUNDERBIRDS, THE
RED FEATHER
| ❏ TH-1 [M] | Meet the Fabulous Thunderbirds | 1964 | 50.00 | 100.00 | 200.00 |

THUNDERCLAP NEWMAN
TRACK
| ❏ SD 8264 | Hollywood Dream | 1970 | 6.25 | 12.50 | 25.00 |

THUNDERPUSSY
M.R.T.
| ❏ 31748 | Documents of Captivity | 1973 | 37.50 | 75.00 | 150.00 |

THUNDERTREE
ROULETTE
| ❏ SR-42038 | Thundertree | 1970 | 7.50 | 15.00 | 30.00 |

TIDE, THE
MOUTH
| ❏ 7237 | Almost Live | 1971 | 12.50 | 25.00 | 50.00 |

TIDES, THE
MERCURY
| ❏ SR-60714 [S] | Limbo Rock | 1962 | 5.00 | 10.00 | 20.00 |
WING
❏ MGW-12265 [M]	Surf City and Other Surfin' Favorites	1963	6.25	12.50	25.00
❏ SRW-16248 [S]	The Best of Bossa Nova	1963	5.00	10.00	20.00
❏ SRW-16265 [S]	Surf City and Other Surfin' Favorites	1963	7.50	15.00	30.00

TIEKEN, FREDDIE, AND THE ROCKERS
I.T.
| ❏ 2301 [M] | By Popular Demand | 1957 | 12.50 | 25.00 | 50.00 |
| ❏ 2304 [M] | Freddie Tieken and the Rockers | 1958 | 12.50 | 25.00 | 50.00 |

TIFFANY SHADE, THE
MAINSTREAM
| ❏ S-6105 | The Tiffany Shade | 1968 | 25.00 | 50.00 | 100.00 |

TIKIS, THE
Probably two different groups.
MINARET
| ❏ TLP-7001 [M] | The Tikis | 196? | 25.00 | 50.00 | 100.00 |
PHILIPS
| ❏ PHM 200-043 [M] | The Tikis | 1962 | 6.25 | 12.50 | 25.00 |
| ❏ PHS 600-043 [S] | The Tikis | 1962 | 7.50 | 15.00 | 30.00 |

TIL, SONNY
Also see THE ORIOLES.
RCA VICTOR
| ❏ LSP-4451 | Sonny Til Returns | 1970 | 5.00 | 10.00 | 20.00 |

TILLIS, MEL
COLUMBIA
| ❏ CL 1724 [M] | Heart Over Mind and Other Big Country Hits | 1962 | 7.50 | 15.00 | 30.00 |
| ❏ CS 8524 [S] | Heart Over Mind and Other Big Country Hits | 1962 | 10.00 | 20.00 | 40.00 |
KAPP
| ❏ KS-3492 [S] | Stateside | 1966 | 5.00 | 10.00 | 20.00 |
| ❏ KS-3514 [S] | Life Turned Her That Way | 1967 | 5.00 | 10.00 | 20.00 |

TILLIS, PAM
WARNER BROS.
| ❏ 23871 | Above and Beyond the Doll of Cutey | 1983 | 6.25 | 12.50 | 25.00 |

Number	Title	Yr	VG	VG+	NM

TILLMAN, FLOYD
CIMARRON
| ❑ C-2003 [M] | Let's Make Memories | 1962 | 12.50 | 25.00 | 50.00 |

HARMONY
| ❑ HL 7316 [M] | Floyd Tillman's Best | 1964 | 6.25 | 12.50 | 25.00 |
| ❑ HS 11297 | I'll Still Be Lovin' You | 1969 | 6.25 | 12.50 | 25.00 |

MUSICOR
❑ MM-2136 [M]	Floyd Tillman's Country	1967	5.00	10.00	20.00
❑ MS-3136 [S]	Floyd Tillman's Country	1967	6.25	12.50	25.00
❑ MS-3157	Dream On	1968	5.00	10.00	20.00

RCA VICTOR
| ❑ LPM-1686 [M] | Floyd Tillman's Greatest | 1958 | 15.00 | 30.00 | 60.00 |

STARDAY
| ❑ SLP-310 [M] | Let's Make Memories | 1965 | 7.50 | 15.00 | 30.00 |

TILLOTSON, JOHNNY
AMOS
| ❑ 7006 | Tears on My Pillow | 1969 | 5.00 | 10.00 | 20.00 |

CADENCE
❑ CLP-3052 [M]	Johnny Tillotson's Best	1961	10.00	20.00	40.00
-- Maroon and silver label					
❑ CLP-3052 [M]	Johnny Tillotson's Best	1962	6.25	12.50	25.00
-- Red and black label					
❑ CLP-3058 [M]	It Keeps Right On a-Hurtin'	1962	7.50	15.00	30.00
❑ CLP-3067 [M]	You Can Never Stop Me Loving You	1963	7.50	15.00	30.00
❑ CLP-25052 [P]	Johnny Tillotson's Best	1961	12.50	25.00	50.00
-- Maroon and silver label					
❑ CLP-25052 [P]	Johnny Tillotson's Best	1962	7.50	15.00	30.00
-- Red and black label					
❑ CLP-25058 [S]	It Keeps Right On a-Hurtin'	1962	10.00	20.00	40.00
❑ CLP-25067 [P]	You Can Never Stop Me Loving You	1963	10.00	20.00	40.00

METRO
| ❑ MS-561 [S] | Johnny Tillotson Sings Tillotson | 1967 | 5.00 | 10.00 | 20.00 |

MGM
❑ E-4188 [M]	Talk Back Trembling Lips	1964	5.00	10.00	20.00
❑ SE-4188 [S]	Talk Back Trembling Lips	1964	6.25	12.50	25.00
❑ E-4224 [M]	The Tillotson Touch	1964	5.00	10.00	20.00
❑ SE-4224 [S]	The Tillotson Touch	1964	6.25	12.50	25.00
❑ E-4270 [M]	She Understands Me	1965	5.00	10.00	20.00
❑ SE-4270 [S]	She Understands Me	1965	6.25	12.50	25.00
❑ E-4302 [M]	That's My Style	1965	5.00	10.00	20.00
❑ SE-4302 [S]	That's My Style	1965	6.25	12.50	25.00
❑ E-4328 [M]	Our World	1965	5.00	10.00	20.00
❑ SE-4328 [S]	Our World	1965	6.25	12.50	25.00
❑ E-4395 [M]	No Love at All	1966	5.00	10.00	20.00
❑ SE-4395 [S]	No Love at All	1966	6.25	12.50	25.00
❑ E-4402 [M]	The Christmas Touch	1966	5.00	10.00	20.00
❑ SE-4402 [S]	The Christmas Touch	1966	6.25	12.50	25.00
❑ E-4452 [M]	Here I Am	1967	5.00	10.00	20.00
❑ SE-4452 [S]	Here I Am	1967	6.25	12.50	25.00
❑ SE-4532	The Best of Johnny Tillotson	1968	5.00	10.00	20.00
❑ ST 90410 [S]	The Tillotson Touch	1965	7.50	15.00	30.00
-- Capitol Record Club edition					
❑ T 90410 [M]	The Tillotson Touch	1965	7.50	15.00	30.00
-- Capitol Record Club edition					

TIMBER CREEK
RENEGADE
| ❑ 95014 | Hellbound Highway | 1975 | 37.50 | 75.00 | 150.00 |

TIMMOTHY
PEAR
| ❑ (# unknown) | Strange But True | 1972 | 50.00 | 100.00 | 200.00 |

TIN HOUSE
EPIC
| ❑ E 30511 | Tin House | 1971 | 5.00 | 10.00 | 20.00 |

TINGLING MOTHER'S CIRCUS
MUSICOR
| ❑ MS-3167 | Circus of the Mind | 1968 | 6.25 | 12.50 | 25.00 |

TINO AND THE REVLONS
DEARBORN
| ❑ 1004 | By Request at the Sway-Zee | 1966 | 50.00 | 100.00 | 200.00 |

TIPTON, CARL
SIMS
| ❑ LP-143 [M] | The Carl Tipton Show | 196? | 10.00 | 20.00 | 40.00 |

TITANS, THE
MGM
| ❑ E-3992 [M] | Today's Teen Beat | 1961 | 7.50 | 15.00 | 30.00 |
| ❑ SE-3992 [S] | Today's Teen Beat | 1961 | 10.00 | 20.00 | 40.00 |

TITUS GROAN
JANUS
| ❑ JLS-3024 | Titus Groan | 1971 | 7.50 | 15.00 | 30.00 |

TITUS OATES
LIPS
| ❑ (no #) | Jungle Lady | 1974 | 50.00 | 100.00 | 200.00 |

TJADER, CAL
CRYSTAL CLEAR
| ❑ 8003 | Huracan | 1978 | 6.25 | 12.50 | 25.00 |
| -- Direct-to-disc recording | | | | | |

FANTASY
❑ 3-9 [10]	The Cal Tjader Trio	1953	37.50	75.00	150.00
-- Any of various non-black vinyl pressings					
❑ 3-9 [10]	The Cal Tjader Trio	1953	25.00	50.00	100.00
-- Black vinyl					
❑ 3-17 [10]	Ritmo Caliente	1954	37.50	75.00	150.00
-- Any of various non-black vinyl pressings					
❑ 3-17 [10]	Ritmo Caliente	1954	25.00	50.00	100.00
-- Black vinyl					
❑ 3202 [M]	Mambo with Tjader	1955	25.00	50.00	100.00
-- Red vinyl					
❑ 3202 [M]	Mambo with Tjader	1956	12.50	25.00	50.00
-- Black vinyl, red label, non-flexible vinyl					
❑ 3202 [M]	Mambo with Tjader	196?	6.25	12.50	25.00
-- Black vinyl, red label, flexible vinyl					
❑ 3211 [M]	Tjader Plays Tjazz	1956	25.00	50.00	100.00
-- Red vinyl					
❑ 3211 [M]	Tjader Plays Tjazz	1956	12.50	25.00	50.00
-- Black vinyl, red label, non-flexible vinyl					
❑ 3216 [M]	Ritmo Caliente	1956	25.00	50.00	100.00
-- Red vinyl					
❑ 3216 [M]	Ritmo Caliente	1956	12.50	25.00	50.00
-- Black vinyl, red label, non-flexible vinyl					
❑ 3216 [M]	Ritmo Caliente	196?	6.25	12.50	25.00
-- Black vinyl, red label, flexible vinyl					
❑ 3221 [M]	Tjader Plays Mambo	1956	25.00	50.00	100.00
-- Red vinyl					
❑ 3221 [M]	Tjader Plays Mambo	1956	12.50	25.00	50.00
-- Black vinyl, red label, non-flexible vinyl					
❑ 3221 [M]	Tjader Plays Mambo	196?	6.25	12.50	25.00
-- Black vinyl, red label, flexible vinyl					
❑ 3227 [M]	Cal Tjader Quartet	1956	25.00	50.00	100.00
-- Red vinyl					
❑ 3232 [M]	The Cal Tjader Quintet	1956	25.00	50.00	100.00
-- Red vinyl					
❑ 3232 [M]	The Cal Tjader Quintet	1956	12.50	25.00	50.00
-- Black vinyl, red label, non-flexible vinyl					
❑ 3232 [M]	The Cal Tjader Quintet	196?	6.25	12.50	25.00
-- Black vinyl, red label, flexible vinyl					
❑ 3241 [M]	Jazz at the Blackhawk	1957	12.50	25.00	50.00
-- Red vinyl					
❑ 3241 [M]	Jazz at the Blackhawk	1957	7.50	15.00	30.00
-- Black vinyl, red label, non-flexible vinyl					
❑ 3250 [M]	Latin Kick	1957	12.50	25.00	50.00
-- Red vinyl					
❑ 3250 [M]	Latin Kick	1957	7.50	15.00	30.00
-- Black vinyl, red label, non-flexible vinyl					
❑ 3262 [M]	Mas Ritmo Caliente	1958	12.50	25.00	50.00
-- Red vinyl					
❑ 3262 [M]	Mas Ritmo Caliente	1958	7.50	15.00	30.00
-- Black vinyl, red label, non-flexible vinyl					
❑ 3271 [M]	San Francisco Moods	1958	12.50	25.00	50.00
-- Red vinyl					
❑ 3271 [M]	San Francisco Moods	1958	7.50	15.00	30.00
-- Black vinyl, red label, non-flexible vinyl					
❑ 3275 [M]	Cal Tjader's Latin Concert	1958	12.50	25.00	50.00
-- Red vinyl					
❑ 3275 [M]	Cal Tjader's Latin Concert	1958	7.50	15.00	30.00
-- Black vinyl, red label, non-flexible vinyl					
❑ 3278 [M]	Tjader Plays Tjazz	1958	12.50	25.00	50.00
-- Red vinyl; reissue of 3211					
❑ 3278 [M]	Tjader Plays Tjazz	1958	7.50	15.00	30.00
❑ 3279 [M]	Latin for Lovers	1958	12.50	25.00	50.00
-- Red vinyl					
❑ 3279 [M]	Latin for Lovers	1958	7.50	15.00	30.00
-- Black vinyl, red label, non-flexible vinyl					
❑ 3283 [M]	A Night at the Blackhawk	1959	12.50	25.00	50.00
-- Red vinyl					

Number	Title	Yr	VG	VG+	NM
❏ 3283 [M]	A Night at the Blackhawk	1959	7.50	15.00	30.00
-- Black vinyl, red label, non-flexible vinyl					
❏ 3289 [M]	Tjader Goes Latin	1959	12.50	25.00	50.00
-- Red vinyl					
❏ 3289 [M]	Tjader Goes Latin	1959	7.50	15.00	30.00
-- Black vinyl, red label, non-flexible vinyl					
❏ 3295 [M]	Concert by the Sea	1959	12.50	25.00	50.00
-- Red vinyl					
❏ 3295 [M]	Concert by the Sea	1959	7.50	15.00	30.00
-- Black vinyl, red label, non-flexible vinyl					
❏ 3299 [M]	Concert on the Campus	1960	10.00	20.00	40.00
-- Red vinyl					
❏ 3299 [M]	Concert on the Campus	1960	6.25	12.50	25.00
-- Black vinyl, red label, non-flexible vinyl					
❏ 3307 [M]	Cal Tjader Quartet	1960	10.00	20.00	40.00
-- Red vinyl					
❏ 3307 [M]	Cal Tjader Quartet	1960	6.25	12.50	25.00
-- Black vinyl, red label, non-flexible vinyl					
❏ 3309 [M]	Demasiado Caliente	1960	10.00	20.00	40.00
-- Red vinyl					
❏ 3309 [M]	Demasiado Caliente	1960	6.25	12.50	25.00
-- Black vinyl, red label, non-flexible vinyl					
❏ 3310 [M]	West Side Story	1960	10.00	20.00	40.00
-- Red vinyl					
❏ 3310 [M]	West Side Story	1960	6.25	12.50	25.00
-- Black vinyl, red label, non-flexible vinyl					
❏ 3313 [M]	Cal Tjader Quintet	1961	10.00	20.00	40.00
-- Red vinyl; evidently a different album than 3232					
❏ 3313 [M]	Cal Tjader Quintet	1961	6.25	12.50	25.00
-- Black vinyl, red label, non-flexible vinyl					
❏ 3315 [M]	Cal Tjader Live and Direct	1961	10.00	20.00	40.00
-- Red vinyl					
❏ 3315 [M]	Cal Tjader Live and Direct	1961	6.25	12.50	25.00
-- Black vinyl, red label, non-flexible vinyl					
❏ 3326 [M]	Mambo	1961	10.00	20.00	40.00
-- Red vinyl					
❏ 3326 [M]	Mambo	1961	6.25	12.50	25.00
-- Black vinyl, red label, non-flexible vinyl					
❏ 3330 [M]	Cal Tjader Plays the Harold Arlen Songbook	1961	10.00	20.00	40.00
-- Red vinyl					
❏ 3330 [M]	Cal Tjader Plays the Harold Arlen Songbook	1961	6.25	12.50	25.00
-- Black vinyl, red label, non-flexible vinyl					
❏ 3339 [M]	Latino	1962	10.00	20.00	40.00
-- Red vinyl					
❏ 3339 [M]	Latino	1962	6.25	12.50	25.00
-- Black vinyl, red label, non-flexible vinyl					
❏ 3341 [M]	Concert by the Sea, Volume 2	1962	10.00	20.00	40.00
-- Red vinyl					
❏ 3341 [M]	Concert by the Sea, Volume 2	1962	6.25	12.50	25.00
-- Black vinyl, red label, non-flexible vinyl					
❏ 8003 [S]	Mas Ritmo Caliente	196?	7.50	15.00	30.00
-- Blue vinyl					
❏ 8003 [S]	Mas Ritmo Caliente	196?	5.00	10.00	20.00
-- Black vinyl, blue label, non-flexible vinyl					
❏ 8014 [S]	Cal Tjader's Latin Concert	196?	7.50	15.00	30.00
-- Blue vinyl					
❏ 8014 [S]	Cal Tjader's Latin Concert	196?	5.00	10.00	20.00
-- Black vinyl, blue label, non-flexible vinyl					
❏ 8016 [S]	Latin for Lovers	196?	7.50	15.00	30.00
-- Blue vinyl					
❏ 8016 [S]	Latin for Lovers	196?	5.00	10.00	20.00
-- Black vinyl, blue label, non-flexible vinyl					
❏ 8017 [S]	San Francisco Moods	196?	7.50	15.00	30.00
-- Blue vinyl					
❏ 8017 [S]	San Francisco Moods	196?	5.00	10.00	20.00
-- Black vinyl, blue label, non-flexible vinyl					
❏ 8019 [S]	Latin for Dancers	196?	25.00	50.00	100.00
-- Blue vinyl; the existence of this has been confirmed. Black vinyl copies of 8019 are unknown.					
❏ 8026 [S]	A Night at the Blackhawk	196?	7.50	15.00	30.00
-- Blue vinyl					
❏ 8026 [S]	A Night at the Blackhawk	196?	5.00	10.00	20.00
-- Black vinyl, blue label, non-flexible vinyl					
❏ 8030 [S]	Tjader Goes Latin	196?	7.50	15.00	30.00
-- Blue vinyl					
❏ 8030 [S]	Tjader Goes Latin	196?	5.00	10.00	20.00
-- Black vinyl, blue label, non-flexible vinyl					
❏ 8033 [S]	Latin Kick	196?	7.50	15.00	30.00
-- Blue vinyl					
❏ 8033 [S]	Latin Kick	196?	5.00	10.00	20.00
-- Black vinyl, blue label, non-flexible vinyl					
❏ 8038 [S]	Concert by the Sea	196?	7.50	15.00	30.00
-- Blue vinyl					
❏ 8038 [S]	Concert by the Sea	196?	5.00	10.00	20.00
-- Black vinyl, blue label, non-flexible vinyl					
❏ 8044 [S]	Concert on the Campus	196?	7.50	15.00	30.00
-- Blue vinyl					
❏ 8044 [S]	Concert on the Campus	196?	5.00	10.00	20.00
-- Black vinyl, blue label, non-flexible vinyl					
❏ 8053 [S]	Demasiado Caliente	196?	7.50	15.00	30.00
-- Blue vinyl					
❏ 8053 [S]	Demasiado Caliente	196?	5.00	10.00	20.00
-- Black vinyl, blue label, non-flexible vinyl					

Number	Title	Yr	VG	VG+	NM
❏ 8054 [S]	West Side Story	196?	7.50	15.00	30.00
-- Blue vinyl					
❏ 8054 [S]	West Side Story	196?	5.00	10.00	20.00
-- Black vinyl, blue label, non-flexible vinyl					
❏ 8057 [S]	Mambo	1962	7.50	15.00	30.00
-- Blue vinyl					
❏ 8057 [S]	Mambo	1962	5.00	10.00	20.00
-- Black vinyl, blue label, non-flexible vinyl					
❏ 8059 [S]	Cal Tjader Live and Direct	1962	7.50	15.00	30.00
-- Blue vinyl					
❏ 8059 [S]	Cal Tjader Live and Direct	1962	5.00	10.00	20.00
-- Black vinyl, blue label, non-flexible vinyl					
❏ 8072 [S]	Cal Tjader Plays the Harold Arlen Songbook	1962	7.50	15.00	30.00
-- Blue vinyl					
❏ 8072 [S]	Cal Tjader Plays the Harold Arlen Songbook	1962	5.00	10.00	20.00
-- Black vinyl, blue label, non-flexible vinyl					
❏ 8077 [R]	Ritmo Caliente	1962	7.50	15.00	30.00
-- Blue vinyl					
❏ 8077 [R]	Ritmo Caliente	1962	5.00	10.00	20.00
-- Black vinyl, blue label, non-flexible vinyl					
❏ 8079 [S]	Latino	1962	7.50	15.00	30.00
-- Blue vinyl					
❏ 8079 [S]	Latino	1962	5.00	10.00	20.00
-- Black vinyl, blue label, non-flexible vinyl					
❏ 8083 [R]	Cal Tjader Quartet	1962	7.50	15.00	30.00
-- Blue vinyl					
❏ 8083 [R]	Cal Tjader Quartet	1962	5.00	10.00	20.00
-- Black vinyl, blue label, non-flexible vinyl					
❏ 8084 [S]	Cal Tjader Quintet	1962	7.50	15.00	30.00
-- Blue vinyl; stereo version of 3313					
❏ 8084 [S]	Cal Tjader Quintet	1962	5.00	10.00	20.00
-- Black vinyl, blue label, non-flexible vinyl					
❏ 8085 [R]	The Cal Tjader Quintet	196?	7.50	15.00	30.00
-- Blue vinyl; stereo version of 3232					
❏ 8085 [R]	The Cal Tjader Quintet	196?	5.00	10.00	20.00
-- Black vinyl, blue label, non-flexible vinyl					
❏ 8096 [R]	Jazz at the Blackhawk	1962	7.50	15.00	30.00
-- Blue vinyl					
❏ 8096 [R]	Jazz at the Blackhawk	1962	5.00	10.00	20.00
-- Black vinyl, blue label, non-flexible vinyl					
❏ 8097 [R]	Tjader Plays Tjazz	1962	7.50	15.00	30.00
-- Blue vinyl					
❏ 8097 [R]	Tjader Plays Tjazz	1962	5.00	10.00	20.00
-- Black vinyl, blue label, non-flexible vinyl					
❏ 8098 [S]	Concert by the Sea, Volume 2	1962	7.50	15.00	30.00
-- Blue vinyl					
❏ 8098 [S]	Concert by the Sea, Volume 2	1962	5.00	10.00	20.00
-- Black vinyl, blue label, non-flexible vinyl					

SAVOY

Number	Title	Yr	VG	VG+	NM
❏ MG-9036 [10]	Cal Tjader -- Vibist	1954	25.00	50.00	100.00
❏ 12054 [M]	Vib-Rations	1956	10.00	20.00	40.00

VERVE

Number	Title	Yr	VG	VG+	NM
❏ V-8419 [M]	In a Latin Bag	1961	5.00	10.00	20.00
❏ V6-8419 [S]	In a Latin Bag	1961	6.25	12.50	25.00
❏ V-8459 [M]	Saturday Night...Sunday Night at the Blackhawk	1962	5.00	10.00	20.00
❏ V6-8459 [S]	Saturday Night...Sunday Night at the Blackhawk	1962	6.25	12.50	25.00
❏ V-8470 [M]	The Contemporary Music of Mexico and Brazil	1962	5.00	10.00	20.00
❏ V6-8470 [S]	The Contemporary Music of Mexico and Brazil	1962	6.25	12.50	25.00
❏ V-8507 [M]	Several Shades of Jade	1963	5.00	10.00	20.00
❏ V6-8507 [S]	Several Shades of Jade	1963	6.25	12.50	25.00
❏ V-8531 [M]	Sona Libre	1963	5.00	10.00	20.00
❏ V6-8531 [S]	Sona Libre	1963	6.25	12.50	25.00
❏ V-8575 [M]	Breeze from the East	1964	5.00	10.00	20.00
❏ V6-8575 [S]	Breeze from the East	1964	6.25	12.50	25.00
❏ V-8585 [M]	Warm Wave	1964	5.00	10.00	20.00
❏ V6-8585 [S]	Warm Wave	1964	6.25	12.50	25.00
❏ V-8614 [M]	Soul Sauce	1965	5.00	10.00	20.00
❏ V6-8614 [S]	Soul Sauce	1965	6.25	12.50	25.00
❏ V-8626 [M]	Soul Bird: Whippenpoof	1965	5.00	10.00	20.00
❏ V6-8626 [S]	Soul Bird: Whippenpoof	1965	6.25	12.50	25.00
❏ V-8637 [M]	Soul Burst	1965	5.00	10.00	20.00
❏ V6-8637 [S]	Soul Burst	1965	6.25	12.50	25.00
❏ V6-8651 [S]	El Soni Do Nuevo -- The New Soul Sound	1966	5.00	10.00	20.00
❏ V6-8671 [S]	Along Comes Cal	1966	5.00	10.00	20.00
❏ V6-8725 [S]	The Best of Cal Tjader	1967	5.00	10.00	20.00
❏ V-8730 [M]	Hip Vibrations	1967	5.00	10.00	20.00

TJADER, CAL, AND STAN GETZ

Also see each artist's individual listings.

FANTASY

Number	Title	Yr	VG	VG+	NM
❏ 3266 [M]	Cal Tjader-Stan Getz Sextet	1958	12.50	25.00	50.00
-- Red vinyl					

Number	Title	Yr	VG	VG+	NM
❑ 3266 [M]	Cal Tjader-Stan Getz Sextet	1958	7.50	15.00	30.00
-- Black vinyl, red label, non-flexible vinyl					
❑ 8005 [S]	Cal Tjader-Stan Getz Sextet	196?	7.50	15.00	30.00
-- Blue vinyl					
❑ 8005 [S]	Cal Tjader-Stan Getz Sextet	196?	5.00	10.00	20.00
-- Black vinyl, blue label, non-flexible vinyl					

TOAD HALL
LIBERTY
❑ LST-7580	Toad Hall	1968	6.25	12.50	25.00

TOAD THE WET SPROCKET
COLUMBIA
❑ C 46060	Pale	1990	7.50	15.00	30.00
-- Marbled white (almost greenish) vinyl					
❑ C 47309	Fear	1991	5.00	10.00	20.00

TOADS, THE
WIGGINS
❑ 64021 [M]	The Toads	1964	75.00	150.00	300.00

TODD, ART AND DOTTY
DART
❑ D-444 [M]	Black Velvet Eyes	1959	10.00	20.00	40.00
DOT
❑ DLP-3742 [M]	Chanson d'Amour (Song of Love)	1966	6.25	12.50	25.00
❑ DLP-25742 [S]	Chanson d'Amour (Song of Love)	1966	7.50	15.00	30.00

TOE FAT
RARE EARTH
❑ RS-511	Toe Fat	1970	6.25	12.50	25.00
❑ RS-525	Toe Fat Two	1971	6.25	12.50	25.00

TOKENS, THE
B.T. PUPPY
❑ BTP-1000 [M]	I Hear Trumpets Blow	1966	5.00	10.00	20.00
❑ BTPS-1000 [S]	I Hear Trumpets Blow	1966	6.25	12.50	25.00
❑ BTPS-1006	Tokens of Gold	1969	6.25	12.50	25.00
❑ BTPS-1012	Greatest Moments	1970	6.25	12.50	25.00
❑ BTPS-1014	December 5th	1971	50.00	100.00	200.00
❑ BTPS-1027	Intercourse	1971	150.00	300.00	600.00
DIPLOMAT
❑ D-2308 [M]	Kings of the Hot Rods	196?	6.25	12.50	25.00
❑ DS-2308 [S]	Kings of the Hot Rods	196?	7.50	15.00	30.00
RCA VICTOR
❑ LPM-2514 [M]	The Lion Sleeps Tonight	1961	20.00	40.00	80.00
❑ LSP-2514 [S]	The Lion Sleeps Tonight	1961	37.50	75.00	150.00
❑ LPM-2631 [M]	We, The Tokens, Sing Folk	1962	10.00	20.00	40.00
❑ LSP-2631 [S]	We, The Tokens, Sing Folk	1962	12.50	25.00	50.00
❑ LPM-2886 [M]	Wheels	1964	20.00	40.00	80.00
❑ LSP-2886 [S]	Wheels	1964	25.00	50.00	100.00
❑ LPM-3685 [M]	The Tokens Again	1966	10.00	20.00	40.00
❑ LSP-3685 [S]	The Tokens Again	1966	12.50	25.00	50.00
WARNER BROS.
❑ W 1685 [M]	It's a Happening World	1967	6.25	12.50	25.00
❑ WS 1685 [S]	It's a Happening World	1967	5.00	10.00	20.00

TOKENS, THE & THE HAPPENINGS
Also see each artist's individual listings.
B.T. PUPPY
❑ BTP-1002 [M]	Back to Back	1967	6.00	10.00	20.00
-- Half this LP is by the Tokens, the other half by the Happenings					
❑ BTPS-1002 [S]	Back to Back	1967	6.25	12.50	25.00

TOLBERT, ISRAEL
WARREN/STAX
❑ STS-2038	Popper Stopper	1971	10.00	20.00	40.00
-- Cover says "Warren Records Distributed by Stax," label is Stax					

TOLKIEN, J.R.R.
CAEDMON
❑ TC 1478	J.R.R. Tolkien Reads and Sings His "The Lord of the Rings"	1975	5.00	10.00	20.00

TOM & JERRY
MERCURY
❑ MG-20626 [M]	Guitar's Greatest Hits	1961	7.50	15.00	30.00
❑ MG-20671 [M]	Guitars Play the Sound of Ray Charles	1962	7.50	15.00	30.00
❑ MG-20756 [M]	Guitar's Greatest Hits, Vol. 2	1962	7.50	15.00	30.00
❑ MG-20842 [M]	Surfin' Hootenanny	1963	10.00	20.00	40.00
❑ SR-60626 [S]	Guitar's Greatest Hits	1961	10.00	20.00	40.00
❑ SR-60671 [S]	Guitars Play the Sound of Ray Charles	1962	10.00	20.00	40.00
❑ SR-60756 [S]	Guitar's Greatest Hits, Vol. 2	1962	10.00	20.00	40.00
❑ SR-60842 [S]	Surfin' Hootenanny	1963	12.50	25.00	50.00

TOM TOM CLUB
Spin-off group from TALKING HEADS.
WARNER BROS.
❑ WBMS-120 [DJ]	Wordy Rapping with the Tom Tom Club	1986	6.25	12.50	25.00
-- Part of "The Warner Bros. Music Show"; promo only					

TOMMY AND THE TWISTERS
REGENT
❑ MG-6104 [M]	Let's All Do the Twist	1961	10.00	20.00	40.00

TOMORROW
SIRE
❑ SES-97912	Tomorrow	1968	15.00	30.00	60.00

TOMPALL AND THE GLASER BROTHERS -- See TOMPALL GLASER.

TONEY, OSCAR, JR.
BELL
❑ 6006 [M]	For Your Precious Love	1967	6.25	12.50	25.00
❑ S-6006 [S]	For Your Precious Love	1967	7.50	15.00	30.00

TONGUE
HEMISPHERE
❑ HIS-101	Tongue	1970	7.50	15.00	30.00

TONGUE AND GROOVE
FONTANA
❑ SRF-67593	Tongue and Groove	1968	5.00	10.00	20.00

TONTO'S EXPANDING HEAD BAND
EMBRYO
❑ SD 732	Zero Time	1971	5.00	10.00	20.00

TOO MUCH JOY
STONEGARDEN
❑ SGN-901	Green Eggs and Crack	1987	50.00	100.00	200.00

TOP DRAWER
WISH BONE
❑ 721207	Solid Oak	1969	100.00	200.00	400.00

TOPSIDERS, THE
JOSIE
❑ JOZ-4000 [M]	Rock Goes Folk	1963	6.25	12.50	25.00

TORME, MEL
ATLANTIC
❑ 8066 [M]	Mel Torme at the Red Hill Inn	1962	7.50	15.00	30.00
❑ SD 8066 [S]	Mel Torme at the Red Hill Inn	1962	10.00	20.00	40.00
❑ 8069 [M]	Comin' Home Baby	1962	7.50	15.00	30.00
❑ SD 8069 [S]	Comin' Home Baby	1962	10.00	20.00	40.00
❑ 8091 [M]	Sunday in New York	1963	7.50	15.00	30.00
❑ SD 8091 [S]	Sunday in New York	1963	10.00	20.00	40.00
AUDIOPHILE
❑ 67	Mel Torme Sings About Love	198?	5.00	10.00	20.00
BETHLEHEM
❑ BCP-34 [M]	It's a Blue World	1956	12.50	25.00	50.00
❑ BCP-52 [M]	Mel Torme and the Marty Paich Dektette	1956	12.50	25.00	50.00
❑ BCP 6013 [M]	Mel Torme Sings Fred Astaire	1957	12.50	25.00	50.00
❑ BCP 6016 [M]	California Suite	1957	12.50	25.00	50.00
❑ BCP 6020 [M]	Mel Torme Live at the Crescendo	1958	12.50	25.00	50.00
❑ BCP 6031 [M]	Songs for Any Taste	1959	12.50	25.00	50.00
CAPITOL
❑ P 200 [10]	California Suite	1950	25.00	50.00	100.00
COLUMBIA
❑ CS 9118 [S]	That's All -- A Lush Romantic Album	1965	5.00	10.00	20.00

Number	Title	Yr	VG	VG+	NM
CORAL					
❑ CRL 57012 [M]	Gene Norman Presents Mel Torme "Live" at the Crescendo	1955	12.50	25.00	50.00
❑ CRL 57044 [M]	Musical Sounds Are the Best Songs	1956	12.50	25.00	50.00
LIBERTY					
❑ LST-7560	A Day in the Life of Bonnie and Clyde	1968	5.00	10.00	20.00
MGM					
❑ E 552 [10]	Songs by Mel Torme	1952	25.00	50.00	100.00
STRAND					
❑ SL-1076 [M]	Mel Torme Sings	1960	5.00	10.00	20.00
❑ SLS-1076 [S]	Mel Torme Sings	1960	6.25	12.50	25.00
TOPS					
❑ L-1615 [M]	Prelude to a Kiss	1958	6.25	12.50	25.00
VERVE					
❑ MGV 2105 [M]	Torme	1958	12.50	25.00	50.00
❑ V-2105 [M]	Torme	1961	5.00	10.00	20.00
-- Reissue					
❑ V6-2105 [S]	Torme	1961	6.25	12.50	25.00
-- Reissue					
❑ MGV 2117 [M]	Ole Torme! Mel Torme Goes South of the Border with Billy May	1959	12.50	25.00	50.00
❑ V-2117 [M]	Ole Torme! Mel Torme Goes South of the Border with Billy May	1961	5.00	10.00	20.00
-- Reissue					
❑ V6-2117 [S]	Ole Torme! Mel Torme Goes South of the Border with Billy May	1961	6.25	12.50	25.00
-- Reissue					
❑ MGV 2120 [M]	Back in Town	1959	12.50	25.00	50.00
❑ V-2120 [M]	Back in Town	1961	5.00	10.00	20.00
-- Reissue					
❑ V6-2120 [S]	Back in Town	1961	6.25	12.50	25.00
-- Reissue					
❑ MGV 2132 [M]	Mel Torme Swings Schubert Alley	1960	12.50	25.00	50.00
❑ V-2132 [M]	Mel Torme Swings Schubert Alley	1961	5.00	10.00	20.00
-- Reissue					
❑ V6-2132 [S]	Mel Torme Swings Schubert Alley	1961	6.25	12.50	25.00
-- Reissue					
❑ MGV 2144 [M]	Swingin' on the Moon	1960	12.50	25.00	50.00
❑ V-2144 [M]	Swingin' on the Moon	1961	5.00	10.00	20.00
-- Reissue					
❑ V6-2144 [S]	Swingin' on the Moon	1961	6.25	12.50	25.00
❑ MGV 2146 [M]	Broadway, Right Now	1961	12.50	25.00	50.00
❑ V-2146 [M]	Broadway, Right Now	1961	5.00	10.00	20.00
-- Reissue					
❑ V6-2146 [S]	Broadway, Right Now	1961	6.25	12.50	25.00
❑ MGV 6015 [S]	Torme	1960	12.50	25.00	50.00
❑ MGV 6058 [S]	Ole Torme! Mel Torme Goes South of the Border with Billy May	1960	12.50	25.00	50.00
❑ MGV 6063 [S]	Back in Town	1960	12.50	25.00	50.00
❑ MGV 6146 [S]	Mel Torme Swings Schubert Alley	1960	12.50	25.00	50.00
❑ V-8440 [M]	My Kind of Music	1962	6.25	12.50	25.00
❑ V6-8440 [S]	My Kind of Music	1962	7.50	15.00	30.00
❑ V-8491 [M]	I Dig the Duke! I Dig the Count!	1962	6.25	12.50	25.00
❑ V6-8491 [S]	I Dig the Duke! I Dig the Count!	1962	7.50	15.00	30.00

TORME, MEL, AND BUDDY RICH

Also see each artist's individual listings.

Number	Title	Yr	VG	VG+	NM
CENTURY					
❑ 1100	Together Again -- For the First Time	1978	6.25	12.50	25.00
-- Direct-to-disc recording					

TORMENTORS, THE

Number	Title	Yr	VG	VG+	NM
ROYAL					
❑ RLP-111 [M]	Hanging Around	1967	50.00	100.00	200.00

TORNADOES, THE

Surf group.

Number	Title	Yr	VG	VG+	NM
JOSIE					
❑ J-4005 [M]	Bustin' Surfboards	1963	50.00	100.00	200.00
❑ JS-4005 [S]	Bustin' Surfboards	1963	75.00	150.00	300.00

TORNADOES, THE

British studio group produced by Joe Meek.

Number	Title	Yr	VG	VG+	NM
LONDON					
❑ LL 3279 [M]	Telstar	1963	50.00	100.00	200.00
❑ LL 3293 [M]	The Sounds of the Tornadoes	1963	50.00	100.00	200.00
-- Basically the same album as above, but with a new cover, one different track and the song order shuffled.					

TOROK, MITCHELL

Number	Title	Yr	VG	VG+	NM
GUYDEN					
❑ GLP-502 [M]	Caribbean	1960	10.00	20.00	40.00
❑ ST-502 [S]	Caribbean	1960	12.50	25.00	50.00

Number	Title	Yr	VG	VG+	NM
REPRISE					
❑ R 6223 [M]	Guitar Course	1966	5.00	10.00	20.00
❑ RS 6223 [S]	Guitar Course	1966	6.25	12.50	25.00

TORQUES, THE

Number	Title	Yr	VG	VG+	NM
LEMCO					
❑ 604	The Torques Live	1966	50.00	100.00	200.00
WIGGINS					
❑ 64010	Zoom!	1967	50.00	100.00	200.00

TOTO

Number	Title	Yr	VG	VG+	NM
COLUMBIA					
❑ AS 577 [DJ]	Special Radio Interview	198?	5.00	10.00	20.00
❑ PD 36813 [PD]	Turn Back	1981	6.25	12.50	25.00
-- Promo-only picture disc					
❑ 8C8 38685 [PD]	Africa/Rosanna	1983	5.00	10.00	20.00
-- Africa-shaped picture disc; numbered like an LP although it has only these two songs on it and is (approximately) 7 inches across					
❑ 9C9 39911 [PD]	Isolation	1984	5.00	10.00	20.00
❑ C 45369	Past to Present 1977-1990	1990	6.25	12.50	25.00
-- Vinyl available only from Columbia House					
❑ HC 47728	Toto IV	198?	10.00	20.00	40.00
-- Half-speed mastered edition					
MOBILE FIDELITY					
❑ 1-250	Toto IV	1996	10.00	20.00	40.00
-- Audiophile vinyl					

TOUCH

Number	Title	Yr	VG	VG+	NM
MAINLINE					
❑ PS-70-116-7	Street Suite	1969	1,000.	1,500.	2,000.

TOUCH, THE

Number	Title	Yr	VG	VG+	NM
COLISEUM					
❑ DS-51004	The Touch	1968	6.25	12.50	25.00

TOUCHSTONE

Number	Title	Yr	VG	VG+	NM
UNITED ARTISTS					
❑ UAS-5563	Tarot	1972	7.50	15.00	30.00

TOUSSAINT, ALLEN

Number	Title	Yr	VG	VG+	NM
RCA VICTOR					
❑ LPM-1767 [M]	The Wild Sounds of New Orleans	1958	75.00	150.00	300.00
-- As "Al Tousan"					
REPRISE					
❑ MS 2062	Life, Love and Faith	1972	6.25	12.50	25.00
SCEPTER					
❑ 24003	Toussaint	1971	6.25	12.50	25.00

TOWER OF POWER

Number	Title	Yr	VG	VG+	NM
DIRECT DISC					
❑ SD 16601	Back to Oakland	1980	6.25	12.50	25.00
-- Audiophile vinyl					
SAN FRANCISCO					
❑ SD 204	East Bay Grease	1971	12.50	25.00	50.00
SHEFFIELD LABS					
❑ 17	Direct	1982	6.25	12.50	25.00
-- Direct-to-disc recording					

TOWNSEND, ED

Number	Title	Yr	VG	VG+	NM
CAPITOL					
❑ ST 1140 [S]	New in Town	1959	7.50	15.00	30.00
❑ T 1140 [M]	New in Town	1959	6.25	12.50	25.00
❑ ST 1214 [S]	Glad to Be Here	1959	7.50	15.00	30.00
❑ T 1214 [M]	Glad to Be Here	1959	6.25	12.50	25.00

TOWNSEND, HENRY

Number	Title	Yr	VG	VG+	NM
BLUESVILLE					
❑ BVLP-1041 [M]	Tired Bein' Mistreated	1962	30.00	60.00	120.00
-- Blue label, silver print					
❑ BVLP-1041 [M]	Tired Bein' Mistreated	1964	7.50	15.00	30.00
-- Blue label, trident logo at side					

TOWNSHEND, PETE

Also see THE WHO.

Number	Title	Yr	VG	VG+	NM
ATCO					
❑ PR 940 [EP]	Deep End Sampler	1986	5.00	10.00	20.00
-- Promo-only sampler from Deep End Live					
DECCA					
❑ 79189	Who Came First	1972	5.00	10.00	20.00
-- With poster (deduct 50% if missing). Evidently a near-simultaneous release with Track 79189					

Number	Title	Yr	VG	VG+	NM

TRACK

Number	Title	Yr	VG	VG+	NM
❏ PR-A-160 [DJ]	Pete Townshend Talks To and About Thunderclap Newman	1970	25.00	50.00	100.00
-- One-sided promo-only interview record					
❏ 79189	Who Came First	1972	5.00	10.00	20.00
-- With poster (deduct 50% if missing)					

TOYS, THE
DYNOVOICE

| ❏ 9002 [M] | The Toys Sing "A Lover's Concerto" and "Attack!" | 1966 | 10.00 | 20.00 | 40.00 |
| ❏ S-9002 [P] | The Toys Sing "A Lover's Concerto" and "Attack!" | 1966 | 12.50 | 25.00 | 50.00 |

TRADE WINDS, THE
KAMA SUTRA

| ❏ KLP-8057 [M] | Excursions | 1967 | 6.25 | 12.50 | 25.00 |
| ❏ KSLP-8057 [S] | Excursions | 1967 | 7.50 | 15.00 | 30.00 |

TRADER HORNE
JANUS

| ❏ JLS-3012 | Morning Way | 1970 | 7.50 | 15.00 | 30.00 |

TRAFFIC
Also see DAVE MASON; STEVE WINWOOD.
ISLAND

| ❏ SMAS-9336 [(2)] | Traffic -- On the Road | 1973 | 5.00 | 10.00 | 20.00 |

MOBILE FIDELITY

| ❏ 1-209 | The Low Spark of High Heeled Boys | 1994 | 6.25 | 12.50 | 25.00 |
| *-- Audiophile vinyl* | | | | | |

UNITED ARTISTS

❏ UAL-3651 [M]	Heaven Is In Your Mind	1967	15.00	30.00	60.00
❏ UAS-5500	Best of Traffic	1969	5.00	10.00	20.00
-- Originals have black and orange labels					
❏ UAS-5504	John Barleycorn Must Die	1970	5.00	10.00	20.00
-- Originals have black and orange labels					
❏ UAS-6651 [S]	Heaven Is In Your Mind	1967	12.50	25.00	50.00
❏ UAS-6651 [S]	Mr. Fantasy	1968	8.75	17.50	35.00
-- Retitled version of "Heaven Is In Your Mind" with old title still on back cover					
❏ UAS-6651 [S]	Mr. Fantasy	1968	6.25	12.50	25.00
-- Retitled version of "Heaven Is In Your Mind" with green strip across top of back with song titles					
❏ UAS-6676	Traffic	1968	5.00	10.00	20.00
-- Originals have purple and orange labels					
❏ UAS-6702	Last Exit	1969	5.00	10.00	20.00
-- Originals have purple and orange labels					

TRAILER, REX, AND THE PLAYBOYS
CROWN

| ❏ CLP-5158 [M] | Country & Western | 1958 | 6.25 | 12.50 | 25.00 |

TRAMLINE
A&M

| ❏ SP-4208 | Somewhere Down the Line | 1969 | 5.00 | 10.00 | 20.00 |

TRAMMELL, BOBBY LEE
ATLANTA

| ❏ 1503 [M] | Arkansas Twist | 1962 | 250.00 | 500.00 | 1,000. |

SOUNCOT

| ❏ SC-1102 | I Dare America to Be Great | 1971 | 5.00 | 10.00 | 20.00 |

TRANSIENTS, THE
HORIZON

| ❏ WP-1633 [M] | The Funky 12 String Guitar | 1963 | 5.00 | 10.00 | 20.00 |
| ❏ WPS-1633 [S] | The Funky 12 String Guitar | 1963 | 6.25 | 12.50 | 25.00 |

TRAPEZE
THRESHOLD

❏ THS 2	Trapeze	1970	10.00	20.00	40.00
❏ THS 4	Medusa	1971	20.00	40.00	80.00
❏ THS 8	You Are the Music, We're Just the Band	1972	10.00	20.00	40.00
❏ THS 11	The Final Swing	1974	10.00	20.00	40.00

TRAPP FAMILY SINGERS, THE
RCA CAMDEN

| ❏ CAL-209 [M] | The Trapp Family Singers Present Christmas and Folk Songs | 195? | 5.00 | 10.00 | 20.00 |

TRASHMEN, THE
GARRETT

| ❏ GA-200 [M] | Surfin' Bird | 1964 | 55.00 | 110.00 | 220.00 |
| ❏ GAS-200 [R] | Surfin' Bird | 1964 | 87.50 | 175.00 | 350.00 |

TRASK, DIANA
COLUMBIA

Number	Title	Yr	VG	VG+	NM
❏ CL 1601 [M]	Diana Trask	1961	6.25	12.50	25.00
❏ CL 1705 [M]	Diana Trask on TV	1961	6.25	12.50	25.00
❏ CS 8401 [S]	Diana Trask	1961	7.50	15.00	30.00
❏ CS 8505 [S]	Diana Trask on TV	1961	7.50	15.00	30.00

TRAVEL AGENCY, THE
VIVA

| ❏ V-36017 | The Travel Agency | 1968 | 6.25 | 12.50 | 25.00 |

TRAVELERS 3, THE
ELEKTRA

❏ EKL-216 [M]	The Travelers 3	1963	6.25	12.50	25.00
❏ EKL-226 [M]	Open House	1963	6.25	12.50	25.00
❏ EKL-236 [M]	Live! Live! Live!	1963	6.25	12.50	25.00

TRAVELING WILBURYS
Also see BOB DYLAN; GEORGE HARRISON; ROY ORBISON; TOM PETTY.
WILBURY

| ❏ 25796 | Traveling Wilburys (Volume One) | 1988 | 5.00 | 10.00 | 20.00 |
| ❏ 26324 | Traveling Wilburys, Vol. 3 | 1990 | 5.00 | 10.00 | 20.00 |

TRAVELLERS, THE
KAPP

| ❏ KL-1157 [M] | Journey with the Travellers | 1960 | 6.25 | 12.50 | 25.00 |
| ❏ KS-3051 [S] | Journey with the Travellers | 1960 | 7.50 | 15.00 | 30.00 |

TRAVIS, MERLE
CAPITOL

❏ T 650 [M]	The Merle Travis Guitar	1956	30.00	60.00	120.00
-- Turquoise or gray label					
❏ T 650 [M]	The Merle Travis Guitar	1959	7.50	15.00	30.00
-- Black colorband label, logo at left					
❏ T 650 [M]	The Merle Travis Guitar	1962	5.00	10.00	20.00
-- Black colorband label, logo at top					
❏ T 891 [M]	Back Home	1957	25.00	50.00	100.00
-- Turquoise or gray label					
❏ T 891 [M]	Back Home	1959	7.50	15.00	30.00
-- Black colorband label, logo at left					
❏ T 891 [M]	Back Home	1962	5.00	10.00	20.00
-- Black colorband label, logo at top					
❏ T 1391 [M]	Walkin' the Strings	1960	20.00	40.00	80.00
-- Black colorband label, logo at left					
❏ T 1391 [M]	Walkin' the Strings	1962	5.00	10.00	20.00
-- Black colorband label, logo at top					
❏ ST 1664 [S]	Travis	1962	12.50	25.00	50.00
-- Black colorband label, logo at left					
❏ ST 1664 [S]	Travis	1962	6.25	12.50	25.00
-- Black colorband label, logo at top					
❏ T 1664 [M]	Travis	1962	5.00	10.00	20.00
-- Black colorband label, logo at top					
❏ T 1664 [M]	Travis	1962	10.00	20.00	40.00
-- Black colorband label, logo at left					
❏ ST 1956 [S]	Songs of the Coal Mines	1963	12.50	25.00	50.00
❏ T 1956 [M]	Songs of the Coal Mines	1963	10.00	20.00	40.00
❏ DT 2662 [R]	The Best of Merle Travis	1967	5.00	10.00	20.00
❏ T 2662 [M]	The Best of Merle Travis	1967	7.50	15.00	30.00
❏ ST 2938	Strictly Guitar	1968	6.25	12.50	25.00

TRAVIS, MERLE, AND JOE MAPHIS
CAPITOL

| ❏ ST 2102 [S] | Merle Travis and Joe Maphis | 1964 | 12.50 | 25.00 | 50.00 |
| ❏ T 2102 [M] | Merle Travis and Joe Maphis | 1964 | 10.00 | 20.00 | 40.00 |

TRAVIS, RANDY
MUSIC VALLEY

❏ (# unknown)	Randy Ray Live at the Nashville Palace	1982	75.00	150.00	300.00
-- With no "Randy Travis" sticker on front cover					
❏ (# unknown)	Randy Ray Live at the Nashville Palace	1986	50.00	100.00	200.00
-- With "Randy Travis" sticker on front cover; the records are the same as the first edition					

WARNER BROS.

| ❏ R 174597 | Heroes and Friends | 1990 | 5.00 | 10.00 | 20.00 |
| *-- Only released on vinyl through BMG Direct Marketing* | | | | | |

TREE
GOAT FARM

| ❏ 580 | Tree | 1970 | 17.50 | 35.00 | 70.00 |

TREMELOES, THE
EPIC

| ❏ LN 24310 [M] | Here Comes My Baby | 1967 | 7.50 | 15.00 | 30.00 |
| ❏ LN 24326 [M] | Even the Bad Times Are Good | 1967 | 6.25 | 12.50 | 25.00 |

(Top left) The Trade Winds (or as they are called on this album, The Tradewinds) were Pete Anders and Vini Poncia. Their big hit was "New York's a Lonely Town" on Red Bird, but they lasted long enough to have an album, *Excursions*, on the Kama Sutra label, based around the later hit song "Mind Excursion." (Top right) Thanks to a licensing dispute, early material by the Troggs came out on two different labels in America – Atco and Fontana. Because Atco lost the battle to keep the Troggs, the material on that label is more sought-after than the Fontana releases. The only Troggs LP on Atco was named after their biggest hit, "Wild Thing." (Bottom left) In 1970, MGM released an entire line of albums it called the "Golden Archive Series," a name also used by Rhino in the 1980s. One of these consisted of early hits of Conway Twitty, when he was a rock 'n' roll singer and not yet a country singer. All the MGM Golden Archive Series albums used the unique prefix "GAS" before a three-digit number. (Bottom right) A promotional gimmick of Cameo and Parkway Records in 1964 was to have a bonus 45 in a see-through sleeve at the front of selected albums. Over the years, most of these 45s became separated from their original LPs. Such was also the case with this album by the Tymes, named after their hit version of "Somewhere."

Number	Title	Yr	VG	VG+	NM
❑ LN 24363 [M]	Suddenly You Love Me	1968	7.50	15.00	30.00
❑ BN 26310 [R]	Here Comes My Baby	1967	5.00	10.00	20.00
❑ BN 26326 [P]	Even the Bad Times Are Good	1967	7.50	15.00	30.00
❑ BN 26363 [R]	Suddenly You Love Me	1968	5.00	10.00	20.00
❑ BN 26388 [S]	World Explosion '58/'68	1968	7.50	15.00	30.00

TRENIERS, THE
DOT
| ❑ DLP-3257 [M] | Souvenir Album | 1960 | 25.00 | 50.00 | 100.00 |
EPIC
| ❑ LG 3125 [M] | The Treniers on TV | 1955 | 50.00 | 100.00 | 200.00 |

TRENT, BUCK
BOONE
| ❑ 1212 | Give Me Five | 1967 | 5.00 | 10.00 | 20.00 |
SMASH
-- Smash LPs as "Charles Trent"
❑ MGS-27002 [M]	The Sound of a Bluegrass Banjo	1962	5.00	10.00	20.00
❑ MGS-27017 [M]	The Sound of a Five String Banjo	1962	5.00	10.00	20.00
❑ SRS-67002 [S]	The Sound of a Bluegrass Banjo	1962	6.25	12.50	25.00
❑ SRS-67017 [S]	The Sound of a Five String Banjo	1962	6.25	12.50	25.00

TREVOR, VAN
BAND BOX
| ❑ (# unknown) | Come On Over to Our Side | 1967 | 5.00 | 10.00 | 20.00 |

TRIANGLE, THE
AMARET
| ❑ 5000 | How Now Brown Cow | 1969 | 6.25 | 12.50 | 25.00 |

TRICHT, EVERT VAN
MERCURY LIVING PRESENCE
| ❑ SR 90403 [S] | Oboe Concerti | 196? | 7.50 | 15.00 | 30.00 |
-- With Kurt Redel/Vienna Symphony Orchestra and Pro Arte Orchestra of Munich; maroon label, no "Vendor: Mercury Record Corporation"

TRICYCLE
ABC
| ❑ S-674 | Tricycle | 1969 | 5.00 | 10.00 | 20.00 |

TRIGGER, VIC
SANCTUARY
| ❑ 12103 | Electronic Wizard | 1977 | 25.00 | 50.00 | 100.00 |

TRIMBLE, BOBB
(NO LABEL)
| ❑ (no #) | Harvest of Dreams | 1982 | 37.50 | 75.00 | 150.00 |
VENGEANCE
| ❑ BT-8458 | Iron Curtain Dream | 1980 | 200.00 | 400.00 | 800.00 |

TRIO
MERCURY
| ❑ 814 320-1 | Trio and Error | 1983 | 5.00 | 10.00 | 20.00 |

TRIPSICHORD MUSIC BOX, THE
JANUS
| ❑ JLS-3016 | The Tripsichord Music Box | 1971 | 50.00 | 100.00 | 200.00 |

TRITT, TRAVIS
WARNER BROS.
| ❑ W1-26589 | It's All About to Change | 1991 | 5.00 | 10.00 | 20.00 |
-- Vinyl available only from Columbia House

TRIZO 50
CAVERN
| ❑ 740142 | Trizo 50 | 197? | 75.00 | 150.00 | 300.00 |

TROGGS, THE
ATCO
| ❑ 33-193 [M] | Wild Thing | 1966 | 12.50 | 25.00 | 50.00 |
| ❑ SD 33-193 [R] | Wild Thing | 1966 | 10.00 | 20.00 | 40.00 |
FONTANA
| ❑ MGF 27556 [M] | Wild Thing/With a Girl Like You | 1966 | 10.00 | 20.00 | 40.00 |
-- Contents identical to the Atco LP; two slightly different cover variations are known
| ❑ SRF 67556 [R] | Wild Thing/With a Girl Like You | 1966 | 7.50 | 15.00 | 30.00 |
-- Contents identical to the Atco LP; two slightly different cover variations are known
| ❑ SRF 67576 [R] | Love Is All Around | 1968 | 7.50 | 15.00 | 30.00 |

TROLL, THE
SMASH
| ❑ SRS-67114 | Animated Music | 1969 | 12.50 | 25.00 | 50.00 |

TROMBONES UNLIMITED
LIBERTY
| ❑ LRP-3472 [M] | You're Gonna Hear from Me | 1966 | 6.25 | 12.50 | 25.00 |
| ❑ LST-7472 [S] | You're Gonna Hear from Me | 1966 | 7.50 | 15.00 | 30.00 |

TROY, DORIS
APPLE
| ❑ ST-3371 | Doris Troy | 1970 | 6.25 | 12.50 | 25.00 |
ATLANTIC
| ❑ 8088 [M] | Just One Look | 1964 | 7.50 | 15.00 | 30.00 |
| ❑ SD 8088 [S] | Just One Look | 1964 | 12.50 | 25.00 | 50.00 |

TROYKA
COTILLION
| ❑ SD 9020 | Troyka | 1970 | 7.50 | 15.00 | 30.00 |

TRUMAN, MARGARET
RCA VICTOR
| ❑ LM-57 [10] | American Songs | 1951 | 20.00 | 40.00 | 80.00 |
| ❑ LM-145 [10] | A Margaret Truman Program | 1952 | 20.00 | 40.00 | 80.00 |

TRUMPETEERS, THE
GRAND
| ❑ 7701 [M] | The Last Supper | 195? | 25.00 | 50.00 | 100.00 |
SCORE
| ❑ SLP-4021 [M] | Milky White Way | 1956 | 75.00 | 150.00 | 300.00 |

TUBB, ERNEST
DECCA
| ❑ DXA 159 [(2) M] | The Ernest Tubb Story | 1959 | 20.00 | 40.00 | 80.00 |
-- Deduct 25 percent if book is missing
❑ DL 4042 [M]	The Ernest Tubb Record Shop	1960	10.00	20.00	40.00
❑ DL 4046 [M]	All Time Hits	1961	7.50	15.00	30.00
❑ DL 4118 [M]	Ernest Tubb's Golden Favorites	1961	7.50	15.00	30.00
❑ DL 4321 [M]	On Tour	1962	6.25	12.50	25.00
❑ DL 4385 [M]	Just Call Me Lonesome	1962	6.25	12.50	25.00
❑ DL 4397 [M]	The Family Bible	1963	6.25	12.50	25.00
❑ DL 4514 [M]	Thanks a Lot	1964	6.25	12.50	25.00
❑ DL 4518 [M]	Blue Christmas	1963	6.25	12.50	25.00
❑ DL 4640 [M]	My Pick of the Hits	1965	6.25	12.50	25.00
❑ DL 4681 [M]	Hittin' the Road	1965	6.25	12.50	25.00
❑ DL 4746 [M]	By Request	1966	6.25	12.50	25.00
❑ DL 4772 [M]	Ernest Tubb Sings Country Hits Old & New	1966	6.25	12.50	25.00
❑ DL 4867 [M]	Another Story	1967	7.50	15.00	30.00
❑ DL 4957 [M]	Ernest Tubb Sings Hank Williams	1968	12.50	25.00	50.00
❑ DL 5301 [10]	Ernest Tubb Favorites	1951	37.50	75.00	150.00
❑ DL 5334 [10]	The Old Rugged Cross	1951	37.50	75.00	150.00
❑ DL 5336 [10]	Jimmie Rodgers Songs Sung by Ernest Tubb	1951	37.50	75.00	150.00
❑ DL 5497 [10]	Sing a Song of Christmas	1954	37.50	75.00	150.00
❑ DXSA 7159 [(2) R]	The Ernest Tubb Story	196?	7.50	15.00	30.00
-- Deduct 25 percent if book is missing
❑ DL 8291 [M]	Ernest Tubb Favorites	1955	17.50	35.00	70.00
❑ DL 8553 [M]	The Daddy of 'Em All	1956	17.50	35.00	70.00
❑ DL 8834 [M]	The Importance of Being Ernest	1959	12.50	25.00	50.00
❑ DL 74042 [S]	The Ernest Tubb Record Shop	1960	12.50	25.00	50.00
❑ DL 74046 [S]	All Time Hits	1961	10.00	20.00	40.00
❑ DL 74118 [S]	Ernest Tubb's Golden Favorites	1961	10.00	2.00	40.00
❑ DL 74321 [S]	On Tour	1962	7.50	15.00	30.00
❑ DL 74385 [S]	Just Call Me Lonesome	1962	7.50	15.00	30.00
❑ DL 74397 [S]	The Family Bible	1963	7.50	15.00	30.00
❑ DL 74514 [S]	Thanks a Lot	1964	7.50	15.00	30.00
❑ DL 74518 [S]	Blue Christmas	1963	7.50	15.00	30.00
❑ DL 74640 [S]	My Pick of the Hits	1965	7.50	15.00	30.00
❑ DL 74681 [S]	Hittin' the Road	1965	7.50	15.00	30.00
❑ DL 74746 [S]	By Request	1966	7.50	15.00	30.00
❑ DL 74772 [S]	Ernest Tubb Sings Country Hits Old & New	1966	7.50	15.00	30.00
❑ DL 74867 [S]	Another Story	1967	6.25	12.50	25.00
❑ DL 74957 [S]	Ernest Tubb Sings Hank Williams	1968	6.25	12.50	25.00
❑ DL 75006	Ernest Tubb's Greatest Hits	1968	6.25	12.50	25.00
❑ DL 75072	Country Hit Time	1968	5.00	10.00	20.00
❑ DL 75122	Saturday Satan, Sunday Saint	1969	5.00	10.00	20.00
❑ DL 75222	A Great Year for the Wine	1970	5.00	10.00	20.00
❑ DL 75252	Ernest Tubb's Greatest Hits, Vol. 2	1970	5.00	10.00	20.00
❑ DL 75301	One Sweet Hello	1971	5.00	10.00	20.00
❑ DL 75345	Say Something Nice to Sarah	1972	5.00	10.00	20.00
❑ DL 75388	Baby, It's So Hard to Be Good	1972	5.00	10.00	20.00
❑ DL 78834 [S]	The Importance of Being Ernest	1959	15.00	30.00	60.00
FIRST GENERATION
❑ LP-0002 [(2)]	The Legend and the Legacy	1979	12.50	25.00	50.00
-- No ads on back cover

Number	Title	Yr	VG	VG+	NM
❏ LP-0002 [(2)]	The Legend and the Legacy	1979	10.00	20.00	40.00
-- With ad for Ernest Tubb Record Shop on back cover					
❏ TV-1033 [(2)]	The Legend and the Legacy	1979	6.25	12.50	25.00
-- Mail-order version					

TUBB, JUSTIN
CUTLASS
| ❏ 123 | Travelin' Singin' Man | 1972 | 7.50 | 15.00 | 30.00 |

DECCA
| ❏ DL 8644 [M] | Country Boy in Love | 1957 | 15.00 | 30.00 | 60.00 |

RCA VICTOR
| ❏ LPM-3339 [M] | Where You're Concerned | 1965 | 5.00 | 10.00 | 20.00 |
| ❏ LSP-3339 [S] | Where You're Concerned | 1965 | 6.25 | 12.50 | 25.00 |

STARDAY
❏ SLP-160 [M]	Star of the Grand Ole Opry	1962	10.00	20.00	40.00
❏ SLP-198 [M]	The Modern Country Sound of Justin Tubb	1962	10.00	20.00	40.00
❏ SLP-334 [M]	The Best of Justin Tubb	1965	6.25	12.50	25.00

TUBB, JUSTIN, AND LORENE MANN
RCA VICTOR
| ❏ LPM-3591 [M] | Together and Alone | 1966 | 7.50 | 15.00 | 30.00 |
| ❏ LSP-3591 [S] | Together and Alone | 1966 | 10.00 | 20.00 | 40.00 |

TUBES, THE
A&M
| ❏ SP-17012 [DJ] | Tubes Live/Edited for Trouble-Free Airplay | 1978 | 6.25 | 12.50 | 25.00 |
| -- Generic cover with sticker; promo only | | | | | |

TUCKER, FAYE
TIME
| ❏ S-2018 [S] | Country & Western Soul | 1963 | 6.25 | 12.50 | 25.00 |
| ❏ 52108 [M] | Country & Western Soul | 1963 | 5.00 | 10.00 | 20.00 |

TUCKER, MAUREEN
Also see THE VELVET UNDERGROUND.
TRASH
| ❏ TLP-1001 | Playin' Possum | 1981 | 7.50 | 15.00 | 30.00 |

TUCKER, TANYA
CAPITOL NASHVILLE
| ❏ 1P 8140 | What Do I Do with Me | 1991 | 5.00 | 10.00 | 20.00 |
| -- Only available on vinyl through Columbia House | | | | | |

TUCKER, TOMMY
CHECKER
❏ LP-2990 [M]	Hi-Heel Sneakers	1964	62.50	125.00	250.00
-- Black label					
❏ LP-2990 [M]	Hi-Heel Sneakers	1965	30.00	60.00	120.00
-- Blue label with checkers					

TURBANS, THE
HERALD
| ❏ 5009 | Presenting the Turbans | 197? | 5.00 | 10.00 | 20.00 |
| -- No such album was released in the 1950s; this is a bootleg that has some collector value. | | | | | |

TURNER, HANK
COLUMBIA
| ❏ CL 1958 [M] | Golden Country and Western Hits | 1963 | 5.00 | 10.00 | 20.00 |
| ❏ CS 8758 [S] | Golden Country and Western Hits | 1963 | 6.25 | 12.50 | 25.00 |

TURNER, IKE
Also see IKE AND TINA TURNER.
CROWN
| ❏ CST-367 [R] | Ike Turner Rocks the Blues | 1963 | 25.00 | 50.00 | 100.00 |
| ❏ CLP-5367 [M] | Ike Turner Rocks the Blues | 1963 | 50.00 | 100.00 | 200.00 |

TURNER, IKE AND TINA
Also see each artist's individual listings.
A&M
| ❏ SP-4178 | River Deep -- Mountain High | 1969 | 6.25 | 12.50 | 25.00 |
| -- Official release of Philles 4011 | | | | | |

KENT
❏ KST-514 [S]	The Ike and Tina Turner Revue Live	1964	10.00	20.00	40.00
❏ KST-519 [S]	The Soul of Ike and Tina	1966	10.00	20.00	40.00
❏ KST-538	Festival of Live Performances	1969	7.50	15.00	30.00
❏ KST-550	Please Please Please	1971	7.50	15.00	30.00
❏ K-5014 [M]	The Ike and Tina Turner Revue Live	1964	7.50	15.00	30.00

Number	Title	Yr	VG	VG+	NM
❏ K-5019 [M]	The Soul of Ike and Tina	1966	7.50	15.00	30.00

LOMA
❏ 5904 [M]	Live! The Ike & Tina Turner Show	1966	6.25	12.50	25.00
❏ 5904 [S]	Live! The Ike & Tina Turner Show	1966	7.50	15.00	30.00
-- Reissue of Warner Bros. 1579?					

MINIT
| ❏ 24018 | In Person | 1969 | 5.00 | 10.00 | 20.00 |

PHILLES
| ❏ PHLP 4011 [M] | River Deep -- Mountain High | 1966 | 2,000. | 4,000. | 8,000. |
| -- Value is for record alone; covers were not printed | | | | | |

POMPEII
❏ SD 6000	So Fine	1968	6.25	12.50	25.00
❏ SD 6004	Cussin', Cryin' and Carryin' On	1969	6.25	12.50	25.00
❏ SD 6006	Get It Together	1969	6.25	12.50	25.00

SUE
❏ LP 1038 [M]	Ike and Tina Turner's Greatest Hits	1965	75.00	150.00	300.00
❏ LP 2001 [M]	The Soul of Ike and Tina Turner	1961	100.00	200.00	400.00
❏ LP 2003 [M]	Ike and Tina Turner's Kings of Rhythm Dance	1962	100.00	200.00	400.00
❏ LP 2004 [M]	Dynamite	1963	100.00	200.00	400.00
❏ LP 2005 [M]	Don't Play Me Cheap	1963	100.00	200.00	400.00
❏ LP 2007 [M]	It's Gonna Work Out Fine	1963	100.00	200.00	400.00

WARNER BROS.
❏ W 1579 [M]	Live! The Ike & Tina Turner Show	1965	7.50	15.00	30.00
❏ WS 1579 [S]	Live! The Ike & Tina Turner Show	1965	10.00	20.00	40.00
❏ WS 1810	Ike & Tina Turner's Greatest Hits	1969	6.25	12.50	25.00

TURNER, JOE
ARHOOLIE
| ❏ 2004 [M] | Jumpin' the Blues | 1962 | 5.00 | 10.00 | 20.00 |

ATLANTIC
❏ 1234 [M]	The Boss of the Blues	1956	30.00	60.00	120.00
-- Black label					
❏ 1234 [M]	The Boss of the Blues	1960	25.00	50.00	100.00
-- White "bullseye" label					
❏ 1234 [M]	The Boss of the Blues	1961	10.00	20.00	40.00
-- White "fan" logo on label					
❏ SD 1234 [S]	The Boss of the Blues	1959	45.00	90.00	180.00
-- Green label					
❏ SD 1234 [S]	The Boss of the Blues	1960	37.50	75.00	150.00
-- White "bullseye" label					
❏ SD 1234 [S]	The Boss of the Blues	1961	12.50	25.00	50.00
-- White "fan" logo on label					
❏ SD 1234 [S]	The Boss of the Blues	1963	5.00	10.00	20.00
-- Black "fan" logo on label					
❏ 1332 [M]	Big Joe Rides Again	1959	37.50	75.00	150.00
-- Black label					
❏ 1332 [M]	Big Joe Rides Again	1960	10.00	20.00	40.00
-- White "fan" logo on label					
❏ SD 1332 [S]	Big Joe Rides Again	1959	50.00	100.00	200.00
-- Green label					
❏ SD 1332 [S]	Big Joe Rides Again	1960	12.50	25.00	50.00
-- White "fan" logo on label					
❏ SD 1332 [S]	Big Joe Rides Again	1963	5.00	10.00	20.00
-- Black "fan" logo on label					
❏ 8005 [M]	Joe Turner	1957	37.50	75.00	150.00
-- Black label					
❏ 8005 [M]	Joe Turner	1961	10.00	20.00	40.00
-- White "fan" logo on label					
❏ 8023 [M]	Rockin' the Blues	1958	30.00	60.00	120.00
-- Black label					
❏ 8023 [M]	Rockin' the Blues	1960	10.00	20.00	40.00
-- White "fan" logo on label					
❏ 8033 [M]	Big Joe Is Here	1959	30.00	60.00	120.00
-- Black label					
❏ 8033 [M]	Big Joe Is Here	1960	10.00	20.00	40.00
-- White "fan" logo on label					
❏ 8033 [M]	Big Joe Is Here	1960	25.00	50.00	100.00
-- White "bullseye" label					
❏ 8081 [M]	The Best of Joe Turner	1963	12.50	25.00	50.00

BLUESTIME
| ❏ 9002 [M] | The Real Boss of the Blues | 196? | 10.00 | 20.00 | 40.00 |
| ❏ 29002 [M] | The Real Boss of the Blues | 196? | 7.50 | 15.00 | 30.00 |

BLUESWAY
| ❏ BL-6006 [M] | Singing the Blues | 1967 | 5.00 | 10.00 | 20.00 |
| ❏ BLS-6006 [S] | Singing the Blues | 1967 | 6.25 | 12.50 | 25.00 |

DECCA
| ❏ DL 8044 [M] | Joe Turner Sings Kansas City Jazz | 1953 | 62.50 | 125.00 | 250.00 |

EMARCY
| ❏ MG-36014 [M] | Joe Turner and Pete Johnson | 1955 | 50.00 | 100.00 | 200.00 |

SAVOY
| ❏ MG-14012 [M] | Blues'll Make You Happy | 1958 | 37.50 | 75.00 | 150.00 |
| ❏ MG-14106 [M] | Careless Love | 1963 | 20.00 | 40.00 | 80.00 |

Number	Title	Yr	VG	VG+	NM

TURNER, SAMMY
BIG TOP
Number	Title	Yr	VG	VG+	NM
❏ 12-1301 [M]	Lavender Blue Moods	1959	75.00	150.00	300.00
-- *May not exist in stereo*					

TURNER, SPYDER
MGM
| ❏ E-4450 [M] | Stand By Me | 1967 | 6.25 | 12.50 | 25.00 |
| ❏ SE-4450 [S] | Stand By Me | 1967 | 7.50 | 15.00 | 30.00 |

TURNER, TINA
Also see IKE AND TINA TURNER.
CAPITOL
| ❏ 1P 8192 [(2)] | Simply the Best | 1991 | 5.00 | 10.00 | 20.00 |
| -- *Columbia House edition (only US vinyl version)* | | | | | |

TURNER, TITUS
JAMIE
| ❏ JLP-3018 [M] | Sound Off | 1961 | 5.00 | 10.00 | 20.00 |
| ❏ JLPS-3018 [S] | Sound Off | 1961 | 7.50 | 15.00 | 30.00 |

TURNER, VELVERT, GROUP
FAMILY PRODUCTIONS
| ❏ FPS-2704 | Velvert Turner Group | 1972 | 12.50 | 25.00 | 50.00 |

TURNER, ZEB
AUDIO LAB
| ❏ AL-1537 [M] | Country Music in the Turner Style | 1959 | 37.50 | 75.00 | 150.00 |

TURNQUIST REMEDY
PENTAGRAM
| ❏ PE-10004 | Turnquist Remedy | 1970 | 6.25 | 12.50 | 25.00 |

TURRENTINE, STANLEY
BLUE NOTE
❏ BLP-4039 [M]	Look Out!	1960	30.00	60.00	120.00
-- *"Deep groove" version (deep indentation under label on both sides)*					
❏ BLP-4039 [M]	Look Out!	1960	20.00	40.00	80.00
-- *Regular version with W. 63rd St. address on label*					
❏ BLP-4039 [M]	Look Out!	1963	6.25	12.50	25.00
-- *With New York, USA address on label*					
❏ BLP-4057 [M]	Blue Hour	1961	20.00	40.00	80.00
-- *With W. 63rd St. addresss on label*					
❏ BLP-4057 [M]	Blue Hour	1963	6.25	12.50	25.00
-- *With New York, USA address on label*					
❏ BLP-4069 [M]	Up at Minton's, Volume 1	1961	20.00	40.00	80.00
-- *With W. 63rd St. addresss on label*					
❏ BLP-4069 [M]	Up at Minton's, Volume 1	1963	6.25	12.50	25.00
-- *With New York, USA address on label*					
❏ BLP-4070 [M]	Up at Minton's, Volume 2	1961	20.00	40.00	80.00
-- *With W. 63rd St. addresss on label*					
❏ BLP-4070 [M]	Up at Minton's, Volume 2	1963	6.25	12.50	25.00
-- *With New York, USA address on label*					
❏ BLP-4081 [M]	Dearly Beloved	1961	18.75	37.50	75.00
-- *With 61st St. address on label*					
❏ BLP-4081 [M]	Dearly Beloved	1963	6.25	12.50	25.00
-- *With New York, USA address on label*					
❏ BLP-4096 [M]	That's Where It's At	1962	15.00	30.00	60.00
-- *With 61st St. address on label*					
❏ BLP-4096 [M]	That's Where It's At	1963	6.25	12.50	25.00
-- *With New York, USA address on label*					
❏ BLP-4129 [M]	Never Let Me Go	1963	7.50	15.00	30.00
❏ BLP-4150 [M]	A Chip Off the Old Block	1963	7.50	15.00	30.00
❏ BLP-4162 [M]	Hustlin'	1964	7.50	15.00	30.00
❏ BLP-4201 [M]	Joyride	1965	6.25	12.50	25.00
❏ BLP-4240 [M]	Rough 'n Tumble	1966	6.25	12.50	25.00
❏ BLP-4256 [M]	The Spoiler	1967	6.25	12.50	25.00
❏ BLP-4268 [M]	Easy Walker	1967	6.25	12.50	25.00
❏ BST-84039 [S]	Look Out!	1960	15.00	30.00	60.00
-- *With W. 63rd St. addresss on label*					
❏ BST-84039 [S]	Look Out!	1963	5.00	10.00	20.00
-- *With New York, USA address on label*					
❏ BST-84057 [S]	Blue Hour	1961	15.00	30.00	60.00
-- *With W. 63rd St. addresss on label*					
❏ BST-84057 [S]	Blue Hour	1963	5.00	10.00	20.00
-- *With New York, USA address on label*					
❏ BST-84069 [S]	Up at Minton's, Volume 1	1961	15.00	30.00	60.00
-- *With W. 63rd St. addresss on label*					
❏ BST-84069 [S]	Up at Minton's, Volume 1	1963	5.00	10.00	20.00
-- *With New York, USA address on label*					
❏ BST-84070 [S]	Dearly Beloved	1961	15.00	30.00	60.00
-- *With 61st St. address on label*					
❏ BST-84070 [S]	Up at Minton's, Volume 2	1961	15.00	30.00	60.00
-- *With W. 63rd St. addresss on label*					
❏ BST-84070 [S]	Dearly Beloved	1963	5.00	10.00	20.00
-- *With New York, USA address on label*					
❏ BST-84070 [S]	Up at Minton's, Volume 2	1963	5.00	10.00	20.00
-- *With New York, USA address on label*					
❏ BST-84096 [S]	That's Where It's At	1962	15.00	30.00	60.00
-- *With 61st St. address on label*					
❏ BST-84096 [S]	That's Where It's At	1963	5.00	10.00	20.00
-- *With New York, USA address on label*					
❏ BST-84129 [S]	Never Let Me Go	1963	7.50	15.00	30.00
-- *With New York, USA address on label*					
❏ BST-84150 [S]	A Chip Off the Old Block	1963	7.50	15.00	30.00
-- *With New York, USA address on label*					
❏ BST-84162 [S]	Hustlin'	1964	7.50	15.00	30.00
-- *With New York, USA address on label*					
❏ BST-84201 [S]	Joyride	1964	6.25	12.50	25.00
-- *With New York, USA address on label*					
❏ BST-84240 [S]	Rough 'n Tumble	1966	5.00	10.00	20.00
-- *With New York, USA address on label*					
❏ BST-84256 [S]	The Spoiler	1967	5.00	10.00	20.00
❏ BST-84268 [S]	Easy Walker	1967	5.00	10.00	20.00
❏ BST-84286	The Look of Love	1968	5.00	10.00	20.00
-- *With "A Division of Liberty Records" on label*					
❏ BST-84298	Always Something There	1968	5.00	10.00	20.00
❏ BST-84315	Common Touch!	1969	5.00	10.00	20.00
❏ BST-84336	Another Story	1969	5.00	10.00	20.00
IMPULSE!
| ❏ AS-9115 | Let It Go | 1967 | 6.25 | 12.50 | 25.00 |
MAINSTREAM
| ❏ S-6041 [S] | Tiger Tail | 1965 | 6.25 | 12.50 | 25.00 |
| ❏ 56041 [M] | Tiger Tail | 1965 | 5.00 | 10.00 | 20.00 |
TIME
| ❏ S-2086 [S] | Stan the Man | 1962 | 10.00 | 20.00 | 40.00 |
| ❏ 52086 [M] | Stan the Man | 1962 | 10.00 | 20.00 | 40.00 |

TURTLES, THE
Also see FLO AND EDDIE.
SIRE
| ❏ SASH-3703 [(2)] | The Turtles' Greatest Hits/ Happy Together Again | 1974 | 5.00 | 10.00 | 20.00 |
WHITE WHALE
❏ WW 111 [M]	It Ain't Me Babe	1965	7.50	15.00	30.00
❏ WW 112 [M]	You Baby	1966	7.50	15.00	30.00
❏ WW 114 [M]	Happy Together	1967	5.00	10.00	20.00
❏ WW 115 [M]	The Turtles! Golden Hits	1967	6.25	12.50	25.00
❏ WWS 7111 [S]	It Ain't Me Babe	1965	10.00	20.00	40.00
❏ WWS 7112 [S]	You Baby	1966	10.00	20.00	40.00
❏ WWS 7114 [S]	Happy Together	1967	6.25	12.50	25.00
❏ WWS 7115 [S]	The Turtles! Golden Hits	1967	5.00	10.00	20.00
❏ WWS 7118	The Turtles Present the Battle of the Bands	1968	6.25	12.50	25.00
❏ WWS 7124	Turtle Soup	1969	6.25	12.50	25.00
❏ WWS 7127	The Turtles! More Golden Hits	1970	5.00	10.00	20.00
❏ WWS 7133	Wooden Head	1970	5.00	10.00	20.00

TUSKEGEE INSTITUTE CHOIR
WESTMINSTER
| ❏ XWM-18080 [M] | Spirituals | 195? | 12.50 | 25.00 | 50.00 |

TUXEDOMOON
TUXEDOMOON
| ❏ EP 45 [EP] | Tuxedomoon | 1978 | 5.00 | 10.00 | 20.00 |
| ❏ EP 79 [EP] | Scream with a View | 1979 | 5.00 | 10.00 | 20.00 |

TWENTIETH CENTURY ZOO, THE
VAULT
| ❏ LPS-122 | Thunder on a Clear Day | 1968 | 15.00 | 30.00 | 60.00 |

$27 SNAP-ON FACE
HETERODYNE
| ❏ 0001 | $27 Snap-On Face | 1977 | 25.00 | 50.00 | 100.00 |
| -- *Blue vinyl; with lyric sheet* | | | | | |

TWINK
SIRE
| ❏ SES-97022 | Think Pink | 1970 | 25.00 | 50.00 | 100.00 |

TWINS, THE
RCA VICTOR
| ❏ LPM-1708 [M] | Teenagers Love the Twins | 1958 | 12.50 | 25.00 | 50.00 |

Number	Title	Yr	VG	VG+	NM

TWISTERS, THE
TREASURE
❑ TLP-890 [M]	Doin' the Twist	1962	7.50	15.00	30.00

TWISTIN' KINGS
MOTOWN
| ❑ M-601 [M] | Twistin' the World Around | 1961 | 75.00 | 150.00 | 300.00 |

TWITTY, CONWAY
DECCA
❑ DL 4724 [M]	Conway Twitty Sings	1965	6.25	12.50	25.00
❑ DL 4828 [M]	Look Into My Teardrops	1966	6.25	12.50	25.00
❑ DL 4913 [M]	Conway Twitty Country	1967	7.50	15.00	30.00
❑ DL 4990 [M]	Here's Conway Twitty	1968	12.50	25.00	50.00
❑ DL 74724 [S]	Conway Twitty Sings	1965	7.50	15.00	30.00
❑ DL 74828 [S]	Look Into My Teardrops	1966	7.50	15.00	30.00
❑ DL 74913 [S]	Conway Twitty Country	1967	7.50	15.00	30.00
❑ DL 74990 [S]	Here's Conway Twitty	1968	7.50	15.00	30.00
❑ DL 75062	Next in Line	1968	6.25	12.50	25.00
❑ DL 75105	Darling, You Know I Wouldn't Lie	1968	5.00	10.00	20.00
❑ DL 75131	I Love You More Today	1969	5.00	10.00	20.00
❑ DL 75172	To See My Angel Cry	1970	5.00	10.00	20.00
❑ DL 75209	Hello Darlin'	1970	5.00	10.00	20.00
❑ DL 75248	Fifteen Years Ago	1970	5.00	10.00	20.00
❑ DL 75276	How Much More Can She Stand	1971	5.00	10.00	20.00
❑ DL 75292	I Wonder What She'll Think About Me Leaving	1971	5.00	10.00	20.00
❑ DL 75335	I Can't See Me Without You	1972	5.00	10.00	20.00
❑ DL 75352	Conway Twitty's Greatest Hits	1972	5.00	10.00	20.00
❑ DL 75361	I Can't Stop Loving You/Last Date	1972	5.00	10.00	20.00
HEARTLAND
| ❑ HL-1088/9 [(2)] The Very Best of Conway Twitty | | 1989 | 5.00 | 10.00 | 20.00 |
MCA
| ❑ 376 | Clinging to a Saving Hand | 1973 | 15.00 | 30.00 | 60.00 |
METRO
| ❑ MS-512 [S] | It's Only Make Believe | 1966 | 5.00 | 10.00 | 20.00 |
MGM
❑ GAS-110	Conway Twitty (Golden Archive Series)	1970	5.00	10.00	20.00
❑ E-3744 [M]	Conway Twitty Sings	1959	25.00	50.00	100.00
-- Yellow label					
❑ E-3744 [M]	Conway Twitty Sings	1960	10.00	20.00	40.00
-- Black label					
❑ E-3744 [M]	Conway Twitty Sings	196?	75.00	150.00	300.00
-- Reissue with orange cover and a clean-cut photo of Conway					
❑ SE-3744 [S]	Conway Twitty Sings	1959	37.50	75.00	150.00
-- Yellow label					
❑ SE-3744 [S]	Conway Twitty Sings	1960	12.50	25.00	50.00
-- Black label					
❑ SE-3744 [S]	Conway Twitty Sings	196?	75.00	150.00	300.00
-- Reissue with orange cover and a clean-cut photo of Conway					
❑ E-3786 [M]	Saturday Night with Conway	1960	17.50	35.00	70.00
❑ SE-3786 [S]	Saturday Night with Conway	1960	25.00	50.00	100.00
❑ E-3818 [M]	Lonely Blue Boy	1960	17.50	35.00	70.00
❑ SE-3818 [S]	Lonely Blue Boy	1960	25.00	50.00	100.00
❑ E-3849 [M]	Conway Twitty's Greatest Hits	1960	17.50	35.00	70.00
-- With poster					
❑ E-3849 [M]	Conway Twitty's Greatest Hits	1960	10.00	20.00	40.00
-- Without poster					
❑ SE-3849 [P]	Conway Twitty's Greatest Hits	1960	20.00	40.00	80.00
-- With poster					
❑ SE-3849 [P]	Conway Twitty's Greatest Hits	1960	12.50	25.00	50.00
-- Without poster					
❑ E-3907 [M]	The Rock and Roll Story	1961	12.50	25.00	50.00
❑ SE-3907 [S]	The Rock and Roll Story	1961	20.00	40.00	80.00
❑ E-3943 [M]	The Conway Twitty Touch	1961	12.50	25.00	50.00
❑ SE-3943 [S]	The Conway Twitty Touch	1961	20.00	40.00	80.00
❑ E-4019 [M]	Portrait of a Fool and Others	1962	10.00	20.00	40.00
❑ SE-4019 [S]	Portrait of a Fool and Others	1962	12.50	25.00	50.00
❑ E-4089 [M]	R & B '63	1963	10.00	20.00	40.00
❑ SE-4089 [S]	R & B '63	1963	12.50	25.00	50.00
❑ E-4217 [M]	Hit the Road	1964	6.25	12.50	25.00
❑ SE-4217 [S]	Hit the Road	1964	7.50	15.00	30.00
WARNER BROS.
| ❑ 23971 | Merry Twismas | 1983 | 5.00 | 10.00 | 20.00 |

TWITTY, CONWAY, AND LORETTA LYNN
Also see each artist's individual listings.
DECCA
| ❑ DL 75251 | We Only Make Believe | 1971 | 5.00 | 10.00 | 20.00 |
| ❑ DL 75326 | Lead Me On | 1972 | 5.00 | 10.00 | 20.00 |
HEARTLAND
| ❑ HL-1059/60 [(2)] The Best of Conway and Loretta | | 1987 | 5.00 | 10.00 | 20.00 |

2PAC
AMARU/JIVE
| ❑ 41628 [(3)] | R U Still Down? (Remember Me) | 1997 | 6.25 | 12.50 | 25.00 |
DEATH ROW/INTERSCOPE
| ❑ INT4-90301 [(4)] Greatest Hits | | 1998 | 7.50 | 15.00 | 30.00 |
| ❑ 524 204-1 [(4)] All Eyez on Me | | 1996 | 7.50 | 15.00 | 30.00 |
INTERSCOPE
| ❑ 92399 [(2)] | Me Against the World | 1995 | 5.00 | 10.00 | 20.00 |

TYLER, ALVIN "RED"
ACE
| ❑ LP-1006 [M] | Rockin' and Rollin' | 1960 | 37.50 | 75.00 | 150.00 |
| ❑ LP-1021 [M] | Twistin' with Mr. Sax | 1962 | 30.00 | 60.00 | 120.00 |

TYLER, T. TEXAS
CAPITOL
❑ ST 1662 [S]	Salvation	1962	7.50	15.00	30.00
❑ T 1662 [M]	Salvation	1962	6.25	12.50	25.00
❑ ST 2344 [S]	The Hits of T. Texas Tyler	1965	6.25	12.50	25.00
❑ T 2344 [M]	The Hits of T. Texas Tyler	1965	5.00	10.00	20.00
KING
❑ 664 [M]	T. Texas Tyler	1959	30.00	60.00	120.00
❑ 689 [M]	The Great Texan	1960	30.00	60.00	120.00
❑ 721 [M]	T. Texas Tyler	1961	20.00	40.00	80.00
❑ 734 [M]	Songs Along the Way	1962	20.00	40.00	80.00
SOUND
| ❑ 607 [M] | Deck of Cards | 1958 | 20.00 | 40.00 | 80.00 |
STARDAY
| ❑ SLP-379 [M] | The Man with a Million Friends | 1966 | 6.25 | 12.50 | 25.00 |
WRANGLER
| ❑ W-1002 [M] | T. Texas Tyler | 1962 | 10.00 | 20.00 | 40.00 |
| ❑ W-31002 [S] | T. Texas Tyler | 1962 | 12.50 | 25.00 | 50.00 |

TYLER, WILLIE, AND LESTER
TAMLA
| ❑ TM-265 [M] | Hello Dummy | 1965 | 50.00 | 100.00 | 200.00 |

TYMES, THE
PARKWAY
❑ P 7032 [M]	So Much in Love	1963	10.00	20.00	40.00
-- With group standing in front-cover photo					
❑ P 7032 [M]	So Much in Love	1963	50.00	100.00	200.00
-- With head-and-shoulders group photo on front cover					
❑ P 7038 [M]	The Sound of the Wonderful Tymes	1963	10.00	20.00	40.00
❑ SP 7038 [S]	The Sound of the Wonderful Tymes	1963	12.50	25.00	50.00
❑ P 7039 [M]	Somewhere	1964	12.50	25.00	50.00
-- Includes bonus single 7039 (deduct 20 percent if missing)					
❑ P 7049 [M]	18 Greatest Hits	1964	10.00	20.00	40.00

TYNER, McCOY
BLUE NOTE
❑ BLP-4264 [M]	The Real McCoy	1967	6.25	12.50	25.00
❑ BST-84264 [S] The Real McCoy		1967	5.00	10.00	20.00
-- With "A Division of Liberty Records" on label					
❑ BST-84275	Tender Moments	1968	5.00	10.00	20.00
-- With "A Division of Liberty Records" on label					
❑ BST-84307	Time for Tyner	1969	5.00	10.00	20.00
-- With "A Division of Liberty Records" on label					
❑ BST-84338	Expansions	1969	5.00	10.00	20.00
-- With "A Division of Liberty Records" on label					
GRP/IMPULSE!
❑ 216	McCoy Tyner Plays Duke	1997	5.00	10.00	20.00
-- Reissue on audiophile vinyl					
❑ 220	Inception	1997	5.00	10.00	20.00
-- Reissue on audiophile vinyl					
❑ 221	Nights of Ballads and Blues	1997	5.00	10.00	20.00
-- Reissue on audiophile vinyl					
IMPULSE!
❑ A-18 [M]	Inception	1962	6.25	12.50	25.00
❑ AS-18 [S]	Inception	1962	6.25	12.50	25.00
❑ A-33 [M]	Reaching Fourth	1963	6.25	12.50	25.00
❑ AS-33 [S]	Reaching Fourth	1963	6.25	12.50	25.00
❑ A-39 [M]	Nights of Ballads and Blues	1963	6.25	12.50	25.00
❑ AS-39 [S]	Nights of Ballads and Blues	1963	6.25	12.50	25.00
❑ A-48 [M]	McCoy Tyner Live at Newport	1963	6.25	12.50	25.00
❑ AS-48 [S]	McCoy Tyner Live at Newport	1963	6.25	12.50	25.00
❑ A-63 [M]	Today and Tomorrow	1964	6.25	12.50	25.00
❑ AS-63 [S]	Today and Tomorrow	1964	6.25	12.50	25.00
❑ A-79 [M]	McCoy Tyner Plays Duke	1965	6.25	12.50	25.00
❑ AS-79 [S]	McCoy Tyner Plays Duke	1965	6.25	12.50	25.00

TYRANNOSAURUS REX -- See T. REX.

U

U2
ISLAND

Number	Title	Yr	VG	VG+	NM
❏ PR 2049 [DJ]	The Joshua Tree Interview... Their Words and Music	1987	6.25	12.50	25.00
❏ PR12 7545-1 [(2)]	PopMart Sampler	1997	5.00	10.00	20.00
-- Promo-only collection of old and new U2 material
❏ 510 347-1	Achtung Baby	1991	10.00	20.00	40.00
-- U.S. LP covers are uncensored (Adam Clayton appears naked without any "X" or shamrock over his appendage)
❏ 518 047-1	Zooropa	1993	6.25	12.50	25.00
-- All "U.S." copies actually are British imports
❏ 524 334-1 [(2)]	Pop	1997	5.00	10.00	20.00

MOBILE FIDELITY

Number	Title	Yr	VG	VG+	NM
❏ 1-207	The Unforgettable Fire	1994	5.00	10.00	20.00
-- Audiophile vinyl

WARNER BROS.

Number	Title	Yr	VG	VG+	NM
❏ WBMS-117 [DJ]	Two Sides Live	1981	30.00	60.00	120.00
-- Promo only, part of "The Warner Bros. Music Show"; legitimate copies are on black vinyl

UFO
RARE EARTH

Number	Title	Yr	VG	VG+	NM
❏ RS 624	UFO 1	1971	6.25	12.50	25.00

UGGAMS, LESLIE
ATLANTIC

Number	Title	Yr	VG	VG+	NM
❏ SD 8128 [S]	Time to Love	1967	5.00	10.00	20.00

COLUMBIA

Number	Title	Yr	VG	VG+	NM
❏ CS 8665 [S]	More Leslie Uggams on TV	1963	5.00	10.00	20.00
❏ CS 8871 [S]	So in Love	1963	5.00	10.00	20.00

ULTIMATE SPINACH
MGM

Number	Title	Yr	VG	VG+	NM
❏ E-4518 [M]	Ultimate Spinach	1968	7.50	15.00	30.00
❏ SE-4518 [S]	Ultimate Spinach	1968	6.25	12.50	25.00
❏ E-4570 [M]	Behold & See	1968	12.50	25.00	50.00
-- Mono is promo only (yellow label)
❏ SE-4570 [S]	Behold & See	1968	6.25	12.50	25.00
❏ SE-4600	Ultimate Spinach	1969	6.25	12.50	25.00

ULTRA VIOLET
CAPITOL

Number	Title	Yr	VG	VG+	NM
❏ ST-11244	Ultra Violet	1973	6.25	12.50	25.00

UMEKI, MIYOSHI
MERCURY

Number	Title	Yr	VG	VG+	NM
❏ MG-20568 [M]	Miyoshi	1958	5.00	10.00	20.00
❏ SR-60228 [S]	Miyoshi	1959	6.25	12.50	25.00

UNBEATABLES, THE
DAWN

Number	Title	Yr	VG	VG+	NM
❏ 5050 [M]	Live at Palisades Park	1964	37.50	75.00	150.00

UNCLE JOSH AND COUSIN JAKE
COTTON TOWN

Number	Title	Yr	VG	VG+	NM
❏ 101 [M]	Just Joshing	1958	25.00	50.00	100.00

UNCLE LAR' AND LIL' TOMMY
WLS

Number	Title	Yr	VG	VG+	NM
❏ WLS-890	Animal Stories	1981	5.00	10.00	20.00
❏ WLS-947	Animal Stories Volume Three	1983	5.00	10.00	20.00
❏ WLS-1000	Animal Stories Volume Two	1982	5.00	10.00	20.00

UNDERGROUND SUNSHINE
INTREPID

Number	Title	Yr	VG	VG+	NM
❏ IT-74003	Let There Be Light	1969	7.50	15.00	30.00

UNDERGROUND, THE
WING

Number	Title	Yr	VG	VG+	NM
❏ MGW-12337 [M]	Psychedelic Visions	1967	20.00	40.00	80.00
❏ SRW-16337 [S]	Psychedelic Visions	1967	25.00	50.00	100.00

UNDISPUTED TRUTH, THE
GORDY

Number	Title	Yr	VG	VG+	NM
❏ G 955L	The Undisputed Truth	1971	6.25	12.50	25.00
❏ G5-959	Face to Face with the Truth	1972	5.00	10.00	20.00
❏ G5-963	Law of the Land	1973	5.00	10.00	20.00
❏ G6-968	Down to Earth	1974	5.00	10.00	20.00
❏ G6-970	Cosmic Truth	1975	5.00	10.00	20.00
❏ G6-972	Higher Than High	1975	5.00	10.00	20.00

UNFOLDING
AUDIO FIDELITY

Number	Title	Yr	VG	VG+	NM
❏ AFLP-2184 [M]	How to Blow Your Mind and Have a Freak-Out Party	1967	17.50	35.00	70.00
❏ AFSD-6184 [S]	How to Blow Your Mind and Have a Freak-Out Party	1967	25.00	50.00	100.00

UNIFICS, THE
KAPP

Number	Title	Yr	VG	VG+	NM
❏ KS-3582	Sittin' In at the Court of Love	1968	6.25	12.50	25.00

UNIQUES, THE
PAULA

Number	Title	Yr	VG	VG+	NM
❏ LP-2190 [M]	Uniquely Yours	1966	6.25	12.50	25.00
❏ LPS-2190 [S]	Uniquely Yours	1966	7.50	15.00	30.00
❏ LP-2194 [M]	Happening Now	1967	6.25	12.50	25.00
❏ LPS-2194 [S]	Happening Now	1967	7.50	15.00	30.00
❏ LP-2199 [M]	Playtime	1968	6.25	12.50	25.00
❏ LPS-2199 [S]	Playtime	1968	6.25	12.50	25.00
❏ LPS-2204	The Uniques	1969	6.25	12.50	25.00
❏ LPS-2208	Golden Hits	1970	6.25	12.50	25.00

UNIT FOUR PLUS TWO
LONDON

Number	Title	Yr	VG	VG+	NM
❏ PS 427 [P]	Unit Four Plus Two #1	1965	12.50	25.00	50.00
❏ LL 3427 [M]	Unit Four Plus Two #1	1965	10.00	20.00	40.00

UNITED STATES DOUBLE QUARTET
Also see THE KIRBY STONE FOUR; THE TOKENS.
B.T. PUPPY

Number	Title	Yr	VG	VG+	NM
❏ BTS-1005	Life Is Groovy	1969	12.50	25.00	50.00

UNITED STATES OF AMERICA, THE
COLUMBIA

Number	Title	Yr	VG	VG+	NM
❏ CL 2814 [M]	The United States of America	1968	25.00	50.00	100.00
-- Mono is promo only
❏ CS 9614 [S]	The United States of America	1968	20.00	40.00	80.00
-- With outer bag
❏ CS 9614 [S]	The United States of America	1968	10.00	20.00	40.00
-- Without outer bag

UNSPOKEN WORD, THE
ASCOT

Number	Title	Yr	VG	VG+	NM
❏ AS 16028	Tuesday, April 19th	1968	5.00	10.00	20.00

UNUSUAL WE
PULSAR

Number	Title	Yr	VG	VG+	NM
❏ 10608	Unusual We	1969	7.50	15.00	30.00

UPCHURCH, PHIL
BOYD

Number	Title	Yr	VG	VG+	NM
❏ B-398 [M]	You Can't Sit Down	1961	20.00	40.00	80.00
❏ BS-398 [S]	You Can't Sit Down	1961	25.00	50.00	100.00

UNITED ARTISTS

Number	Title	Yr	VG	VG+	NM
❏ UAL-3162 [M]	You Can't Sit Down, Part 2	1961	7.50	15.00	30.00
❏ UAL-3175 [M]	Big Hit Dances	1962	6.25	12.50	25.00
❏ UAS-6162 [S]	You Can't Sit Down, Part 2	1961	10.00	20.00	40.00
❏ UAS-6175 [S]	Big Hit Dances	1962	7.50	15.00	30.00

URGE OVERKILL
TOUCH & GO

Number	Title	Yr	VG	VG+	NM
❏ 86 [10]	Stull	1992	6.25	12.50	25.00
-- Whitish vinyl original

Number	Title	Yr	VG	VG+	NM

V

VAGABONDS, THE
UNIQUE
❑ LP-112 [M]	The Vagabonds	1957	6.25	12.50	25.00

VAGRANTS, THE
ARISTA
| ❑ AL-8459 | The Great Lost Vagrants Album | 1987 | 5.00 | 10.00 | 20.00 |

VALE, JERRY
COLUMBIA
❑ CS 8016 [S]	I Remember Russ	1958	5.00	10.00	20.00
-- Originals have red and black "6 eye" labels					
❑ CS 8069 [S]	I Remember Buddy	1959	5.00	10.00	20.00
-- Originals have red and black "6 eye" labels					

VALE, RICKY, AND THE SURFERS
STRAND
| ❑ SL-1104 [M] | Everybody's Surfin' | 1963 | 10.00 | 20.00 | 40.00 |
| ❑ SLS-1104 [S] | Everybody's Surfin' | 1963 | 12.50 | 25.00 | 50.00 |

VALENS, RITCHIE
DEL-FI
❑ DFLP 1201 [M] Ritchie Valens		1959	62.50	125.00	250.00
-- Blue label with black border					
❑ DFLP 1201 [M] Ritchie Valens		1959	37.50	75.00	150.00
-- Black label with "diamonds" border					
❑ DFLP 1206 [M] Ritchie		1959	37.50	75.00	150.00
❑ DFLP 1214 [M] In Concert at Pacoima Jr. High		1960	62.50	125.00	250.00
❑ DFLP 1225 [M] His Greatest Hits		1963	87.50	175.00	350.00
-- Black cover					
❑ DFLP 1225 [M] His Greatest Hits		1963	37.50	75.00	150.00
-- White cover					
❑ DFLP 1247 [M] His Greatest Hits, Volume 2		1965	37.50	75.00	150.00
GUEST STAR
❑ GS-1469 [M]	The Original Ritchie Valens	1963	7.50	15.00	30.00
❑ GSS-1469 [R]	The Original Ritchie Valens	1963	5.00	10.00	20.00
❑ GS-1484 [M]	The Original La Bamba	1963	7.50	15.00	30.00
❑ GSS-1484 [R]	The Original La Bamba	1963	5.00	10.00	20.00
MGM
| ❑ GAS-117 | Ritchie Valens (Golden Archive Series) | 1970 | 7.50 | 15.00 | 30.00 |
RHINO
| ❑ RNBC-2798 [(3)] The History of Ritchie Valens | | 198? | 6.25 | 12.50 | 25.00 |

VALENS, RITCHIE / JERRY KOLE
CROWN
| ❑ CLP-5336 [M] | Ritchie Valens and Jerry Kole | 1963 | 7.50 | 15.00 | 30.00 |

VALENTE, CATERINA
DECCA
❑ DL 4035 [M]	More Schlagerparade	1959	6.25	12.50	25.00
❑ DL 4050 [M]	Caterina A La Carte	1959	6.25	12.50	25.00
❑ DL 4051 [M]	Arriba	1959	6.25	12.50	25.00
❑ DL 4052 [M]	Catarina	1959	6.25	12.50	25.00
❑ DL 4504 [M]	Golden Favorites	1964	5.00	10.00	20.00
❑ DL 8203 [M]	The Hi-Fi Nightingale	1956	6.25	12.50	25.00
❑ DL 8436 [M]	Ole Caterina	1957	6.25	12.50	25.00
❑ DL 8440 [M]	Plenty Valente!	1957	6.25	12.50	25.00
❑ DL 8755 [M]	A Toast to the Girls	1958	6.25	12.50	25.00
RCA VICTOR
❑ LPM-2119 [M]	Classics with a Chaser	1960	5.00	10.00	20.00
❑ LSP-2119 [S]	Classics with a Chaser	1960	6.25	12.50	25.00
❑ LPM-2241 [M]	Superfonics	1961	5.00	10.00	20.00
❑ LSP-2241 [S]	Superfonics	1961	6.25	12.50	25.00

VALENTI, DINO
EPIC
| ❑ LN 24335 [M] | Dino Valenti | 1967 | 5.00 | 10.00 | 20.00 |
| ❑ BN 26335 [S] | Dino Valenti | 1967 | 5.00 | 10.00 | 20.00 |

VALENTINE, HILTON
Also see THE ANIMALS.
CAPITOL
| ❑ ST-330 | All in Your Head | 1969 | 7.50 | 15.00 | 30.00 |

VALENTINE, JIMMIE
JUBILEE
| ❑ LP-9 [10] | Music to Beat By | 1954 | 10.00 | 20.00 | 40.00 |

VALENTINO, MARK
SWAN
| ❑ SLP-508 [M] | Mark Valentino | 1963 | 12.50 | 25.00 | 50.00 |

VALENTYNE, RUDY
ROULETTE
| ❑ R-25299 [M] | And Now… Rudy Valentyne | 1965 | 5.00 | 10.00 | 20.00 |
| ❑ SR-25299 [S] | And Now… Rudy Valentyne | 1965 | 6.25 | 12.50 | 25.00 |

VALHALLA
UNITED ARTISTS
| ❑ UAS-6730 | Valhalla | 1969 | 6.25 | 12.50 | 25.00 |

VALIDS, THE
AMBER
| ❑ 802 [M] | Accapella | 1966 | 6.25 | 12.50 | 25.00 |

VALJEAN
CARLTON
❑ LP-142 [M]	The Theme from Ben Casey	1962	5.00	10.00	20.00
❑ STLP-142 [S]	The Theme from Ben Casey	1962	6.25	12.50	25.00
❑ LP-146 [M]	Mashin' the Classics	1963	5.00	10.00	20.00
❑ STLP-146 [S]	Mashin' the Classics	1963	6.25	12.50	25.00

VALLEE, RUDY
RCA VICTOR
| ❑ LPM-2507 [M] | Young Rudy Vallee | 1961 | 7.50 | 15.00 | 30.00 |
| ❑ LSP-2507 [R] | Young Rudy Vallee | 196? | 5.00 | 10.00 | 20.00 |

VALLEY, JIM
PANORAMA
| ❑ 104-S | Jim "Harpo" Valley | 1968 | 10.00 | 20.00 | 40.00 |

VALLI, FRANKIE
Also see THE FOUR SEASONS.
PHILIPS
❑ PHM 200-247 [M]	Frankie Valli -- Solo	1967	10.00	20.00	40.00
❑ PHS 600-247 [S]	Frankie Valli -- Solo	1967	7.50	15.00	30.00
❑ PHS 600-274	Timeless	1968	6.25	12.50	25.00

VALLI, FRANKIE, AND THE FOUR SEASONS -- See THE FOUR SEASONS.

VAMPIRES, THE
UNITED ARTISTS
| ❑ UAL-3378 [M] | The Vampires at the Monster Ball | 1964 | 6.25 | 12.50 | 25.00 |
| ❑ UAS-6378 [S] | The Vampires at the Monster Ball | 1964 | 7.50 | 15.00 | 30.00 |

VAN DER GRAAF GENERATOR
MERCURY
| ❑ SR-61238 | The Aerosol Grey Machine | 1969 | 25.00 | 50.00 | 100.00 |
PROBE
| ❑ CLP-4515 | The Least We Can Do Is Wave | 1970 | 7.50 | 5.00 | 30.00 |

VAN DERBUR, MARILYN
DECCA
| ❑ DL 8770 [M] | Miss America | 1958 | 10.00 | 20.00 | 40.00 |

VAN DYKE, DICK
COMMAND
| ❑ RS 33-860 [M] | Songs I Like | 1963 | 6.25 | 12.50 | 25.00 |
| ❑ RS 860 SD [S] | Songs I Like | 1963 | 7.50 | 15.00 | 30.00 |

VAN DYKE, EARL, AND THE SOUL BROTHERS
MOTOWN
| ❑ M-631 [M] | The Motown Sound | 1965 | 10.00 | 20.00 | 40.00 |
| ❑ MS-631 [S] | The Motown Sound | 1965 | 12.50 | 25.00 | 50.00 |
SOUL
| ❑ SS-715 | The Earl of Funk | 1970 | 10.00 | 20.00 | 40.00 |

VAN DYKE, LEROY
DOT
| ❑ DLP 3693 [M] | Auctioneer | 1966 | 5.00 | 10.00 | 20.00 |
MERCURY
| ❑ MG-20682 [M] | Walk On By | 1962 | 5.00 | 10.00 | 20.00 |
| ❑ MG-20716 [M] | Movin' Van Dyke | 1963 | 5.00 | 10.00 | 20.00 |

Number	Title	Yr	VG	VG+	NM
❏ MG-20802 [M] Leroy Van Dyke's Greatest Hits		1963	5.00	10.00	20.00
❏ MG-20922 [M] Songs for Mom and Dad		1964	5.00	10.00	20.00
❏ SR-60682 [S] Walk On By		1962	6.25	12.50	25.00
❏ SR-60716 [S] Movin' Van Dyke		1963	6.25	12.50	25.00
❏ SR-60802 [S] Leroy Van Dyke's Greatest Hits		1963	6.25	12.50	25.00
❏ SR-60922 [S] Songs for Mom and Dad		1964	6.25	12.50	25.00
❏ SR-60950 [S] Leroy Van Dyke at the Tradewinds		1964	6.25	12.50	25.00

WARNER BROS.

Number	Title	Yr	VG	VG+	NM
❏ WS 1618 [S] The Leroy Van Dyke Show		1965	5.00	10.00	20.00
❏ WS 1652 [S] Country Hits		1966	5.00	10.00	20.00

VAN DYKES, THE
BELL

Number	Title	Yr	VG	VG+	NM
❏ 6004 [M]	Tellin' It Like It Is	1967	12.50	25.00	50.00
❏ S-6004 [S]	Tellin' It Like It Is	1967	15.00	30.00	60.00

VAN HALEN
WARNER BROS.

Number	Title	Yr	VG	VG+	NM
❏ PRO 705 [DJ]	Looney Tunes	1978	10.00	20.00	40.00
-- Promo-only EP on red vinyl					
❏ 23985 [DJ]	1984	1984	6.25	12.50	25.00
-- Promo on Quiex II vinyl					
❏ W1-26594	For Unlawful Carnal Knowledge	1991	5.00	10.00	20.00
-- The only U.S. vinyl version was released through Columbia House					

VAN HEUSEN, JIMMY
UNITED ARTISTS

Number	Title	Yr	VG	VG+	NM
❏ UAL-3494 [M] Van Heusen Plays Van Heusen		1966	5.00	10.00	20.00
❏ UAS-6494 [S] Van Heusen Plays Van Heusen		1966	6.25	12.50	25.00

VAN RONK, DAVE
CADET

Number	Title	Yr	VG	VG+	NM
❏ CA-50044	Songs for Aging Children	1973	5.00	10.00	20.00

FANTASY

Number	Title	Yr	VG	VG+	NM
❏ 24710 [(2)]	Dave Van Ronk	1972	5.00	10.00	20.00

FOLKLORE

Number	Title	Yr	VG	VG+	NM
❏ FRLP-14001 [M] In the Tradition		1963	7.50	15.00	30.00
❏ FRST-14001 [S] In the Tradition		1963	10.00	20.00	40.00
❏ FRLP-14012 [M] Dave Van Ronk, Folksinger		1963	7.50	15.00	30.00
❏ FRST-14012 [S] Dave Van Ronk, Folksinger		1963	10.00	20.00	40.00
❏ FRLP-14025 [M] Inside Dave Van Ronk		1964	7.50	15.00	30.00
❏ FRST-14025 [S] Inside Dave Van Ronk		1964	10.00	20.00	40.00

FOLKWAYS

Number	Title	Yr	VG	VG+	NM
❏ FA-2383 [M]	Dave Van Ronk Sings Earthy Ballads and Blues	1961	10.00	20.00	40.00
❏ FS-3818 [M]	Dave Van Ronk Sings Ballads, Blues and Spirituals	1959	10.00	20.00	40.00
❏ FTS 31020	Black Mountain Blues	1968	6.25	12.50	25.00

MERCURY

Number	Title	Yr	VG	VG+	NM
❏ MG-20864 [M]	Dave Van Ronk and the Ragtime Jug Stompers	1964	6.25	12.50	25.00
❏ MG-20908 [M]	Just Dave Van Ronk	1964	6.25	12.50	25.00
❏ SR-60864 [S]	Dave Van Ronk and the Ragtime Jug Stompers	1964	7.50	15.00	30.00
❏ SR-60908 [S]	Just Dave Van Ronk	1964	7.50	15.00	30.00

POLYDOR

Number	Title	Yr	VG	VG+	NM
❏ 24-4052	Van Ronk	1972	5.00	10.00	20.00

VERVE FOLKWAYS

Number	Title	Yr	VG	VG+	NM
❏ FV-9006 [M]	Dave Van Ronk Sings the Blues	1965	6.25	12.50	25.00
❏ FVS-9006 [S]	Dave Van Ronk Sings the Blues	1965	7.50	15.00	30.00
❏ FV-9017 [M]	Gambler's Blues	1965	6.25	12.50	25.00
❏ FVS-9017 [S]	Gambler's Blues	1965	7.50	15.00	30.00

VERVE FORECAST

Number	Title	Yr	VG	VG+	NM
❏ FT-3009 [M]	No Dirty Names	1967	6.25	12.50	25.00
❏ FTS-3009 [S]	No Dirty Names	1967	7.50	15.00	30.00
❏ FTS-3041	Dave Van Ronk and the Hudson Dusters	1968	6.25	12.50	25.00

VAN VOOREN, MONIQUE
RCA VICTOR

Number	Title	Yr	VG	VG+	NM
❏ LPM-1553 [M] Mink in Hi-Fi		1958	6.25	12.50	25.00

VAN ZANDT, TOWNES
POPPY

Number	Title	Yr	VG	VG+	NM
❏ PYS-40001	For the Sake of a Song	1968	6.25	12.50	25.00

VANDROSS, LUTHER
EPIC

Number	Title	Yr	VG	VG+	NM
❏ HE 47451	Never Too Much	198?	7.50	15.00	30.00
-- Half-speed mastered edition					

VANILLA FUDGE
ATCO

Number	Title	Yr	VG	VG+	NM
❏ 33-224 [M]	Vanilla Fudge	1967	6.25	12.50	25.00
❏ SD 33-224 [S]	Vanilla Fudge	1967	5.00	10.00	20.00
-- Purple and brown label					
❏ SD 33-237	The Beat Goes On	1968	5.00	10.00	20.00
-- Purple and brown label					
❏ 33-237 [M]	The Beat Goes On	1968	10.00	20.00	40.00
❏ SD 33-244	Renaissance	1968	5.00	10.00	20.00
-- Purple and brown label					

VANILLA ICE
ULTRA

Number	Title	Yr	VG	VG+	NM
❏ ULT 4019	Hooked	1990	7.50	15.00	30.00

VANITY FARE
PAGE ONE

Number	Title	Yr	VG	VG+	NM
❏ 2502	Early in the Morning	1970	5.00	10.00	20.00

VANNELLI, GINO
MOBILE FIDELITY

Number	Title	Yr	VG	VG+	NM
❏ 1-041	Powerful People	1980	5.00	10.00	20.00
-- Audiophile vinyl					

NAUTILUS

Number	Title	Yr	VG	VG+	NM
❏ NR-35	Brother to Brother	198?	6.25	12.50	25.00
-- Audiophile vinyl					

VARIATIONS, THE
JUSTICE

Number	Title	Yr	VG	VG+	NM
❏ JLP-212	Dig 'Em Up	196?	100.00	200.00	400.00

VAUGHAN, FRANKIE
PHILIPS

Number	Title	Yr	VG	VG+	NM
❏ PHM 200-006 [M] Singin' Happy		1962	5.00	10.00	20.00
❏ PHS 600-006 [S] Singin' Happy		1962	6.25	12.50	25.00

VAUGHAN, SARAH
ALLEGRO

Number	Title	Yr	VG	VG+	NM
❏ 1592 [M]	Sarah Vaughan	1955	12.50	25.00	50.00
❏ 1608 [M]	Sarah Vaughan	1955	12.50	25.00	50.00
❏ 3080 [10]	Early Sarah	195?	20.00	40.00	80.00

COLUMBIA

Number	Title	Yr	VG	VG+	NM
❏ CL 660 [M]	After Hours with Sarah Vaughan	1955	12.50	25.00	50.00
❏ CL 745 [M]	Sarah Vaughan in Hi-Fi	1956	12.50	25.00	50.00
❏ CL 914 [M]	Linger Awhile	1956	12.50	25.00	50.00
❏ CL 6133 [10]	Sarah Vaughan	1950	30.00	60.00	120.00

CONCORD

Number	Title	Yr	VG	VG+	NM
❏ 3018 [M]	Sarah Vaughan Concert	1957	7.50	15.00	30.00

EMARCY

Number	Title	Yr	VG	VG+	NM
❏ MG-26005 [10]	Images	1954	20.00	40.00	80.00
❏ MG-36004 [M]	Sarah Vaughan	1955	20.00	40.00	80.00
❏ MG-36058 [M]	In the Land of Hi-Fi	1956	20.00	40.00	80.00
❏ MG-36089 [M]	Sassy	1956	12.50	25.00	50.00
❏ MG-36109 [M]	Swingin' Easy	1957	12.50	25.00	50.00

LION

Number	Title	Yr	VG	VG+	NM
❏ L 70052 [M]	Tenderly	1958	6.25	12.50	25.00

MASTERSEAL

Number	Title	Yr	VG	VG+	NM
❏ MS-55 [M]	Sarah Vaughan Sings	195?	6.25	12.50	25.00

MERCURY

Number	Title	Yr	VG	VG+	NM
❏ MGP-2-100 [(2) M] Great Songs from Hit Shows		1957	15.00	30.00	60.00
❏ MGP-2-101 [(2) M] Sarah Vaughan Sings George Gershwin		1957	15.00	30.00	60.00
❏ MG-20094 [M] Sarah Vaughan at the Blue Note		1956	10.00	20.00	40.00
❏ MG-20219 [M] Wonderful Sarah		1957	10.00	20.00	40.00
❏ MG-20223 [M] In a Romantic Mood		1957	10.00	20.00	40.00
❏ MG-20244 [M] Great Songs from Hit Shows, Vol. 1		1958	7.50	15.00	30.00
❏ MG-20245 [M] Great Songs from Hit Shows, Vol. 2		1958	7.50	15.00	30.00
❏ MG-20310 [M] Sarah Vaughan Sings George Gershwin, Vol. 1		1958	7.50	15.00	30.00
❏ MG-20311 [M] Sarah Vaughan Sings George Gershwin, Vol. 2		1958	7.50	15.00	30.00
❏ MG-20326 [M] Sarah Vaughan and Her Trio at Mr. Kelly's		1958	10.00	20.00	40.00
❏ MG-20370 [M] Vaughan and Violins		1958	10.00	20.00	40.00
❏ MG-20383 [M] After Hours at the London House		1958	10.00	20.00	40.00
❏ MG-20438 [M] The Magic of Sarah Vaughan		1959	7.50	15.00	30.00
❏ MG-20441 [M] No 'Count Sarah		1959	7.50	15.00	30.00
❏ MG-20540 [M] The Divine Sarah Vaughan		1960	6.25	12.50	25.00
❏ MG-20580 [M] Close to You		1960	6.25	12.50	25.00
❏ MG-20617 [M] My Heart Sings		1961	6.25	12.50	25.00
❏ MG-20645 [M] Sarah Vaughan's Golden Hits		1961	5.00	10.00	20.00
❏ MG-20831 [M] Sassy Swings the Tivoli		1962	5.00	10.00	20.00

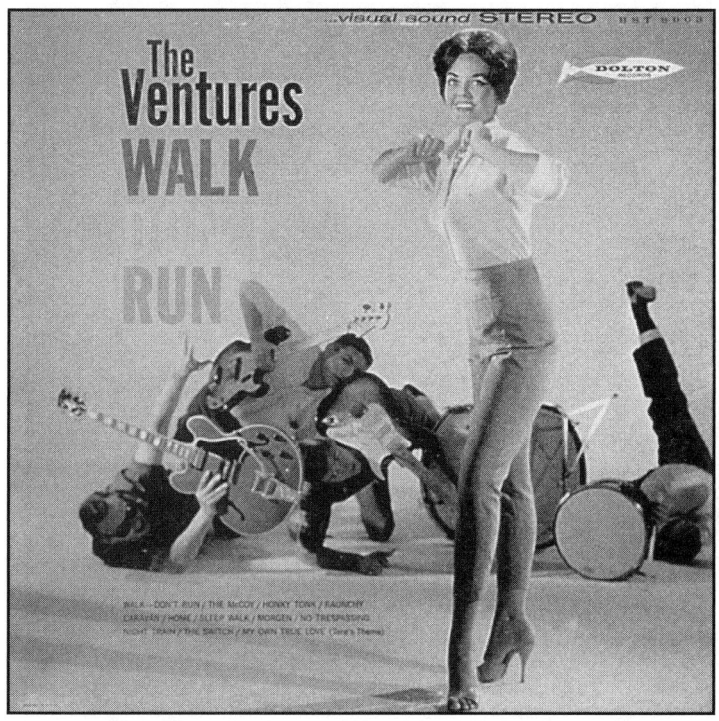

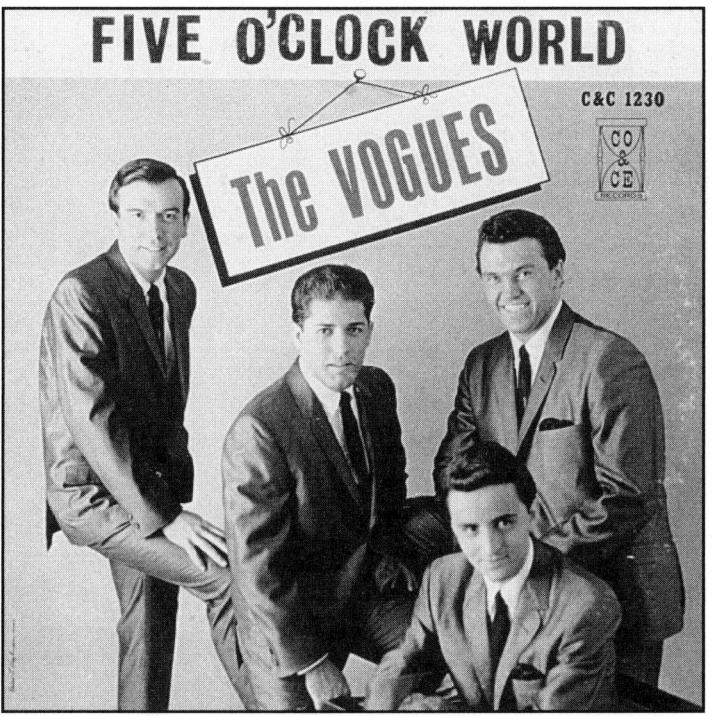

(Top left) One of the many British Invasion groups that tried to have success in the U.S. but never quite made it was Unit Four Plus Two. Their only American album contains their biggest hit, "Concrete and Clay." (Top right) Not as sought-after as their albums on Verve, the Velvet Underground's *Loaded,* their last album as a unit, introduced two of their classics, "Sweet Jane" and "Rock and Roll." An entire 2-CD set of this album, plus outtakes and alternate mixes, was issued by Rhino in 1996. (Bottom left) You have to start somewhere, and this is where the Ventures started their long career as rock's greatest instrumental band. Here is an original stereo pressing of *Walk Don't Run.* (Bottom right) The Vogues had two albums released on the Pittsburgh-based Co & Ce label in 1965 and 1966. This is the second of them, *Five O'Clock World.* Contrary to what you may have seen elsewhere, neither Co & Ce album was released in stereo.

Number	Title	Yr	VG	VG+	NM
❏ MG-20882 [M]	Vaughan with Voices	1963	5.00	10.00	20.00
❏ MG-25188 [10]	Divine Sarah	1955	25.00	50.00	100.00
❏ SR-60020 [S]	After Hours at the London House	1959	10.00	20.00	40.00
❏ SR-60038 [S]	Vaughan and Violins	1959	10.00	20.00	40.00
❏ SR-60041 [S]	Great Songs from Hit Shows, Vol. 1	1959	10.00	20.00	40.00
❏ SR-60045 [S]	Sarah Vaughan Sings George Gershwin, Vol. 1	1959	10.00	20.00	40.00
❏ SR-60046 [S]	Sarah Vaughan Sings George Gershwin, Vol. 2	1959	10.00	20.00	40.00
❏ SR-60078 [S]	Great Songs from Hit Shows, Vol. 2	1959	10.00	20.00	40.00
❏ SR-60110 [S]	The Magic of Sarah Vaughan	1959	10.00	20.00	40.00
❏ SR-60116 [S]	No 'Count Sarah	1959	10.00	20.00	40.00
❏ SR-60240 [S]	Close to You	1960	7.50	15.00	30.00
❏ SR-60255 [S]	The Divine Sarah Vaughan	1960	7.50	15.00	30.00
❏ SR-60617 [S]	My Heart Sings	1961	7.50	15.00	30.00
❏ SR-60645 [S]	Sarah Vaughan's Golden Hits	1961	6.25	12.50	25.00
-- Original black label version					
❏ SR-60831 [S]	Sassy Swings the Tivoli	1962	6.25	12.50	25.00
❏ SR-60882 [S]	Vaughan with Voices	1963	6.25	12.50	25.00
❏ SR-60941 [S]	Viva Vaughan	1964	5.00	10.00	20.00
❏ SR-61009 [S]	Sarah Vaughan Sings the Mancini Songbook	1965	5.00	10.00	20.00
❏ SR-61069 [S]	The Pop Artistry of Sarah Vaughan	1966	5.00	10.00	20.00
❏ SR-61079 [S]	The New Scene	1966	5.00	10.00	20.00
❏ SR-61116 [S]	Sassy Swings Again	1967	5.00	10.00	20.00
❏ SR-61122 [S]	It's a Man's World	1967	5.00	10.00	20.00
❏ 826 320-1 [(6)]	The Complete Sarah Vaughan on Mercury Vol. 1: Great Jazz Years (1954-56)	1986	10.00	20.00	40.00
❏ 826 327-1 [(5)]	The Complete Sarah Vaughan on Mercury Vol. 2: Great American Songs (1956-57)	1986	10.00	20.00	40.00
❏ 826 333-1 [(6)]	The Complete Sarah Vaughan on Mercury Vol. 3: Great Show on Stage (1954-56)	1986	10.00	20.00	40.00
❏ 830 721-1 [(4)]	The Complete Sarah Vaughan on Mercury Vol. 4 Part 1: Live in Europe (1963-64)	1987	10.00	20.00	40.00
❏ 830 726-1 [(5)]	The Complete Sarah Vaughan on Mercury Vol. 4 Part 2: Sassy Swings Again	1987	10.00	20.00	40.00

MGM

Number	Title	Yr	VG	VG+	NM
❏ E-165 [10]	Tenderly	1950	30.00	60.00	120.00
❏ E-544 [10]	Sarah Vaughan Sings	1951	30.00	60.00	120.00
❏ E-3274 [M]	My Kinda Love	1955	12.50	25.00	50.00
-- Combination of two 10-inch LPs on one 12-inch LP					

REMINGTON

Number	Title	Yr	VG	VG+	NM
❏ RLP-1024 [10]	Hot Jazz	1953	50.00	100.00	200.00

RIVERSIDE

Number	Title	Yr	VG	VG+	NM
❏ RLP 2511 [10]	Sarah Vaughan Sings with John Kirby	1955	25.00	50.00	100.00

RONDO-LETTE

Number	Title	Yr	VG	VG+	NM
❏ A-35 [M]	Songs of Broadway	1958	6.25	12.50	25.00
❏ A-53 [M]	Sarah Vaughan Sings	1959	6.25	12.50	25.00

ROULETTE

Number	Title	Yr	VG	VG+	NM
❏ R 52046 [M]	Dreamy	1960	7.50	15.00	30.00
❏ SR 52046 [S]	Dreamy	1960	10.00	20.00	40.00
❏ R 52060 [M]	Divine One	1960	6.25	12.50	25.00
❏ SR 52060 [S]	Divine One	1960	7.50	15.00	30.00
❏ R 52070 [M]	After Hours	1961	6.25	12.50	25.00
❏ SR 52070 [S]	After Hours	1961	7.50	15.00	30.00
❏ R 52082 [M]	You're Mine	1962	6.25	12.50	25.00
❏ SR 52082 [S]	You're Mine	1962	15.00	30.00	60.00
-- Red vinyl					
❏ SR 52082 [S]	You're Mine	1962	7.50	15.00	30.00
-- Black vinyl					
❏ R 52091 [M]	Snowbound	1962	5.00	10.00	20.00
❏ SR 52091 [S]	Snowbound	1962	6.25	12.50	25.00
❏ R 52092 [M]	The Explosive Side of Sarah	1962	5.00	10.00	20.00
❏ SR 52092 [S]	The Explosive Side of Sarah	1962	6.25	12.50	25.00
❏ SR 52100 [S]	Star Eyes	1963	5.00	10.00	20.00
❏ SR 52104 [S]	Lonely Hours	1963	5.00	10.00	20.00
❏ SR 52109 [S]	The World of Sarah Vaughan	1964	5.00	10.00	20.00
❏ SR 52112 [S]	Sweet 'N Sassy	1964	5.00	10.00	20.00
❏ SR 52116 [S]	Sarah Sings Soulfully	1965	5.00	10.00	20.00
❏ SR 52118 [S]	Sarah Plus Two	1965	5.00	10.00	20.00

SPIN-O-RAMA

Number	Title	Yr	VG	VG+	NM
❏ 73 [M]	Sweet, Sultry and Swinging	196?	10.00	20.00	40.00
❏ S-73 [S]	Sweet, Sultry and Swinging	196?	12.50	25.00	50.00
❏ 114 [M]	The Divine Sarah Vaughan	196?	10.00	20.00	40.00
❏ S-114 [S]	The Divine Sarah Vaughan	196?	12.50	25.00	50.00

VAUGHAN, SARAH, AND COUNT BASIE

Also see each artist's individual listings.

ROULETTE

Number	Title	Yr	VG	VG+	NM
❏ R 52061 [M]	Count Basie/Sarah Vaughan	1960	6.25	12.50	25.00
❏ SR 52061 [S]	Count Basie/Sarah Vaughan	1960	7.50	15.00	30.00

VAUGHAN, SARAH, AND BILLY ECKSTINE

Also see each artist's individual listings.

MERCURY

Number	Title	Yr	VG	VG+	NM
❏ MG-20316 [M]	Sarah Vaughan and Billy Eckstine Sing the Best of Irving Berlin	1959	7.50	15.00	30.00
❏ SR-60002 [S]	Sarah Vaughan and Billy Eckstine Sing the Best of Irving Berlin	1959	10.00	20.00	40.00

VAUGHAN, SARAH; DINAH WASHINGTON; & JOE WILLIAMS

Also see each artist's individual listings.

ROULETTE

Number	Title	Yr	VG	VG+	NM
❏ SR 52108 [S]	We Three	1964	5.00	10.00	20.00

VAUGHAN, STEVIE RAY

EPIC

Number	Title	Yr	VG	VG+	NM
❏ 8E8 39609 [PD]	Couldn't Stand the Weather	1984	37.50	75.00	150.00

VAUGHN, BILLY

DOT

Number	Title	Yr	VG	VG+	NM
❏ DLP 3001 [M]	Sweet Music and Memories	1955	6.25	12.50	25.00
-- Maroon label					
❏ DLP 3016 [M]	The Golden Instrumentals	1956	6.25	12.50	25.00
-- Maroon label					
❏ DLP 25100 [S]	Sail Along Silv'ry Moon	1959	5.00	10.00	20.00
❏ DLP 25119 [S]	Billy Vaughn Plays the Million Sellers	1959	5.00	10.00	20.00
❏ DLP 25140 [S]	La Paloma	1959	5.00	10.00	20.00
❏ DLP 25156 [S]	Billy Vaughn Plays	1959	5.00	10.00	20.00
❏ DLP 25165 [S]	Blue Hawaii	1959	5.00	10.00	20.00
❏ DLP 25201 [S]	Golden Hits	1959	5.00	10.00	20.00
❏ DLP 25205 [S]	Golden Saxophones	1959	5.00	10.00	20.00
❏ DLP 25260 [S]	Billy Vaughn Plays Stephen Foster	1960	5.00	10.00	20.00
❏ DLP 25275 [S]	Linger Awhile	1960	5.00	10.00	20.00
❏ DLP 25276 [S]	Theme from A Summer Place	1960	5.00	10.00	20.00
❏ DLP 25280 [S]	Golden Waltzes	1961	5.00	10.00	20.00
❏ DLP 25288 [S]	Great Golden Hits	1960	5.00	10.00	20.00
❏ DLP 25322 [S]	Look for a Star	1960	5.00	10.00	20.00
❏ DLP 25349 [S]	Theme from The Sundowners	1960	5.00	10.00	20.00
❏ DLP 25366 [S]	Orange Blossom Special and Wheels	1961	5.00	10.00	20.00
❏ DLP 25396 [S]	Berlin Melody	1961	5.00	10.00	20.00
❏ DLP 25409 [S]	Greatest String Band Hits	1962	5.00	10.00	20.00
❏ DLP 25424 [S]	Chapel by the Sea	1962	5.00	10.00	20.00
❏ DLP 25442 [S]	The Shifting, Whispering Sands	1962	5.00	10.00	20.00
❏ DLP 25458 [S]	A Swingin' Safari	1962	5.00	10.00	20.00

VAUGHN, ROBERT

MGM

Number	Title	Yr	VG	VG+	NM
❏ E-4488 [M]	Readings from Hamlet	1962	6.25	12.50	25.00
❏ SE-4488 [S]	Readings from Hamlet	1962	7.50	15.00	30.00

VAUGHT, BOB, AND THE RENEGADES

GNP CRESCENDO

Number	Title	Yr	VG	VG+	NM
❏ GNP-83 [M]	Surf Crazy	1963	7.50	15.00	30.00
❏ GNPS-83 [S]	Surf Crazy	1963	10.00	20.00	40.00

VEE, BOBBY

LIBERTY

Number	Title	Yr	VG	VG+	NM
❏ LRP-3165 [M]	Bobby Vee Sings Your Favorites	1960	12.50	25.00	50.00
❏ LRP-3181 [M]	Bobby Vee	1961	10.00	20.00	40.00
❏ LRP-3186 [M]	Bobby Vee With Strings and	1961	10.00	20.00	40.00
❏ LRP-3205 [M]	Bobby Vee Sings Hits of the Rockin' 50's	1961	10.00	20.00	40.00
❏ LRP-3211 [M]	Take Good Care of My Baby	1962	7.50	15.00	30.00
❏ LRP-3228 [M]	Bobby Vee Meets the Crickets	1962	10.00	20.00	40.00
❏ LRP-3232 [M]	A Bobby Vee Recording Session	1962	7.50	15.00	30.00
❏ LRP-3245 [M]	Bobby Vee's Golden Greats	1962	7.50	15.00	30.00
❏ LRP-3267 [M]	Merry Christmas from Bobby Vee	1962	7.50	15.00	30.00
❏ LRP-3285 [M]	The Night Has a Thousand Eyes	1963	7.50	15.00	30.00
❏ LRP-3289 [M]	Bobby Vee Meets the Ventures	1963	10.00	20.00	40.00
❏ LRP-3336 [M]	I Remember Buddy Holly	1963	10.00	20.00	40.00
❏ LRP-3352 [M]	Bobby Vee Sings the New Sound from England!	1964	6.25	12.50	25.00
❏ LRP-3385 [M]	30 Big Hits From the 60's	1964	6.25	12.50	25.00
❏ LRP-3393 [M]	Bobby Vee Live on Tour	1965	6.25	12.50	25.00
❏ LRP-3448 [M]	30 Big Hits From the 60's, Volume 2	1966	6.25	12.50	25.00
❏ LRP-3464 [M]	Bobby Vee's Golden Greats, Volume 2	1966	5.00	10.00	20.00
❏ LRP-3480 [M]	Look at Me Girl	1966	5.00	10.00	20.00
❏ LRP-3534 [M]	Come Back When You Grow Up	1967	5.00	10.00	20.00
❏ LST-7165 [S]	Bobby Vee Sings Your Favorites	1960	20.00	40.00	80.00
❏ LST-7181 [S]	Bobby Vee	1961	12.50	25.00	50.00
❏ LST-7186 [S]	Bobby Vee With Strings and	1961	12.50	25.00	50.00
❏ LST-7205 [S]	Bobby Vee Sings Hits of the Rockin' 50's	1961	12.50	25.00	50.00
❏ LST-7211 [S]	Take Good Care of My Baby	1962	10.00	20.00	40.00
❏ LST-7228 [S]	Bobby Vee Meets the Crickets	1962	12.50	25.00	50.00

Number	Title	Yr	VG	VG+	NM
❏ LST-7232 [S]	A Bobby Vee Recording Session	1962	10.00	20.00	40.00
❏ LST-7245 [S]	Bobby Vee's Golden Greats	1962	10.00	20.00	40.00
❏ LST-7267 [S]	Merry Christmas from Bobby Vee	1962	10.00	20.00	40.00
❏ LST-7285 [S]	The Night Has a Thousand Eyes	1963	10.00	20.00	40.00
❏ LST-7289 [S]	Bobby Vee Meets the Ventures	1963	12.50	25.00	50.00
❏ LST-7336 [S]	I Remember Buddy Holly	1963	12.50	25.00	50.00
❏ LST-7352 [S]	Bobby Vee Sings the New Sound from England!	1964	7.50	15.00	30.00
❏ LST-7385 [S]	30 Big Hits From the 60's Volume 2	1964	7.50	15.00	30.00
❏ LST-7464 [S]	Bobby Vee's Golden Greats, Volume 2	1966	6.25	12.50	25.00
❏ LST-7480 [S]	Look at Me Girl	1966	6.25	12.50	25.00
❏ LST-7534 [S]	Come Back When You Grow Up	1967	6.25	12.50	25.00
❏ LST-7554 [S]	Just Today	1968	6.25	12.50	25.00
❏ LST-7592 [S]	Do What You Gotta Do	1968	7.50	15.00	30.00
❏ LST-7612 [S]	Gates, Grills and Railings	1969	7.50	15.00	30.00

UNITED ARTISTS

Number	Title	Yr	VG	VG+	NM
❏ UA-LA025-G2 [(2)]	Legendary Masters Series	1973	75.00	150.00	300.00
-- Withdrawn before release, but a few copies survived					
❏ UA-LA085-G	Robert Thomas Velline	1973	5.00	10.00	20.00

VEGAS, PAT AND LOLLY
Also see REDBONE.
MERCURY

Number	Title	Yr	VG	VG+	NM
❏ MG-21059 [M]	At the Haunted House	1966	7.50	15.00	30.00
❏ SR-61059 [S]	At the Haunted House	1966	10.00	20.00	40.00

VELASCO, VI
VEE JAY

Number	Title	Yr	VG	VG+	NM
❏ VJ-1135 [M]	The Vi Velasco Album	1965	5.00	10.00	20.00

VELEZ, MARTHA
SIRE

Number	Title	Yr	VG	VG+	NM
❏ SES-97008	Fiends and Angels	1969	7.50	15.00	30.00
-- Jimi Hendrix plays on this album					

VELVET NIGHT
METROMEDIA

Number	Title	Yr	VG	VG+	NM
❏ MD-1028	Velvet Night	1970	7.50	15.00	30.00

VELVET UNDERGROUND, THE
Also see JOHN CALE; LOU REED; MAUREEN TUCKER.
COTILLION

Number	Title	Yr	VG	VG+	NM
❏ SD 9034	Loaded	1970	5.00	10.00	20.00
-- Original pressing has a light blue label					
❏ SD 9034 [DJ]	Loaded	1970	18.75	37.50	75.00
-- White label promo					
❏ SD 9500	Live at Max's Kansas City	1972	5.00	10.00	20.00
-- Original pressing has a light blue label					
❏ SD 9500 [DJ]	Live at Max's Kansas City	1972	18.75	37.50	75.00
-- White label promo					

MERCURY

Number	Title	Yr	VG	VG+	NM
❏ SRM-2-7504 [(2)]	1969 (Live)	1974	12.50	25.00	50.00
-- Originals with red labels					

MGM

Number	Title	Yr	VG	VG+	NM
❏ GAS-131	The Velvet Underground (Golden Archive Series)	1970	10.00	20.00	40.00
❏ SE-4617	The Velvet Underground	1969	12.50	25.00	50.00
❏ SE-4617 [DJ]	The Velvet Underground	1969	75.00	125.00	250.00
-- Yellow label promo					
❏ M3G 4950	Archetypes	1974	5.00	10.00	20.00

VERVE

Number	Title	Yr	VG	VG+	NM
❏ V-5008 [M]	The Velvet Underground and Nico	1967	75.00	150.00	300.00
-- Version 1: With peel-off banana peel, photo of band framed by a male torso (deduct 50% if banana sticker is gone)					
❏ V-5008 [M]	The Velvet Underground and Nico	1967	75.00	150.00	300.00
-- Version 2: With peel-off banana peel, photo of torso obscured by a sticker (deduct 50% if stickers removed)					
❏ V-5008 [M]	The Velvet Underground and Nico	1967	50.00	100.00	200.00
-- Version 3: With peel-off banana peel, torso is airbrushed off the cover (deduct 50% if banana sticker removed)					
❏ V6-5008 [S]	The Velvet Underground and Nico	1967	50.00	100.00	200.00
-- Version 1: With peel-off banana peel, photo of band framed by a male torso (deduct 50% if banana sticker is gone)					
❏ V6-5008 [S]	The Velvet Underground and Nico	1967	50.00	100.00	200.00
-- Version 2: With peel-off banana peel, photo of torso obscured by a sticker (deduct 50% if stickers removed)					
❏ V6-5008 [S]	The Velvet Underground and Nico	1967	37.50	75.00	150.00
-- Version 3: With peel-off banana peel, torso is airbrushed off the cover (deduct 50% if banana sticker removed)					
❏ V6-5008 [S]	The Velvet Underground and Nico	1968	25.00	50.00	100.00
-- Version 4: With unpeelable banana					
❏ V-5046 [M]	White Light/White Heat	1967	37.50	75.00	150.00
-- Version 1: "Skeleton" cover -- a black-on-black skeleton is visible when cover is viewed at an angle					

Number	Title	Yr	VG	VG+	NM
❏ V-5046 [M]	White Light/White Heat	1967	15.00	30.00	60.00
-- Version 2: No "skeleton" on cover					
❏ V-5046 [M/DJ]	White Light/White Heat	1967	75.00	150.00	300.00
-- White label promo					
❏ V6-5046 [S]	White Light/White Heat	1967	20.00	40.00	80.00
-- Version 1: "Skeleton" cover -- a black-on-black skeleton is visible when cover is viewed at an angle					
❏ V6-5046 [S]	White Light/White Heat	1967	10.00	20.00	40.00
-- Version 2: No "skeleton" on cover					
❏ V6-5046 [S/DJ]	White Light/White Heat	1967	62.50	125.00	250.00
-- Yellow label promo					

VELVET, JIMMY
UNITED ARTISTS

Number	Title	Yr	VG	VG+	NM
❏ UAS-6653	A Touch of Velvet	1968	6.25	12.50	25.00

VELVET TONE

Number	Title	Yr	VG	VG+	NM
❏ 501	A Touch of Velvet	1968	15.00	30.00	60.00

VENTURA, RAY
ATLANTIC

Number	Title	Yr	VG	VG+	NM
❏ 8011 [M]	Hi-Fi Music for Young Parisians	1956	12.50	25.00	50.00
-- Black label					

DOT

Number	Title	Yr	VG	VG+	NM
❏ DLP-3120 [M]	La Belle Bardot	1958	12.50	25.00	50.00
-- Brigitte Bardot is the cover model					

VENTURAS, THE
DRUM BOY

Number	Title	Yr	VG	VG+	NM
❏ DBM-1003 [M]	Here They Are	1964	50.00	100.00	200.00
❏ DBS-1003 [S]	Here They Are	1964	75.00	150.00	300.00

VENTURES, THE
DOLTON

Number	Title	Yr	VG	VG+	NM
❏ BLP 2003 [M]	Walk Don't Run	1960	12.50	25.00	50.00
-- Pale blue label with dolphins on top					
❏ BLP 2003 [M]	Walk Don't Run	1963	5.00	10.00	20.00
-- Dark label, logo on left					
❏ BLP 2004 [M]	The Ventures	1961	12.50	25.00	50.00
-- Pale blue label with dolphins on top					
❏ BLP 2004 [M]	The Ventures	1963	5.00	10.00	20.00
-- Dark label, logo on left					
❏ BLP 2006 [M]	Another Smash!!!	1961	12.50	25.00	50.00
-- Pale blue label with dolphins on top					
❏ BLP 2006 [M]	Another Smash!!!	1963	5.00	10.00	20.00
-- Dark label, logo on left					
❏ BLP 2008 [M]	The Colorful Ventures	1961	12.50	25.00	50.00
-- Pale blue label with dolphins on top					
❏ BLP 2008 [M]	The Colorful Ventures	1963	5.00	10.00	20.00
-- Dark label, logo on left					
❏ BLP 2010 [M]	Twist with the Ventures	1962	12.50	25.00	50.00
-- Pale blue label with dolphins on top					
❏ BLP 2010 [M]	Dance!	1963	5.00	10.00	20.00
-- Dark label, logo on left; retitled version of "Twist with the Ventures"					
❏ BLP 2014 [M]	The Ventures' Twist Party, Vol. 2	1962	12.50	25.00	50.00
-- Pale blue label with dolphins on top					
❏ BLP 2014 [M]	Dance with the Ventures	1963	5.00	10.00	20.00
-- Dark label, logo on left' retitled version of "The Ventures' Twist Party, Vol. 2"					
❏ BLP 2016 [M]	Mashed Potatoes and Gravy	1962	7.50	15.00	30.00
❏ BLP 2016 [M]	Beach Party	1963	5.00	10.00	20.00
-- Retitled version of "Mashed Potatoes and Gravy"					
❏ BLP 2017 [M]	Going to the Ventures Dance	1962	7.50	15.00	30.00
❏ BLP 2019 [M]	The Ventures Play Telstar, The Lonely Bull	1962	7.50	15.00	30.00
❏ BLP 2022 [M]	Surfing	1963	6.25	12.50	25.00
❏ BLP 2023 [M]	The Ventures Play the Country Classics	1963	6.25	12.50	25.00
❏ BLP 2024 [M]	Let's Go!	1963	6.25	12.50	25.00
❏ BLP 2027 [M]	(The) Ventures in Space	1964	10.00	20.00	40.00
❏ BLP 2029 [M]	The Fabulous Ventures	1964	6.25	12.50	25.00
❏ BLP 2031 [M]	Walk, Don't Run, Vol. 2	1964	6.25	12.50	25.00
❏ BLP 2033 [M]	The Ventures Knock Me Out!	1965	6.25	12.50	25.00
❏ BLP 2035 [M]	The Ventures on Stage	1965	6.25	12.50	25.00
❏ BLP 2037 [M]	The Ventures A-Go-Go	1965	6.25	12.50	25.00
❏ BLP-2038 [M]	The Ventures' Christmas Album	1965	7.50	15.00	30.00
❏ BLP 2040 [M]	Where the Action Is	1966	5.00	10.00	20.00
❏ BLP 2042 [M]	The Ventures/Batman Theme	1966	7.50	15.00	30.00
❏ BLP 2045 [M]	Go with the Ventures!	1966	5.00	10.00	20.00
❏ BLP 2047 [M]	Wild Things!	1966	5.00	10.00	20.00
❏ BLP 2050 [M]	Guitar Freakout	1967	5.00	10.00	20.00
❏ BST 8003 [S]	Walk Don't Run	1960	15.00	30.00	60.00
-- Pale blue label with dolphins on top					
❏ BST 8003 [S]	Walk Don't Run	1963	6.25	12.50	25.00
-- Dark label, logo on left					
❏ BST 8004 [S]	The Ventures	1961	15.00	30.00	60.00
-- Pale blue label with dolphins on top					
❏ BST 8004 [S]	The Ventures	1963	6.25	12.50	25.00
-- Dark label, logo on left					

Number	Title	Yr	VG	VG+	NM
❏ BST 8006 [S] Another Smash!!!		1961	15.00	30.00	60.00
-- Pale blue label with dolphins on top					
❏ BST 8006 [S] Another Smash!!!		1963	6.25	12.50	25.00
-- Dark label, logo on left					
❏ BST 8008 [S] The Colorful Ventures		1961	15.00	30.00	60.00
-- Pale blue label with dolphins on top					
❏ BST 8008 [S] The Colorful Ventures		1963	6.25	12.50	25.00
-- Dark label, logo on left					
❏ BST 8010 [S] Twist with the Ventures		1962	15.00	30.00	60.00
-- Pale blue label with dolphins on top					
❏ BST 8010 [S] Dance!		1963	6.25	12.50	25.00
-- Dark label, logo on left; retitled version of "Twist with the Ventures"					
❏ BST 8014 [S] The Ventures' Twist Party, Vol. 2		1962	15.00	30.00	60.00
-- Pale blue label with dolphins on top					
❏ BST 8014 [S] Dance with the Ventures		1963	6.25	12.50	25.00
-- Dark label, logo on left' retitled version of "The Ventures' Twist Party, Vol. 2"					
❏ BST 8016 [S] Mashed Potatoes and Gravy		1962	10.00	20.00	40.00
❏ BST 8016 [S] Beach Party		1963	6.25	12.50	25.00
-- Retitled version of "Mashed Potatoes and Gravy"					
❏ BST 8017 [S] Going to the Ventures Dance		1962	10.00	20.00	40.00
❏ BST 8019 [S] The Ventures Play Telstar, The Lonely Bull		1962	10.00	20.00	40.00
❏ BST 8022 [S] Surfing		1963	7.50	15.00	30.00
❏ BST 8023 [S] The Ventures Play the Country Classics		1963	7.50	15.00	30.00
❏ BST 8024 [S] Let's Go!		1963	7.50	15.00	30.00
❏ BST 8027 [S] (The) Ventures in Space		1964	12.50	25.00	50.00
❏ BST 8029 [S] The Fabulous Ventures		1964	7.50	15.00	30.00
❏ BST 8031 [S] Walk, Don't Run, Vol. 2		1964	7.50	15.00	30.00
❏ BST 8033 [S] The Ventures Knock Me Out!		1965	7.50	15.00	30.00
❏ BST 8035 [S] The Ventures on Stage		1965	7.50	15.00	30.00
❏ BST 8037 [S] The Ventures A-Go-Go		1965	7.50	15.00	30.00
❏ BST-8038 [S] The Ventures' Christmas Album		1965	5.00	10.00	20.00
❏ BST 8040 [S] Where the Action Is		1966	6.25	2.50	25.00
❏ BST 8042 [S] The Ventures/Batman Theme		1966	10.00	20.00	40.00
❏ BST 8045 [S] Go with the Ventures!		1966	6.25	12.50	25.00
❏ BST 8047 [S] Wild Things!		1966	6.25	12.50	25.00
❏ BST 8050 [S] Guitar Freakout		1967	6.25	12.50	25.00
❏ BLP 16501 [M] Play Guitar with the Ventures		1965	6.25	12.50	25.00
❏ BLP 16502 [M] Play Guitar with the Ventures, Vol. 2		196?	6.25	12.50	25.00
❏ BLP 16503 [M] Play Guitar with the Ventures, Vol. 3		196?	6.25	12.50	25.00
❏ BLP 16504 [M] Play Guitar with the Ventures, Vol. 4		196?	6.25	12.50	25.00
❏ BST 16504 [S] Play Guitar with the Ventures, Vol. 4		196?	7.50	15.00	30.00
❏ BST 17501 [S] Play Guitar with the Ventures		1965	7.50	15.00	30.00
❏ BST 17502 [S] Play Guitar with the Ventures, Vol. 2		196?	7.50	15.00	30.00
❏ BST 17503 [S] Play Guitar with the Ventures, Vol. 3		196?	7.50	15.00	30.00

LIBERTY

Number	Title	Yr	VG	VG+	NM
❏ LRP-2052 [M] Super Psychedelics		1967	5.00	10.00	20.00
❏ LRP-2053 [M] Golden Greats by the Ventures		1967	5.00	10.00	20.00
❏ LRP-2054 [M] $1,000,000.00 Weekend		1967	5.00	10.00	20.00
❏ LRP-2055 [M] Flights of Fancy		1968	7.50	15.00	30.00
❏ LST-8003 Walk Don't Run		1970	5.00	10.00	20.00
-- Reissue of Dolton 8003 with new front and back covers					
❏ LST-8023 I Walk the Line and Other Giant Hits		1970	5.00	10.00	20.00
-- Reissue of "The Ventures Play the Country Classics"					
❏ LST-8031 Walk, Don't Run, Vol. 2		1970	6.25	12.50	25.00
-- Reissue of Dolton 8031 with new cover					
❏ LST-8050 Revolving Sounds		1970	7.50	15.00	30.00
-- Reissue of "Guitar Freakout"					
❏ LST-8052 [S] Super Psychedelics		1967	6.25	12.50	25.00
❏ LST-8052 [S] Changing Times		1970	10.00	20.00	40.00
-- Reissue of "Super Psychedelics"					
❏ LST-8053 [S] Golden Greats by the Ventures		1967	5.00	10.00	20.00
❏ LST-8054 [S] $1,000,000.00 Weekend		1967	5.00	10.00	20.00
❏ LST-8055 [S] Flights of Fancy		1968	5.00	10.00	20.00
❏ LST-8057 The Horse		1968	5.00	10.00	20.00
❏ LST-8059 Underground Fire		1969	5.00	10.00	20.00
❏ LST-35000 [(2)] The Ventures 10th Anniversary Album		1970	5.00	10.00	20.00

UNITED ARTISTS

Number	Title	Yr	VG	VG+	NM
❏ UA-LA717-F TV Themes		1977	6.25	12.50	25.00

VENUTA, BENAY
MERCURY

Number	Title	Yr	VG	VG+	NM
❏ MG-25006 [10] Old Time Favorites		1949	17.50	35.00	70.00

VERA, BILLY
ATLANTIC

Number	Title	Yr	VG	VG+	NM
❏ 8197 [M] With Pen in Hand		1968	10.00	20.00	40.00
❏ SD 8197 [S] With Pen in Hand		1968	6.25	12.50	25.00

VERA, BILLY, AND JUDY CLAY
ATLANTIC

Number	Title	Yr	VG	VG+	NM
❏ 8174 [M] Storybook Children		1967	6.25	12.50	25.00
❏ SD 8174 [S] Storybook Children		1967	7.50	15.00	30.00

VERDON, GWEN
RCA VICTOR

Number	Title	Yr	VG	VG+	NM
❏ LPM-1152 [M] The Girl I Left Home For		1956	10.00	20.00	40.00

VERITY, JOHN, BAND
ABC DUNHILL

Number	Title	Yr	VG	VG+	NM
❏ DSX-50170 The John Verity Band		1974	5.00	10.00	20.00

VERNE, LARRY
ERA

Number	Title	Yr	VG	VG+	NM
❏ 104 [M] Mister Larry Verne		1961	15.00	30.00	60.00

VERSATONES, THE
RCA VICTOR

Number	Title	Yr	VG	VG+	NM
❏ LPM-1538 [M] The Versatones		1957	25.00	50.00	100.00

VETTES, THE
MGM

Number	Title	Yr	VG	VG+	NM
❏ E-4193 [M] Rev-Up		1963	25.00	50.00	100.00
❏ SE-4193 [S] Rev-Up		1963	30.00	60.00	120.00

VIBRATIONS, THE
CHECKER

Number	Title	Yr	VG	VG+	NM
❏ LP-2978 [M] The Watusi		1961	50.00	100.00	200.00

MANDALA

Number	Title	Yr	VG	VG+	NM
❏ 3006 Taking a New Step		1972	5.00	10.00	20.00

OKEH

Number	Title	Yr	VG	VG+	NM
❏ OKM-12111 [M] Shout		1965	7.50	15.00	30.00
❏ OKM-12112 [M] Misty		1966	7.50	15.00	30.00
❏ OKM-12114 [M] New Vibrations		1967	7.50	15.00	30.00
❏ OKS-14111 [S] Shout		1965	10.00	20.00	40.00
❏ OKS-14112 [S] Misty		1966	10.00	20.00	40.00
❏ OKS-14114 [S] New Vibrations		1967	10.00	20.00	40.00
❏ OKS-14129 The Vibrations' Greatest Hits		1969	7.50	15.00	30.00

VICEROYS, THE
BOLO

Number	Title	Yr	VG	VG+	NM
❏ BLP-8000 [M] The Viceroys at Granny's Pad		1963	10.00	20.00	40.00

VICTIMS OF CHANCE, THE
CRESTVIEW

Number	Title	Yr	VG	VG+	NM
❏ CRS-3052 The Victims of Chance		197?	15.00	30.00	60.00

VIENNA PHILHARMONIC ORCHESTRA (WILHELM FURTWANGLER, CONDUCTOR)
URANIA

Number	Title	Yr	VG	VG+	NM
❏ URLP-7095 [M] Beethoven: Symphony No. 3		195?	125.00	250.00	500.00
-- Withdrawn from the market when it was discovered that the record had been mastered slightly fast					

VIENNA PHILHARMONIC ORCHESTRA (PIERRE MONTEUX, CONDUCTOR)
RCA VICTOR RED SEAL

Number	Title	Yr	VG	VG+	NM
❏ LSC-2316 [S] Beethoven: Symphony No. 6		1959	20.00	40.00	80.00
-- Original with "shaded dog" label					
❏ LSC-2362 [S] Berlioz: Symphonie Fantastique		1960	15.00	30.00	60.00
-- Original with "shaded dog" label					
❏ LSC-2394 [S] Haydn: Symphonies No. 94 and 101		1960	10.00	20.00	40.00
-- Original with "shaded dog" label					
❏ LSC-2491 [S] Beethoven: Symphonies No. 1 and 8		1961	25.00	50.00	100.00
-- Original with "shaded dog" label					

VIENNA PHILHARMONIC ORCHESTRA (FRITZ REINER, CONDUCTOR)
RCA VICTOR RED SEAL

Number	Title	Yr	VG	VG+	NM
❏ LSC-2077 [S] Strauss: Till Eulenspiegel		1959	20.00	40.00	80.00
-- Original with "shaded dog" label					
❏ LSC-2077 [S] Strauss: Till Eulenspiegel		199?	6.25	12.50	25.00
-- Classic Records reissue					

VILLA, PEPE
KING

Number	Title	Yr	VG	VG+	NM
❏ 660 [M] Music of Mexico		1959	7.50	15.00	30.00

Number	Title	Yr	VG	VG+	NM

VILLAGE PEOPLE
CASABLANCA
❑ NBPIX-7064 [PD] Village People	1978	5.00	10.00	20.00

-- *Regular LP released in 1977*

❑ NBPIX-7096 [PD]	Macho Man	1978	5.00	10.00	20.00
❑ NBPIX-7118 [PD]	Cruisin'	1978	5.00	10.00	20.00

VILLAGE STOMPERS, THE
EPIC
❑ BN 26078 [S]	Washington Square	1963	5.00	10.00	20.00
❑ BN 26090 [S]	More Sounds of Washington Square	1964	5.00	10.00	20.00

VINCENT, GENE
CAPITOL
❑ DKAO-380 [R]	Gene Vincent's Greatest	1969	12.50	25.00	50.00
❑ T 764 [M]	Bluejean Bop!	1957	100.00	200.00	400.00

-- *Turquoise label stock copy*

❑ T 764 [M]	Bluejean Bop!	1957	250.00	500.00	1,000.

-- *Black label promo*

❑ T 764 [M]	Bluejean Bop!	1957	250.00	500.00	1,000.

-- *Yellow label promo*

❑ T 811 [M]	Gene Vincent and the Blue Caps	1957	100.00	200.00	400.00

-- *Turquoise label stock copy*

❑ T 811 [M]	Gene Vincent and the Blue Caps	1957	250.00	500.00	1,000.

-- *Black label promo*

❑ T 811 [M]	Gene Vincent and the Blue Caps	1957	250.00	500.00	1,000.

-- *Yellow label promo*

❑ T 970 [M]	Gene Vincent Rocks! And the Blue Caps Roll	1958	100.00	200.00	400.00

-- *Turquoise label stock copy*

❑ T 970 [M]	Gene Vincent Rocks! And the Blue Caps Roll	1958	250.00	500.00	1,000.

-- *Black label promo*

❑ T 970 [M]	Gene Vincent Rocks! And the Blue Caps Roll	1958	250.00	500.00	1,000.

-- *Yellow label promo*

❑ T 1059 [M]	A Gene Vincent Record Date	1958	100.00	200.00	400.00

-- *Turquoise label stock copy*

❑ T 1059 [M]	A Gene Vincent Record Date	1958	250.00	500.00	1,000.

-- *Black label promo*

❑ T 1059 [M]	A Gene Vincent Record Date	1958	250.00	500.00	1,000.

-- *Yellow label promo*

❑ T 1207 [M]	Sounds Like Gene Vincent	1959	75.00	150.00	300.00

-- *Black label with colorband, Capitol logo at left*

❑ ST 1342 [S]	Crazy Times	1960	125.00	250.00	500.00

-- *Black label with colorband, Capitol logo at left*

❑ T 1342 [M]	Crazy Times	1960	75.00	150.00	300.00

-- *Black label with colorband, Capitol logo at left*

DANDELION
❑ 9-102	I'm Back and I'm Proud	1970	12.50	25.00	50.00

KAMA SUTRA
❑ KSBS 2019	Gene Vincent	1970	12.50	25.00	50.00
❑ KSBS 2027	The Day the World Turned Blue	1971	12.50	25.00	50.00

VINSON, EDDIE "CLEANHEAD"
AAMCO
❑ 312 [M]	Cleanhead's Back in Town	196?	10.00	20.00	40.00

BETHLEHEM
❑ BCP-5005 [M]	Eddie "Cleanhead" Vinson Sings	1957	25.00	50.00	100.00

BLUESWAY
❑ BL-6007 [M]	Cherry Red	1967	6.25	12.50	25.00
❑ BLS-6007 [S]	Cherry Red	1967	6.25	12.50	25.00

KING
❑ KS-1087	Cherry Red	1969	6.25	12.50	25.00

RIVERSIDE
❑ RLP-502 [M]	Back Door Blues	1965	10.00	20.00	40.00
❑ RLS-9502 [S]	Back Door Blues	1965	10.00	20.00	40.00

VINSON, EDDIE "CLEANHEAD"/ JIMMY WITHERSPOON
Also see each artist's individual listings.
KING
❑ 634 [M]	Battle of the Blues, Volume 3	1960	375.00	750.00	1,500.

VINTON, BOBBY
EPIC
❑ BN 579 [S]	Dancing at the Hop	1961	12.50	25.00	50.00
❑ BN 597 [S]	Young Man with a Big Band	1961	12.50	25.00	50.00
❑ LN 3727 [M]	Dancing at the Hop	1961	7.50	15.00	30.00
❑ LN 3780 [M]	Young Man with a Big Band	1961	7.50	15.00	30.00
❑ LN 24068 [M]	Blue On Blue	1963	6.25	12.50	25.00

-- *Stock copy on black vinyl*

❑ LN 24068 [M]	Blue On Blue	1963	37.50	75.00	150.00

-- *Promo only on blue vinyl*

❑ BN 26020 [S]	Roses Are Red	1962	5.00	10.00	20.00
❑ BN 26035 [S]	Bobby Vinton Sings the Big Ones	1962	5.00	10.00	20.00
❑ BN 26049 [S]	The Greatest Hits of the Greatest Groups	1963	5.00	10.00	20.00
❑ BN 26068 [S]	Blue On Blue	1963	7.50	15.00	30.00
❑ BN 26068 [S]	Blue Velvet	1963	5.00	10.00	20.00

-- *Retitled version of "Blue On Blue"*

❑ BN 26081 [S]	There! I've Said It Again	1964	5.00	10.00	20.00

VIOLENT FEMMES
WARNER BROS.
❑ PRO-A-3519 [DJ]	3 On 3	1989	6.25	12.50	25.00

-- *Promo-only interviews and music*

VIOLINAIRES, THE
CHECKER
❑ LP-10011 [M]	Stand By Me	1965	6.25	12.50	25.00
❑ LP-10017 [M]	The Fantastic Violinaires	1966	6.25	12.50	25.00
❑ LP-10020 [M]	I'm Going to Serve the Lord	196?	5.00	10.00	20.00
❑ LPS-10020 [S]	I'm Going to Serve the Lord	196?	6.25	12.50	25.00
❑ LP-10030 [M]	Move On Up	196?	5.00	10.00	20.00
❑ LPS-10030 [S]	Move On Up	196?	6.25	12.50	25.00
❑ LP-10040 [M]	Shout!	196?	5.00	10.00	20.00
❑ LPS-10040 [S]	Shout!	196?	6.25	12.50	25.00
❑ LP-10045 [M]	Live the Right Way	196?	6.25	12.50	25.00
❑ LPS-10045 [S]	Live the Right Way	196?	6.25	12.50	25.00
❑ LPS-10053	The Violinaires in Concert	1968	5.00	10.00	20.00
❑ LPS-10057	God's Creation	1969	5.00	10.00	20.00
❑ LP-10060	At His Command	1970	5.00	10.00	20.00
❑ 2CK-10065 [(2)]	Please Answer This Prayer	197?	6.25	12.50	25.00
❑ CK-10067	Groovin' with Jesus	197?	5.00	10.00	20.00

VIRGIN INSANITY
FUNKY
❑ 71411	Illusions of the Maintenance Man	1970	50.00	100.00	200.00

VIRGINIANS, THE
MONUMENT
❑ MLP-8031 [M]	Ballads and Bluegrass	1965	5.00	10.00	20.00
❑ SLP-18031 [S]	Ballads and Bluegrass	1965	6.25	12.50	25.00

UNITED ARTISTS
❑ UAL-3293 [M]	The Wonderful World of Bluegrass Music	1963	5.00	10.00	20.00
❑ UAS-6293 [S]	The Wonderful World of Bluegrass Music	1963	6.25	12.50	25.00

VIRTUE, FRANK
Also see THE VIRTUES.
FAYETTE
❑ 1816 [M]	Frank Virtue and the Virtues	1964	15.00	30.00	60.00

-- *Blue cover*

❑ 1816 [M]	Frank Virtue and the Virtues	1964	10.00	20.00	40.00

-- *White cover*

VIRTUES, THE
Also see FRANK VIRTUE.
STRAND
❑ L-1061 [M]	Guitar Boogie Shuffle	1960	7.50	15.00	30.00
❑ SL-1061 [S]	Guitar Boogie Shuffle	1960	10.00	20.00	40.00

WYNNE
❑ WLP-111 [M]	Guitar Boogie Shuffle	1960	30.00	60.00	120.00
❑ WLP-711 [S]	Guitar Boogie Shuffle	1960	45.00	90.00	180.00

VISCOUNTS, THE
AMY
❑ 8008 [M]	Harlem Nocturne	1965	10.00	20.00	40.00
❑ S-8008 [S]	Harlem Nocturne	1965	12.50	25.00	50.00

MADISON
❑ 1001 [M]	The Viscounts	1960	50.00	100.00	200.00

VISION OF SUNSHINE
AVCO EMBASSY
❑ 33007	Vision of Sunshine	1970	7.50	15.00	30.00

VOGUES, THE
CO & CE
❑ LP-1229 [M]	Meet the Vogues	1965	12.50	25.00	50.00
❑ LP-1230 [M]	Five O'Clock World	1966	12.50	25.00	50.00

-- *Stereo pressings of these two albums are not known to exist!*

Number	Title	Yr	VG	VG+	NM

REPRISE

❏ ST-91559	Turn Around, Look at Me	1968	5.00	10.00	20.00
-- *Capitol Record Club edition*					
❏ SW-93040	The Vogues' Greatest Hits	1970	5.00	10.00	20.00
-- *Capitol Record Club edition*					

VOICE OF THE BEEHIVE
LONDON

| ❏ 828 100-1 | Let It Bee | 1988 | 5.00 | 10.00 | 20.00 |

VON SCHMIDT, ERIC
FOLKLORE

| ❏ FRLP-14005 [M] | Folk Blues | 1964 | 7.50 | 15.00 | 30.00 |
| ❏ FRST-14005 [S] | Folk Blues | 1964 | 10.00 | 20.00 | 40.00 |

PRESTIGE

| ❏ PRLP-7384 [M] | Eric Sings Von Schmidt | 1966 | 5.00 | 10.00 | 20.00 |
| ❏ PRST-7384 [S] | Eric Sings Von Schmidt | 1966 | 6.25 | 12.50 | 25.00 |

SMASH

| ❏ SRS-67124 | Who Knocked the Brains Out of the Sky? | 1969 | 5.00 | 10.00 | 20.00 |

VRONSKY AND BABIN
RCA VICTOR RED SEAL

| ❏ LSC-2417 [S] | 178 Keys | 1960 | 5.00 | 10.00 | 20.00 |
| -- *Original with "shaded dog" label* | | | | | |

W

WADE, ADAM
COED

❏ LPC-902 [M]	And Then Came Adam	1960	12.50	25.00	50.00
❏ LPCS-902 [S]	And Then Came Adam	1960	15.00	30.00	60.00
❏ LPC-903 [M]	Adam and Evening	1961	12.50	25.00	50.00
❏ LPCS-903 [S]	Adam and Evening	1961	15.00	30.00	60.00

EPIC

❏ LN 24019 [M]	Adam Wade's Greatest Hits	1962	6.25	12.50	25.00
❏ LN 24026 [M]	One Is a Lonely Number	1962	6.25	12.50	25.00
❏ LN 24044 [M]	What Kind of Fool Am I?	1963	6.25	12.50	25.00
❏ LN 24056 [M]	A Very Good Year for Girls	1963	6.25	12.50	25.00
❏ BN 26019 [S]	Adam Wade's Greatest Hits	1962	7.50	15.00	30.00
❏ BN 26026 [S]	One Is a Lonely Number	1962	7.50	15.00	30.00
❏ BN 26044 [S]	What Kind of Fool Am I?	1963	7.50	15.00	30.00
❏ BN 26056 [S]	A Very Good Year for Girls	1963	7.50	15.00	30.00

WADSWORTH MANSION
SUSSEX

❏ SXBS-7008	Wadsworth Manison	1971	6.25	12.50	25.00
-- *Some copies of this LP have the above typographical error*					
❏ SXBS-7008	Wadsworth Mansion	1971	5.00	10.00	20.00

WAGNER, DANNY, AND KINDRED SOUL
IMPERIAL

| ❏ LP-12405 | The Kindred Soul of Danny | 1968 | 7.50 | 15.00 | 30.00 |

WAGNER, DAVID -- See CROW.

WAGNER, ROGER, CHORALE
CAPITOL

❏ P 8267 [M]	Songs of Stephen Foster	195?	7.50	15.00	30.00
❏ P 8324 [M]	Folk Songs of the New World	195?	7.50	15.00	30.00
❏ P 8332 [M]	Folk Songs of the Frontier	195?	7.50	15.00	30.00
❏ PBR 8345 [(2) M]	Folk Songs of the Old World	195?	10.00	20.00	40.00
❏ SP 8353 [S]	Joy to the World!	195?	6.25	12.50	25.00
❏ P 8387 [M]	Folk Songs of the World	195?	5.00	10.00	20.00

WAGONER, PORTER
RCA VICTOR

❏ LPM-1358 [M]	A Satisfied Mind	1956	50.00	100.00	200.00
❏ LPM-2447 [M]	A Slice of Life -- Songs Happy 'N' Sad	1962	6.25	12.50	25.00
❏ LSP-2447 [S]	A Slice of Life -- Songs Happy N' Sad	1962	7.50	15.00	30.00
❏ LPM-2650 [M]	The Porter Wagoner Show	1963	6.25	12.50	25.00
❏ LSP-2650 [S]	The Porter Wagoner Show	1963	7.50	15.00	30.00
❏ LPM-2706 [M]	Y'All Come	1963	6.25	12.50	25.00
❏ LSP-2706 [S]	Y'All Come	1963	7.50	15.00	30.00
❏ LPM-2840 [M]	In Person	1964	6.25	12.50	25.00
❏ LSP-2840 [S]	In Person	1964	7.50	15.00	30.00
❏ LPM-2960 [M]	The Bluegrass Story	1964	5.00	10.00	20.00
❏ LSP-2960 [S]	The Bluegrass Story	1964	6.25	12.50	25.00
❏ LPM-3389 [M]	The Thin Man from West Plains	1965	5.00	10.00	20.00
❏ LSP-3389 [S]	The Thin Man from West Plains	1965	6.25	12.50	25.00
❏ LPM-3488 [M]	Grand Old Gospel	1966	5.00	10.00	20.00
❏ LSP-3488 [S]	Grand Old Gospel	1966	6.25	12.50	25.00
❏ LPM-3509 [M]	On the Road	1966	5.00	10.00	20.00
❏ LSP-3509 [S]	On the Road	1966	6.25	12.50	25.00
❏ LPM-3560 [M]	The Best of Porter Wagoner	1966	5.00	10.00	20.00
❏ LSP-3560 [S]	The Best of Porter Wagoner	1966	6.25	12.50	25.00
❏ LPM-3593 [M]	Confessions of a Broken Man	1966	5.00	10.00	20.00
❏ LSP-3593 [S]	Confessions of a Broken Man	1966	6.25	12.50	25.00
❏ LPM-3683 [M]	Soul of a Convict	1967	6.25	12.50	25.00
❏ LSP-3683 [S]	Soul of a Convict	1967	5.00	10.00	20.00
❏ LPM-3797 [M]	The Cold Hard Facts of Life	1967	6.25	12.50	25.00
❏ LSP-3797 [S]	The Cold Hard Facts of Life	1967	5.00	10.00	20.00
❏ LPM-3855 [M]	More Grand Old Gospel	1967	6.25	12.50	25.00
❏ LSP-3855 [S]	More Grand Old Gospel	1967	5.00	10.00	20.00
❏ LPM-3968 [M]	The Bottom of the Bottle	1968	25.00	50.00	100.00
❏ LSP-3968 [S]	The Bottom of the Bottle	1968	5.00	10.00	20.00
❏ LSP-4034	Gospel Country	1968	5.00	10.00	20.00
❏ LSP-4116	The Carroll County Accident	1969	5.00	10.00	20.00
❏ LSP-4181	Me and My Boys	1969	5.00	10.00	20.00
❏ LSP-4286	You Got-ta Have a License	1970	5.00	10.00	20.00
❏ LSP-4321	The Best of Porter Wagoner, Volume 2	1970	5.00	10.00	20.00
❏ LSP-4386	Down in the Alley	1970	5.00	10.00	20.00
❏ LSP-4508	Simple As I Am	1971	5.00	10.00	20.00

Number	Title	Yr	VG	VG+	NM

WAGONER, PORTER, AND DOLLY PARTON
Also see each artist's individual listings.
RCA VICTOR

Number	Title	Yr	VG	VG+	NM
❑ LPM-3926 [M]	Just Between You and Me	1968	25.00	50.00	100.00
❑ LSP-3926 [S]	Just Between You and Me	1968	5.00	10.00	20.00
❑ LSP-4039	Just the Two of Us	1968	5.00	10.00	20.00
❑ LSP-4186	Always, Always	1969	5.00	10.00	20.00
❑ LSP-4305	Porter Wayne and Dolly Rebecca	1970	5.00	10.00	20.00
❑ LSP-4388	Once More	1970	5.00	10.00	20.00
❑ LSP-4490	Two of a Kind	1971	5.00	10.00	20.00
❑ LSP-4556	The Best of Porter Wagoner and Dolly Parton	1971	5.00	10.00	20.00

WAGONER, PORTER, AND SKEETER DAVIS
Also see each artist's individual listings.
RCA VICTOR

Number	Title	Yr	VG	VG+	NM
❑ LPM-2529 [M]	Porter Wagoner and Skeeter Davis Sing Duets	1962	6.25	12.50	25.00
❑ LSP-2529 [S]	Porter Wagoner and Skeeter Davis Sing Duets	1962	7.50	15.00	30.00

WAIKIKIS, THE
KAPP

Number	Title	Yr	VG	VG+	NM
❑ KS-3366 [S]	Hawaii Tattoo	1964	5.00	10.00	20.00
❑ KS-3432 [S]	Hawaii Honeymoon	1965	5.00	10.00	20.00
❑ KS-3437 [S]	Beach Party	1965	5.00	10.00	20.00
❑ KS-3473 [S]	Lollipops and Roses	1966	5.00	10.00	20.00
❑ KS-3484 [S]	A Taste of Hawaii	1966	5.00	10.00	20.00

WAILERS, THE
BELL

Number	Title	Yr	VG	VG+	NM
❑ 6016	Walk Thru the People	1969	7.50	15.00	30.00

ETIQUETTE

Number	Title	Yr	VG	VG+	NM
❑ ALB-01 [M]	The Fabulous Wailers at the Castle	196?	25.00	50.00	100.00
❑ ALB-022 [M]	The Wailers & Company	196?	20.00	40.00	80.00
❑ ALB-023 [M]	Wailers, Wailers, Everywhere	196?	25.00	50.00	100.00
❑ ALB-026 [M]	Out of Our Tree	1966	25.00	50.00	100.00
❑ 22296/7 [(2)]	The Wailers and Their Greatest Hits	1979	6.25	12.50	25.00

GOLDEN CREST

Number	Title	Yr	VG	VG+	NM
❑ CR-3075 [M]	Fabulous Wailers	1959	62.50	125.00	250.00
-- Full-color photo on cover					
❑ CR-3075 [M]	Fabulous Wailers	1962	25.00	50.00	100.00
-- Black and white photo on cover					
❑ CR-3075 [M]	Fabulous Wailers	196?	12.50	25.00	50.00
-- Title, no photo, on cover					

IMPERIAL

Number	Title	Yr	VG	VG+	NM
❑ LP-9262 [M]	Tall Cool One	1964	12.50	25.00	50.00
❑ LP-12262 [S]	Tall Cool One	1964	20.00	40.00	80.00

UNITED ARTISTS

Number	Title	Yr	VG	VG+	NM
❑ UAL-3557 [M]	Outburst!	1966	12.50	25.00	50.00
❑ UAS-6557 [S]	Outburst!	1966	20.00	40.00	80.00

WAINWRIGHT, LOUDON, III
ATLANTIC

Number	Title	Yr	VG	VG+	NM
❑ SD 8260	Loudon Wainwright III	1970	5.00	10.00	20.00
❑ SD 8291	Album II	1971	5.00	10.00	20.00

WAITE, GENEVIEVE
PARAMOUR

Number	Title	Yr	VG	VG+	NM
❑ 5088	Romance Is On the Rise	1974	6.25	12.50	25.00

WAITRESSES, THE
POLYDOR

Number	Title	Yr	VG	VG+	NM
❑ 810 980-1 [DJ]	Bruiseology	1983	6.25	12.50	25.00
-- Promo only on purpleish vinyl					

WAKEFIELD SUN
MGM

Number	Title	Yr	VG	VG+	NM
❑ SE-4626	Wakefield Sun	1969	6.25	12.50	25.00

WAKELY, JIMMY
CAPITOL

Number	Title	Yr	VG	VG+	NM
❑ H 4008 [10]	Songs of the West	195?	30.00	60.00	120.00
❑ H-9004 [10]	Christmas on the Range	1950	37.50	75.00	150.00

DECCA

Number	Title	Yr	VG	VG+	NM
❑ DL 8409 [M]	Santa Fe Trail	1956	20.00	40.00	80.00
❑ DL 8680 [M]	Enter and Rest and Pray	1957	15.00	30.00	60.00

DOT

Number	Title	Yr	VG	VG+	NM
❑ DLP-3711 [M]	Slippin' Around	1966	5.00	10.00	20.00
❑ DLP-3754 [M]	Christmas with Jimmy Wakely	1966	5.00	10.00	20.00
❑ DLP-25711 [S]	Slippin' Around	1966	6.25	12.50	25.00
❑ DLP-25734 [S]	Christmas with Jimmy Wakely	1966	6.25	12.50	25.00

TOPS

Number	Title	Yr	VG	VG+	NM
❑ L-1601 [M]	A Cowboy Serenade	195?	6.25	12.50	25.00

WAKEMAN, RICK
Also see YES.
A&M

Number	Title	Yr	VG	VG+	NM
❑ QU-53621 [Q]	Journey to the Centre of the Earth	1974	6.25	12.50	25.00
❑ QU-54361 [Q]	The Six Wives of Henry VIII	1974	6.25	12.50	25.00
❑ QU-54515 [Q]	The Myths and Legends of King Arthur and the Knights of the Round Table	1975	6.25	12.50	25.00

MOBILE FIDELITY

Number	Title	Yr	VG	VG+	NM
❑ 1-230	Journey to the Centre of the Earth	1995	5.00	10.00	20.00
-- Audiophile vinyl					

SWEET THUNDER

Number	Title	Yr	VG	VG+	NM
❑ 1	Journey to the Centre of the Earth	1981	12.50	25.00	50.00
-- Audiophile vinyl					

WALES, HOWARD, AND JERRY GARCIA
Jerry Garcia was with THE GRATEFUL DEAD.
DOUGLAS

Number	Title	Yr	VG	VG+	NM
❑ Z 30589	Hooteroll	1971	10.00	20.00	40.00

WALKER BROTHERS, THE
Also see SCOTT WALKER.
SMASH

Number	Title	Yr	VG	VG+	NM
❑ MGS-27076 [M]	Introducing the Walker Brothers	1965	12.50	25.00	50.00
❑ MGS-27082 [M]	The Sun Ain't Gonna Shine (Anymore)	1966	10.00	20.00	40.00
❑ SRS-67076 [R]	Introducing the Walker Brothers	1965	10.00	20.00	40.00
❑ SRS-67082 [P]	The Sun Ain't Gonna Shine (Anymore)	1966	12.50	25.00	50.00
-- "The Sun Ain't Gonna Shine (Anymore)" and "When the Lights Go Out" are rechanneled.					

TOWER

Number	Title	Yr	VG	VG+	NM
❑ ST 5026 [S]	I Only Came to Dance with You	1966	5.00	10.00	20.00
-- As "Scott Engel and John Stewart"					

WALKER, BILLY
COLUMBIA

Number	Title	Yr	VG	VG+	NM
❑ CL 1624 [M]	Everybody's Hits But Mine	1961	5.00	10.00	20.00
❑ CS 8424 [S]	Everybody's Hits But Mine	1961	7.50	15.00	30.00
❑ CS 8735 [S]	Billy Walker's Greatest Hits	1963	5.00	10.00	20.00
❑ CS 9006 [S]	Thank You for Calling	1964	5.00	10.00	20.00
❑ CS 9131 [S]	The Gun, the Gold and the Girl/ Cross the Brazos at Waco	1965	5.00	10.00	20.00

WALKER, CHARLIE
COLUMBIA

Number	Title	Yr	VG	VG+	NM
❑ CL 1691 [M]	Charlie Walker's Greatest Hits	1961	5.00	10.00	20.00
❑ CS 8491 [S]	Charlie Walker's Greatest Hits	1961	7.50	15.00	30.00

EPIC

Number	Title	Yr	VG	VG+	NM
❑ LN 24328 [M]	Don't Squeeze My Sharmon	1967	6.25	12.50	25.00
❑ LN 26328 [S]	Don't Squeeze My Sharmon	1967	5.00	10.00	20.00
❑ BN 26137 [S]	Close All the Honky Tonks	1965	5.00	10.00	20.00
❑ BN 26153 [S]	Born to Lose	1965	5.00	10.00	20.00
❑ BN 26209 [S]	Wine, Women and Walker	1966	5.00	10.00	20.00

WALKER, CINDY
MONUMENT

Number	Title	Yr	VG	VG+	NM
❑ MLP-8020 [M]	Words and Music by Cindy Walker	1964	5.00	10.00	20.00
❑ SLP-18020 [S]	Words and Music by Cindy Walker	1964	6.25	12.50	25.00

WALKER, CLINT
WARNER BROS.

Number	Title	Yr	VG	VG+	NM
❑ W 1343 [M]	Inspiration	1959	7.50	15.00	30.00
❑ WS 1343 [S]	Inspiration	1959	10.00	20.00	40.00

WALKER, JERRY JEFF
Also see CIRCUS MAXIMUS.
ATCO

Number	Title	Yr	VG	VG+	NM
❑ SD 33-259	Mr. Bojangles	1968	6.25	12.50	25.00
❑ SD 33-297	Five Years Gone	1969	7.50	15.00	30.00
❑ SD 33-336	Bein' Free	1970	5.00	10.00	20.00

VANGUARD

Number	Title	Yr	VG	VG+	NM
❑ VSD-6521	Driftin' Way of Life	1969	5.00	10.00	20.00

WALKER, JR., AND THE ALL STARS
MOTOWN

Number	Title	Yr	VG	VG+	NM
❑ M7-786 [(2)]	Anthology	1974	5.00	10.00	20.00

Number	Title	Yr	VG	VG+	NM

SOUL

❏ 701 [M]	Shotgun	1965	15.00	30.00	60.00
-- Mostly white label with vertical "Soul" at left					
❏ 701 [M]	Shotgun	1965	5.00	10.00	20.00
-- Purple swirl label with "Soul" at top					
❏ SS-701 [S]	Shotgun	1965	7.50	15.00	30.00
❏ 702 [M]	Soul Session	1966	15.00	30.00	60.00
-- Mostly white label with vertical "Soul" at left					
❏ 702 [M]	Soul Session	1966	5.00	10.00	20.00
-- Purple swirl label with "Soul" at top					
❏ SS-702 [S]	Soul Session	1966	7.50	15.00	30.00
❏ 703 [M]	Road Runner	1966	5.00	10.00	20.00
❏ SS-703 [S]	Road Runner	1966	7.50	15.00	30.00
❏ 705 [M]	"Live"	1967	5.00	10.00	20.00
❏ SS-705 [S]	"Live"	1967	7.50	15.00	30.00
❏ SS-710	Home Cookin'	1969	5.00	10.00	20.00
❏ SS-718	Greatest Hits	1969	5.00	10.00	20.00
❏ SS-721	Gotta Hold On to This Feeling	1969	6.25	12.50	25.00
❏ SS-721	What Does It Take to Win Your Love	1970	5.00	10.00	20.00
-- Retitled version of above					

WALKER, MARTIN
ABC-PARAMOUNT

❏ ABCS-483 [S]	From Scotland with Love	1964	5.00	10.00	20.00

WALKER, NANCY
RCA CAMDEN

❏ CAL-561 [M]	I Hate Men	1960	6.25	12.50	25.00
❏ CAS-561 [S]	I Hate Men	1960	7.50	15.00	30.00

WALKER, PETER
VANGUARD

❏ VSD-79282	Second Poem to Karmela	1968	5.00	10.00	20.00

WALKER, SCOTT
Also see THE WALKER BROTHERS.
SMASH

❏ SRS-67099	Aloner	1968	5.00	10.00	20.00
❏ SRS-67106	Scott, Volume 2	1968	5.00	10.00	20.00
❏ SRS-67121	Scott Walker 3	1969	5.00	10.00	20.00

WALKER, T-BONE
ATLANTIC

❏ 8020 [M]	T-Bone Blues	1959	55.00	110.00	220.00
-- Black label					
❏ 8020 [M]	T-Bone Blues	1960	17.50	35.00	70.00
-- Red and purple label					
❏ SD 8256	T-Bone Blues	1970	5.00	10.00	20.00

BLUE NOTE

❏ BN-LA533-H2 [(2)]	Classics	1975	5.00	10.00	20.00

BLUESTIME

❏ 29004	Everyday I Have the Blues	1968	7.50	15.00	30.00
❏ 29010	Blue Rocks	1969	7.50	15.00	30.00

BLUESWAY

❏ BLS-6008	Stormy Monday Blues	1968	7.50	15.00	30.00
-- Reissue of Wet Soul LP?					
❏ BLS-6014	Funky Town	1968	7.50	15.00	30.00

BRUNSWICK

❏ BL 754126	The Truth	1968	7.50	15.00	30.00

CAPITOL

❏ H 370 [10]	Classics in Jazz	1953	250.00	500.00	1,000.
❏ T 370 [M]	Classics in Jazz	1953	75.00	150.00	300.00
❏ T 1958 [M]	Great Blues Vocal and Guitar	1963	37.50	75.00	150.00
-- Black "The Star Line" label (existence of black colorband label not confirmed)					

DELMARK

❏ D-633 [M]	I Want a Little Girl	1967	10.00	20.00	40.00
❏ DS-633 [S]	I Want a Little Girl	1967	12.50	25.00	50.00

IMPERIAL

❏ LP-9098 [M]	T-Bone Walker Sings the Blues	1959	75.00	150.00	300.00
❏ LP-9116 [M]	Singing the Blues	1960	62.50	125.00	250.00
❏ LP-9146 [M]	I Get So Weary	1961	75.00	150.00	300.00

REPRISE

❏ 2RS 6483 [(2)]	Very Rare	1973	5.00	10.00	20.00

WET SOUL

❏ 1002	Stormy Monday Blues	1967	12.50	25.00	50.00

WALLACE BROTHERS, THE
SIMS

❏ LP-128 [M]	Soul, Soul and More Soul	1965	50.00	100.00	200.00
❏ LPS-128 [S]	Soul, Soul and More Soul	1965	62.50	125.00	250.00

WALLACE, GEORGE, JR.
PORTRAIT

❏ JR 36579	Heroes Like You and Me	1981	6.25	12.50	25.00

WALLACE, JERRY
CHALLENGE

❏ CHL 606 [M]	Just Jerry	1959	15.00	30.00	60.00
❏ CHL 612 [M]	There She Goes	1961	7.50	15.00	30.00
❏ CHS 612 [S]	There She Goes	1961	10.00	20.00	40.00
❏ CHL 616 [M]	Shutters and Boards	1962	7.50	15.00	30.00
❏ CHS 616 [S]	Shutters and Boards	1962	10.00	20.00	40.00
❏ CHL 619 [M]	In the Misty Moonlight	1964	5.00	10.00	20.00
❏ CHS 619 [S]	In the Misty Moonlight	1964	6.25	12.50	25.00

LIBERTY

❏ LST-7545	This One's On the House	1967	5.00	10.00	20.00
❏ LST-7564	Another Time, Another World	1968	5.00	10.00	20.00
❏ LST-7597	Sweet Child of Sunshine	1968	5.00	10.00	20.00

MERCURY

❏ SR-61072 [S]	The Best of Jerry Wallace	1966	5.00	10.00	20.00

UNITED ARTISTS

❏ UXS-95 [(2)]	Jerry Wallace Superpak	1972	5.00	10.00	20.00

WALLER, JIM, AND THE DELTAS
ARVEE

❏ A-432 [M]	Surfin' Wild	1963	20.00	40.00	80.00
❏ AS-432 [S]	Surfin' Wild	1963	25.00	50.00	100.00

WALLIS, RUTH
KING

❏ 265-6 [10]	Rhumba Party	1952	30.00	60.00	120.00
❏ 265-9 [10]	House Party	1952	30.00	60.00	120.00
❏ 395-507 [M]	House Party	1956	25.00	50.00	100.00
❏ 904 [M]	Saucy Hit Parade	1964	7.50	15.00	30.00
❏ 986 [M]	Here's Looking Up Your Hatch	1966	7.50	15.00	30.00
❏ 987 [M]	Davy's Little Dinghy	1966	7.50	15.00	30.00
❏ 988 [M]	Marry Go Round	1966	7.50	15.00	30.00
❏ 989 [M]	Red Lights	1966	7.50	15.00	30.00
❏ 990 [M]	Ubangi Me	1966	7.50	15.00	30.00
❏ 991 [M]	Oil Man from Texas	1966	7.50	15.00	30.00
❏ 992 [M]	He Wants a Little…Pizza	1966	7.50	15.00	30.00
❏ 993 [M]	Bahama Mama	1966	7.50	15.00	30.00

WALLIS ORIGINAL

❏ 2 [M]	Ruth Wallis	1957	10.00	20.00	40.00

WALSH, JOE
Also see EAGLES; THE JAMES GANG.
ABC COMMAND

❏ QD-40016 [Q]	The Smoker You Drink, the Player You Get	1974	5.00	10.00	20.00
❏ QD-40017 [Q]	So What	1975	5.00	10.00	20.00

WALSTON, RAY
VEE JAY

❏ LP-1110 [M]	My Favorite Songs from "Mary Poppins" and Other Songs to Delight	1965	6.25	12.50	25.00
❏ SR-1110 [S]	My Favorite Songs from "Mary Poppins" and Other Songs to Delight	1965	7.50	15.00	30.00

WALT, SHERMAN
RCA VICTOR RED SEAL

❏ LSC-2353 [S]	Vivaldi: The Four Seasons Concertos	1960	7.50	15.00	30.00
-- Original with "shaded dog" label					

WALTON, MERCY DEE -- See MERCY DEE.

WALTON, WADE
BLUESVILLE

❏ BVLP-1060 [M]	Shake 'Em On Down	1963	25.00	50.00	100.00
-- Blue label, silver print					
❏ BVLP-1060 [M]	Shake 'Em On Down	1964	7.50	15.00	30.00
-- Blue label, trident logo at right					

WALTONS, THE -- See "Various Artists Compilations" in back

WANDERERS THREE, THE
DOLTON

❏ BLP 2021 [M]	We Sing Folk Songs	1963	5.00	10.00	20.00
❏ BST 8021 [S]	We Sing Folk Songs	1963	6.25	12.50	25.00

WANDERLEY, WALTER
VERVE

Number	Title	Yr	VG	VG+	NM
❑ V6-8658 [S]	Rain Forest	1966	5.00	10.00	20.00
❑ V-8739 [M]	Kee-Ka-Roo	1967	5.00	10.00	20.00

WAR
UNITED ARTISTS

Number	Title	Yr	VG	VG+	NM
❑ SP-103 [DJ]	Radio Free War	1974	6.25	12.50	25.00
-- Promo only on blue vinyl					

WARD, ALAN
RCA VICTOR RED SEAL

Number	Title	Yr	VG	VG+	NM
❑ LSC-2302 [S]	Gilbert & Sullivan Overtures	1959	12.50	25.00	50.00
-- Original with "shaded dog" label					

WARD, BILLY, AND THE DOMINOES
DECCA

Number	Title	Yr	VG	VG+	NM
❑ DL 8621 [M]	Billy Ward and the Dominoes	1958	50.00	100.00	200.00

FEDERAL

Number	Title	Yr	VG	VG+	NM
❑ 295-94 [10]	Billy Ward and His Dominoes	1955	6,000.	9,500.	13,000.
❑ 548 [M]	Billy Ward and His Dominoes	1958	375.00	750.00	1,500.
❑ 559 [M]	Clyde McPhatter with Billy Ward and His Dominoes	1958	300.00	600.00	1,200.

KING

Number	Title	Yr	VG	VG+	NM
❑ 559 [M]	Clyde McPhatter with Billy Ward and His Dominoes	1958	150.00	300.00	600.00
-- Yellow cover					
❑ 559 [M]	Clyde McPhatter with Billy Ward and His Dominoes	196?	75.00	150.00	300.00
-- Pink cover					
❑ 733 [M]	Billy Ward and His Dominoes Featuring Clyde McPhatter and Jackie Wilson	1961	150.00	300.00	600.00
❑ 952 [M]	24 Songs	1966	12.50	25.00	50.00

LIBERTY

Number	Title	Yr	VG	VG+	NM
❑ LRP-3056 [M]	Sea of Glass	1957	15.00	30.00	60.00
❑ LRP-3083 [M]	Yours Forever	1958	15.00	30.00	60.00
❑ LRP-3113 [M]	Pagan Love Song	1959	15.00	30.00	60.00
❑ LST-7113 [S]	Pagan Love Song	1959	25.00	50.00	100.00

WARD, ROBIN
DOT

Number	Title	Yr	VG	VG+	NM
❑ DLP 3555 [M]	Wonderful Summer	1963	50.00	100.00	200.00
❑ DLP 25555 [S]	Wonderful Summer	1963	75.00	150.00	300.00

WARFIELD, WILLIAM
COLUMBIA MASTERWORKS

Number	Title	Yr	VG	VG+	NM
❑ ML 2206 [M]	Old American Songs and Five Sea Chanties	195?	12.50	25.00	50.00

WARINER, STEVE
ARISTA

Number	Title	Yr	VG	VG+	NM
❑ AL 8691	I Am Ready	1992	5.00	10.00	20.00
-- Vinyl version available only from Columbia House					

WARING, FRED, AND THE PENNSYLVANIANS
CAPITOL

Number	Title	Yr	VG	VG+	NM
❑ T 896 [M]	Now Is the Caroling Season	1957	5.00	10.00	20.00
-- Originals have turquoise labels					
❑ ST 936 [S]	All Through the Night	1958	5.00	10.00	20.00
❑ T 936 [M]	All Through the Night	1958	5.00	10.00	20.00
-- Black colorband label, logo at left					
❑ ST 1260 [S]	The Sounds of Christmas	1959	5.00	10.00	20.00
-- Originals have black label with colorband and "Capitol" logo at 9 o'clock					
❑ ST 1610 [S]	The Meaning of Christmas	1961	5.00	10.00	20.00

DECCA

Number	Title	Yr	VG	VG+	NM
❑ DLP 5004 [10]	Jerome Kern Songs	1950	12.50	25.00	50.00
❑ DLP 5005 [10]	Cole Porter Songs	1950	12.50	25.00	50.00
❑ DLP 5009 [10]	Selections from Miss Liberty	1950	12.50	25.00	50.00
❑ DLP 5021 [10]	'Twas the Night Before Christmas	1950	12.50	25.00	50.00
❑ DLP 5036 [10]	Pleasure Time	1951	10.00	20.00	40.00
❑ DL 5061 [10]	Songs of Devotion, Vol. 1	1950	10.00	20.00	40.00
❑ DL 5062 [10]	Songs of Devotion, Vol. 2	1950	10.00	20.00	40.00
❑ DL 5141 [10]	This Is My Country	1950	10.00	20.00	40.00
❑ DL 5202 [10]	Columbia, the Gem of the Ocean (Patriotic and Service Songs)	1950	10.00	20.00	40.00
❑ DL 5292 [10]	Richard Rodgers and Oscar Hammerstein II Songs, Vol. 1	1950	10.00	20.00	40.00
❑ DL 5293 [10]	Richard Rodgers and Oscar Hammerstein II Songs, Vol. 2	1950	10.00	20.00	40.00
❑ DL 5295 [10]	Christmas Time	1950	10.00	20.00	40.00
❑ DL 8005 [M]	Listening Time	1950	10.00	20.00	40.00
❑ DL 8026 [M]	Program Time	1950	7.50	15.00	30.00
❑ DL 8033 [M]	Song of America	195?	10.00	20.00	40.00
❑ DL 8039 [M]	Songs of Faith, Vols. 1 and 2	195?	7.50	15.00	30.00
❑ DL 8047 [M]	God's Trombones and Other Spirituals	195?	7.50	15.00	30.00
❑ DL 8082 [M]	For Listening Only	1954	6.25	12.50	25.00
❑ DL 8084 [M]	Song of Christmas	1954	6.25	12.50	25.00
❑ DL 8110 [M]	Lullaby Time	1955	5.00	10.00	20.00
❑ DL 8111 [M]	Songs in Reverence	1955	5.00	10.00	20.00
❑ DL 8171 [M]	'Twas the Night Before Christmas	1955	5.00	10.00	20.00
❑ DL 8172 [M]	Christmas Time	1955	5.00	10.00	20.00

WARNES, JENNIFER
Also see JENNIFER.
CYPRESS

Number	Title	Yr	VG	VG+	NM
❑ 661 111-1	Famous Blue Raincoat	1987	7.50	15.00	30.00

ROCK THE HOUSE

Number	Title	Yr	VG	VG+	NM
❑ RTH 5052	Famous Blue Raincoat	1996	12.50	25.00	50.00
-- Classic Records reissue					

WARREN, FRAN
MGM

Number	Title	Yr	VG	VG+	NM
❑ E-3394 [M]	Mood Indigo	1956	12.50	25.00	50.00
-- Yellow label					

TOPS

Number	Title	Yr	VG	VG+	NM
❑ L-1585 [M]	Hey There	195?	5.00	10.00	20.00

VENISE

Number	Title	Yr	VG	VG+	NM
❑ 7019 [M]	Come Rain or Come Shine	195?	6.25	12.50	25.00
❑ 10019 [S]	Come Rain or Come Shine	195?	12.50	25.00	50.00

WARWICK

Number	Title	Yr	VG	VG+	NM
❑ W-2012 [M]	Something's Coming	1960	6.25	12.50	25.00

WARREN, RUSTY
JUBILEE

Number	Title	Yr	VG	VG+	NM
❑ JLP 2024 [M]	Songs for Sinners	1960	6.25	12.50	25.00
❑ JLP 2029 [M]	Knockers Up!	1960	6.25	12.50	25.00
❑ JLP 2034 [M]	Sin-Sational	1961	6.25	12.50	25.00
❑ JGM 2039 [M]	Rusty Warren Bounces Back	1961	6.25	12.50	25.00
❑ JGM 2044 [M]	Rusty Warren in Orbit	1962	6.25	12.50	25.00
❑ JLP 2049 [M]	Banned in Boston?	1963	6.25	12.50	25.00
❑ JLP 2054 [M]	Sex-X-Ponent	1964	6.25	12.50	25.00
❑ JLP 2059 [M]	More Knockers Up!	1965	6.25	12.50	25.00
❑ JGM 2069 [M]	Bottoms Up!	1967	5.00	10.00	20.00
❑ JGM 2074	Look What I've Got for You	1967	5.00	10.00	20.00
❑ JLP 5025 [M]	Portrait of Life	196?	5.00	10.00	20.00
❑ JLPS 5025 [S]	Portrait of Life	196?	5.00	10.00	20.00

WARWICK, DEE DEE
ATCO

Number	Title	Yr	VG	VG+	NM
❑ SD 33-337	Turnin' Around	1970	6.25	12.50	25.00

MERCURY

Number	Title	Yr	VG	VG+	NM
❑ MG-21100 [M]	I Want to Be with You	1967	6.25	12.50	25.00
❑ SR-61100 [S]	I Want to Be with You	1967	6.25	12.50	25.00
❑ SR-61221	Foolish Fool	1968	6.25	12.50	25.00

WARWICK, DIONNE
MOBILE FIDELITY

Number	Title	Yr	VG	VG+	NM
❑ 2-098 [(2)]	Hot! Live and Otherwise	1982	7.50	15.00	30.00
-- Audiophile vinyl					

SCEPTER

Number	Title	Yr	VG	VG+	NM
❑ SS-508 [S]	Presenting Dionne Warwick	1963	5.00	10.00	20.00
❑ SS-517 [S]	Anyone Who Had a Heart	1964	5.00	10.00	20.00
❑ SS-523 [S]	Make Way for Dionne Warwick	1964	5.00	10.00	20.00
❑ SS-528 [S]	The Sensitive Sound of Dionne Warwick	1965	5.00	10.00	20.00
❑ SS-531 [S]	Here I Am	1965	5.00	10.00	20.00
❑ S-565 [M]	Dionne Warwick's Golden Hits, Part One	1967	5.00	10.00	20.00
❑ SS-596 [(2)]	The Dionne Warwicke Story	1971	5.00	10.00	20.00
-- As "Dionne Warwicke"					
❑ SS-598 [(2)]	From Within	1972	5.00	10.00	20.00
-- As "Dionne Warwicke"					

WARNER BROS.

Number	Title	Yr	VG	VG+	NM
❑ BS4 2846 [Q]	Then Came You	1975	5.00	10.00	20.00
-- As "Dionne Warwicke"					

WASHBOARD SAM
RCA VICTOR

Number	Title	Yr	VG	VG+	NM
❑ LPV-577 [M]	Feeling Lowdown	196?	6.25	12.50	25.00

WASHINGTON, BABY
SUE

Number	Title	Yr	VG	VG+	NM
❑ LP-1014 [M]	That's How Heartaches Are Made	1963	37.50	75.00	150.00
❑ LP-1042 [M]	Only Those in Love	1965	37.50	75.00	150.00
❑ LPS-1042 [S]	Only Those in Love	1965	75.00	150.00	300.00

Number	Title	Yr	VG	VG+	NM
VEEP					
❑ VPS-16528	With You in Mind	1968	6.25	12.50	25.00

WASHINGTON, DINAH

Number	Title	Yr	VG	VG+	NM
DELMARK					
❑ DL-451	Mellow Mama	1992	5.00	10.00	20.00
EMARCY					
❑ MG-26032 [10]	After Hours with Miss D	1954	30.00	60.00	120.00
❑ MG-36000 [M]	Dinah Jams	1955	12.50	25.00	50.00
❑ MG-36011 [M]	For Those in Love	1955	12.50	25.00	50.00
❑ MG-36028 [M]	After Hours with Miss D	1955	12.50	25.00	50.00
-- Reissue of 26032					
❑ MG-36065 [M]	Dinah	1956	12.50	25.00	50.00
❑ MG-36073 [M]	In the Land of Hi-Fi	1956	12.50	25.00	50.00
❑ MG-36104 [M]	The Swingin' Miss "D"	1956	12.50	25.00	50.00
❑ MG-36119 [M]	The Fats Waller Songbook	1957	12.50	25.00	50.00
❑ MG-36130 [M]	Dinah Washington Sings Bessie Smith	1957	12.50	25.00	50.00
GRAND AWARD					
❑ GA-33-318 [M]	Dinah Washington Sings the Blues	1955	12.50	25.00	50.00
-- Add 50% if removable wrap-around cover is still there					
MERCURY					
❑ MGP-2-103 [(2) M]	This Is My Story	1963	6.25	12.50	25.00
-- Combines 20788 and 20789 in one package					
❑ MGP-2-603 [(2) S]	This Is My Story	1963	7.50	15.00	30.00
-- Combines 60788 and 60789 in one package					
❑ MG-20119 [M]	Music for a First Love	1957	12.50	25.00	50.00
❑ MG-20120 [M]	Music for Late Hours	1957	12.50	25.00	50.00
❑ MG-20247 [M]	The Best in Blues	1958	12.50	25.00	50.00
❑ MG-20439 [M]	The Queen	1959	7.50	15.00	30.00
❑ MG-20479 [M]	What a Diff'rence a Day Makes!	1960	7.50	15.00	30.00
❑ MG-20523 [M]	Newport '58	1960	7.50	15.00	30.00
❑ MG-20525 [M]	Dinah Washington Sings Fats Waller	1960	7.50	15.00	30.00
-- Reissue of EmArcy 36119					
❑ MG-20572 [M]	Unforgettable	1961	6.25	12.50	25.00
❑ MG-20604 [M]	I Concentrate on You	1961	6.25	12.50	25.00
❑ MG-20614 [M]	For Lonely Lovers	1961	6.25	12.50	25.00
❑ MG-20638 [M]	September in the Rain	1961	6.25	12.50	25.00
❑ MG-20661 [M]	Tears & Laughter	1962	6.25	12.50	25.00
❑ MG-20729 [M]	I Wanna Be Loved	1962	6.25	12.50	25.00
❑ MG-21119 [M]	Dinah Discovered	1967	5.00	10.00	20.00
❑ MG-25060 [10]	Dinah Washington	1950	30.00	60.00	120.00
❑ MG-25138 [10]	Dynamic Dinah	1952	30.00	60.00	120.00
❑ MG-25140 [10]	Blazing Ballads	1952	30.00	60.00	120.00
❑ SR-60111 [S]	The Queen	1959	10.00	20.00	40.00
❑ SR-60158 [S]	What a Diff'rence a Day Makes!	1960	10.00	20.00	40.00
❑ SR-60200 [S]	Newport '58	1960	10.00	20.00	40.00
❑ SR-60202 [S]	Dinah Washington Sings Fats Waller	1960	10.00	20.00	40.00
❑ SR-60232 [S]	Unforgettable	1961	7.50	15.00	30.00
❑ SR-60604 [S]	I Concentrate on You	1961	7.50	15.00	30.00
❑ SR-60614 [S]	For Lonely Lovers	1961	7.50	15.00	30.00
❑ SR-60638 [S]	September in the Rain	1961	7.50	15.00	30.00
❑ SR-60661 [S]	Tears & Laughter	1962	7.50	15.00	30.00
❑ SR-60729 [S]	I Wanna Be Loved	1962	7.50	15.00	30.00
❑ SR-60788 [S]	This Is My Story -- Dinah Washington's Golden Hits, Volume 1	1963	5.00	10.00	20.00
❑ SR-60789 [S]	This Is My Story -- Dinah Washington's Golden Hits, Volume 2	1963	5.00	10.00	20.00
❑ SR-60829 [S]	The Good Old Days	1963	5.00	10.00	20.00
❑ SR-60928 [S]	The Queen and Quincy	1965	5.00	10.00	20.00
ROULETTE					
❑ SR 25170 [S]	Dinah '62	1962	5.00	10.00	20.00
❑ SR 25180 [S]	In Love	1962	5.00	10.00	20.00
❑ SR 25183 [S]	Drinking Again	1962	5.00	10.00	20.00
❑ SR 25189 [S]	Back to the Blues	1963	5.00	10.00	20.00
❑ SR 25220 [S]	Dinah '63	1963	5.00	10.00	20.00
❑ SR 25244 [S]	In Tribute	1963	5.00	10.00	20.00
❑ SR 25253 [S]	A Stranger on Earth	1964	5.00	10.00	20.00
❑ SR 25269 [S]	Dinah Washington	1964	5.00	10.00	20.00
❑ SR 25289 [S]	The Best of Dinah Washington	1965	5.00	10.00	20.00
WING					
❑ PKW-2-121 [(2)]	The Original Queen of Soul	1969	5.00	10.00	20.00

WASHINGTON, DINAH, AND BROOK BENTON

Also see each artist's individual listings.

Number	Title	Yr	VG	VG+	NM
MERCURY					
❑ MG-20588 [M]	The Two of Us	1960	6.25	12.50	25.00
❑ SR-60588 [S]	The Two of Us	1960	7.50	15.00	30.00

WASHINGTON, GINO

Number	Title	Yr	VG	VG+	NM
ATAC					
❑ 2730	Gino Washington's Golden Hits	1969	7.50	15.00	30.00
KAPP					
❑ KL-1415 [M]	Gino Washington's Ram Jam Band	1967	5.00	10.00	20.00
❑ KS-3415 [S]	Gino Washington's Ram Jam Band	1967	6.25	12.50	25.00

WASHINGTON, GROVER, JR.

Number	Title	Yr	VG	VG+	NM
COLUMBIA					
❑ C 48530	Next Exit	1992	5.00	10.00	20.00
KUDU					
❑ KSQX-1213 [(2) Q]	Soul Box	1973	6.25	12.50	25.00
NAUTILUS					
❑ NR-39	Winelight	1981	12.50	25.00	50.00
-- Audiophile vinyl					

WATERS, MUDDY

Number	Title	Yr	VG	VG+	NM
CADET CONCEPT					
❑ CS-314	Electric Mud	1968	6.25	12.50	25.00
❑ CS-320	After the Rain	1969	6.25	12.50	25.00
CHESS					
❑ 127 [(2)]	Fathers and Sons	1969	6.25	12.50	25.00
❑ LP-1427 [DJ]	The Best of Muddy Waters	1957	500.00	1,000.	1,500.
-- White label promo					
❑ LP-1427 [M]	The Best of Muddy Waters	1957	125.00	250.00	500.00
❑ LP-1444 [DJ]	Muddy Waters Sings Big Bill	1960	250.00	500.00	1,000.
-- White label promo					
❑ LP-1444 [M]	Muddy Waters Sings Big Bill	1960	75.00	150.00	300.00
❑ LP-1449 [M]	Muddy Waters at Newport	1962	30.00	60.00	120.00
❑ LP-1483 [M]	Folk Singer	1964	30.00	60.00	120.00
❑ LP-1501 [M]	The Real Folk Blues of Muddy Waters	1965	15.00	30.00	60.00
❑ LP-1507 [M]	Muddy, Brass and Blues	1966	10.00	20.00	40.00
❑ LPS-1507 [S]	Muddy, Brass and Blues	1966	12.50	25.00	50.00
❑ LP-1511 [M]	More Real Folk Blues	1967	12.50	25.00	50.00
❑ LPS-1511 [S]	More Real Folk Blues	1967	10.00	20.00	40.00
❑ LP-1533 [M]	Blues from Big Bill's Copacabana	1968	12.50	25.00	50.00
❑ LPS-1539	Sail On	1969	6.25	12.50	25.00
❑ LPS-1553	They Call Me Muddy Waters	1971	5.00	10.00	20.00
❑ CH-50012	Muddy Waters Live	1972	5.00	10.00	20.00
❑ CH-50023	Can't Get No Grindin'	1973	5.00	10.00	20.00
❑ 2CH-50033 [(2)]	Fathers and Sons	1974	5.00	10.00	20.00
-- Reissue of 127					
❑ 2CH-60006 [(2)]	McKinley Morganfield, A.K.A. Muddy Waters	1971	6.25	12.50	25.00
❑ CH-60013	The London Muddy Waters Sessions	1972	5.00	10.00	20.00
❑ CH6-80002 [(6)]	The Chess Box	1990	12.50	25.00	50.00
MOBILE FIDELITY					
❑ 1-201	Folk Singer	1994	6.25	12.50	25.00
-- Audiophile vinyl					

WATERS, ROGER

Also see PINK FLOYD.

Number	Title	Yr	VG	VG+	NM
COLUMBIA					
❑ FC 39290	The Pros and Cons of Hitch Hiking	1984	5.00	10.00	20.00
-- Original nude cover (later editions have a black rectangle over woman's rear)					
MERCURY					
❑ 846 611-1 [(2)]	The Wall -- Live in Berlin	1990	5.00	10.00	20.00
❑ R 209833 [(2)]	The Wall -- Live in Berlin	1990	5.00	10.00	20.00
-- BMG Direct Marketing version					

WATKINS, LOVELACE

Number	Title	Yr	VG	VG+	NM
MGM					
❑ E-3831 [M]	The Voice of Lovelace Watkins	1960	6.25	12.50	25.00
❑ SE-3831 [S]	The Voice of Lovelace Watkins	1960	10.00	20.00	40.00

WATSON, DOC

Number	Title	Yr	VG	VG+	NM
FOLKWAYS					
❑ FA-2366 [M]	Doc Watson and Family	1963	6.25	12.50	25.00
VANGUARD					
❑ VSD-9/10 [(2)]	Doc Watson On Stage	1970	5.00	10.00	20.00
❑ VSD 45/46 [(2)]	The Essential Doc Watson	1973	5.00	10.00	20.00
❑ VSD 107/8 [(2)]	Old Timey Concert	1977	5.00	10.00	20.00
❑ VRS-9152 [M]	Doc Watson	1964	5.00	10.00	20.00
❑ VRS-9170 [M]	Doc Watson and Son	1965	5.00	10.00	20.00
❑ VSD-79152 [S]	Doc Watson	1964	6.25	12.50	25.00
❑ VSD-79170 [S]	Doc Watson and Son	1965	6.25	12.50	25.00
❑ VSD-79213 [S]	Southbound	1966	5.00	10.00	20.00
❑ VSD-79239 [S]	Home Again	1967	5.00	10.00	20.00

WATSON, JOHNNY "GUITAR"

Number	Title	Yr	VG	VG+	NM
CADET					
❑ LP-4056 [M]	I Cried for You	1967	6.25	12.50	25.00
❑ LPS-4056 [S]	I Cried for You	1967	7.50	15.00	30.00

Number	Title	Yr	VG	VG+	NM
CHESS					
❑ LP-1490 [M]	Blues Soul	1965	17.50	35.00	70.00
❑ LPS-1490 [S]	Blues Soul	1965	20.00	40.00	80.00
KING					
❑ 857 [M]	Johnny Guitar Watson	1963	100.00	200.00	400.00
OKEH					
❑ OKM 12118 [M]	Bad	1967	7.50	15.00	30.00
❑ OKM 12124 [M]	In the Fats Bag	1967	7.50	15.00	30.00
❑ OKS 14118 [S]	Bad	1967	10.00	20.00	40.00
❑ OKS 14124 [S]	In the Fats Bag	1967	10.00	20.00	40.00

WATSON, JOHNNY "GUITAR", AND LARRY WILLIAMS
Also see each artist's individual listings.

Number	Title	Yr	VG	VG+	NM
OKEH					
❑ OKM 12122 [M]	Two for the Price of One	1967	10.00	20.00	40.00
❑ OKS 14122 [S]	Two for the Price of One	1967	15.00	30.00	60.00

WATTS 103RD STREET RHYTHM BAND, THE
-- See CHARLES WRIGHT AND THE WATTS 103RD STREET RHYTHM BAND.

WATTS, ALAN

Number	Title	Yr	VG	VG+	NM
ASCENSION					
❑ (# unknown)	Dhyana: Of the Art of Meditation, Vol. 1	1970	7.50	15.00	30.00
❑ (# unknown)	Dhyana: Of the Art of Meditation, Vol. 2	1970	7.50	15.00	30.00
MEA					
❑ LP-1001 [M]	Haiku Poems	1962	12.50	25.00	50.00
❑ LP-1002 [M]	Zen and Senryu	1962	12.50	25.00	50.00
❑ LP-1007 [M]	This Is It	1962	15.00	30.00	60.00
TOGETHER					
❑ 1025	Why Not Now	1970	6.25	12.50	25.00
WARNER BROS.					
❑ W 1923	The Sounds of Hinduism	1968	6.25	12.50	25.00

WAVE CRESTS, THE

Number	Title	Yr	VG	VG+	NM
VIKING					
❑ VKL-6606 [M]	Surftime U.S.A.	1963	15.00	30.00	60.00
❑ VKS-6606 [S]	Surftime U.S.A.	1963	25.00	50.00	100.00

WAYFARERS, THE

Number	Title	Yr	VG	VG+	NM
RCA VICTOR					
❑ LPM-1213 [M]	The Wayfarers	1956	12.50	25.00	50.00
❑ LPM-2666 [M]	Come Along with the Wayfarers	1963	6.25	12.50	25.00
❑ LSP-2666 [S]	Come Along with the Wayfarers	1963	7.50	15.00	30.00
❑ LPM-2735 [M]	The Wayfarers at the Hungry I	1963	6.25	12.50	25.00
❑ LSP-2735 [S]	The Wayfarers at the Hungry I	1963	7.50	15.00	30.00
❑ LPM-2946 [M]	The Wayfarers at the World's Fair	1964	7.50	15.00	30.00
❑ LSP-2946 [S]	The Wayfarers at the World's Fair	1964	10.00	20.00	40.00

WAYLON AND WILLIE
Also see WAYLON JENNINGS; WILLIE NELSON.

Number	Title	Yr	VG	VG+	NM
RCA VICTOR					
❑ AFL1-2686 [DJ]	Waylon and Willie	1978	6.25	12.50	25.00
-- Promo only on gold vinyl					

WAYNE, FRANCES

Number	Title	Yr	VG	VG+	NM
ATLANTIC					
❑ 1263 [M]	The Warm Sound of Frances Wayne	1957	12.50	25.00	50.00
-- Black label					
❑ 1263 [M]	The Warm Sound of Frances Wayne	1961	5.00	10.00	20.00
-- White "fan" logo at right of label					
BRUNSWICK					
❑ BL 54022 [M]	Frances Wayne	1958	10.00	20.00	40.00
CORAL					
❑ CRL 56019 [10]	Salute to Ethel Waters	195?	15.00	30.00	60.00
EPIC					
❑ LN 3222 [M]	Songs for My Man	1956	12.50	25.00	50.00

WAYNE, JOHN

Number	Title	Yr	VG	VG+	NM
RCA VICTOR					
❑ LSP-4828	America, Why I Love Her	1973	6.25	12.50	25.00

WAYNE, WEE WILLIE

Number	Title	Yr	VG	VG+	NM
IMPERIAL					
❑ LP-9144 [M]	Travelin' Mood	1961	125.00	250.00	500.00

WAZOO

Number	Title	Yr	VG	VG+	NM
ZIG ZAG					
❑ 217	Wazoo	197?	7.50	15.00	30.00

WE FIVE

Number	Title	Yr	VG	VG+	NM
A&M					
❑ SP-138 [M]	Make Someone Happy	1967	5.00	10.00	20.00
❑ SP-4111 [S]	You Were On My Mind	1965	5.00	10.00	20.00

WEASELS, THE

Number	Title	Yr	VG	VG+	NM
WING					
❑ MGW-12282 [M]	The Liverpool Beat	1964	6.25	12.50	25.00
❑ SRW-16282 [S]	The Liverpool Beat	1964	7.50	15.00	30.00

WEATHER REPORT

Number	Title	Yr	VG	VG+	NM
ARC					
❑ HC 47616	Weather Report	1982	10.00	20.00	40.00
-- Half-speed mastered edition					
COLUMBIA					
❑ CQ 32494 [Q]	Mysterious Traveller	1974	5.00	10.00	20.00
❑ HC 44418	Heavy Weather	198?	10.00	20.00	40.00
-- Half-speed mastered edition					
❑ PCQ 33417 [Q]	Tale Spinnin'	1975	5.00	10.00	20.00

WEAVER, CHARLIE

Number	Title	Yr	VG	VG+	NM
COLUMBIA					
❑ CL 1345 [M]	Charlie Weaver Sings for His People	1959	7.50	15.00	30.00
STARLITE					
❑ 6003 [10]	Charlie Weaver Sings	1954	12.50	25.00	50.00

WEAVERS, THE
❑ Also see RONNIE GILBERT; PETE SEEGER.

Number	Title	Yr	VG	VG+	NM
ANALOGUE PRODUCTIONS					
❑ 005	Reunion at Carnegie Hall, 1963	199?	7.50	15.00	30.00
-- Audiophile vinyl					
DECCA					
❑ DXB 173 [(2) M]	The Best of the Weavers	1965	6.25	12.50	25.00
❑ DL 4277 [M]	Weavers' Gold	1962	5.00	10.00	20.00
❑ DL 5285 [10]	Folk Songs of America and Other Lands	1951	25.00	50.00	100.00
❑ DL-5373 [10]	We Wish You a Merry Christmas	1952	25.00	50.00	100.00
❑ DXSB 7173 [(2) R]	The Best of the Weavers	1965	5.00	10.00	20.00
❑ DL 8893 [M]	The Best of the Weavers	1959	10.00	20.00	40.00
❑ DL 8909 [M]	Folk Songs Around the World	1959	10.00	20.00	40.00
VANGUARD					
❑ VSD 2022 [S]	Travelling On with the Weavers	1959	10.00	20.00	40.00
❑ VSD 2030 [S]	The Weavers at Home	1959	10.00	20.00	40.00
❑ VSD 2069 [S]	The Weavers at Carnegie Hall, Vol. 2	1960	10.00	20.00	40.00
❑ VSD 2101 [S]	Almanac	1961	10.00	20.00	40.00
❑ VSD 2150 [S]	Reunion at Carnegie Hall, 1963	1963	7.50	15.00	30.00
❑ SRV-3001 [(2) M]	The Weavers Song Bag	1967	5.00	10.00	20.00
❑ VRS 9010 [M]	The Weavers at Carnegie Hall	1957	10.00	20.00	40.00
❑ VRS 9013 [M]	The Weavers on Tour	1957	10.00	20.00	40.00
❑ VRS 9024 [M]	The Weavers at Home	1959	7.50	15.00	30.00
❑ VRS 9043 [M]	Travelling On with the Weavers	1959	7.50	15.00	30.00
❑ VRS 9075 [M]	The Weavers at Carnegie Hall, Vol. 2	1960	7.50	15.00	30.00
❑ VRS 9100 [M]	Almanac	1961	7.50	15.00	30.00
❑ VRS 9130 [M]	Reunion at Carnegie Hall, 1963	1963	5.00	10.00	20.00
❑ VRS 9161 [M]	Reunion at Carnegie Hall, Part 2	1965	5.00	10.00	20.00
❑ SRV-73001 [(2) S]	The Weavers Song Bag	1967	6.25	12.50	25.00
❑ VSD 79161 [S]	Reunion at Carnegie Hall, Part 2	1965	7.50	15.00	30.00

WEB, THE

Number	Title	Yr	VG	VG+	NM
DERAM					
❑ DES 18018	Fully Interlocking	1968	6.25	12.50	25.00

WEBB, JACK

Number	Title	Yr	VG	VG+	NM
RCA VICTOR					
❑ LPM-1126 [M]	Pete Kelly's Blues	1955	12.50	25.00	50.00
-- Webb narrates; jazz combo plays					
❑ LPM-2053 [M]	Pete Kelly's Blues	1959	7.50	15.00	30.00
-- Reissue of 1126					
❑ LSP-2053(e) [R]	Pete Kelly's Blues	196?	5.00	10.00	20.00
❑ LPM-3199 [10]	Dragnet -- The Christmas Story	1954	37.50	75.00	150.00
WARNER BROS.					
❑ W 1207 [M]	You're My Girl	1958	7.50	15.00	30.00
❑ WS 1207 [S]	You're My Girl	1958	10.00	20.00	40.00

Number	Title	Yr	VG	VG+	NM

WEBB, JAY LEE
DECCA
❑ DL 4933 [M]	I Come Home a-Drinkin'	1967	6.25	12.50	25.00
❑ DL 74933 [S]	I Come Home a-Drinkin'	1967	5.00	10.00	20.00
❑ DL 75121	She's Looking Better by the Minute	1969	5.00	10.00	20.00

WEBB, JIM
EPIC
❑ BN 26401	Jim Webb Sings Jim Webb	1968	5.00	10.00	20.00

WEBSTER, MAMIE
CUB
❑ 8002 [M]	The Blues	1959	37.50	75.00	150.00

WEDGES, THE
TIME
❑ S-2090 [S]	Hang Ten (For Surfers Only)	1963	17.50	35.00	70.00
❑ 52090 [M]	Hang Ten (For Surfers Only)	1963	12.50	25.00	50.00

WEIR, BOB
Also see THE GRATEFUL DEAD.
WARNER BROS.
❑ BS 2627	Ace	1972	10.00	20.00	40.00
-- Color photo on back cover					
❑ BS 2627	Ace	1972	7.50	15.00	30.00
-- Black and white photo on back cover					

WEIRD-OHS, THE
MERCURY
❑ MG-20976 [M]	The Sounds of the Weird-Ohs	1964	37.50	75.00	150.00
❑ SR-60976 [S]	The Sounds of the Weird-Ohs	1964	50.00	100.00	200.00

WEIRDOS
OUT OF DARKNESS
❑ OTD 001 [DJ]	Message from the Underworld	198?	10.00	20.00	40.00
-- Promo-only release					
RHINO
❑ RNEP 508 [EP]	Action Design	1980	5.00	10.00	20.00

WEISBERG, TIM
NAUTILUS
❑ NR-7	Tip of the Weisberg	1980	7.50	15.00	30.00
-- Audiophile vinyl					

WEISSBERG, ERIC, AND MARSHALL BRICKMAN
ELEKTRA
❑ EKL-238 [M]	New Dimensions in Banjo and Bluegrass	1963	5.00	10.00	20.00
❑ EKS-7238 [S]	New Dimensions in Banjo and Bluegrass	1963	6.25	12.50	25.00
-- Mandolin-player label					
❑ EKS-7238 [S]	New Dimensions in Banjo and Bluegrass	1967	5.00	10.00	20.00
-- Tan label with large stylized "E" at top					

WELCH CHORALE, THE
VANGUARD
❑ VRS 428 [M]	A Music Box of Christmas Carols	1954	5.00	10.00	20.00
-- With Music Boxes from the Bornand Collection					

WELCH, LENNY
CADENCE
❑ CLP 3068 [M]	Since I Fell for You	1963	7.50	15.00	30.00
❑ CLP 25068 [S]	Since I Fell for You	1963	12.50	25.00	50.00
COLUMBIA
❑ CL 2430 [M]	Since I Fell for You	1965	5.00	10.00	20.00
-- Reissue of Cadence 3068					
❑ CS 9230 [S]	Since I Fell for You	1965	7.50	15.00	30.00
-- Reissue of Cadence 25068					
KAPP
❑ KS-3457 [S]	Two Different Worlds	1965	5.00	10.00	20.00
❑ KS-3481 [S]	Rags to Riches	1966	5.00	10.00	20.00
❑ KS-3517 [S]	Lenny	1967	5.00	10.00	20.00

WELK, LAWRENCE
CORAL
❑ CXB 5 [(2) M]	The Best of Lawrence Welk	196?	5.00	10.00	20.00
❑ CRL 57011 [M]	Lawrence Welk and His Sparkling Strings	1955	5.00	10.00	20.00

Number	Title	Yr	VG	VG+	NM
❑ CRL 57025 [M]	TV Favorites	1955	5.00	10.00	20.00
❑ CRL 57036 [M]	Shamrocks and Champagne	1955	5.00	10.00	20.00
❑ CRL 57038 [M]	Bubbles in the Wine	1956	5.00	10.00	20.00
❑ CRL 57041 [M]	Say It With Music	1956	5.00	10.00	20.00
❑ CRL 57066 [M]	Lawrence Welk at Madison Square Garden	1956	5.00	10.00	20.00
❑ CRL 57067 [M]	Pick-A-Polka!	1956	5.00	10.00	20.00
❑ CRL 57068 [M]	Moments to Remember	1956	5.00	10.00	20.00
❑ CRL 57078 [M]	Champagne Pops Parade	1956	5.00	10.00	20.00
❑ CRL 57093 [M]	Merry Christmas from Lawrence Welk	1956	5.00	10.00	20.00
❑ CRL 57111 [M]	Show Time	1957	5.00	10.00	20.00
❑ CRL 57113 [M]	The World's Finest Music	1957	5.00	10.00	20.00
❑ CRL 57119 [M]	Waltz with Lawrence Welk	1957	5.00	10.00	20.00
❑ CRL 57146 [M]	Lawrence Welk Plays Dixieland	1957	5.00	10.00	20.00
❑ CRL 57178 [M]	Nimble Fingers	1957	5.00	10.00	20.00
❑ CRL 57186 [M]	Jingle Bells	1957	5.00	10.00	20.00
❑ CRL 757226 [S]	Champagne Dancing Party	1958	5.00	10.00	20.00
❑ CRL 757267 [S]	TV Western Theme Songs	1959	5.00	10.00	20.00

READER'S DIGEST
❑ RDA-07-A [(4)]	Merry Christmas from Lawrence Welk and His Champagne Music Makers	1970	6.25	12.50	25.00
❑ RDA 95 [(6)]	Champagne Music Varieties	196?	6.25	12.50	25.00

WELLS, JUNIOR
BLUE ROCK
❑ 64002	You're Tuff Enough	1968	7.50	15.00	30.00
❑ 64003	Live at the Golden Bear	1969	7.50	15.00	30.00
DELMARK
❑ DL-612 [M]	Hoodoo Man Blues	1966	10.00	20.00	40.00
❑ DS-612 [S]	Hoodoo Man Blues	1966	12.50	25.00	50.00
❑ DS-628	Southside Blues Jam	1967	6.25	12.50	25.00
❑ DS-640	Blue Hit Big Towns	1969	7.50	15.00	30.00
❑ DS-640	Blues Hit the Big Town	1969	6.25	12.50	25.00
VANGUARD
❑ VRS-9231 [M]	It's My Life Baby	1966	7.50	15.00	30.00
❑ VSD-79231 [S]	It's My Life Baby	1966	10.00	20.00	40.00
❑ VSD-79262	Comin' At You	1968	6.25	12.50	25.00

WELLS, KITTY
DECCA
❑ DXB 174 [(2) M]	The Kitty Wells Story	1963	7.50	15.00	30.00
❑ DL 4075 [M]	Seasons of My Heart	1961	7.50	15.00	30.00
❑ DL 4108 [M]	Kitty Wells' Golden Favorites	1961	7.50	15.00	30.00
❑ DL 4141 [M]	Heartbreak U.S.A.	1961	7.50	15.00	30.00
❑ DL 4197 [M]	Queen of Country Music	1962	7.50	15.00	30.00
❑ DL 4270 [M]	Singing on Sunday	1962	7.50	15.00	30.00
❑ DL 4349 [M]	Christmas Day with Kitty Wells	1962	6.25	12.50	25.00
❑ DL 4493 [M]	Especially for You	1964	6.25	12.50	25.00
❑ DL 4554 [M]	Country Music Time	1964	6.25	12.50	25.00
❑ DL 4612 [M]	Burning Memories	1965	6.25	12.50	25.00
❑ DL 4658 [M]	Lonesome Sad and Blue	1965	6.25	12.50	25.00
❑ DL 4679 [M]	Family Gospel Sing	1965	6.25	12.50	25.00
❑ DL 4741 [M]	Kitty Wells Sings Songs Made Famous by Jim Reeves	1966	6.25	12.50	25.00
❑ DL 4776 [M]	Country All the Way	1966	6.25	12.50	25.00
❑ DL 4831 [M]	The Kitty Wells Show	1966	6.25	12.50	25.00
❑ DL 4857 [M]	Love Makes the World Go Around	1967	7.50	15.00	30.00
❑ DL 4929 [M]	Queen of Honky Tonk Street	1967	10.00	20.00	40.00
❑ DXSB 7174 [(2) P]	The Kitty Wells Story	1963	10.00	20.00	40.00
❑ DL 8293 [M]	Kitty Wells' Country Hit Parade	1956	15.00	30.00	60.00
-- Black label, silver print					
❑ DL 8293 [M]	Kitty Wells' Country Hit Parade	1961	7.50	15.00	30.00
-- Black label with color bars					
❑ DL 8552 [M]	Winner of Your Heart	1957	15.00	30.00	60.00
-- Black label, silver print					
❑ DL 8552 [M]	Winner of Your Heart	1961	7.50	15.00	30.00
-- Black label with color bars					
❑ DL 8732 [M]	Lonely Street	1958	15.00	30.00	60.00
-- Black label, silver print					
❑ DL 8732 [M]	Lonely Street	1961	7.50	15.00	30.00
-- Black label with color bars					
❑ DL 8858 [M]	Dust on the Bible	1959	15.00	30.00	60.00
-- Black label, silver print					
❑ DL 8858 [M]	Dust on the Bible	1961	7.50	15.00	30.00
-- Black label with color bars					
❑ DL 8888 [M]	After Dark	1959	15.00	30.00	60.00
-- Black label, silver print					
❑ DL 8888 [M]	After Dark	1961	7.50	15.00	30.00
-- Black label with color bars					
❑ DL 8979 [M]	Kitty's Choice	1960	12.50	25.00	50.00
-- Black label, silver print					
❑ DL 8979 [M]	Kitty's Choice	1961	6.25	12.50	25.00
-- Black label with color bars					
❑ DL 74075 [S]	Seasons of My Heart	1961	10.00	20.00	40.00
❑ DL 74108 [R]	Kitty Wells' Golden Favorites	196?	5.00	10.00	20.00

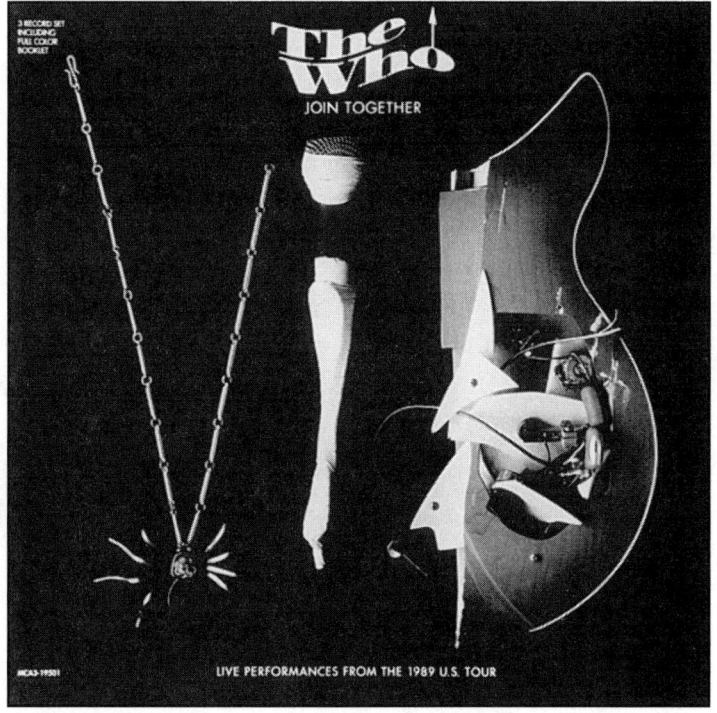

(Top left) *Radio Free War* was sent to radio stations as a promo-only item in 1974. It serves as a good retrospective of their career to that point. It also was issued on blue vinyl. This is the only uncommon War album. (Top right) One of the most valuable records in the world in near-mint condition, the Federal 10-inch LP of *Billy Ward and His Dominoes* is currently quoted at $13,000 in top shape. (Bottom left) Lavishly praised when it was released in 1987, Jennifer Warnes' *Famous Blue Raincoat,* her collection of songs written by Leonard Cohen, quickly became an audiophile favorite, with higher values than your typical 1987 album release as a result. It also has seen reissue on Classic Records, usually an indication of demand among the "golden ears" set. (Bottom right) *Join Together,* a chronicle of one of the Who's many "farewell tours," is not hard to find on CD, but the three-LP vinyl set is another matter altogether.

Number	Title	Yr	VG	VG+	NM
❏ DL 74141 [S]	Heartbreak U.S.A.	1961	10.00	20.00	40.00
❏ DL 74197 [S]	Queen of Country Music	1962	10.00	20.00	40.00
❏ DL 74270 [S]	Singing on Sunday	1962	10.00	20.00	40.00
❏ DL 74349 [S]	Christmas Day with Kitty Wells	1962	7.50	15.00	30.00
❏ DL 74493 [S]	Especially for You	1964	7.50	15.00	30.00
❏ DL 74554 [S]	Country Music Time	1964	7.50	15.00	30.00
❏ DL 74612 [S]	Burning Memories	1965	7.50	15.00	30.00
❏ DL 74658 [S]	Lonesome Sad and Blue	1965	7.50	15.00	30.00
❏ DL 74679 [S]	Family Gospel Sing	1965	7.50	15.00	30.00
❏ DL 74741 [S]	Kitty Wells Sings Songs Made Famous by Jim Reeves	1966	7.50	15.00	30.00
❏ DL 74776 [S]	Country All the Way	1966	7.50	15.00	30.00
❏ DL 74831 [S]	The Kitty Wells Show	1966	7.50	15.00	30.00
❏ DL 74857 [S]	Love Makes the World Go Around	1967	7.50	15.00	30.00
❏ DL 74929 [S]	Queen of Honky Tonk Street	1967	6.25	12.50	25.00
❏ DL 74961	Kitty Wells Showcase	1968	6.25	12.50	25.00
❏ DL 75001	Kitty Wells' Greatest Hits	1968	6.25	12.50	25.00
❏ DL 75067	Cream of Country Hits	1968	6.25	12.50	25.00
❏ DL 75098	Guilty Street	1969	6.25	12.50	25.00
❏ DL 75164	Bouquet of Country Hits	1969	5.00	10.00	20.00
❏ DL 75221	Singin' 'Em Country	1970	5.00	10.00	20.00
❏ DL 75245	Your Love Is the Way	1970	5.00	10.00	20.00
❏ DL 75277	They're Stepping All Over My Heart	1971	5.00	10.00	20.00
❏ DL 75313	Pledging My Love	1971	5.00	10.00	20.00
❏ DL 75325	Heartwarming Gospel Songs	1972	5.00	10.00	20.00
❏ DL 75350	Sincerely	1972	5.00	10.00	20.00
❏ DL 75382	I've Got Yesterday	1972	5.00	10.00	20.00
❏ DL 78293 [R]	Kitty Wells' Country Hit Parade	196?	5.00	10.00	20.00
❏ DL 78552 [R]	Winner of Your Heart	196?	5.00	10.00	20.00
❏ DL 78732 [R]	Lonely Street	196?	5.00	10.00	20.00
❏ DL 78858 [R]	Dust on the Bible	196?	5.00	10.00	20.00
❏ DL 78979 [S]	Kitty's Choice	1960	15.00	30.00	60.00
-- Maroon label, silver print					
❏ DL 78979 [S]	Kitty's Choice	1961	7.50	15.00	30.00
-- Black label with color bars					

WELLS, KITTY, AND JOHNNY WRIGHT
Also see each artist's individual listings.
DECCA

Number	Title	Yr	VG	VG+	NM
❏ DL 75028	We'll Stick Together	1968	6.25	12.50	25.00

WELLS, KITTY, AND RED FOLEY
Also see each artist's individual listings.
DECCA

Number	Title	Yr	VG	VG+	NM
❏ DL 4109 [M]	Golden Favorites	1961	7.50	15.00	30.00
❏ DL 4906 [M]	Together Again	1967	7.50	15.00	30.00
❏ DL 74109 [S]	Golden Favorites	1961	10.00	20.00	40.00
❏ DL 74906 [S]	Together Again	1967	6.25	12.50	25.00

WELLS, MARY
ATCO

Number	Title	Yr	VG	VG+	NM
❏ 33-199 [M]	Two Sides of Mary Wells	1966	6.25	12.50	25.00
❏ SD 33-199 [S]	Two Sides of Mary Wells	1966	7.50	15.00	30.00
JUBILEE					
❏ JGS-8018	Servin' Up Some Soul	1968	6.25	12.50	25.00
MOTOWN					
❏ M 600 [M]	Bye Bye Baby/I Don't Want to Take a Chance	1961	75.00	150.00	300.00
-- White label stock copy					
❏ M 600 [M]	Bye Bye Baby/I Don't Want to Take a Chance	1962	62.50	125.00	250.00
-- With map; label address above the center hole					
❏ M 605 [M]	The One Who Really Loves You	1962	40.00	80.00	160.00
-- With map; label address above the center hole					
❏ M 605 [M]	The One Who Really Loves You	1964	10.00	20.00	40.00
-- With map; label address around lower part of label					
❏ M 607 [M]	Two Lovers and Other Great Hits	1963	30.00	60.00	120.00
-- With map; label address above the center hole					
❏ M 607 [M]	Two Lovers and Other Great Hits	1964	10.00	20.00	40.00
-- With map; label address around lower part of label					
❏ M 611 [M]	Recorded Live On Stage	1963	30.00	60.00	120.00
-- With map; label address above the center hole					
❏ M 611 [M]	Recorded Live On Stage	1964	10.00	20.00	40.00
-- With map; label address around lower part of label					
❏ M 616 [M]	Greatest Hits	1964	10.00	20.00	40.00
❏ MS 616 [S]	Greatest Hits	1964	10.00	20.00	40.00
❏ M 617 [M]	Mary Wells Sings My Guy	1964	12.50	25.00	50.00
❏ M 653 [M]	Vintage Stock	1967	12.50	25.00	50.00
❏ MS 653 [S]	Vintage Stock	1967	12.50	25.00	50.00
MOVIETONE					
❏ 71010 [M]	Ooh	1966	6.25	12.50	25.00
❏ 72010 [S]	Ooh	1966	7.50	15.00	30.00
20TH FOX					
❏ TFM 3171 [M]	Mary Wells	1965	10.00	20.00	40.00
❏ TFM 3178 [M]	Love Songs to the Beatles	1965	20.00	40.00	80.00

Number	Title	Yr	VG	VG+	NM
❏ TFS 4171 [S]	Mary Wells	1965	15.00	30.00	60.00
❏ TFS 4178 [S]	Love Songs to the Beatles	1965	25.00	50.00	100.00

WESLEY, FRED
PEOPLE

Number	Title	Yr	VG	VG+	NM
❏ PE-5601	Food for Thought	1972	20.00	40.00	80.00
❏ PE-5603	Doing It to Death	1973	20.00	40.00	80.00
❏ PE-6602	Damn Right I Am Somebody	1974	5.00	10.00	20.00
❏ PE-6604	Breakin' Bread	1974	5.00	10.00	20.00

WEST
EPIC

Number	Title	Yr	VG	VG+	NM
❏ BN 26380	West	1968	5.00	10.00	20.00
❏ BN 26433	Bridges	1969	5.00	10.00	20.00

WEST COAST POP ART EXPERIMENTAL BAND, THE
AMOS

Number	Title	Yr	VG	VG+	NM
❏ AAS-7004	Where's My Daddy	1969	12.50	25.00	50.00
FIFO					
❏ M 101	West Coast Pop Art Experimental Band	1966	1,000.	1,500.	2,000.
-- With regular cover					
❏ M 101	West Coast Pop Art Experimental Band	1966	125.00	250.00	500.00
-- With plain cardboard cover					
RAZZBERRY SAWFLY					
❏ 800	West Coast Pop Art Experimental Band	1980	25.00	50.00	100.00
-- Reissue of Fifo LP					
REPRISE					
❏ R 6247 [M]	The West Coast Pop Art Experimental Band, Part One	1967	20.00	40.00	80.00
❏ RS 6247 [S]	The West Coast Pop Art Experimental Band, Part One	1967	25.00	50.00	100.00
❏ R 6270 [M]	The West Coast Pop Art Experimental Band, Part Two	1967	20.00	40.00	80.00
❏ RS 6270 [S]	The West Coast Pop Art Experimental Band, Part Two	1967	25.00	50.00	100.00
❏ RS 6298	A Child's Guide to Good and Evil	1968	25.00	50.00	100.00

WEST, BRUCE & LAING
Also see CREAM; MOUNTAIN.
WINDFALL

Number	Title	Yr	VG	VG+	NM
❏ CQ 31929 [Q]	Why Dontcha	1972	5.00	10.00	20.00
❏ CQ 32216 [Q]	Whatever Turns You On	1973	5.00	10.00	20.00

WEST, DOTTIE
RCA VICTOR

Number	Title	Yr	VG	VG+	NM
❏ APD1-0151 [Q]	If It's All Right with You	1973	5.00	10.00	20.00
❏ LPM-3368 [M]	Here Comes My Baby	1965	6.25	12.50	25.00
❏ LSP-3368 [S]	Here Comes My Baby	1965	7.50	15.00	30.00
❏ LPM-3490 [M]	Dottie West Sings	1966	6.25	12.50	25.00
❏ LSP-3490 [S]	Dottie West Sings	1966	7.50	15.00	30.00
❏ LPM-3587 [M]	Suffer Time	1966	6.25	12.50	25.00
❏ LSP-3587 [S]	Suffer Time	1966	7.50	15.00	30.00
❏ LPM-3693 [M]	With All My Heart and Soul	1967	7.50	15.00	30.00
❏ LSP-3693 [S]	With All My Heart and Soul	1967	6.25	12.50	25.00
❏ LPM-3784 [M]	Dottie West Sings Sacred Ballads	1967	7.50	15.00	30.00
❏ LSP-3784 [S]	Dottie West Sings Sacred Ballads	1967	6.25	12.50	25.00
❏ LPM-3830 [M]	I'll Help You Forget Her	1967	7.50	15.00	30.00
❏ LSP-3830 [S]	I'll Help You Forget Her	1967	6.25	12.50	25.00
❏ LPM-3932 [M]	What I'm Cut Out to Be	1968	12.50	25.00	50.00
❏ LSP-3932 [S]	What I'm Cut Out to Be	1968	6.25	12.50	25.00
❏ LSP-4004	Country Girl	1968	6.25	12.50	25.00
❏ LSP-4095	Feminine Fancy	1969	5.00	10.00	20.00
❏ LSP-4154	Dottie Sings Eddy	1969	5.00	10.00	20.00
❏ LSP-4276	Makin' Memories	1970	5.00	10.00	20.00
❏ LSP-4332	Country and West	1970	5.00	10.00	20.00
❏ LSP-4433	Forever Yours	1970	5.00	10.00	20.00
STARDAY					
❏ SLP-302 [M]	Country Girl Singing Sensation	1964	10.00	20.00	40.00

WEST, DOTTIE, AND DON GIBSON
Also see each artist's individual listings.
RCA VICTOR

Number	Title	Yr	VG	VG+	NM
❏ LSP-4131	Dottie and Don	1969	5.00	10.00	20.00

WEST, HEDY
VANGUARD

Number	Title	Yr	VG	VG+	NM
❏ VSD-2124 [S]	Hedy West Accompanying Herself on the 5-String Banjo	1963	6.25	12.50	25.00

Number	Title	Yr	VG	VG+	NM
❏ VSD-2126 [S]	Hedy West, Volume 2	1963	6.25	12.50	25.00
❏ VRS-9124 [M]	Hedy West Accompanying Herself on the 5-String Banjo	1963	5.00	10.00	20.00
❏ VRS-9126 [M]	Hedy West, Volume 2	1963	5.00	10.00	20.00

WEST, LUCRETIA
WESTMISTER
❏ WP-6063 [M]	Spirituals	1957	10.00	20.00	40.00

WEST, MAE
DAGONET
❏ DG-4 [M]	Wild Christmas	1966	7.50	15.00	30.00
❏ DGS-4 [S]	Wild Christmas	1966	10.00	20.00	40.00

DECCA
❏ DL 9016 [M]	The Fabulous Mae West	1955	15.00	30.00	60.00
-- All-black label with silver print					
❏ DL 9016 [M]	The Fabulous Mae West	1960	7.50	15.00	30.00
-- Black label with colorband					

MEZZOTONE
❏ 1 [10]	Mae West Songs, Vol. 1	1952	25.00	50.00	100.00
❏ 2 [10]	Mae West Songs, Vol. 2	1952	25.00	50.00	100.00

MGM
❏ SE-4869	Great Balls of Fire	1972	5.00	10.00	20.00

ROUND
❏ RS-100	Under the Mistletoe with Mae West	1977	5.00	10.00	20.00

TOWER
❏ ST 5028 [S]	Way Out West	1966	10.00	20.00	40.00
❏ T 5028 [M]	Way Out West	1966	7.50	15.00	30.00

WEST, SPEEDY
CAPITOL
❏ T 956 [M]	West of Hawaii	1958	20.00	40.00	80.00
❏ ST 1341 [S]	Steel Guitar	1960	15.00	30.00	60.00
❏ T 1341 [M]	Steel Guitar	1960	10.00	20.00	40.00
❏ ST 1835 [S]	Guitar Spectacular	1962	10.00	20.00	40.00
❏ T 1835 [M]	Guitar Spectacular	1962	7.50	15.00	30.00

WEST, SPEEDY, AND JIMMY BRYANT
CAPITOL
❏ H 520 [10]	Two Guitars Country Style	1954	50.00	100.00	200.00
❏ T 520 [M]	Two Guitars Country Style	1954	30.00	60.00	120.00

WESTERN, JOHNNY
COLUMBIA
❏ CL 1788 [M]	Have Gun, Will Travel	1962	10.00	20.00	40.00
❏ CS 8588 [S]	Have Gun, Will Travel	1962	12.50	25.00	50.00

WESTON, KIM
MGM
❏ E-4477 [M]	For the First Time	1967	7.50	15.00	30.00
❏ SE-4477 [S]	For the First Time	1967	10.00	20.00	40.00
❏ SE-4561	This Is America	1968	10.00	20.00	40.00

VOLT
❏ VOS-6014	Kim, Kim, Kim	1971	6.25	12.50	25.00

WESTON, PAUL
CAPITOL
❏ H 222 [10]	Music for Dreaming	195?	10.00	20.00	40.00

COLUMBIA
❏ CL 6232 [10]	Whispers in the Dark	195?	10.00	20.00	40.00

WHALEFEATHERS, THE
NASCO
❏ 9003	The Whalefeathers Declare	1969	25.00	50.00	100.00
❏ 9005	The Whalefeathers	1970	25.00	50.00	100.00

WHAM!
COLUMBIA
❏ 9C9 40062 [PD]	Make It Big	1985	6.25	12.50	25.00
-- Picture disc					

WHATNAUTS, THE
STANG
❏ 1005	The Whatnauts	1970	5.00	10.00	20.00

WHEELER, BILLY EDD
FOLKWAYS
❏ 31014	When Kentucky Had No Union	196?	5.00	10.00	20.00

KAPP
❏ KL-1533 [M]	Paper Birds	1967	5.00	10.00	20.00
❏ KS-3351 [S]	A New Bag of Songs Written and Sung by Billy Edd Wheeler	1964	5.00	10.00	20.00
❏ KS-3425 [S]	Memories of America/Ode to the Little Brown Shack Out Back	1965	5.00	10.00	20.00
❏ KS-3443 [S]	Wheeler Man	1965	5.00	10.00	20.00
❏ KS-3479 [S]	Goin' Town and Country	1966	5.00	10.00	20.00

MONITOR
❏ MF-354 [M]	Billy Edd U.S.A.	1961	7.50	15.00	30.00
❏ MF-367 [M]	Billy Edd and Bluegrass	1962	7.50	15.00	30.00

WHEELS, BURT, AND THE SPEEDSTERS
CORONET
❏ CX-216 [M]	Sounds of the Big Racers	196?	6.25	12.50	25.00
❏ CXS-216 [S]	Sounds of the Big Racers	196?	7.50	15.00	30.00

WHEELS, THE
MONTGOMERY WARD
❏ 010	Sounds of the Hot Rods	196?	30.00	60.00	120.00

WHISPERS, THE
JANUS
❏ JLS-3041	The Whispers' Love Story	1972	12.50	25.00	50.00
❏ JLS-3046	Life and Breath	1973	10.00	20.00	40.00
❏ 7006	Bingo	1974	10.00	20.00	40.00
❏ 7013	Greatest Hits	1975	7.50	15.00	30.00

SOUL CLOCK
❏ 22001	Planets of Life	1969	25.00	50.00	100.00

WHITCOMB, IAN
TOWER
❏ DT 5004 [R]	You Turn Me On	1965	5.00	10.00	20.00
❏ T 5004 [M]	You Turn Me On	1965	6.25	12.50	25.00
❏ ST 5042 [S]	Mod, Mod Music Hall	1966	5.00	10.00	20.00
❏ ST 5071 [S]	Yellow Underground	1967	5.00	10.00	20.00
❏ ST 5100	Sock Me Some Rock	1968	5.00	10.00	20.00

WHITE BOY
TRADEWIND
❏ MM-11761	The Average Rat Band	1976	37.50	75.00	150.00

WHITE LIGHT
CENTURY
❏ 39955	White Light	1968	75.00	150.00	300.00

WHITE LIGHTNIN'
ABC
❏ S-690	File Under Rock	1969	5.00	10.00	20.00

WHITE TIGER
With Mark St. John, who was briefly a member of KISS.
E.M.C.
❏ EMC-3653	White Tiger	1986	5.00	10.00	20.00

WHITE WITCH
CAPRICORN
❏ CP 0107	White Witch	1973	6.25	12.50	25.00
❏ CP 0129	A Spiritual Greeting	1974	6.25	12.50	25.00

WHITE ZOMBIE
CAROLINE
❏ 1350	Soul Crusher	1988	5.00	10.00	20.00
❏ 1362	Make Them Die Slowly	1989	5.00	10.00	20.00

SILENT EXPLOSION
❏ (# unknown) [EP]	Psycho-Head Blowout	1986	15.00	30.00	60.00
❏ (# unknown)	Soul Crusher	1987	15.00	30.00	60.00

WHITE, BUKKA
ARHOOLIE
❏ 1019 [M]	Sky Songs, Volume 1	1966	7.50	15.00	30.00
❏ 1020 [M]	Sky Songs, Volume 2	1966	7.50	15.00	30.00

BLUE HORIZON
❏ 4604	Blues Masters, Volume 4	1970	6.25	12.50	25.00

HERWIN
❏ 201	Sic 'em Dogs	196?	6.25	12.50	25.00

TAKOMA
❏ C-1001 [M]	Mississippi Blues	196?	7.50	15.00	30.00

Number	Title	Yr	VG	VG+	NM

WHITE, DANNY
GRAND PRIX
❑ 101	Danny White Sings Country	198?	5.00	10.00	20.00

WHITE, JOSH
ABC-PARAMOUNT
❑ ABC-124 [M]	Josh White Stories, Vol. 1	1956	15.00	30.00	60.00
❑ ABC-166 [M]	Josh White Stories, Vol. 2	1957	15.00	30.00	60.00
❑ ABC-407 [M]	Josh White -- Live!	1962	7.50	15.00	30.00
❑ ABCS-407 [S]	Josh White -- Live!	1962	10.00	20.00	40.00

DECCA
❑ DL 5062 [10]	Ballads and Blues	1949	37.50	75.00	150.00
❑ DL 5247 [10]	Ballads and Blues, Vol. 2	195?	30.00	60.00	120.00
❑ DL 8665 [M]	Josh White	1958	10.00	20.00	40.00
-- Black label, silver print					

ELEKTRA
❑ EKL-102 [M]	Josh at Midnight	1956	10.00	20.00	40.00
❑ EKL-114 [M]	Josh, Ballads and Blues	1957	10.00	20.00	40.00
❑ EKL-123 [M]	25th Anniversary Album	1957	10.00	20.00	40.00
❑ EKL-158 [M]	Chain Gang Songs	1958	20.00	40.00	80.00
❑ EKL-193 [M]	Spirituals and Blues	1960	7.50	15.00	30.00
❑ EKL-203 [M]	The House I Live In	1961	7.50	15.00	30.00
❑ EKL-211 [M]	Empty Bed Blues	1962	6.25	12.50	25.00
❑ EKL-701 [(2) 10]	The Story of John Henry/Ballads, Blues and Other Songs	1955	12.50	25.00	50.00
❑ EKS-7158 [S]	Chain Gang Songs	195?	25.00	50.00	100.00
❑ EKS-7193 [S]	Spirituals and Blues	1960	10.00	20.00	40.00
❑ EKS-7203 [S]	The House I Live In	1961	10.00	20.00	40.00
❑ EKS-7211 [S]	Empty Bed Blues	1962	7.50	15.00	30.00

EMARCY
❑ MG-26010 [10]	Strange Fruit	1954	30.00	60.00	120.00

LONDON
❑ LPB-338 [10]	A Josh White Program	195?	30.00	60.00	120.00
❑ LPB-341 [10]	A Josh White Program, Vol. 2	195?	30.00	60.00	120.00
❑ LL 1147 [M]	A Josh White Program	1956	12.50	25.00	50.00
❑ LL 1341 [M]	A Josh White Program, Vol. 2	195?	12.50	25.00	50.00

MERCURY
❑ MG-20203 [M]	Josh White's Blues	1957	15.00	30.00	60.00
❑ MG-20821 [M]	The Beginning	1963	7.50	15.00	30.00
❑ MG-21022 [M]	I'm On My Own Way	1963	7.50	15.00	30.00
❑ MG-25014 [10]	Josh White Sings Blues	1949	37.50	75.00	150.00
❑ SR-60821 [R]	The Beginning	1963	5.00	10.00	20.00
❑ SR-61022 [R]	I'm On My Own Way	1963	5.00	10.00	20.00

PERIOD
❑ SLP-1115 [10]	Josh White Comes a-Visiting	1956	15.00	30.00	60.00

STINSON
❑ SLP-14 [10]	Josh White Sings the Blues	1950	30.00	60.00	120.00
❑ SLP-15 [10]	Josh White Sings Folk Songs	1950	30.00	60.00	120.00

WHITEMAN, PAUL
CAPITOL
❑ T 622 [M]	Classics in Jazz	1955	12.50	25.00	50.00

CORAL
❑ CRL 57021 [M]	The Great Gershwin	1955	5.00	10.00	20.00

GRAND AWARD
❑ GA-208 [S]	Hawaiian Magic	1958	7.50	15.00	30.00
❑ GA-241 [S]	The Night I Played at 666 Fifth	1960	7.50	15.00	30.00
❑ GA-244 [S]	Cavalcade of Music	1960	7.50	15.00	30.00
❑ GA-33-351 [M]	Fiddle on Fire	195?	7.50	15.00	30.00
❑ GA-33-356 [M]	Hawaiian Magic	1958	5.00	10.00	20.00
❑ GA-33-409 [M]	The Night I Played at 666 Fifth	1960	5.00	10.00	20.00
❑ GA-33-412 [M]	Cavalcade of Music	1960	5.00	10.00	20.00
❑ GA-33-502 [M]	Great Whiteman Hits	195?	7.50	15.00	30.00
❑ GA-33-503 [M]	The Greatest Stars of My Life	195?	12.50	25.00	50.00
-- In red velvet jacket					
❑ GA-33-901 [(2) M]	Paul Whiteman/ 50th Anniversary	1956	12.50	25.00	50.00

"X"
❑ LVA-3040 [10]	Paul Whiteman's Orchestra Featuring Bix Beiderbecke	1955	20.00	40.00	80.00

WHITING, MARGARET
CAPITOL
❑ H 163 [10]	South Pacific	1950	12.50	25.00	50.00
❑ H 209 [10]	Margaret Whiting Sings Rodgers and Hart	1950	12.50	25.00	50.00
❑ H 234 [10]	Songs	1950	12.50	25.00	50.00
❑ T 410 [M]	Love Songs	1954	10.00	20.00	40.00
❑ T 685 [M]	For the Starry-Eyed	1955	10.00	20.00	40.00

DOT
❑ DLP 3072 [M]	Goin' Places	1957	6.25	12.50	25.00
❑ DLP 25113 [S]	Margaret	1958	5.00	10.00	20.00
❑ DLP 25176 [S]	Margaret Whiting's Great Hits	1959	5.00	10.00	20.00
❑ DLP 25235 [S]	Ten Top Hits	1960	5.00	10.00	20.00
❑ DLP 25337 [S]	Just a Dream	1960	5.00	10.00	20.00

LONDON
❑ LL 3497 [M]	The Wheel of Hurt	1967	5.00	10.00	20.00
❑ LL 3510 [M]	Maggie Isn't Margaret Anymore	1967	5.00	10.00	20.00

MGM
❑ SE-4006 [S]	Past Midnight	1961	5.00	10.00	20.00

VERVE
❑ V6-4038 [S]	The Jerome Kern Song Book	1960	5.00	10.00	20.00

WHITMAN, SLIM
CLEVELAND INT'L.
❑ AS99-875 [PD]	Songs I Love to Sing	1980	7.50	15.00	30.00
-- Promo-only picture disc					

IMPERIAL
❑ LP-3004 [10]	America's Favorite Folk Artist	1954	150.00	300.00	600.00
❑ LP-9003 [M]	Favorites	1956	12.50	25.00	50.00
-- Maroon label					
❑ LP-9003 [M]	Favorites	1958	7.50	15.00	30.00
-- Black label with stars on top					
❑ LP-9003 [M]	Favorites	1964	5.00	10.00	20.00
-- Black and pink label					
❑ LP-9026 [M]	Slim Whitman Sings	1957	12.50	25.00	50.00
-- Maroon label					
❑ LP-9026 [M]	Slim Whitman Sings	1958	7.50	15.00	30.00
-- Black label with stars on top					
❑ LP-9026 [M]	Slim Whitman Sings	1964	5.00	10.00	20.00
-- Black and pink label					
❑ LP-9056 [M]	Slim Whitman Sings	1958	7.50	15.00	30.00
-- Black label with stars on top					
❑ LP-9056 [M]	Slim Whitman Sings	1958	12.50	25.00	50.00
-- Maroon label					
❑ LP-9056 [M]	Slim Whitman Sings	1964	5.00	10.00	20.00
-- Black and pink label					
❑ LP-9064 [M]	Slim Whitman Sings	1959	7.50	15.00	30.00
-- Black label with stars on top					
❑ LP-9064 [M]	Slim Whitman Sings	1964	5.00	10.00	20.00
-- Black and pink label					
❑ LP-9088 [M]	I'll Walk with God	1960	7.50	15.00	30.00
-- Black label with stars on top					
❑ LP-9088 [M]	I'll Walk with God	1964	5.00	10.00	20.00
-- Black and pink label					
❑ LP-9102 [M]	Million Record Hits	1960	7.50	15.00	30.00
-- Black label with stars on top					
❑ LP-9102 [M]	Million Record Hits	1964	5.00	10.00	20.00
-- Black and pink label					
❑ LP-9135 [M]	Slim Whitman's First Visit to Britain	1960	6.25	12.50	25.00
-- Black label with stars on top					
❑ LP-9137 [M]	Just Call Me Lonesome	1961	6.25	12.50	25.00
-- Black label with stars on top					
❑ LP-9156 [M]	Once in a Lifetime	1961	6.25	12.50	25.00
-- Black label with stars on top					
❑ LP-9163 [M]	Slim Whitman Sings Annie Laurie	1961	6.25	12.50	25.00
-- Black label with stars on top					
❑ LP-9171 [M]	Forever	1961	6.25	12.50	25.00
-- Black label with stars on top					
❑ LP-9194 [M]	Slim Whitman Sings	1962	6.25	12.50	25.00
-- Black label with stars on top					
❑ LP-9209 [M]	Heart Songs and Love Songs	1962	6.25	12.50	25.00
-- Black label with stars on top					
❑ LP-9226 [M]	I'm a Lonely Wanderer	1963	6.25	12.50	25.00
-- Black label with stars on top					
❑ LP-9235 [M]	Yodeling	1963	6.25	12.50	25.00
-- Black label with stars on top					
❑ LP-9245 [M]	Irish Songs The Whitman Way	1963	6.25	12.50	25.00
-- Black label with stars on top					
❑ LP-9252 [M]	All-Time Favorites	1964	7.50	15.00	30.00
-- Black label with stars on top					
❑ LP-12032 [S]	I'll Walk with God	1959	10.00	20.00	40.00
-- Black label with silver top					
❑ LP-12032 [S]	I'll Walk with God	1964	6.25	12.50	25.00
-- Black and pink label					
❑ LP-12032 [S]	I'll Walk with God	1966	5.00	10.00	20.00
-- Black and green label					
❑ LP-12077 [S]	Slim Whitman Sings Annie Laurie	1961	7.50	15.00	30.00
-- Black label with silver top					
❑ LP-12077 [S]	Slim Whitman Sings Annie Laurie	1964	5.00	10.00	20.00
-- Black and pink label					
❑ LP-12194 [S]	Slim Whitman Sings	1962	7.50	15.00	30.00
-- Black label with silver top					
❑ LP-12194 [S]	Slim Whitman Sings	1964	5.00	10.00	20.00
-- Black and pink label					
❑ LP-12268 [S]	Country Songs/City Hits	1964	5.00	10.00	20.00
-- Black and pink label					
❑ LP-12277 [S]	Love Song of the Waterfall	1964	5.00	10.00	20.00
-- Black and pink label					
❑ LP-12288 [S]	Reminiscing	1965	5.00	10.00	20.00
-- Black and pink label					

Number	Title	Yr	VG	VG+	NM
❏ LP-12303 [S]	More Than Yesterday	1965	5.00	10.00	20.00
-- Black and pink label					

RCA CAMDEN

Number	Title	Yr	VG	VG+	NM
❏ CAL-954 [M]	Birmingham Jail	1966	5.00	10.00	20.00

RCA VICTOR

| ❏ LPM-3217 [10] | Slim Whitman Sings and Yodels | 1954 | 75.00 | 150.00 | 300.00 |

WHITNEY SUNDAY
DECCA

| ❏ DL 75239 | Whitney Sunday | 1970 | 5.00 | 10.00 | 20.00 |

WHITNEY, MARVA
KING

❏ KS-1053	I Sing Soul	1969	30.00	60.00	120.00
❏ KS-1062	It's My Thing	1969	30.00	60.00	120.00
❏ KS-1079	Live and Lowdown at the Apollo	1970	50.00	100.00	200.00

WHO, THE
Also see JOHN ENTWISTLE; KEITH MOON; PETE TOWNSHEND.

DECCA

❏ DL 4664 [M]	The Who Sing My Generation	1966	25.00	50.00	100.00
❏ DL 4664 [M-DJ]	The Who Sing My Generation	1966	50.00	100.00	200.00
-- White label promo					
❏ DL 4892 [M]	Happy Jack	1967	12.50	25.00	50.00
❏ DL 4892 [M-DJ]	Happy Jack	1967	37.50	75.00	150.00
-- White label promo					
❏ DL 4950 [M]	The Who Sell Out	1967	25.00	50.00	100.00
❏ DL 4950 [M-DJ]	The Who Sell Out	1967	50.00	100.00	200.00
-- White label promo with songs in the same order as the stock copy					
❏ DL 4950 [M-DJ]	The Who Sell Out	1967	75.00	150.00	300.00
-- White label promo with side 1 banded for airplay and all the commercials on one side					
❏ DL 5064 [M-DJ]	Magic Bus -- The Who on Tour	1968	50.00	100.00	200.00
-- White label promo; no stock copies were released in mono					
❏ DXSW 7205 [(2)]	Tommy	1969	10.00	20.00	40.00
-- With booklet					
❏ DXSW 7205 [(2) DJ]	Tommy	1969	50.00	100.00	200.00
-- White label promo					
❏ DL 74664 [DJ]	The Who Sing My Generation	1966	50.00	100.00	200.00
-- White label promo					
❏ DL 74664 [R]	The Who Sing My Generation	1966	15.00	30.00	60.00
❏ DL 74892 [DJ]	Happy Jack	1967	37.50	75.00	150.00
-- White label promo					
❏ DL 74892 [P]	Happy Jack	1967	12.50	25.00	50.00
-- All stereo except that "Happy Jack" and "Don't Look Away" are rechanneled					
❏ DL 74950 [DJ]	The Who Sell Out	1967	100.00	200.00	400.00
-- White label promo with side 1 banded for airplay and all the commercials on one side					
❏ DL 74950 [DJ]	The Who Sell Out	1967	62.50	125.00	250.00
-- White label promo with songs in the same order as the stock copy					
❏ DL 74950 [S]	The Who Sell Out	1967	12.50	25.00	50.00
❏ DL 75064 [DJ]	Magic Bus -- The Who on Tour	1968	37.50	75.00	150.00
❏ DL 75064 [P]	Magic Bus -- The Who on Tour	1968	12.50	25.00	50.00
-- All rechanneled except "Magic Bus," "I Can't Reach You" and "Tattoo," which are true stereo.					
❏ DL 79175	Live at Leeds	1970	10.00	20.00	40.00
-- With gatefold cover and numerous inserts					
❏ DL 79182	Who's Next	1971	6.25	12.50	25.00
❏ DL 79184	Meaty Beaty Big and Bouncy	1971	7.50	15.00	30.00
-- With poster (deduct 1/3 if missing)					
❏ DL 734586	The Who/The Strawberry Alarm Clock	1969	25.00	50.00	100.00
-- Special Products release for Philco. One side has Who songs, the other, Strawberry Alarm Clock songs					

DIRECT DISC

| ❏ SD 16610 | Who Are You | 1980 | 7.50 | 15.00 | 30.00 |
| -- Audiophile vinyl | | | | | |

LIFE

| ❏ DL 74664 [R] | The Who Sing My Generation | 1967 | 37.50 | 75.00 | 150.00 |

MCA

❏ L33-1987 [DJ]	Who Are You	1978	6.25	12.50	25.00
-- White label promo with sticker "Who Are You Edited for Broadcast" on cover -- the line "Who the fuck are you?" is deleted twice.					
❏ 2044 [R]	The Who Sing My Generation	1974	12.50	25.00	50.00
❏ 2045 [P]	Happy Jack	1974	12.50	25.00	50.00
❏ 4067 [(2) P]	A Quick One/The Who Sell Out	1976	5.00	10.00	20.00
-- Black labels with rainbow					
❏ 4068 [(2) P]	Magic Bus/The Who Sing My Generation	1976	5.00	10.00	20.00
-- Black labels with rainbow					
❏ 11164	Who's Next	1995	6.25	12.50	25.00
-- "Heavy Vinyl" reissue on 180-gram vinyl with gatefold cover					
❏ 19501 [(3)]	Join Together	1990	5.00	10.00	20.00
-- Box set with booklet					

MOBILE FIDELITY

| ❏ 1-115 | Face Dances | 1984 | 6.25 | 12.50 | 25.00 |
| -- Audiophile vinyl | | | | | |

TRACK

| ❏ 2126 | Odds and Sods | 1974 | 6.25 | 12.50 | 25.00 |
| ❏ 2-4067 [(2) P] | A Quick One/The Who Sell Out | 1974 | 6.25 | 12.50 | 25.00 |

Number	Title	Yr	VG	VG+	NM
❏ 2-4068 [(2) P]	Magic Bus/The Who Sing My Generation	1974	6.25	12.50	25.00
❏ 10004 [(2)]	Quadrophenia	1973	5.00	10.00	20.00

WARNER BROS.

❏ WBMS-116 [DJ]	Filling In the Gaps	1981	12.50	25.00	50.00
-- With generic "Warner Bros. Music Show" cover					
❏ WBMS-116 [DJ]	Filling In the Gaps	1981	20.00	40.00	80.00
-- With drawing on cover					
❏ 23731 [DJ]	It's Hard	1982	7.50	15.00	30.00
-- Promo version on Quiex II vinyl					

WICHITA TRAIN WHISTLE, THE
DOT

| ❏ DLP-25861 | Mike Nesmith Presents/ The Wichita Train Whistle Sings | 1968 | 7.50 | 15.00 | 30.00 |

WIGGINS, ROY
STARDAY

❏ SLP-188 [M]	Mister Steel Guitar	1962	7.50	15.00	30.00
❏ SLP-259 [M]	The Fabulous Steel Guitar Artistry of Roy Wiggins	1963	7.50	15.00	30.00
❏ SLP-392 [M]	Nashville Steel Guitar	1965	6.25	12.50	25.00

WIGWAM
VERVE FORECAST

| ❏ FTS-3089 | Tombstone Valentine | 1970 | 5.00 | 10.00 | 20.00 |

WILBURN BROTHERS, THE
DECCA

❏ DL 4058 [M]	The Big Heartbreak	1960	7.50	15.00	30.00
❏ DL 4142 [M]	The Wilburn Brothers Sing	1961	7.50	15.00	30.00
❏ DL 4211 [M]	City Limits	1961	7.50	15.00	30.00
❏ DL 4225 [M]	Folk Songs	1962	5.00	10.00	20.00
❏ DL 4391 [M]	Trouble's Back in Town	1963	5.00	10.00	20.00
❏ DL 4464 [M]	Take Up Thy Cross	1964	5.00	10.00	20.00
❏ DL 4544 [M]	Never Alone	1964	5.00	10.00	20.00
❏ DL 4615 [M]	Country Gold	1965	5.00	10.00	20.00
❏ DL 4645 [M]	I'm Gonna Tie One On Tonight	1965	5.00	10.00	20.00
❏ DL 4721 [M]	The Wilburn Brothers Show	1966	15.00	30.00	60.00
-- With guests Loretta Lynn, Ernest Tubb, Harold Morrison					
❏ DL 4764 [M]	Let's Go Country	1966	5.00	10.00	20.00
❏ DL 4824 [M]	Two for the Show	1967	6.25	12.50	25.00
❏ DL 4871 [M]	Cool	1967	7.50	15.00	30.00
❏ DL 4954 [M]	It's Another World	1968	10.00	20.00	40.00
❏ DL 8576 [M]	The Wilburn Brothers	1957	10.00	20.00	40.00
❏ DL 8774 [M]	Side by Side	1958	10.00	20.00	40.00
❏ DL 8959 [M]	Livin' In God's Country	1959	10.00	20.00	40.00
❏ DL 74058 [S]	The Big Heartbreak	1960	10.00	20.00	40.00
❏ DL 74142 [S]	The Wilburn Brothers Sing	1961	10.00	20.00	40.00
❏ DL 74211 [S]	City Limits	1961	10.00	20.00	40.00
❏ DL 74225 [S]	Folk Songs	1962	7.50	15.00	30.00
❏ DL 74391 [S]	Trouble's Back in Town	1963	7.50	15.00	30.00
❏ DL 74464 [S]	Take Up Thy Cross	1964	6.25	12.50	25.00
❏ DL 74544 [S]	Never Alone	1964	6.25	12.50	25.00
❏ DL 74615 [S]	Country Gold	1965	6.25	12.50	25.00
❏ DL 74645 [S]	I'm Gonna Tie One On Tonight	1965	6.25	12.50	25.00
❏ DL 74721 [S]	The Wilburn Brothers Show	1966	20.00	40.00	80.00
-- With guests Loretta Lynn, Ernest Tubb, Harold Morrison					
❏ DL 74764 [S]	Let's Go Country	1966	6.25	12.50	25.00
❏ DL 74824 [S]	Two for the Show	1967	5.00	10.00	20.00
❏ DL 74871 [S]	Cool	1967	5.00	10.00	20.00
❏ DL 74954 [S]	It's Another World	1968	5.00	10.00	20.00
❏ DL 75173	Little Johnny from Down the Street	1970	5.00	10.00	20.00
❏ DL 75214	Sing Your Heart Out Country Boy	1971	5.00	10.00	20.00
❏ DL 75291	That She's Leaving Feeling	1972	5.00	10.00	20.00
❏ DL 88774 [S]	Side by Side	1959	15.00	30.00	60.00
❏ DL 88959 [S]	Livin' In God's Country	1959	15.00	30.00	60.00

KING

| ❏ 746 [M] | The Wonderful Wilburn Brothers | 1961 | 25.00 | 50.00 | 100.00 |

WILCOX THREE, THE
RCA CAMDEN

| ❏ CAL-669 [M] | The Greatest Folk Songs Ever Sung | 1961 | 5.00 | 10.00 | 20.00 |

WILD BUTTER
UNITED ARTISTS

| ❏ UAS-6766 | Wild Butter | 1970 | 6.25 | 12.50 | 25.00 |

WILD COUNTRY -- See ALABAMA.

WILD MAN STEVE
DICK-ER

| ❏ D 70 | Do Not Disturb | 1972 | 5.00 | 10.00 | 20.00 |

Number	Title	Yr	VG	VG+	NM
WILD ONES, THE					
UNITED ARTISTS					
❏ UAL-3450 [M]	The Arthur Sound	1965	6.25	12.50	25.00
❏ UAS-6450 [S]	The Arthur Sound	1965	7.50	15.00	30.00
WILD, EARL					
-- See BOSTON POPS ORCHESTRA (ARTHUR FIEDLER, COND.)					
WILD, JACK					
BUDDAH					
❏ BDS-5083	Everything's Coming Up Roses	1971	6.25	12.50	25.00
❏ BDS-5110	A Beautiful World	1972	6.25	12.50	25.00
CAPITOL					
❏ SKAO-545	The Jack Wild Album	1970	6.25	12.50	25.00
WILDCATS, THE					
UNITED ARTISTS					
❏ UAL-3031 [M]	Bandstand Record Hop	1958	12.50	25.00	50.00
WILDE, MARTY					
EPIC					
❏ BN 575 [S]	Wilde About Marty	1960	25.00	50.00	100.00
❏ LN 3686 [M]	Bad Boy	1960	20.00	40.00	80.00
❏ LN 3711 [M]	Wilde About Marty	1960	20.00	40.00	80.00
WILDERNESS ROAD					
COLUMBIA					
❏ C 31118	Wilderness Road	1972	5.00	10.00	20.00
REPRISE					
❏ MS 2125	Sold for the Prevention of Disease Only	1973	5.00	10.00	20.00
WILDWEEDS, THE					
VANGUARD					
❏ VSD-6552	The Wildweeds	1970	6.25	12.50	25.00
WILKINSON TRI-CYCLE					
DATE					
❏ TES 4016	Wilkinson Tri-Cycle	1969	10.00	20.00	40.00
WILLETT, SLIM					
AUDIO LAB					
❏ AL-1542 [M]	Slim Willett	1959	25.00	50.00	100.00
WILLIAMS, ANDY					
CADENCE					
❏ CLP 1018 [M]	Andy Williams	1957	12.50	25.00	50.00
❏ CLP 3002 [M]	Andy Williams	1958	12.50	25.00	50.00
-- Cover depicts Andy standing					
❏ CLP 3002 [M]	Andy Williams	1960	5.00	10.00	20.00
-- Cover depicts Andy reclining					
❏ CLP 3005 [M]	Andy Williams Sings Rodgers & Hammerstein	1958	10.00	20.00	40.00
-- Cover depicts a café scene					
❏ CLP 3005 [M]	Andy Williams Sings Rodgers & Hammerstein	1960	5.00	10.00	20.00
-- Cover depicts a close-up of Andy's face					
❏ CLP 3026 [M]	Two Time Winners	1959	5.00	10.00	20.00
❏ CLP 3027 [M]	Andy Williams Sings...Steve Allen	1959	5.00	10.00	20.00
❏ CLP 3029 [M]	To You Sweetheart, Aloha	1959	5.00	10.00	20.00
❏ CLP 3030 [M]	Lonely Street	1960	5.00	10.00	20.00
❏ CLP 3038 [M]	The Village of St. Bernadette	1960	5.00	10.00	20.00
❏ CLP 3047 [M]	Under Paris Skies	1961	5.00	10.00	20.00
❏ CLP 3054 [M]	Andy Williams' Best	1962	5.00	10.00	20.00
❏ CLP 3061 [M]	Million Seller Songs	1962	5.00	10.00	20.00
❏ CLP 25026 [S]	Two Time Winners	1959	20.00	40.00	80.00
-- Red vinyl					
❏ CLP 25026 [S]	Two Time Winners	1959	7.50	15.00	30.00
-- Black vinyl					
❏ CLP 25029 [S]	To You Sweetheart, Aloha	1959	7.50	15.00	30.00
❏ CLP 25030 [S]	Lonely Street	1960	7.50	15.00	30.00
❏ CLP 25038 [S]	The Village of St. Bernadette	1960	7.50	15.00	30.00
❏ CLP 25047 [S]	Under Paris Skies	1961	7.50	15.00	30.00
❏ CLP 25054 [S]	Andy Williams' Best	1962	6.25	12.50	25.00
❏ CLP 25061 [S]	Million Seller Songs	1962	6.25	12.50	25.00
COLUMBIA					
❏ GP 5 [(2)]	The Andy Williams Sound of Music	1969	5.00	10.00	20.00
❏ CS 8551 [S]	Danny Boy And Other Songs I Love to Sing	1962	5.00	10.00	20.00
WILLIAMS, BETTY VAIDEN					
VANGUARD					
❏ VRS-9028 [M]	Folk Songs and Ballads of North Carolina	195?	7.50	15.00	30.00

Number	Title	Yr	VG	VG+	NM
WILLIAMS, BIG JOE					
BLUESVILLE					
❏ BVLP-1056 [M]	Blues for 9 Strings	1962	25.00	50.00	100.00
-- Blue label, silver print					
❏ BVLP-1056 [M]	Blues for 9 Strings	1964	6.25	12.50	25.00
-- Blue label with trident logo					
❏ BVLP-1067 [M]	Big Joe Williams at Folk City	1963	25.00	50.00	100.00
-- Blue label, silver print					
❏ BVLP-1067 [M]	Big Joe Williams at Folk City	1964	6.25	12.50	25.00
-- Blue label with trident logo					
❏ BVLP-1083 [M]	Studio Blues	1964	6.25	12.50	25.00
-- Blue label with trident logo					
❏ BVLP-1083 [M]	Studio Blues	1964	25.00	50.00	100.00
-- Blue label, silver print					
DELMARK					
❏ DL-604 [M]	Blues on Highway 49	1962	15.00	30.00	60.00
❏ DL-609 [M]	Starvin' Chain Blues	1966	6.25	12.50	25.00
FOLKWAYS					
❏ FA-3820 [M]	Mississippi's Big Joe Williams	1962	7.50	15.00	30.00
❏ FAS-3820 [R]	Mississippi's Big Joe Williams	1962	5.00	10.00	20.00
MILESTONE					
❏ 3001 [M]	Classic Delta Blues	1966	6.25	12.50	25.00
WILLIAMS, BILLY					
CORAL					
❏ CRL 57184 [M]	Billy Williams	1957	15.00	30.00	60.00
❏ CRL 57251 [M]	Half Sweet, Half Beat	1959	12.50	25.00	50.00
❏ CRL 57343 [M]	The Billy Williams Revue	1960	12.50	25.00	50.00
❏ CRL 757251 [S]	Half Sweet, Half Beat	1959	20.00	40.00	80.00
❏ CRL 757343 [S]	The Billy Williams Revue	1960	15.00	30.00	60.00
MERCURY					
❏ MG 20317 [M]	Oh Yeah!	1958	15.00	30.00	60.00
MGM					
❏ E-3400 [M]	The Billy Williams Quartet	1957	15.00	30.00	60.00
WING					
❏ MGW-12131 [M]	Vote for Billy Williams	1959	10.00	20.00	40.00
WILLIAMS, BILLY DEE					
PRESTIGE LIVELY ARTS					
❏ 30001 [M]	Let's Misbehave	1962	10.00	20.00	40.00
WILLIAMS, CAMILLA					
MGM					
❏ E-156 [10]	Spirituals	1952	25.00	50.00	100.00
WILLIAMS, DANNY					
UNITED ARTISTS					
❏ UAS-6297 [S]	The Exciting Danny Williams	1963	5.00	10.00	20.00
❏ UAS-6359 [S]	White On White	1964	5.00	10.00	20.00
❏ UAS-6380 [S]	With You in Mind	1964	5.00	10.00	20.00
❏ UAS-6493 [S]	Magic Town	1966	5.00	10.00	20.00
WILLIAMS, DENIECE					
ARC					
❏ AS 1432 [DJ]	Niecy	1982	6.25	12.50	25.00
-- Promo-only picture disc					
❏ HC 47952	Niecy	1983	12.50	25.00	50.00
-- Half-speed mastered edition					
WILLIAMS, DON					
JMI					
❏ 4004	Don Williams	1973	6.25	12.50	25.00
❏ 4006	Don Williams, Vol. 2	1974	5.00	10.00	20.00
WILLIAMS, HANK					
METRO					
❏ M-509 [M]	Hank Williams	1966	5.00	10.00	20.00
❏ M-547 [M]	Mr. and Mrs. Hank Williams	1966	5.00	10.00	20.00
❏ M-602 [M]	The Immortal Hank Williams	1967	5.00	10.00	20.00
MGM					
❏ 3E-2 [(3) M]	36 of Hank Williams' Greatest Hits	1957	50.00	100.00	200.00
-- Yellow labels					
❏ 3E-2 [(3) M]	36 of Hank Williams' Greatest Hits	1960	25.00	50.00	100.00
-- Black labels					
❏ 3E-4 [(3) M]	36 More of Hank Williams' Greatest Hits	1958	50.00	100.00	200.00
-- Yellow labels					
❏ 3E-4 [(3) M]	36 More of Hank Williams' Greatest Hits	1960	25.00	50.00	100.00
-- Black labels					
❏ E-107 [10]	Hank Williams Sings	1952	100.00	200.00	400.00

Number	Title	Yr	VG	VG+	NM
❏ E-168 [10]	Moanin' the Blues	1952	100.00	200.00	400.00
❏ E-202 [10]	Memorial Album	1953	100.00	200.00	400.00
❏ E-203 [10]	Hank Williams as Luke the Drifter	1953	100.00	200.00	400.00
❏ E-242 [10]	Honky Tonkin'	1954	100.00	200.00	400.00
❏ E-243 [10]	I Saw the Light	1954	100.00	200.00	400.00
❏ E-291 [10]	Ramblin' Man	1954	100.00	200.00	400.00
❏ PRO-912 [(3) DJ]	Reflections of Those Who Loved Him	1975	62.50	125.00	250.00
-- Promo-only box set					
❏ E-3219 [M]	Ramblin' Man	1955	25.00	50.00	100.00
-- Yellow label					
❏ E-3219 [M]	Ramblin' Man	1960	10.00	20.00	40.00
-- Black label					
❏ E-3267 [M]	Hank Williams as Luke the Drifter	1955	25.00	50.00	100.00
-- Yellow label					
❏ E-3267 [M]	Hank Williams as Luke the Drifter	1960	10.00	20.00	40.00
-- Black label					
❏ E-3272 [M]	Memorial Album	1955	25.00	50.00	100.00
-- Yellow label					
❏ E-3272 [M]	Memorial Album	1960	10.00	20.00	40.00
-- Black label					
❏ E-3330 [M]	Moanin' the Blues	1956	25.00	50.00	100.00
-- Yellow label					
❏ E-3330 [M]	Moanin' the Blues	1960	10.00	20.00	40.00
-- Black label					
❏ E-3331 [M]	I Saw the Light	1956	50.00	100.00	200.00
-- Yellow label; green cover					
❏ E-3331 [M]	I Saw the Light	1959	25.00	50.00	100.00
-- Yellow label; church on cover					
❏ E-3331 [M]	I Saw the Light	1960	10.00	20.00	40.00
-- Black label					
❏ E-3412 [M]	Honky Tonkin'	1957	25.00	50.00	100.00
-- Yellow label					
❏ E-3412 [M]	Honky Tonkin'	1960	10.00	20.00	40.00
-- Black label					
❏ E-3560 [M]	Sing Me a Blue Song	1957	25.00	50.00	100.00
-- Yellow label					
❏ E-3560 [M]	Sing Me a Blue Song	1960	10.00	20.00	40.00
-- Black label					
❏ E-3605 [M]	The Immortal Hank Williams	1958	25.00	50.00	100.00
-- Yellow label					
❏ E-3605 [M]	The Immortal Hank Williams	1960	10.00	20.00	40.00
-- Black label					
❏ E-3733 [M]	The Unforgettable Hank Williams	1959	25.00	50.00	100.00
-- Yellow label					
❏ E-3733 [M]	The Unforgettable Hank Williams	1960	10.00	20.00	40.00
-- Black label					
❏ E-3803 [M]	The Lonesome Sound of Hank Williams	1960	10.00	20.00	40.00
❏ E-3850 [M]	Wait for the Light to Shine	1960	10.00	20.00	40.00
❏ E-3918 [M]	Hank Williams' Greatest Hits	1961	10.00	20.00	40.00
❏ SE-3918 [R]	Hank Williams' Greatest Hits	1963	5.00	10.00	20.00
-- Black label					
❏ E-3923 [M]	Hank Williams Lives Again	1961	10.00	20.00	40.00
❏ E-3924 [M]	Sing Me a Blue Song	1961	10.00	20.00	40.00
❏ E-3925 [M]	Wanderin' Around	1961	10.00	20.00	40.00
❏ E-3926 [M]	I'm Blue Inside	1961	10.00	20.00	40.00
❏ E-3927 [M]	Luke the Drifter	1961	10.00	20.00	40.00
❏ E-3928 [M]	First, Last and Always	1961	10.00	20.00	40.00
❏ E-3955 [M]	The Spirit of Hank Williams	1961	10.00	20.00	40.00
❏ E-3999 [M]	On Stage! Hank Williams Recorded Live	1962	15.00	30.00	60.00
❏ E-3999 [M]	Hank Williams On Stage Recorded Live	1962	10.00	20.00	40.00
-- Note revised title					
❏ E-4040 [M]	Hank Williams' Greatest Hits, Volume 2	1962	10.00	20.00	40.00
❏ E-4109 [M]	Hank Williams On Stage, Volume 2	1963	10.00	20.00	40.00
❏ SE-4109 [R]	Hank Williams On Stage, Volume 2	1963	5.00	10.00	20.00
-- Black label					
❏ E-4138 [M]	Beyond the Sunset	1963	7.50	15.00	30.00
❏ E-4140 [M]	14 More of Hank Williams' Greatest Hits (Volume 3)	1963	7.50	15.00	30.00
❏ E-4168 [M]	The Very Best of Hank Williams	1963	7.50	15.00	30.00
❏ E-4227 [M]	The Very Best of Hank Williams, Volume 2	1964	7.50	15.00	30.00
❏ E-4254 [M]	Lost Highway (and Other Folk Ballads)	1964	10.00	20.00	40.00
❏ SE-4254 [R]	Lost Highway (and Other Folk Ballads)	1964	5.00	10.00	20.00
-- Black label					
❏ E-4267-4 [(4) M]	The Hank Williams Story	1965	15.00	30.00	60.00
❏ E-4300 [M]	Kaw-Liga and Other Humorous Songs	1965	7.50	15.00	30.00
❏ E-4377 [M]	The Legend Lives Anew -- Hank Williams with Strings	1966	5.00	10.00	20.00
❏ SE-4377 [S]	The Legend Lives Anew -- Hank Williams with Strings	1966	6.25	12.50	25.00
-- Black label					
❏ E-4380 [M]	Movin' On -- Luke the Drifter	1966	7.50	15.00	30.00

Number	Title	Yr	VG	VG+	NM
❏ E-4429 [M]	More Hank Williams and Strings	1966	5.00	10.00	20.00
❏ SE-4429 [S]	More Hank Williams and Strings	1966	6.25	12.50	25.00
-- Black label					
❏ E-4481 [M]	I Won't Be Home No More	1967	7.50	15.00	30.00
❏ SE-4481 [S]	I Won't Be Home No More	1967	5.00	10.00	20.00
-- Black label					
❏ E-4529 [M]	Hank Williams and Strings, Volume 3	1968	10.00	20.00	40.00
❏ SE-4529 [S]	Hank Williams and Strings, Volume 3	1968	5.00	10.00	20.00
❏ E-4576 [M]	Hank Williams In the Beginning	1968	10.00	20.00	40.00
❏ ST-90511 [R]	The Very Best of Hank Williams	1965	5.00	10.00	20.00
-- Capitol Record Club edition					
❏ T-90511 [M]	The Very Best of Hank Williams	1965	10.00	20.00	40.00
-- Capitol Record Club edition					
❏ ST-91115 [S]	The Legend Lives Anew -- Hank Williams with Strings	1968	5.00	10.00	20.00
-- Capitol Record Club edition; blue and gold label					

TIME-LIFE

Number	Title	Yr	VG	VG+	NM
❏ 3003 [(3)]	Country & Western Classics	1981	7.50	15.00	30.00

WILLIAMS, HANK /ROY ACUFF
LAMB AND LION

Number	Title	Yr	VG	VG+	NM
❏ LL-706 [(3)]	Hank Williams, Sr./Roy Acuff "Collector's Item!"	197?	10.00	20.00	40.00
-- Sides 1-4 are reissues of Hank Williams; side 5-6 are Roy Acuff					

WILLIAMS, HANK, AND HANK WILLIAMS, JR.
Also see each artist's individual listings.
MGM

Number	Title	Yr	VG	VG+	NM
❏ E-4276 [M]	Father & Son	1965	5.00	10.00	20.00
❏ SE-4276 [S]	Father & Son	1965	6.25	12.50	25.00
❏ E-4378 [M]	Again	1966	5.00	10.00	20.00
❏ SE-4378 [S]	Again	1966	6.25	12.50	25.00

WILLIAMS, HANK, JR.
CAPRICORN

Number	Title	Yr	VG	VG+	NM
❏ W1-26806	Maverick	1992	5.00	10.00	20.00
-- Columbia House edition (only U.S. vinyl release)					

MGM

Number	Title	Yr	VG	VG+	NM
❏ E-4213 [M]	Sings the Songs of Hank Williams	1964	5.00	10.00	20.00
❏ SE-4213 [S]	Sings the Songs of Hank Williams	1964	6.25	12.50	25.00
❏ E-4260 [M]	Your Cheatin' Heart	1964	5.00	10.00	20.00
❏ SE-4260 [S]	Your Cheatin' Heart	1964	6.25	12.50	25.00
❏ E-4316 [M]	Ballads of the Hills and Plains	1965	5.00	10.00	20.00
❏ SE-4316 [S]	Ballads of the Hills and Plains	1965	6.25	12.50	25.00
❏ E-4344 [M]	Blues My Name	1966	5.00	10.00	20.00
❏ SE-4344 [S]	Blues My Name	1966	6.25	12.50	25.00
❏ E-4391 [M]	Country Shadows	1966	5.00	10.00	20.00
❏ SE-4391 [S]	Country Shadows	1966	6.25	12.50	25.00
❏ E-4428 [M]	In My Own Way	1967	5.00	10.00	20.00
❏ SE-4428 [S]	In My Own Way	1967	6.25	12.50	25.00
❏ E-4513 [M]	The Best of Hank Williams, Jr.	1967	5.00	10.00	20.00
❏ SE-4513 [S]	The Best of Hank Williams, Jr.	1967	6.25	12.50	25.00
❏ SE-4527 [S]	My Songs	1968	6.25	12.50	25.00
❏ SE-4540	A Time to Sing	1968	6.25	12.50	25.00
❏ SE-4559	Luke the Drifter, Jr.	1969	5.00	10.00	20.00
❏ SE-4621	Songs My Father Left Me	1969	5.00	10.00	20.00
❏ SE-4632	Luke the Drifter, Jr. (Vol. 2)	1969	5.00	10.00	20.00
❏ SE-4644	Live at Cobo Hall, Detroit	1969	5.00	10.00	20.00
❏ MG-1-5009	Hank Williams, Jr., and Friends	1975	10.00	20.00	40.00
❏ ST-90695 [S]	Blues My Name	1966	7.50	15.00	30.00
-- Capitol Record Club edition					
❏ T-90695 [M]	Blues My Name	1966	6.25	12.50	25.00
-- Capitol Record Club edition					

WARNER BROS.

Number	Title	Yr	VG	VG+	NM
❏ PRO-A-2092 [DJ]	The Hank Williams, Jr., Interview	1983	6.25	12.50	25.00
❏ R 120612	America (The Way I See It)	1990	5.00	10.00	20.00
-- BMG Music Service edition (no regular vinyl release)					
❏ R 160351	Pure Hank	1991	5.00	10.00	20.00
-- BMG Music Service edition (no regular vinyl release)					

WILLIAMS, HANK, JR., AND LOIS JOHNSON
MGM

Number	Title	Yr	VG	VG+	NM
❏ SE-4750	All for the Love of Sunshine	1971	5.00	10.00	20.00
❏ SE-4857	Send Me Some Lovin'/ Whole Lotta Lovin'	1972	5.00	10.00	20.00

WILLIAMS, JOE
RCA VICTOR

Number	Title	Yr	VG	VG+	NM
❏ LPM-2713 [M]	Jump for Joy	1963	6.25	12.50	25.00
❏ LSP-2713 [S]	Jump for Joy	1963	7.50	15.00	30.00
❏ LPM-2762 [M]	Joe Williams at Newport '63	1963	6.25	12.50	25.00
❏ LSP-2762 [S]	Joe Williams at Newport '63	1963	7.50	15.00	30.00

Number	Title	Yr	VG	VG+	NM
❏ LPM-2879 [M]	Me and the Blues	1964	6.25	12.50	25.00
❏ LSP-2879 [S]	Me and the Blues	1964	7.50	15.00	30.00
❏ LPM-3433 [M]	The Song Is You	1965	5.00	10.00	20.00
❏ LSP-3433 [S]	The Song Is You	1965	6.25	12.50	25.00
❏ LPM-3461 [M]	The Exciting Joe Williams	1965	5.00	10.00	20.00
❏ LSP-3461 [S]	The Exciting Joe Williams	1965	6.25	12.50	25.00

REGENT

Number	Title	Yr	VG	VG+	NM
❏ MG-6002 [M]	Everyday	1956	12.50	25.00	50.00

ROULETTE

Number	Title	Yr	VG	VG+	NM
❏ R-52005 [M]	A Man Ain't Supposed to Cry	1958	7.50	15.00	30.00
❏ SR-52005 [S]	A Man Ain't Supposed to Cry	1958	10.00	20.00	40.00
❏ R-52030 [M]	Joe Williams Sings About You!	1959	7.50	15.00	30.00
❏ SR-52030 [S]	Joe Williams Sings About You!	1959	10.00	20.00	40.00
❏ R-52039 [M]	That Kind of Woman	1960	7.50	15.00	30.00
❏ SR-52039 [S]	That Kind of Woman	1960	10.00	20.00	40.00
❏ R-52066 [M]	Sentimental and Melancholy	1961	7.50	15.00	30.00
❏ SR-52066 [S]	Sentimental and Melancholy	1961	10.00	20.00	40.00
❏ R-52069 [M]	Together	1961	7.50	15.00	30.00
❏ SR-52069 [S]	Together	1961	10.00	20.00	40.00
-- With Harry "Sweets" Edison					
❏ R-52071 [M]	Have a Good Time with Joe Williams	1961	7.50	15.00	30.00
❏ SR-52071 [S]	Have a Good Time with Joe Williams	1961	10.00	20.00	40.00
❏ R-52085 [M]	Swingin' Night at Birdland	1962	6.25	12.50	25.00
❏ SR-52085 [S]	Swingin' Night at Birdland	1962	7.50	15.00	30.00
❏ R-52102 [M]	One Is a Lonesome Number	1963	6.25	12.50	25.00
❏ SR-52102 [S]	One Is a Lonesome Number	1963	7.50	15.00	30.00
❏ R-52105 [M]	New Kind of Love	1964	6.25	12.50	25.00
❏ SR-52105 [S]	New Kind of Love	1964	7.50	15.00	30.00

SOLID STATE

Number	Title	Yr	VG	VG+	NM
❏ SM-17008 [M]	Presenting Joe Williams and the Jazz Orchestra	1967	6.25	12.50	25.00
❏ SS-18008 [S]	Presenting Joe Williams and the Jazz Orchestra	1967	5.00	10.00	20.00
❏ SS-18015 [S]	Something Old, New and Blue	1968	5.00	10.00	20.00

WILLIAMS, LARRY
CHESS

Number	Title	Yr	VG	VG+	NM
❏ LP-1457 [M]	Larry Williams	1961	50.00	100.00	200.00

OKEH

Number	Title	Yr	VG	VG+	NM
❏ OKM-12123 [M]	Larry Williams' Greatest Hits	1967	7.50	15.00	30.00
❏ OKS-14123 [S]	Larry Williams' Greatest Hits	1967	10.00	20.00	40.00

SPECIALTY

Number	Title	Yr	VG	VG+	NM
❏ SP-2109 [M]	Here's Larry Williams	1959	50.00	100.00	200.00
-- Original pressing on thick vinyl with no copyright information on back cover					
❏ SP-7002 [(2)]	Bad Boy	1990	5.00	10.00	20.00

WILLIAMS, LOIS
STARDAY

Number	Title	Yr	VG	VG+	NM
❏ SLP-448	A Girl Named Sam	1970	5.00	10.00	20.00

WILLIAMS, LUCINDA
FOLKWAYS

Number	Title	Yr	VG	VG+	NM
❏ 31066	Ramblin' On My Mind	1979	5.00	10.00	20.00
-- As "Lucinda"					
❏ 31067	Happy Woman Blues	1980	5.00	10.00	20.00
-- As "Lucinda"					

WILLIAMS, MASON
VEE JAY

Number	Title	Yr	VG	VG+	NM
❏ VJ-1103 [M]	Them Poems and Things	1964	5.00	10.00	20.00
❏ VJS-1103 [S]	Them Poems and Things	1964	6.25	12.50	25.00

WILLIAMS, MAURICE, AND THE ZODIACS
HERALD

Number	Title	Yr	VG	VG+	NM
❏ HLP-1014 [M]	Stay	1961	125.00	250.00	500.00

SNYDER

Number	Title	Yr	VG	VG+	NM
❏ 5586 [M]	At the Beach	196?	25.00	50.00	100.00

SPHERE SOUND

Number	Title	Yr	VG	VG+	NM
❏ SR-7007 [M]	Stay	1965	30.00	60.00	120.00
❏ SSR-7007 [R]	Stay	1965	20.00	40.00	80.00

WILLIAMS, MEL
DIG

Number	Title	Yr	VG	VG+	NM
❏ LP-103 [M]	All Thru the Night	1956	150.00	300.00	600.00

WILLIAMS, OTIS, AND HIS CHARMS
DELUXE

Number	Title	Yr	VG	VG+	NM
❏ 570 [M]	Their All Time Hits	1957	250.00	500.00	1,000.

KING

Number	Title	Yr	VG	VG+	NM
❏ 570 [M]	Their All Time Hits	1957	150.00	300.00	600.00
❏ 614 [M]	This Is Otis Williams and His Charms	1959	100.00	200.00	400.00

STOP

Number	Title	Yr	VG	VG+	NM
❏ STLP-1022	Otis Williams and the Midnight Cowboys	1971	6.25	12.50	25.00

WILLIAMS, ROBERT PETE
BLUESVILLE

Number	Title	Yr	VG	VG+	NM
❏ BVLP-1026 [M]	Free Again	1961	25.00	50.00	100.00
-- Blue label, silver print					
❏ BVLP-1026 [M]	Free Again	1964	7.50	15.00	30.00
-- Blue label with trident logo					

FOLK/LYRIC

Number	Title	Yr	VG	VG+	NM
❏ FL-109 [M]	Prison Blues	1960	25.00	50.00	100.00

WILLIAMS, ROGER
KAPP

Number	Title	Yr	VG	VG+	NM
❏ KLE-1 [(3) M]	10th Anniversary/Limited Edition	1964	5.00	10.00	20.00
-- Reissue of Kapp 1088, 1130 and 1172 in one package					
❏ SKLE-1 [(3) S]	10th Anniversary/Limited Edition	1964	6.25	12.50	25.00
❏ KL-1003 [M]	The Boy Next Door	1955	6.25	12.50	25.00
-- Maroon and silver (or blue and silver) labels					
❏ KL-1008 [M]	It's a Big, Wide, Wonderful World	1955	6.25	12.50	25.00
-- Maroon and silver (or blue and silver) labels					
❏ KL-1012 [M]	Roger Williams	1956	6.25	12.50	25.00
❏ KL-1012 [M]	Autumn Leaves	1956	5.00	10.00	20.00
-- Retitled version of above; maroon and silver (or blue and silver) label					
❏ K-1081-S [S]	Till	1959	5.00	10.00	20.00
-- Maroon and silver (or blue and silver) labels					
❏ KS-1112 [S]	Near You	1959	5.00	10.00	20.00
-- Maroon and silver (or blue and silver) labels					
❏ KS-3000 [S]	Waltzes in Stereo	1959	5.00	10.00	20.00
-- Maroon and silver (or blue and silver) labels					
❏ KS-3013 [S]	More Songs of the Fabulous	1959	5.00	10.00	20.00
-- Maroon and silver (or blue and silver) labels					
❏ KS-3030 [S]	With These Hands	1959	5.00	10.00	20.00
-- Maroon and silver (or blue and silver) labels					
❏ KS-3048 [S]	Christmas Time	1959	5.00	10.00	20.00
❏ KS-3056 [S]	Always	1960	5.00	10.00	20.00
-- Maroon and silver (or blue and silver) labels					
❏ KS-3217 [S]	Temptation	1960	5.00	10.00	20.00
❏ KS-3222 [S]	Roger Williams Invites You to Dance	1961	5.00	10.00	20.00
❏ KS-3244 [S]	Yellow Bird	1961	5.00	10.00	20.00
❏ KS-3251 [S]	Songs of the Soaring '60s	1961	5.00	10.00	20.00
❏ KXL-5000 [(2) M]	Songs of the Fabulous Fifties	1957	5.00	10.00	20.00
-- Maroon and silver (or blue and silver) labels					
❏ KXS-5000 [(2) S]	Songs of the Fabulous Fifties	1959	6.25	12.50	25.00
-- Maroon and silver (or blue and silver) labels					
❏ KXS-5000 [(2) S]	Songs of the Fabulous Fifties	1962	5.00	10.00	20.00
-- Any later label variation					
❏ KXL-5003 [(2) M]	Songs of the Fabulous Forties	1957	5.00	10.00	20.00
-- Maroon and silver (or blue and silver) labels					
❏ KXS-5003 [(2) S]	Songs of the Fabulous Forties	1959	6.25	12.50	25.00
-- Maroon and silver (or blue and silver) labels					
❏ KXS-5003 [(2) S]	Songs of the Fabulous Forties	1962	5.00	10.00	20.00
-- Any later label variation					
❏ KXL-5005 [(2) M]	Songs of the Fabulous Century	195?	5.00	10.00	20.00
-- Maroon and silver (or blue and silver) labels					
❏ KXS-5005 [(2) S]	Songs of the Fabulous Century	1959	6.25	12.50	25.00
-- Maroon and silver (or blue and silver) labels					
❏ KXS-5005 [(2) S]	Songs of the Fabulous Century	1962	5.00	10.00	20.00
-- Any later label variation					
❏ KXL-5008 [(2) M]	Tonight! Roger Williams at Town Hall	196?	5.00	10.00	20.00
❏ KXS-5008 [(2) S]	Tonight! Roger Williams at Town Hall	196?	6.25	12.50	25.00

WILLIAMS, TEX
BOONE

Number	Title	Yr	VG	VG+	NM
❏ LP-1210 [M]	The Two Sides of Tex Williams	1966	5.00	10.00	20.00
❏ LSP-1210 [S]	The Two Sides of Tex Williams	1966	6.25	12.50	25.00

CAPITOL

Number	Title	Yr	VG	VG+	NM
❏ ST 1463 [S]	Smoke! Smoke! Smoke!	1960	10.00	20.00	40.00
❏ T 1463 [M]	Smoke! Smoke! Smoke!	1960	7.50	15.00	30.00

DECCA

Number	Title	Yr	VG	VG+	NM
❏ DL 4295 [M]	Country Music Time	1962	5.00	10.00	20.00
❏ DL 5565 [10]	Dance-O-Rama #5	1955	75.00	150.00	300.00
❏ DL 74295 [S]	Country Music Time	1962	7.50	15.00	30.00

IMPERIAL

Number	Title	Yr	VG	VG+	NM
❏ LP-9309 [M]	The Voice of Authority	1966	5.00	10.00	20.00
❏ LP-12309 [S]	The Voice of Authority	1966	6.25	12.50	25.00

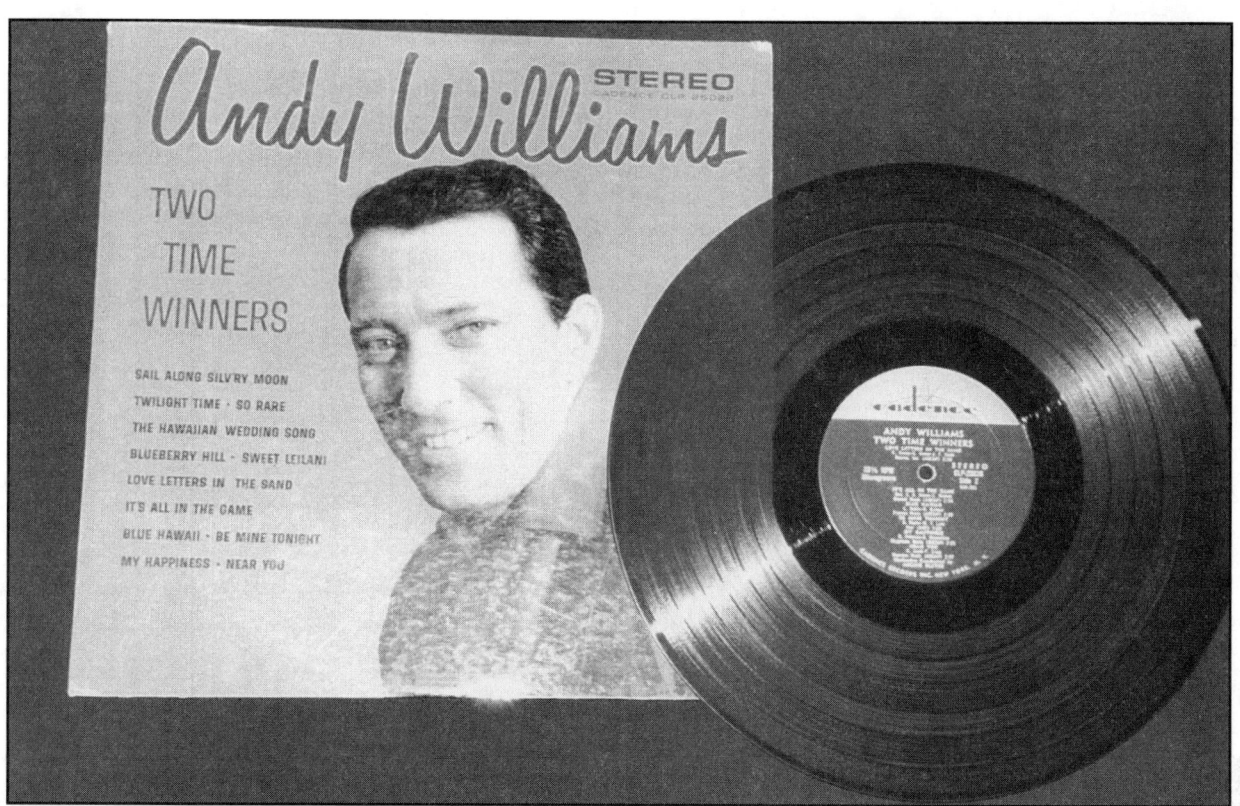

(Top) Is Andy Williams collectible? Well, his albums on Columbia rarely go for more than a few bucks (if that). But his Cadence albums are tough to come by. Perhaps the toughest is this 1959 stereo edition of *Two Time Winners,* which came out on red vinyl in addition to the standard black. (Bottom left) *Their All-Time Hits* by Otis Williams and His Charms was originally issued on the DeLuxe label, later on King. The DeLuxe version can fetch $1,000 in near-mint condition. (Bottom right) One of the more unusual releases from the Motown empire was this 1968 album of harmonica instrumentals by "Eivets Rednow" on the Gordy label. When this album was re-released on the Motown budget-line series in the 1980s, the label spoiled some of the fun by adding a note on the front cover, "What is Stevie Wonder spelled backwards?"

Number	Title	Yr	VG	VG+	NM

LIBERTY
| ❏ LRP-3304 [M] | Tex Williams in Las Vegas | 1963 | 5.00 | 10.00 | 20.00 |
| ❏ LST-7304 [S] | Tex Williams in Las Vegas | 1963 | 7.50 | 15.00 | 30.00 |

MONUMENT
| ❏ Z 30909 | A Man Called Tex | 1971 | 5.00 | 10.00 | 20.00 |

RCA CAMDEN
| ❏ CAL-363 [M] | Tex Williams' Best | 1958 | 6.25 | 12.50 | 25.00 |

WILLIAMS, TONY
The Columbia artist is not the same as the others. Also see THE PLATTERS.

COLUMBIA
| ❏ HC 45705 | Joy of Flying | 198? | 12.50 | 25.00 | 50.00 |
| -- Half-speed mastered edition | | | | | |

MERCURY
| ❏ MG-20454 [M] | A Girl Is a Girl Is a Girl | 1959 | 10.00 | 20.00 | 40.00 |
| ❏ SR-60138 [S] | A Girl Is a Girl Is a Girl | 1959 | 12.50 | 25.00 | 50.00 |

PHILIPS
| ❏ PHM 200-051 [M] | The Magic Touch of Tony | 1962 | 6.25 | 12.50 | 25.00 |
| ❏ PHS 600-051 [S] | The Magic Touch of Tony | 1962 | 7.50 | 15.00 | 30.00 |

REPRISE
| ❏ R-6006 [M] | His Greatest Hits | 1961 | 6.25 | 12.50 | 25.00 |
| ❏ R9-6006 [S] | His Greatest Hits | 1961 | 7.50 | 15.00 | 30.00 |

WILLIAMSON, SONNY BOY (1)
BLUES CLASSICS
| ❏ 3 | Blues Classics by Sonny Boy Williamson | 196? | 6.25 | 12.50 | 25.00 |
| ❏ 20 | Blues Classics by Sonny Boy Williamson, Vol. 2 | 196? | 6.25 | 12.50 | 25.00 |

WILLIAMSON, SONNY BOY (2)
CHECKER
| ❏ LP-1437 [M] | Down and Out Blues | 1959 | 80.00 | 160.00 | 320.00 |

CHESS
❏ 2ACMB-206 [(2)]	Sonny Boy Williamson	1976	5.00	10.00	20.00
-- Reissue of 50027					
❏ LP-1503 [M]	The Real Folk Blues	1966	20.00	40.00	80.00
❏ LP-1509 [M]	More Real Folk Blues	1966	20.00	40.00	80.00
❏ LPS-1536	Bummer Road	1969	6.25	12.50	25.00
❏ 2CH-50027 [(2)]	This Is My Story	1972	6.25	12.50	25.00

WILLIAMSON, SONNY BOY (2), AND THE YARDBIRDS
MERCURY
❏ MG-21071 [M]	Sonny Boy Williamson and the Yardbirds	1965	20.00	40.00	80.00
❏ SR-61071 [R]	Sonny Boy Williamson and the Yardbirds	1965	12.50	25.00	50.00
-- First cover with a picture of the bluesman and the band					
❏ SR-61071 [R]	Sonny Boy Williamson and the Yardbirds	196?	6.25	12.50	25.00
-- Later cover with cartoon artwork on the cover					

WILLING, FOY, AND THE RIDERS OF THE PURPLE SAGE
JUBILEE
| ❏ JL-5028 [M] | The New Sound of American Folk | 1962 | 5.00 | 10.00 | 20.00 |
| ❏ JLS-5028 [S] | The New Sound of American Folk | 1962 | 6.25 | 12.50 | 25.00 |

ROULETTE
| ❏ R-25035 [M] | Cowboy | 1958 | 10.00 | 20.00 | 40.00 |

ROYALE
| ❏ 6032 [10] | The Riders of the Purple Sage | 1952 | 25.00 | 50.00 | 100.00 |

VARSITY
| ❏ 6032 [10] | The Riders of the Purple Sage | 1950 | 30.00 | 60.00 | 120.00 |

WILLIS BROTHERS, THE
STARDAY
❏ SLP-163 [M]	The Willis Brothers in Action	1962	15.00	30.00	60.00
❏ SLP-229 [M]	Code of the West	1963	12.50	25.00	50.00
❏ SLP-306 [M]	Let's Hit the Road	1965	10.00	20.00	40.00
❏ SLP-323 [M]	Give Me 40 Acres	1965	10.00	20.00	40.00
❏ SLP-353 [M]	Road Stop Juke Box Hits	1966	7.50	15.00	30.00
❏ SLP-369 [M]	The Wild Side of Life	1966	7.50	15.00	30.00
❏ SLP-387 [M]	Goin' to Town	1966	7.50	15.00	30.00
❏ SLP-403 [M]	Bob	1967	6.25	12.50	25.00
❏ SLP-428	Hey, Mister Truck Driver	1968	6.25	12.50	25.00
❏ SLP-442	Bummin' Around	1969	6.25	12.50	25.00
❏ SLP-466	The Best of the Willis Brothers	1970	5.00	10.00	20.00
❏ SLP-472	For the Good Times	1971	5.00	10.00	20.00

WILLIS, CHUCK
ATLANTIC
| ❏ 8018 [M] | The King of the Stroll | 1958 | 75.00 | 150.00 | 300.00 |
| -- Black label | | | | | |

❏ 8018 [M]	The King of the Stroll	1960	37.50	75.00	150.00
-- Purple and orange label					
❏ 8079 [M]	I Remember Chuck Willis	1963	37.50	75.00	150.00
❏ SD 8079 [P]	I Remember Chuck Willis	1963	50.00	100.00	200.00

EPIC
| ❏ LN 3425 [M] | Chuck Willis Wails the Blues | 1958 | 125.00 | 250.00 | 500.00 |
| ❏ LN 3728 [M] | A Tribute to Chuck Willis | 1960 | 75.00 | 150.00 | 300.00 |

WILLS, BOB, AND HIS TEXAS PLAYBOYS
ANTONES
❏ 6000 [10]	Old Time Favorites	195?	125.00	250.00	500.00
-- Fan club release					
❏ 6010 [10]	Old Time Favorites	195?	125.00	250.00	500.00
-- Fan club release					

CAPITOL
| ❏ SKBB-11550 [(2)] | Bob Wills and His Texas Playboys In Concert | 1976 | 5.00 | 10.00 | 20.00 |

COLUMBIA
| ❏ CL 9003 [10] | Bob Wills Round-Up | 1949 | 75.00 | 150.00 | 300.00 |
| ❏ KG 32416 [(2)] | Anthology | 1973 | 5.00 | 10.00 | 20.00 |

DECCA
❏ DL 5562 [10]	Dance-O-Rama #2	1955	75.00	150.00	300.00
❏ DL 8727 [M]	Bob Wills and His Texas Playboys	1957	25.00	50.00	100.00
-- Black label, silver print					
❏ DL 8727 [M]	Bob Wills and His Texas Playboys	1961	10.00	20.00	40.00
-- Black label with color bars					
❏ DL 78727 [R]	Bob Wills and His Texas Playboys	196?	5.00	10.00	20.00

HARMONY
❏ HL 7036 [M]	Bob Wills Special	1957	10.00	20.00	40.00
-- Maroon label					
❏ HL 7036 [M]	Bob Wills Special	196?	5.00	10.00	20.00
-- Black label					
❏ HL 7304 [M]	The Best of Bob Wills	1963	6.25	12.50	25.00
❏ HL 7345 [M]	The Great Bob Wills	1965	5.00	10.00	20.00

KAPP
❏ KL-1506 [M]	From the Heart of Texas	1966	5.00	10.00	20.00
❏ KL-1523 [M]	King of Western Swing	1967	6.25	12.50	25.00
❏ KS-3506 [S]	From the Heart of Texas	1966	6.25	12.50	25.00
❏ KS-3523 [S]	King of Western Swing	1967	6.25	12.50	25.00
❏ KS-3542	Here's That Man Again	1968	6.25	12.50	25.00
❏ KS-3569	Time Changes Everything	1969	5.00	10.00	20.00
❏ KS-3587	The Living Legend	1969	5.00	10.00	20.00
❏ KS-3601	The Greatest String Band Hits	1969	5.00	10.00	20.00
❏ KS-3639	Bob Wills In Person	1970	5.00	10.00	20.00
❏ KS-3641	The Best of Bob Wills	1971	5.00	10.00	20.00

LIBERTY
❏ LRP-3173 [M]	Together Again	1960	7.50	15.00	30.00
❏ LRP-3182 [M]	Living Legend	1961	7.50	15.00	30.00
❏ LRP-3194 [M]	Mr. Words and Mr. Music	1961	7.50	15.00	30.00
❏ LRP-3303 [M]	Bob Wills Sings and Plays	1963	7.50	15.00	30.00
❏ LST-7173 [S]	Together Again	1960	10.00	20.00	40.00
❏ LST-7182 [S]	Living Legend	1961	10.00	20.00	40.00
❏ LST-7194 [S]	Mr. Words and Mr. Music	1961	10.00	20.00	40.00
❏ LST-7303 [S]	Bob Wills Sings and Plays	1963	10.00	20.00	40.00

LONGHORN
| ❏ LP-001 [M] | My Keepsake Album | 1965 | 20.00 | 40.00 | 80.00 |

MGM
❏ E-91 [10]	Ranch House Favorites	1951	75.00	150.00	300.00
❏ GAS-141	A Tribute (Golden Archive Series)	1971	6.25	12.50	25.00
❏ E-3352 [M]	Ranch House Favorites	1956	37.50	75.00	150.00

STARDAY
| ❏ SLP-375 [M] | San Antonio Rose | 1965 | 10.00 | 20.00 | 40.00 |

UNITED ARTISTS
❏ UA-LA216-J	For the Last Time	1974	10.00	20.00	40.00
-- Box set with booklet					
❏ UAS-9962 [(2)]	Legendary Masters	1971	6.25	12.50	25.00

VOCALION
| ❏ VL 3735 [M] | Western Swing Band | 1965 | 5.00 | 10.00 | 20.00 |

WILLS, JOHNNY LEE
SIMS
❏ LP-101 [M]	Where There's a Wills, There's a Way	1962	10.00	20.00	40.00
❏ LPS-101 [S]	Where There's a Wills, There's a Way	1962	15.00	30.00	60.00
❏ LP-108 [M]	Johnny Lee Wills at the Tulsa Stampede	1963	7.50	15.00	30.00
❏ LPS-108 [S]	Johnny Lee Wills at the Tulsa Stampede	1963	12.50	25.00	50.00

WILMER AND THE DUKES
APHRODISIAC
| ❏ 6001 | Wilmer and the Dukes | 1969 | 5.00 | 10.00 | 20.00 |

Number	Title	Yr	VG	VG+	NM

WILSON PHILLIPS
SBK
| ❑ 1P-8219 | Shadows and Light | 1992 | 6.25 | 12.50 | 25.00 |

-- Only U.S. vinyl release was through Columbia House

WILSON, AL
SOUL CITY
| ❑ SCS-92006 | Searching for the Dolphins | 1969 | 6.25 | 12.50 | 25.00 |

WILSON, BRIAN
Also see THE BEACH BOYS.
SIRE
| ❑ PRO-A-3248 [DJ] Words and Music | | 1988 | 6.25 | 12.50 | 25.00 |

-- Promo-only music and interview

WILSON, CARL
Also see THE BEACH BOYS.
CARIBOU
| ❑ NJZ 37010 | Carl Wilson | 1981 | 5.00 | 10.00 | 20.00 |
| ❑ ARZ 37970 | Youngblood | 1982 | 5.00 | 10.00 | 20.00 |

WILSON, DENNIS
Also see THE BEACH BOYS.
CARIBOU
| ❑ PZ 34354 | Pacific Ocean Blue | 1977 | 7.50 | 15.00 | 30.00 |

WILSON, FLIP
ATLANTIC
| ❑ 8149 [M] | Cowboys and Colored People | 1967 | 6.25 | 12.50 | 25.00 |
IMPERIAL
| ❑ LP-9155 [M] | Flippin' | 1961 | 6.25 | 12.50 | 25.00 |
SCEPTER
| ❑ S-520 | Flip Wilson's Pot Luck | 1964 | 5.00 | 10.00 | 20.00 |

WILSON, J. FRANK, AND THE CAVALIERS
JOSIE
| ❑ JM-4006 [M] | Last Kiss | 1964 | 18.75 | 37.50 | 75.00 |
| ❑ JS-4006 [S] | Last Kiss | 1964 | 25.00 | 50.00 | 100.00 |

WILSON, JACKIE
BRUNSWICK
❑ BL 54042 [M]	He's So Fine	1959	30.00	60.00	120.00
-- All-black label					
❑ BL 54042 [M]	He's So Fine	1964	6.25	12.50	25.00
-- Black label with color bars					
❑ BL 54045 [M]	Lonely Teardrops	1959	37.50	75.00	150.00
-- All-black label					
❑ BL 54045 [M]	Lonely Teardrops	1964	6.25	12.50	25.00
-- Black label with color bars					
❑ BL 54050 [M]	So Much	1960	25.00	50.00	100.00
-- All-black label					
❑ BL 54050 [M]	So Much	1964	5.00	10.00	20.00
-- Black label with color bars					
❑ BL 54055 [M]	Jackie Sings the Blues	1960	37.50	75.00	150.00
-- All-black label					
❑ BL 54055 [M]	Jackie Sings the Blues	1964	5.00	10.00	20.00
-- Black label with color bars					
❑ BL 54058 [M]	My Golden Favorites	1960	15.00	30.00	60.00
-- All-black label					
❑ BL 54058 [M]	My Golden Favorites	1964	6.25	12.50	25.00
-- Black label with color bars					
❑ BL 54059 [M]	A Woman, a Lover, a Friend	1961	12.50	25.00	50.00
-- All-black label					
❑ BL 54059 [M]	A Woman, a Lover, a Friend	1964	5.00	10.00	20.00
-- Black label with color bars					
❑ BL 54100 [M]	You Ain't Heard Nothin' Yet	1961	12.50	25.00	50.00
-- All-black label					
❑ BL 54100 [M]	You Ain't Heard Nothin' Yet	1964	5.00	10.00	20.00
-- Black label with color bars					
❑ BL 54101 [M]	By Special Request	1961	12.50	25.00	50.00
-- All-black label					
❑ BL 54101 [M]	By Special Request	1964	5.00	10.00	20.00
-- Black label with color bars					
❑ BL 54105 [M]	Body and Soul	1962	12.50	25.00	50.00
-- All-black label					
❑ BL 54105 [M]	Body and Soul	1964	5.00	10.00	20.00
-- Black label with color bars					
❑ BL 54106 [M]	The World's Greatest Melodies	1962	12.50	25.00	50.00
-- All-black label					
❑ BL 54106 [M]	The World's Greatest Melodies	1964	5.00	10.00	20.00
-- Black label with color bars					
❑ BL 54108 [M]	Jackie Wilson at the Copa	1962	12.50	25.00	50.00
-- All-black label					
❑ BL 54108 [M]	Jackie Wilson at the Copa	1964	5.00	10.00	20.00
-- Black label with color bars					
❑ BL 54110 [M]	Baby Workout	1963	12.50	25.00	50.00
-- All-black label					
❑ BL 54110 [M]	Baby Workout	1963	5.00	10.00	20.00
-- Black label with color bars					
❑ BL 54112 [M]	Merry Christmas from Jackie Wilson	1963	7.50	15.00	30.00
❑ BL 54113 [M]	Shake a Hand	1964	6.25	12.50	25.00
❑ BL 54115 [M]	My Golden Favorites, Volume 2	1964	6.25	12.50	25.00
❑ BL 54117 [M]	Somethin' Else	1964	6.25	12.50	25.00
❑ BL 54118 [M]	Soul Time	1965	6.25	12.50	25.00
❑ BL 54119 [M]	Spotlight on Jackie	1965	6.25	12.50	25.00
❑ BL 54120 [M]	Soul Galore	1966	6.25	12.50	25.00
❑ BL 54122 [M]	Whispers	1966	6.25	12.50	25.00
❑ BL 54130 [M]	Higher and Higher	1967	6.25	12.50	25.00
❑ BL 54134 [M]	Manufacturers of Soul	1968	12.50	25.00	50.00
-- With Count Basie					
❑ BL 754050 [S]	So Much	1960	37.50	75.00	150.00
-- All-black label					
❑ BL 754050 [S]	So Much	1964	6.25	12.50	25.00
-- Black label with color bars					
❑ BL 754055 [S]	Jackie Sings the Blues	1960	50.00	100.00	200.00
-- All-black label					
❑ BL 754055 [S]	Jackie Sings the Blues	1964	6.25	12.50	25.00
-- Black label with color bars					
❑ BL 754059 [S]	A Woman, a Lover, a Friend	1961	20.00	40.00	80.00
-- All-black label					
❑ BL 754059 [S]	A Woman, a Lover, a Friend	1964	6.25	12.50	25.00
-- Black label with color bars					
❑ BL 754100 [S]	You Ain't Heard Nothin' Yet	1961	20.00	40.00	80.00
-- All-black label					
❑ BL 754100 [S]	You Ain't Heard Nothin' Yet	1964	6.25	12.50	25.00
-- Black label with color bars					
❑ BL 754101 [S]	By Special Request	1961	20.00	40.00	80.00
-- All-black label					
❑ BL 754101 [S]	By Special Request	1964	6.25	12.50	25.00
-- Black label with color bars					
❑ BL 754105 [S]	Body and Soul	1962	20.00	40.00	80.00
-- All-black label					
❑ BL 754105 [S]	Body and Soul	1964	6.25	12.50	25.00
-- Black label with color bars					
❑ BL 754106 [S]	The World's Greatest Melodies	1962	20.00	40.00	80.00
-- All-black label					
❑ BL 754106 [S]	The World's Greatest Melodies	1964	6.25	12.50	25.00
-- Black label with color bars					
❑ BL 754108 [S]	Jackie Wilson at the Copa	1962	20.00	40.00	80.00
-- All-black label					
❑ BL 754108 [S]	Jackie Wilson at the Copa	1964	6.25	12.50	25.00
-- Black label with color bars					
❑ BL 754110 [S]	Baby Workout	1963	20.00	40.00	80.00
-- All-black label					
❑ BL 754110 [S]	Baby Workout	1963	6.25	12.50	25.00
-- Black label with color bars					
❑ BL 754112 [S]	Merry Christmas from Jackie Wilson	1963	10.00	20.00	40.00
❑ BL 754113 [S]	Shake a Hand	1964	7.50	15.00	30.00
❑ BL 754115 [S]	My Golden Favorites, Volume 2	1964	7.50	15.00	30.00
❑ BL 754117 [S]	Somethin' Else	1964	7.50	15.00	30.00
❑ BL 754118 [S]	Soul Time	1965	7.50	15.00	30.00
❑ BL 754119 [S]	Spotlight on Jackie	1965	7.50	15.00	30.00
❑ BL 754120 [S]	Soul Galore	1966	7.50	15.00	30.00
❑ BL 754122 [S]	Whispers	1966	7.50	15.00	30.00
❑ BL 754130 [S]	Higher and Higher	1967	7.50	15.00	30.00
❑ BL 754134 [S]	Manufacturers of Soul	1968	5.00	10.00	20.00
-- With Count Basie					
❑ BL 754138	I Get the Sweetest Feeling	1968	5.00	10.00	20.00
❑ BL 754140	Jackie Wilson's Greatest Hits	1969	5.00	10.00	20.00
❑ BL 754154	Do Your Thing	1969	5.00	10.00	20.00
❑ BL 754158	It's All a Part of Love	1970	5.00	10.00	20.00
❑ BL 754167	This Love Is Real	1971	5.00	10.00	20.00
❑ BL 754172	You Got Me Walking	1971	5.00	10.00	20.00
EPIC
| ❑ EG 38623 [(2)] The Jackie Wilson Story | | 1983 | 5.00 | 10.00 | 20.00 |

WILSON, JULIE
ARDEN
| ❑ B&S-1 | Julie Wilson at Brothers & Sisters, Vol. 1 | 1976 | 5.00 | 10.00 | 20.00 |
| ❑ B&S-2 | Julie Wilson at Brothers & Sisters, Vol. 2 | 1976 | 5.00 | 10.00 | 20.00 |
CAMEO
| ❑ C-1021 [M] | Meet Julie Wilson | 1962 | 7.50 | 15.00 | 30.00 |
DOLPHIN
| ❑ 6 [M] | Love | 1956 | 12.50 | 25.00 | 50.00 |
VIK
| ❑ LX-1095 [M] | My Old Flame | 1957 | 7.50 | 15.00 | 30.00 |
| ❑ LX-1118 [M] | Julie Wilson at the St. Regis | 1958 | 7.50 | 15.00 | 30.00 |

Number	Title	Yr	VG	VG+	NM

WILSON, LONNIE
STARDAY
❑ SLP-217 [M]	The Playboy Farmer	196?	7.50	15.00	30.00

WILSON, MARIE
DESIGN
❑ DLP-76 [M]	Gentlemen Prefer Marie Wilson	1959	10.00	20.00	40.00

WILSON, MARTY
20TH CENTURY FOX
❑ TF-3101 [M]	Young America Dances to Golden Goodies	1963	5.00	10.00	20.00
❑ TFS-4101 [S]	Young America Dances to Golden Goodies	1963	6.25	12.50	25.00

WILSON, MURRY
CAPITOL
❑ ST 2819 [S]	The Many Moods of Murry Wilson	1967	12.50	25.00	50.00
❑ T 2819 [M]	The Many Moods of Murry Wilson	1967	15.00	30.00	60.00

WILSON, NANCY
CAPITOL
❑ SWBB-256 [(2)]	Close-Up	1969	5.00	10.00	20.00
-- Combines 1828 and 1934 into one package					
❑ STBB-727 [(2)]	For Once in My Life/ Who Can I Turn To	1971	5.00	10.00	20.00
❑ ST 1319 [S]	Like in Love	1960	7.50	15.00	30.00
-- Black label with colorband, Capitol logo on left					
❑ ST 1319 [S]	Like in Love	1960	5.00	10.00	20.00
-- Black label with colorband, Capitol logo on top					
❑ T 1319 [M]	Like in Love	1960	6.25	12.50	25.00
-- Black label with colorband, Capitol logo on left					
❑ ST 1440 [S]	Something Wonderful	1960	7.50	15.00	30.00
-- Black label with colorband, Capitol logo on left					
❑ ST 1440 [S]	Something Wonderful	1960	5.00	10.00	20.00
-- Black label with colorband, Capitol logo on top					
❑ T 1440 [M]	Something Wonderful	1960	6.25	12.50	25.00
-- Black label with colorband, Capitol logo on left					
❑ ST 1524 [S]	The Swingin's Mutual	1961	7.50	15.00	30.00
-- Black label with colorband, Capitol logo on left					
❑ ST 1524 [S]	The Swingin's Mutual	1961	5.00	10.00	20.00
-- Black label with colorband, Capitol logo on top					
❑ T 1524 [M]	The Swingin's Mutual	1961	6.25	12.50	25.00
-- Black label with colorband, Capitol logo on left					
❑ ST 1767 [S]	Hello Young Lovers	1962	6.25	12.50	25.00
❑ T 1767 [M]	Hello Young Lovers	1962	5.00	10.00	20.00
❑ ST 1828 [S]	Broadway My Way	1963	5.00	10.00	20.00
❑ ST 1934 [S]	Hollywood My Way	1963	5.00	10.00	20.00
❑ ST 2012 [S]	Yesterday's Love Songs/ Today's Blues	1964	5.00	10.00	20.00
❑ ST 2082 [S]	Today, Tomorrow, Forever	1964	5.00	10.00	20.00
❑ SKAO 2136 [S]	The Nancy Wilson Show!	1965	5.00	10.00	20.00
❑ ST 2155 [S]	How Glad I Am	1964	5.00	10.00	20.00
❑ ST 2321 [S]	Today -- My Way	1965	5.00	10.00	20.00
❑ ST 2351 [S]	Gentle Is My Love	1965	5.00	10.00	20.00
❑ ST 2433 [S]	From Broadway with Love	1966	5.00	10.00	20.00
❑ ST 2495 [S]	A Touch of Today	1966	5.00	10.00	20.00
❑ ST 2555 [S]	Tender Loving Care	1966	5.00	10.00	20.00
❑ ST 2634 [S]	Nancy -- Naturally	1967	5.00	10.00	20.00
❑ ST 2712 [S]	Just for Now	1967	5.00	10.00	20.00
❑ T 2757 [M]	Lush Life	1967	5.00	10.00	20.00
❑ T 2844 [M]	Welcome to My Love	1968	6.25	12.50	25.00

WILSON, NANCY, AND CANNONBALL ADDERLEY
Also see each artist's individual listings.
CAPITOL
❑ ST 1657 [S]	Nancy Wilson/Cannonball Adderley	1962	7.50	15.00	30.00
-- Black label with colorband, Capitol logo on left					
❑ ST 1657 [S]	Nancy Wilson/Cannonball Adderley	1962	5.00	10.00	20.00
-- Black label with colorband, Capitol logo on top					
❑ T 1657 [M]	Nancy Wilson/Cannonball Adderley	1962	6.25	12.50	25.00
-- Black label with colorband, Capitol logo on left					

WINCHESTER, JESSE
AMPEX
❑ A 10104	Jesse Winchester	1970	5.00	10.00	20.00
BEARSVILLE
❑ PRO 560 [DJ]	The Jesse Winchester Radio Show	1976	10.00	20.00	40.00
❑ PRO-A-693 [(2) DJ]	Live at the Bijou Café Plus a Live Interview at Media College in Montreal	1977	10.00	20.00	40.00

WIND
LIFE
❑ LLPS-2000	Make Believe	1969	5.00	10.00	20.00

WIND HARP, THE
UNITED ARTISTS
❑ UAS-9963 [(2)]	Song from the Hill	1972	5.00	10.00	20.00

WIND IN THE WILLOWS, THE
Debbie Harry, later of BLONDIE, was lead singer.
CAPITOL
❑ SKAO 2956	The Wind in the Willows	1968	12.50	25.00	50.00

WINDING, KAI
COLUMBIA
❑ CL 936 [M]	Trombone Sound	1956	12.50	25.00	50.00
❑ CL 999 [M]	Trombone Panorama	1957	12.50	25.00	50.00
❑ CL 1264 [M]	Swingin' State	1958	12.50	25.00	50.00
❑ CL 1329 [M]	Dance to the City Beat	1959	10.00	20.00	40.00
❑ CS 8062 [S]	Swingin' State	1958	10.00	20.00	40.00
❑ CS 8136 [S]	Dance to the City Beat	1959	7.50	15.00	30.00
IMPULSE!
❑ A 3 [M]	The Incredible Kai Winding Trombones	1960	7.50	15.00	30.00
❑ AS 3 [S]	The Incredible Kai Winding Trombones	1960	6.25	12.50	25.00
-- Orange and black label					
ROOST
❑ LP 408 [10]	Kai Winding All Stars	1952	30.00	60.00	120.00
SAVOY
❑ MG-9017 [10]	New Trends of Jazz	1952	30.00	60.00	120.00
VERVE
❑ V-8427 [M]	Kai Ole	1962	6.25	12.50	25.00
❑ V6-8427 [S]	Kai Ole	1962	6.25	12.50	25.00
❑ V-8493 [M]	Suspense Themes in Jazz	1962	6.25	12.50	25.00
❑ V6-8493 [S]	Suspense Themes in Jazz	1962	6.25	12.50	25.00
❑ V-8525 [M]	Kai Winding Solo	1963	6.25	12.50	25.00
❑ V6-8525 [S]	Kai Winding Solo	1963	6.25	12.50	25.00
❑ V-8551 [M]	More!!!	1963	6.25	12.50	25.00
❑ V6-8551 [S]	More!!!	1963	6.25	12.50	25.00
❑ V-8556 [M]	The Lonely One	1963	6.25	12.50	25.00
❑ V6-8556 [S]	The Lonely One	1963	6.25	12.50	25.00
❑ V-8573 [M]	Mondo Cane #2	1964	6.25	12.50	25.00
❑ V6-8573 [S]	Mondo Cane #2	1964	7.50	15.00	30.00
❑ V6-8602 [S]	Modern Country	1964	5.00	10.00	20.00
❑ V6-8620 [S]	Rainy Day	1965	5.00	10.00	20.00
❑ V6-8639 [S]	The "In" Instrumentals	1965	5.00	10.00	20.00

WINGS -- See PAUL McCARTNEY.

WINNERS, THE
CROWN
❑ CST-394 [S]	Checkered Flag	1963	7.50	15.00	30.00
❑ CLP-5394 [M]	Checkered Flag	1963	6.25	12.50	25.00

WINSTONS, THE
METROMEDIA
❑ MD-1010	Color Him Father	1969	12.50	25.00	50.00

WINTER, EDGAR
BLUE SKY
❑ PZQ 33483 [Q]	Jasmine Nightdreams	1975	5.00	10.00	20.00
❑ PZQ 33798 [Q]	The Edgar Winter Group with Rick Derringer	1975	5.00	10.00	20.00
EPIC
❑ KEG 31249 [(2)]	Roadwork	1972	5.00	10.00	20.00
-- Yellow labels					
❑ EQ 31584 [Q]	They Only Come Out at Night	1973	6.25	12.50	25.00
❑ PEQ 32461 [Q]	Shock Treatment	1974	6.25	12.50	25.00

WINTER, JOHNNY
BLUE SKY
❑ PZQ 33292 [Q]	John Dawson Winter III	1974	5.00	10.00	20.00
BUDDAH
❑ BDS-7513	First Winter	1969	5.00	10.00	20.00
COLUMBIA
❑ CS 9826	Johnny Winter	1969	5.00	10.00	20.00
-- "360 Sound" label					
❑ KCS 9947 [(2)]	Second Winter	1969	6.25	12.50	25.00
-- "360 Sound" labels; record 2 has music on only one side (other side is blank)					
❑ C 30221	Johnny Winter And	1970	5.00	10.00	20.00
-- "360 Sound" label					
❑ CQ 32188 [Q]	Still Alive and Well	1973	6.25	12.50	25.00
❑ CQ 32715 [Q]	Saints and Sinners	1974	6.25	12.50	25.00

Number	Title	Yr	VG	VG+	NM

GRT
❏ 10010	The Johnny Winter Story	1969	5.00	10.00	20.00

IMPERIAL
❏ LP-12431	The Progressive Blues Experiment	1969	12.50	25.00	50.00

JANUS
❏ 3008	About Blues	1970	5.00	10.00	20.00
❏ 3023	Early Times	1970	6.25	12.50	25.00
❏ 3056 [(2)]	Before the Storm	197?	5.00	10.00	20.00

SONOBEAT
❏ RS-1002	The Progressive Blues Experiment	1968	75.00	150.00	300.00

-- Released in plain white cardboard jacket

WINTER, JOHNNY AND EDGAR
BLUE SKY
❏ ASZ 242 [DJ]	Johnny and Edgar Winter Discuss Together	1976	6.25	12.50	25.00

-- Promo-only interview album

WINTER, PAUL
COLUMBIA
❏ CS 8725 [S]	Jazz Meets the Bossa Nova	1962	5.00	10.00	20.00
❏ CS 8797 [S]	Jazz Premiere: Washington	1963	5.00	10.00	20.00
❏ CS 8864 [S]	New Jazz on Campus	1963	5.00	10.00	20.00
❏ CS 8955 [S]	Jazz Meets the Folk Song	1964	5.00	10.00	20.00
❏ CS 9072 [S]	The Sound of Ipanema	1965	5.00	10.00	20.00
❏ CS 9115 [S]	Rio	1965	5.00	10.00	20.00

LIVING MUSIC
❏ LMR-1 [(2)]	Callings	1981	5.00	10.00	20.00

-- With 20-page booklet

❏ LMR-2 [(2)]	Missa Gaia/Earth Mass	1983	5.00	10.00	20.00

WINTERHALTER, HUGO
RCA VICTOR
❏ LPM-1020 [M]	Great Music Themes of TV	1954	6.25	12.50	25.00
❏ LPM-1179 [M]	Always	1955	5.00	10.00	20.00
❏ LPM-1185 [M]	Music by Starlight	1955	5.00	10.00	20.00
❏ LPM-1338 [M]	The Eyes of Love	1956	5.00	10.00	20.00
❏ LPM-1400 [M]	Happy Hunting	1956	5.00	10.00	20.00
❏ LPM-1677 [M]	Hugo Winterhalter Goes... Latin	1957	5.00	10.00	20.00
❏ LSP-1677 [S]	Hugo Winterhalter Goes... Latin	1958	6.25	12.50	25.00
❏ LPM-1904 [M]	Wish You Were Here	1958	5.00	10.00	20.00
❏ LSP-1904 [S]	Wish You Were Here	1958	6.25	12.50	25.00
❏ LPM-1905 [M]	Two Sides of Hugo Winterhalter	1958	5.00	10.00	20.00
❏ LSP-1905 [S]	Two Sides of Hugo Winterhalter	1958	6.25	12.50	25.00
❏ LSP-2167 [S]	Hugo Winterhalter Goes...Gypsy	1960	5.00	10.00	20.00
❏ LSP-2271 [S]	Hugo Winterhalter Goes...South of the Border	1960	5.00	10.00	20.00
❏ LSP-2417 [S]	Hugo Winterhalter Goes...Hawaiian	1961	5.00	10.00	20.00
❏ LSP-2482 [S]	Hugo Winterhalter Goes... Continental	1961	5.00	10.00	20.00
❏ LPM-3100 [10]	Winterhalter Magic	195?	7.50	15.00	30.00
❏ LPM-3101 [10]	Song Hits from "Peter Pan" and "Hans Christian Andersen"	195?	7.50	15.00	30.00
❏ LPM-3132 [10]	Christmas Magic	1954	7.50	15.00	30.00

WINTERS, JONATHAN
COLUMBIA
❏ CL 2811 [M]	Jonathan Winters Wings It!	1968	6.25	12.50	25.00
❏ KG 31985 [(2)]	Jonathan Winters Laughs Live	1972	5.00	10.00	20.00

-- Reissue of 9611 and 9799 in one package

VERVE
❏ MGVS-6099 [S]	The Wonderful World of Jonathan Winters	1960	6.25	12.50	25.00
❏ MGVS-6155 [S]	Down to Earth	1960	6.25	12.50	25.00
❏ MGV-15009 [M]	The Wonderful World of Jonathan Winters	1960	6.25	12.50	25.00
❏ V-15009 [M]	The Wonderful World of Jonathan Winters	1961	5.00	10.00	20.00
❏ V6-15009 [S]	The Wonderful World of Jonathan Winters	1961	5.00	10.00	20.00

-- Reissue of 6099

❏ MGV-15011 [M]	Down to Earth	1960	6.25	12.50	25.00
❏ V-15011 [M]	Down to Earth	1961	5.00	10.00	20.00
❏ V6-15011 [S]	Down to Earth	1961	5.00	10.00	20.00

-- Reissue of 6155

❏ V-15025 [M]	Here's Jonathan	1961	6.25	12.50	25.00
❏ V6-15025 [S]	Here's Jonathan	1961	6.25	12.50	25.00
❏ V-15032 [M]	Another Day, Another World	1962	6.25	12.50	25.00
❏ V-15035 [M]	Humor As Seen Through the Eyes of Jonathan Winters	1963	6.25	12.50	25.00
❏ V6-15035 [S]	Humor As Seen Through the Eyes of Jonathan Winters	1963	6.25	12.50	25.00
❏ V-15037 [M]	Whistle Stopping with Jonathan Winters	1964	5.00	10.00	20.00
❏ V-15041 [M]	Jonathan Winters' Mad, Mad, Mad, Mad World	1964	5.00	10.00	20.00
❏ V-15047 [M]	Great Moments in Comedy	1965	5.00	10.00	20.00
❏ V-15052 [M]	The Best of Frickert and Suggins	1966	5.00	10.00	20.00
❏ V-15057 [M]	Movies Are Better Than Ever	1967	5.00	10.00	20.00

WINWOOD, STEVE
Also see BLIND FAITH; SPENCER DAVIS GROUP; TRAFFIC.
UNITED ARTISTS
❏ UAS-9950 [(2)]	Winwood	1971	6.25	12.50	25.00

-- Collection of tracks Winwood recorded with the Spencer Davis Group, Traffic and Blind Faith; with booklet

WIPERS, THE
PARK AVE.
❏ (# unknown)	Is This Real?	1980	12.50	25.00	50.00
❏ 82802	Youth of America	1981	12.50	25.00	50.00

WISE, CHUBBY
STARDAY
❏ SLP-154 [M]	The Tennessee Fiddler	1961	12.50	25.00	50.00

WISE, CHUBBY, AND MAC WISEMAN
GILLEY'S
❏ 500	Give Me My Smokies & The Tennessee Waltz	197?	5.00	10.00	20.00

WISEMAN, MAC
CAPITOL
❏ ST 1800 [S]	Bluegrass Favorites	1962	10.00	20.00	40.00
❏ T 1800 [M]	Bluegrass Favorites	1962	7.50	15.00	30.00

DOT
❏ DLP-3084 [M]	Tis Sweet to Be Remembered	1958	12.50	25.00	50.00
❏ DLP-3135 [M]	Beside the Still Waters	1959	7.50	15.00	30.00
❏ DLP-3213 [M]	Great Folk Ballads	1959	7.50	15.00	30.00
❏ DLP-3313 [M]	12 Great Hits	1960	7.50	15.00	30.00
❏ DLP-3336 [M]	Keep on the Sunny Side	1960	10.00	20.00	40.00
❏ DLP-3373 [M]	Best Loved Gospel Hymns	1961	7.50	15.00	30.00
❏ DLP-3408 [M]	Fireball Mail	1961	10.00	20.00	40.00
❏ DLP-3697 [M]	This Is Mac Wiseman	1966	5.00	10.00	20.00
❏ DLP-3730 [M]	A Master at Work	1966	5.00	10.00	20.00
❏ DLP-3731 [M]	Bluegrass	1966	5.00	10.00	20.00
❏ DLP-25084 [R]	Tis Sweet to Be Remembered	196?	5.00	10.00	20.00
❏ DLP-25135 [S]	Beside the Still Waters	1959	10.00	20.00	40.00
❏ DLP-25213 [S]	Great Folk Ballads	1959	10.00	20.00	40.00
❏ DLP-25313 [S]	12 Great Hits	1960	10.00	20.00	40.00
❏ DLP-25336 [R]	Keep on the Sunny Side	196?	5.00	10.00	20.00
❏ DLP-25373 [S]	Best Loved Gospel Hymns	1961	10.00	20.00	40.00
❏ DLP-25408 [R]	Fireball Mail	196?	5.00	10.00	20.00
❏ DLP-25697 [S]	This Is Mac Wiseman	1966	6.25	12.50	25.00
❏ DLP-25730 [S]	A Master at Work	1966	6.25	12.50	25.00
❏ DLP-25731 [S]	Bluegrass	1966	6.25	12.50	25.00
❏ DLP-25896	Golden Hits of Mac Wiseman	1968	5.00	10.00	20.00

HAMILTON
❏ HLP-12130 [M]	Sincerely	1964	5.00	10.00	20.00
❏ HLP-12167 [M]	Songs of the Dear Old Days	1965	5.00	10.00	20.00

WITHERS, BILL
SUSSEX
❏ SUX-7006	Just As I Am	1971	5.00	10.00	20.00
❏ SUX-7014	Still Bill	1972	5.00	10.00	20.00
❏ SUX-7025 [(2)]	Bill Withers Live at Carnegie Hall	1973	5.00	10.00	20.00

WITHERSPOON, JIMMY
ABC
❏ 717	Handbags and Gladrags	1970	6.25	12.50	25.00

BLUESWAY
❏ BLS-6026	Blues Singer	1969	6.25	12.50	25.00
❏ BLS-6040	Hunh	1970	6.25	12.50	25.00
❏ BLS-6051	The Best of Jimmy Witherspoon	1970	6.25	12.50	25.00

CONSTELLATION
❏ CM 1422 [M]	Take This Hammer	1964	12.50	25.00	50.00
❏ CMS 1422 [R]	Take This Hammer	1964	7.50	15.00	30.00

CROWN
❏ CST-215 [R]	Jimmy Witherspoon Sings the Blues	1961	20.00	40.00	80.00

-- Red vinyl

❏ CST-215 [R]	Jimmy Witherspoon Sings the Blues	1961	5.00	10.00	20.00

-- Black vinyl

❏ CLP-5156 [M]	Jimmy Witherspoon	1959	20.00	40.00	80.00

-- Black label, silver print

Number	Title	Yr	VG	VG+	NM
❏ CLP-5156 [M]	Jimmy Witherspoon	1961	6.25	12.50	25.00
-- Gray label, black print					
❏ CLP-5192 [M]	Jimmy Witherspoon Sings the Blues	1959	20.00	40.00	80.00
-- Black label, silver print					
❏ CLP-5192 [M]	Jimmy Witherspoon Sings the Blues	1961	6.25	12.50	25.00
-- Gray label, black print					
FANTASY					
❏ 24701 [(2)]	The 'Spoon Concerts	1972	5.00	10.00	20.00
HIFI					
❏ R-421 [M]	At the Monterey Jazz Festival	1959	25.00	50.00	100.00
❏ SR-421 [S]	At the Monterey Jazz Festival	1959	15.00	30.00	60.00
❏ R-422 [M]	Feelin' the Spirit	1959	25.00	50.00	100.00
❏ SR-422 [S]	Feelin' the Spirit	1959	15.00	30.00	60.00
❏ R-426 [M]	Jimmy Witherspoon at the Renaissance	1959	25.00	50.00	100.00
❏ SR-426 [S]	Jimmy Witherspoon at the Renaissance	1959	15.00	30.00	60.00
PRESTIGE					
❏ PRLP-7290 [M]	Baby, Baby, Baby	1963	10.00	20.00	40.00
❏ PRST-7290 [S]	Baby, Baby, Baby	1963	10.00	20.00	40.00
❏ PRLP-7300 [M]	Evenin' Blues	1964	10.00	20.00	40.00
❏ PRST-7300 [S]	Evenin' Blues	1964	10.00	20.00	40.00
❏ PRLP-7314 [M]	Blues Around the Clock	1964	10.00	20.00	40.00
❏ PRST-7314 [S]	Blues Around the Clock	1964	10.00	20.00	40.00
❏ PRLP-7327 [M]	Blue Spoon	1964	10.00	20.00	40.00
❏ PRST-7327 [S]	Blue Spoon	1964	10.00	20.00	40.00
❏ PRLP-7356 [M]	Some of My Best Friends Are the Blues	1965	6.25	12.50	25.00
❏ PRST-7356 [S]	Some of My Best Friends Are the Blues	1965	6.25	12.50	25.00
❏ PRLP-7418 [M]	Spoon in London	1966	6.25	12.50	25.00
❏ PRST-7418 [S]	Spoon in London	1966	6.25	12.50	25.00
❏ PRLP-7475 [M]	Blues for Easy Livers	1967	6.25	12.50	25.00
❏ PRST-7475 [S]	Blues for Easy Livers	1967	5.00	10.00	20.00
❏ PRST-7713	The Best of Jimmy Witherspoon	1969	5.00	10.00	20.00
RCA VICTOR					
❏ LPM-1639 [M]	Goin' to Kansas City Blues	1957	25.00	50.00	100.00
REPRISE					
❏ R-2008 [M]	Spoon	1961	10.00	20.00	40.00
❏ R9-2008 [S]	Spoon	1961	15.00	30.00	60.00
❏ R-6012 [M]	Hey, Mrs. Jones	1961	10.00	20.00	40.00
❏ R9-6012 [S]	Hey, Mrs. Jones	1961	15.00	30.00	60.00
❏ R-6059 [M]	Roots	1962	10.00	20.00	40.00
❏ R9-6059 [S]	Roots	1962	15.00	30.00	60.00
SURREY					
❏ S-1106 [M]	Blues for Spoon and Groove	1965	6.25	12.50	25.00
❏ SS-1106 [S]	Blues for Spoon and Groove	1965	7.50	15.00	30.00
-- Above LP with Groove Holmes					
VERVE					
❏ V-5007 [M]	Blue Point of View	1966	5.00	10.00	20.00
❏ V6-5007 [S]	Blue Point of View	1966	6.25	12.50	25.00
❏ V-5030 [M]	Blues Is Now	1967	6.25	12.50	25.00
❏ V6-5030 [S]	Blues Is Now	1967	5.00	10.00	20.00
❏ V-5050 [M]	A Spoonful of Soul	1968	7.50	15.00	30.00
❏ V6-5050 [S]	A Spoonful of Soul	1968	5.00	10.00	20.00
WORLD PACIFIC					
❏ WP-1267 [M]	Singin' the Blues	1959	25.00	50.00	100.00
❏ WP-1402 [M]	There's Good Rockin' Tonight	1961	15.00	30.00	60.00
-- Reissue of 1267					

WIZARD
PEON

Number	Title	Yr	VG	VG+	NM
❏ 1069	Original Wizard	1971	50.00	100.00	200.00

WIZARDS FROM KANSAS, THE
MERCURY

Number	Title	Yr	VG	VG+	NM
❏ SR-61309	The Wizards from Kansas	1970	37.50	75.00	150.00

WOLFMAN JACK
BREAD

Number	Title	Yr	VG	VG+	NM
❏ 0170	Wolfman Jack and the Wolf Pack	1965	100.00	200.00	400.00
WOODEN NICKEL					
❏ BWS1-0119	Fun and Romance Through the Ages	1974	6.25	12.50	25.00
❏ WNS-1009	Wolfman Jack	1972	7.50	15.00	30.00

WOMACK, BOBBY
MINIT

Number	Title	Yr	VG	VG+	NM
❏ 24014	Fly Me to the Moon	1968	7.50	15.00	30.00
❏ 24027	My Prescription	1969	7.50	15.00	30.00

WOMB
DOT

Number	Title	Yr	VG	VG+	NM
❏ DLP-25933	Womb	1969	5.00	10.00	20.00
❏ DLP-25959	Overdub	1969	5.00	10.00	20.00

WONDER, STEVIE
GORDY

Number	Title	Yr	VG	VG+	NM
❏ GS 932	Eivets Rednow	1968	7.50	15.00	30.00
-- As "Eivets Rednow"					
JOBETE					
❏ JSA-6253 [DJ]	The Wonder of Stevie	1988	5.00	10.00	20.00
-- Publisher's demo with excerpts of 105 (!) Stevie Wonder songs					
MOTOWN					
❏ 31453 0238-1	Conversation Peace [(2) DJ]	1995	6.25	12.50	25.00
-- Vinyl is promo only; white cover with custom sticker					
❏ M-804LP3 [(3)]	Looking Back	1977	6.25	12.50	25.00
-- Withdrawn after Stevie Wonder objected to its release					
❏ 6291 ML	Music from the Movie Jungle Fever	1991	5.00	10.00	20.00
TAMLA					
❏ T 232 [M]	Tribute to Uncle Ray	1962	37.50	75.00	150.00
❏ T 233 [M]	The Jazz Soul of Little Stevie	1962	37.50	75.00	150.00
❏ T 240 [M]	Recorded Live/Little Stevie Wonder/The 12 Year Old Genius	1963	30.00	60.00	120.00
-- The above three LPs as "Little Stevie Wonder"					
❏ T 248 [M]	Workout Stevie, Workout	1963	250.00	500.00	1,000.
-- Canceled; test pressings or acetates may exist					
❏ T 250 [M]	With a Song in My Heart	1964	20.00	40.00	80.00
❏ T 255 [M]	Stevie at the Beach	1964	20.00	40.00	80.00
❏ T 268 [M]	Up-Tight Everything's Alright	1966	6.25	12.50	25.00
❏ TS 268 [S]	Up-Tight Everything's Alright	1966	7.50	15.00	30.00
❏ T 272 [M]	Down to Earth	1966	5.00	10.00	20.00
❏ TS 272 [S]	Down to Earth	1966	6.25	12.50	25.00
❏ T 279 [M]	I Was Made to Love Her	1967	5.00	10.00	20.00
❏ TS 279 [S]	I Was Made to Love Her	1967	6.25	12.50	25.00
❏ T 281 [M]	Someday at Christmas	1967	7.50	15.00	30.00
❏ TS 281 [S]	Someday at Christmas	1967	10.00	20.00	40.00
❏ T 282 [M]	Greatest Hits	1968	7.50	15.00	30.00
❏ TS 282 [S]	Greatest Hits	1968	5.00	10.00	20.00
❏ TS 291	For Once in My Life	1968	5.00	10.00	20.00
❏ TS 296	My Cherie Amour	1969	5.00	10.00	20.00
❏ TS 298	Stevie Wonder Live	1970	5.00	10.00	20.00
❏ TS 304	Signed Sealed & Delivered	1970	5.00	10.00	20.00
❏ TS 308	Where I'm Coming From	1971	5.00	10.00	20.00
❏ TS 313	Stevie Wonder's Greatest Hits, Vol. 2	1971	5.00	10.00	20.00
❏ T 314L	Music of My Mind	1972	5.00	10.00	20.00
❏ T13-340C2 [(2)]	Songs in the Key of Life	1976	5.00	10.00	20.00
-- With booklet and bonus 7-inch EP (deduct 25% if missing)					
❏ T7-362R1	Someday at Christmas	1978	5.00	10.00	20.00
-- Unusual reissue of 281					

WOOD, BOBBY
JOY

Number	Title	Yr	VG	VG+	NM
❏ 1001 [M]	Bobby Wood	1964	10.00	20.00	40.00

WOOD, BRENTON
BRENT

Number	Title	Yr	VG	VG+	NM
❏ S-100 [S]	Introducing Brenton Wood! Boogaloo	1967	15.00	30.00	60.00
-- Four tracks by Brenton Wood, six by other artists					
❏ 5100 [M]	Introducing Brenton Wood! Boogaloo	1967	10.00	20.00	40.00
DOUBLE SHOT					
❏ 1002 [M]	Oogum Boogum	1967	6.25	12.50	25.00
❏ 1003 [M]	Baby You Got It	1967	6.25	12.50	25.00
❏ 5002 [S]	Oogum Boogum	1967	7.50	15.00	30.00
❏ 5003 [S]	Baby You Got It	1967	7.50	15.00	30.00
-- Black vinyl					
❏ 5003 [S]	Baby You Got It	1967	50.00	100.00	200.00
-- Multi-color vinyl					

WOOD, HALLY
ELEKTRA

Number	Title	Yr	VG	VG+	NM
❏ EKL-10 [10]	O Lovely Appearance of Death	1953	12.50	25.00	50.00

WOOD, RONNIE
Also see FACES; THE ROLLING STONES.
WARNER BROS.

Number	Title	Yr	VG	VG+	NM
❏ BS 2819	I've Got My Own Album to Do	1974	5.00	10.00	20.00

Number	Title	Yr	VG	VG+	NM

WOOD, ROY
Also see ELECTRIC LIGHT ORCHESTRA; THE MOVE.
UNITED ARTISTS

Number	Title	Yr	VG	VG+	NM
❏ (# unknown) [DJ] Boulders Folder		1973	10.00	20.00	40.00
-- Promo version of 168 in 13x13 folder with press kit and postcards					

WOODBURY, WOODY
STEREODDITIES

❏ BITOA	Booze Is the Only Answer	1961	10.00	20.00	40.00
-- With record, paperback book and smaller booklets					
❏ MW 1	Woody Woodbury Looks at Love and Life	1960	6.25	12.50	25.00
❏ MW 2	Woody Woodbury's Laughing Room	1960	6.25	12.50	25.00
❏ MW 3	Woody Woodbury's Concert in Comedy	1961	6.25	12.50	25.00
❏ MW 4	Woody Woodbury's Saloonatics	1961	6.25	12.50	25.00
❏ MW 5	The Spice Is Right	1962	6.25	12.50	25.00
❏ MW 6	The Best of Woody Woodbury	1963	5.00	10.00	20.00
❏ MW 7	Through the Keyhole	1964	5.00	10.00	20.00

WOODS, BILL
COUNTRY TOWN

❏ CTR-24803 [M]	Bill Woods from Bakersfield	196?	30.00	60.00	120.00

WOODS, MACEO
VEE JAY

❏ LP-5001 [M]	Amazing Grace	1959	7.50	15.00	30.00
-- Maroon label					
❏ LP-5001 [M]	Amazing Grace	1961	5.00	10.00	20.00
-- Black colorband label					
❏ LP-5010 [M]	The Lord Will Make a Way	1960	7.50	15.00	30.00
-- Maroon label					
❏ LP-5010 [M]	The Lord Will Make a Way	1961	5.00	10.00	20.00
-- Black colorband label					
❏ LP-5053 [M]	Garden of Prayer	1963	5.00	10.00	20.00
❏ SR-5053 [S]	Garden of Prayer	1963	7.50	15.00	30.00

VOLT

❏ VOS-6009	Hello Sunshine	1970	5.00	10.00	20.00
❏ VOS-6013	Step to Jesus	1971	5.00	10.00	20.00

WOODY'S TRUCK STOP
SMASH

❏ SRS-67111	Woody's Truck Stop	1969	6.25	12.50	25.00

WOOFERS, THE
WYNCOTE

❏ SW 9011 [S]	Dragsville	1964	12.50	25.00	50.00
❏ W 9011 [M]	Dragsville	1964	10.00	20.00	40.00

WOOLEY, SHEB
MGM

❏ E-3299 [M]	Sheb Wooley	1956	37.50	75.00	150.00
❏ E-3904 [M]	Songs from the Days of Rawhide	1961	10.00	20.00	40.00
❏ SE-3904 [S]	Songs from the Days of Rawhide	1961	12.50	25.00	50.00
❏ E-4026 [M]	That's My Ma and That's My Pa	1962	7.50	15.00	30.00
❏ SE-4026 [S]	That's My Ma and That's My Pa	1962	10.00	20.00	40.00
❏ E-4117 [M]	Spoofing the Big Ones	1961	10.00	20.00	40.00
❏ SE-4117 [S]	Spoofing the Big Ones	1961	12.50	25.00	50.00
-- MGM 4117 as "Ben Colder"					
❏ E-4136 [M]	Tales of How the West Was Won	1963	7.50	15.00	30.00
❏ SE-4136 [S]	Tales of How the West Was Won	1963	10.00	20.00	40.00
❏ E-4173 [M]	Ben Colder	1963	7.50	15.00	30.00
❏ SE-4173 [S]	Ben Colder	1963	10.00	20.00	40.00
-- MGM 4173 as "Ben Colder"					
❏ E-4275 [M]	The Very Best of Sheb Wooley	1965	5.00	10.00	20.00
❏ SE-4275 [S]	The Very Best of Sheb Wooley	1965	6.25	12.50	25.00
❏ E-4325 [M]	It's a Big Land	1965	5.00	10.00	20.00
❏ SE-4325 [S]	It's a Big Land	1965	6.25	12.50	25.00
❏ E-4421 [M]	Big Ben Strikes Again	1967	5.00	10.00	20.00
❏ SE-4421 [S]	Big Ben Strikes Again	1967	5.00	10.00	20.00
-- MGM 4421 as "Ben Colder"					
❏ E-4482 [M]	Wine, Women and Song	1967	5.00	10.00	20.00
❏ SE-4482 [S]	Wine, Women and Song	1967	5.00	10.00	20.00
-- MGM 4482 as "Ben Colder"					
❏ SE-4530	The Best of Ben Colder	1968	5.00	10.00	20.00
-- As "Ben Colder"					
❏ SE-4614	Harper Valley P.T.A.	1968	5.00	10.00	20.00
-- As "Ben Colder"					
❏ SE-4615	Warm and Wooley	1969	5.00	10.00	20.00

WOOLIES, THE
SPIRIT

❏ 9645-2001	Basic Rock	1971	10.00	20.00	40.00
❏ 9645-2005	Live at Lizards	1973	10.00	20.00	40.00

WORLD OF OZ, THE
DERAM

❏ DES 18022	The World of Oz	1969	12.50	25.00	50.00

WORTH, MARION
COLUMBIA

❏ CL 2011 [M]	Marion Worth's Greatest Hits	1963	5.00	10.00	20.00
❏ CL 2287 [M]	Marion Worth Sings Marty Robbins	1964	5.00	10.00	20.00
❏ CS 8811 [S]	Marion Worth's Greatest Hits	1963	6.25	12.50	25.00
❏ CS 9087 [S]	Marion Worth Sings Marty Robbins	1964	6.25	12.50	25.00

DECCA

❏ DL 4936 [M]	A Woman Needs Love	1967	6.25	12.50	25.00
❏ DL 74936 [S]	A Woman Needs Love	1967	5.00	10.00	20.00

WOULD
PERCEPTION

❏ 24	Would	1972	7.50	15.00	30.00

WRAY, LINK
EPIC

❏ LN 3661 [M]	Link Wray and the Wraymen	1960	62.50	125.00	250.00

POLYDOR

❏ 24-4064	Link Wray	1971	5.00	10.00	20.00
❏ PD-5047	Be What You Want To	1972	5.00	10.00	20.00
❏ PD-6025	The Link Wray Rumble	1974	5.00	10.00	20.00

RECORD FACTORY

❏ 1929	Yesterday and Today	1969	20.00	40.00	80.00

SWAN

❏ SLP-510 [M]	Jack the Ripper	1963	37.50	75.00	150.00

VERMILLION

❏ 1924 [M]	Great Guitar Hits	196?	20.00	40.00	80.00
❏ 1925 [M]	Link Wray Sings and Plays Guitar	196?	20.00	40.00	80.00

WRAY, VERNON
VERMILLION

❏ 1972	Wasted	1972	25.00	50.00	100.00

WRIGHT, BETTY
ATCO

❏ SD 33-260	My First Time Around	1968	6.25	12.50	25.00

WRIGHT, CHARLES, AND THE WATTS 103RD STREET RHYTHM BAND
WARNER BROS.

❏ WS 1741	The Watts 103rd Street Rhythm Band	1968	5.00	10.00	20.00
-- Green label with "W7" logo					
❏ WS 1761	Together	1969	5.00	10.00	20.00
-- Green label with "W7" logo					
❏ WS 1801	In the Jungle, Babe	1969	5.00	10.00	20.00
-- Green label with "W7" logo					

WRIGHT, JOHNNY
DECCA

❏ DL 4698 [M]	Hello Vietnam	1965	6.25	12.50	25.00
❏ DL 4770 [M]	Country Music Special	1966	6.25	12.50	25.00
❏ DL 4846 [M]	Country the Wright Way	1967	6.25	12.50	25.00
❏ DL 74698 [S]	Hello Vietnam	1965	7.50	15.00	30.00
❏ DL 74770 [S]	Country Music Special	1966	7.50	15.00	30.00
❏ DL 74846 [S]	Country the Wright Way	1967	5.00	10.00	20.00
❏ DL 75019	Johnny Wright Sings Country Favorites	1968	5.00	10.00	20.00

WRIGHT, MARVIN "LEFTY"
"X"

❏ LXA-3028 [10]	Boogie Woogie Piano	1954	15.00	30.00	60.00

WRIGHT, O.V.
BACK BEAT

❏ 61 [M]	If It's Only for Tonight	1965	25.00	50.00	100.00
❏ S-61 [S]	If It's Only for Tonight	1965	37.50	75.00	150.00
❏ 66	Eight Men, Four Women	1968	15.00	30.00	60.00
❏ 67	Nucleus of Soul	1969	15.00	30.00	60.00
❏ 70	A Nickel and a Nail and Ace of Spade	1971	15.00	30.00	60.00
❏ 72	Memphis Unlimited	1973	12.50	25.00	50.00

HI

❏ 6001	Into Something	1977	6.25	12.50	25.00
❏ 6008	Bottom Line	1978	6.25	12.50	25.00

Number	Title	Yr	VG	VG+	NM
❏ 6011	We're Still Together	1979	6.25	12.50	25.00

WRIGHT, RICHARD
Also see PINK FLOYD.
COLUMBIA

Number	Title	Yr	VG	VG+	NM
❏ JC 35559	Wet Dream	1978	5.00	10.00	20.00

WRIGHT, SONNY
KAPP

Number	Title	Yr	VG	VG+	NM
❏ KS-3614	I Love You, Loretta Lynn	1968	5.00	10.00	20.00

WRIGHT, WILLIE
ARGO

Number	Title	Yr	VG	VG+	NM
❏ LP-4024 [M]	I'm On My Way	1963	5.00	10.00	20.00
❏ LPS-4024 [S]	I'm On My Way	1963	6.25	12.00	25.00

CONCERT DISC

Number	Title	Yr	VG	VG+	NM
❏ 45 [S]	I Sing Folk Songs	1960	10.00	20.00	40.00
❏ 1045 [M]	I Sing Folk Songs	1960	7.50	15.00	30.00

WYLER, GRETCHEN
JUBILEE

Number	Title	Yr	VG	VG+	NM
❏ JLP-1100 [M]	Wild, Wyler, Wildest	1959	6.25	12.50	25.00
❏ SDJLP-1100 [S]	Wild, Wyler, Wildest	1959	7.50	15.00	30.00

WYMAN, BILL
Also see THE ROLLING STONES.
ROLLING STONES

Number	Title	Yr	VG	VG+	NM
❏ QD 79100 [Q]	Monkey Grip	1974	5.00	10.00	20.00
❏ QD 79103 [Q]	Stone Alone	1976	5.00	10.00	20.00

WYNETTE, TAMMY
EPIC

Number	Title	Yr	VG	VG+	NM
❏ EGP 503 [(2)]	The World of Tammy Wynette	1970	6.25	12.50	25.00
❏ LN 24305 [M]	Your Good Girl's Gonna Go Bad	1967	7.50	15.00	30.00
❏ BN 26305 [S]	Your Good Girl's Gonna Go Bad	1967	5.00	10.00	20.00
❏ BN 26353	Take Me to Your World	1968	5.00	10.00	20.00
❏ BN 26392	D-I-V-O-R-C-E	1968	5.00	10.00	20.00
❏ BN 26423	Inspiration	1969	5.00	10.00	20.00
❏ BN 26451	Stand By Your Man	1969	5.00	10.00	20.00
❏ BN 26486	Tammy's Greatest Hits	1969	5.00	10.00	20.00
❏ BN 26519	The Ways to Love a Man	1970	5.00	10.00	20.00
❏ BN 26549	Tammy's Touch	1970	5.00	10.00	20.00
❏ E 30212	The First Lady	1970	5.00	10.00	20.00
❏ E 30343	Christmas with Tammy	1970	5.00	10.00	20.00
❏ KEG 30358 [(2)]	The First Songs of the First Lady	1970	5.00	10.00	20.00
❏ E 30658	We Sure Can Love Each Other	1971	5.00	10.00	20.00
❏ EQ 30658 [Q]	We Sure Can Love Each Other	1972	7.50	15.00	30.00
❏ E 30733	Tammy's Greatest Hits, Volume II	1971	5.00	10.00	20.00

WYNONNA -- See WYNONNA JUDD.

X

X
SLASH

Number	Title	Yr	VG	VG+	NM
❏ SR-104	Los Angeles	1980	5.00	10.00	20.00

XIT
CANYON

Number	Title	Yr	VG	VG+	NM
❏ 7114	Entrance	197?	12.50	25.00	50.00
❏ 7121	Relocation	197?	10.00	20.00	40.00

RARE EARTH

Number	Title	Yr	VG	VG+	NM
❏ R-536	Plight of the Redman	1972	7.50	15.00	30.00
❏ R-545	Silent Warrior	1973	7.50	15.00	30.00

XTC
GEFFEN

Number	Title	Yr	VG	VG+	NM
❏ WBMS-146 [DJ]	Skylarking Interview	1986	5.00	10.00	20.00
-- Part of "The Warner Bros. Music Show" series					

VIRGIN

Number	Title	Yr	VG	VG+	NM
❏ VA 13134	Drums and Wires	1979	5.00	10.00	20.00
-- With bonus 7-inch record (PR 344) enclosed					

VIRGIN/RSO

Number	Title	Yr	VG	VG+	NM
❏ VR-1-1000	Black Sea	1980	5.00	10.00	20.00
-- With green outer bag (deduct 20% if missing)					

Number	Title	Yr	VG	VG+	NM

Y

Y KANT TORI READ
Lead singer: Tori Amos.
ATLANTIC

Number	Title	Yr	VG	VG+	NM
❑ 81845	Y Kant Tori Read	1989	30.00	60.00	120.00

-- Deduct 20% for albums with a gold promo stamp and cut-out mark

YA HO WA 13
HIGHER KEY

Number	Title	Yr	VG	VG+	NM
❑ 3301	Kohoutek	1973	75.00	150.00	300.00
❑ 3302	Contraction	1974	125.00	250.00	500.00
❑ 3303	Expansion	1974	125.00	250.00	500.00
❑ 3304	All or Nothing at All	1974	100.00	200.00	400.00

-- Above 4 as "Father Yod and the Spirit of '76"

Number	Title	Yr	VG	VG+	NM
❑ 3305	Ya Ho Wa 13	1974	125.00	250.00	500.00
❑ 3306	The Savage Sons of Ya Ho Wa	1974	100.00	200.00	400.00
❑ 3307	Penetration: An Aquarian Symphony	1974	100.00	200.00	400.00
❑ 3308 [(2)]	I'm Gonna Take You Home	1975	200.00	400.00	800.00
❑ 3309	To the Principles For the Children	1975	200.00	400.00	800.00

YACHTSMEN, THE
BUENA VISTA

Number	Title	Yr	VG	VG+	NM
❑ BV-3310 [M]	High and Dry with the Yachtsmen	1961	6.25	12.50	25.00

YAMA AND THE KARMA DUSTERS
MANHOLE

Number	Title	Yr	VG	VG+	NM
❑ 1	Up from the Sewers	1970	50.00	100.00	200.00

YANCEY, MAMA, AND ART RODES
VERVE FOLKWAYS

Number	Title	Yr	VG	VG+	NM
❑ FV-9015 [M]	Blues	1965	5.00	10.00	20.00
❑ FVS-9015 [S]	Blues	1965	6.25	12.50	25.00

YANCY DERRINGER
HEMISPHERE

Number	Title	Yr	VG	VG+	NM
❑ H-15104	Openers	1975	12.50	25.00	50.00

YANKEE DOLLAR, THE
DOT

Number	Title	Yr	VG	VG+	NM
❑ DLP-25874	The Yankee Dollar	1968	30.00	60.00	120.00

YANOVSKY, ZALMAN
Also see THE LOVIN' SPOONFUL.
BUDDAH

Number	Title	Yr	VG	VG+	NM
❑ BDS-5019	Alive and Well in Argentina	1968	10.00	20.00	40.00

KAMA SUTRA

Number	Title	Yr	VG	VG+	NM
❑ KSBS-2030	Alive and Well in Argentina	1971	5.00	10.00	20.00

YARBROUGH, GLENN
Also see THE LIMELITERS.
ELEKTRA

Number	Title	Yr	VG	VG+	NM
❑ EKL-135 [M]	Here We Go, Baby	1957	10.00	20.00	40.00

RCA VICTOR

Number	Title	Yr	VG	VG+	NM
❑ LSP-2905 [S]	One More Round	1964	5.00	10.00	20.00
❑ LSP-3301 [S]	Come Share My Life	1965	5.00	10.00	20.00
❑ LPM-3860 [M]	Honey and Wine	1967	5.00	10.00	20.00
❑ LPM-3951 [M]	The Bitter and the Sweet	1968	7.50	15.00	30.00

TRADITION

Number	Title	Yr	VG	VG+	NM
❑ 1019 [M]	Come Sit By My Side	195?	5.00	10.00	20.00

YARDBIRDS, THE
Also see JEFF BECK; ERIC CLAPTON; JIMMY PAGE; SONNY BOY WILLIAMSON AND THE YARDBIRDS.
COLUMBIA

Number	Title	Yr	VG	VG+	NM
❑ HC 48455	Roger the Engineer	1982	62.50	125.00	250.00

-- "Half-Speed Mastered" edition; regular edition evidently was cancelled, but copies of this exist

COLUMBIA SPECIAL PRODUCTS

Number	Title	Yr	VG	VG+	NM
❑ P 13311 [S]	Live Yardbirds Featuring Jimmy Page	1976	12.50	25.00	50.00

EPIC

Number	Title	Yr	VG	VG+	NM
❑ LN 24167 [DJ]	For Your Love	1965	100.00	200.00	400.00

-- White label promo

Number	Title	Yr	VG	VG+	NM
❑ LN 24167 [M]	For Your Love	1965	75.00	150.00	300.00
❑ LN 24177 [DJ]	Having a Rave Up with the Yardbirds	1965	100.00	200.00	400.00

-- White label promo

Number	Title	Yr	VG	VG+	NM
❑ LN 24177 [M]	Having a Rave Up with the Yardbirds	1965	20.00	40.00	80.00
❑ LN 24210 [DJ]	Over Under Sideways Down	1966	100.00	200.00	400.00

-- White label promo

Number	Title	Yr	VG	VG+	NM
❑ LN 24210 [M]	Over Under Sideways Down	1966	15.00	30.00	60.00
❑ LN 24246 [DJ]	The Yardbirds' Greatest Hits	1966	75.00	150.00	300.00

-- White label promo

Number	Title	Yr	VG	VG+	NM
❑ LN 24246 [M]	The Yardbirds' Greatest Hits	1966	12.50	25.00	50.00
❑ LN 24313 [DJ]	Little Games	1967	75.00	150.00	300.00
❑ LN 24313 [M]	Little Games	1967	20.00	40.00	80.00
❑ BN 26167 [P]	For Your Love	1965	50.00	100.00	200.00

-- The album is in true stereo except for "Sweet Music"

Number	Title	Yr	VG	VG+	NM
❑ BN 26177 [R]	Having a Rave Up with the Yardbirds	1965	12.50	25.00	50.00
❑ BN 26177 [R]	Having a Rave Up with the Yardbirds	1973	7.50	15.00	30.00

-- Reissue with orange label

Number	Title	Yr	VG	VG+	NM
❑ BN 26210 [P]	Over Under Sideways Down	1966	20.00	40.00	80.00

-- "Over Under Sideways Down" is rechanneled

Number	Title	Yr	VG	VG+	NM
❑ BN 26246 [P]	The Yardbirds' Greatest Hits	1966	7.50	15.00	30.00
❑ BN 26313 [S]	Little Games	1967	12.50	25.00	50.00
❑ E 30615 [S]	Live Yardbirds Featuring Jimmy Page	1972	12.50	25.00	50.00
❑ EG 30135 [(2)]	The Yardbirds Featuring Performances by Jeff Beck, Eric Clapton, Jimmy Page	1970	10.00	20.00	40.00
❑ HE 48455 [S]	Yardbirds	1983	25.00	50.00	100.00

-- Half-speed mastered edition

YAZ
SIRE

Number	Title	Yr	VG	VG+	NM
❑ 23737	Upstairs at Eric's	1982	5.00	10.00	20.00

-- First pressing: Band called "Yazoo"

YEARWOOD, TRISHA
MCA

Number	Title	Yr	VG	VG+	NM
❑ 1P-8161	Trisha Yearwood	1991	6.25	12.50	25.00

-- Vinyl edition available only from Columbia House

YELLO
RALPH

Number	Title	Yr	VG	VG+	NM
❑ YL 8059-L	Solid Pleasure	1980	5.00	10.00	20.00
❑ YL 8159	Claro Que Si	1981	5.00	10.00	20.00

YELLOW BALLOON, THE
CANTERBURY

Number	Title	Yr	VG	VG+	NM
❑ CLPM-1502 [M]	The Yellow Balloon	1967	6.25	12.50	25.00
❑ CLPS-1502 [S]	The Yellow Balloon	1967	7.50	15.00	30.00

YELLOW PAYGES, THE
UNI

Number	Title	Yr	VG	VG+	NM
❑ 73045	The Yellow Payges, Volume 1	1969	7.50	15.00	30.00

YES
Also see RICK WAKEMAN.
ARISTA

Number	Title	Yr	VG	VG+	NM
❑ AL 8643	Union	1991	5.00	10.00	20.00

-- U.S. vinyl available only through Columbia House

ATLANTIC

Number	Title	Yr	VG	VG+	NM
❑ PR 260 [DJ]	Yes Solo LP Sampler	1976	6.25	12.50	25.00
❑ PR 285 [DJ]	Yes Music: An Evening with Jon Anderson	1977	12.50	25.00	50.00
❑ SD 2-908 [DJ]	Tales from Topographic Oceans	1974	7.50	15.00	30.00

-- Promo copies banded for airplay

Number	Title	Yr	VG	VG+	NM
❑ 7244 [DJ]	Close to the Edge	1972	12.50	25.00	50.00

-- White label mono copies banded for airplay

Number	Title	Yr	VG	VG+	NM
❑ SD 18122 [DJ]	Relayer	1975	5.00	10.00	20.00

-- Promo copies banded for airplay

MOBILE FIDELITY

Number	Title	Yr	VG	VG+	NM
❑ 1-077	Close to the Edge	1982	15.00	30.00	60.00

-- Audiophile vinyl

YESTERDAY'S CHILDREN
MAP CITY

Number	Title	Yr	VG	VG+	NM
❑ 3012	Yesterday's Children	197?	15.00	30.00	60.00

YESTERDAY'S FOLK
BUDDAH

Number	Title	Yr	VG	VG+	NM
❑ BDS-5035	U.S. 69	1969	5.00	10.00	20.00

YETTI-MEN, THE / THE UPPA TRIO
KAL

Number	Title	Yr	VG	VG+	NM
❑ KB-4348	The Yetti-Men/The Uppa Trio	1967	200.00	400.00	600.00

YOAKAM, DWIGHT
OAK

Number	Title	Yr	VG	VG+	NM
❑ OR 2356 [EP]	Guitars, Cadillacs, Etc.	1984	200.00	400.00	800.00

Number	Title	Yr	VG	VG+	NM

REPRISE

| ❏ R 164310 | If There Was a Way | 1990 | 5.00 | 10.00 | 20.00 |

-- *BMG Direct Marketing edition; only U.S. vinyl version*

YORK BROTHERS, THE
KING

❏ 581 [M]	The York Brothers	1958	25.00	50.00	100.00
❏ 586 [M]	The York Brothers, Volume 2	1958	25.00	50.00	100.00
❏ 820 [M]	16 Great Country & Western Hits	1963	20.00	40.00	80.00

YOU KNOW WHO GROUP, THE
INTERNATIONAL ALLIED

| ❏ 420 [M] | The "You Know Who" Group | 1965 | 12.50 | 25.00 | 50.00 |

YOUNG HEARTS, THE
MINIT

| ❏ LP-24016 [S] | Sweet Soul Shakin'! | 1968 | 6.25 | 12.50 | 25.00 |
| ❏ LP-40016 [M] | Sweet Soul Shakin'! | 1968 | 6.25 | 12.50 | 25.00 |

YOUNG RASCALS, THE -- See THE RASCALS.

YOUNG, BARRY
DOT

| ❏ DLP 3672 [M] | One Has My Name | 1965 | 5.00 | 10.00 | 20.00 |
| ❏ DLP 25672 [S] | One Has My Name | 1965 | 6.25 | 12.50 | 25.00 |

YOUNG, CATHY
MAINSTREAM

| ❏ S-6121 | A Spoonful of Cathy Young | 1968 | 10.00 | 20.00 | 40.00 |

YOUNG, FARON
CAPITOL

❏ T 778 [M]	Sweethearts or Strangers	1957	15.00	30.00	60.00
-- *Turquoise or gray label*					
❏ T 778 [M]	Sweethearts or Strangers	1959	6.25	12.50	25.00
-- *Black colorband label, logo at left*					
❏ T 1004 [M]	The Object of My Affection	1958	12.50	25.00	50.00
❏ T 1096 [M]	This Is Faron Young	1959	12.50	25.00	50.00
❏ T 1185 [M]	My Garden of Prayer	1959	10.00	20.00	40.00
❏ ST 1245 [S]	Talk About Hits	1959	10.00	20.00	40.00
❏ T 1245 [M]	Talk About Hits	1959	7.50	15.00	30.00
❏ ST 1450 [S]	The Best of Faron Young	1960	10.00	20.00	40.00
❏ T 1450 [M]	The Best of Faron Young	1960	7.50	15.00	30.00
❏ ST 1528 [S]	Hello Walls	1961	10.00	20.00	40.00
❏ T 1528 [M]	Hello Walls	1961	7.50	15.00	30.00
❏ ST 1634 [S]	The Young Approach	1961	10.00	20.00	40.00
❏ T 1634 [M]	The Young Approach	1961	7.50	15.00	30.00
❏ DT 1876 [P]	The All-Time Great Hits of Faron Young	1963	5.00	10.00	20.00
❏ T 1876 [M]	The All-Time Great Hits of Faron Young	1963	6.25	12.50	25.00
❏ DT 2037 [R]	Faron Young's Memory Lane	1964	5.00	10.00	20.00
❏ T 2037 [M]	Faron Young's Memory Lane	1964	6.25	12.50	25.00
❏ ST 2307 [S]	Falling in Love	1965	6.25	12.50	25.00
❏ T 2307 [M]	Falling in Love	1965	5.00	10.00	20.00
❏ DT 2536 [R]	If You Ain't Lovin' You Ain't Livin'	1966	5.00	10.00	20.00
❏ T 2536 [M]	If You Ain't Lovin' You Ain't Livin'	1966	6.25	12.50	25.00

MARY CARTER

| ❏ MC 1000 [M] | Faron Young Sings on Stage for Mary Carter Paints | 196? | 15.00 | 30.00 | 60.00 |

-- *Promotional item for sponsor of The Faron Young Show*

MERCURY

❏ MG 20785 [M]	This Is Faron	1963	5.00	10.00	20.00
❏ MG 20840 [M]	Faron Young Aims at the West	1963	5.00	10.00	20.00
❏ MG 20896 [M]	Story Songs for Country Folks	1964	5.00	10.00	20.00
❏ MG 20931 [M]	Country Dance Favorites	1964	5.00	10.00	20.00
❏ MG 20971 [M]	Story Songs of Mountains and Valleys	1965	5.00	10.00	20.00
❏ MG 21007 [M]	Pen and Paper	1965	5.00	10.00	20.00
❏ MG 21047 [M]	Faron Young's Greatest Hits	1965	5.00	10.00	20.00
❏ MG 21058 [M]	Faron Young Sings the Best of Jim Reeves	1966	5.00	10.00	20.00
❏ MG 21110 [M]	Unmitigated Gall	1967	6.25	12.50	25.00
❏ SR 60785 [S]	This Is Faron	1963	6.25	12.50	25.00
❏ SR 60840 [S]	Faron Young Aims at the West	1963	6.25	12.50	25.00
❏ SR 60896 [S]	Story Songs for Country Folks	1964	6.25	12.50	25.00
❏ SR 60931 [S]	Country Dance Favorites	1964	6.25	12.50	25.00
❏ SR 60971 [S]	Story Songs of Mountains and Valleys	1965	6.25	12.50	25.00
❏ SR 61007 [S]	Pen and Paper	1965	6.25	12.50	25.00
❏ SR 61047 [S]	Faron Young's Greatest Hits	1965	6.25	12.50	25.00
❏ SR 61058 [S]	Faron Young Sings the Best of Jim Reeves	1966	6.25	12.50	25.00
❏ SR 61110 [S]	Unmitigated Gall	1967	5.00	10.00	20.00
❏ SR 61143	Greatest Hits Vol. 2	1968	5.00	10.00	20.00

Number	Title	Yr	VG	VG+	NM

❏ SR 61174	Here's Faron Young	1968	5.00	10.00	20.00
❏ SR 61212	I've Got Precious Memories	1969	5.00	10.00	20.00
❏ SR 61241	Wine Me Up	1969	5.00	10.00	20.00
❏ SR 61267	The Best of Faron Young	1970	5.00	10.00	20.00
❏ SR 61275	Faron Young Sings "Occasional Wife" and "If I Ever Fall in Love with a Honky Tonk Girl"	1970	5.00	10.00	20.00
❏ SR 61337	Step Aside	1971	5.00	10.00	20.00

SEARS

| ❏ SPS-124 | Candy Kisses | 1969 | 6.25 | 12.50 | 25.00 |

SESAC

| ❏ (# unknown) [M-DJ] | Church Songs | 196? | 20.00 | 40.00 | 80.00 |

TOWER

| ❏ T 5022 [M] | It's a Great Life | 1966 | 5.00 | 10.00 | 20.00 |

YOUNG, JESSE COLIN
Also see THE YOUNGBLOODS.
CAPITOL

| ❏ T 2070 [M] | The Soul of a City Boy | 1964 | 12.50 | 25.00 | 50.00 |

MERCURY

| ❏ MG 21005 [M] | Young Blood | 1965 | 7.50 | 15.00 | 30.00 |
| ❏ SR 61005 [S] | Young Blood | 1965 | 10.00 | 20.00 | 40.00 |

YOUNG, JOHNNY
ARHOOLIE

| ❏ F-1029 | Johnny Williams and His Chicago Blues Band | 1965 | 6.25 | 12.50 | 25.00 |
| ❏ F-1037 | Chicago Blues | 1966 | 6.25 | 12.50 | 25.00 |

BLUE HORIZON

| ❏ BH-4609 | Blues Masters, Volume 9 | 1969 | 5.00 | 10.00 | 20.00 |

YOUNG, KATHY, AND THE INNOCENTS
INDIGO

| ❏ LP-504 [M] | The Sound of Kathy Young | 1961 | 75.00 | 150.00 | 300.00 |

YOUNG, LEON
ATCO

| ❏ 33-163 [M] | Liverpool Sound for Strings | 1964 | 6.25 | 12.50 | 25.00 |
| ❏ SD 33-163 [S] | Liverpool Sound for Strings | 1964 | 7.50 | 15.00 | 30.00 |

YOUNG, LESTER
ALADDIN

❏ LP-705 [10]	Lester Young Trio	1953	75.00	150.00	300.00
❏ LP-706 [10]	Easy Does It	1954	75.00	150.00	300.00
❏ LP-801 [M]	Volume 1	1956	30.00	60.00	120.00
❏ LP-802 [M]	Volume 2	1956	30.00	60.00	120.00

AMERICAN RECORDING SOCIETY

| ❏ G-417 [M] | Pres and Teddy | 1957 | 12.50 | 25.00 | 50.00 |

CHARLIE PARKER

| ❏ CLP-402 [M] | Pres | 1961 | 12.50 | 25.00 | 50.00 |
| ❏ CLP-405 [M] | Pres Is Blue | 1961 | 12.50 | 25.00 | 50.00 |

CLEF

❏ MGC-104 [10]	The Lester Young Trio	1953	62.50	125.00	250.00
❏ MGC-108 [10]	Lester Young Collates	1953	62.50	125.00	250.00
❏ MGC-124 [10]	Lester Young Collates No. 2	1953	62.50	125.00	250.00
-- *Some copies of this have Mercury covers; no difference in value*					
❏ MGC-135 [10]	The Lester Young Trio No. 2	1953	62.50	125.00	250.00

COMMODORE

| ❏ FL-20021 [10] | Kansas City Style | 1952 | 75.00 | 150.00 | 300.00 |
| ❏ FL-30014 [M] | Kansas City Style | 1959 | 25.00 | 50.00 | 100.00 |

EMARCY

| ❏ MG-26021 [10] | Pres Meets Vice-Pres | 1954 | 62.50 | 125.00 | 250.00 |
| -- *With Paul Quinichette* | | | | | |

EPIC

❏ LN 3107 [M]	Lester Leaps In	1956	25.00	50.00	100.00
❏ LN 3168 [M]	Let's Go to Pres	1956	25.00	50.00	100.00
❏ LN 3576 [M]	Lester Young Memorial Album, Volume 1	1959	12.50	25.00	50.00
❏ LN 3577 [M]	Lester Young Memorial Album, Volume 2	1959	12.50	25.00	50.00
❏ SN 6031 [(2) M]	Lester Young Memorial Album	1959	37.50	75.00	150.00

IMPERIAL

❏ LP-9181-A [M]	The Great Lester Young	1962	12.50	25.00	50.00
❏ LP-9187-A [M]	The Great Lester Young, Volume 2	1962	12.50	25.00	50.00
❏ LP-12181-A [R]	The Great Lester Young	196?	5.00	10.00	20.00
❏ LP-12187-A [R]	The Great Lester Young, Volume 2	196?	5.00	10.00	20.00

INTRO

| ❏ LP-602 [M] | Swinging Lester Young | 1957 | 25.00 | 50.00 | 100.00 |
| ❏ LP-603 [M] | The Greatest | 1957 | 25.00 | 50.00 | 100.00 |

JAZZTONE

| ❏ J-1218 [M] | Tops on Tenor: Pres and Chu | 1956 | 17.50 | 35.00 | 70.00 |
| -- *With Chu Berry* | | | | | |

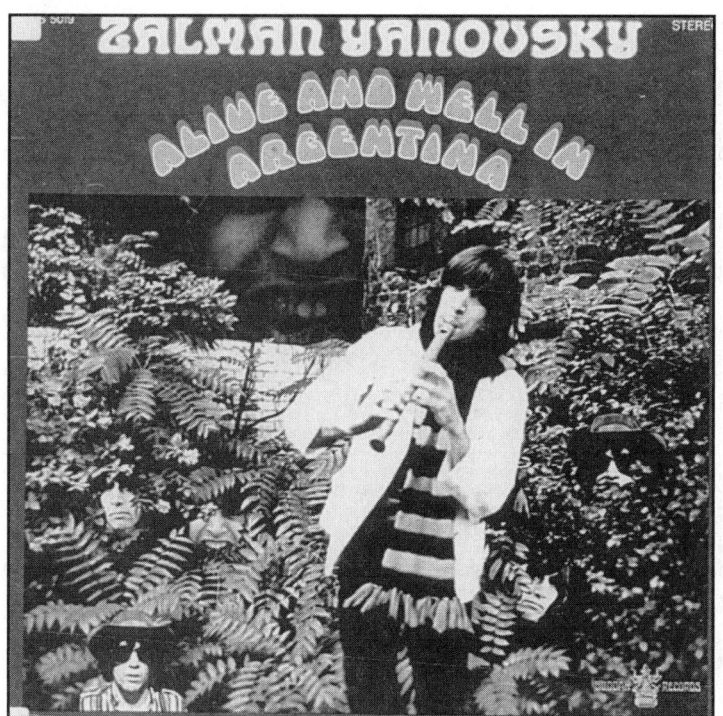

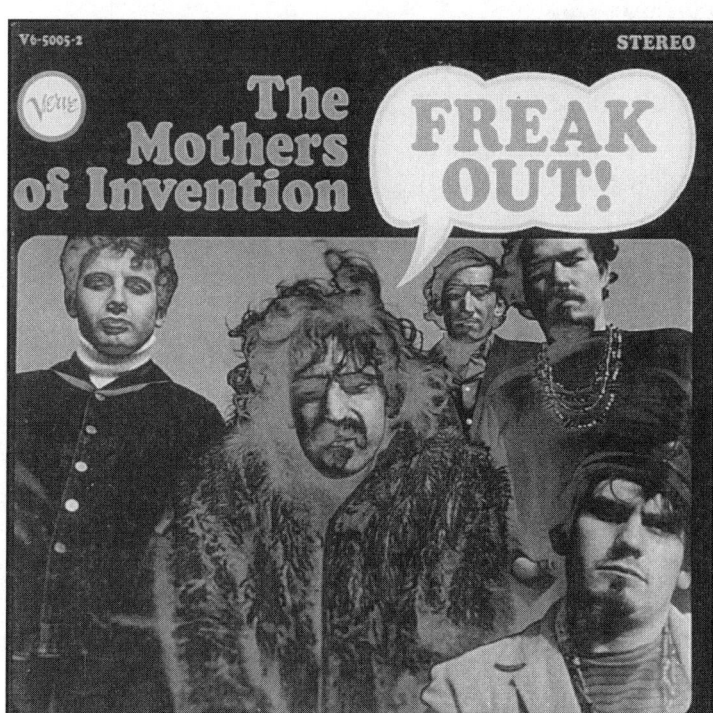

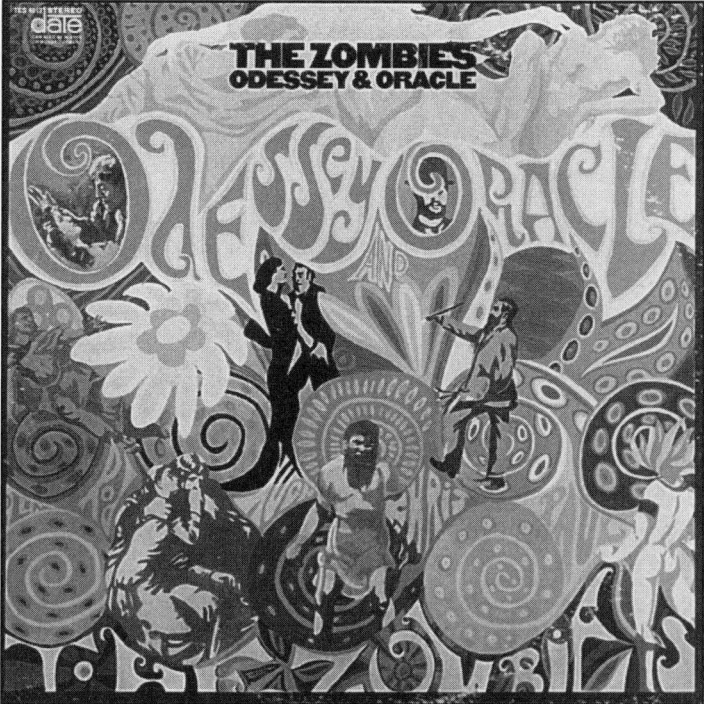

(Top left) Zalman Yanovsky was one of the members of the Lovin' Spoonful. After he left the group, he recorded *Alive and Well in Argentina*, considered something of a cult classic, for the Buddah label. (Top right) *Ragged Glory*, from 1990, became Neil Young's last U.S. vinyl album until 1994's *Sleeps With Angels*. As this was when most chain stores were getting out of vinyl releases and the independent stores had yet to fill the vacuum left behind, this was not an easy record to find at the time. It still isn't. (Bottom left) Who could have thought, when the Mothers of Invention released their first album, *Freak Out!*, that the group's leader, Frank Zappa, would continue to record his iconoclastic music for another 25 years with only one Top 10 hit album (*Apostrophe*) and one Top 40 hit single ("Valley Girl")? (Bottom right) Released in America at the insistence of Al Kooper, who picked up a British copy during a trip over there, the Zombies' *Odessey and Oracle*, featuring "Time of the Season," stands as their finest album.

Number	Title	Yr	VG	VG+	NM

MAINSTREAM

Number	Title	Yr	VG	VG+	NM
❏ 56002 [M]	The Influence of Five	1965	6.25	12.50	25.00
❏ 56004 [M]	Town Hall Concert	1965	6.25	12.50	25.00
❏ 56008 [M]	Chairman of the Board	1965	6.25	12.50	25.00
❏ 56009 [M]	52nd Street	1965	6.25	12.50	25.00
❏ 56012 [M]	Prez	1965	6.25	12.50	25.00

MERCURY

Number	Title	Yr	VG	VG+	NM
❏ MGC-104 [10]	The Lester Young Trio	1951	75.00	150.00	300.00
❏ MGC-108 [10]	Lester Young Collates	1951	75.00	150.00	300.00
❏ MG-25015 [10]	Lester Young Quartet	1950	62.50	125.00	250.00

NORGRAN

Number	Title	Yr	VG	VG+	NM
❏ MGN-5 [10]	Lester Young with the Oscar Peterson Trio No. 1	1954	50.00	100.00	200.00
❏ MGN-6 [10]	Lester Young with the Oscar Peterson Trio No. 2	1954	50.00	100.00	200.00
❏ MGN-1005 [M]	The President	1954	50.00	100.00	200.00
❏ MGN-1022 [M]	Lester Young	1955	50.00	100.00	200.00
❏ MGN-1043 [M]	Pres and Sweets	1955	50.00	100.00	200.00
❏ MGN-1054 [M]	The President Plays with the Oscar Peterson Trio	1955	25.00	50.00	100.00
❏ MGN-1071 [M]	Lester's Here	1956	25.00	50.00	100.00
❏ MGN-1072 [M]	Pres	1956	25.00	50.00	100.00
❏ MGN-1074 [M]	Lester Young and the Buddy Rich Trio	1956	25.00	50.00	100.00
❏ MGN-1093 [M]	Lester Swings Again	1956	25.00	50.00	100.00
❏ MGN-1100 [M]	Lester Young	1956	25.00	50.00	100.00

SAVOY

Number	Title	Yr	VG	VG+	NM
❏ MG-12068 [M]	Blue Lester	1956	20.00	40.00	80.00
❏ MG-12071 [M]	The Master's Touch	1956	20.00	40.00	80.00
❏ MG-12155 [M]	The Immortal Lester Young	1959	15.00	30.00	60.00
❏ MG-9002 [10]	Lester Young (All Star Be Bop)	1951	75.00	150.00	300.00

SCORE

Number	Title	Yr	VG	VG+	NM
❏ SLP-4019 [M]	Lester Young / The King Cole Trio	1958	20.00	40.00	80.00
❏ SLP-4028 [M]	Swinging Lester Young	1958	20.00	40.00	80.00
❏ SLP-4029 [M]	The Great Lester Young	1958	20.00	40.00	80.00

VERVE

Number	Title	Yr	VG	VG+	NM
❏ VSP-27 [M]	The Pres & His Cabinet	1966	6.25	12.50	25.00
❏ VSP-30 [M]	Giants 3	1966	6.25	12.50	25.00
-- With Buddy Rich and Nat King Cole					
❏ MGVS-6054 [S]	Laughin' to Keep from Cryin'	1960	17.50	35.00	70.00
❏ MGV-8134 [M]	Pres and Sweets	1957	15.00	30.00	60.00
❏ V-8134 [M]	Pres and Sweets	1961	6.25	12.50	25.00
❏ MGV-8144 [M]	The President Plays with the Oscar Peterson Trio	1957	15.00	30.00	60.00
❏ V-8144 [M]	The President Plays with the Oscar Peterson Trio	1961	6.25	12.50	25.00
❏ MGV-8161 [M]	Lester's Here	1957	15.00	30.00	60.00
❏ V-8161 [M]	Lester's Here	1961	6.25	12.50	25.00
❏ MGV-8162 [M]	Pres	1957	15.00	30.00	60.00
❏ V-8162 [M]	Pres	1961	6.25	12.50	25.00
❏ MGV-8164 [M]	Lester Young and the Buddy Rich Trio	1957	15.00	30.00	60.00
❏ V-8164 [M]	Lester Young and the Buddy Rich Trio	1961	6.25	12.50	25.00
❏ MGV-8181 [M]	Lester Swings Again	1957	15.00	30.00	60.00
❏ V-8181 [M]	Lester Swings Again	1961	6.25	12.50	25.00
❏ MGV-8187 [M]	It Don't Mean a Thing (If It Ain't Got That Swing)	1957	15.00	30.00	60.00
❏ V-8187 [M]	It Don't Mean a Thing (If It Ain't Got That Swing)	1961	6.25	12.50	25.00
❏ MGV-8205 [M]	Pres and Teddy	1957	15.00	30.00	60.00
❏ V-8205 [M]	Pres and Teddy	1961	6.25	12.50	25.00
❏ MGV-8298 [M]	Going for Myself	1959	15.00	30.00	60.00
❏ V-8298 [M]	Going for Myself	1961	6.25	12.50	25.00
❏ MGV-8308 [M]	The Lester Young Story	1959	15.00	30.00	60.00
❏ V-8308 [M]	The Lester Young Story	1961	6.25	12.50	25.00
❏ MGV-8316 [M]	Laughin' to Keep from Cryin'	1960	15.00	30.00	60.00
❏ V-8316 [M]	Laughin' to Keep from Cryin'	1961	6.25	12.50	25.00
❏ V6-8316 [S]	Laughin' to Keep from Cryin'	1961	7.50	15.00	30.00
❏ MGV-8378 [M]	Lester Young in Paris	1960	15.00	30.00	60.00
❏ V-8378 [M]	Lester Young in Paris	1961	6.25	12.50	25.00
❏ MGV-8398 [M]	The Essential Lester Young	1961	15.00	30.00	60.00
❏ V-8398 [M]	The Essential Lester Young	1961	6.25	12.50	25.00

YOUNG, NEIL

Also see BUFFALO SPRINGFIELD; CROSBY, STILL, NASH & YOUNG.

GEFFEN

Number	Title	Yr	VG	VG+	NM
❏ GHS 2018 [DJ]	Trans	1982	5.00	10.00	20.00
-- Promo on Quiex II audiophile vinyl					
❏ GHS 4013	Everybody's Rockin'	1983	5.00	10.00	20.00
-- Promo on Quiex II audiophile vinyl					

MOBILE FIDELITY

Number	Title	Yr	VG	VG+	NM
❏ 1-252	Old Ways	1996	5.00	10.00	20.00
-- Audiophile vinyl					

NAUTILUS

Number	Title	Yr	VG	VG+	NM
❏ NR-44	Harvest	1982	37.50	75.00	150.00
-- Audiophile vinyl					

REPRISE

Number	Title	Yr	VG	VG+	NM
❏ M 2151 [M-DJ]	Time Fades Away	1973	25.00	50.00	100.00
-- Special mono pressing for radio stations					
❏ MS 2151 [S-DJ]	Time Fades Away	1973	50.00	100.00	200.00
-- With a cardboard inner sleeve, withdrawn after the earliest pressing					
❏ 3RS 2257 [(3)]	Decade	1977	5.00	10.00	20.00
❏ 3RS 2257 [(3) DJ]	Decade	1977	125.00	250.00	500.00
-- Test pressing; "Campaigner" contains extra verse deleted from the final version					
❏ MSK 2266	Comes A Time	1978	18.75	37.50	75.00
-- With "Lotta Love" listed and playing as the last song on side 1					
❏ MSK 2266 [DJ]	Ode to the Wind	1978	250.00	500.00	1,000.
-- Test pressing; plain white jacket with inserts. Title changed to "Comes A Time" for commercial release					
❏ MSK 2283	After the Gold Rush	1978	10.00	20.00	40.00
-- Contains remixed extended version of "When You Dance I Can Really Love." Title on cover in red,"RE 2" in trail-off vinyl					
❏ RS 6317	Neil Young	1968	50.00	100.00	200.00
-- Brown and orange "Reprise/W7" label, no name on front cover, no "RE-1" in trail-off wax					
❏ RS 6317	Neil Young	1969	15.00	30.00	60.00
-- Re-release: Brown and orange "Reprise/W7" label, no name on front cover, four tracks remixed ("RE 1" in trail-off wax)					
❏ RS 6349	Everybody Knows This Is Nowhere	1969	7.50	15.00	30.00
-- Brown and orange "Reprise/W7" label					
❏ RS 6349 [DJ]	Everybody Knows This Is Nowhere	1969	18.75	37.50	75.00
-- White label promo					
❏ RS 6383	After the Gold Rush	1970	8.75	17.50	35.00
-- Brown and orange label; photo of Neil Young appears erroneously printed upside down in gatefold					
❏ RS 6383	After the Gold Rush	1970	10.00	20.00	40.00
-- Brown and orange label; photo of Marc Bolan (of T. Rex) appears erroneously in gatefold					
❏ 2XS 6480 [(2)]	Journey Through the Past (Soundtrack)	1972	5.00	10.00	20.00
❏ 26315	Ragged Glory	1990	5.00	10.00	20.00

WARNER BROS.

Number	Title	Yr	VG	VG+	NM
❏ WBMS-107 [DJ]	The Warner Bros. Music Show	1979	12.50	25.00	50.00
-- Promo-only interview album					

YOUNG-HOLT UNLIMITED

BRUNSWICK

Number	Title	Yr	VG	VG+	NM
❏ BL 54121 [M]	Wack-Wack	1966	5.00	10.00	20.00
-- As "Young-Holt Trio"					
❏ BL 54125 [M]	On Stage	1967	5.00	10.00	20.00
-- As "Young-Holt Trio"					
❏ BL 54128 [M]	The Beat Goes On	1967	7.50	15.00	30.00
❏ BL 754121 [S]	Wack-Wack	1966	5.00	10.00	20.00
-- As "Young-Holt Trio"					
❏ BL 754125 [S]	On Stage	1967	5.00	10.00	20.00
-- As "Young-Holt Trio"					
❏ BL 754128 [S]	The Beat Goes On	1967	5.00	10.00	20.00
❏ BL 754141	Funky But!	1968	5.00	10.00	20.00

YOUNGBLOODS, THE

Also see JESSE COLIN YOUNG.

MERCURY

Number	Title	Yr	VG	VG+	NM
❏ SR-61273	Two Trips	1970	6.25	12.50	25.00
-- Gold border on cover					
❏ SR-61273	Two Trips	1971	5.00	10.00	20.00
-- Red border on cover					

RCA VICTOR

Number	Title	Yr	VG	VG+	NM
❏ LPM-3724 [M]	The Youngbloods	1967	10.00	20.00	40.00
❏ LSP-3724 [S]	The Youngbloods	1967	6.25	12.50	25.00
❏ LPM-3865 [M]	Earth Music	1968	12.50	25.00	50.00
❏ LSP-3865 [S]	Earth Music	1968	6.25	12.50	25.00

YOUNGMAN, HENNY

URANIA

Number	Title	Yr	VG	VG+	NM
❏ UR-9014 [M]	The Horse and Auto Race Game	195?	12.50	25.00	50.00

YUM YUM KIDS, THE

MGM

Number	Title	Yr	VG	VG+	NM
❏ SE-4396 [S]	Yummy in Your Tummy	1966	5.00	10.00	20.00

YURO, TIMI

LIBERTY

Number	Title	Yr	VG	VG+	NM
❏ LRP-3208 [M]	Hurt	1961	10.00	20.00	40.00
❏ LST-7208 [S]	Hurt	1961	12.50	25.00	50.00
❏ LST-7212 [S]	Soul	1962	5.00	10.00	20.00
❏ LST-7234 [S]	Let Me Call You Sweetheart	1962	5.00	10.00	20.00
❏ LST-7263 [S]	What's a Matter Baby?	1963	5.00	10.00	20.00
❏ LST-7286 [S]	The Best of Timi Yuro	1963	5.00	10.00	20.00
❏ LST-7319 [S]	Make the World Go Away	1963	5.00	10.00	20.00

Z

ZABACH, FLORIAN
DECCA

Number	Title	Yr	VG	VG+	NM
❑ DL 5367 [10]	The Hot Canary	1951	12.50	25.00	50.00
❑ DL 8086 [M]	Hour of Love	195?	6.25	12.50	25.00
-- Black label, silver print					
❑ DL 8158 [M]	Dream of Romance	195?	6.25	12.50	25.00
-- Black label, silver print					
❑ DL 8239 [M]	Hi-Fi Fiddle	195?	6.25	12.50	25.00
-- Black label, silver print					

ZACHERLE, JOHN
CRESTVIEW

Number	Title	Yr	VG	VG+	NM
❑ CR 803 [M]	Zacherle's Monster Gallery	1963	10.00	20.00	40.00
❑ CRS 7803 [S]	Zacherle's Monster Gallery	1963	12.50	25.00	50.00

ELEKTRA

❑ EKL-190 [M]	Spook Along with Zacherle	1960	15.00	30.00	60.00
❑ EKS-7190 [S]	Spook Along with Zacherle	1960	20.00	40.00	80.00

PARKWAY

❑ P 7018 [M]	Monster Mash	1962	15.00	30.00	60.00
❑ P 7023 [M]	Scary Tales	1963	15.00	30.00	60.00

ZAGER AND EVANS
RCA VICTOR

Number	Title	Yr	VG	VG+	NM
❑ LSP-4214	2525 (Exordium & Terminus)	1969	5.00	10.00	20.00
❑ LSP-4302	Zager and Evans	1970	5.00	10.00	20.00

WHITE WHALE

❑ WWS-7123	The Early Writings of Zager and Evans	1969	5.00	10.00	20.00

ZANIES, THE
DORE

Number	Title	Yr	VG	VG+	NM
❑ 321	The Zanies	1969	7.50	15.00	30.00

ZAPPA, FRANK
Includes the Mothers of Invention.
BARKING PUMPKIN

Number	Title	Yr	VG	VG+	NM
❑ 7X4-1	The Old Masters Sampler	1984	6.25	12.50	25.00
❑ AS 995 [DJ]	Tinsel Town Rebellion	1981	5.00	10.00	20.00
-- Promo-only sampler					
❑ BPR-1111	Shut Up 'N' Play Yer Guitar	1981	5.00	10.00	20.00
-- Mail-order item only					
❑ BPR-1112	Shut Up 'N' Play Yer Guitar Some More	1981	5.00	10.00	20.00
-- Mail-order item only					
❑ BPR-1113	Return of the Son of Shut Up 'N' Play Yer Guitar	1981	5.00	10.00	20.00
-- Mail-order item only					
❑ AS 1294 [DJ]	You Are What You Is Special Clean Cuts Edition	1981	5.00	10.00	20.00
❑ 7777 [(8)]	The Old Masters, Box 1	1984	15.00	30.00	60.00
-- Boxed set					
❑ 8888 [(8)]	The Old Masters, Box 2	1986	15.00	30.00	60.00
-- Another boxed set					
❑ 8888X	The Old Masters Sampler 2	1986	6.25	12.50	25.00
❑ 9999 [(8)]	The Old Masters, Box 3	1987	15.00	30.00	60.00
-- Still another boxed set					
❑ PW2 37336 [(2)]	Tinsel Town Rebellion	1981	5.00	10.00	20.00
❑ PW2 37537 [(2)]	You Are What You Is	1981	5.00	10.00	20.00
❑ W3X-38290 [(3)]	Shut Up 'N' Play Yer Guitar	1982	6.25	12.50	25.00
-- Box set containing all three "Shut Up 'N' Play Yer Guitar" albums					
❑ SWCO-74201 [(3)]	Thing-Fish	1984	5.00	10.00	20.00
❑ 74206 [(3)]	Joe's Garage, Acts 1, 2 and 3	1986	12.50	25.00	50.00
-- Box set, two gatefolds, with insert					

BIZARRE

❑ MS-2024 [(2)]	Uncle Meat	1969	8.75	17.50	35.00
-- Originals come with a booklet; blue label					
❑ MS-2024 [(2)]	Uncle Meat	1973	5.00	10.00	20.00
-- Reissue with brown Reprise label					
❑ MS-2028	Weasels Ripped My Flesh	1970	6.25	12.50	25.00
-- Blue label original					
❑ MS-2030	Chunga's Revenge	1970	6.25	12.50	25.00
-- Blue label original					
❑ MS 2030 [DJ]	Chunga's Revenge	1970	12.50	25.00	50.00
-- White label promo					
❑ MS-2042	Fillmore East, June 1971	1971	6.25	12.50	25.00
-- Blue label original					
❑ MS 2075	Just Another Band from L.A.	1972	6.25	12.50	25.00
-- Blue label original					
❑ MS 2093	The Grand Wazoo	1972	6.25	12.50	25.00
-- Blue label original					

Number	Title	Yr	VG	VG+	NM
❑ MS 2094	Waka/Jawaka	1972	6.25	12.50	25.00
-- Blue label original					
❑ RS-6356	Hot Rats	1969	12.50	25.00	50.00
-- Blue label original					
❑ RS-6370	Burnt Weenie Sandwich	1970	6.25	12.50	25.00
-- Blue label original; with booklet					

COLUMBIA

❑ (no #) [(4) DJ]	Lather	1977	187.50	375.00	750.00
-- Test pressing only; parts of this LP are on DSK 2291, 2292 and 2294; released as a whole only after Zappa's death, with vinyl only coming out in Japan					

DISCREET

❑ MS 2149	Over-Nite Sensation	1973	5.00	10.00	20.00
❑ MS4 2149 [Q]	Over-Nite Sensation	1973	10.00	20.00	40.00
❑ DS 2175	Apostrophe (')	1974	12.50	25.00	50.00
-- White label promo					
❑ 2DS 2202 [(2)]	Roxy & Elsewhere	1974	6.25	12.50	25.00
❑ 2D 2290 [(2)]	Zappa in New York	1978	62.50	125.00	250.00
-- Stock copy with "Punky's Whips" erroneously listed on jacket					
❑ 2D 2290 [(2)]	Zappa in New York	1978	5.00	10.00	20.00
❑ 2D 2290 [(2)	Zappa in New York	1978	100.00	200.00	400.00
-- Test pressing with "Punky's Whips"					
❑ DS4 2175 [Q]	Apostrophe (')	1974	8.75	17.50	35.00

FOO-EEE

❑ R1-70372 [(11)]	Beat the Boots #2	1992	25.00	50.00	100.00
-- Legitimate box-set release by Rhino of 11 bootlegged concerts					
❑ R1-70907 [(10)]	Beat the Boots	1991	25.00	50.00	100.00
-- Legitimate box-set release by Rhino of eight bootlegged concerts					

MGM

❑ GAS-112	The Mothers of Invention	1970	12.50	25.00	50.00
❑ GAS-112 [DJ]	The Mothers of Invention	1970	25.00	50.00	100.00
-- Yellow label promo					
❑ SE-4754	The Worst of the Mothers	1971	12.50	25.00	50.00
❑ SE-4754 [DJ]	The Worst of the Mothers	1971	37.50	75.00	150.00
-- Yellow label promo					

RHINO/DEL-FI

❑ RNEP-604	Rare Meat: The Early Productions of Frank Zappa	1984	10.00	20.00	40.00
-- With original cover					

RYKO ANALOGUE

❑ RALP 40500 [(2)]	Strictly Commercial: The Best of Frank Zappa	1995	5.00	10.00	20.00
-- Issued with obi					

UNITED ARTISTS

❑ UAS-9956 [(2)]	200 Motels (movie soundtrack)	1971	12.50	25.00	50.00

VERVE

❑ V-5005-2 [(2) M]	Freak Out!	1966	100.00	200.00	400.00
-- White label promo					
❑ V-5005-2 [(2) M]	Freak Out!	1966	50.00	100.00	200.00
-- Cover version 1: Has blurb on inside gatefold on how to get a map of "freak-out hot spots" in L.A.					
❑ V-5005-2 [(2) M]	Freak Out!	1966	37.50	75.00	150.00
-- Cover version 2: Has no blurb inside on getting a map of "freak-out hot spots"					
❑ V6-5005-2 [(2) S]	Freak Out!	1966	75.00	150.00	300.00
-- Yellow label promo					
❑ V6-5005-2 [(2) S]	Freak Out!	1966	20.00	40.00	80.00
-- Cover version 1: Has blurb on inside gatefold on how to get a map of "freak-out hot spots" in L.A.					
❑ V6-5005-2 [(2) S]	Freak Out!	1966	15.00	30.00	60.00
-- Cover version 2: Has no blurb inside on getting a map of "freak-out hot spots"					
❑ V-5013 [M]	Absolutely Free	1967	50.00	100.00	200.00
-- White label promo					
❑ V-5013 [M]	Absolutely Free	1967	30.00	60.00	120.00
❑ V6-5013 [S]	Absolutely Free	1967	15.00	30.00	60.00
❑ V-5045 [M]	We're Only In It for the Money	1968	75.00	150.00	300.00
-- White label promo					
❑ V-5045 [M]	We're Only In It for the Money	1968	37.50	75.00	150.00
-- With sheet of cut-outs a la "Sgt. Pepper's Lonely Hearts Club Band"					
❑ V6-5045 [S]	We're Only In It for the Money	1968	15.00	30.00	60.00
-- Un-censored version, with cut-outs					
❑ V6-5045 [S]	We're Only In It for the Money	1968	37.50	75.00	150.00
-- Censored version: the songs "Who Needs the Peace Corps?" and "Let's Make the Water Turn Black" have lines deleted					
❑ V6-5055	Cruising with Ruben and the Jets	1968	15.00	30.00	60.00
❑ V6-5055 [DJ]	Cruising with Ruben and the Jets	1968	37.50	75.00	150.00
-- Yellow label promo					
❑ V6-5068	Mothermania -- The Best of the Mothers	1969	18.75	37.50	75.00
❑ V6-5068 [DJ]	Mothermania -- The Best of the Mothers	1969	37.50	75.00	150.00
-- Yellow label promo					
❑ V6-5074	The XXXX of the Mothers	1969	12.50	25.00	50.00
❑ V6-5074 [DJ]	The XXXX of the Mothers	1969	37.50	75.00	150.00
-- Yellow label promo					
❑ V6-8741	Lumpy Gravy	1968	12.50	25.00	50.00
❑ V6-8741 [DJ]	Lumpy Gravy	1968	50.00	100.00	200.00
-- Yellow label promo					

ZAPPA

❑ MK-78 [DJ]	Sheik Yerbouti Clean Cuts	1979	8.75	17.50	35.00

Number	Title	Yr	VG	VG+	NM
❏ MK-129 [DJ]	Joe's Garage Acts I, II and III Sampler	1980	8.75	17.50	35.00
❏ SRZ-2-1501	Sheik Yerbouti	1979	5.00	10.00	20.00
❏ SRZ-2-1502	Joe's Garage, Acts II and III	1980	5.00	10.00	20.00

ZAZU
WOODEN NICKEL

Number	Title	Yr	VG	VG+	NM
❏ BWL1-0791	Zazu	1975	5.00	10.00	20.00

ZENITHS, THE
ATLANTIC

Number	Title	Yr	VG	VG+	NM
❏ 8043 [M]	Makin' the Scene	1960	25.00	50.00	100.00
❏ SD 8043 [S]	Makin' the Scene	1960	37.50	75.00	150.00

ZENTNER, SI
SMASH

Number	Title	Yr	VG	VG+	NM
❏ SRS-67007 [S]	Presenting Si Zentner	1961	5.00	10.00	20.00
❏ SRS-67013 [S]	Swing Fever	1962	5.00	10.00	20.00

ZENTNER, SI AND MARTIN DENNY
LIBERTY

Number	Title	Yr	VG	VG+	NM
❏ LSS-14020 [S]	Exotica Suite	1962	5.00	10.00	20.00

ZEPHYR
PROBE

Number	Title	Yr	VG	VG+	NM
❏ 4510	Zephyr	1969	12.50	25.00	50.00

WARNER BROS.

Number	Title	Yr	VG	VG+	NM
❏ WS 1897	Goin' Back to Colorado	1971	10.00	20.00	40.00
❏ BS 2603	Sunset Ride	1972	5.00	10.00	20.00

ZERFAS
700 WEST

Number	Title	Yr	VG	VG+	NM
❏ 730710	Zerfas	1973	200.00	400.00	800.00

ZERO BOYS
NIMROD

Number	Title	Yr	VG	VG+	NM
❏ (# unknown)	Vicious Circle	1982	25.00	50.00	100.00

TOXIC SHOCK

Number	Title	Yr	VG	VG+	NM
❏ TXLP 11	Vicious Circle	1987	6.25	12.50	25.00

-- Reissue of Nimrod release

ZEVON, WARREN
IMPERIAL

Number	Title	Yr	VG	VG+	NM
❏ LP-12456	Wanted Dead or Alive	1970	5.00	10.00	20.00

-- As "Zevon"

ZIG ZAG PEOPLE, THE
DECCA

Number	Title	Yr	VG	VG+	NM
❏ DL 75110	The Zig Zag People Take Bubble Gum Music Underground	1969	6.25	12.50	25.00

ZIP CODES, THE
LIBERTY

Number	Title	Yr	VG	VG+	NM
❏ LRP-3367 [M]	Mustang	1964	37.50	75.00	150.00
❏ LST-7367 [S]	Mustang	1964	50.00	100.00	200.00

ZIPPERS, THE
RHINO

Number	Title	Yr	VG	VG+	NM
❏ RNEP 601 [EP]	Six Song Mini Album	1981	7.50	15.00	30.00

ZIRCONS, THE
SNOWFLAKE

Number	Title	Yr	VG	VG+	NM
❏ 1003	The Crown Kings of Acappella	196?	15.00	30.00	60.00

ZOMBIES, THE
DATE

Number	Title	Yr	VG	VG+	NM
❏ TES-4013	Odessy and Oracle	1968	7.50	15.00	30.00

-- With no mention of "Time of the Season" on front cover

Number	Title	Yr	VG	VG+	NM
❏ TES-4013	Odessy and Oracle	1969	5.00	10.00	20.00

-- With "Time of the Season" mentioned on front cover

EPIC

Number	Title	Yr	VG	VG+	NM
❏ KEG 32861 [(2) B]	Time of the Zombies	1974	5.00	10.00	20.00

-- Record 1 is mono; Record 2 is stereo; orange labels

LONDON

Number	Title	Yr	VG	VG+	NM
❏ PS 557 [P]	Early Days	1969	5.00	10.00	20.00

-- All tracks in true stereo except "Tell Her No"

PARROT

Number	Title	Yr	VG	VG+	NM
❏ PA 61001 [M]	The Zombies	1965	15.00	30.00	60.00
❏ PAS 71001 [R]	The Zombies	1965	10.00	20.00	40.00

ZOO, THE
MERCURY

Number	Title	Yr	VG	VG+	NM
❏ SR-61300	The Zoo	1970	5.00	10.00	20.00

SUNBURST

Number	Title	Yr	VG	VG+	NM
❏ 7500	The Zoo Presents the Chocolate Moose	1968	12.50	25.00	50.00

ZZ TOP
LONDON

Number	Title	Yr	VG	VG+	NM
❏ PS-X-1001 [DJ]	Takin' Texas to the People	1976	12.50	25.00	50.00

Label, Number	Yr	VG	VG+	NM

ORIGINAL CAST RECORDINGS

Includes Broadway, off-Broadway and other similar albums, but not plays staged for television. Those are in the "Television Albums" section.

ALL AMERICAN
- Columbia Masterworks KOS 2160 [S] | 1962 | 7.50 | 15.00 | 30.00
- Columbia Masterworks KOL 5760 [M] | 1962 | 6.25 | 12.50 | 25.00

ANKLES AWEIGHT
- Decca DL 9025 [M] | 1955 | 10.00 | 20.00 | 40.00

ANNIE GET YOUR GUN
- Decca DL 8001 [M] | 1949 | 12.50 | 25.00 | 50.00
-- Original LP issue of the Broadway cast
- Decca DL 9018 [M] | 1955 | 10.00 | 20.00 | 40.00
-- Early reissue of DL 8001; black label with silver print

ANYA
- United Artists UAL-4133 [M] | 1965 | 5.00 | 10.00 | 20.00
- United Artists UAS-5133 [S] | 1965 | 12.50 | 25.00 | 50.00

APPLAUSE
- ABC ABCS-OC-11 | 1970 | 5.00 | 10.00 | 20.00

THE APPLE TREE
- Columbia Masterworks KOS 3020 [S] | 1966 | 6.25 | 12.50 | 25.00
- Columbia Masterworks KOL 6620 [M] | 1966 | 5.00 | 10.00 | 20.00

ARABIAN NIGHTS
- Decca DL 9013 [M] | 1954 | 20.00 | 40.00 | 80.00

THE ATHENIAN TOUCH
- Broadway East OCM-101 [M] | 1964 | 37.50 | 75.00 | 150.00
- Broadway East OCS-101 [S] | 1964 | 50.00 | 100.00 | 200.00

BAJOUR
- Columbia Masterworks KOS 2700 [S] | 1964 | 7.50 | 15.00 | 30.00
- Columbia Masterworks KOL 6300 [M] | 1964 | 6.25 | 12.50 | 25.00

BAKER STREET (A MUSICAL ADVENTURE OF SHERLOCK HOLMES)
- MGM E-7000 [M] | 1965 | 6.25 | 12.50 | 25.00
- MGM SE-7000 [S] | 1965 | 7.50 | 15.00 | 30.00

A BALLAD FOR BIMSHIRE
- London AM 48002 [M] | 1963 | 10.00 | 20.00 | 40.00
- London AMS 78002 [S] | 1963 | 20.00 | 40.00 | 80.00

THE BALLAD OF BABY DOE
- MGM 3GC-1 [(3) M] | 1958 | 37.50 | 75.00 | 150.00
-- Box set

THE BAND WAGON
- "X" LVA-1001 [M] | 1955 | 17.50 | 35.00 | 70.00

BELLS ARE RINGING
- Columbia Masterworks OS 2006 [S] | 1959 | 6.25 | 12.50 | 25.00
-- Re-recording in stereo of OL 5170
- Columbia Masterworks OL 5170 [M] | 1957 | 7.50 | 15.00 | 30.00
-- Gray and black label with six "eye" logos

BEN FRANKLIN IN PARIS
- Capitol SVAS 2191 [S] | 1964 | 7.50 | 15.00 | 30.00
- Capitol VAS 2191 [M] | 1964 | 6.25 | 12.50 | 25.00

BEST FOOT FORWARD
- Cadence CLP-4012 [M] | 1963 | 5.00 | 10.00 | 20.00
- Cadence CLP-24012 [S] | 1963 | 7.50 | 15.00 | 30.00
-- 1963 revival of 1941 play

BEYOND THE FRINGE
- Capitol SW 1792 [S] | 1962 | 7.50 | 15.00 | 30.00
- Capitol W 1792 [M] | 1962 | 6.25 | 12.50 | 25.00

BEYOND THE FRINGE '64
- Capitol SW 2072 [S] | 1964 | 6.25 | 12.50 | 25.00
- Capitol W 2072 [M] | 1964 | 5.00 | 10.00 | 20.00

THE BOY FRIEND
- RCA Victor LOC-1018 [M] | 1954 | 7.50 | 15.00 | 30.00
-- Originals have green labels

THE BOYS IN THE BAND
- A&M SP-6001 [(2)] | 1969 | 6.25 | 12.50 | 25.00

BRAVO, GIOVANNI
- Columbia Masterworks KOS 2200 [S] | 1962 | 5.00 | 10.00 | 20.00

BRIGADOON
- RCA Victor LOC-1001 [M] | 1951 | 7.50 | 15.00 | 30.00
-- Green front cover; green label
- RCA Victor LOC-1001 [M] | 195? | 5.00 | 10.00 | 20.00
-- Photos of kilted dancers on front cover; black "Long Play" label

BY JUPITER
- RCA Victor LOC-1137 [M] | 1967 | 10.00 | 20.00 | 40.00
- RCA Victor LSO-1137 [S] | 1967 | 18.75 | 37.50 | 75.00
-- Above is by a revival cast

BY THE BEAUTIFUL SEA
- Capitol S 531 [M] | 1954 | 17.50 | 35.00 | 70.00

BYE BYE BIRDIE
- Columbia Masterworks KOS 2025 [S] | 1960 | 7.50 | 15.00 | 30.00
-- Gray and black label with six "eye" logos; with gatefold cover
- Columbia Masterworks KOL 5510 [M] | 1960 | 6.25 | 12.50 | 25.00
-- Gray and black label with six "eye" logos; with gatefold cover
- Columbia Masterworks OS 2025 [S] | 196? | 6.25 | 12.50 | 25.00
-- Gray and black label with six "eye" logos; with regular cover
- Columbia Masterworks OL 5510 [M] | 196? | 5.00 | 10.00 | 20.00
-- Gray and black label with six "eye" logos; with regular cover

CABARET
- Columbia Masterworks KOS 3040 [S] | 1966 | 5.00 | 10.00 | 20.00

CABIN IN THE SKY
- Capitol SW 2073 [S] | 1964 | 12.50 | 25.00 | 50.00
- Capitol W 2073 [M] | 1964 | 7.50 | 15.00 | 30.00
-- Above is by a revival cast

CALL ME MADAM
- RCA Victor LOC-1000 [M] | 1950 | 20.00 | 40.00 | 80.00
-- Dinah Shore sings Ethel Merman's part for contractual reasons, otherwise it's by the entire original cast

CAMELOT
- Columbia Masterworks KOS 2031 [S] | 1960 | 6.25 | 12.50 | 25.00
-- Gray and black label with six "eye" logos; gatefold cover
- Columbia Masterworks KOL 5620 [M] | 1960 | 5.00 | 10.00 | 20.00
-- Gray and black label with six "eye" logos

CAN-CAN
- Capitol S 452 [M] | 1953 | 6.25 | 12.50 | 25.00
-- Originals have red labels with Capitol logo at top

CANTERBURY TALES
- Capitol SW-229 | 1969 | 6.25 | 12.50 | 25.00

CAPTAIN JINKS OF THE HORSE MARINES
- RCA Victor ARL2-1727 [(2)] | 1975 | 7.50 | 15.00 | 30.00
-- Box set

CARMEN JONES
- Decca DL 8014 [M] | 1949 | 10.00 | 20.00 | 40.00
-- Black label, gold print
- Decca DL 9021 [M] | 1955 | 5.00 | 10.00 | 20.00
-- Reissue of 8014; black label, silver print

CARNIVAL
- MGM E-3946 [M] | 1961 | 5.00 | 10.00 | 20.00
- MGM SE-3946 [S] | 1961 | 6.25 | 12.50 | 25.00
-- Black label

CAROUSEL
- Command RS-843 SD [M] | 1962 | 5.00 | 10.00 | 20.00
-- Studio cast with Alfred Drake and Roberta Peters, and Enoch Light's orchestra
- Decca DL 8003 [M] | 1949 | 10.00 | 20.00 | 40.00
-- Original LP issue of the Broadway cast
- Decca DL 9020 [M] | 1955 | 7.50 | 15.00 | 30.00
-- Early reissue of DL 8003; black label with silver print

A CHORUS LINE
- Columbia HS 43581 | 1981 | 10.00 | 20.00 | 40.00
-- Half-speed mastered edition

CHRISTINE
- Columbia Masterworks OL 5520 [M] | 1960 | 15.00 | 30.00 | 60.00
- Columbia Masterworks OS 2026 [S] | 1960 | 25.00 | 50.00 | 100.00

CINDY
- ABC-Paramount ABC-OC-2 [M] | 1964 | 7.50 | 15.00 | 30.00
- ABC-Paramount ABC-OCS-2 [S] | 1964 | 12.50 | 25.00 | 50.00

CLOWNAROUND
- RCA Victor LSP-4741 | 1972 | 62.50 | 125.00 | 250.00

CLUB 15
- Decca DL 5155 [10] | 1949 | 15.00 | 30.00 | 60.00

THE COACH WITH THE SIX INSIDES
- ESP-Disk' 1019 [M] | 1967 | 6.25 | 12.50 | 25.00

COCO
- Paramount PMS-1002 | 1969 | 6.25 | 12.50 | 25.00

THE COMMITTEE
- Reprise F-2023 [M] | 1964 | 7.50 | 15.00 | 30.00
- Reprise FS-2023 [S] | 1964 | 10.00 | 20.00 | 40.00

Label, Number	Yr	VG	VG+	NM
COMPANY				
❏ Columbia Masterworks SQ 30993 [Q]	1971	7.50	15.00	30.00
-- *Quadraphonic version has substantially different mixes than the original stereo LP*				
THE CRADLE WILL ROCK				
❏ MGM E-4289-2 [(2) M]	1964	6.25	12.50	25.00
❏ MGM SE-4289-2 [(2) S]	1964	7.50	15.00	30.00
-- *The above is by a revival cast*				
THE CRITIC				
❏ Decca DL 9154 [M]	1967	5.00	10.00	20.00
❏ Decca DL 79154 [S]	1967	5.00	10.00	20.00
CRY FOR US ALL				
❏ Project 3 TS-1000 SD	1970	10.00	20.00	40.00
DAMES AT SEA				
❏ Columbia Masterworks OS 3550	1969	5.00	10.00	20.00
DAMN YANKEES				
❏ RCA Victor LOC-1021 [M]	1955	7.50	15.00	30.00
-- *Green cover*				
❏ RCA Victor LOC-1021 [M]	195?	5.00	10.00	20.00
-- *Orange cover*				
THE DANCERS OF BALI				
❏ Columbia Masterworks ML 4618 [M]	1952	10.00	20.00	40.00
DARLING OF THE DAY				
❏ RCA Victor LOC-1149 [M]	1968	10.00	20.00	40.00
❏ RCA Victor LSO-1149 [S]	1968	15.00	30.00	60.00
DEAR WORLD				
❏ Columbia Masterworks BOS 3260	1969	5.00	10.00	20.00
DEATH OF A SALESMAN				
❏ Decca DX 102 [(2) M]	1951	10.00	20.00	40.00
-- *Two-record boxed set with contents of 9006 and 9007*				
DEATH OF A SALESMAN (PART 1)				
❏ Decca DL 9006 [M]	1951	6.25	12.50	25.00
-- *Black label, gold print*				
DEATH OF A SALESMAN (PART 2)				
❏ Decca DL 9007 [M]	1951	6.25	12.50	25.00
-- *Black label, gold print*				
DESTRY RIDES AGAIN				
❏ Decca DL 9075 [M]	1959	7.50	15.00	30.00
❏ Decca DL 79075 [S]	1959	10.00	20.00	40.00
DO I HEAR A WALTZ?				
❏ Columbia Masterworks KOS 2770 [S]	1965	5.00	10.00	20.00
DO RE MI				
❏ RCA Victor LSO-1105 [S]	1965	5.00	10.00	20.00
-- *Reissue of 2002 with standard red cover*				
❏ RCA Victor LOCD-2002 [M]	1961	7.50	15.00	30.00
-- *In black box with orange sleeve*				
❏ RCA Victor LSOD-2002 [S]	1961	10.00	20.00	40.00
-- *In black box with orange sleeve*				
DOCTOR SELAVY'S MAGIC THEATRE				
❏ United Artists UA-LA196-G	1974	7.50	15.00	30.00
DONNYBROOK!				
❏ Kapp KD-8500-S [S]	1961	6.25	12.50	25.00
❏ Kapp KDL-8500 [M]	1961	5.00	10.00	20.00
DRESSED TO THE NINES				
❏ MGM E-3914 [M]	1960	6.25	12.50	25.00
❏ MGM SE-3914 [S]	1960	10.00	20.00	40.00
THE EARL OF RUSTON				
❏ Capitol ST-465	1971	10.00	20.00	40.00
ERNEST IN LOVE				
❏ Columbia Masterworks OS 2027 [S]	1960	25.00	50.00	100.00
❏ Columbia Masterworks OL 5530 [M]	1960	15.00	30.00	60.00
AN EVENING WITH RICHARD NIXON				
❏ Ode SP-77015	1972	7.50	15.00	30.00
EVITA				
❏ MCA 2-11003 [(2)]	1976	5.00	10.00	20.00
-- *London cast; white cover; with booklet*				
FADE OUT-FADE IN				
❏ ABC-Paramount ABC-OC-3 [M]	1964	6.25	12.50	25.00
❏ ABC-Paramount ABCS-OC-3 [S]	1964	7.50	15.00	30.00
A FAMILY AFFAIR				
❏ United Artists UAL-4099 [M]	1962	7.50	15.00	30.00
❏ United Artists UAS-5099 [S]	1962	12.50	25.00	50.00
FANNY				
❏ RCA Victor LOC-1015 [M]	1954	6.25	12.50	25.00
-- *"Long Play" on label*				
THE FANTASTICKS				
❏ MGM E-3872 [M]	1963	5.00	10.00	20.00
-- *Original non-gatefold cover*				
❏ MGM SE-3872 [S]	1963	6.25	12.50	25.00
-- *Original non-gatefold cover*				
FIDDLER ON THE ROOF				
❏ RCA Victor LSO-1093 [S]	1964	5.00	10.00	20.00
-- *Black label, dog on top*				
FINIAN'S RAINBOW				
❏ Columbia Masterworks ML 4062 [M]	1948	7.50	15.00	30.00
-- *Original cover with no photo; green label*				
FIORELLO!				
❏ Capitol SWAO 1321 [S]	1959	6.25	12.50	25.00
❏ Capitol WAO 1321 [M]	1959	5.00	10.00	20.00
FIRST IMPRESSIONS				
❏ Columbia Masterworks OS 2014 [S]	1959	15.00	30.00	60.00
❏ Columbia Masterworks OL 5400 [M]	1959	7.50	15.00	30.00
FLAHOOLEY				
❏ Capitol S 284 [M]	1951	37.50	75.00	150.00
FLORA, THE RED MENACE				
❏ RCA Victor LOC-1111 [M]	1965	6.25	12.50	25.00
❏ RCA Victor LSO-1111 [S]	1965	7.50	15.00	30.00
FLOWER DRUM SONG				
❏ Columbia Masterworks OS 2009 [S]	1958	6.25	12.50	25.00
-- *Gray and black label with six "eye" logos*				
❏ Columbia Masterworks OL 5350 [M]	1958	5.00	10.00	20.00
-- *Gray and black label with six "eye" logos*				
FLY BLACKBIRD				
❏ Mercury OCM-2206 [M]	1962	7.50	15.00	30.00
❏ Mercury OCS-6206 [S]	1962	15.00	30.00	60.00
FUNNY GIRL				
❏ Capitol SVAS 2059 [S]	1964	5.00	10.00	20.00
A FUNNY THING HAPPENED ON THE WAY TO THE FORUM				
❏ Capitol SWAO 1717 [S]	1962	5.00	10.00	20.00
-- *Gatefold cover*				
THE GAY LIFE				
❏ Capitol SWAO 1560 [S]	1961	12.50	25.00	50.00
❏ Capitol WAO 1560 [M]	1961	6.25	12.50	25.00
GENTLEMEN PREFER BLONDES				
❏ Columbia Masterworks ML 4290 [M]	1949	6.25	12.50	25.00
-- *Original with green label*				
GEORGE M!				
❏ Columbia Masterworks KOS 3200 [S]	1968	5.00	10.00	20.00
❏ Columbia Masterworks KOL 6800 [M]	1968	7.50	15.00	30.00
THE GIRL IN PINK TIGHTS				
❏ Columbia Masterworks ML 4890 [M]	1954	15.00	30.00	60.00
THE GIRL WHO CAME TO SUPPER				
❏ Columbia Masterworks KOL 6020 [M]	1963	6.25	12.50	25.00
❏ Columbia Masterworks KOS 2420 [S]	1963	7.50	15.00	30.00
GIVE 'EM HELL, HARRY!				
❏ United Artists UA-LA540-H2 [(2)]	1975	5.00	10.00	20.00
THE GOLDEN APPLE				
❏ RCA Victor LOC-1014 [M]	1954	25.00	50.00	100.00
GOLDEN BOY				
❏ Capitol SVAS 2124 [S]	1964	7.50	15.00	30.00
❏ Capitol VAS 2124 [M]	1964	6.25	12.50	25.00
GOLDILOCKS				
❏ Columbia Masterworks OS 2007 [S]	1958	15.00	30.00	60.00
❏ Columbia Masterworks OL 5340 [M]	1958	6.25	12.50	25.00
GOODTIME CHARLEY				
❏ RCA Victor ARL1-1011	1975	7.50	15.00	30.00
THE GREAT WALTZ				
❏ Capitol SVAS 2426 [S]	1965	6.25	12.50	25.00
❏ Capitol VAS 2426 [M]	1965	5.00	10.00	20.00
GREENWICH VILLAGE U.S.A.				
❏ 20th Fox TCF-105-2 [(2) M]	1960	15.00	30.00	60.00
-- *With complete show*				
❏ 20th Fox TCF-105-2S [(2) S]	1960	25.00	50.00	100.00
-- *With complete show*				

Label, Number	Yr	VG	VG+	NM
❏ 20th Fox FOX-4005 [M]	1960	10.00	20.00	40.00
-- With excerpts from the show				
❏ 20th Fox SFX-4005 [S]	1960	12.50	25.00	50.00
-- With excerpts from the show				
GREENWILLOW				
❏ RCA Victor LOC-2001 [M]	1960	5.00	10.00	20.00
❏ RCA Victor LSO-2001 [S]	1960	12.50	25.00	50.00
GYPSY				
❏ Columbia Masterworks OL 5420 [M]	1959	5.00	10.00	20.00
-- Original covers are white with drawings				
❏ Columbia Masterworks OS 2017 [S]	1959	6.25	12.50	25.00
-- Original covers are white with drawings				
HAIR				
❏ Philips PHS 600-329	1969	6.25	12.50	25.00
-- Original French cast				
❏ Atco SD 7002	1969	6.25	12.50	25.00
-- Original London cast; not to be confused with US cast recordings on RCA Victor				
HALF A SIXPENCE				
❏ RCA Victor LOC-1110 [M]	1965	5.00	10.00	20.00
❏ RCA Victor LSO-1110 [S]	1965	6.25	12.50	25.00
HALF PAST WEDNESDAY				
❏ Columbia CL 1917 [M]	1962	7.50	15.00	30.00
❏ Columbia CS 8717 [S]	1962	10.00	20.00	40.00
HAMLET				
❏ Columbia Masterworks DOL 302 [(4) M]	1964	6.25	12.50	25.00
-- Boxed set with entire play (Broadway revival)				
❏ Columbia Masterworks DOS 702 [(4) S]	1964	6.25	12.50	25.00
-- Boxed set with entire play (Broadway revival)				
THE HAPPIEST GIRL IN THE WORLD				
❏ Columbia Masterworks KOS 2050 [S]	1961	15.00	30.00	60.00
-- Original covers are yellow				
❏ Columbia Masterworks KOS 2050 [S]	1961	10.00	20.00	40.00
-- Second covers are white				
❏ Columbia Masterworks KOL 5650 [M]	1961	10.00	20.00	40.00
-- Original covers are yellow				
❏ Columbia Masterworks KOL 5650 [M]	1961	7.50	15.00	30.00
-- Second covers are white				
HAPPY HUNTING				
❏ RCA Victor LOC-1026 [M]	1956	10.00	20.00	40.00
HEAR! HEAR!				
❏ Decca DL 9031 [M]	1955	12.50	25.00	50.00
HELLO, DOLLY!				
❏ RCA Victor LOCD-1087 [M]	1964	6.25	12.50	25.00
-- Original cover is black and white on back and spotlights "Come and Be My Butterfly"; this song was deleted from the show, so the cover was changed				
❏ RCA Victor LSOD-1087 [S]	1964	7.50	15.00	30.00
-- Original cover is black and white on back and spotlights "Come and Be My Butterfly"; this song was deleted from the show, so the cover was changed				
❏ RCA Victor LSOD-1087 [S]	1964	5.00	10.00	20.00
-- New back cover is in color and has a photo of Carol Channing; "RE" is on cover				
HENRY, SWEET HENRY				
❏ ABC ABC-OC-4 [M]	1967	7.50	15.00	30.00
❏ ABC ABCS-OC-4 [S]	1967	12.50	25.00	50.00
HERE'S LOVE				
❏ Columbia Masterworks KOS 2400 [S]	1963	10.00	20.00	40.00
❏ Columbia Masterworks KOL 6000 [M]	1963	7.50	15.00	30.00
HIGH BUTTON SHOES				
❏ RCA Camden CAL-457 [M]	1958	7.50	15.00	30.00
❏ RCA Victor LOC-1107 [M]	1964	10.00	20.00	40.00
❏ RCA Victor LSO-1107 [R]	1964	7.50	15.00	30.00
HIGH SPIRITS				
❏ ABC-Paramount ABC-OC-1 [M]	1964	6.25	12.50	25.00
❏ ABC-Paramount ABCS-OC-1 [S]	1964	7.50	15.00	30.00
HOUSE OF FLOWERS				
❏ Columbia Masterworks ML 4969 [M]	1954	10.00	20.00	40.00
-- Blue label original				
❏ United Artists UAS 5180	1968	10.00	20.00	40.00
-- Revival cast				
HOW NOW, DOW JONES				
❏ RCA Victor LOC-1142 [M]	1967	6.25	12.50	25.00
❏ RCA Victor LSO-1142 [S]	1967	7.50	15.00	30.00
HOW TO SUCCEED IN BUSINESS WITHOUT REALLY TRYING				
❏ RCA Victor LOC-1066 [M]	1961	5.00	10.00	20.00
❏ RCA Victor LSO-1066 [S]	1961	6.25	12.50	25.00
-- Black label, dog on top				
HUGHIE				
❏ Columbia Masterworks OS 2760 [S]	1965	7.50	15.00	30.00
❏ Columbia Masterworks OL 6260 [M]	1965	6.25	12.50	25.00

Label, Number	Yr	VG	VG+	NM
I CAN GET IT FOR YOU WHOLESALE				
❏ Columbia Masterworks KOS 2180 [S]	1962	7.50	15.00	30.00
❏ Columbia Masterworks KOL 5780 [M]	1962	6.25	12.50	25.00
I DO! I DO!				
❏ RCA Victor LSO-1128 [S]	1966	5.00	10.00	20.00
-- Black label, dog on top				
I HAD A BALL				
❏ Mercury OCM-2210 [(2) M]	1964	10.00	20.00	40.00
-- Promo-only two-record set with bonus interview record MGD-2-24				
❏ Mercury OCM-2210 [M]	1964	5.00	10.00	20.00
❏ Mercury OCS-6210 [S]	1964	6.25	12.50	25.00
ICE FOLLIES				
❏ Dot DLP-3757 [M]	1967	6.25	12.50	25.00
❏ Dot DLP-25757 [S]	1967	7.50	15.00	30.00
ILLYA DARLING				
❏ United Artists UAL-8901 [M]	1967	5.00	10.00	20.00
❏ United Artists UAS-9901 [S]	1967	5.00	10.00	20.00
INTO THE WOODS				
❏ RCA 6796-1-RC	1988	5.00	10.00	20.00
IRMA LA DOUCE				
❏ Columbia Masterworks OS 2029 [S]	1960	6.25	12.50	25.00
❏ Columbia Masterworks OL 5560 [M]	1960	5.00	10.00	20.00
J.B.				
❏ RCA Victor LD-6075 [(2) M]	1959	15.00	30.00	60.00
❏ RCA Victor LDS-6075 [(2) S]	1959	17.50	35.00	70.00
JACQUES BREL IS ALIVE AND WELL AND LIVING IN PARIS				
❏ Columbia Masterworks D2S 779 [(2)]	1968	5.00	10.00	20.00
-- Box set; gray "360 Sound" labels				
JENNIE				
❏ RCA Victor LOC-1083 [M]	1963	6.25	12.50	25.00
❏ RCA Victor LSO-1083 [S]	1963	12.50	25.00	50.00
JESUS CHRIST SUPERSTAR				
❏ Decca DL 71503	1971	5.00	10.00	20.00
-- Not to be confused with the original studio recording (this is a one-record gatefold)				
JOSEPH AND THE AMAZING TECHNICOLOR DREAMCOAT				
❏ Scepter SPS-588X	1968	5.00	10.00	20.00
-- With gatefold cover and libretto				
❏ Scepter SMAS-93738	197?	6.25	12.50	25.00
-- Capitol Record Club edition				
JOY				
❏ RCA Victor LSO-1166	1970	5.00	10.00	20.00
JUNO				
❏ Columbia Masterworks OS 2013 [S]	1959	17.50	35.00	70.00
❏ Columbia Masterworks OL 5380 [M]	1959	10.00	20.00	40.00
KEAN				
❏ Columbia Masterworks KSO 2120 [S]	1961	10.00	20.00	40.00
❏ Columbia Masterworks KOL 5720 [M]	1961	7.50	15.00	30.00
THE KING AND I				
❏ Decca DL 9008 [M]	1951	6.25	12.50	25.00
-- Black label, gold print				
KWAMINA				
❏ Capitol SW 1645 [S]	1962	12.50	25.00	50.00
❏ Capitol W 1645 [M]	1962	7.50	15.00	30.00
THE LADY'S NOT FOR BURNING				
❏ Decca DL 9508/9 [(2) M]	1951	12.50	25.00	50.00
-- Oversize box set				
LAGINAPPE '59 PRESENTS BE MY GUEST				
❏ (no label) XCTV-10303 [M]	1959	62.50	125.00	250.00
-- Custom pressing for New Trier High School, Illinois. Collectible because the future Ann-Margret sings one track on the LP!				
LEGS DIAMOND				
❏ RCA 7983-1-RC	1989	6.25	12.50	25.00
LES MISERABLES				
❏ Relativity 88561-8140-1 [(2)]	1985	5.00	10.00	20.00
-- Original London cast recording				
LET IT RIDE				
❏ RCA Victor LOC-1064 [M]	1961	5.00	10.00	20.00
❏ RCA Victor LSO-1064 [S]	1961	10.00	20.00	40.00
LI'L ABNER				
❏ Columbia Masterworks OL 5150 [M]	1956	7.50	15.00	30.00
LITTLE ME				
❏ RCA Victor LOC-1078 [M]	1962	5.00	10.00	20.00
❏ RCA Victor LSO-1078 [S]	1962	6.25	12.50	25.00

Label, Number	Yr	VG	VG+	NM
LITTLE SHOP OF HORRORS				
❏ Geffen GHSP-2020	1982	6.25	12.50	25.00
LOOK MA, I'M DANCIN'!				
❏ Decca DL 5231 [M]	1950	25.00	50.00	100.00
LORELEI				
❏ MGM M3G-55	1974	7.50	15.00	30.00
-- Second version, recorded with Broadway cast				
❏ Verve MV-5097-OC	1974	6.25	12.50	25.00
-- First version, recorded before the show hit Broadway				
LOST IN THE STARS				
❏ Decca DL 8028 [M]	1949	12.50	25.00	50.00
THE MAD SHOW				
❏ Columbia Masterworks OS 2930 [S]	1965	25.00	50.00	100.00
❏ Columbia Masterworks OL 6530 [M]	1965	12.50	25.00	50.00
MAGGIE FLYNN				
❏ RCA Victor LSOD-2009	1968	5.00	10.00	20.00
❏ RCA Victor LSOD-2009	1968	6.25	12.50	25.00
THE MAGIC SHOW				
❏ Bell 9003	1974	5.00	10.00	20.00
MAME				
❏ Columbia Masterworks KOS 3000 [S]	1966	5.00	10.00	20.00
-- Gray label with "360 Sound Stereo"				
MAN OF LA MANCHA				
❏ Kapp KRS-4505 [S]	1965	5.00	10.00	20.00
ME AND JULIET				
❏ RCA Victor LOC-1012 [M]	1953	17.50	35.00	70.00
MEDEA				
❏ Decca DLP 9000 [M]	1949	7.50	15.00	30.00
MEGILLA OF ITZIG MANGER				
❏ Columbia Masterworks OS 3270	1968	10.00	20.00	40.00
MERRILY WE ROLL ALONG				
❏ RCA Victor CBL1-4197	1981	7.50	15.00	30.00
THE MERRY WIDOW				
❏ RCA Victor LOC-1094 [M]	1964	5.00	10.00	20.00
❏ RCA Victor LSO-1094 [S]	1964	6.25	12.50	25.00
MEXICAN HAYRIDE				
❏ Decca DL 5232 [10]	1950	30.00	60.00	120.00
MILK AND HONEY				
❏ RCA Victor LOC-1065 [M]	1961	6.25	12.50	25.00
-- With only credits (no picture) on front cover				
❏ RCA Victor LOC-1065 [M]	1961	5.00	10.00	20.00
-- With picture of Tommy Rall and two dancers on front cover				
❏ RCA Victor LSO-1065 [S]	1961	7.50	15.00	30.00
-- With only credits (no picture) on front cover				
❏ RCA Victor LSO-1065 [S]	1961	6.25	12.50	25.00
-- With picture of Tommy Rall and two dancers on front cover				
MISS LIBERTY				
❏ Columbia Masterworks ML 4220 [M]	1949	7.50	15.00	30.00
-- Originals have green labels				
MISS SAIGON				
❏ Geffen GHS 24271 [(2)]	1990	5.00	10.00	20.00
THE MOST HAPPY FELLA				
❏ Columbia Masterworks O3L 240 [(3) M]	1956	12.50	25.00	50.00
-- Box set with entire show				
❏ Columbia Masterworks OL 5118 [M]	1956	7.50	15.00	30.00
-- Gray and black label with six "eye" logos				
MR. PRESIDENT				
❏ Columbia Masterworks KOS 2270 [S]	1962	7.50	15.00	30.00
-- Gatefold with shiny silver cover				
❏ Columbia Masterworks KOL 5870 [M]	1962	5.00	10.00	20.00
-- Gatefold with shiny silver cover				
MR. WONDERFUL				
❏ Decca DL 9032 [M]	1956	12.50	25.00	50.00
MRS. PATTERSON				
❏ RCA Victor LOC-1017 [M]	1954	37.50	75.00	150.00
THE MUSIC MAN				
❏ Capitol SWAO 990 [S]	1957	6.25	12.50	25.00
-- Gatefold cover, white with credits and drawing on front; gray label				
❏ Capitol WAO 990 [M]	1957	5.00	10.00	20.00
-- Gatefold cover, white with credits and drawing on front; gray label				
MY FAIR LADY				
❏ Columbia Masterworks OS 2015 [S]	1959	5.00	10.00	20.00
-- Gray and black label with six "eye" logos; original London cast				
❏ Columbia Masterworks OL 5090 [M]	1956	6.25	12.50	25.00
-- Gray and black label with six "eye" logos				
THE NERVOUS SET				
❏ Columbia Masterworks OS 2018 [S]	1959	15.00	30.00	60.00
❏ Columbia Masterworks OL 5430 [M]	1959	7.50	15.00	30.00
NEW FACES OF 1952				
❏ RCA Victor LOC-1008 [M]	1952	6.25	12.50	25.00
NEW FACES OF 1956				
❏ RCA Victor LOC-1025 [M]	1956	12.50	25.00	50.00
NEW FACES OF 1968				
❏ Warner Bros. BS 2551	1968	7.50	15.00	30.00
THE NEW GIRL IN TOWN				
❏ RCA Victor LOC-1027 [M]	1957	5.00	10.00	20.00
❏ RCA Victor LSO-1027 [S]	1958	12.50	25.00	50.00
❏ RCA Victor LOC-1106 [M]	1965	5.00	10.00	20.00
❏ RCA Victor LSO-1106 [S]	1965	7.50	15.00	30.00
THE NINA, THE PINTA AND THE SANTA MARIA				
❏ Dot DLP-9009 [M]	1960	10.00	20.00	40.00
❏ Dot DLP-29009 [S]	1960	12.50	25.00	50.00
NO STRINGS				
❏ Capitol O 1695 [M]	1962	5.00	10.00	20.00
❏ Capitol SO 1695 [S]	1962	10.00	20.00	40.00
OF THEE I SING				
❏ Capitol S 350 [M]	1952	37.50	75.00	150.00
OH, KAY!				
❏ 20th Fox FOX-4003 [M]	1960	6.25	12.50	25.00
❏ 20th Fox SFX-4003 [S]	1960	12.50	25.00	50.00
OKLAHOMA!				
❏ Decca DLP 8000 [M]	1949	7.50	15.00	30.00
-- Black label, gold print; the first 12-inch LP on Decca				
❏ Decca DL 9017 [M]	1955	5.00	10.00	20.00
-- Reissue of 8000				
❏ Decca DL 9017 [M]	196?	5.00	10.00	20.00
-- Reissue with new cover art				
❏ Decca DL 79017 [R]	1968	5.00	10.00	20.00
-- Special 25th Anniversary edition; cover has yellow drawing, inner sleeve has liner notes				
OLIVER!				
❏ RCA Victor LSOD-2004 [S]	1962	5.00	10.00	20.00
ON A CLEAR DAY YOU CAN SEE FOREVER				
❏ RCA Victor LOCD-2006 [M]	1965	5.00	10.00	20.00
❏ RCA Victor LSOD-2006 [S]	1965	6.25	12.50	25.00
ON YOUR TOES				
❏ Decca DL 9015 [M]	1954	18.75	37.50	75.00
ONCE UPON A MATTRESS				
❏ Kapp KDL-7004 [M]	1959	6.25	12.50	25.00
❏ Kapp KDL-7004-S [S]	1959	7.50	15.00	30.00
110 IN THE SHADE				
❏ RCA Victor LOC-1085 [M]	1963	6.25	12.50	25.00
❏ RCA Victor LSO-1085 [S]	1963	10.00	20.00	40.00
ONE TOUCH OF VENUS				
❏ Decca DL 9122 [M]	1965	6.25	12.50	25.00
❏ Decca DL 79122 [R]	1965	6.25	12.50	25.00
OVER HERE!				
❏ Columbia Masterworks KS 32961	1974	5.00	10.00	20.00
❏ Columbia Masterworks SQ 32961 [Q]	1974	7.50	15.00	30.00
PAINT YOUR WAGON				
❏ RCA Victor LOC-1006 [M]	1951	6.25	12.50	25.00
-- Green label				
❏ RCA Victor LOC-1006 [M]	1955	5.00	10.00	20.00
-- Black label, dog on top, "Long Play" at bottom				
PARADE				
❏ Kapp KDL-7005 [M]	1960	50.00	100.00	200.00
❏ Kapp KDS-7005 [S]	1960	62.50	125.00	250.00
PARIS '90				
❏ Columbia Masterworks ML 4619 [M]	1952	37.50	75.00	150.00
PEACE				
❏ Metromedia MP-33001	1969	7.50	15.00	30.00
PETER PAN				
❏ RCA Victor LOC-1019 [M]	1954	10.00	20.00	40.00
THE PHANTOM OF THE OPERA				
❏ Polydor 831 273-1 [(2)]	1987	5.00	10.00	20.00
-- With libretto; not to be confused with the one-record "Highlights" collection				

Label, Number	Yr	VG	VG+	NM
PIPE DREAM				
❑ RCA Victor LOC-1023 [M]	1955	17.50	35.00	70.00
-- With "Special Advance Edition" sticker on cover				
❑ RCA Victor LOC-1023 [M]	1955	12.50	25.00	50.00
-- Without "Special Advance Edition" sticker on cover				
PLAIN AND FANCY				
❑ Capitol S 603 [M]	1955	6.25	12.50	25.00
-- Red label				
PLAYGIRLS				
❑ Warner Bros. W 1530 [M]	1964	6.25	12.50	25.00
❑ Warner Bros. WS 1530 [S]	1964	7.50	15.00	30.00
PORGY AND BESS				
❑ Decca DL 7006 [10]	1950	7.50	15.00	30.00
-- Reissue of material first released on 78s				
❑ Decca DL 8042 [M]	1950	7.50	15.00	30.00
❑ Decca DL 9024 [M]	1955	6.25	12.50	25.00
-- Reissue of 8042; drawing of Catfish Row on cover				
THE PREMISE				
❑ Vanguard VRS-9092 [M]	1960	10.00	20.00	40.00
PURLIE				
❑ Ampex A-40101	1970	7.50	15.00	30.00
RASHOMON				
❑ Carlton LPX-5000 [M]	1959	6.25	12.50	25.00
❑ Carlton STLPX-5000 [S]	1959	7.50	15.00	30.00
-- Not actually the original cast recording, but the play's incidental music				
REDHEAD				
❑ RCA Victor LOC-1048 [M]	1959	5.00	10.00	20.00
❑ RCA Victor LSO-1048 [S]	1959	12.50	25.00	50.00
-- Without "Essie's Vision"				
THE RIVER WIND				
❑ London AM-48001 [M]	1962	10.00	20.00	40.00
❑ London AMS-78001 [S]	1962	20.00	40.00	80.00
THE ROAR OF THE GREASEPAINT -- THE SMELL OF THE CROWD				
❑ RCA Victor LSO-1109 [S]	1965	5.00	10.00	20.00
THE ROTHSCHILDS				
❑ Columbia Masterworks S 30337	1970	6.25	12.50	25.00
SAIL AWAY				
❑ Capitol SWAO 1643 [S]	1961	7.50	15.00	30.00
❑ Capitol WAO 1643 [M]	1961	5.00	10.00	20.00
ST. LOUIS WOMAN				
❑ Capitol L 355 [10]	1952	20.00	40.00	80.00
SARATOGA				
❑ RCA Victor LOC-1051 [M]	1959	6.25	12.50	25.00
❑ RCA Victor LSO-1051 [S]	1959	12.50	25.00	50.00
SAY, DARLING				
❑ RCA Victor LOC-1045 [M]	1958	10.00	20.00	40.00
❑ RCA Victor LSO-1045 [S]	1958	15.00	30.00	60.00
SELMA				
❑ Cotillion SD 2-110 [(2)]	1976	5.00	10.00	20.00
SEVENTEEN				
❑ RCA Victor LOC-1003 [M]	1951	37.50	75.00	150.00
1776				
❑ Columbia Masterworks BOS 3310	1969	7.50	15.00	30.00
-- The first edition has Howard DaSilva shown as Ben Franklin in credits and synopsis, though he does not appear on the LP				
SEVENTH HEAVEN				
❑ Decca DL 9001 [M]	1955	37.50	75.00	150.00
70 GIRLS, 70				
❑ Columbia Masterworks S 30589	1971	12.50	25.00	50.00
SHE LOVES ME				
❑ MGM E 4118OC-2 [(2) M]	1963	10.00	20.00	40.00
❑ MGM SE 4118OC-2 [(2) S]	1963	12.50	25.00	50.00
SHOW BIZ (FROM VAUDE TO VIDEO)				
❑ RCA Victor LOC-1011 [M]	1954	10.00	20.00	40.00
SHOW BOAT				
❑ Columbia Masterworks ML 4058 [M]	1948	6.25	12.50	25.00
-- From the 1946 revival; paper envelope jacket with its opening on top				
❑ Columbia Masterworks OL 4058 [M]	195?	5.00	10.00	20.00
-- From the 1946 revival; reissue of ML 4058				
SHOW GIRL				
❑ Roulette R-80001 [M]	1961	5.00	10.00	20.00
❑ Roulette SR-80001 [S]	1961	6.25	12.50	25.00

Label, Number	Yr	VG	VG+	NM
SIDE BY SIDE BY SONDHEIM				
❑ RCA Victor CBL2-1851 [(2)]	1976	5.00	10.00	20.00
SILK STOCKINGS				
❑ RCA Victor LOC-1016 [M]	1955	10.00	20.00	40.00
❑ RCA Victor LOC-1102 [M]	1965	5.00	10.00	20.00
-- Reissue; regular cover				
❑ RCA Victor LSO-1102 [R]	1965	5.00	10.00	20.00
SIMPLY HEAVENLY				
❑ Columbia Masterworks OL 5240 [M]	1957	6.25	12.50	25.00
SING OUT, SWEET LAND!				
❑ Decca DL 4304 [M]	1963	5.00	10.00	20.00
❑ Decca DL 8023 [M]	1950	12.50	25.00	50.00
❑ Decca DL 74304 [R]	1963	5.00	10.00	20.00
SKYSCRAPER				
❑ Capitol SVAS 2422 [S]	1965	6.25	12.50	25.00
❑ Capitol VAS 2422 [M]	1965	5.00	10.00	20.00
SNOW WHITE AND THE SEVEN DWARFS				
❑ Buena Vista STER-5009	1979	7.50	15.00	30.00
SONDHEIM: A MUSICAL TRIBUTE				
❑ Warner Bros. 2WS 2705 [(2)]	1973	5.00	10.00	20.00
SONG OF NORWAY				
❑ Columbia CL 1328 [M]	1959	5.00	10.00	20.00
-- 1958 revival cast				
❑ Columbia CS 8135 [S]	1959	12.50	25.00	50.00
-- 1958 revival cast				
❑ Decca DL 8002 [M]	1949	7.50	15.00	30.00
❑ Decca DL 9019 [M]	1955	5.00	10.00	20.00
THE SOUND OF MUSIC				
❑ Columbia Masterworks KOS 2020 [S]	1959	6.25	12.50	25.00
-- Gray and black label with six "eye" logos				
❑ Columbia Masterworks KOL 5450 [M]	1959	5.00	10.00	20.00
-- Gray and black label with six "eye" logos				
SOUTH PACIFIC				
❑ Columbia Masterworks ML 4180 [M]	1949	6.25	12.50	25.00
-- Green or blue label; large anchor on front cover				
STOP THE WORLD-I WANT TO GET OFF				
❑ London AMS 88001 [S]	1962	5.00	10.00	20.00
STREET SCENE				
❑ Columbia Masterworks ML 4139 [M]	1949	7.50	15.00	30.00
-- Paper envelope jacket with its opening on top				
THE SUBJECT WAS ROSES				
❑ Columbia Masterworks DOL 308 [(3) M]	1964	5.00	10.00	20.00
❑ Columbia Masterworks DOS 708 [(3) S]	1964	7.50	15.00	30.00
SUBWAYS ARE FOR SLEEPING				
❑ Columbia Masterworks KOS 2130 [S]	1962	10.00	20.00	40.00
❑ Columbia Masterworks KOL 5730 [M]	1962	6.25	12.50	25.00
THE SURVIVAL OF ST. JOAN				
❑ Paramount PAS-9000 [(2)]	1971	6.25	12.50	25.00
SWEENEY TODD-THE DEMON BARBER OF FLEET STREET				
❑ RCA Victor CBL2-3379 [(2)]	1979	5.00	10.00	20.00
SWEET CHARITY				
❑ Columbia Masterworks KOS 2900 [S]	1966	5.00	10.00	20.00
TAKE ME ALONG				
❑ RCA Victor LSO-1050 [S]	1959	5.00	10.00	20.00
-- Black label				
TAMALPAIS EXCHANGE				
❑ Atlantic SD 8263	1970	7.50	15.00	30.00
TAROT				
❑ United Artists UAS-5563	1970	5.00	10.00	20.00
TENDERLOIN				
❑ Capitol SWAO 1492 [S]	1960	10.00	20.00	40.00
-- With program				
❑ Capitol WAO 1492 [M]	1960	6.25	12.50	25.00
-- With program				
TEVYA AND HIS DAUGHTERS				
❑ Columbia Masterworks OL 5225 [M]	1957	7.50	15.00	30.00
TEXAS, LI'L DARLIN'				
❑ Decca DL 5188 [10]	1950	20.00	40.00	80.00
THIS IS THE ARMY				
❑ Decca DL 5108 [10]	1950	25.00	50.00	100.00
THIS WAS BURLESQUE				
❑ Roulette R-25185 [M]	1962	6.25	12.50	25.00
❑ Roulette SR-25186 [S]	1962	7.50	15.00	30.00

Label, Number	Yr	VG	VG+	NM
THREE TO MAKE MUSIC				
❑ RCA Victor LPM-2012 [M]	1958	6.25	12.50	25.00
❑ RCA Victor LSP-2012 [S]	1958	7.50	15.00	30.00
THREE WISHES FOR JAMIE				
❑ Capitol S 317 [M]	1952	30.00	60.00	120.00
THE THREEPENNY OPERA				
❑ MGM E-3121 [M]	1954	6.25	12.50	25.00
-- Revival cast; yellow label				
❑ Columbia Masterworks PS 34326	1976	5.00	10.00	20.00
-- Another revival cast				
TIME CHANGES				
❑ ABC ABCS-681	1969	7.50	15.00	30.00
A TIME FOR SINGING				
❑ Warner Bros. W 1639 [M]	1966	10.00	20.00	40.00
❑ Warner Bros. WS 1639 [S]	1966	15.00	30.00	60.00
A TIME REMEMBERED				
❑ Mercury MG-20380 [M]	1957	6.25	12.50	25.00
❑ Mercury SR-60023 [S]	1957	10.00	20.00	40.00
-- Music from the dramatic play				
TO BROADWAY WITH LOVE				
❑ Columbia Masterworks OS 2630 [S]	1964	12.50	25.00	50.00
❑ Columbia Masterworks OL 6030 [M]	1964	6.25	12.50	25.00
TOP BANANA				
❑ Capitol S 308 [M]	1952	25.00	50.00	100.00
TOVARICH				
❑ Capitol STAO 1940 [S]	1963	7.50	15.00	30.00
❑ Capitol TAO 1940 [M]	1963	5.00	10.00	20.00
A TREE GROWS IN BROOKLYN				
❑ Columbia Masterworks ML 4405 [M]	1951	7.50	15.00	30.00
-- Blue label				
TWO BY TWO				
❑ Columbia Masterworks S 30338	1970	5.00	10.00	20.00
TWO ON THE AISLE				
❑ Decca DL 8040 [M]	1951	25.00	50.00	100.00
-- Black label, gold print				
❑ Decca DL 8040 [M]	1955	15.00	30.00	60.00
-- Black label, silver print				
❑ Decca DL 8040 [M]	196?	15.00	30.00	60.00
-- Black label with color bars				
TWO'S COMPANY				
❑ RCA Victor LOC-1009 [M]	1952	25.00	50.00	100.00
THE UNSINKABLE MOLLY BROWN				
❑ Capitol SWAO 1509 [S]	1960	6.25	12.50	25.00
❑ Capitol WAO 1509 [M]	1960	5.00	10.00	20.00
UP IN CENTRAL PARK				
❑ Decca DL 8016 [M]	1950	10.00	20.00	40.00
-- Black label, gold print				
❑ Decca DL 8016 [M]	1955	7.50	15.00	30.00
-- Black label, silver print				
WAITING FOR GODOT				
❑ Columbia Masterworks O2L 238 [(2) M]	1956	7.50	15.00	30.00
WEST SIDE STORY				
❑ Columbia Masterworks OS 2001 [S]	1958	7.50	15.00	30.00
-- Gray and black label with six "eye" logos				
❑ Columbia Masterworks OL 5230 [M]	1958	6.25	12.50	25.00
-- Gray and black label with six "eye" logos				
WHAT MAKES SAMMY RUN?				
❑ Columbia Masterworks KSO 2440 [S]	1964	10.00	20.00	40.00
❑ Columbia Masterworks KOL 6040 [M]	1964	7.50	15.00	30.00
WILDCAT				
❑ RCA Victor LOC-1060 [M]	1961	6.25	12.50	25.00
❑ RCA Victor LSO-1060 [S]	1961	10.00	20.00	40.00
WISH YOU WERE HERE				
❑ RCA Victor LOC-1007 [M]	1952	15.00	30.00	60.00
WONDERFUL TOWN				
❑ Decca DL 9010 [M]	1953	7.50	15.00	30.00
-- Black label, gold print				
WORDS AND MUSIC				
❑ RCA Victor LRL1-5079	1974	5.00	10.00	20.00
YOU'RE A GOOD MAN, CHARLIE BROWN				
❑ MGM 1E-9 [M]	1967	5.00	10.00	20.00
❑ MGM S1E-9 [S]	1967	5.00	10.00	20.00

Label, Number	Yr	VG	VG+	NM
YOUR OWN THING				
❑ RCA Victor LOC-1148 [M]	1968	6.25	12.50	25.00
❑ RCA Victor LSO-1148 [S]	1968	5.00	10.00	20.00
ZORBA				
❑ Capitol SO-118	1969	5.00	10.00	20.00

Four original cast albums, selected semi-randomly from among those listed in this guide. (Top left) *The Boys in the Band* is an unusual cast album. Instead of merely releasing the musical numbers or the incidental music, this two-record set contains the complete play! (Top right) *The Gay Life,* which opened in 1961, received four Tony nominations, including best actress (Elizabeth Allen), and won for best costume design. (Bottom left) *The Mad Show,* a highly collectible album, was an attempt to turn the popular satire magazine into a stage play. Jo Ann Worley, who later appeared on the TV show "Rowan and Martin's Laugh-In," was in the original cast. And believe it or not, the music was co-written by Stephen Sondheim! (Bottom right) *Purlie* was the early 1970s musical adaptation of *Purlie Victorious.* Cleavon Little and Melba Moore were among the singers.

Label, Number	Yr	VG	VG+	NM

SOUNDTRACKS

Includes albums released as tie-ins to motion pictures. Most of these fit into three categories: incidental, usually orchestral, music, which generally are the most collectible; all the songs from a movie musical, most (though not all) of which began their lives in the theatre; or a collection of songs in popular styles by various artists.

Many soundtrack composers were recording artists in their own right. Among them are QUINCY JONES; HENRY MANCINI; and LALO SCHIFRIN. Most of their qualifying soundtracks are listed in the main section. If an LP is not listed below, try under the composer's name.

Assuming they meet the minimum-value criteria, the Broadway versions of movie musicals are in the "Original Casts" section. For television movies, miniseries or series, see the next section, "Television Albums."

AARON SLICK FROM PUNKIN CRICK
❑ RCA Victor LPM-3006 [10]	1952	37.50	75.00	150.00

ADVENTURES IN PARADISE
| ❑ ABC-Paramount ABC-329 [M] | 1960 | 7.50 | 15.00 | 30.00 |
| ❑ ABC-Paramount ABCS-329 [S] | 1960 | 10.00 | 20.00 | 40.00 |

ADVISE AND CONSENT
| ❑ RCA Victor LOC-1068 [M] | 1962 | 7.50 | 15.00 | 30.00 |
| ❑ RCA Victor LSO-1068 [S] | 1962 | 15.00 | 30.00 | 60.00 |

AN AFFAIR TO REMEMBER
| ❑ Columbia CL 1013 [M] | 1957 | 10.00 | 20.00 | 40.00 |

AFRICA ADDIO
| ❑ United Artists UAL-4141 [M] | 1966 | 5.00 | 10.00 | 20.00 |
| ❑ United Artists UAS-5141 [S] | 1966 | 6.25 | 12.50 | 25.00 |

THE AGONY AND THE ECSTASY
| ❑ Capitol MAS 2427 [M] | 1965 | 15.00 | 30.00 | 60.00 |
| ❑ Capitol SMAS 2427 [S] | 1965 | 20.00 | 40.00 | 80.00 |

AIRPORT
| ❑ Decca DL 79173 | 1970 | 6.25 | 12.50 | 25.00 |

ALAKAZAM THE GREAT
| ❑ Vee Jay LP-6000 [M] | 1961 | 20.00 | 40.00 | 80.00 |

THE ALAMO
| ❑ Columbia CL 1558 [M] | 1960 | 5.00 | 10.00 | 20.00 |
| ❑ Columbia CS 8358 [S] | 1960 | 6.25 | 12.50 | 25.00 |

ALBERT PECKINPAW'S REVENGE
| ❑ Sidewalk ST 5907 [S] | 1967 | 7.50 | 15.00 | 30.00 |
| ❑ Sidewalk T 5907 [M] | 1967 | 7.50 | 15.00 | 30.00 |

ALEXANDER
| ❑ Polydor 24-7001 | 1970 | 10.00 | 20.00 | 40.00 |

ALEXANDER THE GREAT
| ❑ Mercury MG-20148 [M] | 1956 | 62.50 | 125.00 | 250.00 |

ALIEN
| ❑ 20th Century T-593 | 1979 | 6.25 | 12.50 | 25.00 |

ALIENS
| ❑ Varese Sarabande STV-81283 | 1986 | 6.25 | 12.50 | 25.00 |

ALIKI, MY LOVE
| ❑ Fontana MGF-27523 [M] | 1963 | 6.25 | 12.50 | 25.00 |
| ❑ Fontana SRF-67523 [S] | 1963 | 7.50 | 15.00 | 30.00 |

ALL NIGHT LONG
| ❑ Epic LA 16032 [M] | 1962 | 10.00 | 20.00 | 40.00 |
| ❑ Epic BA 17032 [S] | 1962 | 12.50 | 25.00 | 50.00 |

ALL THE LOVING COUPLES
| ❑ GNP Crescendo GNPS-2051 | 1969 | 10.00 | 20.00 | 40.00 |

ALL THE RIGHT NOISES
| ❑ Buddah BDS-5132 | 1971 | 7.50 | 15.00 | 30.00 |

ALL THIS AND WORLD WAR II
| ❑ 20th Century 2T-522 [(2)] | 1976 | 6.25 | 12.50 | 25.00 |
-- Box set with booklet and flyer

THE ALLNIGHTER
| ❑ Chameleon CHPD 9601 [PD] | 1987 | 7.50 | 15.00 | 30.00 |
-- Picture disc

ALMOST SUMMER
| ❑ MCA 3037 | 1978 | 6.25 | 12.50 | 25.00 |

AMERICA, AMERICA
| ❑ Warner Bros. W 1527 [M] | 1963 | 5.00 | 10.00 | 20.00 |
| ❑ Warner Bros. WS 1527 [S] | 1963 | 6.25 | 12.50 | 25.00 |

AMERICAN HOT WAX
| ❑ A&M SP-6500 [(2)] | 1978 | 5.00 | 10.00 | 20.00 |

AN AMERICAN IN PARIS
| ❑ MGM E-93 [10] | 1951 | 10.00 | 20.00 | 40.00 |

AMERICAN POP
| ❑ MCA 5201 | 1981 | 7.50 | 15.00 | 30.00 |

THE AMOROUS ADVENTURES OF MOLL FLANDERS
| ❑ RCA Victor LOC-1113 [M] | 1965 | 10.00 | 20.00 | 40.00 |
| ❑ RCA Victor LSO-1113 [S] | 1965 | 20.00 | 40.00 | 80.00 |

ANASTASIA
| ❑ Decca DL 8460 [M] | 1956 | 7.50 | 15.00 | 30.00 |

AND GOD CREATED WOMAN
| ❑ Decca DL 8685 [M] | 1957 | 30.00 | 60.00 | 120.00 |

THE ANDROMEDA STRAIN
| ❑ Kapp KRS-5513 | 1971 | 25.00 | 50.00 | 100.00 |
-- Hexagonal cover glued onto silver cardboard
| ❑ Kapp KRS-5513 | 1971 | 10.00 | 20.00 | 40.00 |
-- Regular cover

ANGELS DIE HARD
| ❑ Uni 73091 | 1971 | 7.50 | 15.00 | 30.00 |

ANGELS FROM HELL
| ❑ Tower ST 5128 | 1968 | 15.00 | 30.00 | 60.00 |

THE ANONYMOUS VENETIAN
| ❑ United Artists UAS-5218 | 1971 | 7.50 | 15.00 | 30.00 |

ANOTHER TIME, ANOTHER PLACE
| ❑ Columbia CL 1180 [M] | 1958 | 10.00 | 20.00 | 40.00 |

ANY WEDNESDAY
| ❑ Warner Bros. W 1669 [M] | 1966 | 6.25 | 12.50 | 25.00 |
| ❑ Warner Bros. WS 1669 [S] | 1966 | 10.00 | 20.00 | 40.00 |

THE APARTMENT
| ❑ United Artists UAL-3105 [M] | 1960 | 7.50 | 15.00 | 30.00 |
| ❑ United Artists UAS-6105 [S] | 1960 | 10.00 | 20.00 | 40.00 |

APOCALYPSE NOW
| ❑ Elektra DP-90001 [(2)] | 1979 | 7.50 | 15.00 | 30.00 |

THE APPLE
| ❑ Cannon 1001 | 1980 | 17.50 | 35.00 | 70.00 |

APRIL LOVE
| ❑ Dot DLP-9000 [M] | 1957 | 5.00 | 10.00 | 20.00 |

ARMS AND THE GIRL
| ❑ Decca DL 5200 [10] | 1950 | 25.00 | 50.00 | 100.00 |

AROUND THE WORLD IN 80 DAYS
| ❑ Decca DL 9046 [M] | 1957 | 6.25 | 12.50 | 25.00 |
-- Black label, silver print
| ❑ Decca DL 79046 [S] | 1959 | 10.00 | 20.00 | 40.00 |
-- Maroon label, silver print; cover has "Full Stereo" banner

AROUND THE WORLD UNDER THE SEA
| ❑ Monument MLP-8050 [M] | 1966 | 7.50 | 15.00 | 30.00 |
| ❑ Monument SLP-18050 [S] | 1966 | 12.50 | 25.00 | 50.00 |

ARRIVIDERCI, BABY!
| ❑ RCA Victor LOC-1132 [M] | 1966 | 5.00 | 10.00 | 20.00 |
| ❑ RCA Victor LSO-1132 [S] | 1966 | 10.00 | 20.00 | 40.00 |

AT LONG LAST LOVE
| ❑ RCA Victor ABL2-0967 [(2)] | 1975 | 5.00 | 10.00 | 20.00 |

ATHENA
| ❑ Mercury MG-25202 [10] | 1954 | 37.50 | 75.00 | 150.00 |

AVIATOR
| ❑ Varese Sarabande STV-81240 | 1985 | 5.00 | 10.00 | 20.00 |

BABES IN TOYLAND
| ❑ Buena Vista BV-4022 [M] | 1961 | 7.50 | 15.00 | 30.00 |
| ❑ Buena Vista STER-4022 [S] | 1961 | 10.00 | 20.00 | 40.00 |

BABY DOLL
| ❑ Columbia CL 958 [M] | 1956 | 15.00 | 30.00 | 60.00 |
-- Ads for other Columbia LPs on back cover
| ❑ Columbia CL 958 [M] | 195? | 12.50 | 25.00 | 50.00 |
-- No ads for LPs on back cover

Label, Number	Yr	VG	VG+	NM
BABY FACE NELSON				
❏ Jubilee JLP-2021 [M]	1957	30.00	60.00	120.00
BABY, THE RAIN MUST FALL				
❏ Ava A-53 [M]	1965	10.00	20.00	40.00
❏ Ava AS-53 [S]	1965	12.50	25.00	50.00
❏ Mainstream S-6056 [S]	1965	10.00	20.00	40.00
-- Reissue of Ava AS-53				
❏ Mainstream 56056 [M]	1965	7.50	15.00	30.00
-- Reissue of Ava A-53				
BACK STREET				
❏ Decca DL 9097 [M]	1961	10.00	20.00	40.00
❏ Decca DL 79097 [S]	1961	20.00	40.00	80.00
THE BAD SEED				
❏ RCA Victor LPM-1395 [M]	1956	75.00	150.00	300.00
BAND OF ANGELS				
❏ RCA Victor LPM-1557 [M]	1957	25.00	50.00	100.00
THE BAND WAGON				
❏ MGM E-3051 [M]	1953	7.50	15.00	30.00
-- Yellow label				
❏ MGM E-3051 [M]	1960	5.00	10.00	20.00
-- Black label				
THE BANJOMAN				
❏ Sire SA-7527	1977	5.00	10.00	20.00
BARABBAS				
❏ Colpix CP 510 [M]	1962	10.00	20.00	40.00
❏ Colpix SCP 510 [S]	1962	20.00	40.00	80.00
BARBARELLA				
❏ Dyno Voice DV-31908	1968	12.50	25.00	50.00
THE BARBARIAN AND THE GEISHA				
❏ 20th Fox FOX-3004 [M]	1958	62.50	125.00	250.00
BAREFOOT ADVENTURE				
❏ Pacific Jazz PJ-35 [M]	1961	10.00	20.00	40.00
❏ Pacific Jazz PJS-35 [S]	1961	15.00	30.00	60.00
BAREFOOT IN THE PARK				
❏ Dot DLP-25803 [S]	1967	7.50	15.00	30.00
❏ Dot DLP-3803 [M]	1967	5.00	10.00	20.00
THE BARKLEYS OF BROADWAY				
❏ MGM E-503 [10]	1949	20.00	40.00	80.00
BATMAN				
❏ Warner Bros. 25977	1989	5.00	10.00	20.00
-- Music composed and conducted by Danny Elfman; not to be confused with the Prince LP				
BATMAN FOREVER				
❏ Atlantic PR 6339 [(2)]	1995	5.00	10.00	20.00
-- Promo only generic white cover with sticker				
BATTLE OF THE BULGE				
❏ Warner Bros. W 1617 [M]	1965	10.00	20.00	40.00
❏ Warner Bros. WS 1617 [S]	1965	10.00	20.00	40.00
BEACH BLANKET BINGO				
❏ Capitol ST 2323 [S]	1965	15.00	30.00	60.00
❏ Capitol T 2323 [M]	1965	7.50	15.00	30.00
BEAU JAMES				
❏ Imperial LP-9041 [M]	1957	10.00	20.00	40.00
BECKET				
❏ Decca DL 9117 [M]	1964	7.50	15.00	30.00
❏ Decca DL 79117 [S]	1964	12.50	25.00	50.00
BEDAZZLED				
❏ London MS-82009	1967	20.00	40.00	80.00
BEHOLD A PALE HORSE				
❏ Colpix CP 519 [M]	1964	12.50	25.00	50.00
❏ Colpix SCP 519 [S]	1964	17.50	35.00	70.00
THE BELIEVERS				
❏ Varese Sarabande STV-81328	1987	5.00	10.00	20.00
BELL, BOOK AND CANDLE				
❏ Colpix CP 502 [M]	1959	15.00	30.00	60.00
BELLS ARE RINGING				
❏ Capitol SW 1435 [S]	1960	7.50	15.00	30.00
❏ Capitol W 1435 [M]	1960	6.25	12.50	25.00
BEN-HUR				
❏ MGM 1E1 [M]	1959	10.00	20.00	40.00
-- Boxed edition with hardcover book				
❏ MGM S-1E1 [S]	1959	12.50	25.00	50.00
-- Boxed edition with hardcover book				
BENEATH THE PLANET OF THE APES				
❏ Amos AAS-8001	1970	10.00	20.00	40.00
BEST OF THE BEST				
❏ Relativity 88561 1034 1	1989	5.00	10.00	20.00
BETRAYED				
❏ Varese Sarabande 704.700	1988	7.50	15.00	30.00
BEYOND THE GREAT WALL				
❏ Capitol T 10401 [M]	1965	12.50	25.00	50.00
BEYOND THE VALLEY OF THE DOLLS				
❏ 20th Century Fox TFS-4211	1970	50.00	100.00	200.00
THE BIBLE				
❏ 20th Century Fox TF-3184 [M]	1966	5.00	10.00	20.00
❏ 20th Century Fox TFS-4184 [S]	1966	7.50	15.00	30.00
THE BIG COUNTRY				
❏ United Artists UAL-4004 [M]	1958	6.25	12.50	25.00
❏ United Artists UAS-5004 [S]	1958	12.50	25.00	50.00
THE BIG GUNDOWN				
❏ United Artists UAS-5190	1967	10.00	20.00	40.00
THE BIGGEST BUNDLE OF THEM ALL				
❏ MGM E-4446 [M]	1967	5.00	10.00	20.00
❏ MGM SE-4446 [S]	1967	6.25	12.50	25.00
BILLIE				
❏ United Artists UAL-4131 [M]	1965	5.00	10.00	20.00
❏ United Artists UAS-5131 [S]	1965	6.25	12.50	25.00
THE BILLION DOLLAR BRAIN				
❏ United Artists UAS-5174 [S]	1967	5.00	10.00	20.00
BILLY JACK				
❏ Warner Bros. WS 1926	1971	6.25	12.50	25.00
THE BIRD WITH THE CRYSTAL PLUMAGE				
❏ Capitol ST-642	1970	25.00	50.00	100.00
BLACK AND WHITE IN COLOR				
❏ Buddah BDS-5698	1977	10.00	20.00	40.00
BLACK GIRL				
❏ Fantasy 9420	1973	17.50	35.00	70.00
THE BLACK HOLE				
❏ Buena Vista STER-5008	1979	12.50	25.00	50.00
THE BLACK ORCHID				
❏ Dot DLP-3178 [M]	1959	10.00	20.00	40.00
❏ Dot SLP-25178 [S]	1959	12.50	25.00	50.00
BLACULA				
❏ RCA Victor LSP-4806	1972	15.00	30.00	60.00
BLADE RUNNER				
❏ Full Moon/Warner Bros. 23748	1982	5.00	10.00	20.00
BLESS THE BEASTS AND CHILDREN				
❏ A&M SP-4322	1971	6.25	12.50	25.00
BLOOD AND SAND				
❏ Decca DL 5380 [10]	1952	20.00	40.00	80.00
BLOOMER GIRL				
❏ Decca DL 8015 [M]	1950	7.50	15.00	30.00
BLOW-UP				
❏ MGM E-4447 [M]	1967	10.00	20.00	40.00
❏ MGM SE-4447 [S]	1967	12.50	25.00	50.00
THE BLUE MAX				
❏ Mainstream S-6081 [S]	1966	20.00	40.00	80.00
❏ Mainstream 56081 [M]	1966	10.00	20.00	40.00
BLUE VELVET				
❏ Varese Sarabande STV-81292	1986	6.25	12.50	25.00
BOBO				
❏ Warner Bros. W 1711 [M]	1967	5.00	10.00	20.00
❏ Warner Bros. WS 1711 [S]	1967	5.00	10.00	20.00
BODY HEAT				
❏ Label X LXSE-1-002	1983	30.00	60.00	120.00
BOEING, BOEING				
❏ RCA Victor LOC-1121 [M]	1965	6.25	12.50	25.00
❏ RCA Victor LSO-1121 [S]	1965	7.50	15.00	30.00
BONNIE AND CLYDE				
❏ Warner Bros. W 1742 [M]	1968	10.00	20.00	40.00

Label, Number	Yr	VG	VG+	NM
❏ Warner Bros. WS 1742 [S]	1968	6.25	12.50	25.00
❏ Warner Bros. ST-91414 [S]	1968	7.50	1.00	30.00
-- Capitol Record Club issue				
BORA, BORA				
❏ American Int'l. STA-1029	1970	7.50	15.00	30.00
BORN FREE				
❏ MGM SE-4368 [S]	1966	5.00	10.00	20.00
BORSALINO				
❏ Paramount PAS-5019	1970	7.50	15.00	30.00
THE BOY FRIEND				
❏ MGM 1SE-32	1971	5.00	10.00	20.00
A BOY NAMED CHARLIE BROWN				
❏ Columbia Masterworks OS 3500	1970	5.00	10.00	20.00
BOY ON A DOLPHIN				
❏ Decca DL 8580 [M]	1957	15.00	30.00	60.00
-- Black label with silver print, or pink label with black print (promo)				
❏ Decca DL 8580 [M]	196?	5.00	10.00	20.00
-- Black label with color bars				
THE BOY WHO COULD FLY				
❏ Varese Sarabande STV-81299	1986	5.00	10.00	20.00
THE BOYS FROM SYRACUSE				
❏ Capitol STAO 1933 [S]	1963	7.50	15.00	30.00
❏ Capitol TAO 1933 [M]	1963	6.25	12.50	25.00
BOYZ 'N THE HOOD				
❏ Warner Bros. PRO-A-4996 [DJ]	1991	5.00	10.00	20.00
-- Promo-only vinyl release				
THE BRAVE ONE				
❏ Decca DL 8344 [M]	1956	10.00	20.00	40.00
BROTHER ON THE RUN				
❏ Perception PLP-45	1973	10.00	20.00	40.00
BUCCANEER				
❏ Columbia CL 1278 [M]	1958	6.25	12.50	25.00
❏ Columbia CS 8096 [S]	1958	10.00	20.00	40.00
BULLITT				
❏ Warner Bros. WS 1777	1968	15.00	30.00	60.00
BUNDLE OF JOY				
❏ RCA Victor LPM-1399 [M]	1956	10.00	20.00	40.00
BUNNY LAKE IS MISSING				
❏ RCA Victor LOC-1115 [M]	1965	10.00	20.00	40.00
❏ RCA Victor LSO-1115 [S]	1965	17.50	35.00	70.00
BUNNY O'HARE				
❏ American Int'l. STA-1041	1971	5.00	10.00	20.00
BUONA SERA, MRS. CAMPBELL				
❏ United Artists UAS-5192	1969	7.50	15.00	30.00
THE BURGLARS				
❏ Bell 1105	1971	10.00	20.00	40.00
BUTTERFIELD-8				
❏ MGM E-3952 [M]	1960	5.00	10.00	20.00
❏ MGM SE-3952 [S]	1960	6.25	12.50	25.00
BYE BYE BIRDIE				
❏ RCA Victor LOC-1081 [M]	1963	6.25	12.50	25.00
-- First cover without Ann-Margret on the front				
❏ RCA Victor LOC-1081 [M]	196?	5.00	10.00	20.00
-- Second cover with Ann-Margret on front, but with no credits underneath				
❏ RCA Victor LSO-1081 [S]	1963	7.50	15.00	30.00
-- First cover without Ann-Margret on the front				
❏ RCA Victor LSO-1081 [S]	196?	6.25	12.50	25.00
-- Second cover with Ann-Margret on front, but with no credits underneath				
❏ RCA Victor LSO-1081 [S]	196?	5.00	10.00	20.00
-- Third cover with Ann-Margret on front and with credits underneath				
C'MON, LET'S LIVE A LITTLE				
❏ Liberty LRP-3430 [M]	1966	6.25	12.50	25.00
❏ Liberty LST-7430 [S]	1966	7.50	15.00	30.00
CABARET				
❏ ABC ABCD-752	1972	5.00	10.00	20.00
THE CAINE MUTINY				
❏ RCA Victor LOC-1013 [M]	1954	4,000.	7,000.	10,000.
❏ RCA Victor LOC-1013 [M]	1993	50.00	100.00	200.00
-- Very limited edition (100 copies) reproduction of the original LP				
CALL ME MADAM				
❏ Decca DL 5465 [10]	1953	12.50	25.00	50.00

Label, Number	Yr	VG	VG+	NM
CALL ME MISTER				
❏ Decca DLP 7005 [10]	1950	25.00	50.00	100.00
CAMELOT				
❏ Warner Bros. B 1712 [M]	1967	6.25	12.50	25.00
❏ Warner Bros. BS 1712 [S]	1967	5.00	10.00	20.00
❏ Warner Bros. SW-91347	1968	6.25	12.50	25.00
-- Capitol Record Club edition				
CAN-CAN				
❏ Capitol SW 1301 [S]	1960	7.50	15.00	30.00
❏ Capitol W 1301 [M]	1960	5.00	10.00	20.00
CANDY				
❏ ABC ABCS-OC-9	1968	7.50	15.00	30.00
THE CARDINAL				
❏ RCA Victor LOC-1084 [M]	1963	10.00	20.00	40.00
❏ RCA Victor LSO-1084 [S]	1963	15.00	30.00	60.00
THE CARE BEARS MOVIE				
❏ Kid Stuff 3901	1985	5.00	10.00	20.00
THE CARETAKERS				
❏ Ava A-31 [M]	1963	5.00	10.00	20.00
❏ Ava AS-31 [S]	1963	6.25	12.50	25.00
CAROUSEL				
❏ Capitol SW 694 [S]	1962	5.00	10.00	20.00
-- Black colorband label				
❏ Capitol W 694 [M]	1956	7.50	15.00	30.00
-- Gray label				
❏ Capitol W 694 [M]	1959	5.00	10.00	20.00
-- Black colorband label, logo at left				
THE CARPETBAGGERS				
❏ Ava A-45 [M]	1964	7.50	15.00	30.00
❏ Ava AS-45 [S]	1964	10.00	20.00	40.00
CARRY IT ON				
❏ Vanguard VSD-79313	1971	6.25	12.50	25.00
CASINO ROYALE				
❏ Colgems COMO-5005 [M]	1967	7.50	15.00	30.00
❏ Colgems COSO-5005 [S]	1967	25.00	50.00	100.00
CAT PEOPLE				
❏ Backstreet BSR 6107	1982	5.00	10.00	20.00
A CERTAIN SMILE				
❏ Columbia CL 1194 [M]	1958	10.00	20.00	40.00
❏ Columbia CS 8068 [S]	1958	20.00	40.00	80.00
THE CHAIRMAN				
❏ Tetragrammaton T-5007	1969	7.50	15.00	30.00
CHARLOTTE'S WEB				
❏ Paramount PAS-1008	1973	7.50	15.00	30.00
THE CHASE				
❏ Columbia Masterworks OS 2960 [S]	1966	15.00	30.00	60.00
❏ Columbia Masterworks OL 6560 [M]	1966	10.00	20.00	40.00
CHINATOWN				
❏ ABC ABDP-848	1974	10.00	20.00	40.00
CHITTY CHITTY BANG BANG				
❏ United Artists UAS-5188	1968	6.25	12.50	25.00
THE CHRISTMAS THAT ALMOST WASN'T				
❏ RCA Camden CAL-1086 [M]	1966	6.25	12.50	25.00
❏ RCA Camden CAS-1086 [S]	1966	10.00	20.00	40.00
CINDERELLA				
❏ Disneyland DQ-1207 [M]	1959	10.00	20.00	40.00
-- Second issue, white back cover with ads for nine other LPs				
❏ Disneyland DQ-1207 [M]	1963	7.50	15.00	30.00
-- Third issue, pink back cover				
❏ Disneyland DQ-1207 [M]	1987	6.25	12.50	25.00
-- Fifth issue, high gloss cover with prince putting slipper on Cinderella's foot				
❏ Disneyland 3107 [PD]	1981	7.50	15.00	30.00
-- Fourth issue, picture disc				
❏ Disneyland WDL-4007 [M]	1957	50.00	100.00	200.00
-- Original issue, gatefold cover				
CINDERFELLA				
❏ Dot DLP-8001 [M]	1960	15.00	30.00	60.00
-- Gatefold cover with many extras including game board, spinner, booklet, music stand.				
❏ Dot SLP-38001 [S]	1960	25.00	50.00	100.00
-- Gatefold cover with many extras including game board, spinner, booklet, music stand.				
CLEOPATRA				
❏ 20th Century Fox FXG-5008 [M]	1963	7.50	15.00	30.00
❏ 20th Century Fox SXG-5008 [S]	1963	10.00	20.00	40.00

Label, Number	Yr	VG	VG+	NM
CLEOPATRA JONES				
❑ Warner Bros. BS 2719	1973	7.50	15.00	30.00
CLOSE ENCOUNTERS OF THE THIRD KIND				
❑ Arista AL 9500 [(2)]	1977	6.25	12.50	25.00
-- Includes one 12-inch record and one 7-inch record. Deduct 50 percent if the 7-inch record is missing.				
THE CLOWNS				
❑ Columbia S 30772	1971	10.00	20.00	40.00
COFFY				
❑ Polydor PD-5048	1973	25.00	50.00	100.00
THE COLLECTOR				
❑ Mainstream S-6053 [S]	1965	12.50	25.00	50.00
❑ Mainstream 56053 [M]	1965	7.50	15.00	30.00
COLLEGE CONFIDENTIAL				
❑ Chancellor CHL-5016 [M]	1960	10.00	20.00	40.00
❑ Chancellor CHLS-5016 [S]	1960	12.50	25.00	50.00
THE COLOR PURPLE				
❑ Qwest 25289 [(2)]	1985	6.25	12.50	25.00
-- Box set "limited edition" on purple vinyl with booklet				
❑ Qwest 25336 [(2)]	1985	5.00	10.00	20.00
-- Regular gatefold edition; records are still on purple vinyl				
COMANCHE				
❑ Coral CRL 57046 [M]	1956	100.00	200.00	400.00
COME BACK CHARLESTON BLUE				
❑ Atco SD 7010	1972	7.50	15.00	30.00
COME BLOW YOUR HORN				
❑ Reprise R-6071 [M]	1963	7.50	15.00	30.00
❑ Reprise R9-6071 [S]	1963	12.50	25.00	50.00
COMETOGETHER				
❑ Apple SW-3377	1971	5.00	10.00	20.00
COOLEY HIGH				
❑ Motown M7-840 R2 [(2)]	1975	5.00	10.00	20.00
THE CORRUPT ONES				
❑ United Artists UAL-4158 [M]	1967	10.00	20.00	40.00
❑ United Artists UAS-5158 [S]	1967	10.00	20.00	40.00
COTTON COMES TO HARLEM				
❑ United Artists UAS-5211	1970	7.50	15.00	30.00
THE COURT JESTER				
❑ Decca DL 8212 [M]	1956	17.50	35.00	70.00
-- Black label, silver print, or pink label, black print promo copy				
❑ Decca DL 8212 [M]	196?	7.50	15.00	30.00
-- Black label with color bars				
THE COWBOY				
❑ Decca DL 8684 [M]	1958	15.00	30.00	60.00
-- Black label, silver print, or pink label, black print promo copy				
❑ Decca DL 8684 [M]	196?	5.00	10.00	20.00
-- Black label with color bars				
CRIME IN THE STREETS				
❑ Decca DL 8376 [M]	1956	15.00	30.00	60.00
-- Black label, silver print, or pink label, black print promo copy				
❑ Decca DL 8376 [S]	196?	7.50	15.00	30.00
-- Black label with color bars				
THE CROSS AND THE SWITCHBLADE				
❑ Light LS-5550	1970	7.50	15.00	30.00
CRUISING				
❑ Columbia JS 36410	1980	10.00	20.00	40.00
CUSTER OF THE WEST				
❑ ABC ABC-OC-5 [M]	1968	20.00	40.00	80.00
❑ ABC ABCS-OC-5 [S]	1968	25.00	50.00	100.00
CYCLE SAVAGES				
❑ American Int'l. STA-1033	1970	7.50	15.00	30.00
CYRANO DE BERGERAC				
❑ Capitol S 283 [M]	1951	7.50	15.00	30.00
-- Originals have red labels with Capitol logo at top				
D.O.A.				
❑ Varese Sarabande 704.610	1988	10.00	20.00	40.00
DAMN THE DEFIANT!				
❑ Colpix CP 511 [M]	1962	7.50	15.00	30.00
❑ Colpix SCP 511 [S]	1962	15.00	30.00	60.00
DAMN YANKEES				
❑ RCA Victor LOC-1047 [M]	1958	10.00	20.00	40.00
-- Original pressing with "Long Play" on label				

Label, Number	Yr	VG	VG+	NM
THE DAMNED				
❑ Warner Bros. WS 1829	1969	7.50	15.00	30.00
THE DARK OF THE SUN				
❑ MGM SE-4544	1968	10.00	20.00	40.00
DARLING LILI				
❑ RCA Victor LSPX-1000	1969	5.00	10.00	20.00
DAWN OF THE DEAD				
❑ Varese Sarabande VC-81106	1979	7.50	15.00	30.00
DAY OF ANGER				
❑ RCA Victor LSO-1165	1969	5.00	10.00	20.00
THE DAY OF THE DOLPHIN				
❑ Avco AV-11014	1973	6.25	12.50	25.00
THE DAY THE FISH CAME OUT				
❑ 20th Century Fox TF-3194 [M]	1967	7.50	15.00	30.00
❑ 20th Century Fox TFS-4194 [S]	1967	10.00	20.00	40.00
DAYDREAMER				
❑ Columbia Masterworks OS 2940 [S]	1966	10.00	20.00	40.00
❑ Columbia Masterworks OL 6540 [M]	1966	7.50	15.00	30.00
DAYS OF HEAVEN				
❑ Pacific Arts PAC8-128	1978	10.00	20.00	40.00
DAYS OF THUNDER				
❑ DGC 24294	1990	5.00	10.00	20.00
DE SADE				
❑ Tower ST-5170	1969	7.50	15.00	30.00
DEAD MAN WALKING				
❑ Columbia C3 67989 [(3)]	1997	12.50	25.00	50.00
DEADFALL				
❑ 20th Century Fox S-4203	1968	15.00	30.00	60.00
DEAR JOHN				
❑ Dunhill OCD-55001 [M]	1966	5.00	10.00	20.00
❑ Dunhill OCDS-55001 [S]	1966	6.25	12.50	25.00
THE DECLINE OF WESTERN CIVILIZATION				
❑ Slash 105	1981	5.00	10.00	20.00
DEEP IN MY HEART				
❑ MGM E-3153 [M]	1955	12.50	25.00	50.00
❑ MGM E-3153 [M]	1955	10.00	20.00	40.00
DESIRE UNDER THE ELMS				
❑ Dot DLP-3095 [M]	1958	25.00	50.00	100.00
THE DEVIL AT 4 O'CLOCK				
❑ Colpix CP 509 [M]	1962	10.00	20.00	40.00
❑ Colpix SCP 509 [S]	1962	17.50	35.00	70.00
THE DEVIL IN MISS JONES				
❑ Janus JLS-3059	1973	6.25	12.50	25.00
THE DEVIL'S BRIGADE				
❑ United Artists UAS-6654	1968	5.00	10.00	20.00
DIAMOND HEAD				
❑ Colpix CP-440 [M]	1963	7.50	15.00	30.00
❑ Colpix SCP 440 [S]	1963	15.00	30.00	60.00
DIAMONDS ARE FOREVER				
❑ United Artists UAS-5520	1971	5.00	10.00	20.00
THE DIARY OF ANNE FRANK				
❑ 20th Fox FOX-3012 [M]	1959	12.50	25.00	50.00
❑ 20th Fox SFX-3012 [S]	1959	20.00	40.00	80.00
DIRTY GAME				
❑ Laurie LLP-2034 [M]	1966	6.25	12.50	25.00
❑ Laurie SLP-2034 [S]	1966	7.50	15.00	30.00
DIVORCE AMERICAN STYLE				
❑ United Artists UAL-4163 [M]	1967	5.00	10.00	20.00
❑ United Artists UAS-5163 [S]	1967	5.00	10.00	20.00
DIVORCE ITALIAN STYLE				
❑ United Artists UAL-4106 [M]	1962	10.00	20.00	40.00
❑ United Artists UAS-5106 [S]	1962	12.50	25.00	50.00
DOCTOR DOLITTLE				
❑ 20th Century Fox TCF-5101 [M]	1967	5.00	10.00	20.00
❑ 20th Century Fox TCS-5101 [S]	1967	5.00	10.00	20.00
DOCTOR GOLDFOOT AND THE GIRL BOMBS				
❑ Tower DT 5053 [R]	1966	6.25	12.50	25.00
❑ Tower T 5053 [M]	1966	5.00	10.00	20.00

Label, Number	Yr	VG	VG+	NM
DOCTOR ZHIVAGO				
❑ MGM S1E-6 ST [S]	1965	5.00	10.00	20.00
A DOG OF FLANDERS				
❑ 20th Fox FOX-3026 [M]	1959	20.00	40.00	80.00
❑ 20th Fox SFX-3026 [S]	1959	75.00	150.00	300.00
$ (DOLLARS)				
❑ Reprise MS 2051	1971	5.00	10.00	20.00
DON'T MAKE WAVES				
❑ MGM E-4483 [M]	1967	7.50	15.00	30.00
❑ MGM SE-4483 [S]	1967	7.50	15.00	30.00
THE DOORS				
❑ Elektra E1-61047	1991	5.00	10.00	20.00
-- Only vinyl edition in US was released through Columbia House				
DR. NO				
❑ United Artists UAL-4108 [M]	1963	10.00	20.00	40.00
❑ United Artists UAS-5108 [S]	1963	12.50	25.00	50.00
DR. PHIBES				
❑ American Int'l. A-1040	1971	15.00	30.00	60.00
DRANGO				
❑ Liberty LRP-3036 [M]	1957	37.50	75.00	150.00
A DREAM OF KINGS				
❑ National General NG-1000	1969	7.50	15.00	30.00
DUCK, YOU SUCKER				
❑ United Artists UAS-5221	1972	10.00	20.00	40.00
DUEL AT DIABLO				
❑ United Artists UAL-4139 [M]	1966	6.25	12.50	25.00
❑ United Artists UAS-5139 [S]	1966	7.50	15.00	30.00
DUMBO				
❑ Disneyland DQ-1204 [M]	1959	6.25	12.50	25.00
-- Second issue, back cover has ads for nine other LPs				
❑ Disneyland WDL-4013 [M]	1957	50.00	100.00	200.00
-- Original issue, gatefold cover				
❑ Disneyland ST-4904 [M]	1963	50.00	100.00	200.00
-- Special issue with pop-up figures in gatefold				
DUNE				
❑ Polydor 823 770-1	1984	7.50	15.00	30.00
THE DUNWICH HORROR				
❑ American Int'l. STA-1028	1970	10.00	20.00	40.00
E.T. THE EXTRA-TERRESTRIAL				
❑ MCA 6113 [PD]	1982	6.25	12.50	25.00
-- Picture disc in plastic envelope				
❑ MCA 16014	1982	10.00	20.00	40.00
-- Audiophile edition				
❑ MCA 70000	1982	12.50	25.00	50.00
-- Boxed version with booklet; story narrated by Michael Jackson				
EASTER PARADE				
❑ MGM E-502 [10]	1950	20.00	40.00	80.00
EASY RIDER				
❑ ABC Dunhill DSX-50063	1969	6.25	12.50	25.00
ECCO				
❑ Warner Bros. W 1600 [M]	1965	6.25	12.50	25.00
❑ Warner Bros. WS 1600 [S]	1965	7.50	15.00	30.00
THE EDDY DUCHIN STORY				
❑ Decca DL 8289 [M]	1956	10.00	20.00	40.00
-- Original cover with Tyrone Power and Kim Novak at a piano				
❑ Decca DL 8289 [M]	1959	5.00	10.00	20.00
-- Reissue cover with Tyrone Power and Kim Novak kissing				
❑ Decca DL 78289 [S]	1959	6.25	12.50	25.00
-- Maroon label, silver print, "Full Stereo" on front cover				
THE EDUCATION OF SONNY CARSON				
❑ Paramount PAS-1045	1974	5.00	10.00	20.00
THE EGYPTIAN				
❑ Decca DL 9014 [M]	1954	15.00	30.00	60.00
❑ Decca DL 79014 [R]	196?	5.00	10.00	20.00
EIGHT MEN OUT				
❑ Varese Sarabande 704.600	1988	6.25	12.50	25.00
EL CID				
❑ MGM E-3977 [M]	1962	10.00	20.00	40.00
❑ MGM SE-3977 [S]	1962	12.50	25.00	50.00
EL DORADO				
❑ Epic FLM-13114 [M]	1967	12.50	25.00	50.00
❑ Epic LFS-15114 [S]	1967	17.50	35.00	70.00

Label, Number	Yr	VG	VG+	NM
EL TOPO				
❑ Apple SWAO-3388	1972	10.00	20.00	40.00
ELECTRA GLIDE IN BLUE				
❑ United Artists UA-LA062-H [(2)]	1973	10.00	20.00	40.00
-- With booklet and two posters				
ELEPHANT STEPS				
❑ Columbia Masterworks M2X 33044 [(2)]	1975	5.00	10.00	20.00
ELMER GANTRY				
❑ United Artists UAL-4069 [M]	1960	10.00	20.00	40.00
❑ United Artists UAS-5069 [S]	1960	12.50	25.00	50.00
THE EMPIRE STRIKES BACK				
❑ RSO RS-2-4201 [(2)]	1980	5.00	10.00	20.00
-- With booklet				
ENTER THE DRAGON				
❑ Warner Bros. BS 2727	1973	15.00	30.00	60.00
EVERYTHING I HAVE IS YOURS				
❑ MGM E-187 [10]	1953	10.00	20.00	40.00
EVIL DEAD				
❑ Varese Sarabande STV-81199	1984	5.00	10.00	20.00
EXODUS				
❑ RCA Victor LOC-1058 [M]	1960	5.00	10.00	20.00
-- "Long Play" on label				
❑ RCA Victor LSO-1058 [S]	1960	6.25	12.50	25.00
-- "Living Stereo" on label				
THE EXORCIST				
❑ Warner Bros. W 2774	1974	7.50	15.00	30.00
A FACE IN THE CROWD				
❑ Capitol W 872 [M]	1957	12.50	25.00	50.00
THE FALL OF THE ROMAN EMPIRE				
❑ Columbia Masterworks OS 2460 [S]	1964	15.00	30.00	60.00
❑ Columbia Masterworks OL 6060 [M]	1964	10.00	20.00	40.00
THE FAMILY WAY				
❑ London M 76007 [M]	1967	25.00	50.00	100.00
-- No promo sticker on front cover (deduct 20 percent for promo)				
❑ London ST 82007 [S]	1967	30.00	60.00	120.00
-- No promo sticker on front cover (deduct 20 percent for promo)				
FANNY				
❑ Warner Bros. W 1416 [M]	1961	6.25	12.50	25.00
❑ Warner Bros. WS 1416 [S]	1961	7.50	15.00	30.00
FANTASIA				
❑ Buena Vista 101 [(2) S]	1982	5.00	10.00	20.00
-- Stereo reissue, two records, no booklet				
❑ Buena Vista STER-101 [(3) S]	1961	10.00	20.00	40.00
-- First stereo issue, black and yellow rainbow labels, includes 24-page booklet				
❑ Buena Vista WDX-101 [(3) M]	1961	7.50	15.00	30.00
-- Second issue, blue labels, includes 24-page booklet				
❑ Buena Vista V-104 [(2)]	1982	6.25	12.50	25.00
-- Digitally re-recorded music track, Mickey Mouse as The Sorcerer on cover				
❑ Disneyland WDX-101 [(3)]	1957	15.00	30.00	60.00
-- Original issue, maroon/red labels, includes 24-page booklet				
FANTASIA: NIGHT ON BALD MOUNTAIN; PASTORAL SYMPHONY; AVE MARIA				
❑ Disneyland STER-4101C [S]	1958	7.50	15.00	30.00
❑ Disneyland WDL-4101C [M]	1958	5.00	10.00	20.00
FANTASIA: THE NUTCRACKER SUITE; DANCE OF THE HOURS				
❑ Disneyland STER-4101B [S]	1959	7.50	15.00	30.00
❑ Disneyland WDL-4101B [M]	1958	5.00	10.00	20.00
FANTASIA: RITE OF SPRING; TOCCATA AND FUGUE				
❑ Disneyland STER-4101A [S]	1959	7.50	15.00	30.00
❑ Disneyland WDL-4101A [M]	1958	5.00	10.00	20.00
THE FANTASTIC PLASTIC MACHINE				
❑ Epic BN 26469	1969	6.25	12.50	25.00
FAR FROM THE MADDING CROWD				
❑ MGM S1E-11 [S]	1967	6.25	12.50	25.00
A FAREWELL TO ARMS				
❑ Capitol W 918 [M]	1957	12.50	25.00	50.00
THE FASTEST GUITAR ALIVE				
❑ MGM SE-4475	1968	7.50	15.00	30.00
FATHOM				
❑ 20th Century Fox TFM-4195 [M]	1967	10.00	20.00	40.00
❑ 20th Century Fox TFS-4195 [S]	1967	12.50	25.00	50.00

Label, Number	Yr	VG	VG+	NM
FELLINI SATYRICON				
❏ United Artists UAS-5208	1969	7.50	15.00	30.00
FELLINI'S ROMA				
❏ United Artists UA-LA052-F	1972	7.50	15.00	30.00
THE FEMALE PRISONER				
❏ Columbia Masterworks OS 3320	1969	7.50	15.00	30.00
FIDDLER ON THE ROOF				
❏ United Artists UAS-10900 [(2)]	1971	5.00	10.00	20.00
-- With booklet				
55 DAYS AT PEKING				
❏ Columbia CL 2028 [M]	1963	10.00	20.00	40.00
❏ Columbia CS 8828 [S]	1963	17.50	35.00	70.00
THE FIGHTER				
❏ Decca DL 5414 [10]	1952	20.00	40.00	80.00
THE FINAL COUNTDOWN				
❏ Casablanca NBLP-7232	1980	10.00	20.00	40.00
FINIAN'S RAINBOW				
❏ Warner Bros. BS 2550	1968	5.00	10.00	20.00
FIRE DOWN BELOW				
❏ Decca DL 8597 [M]	1957	17.50	35.00	70.00
A FISTFUL OF DOLLARS				
❏ RCA Victor LOC-1135 [M]	1967	5.00	10.00	20.00
❏ RCA Victor LSO-1135 [S]	1967	7.50	15.00	30.00
-- Black label, dog on top				
FITZWILLY				
❏ United Artists UAL-4173 [M]	1967	5.00	10.00	20.00
❏ United Artists UAS-5173 [S]	1967	6.25	12.50	25.00
FIVE EASY PIECES				
❏ Epic KE 30456	1971	6.25	12.50	25.00
THE FIVE PENNIES				
❏ Dot DLP-9500 [M]	1959	6.25	12.50	25.00
❏ Dot DLP-29500 [S]	1959	12.50	25.00	50.00
THE FLAMINGO KID				
❏ Varese Sarabande STV-81232	1984	10.00	20.00	40.00
-- Original issue (more common version is on Motown)				
A FLEA IN HER EAR				
❏ 20th Century Fox TFS-4200	1968	7.50	15.00	30.00
FLOWER DRUM SONG				
❏ Decca DL 9098 [M]	1961	5.00	10.00	20.00
❏ Decca DL 79098 [S]	1961	6.25	12.50	25.00
THE FOG				
❏ Varese Sarabande STV-81191	1980	6.25	12.50	25.00
FOLIES BERGERE				
❏ Decca DL 8571 [M]	1958	6.25	12.50	25.00
FOLLOW ME				
❏ Uni 73056	1969	7.50	15.00	30.00
FOOTLOOSE				
❏ Columbia 9C9 39404 [PD]	1984	5.00	10.00	20.00
-- Picture disc version				
FOR A FEW DOLLARS MORE				
❏ United Artists UAL-3608 [M]	1967	5.00	10.00	20.00
❏ United Artists UAS-6608 [S]	1967	6.25	12.50	25.00
FOR LOVE OF IVY				
❏ ABC SOC-7	1968	6.25	12.50	25.00
FOR THE FIRST TIME				
❏ RCA Red Seal LSC-2338 [S]	1959	5.00	10.00	20.00
-- With "shaded dog" and smaller RCA Victor lettering				
FOR YOUR EYES ONLY				
❏ Liberty LOO-1109	1981	7.50	15.00	30.00
40 POUNDS OF TROUBLE				
❏ Mercury MG-20784 [M]	1963	7.50	15.00	30.00
❏ Mercury SR-60784 [S]	1963	10.00	20.00	40.00
THE FOUR HORSEMEN OF THE APOCALYPSE				
❏ MGM E-3993 [M]	1962	5.00	10.00	20.00
❏ MGM SE-3993 [S]	1962	6.25	12.50	25.00
FOUR IN THE MORNING				
❏ Roulette OS 805 [M]	1966	10.00	20.00	40.00
❏ Roulette OSS 805 [S]	1966	12.50	25.00	50.00
THE FOX				
❏ Warner Bros. W 1738 [M]	1968	10.00	20.00	40.00
❏ Warner Bros. WS 1738 [S]	1968	6.25	12.50	25.00
THE FOX AND THE HOUND				
❏ Disneyland 3106 [PD]	1981	7.50	15.00	30.00
-- "Disney Picture Disc" series				
❏ Disneyland ST-3823	1981	5.00	10.00	20.00
-- Non-picture disc version				
FOXY BROWN				
❏ Motown M7-811	1974	5.00	10.00	20.00
FRANCIS OF ASSISI				
❏ 20th Fox FOX-3053 [M]	1961	50.00	100.00	200.00
❏ 20th Fox SFX-3053 [S]	1961	62.50	125.00	250.00
THE FRENCH LINE				
❏ Mercury MG-25182 [10]	1954	20.00	40.00	80.00
FRIENDLY PERSUASION				
❏ RKO Unique LP-110 [M]	1956	18.75	37.50	75.00
FRITZ THE CAT				
❏ Fantasy F-9406	1972	7.50	15.00	30.00
FROM RUSSIA WITH LOVE				
❏ United Artists UAL-4114 [M]	1964	5.00	10.00	20.00
❏ United Artists UAS-5114 [S]	1964	6.25	12.50	25.00
THE FUGITIVE KIND				
❏ United Artists UAL-4065 [M]	1959	12.50	25.00	50.00
❏ United Artists UAS-5065 [S]	1959	17.50	35.00	70.00
FUNERAL IN BERLIN				
❏ RCA Victor LOC-1136 [M]	1966	7.50	15.00	30.00
❏ RCA Victor LSO-1136 [S]	1966	12.50	25.00	50.00
FUNNY GIRL				
❏ Columbia Masterworks SQ 30992 [Q]	1971	10.00	20.00	40.00
GAILY, GAILY				
❏ United Artists UAS 5202	1969	6.25	12.50	25.00
THE GAME IS OVER				
❏ Atco 33-205 [M]	1967	5.00	10.00	20.00
❏ Atco SD 33-205 [S]	1967	6.25	12.50	25.00
THE GAMES				
❏ Viking LPS-105	1970	50.00	100.00	200.00
GAY PURR-EE				
❏ Warner Bros. B 1479 [M]	1963	5.00	10.00	20.00
❏ Warner Bros. BS 1479 [S]	1963	7.50	15.00	30.00
GEISHA BOY				
❏ Jubilee JGS-1096 [S]	1959	20.00	40.00	80.00
❏ Jubilee JLP-1096 [M]	1958	12.50	25.00	50.00
THE GENE KRUPA STORY				
❏ Verve MGVS-6105 [S]	1959	25.00	50.00	100.00
-- Original issue				
❏ Verve MGV-15010 [M]	1959	12.50	25.00	50.00
❏ Verve V6-15010 [S]	1963	20.00	40.00	80.00
-- Early reissue				
GENGHIS KHAN				
❏ Liberty LRP-3412 [M]	1965	10.00	20.00	40.00
❏ Liberty LST-7412 [S]	1965	15.00	30.00	60.00
GENTLEMEN MARRY BRUNETTES				
❏ Coral CRL 57013 [M]	1955	17.50	35.00	70.00
GENTLEMEN PREFER BLONDES				
❏ MGM E-208 [M]	1953	30.00	60.00	120.00
GET YOURSELF A COLLEGE GIRL				
❏ MGM E-4273 [M]	1965	5.00	10.00	20.00
❏ MGM SE-4273 [S]	1965	10.00	20.00	40.00
GETTING STRAIGHT				
❏ Colgems COSO-5010	1970	7.50	15.00	30.00
GIANT				
❏ Capitol W 773 [M]	1956	10.00	20.00	40.00
-- Turquoise or gray label				
❏ Capitol W 773 [M]	1959	6.25	12.50	25.00
-- Black colorband label, logo at left				
GIDGET GOES HAWAIIAN				
❏ Colpix CP 418 [M]	1961	12.50	25.00	50.00

Label, Number	Yr	VG	VG+	NM
GIGI				
❑ MGM E-3641 [M]	1958	5.00	10.00	20.00
-- Yellow label				
❑ MGM SE-3641 [S]	1959	6.25	12.50	25.00
-- Yellow label				
GIGOT				
❑ Capitol SW 1754 [S]	1962	10.00	20.00	40.00
❑ Capitol W 1754 [M]	1962	7.50	15.00	30.00
THE GIRL IN THE BIKINI				
❑ Poplar PLP 33-1002 [M]	1952	100.00	200.00	400.00
THE GIRL MOST LIKELY				
❑ Capitol W 930 [M]	1957	15.00	30.00	60.00
GIRL ON A MOTORCYCLE				
❑ Tetragrammaton T-5000	1969	7.50	15.00	30.00
THE GLENN MILLER STORY				
❑ Decca DL 5519 [10]	1954	10.00	20.00	40.00
❑ Decca DL 8226 [M]	1956	7.50	15.00	30.00
❑ Decca DL 9123 [M]	196?	5.00	10.00	20.00
-- Reissue of 8226				
GLORY				
❑ Virgin 91329	1989	7.50	15.00	30.00
❑ Virgin/Classic 91329	1998	5.00	10.00	20.00
-- Audiophile reissue; cover is noticeably less sharp than the originals				
THE GLORY STOMPERS				
❑ Sidewalk DT 5910 [R]	1968	12.50	25.00	50.00
GO, GO, GO WORLD				
❑ Musicor MM-2059 [M]	1965	10.00	20.00	40.00
❑ Musicor MS-3059 [S]	1965	15.00	30.00	60.00
GO, JOHNNY, GO!				
❑ (No label) (no number) [DJ]	1959	250.00	500.00	1,000.
-- Only exists as a promo				
GOD'S LITTLE ACRE				
❑ United Artists UAL-4002 [M]	1958	37.50	75.00	150.00
THE GODFATHER				
❑ Paramount PAS-1003	1972	5.00	10.00	20.00
-- Original cover with triple gatefold				
THE GODFATHER PART II				
❑ ABC ABDP-856	1975	5.00	10.00	20.00
THE GODFATHER PART III				
❑ Columbia C 47078	1990	5.00	10.00	20.00
GOLD				
❑ ABC ABCD-855	1975	7.50	15.00	30.00
THE GOLDEN BREED				
❑ Capitol ST 2886	1967	7.50	15.00	30.00
THE GOLDEN COACH				
❑ MGM E-3111 [M]	1954	37.50	75.00	150.00
THE GOLDEN SCREW				
❑ Atco 33-208 [M]	1967	7.50	15.00	30.00
❑ Atco SD 33-208 [S]	1967	10.00	20.00	40.00
GOLDFINGER				
❑ United Artists UAS-5117 [S]	1964	5.00	10.00	20.00
GOLIATH AND THE BARBARIANS				
❑ American Int'l. 1001-M [M]	1960	10.00	20.00	40.00
❑ American Int'l. 1001-S [S]	1960	17.50	35.00	70.00
GONE WITH THE WAVE				
❑ Colpix CP-492 [M]	1965	10.00	20.00	40.00
❑ Colpix SCP-492 [S]	1965	15.00	30.00	60.00
GONE WITH THE WIND				
❑ MGM 1E-10 [M]	1967	5.00	10.00	20.00
-- Gatefold edition with 32-page booklet				
❑ MGM S1E-10 [S]	1967	5.00	10.00	20.00
-- Gatefold edition with 32-page booklet				
GOOD NEWS				
❑ MGM E-504 [10]	1950	12.50	25.00	50.00
GOODBYE AGAIN				
❑ United Artists UAL-4091 [M]	1961	7.50	15.00	30.00
❑ United Artists UAS-5091 [S]	1961	10.00	20.00	40.00
GOODBYE, CHARLIE				
❑ 20th Century Fox TFM-3165 [M]	1964	6.25	12.50	25.00
❑ 20th Century Fox TFS-4165 [S]	1964	7.50	15.00	30.00

Label, Number	Yr	VG	VG+	NM
GOODBYE, MR. CHIPS				
❑ MGM 1SE-19	1969	5.00	10.00	20.00
GORDON'S WAR				
❑ Buddah BDS-5137	1973	10.00	20.00	40.00
THE GOSPEL ACCORDING TO ST. MATTHEW				
❑ Mainstream S-4000 [S]	1966	25.00	50.00	100.00
❑ Mainstream 54000 [M]	1966	6.25	12.50	25.00
GOTHIC				
❑ Virgin 90607	1987	5.00	10.00	20.00
GOYA				
❑ Decca DL 8236 [M]	1959	37.50	75.00	150.00
GRAND PRIX				
❑ MGM 1E-8 [M]	1967	5.00	10.00	20.00
❑ MGM 1SE-8 [S]	1967	6.25	12.50	25.00
THE GREAT ESCAPE				
❑ United Artists UAL-4107 [M]	1963	6.25	12.50	25.00
❑ United Artists UAS-5107 [S]	1963	7.50	15.00	30.00
THE GREAT GATSBY				
❑ Paramount PAS-2-3001 [(2)]	1974	5.00	10.00	20.00
THE GREATEST SHOW ON EARTH				
❑ RCA Victor LPM-3018 [10]	1952	50.00	100.00	200.00
THE GREATEST STORY EVER TOLD				
❑ United Artists UAL-4120 [M]	1965	6.25	12.50	25.00
❑ United Artists UAS-5120 [S]	1965	7.50	15.00	30.00
GROUNDS FOR MARRIAGE				
❑ MGM E-536 [M]	1950	20.00	40.00	80.00
GUESS WHO'S COMING TO DINNER				
❑ Colgems COM-108 [M]	1968	7.50	15.00	30.00
❑ Colgems COS-108 [S]	1968	7.50	15.00	30.00
GULLIVER'S TRAVELS BEYOND THE MOON				
❑ Mainstream S-4001 [S]	1965	10.00	20.00	40.00
❑ Mainstream 54001 [M]	1965	7.50	15.00	30.00
GUNS FOR SAN SEBASTIAN				
❑ MGM SE-4565	1968	15.00	30.00	60.00
THE GUNS OF NAVARONE				
❑ Columbia CL 1655 [M]	1961	5.00	10.00	20.00
❑ Columbia CS 8455 [S]	1961	12.50	25.00	50.00
GURU				
❑ RCA Victor LSO-1158	1969	5.00	10.00	20.00
GUYS AND DOLLS				
❑ Decca DL 8036 [M]	1950	7.50	15.00	30.00
❑ Decca DL 9023 [M]	1955	5.00	10.00	20.00
-- Reissue of 8036				
GYPSY				
❑ Warner Bros. B 1480 [M]	1962	5.00	10.00	20.00
❑ Warner Bros. BS 1480 [S]	1962	7.50	15.00	30.00
GYPSY GIRL				
❑ Mainstream S-6090 [S]	1966	10.00	20.00	40.00
❑ Mainstream 56090 [M]	1966	7.50	15.00	30.00
HALLELUJAH THE HILLS				
❑ Fontana MGF-27524 [M]	1964	6.25	12.50	25.00
❑ Fontana SRF-67524 [S]	1964	7.50	15.00	30.00
THE HALLELUJAH TRAIL				
❑ United Artists UAL-4127 [M]	1965	5.00	10.00	20.00
❑ United Artists UAS-5127 [S]	1965	6.25	12.50	25.00
HAMMERHEAD				
❑ Colgems COS-110	1968	10.00	20.00	40.00
HAMMERSMITH IS OUT				
❑ Capitol SW-861	1972	7.50	15.00	30.00
HANG 'EM HIGH				
❑ United Artists UAS-5179	1968	6.25	12.50	25.00
THE HAPPENING				
❑ Colgems COMO-5006 [M]	1967	7.50	15.00	30.00
❑ Colgems COSO-5006 [S]	1967	12.50	25.00	50.00
THE HAPPIEST MILLIONAIRE				
❑ Buena Vista STER-5001 [S]	1967	5.00	10.00	20.00
THE HARD RIDE				
❑ Paramount PAS-6005	1971	7.50	15.00	30.00

Label, Number	Yr	VG	VG+	NM
HARPER				
❏ Mainstream S-6078 [S]	1966	6.25	12.50	25.00
❏ Mainstream 56078 [M]	1966	5.00	10.00	20.00
THE HARRAD EXPERIMENT				
❏ Capitol ST-11182	1973	6.25	12.50	25.00
HARRAD SUMMER				
❏ Capitol ST-11338	1974	6.25	12.50	25.00
HAWAII				
❏ United Artists UAL-4143 [M]	1966	5.00	10.00	20.00
❏ United Artists UAS-5143 [S]	1966	6.25	12.50	25.00
❏ United Artists SW-90935 [S]	1966	7.50	15.00	30.00
-- Capitol Record Club issue				
THE HEART IS A LONELY HUNTER				
❏ Warner Bros. WS 1759	1968	7.50	15.00	30.00
HEART OF DIXIE				
❏ A&M SP-3930	1989	5.00	10.00	20.00
HEAVY METAL				
❏ Full Moon/Asylum 5E-547	1981	12.50	25.00	50.00
-- Contains Elmer Bernstein's instrumental music				
❏ Full Moon/Asylum DP-90004 [(2)]	1981	5.00	10.00	20.00
-- Contains two LPs of pop/rock music				
HEAVY TRAFFIC				
❏ Fantasy F-9436	1973	6.25	12.50	25.00
HEIDI'S SONG				
❏ K-Tel NU 5310	1982	5.00	10.00	20.00
THE HELEN MORGAN STORY				
❏ RCA Victor LOC-1030 [M]	1957	15.00	30.00	60.00
HELL TO ETERNITY				
❏ Warwick W 2030 [M]	1960	30.00	60.00	120.00
❏ Warwick WST 2030 [S]	1960	50.00	100.00	200.00
HELL UP IN HARLEM				
❏ Motown M 802V1	1974	7.50	15.00	30.00
HELL'S ANGELS '69				
❏ Capitol SKAO-303	1969	6.25	12.50	25.00
HELL'S ANGELS ON WHEELS				
❏ Smash MGS-27094 [M]	1967	6.25	12.50	25.00
❏ Smash SRS-67094 [S]	1967	7.50	15.00	30.00
HELL'S BELLS				
❏ Sidewalk ST 5919	1969	7.50	15.00	30.00
HELLCATS				
❏ Tower ST 5124	1968	7.50	15.00	30.00
HELLO-GOODBYE				
❏ 20th Century Fox S-4210	1970	10.00	20.00	40.00
HEMINGWAY'S ADVENTURES OF A YOUNG MAN				
❏ RCA Victor LOC-1074 [M]	1962	10.00	20.00	40.00
❏ RCA Victor LSO-1074 [S]	1962	17.50	35.00	70.00
HERCULES				
❏ Varese Sarabande STV-81187	1983	5.00	10.00	20.00
THE HERO				
❏ Capitol SW-11098	1972	5.00	10.00	20.00
HEROES OF TELEMARK				
❏ Mainstream S-6064 [S]	1965	7.50	15.00	30.00
❏ Mainstream 56064 [M]	1965	5.00	10.00	20.00
HEY THERE, IT'S YOGI BEAR!				
❏ Colpix CP-472 [M]	1964	12.50	25.00	50.00
❏ Colpix SCP-472 [S]	1964	20.00	40.00	80.00
HIGH SOCIETY				
❏ Capitol SW 750 [S]	1959	7.50	15.00	30.00
-- Black colorband label, logo at left				
❏ Capitol SW 750 [S]	1962	5.00	10.00	20.00
-- Black colorband label, logo at top				
❏ Capitol W 750 [M]	1956	7.50	15.00	30.00
-- Gray label original				
❏ Capitol W 750 [M]	1959	5.00	10.00	20.00
-- Black colorband label, logo at left				
THE HOBBIT				
❏ Buena Vista 103 [(2)]	1977	7.50	15.00	30.00
❏ Buena Vista 103A [(2)]	1977	10.00	20.00	40.00
-- Special edition sold at Sears stores, with four decals and poster				
❏ Disneyland ST-3819	1978	7.50	15.00	30.00

Label, Number	Yr	VG	VG+	NM
HOLIDAY INN				
❏ Decca DL 4256 [M]	1962	6.25	12.50	25.00
HOMER AND EDDIE				
❏ Apache D1-71654	1989	6.25	12.50	25.00
HOOSIERS				
❏ Polydor 831 475-1	1987	7.50	15.00	30.00
HOOTENANNY HOOT				
❏ MGM E-4172 [M]	1963	5.00	10.00	20.00
❏ MGM SE-4172 [S]	1963	6.25	12.50	25.00
THE HORSE SOLDIERS				
❏ United Artists UAL-4035 [M]	1959	15.00	30.00	60.00
❏ United Artists UAS-5035 [S]	1959	37.50	75.00	150.00
THE HORSEMEN				
❏ Sunflower SNF-5007	1971	10.00	20.00	40.00
THE HOT ROCK				
❏ Prophesy SD 8055	1972	5.00	10.00	20.00
HOT ROD RUMBLE				
❏ Liberty LRP-3048 [M]	1957	37.50	75.00	150.00
HOTEL PARADISO				
❏ MGM E-4419 [M]	1966	5.00	10.00	20.00
❏ MGM SE-4419 [S]	1966	6.25	12.50	25.00
THE HOUR OF THE GUN				
❏ United Artists UAL-4166 [M]	1967	10.00	20.00	40.00
❏ United Artists UAS-5166 [S]	1967	17.50	35.00	70.00
A HOUSE IS NOT A HOME				
❏ Ava A-50 [M]	1964	6.25	12.50	25.00
❏ Ava AS-50 [S]	1964	7.50	15.00	30.00
HOUSEBOAT				
❏ Columbia CL 1222 [M]	1958	12.50	25.00	50.00
HOW SWEET IT IS				
❏ RCA Victor LSP-4037	1968	5.00	10.00	20.00
HOW THE WEST WAS WON				
❏ MGM S1E-5 [S]	1963	5.00	10.00	20.00
HOW TO MURDER YOUR WIFE				
❏ United Artists UAS-5119 [S]	1965	5.00	10.00	20.00
HOW TO SAVE A MARRIAGE AND RUIN YOUR LIFE				
❏ Columbia Masterworks OS 3140	1968	5.00	10.00	20.00
HOW TO STEAL A MILLION				
❏ 20th Century Fox TFM-3183 [M]	1966	10.00	20.00	40.00
❏ 20th Century Fox TFS-4183 [S]	1966	12.50	25.00	50.00
HOW TO STUFF A WILD BIKINI				
❏ Wand 671 [M]	1965	7.50	15.00	30.00
❏ Wand S-671 [S]	1965	10.00	20.00	40.00
HOW TO SUCCEED IN BUSINESS WITHOUT REALLY TRYING				
❏ United Artists UAL-4151 [M]	1967	5.00	10.00	20.00
❏ United Artists UAS-5151 [S]	1967	6.25	12.50	25.00
HOWARD THE DUCK				
❏ MCA 6173	1986	5.00	10.00	20.00
HUGO THE HIPPO				
❏ United Artists UA-LA637-G	1976	5.00	10.00	20.00
THE HUNGER				
❏ Varese Sarabande STV-81184	1983	5.00	10.00	20.00
THE HUNT FOR RED OCTOBER				
❏ MCA 6428	1990	7.50	15.00	30.00
HURRICANE				
❏ Elektra 5E-504	1979	5.00	10.00	20.00
HURRY SUNDOWN				
❏ RCA Victor LOC-1133 [M]	1967	7.50	15.00	30.00
❏ RCA Victor LSO-1133 [S]	1967	10.00	20.00	40.00
THE HUSTLER				
❏ Kapp KL-1264 [M]	1961	15.00	30.00	60.00
❏ Kapp KS-3264 [S]	1961	30.00	60.00	120.00
I LOVE MELVIN				
❏ MGM E-190 [10]	1953	12.50	25.00	50.00
I NEVER SANG FOR MY FATHER				
❏ Bell 1204	1970	10.00	20.00	40.00

Label, Number	Yr	VG	VG+	NM
I WANT TO LIVE				
❑ United Artists UXL 1 [(2) M]	1958	15.00	30.00	60.00
-- Combines 4005 and 4006 into one package				
❑ United Artists UXS 51 [(2) S]	1958	20.00	40.00	80.00
-- Combines 5005 and 5006 into one package				
❑ United Artists UAL-4005 [M]	1958	6.25	12.50	25.00
-- Orchestral music by Johnny Mandel				
❑ United Artists UAL-4006 [M]	1958	7.50	15.00	30.00
-- Jazz music by Gerry Mulligan, Shelly Mann and Art Farmer				
❑ United Artists UAS-5005 [S]	1958	10.00	20.00	40.00
-- Orchestral music by Johnny Mandel				
❑ United Artists UAS-5006 [S]	1958	10.00	20.00	40.00
-- Jazz music by Gerry Mulligan, Shelly Mann and Art Farmer				
I'LL NEVER FORGET WHAT'S 'IS NAME				
❑ Decca DL 9163 [M]	1967	6.25	12.50	25.00
❑ Decca DL 79163 [S]	1967	7.50	15.00	30.00
ICE STATION ZEBRA				
❑ MGM S1E-14 ST	1968	10.00	20.00	40.00
ICEMAN				
❑ Southern Cross SCRS-1006	1983	5.00	10.00	20.00
IF HE HOLLERS, LET HIM GO				
❑ Tower ST 5152	1968	10.00	20.00	40.00
IMITATION OF LIFE				
❑ Decca DL 78879 [S]	1959	20.00	40.00	80.00
❑ Decca DL 8879 [M]	1959	12.50	25.00	50.00
IN A SHALLOW GRAVE				
❑ Varese Sarabande STV-81359	1988	10.00	20.00	40.00
IN HARM'S WAY				
❑ RCA Victor LOC-1100 [M]	1965	10.00	20.00	40.00
❑ RCA Victor LSO-1100 [S]	1965	20.00	40.00	80.00
IN LIKE FLINT				
❑ 20th Century Fox 4193 [M]	1967	10.00	20.00	40.00
❑ 20th Century Fox S-4193 [S]	1967	20.00	40.00	80.00
IN SEARCH OF THE CASTAWAYS				
❑ Disneyland ST-3916 [M]	1962	17.50	35.00	70.00
IN THE GOOD OLD SUMMERTIME				
❑ MGM E-169 [10]	1949	25.00	50.00	100.00
IN THE HEAT OF THE NIGHT				
❑ United Artists UAS-5160 [S]	1967	5.00	10.00	20.00
INCHON				
❑ Regency RI-8502	1982	7.50	15.00	30.00
INDIANA JONES AND THE TEMPLE OF DOOM				
❑ Polydor 821 592-1	1984	5.00	10.00	20.00
THE INDISCRETION OF AN AMERICAN WIFE				
❑ Columbia CL 6277 [10]	1954	20.00	40.00	80.00
THE INN OF THE SIXTH HAPPINESS				
❑ 20th Century Fox FOX-3011 [M]	1958	12.50	25.00	50.00
❑ 20th Century Fox SFX-3011 [S]	1958	17.50	35.00	70.00
INSIDE DAISY CLOVER				
❑ Warner Bros. W 1616 [M]	1965	5.00	10.00	20.00
❑ Warner Bros. WS 1616 [S]	1965	7.50	15.00	30.00
INSPECTOR CLOUSEAU				
❑ United Artists UAS-5186	1968	7.50	15.00	30.00
INTERLUDE				
❑ Colgems COSO-5007	1968	10.00	20.00	40.00
THE INTERNS				
❑ Colpix CP 427 [M]	1962	7.50	15.00	30.00
❑ Colpix SCP 427 [S]	1962	10.00	20.00	40.00
INVITATION TO THE DANCE				
❑ MGM E-3207 [M]	1956	12.50	25.00	50.00
THE IPCRESS FILE				
❑ Decca DL 9124 [M]	1965	7.50	15.00	30.00
❑ Decca DL 79124 [S]	1965	10.00	20.00	40.00
IRMA LA DOUCE				
❑ United Artists UAL-4109 [M]	1963	5.00	10.00	20.00
❑ United Artists UAS-5109 [S]	1963	6.25	12.50	25.00
IS PARIS BURNING?				
❑ Columbia Masterworks OS 3030 [S]	1966	10.00	20.00	40.00
❑ Columbia Masterworks OL 6630 [M]	1966	7.50	15.00	30.00

Label, Number	Yr	VG	VG+	NM
THE ISLAND				
❑ Varese Sarabande VC-81147	1979	5.00	10.00	20.00
THE ISLAND AT THE TOP OF THE WORLD				
❑ Disneyland ST-3814	1974	6.25	12.50	25.00
ISLAND IN THE SKY				
❑ Decca DL 7029 [10]	1953	75.00	150.00	300.00
IT STARTED IN NAPLES				
❑ Dot DLP-3324 [M]	1960	15.00	30.00	60.00
❑ Dot DLP-25324 [S]	1960	25.00	50.00	100.00
IT'S A MAD, MAD, MAD, MAD WORLD				
❑ United Artists UAL-4110 [M]	1963	5.00	10.00	20.00
❑ United Artists UAS-5110 [S]	1963	6.25	12.50	25.00
IT'S ALWAYS FAIR WEATHER				
❑ MGM E-3241 [M]	1955	12.50	25.00	50.00
THE ITALIAN JOB				
❑ Paramount PAS-5007	1969	10.00	20.00	40.00
JACK THE RIPPER				
❑ RCA Victor LPM-2199 [M]	1960	7.50	15.00	30.00
❑ RCA Victor LSP-2199 [S]	1960	12.50	25.00	50.00
JAMBOREE!				
❑ Warner Bros. (no #) [M]	1957	300.00	600.00	1,200.
-- Album has been counterfeited. Originals have front cover slicks and back cover notes printed on the cardboard, and the records have "Jam 1" and "Jam 2" stamped (not etched) in the dead wax.				
JAWS				
❑ MCA 2087	1975	5.00	10.00	20.00
JEAN DE FLORETTE				
❑ TVT 3004	1986	5.00	10.00	20.00
JEREMIAH JOHNSON				
❑ Warner Bros. BS 2902	1972	5.00	10.00	20.00
-- Green label				
JESSICA				
❑ United Artists UAL-4096 [M]	1962	5.00	10.00	20.00
❑ United Artists UAS-5096 [S]	1962	6.25	12.50	25.00
THE JOE LOUIS STORY				
❑ MGM E-221 [10]	1953	20.00	40.00	80.00
JOHN PAUL JONES				
❑ Warner Bros. W 1293 [M]	1959	15.00	30.00	60.00
❑ Warner Bros. WS 1293 [S]	1959	30.00	60.00	120.00
JOHNNY COOL				
❑ United Artists UAL-4111 [M]	1963	5.00	10.00	20.00
❑ United Artists UAS-5111 [S]	1963	6.25	12.50	25.00
JOHNNY TREMAIN				
❑ Disneyland WDL-4014 [M]	1957	12.50	25.00	50.00
JUD				
❑ Ampex A-50101	1971	5.00	10.00	20.00
JUDGMENT AT NUREMBERG				
❑ United Artists UAL-4095 [M]	1961	5.00	10.00	20.00
❑ United Artists UAS-5095 [S]	1961	12.50	25.00	50.00
JUDITH				
❑ RCA Victor LSO-1119 [S]	1966	7.50	15.00	30.00
JULIET OF THE SPIRITS				
❑ Mainstream S-6062 [S]	1965	15.00	30.00	60.00
❑ Mainstream 56062 [M]	1965	6.25	12.50	25.00
JULIUS CAESAR				
❑ MGM E-3033 [M]	1953	10.00	20.00	40.00
JUMBO (BILLY ROSE'S)				
❑ Columbia Masterworks OS 2260 [S]	1962	7.50	15.00	30.00
❑ Columbia Masterworks OL 5860 [M]	1962	5.00	10.00	20.00
THE JUNGLE BOOK				
❑ Disneyland 3105 [PD]	1981	7.50	15.00	30.00
-- "Disney Picture Disc" series				
❑ Buena Vista STER-4041 [S]	1967	6.25	12.50	25.00
❑ Buena Vista STER-4041 [S]	1967	6.25	12.50	25.00
JURASSIC PARK				
❑ MCA/BMG (no #) [PD]	1993	300.00	600.00	1,200.
-- Custom-made picture disc; promo only				
JUSTINE				
❑ Monument SLP-18123	1969	7.50	15.00	30.00

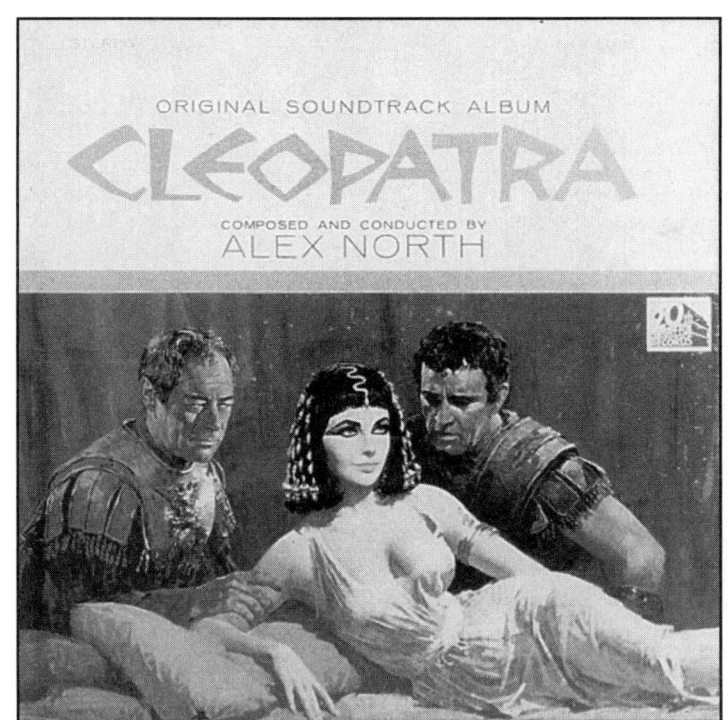

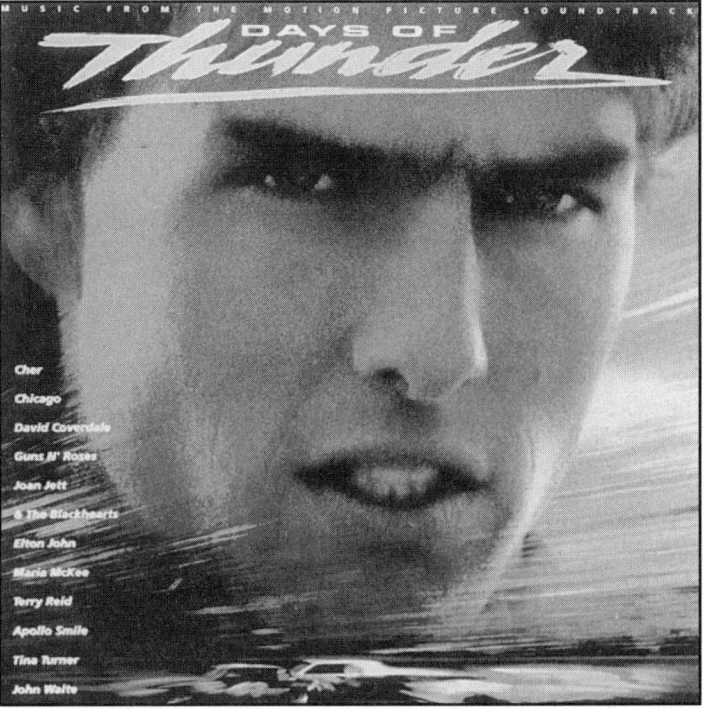

(Top left) *Cleopatra* was one of the most expensive movies of all time at the time of its release in 1963, and, adjusted for inflation, it still is. Alex North's original score, on the above album, was nominated for an Academy Award. (Top right) Finding a complete copy of the soundtrack of *Close Encounters of the Third Kind* is difficult. The original editions came with a one-sided, small-hole, 7-inch record that contained the hit recording of the "Theme from Close Encounters of the Third Kind." Most copies of this album you seem to come across are missing this 7-inch record, which makes up 50 percent of the listed value. (Bottom left) *Damn the Defiant!,* one of many soundtracks to be released on the Colpix label, is much more difficult to track down in stereo than in the mono version, which is pictured above. (Bottom right) The Tom Cruise vehicle *Days of Thunder*, a 1990 hit film, featured a diverse soundtrack with music by artists ranging from Elton John to Guns n' Roses. It is scarce in its vinyl version.

Label, Number	Yr	VG	VG+	NM
KALEIDOSCOPE				
❏ Warner Bros. W 1663 [M]	1966	5.00	10.00	20.00
❏ Warner Bros. WS 1663 [S]	1966	6.25	12.50	25.00
KELLY'S HEROES				
❏ MGM S1E-23	1970	7.50	15.00	30.00
THE KEY				
❏ Columbia CL 1185 [M]	1958	20.00	40.00	80.00
KILLERS THREE				
❏ Tower ST-5141	1968	5.00	10.00	20.00
THE KING AND I				
❏ Capitol SW 740 [S]	1959	5.00	10.00	20.00
-- Black colorband label, logo at left				
❏ Capitol W 740 [M]	1956	6.25	12.50	25.00
-- Gray label				
KING KONG				
❏ Reprise MS 2260	1976	5.00	10.00	20.00
KING KONG LIVES				
❏ MCA 6203	1987	6.25	12.50	25.00
KING OF KINGS				
❏ MGM 1E-2 [M]	1961	7.50	15.00	30.00
-- Boxed version with hardbound book and four 8x10 photos				
❏ MGM S1E-2 [S]	1961	10.00	20.00	40.00
-- Boxed version with hardbound book and four 8x10 photos				
KING RAT				
❏ Mainstream S-6061 [S]	1965	12.50	25.00	50.00
❏ Mainstream 56061 [M]	1965	7.50	15.00	30.00
KING SOLOMON'S MINES				
❏ Restless 72106	1985	5.00	10.00	20.00
KINGS GO FORTH				
❏ Capitol W 1063 [M]	1958	37.50	75.00	150.00
KISMET				
❏ MGM E-3281 [M]	1955	5.00	10.00	20.00
-- Yellow label				
KRULL				
❏ Southern Cross SCRS-1004	1983	5.00	10.00	20.00
LADY AND THE TRAMP				
❏ Disneyland 3103 [PD]	1981	7.50	15.00	30.00
-- "Disney Picture Disc" edition				
❏ Decca DL 5557 [10]	1955	15.00	30.00	60.00
❏ Decca DL 8462 [M]	1957	17.50	35.00	70.00
LADYHAWKE				
❏ Atlantic 81248	1985	5.00	10.00	20.00
THE LANDLORD				
❏ United Artists UAS-5209	1970	5.00	10.00	20.00
THE LAST AMERICAN VIRGIN				
❏ Columbia JS 38279	1982	10.00	20.00	40.00
THE LAST EMBRACE				
❏ Varese Sarabande STV-81166	1983	5.00	10.00	20.00
THE LAST OF THE SECRET AGENTS				
❏ Dot DLP-3714 [M]	1966	5.00	10.00	20.00
❏ Dot DLP-25714 [S]	1966	6.25	12.50	25.00
THE LAST RUN				
❏ MGM 1SE-30	1971	6.25	12.50	25.00
THE LAST STARFIGHTER				
❏ Southern Cross SCRS-1007	1984	6.25	12.50	25.00
LAST SUMMER				
❏ Warner Bros. WS 1791	1969	5.00	10.00	20.00
THE LAST VALLEY				
❏ ABC-Dunhill DSX-50102	1971	10.00	20.00	40.00
LAWRENCE OF ARABIA				
❏ Colpix CP-514 [M]	1962	5.00	10.00	20.00
❏ Colpix SCP-514 [S]	1962	7.50	15.00	30.00
LENNY				
❏ United Artists UA-LA359-H [(2)]	1974	5.00	10.00	20.00
THE LEOPARD				
❏ 20th Century Fox FXG-5015 [M]	1963	7.50	15.00	30.00
❏ 20th Century Fox SXG-5015 [S]	1963	10.00	20.00	40.00
LET THE GOOD TIMES ROLL				
❏ Bell 9002 [(2)]	1973	6.25	12.50	25.00

Label, Number	Yr	VG	VG+	NM
LET'S MAKE LOVE				
❏ Columbia CL 1527 [M]	1960	7.50	15.00	30.00
❏ Columbia CS 8327 [S]	1960	12.50	25.00	50.00
LEVIATHAN				
❏ Varese Sarabande VS-5226	1989	5.00	10.00	20.00
LI'L ABNER				
❏ Columbia Masterworks OS 2021 [S]	1959	10.00	20.00	40.00
-- Credits within photo				
❏ Columbia Masterworks OS 2021 [S]	196?	6.25	12.50	25.00
-- Credits in red strip at bottom of photo				
❏ Columbia Masterworks OL 5460 [M]	1959	7.50	15.00	30.00
-- Credits within photo				
❏ Columbia Masterworks OL 5460 [M]	196?	5.00	10.00	20.00
-- Credits in red strip at bottom of photo				
THE LIFE AND TIMES OF JUDGE ROY BEAN				
❏ Columbia Masterworks S 31948	1972	6.25	12.50	25.00
LIFEFORCE				
❏ Varese Sarabande STV-81249	1985	6.25	12.50	25.00
LIGHT FANTASTIC				
❏ 20th Century Fox FXG-5016 [M]	1963	5.00	10.00	20.00
❏ 20th Century Fox SXG-5016 [S]	1963	6.25	12.50	25.00
LILIES OF THE FIELD				
❏ Epic BN 26094 [S]	1964	7.50	15.00	30.00
❏ Epic LN 24094 [M]	1964	5.00	10.00	20.00
THE LION				
❏ London M-76001 [M]	1962	100.00	200.00	400.00
THE LION IN WINTER				
❏ Columbia Masterworks OS 3250	1969	5.00	10.00	20.00
LIONHEART				
❏ Varese Sarabande STV-81304	1987	5.00	10.00	20.00
LIONHEART (MORE MUSIC FROM THE FILM)				
❏ Varese Sarabande STV-81311	1987	12.50	25.00	50.00
LITTLE BIG MAN				
❏ Columbia Masterworks S 30545	1970	5.00	10.00	20.00
LITTLE SHOP OF HORRORS				
❏ Geffen GHS-24125	1986	5.00	10.00	20.00
LIVE AND LET DIE				
❏ United Artists UA-LA100-G	1973	5.00	10.00	20.00
-- Tan label; cover corner is not clipped off				
❏ United Artists SWAO-95120	1973	7.50	15.00	30.00
-- Longines (formerly Capitol) Record Club edition				
LIVE FOR LIFE				
❏ United Artists UAL-4165 [M]	1967	5.00	10.00	20.00
❏ United Artists UAS-5165 [S]	1967	5.00	10.00	20.00
THE LIVELY SET				
❏ Decca DL 9119 [M]	1964	7.50	15.00	30.00
❏ Decca DL 79119 [S]	1964	10.00	20.00	40.00
LOGAN'S RUN				
❏ MGM MG-1-5302	1976	7.50	15.00	30.00
LOLITA				
❏ MGM E-4050 [M]	1962	5.00	10.00	20.00
❏ MGM SE-4050 [S]	1962	7.50	15.00	30.00
THE LOLLIPOP COVER				
❏ Mainstream S-6067 [S]	1966	7.50	15.00	30.00
❏ Mainstream 56067 [M]	1966	5.00	10.00	20.00
THE LONG HOT SUMMER				
❏ Roulette R-25026 [M]	1958	18.75	37.50	75.00
LONG JOHN SILVER				
❏ RCA Victor LPM-3279 [10]	1954	75.00	150.00	300.00
THE LONG SHIPS				
❏ Colpix CP-517 [M]	1964	12.50	25.00	50.00
❏ Colpix SCP-517 [S]	1964	15.00	30.00	60.00
THE LONGEST DAY				
❏ 20th Century Fox FXG-5007 [M]	1962	5.00	10.00	20.00
❏ 20th Century Fox SXG-5007 [S]	1962	6.25	12.50	25.00
LORD JIM				
❏ Colpix CP-521 [M]	1965	5.00	10.00	20.00
❏ Colpix SCP-521 [S]	1965	6.25	12.50	25.00
LORD LOVE A DUCK				
❏ United Artists UAL-4137 [M]	1966	5.00	10.00	20.00
❏ United Artists UAS-5137 [S]	1966	6.25	12.50	25.00

Label, Number	Yr	VG	VG+	NM
THE LORD OF THE RINGS				
❏ Fantasy LOR-1 [(2)]	1978	5.00	10.00	20.00
❏ Fantasy LOR-PD2 [(2)]	1978	7.50	15.00	30.00
-- Two picture discs				
THE LORDS OF FLATBUSH				
❏ ABC ABCD-828	1974	7.50	15.00	30.00
A LOSS OF INNOCENCE				
❏ Colpix CP-508 [M]	1961	10.00	20.00	40.00
THE LOST CONTINENT				
❏ MGM E-3635 [M]	1957	50.00	100.00	200.00
LOVE IN 4 DIMENSIONS				
❏ Request RLP-8090 [M]	1966	6.25	12.50	25.00
❏ Request SRLP-8090 [S]	1966	7.50	15.00	30.00
LOVERS AND OTHER STRANGERS				
❏ ABC ABCS-OC-15	1970	5.00	10.00	20.00
❏ ABC SW-93479	1971	6.25	12.50	25.00
-- Capitol Record Club edition				
M*A*S*H				
❏ Columbia Masterworks OS 3520	1970	5.00	10.00	20.00
-- Original copies do not have the theme song done by Ahmad Jamal				
MACARTHUR				
❏ MCA 2287	1977	5.00	10.00	20.00
THE MAD ADVENTURES OF RABBI JACOB				
❏ London PS 652	1974	5.00	10.00	20.00
-- Price for intact copies; cut-outs go for maybe 50 percent of this				
MADAME BOVARY				
❏ MGM E-3507 [M]	195?	37.50	75.00	150.00
THE MAGIC CHRISTIAN				
❏ Commonwealth United CU-6004	1970	6.25	12.50	25.00
MAGNIFICENT OBSESSION				
❏ Decca DL 8078 [M]	1954	15.00	30.00	60.00
-- Black label, gold print				
❏ Decca DL 8078 [M]	1955	12.50	25.00	50.00
-- Black label, silver print				
❏ Decca DL 8078 [M]	196?	7.50	15.00	30.00
-- Black label with color bars				
MAJOR DUNDEE				
❏ Columbia Masterworks OS 2780 [S]	1965	7.50	15.00	30.00
❏ Columbia Masterworks OL 6380 [M]	1965	5.00	10.00	20.00
MAKE A WISH				
❏ RCA Victor LOC-1002 [M]	1951	37.50	75.00	150.00
MALAMONDO				
❏ Epic LN 24126 [M]	1964	7.50	15.00	30.00
❏ Epic BN 26126 [S]	1964	10.00	20.00	40.00
MAME				
❏ Warner Bros. PRO 580 [DJ]	1973	12.50	25.00	50.00
-- Promo-only gatefold edition with Lucille Ball in Christmas hat on the cover				
A MAN AND A WOMAN (UN HOMME ET UNE FEMME)				
❏ United Artists UAS-5147 [S]	1966	5.00	10.00	20.00
A MAN CALLED ADAM				
❏ Reprise RS 6180 [S]	1966	5.00	10.00	20.00
A MAN CALLED DAGGER				
❏ MGM SE-4516 [S]	1967	5.00	10.00	20.00
A MAN CALLED FLINTSTONE				
❏ Hanna-Barbera HLP-2055 [M]	1967	25.00	50.00	100.00
A MAN COULD GET KILLED				
❏ Decca DL 74750 [S]	1966	5.00	10.00	20.00
A MAN FOR ALL SEASONS				
❏ RCA Victor VDM-116 [(2) M]	1966	7.50	15.00	30.00
MAN FROM SHAFT				
❏ MGM SE-4836	1972	7.50	15.00	30.00
MAN IN THE MIDDLE				
❏ 20th Century Fox TFM-3128 [M]	1965	7.50	15.00	30.00
❏ 20th Century Fox TFS-4128 [S]	1965	12.50	25.00	50.00
THE MAN OF A THOUSAND FACES				
❏ Decca DL 8623 [M]	1957	12.50	25.00	50.00
-- Black label, silver print, or pink label, black print promos				
❏ Decca DL 8623 [M]	196?	7.50	15.00	30.00
-- Black label with color bars				

Label, Number	Yr	VG	VG+	NM
MAN OF LA MANCHA				
❏ United Artists UAS-9906	1972	5.00	10.00	20.00
-- Price for intact copies; cut-outs go for maybe 50 percent of this				
THE MAN WHO WOULD BE KING				
❏ Capitol SW-11474	1975	5.00	10.00	20.00
THE MAN WITH THE GOLDEN ARM				
❏ Decca DL 8257 [M]	1956	10.00	20.00	40.00
❏ Decca DL 78257 [R]	196?	5.00	10.00	20.00
THE MAN WITH THE GOLDEN GUN				
❏ United Artists UA-LA358-G	1974	5.00	10.00	20.00
MANIAC				
❏ Varese Sarabande STV-81143	1980	5.00	10.00	20.00
MARACAIBO				
❏ Decca DL 8756 [M]	1958	10.00	20.00	40.00
-- Black label, silver print, or pink label, black print promos				
❏ Decca DL 8756 [M]	196?	5.00	10.00	20.00
-- Black label with color bars				
MARCO THE MAGNIFICENT				
❏ Columbia Masterworks OS 2870 [S]	1966	10.00	20.00	40.00
❏ Columbia Masterworks OL 6470 [M]	1966	6.25	12.50	25.00
MARIE WARD				
❏ Varese Sarabande STV-81268	1985	12.50	25.00	50.00
MARJORIE MORNINGSTAR				
❏ RCA Victor LOC-1044 [M]	1958	15.00	30.00	60.00
-- "An Original Soundtrack Recording" on spine				
❏ RCA Victor LOC-1044 [M]	1958	10.00	20.00	40.00
-- "RE" next to label number				
MARRY ME, MARRY ME				
❏ RCA Victor LSO-1160	1969	5.00	10.00	20.00
MARY, QUEEN OF SCOTS				
❏ Decca DL 79186	1972	7.50	15.00	30.00
MASTER OF THE WORLD				
❏ Vee Jay LP-4000 [M]	1961	6.25	12.50	25.00
❏ Vee Jay SR-4000 [S]	1961	10.00	20.00	40.00
MASTERS OF THE UNIVERSE				
❏ Varese Sarabande STV-81333	1987	5.00	10.00	20.00
MCLINTOCK!				
❏ United Artists UAL-4112 [M]	1963	15.00	30.00	60.00
❏ United Artists UAS-5112 [S]	1963	20.00	40.00	80.00
ME AND THE COLONEL				
❏ RCA Victor LOC-1046 [M]	1958	12.50	25.00	50.00
MEDITERRANEAN HOLIDAY				
❏ London M-76003 [M]	1964	12.50	25.00	50.00
❏ London MS-82003 [S]	1964	20.00	40.00	80.00
MEET ME IN ST.LOUIS				
❏ Decca DL 8498 [M]	1957	7.50	15.00	30.00
-- LP reissue of 78 rpm album from 1944; B-side of LP is "The Harvey Girls."				
MEMORIES AUX BRUXELLES				
❏ Carlton LP-112 [M]	1959	6.25	12.50	25.00
❏ Carlton LP-12112 [S]	1959	10.00	20.00	40.00
MEN IN WAR				
❏ Imperial LP-9032 W [M]	1957	37.50	75.00	150.00
MENACE II SOCIETY				
❏ Jive 41522 [(2) DJ]	1993	5.00	10.00	20.00
-- Vinyl is promo only				
MERRY ANDREW				
❏ Capitol T 1016 [M]	1958	12.50	25.00	50.00
MIDNIGHT COWBOY				
❏ United Artists UAS-5198	1969	5.00	10.00	20.00
MIDNIGHT EXPRESS				
❏ Casablanca NBLP-7114	1978	5.00	10.00	20.00
THE MINX				
❏ Amsterdam 12007	1970	30.00	60.00	120.00
THE MISFITS				
❏ United Artists UAL-4087 [M]	1961	12.50	25.00	50.00
❏ United Artists UAS-5087 [S]	1961	25.00	50.00	100.00
MISS SADIE THOMPSON				
❏ Mercury MG-20123 [M]	1956	37.50	75.00	150.00
❏ Mercury MG-25181 [10]	1954	18.75	37.50	75.00

Label, Number	Yr	VG	VG+	NM
THE MISSOURI BREAKS				
❑ United Artists UA-LA623-G	1976	7.50	15.00	30.00
MOBY DICK				
❑ RCA Victor LPM-1247 [M]	1956	30.00	60.00	120.00
MODERN TIMES				
❑ United Artists UAL-4049 [M]	1959	6.25	12.50	25.00
MODESTY BLAISE				
❑ 20th Century Fox TFM-3182 [M]	1966	7.50	15.00	30.00
❑ 20th Century Fox TFS-4182 [S]	1966	12.50	25.00	50.00
MOHAMMAD, MESSENGER OF GOD				
❑ Namara 79001	1977	6.25	12.50	25.00
MONDO CANE				
❑ United Artists UAS-5105 [S]	1963	5.00	10.00	20.00
MONDO CANE NO. 2				
❑ 20th Century Fox TFM-3147 [M]	1964	7.50	15.00	30.00
❑ 20th Century Fox TFS-4147 [S]	1964	10.00	20.00	40.00
MOON OVER PARADOR				
❑ MCA 6249	1988	6.25	12.50	25.00
THE MOON SPINNERS				
❑ Buena Vista BV-3323 [M]	1964	10.00	20.00	40.00
MORE AMERICAN GRAFFITI				
❑ MCA MCA2-11006 [(2)]	1979	5.00	10.00	20.00
-- Tan labels				
MR. MAGOO: 1001 ARABIAN NIGHTS				
❑ Colpix CP-410 [M]	1959	12.50	25.00	50.00
❑ Colpix SCP-410 [S]	1959	37.50	75.00	150.00
MURDER INC.				
❑ Canadian American CALP-1003 [M]	1960	25.00	50.00	100.00
MUSCLE BEACH PARTY PLUS MERLIN JONES AND THE SCRAMBLED EGGHEAD				
❑ Buena Vista BV-3314 [M]	1964	15.00	30.00	60.00
❑ Buena Vista STER-3314 [S]	1964	30.00	60.00	120.00
THE MUSIC MAN				
❑ Warner Bros. BS 1459 [S]	1962	5.00	10.00	20.00
-- Gold label originals				
MUTINY ON THE BOUNTY				
❑ MGM 1E-4 [M]	1962	7.50	15.00	30.00
-- Boxed set with book and painting				
❑ MGM S1E-4 [S]	1962	10.00	20.00	40.00
-- Boxed set with book and painting				
MY GEISHA				
❑ RCA Victor LOC-1070 [M]	1962	12.50	25.00	50.00
❑ RCA Victor LSO-1070 [S]	1962	25.00	50.00	100.00
MY SIDE OF THE MOUNTAIN				
❑ Capitol ST-245	1969	6.25	12.50	25.00
MY WILD IRISH ROSE				
❑ RCA Victor LPM-3036 [10]	1952	10.00	20.00	40.00
NAKED ANGELS				
❑ Straight STS-1056	1969	6.25	12.50	25.00
THE NAKED MAJA				
❑ United Artists UAL-4031 [M]	1959	7.50	15.00	30.00
❑ United Artists UAS-5031 [S]	1959	10.00	20.00	40.00
NANCY GOES TO RIO				
❑ MGM E-508 [10]	1950	15.00	30.00	60.00
NASHVILLE				
❑ ABC ABCD-893	1975	5.00	10.00	20.00
NATIVE SON				
❑ MCA 6198	1986	5.00	10.00	20.00
NAVAJO JOE				
❑ United Artists UA-LA292-G	1974	6.25	12.50	25.00
NED KELLY				
❑ United Artists UAS-5213	1970	6.25	12.50	25.00
NEVADA SMITH				
❑ Dot DLP-3718 [M]	1966	6.25	12.50	25.00
❑ Dot DLP-25718 [S]	1966	10.00	20.00	40.00
THE NEVER ENDING STORY				
❑ EMI America ST-17139	1984	5.00	10.00	20.00
NEVER ON SUNDAY				
❑ United Artists UAS-5070 [S]	1960	5.00	10.00	20.00
❑ United Artists SW-90834 [S]	196?	5.00	10.00	20.00
-- Capitol Record Club edition				
THE NEW INTERNS				
❑ Colpix CP-473 [M]	1964	7.50	15.00	30.00
❑ Colpix SCP-473 [S]	1964	10.00	20.00	40.00
THE NEW MESSIAH				
❑ Columbia KC 31713	1972	5.00	10.00	20.00
NICHOLAS AND ALEXANDRA				
❑ Bell 1103	1971	6.25	12.50	25.00
NIGHT OF THE GENERALS				
❑ Colgems COMO-5002 [M]	1967	10.00	20.00	40.00
❑ Colgems COSO-5002 [S]	1967	17.50	35.00	70.00
THE NIGHT OF THE HUNTER				
❑ RCA Victor LPM-1136 [M]	1955	62.50	125.00	250.00
NINE HOURS TO RAMA				
❑ London M-76002 [M]	1963	75.00	150.00	300.00
NO WAY TO TREAT A LADY				
❑ Dot DLP-25846	1968	6.25	12.50	25.00
NOT WITH MY WIFE, YOU DON'T				
❑ Warner Bros. WS 1668 [S]	1966	5.00	10.00	20.00
NOTHING BUT THE BEST				
❑ Colpix CP-477 [M]	1964	5.00	10.00	20.00
❑ Colpix SCP-477 [S]	1964	6.25	12.50	25.00
A NUN'S STORY				
❑ Warner Bros. B 1306 [M]	1959	15.00	30.00	60.00
❑ Warner Bros. BS 1306 [S]	1959	25.00	50.00	100.00
OBSESSION				
❑ London Phase 4 SPC-21160	1976	6.25	12.50	25.00
OCTOPUSSY				
❑ A&M SP-4967	1983	5.00	10.00	20.00
THE ODD COUPLE				
❑ Dot DLP-25862	1968	5.00	10.00	20.00
ODDS AGAINST TOMORROW				
❑ United Artists UAL-4061 [M]	1959	7.50	15.00	30.00
❑ United Artists UAS-5061 [S]	1959	12.50	25.00	50.00
OF LOVE AND DESIRE				
❑ 20th Century Fox FXG-5014 [M]	1963	6.25	12.50	25.00
❑ 20th Century Fox SXG-5014 [S]	1963	7.50	15.00	30.00
OH DAD, POOR DAD, MAMMA'S HUNG YOU IN THE CLOSET AND I'M FEELIN' SO SAD				
❑ RCA Victor LPM-3750 [M]	1967	5.00	10.00	20.00
❑ RCA Victor LSP-3750 [S]	1967	6.25	12.50	25.00
OH, ROSALINDA!				
❑ Mercury MG-20145 [M]	1957	12.50	25.00	50.00
OIL TOWN, U.S.A.				
❑ RCA Victor LFM-2000 [10]	1953	15.00	30.00	60.00
OKLAHOMA!				
❑ Capitol SWAO 595 [S]	1959	5.00	10.00	20.00
-- Black colorband label, logo at left				
❑ Capitol WAO 595 [M]	1955	6.25	12.50	25.00
-- Purple or dark red label				
❑ Capitol WAO 595 [M]	1956	5.00	10.00	20.00
-- Gray label				
OLD BOYFRIENDS				
❑ Columbia Masterworks JS 36072	1979	12.50	25.00	50.00
THE OLD MAN AND THE SEA				
❑ Columbia CL 1183 [M]	1958	7.50	15.00	30.00
❑ Columbia CS 8013 [S]	1958	15.00	30.00	60.00
OLD YELLER				
❑ Disneyland 1024 [M]	1974	6.25	12.50	25.00
-- Reissue with no prefix				
❑ Disneyland WDL-1024 [M]	1960	10.00	20.00	40.00
-- Second edition				
❑ Disneyland WDL-3024 [M]	1957	12.50	25.00	50.00
-- First edition				
OLIVER AND COMPANY				
❑ Disney 64101	1988	6.25	12.50	25.00

Label, Number	Yr	VG	VG+	NM
ON HER MAJESTY'S SECRET SERVICE				
❏ United Artists UAS-5204	1969	5.00	10.00	20.00
ONCE UPON A TIME IN THE WEST				
❏ RCA Victor LSP-4736	1969	7.50	15.00	30.00
THE ONE AND ONLY, GENUINE, ORIGINAL FAMILY BAND				
❏ Buena Vista STER-5002 [S]	1968	5.00	10.00	20.00
ONE FLEW OVER THE CUCKOO'S NEST				
❏ Fantasy F-9500	1975	5.00	10.00	20.00
THE ONE-EYED JACKS				
❏ Liberty LOM-16001 [M]	1961	7.50	15.00	30.00
❏ Liberty LOS-17001 [S]	1961	12.50	25.00	50.00
101 DALMATIANS				
❏ Disneyland DQ-1308 [M]	1966	5.00	10.00	20.00
❏ Disneyland ST-1908 [M]	1960	6.25	12.50	25.00
❏ Disneyland ST-3931 [M]	1965	10.00	20.00	40.00
❏ Disneyland ST-4903 [M]	1963	37.50	75.00	150.00
-- Gatefold cover with pop-up scene in center				
THE OPTIMISTS				
❏ Paramount PAS-1015	1973	7.50	15.00	30.00
THE OSCAR				
❏ Columbia Masterworks OS 2950 [S]	1966	6.25	12.50	25.00
❏ Columbia Masterworks OL 6550 [M]	1966	5.00	10.00	20.00
OTLEY				
❏ Colgems COS-112	1969	7.50	15.00	30.00
OUR MAN FLINT				
❏ 20th Century Fox TFM-3179 [M]	1966	10.00	20.00	40.00
❏ 20th Century Fox TFS-4179 [S]	1966	15.00	30.00	60.00
OUT OF AFRICA				
❏ MCA 6158	1985	5.00	10.00	20.00
❏ MCA 11327	1995	5.00	10.00	20.00
-- Limited edition on "Heavy Vinyl"				
OUT OF SIGHT				
❏ Decca DL 4751 [M]	1966	5.00	10.00	20.00
❏ Decca DL 74751 [S]	1966	6.25	12.50	25.00
OUTLAND				
❏ Warner Bros. HS 3551	1981	6.25	12.50	25.00
THE OUTLAW JOSEY WALES				
❏ Warner Bros. BS 2956	1976	6.25	12.50	25.00
THE OUTLAW RIDERS				
❏ MGM 1SE-26	1970	5.00	10.00	20.00
PAGAN LOVE SONG				
❏ MGM E-534 [M]	1950	10.00	20.00	40.00
PAINT YOUR WAGON				
❏ Paramount PMS-1001	1969	5.00	10.00	20.00
-- With booklet				
THE PAJAMA GAME				
❏ Columbia Masterworks OL 5210 [M]	1957	7.50	15.00	30.00
-- Gray and black label with six "eye" logos				
PANIC BUTTON				
❏ Musicor MM-2026 [M]	1964	20.00	40.00	80.00
❏ Musicor MS-3026 [S]	1964	30.00	60.00	120.00
PAPER MOON				
❏ Paramount PAS-1012	1973	5.00	10.00	20.00
PAPER TIGER				
❏ Capitol SW-11475	1975	5.00	10.00	20.00
PAPILLON				
❏ Capitol ST-11260	1973	5.00	10.00	20.00
THE PARENT TRAP!				
❏ Buena Vista BV-3309 [M]	1961	10.00	20.00	40.00
❏ Buena Vista STER-3309 [S]	1961	15.00	30.00	60.00
-- B-side of the above two: Camerata Conducts Themes from Great Motion Pictures				
PARIS BLUES				
❏ United Artists UAL-4092 [M]	1961	6.25	12.50	25.00
❏ United Artists UAS-5092 [S]	1961	7.50	15.00	30.00
PARIS HOLIDAY				
❏ United Artists UAL-4001 [M]	1958	12.50	25.00	50.00
PARIS WHEN IT SIZZLES				
❏ Reprise R 6113 [M]	1964	6.25	12.50	25.00
❏ Reprise RS 6113 [S]	1964	10.00	20.00	40.00

Label, Number	Yr	VG	VG+	NM
PARRISH				
❏ Warner Bros. W 1413 [M]	1961	7.50	15.00	30.00
❏ Warner Bros. WS 1413 [S]	1961	20.00	40.00	80.00
-- B-side of the above two: Popular Piano Concertos by George Greeley				
A PATCH OF BLUE				
❏ Mainstream S-6068 [S]	1965	6.25	12.50	25.00
❏ Mainstream 56068 [M]	1965	5.00	10.00	20.00
❏ Mainstream ST-90805 [S]	1965	7.50	15.00	30.00
-- Capitol Record Club edition				
PATTON				
❏ 20th Century Fox S-4208	1970	5.00	10.00	20.00
PATTY				
❏ Stang 1026	1976	5.00	10.00	20.00
PENELOPE				
❏ MGM E-4426 [M]	1966	5.00	10.00	20.00
❏ MGM SE-4426 [S]	1966	7.50	15.00	30.00
PENTHOUSE				
❏ United Artists UAL-4170 [M]	1967	5.00	10.00	20.00
❏ United Artists UAS-5170 [S]	1967	5.00	10.00	20.00
THE PEOPLE NEXT DOOR				
❏ Avco AV-11002	1970	6.25	12.50	25.00
PEPE				
❏ Colpix CP-507 [M]	1960	5.00	10.00	20.00
❏ Colpix SCP-507 [S]	1960	6.25	12.50	25.00
PERFORMANCE				
❏ Warner Bros. WS 1846	1970	7.50	15.00	30.00
-- Original issue				
❏ Warner Bros. BS 2554	1970	5.00	10.00	20.00
-- Second issue				
PETE'S DRAGON				
❏ Capitol SW-11704	1977	5.00	10.00	20.00
PETULIA				
❏ Warner Bros. WS 1755	1968	6.25	12.50	25.00
PEYTON PLACE				
❏ RCA Victor LOC-1042 [M]	1958	7.50	15.00	30.00
-- "Long Play" at bottom of label				
❏ RCA Victor LOC-1042 [M]	1965	6.25	12.50	25.00
-- "Monaural" at bottom of label				
❏ RCA Victor LSO-1042 [S]	1958	25.00	50.00	100.00
-- "Living Stereo" at bottom of label				
❏ RCA Victor LSO-1042 [S]	1965	15.00	30.00	60.00
-- "Stereo" at bottom of label				
PHAEDRA				
❏ United Artists UAL-4102 [M]	1962	5.00	10.00	20.00
❏ United Artists UAS-5102 [S]	1962	7.50	15.00	30.00
THE PHILADELPHIA EXPERIMENT				
❏ Rhino RNSP-306	1984	6.25	12.50	25.00
PICNIC				
❏ Decca DL 8320 [M]	1956	7.50	15.00	30.00
-- Black label, silver print				
❏ Decca DL 78320 [S]	1959	7.50	15.00	30.00
-- Maroon or all-black label				
A PIECE OF THE ACTION				
❏ Curtom CU 5019	1977	5.00	10.00	20.00
PINOCCHIO				
❏ Disneyland DQ-1202 [M]	1959	7.50	15.00	30.00
-- Second edition				
❏ Disneyland DQ-1202MO [M]	1963	5.00	10.00	20.00
-- Third edition				
❏ Disneyland 3102 [PD]	1981	7.50	15.00	30.00
-- "Disney Picture Disc" edition				
❏ Disneyland WDL-4002 [M]	1956	62.50	125.00	250.00
-- Original edition				
❏ Disneyland ST-4905 [M]	1963	37.50	75.00	150.00
-- Gatefold cover with pop-up center graphics				
PIRANHA				
❏ Varese Sarabande STV-81126	1979	5.00	10.00	20.00
THE PIRATE				
❏ MGM E-21 [10]	1951	17.50	35.00	70.00
PLANET OF THE APES				
❏ Project 3 PR-5023 SD	1968	7.50	15.00	30.00
-- Gatefold cover				
❏ Project 3 PR-5023 SD	1968	5.00	10.00	20.00
-- Regular cover				

Label, Number	Yr	VG	VG+	NM
THE PLEASURE SEEKERS				
❏ RCA Victor LOC-1101 [M]	1964	12.50	25.00	50.00
❏ RCA Victor LSO-1101 [S]	1964	25.00	50.00	100.00
POLLYANNA				
❏ Disneyland DQ-1307 [M]	1967	6.25	12.50	25.00
❏ Disneyland ST-1906 [M]	1960	12.50	25.00	50.00
POLTERGEIST				
❏ MGM MG-1-5408	1982	10.00	20.00	40.00
POLTERGEIST III				
❏ Varese Sarabande 704.620	1988	20.00	40.00	80.00
PORGY AND BESS				
❏ Columbia Masterworks OS 2016 [S]	1959	5.00	10.00	20.00
THE POWER				
❏ Cerberus CST-0211	1984	5.00	10.00	20.00
PRET-A-PORTER				
❏ Miramax CAS 6700 [DJ]	1994	6.25	12.50	25.00
-- Promo only vinyl				
PRETTY BOY FLOYD				
❏ Audio Fidelity AFLP-1936 [M]	1960	15.00	30.00	60.00
❏ Audio Fidelity AFSD-5936 [S]	1960	20.00	40.00	80.00
THE PRIDE AND THE PASSION				
❏ Capitol W 873 [M]	1957	15.00	30.00	60.00
THE PRINCESS BRIDE				
❏ Warner Bros. 25610	1987	5.00	10.00	20.00
THE PRISONER OF ZENDA				
❏ United Artists UA-LA374-G	1974	5.00	10.00	20.00
THE PRODUCERS				
❏ RCA Victor LPM-4008 [M]	1968	12.50	25.00	50.00
❏ RCA Victor LSP-4008 [S]	1968	7.50	15.00	30.00
THE PROFESSIONALS				
❏ Colgems COMO-5001 [M]	1966	15.00	30.00	60.00
❏ Colgems COSO-5001 [S]	1966	37.50	75.00	150.00
A PROMISE AT DAWN				
❏ Polydor 24-5502	1970	7.50	15.00	30.00
PROVIDENCE				
❏ DRG SL-9502	1977	5.00	10.00	20.00
PRUDENCE AND THE PILL				
❏ 20th Century Fox S-4199	1968	5.00	10.00	20.00
PSYCHO II				
❏ MCA 6119	1983	5.00	10.00	20.00
Q THE WINGED SERPENT				
❏ Cerberus CST-0206	1983	5.00	10.00	20.00
QUEST FOR FIRE				
❏ RCA Victor ABL1-4274	1982	5.00	10.00	20.00
THE QUIET MAN				
❏ Decca DL 5411 [10]	1952	30.00	60.00	120.00
THE QUILLER MEMORANDUM				
❏ Columbia Masterworks OS 3060 [S]	1966	15.00	30.00	60.00
❏ Columbia Masterworks OL 6660 [M]	1966	7.50	15.00	30.00
QUO VADIS?				
❏ MGM E-103 [10]	1951	10.00	20.00	40.00
-- Music soundtrack only				
❏ MGM E-134 [(2) 10]	1951	15.00	30.00	60.00
-- Box set of two discs; includes dialogue				
RAGTIME				
❏ Elektra 5E-565	1981	5.00	10.00	20.00
RAIDERS OF THE LOST ARK				
❏ DCC Compact Classics LPZ 2-2009 [(2)]	1995	7.50	15.00	30.00
-- Audiophile edition; includes music not on other releases of the soundtrack				
THE RAILWAY CHILDREN				
❏ Capitol SW-871	1972	5.00	10.00	20.00
THE RAINMAKER				
❏ RCA Victor LPM-1434 [M]	1956	25.00	50.00	100.00
RAINTREE COUNTY				
❏ RCA Victor LOC-1038 [M]	1958	7.50	15.00	30.00
❏ RCA Victor LSO-1038 [S]	1958	12.50	25.00	50.00
❏ RCA Victor LOC-6000 [(2) M]	1957	30.00	60.00	120.00

Label, Number	Yr	VG	VG+	NM
RAN				
❏ Fantasy FSP-21004	1985	5.00	10.00	20.00
RED DAWN				
❏ Intrada RVF-6001	1985	10.00	20.00	40.00
RED GARTERS				
❏ Columbia CL 6282 [10]	1954	12.50	25.00	50.00
RED HEAT				
❏ Virgin Movie Music 90891	1988	6.25	12.50	25.00
THE RED PONY				
❏ Columbia Masterworks ML 5983 [M]	196?	6.25	12.50	25.00
❏ Columbia Masterworks MS 6583 [R]	196?	6.25	12.50	25.00
❏ Varese Sarabande STV-81259	1986	6.25	12.50	25.00
THE RED TENT				
❏ Paramount PAS-6019	1971	6.25	12.50	25.00
REDS				
❏ Columbia Masterworks BJS 37960	1981	5.00	10.00	20.00
RENT-A-COP				
❏ Intrada MAS-7002	1988	5.00	10.00	20.00
THE RESCUERS				
❏ Disneyland ST-3816	1977	5.00	10.00	20.00
RETURN TO PARADISE				
❏ Decca DL 5489 [10]	1953	50.00	100.00	200.00
THE REVOLUTION				
❏ United Artists UAS-5185	1968	6.25	12.50	25.00
RHAPSODY OF STEEL				
❏ U.S. Steel JB-502/3	1958	25.00	50.00	100.00
RICH, YOUNG AND PRETTY				
❏ MGM E-86 [10]	1951	10.00	20.00	40.00
RIDER ON THE RAIN				
❏ Capitol ST-584	1970	6.25	12.50	25.00
RIOT ON SUNSET STRIP				
❏ Tower DT 5065 [R]	1967	6.25	12.50	25.00
❏ Tower T 5065 [M]	1967	5.00	10.00	20.00
ROAD TO HONG KONG				
❏ Liberty LOM-16002 [M]	1962	5.00	10.00	20.00
❏ Liberty LOS-17002 [S]	1962	10.00	20.00	40.00
THE ROBE				
❏ Decca DL 9012 [M]	1953	7.50	15.00	30.00
-- Maroon label				
ROBIN AND THE SEVEN HOODS				
❏ Reprise F 2021 [M]	1964	12.50	25.00	50.00
❏ Reprise FS 2021 [S]	1964	15.00	30.00	60.00
ROBIN HOOD				
❏ Disneyland ST-3810	1973	6.25	12.50	25.00
ROCK ALL NIGHT				
❏ Mercury MG-20293 [M]	1957	25.00	50.00	100.00
ROCK, PRETTY BABY				
❏ Decca DL 8429 [M]	1957	30.00	60.00	120.00
-- Black label, silver print; also includes pink label promo				
❏ Decca DL 8429 [M]	196?	7.50	15.00	30.00
-- Black label with color bars				
ROCK, ROCK, ROCK				
❏ (no label) (no #) [M]	1958	375.00	750.00	1,500.
-- Demo version, 20 tracks				
❏ Chess LP-1425 [M]	1958	50.00	100.00	200.00
ROMANCE OF A HORSETHIEF				
❏ Allied Artists AAS-110-100	1971	12.50	25.00	50.00
ROME ADVENTURE				
❏ Warner Bros. W 1458 [M]	1962	5.00	10.00	20.00
❏ Warner Bros. WS 1458 [S]	1962	6.25	12.50	25.00
ROMEO AND JULIET				
❏ Capitol SWDR-289 [(4)]	1969	7.50	15.00	30.00
-- From the 1968 Franco Zeffirelli remake; contains dialogue and music				
❏ Epic LC 3126 [M]	1954	15.00	30.00	60.00
❏ Epic FLM 13104 [M]	1966	7.50	15.00	30.00
-- Reissue of 3126				
❏ Epic FLS 15104 [R]	1966	6.25	12.50	25.00
ROOTS OF HEAVEN				
❏ 20th Fox FOX-3005 [M]	1958	75.00	150.00	300.00

Label, Number	Yr	VG	VG+	NM
ROSE MARIE				
❑ MGM E-229 [10]	1954	10.00	20.00	40.00
THE ROSE TATTOO				
❑ Columbia CL 727 [M]	1955	12.50	25.00	50.00
ROSEMARY'S BABY				
❑ Dot DLP-25875	1968	5.00	10.00	20.00
THE ROYAL WEDDING				
❑ MGM E-543 [10]	1951	12.50	25.00	50.00
THE RULING CLASS				
❑ Avco AV-11003	1972	6.25	12.50	25.00
THE RUN OF THE ARROW				
❑ Decca DL 8620 [M]	1957	15.00	30.00	60.00
-- Black label, silver print, or pink label, black print promo				
❑ Decca DL 8620 [M]	196?	7.50	15.00	30.00
-- Black label with color bars				
RUN WILD, RUN FREE				
❑ SGC SD 5003	1969	5.00	10.00	20.00
RUN, ANGEL, RUN				
❑ Epic BN 26474	1969	5.00	10.00	20.00
RYAN'S DAUGHTER				
❑ MGM 1SE-27	1970	6.25	12.50	25.00
SACCO AND VANZETTI				
❑ RCA Victor LSP-4612	1971	5.00	10.00	20.00
THE SACRED IDOL				
❑ Capitol ST 1293 [S]	1960	7.50	15.00	30.00
❑ Capitol T 1293 [M]	1960	6.25	12.50	25.00
THE SAINT				
❑ Virgin SPRO-12261 [(2) DJ]	1997	6.25	12.50	25.00
-- Promo only vinyl				
SAINT JOAN				
❑ Capitol W 865 [M]	1957	7.50	15.00	30.00
SALLAH				
❑ Philips PHM 200-177 [M]	1965	5.00	10.00	20.00
❑ Philips PHS 600-177 [S]	1965	6.25	12.50	25.00
SALOME				
❑ Decca DL 6026 [10]	1953	30.00	60.00	120.00
SAMSON AND DELILAH				
❑ Decca DL 6007 [10]	1952	15.00	30.00	60.00
THE SAND CASTLE				
❑ Columbia CS 8249 [S]	1961	5.00	10.00	20.00
THE SAND PEBBLES				
❑ 20th Century Fox 3189 [M]	1966	7.50	15.00	30.00
❑ 20th Century Fox S-4189 [S]	1966	12.50	25.00	50.00
THE SANDPIPER				
❑ Mercury MG-21032 [M]	1965	6.25	12.50	25.00
❑ Mercury SR-61032 [S]	1965	7.50	15.00	30.00
SANTA AND THE 3 BEARS				
❑ Mr. Pickwick SPC 1501	196?	5.00	10.00	20.00
-- With "Santa" cutout intact				
SATAN IN HIGH HEELS				
❑ Parker PLP-406 [M]	1962	6.25	12.50	25.00
-- Gatefold cover				
❑ Parker PLP-406S [S]	1962	7.50	15.00	30.00
-- Gatefold cover				
SATAN'S SADISTS				
❑ Smash SRS-67127	1969	7.50	15.00	30.00
THE SAVAGE SEVEN				
❑ Atco 33-245 [M]	1968	7.50	15.00	30.00
❑ Atco SD 33-245 [S]	1968	7.50	15.00	30.00
SAVAGE WILD				
❑ American Int'l. STA-1032	1970	5.00	10.00	20.00
SAY ONE FOR ME				
❑ Columbia CL 1337 [M]	1959	10.00	20.00	40.00
❑ Columbia CS 8147 [S]	1959	20.00	40.00	80.00
SAYONARA				
❑ RCA Victor LOC-1041 [M]	1957	12.50	25.00	50.00
❑ RCA Victor LSO-1041 [S]	1957	17.50	35.00	70.00
THE SCALPHUNTERS				
❑ United Artists UAL-4176 [M]	1968	7.50	15.00	30.00
❑ United Artists UAS-5176 [S]	1968	10.00	20.00	40.00

Label, Number	Yr	VG	VG+	NM
SCARFACE				
❑ MCA 6126	1984	5.00	10.00	20.00
THE SCARLET AND THE BLACK				
❑ Cerberus CEM-0120	1983	6.25	12.50	25.00
SCENT OF MYSTERY				
❑ Ramrod ST-6001 [S]	1960	25.00	50.00	100.00
❑ Ramrod T-6001 [M]	1960	12.50	25.00	50.00
SCROOGE				
❑ Columbia Masterworks S 30258	1970	7.50	15.00	30.00
SEARCH FOR PARADISE				
❑ RCA Victor LOC-1034 [M]	1957	10.00	20.00	40.00
SEASIDE SWINGERS				
❑ Mercury MG-21031 [M]	1965	5.00	10.00	20.00
❑ Mercury SR-61031 [S]	1965	6.25	12.50	25.00
SEBASTIAN				
❑ Dot DLP-25845	1968	5.00	10.00	20.00
THE SECRET OF SANTA VITTORIA				
❑ United Artists UAS-5200	1969	7.50	15.00	30.00
SERGEANTS 3				
❑ Reprise R-2013 [M]	1962	7.50	15.00	30.00
❑ Reprise RS-2013 [S]	1962	12.50	25.00	50.00
THE SERPENT AND THE RAINBOW				
❑ Varese Sarabande STV-81362	1988	10.00	20.00	40.00
SERPICO				
❑ Paramount PAS-1016	1973	6.25	12.50	25.00
SEVEN BRIDES FOR SEVEN BROTHERS				
❑ MGM E-244 [10]	1954	10.00	20.00	40.00
SEVEN GOLDEN MEN				
❑ United Artists UAS-5193	1969	6.25	12.50	25.00
THE SEVEN LITTLE FOYS				
❑ RCA Victor LPM-3275 [10]	1955	17.50	35.00	70.00
1776				
❑ Columbia S 31741	1972	5.00	10.00	20.00
THE SEVENTH DAWN				
❑ United Artists UAL-4115 [M]	1964	7.50	15.00	30.00
❑ United Artists UAS-5115 [S]	1964	10.00	20.00	40.00
THE 7TH VOYAGE OF SINBAD				
❑ Colpix CP-504 [M]	1958	50.00	100.00	200.00
❑ Varese Sarabande STV-81135	1983	5.00	10.00	20.00
SEX AND THE SINGLE GIRL				
❑ Warner Bros. WS 1572 [S]	1964	5.00	10.00	20.00
SHAFT IN AFRICA				
❑ ABC ABCX-793	1973	7.50	15.00	30.00
SHAFT'S BIG SCORE				
❑ MGM 1SE-36	1972	7.50	15.00	30.00
SHAKE HANDS WITH THE DEVIL				
❑ United Artists UAL-4043 [M]	1959	7.50	15.00	30.00
❑ United Artists UAS-5043 [S]	1959	12.50	25.00	50.00
SHALAKO				
❑ Philips PHS 600-286	1968	7.50	15.00	30.00
SHE-DEVIL				
❑ Polydor 841 583-1	1989	7.50	15.00	30.00
SHEBA BABY				
❑ Buddah BDS-5634	1975	7.50	15.00	30.00
SHENANDOAH				
❑ Decca DL 9125 [M]	1965	7.50	15.00	30.00
❑ Decca DL 79125 [S]	1965	10.00	20.00	40.00
THE SHINING				
❑ Warner Bros. HS 3449	1980	5.00	10.00	20.00
THE SHOP ON MAIN STREET				
❑ Mainstream S-6082 [S]	1966	10.00	20.00	40.00
❑ Mainstream 56082 [M]	1966	6.25	12.50	25.00
SHORT EYES				
❑ Curtom CU 5017	1977	6.25	12.50	25.00
SHOW BOAT				
❑ MGM E-559 [10]	1951	7.50	15.00	30.00
THE SICILIAN CLAN				
❑ 20th Century Fox S-4209	1970	12.50	25.00	50.00

Label, Number	Yr	VG	VG+	NM
THE SIDEHACKERS				
❏ Amaret ST-5004	1969	5.00	10.00	20.00
THE SILENCERS				
❏ RCA Victor LOC-1120 [M]	1966	7.50	15.00	30.00
❏ RCA Victor LSO-1120 [S]	1966	12.50	25.00	50.00
SILENT RUNNING				
❏ Decca DL 79188	1972	10.00	20.00	40.00
SILK STOCKINGS				
❏ MGM E-3542 [M]	1957	7.50	15.00	30.00
SILVERADO				
❏ Geffen GHS 24080	1985	5.00	10.00	20.00
SINGIN' IN THE RAIN				
❏ MGM E-113 [10]	1952	7.50	15.00	30.00
SINGLE ROOM FURNISHED				
❏ Sidewalk ST-5917	1968	10.00	20.00	40.00
THE 633 SQUADRON				
❏ United Artists UA-LA305-G	1974	6.25	12.50	25.00
SKATEDANCER				
❏ Mira LP-3004 [M]	1966	5.00	10.00	20.00
❏ Mira LPS-3004 [S]	1966	6.25	12.50	25.00
SKI ON THE WILD SIDE				
❏ MGM E-4439 [M]	1967	7.50	15.00	30.00
❏ MGM SE-4439 [S]	1967	12.50	25.00	50.00
SLAUGHTER ON 10TH AVENUE				
❏ Decca DL 8657 [M]	1957	6.25	12.50	25.00
-- Black label, silver print				
❏ Decca DL 78657 [S]	1957	7.50	15.00	30.00
-- Black label, silver print				
SLAUGHTERHOUSE-FIVE				
❏ Columbia Masterworks S 31333	1972	6.25	12.50	25.00
THE SLAVE TRADE IN THE WORLD TODAY				
❏ London M-76006 [M]	1964	50.00	100.00	200.00
SLAVES				
❏ Skye SK-11	1969	6.25	12.50	25.00
SLEEPING BEAUTY				
❏ Disneyland STER-4018 [S]	1959	10.00	20.00	40.00
❏ Disneyland WDL-4018 [M]	1959	7.50	15.00	30.00
❏ Disneyland STER-4036 [S]	1970	5.00	10.00	20.00
-- Reissue of STER-4018				
SLEUTH				
❏ Columbia Masterworks S 32154	1973	5.00	10.00	20.00
SLUMBER PARTY '57				
❏ Mercury SRM-1-1097	1976	6.25	12.50	25.00
A SMASHING TIME				
❏ ABC ABC-OC-6 [M]	1967	5.00	10.00	20.00
❏ ABC ABCS-OC-6 [S]	1967	6.25	12.50	25.00
❏ ABC SW-91399 [S]	1967	6.25	12.50	25.00
-- Capitol Record Club edition				
SNOOPY COME HOME				
❏ Columbia Masterworks S 31451	1972	5.00	10.00	20.00
THE SNOW QUEEN				
❏ Decca DL 8977 [M]	1959	10.00	20.00	40.00
❏ Decca DL 78977 [S]	1959	15.00	30.00	60.00
SNOW WHITE AND THE SEVEN DWARFS				
❏ Buena Vista 102 [(3)]	1975	12.50	25.00	50.00
-- Entire movie on three LPs; TV mail-order item				
❏ Disneyland DQ-1201 [M]	1959	12.50	25.00	50.00
-- Reissue of 4005; whirlpool-like designs on cover				
❏ Disneyland DQ-1201 [M]	1968	6.25	12.50	25.00
-- Reissue; with same cover as 4005, but no gatefold				
❏ Disneyland DQ-1201 [M]	1987	7.50	15.00	30.00
-- Reissue; high-gloss cover with cel photos on back				
❏ Disneyland 3101 [PD]	1981	7.50	15.00	30.00
-- "Disney Picture Disc" edition				
❏ Disneyland WDL-4005 [M]	1956	50.00	100.00	200.00
-- Gatefold cover				
SNOW WHITE AND THE THREE STOOGES				
❏ Columbia CL 1650 [M]	1961	15.00	30.00	60.00
❏ Columbia CS 8450 [S]	1961	25.00	50.00	100.00
SO THIS IS LOVE				
❏ RCA Victor LOC-3000 [10]	1953	20.00	40.00	80.00

Label, Number	Yr	VG	VG+	NM
SO THIS IS PARIS				
❏ Decca DL 5553 [10]	1955	12.50	25.00	50.00
SODOM AND GOMORRAH				
❏ RCA Victor LOC-1076 [M]	1963	20.00	40.00	80.00
❏ RCA Victor LSO-1076 [S]	1963	25.00	50.00	100.00
SOL MADRID				
❏ MGM SE-4541 ST	1968	7.50	15.00	30.00
SOLOMON AND SHEBA				
❏ United Artists UAL-4051 [M]	1959	12.50	25.00	50.00
-- First cover with silky finish				
❏ United Artists UAL-4051 [M]	1959	6.25	12.50	25.00
-- Second, regular cover				
❏ United Artists UAS-5051 [S]	1959	30.00	60.00	120.00
-- First cover with silky finish				
❏ United Artists UAS-5051 [S]	1959	15.00	30.00	60.00
-- Second, regular cover				
SOME CAME RUNNING				
❏ Capitol SW 1109 [S]	1958	20.00	40.00	80.00
❏ Capitol W 1109 [M]	1958	7.50	15.00	30.00
SOME LIKE IT HOT				
❏ United Artists UAL-4030 [M]	1959	12.50	25.00	50.00
❏ United Artists UAS-5030 [S]	1959	18.75	37.50	75.00
SOMEBODY LOVES ME				
❏ RCA Victor LPM-3097 [10]	1952	12.50	25.00	50.00
SOMEWHERE IN TIME				
❏ MCA 5154	1980	5.00	10.00	20.00
SONG OF THE SOUTH				
❏ Disneyland WDL-4001 [M]	1956	75.00	150.00	300.00
-- Yellow label (first pressing)				
❏ Disneyland WDL-4001 [M]	1957	50.00	100.00	200.00
-- Red/maroon label (second pressing)				
SONG OF THE SOUTH (UNCLE REMUS)				
❏ Disneyland DQ-1205 [M]	1959	6.25	12.50	25.00
SONG WITHOUT END				
❏ Colpix CP-506 [M]	1960	5.00	10.00	20.00
❏ Colpix SCP-506 [S]	1960	6.25	12.50	25.00
THE SONS OF KATIE ELDER				
❏ Columbia Masterworks OS 2820 [S]	1965	25.00	50.00	100.00
❏ Columbia Masterworks OL 6420 [M]	1965	12.50	25.00	50.00
THE SOUL OF NIGGER CHARLEY				
❏ MGM 1SE-46	1973	5.00	10.00	20.00
THE SOUND AND THE FURY				
❏ Decca DL 8885 [M]	1959	7.50	15.00	30.00
❏ Decca DL 78885 [S]	1959	17.50	35.00	70.00
THE SOUND OF MUSIC				
❏ RCA Victor LSOD-2005 [S]	1965	5.00	10.00	20.00
-- With booklet; black label, dog on top				
SOUTH CENTRAL				
❏ Hollywood 61403 [DJ]	1992	5.00	10.00	20.00
-- Vinyl is promo only				
SOUTH PACIFIC				
❏ RCA Victor LOC-1032 [M]	1958	5.00	10.00	20.00
-- "Long Play" on label				
❏ RCA Victor LSO-1032 [S]	1958	6.25	12.50	25.00
-- "Living Stereo" on label				
SOUTHERN STAR				
❏ Colgems COSO-5009	1969	15.00	30.00	60.00
SPACECAMP				
❏ RCA Victor ABL1-5856	1986	10.00	20.00	40.00
A SPANISH AFFAIR				
❏ Dot DLP-3078 [M]	1958	25.00	50.00	100.00
SPARKLE				
❏ Atlantic SD 18176	1976	5.00	10.00	20.00
SPARTACUS				
❏ Decca DL 9092 [M]	1960	5.00	10.00	20.00
-- Black label, silver print				
❏ Decca DL 79092 [S]	1960	6.25	12.50	25.00
-- Maroon label, silver print				
THE SPIRIT OF ST. LOUIS				
❏ RCA Victor LPM-1472 [M]	1957	12.50	25.00	50.00

(Top left) For unclear reasons, two different labels ended up with the rights to release a soundtrack album of *The Flamingo Kid*. The above version, on the Varese Sarabande label, is far more rare than the version that was issued on Motown. (Top right) The 1989 soundtrack of *Heart of Dixie* is collectible in part thanks to Elvis Presley completists. The album includes the King's version of "I Want You, I Need You, I Love You." (Bottom left) The last album Bing Crosby did under contract to Decca – all his future material was leased by Crosby Enterprises to various labels – was the very obscure soundtrack to a TV drama called "High Tor." It is by far the rarest Crosby album on Decca, and near-mint copies can go for figures in the low hundreds. (Bottom right) Speaking of rare soundtracks, this is one of the rarest. Issued as a promotional item by Warner Bros. in 1957, even before there was such a thing as Warner Bros. Records, *Jamboree* contains some classic early rock 'n' roll and trades for over $1,000 in near-mint. The album has been counterfeited, but it's not too difficult to tell the phonies from the real thing (see the listing for *Jamboree* for more details).

Label, Number	Yr	VG	VG+	NM
SPLASH				
❏ Cherry Lane 00301	1984	6.25	12.50	25.00
-- With poster of Daryl Hannah				
THE SPY WHO CAME IN FROM THE COLD				
❏ RCA Victor LOC-1118 [M]	1965	5.00	10.00	20.00
❏ RCA Victor LSO-1118 [S]	1965	10.00	20.00	40.00
THE SPY WITH A COLD NOSE				
❏ Columbia Masterworks OS 3070 [S]	1966	7.50	15.00	30.00
❏ Columbia Masterworks OL 6670 [M]	1966	5.00	10.00	20.00
STAGECOACH				
❏ Mainstream S-6077 [S]	1966	7.50	15.00	30.00
❏ Mainstream 56077 [M]	1966	5.00	10.00	20.00
❏ Mainstream ST-90802 [S]	1966	7.50	15.00	30.00
-- Capitol Record Club edition				
❏ Mainstream T-90802 [M]	1966	6.25	12.50	25.00
-- Capitol Record Club edition				
STAR TREK -- THE MOTION PICTURE				
❏ Columbia JS 36334	1979	5.00	10.00	20.00
STAR!				
❏ 20th Century Fox DTCS-5102	1968	5.00	10.00	20.00
THE STARS AND STRIPES FOREVER				
❏ MGM E-176 [10]	1952	7.50	15.00	30.00
STATE FAIR				
❏ Dot DLP-29011 [S]	1962	7.50	15.00	30.00
❏ Dot DLP-9011 [M]	1962	6.25	12.50	25.00
THE STERILE CUCKOO				
❏ Paramount PAS-5009	1970	5.00	10.00	20.00
STILETTO				
❏ Columbia Masterworks OS 3360	1969	5.00	10.00	20.00
THE STRANGE ONE				
❏ Coral CRL 57132 [M]	1957	17.50	35.00	70.00
THE STRAWBERRY STATEMENT				
❏ MGM 2SE-14 [(2)]	1970	6.25	12.50	25.00
A STREETCAR NAMED DESIRE				
❏ Capitol L 289 [10]	1951	12.50	25.00	50.00
A STUDY IN TERROR				
❏ Roulette OS-801 [M]	1965	10.00	20.00	40.00
❏ Roulette OSS-801 [S]	1965	20.00	40.00	80.00
THE STUNT MAN				
❏ 20th Century T-626	1980	6.25	12.50	25.00
THE SUBTERRANEANS				
❏ MGM E-3812 ST [M]	1960	10.00	20.00	40.00
❏ MGM SE-3812 ST [S]	1960	20.00	40.00	80.00
SUMMER AND SMOKE				
❏ RCA Victor LOC-1067 [M]	1961	12.50	25.00	50.00
❏ RCA Victor LSO-1067 [S]	1961	17.50	35.00	70.00
SUMMER HOLIDAY				
❏ Epic LN 24063 [M]	1963	6.25	12.50	25.00
❏ Epic BN 26063 [S]	1963	7.50	15.00	30.00
SUMMER LOVE				
❏ Decca DL 8714 [M]	1958	15.00	30.00	60.00
-- Black label, silver print, or pink label, black print promo				
❏ Decca DL 8714 [M]	196?	7.50	15.00	30.00
-- Black label with color bars				
SUMMER MAGIC				
❏ Buena Vista BV-4025 [M]	1963	10.00	20.00	40.00
❏ Buena Vista STER-4025 [S]	1963	15.00	30.00	60.00
SUMMER STOCK				
❏ MGM E-519 [10]	1950	10.00	20.00	40.00
THE SUN ALSO RISES				
❏ Kapp KDL-7001 [M]	1957	15.00	30.00	60.00
THE SUNNY SIDE OF THE STREET				
❏ Mercury MG-25100 [10]	1951	15.00	30.00	60.00
SURF PARTY				
❏ 20th Century Fox TFM-3131 [M]	1964	6.25	12.50	25.00
❏ 20th Century Fox TFS-4131 [S]	1964	7.50	15.00	30.00
SURFER GIRLS				
❏ Oakwood SUS-1001	1978	25.00	50.00	100.00
THE SWAN				
❏ MGM E-3399 [M]	1956	17.50	35.00	70.00
THE SWARM				
❏ Warner Bros. BSK 3208	1978	7.50	15.00	30.00
SWEDISH HEAVEN AND HELL				
❏ Ariel ARS-15000	1969	6.25	12.50	25.00
SWEET CHARITY				
❏ Decca DL 71502	1969	5.00	10.00	20.00
THE SWEET RIDE				
❏ 20th Century Fox S-4198	1968	5.00	10.00	20.00
SWEET SWEETBACK'S BADASSSSSS SONG				
❏ Stax STS-3001	1971	7.50	15.00	30.00
SWEPT AWAY				
❏ Peters International PLD 1005	1957	10.00	20.00	40.00
THE SWIMMER				
❏ Columbia Masterworks OS 3210	1968	6.25	12.50	25.00
SWINGER'S PARADISE				
❏ Epic LN 24145 [M]	1965	5.00	10.00	20.00
❏ Epic BN 26145 [S]	1965	6.25	12.50	25.00
A SWINGIN' SUMMER				
❏ Hanna-Barbera HLP-8500 [M]	1966	6.25	12.50	25.00
❏ Hanna-Barbera HST-9500 [S]	1966	7.50	15.00	30.00
SYLVIA				
❏ Mercury MG-21004 [M]	1965	5.00	10.00	20.00
❏ Mercury SR-61004 [S]	1965	7.50	15.00	30.00
TARAS BULBA				
❏ United Artists UAL-4100 [M]	1962	7.50	15.00	30.00
❏ United Artists UAS-5100 [S]	1962	12.50	25.00	50.00
TAXI DRIVER				
❏ Arista AL 4079	1976	5.00	10.00	20.00
TEENAGE REBELLION				
❏ Sidewalk ST-5903 [S]	1967	6.25	12.50	25.00
❏ Sidewalk T-5903 [M]	1967	5.00	10.00	20.00
TELL ME THAT YOU LOVE ME, JUNIE MOON				
❏ Columbia Masterworks OS 3540	1970	5.00	10.00	20.00
THE TEN COMMANDMENTS				
❏ Dot DLP-3054 [M]	1956	10.00	20.00	40.00
❏ Dot DLP-25054 [S]	1959	6.25	12.50	25.00
-- Re-recording of the original soundtrack in stereo				
❏ Paramount PAS-1006	1973	5.00	10.00	20.00
-- Re-release				
TENDER IS THE NIGHT				
❏ 20th Century Fox FOX-3054 [M]	1962	37.50	75.00	150.00
❏ 20th Century Fox SFX-3054 [S]	1962	50.00	100.00	200.00
THE TENTH VICTIM				
❏ Mainstream S-6071 [S]	1965	12.50	25.00	50.00
❏ Mainstream 56071 [M]	1965	10.00	20.00	40.00
THANK GOD IT'S FRIDAY				
❏ Casablanca NBLP-7099-3 [(3)]	1978	5.00	10.00	20.00
-- Two full-length LPs plus a bonus 12-inch single by Donna Summer with blank B-side				
THAT DARN CAT				
❏ Buena Vista BV-3334 [M]	1965	5.00	10.00	20.00
❏ Buena Vista STER-3334 [S]	1965	6.25	12.50	25.00
THAT MAN IN ISTANBUL				
❏ Mainstream S-6072 [S]	1966	6.25	12.50	25.00
❏ Mainstream 56072 [M]	1966	5.00	10.00	20.00
THAT'S ENTERTAINMENT!				
❏ MCA 11002 [(2)]	1974	5.00	10.00	20.00
-- Film credits in small print on back cover, and list of songs omits "That's Entertainment"				
THERE'S NO BUSINESS LIKE SHOW BUSINESS				
❏ Decca DL 8091 [M]	1954	10.00	20.00	40.00
-- Black label, silver print				
❏ Decca DL 8091 [M]	196?	5.00	10.00	20.00
-- Black label with color bars				
THEY SHOOT HORSES, DON'T THEY?				
❏ ABC ABCS-OC-10	1969	5.00	10.00	20.00
THIEF OF HEARTS				
❏ Casablanca 822 942-1	1984	5.00	10.00	20.00
THE THIN BLUE LINE				
❏ Nonesuch 79209-1	1988	5.00	10.00	20.00
THIS COULD BE THE NIGHT				
❏ MGM E-3530 [M]	1957	12.50	25.00	50.00

Label, Number	Yr	VG	VG+	NM
THIS EARTH IS MINE				
❑ Decca DL 8915 [M]	1959	20.00	40.00	80.00
❑ Decca DL 78915 [S]	1959	25.00	50.00	100.00
THIS PROPERTY IS CONDEMNED				
❑ Verve V-8664 [M]	1966	5.00	10.00	20.00
❑ Verve V6-8664 [S]	1966	7.50	15.00	30.00
THE THOMAS CROWN AFFAIR				
❑ United Artists UAS-5182	1968	5.00	10.00	20.00
THOROUGHLY MODERN MILLIE				
❑ Decca DL 1500 [M]	1967	5.00	10.00	20.00
-- With bound-in booklet				
❑ Decca DL 71500 [S]	1967	5.00	10.00	20.00
-- With bound-in booklet				
THOSE GLORIOUS MGM MUSICALS: THE BAND WAGON/KISS ME, KATE				
❑ MGM 2-SES-44-ST [(2)]	1973	5.00	10.00	20.00
THOSE GLORIOUS MGM MUSICALS: THE BARKLEYS OF BROADWAY/ LES GIRLS				
❑ MGM 2-SES-51-ST [(2)]	1973	5.00	10.00	20.00
THOSE GLORIOUS MGM MUSICALS: DEEP IN MY HEART/WORDS AND MUSIC				
❑ MGM 2-SES-54-ST [(2)]	1973	5.00	10.00	20.00
THOSE GLORIOUS MGM MUSICALS: EVERYTHING I HAVE IS YOURS/ SUMMER STOCK/I LOVE MELVIN				
❑ MGM 2-SES-52-ST [(2)]	1973	5.00	10.00	20.00
THOSE GLORIOUS MGM MUSICALS: GOOD NEWS/IN THE GOOD OLD SUMMERTIME/TWO WEEKS WITH LOVE				
❑ MGM 2-SES-49-ST [(2)]	1973	5.00	10.00	20.00
THOSE GLORIOUS MGM MUSICALS: LOVELY TO LOOK AT/ BRIGADOON				
❑ MGM 2-SES-50-ST [(2)]	1973	5.00	10.00	20.00
THOSE GLORIOUS MGM MUSICALS: NANCY GOES TO RIO/RICH, YOUNG AND PRETTY/ROYAL WEDDING				
❑ MGM 2-SES-53-ST [(2)]	1973	5.00	10.00	20.00
THOSE GLORIOUS MGM MUSICALS: THE PIRATE/PAGAN LOVE SONG/HIT THE DECK				
❑ MGM 2-SES-43-ST [(2)]	1973	10.00	20.00	40.00
THOSE GLORIOUS MGM MUSICALS: ROSE MARIE/SEVEN BRIDES FOR SEVEN BROTHERS				
❑ MGM 2-SES-41-ST [(2)]	1973	5.00	10.00	20.00
THOSE GLORIOUS MGM MUSICALS: SHOW BOAT/ANNIE GET YOUR GUN				
❑ MGM 2-SES-42-ST [(2)]	1973	5.00	10.00	20.00
THOSE GLORIOUS MGM MUSICALS: SINGIN' IN THE RAIN/EASTER PARADE				
❑ MGM 2-SES-40-ST [(2)]	1973	5.00	10.00	20.00
THOSE GLORIOUS MGM MUSICALS: TILL THE CLOUDS ROLL BY/ THREE LITTLE WORDS				
❑ MGM 2-SES-45-ST [(2)]	1973	5.00	10.00	20.00
THREE FOR THE SHOW				
❑ Mercury MG-25204 [M]	1955	15.00	30.00	60.00
THREE IN THE ATTIC				
❑ Sidewalk ST-5918	1968	7.50	15.00	30.00
THREE LITTLE WORDS				
❑ MGM E-516 [10]	1959	15.00	30.00	60.00
THE THREE WORLDS OF GULLIVER				
❑ Colpix CP-414 [M]	1960	15.00	30.00	60.00
THE THREEPENNY OPERA				
❑ RCA Victor LOC-1086 [M]	1964	37.50	75.00	150.00
-- With rare original cover: White background, pink and black drawing, characters underneath				
❑ RCA Victor LSO-1086 [S]	1964	50.00	100.00	200.00
-- With rare original cover: White background, pink and black drawing, characters underneath				
❑ RCA Victor LSO-1086 [S]	1964	5.00	10.00	20.00
-- Reissue cover: White background, orange drawing, Sammy Davis Jr. in foreground, "RE" at bottom				
THUNDER ALLEY				
❑ Sidewalk ST-5902 [S]	1967	6.25	12.50	25.00
❑ Sidewalk T-5902 [M]	1967	5.00	10.00	20.00
THUNDERBALL				
❑ United Artists UAL-4132 [M]	1965	5.00	10.00	20.00
❑ United Artists UAS-5132 [S]	1965	7.50	15.00	30.00
❑ United Artists SW-90820 [S]	1965	10.00	20.00	40.00
-- Capitol Record Club edition				

Label, Number	Yr	VG	VG+	NM
TICK...TICK...TICK				
❑ MGM SE-4667 [M]	1970	6.25	12.50	25.00
TILL THE CLOUDS ROLL BY				
❑ MGM E-501 [10]	1950	12.50	25.00	50.00
A TIME TO LOVE AND A TIME TO DIE				
❑ Decca DL 8778 [M]	1958	25.00	50.00	100.00
TO BED... OR NOT TO BED				
❑ London M-76005 [M]	1963	10.00	20.00	40.00
TO KILL A MOCKINGBIRD				
❑ Ava A-20 [M]	1962	6.25	12.50	25.00
❑ Ava AS-20 [S]	1962	7.50	15.00	30.00
TO SIR, WITH LOVE				
❑ Fontana MGF-27569 [M]	1967	5.00	10.00	20.00
❑ Fontana SRF-67569 [S]	1967	6.25	12.50	25.00
TOKYO OLYMPIAD				
❑ Monument SLP-18046 [S]	1966	5.00	10.00	20.00
TOM JONES				
❑ United Artists UAL-4113 [M]	1963	5.00	10.00	20.00
❑ United Artists UAS-5113 [S]	1963	6.25	12.50	25.00
TOM SAWYER				
❑ United Artists UA-LA057-F	1973	5.00	10.00	20.00
TOMMY				
❑ Polydor PD 2 9502 [(2)]	1975	5.00	10.00	20.00
TOO MUCH TOO SOON				
❑ Mercury MG-20381 [M]	1958	7.50	15.00	30.00
❑ Mercury SR-60019 [S]	1958	20.00	40.00	80.00
TOPKAPI				
❑ United Artists UAL-4118 [M]	1964	5.00	10.00	20.00
❑ United Artists UAS-5118 [S]	1964	7.50	15.00	30.00
THE TOUCHABLES				
❑ 20th Century Fox S-4206	1969	5.00	10.00	20.00
THE TRAIN				
❑ United Artists UAL-4122 [M]	1965	5.00	10.00	20.00
❑ United Artists UAS-5122 [S]	1965	10.00	20.00	40.00
THE TRAP				
❑ Atco 33-204 [M]	1966	10.00	20.00	40.00
❑ Atco SD 33-204 [S]	1966	17.50	35.00	70.00
TRAPEZE				
❑ Columbia CL 870 [M]	1956	6.25	12.50	25.00
THE TRAPP FAMILY				
❑ 20th Fox FOX-3044 [M]	1961	6.25	12.50	25.00
❑ 20th Fox STX-3044 [S]	1961	10.00	20.00	40.00
THE TREASURE OF SAN GENNARO				
❑ Buddah BDS-5011	1968	10.00	20.00	40.00
THE TRIP				
❑ Sidewalk ST-5908 [S]	1967	10.00	20.00	40.00
❑ Sidewalk T-5908 [M]	1967	7.50	15.00	30.00
TRIPLE CROSS				
❑ United Artists UAL-4162 [M]	1967	5.00	10.00	20.00
❑ United Artists UAS-5162 [S]	1967	7.50	15.00	30.00
THE TROUBLE WITH ANGELS				
❑ Mainstream S-6073 [S]	1966	20.00	40.00	80.00
❑ Mainstream 56073 [M]	1966	10.00	20.00	40.00
TRUE GRIT				
❑ Capitol ST-263	1969	7.50	15.00	30.00
❑ Capitol ST-8-0263	1969	10.00	20.00	40.00
-- Capitol Record Club edition				
TRUE LIFE ADVENTURES				
❑ Disneyland WDL-4011 [M]	1957	17.50	35.00	70.00
THE TRUE STORY OF THE CIVIL WAR				
❑ Coral CRL 59100 [M]	1958	20.00	40.00	80.00
TWO MULES FOR SISTER SARA				
❑ Kapp KRS-5512	1970	6.25	12.50	25.00
TWO WEEKS WITH LOVE				
❑ MGM E-530 [10]	1950	10.00	20.00	40.00
ULYSSES				
❑ RCA Victor LOC-1138 [M]	1967	6.25	12.50	25.00
❑ RCA Victor LSO-1138 [S]	1967	7.50	15.00	30.00

Label, Number	Yr	VG	VG+	NM
THE UMBRELLAS OF CHERBOURG (LES PARAPLUIES DE CHERBOURG)				
❑ Philips PCC 216 [M]	1965	5.00	10.00	20.00
❑ Philips PCC 616 [S]	1965	7.50	15.00	30.00
THE UNBEARABLE LIGHTNESS OF BEING				
❑ Fantasy FSP-21006	1988	5.00	10.00	20.00
UNCLE TOM'S CABIN				
❑ Philips PHS 600-272	1968	10.00	20.00	40.00
THE UNFORGIVEN				
❑ United Artists UAL-4068 [M]	1960	10.00	20.00	40.00
❑ United Artists UAS-5068 [S]	1960	17.50	35.00	70.00
THE UNSINKABLE MOLLY BROWN				
❑ MGM SE-4232 [S]	1964	5.00	10.00	20.00
UP IN THE CELLAR				
❑ American Int'l. A-1036	1970	5.00	10.00	20.00
UP THE DOWN STAIRCASE				
❑ United Artists UAL-4169 [M]	1967	5.00	10.00	20.00
❑ United Artists UAS-5169 [S]	1967	10.00	20.00	40.00
UP THE JUNCTION				
❑ Mercury SR-61159	1968	6.25	12.50	25.00
VALENTINO				
❑ United Artists UA-LA810-H	1977	6.25	12.50	25.00
VALLEY GIRL				
❑ Epic FE 38623	1983	20.00	40.00	80.00
❑ Roadshow RS-101	1983	30.00	60.00	120.00
VALLEY OF THE DOLLS				
❑ 20th Century Fox TF-4196 [M]	1968	7.50	15.00	30.00
❑ 20th Century Fox TFS-4196 [S]	1968	7.50	15.00	30.00
THE VANISHING POINT				
❑ Amos AAS-8002	1971	5.00	10.00	20.00
THE VANISHING PRAIRIE				
❑ Columbia CL 6332 [10]	1954	20.00	40.00	80.00
VERTIGO				
❑ Mercury MG-20384 [M]	1958	37.50	75.00	150.00
VICTOR/VICTORIA				
❑ MGM MG-1-5407	1982	7.50	15.00	30.00
THE VICTORS				
❑ Colpix CP-516 [M]	1963	5.00	10.00	20.00
❑ Colpix SCP-516 [S]	1963	7.50	15.00	30.00
A VIEW TO A KILL				
❑ Capitol SJ-12413	1985	5.00	10.00	20.00
THE VIKINGS				
❑ United Artists UAL-4003 [M]	1958	7.50	15.00	30.00
❑ United Artists UAS-5003 [S]	1958	10.00	20.00	40.00
VILLA RIDES!				
❑ Dot DLP-25870	1968	10.00	20.00	40.00
VIVA MARIA!				
❑ United Artists UAL-4135 [M]	1965	5.00	10.00	20.00
❑ United Artists UAS-5135 [S]	1965	7.50	15.00	30.00
VIVA MAX!				
❑ RCA Victor LSP-4275	1969	5.00	10.00	20.00
THE VIXEN				
❑ Beverly Hills BHS-22	1968	12.50	25.00	50.00
VOYAGE EN BALLON				
❑ Philips PHM 200-029 [M]	1960	7.50	15.00	30.00
❑ Philips PHS 600-029 [S]	1960	10.00	20.00	40.00
W.W. AND THE DIXIE DANCEKINGS				
❑ 20th Century ST-103	1975	6.25	12.50	25.00
WALK DON'T RUN				
❑ Mainstream S-6080 [S]	1966	10.00	20.00	40.00
❑ Mainstream 56080 [M]	1966	5.00	10.00	20.00
WALK ON THE WILD SIDE				
❑ Ava A-4-ST [M]	1962	5.00	10.00	20.00
❑ Ava AS-4-ST [S]	1962	10.00	20.00	40.00
❑ Choreo A-4-ST [M]	1962	7.50	15.00	30.00
❑ Choreo AS-4-ST [S]	1962	12.50	25.00	50.00
A WALK WITH LOVE AND DEATH				
❑ Citadel CT-6025	1969	20.00	40.00	80.00
THE WANDERERS				
❑ Warner Bros. BSK 3359	1979	7.50	15.00	30.00
WAR AND PEACE				
❑ Columbia CL 930 [M]	1956	6.25	12.50	25.00
❑ Melodiya/Capitol SWAO 2918	1968	10.00	20.00	40.00
THE WAR LORD				
❑ Decca DL 9149 [M]	1965	6.25	12.50	25.00
❑ Decca DL 79149 [S]	1965	12.50	25.00	50.00
THE WARLOCK				
❑ Intrada MAF-7003	1990	5.00	10.00	20.00
WARNING SHOT				
❑ Liberty LRP-3498 [M]	1967	7.50	15.00	30.00
❑ Liberty LST-7498 [S]	1967	10.00	20.00	40.00
WATERLOO				
❑ Paramount PAS-6003	1971	7.50	15.00	30.00
❑ Paramount SW-93729	1971	7.50	15.00	30.00
-- Capitol Record Club edition				
WATERMELON MAN				
❑ Beverly Hills BHS-26	1970	7.50	15.00	30.00
WATERSHIP DOWN				
❑ Columbia JS 35707	1978	6.25	12.50	25.00
WAY...WAY OUT				
❑ 20th Century Fox 3192 [M]	1966	7.50	15.00	30.00
❑ 20th Century Fox S-4192 [S]	1966	10.00	20.00	40.00
WEDDING IN MONACO				
❑ Mercury MG-20149 [M]	1956	62.50	125.00	250.00
WEST SIDE STORY				
❑ Columbia Masterworks OS 2070 [S]	1961	6.25	12.50	25.00
-- Originals have gatefold covers and gray and black labels with six "eye" logos				
❑ Columbia Masterworks OL 5670 [M]	1961	5.00	10.00	20.00
-- Originals have gatefold covers and gray and black labels with six "eye" logos				
WHAT A WAY TO GO!				
❑ 20th Century Fox TFM-3143 [M]	1964	5.00	10.00	20.00
❑ 20th Century Fox TFS-4143 [S]	1964	10.00	20.00	40.00
WHAT'S NEW PUSSYCAT?				
❑ United Artists UAL-4128 [M]	1965	5.00	10.00	20.00
❑ United Artists UAS-5128 [S]	1965	6.25	12.50	25.00
WHEN THE BOYS MEET THE GIRLS				
❑ MGM SE-4334 [S]	1965	7.50	15.00	30.00
WHERE EAGLES DARE				
❑ MGM S1E-16 ST	1969	7.50	15.00	30.00
WHERE'S JACK?				
❑ Paramount PAS-5005	1969	6.25	12.50	25.00
WHERE'S POPPA?				
❑ United Artists UAS-5216	1970	6.25	12.50	25.00
THE WHISPERERS				
❑ United Artists UAL-4161 [M]	1967	5.00	10.00	20.00
❑ United Artists UAS-5161 [S]	1967	7.50	15.00	30.00
WHITE CHRISTMAS				
❑ Decca DL 8083 [M]	1954	12.50	25.00	50.00
WHO FRAMED ROGER RABBIT?				
❑ Buena Vista 64100	1988	5.00	10.00	20.00
WHO'S AFRAID OF VIRGINIA WOOLF?				
❑ Warner Bros. B 1656 [M]	1966	6.25	12.50	25.00
❑ Warner Bros. BS 1656 [S]	1966	7.50	15.00	30.00
❑ Warner Bros. 2B 1657 [(2) M]	1966	10.00	20.00	40.00
-- Above (1657) is the complete film, not just the music and some dialogue				
THE WILD BUNCH				
❑ Warner Bros. WS 1814	1969	25.00	50.00	100.00
THE WILD EYE				
❑ RCA Victor LSP-4003	1968	6.25	12.50	25.00
WILD GEESE				
❑ A&M SP-4730	1978	5.00	10.00	20.00
WILD IN THE STREETS				
❑ Tower SKAO 5099	1968	7.50	15.00	30.00
WILD IS THE WIND				
❑ Columbia CL 1090 [M]	1957	6.25	12.50	25.00
WILD ON THE BEACH				
❑ RCA Victor LPM-3441 [M]	1965	6.25	12.50	25.00
❑ RCA Victor LSP-3441 [S]	1965	10.00	20.00	40.00

Label, Number	Yr	VG	VG+	NM
THE WILD RACERS				
❏ Sidewalk ST-5914	1968	6.25	12.50	25.00
WILD WHEELS				
❏ RCA Victor LSO-1156	1969	5.00	10.00	20.00
WILD, WILD WINTER				
❏ Decca DL 4699 [M]	1966	5.00	10.00	20.00
❏ Decca DL 74699 [S]	1966	7.50	15.00	30.00
WILLIE DYNAMITE				
❏ MCA 393	1974	5.00	10.00	20.00
WILLOW				
❏ Virgin Movie Music 90939	1988	6.25	12.50	25.00
WILLY WONKA AND THE CHOCOLATE FACTORY				
❏ Paramount PAS-6012	1971	10.00	20.00	40.00
THE WITCHES OF EASTWICK				
❏ Warner Bros. 25607	1987	7.50	15.00	30.00
WITH A SONG IN MY HEART				
❏ Capitol L 309 [10]	1952	10.00	20.00	40.00
❏ Capitol T 309 [M]	195?	6.25	12.50	25.00
THE WIZARD OF OZ				
❏ MGM E-3464 [M]	1956	12.50	25.00	50.00
-- Yellow label				
WOMEN OF THE WORLD				
❏ Decca DL 9112 [M]	1963	5.00	10.00	20.00
❏ Decca DL 79112 [S]	1963	7.50	15.00	30.00
WONDERFUL COUNTRY				
❏ United Artists UAL-4050 [M]	1959	12.50	25.00	50.00
❏ United Artists UAS-5050 [S]	1959	25.00	50.00	100.00
WONDERFUL TO BE YOUNG				
❏ Dot DLP-3474 [M]	1962	6.25	12.50	25.00
❏ Dot DLP-25474 [S]	1962	10.00	20.00	40.00
THE WONDERFUL WORLD OF THE BROTHERS GRIMM				
❏ MGM 1E-3 [M]	1962	6.25	12.50	25.00
-- With box and hardback book				
❏ MGM S1E-3 [S]	1962	10.00	20.00	40.00
-- With box and hardback book				
WORDS AND MUSIC				
❏ MGM E-505 [10]	1950	12.50	25.00	50.00
THE WORLD OF SUZIE WONG				
❏ RCA Victor LOC-1059 [M]	1960	5.00	10.00	20.00
❏ RCA Victor LSO-1059 [S]	1960	12.50	25.00	50.00
WRITTEN ON THE WIND				
❏ Decca DL 8424 [M]	1956	10.00	20.00	40.00
-- Black label, silver print, or pink label, black print promo				
❏ Decca DL 8424 [M]	196?	5.00	10.00	20.00
-- Black label with color bars				
THE WRONG BOX				
❏ Mainstream S-6088 [S]	1966	37.50	75.00	150.00
❏ Mainstream 56088 [M]	1966	25.00	50.00	100.00
WUTHERING HEIGHTS				
❏ American Int'l. A-1039	1971	7.50	15.00	30.00
THE YELLOW CANARY				
❏ Verve V-8548 [M]	1963	5.00	10.00	20.00
❏ Verve V6-8548 [S]	1963	6.25	12.50	25.00
THE YELLOW ROLLS-ROYCE				
❏ MGM E-4292 [M]	1965	5.00	10.00	20.00
❏ MGM SE-4292 [S]	1965	7.50	15.00	30.00
YESTERDAY, TODAY AND TOMORROW				
❏ Warner Bros. W 1552 [M]	1964	10.00	20.00	40.00
❏ Warner Bros. WS 1552 [S]	1964	12.50	25.00	50.00
YOJIMBO				
❏ MGM E-4096 [M]	1962	25.00	50.00	100.00
❏ MGM SE-4096 [S]	1962	37.50	75.00	150.00
YOU ARE WHAT YOU EAT				
❏ Columbia Masterworks OS 3240	1968	5.00	10.00	20.00
YOU ONLY LIVE TWICE				
❏ United Artists UAL-4155 [M]	1967	5.00	10.00	20.00
❏ United Artists UAS-5155 [S]	1967	6.25	12.50	25.00
YOUNG BILLY YOUNG				
❏ United Artists UAS-5199	1969	6.25	12.50	25.00
YOUNG DOCTORS IN LOVE				
❏ Regency RI-8501	1982	5.00	10.00	20.00
YOUNG FRANKENSTEIN				
❏ ABC ABCD-870	1975	5.00	10.00	20.00
THE YOUNG GIRLS OF ROCHEFORT				
❏ Philips PCC 2-226 [(2) M]	1968	5.00	10.00	20.00
❏ Philips PCC 2-626 [(2) S]	1968	7.50	15.00	30.00
THE YOUNG LIONS				
❏ Decca DL 8719 [M]	1958	7.50	15.00	30.00
❏ Decca DL 78719 [S]	1958	20.00	40.00	80.00
YOUNG LOVERS				
❏ Columbia Masterworks OS 2510 [S]	1964	6.25	12.50	25.00
❏ Columbia Masterworks OL 7010 [M]	1964	5.00	10.00	20.00
YOUNG MAN WITH A HORN				
❏ Columbia CL 582 [M]	1950	7.50	15.00	30.00
❏ Columbia CL 6106 [10]	1950	12.50	25.00	50.00
THE YOUNG SAVAGES				
❏ Columbia CL 1672 [M]	1961	7.50	15.00	30.00
❏ Columbia CS 8472 [S]	1961	25.00	50.00	100.00
YOUNG WINSTON				
❏ Angel SFO-36901	1972	6.25	12.50	25.00
YOURS, MINE AND OURS				
❏ United Artists UAS-5181	1968	5.00	10.00	20.00
Z				
❏ Columbia Masterworks OS 3370	1970	5.00	10.00	20.00
ZABRISKIE POINT				
❏ MGM SE-4468	1970	5.00	10.00	20.00
ZACHARIAH				
❏ ABC ABCS-OC-13	1970	6.25	12.50	25.00
ZOOT SUIT				
❏ MCA 5267	1981	5.00	10.00	20.00
ZORBA THE GREEK				
❏ 20th Century Fox TFM-3167 [M]	1965	5.00	10.00	20.00
❏ 20th Century Fox TFS-4167 [S]	1965	6.25	12.50	25.00
ZULU				
❏ United Artists UAL-4116 [M]	1964	10.00	20.00	40.00
❏ United Artists UAS-5116 [S]	1964	17.50	35.00	70.00

Label, Number	Yr	VG	VG+	NM

TELEVISION ALBUMS

The following section includes albums with content related to television programs, whether a series, miniseries or one-shot deal. Included are not only soundtracks and incidental music from the shows, but also albums that use the voices and stars from television programs for material created specifically for record. Television-related LPs are usually quite collectible.

Many TV soundtrack composers were recording artists in their own right. Among them are QUINCY JONES; HENRY MANCINI; and LALO SCHIFRIN. Most of their qualifying soundtracks are listed in the main section. If an LP is not listed below, try under the composer's name.

Many cartoon series of the late 1960s and early 1970s featured manufactured musical groups; most of these are found under the "artist" in the main section of the book. See THE ARCHIES; THE BANANA SPLITS; THE BUGALOOS; THE CATANOOGA CATS; GLOBETROTTERS; THE GROOVIE GOOLIES; THE HARDY BOYS; JOSIE AND THE PUSSYCATS; LANCELOT LINK AND THE EVOLUTION REVOLUTION; MULTIPLICATION ROCK; PEBBLES AND BAMM BAMM; PUFNSTUF; THE SUGAR BEARS.

THE ADDAMS FAMILY
❏ RCA Victor LPM-3421 [M]	1965	20.00	40.00	80.00
❏ RCA Victor LSP-3421 [S]	1965	37.50	75.00	150.00

AFRICA
❏ MGM E-4462 [M]	1967	12.50	25.00	50.00
❏ MGM SE-4462 [S]	1967	15.00	30.00	60.00

THE AGE OF TELEVISION -- A CHRONICLE OF THE FIRST 25 YEARS
❏ RCA Victor LL-8	1972	5.00	10.00	20.00
-- With booklet

ALADDIN
❏ Columbia CL 1117 [M]	1958	12.50	25.00	50.00

ALICE THROUGH THE LOOKING GLASS
❏ RCA Victor LOC-1130 [M]	1966	6.25	12.50	25.00
❏ RCA Victor LSO-1130 [S]	1966	7.50	15.00	30.00

AMAHL AND THE NIGHT VISITORS
❏ RCA Red Seal LM-1701 [10]	1952	12.50	25.00	50.00
-- Soundtrack of the 1951 NBC-TV production
| ❏ RCA Red Seal LM-1701 [M] | 1952 | 10.00 | 20.00 | 40.00 |
-- Soundtrack of the 1951 NBC-TV production; 12-inch record in box with booklet

ANDROCLES AND THE LION
❏ RCA Victor LOC-1141 [M]	1967	6.25	12.50	25.00
❏ RCA Victor LSO-1141 [S]	1967	6.25	12.50	25.00

ANNIE GET YOUR GUN
❏ Capitol W 913 [M]	1957	7.50	15.00	30.00
-- Los Angeles/San Francisco production aired on NBC-TV

AT HOME WITH THE MUNSTERS
❏ Golden LP-139 [M]	1964	50.00	100.00	200.00

ATOM ANT IN MUSCLE MAGIC
❏ Hanna-Barbera HLP-2041 [M]	1966	37.50	75.00	150.00

THE AVENGERS
❏ Hanna-Barbera HLP-8506 [M]	1966	15.00	30.00	60.00
❏ Hanna-Barbera HST-9506 [S]	1966	20.00	40.00	80.00

BATMAN
❏ 20th Century Fox TFM-3180 [M]	1966	15.00	30.00	60.00
❏ 20th Century Fox TFS-4180 [S]	1966	25.00	50.00	100.00

THE BEVERLY HILLBILLIES
❏ Columbia CL 2402 [M]	1965	10.00	20.00	40.00
❏ Columbia CS 9202 [S]	1965	15.00	30.00	60.00

THE BIG VALLEY
❏ ABC-Paramount ABC-527 [M]	1965	10.00	20.00	40.00
❏ ABC-Paramount ABCS-527 [S]	1965	12.50	25.00	50.00

THE BORN LOSERS
❏ Tower DT 5082 [R]	1967	5.00	10.00	20.00
❏ Tower T 5082 [M]	1967	6.25	12.50	25.00

THE BORROWERS
❏ Stanyan SRQ-4014 [Q]	1973	12.50	25.00	50.00

BOURBON STREET BEAT
❏ Warner Bros. W 1321 [M]	1960	6.25	12.50	25.00
❏ Warner Bros. WS 1321 [S]	1960	7.50	15.00	30.00

BRIGADOON
❏ Columbia Special Products CSM 385	1968	5.00	10.00	20.00
-- Sold through the mail by broadcast sponsor Armstrong

BURKE'S LAW
❏ Liberty LRP-3374 [M]	1964	15.00	30.00	60.00
❏ Liberty LST-7374 [S]	1964	20.00	40.00	80.00

CAROUSEL
❏ Columbia Special Products CSM 479	1969	5.00	10.00	20.00
-- Sold through the mail by broadcast sponsor Armstrong

A CHARLIE BROWN CHRISTMAS
❏ Charlie Brown 3701	1977	5.00	10.00	20.00
-- Complete soundtrack with dialogue, plus music by VINCE GUARALDI; includes 12-page bound-in booklet with script and illustrations

CHECKMATE
❏ Columbia CL 1591 [M]	1960	10.00	20.00	40.00
❏ Columbia CS 8391 [S]	1960	15.00	30.00	60.00

CINDERELLA
❏ Columbia Masterworks OS 2005 [S]	1959	10.00	20.00	40.00
-- Stage presentation for TV starring Julie Andrews
| ❏ Columbia Masterworks OS 2730 [S] | 1965 | 7.50 | 15.00 | 30.00 |
-- Stage presentation for TV starring Lesley-Ann Warren
| ❏ Columbia Masterworks OL 5190 [M] | 1957 | 7.50 | 15.00 | 30.00 |
-- Stage presentation for TV starring Julie Andrews
| ❏ Columbia Masterworks OL 6330 [M] | 1965 | 6.25 | 12.50 | 25.00 |
-- Stage presentation for TV starring Lesley-Ann Warren

THE COMING OF CHRIST
❏ Decca DL 9093 [M]	1960	10.00	20.00	40.00
❏ Decca DL 79093 [S]	1960	12.50	25.00	50.00

THE CRICKET ON THE HEARTH
❏ RCA Victor LOC-1140 [M]	1967	5.00	10.00	20.00
❏ RCA Victor LSO-1140 [S]	1967	7.50	15.00	30.00

DANGER
❏ MGM E-111 [10]	1951	30.00	60.00	120.00

THE DANGEROUS CHRISTMAS OF RED RIDING HOOD
❏ ABC-Paramount ABCS-536 [S]	1965	6.25	12.50	25.00

DARK SHADOWS
❏ Philips PHS 600-314	1969	7.50	15.00	30.00
-- With poster

DAVID COPPERFIELD
❏ GRT 10008	1970	37.50	75.00	150.00

DENNIS THE MENACE SONGS
❏ Golden LP-59 [M]	1960	20.00	40.00	80.00
-- Black label original

DOGGIE DADDY TELLS AUGGY DOGGIE THE STORY OF PINOCCHIO
❏ Hanna-Barbera HLP-2028 [M]	1965	25.00	50.00	100.00

EAST SIDE, WEST SIDE
❏ Columbia CL 2123 [M]	1963	7.50	15.00	30.00
❏ Columbia CS 8923 [S]	1963	10.00	20.00	40.00

ELEVEN AGAINST THE ICE
❏ RCA Victor LPM-1618 [M]	1958	15.00	30.00	60.00

ELIZABETH TAYLOR IN LONDON
❏ Colpix CP 459 [M]	1963	7.50	15.00	30.00
❏ Colpix SCP 459 [S]	1963	12.50	25.00	50.00

THE EWOK ADVENTURE
❏ Varese Sarabande STV-81281	198?	12.50	25.00	50.00

EXCITING HONG KONG
❏ ABC-Paramount ABC-367 [M]	1961	10.00	20.00	40.00
❏ ABC-Paramount ABCS-367 [S]	1961	12.50	25.00	50.00

FELIX THE CAT
❏ Cricket CR-28 [M]	1958	25.00	50.00	100.00

FENWICK
❏ Fenwick FLP-621	1968	5.00	10.00	20.00
-- Soundtrack to TV special; packaged in oversize (13 1/2 x 13 1/2) sleeve with color cartoon booklet; made especially for Motorola

THE FLINTSTONES
❏ Colpix CP-302 [M]	1961	50.00	100.00	200.00

THE FLINTSTONES AND JOSE JIMENEZ IN THE TIME MACHINE
❏ Hanna-Barbera HLP-2052 [M]	1966	20.00	40.00	80.00

Label, Number	Yr	VG	VG+	NM
THE FLINTSTONES IN S.A.S.F.A.T.P.O.G.O.B.S.O.A.L.T.				
❑ Hanna-Barbera HLP-2047 [M]	1966	25.00	50.00	100.00
THE FLINTSTONES' FLIP FABLES: GOLDI-ROCKS AND THE THREE BEAROSAURUSES				
❑ Hanna-Barbera HLP-2021 [M]	1965	25.00	50.00	100.00
THE FORD 50TH ANNIVERSARY TELEVISION SHOW				
❑ Decca DL 7027 [10]	1953	10.00	20.00	40.00
FOUR ADVENTURES OF ZORRO				
❑ Disneyland WDA-3601 [M]	1958	20.00	40.00	80.00
-- Gatefold with booklet				
FRED FLINTSTONE AND BARNEY RUBBLE SING SONGS FROM MARY POPPINS				
❑ Hanna-Barbera HLP-2035 [M]	1965	25.00	50.00	100.00
FROSTY THE SNOWMAN				
❑ MGM SE-4733	1970	15.00	30.00	60.00
FROSTY'S WINTER WONDERLAND				
❑ Disneyland 1368	1976	5.00	10.00	20.00
GENERAL ELECTRIC THEATER				
❑ Columbia CL 1395 [M]	1959	10.00	20.00	40.00
❑ Columbia CS 8190 [S]	1959	12.50	25.00	50.00
GENERAL MOTORS' 50TH ANNIVERSARY SHOW				
❑ RCA Victor LOC-1037 [M]	1958	25.00	50.00	100.00
GET SMART				
❑ United Artists UAL-3533 [M]	1965	10.00	20.00	40.00
❑ United Artists UAS-6566 [S]	1965	15.00	30.00	60.00
THE GIFT OF LOVE				
❑ Columbia CL 1113 [M]	1958	7.50	15.00	30.00
THE GIFT OF THE MAGI				
❑ United Artists UAL-4013 [M]	1959	10.00	20.00	40.00
❑ United Artists UAS-5103 [S]	1959	12.50	25.00	50.00
THE GIRL FROM U.N.C.L.E.				
❑ MGM E-4410 [M]	1966	10.00	20.00	40.00
❑ MGM SE-4410 [S]	1966	15.00	30.00	60.00
GOOFY'S TV SPECTACULAR				
❑ Disneyland DQ-1252 [M]	1964	5.00	10.00	20.00
THE GREEN HORNET				
❑ 20th Century Fox S-3186 [S]	1966	62.50	125.00	250.00
❑ 20th Century Fox TF-3186 [M]	1966	50.00	100.00	200.00
HANS BRINKER				
❑ Dot DLP-9001 [M]	1958	10.00	20.00	40.00
HANSEL AND GRETEL STARRING THE FLINTSTONES				
❑ Hanna-Barbera HLP-2038 [M]	1965	25.00	50.00	100.00
HAWAII FIVE-O				
❑ Capitol ST-410	1969	10.00	20.00	40.00
HAWAIIAN EYE				
❑ Warner Bros. W 1355 [M]	1959	7.50	15.00	30.00
❑ Warner Bros. WS 1355 [S]	1959	10.00	20.00	40.00
HECTOR, THE STOWAWAY PUP				
❑ Disneyland ST-1921 [M]	1964	7.50	15.00	30.00
HEIDI				
❑ Capitol SKAO 2995	1968	10.00	20.00	40.00
HENNESSEY				
❑ Signature 1049 [M]	1959	15.00	30.00	60.00
❑ Signature SS-1049 [S]	1959	20.00	40.00	80.00
HERE COMES HUCKLEBERRY HOUND				
❑ Colpix CP-207 [M]	1961	45.00	90.00	180.00
HERE'S JOHNNY! MAGIC MOMENTS FROM THE TONIGHT SHOW				
❑ Casablanca SPNB-1296 [(2)]	1976	5.00	10.00	20.00
-- Price for intact copies with poster; cut-outs go for 50-75 percent of this				
HEY THERE, IT'S YOGI BEAR				
❑ Golden LP-124 [M]	1964	10.00	20.00	40.00
HIGH TOR				
❑ Decca DL 8272 [M]	1956	50.00	100.00	200.00
THE HILLBILLY BEARS IN HILLBILLY SHINDIG				
❑ Hanna-Barbera HLP-2044 [M]	1966	37.50	75.00	150.00
HOGAN'S HEROES SING THE BEST OF WWII				
❑ Sunset SUM-1137 [M]	1967	7.50	15.00	30.00
❑ Sunset SUS-5137 [S]	1967	10.00	20.00	40.00

Label, Number	Yr	VG	VG+	NM
HOLOCAUST				
❑ RCA Victor ARL1-2785	1978	6.25	12.50	25.00
HONEY WEST				
❑ ABC-Paramount ABC-532 [M]	1965	10.00	20.00	40.00
❑ ABC-Paramount ABCS-532 [S]	1965	12.50	25.00	50.00
HOW THE GRINCH STOLE CHRISTMAS				
❑ Leo LE-901 [M]	1966	12.50	25.00	50.00
❑ Leo LES-901 [S]	1966	17.50	35.00	70.00
HOWL ALONG WITH HUCKLEBERRY HOUND AND YOGI BEAR				
❑ Golden LP-55 [M]	1959	37.50	75.00	150.00
-- Black label original				
HUCKLEBERRY HOUND AND THE GHOST SHIP				
❑ Colpix CP-210 [M]	1962	25.00	50.00	100.00
HUCKLEBERRY HOUND FOR PRESIDENT				
❑ Golden LP-60 [M]	1960	25.00	50.00	100.00
-- Black label original				
HUCKLEBERRY HOUND TELLS STORIES OF UNCLE REMUS				
❑ Hanna-Barbera HLP-2022 [M]	1965	25.00	50.00	100.00
HUCKLEBERRY HOUND, THE GREAT KELLOGG'S TV SHOW				
❑ Colpix CP-202 [M]	1959	50.00	100.00	200.00
I SPY				
❑ Warner Bros. W 1637 [M]	1965	7.50	15.00	30.00
❑ Warner Bros. WS 1637 [S]	1965	10.00	20.00	40.00
I SPY, VOLUME 2				
❑ Capitol ST 2839	1968	7.50	15.00	30.00
IT'S HOWDY DOODY TIME				
❑ RCA Victor LSP-4546	1971	6.25	12.50	25.00
THE JACKSONS: AN AMERICAN DREAM				
❑ Motown 37463 6356-1 [DJ]	1992	5.00	10.00	20.00
-- Promo only vinyl				
JAMES BOMB STARRING SUPER SNOOPER AND BLABBER MOUSE				
❑ Hanna-Barbera HLP-2036 [M]	1965	25.00	50.00	100.00
JANE EYRE				
❑ Capitol SW-749	1971	7.50	15.00	30.00
THE JETSONS				
❑ Colpix CP-213 [M]	1962	62.50	125.00	250.00
❑ Golden LP-98 [M]	1963	50.00	100.00	200.00
-- Red cover original				
❑ Golden LP-98 [M]	1964	30.00	60.00	120.00
-- Blue cover reissue				
THE JETSONS IN FIRST FAMILY ON THE MOON				
❑ Hanna-Barbera HLP-2037 [M]	1965	37.50	75.00	150.00
THE JIMMY DURANTE TV SHOW				
❑ Royale 1812 [10]	1955	25.00	50.00	100.00
JONNY QUEST IN 20,000 LEAGUES UNDER THE SEA				
❑ Hanna-Barbera HLP-2030 [M]	1965	37.50	75.00	150.00
JOURNEY BACK TO OZ				
❑ Filmation (no #)	1980	12.50	25.00	50.00
KENT STATE				
❑ RCA Victor ABL1-3928	1981	5.00	10.00	20.00
KING KONG				
❑ Golden LP-151 [M]	1965	10.00	20.00	40.00
KISS ME, KATE				
❑ Columbia Special Products CSS 645	1968	6.25	12.50	25.00
-- Sold through the mail by broadcast sponsor Armstrong				
A LOOK AT MONACO				
❑ Columbia CL 2019 [M]	1963	12.50	25.00	50.00
❑ Columbia CS 8819 [R]	1963	12.50	25.00	50.00
LOVE, AMERICAN STYLE				
❑ Capitol ST-11250	1973	10.00	20.00	40.00
MAGILLA GORILLA AND HIS PALS				
❑ Golden LP-120 [M]	1964	12.50	25.00	50.00
MAGILLA GORILLA TELLS OGEE THE STORY OF ALICE IN WONDERLAND				
❑ Hanna-Barbera HLP-2024 [M]	1965	25.00	50.00	100.00
THE MAN FROM INTERPOL				
❑ Top Rank RM-327 [M]	1962	12.50	25.00	50.00
❑ Top Rank RS-627 [S]	1962	15.00	30.00	60.00

Label, Number	Yr	VG	VG+	NM
THE MAN FROM U.N.C.L.E.				
❏ RCA Victor LPM-3475 [M]	1965	15.00	30.00	60.00
❏ RCA Victor LSP-3475 [S]	1965	20.00	40.00	80.00
THE MAN FROM U.N.C.L.E. VOLUME 2				
❏ RCA Victor LPM-3574 [M]	1966	10.00	20.00	40.00
❏ RCA Victor LSP-3574 [S]	1966	12.50	25.00	50.00
MARK TWAIN TONIGHT!				
❏ Columbia Masterworks OS 3080 [S]	1967	5.00	10.00	20.00
MASADA				
❏ MCA 5168	1981	5.00	10.00	20.00
MERRY CHRISTMAS FROM KUKLA, FRAN AND OLLIE				
❏ Decca DL 8192 [M]	1955	20.00	40.00	80.00
MICKEY MOUSE CLUB -- ALL NEW FROM 1977 -- ORIGINAL TV CAST				
❏ Buena Vista 62501	1979	5.00	10.00	20.00
MICKEY MOUSE CLUB MOUSEKEDANCES AND OTHER MOUSEKETEER FAVORITES				
❏ Disneyland DQ-1362 [M]	1974	5.00	10.00	20.00
-- With booklet				
❏ Disneyland STER-1362 [S]	1974	6.25	12.50	25.00
-- With booklet				
MICKEY MOUSE CLUB SONG HITS				
❏ Disneyland ST-3815	1975	10.00	20.00	40.00
-- With 16-page photo album				
MICKEY MOUSE CLUB: THE ALL NEW MICKEY MOUSE CLUB				
❏ Disneyland 2501	1977	5.00	10.00	20.00
MICKEY MOUSE CLUB: FUN WITH MUSIC -- 30 FAVORITE DISNEY SONGS				
❏ Disneyland DQ-1209 [M]	1959	6.25	12.50	25.00
MICKEY MOUSE CLUB: HOLIDAYS WITH THE MOUSEKETEERS (A SONG FOR EVERY HOLIDAY)				
❏ Mickey Mouse Club MM-22	1958	10.00	20.00	40.00
MICKEY MOUSE CLUB: HOW TO BE A MOUSEKETEER				
❏ Disneyland ST-3918	1962	10.00	20.00	40.00
MICKEY MOUSE CLUB: MOUSEKETEERS TALENT ROUNDUP				
❏ Mickey Mouse Club MM-16	1958	10.00	20.00	40.00
MICKEY MOUSE CLUB: MUSICAL HIGHLIGHTS FROM THE MICKEY MOUSE CLUB				
❏ Disneyland DQ-1227 [M]	1962	7.50	15.00	30.00
MICKEY MOUSE CLUB: MUSICAL HIGHLIGHTS FROM THE MICKEY MOUSE CLUB TV SHOW				
❏ Mickey Mouse Club MM-12	1958	20.00	40.00	80.00
MICKEY MOUSE CLUB: SONGS FROM ANNETTE AND OTHER WALT DISNEY SERIALS				
❏ Mickey Mouse Club MM-24	1958	30.00	60.00	120.00
MICKEY MOUSE CLUB: SONGS FROM THE MICKEY MOUSE CLUB SERIALS				
❏ Disneyland DQ-1229 [M]	1962	10.00	20.00	40.00
MICKEY MOUSE CLUB: 27 NEW SONGS FROM THE MICKEY MOUSE CLUB TV SHOW				
❏ Mickey Mouse Club MM-14	1958	12.50	25.00	50.00
MICKEY MOUSE CLUB: A WALT DISNEY SONG FEST				
❏ Mickey Mouse Club MM-20	1958	10.00	20.00	40.00
MICKEY MOUSE CLUB: WE'RE THE MOUSEKETEERS				
❏ Mickey Mouse Club MM-18	1957	10.00	20.00	40.00
THE MIGHTY HERCULES				
❏ Golden LP-109 [M]	1963	50.00	100.00	200.00
MIKADO				
❏ Columbia Masterworks OL 5480 [M]	1960	7.50	15.00	30.00
❏ Columbia Masterworks OS 2022 [S]	1960	25.00	50.00	100.00
THE MISADVENTURES OF DENNIS THE MENACE				
❏ Colpix CP-204 [M]	1960	50.00	100.00	200.00
MR. BROADWAY				
❏ RCA Victor LPM-1520 [M]	1957	7.50	15.00	30.00
MR. ED, THE TALKING HORSE				
❏ Colpix CP-209 [M]	1962	75.00	150.00	300.00
MR. ED: STRAIGHT FROM THE HORSE'S MOUTH				
❏ Golden LP-88 [M]	1962	50.00	100.00	200.00
MR. JINKS, PIXIE AND DIXIE				
❏ Colpix CP-208 [M]	1961	25.00	50.00	100.00
THE MUNSTERS				
❏ Decca DL 4588 [M]	1964	15.00	30.00	60.00
❏ Decca DL 74588 [S]	1964	25.00	50.00	100.00
THE MUSIC FROM M SQUAD				
❏ RCA Victor LPM-2062 [M]	1959	7.50	15.00	30.00
❏ RCA Victor LSP-2062 [S]	1959	10.00	20.00	40.00
THE MUSIC FROM MARLBORO COUNTRY				
❏ United Artists SP-107	1967	12.50	25.00	50.00
NAKED CITY -- A MUSICAL PORTRAIT				
❏ Colpix CP-505 [M]	1958	10.00	20.00	40.00
❏ Colpix SCP-505 [S]	1959	15.00	30.00	60.00
OF THEE I SING				
❏ Columbia S 31763	1972	5.00	10.00	20.00
THE OFFICIAL ALBUM OF NBC'S BAT MASTERSON				
❏ Sea Horse/Chancellor CSH-7002 [M]	1960	20.00	40.00	80.00
ONE STEP BEYOND				
❏ Decca DL 8970 [M]	1960	7.50	1.00	30.00
❏ Decca DL 78970 [S]	1960	10.00	20.00	40.00
ORIGINAL AMATEUR HOUR 25TH ANNIVERSARY ALBUM				
❏ United Artists UXL 2 [(2) M]	1960	10.00	20.00	40.00
THE ORIGINAL TV ADVENTURES OF KING KONG				
❏ Epic LN 24231 [M]	1966	6.25	12.50	25.00
❏ Epic BN 26231 [S]	1966	7.50	15.00	30.00
THE OTHER WORLD OF WINSTON CHURCHILL				
❏ Mercury MG-21033 [M]	1965	7.50	15.00	30.00
❏ Mercury SR-61033 [S]	1965	10.00	20.00	40.00
OZZIE AND HARRIET				
❏ Imperial LP-9049 [M]	1957	50.00	100.00	200.00
PEYTON PLACE				
❏ Epic LN 24147 [M]	1965	7.50	15.00	30.00
❏ Epic BN 26147 [S]	1965	10.00	20.00	40.00
THE PIED PIPER OF HAMELIN				
❏ RCA Victor LPM-1563 [M]	1957	12.50	25.00	50.00
PINOCCHIO				
❏ Columbia CL 1055 [M]	1957	10.00	20.00	40.00
PIXIE AND DIXIE WITH MR. JINKS TELL THE STORY OF CINDERELLA				
❏ Hanna-Barbera HLP-2025 [M]	1965	25.00	50.00	100.00
PRECIOUS PUPP IN HOT ROD GRANNY				
❏ Hanna-Barbera HLP-2045 [M]	1966	37.50	75.00	150.00
QUICK DRAW MCGRAW				
❏ Colpix CP-203 [M]	1960	20.00	40.00	80.00
QUICK DRAW MCGRAW AND HUCKLEBERRY HOUND				
❏ Golden LP-51 [M]	1959	37.50	75.00	150.00
-- Black label original				
QUICK DRAW MCGRAW: THE TREASURE OF SARAH'S MATTRESS				
❏ Colpix CP-211 [M]	1962	30.00	60.00	120.00
THE REPORTER				
❏ Columbia CL 2269 [M]	1964	7.50	15.00	30.00
❏ Columbia CS 9069 [S]	1964	10.00	20.00	40.00
RICH MAN, POOR MAN				
❏ MCA 2095	1976	6.25	12.50	25.00
RICHARD DIAMOND				
❏ Mercury MG-36162 [M]	1959	12.50	25.00	50.00
❏ Mercury SR-80045 [S]	1959	20.00	40.00	80.00
THE RISE AND FALL OF THE THIRD REICH				
❏ MGM 1SE-12	1968	7.50	15.00	30.00
ROBIN HOOD STARRING TOP CAT				
❏ Hanna-Barbera HLP-2031 [M]	1965	25.00	50.00	100.00
ROCKY AND HIS FRIENDS				
❏ Golden LP-64 [M]	1961	50.00	100.00	200.00
-- Gold label original				
THE ROGUES				
❏ RCA Victor LPM-2976 [M]	1964	5.00	10.00	20.00
❏ RCA Victor LSP-2976 [S]	1964	7.50	15.00	30.00
ROOTS				
❏ Warner Bros. 3WS 3048 [(3)]	1978	6.25	12.50	25.00

Label, Number	Yr	VG	VG+	NM
RUDOLPH THE RED-NOSED REINDEER				
❑ Decca DL 4815 [M]	1964	15.00	30.00	60.00
❑ Decca DL 34327 [M]	1965	10.00	20.00	40.00
-- Same as DL 4815; custom products reissue				
❑ Decca DL 74815 [S]	1964	20.00	40.00	80.00
❑ MCA 15003	1973	5.00	10.00	20.00
-- Reissue; black rainbow label				
RUFF AND READY				
❑ Colpix CP-201 [M]	1959	50.00	100.00	200.00
RUGGLES OF RED GAP				
❑ Verve MGV-15000 [M]	1957	12.50	25.00	50.00
THE SAINT				
❑ RCA Victor LPM-3631 [M]	1966	30.00	60.00	120.00
❑ RCA Victor LSP-3631 [S]	1966	50.00	100.00	200.00
SANTA CLAUS IS COMIN' TO TOWN				
❑ MGM SE-4732	1970	15.00	30.00	60.00
SATINS AND SPURS				
❑ Capitol L 547 [10]	1954	17.50	35.00	70.00
SECRET AGENT				
❑ RCA Victor LPM-3630 [M]	1966	62.50	125.00	250.00
❑ RCA Victor LSP-3630 [S]	1966	62.50	125.00	250.00
-- With incorrect title, "Danger Man," on label				
❑ RCA Victor LSP-3630 [S]	1966	75.00	150.00	300.00
-- With correct title on label				
SECRET AGENT MEETS THE SAINT				
❑ RCA Victor LPM-3467 [M]	1965	50.00	100.00	200.00
❑ RCA Victor LSP-3467 [S]	1965	55.00	110.00	220.00
-- Music from both TV shows; pre-dates the individual albums				
SECRET SQUIRREL AND MOROCCO MOLE IN SUPER SPY				
❑ Hanna-Barbera HLP-2046 [M]	1966	37.50	75.00	150.00
77 SUNSET STRIP				
❑ Warner Bros. W 1289 [M]	1959	7.50	15.00	30.00
❑ Warner Bros. WS 1289 [S]	1959	10.00	20.00	40.00
SHOGUN				
❑ RSO RX-1-3088	1981	5.00	10.00	20.00
SHOTGUN SLADE				
❑ Mercury MG-20575 [M]	1960	10.00	20.00	40.00
❑ Mercury SR-60235 [S]	1960	15.00	30.00	60.00
SINBAD JR. IN TREASURE ISLAND				
❑ Hanna-Barbera HLP-2039 [M]	1965	30.00	60.00	120.00
67 MELODY LANE				
❑ Columbia CL 724 [M]	1955	7.50	15.00	30.00
SNAGGLEPUSS TELLS THE STORY OF THE WIZARD OF OZ				
❑ Hanna-Barbera HLP-2026 [M]	1965	25.00	50.00	100.00
SONGS OF THE FLINTSTONES				
❑ Golden LP-66 [M]	1961	62.50	125.00	250.00
-- Gold label original				
SONGS OF YOGI BEAR AND HIS PALS				
❑ Golden LP-70 [M]	1961	20.00	40.00	80.00
-- Gold label original				
THE SOUND OF JAZZ				
❑ Columbia CL 1098 [M]	1958	6.25	12.50	25.00
❑ Columbia CS 8040 [S]	1958	10.00	20.00	40.00
SPACE: 1999				
❑ RCA Victor ABL1-1422	1975	5.00	10.00	20.00
SQUIDDLEY DIDDLEY IN SURFIN' SAFARI				
❑ Hanna-Barbera HLP-2043 [M]	1966	37.50	75.00	150.00
STACCATO (MUSIC FROM JOHNNY STACCATO)				
❑ Capitol ST 1287 [S]	1959	12.50	25.00	50.00
❑ Capitol T 1287 [M]	1959	7.50	15.00	30.00
THE STINGIEST MAN IN TOWN				
❑ Columbia CL 950	1956	5.00	10.00	20.00
-- Music from a television play first aired on The Alcoa Hour				
SUPER SNOOPER AND BLABBER MOUSE IN MONSTER SHINDIG				
❑ Hanna-Barbera HLP-2020 [M]	1965	25.00	50.00	100.00
THRILLER				
❑ Time 52034 [M]	1960	7.50	15.00	30.00
❑ Time S-2034 [S]	1960	10.00	20.00	40.00
TOM SAWYER				
❑ Decca DL 8432 [M]	1957	10.00	20.00	40.00
-- First aired on the U.S. Steel Hour, starring Jimmy Boyd				

Label, Number	Yr	VG	VG+	NM
TOP CAT				
❑ Colpix CP-212 [M]	1963	75.00	150.00	300.00
TOUCHE TURTLE AND DUM-DUM IN THE RELUCTANT DRAGON				
❑ Hanna-Barbera HLP-2029 [M]	1965	25.00	50.00	100.00
' TWAS THE NIGHT BEFORE CHRISTMAS				
❑ Disneyland 1367	1976	5.00	10.00	20.00
THE UNTOUCHABLES				
❑ Capitol ST 1430 [S]	1960	12.50	25.00	50.00
❑ Capitol T 1430 [M]	1960	10.00	20.00	40.00
UP WITH PEOPLE!				
❑ Pace 1101	1965	5.00	10.00	20.00
-- Among the many people on this LP is a young Glenn Close (first name misspelled "Gleen")				
THE VALIANT YEARS				
❑ ABC-Paramount ABC-387 [M]	1962	7.50	15.00	30.00
❑ ABC-Paramount ABCS-387 [S]	1962	10.00	20.00	40.00
VICTORY AT SEA				
❑ Mobile Fidelity 3-150 [(3)]	1984	25.00	50.00	100.00
-- Audiophile vinyl				
❑ RCA Victor LM-1779 [M]	1954	6.25	12.50	25.00
-- Original recording				
❑ RCA Victor LM-2335 [M]	1959	5.00	10.00	20.00
-- Re-recording of 1779				
❑ RCA Victor LSC-2335 [S]	1959	5.00	10.00	20.00
-- Re-recording of 1779 in stereo				
VICTORY AT SEA, VOL. 2				
❑ RCA Victor LM-2226 [M]	1958	5.00	10.00	20.00
❑ RCA Victor LSC-2226 [S]	1958	6.25	12.50	25.00
-- Original with "shaded dog" label				
VICTORY AT SEA, VOL. 3				
❑ RCA Victor LM-2523 [M]	1961	5.00	10.00	20.00
❑ RCA Victor LSC-2523 [S]	1961	6.25	12.50	25.00
WAGON TRAIN				
❑ Mercury MG-20502 [M]	1959	12.50	25.00	50.00
❑ Mercury SR-60179 [S]	1959	20.00	40.00	80.00
WALT DISNEY'S WONDERFUL WORLD OF COLOR				
❑ Disneyland DQ-1245 [M]	1963	7.50	15.00	30.00
WASHINGTON: BEHIND CLOSED DOORS				
❑ ABC AB-1044	1977	6.25	12.50	25.00
WIDE, WIDE WORLD				
❑ RCA Victor LPM-1280 [M]	1956	10.00	20.00	40.00
WILMA FLINTSTONE TELLS THE STORY OF BAMBI				
❑ Hanna-Barbera HLP-2027 [M]	1965	25.00	50.00	100.00
THE WINDS OF WAR				
❑ Varese Sarabande STV-81180	1983	5.00	10.00	20.00
WINSOME WITCH IN IT'S MAGIC				
❑ Hanna-Barbera HLP-2042 [M]	1966	37.50	75.00	150.00
WONDERFUL TOWN				
❑ Columbia Masterworks OL 5360 [M]	1958	5.00	10.00	20.00
❑ Columbia Masterworks OS 2008 [S]	1958	6.25	12.50	25.00
YOGI BEAR AND BOO-BOO				
❑ Colpix CP-205 [M]	1961	30.00	60.00	120.00
YOGI BEAR AND BOO-BOO TELL STORIES OF LITTLE RED RIDING HOOD AND				
JACK AND THE BEANSTALK				
❑ Hanna-Barbera HLP-2023 [M]	1965	25.00	50.00	100.00
YOGI BEAR AND THE THREE STOOGES IN THE MAD, MAD, DR. NO-NO				
❑ Hanna-Barbera HLP-2050 [M]	1966	25.00	50.00	100.00
YOGI BEAR: HOW TO BE A BETTER THAN AVERAGE CHILD				
❑ Golden LP-90 [M]	1962	20.00	40.00	80.00

Label, Number	Yr	VG	VG+	NM

VARIOUS ARTISTS COLLECTIONS

For the most part, this section covers those LPs with three or more artists contained on the same record. There have been tens of thousands of this type of compilation issued; below we merely scratch the surface by listing over 1,000 that qualify for inclusion in this book.

Albums with the same name are grouped together, even if they have different contents! When we know they are different, we indicate that.

A LA CARTE
❑ Warner Bros. PRO-A-794 [(2)]	1978	5.00	10.00	20.00

AFTER HOURS
❑ King 395-528 [M]	1956	125.00	250.00	500.00

AIN'T THAT GOOD NEWS
❑ Specialty SPS-2115	1969	5.00	10.00	20.00

ALAN FREED'S GOLDEN PICS
❑ End LP-313 [M]	1961	15.00	30.00	60.00

ALAN FREED'S MEMORY LANE
❑ End LP-314 [M]	1962	15.00	30.00	60.00

ALAN FREED'S TOP 15
❑ End LP-315 [M]	1962	15.00	30.00	60.00

ALL DAY THUMB SUCKER REVISITED
❑ Blue Thumb BT3-7002 [(3)]	1995	5.00	10.00	20.00

-- Boxed set

ALL GIRL MILLION SELLERS
❑ Ascot AM-13007 [M]	1964	10.00	20.00	40.00
❑ Ascot AS-16007 [P]	1964	10.00	20.00	40.00

ALL MEAT
❑ Warner Bros. PRO 604 [(2)]	1975	5.00	10.00	20.00

ALL SINGING -- ALL TALKING -- ALL ROCKING
❑ Warner Bros. PRO 573 [(2)]	1973	6.25	12.50	25.00

ALL STAR ROCK AND ROLL REVUE
❑ King 395-513 [M]	1956	100.00	200.00	400.00
❑ King 638 [M]	1959	50.00	100.00	200.00

-- Reissue of King 395-513

ALL STAR ROCK, VOLUME 11
❑ Original Sound Recordings OSR-11	1972	10.00	20.00	40.00

-- The first 10 volumes go for much less; this one has an Elvis track on it, thus the higher price

ALL THE HITS BY ALL THE STARS
❑ Parkway P 7013 [M]	1962	10.00	20.00	40.00

ALL THE HITS BY ALL THE STARS, VOL. 2
❑ Parkway P 7016 [M]	1963	7.50	15.00	30.00

ALL THE STARS' BIGGEST HITS
❑ Parkway P-7033 [M]	1963	12.50	25.00	50.00

-- With "pull-off pix" still intact on cover

ALL THE STARS' BIGGEST HITS, VOLUME 2
❑ Parkway P-7034 [M]	1963	12.50	25.00	50.00

-- With "pull-off pix" still intact on cover

ALL THESE THINGS
❑ Instant LP-71000	1969	7.50	15.00	30.00

ALL TIME COUNTRY AND WESTERN HITS
❑ King 537 [M]	1956	37.50	75.00	150.00
❑ King 710 [M]	1961	25.00	50.00	100.00

-- Not a reissue of King 537, but a different collection

ALL TIME HIT SACRED AND GOSPEL SONGS
❑ King 1023 [M]	1967	7.50	15.00	30.00

THE AMAZING METS
❑ Buddah 1969	1969	6.25	12.50	25.00

AMERICAN FOLK BLUES FESTIVAL
❑ Exodus EX-302 [M]	1966	5.00	10.00	20.00
❑ Exodus EXS-302 [S]	1966	6.25	12.50	25.00
❑ Excello LPS-8029	1972	5.00	10.00	20.00

-- A different album than the Exodus release

ANOTHER MONDAY NIGHT AT BIRDLAND
❑ Roulette R 52022 [M]	1959	7.50	15.00	30.00
❑ Roulette SR 52022 [S]	1959	7.50	15.00	30.00

AN ANTHOLOGY OF BRITISH BLUES, VOL. 1
❑ Immediate Z12 52006	1968	7.50	15.00	30.00

AN ANTHOLOGY OF BRITISH BLUES, VOL. 2
❑ Immediate Z12 52014	1968	7.50	15.00	30.00

APOLLO SATURDAY NIGHT
❑ Atco 33-159 [M]	1964	10.00	20.00	40.00
❑ Atco SD 33-159 [S]	1964	12.50	25.00	50.00

APPETIZERS
❑ Warner Bros. PRO 569 [(2)]	1973	6.25	12.50	25.00

APPROVED BY 10,000,000
❑ Teem LP-5004 [M]	196?	7.50	15.00	30.00

ARISTA AOR SAMPLER
❑ Arista ALS 06 [(2) DJ]	1978	5.00	10.00	20.00

ARISTA'S GREATEST HITS: PORTRAIT OF A DECADE 1975-1985
❑ Arista/Silver Eagle SE 10383 [(3)]	1985	5.00	10.00	20.00

THE ARTISTS AND MUSIC THAT STARTED IT ALL
❑ Motown PR-84 [(6) DJ]	1981	50.00	100.00	200.00

-- Promo-only box set; five of the records appeared as "The Motown Story: The First Twenty-Five Years" two years later

AT THE HOOTENANNY
❑ Kapp KL-1330 [M]	1963	5.00	10.00	20.00
❑ Kapp KS-3330 [S]	1963	6.25	12.50	25.00

AT THE HOOTENANNY, VOL. 2
❑ Kapp KL-1343 [M]	1963	5.00	10.00	20.00
❑ Kapp KS-3343 [S]	1963	6.25	12.50	25.00

AT THE HOOTENANNY, VOL. 3
❑ Kapp KL-1344 [M]	1963	5.00	10.00	20.00
❑ Kapp KS-3344 [S]	1963	6.25	12.50	25.00

ATLANTIC BLUES
❑ Atlantic 81713 [(8)]	1987	12.50	25.00	50.00

-- Boxed set; also available as four 2-LP sets

ATLANTIC RECORDS: CLASSIC ROCK
❑ Atlantic 81908 [(4)]	1989	7.50	15.00	30.00

-- Boxed set

ATLANTIC RHYTHM AND BLUES
❑ Atlantic 81620 [(14)]	1986	25.00	50.00	100.00

-- Boxed set; also available as seven 2-LP sets

BALLADS AND BREAKDOWNS OF THE GOLDEN ERA
❑ Columbia CS 9660	1968	5.00	10.00	20.00

BALLROOM BANDSTAND
❑ Columbia CL 611 [M]	1955	6.25	12.50	25.00

BANG AND SHOUT SUPER HITS
❑ Bang BLPS-220 [P]	1969	5.00	10.00	20.00

BANJO COUNTRY STYLE
❑ Audio Lab AL-1569 [M]	1962	20.00	40.00	80.00

BARREL HOUSE PIANO
❑ Brunswick BL 58022 [10]	1951	15.00	30.00	60.00

A BARREL OF OLDIES
❑ Del-Fi DFLP-1219 [M]	1961	12.50	25.00	50.00

BARRY MANN AND CYNTHIA WEIL: SOLID GOLD
❑ Screen Gems/Columbia CPL-712 [DJ]	1975	5.00	10.00	20.00

-- Promo-only compilation of oldies sent to radio to spur airplay on songs owned by this publishing house

BATTLE OF THE GROUPS
❑ End LP-305 [M]	1960	15.00	30.00	60.00

BATTLE OF THE GROUPS, VOLUME 2
❑ End LP-309 [M]	1960	15.00	30.00	60.00

THE BEAT: SOUND WAVE OF THE 80'S
❑ K-Tel TU 5040	1982	5.00	10.00	20.00

THE BELLS OF CHRISTMAS
❑ Book-of-the-Month 90-5677 [(3)]	1973	5.00	10.00	20.00

-- Sold through Book-of-the-Month Records; secondary number is "P3 11972"

THE BEST OF BOMP! VOLUME ONE
❑ Bomp! 4002	1978	5.00	10.00	20.00

-- First pressings on white vinyl

THE BEST OF CHRISTMAS
❑ Capitol STBB 2979 [(2)]	1968	5.00	10.00	20.00

THE BEST OF DISNEY VOL. I
❑ Disneyland 2502	1978	6.25	12.50	25.00

THE BEST OF DISNEY VOL. II
❑ Disneyland 2503	1978	6.25	12.50	25.00

Label, Number	Yr	VG	VG+	NM
BEST OF LIMP, REST OF LIMP				
❑ Limp 1004	1980	10.00	20.00	40.00
-- Numbered edition of 1,000				
BEST OF RALPH				
❑ Ralph RR 8251-2 [(2)]	1982	5.00	10.00	20.00
BEST OF RHYTHM AND BLUES				
❑ Jubilee JLP-1014 [M]	1956	50.00	100.00	200.00
-- Pink label, black vinyl				
❑ Jubilee JLP-1014 [M]	1956	125.00	250.00	500.00
-- Pink label, red vinyl				
❑ Jubilee JLP-1014 [M]	1956	37.50	75.00	150.00
-- Blue label, black vinyl				
❑ Warwick W 2026 [M]	1961	20.00	40.00	80.00
-- Different album than the Jubilee release				
BEST OF THE BLUES, VOLUME 1				
❑ Imperial LP-9257 [M]	1964	6.25	12.50	25.00
❑ Imperial LP-12257 [R]	1964	5.00	10.00	20.00
BEST OF THE BLUES, VOLUME 2				
❑ Imperial LP-9259 [M]	1964	6.25	12.50	25.00
❑ Imperial LP-12259 [R]	1964	5.00	10.00	20.00
THE BEST OF THE KING BISCUIT FLOWER HOUR				
❑ Silver Eagle SE 10674 [(3)]	1988	6.25	12.50	25.00
THE BEST OF THE R AND B GROUPS				
❑ Warwick W 2025 [M]	1961	25.00	50.00	100.00
BEST OF THE SOUNDTRACKS				
❑ Tower ST-5148	1969	6.25	12.50	25.00
THE BEST VOCAL GROUPS IN ROCK 'N' ROLL				
❑ Dooto DL-224 [M]	1957	25.00	50.00	100.00
-- Yellow label				
❑ Dooto DL-224 [M]	196?	7.50	15.00	30.00
-- Multi-color label				
BETHLEHEM'S BEST, VOLUME 1				
❑ Bethlehem BCP-82 [M]	1958	7.50	15.00	30.00
BETHLEHEM'S BEST, VOLUME 2				
❑ Bethlehem BCP-83 [M]	1958	7.50	15.00	30.00
BETHLEHEM'S BEST, VOLUME 3				
❑ Bethlehem BCP-84 [M]	1958	7.50	15.00	30.00
THE BIG BALL				
❑ Warner Bros. PRO 358 [(2)]	1970	6.25	12.50	25.00
-- Originals have green labels				
BIG BAND CONTRAST				
❑ Bethlehem BCP-6037 [M]	1960	7.50	15.00	30.00
BIG COUNTRY HITS				
❑ Pickwick JS-6166	1975	7.50	15.00	30.00
THE BIG HITS				
❑ Columbia CL 1353 [M]	1959	7.50	15.00	30.00
❑ Columbia CS 8161 [S]	1959	10.00	20.00	40.00
THE BIG HITS OF MID-AMERICA				
❑ Soma MG-1245 [M]	1965	20.00	40.00	80.00
THE BIG HITS OF MID-AMERICA VOLUME 2				
❑ Soma MG-1246 [M]	1965	20.00	40.00	80.00
BIG HITS OF MID-AMERICA VOLUME THREE				
❑ Twin/Tone TTTR 7907/8 [(2)]	1979	5.00	10.00	20.00
THE BIG ONES FROM DUKE AND PEACOCK RECORDS				
❑ Peacock PLP-2000 [M]	1967	5.00	10.00	20.00
THE BIG SOUNDS OF THE DRAGS!				
❑ Capitol ST 2001 [S]	1963	6.25	12.50	25.00
❑ Capitol T 2001 [M]	1963	5.00	10.00	20.00
BIG SUR FESTIVAL/ONE HAND CLAPPING				
❑ Columbia KC 31138	1972	5.00	10.00	20.00
BIG SURF HITS				
❑ Del-Fi DFLP-1249 [M]	1964	12.50	25.00	50.00
❑ Del-Fi DFST-1249 [S]	1964	18.75	37.50	75.00
THE BIRDLAND STORY				
❑ Roulette RB-2 [(2) M]	1961	10.00	20.00	40.00
❑ Roulette SRB-2 [(2) S]	1961	10.00	20.00	40.00
BLEECKER AND MACDOUGAL: THE FOLK SCENE OF THE 1960S				
❑ Elektra 60381 [(3)]	1984	5.00	10.00	20.00

Label, Number	Yr	VG	VG+	NM
BLUE CHRISTMAS				
❑ Welk Music Group WM-3002 [DJ]	1984	20.00	40.00	80.00
-- Promo only; compiled by the publisher of "Blue Christmas" and other holiday tunes for radio use				
BLUE RIBBON COUNTRY				
❑ Capitol STBB 2969 [(2)]	1968	6.25	12.50	25.00
BLUE RIBBON COUNTRY, VOL. 2				
❑ Capitol STBB-217 [(2)]	1969	6.25	12.50	25.00
THE BLUES				
❑ Vee Jay VJS-2-1007 [(2)]	1974	5.00	10.00	20.00
❑ Vee Jay LP-1020 [M]	1960	10.00	20.00	40.00
-- Two different compilations				
BLUES 'N' FOLK				
❑ Bethlehem BCP-6071 [M]	1963	15.00	30.00	60.00
BLUES FROM BIG BILL'S COPACABANA				
❑ Chess LP 1533 [M]	1969	6.25	12.50	25.00
-- Possibly a reissue of "Folk Festival of the Blues," Argo 4031				
BLUES LIVE IN BATON ROUGE				
❑ Excello LPS-8021	1971	6.25	12.50	25.00
THE BLUES PROJECT				
❑ Elektra EKL-264 [M]	1964	6.25	12.50	25.00
❑ Elektra EKS-7264 [S]	1964	7.50	15.00	30.00
-- No relation to the band of the same name; on one track, Bob Dylan plays piano under the name "Bob Landy"				
BLUES THAT GAVE AMERICA SOUL				
❑ Duke DLP-82 [M]	1966	5.00	10.00	20.00
❑ Duke DLPS-82 [S]	1966	6.25	12.50	25.00
BLUES UPTOWN: URBAN BLUES, VOLUME 1				
❑ Imperial LP-94002	1968	5.00	10.00	20.00
THE BLUES, VOLUME 1				
❑ Argo LP-4026 [M]	1963	6.25	12.50	25.00
THE BLUES, VOLUME 2				
❑ Argo LP-4027 [M]	1963	6.25	12.50	25.00
THE BLUES, VOLUME 3				
❑ Argo LP-4034 [M]	1964	6.25	12.50	25.00
THE BLUES, VOLUME 4				
❑ Argo LP-4042 [M]	1964	6.25	12.50	25.00
THE BLUES, VOLUME 5				
❑ Cadet LP-4051 [M]	1966	6.25	12.50	25.00
BLUESVILLE				
❑ Bethlehem BCP-6038 [M]	1960	7.50	15.00	30.00
BOOGIE WOOGIE PIANO				
❑ Brunswick BL 58018 [10]	1950	15.00	30.00	60.00
BOPPIN'				
❑ Jubilee JGM-1118 [M]	1960	37.50	75.00	150.00
BOSS GOLDIES -- SOUNDS FROM THE GROOVEYARD				
❑ Columbia CL 2559 [M]	1966	5.00	10.00	20.00
❑ Columbia CS 9339 [S]	1966	6.25	12.50	25.00
BOY MEETS GIRL				
❑ Stax STS 2-2024 [(2)]	1969	5.00	10.00	20.00
BREAKING THE RULES				
❑ Columbia A2S 881 [(2) DJ]	1980	5.00	10.00	20.00
THE BRIGHTEST STARS OF CHRISTMAS				
❑ RCA Special Products DPL1-0086	1974	5.00	10.00	20.00
-- Sold only at JCPenney department stores				
BRITISH GOLD				
❑ Sire R 224095 [(2)]	1978	5.00	10.00	20.00
-- RCA Music Service edition				
BRITISH ROCK CLASSICS				
❑ Sire R 234021 [(2)]	1978	5.00	10.00	20.00
-- RCA Music Service edition				
BRITISH STERLING				
❑ Lakefront LSM 811	1981	6.25	12.50	25.00
BRUNSWICK'S GREATEST HITS				
❑ Brunswick BL 754186	1973	5.00	10.00	20.00
BUBBLE GUM MUSIC IS THE NAKED TRUTH, VOLUME 1				
❑ Buddah BDA 5032	1969	6.25	12.50	25.00
BUDDAH'S 360 DEGREE DIAL-A-HIT				
❑ Buddah BDA 5039	1969	7.50	15.00	30.00
-- With rotating wheel under the front LP cover				

Label, Number	Yr	VG	VG+	NM
A BUMPER CROP OF ALL STARS				
❑ King 753 [M]	1961	25.00	50.00	100.00
BUNCH OF GOODIES				
❑ Chess LP 1441 [DJ]	1960	150.00	300.00	600.00
-- Multi-color splash vinyl				
❑ Chess LP 1441 [M]	1960	30.00	60.00	120.00
-- Black vinyl				
BURBANK				
❑ Warner Bros. PRO 529 [(2)]	1972	6.25	12.50	25.00
-- Originals have green labels				
BURBANK'S GREATEST HITS				
❑ Warner Bros. PRO 548	1973	5.00	10.00	20.00
BYE BYE BIRDIE				
❑ Colpix CP-454 [M]	1963	20.00	40.00	80.00
❑ Colpix SCP-454 [S]	1963	25.00	50.00	100.00
-- Studio version performed by Paul Petersen, Shelley Fabares, James Darren, the Marcels and others				
CALIFORNIA JAM 2				
❑ Columbia PC2 35389 [(2)]	1978	5.00	10.00	20.00
CAN YOU HEAR ME? MUSIC FROM THE DEAF CLUB				
❑ Optional/Walking Dead 001	1980	6.25	12.50	25.00
❑ PVC 7920	1980	5.00	10.00	20.00
CARLOAD O' HITS				
❑ Muse M-500 [M]	1959	50.00	100.00	200.00
A CARNIVAL OF SONGS				
❑ King 819 [M]	1963	25.00	50.00	100.00
CBS TWO-FERS ARE GREAT MUSICAL VALUES!				
❑ CBS A2S 143/4 [(2) DJ]	1975	5.00	10.00	20.00
CELEBRATE THE SEASON WITH TUPPERWARE				
❑ RCA Special Products DPL1-0803	1987	7.50	15.00	30.00
-- Sold only at Tupperware parties				
CHART BUSTERS '62				
❑ Capitol ST 1837 [S]	1963	10.00	20.00	40.00
❑ Capitol T 1837 [M]	1963	7.50	15.00	30.00
CHARTBUSTERS, VOL. 2				
❑ Capitol ST 1945 [S]	1963	10.00	20.00	40.00
❑ Capitol T 1945 [M]	1963	7.50	15.00	30.00
CHARTBUSTERS, VOL. 3				
❑ Capitol ST 2006 [S]	1963	10.00	20.00	40.00
❑ Capitol T 2006 [M]	1963	7.50	15.00	30.00
CHARTBUSTERS, VOL. 4				
❑ Capitol ST 2094 [S]	1964	15.00	30.00	60.00
❑ Capitol T 2094 [M]	1964	10.00	20.00	40.00
CHESS IS BACK!				
❑ Chess CH-333 [DJ]	1982	5.00	10.00	20.00
-- Promo only, distributed by Sugar Hill				
CHICAGO BLUES ANTHOLOGY				
❑ Chess 2CH-60012 [(2)]	1972	5.00	10.00	20.00
A CHRISTMAS CAROL/MUSIC OF CHRISTMAS				
❑ MGM E3222 [M]	1955	7.50	15.00	30.00
-- Expanded version of 10-inch LP (see LIONEL BARRYMORE for original)				
CHRISTMAS CLASSICS				
❑ WCI UN-540 [(4)]	1985	5.00	10.00	20.00
-- Records individually numbered: 1. Capitol Special Markets SL-9309; 2. CBS Special Products P-18335; 3. CBS Special Products P-18334; 4. Capitol Special Markets SL-9308				
CHRISTMAS CLASSICS 1963				
❑ E.F. MacDonald EFMX-63	1963	5.00	10.00	20.00
-- Special album done by the E.F. MacDonald Company, Dayton, Ohio				
CHRISTMAS DAY WITH COLONEL SANDERS				
❑ RCA Victor PRS-274	1968	5.00	10.00	20.00
-- Sold only at Kentucky Fried Chicken restaurants				
CHRISTMAS EVE WITH COLONEL SANDERS				
❑ RCA Victor PRS-256	1967	5.00	10.00	20.00
-- Sold only at Kentucky Fried Chicken restaurants				
CHRISTMAS GIFT 'RAP				
❑ Motown MS-725	1970	5.00	10.00	20.00
-- Reissue of "Merry Christmas from Motown," MS-681				
A CHRISTMAS GIFT FOR YOU FROM PHIL SPECTOR				
❑ Phil Spector/Abkco D1-4005 [M]	1989	5.00	10.00	20.00
-- Last vinyl reissue				

Label, Number	Yr	VG	VG+	NM
A CHRISTMAS GIFT FOR YOU FROM PHILLES RECORDS				
❑ Philles PHLP-4005 [M]	1963	40.00	80.00	160.00
-- First pressings have blue and black labels				
❑ Philles PHLP-4005 [M]	1964	20.00	40.00	80.00
-- Second pressings have yellow and red labels				
CHRISTMAS HITS FROM WARNER BROS.				
❑ Warner Bros. 8467/8 [DJ]	1959	12.50	25.00	50.00
CHRISTMAS PROGRAMMING FROM RCA VICTOR				
❑ RCA Victor SP-33-66 [DJ]	1959	250.00	500.00	1,000.
-- Promo-only collection; has been counterfeited, but originals have color covers				
A CHRISTMAS RECORD				
❑ Ze/Passport PB 6020	1982	5.00	10.00	20.00
CHRISTMAS THROUGH THE YEARS				
❑ Reader's Digest RDA-143 [(5)]	1984	5.00	10.00	20.00
-- Available only through Reader's Digest magazine by mail order				
CHRISTMAS WITH COLONEL SANDERS				
❑ RCA Victor PRS-291	1969	5.00	10.00	20.00
-- Sold only at Kentucky Fried Chicken restaurants				
CHRISTMASTIME IN CAROL AND SONG				
❑ RCA Victor PRM-271 [M]	1968	5.00	10.00	20.00
CLASSIC COUNTRY MUSIC				
❑ RCA Special Products DML6-0914 [(6)]	1990	12.50	25.00	50.00
-- Boxed set; sold only by the Smithsonian				
CLAY COLE'S BIN OF ORIGINAL GOLDEN OLDIES				
❑ Jubilee JGM-5026 [M]	1964	25.00	50.00	100.00
A COLLECTION OF 16 ORIGINAL BIG HITS, VOLUME 2				
❑ Tamla TM 256 [M]	1964	5.00	10.00	20.00
A COLLECTION OF 16 ORIGINAL BIG HITS, VOLUME 3				
❑ Motown MT 624 [M]	1965	5.00	10.00	20.00
❑ Motown MS 624 [S]	1966	6.25	12.50	25.00
A COLLECTION OF 16 ORIGINAL BIG HITS, VOLUME 4				
❑ Motown MS 633 [S]	1965	5.00	10.00	20.00
A COLLECTION OF 16 ORIGINAL BIG HITS, VOLUME 5				
❑ Motown MS 651 [S]	1966	5.00	10.00	20.00
A COLLECTION OF 16 ORIGINAL BIG HITS, VOLUME 6				
❑ Motown M 655 [M]	1967	5.00	10.00	20.00
❑ Motown MS 655 [S]	1967	5.00	10.00	20.00
A COLLECTION OF 16 ORIGINAL BIG HITS, VOLUME 7				
❑ Motown M 661 [M]	1967	5.00	10.00	20.00
❑ Motown MS 661 [S]	1967	5.00	10.00	20.00
A COLLECTION OF 16 ORIGINAL BIG HITS, VOLUME 8				
❑ Motown M 666 [M]	1967	5.00	10.00	20.00
❑ Motown MS 666 [S]	1967	5.00	10.00	20.00
A COLLECTION OF 16 ORIGINAL BIG HITS, VOLUME 9				
❑ Motown MS 668	1968	5.00	10.00	20.00
A COLLECTION OF 16 ORIGINAL BIG HITS, VOLUME 10				
❑ Motown MS 684	1969	5.00	10.00	20.00
A COLLECTION OF 16 ORIGINAL BIG HITS, VOLUME 11				
❑ Motown MS 693	1969	5.00	10.00	20.00
COLLECTOR'S SERIES SAMPLER RECORD				
❑ London LCX 1004 [DJ]	1977	5.00	10.00	20.00
COLLECTUS INTERRUPTUS				
❑ Warner Bros. PRO 726 [(2)]	1977	5.00	10.00	20.00
COLOR ME OBG: STATION WDRC				
❑ Roulette R 25347 [M]	1967	5.00	10.00	20.00
COLUMBIA'S 24 HITS IN THE TOP 20 FOR 1982!				
❑ Columbia A2S 1588 [(2) DJ]	1982	6.25	12.50	25.00
COME CLOSER TO GOD				
❑ Vee Jay LP-5061 [M]	1964	7.50	15.00	30.00
COME TOGETHER: AMERICA SALUTES THE BEATLES				
❑ Liberty 31712	1995	5.00	10.00	20.00
CONCERTS FOR THE PEOPLE OF KAMPUCHEA				
❑ Atlantic SD 2-7005 [(2)]	1981	5.00	10.00	20.00
CONNECTED				
❑ Limp 1005	1981	5.00	10.00	20.00
COOK BOOK				
❑ Warner Bros. PRO 660 [(2)]	1976	5.00	10.00	20.00

Label, Number	Yr	VG	VG+	NM
COUNTRY & WESTERN CLASSICS 1955				
❏ Economic Consultants 1955	1973	5.00	10.00	20.00
COUNTRY & WESTERN CLASSICS 1956				
❏ Economic Consultants 1956	1973	5.00	10.00	20.00
COUNTRY & WESTERN CLASSICS 1957				
❏ Economic Consultants 1957	1973	5.00	10.00	20.00
COUNTRY & WESTERN CLASSICS 1958				
❏ Economic Consultants 1958	1973	5.00	10.00	20.00
COUNTRY AND WESTERN JAMBOREE				
❏ King 697 [M]	1961	37.50	75.00	150.00
COUNTRY CHRISTMAS				
❏ King 811 [M]	1962	25.00	50.00	100.00
❏ Monument SLP-18125	1969	5.00	10.00	20.00
-- Different compilation than the King LP				
❏ Time-Life STL-109 [(3)]	1988	5.00	10.00	20.00
-- Available from Time-Life by mail order only; boxed set; different compilation from either LP above				
COUNTRY FAIR				
❏ Capitol SWBB-562 [(2)]	1970	6.25	12.50	25.00
COUNTRY GOLD				
❏ RCA Special Products DPL1-0561	1980	5.00	10.00	20.00
COUNTRY MUSIC BY THE WAYSIDE				
❏ Wayside 1013	1968	5.00	10.00	20.00
COUNTRY MUSIC HOOTENANNY				
❏ Capitol ST 2009 [S]	1963	7.50	15.00	30.00
❏ Capitol T 2009 [M]	1963	6.25	12.50	25.00
COUNTRY MUSIC SPECTACULAR				
❏ Hickory LPM-116 [M]	1963	6.25	12.50	25.00
COUNTRY SOFT AND MELLOW				
❏ Reader's Digest RB4-200 [(7)]	1989	12.50	25.00	50.00
COUNTRY SPECIAL				
❏ Capitol STBB-402 [(2)]	1969	6.25	12.50	25.00
CROSSROADS: WHITE BLUES IN THE 1960S				
❏ Elektra 60383 [(3)]	1984	5.00	10.00	20.00
CURTAIN UP! AMERICAN DANCE FAVORITES				
❏ Mercury Living Presence SR 90326 [S]	196?	10.00	20.00	40.00
-- Maroon label, no "Vendor: Mercury Record Corporation"				
CURTAIN UP! FAVORITE CONCERT OVERTURES				
❏ Mercury Living Presence SR 90323	196?	15.00	30.00	60.00
-- Maroon label, no "Vendor: Mercury Record Corporation"				
CURTAIN UP! OPERA BALLET FAVORITES				
❏ Mercury Living Presence SR 90327 [S]	196?	7.50	15.00	30.00
-- Maroon label, no "Vendor: Mercury Record Corporation"				
D'OES CRAZY OLDIES				
❏ Oldies 33 OL-8007 [M]	1964	6.25	12.50	25.00
THE D.I.Y. ALBUM				
❏ D.I.Y./JW Productions DIY-0001	1982	12.50	25.00	50.00
-- Band copies on black vinyl				
❏ D.I.Y./JW Productions DIY-0001A	1982	7.50	15.00	30.00
-- Store copies on clear vinyl (3-D pressing was planned but never done)				
DANCE DISCOTHEQUE				
❏ Decca DL 74556 [S]	1964	5.00	10.00	20.00
DANCE ON THE WILD SIDE				
❏ Chancellor CHL-5028 [M]	1962	6.25	12.50	25.00
❏ Chancellor CHLS-5028 [S]	1962	7.50	15.00	30.00
DANCE RHYTHM 'N' ROCK NEW MUSIC SEMINAR MIXER				
❏ Warner Bros. PRO-A-2061 [DJ]	1983	18.75	37.50	75.00
DANCE THE ROCK & ROLL				
❏ Atlantic 8013 [M]	1957	20.00	40.00	80.00
DANCE TUNES FROM THE VAULT, VOLUME 2				
❏ Chess LP 1476 [M]	1962	10.00	20.00	40.00
DARK MUDDY BOTTOM BLUES				
❏ Specialty SPS-2149	1971	5.00	10.00	20.00
A DAY IN THE COUNTRY				
❏ Audio Lab AL-1519 [M]	1959	20.00	40.00	80.00
DAYS OF WINE AND VINYL				
❏ Warner Bros. PRO 540 [(2)]	1973	7.50	15.00	30.00
DEEP EAR				
❏ Warner Bros. PRO 591 [(2)]	1974	6.25	12.50	25.00
DEEP SIX				
❏ C/Z CZ 001	1985	12.50	25.00	50.00
DEF JAM RECORDINGS -- RETAIL TRACKS				
❏ Def Jam CAS 2715 [DJ]	1987	5.00	10.00	20.00
DEL-FI ALBUM SAMPLER				
❏ Del-Fi (no #) [DJ]	1959	125.00	250.00	500.00
-- Green vinyl, promo only, with paper sleeve				
DEL-FI RECORD HOP				
❏ Del-Fi DFLP-1210 [M]	1959	20.00	40.00	80.00
DEMAND PERFORMANCES				
❏ Monument MLP-8010 [M]	1963	6.25	12.50	25.00
❏ Monument SLP-18010 [S]	1963	10.00	20.00	40.00
DESTINATION STEREO				
❏ RCA Victor Red Seal LSC-2307 [S]	1959	7.50	15.00	30.00
DIAL A HIT				
❏ Bell 6030	1969	5.00	10.00	20.00
A DIAMOND HIDDEN IN THE MOUTH OF A CORPSE				
❏ Giomo Poetry Systems 035	1985	7.50	15.00	30.00
DICK CLARK: 20 YEARS OF ROCK N' ROLL				
❏ Buddah BDS 5133 [(2)]	1973	5.00	10.00	20.00
-- Gatefold cover with booklet and bonus 7-inch cardboard record				
DISCO-TEEN '66				
❏ Columbia Record Club D 155 [M]	1966	5.00	10.00	20.00
❏ Columbia Record Club DS 155 [S]	1966	12.50	25.00	50.00
-- The stereo version is sought-after for its otherwise unavailable extended stereo mix of Bob Dylan's "Positively 4th Street"				
DISPLAY CASE #8				
❏ Warner Bros. PRO 532 [(2)]	1972	7.50	15.00	30.00
DISPLAY CASE #9				
❏ Warner Bros. PRO 538 [(2)]	1972	7.50	15.00	30.00
DISPLAY CASE #10				
❏ Warner Bros. PRO 542 [(3)]	1973	7.50	15.00	30.00
DIXIELAND AT CARNEGIE HALL				
❏ Roulette R 25038 [M]	1958	7.50	15.00	30.00
-- Originals have a black label				
❏ Roulette R 25038 [M]	1959	5.00	10.00	20.00
-- Second pressings have a white label with colored spokes				
DOCTOR DEATH'S VOLUME 1				
❏ C'est La Mort 001	1986	7.50	15.00	30.00
DOO WOP				
❏ Specialty SPS-2114	1969	5.00	10.00	20.00
DOUBLE BARREL JAZZ				
❏ Bethlehem BCP-87 [M]	1958	7.50	15.00	30.00
DOWN HOME STOMP: RURAL BLUES, VOLUME 3				
❏ Imperial LP-94006	1968	5.00	10.00	20.00
THE DUTCH EXPLOSION				
❏ White Whale WWS-7130	1970	7.50	15.00	30.00
THE EARLY '60S: THESE WERE OUR SONGS				
❏ Reader's Digest RC4-100 [(7)]	1989	12.50	25.00	50.00
EASY LISTENING HITS OF THE '60S AND '70S				
❏ Reader's Digest RBA-040A [(7)]	1989	12.50	25.00	50.00
ECLIPSE				
❏ Warner Bros. PRO-A-828 [(2)]	1978	5.00	10.00	20.00
18 ALL TIME COUNTRY AND WESTERN HITS				
❏ King 1027 [M]	1968	7.50	15.00	30.00
18 ALL TIME RHYTHM 'N' BLUES HITS				
❏ King 1026 [M]	1968	7.50	15.00	30.00
18 KING-SIZE COUNTRY HITS				
❏ Columbia CL 2668 [M]	1967	5.00	10.00	20.00
❏ Columbia CS 9468 [R]	1967	5.00	10.00	20.00
18 KING-SIZE RHYTHM AND BLUES HITS				
❏ Columbia CL 2667 [M]	1967	7.50	15.00	30.00
❏ Columbia CS 9467 [R]	1967	5.00	10.00	20.00
ELEKTRA'S BEST, VOLUME 1: 1966-1968				
❏ Elektra EB-1 [(2)]	1969	6.25	12.50	25.00
-- Promo only, red labels				
ELEKTROCK: THE SIXTIES				
❏ Elektra 60403 [(4)]	1985	7.50	15.00	30.00

Label, Number	Yr	VG	VG+	NM
THE ELVIS PRESLEY YEARS				
❑ Reader's Digest RBA-236A [(7)]	1991	12.50	25.00	50.00
END OF AN ERA: RHYTHM 'N' BLUES, VOLUME 1				
❑ Imperial LP-94003	1968	5.00	10.00	20.00
ENGLAND'S GREATEST HIT MAKERS				
❑ London LL 3430 [M]	1965	6.25	12.50	25.00
❑ London PS 430 [R]	1965	5.00	10.00	20.00
ENGLAND'S GREATEST HITS				
❑ Fontana MGF 27570 [M]	1967	12.50	25.00	50.00
-- With poster				
❑ Fontana MGF 27570 [M]	1967	10.00	20.00	40.00
-- Without poster				
❑ Fontana SRF 67570 [R]	1967	7.50	15.00	30.00
-- With poster				
❑ Fontana SRF 67570 [R]	1967	5.00	10.00	20.00
-- Without poster				
EVERYBODY'S FAVORITE BLUES				
❑ King 875 [M]	1963	17.50	35.00	70.00
EVERYBODY'S GONE SURFIN'				
❑ Parkway P-7035 [M]	1963	12.50	25.00	50.00
THE EXCELLO STORY				
❑ Excello LPS-8025 [(2)]	1972	6.25	12.50	25.00
THE EXCITING NEW LIVERPOOL SOUND				
❑ Columbia CL 2172 [M]	1964	7.50	15.00	30.00
EXPLOSIVE!				
❑ Liberty MM-412 [DJ]	1962	12.50	25.00	50.00
-- Promo-only release				
FABULOUS FAVORITES OF OUR TIME				
❑ Liberty LRP-3223 [M]	1962	5.00	10.00	20.00
❑ Liberty LST-7223 [S]	1962	6.25	12.50	25.00
THE FAMILY CHRISTMAS COLLECTION				
❑ Time-Life STL-131 [(5)]	1990	7.50	15.00	30.00
-- Available from Time-Life by mail order only				
FAMILY PORTRAIT				
❑ A&M SP-19002	1968	5.00	10.00	20.00
FANFARE OF HITS				
❑ Argo LP-656 [M]	1960	6.25	12.50	25.00
FAVORITE SACRED SONGS				
❑ King 556 [M]	1956	37.50	75.00	150.00
15 FAVORITES				
❑ Hickory LPM-105 [M]	1962	6.25	12.50	25.00
15 GOLDEN HITS				
❑ United Artists UAL-3192 [M]	1962	6.25	12.50	25.00
❑ United Artists UAS-6192 [S]	1962	7.50	15.00	30.00
15 HITS: THE ORIGINAL RECORDINGS (THE ORIGINAL HITS, VOLUME 5)				
❑ Liberty LRP-3235 [M]	1962	5.00	10.00	20.00
50 BELOVED SONGS OF FAITH				
❑ Reader's Digest BMR3-100 [(3)]	1990	6.25	12.50	25.00
50 YEARS OF FILM				
❑ Warner Bros. 3XX 2737 [(3)]	1973	6.25	12.50	25.00
-- Box set with 60-page booklet				
50 YEARS OF FILM MUSIC				
❑ Warner Bros. 3XX 2736 [(3)]	1973	6.25	12.50	25.00
-- Box set with 28-page booklet				
FILLET OF SOUL				
❑ Stax STS 3021	1972	5.00	10.00	20.00
FILLMORE: THE LAST DAYS				
❑ Fillmore Z3X 31390 [(3)]	1972	12.50	25.00	50.00
-- With booklet and bonus 7-inch single				
FILM MUSIC FROM FRANCE				
❑ Philips PHM 200-071 [M]	1962	5.00	10.00	20.00
❑ Philips PHS 600-071 [S]	1962	7.50	15.00	30.00
THE FINEST OF FOLK BLUESMEN				
❑ Bethlehem BCP-6017	197?	5.00	10.00	20.00
-- Despite lower number, this is a reissue of Bethlehem 6071, distributed by RCA				
FINK ALONG WITH MAD				
❑ Big Top 12-1306 [M]	1962	25.00	50.00	100.00
FIRST DECADE				
❑ WEA 10 [(3) DJ]	1981	37.50	75.00	150.00
-- Only 1,000 were made paying tribute to WEA's 10th anniversary				
THE FIRST GREAT ROCK FESTIVALS OF THE SEVENTIES: ISLE OF WIGHT/ATLANTA POP FESTIVAL				
❑ Columbia G3X 30805 [(3)]	1971	6.25	12.50	25.00
5-STRING BANJO PICKIN' AND SINGIN'				
❑ King 994 [M]	1966	10.00	20.00	40.00
FLEX YOUR HEAD				
❑ Dischord 7	1982	12.50	25.00	50.00
-- Includes Teen Idles, Untouchables, Minor Threat, Government Issue, Youth Brigade, etc.				
THE FOLK BOX				
❑ Elektra EKL-9001 [(4)]	1964	12.50	25.00	50.00
FOLK FESTIVAL				
❑ Elektra SMP 2 [M]	1956	7.50	15.00	30.00
FOLK FESTIVAL OF THE BLUES				
❑ Argo LP-4031 [M]	1964	10.00	20.00	40.00
FOLK POPS 'N JAZZ SAMPLER				
❑ Elektra SMP 3 [M]	1957	6.25	12.50	25.00
FOLK SAMPLER FIVE				
❑ Elektra SMP 5 [M]	196?	6.25	12.50	25.00
THE FOLK SCENE				
❑ Elektra SMP 6 [M]	196?	6.25	12.50	25.00
FOLKSONG '65				
❑ Elektra S 78 [S]	1965	6.25	12.50	25.00
❑ Elektra SMP 8 [M]	1965	5.00	10.00	20.00
FOOTPRINTS IN TIME				
❑ White Whale WWS-7125	1970	6.25	12.50	25.00
FOR CHRISTMAS SEALS...A MATTER OF LIFE AND BREATH				
❑ Decca Custom Style E [DJ]	1968	5.00	10.00	20.00
-- Promo-only album for Christmas Seals				
❑ Decca Custom Style F [DJ]	1968	6.25	12.50	25.00
-- Promo-only album for Christmas Seals; four five-minute programs				
FOR TWISTERS ONLY				
❑ Ace LP-1020 [M]	1962	17.50	35.00	70.00
THE FORCE				
❑ Warner Bros. PRO 593	1974	5.00	10.00	20.00
❑ Warner Bros. PRO 596 [(2)]	1974	6.25	12.50	25.00
FOREPLAY #45				
❑ A&M SP-17162 [DJ]	1981	6.25	12.50	25.00
-- Includes 20-minute collage of music from "Urgh! A Music War"				
FORGOTTEN MILLION SELLERS				
❑ King 792 [M]	1962	25.00	50.00	100.00
14 GOLDEN RECORDINGS FROM THE HISTORIC VAULTS OF DUKE-PEACOCK RECORDS				
❑ ABC ABCX-784	1973	5.00	10.00	20.00
14 GOLDEN RECORDINGS FROM THE HISTORIC VAULTS OF DUKE-PEACOCK RECORDS, VOLUME 2				
❑ ABC ABCX-789	1973	5.00	10.00	20.00
14 GREAT ALL TIME C&W WALTZES				
❑ King 890 [M]	1964	17.50	35.00	70.00
14 HIT FLASHBACKS FROM THE GOLDEN GROUP ERA				
❑ King 893 [M]	1964	17.50	35.00	70.00
14 MORE NEWIES BUT GOODIES				
❑ Mercury MG-20493 [M]	1960	7.50	15.00	30.00
❑ Mercury SR-60241 [S]	1960	10.00	20.00	40.00
14 NEWIES BUT GOODIES				
❑ Mercury MG-20493 [M]	1960	7.50	15.00	30.00
❑ Mercury SR-60172 [S]	1960	10.00	20.00	40.00
FORTY GOSPEL GREATS				
❑ Vee Jay VJS-2-19000 [(2)]	1975	6.25	12.50	25.00
FRANK JOHNSON'S FAVORITES				
❑ Ralph 8110	1981	5.00	10.00	20.00
THE FUTURE LOOKS BRIGHT				
❑ SST/Posh Boy PBS 120 [DJ]	1981	7.50	15.00	30.00
-- Vinyl is promo-only				
GALA FAVORITES				
❑ Mercury Living Presence SR 90339 [S]	196?	6.25	12.50	25.00
-- Maroon label, no "Vendor: Mercury Record Corporation"				

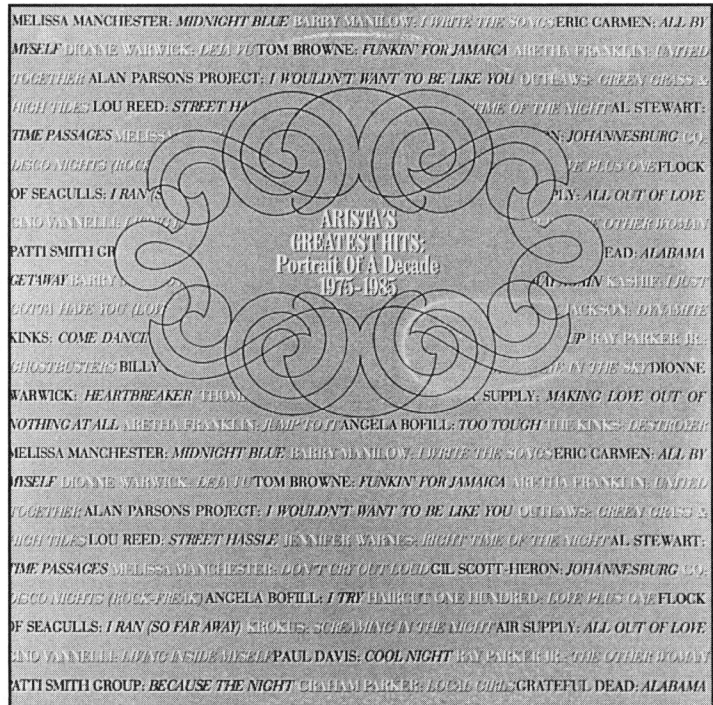

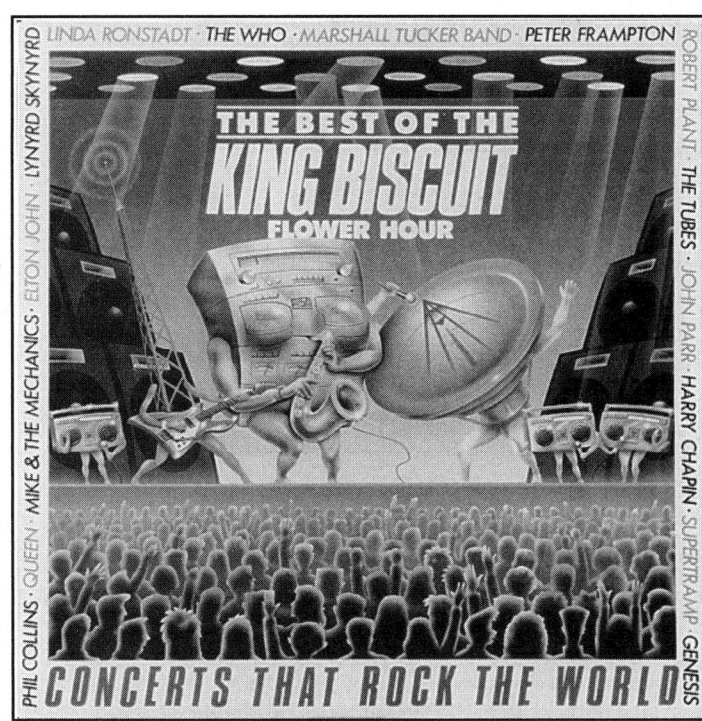

(Top left) The Silver Eagle label was well-known in the 1980s for its television-only collections, some of which were quite interesting. The above 1985 album, *Arista's Greatest Hits: Portrait of a Decade*, was a three-record set containing a little bit of everything that came out on the label in its first 10 years, from Barry Manilow to the Alan Parsons Project to the Kinks to Ray Parker Jr. to Patti Smith. (Top right) Another interesting Silver Eagle TV album was *The Best of the King Biscuit Flower Hour*, the first public issue of many live recordings that had first aired on the legendary radio show. Some of these tracks still haven't been reissued on the new King Biscuit label, which is making even more KBFH live recordings available. (Bottom left) *British Gold* was an RCA Music Service exclusive on Sire, similar to the *History of British Rock* series, and including the Beatles' recording of "Ain't She Sweet." (Bottom right) An amusing Buddah compilation of material from its first year of hits (1968-69), there never was a Volume 2 of *Bubble Gum Music Is the Naked Truth* even though this one is called Volume 1.

Label, Number	Yr	VG	VG+	NM
GARDEN OF DELIGHTS				
❏ Elektra S3 10 [(3)]	1971	5.00	10.00	20.00
-- Butterfly labels, possibly promo only				
GERRY GOFFIN AND CAROLE KING: SOLID GOLD				
❏ Screen Gems/Columbia CPL-713 [DJ]	1975	5.00	10.00	20.00
-- Promo-only compilation of oldies sent to radio to spur airplay on songs owned by this publishing house				
GIANTS OF JAZZ ORGAN				
❏ King 837 [M]	1963	30.00	60.00	120.00
GOIN' UP THE COUNTRY: RURAL BLUES, VOLUME 1				
❏ Imperial LP-94000	1968	5.00	10.00	20.00
GOLD HITS				
❏ Warwick W 2008 [M]	1959	20.00	40.00	80.00
-- Reissue of "Goodies But Oldies, Volume 2"; this title still appears on the label				
GOLD SOUL				
❏ Stax STS 2031	1970	5.00	10.00	20.00
THE GOLDEN AGE OF RHYTHM AND BLUES				
❏ Chess 2CH-50030 [(2)]	1972	6.25	12.50	25.00
THE GOLDEN DAYS OF BRITISH ROCK				
❏ Sire V 6046 [(4)]	1976	10.00	20.00	40.00
GOLDEN ECHOES				
❏ Arvee A-433 [M]	1962	6.25	12.50	25.00
❏ Arvee SA-433 [S]	1962	7.50	15.00	30.00
GOLDEN ENCORES				
❏ Cadence CLP-3043 [M]	1960	10.00	20.00	40.00
GOLDEN GASSERS				
❏ Chess LP 1458 USA [M]	1961	30.00	60.00	120.00
-- National version; see listings in this section under "KYA," "Murray the K" and "WAMO" for regional releases				
GOLDEN GOODIES, VOL. 1				
❏ Roulette R 25207 [M]	1963	6.25	12.50	25.00
GOLDEN GOODIES, VOL. 2				
❏ Roulette R 25210 [M]	1963	6.25	12.50	25.00
GOLDEN GOODIES, VOL. 3				
❏ Roulette R 25218 [M]	1963	6.25	12.50	25.00
GOLDEN GOODIES, VOL. 4: GOODIES FOR A DANCE PARTY				
❏ Roulette R 25209 [M]	1963	6.25	12.50	25.00
GOLDEN GOODIES, VOL. 5				
❏ Roulette R 25215 [M]	1963	6.25	12.50	25.00
GOLDEN GOODIES, VOL. 6				
❏ Roulette R 25216 [M]	1963	6.25	12.50	25.00
GOLDEN GOODIES, VOL. 7				
❏ Roulette R 25212 [M]	1963	6.25	12.50	25.00
GOLDEN GOODIES, VOL. 8				
❏ Roulette R 25214 [M]	1963	6.25	12.50	25.00
GOLDEN GOODIES, VOL. 9				
❏ Roulette R 25213 [M]	1963	6.25	12.50	25.00
GOLDEN GOODIES, VOL. 10				
❏ Roulette R 25217 [M]	1963	6.25	12.50	25.00
GOLDEN GOODIES, VOL. 11				
❏ Roulette R 25219 [M]	1963	6.25	12.50	25.00
GOLDEN GOODIES, VOL. 12				
❏ Roulette R 25211 [M]	1963	6.25	12.50	25.00
GOLDEN GOODIES, VOL. 14				
❏ Roulette R 25239 [M]	1964	5.00	10.00	20.00
GOLDEN GOODIES, VOL. 15				
❏ Roulette R 25240 [M]	1964	5.00	10.00	20.00
GOLDEN GOODIES, VOL. 16				
❏ Roulette R 25241 [M]	1964	5.00	10.00	20.00
GOLDEN GOODIES, VOL. 17				
❏ Roulette R 25242 [M]	1964	5.00	10.00	20.00
GOLDEN GOODIES OF 1963, VOL. 18				
❏ Roulette R 25247 [M]	1964	5.00	10.00	20.00
GOLDEN GREATS				
❏ Liberty LST-7500 [P]	1967	5.00	10.00	20.00
THE GOLDEN GROUPS				
❏ Specialty SPS-2155	1972	5.00	10.00	20.00
GOLDEN HITS FROM THE GANG AT BANG				
❏ Bang BLP-215 [M]	1967	5.00	10.00	20.00
❏ Bang BLPS-215 [P]	1967	6.25	12.50	25.00
GOLDEN INSTRUMENTALS				
❏ Dot DLP-3820 [M]	1967	6.25	12.50	25.00
❏ Dot DLP-25820 [S]	1967	6.25	12.50	25.00
GOLDEN JAZZ INSTRUMENTALS				
❏ Bethlehem BCP-6065 [M]	1962	6.25	12.50	25.00
GOLDEN SOUVENIRS				
❏ United Artists UAL-3317 [M]	1963	6.25	12.50	25.00
❏ United Artists UAS-6317 [S]	1963	7.50	15.00	30.00
GOLDEN TEEN HITS				
❏ Liberty L-5505 [M]	1962	10.00	20.00	40.00
GOLDEN TREASURE CHEST				
❏ United Artists UAL-3314 [M]	1963	6.25	12.50	25.00
❏ United Artists UAS-6314 [S]	1963	7.50	15.00	30.00
GONE BUT NOT FORGOTTEN				
❏ Class LP-5004 [M]	1959	25.00	50.00	100.00
❏ Rendezvous M-1314 [M]	196?	10.00	20.00	40.00
-- Reissue of Class 5004				
GOOD GUY JACK SPECTOR PRESENTS 22 ORIGINAL WINNERS				
❏ Roulette R 25254 [M]	1964	5.00	10.00	20.00
THE GOOD OLD 50'S				
❏ Atco 33-118 [M]	1960	15.00	30.00	60.00
GOODIES BUT OLDIES VOLUME 2				
❏ Warwick W 2008 [M]	1959	30.00	60.00	120.00
-- Original title of LP appears on both cover and label; reissued as "Gold Hits" -- and there was no Volume 1!				
GOSPEL HOOTENANNY				
❏ Imperial LP-9240 [M]	1963	5.00	10.00	20.00
❏ Imperial LP-12240 [S]	1963	6.25	12.50	25.00
GOSPEL STARS IN CONCERT				
❏ Specialty SPS-2153	1971	5.00	10.00	20.00
GRAFFITI GOLD				
❏ Vee Jay VJS-2-9000 [(2)]	1974	5.00	10.00	20.00
THE GREAT GROUP GOODIES				
❏ Atco 33-143 [M]	1962	20.00	40.00	80.00
GREAT GROUP OLDIES				
❏ Oldies 33 OL-8003 [M]	1963	6.25	12.50	25.00
GREAT GROUP OLDIES, VOL. 2				
❏ Oldies 33 OL-8006 [M]	1964	6.25	12.50	25.00
GREAT GROUPS, GREAT RECORDS				
❏ Laurie LLP-2010 [M]	1961	7.50	15.00	30.00
THE GREAT HITS OF 1964 AND SOME GOLDEN OLDIES				
❏ Vee Jay LP-1112 [M]	1965	7.50	15.00	30.00
-- Not known to exist in stereo				
GREAT INSTRUMENTAL R&B HITS				
❏ Imperial LP-12271 [R]	1964	5.00	10.00	20.00
❏ Imperial LP-9271 [M]	1964	6.25	12.50	25.00
GREAT MOMENTS AT THE GRAND OLE OPRY				
❏ RCA Victor CPL2-1904 [(2)]	1977	5.00	10.00	20.00
GREAT MOTION PICTURE THEMES				
❏ United Artists UAS-6122 [S]	1960	5.00	10.00	20.00
GREAT MOTION PICTURE THEMES (MORE ORIGINAL SOUND TRACKS AND HIT MUSIC)				
❏ United Artists UAS-6158 [S]	1961	5.00	10.00	20.00
THE GREAT SOUL HITS				
❏ Brunswick BL 54129 [M]	1968	6.25	12.50	25.00
GREAT SWING BANDS OF THE FORTIES				
❏ Audio Lab AL-1530 [M]	1959	20.00	40.00	80.00
THE GREATEST 15 HITS ON ACE RECORDS				
❏ Ace LP-1012 [M]	1960	17.50	35.00	70.00
GREATEST COUNTRY & WESTERN HITS NO. 3				
❏ Columbia CL 1816 [M]	1962	5.00	10.00	20.00
❏ Columbia CS 8616 [S]	1962	6.25	12.50	25.00
GREATEST COUNTRY & WESTERN HITS NO. 4				
❏ Columbia CL 2081 [M]	1963	5.00	10.00	20.00
❏ Columbia CS 8881 [S]	1963	6.25	12.50	25.00

(Top left) *Bunch of Goodies* was an early compilation put together by Chess Records. It is interesting for several reasons, one of which is the inclusion of the long version of Harvey and the Moonglows' "Ten Commandments of Love," which actually contains a tenth commandment! (Top right) Some special-products Christmas compilations have become collectible in recent years, especially if they happen to have an Elvis Presley track on them. This is one of them. (Bottom left) This promo-only two-record set is exactly what it says it is. The Columbia label had 24 top 20 hits on the *Billboard* Hot 100 in 1982, and they're all here, including two Paul McCartney tracks: "Ebony and Ivory" and the single version of "Take It Away," without the cross-fade from "Tug of War." (Bottom right) The *Dick Clark 20 Years of Rock n' Roll* album was in print for many years and later was a cut-out bin staple. But original copies contain two items missing from later editions: a booklet and a 7-inch square cardboard record of Dick Clark talking about the good old days.

Label, Number	Yr	VG	VG+	NM
THE GREATEST GOLDEN GOODIES				
❏ Laurie LLP-2014 [M]	1962	7.50	15.00	30.00
GREATEST GOSPEL SONGS, VOLUME 1				
❏ Specialty SPS-2144	1970	5.00	10.00	20.00
GREATEST GOSPEL SONGS, VOLUME 2				
❏ Specialty SPS-2145	1970	5.00	10.00	20.00
GREATEST GOSPEL SONGS OF OUR TIMES				
❏ Vee Jay LP-5043 [M]	1963	7.50	15.00	30.00
THE GREATEST HITS FROM ENGLAND				
❏ Parrot PA 61010 [M]	1967	6.25	12.50	25.00
❏ Parrot PAS 71010 [R]	1967	5.00	10.00	20.00
THE GREATEST HITS FROM ENGLAND, VOLUME 2				
❏ Parrot PA 61017 [M]	1968	6.25	12.50	25.00
❏ Parrot PAS 71017 [R]	1968	5.00	10.00	20.00
GREATEST RAP HITS, VOL. 1				
❏ Sugar Hill 9132	1984	5.00	10.00	20.00
THE GREATEST ROCK & ROLL				
❏ Atlantic 8001 [M]	1956	30.00	60.00	120.00
THE GREATEST TEENAGE HITS OF ALL TIME!				
❏ Teem LP-5003 [M]	196?	7.50	15.00	30.00
GREATEST WESTERN HITS				
❏ Columbia CL 1257 [M]	1959	7.50	15.00	30.00
❏ Columbia CS 8776 [R]	1963	5.00	10.00	20.00
GREATEST WESTERN HITS NO. 2				
❏ Columbia CL 1408 [M]	1960	7.50	15.00	30.00
❏ Columbia CS 8777 [R]	1963	5.00	10.00	20.00
GRETSCH DRUM NIGHT AT BIRDLAND				
❏ Roulette R 52049 [M]	1960	7.50	15.00	30.00
❏ Roulette SR 52049 [S]	1960	7.50	15.00	30.00
GRETSCH DRUM NIGHT, VOLUME 2				
❏ Roulette R 52067 [M]	1961	7.50	15.00	30.00
❏ Roulette SR 52067 [S]	1961	7.50	15.00	30.00
GROOVY GOODIES				
❏ Colpix CP-466 [M]	1964	20.00	40.00	80.00
❏ Colpix SCP-466 [S]	1964	25.00	50.00	100.00
GROUP OF GOODIES				
❏ Chess LP 1478 [M]	1963	12.50	25.00	50.00
❏ Chess LPS 1478 [R]	196?	5.00	10.00	20.00
GROUP OF GOODIES, VOLUME 2				
❏ Chess LP 1491 [M]	1965	12.50	25.00	50.00
GUARANTEED TO PLEASE				
❏ Teem LP-5002 [M]	196?	7.50	15.00	30.00
HAPPY HOLIDAYS VOL. 25				
❏ RCA Special Products DPL2-0936 [(2)]	1990	6.25	12.50	25.00
-- Sold only at True Value Hardware stores; the last one on vinyl LP -- and it contains an Elvis track among its 25 selections				
HARD GOODS				
❏ Warner Bros. PRO 583 [(2)]	1974	6.25	12.50	25.00
HARD TO BELIEVE -- A KISS COVERS COMPILATION				
❏ C/Z CZ 024	1990	7.50	15.00	30.00
HARLEM JAZZ 1930				
❏ Brunswick BL 58024 [10]	1951	12.50	25.00	50.00
HAVE YOURSELF A MERRY LITTLE CHRISTMAS				
❏ Reprise 50,001 [M]	1963	6.25	12.50	25.00
-- Red and green cover with ornaments at top; titled on back cover "Top Hollywood Stars Want You to..."				
❏ Reprise R 50001 [M]	1963	6.25	12.50	25.00
-- Wreath cover; titled on back cover "Top Hollywood Stars Want You to..."				
❏ Reprise R 50001 [M]	1963	6.25	12.50	25.00
-- Christmas tree cover; titled "Frank Sinatra and His Friends Want You to..."				
❏ Reprise R9-50,001 [S]	1963	7.50	15.00	30.00
-- Christmas tree cover; titled "Frank Sinatra and His Friends Want You to..."				
HAVING A BALL				
❏ End LP-302 [M]	1958	125.00	250.00	500.00
-- Original cover with groups pictured on a record				
HEAVY HEADS				
❏ Chess LP 1522 [M]	1967	6.25	12.50	25.00
❏ Chess LPS 1522 [P]	1967	6.25	12.50	25.00
HEAVY HEADS, VOYAGE 2				
❏ Chess LP 1528 [M]	1969	5.00	10.00	20.00
HEAVY METAL (SUPERSTARS OF THE 70S, VOLUME 2)				
❏ Warner Special Products SP-2001	1974	5.00	10.00	20.00

Label, Number	Yr	VG	VG+	NM
HERALD THE BEAT				
❏ Herald HLP-0110 [M]	195?	37.50	75.00	150.00
-- Yellow label				
❏ Herald HLP-0110 [M]	1957	75.00	150.00	300.00
-- Black label				
HERE ARE THE HITS!				
❏ Fire FLP-100 [M]	1959	100.00	200.00	400.00
-- Reissued as "Memory Lane, Hits by the Original Groups" with the same label and number				
HILLBILLY HOUSE PARTY				
❏ Imperial LP-9214 [M]	1963	6.25	12.50	25.00
❏ Imperial LP-12214 [R]	1963	5.00	10.00	20.00
HISTORY OF BRITISH BLUES, VOLUME 1				
❏ Sire SASH-3701 [(2)]	1973	5.00	10.00	20.00
HISTORY OF BRITISH ROCK				
❏ Sire 2P 6547 [(2)]	1975	5.00	10.00	20.00
-- Columbia House edition				
❏ Sire SASH-3702 [(2)]	1974	5.00	10.00	20.00
HISTORY OF BRITISH ROCK, VOL. 2				
❏ Sire SASH-3705 [(2)]	1974	5.00	10.00	20.00
HISTORY OF BRITISH ROCK, VOLUME 3				
❏ Sire SASH-3712 [(2)]	1975	5.00	10.00	20.00
HISTORY OF RHYTHM & BLUES, VOLUME 1/THE ROOTS 1947-52				
❏ Atlantic SD 8161	1968	5.00	10.00	20.00
HISTORY OF RHYTHM & BLUES, VOLUME 2/THE GOLDEN YEARS 1953-55				
❏ Atlantic SD 8162	1968	5.00	10.00	20.00
HISTORY OF RHYTHM & BLUES, VOLUME 3/ROCK & ROLL 1956-57				
❏ Atlantic SD 8163	1968	5.00	10.00	20.00
HISTORY OF RHYTHM & BLUES, VOLUME 4/THE BIG BEAT 1958-60				
❏ Atlantic SD 8164	1968	5.00	10.00	20.00
THE HIT MAKERS AND THEIR RECORD BREAKERS				
❏ King 737 [M]	1961	25.00	50.00	100.00
HIT SOUNDS OF MERRIE MELODIES				
❏ Warner Bros. PRO 550 [(2)]	1973	6.25	12.50	25.00
HITCHHIKER 2				
❏ Columbia CAS 1826 [DJ]	1989	6.25	12.50	25.00
-- Includes music and interviews				
THE HITCHHIKER COLLEGE RADIO HOUR				
❏ Columbia CAS 1598 [DJ]	1989	6.25	12.50	25.00
HITS FROM THE SOUTH PRESENTED BY NICK CHARLES				
❏ Stax 702 [M]	1962	25.00	50.00	100.00
-- Has the same number as "Walk Right In" by Gus Cannon, but this LP doesn't have any mention of Atlantic distribution				
HITS I FORGOT TO BUY				
❏ Swan SLP-512 [M]	1963	12.50	25.00	50.00
HITS OF THE HOPS				
❏ Warner Bros. W 1448 [M]	1962	7.50	15.00	30.00
❏ Warner Bros. WS 1448 [S]	1962	10.00	20.00	40.00
HITS THAT JUMPED				
❏ Checker LP 2975 [M]	1959	30.00	60.00	120.00
HITSVILLE				
❏ Coral CRL 57269 [M]	1959	20.00	40.00	80.00
❏ Coral CRL 757269 [S]	1959	25.00	50.00	100.00
HITSVILLE U.S.A.				
❏ Imperial LP-9084 [M]	1959	10.00	20.00	40.00
HITSVILLE U.S.A., VOLUME 2				
❏ Imperial LP-9099 [M]	1960	10.00	20.00	40.00
HOLLAND-DOZIER-HOLLAND: YESTERDAY, TODAY AND FOREVER				
❏ Jobete PRO-9 [(3) DJ]	1977	12.50	25.00	50.00
-- Promo-only publisher's demo				
HOME FOR CHRISTMAS: A JOYOUS EVENING OF YULETIDE MUSIC				
❏ RCA Victor CSP-109 [S]	1964	5.00	10.00	20.00
HOME OF THE BLUES				
❏ Minit LP-0001 [M]	1961	12.50	25.00	50.00
HOME OF THE BLUES, VOLUME 2				
❏ Minit LP-0004 [M]	1963	12.50	25.00	50.00
❏ Minit LP-24004 [R]	1964	5.00	10.00	20.00
❏ Minit LP-40004 [M]	1964	6.25	12.50	25.00
-- Reissue of 0004				

Label, Number	Yr	VG	VG+	NM
HOMESPUN HUMOR				
❏ King 726 [M]	1961	25.00	50.00	100.00
HOT PLATTERS				
❏ Warner Bros. PRO 474 [(2)]	1971	6.25	12.50	25.00
-- Originals have green labels				
HYMNS OF FAITH				
❏ Colpix CP-408 [M]	1959	7.50	15.00	30.00
I DIDN'T KNOW THEY STILL MADE RECORDS LIKE THIS				
❏ Warner Bros. PRO 608 [(2)]	1975	5.00	10.00	20.00
I DIG ROCK AND ROLL				
❏ Score SLP-4002 [M]	1957	50.00	100.00	200.00
-- Reissue of "Rock & Roll with Rhythm & Blues," Aladdin 710				
I LIKE JAZZ!				
❏ Columbia JZ 1	1955	7.50	15.00	30.00
IMPERIAL SAMPLER				
❏ Imperial DJLP-1 [10]	195?	25.00	50.00	100.00
-- Promo-only item				
THE IMPOSSIBLE DREAM -- THE STORY OF THE 1967 BOSTON RED SOX				
❏ Fleetwood FCLP 3024	1967	5.00	10.00	20.00
IN CONCERT				
❏ RCA Victor CPL2-1014 [(2)]	1975	5.00	10.00	20.00
IN LOVING MEMORY				
❏ Motown M 642 [M]	1968	62.50	125.00	250.00
-- Without song titles on cover				
❏ Motown M 642 [M]	1968	37.50	75.00	150.00
-- With song titles on cover				
❏ Motown M 642 [DJ]	1969	125.00	250.00	500.00
-- With custom silver cover; Loucye Gordy Wakefield Scholarship Fund benefit giveaway				
❏ Motown MS 642 [S]	1968	62.50	125.00	250.00
-- Without song titles on cover				
❏ Motown MS 642 [S]	1968	37.50	75.00	150.00
-- With song titles on cover				
INCENSE AND OLDIES				
❏ Buddah BDS 5014	1969	5.00	10.00	20.00
INSTRUMENTAL GOLDEN GOODIES, VOL. 13				
❏ Roulette R 25238 [M]	1964	5.00	10.00	20.00
INTRODUCTION TO RARE EARTH RECORDS				
❏ Rare Earth RS-505 to 509 [(5) DJ]	1969	50.00	100.00	200.00
-- Promo-only box set with rounded top; contains the first five LPs on the Rare Earth label				
THE ISLAND STORY				
❏ Island R 243395 [(2)]	1988	5.00	10.00	20.00
-- Same as Island 90684; BMG Direct Marketing edition				
IT'S DANCE TIME				
❏ Cameo C-1068 [M]	1964	7.50	15.00	30.00
ITAL CHRISTMAS				
❏ Top Ranking (no #)	197?	6.25	12.50	25.00
-- Jamaican import				
JACKPOT OF HITS				
❏ Apollo LP-490 [M]	1959	37.50	75.00	150.00
JAM SESSION AT CARNEGIE HALL				
❏ Columbia CL 557 [M]	1954	6.25	12.50	25.00
JAMES BOND -- 10TH ANNIVERSARY				
❏ United Artists UXS-91 [(2)]	1972	7.50	15.00	30.00
JAZZ FESTIVAL				
❏ Imperial LP-9233 [M]	1963	5.00	10.00	20.00
❏ Imperial LP-12233 [S]	1963	6.25	12.50	25.00
JAZZ FESTIVAL, VOLUME 2				
❏ Imperial LP-9238 [M]	1963	5.00	10.00	20.00
❏ Imperial LP-12238 [S]	1963	6.25	12.50	25.00
JAZZ IN HOLLYWOOD				
❏ Liberty LRP-6001 [M]	1955	7.50	15.00	30.00
JAZZ MONTAGE				
❏ Liberty LST-7292 [S]	1963	5.00	10.00	20.00
JAZZ MUSIC FOR PEOPLE WHO DON'T CARE ABOUT MONEY				
❏ Bethlehem BCP-88 [M]	1958	7.50	15.00	30.00
JAZZ OF THE SIXTIES				
❏ Vee Jay VJS-2-1008 [(2)]	1974	5.00	10.00	20.00
JAZZ TIME U.S.A. -- VOLUME 2				
❏ Brunswick BL 54001 [M]	1953	7.50	15.00	30.00

Label, Number	Yr	VG	VG+	NM
JAZZ TIME U.S.A. -- VOLUME 3				
❏ Brunswick BL 54002 [M]	1954	7.50	15.00	30.00
JAZZ VOCALS AWARD ALBUM				
❏ Bethlehem BCP-6068 [M]	1963	6.25	12.50	25.00
JESUS CHRIST SUPERSTAR				
❏ Decca DXA 7206 [(2)]	1970	7.50	15.00	30.00
-- Box set with booklet				
❏ Decca DXSA 7206 [(2)]	1970	6.25	12.50	25.00
-- Gatefold cover with booklet				
JINGLE BELL JAZZ				
❏ Columbia CL 1893 [M]	1962	5.00	10.00	20.00
JINGLE BELL ROCK				
❏ Time-Life SRNR-XM [(2)]	1987	5.00	10.00	20.00
-- Available from Time-Life by mail order only; boxed set				
JOY TO THE WORLD (30 CLASSIC CHRISTMAS MELODIES)				
❏ Columbia Special Products P3 14654 [(3)]	1978	5.00	10.00	20.00
-- Box set; produced for Murray Hill Records				
THE JOYFUL SOUND OF CHRISTMAS				
❏ RCA Record Club CSP-0601 [(2)]	1969	5.00	10.00	20.00
-- Available only through the RCA Record Club				
JOYOUS MUSIC FOR CHRISTMAS TIME				
❏ Reader's Digest RD 45-M [(4) M]	1963	5.00	10.00	20.00
-- Available only through Reader's Digest magazine by mail order				
❏ Reader's Digest RD 45-S [(4) S]	1963	5.00	10.00	20.00
-- Same as above, but in stereo				
JOYOUS NOEL				
❏ Reader's Digest RDA-57A [(4)]	1966	5.00	10.00	20.00
-- Available only through Reader's Digest magazine by mail order				
JUBILEE MONAURAL SAMPLER: VOCALS AND INSTRUMENTALS				
❏ Jubilee MSJLP-803 [M]	1959	7.50	15.00	30.00
JUBILEE STEREOSONIC VOCAL SAMPLER, VOLUME 2				
❏ Jubilee SSJLP-802 [S]	1959	10.00	20.00	40.00
JUBILEE SURPRISE PARTY				
❏ Jubilee JGM-1107 [M]	1959	37.50	75.00	150.00
❏ Jubilee JGS-1107 [S]	1959	50.00	100.00	200.00
JUST JAZZ				
❏ Imperial LP-9246 [M]	1963	5.00	10.00	20.00
❏ Imperial LP-12246 [S]	1963	6.25	12.50	25.00
K-BOX DUSTY DISCS				
❏ Roulette R 25338 [M]	1966	5.00	10.00	20.00
KATS KARAVAN (OLD FAVORITES WITH JIM LOWE)				
❏ Vee Jay LP-100 [M]	1957	12.50	25.00	50.00
-- Gold label, black print				
KEATS RIDES A HARLEY				
❏ Happy Squid HS 002	1981	5.00	10.00	20.00
KGFJ SOUNDS OF SUCCESS				
❏ Roulette R 25349 [M]	1967	5.00	10.00	20.00
THE KINGS SING THE BLUES				
❏ Teem LP-5005 [M]	196?	7.50	15.00	30.00
KPOI'S BATTLE OF THE SURFING BANDS				
❏ Del-Fi DFLP-1235 [M]	1964	15.00	30.00	60.00
❏ Del-Fi DFST-1235 [S]	1964	25.00	50.00	100.00
-- Honolulu version of the above LP				
KTLA'S BATTLE OF THE SURFING BANDS				
❏ Del-Fi DFLP-1235 [M]	1964	12.50	25.00	50.00
❏ Del-Fi DFST-1235 [S]	1964	20.00	40.00	80.00
-- Los Angeles version of the above LP				
KYA GOLDEN GATE GREATS				
❏ Chess LP 1458 SF [M]	1961	37.50	75.00	150.00
-- San Francisco version of "Golden Gassers," Chess 1458				
KYA'S BATTLE OF THE SURFING BANDS				
❏ Del-Fi DFLP-1235 [M]	1964	12.50	25.00	50.00
❏ Del-Fi DFST-1235 [S]	1964	20.00	40.00	80.00
-- San Francisco version of the above LP, with slightly different contents				
KYA'S MEMORIES OF THE COW PALACE				
❏ Autumn LP 101 [M]	1963	17.50	35.00	70.00
THE LAST RECORD ALBUM				
❏ A&M (# unknown)	1989	10.00	20.00	40.00
LATE MUSIC, VOLUME I				
❏ Columbia CL 541 [M]	1954	6.25	12.50	25.00

Label, Number	Yr	VG	VG+	NM
LATE MUSIC, VOLUME II				
❏ Columbia CL 542 [M]	1954	6.25	12.50	25.00
LATE MUSIC, VOLUME III				
❏ Columbia CL 543 [M]	1954	6.25	12.50	25.00
THE LAUGHTOUR				
❏ Sire PRO-A-3931 [EP]	1990	5.00	10.00	20.00
-- Promo only				
LAURIE GOLDEN GOODIES				
❏ Laurie SLLP-2041 [P]	1967	6.25	12.50	25.00
LEONARD FEATHER'S ENCYCLOPEDIA OF JAZZ				
❏ Vee Jay VJSP-400 [(2)]	1977	6.25	12.50	25.00
LEONARD FEATHER'S ENCYCLOPEDIA OF JAZZ, VOLUME ONE: GIANTS OF THE SAXOPHONE				
❏ Vee Jay LP-2501 [M]	1964	5.00	10.00	20.00
-- Not known to exist in stereo				
LET THEM EAT JELLYBEANS				
❏ Alternative Tentacles VIRUS 4	1982	6.25	12.50	25.00
LET'S HAVE A DANCE PARTY				
❏ Ace LP-1019 [M]	1961	17.50	35.00	70.00
LET'S SING ABOUT FREEDOM				
❏ Vee Jay LP-5044 [M]	1963	7.50	15.00	30.00
LIBERTY PREMIER SERIES SPECTACULAR				
❏ Liberty L-5504 [M]	1962	5.00	10.00	20.00
❏ Liberty S-6604 [S]	1962	7.50	15.00	30.00
LIBERTY PROUDLY PRESENTS STEREO -- THE VISUAL SOUND				
❏ Liberty LST-100 [S]	1959	10.00	20.00	40.00
LIFE IS BEAUTIFUL, SO WHY NOT EAT HEALTH FOOD?				
❏ New Underground 44	1981	5.00	10.00	20.00
LIFE IS UGLY, SO WHY NOT KILL YOURSELF?				
❏ New Underground 11	1981	5.00	10.00	20.00
THE LIFE TREASURY OF CHRISTMAS MUSIC				
❏ Project/Capitol TL 100 [M]	1963	5.00	10.00	20.00
-- Designed as a supplement to the Life Book of Christmas; selections performed by anonymous chorus and orchestra and Boy Choristers from the Church of the Transfiguration (NY)				
LIKE 'ER RED HOT				
❏ Duke DLP-73 [M]	1960	30.00	60.00	120.00
-- Purple and yellow label				
❏ Duke DLP-73 [M]	196?	12.50	25.00	50.00
-- Orange label				
❏ Duke DLP-73 [M]	196?	7.50	15.00	30.00
-- Green label, "Distributed by ABC-Dunhill"				
LIMO				
❏ Warner Bros. PRO 691 [(2)]	1977	5.00	10.00	20.00
LISTEN TO OUR STORY				
❏ Brunswick BL 59001 [10]	1950	15.00	30.00	60.00
A LITTLE ROCK AND ROLL FOR EVERYBODY				
❏ Audio Lab AL-1567 [M]	1960	50.00	100.00	200.00
THE LITTLEST ANGEL/LULLABY OF CHRISTMAS				
❏ Decca DLP 8009 [M]	1949	10.00	20.00	40.00
LIVE AT CBGB'S				
❏ CBGB/Omfug 315 [(2)]	1976	7.50	15.00	30.00
❏ Atlantic SD2-508 [(2)]	1976	5.00	10.00	20.00
-- Same album as CBGB/Omfug release				
LIVE AT TARGET				
❏ Subterranean 3	1980	6.25	12.50	25.00
LIVE AT THE WHISKEY A-GO-GO				
❏ Vee Jay LP-1100 [M]	1964	7.50	15.00	30.00
-- Not known to exist in stereo				
LOOK WHO'S SURFIN' NOW!				
❏ King 882 [M]	1964	37.50	75.00	150.00
LOONEY TUNES AND MERRIE MELODIES				
❏ Warner Bros. PRO 423 [(3)]	1970	25.00	50.00	100.00
-- Box set with booklet of liner notes; originals have green labels				
A LOT OF YARN BUT A WELL-KNITTED JAZZ ALBUM				
❏ Bethlehem BCP-91 [M]	1958	7.50	15.00	30.00
LOVE ME TENDER				
❏ Time-Life STL-133 [(2)]	1991	6.25	12.50	25.00

Label, Number	Yr	VG	VG+	NM
LOVE THOSE GOODIES				
❏ Checker LP 2973 [DJ]	1959	125.00	250.00	500.00
-- White label, multi-color splash vinyl				
❏ Checker LP 2973 [M]	1959	30.00	60.00	120.00
MAD "TWISTS" ROCK 'N' ROLL				
❏ Big Top 12-1305 [M]	1962	25.00	50.00	100.00
THE MAGIC OF CHRISTMAS				
❏ Columbia Musical Treasury P3S 5806 [(3)]	1972	5.00	10.00	20.00
THE MAGICAL MUSIC OF WALT DISNEY				
❏ Ovation OV-5000 [(4)]	1978	15.00	30.00	60.00
-- Box set				
MAGNAVOX ALBUM OF CHRISTMAS MUSIC				
❏ Columbia Special Products CSQ 11093 [Q]	1972	5.00	10.00	20.00
-- Sold only at Magnavox dealers; yes, this is in quadraphonic!				
MAX'S KANSAS CITY 1976				
❏ Ram 1213	1976	5.00	10.00	20.00
MAX'S KANSAS CITY PRESENTS NEW WAVE HITS FOR THE '80S				
❏ Max's Kansas City 19801	1981	5.00	10.00	20.00
-- Compilation of first two Max's Kansas City albums plus new tracks				
MEMORIES ARE MADE OF HITS				
❏ Liberty LRP-3200 [M]	1961	6.25	12.50	25.00
-- Reissued as "The Original Hits, Volume 4"				
MEMORY LANE, HITS BY THE ORIGINAL GROUPS				
❏ Fire FLP-100 [M]	1959	50.00	100.00	200.00
-- Reissue of "Here Are the Hits!" with the same label and number				
MEMPHIS GOLD				
❏ Stax 710 [M]	1966	6.25	12.50	25.00
❏ Stax S710 [S]	1966	7.50	15.00	30.00
MEMPHIS GOLD VOLUME 2				
❏ Stax 726 [M]	1967	5.00	10.00	20.00
❏ Stax S726 [S]	1967	6.25	12.50	25.00
MERCURY LIVING PRESENCE				
❏ Mercury Living Presence SR 90293 [S]	196?	30.00	60.00	120.00
-- Maroon label, no "Vendor: Mercury Record Corporation"; contains music by groups conducted by Paul Paray, Antal Dorati and Frederick Fennell				
MERRY CHRISTMAS				
❏ Coral CRL 56080 [10]	1952	20.00	40.00	80.00
MERRY CHRISTMAS BABY (CHRISTMAS MUSIC FOR YOUNG LOVERS)				
❏ Hollywood HLP 501 [M]	1956	30.00	60.00	120.00
MERRY CHRISTMAS FROM MOTOWN				
❏ Motown MS-681	1968	7.50	15.00	30.00
MERRY CHRISTMAS FROM...				
❏ King 680 [M]	1959	50.00	100.00	200.00
❏ Reader's Digest RD4-83 [(4)]	1969	5.00	10.00	20.00
-- Available only through Reader's Digest magazine by mail order				
MERRY CHRISTMAS MUSIC/CHRISTMAS FAVORITES				
❏ Plymouth P12-59 [M]	1952	5.00	10.00	20.00
-- Artists not mentioned on jacket or label				
MERRY CHRISTMAS TO YOU				
❏ Capitol T 9030 [M]	1955	12.50	25.00	50.00
MGM RECORDS PARADE OF STARS				
❏ MGM NP 90569 [M]	1965	5.00	10.00	20.00
-- Capitol Record Club sampler of 12 MGM artists and soundtracks				
MICHIGAN ROCKS				
❏ Seeds and Stems 77001 [(2)]	1977	6.25	12.50	25.00
MICKEY MOST PRESENTS BRITISH GO-GO				
❏ MGM E 4306 [M]	1965	7.50	15.00	30.00
❏ MGM SE 4306 [R]	1965	7.50	15.00	30.00
MICKEY MOST PRESENTS ENGLISH IN-GROUPS				
❏ Metro 577 [M]	1966	5.00	10.00	20.00
❏ Metro MS-577 [R]	1966	5.00	10.00	20.00
MIDDLE OF THE ROAD				
❏ Warner Bros. PRO 525 [(2)]	1972	7.50	15.00	30.00
-- Originals have green labels				
A MILLION OR MORE				
❏ ABC-Paramount ABC-216 [M]	1959	20.00	40.00	80.00
MILLION PERFORMANCE SONGS, VOLUME 1				
❏ Jobete JSA-6251 [DJ]	1988	5.00	10.00	20.00
-- Promo-only publisher's demo				

Label, Number	Yr	VG	VG+	NM
MILLION PERFORMANCE SONGS, VOLUME 2				
❑ Jobete JSA-6252 [DJ]	1988	5.00	10.00	20.00
-- Promo-only publisher's demo				
MILLION SELLER DANCE HITS				
❑ Parkway P-7028 [M]	1963	7.50	15.00	30.00
THE MILLION-AIRS				
❑ Coral CRL 57310 [M]	1959	6.25	12.50	25.00
MOMENTS OF MOTOWN				
❑ Motown PR-122 [DJ]	1983	12.50	25.00	50.00
-- Promo-only item with narration and song snippets				
MONDAY NIGHT AT BIRDLAND				
❑ Roulette R 52015 [M]	1958	7.50	15.00	30.00
❑ Roulette SR 52015 [S]	1959	7.50	15.00	30.00
MONSTERS				
❑ Warner Bros. PRO-A-796 [(2)]	1978	5.00	10.00	20.00
MONUMENTAL COUNTRY HITS				
❑ Monument SLP-18095	1968	5.00	10.00	20.00
MONUMENTAL POP HITS				
❑ Monument SLP-18096	1968	5.00	10.00	20.00
MORE FOR YOUR MONEY				
❑ Bell 6009	1968	5.00	10.00	20.00
MORE GOLD HITS, VOLUME 2				
❑ Warwick W 2044 [M]	1961	20.00	40.00	80.00
MORE GOLDEN GREATS				
❑ Liberty LRP-3548 [M]	1967	5.00	10.00	20.00
MORE GREAT HITS OF 1964 AND OTHER GOLDEN GOODIES				
❑ Vee Jay LP-1136 [M]	1965	7.50	15.00	30.00
-- Not known to exist in stereo				
MORE SOLID GOLD PROGRAMMING				
❑ Screen Gems/Columbia CPL-716/7 [(2) DJ]	1975	7.50	15.00	30.00
-- Promo-only compilation of oldies sent to radio to spur airplay on songs owned by this publishing house; contains three Beatles recordings				
THE MOST OF THE TWIST				
❑ Roulette R 25176 [M]	1962	6.25	12.50	25.00
-- Originals have a white label with colored spokes				
THE MOST, VOLUME 1				
❑ Roulette R 52050 [M]	1960	5.00	10.00	20.00
❑ Roulette SR 52050 [S]	1960	6.25	12.50	25.00
THE MOST, VOLUME 2				
❑ Roulette R 52053 [M]	1960	5.00	10.00	20.00
❑ Roulette SR 52053 [S]	1960	6.25	12.50	25.00
THE MOST, VOLUME 3				
❑ Roulette R 52057 [M]	1961	5.00	10.00	20.00
❑ Roulette SR 52057 [S]	1961	6.25	12.50	25.00
THE MOST, VOLUME 4				
❑ Roulette R 52062 [M]	1961	5.00	10.00	20.00
❑ Roulette SR 52062 [S]	1961	6.25	12.50	25.00
THE MOST, VOLUME 5				
❑ Roulette R 52075 [M]	1961	5.00	10.00	20.00
❑ Roulette SR 52075 [S]	1961	6.25	12.50	25.00
THE MOTOR-TOWN REVIEW, VOL. 1				
❑ Motown MT 609 [M]	1963	10.00	20.00	40.00
THE MOTOR-TOWN REVIEW, VOL. 2				
❑ Motown MT 615 [M]	1964	7.50	15.00	30.00
THE MOTORTOWN REVIEW IN PARIS				
❑ Tamla T 264 [M]	1965	6.25	12.50	25.00
❑ Tamla TS 264 [S]	1965	7.50	15.00	30.00
THE MOTORTOWN REVUE LIVE!				
❑ Motown MS-688	1969	6.25	12.50	25.00
A MOTOWN CHRISTMAS				
❑ Motown M-795V2 [(2)]	1973	5.00	10.00	20.00
MOTOWN INSTRUMENTALS				
❑ Natural Resources NR 4002T1	1978	5.00	10.00	20.00
MOTOWN SHOW TUNES				
❑ Natural Resources NR 4003T1	1978	5.00	10.00	20.00
MOTOWN SPECIAL				
❑ Motown M 603 [M]	1962	20.00	40.00	80.00

Label, Number	Yr	VG	VG+	NM
THE MOTOWN STORY: THE FIRST DECADE				
❑ Motown MS-726 [(5)]	1971	7.50	15.00	30.00
THE MOTOWN STORY: THE FIRST 25 YEARS				
❑ Motown PR-121 [(7) DJ]	1983	62.50	125.00	250.00
-- Promo-only box set with extra record not on the commercial release; labels are white				
THE MOTOWN STORY: THE FIRST TWENTY-FIVE YEARS				
❑ Motown 6048 ML5 [(5)]	1983	7.50	15.00	30.00
MOTOWN WINNER'S CIRCLE: #1 HITS, VOL. 1				
❑ Gordy GS-935	1969	6.25	12.50	25.00
MOTOWN WINNER'S CIRCLE: #1 HITS, VOL. 2				
❑ Gordy GS-936	1969	6.25	12.50	25.00
MOTOWN WINNER'S CIRCLE: #1 HITS, VOL. 3				
❑ Gordy GS-943	1969	6.25	12.50	25.00
MOTOWN WINNER'S CIRCLE: #1 HITS, VOL. 4				
❑ Gordy GS-946	1969	6.25	12.50	25.00
MOTOWN WINNER'S CIRCLE: #1 HITS, VOL. 5				
❑ Gordy GS-950	1970	6.25	12.50	25.00
MOTOWN'S GREAT INTERPRETATIONS				
❑ Natural Resources NR 4001T1	1978	5.00	10.00	20.00
MOUNTAIN FROLIC				
❑ Brunswick BL 59000 [10]	1950	15.00	30.00	60.00
MURRAY THE "K'S" SING ALONG WITH THE ORIGINAL GOLDEN GASSERS				
❑ Roulette R 25159 [M]	1961	7.50	15.00	30.00
MURRAY THE K -- LIVE FROM THE BROOKLYN FOX				
❑ KFM 1001 [M]	1963	10.00	20.00	40.00
MURRAY THE K PRESENTS GOLDEN GASSERS FOR A DANCE PARTY				
❑ Roulette R 25192 [M]	1962	6.25	12.50	25.00
MURRAY THE K PRESENTS GOLDEN GASSERS FOR HAND HOLDERS				
❑ Roulette R 25191 [M]	1962	6.25	12.50	25.00
MURRAY THE K'S BLASTS FROM THE PAST				
❑ Chess LP 1461 [M]	1961	10.00	20.00	40.00
MURRAY THE K'S GASSERS FOR SUBMARINE RACE WATCHERS				
❑ Chess LP 1470 [M]	1962	10.00	20.00	40.00
MURRAY THE K'S GOLDEN GASSERS				
❑ Chess LP 1458 NYC [M]	1961	37.50	75.00	150.00
-- New York version of "Golden Gassers," Chess 1458				
MURRAY THE K'S NINETEEN-SIXTY TWO BOSS GOLDEN GASSERS				
❑ Scepter SP-510 [M]	1963	5.00	10.00	20.00
❑ Scepter SPS-510 [P]	1963	6.25	12.50	25.00
MUSIC AND PLUNK, TINKLE, TING-A-LING				
❑ Mercury Living Presence SR 90338 [S]	196?	12.50	25.00	50.00
-- Maroon label, no "Vendor: Mercury Record Corporation"				
MUSIC AND RHYTHM SAMPLER				
❑ PVC EP 2 [DJ]	1982	6.25	12.50	25.00
MUSIC FOR FRUSTRATED CONDUCTORS				
❑ RCA Victor Red Seal LSC-2325 [S]	1959	12.50	25.00	50.00
-- Original with "shaded dog" label				
THE MUSIC PEOPLE				
❑ Columbia C3X 31280 [(3)]	1972	6.25	12.50	25.00
MUSIC TO READ JAMES BOND BY				
❑ United Artists UAL-3415 [M]	1965	5.00	10.00	20.00
❑ United Artists UAS-6415 [S]	1965	6.25	12.50	25.00
MUSIC TO READ JAMES BOND BY, VOL. 2				
❑ United Artists UAL-3541 [M]	1966	5.00	10.00	20.00
❑ United Artists UAS-6541 [S]	1966	6.25	12.50	25.00
MY SON THE SURF NUT				
❑ Capitol ST 1939 [S]	1963	15.00	30.00	60.00
❑ Capitol T 1939 [M]	1963	12.50	25.00	50.00
NASCAR GOES COUNTRY				
❑ MCA 474	1975	7.50	15.00	30.00
NASHVILLE BANDSTAND				
❑ King 813 [M]	1962	25.00	50.00	100.00
NASHVILLE BANDSTAND, VOLUME 2				
❑ King 847 [M]	1963	20.00	40.00	80.00
NEIGHBORHOOD RHYTHMS				
❑ Freeway 213 [(2)]	1984	10.00	20.00	40.00

Label, Number	Yr	VG	VG+	NM
NEW ORLEANS BOUNCE: URBAN BLUES, VOLUME 2				
❑ Imperial LP-94004	1968	5.00	10.00	20.00
NEW ORLEANS, OUR HOME TOWN				
❑ Imperial LP-9260 [M]	1964	6.25	12.50	25.00
❑ Imperial LP-12260 [R]	1964	5.00	10.00	20.00
A NIGHT AT THE BOULEVARD				
❑ Felsted FL-7503 [M]	1960	10.00	20.00	40.00
THE 1969 WARNER/REPRISE RECORD SHOW				
❑ Warner Bros./Seven Arts PRO 336 [(2)]	1969	7.50	15.00	30.00
-- Originals have "W7" logos on labels				
THE 1969 WARNER/REPRISE SONGBOOK				
❑ Warner Bros./Seven Arts PRO 331 [(2)]	1969	7.50	15.00	30.00
-- The first of the famous Warner/Reprise "Loss Leaders" mail-order series; originals have "W7" logos on labels				
THE NITTY GRITTY				
❑ Vee Jay LP-1084 [M]	1964	7.50	15.00	30.00
-- Not known to exist in stereo				
NO NUKES: THE MUSE CONCERTS FOR A NON-NUCLEAR FUTURE				
❑ Asylum ML-801 [(3)]	1979	6.25	12.50	25.00
NO SOUR GRAPES, JUST PURE JAZZ				
❑ Bethlehem BCP-92 [M]	1958	7.50	15.00	30.00
NO WAVE				
❑ A&M PR 4738 [DJ]	1978	6.25	12.50	25.00
-- White label promo on watercolor blue vinyl; numbered sticker on generic cover				
NON DAIRY CREAMER				
❑ Warner Bros. PRO 443	1971	6.25	12.50	25.00
-- Originals have green labels				
NOT SO QUIET ON THE WESTERN FRONT				
❑ Alternative Tentacles VIRUS 14 [(2)]	1982	6.25	12.50	25.00
NOTHING CHEESY ABOUT THIS JAZZ				
❑ Bethlehem BCP-85 [M]	1958	7.50	15.00	30.00
NOVA SCOTIA FOLK SONGS				
❑ Elektra EKL-23 [10]	1954	10.00	20.00	40.00
NUGGETS				
❑ Elektra 7E-2006 [(2)]	1972	10.00	20.00	40.00
O LOVE IS TEASIN': ANGLO-AMERICAN MOUNTAIN BALLADRY				
❑ Elektra 60402 [(3)]	1985	5.00	10.00	20.00
O. HENRY'S THE GIFT OF THE MAGI				
❑ E.F. MacDonald EFMX-62	1962	5.00	10.00	20.00
-- Special album done by the E.F. MacDonald Company, Dayton, Ohio				
OCTOBER '61 POP SAMPLER				
❑ RCA Victor SPS-33-141 [DJ]	1961	150.00	300.00	600.00
-- Promo-only collection.				
OCTOBER 1960 POPULAR STEREO SAMPLER				
❑ RCA Victor SPS-33-96 [DJ]	1960	150.00	300.00	600.00
-- Promo-only collection				
OCTOBER CHRISTMAS SAMPLER 59-40-41				
❑ RCA Victor SPS-33-54 [DJ]	1959	150.00	300.00	600.00
-- Promo-only collection				
THE OFFICIAL GRAMMY AWARDS ARCHIVE COLLECTION (ALBUM OF THE YEAR)				
❑ Franklin Mint GRAM-14 [(4)]	1985	15.00	30.00	60.00
THE OFFICIAL GRAMMY AWARDS ARCHIVE COLLECTION (ALL-TIME WINNERS)				
❑ Franklin Mint GRAM-2 [(4)]	1985	15.00	30.00	60.00
THE OFFICIAL GRAMMY AWARDS ARCHIVE COLLECTION (BEST NEW ARTIST)				
❑ Franklin Mint GRAM-6 [(4)]	1985	15.00	30.00	60.00
THE OFFICIAL GRAMMY AWARDS ARCHIVE COLLECTION (THE BIG BAND SOUND)				
❑ Franklin Mint GRAM-7 [(4)]	1985	15.00	30.00	60.00
THE OFFICIAL GRAMMY AWARDS ARCHIVE COLLECTION (FOLK PERFORMANCES)				
❑ Franklin Mint GRAM-10 [(4)]	1985	15.00	30.00	60.00
THE OFFICIAL GRAMMY AWARDS ARCHIVE COLLECTION (GREAT PERFORMANCES OF THE ROCK ERA, VOL. 1)				
❑ Franklin Mint GRAM-3 [(4)]	1985	15.00	30.00	60.00

Label, Number	Yr	VG	VG+	NM
THE OFFICIAL GRAMMY AWARDS ARCHIVE COLLECTION (THE GREAT SINGERS)				
❑ Franklin Mint GRAM-4 [(4)]	1985	37.50	75.00	150.00
THE OFFICIAL GRAMMY AWARDS ARCHIVE COLLECTION (JAZZ VOCALISTS)				
❑ Franklin Mint GRAM-13 [(4)]	1985	15.00	30.00	60.00
THE OFFICIAL GRAMMY AWARDS ARCHIVE COLLECTION (POP PERFORMANCES, VOL. 1)				
❑ Franklin Mint GRAM-5 [(4)]	1985	15.00	30.00	60.00
THE OFFICIAL GRAMMY AWARDS ARCHIVE COLLECTION (THE PRODUCER'S CHOICE)				
❑ Franklin Mint GRAM-12 [(4)]	1985	15.00	30.00	60.00
THE OFFICIAL GRAMMY AWARDS ARCHIVE COLLECTION (RECORD OF THE YEAR)				
❑ Franklin Mint GRAM-1 [(4)]	1985	15.00	30.00	60.00
THE OFFICIAL GRAMMY AWARDS ARCHIVE COLLECTION (RHYTHM AND BLUES, VOL. 1)				
❑ Franklin Mint GRAM-8 [(4)]	1985	17.50	35.00	70.00
THE OFFICIAL GRAMMY AWARDS ARCHIVE COLLECTION (SONG OF THE YEAR)				
❑ Franklin Mint GRAM-9 [(4)]	1985	15.00	30.00	60.00
THE OFFICIAL GRAMMY AWARDS ARCHIVE COLLECTION (STAGE & ORIGINAL CAST RECORDINGS)				
❑ Franklin Mint GRAM-11 [(4)]	1985	30.00	60.00	120.00
OLD 'N GOLDEN				
❑ Jamie JLPS-3031	1968	5.00	10.00	20.00
OLD AND HEAVY GOLD 1955				
❑ Economic Consultants 1955	1973	5.00	10.00	20.00
OLD AND HEAVY GOLD 1956				
❑ Economic Consultants 1956	1973	7.50	15.00	30.00
OLD AND HEAVY GOLD 1957				
❑ Economic Consultants 1957	1973	7.50	15.00	30.00
OLD AND HEAVY GOLD 1958				
❑ Economic Consultants 1958	1973	7.50	15.00	30.00
OLD AND HEAVY GOLD 1959				
❑ Economic Consultants 1959	1973	5.00	10.00	20.00
OLD AND HEAVY GOLD 1960				
❑ Economic Consultants 1960	1973	7.50	15.00	30.00
OLD AND HEAVY GOLD 1961				
❑ Economic Consultants 1961	1973	7.50	15.00	30.00
OLD AND HEAVY GOLD 1962				
❑ Economic Consultants 1962	1973	7.50	15.00	30.00
OLD AND HEAVY GOLD 1963				
❑ Economic Consultants 1963	1973	5.00	10.00	20.00
OLD AND HEAVY GOLD 1964				
❑ Economic Consultants 1964	1973	5.00	10.00	20.00
-- Original magazine ads claimed that six Beatles tracks would appear on this LP; they were replaced before release				
OLD AND HEAVY GOLD 1965				
❑ Economic Consultants 1965	1973	5.00	10.00	20.00
-- Original magazine ads claimed that three Beatles tracks would appear on this LP; they were replaced before release				
OLD AND HEAVY GOLD 1966				
❑ Economic Consultants 1966	1973	5.00	10.00	20.00
OLD AND HEAVY GOLD 1967				
❑ Economic Consultants 1967	1973	5.00	10.00	20.00
-- Original magazine ads claimed that a Beatles track would appear on this LP; it was replaced with another track before release				
OLD AND HEAVY GOLD 1968				
❑ Economic Consultants 1968	1973	5.00	10.00	20.00
-- Original magazine ads claimed that a Beatles track would appear on this LP; it was replaced with another track before release				
OLD AND HEAVY GOLD 1969				
❑ Economic Consultants 1969	1973	5.00	10.00	20.00
-- Original magazine ads claimed that a Beatles track would appear on this LP; it was replaced with another track before release				
OLD AND HEAVY GOLD 1970				
❑ Economic Consultants 1970	1973	5.00	10.00	20.00
-- Original magazine ads claimed that a Beatles track would appear on this LP; it was replaced with another track before release				

Label, Number	Yr	VG	VG+	NM
OLD AND HEAVY GOLD 1971				
❏ Economic Consultants 1971	1973	5.00	10.00	20.00
-- *Original magazine ads claimed that a Paul McCartney track would appear on this LP; it was replaced with another track before release*				
AN OLD FASHIONED CHRISTMAS				
❏ Reader's Digest RDA 216-A [(6)]	197?	5.00	10.00	20.00
-- *Available only through Reader's Digest magazine by mail order*				
OLD TIME BANJO PROJECT				
❏ Elektra EKL-276 [M]	1964	5.00	10.00	20.00
❏ Elektra EKS-7276 [S]	1964	6.25	12.50	25.00
OLDIES BUT GOODIES				
❏ Original Sound LPM-5001 [M]	1959	12.50	25.00	50.00
-- *Original pressing with no reference to other volumes on the back cover*				
OLDIES BUT GOODIES, VOL. 2				
❏ Original Sound LPM-5003 [M]	1960	10.00	20.00	40.00
-- *Original pressing with no reference to later volumes on the back cover*				
OLDIES BUT GOODIES, VOL. 3				
❏ Original Sound LPM-5004 [M]	1961	7.50	15.00	30.00
-- *Original pressing with no reference to later volumes on the back cover*				
OLDIES BUT GOODIES, VOL. 4				
❏ Original Sound LPM-5005 [M]	1962	7.50	15.00	30.00
-- *Original pressing with no reference to later volumes on the back cover*				
OLDIES BUT GOODIES, VOL. 5				
❏ Original Sound LPM-5007 [M]	1963	5.00	10.00	20.00
-- *Original pressing with no reference to later volumes on the back cover*				
OLDIES BUT GOODIES, VOL. 6				
❏ Original Sound LPM-5011 [M]	1963	5.00	10.00	20.00
-- *Original pressing with no reference to later volumes on the back cover*				
OLDIES BUT GOODIES, VOL. 7				
❏ Original Sound LPM-5012 [M]	1964	5.00	10.00	20.00
-- *Original pressing with no reference to later volumes on the back cover*				
OLDIES BY THE DOZEN				
❏ Parkway P-7035 [M]	1963	7.50	15.00	30.00
OLDIES BY THE DOZEN, VOLUME 2				
❏ Parkway P-7041 [M]	1964	12.50	25.00	50.00
-- *With bonus 45 of "The Twist" by Chubby Checker on on side and "Mashed Potato Time" by Dee Dee Sharp on the other; deduct 40 percent if missing*				
OLDIES DANCE PARTY, VOLUME 1				
❏ Oldies 33 OL-8001 [M]	1963	5.00	10.00	20.00
OLDIES DANCE PARTY, VOLUME 2				
❏ Oldies 33 OL-8002 [M]	1963	5.00	10.00	20.00
OLDIES IN HI-FI				
❏ Chess LP 1439 [DJ]	1959	150.00	300.00	600.00
-- *Multi-color splash vinyl*				
❏ Chess LP 1439 [M]	1959	75.00	150.00	300.00
-- *Black vinyl*				
ONE DOZEN GOLDIES				
❏ Carlton LP 12-121 [M]	1960	12.50	25.00	50.00
OPENING NIGHTS AT THE MET				
❏ RCA Victor Red Seal LM-6171 [(3) M]	1966	5.00	10.00	20.00
OPERA FOR PEOPLE WHO HATE OPERA				
❏ RCA Victor Red Seal LSC-2391 [S]	1960	5.00	10.00	20.00
-- *Originals with "shaded dog" label*				
THE ORGAN PLAYS MUSIC FOR A MERRY CHRISTMAS				
❏ Reader's Digest RDA 42-A [(4)]	1966	5.00	10.00	20.00
-- *Available only through Reader's Digest magazine by mail order*				
THE ORIGINAL COUNTRY HITS #1				
❏ Liberty LRP-3305 [M]	1963	5.00	10.00	20.00
THE ORIGINAL COUNTRY HITS #2				
❏ Liberty LRP-3345 [M]	1964	5.00	10.00	20.00
THE ORIGINAL COUNTRY HITS #3				
❏ Liberty LRP-3382 [M]	1964	5.00	10.00	20.00
ORIGINAL GOLDIES FROM THE FABULOUS '50S, VOLUME 1				
❏ Josie JM-4002 [M]	1963	15.00	30.00	60.00
ORIGINAL GOLDIES FROM THE FABULOUS '50S, VOLUME 2				
❏ Josie JM-4003 [M]	1963	15.00	30.00	60.00
ORIGINAL GOLDIES FROM THE FABULOUS '50S, VOLUME 3				
❏ Josie JM-4004 [M]	1963	15.00	30.00	60.00
ORIGINAL HIT RECORDS				
❏ Roulette R 25106 [M]	1960	7.50	15.00	30.00
-- *Originals have a white label with colored spokes*				
THE ORIGINAL HITS, PAST & PRESENT				
❏ Liberty LRP-3178 [M]	1960	5.00	10.00	20.00
THE ORIGINAL HITS, VOLUME TWO: PAST & PRESENT				
❏ Liberty LRP-3180 [M]	1961	5.00	10.00	20.00
THE ORIGINAL HITS, VOLUME 3: PAST & PRESENT				
❏ Liberty LRP-3187 [M]	1961	5.00	10.00	20.00
THE ORIGINAL HITS, VOLUME 4				
❏ Liberty LRP-3200 [M]	1962	5.00	10.00	20.00
-- *Reissue of "Memories Are Made of Hits"; for "The Original Hits, Volume 5," see "15 Hits: The Original Recordings"*				
THE ORIGINAL HITS, VOLUME 6				
❏ Liberty LRP-3260 [M]	1962	5.00	10.00	20.00
THE ORIGINAL HITS, VOLUME 7: ALL-TIME HIT INSTRUMENTALS				
❏ Liberty LRP-3274 [M]	1963	5.00	10.00	20.00
THE ORIGINAL HITS, VOLUME 8				
❏ Liberty LRP-3288 [M]	1963	5.00	10.00	20.00
THE ORIGINAL HITS, VOLUME 9				
❏ Liberty LRP-3325 [M]	1963	5.00	10.00	20.00
THE ORIGINAL HITS, VOLUME 10				
❏ Liberty LRP-3344 [M]	1964	5.00	10.00	20.00
THE ORIGINAL HITS, VOLUME 11				
❏ Liberty LRP-3418 [M]	1965	5.00	10.00	20.00
❏ Liberty LST-7418 [P]	1965	5.00	10.00	20.00
THE ORIGINAL HOOTENANNY				
❏ Crestview CRS 7806 [S]	1963	6.25	12.50	25.00
❏ Crestview CRV 806 [M]	1963	5.00	10.00	20.00
ORIGINAL MEMPHIS ROCK AND ROLL, VOLUME 1				
❏ Sun 116	1970	5.00	10.00	20.00
ORIGINAL MOTION PICTURE HIT THEMES				
❏ United Artists UAS-6197 [S]	1962	5.00	10.00	20.00
THE ORIGINAL R&B HITS, VOLUME 1				
❏ Liberty LRP-3381 [M]	1964	5.00	10.00	20.00
ORIGINAL RECORDINGS BY THE ARTISTS WHO MADE THEM HITS				
❏ Flip 1002 [M]	1960	100.00	200.00	400.00
ORIGINAL ROCK OLDIES, VOLUME 1				
❏ Specialty SPS-2129	1970	5.00	10.00	20.00
ORIGINAL ROCK OLDIES, VOLUME 2				
❏ Specialty SPS-2130	1970	5.00	10.00	20.00
ORIGINAL SURFIN' HITS				
❏ GNP Crescendo GNP-84 [M]	1963	10.00	20.00	40.00
-- *With bonus photos; deduct 25-50 percent if missing*				
❏ GNP Crescendo GNPS-84 [S]	1963	12.50	25.00	50.00
-- *With bonus photos; deduct 25-50 percent if missing*				
OUR BEST TO YOU				
❏ Everlast ELP-201 [M]	1960	50.00	100.00	200.00
OUR SIGNIFICANT HITS				
❏ Specialty SP-2112 [M]	1960	30.00	60.00	120.00
-- *Gold and black label*				
OUR SINGING HERITAGE, VOL. 1				
❏ Elektra EKL-151 [M]	1958	6.25	12.50	25.00
OUR SINGING HERITAGE, VOL. 2				
❏ Elektra EKL-152 [M]	1958	6.25	12.50	25.00
A PACKAGE OF 16 BIG HITS				
❏ Motown MS 614 [S]	1966	7.50	15.00	30.00
-- *No "package" on cover; contains alternate stereo versions of "Please Mr. Postman" by the Marvelettes and "Do You Love Me" by the Contours*				
❏ Motown MT 614 [M]	1964	25.00	50.00	100.00
-- *"Package" cover*				
❏ Motown MT 614 [M]	1966	5.00	10.00	20.00
-- *No "package" on cover*				
PAJAMA PARTY				
❏ Forum F-9006 [M]	196?	7.50	15.00	30.00
-- *Reissue of Roulette 25021*				
❏ Forum SF-9006 [R]	196?	5.00	10.00	20.00
❏ Roulette R 25021 [M]	1958	10.00	20.00	40.00
-- *Originals have a black label*				
❏ Roulette R 25021 [M]	1959	6.25	12.50	25.00
-- *Second pressings have a white label with colored spokes*				
PEACHES: "PICK OF THE CROP"				
❏ Capricorn PRO 588 [(2)]	1974	6.25	12.50	25.00

Label, Number	Yr	VG	VG+	NM
THE PEOPLE'S RECORD				
❏ Warner Bros. PRO 645 [(2)]	1976	5.00	10.00	20.00
PETAL PUSHERS				
❏ Chess LP 1520 [M]	1967	6.25	12.50	25.00
❏ Chess LPS 1520 [S]	1967	6.25	12.50	25.00
THE PHIL SPECTOR SPECTACULAR				
❏ Philles PHLP 100 [DJ]	197?	375.00	750.00	1,500.
-- Not issued with cover				
PHIL SPECTOR'S CHRISTMAS ALBUM				
❏ Apple SW 3400 [M]	1972	7.50	15.00	30.00
-- Reissue of "A Christmas Gift for You from Philles Records," PHLP-4005				
PHIL SPECTOR: BACK TO MONO 1958-1969				
❏ Phil Spector/Abkco 7118-1 [(5)]	1991	20.00	40.00	80.00
-- Box set				
PHIL SPECTOR'S GREATEST HITS				
❏ Warner/Spector 2SP 9104 [(2)]	1977	10.00	20.00	40.00
PIANO JAZZ, VOLUME 1				
❏ Brunswick BL 54014 [M]	1955	7.50	15.00	30.00
PIANO JAZZ, VOLUME 2				
❏ Brunswick BL 54015 [M]	1955	7.50	15.00	30.00
PIANO VARIATIONS				
❏ King 540 [M]	1956	37.50	75.00	150.00
PICK HITS OF THE RADIO GOOD GUYS				
❏ Laurie LLP-2021 [M]	1963	7.50	15.00	30.00
PICK HITS OF THE RADIO GOOD GUYS, VOLUME 2				
❏ Laurie LLP-2026 [M]	1964	6.25	12.50	25.00
PITTSBURGH'S GREATEST HITS				
❏ Itzy 101 [(2)]	1966	12.50	25.00	50.00
PLAYBOY MUSIC HALL OF FAME WINNERS				
❏ Playboy PB-7473 [(3)]	1978	50.00	100.00	200.00
-- One of very few compilation LPs to contain both an Elvis and a Beatles track!				
POLKAS				
❏ Audio Lab AL-1543 [M]	1959	10.00	20.00	40.00
POP ORIGINS				
❏ Chess LP 1544 [M]	1969	6.25	12.50	25.00
POP SHOPPER				
❏ RCA Victor SPL-12/13 [M]	1955	7.50	15.00	30.00
THE POPULAR GOLD ALBUM				
❏ Capitol T 972 [M]	1958	7.50	15.00	30.00
A POT OF FLOWERS				
❏ Mainstream S-6100 [S]	1967	25.00	50.00	100.00
❏ Mainstream 56100 [M]	1967	20.00	40.00	80.00
POT OF GOLDEN GOODIES				
❏ Herald HLP-1015 [M]	1962	37.50	75.00	150.00
THE POWER AND THE MAJESTY: RAIN 'N' TRAIN DEMONSTRATION DISC				
❏ Mobile Fidelity 1-004	1979	12.50	25.00	50.00
-- Audiophile vinyl				
THE PROGRESSIVES				
❏ Columbia KG 31574 [(2)]	1973	5.00	10.00	20.00
PROPAGANDA				
❏ A&M SP-4786	1979	5.00	10.00	20.00
-- Includes poster				
PUMPING VINYL				
❏ Warner Bros. PRO 773 [(2)]	1977	5.00	10.00	20.00
PURE MAGIC: THE SONGS OF PAM SAWYER & MARILYN MCLEOD				
❏ Jobete PRO-1A [DJ]	1978	10.00	20.00	40.00
-- Promo-only publisher's demo with short excerpts of songs				
QSP PRESENTS A GIFT OF MUSIC				
❏ RCA Special Products QSP1-0034	1984	12.50	25.00	50.00
RADAR BLUES				
❏ King KLP-1050 [M]	1969	7.50	15.00	30.00
RADIO RADIO/SOUL TWIST/YOU'VE GOTTA BE CRUEL TO BE KIND				
❏ Columbia AS 443 [DJ]	1979	10.00	20.00	40.00
-- Promo-only 3-song sampler on orange vinyl				
RADIO SMASH FLASHBACKS: DRIVE TIME				
❏ Laurie LLP-2028 [M]	1964	6.25	12.50	25.00
RADIO SMASH FLASHBACKS: PRIME TIME				
❏ Laurie LLP-2029 [M]	1964	6.25	12.50	25.00
RAILROAD SONGS				
❏ King 869 [M]	1963	17.50	35.00	70.00
RAT MUSIC FOR RAT PEOPLE				
❏ Go 003	1982	5.00	10.00	20.00
THE RCA VICTOR ENCYCLOPEDIA OF RECORDED JAZZ, ALBUM 1				
❏ RCA Victor LEJ-1 [10]	195?	10.00	20.00	40.00
THE RCA VICTOR ENCYCLOPEDIA OF RECORDED JAZZ, ALBUM 2				
❏ RCA Victor LEJ-2 [10]	195?	10.00	20.00	40.00
THE RCA VICTOR ENCYCLOPEDIA OF RECORDED JAZZ, ALBUM 3				
❏ RCA Victor LEJ-3 [10]	195?	10.00	20.00	40.00
THE RCA VICTOR ENCYCLOPEDIA OF RECORDED JAZZ, ALBUM 4				
❏ RCA Victor LEJ-4 [10]	195?	10.00	20.00	40.00
THE RCA VICTOR ENCYCLOPEDIA OF RECORDED JAZZ, ALBUM 5				
❏ RCA Victor LEJ-5 [10]	195?	10.00	20.00	40.00
THE RCA VICTOR ENCYCLOPEDIA OF RECORDED JAZZ, ALBUM 6				
❏ RCA Victor LEJ-6 [10]	195?	10.00	20.00	40.00
THE RCA VICTOR ENCYCLOPEDIA OF RECORDED JAZZ, ALBUM 7				
❏ RCA Victor LEJ-7 [10]	195?	10.00	20.00	40.00
THE RCA VICTOR ENCYCLOPEDIA OF RECORDED JAZZ, ALBUM 8				
❏ RCA Victor LEJ-8 [10]	195?	10.00	20.00	40.00
THE RCA VICTOR ENCYCLOPEDIA OF RECORDED JAZZ, ALBUM 9				
❏ RCA Victor LEJ-9 [10]	195?	10.00	20.00	40.00
THE RCA VICTOR ENCYCLOPEDIA OF RECORDED JAZZ, ALBUM 10				
❏ RCA Victor LEJ-10 [10]	195?	10.00	20.00	40.00
THE RCA VICTOR ENCYCLOPEDIA OF RECORDED JAZZ, ALBUM 11				
❏ RCA Victor LEJ-11 [10]	195?	10.00	20.00	40.00
THE RCA VICTOR ENCYCLOPEDIA OF RECORDED JAZZ, ALBUM 12				
❏ RCA Victor LEJ-12 [10]	195?	10.00	20.00	40.00
REACH OUT AND TOUCH				
❏ Reader's Digest RBA-037A [(7)]	1991	12.50	25.00	50.00
THE REAL BLUES				
❏ Excello LPS-8011 [R]	1969	5.00	10.00	20.00
REBIRTH OF BEALE STREET				
❏ Beale Street BS-1	1983	50.00	100.00	200.00
-- Limited edition of 1,000 made for the city of Memphis				
RED BIRD GOLDIES				
❏ Red Bird LP 20-102 [M]	1965	20.00	40.00	80.00
REGGAE CHRISTMAS BY THE JOE GIBBS FAMILY OF ARTISTS				
❏ Joe Gibbs Music 8077	1982	5.00	10.00	20.00
REMEMBER THE OLDIES				
❏ Argo LP-649 [M]	1963	10.00	20.00	40.00
-- Black vinyl				
❏ Argo LP-649 [M]	1963	100.00	200.00	400.00
-- Multi-color splash vinyl; white label promo				
REQUESTED BY YOU				
❏ Columbia CL 607 [M]	1955	6.25	12.50	25.00
RICHARD NADER/LET THE GOOD TIMES ROLL				
❏ Bell 9002 [(2)]	1973	5.00	10.00	20.00
RIVERBOAT JAZZ				
❏ Brunswick BL 58026 [10]	1951	12.50	25.00	50.00
ROBERT W. SARNOFF -- 25 YEARS OF RCA LEADERSHIP				
❏ RCA Victor RWS-0001 [DJ]	1973	1,000.	1,500.	2,000.
-- Souvenir record handed out at Sarnoff's retirement party				
ROCK & ROLL FOREVER				
❏ Atlantic 1239 [M]	1956	37.50	75.00	150.00
ROCK & ROLL JAMBOREE				
❏ End LP-302 [M]	1959	30.00	60.00	120.00
-- Second cover and title with puppet and a guitar				
ROCK & ROLL WITH RHYTHM & BLUES				
❏ Aladdin LP-710 [M]	195?	375.00	750.00	1,500.
ROCK 'N' ROLL SOCK HOP				
❏ Score SLP-4018 [M]	1958	50.00	100.00	200.00
ROCK AND ROLL BANDSTAND				
❏ Roulette R 25093 [M]	1959	7.50	15.00	30.00
-- Originals have a white label with colored spokes				

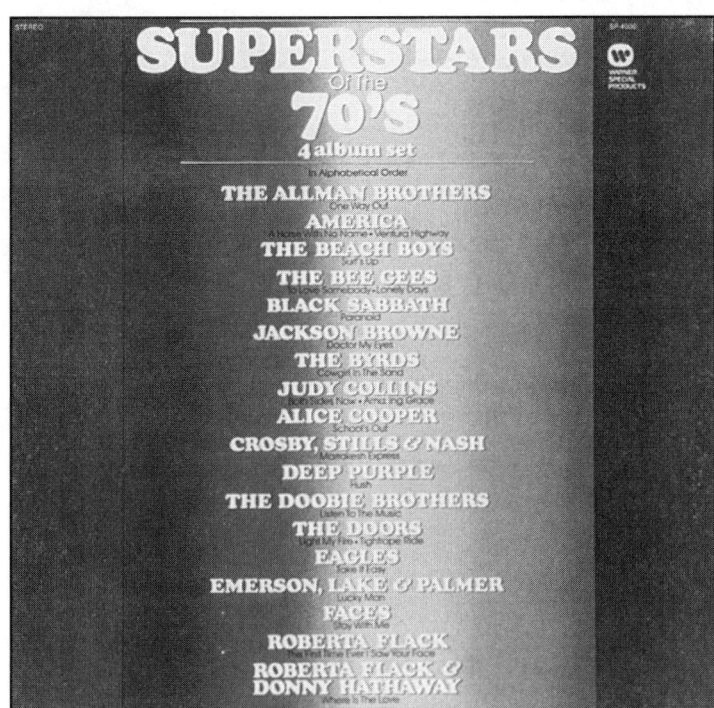

(Top left) *Disco Teen '66,* which was only available from the Columbia Record Club, contains a bonus in its stereo version, pictured above. This album has the first true stereo mix of Bob Dylan's "Positively Fourth Street," and it has a much longer fade than either the single version or the later stereo mix that appeared on *Bob Dylan's Greatest Hits.* (Top right) *The Greatest Hits From England* is a good sampler of some of the British Invasion acts whose records came out on London, Parrot or Press in the United States. (Bottom left) When it was released in 1973, *Superstars of the 70's* was heavily promoted on television and was sold in discount stores. But its price, $10.98, turned off a lot of people – that was a lot for 1973, even for a four-record set. Today, it's a hard collection to find, but a sought-after one, as much for some of the artists who rarely appear on compilations (the Rolling Stones and Led Zeppelin, to name two) as anything else. (Bottom right) *Winter Warnerland* was one of two promo-only collections of Christmas music and messages Warner Bros. released to radio in the late 1980s. This one is special because it contains an otherwise unavailable performance of "Deck the Halls" by R.E.M.

Label, Number	Yr	VG	VG+	NM
ROCK AND ROLL DANCE PARTY				
❑ King 536 [M]	1956	75.00	150.00	300.00
ROCK AND ROLL RECORD HOP				
❑ Roulette R 25059 [M]	1959	7.50	15.00	30.00
-- Originals have a white label with colored spokes				
ROCK AND ROLL REVUE, VOLUME 2				
❑ King 654 [M]	1959	37.50	75.00	150.00
ROCK AND ROLL VS. RHYTHM AND BLUES				
❑ Dooto DTL-223 [M]	1957	25.00	50.00	100.00
ROCK AND ROLL: THE EARLY DAYS				
❑ RCA Victor AFM1-5463	1985	5.00	10.00	20.00
ROCK'S GREATEST HITS				
❑ Columbia GP 11 [(2)]	1969	5.00	10.00	20.00
ROCK-A-BALLADS				
❑ Cadence CLP-3041 [M]	1960	10.00	20.00	40.00
ROCK-A-HITS				
❑ Cadence CLP-3042 [M]	1960	10.00	20.00	40.00
ROCK-O-RAMA				
❑ Abkco AB 4222 [(2)]	1972	5.00	10.00	20.00
ROCK-O-RAMA, VOLUME 2				
❑ Abkco AB 4223 [(2)]	1972	5.00	10.00	20.00
ROCKIN' SLUMBER PARTY				
❑ Famous LP-501 [M]	1961	7.50	15.00	30.00
ROCKIN' TOGETHER				
❑ Atco 33-103 [M]	1958	25.00	50.00	100.00
A ROCKING CHRISTMAS STOCKING				
❑ Capitol SPRO 9303/4/5/6 [(2) DJ]	1984	5.00	10.00	20.00
ROOST 5TH ANNIVERSARY ALBUM				
❑ Roost RST-1201 [M]	1955	12.50	25.00	50.00
ROOTS OF BRITISH ROCK				
❑ Sire SASH-3711 [(2)]	1975	5.00	10.00	20.00
ROULETTE PRESENTS A DEMONSTRATION OF THE NEW DIMENSIONAL SOUND OF DYNAMIC STEREO				
❑ Roulette SR-100 [S]	1958	7.50	15.00	30.00
RUMBLE				
❑ Jubilee JGM-1114 [M]	1959	37.50	75.00	150.00
SATURDAY NIGHT AT THE UPTOWN				
❑ Atlantic 8101 [M]	1964	6.25	12.50	25.00
❑ Atlantic SD 8101 [S]	1964	7.50	15.00	30.00
SATURDAY NIGHT FUNCTION: RURAL BLUES, VOLUME 2				
❑ Imperial LP-94001	1968	5.00	10.00	20.00
SATURDAY NIGHT MOOD				
❑ Columbia CL 599 [M]	1954	6.25	12.50	25.00
SAXOMANIAC				
❑ Apollo LP-477 [M]	1958	25.00	50.00	100.00
SCHLAGERS!				
❑ Warner Bros. PRO 359 [(2)]	1970	7.50	15.00	30.00
-- Originals have green labels				
SEASON'S GREETINGS FROM BARBRA STREISAND...AND FRIENDS				
❑ Columbia Special Products CSS 1075	1969	5.00	10.00	20.00
-- Created exclusively for Maxwell House Coffee				
SEASONS GREETINGS (A CHRISTMAS FESTIVAL OF STARS)				
❑ Columbia CL 1394 [M]	1959	5.00	10.00	20.00
❑ Columbia CS 8189 [S]	1959	6.25	12.50	25.00
SHUT DOWN				
❑ Capitol ST 1918 [S]	1963	12.50	25.00	50.00
❑ Capitol T 1918 [M]	1963	10.00	20.00	40.00
SHUT DOWNS AND HILL CLIMBS				
❑ Liberty LRP-3366 [M]	1964	10.00	20.00	40.00
❑ Liberty LST-7366 [S]	1964	12.50	25.00	50.00
THE SINATRA FAMILY WISH YOU A MERRY CHRISTMAS				
❑ Reprise FS-1026	1969	12.50	25.00	50.00
SING A SONG OF SOUL				
❑ Checker LP 2998 [M]	1966	20.00	40.00	80.00
❑ Checker LPS 2998 [S]	1966	25.00	50.00	100.00
THE SINGER-SONGWRITER PROJECT				
❑ Elektra EKL-299 [M]	1965	6.25	12.50	25.00
-- With 13 tracks				
❑ Elektra EKL-299 [M]	1965	5.00	10.00	20.00
-- With 11 tracks, though the label and cover claim there are 13				
❑ Elektra EKS-7299 [S]	1965	7.50	15.00	30.00
-- With 13 tracks				
❑ Elektra EKS-7299 [S]	1965	5.00	10.00	20.00
-- With 11 tracks, though the label and cover claim there are 13				
THE SIREN				
❑ Posh Boy PBS-103	1980	5.00	10.00	20.00
16 GOODIES -- BLASTS FROM THE PAST				
❑ Blast LP-6805 [M]	1964	10.00	20.00	40.00
60 CHRISTMAS CLASSICS				
❑ Sessions DVL2-0723 [(4)]	1985	5.00	10.00	20.00
-- Record 3 is numbered "P18827" and Record 4 is numbered "P18828"				
60 FLASH-BACK GREATS OF THE SIXTIES				
❑ K-Tel TU 229 [(4)]	1972	10.00	20.00	40.00
-- One of the few sought-after K-Tel collections, among its contents is a Beatles track ("My Bonnie")				
60 YEARS OF MUSIC AMERICA LOVES BEST				
❑ RCA Victor LM-6074 [(2)]	1959	7.50	15.00	30.00
60 YEARS OF MUSIC AMERICA LOVES BEST, VOLUME II				
❑ RCA Victor LM-6088 [(2)]	1960	7.50	15.00	30.00
60 YEARS OF MUSIC AMERICA LOVES BEST, VOLUME III (POPULAR)				
❑ RCA Victor LOP-1509	1961	5.00	10.00	20.00
60 YEARS OF MUSIC AMERICA LOVES BEST, VOLUME III (RED SEAL)				
❑ RCA Victor Red Seal LM-2574	1961	5.00	10.00	20.00
$64,000 JAZZ				
❑ Columbia CL 777 [M]	1955	12.50	25.00	50.00
SMART, LUSCIOUS, BEAUTIFUL				
❑ Bethlehem BCP-6034 [M]	1960	7.50	15.00	30.00
SOLID GOLD HITS				
❑ Imperial LP-12230 [R]	1963	5.00	10.00	20.00
❑ Imperial LP-9230 [M]	1963	6.25	12.50	25.00
SOLID GOLD PROGRAMMING				
❑ Screen Gems/Columbia CPL-711 [DJ]	1975	5.00	10.00	20.00
-- Promo-only compilation of oldies sent to radio to spur airplay on songs owned by this publishing house				
❑ Screen Gems/Columbia CPL-715 [DJ]	1975	5.00	10.00	20.00
-- Same concept as above album, but completely different contents, and mostly in stereo				
SOLID GOLD SONGS INSTRUMENTALLY				
❑ Screen Gems/Columbia CPL-714 [DJ]	1975	5.00	10.00	20.00
-- Promo-only compilation of oldies sent to radio to spur airplay on songs owned by this publishing house				
SOLID GOLD SOUL				
❑ Atlantic SD 8116 [S]	1966	5.00	10.00	20.00
SOLO SPOTLIGHTS				
❑ King 745 [M]	1961	25.00	50.00	100.00
SONGS FOR A SUMMER NIGHT				
❑ Columbia PM 2 [(2) M]	1963	5.00	10.00	20.00
❑ Columbia PMS 2 [(2) S]	1963	6.25	12.50	25.00
THE SONGS OF ASHFORD AND SIMPSON				
❑ Jobete PRO-3 [DJ]	1974	10.00	20.00	40.00
-- Promo-only publisher's demo with short excerpts of songs				
SONGS OF FAITH				
❑ Audio Lab AL-1504 [M]	1959	20.00	40.00	80.00
SONGS OF FAITH AND INSPIRATION				
❑ Time-Life STL-127 [(3)]	1989	6.25	12.50	25.00
SONGS OF FAITH VOLUME 2				
❑ Audio Lab AL-1523 [M]	1959	20.00	40.00	80.00
THE SONGS OF HOLLAND-DOZIER-HOLLAND				
❑ Jobete PRO-4 [DJ]	1974	10.00	20.00	40.00
-- Promo-only publisher's demo with short excerpts of songs				
THE SONGS OF JOHNNY BRISTOL-FRANK WILSON-MICKEY STEVENSON AND FREDDIE PERREN				
❑ Jobete PRO-8 [DJ]	1976	10.00	20.00	40.00
-- Promo-only publisher's demo with short excerpts of songs				
THE SONGS OF MARVIN GAYE				
❑ Jobete PRO-6 [DJ]	1974	10.00	20.00	40.00
-- Promo-only publisher's demo with short excerpts of songs				

Label, Number	Yr	VG	VG+	NM
THE SONGS OF NORMAN WHITFIELD				
❑ Jobete PRO-7 [DJ]	1976	10.00	20.00	40.00
-- *Promo-only publisher's demo with short excerpts of songs*				
SONGS OF RIVERS, OCEANS AND SEAS				
❑ King 871 [M]	1963	17.50	35.00	70.00
THE SONGS OF SMOKEY ROBINSON				
❑ Jobete PRO-2 [DJ]	1972	10.00	20.00	40.00
-- *Promo-only publisher's demo with short excerpts of songs; there are two versions of this LP, both with the same number; each is of equal value*				
THE SONGS OF STEVIE WONDER				
❑ Jobete PRO-5 [DJ]	1974	10.00	20.00	40.00
-- *Promo-only publisher's demo with short excerpts of songs*				
SONGS OF THE HILLS				
❑ Audio Lab AL-1515 [M]	1959	20.00	40.00	80.00
SOUL CHRISTMAS				
❑ Atco SD 33-269	1968	7.50	15.00	30.00
SOUL EXPLOSION				
❑ Stax STS 2-2007 [(2)]	1969	5.00	10.00	20.00
SOUL MEETING SATURDAY NIGHT HOOTENANNY STYLE				
❑ Vee Jay LP-1074 [M]	1963	7.50	15.00	30.00
-- *Not known to exist in stereo*				
THE SOUL OF JAZZ PERCUSSION				
❑ Warwick W 5003 [M]	1961	7.50	15.00	30.00
❑ Warwick W 5003ST [S]	1961	10.00	20.00	40.00
SOULED OUT				
❑ Chess LPS 1546 [S]	1969	12.50	25.00	50.00
SOULFUL OLDIES				
❑ Oldies 33 OL-8005 [M]	1964	6.25	12.50	25.00
THE SOUND OF GENIUS				
❑ Columbia Masterworks SGM 1 [(2) M]	1963	5.00	10.00	20.00
❑ Columbia Masterworks SGS 1 [(2) S]	1963	6.25	12.50	25.00
SOUNDS OF SUCCESS				
❑ Jamie JLP-3017 [M]	1961	6.25	12.50	25.00
❑ Jamie JLPS-3017 [S]	1961	7.50	15.00	30.00
SPECIAL COLLECTOR'S EDITION ALBUM FROM ROCKIN' RECORDS				
❑ Sun 1032	1986	7.50	15.00	30.00
-- *Limited edition of 600 copies*				
SPIN TIME WITH LIBERTY				
❑ Liberty MM-417 [DJ]	1962	12.50	25.00	50.00
-- *Promo-only release*				
SPIRITUALS				
❑ King 951 [M]	1966	12.50	25.00	50.00
-- *Reissue of "Spirituals, Volume 5," King 576*				
SPIRITUALS, VOLUME 5				
❑ King 576 [M]	1957	37.50	75.00	150.00
STARS				
❑ Sun 148	1982	5.00	10.00	20.00
-- *Includes two early Alabama tracks*				
STARS FOR A SUMMER NIGHT				
❑ Columbia PM 1 [(2) M]	1961	6.25	12.50	25.00
❑ Columbia PMS 1 [(2) S]	1961	7.50	15.00	30.00
THE STARS OF CHRISTMAS				
❑ RCA Special Products DPL1-0842	1988	5.00	10.00	20.00
-- *Sold only through Avon dealers*				
THE STARS OF HEE HAW				
❑ Capitol ST-437	1970	5.00	10.00	20.00
STARS OF THE GRAND OLE OPRY 1926-1974				
❑ RCA Victor CPL2-0466 [(2)]	1974	5.00	10.00	20.00
START SWIMMING				
❑ Stiff SINK 1	1981	5.00	10.00	20.00
STAX...ONCE YOU'VE BEEN THERE, YOU KNOW YOU'RE HOME				
❑ Stax STS 1 [(2) DJ]	1971	10.00	20.00	40.00
-- *Promo only in blank white gatefold cover*				
THE STAX/VOLT REVUE -- LIVE IN LONDON				
❑ Stax 721 [M]	1967	5.00	10.00	20.00
❑ Stax S721 [S]	1967	6.25	12.50	25.00
THE STAX/VOLT REVUE -- LIVE IN LONDON, VOLUME 2				
❑ Stax 722 [M]	1967	5.00	10.00	20.00
❑ Stax S722 [S]	1967	6.25	12.50	25.00

Label, Number	Yr	VG	VG+	NM
STAY IN SCHOOL -- DON'T BE A DROP OUT				
❑ Stax A-11 [DJ]	1967	125.00	250.00	500.00
STEREOSONIC JUBILEE SAMPLER, VOLUME 1				
❑ Jubilee SSJLP-801 [S]	1959	10.00	20.00	40.00
STERLING BALL 1971				
❑ Motown M 739 [DJ]	1971	62.50	125.00	250.00
-- *Loucye Gordy Wakefield Scholarship Fund benefit giveaway*				
STILL MORE GOLD HITS, VOLUME 3				
❑ Warwick W 2048 [M]	1962	20.00	40.00	80.00
STREET BEAT				
❑ Sugar Hill 9228 [(2)]	1984	6.25	12.50	25.00
THE STRING BAND PROJECT				
❑ Elektra EKL-292 [M]	1965	5.00	10.00	20.00
❑ Elektra EKS-7292 [S]	1965	6.25	12.50	25.00
SUB POP 100				
❑ Sub Pop 10	1986	12.50	25.00	50.00
SUB POP 200				
❑ Sub Pop 25 [(3) EP]	1988	12.50	25.00	50.00
SUMMER FESTIVAL				
❑ RCA Victor Red Seal LM-6097 [(2) M]	1962	5.00	10.00	20.00
❑ RCA Victor Red Seal LSC-6097 [(2) S]	1962	6.25	12.50	25.00
SUMMER SOUVENIRS				
❑ Bell 6035	1969	5.00	10.00	20.00
SUMMIT MEETING				
❑ Vee Jay LP-3026 [M]	1961	5.00	10.00	20.00
❑ Vee Jay SR-3026 [S]	1961	6.25	12.50	25.00
THE SUN STORY				
❑ Rhino RNDA-71103 [(2)]	1986	5.00	10.00	20.00
SUN'S GOLD HITS				
❑ Sun LP-1250 [M]	1961	50.00	100.00	200.00
SUNDAY MORNING				
❑ Vee Jay LP-5016 [M]	1961	7.50	15.00	30.00
SUPER GOLDEN HITS				
❑ Jubilee JGS-8019	1968	25.00	50.00	100.00
-- *Despite the stereo prefix, this LP is mono*				
SUPER GOLDEN HITS, VOLUME 2				
❑ Jubilee JGS-8023	1969	25.00	50.00	100.00
-- *Reissue of "Clay Cole's Bin of Original Golden Oldies," Jubilee 5026; again, despite the stereo prefix, this LP is mono*				
SUPER GROUPS				
❑ Warner Bros. PRO 630 [(2)]	1976	5.00	10.00	20.00
THE SUPER GROUPS				
❑ Atco SD 33-279	1969	5.00	10.00	20.00
THE SUPER GROUPS FROM HOLLAND				
❑ White Whale WWS-7129	1970	6.25	12.50	25.00
THE SUPER HITS				
❑ Atlantic Group 501 [M]	1967	5.00	10.00	20.00
❑ Atlantic Group SD 501 [S]	1967	5.00	10.00	20.00
THE SUPER HITS, VOL. 2				
❑ Atlantic SD 8188	1968	5.00	10.00	20.00
THE SUPER HITS, VOL. 3				
❑ Atlantic SD 8203	1968	5.00	10.00	20.00
THE SUPER HITS, VOL. 4				
❑ Atlantic SD 8224	1969	5.00	10.00	20.00
THE SUPER HITS, VOL. 5				
❑ Atlantic SD 8274	1970	5.00	10.00	20.00
SUPER OLDIES/VOL. 1				
❑ Capitol ST 2562 [S]	1966	6.25	12.50	25.00
❑ Capitol T 2562 [M]	1966	5.00	10.00	20.00
SUPER OLDIES/VOL. 2				
❑ Capitol ST 2565 [S]	1966	6.25	12.50	25.00
❑ Capitol T 2565 [M]	1966	5.00	10.00	20.00
SUPER OLDIES/VOL. 3				
❑ Capitol STBB 2910 [(2)]	1968	5.00	10.00	20.00
SUPER OLDIES/VOL. 4				
❑ Capitol STBB-149 [(2)]	1969	5.00	10.00	20.00
SUPER OLDIES/VOL. 5				
❑ Capitol STBB-216 [(2)]	1969	5.00	10.00	20.00

Label, Number	Yr	VG	VG+	NM
THE SUPER SOUL-DEES				
❏ Capitol ST 2798 [S]	1967	5.00	10.00	20.00
❏ Capitol T 2798 [M]	1967	5.00	10.00	20.00
THE SUPER SOUL-DEES, VOL. 2				
❏ Capitol STBB-2911 [(2)]	1968	5.00	10.00	20.00
THE SUPER SOUL-DEES, VOL. 3				
❏ Capitol STBB-178 [(2)]	1969	5.00	10.00	20.00
SUPERSTARS OF THE '70S				
❏ Warner Special Products SP-4000 [(4)]	1973	10.00	20.00	40.00
-- Box set with booklet of liner notes				
SURF'S UP AT BANZAI PIPELINE				
❏ Northridge NM-101 [M]	1963	50.00	100.00	200.00
-- Original pressing of LP reissued on Reprise				
❏ Reprise R 6094 [M]	1963	25.00	50.00	100.00
❏ Reprise RS 6094 [S]	1963	37.50	75.00	150.00
SURF'S UP! AT BANZAI PIPELINE				
❏ Northridge NM-101 [M]	1963	37.50	75.00	150.00
SURFIN' ON WAVE NINE				
❏ King 855 [M]	1963	20.00	40.00	80.00
SWAMP BLUES VOLUME 1				
❏ Excello LPS-8015 [R]	1970	5.00	10.00	20.00
SWAMP BLUES VOLUME 2				
❏ Excello LPS-8016 [R]	1970	5.00	10.00	20.00
SWEET 'N' GREASY: RHYTHM 'N' BLUES, VOLUME 2				
❏ Imperial LP-94005	1968	5.00	10.00	20.00
SWEET ADELINES MEDALIST QUARTETS OF 1958				
❏ Cadence CLP-3018 [M]	1959	10.00	20.00	40.00
SWEET ADELINES MEDALISTS OF 1957				
❏ Cadence CLP-3009 [M]	1958	10.00	20.00	40.00
SWEET DREAMS OF COUNTRY				
❏ Reader's Digest RBA-049A [(7)]	1990	12.50	25.00	50.00
SWING BILLIES				
❏ Audio Lab AL-1546 [M]	1960	30.00	60.00	120.00
SWING BILLIES VOLUME 2				
❏ Audio Lab AL-1566 [M]	1960	30.00	60.00	120.00
SWITCHED ON BLUES				
❏ Soul SS-720	1969	37.50	75.00	150.00
TAME YOURSELF				
❏ Rhino 90082	1991	6.25	12.50	25.00
TAMLA SPECIAL #1				
❏ Tamla TM 224 [M]	1962	37.50	75.00	150.00
-- White label				
❏ Tamla TM 224 [M]	1963	17.50	35.00	70.00
-- Yellow label				
TASTE TEST #1 -- LIVE FROM BRAIN COOKIES				
❏ New Alliance 045 [(2)]	1990	6.25	12.50	25.00
TEEN DELIGHTS				
❏ Vee Jay LP-1021 [M]	1960	7.50	15.00	30.00
TEEN DELIGHTS, VOLUME 2				
❏ Vee Jay LP-1036 [M]	1961	7.50	15.00	30.00
TEENAGE PARTY				
❏ Gee GLP-702 [M]	1958	50.00	100.00	200.00
-- Red label				
❏ Gee GLP-702 [M]	196?	15.00	30.00	60.00
-- Gray label				
TEENSVILLE				
❏ Liberty L-5503 [M]	1962	10.00	20.00	40.00
TEN TUNES OF CHRISTMAS				
❏ Candee 50-50	195?	5.00	10.00	20.00
-- Sold through "The 50-50 Club," a Cincinnati radio and TV show; all the artists have Cincinnati ties				
TENNESSEE				
❏ Design DLP-611 [M]	1962	5.00	10.00	20.00
THEMES LIKE OLD TIMES				
❏ Viva 36018 [(2)]	1969	5.00	10.00	20.00
30 FAVORITE SONGS OF CHRISTMAS WITH CHIMES AND CHORUS				
❏ Disneyland DQ-1329 [M]	1963	5.00	10.00	20.00
-- Performed by anonymous musicians				
30 YEARS OF NO. 1 COUNTRY HITS				
❏ Reader's Digest RBA-215-A [(7)]	1986	12.50	25.00	50.00
THIS IS HOW IT ALL BEGAN: THE SPECIALTY STORY, VOLUME 1				
❏ Specialty SPS-2117	1970	5.00	10.00	20.00
THIS IS HOW IT ALL BEGAN: THE SPECIALTY STORY, VOLUME 2				
❏ Specialty SPS-2118	1970	5.00	10.00	20.00
THIS IS SOUL				
❏ Atlantic SD 8170	1968	5.00	10.00	20.00
THIS IS STEREO				
❏ Liberty LST-101 [S]	1960	10.00	20.00	40.00
-- Black vinyl				
❏ Liberty LST-101 [S]	1960	30.00	60.00	120.00
-- Red vinyl				
THREADS OF GLORY -- 200 YEARS OF AMERICA IN WORDS & MUSIC				
❏ London Phase 4 6SP 14000 [(6)]	1975	7.50	15.00	30.00
A TIME FOR PRAYER				
❏ Audio Lab AL-1518 [M]	1959	20.00	40.00	80.00
THE TIME-LIFE TREASURY OF CHRISTMAS				
❏ Time-Life STL-107 [(3)]	1986	5.00	10.00	20.00
-- Available from Time-Life by mail order only; boxed set				
THE TIME-LIFE TREASURY OF CHRISTMAS, VOLUME TWO				
❏ Time-Life STL-108 [(3)]	1987	5.00	10.00	20.00
-- Available from Time-Life by mail-order only; all known copies are boxed sets				
TODAY'S HITS				
❏ Philles PHLP 4004 [M]	1963	100.00	200.00	400.00
-- First pressings have blue and black labels				
❏ Philles PHLP 4004 [M]	1964	50.00	100.00	200.00
-- Second pressings have yellow and red labels				
TOGETHER				
❏ Warner Bros. PRO 486	1972	5.00	10.00	20.00
-- Originals have green labels				
TOGETHER AT CHRISTMAS (READER'S DIGEST FAMILY ALBUM OF CHRISTMAS MUSIC)				
❏ Reader's Digest RDA 151-A [(5)]	1974	5.00	10.00	20.00
-- Available only through Reader's Digest magazine by mail order				
TOMORROW'S HITS				
❏ Vee Jay LP-1042 [M]	1962	7.50	15.00	30.00
THE TOP 10 STORY IN SOUND				
❏ Jobete PRO-1 [(2) DJ]	1972	10.00	20.00	40.00
-- Promo-only publisher's demo with short excerpts of songs				
TOP R&B ARTISTS SING COUNTRY SONGS				
❏ King 884 [M]	1964	20.00	40.00	80.00
TRADITIONAL CHRISTMAS SONGS				
❏ Audio Lab AL-1517 [M]	1959	20.00	40.00	80.00
TREASURE ALBUM				
❏ Hickory LPS-154	1970	10.00	20.00	40.00
TREASURE CHEST GOODIES				
❏ Stax 703 [M]	1963	10.00	20.00	40.00
-- National version of "Hits from the South Presented by Nick Charles" with rearranged contents				
TREASURE CHEST OF HITS				
❏ Swan LP-501 [M]	1960	20.00	40.00	80.00
A TREASURE CHEST OF SONG HITS				
❏ Columbia CL 613 [M]	1955	6.25	12.50	25.00
TREASURE TUNES FROM THE VAULT (AS ADVERTISED ON WLS)				
❏ Chess LP 1474 [M]	1962	10.00	20.00	40.00
A TREASURY OF CHRISTMAS				
❏ Columbia Record Club P4S 5022 [(4)]	1965	7.50	15.00	30.00
A TREASURY OF GOLDEN CHRISTMAS SONGS				
❏ Vee Jay LP-5045 [M]	1963	7.50	15.00	30.00
TROMBONE BAND STAND				
❏ Bethlehem BCP-6036 [M]	1960	7.50	15.00	30.00
TROUBLEMAKERS				
❏ Warner Bros. PRO-A-857 [(2) DJ]	1978	5.00	10.00	20.00
TRUCK DRIVER SONGS				
❏ King 866 [M]	1963	17.50	35.00	70.00
TUNES TO BE REMEMBERED				
❏ Excello LP-8001 [M]	1960	37.50	75.00	150.00
-- Original cover is green with black records that list the title and artist of each selection				
TURN BACK THE CLOCK				
❏ King 859 [M]	1963	17.50	35.00	70.00

Label, Number	Yr	VG	VG+	NM
12 + 3 = 15 HITS				
❏ End LP 310 [M]	1961	15.00	30.00	60.00
12 FLIP HITS				
❏ Flip 1001 [M]	1959	75.00	150.00	300.00
THE 12 GREATEST OLDIES IN THE WHOLE WORLD, EVER				
❏ Parkway P-7031 [M]	1963	7.50	15.00	30.00
12 MILLION SELLERS				
❏ Forum F-9057 [M]	1963	5.00	10.00	20.00
12 SONGS OF CHRISTMAS				
❏ Reprise F-2022 [M]	1964	5.00	10.00	20.00
12 TOP TEEN DANCES 1961-1962				
❏ Cameo C-1016 [M]	1962	7.50	15.00	30.00
20 ALL TIME NO. 1 HITS				
❏ Roulette R 25290 [M]	1965	5.00	10.00	20.00
20 BIG BOSS FAVORITES: 10 GREAT HITS OF 1964 -- 10 GREAT OLDIES HITS				
❏ Roulette R 25304 [M]	1965	5.00	10.00	20.00
20 GREAT COUNTRY HITS				
❏ RCA Victor CPL2-1286 [(2)]	1975	5.00	10.00	20.00
20 ORIGINAL WINNERS OF 1964				
❏ Roulette R 25293 [M]	1965	5.00	10.00	20.00
20 ORIGINAL WINNERS, VOLUME 1				
❏ Roulette R 25249 [M]	1964	5.00	10.00	20.00
20 ORIGINAL WINNERS, VOLUME 2				
❏ Roulette R 25251 [M]	1964	5.00	10.00	20.00
20 ORIGINAL WINNERS, VOLUME 3				
❏ Roulette R 25263 [M]	1965	5.00	10.00	20.00
20 ORIGINAL WINNERS, VOLUME 4				
❏ Roulette R 25264 [M]	1965	5.00	10.00	20.00
20 SOULFUL OLDIES, VOLUME 1				
❏ Vee Jay VJVS-1001 [R]	1972	5.00	10.00	20.00
20 SOULFUL OLDIES, VOLUME 2				
❏ Vee Jay VJVS-1002 [R]	1972	5.00	10.00	20.00
20 SOULFUL OLDIES, VOLUME 3				
❏ Vee Jay VJVS-1003 [R]	1972	5.00	10.00	20.00
20 SOULFUL OLDIES, VOLUME 4				
❏ Vee Jay VJVS-73-1006/7 [R]	1973	5.00	10.00	20.00
20 SOULFUL OLDIES, VOLUME 5				
❏ Vee Jay VJVS-73-1008/9 [R]	1973	5.00	10.00	20.00
20 SOULFUL OLDIES, VOLUME 6				
❏ Vee Jay VJVS-73-1010/11 [R]	1973	5.00	10.00	20.00
20 YEARS OF NO. 1 HITS (1956-1975)				
❏ Reader's Digest RBA-243A [(7)]	1986	12.50	25.00	50.00
24 SACRED SONGS				
❏ King 965 [M]	1966	12.50	25.00	50.00
25 YEARS OF C&W HITS				
❏ King 1006 [M]	1966	7.50	15.00	30.00
25 YEARS OF COUNTRY AND WESTERN AND SACRED				
❏ King 807 [M]	1962	25.00	50.00	100.00
25 YEARS OF POPULAR MUSIC				
❏ King 1008 [M]	1966	7.50	15.00	30.00
25 YEARS OF R&B HITS				
❏ King 1004 [M]	1966	7.50	15.00	30.00
25 YEARS OF R&B HITS, VOLUME 1				
❏ King 725 [M]	1961	25.00	50.00	100.00
25 YEARS OF R&B HITS, VOLUME 2				
❏ King 749 [M]	1961	25.00	50.00	100.00
TWISTIN' ALL NIGHT LONG				
❏ Swan LP-506 [M]	1962	30.00	60.00	120.00
TWO ROOMS: CELEBRATING THE SONGS OF ELTON JOHN & BERNIE TAUPIN				
❏ Polydor P1-47570 [(2)]	1990	6.25	12.50	25.00
-- U.S. vinyl available only through Columbia House				
THE UNAVAILABLE 16				
❏ Vee Jay LP-1051 [M]	1962	10.00	20.00	40.00
THE UNFORGETTABLE FIFTIES				
❏ Heartland 1072 [(4)]	1988	5.00	10.00	20.00
THE UP ANOTHER OCTAVE TRANSMISSION				
❏ Up Another Octave (no #)	1981	6.25	12.50	25.00
-- Includes early Berlin				
A VARIETY OF COUNTRY SACRED SONGS				
❏ Audio Lab AL-1557 [M]	1960	15.00	30.00	60.00
A VERY MERRY CHRISTMAS				
❏ Columbia Special Products CSS 563	1967	5.00	10.00	20.00
-- Sold only at Grants stores				
VOICES OF HAITI				
❏ Elektra EKL-5 [10]	1953	10.00	20.00	40.00
VOLUNTEER JAM III AND IV				
❏ Epic E2 35368 [(2)]	1978	5.00	10.00	20.00
WALKIN' BY MYSELF				
❏ Chess LP 1446 [M]	1960	20.00	40.00	80.00
WAMO'S GOLDEN GASSERS				
❏ Chess LP 1458 PGH [M]	1961	37.50	75.00	150.00
-- Pittsburgh version of "Golden Gassers," Chess 1458				
THE WARNER/REPRISE RADIO SHOW				
❏ Warner Bros. PRO 463	1971	6.25	12.50	25.00
-- Originals have green labels				
WAVES				
❏ Bomp! 4003	1979	6.25	12.50	25.00
-- Originals on blue vinyl				
WE CUT THIS ALBUM FOR BREAD				
❏ Bethlehem BCP-86 [M]	1958	7.50	15.00	30.00
WE LIKE BOYS/GREAT BOY OLDIES				
❏ Oldies 33 OL-8004 [M]	1964	6.25	12.50	25.00
WE SING THE BLUES				
❏ Minit LP-0003 [M]	1962	12.50	25.00	50.00
WE WISH YOU A MERRY CHRISTMAS				
❏ Warner Bros. W 1337 [M]	1960	6.25	12.50	25.00
❏ Warner Bros. WS 1337 [S]	1960	7.50	15.00	30.00
WE'VE BUILT A JAZZ ALBUM FOR YOU				
❏ Bethlehem BCP-89 [M]	1958	7.50	15.00	30.00
WESTERN SWING				
❏ King 876 [M]	1963	17.50	35.00	70.00
WFUN GOOD GUYS				
❏ Roulette R 25273 [M]	1965	5.00	10.00	20.00
WHAT'S NEW? ON CAPITOL STEREO, VOL. 1				
❏ Capitol SN-1 [S]	1959	6.25	12.50	25.00
WHAT'S SHAKIN'				
❏ Elektra EKL-4002 [M]	1966	10.00	20.00	40.00
-- Deduct 25 percent if booklet is missing				
❏ Elektra EKS-74002 [S]	1966	12.50	25.00	50.00
-- Deduct 25 percent if booklet is missing				
WHITE MANSIONS				
❏ A&M SP 6004 [(2)]	1978	5.00	10.00	20.00
WHK GOOD GUYS				
❏ Roulette R 25295 [M]	1965	5.00	10.00	20.00
THE WHO'S WHO OF COUNTRY AND WESTERN MUSIC				
❏ Capitol ST 2538 [S]	1966	5.00	10.00	20.00
❏ Capitol T 2538 [M]	1966	5.00	10.00	20.00
THE WHOLE BURBANK CATALOG				
❏ Warner Bros. PRO 512 [(2)]	1972	5.00	10.00	20.00
-- Originals have green labels				
A WHOLE LOT OF BLOWIN'				
❏ Audio Lab AL-1539 [M]	1959	15.00	30.00	60.00
WHOPPERS				
❏ Jubilee JGM-1119 [M]	1960	25.00	50.00	100.00
-- Reissue of "Best of Rhythm and Blues," Jubilee 1014				
WILD WILDWOOD RECORDED LIVE				
❏ Chancellor CHL-5017 [M]	1960	6.25	12.50	25.00
❏ Chancellor CHLS-5017 [S]	1960	7.50	15.00	30.00
WING LIVELY GUYS				
❏ Roulette R 25307 [M]	1965	5.00	10.00	20.00

Label, Number	Yr	VG	VG+	NM
WINTER WARNERLAND				
❏ Warner Bros. PRO-A-3328 [(2)]	1988	10.00	20.00	40.00
-- *Promo-only set; Record 1 is red vinyl, Record 2 is green vinyl*				
WMAK JET SET-22 WINNERS				
❏ Roulette R 25291 [M]	1965	5.00	10.00	20.00
WOL SOUL BROTHERS				
❏ Roulette R 25337 [M]	1966	5.00	10.00	20.00
-- *Same LP as "WWIN Astro Jocks"*				
WONDERFUL MEMORIES FROM THE FAMILY PRAYER BOOK				
❏ Vee Jay LP-5066 [M]	1964	7.50	15.00	30.00
WOODSTOCK				
❏ Cotillion SD 3-500 [(3)]	1970	5.00	10.00	20.00
-- *Pale blue labels*				
❏ Mobile Fidelity 5-200 [(5)]	1985	50.00	100.00	200.00
-- *Audiophile vinyl*				
WOODSTOCK TWO				
❏ Cotillion SD 2-400 [(2)]	1971	5.00	10.00	20.00
THE WORKS				
❏ Warner Bros. PRO 610 [(2)]	1975	6.25	12.50	25.00
A WORLD OF BLUES				
❏ Imperial LP-9210 [M]	1963	7.50	15.00	30.00
❏ Imperial LP-12210 [R]	1963	5.00	10.00	20.00
THE WORLD OF COUNTRY MUSIC				
❏ Capitol NPB-5 [(3)]	1965	7.50	15.00	30.00
WRCA PLAYS THE HITS FOR YOUR CUSTOMERS				
❏ RCA Victor DJL1-1785 [DJ]	1976	50.00	100.00	200.00
WWIN ASTRO JOCKS				
❏ Roulette R 25337 [M]	1966	5.00	10.00	20.00
-- *Same LP as "WOL Soul Brothers"*				
YES L.A.				
❏ Dangerhouse EW 79 [PD]	1979	20.00	40.00	80.00
-- *One-sided clear picture disc*				
YOUR FAVORITE GROUPS AND THEIR GOLDEN GOODIES, VOL. 19				
❏ Roulette R 25248 [M]	1964	5.00	10.00	20.00
YOUR FAVORITE SINGING GROUPS				
❏ Hull 1002 [M]	1962	375.00	750.00	1,500.
YOUR INTRODUCTION TO THE SOUND OF THE 'SIXTIES				
❏ Liberty MM-403 [DJ]	1960	7.50	15.00	30.00
-- *Promo-only release*				
YOUR MUSICAL SOUVENIR FROM QSP				
❏ RCA Special Products QSP1-0042	1986	15.00	30.00	60.00
YOUR OLD FAVORITES ON OLD TOWN				
❏ Old Town LP-101 [M]	1959	50.00	100.00	200.00
YOUR SPECIAL MUSICAL SOUVENIR FROM QSP				
❏ RCA Special Products QSP1-0047	1986	15.00	30.00	60.00
YULESVILLE				
❏ Warner Bros. PRO-A-2896	1987	6.25	12.50	25.00
-- *Promo-only on red vinyl*				
ZENITH PRESENTS ALL STAR HOOTENANNY				
❏ Columbia Special Products XSV 88914/5 [M]	1963	12.50	25.00	50.00
-- *With three early Bob Dylan tracks credited to "Bobby Dylan," including "Corrina, Corrina," the B-side of his first single*				
ZIG ZAG FESTIVAL				
❏ Mercury SRD-2-29 [DJ]	1970	6.25	12.50	25.00
ZOO'S NEXT -- WMMR MORNING ZOO				
❏ Comedy Spotlight (no #)	1986	5.00	10.00	20.00

Label, Number	Yr	VG	VG+	NM

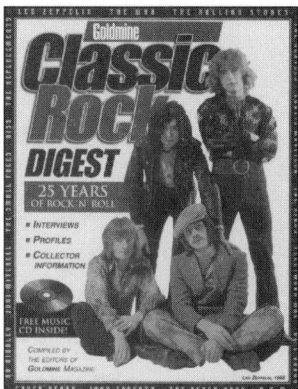

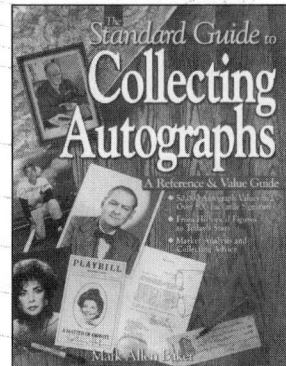